1998
WRITER'S
MARKET

WHERE & HOW TO SELL WHAT YOU WRITE

EDITOR
KIRSTEN C. HOLM

ASSISTANT EDITOR
DON PRUES

WRITER'S DIGEST BOOKS
CINCINNATI, OHIO

The cover illustration is a detail of a painting by Berge Missakian. Missakian is a Canadian artist from Montreal. He has studied art at the American University of Beruit; Cornell University, Ithaca, NY; and Concordia University, Montreal, Canada. Illusion, imagination and fantasy appear in his paintings and unify his compositions with explosively brilliant shapes of color. Missakian, who is listed in several books on art, including *Who's Who in American Art* (22nd edition), exhibits internationally. He celebrates passion over passivity, movement over inertia and joy over melancholic outlook. His internet URL is http://www.generation.net/studiom1

Serenade in Red
20″ × 16″
acrylic on canvas

Managing Editor, Market Books Department: Constance J. Achabal
Supervisory Editor: Mark Garvey
Production Editor: Andrew Lucyszyn

Writer's Market. *Copyright © 1997 by Writer's Digest Books. Published by F&W Publications, 1507 Dana Ave., Cincinnati, Ohio 45207. Printed and bound in the United States of America.* *All rights reserved. No part of this book may be reproduced in any form or by any electronic or mechanical means including information storage and retrieval systems without written permission from the publisher. Reviewers may quote brief passages to be printed in a magazine or newspaper.*

Library of Congress Catalog Number 31-20772
International Standard Serial Number 0084-2729
International Standard Book Number 0-89879-792-6

Special thanks to SRDS for allowing us to use their editorial descriptions for publications that did not respond to our request for information.

Cover design by Sandy Kent and Angela Lennert Wilcox

Attention Booksellers: This is an annual directory of F&W Publications. Return deadline for this edition is December 31, 1998.

Contents

Getting Published

Before Your First Sale 4

*The basics of writing for publication. Insider Reports offer insights for new writers. **Elaine DePrince** shares the struggle she had finding a publisher for her investigative and personal look at a family tragedy on **page 6**. **Cindy Brown** talks about her excitement at her first magazine article assignment on **page 12**. **J. Kevin Wolfe** discusses the path he took through self-publishing that led to a contract with a major publisher on **page 16**.*

Analyzing a Magazine From the Outside In, by Lisa Collier Cool 19

*You have the sample copies, now what do you do? An experienced writer shares tips on how to study a magazine for clues about its readers that help you target your articles appropriately. An Insider Report with **Kate Greer**, editor of the newly redesigned* Weight Watchers Magazine, *examines the philosophical, editorial and visual changes she has made, and what this means for potential freelancers on **page 22**.*

Query Letter Clinic, by Don Prues 25

Five magazine editors offer specific, real-life examples of queries that succeeded and queries that failed, with plenty of comments to help you understand why. A quick checklist of items a good query should contain is also included.

The Business of Writing

Minding the Details 40

*Information for the more experienced writer on negotiating and securing fair agreements, managing your rights and handling your earnings legally. **Dan Dieterich**, a writing consultant, offers tips on how writers can make money from selling their writing abilities, as well as their writing on **page 38**.*

Smooth Starting for Fulltime Freelancing, by John Lauerman 47

*What should you know before you make the leap? Important tips from how to stock your office to how to snag your clients from a successful author who faces the same questions in his own freelance career. Author **David Wright** talks about the various places his freelance career has taken him on **page 54**.*

How Much Should I Charge?, by Robin Gee 56

Robin Gee, a freelance writer/editor and former Writer's Digest Books editor, updates our annual guide to typical pay ranges for freelance jobs with tips and trends in the current market.

Interactive Writing, by Anthony Tedesco 68

Online magazines not only look and sound different, they are different from their print counterparts. One of Virtual City *magazine's top "Cyberstars," Tedesco offers practical advice on getting your work published online. An Insider Report on* **page 77** *revisits* **Randi Benton***, president of New Media for Random House, to find out how electronic book publishing is changing, moving away from CD-ROM and towards online publishing.*

Important Listing Information and Complaint Procedure 79

The Markets

Book Publishers 80

From A&B Publishers to Zondervan, hundreds of places to sell your book ideas. The introduction to this section helps you refine your approach to publishers. In an interview on **page 222***,* **Laura Minchew***, editorial director of the new Thomas Nelson imprint, Tommy Nelson, predicts that the children's Christian fiction market may offer a few surprises—it's not just Bible stories anymore! On* **page 264***,* **Kelli Spenser** *of Sams Publishing, a division of Macmillan Computer Publishing, talks about the opportunities for writers in technical publishing, when the manuscript must be right—and right on time.*

Canadian and International Book Publishers 316

The introduction to this section covers how to submit your work to international markets.

Small Presses 341

Companies publishing three or fewer books per year are listed here. Small presses often have narrowly tailored subjects—be sure to read the listing closely.

Book Producers 359

Book producers, or packagers as they are sometimes called, assemble the elements of books (writers, editors, designers and illustrators) for publishers.

Consumer Magazines 367

This section offers plentiful opportunities for writers with hundreds of listings for magazines on nearly every subject under the sun. The introduction offers tips on approaching consumer magazine markets and includes an interview with **Adrienne Brodeur***, editor of* Zoetrope*, one of the hottest new fiction magazines on* **page 577***.*

Trade, Technical and Professional Journals 795

Magazines listed in this section serve a wide variety of trades and professions. The introduction tells how to break in and establish yourself in the trades.

Scriptwriting 927

Markets for film and television scripts and stageplays are listed here.

Syndicates 968

Newspaper syndicates distribute writers' works around the nation and the world. The introduction offers advice for breaking into this market.

Greeting Cards & Gift Ideas 971

Greeting card and gift markets provide outlets for a wide variety of writing styles. The introduction to this section tells you how to approach these companies professionally.

Contests and Awards 982

Contests and awards offer many opportunities for writers, and can launch a successful writing career.

Resources

Publications of Interest 1042

Organizations of Interest 1044

Websites of Interest 1052

Glossary 1054

Book Publishers Subject Index 1058

General Index 1085

This edition is dedicated to the Managing Editor of the Market Books Department,

❧ Constance J. Achabal ☙

*We all have collective memories of Connie: the amazingly hot and
spicy foods she ate at our lunches out; her love of her garden;
the wonderful birthday cakes she baked for our birthdays.
We each also have private memories of her friendship:
her generous spirit, sense of humor and quiet grace.*

*Work will not be the same without Connie.
And we are not the same for having worked with her.*

From the Editors

Did you do a doubletake?

"This can't be *Writer's Market*. It's bigger. It's thicker. It's (gasp) . . . *paperback*!" Without even cracking the book, you know already that it's not your father's *Writer's Market*.

The 1998 edition started with a vision. We started by defining The Ideal Writer's Market: complete, comprehensive, reliable. It would provide more listings, more information in each listing, and more helpful reference material than any other directory.

With this vision in mind, we set out to make the best even better.

In U.S. Book Publishers, an editorial mission statement distinguishes one publishing house from another, so you can better target your submissions. More acquisitions editors' names, with specific areas of interest, help you get your work to the right person. More information on royalty rates and advances lets you know what to expect when you make the sale.

For the Consumer Magazine section, we did what all good freelancers do—requested writer's guidelines and sample copies. We added substantial information to many listings, particularly in the areas of pay rates, columns and departments, word lengths and expanded tips. The additional information gives a fuller view of the opportunities in each market.

We waged an aggressive campaign to obtain information on important publishers and magazines that may not have responded to our requests in the past. For those "must" listings, we present (at minimum) a name, address, phone number and contact person; an editorial thrust; the freelance submission policy; and payment information. While a number of these "musts" do not accept unsolicited submissions or rely on a pool of veteran freelancers, we felt that providing some information on these major markets presents a more comprehensive overview, giving less experienced readers a broader understanding of the publishing world while providing additional opportunities for more experienced and/or agented writers who use *Writer's Market*.

Compiling *Writer's Market* is never easy. But this year has been particularly challenging. A small army was gathered—busy phoning, faxing and filing until the book was bursting at the seams—to help us assemble an exceptional depth and breadth of information. Our goal has been to make the best even better. We welcome your comments at writersmarket@fwpubs.com.

On the first day of the recent American Library Association convention, several librarians told our marketing representative that *Writer's Market* was one of the books most frequently stolen from libraries. On the second day, several copies were missing from our display.

We want the 1998 *Writer's Market* to be your most timely, informative and comprehensive writing resource ever. Our vision was to create the market reference book you would reach for first. Apparently a few librarians agree with our vision!

Wishing you the best of luck and a successful year,

Kirsten Campbell Holm
Editor

Don Prues
Assistant Editor

Using Your *Writer's Market* to Sell Your Writing

Writer's Market is here to help you decide where and how to submit your writing to appropriate markets. Each listing contains information about the editorial focus of the market, how it prefers material to be submitted, payment information and other helpful tips.

IF YOU'VE BOUGHT *WRITER'S MARKET* BEFORE . . .

We've added a number of new features in this edition you should know about.

In the Book Publishers section, the contact persons are listed after the word **Acquisitions** and editors' areas of special interest follow their names. An editorial mission statement for each publisher sums up the philosophy underlying its publishing program. Imprints are listed under a new subhead, **Imprint(s)**; a name in boldface indicates a separate listing with more information specific to that individual imprint.

In magazines we have included substantial additional information this year, particularly in the area of columns and departments and updated pay rates. The **Reprints** heading provides information on approaching markets accepting previously published submissions.

Be sure to check out the new articles geared to more experienced writers in Minding the Details. In Smooth Starting for Fulltime Freelancing, John Lauerman helps you weigh the pros and cons of fulltime freelancing before you take the plunge. Anthony Tedesco's article, Interactive Writing, points out the verbal, visual and technical differences in writing for the exploding online market (and gives you the inside scoop on ten hot online magazines).

IF *WRITER'S MARKET* IS NEW TO YOU . . .

A quick look at the Table of Contents will familiarize you with the arrangement of *Writer's Market*. The three largest sections of the book are the market listings of Book Publishers; Consumer Magazines; and Trade, Technical and Professional Journals. You will also find sections for scriptwriting markets, syndicates, greeting card publishers and contests and awards. The section introductions contain specific information about trends, submission methods and other helpful resources for the material included in that section.

NARROWING YOUR SEARCH

After you've identified the market categories you're interested in, you can begin researching specific markets within each section.

Book Publishers are categorized, in the Book Publishers Subject Index, according to types of books they are interested in. If, for example, you plan to write a book on a religious topic, simply turn to the Book Publishers Subject Index and look under the Religion subhead in Nonfiction for the names and page numbers of companies that publish such books.

Consumer Magazines and Trade, Technical and Professional Journals are categorized by subject to make it easier for you to identify markets for your work. If you want to publish an article dealing with some aspect of retirement, you could look under the Retirement category of Consumer Magazines to find an appropriate market. You would want to keep in mind, however, that magazines in other categories might also be interested in your article (for example, women's magazines publish such material as well). Keep your antennae up while studying the markets: less obvious markets often offer the best opportunities.

INTERPRETING THE MARKETS

Once you've identified companies or publications that cover the subjects you're interested in, you can begin evaluating specific listings to pinpoint the markets most receptive to your work and most beneficial to you.

In evaluating an individual listing, first check the location of the company, the types of material it is interested in seeing, submission requirements, and rights and payment policies. Depending upon your personal concerns, any of these items could be a deciding factor as you determine which markets you plan to approach. Many listings also include a reporting time, which lets you know how long it will typically take for the publisher to respond to your initial query or submission. (We suggest that you allow an additional month for a response, just in case your submission is under further review or the publisher is backlogged.)

Check the Glossary at the back of the book for unfamiliar words. Specific symbols and abbreviations are explained in the table below. The most important abbreviation is SASE—self-addressed, stamped envelope. Always enclose one when you send unsolicited queries, proposals or manuscripts. This requirement is not included in most of the individual market listings because it is a "given" that you must follow if you expect to receive a reply.

A careful reading of the listings will reveal that many editors are very specific about their needs. Your chances of success increase if you follow directions to the letter. Often companies do not accept unsolicited manuscripts and return them unread. Read each listing closely, heed the tips given, and follow the instructions. Work presented professionally will normally be given more serious consideration.

Whenever possible, obtain writer's guidelines before submitting material. You can usually obtain them by sending a SASE to the address in the listing. You should also familiarize yourself with the company's publications. Many of the listings contain instructions on how to obtain sample copies, catalogs or market lists. The more research you do upfront, the better your chances of acceptance, publication and payment.

ADDITIONAL HELP

The book contains many articles on a variety of helpful topics. Insider Reports—interviews with writers, editors and publishers—offer advice and an inside look at publishing. Some listings contain editorial comments, indicated by a bullet (●), that provide additional information discovered during our compilation of this year's *Writer's Market*. E-mail addresses and websites have been included for many markets. Websites of Interest in the Resources section points you to writing-related material on the Web.

Newer or unpublished writers should read Before Your First Sale. Minding the Details offers valuable information about rights, taxes and other practical matters. There is also a helpful section titled How Much Should I Charge? that offers guidance for setting your freelance fees.

KEY TO SYMBOLS AND ABBREVIATIONS

●—Comment offering additional market information from the editors of *Writer's Market*
‡—New listing in all sections
□—Cable TV market in Scriptwriting section
ms—manuscript; **mss**-manuscripts
b&w—black and white (photo)
SASE—self-addressed, stamped envelope; **SAE**—self-addressed envelope
IRC—International Reply Coupon, for use on reply mail in countries other than your own.

See Glossary for definitions of words and expressions used in writing and publishing.

Getting Published

Before Your First Sale

Many writers new to the craft feel that achieving publication—and getting paid for their work—is an accomplishment so shrouded in mystery and magic that there can be little hope it will ever happen to *them*. Of course, that's nonsense. All writers were newcomers once. Getting paid for your writing is not a matter of insider information or being handed the one "key" to success. There's not even a secret handshake.

Making money from your writing will require three things of you:
- Good writing;
- Knowledge of writing markets (magazines and book publishers) and how to approach them professionally;
- Persistence.

Good writing without marketing know-how and persistence might be art, but who's going to know if it never sells? A knowledge of markets without writing ability or persistence is pointless. And persistence without talent and at least a hint of professionalism is simply irksome. But a writer who can combine the above-mentioned virtues stands a good chance of not only selling a piece occasionally, but enjoying a long and successful writing career.

You may think a previously unpublished writer has a difficult time breaking into the field. As with any profession, experience is valued, but that doesn't mean publishers are closed to new writers. While it is true some editors prefer working with established writers, most are open to professional submissions and good ideas from any writer, and quite a few magazine editors like to feature different styles and voices.

In nonfiction book publishing, experience in writing or in a particular subject area is valued by editors as an indicator of the author's ability and expertise in the subject. As with magazines, the idea is paramount, and new authors break in every year with good, timely ideas.

As you work in the writing field, you may read articles or talk to writers and editors who give conflicting advice. There are some norms in the business, but they are few. You'll probably hear as many different routes to publication as writers you talk to.

The following information on submissions has worked for many writers, but it's not the *only* method you can follow. It's easy to get wrapped up in the specifics of submitting (should my name go at the top left or right of the manuscript?) and fail to consider weightier matters (is this idea appropriate for this market?). Let common sense and courtesy be your guides as you work with editors, and eventually you'll develop your own most effective submission methods.

TARGETING YOUR IDEAS

Writers often think of an interesting story, complete the manuscript and then begin the search for a suitable publisher or magazine. While this approach is common for fiction, poetry and screenwriting, it reduces your chances of success in many other writing areas. Instead, try choosing categories that interest you and study those sections in *Writer's Market*. Select several listings that you consider good prospects for your type of writing. Sometimes the individual listings will even help you generate ideas.

Next, make a list of the potential markets for each idea. Make the initial contact with markets using the method stated in the market listings. If you exhaust your list of possibilities, don't give up. Reevaluate the idea, revise it or try another angle. Continue developing ideas and approaching markets with them. Identify and rank potential markets for an idea and continue the process.

As you submit to the various periodicals listed in *Writer's Market*, it's important to remember that every magazine is published with a particular slant and audience in mind. Probably the number one complaint we hear from editors is that writers often send material and ideas that are completely wrong for their magazines. The first mark of professionalism is to know your market well. That knowledge starts here in *Writer's Market*, but you should also search out back issues of the magazines you wish to write for and learn what specific subjects they have published in past issues and how those subjects have been handled.

Prepare for rejection and the sometimes lengthy wait. When a submission is returned, check your file folder of potential markets for that idea. Cross off the market that rejected the idea and immediately mail an appropriate submission to the next market on your list. If the editor has given you suggestions or reasons as to why the manuscript was not accepted, you might want to incorporate these when revising your manuscript.

About rejection. Rejection is a way of life in the publishing world. It's inevitable in a business that deals with such an overwhelming number of applicants for such a limited number of positions. Anyone who has published has lived through many rejections, and writers with thin skin are at a distinct disadvantage. The key to surviving rejection is to remember that it is not a personal attack—it's merely a judgment about the appropriateness of your work for that particular market at that particular time. Writers who let rejection dissuade them from pursuing their dream or who react to each editor's "No" with indignation or fury do themselves a disservice. Writers who let rejection stop them do not publish. Resign yourself to facing rejection now. You will live through it, and you will eventually overcome it.

QUERY AND COVER LETTERS

A query letter is a brief but detailed letter written to interest an editor in your manuscript. It is a tool for selling both nonfiction magazine articles and nonfiction books. With a magazine query you are attempting to interest an editor in buying your article for her periodical. A book query's job is to get an editor interested enough to ask you for either a full proposal or the entire manuscript. (Note: Some book editors accept proposals on first contact. Refer to individual listings for contact guidelines.) Some beginners are hesitant to query, thinking an editor can more fairly judge an idea by seeing the entire manuscript. Actually, most nonfiction editors prefer to be queried.

There is no query formula that guarantees success, but there are some points to consider when you begin. Queries should:

- Be limited to one page, single-spaced, and address the editor by name (Mr. or Ms. and the surname).
- Grab the editor's interest with a strong opening. Some magazine queries begin with a paragraph meant to approximate the lead of the intended article.
- Indicate how you intend to develop the article or book. Give the editor some idea of the work's structure and contents.
- Let the editor know if you have photos available to accompany your magazine article (never send original photos—send duplicates).
- Mention any expertise or training that qualifies you to write the article or book. If you've published before, mention it; if not, don't.
- End with a direct request to write the article (or, if you're pitching a book, ask for the go-ahead to send in a full proposal or the entire manuscript). Give the editor an idea of the expected length and delivery date of your manuscript.

Some writers state politely in their query letters that after a specified date (slightly beyond the listed reporting time), they will assume the editor is not currently interested in their topic and

INSIDER REPORT

Don't be intimidated, be persistent

Elaine DePrince

Mother, author, and AIDS education activist Elaine De-Prince knows the value of hanging on. As a special education teacher, and the mother of five boys, she enjoyed the daily adventures and tribulations of childhood. When her sons Michael and Cubby developed HIV from contaminated blood products, she helped them hang on and savor life for as long as they could. After their deaths, she began to tell the story of how they and thousands of other hemophiliacs contracted HIV/AIDS through unregulated contaminated blood products. Her perseverance led to the publication of *Cry Bloody Murder* (Random House, 1997), a story she calls an indictment of corporate greed and governmental indifference.

In 1993, after the death of her son Cubby, DePrince lectured to audiences about the link between AIDS and blood clotting disorders. At one lecture, she asked the audience to define the term "hemophiliac." "This young woman raised her hand," DePrince recalls, "and said 'It sounds like homosexual, and it sounds like pedophilia. Is it a sexual disorder?' " DePrince says that innocent question prompted her to start writing about what she calls the greatest medical tragedy in the history of our nation.

"I was a first-time author with no credentials," she admits. "I was no journalist, I had won no Pulitzer Prize, but I *had* a story to tell." Although DePrince had written children's stories, she had no investigative experience. But she was determined to tell this story, and she started with the people she met during her sons' illnesses.

"I interviewed everyone I could," she says. "Scientists, consumers, families affected by this. I sent questionnaires throughout the country to doctors at hemophilia centers." As she sorted through the pieces of the story, DePrince began to receive documents anonymously through the mail that had been introduced as evidence in hemophilia/AIDS court cases around the country. The book began to come together.

The process was not easy. DePrince enjoys writing and the academic discipline of pulling a coherent narrative out of a jumble of impressions, interviews and documents. She was also angry about what had happened to her sons, and that anger fueled her energy. But when it came to writing about her own family, the process became much more difficult. "I had to write in the middle of the night, without interruption. I would have been a bear to live with if I'd tried to write about our experiences during the day, because of the emotional roller coaster."

As difficult as the book was to write, looking for a publisher was even more difficult. Finding an agent to represent the book was even harder. DePrince listened in amazement while agent after agent told her the book was too heavy, too limited, or too long. Several agents accepted the manuscript, only to let it lie in a desk drawer for weeks. "I really could have crumbled at that point," DePrince says, "just figure I gave it my best shot and go on my way." Instead, she began her own assault on the publishing industry.

INSIDER REPORT, *DePrince*

"I sent out 96 query letters," she recalls. The only positive responses came from academic publishers, and she finally sent the manuscript to Vanderbilt University Press, who turned it over to an outside reader, Robert K. Massie. Massie's own books on the Russian royal family, *Nicholas and Alexandra* and *The Romanovs*, as well as personal experience, gave him some insight on hemophilia. He wasted no time and called DePrince immediately.

"He was just hysterical," DePrince says with relish. "He said 'What are you doing? You've got to send this book to a commercial publisher.' " Armed with the name of Massie's editor but prepared for rejection, DePrince sent the manuscript, complete with academic footnotes and annotations, to Random House. She was unprepared for the reception she got.

"They loved it," she says. Her editor had a few suggestions: drop the academic annotations, include more information about her own family, but DePrince says the process was much easier than she had anticipated. "My editor gave me a lot of leeway. She was very light-handed, because she felt I was a good writer and I had a good book. Which I appreciated, but it amazed me, because it was so unlike the response I'd gotten from others."

The book was published in July 1997, almost exactly four years after the death of her son Cubby. Even before the book was released, Massie printed an almost unheard of eight-page review in *The New Yorker*. DePrince says the magazine's reputation for rigorous fact-checking gave her book an added authority. "People knew I wasn't some hysterical mother making unsubstantiated claims, but that I had solid information." A starred review in the well-respected *Kirkus Reviews* also helped validate DePrince's work. DePrince has written a screenplay based on the book and is working with an agent and a major studio. "I think part of the interest here is how I was able to stick with this," she says.

In retrospect, she thinks the process taught her a lot about what *not* to do with agents and publishers. "I wish someone had told me you don't let an agent just hold on to a manuscript for eight weeks," she says. "I wish someone had told me to be more aggressive from the very beginning, because I lost a lot of time just waiting around."

DePrince's success with the investigative research in her book has led to other offers. The New Jersey chapter of the American Trial Lawyers Association has asked her to research the use of court-sealed documents in product liability cases. DePrince says the prospect intrigues her, and she'd like to work on it—eventually. After the emotional strain of *Cry Bloody Murder*, she wants to write something lighter as a "mental health break." She has already begun her first novel, *My Benjamin*. Set in 18th century New Jersey, the novel is about a child born with severe cranio-facial anomalies and his relationship with his mother, his family, and the rest of his world. "The theme of the book is the love the family has for this less-than-perfect child." DePrince drew her inspiration from the families of disabled children she met through her sons. While she concedes the novel sounds heavy, she promises "it has a really great ending!"

DePrince continues to write and lead AIDS awareness presentations, and she and her husband have established a non-profit foundation in New Jersey to help children with medical disorders deal with the discrimination they face.

DePrince insists perseverance made her book possible, and it is advice she readily gives to other authors. While searching for a publisher she met a newspaper reporter who had written a powerful series about hemophiliacs and AIDS. He had tried to write a book and had sent out 20 query letters. But he concluded there was no interest in such a book and

---

INSIDER REPORT, *continued*

warned her about getting too wrapped up in her crusade to find a publisher. DePrince says her willingness to send out nearly 100 queries and her refusal to give up were the reasons she succeeded.

"If you truly believe you have something of value to share, don't give up," DePrince says. The publishing world can be an intimidating place, she warns, and it pays to do your research and be prepared. But in the end there is no substitute for persistence. "Don't be intimidated," she advises, "be persistent. And just hang on."

—Alison Holm

---

will submit the query elsewhere. It's a good idea to do this only if your topic is a timely one that will suffer if not considered quickly.

A brief single-spaced cover letter enclosed with your manuscript is helpful in personalizing a submission. If you have previously queried the editor on the article or book, the cover letter should be a brief reminder, not a sales pitch. "Here is the piece on goat herding, which we discussed previously. I look forward to hearing from you at your earliest convenience."

If you are submitting to a market that considers unsolicited complete manuscripts, your cover letter should tell the editor something about your manuscript and about you—your publishing history and any particular qualifications you have for writing the enclosed manuscript.

Once your manuscript has been accepted, you may offer to get involved in the editing process, but policy on this will vary from magazine to magazine. Most magazine editors don't send galleys to authors before publication, but if they do, you should review the galleys and return them as soon as possible. Book publishers will normally involve you in rewrites whether you like it or not.

See the article Query Letter Clinic in this edition of *Writer's Market* for specific real-life examples of query letters that worked (and some that didn't), along with editors' comments. For more information about writing query letters, read *How To Write Attention-Grabbing Query & Cover Letters*, by John Wood (Writer's Digest Books).

Querying for Fiction

Fiction is sometimes queried, but most fiction editors don't like to make a final decision until they see the complete manuscript. Most editors will want to see a synopsis and sample chapters for a book, or a complete short story manuscript. Consult individual listings for specific fiction guidelines. If a fiction editor does request a query, briefly describe the main theme and story line, including the conflict and resolution.

BOOK PROPOSALS

Most nonfiction books are sold by book proposal, a package of materials that details what your book is about, who its intended audience is, and how you intend to write it. Most fiction is sold either by complete manuscript, especially for first-time authors, or by two or three sample chapters. Take a look at individual listings to see what submission method editors prefer.

The nonfiction book proposal includes some combination of a cover or query letter, an overview, an outline, author's information sheet and sample chapters. Editors also want to see information about the audience for your book and about titles that compete with your proposed book.

If a listing does not specify, send as much of the following information as you can.

• The cover or query letter should be a short introduction to the material you include
  in the proposal.

- An overview is a brief summary of your book. For nonfiction, it should detail your book's subject and give an idea of how that subject will be developed. If you're sending a synopsis of a novel, cover the basic plot.
- An outline covers your book chapter by chapter. The outline should include all major points covered in each chapter. Some outlines are done in traditional outline form, but most are written in paragraph form.
- An author's information sheet should—as succinctly and clearly as possible—acquaint the editor with your writing background and convince her of your qualifications to write about the subject.
- Many editors like to see sample chapters, especially for a first book. In fiction it's essential. In nonfiction, sample chapters show the editor how well you write and develop the ideas from your outline.
- Marketing information—i.e., facts about how and to whom your book can be successfully marketed—is now expected to accompany every book proposal. If you can provide information about the audience for your book and suggest ways the book publisher can reach those people, you will increase your chances of acceptance.
- Competitive title analysis is an integral part of the marketing information. Check the *Subject Guide* to *Books in Print* for other titles on your topic. Write a one- or two-sentence synopsis of each. Point out how your book differs and improves upon existing titles.

A WORD ABOUT AGENTS

An agent represents a writer's work to publishers, negotiates publishing contracts, follows up to see that contracts are fulfilled and generally handles a writer's business affairs, leaving the writer free to write. Effective agents are valued for their contacts in the publishing industry, their savvy about which publishers and editors to approach with which ideas, their ability to guide an author's career and their business sense.

While most book publishers listed in *Writer's Market* publish books by unagented writers, some of the larger ones are reluctant to consider submissions that have not reached them through a literary agent. Companies with such a policy are so noted in the listings.

For more information about finding and working with a literary agent, see *Guide to Literary Agents* (Writer's Digest Books). The *Guide* offers listings of agents as well as helpful articles written by professionals in the field.

PROFESSIONALISM AND COURTESY

Publishers are as crunched for time as any other business professional. Between struggling to meet deadlines without exceeding budgets and dealing with incoming submissions, most editors find that time is their most precious commodity. This state of affairs means an editor's communications with new writers, while necessarily a part of his job, have to be handled efficiently and with a certain amount of bluntness.

But writers work hard too. Shouldn't editors treat them nicely? Shouldn't an editor take the time to point out the *good* things about the manuscript he is rejecting? Is that too much to ask? Well, in a way, yes. It *is* too much to ask. Editors are not writing coaches; much less are they counselors or therapists. Editors are in the business of buying workable writing from people who produce it. This, of course, does not excuse editors from observing the conventions of common business courtesy. Good editors know how to be polite (or they hire an assistant who can be polite for them).

The best way for busy writers to get along with (and flourish among) busy editors is to develop professional business habits. Correspondence and phone calls should be kept short and to the point. Don't hound editors with unwanted calls or letters. Honor all agreements, and give every assignment your best effort. Pleasantness, good humor, honesty and reliability will serve you as well in publishing as they will in any other area of life.

You will occasionally run up against editors and publishers who don't share your standard of business etiquette. It is easy enough to withdraw your submissions from such people and avoid them in the future.

WRITING TOOLS

Typewriters and computers. For many years, *the* tool of the writer's trade was the typewriter. While many writers continue to produce perfectly acceptable material on their manual or electric typewriters, more and more writers have discovered the benefits of writing on a computer. Editors, too, have benefited from the change; documents produced on a computer are less likely to present to the editor such distractions as typos, eraser marks or globs of white correction fluid. That's because writing composed on a computer can be corrected before it is printed out.

If you think computers are not for you, you should reconsider. A desktop computer, running a good word processing program, can be the greatest boon to your writing career since the dictionary. For ease of manipulating text, formatting pages and correcting spelling errors, the computer handily outperforms the typewriter. Many word processing programs will count words for you, offer synonyms from a thesaurus, construct an index and give you a choice of typefaces to print out your material. Some will even correct your grammar (if you want them to). When you consider that the personal computer is also a great way of tracking your submissions and staying on top of all the other business details of a writing career—and a handy way to do research if you have a modem—it's hard to imagine how we ever got along without them.

Many people considering working with a computer for the first time are under the mistaken impression that they face an insurmountable learning curve. That's no longer true. While learning computer skills once may have been a daunting undertaking, today's personal computers are much more user-friendly than they once were.

Whether you're writing on a computer or typewriter, your goal should be to produce pages of clean, error-free copy. Stick to standard typefaces, avoiding such unusual styles as script or italic. Your work should reflect a professional approach and consideration for your reader. If you are printing from a computer, avoid sending material printed from a low-quality dot-matrix printer, with hard-to-read, poorly shaped characters. Many editors are unwilling to read these manuscripts. New laser and ink jet printers, however, produce high-quality pages that *are* acceptable to editors. Readability is the key.

Electronic submissions. Many publishers are accepting or even requesting that final manuscript submissions be made on computer disk. This saves the magazine or book publisher the expense of having your manuscript typeset, and can be helpful in the editing stage. The publisher will simply download your finished manuscript into the computer system they use to produce their product. Be sure to mention if you are able to submit the final manuscript on disk. The editors will let you know what computer format they use and how they would like to receive your material.

Some publishers who accept submissions on disk also will accept electronic submissions by modem. Modems are computer components that can use your phone line to send computerized files to other computers with modems. It is an extremely fast way to get your manuscript to the publisher. You'll need to work out submission information with the editor before you send something via modem.

Fax machines and e-mail. Fax machines transmit copy across phone lines. E-mail addresses are for receiving and sending electronic mail over a computer network, most commonly the Internet. Those publishers who wanted to list their fax machine numbers and e-mail addresses have done so.

Between businesses, the fax has come into standard daily use for materials that have to be sent quickly. In addition, some public fax machines are being installed in airports, hotels, libraries and even grocery stores. However, do not fax or e-mail queries, proposals or entire manscripts to editors unless they specifically request it. A proposal on shiny fax paper curling into itself on the editor's desk makes an impression—but not the one you want. If your proposal is being considered, it will probably be routed to a number of people for their reactions. Fax paper won't stand up well to that amount of handling. Writers should continue to use traditional means for sending manuscripts and queries and use the fax number or e-mail address we list only when an editor asks to receive correspondence by this method.

Letters and manuscripts sent to an editor for consideration should be neat, clean and legible. That means typed (or computer-printed), double spaced, on $8\frac{1}{2} \times 11$ inch paper. Handwritten materials will most often not be considered at all. The typing paper should be at least 16 lb. bond (20 lb. is preferred). Very thin papers and erasable bond papers are not recommended for manuscripts.

The first impression an editor has of your work is its appearance on the page. Why take the chance of blowing that impression with a manuscript or letter that's not as appealing as it could be?

You don't need fancy letterhead for your correspondence with editors. Plain bond paper is fine. Just type your name, address, phone number and the date at the top of the page—centered or in the right-hand corner. If you want letterhead, make it as simple and businesslike as possible. Many quick print shops have standard typefaces and can supply letterhead stationery at a relatively low cost. Never use letterhead for typing your manuscripts. Only the first page of queries, cover letters and other correspondence should be typed on letterhead.

MANUSCRIPT FORMAT

When submitting a manuscript for possible publication, you can increase its chances of making a favorable impression by adhering to some fairly standard matters of physical format. Many professional writers use the format described here. Of course, there are no "rules" about what a manuscript must look like. These are just guidelines—some based on common sense, others more a matter of convention—that are meant to help writers display their work to best advantage. Strive for easy readability in whatever method you choose and adapt your style to your own personal tastes and those of the editors to whom you submit. Complete information on formats for books, articles, scripts, proposals and cover letters, with illustrated examples, is available in *The Writer's Digest Guide to Manuscript Formats*, by Dian Dincin Buchman and Seli Groves (Writer's Digest Books).

Most manuscripts do not use a cover sheet or title page. Use a paper clip to hold pages together, not staples. This allows editors to separate the pages easily for editing. Scripts should be submitted with plain cardstock covers front and back, held together by Chicago or Revere screws.

The upper corners of the first page of an article manuscript contain important information about you and your manuscript. This information should be single-spaced. In the upper *left* corner list your name, address and phone number. If you are using a pseudonym for your byline, your legal name still must appear in this space. In the upper *right* corner, indicate the approximate word count of the manuscript, the rights you are offering for sale and your copyright notice (© 1998 Ralph Anderson). A handwritten copyright symbol is acceptable. (For more information about rights and copyright, see Minding the Details on page 40.) For a book manuscript include the same information with the exception of rights. Do not number the first page of your manuscript.

Center the title in capital letters one-third of the way down the page. Set your typewriter to double-space. Type "by" and your name or pseudonym centered one double-space beneath that.

After the title and byline, drop down two double-spaces, paragraph indent, and begin the body of your manuscript. Always double-space your manuscript and use standard paragraph

INSIDER REPORT

Shelving her shoes to make a first sale

Cindy Brown

In Saginaw, Michigan, people know Cindy Brown for her dancing and videography, not her writing. No surprise there: For years Brown has spent most of her time on her singing telegram service, Rainbow Grams, and the television show she films, *Adventures with Ol' Grizz* (Ol' Grizz is her husband). Recently, however, Brown has shelved her dancing shoes in pursuit of bylines.

Although Brown has written press releases for newspapers and magazines for years, she's never been happy with the way other writers worked her material into print. "Reporters would take my promotional materials to write their own article, but they would really just copy a few paragraphs of mine and print them, often way out of context."

In June of 1996, Brown launched a publicity campaign for *Adventures with Ol' Grizz* and read Marcia Yudkin's *Six Steps to Free Publicity* (Plume, 1994). Yudkin advised that to get an article written the way you envisioned, you should write it yourself. Considering Brown's past disappointments with promotional pieces she'd passed on to others, Yudkin's advice struck her profoundly. "I thought, I can do this, and then I won't have to worry about being misquoted and taken out of context." So she did.

While working on *Adventures with Ol' Grizz*, Brown tested and was so impressed with a new weatherproof camcorder system (the LJ&L) she decided to write something to publicize it. "I loved the LJ&L and I thought, 'The guy who came up with this should get some publicity.' So I started out writing a press release, but that graduated to a 400-word article, thanks to all the advice and encouragement I found in Yudkin's book."

In July, Brown sent simultaneous queries to *Camcorder* and *Videomaker* magazines. Two months later she received a "no" from *Videomaker* and a "yes" from *Camcorder*. Bob Wolenik, editor at *Camcorder*, obviously liked Brown's query, but Brown doesn't think it was that exceptional. "The writing in my query letter wasn't too funny or catchy. I think he liked the idea more than anything." He obviously liked something, because he asked Brown if she could expand the proposed piece from 400 to 2,000 words.

"To tell you the truth," says Brown. "I had no idea how long 2,000 words would be but I was so delighted I impulsively said, 'Sure, I'll expand it.' He wanted more information about how I used the camera and other anecdotes. I was really excited by his request."

Brown was so excited, in fact, she forgot to ask what she'd get paid for the piece. Unsure how to go about finding out, she called our offices at *Writer's Market* to ask what *Camcorder* pays. We obviously couldn't offer her a specific figure, as each deal is negotiated individually, so we suggested she give the editor a call. "In a calm voice I told Mr. Wolenik that we forgot to discuss my fee," says Brown. She negotiated and was paid $300—not bad for a first sale. But $300 isn't all Brown made from this piece.

Smart freelance writers make the most of their time by recycling stories. Brown learned

INSIDER REPORT, *Brown*

this early and has successfully reworked that first piece into additional sales to hunting magazines. "I realized this camcorder can appeal to a variety of people other than video techies who read *Camcorder* magazine," she says. "Hunters, lodge-owners, drug-enforcement officers, department store security, anyone wanting a revolutionary surveillance camera, would be interested in the LJ&L."

In addition to learning how to make more than one sale from a single article, Brown has learned another key way to get the most from her writing: adding photographs. "I've found that I've got to be a photographer as well as a writer," she says. "Editors really seem to like it, especially at the smaller publications, when you can provide your own pictures. It saves them the extra trouble of finding and paying a professional photographer." Offering photos not only makes a writer more marketable but it can also bring in more money, as most magazines pay extra for photos they run with a piece.

Brown attributes much of her first-sale success to research she conducted before submitting her queries. "I think it's so important for writers to learn the business of writing. Because most of them probably know the craft of writing, what's holding them back is the business know-how. Lots of what I've learned about getting published came from reading books on writing and publishing. Writers, no matter how great, need to understand the business and present their writing properly."

Now that Brown has placed a few articles, she's overcoming her fear of rejection. "I know I'm going to be rejected, but that's just part of this business. I also know I won't make any hits if I don't go for it."

Hence her parting advice for those who seek publication but fear the rejection that goes along with it: "If you want to do it, do it. Nobody is going to beat you up or put you in jail for not liking what you offer. All they can do is say no. It's no big deal. I once heard this saying that still impresses me: 'A ship in the harbor is safe in the harbor, but that's not what ships are built for.' You don't want to look back when you're 90 and say, 'Gosh, I wish I had become a writer.' "

—*Don Prues*

indentations of five spaces. Margins should be about 1½ inches on all sides of each full page of typewritten manuscript.

On every page after the first, type your last name, a dash and the page number in either the upper left or right corner. The title of your manuscript may, but need not, be typed on this line or beneath it. Page number two would read: Anderson—2. Follow this format throughout your manuscript.

If you are submitting novel chapters, leave the top one-third of the first page of each chapter blank before typing the chapter title. Subsequent pages should include the author's last name, the page number, and a shortened form of the book's title: Anderson—2—Skating. (In a variation on this, some authors place the title before the name on the left side and put the page number on the right-hand margin.)

When submitting poetry, the poems should be typed single-spaced (double-space between stanzas), one poem per page. For a long poem requiring more than one page, paper clip the pages together. You may want to write "continued" at the bottom of the page, so if the pages are separated, editors, typesetters and proofreaders won't assume your poem ends at the bottom of the first page.

ESTIMATING WORD COUNT

Many computers will provide you with a word count of your manuscript. Your editor will count again after editing the manuscript. Although your computer is counting characters, an editor or production editor is more concerned with the amount of space the text will occupy on a page. Several small headlines, or subheads, for instance, will be counted the same by your computer as any other word of text. An editor may count them differently to be sure enough space has been estimated for larger type.

For short manuscripts, it's often quickest to count each word on a representative page and multiply by the number of pages. You can get a very rough count by multiplying the number of pages in your manuscript by 250 (the average number of words on a double-spaced typewritten page). Do not count words for a poetry manuscript or put the word count at the top of the manuscript.

To get a more precise count, add the number of characters and spaces in an average line and divide by six for the average words per line. Then count the number of lines of type on a representative page. Multiply the words per line by the lines per page to find the average number of words per page. Then count the number of manuscript pages (fractions should be counted as fractions, except in book manuscript chapter headings, which are counted as a full page). Multiply the number of pages by the number of words per page you already determined. This will give you the approximate number of words in the manuscript.

PHOTOGRAPHS AND SLIDES

The availability of good quality photos can be a deciding factor when an editor is considering a manuscript. Many publications also offer additional pay for photos accepted with a manuscript. Check the magazine's listing when submitting black & white prints for the size an editor prefers to review. The universally accepted format for transparencies is 35mm; few buyers will look at color prints. Don't send any transparencies or prints with a query; wait until an editor indicates interest in seeing your photos.

On all your photos and slides, you should stamp or print your copyright notice and "Return to:" followed by your name, address and phone number. Rubber stamps are preferred for labeling photos since they are less likely to cause damage. You can order them from many stationery or office supply stores. If you use a pen to write this information on the back of your photos, be careful not to damage the print by pressing too hard or by allowing ink to bleed through the paper. A felt tip pen is best, but you should take care not to put photos or copy together before the ink dries.

Captions can be typed on a sheet of paper and taped to the back of the prints. Some writers, when submitting several transparencies or photos, number the photos and type captions (numbered accordingly) on a separate 8½ × 11 sheet of paper.

Submit prints rather than negatives or consider having duplicates made of your slides or transparencies. Don't risk having your original negative or slide lost or damaged when you submit it.

PHOTOCOPIES

Make copies of your manuscripts and correspondence before putting them in the mail. Don't learn the hard way, as many writers have, that manuscripts get lost in the mail and that publishers sometimes go out of business without returning submissions. You might want to make several good quality copies of your manuscript while it is still clean and submit them while keeping the original manuscript as a file copy.

Some writers include a self-addressed postcard with a photocopied submission and suggest in the cover letter that if the editor is not interested in the manuscript, it may be tossed out and a reply returned on the postcard. This practice is recommended when dealing with international markets. If you find that your personal computer generates copies more cheaply than you can pay to have them returned, you might choose to send disposable manuscripts. Submitting a disposable manuscript costs the writer some photocopy or computer printer expense, but it can save on large postage bills.

MAILING SUBMISSIONS

No matter what size manuscript you're mailing, always include a self-addressed, stamped envelope (SASE) with sufficient return postage that is large enough to contain your manuscript if it is returned.

A manuscript of fewer than six pages may be folded in thirds and mailed as if it were a letter using a #10 (business-size) envelope. The enclosed SASE can be a #10 folded in thirds or a #9 envelope which will slip into the mailing envelope without being folded. Some editors also appreciate the convenience of having a manuscript folded into halves in a 6×9 envelope. For manuscripts of six pages or longer, use 9×12 envelopes for both mailing and return. The return SASE may be folded in half.

A book manuscript should be mailed in a sturdy, well-wrapped box. Enclose a self-addressed mailing label and paper clip your return postage to the label.

Always mail photos and slides First Class. The rougher handling received by standard mail could damage them. If you are concerned about losing prints or slides, send them certified or registered mail. For any photo submission that is mailed separately from a manuscript, enclose a short cover letter of explanation, separate self-addressed label, adequate return postage and an envelope. Never submit photos or slides mounted in glass.

To mail up to 20 prints, you can buy photo mailers that are stamped "Photos—Do Not Bend" and contain two cardboard inserts to sandwich your prints. Or use a 9×12 manila envelope, write "Photos—Do Not Bend" and make your own cardboard inserts. Some photography supply shops also carry heavy cardboard envelopes that are reusable.

When mailing a number of prints, say 25-50 for a book with illustrations, pack them in a sturdy cardboard box. A box for typing paper or photo paper is an adequate mailer. If, after packing both manuscript and photos, there's empty space in the box, slip in enough cardboard inserts to fill the box. Wrap the box securely.

To mail transparencies, first slip them into protective vinyl sleeves, then mail as you would prints. If you're mailing a number of sheets, use a cardboard box as for photos.

Types of Mail Service

- First Class is an expensive way to mail a manuscript, but many writers prefer it. First Class mail generally receives better handling and is delivered more quickly. Mail sent First Class is also forwarded for one year if the addressee has moved, and is returned automatically if it is undeliverable.
- Priority mail reaches its destination within 2-3 days. To mail a package of up to 2 pounds costs $3, less than either United Parcel Service or Federal Express. First Class mail over 11 ounces is classified Priority.
- Standard mail rates are available for packages, but be sure to pack your materials carefully because they will be handled roughly. To make sure your package will be returned to you if it is undeliverable, print "Return Postage Guaranteed" under your address.
- Certified Mail must be signed for when it reaches its destination. If requested, a signed receipt is returned to the sender. There is a $1.35 charge for this service, in addition to the required postage, and a $1.10 charge for a return receipt.
- Registered Mail is a high-security method of mailing where the contents are insured. The package is signed in and out of every office it passes through, and a receipt is returned to the sender when the package reaches its destination. The cost depends on the weight, destination and whether you obtain insurance.

INSIDER REPORT

Cooking up something good

In cooking, as in publishing, there are many different approaches, depending on your confidence. The timid chef can pick up a microwave entree on the way home from work, while the bold cook may start with homemade mayonnaise and secret blends of spices. When J. Kevin Wolfe decided to publish his first cookbook, he took the adventurous route, starting from scratch.

J. Kevin Wolfe

Wolfe, who produces a successful Cincinnati radio show, always knew he wanted to write a cookbook. Both parents were accomplished cooks, and he grew up surrounded by good food. "But you need a hook," he says. "I couldn't just come out with 'Kevin Wolfe's Cookbook.'" In 1992 he went on a low-fat diet to lose weight. Rather than limit himself to rabbit food and broiled chicken breasts, he began to tinker with recipes, trying to replicate the tastes he craved. When he shared his concoctions with a friend in the publishing business, he realized he'd found the hook. And the *Low-Fat Junk Food Cookbook* was born.

But writing the book was only the first step. As the manuscript took shape, Wolfe began seeking advice from other friends in the publishing industry. He began to consider self-publishing when he realized what a small profit authors realize with conventional arrangements. "With a first book, you're talking about a six percent figure," he says, "minus your literary agent's 15 percent. For a $15 dollar book, you're suddenly making less than $1 a copy."

Preparation is as essential in publishing as in cooking, and Wolfe did his research carefully. In addition to talking to everyone he could, he consulted *The Complete Guide to Self-Publishing* (Writer's Digest Books, 1994), by Marilyn and Tom Ross, "the Bible of self-publishing," as he calls it. Wolfe says the advice helped him avoid some obstacles, and gave him some much-needed encouragement. For example, "the process of laying out the book was much more than I'd bargained for," he says ruefully. Working on a vintage word processor, he had to draft each page separately, and every correction and addition meant starting over again.

Finally, completed manuscript in hand, he began shopping for printers. He planned a small run of 500-1,000 copies, but the quotes from local printers sent him into "sticker shock." "I had read that you need to make your book cost 20 percent of the retail price," he recalls. "And I was getting $11 quotes for a $15 book. It occurred to me I could print the book in my basement for half that." So he took the next step, and plunged himself into the world of printing.

"I bought a Yugo-sized copier and put it in the basement," he says, along with a binder, paper cutter and other paraphernalia. His initial investment was about $6,000, but he points out that the cost of each successive book went down. He printed an initial run in the basement and began selling them out of his home. At the same time he undertook distribu-

INSIDER REPORT, *Wolfe*

tion and promotion as well.

Initial sales came from newspaper articles, but he quickly realized he needed a more effective sales strategy. "I knew I wasn't going to get into the food section of every paper in the country," he says. So he turned to local bookstores, offering them a 20 percent discount. Sales of the books began to take off, and he was confronted with an unexpected problem.

"At one point I had 1,200 orders in my hands," he recalls, "and no books to send people." Despite the best efforts of his basement copier, he simply couldn't keep up with demand. He did a time analysis of his production methods and determined it took him six to ten minutes to produce a single copy. At that rate he realized he was producing fewer than 50 copies a day. So he returned to local printers, this time with an order for 10,000 copies.

"That made the difference," he says. Because of the larger run, the cost per book dropped to about $2. And the printer delivered the books within a week, freeing Wolfe to concentrate on publicity and promotion.

Despite the obstacles, Wolfe enjoyed the experience. So much so that, two years later, he came out with the *Low-Fat Real Food Cookbook*, based on the same successful formula. In addition to developing the recipes, writing the text and inking the humorous line drawings that illustrate the chapter headings, he handled much of the distribution and publicity himself. He says negotiating his own contracts gave him a sense of control, even if it did create some headaches.

"At one time I turned down a pretty lucrative deal from a really large book company," he recalls. Despite a very appealing initial offer, the company seemed ambiguous about what it wanted, and what it would do. "So I turned down a fairly good deal, but probably saved myself a lot of heartache in the process," Wolfe acknowledges.

Eventually he negotiated a contract with Crown Books. Even there, his experience as his own publisher and printer stood him in good stead. "I've had friends in the business tell me I got a good contract," he says, "better than they would have gotten." And the Yugo-sized copier in his basement is still getting some exercise. When Wolfe wanted to test the market for a collection of recipes developed with his five-year-old son Tristan, he ran off several hundred copies for Christmas, 1996. That gave him the information he needed to decide whether to market the book more aggressively.

Although he now has an agent and a contract with Crown Books, Wolfe says his experience with self-publishing was invaluable. And he says "doing-it-yourself" is sometimes the only option open to first-time authors. "It's an unfortunate reality," Wolfe says, "but getting in with a literary agent is just as difficult as getting your book on the desk of a publisher."

Wolfe says there is no substitute for market research, and asking others to take a good, hard look at your manuscript. And he says the maxim "Don't quit your day job" is trite but true. "Things are very shaky," he warns. "Some weeks you may have a lot of orders, and some weeks you have nothing."

Wolfe says he's out of the self-publishing business now, preferring to leave that to the experts. But he's holding onto his basement copier. "You never know," he laughs, "there may be some book project in the future where I say, 'Hmmm, I really need 200 copies of that . . .' "

—Alison Holm

- If you're in a hurry to get your material to your editor, you have a lot of choices these days. In addition to fax and computer technologies mentioned earlier, overnight and two-day mail services are provided by both the U.S. Postal Service and several private firms. More information on next day service is available from the U.S. Post Office in your area, or check your Yellow Pages under "Delivery Services."

Other Correspondence Details

Use money orders if you are ordering sample copies or supplies and do not have checking services. You'll have a receipt, and money orders are traceable. Money orders for up to $700 can be purchased from the U.S. Postal Service for an 85 cents service charge. Banks, savings and loans, and some commercial businesses also carry money orders; their fees vary. *Never* send cash through the mail for sample copies.

Insurance is available for items handled by the U.S. Postal Service but is payable only on typing fees or the tangible value of the item in the package—such as typing paper—so your best insurance when mailing manuscripts is to keep a copy of what you send. Insurance is 75 cents for $50 or less and goes up to a $45.70 plus postage maximum charge for $5,000.

When corresponding with publishers in other countries, International Reply Coupons (IRCs) must be used for return postage. Surface rates in other countries differ from those in the U.S., and U.S. postage stamps are of use only within the U.S. Currently, one IRC costs $1.05 and is sufficient for one ounce traveling at surface rate. Canadian writers pay $3.50 for an IRC which is redeemable for 46 cents in postage.

Because some post offices don't carry IRCs (or because of the added expense), many writers dealing with international mail send photocopies and tell the publisher to dispose of them if the manuscript is not appropriate. When you use this method, it's best to set a deadline for withdrawing your manuscript from consideration, so you can market it elsewhere.

International money orders are also available from the post office for a $3 charge.

RECORDING SUBMISSIONS

Once you begin submitting manuscripts, you'll need to manage your writing business by keeping copies of all manuscripts and correspondence, and by recording the dates of submissions.

One way to keep track of your manuscripts is to use a record of submissions that includes the date sent, title, market, editor and enclosures (such as photos). You should also note the date of the editor's response, any rewrites that were done, and, if the manuscript was accepted, the deadline, publication date and payment information. You might want to keep a similar record just for queries.

Also remember to keep a separate file for each manuscript or idea along with its list of potential markets. You may want to keep track of expected reporting times on a calendar, too. Then you'll know if a market has been slow to respond and you can follow up on your query or submission. It will also provide you with a detailed picture of your sales over time.

Analyzing a Magazine From the Outside In

BY LISA COLLIER COOL

What's the best way to identify promising markets for your article ideas? The secret is knowing how to size up unfamiliar publications quickly—by learning to read them as a prospective writer. A *reader* skims through a magazine reading the articles that strike his fancy and skipping the rest. A *writer* analyzes everything in the magazine from the ads to the articles, looking for clues that will show him how to sell to that magazine. This attitude is what will give you that extra edge over the competition, making points with editors and ultimately paying off in sales.

WHAT TO STUDY

The cover. While you can judge a magazine by its cover, you're likely to get a superficial impression. *New York* magazine is obviously a regional publication, but with eight million stories in the "naked city," which one should you pitch? Let's take a closer look at that cover; two stories are featured as I write this: "Clinton: Fire Your Lawyer," and "Summer Fun: The Hottest Beaches, Sports, Fashion, Shopping, Books, Food, Movies, Kid Stuff, and More." Since cover stories are the ones editors see as the most important in that particular issue, right off we know these editors are interested in politics, current events, recreation, fashion, food and trends—possible areas to consider for your submissions to this publication.

The table of contents. Since considerable creativity goes into composing the contents, often writers are confused by the differing terms and are unable to distinguish staff-written material from freelance pieces, or they waste time scrutinizing staff-written magazines that are not potential markets for their material. In the table of contents, staff-written pieces often appear without author bylines, while titles of freelance pieces are normally credited to their authors. If *no* bylines appear in the table of contents, the magazine is almost certainly staff-written; for further confirmation compare bylines of the actual articles with the list of "contributing editors" or "staff writers" in the masthead of the magazine. (If no bylines accompany the articles either, the magazine is definitely staff-written.) Checking for author biographies (usually called "bios" by editors) at the end of published articles will also help you identify freelance articles. "Joan Smith owns Renovations Unlimited and is currently writing a book on home renovations" implies that the author does not work for the magazine regularly.

The table of contents is likely to be divided into at least two categories, one containing "articles" and "features" and another listing "columns" and "departments." While some magazines favor more fanciful terms, or group material by subject, your goal should be to learn which articles are regular, monthly features ("Cosmo Tells All") and which are one-shots ("Birth Control Update"). While the majority of freelance work will appear in the articles and features sections, some regular columns and departments also buy freelance material. Others are completely staff-written. To determine which columns or departments are potential markets for you, compare each bylined name with the masthead—if the writer works for the magazine, the column

---

LISA COLLIER COOL *is an award-winning medical journalist and co-author of* Bad Boys: Why We Love Them, How to Live With Them and When to Leave Them (*Dutton, 1997*).

isn't open to freelance work. Another test is to check two or more issues. If a byline appears each month, the column is probably done by freelancers. Also look for small print at the end of the column—some magazines include writing tips and prices paid to encourage submissions.

The articles. Having several issues on hand is particularly helpful since some article types may not appear in each issue. You'll want to note *length* (one printed magazine page with no ads is usually about 1,000 words; or count the number of words in one inch of columns and measure the article with a ruler to get a more exact count). Then look at what kind of *research* is favored: numerous quotes from experts, book references, news breaking reportage, popularization of scientific research, personal experience, author expertise, or intellectual analysis of ideas. Now consider *tone*: witty, practical, sophisticated, intellectual, sexy, step-by-step how-to, emotional, or chatty. Finally, look for *distribution* of subject matter: if the last three issues contain ten self-help articles and one humor piece, you'll have some idea of the relative demand for these two article types. Knowing the magazine's editorial standards will help you structure suitable queries.

The columns and departments. In addition to being possible markets for your writing, these can also indicate what *not* to write about. A column may completely satisfy the magazine's need for a certain kind of material, or it may limit submission possibilities for a particular topic. While some magazines buy freelance book or record reviews, for example, freelance sales are unlikely if a regular column already covers new releases. Sometimes taking a specialized angle may overcome this problem: "The All-Time Best Love Songs," or "Finding Nonsexist Children's Books." If a column covers a very broad subject area like travel, check several recent issues before making submissions in the same area. Freelance articles on the subject, if any, are likely to be either longer or more specialized. Being aware of recent coverage also prevents you from making overlapping submissions.

The regular features can also help you construct a profile of the typical reader. Consider what these departments tell you about the *Cosmopolitan* reader: "Cosmo Body," "Cosmo Health," "Cosmo Diet," "Style Counsel," "Beauty Q and A," "Cosmo Tells All," "Best Gets" (fashion update), "Inside Hollywood," "Cosmo Careers," "Cosmo Controversy," "Agony" (self-help advice), "Cosmo Cash," "Dating and Relating," "Decorating," and "Bedside Astrologer." Right off you see the Cosmo girl is quite interested in her looks, her body and her mind. She's upwardly mobile ("Cosmo Careers" and "Cosmo Cash"), but immersed in pop culture ("Bedside Astrologer," "Inside Hollywood"), and probably single (the horoscope is for her *man*, not her husband). Extrapolating from this, you can imagine the typical reader as an upwardly mobile administrative assistant searching for her male counterpart.

The ads. Since advertisers spend vast sums to pinpoint appropriate markets for their products, put this valuable research to use by learning all you can about the demographics of the readership: age, sex, lifestyle, income level, social class and interests. Let's take a look at *Child* magazine. Its name immediately identifies children as the reader's most salient interest, but who exactly is that reader? A quick glance at the ads: Huggies diapers, Ford Windstar minivan, swimming pool covers, Baby Magic lotions, Claritan antihistamine syrup, suggests that the main audience is women—mothers—with above-average income (hence the swimming pool covers and $20,000 minivan). With this in mind, finding suitable angles on articles slated for this publication is much simpler.

Scrutiny of the ads can also suggest *topics* to write about. Since *Child* has many ads for diapers, baby food, infant toys, and children's medicines, good articles might be: "The Best Over-the-Counter Remedies for Your Child," "Starting Your Baby on Solid Food," and "What to Do About Diaper Rash."

The editor's page. Though some magazines don't carry one, this page is your opportunity to meet the top editor "up close and personal," as sportscasters say. Often the editor either discusses what interests him/her about some of the major articles, or imparts philosophical reflections about the magazine's subject matter. Both give you insights into the editor's mental outlook and interests that can be reflected in your queries. In a recent issue of *PC: The Independent Guide to IBM Personal Computers*, "From the Editor-in-Chief" talked about the long hours devoted to two features in the magazine as well the editor's curiosity about the new directions of computer technology—either for good or evil (think Big Brother). What this suggests to me as a writer is that this editor is looking for thoroughly researched, thought-provoking stories about IBM PC-related hardware and software.

In a recent issue of *Child*, editor Pamela Abrams wrote about her husband being honored for volunteering at their nine-year-old's school, and how expert he is at packing a diaper bag for their younger son. A writer might follow up these leads with such article proposals as "Balancing Work and Fatherhood" or "Mothers and Sons," ideas that should strike a chord with this editor.

Letters to the editor. If the magazine runs reader mail, two helpful nuggets can be gleaned from it. First, you can infer subject matter of previous articles you might have missed, broadening your understanding of the magazine's emphasis. Second, the readers' reactions both tell you what does and doesn't work in this magazine. The readers' comments can sometimes suggest affiliated article topics to consider for future queries: if reader X complains that something wasn't covered, your query might focus on that subject.

"In the next issue" announcements. Like letters to the editor, this clues you in to additional topics that interest the magazine and shows the editor's priorities as major articles are emphasized in such announcements.

As you sharpen your skill to size up market needs, you'll soon find the process becomes automatic—so even a casual read turns up ideas or approaches that can open more markets for your writing. Once you make reading like a writer a habit, you could soon find that your favorite magazine's next cover story is . . . *your* article!

INSIDER REPORT

Zeroing in on changing markets

Targeting your markets is not as easy as it seems. Sure, some writers will send off the same query letter to 20 magazines in a given category, hoping at least one editor will want the article. The judicious writer, however, discerns the subtle differences among magazines and tailors the query accordingly. But if you are one of those writers who thinks all magazines in a category are "basically the same," perhaps it's time to reevaluate your stance—especially if you haven't been generating many sales.

Photo by Bob Levy

Kate Greer

Magazines make strategic changes to set themselves apart from their competitors. That's why writers are constantly told to examine the past few issues of a magazine before submitting, even if it's one they've been reading for years. How many writers do this? According to editors, not many. Desperately busy trying to make sales, frustrated writers adopt the I've-seen-50-issues-of-this-magazine-over-the-years-and-I-don't-need-to-see-another attitude. They query the magazine, failing to notice what's changed in recent issues. Can anything *that* radical happen to a magazine that's been around for so long? Yes. Because it's a volatile business: New magazines launch. Outmoded magazines die. Existing magazines change.

The gears definitely are changing at *Weight Watchers Magazine*. Southern Progress (*Southern Living, Cooking Light*) recently bought it from Weight Watchers International, and momentous changes have followed. Most notably, the magazine has a new editor, Kate Greer, who's making so many burly improvements that *Weight Watchers* is literally bursting at its seams. Small isn't always beautiful.

And maintaining a magazine isn't improving it, which is why Southern Progress put *Weight Watchers* in Greer's hands. For 17 years, Greer served as an editor at *Better Homes & Gardens* until she moved to Pace Communications and totally revamped United Airlines' in-flight magazine, even changing the magazine's name. Under Greer's command, *Hemispheres* has won numerous editorial and design awards since its inception in 1992. Greer also served as an editor at *Reader's Digest*.

A new editor at a magazine is more than just a name change on the masthead. In Greer's case, aside from the title, the entirety of *Weight Watchers* has been overhauled, from design, layout and page count to editorial content and advertising. Why all the changes? As Greer puts it, "Although *Weight Watchers* had a circulation of one million before the buyout, it wasn't really much of a magazine. It had been what we call underpublished. It had become more of a promotional extension of the company [Weight Watchers International] than it was a real magazine for readers. We wanted to change that."

One major change since Greer's takeover has been the inclusion of an editor's column. It's not just an introduction to the Table of Contents (or a long-winded, text version of it). "I hate an editor's column that is nothing more than a duplication of the Table of Contents,

INSIDER REPORT, *Greer*

or that tells how difficult it was to get a story or photograph. Knowing these things doesn't help the reader." Obviously for Greer, some magazines are better without an editor's introduction. Not *Weight Watchers*. "It's important to have an editor's note in a magazine like *Weight Watchers* because there is such an emotional bond with readers, and the editor has to become a persona who talks directly to them. I sit down to write it and it's like writing a letter to a friend."

In addition to the editor's column, Greer has made wholesale changes to the magazine's design. All one needs to do is look at the last issue (October, 1996) published by the former owners and compare it to an issue published under Greer. "They [Weight Watchers International] weren't approaching it so much as publishers," she says. "They restricted who could advertise in it by not taking advertisements for products that competed with Weight Watchers International Foods. There was no Lean Cuisine, no Healthy Choice, for instance. Also, the editorial was spotty and the design and artwork were dated. In effect, for us it's been like a start up."

A major focus of Greer's "start up" has been enhancing the design and feel of *Weight Watchers*, because she believes the graphics should be consistent with the message in the words. "The quality or the level of information provided should be in an environment that reflects the same quality," says Greer. "A picture really is worth a thousand words. I want this to be a magazine readers will be proud of. I want them to feel good when and about reading it. I want advertisers to feel their ads are in a good environment. And I want the writers and photographers who work with us to feel proud when they see their work in our publication."

When analyzing a magazine, writers can't ignore the importance of its cover, particularly when the magazine's aesthetic has evolved. With *Weight Watchers*, the difference between the new and old covers is striking: The new covers do not have close-ups of thin, blonde models posing with hands on hips. Instead, they showcase active women who are only a small part of the cover's larger landscape. "Women can look at

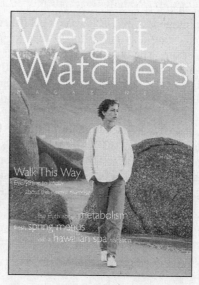

INSIDER REPORT, *continued*

our cover photos and identify with them. A model standing there staring at you with her hands on her hips doesn't reflect anything of my life as a reader. With the new *Weight Watchers*, we're telling readers this magazine is for and about them." Greer wasted no time getting her point across, as the January/February 1997 cover featured a woman smeared in mud—an image you would never find on the cover of the old *Weight Watchers*. Says Greer, "That sent the signal we wanted to send: THIS IS A DIFFERENT MAGAZINE."

By now it's easy to see how the new *Weight Watchers* differs from the old, but how can writers discern what distinguishes *Weight Watchers* from other diet-related magazines? Analyzing the editorial slant of the articles is one way to detect subtle distinctions. Ask yourself: What is this editor trying to do to make this magazine stand out from its competitors? If you look hard enough, you'll find answers.

For example, according to Greer *Weight Watchers* is the only magazine that directly focuses on living a healthy life by means of weight control. "People compare us to *Cooking Light*, but that's an epicurean magazine for people who love to cook. Ours is not; it's about weight control. Sure, every month almost every woman's magazine is going to have something about weight loss or shaping up. But no one else has our mix of psychology, motivation and information. We're approaching the reader holistically, not just about issues of weight. For us many other factors enter into the picture, such as mindset, which is so important, as is nutrition and exercise. Professionals are making great advances in nutrition sciences and we let our readers in on the scientific information, but the writing and presentation are clear and not couched in jargon."

Writers also should discern a magazine's tone. Is it academic, sarcastic, chatty, humorous, belligerent, stiff, quirky? "I think the voice of our magazine is pretty darn clear, and professional writers pick up on that," says Greer. "They should also be able to tell that I respect the reader. I also like to include illustrations that complement the tone of the articles. Writers are basic to the magazine and we are predominantly freelance-written. Writers are our lifeblood. I treasure them and want them to look at the magazine and know that."

While in the past *Weight Watchers* published numerous articles on looking thin, losing weight and eating only fatless foods, such topics are not what Greer's *Weight Watchers* is primarily about. The new *Weight Watchers* concentrates on managing health, not losing weight—a healthy body makes a beautiful body for Greer. "The message I want repeated is not thinness and weight loss but getting to and maintaining a healthy weight, and that's clear in our articles," she emphasizes. The title is, after all, *Weight Watchers* not *Weight Losers*.

Without analyzing recent issues of *Weight Watchers*, chances are you'd be submitting material that's slightly "off" to an editor who's no longer there for a magazine that doesn't exist. So forgo rapid-fire shots in the dark and target your submissions appropriately. Although it might take a little time upfront, studying recent issues of a magazine before querying will put you more than a few steps closer to the bull's-eye. Then it's time to fire away.

—*Don Prues*

Query Letter Clinic

by Don Prues

The most indispensable companion to an unsold piece of writing is its query letter. Whether you're trying to sell a 100-word sidebar, a 4,000-word feature article, a 60,000-word nonfiction book or a 100,000-word novel, you need a darn good query letter to go with it. Period.

The *Writer's Encyclopedia* defines a query letter as "a sales letter to an editor that is designed to interest him in an article or book idea." The query is your opportunity to quickly convince an editor to buy your piece. With so many submissions to evaluate, editors tend to make fast judgments. So you must pitch a tight and concise query that explains the gist of your piece, why readers will want to read it, and why you're the perfect person to write it. Otherwise you're likely to sabotage your submission.

PRE-QUERY PROVISIONS

Identifying what to omit and what to include in your query can mean the difference between earning a sale or receiving a rejection. Before you end up making some serious query writing mistakes, take some precautions before submitting.

Trust the editor and suppress your paranoia. Some writers exclude important information from a query fearing the editor will "steal" their idea. Bad move. Editors aren't thieves, and leaving important information out of your query will only increase your chances of keeping yourself out of print. As will mentioning fees in your query; it will send your query straight to the can. If you're an unpublished writer, don't mention that either. Finally, never include a separate cover letter with your query letter. The query is your cover letter, your letter of inquiry, and your letter of intent—all packed into one tightly-wrapped, single-spaced page.

While some rules are meant to be broken, the rule of keeping a query to one page remains intact. Editors want to ensure it stays that way. The one-page query is not just a minor formality; it makes a lot of sense editorially. If you can't explain your idea in less than a page, you're probably not too clear about the idea itself.

Just because a query is simply one page don't assume it is simple to compose. A saleable query demands you include all the right information in a small space. Addressing your query to the appropriate editor is most important. Ensure this by calling the editorial office and asking who handles the type of material you're submitting. If you want to write a travel piece for a magazine, call and ask for the name and title of the travel editor. That's it. Don't ask to speak with the travel editor; merely get the correct spelling of his name. Always type or word process your query and put it on simple letterhead—editors want good ideas, not fancy fonts and cute clip art. Make your salutation formal; no "Dear Jim" or "Hello" (just today I saw two queries with these exact salutations!). And always offer an estimated word count and delivery date.

COMPOSING THE QUERY

You're ready to write your letter. Introduce your idea in a sentence or two that will make the editor curious, such as an interesting fact, an intriguing question, or maybe something humorous. Then state your idea in one crisp sentence to grab the editor's attention. But don't stop there. Reel in the editor with one or two paragraphs expounding upon your idea. Walk through the steps of your project and explain why you're the perfect person to write what you're proposing. List your sources, particularly if you have interviews lined up with specialists on your topic, as this will help establish the credibility of your work.

The Ten Query Commandments	The Ten Query Sins
Each query letter must be:	No query letter must ever be:
1. Professional (includes SASE, is error-free, is addressed to the right editor, etc.).	1. Wordy (text rambles; length exceeds one-and-a-half pages).
2. New (idea is fresh, set off, and up front).	2. Sketchy (idea isn't fleshed out enough).
3. Provocative (lead pulls you in).	3. Presumptuous (tone is too cocky).
4. Creative (presentation is offbeat).	4. Egotistical (topic is yourself).
5. Focused (story is narrowed down, length is kept to one page).	5. Reluctant (lame reason why you're doing it).
6. Customized (slanted to that magazine).	6. Loose-lipped (article is offered on spec).
7. Multifaceted (offers several options on how it could be done).	7. Stubborn (prior rejects from same editor haven't given you the hint).
8. Realistic (instills confidence that you're reliable and the project's doable).	8. Intrusive (phone call precedes or supplants query).
9. Accredited (includes your clips, credits, and qualifications).	9. Inappropriate (clips don't match the idea).
10. Conclusive (confirms that you're the best and only writer to do it).	10. Careless (faults are mentioned or major gaffe is made).

*From *How To Write Attention-Grabbing Query & Cover Letters,* by John Wood (Writer's Digest Books)

The tone of your writing is also important. Create a catchy query laden with confidence but devoid of cockiness. Include personal information only if it will help sell your piece, such as previous writing experience with the topic and relevant sample clips. And never forget a SASE. (Before sending your queries, use Andrew Scheers's Query Letter Checklist on page 27.)

Most questions about queries revolve around whether to send simultaneous submissions. There's no clear-cut way to wisdom here. Sending simultaneous queries to multiple editors is typically okay if you inform all editors you're doing so. But beware: Some editors refuse to read simultaneous queries (*Writer's Market* listings indicate whether an editor is not receptive to them) because they want an exclusive option to accept or reject your submission. This can be a problem if these editors do not respond quickly; it leaves you hanging and keeps you from submitting to other markets. The two clear advantages to sending simultaneous queries are that you have many lines in the water at once and it prompts a rapid reply—an editor excited by your query will be more apt to get back to you knowing the competition could get to you first.

Something else you must keep in mind: The query letter, however important, should not be better than the manuscript. Be sure your piece can deliver what you propose. All too often editors receive promising queries, make the assignment, and then receive something they can't publish. While a bad query can prevent an editor from considering your idea, an exaggerated, misleading query that does not fulfill its promises will guarantee you won't be offered another assignment.

Unpublished writers wonder how published writers break into print. It's not just a matter of luck; published writers construct compelling queries. What follows are eight actual queries submitted to editors. Four queries are strong; four are not. Detailed comments from the editors show what the writer did and did not do to secure a sale. As you'll see, there's no such thing as a boilerplate "good" query; every winning query works its own magic. Study the following examples so you can both avoid the pitfalls of those that failed and learn from those that went on to publication.

ANDREW SCHEER'S QUERY LETTER CHECKLIST

CONTENT
1. Working title (to help editors grasp your idea quickly)
2. Summary of topic or theme
3. Intended reader application (takeaway value)
4. Approximate article length (e.g., 800 words, 1,500 words)
5. Sample paragraph: lead or key segment (a big help in assessing your writing)
6. Paragraph summarizing key supporting material (e.g., anecdotes, interviews)
7. Your qualifications to write on this topic (incl. writing experience, if applicable)

MECHANICS
1. Current magazine title
2. Current magazine address
3. Correct editor (when in doubt, ask first)
4. Correct spelling of editor's name
5. Neat, error-free typing
6. One page, single-spaced
7. Self-addressed, stamped envelope (SASE) (hint: fold it in thirds)
8. Mailed in #10 business envelope

INFORMATION ABOUT YOU
1. Your name
2. Your title (Miss, Ms., Mrs., Mr., Dr., etc.)
3. Your address
4. Your day phone number (fax, e-mail if available)

INFORMATION ABOUT YOUR ARTICLE
1. Approximate article length (e.g., 500 words, 1,200 words)
2. When article is available (e.g., immediately, in 4 weeks)
3. Rights available (first, one-time, or reprint)

OPTIONAL (in descending order of potential usefulness)
1. Samples (include only if applicable/impressive to this publication)
2. Reply Postcard
3. Letterhead (avoid unconventional stock or too many dingbats)
4. Business Card

DON'TS
1. Phone or fax (unless urgent article, e.g., L.A. earthquake story on 1/18/95)
2. Unrealistic deadline ("If I don't hear from you in one week...")
3. Query for a topic that's just been given major coverage
4. Confess unfamiliarity with the magazine
5. Request guidelines as part of your query
6. "Dear Editor"/"Occupant" letter
7. Long or vague letter
8. Bad attitude (antagonistic, defeatist)
9. Query for type of articles the magazine doesn't print

There's no special format that results in a yes; let it reflect you and the nature of your topic.

Clean, simple letterhead

(Good Query)

Hugh Arclose
1234 Good Query Rd.
Almost, OH 45209
(513)555-8781

Frank Murray, Editor
Better Nutrition for Today's Living
6255 Barfield Road
Atlanta, GA 38328

April 3, 1995

Unusual placement of date but not a big deal.

Dear Mr. Murray:

Here are some interesting facts:

A very stimulating start, especially since the info is actually interesting. It's also brief, factual, clean and structured—very to the point.

- Pineapple contains bromelain, a natural anti-inflammatory that relieves muscoskeletal injuries.

- Tea contains polyhydroxy phenolic compounds that inhibit tumors and reduce the risk of lung cancer.

- The herb St. John's Wort is proving itself a natural antidepressant that's proven to elevate serotonin levels in the brain.

- Women who drink two or more cups of coffee a day are 60 percent less likely to commit suicide.

This is good: "I propose an article meeting your exact specifications." Writer knows exactly where he's going.

I propose a 1500 word article that outlines and explains some highly surprising results from recent research on fruits, vegetables and herbs. I can offer you charts showing the compounds various foods contain and what benefits each provides.

"Here's where I will obtain my information." All reputable sources.

My sources include studies from *JAMA*, the *Journal of the National Cancer Institute*, the *Australian Journal of Medical Herbalism*, *British Medical Journal* and the *Japanese Journal of Cancer Research*.

"This is not just a hobby of mine. I work at it full-time. Here's who I am and why I'm qualified."

I write fulltime and have published over 150 articles in such national health and fitness magazines as *Your Health*, *Weight Watchers*, *Remedy Magazine*, *Nourish*, *Better Health* and *Fit*. Other credits include *Time* and *Discover* magazines. Enclosed are clips and a writing résumé.

(May I write this article for you?) Thank you and I look forward to hearing from you soon.

A little weak, but he closes the query acceptably.

Sincerely,

Hugh Arclose

—All bases are covered completely in line with our normal coverage.

—Makes me interested to see the piece.

—Sale? No, because letter was addressed to previous editor and all our freelance spots were filled. But if letter was sent to me now, I would give writer a call.

John Denied
1234 Sorry Lane
Nowhere, Ohio 49382

March 19, 1997

Better Nutrition
13th Floor
5 Penn Plaza — *Basic Rules of Address not followed.*
New York, NY 10001
Attn: Article Editor — *Immediately this triggers "Rejectable" b/c writer doesn't take time to get my name.*

   Subj: The attached article submission — *My suspicions tell me this, somehow. Not a memo.*

Dear Editor: — *Can't take time to get my name?*

   It has come to my understanding that your publication accepts material submitted by freelance writers concerning recipes for new healthy and tasty dishes. For your consideration, I have enclosed two article submissions concerning sweet desserts that are also quite healthy.

This is a terribly wordy and formal opening. Very uninteresting and strangely worded. Poorly written with unnecessary and repeated verbiage. Concerning recipes?

   Included you will also find my published credits that highlight some of the successes I have enjoyed as a freelance writer over the past fifteen years. If you want a detailed résumé or biography regarding my writing career, I would be happy to provide one at your earliest request.

   I have many ideas for other articles which may interest you in the future. May I submit to you other material which may interest your readers? As is customary, I've enclosed a SASE for your convenience and will look forward to hearing from you at your earliest opportunity. Thank you.

Such as...Tell me these ideas. Is one skiing in the French Alps? If you can't interest me how will you interest our readers? Too vague.

All this "At your earliest convenience," "may," "concerning" is double-duty of simple words & phrases.

                                    Sincerely,

                                    John Denied
                                    Freelance Writer

Enclosure

Why does he feel the need to tell me this? Unnecessary occupational "title," which can give a juvenile impression.

—*Are words and phrases at a premium today? Apparently.*

—*This query is flat and unclear and uninformative. Not enticing at all.*

Great Query!

Judy Published
1234 Winning Query Lane
Somewhere, Ohio 45207

July 11, 1995

Mary Lou Carney
Guideposts for Kids
16 East 34th Street
New York, NY 10016

Dear Ms. Carney:

Readers can identify with him.

Philip Newberry is a typical ten-year-old boy. He enjoys bouncing on a trampoline, throwing a spiral football pass, swinging a bat, and playing soccer. On a recent Saturday, the opening game whistle blew. Philip raced forward, and kicked the soccer ball. It sailed 30 feet; his leg flew after it. No big deal. Philip reattached his prosthetic leg while his team-mates pressed into action to take advantage of the diversion.

Wow! Surprise! I will keep reading.

Humor—always welcome. This will not be a "pity piece" or a sermon.

Philip laughs about the one time a referee called "hands" on him. He held up his stubby arms and yelled, "They called hands on me!"

When Philip was two years old, meningitis turned his limbs black. Close to death, doctors amputated his left hand to the elbow, his right hand at the wrist, and both legs just below the knees. The surgery saved his life.

Positive role model—just the kind of "positive thinking" GP4K loves!

Philip believes that he can still do anything he sets his mind to. He shares this message with other children who face the challenges of a handicap. He is featured on a video for Scottish Rite Children's Hospital in Dallas, Texas.

she knows our magazine.

I believe that Philip Newberry is a perfect candidate for your "Featuring Kids" column. I have interviewed him and attended one of his YMCA soccer games. I have color snapshots taken during the game.

Photo reference available—helpful to art/production depts.

I am proposing a 300-word profile. I look forward to your reaction to this submission.

Right length for us.

I have written feature articles for Focus on the Family's *Single Parent Family* and *Christian Single* magazines.

Sincerely,

she's a published professional.

Judy Published

This turned out to be a great profile. We did our own photo shoot, and this became our cover story.

Mary Rejected
1234 Sorry Lane
Nowhere, Ohio 49382

Mary Lou Carney, Editor
℅ Guidepost ——— *Doesn't even know the*
747 Third Avenue   *name of my magazine!*
NY, NY 10017

Dear Mary Lou: *If you have to tell me*   *A one-size-fits-all story? We*
                   this, they probably are.   *are a publication for kids.*

Enclosed you will find four short stories about Alice, Andrew, Cindy and Tara.
These are not preachy stories, but I do believe they may have a message for
children as well as parents.
                   Don't tell me more   *Does she really consider*
                   than you need to!   *this as "published"?*   *— Did I need to know*
                                                                              this?

Although I've never had anything published other than want ads and my education is limited, my life experiences have taught me much about the nature of
children. My home has always been a kid magnet and I can write about them. I
have taught my children and my grandchildren to love books and reading. My
dream is that someday they will see something of mine in print.

— Laughable
image—kids
clinging to the
side of her house.

— Ack! The guilt
factor. If I
refuse...

I thank you sincerely for considering my stories.

                                Sincerely yours,

                                Mary Rejected

P.S. Please excuse my handwriting, my typewriter is in the shop.

                        Borrow one! Go to the
                        library! Wait until
                        you get it back!

Everything about this query marked
her as a novice—a novice too lazy to
present her or her writing in the best
possible light. No sell here!

Great Query!

Chris Sold
1234 Published Lane
Somewhere, Ohio 45207

July 9, 1996

Ms. Kimberly Ridley
Hope Magazine
Box 160
Brooklin, ME 04616

Dear Ms. Ridley:

This starts off great, showing she's read the magazine. Very important!

After reading founder Jon Wilson's Dec. 1996 editorial "Home and Family" and his call for ideas/activities that could make a difference in the lives of the homeless, I thought you might be interested in "Cooking Up Comfort" for your front-of-the-magazine section.

Good to specify title and to target specific section. Good hook. I'm curious.

Briefly: At the same time that they're mastering the intricacies of preparing appetizing meals, 640 aspiring chefs at the prestigious culinary school at Johnson & Wales University in Providence, RI, are learning lessons in life. While they prepare for careers at some of the nation's top restaurants, they must also, thanks to an unusual scholastic requirement, contribute their developing skills to people more concerned with where their next meal may be coming from than with gourmet elegance or eye-catching presentation. To help low-income, often homeless residents, each student donates 24 hours of their time a year to cooking—and serving up—meals at four soup kitchens in their city.

Strong synopsis with pertinent & interesting details.

While they contributed 15,360 hours of slicing, dicing, broiling and baking this year, coming up with nutritious meals is only part of the challenge. Instead of the fine meats and foodstuffs they deal with in their state-of-the-art school kitchens, they usually face a haphazard potpourri of donated canned food and leftovers from local restaurants. They also witness the effects of poverty close up. At the same time that they manage to conjure up good meals from accidental ingredients (lunch might include stir-fried beef with mushrooms, onions and sauteed vegetables), many report increased compassion and understanding.

Offers a good sense of those helping and those in need.

Excellent! We love them.

In 1,000 words and with strong emphasis in anecdotes, I would also include:
—Information on how and why the program was started.
—Quotes from students on what they have learned from their experiences.
—The perspective of the schools' professors, as well as community leaders' views, on the value of the students' efforts.

This too is great. It shows the writer has thought through her approach.

I am a national award-winning freelance writer with 15 years' experience and credits from national, regional and local publications. Clips are available upon request. I look forward to hearing from you.

Establishes her credibility.

Always essential.

Sincerely,

Great query that grasps our mission and offers a focused synopsis of subject, why it matters and how she'll approach it. She's done her homework by doing background work and thinking a lot about her story before pitching it.

Chris Sold

No Sale

Al Tryagain
1234 Sorry Lane
Nowhere, Ohio 49382

November 28, 1996

Editorial Director — *Can't get my name?*
Icon Thoughtstyle Magazine
595 Broadway
New York, NY 10012

Dear Sir, — *Who's this? Bad to assume editor is a man.*

Not ICON! We aren't interested in "easy guides."

Query re: ''A Beginner's Guide to Brandy''

So you want to impress your boss with an after-dinner brandy but you think a snifter is a kind of dog? Then ''A Beginner's Guide to Brandy'' is for you.

We would never care about impressing people in such a superficial manner.

The article would describe the unique vocabulary of brandies and the difference between a VS, VSOP, and an XO brandy. It will also detail how brandies are produced, how they are aged, how they should be stored, how to drink them (yes, there is a proper way), and how to choose a snifter. It is aimed as a department piece for *ICONnoisseur*.

What department?

I am a freelance writer and ardent wine lover, the author of four books and over fifty magazine articles, including pieces in *Wine Tidings, Leisure World, Southwest Art, Country Journal, Discovery* and many others. Sample clips are enclosed. The article would run about 1500 words and could be ready within four weeks. I would appreciate receiving a copy of your writer's guidelines.

This is good to know if we wanted to run the article.

Thank you for your time in reviewing this idea. I look forward to your response (and congratulations on the new magazine).

Sincerely,

Al Tryagain

This stuff is fine and written well, but it needs a hook. He includes all the right information about his credentials and his proposed piece—except why we need to publish it.

—*The biggest problem with this query is its first sentence. We want to interest people, not impress them.*

—*While this guy seems like a great writer, the piece sounds a bit dry, and lacks a human interest angle— we need such an angle to grab our readers' attention.*

—*We avoid all things like "A Beginners Guide." It's too simple. We need something unique/interesting about this topic.*

Debra Inprint — *A familiar*
1234 Published Lane   *name from*
Somewhere, OH 45207   *past successful*
(604)333-0000   *articles.*

September 30, 1994

Andrew Scheer
Moody Magazine
820 N. LaSalle Dr.,
Chicago, IL 60610

Dear Mr. Scheer,

Wow! A real attention grabber. It's good to get right into a strong quote from the piece.

Mom cleared her throat. "Before I sign anything, I want to make certain that no black families can buy my house." My jaw dropped open. She had just been telling the agent how we were all Christians! What would he think about Christians now?

shows her position and lets me know a bit about her.

I was appalled by Mom's blatant racism, not only here, but in many areas. I knew the Lord was not pleased either. Worse, she was combining it with her witness for Christ. I tried arguing, reasoning from Scripture, and praying, but to no avail. My husband, Tom, thought my efforts were probably hopeless.

Writing with punch!

"Maybe it's too late for your Mom to change here on earth. Seventy years is a long time to believe something, even if it is garbage." Then he sighed, "The Lord will set her straight some day. There sure won't be any segregation in heaven!"

But the Lord had the situation well in hand. A stroke. An adult family home. A loving black family. Mom changed. I changed. When Mom graduated to heaven in the arms of her adopted black sister, I knew the Lord had performed a miracle of love.

Key elements for our magazine.

I remember them well, but it certainly doesn't hurt to let me know.

Similar to my other family stories, "Allison's Prayers," (January 91) and "the Truth About Death," (April 1992), *Moody* readers will also enjoy "My Impossible Mom." Imbedded in the story are the Scriptural principles I learned about racism and about trusting God to defend His own reputation. I believe God can use my experience to challenge readers to pray with renewed faith for the "impossible" people in their lives.

"Impossible Mom" weighs in at 2,400 words. My other stories and articles have appeared in *Discipleship Journal, Christian Parenting, Virtue, Plus, Lutheran Digest, Power for Living,* and others. May I send you "Impossible Mom" on speculation?

Good references.

Nice note to end with. No "hard sell."

Thank you for your kind attention. I hope you, your wife and your "small fry" are well and thriving.

Yours in Christ,

This query is the right length and includes everything a query needs to get the go ahead for publication.

Debbie Inprint

Megan Nosale
1234 Sorry Lane
Nowhere, Ohio 49382

March 14, 1994

Mr. Andrew Scheer
Moody Magazine
820 N. LaSalle Blvd.
Chicago, Illinois 60610-3284

(Definite NO)

Dear Mr. Scheer,

I would like you to take the time to accept this correspondence as a query letter
requesting consideration of an article for your publication. "A Giving Christmas"
is written to present the importance of God and giving at Christmas. By seeing
that we receive when we give and that we give when we gratefully receive, the
reader will discover truly what God wants to give us and what He deserves from
us. The article is 1500 words in length.

This windy, stilted first sentence is a sure turn-off.

A shame to have a good topic fall in the hands of a poor writer.

You see our whole family likes it when the children (rent open) their boxes of new
toys and play until mother or father reminds them that there is more to open. And
then mom and dad open and enjoy their new presents. Coming together and enjoying the gifts and each other is the (final culmination) of giving and receiving that
God wants us to appreciate. It is the annual ritual we all benefit from.

The redundancies and awkward prose do nothing to change my impression from the lead paragraph.

Not this time!
Sometimes, maybe even (oftentimes,) we think about the cause of this tradition.
We think of three kings bearing gifts to the Christ child. Sadly, we often emulate
the expense of their gift and not the spirit of their worship...

All givers and receivers should get joy and love from exchanging gifts. What gifts
do we want from God and what does God want from us? As a believer, who
accepted Christ as His Savior many years ago, I realize that I too need to remember
all that God desires for His children and from His children. Regarding my writing
experiences professionally, I can only claim to have written an article published
years ago.

Don't tell me this because it's not convincing. Why haven't you had anything published recently? Better for me to think you're a new writer.

I trust that the information I have supplied will satisfy your requirements. If more
is necessary please contact me at your convenience. Thank you.

Sincerely,

It did. It tells me I'm making the right decision in saying NO.

Megan Nosale

3 strikes:
—Multiple redundancies
—Ponderous style
—No SASE

Looking for a Few Good Ideas?

BY PATRICIA L. FRY

When my writing students find out that I submit about 50 queries a month, the first question they ask isn't how much money I make or even how I handle rejection. They ask, "Don't you ever run out of ideas?"

To writers who claim they can't come up with good ideas, I say, "You aren't paying attention." Thousands of article ideas are all around you. Still at a loss? I'll show you where to look.

EXPERIENCE COUNTS

One of the first maxims budding writers hear is "write what you know." You may feel you've been there and done that, but have you truly explored all your personal expertise?

What kind of work experience have you had? Perhaps you're an office manager in a small company, a sales representative, a secretary or an auto mechanic. Nothing to write home about, you say? Think again. The lessons you've learned, the contacts you've made and the insights you have can be turned into ideas—and sales.

For example, maybe your worst work nightmare is the customer complaint. Add a little research to what you've learned about handling irate customers and create a how-to article for a business or communications magazine.

Perhaps your employer is particularly careful about wastefulness. Your observations, along with an interview or two, might result in a great piece on office or industrial recycling.

Explore some of the changes taking place in your industry and report on an aspect of them for inhouse or union publications. What's really behind the paper shortage? Which mid-management positions are likely to get the ax?

On a more personal level, what are your interests and hobbies? Do you volunteer in your community? What aspect of your life do friends ask about? Your karate classes? Your five-year-old triplets? The family reunion you're planning at the site where your first ancestor in America landed?

When I started writing for publication, horses were my primary interest. As a family we often took horse pack trips into the wilderness, and our daughters participated in horse shows. It made sense for me to start my career by writing horse-oriented articles. I was already familiar with the popular horse magazines, but I now studied them with a fresh eye, looking for a void I could fill. I found that no one else seemed to be writing from a really basic, practical standpoint.

So, from my own curiosity and frustration I wrote a piece featuring ideas for exhibiting and using horse show ribbons. I even traveled around and photographed creative home displays, quilts and horse blankets that folks had made from their ribbons. That was the first article I wrote—and I sold it to *Horse and Horseman*. After that, I sold articles about how to make show chaps, easy horse show hairdos, what to expect when expecting a foal, and wilderness riding tips to magazines such as *Spur*, *Horse Illustrated* and *Western Horse*. I even sold a humor piece about horse show mothers.

PATRICIA L. FRY *has been writing for publication for 23 years. Her articles have appeared in such publications as* Kiwanis Magazine, The World & I, Complete Woman *and* Cats Magazine. *She's also the author of six books, including* The Mainland Luau *and* Quest for Truth, *both from Matilija Press.*

EXPAND YOUR MARKETS

A student in my Business of Writing class was publishing technical articles in architectural publications, but wanted to break into mainstream publications. I suggested she refocus. As an architect, she could offer expert home remodeling and decorating ideas, or provide plans and instruction for building a dog house or patio deck. She could also promote her profession in college publications.

The point is this: Explore other levels of potential interest relating to your area of expertise.

COLLECT INTERESTING PEOPLE

We all know people worth writing about, and most of them love to be placed in the limelight for personal or professional reasons. Make it a point to seek out these people in your life.

I have an artistically talented brother and sister-in-law who discovered their skills later in life. He creates cowboy sculptures from horseshoes, and she paints charming folk art. They make good copy, and I make good money.

I once ordered a couple of African violet plants from a woman who sells these blooming beauties through mail order from her ranch home in Montana. I became interested in her story and interviewed her. Two articles resulted, netting me nearly $1,000. *Cooperative Partners*, a farm magazine, published a piece featuring Angelika and her at-home business, and *Lady's Circle* ran my article on how to grow African violets.

Look around your community for interesting stories. A few years ago, a local woman started a cemetery clean-up program in her deceased father's memory. She now has more than 200 volunteers hoeing weeds, planting flowers, replacing broken or missing markers—and I have something worth writing about.

EXAMINE YOUR BELIEFS

Share your convictions. Air your pet peeves. Whether your cause is big or small, if you're passionate about it, write about it.

Maybe your cousin lives on the streets, and you have a particular perspective about the homeless that you'd like to share with the world, or it irritates you to see shoppers buying heavily packaged products, and you want to educate them through your writing.

I'm concerned we are neglecting to instill in our kids a sense of responsibility. The articles I've generated from that concern—essays and how-to pieces—have netted nearly $2,000 so far. I've sold articles about how to teach children a sense of responsibility to *St. Anthony Messenger*; teaching children responsibility through pet ownership to *I Love Cats*, *Paint Horse Journal* and *Chronicle of a Horse*; and pieces on preparing today's children for tomorrow's workplace to *Kiwanis Magazine*, *Home Life* and *The World & I*.

WHAT DO YOU WANT TO KNOW?

Is there something about which you want more information? Interest a magazine editor in an article on that subject. Maybe you want to know how to compost, or you're looking for some good fund-raising ideas. Elicit an article assignment and learn as you write.

For example, I've received many chain letters and have always been fascinated by the concept: They ask you to send $1 or a recipe, for instance, and promise you'll receive thousands of them in return.

When yet another chain letter arrived last year, I again wondered, "Can they really work?" I found an editor who was also interested in these questions and was willing to pay me to research and write the piece.

One summer, I visited the Denver Zoo where I met up with a pair of Pallas cats. Fascinated by their uniqueness, I began researching this rare breed of wild cat. My effort resulted in a sale to *Cats Magazine*.

KEEP YOUR EARS OPEN

You'll also find article ideas through your conversations. Idle conversation will never be the same once you learn how to extract tidbits of information to use in developing potential articles. A conversation with a neighbor about his yard's infestation of snails might lead to a piece on ancient remedies for discouraging these pests. Overhearing someone complain about waiting in line might be the impetus for "Ten Things You Can Do While Waiting" or "How to Make Waiting Work for You." A friend told of a particularly miserable time he had on a trip because nothing went as planned. His tale of woe prompted me to write an article on how to have a wonderful vacation *despite* the unexpected. I sold it to *Tours and Resorts Magazine* and have since sold numerous reprints.

EXTRA! EXTRA! READ ALL ABOUT IT

Talk shows and newspaper and magazine articles are great sources for ideas. Find out what's happening, establish your own slant and you've got an idea.

A news report about home-schooling might inspire you to write on how to decide whether to home-school a child. A magazine article featuring three women who returned to work after raising their children may prompt you to write "How to Prepare a Housewife's Résumé."

After reading a newspaper article reporting the rising number of seniors in the work force, I wrote a piece featuring seniors who started their own businesses after retirement, and another about people who turned their hobbies into businesses. Both found a home in *Grit*.

START SPINNING OFF

Don't look at your finished articles as the end of an idea. Milk them for all they're worth. You've already done the research, after all.

From a piece about healthy grieving, for example, you could develop articles about how to help a friend through the grieving process, what to tell a child in a family crisis and how a community copes with grief in a major disaster.

Maybe you've done a comparison study of Internet systems for a computer magazine. Now, break down your information to create articles on computer pen pals for kids or how writers can use the Internet as a research tool.

I recently wrote a piece about long-distance grandparenting for *Columbia Magazine*. This led to another article featuring the changing roles of today's grandparents and a third about organized activities throughout the U.S. designed to promote grandparenting.

Earlier, I mentioned my interest in the woman who started the Adopt-a-Grave program in her community. From my interview with her, I developed and sold an informational piece about the program to *Woman's Day*, a how-to article on starting a similar program to *Country Journal*, and a profile of the program's founder to *Successful Retirement*. I also self-published a book on the history of the cemetery.

REUSE YOUR RESOURCES

Many interviews have the potential to generate articles on more than one topic. As an example, while interviewing a woman for a piece about how to avoid becoming a workaholic, she mentioned office politics. I noted the term and later solicited her help in developing an article around that theme. My encounter with her resulted in original articles for *Entrepreneur Magazine*, *Career Woman* and *Communication Briefings*.

During an interview with the former vice president of the National Stepfamily Association for an article exploring the role of each member in a stepfamily came the spark of an idea for another piece on how to give and receive emotional support. *St. Anthony Messenger* bought both articles.

RANDOM NOTES

Meditate, relax or lose yourself in a physical activity for ten minutes to an hour each day. Clear your mind of all the get-through-the-day thoughts and allow random thoughts in. You may be surprised at how many great ideas come when you allow them.

During these times I've come up with ideas that have resulted in articles on a variety of subjects, including simple and inexpensive decorating tips for *Grit*; the concept of relationships in transition for *Body, Mind and Spirit*; self-abuse for *Complete Woman*; and avoiding the Monday blues for *Woman's Own*. After a day-long trip on Amtrak with five grandchildren, I wrote a how-to article for *L.A. Parent Magazine* about traveling with kids. While watching one of my grandson's Little League games, I met a father who tells stories for a living. That connection resulted in a feature piece on storytelling as therapy for *The World & I*.

Be on guard. Any place, any time is fair game for finding article ideas. Never let down your guard. Carry a note pad and pencil or tape recorder wherever you go. Start an idea file to keep your notes in, as well as newspaper and magazine clippings. Do this faithfully and you'll always find some fresh ideas waiting in your file to pitch to editors.

Idea block? No way. All you have to do is pay attention.

The Business of Writing
Minding the Details

Writers who have had some success in placing their work know that the effort to publish requires an entirely different set of skills than does the act of writing. A shift in perspective is required when you move from creating your work to selling it. Like it or not, successful writers—*career* writers—have to keep the business side of the writing business in mind as they work.

Each of the following sections discusses a writing business topic that affects anyone selling his writing. We'll take a look at contracts and agreements—the documents that license a publisher to use your work. We'll consider your rights as a writer and sort out some potentially confusing terminology. We'll cover the basics of copyright protection—a topic of perennial concern for writers. And for those of you who are already making money with your writing, we'll offer some tips for keeping track of financial matters and staying on top of your tax liabilities.

Our treatment of the business topics that follow is necessarily limited. Look for complete information on each subject at your local bookstore or library—both in books (some of which we mention) and periodicals aimed at writers. Information is also available from the federal government, as indicated later in this article.

CONTRACTS AND AGREEMENTS

If you've been freelancing even a short time, you know that contracts and agreements vary considerably from one publisher to another. Some magazine editors work only by verbal agreement; others have elaborate documents you must sign in triplicate and return before you begin the assignment. As you evaluate any contract or agreement, consider carefully what you stand to gain and lose by signing. Did you have another sale in mind that selling all rights the first time will negate? Does the agreement provide the publisher with a number of add-ons (advertising rights, reprint rights, etc.) for which they won't have to pay you again?

In contract negotiations, the writer is usually interested in licensing the work for a particular use but limiting the publisher's ability to make other uses of the work in the future. It's in the publisher's best interest, however, to secure rights to use the work in as many ways as possible, both now and later on. Those are the basic positions of each party. The negotiation is a process of compromise and capitulation on questions relating to those basic points—and the amount of compensation to be given the writer for his work.

A contract is rarely a take-it-or-leave-it proposition. If an editor tells you that his company will allow *no* changes on the contract, you will then have to decide how important the assignment is to you. But most editors are open to negotiation, and you should learn to compromise on points that don't matter to you while maintaining your stand on things that do.

When it's not specified, most writers assume that a magazine publisher is buying first rights. Some writers' groups can supply you with a sample magazine contract to use when the publisher doesn't supply one, so you can document your agreement in writing. Members of The Authors

Guild are given a sample book contract and information about negotiating when they join. For more information about contracts and agreements, see *Business and Legal Forms for Authors & Self-Publishers*, by Tad Crawford (Allworth Press, 1990); *From Printout to Published*, by Michael Seidman (Carroll & Graf, 1992) or *The Writer's Guide to Contract Negotiations*, by Richard Balkin (Writer's Digest Books, 1985), which is out of print but should be available in libraries.

RIGHTS AND THE WRITER

A creative work can be used in many different ways. As the originator of written works, you enjoy full control over how those works are used; you are in charge of the rights that your creative works are "born" with. When you agree to have your work published, you are giving the publisher the right to use your work in one or more ways. Whether that right is simply to publish the work for the first time in a periodical or to publish it as many times as he likes and in whatever form he likes is up to you—it all depends on the terms of the contract or agreement the two of you arrive at. As a general rule, the more rights you license away, the less control you have over your work and the more money you should be paid for the license. We find that writers and editors sometimes define rights in different ways. For a classification of terms, read Types of Rights, below.

Sometimes editors don't take the time to specify the rights they are buying. If you sense that an editor is interested in getting stories but doesn't seem to know what his and the writer's responsibilities are regarding rights, be wary. In such a case, you'll want to explain what rights you're offering (preferably one-time or first serial rights only) and that you expect additional payment for subsequent use of your work.

You should strive to keep as many rights to your work as you can from the outset, otherwise, your attempts to resell your writing may be seriously hampered.

The Copyright Law that went into effect January 1, 1978, said writers were primarily selling one-time rights to their work unless they—and the publisher—agreed otherwise in writing. Book rights are covered fully by the contract between the writer and the book publisher.

TYPES OF RIGHTS

- First Serial Rights—First serial rights means the writer offers a newspaper or magazine the right to publish the article, story or poem for the first time in any periodical. All other rights to the material remain with the writer. The qualifier "North American" is often added to this phrase to specify a geographical limit to the license.

  When material is excerpted from a book scheduled to be published and it appears in a magazine or newspaper prior to book publication, this is also called first serial rights.
- One-Time Rights—A periodical that licenses one-time rights to a work (also known as simultaneous rights) buys the *nonexclusive* right to publish the work once. That is, there is nothing to stop the author from selling the work to other publications at the same time. Simultaneous sales would typically be to periodicals without overlapping audiences.
- Second Serial (Reprint) Rights—This gives a newspaper or magazine the opportunity to print an article, poem or story after it has already appeared in another newspaper or magazine. Second serial rights are nonexclusive—that is, they can be licensed to more than one market.
- All Rights—This is just what it sounds like. If you license away all rights to your work, you forfeit the right to ever use it again. If you think you'll want to use the material later, you must avoid submitting to such markets or refuse payment and withdraw your material. Ask the editor whether he is willing to buy first

rights instead of all rights before you agree to an assignment or sale. Some editors will reassign rights to a writer after a given period, such as one year. It's worth an inquiry in writing.

- Subsidiary Rights—These are the rights, other than book publication rights, that should be covered in a book contract. These may include various serial rights; movie, television, audiotape and other electronic rights; translation rights, etc. The book contract should specify who controls these rights (author or publisher) and what percentage of sales from the licensing of these sub rights goes to the author.
- Dramatic, Television and Motion Picture Rights—This means the writer is selling his material for use on the stage, in television or in the movies. Often a one-year option to buy such rights is offered (generally for 10% of the total price). The interested party then tries to sell the idea to other people—actors, directors, studios or television networks, etc. Some properties are optioned over and over again, but most fail to become dramatic productions. In such cases, the writer can sell his rights again and again—as long as there is interest in the material. Though dramatic, TV and motion picture rights are more important to the fiction writer than the nonfiction writer, producers today are increasingly interested in nonfiction material; many biographies, topical books and true stories are being dramatized.

SELLING SUBSIDIARY RIGHTS

The primary right in the world of book publishing is the right to publish the book itself. All other rights (such as movie rights, audio rights, book club rights, electronic rights and foreign rights) are considered secondary, or subsidiary, to the right to print publication. In contract negotiations, authors and their agents traditionally try to avoid granting the publisher subsidiary rights that they feel capable of marketing themselves. Publishers, on the other hand, typically hope to obtain control over as many of the sub rights as they can. Philosophically speaking, subsidiary rights will be best served by being left in the hands of the person or organization most capable of—and interested in—exploiting them profitably. Sometimes that will be the author and her agent, and sometimes that will be the publisher.

Larger agencies have experience selling foreign rights, movie rights and the like, and many authors represented by such agents prefer to retain those rights and let their agents do the selling. Book publishers, on the other hand, have subsidiary rights departments, which are responsible for exploiting all sub rights the publisher was able to retain during the contract negotiation.

That job might begin with a push to sell foreign rights, which normally bring in advance money which is divided among author, agent and publisher. Further efforts then might be made to sell the right to publish the book as a paperback (although many book contracts now call for hard/soft deals, in which the original hardcover publisher buys the right to also publish the paperback version).

Any other rights which the publisher controls will be pursued, such as book clubs and magazines. Publishers usually don't control movie rights to a work, as those are most often retained by author and agent.

The marketing of electronic rights to a work, in this era of rapidly expanding capabilities and markets for electronic material, can be tricky. With the proliferation of electronic and multimedia formats, publishers, agents and authors are going to great pains these days to make sure contracts specify exactly *which* electronic rights are being conveyed (or retained).

Compensation for these rights is a major source of conflict between writers and publishers, as many book publishers seek control of them and many magazines routinely include electronic rights in the purchase of all rights, often with no additional payment. Alternative ways of handling this issue include an additional 15% added to the amount to purchase first rights to a royalty system based on the number of times an article is accessed from an electronic database.

COPYRIGHT

Copyright law exists to protect creators of original works. It is engineered to encourage creative expression and aid in the progress of the arts and sciences by ensuring that artists and authors hold the rights by which they can profit from their labors.

Copyright protects your writing, unequivocally recognizes you (its creator) as its owner, and grants you all the rights, benefits and privileges that come with ownership. The moment you finish a piece of writing—whether it is a short story, article, novel or poem—the law recognizes that only you can decide how it is to be used.

The basics of copyright law are discussed here. More detailed information can be obtained from the Copyright Office and in the books mentioned at the end of this section.

Copyright law gives you the right to make and distribute copies of your written works, the right to prepare derivative works (dramatizations, translations, musical arrangements, etc.—any work based on the original) and the right to perform or publicly display your work. With very few exceptions, anything you write today will enjoy copyright protection for your lifetime plus 50 years. Copyright protects "original works of authorship" that are fixed in a tangible form of expression. Titles, ideas and facts can *not* be copyrighted.

Some people are under the mistaken impression that copyright is something they have to send away for, and that their writing is not properly protected until they have "received" their copyright from the government. The fact is, you don't have to register your work with the Copyright Office in order for your work to be copyrighted; any piece of writing is copyrighted the moment it is put to paper. Registration of your work does, however, offer some additional protection (specifically, the possibility of recovering punitive damages in an infringement suit) as well as legal proof of the date of copyright.

Registration is a matter of filling out a form (for writers, that's generally form TX) and sending the completed form, a copy of the work in question and a check for $20 to the Register of Copyrights, Library of Congress, Washington DC 20559. If the thought of paying $20 each to register every piece you write does not appeal to you, you can cut costs by registering a group of your works with one form, under one title for one $20 fee.

Most magazines are registered with the Copyright Office as single collective entities themselves; that is, the individual works that make up the magazine are *not* copyrighted individually in the names of the authors. You'll need to register your article yourself if you wish to have the additional protection of copyright registration. It's always a good idea to ask that your notice of copyright (your name, the year of first publication, and the copyright symbol ©) be appended to any published version of your work. You may use the copyright notice regardless of whether or not your work has been registered.

One thing writers need to be wary of is "work for hire" arrangements. If you sign an agreement stipulating that your writing will be done as work for hire, you will not control the copyright of the completed work—the person or organization who hired you will be the copyright owner. Work for hire arrangements and transfers of exclusive rights must be in writing to be legal, but it's a good idea to get every publishing agreement in writing before the sale.

You can obtain more information about copyright from the Copyright Office, Library of Congress, Washington DC 20559. To get answers to specific questions about copyright, call the Copyright Public Information Office at (202)707-3000 weekdays between 8:30 a.m. and 5 p.m. eastern standard time. To order copyright forms by phone, call (202)707-9100. Forms can also be downloaded from the Library of Congress website at http://lcweb.loc.gov/copyright. The website also includes information on filling out the forms, general copyright information and links to other websites related to copyright issues. A thorough (and thoroughly enjoyable) discussion of the subject of copyright law as it applies to writers can be found in Stephen Fishman's *The Copyright Handbook: How to Protect and Use Written Works* (Nolo Press, 1994). A shorter

INSIDER REPORT

Consider consulting, a growing concern

Dan Dieterich

"If you are an expert in written communication, you can apply that expertise in many places, and there are many people who need that type of help—bankers, social workers, sheriffs, accountants," says Dan Dieterich, a Wisconsin-based writing consultant. "Not being in a particular field can be an asset. For example, if an accountant asks for your help, you shouldn't fear that you know nothing about accounting. What that accountant wants is not accounting, it's an effective way to convey his or her message and that's your area of expertise."

Businesses and governmental organizations are in constant need of writing help, says Dieterich. "Businesses are hungry for our help. When a business goes bellyup, the problem is usually communication—to customers, to suppliers. Many business people know this, too. Good written communication can be the key to success. The same thing applies to government and nonprofit organizations."

According to Dieterich, the term "writing consultant" can mean different things to different people. Generally, consulting involves helping a business or individual with any form of communication. Consultants help with ad copy and direct mail pieces, but they may also give advice on business letters, speeches, forms, annual reports and company newsletters. Some teach workshops on grammar, others teach advanced communication skills.

"It takes a little guts but not a terrible financial outlay," says Dieterich, who started consulting in 1978. "Networking is the key. You just have to do an outstanding job with that first client. After that a lot of business will come by word of mouth."

Finding the first client is usually pretty simple, he says. "We all know hundreds of people who might need writing help. They could be family friends, your church group, people in clubs and organizations. I once had a student in my writing class refer her father to me. I know one consultant who got all his contacts through a fraternal organization."

Advertising in the yellow pages or a local business newspaper can also help spread the word. Many consultants use direct mail advertising to promote themselves. Promotional materials are a direct reflection of your level of expertise, says Dieterich, so a professional presentation is a must.

"You should present a professional appearance in everything you do, including your stationery and business cards as well as your appearance. But it doesn't have to cost a lot of money. You could hire a graphic designer to do your letterhead and business cards, but companies like Paper Direct now offer professional-looking products that can make you look very good."

but no less enlightening treatment is Ellen Kozak's *Every Writer's Guide to Copyright & Publishing Law* (Henry Holt, 1990).

FINANCES AND TAXES

As your writing business grows, so will your obligation to keep track of your writing-related finances and taxes. Keeping a close eye on these details will help you pay as little tax as possible and keep you apprised of the state of your freelance business. A writing business with no systematic way of tracking expenses and income will soon be no writing business at all. If you dislike handling finance-related tasks, you can always hire someone else to handle them for a fee. If you do employ a professional, you must still keep the original records with an eye to providing the professional with the appropriate information.

If you decide to handle these tasks yourself—or if you just want to know what to expect of the person you employ—consider these tips:

Accurate records are essential, and the easiest way to keep them is to separate your writing income and expenses from your personal ones. Most professionals find that separate checking accounts and credit cards help them provide the best and easiest records.

Get in the habit of recording every transaction (both expenses and earnings) related to your writing. You can start at any time; you don't need to begin on January 1. Because you're likely to have expenses before you have income, start keeping your records whenever you make your first purchase related to writing—such as this copy of *Writer's Market.*

Any system of tracking expenses and income will suffice, but the more detailed it is, the better. Be sure to describe each transaction clearly—including the date; the source of the income (or the vendor of your purchase); a description of what was sold or bought; whether the payment was by cash, check or credit card; and the amount of the transaction.

The other necessary component of your financial record-keeping system is an orderly way to store receipts related to your writing. Check stubs, receipts for cash purchases, credit card receipts and similar paperwork should all be kept as well as recorded in your ledger. Any good book about accounting for small business will offer specific suggestions for ways to track your finances.

Freelance writers, artists and photographers have a variety of concerns about taxes that employees don't have, including deductions, self-employment tax and home office credits. Many freelance expenses can be deducted in the year in which they are incurred (rather than having to be capitalized, or depreciated, over a period of years). For details, consult the IRS publications mentioned later. Keep in mind that to be considered a business (and not a hobby) by the IRS you need to show a profit in three of the past five years. Hobby losses are deductible only to the extent of income produced by the activity.

There also is a home office deduction that can be claimed if an area in your home is used *exclusively* and *regularly* for business. Contact the IRS for information on requirements and limitations for this deduction. If your freelance income exceeds your expenses, regardless of the amount, you must declare that profit. If you make $400 or more after deductions, you must pay Social Security tax and file Schedule SE, a self-employment form, along with your Form 1040 and Schedule C tax forms.

While we cannot offer you tax advice or interpretations, we can suggest several sources for the most current information.

- Check the IRS website, http://www.irs.ustreas.gov/. Full of helpful tips and information, the site also provides instant access to important IRS forms and publications.
- Call your local IRS office. Look in the white pages of the telephone directory under U.S. Government—Internal Revenue Service. Someone will be able to respond to your request for IRS publications and tax forms or other information. Ask about the IRS Tele-tax service, a series of recorded messages you can hear by dialing on a touch-tone phone. If you need answers to complicated questions, ask to speak with a Taxpayer Service Specialist.
- Obtain the basic IRS publications. You can order them by phone or mail from any IRS office; most are available at libraries and some post offices. Start with *Your Federal Income Tax* (Publication 17) and *Tax Guide for Small Business* (Publication 334). These are both comprehensive, detailed guides—you'll need to find the regulations that apply to you and ignore the rest. There are many IRS publications relating to self-employment and taxes; Publication 334 lists many of these publications—such as *Business Use of Your Home* (Publication 587) and *Self-Employment Tax* (Publication 533).
- Consider other information sources. Many public libraries have detailed tax instructions available on tape. Some colleges and universities offer free assistance in preparing tax returns. And if you decide to consult a professional tax preparer, the fee is a deductible business expense on your tax return.

Smooth Starting for Fulltime Freelance Writing

BY JOHN F. LAUERMAN

At 7 a.m. I rise smiling and unblinking from my bed and begin preparing for another day of the life of a freelancer. First there's a hearty breakfast, a few minutes of play with Hanna and James, and then a long, hot shower.

At 8:30, dressed in mismatched socks, a torn sweatshirt, jeans and high-top sneakers (who cares what I wear?) I make my way downstairs to the office where my computer hums expectantly. My to-do list beckons: an op-ed piece for the *Times*, a 6,500-word article on chaos for *The New Yorker*, a speech for the president of General Motors (due tomorrow), and the script for a "Nova" episode on the physics of baseball.

Like a Top Gun pilot strapping into the cockpit, I take the controls of my word processor and begin meticulously crafting sentences, paragraphs, pages, chapters. A full two hours pass before I even glance away from the screen, but when I do, holy cow! The sun is out, it's a beautiful day, and it's still only 10:30.

"Golf!" I yelp, and hurriedly add the Pings to the collection of sports equipment in the Miata's trunk. As I race to tee off, the cell phone rings. It's my agent: the six-figure book deal has come through. "Check's in the mail!" she says. "Don't spend it all in one place."

Wow, I love this job!

WHAT KIND OF PERSON FREELANCES?

Well, it isn't always like that. As a matter of fact, it's almost never like that, and to be absolutely truthful I would have to admit that I can't remember a single day of freelancing that was even remotely like that. Sure, I take some days off. Yes, it's true that I seldom dress up for work. Given, some of the jobs are exciting. But all in all, the freedom of freelancing has been greatly exaggerated. Most freelancers have offices, and most of them spend their 9-to-5 day in that office, trying to make a living.

Being a successful freelancer doesn't necessarily mean having time to work on your golf game, or writing for high-profile national magazines. I once read that a good farmer is one who can make enough money to keep on farming. The same is true of freelance writing: if you're making enough money to keep afloat, you must be doing okay.

I often think of a freelancer as an artisan, not unlike the coppersmith Paul Revere: He lived upstairs, worked downstairs, and was as active in the community as he was in his own profession. Before the birth of large corporations, virtually everyone's work life was organically related to life in the community, by both proximity and function. As it happens, today's economic climate allows for a certain amount of artisanship in the field of writing; people who can fill that niche are able to make a living.

That being said, there are lots of talented people who have tried freelancing and returned to

---

JOHN F. LAUERMAN is a freelance writer working in Brookline, Mass. under the watchful eyes of his wife, Judi, and children, Hanna and James. His book, Diabetes, *co-written with Dr. David M. Nathan, was published by Random House in March. He is currently trying to find a publisher who will pay him enough to write another book.*

office work; likewise, there are others who have left the daily grind and high-tailed it back to the home office. I began freelancing while on a science writing fellowship at the University of California, Berkeley, doing pieces for the *San Francisco Examiner* and the *San Jose Mercury News*. Later, when I took a job with the Harvard Medical School news office, I continued to do occasional articles for the *Boston Globe*, the *Quincy Patriot Ledger*, the *Boston Herald*, as well as other publications.

The notion of fulltime freelancing—as opposed to after-hours, weekend freelancing—occurred to me in the same idealized way that it strikes a lot of people: "be your own boss," "more time for writing fiction," "tennis at 3." These were the ideas floating around in my head. Two children, a mortgage and a car loan have dashed those dreams, but I'm still a thriving small businessman, I still decide more or less how I'm going to spend each day—as long as I spend it working—and I still have the sense of artisanry and identification with my work that I think only freelancing can provide.

As I think I've proven often enough, you don't have to be a gifted writer to freelance. You just need to be willing to gather information and write it up clearly. That, in a nutshell, is what most freelancers provide: fresh information served hot. (See the sidebar on specialization.) However, the news that many writers aren't prepared for is that freelancing is hard work, and it requires planning, risk-taking, and doing a few things most people aren't used to doing on a daily basis:

• working alone,
• marketing your services,
• editing your own work,
• motivating yourself,
• being your own office manager,
• and doing other work for which you have no training.

Are you prepared to do these things? Erin Martin was a public information officer at a large Boston teaching hospital until a merger forced her to reconsider her position. She knew freelancers who were making $100 an hour writing public relations copy for local firms, and decided to take a stab at it herself.

"The work was there," says Martin, "but I didn't like the isolation. The telephone man came to install a new line and I wanted to have lunch with the guy. I didn't like freelancing very much. I'm much more comfortable in an environment where I interact with other people."

Luckily for Martin, she managed to find another position quickly, where she now hires many freelancers. However, many would-be freelancers find they have difficulty getting adequate work. I receive any number of calls from people who are simply looking for new clients, or advice on how to find them. The reality is that the vast majority of assignments come by referral, and that the best time to develop a client base is before you go out on your own.

Marketing your services is an unending part of the life of a freelancer. As long as you're peddling your own services, you will need to put your products and abilities in front of the people with the power to buy them. This means going to professional meetings, having lunch, making calls, small talk, and friends. Keep in mind that none of this is a replacement for good writing and editing, the most important components of a good marketing effort. But personal relations with editors and managers make getting repeat business much more likely.

Many freelancers are unprepared for the level of writing and reporting they will have to reach to satisfy their clients. Bob Whitaker, editor of *CenterWatch*, a newsletter that follows the clinical drug trials scene, says that many freelancers are surprised when he asks them to go back for additional reporting.

"Some freelancers think they can do a couple quick interviews without really understanding the subject," he says, "and then use their writing skills to cover that up. I need someone who can report stories in a thorough manner."

TO SPECIALIZE OR NOT . . .

Building a specialty can be vital to maintaining your freelance career. In fact, many freelancers start out with a specialty interest, and the desire to write about it. I've been writing about science and medicine for more than ten years, and here are a few observations:

• Specializing can be important to financial and career survival. If you can say "I know architecture, I've been writing about it for years," it's helpful when you're looking for jobs, or when you're trying to sell yourself. The best markets in freelancing are for up-to-the-minute, accurate, understandable information about specific fields. The best way to do that is via specialization.

• Don't be intimidated by specializing. That is, you don't need to be an architect to write about architecture. Sure, it helps to know something about it, and have more than a passing interest. But the important thing is to become familiar with the terminology, be able to communicate familiar concepts and cultivate contacts in the field.

• Once you do specialize, the world tends to get very small. Treat your sources as well as you can, particularly when you're starting out. Some sources will want you to read quotes back to them. Depending on the type of assignment you're working on, you may want to accommodate them, or at least negotiate something with them. Calling people back to comment on what you've written also gives you a chance to do more reporting, and to cultivate them as regular sources. Many of your sources, particularly the higher-placed ones, will be very concerned about whether they can trust you, and they will remember if they think they've been burned.

Then there's the Big Mo: motivation. I can't tell you how often people ask me how I motivate myself to go to work in the morning. My answer is that there's no better motivator than a mailbox with a paycheck in it. However, I find many people can't make the connection between working in December and eating in January; if you're one of those people, keep commuting.

One of the hardest things to get up for is the everyday running of your office. I often tell new freelancers that their most important job is collecting receipts, so they can keep track of their expenses. Those receipts are worth money, and when I started off, I collected everything, even if it was for a cup of coffee. Now I'm a little more selective, but I'm always thinking about my expenses, and how they'll affect my earnings and taxes. (See the sidebar on financial habits.) As I write this, I'm getting ready to prepare my taxes, something I never look forward to. I also have to make all the decisions about what equipment to buy, when to buy it, and when to get rid of it. It gives one a whole new appreciation of the job an office manager has to perform.

Office management may sound imposing enough, but this may not even compare with some of the professional work you'll do. In the quest to keep a steady stream of clients, and to find interesting and rewarding work, I've written all kinds of things I'd had no experience writing before: market analyses, video scripts, slide shows, advertising copy, you name it. If you need work, you may have to expand beyond your comfortable area of expertise and try some new things.

If you're ready to do all these things, and take some unforeseen chances, then you have what I consider the basic traits to become a freelance writer. Now let's take a look at some of the more concrete requirements that must be fulfilled, starting with equipment.

TOOLS OF THE TRADE

The time is gone when a freelancer could make a living with an Underwood typewriter and a stack of white paper. Now writers must have a computer, fax, modem, an Internet account, and other business basics that will be mentioned later. So before you start your new freelance career know that purchasing office equipment is a big investment at first, but keep in mind that

SOME FINANCIAL ADVICE

My late mentor, Lillian Blacker, gave me one piece of important financial advice: "Always keep your milk money tucked into your mittens." Here I'm adding a few more tips for beginning fulltime freelancers:

• Keep track of your expenses. Have a good idea of how much money you need to meet your monthly expenses.

• Keep some emergency money in the bank. This admonition may sound hackneyed and unrealistic, but most family financial advisers recommend a cash reserve equal to three months of your income—and they're talking about people who already have jobs! Your ability to continue freelancing will depend on whether you can get through tough times.

• This may be the most important sentence in this article: Save your receipts. Every dollar you can legally deduct from your taxable income is more money you can keep. The current tax situation is not particularly friendly to freelancers, so keep track of every dollar you spend; then find out from a tax expert what you can legally deduct.

• Save for the future. If you figure to be freelancing for a long period of time you must think realistically about your retirement income. Take advantage of things like self-employment IRAs and other tax-exempt savings opportunities. That leads me to an important point: If you have children, set up a savings account for their education.

• If you feel you need to know more about finances, learn it! "I read all kinds of books and went to one-day seminars on small business administration," says Judi Norkin, a freelancer in Newtown, Pennsylvania. "I am always actively teaching myself about the business side."

• Get an accountant. It may cost more in the short run, but if you are ever audited, it may be very useful to have someone with you at your elbow as you face the IRS. An accountant can objectively evaluate all your deductions and tell you how the IRS is going to look at them, which could save you quite a bit of money.

you're equipping yourself for a business that promises to make you thousands of dollars in the years to come. Although there may be a temptation to get the cheapest equipment possible, remember that you'll be using these devices every day, so make sure you get something reliable and durable. There's no worse feeling than losing a 100-page manuscript when your computer crashes, pulling down all your documents with it. Poor equipment can waste thousands of hours—make sure you put time into selecting your equipment and ensuring that it works as advertised:

• First is a computer. There are lots of computers on the market now that come loaded with all kinds of software that's terrific for freelancers, and just about all of them also have some kind of built-in communications program. Make sure that yours does; this will make it easier to get online. Being online is becoming a must for many freelancers, both for communicating with and sending copy to clients. Also, make sure you have some kind of a CD drive built into your computer, because a lot of the new software will run only from CDs. I recently bought a Mac Performa system with all of the above for about $1,600, including a printer.

• I couldn't be a freelancer without an answering machine but would an answering service work better? I don't know. The answering machine is a one-time expense at about $75. You need to be able to pick up your messages from remote phones. I had a beeper for a while, but found that it offered me very little. I don't think anyone absolutely needs a cellular phone, but I suppose it could come in handy.

• A fax machine, on the other hand, is an absolute necessity. I've used the fax machines that have come built into my computers for years, although this does have some drawbacks, in that you can only fax out documents that are already on the computer. This means that you can't sign and fax a contract, unless you also have a stand-alone fax alongside your fax machine (cost, maybe $200). I've found that it's very helpful to have one separate line for fax and modem, so I can communicate without tying up my telephone line. When you're writing, reporting, and looking for work all at the same time, a lot depends on having a telephone line that's as free as possible.

• Desk and file cabinets. These things are important to have, but I don't think people realize how cheaply they can be had at used furniture stores. If they're just for your office, save yourself a couple hundred dollars and try to find these things used.

• It's best to have a couple of hand-held tape recorders. They only cost about $30 apiece. I personally don't think it's necessary to get the micro models, and I always look for something that can use a rechargeable battery.

• Software changes so quickly that it's impossible for someone like me to keep current with the market. I think that if you've found something you're comfortable with, you may as well keep using it as a freelancer, because it's usually very easy to convert to whatever your clients are using. Surprisingly, a lot of my clients use Apple computers, and I can e-mail them Microsoft Word documents without converting. The main programs you need are a word processor, a good database, a program to keep track of finances, and a communications program that will take care of faxes and get you online.

• Your office. Now, where are you going to put all this stuff? If possible, set up a separate room in your home as an office. If you have kids, you absolutely need a door that closes. Because of the way my house is built, my office is separated from my home by two flights of stairs, and two closed doors. Not everyone can do that, but do whatever you can to separate your home life from your work life. It's important for tax reasons, since the IRS doesn't think a freelance writer's office needs to be equipped with a home theater system, for example (unless you're involved in script-writing). And it's also important because you'll find that, if you're available, people will make demands on your time, no matter how busy you are.

MYTHS BUSTED: THE BUSINESS PLAN

A few years ago, when I was starting out fulltime, I felt that there were some important gaps in my understanding of how to make the freelance business work. Naturally, the most important thing I was concerned with was cash flow. I decided to attend a seminar on the business of freelancing to see how other people handled their finances, and perhaps get some expert advice that would help maximize my income. At the course, we students sat in an attentive circle, waiting to hear what pearls of wisdom would fall from the mouth of our instructor.

"First of all," he instructed, "you need a business plan."

Everyone in the circle quickly wrote down "Business plan!" I felt naive and embarassed; I had never had a business plan. How would I ever get ahead in life without a business plan? However, I wasn't sure what a business plan was, so I decided to take a reporting tack. I raised my hand.

"What did your business plan say when you started out?" I asked.

"Well," admitted our instructor, "I never actually had a business plan myself, but this syllabus I'm using says you should have one."

It was a telling moment, but in looking back, I'm not that surprised. Almost no one I've ever talked to had a business plan before beginning their freelancing career. Most successful freelancers I've spoken to went out on their own because they just couldn't stand another day of business-as-usual and office politics. Rob Dinsmoor, a good friend of mine who's been freelancing almost as long as I have, got started in a fit of temper.

"My employers were about to publish a table in 8-point type, and I knew no one was going to be able to read it," he recalls. "They had done it before, and I thought that if no one said anything they would do it again. So I started shouting and before I knew it I was having a tantrum. The next day I was so ashamed, I gave my notice. But I started picking up freelance work right away, before I even had time to look for a fulltime job."

Rob didn't have a business plan either, but he did have what he really needed: paying clients. As a freelancer, having clients is your number one concern; my idea of a business plan is that you know where the money is coming from. Rob was lucky enough to have enough contacts—including his former employer—to generate the income he needed to cover his bills. If you know you have enough business to cover your expenses before you go out on your own, you've basically won the battle before a shot has been fired. A common fatal error committed by freelancers is they start their business without any idea who their clients will be.

To start off with, new freelancers should optimally have one big client or several small clients. I began with one medium-sized client, a medical alumni magazine. A friend of mine was obligated by circumstances (the birth of her first child) to take a three-month maternity leave. So, my first freelance assignment was to fill in during her convalescence. This gave me three months of steady, paid work during which I could look for additional clients.

How many clients do you need to start with? You can never have too many clients, but you want to be assured of enough business to pay your bills. Aspiring freelancers come to me all the time asking how much they should charge for their services. The answer is: enough to pay your bills.

There's an easy way to figure this out, which I actually picked up from a freelancing seminar. To figure out how much you need to earn each hour, try this exercise:
- Sum up your annual expenses: rent, groceries, clothing, car payment, utilities, opera tickets, greens fees . . . everything. Add in the costs of running your own business, like office supplies and telephone bills that formerly would have been charged to your office. Also add in things like health insurance, and your contribution to a retirement fund. Then figure that if you make enough money to cover all these expenses, you'll have to pay about one-third that amount in taxes. So add up all those expenses, plus one-third more: that's the amount of money you need to get by each year. Let's say—very conservatively—it's $35,000.
- All right, time is money. Let's see how much time you have to earn your annual $35,000. There are 52 weeks in a year.

Say you're a tough boss to start off with, and you only give yourself two weeks vacation. Plus you take the major holidays and your own religious or cultural holidays. If you're an uncultured atheist, this adds up to five days, but for other people it could be more. Take another five days for sickness and personal matters. Let's say we have 47 weeks left for you to work 40 hours in: $47 \times 40 = 1880$.
- Of course, you won't spend all that time working on projects you can bill for. Your main activities in your office will be (from greatest to smallest, we hope) working, looking for work, and office management. In your first year of freelancing, you could spend as much as 30 percent of your time actually looking for work, and 5 percent managing your office. That means that with any luck you'll spend (65 percent of 1880) 1222 hours or 152.75 days working. So, in order to make $35,000, you'll have to charge about $30 an hour for your services.
- So, the first sentence of your realistic business plan should read something like this: find enough clients to give me 152.75 full days of work paying at least $30 an hour.

Don't interpret all this as saying you should try to earn just enough money to keep you out of poverty. Far from it! My own hourly rate is more than double the figure I've suggested here, but for reasons I'll explain in the next section, that doesn't mean I earn more than $70,000 annually. My point is that your business plan should tell you how much money you need and how much time you'll need to get it. While that makes your planning process a little simpler, it doesn't solve all your problems.

REALITY BITES

That little exercise only took a couple of minutes, and it made everything sound so simple. Well, the unfortunate reality is that nothing is simple, least of all starting your own business.

For starters, almost none of my clients allow me to charge my hourly rate, with the consistent exception of PR companies. However, it's not like driving a cab—as a freelancer, you can't just turn the meter on and charge whatever it says when you get to the airport. Even PR clients have a budget for each project, and you start off with an understanding that you'll spend a limited number of hours on the project and charge within the budget.

Most of my newsletter, newspaper and magazine clients, on the other hand, pay on a "per-word" basis, which is similar to a project basis in that you've agreed ahead of time how many words the project will be. So no matter how many words you actually write, the project will pay the same amount of money.

Unfortunately, you can't assume that if you work longer hours and do a better job on a project, you'll be rewarded for it. But there are two things you can do: look for better-paying clients, and negotiate. If you hustle, chances are you'll find lots of clients, and work on many different kinds of projects. As you'll see, some types of projects tend to pay more than others, although not always. However, you can quickly identify the clients who pay well and on time. My advice is, phase out those clients who pay poorly—with the exception of those who can give you good exposure—and go with the clients who can pay your bills.

Negotiation on price is also extremely important. This process is something that many free-lancers are not too familiar with. It can be extremely uncomfortable at first, but eventually you may find it very rewarding. Although there are no hard and fast rules to this, here are three important things to remember:

- Recognize your strengths. Clients are calling because they need you. Don't assume they're doing you a favor by giving you work.
- You can always negotiate down, but you can never negotiate up. Think before you bid on a project, and always start higher than you think the project is worth.
- Don't take professional negotiations personally. Understand that it's your client's job to try to get good services at low prices. Remember that it's your job—not your client's—to make sure that you're fairly reimbursed.

GET GOING!

Every time I teach my course in freelance writing, we run out of time long before everyone's questions are answered, and I usually stand at the front of the class for several minutes doling out advice and encouragement. No one can tell you everything you need to know about freelancing in one 4,000-word article, even with ample sidebar space. There are so many more things that could be discussed in detail, such as marketing your services, writing good query letters, client relations, how to choose jobs, and more.

One final note is for you to remember the best reason to become a fulltime freelance writer: the enjoyment. You have to like being at home and being with the people who live with you at home. Make sure you discuss your plans for fulltime freelancing with your spouse, significant other, and children before making the move. Let them know their support is important to you, and there may be some tough times ahead.

From my standpoint, it's worth it. Nothing you learn as a fulltime freelancer will ever be wasted, especially the feeling of freedom and satisfaction that naturally comes from independence. It's like learning to fish; it's a skill that can put food on the table for a lifetime.

As my fellow freelancer, P.J. Skerret, says, "The beauty of having freelanced successfully is knowing that, no matter what happens, you will always have a job you can fall back on."

INSIDER REPORT

"I have no illusions"

"I have no illusions that what I do is an art, but if you can turn a nice phrase, you can write about almost anything," says author and freelancer David Wright. The author of 36 books ranging from company histories to children's social studies books to travel guides, Wright says he takes a pragmatic approach.

"There is nothing wrong with writing anything that pays well. It will make you a better writer even if you hate direct mail or business writing. No matter what you are writing, the practice will help make your writing faster, tighter, better and more original," he says. Before embarking on his career as a fulltime freelance writer and author, Wright worked in public relations and spent six years writing and editing for daily newspapers including the *Chicago Tribune* and *The Beaver County Times* in Pennsylvania. There are many unique oppor-

David Wright

tunities for freelancers out there, says Wright, but you must be willing to try. "A lot of people seem to need to think twice before going out to the store, but I know one freelancer who moved to Bangkok. He doesn't even know the language, but he is regularly selling material. He lives simply, but he can make a living. For some of those smaller countries, if a freelancer isn't sending out news from there, no news is getting out."

Choosing what to write is an important decision, Wright says, and there are generally two ways to go. "You either have to do everything or become the ultimate expert in one small area. You can be a mile wide and an inch deep like I am or you can be 'the source.' "

Although Wright is a generalist who writes for magazines, book publishers and electronic formats, he has had most success writing short nonfiction books. His first book assignment was a company history of Harley Davidson published in 1983. The book sold 85,000 copies in three editions. Later, Wright began writing children's books known as "school and library books" for both book publishers and packagers. "As a kid I was sent to Vietnam and became interested in southeast Asia. I hounded children's book publishers to let me do social studies books about the area." He wrote books on Malaysia and Cambodia and later branched out to other topics of interest to the 12- to 14-year-old set including short biographies of John Lennon and Arthur Ashe.

"Social studies books are so much better today. It's no longer about how many pounds of bauxite a country produces but how other kids live."

With social studies books and with travel, another area in which Wright has published extensively, photography and illustration are an important part of the package. He has taken photos himself, but Wright often does photo research to find free or inexpensive images. Sometimes this takes a little creativity, he says. For the book on Ashe, he contacted sporting goods companies to find photos of the tennis great taken for various ad campaigns. When approaching a publisher with an idea for a book that will need photos, send color copies, he says.

INSIDER REPORT, *Wright*

For those interested in writing for school-age children, Wright has this advice: "Sixth-graders are a tough audience. You need to blow them away right from the start. You can't back into a book with kids or you're sunk. It says to them go watch TV or turn on a computer instead.

"With kids' books every chapter has to grab them, pull them in, but this would apply to books for adults too. And it would apply to any written media—books or even the Web."

Your lead is your key to opening publishers' doors, he says. "Your first sentence is not the most important sentence—it's your *only* sentence. Try never to start a piece with a sentence that reads like an 'editor's note.' Your first sentence has to absolutely slay them."

Once you get an assignment, says Wright, follow through is equally important. "Never turn anything in late. I feel I can't afford to let people wait. It can throw off the whole production process. With writing, time is money. If you have to put a lot of time into an article and compare it to the money, you may find it's not much money. That's why it's important to try to be fast. After I've talked to someone for a piece, I'm thinking about the lead right away in the car on the way home."

In book publishing, consolidation is eating up many opportunities, says Wright. "I've had to work more hours and it's getting harder." Again, he says the speed with which he completes projects helps him stay competitive.

"The market is changing," says Wright. "It seems to be in a downturn right now. I've been doing this 18 years and it's only been in the last two that I've been scratching for work. I think it's because we are in a post-pulp society—all the words are becoming electronic."

Yet, he says, the new electronic media presents some promising opportunities for writers. He recently worked on a series of travel guides done on CD-ROM format. "It was like a big fill-in-the-blanks project. I was limited to 250 words to give an overview of a city, but with those 250 words I almost could write whatever I wanted. Rather than think of a new format as limiting, you should approach it with enthusiasm."

Whether working on a CD-ROM project, a children's nonfiction book or an article, Wright says good research is important and being able to synthesize the research is even more important. "One thing newspapers taught me was to get the big overview of things, to read up on things and then to have the confidence to draw conclusions. I ask myself, 'What does the reader want to take away from this, what can he or she learn from this?' "

While Wright admits the market is particularly tough right now, he urges writers to pursue their dreams. "I tell people somebody's going to be doing it, it might as well be you."

—*Robin Gee*

How Much Should I Charge?

BY ROBIN GEE

More and more writers are making the switch from a fulltime job to a combination of a part-time job and freelance work or a fulltime freelance career. Economic factors play a part, of course, as employers continue to downsize, but many choose the freelance life for a variety of reasons—for more freedom, to have more time with their families, to have more control over their careers, and, simply, because they want to make a living doing what they love.

One of the first questions new freelancers ask is, "How much should I charge?" Unfortunately, there is not one set of standard, agreed-upon rates. Many factors play a part in how fees are set. Freelancers must take into account their overhead and the costs of doing business, their level of experience, area of expertise and the kind of work they do. Sometimes location plays a part, as does the nature and size of a client's business.

PRICING IN THE FREELANCE MARKET

The information supplied in this section is designed to give new freelancers and those interested in trying other areas of freelance an idea of what other freelancers are charging. Based on research—surveys and interviews with freelancers, clients and writers' organizations in the U.S. and Canada—we've compiled a list of typical freelance projects or services and typical ranges. Some of the ranges are quite broad because fees vary widely depending on location (generally more on either coast), the nature of the client (nonprofits and small businesses pay less than large corporations) and the size or complexity of the job (highly skilled or technical tasks pay more than more generalized work).

Knowing what the market will bear is an important part of establishing a viable fee schedule. The most common mistake freelancers make is selling themselves short, underestimating the value of good writing and editing skills to business and others in need of such services. On the other hand, you don't want to price yourself out of the market.

Networking with other writers in your area is the best way to learn how much to charge for your level of expertise and location. Not only can talking to other writers help you determine how much you can charge for a particular service, it can also help you learn of new opportunities as well as combat the isolation that can come from working alone. The grapevine is also very useful in identifying problem clients and areas of concern.

FREELANCERS' ORGANIZATIONS

Most freelancers belong to at least one writers' or freelancers' organization. The National Writers Association and the Freelance Editorial Association are two national groups working for the best interests of freelance writers and editors. If you specialize in a particular area such as translation or indexing there are a number of professional organizations for those working in these areas. Check the Organizations of Interest section in *Writer's Market* or in the *Literary Market Place* publishing trade directory for names and addresses of writers' organizations. Just as important are regional and local associations—not just for writers and editors—but also chambers of commerce and business groups in which you are likely to meet potential contacts.

ROBIN GEE *is former editor of* Novel & Short Story Writer's Market *and is currently a freelance writer and editor in Madison, Wisconsin.*

"At least 25 percent of my new business comes from networking," says Colorado-based freelancer Carole Williams, who went from a full-time career as the director of information for a nonprofit organization to freelancing. Williams is a member of the National Writers Association, her local Chamber of Commerce, the Denver Women's Press Club and the Colorado Independent Publishers Association, where she meets many self-publishers looking for help with promotion.

"I've also received many wonderful referrals from graphic designers and other writers," she says. In fact, she and other writers sometimes subcontract work on large jobs to each other. "In this business it's better to be open to working with and referring others rather than to be highly competitive."

SETTING YOUR FEES

Take what you've learned from others in the field and the ranges provided here as starting points for establishing your own fees. You must also assess how much your particular client is willing or able to pay. In general, working in advertising or for businesses pays better than writing for magazines or editing books. Yet many freelancers prefer to work in the publishing industry because it can be steady and interesting. If, after you've studied the market, you are still unsure about a particular client, try to find out what the budget is for a project and work from there.

Location used to play a larger part in influencing fees. Although East and West Coast clients still tend to pay more, the rest of the country is catching up. Thanks to fax machines, e-mail and other technology, where you live is less important for many businesses. You may live in the South or Midwest and end up working for an East Coast publisher accustomed to paying higher rates. On the other hand, living near a small business or publisher may give you the edge and create a steady income even though your clients may not pay as much as those far away.

While you can quote flat fees for various projects, experienced freelancers say the best way to start out is to charge hourly rates until you are certain how long a particular type of job should take. Still, there are surprises. Before taking on any new project, it's best to take a good look at it first. Ask if you can do a sample—a few pages—so you and the client can be certain you understand exactly what the job entails, and you can get a feel for how long it is likely to take.

One way to determine an hourly fee is to determine how much a company might pay per hour for someone on staff to do the same job. If, for example, you think a client would have to pay a staff person $26,000/year, divide that by 2,000 (approximately 40 hours a week for 50 weeks) and you would get $13/hour.

Next, add another 33 percent to cover the cost of fringe benefits that an employer would normally pay in Social Security, unemployment insurance, hospitalization, retirement funds, etc. This figure varies from employer to employer but the U.S. Chamber of Commerce reports that the U.S. average paid by employers is 37.6 percent of an employee's salary.

Then add a dollars-per-hour figure to cover your actual overhead expenses for office space, equipment, supplies plus time spent for professional meetings, research and soliciting new business. (To get this figure, add one year's expenses and divide by the number of hours per year you have been freelancing.) In the beginning (when you have large investments such as a computer) you may have to adjust this amount to avoid pricing yourself out of the market. Finally, you may wish to figure in a profit percentage to be useful for capital investments or future growth.

It's useful to take this figure and compare it to the ranges provided here or those suggested by the different freelance organizations. Many freelancers temper the figure from the above formula with what they've learned from suggested ranges and networking. Keep in mind, too, that few fulltime freelancers bill 2,000 hours per year. Most who consider themselves fulltime bill about half that many hours. Some freelancers start with the amount they'd like to make in a year and work down to determine how many projects they need to do and what rate to charge.

Here's an example:
$26,000 (salary) ÷ 2,000 (hours) = $13.00 per hour
+ 4.29 (33% to cover fringe benefits, taxes, etc.)
+ 2.50 (overhead based on annual expenses of $5,000)
+ 1.30 (10% profit margin)
$21.09 per hour charge

No matter how you determine your fees initially, you will need to consider your experience, your client's budget and the current market value of your service.

Once you and your client have come to an agreement on how much to charge and the details of your assignment, make sure you follow up with a written contract or letter of agreement signed by both parties outlining exactly what is to be done. Experienced freelancers say this is the best way to avoid misunderstandings down the line. If there is any question about how long a job should take, be sure the agreement indicates that you are estimating the time and that your project fee is based on a certain number of hours. If you quote a flat fee, you should stipulate in the agreement that a higher rate might be charged for overtime hours or late changes in the project.

Communication is important in dealing with clients. Make sure they know right away if you find the project is more complex and will take more time than you anticipated. Leave yourself open to renegotiation and, again, be sure to put any renegotiated fees in writing. On big jobs, some freelancers ask for partial payment at different stages of the project.

Freelancers who deal with businesses (especially those working in public relations and advertising) are careful to outline additional expenses that might be charged. Some figure this into their flat fees, but if you require reimbursement for extensive photocopying, postage, gas mileage, etc., it's best to make sure your client knows upfront and that you get it in writing that these expenses will be paid. The bottom line: clear communication and mutual respect between you and your client is an important factor in building your credibility and your business.

FREELANCE TRENDS

"How Much Should I Charge" has become a regular feature in this book and you will notice this year we've streamlined and reorganized some of the categories to better reflect changes in the field. We've noticed a few trends worth mentioning, too. Several freelance writers and editors have come to think of themselves as consultants. Writing consultants used to deal mostly with training others to improve their writing and editing skills. This is still a primary focus of many consultants, but others have added editing, manuscript evaluation and various writing projects to their list of services. In fact, the Professional Writing Consultants organization recently changed its name to the Association of Professional Communications Consultants to better reflect the growing diversity in their field.

Consultant Dan Dieterich says consulting is well suited to writers or editors who are comfortable working in front of a group and who enjoy teaching others how to improve their writing skills (see Insider Report with Dieterich on page 54). Some beginning consultants fear selling themselves as trainers. Yet, he says, keep in mind that if you develop a good program you will be benefiting a large group of people as well as yourself.

"Many consultants get into the business through academia, a place where we teach for the love of learning, so we tend to undercharge for our services. Good communication skills can make the difference between success and failure in business and many organizations are willing to pay for help in these areas accordingly," he says. Deiterich has done a variety of work for various businesses including business communication development and proposal evaluation, but he enjoys teaching others best. Some of the training he's done includes helping school teachers eliminate sexist language from their communications, assisting business people assess their needs in order to write better proposals, and helping businesses develop their own inhouse training programs.

Another growing area is technical writing. Ever since computers became commonplace there has been a need for writers and editors who can help develop clear training manuals and documentation, but the World Wide Web and an explosion in software has added even more opportunities for those with computer savvy. Indexing skills are needed for computer database archiving, and editors or writers who can identify key words and write clearly may find a number of projects developing online help programs for various software.

Writers and designers are needed for webpage development and editing for almost every type of business. Since this is such a new area, we took the average rate range, but have heard of freelancers receiving everything from $10-12/hour for a small organization's webpage to charging more than $10,000 for a large corporate site.

This type of work, however, usually requires expertise in writing in the HTML computer language and often jobs include graphic-design skills. Training in this area is becoming more available. Kurt Foss, professor of journalism at the University of Wisconsin, teaches a multimedia publishing course designed to prepare students for changes in technology. He says businesses are beginning to understand that they may need to hire writers and designers separately for webpage jobs. Yet, even if design is not included, writers will have to learn new skills to write effectively for webpages and software programs.

"There's a whole new area called multimedia reporting. Writers need to write in a nonlinear fashion," says Foss. People using websites and CD-ROM programs can start at different places and move about at random within the program so writing must be self-contained on each subject. Also writers need to think in terms of a variety of media. When interviewing, Foss thinks of sound clips from his taped interviews and possibilities for visuals.

Even in established areas of freelancing there have been some changes. In the public relations field more and more companies are outsourcing all their PR services. They may hire on an as-needed basis or hire someone who works on a retainer. Many former public relations employees are taking their skills into the freelance marketplace.

Again, keep in mind that reading the ranges in this book or looking at those provided by some of the professional organizations is only a first step in determining how much you should charge. Networking and studying the ever-changing market will help you remain competitive and motivated.

ADVERTISING, COPYWRITING & PR

Advertising copywriting: $35-100/hour; $250 and up per day; $500 and up per week; $1,000-$2,000 as a monthly retainer. Flat-fee-per-ad rates could range from $100 and up per page depending on the size and kind of client. In Canada rates range from $40-80/hour.

Advertorials: $25-35/hour; up to $1/word or by flat fee ($300 for about 700 words is typical). In Canada, 40-80¢/word; $35-75/hour.

Book jacket copywriting: $100-600 for front cover jacket plus flaps and back jacket copy summarizing content and tone of the book.

Catalog copywriting: $25-$45/hour or $85 and up per project.

Copyediting for advertising: $25-35/hour.

Direct-mail copywriting: $25-45/hour; $75 and up per item or $60-1,000/page.

Direct-mail packages: This includes copywriting direct mail letter, response card and advertising materials. Up to $85/hour or $500-3,000/project, depending on complexity of the project. Additional charges for production such as desktop publishing, addressing, etc.

Direct mail response card for a product: $250-500/project.

Fundraising campaign brochure: $50-75 for research (20 hours) and copywriting (30 hours);

up to $5,000 for major campaign brochure, including research, writing and production (about 50 hours of work).

New product release: $20-35/hour or $300-500/release.

News release: *See Press release.*

Political campaigns, public relations: Small town or state campaigns, $10-50/hour; congressional, gubernatorial or other national campaigns, $25-100/hour or up to 10 percent of campaign budget.

Promotion for events: $20-30/hour. For conventions and longer events, payment may be per diem or a flat fee of $500-2,500. *See also Press release.*

Press kits: $500-3,000/project.

Press release: $20-30/hour or $200-500/release.

Print advertisement: $200-500/project. In Canada, $100-200/concept. *See also Advertising copywriting*

Product information: $30-60/hour; $400-500/day or $100-300/page. *See also Sales and services brochures and fliers for smaller projects.*

Promotion for tourism, museums, art shows, etc.: $20-$50 and up per hour for writing or editing promotion copy. Additional charges for production, mailings, etc.

Public relations for businesses: $250-600/day plus expenses average—more for large corporations.

Public relations for government: $25-50/hour or a monthly retainer based on number of hours per period. Lower fees for local government agencies, higher for state-level and above.

Public relations for organizations or nonprofits: $15-35/hour. If working on a monthly retainer, $100-500/month.

Public relations for schools or libraries: $15-20/hour for small districts or libraries; up to $35 for larger districts.

Radio advertisement: $50-100/script; $200-400/week for part-time positions writing radio ads, depending on the size of the city (and market).

Sales and services brochures and fliers: $20-$600/published page or from $100 to $7,500/project depending on size and type of business (small nonprofit organization to a large corporation) and on the number of pages (usually from 1-16) and complexity of the job.

Sales letters: $350-1,000 for 1-2 pages.

Speech editing or evaluation: $20/hour and up.

Speechwriting (general): $30-85/hour. In Canada, $75-125/hour or $70-100/minute of speech.

Speechwriting for business owners or executives: Up to $80/hour or a flat fee of about $100 for a short (6- or 7- minute speech); $500-3,000 for up to 30 minutes. Rates also depend on size of the company and the event.

Speechwriting for government officials: $4,000 for 20 minutes plus up to $1,000 for travel and expenses.

Speechwriting for political candidates: $250 and up for local candidates (about 15 minutes); $375-800 for statewide candidates and $1,000 or more for national congressional candidates.

TV commercial: $60-375/finished minute; $1,000-2,000/finished project. In Canada, $60-130/minute of script (CBC pays Writers Guild rates, CTV pays close to that and others pay less. For example, TV Ontario pays $70-100/script minute).

AUDIOVISUALS & ELECTRONIC COMMUNICATIONS

Audiocassette scripts: $10-50/scripted minute, assuming written from existing client materials, with no additional research or meetings; otherwise $75-100/minute, $750 minimum.

Audiovisuals: For writing, $250-350/requested scripted minute; includes rough draft, editing conference with client, and final shooting script. For consulting, research, producing, directing, soundtrack oversight, etc. $400-600/day plus travel and expenses. Writing fee is sometimes 10% of gross production price as billed to client. Some charge flat fee of $1,500-2,100/package.

Book summaries for film producers: $50-100/book. *Note: You must live in the area where the business is located to get this kind of work.*

Business film scripts (training and information): $200-250/day.

Copyediting audiovisuals: $20-25/hour.

Industrial product film: $125-150/minute; $500 minimum flat fee.

Novel synopsis for film producer: $150 for 5-10 pages typed, single spaced.

Radio continuity writing: $5/page to $150/week, part-time. In Canada, $40-80/minute of script; $640/show for a multi-part series.

Radio copywriting: *See Advertising, Copywriting & PR.*

Radio documentaries: $258 for 60 minutes, local station.

Radio editorials: $10-30 for 90-second to two-minute spots.

Radio interviews: For National Public Radio, up to 3 minutes, $25; 3-10 minutes, $40-75; 10-60 minutes, $125 to negotiable fees. Small radio stations would pay approximately 50% of the NPR rate; large stations, double the NPR rate.

Script synopsis for business: $40/hour.

Script synopsis for agent or film producer: $75 for 2-3 typed pages, single-spaced.

Scripts for nontheatrical films for education, business, industry: Prices vary among producers, clients, and sponsors and there is no standardization of rates in the field. Fees include $75-120/minute for one reel (10 minutes) and corresponding increases with each successive reel; approximately 10% of the production cost of films that cost the producer more than $1,500/release minute.

Screenwriting: $6,000 and up per project.

Slide presentation: Including visual formats plus audio, $150-600 for 10-15 minutes.

Slide/single image photos: $75 flat fee.

Slide/tape script: $75-100/minute, $750 minimum.

TV commercial: *See Advertising, Copywriting & PR.*

TV documentary: 30-minute 5-6 page proposal outline, $1,839 and up; 15-17 page treatment, $1,839 and up; less in smaller cities. In Canada research for a documentary runs about $6,500.

TV editorials: $35 and up for 1-minute, 45 seconds (250-300 words).

TV filmed news and features: From $10-20/clip for 30-second spot; $15-25 for 60-second clip; more for special events.

TV information scripts: Short 5- to 10-minute scripts for local cable TV stations, $10-15/hour.

TV news film still photo: $3-6 flat fee.

TV news story: $16-25 flat fee.

TV, national and local public stations: For programs, $35-100/minute down to a flat fee of $5,000 and up for a 30- to 60-minute script.

TV scripts: (Teleplay only), 60 minutes; network prime time, Writers Guild rates: $14,048; 30 minutes, $10,414. In Canada, $60-130/minute of script.

BOOK PUBLISHING

Abstracting and abridging: Up to $75/hour for nonfiction; $30-35/hour for reference and professional journals.

Anthology editing: Variable advance plus 3-15 percent of royalties. Advance should cover reprint fees or fees are handled by the publisher. Flat-fee-per-manuscript rates range from $500-5,000 and up.

Book proposal consultation: $20-75/hour or a flat rate of $100-250.

Book proposal writing: Up to $150/page or a flat rate of $175-3,000 depending on length and whether the client provides full information or the writer must do research, and whether a sample chapter is required.

Book query critique: $50 for critique of letter to the publisher and outline.

Book summaries for book clubs: $50-100/book.

Content editing: $20-50/hour or $600-5,000/manuscript, based on the size and complexity of the project.

Copyediting: $16-40/hour or $2-4/page. Lower-end rates charged for light copyedit (3-10 pages per hour) of general, trade material. Higher-end rates charged for substantive copyediting or for textbooks and technical material (2-5 pages per hour).

Ghostwriting, as told to: This is writing for a celebrity or expert either for a self-published book or for a publisher. Author gets full advance plus 50 percent of royalties. Hourly rates for subjects who are self-publishing are $25-80/hour. In Canada, author also gets full advance and 50 percent of royalties or $10,000-20,000 flat fee per project. Research time is charged extra.

Ghostwriting, no credit: Projects may include writing for an individual planning to self publish or for a book packager, book producer, publisher, agent or corporation. Rates range from $5,000-35,000 and up (plus expenses) per project; packagers pay flat fee or combination of advance plus royalties. For self-published clients, ask for one-fourth down payment, one-fourth when book is half-finished, one-fourth at the three-quarters mark and one-fourth upon completion.

Indexing: $20-40/hour; charge higher hourly rate if using a computer index program that takes fewer hours. Also can charge $2-6/indexable page; 40-70 cents per line of index or a flat fee of $250-500 depending on length.

Jacket copywriting: *See Advertising, Copywriting & PR.*

Manuscript evaluation and critique: $150-200 for outline and first 20,000 words; $300-500 for up to 100,000 words. Also $15-35/hour for trade books, slightly less for nonprofits. Page rates run from $1.50-2.50/page.

Movie novelization: $3,500-15,000, depending on writer's reputation, amount of work to be done and amount of time writer is given.

Novel synopsis for a literary agent: $150 for 5-10 pages typed, single-spaced.

Page layout (desktop publishing): $20-35/hour or $5-15/page. Higher per page rates may be charged if material involves complex technical material and graphics.

Production editing/project management: This is overseeing the production of a project, coordinating editing and production stages, etc. $25-50/hour.

Proofreading: $12-30/hour or $1.50-3.50/page. High-end rates are charged for technical, scientific and reference material.

Research for writers or book publishers: $20-40/hour and up; $150 and up per day plus expenses. A flat rate of $300-500 may be charged, depending on complexity of the job.

Rewriting: $18-50/hour; $5-7/page. Some writers receive royalties on book projects.

Translation (literary): $30-35/hour; also $95-125 per 1,000 English words.

Typesetting: $20-35/hour or $4-7/page.

BUSINESS

Annual reports: A brief report with some economic information and an explanation of figures, $25-60/hour; 12- to 16-page report, $600-1,500 flat fees for editing. If extensive research and/or writing is involved in a large project, rates could go as high as $5,000-10,000/project. A report that must meet Securities and Exchange Commission (SEC) standards and reports requiring legal language could bill $40-85/hour. Bill separately if desktop publication (typesetting, page layout, etc.) is involved (some smaller firms and nonprofits may ask for writing/production packages).

Associations and organizations (writing for): $15-25/hour for small organizations; up to $50/hour for larger associations or a flat fee depending on the length and complexity of the project.

For example, $500-1,000 for association magazine article (2,000 words) or $1,000-1,800 for a 10-page informational booklet.

Audiovisuals/audiocassette scripts: *See Audiovisuals & Electronic Communications.*

Book summaries for businesses: $25-50/page or $20-35/hour.

Brochures, fliers, booklets for business: $25-40/hour for writing or from $500-$4,000 and up per project (12-16 pages and more). Additional charges for desktop publishing, usually $20-40/hour; $20-30/page or a flat fee per project. *See also Copyediting for business or Manuscript editing/evaluation for business in this section.*

Business editing (general): $25-50/hour.

Business letters: For letters such as form letters designed to improve customer relations or interoffice communications, $100-500/letter depending on the size of the business and the length/complexity of the material.

Business plan: $1/word; $200/manuscript page or up to $1,500/project. High-end rates are charged if extensive research is involved. Sometimes research is charged separately per hour or per day.

Business writing (general): $30-80/hour. In Canada, $1-2/word or $50-100/hour. *See other entries in this section and in Advertising, Copywriting & PR for specific projects such as brochures, copywriting, speechwriting, brochures or business letters. For business film script-writing see Audiovisuals & Electronic Communications.*

Business writing seminars: $500 for a half-day seminar, plus travel expenses or $1,000-5,000/day. Rates depend on number of participants as well as duration. Average per-person rate is $50/person for a half-day seminar. *See also Educational and Literary Services.*

Catalogs for business: $25-40/hour or $25-600/printed page; more if tables or charts must be reworked for readability or consistency. Additional charges for desktop publishing ($20-40/hour is average).

Collateral materials for business: *See individual pieces (brochures, catalogs, etc.) in this section and in Advertising, Copywriting & PR.*

Commercial reports for business, insurance companies, credit agencies: $6-15/page.

Consultation on communications: $300-2,000/day. Lower-end fees charged to nonprofits and small businesses.

Consumer complaint letters (answering): $25-30/letter.

Copyediting for business: $20-40/hour or $20-50/manuscript page, up to $40/hour for business proposals. Charge lower-end fees ($15-25/hour) to nonprofits and very small businesses.

Corporate histories: $1,000-2,000 flat fee.

Corporate periodicals, editing: $30-75/hour.

Corporate periodicals, writing: $30-100/hour, depending on size and nature of the corporation. Also 50¢ to $1/word. In Canada, $1-2/word or $40-90/hour.

Corporate profile: $1,250-2,500 flat fee for up to 3,000 words or charge on a per word basis, up to $1/word.

Financial presentation: $1,500-4,500 for a 20-30 minute presentation.

Fundraising campaign brochure: *See Advertising, Copywriting & PR.*

Ghostwriting for business (usually trade magazine articles or business columns): $25-100/hour; $200 or more per day plus expenses (depending on amount of research involved, length of project).

Government research: $35-50/hour.

Government writing: $30-50/hour. In Canada, $50-80/hour.

Grant proposal writing for nonprofits: $30-100/hour or flat fee.

Indexing for professional journals: $20-40/hour.

Industrial/service business training manual: $25-40/hour; $50-100/manuscript page or a flat fee, $1,000-4,000, depending on number of pages and complexity of the job.

Industry training film scripts: *See Business film scripts in Audiovisuals & Electronic Communications.*

Industrial product film script: *See Audiovisuals & Electronic Communications.*

Job application letters: $20-40/letter.

Manuals/documentation: $25-60/hour. *See also Computers, Science and Technical Writing.*

Manuscript editing/evaluation for trade journals: $20-40/hour.

Market research survey reports: $25-50/hour or $500-1,500/day; also flat rates of $500-2,000/ project.

Newsletters, abstracting: $30/hour.

Newsletters, desktop publishing/production: $20-60/hour. Higher-end rates for scanning photographs, advertising layout, illustration or design. Editing charged extra.

Newsletters, editing: $25-45/hour; $50-500/issue. Higher-end fees charged if writing or production is included. Editors who produce a regular newsletter on a monthly or quarterly basis tend to charge per month or per issue—and find them easier to do after initial set up.

Newsletters, writing: $25-45/hour; 25¢ to $1/word; $25-300/page; $35-2,500/story or $375-2,500/issue. In Canada, $45-70/hour.

Programmed instruction consultation fees: *See Educational & Literary Services.*

Programmed instruction materials for business: *See Educational & Literary Services.*

Proofreading for business: $15-50/hour; low-end fees for nonprofits.

Public relations: *See Advertising, Copywriting and PR.*

Retail newsletters for customers: Charge regular newsletter rates or $175-300 per 4-page project. Additional charges for desktop publishing.

Sales brochures, fliers, letters, other advertising materials: *See Advertising, Copywriting & PR.*

Scripts for business/training films: *See Audiovisuals & Electronic Communications.*

Translation, commercial: $30-45/hour; $115-125 per 1,000 words. Higher-end fees for non-European languages into English.

Translation for government agencies: $30-45; up to $125 per 1,000 words. Higher-end fees for non-European languages into English.

Translation through translation agencies: Agencies by 33⅓ percent average less than end-user clients and mark up translator's prices by as much as 100 percent or more.

Translation, technical: $30-45/hour; $125 and up per 1,000 words, depending on complexity of the material.

COMPUTER, SCIENTIFIC & TECHNICAL

Computer documentation, general (hard copy): $30-75/hour; $20-30/page. *See also Software manual writing in this section.*

Computer documentation (on line): $30-35/hour; $15-25/screen.

Demonstration software: $70 and up per hour.

Legal/government editing: $20-65/hour.

Legal/government writing: $30-65/hour.

Medical and science editing: $20-65/hour, depending on the complexity of the material and the expertise of the editor.

Medical and science proofreading: $15-30/hour.

Medical and science writing: $30-65/hour; $20-30/page, depending on the complexity of the project and the writer's expertise.

Online editing: $30-35/hour.

Software manual writing: $35-50/hour for research and writing.

Technical editing: $20-60/hour or $150-1,000/day.

Technical typesetting: $4-7/page; $25-35/hour; more for inputting of complex material.

Technical writing: $30-75/hour; $20-30/page. *See Computer documentation and Software manual writing in this section.*

Technical translation: *See item in Business section.*

Webpage design: $50-100/page.

Webpage editing: $30/page and up.

EDITORIAL/DESIGN PACKAGES

Business catalogs: *See Business.*

Desktop publishing: For 1,000 dots-per-inch type, $5-15/camera-ready page of straight type; $30/camera-ready page with illustrations, maps, tables, charts, photos; $100-150/camera-ready page for oversize pages with art. Also $20-40/hour depending on graphics, number of photos, and amount of copy to be typeset. Packages often include writing, layout/design, and typesetting services.

Greeting cards ideas (with art included): Anywhere from $30-300, depending on size of company.

Newsletters: *See Desktop Publishing (this section) and Newsletters (Business).*

Picture editing: $20-40.

Photo brochures: $700-15,000 flat fee for photos and writing.

Photo research: $15-30/hour.

Photography: $10-150/b&w photo; $25-300/color photo; also $800/day.

EDUCATIONAL & LITERARY SERVICES

Business writing seminars: *See Business.*

Consultation for individuals (in business): $250-1,000/day.

Consultation on communications: *See Business.*

Developing and designing courses for business or adult education: $250-$1,500day or flat fee.

Editing for individual clients: $10-50/hour or $2-7/page.

Educational consulting and educational grant and proposal writing: $250-750/day or $30-75/hour.

Lectures at national conventions by well-known authors: $2,500-20,000 and up, plus expenses; less for panel discussions.

Lectures at regional writers' conferences: $300 and up, plus expenses.

Lectures to local groups, librarians or teachers: $50-150.

Lectures to school classes: $25-75; $150/day; $250/day if farther than 100 miles.

Manuscript evaluation for theses/dissertations: $15-30/hour.

Poetry manuscript critique: $25 per 16-line poem.

Programmed instruction consultant fees: $300-1,000/day, $50-75/hour.

Programmed instruction materials for business: $50/hour for inhouse writing and editing; $500-1,000/day plus expenses for outside research and writing. Alternate method: $2,000-5,000/hour of programmed training provided depending on technicality of subject.

Public relations for schools: *See Advertising, Copywriting & PR.*

Readings by poets, fiction writers: $25-600 depending on author.

Scripts for nontheatrical films for education: *See Audiovisuals & Electronic Communications.*

Short story manuscript critique: 3,000 words, $40-60.

Teaching adult education course: $10-60/class hour; fee usually set by school, not negotiated by teachers.

Teaching adult seminar: $400 plus mileage and per diem for a 6- or 7-hour day; plus 40% of the tuition fee beyond the sponsor's break-even point. In Canada, $35-50/hour.

Teaching Business writing to company employees: *See Consultation on communications in Business section.*

Teaching college course or seminar: $15-70/class hour.

Teaching creative writing in school: $15-70/hour of instruction, or $1,500-2,000 per 12-15 week semester; less in recessionary times.

Teaching elementary and middle school teachers how to teach writing to students: $75-150 for a 1- to 1½ hour session.

Teaching home-bound students: $5-15/hour.

Tutoring: $25 per 1- to 1½ hour private session.

TV instruction taping: $150 per 30-minute tape; $25 residual each time tape is sold.

Writer-in-schools: Arts council program, $130/day; $650/week. Personal charges plus expenses vary from $25/day to $100/hour depending on school's ability to pay.

Writer's workshop: Lecturing and seminar conducting, $50-150/hour to $750/day plus expenses; local classes, $35-50/student for 10 sessions.

Writing for individual clients: $25-100/hour, depending on the situation. *See also Business writing in Business section.*

Writing for scholarly journals: $75/hour.

MAGAZINES & TRADE JOURNALS

Abstracting: $20-30/hour for trade and professional journals; $8 per abstract for scholarly journals.

Article manuscript critique: 3,000 words, $40.

Arts reviewing: $35-100 flat fee or 20-30¢/word, plus admission to events or copy of CD (for music).

Book reviews: $50-300 flat fee and copy of book.

Consultation on magazine editorial: $1,000-1,500/day plus expenses.

Copyediting magazines: $16-30/hour.

Editing: General, $25-500/day or $250-2,000/issue; Religious publications, $200-500/month or $15-30/hour.

Fact checking: $17-25/hour or 75¢ to $1/item.

Feature articles: Anywhere from 20¢ to $4/word; or $200-2,000 per 2,000 word article, depending on size (circulation) and reputation of magazine.

Ghostwriting articles (general): Up to $2/word; or $300-3,000/project.

Indexing: $15-40/hour.

Magazine, city, calendar of events column: $50-150/column.

Magazine column: 200 words, $40; 800 words, $400. Also $1/word. Larger circulation publications pay fees related to their regular word rate.

Manuscript consultation: $25-50/hour.

Manuscript criticism: $40-60 per article or short story of up to 3,000 words. Also $20-25/hour.

Picture editing: *See Editorial/Design Packages.*

Permission fees to publishers to reprint article or story: $75-500; 10-15¢/word; less for charitable organizations.

Production editing: $15-30/hour.

Proofreading: $12-25/hour.

Research: $20-25/hour.

Rewriting: Up to $80/manuscript page; also $100/published page.

Science writing for magazines: $2,000-5,000/article. *See also Computer, Scientific & Technical Writing.*

Special news article: For a business's submission to trade publication, $250-500 for 1,000 words. In Canada, 25-45¢/word.

Stringing: 20¢ to $1/word based on circulation. Daily rate: $150-250 plus expenses; weekly rate: $900 plus expenses. Also $10-35/hour plus expenses; $1/column inch.

Trade journal ad copywriting: *See Advertising, Copywriting & PR.*

Trade journal feature article: For business client, $400-1,000. Also $1-2/word.

NEWSPAPERS

Ads for small business: $25 for a small, one-column ad, or $10/hour and up. *See also Advertising, Copywriting & PR.*

Arts reviewing: For weekly newspapers, $15-35 flat fee; for dailies, $45 and up; for Sunday supplements, $100-400. Also admission to event or copy of CD (for music).

Book reviews: For small newspapers, byline and the book only; for larger publications, $35-200. Also copy of the book.

Column, local: $10-20 for a weekly; $15-30 for dailies of 4,000-6,000 circulation; $35-50 for 7,000-10,000 dailies; $40-75 for 11,000-25,000 dailies; and $100 and up for larger dailies. Also 15-80¢/word depending on circulation.

Copyediting: $10-30/hour; up to $40/hour for large daily paper.

Copywriting: *See Advertising, Copywriting & PR.*

Dance criticism: $25-400/article.

Drama criticism: Local, newspaper rates; non-local, $50 and up per review.

Editing/manuscript evaluation: $25/hour.

Fact checking: *See Magazines & Trade Journals.*

Feature: $25-35/article plus mileage for a weekly; $40-500 for a daily (depending on size of paper). Also 10-30¢/word. In Canada $15-40/word, but rates vary widely.

Obituary copy: Where local newspapers permit lengthier than normal notices paid for by the funeral home (and charged to the family), $15-25. Writers are engaged by funeral homes.

Picture editing: *See Editorial/Design Packages.*

Proofreading: $16-20/hour.

Science writing for newspapers: *See Computer, Scientific & Technical Writing.*

Stringing: Sometimes flat rate of $20-35 to cover meeting and write article; sometimes additional mileage payment.

Syndicted column, self-promoted: $5-10 each for weeklies; $10-25/week for dailies, based on circulation.

MISCELLANEOUS

Comedy writing for night club entertainers: Gags only, $5-25 each. Routines, $100-1,000 per minute. Some new comics may try to get a 5-minute routine for $150; others will pay $2,500 for a 5-minute bit from a top writer.

Comics writing: $35-50/page and up for established comics writers.

Contest judging: Short manuscripts, $10/entry; with one-page critique, $15-25. Overall contest judging: $100-500.

Corporate comedy skits: $300-800 for half-hour skit (used at meetings, conventions).

Craft ideas with instructions: $50-200/project.

Encyclopedia articles: Entries in some reference books, such as biographical encyclopedias, 500-2,000 words; pay ranges from $60-80 per 1,000 words. Specialists' fees vary.

Family histories: Fees depend on whether the writer edits already prepared notes or does extensive research and writing; and the length of the work, $500-15,000.

Institutional (church, school) history: $200-1,000 for 15-50 pages, or $20-35/hour.

Manuscript typing: Depending on manuscript length and delivery schedule, $1.25-2/page with one copy; $15/hour.

Party toasts, limericks, place card verses: $1.50/line.

Research for individuals: $5-30/hour, depending on experience, geographic area and nature of work.

Special occasion booklet: Family keepsake of a wedding, anniversary, Bar Mitzvah, etc., $120 and up.

Interactive Writing

BY ANTHONY TEDESCO

Let's get one thing straight. If you're looking to learn all those geek-speak emoticon hieroglyphic winkey-smiley code symbols, you've come to the wrong article. This is not about cyber-centric parlance. There will be no 12-letter acronyms in lieu of conversational phrases. There will be no obscure technical references ending with three exclamation points denoting excitement about said obscure technical references.

Sure there are some Net users who communicate almost exclusively in this cryptic high-tech vernacular, but they're the same people you spent most of your junior high school years beating up. Well, razzing at least. And the majority of today's online writers and publishers spent their junior high school years razzing them too (okay, some of us semi-juvenile ones still do).

Point is: Most online writers aren't techies writing for techies about techie things. We're just opportunists who've tapped a new market—25 million readers strong and growing faster than any other mass medium. For us, technology is a means not an end. We've supplemented our newsstand options with the Net, but we're still writing and selling the same cultural/comical/whatever-ical pieces we've been writing for traditional media.

Maybe not *exactly* the same. The same topics, yes. But writing for the Internet and the Internet's audience does have its distinct nuances, and knowing these nuances will help you sell articles online. Here are some tips, traps and tricks (try saying that ten times fast) that I've learned from being on both sides of the online magazine query letter for the last four years.

KNOW YOUR READERS

Now that I've hopefully established that all Net users aren't (necessarily) quintessential tech weenies, let's take a quick look at the official landscape of online readers, care of the research firms gathered at CyberAtlas (www.cyberatlas.com):

- the average Internet user is 32 years old;
- 64 percent of all Internet users have at least a college degree (Nielsen Media Research);
- 42 percent of Internet users are female;
- Internet users have a median household income of $59,000 (GVU).

Those are a few stats, but the bottom line is that online readers are really whoever you want them to be. With personal Net access costing less than $20 per month, and free access being provided by everyone from public and private schools to public libraries and employers, there are just so many different people online—people of all ages, academic backgrounds, incomes, and cultures—that you can easily find readers interested in topics that interest you, as well as online magazines catering to those interests.

FIND YOUR TARGET MAGAZINES

The trick, of course, is finding online magazines catering to your interests that also pay writers for content. A few of those magazines are listed with submission guidelines following this

ANTHONY TEDESCO (anthony@crispzine.com) is editorial director of Crisp (http://www.crispzine.com), as well as a freelance writer for both online and offline publications, and co-author of Insider's Guide to Interactive Writing and Publishing, along with co-authors Paul Tedesco and Thomas Elia, both of whom contributed to this article.

article. Another resource is forthcoming in a book I've co-authored (shameless-yet-pertinent plug) entitled *Insider's Guide to Interactive Writing and Publishing* which will include a comprehensive list of online markets and submission guidelines. Until then, all it takes is a little foraging to customize your own list of potential online publications.

A good place to start is on the pages of the very same markets you've targeted in traditional media. Most print publications have companion online magazines that feature high percentages of original online writing. Check the masthead page for their corresponding URL (Internet address), or peruse the advertising pages for website promotions. Even publishing companies with the resources of many magazines usually opt for creating original online brands merely rooted in their print counterparts. Condé Nast, for example, publishes the "online versions" of its magazines *Gourmet* and *Bon Appetit* under the online brand Epicurious Food (http://www.epicurious.com), with 80 percent original online content.

You can occasionally find a print publication's online version by simply typing the publication's title into the Internet address (http://www.thetitle.com). If that fails, try entering the title into one of the Internet's many search engines.

Here are a few pervasive print publications with sister online ventures:

- *Boston Globe* online (http://www.boston.com)
- *USA Today* online (http://www.usatoday.com)
- *New York Times Interactive* (http://www.nytimes.com)
- *Internet World* online (http://www.iworld.com)
- *Advertising Age* online (http://www.adage.com)
- *The Village Voice* online (http://www.villagevoice.com)
- *GQ, Mademoiselle, Glamour,* and *Details* online (http://www.swoon.com)
- *Elle* online (http://www.ellemag.com)
- *Playboy* online (http://www.playboy.com)
- *Gourmet* and *Bon Appetit* online (http://www.epicurious.com)
- *Wired* online (http://www.hotwired.com)
- *The Wall Street Journal Interactive Edition* (http://www.wsj.com)

Another way to locate online magazines with your target readers are directories and electronic newsstands, though there are so many online magazines on the Internet that it's easy to get overwhelmed with options, and without actually querying the editor it's also often difficult to discern whether they pay their freelancers. The good news: If you can muster the perseverance, the Internet is your best shot at securing a patron publication for your most idiosyncratic of interests. Here are some resources:

- John Labovitz's E-Zine List (http://www.meer.net/~johnl/e-zine-list/index.html) touts almost 2,000 online magazines searchable by title, subject or even keywords.
- F5 Ezine Archive (http://www.well.com/conf/f5/ezines.html) features links to other online magazine archives.
- Etext Archives (http://www.etext.org) is home to electronic texts of all kinds.
- Ezine Newsgroup (alt.ezines) is a good place to query the ezine community about any genre of magazine.
- The Well's Publications Area (gopher://gopher.well.com/11/Publications) offers information on the full gamut of online magazines.

ADAPTING YOUR WRITING TO THE WEB

Once you're armed/dangerous with your target list of online markets, you should consider adapting your writing muse to the nuances of the World Wide Web.

Local writing for a global audience

The words "World" and "Wide" make this first tip so obvious that writers often overlook it. Readers on the Internet hail from all over the world. English is still the standard, but English doesn't mean U.S.-centric. It's just as easy for someone in Sri Lanka to read a particular online magazine as it is for someone from Seattle. Your articles should reflect that diversity without watering down the distinctions that make it real. Think local details with global appeal.

Take, for example, one of our columns at *Crisp* (http://www.crispzine.com) entitled "Actor's Journal: Amy Carle rants and rambles about trying to balance her office day job with her theater-group dream job." Amy's writing is so engaging because, well, a) she's an engaging writer/person; and b) she infuses her journal entries with personal details such as her coworker's compulsion with keeping the workplace temperature at a brisk sub-zero, or the high, clunky and undoubtedly dangerous heels that she's agreed to dance in for the full run of Chicago-based Roadwork's rendition of *Orestes*.

Is Mr. Sri Lanka going to make it to the show to see the heels? Probably not (his loss). Is it cold in your workplace? I don't know, I don't work with you. But Amy balances these animated details with the bigger picture that people all around the world can relate to: making sacrifices in the pursuit of your passions; dealing with quirky (freaky) coworkers at a job that means little more to you than money for bills while pursuing those passions.

Use your own voice

Along the same lines of personal details, Net readers have a penchant for wanting to know people, real people, real regular Joe/Jody individuals, you. I think it stems from the fact that regular Joe/Jody has always had equal billing to corporate behemoths. Homepages are as accessible as high-falutin' sites, and Net users still prize themselves as anti-establishment, give or take an establishment.

Also, although the Internet is a global gathering, it's a gathering that empowers and connects individuals. This subtle dichotomy was best demonstrated by a Net-spawned amateur exhibitionist who was adamant about her being shy, despite her nude pictures posted on her site at . . . (sorry). (Please note: I, of course, merely read about her site in a recent issue of *Details*.) Anyway, she explained that the only reason she was able to, um, exhibit herself in front of so many people was that she wasn't doing it in front of all those people at once. Each person experienced her "art" individually, at his or her own computer.

Okay, that was a dangerous example but one worth illustrating this most pivotal aspect of interactive writing: Although it feels like you're writing for a mass audience called Net users, you're actually communicating with people on a one-to-one basis.

So stay away from third person, which says "corporate," "faux" "disinterested." The collective "We" addressing the collective "You." Opt instead for first person, and don't shy away from your opinions (not that you have to bash them with your cyber-soapbox either; impassioned doesn't have to mean belligerent).

Write in your own voice, not standard written English. Let your vernacular and personality show through, even if you're pitching a service-oriented piece such as a book review or an interview. I want to know less about the book and more about how the book made you feel.

Were you reading the book at your desk or in a hammock sipping makeshift coladas? Why did you choose the book? Were you feeling down about your best friend, Frank Botts, who gave your Yankees seat to some girl-of-the-week he's trying to impress, as if she'll stick around after watching him inhale eight hot dogs? Were you extra nervous interviewing Bo Derek not only because of her epic beauty but because you spent ages 10 through 16, all right, 18, drooling at the poster of her that you nailed, roped and scotch-taped to the ceiling? Did your dad get pissed about the ceiling damage?

Net readers want to know you. Let your article be a window into you as a person and not as a press release.

Service-oriented content, brevity and pace

Because many people use the Internet as an informational or instructional resource, editors are always looking for functional pieces—with personality, of course. Also, quick-reference tips cater to the Net's need for brevity.

Fast-paced and brief writing is more effective because Net users have so many other options online. You have to hook them and hook them fast, complementing the visually-oriented medium with soundbite-esque copy. Also, computer screens are more difficult to read than traditional pages. The screen is small and the area for your text is even smaller. Net users don't want to scroll and scroll to finish a piece. They even go so far as to liken excessive scrolling to a drowning feeling, having to go deeper and deeper into a Web page. (You wouldn't want to drown cute little Net users, now would you?)

Brevity is also important to keep download times low (the time readers have to sit around waiting for a page to load onto their screens). Text is data, and while not as cumbersome as images/video/sound, long text files can cause similar delays.

Getting involved

Interactivity is a buzzword for all publishers. Netizens want to be vehicles, not just voyeurs. Writers must find ways to let their audience participate in their contents, because they expect it. The Web provides and promotes immediate interaction, whether readers contribute opinion posts, additional resources and links, instant surveys and form responses, or actual real-time chats with writers.

Incorporating technology

When writing for such a technologically cutting-edge medium as the Internet, there are two things to consider: a) it's not print; and b) it's not print. Once you understand that, the next step is: c) it's not print. Kidding (not very well). No, fine, extremely patient folks, c) is actually: Understanding what this medium offers that print doesn't, and incorporating those technologies into your creative process and editorial pitches.

Note: You don't have to know the mechanisms that make the technologies work. (We'd love it if you did, but then we'd love you to do the rest of our jobs too so we could just lounge poolside.) All you have to know is what's out there, what available technology *could* be used to enhance your article. (And how much fatter your freelance check should be for coming up with such a tech-savvy sidebar.)

Here are a few technologies that could enhance your article:

Audio and video. Yes, you can incorporate high-quality audio and video right into online articles. Although the download times and streaming advantages are cutting the waiting time for the reader, your best bet is to limit yourself to short clips. An article about dining on the Italian Riviera could include not only key phrases for ordering, but actual audio clips of the phrases so readers can hear how they are pronounced. In *Crisp*, instead of merely including photos of clothing from the innovative, up-and-coming designers of Space Girl, we added short video clips from their fashion show so readers could see how the clothes move on the body.

Hyperlinks. Hyperlinks are words or images that can be "clicked" on to send Net Users to another page or site. Almost every company or institution is on the Web now, so if you make reference to one, you can link its name to its site. This concept also goes for references and official homepages of celebrities. If you're writing about it, chances are there is another related article or image out on the Web somewhere that can be linked to, so just as you would do conventional research for any article, search the web for related sites/pages relevant to your piece. The Web is an extremely large database that can be accessed and utilized by the click of a button for the good of your article/humankind.

An interview with Pamela Anderson could include a sidebar of links to all 14 billion of her fan sites. An article on ginger (I don't know, maybe ginger has some healing qualities) could include links to recipes with ginger available at the many food sites on the Internet.

Chats and bulletin boards. Chats and bulletin boards are some of the most widely used aspects of the Web because, at the root of it all, the Web is chock full of people who like to talk and share and complain with other people. If you interview someone, get them to participate in a live chat with readers/fans for a half-hour or field questions over a short period on a bulletin board (to plug their latest starry project, of course).

Java. Four months with Michael Daconta's expert book, Java for C/C++ Programmers (Wiley) and the high-tech behind this technology still looks like gibberish to me. I'm just not cut out for programming. Although I do know some ways Java can enhance your article, such as real-time stock tickers of each business in your article on "Top Businesses for Writers Who Don't Know a Thing About Investing," your best bet is to get in touch with/peruse the Java experts at Gamelan (http://www.gamelan.com). They not only know the programming, they know the uses of it, and can link you to the sites making the most of their precious programmers.

Cybercasts. You can not only review a concert or band, you can broadcast it live over the Internet with your article. Check out Sonic Net (http://www.sonicnet.com) for inspiration.

QUERYING ONLINE EDITORS

Okay, you've found the online magazine that makes your heart go "thump," and you've honed your Pulitzer prize winner. Now what?

At the risk of sounding redundant: Remember to read through the online magazine that made your heart go "thump" before sending your article. Online editors are just like print editors, only a little cooler (kidding): We don't want a 12,000-word fiction book excerpt if all we publish is poetry.

Query us first with a short e-mail. You don't have to pay postage, and you don't have to wait for delivery. It still may take a few days for an editor to respond, but the entire process usually takes much less time than with print queries.

Obviously it's best to send your e-mail directly to the appropriate editor. Sometimes, however, his or her address isn't listed on the masthead of the magazine. Fret not. You still have a few options.

You can rummage through the site until you find a general editorial e-mail address (e.g., "editorial@thetitle.com" or "feedback@thetitle.com") or even the ubiquitous e-mail address of the site's Webmaster (technical overseer) who will probably do you the favor of forwarding your query unless he or she is particularly busy doing [insert obscure technical task] or he or she just doesn't feel like it. Let's face it, with a title like Webmaster and the perceived power to crash your computer and then charge a celebratory bottle of Dom to your credit card, he or she can do whatever he or she wants, whenever he or she wants.

Option Two shows a little resourcefulness of your own, though don't tell anyone I showed you. Even though an editor's e-mail address might not be listed in the magazine's masthead, that doesn't mean it doesn't exist, and that you can't find it. Sites such as WhoWhere? (http://www.whowhere.com) and Four11 (http://www.four11.com) have gathered millions of e-mail addresses from the Internet so you can get in touch with your long-lost best high school pal or fave celebrity, as well as, of course, the editor who's going to jump for joy after reading your revolutionary query.

Yes, the non-joy-jumping editor in me says you shouldn't send me e-mails directly. I'm busy, and you shouldn't risk simultaneous submissions, and you shouldn't pitch to me over the phone. But then I'm also a freelance writer doing all of those things for the advantages they provide.

Make your own decision, and mum's the word.

STYLE MANUAL

Despite lofty intentions toward a universal Net style, each publication usually exercises its right to reek of quirkiness (I mean, branding), a lot more so than in print media. The bottom line is that it's tough to look bad grammatically. The onus is usually on the editor because there's really no *AP Style Manual*-esque rulebook governing Net publishing. (Yet.)

Of course, if someone could pull it off, I'd put my little e-dollars on those gifted techno-geek guru digerati at *Wired* magazine, revered keepers of all cryptic netspeak, purveyors of digi-panache, and (you get the picture, but I'm still going) undisputed virtual-weight champs of neo-neologisms. Although your editor-to-hopefully-be should be the one purchasing *Wired*'s book as a style manual, you could definitely score some tech-savvy points with him or her by perusing your own copy (especially if you're targeting online publications focused on technology). Their book is called *Wired Style: Principles of English Usage in the Digital Age* (HardWired), edited by Constance Hale, with the editors of *Wired*.

SENDING YOUR QUERY

When you do finally send the article, plee-ease don't send those 12,000 words, et al, to us as an e-mail attachment unless we've requested it. All it took was one writer with one jumbled photo attachment to crash my computer, and all the files I hadn't backed up, a.k.a., all my files. It then took three days, lots of cash and numerous sacrifices to the hard-drive deities to get things working again.

Even big attachments that don't crash my system still take years-or-so to come across my humble Internet connection, which means for years-or-so I have to watch that little "percentage completed" line inch and inch (and inch) its way to completion in the middle of my morning e-mails. Just save the article as "text-only" and paste it into your e-mail message. Or at least get permission to send it as an attachment. (Okay, I'm done whining.)

(Okay, not yet.) If you do choose to paste the article into your e-mail message, remember to save it as text-only (yes, it was worth repeating). Many writers forget, sending formatted articles (with bolds, italics, indents, accents, hooked quotation marks, etc.) via e-mail which is text-only. The result is that the aforementioned article arrives spotted with awry symbols—not awry enough to make it illegible, just enough to make you (me) crazy trying to read it. Consider sending all e-mail to yourself first to make sure they're formatted how you want them. (Whining completed.)

AND IN THE END . . .

Best of luck with the freelance process. A little extra effort understanding the Internet and the Internet's readers (and editors) will go a long way to tapping this promising new market.

Online Markets

There are many online markets; the problem is that many don't pay writers. But with a little creative Net foraging you can customize a list of patron publications that cater to your most idiosyncratic interests. Here are ten perennial well-paying markets to take a look at.

CYBERTIMES, http://www.nytimes.com/yr/mo/day/cyber/index.html
The New York Times on the Web, 1120 Avenue of the Americas, New York NY 10036. (212)597-8023. Fax: (212)597-8014. E-mail: cybertimes@nytimes.com. Contact: Rob Fixmer, editor. 60-70% freelance written. "*CyberTimes* is the interactive daily newspaper of cyberspace, focusing on the social, cultural, political and economic implications of the Internet." Estab. January 1996. Circ. 200,000 visitors/month. Pays on publication. Byline given. Buys all world rights, print and electronic, in perpetuity. Accepts submissions via e-mail. Reports in 1 day on queries; 1-3 days on mss.
Nonfiction: Contact: John Haskins, deputy editor. Humor, expose, interview/profile, new product, historical/nostalgic. "No articles about technology or the technology industries." Query with or without published clips. Length: 600-800 words. Pays $400-600. Pays expenses of writers on assignment.
Photos: State availability of photos with submission. Negotiates payment individually. Captions, identification of subjects required. Buys one-time electronic rights, permanently archived.
Tips: "*CyberTimes*, a web-only section of *The New York Times*, is the interactive daily newspaper of cyberspace. It is

not a technology publication. We are looking for features and news articles that place computer and Internet technologies in a human and social context and describe new dimensions of the networked experience, from simple fun and games to the most serious endeavors in science, politics and culture. Keep in mind that this is a *New York Times* publication. *CyberTimes* adheres to the same journalistic standards and most of the style dictates of the print edition of the newspaper."

FEED MAGAZINE, http://www.feedmag.com
FEED, Inc., *FEED* Magazine c/o Power and Light, 11 Broadway, 3rd Floor, New York, NY 10004. E-mail: lipsyte@feed mag.com. Contact: Sam Lipsyte, senior editor. 60% freelance written. "*FEED* is a Web-only magazine (though we may eventually be syndicated in print) of culture, politics and technology. We are most frequently compared with magazines like *The New Republic* and *Harper's* and *Wired*. We like to publish a wide variety of perspectives, especially in the Dialog section where a disparate-minded panel of four hash it out. Our contributors range in social and political attitudes from John Perry Barlow and Katha Pollitt to Laura Ingraham and Senator Exon." Estab. May 1995. Circ. 40,000 visitors/month. Pays within 60 days after publication. Byline given. Buys electronic and print rights for specified periods of time. Editorial lead time 1 week-1 month. Accepts simultaneous submissions and electronic submissions via e-mail. Reports in 2 weeks on queries and mss.
Nonfiction: Book excerpts, essays, expose, general interest, technical, opinion. "We don't want anything that isn't high-caliber writing, with thoughtful analysis of relevant ideas." Query with or without published clips; query by e-mail preferred. Length: 1,000-4,000 words. Pays $400-1,500. Sometimes pays expenses of writers on assignment.
Reprints: Accepts previously published submissions occasionally.
Columns/Departments: Feature (2,000-4,000 words); Feedline (1,000-1,500 words); Filter (editorial); Document (annotation of book passage, graphics, etc.); Dialog (panel members discuss an issue in three rounds of commentary, of at least 300 words each).
Tips: "If writing about a well-known cultural, political or technological phenomenon, it is important to have a new take on the subject, to risk being a little off-beat. Proposals by e-mail are preferred."

HOTWIRED NETWORK, http://www.hotwired.com
Wired Ventures, Inc.. 650 Third St., 4th Floor, San Francisco CA 94107. (415)276-8400. Fax: (415)276-8499. Contact: Mark Ricci, editorial executive assistant. 25% freelance written. "*HotWired* is a collection of websites, each focusing on a different aspect of the phenomenon of the 'digital devolution.' (*HotWired Network* is currently undergoing a change to *Wired Digital*, including *HotWired*, *Wired News* and *HotBot*.) Our audience on average is similar to that of the Internet as a whole. Due to the varied aspects of the different channels on *HotWired*, we draw a very diverse audience spanning all age groups. The demographics for *Webmonkey* (http://www.webmonkey.com) for instance vary greatly from that of our interactive chat space, *Talk.com* (http://www.talk.com)." Estab. October 1995. Circ. 3 million visitors/month (includes multiple sites). Pays on publication, unless there is a contractual arrangement set up for regular contributions and payments, or a kill fee is paid. Byline given. Offers $50 kill fee. Buys exclusive ownership of work produced including reprint rights. Editorial lead time varies from several hours to several weeks. Accepts electronic submissions via e-mail to submit@wired.com. "Editorial staff will review the submission for quality and relevance to determine where it would best fit into our format and will forward as appropriate."
Nonfiction: Humor, personal experience, essays, expose, technical, opinion, new product, interview/profile, historical/nostalgic. "All of these are appropriate aspects for submission to *HotWired*. The variety of interpretations of 'digital culture' and its manifestations allow for and demand a variety of writing styles, incorporating all of the aforementioned formats. Although *Wired* is very open toward what it will consider, we don't want anything that duplicates what you can read elsewhere." Send complete ms. Length: no set requirements. Pays $75-$600, sometimes more. Pays expenses of writers on assignment.
Reprints: Accepts previously published submissions occasionally.
Photos: State availability of photos with submission. Reviews contact sheets, negatives, transparencies and prints. Negotiates payment individually. Captions, identification of subjects required. Buys one-time rights.
Columns/Departments: Wired News (reporting on business, technology, culture & politics); Netizen (political commentary).
Tips: "E-mail is the best way to submit work or contact anyone here at *Wired*. I am generally the contact person for information about contributors and our Editorial staff. I respond to or forward e-mail inquiries and résumés to the appropriate editors or departments. I can be reached at markr@wired.com. Submissions should be sent to submit@wired.com."

THE NETLY NEWS, http://www.netlynews.com
Time, Inc., 1271 Avenue of the Americas, New York NY 10020. (212) 522-5876. Fax: (212)522-3063. E-mail: thenetlyne ws@pathfinder.com. Contact: Noah Robischon, editor. 60% freelance written. "*The Netly News* covers digital culture. Stories must include URLs and pertain to issues, personalities and the politics of the online world. Reporting, rather than just opinion, is stressed." Estab. October 1995. Circ. 80,000 visitors/month. Pays on publication. Byline given. Buys online rights only. Accepts simultaneous submissions, electronic submissions via e-mail only; *no snail mail please!* Reports on queries and mss within a few days.
Nonfiction: Humor, personal experience, essays, expose, interview/profile, new product, technical, opinion. "Don't send highly technical stuff. Our audience is generally Web-savvy, but not interested in trade magazine-type stuff." Query. Length: 600-800 words. Pays $150-300. Sometimes pays expenses of writers on assignment.

NEWYORK.SIDEWALK, http://www.newyork.sidewalk.com
Microsoft, 825 Eighth Ave., 18th Floor, New York NY 10019. (212)621-7091. Fax: (212)246-3398. E-mail: vanessah@m
icrosoft.com. Contact: Vanessa Heau, associate producer. 85% freelance written. "Guide to arts and entertainment in
New York City." Estab. May 1997. **Pays on acceptance.** Byline given. Buys all rights. Editorial lead time 2-3 weeks.
Accepts simultaneous submissions. Reports in 1 week on queries and mss.
Nonfiction: Contact: Kate O'Hara, calendar producer. Reviews/previews of NYC events. Query with published clips.
Length: 25-100 words. Pays flat weekly rate for contributors. Sometimes pays expenses of writers on assignment.
Photos: Send photos with submission. Reviews contact sheets, transparencies, prints. Negotiates payment individually.
Captions, model releases, identification of subjects required. Buys all, universal rights.
Columns/Departments: Contact: Ben Cosgrove, Today Page producer. What to Do This Week, Block by Block,
Clerks, The Essential. Length: 75-200 words.
Tips: "Call Kate O'Hara at (212)621-7138 or Ben Cosgrove at (212)621-7087 for more information."

PARENT SOUP, http://www.parentsoup.com
Village, 170 Fifth Ave., New York NY 10010. Fax: (212)604-9133. Contact: Kellie Krumplitsch, editor. 10% freelance
written. "*Parent Soup* is the number one online community for parents. Articles generally focus on information for
parents of all ages, from expecting parents to grandparents." Estab. January 1996. Circ.150,000 visitors/month. **Pays
on acceptance.** Byline given. Buys negotiated rights. Accepts simultaneous submissions, electronic submissions via e-
mail to PSArticles@aol.com. Reports in 2 weeks on queries and mss.
Nonfiction: Book excerpts, humor, personal experience, essays, inspirational, interview/profile, historical/nostalgic.
Query with published clips or send complete ms. Length: 200-1,500 words. Negotiates payment individually.
Reprints: Accepts previously published submissions.
Tips: "Please be familiar with *Parent Soup* before submitting article ideas. We are interested in either humor or educating
parents about all things concerning the family, including but not limited to health, education, activities, finance, sports,
parenting styles, entertainment, technology, holidays and the ages and stages of children."

SALON MAGAZINE, http://www. salonmagazine.com
Salon Internet, Inc., 185 Berry St., Suite 4811, San Francisco CA 94107. E-mail: salon@salonmagazine.com. Contact:
salon@salon1999.com. 50% freelance written. "Every day, *Salon* publishes stories about books, arts, entertainment,
politics and society, featuring original reviews, interviews, and commentary on topics ranging from technology and
travel to parenting and sex." Estab. November 1995. Circ. 300,000 visitors/month. Pays on publication. Byline given.
Purchases exclusive rights for 60 days from the date of the initial publication, unless otherwise negotiated. Editorial
lead time varies. Accepts electronic submissions via e-mail to salon@salon1999.com. Reports in 3 weeks on mss.
Nonfiction: Book excerpts, essays, expose, general interest, high-tech, humor, interview/profile, media, news-related,
opinion, personal experience, politics, religious, technical, travel, book reviews, music reviews. Query with published
clips. Length: 500-2,000 words. Pays $100-1,000. Sometimes pays expenses of writers on assignment.
Photos: State availability of photos with submission. Reviews prints. Pays $25-75/photo. Captions, model releases,
identification of subjects required. Buys one-time rights.
Columns/Departments: Wanderlust (travel column); 21st (technology); Media Circus (critical updates); NewsReal
(national and international stories). Length: under 1,000 words.
Fiction: Accepts all kinds of fiction.
Tips: "Submit a query or pitch letter to the general editor box. It will be forwarded to the appropriate editor. Note: Our
office is moving; our mailing address is going to change at that time. Use the e-mail address for submissions to guarantee
their consideration."

SUCK, http://www.suck.com
Wired Ventures, 660 Third Street, San Francisco CA 94107. (415) 276-8788. Fax: (415)276-8499. E-mail: sucksters@suc
k.com. Contact: Ana Marie Cox, executive editor. 65-70% freelance written. "*Suck* specializes in detonating media
myths. The journalistic equivalent of running with scissors, *Suck*'s daily posts are too literate to be called rants, too
obsessed with popular culture to be considered academic and too funny to be taken seriously. We are not afraid to take
on an easy target: public television, Anthony Robbins, Canada, cyberdelia, Tiger Woods. Our readers are probably
smarter than we are but we try not make them feel bad about it—they look to us for cheap laughs and juvenile finger
pointing. We rarely disappoint." Estab. August 1995. Circ. 190,000 visitors/month. Pays on publication. Byline not
given; "most *Suck* contributors prefer to remain anonymous. (Would you want your parents to know you wrote for
Suck?) All bylines are pseudonyms, but every author gets a bio page where he/she may reveal their true identity. Why
they'd want to is, of course, a mystery." Buys exclusive rights for 60 days, shared after that. Editorial lead time 2 days.
Accepts simultaneous submissions, electronic submissions via e-mail. "We accept only electronic submissions." Reports
in a couple of weeks at the very longest, usually within a couple of days on queries and mss.
Nonfiction: Humor, personal experience, essays, expose, historical/nostalgic, opinion. "We don't want anything about
how Microsoft is evil, how the web sucks, why advertising is bad or what's wrong with newbies on the net. No website
reviews. No music reviews. Don't use the the word 'suck' in a clever pun." Send complete ms via e-mail. Length: 600-
1,200 words. Pays $600 for assigned articles; $450 for unsolicited articles. Sometimes pays expenses of writers on
assignment.
Tips: "Submit via e-mail, put the essay in the body of the message, that it is a 'submission' in the subject line. Include
a phone number and e-mail address where you can reliably be reached. Don't worry about including clever links or

submitting it with HTML tags. Unadorned insight will be impressive enough. A chimp can put it into HTML format, and his brother could find links. If you have a chimp available for these duties, of course, let us know."

WOMEN'S WIRE, http://www.women.com
Wire Networks, Inc., 1820 Gateway Dr., Suite 150, San Mateo CA 94404. Contact: Laurie Kretchmar, editor-in-chief. 75% freelance written. "*Women's Wire* is the leading online magazine for women. *Women's Wire* covers news, health, work, relationships, entertainment, fitness, money, fashion, shopping and more. Updated daily. Estab. August 1995. **Pays on acceptance.** Byline given sometimes. Buys all rights. Editorial lead time 1-3 months. Accepts electronic submissions via e-mail to editor@women.com. Reports in a few weeks on queries. *No unsolicited mss.*
Nonfiction: Personal experience (first person OP/EDs), essays, interview/profile (female movers & shakers, celebrity and otherwise), general interest (features). "We don't want long articles." Query with published clips. Length: 300-1,000 words. Negotiates payment individually.
Tips: "Be sure to visit *Women's Wire* before you make any queries. See what kinds of things are featured already. When pitching an idea, make web-specific suggestions, i.e., about how you'd lay it out or illustrate it, how it's interactive. Think very visually about your piece. Note that unsolicited manuscripts are not accepted. And note that *Women's Wire* is flooded with inquiries; editors look for published writers who have written for national publications and who have web experience, great clips and original ideas."

WORD, http://www.word.com
ICon CMT Corp. c/o ICon New Media, 1700 Broadway, 9th Floor, New York NY 10019. (800)572-4266. Contact: Lisa Webster, managing editor. 80% freelance written. "*Word* is an intelligent, witty, general-interest publication for men and women in their 20s and 30s which features primarily what we call 'creative nonfiction.' *Word* doesn't publish reviews, celebrity or lifestyle stories, or anything self-consciously trendy. *Word* does publish irreverent and insightful personal essays and eccentric humor pieces." Estab. July 1995. Circ. 80,000 visitors/month. **Pays on acceptance.** Byline given. Buys exclusive electronic rights for 60 days, non-exclusive thereafter. Editorial lead time varies, generally 1-3 months. Accepts simultaneous submissions, electronic submissions via e-mail to word editor@word.com. Reports in 2 weeks on queries; 6 weeks on mss.
Nonfiction: Book excerpts, essays, expose, general interest, historical/nostalgic, inspirational, interview/profile, humor, opinion, personal experience, photo feature, religious, travel. "We do not want straight journalism, reviews, celebrity stories, stories about the media, product reviews, or stories about the Internet or digital media." Query with or without published clips, or send complete ms. Length: 400-3,000 words. Pays $200-1,500 for assigned articles; $100-1,000 for unsolicited articles.
Photos: State availability of photos with submission. Reviews contact sheets. Negotiates payment individually. Buys exclusive electronic rights for 60 days, non-exclusive thereafter.
Columns/Departments: Work (people talking about their jobs); Money (real-life situations involving the drama of money); both 1,500 words.
Fiction: "We publish fiction only by well-known writers."
Tips: "For aspiring *Word* writers, we have two pieces of advice: 1) Read the magazine before you submit a query, and 2) Don't write in a typical, glib, 'professional' magazine voice—we hate that. *Word* has a very particular 'voice,' and many different subject areas are permissible, as long as they're written in the right kind of voice. Written material is best submitted through e-mail or on disk (but note that disks cannot be returned). Please try to keep text submissions under 2,000 words. Photos, video and audio cassettes, and other art pieces should include a SASE if you want us to return them. Our official submissions page is at http://www.word.com/info/submit.html."

INSIDER REPORT

Pursuing profits in electronic media

As President of New Media at Random House, Randi Benton is charged with developing and overseeing her company's presence in the worldwide electronic media explosion. In the few years she's been in that position, the communications world has undergone a sea change.

"What is going on is revolutionary in the most extreme sense," she says, referring to the prolific and seemingly boundless expansion of computerized media. "To me, it's similar to the invention of the printing press or the telephone—it's that significant."

The challenge to Benton and others in similar positions at major communications, publishing and entertainment companies is to unearth the business models by which the new technology can be harnessed and put to work supplying "content" to consumers in a profitable way.

Randi Benton

CD-ROM is one way Random House markets new media to consumers, but the CD-ROM market has not turned out to be the profit generator most publishers had hoped it would be.

"It was a little bit like the gold rush, at first," Benton says of the initial push by publishers to market CD-ROM products. "People were throwing everything onto CD-ROM because it seemed the obvious thing to do, but that turned out to be the wrong way to go about it. There were way too many titles out there, many of them of questionable quality." The result, according to Benton, was a "shakeout" in that market and a consolidation of companies manufacturing and marketing CD-ROMs. "It is a marketplace where a lot of people suffered and were not successful. It's turned out to be a limited opportunity—much smaller than we would have hoped." Still, she says, it's a market worth staying in, particularly for companies that control properties with strong "brand" identification among consumers. "At the end of the day, people are still buying software. They may not be buying as many titles per year as we had hoped, but they're still buying these products. The marketplace may have evolved differently than we had hoped, but it's still a real marketplace and people make money on titles. That's harder to say about the Web."

Benton's New Media group is using the World Wide Web primarily as a supplement to Random House's more traditional marketing and public relations efforts, another means by which to enhance the company's sales of print products. At the Random House website (www.randomhouse.com), visitors can browse and order from the publisher's current catalog and backlist, participate in a variety of interactive forums, read author interviews, link to selected authors' own websites, play games and enter contests.

As a profit center, however, the World Wide Web poses a considerable challenge, chiefly because the very question of what the Web might become as a retailing channel is as yet unanswered.

"What we're trying to do now is very different from what I was doing when I started

INSIDER REPORT, *continued*

in this job," Benton says. "At that time, the question was, 'Which of our print products would make good digital products?' And we could have picked right or wrong and we could have done a good job making the products or not. The business model in place for those kinds of decisions was clear—it was not that dissimilar from book publishing. We shipped product, and consumers either bought it or they didn't. With the web, we are presented with a medium in which it's very unclear what business model will eventually work. What will consumers eventually want to do on this medium? And who's going to pay for what? How will money exchange hands? Are advertisers going to support things? Are consumers going to pay for things?"

While the answers to those questions come slowly into focus, Benton and her group experiment in an attempt to "figure out where the opportunities are." One current exploration involves a section of the Random House website known as "The Lurker Files." "In that area," Benton explains, "one of our authors actually posts original fiction twice a week. It's an ongoing serialization; we built a whole community around it, and we've since published books based on that property. It has been, I think, a very good experience for us; we've learned how to manage and market editorial product on the Web, but at the same time it's very unclear to us how to make money at this other than by eventually publishing and selling books."

The selling of print products via the Web, according to Benton, shows a good deal of promise. Pointing to the success of online bookstore Amazon.com, Benton says that as more people warm to the idea of shopping online, consumers and publishers will both benefit from the ease, speed and economic efficiency of conducting business electronically.

Benton suggests that writers hoping to work on and profit from the Web do the same thing Random House is doing—keep their eyes and ears open and be willing to experiment. "Clearly the Web is a medium for communication and for community building," she says. "There are going to be certain types of experiences and opportunities that will evolve in this medium, and the only way we'll find those ideas, those experiences, is through people experimenting. If writers are looking for an established model or a blueprint for how to work, they probably shouldn't go into this yet. It's definitely a medium for pioneers."

—*Mark Garvey*

IMPORTANT LISTING INFORMATION

• Listings are based on editorial questionnaires and interviews. They are not advertisements; publishers do not pay for their listings. The markets are not endorsed by *Writer's Market* editors.
• All listings have been verified before publication of this book. If a listing has not changed from last year, then the editor told us the market's needs have not changed and the previous listing continues to accurately reflect its policies. We require documentation in our files for each listing.
• *Writer's Market* reserves the right to exclude any listing.
• When looking for a specific market, check the index. A market may not be listed for one of these reasons.

1. It doesn't solicit freelance material.
2. It doesn't pay for material.
3. It has gone out of business.
4. It has failed to verify or update its listing for the 1998 edition.
5. It was in the middle of being sold at press time, and rather than disclose premature details, we chose not to list it.
6. It hasn't answered *Writer's Market* inquiries satisfactorily. (To the best of our ability, and with our readers' help, we try to screen out fraudulent listings.)
7. It buys few manuscripts, constituting a very small market for freelancers.

• Individual markets that appeared in last year's edition but are not listed in this edition are included in the general index, with a notation giving the basis for their exclusion.

COMPLAINT PROCEDURE

If you feel you have not been treated fairly by a listing in *Writer's Market*, we advise you to take the following steps:
• First try to contact the listing. Sometimes one phone call or a letter can quickly clear up the matter.
• Document all your correspondence with the listing. When you write to us with a complaint, provide the details of your submission, the date of your first contact with the listing and the nature of your subsequent correspondence.
• We will enter your letter into our files and attempt to contact the listing.
• The number and severity of complaints will be considered in our decision whether or not to delete the listing from the next edition.

The Markets
Book Publishers

The book business, for the most part, runs on hunches. Whether the idea for a book comes from a writer, an agent or the imagination of an acquiring editor, it is generally expressed in these terms: "This is a book that I *think* people will like. People will *probably* want to buy it." The decision to publish is mainly a matter of the right person, or persons, agreeing that those hunches are sound.

THE PATH TO PUBLICATION

Ideas reach editors in a variety of ways. They arrive unsolicited every day through the mail. They come by phone, sometimes from writers but most often from agents. They arise in the editor's mind because of his daily traffic with the culture in which he lives. The acquisitions editor, so named because he is responsible for securing manuscripts for his company to publish, sifts through the deluge of possibilities, waiting for a book idea to strike him as extraordinary, inevitable, profitable.

In some companies, acquisitions editors possess the authority required to say, "Yes, we will publish this book." In most publishing houses, though, the acquisitions editor must prepare and present the idea to a proposal committee made up of marketing and administrative personnel. Proposal committees are usually less interested in questions of extraordinariness and inevitability than they are in profitability. The editor has to convince them that it makes good business sense to publish this book.

Once a contract is signed, several different wheels are set in motion. The author, of course, writes the book if he hasn't done so already. While the editor is helping to assure that the author is making the book the best it can be, promotion and publicity people are planning mailings of review copies to influential newspapers and review periodicals, writing catalog copy that will help sales representatives push the book to bookstores, and plotting a multitude of other promotional efforts (including interview tours and bookstore signings by the author) designed to dangle the book attractively before the reading public's eye.

When the book is published, it usually receives a concerted promotional push for a month or two. After that, the fate of the book—whether it will "grow legs" and set sales records or sit untouched on bookstore shelves—rests in the hands of the public. Publishers have to compete with all of the other entertainment industries vying for the consumer's money and limited leisure time. Successful books are reprinted to meet the demand. Unsuccessful books are returned from bookstores to publishers and are sold off cheaply as "remainders" or are otherwise disposed of.

THE STATE OF THE BUSINESS

The book publishing industry is beginning to recover from the difficulties experienced in the last year or two. Publishers sell their products to bookstores on a returnable basis, which means the stores usually have 120 days to either pay the bill or return the order. With independent bookstores continuing to close and superstores experiencing setbacks as well, many publishers were hit with staggering returns. This has slowed somewhat, but continues to be a concern. While there are many more outlets to *buy* books, including online bookstores such as Amazon.com and

Barnes & Noble, this doesn't necessarily translate into more books being *bought*. Some feel the superstore phenomenon has proved a mixed blessing. The greater shelf area means there are more materials available, but also drives a need for books as "wallpaper" that is continually refreshed by returning older books and restocking with newer ones.

But that's not to say publishers are rushing to bring esoteric or highly experimental material to the marketplace. The blockbuster mentality—publishing's penchant for sticking with "name brand" novelists—still drives most large publishers. It's simply a less risky venture to continue publishing authors whom they know readers like. On the other hand, the prospects for nonfiction authors are perhaps better than they have been for years. The boom in available shelf space has provided entree to the marketplace for books on niche topics that heretofore would not have seen the light of day in most bookstores. The superstores position themselves as one-stop shopping centers for readers of every stripe. As such, they must carry books on a wide range of subjects.

Paper costs continue to be an area of concern for publishers, although prices are predicted to remain relatively stable and supply is estimated to grow slightly yet steadily over the next several years. Most publishers have laid in a supply that would get them through any price increases without upsetting their budgets.

The publishing community as a whole seems to be stepping back from the multimedia "hysteria" of the past few years, and approaching the market a little more cautiously. While the possibilities of CD-ROM are still being explored, the number of unsuccessful products in this area is a warning that the content must fit the format in order to sell.

The publishing community as a whole is stepping back from the multimedia hype and approaching the market more cautiously, if not abandoning it entirely. While the possibilities offered by CD-ROM technology still exist, publishers realize that marrying format and content are crucial for a successful, profitable product. Online publishing seems to offer promise, if only publishers can figure out how to make money from this new and different format. See the interview with Randi Benton of Random House New Media for an inside look at the search for the "business model" that will make online publishing lucrative and more widespread.

HOW TO PUBLISH YOUR BOOK

The markets in this year's Book Publishers section offer opportunities in nearly every area of publishing. Large, commercial houses are here as are their smaller counterparts; large and small "literary" houses are represented as well. In addition, you'll find university presses, industry-related publishers, textbook houses and more.

The Book Publishers Subject Index is the place to start. You'll find it in the back of the book, before the General Index. Subject areas for both fiction and nonfiction are broken out for the more than 1,250 total book publisher listings. Not all of them buy the kind of book you've written, but this Index will tell you which ones do.

When you have compiled a list of publishers interested in books in your subject area, read the detailed listings. Pare down your list by cross-referencing two or three subject areas and eliminating the listings only marginally suited to your book. When you have a good list, send for those publishers' catalogs and any manuscript guidelines available. You want to make sure your book idea is not a duplicate of something they've already published. Visit bookstores and libraries to see if their books are well represented. When you find a couple of books they have published that are similar to yours, write or call the company to find out who edited these books. This last, extra bit of research could be the key to getting your proposal to precisely the right editor.

Publishers prefer different kinds of submissions on first contact. Most like to see a one-page query with SASE, especially for nonfiction. Others will accept a brief proposal package that might include an outline and/or a sample chapter. Some publishers will accept submissions from agents only. Virtually no publisher wants to see a complete manuscript on initial contact, and sending one when they prefer another method will signal to the publisher "this is an amateur's submission." Editors do not have the time to read an entire manuscript, even editors at small presses who receive fewer submissions. Perhaps the only exceptions to this rule are children's book manuscripts and poetry manuscripts, which take only as much time to read as an outline and sample chapter anyway.

In your one-page query, give an overview of your book, mention the intended audience, the competition (check *Books in Print* and local bookstore shelves), and what sets your book apart. Detail any previous publishing experience or special training relevant to the subject of your book. All of this information will help your cause; it is the professional approach.

Only one in a thousand writers will sell a book to the first publisher they query, especially if the book is the writer's first effort. Make a list of a dozen or so publishers that might be interested in your book. Try to learn as much about the books they publish and their editors as you can. Research, knowing the specifics of your subject area, and a professional approach are often the difference between acceptance and rejection. You are likely to receive at least a few rejections, however, and when that happens, don't give up. Rejection is as much a part of publishing, if not more, than signing royalty checks. Send your query to the next publisher on your list. Multiple queries can speed up the process at this early stage.

Personalize your queries by addressing them individually and mentioning what you know about a company from its catalog or books you've seen. Never send a form letter as a query. Envelopes addressed to "Editor" or "Editorial Department" end up in the dreaded slush pile.

If a publisher offers you a contract, you may want to seek advice before signing and returning it. An author's agent will very likely take 15% if you employ one, but you could be making 85% of a larger amount. Some literary agents are available on an hourly basis for contract negotiations only. For more information on literary agents, contact the Association of Author's Representatives, 10 Astor Place, 3rd Floor, New York NY 10003, (212)353-3709. Also check the current edition of *Guide to Literary Agents* (Writer's Digest Books). Attorneys will only be able to tell you if everything is legal, not if you are getting a good deal, unless they have prior experience with literary contracts. If you have a legal problem, you might consider contacting Volunteer Lawyers for the Arts, 1 E. 53rd St., 6th Floor, New York NY 10022, (212)319-2787.

AUTHOR-SUBSIDY PUBLISHER'S LISTINGS ELIMINATED

In previous editions a section of Subsidy/Royalty publishers was included in *Writer's Market*. Subsidy publishing involves paying money to a publishing house to publish a book. The source of the money could be a government, foundation or university grant, or it could be the author of the book. Beginning with the 1997 edition, listings for book publishers offering author-subsidy arrangements were eliminated. Publishers offering nonauthor-subsidized arrangements have been included in the appropriate section.

Writer's Market is a reference tool to help you sell your writing, and we encourage you to work with publishers that pay a royalty. If one of the publishers listed here offers you an author-subsidy arrangement (sometimes called "cooperative publishing," "co-publishing" or "joint venture"), asks you to pay for all or part of the cost of any aspect of publishing (printing, advertising, etc.) or to guarantee the purchase of any number of the books yourself, we would like you to let us know about that company immediately.

Publishers are offering more author-subsidy arrangements than ever before. Some publishers feel they must seek them to expand their lists beyond the capabilities of their limited resources. This may be true, and you may be willing to agree to it, but we choose to list only those publishers paying a royalty without requiring a financial investment from the author.

WHAT'S NEW THIS YEAR

With this edition we have provided additional information to help you in your search for the right publisher for your work. First off, the number of listings has increased dramatically. Some entries are entirely new. This edition also provides detailed information in individual listings for as many of the larger imprints as possible, since the philosophical thrust can vary greatly from one imprint to another, particularly at the major houses. We have included "umbrella listings" for these larger houses, that list the imprints under the company name. An imprint listed in boldface type means there is an independent listing arranged alphabetically within this section.

Each listing includes a summary of the editorial mission of the house, an overarching principle that ties together what they publish. Under the heading **Acquisitions:** we list many more editors, often with their specific areas of expertise. We have also increased the number of recent titles to help give you an idea of the publishers' scope. We have included the royalty rates for those publishers willing to disclose them, but contract details are closely guarded and a number of larger publishers are reluctant to publicly state these terms. Standard royalty rates for paperbacks generally range from 7½ to 12½ percent, for hardcovers from 10 to 15 percent. Royalty rates for children's books are often lower, generally ranging from 5 to 10 percent.

Finally, we have listed a number of publishers who only accept agented submissions. This benefits the agents who use *Writer's Market*, those writers with agents who use the book themselves, and those as yet unagented writers who want to know more about a particular company.

For a list of publishers according to their subjects of interest, see the nonfiction and fiction sections of the Book Publishers Subject Index. Information on book publishers and producers listed in the previous editions but not included in this edition of *Writer's Market* can be found in the General Index.

‡**A&B PUBLISHERS GROUP**, 1000 Atlantic Ave., Brooklyn NY 11238. **Acquisitions:** Maxwell Taylor, editor. Publishes hardcover originals and trade paperback originals and reprints. Publishes 12 titles/year. Receives 180 queries and 75 mss/year. 20% of books from first-time authors; 40% from unagented writers. Pays 5-12% royalty on retail price. Offers $500-2,500 advance. Publishes book 8 months after acceptance of ms. Accepts simultaneous submissions. Reports in 2 months on queries and proposals, 5 months on mss. Book catalog free.
Nonfiction: Children's/juvenile, coffee table book, cookbook, illustrated book. Subjects include cooking/foods/nutrition, history. "We have published no fiction, but may start in fall '97." Query. Reviews artwork/photos as part of ms package. Send photocopies.
Tips: Audience is children and adult African-Americans. "Read, read, read. The best writers are developed from good reading. There is not enough attention to quality."

‡**ABBEVILLE KIDS**, Imprint of Abbeville Publishing Group, 488 Madison Ave., New York NY 10022. (212)888-1969. Fax: (212)644-5085. **Acquisitions:** Susan Costello, editorial director/editor-in-chief. Abbeville Kids publishes children's fiction and nonfiction with an emphasis on illustrations and picture books. Publishes hardcover and trade paperback originals. 75% of books from unagented writers. Pays royalty. Advance varies. Publishes book 18 months after acceptance of ms. Accepts simultaneous submissions. Reports in 3 months on queries. Book catalog and ms guidelines free; call customer service.
Nonfiction: Children's/juvenile, illustrated book. Subjects include art/architecture. Rarely publishes unsolicited material. Query with outline, TOC, CV, cover letter describing scope of project and SASE. Reviews artwork/photos as part of the ms package. Send photocopies.
Recent Nonfiction Title(s): *Heroes: Great Men Through the Ages*, written and illustrated by Rebecca Hazell.
Fiction: Juvenile, picture books. Rarely publishes unsolicited material. Query with full ms and SASE.
Recent Fiction Title(s): *Felix Explores Planet Earth*, by Annette Langen and Constanza Droop; The *Silly Shapes* series, by Sophie Fatus.

‡**ABBEVILLE PRESS**, Imprint of Abbeville Publishing Group, 488 Madison Ave., New York NY 10022. (212)888-1969. Fax: (212)644-5085. **Acquisitions:** Susan Costello, editorial director/editor-in-chief. Abbeville publishes high-quality trade nonfiction with an emphasis on illustrations. Publishes nonfiction hardcover and trade paperback originals. Publishes 100 titles/year. 5% of books from first-time authors; 75% from unagented writers. Pays royalty. Advance varies. Publishes book 18 months after acceptance of ms. Accepts simultaneous submissions. Reports in 3 months on queries. Book catalog and ms guidelines free; call customer service.
Nonfiction: Coffee table book, cookbook, gift book, how-to, illustrated book. Subjects include art/architecture, cooking/food/nutrition, gardening, fashion, history, photography. Rarely publishes unsolicited material. Query with outline, TOC, CV, cover letter describing scope of project and SASE. Reviews artwork/photos as part of the ms package. Send photocopies.
Recent Nonfiction Title(s): *A History of Women Photographers*, by Naomi Rosenblum; *Holy Terrors: Gargoyles on*

Medieval Buildings, by Janetta Rebold Benton; *The Civil Rights Movement: A Photographic History, 1954-68*, by Steven Kasher.

‡ABBEVILLE PUBLISHING GROUP, 488 Madison Ave., New York NY 10022. (212)888-1969. Fax: (212)644-5085. **Acquisitions:** Susan Costello, editorial director and editor-in-chief. Publishes hardcover and trade paperback originals. Pays royalty. Publishes book 18 months after acceptance of ms. Accepts simultaneous submissions. Reports in 3 months on queries. Book catalog and ms guidelines free; call customer service.
Imprint(s): Abbeville Kids, Abbeville Press, Artabras (promotional books), Canopy Books, Cross River Press.

ABBOTT, LANGER & ASSOCIATES, 548 First St., Crete IL 60417-2199. (708)672-4200. **Acquisitions:** Dr. Steven Langer, president. Estab. 1967. Publishes trade paperback originals, loose-leaf books. Publishes 25 titles/year, mostly prepared inhouse. Receives 25 submissions/year. 10% of books from first-time authors; 90% of books from unagented writers. Pays 10-15% royalty. Offers advance. Publishes book 18 months after acceptance. Book catalog for 6×9 SAE with 2 first-class stamps. Reports in 1 month on queries, 3 months on mss.
Nonfiction: How-to, reference, technical on some phase of human resources management, security, sales management, etc. Especially needs "a very limited number (3-5) of books dealing with very specialized topics in the field of human resource management, wage and salary administration, sales compensation, recruitment, selection, etc." Publishes for human resources directors, wage and salary administrators, sales/marketing managers, security directors, etc. Query with outline. Reviews artwork/photos.
Recent Nonfiction Title(s): *Security Survey*, by William Floyd; *Fire Safety & Hihg Rise Buildings*, by Harry Azoni.
Tips: "A writer has the best chance selling our firm a how-to book in human resources management, sales/marketing management or security management."

ABC-CLIO, INC., 501 S. Cherry St., Suite 350, Denver CO 80222. (303)333-3003. Fax: (303)333-4037. Subsidiaries include ABC-CLIO Ltd. President: Heather Cameron. **Acquisitions:** Rolf A. Janke, editorial director. Estab. 1955. ABC-CLIO publishes "easy-to-use, authoritative sources on high-interest topics." Publishes hardcover originals. Publishes 45 titles/year. Receives 500 submissions/year. 20% of books from first-time authors; 95% from unagented writers. Pays royalty on net receipts. Offers advance. Publishes ms 10 months after acceptance. Reports in 2 months on queries. Book catalog and ms guidelines free.
Nonfiction: Reference. Subjects include art/architecture, education, environmental issues, government/politics, history, literary studies, multicultural studies, mythology, science, women's issues/studies. "Looking for reference books on current world issues, women's issues, and for subjects compatible with high school curriculum. No monographs or textbooks." Query or submit outline and sample chapters.
Recent Nonfiction Title(s): *The Encyclopedia of World Sport*, by David Levinson and Karen Christensen; *Encyclopedia of Satirical Literature*, by Mary Ellen Snodgrass.

THE ABERDEEN GROUP, 426 S. Westgate St., Addison IL 60101. (630)543-0870. Fax: (630)543-3112. **Acquisitions:** Mark DiCicco, publisher; Kari Moosmann, managing editor. "We seek to strengthen and grow the concrete and masonry industries worldwide by striving to be the world's foremost information provider for these industries." Publishes 6 titles/year. Receives 75 queries and 12 mss/year. 10% of books from first-time authors; 100% from unagented writers. Pays 6-18% royalty on retail price. Offers $1,000-2,000 advance. Publishes book 6 months after acceptance of ms. Accepts simultaneous submissions. Reports in 1 month on queries and proposals, 2 months on mss. Book catalog free.
Nonfiction: How-to, technical (primarily in the concrete and masonry fields.) Subjects include architecture, construction, general engineering and construction business. Query with outline, 2-3 sample chapters, definition of topic, features, market analysis.
Recent Nonfiction Title(s): *Concrete Construction Handbook* (how-to); *Nondestructive Testing: Evaluation of Masonry Structures*, by Supernant/Schueller (how-to/technical).

ABINGDON PRESS, Imprint of The United Methodist Publishing House, P.O. Box 801, Nashville TN 37202-0801. (615)749-6301. Fax: (615)748-6512. Website: http://www.abingdon.org. President/Publisher: Neil M. Alexander. Vice President/Editorial Director: Harriett Jane Olson. **Acquisitions:** Michael E. Lawrence, director, academic/professional unit; Mary Catherine Dean, senior editor (general interest books); Rex Mathews, senior editor (academic books); J. Richard Peck, senior editor, United Methodist Newscope; Robert Ratcliff, senior editor (professional products); Jack Keller, senior editor (reference books); Gary A. Smith, senior editor (music). Estab. 1789. "Abingdon Press, America's oldest theological publisher, provides an ecumenical publishing program dedicated to serving the Christian community—clergy, scholars, church leaders, musicians and general readers—with quality resources in the areas of Bible study, the practice of ministry, theology, devotion, spirituality, inspiration, prayer, music and worship, reference, Christian education and church supplies." Publishes hardcover and paperback originals and reprints; church supplies. Publishes 130 titles/year. Receives approximately 2,500 submissions/year. Few books from first-time authors; 90-95% of books from unagented writers. Average print order for a first book is 4,000-5,000. Pays royalty. Publishes book 2 years after acceptance. Manuscript guidelines for SASE. Reports in 3 months.
Imprint(s): Dimensions for Living, Cokesbury.
Nonfiction: Religious-lay and professional, children's religious books, academic texts. Length: 32-300 pages. Query with outline and samples only.

Recent Nonfiction Title(s): *The New Interpreter's Bible: A Commentary in Twelve Volumes*; *Tattered Trust*, by Lyle E. Schaller; *Selling Out the Church*, by Philip D. Kenneson and James L. Street.

HARRY N. ABRAMS, INC., Subsidiary of Groupe Latingy, 100 Fifth Ave., New York NY 10011. (212)206-7715. President/Publisher/Editor-in-Chief: Paul Gottlieb. **Acquisitions:** Margaret Chase, managing editor. Estab. 1949. "We publish *only* high-quality illustrated art books, i.e., art, art history, museum exhibition catalogs, written by specialists and scholars in the field." Publishes hardcover and "a few" paperback originals. Publishes 100 titles/year. Pays royalty. Offers variable advance. Publishes book 2 years after acceptance. Reports in 3 months. Book catalog for $5.
 • Abrams was sold by Times Mirror in May, 1997.
Nonfiction: Art, nature and science, outdoor recreation. Requires illustrated material for art and art history, museums. Submit outline, sample chapters and illustrations. Reviews artwork/photos as part of ms package.
Tips: "We are one of the few publishers who publish almost exclusively illustrated books. We consider ourselves the leading publishers of art books and high-quality artwork in the U.S. Once the author has signed a contract to write a book for our firm the author must finish the manuscript to agreed-upon high standards within the schedule agreed upon in the contract."

‡ABSEY & CO., 5706 Root Rd., Suite #5, Spring TX 77389. E-mail: abseyandco@aol.com. **Acquisitions:** Karen Foster, editorial director. "We are looking primarily for education books, especially those with teaching strategies based upon research." Publishes hardcover, trade paperback and mass market paperback originals. Publishes 5-10 titles/year. 50% of books from first-time authors; 50% from unagented writers. Pays 8-15% royalty on wholesale price. Publishes book 1 year after acceptance of ms. Accepts simultaneous submissions. Reports in 3 months on queries. Manuscript guidelines for #10 SASE.
Nonfiction: Children's/juvenile, how-to for teachers. Education subjects. Query with outline and 1-2 sample chapters. Reviews artwork/photos as part of ms package. Send photocopies, transparencies, etc.
Recent Nonfiction Title(s): *Amazing Jones*, by Deanna Cera; *Ancient Egyptian Jewelry*, by Carol Andrews.
Fiction: Juvenile, mainstream/contemporary, short story collections. "Since we are a small, new press, we are looking for good manuscripts with a firm intended audience. As yet, we haven't explored this market. We feel more comfortable starting with nonfiction—educational. A mistake we often see in submissions is writers underwrite or overwrite—a lack of balance." Query with SASE.
Poetry: "We are primarily interested in narrative poems." Submit 6 sample poems or complete ms.
Recent Poetry Title(s): *Poems After Lunch*, edited by Joyce Armstrong Carroll and Edward E. Wilson (primarily narrative).

ACA BOOKS, American Council for the Arts, 1 E. 53rd St., 3rd Floor, New York NY 10022. (212)223-2787. E-mail: djones@artsusa.org. Website: http://www.artsusa.org. **Acquisitions:** J.R. Wells. "ACA Books and the American Council for the Arts strive to make art accessible to all adults and children." Publishes trade paperback originals and reprints. Publishes 2 titles/year. Receives 60 queries and 30 mss/year. 100% of mss from unagented writers. Publishes book 1 year after acceptance of ms. Accepts simultaneous submissions. Reports in 3 months on queries. Book catalog free.
Nonfiction: Reference, textbook. Subjects include art, education and government/politics. "We do *not* publish art books (i.e. studies of artwork, coffee table books). We are most interested in books on careers in the arts, arts policy, arts education, arts fundraising and management." Query.
Recent Nonfiction Title(s): *Amusement Taxes for the Arts*, by the Institute for Community Development; *Artist in the Community: Training Artists to Work in Alternative Settings*, by Grady Hillman.

ACADEMY CHICAGO, 363 W. Erie St., Chicago IL 60610-3125. (312)751-7300. **Acquisitions:** Anita Miller, editorial director/senior editor. Estab. 1975. "We are known for our women's studies." Publishes hardcover and paperback originals and reprints. Publishes 20 titles/year. Receives approximately 2,000 submissions/year. Average print order for a first book is 1,500-5,000. Pays 7-10% royalty. Modest advances. Publishes book 18 months after acceptance. Book catalog for 9×12 SAE with 5 first-class stamps. Manuscript guidelines for #10 SASE. Query with first 4 chapters and SASE. Reports in 2 months. "No electronic submissions."
Nonfiction: Adult, biography, historical, travel, true crime, reprints. No how-to, cookbooks, self-help, etc. Query and submit first 4 consecutive chapters.
Recent Nonfiction Title(s): *The Quest for Author's Britain*, by Geoffrey Ashe; *Chicago By Gaslight*, by Richard Lindberg (history); *Titanic: A Survivor's Story*, by Colonel Archibald Gracie.
Fiction: Mainstream novels, mysteries. No romantic, children's, young adult, religious or sexist fiction; nothing avant-garde. Query with first 3 chapters.
Recent Fiction Title(s): *Circling Eden*, by Carol Magun; *The Perfect Murder*, by H.R.F. Keating; *The Fat Woman's Joke*, by Fay Weldon.
Tips: "At the moment, we are looking for good nonfiction; we certainly want excellent original fiction, but we are swamped. No fax queries, no disks. We are always interested in reprinting good out-of-print books."

ACCENT ON LIVING, Subsidiary of Cheever Publishing, Inc., P.O. Box 700, Bloomington IL 61702. (309)378-2961. Fax: (309)378-4420. Editor: Betty Garee. Accent on Living publishes books pertaining to the physically disabled. Publishes 4 titles/year. Receives 300 queries and 150 mss/year. 50% of books from first-time authors; 95% from unagented writers. Pays 6% royalty on retail price or makes outright purchase. Publishes book 3 months after acceptance of ms. Accepts simultaneous submissions. Reports on queries in 1 month. *Writer's Market* recommends allowing 2 months for reply. Book catalog for 8×10 SAE with 2 first-class stamps. Manuscript guidelines for #10 SASE.

Nonfiction: How-to, humor, self-help. Subjects include business/economics, child guidance/parenting, cooking/foods/ nutrition, education, gardening, money/finance, recreation, religion, travel. All pertaining to physically disabled. Query. Reviews artwork/photos as part of ms package. Send snapshots or slides.

Recent Nonfiction Title(s): *If It Weren't for the Honor, I'd Rather Have Walked*, by Jan Little.

ACCENT PUBLICATIONS, Cook Communications Ministries, P.O. Box 36640, Colorado Springs CO 80936-3664. (719)536-0100 ext. 3337. **Acquisitions:** Mary B. Nelson. Estab. 1947. Publishes evangelical church resource products. Publishes 6-8 titles/year. 100% of books from unagented writers. Pays royalty on retail price or makes outright purchase. Publishes book within 1 year of acceptance. Query with brief synopsis and chapter outline. Do not submit full ms unless requested. No phone calls, please. Reports in 3 months. Manuscript guidelines for #10 SASE.

Nonfiction: "We are currently soliciting only Church Resources for the programmed ministries of the local church such as VBS, clubs, and children's church (no children's sermons). We would consider Bible study series and ancillary curriculum programs, or children's programs for the King James Version church market. We do not consider games, puzzles, puppet books, fiction for children, youth, or adults. We do not consider devotionals, poetry, biographies, autobiographies, personal experience stories, manuscripts with a charismatic emphasis, or general Christian living."

Nonfiction Title: *Celebrating the Heart of Marriage*, by Kathy Collard Miller (Women's Bible study).

ACE SCIENCE FICTION AND FANTASY, (formerly Ace Science Fiction), Imprint of The Berkley Publishing Group, Division of Penguin Putnam Inc., 200 Madison Ave., New York NY 10016. (212)686-9820. E-mail: acebooks@ge nie.com. Website: http://www.berkley.com. Editor: Anne Sowards. Estab. 1953. Ace publishes exclusively science fiction and fantasy. Publishes hardcover, paperback and trade paperback originals and reprints. Publishes 75 titles/year. Reports in 6 months. Manuscript guidelines for #10 SASE.

• This publisher accepts agented submissions only. Ace Science Fiction and Fantasy has reduced their number of books published from 96 to 75 titles/year.

Fiction: Science fiction, fantasy. Query first with SASE.

Recent Fiction Title(s): *Resurrection Man*, by Sean Stewart; *Neuromancer*, by William Gibson.

‡ACROPOLIS BOOKS, INC., 747 Sheridan Blvd., #1A, Lakewood CO 80214-2551. (303)231-9923. Fax: (303)231-0492. E-mail: acropolisbooks@worldnet.att.net. Website: acropolisbooks.com. **Acquisitions:** Constance J. Wilson, vice president of operations. "It is the mission of Acropolis Books to publish books at the highest level of consciousness, commonly referred to as mysticism. This was the consciousness demonstrated by revelators of every religion in the world." Publishes hardcover and trade paperback originals and reprints. Publishes 20 titles/year. Imprint publishes 5-10 titles/year. Receives 150 queries and 80 mss/year. 30% of books from first-time authors; 90% from unagented writers. Royalties or outright purchases negotiable. Advances negotiable. Publishes book an average of 1 year after acceptance of ms. Reports in 1 month on queries and proposals, 2 months on mss. Book catalog and ms guidelines for #10 SASE.

Imprint(s): I-Level, Awakening and Flashlight.

• Acropolis Books has published such authors as Joel Goldsmith, Jim Rosemergy and Jefferson Bates.

Nonfiction: Inspirational. Subjects include philosophy, religion and mysticism. "We publish books of higher consciousness and books that are a bridge to higher consciousness, and writers must understand our focus on mysticism and higher consciousness." Submit 4 sample chapters with SASE. Reviews artwork/photos as part of ms package. Send photocopies.

Recent Nonfiction Title(s): *Secret Splendor*, Charles E. Essert (New Age).

Fiction: Mysticism/inspirational. "Our books encompass the spiritual principles of Omnipresence, Omnipotence and Omniscience; and further bring home the mystical realization that everyone in this world is an individual instrument of God in expression." Submit 4 sample chapters with SASE.

Recent Fiction Title(s): *Bunny Bu*, by Dianne Baker (children's book).

Poetry: Submit complete ms.

Recent Poetry Title(s): *The Oxford Book of English Mystical Verse*, by DHS Nicholson/AHE Lee (mystical).

Tips: "Clearly understand our focus by reading or understanding books that we have published."

ACTA PUBLICATIONS, 4848 N. Clark St., Chicago IL 60640-4711. Fax: (773)271-7399. E-mail: acta@one.org. **Acquisitions:** Gregory F. Augustine Pierce, copublisher. Copublisher: Thomas R. Artz. Estab. 1958. "We publish non-academic, practical books aimed at the mainline religious market." Publishes trade paperback originals. Publishes 10 titles/year. Receives 50 queries and 15 mss/year. 50% of books from first-time authors; 90% from unagented writers. Pays 10-12½% royalty on wholesale price. Publishes book 1 year after acceptance of ms. Reports in 2 months on proposals. Book catalog and author guidelines for SASE.

Nonfiction: Religion. Submit outline and 1 sample chapter. Reviews artwork/photos. Send photocopies.

Recent Nonfiction Title(s): *Daily Meditations (with Scripture), for Busy Moms*, by Patricia Robertson (spirituality); *The Legend of the Bells and Other Tales*, by John Shea (spirituality).

Tips: "Don't send a submission unless you have read our catalog or one of our books."

ACTIVE PARENTING PUBLISHERS, INC., 810-B Franklin Court, Marietta GA 30067. Fax: (770)429-0334. E-mail: cservice@activeparenting.com. Website: http://www.activeparenting.com. Editorial Manager: Shelly Cox. **Acqui-**

sitions: Michele Cox, associate editor. "Our aim is to develop human potential by producing quality programs and training which provide value to our customers and offer creative solutions to our needs." Publishes 4 titles/year.
Nonfiction: Self-help, textbook, educational. Subjects include child guidance/parenting, psychology, loss, self-esteem. Nonfiction work; mainly parent education and family issues. *Does not accept unsolicited mss.*
Recent Nonfiction Title(s): *Parenting Your 1- to 4-Year-Old*, by Michael H. Popkin, Ph.D.; contributing authors: Betsy Gard, Ph.D. and Marilyn Montgomery, Ph.D. (self-help).

ADAMS MEDIA CORPORATION, 260 Center St., Holbrook MA 02343. (617)767-8100. Fax: (617)767-0994. Website: http://www.adamsonline.com. Editor-in-Chief: Edward Walters. **Acquisitions:** Anne Weaver; Pam Liflander. "We publish commercial nonfiction, not scholarly or literary material." Publishes hardcover originals, trade paperback originals and reprints. Publishes 100 titles/year. Receives 1,500 queries and 500 mss/year. 25% of books from first-time authors; 25% from unagented writers. Pays standard royalty or makes outright purchase. Offers variable advance. Publishes book 1 year after acceptance of ms. Accepts simultaneous submissions. Reports in 3 months. Book catalog for SAE with 4 first-class stamps.
Nonfiction: Biography, children's/juvenile, cookbook, gift book, how-to, humor, illustrated book, reference, self-help. Subjects include Americana, animals, business/economics, child guidance/parenting, cooking/foods/nutrition, gardening, government/politics, health/medicine, history, hobbies, language/literature, military/war, money/finance, nature/environment, psychology, regional, science, sports, women's issues/studies. Submit outline.
Recent Nonfiction Title(s): *Knock 'em Dead*, by Martih Yate (careers); *Old Soldiers Never Die: The Life of Douglas MacArthur*, by Geoffrey Perret (biography); *Really Reading!*, by Janet Gardner and Lora Myers (parenting).

ADAMS-BLAKE PUBLISHING, 8041 Sierra St., Fair Oaks CA 95628. (916)962-9296. Vice President: Paul Raymond. **Acquisitions:** Monica Blane, senior editor. "We are looking for business, technology and finance titles as well as data that can be bound/packaged and sold to specific industry groups at high margins. We are especially looking for 'high ticket' items that sell to the corporate market for prices between $100-300." Publishes trade paperback originals and reprints. Publishes 10-15 titles/year. Receives 150 queries and 90 mss/year. 90% of books from first-time authors; 90% from unagented writers. Pays 10% royalty on wholesale price. Publishes book 6 months after acceptance of ms. Accepts simultaneous submissions. Reports in 1 month on mss. *Writer's Market* recommends allowing 2 months for reply.
Nonfiction: How-to, technical. Subjects include business/economics, computers/electronics, health/medicine, money/finance, software. Query with sample chapters or complete ms. Reviews artwork/photos as part of ms package. Send photocopies.
Recent Nonfiction Title(s): *Silver Pen*, by A. Canton; *Apartment Manager's Desk Reference*, by John Maciha.
● Addison Wesley Longman has discontinued publishing hitory and politics titles.
Tips: "We will take a chance on material the big houses reject. Since we sell the majority of our material directly, we can publish material for a very select market. This year we seek niche market material that we can Douctech™ and sell direct to the corporate sector. Author should include a marketing plan. Sell us on the project!"

ADDICUS BOOKS, INC., P.O. Box 45327, Omaha NE 68145. **Acquisitions:** Rod Colvin, president. E-mail: addicusb ks@aol.com Website: http://members.aol.com/addicusbks. Seeks high-quality mss with national or strong regional appeal. Publishes trade paperback originals. Publishes 8-10 titles/year. 70% of books from first-time authors; 60% from unagented writers. Pays royalty on retail price. Publishes book 9 months after acceptance of ms. Accepts simultaneous submissions. Reports in 1 month on proposals. Guidelines for #10 SASE.
Nonfiction: How-to, self-help. Subjects include Americana, business/economics, health/medicine, psychology, regional, true-crime. Query with outline and 3-4 sample chapters.
Recent Nonfiction Title(s): *The Family Compatibility Test*, by Susan Adams (family communication); *The ABCs of Gold Investing*, by Michael Kosares (business); *First Impressions*, by Joni Craighead (beauty/health).
Tips: "With health titles, we're looking for high-quality manuscripts from authors who have done their market research. In addition to books with national appeal, we will consider titles with strong regional appeal, such as true-crime. Here, we're looking for well-written, well-researched manuscripts with interesting stories behind the crimes."

ADDISON WESLEY LONGMAN, INC., General Publishing Group, One Jacob Way, Reading MA 01867. (617)944-3700. Fax: (617)944-8243. Website: http://www.aw.com. Publisher: David Goehring. **Acquisitions:** Nicholas Philipson, executive editor (business); Elizabeth Maguire, executive editor (psychology, social issues); Henning Gutmann, senior editor (economics, current affairs, international affairs); John Bell, editor (health); Sharon Broll, associate editor (health, biography); Jeffrey Robbins, executive editor (sciences); Beth Wolfensberger Singer, editor (children's). Estab. 1942. "Addison Wesley Longman is a premiere educational publisher, selling books, multimedia and learning programs in all major academic disciplines to the primary, secondary, higher education and professional markets throughout the world." Publishes hardcover and paperback originals. Publishes 125 titles/year. Pays royalty.
Imprint(s): Addison-Wesley, **Helix Books**, **Merloyd Lawrence Books**, **Planet Dexter**.
Nonfiction: Publishes general nonfiction, business, science, health, parenting/child care, psychology, current affairs, biography/memoir, social science, narrative nonfiction, children's multimedia. No fiction. Query by letter or phone, then submit synopsis and 1 sample chapter.
● Addison Wesley Longman has published such well-known authors as Robert Bly, T. Berry Brazelton and Richard P. Feynman.

Recent Nonfiction Title(s): *The Temple Bombing*, by Melissa Fay Greene; *Banishing Bureaucracy*, by David Osborne and Peter Plastrik; *Customers Mean Business*, by James A. Unruh.

AEGIS PUBLISHING GROUP, 796 Aquidneck Ave., Newport RI 02842-7246. (401)849-4200. **Acquisitions:** Robert Mastin, publisher. Estab. 1992. "Our specialty is telecommunications books targeted to small businesses, entrepreneurs and telecommuters—how they can benefit from the latest telecom products and services." Publishes trade paperback originals and reprints. Publishes 5 titles/year. Pays 12% royalty on net sales. Offers $1,000-4,000 advance. Reports in 2 months on queries.
Nonfiction: Reference, technical. Subjects include business/economics, computers/electronics. "Author must be an experienced authority in the subject, and the material must be very specific with helpful step-by-step advice." Query with outline and SASE.
Recent nonfiction title: *Winning Communications Strategies*, by Jeffrey Kagan (trade paperback).

AKTRIN FURNITURE RESEARCH, 164 S. Main St., P.O. Box 898, High Point NC 27261. (910)841-8535. Fax: (910)841-5435. Website: http://www.aktrin.com. **Acquisitions:** Carlene Damba, director of operations. "AKTRIN is a full-service organization dedicated to the furniture industry. Our focus is on determining trends, challenges and opportunities, while also identifying problems and weak spots." Publishes trade paperback originals. Publishes 8 titles/year. Receives 5 queries/year. 20% of books from first-time authors; 20% from unagented writers. Makes outright purchase of $1,500 minimum. Offers $300-600 advance. Publishes book 2 months after acceptance. Accepts simultaneous submissions. Reports in 1 month. *Writer's Market* recommends allowing 2 months for reply. Book catalog free.
Imprint(s): AKTRIN Furniture Research-Canada. 151 Randall St., Oakville, Ontario L6J 1P5 Canada. (905)845-3474. Contact: Stefan Wille.
Nonfiction: Reference. Subjects include business/economics. "Have an understanding of business/economics. We are writing only about the furniture industry." Query.
Recent Nonfiction Title(s): *Standards in the Furniture Industry*, by Sean Fegan (business); *Wood Material Use in the US Furniture and Cabinet Industry*; *The Furniture Industry*, in the European Union.
Tips: Audience is executives of furniture companies (manufacturers and retailers) and suppliers to the furniture industry.

‡ALBA HOUSE, 2187 Victory Blvd., Staten Island NY 10314-6603. (718)761-0047. **Acquisitions:** Edmund C. Lane, S.S.P., editor. Alba House is the North American publishing division of the Society of St. Paul, an International Roman Catholic Missionary Religious Congregation dedicated to spreading the Gospel message via the media of communications. Publishes hardcover, trade paperback and mass market paperback originals. Publishes 24 titles/year. Receives 300 queries and 150 mss/year. 20% of books from first-time authors; 100% from unagented writers. Pays 7-10% royalty. No advance. Publishes book 9 months after acceptance of ms. Reports in 1 month on queries and proposals, 2 months on mss. Book catalog and ms guidelines free.
Nonfiction: Reference, textbook. Religious subjects. Manuscripts which contribute, from a Roman Catholic perspective, to the personal, intellectual and spiritual growth of individuals in the following areas: Scripture, theology and the Church, saints-their lives and teachings, spirituality and prayer, religious life, marriage and family life, liturgy and homily preparation, pastoral concerns, religious education, bereavement, moral and ethical concerns, philosophy, psychology. Reviews artwork/photos as part of ms package. Send photocopies.
Recent Nonfiction Title(s): *Living The Truth In Love*, by Benedict Ashley, O.P. (moral theology textbook); *Synoptic Gospels*, by Joseph Kudasiewicz (scripture textbook); *All Things Made New*, by Harold A Buetow (homily helps).

‡ALETHEIA PUBLICATIONS, 38-15 Corporal Kennedy St., Bayside NY 11361. **Acquisitions:** Carolyn Smith, publisher. Publishes trade paperback originals and reprints. Publishes 4 titles/year. Imprint publishes 2 titles/year. Receives 10 queries and 3 mss/year. 90% of books from first-time authors; 100% from unagented writers. Pays 10-12% royalty on retail price. No advance. Publishes book 8 months after acceptance of ms. Accepts simultaneous submissions. Reports in 1 month on queries, 2 months on proposals, 3 months on mss.
Imprint(s): Social Change Press.
Nonfiction: Subjects include psychology, sociology, editing. "We seek manuscripts about freelance editing and writing." Submit proposal package, including rationale, sample chapters, table of contents and SASE.
Recent Nonfiction Title(s): *The Unknown Ambassadors*, by Phyllis Michaux; *Military Brats*, by Mary Wertsch; *Editorial Freelancing*, by Trumbull Rogers; *Falling Through the Cracks: AIDS and the Urban Poor*, by Victor Ayala.
Tips: Audience for Aletheia Publications: Americans who have lived overseas and freelance editors and writers. Audience for Social Change Press is sociologists interested in urban problems and culture.

‡ALEXANDER BOOKS, Subsidiary of Creativity, Inc., 65 Macedonia Rd., Alexander NC 28701. (704)252-9515. **Acquisitions:** Vivian Terrell, executive editor. Publishes hardcover originals, and trade paperback and mass market paperback originals and reprints. Publishes 8-10 titles/year. Receives 200 queries and 100 mss/year. 10% of books from first-time authors; 75% from unagented writers. Pays 12-15% royalty on wholesale price. Advances seldom given (minimum $100). Publishes book 1 year after acceptance of ms. Reports in 1 month on queries, 2 months on proposals, 3 months on mss. Book catalog and ms guidelines for #10 SASE with 2 first-class stamps.
Imprint(s): Farthest Star (Ralph Roberts, publisher).
Nonfiction: Biography, how-to, reference, self-help. Subjects include computers/electronics, government/politics, history, psychology, regional, religion, travel. "We are interested in large niche markets. Do not seek immediate publishing."

Query or submit 3 sample chapters and proposal package, including marketing plans with SASE. Reviews artwork/ photos as part of ms package. Send photocopies.
Recent Nonfiction Title(s): *The Father Quest*, by Bud Harris, PhD (psychology); *Like Gold Through Fire*, by Bud Harris, PhD (psychology); *The Sanders Price Guide to Autographs*, by George Sanders, Helen Sanders, Ralph Roberts.
Fiction: Historical, mainstream/contemporary, mystery, science fiction, western. "We prefer local or well-known authors or local interest settings". Query or submit synopsis and 3 sample chapters with SASE.
Recent Fiction Title(s): *Six-Gun Ladies*, by Talmage Powell (western); *Compleat Chance Perdue*, by Ross H. Spencer (mystery); *The Giant Rat of Sumatra*, by Rick Boyer (mystery).
Tips: "Always send well-proofed manuscripts in final form. We will not read first rough drafts. Know your market."

‡**ALGONQUIN BOOKS OF CHAPEL HILL**, Subsidiary of Workman Publishing, 307 W. Weaver St., Carrboro NC 27510. (919)767-0108. Fax: (919)933-0272. E-mail: mged@workman.com. Website: http://www.workman.com.
Acquisitions: Elisabeth Scharlatt, publisher. "We're a very small company that tries to give voice to new writers." Publishes hardcover originals, trade paperback originals and reprints. Publishes 24 titles/year. Pays 7½-15% royalty.
Imprint(s): Front Porch Paperbacks.
Nonfiction: Subjects include biography, computers/electronics, cooking/foods/nutrition, gardening, history, military/ war, nature/environment, regional, sports. Query with outline and description of book, sample chapters and SASE. Reviews artwork/photos as part of ms package. Send good color copies; prefers transparencies or duplicate slides.
Fiction: Literary, mainstream/contemporary, short story collections. Query with SASE.

ALLEN PUBLISHING CO., 7324 Reseda Blvd., Reseda CA 91335. (818)344-6788. **Acquisitions:** Michael Wiener, owner/publisher. Estab. 1979. "Our books are primarily aimed at opportunity seekers—people who are looking for an opportunity (usually a business) to improve their financial condition. Our books are not aimed at sophisticated entrepreneurs." Publishes mass market paperback originals. Publishes 4 titles/year. Receives 50-100 submissions/year. 50% of books from first-time authors; 90% from unagented writers. Makes outright purchase for negotiable sum. Publishes book 6 months after acceptance. Accepts simultaneous submissions. Reports in 2 weeks. *Writer's Market* recommends allowing 2 months for reply. Book catalog and writer's guidelines for #10 SASE.
● This publisher reports having received many manuscripts outside its area of interest. Writers are encouraged to follow the publisher's subject matter guidelines.
Nonfiction: How-to, self-help. Subjects include how to start various businesses and how to improve your financial condition. "We want self-help material, 25,000 words approximately, aimed at wealth-builders, opportunity seekers, aspiring entrepreneurs. We specialize in material for people who are relatively inexperienced in the world of business and have little or no capital to invest. Material must be original and authoritative, not rehashed from other sources. All our books are marketed exclusively by mail, in soft-cover, 8½×11 format. We are a specialty publisher and will not consider anything that does not exactly meet our needs." Query. Reviews artwork/photos as part of ms package.
Recent Nonfiction Title(s): *751 Ways To Save Money On Just About Everything*, by Mike Wiener.
Tips: "We are a specialty publisher, as noted above. If your subject does not match our specialty, do not waste your time and ours by submitting a query we cannot possibly consider."

ALLWORTH PRESS, 10 E. 23rd St., New York NY 10010-4402. Fax: (212)777-8261. E-mail: pub@allworth.com. Website: http://www.arts~online.com/allworth/home.html. **Acquisitions:** Ted Gachot, editor. Tad Crawford, publisher. Estab. 1989. "We are trying to give ordinary people advice to better themselves in practical ways—as well as helping creative people in the fine and commercial arts." Publishes trade paperback originals. Publishes 20 titles/year. Pays 6-7½% royalty (for paperback) on retail price. Reports in 1 month on queries and proposals. *Writer's Market* recommends allowing 2 months for reply. Book catalog and ms guidelines free on request.
● Allworth has published such authors as Nelson Aldrich, John Ruskin, and Steven Heller (*Design Literacy— with Waren Pomeroy*).
Nonfiction: How-to, reference. Subjects include the business aspects of art, design, photography, performing arts, writing, as well as legal guides for the public. Query.
Recent Nonfiction Title(s): *Lectures on Art*, by John Ruskin (aesthetics); *Artists Communities*, by Alliance of Artist's Communities (directory); *The Internet Publicity Guide*, by V.A. Shiva (Internet/business).

‡**ALLYN & BACON**, Division of Simon & Schuster, 160 Gould St., Needham Heights MA 02194-2310. (617)455-1200. Website: http://www.abacon.com. **Acquisitions:** Sandi Kirshner, editorial director. *Education:* Virginia Lanigan, editor (foundations, curriculum, reading/emergent literacy, language arts, children's literature, ESL/bilingual methods, vocational-ed methods); Frances Helland, editor (C&L, social studies, multicultural ed, math & science, early childhood; Nancy Forsyth, editor (ed psych, ed tech); Ray Short, editor (special ed, counseling, ed administration); Steve Dragin, editor (special-path, aud, deaf study/ed, higher ed). *English:* Joe Opiela, editor (English comp plus developmental, authors with last name A-K and all developmental authors); Eben Ludlow, editor (English comp, authors with last name L-Z). *Communication:* Joe Terry, editor (mass communication, journalism); Paul Smith, editor (speech communication, theater, music, professional drama & speech). *Political Science:* Joe Terry, editor. Psychology: Sean Wakely, editor (intro, indstr/organztnl, human relations/human factors/group process, enviro/evolutionary); Carolyn Merrill, editor (intro, experimental-except statistics/methods, developmental, physio, social and applied); Carla Daves, editor (clinical psych, assessment, professional psych, statistics/methods); Suzy Spivey, editor (health, phys ed, dance). *Sociology:* Karen Hanson, editor (sociology/intro, crime, criminal justice); Judy Fifer, editor (social work, family therapy); Sarah

Dunbar, editor (advanced sociology, anthropology). *First-year Orientation:* Nancy Forsyth, editor. Allyn & Bacon publishes college texts, freshman through graduate level, and professional reference books. Publishes hardcover and trade paperback originals. Publishes 300 titles/year. 5-10% of books from first-time authors; 95% from unagented writers. Pays 12-15% royalty on net price. Advance varies. Publishes book 1-3 years after acceptance of ms. Accepts simultaneous submissions. Reports in 2 months on queries. Book catalog and ms guidelines free; also available online.
Nonfiction: Reference, technical, textbook; primarily college texts; some titles for professionals. Subjects include education, government/politics, health/medicine, psychology, sociology, criminal justice, social work, speech, mass communication. "We focus on a few areas and cover them thoroughly; publishing vertically, from freshman level through graduate level. We also publish a number of titles within each discipline, same area but different approach. So, just because we have titles in an area already, it doesn't mean we aren't interested in more." Query with outline, 2-3 sample chapters, table of contents, author's vita and SASE. Reviews artwork/photos. Send photocopies.
Recent Nonfiction Title(s): *Educational Psychology*, by Anita Woolfolk (textbook); *Sociology: A Down to Earth Approach*, by James Henslin (textbook); *Psychology*, by Lester Lefton (textbook).

ALMAR PRESS, 4105 Marietta Dr., Vestal NY 13850-4032. (607)722-0265. Fax: (607)722-3545. Editor-in-Chief: A.N. Weiner. **Acquisitions:** M.F. Weiner, managing editor. Estab. 1977. *Almar Reports* are business and technology subjects published for management use and prepared in 8½×11 book format. Reprint publications represent a new aspect of our business. We expanding our books on avoiding crime problems in business and personal life, and books covering unusual business topics—*not* the usual 'How to succeed in business,' or 'How I made a fortune in business.' " Publishes hardcover and paperback originals and reprints. Publishes 8 titles/year. Receives 200 submissions/year. 75% of books from first-time authors; 100% from unagented writers. Average print order for a first book is 2,000. Pays 10% royalty. No advance. Publishes book 6 months after acceptance. Prefers exclusive submissions; however, accepts simultaneous submissions, if so noted. Reports within 2 months. Book catalog for #10 SAE with 2 first-class stamps. Submissions *must* include SASE for reply.
Nonfiction: Publishes business, technical, regional, consumer books and reports. "Main subjects include general business, financial, travel, career, technology, personal help, Northeast regional, hobbies, general medical, general legal, how-to. Submit outline and sample chapters. Reviews artwork/photos as part of ms package.
Recent Nonfiction Title(s): *A Picture Postcard History of Baseball*, by R. Menchine (baseball).
Tips: "We are open to any suggested topic. This type of book will be important to us. We look for timely subjects. The type of book the writer has the best chance of selling to our firm is something different or unusual—*no* poetry or fiction, also *no* first-person travel or family history. The book must be complete and of good quality."

ALPINE PUBLICATIONS, 225 S. Madison Ave., Loveland CO 80537. **Acquisitions:** Ms. B.J. McKinney, publisher. "Our audience is pet owners, breeders and exhibitors, veterinarians, animal trainers, animal care specialists, judges." Publishes 6-10 titles/year. 30% of books from first-time authors; 95% from unagented writers. Pays 7-15% royalty on wholesale price. Publishes hardcover and trade paperback originals and reprints. Publishes book 18 months after acceptance. Accepts simultaneous submissions. Reports in 1 month on queries; 3 months on mss. Book catalog free. Manuscript guidelines for #10 SASE.
Imprint(s): Blue Ribbon Books.
Nonfiction: Animal subjects. "Alpine specializes in books that promote the enjoyment of and responsibility for companion animals with emphasis on dogs and horses." Submit 2-3 sample chapters, summary, outline with SASE. Reviews artwork/photos as part of ms package. Send photocopies.
Recent Nonfiction Title(s): *The Mentally Sound Dog*, by Clark (dog behavior modification).
Tips: "We prefer to work directly with authors, not through agents. Look up some of our titles before you submit. See what is unique about our books. Write your proposal to suit our guidelines."

AMACOM BOOKS, Imprint of American Management Association, 1601 Broadway, New York NY 10019-7406. (212)903-8081. Managing Director: Weldon P. Rackley. **Acquisitions:** Hank Kennedy, publisher. Estab. 1923. "We publish practical books on business issues, strategies, and tasks for the business sector." Publishes hardcover and trade paperback originals and trade paperback reprints. Publishes 68 titles/year. Receives 200 submissions/year. 50% of books from first-time authors; 90% from unagented writers. Pays 10-15% royalty on net receipts by the publisher. Publishes book 9 months after acceptance. Reports in 2 months. Book catalog and proposal guidelines free.
Nonfiction: Publishes business books of all types, including management, marketing, technology (computers), career, professional skills, small business. Retail, direct mail, college, corporate markets. Query. Submit outline/synopsis, sample chapters, résumé/vita.

AMERICA WEST PUBLISHERS, P.O. Box 2208, Carson City NV 89702-2208. (702)585-0700. Fax: (702)367-1338. **Acquisitions:** George Green, president. Estab. 1985. America West Publishers seek research and proof of the "other side of picture" and new health alternatives. Publishes hardcover and trade paperback originals and reprints. Publishes 20 titles/year. Receives 150 submissions/year. 90% of books from first-time authors; 90% from unagented writers. Pays 10% on wholesale price. Offers $300 average advance. Publishes book 6 months after acceptance. Accepts simultaneous submissions. Reports in 1 month. *Writer's Market* recommends allowing 2 months for reply. Book catalog and ms guidelines free.
Nonfiction: UFO—metaphysical. Subjects include health/medicine (holistic self-help), political (including cover-up), economic. Submit outline/synopsis and sample chapters. Reviews artwork/photos as part of ms package.

Recent Nonfiction Title(s): *Project Seek*, by Gerald Carroll; *Conspirators Hierarchy*, by Dr. John Coleman.
Tips: "We currently have materials in all bookstores that have areas of UFOs; also political and economic nonfiction."

AMERICAN ASTRONAUTICAL SOCIETY, Univelt, Inc., Publisher, P.O. Box 28130, San Diego CA 92198.
(619)746-4005. Fax: (619)746-3139. **Acquisitions:** Robert H. Jacobs, editorial director. Estab. 1970. "Our books must be space-oriented or space-related. They are meant for technical libraries, research establishments and the aerospace industry worldwide." Publishes hardcover originals. Publishes 8 titles/year. Receives 12-15 submissions/year. 5% of books from first-time authors; 5% from unagented writers. Average print order for a first book is 300-1,500. Pays 10% royalty on actual sales. Publishes book 4 months after acceptance. Accepts simultaneous submissions. Reports in 1 month. Book catalog and ms guidelines for 9×12 SAE with 3 first-class stamps.
Nonfiction: Proceedings or monographs in the field of astronautics, including applications of aerospace technology to Earth's problems. Call first, then submit outline and 1-2 sample chapters. Reviews artwork/photos as part of ms package.
Recent Nonfiction Title(s): *Strategies for Mars: A Guide to Human Exploration*, edited by Carol R. Stoker, Carter Emmart.

AMERICAN ATHEIST PRESS, P.O. Box 140195, Austin TX 78714-0195. (512)458-1244. Fax: (512)467-9525
Acquisitions: Frank Zindler, editor. Estab. 1959. "We are interested in hard-hitting and original books expounding the lifestyle of atheism and criticizing religion." Publishes trade paperback originals and reprints. Publishes 12 titles/year. Receives 200 submissions/year. 40-50% of books from first-time authors; 100% from unagented writers. Pays 5-10% royalty on retail price. Publishes book 2 years after acceptance. Accepts simultaneous submissions. Reports in 4 months on queries. Book catalog for $6\frac{1}{2} \times 9\frac{1}{2}$ SAE. Writer's guidelines for 9×12 SAE.
Imprint(s): Gustav Broukal Press.
Nonfiction: Biography, reference, general. Subjects include history (of religion and atheism, of the effects of religion historically); philosophy and religion (from an atheist perspective, particularly criticism of religion); politics (separation of state and church, religion and politics); atheism (particularly the lifestyle of atheism; the history of atheism; applications of atheism). "We would like to see more submissions dealing with the histories of specific religious sects, such as the L.D.S., the Worldwide Church of God, etc." Submit outline and sample chapters. Reviews artwork/photos.
Recent Nonfiction Title(s): *Manual of a Perfect Atheist*, by Rios.
Fiction: Humor (satire of religion or of current religious leaders); anything of particular interest to atheists. "We rarely publish any fiction. But we have occasionally released a humorous book. No mainstream. For our press to consider fiction, it would have to tie in with the general focus of our press, which is the promotion of atheism and free thought." Submit outline/synopsis and sample chapters.
Tips: "We will need more how-to types of material—how to argue with creationists, how to fight for state/church separation, etc. We have an urgent need for literature for young atheists."

‡AMERICAN BAR ASSOCIATION BOOK PUBLISHING, 750 N. Lake Shore Dr., Chicago IL 60611. **Acquisitions:** J. Weintraub, director of book development and marketing; Jane L. Johnston, executive editor. "We are interested in books that will help lawyers practice law more effectively whether it's help in handling clients, structuring a real estate deal or taking an antitrust case to court." Publishes hardcover and trade paperback originals. Publishes 100 titles/year. Receives 50 queries/year. 20% of books from first-time authors; 95% from unagented writers. Pays 5-15% royalty on wholesale or retail price. Publishes book 18 months after acceptance of ms. Accepts simultaneous submissions. Reports in 1 months on queries and proposals, 3 months on mss. Book catalog for $5.95. Ms guidelines free.
Nonfiction: How-to (in the legal market), reference, technical. Subjects include business/economics, computers/electronics, money/finance, software, legal practice. "Our market is not, generally, the public. Books need to be targeted to lawyers who are seeking solutions to their practice problems. We also rarely publish scholarly treatises." Query with SASE.
Recent Nonfiction Title(s): *The Complete Guide to Mediation*, by Forrest Mosten (professional); *Connecting with Your Client*, by Noelle Nelson (practice/guide); *The Portable UCC*, by Corinne Cooper (professional).

‡AMERICAN COLLEGE OF PHYSICIAN EXECUTIVES, (ACPE PUBLICATIONS), 4890 W. Kennedy Blvd., Suite 200, Tampa FL 33609. (813)287-2000. **Acquisitions:** Wesley Curry, managing editor. Publishes hardcover and trade paperback originals. Publishes 12-15 titles/year. Receives 6 queries and 3 mss/year. 80% of books from first-time authors; 100% from unagented writers. Pays 10-15% royalty on wholesale price or makes outright purchase of $1,000-4,000. Publishes book 8 months after acceptance of ms. Reports in 1 month on queries and ms, 2 months on proposals. Book catalog and ms guidelines free.
Nonfiction: Technical, textbook. Subjects include business/economics, health/medicine. Query and submit outline. Reviews artwork/photos as part of ms package. Send photocopies.
Recent Nonfiction Title(s): *Hope for the Future*, by Barbara Linney (career guide); *So You've Been Integrated*, by Richard Thompson, M.D. (business); *Issues and Trends in Liability*, edited by Todd Sagin, M.D., J.D. (law).
Tips: Audience is physicians in management and physicians interested in management.

AMERICAN CORRECTIONAL ASSOCIATION, 4380 Forbes Blvd., Lanham MD 20706. (301)918-1800. Fax: (301)918-1896. E-mail: afins@aca.com. Website: http://www.corrections.com/aca. **Acquisitions:** Alice Fins, managing editor. Estab. 1870. American Correctional Association provides practical information on jails, prisons, boot camps, probation, parole, community corrections, juvenile facilities and programs rehabilitation, substance abuse programs and other areas of corrections. Publishes hardcover and trade paperback originals. Publishes 18 titles/year. Receives 40 submissions/year. 90% of books from first-time authors; 100% from unagented writers. Pays 10% royalty on net sales. Publishes book 6-12 months after acceptance. Reports in 4 months. Book catalog and ms guidelines free.

● This publisher advises out-of-town freelance editors, indexers and proofreaders to refrain from requesting work from them.

Nonfiction: How-to, reference, technical, textbook, correspondence courses. "We are looking for practical, how-to texts or training materials written for the corrections profession. No true-life accounts by current or former inmates or correctional officers, theses, or dissertations." Query. Reviews artwork/photos as part of ms package.

Recent Nonfiction Title(s): *Reform & Retribution: An Illustrated History of American Prisons*, by John Roberts, Ph.D; *Women Behind Bars*, by Raymond Wojda and Judy Rowse, photos by Grace Wojda; *Managing Delinquency Programs that Work*, by Barry Glick, Ph.D. and Arnold Goldstein, Ph.D.

Tips: "Our audience is made up of corrections professionals and criminal justice students."

AMERICAN DIABETES ASSOCIATION, 1660 Duke St., Alexandria VA 22314. (703)549-1500. Website: http://www.diabetes.org. **Acquisitions:** Susan Reynolds, acquisitions editor. "The mission of the American Diabetes Association is to prevent and cure diabetes and to improve the lives of all people affected by diabetes." Publishes hardcover originals and trade paperback originals. Publishes 15 titles/year. Receives 60 queries and 20 mss/year. 10% of books from first-time authors; 80% from unagented writers. Pays 7-10% royalty on retail price. Offers $3,000 advance. Publishes book 9 months after acceptance of ms. Reports in 2 months. Book catalog free.

Nonfiction: Children's/juvenile, cookbook, how-to, reference, self-help. Subjects include child guidance/parenting, cooking/foods/nutrition, health/medicine, psychology. "Our books are written for people with diabetes and their families. We are interested in the medical, nutritional and psychosocial aspects of living with diabetes." Query with outline and 2 sample chapters. Reviews artwork/photos as part of ms package. Send photocopies.

Recent Nonfiction Title(s): *American Diabetes Association Complete Guide to Diabetes* (information); *Flavorful Seasons Cookbook*, by Robyn Webb (menus with healthy recipes); *How to Get Great Diabetes Care*, by Irl Hirsch, MD (information on medical care and benefits).

Fiction: Juvenile. "We publish very little fiction—all for juveniles with diabetes." Query with synopsis and 2 sample chapters.

Recent Fiction Title(s): *The Dinosaur Tamer*, by Marcia Levine Mazur (juvenile fiction).

Tips: "Our audience consists primarily of consumers with diabetes who want to better manage their illness. Obtain a few of our books to better understand our target audience and appropriate reading level."

AMERICAN EAGLE PUBLICATIONS INC., P.O. Box 1507, Show Low AZ 85901. Phone/fax: (520)367-1621. E-mail: ameagle@whitemtns.com. **Acquisitions:** Mark Ludwig, publisher. Estab. 1988. Publishes hardcover and trade paperback originals and reprints. Publishes 8 titles/year. 50% of books from first-time authors; 100% from unagented writers. Pays 5-12% royalty on retail price. Offers $1,000 average advance. Publishes book 6 months after acceptance of ms. Accepts simultaneous submissions. Reports in 2 months. Catalog for #10 SASE.

● Publisher reports no interest in seeing military or other autobiographies.

Nonfiction: Historical biography, technical. Subjects include computers/electronics (security), military/war and science (computers and artificial intelligence). "We are highly specialized in nonfiction. Writers should call and discuss what they have first." Query. Reviews artwork/photos as part of freelance ms package. Send photocopies.

Recent Nonfiction Title(s): *The Quest for Water Planets*, by Ray Halyard (science); *Civil War II* (socio-political).

Tips: Audience is "scholarly, university profs, (some used as textbooks), very technical programmers and researchers, military, very international. No autobiographies."

AMERICAN FEDERATION OF ASTROLOGERS, P.O. Box 22040, Tempe AZ 85285. (602)838-1751. Fax: (602)838-8293. E-mail: afa@msn.com. **Acquisitions:** Kris Brandt Riske, publications manager. American Federation of Astrologers publishes only astrology books, software, calendars, charts and related aids. Publishes trade paperback originals and reprints. Publishes 15-20 titles/year. Receives 10 queries and 20 mss/year. 30% of books from first-time authors; 100% from unagented writers. Pays 10% royalty. Publishes book 10 months after acceptance of ms. Accepts simultaneous submissions. Reports in 6 months on mss. Book catalog for $2. Manuscript guidelines free.

Nonfiction: Astrology. Submit complete ms.

Recent Nonfiction Title(s): *The Astrologer's Forecasting Workbook*, by Lloyd Cope.

AMERICAN HOSPITAL PUBLISHING, INC., American Hospital Association, 737 N. Michigan Ave., Chicago IL 60611-2615. (312)440-6800. Fax: (312)951-8491. **Acquisitions:** Division Director. Estab. 1979. "We publish books for senior and middle management of health care institutions." Publishes trade paperback originals. Publishes 20-30 titles/year. Receives 75-100 submissions/year. 20% of books from first-time authors; 100% from unagented writers. Pays 10-12% royalty on retail price. Offers $1,000 average advance. Publishes book 1 year after acceptance. Reports in 3 months. Book catalog and ms guidelines for 9×12 SAE with 7 first-class stamps.

Nonfiction: Reference, technical, textbook. Subjects include business/economics (specific to health care institutions); health/medicine (never consumer oriented). Need field-based, reality-tested responses to changes in the health care field directed to hospital CEO's, planners, boards of directors, or other senior management. No personal histories, untested health care programs or clinical texts. Query.

Tips: "The successful proposal demonstrates a clear understanding of the needs of the market and the writer's ability to succinctly present practical knowledge of demonstrable benefit that comes from genuine experience that readers will recognize, trust and accept."

‡AMERICAN INSTITUTE OF CERTIFIED PUBLIC ACCOUNTANTS, Harborside Financial Center, 201 Plaza Three, Jersey City NJ 07711-3881. **Acquisitions:** Marie Bareille, senior manager. Publishes hardcover and trade paperback originals. Publishes 104 titles/year. Receives 5 queries/year; 3 mss/year. 10% of books are from first-time authors; 100% from unagented writers. Pays 10-15% royalty on retail price. Offers $500-2,000 advance. Publishes book 5 months after acceptance of ms. Reports in 1 month on queries, 3 months on proposals and mss. Book catalog and ms guidelines free.
Nonfiction: Technical. Subjects include business/economics, computers/electronics, accounting, taxation, personal financial planning. "We are interested in expanding in topics for corporate accountants, consultants and computers." Submit proposal package including table of contents and outline.
Recent Nonfiction Title(s): *Manual for Mobile CPAs* (how-to); *Top Ten Technologies for Business Professionals* (information roundup); *The Marketing Advantage* (how-to for CPA firms).
Tips: Audience is CPAs in public accounting firms and corporate accountants.

AMERICAN NURSES PUBLISHING, American Nurses Foundation, #100 W. 600 Maryland Ave., Washington DC 20024. (202)651-7213. **Acquisitions:** Mandy Mikulencak, publishing manager. American Nurses publishes books designed to help professional nurses in their work and careers. Publishes trade paperback originals and reprints. Publishes 20 titles/year. Receives 20 queries and 10 mss/year. 75% of books from first-time authors; 100% from unagented writers. Pays 10% royalty on retail price. Publishes book 6 months after acceptance of ms. Reports in 6 months on proposals and mss. Catalog and ms guidelines free.
Nonfiction: Reference, technical and textbook. Subjects include business/economics, education, health/medicine, money/finance, psychology, science, women's issues/studies pertaining to nursing. Submit outline and 1 sample chapter. Reviews artwork/photos as part of ms package. Send photocopies.
Recent Nonfiction Title(s): *Managed Care and Case Management: Roles for Professional Nursing*, by Cheryl May (reference/text).
Tips: Audience is nurses.

AMERICAN PRESS, 520 Commonwealth Ave., Boston MA 02215-2605. **Acquisitions:** Marcy Taylor, editor. Publishes college textbooks. Publishes 25 titles/year. Receives 350 queries and 100 mss/year. 50% of books from first-time authors; 90% from unagented writers. Pays 5-15% royalty on wholesale price. Publishes book 9 months after acceptance of ms. Reports in 3 months. Book catalog free.
Nonfiction: Technical, textbook. Subjects include agriculture/horticulture, anthropology/archaeology, art/architecture, business/economics, education, government/politics, health/medicine, history, music/dance, psychology, science, sociology, sports. "We prefer that our authors actually teach courses for which the manuscripts are designed." Query or submit outline with tentative table of contents. No complete mss.

‡THE AMERICAN PSYCHIATRIC PRESS, INC., 1400 K St. NW, Washington DC 20005. (202)682-6231. **Acquisitions:** Carol C. Nadelson, editor-in-chief. Estab. 1981. American Psychiatric Press publishes professional, authoritative reference books and general nonfiction on psychiatry only. Publishes hardcover and trade paperback originals and hardcover reprints. Publishes 50 titles/year. Receives 200 queries/year. 25% of books from first-time authors; 90% from unagented writers. Pays 10-15% royalty on net sales. Offers $3,000 advance. Publishes book 1 year after acceptance of ms. Accepts simultaneous submissions, but this must be mentioned in the submission. Reports in 1 month on queries, 2 months on proposals. Book catalog, author questionnaire and proposal guidelines free.
Nonfiction: Reference (psychiatry), textbook (psychiatry), handbooks, manuals, study guides, assessment/interview booklets, clinical and research aspects. All psychiatry-related. "Projects with significant clinical applications in psychiatry will be given the highest priority. We are also interested in authoritative books that interpret the scientific and medical aspects of serious mental illness for the lay public. Request and submit a completed author questionnaire. Do not submit an entire manuscript. American Psychiatric press prefers to consider proposals." Submit outline and 1 sample chapter and proposal package, including Author Questionnaire, table of contents, author's curriculum vitae with SASE. Reviews artwork/photos as part of the proposal package. Send photocopies.
Recent Nonfiction Title(s): *Time-Managed Group Psychotherapy: Effective Clinical Applications*, by K. Roy MacKenzie, M.D. (professional); *Cognitive Rehabilitation for Neuropsychiatric Disorders*, edited by P. Corrigan, Psy. D., and S. Yudofsky, M.D. (professional); *The Selfish Brain: Learning from Addiction*, by Robert L. Dupont, M.D. (trade).
Tips: "Primary audience is psychiatrists and other mental health professionals. Secondary audience is primary care physicians and other health care professionals.

AMERICAN SOCIETY OF CIVIL ENGINEERS PRESS, (formerly American Society of Civil Engineers), ASCE, 345 E. 47th St., New York NY 10017-2398. (212)705-7689. Fax: (212)705-7712. E-mail: mluke@ny.asce.org. Website: http://www.asce.org. **Acquisitions:** Mary Grace Luke-Stefanchik, book acquisitions editor: . Estab. 1988. ASCE Press is the non-committee-sponsored book publishing program of the American Society of Civil Engineers. "We publish books by individual authors to advance the civil engineering profession." Publishes 15-20 titles/year. 50% of books from first-time authors; 100% from unagented writers. Pays 10% royalty. No advance. Accepts simultaneous submissions. Request proposal guidelines.

• ASCE Press has increased their publication program from 10 to 15-20 titles per year.
Nonfiction: Civil engineering. "We are looking for topics that are useful and instructive to the engineering practitioner." Query with outline, sample chapters and cv.
Recent Nonfiction Title(s): *Historic American Covered Bridges*, by McKee (engineering history); *Building on Sinkholes*, by Sowers (engineering practice); *Lessons from the Oklahoma City Bombing*, by Hinman & Hammond (engineering practice).
Tips: "ASCE is a not-for-profit organization, so we've always been cost conscious. We produce inexpensive professional books on a tight budget. We have increased the number of new books that we are producing by about 50-100%."

‡AMERICAN WATER WORKS ASSOCIATION 6666 W. Quincy Ave., Denver CO 80235. (303)794-7711.
Acquisitions: Mead L. Noss, manager of business and product development. Publishes hardcover and trade paperback originals. Publishes 100 titles/year. Receives 200 queries and 35 mss/year. 30% of books from first-time authors; 100% from unagented writers. Pays 15% royalty on wholesale or retail price. No advance. Publishes book 1 year after acceptance of ms. Book catalog and manuscript guidelines free.
Nonfiction: Multimedia (format MS/Windows), technical. Subjects include nature/environment, science, software, drinking water-related topics. Query or submit outline, 3 sample chapters and author biography. Reviews artwork/photos as part of ms package. Send photocopies.
Recent Nonfiction Title(s): *Xeriscape Plant Guide*, by Denver Water/AWWA/Fulcrum Publishing (low-water gardening); *The Story of Drinking Water* (children's educational); *A Consumer's Guide to Water Conservation*, by Mark Obmascik (light-hearted consumer tips).

AMHERST MEDIA, INC., P.O. Box 586, Amherst NY 14226-1219. (716)874-4450. Fax: (716)874-4508. Publisher: Craig Alesse. **Acquisitions:** Richard Lynch, senior editor. Estab. 1974. "We publish how-to photography books." Publishes trade paperback originals and reprints. Publishes 10 titles/year. Receives 50 submissions/year. 80% of books from first-time authors; 100% from unagented writers. Pays 8% royalty on retail price. Publishes book 1 year after acceptance. Accepts simultaneous submissions. Reports in 2 months. Book catalog and ms guidelines free on request.
Nonfiction: How-to photography. Looking for well-written and illustrated photo books. Query with outline, 2 sample chapters and SASE. Reviews artwork/photos as part of ms package.
Recent Nonfiction Title(s): *Wide-Angle Photography*, by Joseph Paduano; *Wedding Photographer's Handbook*, by Robert Hurth; *Handcoloring Photographs Step-by-Step*, by Sandra Laird and Carey Chambers.
Tips: "Our audience is made up of beginning to advanced photographers. If I were a writer trying to market a book today, I would fill the need of a specific audience and self-edit in a tight manner."

THE AMWELL PRESS, P.O. Box 5385, Clinton NJ 08809-0385. (908)537-6888. President: James Rikhoff. **Acquisitions:** Monica Sullivan, vice president. Corporate Secretary: Genevieve Symonds. Estab. 1976. Publishes hardcover originals. Publishes 6 titles/year. Publishes book 18 months after acceptance. Reports in 2 months on queries.
Nonfiction: Hunting and fishing stories/literature (not how-to). Mostly limited editions. Query.
Recent Nonfiction Title(s): *Taking Your Chances in the High Country*, anthology compiled by Jim Rikhoff.

‡ANCESTRY INCORPORATED, P.O. Box 476, Salt Lake City UT 84110-0476. (801)531-1790. Fax: (801)531-1798. E-mail: gbdc96a@prodigy.com. Book Editor: Matt Grove. *Ancestry* magazine Editor: Lynda Angelastro. **Acquisitions:** Loretto Szucs, managing editor. Estab. 1983. "Our publications are aimed exclusively at the genealogist. We consider everything from short monographs to book length works on immigration, migration, record collections and heraldic topics." Publishes hardcover, trade and paperback originals and *Ancestry* magazine. Publishes 6-8 titles/year. Receives over 100 submissions/year. 70% of books from first-time authors; 100% from unagented writers. Pays 8-12% royalty or makes outright purchase. No advance. Publishes book 1 year after acceptance. Accepts simultaneous submissions for books. Reports in 2 months. Book catalog for 9×12 SAE with 2 first-class stamps.
Nonfiction: How-to, reference, genealogy. Subjects include Americana, historical methodology and genealogical research techniques. No mss that are not genealogical or historical. Query, or submit outline/synopsis and sample chapters. Reviews artwork/photos.
Recent Nonfiction Title(s): *U.S. Miltary Records*, by James C. Neagles; *The Source*, by L. Szucs and S. Luebking.
Tips: "Genealogical reference, how-to, and descriptions of source collections have the best chance of selling to our firm. Be precise in your description. Please, no family histories or genealogies."

ANCHORAGE PRESS, INC., P.O. Box 8067, New Orleans LA 70182-8067. (504)283-8868. Fax: (504)866-0502. **Acquisitions:** Orlin Corey, editor. Publishes hardcover originals. Estab. 1935. "We are an international agency for plays for young people. First in the field since 1935." Publishes 10 titles/year. Receives 450-900 submissions/year. 50% of books from first-time authors; 80% from unagented writers. Pays 10-15% royalty on retail price. Playwrights also receive 50-75% royalties. Publishes book 1-2 years after acceptance. Reports in 1 month on queries, 4 months on mss. Book catalog and ms guidelines free.
Nonfiction: Textbook, plays. Subjects include education, language/literature, plays. "We are looking for play anthologies; and texts for teachers of drama/theater (middle school and high school.)" Query. Reviews artwork/photos as part of ms package.
Recent Nonfiction Title(s): *The Theater of Aurand Harris*, by Lowell Swortzell; *Bambi: A Life in the Woods*, play by De Vita; *Boy Who Tripped the Moon*, by Grarer.

Fiction: Plays of juvenile/young people's interest. Query.

ANDREWS McMEEL UNIVERSAL, (formerly Andrews & McMeel), 4520 Main St., Kansas City MO 64111-7701. **Acquisitions:** Christine Schillig, vice president/editorial director. (816)932-6700. Andrews McMeel publishes general trade books, humor books, miniature gift books, calendars, greeting cards, and stationery products. Publishes hardcover and paperback originals. Publishes 300 titles/year. Pays royalty on retail price. Offers advance.
  • This publisher accepts agented submissions only.
Nonfiction: General trade, humor, how-to, journalism, juvenile, consumer reference books. Also produces gift books, posters and kits. Query only. *Accepts only agented material.*
Recent Nonfiction Title(s): *Forever Erma*, by Erma Bombeck; *The Ultimate Answering Machine Message-Book*, by Marnie Winston-Macauley; *Inside the Brain*, by Ronald Kotulak.
Recent Fiction Title(s): *Casual Day Has Gone Too Far*, by Scott Adams; *The Man Who Loved God*, by William X. Kienzle (mystery).

APOLLO BOOKS, 151 Tiremont St., Boston MA 02116. (617)350-7821. Fax: (617)350-7822. **Acquisitions:** Gregory Morson, owner. Estab. 1994. Publishes 8 titles/year. Receives 100 submissions/year. Publishes book 6 months after acceptance. Simultaneous submissions OK. Reports in 2 months. Book catalog for 9×12 SAE with 4 first-class stamps.
  • Apollo Books is not accepting new mss or submissions.
Nonfiction: Biography, coffee table book and reference. Subjects include art/architecture and gardening. Query. Reviews artwork as part of ms package.
Recent Nonfiction Title(s): *Chinese and Other Far Eastern Art*.

APPALACHIAN MOUNTAIN CLUB BOOKS, 5 Joy St., Boston MA 02108. **Acquisitions:** Gordon Hardy, editor/publisher. "We publish hiking guides, water-recreation guides (non-motorized), nature, conservation and mountain-subject guides for America's Northeast. We connect recreation to conservation." Publishes trade paperback originals. Publishes 6-10 titles/year. Receives 200 queries and 20 mss/year. 30% of books from first-time authors; 90% from unagented writers. Pays 6-10% royalty on retail price. Offers modest advance. Publishes book 10 months after acceptance of ms. Accepts simultaneous submissions. Reports in 2-3 months on proposals. Book catalog for 8½×11 SAE with 4 first-class stamps. Manuscript guidelines for #10 SASE.
Nonfiction: How-to, guidebooks. Subjects include history (mountains, Northeast), nature/environment, recreation, regional (Northeast outdoor recreation). Writers should avoid submitting: proposals on Appalachia (rural southern mountains); not enough market research; too much personal experience—autobiography." Query. Reviews artwork/photos as part of ms package. Send photocopies and transparencies "at your own risk."
Recent Nonfiction Title(s): *Quiet Water Canoe Guide: New York*; *Exploring Boston on Bike & Foot*; *Nature Walks in/around New York City.*
Tips: "Our audience is outdoor recreationalists, conservation-minded hikers and canoeists, family outdoor lovers, armchair enthusiasts. Our guidebooks have a strong conservation message."

‡A-R EDITIONS, INC., 801 Deming Way, Madison WI 53717. (608)836-9000. Website: http://www.areditions.com. **Acquisitions:** Paul Corneilson, managing editor, recent researches (music editions); James L. Zychowicz, managing editor, digital audio series. Publishes 16 titles/year. Receives 12 queries and 8 mss/year. 50% of books from first-time authors; 100% from unagented writers. Pays royalty or honoraria. Reports in 1 month on queries, 3 months on proposals and 4 months on mss. Book catalog free. Manuscript guidelines free (check website).
Nonfiction: Computer and electronics, historical music editions, software; also titles related to computer music and digital audio. Query. Submit outline with SASE.
Recent Nonfiction Title(s): *General Midi*, by Stanley Jungleib (computer music); *Experiments in Musical Intelligence*, by David Cope (music/AI); *The Music and Scripts for In Dahomey*, edited by Thomas Riis.

ARABESQUE, Imprint of Kensington, 850 Third Ave., 16th Floor, New York NY 10022. (212)407-1500. **Acquisitions:** Monica Harris, senior editor. "Arabesque publishes contemporary romances about African-American couples." Publishes mass market paperback originals. Publishes 48 titles/year. 30-50% of books from first-time authors; 50% from unagented writers. Pays royalty on retail price, varies by author. Advance varies by author. Publishes book 18 months after acceptance of ms. Accepts simultaneous submissions. Reports in 3 months on mss. Book catalog for #10 SASE.
Fiction: Multicultural romance. Query with synopsis and SASE. "We are not accepting unsolicited mss at this time."
Recent Fiction Title(s): *Legacy*, by Shirley Hailstock; *Silken Betrayal*, by Francis Ray.

ARCADE PUBLISHING, 141 Fifth Ave., New York NY 10010. (212)475-2633. **Acquisitions:** Cal Barksdale; Timothy Bent; Sean McDonald; Richard Seaver, publisher; Jeannette Seaver, associate publisher; David Martyn. Arcade prides itself on publishing top-notch commercial nonfiction, literary fiction and poetry. Publishes hardcover originals, trade paperback originals and reprints. Publishes 40 titles/year. 5% of books from first-time authors. Pays royalty on retail price. Offers $1,000-100,000 advance. Publishes book within 18 months after acceptance of ms. Reports in 3 months on queries.
  • Arcade accepts agented submissions only.
Nonfiction: Biography, cookbook, general nonfiction. Subjects include cooking/foods/nutrition, government/politics, history, nature/environment and travel. Query. Reviews artwork/photos as part of ms package. Send photocopies.

Recent Nonfiction Title(s): *Ivy League Stripper*, by Heidi Mattson; *Prohibition: Thirteen Years That Changed America*, by Edward Behr.
Fiction: Ethnic, historical, humor, literary, mainstream/contemporary, mystery, short story collections, suspense. Query. *Agented submissions only.*
Recent Fiction Title(s): *Trying to Save Piggy Sneed*, by John Irving; *The Lost Son*, by Brent Spencer; *Death by Publication*, by J.J. Fletcher.
Poetry: "We do not publish poetry as a rule; since our inception we have published only a few volumes of poetry." Query.

ARCHWAY PAPERBACKS, Imprint of Pocket Books for Young Readers, Imprint of Simon & Schuster, 1230 Avenue of the Americas, New York NY 10020. (212)698-7669. Fax: (212)698-7007. Vice President/Editorial Director: Patricia MacDonald. **Acquisitions:** send all submissions Attn: Manuscript Proposals. Archway Paperbacks publishes fiction and current nonfiction for young adult readers ages 12-18. Publishes mass market paperback originals and reprints. Publishes 80 titles/year. Receives over 1,000 submissions/year. Pays 6-8% royalty on retail price. Publishes book 2 years after acceptance. Reports in 3 months. SASE for all material necessary or query not answered.
Nonfiction: Young adult, ages 12-18. Subjects include current popular subjects or people, sports. Query with outline/synopsis, 2 sample chapters and SASE. Reviews artwork/photos as part of ms package. Send photocopies.
Fiction: Young adult horror, mystery, suspense thrillers, contemporary fiction, romances for YA, ages 12-18. Query with outline/synopsis, sample chapters and SASE.
Recent Fiction Title(s): *Fear Street: The New Boy*, by R.L. Stine; *Aliens Ate My Homework*, by Bruce Coville.

ARDEN PRESS INC., P.O. Box 418, Denver CO 80201-0418. (303)697-6766. **Acquisitions:** Susan Conley, publisher. Estab. 1980. "We sell to general and women's bookstores and public and academic libraries. Many of our titles are adopted as texts for college courses." Publishes hardcover and trade paperback originals and reprints. 95% of books are originals; 5% are reprints. Publishes 4-6 titles/year. Receives 600 submissions/year. 20% of books from first-time authors; 80% from unagented writers. Pays 8-15% royalty on wholesale price. Offers $2,000 average advance. Publishes book 6 months after acceptance. Accepts simultaneous submissions. Reports in 2 months on queries. Manuscript guidelines free.
Nonfiction: Practical guides in many subjects, biography, reference, textbooks. Subjects include women's issues/studies and video selection guides. No personal memoirs or autobiographies. Query with outline/synopsis and sample chapters.
Recent Nonfiction Title(s): *Women Gardeners: A History*, by Cuthbertson; *Women & the Italian Resistance*, by Slaughter; *Adventures in Video: The Best Instructional Videos for Children*, by Wendling (general reference).
Tips: "Writers have the best chance selling us nonfiction on women's subjects. If I were a writer trying to market a book today, I would learn as much as I could about publishers' profiles *then* contact those who publish similar works."

ARDSLEY HOUSE PUBLISHERS, INC., 320 Central Park West, New York NY 10025. (212)496-7040. **Acquisitions:** Karyn Bianco. "We publish only college-level textbooks—particularly in the areas of music, philosophy, history, and film." Publishes hardcover and trade paperback originals and reprints. Publishes 5-8 titles/year. 25% of books from first-time authors; 100% from unagented writers (all are college professors). Pays generally by royalty. No advance. Publishes book 15 months after acceptance of ms. Reports in 1 month on queries, 2 months on proposals, 3 months on mss. Book catalog free.
Nonfiction: Textbook (college). Subjects include Americana, history, music/dance, philosophy, film. "We don't accept any other type of manuscript." Query with proposal package, including outline, 2-3 sample chapters, prospectus, author's résumé and SASE. Reviews artwork/photos as part of ms package. Send photocopies.
Recent Nonfiction Title(s): *Twelve Great Philosophers*, by Wayne Pomerleau; *Functional Hearing: A Contextual Method for Ear Training*, by Arthur Gottschalk and Phillip Kloeckner.

‡**ARKANSAS RESEARCH**, P.O. Box 303, Conway AR 72033. (501)470-1120. Fax: (501)470-1120. E-mail: desmond @intellinet.com. **Acquisitions:** Desmond Walls Allen, owner. "Our company opens a world of information to researchers interested in the history of Arkansas." Publishes hardcover originals and trade paperback originals and reprints. Publishes 20 titles/year. 90% of books from first-time authors; 100% from unagented writers. Pays 5-10% royalty on retail price. Offers no advance. Publishes book 2 months after acceptance of ms. Reports in 1 month. Book catalog for $1. Manuscript guidelines free.
Imprint(s): Research Associates.
Nonfiction: How-to (genealogy), reference, self-help. Subjects include Americana, ethnic, history, hobbies (genealogy), military/war, regional, all Arkansas-related. "We don't print autobiographies or genealogies about one family." Query with SASE. Reviews artwork/photos as part of ms package. Send photocopies.
Recent Nonfiction Title(s): *Extracts from the Pilot Newspaper*, by Cathy Barnes (reference); *Civil War Soldiers Buried in Arkansas' National Cemeteries*, by Rena Knight.

JASON ARONSON, INC., 230 Livingston St., Northvale NJ 07647-1726. (201)767-4093. Fax: (201)767-4330. Website: http://www.aronson.com. Editor-in-chief: Arthur Kurzweil. **Acquisitions:** Michael Moskowitz (psychology); Arthur Kurzweil (Judaica). Estab. 1967. "We are looking for high quality books in two fields: psychotherapy and Judaica." Publishes hardcover and trade paperback originals and reprints. Publishes 250 titles/year. 50% of books from first-time authors; 95% from unagented writers. Pays 10-15% royalty on retail price. Offers $250-$2500 advance.

Publishes book an average of 1 year after acceptance. Reports in 1 month. *Writer's Market* recommends allowing 2 months for reply. Catalog and ms guidelines free.
Nonfiction: Subjects include history, philosophy, psychology, religion translation. Query or submit outline and sample chapters. Reviews artwork/photos as part of ms packages. Send photocopies.
Recent Nonfiction Title(s): *Borderline Conditions*, by Otto Kernberg (psychotherapy).

ART DIRECTION BOOK COMPANY, INC., 456 Glenbrook Rd., Glenbrook CT 06096-1800. (203)353-1441. Fax: (203) 353-1371. **Acquisitions:** Don Barron, editorial director. "We are interested in books for the professional advertising art field—books for art directors, designers, etc.; also entry level books for commercial and advertising art students in such fields as typography, photography, paste-up, illustration, clip-art, design, layout and graphic arts." Publishes hardcover and paperback originals. Publishes 6 titles/year. Pays 10% royalty on retail price. Offers average $1,000 advance. Publishes book 1 year after acceptance. Reports in 3 months. Book catalog for 6×9 SASE.
Imprint(s): Infosource Publications.
Nonfiction: Commercial art, ad art how-to and textbooks. Query with outline and 1 sample chapter. Reviews artwork/photos as part of ms package.

‡ARTE PUBLICO PRESS, University of Houston, Houston TX 77204-2090. (713)743-2841. Fax (713)743-2847. **Acquisitions:** Nicolas Kanellos, editor. Estab. 1979. "We are a showcase for Hispanic literary creativity, arts and culture. Our endeavor is to provide a national forum for Hispanic literature." Publishes hardcover originals, trade paperback originals and reprints. Publishes 36 titles/year. Receives 1,000 queries and 500 mss/year. 50% of books from first-time authors; 80% from unagented writers. Pays 10% royalty on wholesale price. Offers $1,000-3,000 advance. Publishes book 2 years after acceptance of ms. Accepts simultaneous submissions. Reports in 1 month on queries and proposals; 4 months on mss. Book catalog free. Manuscript guidelines for #10 SASE.
Imprint(s): Pinata Books.
Nonfiction: Children's/juvenile, reference. Subjects include ethnic, language/literature, regional, translation, women's issues/studies. "Our nonfiction is definitely not our major area of publishing." Query with outline/synopsis, 2 sample chapters and SASE. "Include cover letter explaining why your manuscript is unique and important, why we should publish it, who will buy it, etc."
Recent Nonfiction Title(s): *Spared Angola: Memories from a Cuban-American Childhood*, by Virgil Suarez (memoir); *Chicano! The History of the Mexican American Civil Rights Movement*, by F. Arturo Rosales (history).
Fiction: Ethnic, literary, mainstream/contemporary. Query with synopsis, 2 sample chapters and SASE.
Recent Fiction Title(s): *Project Death*, by Richard Bertematti (novel/mystery); *A Matter of Pride and Other Stories*, by Nicolasa Mohr (short story collection); *The Old Gents*, by Jose Yglesias (novel).
Poetry: Submit 10 sample poems.
Recent Poetry Title(s): *I Used to Be a Superwoman*, by Gloria Velasquez (poetry collection/inspirational); *They Say That I Am Two*, by Marcus Villatroro (bicultural identity)

ASA, AVIATION SUPPLIES & ACADEMICS, 7005 132nd Place SE, Newcastle WA 98059. (206)235-1500. Director of Operations: Mike Lorden. Editor: Jennifer Trerise. **Acquisitions:** Fred Boyns, controller. Publishes 25-40 titles/year. 100% of books from unagented writers. Publishes book 9 months after acceptance. Reports in 3 months on proposals. Book catalog free.
Nonfiction: How-to, humor, technical, education. All subjects must be related to aviation. "We are primarily an aviation publisher. Educational books in this area are great; other aviation books will be considered." Query with outline. Send photocopies.
Recent Nonfiction Title(s): *Say Again, Please*, by Bob Gardner (guide to aviation radio communications).
Fiction: Aviation. *Writer's Market* recommends sending a query with SASE first.
Tips: "We have a new series that we are looking for titles to include: ASA's *Focus Series*. These will be books on *specific* aviation topics, which we decide need their own, more detailed and *focused* approach."

ASIAN HUMANITIES PRESS, Imprint of Jain Publishing Co., P.O. Box 3523, Fremont CA 94539. (510)659-8272. Fax: (510)659-0501. E-mail: mail@jainpub.com. Website: http://www.jainpub.com. **Acquisitions:** M.K. Jain, editor in chief. Estab. 1989. Asian Humanities Press seeks "to provide quality reading material at reasonable prices" in the areas of Asian culture, psychology and literature. Publishes hardcover and trade paperback originals and reprints. Publishes 6 titles/year. Receives 200 submissions/year. 100% of books from unagented authors. Pays up to 10% royalty on net sales. Publishes book 1-2 years after acceptance. Reports in 3 months on mss. Book catalog for 6×9 SAE with 2 first-class stamps. Manuscript guidelines for #10 SASE. Book catalog and ms guidelines can also be viewed on website.
  • Publisher reports an increased emphasis on undergraduate-level textbooks.
Nonfiction: Reference, textbooks, general trade books. Subjects include Asian classics, language/literature (Asian), philosophy/religion (Asian and East-West), psychology/spirituality (Asian and East-West), art/culture (Asian and East-West). Submit proposal package, including vita, list of prior publications and SASE. Reviews artwork/photos as part of ms package. Send photocopies.
Recent Nonfiction Title(s): *Buddhism: A History*, by Noble Ross Reat (textbook).

‡ASPHODEL PRESS, Imprint of Moyer Bell, Kymbolde Way, Wakefield RI 02879. (401)789-0074. Fax: (401)789-3793. **Acquisitions:** Jennifer Moyer, editor. "Asphodel publishes fine art and literary titles." Publishes trade paperback

originals. Publishes 4 titles/year. 1% of books from first-time authors; 90% from unagented writers. Pays royalty on retail price. No advance. Publishes book 1-2 years after acceptance of ms. Reports in 1 month on queries, 6 months on mss. Book catalog for #10 SASE.
Nonfiction: Biography, reference, literary criticism. Subjects include art/architecture. Query with 1-2 sample chapters and SASE.
Recent Nonfiction Title(s): *Directory of Literary Magazines*, edited by The Council of Literary Magazines and Presses (reference); *In Plain Sight: Obsessions, Morals and Domestic Laughter*, by Michael Anania (literary criticism).
Recent Poetry Title(s): *Storyville: A Hidden Mirror*, by Brooke Bergon; *Shadow of a Soul: Collected Poems*, by Bella Dizhur (translation).

ATHENEUM BOOKS FOR YOUNG READERS, Imprint of Simon & Schuster, 1230 Avenue of the Americas, New York NY 10020. (212)698-7000. Associate Publisher, Vice President/Editorial Director: Jonathan J. Lanman.
Acquisitions: Marcia Marshall, executive editor; Ana Cerro, editor; Anne Schwartz, editorial director, Anne Schwartz Books; and Jean Karl, editor of Jean Karl books. Estab. 1960. "Our books are aimed at children from pre-school age, up through high school." Publishes hardcover originals. Publishes 70 titles/year. Receives 15,000 submissions/year. 8-12% of books from first-time authors; 50% from unagented writers. Pays 10% royalty on retail price. Offers $2,000-3,000 average advance. Publishes book 18 months after acceptance. Reports within 3 months. Manuscript guidelines for #10 SASE.
Nonfiction: Biography, history, science, humor, self-help, all for juveniles. Subjects include: Americana, animals, art, business/economics, health, music, nature, photography, politics, psychology, recreation, religion, sociology, sports and travel. "Do remember, most publishers plan their lists as much as two years in advance. So if a topic is 'hot' right now, it may be 'old hat' by the time we could bring it out. It's better to steer clear of fads. Some writers assume juvenile books are for 'practice' until you get good enough to write adult books. Not so. Books for young readers demand just as much 'professionalism' in writing as adult books. So save those 'practice' manuscripts for class, or polish them before sending them." Query only.
Fiction: Adventure, ethnic, experimental, fantasy, gothic, historical, horror, humor, mainstream, mystery, science fiction, suspense, western, all in juvenile versions. "We have few specific needs except for books that are fresh, interesting and well written. Again, fad topics are dangerous, as are works you haven't polished to the best of your ability. (The competition is fierce.) We've been inundated with dragon stories (misunderstood dragon befriends understanding child), unicorn stories (misunderstood child befriends understanding unicorn), and variations of 'Ignatz the Egg' (Everyone laughs at Ignatz the egg [giraffe/airplane/accountant] because he's square [short/purple/stupid] until he saves them from the eggbeater [lion/storm/I.R.S. man] and becomes a hero). Other things we don't need at this time are safety pamphlets, ABC books, coloring books, board books, and rhymed narratives. In writing picture book texts, avoid the coy and 'cutesy.' " Query only for all submissions. Reviews artwork as part of ms package. Send photocopies.
Recent Fiction Title(s): *The Watcher*, by James Howe.
Poetry: "At this time there is a growing market for children's poetry. However, we don't anticipate needing any for the next year or two, especially rhymed narratives."

‡AUBURN HOUSE, Imprint of Greenwood Publishing Group, 88 Post Rd. W., Westport CT 06881. (203)226-3571. Fax: (203)222-1502. Website: http://www.greenwood.com. Executive Vice President: Jim Sabin. **Acquisitions:** Editorial Offices. "Auburn publishes books and advanced texts in health studies, education and social policy." Publishes hardcover and trade paperback originals. Publishes 16 titles/year. Pays variable royalty on net price. Rarely offers advance. Publishes book 1 year after acceptance of ms. Accepts simultaneous submissions. Reports in 6 months on queries and proposals. Book catalog and ms guidelines online.
• Greenwood Publishing maintains an excellent website offering catalog, ms guidelines and editorial contacts.
Nonfiction: Subjects include business/economics, government/politics, health/medicine. Query with proposal package, including: scope, whether a complete ms is available or when it will be, CV or résumé and SASE. *No unsolicited mss.*
Recent Nonfiction Title(s): *Adoption Policy and Special Needs Children*, edited by Rosemary Avery (sociology).

AUGSBURG BOOKS, Imprint of Augsburg Fortress, Publishers, P.O. Box 1209, 426 S. Fifth St., Minneapolis MN 55440. Director of Publications: Ronald Klug. **Acquisitions:** Robert Klausmeier, senior acquisitions editor. "We publish for the mainline Christian market." Publishes trade and mass market paperback originals and reprints. Publishes 37 titles/year. 2-3% of books from first-time authors. Pays royalty. Publishes book 18 months after acceptance of ms. Reports in 3 months. Book catalog for 8½×11 SAE with 3 first-class stamps. Manuscript guidelines for #10 SASE.
Nonfiction: Children's/juvenile, self-help. Subjects include religion, adult spirituality, life issues, devotions, "over 50" titles, men's and women's books, family, Christmas, Lent/Easter. Submit outline and 1-2 sample chapters if requested. Overstocked in children's book mss.

Recent Nonfiction Title(s): *Inspirations: Glimpses of God*, by Scott Walker; *Family Parenting* Series, by Donna Frickson; *Moving Into a New Now*, by Mildred Tengbom.

AUTONOMEDIA, P.O. Box 568, Williamsburgh Station, Brooklyn NY 11211. (718)963-2603. **Acquisitions:** Jim Fleming, editor (Semiotext(e)); Peter Lamborn Wilson, editor (New Autonomy). Autonomedia publishes radical and marginal books on culture and politics. Publishes trade paperback originals and reprints. Publishes 25 titles/year. Receives 350 queries/year. 30% of books from first-time authors; 90% from unagented writers. Pays variable royalty. Offers $100 advance. Publishes book 6 months after acceptance of ms. Accepts simultaneous submissions. Reports in 2 months. Book catalog for $1.
Imprint(s): Semiotext(e); New Autonomy.
Nonfiction: Subjects include anthropology/archaeology, art/architecture, business/economics, gay/lesbian, government/politics, history, nature/environment, philosophy, religion, translation, women's issues/studies. Submit outline with SASE. Reviews artwork/photos as part of ms package. Send photocopies.
Recent Nonfiction Title(s): *Foucault Live*, by Michel Foucault (interviews).
Fiction: Erotica, experimental, feminist, gay/lesbian, literary, mainstream/contemporary, occult, science fiction, short story collections. Submit synopsis with SASE.
Recent Fiction Title(s): *Cutmouth Lady*, by Romy Ashby (contemporary).
Poetry: Submit sample poems.
Recent Poetry Title(s): *Not Me*, by Eileen Myles (lesbian).

AVALON BOOKS, Imprint of Thomas Bouregy & Co., Inc., 401 Lafayette St., New York NY 10003-7014. **Acquisitions:** Marcia Markland, vice president/publisher. Estab. 1950. "We publish wholesome fiction. We're the Family Channel of publishing. We try to make what we publish suitable for anybody in the family." Publishes 60 titles/year. 10% of books from unagented writers. Pays royalty; contracts negotiated on an individual basis. Manuscript published 6 months after acceptance. Reports in 6 months. Manuscript guidelines for #10 SASE.
Fiction: "We publish wholesome romances, mysteries, westerns. Our books are read by adults as well as teenagers, and their characters are all adults. All the romances and mysteries are contemporary; all the westerns are historical." Length: 40,000-50,000 words. Submit first chapter, a brief, but complete summary of the book and SASE.
Recent Fiction Title(s): *Frontier Justice*, by Don Hepler (western); *Milwaukee Winters Can Be Murder*, by Kathy Barrett (mystery).
Tips: "We are looking for love stories, heroines who have interesting professions, and we are actively seeking ethnic fiction. We do accept unagented manuscripts, and we do publish first novels. Right now we are concentrating on finding talented new mystery and romantic suspense writers."

AVANYU PUBLISHING INC., P.O. Box 27134, Albuquerque NM 87125. (505)266-6128. Fax: (505)821-8864. **Acquisitions:** J. Brent Ricks, president. Estab. 1984. Avanyu publishes highly-illustrated, history-oriented books and contemporary Indian/Western art. "Our audience consists of libraries, art collectors and history students. Publishes hardcover and trade paperback originals and reprints." Publishes 4 titles/year. Receives 40 submissions/year. 30% of books from first-time authors; 90% from unagented writers. Pays 8% maximum royalty on wholesale price. No advance. Publishes book 1 year after acceptance. Reports in 6 weeks. *Writer's Market* recommends allowing 2 months for reply. Book catalog for #10 SASE.
Nonfiction: Biography, illustrated book, reference, Southwest Americana. Subjects include Americana, anthropology/archaeology, art/architecture, ethnic, history, photography, regional, sociology. Query. Reviews artwork/photos as part of ms package.

‡AVERY PUBLISHING GROUP, INC., 120 Old Broadway, Garden City Park NY 11040. (516)741-2155. **Acquisitions:** Rudy Shur, managing editor. "Avery specializes in alternative medicine, natural medicine, health, healthy cooking, health reference, childcare and childbirth." Publishes trade paperback originals. Publishes 50 titles/year. Receives 3,000 queries and 1,000 mss/year. 70% of books from first-time authors; 90% from unagented writers. Pays royalty. Offers no advance. Publishes book 1 year after acceptance of ms. Accepts simultaneous submissions. Reports in 2 weeks on queries, 3 weeks on proposals and manuscripts. *Writer's Market* recommends allowing 2 months for reply. Book catalog and ms guidelines free.
Nonfiction: Cookbook, reference, self-help. Subjects include business/economics, child guidance/parenting, cooking, foods and nutrition, gardening, health/medicine, money/finance. "We generally do not publish personal accounts of health topics unless they outline a specific plan that covers all areas of the topic." Submit outline with proposal package, including cover letter, author biography, table of contents, preface with SASE.
Recent Nonfiction Title(s): *Sharks Still Don't Get Cancer*, by Dr. I. William Lane and Linda Comac (medicine); *Prescription for Nutritional Healing*, by James F. Balch and Phyllis A. Balch (health); *Secrets of Fat-Free Cooking*, by Sandra Woodruff (cooking).

‡AVISSON PRESS, INC., 3007 Taliaferro Rd., Greensboro NC 27408. **Acquisitions:** M.L. Hester, editor. Publishes hardcover originals and trade paperback originals and reprints. Publishes 12-15 titles/year. Receives 600 queries and 400 mss/year. 5% of books from first-time authors; 75% from unagented writers. Pays 8-10% royalty on wholesale price or a percentage of print run (for poetry). Offers $200-500 advance. Publishes book 9 months after acceptance of ms. Accepts simultaneous submissions if so noted. Reports in 1 week on queries and proposals, 1-3 months on mss. Book catalog for #10 SASE.

Nonfiction: Biography, reference, self-help (senior citizens and teenagers), regional or North Carolina, textbook (creative writing text). Subjects include history (Southeast or North Carolina), language/literature, psychology, regional, sports, women's issues/studies. "We need helpful nonfiction for senior citizens, minority topics and young adult biographies (African-American, women). Study the market." Query or submit outline and 1-3 sample chapters.

Recent Nonfiction Title(s): *Miller, Bukowski & Their Enemies*, by William Joyce (literature/essays); *Hunting the Snark*, by Robert Peters (criticism/textbook); *The Tiger Woods Story*, by A. Teague (young adult biography).

Fiction: Ethnic, historical, literary. "Upcoming and future titles are market-driven." Query or submit synopsis and 3 sample chapters (30-50 pages).

Recent Fiction Title(s): *Constellation*, by Greg Mulenhey (novel); *Faith In What?, by Richard Krawiec (novel); In Bed With The Exotic Enemy*, by Daniela Gioseffi (stories/novella).

Poetry: "Very limited—'name' authors only." Query only.

Recent Poetry Title(s): *The Firewalkers*, by Charles Fishman (literary); *Heroics*, by Joanne Lowery (literary); *The Invention of Ice Skating*, by William F. Van Wert (literary).

Tips: Audience is public and school libraries.

AVON BOOKS, Division of the Hearst Corp., 1350 Avenue of the Americas, New York NY 10019. **Acquisitions:** Alice Webster-Williams. Estab. 1941. Publishes trade and mass market paperback originals and reprints. Publishes 400 titles/year. Royalty and advance negotiable. Publishes ms 2 years after acceptance. Accepts simultaneous submissions. Reports in 3 months. Guidelines for SASE.

Imprint(s): Avon Flare, Avon Science Fiction, Camelot, Confident, Equinox.

Nonfiction: How-to, popular psychology, self-help, health, history, war, sports, business/economics, biography, politics. No textbooks. Query only with SASE.

Recent Nonfiction Title(s): *Model: The Ugly Business of Beautiful Women*, by Michael Gross; *Skygods: The Fall of Pan Am*, by Robert Gandt; *A Gift of Irish Wisdom*, by Cyril and Renee Reilly.

Fiction: Romance (contemporary, historical), science fiction, fantasy, men's adventure, suspense/thriller, mystery, western. Query only with SASE.

Recent Fiction Title(s): *Memoir from Antproof Case*, by Mark Halprin; *Butterfly*, Kathryn Harvey; *So Worthy My Love*, by Kathleen Woodwiss.

AVON FLARE BOOKS, Imprint of Avon Books, Division of the Hearst Corp., 1350 Avenue of the Americas, New York NY 10019. (212)261-6817. Fax: (212)261-6895. **Acquisitions:** Elise Howard, executive editorial director. Publishes mass market paperback originals and reprints. Imprint publishes 115 new titles/year. 25% of books from first-time authors; 15% from unagented writers. Pays 6-8% royalty. Offers $2,500 minimum advance. Publishes book 2 years after acceptance. Accepts simultaneous submissions. Reports in 4 months. Book catalog and ms guidelines for 8×10 SAE with 5 first-class stamps.

Nonfiction: General. Submit outline/synopsis and sample chapters. "*Very* selective with young adult nonfiction."

Recent Nonfiction Title(s): *Help! My Heart is Breaking*, by Meg Schneider; *The Worst Joke Book Ever*, by Paul Brewer.

Fiction: Adventure, ethnic, humor, mainstream, mystery, romance, suspense, contemporary. "Very selective with mystery." Manuscripts appropriate to ages 12-18. Query with sample chapters and synopsis.

Recent Fiction Title(s): *The Dark Shore*, by Adam Lee; *Angela & Diabola*, by Lynne Reidbanks.

Tips: "The YA market is not as strong as it was five years ago. We are very selective with young adult fiction. *Avon does not publish picture books,* nor do we use freelance readers."

‡**AVON SCIENCE FICTION**, (formerly AvoNova), Imprint of Avon Books, 1350 Avenue of the Americas, New York NY 10019. (212)261-6800. Website: http://www.williammorrow.com. **Acquisitions:** Amy Goldschlager, editorial assistant to Jennifer Brehl, senior editor. "We are a 'small big company.' We can't be all things to all people. We put out a cutting-edge literary science fiction/fantasy line that appeals to people who want to read good books." Publishes hardcover originals, trade paperback and mass market paperback originals and reprints. Publishes 70 titles/year. Receives 2,500 queries and 800 mss/year. 25% of books from first-time authors; 5% from unagented writers. Pays royalty on retail price, range varies. Publishes book 18 months after acceptance of ms. Accepts simultaneous submissions if so noted, "but we discourage it." Reports in 6 months. Book catalog for 9×12 SAE with 7 first-class stamps. Manuscript guidelines for #10 SASE.

Fiction: Fantasy, science fiction. No horror or juvenile topics. "We look for cutting-edge, original work that will break traditional boundaries of this genre." Query with full synopsis of book, 3 sample chapters and SASE.

Recent Fiction Title(s): *Rage of a Demon King*, by Raymond Feist (fantasy); *The Family Tree*, by Sheri Tepper (science fiction); *An Exchange of Hostages*, by Susan R. Matthews (science fiction).

Tips: "Having an agent is a good thing. Don't send clones of other books. If you're going to take the time to write a whole book, please submit following our guidelines to the detail. Make sure information is up to date."

‡**BACKCOUNTRY**, Imprint of The Countryman Press, Divison of W.W. Norton & Co., P. O. Box 748, Woodstock VT 05091-0748. (802)457-4826. Fax: (802)457-1678. **Acquisitions:** Laura Jorstad, managing editor. "Our aim is to publish guidebooks of the highest quality that encourage physical fitness and appreciation for and understanding of the

natural world, self-sufficiency and adventure." Publishes trade paperback originals. Publishes 15 titles/year. Receives 1,000 queries and a few mss/year. 25% of books from first-time authors; 75% from unagented writers. Pays 7-10% royalty on retail price. Offers $1,500-2,500 advance. Publishes book 18 months after acceptance of ms. Accepts simultaneous submissions. Returns submissions only with SASE. Reports in 2 months on proposals. Book catalog free. Manuscript guidelines for #10 SASE.
Nonfiction: Subjects include animals, nature/environment, recreation, guide books and series. "Look at existing series of guidebooks to see how your proposal fits in." Query with outline, 50 sample pages and proposal package including market analysis and SASE.
Recent Nonfiction Title(s): *Mid-Atlantic Trout Streams*, by Charles Meck; *50 Hikes in the Adirondacks*, by Barbara McMartin (recreation).

BAEN PUBLISHING ENTERPRISES, P.O. Box 1403, Riverdale NY 10471-0671. (718)548-3100. Website: http://baen.com. **Acquisitions:** Toni Weisskopf, executive editor. Estab. 1983. "We publish books at the heart of science fiction and fantasy." Publishes hardcover, trade paperback and mass market paperback originals and reprints. Publishes 120 titles/year. Receives 5,000 submissions/year. 5% of books from first-time authors; 50% from unagented writers. Pays royalty on retail price. Reports in 6-8 months on queries and proposals, 6 months on complete mss. Queries not necessary. *Writer's Market* recommends sending a query with SASE first. Book catalog free. Manuscript guidelines for #10 SASE.
  • Baen has published such authors as Lois McMaster Bujold, David Drake, Mercedes Lachey, Marion Zimmer Bradley and James P. Hogan.
Fiction: Fantasy, science fiction. Submit outline/synopsis and sample chapters or complete ms.
Recent Fiction Title(s): *Once a Hero*, by Elizabeth Moon; *Honor Among Enemies*, by David Weber; *Glenraven*, by Marion Zimmer-Bradley and Holly Cisle.
Tips: "See our books before submitting. Send for our writers' guidelines."

BAKER BOOK HOUSE COMPANY, P.O. Box 6287, Grand Rapids MI 49516-6287. (616)676-9185. Fax: (616)676-9573. Website: http://www.bakerbooks.com.
Imprints: Baker Books, Chosen, Fleming H. Revell.

BAKER BOOKS, Division of Baker Book House Company, P.O. Box 6287, Grand Rapids MI 49516-6287. (616)676-9185. Fax: (616)676-9573. E-mail: tbennett@bakerbooks.com. Website: http://www.bakerbooks.com. Director of Publications: Allan Fisher. **Acquisitions:** Jane Schrier, assistant to the director of publications. Estab. 1939. "Baker Books publishes popular religious nonfiction and fiction, children's books, academic and reference books, and professional books for church leaders." Publishes hardcover and trade paperback originals. Publishes 120 titles/year. 10% of books from first-time authors; 85% from unagented writers. Pays 14% royalty on net receipts. Publishes book within 1 year after acceptance. Accepts simultaneous submissions, if so noted. Reports in 2 months on proposals. Book catalog for 9×12 SAE with 6 first-class stamps. Manuscript guidelines for #10 SASE, also online.
  • Baker Books has published such authors as R.C. Sproul, James Montgomery Boice and Ruth Bell Graham.
Imprint(s): Hamewith, Hourglass, Labyrinth, Raven's Ridge, **Spire Books.**
Nonfiction: Contemporary issues, women's concerns, parenting, singleness, seniors' concerns, self-help, children's books, Bible study, Christian doctrine, reference books, books for pastors and church leaders, textbooks for Christian colleges and seminaries. Query with proposal, including chapter summaries or outlines, 1-2 sample chapters, CV, letter of recommendation and SASE. *No unsolicited mss.* Reviews artwork as part of ms package. Send 1-2 photocopies.
Recent Nonfiction Title(s): *Faith Alone*, by R.C. Sproul (theology); *Excuse Me? I'll Take My Piece of the Planet Now*, by Joey O'Connor (grad book); *Jumping Hurdles*, by Steve Brown (Christian living).
Fiction: Literary novels focusing on women's concerns, mainstream/contemporary, religious, mysteries. Query with synopsis/outline, 1-2 sample chapters, résumé and SASE. *No unsolicited mss.*
Recent Fiction Title(s): *Praise Jerusalem*, by Augusta Trobaugh; *The Secrets of Barneveld Calvary*, by James Calvin Schaap; *Sweetbriar Summer*, by Brenda Wilber.
Tips: "Most of our authors and readers are evangelical Christians, and our books are purchased from Christian bookstores, mail-order retailers, and school bookstores."

BALLANTINE BOOKS, Division of Random House, Inc., 201 E. 50th St., New York NY 10022. (212)572-4910. Publishes wide variety of nonfiction and fiction. Publishes hardcover, trade paperback and mass market originals.
Acquisitions: Doug Grad, editor (sports and business nonfiction, historical and thriller fiction); Leona Nevler, editor (all kinds of fiction and nonfiction); Peter Borland, executive editor (commercial fiction, pop culture); Elisa Wares, senior editor (romance, health, parenting, mystery); Joe Blades, associate publisher (mystery); Susan Randol, senior editor (business, motivational, true medicine, true crime, mystery); Elizabeth Zack, editor (motivational, inspirational, sports [women]; career, seasonal tie-ins); Joanne Wycoff, senior editor (religion, spirituality, nature/pets, psychology); Andrea Schulz, associate editor (literary fiction, travel, women's studies, narrative nonfiction).
  • Also see the listing for Random House, Inc.
Nonfiction: How-to, humor, illustrated book, reference, self-help. Subjects include animals, child guidance/parenting, cooking/foods/nutrition, health/medicine. Submit proposal and 100 ms pages with SASE. Reviews artwork/photos as part of ms package. Send photocopies.

Recent Nonfiction Title(s): *The Mom & Dad Conservation Piece: Creative Questions to Honor the Family,* by Bret Nicholaus and Paul Lowrie: *The Secret to Tender Pie,* by Mindy Marin; *Five Lost Classics: Tao, Huang-Lao, and Yin-yang in Han China,* translated by Robin D.S. Yates.
Fiction: Historical fiction, women's mainstream, multicultural and general fiction. Submit query letter or brief synopsis, first 100 pages of ms and SASE of proper size to Louis Mendez. Responds promptly to queries; 5 months on mss.
Recent Fiction Title(s): *Dean's List,* by John Hassler; *Stray Dogs,* by John Ridley; *State of Mind,* by John Katzenbach.

BANTAM BOOKS, Subsidiary of Bantam Doubleday Dell, Dept. WM, 1540 Broadway, New York NY 10036. (212)354-6500. Publishes hardcover, trade paperback and mass market paperback originals, trade paperback; mass market paperback reprints and audio. Publishes 350 titles/year. Publishes book an average of 8 months after ms is accepted. Accepts simultaneous submissions from agents.
Imprint(s): Bantam Classics (reprints), Crime Line, Fanfare, **Loveswept**, **Spectra**.
Nonfiction: Biography, how-to, cookbook, humor, illustrated book, self-help. Subjects include Americana, business/economics, child care/parenting, diet/fitness, education, cooking/foods/nutrition, gay/lesbian, government/politics, health/medicine, history, language/literature, military/war, mysticism/astrology, nature, philosophy/mythology, psychology, religion/inspiration, science, sociology, spirituality, sports, true crime, women's studies.
Fiction: Adventure, fantasy, feminist, gay/lesbian, historical, horror, juvenile, literary, mainstream/contemporary, mystery, romance, science fiction, suspense, western. Query or submit outline/synopsis. All unsolicited mss returned unopened.

BANTAM DOUBLEDAY DELL, 1540 Broadway, New York NY 10036. (212)354-6500. Publishes hardcover originals and reprints, trade paperback originals and reprints, mass market paperback originals and reprints.
Imprint(s): Divisions include: *Bantam Doubleday Dell Books for Young Readers* (Delacorte Books for Young Readers, Doubleday Books for Young Readers, Laurel Leaf, Skylark, Yearling), *Bantam Books* (**Bantam Books**, Crime Line, Fanfare, **Loveswept**, **Spectra**); *Doubleday* (Anchor Books, **Currency**, **Doubleday**, **Image Books**, **Main Street Books**, **Nan A. Talese**); *Dell Publishing* (**Delacorte Press**, **Dell**, Dell Abyss, **Dell Publishing Island**, **Dell Trade Paperbacks**, Delta Trade Paperbacks, **Dial Press**, Laurel); **Broadway Books**.

‡**BANTAM DOUBLEDAY DELL BOOKS FOR YOUNG READERS**, Division of Bantam Doubleday Dell, 1540 Broadway, New York NY 10036. (212)354-6500. Fax: (212)302-7985. Website: http://www.bdd.com. Contact: Michelle Poploff, editorial director. "Bantam Doubleday Dell Books for Young Readers publishes award-winning books by distinguished authors and the most promising new writers." Publishes hardcover, trade paperback and mass market paperback originals, trade paperback reprints. Publishes 300 titles/year. Receives thousands of queries/year. 10% of books from first-time authors; none from unagented writers. Pays royalty. Advance varies. Publishes book 2 years after acceptance of ms. Reports in 4 months. Book catalog free.
Imprint(s): Delacorte Press Books for Young Readers, Doubleday Books for Young Readers, Laurel Leaf, Skylark, Yearling.
Nonfiction: "Bantam Doubleday Dell Books for Young Readers publishes a very limited number of nonfiction titles."
Fiction: Adventure, fantasy, humor, juvenile, mainstream/contemporary, mystery, picture books, suspense, young adult. Query with SASE. "No unsolicited mss accepted. Even queries are being discouraged for the present."
Recent Fiction Title(s): *The Lizard and the Sun,* by Alma Flor Ada (folktale picture book); *The Suitcase Kid,* by Jacqueline Wilson (ages 8-12); *Talk to Me,* by Carol Dines (young adult stories/novella); *Facing the Music,* by Margaret Willey (young adult); *Tales from the Brothers Grimm and the Sisters Weird,* by Vivian Van Velde, *Scarface,* by Robert D. San Souci (picture book).
Tips: Audience is children to young adults.

BARBOUR & CO., P.O. Box 719, Uhrichsville OH 44683. **Acquisitions:** Susan Johnson, managing editor (all areas). Barbour & Co. publishes and distributes Christian fiction and nonfiction. Barbour Books covers many areas; Heartsong Presents publishes Christian romance. "We're a Christian evangelical publisher." Publishes hardcover, trade paperback and mass market paperback originals and reprints. Publishes 75 titles/year. Receives 300 queries and 150 mss/year. 40% of books from first-time authors; 99% from unagented writers. Nonauthor-subsidy publishes .5% of books. Makes outright purchase of $750-2,500. Offers half of payment in advance. Publishes book 1 year after acceptance of ms. Accepts simultaneous submissions. Reports in 1 month on queries, 3 months on proposals and mss. Book catalog for $2. Manuscript guidelines for #10 SASE.
Imprints: Barbour Books (general nonfiction), Heartsong Presents (Christian romance).
Nonfiction: Biography, humor, children's/juvenile. Religious subjects. Query.
Recent Nonfiction Title(s): *When I'm On My Knees,* by Anita Donihue (prayer); *C.S. Lewis,* by Sam Wellman (biography).
Recent Fiction Title(s): *Summer Dreams,* by several authors (inspirational romance); *Mysterious Monday,* Colleen Reece (juvenile mystery).
Tips: "Having a great agent won't help here. A great idea or book will catch our attention. Our goal is to distribute great Christian books by the millions at bargain prices."

‡**BARNEGAT LIGHT PRESS**, P.O. Box 305, Barnegat Light NJ 08006. (609)494-3154. Fax: (609)494-6092. **Acquisitions:** R. Marilyn Schmidt, publisher. "We are a regional publisher emphasizing the mid-Atlantic region. Areas

concerned are gardening and cooking." Publishes trade paperback originals. Publishes 8 titles/year. Receives 12 queries and 10 mss/year. 0% of books from first-time authors; 100% from unagented writers. Makes outright purchase. Publishes book 6 months after acceptance of ms. Reports in 1 month. *Writer's Market* recommends allowing 2 months for reply. Book catalog free.

Imprint(s): Pine Barrens Press.

Nonfiction: Cookbook, how-to. Subjects include cooking/foods/nutrition, gardening, regional, travel, all New Jersey-oriented. Query.

Recent Nonfiction Title(s): *Exploring the Pine Barrens of NJ*, by R.M. Schmidt (travel guide); *Seashore Gardening with Native Plants*, by R. Marilyn Schmidt.

BARRICADE BOOKS INC., 150 Fifth Ave., Suite 700, New York NY 10011-4311. **Acquisitions:** Carole Stuart, publisher. "We look for nonfiction, mostly of the controversial type, and books we can promote with authors who can talk about their topics on radio and television and to the press." Publishes hardcover and trade paperback originals and trade paperback reprints. Publishes 30 titles/year. Receives 200 queries and 100 mss/year. 80% of books from first-time authors; 50% from unagented writers. Pays 10-12% royalty on retail price for hardcover. Advance varies. Publishes book 18 months after acceptance of ms. Simultaneous submissions not encouraged. Reports in 1 month on queries. Book catalog for $3.

Nonfiction: Biography, how-to, reference, self-help. Subjects include business/economics, child guidance/parenting, ethnic, gay/lesbian, government/politics, health/medicine, history, nature/environment, psychology, sociology, women's issues/studies. Query with outline and 1-2 sample chapters with SASE or material will not be returned. Reviews artwork/photos as part of ms package. Send photocopies.

Recent Nonfiction Title(s): *Grave Exodus*, by Xavier Cronin (dealing with death in the 20th Century).

Tips: "Do your homework. Visit bookshops to find publishers who are doing the kinds of books you want to write. Always submit to a *person*—not just 'editor.' *Always enclose SASE.*"

BARRON'S EDUCATIONAL SERIES, INC., 250 Wireless Blvd., Hauppauge NY 11788. Fax: (516)434-3217. **Acquisitions:** Grace Freedson, managing editor/director of acquisitions. "Barron's tends to publish series of books, both for adults and children." Publishes hardcover and paperback originals and software. Publishes 170 titles/year. 10% of books from first-time authors; 90% from unagented writers. Pays royalty on both wholesale and retail price. Publishes book 1 year after acceptance. Accepts simultaneous submissions. Reports in 8 months. Book catalog free.

Nonfiction: Adult education, art, business, cookbooks, crafts, foreign language, review books, guidance, pet books, travel, literary guides, parenting, health, juvenile, young adult sports, test preparation materials and textbooks. Reviews artwork/photos as part of ms package. Query or submit outline/synopsis and 2-3 sample chapters. Accepts nonfiction translations.

Recent Nonfiction Title(s): *Dictionary of Modern Biology*, by Norah Rudin, Ph.D.; *Dictionary of Healthful Food Terms*, by Bev Bennett and Virginia Van Vynckt (health foods and nutrition).

Tips: "The writer has the best chance of selling us a book that will fit into one of our series. SASE must be included for the return of all materials."

‡BASKERVILLE PUBLISHERS, INC., 7616 LBJ Freeway, Suite 510, Dallas TX 75251. (214)934-3451. **Acquisitions:** Same Chase, acquisitions editor. Estab. 1992. Baskerville specializes in literary fiction with a commercial edge. Publishes hardcover originals, trade paperback originals and reprints. Publishes 10-14 titles/year. Receives 500-600 queries/yar. 50% of books from first-time authors; 50% from unagented writers. Pays royalty on retail price. Offers $3,000 average advance. Publishes book 18 months after acceptance of ms. Accepts simultaneous submissions if so noted. Reports in 7 months on queries. Book catalog for 6×9 SAE with 65¢ postage. Manuscript guidelines for #10 SASE.

Nonfiction: Biography of opera singers. "Very interested in (original) biographies of opera singers." Query only with SASE.

Recent Nonfiction Title(s): *Tebaldi: The Voice Of An Angel* (translation), by Carlamaria Casanova.

Fiction: Literary. "Interested in wonderful characters and wonderful writing." Not interested in short story collections, romances, poetry; no genre literature. Query only with SASE.

‡BATTELLE PRESS, Imprint of Battelle Memorial Institute, 505 King Ave., Columbus OH 43201. (614)424-6393. Fax: (614)424-3819. E-mail: press@battelle.org. Website: http://www.battelle.org. **Acquisitions:** Joe Sheldrick. "Battelle Press strives to be a primary source of books and software on science and the management of science." Publishes hardcover and paperback originals and markets primarily by direct mail. Website: http://www.battelle.org. Publishes 10 titles/year. Pays 10% royalty on retail price. No advance. Publishes book 6 months after acceptance of ms. Accepts simultaneous submissions. Returns submissions with SASE only by writer's request. Reports in 1 month. Book catalog free.

Nonfiction: "We are looking for management, leadership, project management and communications books specifically targeted to engineers and scientists." Reviews artwork/photos as part of ms package. Send photocopies.

Recent Nonfiction Title(s): *Keeping Abreast of Science & Technology: Technical Intelligence for Business*, edited by W.B. Ashton and R.A. Klaven; *Biomacromolecules: From 3-D Structure to Applications*, edited by Rick L. Ornstein.

Tips: Audience consists of engineers, researchers, scientists and corporate researchers and developers.

‡**BAYWOOD PUBLISHING CO., INC.**, 26 Austin Ave., Amityville NY 11701. (516)691-1270. Fax: (516)691-1770. E-mail: baywood@baywood.com. Website: http://baywood.com. **Acquisitions:** Stuart Cohen, managing editor. "We publish original and innovative books in the humanities and social sciences, including areas such as health sciences, gerontology, death and bereavement, psychology, technical communications and archaeology." Publishes 25 titles/year. Pays 7-15% royalty on retail price. Publishes book within 1 year after acceptance of ms. Catalog and ms guidelines free.
  • Baywood Publishing Co. has published Vicente Navarro, Jon Hendricks and Robert Kastenbaum.
Nonfiction: Technical, scholarly. Subjects include anthropology/archaeology, computers/electronics, gerontology, imagery, labor relations, education, death/dying, drugs, nature/environment, psychology, public health/medicine, sociology, technical communications, women's issues/studies. Submit outline/synopsis and sample chapters.
Recent Nonfiction Title(s): *The Memorial Rituals Book for Healing and Hope* (death and bereavement); *Decisions: A Call to Action* (drug education); *Surviving Dependence: Voices of African American Elders* (*Society and Aging* series).

BEACHWAY PRESS, 9201 Beachway Lane, Springfield VA 22153. **Acquisitions:** Scott Adams, publisher. "Our books are designed to open up new worlds of experiences for those anxious to explore, and to provide the detailed information necessary to get them started." Publishes 10-15 titles/year. Pays 10-15% royalty on wholesale price. Offers $1,500 advance. Publishes book 1 year after acceptance of ms. Reports in 2 months on queries and proposals. Manuscript guidelines for #10 SASE.
  • Beachway Press has increased their number of books published from 2-3 titles/year to 10-15 titles/year.
Nonfiction: Innovative outdoor adventure and travel guidebooks. "We welcome ideas that explore the world of adventure and wonder; from day hikes to mountain bikes, from surf to skis." Query with outline, 2 sample chapters, methods of research and SASE. Reviews artwork/photos as part of ms package. Send proof prints.
Recent Nonfiction Title(s): *Mountain Bike Vermont*, by Jen Mynter (guidebook).
Tips: "Someone interested in writing for us should be both an avid outdoors person and an expert in their area of interest. This person should have a clear understanding of maps and terrain and should enjoy sharing their adventurous spirit and enthusiasm with others."

BEACON HILL PRESS OF KANSAS CITY, Book Division of Nazarene Publishing House, P.O. Box 419527, Kansas City MO 64141. Fax: (816)753-4071. E-mail: bjp@bhillkc.com. **Acquisitions:** Bonnie Perry, managing editor. Estab. 1912. "Beacon Hill Press is a Christ-centered publisher that provides authentically Christian resources that are faithful to God's word and relevant to life." Publishes hardcover and paperback originals. Publishes 30 titles/year. Standard contract is 12% royalty on net sales for first 10,000 copies and 14% on subsequent copies. (Sometimes makes flat rate purchase.) Publishes book within 1 year after acceptance. Reports within 3 months. Accent on holy living; encouragement in daily Christian life. Query or proposal preferred. Average ms length: 30,000-60,000 words.
  • Beacon Hill has published such authors as Grace Ketterman, Stan Toler and Neil Wiseman.
Nonfiction: Inspirational, Bible-based. Doctrinally must conform to the evangelical, Wesleyan tradition. No autobiography, poetry, short stories or children's picture books. Contemporary issues acceptable.
Recent Nonfiction Title(s): *If God is God...Then Why*, by Al Truesdale; *The Untamed God* (recovering the supernatural in the body of Christ); *Spiritual Secrets of Faithful Fathers*, by Ken Canfield.
Fiction: Wholesome, inspirational. Considers historical and Biblical fiction, Christian romance, but no teen or children's.
Recent Fiction Title(s): *Turn Northward, Love*, by Ruth Glover; *Fly Away*, by Lynn Austin.

BEACON PRESS, 25 Beacon St., Boston MA 02108-2892. (617)742-2110. Fax: (617)723-3097. E-mail: candrews@beacon.org. Website: http://www.beacon.org/Beacon. Director: Helene Atwan. **Acquisitions:** Editorial Director (African-American, Asian-American, Native American, Jewish and gay and lesbian studies, anthropology); Deanne Urmy, executive editor, (child and family issues, environmental concerns); Marya Van't Hul, editor (women's studies, legal studies); Susan Worst, editor (religion, Irish studies); Andrew Hrycyna, editor (education, current affairs, philosophy, Latino studies). Estab. 1854. "Beacon Press publishes general interest books that promote the following values: the inherent worth and dignity of every person; justice, equity, and compassion in human relations; acceptance of one another; a free and responsible search for truth and meaning; the goal of world community with peace, liberty and justice for all; respect for the interdependent web of all existence." Publishes hardcover originals and paperback reprints. Publishes 60 titles/year. Receives 4,000 submissions/year. 10% of books from first-time authors; 70% from unagented writers. Pays royalty. Advance varies. Accepts simultaneous submissions. Reports in 3 months.
Imprint(s): Black Women Writers Series (Tisha Hooks, editor), Concord Library (Deanne Urmy, editor).
  • Beacon Press has published such authors as Marian Wright Edelman, Leslie Feinberg and Sidney Mintz.
Nonfiction: General nonfiction including works of original scholarship, religion, women's studies, philosophy, current affairs, anthropology, environmental concerns, African-American, Asian-American, Native American, Latino and Jewish studies, gay and lesbian studies. education, legal studies, child and family issues, Irish studies. Query with outline/synopsis, cv or résumé and sample chapters with SASE.
Recent Nonfiction Title(s): *The Opening of the American Mind: Canons, Culture, and History*, by Lawrence W. Levine (history/education); *In the Name of the Family: Rethinking Family Values in the Postmodern Age*, by Judith Stacey (current affairs/sociology); *Bridging the Glass Divide: and Other Lessons for Grassroots Organizing* by Linda Stout (current affairs/memoir).
Tips: "We probably accept only one or two manuscripts from an unpublished pool of 4,000 submissions per year. No fiction, children's book, or poetry submissions invited. Authors should have academic affiliation."

BEHRMAN HOUSE INC., 235 Watchung Ave., West Orange NJ 07052-9827. (201)669-0447. Fax: (201)669-9769. **Acquisitions:** Adam Siegel, editor. Managing Editor: Adam Bengal. Estab. 1921. "Behrman House publishes quality books of Jewish content—history, Bible, philosophy, holidays, ethics—for children and adults." Publishes 20 titles/year. Receives 200 submissions/year. 20% of books from first-time authors; 95% from unagented writers. Pays 2-10% on wholesale price or retail price or makes outright purchase of $500-10,000. Offers $1,000 average advance. Publishes book 18 months after acceptance. Accepts simultaneous submissions. Reports in 2 months. Book catalog free.
Nonfiction: Juvenile (1-18), reference, textbook. Subjects include religion. "We want Jewish textbooks for the el-hi market." Query with outline and sample chapters.
Recent Nonfiction Title(s): *Partners with God*, by Gila Gevirtz (theology); *Jewish Heroes, Jewish Values*, by Barry Schwartz (heroes); *Women of Valor*, by Sheila Segal (women's biography).

FREDERIC C. BEIL, PUBLISHER, INC., 609 Whitaker St., Savannah GA 31401. Phone/fax: (912)233-2446. E-mail: beilbook@beil.com. Website: http://www.beil.com. **Acquisitions:** Mary Ann Bowman, editor. "Our objectives are (1) to offer to the reading public carefully selected texts of lasting value; (2) to adhere to high standards in the choice of materials and in bookmaking craftsmanship; (3) to produce books that exemplify good taste in format and design; and (4) to maintain the lowest cost consistent with quality." Publishes hardcover originals and reprints. Publishes 7 titles/year. Receives 700 queries and 9 mss/year. 15% of books from first-time authors; 80% from unagented writers. Pays 7½% royalty on retail price. Publishes book 20 months after acceptance. Accepts simultaneous submissions. Reports in 1 month on queries. Book catalog free.
Imprint(s): The Sandstone Press.
● Frederic C. Beil has published such well-known authors as Robert Metzger, Peter Taylor, Ruth Koenig, Helen Binyon and Madison Jones.
Nonfiction: Biography, general trade, illustrated book, juvenile, reference. Subjects include art/architecture, history, language/literature, book arts. Query. Reviews artwork/photos as part of ms package. Send photocopies.
Recent Nonfiction Title(s): *Anthony Trollope: A Victorian in His World*, by Richard Mullens.
Fiction: Historical and literary. Query.
Recent Fiction Title(s): *The Magicians*, by J.B. Priestley.

ROBERT BENTLEY, INC., Automotive Publishers, 1033 Massachusetts Ave., Cambridge MA 02138. (617)547-4170. Publisher: Michael Bentley. **Acquisitions:** Fred Newcomb, sales marketing director. Estab. 1949. Robert Bentley publishes books for automotive enthusiasts. Publishes hardcover and trade paperback originals and reprints. Publishes 15-20 titles/year. 20% of books are from first-time authors; 95% from unagented writers. Pays 10-15% royalty on net price or makes outright purchase. Advance negotiable. Publishes book 1 year after acceptance. Reports in 6 weeks. Book catalog and ms guidelines for 9×12 SAE with 4 first-class stamps.
Nonfiction: How-to, technical, theory of operation, coffee table. Automotive subjects only; this includes motor sports. Query or submit outline and sample chapters. Reviews artwork/photos as part of ms package.
Recent Nonfiction Title(s): *Race Car Aerodynamics*, by Joe Katz; *Toyota Truck Land Cruiser*, by Moses Ludel.
Tips: "We are excited about the possibilities and growth in the automobile enthusiast book market. Our audience is composed of serious, intelligent automobile, sports car, and racing enthusiasts, automotive technicians and high-performance tuners."

‡BERGIN & GARVEY, Imprint of Greenwood Publishing Group, 88 Post Rd. W., Westport CT 06881. (203)226-3571. Fax: (203)222-1502. Website: http://www.greenwood.com. Executive Vice President: Jim Sabin. **Acquisitions:** Editorial Offices. Publishes hardcover and trade paperback original nonfiction in the areas of education, anthropology, alternative medicine and parenting for libraries, educational groups and university scholars. Publishes 25 titles/year. Receives 1000s of queries/year. 50% of books from first-time authors. Pays variable royalty on net price. Rarely offers advance. Publishes book 1 year after acceptance of ms. Accepts simultaneous submissions. Reports in 6 months on queries and proposals. Book catalog and ms guidelines online.
● See Greenwood Publishing's Website for catalog, ms guidelines and editorial contacts.
Nonfiction: Subjects include anthropology/archaeology, child guidance/parenting, education. Query with proposal package, including scope, organization, length of project, whether a complete ms is available or when it will be, CV or résumé and SASE. *No unsolicited mss.*

THE BERKLEY PUBLISHING GROUP, Division of the Penguin Putnam Inc., 200 Madison Ave., New York NY 10016. (212)951-8400. Editorial Director: Judy Palais. Editor-in-Chief: Leslie Gelbman. Estab. 1954. "The Berkley Publishing Group is a full-line publisher. We do a variety of general nonfiction and fiction including the traditional categories of romance, mystery and science fiction, and Jove Books publishes the Prime Crime mystery imprint. We run the gamut and we're exciting." Publishes paperback and mass market originals and reprints. Publishes approximately 800 titles/year. Small percentage of books from first-time authors. 1% from unagented writers. Pays 4-15% royalty on retail price. Offers advance. Publishes book 2 years after acceptance. Reports in 4-6 weeks on queries.
Imprint(s): Berkley, Jove, **Ace Science Fiction, Boulevard**, Prime Crime.
Nonfiction: Biography, reference, self-help, how-to. Subjects include business management, job-seeking communication, positive thinking, gay/lesbian, health/fitness, psychology/self-help, women's issues/studies, general commercial publishing. "We prefer agented submissions." Query with SASE.
Recent Nonfiction Title(s): *Webster's Dictionary* (reference), *The Aladdin Factor*, by Jack Canfield and Mark Victor

Hansen (trade paperback general nonfiction mass market).
Fiction: Mystery, romance, western, young adult. We prefer agented material. Query with SASE.
Recent Fiction Title(s): *Goose in the Pond*, by Earlene Fowler (mystery); *Troubled Waters*, by Carolyn Wheat (mystery).
Tips: General audience. No longer seeking adventure or occult fiction. Does not publish memoirs or personal stories. "Read our books and submit through the Berkley Publishing group."

BERKSHIRE HOUSE PUBLISHERS, INC., 480 Pleasant St., Suite #5, Lee MA 01238. (413)243-0303. Fax: (413)243-4737. President: Jean J. Rousseau. **Acquisitions:** Philip Rich, managing editor. Estab. 1989. "All our books have a strong Berkshires or New England orientation—no others, please." Publishes 12-15 titles/year. Receives 100 queries and 6 mss/year. 50% of books from first-time authors; 80% from unagented writers. Pays 5-10% royalty on retail price. Offers $500-5,000 advance. Publishes book 18 months after acceptance. Accepts simultaneous submissions. Reports in 1 month on proposals. Book catalog free.
Nonfiction: Biography, cookbook. Subjects include Americana, history, nature/environment, recreation (outdoors), wood crafts, regional. "To a great extent, we choose our topics then commission the authors, but we don't discourage speculative submissions. We just don't accept many. Don't overdo it; a well-written outline/proposal is more useable than a full manuscript. Also, include a cv with writing credits."
Recent Nonfiction Title(s): *Old Barns in the New World*, by Richard Babcock and Lauren Stevens.
Tips: "Our readers are literate, active, prosperous, interested in travel, especially in selected 'Great Destinations' areas and outdoor activities and cooking."

‡BETHANY HOUSE PUBLISHERS, Subsidiary of Bethany Fellowship, Inc., 11300 Hampshire Ave. S., Minneapolis MN 55438. (612)829-2500. **Acquisitions:** Cindy M. Alewine, review department. "The purpose of Bethany House Publishers' publishing program is to relate biblical truth to all areas of life—whether in the framework of a well-told story, of a challenging book for spiritual growth, or of a Bible reference work." Publishes hardcover and trade paperback originals, mass market paperback reprints. Publishes 120-150 titles/year. 93% of books are from unagented writers. Pays negotiable royalty on wholesale price. Offers negotiable advance. Publishes ms 1 year after acceptance of ms. Accepts simultaneous submissions. Reports in 3 months. Book catalog for 9×12 SAE with 5 first-class stamps. Manuscript guidelines free.
Imprint(s): Portraits (Barbara Lilland, editor).
Nonfiction: Biography, gift book, how-to, references, self-help. Subjects include child guidance/parenting, ethnic, psychology, religion, sociology, women's issues/studies, devotionals, men's issues, apologetics, contemporary issues, deeper life. "Prospective authors must have credentials, credibility and well-honed writing." Submit proposal package including outline, 3 sample chapters, author information, and qualifications for writing with SASE. Reviews artwork/photos as part of ms package. Send photocopies.
Recent Nonfiction Title(s): *Becoming a Vessel God Can Use*, by Donna Partow (self-help); *The Compact Guide to World Religions*, by Dean C. Halverson (reference); *When God Says No*, by Leith Anderson (meditation and prayer).
Fiction: Adventure, historical, mainstream/contemporary, religious/romance, young adult. Submit proposal package including synopsis, 3 sample chapters, author information, educational background and writing experience with SASE.
Recent Fiction Title(s): *Drums of Change*, by Janet Oke; *The Shunning*, by Beverly Lewis; *Mandie & the Courtroom Battle*, by Lois Gladys Leppard.

BETTERWAY BOOKS, Imprint of F&W Publications, 1507 Dana Ave., Cincinnati OH 45207. (513)531-2690. **Acquisitions:** Acquisitions Coordinator. David Lewis (home decorating and remodeling, lifestyle (including home organization), woodworking, small business and personal finance, hobbies and collectibles); William Brohaugh (genealogy, reference books and handbooks, theater and the performing arts). Estab. 1982. "Betterway books are instructional books that are to be *used*. We like specific step-by-step advice, charts, illustrations, and clear explanations of the activities and projects the books describe." Publishes hardcover and trade paperback originals, trade paperback reprints. Publishes 30 titles/year. Pays 10-20% royalty on net receipts. Offers $3,000-5,000 advance. Accepts simultaneous submissions, if so noted. Publishes book an average of 18 months after acceptance. Reports in 1 month. Book catalog for 9×12 SAE with 6 first-class stamps.
Nonfiction: How-to, illustrated book, reference and self-help in 7 categories. "Genealogy and family traditions are topics that we're particularly interested in. We are interested mostly in original material, but we will consider republishing self-published nonfiction books and good instructional or reference books that have gone out of print before their time. Send a sample copy, sales information, and reviews, if available. If you have a good idea for a reference book that can be updated annually, try us. We're willing to consider freelance compilers of such works." No cookbooks, diet/exercise, psychology self-help, health or parenting books. Query with outline and sample chapters. Reviews artwork/photos as part of ms package.
Recent Nonfiction Title(s): *Family History Logbook*, by Reinhard Klein (genealogy); *How to Have a Big Wedding on a Small Budget, 3rd edition*, by Diane Warner; *Encyclopedia of Acting Techniques*, by John Perry (how-to).
Tips: "Keep the imprint name well in mind when submitting ideas to us. What is the 'better way' you're proposing? How will readers benefit *immediately* from the instruction and information you're giving them?"

BIRCH LANE PRESS, Imprint of Carol Publishing, 120 Enterprise Ave., Secaucus NJ 07094. (201)866-0490. Fax: (201)866-8159. **Acquisitions:** Hillel Black, executive editor. Birch Lane publishes general interest nonfiction for an adult audience. Publishes hardcover originals. Publishes 100 titles/year. 10% of books first-time authors; 10% from unagented writers. Pays 5-15% royalty on retail price. Offers $5,000-10,000. Publishes book 1 year after acceptance of ms. Accepts simultaneous submissions. Reports in 2 months on proposals.

Nonfiction: Subjects include business/economics, cooking/foods/nutrition, government/politics, history, humor, music/dance, popular culture. Query with outline, 2-3 sample chapters and SASE. Reviews artwork/photos as part of ms package. Send photocopies.

Recent Nonfiction Title(s): *The Financially Independent Woman*, by Barbara Lee (investment); *Torvill and Dean*, by Jayne Torvill & Christopher Dean (autobiography).

BLACK HERON PRESS, P.O. Box 95676, Seattle WA 98145. **Acquisitions:** Jerry Gold, publisher. Publishes hardcover and trade paperback originals. Publishes 4 titles/year. Pays 8-10% royalty on retail price. Reports in 3 months on queries, 6 months on proposals and mss.
  • Black Heron Press is not looking at new material until 1998.
Fiction: High quality, innovative fiction. Query with outline, 3 sample chapters and SASE.
Recent Fiction Title(s): *The Rat and The Rose*, by Arnold Rabin (surrealistic humorous novel); *Charlie And The Children*, by Joanna C. Scott (Vietnam War); *The Fruit 'N Food*, by Leonard Chang (interethnic conflict).
Tips: "Readers should look at some of Black Heron's Books before submitting—they are easily available. Most submissions we see are competently done, but have been sent to the wrong press. We do not publish self-help books."

BLACKBIRCH PRESS, INC., P.O. Box 3573, Woodbridge CT 06525. **Acquisitions:** Bruce Glassman, editorial director. Senior Editor: Deborah Kops. Blackbirch Press publishes juvenile and young adult nonfiction titles. Publishes hardcover and trade paperback originals. Publishes 30 titles/year. Receives 400 queries and 75 mss/year. 100% of books from unagented writers. Pays 4-8% royalty on wholesale price or makes outright purchase. Offers $1,000-5,000 advance. Publishes book 1 year after acceptance of ms. Accepts simultaneous submissions. Reports in 2 months. Manuscript guidelines free.
  • Blackbirch Press will be launching a fiction list "in the near future." Subjects include historical, humor, juvenile, picture books, young adult. Query.
Nonfiction: Biography, illustrated books, children's/juvenile, reference. Subjects include animals, anthropology/archeology, art/architecture, education, health/medicine, history, nature/environment, science, sports, travel, women's issues/studies. Publishes in series—6-8 books at a time. Query. *No unsolicited mss or proposals.* Cover letters and résumés are useful for identifying new authors. Reviews artwork/photos as part of ms package. Send photocopies. No adult proposals, please.
Recent Nonfiction Title(s): *The Seattle Space Needle*, by Katherine and Craig Doherty (Americana); *Lennon & McCartney*, by Bruce Glassman (biography); *Earthworms*, by Elaine Padscoe (science).

JOHN F. BLAIR, PUBLISHER, 1406 Plaza Dr., Winston-Salem NC 27103-1470. (910)768-1374. Fax: (910)768-9194. **Acquisitions:** Carolyn Sakowski, editor. Estab. 1954. "John F. Blair publishes hardcover and trade paperback fiction and nonfiction originals in the areas of travel, history, folklore and the outdoors for a general trade audience, most of whom live or travel in the southeastern U.S. Publishes hardcover originals and trade paperbacks." Publishes 15 titles/year. Receives 5,000 submissions/year. 20-30% of books from first-time authors; 90% from unagented writers. Average print order for a first book is 5,000. Royalty negotiable. Publishes book 18 months after acceptance. Reports in 3 months. Book catalog and ms guidelines for 9×12 SAE with 5 first-class stamps.
Nonfiction: Especially interested in travel guides dealing with the Southeastern US. Also interested in Civil War, outdoors, travel and Americana; query on other nonfiction topics. Looks for utility and significance. Submit outline and first 3 chapters. Reviews artwork/photos as part of ms package.
Fiction: "We are interested only in material related to the Southeastern U.S." No category fiction, juvenile fiction, picture books or poetry. *Writer's Market* recommends sending a query with SASE first.

BLOOMBERG PRESS, Imprint of Bloomberg L.P., 100 Business Park Dr., P.O. Box 888, Princeton NJ 08542-0888. Website: http://www.bloomberg.com. **Acquisitions:** Jared Kieling, editorial director. "Bloomberg Press publishes books both for dedicated professionals in the financial markets and for informed personal investors and consumers." Publishes hardcover and trade paperback originals. Publishes 12 titles/year. Receives 60 queries and 25 mss/year. 5% of books from first-time authors; 45% from unagented writers. Pays royalty on net receipts. Offers negotiable advance. Publishes book 9 months after acceptance of ms. Accepts simultaneous submissions. Reports in 1 month on queries. Book catalog for 10×13 SAE with 5 first-class stamps.
Imprint(s): Bloomberg Personal Bookshelf, Bloomberg Professional Library, Bloomberg Small Business.
Nonfiction: How-to, reference, technical. Subjects include small business, money/finance, personal finance for consumers, professional books on finance, investment and financial services. Submit outline, sample chapters with SASE.
Recent Nonfiction Title(s): *A Commonsense Guide to Mutual Funds*, by Mary Rowland (personal finance).
Tips: *Bloomberg Professional Library*: Audience is upscale financial professionals—traders, dealers, brokers, company executives, sophisticated investors, such as people who lease a BLOOMBERG terminal system. *Bloomberg Personal Bookshelf*: Audience is upscale consumers and individual investors, as well as all categories listed for the Professional Library—readers of our magazine *Bloomberg Personal*. "Authors are experienced business and financial journalists and/or financial professionals prominent in their specialty for some time. Do research on Bloomberg and look at our

specially formatted books in a library or bookstore, read *Bloomberg Personal* and *Bloomberg* magazines and peruse our website."

‡**BLUE HERON PUBLISHING**, 24450 NW Hansen Rd., Hillsboro OR 97124. (503)621-3911. **Acquisitions:** Dennis Stovall, president; Linny Stovall, vice president. Estab. 1985. Publishes trade paperback originals and reprints. Averages 6 titles/year. Reports in 6 weeks. Book catalog for #10 SASE.
Nonfiction: Looking for books that sell in educational markets as well as the trade. Query with SASE.
Tips: "We publish Northwest writers *only*."

BLUE MOON BOOKS, INC., North Star Line, 61 Fourth Ave., New York NY 10003. (212)505-6880. Fax: (212)673-1039. E-mail: bluoff@aol.com. **Acquisitions:** Barney Rosset, publisher/editor. "Blue Moon Books is strictly an erotic press; largely fetish-oriented material, B&D, S&M, etc." Publishes trade paperback and mass market paperback originals. Publishes 30-40 titles/year. Receives 1,000 queries and 500 mss/year. Pays 7½-10% royalty on retail price. Offers $500 and up advance. Publishes book 1 year after acceptance of ms. Accepts simultaneous submissions. Reports in 2 months. Book catalog free. Manuscript guidelines for #10 SASE.
Imprint(s): North Star Line.
Nonfiction: Trade erotic and sexual nonfiction. Query or submit outline and 3-6 sample chapters with SASE. Reviews artwork/photos as part of ms package if part of story. Color photocopies best but not necessary.
Recent Nonfiction Title(s): *Patong Sisters: An American Woman's View of the Bangkok Sex World*, by Cleo Odzer.
Fiction: Erotica. Query or submit synopsis and 1-2 sample chapters with SASE.
Recent Fiction Title(s): *J and Seventeen*, by Kenzaburo Oe; *The Love Run*, by Jay Parini.

BLUE POPPY PRESS, 1775 Linden Ave., Boulder CO 80304-1537. (303)442-0796. Fax: (303)447-0740. E-mail: 102151.1614@compuserve.com. **Acquisitions:** Bob Flaws, editor-in-chief. "Blue Poppy Press is dedicated to expanding and improving the English language literature on acupuncture and Asian medicine for both professional practitioners and lay readers." Publishes hardcover and trade paperback originals. Publishes 9-12 titles/year. Receives 50-100 queries and 20 mss/year. 40-50% of books from first-time authors; 100% from unagented writers. Pays 10-15% royalty "of sales price at all discount levels." Publishes book 1 year after acceptance. Reports in 1 month. Book catalog and ms guidelines free.
Nonfiction: Self-help, technical, textbook related to acupuncture and Oriental medicine. "We only publish books on acupuncture and Oriental medicine by authors who can read Chinese and have a minimum of five years clinical experience. We also require all our authors to use Wiseman's *Glossary of Chinese Medical Terminology* as their standard for technical terms." Query or submit outline, 1 sample chapter and SASE.
Recent Nonfiction Title(s): *The Pulse Classic*, by Wang Shu-he (Chinese Pulse diagnosis); *The Treatment of Disease in TCM*, by Philippe Sconneau (clinical manual); *The Secret of Chinese Pulse Diagnosis*, by Bob Flaws.
Tips: Audience is "practicing accupuncturists, interested in alternatives in healthcare, preventive medicine, Chinese philosophy and medicine."

THE BLUE SKY PRESS, Imprint of Scholastic Inc., 555 Broadway, New York NY 10012. (212)343-6100. Fax: (212)343-4535. Website: http://www.scholastic.com. **Acquisitions:** The Editors. Blue Sky Press publishes primarily juvenile picture books. Publishes hardcover and trade paperback originals. Publishes 15-20 titles/year. Receives 2,500 queries/year. 1% of books from first-time authors; 75% from unagented writers. Pays 10% royalty on wholesale price, between authors and illustrators. Publishes book 2 1/2 years after acceptance of ms. Reports in 6 months on queries.
  ● Because of a long backlog of books, The Blue Sky Press is not accepting unsolicited submissions.
Fiction: Juvenile: adventure, fantasy, historical, humor, mainstream/contemporary, picture books, multicultural, folktales.
Recent Fiction Title(s): *True North*, by Kathryn Lasky (novel); *Goose*, by Molly Bang (picture book); *When Birds Could Talk & Bats Could Sing*, by Virginia Hamilton (folktales).

BLUE STAR PRODUCTIONS, Division of Bookworld, Inc., 9666 E. Riggs Rd., #194, Sun Lakes AZ 85248. (602)895-7995. Fax: (602)895-6991. E-mail: bkworld@aol.com. Website: http://www.bkworld.com. **Acquisitions:** Barbara DeBolt, editor. Blue Star Productions publishes metaphysical fiction and nonfiction titles on specialized subjects. "Our mission is to aid in the spiritual growth of mankind." Publishes trade and mass market paperback originals. Publishes 10-12 titles/year. Receives 500 queries and 400-500 mss/year. 75% of books from first-time authors; 99% from unagented writers. Pays 10% royalty on wholesale or retail price. No advance. Reports in 1 month on queries, 2 months on proposals, 6 months on mss. Book catalog free. Manuscript guidelines for #10 SASE.
  ● Blue Star has published such authors as Laura Leffers and Aaron Pryor.
Nonfiction: Subjects include philosophy, ufology, spiritual (metaphysical), self-help. Query with SASE. No response without SASE. No phone queries. Reviews artwork/photos as part of the ms package. Send photocopies.
Recent Nonfiction Title(s): *Cataclysms: A New Look at Earth Changes*, by Norma Hickox; *The Ascent: Doorway to Eternity*, by C.L. Cross; *365 Days of Prosperity*, by Patricia Telesco.
Fiction: Fantasy, spiritual (metaphysical), UFO's. Query or submit synopsis and the first 3 chapters. SASE a must.
Recent Fiction Title(s): *The Best Kept Secrets*, by Charles Wright; *The Antilles Incident*, by Donald Todd.
Tips: "Know our guidelines. We have temporarily restricted our needs to those manuscripts whose focus is metaphysical,

ufology, time travel and Native American. Query to see if this restriction has been lifted before submitting other material."

BNA BOOKS, Division of The Bureau of National Affairs, Inc., 1250 23rd St. NW, Washington DC 20037-1165. (202)833-7470. Fax: (202)833-7490. E-mail: books@bna.com. Website: http://www.bna.com. Administrative Assistant: Esther H. Marshall. **Acquisitions:** Tim Darby, acquisitions manager; Jim Fattibene (environment and intellectual property). Estab. 1929. "BNA Books publishes professional reference books written by lawyers, for lawyers." Publishes hardcover and softcover originals. Publishes 35 titles/year. Receives 200 submissions/year. 20% of books from first-time authors; 95% from unagented writers. Pays 5-15% royalty on net cash receipts. Offers $500 average advance. Publishes book 1 year after acceptance. Accepts simultaneous submissions. Reports in 3 months on queries. Book catalog and ms guidelines free.
Nonfiction: Reference, professional/scholarly. Subjects include labor and unemployment law, environmental law, legal practice, labor relations and intellectual property law. No biographies, bibliographies, cookbooks, religion books, humor or trade books. Submit detailed table of contents or outline.
Recent Nonfiction Title(s): *Downsizing* (with disk), by Ethan Lipsig (layoffs, RIFs, exit incentives); *How to Prepare/Present A Labor Arbitration Case*, by Charles S. Loughran; *Equal Employment Law Updates*, by Richard T. Seymour and Barbara Beris Brown.
Tips: "Our audience is made up of practicing lawyers and business executives; managers, federal, state, and local government administrators; unions; and law libraries. We look for authoritative and comprehensive works that can be supplemented or revised every year or two on subjects of interest to those audiences."

‡BOA EDITIONS, LTD., 260 East Ave., Rochester NY 14604. **Acquisitions:** Steven Huff, publisher/managing editor. "BOA Editions publishes frontlist and backlist collections of poetry and poetry in translation." Publishes hardcover and trade paperback originals. Publishes 6 titles/year. Receives 1,000 queries and 700 mss/year. 15% of books from first-time authors; 90% from unagented writers. Pays 7½-10% royalty on retail price. Advance varies, usually $500. Publishes book 18 months after acceptance of ms. Accepts simultaneous submissions. Reports in 1 month on queries, 3-4 months on mss. Book catalog and ms guidelines free.
Poetry: "We are currently accepting manuscripts for publication in 1999 and beyond." Query or submit 10 sample poems with SASE.
Recent Poetry Title(s): *The Quicken Tree*, by Bill Knott.
Tips: "Readers who, like Whitman, expect of the poet to 'indicate more than the beauty and dignity which always attach to dumb real objects . . . they expect him to indicate the path between reality and their souls,' are the audience of BOA's books.

BONUS BOOKS, INC., Parent of Precept Press, 160 E. Illinois St., Chicago IL 60611. (312)467-0580. Fax: (312)467-9271. E-mail: rachel@bonus-books.com. Website: http://www.bonus-books.com. Managing Editor: Rachel Drzewicki. **Acquisitions:** Assistant Editor. Estab. 1985. Bonus Books is a publishing and audio/video company featuring subjects ranging from human interest to sports to gambling. Publishes hardcover and trade paperback originals and reprints. Publishes 30 titles/year. Receives 400-500 submissions/year. 40% of books from first-time authors; 60% from unagented writers. Royalties vary. Advances are not frequent. Publishes book 8 months after acceptance. Accepts simultaneous submissions, if so noted. Reports in 2 months on queries. Book catalog for 9 × 11 SASE. Manuscript guidelines for #10 SASE. All submissions and queries must include SASE.
Nonfiction: Subjects include automotive/self-help, biography/current affairs, broadcasting, business/self-help, Chicago people and places, collectibles, cookbooks, education/self-help, fund raising, handicapping winners, home and health, humor, entertainment, regional, sports and women's issues/studies. Query with outline, sample chapters and SASE. Reviews artwork/photos as part of ms package.
Recent Nonfiction Title(s): *Spin Roulette Gold*, by Frank Scoblete (win at roulette); *Shock Marketing*, by Joe Marconi (advertising, influence and family values); *Legal Guide to Buying & Selling Art and Collectibles*; by Armen Vartian.

BOOKCRAFT, INC., 1848 West 2300 South, Salt Lake City UT 84119. (801)972-6180. **Acquisitions:** Cory H. Maxwell, editorial manager. Estab. 1942. Imprint is Parliament. Publishes mainly hardcover and trade paperback originals closely oriented to the faith and practices of the Latter-Day Saints. Publishes 40-45 titles/year. Receives 500-600 submissions/year. 20% of books from first-time authors; virtually 100% from unagented writers. Pays standard 7½-10-12½-15% royalty on retail price. Rarely gives advance. Publishes book 6 months after acceptance. Accepts simultaneous submissions. Reports in about 2 months. Book catalog and ms guidelines for #10 SASE.
Imprint: Parliament.
Nonfiction: "We publish for members of The Church of Jesus Christ of Latter-Day Saints (Mormons) and our books are closely oriented to the faith and practices of the LDS church, and we will be glad to review such mss. Those which have merely a general religious appeal are not acceptable. Ideal book lengths range from about 100-300 pages or so, depending on subject, presentation, and age level. We look for a fresh approach—rehashes of well-known concepts or doctrines not acceptable. Manuscripts should be anecdotal unless truly scholarly or on a specialized subject. We do not publish anti-Mormon works. We also publish short and moderate length books for children and young adults, and fiction as well as nonfiction. These reflect LDS principles without being 'preachy'; must be motivational. 30,000-45,000 words is about the right length, though good, longer manuscripts are not ruled out. We publish only 5 or 6 new juvenile titles annually. No poetry, plays, personal philosophizings, or family histories." Biography, childrens/juvenile, coffee table

book, how-to, humor, reference, self-help. Subjects include: child guidance/parenting, history, religion. Query with full ms and SASE. *Writer's Market* recommends sending a query with SASE first. Reviews artwork/photos as part of ms package. Send photocopies.

Recent Nonfiction Title(s): *Sunshine* by Elaine Cannon (inspirational).

Fiction: Should be oriented to LDS faith and practices. Adventure, historical, juvenile, literary, mainstream/contemporary, mystery, religious, romance, short story collections, suspense, western, young adult. Submit full ms with SASE. *Writer's Market* recommends sending a query with SASE first.

Recent Fiction Title(s): *The Work and the Glory: Praise to the Man*, volume 7, by Gerald N. Lund.

Tips: "The competition in the area of fiction is much more intense than it has ever been before. We receive two or three times as many quality fiction manuscripts as we did even as recently as five years ago."

BOOKHAVEN PRESS, P.O. Box 1243, 401 Amherst Ave., Moon Township PA 15108. (412)262-5578. Orders: (800)782-7424. Fax: (412)262-5147. Website: http://www.members@aol.com//bookhaven. Publisher: Dennis Damp. **Acquisitions:** Victor Richards, editorial manager. Publishes trade paperback originals. Publishes 8 titles/year. Receives 36 queries and 15 mss/year. 100% of books from first-time authors; 100% from unagented writers. Pays 7-12% royalty on wholesale price. No advance. Publishes book 6 months after acceptance of ms. Accepts simultaneous submissions. Does not return submissions. Form letter for rejection, destroys originals. Reports in 3 months on queries, 1 month on proposals, 2 months on mss. Book catalog free.

Nonfiction: How-to, reference. Subjects include business/economics, education, money/finance and careers. "We look for well developed manuscripts from computer literate writers. All manuscripts must be available in IBM computer format (Word Perfect Preferred)." Submit outline and 2 sample chapters. Reviews artwork/photos as part of ms package. Send photocopies.

Recent Nonfiction Title(s): *How to Raise A Family and A Career Under One Roof*, by Lisa Roberts.

‡BOOKS IN MOTION, 9212 E. Montgomery, #501, Spokane WA 99206. (509)922-1646. **Acquisitions:** Gary Challender, president. Publishes unabridged audiobook originals. Publishes 70-80 titles/year. 25% of books from first-time authors; 90% from unagented writers. Pays 10% royalty on wholesale or retail price. No advance. Publishes book 3 months after acceptance of ms. Accepts simultaneous submissions. Reporting time varies. Book catalog and ms guidelines on request.

Fiction: Adventure, fantasy, historical, horror, humor, mainstream/contemporary, mystery, religious, science fiction, suspense, western. "Minimal profanity and no gratuitous sex. We like series using the same charismatic character." Query with synopsis and first chapter.

Recent Fiction Title(s): *Counterfeit Wife*, by Tom Neet (detective mystery); *Timegap*, by Loren Robinson (science fiction); *Apache Moon*, by Audra McWilliams (western).

Tips: "Our audience is 20% women, 80% men. Many of our audience are truck drivers, who want something interesting to listen to."

THE BORGO PRESS, P.O. Box 2845, San Bernardino CA 92406-2845. (909)884-5813. Fax: (909)888-4942. E-mail: borgopr@gte.net. Website: http://www.borgopress.com. **Acquisitions:** Robert Reginald, Mary A. Burgess, publishers. Estab. 1975. "We publish quality books on literature, the theater, films and related topics for the library and academic market." Publishes hardcover and paperback originals. Publishes 25 new titles/year, plus 100 new distributed books. Receives 500 submissions/year. 90% of books from first-time authors; 100% from unagented writers. Pays 10% royalty on retail price. No advance. Publishes book 3 years after acceptance. "99% of our sales go to the academic library market; we do not sell to the trade (i.e., bookstores)." Reports in 3 months. Book catalog for 9×12 SAE with 6 first-class stamps.

• The Borgo Press has published such authors as L. Sprague de Camp, Algis Budrys, Henry Miller, Ross MacDonald, Brian Stableford and Colin Wilson.

Nonfiction: Publishes literary critiques, bibliographies, film critiques, theatrical research, interview volumes, scholarly literary biographies and reference works for the academic library market only. Query with letter or outline/synopsis and 1 sample chapter. "All of our proprietary books, without exception, are published in open-ended, numbered, monographic series. Do not submit proposals until you have looked at actual copies of recent Borgo Press publications (*not our catalog*). We are *not* a market for fiction, poetry, popular nonfiction, artwork, or anything else except scholarly monographs in the humanities. We discard unsolicited manuscripts from outside of our subject fields that are not accompanied by SASE. The vast majority of proposals we receive are clearly unsuitable and are a waste of both our time and the prospective author's."

Recent Nonfiction Title(s): *A Subtler Magick*, by Joshi (critique); *Confessions of a Trekoholic*, by Palencar (TV critique); *Discovering Classic Fantasy Fiction*, edited by Schweitzer.

BOULEVARD, Imprint of Penguin Putnam Inc., 200 Madison Ave., New York NY 10016. (212)951-8400. Fax: (212)545-8917. **Acquisitions:** Elizabeth Beier, editorial director. Estab. 1995. Publishes trade paperback and mass market paperbacks originals and reprints. Publishes 85 titles/year.

Recent Nonfiction Title(s): *Asian Cult Cinema*, by Thomas Wisser (reference/movie guide); *Penn & Teller's How to Play in Traffic*, by Penn Jillette & Teller (humor).

Recent Fiction Title(s): *Xena: The Thief of Hermes*, by Ru Emerson; *Quantum Leap: Obsessions*, by Carol Davis; *Dante's Peak*, by Dewey Gram.

BOWLING GREEN STATE UNIVERSITY POPULAR PRESS, Bowling Green State University, Bowling Green OH 43403-1000. (419)372-7866. Fax: (419)372-8095. **Acquisitions:** Ms. Pat Browne. Estab. 1967. Publishes hardcover originals and trade paperback originals and reprints. Publishes 25 titles/year. Receives 400 submissions/year. 50% of books from first-time authors; 100% from unagented writers. Pays 5-12% royalty on wholesale price or makes outright purchase. Publishes book 9 months after acceptance. Reports in 3 months. Book catalog and ms guidelines free.
Nonfiction: Biography, reference, textbook. Subjects include Americana, art/architecture, ethnic, history, language/literature, regional, sports, women's issues/studies. Submit outline and 3 sample chapters.
Recent Nonfiction Title(s): *Stephen King's America*, by Jonathan Davis.
Tips: "Our audience includes university professors, students, and libraries."

BOYDS MILLS PRESS, Division of *Highlights for Children*, 815 Church St., Honesdale PA 18431-1895. (800)490-5111. **Acquisitions:** Beth Troop, manuscript coordinator. Estab. 1990. "We publish a wide range of quality children's books of literary merit, from preschool to young adult." Publishes hardcover originals. Publishes 50 titles/year. Receives 10,000 queries and mss/year. 20% of books are from first-time authors; 75% from unagented writers. Pays varying royalty on retail price. Advance varies. Accepts simultaneous submissions. Reports in 1 month. *Writer's Market* recommends allowing 2 months for reply. Manuscript guidelines free. Book catalog for 9 × 12 SASE with 7 first-class stamps.
• Boyds Mills Press published one 1996 Junior Library Guild Selection, *Leah's Pony*, by Elizabeth Friedrich. Boyds Mills Press has also published such authors as Jane Yolen, Eve Bunting, Lee Bennett Hopkins and Laurence Pringle.
Imprint(s): Wordsong (poetry).
Nonfiction: Juvenile on all subjects. "Boyds Mills Press is not interested in manuscripts depicting violence, explicit sexuality, racism of any kind or which promote hatred. We also are not the right market for self-help books." Submit outline and sample chapters. Reviews artwork/photos as part of ms package.
Recent Nonfiction Title(s): *Horsepower*, by Cris Peterson (draft horses); *Everybody Has a Bellybutton*, by Laurence Pringle (the role of the bellybutton during life in the womb).
Fiction: Juvenile—picture book, middle grade, young adult, poetry. Submit outline/synopsis and sample chapters for novel or complete ms for picture book.
Recent Fiction Title(s): *Read for Me, Mama*, by Vashanti Rahaman (family love and literacy); *Secret Signs*, by Anita Riggio (the Underground Railroad).
Recent Poetry Title(s): *Bicycle Riding*, by Sandra Olson Liatsos (the mysteries and joys of nature).
Tips: "Our audience is pre-school to young adult. Concentrate first on your writing. Polish it. Then—and only then—select a market. We need primarily picture books with fresh ideas and characters—avoid worn themes of 'coming-of-age,' 'new sibling,' and self-help ideas. We are always interested in multicultural settings. Please—no anthropomorphic characters."

BRANDEN PUBLISHING CO., INC., 17 Station St., Box 843, Brookline Village MA 02147. Fax: (617)734-2046. E-mail: branden@branden.com. Website: http://www.branden.com. **Acquisitions:** Adolph Caso, editor. Estab. 1965. "Branden publishes only manuscripts determined to have a significant impact on modern society." Subsidiaries include International Pocket Library and Popular Technology, Four Seas and Brashear. Publishes hardcover and trade paperback originals, reprints and software. Publishes 15 titles/year. Receives 1,000 submissions/year. 80% of books from first-time authors; 90% from unagented writers. Average print order for a first book is 3,000. Pays 5-10% royalty on net. Offers $1,000 maximum advance. Publishes book 10 months after acceptance. Reports in 1 month. *Writer's Market* recommends allowing 2 months for reply.
Nonfiction: Biography, illustrated book, juvenile, reference, technical, textbook. Subjects include Americana, art, computers, health, history, music, photography, politics, sociology, software, classics. Especially looking for "about 10 manuscripts on national and international subjects, including biographies of well-known individuals." No religion or philosophy. Paragraph query only with author's vita and SASE. *No unsolicited mss.* No telephone inquiries. No e-mail or fax inquiries. Reviews artwork/photos as part of ms package.
Recent Nonfiction Title(s): *Jews*, by George E. Berkley (history); *Escape of the Pacific Clipper*, by George L. Flynn (history); *Trial of the Century—Obstruction of Justice: Viewpoint of a Trial Watcher*, by Loretta Justice (law).
Fiction: Ethnic (histories, integration); religious (historical-reconstructive). No science, mystery or pornography. Paragraph query only with author's vita and SASE. *No unsolicited mss.* No other inquiries.
Recent Fiction Title(s): *The Straw Obelisk*, by Caso (World War II); *Blood Games*, by Woody Tanger (thriller).
Tips: "Our audience is a well-read general public, professionals, college students, and some high school students. If I were a writer trying to market a book today, I would thoroughly investigate the number of potential readers interested in the content of my book. We like books by or about women."

BRASSEY'S, INC., Division of Brassey's Ltd. (London), 1313 Dolley Madison Blvd., Suite #401, McLean VA 22101. (703)442-4535. Fax: (703)442-9848. Website: http://www.brasseys.com. **Acquisitions:** Don McKeon, editorial director. Brassey's is a U.S. publisher specializing in national and international affairs, military history, biography, intelligence, foreign policy and defense. Publishes hardcover and trade paperback originals and reprints. Publishes 40 titles/year. Receives 900 queries/year. 30% of books from first-time authors; 80% from unagented writers. Pays 6-12% royalty on wholesale price. Offers $50,000 maximum advance. Publishes book 1 year after acceptance of ms. Accepts simultaneous submissions. Reports in 2 months on proposals. Book catalog and ms guidelines for 9 × 12 SASE.

• Brassey's, Inc. has published such authors as Bill Clinton, Jim Wright, John Tower, Les Aspin, Perry Smith, Georgie Anne Geyer, Donald M. Goldstein, Jack Galvin and Roy Godson.

Nonfiction: Biography, coffee-table book, reference, textbook. Subjects include government/politics, national and international affairs, history, military/war, intelligence studies and sports. "We are seeking to build our biography, military history and national affairs lists and have also created a new imprint, Brassey's Sports." When submitting nonfiction, be sure to include sufficient biographical information (e.g., track records of previous publications), and "make clear in proposal how your work might differ from other such works already published and with which yours might compete." Submit proposal package, including outline, 1 sample chapter, bio, analysis of book's competition, return postage and SASE. Reviews artwork/photos as part of ms package. Send photocopies.

Recent Nonfiction Title(s): *The U.S. Military Online: A Directory for Internet Access to the Department of Defense*, by William M. Arkin; *When Dreams Came True: The GI Bill and The Making of Modern America*, by Michael J. Bennett (GI Bill and postwar US); *One Day of the Civil War: America in Conflict, April 10, 1863*, by Robert L. Willett (a day at war's midpoint).

Tips: "Our audience consists of military personnel, government policymakers, and general readers with an interest in military history, biography, national and international affairs, defense issues, intelligence studies and sports." Brassey's, Inc. is no longer considering fiction.

‡**GEORGE BRAZILLER, INC.**, 171 Madison Ave., Suite 1103, New York NY 10016. (212)889-0909. **Acquisitions:** Adrienne Baxter, editor. Publishes hardcover originals, trade paperback originals and reprints. Publishes 10-15 titles/year. Receives 300 queries and 60 mss/year. 2% of books from first-time authors; 80% from unagented writers. Pays 2-10% royalty on retail price, or makes outright purchase of $2,000-6,000. Offers $2,500-6,000 advance. Publishes book 10 months after acceptance of ms. Reports in 3 months on proposals. Book catalog and ms guidelines free.

Nonfiction: Biography, coffee table book, illustrated book. Subjects include art/architecture, history, language/literature. "We do very little nonfiction but, as we don't publish in specific categories only, we are willing to consider a wide range of subjects." Submit outline with 4 sample chapters and SASE. Reviews artwork/photos as part of ms package. Send photocopies.

Recent Nonfiction Title(s): *Mosaics of Roman Africa*, by M. Blanchard Lemee et al (art); *Michelangelo: The Sistine Chapel Ceiling, Rome*, by Loren Partridge (art); *Sexuality and Catholicism*, by Thomas C. Fox (religion/sexuality).

Fiction: Ethnic, gay/lesbian, literary. "We rarely do fiction but when we have published novels, they have mostly been literary novels." Submit 4-6 sample chapters with SASE.

Recent Fiction Title(s): *Blindsight*, by Herve Guibert; *Papa's Suitcase*, by Gerhard Kopf (literary fiction).

BREVET PRESS, INC., P.O. Box 1404, Sioux Falls SD 57101. **Acquisitions:** Donald P. Mackintosh, publisher (business); Peter E. Reid, managing editor (technical); A. Melton, editor (Americana); B. Mackintosh, editor (history). Estab. 1972. Brevet Books seeks nonfiction with "market potential and literary excellence." Publishes hardcover and paperback originals and reprints. Publishes 15 titles/year. Receives 40 submissions/year. 50% of books from first-time authors; 100% from unagented writers. Average print order for a first book is 5,000. Pays 5% royalty. Offers $1,000 average advance. Publishes book 1 year after acceptance. Accepts simultaneous submissions. Reports in 2 months. Book catalog free.

Nonfiction: Specializes in business management, history, place names, and historical marker series. Americana, business, history, technical books. Query. "After query, detailed instructions will follow if we are interested." Reviews artwork/photos as part of ms package. Send photocopies.

Tips: "Keep sexism out of the manuscripts."

BREWERS PUBLICATIONS, Division of Association of Brewers, 736 Pearl St., Boulder CO 80302. (303)447-0816. Fax: (303)447-2825. E-mail: bp@aob.org. Website: http://beertown.org. **Acquisitions:** Toni Knapp, publisher. Estab. 1986. "Brewers Publications is the largest publisher of books on beer and brewing. In operation since 1986, Brewers Publications is a nonprofit, educational publisher dedicated to providing quality books for the home brewer, professional brewer and beer enthusiast." Publishes trade paperback and mass market paperback originals. Publishes 5 titles/year. Receives 50 queries and 4 mss/year. 50% of books from first-time authors; 100% from unagented writers. Pays 2-10% royalty on net receipts. Offers $500 maximum advance. Publishes book within 18 months of acceptance of ms. Accepts simultaneous submissions. Reports in 3 months. Book catalog free.

Nonfiction: "We only publish books about beer and brewing—for professional brewers, home brewers and beer enthusiasts." Query first, then submit outline if requested. Reviews artwork/photos only after a ms is accepted.

Recent Nonfiction Title(s): *Designing Great Beers*, by Ray Daniels (home brewing and craft brewing); *Brewery Planner*, 2nd edition, compiled by Brewers Publications (business); *Stout*, by Michael Lewis (beer and brewing).

MARKET CONDITIONS are constantly changing! If this is 1999 or later, buy the newest edition of *Writer's Market* at your favorite bookstore or order directly from Writer's Digest Books.

‡**BRIDGE WORKS PUBLISHING CO.**, Box 1798, Bridge Lane, Bridgehampton NY 11932. (516)537-3418. Fax: (516)537-5092. **Acquisitions:** Barbara Phillips, editor/publisher. "We are a very small press dedicated to quality fiction and nonfiction. Like a university press, we are not interested in mass market material, but look for writing that is original and inventive, as well as entertaining." Publishes hardcover originals and reprints. Publishes 4-6 titles/year. Receives 100 queries and 200 mss/year. 50% of books from first-time authors; 80% from unagented writers. Pays 10% royalty on retail price. Offers $1,000 advance. Publishes book 1 year after acceptance of ms. Reports in 1 month on queries and proposals, 2 months on mss. Book catalog and ms guidelines for #10 SASE.
Nonfiction: Biography, reference, memoirs, essays. Subjects include history, language/literature, philosophy, psychology, sociology. "We *do not* accept multiple submissions. We prefer a proposal first of all, and the subjects should have either a national or universal significance." Query or submit outline and proposal package with SASE. Reviews artwork/photos as part of ms package. Send photocopies.
Recent Nonfiction Title(s): *The Woman Who Ran For President*, by Lois Underhill (history).
Fiction: Feminist, historical, literary, short story collections. "Query with SASE before submitting ms. First-time authors should have mss vetted by freelance editors before submitting them to publishers. We do not accept or read multiple submissions." Query or submit synopsis and 2 sample chapters with SASE.
Recent Fiction Title(s): *Zip Six*, by Jack Gantos (prison life novel as narrated by teenage drug smuggler).
Poetry: "We publish only *one* collection every 5 years." Query or submit sample poems.
Recent Poetry Title(s): *Look For a Field to Land*, by Elaine Preston (modern).
Tips: "Since we publish so few books a year, we look for literate or literary works. The subject does not matter, *but* we are not mass market. Query letters should be one page, giving general subject or plot of the book and stating who the writer feels is the audience for the work. In the case of novels or poetry, a small portion of the work could be enclosed."

‡**BRISTOL FASHION PUBLICATIONS**, P.O. Box 20, Enola PA 17025. **Acquisitions:** John Kaufman, publisher; Robert "Bob" Lollo, managing editor. Publishes hardcover and trade paperback originals. Publishes 6-8 titles/year. Receives 20 queries and 4 mss/year. 80% of books from first-time authors; 100% from unagented writers. Pays 7-11% royalty on retail price. Splits royalty or makes outright purchase for portions to be included with other's work. Offers $500-2,500 advance based on writer and project. Usually offers no advance to unpublished authors. Publishes books 6 months after acceptance of ms. Accepts simultaneous submissions. Reports in 1 month on queries and proposals, 2 months on mss. Book catalog for 9½×12 SAE and $1.01 postage. Manuscript guidelines for #10 SASE.
Nonfiction: How-to, reference. Nautical/marine subjects only. "All titles are how to repair, maintain and restore boats over 25 feet. Query for specific needs with a list of your ideas. Include phone number. This is a fast changing market. We make no long range title plans. We prefer good technical knowledge with simple to understand, step-by-step writing. K.I.S.S." Query first, then submit proposal package, including outline, writing samples, tearsheets, with SASE. Reviews artwork/photos as part of the ms package. Send photocopies of b&w prints and/or line art.
Recent Nonfiction Title(s): *Boat Repair Made Easy* series: *Systems, Haul Out, Engines, Troubleshooting, Finishes.*
Tips: "Audience is boaters with vessels over 25 feet who want to learn how to do their own work, new boaters, boaters who have recently purchased a larger vessel, cruising boaters or in general, the non-handy. No agents. Period!!! Keep it simple and easy to follow. Use nautical terms where appropriate. Do not use complicated technical terms or formulas. Start from the very basic and work towards the larger projects. Write for guidelines and include any ideas you may have for a title. Use good craftsman as a resource."

BROADMAN & HOLMAN PUBLISHERS, 127 Ninth Ave. N, Nashville TN 37234. **Acquisitions:** Vicki Crumpton, Matt Jacobson, acquisitions and development editors. "Broadman & Holman will be the best provider of distinctive, relevant, high-quality products and services that lead individuals toward: a personal faith in Jesus Christ, a lifestyle of practical discipleship, a world view that is consistent with the historic, Christian Faith. We will accomplish this in a manner that glorifies God and serves His Kingdom while making a positive financial contribution." Publishes hardcover and paperback originals. Publishes 48 titles/year. Pays negotiable royalty. Reports in 2 months. Writer's guidelines for #10 SAE with 2 first-class stamps.
● Broadman & Holman has published such authors as Henry Blackaby, Bob Briner, J. Keith Miller.
Nonfiction: Religion. "We are open to freelance submissions in all areas. Materials in these areas must be suited for an evangelical Christian readership." No poetry, biography, sermons, or art/gift books. Query with outline/synopsis and sample chapters.
Recent Nonfiction Title(s): *The Father Connection*, by Josh McDowell (parenting); *The Financially Confident Woman*, by Mary Hunt (women/finance); *Moral of the Story*, by Jerry Newcombe (Christian literature).
Fiction: Religious. "We publish a limited number of fiction titles. We want not only a very good story, but also one that sets forth Christian values. Nothing that lacks a positive Christian emphasis; nothing that fails to sustain reader interest."
Recent Fiction Title(s): *Anonymous Tip*, by Michael Farris (current issues).
Tips: "Please study competing titles and be able to identify the unique, compelling features of your proposed book."

BROADWAY BOOKS, Division of Bantam Doubleday Dell Publishing Group, Inc. 1540 Broadway, New York NY 10036. (212)354-6500. Publisher: William Shinker. Editor-in-Chief: John Sterling. **Acquisitions:** Harriet Bell, executive editor (cookbooks); Janet Goldstein, vice president and executive editor (women's and family issues, psychology, self-help); John Sterling, vice president and editor-in-chief (literary fiction, nonfiction); Lauren Marino, editor (pop culture, entertainment, spirituality); Suzanne Oaks, editor (business); Tracy Behar, managing editor and special projects editor (illustrated books, consumer reference, health); Charles Conrad, vice president and executive editor (general nonfiction). Broadway publishes general interest nonfiction and fiction for adults. Publishes hardcover and trade paperback originals and reprints.

• This publisher accepts agented submissions only.

Nonfiction: General interest adult books. Subjects include biography/memoirs, business, child care/parenting, cookbooks, current affairs, diet/nutrition, health, history, illustrated books, New Age/spirituality, money/finance, politics, popular culture, psychology, women's issues/studies, multicultural studies, gay and lesbian, sex/erotica, consumer reference, golf. Agented submissions only.

Recent Nonfiction Title(s): *The Fourth Turning*, by William Strauss and Neil Howe.

Fiction: Publishes commercial literary fiction.

Recent Fiction Title(s): *A Face at the Window*, by Dennis McFarland.

BROOKLINE BOOKS, P.O. Box 1047, Cambridge MA 02238. (617)868-0360. Fax: (617)868-1772. E-mail: brooklin ebks@delphi.com. Website: http://people.delphi.com/brooklinebks. **Acquisitions:** Milt Budoff, editor. "Brookline publishes books for parents, families and professionals whose lives were affected by disabilities, and the need for special education." Publishes trade and professional paperback originals and reprints. Publishes 8-12 titles/year. Receives 50-100 queries and 30-50 mss/year. 30% of books from first-time authors; majority from unagented writers. Pays 10-15% royalty on wholesale price. Publishes book 8 months after acceptance of ms. Accepts simultaneous submissions. Reports in 1 month on queries, 2 months on proposals and mss. Book catalog and ms guidelines free.

Imprint(s): Lumen Editions (Sadi Ranson, editor, trade fiction and nonfiction).

• Brookline has published authors such as Hans Koning, Nadia Tesich and Steven Crower.

Nonfiction: Reference, technical, textbook, professional. Subjects include child guidance/parenting, education, health/medicine, language/literature, psychology, translation, special needs/disabilities. Query or submit outline, 3 sample chapters and SASE. Reviews artwork/photos as part of ms package. Send photocopies.

Recent Nonfiction Title(s): *New Voices*, by G. Dybwad and H. Bercani (self-advocacy among persons with mental retardation).

Fiction: First time translations of Latin American, European and Asian literary fiction and nonfiction. Query or submit synopsis, 3 sample chapters and SASE.

Recent Fiction Title(s): *Urban Oracles*, by Mayra Santos-Febres (stories of lives of Puerto Rican women).

Recent Poetry Title(s): *Dialogues for Left and Right Hand*, by Steven Crower.

BRYANT & DILLON PUBLISHERS, INC., P.O. Box 39, Orange NJ 07050. (201)675-5668. Fax: (201)675-8443). **Acquisitions:** Gerri Dillon. "We publish books that speak to an African-American audience." Publishes hardcover and trade paperback originals. Publishes 8-10 titles/year. Receives 800 queries and 1,200 mss/year. 100% of books from first-time authors; 90% from unagented writers. Pays 6-10% royalty on retail price. Publishes book 1 year after acceptance of ms. Accepts simultaneous submissions. Reports in 3 months on proposals.

Nonfiction: Biography, how-to, self-help. Subjects include Black studies, business/economics, education, ethnic, film, government/politics, history, language/literature, money/finance, women's issues/studies. "Must be on subjects of interest to African-Americans." Submit cover letter, author's information sheet, marketing information, outline and 3 sample chapters with SASE (envelope large enough for contents sent).

Recent Nonfiction Title(s): *Breaking the Glass Ceiling*, by Anthony Stith (business); *A Stranger in My Bed*, by Kevin Luttery (relationships).

Fiction: Ethnic, mystery, romance, suspense. Main characters must be African-American/or African-American themes. Submit cover letter, author's information sheet, marketing information, synopsis and 3 sample chapters with SASE (envelope large enough for contenst sent).

Recent Fiction Title(s): *Forever Mine*, by Kathryn Williams-Platt (novel); *Ebony Blood*, by Claire Luna (novel).

Tips: "No faxes or phone calls, please!" Audience is majority African-American. No poetry or children's books.

BUCKNELL UNIVERSITY PRESS, Lewisburg PA 17837. (717)524-3674. Fax: (717)524-3797. E-mail: clingham@bucknell.edu. **Acquisitions:** Greg Clingham, director. Estab. 1969. "In all fields, our criterion is scholarly presentation; manuscripts must be addressed to the scholarly community." Publishes hardcover originals. Publishes 25 titles/year. Receives 150 inquiries and submissions/year. 20% of books from first-time authors; 99% from unagented writers. Pays royalty. Publishes accepted works within 2 years of delivery of finished ms. Reports in 1 month on queries. *Writer's Market* recommends allowing 2 months for reply. Book catalog free.

Nonfiction: Subjects include scholarly art history, history, literary criticism, music, philosophy, political science, psychology, religion, sociology. Query.

Recent Nonfiction Title(s): *The Play in the Mirror: Lacanian Perspectives on Spanish Baroque Theater*, by Matthew D. Stroud.

Tips: "An original work of high-quality scholarship has the best chance. We publish for the scholarly community."

‡BULFINCH PRESS, Imprint of Little, Brown & Co., 34 Beacon St., Boston MA 02108. (617)227-0730. Fax: (617)227-0790. Website: http://www.littlebrown.com. *Acquisitions:* Melissa Lotfy, department assistant. "Bulfinch Press publishes large format art books using the finest quality reproduction." Publishes hardcover and trade paperback originals. Publishes 60-70 titles/year. Receives 500 queries/year. Pays variable royalty on wholesale price. Advance varies.

Publishes book 18 months after acceptance of ms. Accepts simultaneous submissions. Reports in 2 months on proposals.
Nonfiction: Coffee table book, gift book, illustrated book. Subjects include art/architecture, gardening, photography. Query with outline, 1 sample chapter and SASE. Reviews artwork as part of ms package. Send color photocopies or laser prints.
Recent Nonfiction Title(s): *Lillian Bassman* (fashion photography); *Colefax & Fowlers Interior Inspirations*, by Roger Banks-Pye and Nonie Nieseward (interior decorating).

THE BUREAU FOR AT-RISK YOUTH, P.O. Box 760, Plainview NY 11803-0760. **Acquisitions:** Sally Germain, editor-in-chief. Publishes booklets, pamphlets, curriculum and other educational materials for educators, parents, mental health and juvenile justice professionals. Publishes 25-50 titles/year. Receives 50-100 queries and 30-50 mss/year. Most books from first-time authors; 100% from unagented writers. Pays royalty of 10% maximum on selling price. Advance varies. Publication 6 months after acceptance of ms. Accepts simultaneous submissions. Reports on queries, proposals, mss in 1-8 months. Book catalog free if appropriate after communication with author.
Nonfiction: Educational materials for parents, educators and other professionals who work with youth. Subjects include child guidance/parenting, education. "The materials we publish are curriculum, book series or how-to oriented pieces tailored to our audience. They are generally not single book titles and are rarely book length." Query.
Recent Nonfiction Title(s): *C.O.L.O.R.S: Crossing Over Lines of Racial Stereotypes*, by Michelle Jackson, Ph.D. (race relations curriculum); *Speaking of Sex*, by Dale Zevin, M.A. (pamphlet series on sexuality).
Tips: "Publications are sold exclusively through direct mail catalog. We do not publish book-length pieces. Writers whose expertise is appropriate to our customers should send query or proposal since we tailor everything very specifically to meet our audience's needs."

‡**BUSINESS & LEGAL REPORTS, INC.**, 39 Academy St., Madison CT 06443-1513. (203)245-7448. Fax: (203)245-2559. **Acquisitions:** Daniel Schwartz, editor-in-chief. Estab. 1978. Business & Legal Reports publishes administrative and management titles for business. Publishes loose leaf and soft cover originals. Averages 20 titles/year. Receives 100 submissions/year. Pays 2½-5% royalty on retail price, or makes outright purchase for $1,000-5,000. Offers $3,000 average advance. Publishes book an average of 6 months after acceptance. Accepts simultaneous submissions. Book catalog free.
Nonfiction: Reference. Subjects include human resources, management, safety, environmental management. Query.
   ● Publisher reports a special interest in "how-to" compliance guides.

BUSINESS McGRAW-HILL, The McGraw Hill Companies, 11 W. 19th St., New York NY 10011. (212)337-4098. Fax: (212)337-5999. Publisher: Philip Ruppel. **Acquisitions:** Betsy Brown, senior editor; Nancy Caraccilo, editorial assistant; Robin Gardner, editorial assistant. "McGraw Hill's business division is the world's largest business publisher, offering nonfiction trade and paperback originals in more than ten areas, including management, sales and marketing, careers, self-help, training, finance, personal finance and manufacturing operations." Publishes 100 titles/year. Receives 1,200 queries and 1,200 mss/year. 30% of books from first-time authors; 60% from unagented writers. Pays 5-17% royalty on net price. Offers $1,000-100,000 advance. Publishes book 6 months after acceptance of ms. Accepts simultaneous submissions. Reports in 3 months. Book catalog and ms guidelines free on request with SASE.
Nonfiction: How-to, reference, self-help, technical. Subjects include business/economics, government/politics, money/finance. "Current, up-to-date, original ideas are needed. Good self-promotion is key." Submit proposal package, including outline, table of contents, concept.
Recent Nonfiction Title(s): *Informed Consent*, by John Byrne (general interest); *Business Speak*, by Suzette Haden Elgin; *The Dark Side of Making Money*, by Gene Marcial.

BUTTERWORTH-HEINEMANN, Division of Reed-Elsevier, 313 Washington St., Newton MA 02158-1626. Publishing Director: Karen Speerstra. **Acquisitions:** Karen Speerstra, business (books on transforming business); Marie Lee, senior editor (Focal Press); Mike Cash, publisher (Digital Press); Susan Pioli, publishing director (Medical). "Butterworth-Heinemann has been serving professionals and students for over five decades. We remain committed to publishing materials that forge ahead of rapidly changing technology and reinforce the highest professional standards. Our goal is to give you the competitive advantage in this rapidly changing digital age." Publishes hardcover and trade paperback originals. Publishes 150 titles/year. Each imprint publishes 25-30 titles/year. 25% of books from first-time authors; 95% from unagented writers. Pays 10-12% royalty on wholesale price. Offers modest advance. Publishes book 9 months after acceptance of ms. Reports in 1 month on proposals. Book catalog and ms guidelines free.
Imprint(s): Focal Press, International Digital Press, **Butterworth-Heinemann**, Medical.
Nonfiction: How-to (in our selected areas), reference, technical, textbook. Subjects include business, computers/electronics, health/medicine, photography, security/criminal justice, audio-video broadcast, communication technology. "We publish technical professional and academic books; no fiction." Submit outline, 1-2 sample chapters, competing books and how yours is different/better with SASE. Reviews artwork/photos as part of ms package. Send photocopies.

‡**C Q BOOKS**, Imprint of CQ, Inc., 1414 22nd St. NW, Washington DC 20037. (202)887-8645. Fax: (202)822-6583. Website: http://books.cq.com. **Acquisitions:** Shana Wagger, acquisitions editor. C Q Books publishes authoritative reference works on American and international government and politics. Publishes 15-20 hardcover and paperback titles/year. 95% of books from unagented writers. Pays royalty or makes work-for-hire arrangements. Accepts simultaneous submissions. Reports in 3 months. Book catalog free.

Nonfiction: All types of reference works on US and international government, politics, and public policies. Submit proposal, outline and bio.

C Q INC., Imprint of Congressional Quarterly, Inc., 1414 22nd St. NW, Washington DC 20037. (202)887-8640 or 8645. Fax: (202)822-6583. E-mail: swagger@cqalert.com or dtarr@cqalert.com. **Acquisitions:** David Tarr, Shana Wagger, acquisitions editors. Publishes 50-70 hardcover and paperback titles/year. 95% of books from unagented writers. Pays royalties on net receipts. Sometimes offers advance. Publishes book an average of 1 year after acceptance. Accepts simultaneous submissions. Reports in 3 months. Book catalog free.
Nonfiction: Reference books, information directories on federal and state governments, national elections, international/state politics and governmental issues. Submit prospectus, writing sample and cv.
Tips: "Our books present important information on American government and politics, and related issues, with careful attention to accuracy, thoroughness and readability."

C Q PRESS, Imprint of CQ, Inc., 1414 22nd St. NW, Washington DC 20037. (202)887-8641. Fax: (202)822-6583. Website: http://books.cq.com. **Acquisitions:** Brenda Carter, acquisitions editor. C Q Press seeks "to educate the public by publishing authoritative works on American and international government and politics." Publishes 20-30 hardcover and paperback titles/year. 95% of books from unagented writers. Pays standard college royalty on wholesale price. Offers college text advance. Publishes book 6 months after acceptance of final ms. Accepts simultaneous submissions. Reports in 3 months. Book catalog free.
   • C Q Press has published such authors as Marcy Kaptur, Seymour Martin Lipset and the Supreme Court Historical Society.
Nonfiction: All levels of college political science texts. "We are interested in American government, public administration, comparative government, and international relations." Submit proposal, outline and bio.
Recent Nonfiction Title(s): *Guide to the Presidency*, edited by Nelson (government/law); *Encyclopedia of Democracy*, (four-volume set of essays on democracy).

CADDO GAP PRESS, 317 S. Division St., Suite 2, Ann Arbor MI 48104. (313)662-0886. Fax: (313)668-7672. E-mail: caddogap@aol.com. **Acquisitions:** Alan H. Jones, publisher. Caddo Gap publishes works on education for teachers. Estab. 1989. Publishes trade paperback originals and educational journals and newsletters. Publishes 4 titles/year. Receives 20 queries and 10 mss/year. 50% of books from first-time authors; 100% from unagented writers. Pays 10% royalty on wholesale price. Publishes book 1 year after acceptance of ms. Accepts simultaneous submissions. Reports in 2 months on proposals.
Nonfiction: Subjects limited to teacher education, social foundations of education, and multicultural education. Query.
Recent Nonfiction Title(s): *Schoolmarms: Women in America's Schools*, by Edwina Walsh.

CAMBRIDGE EDUCATIONAL, P.O. Box 2153, Charleston WV 25328-2153. (800)468-4227. Fax: (304)744-9351. Subsidiaries include: Cambridge Parenting and Cambridge Job Search. President: Edward T. Gardner, Ph.D. **Acquisitions:** Amy Pauley, managing editor. Estab. 1981. Publishes supplemental educational products. "We are known in the education industry for guidance-related and career search programs." Publishes 30-40 titles/year. Receives 200 submissions/year. 20% of books from first-time authors; 90% from unagented writers. Makes outright purchase of $1,500-4,000. Occasional royalty arrangement. Publishes book 8 months after acceptance. Accepts simultaneous submissions.
   • Publisher reports a greater focus on social studies and science.
Nonfiction: Subjects include child guidance/parenting, cooking/foods/nutrition, education, health/medicine, money/finance, career guidance, social studies and science. "We are looking for scriptwriters in the same subject areas and age group. We only publish books written for young adults and primarily sold to libraries, schools, etc. We do not seek books targeted to adults or written at high readability levels." Query or submit outline/synopsis and sample chapters. Reviews artwork/photos as part of ms package. No response unless interested.
Recent Nonfiction Title(s): *Job Search Tactics*; *The X-Offenders Job Search Companion*.
Tips: "We encourage the submission of high-quality books on timely topics written for young adult audiences at moderate to low readability levels. Call and request a copy of all our current catalogs, talk to the management about what is timely in the areas you wish to write on, thoroughly research the topic, and write a manuscript that will be read by young adults without being overly technical. Low to moderate readibility yet entertaining, informative and accurate."

CAMBRIDGE UNIVERSITY PRESS, 40 W. 20th St., New York NY 10011-4211. **Acquisitions Editors:** Frank Smith (history, social sciences); Mary Vaughn (English as second language); Deborah Goldblatt (English as a second language); Sidney Landau (reference); Lauren Cowles (mathematics, computer science); Scott Parris (economics); Julia Hough (developmental and social psychology, cognitive science); Alex Holzman (politics, history of science); Beatrice Rehl (fine arts, film studies); Robin Smith (life sciences); Catherine Flack (earth sciences); Alan Harvey, (applied mathematics); Florence Padgett, (engineering, materials science); Terence Moore (philosophy); Ann Sandow (American literature, Latin American literature); Elizabeth Neal (sociology, East Asian studies). Estab. 1534. "Cambridge University Press publishes scholarly and general interest hardcover and paperback nonfiction originals on a wide range of subjects for a general and academic readership." Publishes 1,300 titles/year. Receives 1,000 submissions annually. 50% of books from first-time authors; 99% from unagented writers. Pays 10% royalty on receipts; 8% on paperbacks. Publishes book an average of 1 year after acceptance. Reports in 4 months.
Nonfiction: Anthropology, archeology, economics, life sciences, medicine, mathematics, psychology, physics, art his-

tory, upper-level textbooks, academic trade, scholarly monographs, biography, history, and music. Looking for academic excellence in all work submitted. Query. Reviews artwork/photos.

CAMELOT BOOKS, Imprint of Avon Books, Division of The Hearst Corp., 1350 Avenue of the Americas, New York NY 10019. (212)261-6817. Fax: (212)261-6895. **Acquisitions**: Elise Howard, editorial director; Stephanie Seigel, assistant editor. Camelot publishes fiction for children ages 8-12. Publishes paperback originals and reprints. Publishes 80-100 titles/year. Pays 6-8% royalty on retail price. Offers $2,000 minimum advance. Publishes book 2 years after acceptance. Book catalog and ms guidelines for 8×10 SAE with 5 first-class stamps.
Imprint(s): Avon Flare (for ages 12 and up).
Fiction: Subjects include adventure, humor, juvenile (Camelot, 8-12) mainstream, mystery, ("very selective with mystery"), suspense. Avon does not publish picture books. Submit query letter *only*. Reports back in 3 months.
Recent Fiction Title(s): *Honus & Me*, by Dan Gutman; *Christie & Company*, by Katherine Hall Page (mystery).

CAMINO BOOKS, INC., P.O. Box 59026, Philadelphia PA 19102. (215)732-2491. **Acquisitions**: E. Jutkowitz, publisher. Estab. 1987. Camino publishes nonfiction of regional interest to the Mid-Atlantic states. Publishes hardcover and trade paperback originals. Publishes 8 titles/year. Receives 500 submissions/year. 20% of books from first-time authors. Pays 6-12% royalty on net price. Offers $1,000 average advance. Publishes book 1 year after acceptance. Reports in 2 weeks on queries. *Writer's Market* recommends allowing 2 months for reply.
Nonfiction: Biography, cookbook, how-to, juvenile. Subjects include agriculture/horticulture, Americana, art/architecture, child guidance/parenting, cooking/foods/nutrition, ethnic, gardening, government/politics, history, regional, travel. Query with outline/synopsis and sample chapters with SASE.
Tips: "The books must be of interest to readers in the Middle Atlantic states, or they should have a clearly defined niche, such as cookbooks."

‡CANDLEWICK PRESS, Subsidiary of Walker Books Ltd. (London), 2067 Massachusetts Ave., Cambridge MA 02140. (617)661-3330. Fax: (617)661-0565. **Acquisitions:** Liz Bicknell, editor-in-chief (nonfiction/fiction); Mary Lee Donovan, senior editor (nonfiction/fiction); Gale Pryor, editor (nonfiction/fiction); Susan Halperin, editor (fiction for ya, middle grades); Amy Ehrlich, consulting editor (picture books). Candlewick Press publishes high-quality illustrated children's books for ages infant through young adult. "We are a truly child-centered publisher." Estab. 1991. Publishes hardcover originals, trade paperback originals and reprints. Publishes 200 titles/year. Receives 1,000 queries and 1,000 mss/year. 5% of books from first-time authors; 20% from unagented writers. Pays 10% royalty on retail price. Advance varies. Publishes book 3 years after acceptance of ms for illustrated books, 1 year for others. Accepts simultaneous submissions, if so noted. Reports in 10 weeks on mss.
• Candlewick Press accepts agented submissions only.
Nonfiction: Children's/juvenile. "Good writing is essential; specific topics are less important than strong, clear writing." Agented submissions only.
Recent Nonfiction Title(s): *Kennedy Assassinated*, by Wilborn Hampton (history); *The Explorer's News* (history in newspaper format).
Fiction: Juvenile. Agented submissions only.
Recent Fiction Title(s): *What Do Fish Have To Do With Anything*, by Avi; *Lone Wolf*, by Kristine Franklin.
Poetry: Looking for poetry for middle grades. Submit 1-10 sample poems.
Recent Poetry Title(s): *My Very First Mother Goose*, edited by Iona Opie.

C&T PUBLISHING, 5021 Blum Rd., #1, Martinez CA 94553. (510)370-9600. Fax: (510)370-2499. E-mail: ctinfo@ct pub.com. Website: http://www.ctpub.com. **Acquisitions:** Liz Aneloski and Barb Kuhn, editors. Estab. 1983. "We want to publish well-written, beautifully designed books that appeal to our projected audience." Publishes hardcover and trade paperback originals. Publishes 12-14 titles/year. Receives 60 submissions/year. 10% of books from first-time authors; 100% from unagented writers. Pays 5-10% royalty on retail price. Offers $1,000 average advance. Accepts simultaneous submissions. Reports in 2 months. Free book catalog and proposal guidelines.
• C&T has published such authors as Judith Baker Montano, Harriet Hargrave, Joen Wolfrom, Elly Sienkiewicz.
Nonfiction: Quilting books, primarily how-to, occasional quilt picture books, children's books relating to quilting, quilt-related crafts, wearable art, needlework, fiber and surface embellishments, other books relating to fabric crafting. "Please call or write for proposal guidelines."
Recent Nonfiction Title(s): *Say It With Quilts*, by Diana McClun and Laura Nownes; *Anatomy of a Doll*, by Susanna Oroyan; *Art & Inspirations,* by Ruth B. McDowell.
Tips: "In our industry, we find that how-to books have the longest selling life. Quiltmakers, sewing enthusiasts, needle artists and fiber artists are our audience."

CARADIUM PUBLISHING, Division of I.L.I, 2503 Del Prado Blvd S., #435, Cape Coral FL 33904. **Acquisitions:** Troy Dunn, product evaluation. Estab. 1989. "We want to discover unknown experts in fields that are of interest to business owners and entrepreneurs." Publishes hardcover, trade and mass market paperback originals. Publishes 15-20 titles/year. Receives 300 queries and 250 mss/year. 50% of books from first-time authors; 90% from unagented writers. Pays 15-20% royalty on retail price or makes outright purchase of $100 minimum. Offers $0-5,000 advance. Publishes book 6 months after acceptance of ms. Accepts simultaneous submissions. Does not return submissions; mss remain on file or destroyed. Reports on queries in 2 months.

Nonfiction: Business related: how-to, reference, self-help. Subjects include business/economics (motivation and how-to), money/finance. "We specialize in infomercials for our products." Query with outline and 3 sample chapters. Reviews artwork/photos as part of ms package. Send photocopies.
Recent Nonfiction Title(s): *The Locator*, by Klunder/Dunn (missing persons locating).
Tips: "Know the market you want to reach statistically and be creative in your submissions. We are seeking self-help books with action plans in them, not theory or story telling. How-to manuscripts, we consider *gold* while fluffy, pointless, motivational books leave us cold."

CARDOZA PUBLISHING, 132 Hastings St., Brooklyn NY 11235. (718)743-5229. **Acquisitions:** Rose Swann, acquisitions editor. Publishes 175 titles/year. Receives 175 queries and 70 mss/year. 50% of books from first-time authors; 90% from unagented writers. Pays 5% royalty on retail price. Offers $500-2,000 advance. Publishes book 6 months after acceptance of ms. Accepts simultaneous submissions. Reports in 2 months on queries.
Imprint(s): Gambling Research Institute and Word Reference Library. Publishes trade paperback originals, mass market paperback originals and reprints.
Nonfiction: How-to, reference. Subjects include gaming, gambling, health/fitness, publishing, reference/word, travel. "The world's foremost publisher of gaming and gambling books is expanding into how-to books by qualified and knowledgeable writers. We're also actively seeking travel guides for our sister company Open Road Publishing and multimedia and software titles on all subjects for our sister company, Cardoza Entertainment." Submit outline, table of contents and 2 sample chapters.
Recent Nonfiction Title(s): *Silberstang's Encyclopedia of Games & Gambling*, by Edwin Silberstang.
Tips: "The best manuscripts target the audience and appeal to readers in clear, easy-to-read writing."

‡**THE CAREER PRESS, INC.**, Box 687, 3 Tice Rd., Franklin Lakes NJ 07417. (201)848-0310. Fax: (201)848-1727. **Acquisitions:** Betsy Sheldon, editor-in-chief. Career Press publishes primarily paperback and some hardcover nonfiction originals in the areas of job hunting and career improvement, including reference and education; as well as management philosophy titles for a small business and management audience. Career Press also offers a line of personal finance titles for a general readership. Publishes 50 titles/year. Receives 100 queries and 200 mss/year. 50% of books from first-time authors; 50% from unagented writers. Pays royalty on retail price. Publishes book 6 months after acceptance of ms. Accepts simlultaneous submissions. Reports in 2 months on queries, 3 months on mss. Book catalog and ms guidelines free.
Nonfiction: Coffee table book, how-to, reference, self-help. Subjects include business/economics, money/finance, recreation, financial planning/careers. "Look through our catalog; become familiar with our publications. We like to select authors who are specialists on their topic." Query with outline, 1-2 sample chapters and SASE.
Recent Nonfiction Title(s): *Every Woman's Guide to Financial Security*, by Ann Peterson and Stephen Rosenberg (financial planning); *Taking Your Business Global*, by James Wilfong and Toni Seger (business); *50 Fabulous Places to Retire in America*, by Ken Stern (reference).

CAREER PUBLISHING, INC., P.O. Box 5486, Orange CA 92863-5486. (714)771-5155. Fax: (714)532-0180. **Acquisitions:** Marilyn M. Martin, editor-in-chief. Career publishes educational, career-related texts and software for vocational schools and community colleges. Publishes paperback originals and software. Publishes 6-20 titles/year. Receives 300 submissions/year. 80% of books from first-time authors; 90% of books from unagented writers. Average print order for a first book is 3,000-10,000. Pays 10% royalty on actual amount received. No advance. Publishes book 1 year after acceptance. Accepts simultaneous submissions (if informed of names of others to whom submissions have been sent). Reports in 2 months. Book catalog and ms guidelines for 9 × 12 SAE with 2 first-class stamps.
Nonfiction: Software related to work experience, allied health and medical, and transportation (trucking business, etc.) "Textbooks should provide core upon which class curriculum can be based: textbook, workbook or kit with 'hands-on' activities and exercises, and teacher's guide. Should incorporate modern and effective teaching techniques. Should lead to a job objective. We also publish support materials for existing courses and are open to unique, marketable ideas with schools (secondary and post secondary) in mind. Reading level should be controlled appropriately—usually 7th-10th grade equivalent for vocational school and community college level courses. Any sign of sexism or racism will disqualify the work. No career awareness masquerading as career training." Submit outline, 2 sample chapters and table of contents. Reviews artwork/photos as part of ms package. If material is to be returned, enclose SAE and return postage.
Recent Nonfiction Title(s): *Become a 911 Dispatcher: Your Personal Career Guide*, by Capt. Richard Callen.
Tips: "Authors should be aware of vocational/career areas with inadequate or no training textbooks and submit ideas and samples to fill the gap. Trends in book publishing that freelance writers should be aware of include education—especially for microcomputers."

CAROL PUBLISHING, 120 Enterprise Ave., Secaucus NJ 07094. (201)866-0490. Fax: (201)866-8159. Publisher: Steven Schragis. **Acquisitions:** Beth Derochea, editorial assistant; Hillel Black (Birch Lane Press); Allen Wilson (Lyle Stuart); Jim Ellison (University Books, Citadel Press); Michael Lewis (Citadel Press); Lisa Kaufman (Birch Lane Press, Citadel Press). Carol has a reputation for publishing unauthorized celebrity biographies for a general audience. Publishes hardcover originals, trade paperback originals and mass market paperback reprints. Publishes 180 titles/year. Receives 2,000 submissions/year. 10% of books from first-time authors; 10% from unagented writers. Pays 5-15% royalty on retail price. Offers $3,000-50,000 advance. Publishes book 1 year after acceptance. Accepts simultaneous submissions. Reports in 2 months.

Imprint(s): Birch Lane Press; Citadel Press; Lyle Stuart.
Nonfiction: Biography, cookbook, gift book, how-to, humor, self-help. Subjects include Americana, animals, art/architecture, business/economics, computers/electronics, cooking/foods/nutrition, education ethnic, film, gay/lesbian, government/politics, health/medicine, history, hobbies, language/literature, military/war, money/finance, music/dance, nature/environment, philosophy, psychology, recreation, regional, science, sports, travel, women's issues/studies. Submit outline/synopsis, sample chapters and SASE. Reviews artwork as part of ms package. Send photocopies.
Recent Nonfiction Title(s): *Wizard: Biography of N. Tesla*, by Marc J. Seifer; *The Mad King: Biography of Ludwig II*, by Greg King; *The Films of Tom Hanks*, by L. Pfeiffer and M. Lewis.
Fiction: Not considering any fiction.

CAROLRHODA BOOKS, INC., Imprint of Lerner Publications Co., 241 First Ave. N., Minneapolis MN 55401. (612)332-3344. Fax: (612)332-7615. **Acquisitions:** Rebecca Poole, submissions editor. Estab. 1969. Carolrhoda Books seeks creative children's nonfiction and historical fiction with unique and well-developed ideas and angles. Publishes hardcover originals. Publishes 50-60 titles/year. Receives 2,000 submissions/year. 10% of books from first-time authors; 90% from unagented writers. Pays royalty on wholesale price, makes outright purchase or negotiates payments of advance against royalty. Advance varies. Publishes book 18 months after acceptance. Accepts simultaneous submissions. Include SASE for return of ms. Reports in 3 months on queries, 5 months on mss. Book catalog and ms guidelines for 9×12 SASE with $3 in postage. No phone calls.
Nonfiction: Children's/juvenile (pre-kindergarten to 3rd grade). Subjects include biography, ethnic, nature/environment, science, sports. "We are always interested in adding to our biography series. Also seeking books on math and hard sciences." Query with SASE. Reviews artwork/photos as part of ms package. Send photocopies.
Recent Nonfiction Title(s): *Up in the Air: The Story of Bessie Coleman*, by Philip S. Hart (biography); *Bridges Connect*, by Lee Sullivan Hill (photoessay); *The Sunflower Family*, by Cherie Winner (natural science).
Fiction: Juvenile, historical, picture books. "We continue to add fiction for middle grades and 1-2 picture books per year. Not looking for folktales or anthropomorphic animal stories." Query with SASE or send complete ms for picture books.
Recent Fiction Title(s): *Come Morning*, by Leslie Davis Guccione (historical); *Fire in the Sky*, by Candice Ransom (historical); *Fire at the Triangle Factory*, by Holly Littlefield (easy reader historical).
Tips: "Our audience consists of children ages four to eleven. We publish very few picture books. Nonfiction science topics, particularly nature, do well for us, as do biographies, photo essays, and easy readers. We prefer manuscripts that can fit into one of our series. Spend time developing your idea in a unique way or from a unique angle; avoid trite, hackneyed plots and ideas."

‡CARROLL & GRAF PUBLISHERS INC., 19 W. 21st St., Suite 601, New York NY 10010. (212)889-8772. Fax: (212)545-7909. **Acquisitions:** Kent Carroll, publisher/executive editor. Estab. 1983. "Carroll and Graf Publishers offers quality hardcover, trade paperback, and mass market fiction (literary, popular, mystery and crime) and nonfiction (biography, history, self-help and current events) for a general readership. Carroll and Graf is one of the few remaining independent trade publishers and is therefore able to publish successfully and work with first-time authors and novelists." Publishes hardcover and trade paperback originals. Publishes 120 titles/year. 10% of books from first-time authors. Pays 10-15% royalty on retail price for hardcover, 15% for paperback. Offers $5,000-100,000 advance. Publishes book 9 months after acceptance of ms. Accepts simultaneous submissions, but prefers not to. Reports in 1 month on queries. Book catalog free.
   • Carroll & Graf accepts agented submissions only.
Nonfiction: Biography, reference, self-help. Subjects include business/economics, history, contemporary culture, true crime. Publish general trade listings; are interested in developing long term relations with authors. Query.
Recent Nonfiction Title(s): *Kurt Cobain*, by Christopher Sanford (biography).
Fiction: Erotica, literary, mystery, science fiction, suspense, thriller. Agented submissions only.
Recent Fiction Title(s): *Every Man for Himself*, by Beryl Bainbridge.

‡CARSTENS PUBLICATIONS, INC., Hobby Book Division, P.O. Box 700, Newton NJ 07860-0700. (201)383-3355. Fax: (204)383-4064. **Acquisitions:** Harold H. Carstens, publisher. Estab. 1933. Carstens specializes in books about railroads and model railroads and airplanes for hobbyists. Publishes paperback originals. Averages 8 titles/year. 100% of books from unagented writers. Pays 10% royalty on retail price. Offers advance. Publishes book 1 year after acceptance. *Writer's Market* recommends allowing 2 months for reply. Book catalog for SASE.
Nonfiction: Model railroading, toy trains, model aviation, railroads and model hobbies. "We have scheduled or planned titles on several railroads as well as model railroad and model airplane books. Authors must know their field intimately because our readers are active modelers. Our railroad books presently are primarily photographic essays on specific railroads. Writers cannot write about somebody else's hobby with authority. If they do, we can't use them." Query. Reviews artwork/photos as part of ms package.
Recent Nonfiction Title(s): *Electrical Handbook for Model Railroads*, by P. Mallery and *Track Design*, by H. Carstens (model railroading); *The Final Years of the NYO&W*, by J. Krause (railroads).
Tips: "We need lots of good photos. Material must be in model, hobby, railroad and transportation field only."

‡CARTWHEEL BOOKS, Imprint of Scholastic, Inc., 555 Broadway, New York NY 10012. (212)343-6100. Fax: (212)343-4444. Website: http://www.scholastic.com. **Acquisitions:** Bernette Ford, vice president/editorial director. Estab. 1991. "Cartwheel Books publishes innovative books for children, ages 3-9. We are looking for 'novelties' that are books first, play objects second. Even without its gimmick, a Cartwheel Book should stand alone as a valid piece of children's literature." Publishes hardcover originals. Publishes 85-100 titles/year. Receives 250 queries/year; 1,200 mss/year. 1% of books from first-time authors; 50% from unagented writers. Pays royalty on retail price. Offers advance. Publishes book 2 years after acceptance of ms. Accepts simultaneous submissions. Reports in 2 months on queries; 3 months on proposals; 6 months on mss/ Book catalog for 9 × 12 SAE. Manuscript guidelines free.

Nonfiction: Children's/juvenile. Subjects include animals, history, music/dance, nature/environment, recreation, science, sports. "Cartwheel Books publishes for the very young, therefore nonfiction should be written in a manner that is accessible to preschoolers through 2nd grade. Often writers choose topics that are too narrow or 'special' and do not appeal to the mass market. Also, the text and vocabulary are frequently too difficult for our young audience." Agented submissions or previously published authors only. Reviews artwork/photos as part of ms package.

Recent Nonfiction Title(s): *K is for Kwanzaa*, by Juwanda G. Ford (picture book); *Peek-A-Boo!*, by Roberta Grobel Intrater (photographs).

Fiction: Fantasy, humor, juvenile, mystery, picture books, science fiction. "Again, the subject should have mass market appeal for very young children. Humor can be helpful, but not necessary. Mistakes writers make are a reading level that is too difficult, a topic of no interest or too narrow, or manuscripts that are too long." Agented submissions or previously published authors only.

Recent Fiction Title(s): *Little Bill (series)*, by Bill Cosby (picture book); *Dinofours* (series), by Steve Metzger (picture book); *The Haunted House*, by Fiona Conboy (3-D puzzle storybook).

Poetry: Agented submissions or previously published authors only.

Recent Poetry Title(s): *Boo Who? A Spooky Lift-the-Flap Book*, by Joan Holub; *Pumpkin Faces*, by Emma Rose (glow in the dark book).

Tips: Audience is young children, ages 3-9. "Know what types of books the publisher does. Some manuscripts that don't work for one house may be perfect for another. Check out bookstores or catalogs to see where your writing would 'fit' best."

CATBIRD PRESS, 16 Windsor Rd., North Haven CT 06473-3015. (203)230-2391. E-mail: catbird@pipeline.com. **Acquisitions:** Robert Wechsler, publisher. Estab. 1987. Catbird publishes sophisticated, humorous, literary fiction and nonfiction with fresh styles and approaches. Publishes hardcover and trade paperback originals and trade paperback reprints. Publishes 4-5 titles/year. Receives 1,000 submissions/year. 5% of books from first-time authors. 100% from unagented writers. Pays 2½-10% royalty on retail price. Offers $2,000 average advance. Publishes book 1 year after acceptance. Accepts simultaneous submissions, if so noted. Reports in 1 month on queries if SASE is included. *Writer's Market* recommends allowing 2 months for reply. Book catalog free. Manuscript guidelines for #10 SASE.

Imprint(s): Garrigue Books (Czech works in translation).

● Catbird has published such authors as Karel Capek, Daniel R. White and Stephen Longstreet.

Nonfiction: Humor, law, general. "We are looking for up-market prose humorists. No joke or other small gift books. We are also interested in very well-written general nonfiction that takes fresh, sophisticated approaches." Submit outline, sample chapters and SASE.

Recent Nonfiction Title(s): *The Breath of an Unfee'd Lawyer—Shakespeare on Lawyers and the Law*, edited by Edward J. Bander.

Fiction: Humor, literary. translations. "We are looking for writers of well-written literature who have a comic vision, take a fresh approach, and have a fresh, sophisticated style. No genre, wacky, or derivative mainstream fiction." Submit outline/synopsis, sample chapter and SASE.

Recent Fiction Title(s): *The Third Lion*, by Floyd Kemske (novel); *It Came with the House*, by Jeffrey Shaffer (humorous stories); *The Royalscope Fe-As-Ko*, by Randall Beth Platt.

Tips: "First of all, we want writers, not books. Second, we only are interested in writing that is not like what is out there already. The writing should be highly sophisticated, but not obscure; the approach or, better, approaches should be fresh and humorous and ethical rather than moralistic. If a writer is more interested in content than in style, that writer should look elsewhere."

CATHOLIC UNIVERSITY OF AMERICA PRESS, 620 Michigan Ave. NE, Washington DC 20064. (202)319-5052. Fax: (202)319-4985. E-mail: mcgonagle@cua.edu. **Acquisitions:** Dr. David J. McGonagle, director. Estab. 1939. Marketing Manager: Beth Benevides. Publishes 15-20 titles/year. Receives 100 submissions/year. 50% of books from first-time authors; 100% from unagented writers. Average print order for a first book is 750. Pays variable royalty on net receipts. Publishes book 1 year after acceptance. Reports in 3 months. Book catalog for SASE.

Nonfiction: Publishes history, languages and literature, philosophy, religion, church-state relations, political theory. No unrevised doctoral dissertations. Length: 80,000-200,000 words. Query with outline, sample chapter, cv and list of previous publications.

Tips: "Freelancer has best chance of selling us scholarly monographs and works suitable for adoption as supplementary reading material in courses."

CATO INSTITUTE, 1000 Massachusetts Ave. NW, Washington DC 20001. (202)842-0200. Executive Vice President: David Boaz. **Acquisitions:** Tom Palmer, director of special projects. Estab. 1977. "We publish books on public policy issues from a free-market or libertarian perspective." Publishes hardcover originals, trade paperback originals and reprints. Publishes 12 titles/year. Receives 50 submissions/year. 25% of books from first-time authors; 90% from un-

agented writers. Makes outright purchase of $1,000-10,000. Publishes book 9 months after acceptance. Accepts simultaneous submissions. Reports in 3 months. Book catalog free.
Nonfiction: Public policy *only*. Subjects include foreign policy, economics, education, government/politics, health/medicine, monetary policy, sociology. Query.

CAVE BOOKS, 756 Harvard Ave., St. Louis MO 63130-3134. (314)862-7646. **Acquisitions:** Richard Watson, editor. Estab. 1980. "We publish only books on caves, karst, and speleology." Publishes hardcover and trade paperback originals and reprints. Publishes 4 titles/year. Receives 20 queries and 10 mss/year. 75% of books from first-time authors; 100% from unagented writers. Pays 10% royalty on retail price. Publishes book 18 months after acceptance. Accepts simultaneous submissions. Reports in 3 months on mss.
Nonfiction: Biography, technical (science), adventure. Subjects are Americana, animals, anthropology/archaeology, history, nature/environment, photography, recreation, regional, science, sports (cave exploration), travel. Send complete ms. Reviews artwork/photos as part of ms package. Send photocopies.
Recent Nonfiction Title(s): *Caverns Measureless to Man*, by Sheck Exley (memoirs of the world's greatest cave diver).
Fiction: Adventure, historical, literary. "Must be realistic and centrally concerned with cave exploration. No gothic, science fiction, fantasy, romance, mystery or poetry. No novels that are not entirely about caves. The cave and action in the cave must be central, authentic, and realistic." Send complete ms.
Tips: "Our readers are interested only in caves, karst, and speleology. Please do not send manuscripts on other subjects. Query with outline and SAE first."

THE CAXTON PRINTERS, LTD., 312 Main St., Caldwell ID 83605-3299. (208)459-7421. Fax: (208)459-7450. Website: caxtonprinters.com. President: Gordon Gipson. **Acquisitions:** Wayne Cornell, editor. Estab. 1907. "Books to us never can or will be primarily articles of merchandise to be produced as cheaply as possible and to be sold like slabs of bacon or packages of cereal over the counter. If there is anything that is really worthwhile in this mad jumble we call the twentieth century, it should be books." Publishes hardcover and trade paperback originals. Publishes 6-10 titles/year. Receives 250 submissions/year. 50% of books from first-time authors; 60% from unagented writers. Pays royalty. Offers $500-2,000 advance. Publishes book 18 months after acceptance. Accepts simultaneous submissions. Reports in 3 months. Book catalog for 9 × 12 SASE.
Nonfiction: Coffee table, Americana, Western Americana. "We need good Western Americana, especially the Northwest, preferably copiously illustrated with unpublished photos." Query. Reviews artwork/photos as part of ms package.
Recent Nonfiction Title(s): *Traveler's History of Washington*, by Bill Gulick (history/travel); *Hatchet, Hands & Hoe*, by Erica Calkins (heritage gardening/history); *River Tales of Idaho*, by Darcy Williamson (Idaho history/recreation).
Tips: "Audience includes Westerners, students, historians and researchers."

CCC PUBLICATIONS, 9725 Lurline Ave., Chatsworth CA 91311. (818)718-0507. **Acquisitions:** Cliff Carle, editorial director. Estab. 1983. "CCC publishes humor that is 'today' and will appeal to a wide demographic." Publishes trade paperback and mass market paperback originals. Publishes 25-30 titles/year. Receives 400-600 mss/year. 50% of books from first-time authors; 50% of books from unagented writers. Pays 7-12% royalty on wholesale price. Publishes book 6 months after acceptance. Accepts simultaneous submissions. Reports in 3 months. Catalog for 10 × 13 SAE with 2 first-class stamps.
  ● CCC is looking for short, punchy pieces with *lots* of cartoon illustrations. They have published such authors as Jerry King, Ed Strnad and Jan King.
Nonfiction: Humorous how-to/self-help. "We are looking for *original, clever* and *current* humor that is not too limited in audience appeal or that will have a limited shelf life. All of our titles are as marketable five years from now as they are today. No rip-offs of previously published books, or too special interest manuscripts." Query or complete manuscript with SASE. Reviews artwork/photos as part of ms package.
Recent Nonfiction Title(s): *The Better Half*, by Randy Glasberger (marriage humor); *The Little Book of Romantic Lies*, by Bruce T. Smith (relationship humor); *Golfaholics*, by Bob Zahn (golf humor).
Tips: "Humor—we specialize in the subject and have a good reputation with retailers and wholesalers for publishing super-impulse titles. SASE is a must!"

CELESTIAL ARTS, Division of Ten Speed Press, P.O. Box 7123, Berkeley CA 94707. (510)559-1600. Fax: (510)524-1052. Publisher: David Hinds. **Acquisitions**: Veronica Randall, managing editor. Publishes hardcover and trade paperback originals, trade paperback reprints. "Celestial Arts publishes nonfiction for a forward-thinking, open-minded audience interested in psychology, sociology and related topics." Publishes 40 titles/year. Receives 500 queries and 200 mss/year. 30% of books from first-time authors; 10% from unagented writers. Pays 7½-12½ royalty on wholesale price. No advance. Publishes book 6 months after acceptance of ms. Accepts simultaneous submissions. Reports in 6 weeks on queries, 3 months on proposals and mss. Book catalog and ms guidelines free.
Nonfiction: Cookbook, how-to, reference, self-help. Subjects include child guidance/parenting, cooking/foods/nutrition, education, gay/lesbian, health/medicine, New Age, psychology, women's issues/studies. "We specialize in parenting, women's issues, health and family/parenting. On gay/lesbian topics, we publish nonfiction only. And please, no poetry!" Submit proposal package, including: outline, 1-2 sample chapters, author background and SASE. Reviews artwork/photos as part of ms package. Send photocopies.
Recent Nonfiction Title(s): *Raising A Family: Living on Planet Parenthood*, by Don and Jeanne Elium (parenting);

Herbal Medicine Cabinet, by Debra St. Clair (medicine); *Detox Diet*, by Elson Hass (self-help).
Tips: Audience is fairly well-informed, interested in psychology and sociology related topics, open-minded, innovative, forward-thinking. "The most completely thought-out (developed) proposals earn the most consideration."

‡**CENTENNIAL PUBLICATIONS**, 256 Nashua Ct., Grand Junction CO 81503. (970)243-8780. **Acquisitions:** Dick Spurr, publisher. Publishes hardcover and trade paperback originals and reprints. Publishes 4-5 titles/year. Receives 20 queries and 10 mss/year. 80% of books from first-time authors; 100% from unagented writers. Pays 8-10% royalty on retail price. Offers average of $1,000 advance. Publishes book 8 months after acceptance of ms. Reports in 1 week on queries, 2 weeks on proposals, 1 month on mss. Book catalog free.
Nonfiction: Biography, how-to, humor. Subjects include Americana, cooking/foods/nutrition, history, hobbies, recreation, regional, sports. "A phone call is easiest way to determine suitability of topic. No poorly researched topics." Submit proposal package, including outline and sample chapters. Reviews artwork/photos as part of the ms package. Send photocopies.
Recent Nonfiction Title(s): *Bamboo Rod Restoration*, Michael Sinclair (how-to).
Fiction: Humor, mystery. "We are very selective in this market." Submit synopsis.
Recent Fiction Title(s): *In Over My Waders*, by Jack Sayer (humor).

CENTERSTREAM PUBLICATIONS, P.O. Box 17878, Anaheim Hills CA 92807. (714)779-9390. Fax: (714)779-9390. **Acquisitions:** Ron Middlebrook, Cindy Middlebrook, owners. Estab. 1980. Centerstream publishes music history and instructional books. Publishes hardcover and mass market paperback originals, trade paperback and mass market paperback reprints. Publishes 12 titles/year. Receives 15 queries and 15 mss/year. 80% of books from first-time authors; 100% from unagented writers. Pays 10-15% royalty on wholesale price. Offers $300-3,000 advance. Publishes book 8 months after acceptance of ms. Accepts simultaneous submissions. Reports in 3 months on queries. Book catalog and ms guidelines for #10 SASE.
Nonfiction: Currently publishing only music history and music instructional book. Query with SASE.
Recent Nonfiction Title(s): *The Hawaiian Steel Guitar and Its Great Hawaiian Musicians*, by Lorene Ruymar (music history); *The Ultimate Musician's Reference Handbook*, by Brent E. Kick (reference).

CHAMPION BOOKS INC., P.O. Box 636, Lemont IL 60439. (800)230-1135. **Acquisitions:** Rebecca Rush, president. "In their prime, Kerouac and Ginsberg were never literary stars. They were the unknown and unheard, speaking their minds and breaking new ground. Champion Books seeks obscure and unrenowned authors interested not in following the footsteps of others, but in creating their own new shoes to walk in." Publishes trade paperback originals. Publishes 5 titles/year. 100% of books from first-time authors; 100% from unagented writers. Pays 8-10% royalty on retail price. Publishes book 5 months after acceptance of ms. Accepts simultaneous submissions. Reports in 4 months on mss. Book catalog and ms guidelines for SASE.
Imprint(s): New Shoes Series.
Fiction: Literary, poetry, short story collections. *Writer's Market* recommends sending a query with SASE first.
Recent Fiction Title(s): *Warning This is Not a Book*, by Pete Babones.
Recent Poetry Title(s): *My Gradual Demise & Honeysuckle*, by Douglas A. Martin.
Tips: "We are seeking works that deal with contemporary American Society with an emphasis on counterculture and alternative lifestyles."

‡**CHAPTERS PUBLISHING LTD.**, Division of Houghton-Mifflin Co., 2031 Shelbourne Rd., Shelbourne VT 05482. (802)985-8700. Fax: (802)985-8787. **Acquisitions:** Alesia Rowley, editorial assistant. Estab. 1991. "We want to publish useful books that pass our ultimate test. Would you take this book home and use it in your own cooking, weekend building or nature excursions? Would you reccomend this book to your best friend?" Publishes hardcover and trade paperback originals. Publishes 20 titles/year. 60% of books from first-time authors. Pays royalty on retail price. Advance varies. Publishes book 2 years after acceptance of ms. Reports in 3 months on queries.
● This publisher accepts agented submissions only.
Nonfiction: Subjects include cooking/foods/nutrition, gardening, health/medicine, nature/environment, regional. Query.

CHARIOT CHILDREN'S BOOKS, Imprint of Chariot Victor Publishing, 4050 Lee Vance View, Colorado Springs CO 80918. (719)536-3271. Fax: (719)536-3269. **Acquisitions:** Liz Duckworth, managing editor. "Chariot Children's Books publishes works of children's inspirational titles, ages 1-12, with a strong underlying Christian theme or clearly stated Biblical value." Publishes hardcover and trade paperback originals. Publishes 50 titles/year. Receives 200 queries and 1,500-2,000 mss/year. 15-20% of books from first-time authors; 95% from unagented writers. Pays variable royalty on retail price. Offers advance, $1,000 for picture books, $2,500 for juvenile fiction. Publishes book 2 years after acceptance of ms. Accepts simultaneous submissions if so noted. Reports in 4 months on queries. Book catalog on request. Manuscript guidelines for #10 SASE.
● Chariot Children's Books is not accepting unsolicited submissions at this time.
Nonfiction: Biography, children's/juvenile. Subjects include religion. Query with SASE.
Recent Nonfiction Title(s): *Volcanoes and Earthquakes*, written and illustrated by Michael Carroll.
Fiction: Historical, juvenile, picture books, religious. "Our age range is 8-12 years old. We're particularly interested in historical Christian juvenile fiction and series." Does not want teen fiction; currently overwhelmed with contemporary fiction. Query with SASE. Queries from previously published authors only.

Recent Fiction Title(s): *Dance of Darkness*, by Sigmund Brouwer (Winds of Light series).

‡CHARIOT/VICTOR PUBLISHING, Division of Cook Communications Ministries, 4050 Lee Vance View, Colorado Springs CO 80918. (719)536-3271. Fax: (719)536-3269. **Acquisitions:** Lee Hough, senior acquisitions editor. Chariot/Victor books "must have strong underlying Christian themes or clearly stated Biblical value." Publishes hardcover and trade paperback originals, both children's and adult. Publishes 150 titles/year. 10% of books from first-time authors; 50% from unagented writers. Pays variable royalty on net price. Advance varies. Publishes book 1-2 years after acceptance of ms. Accepts simultaneous submissions, if so noted. Reports in 2 months on queries. Send SASE and query to senior acquisitions editor on adult fiction or nonfiction; no unsolicited children's/juvenile mss accepted. Manuscript guidelines for #10 SASE.
Imprint(s): Rainfall (Judith Barnes); **Chariot Children's Books**; **Lion Publishing**.
Nonfiction: Biography, children's/juvenile. Subjects include child guidance/parenting, history, religion. Query with SASE.
Fiction: Historical, mainstream/contemporary, religious. Query with SASE.

CHARLES RIVER PRESS, 427 Old Town Court, Alexandria VA 22314-3544. (703)519-9197. **Acquisitions:** Lynn Page Whittaker, editor-in-chief. "Charles River Press is a small, independent publishing house committed to bringing to readers the personal stories that illustrate and illuminate historical events and current issues. Our accent is on narrative nonfiction in the areas of race relations, women and multi-cultural history from U.S. and global perspectives." Publishes trade paperback originals and reprints. Publishes 5 titles/year. Pays 5-15% royalty on wholesale price. Offers $0-1,000 advance. Reports in 1 month on proposals. *Writer's Market* recommends allowing 2 months for reply.
Nonfiction: Biography and general nonfiction. Subjects include Americana, ethnic, history (especially African-American), women's issues/studies (especially women's stories), travel memoirs, race relations. Submit proposal package, including outline, 1 sample chapter, letter saying why you have written the book, audience for it, bio and SASE. No phone calls, please.
Recent Nonfiction Title: *I Have Arrived Before My Words: Autobiographical Writing of Homeless Women*, by Deborah Pugh and Jeanie Tietjen.
Tips: "I'm interested in personal stories by writers who have achieved deep understanding and insights into those stories and their meaning. I am especially interested in stories of individuals that illustrate historical events and social issues and in academic work that can be adapted to a general audience. In 1998 we will publish an author that came to us through *Writer's Market*. What stood out? An original story (the author was with the Peace Corp in the Ukraine), a good sense of narrative structure, and fabulous writing."

‡CHARLESBRIDGE PUBLISHING, 85 Main St., Watertown MA 02172. (617)926-0329. **Acquisitions:** Elena Dworkin Wright, editorial director. Estab. 1980. "We are looking for fiction to use as literature in the math curriculum and activity books for kids to make or do some project (not coloring)." Publishes school programs and hardcover and trade paperback originals. Publishes 20 books/year. Receives 1,000 submissions/year. 10% of books from first-time authors, 100% from unagented writers. Publishes books 1 year after acceptance of ms. Reports in 2 months.
Imprint: Talewinds (fiction).
Nonfiction: School or craft books that involve problem solving, building, projects, crafts, and are written with humor and expertise in the field. Submit complete mss with vita and SASE.
Recent Nonfiction Title(s): *Insights: Strategies for Reading with a Purpose*, edited by E.D. Wright (grades 3-8).
Fiction: Math concepts in nonrhyming story.
Recent Fiction Title(s): *Sir Cumference and the First Round Table*, by Cindy Neuschwander (a math adventure/picture book).
Tips: "We market through schools, book stores and specialty stores at museums, science centers, etc."

CHATHAM PRESS, Box A, Old Greenwich CT 06870. Fax: (203)531-7755. **Acquisitions:** Editor. Estab. 1971. Chatham Press publishes mostly illustrated regional history and natural history, involving mainly the Northeast seaboard to the Carolinas with an emphasis on conservation and outdoor recreation. Publishes hardcover and paperback originals, reprints and anthologies. Publishes 10 titles/year. Receives 50 submissions annually. 25% of books from first-time authors; 75% from unagented writers. Nonauthor subsidy publishes 10% of books, mainly poetry or ecological topics. "Standard book contract does not always apply if the book is heavily illustrated. Average advance is low." Publishes book 6 months after acceptance. Reports in 1 month. *Writer's Market* recommends allowing 2 months for reply. Book catalog and ms guidelines for 6×9 SAE with 6 first-class stamps.
 ● Due to the current economy this press indicates their need for freelance material has lessened.
Nonfiction: Illustrated books subjects include regional history (Northeast seaboard), natural history, nature/environment, recreation. Accepts nonfiction translations from French and German. Query with outline and 3 sample chapters. Reviews artwork/photos as part of ms package.
Tips: "Illustrated New England-relevant titles have the best chance of being sold to our firm. We have a slightly greater (15%) skew towards cooking and travel titles."

CHESS ENTERPRISES, 107 Crosstree Rd., Caraopolis PA 15108-2607. Fax: (412)262-2138. E-mail: dudley@robert-morris.edu. **Acquisitions:** Bob Dudley, owner. Estab. 1981. Chess Enterprises publishes books on how to play the game of chess. Publishes trade paperback originals. Publishes 10 titles/year. Receives 20 queries and 12 mss/year. 10% of

books from first-time authors; 100% from unagented writers. Makes outright purchase of $500-3,000. No advance. Publishes book 4 months after acceptance of ms. Accepts simultaneous submissions. Reports in 1 month.
 ● Chess Enterprises has published such authors as Michael Botuinnik, Edmar Mednis, Larry Christianson, George Koltanowski.
Nonfiction: Game of chess only. Query.
Recent Nonfiction Title(s): *Advanced Endgame Strategies*, by Edmar Mednis (complicated endgame play); *Learn to Attack with Rudolf Spielman*, by Eric Schiller (collection of chess games).
Tips: "Books are targeted to chess tournament players, book collectors."

CHICAGO REVIEW PRESS, 814 N. Franklin, Chicago IL 60610-3109. **Acquisitions**: Cynthia Sherry, editorial director. Estab. 1973. Chicago Review Press publishes intelligent nonfiction on timely subjects for educated readers with special interests. Publishes hardcover and trade paperback originals and trade paperback reprints. Publishes 25 titles/year. Receives 300 queries and 300 manuscripts/year. 30% of books from first-time authors; 50% from unagented writers. Pays 7½-12½% royalty. Offers $1,000 average advance. Publishes book 15 months after acceptance. Accepts simultaneous submissions. Reports in 2 months. Book catalog for 9×12 SAE with 10 first-class stamps. Manuscript guidelines for #10 SASE.
Nonfiction: Children's/juvenile (activity books only), cookbooks (specialty only), how-to, child guidance/parenting/ pregnancy, education, gardening (regional), history, hobbies, regional. Submit outline and 1-2 sample chapters or proposal package (see our guidelines). Reviews artwork/photos.
Recent Nonfiction Title(s): *Westward Ho: An Activity Guide to the Wild West*, by Laurie Carlson.
Tips: "Please send for our guidelines and read them carefully."

‡**CHICAGO SPECTRUM PRESS**, 1571 Sherman Ave., Annex C, Evanston, IL 61201. (847)492-1911. **Acquisitions:** Wanda Johnson-Hall, office administrator. Publishes hardcover and trade paperback originals. Publishes 20 titles/year. Receives 100 queries/year. 95% of books from first-time authors; 95% from unagented writers. Pays royalty on retail price. Offers no advance. Publishes book 2 months after acceptance of ms. Reports in 1 month. Book catalog free.
Nonfiction: Biography, children's/juvenile, gift book, how-to, humor, self-help, technical. Subjects include child guidance/parenting, cooking/foods/nutrition, ethnic, history, language/literature, music/dance, psychology, travel, women's issues/studies. Query with SASE.
Recent Nonfiction Title(s): *Show Him Your Love*, by Haya Gil-Lubin (gift book); *Travel Alone and Love It*, by Sharon Wingler (travel); *Keeping Our Heads on Straight*, ed. by Eleanor Perry (journal writing).
Fiction: Ethnic, feminist, historical, humor, juvenile, literary, mainstream/contemporary, mystery, science fiction, short story collections, suspense, young adult. Query.
Recent Fiction Title(s): *Deadly Prayer*, by Pascal Littman (mystery); *Beaned in Boston*, by Gail Farrelley (mystery); *Into the Arena*, by Corey Kinczewski (politics).
Poetry: Query.
Recent Poetry Title(s): *That's What Grandmothers Are For*, by Arlene Vslander (children's); *New Wrinkles*, by Roger Lewin (life's Lessons); *I've Got Cancer*, by Barbara Whipple (cancer survival).

CHILD WELFARE LEAGUE OF AMERICA, 440 First St. NW, Third Floor, Washington DC 20001. (202)638-2952. Fax: (202)638-4004. **Acquisitions:** Susan Brite, director, publications. Child Welfare League of America publishes books on guarding children's rights and serving children's needs. Publishes hardcover and trade paperback originals. Publishes 10-12 titles/year. Receives 60-100 submissions/year. 95% of books from unagented writers. 50% of books are nonauthor-subsidy published. Pays 0-10% royalty on net domestic sales. Publishes book 1 year after acceptance. Reports on queries in 3 months. Book catalog and ms guidelines free.
Imprint(s): CWLA Press (child welfare professional publications), Child & Family Press (children's books and parenting books for the general public).
Nonfiction: Child welfare. Subjects include children's books, child guidance/parenting, sociology. Submit outline and sample chapters.
Recent Nonfiction Title(s): *Working with Traumatized Children*, by Kathryn Brohl (guide for anyone who works with children who have been through a traumatic experience).
Recent Fiction Title(s): *Sassafras*, by Audrey Penn (children's picture book on self-esteem).
Tips: "Our audience is child welfare workers, administrators, agency executives, parents, children, etc. We also publish training curricula, including videos."

CHILDREN'S PRESS, Division of Grolier Publishing, Sherman Turnpike, Danbury CT 06813. (203)797-6802. Fax: (203)797-6986. E-mail: rprimm@grolier.com. Website: http://www.grolier.com. Editorial Director: E. Russell Primm. **Acquisitions**: Dana Rau, assistant editor (nonfiction), Mark Friedman, senior editor (nonfiction). "Children's Press publishes nonfiction for the school and library market. Our books support textbooks and closely relate to the elementary and middle-school curriculum." Publishes nonfiction hardcover originals. Publishes 200 titles/year. Makes outright purchase for $500-1,000. No advance. Publishes book 20 months after acceptance. Book catalog available.
 ● Children's Press has published such authors as Larry Dane Brimmer, Charnan Simon and Elaine Landau.
Nonfiction: Children's/juvenile. Subjects include animals, anthropology/archaeology, art/architecture, ethnic, health/ medicine, history, hobbies, music/dance, nature/environment, science and sports. "We publish nonfiction books that supplement the elementary school curriculum." Not accepting unsolicited mss.

Recent Nonfiction Title(s): *Extraordinary People with Disabilities*, by Kate Quinlan and Debra Kent.
Recent Fiction Title(s): *Sam the Garbage Hound*, by Charnan Simon; *Firehouse Sal*, by Larry Dane Brimmer.

‡**CHINA BOOKS & PERIODICALS, INC.**, 2929 24th St., San Francisco CA 94110-4126. (415)282-2994. Fax: (415)282-0994. Website: http://www.chinabooks.com. **Acquisitions:** Greg Jones, editor. Estab. 1960. "China Books is the main importer and distributor of books and magazines from China, providing an ever-changing variety of useful tools for travelers, scholars and others interested in China and Chinese culture." Publishes hardcover and trade paperback originals. Averages 5 titles/year. Receives 300 submissions/year. 10% of books from first-time authors; 95% from unagented writers. Pays 6-8% royalty on net receipts. Offers $1,000 average advance. Publishes book 1 year after acceptance. Accepts simultaneous submissions. Query for electronic submissions. Reports in 3 months on queries. Book catalog free. Manuscript guidelines for #10 SASE.
Nonfiction: "*Important*: *All* books *must* be on topics related to China or East Asia, or Chinese-Americans. Books on China's history, politics, environment, women, art, architecture; language textbooks, acupuncture and folklore." Biography, coffee table book, cookbook, how-to, juvenile, self-help, textbook. Subjects include agriculture/horticulture, art/architecture, business/economics, cooking/foods/nutrition, ethnic, gardening, government/politics, history, language/literature, nature/environment, religion, sociology, translation, travel, women's issues/studies. Query with outline and sample chapters. Reviews artwork/photos as part of ms package.
Fiction: Ethnic, experimental, historical, literary. "*Must* have Chinese, Chinese-American or East Asian theme. We are looking for high-quality fiction with a Chinese or East Asian theme or translated from Chinese that makes a genuine literary breakthrough and seriously treats life in contemporary China or Chinese-Americans. No fiction that is too conventional in style or treats hackneyed subjects. No fiction without Chinese or Chinese-American or East Asian themes, please." Query with outline/synopsis and sample chapters.
Recent Fiction Title(s): *The Banker*, by Cheng Naishan.
Tips: "We are looking for original ideas, especially in language study, children's education, adoption of Chinese babies, or health issues relating to Traditional Chinese medicine. See our website for author guidelines."

CHOSEN BOOKS PUBLISHING CO., LTD., Division of Baker Book House Company, 3985 Bradwater St., Fairfax VA 22031-3702. (703)764-8250. Fax: (703)764-3995. E-mail: jecampbell@aol.com. (No e-mail submissions; query only by e-mail). Website: http://www.bakerbooks.com. **Acquisitions:** Jane Campbell, editor. Estab. 1971. "We publish well-crafted books that recognize the gifts and ministry of the Holy Spirit, and help the reader live a more empowered and effective life for Jesus Christ." Publishes hardcover and trade paperback originals. Publishes 6-8 titles/year. Receives 500 submissions/year. 15% of books from first-time authors; 99% from unagented writers. Pays royalty on net receipts. Publishes book 18 months after acceptance. Accepts simultaneous submissions. Reports in 3 months. Manuscript guidelines for #10 SASE.
● Chosen Books Publishing Co., Ltd., has published such authors as Derek Prince and David Wilkerson.
Nonfiction: Expositional books on narrowly focused themes. "We publish books reflecting the current acts of the Holy Spirit in the world, books with a charismatic Christian orientation." No New Age, poetry, fiction, autobiographies, academic or children's books. Submit synopsis, chapter outline, résumé, 2 sample chapters and SASE. No complete mss. No response without SASE.
Recent Nonfiction Title(s): *Deliverance from Evil Spirits*, by Francis MacNutt (expositional nonfiction); *The River Is Here*, by Melinda Fish (present-day renewal); *Jesus Reigns in Me!*, by Sarah Hornsby (daily devotional).
Tips: "We look for solid, practical advice for the growing and maturing Christian from authors with professional or personal experience platforms. No conversion accounts or chronicling of life events, please. State the topic or theme of your book clearly in your cover letter."

‡**CHRISTIAN LITERATURE CRUSADE**, 701 Pennsylvania Ave., P.O. Box 1449, Fort Washington PA 19034-8449. (215)542-1242. Fax: (215)542-7580. **Acquisitions:** Willard Stone, publications coordinator. "Publications are carefully selected to conform to our constitutional statement of only producing and distributing books which are true to the inerrant Word of God and the fundamentals of the faith as commonly held by all evangelical believers." Publishes mass market and trade paperback originals and reprints. Publishes 6-8 titles/year. Receives 50-100 queries and 80-100 mss/year. 90% of books from first-time authors; 100% from unagented writers. Pays 5-10% on retail price. Offers $300-500 advance, may be negotiated. Publishes book 1 year after acceptance of ms. Accepts simultaneous submissions. Reports in 3 months on proposals. Book catalog free. Manuscript guidelines for #10 SASE.
● Christian Literature Crusade has published such authors as Andrew Murray, F.B. Meyer, Jessie Penn Lewis, Amy Carmichael and Oswald Chambers.
Nonfiction: Biography. Subjects include religion. Writers must send query before submitting ms. Query or submit outline with 3 sample chapters with SASE.
Recent Nonfiction Title(s): *Marching to a Different Drummer*, by J. Raymo (missions challenge).; *The Marriage Ring*, by D. Talmadge (marriage, morality, family).
Tips: "We publish books which deal with the following areas: Evangelism, Discipleship, Deeper Spiritual Life and Mission. Our audience consists of 'Deeper Life' readers; missions, adults, and junior high students. Query or send a proposal first."

CHRISTIAN PUBLICATIONS, INC., 3825 Hartzdale Dr., Camp Hill PA 17011. (717)761-7044. Fax: (717)761-7273. E-mail: editors@cpi~horizon.com. Website: cpi~horizon.com. Managing Editor: David E. Fessenden. **Acquisi-**

tions: George McPeek, editorial director. "Our purpose is to propagate the gospel of Jesus Christ through evangelistic, deeper life and other publishing, serving our denomination and the wider Christian community." Publishes hardcover originals and trade paperback originals and reprints. Publishes 48 titles/year (about 50% are reprints of classic authors). Receives 600 queries and 800 mss/year. 25% of books from first-time authors; 80% from unagented writers. Pays variable royalty or makes outright purchase. Publishes book 18 months after acceptance of ms. Accepts simultaneous submissions; "We do *not* reprint other publishers' material." Book catalog for 9 × 12 SAE with 7 first-class stamps. Manuscript guidelines for #10 SASE.
Imprint(s): Christian Publications, Inc., Horizon Books.
Nonfiction: How-to, reference (reprints *only*), self-help. Subjects include religion (Evangelical Christian perspective). "We are owned by The Christian and Missionary Alliance denomination; while we welcome and publish authors from various denominations, their theological perspective must be compatible with The Christian and Missionary Alliance. We are especially interested in fresh, practical approaches to deeper life—sanctification with running shoes on." Submit proposal package, including chapter synopsis, 2 sample chapters (including chapter 1), audience and market ideas, author bio.
Recent Nonfiction Title(s): *Ten Foolish Things Christians Do to Stunt Their Growth*, by Tom Allen (church life/ growth); *Out of the Locker Room of the Male Soul*, by Steve Masterson, with George McPeek (men's issues); *Single, Whole and Holy: Christian Women and Sexuality*, by Joy Jacobs and Deborah Strubel (women's issues).
Fiction: "At the present time, we are not accepting unsolicited fiction, poetry or children's books."
Tips: "Take time with your proposal—make it thorough, concise, complete. Authors who have done their homework regarding our message and approach have a much better chance of being accepted."

CHRONICLE BOOKS, Chronicle Publishing Co., 85 Second St., San Francisco CA 94105. (415)537-3730. Fax: (415)537-4440. E-mail: frontdesk@chronbooks.com. Website: http://www.chronbooks.com. President: Jack Jensen. Publishing Director: Caroline Herter. Associate Publishers: Nion McEvoy, Victoria Rock, Christine Carswell. **Acquisitions:** Jay Schaefer, editor (fiction); Bill LeBlond, editor (cookbooks); Annie Barrows, editor (general); Victoria Rock, editor (children's); Debra Lande, editor (ancillary products); Nion McEvoy, editor (multimedia); Leslie Jonath, editor (gardening); Karen Silver, editor (regional). "Chronicle Books specializes in high-quality, reasonably priced books for adults and children. Our titles include best-selling cookbooks; fine art, design, photography, and architecture titles; full-color nature books; award-winning poetry and literary fiction; regional and international travel guides; and gift and stationery items." Publishes hardcover and trade paperback originals. Publishes 200 titles/year. Receives 22,500 submissions/year. 20% of books from first-time authors. 15% from unagented writers. Publishes book 18 months after acceptance. Accepts simultaneous submissions. Reports in 3 months on queries. Book catalog for 11 × 14 SAE with 5 first-class stamps.
Imprint(s): Chronicle Books for Children, GiftWorks (ancillary products, such as stationery, gift books).
Nonfiction: Coffee table book, cookbook, regional California, architecture, art, design, gardening, gift, health, nature, nostalgia, photography, recreation, travel. Query or submit outline/synopsis with artwork and sample chapters.
Recent Nonfiction Title(s): *Living Happily Ever After*, by David Collier and Laurie Wagner (gift/relationships); *Star Wars Chronicles*, by Deborah Fine and Aeon Inc. (film/popular culture); *Fresh from the Farmer's Market*, by Janet Fletcher (food).
Fiction: Novels, novellas, short story collections. Submit complete ms and synopsis; do not query.
Recent Fiction Title(s): *The Venetian's Wife*, by Nick Bantock (illustrated novel); *Paris Out of Hand*, by Karen Elizabeth Gordon; *The Loneliest Road in America*, by Roy Parrin (short story collection).
Recent Poetry Title(s): *Junior College*, by Gary Soto.

‡**CHRONICLE BOOKS FOR CHILDREN**, Imprint of Chronicle Books, 85 Second St., San Francisco CA 94105. (415)537-3730. Fax: (415)537-4460. E-mail: frontdesk@chronbooks.com. Website: http://www.chronbooks.com. **Acquisitions:** Victoria Rock, director of Children's Books (nonfiction/fiction); Erica Jacobs, editor (nonfiction/fiction plus novelty, packaged, buy-ins); Amy Novesky, assistant editor (nonfiction/fiction plus middle grade and young adult). "Chronicle Books for Children publishes an eclectic mixture of traditional and innovative children's books. We're looking for quirky, bold artwork and subject matter." Publishes hardcover and trade paperback originals. Publishes 40-50 titles/year. Receives 20,000 submissions/year. 5% of books from first-time authors; 25% from unagented writers. Pays 8% royalty. Advance varies. Publishes book 18 months after acceptance of ms. Accepts simultaneous submissions if so noted. Reports in 2-18 weeks on queries; 5 months on mss. Book catalog for 9 × 12 SAE and 3 first-class stamps. Manuscript guidelines for #10 SASE.
Nonfiction: Biography, children's/juvenile, illustrated book, nonfiction books for ages 8-12 years, and nonfiction picture books for ages up to 8 years. Subjects include animals, multicultural and bilingual, nature/environment, art, science. Query with outline and SASE. Reviews artwork/photos as part of the ms package.
Recent Nonfiction Title(s): *Creeps From The Deep*, by Leighton Taylor (science/natural history); *Beneath The Waves*, by Norbert Wu (science/natural history); *Artist in Overalls: The Story of Grant Wood*, by John Duggelby (biography).
Fiction: Fiction picture books, middle grades fiction, young adult projects. Mainstream/contemporary, multicultural, picture books, young adult, chapter books. Query with synopsis and SASE. Send complete ms for picture books.
Recent Fiction Title(s): *The Eyes of Graywolf*, by Jonathan London; *Dem Bones*, by Bob Banner; *Hush Little Baby*, by Sylvia Long.
Tips: "We are interested in projects that have a unique bent to them—be it in subject matter, writing style, or illustrative

technique. As a small list, we are looking for books that will lend our list a distinctive flavor. Primarily we are interested in fiction and nonfiction picture books for children ages up to eight years, and nonfiction books for children ages up to twelve years. We publish board, pop-up, and other novelty formats as well as picture books. We are also interested in early chapter books, middle grade fiction, and young adult projects."

‡**CHRONIMED PUBLISHING**, 13911 Ridgedale Dr., Suite 250, Minnetonka MN 55305. (612)541-0239. Fax: (612)513-6170. Website: http://www.chronimed.com. Director of Publishing: Cheryl Kimball. **Acquisitions**: Jeff Braun, editorial manager. Estab. 1986. Chronicle Publishing publishes authoritative health and disease management titles. Publishes hardcover originals and trade paperback originals and reprints. Publishes 30-40 titles/year. Receives 600 submissions/year. 30% of books are from first-time authors; 60% from unagented writers. Pays 7-12% royalty on retail price. Offers $1,000-5,000 advance. Publishes ms an average of 6 months after acceptance of ms. Accepts simultaneous submissions. Reports in 2 months on queries, 3 months on proposals and mss. Book catalog free. Manuscript guidelines free or from our website.
Nonfiction: Cookbook, how-to, reference, self-help. Subjects include child guidance/parenting, cooking/foods/nutrition, health/medicine. "We are seeking manuscripts relating to health and chronic disease management from authoritative sources. No New Age material." Query or submit proposal including outline and 1-2 sample chapters. Reviews artwork/photos as part of ms package. Send photocopies.
Recent Nonfiction Title(s): *Diabetic Low-Fat and No-Fat Meals in Minutes!*, by M.J. Smith, R.D.; *A Cancer Survivor's Almanac*, edited by Barbara Hoffman; *Quick Meals for Healthy Kids and Busy Parents*, by Sandra Nissenberg.
Tips: Audience is "general consumers concerned about overall good health and people with a chronic illness interested in specific information from medical professionals. Be clear about your book's topic—better to be specific when it comes to writing about health-related issues. Cookbook authors be sure to tell what your recipe-testing process is."

CHURCH GROWTH INSTITUTE, P.O. Box 7000, Forest VA 24551. (804)525-0022. Fax: (804)525-0608. **Acquisitions**: Cindy Spear, director of resource development. Estab. 1984. "Our mission is to provide cutting-edge seminars and publish practical resources to help pastors, churches and individuals reach their potential for Christ; to promote spiritual and numerical growth in churches, thereby leading Christians to maturity and lost people to Christ; and to equip pastors so they can equip their church members to do the work of the ministry." Publishes trade paperback originals. Publishes 10 titles/year. Pays 5% royalty on retail price. Publishes book 1 year after acceptance of ms. Accepts simultaneous submissions. Reports in 3 months on queries. Resource catalog for 9×12 SAE with 4 first-class stamps. Manuscript guidelines given after query and outline is received.
Nonfiction: How-to, manuals. Subjects include religious education (church-growth related). "Material should originate from a conservative Christian view and cover topics that will help churches grow, through leadership training, new attendance or stewardship programs, and new or unique ministries, plus drama/skits for worship services and other such aids to enhance existing ministries. Accepted manuscripts will be adapted to our resource packet format. All material must be practical and easy for the *average* Christian to understand." Query or submit outline and brief explanation of what the packet will accomplish in the local church and whether it is leadership or lay-oriented. Reviews artwork/photos as part of ms package. Send photocopies or transparencies.
Recent Nonfiction Title(s): *How to Establish a Local Church Men's Ministry*, by Dr. Ron Jenson and Dr. Glen Martin; *Fasting for Spiritual Breakthrough*, by Dr. Elmer Towns; *Easter Services: Dramatic Events That Share the Message*, by Dr. Robert Kintigh.
Tips: "We are not publishing many *textbooks*. Concentrate on how-to manuals, video curriculum for small group studies and complete resource packets (planning a campaign, program or ministry, step-by-step agenda, resource list, etc., plus audio- or video-cassettes)."

CIRCLET PRESS INC., P.O. Box 15143, Boston MA 02215-0143. E-mail: circlet-info@circlet.com. Website: http://www.circlet.com/circlet/home.html. **Acquisitions:** Cecilia Tan, publisher/editor. "Circlet Press publishes science fiction/fantasy which is too erotic for the mainstream and to promote literature with a positive view of sex and sexuality, which celebrates pleasure and diversity." Publishes hardcover and trade paperback originals. Publishes 6-10 titles/year. Receives 50-100 queries and 500 mss/year. 50% of stories from first-time authors; 90% from unagented writers. Pays 4-12% royalty on retail price or makes outright purchase (depending on rights); also pays in books if author prefers. Publishes stories 12-18 months after acceptance. Accepts simultaneous submissions. Reports in 1 month on queries, 6-12 months on mss. Book catalog and ms guidelines for #10 SASE.
  ● Circlet Press currently accepts manuscripts between April 15 and August 31. Manuscripts received outside this reading period are discarded. They have published such authors as Shariann Lewitt, Lawrence Schimel, Thomas S. Roche, Gary Bowen and Cecilia Tan.
Imprint(s): The Ultra Violet Library (specifically gay and lesbian science fiction and fantasy. "These books will not be as erotic as our others.")
Fiction: Erotic science fiction and fantasy short stories only. Gay/lesbian stories needed but all persuasions welcome. "Fiction must combine both the erotic and the fantastic. The erotic content needs to be an integral part of a science fiction story, and vice versa. Writers should not assume that any sex is the same as erotica." Submit full short stories up to 10,000 words. *Writer's Market* recommends sending a query with SASE first. Queries only via e-mail.
Recent Fiction Title(s): *Genderflex*, edited by Cecilia Tan (anthology of erotic science fiction/fantasy stories); *The Drag Queen of Elfland*, by Lawrence Schimel (collection of short science fiction/fantasy stories); *Erotica Vampirica*, edited by Cecilia Tan (erotic vampire stories).

Tips: "Our audience is adults who enjoy science fiction and fantasy, especially the works of Anne Rice, Storm Constantine, Samuel Delany, who enjoy vivid storytelling and erotic content. Seize your most vivid fantasy, your deepest dream and set it free onto paper. That is at the heart of all good speculative fiction. Then if it has an erotic theme as well as a science fiction one, send it to me. No horror, rape, death or mutilation! I want to see stories that *celebrate* sex and sexuality in a positive manner. Please write for our guidelines as each year we have a specific list of topics we seek."

CITADEL PRESS, Imprint of Carol Publishing Group, 120 Enterprise, Secaucus NJ 07094. Fax: (201)866-8159. E-mail: info@citadelpublishing.com. Website: http://www.citadelpublishing.com. **Acquisitions**: Alan Wilson, executive editor; Hillel Black, executive editor; Marcy Swingler, associate editor. Estab. 1945. "We concentrate on biography, popular interest, and film, with limited fiction (no romance, religion, poetry, music)." Publishes hardcover originals and paperback reprints. Publishes 60-80 titles/year. Receives 800-1,000 submissions/year. 7% of books from first-time authors; 50% from unagented writers. Average print order for a first book is 5,000. Pays 10% royalty on hardcover, 5-7% on paperback. Offers average $7,000 advance. Publishes book 1 year after acceptance. Accepts simultaneous submissions. Reports in 2 months. Book catalog for $1.
 • Citadel Press also publishes books in conjunction with the Learning Annex, a popular adult education and self-improvement school in New York City. Citadel has published such authors as C. David Heymann, Fred Guiles and John Patrick.
Nonfiction: Biography, film, psychology, humor, history. Also seeks "off-beat material, but no fiction, poetry, religion, politics." Accepts nonfiction translations. Query or submit outline/synopsis and 3 sample chapters. Reviews artwork/photos as part of ms package. Send photocopies with SASE.
Recent Nonfiction Title(s): *Hitler's Secret Bankers*, by Adam Lebor (history); *The Mad King*, by Greg King (biography of Ludwig II of Bavaria); *Wizard*, by Marc J. Seifer (biography of Nikola Tesla).

CLARION BOOKS, Imprint of Houghton Mifflin Company, 215 Park Ave. S., New York NY 10003. **Acquisitions**: Dorothy Briley, editor/publisher; Dinah Stevenson, executive editor; Nina Ignatowicz, senior editor. Estab. 1965. Clarion is a strong presence when it comes to books for young readers. Publishes hardcover originals. Publishes 50 titles/year. Pays 5-10% royalty on retail price. Advances from $4,000. Prefers no multiple submissions. Reports in 2 months. Publishes book 2 years after acceptance. Manuscript guidelines for #10 SASE.
 • Clarion is swamped with submissions and is not accepting manuscripts at this time.
Nonfiction: Americana, biography, history, holiday, humor, nature, photo essays, word play. Prefers books for younger children. *No unsolicited mss.* Reviews artwork/photos as part of ms package. Send photocopies.
Fiction: Adventure, humor, mystery, strong character studies, suspense. "We would like to see more distinguished short fiction for readers seven to ten." Accepts fiction translations. *No unsolicited mss.*
Tips: Looks for "freshness, enthusiasm—in short, life" (fiction and nonfiction).

CLARKSON POTTER, Imprint of The Crown Publishing Group, Division of Random House, 201 E. 50th St., New York NY 10022. **Acquisitions**: Lauren Shakely, editorial director. Clarkson Potter specializes in publishing cooking books, decorating and other around-the-house how-to subjects. Publishes hardcover and trade paperback originals. Publishes 55 titles/year. 15% of books from first-time authors. Reports in 2-3 months on queries and proposals.
Nonfiction: Publishes art/architecture, biography, child guidance/parenting, crafts, cooking and foods, decorating, design gardening, how-to, humor, photography, and popular psychology. Query or submit outline and sample chapter with tearsheets from magazines and artwork copies (e.g.—color photocopies or duplicate transparencies).

CLEAR LIGHT PUBLISHERS, 823 Don Diego, Santa Fe NM 87501-4224. (505)989-9590. E-mail: clpublish@aol.com. **Acquisitions:** Harmon Houghton, publisher. Estab. 1981. Publishes hardcover and trade paperback originals. Publishes 12 titles/year. Receives 100 queries/year. 10% of books from first-time authors; 50% from unagented writers. Pays 10% royalty on wholesale price. Offers advance, a percent of gross potential. Publishes book 1 year after acceptance of ms. Accepts simultaneous submissions. Reports in 3 months on queries. Book catalog free.
Nonfiction: Biography, coffee table book, cookbook, humor. Subjects include Americana, anthropology/archaelogy, art/architecture, cooking/foods/nutrition, ethnic, history, nature/environment, philosophy, photography, regional (Southwest). Query with SASE. Reviews artwork/photos as part of ms package. Send photocopies (no originals).
Recent Nonfiction Title(s): *One Nation Under God*, by Huston Smith (Native American Church).

CLIFFS NOTES, INC., P.O. Box 80728, Lincoln NE 68501. (402)423-5050. Website: http://www.cliffs.com. General Editor: Michele Spence. **Acquisitions:** Gary Carey, notes editor; Richard Guittar, studyware editor. Estab. 1958. "We publish self-help study aids directed to junior high through graduate school audience. Publications include *Cliffs Notes*, *Cliffs Test Preparation Guides*, *Cliffs Quick Reviews*, *Cliffs StudyWare*, and other study guides." Publishes trade paperback originals and educational software. Averages 20 titles/year. 100% of books from unagented writers. Pays royalty on wholesale price. Buys majority of mss outright; "full payment on acceptance of ms." Publishes book 1 year after acceptance. Reports in 1 month. *Writer's Market* recommends allowing 2 months for reply. "We provide specific guidelines when a project is assigned."
Imprint(s): Centennial Press.
Nonfiction: Self-help, textbook. "Most authors are experienced teachers, usually with advanced degrees. Some books also appeal to a general lay audience. Query.
Recent Nonfiction Title(s): Cliffs *Quick Review Microbiology*.

COBBLEHILL BOOKS, Imprint of Dutton Children's Books, Division of Penguin Putnam Inc. Children's, 375 Hudson St., New York NY 10014. (212)366-2000. **Acquisitions:** Joe Ann Daly, editorial director; Rosanne Lauer, executive editor. Pays royalty. Publishes fiction and nonfiction for young readers, middle readers and young adults, and picture books. Query for mss longer than picture book length; submit complete ms for picture books. Reports in 1 month. *Writer's Market* recommends allowing 2 months for reply. Accepts simultaneous submissions, if so noted.
  • At press time, Dutton Children's Books was being restructured. Verify current information.
Recent Picture Book Title: *The Fiddler of the Northern Lights*, by Natalie Kinsey-Warnock, illus. by Leslie Bowman.

COFFEE HOUSE PRESS, 27 N. Fourth St., Suite 400, Minneapolis MN 55401. Fax: (612)338-4004. **Acquisitions:** Chris Fischbach, associate editor. Estab. 1984. Publishes hardcover and trade paperback originals. Publishes 14 titles/ year. Receives 5,000 queries and mss/year. 95% of books are from unagented writers. Pays 8% royalty on retail price. No advance. Publishes book 18 months after acceptance. Reports in 1 month on queries or samples, 4-6 months on mss. Book catalog and ms guidelines for #10 SAE with 2 first-class stamps.
  • Coffee House Press has published such authors as Paul Metcalf, Anne Waldman, Russel Edson.
Fiction: Literary novels, short story collections, short-short story collections. No genre. Query first with samples and SASE.
Recent Fiction Title(s): *American Heaven*, by Maxine Chernoff; *Dog People*, by Chris Mazza.
Recent Poetry Title(s): *Avalanche*, by Quincy Troupe; *Iovis*, by Anne Waldman.
Tips: Look for our books at stores and libraries to get a feel for what we like to publish. Please, no calls or faxes.

COLLECTOR BOOKS, Division of Schroeder Publishing Co., Inc., 5801 Kentucky Dam Rd., P.O. Box 3009, Paducah KY 42002-3009. **Acquisitions:** Lisa Stroup, editor. Estab. 1974. "Collector Books publishes books on antiques and collectibles." Publishes hardcover and paperback originals. Publishes 65 titles/year. 50% of books from first-time authors; 100% of books from unagented writers. Average print order for a first book is 5,000-10,000. Pays 5% royalty on retail price. No advance. Publishes book 9 months after acceptance. Reports in 1 month. Book catalog for 9×12 SAE with 4 first-class stamps. Manuscript guidelines for #10 SASE.
  • Collector Books has increased their number of books published from 35 to 65 in the past year.
Nonfiction: "We require our authors to be very knowledgeable in their respective fields and have access to a large representative sampling of the particular subject concerned." Query with outline and 2-3 sample chapters. Reviews artwork/photos as part of ms package.
Tips: "Common mistakes writers make include making phone contact instead of written contact and assuming an accurate market evaluation."

THE COLLEGE BOARD, Imprint of College Entrance Examination Board, 45 Columbus Ave., New York NY 10023-6992. (212)713-8000. Website: http://www.collegeboard.org. **Acquisitions:** Carolyn Trager, director of publications. "We publish guidance information for college-bound students." Publishes trade paperback originals. Publishes 30 titles/ year; imprint publishes 12 titles/year. Receives 50-60 submissions/year. 25% of books from first-time authors; 50% from unagented writers. Pays royalty on retail price of books sold through bookstores. Offers advance based on anticipated first year's earnings. Publishes book 9 months after acceptance. Reports in 6 weeks on queries. *Writer's Market* recommends allowing 2 months for reply. Book catalog free.
Nonfiction: Education-related how-to, reference, self-help. Subjects include college guidance, education, language/ literature, science. "We want books to help students make a successful transition from high school to college." Query or send outline and sample chapters.
Recent Nonfiction Title(s): *Internet Guide for College Bound Students*, by Kenneth Hartman.
Tips: "Our audience consists of college-bound high school students, beginning college students and/or their parents."

COMMUNE-A-KEY PUBLISHING, P.O. Box 58637, Salt Lake City UT 84158. (801)581-9191. Fax: (801)581-9196. E-mail: keypublish@lgcy.com. **Acquisitions:** Caryn Summers, editor-in-chief. Commune-A-Key's mission statement is: "Communicating Keys to Growth and Empowerment." Publishes trade paperback originals and reprints and audiotapes. Publishes 4-6 titles/year. 40% of books from first-time authors; 75% from unagented writers. Pays 7-8% royalty on retail price. Publishes book 1 year after acceptance of ms. Accepts simultaneous submissions. Reports in 1 month on queries and proposals, 2 months on mss. Book catalog and ms guidelines free.
Nonfiction: Gift book/inspirational, humor, self-help/psychology, spiritual. Subjects include health/medicine, psychology, men's or women's issues/studies, recovery, Native American. Query. Reviews artwork/photos as part of ms package. Send photocopies.
Recent Nonfiction Title(s): *Earth Dance Drum*, by Blackwolf and Gina Jones (Native American/spirituality); *Compassionate Laughter: Jest for Your Health*, by Patty Wooten, R.N. (health psychology).

 THE DOUBLE DAGGER before a listing indicates that the listing is new in this edition. New markets are often more receptive to freelance submissions.

COMPANION PRESS, P.O. Box 2575, Laguna Hills CA 92654. E-mail: sstewart@companionpress.com. Website: http://www.companionpress.com. **Acquisitions**: Steve Stewart, publisher. "We are interested in movie and video guides written for the general reader, rather than the academic." Publishes trade paperback originals. Publishes 6 titles/year. Receives 50 queries and 25 mss/year. 50% of books from first-time authors; 100% from unagented writers. Pays 7-9% royalty on retail price or makes outright purchase. Offers $500-1,000 advance. Publishes book 9 months after acceptance of ms. Reports in 1 month. *Writer's Market* recommends allowing 2 months for reply. Book catalog and manuscript guidelines for #10 SASE.
Nonfiction: Movie and video guides. Subjects include: adult, bisexuality, erotic, fetishes, homosexuality, nudity and sex in the movies. Query. Reviews artwork/photos as part of ms package. Send photocopies.
Recent Nonfiction Title(s): *Superstars—Gay Adult Video Guide*, by Jamoo.

‡COMPASS AMERICAN GUIDES INC., Imprint of Fodor's, Division of Random House. 5332 College Ave., Suite 201, Oakland CA 94618. **Acquisitions:** Kit Duane, managing editor; Christopher Burt, creative director. "We publish guides to U.S. and Canadian states, provinces or cities." Publishes trade paperback originals. Publishes 10 titles/year. Receives 50 queries and 5 mss/year. 5% of books from first-time authors; 90% from unagented writers. Makes outright purchase of $5,000-10,000. Offers $1,500-3,000 advance. Publishes book an average of 8 months after acceptance of ms. Accepts simultaneous submissions. Reports in 6 months. Book catalog for $1.
   • Query this publisher about its specific format.
Nonfiction: Travel guides. "We cannot guarantee the return of any submissions." Reviews artwork/photos as part of ms package. Photographers should send duplicate slides.

COMPUTER SCIENCE PRESS, Imprint of W.H. Freeman and Company, 41 Madison Ave., New York NY 10010. (212)576-9451. Fax: (212)689-2383. E-mail: rjbonacci@whfreeman.com. Website: http://www.whfreeman.com. **Acquisitions:** Richard J. Bonacci, publisher. Estab. 1974. "Computer Science Press publishes technical books in all aspects of computer science, computer engineering, information systems and telecommunications." Publishes hardcover and paperback originals. Publishes 5 titles/year. 25% of books from first-time authors; 98% of books from unagented writers. All authors are recognized subject area experts. Pays royalty on net price. Publishes book 6-9 months after acceptance. Reports ASAP.
Nonfiction: Primarily textbooks. Subjects include computer science, computer engineering, information systems and telecommunications. Also considers public appeal 'trade' books in computer science, manuscripts and diskettes." Query or submit sample chapters of ms. Looks for "technical accuracy of the material and an explanation of why this approach was taken. We would also like a covering letter stating what the author sees as the competition for this work and why this work is superior or an improvement on previous available material."
Recent Nonfiction Title(s): *Programming Visual Basic*, by Gersting (textbook).
Tips: "We are looking for more trade titles on technology's effect on society, politics or business."

COMPUTING McGRAW-HILL, Imprint of McGraw Hill Publishing Group, 11 W. 19th St., New York NY 10011. (212)337-4098. Website: http://www.mcgraw-hill.com. **Acquisitions:** Mike Hays, editor. Estab. 1992. "Computing McGraw-Hill publishes computer titles for professionals. We're especially strong in emerging technologies." Publishes hardcover and trade paperback originals. Publishes 120 titles/year. Receives 500 queries/year. 25% of books from first-time writers. 25% from unagented writers. Pays 7½-15% royalty on net price. Advance varies. Publishes book 9 months after acceptance of ms. Accepts simultaneous submissions. Reports in 1 month on proposals. Book catalog and ms guidelines not available.
Nonfiction: Reference, textbook. Subjects include computers/electronics, data communications. "Writers should keep two things in mind. First: what is the purpose of this book, as distinct from the topic. Second: a clear statement of who the book is intended for." Query with outline, 1 sample chapter and SASE.
Recent Nonfiction Title(s): *ATM*, by McDyson & Stone (data communications); *Novelle CNA CNE*, by Mueller (programming).

CONARI PRESS, 2550 Ninth St., Suite 101, Berkeley CA 94710. (510)649-7175. Fax: (510)649-7190. E-mail: conaripub@aol.com. Website: http://www.readersndex.com/conari. **Acquisitions:** Mary Jane Ryan, executive editor; Claudia Schaab, editorial associate. Estab. 1987. "Conari Press publishes books that make a difference. We value integrity, process, compassion and receptivity, both in the books we publish and in our internal workings." Publishes hardcover and trade paperback originals. Publishes 26 titles/year. Receives 1,000 submissions/year. 50% of books from first-time authors; 50% from unagented writers. Pays 7½-15% royalty on list price. Offers $2,000 average advance. Publishes book 1-3 years after acceptance. Accepts simultaneous submissions. Reports in 3 months. Manuscript guidelines for 6×9 SASE.
   • Conari Press has published such authors as Daphne Rose Kingma, Andrew Harvey and Adair Lara.
Nonfiction: Psychology, spirituality, women's issues, parenting. Submit outline and sample chapters, attn: Claudia Schaab. Reviews artwork/photos as part of ms package.
Recent Nonfiction Title(s): *Chore Wars*, by Jim Thornton; *Simple Pleasures*, by R. Taylor, S. Seton, D. Grev (lifestyle/spiritual); *Honor Thy Children*, by M. Furnice (parenting/gay and lesbian).
Tips: "Writers should send us well-targeted, specific and focused manuscripts. No recovery issues."

CONCORDIA PUBLISHING HOUSE, 3558 S. Jefferson Ave., St. Louis MO 63118-3968. (314)268-1000. Fax: (314)268-1329. Family and Children's Editor: Ruth Geisler. **Acquisitions:** Dawn Weinstock. Estab. 1869. "We publish

Protestant, inspirational, theological, family and juveniles. All manuscripts must conform to the doctrinal tenets of The Lutheran Church—Missouri Synod." Publishes hardcover and trade paperback originals. Publishes 80 titles/year. Receives 2,000 submissions/year. 10% of books from first-time authors; 95% from unagented writers. Pays royalty or makes outright purchase. Publishes book 1 year after acceptance. Simultaneous submissions discouraged. Reports in 2 months on queries. Manuscript guidelines for #10 SASE.

• Concordia has increased their number of books published from 60 to 80 in the past year.

Nonfiction: Juvenile, adult. Subjects include child guidance/parenting (in Christian context), inspirational, how-to, religion. *Writer's Market* recommends sending a query with SASE first.

Recent Nonfiction Title(s): *Lessons in Dadhood*, by Tim Wesemann (devotional for men).

Fiction: Juvenile. "We will consider preteen and children's fiction and picture books. All books must contain Christian content. No adult Christian fiction." *Writer's Market* recommends sending a query with SASE first.

Recent Fiction Title(s): *The Great Meow Mystery*, by Dandi Mackall.

Tips: "Our needs have broadened to include writers of books for lay adult Christians and of Christian novels (low-key, soft-sell) for pre-teens and teenagers."

THE CONSULTANT PRESS, 163 Amsterdam Ave., #201, New York NY 10023-5001. (212)838-8640. Fax: (212)873-7065. **Acquisitions:** Bob Persky, publisher. Estab. 1980. "Our prime areas of interest are books on the business of art and photography." Publishes trade paperback originals. Publishes 7 titles/year. Receives 25 submissions/year. 20% of books from first-time authors; 75% from unagented writers. Pays 7-12% royalty on receipts. Offers $500 average advance. Publishes book 6 months after acceptance. Reports in 3 weeks. *Writer's Market* recommends allowing 2 months for reply. Book catalog free.

Imprint(s): The Photographic Arts Center.

Nonfiction: How-to, reference, art/architecture, business/economics of the art world and photography. "Writers should check *Books In Print* for competing titles." Submit outline and 2 sample chapters.

Recent Nonfiction Title(s): *Art of Displaying Art*, by Lawrence B. Smith (displaying art in homes, offices and galleries).

Tips: "Artists, photographers, galleries, museums, curators and art consultants are our audience."

CONSUMER PRESS, 13326 SW 28 St., Suite 102, Ft. Lauderdale FL 33330. **Acquisitions**: Joseph Pappas, editorial director. Publishes trade paperback originals. Publishes 2-5 titles/year. Receives 500 queries and 250 mss/year. 50% of books from first-time authors; 70% from unagented writers. Pays royalty on wholesale price or on retail price, as per agreement. Publishes book 6 months after acceptance of ms. Accepts simultaneous submissions. Book catalog free.

Imprint(s): Women's Publications.

Nonfiction: How-to, self-help. Subjects include child guidance/parenting, health/medicine, money/finance, women's issues/studies. Query with outline and SASE. Reviews artwork/photos as part of ms package. Send photocopies.

Recent Nonfiction Title(s): *The Ritalin Free Child*, by Diana Hunter.

COPPER CANYON PRESS, P.O. Box 271, Port Townsend WA 98368. (360)385-4925. **Acquisitions:** Sam Hamill, editor. "Copper Canyon Press has remained dedicated to publishing poetry in a wide range of styles and from a full range of the world's many cultures." Publishes trade paperback originals and occasional clothbound editions. Publishes 8 titles/year. Receives 1,500 queries/year and 500 mss/year. 10% of books from first-time authors; 95% from unagented writers. Pays 7-10% royalty on retail price. Publishes book 18 months after acceptance of ms. Reports in 1 month. Book catalog and ms guidelines free.

• Copper Canyon Press publishes such authors as Pablo Neruda, Carolyn Kizer and W.S. Merwin.

Poetry: *No unsolicited mss.* Query with 5-7 sample poems and SASE.

Recent Poetry Title(s): *Scrambled Eggs & Whiskey*, by Hayden Carruth.

CORNELL MARITIME PRESS, INC., P.O. Box 456, Centreville MD 21617-0456. (410)758-1075. Fax: (410)758-6849. **Acquisitions:** Charlotte Kurst, managing editor. Estab. 1938. "Cornell Maritime Press publishes books for the merchant marine and a few recreational boating books." Publishes hardcover originals and quality paperbacks for professional mariners and yachtsmen. Publishes 7-9 titles/year. Receives 150 submissions/year. 41% of books from first-time authors; 99% from unagented writers. "Payment is negotiable but royalties do not exceed 10% for first 5,000 copies, 12½% for second 5,000 copies, 15% on all additional. Royalties for original paperbacks are invariably lower. Revised editions revert to original royalty schedule." Publishes book 1 year after acceptance. Query first, with writing samples and outlines of book ideas. Reports in 2 months. Book catalog for 10×13 SAE with 5 first-class stamps.

Nonfiction: Marine subjects (highly technical), manuals, how-to books on maritime subjects. Tidewater imprint publishes books on regional history, folklore and wildlife of the Chesapeake Bay and the Delmarva Peninsula.

Recent Nonfiction Title(s): *Modern Marine Salvage*, by William I. Milwee, Jr.; *Making Money with Boats*, by Fred Edwards (business; *Applied Naval Architecture*, by Robert Zubaly.

CORWIN PRESS, INC., 2455 Teller Rd., Thousand Oaks CA 91320. (805)499-9734. **Acquisitions:** Ann McMartin, editor. Alice Foster, editor. Corwin Press, Inc. publishes leading-edge, user-friendly publications for education professionals. Publishes hardcover and paperback originals. Publishes 70 titles/year. Pays 10% royalty on net sales. Publishes book 7 months after acceptance of ms. Reports on queries in 1 month. *Writer's Market* recommends allowing 2 months for reply. Manuscript guidelines for #10 SASE.

Nonfiction: Professional-level publications for administrators, teachers, school specialists, policymakers, researchers and others involved with K-12 education. Seeking fresh insights, conclusions and recommendations for action. Prefers theory or research based books that provide real-world examples and practical, hands-on strategies to help busy educators be successful. No textbooks that simply summarize existing knowledge or mass-market books. Query.

COTTONWOOD PRESS, INC., 305 W. Magnolia, Suite 398, Fort Collins CO 80521. **Acquisitions:** Cheryl Thurston, editor. "We believe English should be everyone's favorite subject. We publish creative and practical materials for English and language arts teachers, grades 5-12." Publishes trade paperback originals. Publishes 2-8 titles/year. Receives 50 queries and 400 mss/year. 50% of books from first-time authors; 100% from unagented writers. Pays 10-12% royalty on net sales. Publishes book 1 year after acceptance. Accepts simultaneous submissions, if so noted. Reports in 1 month on queries and proposals, 3 months on mss. Book catalog for 6×9 SAE with 2 first-class stamps. Manuscript guidelines for #10 SASE.
Nonfiction: Textbook. Subjects include education, language/literature. "We publish *only* supplemental textbooks for English/language arts teachers, grades 5-12, with an emphasis upon middle school and junior high materials. Don't assume we publish educational materials for all subject areas. We do not. Never submit anything to us before looking at our catalog. We have a very narrow focus and a distinctive style. Writers who don't understand that are wasting their time." Query with outline and 1-3 sample chapters. "We are always looking for truly original, creative materials for teachers."
Recent Nonfiction Title(s): *A Month of Fundays—A whole year of games and activities for just about every holiday*; *Beyond Roses Are Red, Violets Are Blue—A practical guide for helping students write free verse.*

‡COUNCIL FOR INDIAN EDUCATION, 2032 Woody Dr., Billings MT 59102-2852. (406)248-3465, MTWF, 1-5 pm Mountain Time. Fax: % (406)652-0536. **Acquisitions:** Hap Gilliland, president and editor. Estab. 1963. "We publish authentic Native American information that is well-written, for Native American and non-Indian readers alike." Publishes hardcover and trade paperback originals. Publishes 6 titles/year. Receives 200 queries/year. 75% of books from first-time authors; 100% from unagented writers. Pays 10% (book mss) on wholesale price or makes outright purchase of short stories. Publishes book 1 year after acceptance of ms. Accepts simultaneous submissions. Reports in 3 months on queries. Book catalog and ms guidelines for #10 SASE.
Nonfiction: Biography, how-to, humor, illustrated book, children's/juvenile. Subjects include anthropology/archaeology, education, ethnic, history, hobbies, nature/environment, recreation related to Indian life. Query. Reviews artwork/photos as part of the freelance ms package. Writers should send photocopies with SASE.
Recent Nonfiction Title(s): *Phillip Johnston and the Navajo Code Talkers*, by Sybil Lagerquist (history); *James Joe*, as told to Susan Thompson (autobiography).
Fiction: Adventure, ethnic, historical, humor, juvenile, mystery, picture books, short story collections, Western. Main character(s) must be authentic Native American. Submit synopsis or complete mss.
Recent Fiction Title(s): *Storypole Legends*, by Emerson N. Matson (NW Indian legends); *Journey to Center Place*, by Viola R. Gates; *Signs of Spring*, by Patrick Quinn.
Poetry: "We publish one poetry book every year or two—all poems related to Indian life must be upbeat, positive—no complaining." Submit individual poems or submit complete ms with SASE.
Tips: "Our books are for students, kindergarten through high school. Many are American Indian. We buy *only* books related to Native American life and culture, suitable for use in schools (all levels but mainly elementary). We accept no manuscripts June thru September."

COUNTERPOINT, 1627 I St. NW, Suite 850, Washington DC 20006. Fax: (202)887-0562. **Acquisitions**: Jack Shoemaker, editor-in-chief. "Counterpoint publishes serious literary work, with particular emphasis on natural history, science, philosophy and contemporary thought, history, art, poetry and fiction. All of our books are printed on acid-free paper, with cloth bindings sewn. In this multimedia age, we are committed to the significant readership that still demands and appreciates well-published and well-crafted books." Publishes hardcover and trade paperback originals and reprints. Publishes 20-25 titles/year. Receives 10 queries/week, 250 mss/year. 2% of books from first-time authors; 2% from unagented writers. Pays 7.5-15% royalty on retail price. Publishes book 18 months after acceptance of ms. Accepts simultaneous submissions. Reports in 2 months.
   ● Counterpoint accepts agented submissions only.
Nonfiction: Biography, coffee table book, gift book. Subjects include agriculture/horticulture, art/architecture, history, language/literature, nature/environment, philosophy, religion, science, translation. Agneted submissions only.
Recent Nonfiction Title(s): *Tube: The Invention of Television*, by David E. Fisher and Marshall John Fisher (history of science).
Fiction: Historical, humor, literary, mainstream/contemporary, religious, short story collections. Agented submissions only.
Recent Fiction Title(s): *Women in Their Beds*, by Gina Berriault (short stories).

‡THE COUNTRYMAN PRESS, Division of W.W. Norton & Co., Inc., P.O. Box 748, Woodstock VT 05091-0748. (802)457-4826. Fax: (802)457-1678. **Acquisitions:** Laura Jorstad, managing editor. "We aim to publish books of the highest quality that encourage physical fitness and appreciation for and understanding of the natural world, self-sufficiency and adventure." Publishes hardcover originals, trade paperback originals and reprints. Publishes 12 titles/year. Receives 1,000 queries/year. 30% of books from first-time authors; 70% from unagented writers. Pays 5-15% royalty on retail price. Offers $1,000-5,000 advance. Publishes book 18 months after acceptance of ms. Accepts simultaneous submissions. Reports in 2 months on proposals. Book catalog free. Manuscript guidelines for #10 SASE.

Imprint(s): Backcountry Publications.

Nonfiction: How-to, guidebooks, general nonfiction. Subjects include gardening, nature/environment, recreation, regional, travel, country living. "We publish several series of regional recreation guidebooks—hiking, bicycling, walking, fly-fishing—and are looking to expand them. We're also looking for books of national interest on travel, gardening, rural living, nature, and especially all types of fly-fishing." Submit proposal package including outline, 3 sample chapters, market information, author bio with SASE. Reviews artwork/photos as part of ms package. Send photocopies.

Recent Nonfiction Title(s): *Living with Herbs*, by Jo Ann Gardner (gardening); *Reading the Forested Landscape*, by Tom Wessels and Brian Cohen (natural history); *Tailwater Trout in the South*, by Jimmy Jacobs (fishing guidebook).

   ● Countryman Press no longer publishes fiction.

COUNTRYSPORT PRESS, 1515 Cass, P.O. Box 1856, Traverse City MI 49685. **Acquisitions:** Art DeLaurier Jr., editorial director. "Our audience is upscale sportsmen with interests in wingshooting, fly fishing, and other outdoor activities." Publishes hardcover originals and reprints. Publishes 12 titles/year. 20% of books from first-time authors; 90% from unagented writers. Pays royalty on wholesale price. Advance varies by title. Publishes book 1 year after acceptance of ms. Accepts simultaneous submissions. Reports in 1 month on queries; 3 months on proposals and mss. Book catalog free.

Nonfiction: Coffee table book, how-to, illustrated book, other. Subjects include wingshooting, fly fishing, outdoor-related subjects. "We are looking for high-quality writing that is often reflective, anecdotal, and that offers a complete picture of an outdoor experience." Query with outline and 3 sample chapters.

Recent Nonfiction Title(s): *Passing a Good Time*, by Gene Hill (outdoor stories).

CRAFTSMAN BOOK COMPANY, 6058 Corte Del Cedro, Carlsbad CA 92009-9974. (760)438-7828 or (800)829-8123. Fax: (760)438-0398. Website: http://www.craftsman-book.com. **Acquisitions:** Laurence D. Jacobs, editorial manager. Estab. 1957. Publishes paperback originals. Publishes 50 submissions/year. 85% of books from first-time authors; 98% from unagented writers. Pays 7½-12½% royalty on wholesale price or retail price. Publishes book 18 months after acceptance. Accepts simultaneous submissions. Reports in 1 month on queries. *Writer's Market* recommends allowing 2 months for reply. Book catalog and ms guidelines free.

   ● Craftsman publishes such authors as John Traister, Howard Massey and Jack Hageman.

Nonfiction: How-to, technical. All titles are related to construction for professional builders. Query. Reviews artwork/photos as part of ms package.

Recent Nonfiction Title(s): *Plumbing & HVAC Manhour Estimates*, by Ray Prescher; *Builder's Guide to Room Additions*, by Jack Jones; *Renovating & Restyling Vintage Homes*, by Lawrence Dworin.

Tips: "The book should be loaded with step-by-step instructions, illustrations, charts, reference data, forms, samples, cost estimates, rules of thumb, and examples that solve actual problems in the builder's office and in the field. The book must cover the subject completely, become the owner's primary reference on the subject, have a high utility-to-cost ratio, and help the owner make a better living in his chosen field."

CREATION HOUSE, Subsidiary of Strang Communications, 600 Rinehart Rd., Lake Mary FL 32746. (407)333-3132. **Acquisitions:** Ginger Schmaus, submissions coordinator. "Our target market is Pentecostal/charismatic Christians." Publishes hardcover and trade paperback originals. Publishes 25-30 titles/year. Receives 100 queries and 600 mss/year. 2% of books from first-time authors; 95% from unagented writers. Pays 4-18% royalty on retail price. Offers $1,500-5,000 advance. Publishes book 9 months after acceptance of ms. Accepts simultaneous submissions. Reports in 2 months on proposals, 3 months on mss. Manuscript guidelines for #10 SASE.

Nonfiction: Christian, spirit-filled interest, charismatic, cookbook, giftbook. Subjects include religion, spirituality (charismatic). Query with outline, 3 sample chapters, author bio and SASE.

Recent Nonfiction Title(s): *Multiplication*, by Tommy Barnett; *I'm Mad About You*, by Mack & Brenda Timberlake (Christian living); *Praying with Smith Wigglesworth*, by Larry Keefauver (devotional gift book).

CREATIVE PUBLISHING CO., The Early West, Box 9292, College Station TX 77842-0292. (409)775-6047. Fax: (409)764-7758. **Acquisitions:** Theresa Earle. Estab. 1978. Publishes hardcover originals. Receives 20-40 submissions/year. 50% of books from first-time authors; 100% from unagented writers. Royalty varies on wholesale price. Publishes book 8 months after acceptance. *Writer's Market* recommends allowing 2 months for reply. Free book catalog.

Nonfiction: Biography. Subjects include Americana (western), history. No mss other than 19th century Western America. Query. Reviews artwork/photos as part of ms package.

Recent Nonfiction Title(s): *Goodbye Billy the Kid*, by Harold Edwards.

CRESTWOOD HOUSE, Imprint of Silver Burdett Press, Division Simon & Schuster, 299 Jefferson Rd., Parsippany NJ 07054. (201)236-7000. Fax: (201)326-8606. **Acquisitions:** Debbie Biber, acquisitions editor. Publishes hardcover and trade paperback originals. Publishes 15-20 titles/year. 10% of books from first-time authors; 80% from unagented writers. Pays 3-7½% royalty on retail price. Advance varies. Publishes book 2-3 years after acceptance of ms. Accepts simultaneous submissions. Reports in 6 months on queries, 1 year on mss.

Nonfiction: Childrens/juvenile. Subjects include high-lo, biographies. Books must be accessible to reluctant readers, a casual style. *Not accepting unsolicited submissions at this time.*

CROSS CULTURAL PUBLICATIONS, INC., P.O. Box 506, Notre Dame IN 46556. Fax: (219)273-5973. **Acquisitions**: Cyriac Pullapilly, general editor. "We publish scholarly books that deal with intercultural topics—regardless of discipline." Publishes hardcover and software originals. Publishes 15-20 titles/year. Receives 3,000 queries and 1,000 mss/year. 25% of books from first-time authors; 99% from unagented writers. Pays 10% royalty on wholesale price. Publishes book 6 months after acceptance of ms. Accepts simultaneous submissions. Reports in 1 month on queries. *Writer's Market* recommends allowing 2 months for reply. Book catalog free.
Nonfiction: Biography. Subjects include government/politics, history, philosophy, religion, sociology, scholarly. "Books pushing into new horizons are welcome, but they have to be intellectually sound and balanced in judgement." Query.
Recent Nonfiction Title(s): *An Agenda for Sustainability: Fairness in a World of Limits*, by William M. Bueler (environmental); *Your Neighbor As Yourself: Race, Religion and Region in North America Into the 21st Century*, by Brian A. Brown (Canadian-American relations).

THE CROSSING PRESS, 97 Hangar Way, Watsonville CA 95019. **Acquisitions:** Elaine Goldman Gill, publisher. The Crossing Press publishes women's interest titles with an emphasis on health and spiritual growth and healing. Publishes trade paperback originals. Publishes 50 titles/year. Receives 1,600 submissions/year. 10% of books from first-time authors; 75% from unagented writers. Pays royalty. Publishes book 18 months after acceptance. Accepts simultaneous submissions. Reports in 2 months on queries. Book catalog free.
Nonfiction: Cookbook, women's interest. Subjects include alternative health, New Age (astrology, magic, psychic healing, spiritual growth). Submit outline and sample chapter.
Recent Nonfiction Title(s): *Sacrificing Our Selves for Love*, by Jane Hyman and Esther Rome.
Tips: "Simple intelligent query letters do best. No come-ons, no cutes. It helps if there are credentials. Authors should research the press first to see what sort of books it publishes."

CROSSWAY BOOKS, Division of Good News Publishers, 1300 Crescent St., Wheaton IL 60187-5800. Fax: (630)682-4785. Vice President, Editorial and Editor-in-Chief: Leonard G. Goss. **Acquisitions:** Jill Carter. Estab. 1938. " 'Making a difference in people's lives for Christ' as its maxim, Crossway Books lists titles written from an evangelical Christian perspective. Both its expansive fiction line and its nonfiction list present a Christian worldview." Publishes hardcover and trade paperback originals. Publishes 50 titles/year. Receives 3,000 submissions/year. 5% of books from first-time authors; 75% from unagented writers. Average print order for a first book is 5,000-10,000. Pays negotiable royalty. Offers negotiable advance. Publishes book 1 year after acceptance. No phone queries. Reports in up to 9 months. Book catalog and ms guidelines for 9×12 SAE with 6 first-class stamps.
• Crossway Books has published such authors as Frank Peretti, Max Lucardo and Tony Evans.
Nonfiction: "Books that provide fresh understanding and a distinctively Christian examination of questions confronting Christians and non-Christians in their personal lives, families, churches, communities and the wider culture. The main types include: (1) Issues books that typically address critical issues facing Christians today; (2) Books on the deeper Christian life that provide a deeper understanding of Christianity and its application to daily life; and, (3) Christian academic and professional books directed at an audience of religious professionals." Query with SASE.
Recent Nonfiction Title(s): *A Heart Like His*, by Rebecca Manley Pippert (Christian living); *The Glory of Heaven*, by John F. MacArthur (theology); *Billy: A Personal Look at the World's Best Loved Evangelist*, by Sherwood Eliot Wirt.
Fiction: "We publish fiction that falls into these categories: (1) Christian realism, or novels set in modern, true-to-life settings as a means of telling stories about Christians today in an increasingly post-Christian era; (2) Supernatural fiction, or stories typically set in the 'real world' but that bring supernatural reality into it in a way that heightens our spiritual dimension; (3) Historical fiction, using historical characters, times and places of interest as a mirror for our own times; (4) Some genre-technique fiction (mystery, western); and (5) Children's fiction." Query with SASE.
Recent Fiction Title(s): *Lethal Mercy*, by Harry Lee Kraus Jr. (medical thriller); *In Honor Bound*, by DeAnna Dodson (historical); *Tell Me the Promises*, by Joni Eaveckson Toda.
Tips: "We are not interested in romance novels, horror novels, biblical novels (i.e., stories set in Bible times that fictionalize events in the lives of prominent biblical characters), issues novels (i.e., fictionalized treatments of contemporary issues), and end times/prophecy novels. We do not accept full manuscripts or electronic submissions."

CROWN PUBLISHING GROUP, Division of Random House, 201 E. 50th St., New York NY 10022. General interest publisher of hardcover and trade paperback originals. Publishes 277 titles/year.
Imprint(s): Bell Tower, **Clarkson Potter**, Crown Arts & Letters, Crown Books for Young Readers, Harmony Books, Living Language, Prince Paperbacks, Carol Southern Books.

‡**CSLI PUBLICATIONS**, The Center for the Study of Language and Information, Stanford University, Ventura Hall, Stanford CA 94305. (415)723-1839. **Acquisitions:** Tony Gee, editorial associate. "We prefer works recommended by professors and researchers in the field of linguistics." Publishes hardcover and trade paperback originals. Publishes 10 titles/year. Receives 75-100 queries and 23-35 mss/year. 50% of books from first-time authors; 100% from unagented writers. Pays 5-10% royalty on retail price or makes outright purchase for books. Offers $150-250 advance. Publishes book 1 year after acceptance of ms. "We do not accept simultaneous submissions." Does not return submissions. Reports in 3 months on queries, 1 year on proposals and mss.
Nonfiction: Textbook, other academic books. Subjects include linguistics, computer science. Query. "We only accept

camera-ready copy."
Recent Nonfiction Title(s): *Perspectives In Phonology,* by Jennifer Cole and Charles Kisseberth (linguistics text).

‡**CUMBERLAND HOUSE PUBLISHING,** 2200 Abbott Marten Rd., Suite 102, Nashville TN 37215. (615)385-2444. Fax: (615)385-3772. E-mail: cumbhouse@aol.com. **Acquisitions:** Ron Pitkin, president; Julia M. Pitkin (cooking/lifestyle). "We look for unique titles with clearly defined audiences." Publishes hardcover and trade paperback originals, and hardcover and trade paperback reprints. Publishes 35 titles/year. Imprint publishes 5 titles/year. Receives 1,000 queries and 400 mss/year. 30% of books from first-time authors; 80% from unagented writers. Pays 10-20% royalty on wholesale price. Offers $1,000-25,000 advance. Publishes book an average of 8 months after acceptance. Accepts simultaneous submissions. Reports in 2 months on queries and proposals, 4 months on mss. Book catalog for 8×10 SAE and 4 first-class stamps. Manuscript guidelines free.
Imprint(s): Cumberland House Hearthside: Julia M. Pitkin, editor-in-chief.
● Cumberland House has published such authors as William F. Buckley, Jr., Arnold Palmer and Steve Cox.
Nonfiction: Cookbook, gift book, how-to, humor, illustrated book, reference. Subjects include Americana, business/economics, cooking/foods/nutrition, government/politics, history, hobbies, military/war, money/finance, recreation, regional, sports, travel. Query or submit outline. Reviews artwork/photos as part of ms package. Send photocopies.
Recent Nonfiction Title(s): *Blue Plate Special,* by Liz McKeon (cookbook); *The Munchkins of Oz,* by Steve Cox (entertainment); *Bringing Out the Winner in Your Child,* by John Croyle (parenting).
Fiction: Mystery, western. Writers should know "the odds are really stacked against them." Query.
Recent Fiction Title(s): *A Rumor of Bones,* by Beverly Connor (mystery); *The Broncbuster,* by Mike Flanagan.
Tips: Audience is "adventuresome people who like a fresh approach to things. Writers should tell what their idea is, why it's unique and why somebody would want to buy it—but don't pester us."

‡**CUMMINGS & HATHAWAY,** 422 Atlantic Ave., East Rockaway NY 11518. (800)344-7579. **Acquisitions:** William Burke, director of publications. "We are a 'teacher's publisher.'" Publishes textbooks, paperback originals and reprints. Publishes 20-25 titles/year. Receives 75-100 queries and 10-15 unsolicited mss/year. 99% of books from first-time authors; 99% from unagented writers. Pays 10-25% royalty on wholesale price. Offers $500 maximum advance rarely. Publishes book 4 months after acceptance of ms. Reports in 1 month on queries. Manuscript guidelines free.
Nonfiction: Biography, reference, technical, textbook. Subjects include anthropology/archaeology, business/economics, computers/electronics, education, ethnic, gay/lesbian, government/politics, health medicine, history, language/literature, military/war, money/finance, music/dance, philosophy, psychology, regional, religion, sociology, women's issues/studies. "We publish texts for college courses controlled by the author and for which he/she can assure us of 100 copies sold within first year. Manuscript must be original. We do not publish collections requiring extensive permissions." Query.
Recent Nonfiction Title(s): *Road Map of Head & Neck Anatomy,* by Rumy Hilloowala (textbook/reference); *Handbook of Public Speaking,* by Richard Letteri (textbook); *Macroeconomics in Brief,* by Peter M. Gutmann (textbook).

‡**CURRENCY,** Imprint of Doubleday, 1540 Broadway, New York NY 10036. (212)354-6500. Fax: (212)782-8911. **Acquisitions:** Harriet Rubin, executive editor; Kathleen Berger, assistant editor. Estab. 1989. Currency publishes "books for people who want to make a difference, not just a living." Pays 7½-15% royalty on net price. Offers advance. Publishes book 1 year after acceptance of ms.
● This publisher accepts agented submissions only.
Nonfiction: Subjects include business/economics. Agented submissions only.
Recent Nonfiction Title(s): *The Princessa: Macchiavelli for Women,* by Harriet Rubin (business/women's studies); *The Compleat Perfectionist,* by Juan Ramon Jiminez (philosophy/self-help); *Dig Well Before You're Thirst,* by Harvey Mackay (business/management).

CURRENT CLINICAL STRATEGIES PUBLISHING, 27071 Cabot Rd., Suite 126, Laguna Hills CA 92653. E-mail: ccspublishing@msn.com. Website: http://www.ccspublishing.com. **Acquisitions:** Camille deTonnancour, editor. "We are a medical publisher for healthcare professionals." Publishes trade paperback originals. Publishes 20 titles/year. Receives 10 queries and 10 mss/year. 50% of books from first-time authors; 80% from unagented writers. Pays royalty. Publishes book 6 months after acceptance of ms.
Nonfiction: Technical. Subjects include health/medicine. Submit 6 sample chapters. Reviews artwork/photos as part of ms package. Send photocopies.
Recent Nonfiction Title(s): *Current Clinical Strategies, Gynecology and Obstetrics, 3rd ed.,* by Paul D. Chan and Christopher R. Winkle (medical reference).

‡**CURTIS/STRONGMEN PUBLISHING,** P.O. Box 4306, Grand Central Station, New York NY 10163. (212)544-8592. **Acquisitions:** Antonio M. Monaco, editor. Publishes hardcover, trade paperback and mass market paperback originals. Publishes 11 titles/year, 5-6 imprint titles/year. Receives 120 queries and 25 mss/year. Pays 5-12% royalty on wholesale price. Offers negotiable advance. Publishes book 5 months after acceptance of ms. Accepts simultaneous submissions. Reports in 1 month on queries and proposals, 2 months on mss. Book catalog free. Manuscript guidelines for #10 SASE.
Imprint(s): Curtis (James J. Izzo, publisher), Strongmen (Antonio M. Monaco, editor).
Nonfiction: Biography, self-help. "We publish quality masculine gay nonfiction." Query or submit outline and 10-12 sample pages with SASE. Reviews artwork/photos as part of ms package. Send photocopies.

Fiction: "We publish quality (and racy) masculine gay fiction. Don't send lengthy sample material." Query or submit synopsis amd 10-12 sample pages with SASE.
Tips: Audience is "mainstream gay males, their friends and families. Keep within our guidelines and only submit material consistent with Curtis/Strongmen themes. Most importantly—keep writing!"

DANCE HORIZONS, Imprint of Princeton Book Co., Publishers, P.O. Box 57, 12 W. Delaware Ave., Pennington NJ 08534. (609)737-8177. Fax: (609)737-1869. Publicity Manager: Frank Bridges. **Acquisitions:** Charles Woodford, president. Estab. 1976. Publishes hardcover and paperback originals, paperback reprints. Publishes 10 titles/year. Receives 25-30 submissions/year. 50% of books from first-time authors; 98% of books from unagented writers. Pays 10% royalty on net receipts. No advance. Publishes book 10 months after acceptance. Accepts simultaneous submissions. Reports in 3 months. Book catalog free.
Nonfiction: Dance and children's movement subjects only. *Writer's Market* recommends sending a query with SASE.
Recent Nonfiction Title(s): *Lugi's Jazz Warm Up*, by Lugi Loraine Kriegel and Francis Roach.
Tips: "We're very careful about the projects we take on. They have to be, at the outset, polished, original and cross-marketable."

DANTE UNIVERSITY OF AMERICA PRESS, INC., P.O. Box 843, Brookline Village MA 02147-0843. Fax: (617)734-2046. E-mail: danteu@usa1.com. Website: http://www1.usa1.com/~danteu/. **Acquisitions:** Adolph Caso, president. "The Dante University Press exists to bring quality, educational books pertaining to our Italian heritage as well as the historical and political studies of America. Profits from the sale of these publications benefit the Foundation, bringing Dante University closer to a reality." Estab. 1975. Publishes hardcover and trade paperback originals and reprints. Publishes 5 titles/year. Receives 50 submissions/year. 50% of books from first-time authors; 50% from unagented writers. Average print order for a first book is 3,000. Pays royalty. Negotiable advance. Publishes book 10 months after acceptance. Query only with SASE. Reports in 2 months.
Nonfiction: Biography, reference, reprints, translations from Italian and Latin. Subjects include general scholarly nonfiction, Renaissance thought and letter, Italian language and linguistics, Italian-American history and culture, bilingual education. Query first with SASE. Reviews artwork/photos as part of ms package.
Fiction: Translations from Italian and Latin. Query first with SASE.
Recent Fiction Title(s): *Rogue Angel*, by Carol Damioli.
Poetry: "There is a chance that we would use Renaissance poetry translations."
Recent Poetry Title(s): *Italian Poetry 1950-1990*.

DARLINGTON PRODUCTIONS, INC., P.O. Box 5884, Darlington MD 21034. (410)457-5400. E-mail: dpi14@aol.com. **Acquisitions:** Jeffrey D. McKaughan, president. Darlington publishes military history/war reference and illustated titles. Publishes hardcover originals, trade paperback originals and reprints. Publishes 9 titles/year. Receives 20 queries/year. 75% of books published are from first-time writers; 100% from unagented writers. Pays 10% royalty on retail price and small bulk fee at time of release. No advance. Publishes book 6 months after acceptance. Accepts simultaneous submissions. Reports in 1 month on queries and proposals, 3 months on mss. Book catalog and ms guidelines free.
Nonfiction: Illustrated book, reference, technical. Military history/war subjects. Query with outline. Reviews artwork/photos as part of ms package. Send photocopies.
Recent Nonfiction Title(s): *Panzerkampfwagen MAUS*, by Thomas Jentz (WWII); *IS-III Soviet Heavy Tank*, by Steve Zaloga (AFV study); *British Firefly*, by David Fletcher (WWII AFV study).

DATABOOKS, Subsidiary of Rainbow New England Corp., 335 Chandler St., Worcester MA 01602. (508)756-7644. Fax: (508)756-9425. E-mail: databooks@tatnuck.com. Website: http://www.tatnuck.com. Publisher: Lawrence J. Abramoff. **Acquisitions:** Jennifer Goguen, publishing assistant. Databooks is a general interest nonfiction publisher. Publishes hardcover and trade paperback originals and reprints. Publishes 12-15 titles/year. Receives 200 queries and 50 mss/year. 50% of books from first-time authors; 70% from unagented writers. Pays royalty on retail price or makes outright purchase. Publishes book 1 year after acceptance of ms. Accepts simultaneous submissions. Reports in 1 month. *Writer's Market* recommends allowing 2 months for reply. Book catalog and manuscript guidelines free.
Imprint(s): Tatnuck Bookseller Press, Professional Development Press.
Nonfiction: Biography, cookbook, gift book, how-to, illustrated book, reference, self-help, technical. Subjects include Americana, cooking/foods/nutrition, history, military/war, recreation, regional, science, sports, travel. Submit outline, 1-3 sample chapters and SASE. Reviews artwork/photos as part of ms package. Send photocopies.
Recent Nonfiction Title(s): *Affirmations of Wealth, 101 Secrets of Daily Success*, by V. John Alexandrov (motivational, self-help); *The Worcester Account*, by S.N. Behrman (autobiography).
Fiction: Historical.

MAY DAVENPORT, PUBLISHERS, 26313 Purissima Rd., Los Altos Hills CA 94022. (415)948-6499. Fax: (415)948-6499. **Acquisitions:** May Davenport, editor/publisher. Estab. 1976. "We prefer books which can be *used* in high schools as supplementary readings in English or creative writing courses. Reading skills have to be taught, and novels by humorous authors can be more pleasant to read than Hawthorne's or Melville's novels, war novels, or novels about past generations. Humor has a place in literature." Imprint is md Books (nonfiction and fiction). Publishes hardcover and trade paperback originals. Publishes 4 titles/year. Receives 1,500 submissions/year. 95% of books from first-time authors; 100% from unagented writers. Pays 15% royalty on retail price. No advance. Publishes book 1 year after acceptance. Reports in 1 month. *Writer's Market* recommends allowing 2 months for reply. Book catalog and ms guidelines for #10 SASE.

Nonfiction: Subjects include: Americana, language/literature, humorous memoirs for children/young adults. "For children ages 6-8: stories to read with pictures to color in 500 words. For preteens and young adults: exhibit your writing skills and entertain them with your literary tools. Query with SASE.

Recent Nonfiction Title(s): *Grandpa McKucheon's Kangaroomatic Rocking Chair*, by Jonathan Middleton.

Fiction: Humor, literary. Novels: "We want to focus on novels junior and senior high school teachers can share with their reluctant readers in their classrooms."

Recent Fiction Title(s): *Drivers Ed is Dead*, by Pat Delgado; *The Newman Assignment*, by Kurt Haberl; *When the Dancing Ends*, by Judy Hairfield.

Tips: "Since the TV-oriented youth in schools today do not like to read or to write, why not create books for that impressionable and captive audience? Great to work with talented writers especially when writers are happy and inspired within themselves."

JONATHAN DAVID PUBLISHERS, INC., 68-22 Eliot Ave., Middle Village NY 11379-1194. Fax: (718)894-2818. **Acquisitions:** Alfred J. Kolatch, editor-in-chief. Estab. 1948. Jonathan David publishes "popular Judaica." Publishes hardcover and trade paperback originals and reprints. Publishes 20-25 titles/year. 50% of books from first-time authors; 90% from unagented writers. Pays royalty or makes outright purchase. Publishes book 18 months after acceptance of ms. Reports in 2 months on queries. Book catalog for 6×9 SAE with 4 first-class stamps.

• This publisher has expressed an interest in seeing more projects geared toward children.

Nonfiction: Cookbook, how-to, reference, self-help. Submit outline, 1 sample chapter and SASE.

Recent Nonfiction Title(s): *Great Jewish Men*, by Elinor Slater and Robert Slater.

HARLAN DAVIDSON, INC., 773 Glenn Ave., Wheeling IL 60090-6000. (847)541-9720. Fax: (847)541-9830. E-mail: harlandavidson@harlandavidson.com. Website: http://www.harlandavidson.com. **Acquisitions:** Andrew J. Davidson, publisher. Harlan Davidson publishes college textbooks in American, biographical, women's and European history, drama, literature and political science. Estab. 1972. Publishes college texts, both hardcover and paperback. Publishes 6-15 titles/year. Receives 100 queries and 15 mss/year. 100% of books from unagented writers. Manuscripts contracted as work for hire. Pays royalty on net. Publishes book 10 months after acceptance of ms. Accepts simultaneous submissions. Reports in 3 months on proposals. Book catalog free.

Imprint(s): Forum Press, Inc.; Crofts Classics.

Nonfiction: Textbooks. Subjects include business, education, ethnic history, government, history (main list), biographical history, literature, philosophy, regional and state histories, women's issues/studies. "Because we are a college textbook publisher, academic credentials are extremely important. We usually find our own authors for a need in the field that we identify, but we are also receptive to ideas brought to us by qualified professionals, in history, especially." Submit proposal package, including outline, brief description of proposed book, its market and competition and a recent vita.

Recent Nonfiction Title(s): *And Still They Come: Immigrants & American Society, 1920 to the 1990s*, by Elliott Robert Barkan; *The History of Texas*, 2E, by Robert A. Calvert and Arnoldo DeLeón; *Hitler, Stalin, & Mussolini: Totalitarianism in the Twentieth Century*, by Bruce F. Pauley.

DAVIS PUBLICATIONS, INC., 50 Portland St., Worcester MA 01608. (508)754-7201. Fax: (508)753-3834. **Acquisitions:** Claire Mowbray Golding, editorial director (grades K-8); Helen Ronan, editorial director (grades 9-12). Estab. 1901. Davis publishes art, design and craft books for the elementary and high school markets. Publishes 5-10 titles/year. Pays 10-12% royalty. Publishes book 1 year after acceptance. Book catalog for 9×12 SAE with 2 first-class stamps. Authors guidelines for SASE.

Nonfiction: Publishes technique-oriented art, design and craft books for the educational market, as well as books dealing with art and culture, and art history. "Keep in mind the intended audience. Our readers are visually oriented. All illustrations should be collated separately from the text, but keyed to the text. Photos should be good quality transparencies and black and white photographs. Well-selected illustrations should explain, amplify, and enhance the text. We average 2-4 photos/page. We like to see technique photos as well as illustrations of finished artwork, by a variety of artists, including students. Recent books have been on printmaking, clay sculpture, design, jewelry, drawing and watercolor painting." Submit outline, sample chapters and illustrations. Reviews artwork/photos as part of ms package.

Recent Nonfiction Title(s): *Pioneering Spirits*, by Abby Remer (women artists); *Humor in Art*, by Nicholas Roukes (visual wit).

DAW BOOKS, INC., Division of Penguin Putnam Inc., 375 Hudson St., 3rd Floor, New York NY 10014-3658. **Acquisitions:** Peter Stampfel, submissions editor. Estab. 1971. Publishes science fiction and fantasy hardcover and paperback originals and reprints. Publishes 60-80 titles/year. Pays in royalties with an advance negotiable on a book-by-book basis. Sends galleys to author. Simultaneous submissions "returned unread at once, unless prior arrangements are made by agent." Reports in 6 weeks "or longer, if a second reading is required." Book catalog free.

Fiction: "We are interested in science fiction and fantasy novels. We need science fiction more than fantasy right now, but we're still looking for both. We're not looking for horror novels, but we are looking for mainstream suspense thrillers. We accept both agented and unagented manuscripts. We are not seeking collections of short stories or ideas

for anthologies. We do not want any nonfiction manuscripts." Submit complete ms. *Writer's Market* recommends sending a query with SASE first.
Recent Fiction Title(s): *King's Dragon*, by Kay Elliott; *The Made Born Trader*, by Melanie Rawn.

DAWN PUBLICATIONS, 14618 Tyler Foote Rd., Nevada City CA 95959. (800)545-7475. Website: http://www.dawnpub.com. **Acquisitions:** Glenn J. Hovemann, editor. "Dawn Publications is dedicated to inspiring in children a sense of appreciation for all life on earth." Publishes hardcover and trade paperback originals. Publishes 6 titles/year. Receives 250 queries and 1,500 mss/year. 35% of books from first-time authors; 100% from unagented writers. Pays royalty on wholesale price. Publishes book 1 year after acceptance of ms. Accepts simultaneous submissions. Reports in 2 months. Book catalog and ms guidelines for #10 SASE.
Nonfiction: Children's/juvenile. Nature awareness and inspiration. Query with SASE.
Recent Nonfiction Title(s): *Lifetimes*, by David Rice (some of nature's longest, shortest, most unusual lifetimes).
Fiction: Children's juvenile. Nature awareness and inspiration. Query with SASE.
Recent Fiction Title(s): *Walking with Mama*, by Barbara Stynes (shows the sweetness and intimacy of a walk in nature by toddler and mother).

‡DAYBREAK BOOKS, Imprint of Rodale Press, Inc., 733 Third Ave., 15th Floor, New York NY 10017-3204. **Acquisitions:** Karen Kelly, editorial director. Publishes hardcover originals. Publishes 10-15 titles/year. Pays 6-15% royalty on retail price. Publishes book 12-18 months after acceptance of ms. Accepts simultaneous submissions. Reports in 1 month on queries, 2 months on proposals and mss. Book catalog and ms guidelines free.
Nonfiction: "Daybreak Books explore all aspects of spirituality and humanity through a variety of voices, viewpoints and approaches." Query with outline, 1-2 sample chapters and proposal package including author's résumé.
Recent Nonfiction Title(s): *12 Lessons on Life I Learned from My Garden*, by Vivian Elisabeth Glyck and *Gift of Life: A Spiritual Companion for the Mother-To-Be*, by Joan Swirsky (spirituality).

‡DEAD LETTER, Imprint of St. Martin's Press, 175 Fifth Ave., New York NY 10010. (212)674-5151. **Acquisitions:** Joe Veltre, editor. Publishes trade paperback originals and reprints, mass market paperback originals and reprints. Publishes 36 titles/year. 15% of books from first-time authors; 7% from unagented writers. Pays variable royalty on net price. Advance varies. Accepts simultaneous submissions. Book catalog and ms guidelines not available.
Fiction: Mystery. Query with synopsis, 3 sample chapters and SASE.
Recent Fiction Title(s): *A Stiff Risotto*, by Lou Jane Temple; *Mortal Causes*, by Ian Rankin.

DEARBORN FINANCIAL PUBLISHING, INC., 155 N. Wacker Dr., Chicago IL 60606-1719. (312)836-4400. Fax: (312)836-1021. Website: http://www.dearborn.com. **Acquisitions:** Diana Faulhaber (real estate); Cynthia Zigmund (finance); Anne Shropshire (insurance). Estab. 1959. "We provide products and services for information, education and training globally. We are highly focused in niche markets and expect to be a recognized leader in each market segment we serve." Publishes hardcover and paperback originals. Publishes 200 titles/year. Receives 200 submissions/year. 50% of books from first-time authors; 50% from unagented writers. Pays 1-15% royalty on wholesale price. Publishes book 6 months after acceptance. Accepts simultaneous submissions. Reports in 1 month. *Writer's Market* recommends allowing 2 months for reply. Book catalog and ms guidelines free.
Imprint(s): Upstart Publishing Co.
   ● Dearborn Financial Publishing has published such authors as Jordan Goodman, Carol Kleiman and Edith Lank.
Nonfiction: How-to, reference, textbooks. Subjects include small business, real estate, insurance, banking, securities, money/finance. Query.
Recent Nonfiction Title(s): *Wall Street's Picks For 1997*, by Kirk Kazanjian (investments); *Annuities, 2nd edition*, by David Shapiro, Thomas Streiff (insurance); *Modern Real Estate Practice, 14th edition*, by Galaty, Allaway, Kyle.
Tips: "People seeking real estate, insurance, broker's licenses are our audience; also professionals in these areas. Additionally, we publish for consumers who are interested in buying homes, managing their finances; and people interested in starting and running a small business."

IVAN R. DEE, INC., 1332 N. Halsted St., Chicago IL 60622-2637. (312)787-6262. Fax: (312)787-6269. **Acquisitions:** Ivan R. Dee, president. Estab. 1988. Ivan R. Dee publishes serious nonfiction for general informed readers. Publishes hardcover originals and trade paperback originals and reprints. Publishes 25 titles/year. 10% of books from first-time authors; 75% from unagented writers. Pays royalty. Publishes book 9 months after acceptance. Reports in 1 month on queries. *Writer's Market* recommends allowing 2 months for reply. Book catalog free.
Imprint(s): Elephant Paperbacks.
Nonfiction: History, literature and letters, biography, politics, contemporary affairs, theater. Submit outline and sample chapters. Reviews artwork/photos as part of ms package.
   ● Ivan R. Dee has published such authors as Anthony Burgess, Gertrude Himmelfarb and Aldous Huxley.
Recent Nonfiction Title(s): *Passage to Union*, by Sarah H. Gordon (American history); *The Politics of Memory*, by Raul Hilberg (memoir); *To Sleep with the Angels*, by David Cowan and John Kuenster (history).
Tips: "We publish for an intelligent lay audience and college course adoptions."

DEL REY BOOKS, Imprint of Ballantine Books, Division of Random House, 201 E. 50th St., New York NY 10022-7703. (212)572-2677. E-mail: delrey@randomhouse.com. Website: http://www.randomhouse.com/delrey/. Executive

Editor: Shelly Shapiro. Senior Editor: Veronica Chapman. **Acquisitions:** Jill Benjamin. Estab. 1977. Del Rey publishes top level fantasy and science fiction. "In terms of mass market, we basically created the field of fantasy bestsellers. Not that it didn't exist before, but we put the mass into mass market." Publishes hardcover, trade paperback, and mass market originals and mass market paperback reprints. Publishes 60 titles/year. Receives 1,900 submissions/year. 10% of books from first-time authors; 40% from unagented writers. Pays royalty on retail price. Offers competitive advance. Publishes book 1 year after acceptance. Reports in 6 months, occasionally longer. Writer's guidelines for #10 SASE.
Fiction: Fantasy ("should have the practice of magic as an essential element of the plot"), science fiction ("well-plotted novels with good characterization, exotic locales, and detailed alien cultures"). Query first to Jill Benjamin with detailed outline and synopsis of story from beginning to end. *Does not accept unsolicited mss.*
Recent Fiction Title(s): *First King of Shamara*, by Terry Brooks; *Worldwar: Upsetting the Balance*, by Harry Turtledove; *The Wind After Time*, by Chris Bunch.
Tips: "Del Rey is a reader's house. Our audience is anyone who wants to be pleased by a good, entertaining novel. Pay particular attention to plotting and a satisfactory conclusion. It must be/feel believable. That's what the readers like."

DELACORTE PRESS, Imprint of Dell Publishing, Division of Bantam Doubleday Dell, 1540 Broadway, New York NY 10036. (212)354-6500. Editor-in-Chief: Leslie Schnur. **Acquisitions:** (Ms.) Jackie Cantor (women's fiction); Steve Ross (commercial nonfiction and fiction). Publishes hardcover and trade paperback originals. Publishes 36 titles/year. Pays 7½-12½% royalty. Advance varies. Publishes book 2 years after acceptance, but varies. Accepts simultaneous submissions. Reports in 3-4 months. Guidelines for 9×12 SASE.
   • Delacorte has published such authors as Barbara De Angelis, Elmore Leonard, Danielle Steel and Nicholas Evans.
Nonfiction and Fiction: Query with outline, first 3 chapters or brief proposal. No mss for children's or young adult books accepted in this division. No poetry accepted.
Recent Nonfiction Title(s): *A Day in the Life: The Music and Artistry of the Beatles*, by Mark Hetsgaard; *Real Moments for Lovers*, by Barbara De Angelis.
Recent Fiction Title(s): *The Horse Whisperer*, by Nicholas Evans; *Hardcase*, by Bill Pronzin; *The Magic Bullet*, by Harry Stein.

DELL PUBLISHING, Division of Bantam Doubleday Dell, Inc., 1540 Broadway, New York NY 10036. General interest publisher of all categories of fiction and nonfiction. Publishes approximately 40 books/month. Query Editorial Department before submitting. Unsolicited and unagented mss will not receive a response for 4 months.
Imprint(s): Delacorte Press, Dell Abyss, Dell Books, **Dell Publishing Island**, **Delta Trade Paperbacks**, **Dial Books**, Bland Books, Laurel Books.

‡**DELL PUBLISHING ISLAND**, Imprint of Dell Publishing, Division of Bantam Doubleday Dell, 1540 Broadway, New York NY 10036. (212)354-6500. **Acquisitions**: Leslie Schnur, editor-in-chief. Publishes trade paperback originals and reprints. Publishes bestseller fiction and nonfiction. Publishes 12 titles/year. 15% of books from first-time authors; 5% from unagented writers. Pay 7½-12½% royalty on retail price. Advance varies. Publishes book 1 year after acceptance of ms. Accepts simultaneous submissions. Reports in 4-6 months on queries. Book catalog for 9×12 SAE and 3 first class stamps.
Nonfiction: subjects include government/politics, health/medicine, history, psychology. Query with synopsis, 2-3 sample chapters and SASE.
Fiction: Mystery, romance, suspense.
Recent Fiction Title(s): *Runaway Jury*, by John Grisham (suspense).

‡**DELL TRADE PAPERBACKS**, Imprint of Dell Publishing, Division of Bantam Doubleday Dell, 1540 Broadway, New York NY 10036. (212)354-6500. **Acquisitions**: Leslie Schnur, editor-in-chief. Publishes trade paperback originals, mostly light, humorous material and books on pop culture. Publishes 36 titles/year. 15% of books from first-time authors; 5% from unagented writers. Pays 7½-12½% royalty on retail price. Advance varies. Publishes book 1 year after acceptance of ms. Accepts simultaneous submissions. Reports in 4-6 months on queries. Book catalog for 9×12 SAE and 3 first class stamps.
Nonfiction: Humor, self-help, pop culture. Query with synopsis, 2-3 sample chapters and SASE.
Recent Nonfiction Title(s): *Real Moments*, by Barbara Deangelis (self-help); *Seven Weeks to Better Sex*, by Domeena Renshan.

‡**DELTA TRADE PAPERBACKS**, Imprint of Dell Publishing, Division of Bantam Doubleday Dell, 1540 Broadway, New York NY 10036. (212)354-6500. **Acquisitions**: Leslie Schnur, editor-in-chief. Publishes trade paperback originals, mostly light, humorous material and books on pop culture. Publishes 36 titles/year. 15% of books from first-time authors; 5% from unagented writers. Pays 7½-12½% royalty on retail price. Advance varies. Publishes book 1 year after acceptance of ms. Accepts simultaneous submissions. Reports in 4-6 months on queries. Book catalog for 9×12 SAE and 3 first class stamps.
Nonfiction: Biography, memoir. Subjects include child guidance/parenting, ethnic, health/medicine, music/dance. Query with synopsis, 2-3 sample chapters and SASE.
Recent Nonfiction Title(s): *Oasis: What's the Story*, by Ian Robertson (music); *What Your Kindergartner Needs to*

Know, edited by E.D. Hirsch, Jr. and John Holdren (parenting).

Fiction: Erotica, literary, short story collections. Query with synopsis, 2-3 sample chapters or complete ms and SASE.

Recent Fiction Title(s): *Fast Greens*, by Turk Pipkin; *Last Days of the Dog Men*, by Brad Watson (stories); *Sacred Dust*, by David Hill.

THE DENALI PRESS, P.O. Box 021535, Juneau AK 99802-1535. (907)586-6014. Fax: (907)463-6780. E-mail: denalipr@alaska.net. Website: http://www.alaska.net/~denalipr/index.html. **Acquisitions:** Alan Schorr, editorial director. Editorial Associate: Sally Silvas-Ottumwa. Estab. 1986. The Denali Press looks for reference works suitable for the educational, professional and library market.Publishes trade paperback originals. Publishes 5 titles/year. Receives 120 submissions/year. 50% of books from first-time authors; 80% from unagented writers. Pays 10% royalty on wholesale price or makes outright purchase. Publishes book 1 year after acceptance. Accepts simultaneous submissions. Reports in 1 month. *Writer's Market* recommends allowing 2 months for reply. Prefers letter of inquiry. Book catalog free.

Nonfiction: Reference. Subjects include Americana, Alaskana, anthropology, ethnic, government/politics, history, recreation. "We need reference books—ethnic, refugee and minority concerns." Query with outline and sample chapters. All unsolicited mss are tossed. Author must contact prior to sending ms.

Recent Nonfiction Title(s): *Hispanic Resource Directory, 3rd ed.*; *Judaica Reference Sources, 2nd ed.*; *Refugee & Immigrant Resource Directory, 4th ed.*

T.S. DENISON & CO., INC., 9601 Newton Ave. S., Minneapolis MN 55431-2590. (612)888-6404. Fax: (612)888-6318. Director of Product Development: Sherrill B. Flora. **Acquisitions:** Danielle de Gregory, acquisitions editor. Estab. 1876. T.S. Denison publishes supplemental educational materials; teacher aid materials. Receives 1,500 submissions/year. 20% of books from first-time authors; 100% from unagented writers. Average print order for a first book is 3,000. No advance. Makes outright purchase. Publishes book 2 years after acceptance. Reports in 2 months. Book catalog and ms guidelines for 9 × 12 SASE with 3 first-class stamps.

Nonfiction: Specializes in early childhood, elementary and middle school teaching aids. Submit complete ms. *Writer's Market* recommends query with SASE first. Reviews artwork/photos as part of ms package. Send prints.

Recent Nonfiction Title(s): *Teaching Real Painting*, by Darry Bell-Myers (art projects for elementary students that teach art, not crafts); Math Topics; Center Activities for Early Childhood.

DENLINGERS PUBLISHERS, LTD., P.O. Box 2300, Centreville VA 20122-8445. **Acquisitions:** William W. Denlinger. Publishes hardcover and trade paperback originals. Publishes 10 titles/year. Receives 100 queries and 10 mss/year. 90% of books from first-time authors; 100% of books from unagented writers. Pays 5-10% royalty on wholesale price or makes outright purchase of $300-3,000. Publishes book 1 year after acceptance of ms. Reports in 1 week on queries, 2 months on mss. Book catalog for #10 SASE.

Nonfiction: Biography, how-to. Subjects include Americana, animals. "We will consider all queries to relative subjects." Query or submit outline with SASE. Reviews artwork/photos as part of ms package. Send photocopies.

Recent Nonfiction Title(s): *Victory*, by Victory Lanse (autobiography).

Fiction: Adventure, feminist, historical, mainstream/contemporary, suspense. "We may consider other subjects. We are always looking for outstanding material." Query with SASE.

Tips: "We only accept manuscripts that are written on a computer and have a disk available in a program that we can use or convert."

‡DERRYNANE PRESS, 348 Hartford Turnpike, Hampton CT 06247. (860)455-0039. **Acquisitions:** Peter Cherici, executive editor. Publishes hardcover and trade paperback originals and reprints. Publishes 4 titles/year, 1 imprint title/year. Receives 400 queries and 250 mss/year. 20% of books from first-time authors; 100% from unagented writers. Pays 8-12% royalty on wholesale price on discounts of 55% or more. Offers $500-1,000 advance. Publishes book 9 months after acceptance of ms. Accepts simultaneous submissions. Reports in 1 month on queries, proposals and mss. *Writer's Market* recommends allowing 2 months for reply. Book catalog free.

Imprint(s): Golden Grove Books.

Nonfiction: Biography. Subjects include ethnic, history, military/war. "We specialize in Irish and Celtic themes." Submit outline and 2 sample chapters with SASE. Reviews artwork/photos as part of ms package. Send photocopies.

Recent Nonfiction Title(s): *Wandering Irish in Europe*, by Matthew Culligan (history); *The Patriots*, by Peter Cullum (history).

Fiction: Historical, literary. "Irish and Celtic themes only." Submit synopsis and 2 sample chapters with SASE.

Recent Fiction Title(s): *Under Pegasus*, by David Beckman.

Tips: "We have an Irish-American ethnic audience, and material must be attuned to our market."

DIAL BOOKS FOR YOUNG READERS, Imprint of Penguin Putnam Inc., 375 Hudson St., 3rd Floor, New York NY 10014. (212)366-2800. Editorial Assistant: Victoria Wells. **Acquisitions:** Submissions Editor. Dial publishes lively, believable novels for middle readers and young adults, quality picture books and well-researched manuscripts for young adults and middle readers. Publishes hardcover originals. Publishes 80 titles/year. Receives 8,000 submissions/year. 10% of books from first-time authors. Pays variable royalty and advance. Reports in 4 months.

Imprint(s): Dial Easy-to-Read Books, Dial Very First Books, Pied Piper Books (paperback Dial reprints), Pied Piper Giants (1½ feet tall reprints).

• This publisher accepts agented manuscripts only.

Nonfiction: Juvenile picture books, young adult books. Especially looking for "quality picture books and well-researched young adult and middle-reader manuscripts." Not interested in alphabet books, riddle and game books, and early concept books. Agented mss only. *No unsolicited mss.*

Fiction: Juvenile picture books, young adult books. Adventure, fantasy, historical, humor, mystery, YA romance, suspense. Especially looking for "lively and well written novels for middle grade and young adult children involving a convincing plot and believable characters. The subject matter or theme should not already be overworked in previously published books. The approach must not be demeaning to any minority group, nor should the roles of female characters (or others) be stereotyped, though we don't think books should be didactic, or in any way message-y. No topics inappropriate for the juvenile, young adult, and middle grade audiences. No plays." Agented mss only.

Tips: "Our readers are anywhere from preschool age to teenage. Picture books must have strong plots, lots of action, unusual premises, or universal themes treated with freshness and originality. Humor works well in these books. A very well thought out and intelligently presented book has the best chance of being taken on. Genre isn't as much of a factor as presentation."

‡DIAL PRESS, Imprint of Dell Publishing, 1540 Broadway, New York NY 10036. (212)354-6500. Fax: (212)782-9698. Website: http://www.bbd.com. **Acquisitions:** Susan Kamil, vice president, editorial director. Estab. 1924. "Dial Press is dedicated to the publication of quality fiction and nonfiction." Publishes 6 titles/year. Receives 200 queries and 450 mss/year. 75% of books from first-time authors. Pays royalty on retail price. Offers $25,000-500,000 advance. Publishes book 1-2 years after acceptance of ms. Accepts simultaneous submissions. Reports in 2 months.
  • Dial Press accepts agented submissions only.

Nonfiction: Biography, memoirs, serious nonfiction, cultural criticism. Subjects include Americana, art/architecture, government/politics, health/medicine, history, psychology, women's issues/studies. Agented submissions only. Query by letter with SASE.

Recent Nonfiction Title(s): *Light Fantastic*, by John Lehr (theater criticism essay); *The Last Gift of Time*, by Carolyn Heilbrun (essays).

Fiction: Ethnic, literary. Agented submissions only. Query with SASE.

Recent Fiction Title(s): *Drinking: A Love Story*, by Caroline Knapp (memoir); *The Giant's House*, by Elizabeth McCracken; *Animal Husbandry*, by Laura Zigman (humorous novel).

DILLON HOUSE, Division of Simon & Schuster, Imprint of Silver Burdett Press, 299 Jefferson Rd., Parsippany NJ 07054. (201)236-7000. Fax: (201)326-8606. **Acquisitions:** Debbie Biber, acquisitions editor. Publishes hardcover and trade paperback originals. Publishes 20-25 titles/year. 10% of books from first-time authors; 80% from unagented writers. Pays 3-7½% royalty on retail price. Advance varies. Publishes book 2-3 years after acceptance of ms. Accepts simultaneous submissions. Reports in 6 months on queries, 1 year on mss.

Nonfiction: Children's/juvenile, grades 5-8. Subjects include biography, social studies, current history. "We look for current, topical subjects and clear, straightforward writing, appealing to young readers." *Not accepting unsolicited submissions at this time.*

DIMI PRESS, 3820 Oak Hollow Lane, SE, Salem OR 97302-4774. (503)364-7698. Fax: (503)364-9727. E-mail: dickbook@aol.com. Website: http://www.open.org/dicklutz/DIMI_PRESS.html. **Acquisitions:** Dick Lutz, president. "Dimi Press publishes books that help people solve problems in their lives." Publishes trade paperback originals. Publishes 5 titles/year. Receives 100-150 queries and 20-25 mss/year. 80% of books from first-time authors; 100% from unagented writers. Pays 10% royalty on net receipts. No advance. Publishes book 9 months after acceptance of ms. Accepts simultaneous submissions. Reports in 2 weeks on queries and proposals, 1 month on mss. *Writer's Market* recommends allowing 2 months for reply. Book catalog and ms guidelines for #10 SASE.

Nonfiction: How-to, self-help. Subjects include child guidance/parenting, health/medicine, hobbies, money/finance, natural history, nature/environment, psychology, travel. "We are interested in practical, hands-on material." Query with outline and 1 sample chapter and SASE, if answer is desired. Reviews artwork/photos as part of ms package. Send photocopies.

Recent Nonfiction Title(s): *All About Your Car*, by David Kline and Jamie Robertson (how-to); *Komodo, the Living Dragon*, (Revised Edition), by Dick Lutz and J. Marie Lutz (nature).

Tips: "Audience is adults who wish to learn something, save money, solve a problem, etc. Please send for guidelines before submitting."

DISCIPLESHIP RESOURCES, 1908 Grand Ave., Box 840, Nashville TN 37202-0840. (615)340-7068. Fax: (615)340-1789. Publisher: Alan K. Waltz. **Acquisitions:** Hank Pieterse, editor; Deb Smith, editor. "Discipleship Resources publishes books focused on specific ministries of the church, in particular The United Methodist Church." Publishes trade paperback originals and reprints. Publishes 15 titles/year. Receives 200 queries and 100 mss/year. 20% of books from first-time authors; 100% from unagented writers. Pays 5-10% royalty on net sales. Publishes book 9 months after acceptance of ms. Reports in 2 months on queries. Book catalog and ms guidelines for #10 SASE.

Nonfiction: Subjects include theology of ministry, evangelism, worship, stewardship, ministry of laity, family ministry, Christian education, ethnic (church), history (Methodist/church), nature/environment (ecology), recreation (leisure ministry), Christian biography (ecclesiastical). Query with proposal package, including outline, sample chapter, description of audience. Reviews artwork/photos as part of ms package. Send photocopies.

Tips: "Focus on ministry, write simply, and do more research."

DORCHESTER PUBLISHING CO., INC., 276 Fifth Ave., Suite 1008, New York NY 10001-0112. (212)725-8811. Fax: (212)532-1054. E-mail: timdy@aol.com.
Imprints: Love Spell (romance), **Leisure Books.**

‡DOUBLEDAY ADULT TRADE, Division of Bantam Doubleday Dell, 1540 Broadway, New York NY 10036. (212)782-9911. Fax: (212)782-9700. Website: http://www.bdd.com. **Acquisitions:** Patricia Mulcahy, vice president/ editor-in-chief. Estab. 1897. "Doubleday publishes the best in quality fiction and nonfiction." Publishes hardcover and trade paperback originals and reprints. Publishes 200 titles/year. Receives thousands of queries and mss/year. 30% of books from first-time authors; 1% from unagented writers. Pays royalty on retail price. Advance varies. Publishes book 1 year after acceptance of ms. Accepts simultaneous submissions. Reports in 6 months on queries.
● Doubleday accepts agented submissions only.
Imprint(s): Anchor Press (contact Martha Lewis); **Currency** (contact Harriet Rubin); **Main Street** (contact Bruce Tracy); **Nan A. Talese** (contact Nan A. Talese); **Religious Division** (contact Eric Major); **Image** (contact Trace Murphy).
Nonfiction: Biography, cookbook, gift book, how-to, humor, illustrated book, self-help. Subjects include agriculture/ horticulture, Americana, animals, anthropology, art/architecture, business/economics, child guidance/parenting, computers/electronics, cooking/foods/nutrition, education, ethnic, gardening, gay/lesbian, government/politics, health/medicine, history, hobbies, language/literature, military/war, money/finance, music/dance, nature/environment, philosophy, photography, psychology, recreation, regional, religion, science, sociology, software, sports, translation, travel, women's issues/ studies. Agented submissions only. Reviews artwork/photos as part of ms package. Send photocopies.
Recent Nonfiction Title(s): *Mothers and Daughters*, by Saline and Wohlmuth (photo essay); *A Lifelong Passion*, by Maylunas and Mironenko (letters/biography); *Boys to Men*, by Greg Alan-Williams (parenting).
Fiction: Adventure, confession, erotica, ethnic, experimental, feminist, gay/lesbian, historical, horror, humor, literary, mainstream/contemporary, mystery, picture books, religious, short story collections, suspense.
Recent Fiction Title(s): *Alias Grace*, by Margaret Atwood; *The Partner*, by John Grisham; *The Speed Queen*, by Stewart O'Nan (novels).

‡DOUBLEDAY RELIGIOUS DIVISION, Imprint of Doubleday Books, 1540 Broadway, New York NY 10036. Fax: (212)782-8911. Website: http://www.bdd.com. **Acquisitions**: Eric Major, vice president, religious division. Estab. 1897. "Doubleday's diverse religious booklist offers breadth and strength in depth that gives it its unique place in religious publishing. Publishes hardcover originals and reprints, trade paperback originals and reprints, mass market paperback originals and reprints. Publishes 36 titles/year; each imprint publishes 12 titles/year. Receives 700 queries/ year; receives 500 mss/year. 5% of books are from first-time authors; 1% from unagented writers. Pays 7½-15% royalty on net price. Advance varies. Publishes book 13 months after acceptance of ms. Accepts simultaneous submissions. Reports in 3 months on proposals. Book catalog for SAE with 3 first-class stamps.
● Doubleday Press accepts agented submissions only.
Nonfiction: Biography, cookbook, gift book, how-to, humor, illustrated book, reference, self-help. Subjects include child guidance/parenting, history, language/literature, religion. Agented submissions only.
Imprint(s): Image, Anchor Bible Commentary, Anchor Bible Reference, Anchor Bible Dictionary.
Recent Nonfiction Title(s): *The Celtic Way of Prayer*, by Esther de Waal (spirituality/prayer); *His Holiness*, by Carl Bernstein and Marco Politi (bio of John Paul II).

DOVER PUBLICATIONS, INC., 31 E. Second St., Mineola NY 11501. **Acquisitions:** Mary Carolyn Waldrep, crafts editor. Publishes trade paperback originals and reprints. Publishes 500 titles/year. Makes outright purchase. Book catalog free.
Nonfiction: Biography, children's/juvenile, coffee table book, cookbook, how-to, humor, illustrated book, textbook. Subjects include agriculture/horticulture, Americana, animals, anthropology/archaeology, art/architecture, cooking, food & nutrition, health/medicine, history, hobbies, language/literature, music/dance, nature/environment, philosophy, photography, religion, science, sports, translation, travel. Publishes mostly reprints. Accepts original paper doll collections, game books, coloring books (juvenile). Query. Reviews artwork/photos as part of ms package.
Recent Nonfiction Title(s): *Wild Animals Stained Glass Pattern Book*, by C.C. Eaton (craft); *Victorian Angels Punch-Out Gift Cards*, by C.B. Grafton (stationery); *Medieval Knights Paper Soldiers*, by A.G. Smith (toy).

DOWLING PRESS, INC., 1110 17th Ave. S., #4, Nashville TN 37212. (615)340-0967. **Acquisitions:** Maryglenn McCombs. Publishes hardcover, trade paperback and mass market paperback originals. Publishes 5 titles/year. Receives 150 queries and 100 mss/year. Pays 10% royalty on retail price. No advance. Reports in 3 months on queries and proposals, 6 months on mss. Manuscript guidelines free.
Nonfiction: Biography, cookbook, gift book, how-to, humor, self-help. Subjects include Americana, cooking/foods/ nutrition, gardening, gay/lesbian, hobbies, music/dance, women's issues/studies. Query with SASE.
Recent Nonfiction Title(s): *The Walrus Was Paul: The Great Beatle Death Clues of 1969*, by R. Gary Patterson (music/mystery); *Ticket To Ride: The Extraordinary Diary of The Beatles' Last Tour*, by Barry Tashian (music/nonfiction); *A Lifetime of Rules on Dating Women*, by Gavin Reily and Louis Vale (self-help/humor).
Tips: Audience is 18-40 year olds, middle class. "Please proofread! There is nothing worse than carelessness (especially in a cover letter). Don't call us a day after we've received the manuscript to ask what we think! Be patient."

DOWN EAST BOOKS, Division of Down East Enterprise, Inc., P.O. Box 679, Camden ME 04843-0679. Fax: (207)594-7215. E-mail: adevine@downeast.com. Managing Editor: Karin Womer. **Acquisitions:** Acquisitions Editor.

Estab. 1954. "We are primarily a regional publisher concentrating on Maine or New England." Publishes hardcover and trade paperback originals, trade paperback reprints. Publishes 20-24 titles/year. Receives 600 submissions/year. 50% of books from first-time authors; 90% from unagented writers. Average print order for a first book is 3,000. Pays 10-15% on receipts. Offers $200 average advance. Publishes book 1 year after acceptance. Accepts simultaneous submissions. Reports in 2 months. Manuscript guidelines for 9 × 12 SAE with 3 first-class stamps.

• Down East Books has published Elisabeth Ogilvie, Michael McIntosh, Robin Hansen, Peter F. Stevens, Lee Wulff.

Imprint(s): Silver Quill (outdoor sportsmen market).

Nonfiction: Books about the New England region, Maine in particular. Subjects include Americana, history, nature, guide books, crafts, recreation. "All of our books must have a Maine or New England emphasis." Query. Reviews artwork/photos as part of ms package.

Recent Nonfiction Title(s): *The Forgotten Nature of New England*, by Dean Bennett (a search for traces of the original wilderness); *A Birder's Guide to Maine*, by Elizabeth C. and Jan Erik Pierson and Peter Vickery (guidebook); *Maine—A View from Above*, Charles Feil (aerial photography).

Fiction: "We publish 1-2 juvenile titles/year (fiction and non-fiction), and 1-2 adult fiction titles/year." *Writer's Market* recommends sending a query with SASE first.

Recent Fiction Title(s): *A Show of Hands*, by David Crossman (regional mystery); *A Penny for a Hundred*, by Ethel Pochocki (juvenile); *Saturday Night at Moody's Diner*, by Tim Sample (humor).

DOWN HOME PRESS, P.O. Box 4126, Asheboro NC 27204. (910)672-6889. Fax: (910)672-2003. **Acquisitions:** Jerry Bledsoe, editor-in-chief. Down Home Press publishes books about the Carolinas and the South. Publishes hardcover originals and trade paperback originals and reprints. Publishes 8-10 titles/year. Receives 250 queries and 100 mss/year. 95% of books from unagented writers. Pays 8-15% royalty on wholesale price. Offers $500 advance. Publishes book 1 year after acceptance of ms. Reports in 3 months on queries, 6 months on proposals and mss. Book catalog for 9 × 12 SAE with 5 first-class stamps. Manuscript guidelines for #10 SASE.

Imprint(s): Imprimatur Books.

Nonfiction: Biography, cookbook, how-to, humor, illustrated book. Subjects include agriculture/horticulture, cooking/foods/nutrition, gardening, government/politics, history, hobbies, language/literature, nature/environment, photography, recreation, regional, sports, travel, Carolinas and South. Query. Submit outline and 1 sample chapter with SASE. Reviews artwork/photos as part of ms package. Send photocopies.

Recent Nonfiction Title(s): *Ocracoke Wild*, by Pat Garber (nature/travel); *The Heart of Dixie*, by F. Gaillard (essays on Southern people); *Books of Passage*, edited by D. Perkins (essays by North Carolina writers).

Recent Fiction Title(s): *The Angel Doll*, by Jerry Bledsoe (Christmas); *Pete & Shirley*, edited by David Perkins.

Tips: Audience is mostly Southerners and Carolinians.

DRAMA PUBLISHERS, 260 Fifth Ave., New York NY 10001. (212)725-5377. Fax: (212)725-8506. E-mail: info@dramapublishers.com. Website: http://www.dramapublishers.com. **Acquisitions:** Ina Kohler, acquisitions/rights; Ralph Pine, editor-in-chief. Estab. 1967. Drama Publishers publishes books and new media in the performing arts and costume and fashion. Publishes hardcover and paperback originals and reprints. Publishes 4-15 titles/year. Receives 420 submissions/year. 70% of books from first-time authors; 90% from unagented writers. Royalty varies. Advance negotiable. Publishes book 18 months after acceptance. Reports in 2 months.

• Drama Publishers has published such authors as Richard Pilbrow, Kristin Linklater, William Ball.

Nonfiction: Texts, guides, manuals, directories, reference and multimedia—for and about performing arts theory and practice: acting, directing; voice, speech, movement; makeup, masks, wigs; costumes, sets, lighting, sound; design and execution; technical theater, stagecraft, equipment; stage management; producing; arts management, all varieties; business and legal aspects; film, radio, television, cable, video; theory, criticism, reference; playwriting; theatre and performance history; costume and fashion. Accepts nonfiction and technical works in translations also. Query with 1-3 sample chapters; no complete mss. Reviews artwork/photos as part of ms package.

Recent Nonfiction Title(s): *Wearing of Costume*, by Green.

‡**LISA DREW BOOKS**, Imprint of Scribner, Unit of Simon & Schuster, 1230 Avenue of the Americas, New York NY 10020. (212)698-7000. **Acquisitions:** Lisa Drew, publisher. "We publish *reading* books; nonfiction that tells a story, not '14 ways to improve your marriage.' " Publishes hardcover and trade paperback originals. Publishes 10-14 titles/year. Receives 600 queries/year. 10% of books from first-time authors; 10% from unagented writers. Pays royalty on retail price, varies by author and project. Advance varies. Publishes book 1 year after acceptance of ms. Accepts simultaneous submissions, if so noted. Reports in 1 month on queries. Book catalog free through Scribner (same address).

Nonfiction: Subjects include government/politics, history, women's issues/studies, law, entertainment. Query with outline, 2 sample chapters and SASE. Reviews artwork/photos with ms package. Send photocopies.

DUKE PRESS, Division of Duke Communications International, 221 E. 29th St., Loveland CO 80538. (970)663-4700. Fax: (970)667-2321. E-mail: dbernard@duke.com. Website: http://www.dukepress.com. **Acquisitions:** David R. Bernard, publisher, AS/400; Mick Gusinde-Duffy, acquisitions editor, Windows NT. "Readers are MIS managers, students, programmers, and system operators working on an IBM AS/400 midrange computer or a Windows NT platform; financial controllers." Publishes trade paperback originals. Publishes 20-25 titles/year. Receives 20 queries and 5 mss/year. 75% of books from first-time authors; 90% from unagented writers. Pays 10-15% royalty on wholesale price.

Offers no advance. Publishes book 4 months after acceptance of ms. Accepts simultaneous submissions. Reports in 1 month on proposals. Book catalog and ms guidelines free.

● Duke Press has published such authors as Paul Conte, Frank Soltis and Judy Yaeger.

Nonfiction: Technical, textbook, multimedia (CD-ROM). Subjects include IBM AS/400 midrange computer, accounting software and Windows NT operating system. Submit proposal package including overview, table of contents, sample chapter, schedule, target audience, competing products, marketing plan, personal information, résumé, list of previous publications.

Recent Nonfiction Title(s): *Database Design & Programming for DB2/400*, by Paul Conte; *Mastering AS/400 Performance*, by Alan Arnold, Charley Jones, Jim Stewart and Rick Turner; *RPG IV Jump Start, 2nd Ed.*, by Bryan Meyers; *Migrating to Windows NT 4.0*, by Sean Daily.

Tips: "Authors must have technical knowledge and experience on an IBM AS/400 or Windows NT."

‡DUMMIES TRADE PRESS, Imprint of IDG Books, 645 N. Michigan Ave., Chicago IL 60611. (312)482-8460. Fax: (312)482-8561. E-mail: kwelton@idgbooks.com. Website: www.dummies.com. **Acquisitions:** Kathleen A. Welton, vice president/publisher (animals/pets; home improvement/nature); Sarah Kennedy, executive editor (gardening; food/wine; sports); Tami Booth, executive editor (diet/health/fitness; photography); Mark Butler (business). "Dummies Trade Press dedicates itself to publishing innovative, high-quality "For Dummies®" titles on the most popular business and general reference topics." Publishes trade paperback originals. Publishes 50 titles/year. Receives 1,000 queries/year. 30% of books from first-time authors; 50% from unagented writers. Pays 10-15% royalty. Offers $0-25,000 advance. Publishes book 3 months after acceptance of ms. Accepts simultaneous submissions. Reports in 1-2 months. Manuscript guidelines free.

Nonfiction: Cookbook, gift book, how-to, illustrated book, reference, self-help. Subjects include animals, art/architecture, business/economics, child guidance/parenting, cooking, diet/health/medical, food & nutrition, gardening, government/politics, hobbies, money/finance, music/dance, nature/environment, photography, recreation, sports, travel. Query with outline. Reviews artwork/photos as part of ms package. Send photocopies.

Recent Nonfiction Title(s): *Wine for Dummies*, by Ed McCarthy and Mary Ewing-Mulligan; *Golf for Dummies*, by Gary McCord; *Dogs for Dummies*, by Gina Spadafori.

‡THOMAS DUNNE BOOKS, Imprint of St. Martin's Press, 175 Fifth Ave., New York NY 10010. (212)674-5151. **Acquisitions:** Tom Dunne. Publishes wide range of fiction and nonfiction. Publishes hardcover originals, trade paperback originals and reprints. Publishes 90 titles/year. Receives 1,000 queries/year. 20% of books from first-time authors; less than 5% from unagented writers. Pays 10-15% royalty on retail price for hardcover, 7½% for paperback. Advance varies with project. Publishes book 1 year after acceptance of ms. Accepts simultaneous submissions. Reports in 2 months on queries. Book catalog and ms guidelines free.

Nonfiction: Biography. Subjects include government/politics, history, political commentary. "Author's attention to detail is important. We get a lot of manuscripts that are poorly proofread and just can't be considered." Query or submit outline and 100 sample pages with SASE. Reviews artwork/photos as part of ms package. Send photocopies.

Recent Nonfiction Title(s): *Beyond The Wild Blue: A History of The United States Air Force*, by Walter Boyne (military history); *Rhodes: The Race For Africa*, by Antony Thomas (history).

Fiction: Mainstream/contemporary, mystery, suspense, "women's" thriller. Query or submit synopsis and 100 sample pages with SASE.

Recent Fiction Title(s): *Brandenburg*, by Glenn Meade (thriller); *Birds of Prey*, by Wilbur Smith.

‡DUQUESNE UNIVERSITY PRESS, 600 Forbes Ave., Pittsburgh PA 15282-0101. (412)396-6610. Fax: (412)396-5984. Website: http://www.duq.edu/dupress. **Acquisitions:** Susan Wadsworth-Booth, senior editor. Publishes hardcover and trade paperback originals. Publishes 8-12 titles/year. Receives 500 queries and 75 mss/year. 30% of books from first-time authors; 95% from unagented writers. Pays royalty on retail price. Publishes book 1 year after acceptance of ms. Reports in 1 month on proposals, 3 months on mss. Book catalog and ms guidelines free.

Nonfiction: Creative nonfiction, scholarly/academic. Subjects include language/literature, philosophy, religion. "Duquesne publishes scholarly monographs in the fields of literary studies (medieval & Renaissance), philosophy, ethics, religious studies and psychology. We look for quality of scholarship. We also publish a series, *Emerging Writers in Creative Nonfiction*, for first-time authors of creative nonfiction for a general readership. For the *Emerging Writers in Creative Nonfiction* series, two copies of the manuscript and a $20 reading fee are required for submissions." Query or submit outline with 1 sample chapter and SASE.

Recent Nonfiction Title(s): *Born Southern and Restless*, by Kat Meads (personal essays); *The Balloon Lady and Other People I Know*, by Jeanne Maries Laskas (profiles).

DUTTON, Division of Penguin Putnam Inc., 375 Hudson St., New York NY 10014. (212)366-2000. Publisher: Elaine Koster. **Acquisitions:** Rosemary Ahern, senior editor (scholarly books, literary fiction); Matthew Carnicelli, editor (general nonfiction, business); Joe Pittman, editor (mystery); Diedre Mullane, senior editor (nonfiction, science, multicultural literary fiction); Audrey LaFehr, executive editor (women's fiction); Micheala Hamilton, editorial director (psychology, true crime, fiction). Estab. 1852. Dutton publishes hardcover, original, mainstream, and contemporary fiction and nonfiction in the areas of biography, self-help, politics, psychology, and science for a general readership. Publishes 500 titles/year. Receives 20,000 queries and 10,000 mss/year. 30-40% of books from first-time authors; 2% from unagented writers. Royalty and advance negotiable. Publishes book 18 months after acceptance. Reports in 6 months.

Imprint(s): Signet, Onyx, Topaz, NAL, Plume.
• This publisher accepts agented mss only.
Nonfiction: Biography, cookbook, gift book, how-to, humor, reference, self-help. Subjects include agriculture/horticulture, Americana, animals, anthropology/archaeology, art/architecture, business/economics, child guidance/parenting, cooking/foods/nutrition education, ethnic, gardening, gay/lesbian, government/politics, health/medicine, history, hobbies, language/literature, military/war, money/finance, music/dance, nature/environment, philosophy, photography, psychology, recreation, regional, religion, science, sociology, sports, translation, women's issues/studies. "Author's credentials are essential. Many writers don't know the difference between a good book idea and a good idea for a magazine article. Query with outline and proposal package, including overview and 3 sample chapters. Agented submissions only. Reviews artwork/photo as part of ms package. Send photocopies.
Recent Nonfiction Title(s): *Foster Child: A Biography of Jodie Foster*, by Buddy Foster and Leon Wagener (celebrity biography); *How to Stay Lovers for Life*, by Sharyn Wolf (how-to); *The Indian Spice Kitchen*, by Monisha Bharadwaj (cookbook).
Fiction: Adventure, erotica, ethnic, fantasy, gay/lesbian, historical, horror, literary, mainstream/contemporary, mystery, occult, romance, science fiction, short story collections, suspense, western. "We are looking for novelists who can write a book a year with consistent quality." Agented submissions only. All unsolicited mss returned unopened.
Recent Fiction Title(s): *Ordeal*, by Deanie Francis Mills (suspense); *Le Divorce*, by Diane Johnson (literary); *The Men from the Boys*, by William J. Mann (gay).
Tips: "Write the complete manuscript and submit it to an agent or agents. We publish The Trailsman, Battletech and other western and science fiction series—all by ongoing authors. Receptive to ideas for new series in commercial fiction."

DUTTON CHILDREN'S BOOKS, Imprint of Penguin Putnam Inc., 375 Hudson St., New York NY 10014. (212)366-2000. **Acquisitions:** Lucia Monfried, editor-in-chief. Estab. 1852. Dutton Children's Books publishes fiction and nonfiction for readers ranging from preschoolers to young adults on a variety of subjects. Publishes hardcover originals. Publishes 70 titles/year. 15% from first-time authors. Pays royalty on retail price.
• At press time, Dutton Children's Books was being restructured. Verify current information.
Nonfiction: For preschoolers to middle-graders; including animals/nature, U.S. history, science and photo essays. Query with SASE.
Recent Nonfiction Title(s): *Our Journey From Tibet*, by Laurie Dolphin.
Fiction: Dutton Children's Books has a complete publishing program that includes picture books; easy-to-read books; and fiction for all ages, from "first-chapter" books to young adult readers. Query with SASE.
Recent Fiction Title(s): *The Iron Ring*, by Lloyd Alexander.

EAGLE'S VIEW PUBLISHING, 6756 N. Fork Rd., Liberty UT 84310. Fax: (801)745-0903. E-mail: porsturbo@aol.com. **Acquisitions:** Denise Knight, editor-in-chief. Estab. 1982. "We publish nonfiction only. Primarily how-to craft books with a subject related to historical or contemporary Native American/Mountain Man/frontier crafts." Publishes trade paperback originals. Publishes 4-6 titles/year. Receives 40 queries and 20 mss/year. 90% of books from first-time authors; 100% from unagented writers. Pays 8-10% royalty on net selling price. Publishes book 1 year or more after acceptance of ms. Accepts simultaneous submissions. Reports in 1 year on proposals. Book catalog and ms guidelines for $2.
Nonfiction: How-to, Indian, mountain man and American frontier (history and craft). Subjects include anthropology/archaeology (Native American crafts), ethnic (Native American), history (American frontier), hobbies (crafts, especially beadwork, earrings). "We are expanding from our Indian craft base to more general but related crafts." Submit outline and 1-2 sample chapters. Reviews artwork/photos as part of ms package. Send photocopies or sample illustrations. "We prefer to do photography in house."
Recent Nonfiction Title(s): *Beaded Treasure Purses*, by Deon DeLange (how-to).
Tips: "We will not be publishing any new beaded earrings books for 1 to 2 years. We are interested in other craft projects using seed beads, especially books that feature a variety of items, not just different designs for one type of item."

EAKIN PRESS/SUNBELT MEDIA, INC., P.O. Box 90159, Austin TX 78709-0159. (512)288-1771. Fax: (512)288-1813. **Acquisitions:** Edwin M. Eakin, editorial director; Melissa Roberts, Virginia Messer. Estab. 1978. Eakin specializes in Texana and Western Americana for adults and juveniles. Publishes hardcover and paperback originals and reprints. Publishes 35 titles/year. Receives 1,500 submissions/year. 50% of books from first-time authors; 90% from unagented writers. Average print order for a first book is 2,000-5,000. Pays 10-12-15% royalty on net sales. Publishes book 18 months after acceptance. Accepts simultaneous submissions. Reports in 3 months. Book catalog for $1.25. Manuscript guidelines for #10 SASE.
Imprint(s): Eakin Press and Nortex Press.
Nonfiction: Adult nonfiction categories include Western Americana, African American studies, business, sports, biographies, Civil War, regional cookbooks, Texas history, World War II. Juvenile nonfiction includes biographies of historic personalities, prefer with Texas or regional interest, or nature studies. Easy-read illustrated books for grades 1-3. Query with SASE.
Recent Nonfiction Title(s): *Farewell, Jimmy the Greek, Wizard of Odds*, by Ginger Wadsworth.
Fiction: No longer publishes adult fiction. Juvenile fiction for grades 4-7, preferably relating to Texas and the southwest

or contemporary. Query or submit outline/synopsis and sample chapters.

‡EASTERN NATIONAL ASSOCIATION, (formerly Eastern National Park & Monument Association), 446 North Lane, Conshohocken PA 19428. (610)832-0555. Fax: (610)832-0242. **Acquisitions:** Patti Plummer, production coordinator. Estab. 1948. "Our mission is to continue to strengthen our relationship with the National Park Service and other partners." Publishes trade paperback originals and reprints. Publishes 50-60 titles/year. Receives 20 queries and 10 mss/year. 5% of books from first-time authors; 50% from unagented writers. Pays 1-10% royalty on retail price or makes outright purchase of $6,000 maximum. Publishes book 2 years after acceptance of ms. Reports in 1 month on queries. *Writer's Market* recommends allowing 2 months for reply. Book catalog free.
Imprint(s): Eastern Acorn Press.
Nonfiction: Biography, children's/juvenile. Subjects include Americana, history, military/war and nature/environment. "Requests for editorial plans are only accepted from member agencies." Query. All unsolicited mss are returned unopened.
Recent Nonfiction Title(s): *Life in Civil War America*, by Catherine Clinton; *Black Soldier in the Civil War*, by Joseph Glatthaar.

THE ECCO PRESS, 100 W. Broad St., Hopewell NJ 08525. (609)466-4748. Editor-in-Chief: Daniel Halpern. **Acquisitions:** Ruth Greenstein. Publishes hardcover and mass market paperback originals and reprints and trade paperback reprints. Publishes 60 titles/year. Receives 1,200 queries/year. Pays 7½-15% royalty. Offers $250-5,000 advance. Publishes book 1 year after acceptance of ms. No unsolicited mss. Book catalog and ms guidelines free.
Nonfiction: Biography, coffee table book, cookbook. Subjects include Americana, art/architecture, cooking/foods/nutrition, government/politics, history, language/literature, music/dance, regional, translation, travel. Query. Reviews artwork/photos as part of ms package. Send transparencies.
Recent Nonfiction Title(s): *The Roaring Stream*, edited by Nelson Foster and Jack Shoemaker.
Fiction: Ethnic, historical, literary, plays, short story collections.
Recent Fiction Title(s): *Snake*, by Kate Jennings.
Poetry: Submit 10 sample poems.
Recent Poetry Title(s): *Sun Under Wood*, by Robert Haass.

‡EDGE BOOKS, Imprint of Henry Holt & Co., 115 W. 18th St., New York NY 10011. (212)886-9200. **Acquisitions:** Marc Aronson, executive editor. Publishes hardcover originals. Publishes 4-5 titles/year. 80% of books from first-time authors. Pays 6-7½% royalty on retail price. Advance varies. Publishes book 18 months after acceptance of ms. Accepts simultaneous submissions. Reports in 4 months on queries. Book catalog free from Henry Holt (same address).
Nonfiction: Young adult. Query with outline, 1 sample chapter, market analysis and SASE.
Recent Nonfiction Title(s): *We Are Witnesses*, by Jacob Boaz (memoir); *The Beautiful Days of My Youth*, by Ana Novac (Holocaust diary).
Fiction: Young adult. Query or submit complete ms.
Recent Fiction Title(s): *Shizko's Daughter*, by Kyoko Mori and *The Long Season of Rain*, by Helen Kim (novels).
Tips: "All our titles are international or multicultural coming-of-age fiction and nonfiction. We are very open to new authors, but because we publish so few titles, the standards are very high. The emphasis is on voice and literary quality, rather than subject."

THE EDUCATION CENTER, INC., 3511 W. Market St., Greensboro NC 27403. Fax: (910)547-1590. Estab. 1973. Publishes supplementary resource books for elementary teachers: preschool/grade 6. Publishes 40 titles/year. Receives 300 queries and 100 mss/year. Under 5% of books from first-time authors; 100% from unagented writers. Pays 2-6% royalty on wholesale price (on books sold through dealers); 2-6% royalty on retail price (on books sold through direct mail). "Payment schedule and amount negotiated when contract signed." Publishes book 1 year after acceptance of ms (depending on condition of ms). Reports in 3 months on proposals.
● The Education Center is looking for more preschool books in a series.
Nonfiction: Teacher resource/supplementary materials. Subjects include education P/K-6, language/literature. "We place a strong emphasis on materials that teach the basic language arts and math skills. We are also seeking materials for teaching science and geography, literature-based activities for the whole language classroom, cooperative learning ideas and multicultural materials. Technical, complex or comprehensive manuscripts (such as textbooks and theory/practice articles) are not accepted." Submit outline and 1 sample chapter.
Recent Nonfiction Title(s): *Arts & Crafts for Little Hands*, by Jennifer Overend.

WILLIAM B. EERDMANS PUBLISHING CO., 255 Jefferson Ave. SE, Grand Rapids MI 49503. (616)459-4591. Fax: (616)459-6540. **Acquisitions:** Jon Pott, editor-in-chief; Anne Salsich, assistant to the editor; Charles Van Hof,

 A BULLET introduces comments by the editors of *Writer's Market* indicating special information about the listing.

managing editor (history); Amy DeVries, children's book editor. Estab. 1911. "Approximately 80% of our publications are religious and largely of the more academic or theological variety (as opposed to the devotional, inspirational or celebrity-conversion books). Our history and social issues titles aim, similarly, at an educated audience." Publishes hardcover and paperback originals and reprints. Publishes 120-130 titles/year. Receives 3,000-4,000 submissions/year. 10% of books from first-time authors; 95% from unagented writers. Average print order for a first book is 4,000. Pays 7½-10% royalty on retail price. Publishes book 1 year after acceptance. Accepts simultaneous submissions if noted. Reports in 6 weeks on queries. *Writer's Market* recommends allowing 2 months for reply. Book catalog free.
Imprint(s): Eerdmans Books for Young Readers (Amy DeVries, editor).
 • William B. Eerdmans has published such authors as Martin E. Marty, Lewis B. Smedes and C.S. Lewis.
Nonfiction: Religious, reference, textbooks, monographs, children's books. Subjects include ethics, religious literature, history, philosophy, psychology, religion, sociology, regional history. "We prefer that writers take the time to notice if we have published anything at all in the same category as their manuscript before sending it to us." Accepts nonfiction translations. Query with outline, 2-3 sample chapters and SASE for return of ms. Reviews artwork/photos.
Recent Nonfiction Title(s): *The Dead Sea Scrolls*, translated by Florentino Garcia Martinez (Biblical studies); *The Man Who Created Narnia*, by Michael Coren (biography); *People of the Book*, by David Jeffrey (arts and literature).

‡**ELEMENT BOOKS**, Subsidiary of Element Books Ltd. (UK), 21 Broadway, Rockport MA 01966. (508)546-1040. Fax: (508)546-9882. E-mail: element@cove.com. **Acquisitions:** Roberta Scimone, editorial director. Estab. 1975. "We publish high-quality, accessible books on spiritual traditions, complimentary health and inner wisdom." Publishes hardcover originals. Publishes 15-20 titles/year. Receives 600 queries/year. 50% of books from first-time authors; 80% from unagented writers. Pays 15-20% royalty on retail price. Offers $3,000 average advance. Publishes book 1 year after acceptance of ms. Accepts simultaneous submissions. Reports in 2 months on proposals. Book catalog and ms guidelines free.
Imprint(s): One World (UK).
Nonfiction: Reference, self-help. Subjects include business/economics, health/medicine, philosophy, psychology, regional. Query with outline, 2-3 sample chapters, table of contents, author's bio and SASE. Reviews artwork/photos as part of ms package. Send photocopies.
Recent Nonfiction Title(s): *Dr. Hirsch's Guide to Scentsational Weight Loss*, by Dr. Alan Hirsch (self-help); *The Tao of Sales*, by E. Thomas Behr (business).

‡**ELEPHANT BOOKS**, Subsidiary of Creativity, Inc., 65 Macedonia Rd., Alexander NC 28701. (704)252-9515. **Acquisitions:** Vivian Terrell, executive editor. Publishes trade paperback originals and reprints. Publishes 4 titles/year. Receives 20 queries and 15 mss/year. 90% of books from first-time authors; 80% from unagented writers. Pays 12-15% royalty on wholesale price. Seldom offers advance. Publishes book 1 year after acceptance of ms. Reports in 1 month on queries, 2 months on proposals, 3 months on mss. Book catalog and manuscript guidelines for #10 SASE with 2 first-class stamps.
Imprint(s): Blue/Gray Books (Ralph Roberts, publisher).
Nonfiction: Cookbook. History subjects. Interested in Civil War and innovative cookbooks. Query or submit outline with 3 sample chapters and proposal package, including potential marketing plans with SASE. Reviews artwork/photos as part of ms package. Send photocopies.

ELLIOTT & CLARK PUBLISHING, Imprint of Black Belt Communications Group, P.O. Box 551, Montgomery AL 36101. (334)265-6753. Fax: (334)265-8880. E-mail: jeff_slaton@black-belt.com. **Acquisitions:** Jeff Slaton, editor; Ashley Gordon, editor (gardening). Elliott & Clark specializes in illustrated histories. Publishes hardcover and trade paperback originals. Publishes 5 titles/year. 50% of books from first-time authors; 90% from unagented writers. Pays royalty on wholesale price. Offers variable advance. Accepts simultaneous submissions. Reports in 3 months on proposals. Manuscript guidelines free.
 • Elliott & Clark has published such authors as Kathryn Tucker Windham.
Nonfiction: Subjects include Americana, art/architecture, biography, gardening, history, nature/environment, photography. "We specialize in illustrated histories—need to think of possible photography/illustration sources to accompany manuscript. Submit an analysis of audience or a discussion of possible sales avenues beyond traditional book stores (such as interest groups, magazines, associations, etc.)." Submit proposal package, including possible illustrations (if applicable), outline, sales avenues. Reviews artwork/photos as part of ms package. Send transparencies. SASE must be included for response and returned materials.
Recent Nonfiction Title(s): *Drawn & Quartered: The History of American Political Cartoons*, by Stephen Hess and Sandy Northrop; *Outlaws*, by Marley Brandt (James/Younger Gang, Jesse James et. al.).
Tips: "We prefer proactive authors who are interested in providing marketing and the right leads."

ENGINEERING & MANAGEMENT PRESS, 25 Technology Park, Norcross GA 30092. (770)449-0461. Fax: (770)263-8532. E-mail: falexander@www.iienet.org. Website: http://www.iienet.org. **Acquisitions:** Eric Torrey, director; Forsyth Alexander, book editor (engineering and management). "Enginnering & Management Press seeks to publish quality books that cover timely, crucial topics of importance to engineering and management professionals and businesses today." Publishes hardcover and trade paperback originals. Publishes 6-10 titles/year. Receives 60-80 queries and 40-50 mss/year. 75% of books from first-time authors; 100% from unagented writers. Pays 10-15% royalty. Offers up to $1,000 advance. Publishes book 1 year after acceptance of ms. Accepts simultaneous submissions. Reports in 3 months on mss. Book catalog and ms guidelines free.

Nonfiction: Reference, technical, textbook. Subjects include business, computers/electronics, health/medicine (healthcare administration), industrial engineering and related topics. All books relate to industrial engineering disciplines. Submit proposal package, including outline, 2 sample chapters, competitive analysis and what makes your book unique. Reviews artwork/photos as part of ms package. Send photocopies.

Recent Nonfiction Title(s): *Facilities and Workplace Design*, by Quarterman Lee (engineering); *Manufacturing and the Internet*, Richard Mathieu (Internet); *Work Simplification*, by Pierre Thériault (business/management).

Tips: Audience is professionals working in the fields of industrial engineering and management.

ENSLOW PUBLISHERS INC., 44 Fadem Rd., P.O. Box 699, Springfield NJ 07081. (201)379-8890. **Acquisitions:** Brian D. Enslow, editor. Estab. 1977. Enslow publishes nonfiction for children and young adults in a variety of subjects including science, history, reference and biographies. Publishes hardcover originals. Publishes 120 titles/year. 30% require freelance illustration. Pays royalty on net price. Offers advance. Publishes book 1 year after acceptance. Reports in 1 month. *Writer's Market* recommends allowing 2 months for reply. Book catalog for $2 and 9×12 SAE with 3 first-class stamps. Writer's guidelines for SASE.

● This publisher is especially interested in ideas for series. It does not publish fiction, fictionalized history or educational materials. Enslow Publishers has increased their numbers of books published from 90 to 120 titles/year.

Nonfiction: Interested in nonfiction mss for young adults and children. Some areas of special interest are science, social issues, biography, reference topics, recreation. Query with information on competing titles and writer's résumé.

Recent Nonfiction Title(s): *The Alamo in American History*, by Roy Sorrels; *Toni Morrison: Nobel Prize-Winning Author*, by Barbara Kramer; *Bizarre Insects*, by Margaret J. Anderson (science).

EPICENTER PRESS INC., P.O. Box 82368, Kenmore WA 98028. (206)485-6822. Fax: (206)481-8253. E-mail: gksturgis@aol.com. **Acquisitions:** Lael Morgan, acquisitions editor; Kent Sturgis, publisher; Christine Ummel, associate editor. "We are a regional press founded in Alaska whose interests include but are not limited to the arts, history, environment, and diverse cultures and lifestyles of the North Pacific and high latitudes." Publishes hardcover and trade paperback originals. Publishes 10 titles/year. Receives 200 queries and 100 mss/year. 90% of books from first-time authors; 90% from unagented writers. Advance negotiable. Publishes book 2 years after acceptance of ms. Reports in 2 months on queries. Book catalog and ms guidelines free.

● Epicenter Press has published such authors as Tim Jones, Barbara Lavallee, Jon Van Zyle.

Imprint(s): Umbrella Books.

Nonfiction: Biography, coffee table book, gift books, humor. Subjects include animals, art/architecture, ethnic, history, nature/environment, photography, recreation, regional, travel, women's issues/studies. "Our focus is the Pacific Northwest and Alaska. We do not encourage nonfiction titles from outside Alaska and the Pacific Northwest, nor travel from beyond Alaska, Washington, Oregon and California." Submit outline and 3 sample chapters. Reviews artwork/photos as part of ms package. Send photocopies.

Recent Nonfiction Title(s): *Bird Girl and the Man who Followed the Sun*, by Velma Wallis; *Cold Starry Night*, by Claire Fejes (memoir); *Strange Stories of Alaska and the Yukon*, by Ed Ferrell.

PAUL S. ERIKSSON, PUBLISHER, P.O. Box 62, Forest Dale VT 05745-4210. (802)247-4210. Fax: (802)247-4256. **Acquisitions:** Paul S. Eriksson, publisher/editor; Peggy Eriksson, associate publisher/co-editor. Estab. 1960. "We look for intelligence, excitement and saleability." Publishes hardcover and paperback trade originals, paperback trade reprints. Publishes 5 titles/year. Receives 1,500 submissions/year. 25% of books from first-time authors; 95% from unagented writers. Average print order for a first book is 3,000-5,000. Pays 10-15% royalty on retail price. Offers advance if necessary. Publishes book 6 months after acceptance. *Writer's Market* recommends allowing 2 months for reply. Catalog for #10 SASE.

Nonfiction: Americana, birds (ornithology), art, biography, business/economics, cooking/foods/nutrition, health, history, hobbies, how-to, humor, nature, politics, psychology, recreation, self-help, sociology, sports, travel. Query with SASE.

Recent Nonfiction Title(s): *Papers From The Headmaster*, by Richard A. Hawley; *The Hunt for the Whooping Cranes*, by J.J. McCoy (natural history); *The Revenge of the Fishgod*, by Carl von Essen, M.D. (fishing).

Fiction: Serious, literary. Query with SASE.

ETC PUBLICATIONS, 700 E. Vereda Sur, Palm Springs CA 92262-4816. (760)325-5352. Fax: (760)325-8841. **Acquisitions:** Dr. Richard W. Hostrop, publisher (education and social sciences); Lee Ona S. Hostrop, editorial director (history and works suitable below the college level). Estab. 1972. ETC publishes works that "further learning as opposed to entertainment." Publishes hardcover and paperback originals. Publishes 6-12 titles/year. Receives 100 submissions/year. 75% of books from first-time authors; 90% from unagented writers. Average print order for a first book is 2,500. Offers 5-15% royalty, based on wholesale and retail price. No advance. Publishes book 9 months after acceptance. *Writer's Market* recommends allowing 2 months for reply.

Nonfiction: Educational management, gifted education, futuristics, textbooks. Accepts nonfiction translations in above areas. Submit complete ms with SASE. Query with SASE. Reviews artwork/photos as part of ms package.

Recent Nonfiction Title(s): *Our Golden California*, by Juanita Houston (Christian-oriented text for elementary

school age children); *Corresponding With History*, by John E. Schlimm II (art and benefits of autograph collecting).
Tips: "ETC will seriously consider textbook manuscripts in any knowledge area in which the author can guarantee a first-year adoption of not less than 500 copies. Special consideration is given to those authors who are capable and willing to submit their completed work in camera-ready, typeset form. We are particularly interested in works suitable for *both* the Christian school market and homeschoolers; e.g., state history texts below the high school level with a Christian-oriented slant."

M. EVANS AND CO., INC., 216 E. 49th St., New York NY 10017-1502. Fax: (212)486-4544. **Acquisitions:** Betty Ann Crawford, senior editor. Editor-in-Chief: George C. deKay. Estab. 1960. "We publish a general trade list of adult fiction and nonfiction, cookbooks and semi-reference works. The emphasis is on selectivity, publishing commercial works with quality." Publishes hardcover originals. Pays negotiable royalty. Publishes 30-40 titles/year. 5% of books from unagented writers. Publishes book 8 months after acceptance. No unsolicited mss. Reports in 2 months. Book catalog for 9×12 SAE with 3 first-class stamps.
Nonfiction: "Our most successful nonfiction titles have been related to health and the behavioral sciences. No limitation on subject." Query.
Recent Nonfiction Title(s): *An Inquiry Into the Existence of Guardian Angels*, by Pierre Jovanovic.
Fiction: "Our very small general fiction list represents an attempt to combine quality with commercial potential." Query.
Recent Fiction Title(s): *A Fine Italian Hand*, by William Murray (mystery).
Tips: "A writer should clearly indicate what his book is all about, frequently the task the writer performs least well. His credentials, although important, mean less than his ability to convince this company that he understands his subject and that he has the ability to communicate a message worth hearing. Writers should review our book catalog before making submissions."

‡EXCELSIOR CEE PUBLISHING, P.O. Box 5861, Norman OK 73070. (405)329-3909. **Acquisitions:** J.C. Marshall. Publishes hardcover and trade paperback originals. Publishes 8 titles/year. Receives 100 queries/year. Pays royalty or makes outright purchase (both negotiable). Offers no advance. Publishes book 1 year after acceptance of ms. Accepts simultaneous submissions. Reports in 1 month. *Writer's Market* recommends allowing 2 months for reply. Book catalog for #10 SASE.
Nonfiction: Biography, coffee table book, how-to, humor, self-help, textbook. Subjects include Americana, education, history, hobbies, language/literature, women's issues/studies, writing. Query with SASE.
Recent Nonfiction Title(s): *Anyone Can Write—Just Let It Come Out* and *How to Record Your Family History*, both by Jimmie Blaine Marshall.
Tips: "We have a general audience, book store browser interested in nonfiction reading. We publish titles that have a mass appeal and can be enjoyed by a large reading public. We publish very few unsolicited manuscripts, and our publishing calendar is 75% full up to 1 year in advance."

‡EXPLORER'S GUIDE PUBLISHING, 4843 Apperson Dr., Rhinelander WI 54501. Phone/fax: (715)362-6029. E-mail: explore@newnorth.net. Website: http://www.desocom.com/. **Acquisitions:** Gary Kulibert, managing editor. "Our mission is to provide quality outdoor-related books at a good price." Publishes trade paperback originals. Publishes 6 titles/year. Receives 50 queries and 10 mss/year. 50% of books from first-time authors; 100% from unagented writers. Pays 7-15% royalty on wholesale price. Publishes book 9 months after acceptance of ms. Accepts simultaneous submissions. Reports in 2 months on queries. Book catalog for SASE.
Nonfiction: Outdoor cookbooks, outdoor-related children's/juvenile, guide books. Subjects include cooking, nature/environment, recreation, regional, travel. "Our main emphasis is outdoor recreation and related activities. We are looking for helpful and entertaining proposals with b&w photos, drawings, maps and other graphic elements. No coffee table books." Query with outline, 2 sample chapters, author qualifications, proposed market. Reviews artwork/photos as part of ms package. Send photocopies.
Recent Nonfiction Title(s): *Pudgie Pie*, by Heidi Kulibert (cooking); *Foil Cookery*, by Lori Heral (cooking).
Recent Fiction Title(s): *A Walk in the Woods*, by Eric Larsen (children's).

FABER & FABER, INC., Division of Faber & Faber, Ltd., London, England; 53 Shore Rd., Winchester MA 01890. (617)721-1427. Fax: (617)729-2783. **Acquisitions:** Ms. Adrian Wood. Estab. 1976. "Faber and Faber publishes adult trade titles only, fiction and non-fiction." Publishes hardcover and trade paperback originals. Publishes 30 titles/year. Receives 1,200 submissions/year. 10% of books from first-time authors; 10% from unagented writers. Pays royalty on retail price. Advance varies. Publishes book 1 year after acceptance. Accepts simultaneous submissions. Reports in 3 months on queries. Writer's guidelines for #10 SASE.
Nonfiction: Anthologies, biography, contemporary culture, film and screenplays, history and natural history, cooking, popular science. Query with synopsis, outline; Faber will contact author if interested in pursuing project.
Recent Nonfiction Title(s): *Knowing Hepburn*, by James Prideaux.
Fiction: "Currently we are not reviewing poetry, children's books, young adult titles, mass-market romances or mysteries, how-to books, photo/art books, or humor."
Recent Fiction Title(s): *Leaning Towards Infinity*, by Sue Woolfe.
Tips: "Subjects that have consistently done well for us include popular culture; serious, intelligent biographies and history books; and literary, somewhat quirky fiction. Please send only synopsis and outline. We will contact you if we

wish to see more or your project. No calls regarding the status of your submission, please."

FACTS ON FILE, INC., 11 Penn Plaza, New York NY 10001. (212)967-8800. Fax: (212)967-9196. E-mail: factsonfile .com. **Acquisitions:** Laurie Likoff, editorial director; Eleanora Von Dehsen (multi-volume reference); Nicole Bowen, senior editor (young adult reference); Hilary Poole, assistant editor (health, pop culture). Estab. 1941. "We produce high-quality reference materials for the school library market and the general nonfiction trade." Publishes hardcover originals and reprints. Publishes 135 titles/year. Receives approximately 2,000 submissions/year. 25% of books from unagented writers. Pays 10-15% royalty on retail price. Offers $10,000 average advance. Accepts simultaneous submissions. Reports in 2 months on queries. Book catalog free.
  ● Facts On File has published such authors as Alan Axelrod, Doris Weatherford and Ken Bloom.
Nonfiction: Reference. Informational books on health, history, entertainment, natural history, philosophy, psychology, recreation, religion, language, sports, multicultural studies, science, popular culture. "We need serious, informational books for a targeted audience. All our books must have strong library interest, but we also distribute books effectively to the book trade. Our books fit the junior and senior high school curriculum." No computer books, technical books, cookbooks, biographies (except YA), pop psychology, humor, do-it-yourself crafts, fiction or poetry. Query or submit outline and sample chapter with SASE. No submissions returned without SASE.
Recent Nonfiction Title(s): *People of Africa*, by Diagram Group (African history); *Encyclopedia of Black Women in America*, by Darlene Clark Hine; *Encyclopedia of Nutrition & Good Health*, by R. Ronzio (health).
Tips: "Our audience is school and public libraries for our more reference-oriented books and libraries, schools and bookstores for our less reference-oriented informational titles."

FAIRLEIGH DICKINSON UNIVERSITY PRESS, 285 Madison Ave., Madison NJ 07940. Phone/fax: (201)443-8564. E-mail: fdupress@fdu.edu. **Acquisitions:** Harry Keyishian, director. Estab. 1967. Publishes hardcover originals. Publishes 45 titles/year. Receives 300 submissions/year. 33% of books from first-time authors; 95% from unagented writers. Average print order for a first book is 1,000. "Contract is arranged through Associated University Presses of Cranbury, New Jersey. We are a *selection* committee only." Nonauthor subsidy publishes 2% of books. Publishes book 1 year after acceptance. Reports in 2 weeks on queries. *Writer's Market* recommends allowing 2 months for reply.
Nonfiction: Reference, scholarly books. Subjects include art, business/economics, Civil War, film, history, Jewish studies, literary criticism, music, philosophy, politics, psychology, sociology, women's studies. Looking for scholarly books in all fields; no nonscholarly books. Query with outline and sample chapters. Reviews artwork/photos as part of ms package.
Recent Nonfiction Title(s): *Mary Wollstonecraft and the Language of Sensibility*, by Syndy McMillen Conger.
Tips: "Research must be up to date. Poor reviews result when authors' bibliographies and notes don't reflect current research. We follow *Chicago Manual of Style* (14th edition) style in scholarly citations."

FAIRVIEW PRESS, 2450 Riverside Ave. S., Minneapolis MN 55454. (800)544-8207. Fax: (612)672-4980. Website: http://www.press.fairview.org. **Acquisitions:** Lane Stiles, senior editor. "Fairview Press publishes books and related materials that educate families and individuals about their physical and emotional health, and motivate them to seek positive changes in themselves and their communities." Publishes hardcover and trade paperback originals and reprints. Publishes 24-30 titles/year. Imprint publishes 8-10 titles/year. Receives 1,000 queries and 200 mss/year. 40% of books from first-time authors; 65% from unagented writers. Pays 16-22% royalty on wholesale price. Offers $500-2,500 advance. Publishes book 1 year after acceptance of ms. Accepts simultaneous submissions. Reports in 3 months on proposals. Book catalog and manuscript guidelines free.
  ● Fairview Press has published such authors as Bob Keeshan (TV's Captain Kangaroo), Slim Goodbody and Robyn Spizman.
Imprint(s): Growing & Reading with Bob Keeshan (Acquisitions: Jessica Thoreson, children's book editor).
Nonfiction: Children's/juvenile, how-to, reference, self-help. Subjects include child guidance/parenting, psychology, sociology, social and family issues. "We publish books on issues that impact families and the communities in which they live. Manuscripts that are essentially one person's story are rarely saleable." Submit proposal package, including outline, 2 sample chapters, author information, marketing ideas and SASE. Reviews artwork/photos as part of ms package. Send photocopies.
Recent Nonfiction Title(s): *Our Stories of Miscarriage*, edited by Rachel Faldet and Karen Fitton (women's studies/health); *Street Gang Awareness*, by Steven Sachs (reference/social science); *Kids-on-Board: Fun Things to Do While Commuting or Road Tripping with Children*, by Robyn Spizman (childcare/parenting/games and hobbies).
Tips: Audience is general reader, especially families. "Tell us what void your book fills in the market; give us an angle. Tell us who will buy your book. We have moved away from recovery books and have focused on social, community and family issues."

‡FALCON PRESS PUBLISHING CO. INC., Box 1718, Helena MT 59624. (406)442-6597. Fax: (406)442-2995. E-mail: falconbk@ix.netcom. **Acquisitions:** Neil Sexton, editorial assistant. Estab. 1978. "Falcon Press is primarily interested in ideas for recreational guidebooks and books on regional outdoor subjects." Publishes hardcover and trade paperback originals. Publishes 60 titles/year. Receives 350 queries and 30 mss/year. 20% of books from first-time authors; 80% from unagented writers. Pays royalty on retail price. Publishes book 1-2 years after acceptance of ms. Accepts simultaneous submissions. Reports in 2 months on queries. Book catalog for $1.93.
Imprint: Two Dot.

Nonfiction: Illustrated book, reference, guide books. Subjects include nature/environment, recreation, travel. Query with SASE. "We can only respond to queries submitted on the topics listed above. No fiction, no poetry." Reviews artwork/photos as part of the ms package. Send transparencies.
Recent Nonfiction Title(s): *Becoming An Outdoors Woman: My Outdoor Adventure*, by Christine Thomas; *Food Festivals of Northern California: A Travellers Guide and Cookbook*, by Bob Carter.

‡FANFARE, Imprint of Bantam Books, Division of Bantam Doubleday Dell, 1540 Broadway, New York NY 10036. (212)354-6500. Fax: (212)782-9523. **Acquisition:** Beth de Guzman, senior editor; Wendy McCurdy, senior editor; Stephanie Kip, associate editor; Cassie Goddard, associate editor. Fanfare's mission is "to publish a range of the best voices in women's fiction from brand new to established authors." Published 30 titles/year. 10-15% of books from first-time authors; less than 5% from unagented writers. Royalty and advance negotiable. Publishes book 12 months after acceptance of ms. Accepts simultaneous submissions. Reports in 2-3 months on queries; 3-4 months on proposals and mss (accepted only upon request).
● This publisher is open to agented submissions only.
Fiction: Publishes only romance and women's contemporary fiction. Adventure/romance, historical/romance, suspense/romance, western/romance. Length: 90,000-120,000 words. Query with SASE. *No unsolicited mss.*
Recent Fiction Title(s): *The Unlikely Angel*, by Betina Krahn (historical romance); *Long After Midnight*, by Iris Johansen (romantic suspense); *Stolen Hearts*, by Michelle Martin (contemporary romance).
Tips: "Be aware of what we publish and what our needs are in terms of length and content of manuscripts."

‡FARRAR STRAUS & GIROUX BOOKS FOR YOUNG READERS, Imprint of Farrar Straus Giroux, Inc., 19 Union Sq., New York NY 10003. (212)741-6900. Fax: (212)633-2427. E-mail: remayes@fsgee.com. **Acquisitions:** Margaret Ferguson, editor-in-chief. Estab. 1946. "We publish original and well-written material for all ages." Publishes hardcover and trade paperback originals. Publishes 50 titles/year. Receives 6,000 queries and mss/year. 10% of books from first-time authors; 50% from unagented writers. Pays 6% royalty on retail price. Offers $3,000-15,000 advance. Publishes book 18 months after acceptance of ms. Accepts simultaneous submissions, if informed. Reports in 2 months on queries, 3 months on mss. Book catalog for 9×12 SASE with 3 first-class stamps. Manuscript guidelines for #10 SASE.
Imprint(s): Aerial Fiction, Mirasol/libros juveniles, Sunburst.
Fiction: Juvenile, picture books, young adult. Query with SASE; considers complete ms. "We still look at unsolicited manuscripts, but for novels we prefer synopsis and sample chapters. Always enclose SASE for any materials author wishes returned. Query status of submissions in writing—no calls, please."
Recent Fiction Title(s): *Children of Summer: Henri Fabre's Insects*, by Margaret J. Anderson, illustrated by Marie LeGlatin Keis (ages 8-up); *Tangle Town*, by Kurt Cyrus (picture book, ages 4-8); *Belle Prater's Boy*, by Ruth White—won Newbery Honor (novel, ages 9-12).
Tips: Audience is full age range, preschool to young adult. Specializes in literary fiction.

FARRAR, STRAUS & GIROUX, INC., 19 Union Square West, New York NY 10003. Fax: (212)633-2427. **Acquisitions:** John Glusman, executive editor; Elizabeth Dyssegard, executive editor, (Noonday Press); Elisabeth Sifton, publisher (Hill and Wang); Ethan Nosowsky, editor (North Point Press). Farrar, Straus & Giroux is one of the most respected publishers of top-notch commercial-literary fiction and specialized nonfiction, as well as cutting-edge poetry. Publishes hardcover originals. Publishes 120 titles/year. Receives 5,000 submissions/year. Pays royalty. Offers advance. Publishes book 18 months after acceptance. Reports in 3 months. Catalog for 9×12 SAE with 3 first-class stamps.
● Farrar, Straus & Giroux has published such authors as John McPhee, Tom Wolfe, Susan Sontag, Scott Turow and Calvin Trillin.
Imprint(s): Farrar Straus & Giroux Books for Young Readers (Sunburst Books, Aerial Fiction, Mirasol), **Noonday Press**, **Hill & Wang**, **North Point Press**.
Nonfiction and Fiction: Submit outline/synopsis and sample chapters. Reviews copies of artwork/photos as part of ms package.
Recent Nonfiction Title(s): *Television*, by Carter Merbreier (behind-the-scenes, illustrated).
Recent Fiction Title(s): *Dove and Sword*, by Nancy Garden (historical fiction); *The Golden Plough*, by James Buchan; *Flesh and Blood*, by Michael Cunningham.
Recent Poetry Title(s): *The Man With Night Sweats*, by Thom Gunn.
Tips: "Study our style and our list."

‡FARTHEST STAR, Imprint of Alexander Books, 65 Macedonia Rd., Alexander NC 28701. (704)252-9515. **Acquisitions:** Ralph Roberts, publisher. Publishes trade paperback originals and reprints. Publishes 4 titles/year. Pays 12-15% royalty on wholesale price. Seldom offers advance. Publishes book 1 year after acceptance of ms. Accepts simultaneous submissions. Reports in 1 month on queries, 2 months on proposals, 3 months on mss. Book catalog for #10 SASE with 2 first-class stamps. Manuscript guidelines for #10 SASE with 2 first-class stamps.
Fiction: Science fiction. Query or submit 3 sample chapters with SASE.
Recent Fiction Title(s): *Birthright: The Book of Man*, by Mike Resnick (science fiction reprint).

FAWCETT JUNIPER, 201 E. 50th St., New York NY 10022. (212)751-2600. **Acquisitions:** Leona Nevler, editor. Publishes 24 titles/year. Pays royalty. Offers advance. Publishes book 1 year after acceptance. Accepts simultaneous submissions. Reports in 6 months on queries.

Nonfiction: Adult books.
Recent Nonfiction Title(s): *My Life: Magic Johnson*, by Magic Johnson.
Fiction: Mainstream/contemporary, young adult (12-18). No children's books. Query.
Recent Fiction Title(s): *The Genesis Code*, by John Case.

THE FEMINIST PRESS AT THE CITY UNIVERSITY OF NEW YORK, 311 E. 94th St., 2nd Floor, New York NY 10128. (212)360-5790. Fax: (212)348-1241. **Acquisitions:** Jean Casella, senior editor. Estab. 1970. "Our primary mission is to publish works of fiction by women which preserve and extend women's literary traditions. We emphasize work by multicultural /international women writers." Publishes hardcover and trade paperback originals and reprints. Publishes 10-12 titles/year. Receives 1,000 submissions/year. 20% of books from first-time authors; 80% from unagented writers. Pays royalty on net price. Offers $250 average advance. Accepts simultaneous submissions. Reports in 4 months on proposals. Book catalog free; ms guidelines for #10 SASE.
   ● The Feminist Press publishes such authors as Valerie Miner and Shirley Lim.
Nonfiction: "We look for nonfiction work which challenges gender-role stereotypes and documents women's historical and cultural contributions. No monographs. Note that we generally publish for the college classroom as well as the trade." Children's (ages 8 and up)/juvenile, primary materials for the humanities and social science classroom and general readers. Subjects include ethnic, gay/lesbian, government/politics, health/medicine, history, language/literature, music, sociology, translation, women's issues/studies and peace, memoir, international. Send proposal package, including materials requested in guidelines. Reviews artwork/photos as part of ms package. Send photocopies and SASE.
Recent Nonfiction Title(s): *Across Boundaries: The Journey of a South African Woman Leader*, by Mamphela Ramphele (memoir).
Fiction: "The Feminist Press publishes fiction reprints only. No original fiction is considered."
Tips: "Our audience consists of college students, professors, general readers. It is essential to look at our catalog and guidelines before submitting."

J.G. FERGUSON PUBLISHING COMPANY, 200 W. Madison, Suite 300, Chicago IL 60606. **Acquisitions:** Holli Cosgrove, editorial director. Estab. 1940. "We are primarily a career education publisher that publishes for schools and libraries." Publishes hardcover originals. Publishes 15 titles/year. Reports in 3 months on queries. Pays by project.
Nonfiction: Reference. "We publish work specifically for the junior high/high school/college library reference market. Works are generally encyclopedic in nature. Our current focus is career encyclopedias. No mass market, scholarly, or juvenile books, please." Query or submit outline and 1 sample chapter.
Recent Nonfiction Title(s): *Career Discovery Encyclopedia*, edited by Holli Cosgrove.
Tips: "We like writers who know the market—former or current librarians or teachers or guidance counselors."

FILTER PRESS, P.O. Box 95, Palmer Lake CO 80133-0095. (719)481-2420. President: Doris Baker. Estab. 1956. Publishes trade paperback originals and reprints. Publishes 4-6 titles/year. Pays 10-12% royalty on wholesale price. Publishes ms an average of 8 months after acceptance.
   ● Filter Press has increased their number of books published from 2-3 to 4-6 titles/year.
Nonfiction: Subjects include Americana, anthropology/archaeology, cooking/foods/nutrition, crafts and crafts people of the Southwest, women writers of the West. "We're interested in the history and natural history of the West, history of place names, etc. We will consider some Western Americana. We are interested in women anthropologists who did field work in the American Southwest in early 20th century. Interested in women in the West in general: settlers, Native-American, Chicanas." Query with outline and SASE. Reviews artwork/photos as part of ms package.
Recent Nonfiction Title(s): *Gold Panning in New Mexico*, by Robert Wilson.

DONALD I. FINE BOOKS, Division of Penguin Putnam Inc., 375 Hudson St., New York NY 10014. (212)366-2570. Fax: (212)366-2933. **Acquisitions:** Tom Burke, editor. Publishes hardcover originals and trade paperback originals and reprints. Publishes 20 titles/year. Receives 1,000 submissions/year. 30% of books from first-time authors. Pays royalty on retail price. Advance varies. Publishes book 1 year after acceptance.
   ● Donald I. Fine has published such authors as Bruce Jay Friedman and Copeland Marks.
Imprint(s): Primus Library of Contemporary Americana.
Nonfiction: Biography, cookbook, self-help. Subjects include history, military/war, sports. Agented submissions only. All unsolicited mss returned unopened. Reviews artwork/photos as part of ms package.
Recent Nonfiction Title(s): *Showtime: A Biography*, by Jerry Herman.
Fiction: Adventure, ethnic, historical, literary, mainstream/contemporary, mystery, suspense. Agented submissions only. All unsolicited mss returned unopened.
Recent Fiction Title(s): *Grand Jury*, by Philip Friedman (thriller).
Tips: *"We do not accept unagented mss."*

‡FIRE ENGINEERING BOOKS & VIDEOS, Division of PennWell Publishing Co., Park 80 W., Plaza 2, Saddle Brook NJ 07663. (201)845-0800. Fax: (201)845-6275. E-mail: 74677.1505@compuserve.com. Website: http://www.fire engineering.com. **Acquisitions:** William Manning, editor; Diane Feldman, managing editor; James Bacon, book editor. Fire Engineering publishes textbooks relevant to firefighting and training. Publishes hardcover originals. Publishes 10 titles/year. Receives 24 queries/year. 75% of books from first-time authors; 100% from unagented writers. Pays 7-10%

royalty on net sales. Publishes book 1 year after acceptance of ms. No simultaneous submissions. Reports in 3 months on proposals. Book catalog free.

• Fire Engineering has published such authors as Ray Downey, Tom Brennan, Vinnie Dunn.

Nonfiction: Reference, technical, textbook. Subjects include firefighter training, public safety. Submit outline and 2 sample chapters.

Recent Nonfiction Title(s): *The Common Sense Approach to Hazardous Materials*, by Frank Fire (Haz-mot training); *Incident Management for the Street Smart Officer*, by Skip Coleman (tactical chain of command).

FIREBRAND BOOKS, 141 The Commons, Ithaca NY 14850. (607)272-0000. **Acquisitions:** Nancy K. Bereano, publisher. Estab. 1985. "Our audience includes feminists, lesbians, ethnic audiences, and other progressive people." Publishes hardcover and trade paperback originals. Publishes 6-8 titles/year. Receives 400-500 submissions/year. 50% of books from first-time authors; 90% from unagented writers. Pays 7-9% royalty on retail price, or makes outright purchase. Publishes book 18 months after acceptance. Accepts simultaneous submissions, if so noted. Reports in 1 month on queries. *Writer's Market* recommends allowing 2 months for reply. Book catalog free.

Nonfiction: Personal narratives, essays. Subjects include feminism, lesbianism. Submit complete ms.

Fiction: Considers all types of feminist and lesbian fiction.

FISHER BOOKS, 4239 W. Ina Road, Suite 101, Tucson AZ 85741. (520)744-6110. Fax: (520)744-0944. Website: http://www.fisherbooks.com. **Acquisitions:** Sarah Trotta, managing editor. Estab. 1987. Publishes trade paperback originals and reprints. Publishes 16 titles/year. 25% of books from first-time authors; 75% from unagented writers. Pays 10-15% royalty on wholesale price. Accepts simultaneous submissions. Reports in 3 months. Book catalog for 8½×11 SAE with 3 first-class stamps.

Nonfiction: Subjects include automotive, business, cooking/foods/nutrition, regional gardening, family health, self-help. Submit outline and sample chapter, not complete ms. Include SAE and return postage.

Recent Nonfiction Title(s): *Your Pregnancy After 30*, by Glade B. Curtis, M.D. (health).

FJORD PRESS, P.O. Box 16349, Seattle WA 98116. (206)935-7376. Fax: (206)938-1991. E-mail: fjord@halcyon.com. Website: http://www.fjordpress.com/fjord. **Acquisitions:** Steven T. Murray, editor-in-chief. "We publish only literary novels of the highest quality." Publishes trade paperback originals and reprints. Publishes 4-8 titles/year. Receives 500 queries and 100 mss/year. 3% of books from first-time authors; 97% from unagented writers. Pays 10-15% royalty on retail price or small advance and royalty. Offers $100-1,000 advance. Publishes book up to 2 years after acceptance of ms. Accepts simultaneous submissions. Reports in 2 months on queries. Book catalog for #10 SASE.

Fiction: Ethnic, feminist (but not anti-male), literary, mainstream/contemporary, mystery, suspense (international thrillers, but no military or techno), literature in translation. "Topics we do not do: WWII, child abuse, anything medical or religious, fantasy or science fiction, romance, gore, kinky sex." Query or submit 1 sample chapter (not over 20 pages) and SASE.

Recent Fiction Title(s): *Runemaker*, by Tiina Nunnally (ethnic mystery); *The Summer Book*, by Tove Jansson (translation); *Nelio*, by Henning Mankell (translation).

Tips: Audience is literate readers looking for something different and willing to take a chance on an unfamiliar author. "If your fiction isn't as good as what's out there on the market, save your postage and keep practicing. If you expect to get rich by selling your book to Hollywood, write a screenplay instead. We want serious and entertaining novels (50,000-100,000 words) with well-rounded characters we can remember. Looking for new voices from both the African-American and white, Gen-X, angst communities, especially writers who love music and have a sense of rhythm in their prose. Some of our favorite writers are: Kafka, E. Leonard, Mosley, Morrison, Mowry, T. Wolff—get the idea?"

FOCAL PRESS, Subsidiary of Butterworth Heinemann, Division of Reed Elsevier (USA) Inc., 313 Washington St., Newton MA 02158-1630. Fax: (617)928-2640. Website: http://www.bh.com/fp/. **Acquisitions:** Marie Lee, senior editor. (media technology, broadcast, film/video, audio and sound technology, media writing, multimedia. E-mail: marie.lee@repp.com.); Tammy Harvey, associate acquisitions editor (photography/digital imaging, theater/live performance. E-mail: tammy.harvey@repp.com.). Estab. US, 1981; UK, 1938. "Focal Press, an imprint of Butterworth-Heinemann, is based on over 50 years of quality publishing in all areas of the media. From audio, broadcasting, and cinematography, through to journalism, radio, television, video, and writing, Focal Press books provide a comprehensive library of reference material for anyone involved in these varied fields." Imprint publishes hardcover and paperback originals and reprints. Publishes 40-45 UK-US titles/year; entire firm publishes 200 titles/year. Receives 500-700 submissions/year. 25% of books from first-time authors; 90% from unagented writers. Pays 10-12% royalty on wholesale price. Offers modest advance. Publishes book 9 months after acceptance. Accepts simultaneous submissions. Reports in 2 months. Book catalog and ms guidelines for SASE.

• Focal Press has published such authors as Carson Graves, Tom Ohanian and David Samuelson.

Nonfiction: How-to, reference, technical and textbooks in media arts: photography, film and cinematography, broadcasting, theater and performing arts. High-level scientific/technical monographs are also considered. "We do not publish collections of photographs or books composed primarily of photographs. Our books are text-oriented, with artwork serving to illustrate and expand on points in the text." Query preferred, or submit outline and sample chapters. Reviews artwork/photos as part of ms package.

Recent Nonfiction Title(s): *What is Theatre?* by John Russell Brown (theater); *Writing for Multimedia*, by Timothy Garrand (multimedia); *The Variable Contrast Printing*, by Steve Anchell (photography manual).

Tips: "We are publishing fewer photography books. Our advances and royalties are more carefully determined with an eye toward greater profitability for all our publications."

FOCUS ON THE FAMILY BOOK PUBLISHING, 8605 Explorer Dr., Colorado Springs CO 80920. **Acquisitions:** Editor. "We are the publishing arm of Focus on the Family, an evangelical Christian organization. Authors need to be aware that our book publishing is closely related to the focus of the organization, which is the strengthening and preservation of family and marriages." Publishes hardcover and trade paperback originals. Publishes 15-20 titles/year. 25% of books from first-time authors; 25% from unagented writers. Pays royalty. Offers advance. Publishes book 1 year after acceptance of ms. Accepts simultaneous submissions. Reports in 1 month on queries, 2 months on proposals. Book catalog free. Manuscript guidelines for #10 SASE.
Nonfiction: How-to, juvenile, self-help. Subjects include child guidance/parenting, money/finance, women's issues/ studies. Query before submitting ms.
Tips: Our audience is "families and the people who make up families. Know what we publish before submitting query."

‡FOCUS PUBLISHING, INC., 1375 Washington Ave. S., Bemidji MN 56601. (218)759-9817. Website: http:// www.paulbunyan.net/focus. **Acquisitions:** Jan Haley, vice president. "Focus Publishing is a small press primarily devoted to Christian books and secular titles appropriate to children and home-schooling families." Publishes hardcover and trade paperback originals and reprints. Publishes 4-6 titles/year. Receives 10 queries and 10 mss/year. 90% of books from first-time authors; 100% from unagented writers. Pays 7-10% royalty on retail price. Publishes book 1 year after acceptance of ms. Reports in 2 months. Book catalog free.
Nonfiction: Children's/juvenile. Subjects include religion, women's issues/studies. Submit proposal package, including marketing ideas with SASE. Reviews artwork/photos as part of the ms package. Send photocopies.
Recent Nonfiction Title(s): *The Excellent Wife*, by Martha Peace (women's issues/religious); *Three to Get Ready*, by Dr. Howard Eyrich (Christian Marriage counseling); *Flying Higher*, by Capt. Paul Read (parables of flying).
Fiction: Juvenile, picture books, religious, young adult. "We are looking for Christian books for men and young adults. Be sure to list your target audience." Query and submit synopsis.
Recent Fiction Title(s): *Butch & the Rooster*, by Judy Hess (children's picture book).
Poetry: "We are not especially interested in poetry at this time." Query.
Recent Poetry Title(s): *Poems From The Heart*, by Ruth Martindale (spiritual).
Tips: "I prefer SASE inquiries, synopsis and target markets. Please don't send 5 lbs. of paper with no return postage."

‡FORDHAM UNIVERSITY PRESS, University Box L, Bronx NY 10458. (718)817-4782. **Acquisitions:** Mary Beatrice Schulte, executive editor. Publishes hardcover and trade paperback originals and reprints. Publishes 30 titles/ year. Receives 100 queries and 50 mss/year. 25% of books from first-time authors; 75% from unagented writers. Pays 4-7% royalty on retail price. No advance Publishes book 6-24 months after acceptance of ms. Reports in 2 months on proposals and mss. Book catalog and ms guidelines free.
Nonfiction: Biography, textbook. Subjects include Americana, anthropology/archaeology, art/architecture, government/ politics, history, language/literature, military/war, philosophy, regional, religion, sociology, translation. "We are a publisher in humanities, accepting scholarly monographs, collections, occasional reprints and general interest titles for consideration." Submit outline with 2-5 sample chapters.
Recent Nonfiction Title(s): *Wordsworth: A Poetic Life*, by John L. Mahoney (biography/literary studies); *Deconstruction in a Nutshell: A Conversation with Jacques Derrida*, by J. Derrida (philosophy); *Hudson River Guidebook*, by Arthur G. Adams (regional/travel).
Tips: "We have an academic and general audience."

FOREIGN POLICY ASSOCIATION, 470 Park Ave. S., New York NY 10016. (212)481-8100. **Acquisitions:** Nancy Hoepli-Phalon, editor-in-chief. "The Foreign Policy Association, a nonpartisan, not-for-profit educational organization founded in 1918, is a catalyst for developing awareness, understanding of and informed opinion on U.S. foreign policy and global issues. Through its balanced, nonpartisan publications, FPA seeks to encourage individuals in schools, communities and the workplace to participate in the foreign policy process." Publishes 2 periodicals and an occasional hardcover and trade paperback original. Publishes 5-6 titles/year. Receives 12 queries and 6 mss/year, 99% from unagented writers. No advance. Pays outright purchase of $2,500-4,000. Publishes periodical article 9 months after acceptance. Maximum length: 16,000 words. Accepts simultaneous submissions. Reports in 2 months. Catalog free.
Imprint(s): Headline Series (quarterly), Great Decisions (annual).
Nonfiction: Reference and textbook. Subjects include foreign policy, government/politics, history and social studies. "We are a nonpartisan educational organization. Audience: students, educators, general public with an interest in international relations." Query. Submit outline.
Recent Nonfiction Title(s): *Hong Kong and China: 'One Country, Two Systems'?*, by Frank Ching.
Tips: Audience is students and people with an interest, but not necessarily any expertise, in foreign policy and international relations.

‡FORGE, Subsidiary of Tom Doherty Associates, Inc., Imprint of St. Martin's Press, 175 Fifth Ave., 14th Floor, New York NY 10010. (212)388-0100. Fax: (212)388-0191. **Acquisitions:** Melissa Ann Singer, senior editor; Natalia Aponte, editor. Publishes hardcover, trade paperback and mass market paperback originals, trade and mass market paperback reprints. Receives 5,000 mss/year. 2% of books from first-time authors; a few from unagented writers. Royalties:

paperback, 6-8% first-time authors, 8-10% established authors; hardcover, 10% first 5,000, 12½% second 5,000, 15% thereafter. Offers $7,500 and up advance. Reports in 4 months on proposals. Book catalog for 9×12 SASE with 2 first-class stamps.
Nonfiction: Subjects include health/medicine, women's issues/studies. Query with outline and 3 sample chapters.
Recent Nonfiction Title(s): *Hard Labor*, by Susan L. Diamond (childbirth/medical guide).
Fiction: Historical, horror, mainstream/contemporary, mystery, suspense, thriller; general fiction of all sorts. "We handle a wide range of books; if you're not sure if a project is right for us, phone us and ask." Query with synopsis and 3 sample chapters.
Recent Fiction Title(s): *1812*, by David Niven (historical novel); *People of the Silence*, by Kathleen O'Neal Gear and W. Michael Gear (historical novel).

‡FORTRESS PRESS, Imprint of Augsburg Fortress Publishers. Box 1209, 426 S. Fifth St., Minneapolis MN 55440. (612)330-3300. Fax: (612)330-3455. E-mail: afp_bookstore.topic@ecunet.org. Website: http://www.elca.org/afp/fortres. html. **Acquisitions:** Marshall Johnson, director of publishing. Estab. 1855. Fortress Press publishes academic books in Biblical studies, theology, Christian ethics, church history. Publishes hardcover and trade paperback originals. Publishes 35 titles/year. Receives 500-700 queries/year. 5-10% of books from first-time authors; prefers established authors. Pays royalty on retail price. No advance. Publishes book 1 year after acceptance of ms. Accepts simultaneous submissions. Reports in 3 months on proposals. Book catalog free. Call 1-800-328-4648. Manuscript guidelines available on line.
Nonfiction: Subjects include government/politics, history, religion, women's issues/studies. Query with annotated TOC, brief CV, sample chapter (introduction) and SASE. Please study guidelines before submitting.
Recent Nonfiction Title(s): *Intro to the History of Christianity*, by Tim Dewley; *Ethics in Business*, by James M. Childs, Jr.; *God, Creation & Contemporary Physics*, by Mark William Worthy.

‡FORUM, Imprint of Prima Publishing, 3875 Atherton Rd., Rocklin CA 95765. (916)632-4400. Fax: (916)632-4403. **Acquisitions:** Steven Martin, managing editor. "Forum publishes books that contribute to the marketplace of ideas." Publishes hardcover originals and reprints, trade paperback originals and reprints. Publishes 10-15 titles/year. 25% of books from first-time authors; 5% from unagented writers. Pays 15-22% royalty on wholesale price. Advance varies. Publishes book 1 year after acceptance of ms. Accepts simultaneous submissions. Reports in 1 month on queries and proposals, 2 months on mss.
Nonfiction: Subjects include libertarian/conservative thought, business/economics, government/politics, history, religion, current affairs, individual empowerment. Query with outline, 1 sample chapter and SASE.
Recent Nonfiction Title(s): *God: The Evidence*, Patrick Glynn (religion); *The Race Card*, edited by Peter Collier and David Horowitz (current affairs); *Churchill on Leadership*, by Steven Hayward (business).

FORWARD MOVEMENT PUBLICATIONS, 412 Sycamore St., Cincinnati OH 45202. Fax: (513)421-0315. E-mail: forward.movement@ecunet.org. Website: http://www.dfms.org/forward-movement. **Acquisitions:** Edward S. Gleason, editor and director. "Forward Movement was established in 1934 'to help reinvigorate the life of the church.' Many titles focus on the life of prayer, where our relationship with God is centered, death, marriage, baptism, recovery, joy, the Episcopal Church and more." Publishes trade paperback originals. Publishes 12 titles/year. 50% of books from first-time authors; 100% from unagented writers. Pays one-time honorarium. Reports in 1 month on queries and proposals, 2 months on mss. Book catalog for 9×12 SAE with $1.47 postage.
Nonfiction: Essays. Religious subjects. "We publish a variety of types of books, but they all relate to the lives of Christians. We are an agency of the Episcopal Church." Query with SASE.
Recent Nonfiction Title(s): *Building Up the Church*, by selected authors.
Tips: Audience is primarily members of mainline Protestant churches.

‡WALTER FOSTER PUBLISHING, INC., A Quarto Group Company, 23062 La Cadena Dr., Laguna Hills CA 92653. **Acquisitions:** Sheena Needham, creative director. "We publish instructional 'how to' art/craft instruction only." Publishes trade paperback originals. Publishes 40-100 titles/year. Receives 10-20 queries/year. 50% of books from first-time authors; 100% from unagented writers. Makes outright purchase. No advance. Publishes book 1-2 years after acceptance of ms. Accepts simultaneous submissions. Reports in 2 months on queries, 6 months on proposals and mss. Book catalog free.
Nonfiction: How-to. Subjects include art, craft. "Send enough samples of your artwork to prove your qualifications." Submit proposal package, including query letter, color photos/examples of artwork. Reviews artwork/photos as part of ms package. Send color photocopies or color photos.
Recent Nonfiction Title(s): *How to Draw Bugs Bunny & Friends* (art instruction); *Papier-Mâché* (art instruction).
Tips: Audience is all ages. "Don't call us, we'll call you."

‡FOUL PLAY, Imprint of W.W. Norton, 500 Fifth Ave., New York NY 10110. (212)354-5500. Fax: (212)869.0856. Website: http://www.wwnorton.com. **Acquisitions:** Candace Watt, editor. Estab. 1996. "We publish a broad range of mysteries, from cozies to hard-boiled to traditional." Publishes hardcover originals and reprints. Publishes 6 titles/year. Receives hundreds of queries/year. A small percentage of books from first-time authors; 10% from unagented writers. Pays 10-12½-15% royalty on retail price. Advance varies. Publishes book 6 months after acceptance of ms. Accepts simultaneous submissions. Reporting time varies. Book catalog free from W.W. Norton (same address).
Fiction: Mystery, suspense. Query with synopsis, 1 sample chapter and SASE.

Recent Fiction Title(s): *Death of a Sunday Writer*, by Eric Wright; *Gospel*, by Bill James (mysteries).

FOUR WALLS EIGHT WINDOWS, 39 W. 14th St., Room 503, New York NY 10011. Website: users.aol.com/specpress/fourwalls.htm. **Acquisitions**. Dan Simon, editor or John Oakes, editor. Estab. 1987. "Emphasizing fine literature and quality nonfiction, Four Walls Eight Windows has a reputation for carefully edited and distinctive books." Publishes hardcover originals, trade paperback originals and reprints. Publishes 20 titles/year. Receives 3,000 submissions/year. 15% of books from first-time authors; 50% from unagented writers. Pays royalty on retail price. Advance varies widely. Publishes book 1-2 years after acceptance. Reports in 2 months on queries. Book catalog for 6×9 SAE with 3 first-class stamps.
Nonfiction: Political, investigative. Subjects include art/architecture, government/politics, history, language/literature, nature/environment, science. "We do not want New Age works." Query first with outline and SASE. All sent without SASE discarded.
Recent Nonfiction Title(s): *Bike Cult*, by David Perry.
Fiction: Ethnic, feminist, literary. "No romance, popular." Query first with outline/synopsis and SASE.
Recent Fiction Title(s): *Ribofunk*, by Paul DiFilippo.
Tips: No longer accepts unsolicited submissions.

FOX CHAPEL PUBLISHING, 1970 Broad St., East Petersburg PA 17520. **Acquisitions:** John Alan. Fox Chapel publishes woodworking and woodcarving titles for professionals and hobbyists. Publishes hardcover and trade paperback originals and trade paperback reprints. Publishes 12-20 titles/year. 80% of books from first-time authors; 100% from unagented writers. Pays royalty or makes outright purchase. Advance varies. Publishes book 6 months after acceptance of ms. Accepts simultaneous submissions. Reports in 2 months on queries.
Nonfiction: Woodworking, woodcarving and related titles. Query. Reviews artwork/photos as part of ms package. Send photocopies.
Recent Nonfiction Title(s): *Complete Beginners Woodcarvers Workbook*, by Gulden (how-to/crafts); *Making Classic Chairs: A Chippendale Reference*, by Ron Clarkson.
Tips: "We're looking for knowledgeable artists, woodworkers first, writers second to write for us. Our market is for avid woodworking hobbyists and professionals."

‡**FPMI COMMUNICATIONS, INC.**, 707 Fiber St., NW, Huntsville AL 35801-5833. (205)539-1850. Fax: (205)539-0911. **Acquisitions:** Ralph Smith, president. Estab. 1985. "Our primary audience is federal managers and supervisors—particularly first and second level." Publishes trade paperback originals. Averages 4-6 titles/year. Receives 4-5 submissions/year. 60% of books from first-time authors; 100% from unagented writers. Pays 15% on retail price. Publishes book an average of 1 year after acceptance. Simultaneous submissions OK. Query for electronic submissions. Reports in 3 weeks on queries, 2 months on mss. Free book catalog.
Nonfiction: Technical. Subjects include government/politics, labor relations, personnel issues. "We will be publishing books for government and business on topics such as sexual harassment, drug testing, and how to deal with leave abuse by employees. Our books are practical, how-to books for a supervisor or manager. Scholarly theoretical works do not interest our audience." Submit outline/synopsis and sample chapters or send complete ms.
Tips: "We are interested in books that are practical, easy-to-read and less than 150 pages. If I were a writer trying to market a book today, I would emphasize practical topics with plenty of examples in succinct, concrete language."

FRANCISCAN UNIVERSITY PRESS, University Blvd., Steubenville OH 43952. Fax: (614)283-6427. Website: http://esoptron.umd.edu/fusfolder/press.html. **Acquisitions:** James Fox, executive director. "We seek to further the Catholic and Franciscan mission of Franciscan University of Steubenville by publishing quality popular-level Catholic apologetics and biblical studies. In this manner we hope to serve Pope John Paul II's call for a new evangelization of today's Catholics." Publishes trade paperback originals and reprints. Publishes 7 titles/year. 5% of books from first-time authors; 100% from unagented writers. Pays 5-15% royalty on retail price. Publishes book 1 year after acceptance of ms. Reports in 3 months on proposals. Book catalog and ms guidelines free.
Nonfiction: Popular level Catholic theology. Subjects include catechetics, scripture, Catholic apologetics. Submit proposal package, including outline, 3 sample chapters, author cv.
Recent Nonfiction Title(s): *If Your Mind Wanders at Mass*, by Thomas Howard (religion/liturgy).
Tips: "95% of our publications are solicited."

THE FREE PRESS, Imprint of Simon & Schuster, 1230 Avenue of the Americas, New York NY 10020. (212)698-7000. Fax: (212)632-4989. **Acquisitions:** Liz McGuire, editorial director; Robert Wallace, senior editor (business); Bruce Nichols, senior editor (history); Susan Arellano, senior editor (psychology, education); Mitch Horowitz, senior editor (current events/politics); Philip Rapapport, editor (psychology/social work); Janet Coleman, senior editor (business/culture). Estab. 1947. The Free Press publishes serious adult nonfiction. Publishes 120 titles/year. Receives 3,000 submissions/year. 15% of books from first-time authors; 50% from unagented writers. Pays variable royalty. Publishes book 1 year after acceptance of ms. Reports in 2 months.
● The Free Press has published such authors as Gary Hart, Dinesh D'Souza, Irving Kristol.
Nonfiction: professional books and college texts in the social sciences, humanities and business. Reviews artwork/photos as part of ms package "but we can accept no responsibility for photos or art. Looks for identifiable target

audience, evidence of writing ability." Accepts nonfiction translations. Query with 1-3 sample chapters, outline before submitting mss.

FREE SPIRIT PUBLISHING INC., 400 First Ave. N., Suite 616, Minneapolis MN 55401-1730. (612)338-2068. Fax: (612)337-5050. E-mail: help4kids@freespirit.com. **Acquisitions:** Elizabeth H. Verdick, editor. "We believe passionately in empowering kids to learn to think for themselves and make their own good choices." Publishes trade paperback originals and reprints. Publishes 20 titles/year. 10% of books from first-time authors; 90% from unagented writers. Offers advance. Book catalog and ms guidelines free.
Imprint(s): Self-Help for Kids®, Free Spirited Classroom® Series.
 • Free Spirit has published such authors as Barbara A. Lewis.
Nonfiction: Self-Help for Kids ®. Subjects include child guidance/parenting, education (pre-K-12, but not textbooks or basic skills books like reading, counting, etc.), health (mental/emotional health—*not* physical health—for/about children), psychology (for/about children), sociology (for/about children). Query with outline, 2 sample chapters and SASE. Send photocopies. "Many of our authors are teachers, counselors or others involved in helping kids."
Recent Nonfiction Title(s): *Taking Charge of My Mind and Body, A Girl's Guide to Outsmarting Alcohol, Drug, Smoking, and Eating Problems*, by Folkers and Engelmann.
Tips: "Our audience is children, teens, teachers, parents and youth counselors. We are concerned with kids' mental/ emotional well-being. We are not looking for academic or religious materials, nor books that analyze problems with the nation's school systems. Instead we want books that offer practical, positive advice so kids can help themselves."

FRIENDS UNITED PRESS, 101 Quaker Hill, Richmond IN 47374. (317)962-7573. Fax: (317)966-1293. **Acquisitions:** Ardith Talbot, editor/manager. Estab. 1968. "Friends United Press commits itself to energise and equip Friends and others through the power of the Holy Spirit to gather people into fellowship where Jesus Christ is known, loved and obeyed as teacher and Lord." Publishes 5 titles/year. Receives 100 queries and 80 mss/year. 50% of books from first-time authors; 99% from unagented writers. Pays 7½% royalty. Publishes ms 1 year after acceptance of ms. Accepts simultaneous submissions. Reports in 16 months. Book catalog and ms guidelines free.
Nonfiction: Biography, humor, children's/juvenile, reference, textbook. Religious subjects. "Authors should be Quaker and should be familiar with Quaker history, spirituality and doctrine." Submit proposal package. Reviews artwork/ photos as part of ms package. Send photocopies.
Recent Nonfiction Title(s): *A Life of Search*, by D. Elton Trueblood (spirituality); *Beatitudes of Christmas*, by Jay Marshall (spirituality).
Fiction: Historical, juvenile, religious. "Must be Quaker-related." Query.
Tips: "Spirituality manuscripts must be in agreement with Quaker spirituality."

‡FROMM INTERNATIONAL PUBLISHING CORPORATION, 560 Lexington Ave., New York NY 10022. **Acquisitions:** Fred Jordan, executive director; Matthew McGowan, assistant editor. Publishes hardcover originals, trade paperback originals and reprints. Publishes 20-25 titles/year. Receives 200 mss/year. 10% of books from first-time authors; 10% from unagented writers. Pays 10-15% royalty. Offers $2,500 advance. Publishes book 1 year after acceptance of ms. Accepts simultaneous submissions. Reports in 1 month on queries and proposals, 2 months on mss. Book catalog free.
Nonfiction: Biography, illustrated book, reference. Subjects include Americana, art/architecture, health/medicine, history, language/literature, psychology. Submit 3 sample chapters and table of contents with SASE. Reviews artwork/ photos as part of ms package. Send photocopies.
Recent Nonfiction Title(s): *The Story of Britain*, by Roy Strong (history); *Hermann Hesse: Pilgrim of Crisis*, by Ralph Freedman (biography); *Bauhaus: Crucible of Modernism*, by Elaine S. Hochman (art/history).
Tips: Audience is the general trade, both popular and "high brow."

‡GATEWAY PUBLISHERS, P.O. Box 1749, Newark NJ 07101. (201)824-7207. Fax: (201)824-1531. E-mail: gway-pub@ix.netcom.com. **Acquisitions:** Andrea Walker/Arthur Walker, vice president/editors. "Gateway's mission is to publish parenting books with business themes and books that help parents give their kids the skills they need to get ahead in the world—business skills, computer skills, etiquette, etc." Publishes hardcover and trade paperback originals. Publishes 5 titles/year. Receives 40 queries/year. 100% of books from unagented writers. Pays 5-12% royalty on whole-sale price, may also make outright purchase. Offers $500-1,000 advance. Publishes book 9 months after acceptance of ms. Accepts simultaneous submissions. Reports in 1 month on queries, 2 months on proposals.
Nonfiction: How-to. Subjects include business/economics, child guidance/parenting, education, hobbies, money/finance. "Gateway Publishers is launching a new series called 'Getting Your Kids Started.' The series will feature books to help parents teach kids financial, business, entrepreneurial, computer, social skills and other important 'life skills.' We are looking for books that will help parents teach their kids 'real skills.' We are not looking for fluff." Query with outline, 2 sample chapters, proposal package and SASE. Reviews artwork/photos as part of ms package. Send photocopies.
Recent Nonfiction Title(s): *The Lemonade Stand: A Guide to Encouraging the Entrepreneur in Your Child*, by Emmanuel Modu (business/parenting/how-to).
Tips: "We envision an audience of parents with children between the ages of ten and seventeen."

GAY SUNSHINE PRESS and LEYLAND PUBLICATIONS, P.O. Box 410690, San Francisco CA 94141-0690. **Acquisitions:** Winston Leyland, editor. Estab. 1970. "We seek innovative literary nonfiction and depicting gay themes and lifestyles." Publishes hardcover originals, trade paperback originals and reprints. Publishes 6-8 titles/year. Pays royalty or makes outright purchase. Reports in 6 weeks on queries. Book catalog for $1.

Nonfiction: How-to and gay lifestyle topics. "We're interested in innovative literary nonfiction which deals with gay lifestyles." No long personal accounts, academic or overly formal titles. Query. "After query is returned by us, submit outline and sample chapters with SASE. All unsolicited manuscripts are returned unopened."

Fiction: Erotica, ethnic, experimental, historical, mystery, science fiction, translation. "Interested in well-written novels on gay themes; also short story collections. We have a high literary standard for fiction." Query. "After query is returned by us, submit outline/synopsis and sample chapters with SASE. All unsolicited manuscripts are returned unopened."

Recent Fiction Title(s): *Out of the Blue: Russia's Hidden Gay Literature*; *Partings at Dawn: An Anthology of Japanese Gay Literature.*

GEM GUIDES BOOK COMPANY, 315 Cloverleaf Dr., Suite F, Baldwin Park CA 91706-6510. (818)855-1611. Fax: (818)855-1610. **Acquisitions:** Robin Nordhues, editor. Gem Guides specializes in books on earth sciences, nature books, also travel/local interest titles for the Western U.S. Publishes trade paperback originals. Publishes 6-8 titles/year. Receives 40 submissions/year. 30% of books from first-time authors; 100% from unagented writers. Pays 6-10% royalty on retail price. Publishes book 8 months after acceptance. Accepts simultaneous submissions. Reports in 1 month. *Writer's Market* recommends allowing 2 months for reply.

Imprint(s): Gembooks.

Nonfiction: Regional books for the Western U.S. Subjects include hobbies, Western history, nature/environment, recreation, travel. "We are looking for " Query with outline/synopsis and sample chapters. Reviews artwork/photos as part of ms package.

Recent Nonfiction Title(s): *The Rockhound's Handbook*, by James R. Mitchell.

Tips: "We have a general audience of people interested in recreational activities. Publishers plan and have specific book lines in which they specialize. Learn about the publisher and submit materials compatible with that publisher's product line."

GENERAL PUBLISHING GROUP, 2701 Ocean Park Blvd., Suite 140, Santa Monica CA 90405. (310)314-4000. Fax: (310)314-8080. E-mail: gpgedit@aol.com. **Acquisitions:** Peter Hoffman, editorial director. General Publishing Group specializes in popular culture, entertainment, politics and humor titles. Publishes hardcover and trade paperback originals. Publishes 50 titles/year. Pays royalty. Publishes ms 8 months after acceptance. Accepts simultaneous submissions. Reports in 4 months on queries. Book catalog free.

● General Publishing Group has increased their number of books published from 30 to 50 titles/year.

Nonfiction: Biography, coffee table book, gift book, humor, illustrated book. Subjects include Americana, art/architecture, music/dance, photography, entertainment/media, politics. Query with proposal package, including sample chapters, toc and SASE. Reviews artwork as part of ms package. Send photocopies.

Recent Nonfiction Title(s): *Frank Sinatra: An American Legend*, by Nancy Sinatra; *The Playmate Book.*

‡LAURA GERINGER BOOKS, Imprint of HarperCollins Children's Books, 10 E. 53rd St., New York NY 10022. (212)207-7000. Website: http://www.harpercollins.com. **Acquisitions:** Laura Geringer, editorial director. "We look for books that are out of the ordinary, authors who have their own definite take, and artists that add a sense of humor to the text." Publishes hardcover originals. Publishes 15-20 titles/year. 5% of books from first-time authors; 25% from unagented writers. Pays 10-12½% on retail price. Advance varies. Publishes ms 6-12 months after acceptance of ms for novels, 1-2 years after acceptance of ms for picture books. Reports in 2 weeks on queries, 1 month on proposals, 4 months on mss. Book catalog for 8×10 SAE with 3 first-class stamps. Manuscript guidelines for #10 SASE.

Fiction: Adventure, fantasy, historical, humor, literary, picture books, young adult. "A mistake writers often make is failing to research the type of books an imprint publishes, therefore sending inappropriate material." Query with SASE for picture books; submit complete ms with SASE for novels.

Recent Fiction Title(s): *Zoe Rising*, by Pam Conrad (novel); *The Leaf Men*, by William Joyce (picture book).

‡GESSLER PUBLISHING CO., INC., 10 E. Church Ave., Roanoke VA 24011. (540)345-1429. Fax: (540)342-7172. E-mail: gesslerco@aol.com. Website: http://www.gessler.com/gessler/. **Acquisitions:** Richard Kurshan, CEO. Estab. 1932. "We provide high-quality language-learning materials for the education market." Publishes trade paperback originals and reprints. Publishes 75 titles/year. Receives 50 queries and 25 mss/year. 5% of books from first-time authors; 90% from unagented writers, "very few, if any, are agented." Pays 10-20% royalty on retail price. Offers $250-500 advance. Publishes book 9 months after acceptance of ms. Accepts simultaneous submissions. Reports in 3 days on queries, 3 weeks on mss. *Writer's Market* recommends allowing 2 months for reply. Book catalog free.

Nonfiction: Textbook. Subjects include education, language/literature, multicultural. "We publish supplementary language learning materials. Our products assist teachers with foreign languages, ESL, and multicultural activities." Query first, then submit outline/synopsis with 2-3 sample chapters or complete ms with cover letter and SASE. Reviews artwork/photos as part of ms package. Send photocopies.

Recent Nonfiction Title(s): *Parabienes*, by Richard Sandford (Spanish reader); *Buenviaje*, by Maria Koonce (Spanish workbook).

Tips: Middle school/high school audience. "Writers need to be more open-minded when it comes to understanding not everyone learns the same way. They may have to be flexible when it comes to revising their work to accommodate broader teaching/learning methods."

GLENBRIDGE PUBLISHING LTD., 6010 W. Jewell Ave., Denver CO 80232-7106. Fax: (303)987-9037. **Acquisitions:** James A. Keene, editor. Estab. 1986. Glenbridge is a general interest publisher. Publishes hardcover originals and reprints, trade paperback originals. Publishes 6-8 titles/year. Pays 10% royalty. Publishes book 1 year after acceptance. Accepts simultaneous submissions. Reports in 2 months on queries. Book catalog for 6×9 SASE. Manuscript guidelines for #10 SASE.
Nonfiction: Subjects include Americana, business/economics, history, music, philosophy, politics, psychology, sociology, cookbooks. Query with outline/synopsis, sample chapters and SASE.
Recent Nonfiction Title(s): *Cooking With the Ancients: The Bible Food Book*; *Flying the Stock Market: Pilot Your Dollars to Success*; *Three Minute Therapy: Change Your Thinking, Change Your Life*.

THE GLOBE PEQUOT PRESS, INC., P.O. Box 833, Old Saybrook CT 06475-0833. (860)395-0440. Fax: (203)395-1418. **Acquisitions:** Laura Strom, submissions editor. Estab. 1947. "Globe Pequot is among the top sources for travel books in the United States and offering the broadest selection of travel titles of any vendor in this market." Publishes hardcover originals, paperback originals and reprints. Publishes 110 titles/year. Receives 1,500 submissions/year. 30% of books from first-time authors; 70% from unagented writers. Average print order for a first book is 4,000-7,500. Makes outright purchase or pays 10% royalty on net price. Offers advance. Publishes book 1 year after acceptance. Accepts simultaneous submissions. Reports in 3 months. Book catalog for 9×12 SASE.
Imprint(s): Voyager Books and East Woods Books.
• Globe Pequot Press has increased their number of books published from 80 to 110 titles/year.
Nonfiction: Travel guidebooks (regional OK) and outdoor recreation. No doctoral theses, fiction, genealogies, memoirs, poetry or textbooks. Submit outline, table of contents, sample chapter and résumé/vita. Reviews artwork/photos.
Recent Nonfiction Title(s): *Oregon: Off the Beaten Path*, by Myrna Oakley; *Quick Escapes from New York City, 2nd Edition*, by Susan Farewell.

DAVID R. GODINE, PUBLISHER, INC., P.O. Box 9103, Lincoln MA 01773. Fax: (617)259-9198. Website: http://www.godine.com. **Acquisitions:** Mark Polizzotti, editorial director. Estab. 1970. "We publish books that matter for people who care." Publishes hardcover and trade paperback originals and reprints. Publishes 30 titles/year. Pays royalty on retail price. Publishes book 3 years after acceptance of ms. Book catalog for 5×8 SAE with 3 first-class stamps.
• David R. Godine has published such authors as Andre Dubus, Leslie Fiedler, Ron Padgett, William Gass, William Maxwell, Stanley Elkin and Georges Perec.
Nonfiction: Biography, coffee table book, cookbook, illustrated book, children's/juvenile. Subjects include Americana, art/architecture, gardening, nature/environment, photography, literary criticism and current affairs. *Writer's Market* recommends sending a query with SASE first.
Recent Nonfiction Title(s): *Tyranny of the Normal*, by Leslie Fiedler (essays).
Fiction: Literary, novel, short story collection, children's/juvenile. "We are not considering unsolicited manuscripts."
Recent Fiction Title(s): *Last Trolley from Beethovenstraat*, by Grete Weil (novel); *The Last Worthless Evening*, by Andre Dubus (short stories).
Poetry: "Our poetry list is filled through 1998."
Recent Poetry Title(s): *New and Selected Poems*, by Ron Padgett.

GOLDEN WEST PUBLISHERS, 4113 N. Longview, Phoenix AZ 85014. (602)265-4392. Fax: (602)279-6901. **Acquisitions:** Hal Mitchell, editor. Estab. 1973. "We seek to provide quality, affordable cookbooks and books about the Southwest to the marketplace." Publishes trade paperback originals. Publishes 15-20 titles/year. Receives 200 submissions/year. 50% of books from first-time authors; 100% from unagented writers. Average print order for a first book is 5,000. Prefers mss on work-for-hire basis. No advance. Publishes book an average of 6 months after acceptance. Accepts simultaneous submissions. Reports in 1 month on queries, 2 months on mss.
• Golden West Publishers has increased their number of books published from 5-6 to 15-20 titles/year. They have published such authors as Marshall Trimble.
Nonfiction: Cookbooks, books on the Southwest and West. Subjects include cooking/foods, Southwest history and outdoors, travel. Query. Reviews artwork/photos as part of ms package.
Recent Nonfiction Title(s): *Grand Canyon Cookbook*, by Fischer; *Arizona Trivia* by Trimble (history/trivia).
Tips: "We are interested in Arizona and Southwest material, and regional and state cookbooks for the entire country, and welcome material in these areas."

‡**GOVERNMENT INSTITUTES, INC.**, 4 Research Place, Suite 200, Rockville MD 20850-3226. (301)921-2355. Fax: (301)921-0373. E-mail: giinc@aol.com. **Acquisitions:** Alexander M. Padro (occupational and environmental safety, health and engineering) and Charlene Ikonomou (environmental compliance and natural resources, telecommunications), editors. Estab. 1973. "Our mission is to be the leading global company providing practical, accurate, timely and authoritative information desired by people concerned with environment, health and safety, telecommunications, and other regulatory and technical topics." Publishes hardcover and softcover originals and CD-ROM/disk products. Averages 45 titles/year. Receives 100 submissions/year. 50% of books from first-time authors; 100% from unagented writers. Pays royalty or makes outright purchase. Publishes book 2 months after acceptance. Accepts simultaneous submissions, if so noted. Reports in 1 month. *Writer's Market* recommends allowing 2 months for reply. Book catalog free.
Nonfiction: Reference, technical. Subjects include environmental law, occupational safety and health, environmental engineering, telecommunications, employment law, FDA matters, industrial hygiene and safety, real estate with an

environmental slant. Needs professional-level titles in those areas. Also looking for international environmental topics. Submit outline and at least 1 sample chapter.
Recent Nonfiction Title(s): *Fundamentals of Occupational Safety and Health*, by James P. Kohn et al; *Environmental Law Handbook*, Thomas F.P. Sullivan; *ISO 14000: Understanding the Environmental Standards*, by W.M. van Zharen.
Tips: "We also conduct courses. Authors are frequently invited to serve as instructors."

THE GRADUATE GROUP, P.O. Box 370351, West Hartford CT 06137-0351. **Acquisitions:** Mara Whitman, president; Robert Whitman, vice president. The Graduate Group "helps college and graduate students better prepare themselves for rewarding careers and helps people advance in the workplace." Publishes trade paperback originals. Publishes 30 titles/year. Receives 100 queries and 70 mss/year. 60% of books from first-time authors; 85% from unagented writers. Pays 20% royalty on retail price. Publishes book 3 months after acceptance of ms. Accepts simultaneous submissions. Reports in 1 month. *Writer's Market* recommends allowing 2 months for reply. Book catalog and ms guidelines free.
  ● The Graduate Group has published such authors as Lt. Jim Nelson and Josh Hoekstra.
Nonfiction: Reference. Subjects include career/internships, law, medicine, law enforcement, corrections, how to succeed, self-motivation.
Recent Nonfiction Title(s): *Outstanding Résumés for College, Business And Law Graduates*, by Robert Whitman (reference); *Confidence at Work*, by Frank Doerger.
Tips: Audience is career planning offices, college and graduate school libraries and public libraries. "We are open to all submissions, especially those involving career planning, internships and other nonfiction titles. Looking for books on law enforcement, books for prisoners and reference books on subjects/fields students would be interested in."

GRAPHIC ARTS TECHNICAL FOUNDATION, 200 Deer Run Rd., Sewickley PA 15143-2328. (412)741-6860. Fax: (412)741-2311. E-mail: poresick@aol.com. Website: http://www.gatf.lm.com. **Acquisitions:** Peter Oresick, director of publications. Technical Editor: Pamela J. Groff. Estab. 1924. "We publish college and adult general texts about printing technology, computers and electronic publishing techniques." Publishes trade paperback originals and hardcover reference texts. Publishes 15 titles/year. Receives 25 submissions/year. 50% of books from first-time authors; 100% from unagented writers. Pays 5-15% royalty on retail price. Publishes book 4-6 months after acceptance. Reports in 1 month on queries. *Writer's Market* recommends allowing 2 months for reply. Book catalog for 9 × 12 SAE with 2 first-class stamps. Manuscript guidelines for #10 SASE.
Nonfiction: How-to, reference, technical, textbook. Subjects include printing/graphic communications and electronic publishing. "We primarily want textbook/reference books about printing and related technologies. However, we are expanding our reach into general computing and electronic communications." Query with SASE or submit outline, sample chapters and SASE. Reviews artwork/photos as part of ms package.
Recent Nonfiction Title(s): *Digital Photography Primer*; *The Magazine*, by Leonard Mogel (understanding magazine publishing); *Understanding Electronic Communications*, by A'isha Ajayi and Pamela Groff (computers Internet).
Tips: "We are publishing titles that are updated more frequently, such as *Understanding Electronic Communications*. Our scope now includes reference titles geared toward general audiences interested in computers, imaging, and Internet as well as print publishing."

‡GRAYWOLF PRESS, 2402 University Ave., Suite 203, St. Paul MN 55114. (612)641-0077. Fax: (612)641-0036. Website: http://www.graywolfpress.org. Director: Fiona McCrae. **Acquisitions:** Jeffrey Shotts. Estab. 1974. "Graywolf Press is an independent, nonprofit publisher dedicated to the creation and promotion of thoughtful and imaginative contemporary literature essential to a vital and diverse culture." Publishes trade cloth and paperback originals and reprints. Publishes 16 titles/year. Receives 2,500 queries/year. 20% of books from first-time authors; 50% from unagented writers. Pays royalty on retail price. Offers $1,000-6,000 advance on average. Publishes book 18 months after acceptance of ms. Reports in 2 months on queries. Book catalog free. Manuscript guidelines for #10 SASE.
Nonfiction: Language/literature/culture. Query with SASE.
Recent Nonfiction Title(s): *Tolstoy's Dictaphone: Technology & the Muse*, edited by Sven Birkerts (essays); *North Enough: AIDS and Other Clear-Cuts*, by Jan Zita Grover (ecology/memoir).
Fiction: Literary. "Familiarize yourself with our list first." Query with SASE.
Recent Fiction Title(s): *Characters on the Loose*, by Janet Kauffman (short stories); *Night Talk*, by Elizabeth Cox (novel/race); *The Apprentice*, by Lewis Libby (novel).
Poetry: "We are interested in linguistically challenging work." Query sample with SASE.
Recent Poetry Title(s): *Otherwise New & Selected Poems*, by Jane Kenyon; *Wise Poison*, by David Rivard.

GREAT QUOTATIONS PUBLISHING, 1967 Quincy Ct., Glendale Heights IL 60139. (630)582-2800. Fax: (630)582-2813. **Acquisitions:** Patrick Caton, acquisitions editor. Estab. 1991. "Great Quotations seeks original material for the following general categories: humor, inspiration, motivation, success, romance, tributes to mom/dad/grandma/grandpa, etc." Publishes 30 titles/year. Receives 1,500 queries and 1,200 mss/year. 50% of books from first-time authors; 80% from unagented writers. Pays 3-10% royalty on net sales or makes outright purchase of $300-3,000. Offers $200-1,200 advance. Publishes book 6 months after acceptance of ms. "We publish new books twice a year, in July and in January." Accepts simultaneous submissions. "Usually we return submissions, but we do not guarantee 100% that they will be returned." Reports in 2 months. Book catalog for $1.50. Manuscript guidelines for #10 SASE.
Nonfiction: Humor, illustrated book, self-help, quotes. Subjects include business/economics, child guidance/parenting, nature/environment, religion, sports, women's issues/studies. "We look for subjects with identifiable markets, appeal

to the general public. We do not publish children's books or others requiring multicolor illustration on the inside. Nor do we publish highly controversial subject matter." Submit outline and 2 sample chapters. Reviews artwork/photos as part of ms package. Send photocopies, transparencies.
Recent Nonfiction Title(s): *Secret Language of Men*, by Shearer Weaver (gift book).
Poetry: "We would be most interested in upbeat and juvenile poetry."
Tips: "Our books are physically small, and generally a very quick read. They are available at gift shops and book shops throughout the country. We are very aware that most of our books are bought on impulse and given as gifts. We need very strong, clever, descriptive titles; beautiful cover art, and brief, positive, upbeat text. Be prepared to submit final manuscript on computer disk, according to our specifications. (It is not necessary to try to format the typesetting of your manuscript to look like a finished book.)"

GREENE BARK PRESS, P.O. Box 1108, Bridgeport CT 06601. (203)372-4861. **Acquisitions:** Thomas J. Greene, publisher. "We only publish children's fiction—all subjects, but in reading picture book format appealing to ages 3-9 or all ages." Publishes hardcover originals. Publishes 5 titles/year. Receives 100 queries and 6,000 mss/year. 60% of books from first-time authors; 100% from unagented writers. Pays 10-15% royalty on wholesale price. Publishes book 1 year after acceptance of ms. Accepts simultaneous submissions. Reports in 3 months on mss. Book catalog and ms guidelines with SASE.
Fiction: Juvenile. Submit entire ms with SASE. Does not accept queries or ms by e-mail.
Recent Fiction Title(s): *The Butterfly Bandit*, by Ester Hauser Laurence (hardcover picture book).
Tips: Audience is "children who read to themselves and others. Mothers, fathers, grandparents, godparents who read to their respective children, grandchildren. Include SASE, be prepared to wait, do not inquire by telephone."

‡GREENWILLOW BOOKS, Imprint of William Morrow & Co., Division of Hearst Books, 1350 Avenue of the Americas, New York NY 10019. (212)261-6500. Website: http://www.williammorrow.com. Estab. 1974. "Greenwillow Books publishes quality hardcover books for children." Publishes hardcover originals and reprints. Publishes 70-80 titles/year. 1% of books from first-time authors; 30% from unagented writers. Pays 10% royalty on wholesale price for first-time authors. Advance varies. Publishes ms 2 years after acceptance of ms. Accepts simultaneous submissions. Reports in 3 months on mss. Book catalog for $2 and 9×12 SAE. Manuscript guidelines for #10 SASE.
Fiction: Juvenile, picture books: fantasy, historical, humor, literary, mystery.
Recent Fiction Title(s): *Lilly's Purple Plastic Purse*, by Kevin Henkes; *Under the Table*, by Marisabina Russo; *The Missing Sunflowers*, Maggie Stern.

‡GREENWOOD PRESS, Imprint of Greenwood Publishing Group, 88 Post Rd. W., Westport CT 06881. (203)226-3571. Fax: (203)222-1502. Website: http://www.greenwood.com. **Acquisitions:** Cynthia Harris, executive editor. "Greenwood Press publishes reference materials for the entire spectrum of libraries, as well as scholarly monographs in the humanities and the social and behavioral sciences." Publishes hardcover and trade paperback originals. Publishes 300 titles/year. Receives 1,000 queries/year. 50% of books from first-time authors. Pays variable royalty on net price. Offers advance rarely. Publishes book 1 year after acceptance of ms. Accepts simultaneous submissions. Reports in 6 months on queries. Book catalog and ms guidelines online.
Nonfiction: Reference. Query with proposal package, including scope, organization, length of project, whether a complete ms is available or when it will be, CV or résumé and SASE. *No unsolicited mss.*
Recent Nonfiction Title(s): *New Religious Movement in Western Europe*, by Elisabeth Arweck and Peter B. Clarke; *John Grisham: A Critical Companion*, by Mary Beth Pringle.

‡GREENWOOD PUBLISHING GROUP, Division of Reed-Elsevier, 88 Post Rd. W, Westport CT 06881. (203)226-3571. Fax: (203)222-1502. Website: http://www.greenwood.com. Executive Vice President: Jim Sabin. **Acquisitions:** Reference Publishing: Academic Reference—Cynthia Harris (history and economics, ext. 460 ‹charris@greenwood.com›); George Butler (anthropology, education, literature, drama and sociology, ext. 461‹gbutler@greenwood.com›); Alicia Merritt (art and architecture, music and dance, philosophy and religion, popular culture, ext. 443 ‹amerritt@greenwood.com›); Nita Romer (multicultural and women's studies, gerontology, media, political science and law, psychology, ext. 445 ‹nromer@greenwood.com›); Interdisciplinary studies, such as African-American studies are handled by all editors; contact js@greenwood.com. Secondary School Reference—Barbara Rader (literature, history, women's studies, school librarianship, ext. 442 ‹brader@greenwood.com›); Emily Birch (sociology, psychology, arts, religion, sports and recreation, ext. 448 ‹ebirch@greenwood.com›). Academic and Trade: Alan Sturmer (economics, business, law, ext. 475 ‹asturmer@greenwood.com›); Dan Eades (history and military studies, ext. 479 ‹deades@greenwood.com›); Jane Garry (library science, pregnancy, parenting, alternative medicine, education, and anthropology, ext. 480 ‹jgarry@greenwood.com›). Professional Publishing: Eric Valentine (Quorum Books, ext. 471 ‹evalentine@greenwood.com›). "The Greenwood Publishing Group consists of five distinguished imprints with one unifying purpose: to provide the best possible reference, professional, text, and scholarly resources in the humanities and the social and behavioral sciences." Publishes hardcover and trade paperback originals. Publishes 700 titles/year. Pays royalty on net price. Offers advance rarely. Publishes book 1 year after acceptance of ms. Accepts simultaneous submissions. Book catalog and ms guidelines online.
  ● Greenwood Publishing maintains an excellent website, providing complete catalog, ms guidelines and editorial contacts.
Imprint(s): Auburn House, Bergin & Garvey, Greenwood Press, Praeger Publishers, Quorum Books.

Nonfiction: Reference, textbook. Subjects include anthropology/archaeology, business/economics, child guidance/parenting, education, government/politics, history, language/literature, military/war, music/dance, philosophy, psychology, religion, sociology, sports, women's issues/studies. Query with proposal package, including scope, organization, length of project, whether a complete ms is available or when it will be, cv or résumé and SASE. *No unsolicited mss.*
Recent Nonfiction Title(s): *From the Unthinkable to the Unavoidable*, edited by Carol Rittner and John Roth (religion/Holocaust studies); *The Feminist Encyclopedia of German Literature*, edited by Friederike Eigler and Susanne Kord; *The Fighting Pattons*, by Brian Sobel (military).
Tips: "No interest in fiction, drama, poetry—looking for serious, scholarly, analytical studies of historical problems."

‡**GROLIER PUBLISHING**, Grolier Inc., Sherman Turnpike, Danbury CT 06813. (203)797-3500. Fax: (203)797-3197. Estab. 1895. "Grolier Publishing is a leading publisher of reference, educational and children's books. We provide parents, teachers and librarians with the tools they need to enlighten children to the pleasure of learning and prepare them for the road ahead." Publishes hardcover and trade paperback originals. 5% of books from first-time authors; 95% from unagented writers. Prefers to work with unagented authors. Pays royalty for established authors; makes outright purchase for first-time authors. Advance varies. Publishes book 18 months after acceptance of ms. Accepts simultaneous submissions. Reports in 4 months on proposals. Book catalog for 9×12 SAE and $3 postage. Manuscript guidelines free.
Imprint(s): Children's Press, Franklin Watts, Orchard Books.
Nonfiction: Children's/juvenile, illustrated book, reference. Query with outline and SASE.
Recent Nonfiction Title(s): *Electoral College*, by Christopher Henry; *North American Biographies* series.
Fiction: Juvenile, picture books.

‡**GROSSET**, Imprint of Putnam Adult, Division of Penguin Putnam Inc., 200 Madison Ave., New York NY 10016. (212)951-8610. Website: http://www.putnam.com. **Acquisitions:** Dolores McMullan, assistant editor. Estab. 1991. "Grosset offers hardcover nonfiction for a highly literate audience." Publishes hardcover originals. Publishes 6-10 titles/year. Receives 20-30 queries/year. 5% of books from first-time authors; 30% from unagented writers. Pays variable royalty on net price. Advance varies. Publishes book 18 months after acceptance of ms. Accepts simultaneous submissions. Reports in 3 months on proposals.
Nonfiction: General adult nonfiction. Subjects include anthropology/archaeology, education, government/politics, health/medicine, nature/environment, philosophy, psychology, religious studies, science, sociology, women's issues/studies. "The people we publish tend to be experts in their fields, with academic credentials." Query with proposal package including detailed synopsis, sample chapters and cover letter, with SASE.
Recent Nonfiction Title(s): *Violence*, by James Gilligan, MD (social theory); *The Shelter of Each Other*, by Mary Pipher (family psychology); *The New Men*, by Brian Murphy (religious studies).

GROSSET & DUNLAP PUBLISHERS, Imprint of Penguin Putnam Inc., 200 Madison Ave., New York NY 10016. **Acquisitions:** Jane O'Connor, president. VP/Art Director: Ronnie Ann Herman. Estab. 1898. Grosset & Dunlap publishes children's books that examine new ways of looking at the world of a child. Publishes hardcover and paperback originals. Publishes 75 titles/year. Receives more than 3,000 submissions/year. Publishes book 18 months after acceptance. Accepts simultaneous submissions. Reports in 2 months.
Imprint(s): Tuffy Books, Platt & Munk.
Nonfiction: Juveniles. Subjects include nature, science. No unsolicited submissions; agented submissions only.
Recent Nonfiction Title(s): *The Clear and Simple Thesaurus Dictionary*.
Fiction: Juveniles. No unsolicited submissions; agented submissions only.
   ● Grosset & Dunlap accepts agented submissions only.
Tips: "Nonfiction that is particularly topical or of wide interest in the mass market; new concepts for novelty format for preschoolers; and very well-written easy readers on topics that appeal to primary graders have the best chance of selling to our firm."

GROUP PUBLISHING, INC., 1515 Cascade Ave., Loveland CO 80538. Fax: (970)669-1994. E-mail: greditor@aol.com. Website: http://www.grouppublishing.com. **Acquisitions:** Kerri Nance, editorial assistant; Paul Woods (curriculum); Michael Warden (children's books and adult); Amy Simpson (youth books). "Our mission is to encourage Christian growth in children, youth and adults." Publishes trade paperback originals. Publishes 20-30 titles/year. Receives 200-400 queries and 300-500 mss/year. 30% of books from first-time authors; 95% from unagented writers. Pays up to 10% royalty on wholesale price or makes outright purchase. Offers up to $1,000 advance. Publishes book 18 months after acceptance of ms. Accepts simultaneous submissions. Reports in 2 months on queries, 6 months on proposals. Book catalog for 9×12 SAE with 2 first-class stamps. Manuscript guidelines for #10 SASE.
Nonfiction: How-to, adult, youth and children's ministry resources. Subjects include education, religion and any subjects pertinent to adult, youth or children's ministry in a church setting. "We're an interdenominational publisher of resource materials for people who work with adults, youth or children in a Christian church setting. We also publish materials for use directly by youth or children (such as devotional books, workbooks or stories). Everything we do is based on concepts of active and interactive learning as described in *Why Nobody Learns Much of Anything at Church: And How to Fix It* by Thom and Joani Schultz. We need new, practical, hands-on, innovative, out-of-the-box ideas— things that no one's doing . . . yet." Submit proposal package, including outline, 2 sample chapters, introduction to the book (written as if the reader will read it), and sample activities if appropriate.

Recent Nonfiction Title(s): *Core Belief Bible Study Series*™, by various authors (youth/junior and senior curriculum); *You Can Double . . .* , by Josh Hunt (church leaders); *Saving Your Sanity*, by Susan L. Lingo (preschool teachers).
Tips: "We're seeking proposals for CD-ROM projects."

‡**GROVE/ATLANTIC, INC.**, 841 Broadway, New York NY 10003. (212)614-7850, 7860. Fax: (212)614-7886, 7915. **Acquisitions:** Jim Moser, executive editor. "Grove/Atlantic publishes serious nonfiction and literary fiction." Publishes hardcover originals, trade paperback originals and reprints. Publishes 60-70 titles/year. Receives 1000s queries/year. 10-15% of books from first-time authors; "very few" from unagented writers. Pays 7½-15% royalty on retail price. Advance varies considerably. Publishes book 1 year after acceptance of ms. Accepts simultaneous submissions. "Because of volume of queries, Grove/Atlantic can only respond when interested—though SASE might generate a response." Book catalog free.
Imprint(s): Grove Press (Estab. 1952), Atlantic Monthly Press (Estab. 1917).
Nonfiction: Biography. Subjects include art/architecture, cooking/foods/nutrition, government/politics, history, language/literature, travel. Query with SASE. No unsolicited mss.
Recent Nonfiction Title(s): *Ché*, by Jon Lee Anderson (biography); *Howard Hawks*, by Todd McCarthy (biography).
Fiction: Experimental, literary. Query with SASE. No unsolicited mss.
Recent Fiction Title(s): *The Ordinary Seaman*, by Francisco Goldman; *Cold Mountain*, by Charles Frasier.
Poetry: "We try to publish at least one volume of poetry every list." Query. No unsolicited mss.
Recent Poetry Title(s): *For a Modest God*, by Eric Ormsby.

GRYPHON HOUSE, INC., P.O. Box 207, Beltsville MD 20704. (301)595-9500. Fax: (301)595-0051. **Acquisitions:** Kathy Charner, editor-in-chief. Gryphon House publishes creative educational activities for parents and teachers to do with children ages 1-5. Publishes trade paperback originals. Publishes 6 titles/year. Pays royalty on wholesale price. Reports in 3 months.
Nonfiction: How-to, education. Submit outline, 2-3 sample chapters and SASE.
Recent Nonfiction Title(s): *Preschool Art*, by Maryann Kohl (open-ended art activities for young children); *300 Three Minute Games*, by Jackie Silberg.

‡**GULF PUBLISHING COMPANY**, 3301 Allen Parkway, Houston TX 77019-1896. (713)520-4441. **Acquisitions:** Claire Blondeau, acquisitions editor. Gulf publishes business, travel, nature, cooking and other nonfiction subjects of interest primarily to a regional audience in Texas, California and Florida. Publishes hardcover and trade paperback originals and reprints. Publishes 75 titles/year. 60% of books from first-time authors; 80% from unagented writers. Pays royalty on wholesale price or offers fee for hire. Offers advance upon justification of expenses. Publishes book within 2 years after receipt of ms. Accepts simultaneous submissions. Reports in 2 months on queries, 3 months on proposals, 4 months on mss. Book catalog free.
Nonfiction: Regional cookbook, gift book, humor, illustrated book, multimedia (cassette, computer disk), reference, technical, textbook. Subjects include Americana (Texana), archaeology, business, human resources development, cooking, gardening, nature/environment, regional (Texas, California or Florida only), science, translation (engineering and business topics), travel (guidebooks), engineering, bird watching. "We are not considering regional, nature or archaeology outside of Texas, California, Florida. Business topics are human resources, development and training and multicultural development-oriented. Writers pay their own permissions in most cases. Writers often do not include enough information about their book or previous experience. Send illustration and photo samples." Submit outline with 2 sample chapters and proposal package, including illustrations, résumé, purpose of book. Reviews artwork/photos as part of ms package. Send transparencies, slides, photos or camera-ready samples.
Recent Nonfiction Title(s): *America's Regional Cookbook*, by Betty Evans; *Rules of Thumb for Mechanical Engineers*, edited by J. Edward Pope.
Tips: "Call before sending a proposal. We can usually give you an opinion over the phone if your proposal will be considered."

HALF HALT PRESS, INC., P.O. Box 67, Boonsboro MD 21713. (301)733-7119. Fax: (301)733-7408. **Acquisitions:** Elizabeth Carnes, publisher. Estab. 1986. "We publish high-quality nonfiction on equestrian topics, books that help riders and trainers do something better." Publishes 90% hardcover and trade paperback originals and 10% reprints. Publishes 15 titles/year. Receives 150 submissions/year. 25% of books from first-time authors; 50% from unagented authors. Pays 10-12½% royalty on retail price. Offers advance by agreement. Publishes book 1 year after acceptance. Reports in 1 month on queries. *Writer's Market* recommends allowing 2 months for reply. Book catalog for 6×9 SAE with 2 first-class stamps.
Nonfiction: Instructional: horse and equestrian related subjects only. "We need serious instructional works by authori-

FOR INFORMATION on book publishers' areas of interest, see the nonfiction and fiction sections in the Book Publishers Subject Index.

ties in the field on horse-related topics, broadly defined." Query. Reviews artwork/photos as part of ms package.

Recent Nonfiction Title(s): *Equestrian Excellence: The Stories of Our Olympic Equestrian Medal Winners, From Stockholm 1912 thru Atlanta 1996,* by Barbara Wallace Shambach; *Masters of Horsemanship Series, Book 1: Dressage: A Guidebook to the Road to Success,* by Alfred Knopfhart.

Tips: "Writers have the best chance selling us well-written, unique works that teach serious horse people how to do something better. If I were a writer trying to market a book today, I would offer a straightforward presentation, letting work speak for itself, without hype or hard sell. Allow publisher to contact writer, without frequent calling to check status. They haven't forgotten the writer but may have many different proposals at hand; frequent calls to 'touch base,' multiplied by the number of submissions, become an annoyance. As the publisher/author relationship becomes close and is based on working well together, early impressions may be important, even to the point of being a consideration in acceptance for publication."

ALEXANDER HAMILTON INSTITUTE, 70 Hilltop Rd., Ramsey NJ 07446-1119. (201)825-3377. Fax: (201)825-8696. **Acquisitions:** Brian L.P. Zevnik, editor-in-chief. Estab. 1909. Alexander Hamilton Institute publishes "non-traditional" management books for upper-level managers and executives. Publishes 3-ring binder and paperback originals. Publishes 10-15 titles/year. Receives 50 queries and 10 mss/year. 25% of books from first-time authors; 95% from unagented writers. Pays 5-8% royalty on retail price or makes outright purchase ($3,500-7,000). Offers $3,500-7,000 advance. Publishes book 10 months after acceptance. Reports in 1 month on queries, 2 months on mss.

Nonfiction: Executive/management books for 2 audiences. The first is overseas, upper-level manager. "We need how-to and skills building books. *No* traditional management texts or academic treatises." The second audience is US personnel executives and high-level management. Subject is legal personnel matters. "These books combine court case research and practical application of defensible programs." Submit outline, 3 paragraphs on each chapter, examples of lists, graphics, cases.

Recent Nonfiction Title(s): *Performance Appraisals: Building a High Performance Lawsuit-Free Workplace*; *The Employee Problem Solver*; *Effective Interviews for Every Situation.*

Tips: "We sell exclusively by direct mail to managers and executives around the world. A writer must know his/her field and be able to communicate practical systems and programs."

HANCOCK HOUSE PUBLISHERS LTD., 1431 Harrison Ave., Blaine WA 98230-5005. (604)538-1114. Fax: (604)538-2262. E-mail: hancock@uniserve.com. **Acquisitions:** David Hancock, publisher; Myron Shutty, editor. Estab. 1971. Hancock House Publishers Ltd., seeks aviculture, natural history, animal husbandry, conservation and popular science titles with a regional (Pacific Northwest), national or international focus. Publishes hardcover and trade paperback originals and reprints. Publishes 12 titles/year. Receives 400 submissions/year. 50% of books from first-time authors; 90% from unagented writers. Pays 10% royalty. Accepts simultaneous submissions. Publishes book up to 1 year after acceptance. Reports in 6 months. Book catalog free. Manuscript guidelines for #10 SASE.

Nonfiction: Biography, how-to, reference, technical. Pacific Northwest history and biography, nature guides, native culture, and international natural history. "Centered around Pacific Northwest, local history, nature guide books, international ornithology and Native Americans." Submit outline, 3 sample chapters and proposal package, including selling points with SASE. Reviews artwork/photos as part of ms package. Send photocopies.

Recent Nonfiction Title(s): *Understanding the Bird of Prey,* by Nick Fox (ornithology, technical); *Rumors of Existence,* by Matthew Bille (animals); *Bush Flying: The Romance of the North,* by Robert Grant (biography/history).

HANSER GARDNER PUBLICATIONS, 6915 Valley Ave., Cincinnati OH 45244. (513)527-8977. Fax: (513)527-8950. Website: http://www.gardnerweb.com. **Acquisitions:** Woody Chapman. Hanser Gardner publishes training and practical application titles for metalworking, machining and finishing shops/plants. Publishes hardcover and paperback originals and reprints. Publishes 5-10 titles/year. Receives 40-50 queries and 5-10 mss/year. 75% of books from first-time authors; 100% from unagented writers. Pays 10-15% royalty on net receipts. No advance. Publishes book 10 months after acceptance of ms. Accepts simultaneous submissions. Reports in 2 weeks on queries, 1 month on proposals and mss. Book catalog and ms guidelines free.

Nonfiction: How-to, technical, textbook. Subjects include metalworking and finishing processes, and related management topics. "Our books are primarily basic introductory-level training books, and books that emphasize practical applications. Strictly deal with subjects shown above." Query with résumé, preface, outline, sample chapter, comparison to competing or similar titles. Reviews artwork/photos as part of ms package. Send photocopies.

Recent Nonfiction Title(s): *Industrial Painting,* by Norman R. Roobol (industrial reference).

Tips: "Our readers and authors occupy various positions within small and large metalworking, machining and finishing shops/plants. We prefer that interested individuals write, call, or fax us with their queries first, so we can send them our proposal guideline form."

HARBOR PRESS, 5713 Wollochet Dr. NW, Gig Harbor WA 98335. Fax: (206)851-5191. President/Publisher: Harry R. Lynn. **Acquisitions:** Deborah Young, acquisitions editor. Harbor Press publishes consumer-oriented health and cooking titles for both trade and mail-order markets. Publishes hardcover and trade paperback originals and reprints. Publishes 8-10 titles/year. Negotiates competitive royalties on wholesale price or makes outright purchase.

Nonfiction: Cookbook, self-help. Subjects include cooking/foods/nutrition, health/medicine. Query with proposal package, including outline, 3 sample chapters, synopsis and SASE. Reviews artwork/photos. Send photocopies.

Recent Nonfiction Title(s): *Ancient Secret of the Fountain of Youth* (health/exercise).

HARCOURT BRACE & COMPANY, Children's Books Division, 525 B St., Suite 1900, San Diego CA 92101. (619) 699-6810. Fax: (619)699-6777. E-mail: lpelan@harcourtbrace.com. **Acquisitions:** Manuscript Submissions. "Harcourt Brace & Company owns some of the world's most prestigious publishing imprints—which distinguish quality products for the juvenile, educational, scientific, technical, medical, professional and trade markets worldwide." Publishes hardcover originals and trade paperback reprints. Query. No phone calls.
Imprint(s): Gulliver Books, Gulliver Green, Browndeer Press, Red Wagon, Voyager and Odyssey Paperbacks, Magic Carpet and Libros Viajeros.
   • Harcourt Brace & Company has published such authors as Nancy Willard, Jane Yolen and Eve Bunting. This publisher accepts agented submissions or query letters only with SASE.
Recent Nonfiction Title(s): *I Want to Be an Astronaut*, by Stephanie Maze and Catherine O'Neill Grace (nonfiction picture book); *Lives of the Athletes*, by Kathleen Krull (little-known facts about athletes, middle grade).
Recent Fiction Title(s): *Tangerine*, by Edward Bloor (young adult); *Littlejim's Dreams*, by Gloria Houston (middlegrade); *The Last Rainmaker*, by Sherry Garland (young adult).
Recent Poetry Title(s): *Worksong*, by Gary Paulsen (poetry picture book); *In the Swim*, by Douglas Florian (favorite underwater creature).

HARCOURT BRACE & COMPANY, Trade Division, 525 B St., Suite 1900, San Diego, CA 92101. (619)699-6560. **Acquisitions**: Marsha Brubaker. "Harcourt Brace & Company owns some of the world's most prestigious publishing imprints—imprints which distinguish quality products for the juvenile, educational, scientific, technical, medical, professional and trade markets worldwide." No unsolicited mss from individuals, only literary agents. Query letters accepted, but MUST be accompanied by SASE.
Nonfiction: Publishes all categories except business/finance (university texts), cookbooks, self-help, sex.
Recent Nonfiction Title(s): *The Western Canon*, by Harold Bloom; *In Light of India*, by Octavio Paz (memoir); *The Fight in the Fields: Cesar Chavez and the Farmworkers Movement*, by Susan Ferris and Ricardo Sandoval.
Recent Fiction Title(s): *Snow Falling on Cedars*, by David Guterson; *Ingenious Pain*, by Andrew Miller; *Margaret Cape*, by Wylene Dunbar.

‡**HARKEY MULTIMEDIA**, P.O. Box 20001, Seattle WA 98102. **Acquisitions:** Charlotte Bosarge, editor/art director. Publishes hardcover and trade paperback originals. Publishes 3-6 titles/year. Receives 100 queries and 50 mss/year. 95% of books from first-time authors; 95% from unagented writers. Pays 6-12% royalty on retail price. Publishes book 6 months after acceptance of ms. Accepts simultaneous submissions. Reports in 1 month on queries and mss. Book catalog not available; ms guidelines for #10 SASE.
Nonfiction: Children's/juvenile, coffee table book, cookbook, humor, multimedia (CD-ROM), self-help. Subjects include art/architecture, language/literature, philosophy, science. Query with outline and 1-3 sample chapters. Reviews artwork/photos as part of the ms package. Send photocopies, color prints, even sketches.
Recent Nonfiction Title(s): *The High-Fat Cookbook*, by Meg Walters (cookbook).
Fiction: Adventure, confession, experimental, horror, humor, mystery, picture books, religious, romance, science fiction, young adult. "Fiction writing is your chance to be free and express yourself and try something new! Show us who you really are and we are more likely to be interested in your work." Query with synopsis and 1-3 sample chapters.

‡**HARPER BUSINESS**, Imprint of HarperCollins Publishers, 10 E. 53rd St., New York NY 10036. (212)207-7006. Website: http://www.harpercollins.com. **Acquisitions:** Framji Minwalla, editorial coordinator. Estab. 1991. Harper Business publishes "the inside story on ideas that will shape business practices and thinking well into the next millenium, with cutting-edge information and visionary concepts." Publishes hardcover, trade paperback and mass market paperback originals, hardcover and trade paperback reprints. Publishes 50-55 titles/year. Receives 500 queries and mss/year. 1% of books from first-time authors; 10% from unagented writers. Pays royalty on retail price; varies. Offers $15,000 and up advance. Publishes book 1 year after acceptance of ms. Accepts simultaneous submissions. Reports in 2 months on proposals and mss. Book catalog free.
Nonfiction: Biography (economics); business/economics, marketing subjects. "We don't publish how-to, textbooks or things for academic market; no reference (tax or mortgage guides), our reference department does that. Proposals need to be top notch, especially for unagented writers. We tend not to publish people who have no business standing. Must have business credentials." Submit proposal package with SASE.
Recent Nonfiction Title(s): *The Dilbert Principle*, by Scott Adams (business/humor); *Unbridled Power*, by Shelly Davis (exposé on IRS); *Rocking the Ages*, by Jay Walker Smith and Ann Clusman (marketing).
Tips: Business audience: managers, CEOs, consultants, some academics. "We accept more unagented proposals, but they tend to come from authors who are already well established in their fields."

‡**HARPER LIBROS**, Imprint of HarperCollins Publishers, 10 E. 53rd St., New York NY 10022. (212)207-7000. Fax: (212)207-7145. Website: http://www.harpercollins.com. **Acquisitions:** Terry Karten, editorial director. Estab. 1994. "Harper Libros offers Spanish language editions of selected HarperCollins titles, sometimes reprints, sometimes new books that are published simultaneously in English and Spanish. The list mirrors the English-language list of HarperCollins in that we publish both literary and commercial fiction and nonfiction titles including all the different HarperCollins categories, such as self-help, spirituality, etc." Publishes hardcover and trade paperback originals. Publishes 10 titles/year. Receives 250 queries/year. 30% of books from first-time authors. Pays variable royalty on net price. Advance varies. Publishes book 1 year after acceptance of ms.

Imprint(s): Harper Arco Iris (Jennifer Pasanen) (children's).
Nonfiction: How-to, self-help. Subjects include business/economics, ethnic, spirituality, women's health. Query. *No unsolicited mss.*
Recent Nonfiction Title(s): *Salud: A Latina's Guide to Total Health*, by Jane Delgado, MD (women's health); *The Dilbert Principle*, by Scott Adams (business).
Fiction: Literary. Query. *No unsolicited mss.*
 ● Harper Libros has published such authors as Isabal Allende and Paulo Coelho.

‡**HARPER PERENNIAL**, Imprint of HarperCollins Publishers, 10 E. 53rd St., New York NY 10036. (212)207-7000. Website: http://www.harpercollins.com. **Acquisitions:** Hugh Van Dusen, vice president/executive editor. Estab. 1963. "Harper Perennial publishes a broad range of adult fiction and nonfiction paperbacks." Publishes trade paperback originals and reprints. Publishes 100 titles/year. Receives 500 queries/year. 5% of books from first-time authors; 2% from unagented writers. Pays 5-7½% royalty. Advance varies. Publishes book 6 months after acceptance of ms. Reports in 2 weeks on queries, 1 month on mss. *Writer's Market* recommends allowing 2 months for a reply. Book catalog free.
Nonfiction: Biography, cookbook, how-to, humor, illustrated book, reference, self-help. Subjects include Americana, animals, art/architecture, business/economics, child guidance/parenting, computers/electronics, education, ethnic, gardening, gay/lesbian,history, hobbies/antiques/collectibles, language/literature, mental health, military/war, money/finance, music/dance, nature/environment, philosophy, psychology/self-help psychotherapy, recreation, regional, religion/spirituality, science, sociology, sports, translation, travel, women's issues/studies. "We publish trade paperbacks, many of which come from hardcover originals. Our focus is ever-changing, adjusting to the marketplace. Mistakes writers often make are not giving their background and credentials—why they are qualified to write the book. A proposal should explain why the author wants to write this book; why it will sell; and why it is better or different from others of its kind." Query with cover letter, complete ms and SASE. Reviews artwork/photos as part of ms package. Reviews prints.
Recent Nonfiction Title(s): *Care of the Soul*, by Thomas Moore (self-help/spirituality); *Fanny at Chez Panisse*, by Alice Waters (cookbook); *Downsize This!*, by Michael Moore (current affairs/humor).
Fiction: Ethnic, feminist, literary. "Don't send us novels—go through hardcover." Agented submissions only.
Recent Fiction Title(s): *Lying On the Couch*, by Irwin D. Yalom (psycho-thriller novel); *American Pie*, by Michael Lee West (novel); *Bird Girl and the Man Who Followed the Sun*, by Velma Wallis (fiction/native American studies).
Poetry: Don't send poetry unless you have been published in several established literary magazines already. Query with 10 sample poems.
Recent Poetry Title(s): *The Lines of the Heart*, by Jane Hirshfield; *Falling Water*, by John Koethe; *Selected Poems*, by Allen Ginsberg.
Tips: Audience is general reader—high school, college. "Call and get the name of an editor and they will look at it. Usually an editor is listed in a book's acknowledgments. You should address your submission to an editor or else it will probably be returned."

HARPERACTIVE, Imprint of HarperCollins, 10 E. 53rd St., New York NY 10022. (212)207-7000. **Acquisitions:** Hope Innelli, editorial director/vice president. Estab. 1997. "A newly formed imprint, HarperActive is dedicated to publishing the hottest properties in biographies, sports, movie and tv tie-ins, anything that reflects trends in pop culture." 40% of books from first-time authors. Pays royalty. Advance varies. Reports in 3-12 months on mss. Book catalog and mss. guidelines not available.
Nonfiction: Children's/juvenile, biographies, spoofs, movie and t.v.-tie ins. "The bulk of our work is done by experienced writers for hire, but we are open to original ideas." Query with outline and SASE.
Fiction: Humor, juvenile, movie and t.v. tie-ins. Query with synopsis and SASE.

‡**HARPERCOLLINS CHILDREN'S BOOKS**, Imprint of HarperCollins Publishers, 10 E. 53rd St., New York NY 10022. (212)207-7000. Website: http://www.harpercollins.com. **Acquisitions:** Laura Geringer, editorial director. "We have no rules for subject matter, length or vocabulary, but look instead for ideas that are fresh and imaginative, good writing that involves the reader is essential." Publishes hardcover originals. Publishes 350 titles/year. Receives 200 queries and 5,000 mss/year. 5% of books from first-time authors; 25% from unagented writers. Pays 10-12½% royalty on retail price. Advance varies. Publishes novel 1 year, picture books 2 years after acceptance of ms. Accepts simultaneous submissions. Reports in 1 month on queries and proposals, 4 months on mss. Book catalog for 8×10 SASE with 3 first-class stamps. Manuscript guidelines for #10 SASE.
Imprint(s): Laura Geringer Books (Laura Geringer, editorial director); Joanna Cotler Books.
Fiction: Adventure, fantasy, historical, humor, juvenile, literary, picture books, young adult. Query only with SASE for picture books; send novel ms with SASE.
Recent Fiction Title(s): *Zoe Rising*, by Pam Conrad (novel); *The Leaf Men*, by William Joyce (picture book); *Follow the Moon*, by Sarah Weeks (picture book with tape).

HARPERCOLLINS PUBLISHERS, 10 E. 53rd St., New York NY 10022. (212)207-7000. Website: http://www.harpercollins.com. **Acquisitions**: Joelle Del Bourgo, vice president/editorial director. "HarperCollins, one of the largest English language publishers in the world, is a broad-based publisher with strengths in academic, business and professional, children's, educational, general interest, and religious and spiritual books, as well as multimedia titles." Publishes hardcover and paperback originals and paperback reprints. Trade publishes more than 500 titles/year. Pays standard royalties. Advance negotiable. *No unsolicited queries or mss.* Reports on solicited queries in 6 weeks. *Writer's Market* recommends allowing 2 months for reply.

Imprint(s): Harper Adult Trade; Harper Audio, **Harper Business**, **HarperActive**, **Harper Libros**, Harper Paperback, **Harper Perennial**, **HarperCollins Children's Books**, **HarperCollins San Francisco**, **Regan Books**, **Westview Press**, **Zondervan Publishing House**.

• This publisher accepts agented submissions only.

Nonfiction: Americana, animals, art, biography, business/economics, current affairs, cookbooks, health, history, how-to, humor, music, nature, philosophy, politics, psychology, reference, religion, science, self-help, sociology, sports, travel. Agented submissions only.

Recent Nonfiction Title(s): *10 Stupid Things Men Do to Mess Up Their Lives*, by Dr. Laura Schlessinger (psychology); *Handmade Cigar Collectors Guide*, by Tom Connor; *Junior*, by Ken Griffey (sports).

Fiction: Adventure, fantasy, gothic, historical, mystery, science fiction, suspense, western, literary. "We look for a strong story line and exceptional literary talent." Agented submissions only.

Recent Fiction Title(s): *Monkey King*, by Patricia Chao; *The House of Forgetting*, by Benjamin Saenz; *Trading Reality*, by Michael Ridpath (thriller).

Tips: "We do not accept any unsolicited material."

HARPERSANFRANCISCO, Imprint of HarperCollins, 1160 Battery St., 3rd Floor, San Francisco CA 94111-1213. (415)477-4400. Fax: (415)477-4444. E-mail: hcsanfrancisco@harpercollins.com. Publisher: Diane Gedymin. **Acquisitions:** Lisa Bach, editor (women's studies, psychology, alternative spirituality); Kevin Bentley, editor (gay/lesbian studies, memoirs, general nonfiction); Mark Chimsky, editorial director (religious studies, popular spirituality, popular culture); Thomas Grady, executive editor (world religions, Christian and alternative spirituality); Patricia Klien, senior editor (Christian life, spirituality, devotional); John Loudon, executive editor (religious studies, psychology/personal growth, Eastern religious); Caroline Pincus, editor (psychology/self-help, Jewish spirituality, alternative and contemporary health, multicultural studies). Estab. 1817. Harper San Francisco publishes books that "nurture the mind, body and spirit; support readers in their ongoing self-discovery and personal growth; explore the essential religious and philosophical issues of our time; and present the rich and diverse array of the wisdom traditions of the world to a contemporary audience." Publishes hardcover originals, trade paperback originals and reprints. Publishes 125 titles/year. Receives about 10,000 submissions/year. 5% of books from first-time authors; 30% from unagented writers. Pays royalty. Publishes book 18 months after acceptance. Accepts simultaneous submissions, if so noted. Reports in 3 months on queries. Manuscript guidelines free.

Nonfiction: Biography, how-to, reference, self-help. Subjects include psychology, religion, self-help, spirituality. Query or submit outline and sample chapters with SASE.

Recent Nonfiction Title(s): *Honest Jesus*, by Robert Funk; *The Historical Jesus*, by John Dominic Crossan (religious studies); *Martyrs*, by Susan Bergman (essays).

‡**HARVARD BUSINESS SCHOOL PRESS**, Division of Harvard Business School Publishing Corporation, 60 Harvard Way, Boston MA 02163. (617)495-6700. **Acquisitions:** Marjorie Williams, executive editor. "The Harvard Business School Press publishes primarily research-based books for an audience of senior and general managers and business scholars." Publishes hardcover originals. Publishes 35-45 titles/year. Receives 500 queries and 300 mss/year. 25% of books from first-time authors; 5% from unagented writers. Pays 10% royalty on retail price. Advances vary widely depending on author and market for the book. Publishes book 18 months after acceptance of ms. Accepts simultaneous submissions. Reports in 1 month on proposals and mss. Book catalog and ms guidelines free.

• This publisher accepts agented submissions only.

Nonfiction: Subjects include business/economics. "Do not submit projects which are too prescriptive or 'how-to' in format or emphasis, too policy-based or are based on dissertations." Submit outline with proposal package, including several sample chapters or ms.

Recent Nonfiction Title(s): *Leading Change*, by John P. Kotter (trade); *The Development Factory*, by Gary P. Pisano (professional); *Technology Fountainheads*, by E. Raymond Corey (scholarly).

Tips: "Take care to really look into the type of business books we publish. They are generally not handbooks, how-to manuals, policy-oriented, dissertations, edited collections, or personal business narratives."

THE HARVARD COMMON PRESS, 535 Albany St., Boston MA 02118-2500. (617)423-5803. Fax: (617)423-0679 or (617)695-9794. **Acquisitions:** Bruce P. Shaw, president/publisher. Associate Publisher: Dan Rosenberg. Estab. 1976. "We want strong, practical books that help people gain control over a particular area of their lives." Publishes hardcover and trade paperback originals and reprints. Publishes 8 titles/year. Receives 1,000 submissions/year. 50% of books from first-time authors; 75% of books from unagented writers. Average print order for a first book is 10,000-20,000 copies. Pays royalty. Offers average $4,000 advance. Publishes book 1 year after acceptance. Accepts simultaneous submissions. Reports in 2 months. Book catalog for 9×12 SAE with 3 first-class stamps. Manuscript guidelines for SASE.

Imprint(s): Gambit Books.

• Harvard Common Press has changed subject focus from family matters to childcare.

Nonfiction: Cooking, childcare and parenting, travel. "An increasing percentage of our list is made up of books about cooking, child care and parenting; in these areas we are looking for authors who are knowledgeable, if not experts, and who can offer a different approach to the subject. We are open to good nonfiction proposals that show evidence of

strong organization and writing, and clearly demonstrate a need in the marketplace. First-time authors are welcome."
Accepts nonfiction translations. Submit outline and 1-3 sample chapters. Reviews artwork/photos.
Recent Nonfiction Title(s): *The Nursing Mother's Companion*, (4th ed.), by Huggins (childcare).
Tips: "We are much more demanding about the quality of proposals; in addition to strong writing skills and thorough knowledge of the subject matter, we require a detailed analysis of the competition."

‡**HARVARD UNIVERSITY PRESS**, 79 Garden St., Cambridge MA 02138. (617)495-2600. Fax: (617)495-5898. Website: http://www.hup.harvard.edu. **Acquisitions:** Aïda D. Donald, assistant director/editor-in-chief (history, sociology with historical emphasis, women's studies with historical emphasis); Lindsay Waters, executive editor for the humanities (literary criticism, philosophy); Michael G. Fisher, executive editor for science and medicine (medicine, neuroscience, science—except astronomy); Joyce Seltzer, senior executive editor (history, contemporary affairs); Michael Aronson, senior acquisitions editor for social sciences (sociology, economics, law, political science); Margaretta Fulton, general editor for the humanities (classics, religion, music, art, Jewish studies, women's studies); Angela von der Lippe, senior editor for the behavioral sciences (behavioral sciences, earth sciences, astronomy, neuroscience, education); Elizabeth Suttell, senior editor (East Asian studies). "Harvard University Press publishes scholarly books and works of general interest in the humanities, the social and behavioral sciences, the natural sciences, and medicine. Does not normally publish poetry, fiction, festschriften, memoirs, symposia, or unrevised doctoral dissertations." Publishes 130 titles/year. "Doesn't want first-time authors."
Imprint(s): The Belknap Press.
Nonfiction: Reference. Subjects include art/architecture, business/economics, ethnic, government/politics, history, language/literature, music/dance, philosophy, psychology, religion, science, sociology, women's issues/studies. Query with SASE. "We discourage unsolicited mss."
Recent Nonfiction Title(s): *Florence: A Portrait*, by Michael Levey (history); *Harvard Biographical Dictionary of Music*, by Don Michael Marling; *Graceland: Going Home with Elvis*, by Karal Ann Marling (cultural history).

HARVEST HOUSE PUBLISHERS, 1075 Arrowsmith, Eugene OR 97402-9197. (541)343-0123. Fax: (541)342-6410. **Acquisitions:** Kristi Hirte, manuscript coordinator. Manager: LaRae Weikert. Estab. 1974. "The foundation of our publishing program is to publish books that 'help the hurts of people' and nurture spiritual growth." Publishes hardcover, trade paperback and mass market originals and reprints. Publishes 70-80 titles/year. Receives 3,500 submissions/year. 10% of books from first-time authors; 90% from unagented writers. Pays 14-18% royalty on wholesale price. Publishes book 1 year after acceptance. Accepts simultaneous submissions. Reports in 10 weeks. Book catalog for 9×12 SAE with 2 first-class stamps. Manuscript guidelines for SASE.
Imprint(s): Harvest House Books for Children and Young Adults.
  • Harvest House has published such authors as Kay Arthur, Peter Lalonde, Emilie Barnes, Thomas Kinkade (artist) and John Ankerberg.
Nonfiction: Self-help, current issues, women's and family on Evangelical Christian religion, Bible study. No cookbooks, theses, dissertations, music, or poetry. Query or submit outline and sample chapters.
Recent Nonfiction Title(s): *The Common Made Holy*, by Neil Anderson and Robert Saucy; *What to Do Until Love Finds You*, by Michelle McKinney-Hammond.
Fiction: Historical, mystery, religious. No short stories. Query or submit outline/synopsis and sample chapters.
Recent Fiction Title(s): *To Know Her By Name*, by Lori Wick (romance, Rocky Mountain Memory Series #3); *Love's Ransom*, by Lisa Samson (The Abbey Series #2).
Tips: "Audience is primarily women ages 25-40—evangelical Christians of all denominations." Harvest House is no longer interested in manuscripts dealing with counseling, children's books or juvenile fiction.

HASTINGS HOUSE, Eagle Publishing Corp., Division of United Publishers Group, 50 Washington St., 7th Floor, Norwalk CT 06854. (203)838-4083. Fax: (203)838-4084. Editor/Publisher: Henno Lohmeyer. **Acquisitions:** Hy Steirman. "We are looking for books that address consumer needs." Publishes hardcover and trade paperback originals and reprints. Publishes 40 titles/year. Receives 700 queries and 750 mss/year. 5% of books from first-time authors; 40% from unagented writers. Pays 8-10% royalty on retail price on trade paperbacks. Offers $1,000-10,000 advance. Publishes book 10 months after acceptance of ms. Reports in 1 month. *Writer's Market* recommends allowing 2 months for reply.
Nonfiction: Biography, coffee table book, cookbook, how-to, humor, reference, self-help, consumer. Subjects include business/economics, cooking/foods/nutrition, health/medicine, psychology, travel, writing. Query or submit outline.
Recent Nonfiction Title(s): *Lincoln's Unknown Private Life*; *Day Trip to Florida*, by Earl Steinbecker.

HATHERLEIGH PRESS, 1114 First Ave., New York NY 10021. (212)832-1584. Fax: (212)308-7930. E-mail: hatherle i@aol.com. Website: www.hatherleigh.com. Editor-In-Chief: Frederic Flach, M.D. **Acquisitions:** Adam Cohen, managing editor. Hatherleigh Press publishes general self-help titles and reference books for mental health professionals. Publishes hardcover originals, trade paperback originals and reprints. Publishes 10-12 titles/year. Receives 20 queries and 20 mss/year. Pays 5-15% royalty on retail price or makes outright purchase. Offers $500-5,000 advance. Publishes book 6 months after acceptance of ms. Reports in 2 months on queries. Book catalog free.
Imprint(s): Red Brick Books—new fiction imprint (Kevin J. Moran, acquisitions editor).
Nonfiction: Reference, self-help, technical. Subjects include health/medicine, psychology. Submit outline and 1 sample chapter with SASE. Reviews artwork/photos as part of ms package. Send photocopies.
Recent Nonfiction Title(s): *Climb A Fallen Ladder: How To Survive (And Thrive!) In A Downsized America*, by

Rochelle H. Gordon, M.D. and Catherine E. Harold; *The Secret Strength of Depression*, by Frederic Flach, M.D.; *The Hatherleigh Guides to Mental Health Care*.

Tips: Audience is mental health professionals, general (self-help, etc.). Submit a clear outline that includes the market and audience for your book.

‡THE HAWORTH PRESS, INC., 10 Alice St., Binghamton NY 13904. **Acquisitions:** Bill Palmer, managing editor. The Haworth Press is primarily a scholarly press. Publishes hardcover and trade paperback originals. Publishes 100 titles/year. Receives 500 queries and 250 mss/year. 60% of books from first-time authors; 98% from unagented writers. Pays 7½-15% royalty on wholesale price. Offers $500-1,000 advance. Publishes book 1 year after acceptance of ms. Reports in 2 months on proposals. Manuscript guidelines free.

Imprint(s): The Harrington Park Press, Haworth Pastoral Press, Haworth Food Products Press.

Nonfiction: Reference, textbook. Subjects include agriculture/horticulture, business/economics, child guidance/parenting, cooking/foods/nutrition, gay/lesbian, health/medicine, money/finance, psychology, sociology, women's issues/studies. "No 'pop' books." Submit outline and 1-3 sample chapters and proposal package, including author biography. Reviews artwork/photos as part of ms package. Send photocopies.

Recent Nonfiction Title(s): *Group Psychotherapy with Addicted People*, by Philip Flores, Ph.D. (textbook); *Feminist Theories and Social Work*, by Christian Saulnier, Ph.D. (textbook); *Reviving the Tribe*, by Eric Rofes (gay & lesbian trade).

Tips: Audience is "scholarly, professional and intelligent lay persons."

HAY HOUSE, INC., P.O. Box 5100, Carlsbad CA 92018-5100. (619)431-7695. Fax: (619)431-6948. E-mail: editorjk @aol.com. Website: http://www.hayhouse.com. **Acquisitions:** Jill Kramer, editorial director. Estab. 1985. "We publish books, audios and videos that help heal the planet." Publishes hardcover originals, trade paperback originals and reprints. Publishes 30 titles/year. Receives 1,200 submissions/year. 10% of books are from first-time authors; 25% from unagented writers. Pays standard royalty. Publishes book 10-15 months after acceptance. Accepts simultaneous submissions. Reports in 3 weeks. *Writer's Market* recommends allowing 2 months for reply. Book catalog free. Does not respond or return mss without SASE.

● Hay House has published such authors as Barbara De Angelis, Louise Hay and John Randolph Price.

Imprint(s): Astro Room.

Nonfiction: Self-help, primarily. Subjects include relationships, mind/body health, nutrition, education, astrology, environment, health/medicine, money/finance, nature, philosophy/New Age, psychology, spiritual, sociology, women's and men's issues/studies. "Hay House is interested in a variety of subjects so long as they have a positive self-help slant to them. No poetry, children's books, or negative concepts that are not conducive to helping/healing ourselves or our planet." Query or submit outline, sample chapters and SASE.

Recent Nonfiction Title(s): *The Western Guide to Feng Shui*, by Terah Kathryn Collins; *Empowering Women*, by Louise L. Hay.; *Deep Healing*, by Emmett Miller, M.D. (mind/body health).

Tips: "Our audience is concerned with our planet, the healing properties of love, and general self-help principles. Hay House has noticed that our reader is interested in taking more control of his/her life. A writer has a chance of selling us a book with a unique, positive message. If I were a writer trying to market a book today, I would research the market thoroughly to make sure that there weren't already too many books on the subject I was interested in writing about. Then I would make sure that I had a unique slant on my idea. SASE a must!"

HEALTH COMMUNICATIONS, INC., 3201 SW 15th St., Deerfield Beach FL 33442. (954)360-0909. E-mail: 102450.722@compuserve.com. Website: http://www.hci-online.com. **Acquisitions:** Christine Belleris, editorial director; Matthew Diener, editor; Allison Janse, editorial assistant. "We are the Life Issues Publisher. Health Communications, Inc., strives to help people grow mentally, emotionally and spiritually." Publishes hardcover and trade paperback originals. Publishes 40 titles/year. 20% of books from first-time authors; 90% from unagented writers. Pays 15-20% royalty on retail price. Publishes book 9 months after acceptance of ms. Accepts simultaneous submissions. Reports in 1 month on queries, 3 months on proposals and mss. Book catalog for 8½×11 SASE. Manuscript guidelines for #10 SASE.

● Health Communications publishes such authors as John Bradshaw, Janet Woititz and Charles Whitfield.

Nonfiction: Gift book, self-help. Subjects include child guidance/parenting, inspiration, psychology, spirituality, women's issues/studies, recovery. Submit proposal package, including outline, 2 sample chapters, vitae, marketing study and SASE. Reviews artwork/photos as part of ms package. Send photocopies. No phone calls.

Recent Nonfiction Title(s): *Chicken Soup for the Soul*, by Jack Canfield and Mark Victor Hansen (self-help/inspiration); *Meetings*, by Jess Stern (inspiration).

Tips: Audience is composed primarily of women, aged 25-60, interested in personal growth and self-improvement. "Please do your research in your subject area. We publish general self-help books, and are expanding to include new subjects such as business self-help and possibly alternative healing. We need to know why there is a need for your book, how it might differ from other books on the market and what you have to offer to promote your work."

‡HEALTH INFORMATION PRESS (HIP), Imprint of PMIC (Practice Management Information Corp.), 4727 Wilshire Blvd., Los Angeles CA 90010. (213)954-0224. Fax: (213)954-0253. E-mail: pmiceditor@aol.com. Website: http://medicalbookstore.com. **Acquisitions:** Kathryn Swanson, managing editor. "Audience is consumers who are interested in taking an active role in their health care." Publishes hardcover originals, trade paperback originals and reprints.

Publishes 8-10 titles/year. Receives 10 queries and 25-50 mss/year. 20% of books from first-time authors; 90% from unagented writers. Pays 10-15% royalty on net receipts. Offers $1,500-5,000 average advance. Publishes books 18 months after acceptance of ms. Reports in 3 months. Book catalog and ms guidelines for #10 SASE.

Nonfiction: How-to, illustrated book, reference, self-help. Subjects include health/medicine, psychology, science. "We seek to provide consumer health information." Submit proposal package, including outline, 3-5 sample chapters, curriculum vitae or résumé and letter detailing who would buy the book and the market/need for the book. Reviews artwork/photos as part of the ms package.

Recent Nonfiction Title(s): *Questions & Answers on AIDS*, by Lyn Frumkin, M.D., Ph.D. and John Leonard, M.D.; *Medicine Made Simple*, by Denise Knaus.

HEINEMANN, Division of Reed Elsevier, 361 Hanover St., Portsmouth NH 03801. **Acquisitions:** Cheryl Kimball, publisher (Trade Division). Heinemann specializes in theater, world literature and education titles. "Our goal is to offer a wide selecton of books that satisfy the needs and interests of educators from kindergarten to college." Publishes hardcover and trade paperback originals. Publishes 80-100 titles/year. 50% of books from first-time authors; 75% from unagented writers. Pays royalty on wholesale price. Advance varies widely. Publishes book 9 months after acceptance of ms. Accepts simultaneous submissions. Reports in 3 months on proposals. Book catalog free. Manuscript guidelines for #10 SASE.

Imprint(s): Butterworth-Heinemann, Focal Press, Digital Press.

Nonfiction: How-to, reference. Subjects include parenting as it relates to school education, education, gay/lesbian issues, language arts, women's issues/studies, African studies, drama. "We publish very strictly within our categories. We do not publish classroom textbooks." Query. Submit proposal package, including table of contents, outline, 1-2 sample chapters.

Recent Nonfiction Title(s): *Acting: Thought Into Action*, by Kurt Daw, illustrated by Rosemary Ingham; *Against the Current*, by Michael Brosnam (at-risk teens).

Tips: "Keep your queries (and manuscripts!) short, study the market, be realistic prepared to promote your book!"

‡HELIX BOOKS, Addison-Wesley Longman, Inc. One Jacob Way, Reading MA 01867 (617)944-3700. Fax: (617)944-8243. Website: http://www.aw.com. **Acquisitions**: Jeffrey Robbins, executive editor; Amanda Cook, assistant editor. Estab. 1992. "Helix Books presents the world's top scientists and science writers sharing with the general public the latest discoveries and their human implications, across the full range of scientific disciplines. Publishes hardcover and trade paperback originals. Publishes 10 titles/year. Receives 160 queries/year. 50% of books from first-time authors; 70% from unagented writers. Pays 7½-15% royalty on retail price "sliding scale based on number of copies sold." Offers $5,000 and up advance. Publishes book 1 year after acceptance of ms. Accepts simultaneous submissions but prefer exclusive. Reports in 1 month on queries. Book catalog free.

Nonfiction: Science. Query or submit outline, 2 sample chapters and proposal package, including market analysis, competition analysis, audience description, chapter outlines/table of contents, why topic is hot, why author is the one to write this book, 25-word synopsis that explains why the proposed book will be the best ever written about this topic.

Recent Nonfiction Title(s): *The Inflationary Universe: The Quest for a New Theory of Cosmic Origin*, by Guth (cosmology); *Six Not So Easy Pieces: Einstein's Relativity, Symmetry, and Space-Time*, by Richard P. Feynman (physics).

‡HELLGATE PRESS, PSI Research, 300 N. Valley Dr., Grants Pass OR 97526. (503)479-9464. Fax: (503)476-1479. **Acquisitions:** Emmett Ramey, president. Estab. 1996. "Hellgate Press specializes in military history and other military topics." Publishes 6-8 titles/year. Pays royalty. Publishes books 6 months after acceptance of ms. Accepts simultaneous submissions. Reports in 2 months on queries. Book catalog and ms guidelines for #10 SASE.

Nonfiction: Subjects include history, military/war, travel. Query with outline, sample chapter and SASE. Reviews artwork/photos as part of the ms package. Send photocopies.

Recent Nonfiction Title(s): *Gulf War Debriefing Book*, by Andrew Leyden; *Army Museums West of the Mississippi*, by Fred Bell.

HENDRICK-LONG PUBLISHING CO., INC., P.O. Box 25123, Dallas TX 75225-1123. (214)358-4677. Fax: (214)352-4768. **Acquisitions:** Joann Long. Estab. 1969. Hendrick-Long publishes historical fiction and nonfiction primarily about Texas and the Southwest for children and young adults. Publishes hardcover and trade paperback originals and hardcover reprints. Publishes 8 titles/year. Receives 500 submissions/year. 90% of books from unagented writers. Pays royalty on selling price. Publishes book 18 months after acceptance. Reports in 1 month on queries, 2 months if more than query sent. *Writer's Market* recommends allowing 2 months for reply. Book catalog for 8½×11 or 9×12 SAE with 4 first-class stamps. Manuscript guidelines for #10 SASE.

● Hendrick-Long has published such authors as Mary Blount Christian, Betsy Warren and Ruby Tolliver.

Nonfiction: Biography, history. Needs Texas and Southwest focused material for children and young adults. Query or submit outline and 2 sample chapters. Reviews artwork/photos as part of ms package; copies of material are acceptable. Do not send original art.

Recent Nonfiction Title(s): *Texas Granite: Story Of A World War II Hero*, by Mary Hartman (young adult); *Lone Star Justice: Supreme Court Justice Tom C. Clark*, by Evan Young (young adult).

Fiction: Texas and the Southwest for kindergarten through young adult. Query or submit outline/synopsis and 2 sample chapters.

Recent Fiction Title(s): *The Confederate Fiddle*, by Jeanne Williams (young adult/civil war); *I Know An Old Texan*

Who Swallowed A Fly, by Donna Cooner, illustrated by Ann Rife (animals, ages 4-8).

HENDRICKSON PUBLISHERS, INC., 140 Summit St., P.O. Box 3473, Peabody MA 01961-3473. Fax: (508)531-8146. E-mail: DPenwell@hendrickson.com or PAlexander@hendrickson.com. **Acquisitions:** Dan Penwell, manager of products; Patrick Alexander, editorial director (academic). Estab. 1983. Hendrickson publishes "books that give insight into Bible understanding (academically) and encourage spiritual growth (popular trade)." Publishes hardcover and trade paperback originals and reprints. Publishes 35 titles/year. Receives 200 submissions/year. 10% of books from first-time authors; 100% from unagented writers. Publishes book an average of 1 year after acceptance. Accepts simultaneous submissions (if so notified). Reports in 2 months. Book catalog and ms guidelines for SASE.
Nonfiction: Religious. "We will consider any quality manuscript within the area of religion specifically related to biblical studies and related fields. Also, nonfiction books in a more popular vein that give a hunger to studying, understanding and applying Scripture; books that encourage spiritual growth, such as personal devotionals." Submit outline and sample chapters.
Recent Nonfiction Title(s): *Paul, the Spirit and the People of God*, by Gordon Fee; *Theological Lexicon of the Old Testament*, by Mark Biddle (translator studies); *A Body Broken for a Broken People*, by Frances J. Moloney.

‡**JOSEPH HENRY PRESS**, Imprint of National Academy Press, 2101 Constitution Ave. NW, Washington DC 20418. (202)334-3313. E-mail: american@nas.edu. **Acquisitions:** Stephen Mautner, executive editor. Estab. 1993. "The Joseph Henry Press seeks manuscripts in general science and technology that will appeal to young scientists and established professionals or to interested lay readers within the overall categories of science, technology, and health. We'll be looking at everything from astrophysics to the environment to nutrition." Publishes hardcover and trade paperback originals. Publishes 15-20 titles/year. Receives 200 queries and 50-60 mss/year. 40% of books from first-time authors; 80% from unagented writers. Pays 10% royalty of net. Offers advance occasionally; varies with author. Publishes book 18 months after acceptance of ms. Accepts simultaneous submissions. Reports in 1 month on queries.
Nonfiction: Technical. Subjects include cooking/foods/nutrition, health/medicine, nature/environment, psychology, science, technology. Query with proposal package, including contents, prospectus, author's bio and SASE.
Recent Nonfiction Title(s): *Biodiversity 2: Understanding and Protecting Our Biological Resources*, edited by Marjorie Reak-Kudla, Don Wilson, Edward O. Wilson (environment); *A Miracle And A Privilege: A Half Century Of Surgical Advances*, by Francis D. Moore (medical)..

VIRGIL HENSLEY PUBLISHING, 6116 E. 32nd St., Tulsa OK 74135-5494. (918)664-8520. **Acquisitions:** Terri Kalfas, editor. Estab. 1965. "We serve an interdenominational market—all Christian persuasions." Publishes hardcover and paperback originals. Publishes 5-10 titles/year. Receives 800 submissions/year. 50% of books from first-time authors; 50% from unagented writers. Pays 5% minimum royalty on gross sales or makes outright purchase of $250 minimum for study aids. Publishes ms 18 months after acceptance. Reports in 2 months on queries. Manuscript guidelines for #10 SASE.
Nonfiction: Bible study curriculum. Subjects include child guidance, parenting, money/finance, men's and women's Christian education, prayer, prophecy, Christian living, large and small group studies, discipleship, adult development, parenting, personal growth, pastoral aids, church growth, family. "We do not want to see anything non-Christian." Actively seeking nonfiction other than Bible studies. No New Age, poetry, plays, sermon collections. Query with synopsis and sample chapters.
Recent Nonfiction Title(s): *How to Reach Your Church's Financial Goals This Year*, by Virgil Hensley.
Tips: "Submit something that crosses denominational lines directed toward the large Christian market, not small specialized groups."

HERITAGE BOOKS, INC., 1540-E Pointer Ridge Place, Bowie MD 20716-1859. (301)390-7708. Fax: (301)390-7193. **Acquisitions:** Leslie Towle, editorial supervisor. Estab. 1978. "We particularly desire to publish nonfiction titles dealing with history and genealogy." Publishes hardcover and paperback originals and reprints. Publishes 100 titles/year. Receives 300 submissions/year. 25% of books from first-time authors; 100% from unagented writers. Pays 10% royalty on list price. No advance. Accepts simultaneous submissions. Reports in 1 month. *Writer's Market* recommends allowing 2 months for reply. Book catalog for SAE.
Nonfiction: History and genealogy including how-to and reference works, as well as conventional histories and genealogies. "Ancestries of contemporary people are not of interest. The titles should be either of general interest or restricted to Eastern U.S. and Midwest, United Kingdom, Germany. Material dealing with the present century is usually not of interest." Query or submit outline. Reviews artwork/photos.
Tips: "The quality of the book is of prime importance; next is its relevance to our fields of interest."

HEYDAY BOOKS, Box 9145, Berkeley CA 94709-9145. Fax: (510)549-1889. E-mail: heyday@heydaybooks.com. **Acquisitions:** Malcolm Margolin, publisher. Estab. 1974. "Heyday Books publishes nonfiction books with a strong California focus." Publishes hardcover originals, trade paperback originals and reprints. Publishes 8-10 titles/year. Receives 200 submissions/year. 50% of books from first-time authors; 90% from unagented writers. Pays 8-15% royalty on net price. Publishes book 8 months after acceptance. Reports in 1 week on queries, 5 weeks on mss. *Writer's Market* recommends allowing 2 months for reply. Book catalog for 7×9 SAE with 2 first-class stamps.
• Heyday Books has published anthologies of such well-known writers as Maxine Hong Kingston, Richard Rodriquez, Gary Snyder and Joan Didion.

Nonfiction: Books about California only. Subjects include Americana, history, nature, travel. "We publish books about native Americans, natural history, history, and recreation, with a strong California focus." Query with outline and synopsis. Reviews artwork/photos.
Recent Nonfiction Title(s): *Highway 99*, edited by Stan Yogi (literary anthology); *Fine Art of California Indian Basketry*, by Brian Bibby (basket weaving); *First & Foremost*, by Charlene Akers (guide to California bookstores).

HIGH PLAINS PRESS, P.O. Box 123, 539 Cassa Rd., Glendo WY 82213. Fax: (307)735-4590. **Acquisitions:** Nancy Curtis, publisher. "What we sell best is history of the Old West, focusing on Wyoming. We also publish one book of poetry a year in our Poetry of the American West series." Publishes hardcover and trade paperback originals. Publishes 4 titles/year. Receives 300 queries and 200 mss/year. 80% of books from first-time authors; 95% from unagented writers. Pays 10% royalty on wholesale price. Offers $100-600 advance. Publishes book 2 years after acceptance. Accepts simultaneous submissions. Reports in 1 month on queries and proposals, 3 months on mss. Book catalog and ms guidelines for 8½×10 SASE.
Nonfiction: Biography, Western Americana, Americana, art/architecture, history, nature/environment, regional. "We focus on books of the American West, particularly history." Submit outline. Reviews artwork/photos as part of ms package. Send photocopies.
Recent Nonfiction Title(s): *Wagon Wheels: A Contemporary Journey on the Oregon Trail*, by Candy Moulton and Ben Kern; *Thunder & Mud: A Pioneer Childhood on the Prairie*, by Julia Brown Tobias.
Poetry: "We only seek poetry closely tied to the Rockies. Do not submit single poems." Query with complete ms.
Recent Poetry Title(s): *Glass-eyed Paint in the Rain*, by Laurie Wagner Buyer.

HIGHSMITH PRESS, P.O. Box 800, Fort Atkinson WI 53538-0800. (414)563-9571. Fax: (414)563-4801. E-mail: hpress@highsmith.com. Website: http://www.hpress.highsmith.com. **Acquisitions:** Donald J. Sager, publisher. "Highsmith Press emphasizes library reference and professional books that meet the practical needs of librarians, educators and the general public." Publishes hardcover and paperback originals. Publishes 20 titles/year. Receives 500-600 queries and 400-500 mss/year. 30% of books from first-time authors; 100% from unagented writers. Pays 10-12% royalty on net sales price. Offers $250-2,000 advance. Publishes book 6 months after acceptance of ms. Accepts simultaneous submissions. Reports in 1 month on queries, 2 months on proposals, 3 months on mss. Catalog and ms guidelines free.
Imprint(s): Alleyside Press (creative, time-saving, low-cost resources for teachers and librarians).
Nonfiction: Reference and professional. Subjects include education, language/literature, multicultural, professional (library science), teacher activity. "We are primarily interested in reference and library professional books, multicultural resources for youth, library and study skills, curricular and activity books for teachers and others who work with preschool through high school youth." Query with outline and 1-2 sample chapters. Reviews artwork/photos.
Recent Nonfiction Title(s): *Reading Resources and Activities That Work*, by Phyllis Perry (reading activities); *Don't Knock It, or How to Care for Your Library Books*, by Karen Books (library skills).
Fiction: No longer accepting children's picture book ms. "Our current emphasis is on storytelling collections for preschool-grade 6. We prefer stories that can be easily used by teachers and children's librarians, multicultural topics, and manuscripts that feature fold and cut, flannelboard, tangram, or similar simple patterns that can be reproduced."
Recent Fiction Title(s): *Storyteller's Sampler*, by Valerie Marsh.

‡HILL AND WANG, Division of Farrar Straus & Giroux, Inc., 19 Union Square W., New York NY 10003. (212)741-6900. Fax: (212)633-9385. **Acquisitions:** Elisabeth Sifton, publisher; Lauren Osborne, editor. Publishes hardcover and trade paperback originals. Publishes 12 titles/year. Receives 1,500 queries/year. 5% of books from first-time authors; 50% from unagented writers. Pays 7½% royalty on retail price. Advances "vary widely from a few hundred to several thousand dollars." Publishes book 1 year after acceptance of ms. Accepts simultaneous submissions. Reports in 2 months. Book catalog free.
Nonfiction: Cross-over academic and trade books. Subjects include government/politics, history (primarily American, some European and African history), public policy, sociology, women's issues, some drama. Submit outline, sample chapters, letter explaining rationale for book and SASE. Reviews artwork/photos as part of ms package. Send samples.
Recent Nonfiction Title(s): *First Generations: Women of Colonial America*, by Carol Berkin; *Prague in Black & Gold*, by Peter Demetz; *Neglected Stories: The Constitution and Family Values*, by Peggy Cooper Davis.
Fiction: "Fiction list inactive; maintaining backlist of fiction and drama, but *not* considering new material."

HIPPOCRENE BOOKS INC., 171 Madison Ave., New York NY 10016. (212)685-4371. Fax: (212)779-9338. E-mail: hippocre@ix.netcom.com. **Acquisitions:** George Blagowidow, president. Publisher: Jacek Galazka. Estab. 1971. "We publish reference books of international interest, often bilingual, in the fields of cookery, travel, language and literature." Publishes hardcover and trade paperback originals. Publishes 100 titles/year. Receives 250 submissions/year. 10% of books from first-time authors; 95% from unagented writers. Pays 6-10% royalty on retail price. Offers $2,000 advance. Publishes book 16 months after acceptance. Accepts simultaneous submissions. Reports in 2 months. Book catalog for 9×12 SAE with 5 first-class stamps. Manuscript guidelines for #10 SASE.
Nonfiction: Reference. Subjects include foreign language, Judaic reference, ethnic and special interest travel, military history, bilingual love poetry, bilingual proverbs, international cookbooks, Polish interest, foreign language, dictionaries and instruction. Submit outline, 2 sample chapters, toc.
Recent Nonfiction Title(s): *Uncertain Glory: Lee's Generalship Re-Examined*, by John D. McKenzie (Civil War);

Under the Wedding Canopy, by David and Esther Gross (Jewish wedding traditions); *Cuisine of Armenia*, by Sonia Uzvezian (Armenian cookbook).

Recent Poetry Title(s): *Irish Love Poems: Dánta Grá* (anthology of Irish poetry); *Treasury of French Love Poems, Quotations & Proverbs* (bilingual); *Treasury of Arabic Love Poems, Quotations & Proverbs* (bilingual).

Tips: "Our recent successes in publishing general books considered midlist by larger publishers is making us more of a general trade publisher. We continue to do well with reference books like dictionaries, atlases and language studies. We ask for proposal, sample chapter, and table of contents. We then ask for material if we are interested."

‡HOHM PRESS, P.O. Box 2501, Prescott AZ 86302. **Acquisitions:** Regina Sara Ryan, managing editor. "Our offerings include a range of titles in the areas of psychology and spirituality, herbistry, alternative health methods and nutrition, as well as distinctive children's books. Hohm Press is proud to present authors from the U.S. and Europe who have a clarity of vision and the mastery to communicate that vision." Publishes hardcover and trade paperback originals. Publishes 6-10 titles/year. 50% of books from first-time authors. Pays 10-15% royalty on net sales. No advance. Publishes book 18 months after acceptance of ms. Accepts simultaneous submissions. Reports in 3 months on queries. Book catalog for $1.50.

Nonfiction: Self-help. Subjects include child guidance/parenting, health/medicine, philosophy, religious (Hindu, Buddhist, Sufi or translations of classic texts in major religious traditions). "We look for writers who have an established record in their field of expertise. The best buy of recent years came from two women who fully substantiated how they could market their book. We believed they could do it. We were right." Query with SASE.

Recent Nonfiction Title(s): *Your Body Can Talk*, by Susan Levy D.C. and Carol Lehr (health); *When Sons and Daughters Choose Alternative Lifestyles*, by Mariana Caplan; *10 Essential Foods*, by Lalitha Thomas.

Recent Poetry Title(s): Rending The Veil—RUMI, translated by Shahram T. Shiva (Sufic/religious).

HOLIDAY HOUSE INC., 425 Madison Ave., New York NY 10017. (212)688-0085. Fax: (212)421-6134. **Acquisitions:** Allison Cunningham, assistant editor. Estab. 1935. Publishes children's and young adult books for the school and library markets. "Holiday House has a commitment to publishing first-time authors and illustrators." Publishes hardcover originals. Publishes 50 titles/year. Receives 3,000 submissions/year. 2-5% of books from first-time authors; 50% from unagented writers. Pays royalty on list price, range varies. Offers $2,000-10,000 advance. Publishes book 1-2 years after acceptance. Accepts simultaneous submissions. Reports in 1 month on queries, 3 months on mss. Manuscripts not returned without SASE. Book catalog for 9×12 SAE with 7 first-class stamps. Manuscript guidelines for #10 SASE.

Nonfiction: Biography, children's/juvenile, humor, illustrated book, young adult. Subjects include animals, art/architecture, history, sports. "We are looking for manuscripts for picture books with new and different approaches. We don't want anything that combines fiction and nonfiction." Submit outline and 2-3 sample chapters; submit complete ms for picture books only. Reviews artwork/photos as part of ms package. Send photocopies.

Recent Nonfiction Title(s): *The Life and Death of Crazy Horse*, by Russell Freedman; *The Picture Book Biography Series*, by David Adler (5-8, early elementary).

Fiction: Adventure, ethnic, historical, humor, juvenile, picture books, easy readers. "We are not looking for young adult at this point. We are looking for young picture books and middle-grade fiction." Send full ms for picture book; send 3 chapters and outline for chapter books.

Recent Fiction Title(s): *Hey, Dad, Get A Life!*, by Todd Strasser; *Rum-a-Tum-Tum*, by Angela Medearis (4-8); *Shooting Star*, by Sheila Solomon Klass (8-12).

Tips: "We are not geared toward the mass market, but toward school and library markets. We need picturebook texts with strong stories and writing. We are not interested in folktales or poetry. We do not publish board books."

HOLLOW EARTH PUBLISHING, P.O. Box 1355, Boston MA 02205-1355. (617)746-3130. E-mail: hep2@aol.com. **Acquisitions:** Helian Yvette Grimes, editor/publisher. Publishes hardcover, trade and mass market paperback originals and reprints. Publishes 6 titles/year. Receives 250 submissions/year. 30% of books from first-time authors. Pays 5-15% royalty on wholesale price. Publishes book 6 months after acceptance. Reports in 3 weeks on queries . *Writer's Market* recommends allowing 2 months for reply. Book catalog for 9×12 SAE with 3 first-class stamps. Manuscript guidelines for #10 SASE.

Nonfiction: How-to, reference, technical (computer), mythology. Subjects include architecture, computers/electronics, photography, religion/mythology and travel. "We are currently interested in books on technical aspects of photography and computer and Internet-related topics." Query. All unsolicited mss are returned unopened. Reviews artwork/photos as part of ms package.

Fiction: Fantasy, literary, mystery, science fiction. Submit outline/synopsis and sample chapters. All unsolicited mss are returned unopened.

Tips: "Computer books are fairly easy to publish because they can be marketed specifically."

HOLMES & MEIER PUBLISHERS, INC., East Building, 160 Broadway, New York NY 10038. (212)374-0100. Fax: (212)374-1313. **Acquisitions:** Katharine Turok, executive editor. Publisher: Miriam H. Holmes. Estab. 1969. "We are noted as an academic publishing house and are pleased with our reputation for excellence in the field. However, we are also expanding our list to include books of more general interest." Publishes hardcover and paperback originals. Publishes 20 titles/year. Pays royalty. Publishes book an average of 18 months after acceptance. Reports in up to 6 months. Query with SASE. Book catalog free.

Imprint(s): Africana Publishing Co.

Nonfiction: Africana, art, biography, business/economics, history, Judaica, Latin American studies, literary criticism, politics, reference and women's studies. Accepts translations. Query first with outline, sample chapters, cv and idea of intended market/audience.

HOLMES PUBLISHING GROUP, P.O. Box 623, Edmonds WA 98020. E-mail: jdh@jdh.seanet.com. CEO: J.D. Holmes. **Acquisitions:** L.Y. Fitzgerald. Holmes publishes informative spiritual health titles on philosophy, metaphysical and religious subjects. Publishes hardcover and trade paperback originals and reprints. Publishes 40 titles/year. Receives 120 queries and 80 mss/year. 20% of books from first-time authors; 20% from unagented writers. Pays 10% royalty on wholesale price. Publishes book 4 months after acceptance of ms. Reports in 2 months.
Imprint(s): Alchemical Press, Sure Fire Press, Contra/Thought, Alexandria Press.
Nonfiction: Self-help. Subjects include health/medicine, occult, philosophy, religion, metaphysical. "We do not publish titles that are more inspirational than informative." Query or submit complete ms with SASE. Reviews artwork/photos as part of ms package. Send photocopies.
Recent Nonfiction Title(s): *Complete Golden Cipher Manuscript*, by Darcy Küntz (alchemy, magic, occult).
Fiction: Metaphysical, occult. Query.

‡**HENRY HOLT & COMPANY BOOKS FOR YOUNG READERS**, Imprint of Henry Holt & Co., Inc., 115 W. 18th St., New York NY 10011. (212)886-9200. Fax: (212)633-0748. **Acquisitions:** Laura Godwin, associate publisher. Marc Aronson, senior editor (ya nonfiction and fiction); Christy Ottaviano (picture books, middle grade fiction). Estab. 1866 (Holt). Henry Holt Books for Young Readers publishes excellent books of all kinds (fiction, nonfiction, illustrated) for all ages, from the very young to the young adult. Publishes hardcover and trade paperback originals. Publishes 50-60 titles/year. Over 50% of books from first-time authors; 50% from unagented writers. Pays royalty on retail price, 6% minimum for paperback, 10% minimum for hardcover. Offers $2,500 and up advance. Publishes book 18 months after acceptance of ms. Accepts simultaneous submissions. Reports in 5 months on queries and mss. Book catalog and ms guidelines free.
Imprint(s): Edge Books (Marc Aronson, senior editor, "a high caliber ya fiction imprint"); Red Feather Books (Christy Ottaviano, editor, "covers a range between early chapter and younger middle grade readers"); Owlet Paperbacks.
Nonfiction: Children's/juvenile, illustrated book. Query with SASE.
Recent Nonfiction Title(s): *Night Driving*, by John Coy (picture book); *Clown*, by Quentin Blake (picture book).
Fiction: Juvenile: adventure, animal, contemporary, fantasy, history, humor, multicultural, religion, sports, suspense/mystery. Picture books: animal, concept, history, humor, multicultural, religion, sports. Young adult: contemporary, fantasy, history, multicultural, nature/environment, problem novels, sports. Query with SASE.
Recent Fiction Title(s): *Long Season of Rain*, by Helen Kim; *Winning Ways*, by Sue Macy (both ya).

‡**HENRY HOLT & COMPANY, INC.**, 115 W. 18th St., New York NY 10011. (212)886-9200. Editor-in-Chief: William Strachan. **Acquisitions**: Sara Bershtel, editorial director (Metropolitan); Bryan Oettel, editor (nonfiction); Elizabeth Crossman, editor (cooking); Allen Peacock, senior editor (fiction); David Sobel, senior editor (science, culture, history, health). General interest publisher of both fiction and nonfiction. Query before submitting.
Imprint(s): John Macrae Books, Metropolitan Books, **MIS: Press, M&T Books, Owl Books**, Marian Wood Books, **Henry Holt & Company Books for Young Readers** (**Edge Books**, Books by Michael Hague, Books by Bill Martin Jr. and John Archambault, Owlet Paperbacks, Redfeather Books, W5 Reference).
Recent Nonfiction Title(s): *The Strange Death of the Soviet Empire*, by David Pryce-Jones.
Recent Fiction Title(s): *Give Us a Kiss: A Country Noir*, by Daniel Woodrell.

‡**HONOR BOOKS**, P.O. Box 55388, Tulsa OK 74155. (918)496-9007. **Acquistions:** Cristine Bolley, acquisition director. "We are a Christian publishing house with a mission to inspire and encourage people to draw near to God and to enjoy His love and grace." Publishes hardcover and trade paperback originals. Publishes 60 titles/year. Receives 1,000 queries and 500 mss/year. 2% of books from first-time authors. 90% of books from unagented writers. Pays royalty on wholesale price, makes outright purchase or assigns work for hire. Offers advance. Publishes book 1 year after acceptance of ms. Accepts simultaneous submissions. Reports in 1 month on queries, 3 months on proposals. Manuscript guidelines for #10 SASE.
Nonfiction: Gift book, humor, seasonal/holiday gift books, inspirational. Subjects include hobbies (devotional or inspirational in format), religion, devotional. "We aren't looking for testimony books, but we do welcome personal experience stories that illustrate specific principles that are central to the theme of the book and which accomplish our publishing mission." Query with outline, 1-2 sample chapters and proposal package, including table of contents, synopsis and author bio, SASE. Reviews artwork/photos as part of the ms package. Send photocopies.
Recent Nonfiction Title(s): *What My Cat Taught Me About Life*, by Niki Anderson (gift); *God's Little Devotional Books* (series); *The Golfer's Tee Time Devotional*.
Tips: "Our books are for busy, achievement-oriented people who are looking for balance between reaching their goals and knowing that God loves them unconditionally. Our books should challenge spiritual growth, victorious living and an intimate knowledge of God. Write about what you are for and not what you are against. We look for scripts that are biblically correct and which edify the reader."

‡**HOOVER'S, INC.**, Affiliate of Time Warner Books, 1033 La Posada Dr., Suite 250, Austin TX 78752. (512)374-4500. Fax: (512)374-4501. Website: http://www.hoovers.com. **Acquisitions:** George Sutton, senior managing editor.

Estab. 1990. "Hoover's publishes business information in a variety of electronic and print media; information on the operations, strategies, histories, financial performance and products of major U.S. and global public and private enterprises, for executives, investors, salespeople, consumers and scholars—anyone who needs to know about companies." Publishes 12 titles/year. Royalty and advance negotiable. Accepts simultaneous submissions. Reports in 2 months on queries. Book catalog free.

● Hoover's, Inc. is open to submissions; however, virtually all titles are produced in-house.

Nonfiction: Reference. Subjects include business/economics, investment. Query with outline and SASE.
Recent Nonfiction Title(s): *Hoover's Handbook of American Business 1997* (reference); *Hoover's Guide to Media Companies* (reference); *Cyberstocks: An Investor's Guide to Internet Companies*.

HOUGHTON MIFFLIN BOOKS FOR CHILDREN, Imprint of Houghton Mifflin Company, 222 Berkeley St., Boston MA 02116. (617)351-5959. Fax: (617)351-1111. Website: http://www.hmco.com. **Acquisitions:** Sarah Hines-Stephens, submissions coordinator. "Houghton Mifflin gives shape to ideas that educate, inform, and above all, delight." Publishes hardcover and trade paperback originals and reprints. Firm publishes 100 titles/year. Receives 5,000 queries and 12,000 mss/year. 10% of books from first-time authors; 70% from unagented writers. Pays 5-10% royalty on retail price. Advance dependent on many factors. Publishes book 18 months after acceptance of ms. Accepts simultaneous submissions. Reports in 2 months. Book catalog for 9×12 SASE with 3 first-class stamps. Manuscript guidelines for 8×10 SASE.

Nonfiction: Biography, children's/juvenile, humor, illustrated book. Subjects include agriculture/horticulture, Americana, animals, anthropology, art/architecture, ethnic, gardening, history, language/literature, music/dance, nature/environment, recreation, regional, science, sports, travel. Interested in "innovative science books, especially about scientists 'in the field' and what they do." Submit outline and 2 sample chapters with SASE. Mss will not be returned without appropriate-sized SASE. Reviews artwork/photos as part of ms package. Send photocopies.
Recent Nonfiction Title(s): *The Nine-Ton Cat: Behind the Scenes in an Art Museum*, by Peggy Thomson; *The Life & Times of the Peanut*, by Charles Micucci; *Old Ironsides*, by David Weitzman (history).
Fiction: Adventure, ethnic, historical, humor, juvenile (early readers), literary, mystery, picture books, suspense, young adult, board books. Submit full ms with appropriate-sized SASE.
Recent Fiction Title(s): *Where Are You, Little Zack?*, by Enderle/Tessler (picture book, humorous); *The Woman in the Wall*, by Patrice Kindl (novel); *Three Stories You Can Read to Your Cat*, by Miller (early reader with illustrations).
Tips: "Faxed manuscripts and proposals are not considered."

HOUGHTON MIFFLIN COMPANY, 222 Berkeley St., Boston MA 02116. (617)351-5940. Fax: (617)351-1202. Website: http://www.hmco.com. **Acquisitions:** Christine Corcoran, assistant to editorial director. Estab. 1832. "Houghton Mifflin gives shape to ideas that educate, inform and delight. In a new era of publishing, our legacy of quality thrives as we combine imagination with technology, bringing you new ways to know." Publishes hardcover and trade paperback originals and reprints. Publishes 60 hardcovers, 30-40 paperbacks/year. 10% of books from first-time authors; 20% from unagented writers. Hardcover: pays 10-15% royalty on retail price, sliding scale or flat rate based on sales; paperback: 7 1/2% flat fee, but negotiable. Advance varies. Publishes book 1-2 years after acceptance of ms. Accepts simultaneous submissions. Reports in 3 months. Book catalog and ms guidelines free.

● Houghton Mifflin published such authors as Robert Stone, David Leavitt, John Kenneth Galbraith, JRR Tolkein, Margaret Atwood and Rachel Carson.

Imprint(s): Chapters Publishing Ltd., Clarion Books, Peter Davison Books, Marc Jaffe Books, Walter Lorraine Books, **Houghton Mifflin Books for Children**, Mariner Paperbacks, Sandpiper Paperbacks.
Nonfiction Biography, childrens/juvenile, coffee table hobbies, language/literature, military/war, money/finance, music/dance, nature/environment, philosophy, photography, psychology, recreation, regional, religion, science, sociology, sports, travel, women's issues/studies. "We are not a mass market publisher. Our main focus is serious nonfiction. We do practical self-help but not pop psychology self-help." Query with outline, 1 sample chapter and SASE. Reviews artwork/photos as part of ms package. Send photocopies.
Recent Nonfiction Title(s): *Bogart: A Life in Hollywood*, by Jeffrey Myers (biography); *Promised Land, Crusades State*, by Walter McDougall (American history); *The Haygoods of Columbus: A Love Story*, by Wil Haygood (memoir).
Fiction: Adventure, confession, erotica, ethnic, fantasy, feminist, gay/lesbian, historical, humor, literary, mainstream/contemporary, mystery, romance (but not mass-market), short story collections, suspense. "We are not a mass market publisher. Study the current list." Query with 3 sample chapters or complete mss and SASE.
Recent Fiction Title(s): *American Pastoral*, by Philip Roth (literary novel); *Reality and Dreams*, by Muriel Spark (novel); *My Other Life*, by Paul Theroux (novel).
Poetry: "At this point we have an established roster of poets we use. It is hard for first-time poets to get published by

---

MARKET CONDITIONS are constantly changing! If this is 1999 or later, buy the newest edition of *Writer's Market* at your favorite bookstore or order directly from Writer's Digest Books.

Houghton Mifflin." Query with 10 sample poems.
Recent Poetry Title(s): *The Old Life*, by Donald Hall; *The Alamo*, by Michael Lind; *West Wind*, by Mary Oliver.

‡**HOUSE OF COLLECTIBLES**, Imprint of Ballantine Publishing, 201 E. 50th St., New York NY 10022. Website: http://www.randomhouse.com. **Acquisitions:** Randy Ladenheim-Gil, editor. "One of the premier publishing companies devoted to books on a wide range of antiques and collectibles, House of Collectibles publishes books for the seasoned expert and the beginning collector alike. We have been publishing price guides and other books on antiques and collectibles for over 35 years and plan to meet the needs of collectors, dealers and appraisers well into the 21st century." Publishes trade and mass market paperback originals. Publishes 25-28 titles/year. Receives 200 queries/year. 1% of books from first-time authors; 85% from unagented writers. Pays royalty on retail price, varies. Offers advance against royalties, varies. Publishes book 6 months after acceptance of ms. Accepts simultaneous submissions, if so noted. Reports in 3 months on queries. Book catalog free from Ballantine.
Imprint(s): Official Price Guide series.
Nonfiction: Coffee table book, how-to (related to collecting antiques and coins). Subjects include hobbies, recreation. "We are happy to hear from collectors with a particular expertise. Something may strike us, or be timely. We are expanding beyond price guides." Query or submit outline, 3 sample chapters with SASE.
Recent Nonfiction Title(s): *The Official Harry L. Rinker Guide to Collectibles* (reference); *The One Minute Coin Expert*, by Scott Travers (reference); *The Official R.L. Wilson Price Guide to Firearms* (reference).

‡**HOWELL BOOK HOUSE**, Imprint of Macmillan General Reference, Subsidiary of Simon & Schuster, 1633 Broadway, New York NY 10019. (212)654-8500. **Acquisitions**: Sean Frawley, publisher; Don Stevens, associate publisher; Seymour Weiss, editor-in-chief; Madeleine Larsen, equine editor. "Our mission is to publish the highest quality and most useful information and reference books on pet and animal subjects." Publishes hardcover originals, trade paperback originals and reprints. Publishes 60-100 titles/year. Receives 3,000 queries/year. 15% of books from first-time authors; 5% from unagented writers. Pays royalty on retail price or net sales, or makes outright purchase or work-for-hire assignments. Offers variable advance. Publishes book 1 year after acceptance of ms. Accepts simultaneous submissions. Reports in 2 months on queries and mss, 1 month on proposals.
Nonfiction: How-to, reference. Subjects include animals, recreation. Submit outline with 1 sample chapter and proposal package, including table of contents, author's credentials, target audience and market analysis. Reviews artwork/photos as part of ms package. Send photocopies. SASE for returns.
Recent Nonfiction Title(s): *Dressage by the Letter*, by Moira C. Harris; *All Dogs Need Some Training*, by Liz Polkia; *Breeding Pedigree Cats*, by Carolyn Vella and John McGonagle Jr.

HOWELL PRESS, INC., 1147 River Rd., Suite 2, Charlottesville VA 22901-4172. (804)977-4006. Fax: (804)971-7204. E-mail: howellpres@aol.com. **Acquisitions:** Ross A. Howell, president. Estab. 1985. "Howell Press publishes and distributes books in the categories of history, transportation, gardening and cooking." Publishes 6 titles/year. Receives 500 submissions/year. 10% of books from first-time authors; 80% from unagented writers. Pays 5-7% royalty on net retail price. "We generally offer an advance, but amount differs with each project and is generally negotiated with authors on a case-by-case basis." Publishes book 18 months after acceptance. Reports in 2 months. Book catalog for 9×12 SAE with 4 first-class stamps. Manuscript guidelines for #10 SASE.
Nonfiction: Illustrated books, historical texts. Subjects include aviation, military history, cooking, maritime history, motorsports, gardening. "Generally open to most ideas, as long as writing is accessible to average adult reader. Our line is targeted, so it would be advisable to look over our catalog before querying to better understand what Howell Press does." Query with outline and sample chapters. Reviews artwork/photos as part of ms package. Does not return mss without SASE.
Recent Nonfiction Title(s): *Stuck on Cactus: A Beginning Grower's Guide*, by David Wright; *Corvette GTP*, by Alex Gabbard (auto racing); *Magic Motors 1930*, by Brooks Brierley (classic cars).
Tips: "Focus of our program has been illustrated books, but we will also consider nonfiction manuscripts that would not be illustrated. Selections limited to history, transportation, cooking and gardening."

HOWELLS HOUSE, P.O. Box 9546, Washington DC 20016-9546. (202)333-2182. **Acquisitions:** W.D. Howells, publisher. Estab. 1988. "Our interests are institutions and institutional change." Publishes hardcover and trade paperback originals and reprints. Publishes 4 titles/year; each imprint publishes 2-3 titles/year. Receives 2,000 queries and 300 mss/year. 50% of books from first-time authors; 60% from unagented writers. Pays 15% net royalty or makes outright purchase. May offer advance. Publishes book 8 months after ms development completed. Reports in 2 months on proposals.
Imprint(s): The Compass Press, Whalesback Books.
Nonfiction: Biography, illustrated book, textbook. Subjects include Americana, anthropology/archaeology, art/architecture, business/economics, education, government/politics, history, military/war, photography, science, sociology, translation. Query.
Fiction: Historical, literary, mainstream/contemporary. Query.

‡**HRD PRESS, INC.**, 22 Amherst Rd., Amherst MA 01002. (413)253-3488. Fax: (413)253-3490. **Acquisitions:** Robert W. Carkhuff, publisher. Estab. 1970. "We publish mostly business oriented titles, training and the development of

human resources." Publishes hardcover and trade paperback originals. Averages 15-20 titles/year. Receives 300-400 submissions/year. 25% of books from first-time authors; 100% from unagented writers. Pays 10-15% royalty on wholesale price. Offers $1,000 average advance. Publishes book an average of 6 months after acceptance. Accepts simultaneous submissions. Reports in 1 month on queries. *Writer's Market* recommends allowing 2 months for reply. Book catalog and ms guidelines free.

Nonfiction: Reference, software, technical. Business subjects. Submit outline and sample chapters.

Tips: "We are no longer seeking juvenile nonfiction or psychology titles."

HUDSON HILLS PRESS, INC., 230 Fifth Ave., Suite 1308, New York NY 10001-7704. (212)889-3090. Fax: (212)889-3091. **Acquisitions:** Paul Anbinder, president/publisher. Estab. 1978. "We only publish books about art and photography, including monographs." Publishes hardcover and paperback originals. Publishes 10 titles/year. Receives 50-100 submissions/year. 15% of books from first-time authors; 90% from unagented writers. Average print order for a first book is 3,000. Pays 4-6% royalty on retail price. Offers $3,500 average advance. Publishes book 1 year after acceptance. Reports in 2 months. Book catalog for 6×9 SAE with 2 first-class stamps.

Nonfiction: Art, photography. Query first, then submit outline and sample chapters. Reviews artwork/photos.

HUMAN KINETICS PUBLISHERS, INC., P.O. Box 5076, Champaign IL 61825-5076. (217)351-5076. Fax: (217)351-2674. **Acquisitions:** Ted Miller, director (trade); Loarn Robertson, director (academic). Publisher: Rainer Martens. Estab. 1974. "We publish books which accurately interpret sport sciences and health research to coaches, athletes and fitness enthusiasts." Publishes hardcover and paperback text and reference books, trade paperback originals, software and audiovisual. Publishes 100 titles/year. Receives 300 submissions/year. 50% of books from first-time authors; 97% of books from unagented writers. Pays 10-15% royalty on net income. Publishes book an average of 18 months after acceptance. Accepts simultaneous submissions. Reports in 2 months. Book catalog free.

Imprint(s): HK Trade, HK Academic.

Nonfiction: How-to, reference, self-help, technical and textbook. Subjects include health, recreation, sports, sport sciences and sports medicine, and physical education. Especially interested in books on fitness; books on all aspects of sports technique or how-to books and coaching books; books which interpret the sport sciences and sports medicine, including sport physiology, sport psychology, sport pedagogy and sport biomechanics. No sport biographies, sport record or statistics books or regional books. Submit outline and sample chapters. Reviews artwork/photos as part of ms package.

Recent Nonfiction Title(s): *Complete Home Fitness Handbook, 2nd edition*, by Edmund R. Burke.

‡HUMANICS CHILDREN'S HOUSE, Imprint of Humanics Publishing, 1482 Mecaslin St. NW, Atlanta GA 30309. (404)874-2176. **Acquisitions:** Shattuck Groom, director of trade division. Estab. 1977. "We publish picture books for young children that incorporate a small message about self-development." Publishes hardcover and trade paperback originals and reprints. Publishes 8 titles/year. Receives 1,200 queries and 1,300 mss/year. 90% of books from unagented writers. Pays 5-13% royalty on net receipts. Offers $500-1,000 advance. Publishes book 6-24 months after acceptance of ms. Accepts simultaneous submissions, if so noted. Reports in 1 month. Book catalog for 9×12 SAE with 7 first-class stamps. Manuscript guidelines for #10 SASE.

Fiction: Picture books. "We do not publish many unsolicited manuscripts." Query or submit ms with SASE.

Recent Fiction Title(s): *Giggle E. Goose*, by Al Newman and *Paz in the Land of Numbers*, by Miriam Bowden.

Tips: Audience is young children who need to be read to, or are beginning to read a little. "No phone calls, please."

‡HUMANICS LEARNING, Imprint of Humanics Publishing Group, 1482 Mecaslin St. NW, Atlanta GA 30309. (404)874-2176. Fax: (404)874-1976. **Acquisitions:** Shattuck Groom, director of trade division. Estab. 1977. "Our goal is to furnish teachers, home schoolers, daycare facilitators and other instructors with the best teacher resource guides available to help improve curriculum." Publishes hardcover and trade paperback originals and reprints. Publishes 8 titles/year. Receives 1,500 queries and 1,300 mss/year. 90% of books from unagented writers. Pays 5-13% royalty on net receipts. Offers $500-1,000 advance. Publishes book 1-6 months after acceptance of ms. Accepts simultaneous submissions, if so noted. Reports in 1 month. Book catalog for 9×12 SAE with 7 first-class stamps. Manuscript guidelines for #10 SASE.

Nonfiction: How-to, teacher resource guides. Subjects include child guidance/parenting, education, ethnic, health, language, music/dance, nature/environment, psychology, self-esteem, science. "Know our focus." Query and/or submit outline and 3 sample chapters with SASE. Reviews artwork/photos as part of ms package. Send photocopies.

Recent Nonfiction Title(s): *Pre-K Science*, by Cynthia Marthy (teacher resource).

Tips: "Request a catalog."

HUMANICS PUBLISHING GROUP, 1482 Mecaslin St. NW, Atlanta GA 30309. (404)874-2176. Fax: (404)874-1976. E-mail: humanics@mindspring.com. **Acquisitions:** W. Arthur Bligh, editor. Estab. 1976. Humanics Trade pub-

FOR EXPLANATION of symbols, see the Key to Symbols and Abbreviations. For unfamiliar words, see the Glossary.

lishes "books for the mind, body and spirit." Publishes hardcover and trade paperback originals. Publishes 22 titles/year; imprints: Humanics Trade, 2; Humanics Children's House, 2; Humanics Learning,10. Receives 5,000 queries/year. 70% of books from first-time authors. Pays 10% royalty on wholesale price. Offers $500-3,000 advance. Publishes book 1-12 months after acceptance of ms. Accepts simultaneous submissions, if so noted. Responds only if interested. Book catalog free. Manuscript guidelines for #10 SASE.
Imprint(s): Humanics Trade, **Humanics Learning**, **Humanics Children's House**.
Nonfiction: Children's/juvenile, illustrated book, self-help. Subjects include child guidance/parenting, philosophy, spirituality (e.g., taoism). Query with outline, 1 sample chapter and SASE.
Recent Nonfiction Title(s): *Zen of Magic*, by Inez Stein.
Tips: "For our activity books, audience is parents and educators looking for books which will enrich their children's lives. For our trade books, audience is anyone interested in positive, healthy self-development. We are looking for quality and creativity. As a small publisher, we don't waste our time or an author's time on books that are not of lasting importance or value. Taoism and Zen high interest."

‡HUMANITIES PRESS INTERNATIONAL INC., 165 First Ave., Atlantic Highlands NJ 07716. (908)872-1441.
Acquisitions: Keith Ashfield, publisher (history, politics, philosophy); Melanie Hawley, assistant; Terry Mares, acquisitions editor (sociology, politics). "We publish books suitable for use in college courses." Publishes hardcover originals and trade paperback originals and reprints. Publishes 35 titles/year. 25% of books from first-time authors; 99% from unagented writers. Pays 5-10% royalty on retail price. Offers $0-1,000 advance. Publishes book 15 months after acceptance of ms. Reports in 1 month on queries and proposals, 3 months on mss. Book catalog and ms guidelines free.
Nonfiction: Textbook (college level). Subjects include political theory, history, philosophy, religion, sociology. "Junior/senior undergrad level and up. All authors will be post doctoral, holding a current academic position."
Recent Nonfiction Title(s): *Defending Rights*, by Frank Arkin, General Counsel ACLU (civil rights); *Dead Reckonings*, by John Kurt Jacobsen (politics); *Some Chose to Stay*, by Alan Merman (contemporary philosophy/ethics).

‡HUNGRY MIND PRESS, 1648 Grand Ave., St. Paul MN 55105. Fax: (612)699-7190. E-mail: hmindpress@aol.com.
Acquisitions: Pearl Kilbride. "We publish adult-level, literary nonfiction." Publishes hardcover originals, trade paperback originals and reprints. Publishes 8-10 titles/year. Receives 200 queries and 300 mss/year. 25% of books from unagented writers. Royalties and advances vary. Publishes book 10 months after acceptance of ms. Accepts simultaneous submissions. Reports in 2 months on proposals. Book catalog for 6×9 SAE and 2 first-class stamps. Manuscript guidelines for #10 SASE.
Nonfiction: Biography, gift book, humor, literary nonfiction. Subjects include history, language/literature, nature/environment, philosophy (nonacademic), travel, women's issues/studies, memoirs, current events, agriculture/horticulture, art/architecture, cooking/foods/nutrition, education, ethnic, gardening, gay/lesbian, regional, religion, science, sociology. "We do not accept how-to or self-help/instructional mss." Submit proposal package, including letter, outline and at least one sample chapter with SASE.
Recent Nonfiction Title(s): *Hope, Human and Wild*, by Bill McKibben (environmental); *Perfection of the Morning*, by Sharon Butala (memoir/nature); *Crossing the Moon*, by Paulette Bates Awen (memoir/infertility).

HUNTER HOUSE, P.O. Box 2914, Alameda CA 94501. Website: http://www.hunterhouse.com. **Acquisitions:** Editor. "We are looking for manuscripts that will flesh out our three specific lines—health, family, community." Publishes hardcover and trade paperback originals and reprints. Publishes 10 titles/year. Receives 200-300 queries and 100 mss/year. 50% of books from first-time authors; 80% from unagented writers. Pays 12% royalty on net receipts, defined as selling price. Offers $0-2,000 advance. Publishes book 1-2 years after acceptance of final ms. Accepts simultaneous submissions. Reports in 2 months on queries, 3 months on proposals, 6 months on mss. Book catalog and ms guidelines for 8½×11 SAE with 3 first-class stamps.
Nonfiction: Reference, (only health reference); self-help, social issues. Subjects include education, health/medicine, women's issues/studies, sexuality, aging, family. Query with proposal package, including outline, 1 sample chapter, target audience info, relevant statistics, competition. Reviews artwork/photos as part of ms package. Send photocopies.
Recent Nonfiction Title(s): *Menopause Without Medicine*, by Linda Ojeda, Ph.D. (health).
Tips: Audience is "relatively savvy, concerned and sensitive people who are looking to educate themselves and their community about real-life issues that affect them. Please send as much information as possible about *who* your audience is, *how* your book addresses their needs, and *how* a publisher can reach that audience."

HUNTER PUBLISHING, INC., 300 Raritan Center Pkwy., Edison NJ 08818. Fax: (561)546-8040. E-mail: hunterpub @emi.net. Website: http://www.hunterpublishing.com. **Acquisitions:** Kim André, editor; Lissa Dailey; Nikki Krider. President: Michael Hunter. Estab. 1985. "We publish practical guides for travelers." Publishes 100 titles/year. Receives 300 submissions/year. 10% of books from first-time authors; 75% from unagented writers. Pays royalty. Offers negotiable advance. Publishes book 5 months after acceptance. Accepts simultaneous submissions. Reports in 3 weeks on queries, 1 month on ms. Book catalog for #10 SAE with 4 first-class stamps.
Imprint(s): Adventure Guides, Romantic Weekends Guides.
Nonfiction: Reference, travel guides. "We need travel guides to areas covered by few competitors: Caribbean Islands, South and Central America, Mexico, regional US from an active 'adventure' perspective." No personal travel stories or books not directed to travelers. Query or submit outline/synopsis and sample chapters. Reviews artwork/photos.
Recent Nonfiction Title(s): *Adventure Guide to the Georgia and Carolina Coasts,* by Howard; *Romantic Weekends*

in Virginia and Washington, DC, by Renouf; *The Amazon Up Close*, by Bloom.
Tips: "Guides should be destination-specific, rather than theme-based alone. Thus, 'travel with kids' is too broad; 'Florida with Kids' is OK. Make sure the guide doesn't duplicate what other guide publishers do. We need active adventure-oriented guides and more specialized guides for travelers in search of the unusual."

HUNTINGTON HOUSE PUBLISHERS, P.O. Box 53788, Lafayette LA 70505-3788.(318)237-7049. **Acquisitions:** Mark Anthony, editor-in-chief. Estab. 1982. "The company's goal is to educate and keep readers abreast of critical current events." Publishes hardcover, trade paperback and mass market paperback originals, trade paperback reprints. Publishes 10 titles/year. Receives 1,500 submissions/year. 25% of books from first-time authors; 90% from unagented writers. Average print order for a first book is 3,000-5,000. Pays up to 10% royalty on sale price. Publishes book 1 year after acceptance. Accepts simultaneous submissions. Reports in 4 months. Manuscript guidelines free.
Nonfiction: Current social and political issues, especially the globalist movement, conspiracy theories and New Age topics. Query with descriptive outline.
Recent Nonfiction Title(s): *Global Bondage*, by Cliff Kincaid; *Do Angels Really Exist?*, by David Dykes.
Tips: "Write clear, crisp, exciting mss that grab the reader. Published authors should expect a heavy publicity schedule."

HYPERION, Division of Disney Book Publishing, Inc., 114 Fifth Ave., New York NY 10011. **Acquisitions**: Leslie Wells, executive editor; Rick Kot, executive editor; Laurie Abkemeier, editor; Wendy Lefkon, executive editor. General interest publisher of both fiction and nonfiction. Publishes hardcover and trade paperback originals.
Imprint(s): Miramax Books, **Hyperion Books for Children**, Disney Press.
Nonfiction: Current events, humor, international affairs, popular culture, psychology, self-help. Query before submitting. *No unsolicited mss.*
Recent Nonfiction Title(s): *In Heaven as on Earth: A Vision of the Afterlife*, by M. Scott Peck; *Knee Deep in Paradise*, by Brett Butler.
Fiction: Mainstream, literary, juvenile, young adult. Query before submitting. *No unsolicited mss.*
Recent Fiction Title(s): *Burning Angel*, by James Lee Burke; *Sunset Express*, by Robert Crais.

‡HYPERION BOOKS FOR CHILDREN, Imprint of Hyperion, 114 Fifth Ave., New York NY 10011. (212)633-4400. Fax: (212)633-4833. **Acquisitions:** Lisa Holton, vice president/publisher. "The aim of Hyperion Books for Children is to create a dynamic children's program informed by Disney's creative vision, direct connection to children, and unparalleled marketing and distribution." Publishes hardcover and trade paperback originals. Publishes 210 titles/year. Receives 2,000 queries and mss/year. 50% of books from first-time authors. Pays royalty, "varies too widely to generalize." Advance varies. Publishes book 1 year after acceptance of ms. Accepts simultaneous submissions. Reports in 1 month. Book catalog and ms guidelines free.
 • This publisher accepts agented submissions only.
Nonfiction: Biography, children's/juvenile, illustrated book. Subjects include government/politics, history. Agented submissions only. Reviews artwork/photos as part of the ms package.
Recent Nonfiction Title(s): *Anastasia's Album*, by Hugh Brewster (picture book).
Fiction: Juvenile, picture books, young adult. Agented submissions only.
Recent Fiction Title(s): *McDuff*, by Rosemary Wells and Susan Jeffers (picture book); *Split Just Right*, by Adele Griffin (middle grade).
Tips: "Hyperion Books for Children are meant to appeal to an upscale children's audience. Study your audience. Look at and research current children's books. Who publishes what you like? Approach them. We are Disney, and are always looking for Disney material."

‡ICC PUBLISHING, INC., Subsidiary of International Chamber of Commerce, 156 Fifth Ave., Suite 308, New York NY 10010. (212)206-1150. Fax: (212)633-6025. E-mail: iccpub@interport.net. Website: http://www.iccwbo.org. **Acquisitons:** Rachelle Bijou, director. "We publish essential books and reference materials on all facets of international banking and business including letters of credit, collections, incoterms, law and arbitration and environmental business matters." Publishes paperback originals. Publishes 10 titles/year. Pays royalty or makes outright purchase. Publishes book approximately 1 year after acceptance of ms. Accepts simultaneous submissions. Reports in 1 month on queries and proposals. *Writer's Market* recommends allowing 2 months for reply. Book catalog and ms guidelines free.
 • ICC has published such authors as Charles del Busto, Jan Ramberg, and Nick Douch.
Nonfiction: Reference, technical. Subjects include international trade and business. Query or submit proposal package, including outline, table of contents and 3 sample chapters with SASE.
Recent Nonfiction Title(s): *Intellectual Property and International Trade*, ICC (author); *Keywords in International Trade*, ICC (author); *Bills of Exchange*, by Uwe Jahn.

‡ICON EDITIONS, Imprint of Westview Press, 10 E. 53rd St., New York NY 10036. (212)207-7000. **Acquisitions:** Cass Canfield, editor. Estab. 1973. "Icon Editions focuses on books in art history and art criticism for the academic and semi-academic market, college and university market." Publishes hardcover and trade paperback originals and reprints. Publishes 6-8 titles/year. Receives hundreds of queries/year. 25% of books from first-time authors; 80% from unagented writers. Royalty and advance vary. Publishes book 1 year after acceptance of ms. Accepts simultaneous submissions, if so noted. Returns submissions with SASE if author requests. Book catalog free.
Nonfiction: Books for academic and semi-academic market. Subjects include art/architecture, art history. Query with

SASE. Reviews artwork/photos as part of ms package "if we're interested." Send photocopies.
Recent Nonfiction Title(s): *Titian and Venetian Painting*, by Bruce Cole (art history); *The Methodologies of Art*, by Laurie Schneider-Adams; *Understanding Architecture*, by Leland M. Roth.

ICS BOOKS, INC., 1370 E. 86th Place, Merrillville IN 46410. (219)769-0585. Fax: (219)769-6085. E-mail: booksics @aol.com. Website: http://www.icsbooks.com. **Acquisitions:** Thomas A. Todd, publisher/editor. "We have been providing books for outdoor enthusiasts, sport and game players and gift-givers since 1979." Publishes trade paperback originals. Publishes 30-35 titles/year. 40% of books from first-time authors; 95% from unagented writers. Pays 10% royalty on net receipts. Publishes book 9 months after acceptance of ms. Accepts simultaneous submissions. Reports in 3 months on mss. Book catalog and ms guidelines available for $2.62 with SASE.
● ICS Books has published such authors as John Long, Michael Hodgson and Cliff Jacobson.
Nonfiction: Children's/juvenile, coffee table book, cookbook, gift book, how-to, humor, illustrated book. Subjects include animals, cooking/foods/nutrition, government/politics, health/medicine, nature/environment, photography, recreation, sports, travel, women's issues/studies. Send proposal package, including cover letter, outline, 3-5 sample chapters and SASE. Reviews artwork/photos as part of ms package. Query with SASE.
Recent Nonfiction Title(s): *Compass & Map Navigator*, by Michael Hodgson; *Dog Adoption*, by Joan Hustace Walker; *Billiards for Beginners*, by Steve Mizerak.
Tips: "Send a thoughtful proposal with cover letter, table of contents and synopsis. Include number of words, submission date and retail preference. We are looking for 15,000- to 18,000-word manuscripts on team sports and components of each sport (i.e., base stealing, hitting, passing, pitching, darts and billiards)." Query with SASE.

ICS PUBLICATIONS, Institute of Carmelite Studies, 2131 Lincoln Rd. NE, Washington DC 20002. (202)832-8489. Fax: (202)832-8967. Website: http://www.ocd.or.at/ics. **Acquisitions:** Steven Payne, O.C.D., editorial director. "Our audience consists of those interested in the Carmelite tradition or in developing their life of prayer and spirituality." Publishes hardcover and trade paperback originals and reprints. Publishes 8 titles/year. Receives 10-20 queries and 10 mss/year. 10% of books from first-time authors; 90-100% from unagented writers. Pays 2-6% royalty on retail price or makes outright purchase. Offers $500 advance. Publishes book 2 years after acceptance. Accepts simultaneous submissions, if so noted. Reports in 2 months on proposals. Book catalog for 7×10 SAE with 2 first-class stamps. Writer's guidelines for #10 SASE.
Nonfiction: Religious (should relate to Carmelite spirituality and prayer). "We are looking for significant works on Carmelite history, spirituality, and main figures (Saints Theresa, John of the Cross, Therese of Lisieux, etc.). Also open to more general works on prayer, spiritual direction, etc. Too often we receive proposals for works that merely repeat what has already been done, or are too technical for a general audience, or have little to do with the Carmelite tradition and spirit." Query or submit outline and 1 sample chapter.
Recent Nonfiction Title(s): *The Poetry of St. Thérese of Lisieux* (religious poetry); *Temptation and Discernment*, by Segundo Galilea (discernment of spirits).

IDE HOUSE PUBLISHERS, 4631 Harvey Dr., Mesquite TX 75150-1609. (214)686-5332. **Acquisitions:** Ryan Idol, senior editor (gay/lesbian studies); Geofferoi de Struckette, liberal studies coordinator; Nalinda Downs, senior editor (women's studies); David Ashford, associate editor (U.S. politics); Mary Meeks, associate editor (Third World politics); James Davidson, associate editor (European politics). "We publish books that reflect choice for mortals and reject all religious and political interference in the evolution of life and instill the reality of people's obligation to live with nature." Publishes hardcover and trade paperback originals. Publishes 10 titles/year. Receives 300 queries and 500 mss/year. 70% of books from first-time authors; 100% from unagented writers. Pays 4-7% royalty on retail price. Publishes book 1 year after acceptance of ms. Reports in 1 month on queries and proposals, 4 months on mss. Book catalog for 6×9 SAE with 5 first-class stamps. Manuscript guidelines for #10 SASE.
Imprint(s): Hercules Press (Bryan Estevez, executive senior vice president/editor).
Nonfiction: Women's history. Subjects include gay/lesbian, government/politics (liberal only), history, women's issues/studies. "We accept only nonsexist/nonhomophobic scholarly works." Query with outline and 2 sample chapters. All unsolicited mss returned unopened.
Recent Nonfiction Title(s): *Healing a Catholic Girlhood*, by Ann Dornblazer (rejecting patriarchy); *Oriental Women*, by Jid Lee (women's studies/literature); *What America Wants, America Gets*, by Joe Sharpnack (politics/humor).
Recent Poetry Title(s): *Darvik*, by Tim Oates (3rd world poetry/epic).
Tips: "Inaugurating poetry branch. We are emphasizing a quest for liberal politics and have budgeted for 100 titles in 1996-1998."

IDEALS CHILDREN'S BOOKS, Imprint of Hambleton-Hill Publishing, Inc., 1501 County Hospital Rd., Nashville TN 37218. **Acquisitions:** Suzanne Smith, copy editor. Ideals Children's Books publishes nonfiction, fiction and poetry for toddlers to 10-year-olds. Publishes children's hardcover and trade paperback originals. Publishes 40 titles/year. Receives 300 queries and 2,000-2,500 mss/year. 10% of books from first-time authors; 80% from unagented writers. Pay determined by individual contract. Publishes book up to 2 years after acceptance of ms. Reports in 6 months on queries, proposals and mss. Book catalog for 9×12 SASE with 11 first-class stamps. Manuscript guidelines for #10 SASE.
● This publisher only accepts unsolicited mss from agents and members of the Society of Children's Book

Writers & Illustrators, and previously published book authors may submit with a list of writing credits. They have published such authors as Carol Heyer and Donna Guthrie.

Nonfiction: Children's. Subjects include Americana, animals, art/architecture, nature/environment, science, sports. No middle-grade or young adult novels. Submit proposal package. Reviews artwork/photos as part of ms package. Send photocopies.

Recent Nonfiction Title(s): *What Do Animals Do in Winter?*, by Melvin and Gilda Berger (easy reader).

Fiction: Query or submit complete ms with SASE.

Recent Fiction Title(s): *The Sea Maidens of Japan*, by Lili Bell (Japanese culture, parent-child relationships); *Sing, Henrietta! Sing!*, by Lynn Downey (friendship/gardening).

Poetry: Query or submit complete ms with SASE.

Recent Poetry Title(s): *Let's Play as a Team!*, by P.K. Hallinan (teamwork); *Let's Care About Sharing!*, by P.K. Hallinan (cooperation/sharing).

Tips: Audience is children in the toddler to 10-year-old range. "We are seeking original, child-centered fiction for the picture book format. Innovative nonfiction ideas for easy readers are also being sought."

IDEALS PUBLICATIONS INC., 535 Metroplex Dr., Suite 250, Nashville TN 37211. (615)333-0478. Publisher: Patricia Pingry. Editor: Lisa Ragan. **Acquisitions:** Michelle Burke, copy editor. Estab. 1944. Publishes highly-illustrated seasonal and nostalgic hardbound books. Uses short prose and poetry. Also publishes *Ideals* magazine. Publishes 4 hardbound books, 6 *Ideals*, 1-2 others titles/year. Payment varies. Accepts simultaneous submissions. Accepts previously published material. Send information about when and where the piece previously appeared. Reports in 2 months. Manuscript guidelines free with SASE.

• No longer publishing children's titles.

IDYLL ARBOR, INC., P.O. Box 720, Ravensdale WA 98051. (206)432-3231. Fax: (206)432-3726. E-mail: idyarbor@ix.netcom.com. **Acquisitions:** Tom Blaschko. "Our books provide practical information on the current state and art of health care practice." Publishes hardcover and trade paperback originals and trade paperback reprints. Publishes 6 titles/year. 50% of books from first-time authors; 100% from unagented writers. Pays 8-20% royalty on wholesale price or retail price. Publishes book 6 months after acceptance of ms. Accepts simultaneous submissions. Reports in 1 month on queries, 2 months on proposals, 4 months on mss. Book catalog and ms guidelines free.

Nonfiction: Technical, textbook. Subjects include agriculture/horticulture (used in long term care activities or health care—therapy), health/medicine (for therapists, social service providers and activity directors), recreation (as therapy). "We look for manuscripts from authors with recent clinical experience. Good grounding in theory is required, but practical experience is more important." Query preferred with outline and 1 sample chapter. Reviews artwork/photos as part of ms package. Send photocopies.

Recent Nonfiction Title(s): *Quality Assurance*, by Cunningham and Martini (health care text); *Assessment Tools for Recreational Therapy, 2nd Edition*, by Joan Burlingame and Thomas M. Blaschko.

Tips: "We currently emphasize therapies (recreational, occupational, music, horticultural), activity directors in long term care facilities, and social service professionals. The books must be useful for the health practitioner who meets face to face with patients *or* the books must be useful for teaching undergraduate and graduate level classes. We are especially looking for therapists with a solid clinical background to write on their area of expertise."

‡ILR PRESS, Imprint of Cornell University Press, Sage House, 512 E. State St., Cornell University Press, Ithaca NY 14850. (607)277-2338 ext. 232. Fax: (607)277-2374. **Acquisitions:** F. Benson, editor. Estab. 1945. "We are interested in manuscripts with innovative perspectives on current workplace issues that concern both academics and the general public." Publishes hardcover and trade paperback originals and reprints. Publishes 12-15 titles/year. Pays royalty. Reports in 2 months on queries. Book catalog free.

Nonfiction: All titles relate to industrial relations and/or workplace issues including relevant work in the fields of history, sociology, political science, economics, human resources, and organizational behavior. Needs for the next year include "manuscripts on workplace problems, employment policy, immigration, current history, and dispute resolution that will interest academics and practitioners." Query or submit outline and sample chapters.

Recent Nonfiction Title(s): *On the Line at Subaru-Isuzu: The Japanese Model and the American Worker*, by Laurie Graham.

Tips: "Manuscripts must be well documented to pass our editorial evaluation, which includes review by academics in related fields."

‡IMAGE BOOKS, Imprint of Doubleday Books, 1540 Broadway, New York NY 10036. (22)354-6500. Fax: (212)782-8911. Website: http://www.bdd.com. **Acquisitions:** Trace Murphy, editor. Estab. 1956. "Image Books has grown from a classic Catholic list to include a variety of current and future classics, maintaining a high standard of quality as the finest in religious paperbacks." Publishes hardcover originals and reprints, trade paperback originals and reprints, mass market paperback originals and reprints. Publishes 12 titles/year. Receives 500 queries/year; receives 300 mss/year. 10% of books from first-time writers; no unagented writers. Pays royalty on net price. Advance varies. Publishes book 18 months after acceptance of ms. Accepts simultaneous submissions. Reports in 3 months on proposals. Book catalog for 9 × 12 SAE with 3 first-class stamps.

Nonfiction: Biography, cookbook, gift book, how-to, humor, illustrated book, reference, self-help. Subjects include

philosophy, psychology, religious/inspirational, world wisdom traditions, women's issues/studies. Query. Prefers agented submissions. Reviews artwork as part of ms package. Send photocopies.
Recent Nonfiction Title(s): *The Way of Woman*, by Helen Luke (meditations/psychology/spirituality); *The Rainbow People of God*, by Desmond Tutu (history/ethnic); *Tying Rocks to Clouds*, by William Elliott (spirituality).

INCENTIVE PUBLICATIONS, INC., 3835 Cleghorn Ave., Nashville TN 37215-2532. (615)385-2934. **Acquisitions:** Catherine Aldy, assistant to the president. Editor: Anna Quinn. Estab. 1970. "Incentive publishes developmentally appropriate instructional aids for tots to teens." Publishes paperback originals. Publishes 25-30 titles/year. Receives 350 submissions/year. 25% of books from first-time authors; 95% from unagented writers. Pays royalty or makes outright purchase. Publishes book an average of 1 year after acceptance. Reports in 1 month on queries. *Writer's Market* recommends allowing 2 months for reply.
Nonfiction: Teacher resource books in pre-K through 8th grade. Query with synopsis and detailed outline.
Recent Nonfiction Title(s): *180 Icebreakers to Strengthen Critical Thinking and Problem-Solving Skills*, by Forte and Schurr; *Risk It!*, by Newton (positive risk-taking); *A Is For Algebra*, by Breeden and Ralph.

INDEX PUBLISHING GROUP, INC., 3368 Governor Dr., Suite 273, San Diego CA 92122. (619)455-6100. Fax: (619)552-9050. E-mail: ipqbooks@indexbooks.com. Website: http://www.electriciti.com/~ipgbooks. **Acquisitions:** Linton M. Vandiver, publisher (casino gambling, privacy, identity changes); Henry L. Eisenson, vice president, editorial (radios and electronics). "We publish nonfiction, for both trade and special markets, with emphasis on casino gambling, communication electronics (scanners, ham radio, cellular telephones), and gray areas (e.g., identity, privacy, etc.)." Publishes hardcover and trade paperback originals. Publishes 25 titles/year. Receives 100 queries and 40 mss/year. 40% of books from first-time authors; 100% from unagented writers. Pays 6-20% royalty on price. Publishes book 4 months after acceptance. Accepts simultaneous submissions. Reports in 1 week on queries, 2 weeks on proposals. *Writer's Market* recommends allowing 2 months for reply. Book catalog and ms guidelines free and on website.
Nonfiction: Reference, technical, trade nonfiction. Subjects include gambling, computers/electronics, hobbies (consumer electronics: ham radio, scanners), electronic crime: cellular telephones, computer hacking, etc. "Index Publishing specializes in trade nonfiction (paper and hardcover) in three broad areas: (1) communication electronics, especially ham radio, scanning and radio monitoring, cellular telephones, computer hacking, etc.; (2) controversial topics such as eavesdropping, cable and satellite TV signal piracy, identity changes, electronic crime prevention; (3) gambling, especially casino gambling and gaming theory." Query.
Recent Nonfiction Title(s): *Smart Casino Gambling*, by Olaf Vancura, Ph.D.; *Radio Monitoring: The How-To Guide*, by T.J. Arey WBZGHA (shortwave, ham and scanners); *How to Investigate Your Friends, Enemies, and Lovers*.

INDIANA UNIVERSITY PRESS, 601 N. Morton St., Bloomington IN 47404-3796. (812)855-4203. Fax: (812)855-7931. E-mail: jgallman@indiana.edu. **Acquisitions:** Bob Sloan (religion, criminal justice); Janet Rabinowitch (art, African studies, Jewish studies, philosophy); John Gallman (Asian studies, politics); Joan Catapomo (Black studies, film, women's studies); Jeff Ankrom (music). Estab. 1951. Publishes hardcover originals, paperback originals and reprints. Publishes 175 titles/year. 30% of books from first-time authors; 98% from unagented writers. Average print order for a first book varies depending on subject. Nonauthor subsidy publishes 9% of books. Pays maximum 10% royalty on retail price. Offers occasional advance. Publishes book 1 year after acceptance. Reports in 2 months. Book catalog and ms guidelines free.
Nonfiction: Scholarly books on humanities, history, philosophy, religion, Jewish studies, Black studies, criminal justice, translations, semiotics, public policy, film, music, philanthropy, social sciences, regional materials, African studies, Russian Studies, women's studies, and serious nonfiction for the general reader. Also interested in textbooks and works with course appeal in designated subject areas. Query with outline and sample chapters. "Queries should include as much descriptive material as is necessary to convey scope and market appeal to us." Reviews artwork/photos.
Recent Nonfiction Title(s): *The Making of a Conservative Environmentalist*, by Gordon Durnil.
Tips: Looking for fewer, better-selling books. "We have been a bit more cautious about specialized monographs."

INNER TRADITIONS INTERNATIONAL, P.O. Box 388, 1 Park St., Rochester VT 05767. (802)767-3174. Fax: (802)767-3726. **Acquisitions:** Jon Graham, editor. Estab. 1975. "We are interested in the relationship of the spiritual and transformative aspects of world cultures." Publishes hardcover and trade paperback originals and reprints. Publishes 40 titles/year. Receives 2,000 submissions/year. 5% of books from first-time authors; 5% from unagented writers. Pays 8-10% royalty on net receipts. Offers $1,000 average advance. Publishes book 1 year after acceptance. Reports in 3 months on queries, 6 months on mss. Book catalog and ms guidelines free.
Imprint(s): Inner Traditions, Destiny Books, Healing Arts Press, Park Street Press, Destiny Recordings, Destiny Audio Editions, Inner Traditions En Espanol, Inner Traditions India.
Nonfiction: Subjects include anthropology/archaeology, natural foods, cooking, nutrition, health/alternative medicine, history and mythology, indigenous cultures, music/dance, nature/environment, esoteric philosophy, psychology, world religions, women's issues/studies, New Age. Query or submit outline and sample chapters with SASE. Does not return mss without SASE. Reviews artwork/photos as part of ms package.
Recent Nonfiction Title(s): *Chi Kung: The Chinese Art of Mastering Energy*, by Yves Réquéna (Eastern traditions); *Light & Shadow Tarot*, Brian Williams and Michael Gosaferd (tarot); *Meals That Heal*, Lisa Turner (health/cooking).
Tips: "We are not interested in autobiographical stories of self-transformation. We do not accept any electronic submissions (via e-mail)."

‡INNISFREE PRESS, (formerly LuraMedia), 136 Roumfort Rd., Philadelphia PA 19119. (215)247-4085. Fax: (215)247-2343. E-mail: InnisfreeP@aol.com. **Acquisitions:** Marcia Broucek, publisher. "Innisfree's mission is to publish books that nourish individuals both emotionally and spiritually; to offer books that 'call to the deep heart's core' " Publishes trade paperback originals. Publishes 6-8 titles/year. Receives 500 queries and 300 mss/year. 50% of books from first-time authors; 90% from unagented writers. Pays 10-15% royalty on wholesale price. Publishes book 1 year after acceptance of ms. Accepts simultaneous submissions. Reports in 1 month on queries; 2 months on proposals; 3 months on mss. Book catalog and ms guidelines free.
   • Innisfree Press has published such authors as Judith Duerk, Renita Weems and Ted Loder.
Nonfiction: Gift book, self-help, books for discussion groups. Subjects include child guidance/parenting, health/medicine, holistic body/mind/spirit, nature/environment, psychology, religion, women's issues/studies. Query with proposal package, including outline, 2 sample chapters, potential audience, and what makes the book unique, with SASE. Reviews artwork/photos as part of ms package. Send photocopies.
Recent Nonfiction Title(s): *Success Redefined: Notes to a Working Woman*, by Lori Giovannoni (motivational); *Silence: Making the Journey to Inner Quiet*, by Barbara Erakko Taylor (personal growth); *Spiritual Lemons: Biblical Women, Irreverent Laughter, Righteous Rage*, by Lyn Brakeman (biblical study).

INSIGHT BOOKS TRADE, Imprint of Plenum Publishing Corp., 233 Spring St., New York NY 10013-1578. (212)620-8000. Fax: (212)463-0742. E-mail: frankd@plenum.com. Website: http://www.plenum.com. **Acquisitions:** Frank K. Darmstadt, editor. Plenum estab. 1946. "Insight Books are to-the-point, unafraid to address important or controversial issues, and its authors are qualified to promote their work." Publishes trade nonfiction hardcover and paperback originals. Publishes 12 titles/year. Receives 1,000 submissions/year. 50% of books from first-time authors; 75% from unagented writers. Prefers proposals from agents. Pays royalty. Advance varies. Publishes book 1-2 years after acceptance. Accepts simultaneous submissions. Reports in 2 months. Book catalog free.
Nonfiction: Self-help, how-to, treatises. Subjects include anthropology, business/economics, education, ethnic, gay and lesbian studies, government/politics, health/medicine, money/finance, nature/environment, psychology, science, sociology, women's issues/studies. Submit outline, sample chapters and résumé. No e-mail proposals.
Recent Nonfiction Title(s): *Success with Heart Failure*, by Dr. M. Silver (health); *HIV-Negative*, by W. Johnston (AIDS/gay studies); *The Tough-on-Crime Myth*, by P. Elikann (social issues).
Tips: "Writers have the best chance selling authoritative, well-written, serious information in areas of health, mental health, social sciences, education and contemporary issues. Our audience consists of informed general readers as well as professionals and students in human, life and social sciences. If I were a writer trying to market a book today, I would say something interesting, important and useful, and say it well."

‡INSIGNIA PUBLISHING, 1429 G St. NW, Washington DC 20005. (301)540-4413. **Acquisitions:** Bruce W. Kletz, president. Publishes hardcover and trade paperback originals. 100% of books from first-time authors; 100% from unagented writers. Pays 8-15% royalty on retail price. Reports in 2 months on proposals. Manuscript guidelines free.
Nonfiction: Biography, coffee table book, reference. Subjects include government/politics, history, military/war. "We're looking for Gulf War topics, historical/military biography, professional military education." Query with outline (annotated), 1 sample chapter or writing sample for new authors and SASE. Reviews artwork/photos as part of ms package. Send photocopies.
Recent Nonfiction Title(s): *Gassed in the Gulf: The Inside Story of the Pentagon-CIA Cover-up of Gulf War Syndrome*, by Patrick E. Eddington.

INSTITUTE OF POLICE TECHNOLOGY AND MANAGEMENT, University of North Florida, 4567 St. Johns Bluff Rd., S., Jacksonville FL 32224-2645. (904)646-2722. **Acquisitions:** Richard C. Hodge, editor. "Our publications are principally for law enforcement. Our authors are almost all present or retired law enforcement officers with excellent, up-to-date knowledge." Publishes trade paperback originals. Publishes 8 titles/year. Receives 30 queries and 12 mss/year. 50% of books from first-time authors; 100% from unagented writers. Pays 25% royalty on retail price or makes outright purchase of $300-2,000 (may be some combination of above). No advance. Publishes book 2 months after acceptance of ms. Accepts simultaneous submissions. Reports in 1 month.
Nonfiction: Illustrated book, reference, technical, textbook. Subjects include law enforcement. "Our authors are not necessarily persons whose works have been published. Manuscripts should *not* be submitted until the author has talked with the editor on the telephone. The best procedure is to have this talk before beginning to write. Articles and short handbooks are acceptable as well as longer manuals." Query by phone first. Reviews artwork/photos as part of ms package. Send photocopies.
Recent Nonfiction Title(s): *DWI Mobile Videotaping for Police and Prosecutors: Policy, Procedures and Law*, by Jim Kuboviak and Chester Quarles.
Tips: Audience is law enforcement, private investigators, personal injury attorneys, insurance investigators and adjustors.

‡INTER TRADE CORPORATION, 6767-B Peachtree Ind. Blvd., Norcross GA 30092. (770)446-2650. Fax: (770)446-2685. E-mail: editor@superchoice.com. Website: www.superchoice.com. **Acquisitions:** Susan Mayer, vice president. "We produce personal and professional development books." Publishes trade paperback originals. Publishes 5-10 titles/year. Receives 20 queries and 5 mss/year. 30% of books from first-time authors; 30% from unagented writers. Makes outright purchase. Publishes book 6 months after acceptance of ms. Accepts simultaneous submissions. Reports in 1 month. *Writer's Market* recommends allowing 2 months for reply. Book catalog free.

Nonfiction: How-to, reference, self-help. Subjects include business/economics, computers/electronics, education, money/finance, software. Submit outline.
Recent Nonfiction Title(s): *PC GUIDE Introduction to Computers*; *PC GUIDE for Windows 95.*

INTERCULTURAL PRESS, INC., P.O. Box 700, Yarmouth ME 04096. (207)846-5181. Fax: (207)846-5181. E-mail: interculturalpress@internetmci.com. **Acquisitions:** Judy Carl-Hendrick, managing editor. Estab. 1980. Intercultural Press publishes materials related to intercultural relations, including the practical concerns of living and working in foreign countries, the impact of cultural differences on personal and professional relationships and the challenges of interacting with people from unfamiliar cultures, whether at home or abroad. Publishes hardcover and trade paperback originals. Publishes 10-15 titles/year. Receives 50-80 submissions/year. 50% of books from first-time authors; 95% of books from unagented writers. Pays royalty. Offers small advance occasionally. Publishes book within 2 years after acceptance. Accepts simultaneous submissions. Reports in 2 months. Book catalog and ms guidelines free.
Nonfiction: Reference, textbook and theory. "We want books with an international or domestic intercultural or multicultural focus, especially those on business operations (how to be effective in intercultural business activities), education (textbooks for teaching intercultural subjects, for instance) and training (for Americans abroad or foreign nationals coming to the United States). Our books are published for educators in the intercultural field, business people engaged in international business, managers concerned with cultural diversity in the workplace, and anyone who works in an occupation where cross-cultural communication and adaptation are important skills. No mss without intercultural focus." Accepts nonfiction translations. Query with outline or proposal. No unsolicited mss.
Recent Nonfiction Title(s): *Survival Kit for Multicultural Living*, by Elen Summerfield; *The Color of Words*, by Phil Herbst (reference); *Understanding Arabs*, by Nydell (cross-cultural interaction).

INTERLINK PUBLISHING GROUP, INC., 46 Crosby St., Northampton MA 01060. (413)582-7054. Fax: (413)582-7057. E-mail: interpg@aol.com. **Acquisitions:** Michel Moushabeck, publisher. "Interlink publishes a general trade list of adult fiction and nonfiction with an emphasis on books that have a wide appeal while also meeting high intellectual and literary standards." Publishes hardcover and trade paperback originals. Publishes 30 titles/year. Receives 200 submissions/year. 30% of books from first-time authors; 50% from unagented writers. Pays 5-7% royalty on retail price. Publishes book 18 months after acceptance. Accepts simultaneous submissions. Reports in 1 month on queries. *Writer's Market* recommends allowing 2 months for reply. Book catalog and ms guidelines free.
Imprint(s): Interlink Books, Crocodile Books, USA, Olive Branch Press.
● Interlink is looking for folktale collections to add to its International Folk Tale series; also political/current affairs titles for new Voices & Visions series as well as titles on world travel.
Nonfiction: World travel, world history and politics, ethnic cooking. Submit outline and sample chapters for adult nonfiction; complete ms for juvenile titles. Reviews artwork/photos as part of ms package.
Recent Nonfiction Title(s): *A Traveller's History of China*, by Stephen Haw (travel/history); *A Traveller's Wine Guide to France*, by Christopher Felden.
Fiction: Ethnic, international feminist. "Adult fiction—We are looking for translated works relating to the Middle East, Africa or Latin America. Juvenile/Picture Books—Our list is full for the next two years. No science fiction, romance, plays, erotica, fantasy, horror. Submit outline/synopsis and sample chapters.
Recent Fiction Title(s): *Samarkand*, by Amin Maalouf (translated fiction).
Recent Poetry Title(s): *On Entering the Sea*, by Nizar Qabbani (translated poetry).
Tips: "Any submissions that fit well in our International Folktale, Emerging Voices: New International Fiction Series or The Independent Walker Series will receive careful attention."

INTERNATIONAL CITY/COUNTY MANAGEMENT ASSOCIATION, 777 N. Capitol St., NE, Suite 500, Washington DC 20002. (202)962-3648. **Acquisitions:** Verity Weston-Truby, senior editor; Christine Ulrich, senior editor. "Our mission is to enhance the quality of local government and to support and assist professional local administrators in the United States and other countries." Publishes hardcover and paperback originals. Publishes 10-15 titles/year. Receives 50 queries and 20 mss/year. 20% of books from first-time authors; 100% from unagented writers. Makes negotiable outright purchase. Publishes book 18 months after acceptance of ms. Reports in 1 month. *Writer's Market* recommends allowing 2 months for reply. Book catalog and ms guidelines free.
Nonfiction: Reference, textbook, training manuals. Subjects include local government. Query with outline and 1 sample chapter. Reviews artwork/photos as part of ms package. Send photocopies.
Recent Nonfiction Title(s): *Records Management*, by Julian L. Mims; *Telecommunications: Planning for the Future*; *Accountability for Performance*, edited by David N. Ammons (performance measurement).

INTERNATIONAL FOUNDATION OF EMPLOYEE BENEFIT PLANS, P.O. Box 69, Brookfield WI 53008-0069. (414)786-6700. Fax: (414)786-8670. E-mail: books@ifebp.org. Website: http://www.ifebp.org. **Acquisitions:** Dee Birschel, senior director of publications. Estab. 1954. "We publish general and technical monographs on all aspects of employee benefits—pension plans, health insurance, etc." Publishes hardcover and trade paperback originals. Publishes 10 titles/year. Receives 20 submissions/year. 15% of books from first-time authors; 80% from unagented writers. Pays 5-15% royalty on wholesale and retail price. Publishes book 1 year after acceptance. Reports in 3 months on queries. Book catalog free. Manuscript guidelines for SASE.
Nonfiction: Reference, technical, consumer information, textbook. Subjects limited to health care, pensions, retirement planning, and employee benefits. Query with outline.

Recent Nonfiction Title(s): *Managed Vision Benefits*, by Jessie Rosenthal; *New Era of Benefits Communication*, by Ann Black; *Health Care Cost Management—A Basic Guide, Third Edition*, by Madelon Lubin.
Tips: "Be aware of interests of employers and the marketplace in benefits topics, for example, how AIDS affects employers, health care cost containment."

INTERNATIONAL MARINE, Division of the McGraw-Hill Companies, P.O. Box 220, Camden ME 04843-0220. Fax: (207)236-6314. **Acquisitions:** Jonathan Eaton, editorial director. Estab. 1969. International Marine publishes "good books about boats." Publishes hardcover and paperback originals. Publishes 40 titles/year. Receives 500-700 mss/year. 30% of books from first-time authors; 80% from unagented writers. Pays standard royalties based on net price. Offers advance. Publishes book 1 year after acceptance. Reports in 2 months. Book catalog and ms guidelines for SASE.
Imprint(s): Ragged Mountain Press.
Nonfiction: "Marine nonfiction. A wide range of subjects include: boatbuilding, boat design, yachting, seamanship, boat maintenance, maritime history, etc." All books are illustrated. "Material in all stages welcome." Query first with outline and 2-3 sample chapters. Reviews artwork/photos as part of ms package.
Recent Nonfiction Title(s): *Inspecting the Aging Sailboat*, by Don Casey (how-to); *Nautical Knots & Lines Illustrated*, by Snyder and Snyder (how-to); *The International Guide to Fly-Tying Materials*, by Clarke and Spaight.
Tips: "Writers should be aware of the need for clarity, accuracy and interest. Many progress too far in the actual writing, with an unsaleable topic."

INTERNATIONAL MEDICAL PUBLISHING, P.O. Box 479, McLean VA 22101-0479. (703)519-0807. Fax: (703)519-0806. E-mail: masterso@patriot.net. **Acquisitions:** Thomas Masterson, MD, editor. Publishes mass market paperback originals. Publishes 11 titles/year. Receives 20 queries and 2 mss/year. 5% of books from first-time authors; 100% from unagented writers. Pays royalty on gross receipts. Publishes book 8 months after acceptance. Reports in 2 months on queries. Book catalog free.
Nonfiction: Reference, textbook. Health/medicine subjects. "We distribute only through medical and scientific bookstores. Look at our books. Think about practical material for doctors-in-training. We are interested in handbooks. Keep prose simple when dealing with very technical subjects." Query with outline.
Recent Nonfiction Title(s): *How to Be a Truly Excellent Medical Student*, by Robert Lederman (medical).
Tips: Audience is medical students, physicians and nurses.

INTERNATIONAL PUBLISHERS CO., INC., P.O. Box 3042, New York NY 10116-3042. (212)366-9816. Fax: (212)366-9820. **Acquisitions:** Betty Smith, president. Estab. 1924. International Publishers Co., Inc., emphasizes books based on Marxist science. Publishes hardcover originals, trade paperback originals and reprints. Publishes 5-6 titles/ year. Receives 50-100 mss/year. 10% of books from first-time authors. Pays 5-7½% royalty on paperbacks; 10% royalty on cloth. No advance. Publishes book 6 months after acceptance. Accepts simultaneous submissions. Reports in 1 month on queries with SASE, 6 months on mss. Book catalog and ms guidelines for SAE with 2 first-class stamps.
   ● This publisher has reduced their number of books published from 10-15 titles/year to 5-6 titles/year.
Nonfiction: Biography, reference, textbook. Subjects include Americana, economics, history, philosophy, politics, social sciences, Marxist-Leninist classics. "Books on labor, black studies and women's studies based on Marxist science have high priority." Query or submit outline, sample chapters and SASE. Reviews artwork/photos as part of ms package.
Recent Nonfiction Title(s): *Economics of Racism, II*, by Victor Penlo and others.
Tips: No fiction or poetry.

INTERNATIONAL WEALTH SUCCESS, P.O. Box 186, Merrick NY 11570-0186. (516)766-5850. Fax: (516)766-5919. **Acquisitions:** Tyler G. Hicks, editor. Estab. 1967. "We publish useful hands-on self-help books for people seeking to start, and succeed in, their own business." Publishes 10 titles/year. Receives 100 submissions/year. 100% of books from first-time authors; 100% from unagented writers. Average print order for a first book "varies from 500 and up, depending on the book." Pays 10% royalty on wholesale or retail price. Buys all rights. Offers usual advance of $1,000, but this varies depending on author's reputation and nature of book. Publishes book 4 months after acceptance. Reports in 1 month. Book catalog and ms guidelines for 9 × 12 SAE with 3 first-class stamps.
Nonfiction: Self-help, how-to. "Techniques, methods, sources for building wealth. Highly personal, how-to-do-it with plenty of case histories. Books are aimed at wealth builders and are highly sympathetic to their problems." Financing, business success, venture capital, etc. Length: 60,000-70,000 words. Query. Reviews artwork/photos.
Recent Nonfiction Title(s): *How to Run a Profitable Child-Care Referral Service*, by William Frederick.
Tips: "With the mass layoffs in large and medium-size companies there is an increasing interest in owning your own business. So we will focus on more how-to hands-on material on owning—and becoming successful in—one's own business of any kind. Our market is the BWB—Beginning Wealth Builder. This person has so little money that financial planning is something they never think of. Instead, they want to know what kind of a business they can get into to make some money without a large investment. Write for this market and you have millions of potential readers. Remember—there are a lot more people *without* money than *with* money."

INTERWEAVE PRESS, 201 E. Fourth St., Loveland CO 80537. (667)669-7672. Fax: (970)669-8317. **Acquisitions:** Judith Durant, book editor. Estab. 1975. Interweave Press publishes instructive and inspirational titles relating to the fiber arts and herbal topics. Publishes hardcover and trade paperback originals. Publishes 8-12 titles/year. Receives 50 submissions/year. 60% of books from first-time authors; 98% from unagented writers. Pays 10% royalty on net receipts.

Offers $500 average advance. Publishes book 1 year after acceptance. Accepts simultaneous submissions, if so noted. Reports in 2 months. Book catalog and ms guidelines free.

Nonfiction: How-to, technical. Subjects limited to fiber arts—basketry, spinning, knitting, dyeing and weaving, and herbal topics—gardening, cooking, and lore. Submit outline/synopsis and sample chapters. Reviews artwork/photos.

Recent Nonfiction Title(s): *Ask the Doctor: Herbs and Supplements for Better Health*, by Dr. Derrick Desilva; *Navajo Weaving Way*, by Noel Bennett (crafts); *Enchanted Knitting*, by Catherine Cartwright-Jones and Roy Jones.

Tips: "We are looking for very clear, informally written, technically correct manuscripts, generally of a how-to nature, in our specific fiber and herb fields only. Our audience includes a variety of creative self-starters who appreciate inspiration and clear instruction. They are often well educated and skillful in many areas."

IOWA STATE UNIVERSITY PRESS, 2121 S. State Ave., Ames IA 50014-8300. (515)292-0140. Fax: (515)292-3348. E-mail: acqisup@netins.net. **Acquisitions:** Gretchen Van Houten, editor-in-chief (veterinary medicine and animal science); Jim Ice (agriculture), editor; Judy Brown (journalism, mass communications), editor; Linda Speth (Iowa trade), editor; Sally Clayton (aviation), marketing manager. Estab. 1924. "Iowa State University Press focuses on the areas of agriculture, aviation, journalism and mass communications, veterinary medicine and to a limited extent Iowa trade books." Publishes hardcover and paperback originals. Publishes 55 titles/year. Receives 450 submissions/year. 98% of books from unagented writers. Average print order for a first book is 1,000. Nonauthor-subsidy publishes some titles, based on sales potential of book and contribution to scholarship on monographs. Pays 10% or less royalty for trade books on wholesale price. No advance. Publishes book 1 year after acceptance. Accepts simultaneous submissions, if so noted. Reports in up to 6 months. Book catalog free. Manuscript guidelines for SASE.

Nonfiction: Publishes agriculture, food and nutrition, economics, aviation, journalism, veterinary sciences. Submit outline and several sample chapters, preferably not in sequence. Looks for "unique approach to subject."

Recent Nonfiction Title(s): *Equine Color Genetics*, by D. Philip Sponenberg (veterinary medicine).

IRI/SKYLIGHT TRAINING AND PUBLISHING, INC., 2626 Clearbrook Dr., Arlington Heights IL 60005. (800)348-4474. E-mail: info@iriskylight.com. Website: http://www.iriskylight.com. **Acquisitions:** T.B. Zaban, managing editor. "We seek books that provide a bridge from the theory to practice in the classroom." Publishes 20-25 titles/year. Receives 100 queries and 60 mss/year. 40% of books from first-time authors; 100% from unagented writers. Pays 5-10% royalty on retail price. No advance. Publishes book 9 months after acceptance of ms. Reports in 1 month on queries, 4 months on proposals and mss. Book catalog and ms guidelines free.

Nonfiction: Educational how-to for K-12 classroom practitioners. Multiple intelligences, integrated curriculum, year-round education, multi-age classroom, diversity, inclusion, cooperative learning, higher-level thinking and technology in the classroom. Submit outline with brief synopsis of each chapter and 2 sample chapters. Reviews artwork/photos as part of ms package. Send photocopies.

Recent Nonfiction Title(s): *A Multiple Intelligences Road to a Quality Classroom*, by Sally Berman (activity-based classroom lessons).

Tips: "Target K-12 classroom practitioners, staff developers, school administrators, education students. We are interested in research-based books that tell teachers in a clear, friendly, direct manner how to apply educational best practices to their classrooms. We are especially interested in books that give teachers the tools to create lessons on their own, no matter what subject area they teach."

ITALICA PRESS, 595 Main St., Suite 605, New York NY 10044-0047. (212)935-4230. Fax: (212)838-7812. E-mail: italica@aol.com. **Acquisitions:** Ronald G. Musto, publisher. Estab. 1985. Italica Press publishes English translations of modern Italian fiction and medieval and Renaissance nonfiction. Publishes trade paperback originals. Publishes 6 titles/year. Receives 75 queries and 20 mss/year. 50% of books from first-time authors; 100% from unagented writers. Pays 7-15% royalty on wholesale price. Publishes book 1 year after acceptance of ms. Accepts simultaneous submissions. Reports in 1 month on queries. *Writer's Market* recommends allowing 2 months for reply. Book catalog free.

Nonfiction: "We publish *only* English translations of medieval and Renaissance source materials and English translations of modern Italian fiction." Query. Reviews artwork/photos as part of ms package. Send photocopies.

Tips: "We are interested in considering a wide variety of medieval and Renaissance topics (not historical fiction), and for modern works we are only interested in translations from Italian fiction."

J & L LEE CO., P.O. Box 5575, Lincoln NE 68505. **Acquisitions:** James L. McKee, publisher. "Virtually everything we publish is of a Great Plains nature." Publishes trade paperback originals and reprints. Publishes 5 titles/year. Receives 25 queries and 5-10 mss/year. 20% of books from first-time authors; 60% from unagented writers. Pays 10% royalty on retail price or makes outright purchase of $100 minimum. Rarely offers advance. Publishes book 10 months after acceptance of ms. Accepts simultaneous submissions. Reports in 6 months on queries and mss, 1 month on proposals. Book catalog free.

Imprint(s): Salt Creek Press, Young Hearts.

Nonfiction: Biography, reference. Subjects include Americana, history, regional. Query.

Recent Nonfiction Title(s): *Luther North, Frontier Scout*, by Jeff O'Donnell (history); *Nebraska Place Names*, by Elton Perkey (history).

Recent Fiction Title(s): *How Cold Is It?*, by Roger Welsch & Paul Fell (humor).

JAIN PUBLISHING CO., P.O. Box 3523, Fremont CA 94539. (510)659-8272. Fax: (510)659-0501. E-mail: mail@jainpub.com. Website: http://www.jainpub.com. **Acquisitions:** M.K. Jain, editor-in-chief. Estab. 1989. "Our goal is to

provide quality reading material at reasonable prices." Publishes hardcover and trade paperback originals and reprints. Publishes 10 titles/year. Receives 500 queries/year. 20% of books from first-time authors; 100% from unagented writers. Pays up to 10% royalty on net sales. Offers occasional advance. Publishes book 1-2 years after acceptance. Reports in 3 months on mss. Book catalog for 6×9 SAE with 2 first-class stamps. Manuscript guidelines for #10 SASE. "Book catalog and ms guidelines can also be viewed on our website."
Imprint(s): Asian Humanities Press.
  • Jain has published such authors as Archie J. Bahm, Paul L. Leppert and Noble Ross Reat.
Nonfiction: Self-help, motivational/inspirational, how-to, foods/nutrition (vegetarian), health/fitness, gift books, guides and handbooks, computer/internet books (general purpose), business/management, reference, textbooks. "Manuscripts should be related to our subjects and written in an 'easy to read' and understandable format. Preferably between 60,000-80,000 words." Submit proposal package, including cv and list of prior publications with SASE. Reviews artwork/photos as part of ms package. Send photocopies.
Recent Nonfiction Title(s): *Common Sense Management*, by Milt Thomas (business/management); *Hands on Website Design*, by Andreas Ramos (computers/Internet).
Tips: Jain is putting more emphasis on general purpose computer/internet books and books dealing with health/fitness and business/management. Continued emphasis on undergraduate textbooks. "We're interested more in user-oriented books than general treatises."

‡JAMESON BOOKS INC., 722 Columbus St., P.O. Box 738, Ottawa IL 61350. (815)434-7905. Fax: (815)434-7907. **Acquisitions:** Jameson G. Campaigne, publisher/editor. Estab. 1986. "Jameson Books publishes conservative, even libertarian politics and economics; Chicago area history and biographies." Publishes hardcover originals. Publishes 12 titles/year. Receives 500-1,000 queries/year; 300 mss/year. 33% of books from first-time authors; 33% from unagented writers. Pays 6-15% royalty on retail price. Offers $1,000-25,000 advance. Publishes book 1-12 months after acceptance. Accepts simultaneous submissions. Reports in 6 months on queries. Book catalog for 8×10 SASE.
Nonfiction: Biography. Subjects include business/economics, history, regional (Chicago area). Query with 1 sample chapter and SASE (essential). *Submissions are not returned without an SASE.*
Recent Nonfiction Title(s): *Capitalism*, by George Reisman (economics); *The Thing of It Is . . .* , by John Calloway (essays); *Politics as a Noble Calling*, by F. Clifton White (memoirs).
Fiction: Frontier. Interested in pre-cowboy frontier fiction. Query with 1 sample chapter and SASE.
Recent Fiction Title(s): *Carry the Wind*, by Terry Johnston; *Yellowstone Kelly: Gentleman and Scout*, by Peter Bowen; *The Woodsman*, by Don Right.

THOMAS JEFFERSON UNIVERSITY PRESS, MC111L, 100 E. Normal St., Kirksville MO 63501-4221. (816)785-4665. Fax: (816)785-4181. E-mail: tjup@truman.edu. Website: http://www.truman.edu/tjup. **Acquisitions:** Robert V. Schnucker, director. Thomas Jefferson University Press publishes books in the humanities and social sciences with high standards of production quality. Publishes 4-6 titles/year. Pays 25% maximum royalty on net sales.
Nonfiction: Biography, illustrated book, textbook and monographs on Americana, anthropology/archaeology, art/architecture, government/politics, history, language/literature, military/war, philosophy, religion, sociology and translation.
Recent Nonfiction Title(s): *Bethsaida*, by Aran/Freund (archaeology); *Naked Heart*, by Pagliaro (biography/history).
Poetry: Original poetry and translations.
Recent Poetry Title(s): *Burning of Los Angeles*, by Samuel Maio; *Kangaroo Paws*, by David Ray.

JEWISH LIGHTS PUBLISHING, LongHill Partners, Inc., P.O. Box 237, Sunset Farms Offices, Rt. 4, Woodstock VT 05091. (802)457-4000. **Acquisitions:** Jennifer P. Goneau, editorial assistant. "We publish books which fall under the category of religion, theology, philosophy, history and spirituality which can be read by people of all faiths and all backgrounds." Publishes hardcover and trade paperback originals, trade paperback reprints. Publishes 12 titles/year. Receives 500 queries and 250 mss/year. 25% of books from first-time authors; 90% from unagented writers. Pays royalty on net sales, 10% on first printing, then increases. Publishes book 1 year after acceptance of ms. Accepts simultaneous submissions. Reports in 3 months. Book catalog and ms guidelines free.
Nonfiction: Children's/juvenile, illustrated book, reference, self-help, spirituality, inspiration. Subjects include business/economics (with spiritual slant, finding spiritual meaning in one's work), health/medicine, healing/recovery, wellness, aging, life cycle, history, nature/environment, philosophy, theology, religion, women's issues/studies. "We do *not* publish haggadot, biography, poetry, cookbooks or books aiming to be most successfully sold during any specific holiday season." Submit proposal package, including cover letter, table of contents, 2 sample chapters and SASE. (Postage must cover weight of ms.) Reviews artwork/photos as part of ms package. Send photocopies.
Recent Nonfiction Title(s): *How to Be A Perfect Stranger: A Guide to Etiquette in Other People's Religious Ceremonies, Vol. 2*, edited by Stuart M. Matlins and Arthur J. Magida (spirituality/reference); *Lifecycles, Vol. 2: Jewish Women on Biblical Themes in Contemporary Life*, edited by Rabbi Debra Orenstein and Rabbi Jane Rachel Litman.
Tips: "We publish books for all faiths and backgrounds. Many also reflect the Jewish wisdom tradition."

JEWISH PUBLICATION SOCIETY, 1930 Chestnut St., Philadelphia PA 19103. (215)564-5925. **Acquisitions**: Dr. Ellen Frankel, editor-in-chief; Bruce Black, children's editor. "We are interested in books of Judaica for a college-educated readership." Publishes hardcover and trade paperback originals, trade paperback reprints. Publishes 12 titles/year. 20% of books from first-time authors; 75% from unagented writers. Pays 10-15% royalty on wholesale price.

Offers $1,000-4,000 advance. Publishes book 18 months after acceptance. Accepts simultaneous submissions, if noted. Reports in 3 months on proposals. Book catalog free.

Nonfiction: Children's/juvenile, reference, trade books. Subjects include history, language/literature, religion, women's issues/studies. "No monographs or textbooks. We do not accept memoirs, biographies, art books, coffee-table books." Children's books include picture books, biography, history, religion, young middle readers; young adult include biography, history, religion, sports. Query with proposal package including outline, description and proposed table of contents, curriculum vitae with SASE.

Recent Nonfiction Title(s): *Biblical Women Unbound: Counter-Tales*, by Norma Rosen; *The Kids' Catalog of Jewish Holidays*, by David A. Adler.

Poetry: "We publish no original poetry in English. We would consider a topical anthology on a Jewish theme." Query.

Recent Poetry Title(s): *Modern Poems on the Bible*, edited by David Curzon (responses to biblical texts - 20 C.).

Tips: "Our audience is college-educated Jewish readers interested in Bible, Jewish history or Jewish practice, as well as young readers."

JIST WORKS, INC., 720 N. Park Ave., Indianapolis IN 46202-3431. (317)264-3720. Fax: (317)264-3763. E-mail: jistworks@aol.com. Website: http://www.jistworks.com. **Acquisitions:** James Irizarry (trade/institutional); Sara Hall (trade). Estab. 1981. "Our purpose is to provide quality career, job search, and other living skills information, products, and services that help people manage and improve their lives—and the lives of others." Publishes trade paperback originals and reprints. Publishes 40 titles/year. Receives 300 submissions/year. 60% of books from first time authors; 100% from unagented writers. Pays 5-12% royalty on wholesale price or makes outright purchase (negotiable). Publishes book 1 year after acceptance. Accepts simultaneous submissions. Reports in 3 months on queries. Book catalog and ms guidelines for 9×12 SAE with 6 first-class stamps.

• Jist Works has published such authors as LaVerne L. Ludden, Patricia Westheimer and Bernard Haldane.

Imprint(s): Park Avenue Publications (business and self-help mss outside of the JIST topical parameters.)

Nonfiction: How-to, career, reference, self-help, software, video, textbook. Specializes in job search, self-help and career related topics. "We want text/workbook formats that would be useful in a school or other institutional setting. We also publish trade titles, all reading levels. Will consider books for professional staff and educators, appropriate software and videos." Query with SASE. Reviews artwork/photos as part of ms package.

Recent Nonfiction Title(s): *The Very Quick Job Search*, by J. Michael Farr; *We've Got To Start Meeting Like This*, by Robert B. Nelson and Roger K. Mosvick (business); *The Working Parents Handbook*, by Katherine Murray.

Tips: "Institutions and staff who work with people of all reading and academic skill levels, making career and life decisions or people who are looking for jobs are our primary audience, but we're focusing more on business and trade topics for consumers."

JOHNSON BOOKS, Johnson Publishing Co., 1880 S. 57th Court., Boulder CO 80301. (303)443-9766. Fax: (303)443-1106. **Acquisitions:** Stephen Topping, editorial director. Estab. 1979. Johnson Books specializes in books on the American West, primarily outdoor, "useful" titles that will have strong national appeal. Publishes hardcover and paperback originals and reprints. Publishes 10-12 titles/year. Receives 500 submissions/year. 30% of books from first-time authors; 90% from unagented writers. Average print order for a first book is 5,000. Royalties vary. Publishes book 1 year after acceptance. Reports in 3 months. Book catalog and ms guidelines for 9×12 SAE with 5 first-class stamps.

• Johnson has published such authors as Gregory McNamee, Roderick Nash and Paul Jorgensen.

Imprint(s): Spring Creek Press.

Nonfiction: General nonfiction, books on the West, environmental subjects, natural history, paleontology, geology, archaeology, travel, guidebooks, outdoor recreation. Accepts nonfiction translations. "We are primarily interested in books for the informed popular market, though we will consider vividly written scholarly works." Submit outline/synopsis and 3 sample chapters. Looks for "good writing, thorough research, professional presentation and appropriate style. Marketing suggestions from writers are helpful."

Recent Nonfiction Title(s): *Army Wives On The American Frontier*, by Anne B. Eales (western history); *Desert Bestiary*, by Gregory McNamee (nature); *Due North Of Montana*, by Cyris Dawson (fly-fishing).

Tips: "We are looking for titles with broad national, not just regional, appeal. We are especially interested in 'useful' books with strong backlist potential."

BOB JONES UNIVERSITY PRESS BOOKS FOR YOUNG READERS, Greenville SC 29614-0001. **Acquisitions:** Ms. Gloria Repp, acquisitions editor. Estab. 1974. Bob Jones publishes nonfiction and fiction "reflecting a Christian perspective." Publishes trade paperback originals and reprints. Publishes 11 titles/year. Receives 180 queries and 480 mss/year. 40% of books from first-time authors; 100% from unagented writers. Makes outright purchase of $500-1,250; royalties to established authors. Publishes book 18 months after acceptance. Accepts simultaneous submissions. Reports in 2 months on mss. Book catalog and ms guidelines free.

Nonfiction: Biography (for teens), children's/juvenile. Subjects include animals, gardening, health/medicine, history, nature/environment, sports. "We're looking for concept books on almost any subject suitable for children. We also like biographies." Submit outline and 3 sample chapters.

Fiction: Juvenile, young adult. "We're looking for well-rounded characters and plots with plenty of action suitable for a Christian audience. Avoid being preachy." Submit synopsis and 5 sample chapters or complete ms.

Recent Nonfiction Title(s): *Dust of the Earth*, by Donna Hess (biographical fiction ages 12+).

Tips: "Our readers are children ages two and up, teens and young adults. We're looking for high-quality writing that reflects a Christian perspective and features well-developed characters in a convincing plot. Most open to: first chapter books; adventure; biography."

‡JOSSEY-BASS/PFEIFFER, Imprint of Simon & Schuster, 350 Sansome St., San Francisco CA 94104. (415)433-1740. **Acquisitions**: Josh Blatter, editor. "Jossey-Bass/Pfeiffer specializes in human resource development titles in the fields of business, management, politics, education, and current affairs." Publishes 25 titles/year. 30% of books from first-time authors; 95% of books from unagented writers. Pays 10% average royalty. Publishes book 1 year after acceptance of manuscript. Accepts simultaneous submissions. Reports in 1-2 months on queries.
Nonfiction: How-to, self-help. Subjects include education, government/politics, psychology, religion, management, human resource development, current affairs. Query with SASE.
Recent Nonfiction Title(s): *The New Leaders: Leadership Diversity*, by Ann Morrison (business/management); *Workplace by Design*, by Franklin Becker and Fritz Steele (business/design).

‡JUDAICA PRESS, 123 Ditmas Ave., Brooklyn NY 11218. **Acquisitions:** Bonnie Goldman, senior editor. "We cater to the traditional, Orthodox Jewish market." Publishes hardcover and trade paperback originals and reprints. Publishes 8 titles/year. No advance. Reports in 3 months on queries.
Nonfiction: "We're looking for very traditional Judaica—especially children's books." Query with outline and 1 sample chapter.
Recent Nonfiction Title(s): *The Annihilation of Lithuanian Jewry*, by Rabbi Oshry (Holocaust memoir); *The Complete Torah Reading Handbook*; *A New Translation of Shemos*.

JUDSON PRESS, P.O. Box 851, Valley Forge PA 19482-0851. (610)768-2118. Fax: (610)768-2441. E-mail: judsonpress@juno.com. Website: http://www.judsonpress.com. Publisher: Harold W. Rast. **Acquisitions:** Kristy Pullen. Editorial Manager: Mary Nicol. Estab. 1824. "Our audience is mostly church members and leaders who seek to have a more fulfilling personal spiritual life and want to serve Christ in their churches and other relationships." Publishes hardcover and paperback originals. Publishes 15-20 titles/year. Receives 750 queries/year. Average print order for a first book is 5,000. Pays royalty or makes outright purchase. Publishes book 15 months after acceptance. Accepts simultaneous submissions. Reports in 6 months. Enclose return postage. Book catalog for 9×12 SAE with 4 first-class stamps. Manuscript guidelines for #10 SASE.
Nonfiction: Adult religious nonfiction of 30,000-80,000 words. Query with outline and sample chapter.
Recent Nonfiction Title(s): *We Have This Ministry*, by Samuel Proctor and Gardner Taylor (pastoral ministry); *Women at the Well*, edited by Mary Mild (devotions on healing and wholeness); *Cherish the Gift*, by Cindy Causey (earth stewardship for congregations).
Tips: "Writers have the best chance selling us practical books assisting clergy or laypersons in their ministry and personal lives. Our audience consists of Protestant church leaders and members. Be sensitive to our workload and adapt to the market's needs. Books on multicultural issues are very welcome."

JUST US BOOKS, INC., 356 Glenwood Ave., 3rd Floor, East Orange NJ 07017. Fax: (201)677-7570. E-mail: justusbook@aol.com. Publisher: Cheryl Willis Hudson. **Acquisitions:** Allyson Sherwood, submissions manager. Publishes hardcover and trade paperback and mass market paperback originals. Publishes 3-5 titles/year. Receives 300 queries and 500 mss/year. 33% of books from first-time authors; 33% from unagented writers. Pays royalty or makes outright purchase. Offers variable advance. Publishes book 18 months after acceptance of ms. "Currently accepts queries *only*. Due to proliferation of unsuitable manuscripts, prospective writers must send for guidelines and catalog. Unsolicited manuscripts will be returned *unread*." Book catalog and ms guidelines for 6×9 SAE with 2 first-class stamps.
Imprint(s): Afro-Bets®.
Nonfiction: Biography, children's/juvenile, illustrated books, middle readers and young adult. Emphasis on African-American subjects. Concentrate on young adult readers—no picture books. Query with SASE. Reviews artwork/photos as part of ms package. Send photocopies, transparencies or color or b&w sketches that may be kept on file..
Recent Nonfiction Title(s): *In Praise of Our Fathers and Our Mothers: An Anthology*; *Kids' Book of Wisdom*, compiled by Cheryl and Wade Huston.
Fiction: For middle readers and young adults. Looking for "contemporary, realistic, appealing fiction for readers aged 9-12, especially stories involving boys. Stories may take the form of chapter books with a range of 5,000-20,000 words." Query with SASE. Unsolicited mss will be returned unread.
Recent Fiction Title(s): *Ziggy and the Black Dinosaurs: Lost in the Tunnel of Time*, by Sharon M. Draper (mystery); *Annie's Gifts*, by Angela Shelf Medearis, illustrated by Anna Rich.
Tips: "We want stories for middle readers that appeal to both girls and boys (ages 9-12). This group still has higher priority for us than acquiring picture books."

KALMBACH PUBLISHING CO., 21027 Crossroads Circle, P.O. Box 1612, Waukesha WI 53187-1612. Fax: (414)796-1142. E-mail: tspohn@kalmbach.com. Website: http://books.kalmbach.com. **Acquisitions:** Terry Spohn, senior acquisitions editor (railroading, astronomy, scale modeling, miniatures, radio control); Kent Johnson, acquisitions editor (model railroading, toys trains); Roger Carp, acquisitions editor (toy trains, toys). Estab. 1934. "Kalmbach publishes books covering hobby, special interest, and leisure-time subjects." Publishes hardcover and paperback originals, paperback reprints. Publishes 15-20 titles/year. Receives 100 submissions/year. 85% of books from first-time authors; 100% from unagented writers. Pays 10% royalty on net. Offers $1,500 average advance. Publishes book 18 months after acceptance. Reports in 2 months.

Nonfiction: Hobbies, how-to, amateur astronomy, railroading. "Our book publishing effort is in amateur astronomy, railroading and hobby how-to-do-it titles *only*." Query first. "I welcome telephone inquiries. They save me a lot of time, and they can save an author a lot of misconceptions and wasted work." In written query, wants detailed outline of 2-3 pages and a complete sample chapter with photos, drawings, and how-to text. Reviews artwork/photos.

Recent Nonfiction Title(s): *Eight Easy Observing Projects*, by Hendrickson/Cortner (astronomy); *Wisconsin Central: Railroad Success Story*, by Dobnick and Glischinski (railroading); *Freight Car Projects & Ideas* (model railroading).

Tips: "Our books are about half text and half illustrations. Any author who wants to publish with us must be able to furnish good photographs and rough drawings before we'll consider contracting for his book."

KAYA PRODUCTION, 133 W. 25th St. #3E, New York NY 10001. (212)352-9220. Fax: (212)352-9221. E-mail: kaya@panix.com. Website: http://www.kaya.com. **Asquistions:** Sunyoung Lee, associate editor. "Kaya is a small independent press dedicated to the publication of innovative literature from the Asian diaspora." Publishes hardcover originals and trade paperback originals and reprints. Accepts simultaneous submissions. Reports in 6 months on mss. Book catalog free. Manuscript guidelines for #10 SASE.
 ● Kaya has published such authors as Kimiko Hahn, Sesshu Foster and R. Zamora Linmark.
Nonfiction: Submit proposal package, including outline, sample chapters, previous publications with SASE. Reviews artwork/photos as part of ms package. Send photocopies.
Recent Nonfiction Title(s): *Collapsing New Buildings: MUAEZ*, edited by Lawrence Chua.
Fiction: "Kaya publishes Asian, Asian-American and Asian diasporic materials. We are looking for innovative writers with a commitment to quality literature." Submit synopsis and 2-4 sample chapters with SASE.
Recent Fiction Title(s): *East Goes West*, by Younghill Kang (novel reprint).
Poetry: Submit complete ms.
Recent Poetry Title(s): *City Terrace Field Manual*, by Sesshu Foster (prose poetry collection).
Tips: Audience is people interested in a high standard of literature and who are interested in breaking down easy approaches to multicultural literature.

‡KENSINGTON, 850 Third Ave., 16th Floor, New York NY 10022. (212)407-1500. Fax: (212)935-0699. **Acquisitions:** Ann LaFarge, executive editor (romance, fiction); Tracy Bernstein, executive editor (trivia, health); Paul Dinas, editor-in-chief (true crime, expose); Kate Duffy, senior editor (historical, regency, romance); John Scognamiglio, senior editor (romance, mystery); Monica Harris, senior editor (multicultural romance). "Kensington focuses on profitable niches and uses aggressive marketing techniques to support its books." Publishes hardcover originals, trade paperback originals and reprints. Kensington publishes 300 titles/year; Pinnacle 60; Zebra 140-170; Arabesque 48. Receives 6,000 queries/year. 3-5% of books from first-time authors. Pays royalty on retail price, varies by author and type of book. Advance varies by author and type of book. Publishes book 18 months after acceptance of ms. Accepts simultaneous submissions. Reports in 1 month on queries; 3 months on mss. Book catalog for #10 SASE.
 ● Kensington has published such authors as Mike Lupica, Joyce Carol Oates and Roxanne Pulitzer. This publisher is no longer accepting unsolicited manuscripts or unagented writers.
Imprint(s): Zebra, Pinnacle, Arabesque.
Nonfiction: Self-help. Subjects include health/medicine, pop culture. Query with outline and SASE. "We are no longer accepting unsolicited manuscripts or unagented writers." Reviews artwork/photos as part of the ms package, if integral to project. Send photocopies.
Recent Nonfiction Title(s): *The Arthritic's Cookbook*, by Dr. Colin Dong (cookbook); *Star Wars Trilogy Trivia Challenge*, by James Natfield, George Burt (pop culture); *Bad Blood*, by Judith Reitman (crisis in the Red Cross).
Fiction: Mystery, romance, suspense, women's. Query with synopsis and SASE. "We are no longer accepting unsolicited manuscripts or unagented writers."
Recent Fiction Title(s): *Vegas*, by Fern Michaels (novel); *Princess Charming*, by Jane Heller (novel).

KENT STATE UNIVERSITY PRESS, P.O. Box 5190, Kent OH 44242-0001. (330)672-7913. Fax: (330)672-3104. Director: John T. Hubbell. **Acquisitions:** Julia Morton, editor-in-chief. Estab. 1965. Kent State publishes primarily scholarly works and titles of regional interest. Publishes hardcover and paperback originals and some reprints. Publishes 20-25 titles/year. Nonauthor subsidy publishes 20% of books. Standard minimum book contract on net sales. Offers advance rarely. Reports in 3 months. Enclose return postage. Book catalog free.
Nonfiction: Especially interested in "scholarly works in history and literary studies of high quality, any titles of regional interest for Ohio, scholarly biographies, archaeological research, the arts, and general nonfiction. Always write a letter of inquiry before submitting manuscripts. We can publish only a limited number of titles each year and can frequently tell in advance whether or not we would be interested in a particular manuscript. This practice saves both our time and that of the author, not to mention postage costs. If interested we will ask for complete manuscript. Decisions based on inhouse readings and two by outside scholars in the field of study."
Recent Nonfiction Title(s): *Ironclad Captain*, by Jay Slagle (US history); *Containing Coexistence: America, Russia and the "Finnish Situation,"* 1945-1956, by Jussi M. Hanhimäki (history); *The Romance of History*, edited by Scott Bills and E. Timothy Smith.
Recent Fiction Title(s): *Tales from the Irish Club*, by Lester Goran (original short stories).
Recent Poetry Title(s): *Likely*, by Lisa Coffman; *In the Arbor*, by Nancy Kuhl; *white*, by Mary Weems.

Tips: "We are cautious about publishing heavily-illustrated manuscripts."

MICHAEL KESEND PUBLISHING, LTD., 1025 Fifth Ave., New York NY 10028. (212)249-5150. **Acquisitions:** Judy Wilder, editor. Estab. 1979. Michael Kesend publishes guidebooks and other nonfiction titles for sale in museum stores, parks or similar outlets. Publishes hardcover and trade paperback originals and reprints. Publishes 4-6 titles/year. Receives 300 submissions/year. 20% of books from first-time authors; 40% from unagented writers. Pays 6% royalty on wholesale price. Advance varies. Publishes book 18 months after acceptance. Reports in 2 months on queries. Guidelines for #10 SASE.
Nonfiction: Biography, how-to, illustrated book, self-help, sports. Subjects include animals, health, history, hobbies, nature, sports, travel, the environment, guides to several subjects. Needs sports, health self-help and environmental awareness guides. No photography mss. Submit outline and sample chapters. Reviews artwork/photos as part of ms package.
Recent Nonfiction Title(s): *Walks in Welcoming Place*, by Harrison (regional guide for seniors and disabled); *A Guide to the Sculpture Parks and Gardens of America*, by McCarthy & Epstein (national guidebook).
Tips: "Looking for national guides, outdoor travel guides, sports nonfiction, art or garden-related guides and/or others suitable for museum stores, natural history and national or state park outlets."

KINSEEKER PUBLICATIONS, P.O. Box 184, Grawn MI 49637-0184. (616)276-6745. E-mail: ab0764@traverse.lib. mi.us. Website: http://www.angelfire.com/biz/Kinseeker/index.html. **Acquisitions:** Victoria Wilson, editor. Estab. 1986. "We publish books to help people researching their family histories." Publishes trade paperback originals. Publishes 6 titles/year. 100% of books from unagented writers. Pays 10-25% royalty on retail price. No advance. Publishes book 8 months after acceptance. Accepts simultaneous submissions. Reports in 3 months. Book catalog and ms guidelines for #10 SASE.
Imprint(s): Roundsky Press.
Nonfiction: How-to, reference books. Subjects are local history and genealogy. Query or submit outline and sample chapters. Reviews artwork/photos as part of ms package.
Recent Nonfiction Title(s): *Spiritual Genealogy*, by Rola Langell; *Digging in the Dirt*, by Janet Elaine Smith; *Finding Families*, by Sally Landreville (all genealogy how-to).

‡**KITCHEN SINK PRESS**, Subsidiary of Kitchen Sink Entertainment, Inc., 320 Riverside Dr., Northampton MA 01060. (413)586-9525. Fax: (413)586-7040. Website: kitchensp@aol.com. **Acquisitions**: N.C. Christopher Couch, editor; Robert Boyd, editor; Catherine Garnier, associate editor. Estab. 1969. "Kitchen Sink Press publishes graphic novels and comics. It also publishes historical and analytical works on comics, artists, film and animation." Publishes trade paperback originals. Publishes 20 titles/year. Receives 1,000 queries/year and 500 mss/year. 10% of books from first-time authors; 90% from unagented writers. Authors paid royalty on original work; stories based on licensed characters treated as work-for-hire. Publishes book 18 months after acceptance of ms. Accepts simultaneous submissions. Reports in 3 months on queries. For book catalog call (800)672-7862 or fax request to (413)582-7116. Manuscript guidelines for #10 SASE.
Imprint(s): Kitchen Sink Comix (comic books), Kitchen Sink Kids (children's titles).
Nonfiction: Illustrated book. Subjects include comics, film animation. Query with SASE. Reviews artwork/photos as part of the ms package. Send photocopies.
Recent Nonfiction Title(s): *The Great Women Superheroes*, by Trina Robbins (art history); *Understanding Comics*, by Scott McCloud (art); *Will Eisner: Comics and Sequential Art*.
Fiction: Graphic novels, comics. Holds license for Will Eisner's *The Spirit*, J. O'Barr's *The Crow*. "We are not interested in superheroes. Check current catalog and works by Will Eisner, Alan Moore to get a feel for what we want." Query with 1 sample chapter for graphic novels, several pages for comics, and SASE.
Recent Fiction Title(s): *From Hell*, by Alan Moore; *Cages*, by Dave McKean; *Xenozoic Tales*, by Mark Schultz.

‡**ALFRED A. KNOPF AND CROWN BOOKS FOR YOUNG READERS**, Imprint of Random House, 201 E. 50th St., New York NY 10022. (212)751-2600. Website: http://www.randomhouse.com/knopf/index. Senior Editor: Tracy Gates. Associate Publisher: Andrea Cascardi. **Acquisitions:** send mss to Crown/Knopf Editorial Department. "Knopf is known for high quality literary fiction, and is willing to take risks with writing styles. It publishes for children ages 5 and up. Crown is known for books young children immediately use and relate to. It publishes work for children ages 2-5." Publishes hardcover originals, trade paperback reprints. Publishes 60 titles/year. 10% of books from first-time authors; 40% from unagented writers. Pays 4-10% royalty on retail price. Offers advance of $3,000 and up. Publishes book 1-2 years after acceptance of ms. Accepts simultaneous submissions. Reports in 3 months on manuscripts. Book catalog for 9×12 SASE. Manuscript guidelines free.
Imprint(s): Alfred A. Knopf Books for Young Readers (Andrea Cascardi), Crown Books for Young Readers (Andrea Cascardi), Knopf Paperbacks (Joan Slattery, executive editor), Dragonfly (Joan Slattery, executive editor).
Nonfiction: Children's/juvenile, biography. Subjects include ethnic, history, nature/environment, science. Query with entire ms and SASE.
Recent Nonfiction Title(s): *Me On the Map*, by Joan Sweeney (science—Crown); *It's a Girl Thing*, by Mavis Jukes (culture—Knopf).
Fiction: Juvenile, literary, picture books, young adult. Query with entire ms and SASE.
Recent Fiction Title(s): *My Little Sister Ate One Hair*, by Bill Grossman (picture book—Crown); *Wrestling Stur-*

bridge, by Rich Wallace (middle grade novel—Knopf).
Tips: "Request catalogs. Familiarize yourself with the most recent titles from the publishers you're interested in."

ALFRED A. KNOPF, INC., Division of Random House, 201 E. 50th St., New York NY 10022. (212)751-2600.
Acquisitions: Senior Editor or Children's Book Editor. Vice President: Judith Jones. Publishes hardcover and paperback originals. Averages 200 titles/yearly. 15% of books from first-time authors; 30% from unagented writers. Royalty and advance vary. Publishes book 1 year after acceptance. Accepts simultaneous submissions if so informed. Reports in 3 months. Book catalog for 7½×10½ SAE with 5 first-class stamps.
  ● Knopf has published such authors as Richard Ford, Ann Beattie, James Ellroy, Anne Rice, John Updike, Toni Morrison and Michael Crichton.
Nonfiction: Book-length nonfiction, including books of scholarly merit. Preferred length: 50,000-150,000 words. "A good nonfiction writer should be able to follow the latest scholarship in any field of human knowledge, and fill in the abstractions of scholarship for the benefit of the general reader by means of good, concrete, sensory reporting." Query. Reviews artwork/photos as part of ms package.
Recent Nonfiction Title(s): *River*, by Colin Fletcher; *The Wisdom of the Body*, by Sherwin B. Nuland.
Fiction: Publishes book-length fiction of literary merit by known or unknown writers. Length: 40,000-150,000 words. *Writer's Market* recommends writers query with sample chapters.
Recent Fiction Title(s): *I Was Amelia Earhart*, by Jane Mendelsohn; *Gut Symmetries*, by Jeannette Winterson; *The Putter-Messer Papers*, by Cynthia Ozick.

KNOWLEDGE, IDEAS & TRENDS, INC. (KIT), 1131-0 Tolland Turnpike, Suite 175, Manchester CT 06040. (860)646-0745. **Acquisitions:** Ruth Kimball-Bailey, editor. Publishes hardcover and trade paperback originals. Publishes 4-5 titles/year. 80% of books from first-time authors; 100% from unagented writers. Pays royalty on wholesale price or advance against royalty. Advance varies. Publishes book 18 months after acceptance. Accepts simultaneous submissions. Reports in 3 months on mss. Book catalog and ms guidelines free.
Nonfiction: Biography, humor, reference, self-help. Subjects include anthropology/archaeology, history, psychology, sociology, women's issues/studies. Send outline and 3 sample chapters to Editor. Reviews artwork/photos. Send photocopies.
Recent Nonfiction Title(s): *From the Realm of the Ancestors: An Anthology in Honor of Marija Combutas*, edited by Joan Marler (archaeology/women's studies).
Recent Fiction Title(s): *Button, Button, Who Has the Button*, by Ruth Harriet Jacobs, Ph.D. (drama).
Tips: "Audience is general readers, academics, older women, sociologists."

‡KQED BOOKS, 555 DeHaro St., San Francisco CA 94107. (415)252-4350. **Acquisitions**: Pamela Byers, editorial director. Publishes hardcover originals, trade paperback originals and reprints. Publishes 10 titles/year. Receives 20 queries/year. 70% of books from first-time authors. Royalties vary substantially. Offers $0-25,000 advance. Publishes book 6 months after acceptance of ms. Accepts simultaneous submissions. Reports in 1 month. *Writer's Market* recommends allowing 2 months for reply. Book catalog for 9×12 SASE and 3 first-class stamps.
Nonfiction: Coffee table book, cookbook, gift book, how-to, humor, illustrated book. Subjects include Americana, child guidance/parenting, cooking, food & nutrition, education, health/medicine, history, hobbies, nature/environment, religion, travel (Armchair Travel), cable/PBS series companions. "We only publish titles related to public and cable television series." Query.
Recent Nonfiction Title(s): *Jacques Pepin's Kitchen: Cooking with Claudine*, by Jacques Pepin; *Mystery! A Celebration*, by Ron Miller (coffee table); *Are You Being Served?: The Inside Story*, by Rigelsford, et al (humor).
Tips: "Audience is people interested in Public Broadcasting subjects: history, cooking, how-to, armchair travel, etc."

KREGEL PUBLICATIONS, Kregel, Inc., P.O. Box 2607, Grand Rapids MI 49501. E-mail: kregelpub@aol.com.
Acquisitions: Dennis R. Hillman, publisher. "Our mission as an evangelical Christian publisher is to provide—with integrity and excellence—trusted, biblically-based resources that challenge and encourage individuals in their Christian lives." Publishes hardcover and trade paperback originals and reprints. Publishes 80 titles/year. Receives 150 queries and 100 mss/year. 5% of books from first-time authors; 100% from unagented writers. Pays 8-14% royalty on wholesale price or makes outright purchase of $500-1,000. Offers negotiated advance. Publishes book 1 year after acceptance of ms. Accepts simultaneous submissions. Reports in 1 month on queries and proposals, 3 months on mss. Book catalog for 9×12 SAE with 3 first-class stamps. Manuscript guidelines for #10 SASE.
Imprint(s): Kregel Resources, Kregel Classics.
Nonfiction: Biography (Christian), reference, textbook. Subjects include religion. "We serve evangelical Christian readers and those in career Christian service." Query with outline, 2 sample chapters, bio and market comparison.
Recent Nonfiction Title(s): *52 Ways to Keep Your Promises*, by Wayne and Judith Rolfs; *The Labor of Love*, by Timothy Hall.
Tips: "Looking for titles with broad appeal in the area of biblical studies and spiritual living."

KRIEGER PUBLISHING CO., P.O. Box 9542, Melbourne FL 32902-9542. (407)724-9542. Fax: (407)951-3671. E-mail: info@krieger-pub.com. **Acquisitions:** Elaine Harland (natural history); Michael W. Galbraith (Professional Practices Series); Gordon Patterson (Open Forum Series); Donald M. Waltz (Orbit Series); Hans Trefousse (Anvil Series). "We provide accurate and well documented titles for text and reference use, college level and higher." Publishes

hardcover and paperback originals and reprints. Publishes 60 titles/year. Receives 50-60 submissions/year. 30% of books from first-time authors; 100% from unagented writers. Pays royalty on net realized price. Publishes book 8 months after acceptance. Reports in 1 month. *Writer's Market* recommends allowing 2 months for reply. Book catalog free.
Imprint(s): Orbit Series, Anvil Series and Public History.
Nonfiction: College reference, technical, textbook. Subjects include history, music, philosophy, psychology, space science, herpetology, chemistry, physics, engineering, medical. Query. Reviews artwork/photos as part of ms package.
Recent Nonfiction Title(s): *Where Do You Go After You've Been to the Moon? A Case Study of NASA's Pioneer Efforts at Change*, by Francis T. Hoban; *Maritime History Volume 2: The Eighteenth Century and the Classic Age of Sail*, edited by John B. Hattendorf; *Transforming Your Community: Empowering for Change*, by Allen B. Moore.

KROSHKA BOOKS, (formerly Nova Science Publishers Inc.), 6080 Jericho Turnpike, Suite 207, Commack NY 11725-2808. (516)499-3103. Fax: (516)499-3146. E-mail: novascience@earthlink.net. **Acquisitions:** Frank Columbus, editor-in-chief; Nadya Columbus, editor. "Virtually all areas of human endeavor fall within our scope of interest. We have two major lines of activity: academic and scholarly books; and trade books dealing with every type of book known to mankind." Publishes hardcover and paperback originals. Publishes 150 titles/year. Receives 1,000 queries/year. Pays royalty. Publishes book 1 year after acceptance. Accepts simultaneous submissions. Reports in 1 month.
 ● Kroshka Books has published such authors as Senator Terry Sanford, David Lester and Craig Scott Rice.
Nonfiction: Biography, novels, self-help, technical, textbook. Subjects include Americana, anthropology, business/economics, computers/electronics, nutrition, education, government/politics, health/medicine, history, money/finance, nature/environment, philosophy, poetry, psychology, recreation, religion, science, sociology, software, sports, childhood development. Query. Reviews artwork/photos as part of ms package. Send photocopies.
Recent Nonfiction Title(s): *Firemania*, by Carl Chiarelli; *U.S. Presidents In Perspective*.
Recent Poetry Title(s): *Tests of Being*, by Nur Cheyenne.

‡KUMARIAN PRESS, INC., 14 Oakwood Ave., West Hartford CT 06119-2127. (860)233-5895. **Acquisitions:** send mss to Acquisitions Editor. "We publish books for professionals, academics, students interested in global affairs." Publishes hardcover and trade paperback originals. Publishes 8-12 titles/year; imprints publish 4-6 titles/year. Receives 200 queries and 150 mss/year. 10% of books from first-time authors; 100% from unagented writers. Pays royalty of 7-10% of net. Publishes book 1 year after acceptance of ms. Accepts simultaneous submissions, if so noted. Reports in 1 month on queries and proposals. Book catalog and ms guidelines free.
Imprint(s): Kumarian Press Books on International Development.
Nonfiction: Professional, academic. Subjects include anthropology, business/economics, government/politics, nature/environment, sociology, women's issues/studies, microenterprise, globalization, international health. "Kumarian Press is looking for manuscripts that address world issues and promote change. Areas of interest include, but are not limited to: international development, peace and conflict resolution, gender, NGOs, Third World studies, environment and works that link the shared problems faced by both the North and the South." Submit outline, 1-2 sample chapters, cv or resume, description of intended readership, detailed table of contents and projected word count with SASE.
Recent Nonfiction Title(s): *When Corporations Rule the World*, by David C. Korten (politics, economics, business); *Promises Not Kept, Third Edition*, by John Isbister (Third World studies).

LAKE VIEW PRESS, P.O. Box 578279, Chicago IL 60657. **Acquisitions:** Paul Elitzik, director. "We are mainly interested in scholarly nonfiction written in a manner accessible to a nonprofessional reader." Publishes hardcover and trade paperback originals. Publishes 5 titles/year. Receives 100 queries and 10 mss/year. 100% of books from unagented writers. Pays 6-10% royalty on wholesale price. Publishes book 1 year after acceptance of ms. Reports in 1 month on queries. *Writer's Market* recommends allowing 2 months for reply. Query with toc, c.v. and SASE. No sample chapters. Book catalog for #10 SASE.
Nonfiction: Biography, reference, technical. Subjects include government/politics, history, language/literature, sociology, women's issues/studies. Query.
Recent Nonfiction Title(s): *Forsaking our Children: Bureaucracy & Reform in the Child Welfare System*, by John M. Hagedorn (scholarly); *The Political Companion to American Film*, edited by Gary Crowdus.

PETER LANG PUBLISHING, Subsidiary of Peter Lang AG, Bern, Switzerland, 275 Seventh Ave., New York NY 10001. (212)647-7700. Fax: (212)647-7707. Website: http://www.peterlang.com. Managing Director: Christopher S. Myers. Senior Editor: Heidi Burns, Ph.D. **Acquisitions:** Owen Lancer, editor. Estab. 1952. "We publish scholarly textbooks and monographs in the humanities and social sciences." Publishes mostly hardcover originals. Publishes 300 titles/year. 75% of books from first-time authors; 98% from unagented writers. Write or call for submission requirements. Pays 10-20% royalty on net price. Translators get flat fee plus percentage of royalties. No advance. Publishes book 1 year after acceptance. Reports in 2 months. Book catalog free.
Nonfiction: Reference works, scholarly monographs. Subjects include literary criticism, Germanic and Romance lan-

---

ALWAYS ENCLOSE a self-addressed, stamped envelope (SASE) with all your queries and correspondence.

guages, art history, business/economics, American and European political science, history, music, philosophy, psychology, religion, sociology, biography. All books are scholarly monographs, textbooks, reference books, reprints of historic texts, critical editions or translations. No mss shorter than 200 pages. Submit complete ms. *Writer's Market* recommends sending a query with SASE first. Fully refereed review process.

Recent Nonfiction Title(s): *Scottish Literature: An Anthology, Vols. I & II*, by David McCordick (English literature); *Pedagogy, Technology and the Body*, by McWilliam and Taylor (education); *Opening Nights: 25 Years of the Manhattan Theatre Club*, by John W. Pereira.

Fiction and Poetry: "We do not publish original fiction or poetry. We seek scholarly and critical editions only. Submit complete manuscript." *Writer's Market* recommends sending a query with SASE first.

Tips: "Besides our commitment to specialist academic monographs, we are one of the few US publishers who publish books in most of the modern languages. A major advantage for Lang authors is international marketing and distribution of all titles. Translation rights sold for many titles."

LANGENSCHEIDT PUBLISHING GROUP, 46-35 54th Rd., Maspeth NY 11378. (800)432-MAPS. Fax: (718)784-0640. E-mail: kroche@langenscheidt.com. **Acquisitions:** Christine Cardone, editor. "We publish map and foreign language dictionary products." Publishes hardcover, trade paperback and mass market paperback originals. Publishes over 100 titles/year; each imprint publishes 20 titles/year. Receives 25 queries and 15 mss/year. 100% of books from unagented writers. Pays royalty or makes outright purchase. Publishes book 6 months after acceptance of ms. Accepts simultaneous submissions. Reports in 2 months on proposals. Book catalog free.

Imprint(s): Hagstrom Map, American Map, Trakker Map, Arrow Map, Creative Sales.

Nonfiction: Reference. Subjects include foreign language. "Any foreign language that fills a gap in our line is welcome." Submit outline and 2 sample chapters (complete ms preferred.)

Recent Nonfiction Title(s): *Pocket Webster* (reference); *Diccionario Universal (foreign language); Diccionario Moderno* (foreign languages), all by Langenscheidt.

Tips: "Any item related to our map and foreign language dictionary products could have potential for us."

LARK BOOKS, Altamont Press, 50 College St., Asheville NC 28801. **Acquisitons:** Rob Pulleyn, publisher. Estab. 1976. "We publish high quality, highly illustrated books, primarily in the crafts/leisure markets. We work closely with bookclubs. Our books are either how-to, 'gallery' or combination books." Publishes hardcover and trade paperback originals and reprints. Publishes over 40 titles/year. Sterling publishes 25; Lark publishes 15. Receives 300 queries and 100 mss/year. 80% of books from first-time authors; 100% from unagented writers. Offers up to $2,500 advance. Publishes book 1 year after acceptance of ms. Accepts simultaneous submissions. Reports in 2 months.

Imprint(s): Sterling/Lark Books.

Nonfiction: Coffee table book, cookbook, how-to, illustrated book, nonfiction children's/juvenile. Subjects include cooking, gardening, hobbies, nature/environment, crafts. Submit outline and 1 sample chapter, sample projects, table of contents. Reviews artwork/photos as part of ms package. Send transparencies if possible.

Recent Nonfiction Title(s): *Handmade Tiles*, by Frank Giorgini (how-to and gallery book, all color, technique, projects, portfolio).

LARSON PUBLICATIONS/PBPF, 4936 Rt. 414, Burdett NY 14818-9729. (607)546-9342. **Acquisitions:** Paul Cash, director. Estab. 1982. "We look for studies of comparative spiritual philosophy or personal fruits of independent (transsectarian viewpoint) spiritual research/practice." Publishes hardcover and trade paperback originals. Publishes 4-5 titles/year. Receives 1,000 submissions/year. 5% of books from first-time authors. Pays 7½% royalty on retail price or 10% cash received. Rarely offers advance. Publishes book 1 year after acceptance. Accepts simultaneous submissions. Reports in 4 months on queries. Book catalog for 9×12 SAE with 3 first-class stamps.

Nonfiction: Spiritual philosophy. Subjects include philosophy, psychology and religion. Query or submit outline and sample chapters. *No unsolicited mss.* Reviews artwork/photos as part of ms package.

Recent Nonfiction Title(s): *The Art of Napping*, by William Anthony.

‡LAUREL BOOKS, Imprint of Dell Publishing, Division of Bantam Doubleday Dell, 1540 Broadway, New York NY 10036. (212)354-6500. **Acquisitions:** Leslie Schnur, editor-in-chief. Publishes trade paperback originals, mostly light, humorous material and books on pop culture. Publishes 4 titles/year. 15% of books from first-time authors; less than 5% from unagented writers. Pay 7½-12½% royalty on retail price. Advance varies. Publishes book 1 year after acceptance of ms. Accepts simultaneous submissions. Reports in 4-6 months on queries. Book catalog for 9x12 SAE and 3 first class stamps.

Nonfiction: Textbook. Subjects include education, government/politics, history, philosophy, psychology, science, sociology. Query with synopsis, 2-3 sample chapters and SASE.

Fiction: Literary. Query with synopsis, 2-3 sample chapters or complete ms and SASE.

MERLOYD LAWRENCE BOOKS, Imprint of Addison Wesley-Longman, 102 Chestnut St., Boston MA 02108. **Acquisitions:** Merloyd Lawrence, president. Estab. 1982. Publishes hardcover and trade paperback originals. Publishes 7-8 titles/year. Receives 400 submissions/year. 25% of books from first-time authors; 20% from unagented writers. Pays royalty on retail price. Publishes book 1 year after acceptance. Accepts simultaneous submissions. No unsolicited mss read. Book catalog available from Addison Wesley.

Nonfiction: Biography, child development, health/medicine, nature/environment, psychology. Query with SASE. *All*

queries with SASE read and answered.
Recent Nonfiction Title(s): *The Power of Mindful Learning*, by Ellen J. Langer (psychology); *Helen and Teacher*, by Joseph P. Lash (biography); *Walking Towards Walden*, by John Hanson Mitchell (natural history).

LAWYERS & JUDGES PUBLISHING CO., P.O. Box 30040, Tucson AZ 85751-0040. (520)323-1500. Fax: (520)323-0055. E-mail: lj_publ@azstarnet.com. **Acquisitions:** Steve Weintraub, president. "We are a highly specific publishing company, reaching the legal and insurance fields and accident reconstruction." Publishes professional hardcover originals. Publishes 15 titles/year. Receives 200 queries and 30 mss/year. 5% of books from first-time authors; 100% from unagented writers. Pays 7-10% royalty on retail price. Publishes book 5 months after acceptance of ms. Accepts simultaneous submissions. Reports in 2 months. Book catalog free.
Nonfiction: Reference. Legal/insurance subjects. "Unless a writer is an expert in the legal/insurance areas, we are not interested." Submit proposal package, including full or *very* representative portion of ms. *Writer's Market* recommends query with SASE first.
Recent Nonfiction Title(s): *Motorcycle Accident Reconstruction and Litigation, Second Edition*, by Kenneth Obenski and Paul Hill; *Forensic Aspects of Vision and Highway Safety*, by Allen, Abrams, Ginsburg and Weintraub; *Whiplash Injuries*, by Stephen Foreman and Arthur Croft.

LEADERSHIP PUBLISHERS, INC., Talented and Gifted Education, P.O. Box 8358, Des Moines IA 50301-8358. (515)278-4765. Fax: (515)270-8303. **Acquisitions:** Lois F. Roets, editorial director. Estab. 1982. "We publish enrichment/supplementary educational programs and teacher reference books; our specialty is education of the talented and gifted." Publishes trade paperback originals. Publishes 5 titles/year. Receives 25 queries and 10 mss/year. Pays 10% royalty of sales. Publishes book 1 year after acceptance of ms. Reports in 3 months. Book catalog and ms guidelines for 9×12 SAE with 2 first-class stamps.
Nonfiction: Textbook. Education subjects. Submit outline and 2 sample chapters. Reviews artwork/photos as part of ms package. Send photocopies.

‡LEARNING PUBLICATIONS, INC., 5351 Gulf Dr., Holmes Beach FL 34217. (941)778-6651. Fax: (941)778-6818. E-mail: lpi@bhip.infi.net. Website: http://www.bhip.infi.net/~lpi. **Acquisitions:** Tomara Kafka, editor. "We specifically market by direct mail to education and human service professionals materials to use with students and clients." Publishes trade paperback originals and reprints. Publishes 10-15 titles/year. Receives 150 queries and 50 mss/year. 50% of books from first-time authors; 100% from unagented writers. Pays 5-10% royalty. Publishes book 1 year after acceptance of ms. Accepts simultaneous submissions. Reports in 1 month on queries and proposals, 4 months on mss. Book catalog free. Manuscript guidelines for #10 SASE.
● Learning Publications has published such authors as Adele Mayer, Ph.D.; Robert Ackerman, Ph.D.; Wilbur Broohover, Ph.D.; and Andrea Parrot, Ph.D.
Nonfiction: Reference, textbook, curricula and manuals for education and human service professionals. Subjects include education, psychology, sociology, women's issues/studies. "Writers interested in submitting manuscripts should request our guidelines first." Query with outline and/or table of contents, 1 sample chapter, one-page synopsis and résumé with SASE. Reviews artwork/photos as part of ms package. Send photocopies.
Recent Nonfiction Title(s): *Process-Oriented Group Therapy for Men and Women Sexually Abused as Children*, by Carolyn Knight, Ph.D. (psychology/therapy); *School Crisis Management Manual: Guidelines for Administrators*, by Judie Smith (education).
Tips: "Learning Publications has a limited, specific market. Writers should be familiar with who buys our books."

LEE & LOW BOOKS, 95 Madison Ave., New York NY 10016. (212)779-4400. Publisher: Philip Lee. Editor-in-Chief: Elizabeth Szabla. **Acquisitions:** Renee Schultz. Estab. 1991. "Our goals are to meet a growing need for books that address children of color, and to present literature that all children can identify with. We only consider multicultural children's picture books. Of special interest are stories set in contemporary America. We are interested in fiction as well as nonfiction. We do not consider folktales, fairy tales or animal stories." Publishes 12 titles/year. Send complete ms with SASE. Reports in 3 months. Encourages new writers.
● Lee & Low has published such authors as Pat Mora, Rosa Parks and William Miller.
Recent Nonfiction Title(s): *Passage to Freedom*, by Ken Mochizuki (Holocaust); *America: My Land, Your Land, Our Land*, by W. Nikola-Lisa.
Recent Fiction Title(s): *The Birthday Swap*, by Loretta Lopez (a surprise party); *A House by the River*, by William Miller, illustrated by Cornelius Van Wright and Ying-Hwa Hu.
Recent Poetry Title(s): *The Palm of My Heart: Poetry by African American Children.*

LEHIGH UNIVERSITY PRESS, Linderman Library, 30 Library Dr., Lehigh University, Bethlehem PA 18015-3067. (610)758-3933. Fax: (610)974-2823. E-mail: inlup@lehigh.edu. **Acquisitions:** Philip A. Metzger, director. Estab. 1985. "The LUP is a conduit for nonfiction works of scholarly interest. LUP bases its selection criteria on a manuscript's contribution to the world of ideas." Publishes hardcover originals. Publishes 10 titles/year. Receives 30 queries and 25 mss/year. 70% of books from first-time authors; 100% from unagented writers. Pays royalty. Publishes book 18 months after acceptance of ms. Accepts simultaneous submissions. Reports in 3 months. Book catalog and ms guidelines free.
Nonfiction: Biography, reference, academic. Subjects include Americana, art/architecture, history, language/literature, science. "We are an academic press publishing scholarly monographs. We are especially interested in works on 18th

century studies and the history of technology, but consider works of quality on a variety of subjects." No fiction, poetry or textbooks. Submit 1 sample chapter and proposal package.
Recent Nonfiction Title(s): *Leonardo de Vinci's Sporza Monument Horse: The Art and the Engineering*, by Deane Cole Ahl; *John Wesley and Marriage*, by Buford W. Coe; *B.F. Skinner and Behaviorism in American Culture*, by Laurence Smith and William R. Woodward.

LEISURE BOOKS, Imprint of Dorchester Publishing Co., 276 Fifth Ave., Suite 1008, New York NY 10001-0112. (212)725-8811. Fax: (212)532-1054. E-mail: timdy@aol.com. **Acquisitions:** Mira Son, editorial assistant; Christopher Keeslar, assistant editor. Estab. 1970. Leisure Books is seeking time-travel or futuristic romances, westerns, horror and techno-thrillers. Publishes mass market paperback originals and reprints. Publishes 160 titles/year. Receives thousands of submissions/year. 20% of books from first-time authors; 20% from unagented writers. Pays royalty on retail price. Advance negotiable. Publishes book 18 months after acceptance. Reports in 4 months on queries. Book catalog and ms guidelines for #10 SASE.
Nonfiction: "Our needs are minimal as we publish perhaps two nonfiction titles a year." Query.
Fiction: Historical romance (115,000 words); time-travel romance (90,000 words); futuristic romance (90,000 words); westerns (75,000-115,000 words); horror (90,000 words); techno-thrillers (90,000 words). "We are strongly backing historical romance. No sweet romance, gothic, science fiction, erotica, contemporary women's fiction, mainstream or action/adventure." Query or submit outline/synopsis and sample chapters. "No material will be returned without SASE."
Recent Fiction Title(s): *Shadow Walker*, by Connie Mason (historical romance); *Feather In the Wind*, by Madeline Baker (historical romance); *Rejar*, by Dara Joy (time-travel romance).

LERNER PUBLICATIONS COMPANY, Division of Lerner Publications Group, 241 First Ave. N., Minneapolis MN 55401. (612)332-3344. **Acquisitions:** Jennifer Martin, editor. Estab. 1959. "Our goal is to publish books that educate, stimulate and stretch the imagination, foster global awareness, encourage critical thinking and inform, inspire and entertain." Publishes hardcover originals, trade paperback originals and reprints. Publishes 150-175 titles/year; First Avenue Edition, 30; Carolrhoda, 50-60; Runestone Press, 3. Receives 1,000 queries and 300 mss/year. 20% of books from first-time authors; 95% from unagented writers. Pays 3-8% royalty on retail price (approximately 60% of books) or makes outright purchase of $1,000-3,000 (for series and work-for-hire). Offers $1,000-3,000 advance. Publishes book 2 years after acceptance of ms. Accepts simultaneous submissions. Reports in 4 months on proposals. Catalog for 9×12 SAE with 6 first-class stamps. Manuscript guidelines for #10 SASE.
Imprint(s): Carolrhoda Books, First Avenue Editions (paperback reprints for hard/soft deals only), Runestone Press.
Nonfiction: Children's/juvenile (grades 3-10). Subjects include art/architecture, ethnic, history, nature/environment, science, sports, aviation, geography. Query with outline, 1-2 sample chapters, SASE.
Recent Nonfiction Title(s): *A Sure Thing? Sports and Gambling*, by Jeff Savage; *We Have Marched Together: The Working Children's Crusade*, by Stephen Curry (history); *Songs from the Loom: A Navajo Girl Learns to Weave*, by Monty Ruessel (cultural studies).
Fiction: Juvenile (middle grade). "We are not actively pursuing fiction titles." Query with synopsis, 1-2 sample chapters and SASE.
Recent Fiction Title(s): *Mystery in Miami Beach*, by Harriet Feder (mystery).

‡ARTHUR LEVINE BOOKS, Imprint of Scholastic Inc.,%555 Broadway, New York NY 10012. (212)343-6100. **Acquisitions:** Arthur Levine, publisher. "Arthur Levine Books is looking for distinctive literature, for whatever's extraordinary. This is the first year for our list; we plan to focus on fiction." Publishes 8-10 titles/year. "We are willing to work with first-time authors, with or without agent." Pays variable royalty on retail price. Advance varies. Book catalog for 9×12 SASE.
Fiction: Juvenile, picture books. Query only, include SASE.
Recent Fiction Title(s): *When She Was Good*, by Norma Fox Mazer.

LEXIKOS, P.O. Box 296, Lagunitas CA 94938. (415)488-0401. Fax: (415)488-0401. **Acquisitions:** Mike Witter, editor. Estab. 1981. Lexikos specializes in anecdotal regional history and Americana for a general audience with a long-lasting appeal. Publishes hardcover and trade paperback originals and trade paperback reprints. Publishes 8 titles/year. Receives 200 submissions/year. 50% of books from first-time authors; 90% from unagented writers. Average print order for a first book is 5,000. Royalties vary from 8-12½% according to books sold. "Authors asked to accept lower royalty on high discount (50% plus) sales." Offers $1,000 average advance. Publishes book 10 months after acceptance. Accepts simultaneous submissions. Reports in 1 month. *Writer's Market* recommends allowing 2 months for reply. Book catalog and ms guidelines for 6×9 SAE with 2 first-class stamps.
Imprint(s): Don't Call It Frisco Press.
Nonfiction: Coffee table book, illustrated book. Subjects include regional, outdoors, oral histories, Americana, history, nature. Especially looking for 50,000-word "city and regional histories, anecdotal in style for a general audience; books of regional interest about *places*; adventure and wilderness books; annotated reprints of books of Americana; Americana in general." No health, sex, European travel, diet, broad humor, fiction, quickie books ("We stress backlist vitality"), religion, children's or nutrition. Submit outline and sample chapters. Reviews artwork/photos as part of ms package.
Recent Nonfiction Title(s): *Confessions of a Fundraiser*, by Scottow (memoir).
Tips: "A regional interest or history book has the best chance of selling to Lexikos. Submit a short, cogent proposal; follow up with letter queries. Give the publisher reason to believe you will help him *sell* the book (identify the market,

point out the availability of mailing lists, distinguish your book from the competition). Avoid grandiose claims."

THE LIBERAL PRESS, P.O. Box 140361, Las Colinas TX 75014. (972)686-5332. **Acquisitions:** Rick Donovon, executive vice president; Rockod Reinald, senior editor; Lynda Lucilton, editor; Jana Johnson, associate editor. "The Liberal Press seeks to publish well-researched books on liberal politics, humanist studies, and personal freedom." Publishes trade paperback originals. Publishes 4 titles/year. Receives 250 queries and 100 mss/year. 50% of books from first-time authors; 100% from unagented writers. Pays 4% royalty on retail price. Publishes book 1 year after acceptance of ms. Reports in 1 month on queries, 4 months on mss. Book catalog for 6×9 SAE with 5 first-class stamps. Manuscript guidelines for #10 SASE.

• The Liberal Press has published such authors as J. Michael Clark and Arthur Frederick Ide.

Nonfiction: Textbook. Subjects include gay/lesbian, government/politics (liberal only), history, women's issues/studies. "Work must be gender-free nonsexist, historical/factual with necessary bibliographic material (footnote/bibliography)." Query with outline and 2 sample chapters. All unsolicited mss returned unopened.

Recent Nonfiction Title(s): *An Ambitious Sort of Grief*, by Marion Cohen (neo-natal loss).

LIBRARIES UNLIMITED, INC., P.O. Box 6633, Englewood CO 80155. (303)770-1220. Fax: (303)220-8843. E-mail: lu-editorial@lu.com. **Acquisitions:** Susan Zernial, editor. Audience is librarians (school, public, academic and special) and teachers (K-12). Publishes hardcover originals. Publishes 75 titles/year; Ukranian, 45; Teacher Ideas, 30. Receives 100 queries and 75 mss/year. 75% of books from first-time authors; 100% from unagented writers. Pays 8-15% royalty on wholesale price. Publishes book 1 year after acceptance of ms. Accepts simultaneous submissions. Reports in 1 month on queries, 2 months on proposals and mss. Book catalog and manuscript guidelines free.

Imprint(s): Teacher Ideas Press (Susan Zernial, acquisitions editor); Ukranian Academic Press.

Nonfiction: Reference, textbook, teacher resource and activity books. Reference books on these topics for libraries: agriculture/horticulture, anthropology/archaeology, art/architecture, business/economics, education, ethnic, health/medicine, history, language/literature, military/war, music/dance, philosophy, psychology, religion, science, sociology, women's issues/studies. Interested in reference books of all types (annotated bibliographies, sourcebooks and handbooks; curriculum enrichment/support books for teachers K-12 and school librarians. Submit proposal package, including brief description of book, outline, 1 sample chapter, author credentials, comparison with competing titles, audience and market. Reviews artwork/photos as part of ms package. Send photocopies.

Recent Nonfiction Title(s): *Video Projects for Elementary and Middle Schools*, by Keith Kyker and Christopher Curchy (how-to); *The Humanities: A Selective Guide to Information Sources*, by Ron Blazek and Elizabeth Aveisa (annotated bibliography); *Science Through Children's Literature: An Integrated Approach*, by Carol Butzow and John Butzow (curriculum ideas and activities for teachers).

Tips: "We welcome any ideas that combine professional expertise, writing ability, and innovative thinking."

LIFETIME BOOKS, INC., 2131 Hollywood Blvd., Hollywood FL 33020. (954)925-5242, ext. 13. Fax: (954)925-5244. E-mail: lifetime@shadow.net. Website: http://www.lifetimebooks.com. **Acquisitions:** Brian Feinblum, senior editor. "We are interested in material on business, health and fitness, self-improvement and reference. We will not consider topics that only appeal to a small, select audience." Publishes hardcover and trade paperback originals and reprints. Publishes 30 titles/year. Receives 3,500 queries and 1,500 mss/year. 60% of books from first-time authors; 50% from unagented writers. Pays 6-15% royalty on retail price. Offers advance of $500-10,000. Publishes book 9 months after acceptance. Accepts simultaneous submissions. Reports in 1 month on queries, 2 months on mss. Book catalog and ms guidelines for 9×12 SAE with 5 first-class stamps.

• Lifetime Books, Inc. is no longer accepting fiction.

Imprint(s): Fell Publishers, Compact Books, (contact Donald Lessne); Lifetime Periodicals.

Nonfiction: How-to, self-help. Subjects include business and sales, psychology, cookbooks, foods/nutrition, medical, hobbies, Hollywood bio/exposé, money/finance. Submit outline, author bio, publicity ideas and 1 sample chapter. Reviews artwork as part of ms package. Send photocopies. No poetry, no fiction, no short stories, no children's.

Recent Nonfiction Title(s): *How to Control Diabetes*, by Seymour Alterman, F.A.C.R.; *How to Develop Your ESP Power*, by Jane Roberts; *How to Make a Good Speech*, by LeRoy Brown.

Tips: "We are most interested in well-written, timely nonfiction with strong sales potential. Our audience is very general. Learn markets and be prepared to help with sales and promotion. Show us how your book is unique, different or better than the competition."

LIGUORI PUBLICATIONS, One Liguori Dr., Liguori MO 63057. (314)464-2500. Fax: (314)464-8449. E-mail: 104626.1563@compuserve.com. Website: http://www.liguori.org. Thomas M. Santa, C.SS.R., publisher. **Acquisitions:** Anthony Chiffolo, managing editor (Trade Group); Patricia Kossman, executive editor (Trade Group, New York office (516)759-7402, fax: (516)759-8619.); Kass Dotterweich, managing editor (Pastoral Resource Materials Group); Terry Matz, director (Electronic Publishing). "Liguori Publications, faithful to the charisma of Saint Alphonsus, is an apostolate within the mission of the Denver Province. Its mission, a collaborative effort of Redemptorists and laity, is to spread the gospel of Jesus Christ primarily through the print and electronic media. It shares in the Redemptorist priority of giving special attention to the poor and the most abandoned." The Trade Group publishes hardcover and trade paperback originals and reprints under the Liguori and Triumph imprints. Publishes 20 titles/year. Royalty varies. Advance varies. Reports in 2 months. The Pastoral Resource Materials Group publishes paperback originals and reprints under the Liguori and Libros Liguori imprints. Publishes 50 titles/year, including Spanish-language titles. Royalty varies or purchases outright. Publishes 2 years after acceptance of ms. Prefers no simultaneous submissions. Reports in 2 months on queries and proposals, 3 months on mss. Author guidelines on request. The New Media Division publishes 4 titles/year. under the Faithware® imprint. Query for CD-ROM and Internet publishing. Publishes very few electronic products received unsolicited.

Imprint(s): Liguori Books, Libros Liguori, Faithware®, Triumph Books.

Nonfiction: Inspirational, devotional, prayer, Christian-living, self-help books. Religious subjects. Mostly adult audience; limited children/juvenile. Query with annotated outline, 1 sample chapter, SASE. For CD-ROM and Internet products, query with outline, software sample, SASE.

Recent Nonfiction Title(s): Trade Group: *Mother Teresa: In My Own Words*: Pastoral Resource Materials Group: *The Way of Mary*: New Media Division: *Scripture Sleuth*.

LIMELIGHT EDITIONS, Imprint of Proscenium Publishers Inc., 118 E. 30th St., New York NY 10016. Fax: (212)532-5526. E-mail: jjlmlt@haven.ios.com. **Acquisitions:** Melvyn B. Zerman, president; Jenna Johnson, administrative assistant. "We are committed to publishing books on film, theater, music and dance that make a strong contribution to their fields and deserve to remain in print for many years." Publishes hardcover and trade paperback originals, trade paperback reprints. Publishes 14 titles/year. Receives 150 queries and 40 mss/year. 15% of books from first-time authors; 20% from unagented writers. Pays 7½ (paperback)-10% (hardcover) royalty on retail price. Offers $500-2,000 advance. Publishes book 10 months after acceptance of ms. Reports in 1 month on queries and proposals, 3 months on mss. Book catalog and ms guidelines free.

● Limelight Editions has published such authors as John Lahr, Pauline Kael and Patricia Bosworth.

Nonfiction: Biography, historical, humor, instructional—most illustrated—on music/dance or theater/film. "All books are on the performing arts *exclusively*." Query with proposal package, including 2-3 sample chapters, outline. Reviews artwork/photos as part of ms package. Send photocopies.

Recent Nonfiction Title(s): *Film Noir Reader*, by Silver & Ursini (film); *Making It Big: The Diary of a Broadway Musical*, by B. Isenberg (theater); *Hamlet: A User's Guide*, by M. Pennington (theater).

LION BOOKS, Subsidiary of Sayre Ross Co., 210 Nelson Rd., Scarsdale NY 10583. (914)725-3572. **Acquisitions:** Harriet Ross, editor. Publishes hardcover originals and reprints, trade paperback reprints. Publishes 14 titles/year. Receives 60-150 queries and 50 mss/year. 60% of books from first-time authors. Pays 7-15% royalty on wholesale price or makes outright purchase of $500-5,000. Publishes book 5 months after acceptance of ms. Reports in 1 week on queries, 1 month on mss.

Nonfiction: Biography, how-to. Subjects include Americana, ethnic, government/politics, history, recreation, sports. Submit complete mss with SASE.

LION PUBLISHING, Imprint of Chariot Victor Publishing, 4050 Lee Vance View, Colorado Springs CO 80918-7102. (719)536-3271. **Acquisitions**: Liz Duckworth, managing editor (children's); Greg Clouse, executive editor (adult). "Lion Publishing's books are more 'seeker-sensitive' than Chariot; less Christian jargon, more accessible to the 'unchurched.' " Publishes hardcover and trade paperback originals. Published 10 titles/year. Pays variable royalty on wholesale price. Advance varies. Publishes book 18 months after acceptance of ms. Accepts simultaneous submissions, if so noted. Reports in 3 months on queries.

● Lion Publishing originates and distributes books in the United Kingdom and the United States. The numbers listed above do not include titles originating in and distributed solely in U.K.

Nonfiction: Biography, gift book, devotional. Subjects include child guidance/parenting, religion, marriage/family, inspirational, Christian living. Query or submit outline, 1 sample chapter with SASE.

Recent Nonfiction Title(s): *The Lion Storyteller Bible*, by Bob Hartman.

Fiction: Religious. Query with complete ms. *Writer's Market* recommends query with SASE first.

Recent Fiction Title(s): *Mitford Chronicles*, by Jan Karon; *Star of Wonder* (anthology of Christmas stories).

Tips: "All Lion books are written from a Christian perspective. However, they must speak primarily to a general audience. Half of our titles are children's books, yet we receive few manuscripts of publishable quality and almost no nonfiction of *any* kind. In short, we need high-quality nonfiction of all types that fit our guidelines."

‡LIPPINCOTT, Imprint of Lippincott-Raven Publishers, Subsidiary of Wolters Kluwer, 227 E. Washington, Philadelphia PA 19106.(215)238-4200. Fax:(215)238-4411. Website: http://www.lrpub.com. **Acquisitions:** Kathleen Mowery, secretary; Donna Hilton, vice president, publisher. Estab. 1792. Lippincott publishes high-quality nursing and allied health texts and reference books for healthcare students and practitioners. Publishes hardcover and trade paperback originals and reprints. Publishes 50 titles/year. Receives 500 queries and 20 proposals/year. 75% of books from first-time authors; 100% from unagented writers. Pays 10-18% royalty on wholesale price. Offers $2,000-10,000 advance. Publishes book 1 year after acceptance of ms (2 years from initiation of project and development of ms). Accepts simultaneous submissions. Reports in 2 months on proposals. Book catalog and ms guidelines free.

Nonfiction: Reference, textbook, healthcare practitioner books. Subjects include health/medicine, science, women's issues/studies. Query or submit outline, 2 sample chapters and proposal package, including purpose, market and table of contents with SASE. Reviews artwork/photos as part of ms package. Send originals.

Recent Nonfiction Title(s): *Handbook of Nursing Diagnosis*, by Linda Carpenito; *American Journal of Nursing*.

‡LIPPINCOTT-RAVEN PUBLISHERS, Subsidiary of Wolters Kluwer, 227 E. Washington Sq., Philadelphia PA 19106. (215)238-4200. Fax: (215)238-4227. Website: http://www.LRPUB.com. **Acquisitions:** Kathey Alexander, vice president/editor-in-chief, medical; Donna Hilton, vice president/editor-in-chief, nursing. Estab. 1792. "The mission of Lippincott-Raven is to disseminate healthcare information, including basic science, for medical and nursing students and ongoing education for practicing clinicians." Publishes hardcover originals. Publishes 180 titles/year. Pay rates vary depending on type of book, whether the author is the principal or contributing author and amount of production necessary. Accepts simultaneous submissions, if so noted. Reports in 3 months on proposals.

Imprint(s): Lippincott.

Nonfiction: Textbook. Health/medicine subjects. "We do not publish for the layperson." Query with proposal package including outline, table of contents, cv, proposed market and how your ms differs, estimate number of trim size pages and number and type of illustrations (line drawing, half-tone, 4-color).

Recent Nonfiction Title(s): *A Guide to Physical Exam and History Taking*, edited by Barbara Bates (nursing); *The Lippincott Manual of Nursing Practice*, edited by Nettina (nursing).

Tips: Audience is medical and nursing students and practicing clinicians.

LITTLE, BROWN AND CO., INC., Division of Time Warner Inc., 1271 Avenue of the Americas, New York NY 10020. (212)522-8700. **Acquisitions:** Editorial Department, Trade Division. Estab. 1837. "The general editorial philosophy for all divisions continues to be broad and flexible, with high quality and the promise of commercial success as always the first considerations." Publishes hardcover originals and paperback originals and reprints. Publishes 100 titles/year. "Royalty and advance agreements vary from book to book and are discussed with the author at the time an offer is made. Submissions from literary agents only. No unsolicited mss or proposals."

Imprint(s): Back Bay Books; **Bulfinch Press**; **Little, Brown and Co. Children's Books**.

● This publisher accepts agented submissions only.

Nonfiction: "Issue books, autobiography, biographies, culture, cookbooks, history, popular science, nature, and sports." Query *only. No unsolicited mss or proposals.*

Recent Nonfiction Title(s): *Joan Lunden's Healthy Cooking*, by Joan Lunden and Laura Morton; *A Change of Heart*, by Claire Sylvia with William Novak (memoir); *Cobain*, by the editors of *Rolling Stone*.

Fiction: Contemporary popular fiction as well as fiction of literary distinction. Query *only.*

Recent Fiction Title(s): *The Art of Breaking Glass*, by Matthew Hall (thriller); *Purple America*, by Rick Moody; *King Suckerman*, by George P. Pelecanos.

LITTLE, BROWN AND CO., CHILDREN'S BOOK DIVISION, 34 Beacon St., Boston MA 02108. (617)227-0730. **Acquisitions:** Erica Stahler, assistant editor; Maria Modugno, editor-in-chief; Megan S. Tingley, senior editor; Stephanie Peters, editor. Estab. 1837. "We publish books on a wide variety of nonfiction topics which may be of interest to children and are looking for strong writing and presentation, but no predetermined topics." Publishes hardcover originals, trade paperback originals and reprints. Firm publishes 60-70 titles/year. Pays royalty on retail price. Offers advance to be negotiated individually. Publishes book 2 years after acceptance of ms. Accepts simultaneous submissions, if so noted. Reports in 1 month on queries, 2 months on proposals and mss.

● This publisher accepts agented submissions only.

Nonfiction: Children's/juvenile, middle grade and young adult. Subjects include animals, art/architecture, ethnic, gay/lesbian, history, hobbies, nature/environment, recreation, science, sports. Writers should avoid "looking for the 'issue' they think publishers want to see, choosing instead topics they know best and are most enthusiastic about/inspired by." Submit outline and 3 sample chapters or proposal package, including "most complete outline, possible samples and background info (if project is not complete due to necessary research)." Reviews artwork/photos as part of package. Send photocopies (color if possible).

Recent Nonfiction Title(s): *Breaking Into Print*, by Stephen Krensky (history, ages 7-10); *Voices from the Streets*, by S. Beth Atkin (young former gang members tell their stories); *The Girls' Guide to Life: How to Take Charge of the Issues that Affect YOU*, by Catherine Dee.

Fiction: All juvenile/young adult; picture books. Categories include adventure, ethnic, fantasy, feminist, gay/lesbian, historical, humor, mystery, science fiction and suspense. "We are looking for strong fiction for children of all ages in any area, including multicultural. We always prefer full manuscripts for fiction."

Recent Fiction Title(s): *Lunch Bunnies*, by Kathryn Lasky (ages 4-8); *Painting the Wind*, by Michelle Dionetti (ages 6-10); *The Dark Side of Nowhere*, by Neal Shusterman (young adult thriller).

Recent Poetry Title(s): *Poems for Youth*, by Emily Dickinson (illustrated collection of poems); *Animal Crackers*, illustrated by Jane Dyer (anthology for the very young).

Tips: "Our audience is children of all ages, from preschool through young adult. We are looking for quality material that will work in hardcover—send us your best."

‡LITTLE SIMON, Imprint of Simon & Schuster Children's Publishing Division, 1230 Avenue of the Americas, New York NY 10020. (212)698-7200. Website: http://www.simonandschuster.com. **Acquisitions:** Robin Corey, editor. "Our goal is to provide fresh material in an innovative format for pre-school age. Our books are often, if not exclusively, illustrator driven." Publishes hardcover originals. Publishes 120 titles/year. 5% of books from first-time authors; 5% from unagented writers. Pays 2-5% royalty on retail price for first time, non-licensed. Publishes book 6 months after acceptance of ms. Accepts simultaneous submissions. Accepts queries only; reports in 8 months.

Nonfiction: Children's/juvenile, novelty books. "Novelty books include many things that do not fit in the traditional hardcover or paperback format, like pop-up, board book, scratch and sniff, glow in the dark, open the flap, etc." Query only with SASE. *All unsolicited mss returned unopened.*

Recent Nonfiction Title(s): *12 Days of Christmas*, by Robert Sabuda; *Bugs*, by David Carter (pop-up).

‡**LITTLE TIGER PRESS**, % XYZ Distributors, 12221 W. Feerick St., Wauwatosa WI 53222. (414)466-6900. **Acquisitions**: Amy Mascillino. Publishes hardcover originals. Publishes 8-10 titles/year. Receives 100 queries and 1,200 mss/year. 75% of books from first-time authors; 85% from unagented writers. Pays 7½-10% royalty on retail price or for first-time authors makes outright purchase of $800-2,500. Offers $2,000 minimum advance. Publishes book 1 year after acceptance of ms. Accepts simultaneous submissions. Reports in 2 months on queries and proposals, 3 months on mss. Book catalog for #10 SASE with 3 first-class stamps. Manuscript guidelines for #10 SASE.
Fiction: Humor, juvenile, picture books. "Humorous stories, stories about animals, children's imagination, or realistic fiction are especially sought." Send ms with SASE.
Recent Fiction Title(s): *Lazy Ozzie*, by Michael Coleman, illustrated by Gwyneth Williamson; *Shhh!*, by Julie Sykes, illustrated by Tim Warnes; *Dora's Eggs*, by Julie Sykes, illustrated by Jane Chapman.
Tips: "Audience is children 3-8 years old. We are looking for simple, basic picture books, preferably humorous, that children will enjoy again and again. We do not have a multicultural or social agenda."

LIVING THE GOOD NEWS, a division of the Morehouse Group, 600 Grant St., Suite #400. Denver CO 80203. Fax: (303)832-4971. **Acquisitions:** Liz Riggleman, editorial administrator. "Living the Good News is looking for books on practical, personal, spiritual growth for children, teens, families and faith communities." Publishes hardcover and trade paperback originals. Publishes 15 titles/year. Pays royalty. Publishes book 1 year after acceptance of ms. Accepts simultaneous submissions. Reports in 2 months on proposals. Book catalog for 9×12 SAE and 4 first-class stamps. Manuscript guidelines for #10 SASE.
Nonfiction: Children's/juvenile, gift book, how-to, illustrated book, self-help. Subjects include child guidance/parenting, grandparenting, education, religion (prayer, scripture, saints, ritual and celebration), storytelling, contemporary issues. No poetry or drama. Query. Submit proposal package, including cover letter, chapter outline, sample chapter, author information and SASE. Reviews artwork/photos as part of ms package. Send photocopies.
Recent Nonfiction Title(s): *Children and Christian Initiation: A Practical Guide*, by Kathy Coffey (leader's guide).
Fiction: Juvenile, picture books, religious, young adult. Query. Submit synopsis with SASE.
Tips: Audience is those seeking to enrich their spiritual journey, typically from mainline and liturgical church backgrounds. "We look for original, creative ways to build connectedness with self, others, God and the earth."

LIVINGSTON PRESS, Station 22, University of West Alabama, Livingston AL 35470. **Acquisitions:** Joe Taylor, director. Livingston Press seeks literary or experimental fiction and nonfiction. Publishes hardcover and trade paperback originals. Publishes 4-6 titles/year; imprint publishes 1 title/year. 20% of books from first-time authors; 90% from unagented writers. Pays 12½% of book run. Publishes book 18 months after acceptance of ms. Accepts simultaneous submissions. Reports in 1 month on queries; 1 year on mss.
Imprint(s): Swallow's Tale Press.
Nonfiction: Local history, folklore only. All unsolicited mss returned.
Fiction: Experimental, literary, short story collections. Query with SASE.
Recent Fiction Title(s): *Sixteen Reasons Why I Killed Richard M. Nixon*, by L.A. Heberlein; *Don Quickshot*, by William F. Van Wert; *Gabr'l Blow Sof': Sumter County, Alabama Slave Narratives*, edited by David Taylor and Alan Brown.
Poetry: "We publish very little poetry, mostly books we have asked to see." Query with SASE.
Recent Poetry Title(s): *Flight From Valhalla*, by Michael Bugeja (poetry); *Hunter-Gatherer*, by R.T. Smith.
Tips: "Our readers are interested in literature, often quirky literature."

LLEWELLYN PUBLICATIONS, Subsidiary of Llewellyn Worldwide, Ltd., P.O. Box 64383, St. Paul MN 55164-0383. (612)291-1970. Fax: (612)291-1908. E-mail: lwlpc@llewellyn.com. **Acquisitions:** Nancy J. Mostad, acquisitions manager. Estab. 1901. Llewellyn publishes New Age fiction and nonfiction exploring "new worlds of mind and spirit." Publishes trade and mass market paperback originals. Publishes 72 titles/year. Receives 500 submissions/year. 30% of books from first-time authors; 90% from unagented writers. Pays 10% royalty on moneys received both wholesale and retail. Accepts simultaneous submissions. Reports in 3 months. Book catalog for 9×12 SAE with 4 first-class stamps. Manuscript guidelines for SASE.
• Llewellyn has had a 20% growth rate in sales each year for the past six years.
Nonfiction: How-to, self-help. Subjects include nature/environment, health and nutrition, metaphysical/magic, psychology, women's issues/studies. Submit outline and sample chapters. Reviews artwork/photos as part of ms package.
Recent Nonfiction Title(s): *Creator, Protector, Destroyer: Discover That You Are God*, by J.R. Picksen, Ph.D., M.D.; *Pet Loss: A Spiritual Guide*, by Eleanor L. Harris; *Scrying for Beginners*, by Donald Tyson.
Fiction: Metaphysical/occult, which is authentic and educational, yet entertaining.
Recent Fiction Title(s): *Soothslayer*, by D.J. Conway (fantasy); *Ronin*, by D.A. Heeley (science-fiction/fantasy).

LOCUST HILL PRESS, P.O. Box 260, West Cornwall CT 06796-0260. (860)672-0060. Fax: (860)672-4968. **Acquisitions:** Thomas C. Bechtle, publisher. Locust Hill Press specializes in scholarly reference and bibliography works for college and university libraries worldwide. Publishes hardcover originals. Publishes 12 titles/year. Receives 150 queries and 20 mss/year. 100% of books from unagented writers. Pays 12-18% royalty on retail price. Publishes book 6 months after acceptance of ms. Accepts simultaneous submissions. Reports in 1 month on queries. *Writer's Market* recommends allowing 2 months for reply. Book catalog free.

• Locust Hill has published such authors as David V. Erdman, M. Thomas Inge and Germaine Greer.

Nonfiction: Reference. Subjects include ethnic, language/literature, women's issues/studies. "Since our audience is exclusively college and university libraries (and the occasional specialist), we are less inclined to accept manuscripts in 'popular' (i.e., public library) fields. While bibliography has been and will continue to be a specialty, our Locust Hill Literary Studies is gaining popularity as a series of essay collections and monographs in a wide variety of literary topics." Query.

Recent Nonfiction Title(s): *Juan Benet: A Critical Reappraisal of His Fiction*, edited by John B. Margenot III; *Henry James in the Periodicals*, by Arthur Sherbo; *"The Muses Females Are": Martha Moulsworth and Other Women Writers*, edited by Robert C. Evans and Anne C. Little.

Tips: "Remember that this is a small, very specialized academic publisher with no distribution network other than mail contact with most academic libraries worldwide. Please shape your expectations accordingly. If your aim is to reach the world's scholarly community by way of its libraries, we are the correct firm to contact. But *please*: no fiction, poetry, popular religion, or personal memoirs."

LODESTAR BOOKS, Imprint of Penguin Putnam Inc., 375 Hudson St., New York NY 10014. (212)366-2627. Fax: (212)366-2011. **Acquisitions:** Virginia Buckley, editorial director. Rosemary Brosnan, executive editor. "Lodestar Books publishes a small, quality juvenile hardcover list aimed at the institutional and retail markets." Publishes hardcover originals: juveniles, young adults, fiction, nonfiction and picture books. Publishes 20-25 titles/year. Receives 1,000 submissions/year. 10-20% of books from first-time authors; 25-30% from unagented writers. Average print order for a first novel or nonfiction is 4,000-5,000; picture book print runs are higher. Pays royalty on invoice list price. Offers advance. Publishes book 18 months after acceptance. Reports in 3 months. Manuscript guidelines for SASE.

Nonfiction: Query letters only. State availability of photos and/or illustrations. Reviews artwork/photos.

Recent Nonfiction Title(s): *A Soldier's Life*, by Andrew Robertshaw (soldiers through history); *Hell Fighters*, by Michael Cooper (African-American soldiers in World War I); *Journey for Peace: The Story of Rigoberta Menchu*, by Marlene Targ Brill.

Fiction: Publishes for young adults (middle grade) and juveniles (ages 5-17). Subjects include adventure, contemporary, fantasy, historical, humorous, multicultural, mystery, science fiction, suspense, western books, picture books. Query only.

Recent Fiction Title(s): *Jip: His Story*, by Katherine Paterson (a young boy learns his identity); *The Sin Eater*, by Gary Schmidt (heritage/identity); *So Loud a Silence*, by Lyll Becerra de Jenkins (multicultural).

Recent Poetry Title(s): *Who Killed Mr. Chippendale?*, by Mel Glenn (mystery in poems).

Tips: "A young adult or middle-grade novel that is literary, fast-paced, well-constructed (as opposed to a commercial novel); well-written nonfiction on contemporary issues, photographic essays, and nonfiction picture books have been our staples. We do only a select number of picture books, which are very carefully chosen."

LONE EAGLE PUBLISHING CO., 2337 Roscomare Rd., Suite 9, Los Angeles CA 90077-1851. (310)471-8066. Toll Free: 1-800-FILMBKS. Fax: (310)471-4969. E-mail: info-le@loneeagle.com. **Acquisitions:** Joan V. Singleton, president; Beth Ann Wetzel, editorial vice president; Jeff Black. Estab. 1982. "Lone Eagle publishes directories, books and software for the entertainment industry." Publishes perfectbound and trade paperback originals. Publishes 15 titles/year. Receives 100 submissions/year. 80% of books from unagented writers. Pays 10% royalty minimum on net income wholesale and retail. Offers $500-1,000 average advance. Publishes book 1 year after acceptance. Accepts simultaneous submissions. Reports quarterly on queries. Book catalog free.

Nonfiction: Technical, how-to, reference. Film and television subjects. "We are looking for technical books in film and television. No unrelated topics or biographies." Submit outline and sample chapters. Reviews artwork/photos as part of ms package.

Recent Nonfiction Title(s): *Breaking and Entering: Landing Your First Job in Film Production*, by April Fitzsimmons; *Film Directing: Killer Style and Cutting Edge Technique*, by Renee Harmon.

Tips: "A well-written, well-thought-out book on some technical aspect of the motion picture (or video) industry has the best chance: for example, script supervising, editing, special effects, costume design, production design. Pick a subject that has not been done to death, make sure you know what you're talking about, get someone well-known in that area to endorse the book and prepare to spend a lot of time publicizing the book."

LONELY PLANET PUBLICATIONS, 155 Filbert St., Suite 251, Oakland CA 94607-2538. Fax: (510)893-8563. E-mail: info@lonelyplanet.com. Website: http://www.lonelyplanet.com. **Acquisitions:** Caroline Liou, publishing manager. Estab. 1973. Publishes trade paperback originals. Publishes 30 titles/year. Receives 500 queries and 100 mss/year. 5% of books from first-time authors; 50% from unagented writers. Makes outright purchase or negotiated fee—⅓ on contract, ⅓ on submission, ⅓ on approval. Publishes book 2 years after acceptance of ms. Accepts simultaneous submissions. Reports in 3 months on queries. Book catalog free.

Nonfiction: Travel guides, phrasebooks atlases and travel literature exclusively. "Writers should request our catalog first to make sure we don't already have a book similar to what they have written or would like to write. Also they should call and see if a similar book is on our production schedule." Submit outline or proposal package. Reviews artwork/photos as part of ms package. Send photocopies. "Don't send unsolicited transparencies!"

Recent Nonfiction Title(s): *Pacific Northwest USA*, by Bill McRae (travel guide).

Recent Fiction Title(s): *The Gates of Damascus*, by Lieve Joris.

LONGSTREET PRESS, INC., 2140 Newmarket Parkway, Suite 122, Marietta GA 30067. (770)980-1488. Fax: (770)859-9894. **Acquisitions:** Abby Barr. Estab. 1988. "We want serious journalism-oriented nonfiction on subjects appealing to a broad, various audience or popular fiction that's exceptionally well done. The audience for our books has a strong sense of intellectual curiosity and a functioning sense of humor." Publishes hardcover and trade paperback originals. Publishes 45 titles/year. Receives 2,500 submissions/year. 25-30% of books from first-time authors. Pays royalty. Publishes book 1 year after acceptance. Accepts simultaneous submissions. Reports in 3 months. Book catalog for 9×12 SAE with 4 first-class stamps. Manuscript guidelines for #10 SASE.
Nonfiction: Biography, coffee table book, cookbook, humor, illustrated book, reference. Subjects include Americana, cooking/foods/nutrition, gardening, history, language/literature, nature/environment, photography, regional, sports, women's issues/studies. "No poetry, how-to, religious or inspirational, scientific or highly technical, textbooks of any kind, erotica." Query or submit outline and sample chapters. Reviews artwork as part of ms package.
Fiction: Literary, mainstream/contemporary. Agented fiction only. "We are not interested in formula/genre novels."
Recent Fiction Title(s): *Jenny Dorset*, by Phillip Lee Williams; *Too Blue To Fly*, by Judith Richards.
Tips: "Midlist books have a harder time making it. The nonfiction book, serious or humorous, with a clearly defined audience has the best chance. If I were a writer trying to market a book today, I would do thorough, professional work aimed at a clearly defined and reachable audience."

LOOMPANICS UNLIMITED, P.O. Box 1197, Port Townsend WA 98368-0997. Fax: (360)385-7785. E-mail: loompanx@olympus.net. Website: http://www.loompanics.com. President: Michael Hoy. **Acquisitions:** Dennis P. Eichhorn, editorial director. Estab. 1975. The mission statement offered by Loompanics is "no more secrets—no more excuses—no more limits!" Publishes trade paperback originals. Publishes 15 titles/year. Receives 500 submissions/year. 40% of books from first-time authors; 100% from unagented writers. Average print order for a first book is 2,000. Pays 10-15% royalty on wholesale or retail price or makes outright purchase of $100-1,200. Offers $500 average advance. Publishes book 1 year after acceptance. Accepts simultaneous submissions. Reports in 2 months. Author guidelines free. Book catalog for $5, postpaid.
● Loompanics Unlimited has published such authors as Michael Newton, Jim Hogshire and Douglas Rushkoff.
Nonfiction: How-to, reference, self-help. "In general, works about outrageous topics or obscure-but-useful technology written authoritatively in a matter-of-fact way." Subjects include the underground economy, crime, drugs, privacy, self-sufficiency, anarchism and "beat the system" books. "We are looking for how-to books in the fields of espionage, investigation, the underground economy, police methods, how to beat the system, crime and criminal techniques. We are also looking for similarly-written articles for our catalog and its supplements. No cookbooks, inspirational, travel, management or cutesy-wutesy stuff." Query or submit outline/synopsis and sample chapters. Reviews artwork/photos.
Recent Nonfiction Title(s): *Politics of Consciousness*, by Steve Kubby (philosophy of drug use); *How to Clear Your Adult and Juvenile Criminal Records*, by William A. Rinehart; *101 Things to Do 'Til the Revolution*, by Claire Wolfe.
Tips: "Our audience is young males looking for hard-to-find information on alternatives to 'The System.' Your chances for success are greatly improved if you can show us how your proposal fits in with our catalog."

LOTHROP, LEE & SHEPARD BOOKS, Imprint of William Morrow & Co., Division of The Hearst Corp., 1350 Avenue of the Americas, New York NY 10019. (212)261-6640. Fax: (212)261-6648. **Acquisitions:** Susan Pearson, editor-in-chief; Melanie Donovan, senior editor. Estab. 1859. Lothrop, Lee & Shepard publishes children's books only and is currently emphasizing picture books. Publishes hardcover originals only. Royalty and advance vary. Publishes 30 titles/year. Fewer than 2% of books from first-time authors; 25% of books from unagented writers. Average print order for a first book is 6,000-10,000. Publishes book within 2 years of acceptance. Reports in 3 months.
Imprint(s): Morrow Junior Books, Greenwillow Books.
● Lothrop, Lee & Shepard has published such authors as Laura Melmed and Ted Lewin and artists such as Henri Sorensen.
Fiction and Nonfiction: Publishes picture books, general nonfiction, and novels. Emphasis is on picture books. Looks for "organization, clarity, creativity, literary style." Query *only*. No unsolicited mss.
Recent Nonfiction Title(s): *The Voice of the People*, by Betsy and Giulio Maestro; *Market!*, by Ted Lewin.
Recent Fiction Title(s): *Harvey Potter's Balloon Farm*, by Jerdine Nolen, illustrated by Mark Buehner (picture book); *The Rainbabies*, by Laura Krauss Melmed, illustrated by Jim LaMarche.
Recent Poetry Title(s): *Maples in the Mist*, by Minfong Ho; *Advice for a Frog*, by Alice Schertle.

‡LOVE SPELL, Imprint of Dorchester Publishing Co., Inc., 276 Fifth Ave., Suite 1008, New York NY 10001-0112. (212)725-8811. **Acquisitions:** Mira Son, editorial assistant. "Love Spell publishes the quirky sub-genres of romance: time-travel, paranormal, futuristic. Despite the exotic settings, we are still interested in character driven plots." Publishes mass market paperback originals. Publishes 48 titles/year. Receives 1,500-2,000 queries and 150-500 mss/year. 30% of books from first-time authors; 25-30% from unagented writers. Pays 4% royalty on retail price for new authors. Offers $2,000 average advance for new authors. Publishes book 1 year after acceptance of ms. Reports in 6 months on mss. Book catalog free (800)481-9191. Manuscript guidelines for #10 SASE.
Fiction: Romance: time travel, paranormal, futuristic, angel. Query with synopsis, 3 sample chapters and SASE. "Books industry-wide are getting shorter; we're interested in 90,000 words."
Recent Fiction Title(s): *Rose Red*, by Flora Speer (fairy tale romance); *Rejar*, by Dara Joy (time travel romance);

Deeper Than The Night, by Amanda Ashley (paranormal romance).

‡**LOVESWEPT**, Imprint of Bantam Books/Bantam Doubleday Dell, 1540 Broadway, New York NY 10036. (212)354-6500. Website: http://www.bdd.com. **Acquisitions:** Joy Abella, administrative editor. Estab. 1983. "Our goal is to give you, the reader, stories of consistently high quality that sometimes make you laugh, make you cry, but are always fresh and creative and contain many delightful surprises within their pages." Publishes mass market paperback originals. Publishes 48 titles/year. 5% of books from first-time authors; 65% from unagented writers. Royalty and advance vary. Accepts simultaneous submissions, if so noted, "but would rather not." Reports in 1 month on queries, 8 months on proposals and mss. Book catalog free from Bantam Books (same address). Manuscript guidelines free and on the Web.
Fiction: Romance. "Review titles we have published during the last few years. No bodice rippers. Traditional conservative romance with happy endings. No more than 60,000 words." Query with synopsis, no more than 3 pages covering character and plot basics and SASE. "Don't submit sample chapters unless we ask for them."
Recent Fiction Title(s): *The Last Arrow*, by Marsha Canham; *Once a Warrior*, by Caryn Monk; *Charmed and Dangerous*, by Jill Shaluis; (romance novels).
Tips: Audience is "women, teenagers to elderly, but we do have a few male readers."

LRP PUBLICATIONS, INC., P.O. Box 980, Horsham PA 19044-0980. **Acquisitions:** Gail M. Richman, director of publishing. LRP Publications, Inc., publishes reference books for human resource managers, attorneys, risk managers, school administrators, consulting experts in litigation. Publishes hardcover and trade paperback originals. Publishes 10 titles/year. Receives 15 queries and 12 mss/year. 95% of books from first-time authors; 100% from unagented writers. Royalties vary. Offers $0-1,000 advance. Publishes book 9 months after acceptance of ms. Reports in 1 month on queries, 2 months on proposals, 3 months on mss. Book catalog and manuscript guidelines free.
Nonfiction: Reference. Subjects include education, law, workers compensation, bankruptcy, employment. Submit proposal package, including outline, cv, market analysis, competition.
Recent Nonfiction Title(s): *Preventing and Responding to Workplace Sexual Harassment*, by Christopher McNeill.

LUCENT BOOKS, P.O. Box 289011, San Diego CA 92198-9011. (619)485-7424. Fax: (619)485-9549. **Acquisitions:** Bonnie Szumski, managing editor; David M. Haugen, editor. Estab. 1988. "Lucent publishes nonfiction for a middle school audience. Our goal is to provide middle grade students with resource material for academic studies and for independent learning." Publishes hardcover educational supplementary materials and (nontrade) juvenile nonfiction. Publishes 75 books/year. All are works for hire, done by assignment only. 5% of books from first-time authors; 95% from unagented writers. Makes outright purchase of $2,500-3,000. No unsolicited mss. Query for book catalog and ms guidelines; send 9×12 SAE with 3 first-class stamps.
Nonfiction: Juvenile. "We produce tightly formatted books for middle grade readers. Each series has specific requirements. Potential writers should familiarize themselves with our material." History, current events and social issues series.
Recent Nonfiction Title(s): *The Rebuilding of Bosnia*, by James P. Reger (contemporary issues); *The Scopes Trial*, by Don Nardo (history); *James Baldwin*, by James Tackach (biography).
Tips: "We expect writers to do thorough research using books, magazines and newspapers. Biased writing—whether liberal or conservative—has no place in our books. We prefer to work with writers who have experience writing nonfiction for middle grade students."

THE LYONS PRESS, (formerly Lyons & Burford, Publishers, Inc.), 31 W. 21st St., New York NY 10010. (212)620-9580. Fax: (212)929-1836. **Acquisitions:** Lilly Golden, editor. Publisher: Peter Burford. Estab. 1984. "We want practical, well-written books on any aspect of the outdoors." Publishes hardcover and trade paperback originals and reprints. Publishes 40-50 titles/year. 50% of books from first-time authors; 75% from unagented writers. Pays varied royalty on retail price. Publishes book 1 year after acceptance. Accepts simultaneous submissions. Reports in 2 weeks on queries. *Writer's Market* recommends allowing 2 months for reply. Book catalog free.
Nonfiction: Subjects include agriculture/horticulture, Americana, animals, art/architecture, cooking/foods/nutrition, gardening, hobbies, nature/environment, science, sports, travel. Query.
Recent Nonfiction Title(s): *The Wolf Almanac*, by Robert Busch; *Spy on the Roof of the World*, by Sydney Wignall (history); *Equinox: Life, Love and Birds of Prey*, by Dan O'Brien (nature).
Recent Fiction Title(s): *Dry Rain*, by Pete Fromm; *Travers Corners*, by Scott Waldie.

‡**M & T**, Imprint of MIS Press, 115 W. 18th St., New York NY 10011. (212)886-9210. Fax: (212)807-6654. Website: http://www.mispress.com. Associate Publisher: Paul Farrell. **Acquisitions:** Ann Lush, assistant to the publisher. Estab. 1984. "M & T Books provides high-level guides to advanced programmers using commercial developing environments and more basic programming techniques, as well as the latest innovations in programming techniques." Publishes trade paperback originals and reprints. Publishes 25 titles/year. Receives 250 queries/year. 20% of books from first-time authors; 50% of books from unagented writers. Pays 5-15% royalty on net receipts. Offers $8,000 average advance. Publishes book 4 months after acceptance of ms. Accepts simultaneous submissions. Reports in 2 months on queries. Book catalog free.
Nonfiction: How-to, technical, networking, programming, databases, operating systems. Computer books for advanced users. "We are not about 'business management theory,' but we are about the practical and usable. Beware of poor grammar, spelling and writing in proposals." Query with outline and SASE.

Recent Nonfiction Title(s): *Analyzing Broadband Networks*, by Mark A. Miller (network administrators); *Lotus Domino Server*, by Steve Longerden (advanced administrators).
Tips: "Audience is computer users and network administrators."

McDONALD & WOODWARD PUBLISHING CO., 6414 Riverland Dr., Fort Pierce FL 34982-7644. (561)468-6361. Fax: (561)468-6571. **Acquisitions:** Jerry N. McDonald, managing partner/publisher. Estab. 1986. "McDonald & Woodward publishes books in natural and cultural history that are well organized, clearly written and substantive." Publishes hardcover and trade paperback originals. Publishes 8 titles/year. Receives 100 queries and 20 mss/year. 50% of books from first-time authors; 100% from unagented writers. Pays 10% royalty on net receipts. Publishes book 1 year after acceptance of ms. Accepts simultaneous submissions. Reports in 2 months. Catalog free.
Nonfiction: Biography, coffee table book, how-to, illustrated book, self-help. Subjects include Americana, animals, anthropology, ethnic, history, nature/environment, science, travel. Query or submit outline and sample chapters. Reviews artwork/photos as part of ms package. Send photocopies.
Recent Nonfiction Title(s): *An Old House in Greenville, Virginia: A Study of Human Intention in Vernacular Architecture*, by Michael S. Shutty, Jr. (vernacular architecture/material culture); *An Alien in Antarctica*, by Charles Swithinbank (Antarctica/history of science).
Tips: "We are especially interested in additional titles in our 'Guides to the American Landscape' series. Should consult titles in print for guidance. We want well-organized, clearly written, substantive material."

MARGARET K. McELDERRY BOOKS, Imprint of Simon & Schuster Children's Publishing Division, Division of Simon & Schuster, 1230 Sixth Ave., New York NY 10020. (212)698-2761. Fax: (212)698-2796. Vice President/Publisher: Margaret K. McElderry. **Acquisitions:** Emma D. Dryden, editor. Estab. 1971. Publishes quality material for preschoolers to 16-year-olds, but publishes only a few YAs. "We are more interested in superior writing and illustration than in a particular 'type' of book." Publishes hardcover originals. Publishes 25 titles/year. Receives 5,000 queries/year. 10% of books from first-time authors; 66% from unagented writers. Average print order is 4,000-6,000 for a first teen book; 8,000-10,000 for a first picture book. Pays royalty on retail price: 10% fiction; picture book, 5% author, 5% illustrator. Offers $5,000-6,000 advance for new authors. Publishes book 18 months after contract signing. Manuscript guidelines for #10 SASE.
● Margaret K. McElderry Books has published such authors as Susan Cooper, Nancy Bond and Niki Daly.
Nonfiction: Children's/juvenile, adventure, biography, history. "Read. The field is competitive. See what's been done and what's out there before submitting. Looks for originality of ideas, clarity and felicity of expression, well-organized plot and strong characterization (fiction) or clear exposition (nonfiction); quality. *We do not accept any unsolicited manuscripts.* We will accept one-page query letters for picture books or novels."
Recent Nonfiction Title(s): *The Planet Hunters: The Search for Other Worlds*, by Denis Fraydin; *How It Was with Dooms: A True Story from Africa*, by Carol Hopcraft.
Fiction: Juvenile only. Adventure, fantasy, historical, mainstream/contemporary, mystery, science fiction. Query with SASE. *No unsolicited mss.*
Recent Fiction Title(s): *The Boggart and the Monster*, by Susan Cooper; *Goodbye Buffalo Sky*, by John Loveday.
Poetry: Query with 3 sample chapters.
Recent Poetry Title(s): *Cricket Never Does*, by Myra Cohn Livingston (haiku).
Tips: "Freelance writers should be aware of the swing away from teen-age novels to books for younger readers and of the growing need for beginning chapter books for children just learning to read on their own."

McFARLAND & COMPANY, INC., PUBLISHERS, Box 611, Jefferson NC 28640. (910)246-4460. Fax: (910)246-5018. E-mail: mcfarland@skybest.com. Website: www.mcfarlandpub.com. **Acquisitions:** Robert Franklin, editor-in-chief; Steve Wilson, editor; Rhonda Herman, vice president; Virginia Tobiassen, editor. Estab. 1979. Publishes reference books and scholarly, technical and professional monographs. "We will consider any scholarly book—with authorial maturity and competent grasp of subject." Publishes mostly hardcover and a few "quality" paperback originals; a non-"trade" publisher. Publishes 135 titles/year. Receives 1,000 submissions/year. 70% of books from first-time authors; 95% from unagented writers. Average first printing for a book is 750. Pays 10-12½% royalty on net receipts. No advance. Publishes book 10 months after acceptance. Reports in 2 weeks. *Writer's Market* recommends allowing 2 months for reply.
Nonfiction: Reference books and scholarly, technical and professional monographs. Subjects include African American studies (very strong), art, business, chess, Civil War, drama/theater, cinema/radio/TV (very strong), health, history, librarianship (very strong), music, pop culture, sociology, sports/recreation (very strong), women's studies (very strong), world affairs (very strong). Reference books are particularly wanted—fresh material (i.e., not in head-to-head competition with an established title). "We prefer manuscripts of 250 or more double-spaced pages. Our market is worldwide and libraries are an important part." No New Age, exposés, poetry, children's books, devotional/inspirational works or personal essays. Query with outline and sample chapters. Reviews artwork/photos.
Recent Nonfiction Title(s): *The British Empire: An Encyclopedia of the Crown's Holdings, 1493 through 1995*, by John Stewart.
Tips: "We do not accept novels or fiction of any kind or personal Bible studies. What we want is well-organized knowledge of an area in which there is not good information coverage at present, plus reliability so we don't feel we have to check absolutely everything."

McGRAW-HILL COMPANIES, 1221 Avenue of the Americas, New York NY 10020. Divisions include **Business McGraw Hill**; **Computing McGraw Hill**; McGraw Hill Inc./TAB Books; McGraw-Hill Ryerson (Canada), Osborne/McGraw-Hill, Professional Book Group. General interest publisher of fiction and nonfiction. Query before submitting.

THE McGRAW-HILL COMPANIES, Professional Book Group Division, 11 W. 19th St., New York NY 10011. (212)512-2000. **Acquisitions**: David Conte, editorial director. Publishes hardcover and trade paperback originals and reprints. Publishes 800 titles/year. 30% of books from first-time authors; 70% from unagented writers. Pays royalty. Offers $3,000 and up advance. Publishes book 10 months after acceptance of ms. Accepts simultaneous submissions. Reports in 1 month on queries. Book catalog and ms guidelines free.
Imprint(s): Engineering & Science (contact Sybil Parker); **Business McGraw-Hill** (contact Philip Ruppel); **Computing McGraw-Hill** (contact Mike Hayes); **International Marine** and **Ragged Mountain Press** (contact John Eaton).
Nonfiction: How-to, multimedia (disk and CD ROM), reference, self-help, technical, professional. Subjects include art/architecture, business/economics, computers/electronics, money/finance, science, software, sports, technical engineering, boating. Query with proposal package, including outline, sample chapters, author bio, marketing information. Reviews artwork/photos as part of ms package.
Recent Nonfiction Title(s): *Heart at Work*, by Jack Canfield; *The Art of Architectural Illustration*, by Gordon Grice; *In the Company of Giants*, by Rama Dev Jager and Rafael Ortiz (business/computers).

‡**McGREGOR PUBLISHING**, 118 S. Westshore Blvd., Suite 233, Tampa FL 33609. (813)254-2665 or (888)405-2665. **Acquisitions:** Dave Rosenbaum, acquisitions editor. Publishes hardcover and trade paperback originals. Publishes 4-6 titles/year. Receives 20 queries and 12 mss/year. 75% of books from first-time authors; 100% from unagented writers. Pays 10-12% on retail price; 13-16% on wholesale price. Advances vary. Publishes book 1 year after acceptance of ms. Accepts simultaneous submissions. Reports in 1 month on queries and proposals, 2 months on mss. Book catalog and ms guidelines free.
Nonfiction: Biography, how-to, self-help. Subjects include business/economics, ethnic, history, money/finance, regional, sports. "We're always looking for regional nonfiction titles, and especially for sports, biographies, true crime, self-help and how-to books." Query or submit outline with 2 sample chapters.
Recent Nonfiction Title(s): *Miami Ice: Winning the NHL Rat Race with the Florida Panthers*, by Dave Rosenbaum (sports/nonfiction).
Fiction: Mystery, suspense. Query or submit synopsis with 2 sample chapters.
Tips: "We work closely with an author to produce quality product with strong promotional campaigns."

McGUINN & McGUIRE PUBLISHING INC., P.O. Box 20603, Bradenton FL 34203-0603. **Acquisitions:** Christopher Carroll, managing editor. Estab. 1991. Publishes hardcover and trade paperback originals. Publishes 6 titles/year. Receives 500 queries and 75 mss/year. 50% of books from first-time authors; 100% from unagented writers. Pays 10-15% royalty on net receipts. Offers $250 advance. Publishes book 1 year after acceptance of ms. Accepts simultaneous submissions. Reports in 1 month on queries and proposals, 2 months on mss. Book catalog and ms guidelines for #10 SASE.
Nonfiction: Biography. Subjects include business, history. "We are not interested in religious materials, memoirs, books relating a personal philosophy, diet books, or investment books. Author should be able to demonstrate how his/her book fills a void in the market." Query or submit outline and 3 sample chapters. Will not return submissions without SASE. Reviews artwork/photos as part of the ms package. Send photocopies.
Recent Nonfiction Title(s): *Encyclopedia of Ancient Deities*, by Charles Russell Coulter and Patricia Turner; *Women Pioneers in Television*, by Cary O'Dell.
Tips: "Always include a word count with queries and proposals. We will only consider books which are at least 50,000 words. Our audience consists of college-educated adults who look for books written by experts in their field. We are particularly interested in reviewing business books which help managers improve their business skills."

‡**MACMILLAN BOOKS**, Imprint of Macmillan General Reference, Subsidiary of Simon & Schuster, 1633 Broadway, New York NY 10019. (212)654-8500. **Acquisitions**: Natalie Chapman, publisher (popular reference, history, social sciences, illustrated reference, atlases); Mary Ann Lynch, senior editor (illustrated books, topical nonfiction, women, current affairs, arts, popular culture); Jennifer Griffin, senior editor (cookbooks); Amy Gordon, assistant editor (cookbooks); Ken Samelson, editor (sports); Betsy Thorpe, associate editor (health, psychology, parenting, self-help, popular reference). "Our mission is to publish the highest quality and most useful information and reference books." Publishes hardcover originals, trade paperback originals and reprints. Publishes 60-100 titles/year. Receives 3,000 queries/year. 15% of books from first-time authors; 5% from unagented writers. Pays royalty on retail price or net sales, makes outright purchase or work-for-hire assignments. Offers wide-ranging advance. Publishes book 1 year after acceptance of ms. Accepts simultaneous submissions. Reports in 2 months on queries and mss, 1 on proposals.
Nonfiction: Biography, how-to, reference, self-help. Subjects include child guidance/parenting, cooking/foods/nutrition, health/medicine, history, language/literature, psychology, recreation, science, sports, writing, atlases. Authors must have interesting and original ideas, good credentials and writing skills and an understanding of their market and audience. Submit outline, 1 sample chapter and proposal package, including table of contents, author credentials, target audience and market analysis. Reviews artwork/photos as part of ms package. Send photocopies.
Recent Nonfiction Title(s): *The New York Yankee Encyclopedia*, edited by Harvey Frommer (sports reference); *Encyclopedia Mysterios*, by William L. Deandrea (literary reference); *Easy Exercises for Pregnancy*, by Janet Balaskas.

‡MACMILLAN BRANDS, Imprint of Macmillan General Reference, subsidiary of Simon & Schuster, 1633 Broadway, New York NY 10019. (212)654-8500. **Acquisitions**: Susan Clarey, publisher; Anne Ficklen, senior editor (Weight Watchers, Betty Crocker); Barbara Berger, assistant editor (Burpee gardening). MacMillan Brands publishes cooking and gardening reference titles. Publishes hardcover originals, trade paperback originals and reprints. Publishes 60-100 titles/year. Receives 3,000 queries/year. 15% of books from first-time authors; 5% from unagented writers. Pays royalty on retail price or net sales, or makes outright purchase or work-for-hire assignments. Offers variable advance. Publishes book 1 year after acceptance of ms. Accepts simultaneous submissions. Reports in 2 months on queries and mss, 1 month on proposals.

Nonfiction: Cookbook, how-to, reference. Subjects include cooking/foods/nutrition, gardening. Submit outline, 1 sample chapter and proposal package, including table of contents, author credentials, target audience and market analysis. Reviews artwork/photos as part of ms package. Send photocopies.

Recent Nonfiction Title(s): *Jamaican Cooking*, by Lucinda Scala Quinn; *Ferns for American Gardens*, by John Mickel; *Betty Crocker's Great Grilling*.

‡MACMILLAN COMPUTER PUBLISHING, Division of Simon & Schuster, 201 W. 103rd St., Indianapolis IN 46290. (317)581-3500.

Imprint(s): Brady Games (by invitation), Hayden Books, **Que Publishing**, **New Riders Publishing**, Sams Publishing.

‡MACMILLAN CONSUMER INFORMATION GROUP, Macmillan General Reference, Subsidiary of Simon & Schuster, 1633 Broadway, New York NY 10019. (212)654-8500. **Acquisitions:** Theresa Murtha, publisher. Publishes hard originals cover and trade paperback originals and reprints. Publishes 60-100 titles/year. Receives 3,000 queries/year. 15% of books from first-time authors; 5% from unagented writers. Pays royalty on retail price or net sales or makes outright purchase or work-for-hire assignments. Offers variable advance. Publishes book 1 year after acceptance of ms. Accepts simultaneous submissions. Reports in 2 months on queries and mss, 1 month on proposals.

Nonfiction: How-to, reference, self-help. Subjects include animals, business/economics, child guidance/parenting, cooking/foods/nutrition, language/literature, music/dance, recreation, religion, sports, relationships, personal finance, games, weddings, law, careers, dictionaries, college, test guides, writing. Publishes popular reference books for seekers of practical information in Complete Idiot's Guides, Spectrum, Webster's New World and ARCO series. Submit outline, 1 sample chapter and proposal package, including table of contents, author's credentials, target audience and market analysis. Reviews artwork/photos as part of ms package. Send photocopies.

Recent Nonfiction Title(s): *The Complete Idiot's Guide to Chess*, by Murray Fisher and Patrick Wolfe; *Webster's New World College Dictionary, 3rd edition*; *J.K. Lasser's Your Income Tax 1997*, by the J.K. Lasser Institute.

‡MACMILLAN GENERAL REFERENCE, Subsidiary of Simon & Schuster, 1633 Broadway, New York NY 10019. (212)654-8500. Fax: (212)654-4850. Website: http://www.mcp.com/mgr. **Acquisitions**: Mary Ann Lynch, senior editor. "We publish popular reference in travel, pet books, consumer information, careers, test preparation, tax guides, cooking, gardening, sports, health, history, psychology, parenting, writing guides, atlases, dictionaries, music, the arts, business, parenting, science, religion." Publishes hardcover originals, trade paperback originals and reprints. Publishes 400-500 titles/year. Receives 10,000 queries/year. 15% of books from first-time authors; 5% from unagented writers. Pays royalty on retail price or net sales or makes outright purchase or work-for-hire assignments. Offers $1,000-1,000,000 advance depending on imprint. Publishes book 1 year after acceptance of ms. Accepts simultaneous submissions. Reports in 2 months on queries and mss, 1 month on proposals.

Imprint(s): Macmillan Books, Macmillan Travel, Consumer Information Group, Macmillan Brands, Howell Book House.

Nonfiction: Biography, cookbook, gift book, how-to, illustrated book, multimedia (disk/CD-ROM/cassette with book), reference, self-help. Subjects include Americana, animals, anthropology/archaeology, art/architecture, business/economics, child guidance/parenting, computers/electronics, cooking/foods/nutrition, education, ethnic, gardening, gay/lesbian, government/politics, health/medicine, history, hobbies, language/literature, military/war, money/finance, music/dance, nature/environment, psychology, recreation, religion, science, sociology, software, sports, travel, women's issues/studies, pets, consumer affairs. Submissions must have an original and interesting idea, good credentials and writing skills and an understanding of the market, and audience. Submit outline, 1 sample chapter and proposal package, including table of contents, author credentials, market competition and audience assessment. Reviews artwork/photos as part of ms package. Send photocopies.

Tips: Audience is "people who want practical information."

‡MACMILLAN TRAVEL, Imprint of Macmillan General Reference, subsidiary of Simon & Schuster, 1633 Broadway, New York NY 10019. (212)654-8500. **Acquisitions**: Michael Spring, publisher. Macmillan Travel publishes regional travel guides for Europe, America and Australia. Publishes hardcover originals, trade paperback originals and reprints. Publishes 60-100 titles/year. Receives 3,000 queries/year. 15% of books from first-time authors. Pays royalty on retail price or net sales, or makes outright purchase. Offers variable advance. Publishes book 1 year after acceptance of ms. Accepts simultaneous submissions. Reports in 2 months on queries and mss, 1 month on proposals.

  • Agented submissions only.

Nonfiction: Subjects include regional, travel. Submit outline, 1 sample chapter, table of contents, author credentials, target audience and market analysis. Reviews artwork/photos as part of ms package. Send photocopies.

Recent Nonfiction Title(s): *Frommer's France's Best Loved Driving Tours, 3rd edition; Frommer's Australia from*

$50 a Day, 10th edition; America on Wheels: Florida.

‡**MACMURRAY & BECK**, 1649 Downing St., Denver CO 80218. Fax: (303)832-2158. E-mail: ramey@macmurraybeck.com. Website: http://macmurraybeck.com. **Acquisitions:** Frederick Ramey, executive editor. "We are interested in reflective personal narrative of high literary quality both fiction and nonfiction." Publishes hardcover and trade paperback originals. Publishes 5-8 titles/year. 90% of books from first-time authors; 20% from unagented writers. Pays 8-12% royalty on retail price. Offers $2,000-8,000 advance. Publishes book 18 months after acceptance of ms. Accepts simultaneous submissions. Reports in 3 months on queries and proposals, 4 months on mss. Catalog and ms guidelines free.
 • MacMurray & Beck has published such authors as Laura Hendrie, Cathryn Alpert and Rick Collignon.
Nonfiction: Philosophy (non-academic), psychology (non-academic), sociology (non-academic), women's issues/studies. "We are looking for personal narratives and extraordinary perspectives." Submit outline and 2 sample chapters with SASE. Reviews artwork/photos as part of ms package. Send photocopies.
Recent Nonfiction Title(s): *Immortelles: Memoir of a Will-o'-the-Wisp*, by Mireille Marokvia; *Reeling & Writhing*, by Candida Lawrence (memoir).
Fiction: Literary. "We are most interested in debut novels of life in the contemporary West. But we select for voice and literary merit far more than for subject or narrative." Writers often make the mistake of "submitting genre fiction when we are in search of strong literary fiction." Submit synopsis and 3 sample chapters with SASE.
Recent Fiction Title(s): *St. Burl's Obituary*, by Daniel Akst; *Journal of Antonio Montoya*, by Rick Collignon.
Tips: "Our books are for thinking readers in search of new ideas and new voices."

‡**JOHN MACRAE BOOKS**, Imprint of Henry Holt & Co., Inc., 115 W. 18th St., New York NY 10011. (212)886-9200. **Acquisitions:** John Macrae, executive editor. Estab. 1991. "We publish literary fiction and nonfiction. Our primary interest is in language; strong, compelling writing." Publishes hardcover and trade paperback originals. Publishes 20-25 titles/year. 5% of books from first-time authors; 2% from unagented writers. Pays 6-7½% royalty on retail price. Advance varies. Publishes book 1 year after acceptance of ms. Accepts simultaneous submissions. Reports in 2 months on queries.
Nonfiction: Subjects include art/architecture, history, nature/environment, biography. Query only with SASE.
Recent Nonfiction Title(s): *Serpents of Paradise*, by Edward Abby.
Fiction: Literary, mainstream/contemporary. Query only with SASE.
Recent Fiction Title(s): *Burning Your Boats*, by Angela Carter (novel).

MADISON BOOKS, 4720 Boston Way, Lanham MD 20706. (301)459-3366. Fax: (301)459-2118. **Acquisitions:** James E. Lyons, publisher; Julie Kirsch, managing editor. Estab. 1984. Publishes hardcover originals, trade paperback originals and reprints. Publishes 40 titles/year. Receives 1,200 submissions/year. 15% of books from first-time authors; 65% from unagented writers. Pays 10-15% royalty on net price. Publishes ms 1 year after acceptance. *Writer's Market* recommends allowing 2 months for reply. Book catalog and ms guidelines for 9×12 SAE with 4 first-class stamps.
Nonfiction: History, biography, contemporary affairs, trade reference. Query or submit outline and sample chapter. No complete mss.

MAGE PUBLISHERS INC., 1032 29th St. NW, Washington DC 20007. Fax: (202)342-9269. E-mail: mage1@access.digex.com. Website: http://www.mage.com. **Acquisitions:** Amin Sepehri, assistant to publisher. "We only publish books which relate to Persian/Iranian culture." Publishes hardcover originals and reprints, trade paperback originals. Publishes 4 titles/year. Receives 40 queries and 20 mss/year. 10% of books from first-time authors; 95% from unagented writers. Pays variable royalty. Offers $250-1,500 advance. Publishes book 8-16 months after acceptance of ms. Accepts simultaneous submissions. Reports in 1 month on queries and proposals, 3 months on mss. Book catalog free.
Nonfiction: Biography, children's/juvenile, coffee table book, cookbook, gift book, illustrated book. Subjects include anthropology/archaeology, art/architecture, cooking/foods/nutrition, ethnic, history, language/literature, music/dance, sociology, translation. Query. Reviews artwork/photos as part of ms package. Send photocopies.
Recent Nonfiction Title(s): *Pivot of the Universe*, by Abbas Amanat (history/biography); *Lost Treasures of Persia*, by V. Lukonin (Persian art); *Tales of Two Cities*, by Abbas Milani (memoir).
Fiction: Ethnic, feminist, historical, literary, mainstream/contemporary, short story collections. Must relate to Persian/Iranian culture. Query.
Recent Fiction Title(s): *My Uncle Napoleon*, by I. Pezeshkzad (translation).
Poetry: Must relate to Persian/Iranian culture. Query.
Recent Poetry Title(s): *Borrowed Ware* (medieval Persian).
Tips: Audience is the Iranian-American community in America interested in the Middle East.

‡**MAIN STREET BOOKS**, Imprint of Doubleday Adult Trade, 1540 Broadway, New York NY 10036. (212)354-6500. **Acquisitions:** Bruce Tracy, editorial director. Estab. 1992. "Main Street Books continues the tradition of Dolphin Books of publishing backlists, but we are focusing more on 'up front' books and big sellers in the areas of self-help, fitness and popular culture." Publishes hardcover originals, trade paperback originals and reprints. Publishes 20-30 titles/year. Receives 600 queries, 200 mss/year. 25% of books from first-time authors. Offers advance and royalties. Publishes book 18 months after acceptance of ms. Accepts simultaneous submissions, if so noted. Reports in 1 month on queries, 6 months on mss. Doubleday book catalog and ms guidelines free.
 • Main Street Books accepts agented submissions only.

Nonfiction: Cookbook, gift book, how-to, humor, illustrated book, self-help. Subjects include Americana, animals, business/economics, child guidance/parenting, cooking/foods/nutrition, education, ethnic, gay/lesbian, health/fitness, money/finance, music/dance, nature/environment, pop psychology, pop culture. Query with SASE, but agented submissions only of manuscripts. Reviews artwork/photos as part of ms package, "but never send unless requested."
Recent Nonfiction Title(s): *Easy As 1-2-3 Cooking Chinese*, by Deh-Ta Hsiung (cookbook); *Checklist for Your First Baby*, by Susan Kagen Podell, M.S., R.D. (parenting/childcare).
Fiction: Literary, pop and commercial. Agented submissions only.
Recent Fiction Title(s): *Outside Providence*, by Peter Farrelly; *Beeperless Remote*, by Van Whitfield.
Tips: "We have a general interest list."

MAISONNEUVE PRESS, P.O. Box 2980, Washington DC 20013-2980. (301)277-7505. Fax: (301)277-2467. E-mail: rmerrill@mica.edu. **Acquisitions:** Robert Merrill, editor (politics, literature, philosophy); Dennis Crow, editor (architecture, urban studies, sociology). "Maisonneuve provides solid, first-hand information for serious adult readers: academics and political activists." Publishes hardcover and trade paperback originals. Publishes 6 titles/year. 5% of books from first-time authors; 100% from unagented writers. Pays 2-9% royalty on wholesale price or $2,000 maximum outright purchase. Publishes book 1 year after acceptance. Accepts simultaneous submissions. Reports in 1 month on queries; 2 months on proposals; 5 months on mss. Book catalog free. Send letter for guidelines; individual response.
• This publisher is not considering any new manuscripts in 1997. They are already over-booked with projects.
Nonfiction: Biography, philosophy, literary criticism, social theory. Subjects include education, ethnic, gay/lesbian, government/politics, history, language/literature, military/war, philosophy, psychology, sociology, translation, women's issues/studies, politics, economics, essay collections. "We make decisions on completed mss only. Will correspond on work in progress. Some books submitted are too narrowly focused; not marketable enough." Query; then send completed ms. Reviews artwork/photos as part of ms package. Send photocopies.
Recent Nonfiction Title(s): *Positively Postmodern: The Multi-Media Muse in America*, ed. by Nicholas Zurburgg.

MARCH STREET PRESS, 3413 Wilshire, Greensboro NC 27408. Website: http://users.aol.com/marchst/msp.html. **Acquisitions:** Robert Bixby, editor/publisher. "We want to support good work by drawing attention to it and to help poets create a lasting legacy beyond reading." Publishes literary chapbooks. Publishes 6-10 titles/year. Receives 12 queries and 30 mss/year. 50% of books from first-time authors; 100% from unagented writers. Pays 15% on royalty. Offers advance of 10 copies. Publishes book 6 months after acceptance of ms. Accepts simultaneous submissions. Reports in 3 months on mss. Book catalog and ms guidelines for #10 SASE.
• March Street has published such authors as Judith Minty, Kelly Cherry and Arnold Johnston.
Poetry: "My plans are based on the submissions I receive, not vice versa." Submit complete ms.
Recent Poetry Title(s): *Everything I Need*, by Keith Taylor; *Jailer's Inn*, by Deborah Bayer.
Tips: "Audience is extremely sophisticated, widely read graduates of MA, MFA and PhD programs in English and fine arts. Also lovers of significant, vibrant and enriching verse regardless of field of study or endeavor. Most beginning poets, I have found, think it beneath them to read other poets. This is the most glaring flaw in their work. My advice is to read ceaselessly. Otherwise, you may be published, but you will never be accomplished."

‡**MARINER BOOKS**, Imprint of Houghton Mifflin, 222 Berkeley St., Boston MA 02116. (617)351-5000. Fax: (617)351-1202. Website: http://www.hmco.com. **Acquisitions:** John Radziewicz. Estab. 1997. "Houghton Mifflin books give shape to ideas that educate, inform and delight. Mariner is an eclectic list that notably embraces fiction." Publishes trade paperback originals and reprints. Pays 6% royalty on retail price or makes outright purchase. Advance varies. Accepts simultaneous submissions. Reports in 2 months on mss. Book catalog free.
Nonfiction: Subjects include biography, business/economics, education, government/politics, history, military/war, philosophy, political thought, sociology. Query with SASE.
Recent Nonfiction Title(s): *An American Requiem*, by James Carroll (family memoir/history); *The Great Crash*, by John Kenneth Galbraith (financial history); *Ancestors*, by Jim & Terry Willard (tie-in with PBS show/family history).
Fiction: Literary, mainstream/contemporary. Submit synopsis with SASE. Prefers agented submissions.
Recent Fiction Title(s): *The Blue Flower*, by Penelope Fitzgerald (historical fiction).
Recent Poetry Title(s): *The Old Life*, by Donald Hall; *Things That Happen Once*, by Rodney Jones.

‡**MARIPOSA**, Imprint of Scholastic Inc., 555 Broadway, New York NY 10012. (212)343-6100. Website: http://www.scholastic.com. **Acquisitions:** Susana Pasternac, editor. "There is a great need for children's Spanish-language literature, work that is well done and authentic, that fills a *need*, not just a space." Publishes trade paperback originals and reprints. Publishes 20-25 titles/year (2-3 original titles/year). Receives 40 queries/year. Pays royalty on retail price, varies. Publishes book 1 year after acceptance of ms. Accepts simultaneous submissions. Reports in 3 months on mss. Book catalog for #10 SASE.
Nonfiction: Children's/juvenile, all areas. "We are introducing more nonfiction; looking for titles that don't have nationalities, that are interesting to everybody." Query with completed ms and SASE. Reviews artwork/photos as part of ms package if important to ms. Send photocopies.
Fiction: Juvenile, picture books, young adult. Query with completed ms and SASE. "We do Spanish-language translations of the Magic School Bus and Goosebumps series."
Recent Fiction Title(s): *Abuela and the Three Bears*, by Jerry Gello and Anna Lopez Escriva (bilingual picture book).

MARLOR PRESS, INC., 4304 Brigadoon Dr., St. Paul MN 55126. (612)484-4600. Fax: (612)490-1182. **Acquisitions:** Marlin Bree, publisher. Estab. 1981. "We publish nonfiction trade paperback books that fit a perceived market need." Publishes trade paperback originals. Publishes 6 titles/year. Receives 100 queries and 25 mss/year. Pays 10% royalty on wholesale price. Publishes book 8 months after final acceptance. Reports in 2 months on queries and proposals, 3 months on mss. Book catalog for 6×9 SAE with 2 first-class stamps. Manuscript guidelines for #10 SASE.
Nonfiction: Travel, boating, children's and gift books. Query first; submit outline with sample chapters only when requested. Do not send full ms. Reviews artwork/photos as part of ms package.
Recent Nonfiction Title(s): *The Stormy Voyage of Father's Day: Solo Across the North Atlantic in the Smallest Sailboat Ever!,* by Hugo Vihlen with Joanne Kimberlin; *New York for the Independent Traveler,* by Ruth Humlekev (travel).
Tips: "We only look for nonfiction titles and want more general interest boating and how-to travel books.

‡**MARLOWE & COMPANY,** Imprint of Marlowe & Thunder's Mouth, 632 Broadway, New York NY 10012. (212)780-0380. **Acquisitions:** John Webber, publisher. "We feature challenging, entertaining and topical titles in our extensive publishing program." Publishes hardcover and trade paperback originals and reprints. Publishes 50 titles/year. Receives 200 queries/year. 5% of books from first-time authors; 5% from unagented writers. Pays 10% royalty on retail price for hardcover, 6% for paperback. Offers advance of 50% of anticipated first printing. Publishes book 1 year after acceptance of ms. Accepts simultaneous submissions. Reports in 2 months on queries. Book catalog free.
Nonfiction: Self-help. Subjects include government/politics, health/medicine, history, New Age, public policy. Query. "We do not accept unsolicited submissions."
Recent Nonfiction Title(s): *Legal Lynching,* by Rev. Jesse Jackson (public policy); *Mystic Warriors of the Plains,* by Thomas Mails (history).
Fiction: Literary. "We are looking for literary, rather than genre fiction." Query with SASE. "We do not accept unsolicited submissions."
Recent Fiction Title(s): *Fata Morgana,* by William Kotzwinkle; *Heart's Journey In Winter,* by James Buchaw (winner of the Guardian Fiction Prize).

‡**MARSHALL & SWIFT, L.P.,** 911 Wilshire Blvd., Suite 1600, Los Angeles CA 90017. (213)683-9000. **Acquisitions:** C.L. Capell, editor-in-chief. "We focus exclusively on the appraisal, assessment, real estate and construction industries; providing data-related books and products to that market." Publishes hardcover and trade paperback originals. Publishes 11 titles/year. Receives 15 queries and 10 mss/year. 5% of books from first-time authors; 100% from unagented writers. Pays royalty on wholesale price. Offers $1,000-5,000 advance. Publishes book 6 months after acceptance of ms. Accepts simultaneous submissions. Reports in 1 month on queries and proposals, 2 months on mss. Book catalog free.
Imprint(s): Valuation Press.
Nonfiction: Construction cost-related business subjects. Query or submit 3 sample chapters.
Recent Nonfiction Title(s): *Winning More Bids,* by Dodge Woodson (construction/business); *Home Builder's Handbook,* by Dodge Woodson; Winning Strategies for Negotiating Claims, Kevin Quinley.

MASTERS PRESS, 2647 Waterfront Pkwy., Suite 100, Indianapolis IN 46214-2041. (317)298-5706. Fax: (317)298-5604. **Acquisitions:** Thomas H. Bast, director; Holly Kondras, managing editor. Estab. 1986. "Our audience is sports enthusiasts and participants, people interested in fitness." Publishes hardcover and trade paperback originals. Publishes 45-50 titles/year; imprint publishes 20 titles/year. Receives 60 queries and 50 mss/year. 25% of books from first-time authors; 75% from unagented writers. Pays 10-15% royalty. Offers $1,000-5,000 advance. Publishes book 1 year after acceptance. Accepts simultaneous submissions. Reports in 2 months on proposals. Book catalog free.
Imprint(s): Spalding Sports Library.
● Masters Press has increased their number of books published from 30-40 to 45-50 titles/year.
Nonfiction: Biography, how-to, reference, self-help. Subjects include recreation, sports, fitness. Submit outline, 2 sample chapters, author bio and marketing ideas.
Recent Nonfiction Title(s): *Ted Williams' Hit List,* by Ted Williams and Jim Prime; *Etched in Gold: The Story of America's First-Ever Olympic Gold Medal Winning Softball Team,* by Ron Babb and the Amateur Softball Association.

MAUPIN HOUSE PUBLISHING INC., P.O. Box 90148, Gainesville FL 32607-0148. Fax: (352)373-5588. E-mail: jgraddy@maupinhouse.com. **Acquisitions:** Julia Graddy, co-publisher. "We are focusing on teacher resource books for language arts teachers K-12." Publishes trade paperback originals and reprints. Publishes 7 titles/year. Pays 5-10% royalty on retail price. Reports in 1 month on queries. *Writer's Market* recommends allowing 2 months for reply.
● Maupin House has increased its number of titles published from 3 to 7 in the past year.
Nonfiction: Publishes nonfiction books on language art education, regional (Florida). "We are looking for practical,

MARKETS THAT WERE listed in the 1997 edition of *Writer's Market* but do not appear this year are listed in the General Index with a notation explaining why they were omitted.

in-classroom resource materials. Classroom teachers are our top choice as authors." Query with SASE.
Recent Nonfiction Title(s): *Listen to This: Developing an Ear for Expository*, by Marci Freeman (teacher resource for 4th-10th grades).

MAXIMUM PRESS, 605 Silverthorn Rd., Gulf Breeze FL 32561. (904)934-0819. **Acquisitions:** Jim Hoskins, publisher. "Maximum Press is a premier publisher of books that help readers apply technology efficiently and profitably. Special emphasis is on books that help individuals and businesses increase revenue and reduce expenses through the use of computers and other low-cost information tools." Publishes trade paperback originals. Publishes 10-12 titles/year. Receives 10 queries and 10 mss/year. 40% of books from first-time authors; 100% from unagented writers. Pays 7½-15% royalty on wholesale price. Offers $1,000-2,500 advance. Publishes book 3 months after acceptance of ms. Reports in 1 month. *Writer's Market* recommends allowing 2 months for reply. Book catalog free.
Nonfiction: How-to, technical. Subjects include business, computers and Internet. Query with proposal package, including credentials.
Recent Nonfiction Title(s): *Marketing on the Internet*, by Michael Mathiesen (computer/Internet); *Exploring IBM AS/400 Computers*, by Jim Hoskins and Roger Dimmick.

MAYFIELD PUBLISHING COMPANY, 1280 Villa St., Mountain View CA 94041. **Acquisitions:** Richard Greenberg, president/CEO. Mayfield Publishing Company publishers college textbooks on a variety of subjects. Publishes 60-70 titles/year. Accepts simultaneous submissions. Manuscript guidelines free.
Nonfiction: Textbook (*college only*). Subjects include anthropology/archaeology, art, child guidance/parenting, communications/theater, ethnic, health/physical education, language/literature, music/dance, philosophy, psychology, religion, sociology, women's studies. Submit proposal package including outline, table of contents, sample chapter, description of proposed market.
Recent Nonfiction Title(s): *The Mayfield Handbook of Technical and Scientific Writing*, by Barrett, Paradis and Perelman; *The Moral of the Story: An Introduction to Ethics*, by Nina Rosenstand (philosophy).

MEADOWBROOK PRESS, 5451 Smetana Dr., Minnetonka MN 55343. (612)930-1100. Fax: (612)930-1940. **Acquisitions:** Jason Sanford, submissions editor. Estab. 1975. "We look for fresh approaches to overcoming traditional problems (e.g. potty training)." Publishes trade paperback originals and reprints. Publishes 12 titles/year. Receives 1,500 queries/year. 15% of books from first-time authors. Publishes book 1 year after acceptance. Accepts simultaneous submissions. Reports in 3 months on queries. Book catalog and ms guidelines for #10 SASE.
• Meadowbrook has a need for parenting titles, humorous children's poetry and juvenile fiction (send for guidelines).
Nonfiction: How-to, humor, reference. Subjects include baby and childcare, senior citizens, children's activities, relationships. No academic or autobiography. Query with outline and sample chapters. "We prefer a query first; then we will request an outline and/or sample material."
Recent Nonfiction Title(s): *The Best Wedding Shower Book*, by Courtney Cooke (wedding guide); *Child Care A to Z*, by Dr. Richard C. Woolfson; *How to Pamper Your Pregnant Wife*, by Ron and Sam Schultz.
Recent Fiction Title(s): *Girls to the Rescue*, Book #3, edited by Bruce Lansky (a collection of stories featuring courageous, clever and determined girls).
Recent Poetry Title(s): *Poetry Party*, by Bruce Lansky (humorous poems for children); *Kids Pick the Funniest Poems*; *A Bad Case of the Giggles*; selected by Bruce Lansky, illustrated by Stephen Carpenter.
Tips: "We like how-to books in a simple, accessible format and any new advice on parenting."

‡MEDICAL PHYSICS PUBLISHING, 4513 Vernon Blvd., Madison WI 53705. (608)262-4021. Fax: (608)265-2121. E-mail: mpp@medicalphysics.org. Website: http://www.medicalphysics.org. **Acquisitions:** John Cameron, vice president; Elizabeth Seaman, managing editor. "We are a nonprofit, membership organization founded in 1985 to provide affordable books in medical physics and related fields." Publishes hardcover and trade paperback originals and reprints. Publishes 8-10 titles/year; imprint publishes 3-5 titles/year. Receives 10-20 queries/year. 100% of books from unagented writers. Pays 10% royalty on wholesale price. Publishes book 6 months after acceptance of ms. Accepts simultaneous submissions. Reports in 2-6 months on mss. Book catalog free.
Imprint(s): Cogito Books.
Nonfiction: Reference books, textbooks, and symposium proceedings in the fields of medical physics and radiology. Also distribute Ph.D. theses in these fields. Submit entire ms. *Writer's Market* recommends sending a query first. Reviews artwork/photos as part of ms package. Send disposable copies.
Recent Nonfiction Title(s): *The Physics of Radiotherapy X-Rays from Linear Accelerators*, by Metcalfe, Kron and Hoban; *A Practical Manual of Brachytherapy*, edited by Pierquin and Marinello and translated by Wilson, Erickson and Cunningham.

MERCURY HOUSE, INC., 785 Market St., Suite 1500, San Francisco CA 94103. (415)974-0729. Fax: (415)974-0832. **Acquisitions:** Tom Christensen, executive director; Janene-Nelson, managing editor. "Mercury House is a nonprofit corporation guided by a dedication to literary values. It exists to promote professional publishing services, to writers largely abandoned by market-driven commercial presses. Our purpose is to promote the free exchange of ideas, including minority viewpoints, by providing our writers with both an enduring format and the widest possible audience for their work." Publishes hardcover originals and trade paperbacks originals and reprints. Averages 10 titles/year. Pays

10-20% royalty on retail price. Offers $3,000-6,000 advance. Publishes book 1 year after acceptance of ms. Reports in 3 months. Catalog for 55¢ postage. "We no longer accept unsolicited manuscripts."

Nonfiction: Biography, essays, memoirs. Subjects include anthropology, ethnic, gay/lesbian, politics/current affairs, language/literature, literary current affairs, nature/environment, philosophy, translation, literary travel, women's issues/studies, human rights/indigenous peoples. "Within the subjects we publish, we are above all a literary publisher looking for high quality writing and innovative book structure, research, etc." Query with 1 sample chapter.

Recent Nonfiction Title(s): *In Few Words/En Pocas Palabras*, by José Antino Bureiago (Latino folk wit and wisdom).

Fiction: Ethnic, experimental, feminist, gay/lesbian, historical, literary, short story collections, literature in translation. "Very limited spots. We prefer sample chapters to determine writing style. It's very important to submit only if the subject is appropriate (as listed), though we do enjoy mutations/blending of genres (high quality, thoughtful work!). We do not publish mainstream, thrillers, sexy books. We look for a well-written cover letter."

Recent Fiction Title(s): *Ledoyt*, by Emshwiller.

Tips: "Our reader is a person who is discriminating about his/her reading material, someone who appreciates the extra care we devote to design, paper, cover, and exterior excellence to go along with the high quality of the writing itself. Be patient with us concerning responses: it's easier to reject the manuscript of a nagging author than it is to decide upon it. The manner in which an author deals with us (via letter or phone) gives us a sense of how it would be to work with this person for a whole project; good books with troublesome authors are to be avoided."

MERIWETHER PUBLISHING LTD., 885 Elkton Dr., Colorado Springs CO 80907-3557. (719)594-4422. **Acquisitions:** Arthur Zapel, Theodore Zapel, Rhonda Wray, editors. Estab. 1969. Meriwether publishes theater books, games and videos; speech resources; plays, skits and musicals; and resources for gifted students. Publishes trade paperback originals and reprints. Publishes 10-12 books/year; 50-60 plays/year. Receives 1,200 submissions/year. 50% of books from first-time authors; 90% from unagented writers. Pays 10% royalty on retail price or makes outright purchase. Publishes book 6 months after acceptance. Accepts simultaneous submissions. Reports in 2 months. Book catalog and ms guidelines for $2.

• Meriwether is looking for books of short scenes and textbooks on directing, staging, make-up, lighting, etc.

Nonfiction: How-to, reference, educational, humor. Also textbooks. Subjects include art/theatre/drama, music/dance, recreation, religion. "We publish unusual textbooks or trade books related to the communication or performing arts and how-to books on staging, costuming, lighting, etc. We are not interested in religious titles with fundamentalist themes or approaches—we prefer mainstream religion titles." Query or submit outline/synopsis and sample chapters.

Recent Nonfiction Title(s): *Playing Scenes From Classic Literature*, edited by Joellen Bland; *Playing Contemporary Scenes*, edited by Gerald Lee Ratliff; *Multicultural Theatre*, edited by Roger Ellis.

Fiction: Plays and musicals—humorous, mainstream, mystery, religious, suspense.

Tips: "Our educational books are sold to teachers and students at college and high school levels. Our religious books are sold to youth activity directors, pastors and choir directors. Our trade books are directed at the public with a sense of humor. Another group of buyers is the professional theatre, radio and TV category. We focus more on books of plays and theater texts."

THE MESSAGE COMPANY, 4 Camino Azul, Sante Fe NM 87505. (505)474-0998. **Acquisitions:** James Berry, president. The Message Company packages alternative topics for the mainstream market. Publishes trade paperback originals and reprints. Publishes 6-8 titles/year. Receives 20 queries and 12 mss/year. 80% of books from first-time authors; 100% from unagented writers. Pays 6-8% royalty on retail price or makes outright purchase of $500-2,000. No advance. Publishes book 3 months after acceptance of ms. Accepts simultaneous submissions. Reports in 1 month on mss. *Writer's Market* recommends allowing 2 months for reply. Book catalog for 6×9 SAE with 2 first-class stamps.

Nonfiction: How-to. Subjects include business/economics (spirituality in business-related only), government/politics (freedom/privacy issues only), science (new energy/new science only). Submit proposal package, including outline and sample chapters. Reviews artwork/photos as part of ms package. Send photocopies.

Recent Nonfiction Title(s): *Spiritual Vampires*, by Marty Raphael (trade paperback); *Law and the Heart: A Practical Guide for Successful Lawyer/Client Relationships*, by Merit Bennett, J.D.

JULIAN MESSNER, Imprint of Silver Burdett Press, Division of Simon & Schuster, 250 James St., Morristown NJ 07960. Publishes hardcover and trade paperback originals. Publishes 15 titles/year. Pays 3-7½% royalty. Average advance $4,000. Publishes book 2-3 years after acceptance of ms. Book catalog for 9×12 SASE with $2.60 postage.

• Julian Messner is not accepting any unsolicited material.

Nonfiction: Children's/juvenile, grades 5-9. Subjects include science, sociology, social studies. All unsolicited mss returned unopened. Not accepting any unsolicited material.

METAL POWDER INDUSTRIES FEDERATION, 105 College Rd. E., Princeton NJ 08540. (609)452-7700. Fax: (609)987-8523. **Acquisitions:** Cindy Jablonowski, publications manager; Peggy Lebedz, assistant publications manager. Estab. 1946. "We publish monographs, textbooks, handbooks, design guides, conference proceedings, standards, and general titles in the field of powder metullary or particulate materials." Publishes hardcover originals. Publishes 10 titles/year. Pays 3-12½% royalty on wholesale or retail price. Offers $3,000-5,000 advance. Reports in 1 month. *Writer's Market* recommends allowing 2 months for reply.

Nonfiction: Work must relate to powder metallurgy or particulate materials.

Recent Nonfiction Title(s): *Advances in Powder Metallurgy and Particulate Materials* (conference proceeding).

METAMORPHOUS PRESS, P.O. Box 10616, Portland OR 97296-0616. (503)228-4972. Fax: (503)223-9117. E-mail: metabooks@msn.com. Publisher: David Balding. Editorial Director: Lori Vannorsdel. **Acquisitions:** Nancy Wyatt-Kelsey, acquisitions editor. Estab. 1982. "Our primary editorial screen is 'will this (behavioral science) book further define, explain or support the concept that we are responsible for our reality or assist people in gaining control of their lives?' " Publishes trade paperback originals and reprints. Publishes 4-5 titles/year. Receives 2,500 submissions/year. 90% of books from first-time authors; 90% from unagented writers. Average print order for a first book is 2,000-5,000. Pays minimum 10% profit split on wholesale prices. No advance. Publishes book 1 year after acceptance. Accepts simultaneous submissions. Reports in 3 months. Book catalog and ms guidelines for 9×12 SAE with 3 first-class stamps.
Imprint(s): Grinder & Associates (Lori Vannorsdel, editorial director).
  ● Metamorphous Books has published such authors as Robert Dilts and John Cantwell Kiley, M.D., Ph.D.
Nonfiction: How-to, reference, self-help, technical, textbook—all related to behavioral science and personal growth. Subjects include business and sales, health, psychology, sociology, education, science and new ideas in behavioral science. "We are interested in any well-proven new idea or philosophy in the behavioral science areas." Submit idea, outline, and table of contents only. Reviews artwork/photos as part of ms package.
Recent Nonfiction Title(s): *Enneagram Spectrum of Personality Styles*, by Wagner; *Framework of Excellence*, by C. Miliner; *Patterns of Therapeutic Technology of Milton Erickson, vols 1-2*, by Bandler & Grinder (hypnotherapy).

MICHIGAN STATE UNIVERSITY PRESS, 1405 S. Harrison Rd., Suite 25, East Lansing MI 48823-5202. (517)355-9543. Fax: (800)678-2120; local/international (517)432-2611. E-mail: msp05@msu.edu Website: http://web.msu.edu/press. **Acquisitions:** Martha Bates, acquisitions editor. Estab. 1947. Michigan State University Press looks for "scholarship that addresses the social and political concerns of the late 20th century." Publishes hardcover and softcover originals. Publishes 30 titles/year. Receives 400 submissions/year. 75% of books from first-time authors; 100% from unagented writers. Royalties vary. Publishes ms 18 months after acceptance. Catalog and ms guidelines for 9×12 SASE.
  ● Michigan State University Press has published such authors as Richard Seltzer, Jim Harrison and Dan Gerber.
Nonfiction: Reference, technical, scholarly. Subjects include Afro-American Studies, American history, American Studies, business/economics, Canadian Studies, Civil War history, communication and speech, Great Lakes Regional Studies, literature, Native American Studies, philosophy, politics, Women's Studies. Series: Canadian Series, Lotus Poetry Series, Schoolcraft Series, Rhetoric and Public Affairs Series, Native American Series, Colleagues Books. Selected titles from Carleton University Press. Query with outline and sample chapters. Reviews artwork/photos.
Recent Nonfiction Title(s): *Death Stalks The Vakama: Epidemiological Transitions and Mortality on the Vakama Indian Reservation, 1888-1964*, by Clifford E. Trafzer; *To Tilt at Windmills* (Spanish Civil War).
Recent Poetry Title(s): *An American South*; *Walking North*.

MID-LIST PRESS, Imprint of Jackson, Hart & Leslie, 4324 12th Ave S., Minneapolis MN 55407-3218. Estab. 1989. Mid-List Press is an independent press. "Mid-List Press publishes books of high literary merit and fresh artistic vision by new and emerging writers ignored, marginalized, or excluded from publication by commercial and mainstream publishers. In addition to publishing the annual winners of the Mid-List Press First Series Awards, Mid-List Press publishes general interest fiction and nonfiction by first-time and established writers. Publishes hardcover and trade paperback originals. Publishes minimum 4 titles/year. Pays 40-50% royalty of profits. Offers $500-1,000 advance. Send SASE for First Series guidelines and/or general submission guidelines.
Recent Fiction Title(s): *Part of His Story*, by Alfred Corn (novel); *The Sincere Cafe*, by Leslee Becker (short stories).
Recent Poetry Title(s): *A Step in the Dark*, by Stephen C. Behrendt.

MILKWEED EDITIONS, 430 First Ave. N, Suite 400, Minneapolis MN 55401-1743. (612)332-3192. **Acquisitions:** Emilie Buchwald, publisher; Elisabeth Fitz, manuscript coordinator. Estab. 1980. "Milkweed Editions publishes with the intention of making a humane impact on society in the belief that literature is a transformative art uniquely able to convey the essential experiences of the human heart and spirit." Publishes hardcover originals and paperback originals and reprints. Publishes 20 titles/year. Receives 1,560 submissions/year. 30% of books from first-time authors; 70% from unagented writers. Pays 7½% royalty on list price. Advance varies. Publishes work 1 year after acceptance. Accepts simultaneous submissions. Reports in 6 months. Book catalog for $1.50. Manuscript guidelines for SASE.
  ● Milkweed Editions has published such authors as Carol Bly, Larry Watson and Bill Holm.
Nonfiction: Literary. Subjects include government/politics, history, language/literature, nature/environment, women's issues/studies, education. Query with SASE.
Recent Nonfiction Title(s): *Chasing Hellhounds: A Teacher Learns from His Students*, by Marvin Hoffman (urban education).
Fiction: Literary. Novels for readers aged 8-14. High literary quality. Query with SASE.
Recent Fiction Title(s): *The Empress of One*, by Faith Sullivan.
Recent Poetry Title(s): *Invisible Horses*, by Patricia Goedicke.
Tips: "We are looking for excellent writing in fiction, nonfiction, poetry and children's novels, with the intent of making a humane impact on society. Send for guidelines. Acquaint yourself with our books in terms of style and quality before submitting. Many factors influence our selection process, so don't get discouraged. Nonfiction is taking a predominantly environmental as well as educational focus. We no longer publish children's biographies."

‡MILKWEEDS FOR YOUNG READERS, Imprint of Milkweed Editions, 430 First Ave. N., Suite 400, Minneapolis MN 55401-1743. (612)332-3192. Fax: (612)332-6248. **Acquisitions:** Elisabeth Fitz, children's reader. Estab. 1984. "Milkweeds for Young Readers are works that embody humane values and contribute to cultural understanding." Publishes hardcover and trade paperback originals. Publishes 1 title/year. 25% of books from first-time authors; 70% from unagented writers. Pays 7½% royalty on retail price. Advance varies. Publishes book 1 year after acceptance of ms. Accepts simultaneous submissions. Reports in 2 months on queries, 6 months on mss. Book catalog for $1.50. Manuscript guidelines for #10 SASE.
Fiction: For ages 8-12: adventure, animal, fantasy, historical, humor, juvenile, mainstream/contemporary, religious, romance, sports. Query with 2-3 sample chapters and SASE.
Recent Fiction Title(s): *Behind the Bedroom Wall*, by Laura E. Williams (historical); *The Boy with Paper Wings*, by Susan Lowell; *Summer of the Bonepile Monster*, by Aileen Kilgore Henderson (adventure).

‡THE MILLBROOK PRESS INC., 2 Old New Milford Rd., Brookfield CT 06804. Website: http://www.neca.com/mall/millbrook. **Acquisitions:** Dottie Carlson, manuscript coordinator. Estab. 1989. "Millbrook Press publishes quality children's books that educate and entertain." Publishes hardcover and paperback originals. Publishes 150 titles/year. Pays varying royalty on wholesale price or makes outright purchase. Advance varies. Publishes book 1 year after acceptance of ms. Reports in 1 month on queries and proposals. Book catalog for 9 × 12 SAE with 4 first-class stamps. Manuscript guidelines for #10 SASE.
Nonfiction: Children's/juvenile. Subjects include animals, anthropology/archaeology, ethnic, government/politics, health/medicine, history, hobbies, nature/environment, science, sports. "We publish curriculum-related nonfiction for the school/library market. Mistakes writers most often make when submitting nonfiction are failure to research competing titles and failure to research school curriculum." Query or submit outline and 1 sample chapter.
Recent Nonfiction Title(s): *The Young People's Atlas of the World*, by Jon Richards, illustrated by Stephen Sweet; *Ancient Egyptian People*, by Sarah McNeill; *Sidewalk Games Around the World*, by Arlene Erlbach.

‡MILLENIUM PRESS, Subsidiary of Skeptics Society, P.O. Box 338, Altadena CA 91001. (818)794-3119. **Acquisitions:** Michael Shermer, editor. "Millenium Press strives to publish skeptical/scientific books supporting and embodying the scientific method and critical thinking." Publishes hardcover and trade paperback originals. Publishes 4 titles/year. Receives 100 queries and 10 mss/year. 30% of books from first-time authors; 100% from unagented writers. Pays 10% or negotiable royalty on retail price. Offers negotiable advance. Publishes book 8 months after acceptance of ms. Accepts simultaneous submissions. Reports in 1 month on queries, 2 months on proposals, 3 months on mss. Book catalog and ms guidelines free.
Imprint(s): *Skeptic Magazine*.
Nonfiction: Reference, technical. Subjects include history, religion, science. Submit outline, 1 sample chapter, proposal package, including table of contents and author biography. Reviews artwork/photos. Send photocopies.
Recent Nonfiction Title(s): *Bible Prophecy: Failure or Fulfillment?*, by Tim Callahan; *Who Wrote the Gospels?*, by Randel Helms; *Creationism*, by Tom McIver.

MINNESOTA HISTORICAL SOCIETY PRESS, Minnesota Historical Society, 345 Kellogg Blvd. W., St. Paul MN 55102-1906. (612)297-4457. Fax: (612)297-1345. Website: http://www.mnhs.org. **Acquisitions:** Ann Regan, managing editor. Minnesota Historical Society Press publishes both scholarly and general interest books that contribute to the understanding of Minnesota and Midwestern history. Publishes hardcover and trade paperback originals, trade paperback reprints. Publishes 10 titles/year (5 for each imprint). Receives 100 queries and 25 mss/year. 50% of books from first-time authors; 100% from unagented writers. Royalties are negotiated. Publishes book 14 months after acceptance. Reports in 1 month on queries. *Writer's Market* recommends allowing 2 months for reply. Book catalog free.
● Minnesota Historical Society Press is getting many inappropriate submissions from their listing. A regional connection is required.
Imprint(s): Borealis Books (reprints only).
Nonfiction: Regional works only: biography, coffee table book, cookbook, illustrated book, reference. Subjects include anthropology/archaeology, art/architecture, history, memoir, photography, regional, women's issues/studies, Native American studies. Query with proposal package including letter, outline, vita, sample chapter. Reviews artwork/photos as part of ms package. Send photocopies.
Recent Nonfiction Title(s): *In the Company of Women: Voices from the Women's Movement*, by Bonnie Watkins and Nina Rothchild, with a foreword by Gloria Steinem; *Twin Cities: Then and Now*, by Larry Millett, photography by Jerry Mathiason; *From the Hidewood: Memories of a Dakota Neighborhood*, by Robert Amerson.

‡MINSTREL BOOKS, Imprint of Pocket Books for Young Readers, Imprint of Simon & Schuster, 1230 Avenue of the Americas, New York NY 10020. (212)698-7000. Fax: (212698-7007). Website: http://www.simonandschuster.com. Editorial director: Patricia McDonald. **Acquisitions:**Attn: Manuscript proposals. Estab. 1986. "Minstrel publishes fun, kid-oriented books, the kinds kids pick for themselves, for middle grade readers, ages 8-12. " Publishes hardcover originals and reprints, trade paperback originals. Publishes 125 titles/year. Receives 1,200 queries/year. Less than 25% from first-time authors; less than 25% from unagented writers. Pays 6-8% royalty on retail price. Advance varies. Publishes book 2 years after acceptance of ms. Accepts simultaneous submissions. Reports in 3 months on queries. Book catalog and ms guidelines free.
Nonfiction: Children's/juvenile—middle grades, ages 8-12. Subjects include celebrity biographies and books about

TV shows. Query with outline, sample chapters and SASE.
Recent Nonfiction Title(s): *Nickelodeon® The Big Help™ Book: 365 Ways You Can Make a Difference Volunteering*, by Alan Goodman; *My Life with the Chimpanzees*, by Jane Goodall.
 • Minstrel Books publishes many books in series, such as Nancy Drew and The Hardy Boys. Many are based on TV shows such as Nickelodeon, Full House, Clarissa, Star Trek.
Fiction: Middle grade fiction for ages 8-12: animal stories, fantasy, humor, juvenile, mystery, suspense. No picture books. "Thrillers are very popular, and 'humor at school' books." Query with synopsis/outline, sample chapters and SASE.
Recent Fiction Title(s): *R.L. Stine's Ghosts of Fear Street*, by R.L. Stine; *Aliens Ate My Homework*, by Bruce Coville.
Tips: "Hang out with kids to make sure your dialogue and subject matter are accurate."

‡MIRAMAX BOOKS, Imprint of Hyperion, 114 Fifth Ave., New York NY 10011. (212)721-8357. **Acquisitions:** Susan Dalsimer, vice president of publishing. Miramax Books publishes movie tie-ins with Miramax films. Publishes trade paperback originals. Publishes 25-30 titles/year. Receives 50 queries/year. 5% of books from first-time authors. Pays royalty on retail price. Advance varies. Publishes book 1-12 months after acceptance of ms. Accepts simultaneous submissions. Reports in 2 months. Manuscript guidelines free.
 • Miramax Books accepts agented submissions only.

MIS: PRESS, Imprint of Henry Holt & Co., 115 W. 18th St., New York NY 10011. (212)886-9210. Fax: (212)807-6654. Website: http://www.mispress.com. **Acquisitions:** Paul Farrell, associate publisher. "MIS: Press provides practical guides to the general PC user on how to use their PC, including updating and maintaining hardware, how to use software packages and applications like Microsoft Office 97 and Windows 95, and guides to the Internet and the World Wide Web." Publishes trade paperback originals. Publishes 60 titles/year. Receives 250 queries/year. 20% of books from first-time authors; 50% from unagented writers. Pays 5-15% royalty on net price received (receipts), or makes outright purchase of $5,000-20,000. Offers $5,000-10,000 advance. Publishes book 4 months after acceptance. Accepts simultaneous submissions. Book catalog and ms guidelines free.
Nonfiction: Technical, computer, electronic, internet, World Wide Web. "MIS: publishes titles related to computer software or hardware." Submit outline and proposal package.
Recent Nonfiction Title(s): *The Windows 95 Registry*, by John Woram; *Teach Yourself Windows 95*, by Al Stevens.
Tips: "Our audience consists of low-level, brand new computer users. Beginners. A more mass market appeal."

MITCHELL LANE PUBLISHERS, P.O. Box 200, Childs MD 21916. Fax: (410)392-4781. **Acquisitions:** Barbara Mitchell, publisher. "We only publish multicultural biographies." Publishes hardcover and trade paperback originals. Publishes 4-6 titles/year. 10% of books from first-time authors; 100% from unagented writers. Makes outright purchase. Looking for freelance writers on work-for-hire basis to research, interview subjects and write multicultural biographies for children and young adults. No advance. Publishes book 1 year after acceptance of ms. Reports in 1 month. *Writer's Market* recommends allowing 2 months for reply. Book catalog free.
Nonfiction: Biography, multicultural. Ethnic subjects. Query with SASE.
Recent Nonfiction Title(s): *Famous People of Hispanic Heritage*, by B. Marvis (biography collection); *Rafael Palmeiro: Living the American Dream*, by E. Brandt (biography).

MODERN LANGUAGE ASSOCIATION OF AMERICA, Dept. WM, 10 Astor Pl., New York NY 10003. (212)475-9500. Fax: (212)477-9863. **Acquisitions:** Joseph Gibaldi, director of book acquisitions and development. Director of MLA Book Publications: Martha Evans. Estab. 1883. Publishes on current issues in literary and linguistic research and teaching of language and literature at postsecondary level. Publishes hardcover and paperback originals. Publishes 15 titles/year. Receives 125 submissions/year. 100% of books from unagented writers. Pays 5-10% royalty on net proceeds. Publishes book 1 year after acceptance. Reports in 2 months on mss. Book catalog free.
Nonfiction: Scholarly, professional. Language and literature subjects. No critical monographs. Query with outline/synopsis.

‡MONACELLI PRESS, 10 E. 92nd St., New York NY 10128. (212)831-0248. **Acquisitions:** Andrea Monfried, editor. Estab. 1994. "Monacelli Press produces high-quality art books in architecture, fine arts, decorative arts, landscape and photography." Publishes hardcover and trade paperback originals. Publishes 25-30 titles/year. Receives over 100 queries and mss/year. 10% of books from first-time authors; 90% from unagented writers. Pays royalty on retail price. Offers occasional advance. Amount negotiable. Publishes book 18 months after acceptance of ms. Accepts simultaneous submissions. Reports in 3 months on queries. Book catalog free.
Nonfiction: Coffee table book. Subjects include art/architecture. Query with outline, 1 sample chapter and SASE. Reviews artwork/photos as part of ms package. Send transparencies, duplicate slides best. (Monacelli does not assume responsibility for unsolicited artwork; call if you are uncertain about what to send.)
Recent Nonfiction Title(s): *Thomas Jefferson's Monticello: A Photographic Portrait*, photographs by Robert C. Lautman; *The New York Waterfront: Evolution and Building Culture of the Port and Harbor*, edited by Kevin Bone.

‡MOODY PRESS, Subsidiary of Moody Bible Institute, 820 N. LaSalle Blvd., Chicago IL 60610. (312)329-2101. Fax: (312)329-2144. **Acquisitions:** Acquisitions Coordinator. Estab. 1894. "The mission of Moody Press is to educate and edify the Christian and to evangelize the nonChristian by ethically publishing conservative, evangelical Christian literature and other media for all ages around the world; and to help provide resources for Moody Bible Institute in its training of future Christian leaders." Publishes hardcover, trade and mass market paperback originals and hardcover and mass market paperback reprints. Publishes 60 titles/year; imprint publishes 5-10 titles/year. Receives 1,500 queries and 2,000 mss/year. Less than 1% of books from first-time authors; 99% from unagented writers. Royalties and advances vary. Offers $500-50,000 advance. Publishes book 6 months after acceptance of ms. Reports in 2 months. Book catalog for 9×12 SAE with 4 first-class stamps. Manuscript guidelines for #10 SASE.

• Moody Press has published such authors as Erwin Lutzer, Larry Burkett, and Dr. Joseph Stowell.

Imprint(s): Northfield Publishing.

Nonfiction: Children's/juvenile, gift book, general Christian living. Subjects include child guidance/parenting, money/finance, religion, women's issues/studies. "Look at our recent publications, and convince us of what sets your book apart from all the rest on bookstore shelves and why it's consistent with our publications. Many writers don't do enough research of the market or of our needs. Query with outline, 3 sample chapters, table of contents, author's own market study showing why book will be successful and SASE.

Recent Nonfiction Title(s): *Keep Believing*, by Ray Pritchard (Christian living); *Growing Little Women*, by Donna J. Miller (women/family).

Fiction: Religious. "We are not currently accepting fiction submissions."

Tips: "Our audience consists of general, average Christian readers, not scholars. Know the market and publishers. Spend time in bookstores researching. Right now the market is saturated with Christian fiction. We are not currently seeking more fiction."

MOON PUBLICATIONS, INC., P.O. Box 3040, Chico CA 95927-3040. (916)345-3778. Fax: (916)345-6751. E-mail: tmarch@moon.com. Website: http://www.moon.com. **Acquisitions:** Taran March, executive editor. Estab. 1973. "Moon Publications publishes comprehensive, articulate travel information to North and South America, Asia and the Pacific." Publishes trade paperback originals. Publishes 15 titles/year. Receives 100-200 submissions/year. 50% from first-time authors; 95% from unagented writers. Pays royalty on net price. Offers advance of up to $10,000. Publishes book an average of 9 months after acceptance. Accepts simultaneous submissions. Reports in 2 months. Book catalog and proposal guidelines for 7½×10½ SAE with 2 first-class stamps.

• Moon is putting increased emphasis on acquiring writers who are experts in a given destination and demonstrate above-average writing ability.

Nonfiction: "We specialize in travel guides to Asia and the Pacific Basin, the United States, Canada, the Caribbean, Latin America and South America, but are open to new ideas. Our guides include in-depth cultural and historical background, as well as recreational and practical travel information. We prefer comprehensive guides to entire countries, states, and regions over more narrowly defined areas such as cities, museums, etc. Writers should write first for a copy of our guidelines. Proposal required with outline, table of contents, and writing sample. Author should also be prepared to provide photos, artwork and base maps. No fictional or strictly narrative travel writing; no how-to guides." Reviews artwork/photos as part of ms package.

Recent Nonfiction Title(s): *New York Handbook*, by Christiane Bird (travel); *Tennessee Handbook*, by Jeff Bradley (travel); *Dominican Republic Handbook*, by Gaylord Dold (travel).

Tips: "Moon Travel Handbooks are designed by and for independent travelers seeking the most rewarding travel experience possible. Our Handbooks appeal to all travelers because they are the most comprehensive and honest guides available. Check our website."

MOREHOUSE PUBLISHING CO., 871 Ethan Allen Hwy., Ridgefield CT 06877-2801. Fax: (203)431-3964. E-mail: eakelley@aol.com. **Acquisitions:** E. Allen Kelley, publisher; Deborah Grahame, senior editor. Estab. 1884. Morehouse publishes a wide variety of religious nonfiction and fiction with an emphasis on the Anglican faith. Publishes hardcover and paperback originals. Publishes 15 titles/year. Receives 500 submissions/year. 40% of books from first-time authors; 75% from unagented writers. Pays 7-10% royalty. Offers $500-1,000 advance. Publishes book 8 months after acceptance. Accepts simultaneous submissions. Reports in 4 months. Book catalog for 9×12 SAE with $1.01 in postage stamps.

Nonfiction: Specializes in Christian publishing (with an Anglican emphasis). Theology, spirituality, ethics, church history, pastoral counseling, liturgy, religious education activity and gift books, and children's books (preschool-teen). No poetry or drama. Submit outline/synopsis and 1-2 sample chapters. Reviews artwork/photos as part of ms package. Send photocopies, color for color photos.

Recent Nonfiction Title(s): *The Spirituality of St. Patrick*, by Lesley Whiteside; *Glendalough: A Celtic Pilgrimage*, by Michael Rodgers and Marcus Losak; *Spiritual Care of Dying and Bereaved People*, by Penelope Wilcock.

Fiction: Juvenile, picture books, religious, young adult. Small children's list. Artwork essential. Query with synopsis, 2 chapters, intro and SASE. Note: Manuscripts from outside the US will not be returned. Please send copies only.

Recent Fiction Title(s): *Bless All Creatures Here Below*, by Judith Gwyn Brown; *Angel and Me*, by Sara Maitland.

WILLIAM MORROW AND CO., 1350 Avenue of the Americas, New York NY 10019. (212)261-6500. Fax: (212)261-6595. Editorial Director: Betty Nichols Kelly. Managing Editor: Michael Beacon. **Acquisitions:** Ann Bramson, editorial director (Hearst Books, Hearst Marine Books); Amy Cohn (Beech Tree Books, Mulberry Books); Susan Pearson, editor-in-chief (Lothrop, Lee & Shepard Books); David Reuther, editor-in-chief (Morrow Junior Books); Toni Sciarra, editor (Quill Trade Paperbacks); Elizabeth Shub (Greenwillow Books). Estab. 1926. Morrow publishes a wide range of titles that receive much recognition and prestige. A most selective house. Publishes 200 titles/year. Receives 10,000 submissions/year. 30% of books from first-time authors; 5% from unagented writers. Pays standard royalty on retail price. Advance varies. Publishes book 2 years after acceptance. Reports in 3 months. Query letter on all books. *No unsolicited mss or proposals.*

• William Morrow accepts agented submissions only.

Imprint(s): Hearst Books, Hearst Marine Books, Quill Trade Paperbacks, Beech Tree Books (juvenile); **Greenwillow Books** (juvenile); **Lothrop, Lee & Shepard Books** (juvenile); **Morrow Junior Books** (juvenile); Mulberry Books (juvenile).

Nonfiction and Fiction: Adult fiction, nonfiction, history, biography, arts, religion, poetry, how-to books, cookbooks. Length: 50,000-100,000 words. Query only; mss and proposals should be submitted only through an agent.

Recent Nonfiction Title(s): *The Last Party: The Life and Times of Studio 54*, by Anthony Haden-Guest (social history); *Right in the Old Gazoo*, by Alan K. Simpson (politics); *Bogart*, by A.M. Sperber and Eric Lax (biography).

Recent Fiction Title(s): *Van Gogh's Bad Cafe*, by Frederic Tuten; *Playing for Thrills*, by Wang Shuo (translation).

Recent Poetry Title(s): *Love Poems*, by Nikki Giovanni.

MORROW JUNIOR BOOKS, Imprint of William Morrow and Co., Division of The Hearst Corp., 1350 Avenue of the Americas, New York NY 10019. (212)261-6691. **Acquisitions:** David L. Reuther, editor-in-chief; Meredith Carpenter, executive editor; Andrea Curley, senior editor. "Morrow is one of the nation's leading publishers of books for children, including bestselling fiction and nonfiction." Publishes hardcover originals. Publishes 50 titles/year. All contracts negotiated individually. Offers variable advance. Book catalog and guidelines for 9×12 SAE with 3 first-class stamps.

• William Morrow has published such authors as Beverly Cleary, Michael Hague, Kevin Henkes, and James Stevenson. Many Morrow books have won awards including the prestigious Newbery and Caldecott Medals.

Nonfiction: Juveniles (trade books). No textbooks. Query. No unsolicited mss.

Recent Nonfiction Title(s): *I'm a Big Brother*; *I'm a Big Sister*; by Joanna Cole, illustrated by Maxie Chambliss; *The Honey Makers*, by Gail Gibbons (nature).

Fiction: Juveniles (trade books). Query. No unsolicited mss.

Recent Fiction Title(s): *Rumpelstiltskin's Daughter*, by Diane Stanley; *Engelbert Joins the Circus*, by Tom Paxton; illustrated by Roberta Wilson; *Flood*, by Mary Calhoun, illustrated by Erick Ingraham.

MOTORBOOKS INTERNATIONAL, 729 Prospect Ave., Osceola WI 54020. Fax: (715)294-4448. E-mail: mbibks @win.bright.net. Publishing Director: Jack Savage. **Acquisitions:** Zack Miller, senior editor. Estab. 1973. "We are a transportation-related publisher: Cars, motorcycles, racing, trucks, tractors—also aviation and military history." Publishes hardcover and paperback originals. Publishes 100 titles/year. 95% of books from unagented writers. Pays 12% royalty on net receipts. Offers $3,000 average advance. Publishes book 1 year after acceptance. Accepts simultaneous submissions. Reports in 3 months. Free book catalog. Manuscript guidelines for #10 SASE.

Imprint(s): Bicycle Books, Crestline, Zenith Books.

Nonfiction: History, how-to, photography (as they relate to cars, trucks, motorcycles, motor sports, aviation—domestic, foreign and military). Accepts nonfiction translations. Submit outline, 1-2 sample chapters and sample of illustrations. "State qualifications for doing book." Reviews artwork/photos as part of ms package.

Recent Nonfiction Title(s): *The American Barn*, by Randy Leffingwell.

‡MOUNTAIN N'AIR BOOKS, P.O. Box 12540, La Crescenta CA 91224. (818)951-4150. **Acquisitions:** Gilberto d'Urso, owner. Publishes trade paperback originals. Publishes 6 titles/year. Receives 50 queries and 35 mss/year. 75% of books from first-time authors; 100% from unagented writers. Pays 5-10% royalty on retail price or makes outright purchase. No advance. Publishes book 6 months after acceptance with ms. Reports in 2 weeks on queries and 2 months on mss. Manuscript guidelines free.

Imprint(s): Bearly Cooking.

Nonfiction: Biography, cookbook, how-to. Subjects include cooking/foods/nutrition, nature/environment, recreation, travel/adventure. Submit outline with 2 sample chapters. Reviews artwork/photos. Send photocopies.

Recent Nonfiction Title(s): *The Nose Knows*, by Battista (restaurant guide); *Best Hikes of Marble Mt.*, by A. Bernstein (hiking guide).

Tips: Audience is generally interested in the outdoors and travel.

‡MOUNTAIN PRESS PUBLISHING COMPANY, P.O. Box 2399, Missoula MT 59806-2399. (406)728-1900. Fax: (406)728-1635. E-mail: mtpresspub@aol.com. **Acquisitions:** Daniel Greer, editor (history); Kathleen Ort, editor (natural history); Gwen McKenna, assistant editor. Estab. 1948. "We are expanding our Roadside Geology and Roadside History series (done on a state by state basis). We are interested in how-to books (about horses) and well-written regional outdoor guides—plants, flowers and birds." Publishes hardcover and trade paperback originals. Publishes 15 titles/year. Receives 250 submissions/year. 50% of books from first-time authors; 90% from unagented writers. Pays 7-12% on wholesale price. Publishes book 2 years after acceptance. Reports in 3 months on queries. Book catalog free.

Imprint(s): Roadside Geology Series, Roadside History Series, Tumbleweed Series, Classics of the Fur Trade.

Nonfiction: Western history, Americana, nature/environment, regional, earth science, travel. "No personal histories or journals." Query or submit outline and sample chapters. Reviews artwork/photos as part of ms package.

Recent Nonfiction Title(s): *The Journal and Account Book of Patrick Gass, Member of the Lewis and Clark Expedition*, edited and annotated by Carol Lynn MacGregor (history); *Edible and Medicinal Plants of the West*, by Gregory M. Tilford (nature); *Mountain Flowers of New England*, by Jeff Wallner and Mario J. DiGregorio (nature).

Tips: "It is obvious that small- to medium-size publishers are becoming more important, while the giants are becoming less accessible. If I were a writer trying to market a book today, I would find out what kind of books a publisher was interested in and tailor my writing to them; research markets and target my audience. Research other books on the same subjects. Make yours different. Don't present your manuscript to a publisher—*sell* it to him. Give him the information he needs to make a decision on a title."

THE MOUNTAINEERS BOOKS, 1001 SW Klickitat Way, Suite 201, Seattle WA 98134-1162. (206)223-6303. Fax: (206)223-6306. E-mail: mbooks@mountaineers.org. **Acquisitions:** Margaret Foster, editor-in-chief; Thom Votteler, senior acquisitions editor. Estab. 1961. "We specialize in expert, authoritative books dealing with mountaineering, hiking, backpacking, skiing, snowshoeing, canoeing, bicycling, etc. These can be either how-to-do-it or where-to-do-it (guidebooks)." Publishes 95% hardcover and trade paperback originals and 5% reprints. Publishes 40 titles/year. Receives 150-250 submissions/year. 25% of books from first-time authors; 98% from unagented writers. Average print order for a first book is 5,000-7,000. Pays royalty on net sales. Offers advance. Publishes book 1 year after acceptance. Reports in 3 months. Book catalog and ms guidelines for 9 × 12 SAE with 3 first-class stamps.
  ● Mountain Books is looking for manuscripts with more emphasis on regional conservation and natural history. See the Contests and Awards section for information on the Barbara Savage/"Miles From Nowhere" Memorial Award offered by Mountain Books.
Nonfiction: Guidebooks for national and international adventure travel, recreation, natural history, conservation/environment, non-competitive self-propelled sports, outdoor how-to, and some children's books. Does *not* want to see "anything dealing with hunting, fishing or motorized travel." Submit author bio, outline and minimum of 2 sample chapters. Accepts nonfiction translations. Looks for "expert knowledge, good organization." Also interested in nonfiction adventure narratives. Ongoing award—The Barbara Savage/"Miles from Nowhere" Memorial Award for outstanding adventure narratives is offered.
Recent Nonfiction Title(s): *Conditioning for Outdoor Fitness*, edited by David Musnick and Sandra Kay Elliot; *Backcountry Bear Basics*, by David Smith; *Trekking in Bolivia*, by Yossi Brain.
Fiction: "We might consider an exceptionally well-done book-length manuscript on mountaineering." No poetry or mystery. Query first.
Tips: "The type of book the writer has the best chance of selling our firm is an authoritative guidebook (*in our field*) to a specific area not otherwise covered; or a how-to that is better than existing competition (again, *in our field*)."

‡MOYER BELL, Kymbolde Way, Wakefield RI 02879. (401)789-0074. Fax: (401)789-3793. **Acquisitions:** Jennifer Moyer, editor. Estab. 1984. "Moyer Bell was established to publish literature, reference and art books." Publishes hardcover originals, trade paperback originals and reprints. Publishes 25 titles/year; imprint publishes 4 titles/year. Receives 500 queries and 1,500 mss/year. 1% of books from first-time authors; 90% from unagented writers. Pays royalty on retail price. No advance. Publishes book 1-2 years after acceptance of ms. Accepts simultaneous submissions. Reports in 1 month on queries and proposals; 6 months on mss. Book catalog for #10 SASE.
Imprint(s): Asphodel Press.
Nonfiction: Biography, self-help. Subjects include art/architecture, current affairs, politics. Query with outline, 1-2 sample chapters and SASE.
Recent Nonfiction Title(s): *World Enough And Time: A Historical Chronicle*, by Jonathan Schell (politics); *In The Wake of Death: Surviving The Loss Of A Child*, by Mark Cosman (self-help).
Fiction: Literary. Query with synopsis, 1-2 sample chapters and SASE.
Recent Fiction Title(s): *The Orchard On Fire*, by Shena Mackay (novel); *The Only Piece Of Furniture In The House*, by Diane Glancy (novel).

‡JOHN MUIR PUBLICATIONS, Subsidiary of Agever Inc., P.O. Box 613, Santa Fe NM 87504. (505)982-4078. Fax: (505)988-1680. **Acquisitions:** Cassandra Conyers, acquisitions editor. John Muir Publications seeks to "enrich independent spirits." Publishes trade paperback originals. Publishes 60-70 titles/year. Receives 1,000 queries and 50 mss/year. 60% of books from first-time authors; 90% from unagented writers. Pays 3½-10% royalty on wholesale price or makes outright purchase occasionally. Offers $1,000-2,500 advance. Publishes book 1 year after acceptance of ms. Accepts simultaneous submissions if noted in cover letter. Reports in 6 weeks on queries, 4 months on proposals. Book catalog for 9 × 12 SAE and 3 first-class stamps. Manuscript guidelines for #10 SASE.
Nonfiction: Adult/juvenile, self-help, nature/environment, child guidance/parenting, travel, travel-related and alternative health. "We are continuing our commitment to adult travel titles and seeking unique travel-related manuscripts for children 6-10 or 8-12-year olds. We are refining our list; we're particularly interested in travel, juvenile and alternative health. Do your homework to see what kinds of books we publish." Query or submit outline, 1-2 sample chapters and proposal package, including competition, résumé, marketing ideas with SASE. Reviews artwork/photos as part of ms package. Send photocopies or transparencies.
Recent Nonfiction Title(s): *Saddle Up!*, by Ute Haker (guide for horseback vacations); *American Southwest*, by Richard Harris (road guide); *Kids Explore Kids Who Make a Difference*, by Westridge Young Writer's Workshop.
Tips: "Audience is adults interested in independent travel and wanting to share enthusiasm with their children. They are environmentally-minded, somewhat adventurous and interested in multicultural themes. Know that John Muir publishes nonfiction, so don't send us your great fiction idea. Check the competition. We don't want to see your idea if it's already on the store shelves."

MUSTANG PUBLISHING CO., P.O. Box 3004, Memphis TN 38173-0004. (901)521-1406. **Acquisitions:** Rollin Riggs, editor. Estab. 1983. Mustang publishes general interest nonfiction for an adult audience. Publishes hardcover and trade paperback originals. Publishes 10 titles/year. Receives 1,000 submissions/year. 50% of books from first-time authors; 90% of books from unagented writers. Pays 6-8% royalty on retail price. Publishes book 1 year after acceptance. Accepts simultaneous submissions. Reports in 1 month. *Writer's Market* recommends allowing 2 months for reply. Book catalog for $2 and #10 SASE. No phone calls, please.
Nonfiction: How-to, humor, self-help. Subjects include Americana, hobbies, recreation, sports, travel. "Our needs are very general—humor, travel, how-to, etc.—for the 18-to 45-year-old market." Query or submit outline and sample chapters with SASE.
Recent Nonfiction Title(s): *Dear Elvis: Graffiti From Graceland*, by Wright (pop culture); *Luck Pants & Other Golf Myths*, by Kohl (humor).
Tips: "From the proposals we receive, it seems that many writers never go to bookstores and have no idea what sells. Before you waste a lot of time on a nonfiction book idea, ask yourself, 'How often have my friends and I actually *bought* a book like this?' Know the market, and know the audience you're trying to reach."

THE MYSTERIOUS PRESS, Imprint of Warner Books, 1271 Avenue of the Americas, New York NY 10020. (212)522-5144. Fax: (212)522-7994. Website: http://www.twep.timeinc.com/twep/mysterious_press. **Acquisitions:** William Malloy, editor-in-chief; Sara Ann Freed, executive editor; Susanna Einstein, editorial assistant. Estab. 1976. The Mysterious Press seeks "well-written crime/mystery/suspense fiction." Publishes hardcover and mass market editions. Averages 50 titles/year. Accepts no unagented mss. Pays standard, but negotiable, royalty on retail price. Amount of advance varies widely. Publishes book an average of 1 year after acceptance. Reports in 2 months.
 • This publisher considers agented submissions only. The Mysterious Press has reduced their list to 50 titles/year. They have published such authors as James Crumley, Marcia Muller and Aaron Elkins.
Fiction: Mystery, suspense. "We will consider publishing any outstanding crime/suspense/detective novel that comes our way. No short stories." Query. Agented submissions only.
Recent Fiction Title(s): *The Ragman's Memory*, by Archer Mayor; *Up Jumps the Devil*, by Margaret Maron.
Tips: "We do not read unagented material. Agents only, please."

MYSTIC SEAPORT MUSEUM, 75 Greenmanville Ave., Mystic CT 06355-0990. (203)572-0711. Fax: (203)572-5326. **Acquisitions:** Joseph Gribbins, publications director. Estab. 1970. Publishes hardcover and trade paperback originals and reprints. Publishes 4-6 titles/year. Pays 15% royalty on wholesale price. Offers up to $10,000 advance. Reports in 3 months.
Imprint(s): American Maritime Library.
Nonfiction: "We need serious, well-documented biographies, studies of economic, social, artistic, or musical elements of American maritime (not naval) history; books on traditional boat and ship types and construction (how-to). We are now interested in all North American maritime history—not, as in the past, principally New England. We like to see anything and everything, from queries to finished work." Query with outline and 3 sample chapters and SASE.
Recent Nonfiction Title(s): *Letters from China*, edited by Phyllis Forbes Kerr (China-trade correspondence-1840).

THE NAIAD PRESS, INC., P.O. Box 10543, Tallahassee FL 32302. (904)539-5965. Fax: (904)539-9731. **Acquisitions:** Barbara Grier, editorial director. Estab. 1973. "We publish lesbian fiction, preferably lesbian/feminist fiction." Publishes paperback originals. Publishes 31 titles/year. Receives over 1,500 submissions/year. 20% of books from first-time authors; 99% from unagented writers. Average print order for a first book is 8,000. Pays 15% royalty on wholesale or retail price. No advance. Publishes book 2 years after acceptance. Reports in 4 months. Book catalog and ms guidelines for 6×9 SAE and $1.50 postage and handling
 • Naiad Press has published such authors as Gertrude Stein, Isabel Miller and Teresa Stores.
Recent Nonfiction Title(s): *The Loving Lesbian*, edited by Claire McNab and Sharon Gedan (long-term relationships); *Sapphistry: The Book of Lesbian Sexuality, 3rd Edition.*
Fiction: "We are not impressed with the 'oh woe' school and prefer realistic (i.e., happy) novels. We emphasize fiction and are now heavily reading manuscripts in that area. We are working in a lot of genre fiction—mysteries, short stories, fantasy—all with lesbian themes, of course. We have instituted an inhouse anthology series, featuring short stories only by our own authors (i.e. authors who have published full length fiction with us or those signed to do so)." Query.
Recent Fiction Title(s): *Sea to Shining Sea*, by Lisa Shapiro (lesbian romance); *Second Fiddle*, by Kate Calloway (mystery); *Devil's Leg Crossing*, by Kaye Davis (mystery).
Tips: "There is tremendous world-wide demand for lesbian mysteries from lesbian authors published by lesbian presses, and we are doing several such series. We are no longer seeking science fiction. Manuscripts under 50,000 words have twice as good a chance as over 50,000."

NASW PRESS, Division of National Association of Social Workers, 750 First St. NE, Suite 700, Washington DC 20002-4241. Fax: (202)336-8312. E-mail: press@naswdc.org. Website: http://www.naswpress.org. Executive Editor: Nancy Winchester. **Acquisitions**: Chanté Lampton, acquisitions associate. Estab. 1956. NASW Books "provides outstanding information tools for social workers and other human service professionals to advance the knowledge base in social work and social welfare." Publishes 10-15 titles/year. Receives 100 submissions/year. 20% of books from first-time authors; 100% from unagented writers. Pays 10-15% royalty on net prices. Publishes book 8 months after acceptance of ms. Reports within 4 months on submissions. Book catalog and ms guidelines free.

• NASW will be putting more emphasis on publishing health, policy, substance abuse and aging books.
Nonfiction: Textbooks of interest to professional social workers. "We're looking for books on social work in health care, mental health, multicultural competence and substance abuse. Books must be directed to the professional social worker and build on the current literature." Submit outline and sample chapters. Rarely reviews artwork/photos as part of ms package.
Recent Nonfiction Title(s): *Multicultural Issues in Social Work* (diversity); *Who We Are: A Second Look*, by Gibelman and Schervish (professional); *Risk and Resilience in Childhood*, edited by Mark Fraser (children and families).
Tips: "Our audience includes social work practitioners, educators, students and policy makers. They are looking for practice-related books that are well grounded in theory. The books that do well have direct application to the work our audience does. New technology, AIDS, welfare reform and health policy will be of increasing interest to our readers. We are particularly interested in manuscripts for fact-based practice manuals that will be very user-friendly."

NATIONAL TEXTBOOK CO., Imprint of NTC/Contemporary Publishing Group, 4255 W. Touhy Ave., Lincolnwood IL 60646. (847)679-5500. Fax: (847)679-2494. President/CEO: Mark R. Pattis. **Acquisitions:** N. Keith Fry, executive editor (foreign language and ESL); Anne Knudsen, executive editor (Quilt Digest Press, nonfiction books on quilting, 5 titles/year); Betsy Lancefield executive editor (VGM Career Horizons); Richard Hagle (NTC Business Books). Publishes original textbooks for education and trade market, and software. Publishes 100-150 titles/year. Receives 1,000 submissions/year. 10% of books from first-time authors. 75% from unagented writers. Manuscripts purchased on either royalty or fee basis. Publishes book 1 year after acceptance. Reports in 3 months. Book catalog and ms guidelines for 6×9 SAE and 2 first-class stamps.
Nonfiction: Textbooks. Major emphasis being given to foreign language and language arts classroom texts, especially secondary level material, and business and career subjects (marketing, advertising, sales, etc.). Editorial group director: John T. Nolan. Send sample chapter and outline or table of contents.
Recent Nonfiction Title(s): *Beginner's Kana Workbook* (Japanese); *Hammer's German Grammar and Usage*; *Cybermarketing*.

NATUREGRAPH PUBLISHERS, INC., P.O. Box 1075, Happy Camp CA 96039. (916)493-5353. Fax: (916)493-5240. **Acquisitions:** Barbara Brown, editor. Estab. 1946. "Our primary niches are nature and Native American subjects with adult level, non-technical language and scientific accuracy." Publishes trade paperback originals. Publishes 5 titles/year. Pays 8-10% royalty on wholesale price. No advance. Reports in 1 month on queries, 2 months on proposals and mss. Book catalog free.
Nonfiction: Primarily publishes nonfiction for the layman in 6 general areas: natural history (biology, geology, ecology, astronomy); American Indian (historical and contemporary); outdoor living (backpacking, wild edibles, etc.); land and gardening (modern homesteading); crafts and how-to; holistic health (natural foods and healing arts). "Send for our catalog. Study what kind of books we have already published." Submit outline, 2 sample chapters and SASE.
Recent Nonfiction Title(s): *Tricks of the Trail: Modern Backpacking*, by Roy Santoro (outdoor); *Welcome to the Moon: Twelve Lunar Expeditions for Small Telescopes*, by Robert Bruce Kelsey (astronomy); *Making an Accurate Modern Sundial: Timepiece and Teacher for the Modern Hemisphere*, by Sam Muller.
Tips: "Please—always send a stamped reply envelope. Publishers get hundreds of manuscripts yearly; not just yours."

THE NAUTICAL & AVIATION PUBLISHING CO., 8 W. Madison St., Baltimore MD 21201. (410)659-0220. Fax: (410)539-8832. President/Publisher: Jan Snouck-Hurgronje. **Acquisitions:** Rebecca Irish, editor. Estab. 1979. "We are publishers of military history." Publishes hardcover originals and reprints. Publishes 10-12 titles/year. Receives 125 submissions/year. Pays 10-15% royalty on net selling price. Rarely offers advance. Accepts simultaneous submissions. Book catalog free.
• The Nautical & Aviation Publishing Company has published such authors as Admiral William P. Mack and C.S. Forester.
Nonfiction: Reference. Subjects include history, military/war. Query with synopsis and 3 sample chapters. Reviews artwork/photo as part of package.
Recent Nonfiction Title(s): *The Battle for Baltimore: 1814*, by Joseph A. Whitehorne; (War of 1812 on the Chesapeake Bay); *The Battle of Tassafaronga*, by Captain Russell Crenshaw; *The Essex Aircraft Carriers*, by Andrew Faltum.
Fiction: Historical. Submit outline/synopsis and sample chapters.
Recent Fiction Title(s): *The Black Flower: Angel of the Civil War*, by Howard Bahr, (Battle of Franklin, TN).
Tips: "We are primarily a nonfiction publisher, but will review historical fiction of military interest."

NAVAL INSTITUTE PRESS, Imprint of U.S. Naval Institute, 118 Maryland Ave., Annapolis MD 21402-5035. Fax: (410)269-7940. E-mail: esecunda@usni.org. Website: http://www.usni.org. Press Director: Ronald Chambers. **Acquisitions:** Paul Wilderson, executive editor; Mark Gatlin, senior acquisitions editor; Scott Belliveau, acquisitions editor. Estab. 1873. The U.S. Naval Institute Press publishes general and scholarly books of professional, scientific, historical and literary interest to the naval and maritime community. Publishes 80 titles/year. Receives 400-500 submissions/year. 50% of books from first-time authors; 85% from unagented writers. Average print order for a first book is 2,000. Pays 5-10% royalty on net sales. Publishes book 1 year after acceptance. Query letter strongly recommended. *Writer's Market* recommends allowing 2 months for reply. Book catalog free with 9×12 SASE. Manuscript guidelines for #10 SASE.
Imprint(s): Bluejacket Books (paperback reprints).
• Naval Institute Press has increased their number of books published from 65 to 80 titles/year.

Nonfiction: "We are interested in naval and maritime subjects and in broad military topics, including government policy and funding. Specific subjects include: tactics, strategy, navigation, history, biographies, aviation, technology and others."
Recent Nonfiction Title(s): *Missile Inbound: The Attack on the Stark in the Persian Gulf*, by Jeffrey L. Levinson and Randy L. Edwards; *Japanese Cruises of the Pacific War*, by Eric Lacroix and Linton Wells II (World War II history).
Fiction: Limited fiction on military and naval themes.
Recent Fiction Title(s): *Rising Wind*, by Dick Couch (modern military thriller).

NEAL-SCHUMAN PUBLISHERS, INC., 100 Varick St., New York NY 10013. (212)925-8650. Fax: (212)219-8916. E-mail: ctharmon@aol.com. **Acquistions:** Charles Harmon, editorial director. "Neal-Schuman publishes books about libraries, information science and the use of information technology, especially in education and libraries." Publishes hardcover and trade paperback originals. Publishes 30 titles/year. Receives 80 submissions/year. 75% of books from first-time authors; 80% from unagented writers. Pays 10% royalty on net sales. Offers advances infrequently. Publishes book 1 year after acceptance. Reports in 1 month on proposals. *Writer's Market* recommends allowing 2 months for reply. Book catalog and ms guidelines free.
Nonfiction: Reference, software, technical, textbook, texts and professional books in library and information science. Subjects include computers/electronics, education, gay/lesbian, language/literature, software. "We are looking for books about the Internet." Submit proposal package, including vita, outline, preface and sample chapters.
Recent Nonfiction Title(s): *Technology and Copyright Law: A Guidebook for the Library, Research and Teaching Professions*, by Arlene Bielefield and Lawrence Cheeseman; *The Internet for Teachers and School Library Media Specialists*, edited by Edward Valauskas and Monica Ertel; *The New Library Legacy*, edited by Susan Lee.

THOMAS NELSON PUBLISHERS, Nashville TN. Corporate address does not accept unsolicited manuscripts. No phone queries. **Acquisitions:** Janet Thoma (Janet Thoma Books, 1157 Molokai, Tega Cay SC 29715, fax: (803)548-2684); Victor Oliver (Oliver-Nelson Books, 1360 Center Dr., Suite 102-B, Atlanta GA 30338, fax: (770)391-9784); Mark Roberts, (reference and religious studies, P.O. Box 1410000, Nashville TN 37214, fax: (615)391-5225). Publishes Christian lifestyle nonfiction and fiction. Publishes 150-200 titles/year. Pays variable royalty on net sales. Books published 1-2 years after acceptance. Reports in 3 months. Accepts simultaneous submissions, if so noted.
Imprint(s): Janet Thoma Books, Oliver-Nelson Books, **Tommy Nelson**.
Nonfiction: Adult inspirational, motivational, devotional, self-help, Christian living, prayer and evangelism, reference/Bible study. Send brief, prosaic résumé, 1-page synopsis and 1 sample chapter to one of the acquisitions editors at the above locations with SASE.
Recent Nonfiction Title(s): *The Big Book of Bible People*, by Mark Walter, illustrated by Graham Round; *Angels in Action: What the Bible Says About Angels*, by Helen Haidle, illustrated by David Haidle.
Fiction: Seeking successfully published commercial fiction authors who write for adults from a Christian perspective. Send brief, prosaic résumé, 1-page synopsis and 1 sample chapter to one of the acquisitions editors at the above locations with SASE.
Recent Fiction Title(s): *Spine Chillers*, by Fred E. Katz (thriller series).

‡TOMMY NELSON, Thomas Nelson, Inc. Publishers, 404 BNA Dr., Bldg. 200, Suite 508, Nashville TN 37217. **Acquisitions**: Laura Minchew, acquisitions editor. Tommy Nelson publishes children's Christian nonfiction and fiction for boys and girls up to age 14. Publishes hardcover and trade paperback originals. Publishes 50-75 titles/year. Receives 200 queries and 1,000 mss/year. 5% of books from first-time authors; 50% from unagented writers. Pays royalty on wholesale price or makes outright purchase. Pays $1,000 minimum advance. Publishes book 18 months after acceptance of ms. Accepts simultaneous submissions but prefers not to. Reports in 1 month on queries, 3 months on proposals and mss. Manuscript guidelines for #10 SASE.
Nonfiction: Children's/juvenile. Religious subjects (Christian evangelical). Submit outline, 3 sample chapters and SASE.
Recent Nonfiction Title(s): *Tiny Talks*, by Robert J. Morgan, illustrated by Ann Hagne (devotion, ages 3-7); *The Toddler's ABC Books*, by Andy and Sandra Stanley (board book).
Fiction: Adventure, juvenile, mystery, picture books, religious. "No stereotypical characters without depth." Submit synopsis with 3 sample chapters.
Recent Fiction Title(s): *The Parable of the Lily*, by Liz Curtis Higgs, illustrated by Nancy Munger (picture book, ages 3-7); *The Younguns of Mansfield*, by Thomas L. Tedrow (fiction, ages 10-14).
Tips: "Know the CBA market. Check out the Christian bookstores to see what sells and what is needed." Note: Nelson Children's Books and Word Children's books are now Tommy Nelson.

NELSON-HALL PUBLISHERS, 111 N. Canal St., Chicago IL 60606. (312)930-9446. General Manager: Richard O. Meade. **Acquistions:** Editorial Director. Estab. 1909. Nelson-Hall publishes college textbooks and general scholarly books in the social sciences. Publishes hardcover and paperback originals. Publishes 30 titles/year. Receives 200 queries and 20 mss/year. 90% of books submitted by unagented writers. Pays 5-15% royalty on wholesale price. Publishes book 1 year after acceptance. Accepts simultaneous submissions. Reports in 1 month on queries. *Writer's Market* recommends allowing 2 months for reply.

Nonfiction: Subjects include anthropology/archaeology, government/politics, music/dance, psychology, sociology. Query with outline, 2 sample chapters, cv.
Recent Nonfiction Title(s): *The Rich Get Richer*, by Denny Braun, Ph.D.

‡**NEW DIRECTIONS PUBLISHING CORP.**, 80 Eighth Ave., New York NY 10011. (212)255-0230. Fax: (212)255-0231. Website: http://www.wwnorton.com. **Acquisitions:** (Mr.) Declan Spring, managing editor. Estab. 1936. "New Directions publishes experimental, avant-garde works." Publishes hardcover and trade paperback originals and reprints. Publishes 30-35 titles/year. Receives 500 queries/year. 1% of books from first-time authors; 5% from unagented writers. Pays royalty on retail price. Offers $200-2,000 advance. Publishes book 18 months after acceptance of ms. Reports in 4 months.
Fiction: Experimental, avant-garde. "Become familiar with our catalog before deciding to submit." Query.
Poetry: Experimental. Query.
Recent Poetry Title(s): *At Passages*, by Michael Palmer; *Cantos*, by Ezra Pound (reprint).

‡**THE NEW ENGLAND PRESS, INC.**, P.O. Box 575, Shelburne VT 05482. (802)863-2520. Fax: (802)863-1510. E-mail: nep@together.net. **Acquisitions:** Mark Wanner, managing editor. The New England Press publishes regional nonfiction and regional/historical young adult fiction. Publishes hardcover and trade paperback originals. Publishes 6-8 titles/year. Receives 500 queries and 200 mss/year. 50% of books from first-time authors; 90% from unagented writers. Pays royalty on wholesale price. No advance. Publishes book 15 months after acceptance of ms. Accepts simultaneous submissions. Reports in 3 months on proposals. Book catalog free.
Nonfiction: Biography, children's/juvenile, illustrated book. Subjects include gardening, history, regional, Vermontiana. "Nonfiction submissions must be based in Vermont and have northern New England topics. No memoirs or family histories. Identify potential markets and ways to reach them in cover letter." Submit outline and 2 sample chapters with SASE. Reviews artwork/photos as part of the ms package. Send photocopies.
Recent Nonfiction Title(s): *A Pinprick of Light*, by Carl Byron (history).
Fiction: "We look for very specific subject matters based on Vermont history and heritage. We are also interested in historical novels for young adults based in New Hampshire and Maine. We do not publish contemporary adult fiction of any kind." Submit synopsis and 2 sample chapters with SASE.
Recent Fiction Title(s): *The Black Bonnet*, by Louella Bryant (young adult/Vermont history.)
Tips: "Our readers are interested in all aspects of Vermont and northern New England, including hobbyists (railroad books) and students (young adult fiction and biography). No agent is needed, but our market is extremely specific and our volume is low, so send a query or outline and writing samples first. Sending the whole manuscript is discouraged. We will not accept projects that are still under development or give advances."

NEW HARBINGER PUBLICATIONS, 5674 Shattuck Ave., Oakland CA 94609. Fax: (510)652-5472. E-mail: newharbpub@aol.com. Website: http://www.newharbinger.com. **Acquisitions:** Kristin Beck, acquisitions editor. "We look for psychology and health self-help books that teach the average reader how to master essential skills. Our books are also read by mental health professionals who want simple, clear explanations of important psychological techniques and health issues." Publishes 26 titles/year. Receives 750 queries and 200 mss/year. 60% of books from first-time authors; 95% from unagented writers. Pays 12% royalty on wholesale price. Offers $0-3,000 advance. Publishes book 1 year after acceptance of ms. Accepts simultaneous submissions. Reports in 1 month on queries and proposals, 2 months on mss. Book catalog and ms guidelines free.
● New Harbinger has published such authors as Matthew McKay, Ph.D.; Patrick Fanning and Ed Bourne, Ph.D..
Nonfiction: Self-help (psychology/health), textbooks. Subjects include anger management, anxiety, coping, health/medicine, psychology. "Authors need to be a qualified psychotherapist or health practitioner to publish with us." Submit proposal package, including outline, 3 sample chapters, competing titles and why this one is special.
Recent Nonfiction Title(s): *The Body Image Workbook*, by Thomas F. Cash, Ph.D. (psychology/self-help); *Living with ADD: A Workbook for Adults with Attention Deficit Disorder*, by M. Susan Roberts/Gerard Jansen, Ph.D. (psychology/self-help).
Tips: Audience includes psychotherapists and lay readers wanting step-by-step strategies to solve specific problems.

NEW HOPE, Woman's Missionary Union, P.O. Box 12065, Birmingham AL 35202-2065. (205)991-8100. Fax: (205)991-4990. Website: http://www.wmu.com/wmu. **Acquisitions:** Cindy McClain, editorial director. "Our goal is to provide missions-related programs, information, resources and training to motivate and enable churches and believers to meet spiritual, physical and social needs, locally and globally." Publishes 15 titles/year. Receives 100 queries and 60 mss/year. 25% of books from first-time authors; 98% from unagented writers. Pays 7-10% royalty on retail price or makes outright purchase. Publishes book 2 years after acceptance of ms. Reports in 6 months on mss. Book catalog for 9×12 SAE with 3 first-class stamps. Manuscript guidelines for #10 SASE.
● New Hope has published such authors as Esther Burroughs, Jennifer Kenedy Dean and Barbara Joiner.
Imprint(s): New Hope, Woman's Missionary Union.
Nonfiction: How-to, children's/juvenile (religion), personal spiritual growth. Subjects include child guidance/parenting (from Christian perspective), education (Christian church), religion (Christian faith—must relate to missions work, culture and multicultural issues, Christian concerns, Christian ethical issues, spiritual growth, etc.), women's issues/studies from Christian perspective. "We publish Christian education materials that focus on missions work or educational work in some way. Teaching helps, spiritual growth material, ideas for working with different audiences in a church,

INSIDER REPORT

Growing Christian market offers unexpected outlet for children's writers

If you think Christian children's publishers produce only kids' Bible story books, Christmas stories and parables, you'll be surprised paging through a Tommy Nelson catalog.

Laura Minchew

A Division of Thomas Nelson, Inc. (resulting from a marriage of Nelson's children's line to Word Kids!), Tommy Nelson offers a diverse list including a series of scary mysteries, a book of money-making ideas for kids, and an adventure series of futuristic fiction including virtual reality and time travel, along with traditional Biblical tales.

"Bible stories are very important to Christians," says Laura Minchew, vice president of editorial acquisitions for Tommy Nelson. "They also live the rest of the day just like everyone else, so we're trying to offer Bible story books along with adventure books and fun books for casual reading."

An adventure story from a Christian publisher does differ somewhat from an adventure story from a general children's publisher. "Our books have a take-away value," explains Minchew. "There are some delightful stories in trade bookstores that are simply fun to read, but there's nothing really to take away at the end of the day. In the inspirational market, readers come away with something they've learned about life, a value, something that inspires them, a moral."

For example, the Tommy Nelson title *50 Money Making Ideas for Kids*, by Larry Burkett, "actually teaches some stewardship principles—such as 'with ownership comes responsibility'—which you would find in other financial books, but which are actually based in the Bible."

Writers may wonder how Tommy Nelson's SpineChillers Mysteries line of scary stories could fit the needs of an inspirational publisher. These titles certainly are not clones of R.L. Stine's books. "There are mystery elements to these books; there are scary things in these books, but the difference is that by the end of our books, everything is explained rationally or scientifically—there's no supernatural. These are not nightmare books."

For example, in the SpineChillers title *Attack of the Killer House*, a couple of kids are "terrorized" by out-of-control home appliances—a hair dryer chases them, an electric blanket rolls them up, a video game shoots back. It's pretty scary, but there are no ghosts involved. It turns out that their dad is a computer guy and has all the appliances wired to a central system. When the house is struck by lightning in the beginning of the book, the fried computer system sends mixed-up commands throughout the household, causing all the appliances to "attack."

INSIDER REPORT, *Minchew*

These "kinder, gentler Goosebumps" books may be just what some parents seek for their children's bookshelves. "We're trying to offer an alternative to parents, so they don't have to say, 'You can't read anything scary.' SpineChillers offer a nice combination of elements that a child is looking for and the things that a parent is going to feel good about them reading," says Minchew.

There is one pitfall writers should avoid when submitting to the Christian children's market—preachiness. Books can have a spiritual bent without talking down to kids, pointing fingers at them, or shoving lessons down their throats. "As an adult, I don't like someone telling me, 'This is what you will think and this is what you will do.' To me that's really offensive. We see kids in a lot of our books for whom Christianity is a way of life. They act as Christians would act, they talk as Christians would talk. They don't go around preaching to everyone they see—it's more natural," says Minchew.

This light touch may explain why sales of books from inspirational publishers are not limited to the Christian market. One humorous Tommy Nelson series, The Incredible Worlds of Wally MacDoogle, written by Bill Myers, has sold over a quarter million units in CBA (Christian Booksellers Association), ABA (American Booksellers Association) and mass market outlets. "I think the sales figures of some of our books would be surprising to people," says Minchew. In fact, a recent consumer research study shows, out of all book categories, juvenile religious fiction has had the second highest growth in market share in recent years.

Sales potential is certainly an important factor for writers to consider when preparing a submission package. "When I present a book to a sales rep, I have to have a hook," says Minchew. "I was talking to an author today, and I said, 'What differentiates your series from these other two series that sound very similar?' He said, 'I'm a better writer.' Okay, good. You are a better writer. That will help sell book number six in your series. But tell me—when I'm going to sell book number one, what's the marketing hook? What's the angle? What differentiates this book from everything else?

"I get submissions from authors that say, 'I've always wanted to write a children's book, and this is a nice little story.' Well, am I supposed to say to a sales rep, 'Hey look— here's a nice little story'; then they're supposed say that to the book seller; and the book seller is supposed to say that to the customer? There has to be something to motivate the buyer. There's either a felt need, or something really unique about the book. I know writers feel very strongly about their books, and it's amazing how often they don't tell me why they feel strongly. They expect me to dig through 200 pages to figure out why."

Another Tommy Nelson series, CyberQuest, is a perfect example of an author with a great marketing concept. The first book in this series by Sigmund Brouwer is selling for 99 cents, "seeding the market." Each book in the six-book series is an independent story, but the end of each book teases the next one, and they're all a serial—at the end, kids can read them all through as a straight story. Brouwer has also taken an ultra hip element— virtual reality—and woven it into a series of adventures following Mok, a futuristic hero, as he travels through time to save his race from annihilation by the evil Technocrats. Throughout his travels through virtual time, "this person from the future is seeing how Jesus impacted people's lives and thinking in every time period and throughout every part of history." says Minchew. "Sigmund Brouwer is one of our most fun authors. He is in schools constantly, so he really knows where kids are, what they like and what they're thinking."

For Minchew, this audience familiarity is important. "There are four million children

---

INSIDER REPORT, *continued*

born each year. There are more preschoolers now than in any time in history since the early 1960s. Fifty-one million people in the U.S. are preteens. At Tommy Nelson, we wake up and we go to sleep thinking children."

In addition to knowing your audience, Minchew feels the most important thing a writer can do is know the companies she's submitting to and target manuscripts appropriately. "We get about 50 manuscripts a week right now—it's unbelievable to try to get through. The vast majority are not what we're looking for. If you don't have something that's inspirational in nature, don't send it to us saying, 'This isn't really what you want, but here's a nice story.' "

—Alice. P. Buening

---

etc.—missions work overseas or church work in the U.S., women's spiritual issues, guiding children in Christian faith." Submit outline and 3 sample chapters for review. Submit complete ms for acceptance decision.
Recent Nonfiction Title(s): *Precious in His Sight,* by Diana Garland (child advocacy); *Lose the Halo, Keep the Wings (Great Advice for Ministers' Wives),* by Virginia Wilson; *One Common Need* (advocacy).
Recent Fiction Title(s): *Clay Homes,* by Judy Langley.

NEW LEAF PRESS, INC., P.O. Box 726, Green Forest AR 72638-0726. Fax: (501)438-5120. **Acquisitions:** Editorial Board. Estab. 1975. "We are known for our prophecy books, Christian living books and our inspirational gift line." Publishes hardcover and paperback originals. Publishes 15-20 titles/year. Receives 500 submissions/year. 15% of books from first-time authors; 90% from unagented writers. Average print order for a first book is 10,000. Pays variable royalty once per year. No advance. Publishes book 10 months after acceptance. Accepts simultaneous submissions. Reports in 3 months. Book catalog and ms guidelines for 9×12 SAE with 5 first-class stamps.
Nonfiction: How to live the Christian life, humor, self-help, devotionals. Length: 100-400 pages. Submit complete ms. *Writer's Market* recommends sending a query with SASE first. Reviews artwork/photos as part of ms package. Send photos and illustrations to accompany ms.
Recent Nonfiction Title(s): *The Moment to Give,* by Robert Strand (series); *A Bouquet From Heaven,* by Melva Lard; *Signs of His Coming,* by David Allan Lewis.
Tips: "Quality Christian writing is still the measuring stick, so writers should submit accordingly."

THE NEW LEXINGTON PRESS, Imprint of Jossey-Bass Publishers, Inc., Division of Simon & Schuster, 350 Sansome St., Fifth Floor, San Francisco CA 94104-1342. (415)433-1740. Fax: (415)433-0499. Website: www.newlex.com. **Acquisitions:** William H. Hicks, editor/publisher (management); Leslie Berriman, editor (psychology). "We publish cutting-edge scholarly books for researchers, academics, advanced graduate students and thinking professionals." Imprint publishes 40 titles/year. Receive 500 queries and 100 mss/year. 80% from unagented writers. Pays 7½-15% royalty on wholesale price. Publishes books within 1 year after acceptance of ms. Accepts simultaneous submissions. Reports in 1 month on proposals. *Writer's Market* recommends allowing 2 months for reply. Manuscript guidelines for SASE.
Nonfiction: Scholarly/academic. Subjects include business management, organization and management sciences, social and behavioral sciences, psychology, research methods. Query with market analysis for the book and SASE.
Recent Nonfiction Title(s): *Cooperative Strategy Series,* by Paul Beamish (international business); *Environment, Ethics & Behavior,* by Max Bazerman (psychology).

NEW RIVERS PRESS, 420 N. Fifth St., Suite 910, Minneapolis MN 55401. **Acquisitions:** Phyllis Jendor, executive director. "New Rivers publishes the best poetry, fiction and creative nonfiction from new and emerging writers from the upper Midwest." Publishes trade paperback originals. Publishes 8-10 titles/year. Receives 500 queries and 1,000 mss/year. 95% of books from first-time authors; 99.9% from unagented writers. Pays royalty. Publishes book 2 years after acceptance. Book catalog free. Manuscript guidelines to Minnesota Voices Project.
Nonfiction: Creative prose. "We publish memoirs, essay collections, and other forms of creative nonfiction." Query.
Recent Nonfiction Title(s): *Tanzania on Tuesday,* edited by Kathleen Coskran and C.W. Truesdale (writing by American women abroad); *The House on Via Gombito,* edited by Madelon Sprengnether and C.W. Truesdale (travel writing by American women abroad); *Remembering China: 1935-1945,* by Bea Exner Liu (memoir).
Fiction: Literary and short story collections. Query with synopsis and 2 sample chapters.
Recent Fiction Title(s): *Laundromat Blues,* by Lupe Solis; *The Natural Father,* by Robert Lacy.
Poetry: Submit 10-15 sample poems.
Recent Poetry Title(s): *Fishing for Myth,* by Heid E. Erdrich; *Sustenance,* by Aaron Anstett.

NEW VICTORIA PUBLISHERS, P.O. Box 27, Norwich VT 05055-0027. Phone/fax: (802)649-5297. E-mail: newvic@aol.com. Website: http://www.opendoor.com/NewVic/. **Acquisitions:** Claudia Lamperti, editor; ReBecca Béguin, editor. Estab. 1976. "New Victoria is a nonprofit literary and cultural organization producing the finest in lesbian fiction and nonfiction." Publishes trade paperback originals. Publishes 8-10 titles/year. Receives 100 submissions/year. 50% of books from first-time authors; most books from unagented writers. Pays 10% royalty. Publishes book 1 year after acceptance. Reports on queries in 1 month. *Writer's Market* recommends allowing 2 months for reply. Book catalog free.
• New Victoria has published such authors as Sarah Dreher and Leslia Newman.
Nonfiction: History. "We are interested in feminist history or biography and interviews with or topics relating to lesbians. No poetry." Submit outline and sample chapters.
Recent Nonfiction Title(s): *Off The Rag: Lesbians Writing on Menopause*, edited by Lee Lynch and Akia Woods; *Orlando's Sleep*, by Jennifer Spry (autobiography).
Fiction: Adventure, erotica, fantasy, historical, humor, mystery, romance, science fiction, western. "We will consider most anything if it is well written and appeals to lesbian/feminist audience." Submit outline/synopsis and sample chapters. "Hard copy only—no disks."
Recent Fiction Title(s): *Takes One To Know One*, by Kate Allen (mystery); *Outside In*, by Nanisi Barrett d'Amuk (mystery); *Cemetery Murders*, by Jean Marcy.
Recent Poetry Title(s): *I Change, I Change*, by Barbara Deming; *A Fire Is Burning/It Is In Me: The Life and Writings of Michiyo Fukaya*, edited by Gwendolyn L. Shervington.
Tips: "Try to appeal to a specific audience and not write for the general market. We're still looking for well-written, hopefully humorous, lesbian fiction and well-researched biography or nonfiction."

NEW WORLD LIBRARY, Subsidiary of Whatever Publishing, Inc., 14 Pamaron Way, Novato CA 94949. (415)884-2100. Fax: (415)884-2199. E-mail: becky@nwlib.com. Website: http://www.nwlib.com. Publisher: Marc Allen. **Acquisitions:** Becky Benenate, editorial director. 'NWO is dedicated to publishing books and cassettes that inspire and challenge us to improve the quality of our lives and our world." Publishes hardcover and trade paperback originals and reprints. Publishes 25 titles/year. 10% of books from first-time authors; 50% from unagented writers. Pays 12-16% royalty on wholesale price. Offers $0-200,000 advance. Publishes book 1 year after acceptance of ms. Accepts simultaneous submissions. Reports in 2 months. Book catalog and ms guidelines free.
• New World has published such authors as Deepak Chopra, Richard Carlson and Benjamin Shields. New World Library also has an extensive audio program.
Nonfiction: Gift book, self-help. Subjects include business/prosperity, cooking/foods/nutrition, ethnic (African-American, Native American), money/finance, nature/environment, personal growth, psychology, religion, women's issues/studies. Query or submit outline, 1 sample chapter and author bio with SASE. Reviews artwork/photos as part of ms package. Send photocopies.
Recent Nonfiction Title(s): *No Greater Love*, by Mother Teresa (inspiration/religion); *A Haunting Reverence*, by Kent Nerburn (nature); *5 Steps to Selecting the Best Alternative Medicine*, by Mary and Michael Morton (health).
Recent Fiction Title(s): *Papa's Angels*, by Collin Wilcox-Paxton (Christmas).
Recent Poetry Title(s): *Passionate Hearts*, by Wendy Maltz.

‡NEW YORK UNIVERSITY PRESS, 70 Washington Square, New York NY 10012. (212)998-2575. Fax: (212)995-3833. E-mail: nyupmark@elmer2.bobst.nyu.edu. Website: http://www.nyu.edu/pages/nyupress/index.html. **Acquisitions:** Tim Bartlett (psychology, literature); Eric Zinner (cultural studies); Jennifer Hammer (Jewish studies, women's studies); Niko Pfund (business, history, law). Estab. 1916. "New York University Press embraces ideological diversity. We often publish books on the same issue from different poles to generate dialogue, engender and resist pat categorizations." Hardcover and trade paperback originals. Publishes 200 titles/year. Receives 800-1,000 queries/year. 30% of books from first-time authors; 90% from unagented writers. Advance and royalty on net receipts varies. Publishes book 8 months after acceptance of ms. Accepts simultaneous submissions. Reports in 1 month on proposals.
Nonfiction: Subjects include anthropology/archaeology, art/architecture, business/economics, computers/electronics, education, ethnic, gay/lesbian, government/politics, health/medicine, history, language/literature, military/war, money/finance, music/dance, nature/environment, philosophy, photography, psychology, regional, religion, sociology, sports, travel, women's issues/studies. Submit outline, 1 sample chapter and proposal backage, including author's C.V. with SASE. Reviews artwork/photos as part of the ms package. Send photocopies.
Recent Nonfiction Title(s): *Black Rage Confronts The Law*, by Paul Harris (social history); *Net. Wars*, by Wendy M. Grossman (computers).
Fiction: Literary. "We publish only 1 fiction title per year and don't encourage fiction submissions." Submit synopsis and 1 sample chapter with SASE.
Recent Fiction Title(s): *Bird-Self Accumulated*, by Don Judson (novella).
Poetry: "We publish only 1 poetry title per year and don't encourage poetry submissions." Submit 3-5 sample poems.
Recent Poetry Title(s): *Flying Out With The Wounded*, by Anne Caston; *Rodent Angel*, by Debra Weinstein.

NEWJOY PRESS, P.O. Box 3437, Ventura CA 93006. (800)876-1373. Fax: (805)984-0503. E-mail: njpublish@aol.com. **Acquisitions:** Joy Nyquist, publisher. "Our plan is to focus on traveler's aid books and substance abuse treatment for therapists and lay people. We will also consider self-help books in assertiveness and personal responsibility." Publishes trade paperback originals. Publishes 7-10 titles/year. Pays 10-15% royalty on retail price. Reports in 4 months.

• Newjoy Press has increased their number of books published from 3-5 to 7-10 titles per year.

Nonfiction: Publishes chemical dependency recovery, self-help, travel. Subjects include travel health, assertiveness/self-esteem, travelers' aid (not guidebooks), substance abuse (especially relapse) treatment and self-help. Submit proposal package including outline, 1 sample chapter, marketing plans and author's qualifications with SASE.

Recent Nonfiction Title(s): *Trust the Process: How to Enhance Recovery & Prevent Relapse*, by Linda Free-Gardiner; *Traveling to Europe Like a Pro*, by Analu (travel).

Tips: "We are not interested in first person accounts of their lives and/or issues. We want books from qualified professionals in their fields who offer information based on their expertise. No phone, fax or e-mail proposals wanted."

NICHOLS PUBLISHING, P.O. Box 6036, E. Brunswick NJ 08816. (908)297-2862. Fax: (908)940-0549. Vice President and Publisher: Fran Van Dalen. **Acquisitions:** Fran Lubrano, editorial director. Estab. 1979. Nichols publishes training and management reference books. Publishes hardcover and paperback originals. Publishes 50 titles/year. 15% of books from first-time authors; 98% from unagented writers. Pays 5-15% royalty on wholesale price. Offers $300-500 average advance. Publishes book 9 months after acceptance. Simultaneous submissions OK. Reports on queries in 1 month. *Writer's Market* recommends allowing 2 months for reply. Book catalog and ms guidelines free.

Nonfiction: Reference, technical. Subjects include management, education, training. Submit outline and sample chapters. "We need more books on training."

Recent Nonfiction Title(s): *Assembling Course Materials*, by Nicolay and Barrett.

Tips: "No longer seeking books on architecture, computers/electronics, or engineering."

‡NIGHTSHADE PRESS, P.O. Box 76, Troy ME 04987. (207)948-3427. Fax: (207)948-5088. E-mail: potatoeyes@uni net.net. Publishes hardcover and trade paperback originals. Publishes 4-5 titles/year. Pays royalty on retail price. No advance. Reports in 2 months on queries and proposals, 3 months on mss.

• Nightshade Press also publishes the literary magazine *Potato Eyes*.

Fiction: Contemporary, feminist, humor/satire, literary, mainstream, regional. No religious, romance, preschool, juvenile, young adult, psychic/occult. Query with SASE.

Recent Fiction Title(s): *Every Day A Visitor*, by Richard Abrons (short story collection).

Poetry: Submit 3-5 poems with SASE.

Recent Poetry Title(s): *Bone Music*, by Howard Nelson; *Androscoggin Two*, by Robert M. Chute.

NO STARCH PRESS, 401 China Basin St., Suite 108, San Francisco CA 94107. (415)284-9900. Fax: (415)284-9955. **Acquisitions:** William Pollock, publisher. No Starch Press publishes "computer books for non-computer people." Publishes trade paperback originals. Publishes 6-10 titles/year. Receives 100 queries and 5 mss/year. 80% of books from first-time authors; 90% from unagented writers. Pays 10-15% royalty on wholesale price. Offers negotiable advance. Publishes book 4 months after acceptance of ms. Accepts simultaneous submissions. Book catalog free.

Imprint(s): No Starch Comix.

Nonfiction: How-to, reference, technical. Subjects include computers/electronics, hobbies, software. Only considers computer-related books or underground comics. Submit outline, 1 sample chapter, bio, market rationale. Reviews artwork/photos as part of ms package. Send photocopies.

Recent Nonfiction Title(s): *The World's Weirdest Web Pages*, by Hank Duderstadt; *The Guide to the Jewish Internet*, by Michael Levin; *Dr. Bob's Painless Guide to the Internet*, by Bob Rankin.

Tips: "No fluff—content, content, content or just plain fun. Understand how your book fits into the market. Tell us why someone, anyone, will buy your book. Be enthusiastic."

NODIN PRESS, Imprint of Micawber's Inc., 525 N. Third St., Minneapolis MN 55401. (612)333-6300. Fax: (612)341-3065. **Acquisitions:** Norton Stillman, publisher. "We publish Minnesota guidebooks." Publishes hardcover and trade paperback originals. Publishes 4 titles/year. Receives 20 queries and 20 mss/year. 75% of books from first-time authors; 100% from unagented writers. Pays 10% royalty. Offers $250-1,000 advance. Publishes book 20 months after acceptance of ms. Accepts simultaneous submissions. Reports in 6 months on queries. Book catalog or ms guidelines free.

Nonfiction: Biography, regional guide book. Subjects include ethnic, history, sports, travel. Query.

Recent Nonfiction Title(s): *Hi Everybody*, by Herb Carneal (autobiography); *Railtrail Handbooks*, by Bruce Blair (trails on discontinued railroad beds); *Exploring the Twin Cities with Children* (new edition), by E. French.

Recent Fiction Title(s): *Lessons on the Journey*, by David Nimmer (collection of short fiction).

‡NOLO PRESS, 950 Parker St., Berkeley CA 94710. (510)549-1976. Fax: (510)548-5902. E-mail: info@nolo.com. Website: http://www.nolo.com. **Acquisitions:** Barbara Tate Repa. Estab. 1971. "Our goal is to publish 'plain English' self-help law books for the average consumer." Publishes trade paperback originals. Publishes 10 titles/year. 25% of books from first-time authors; 5% from unagented writers. Pays 7½-10% royalty on retail price. Offers $500 advance. Accepts simultaneous submissions. Reports in 1 month on queries..

Nonfiction: How-to, reference, self-help. Subjects include law, business/economics, money/finance, legal guides. "We do some business and finance titles, but always from a legal perspective, i.e., bankruptcy law." Query with outline, 1 sample chapter and SASE. Welcome queries but majority of titles are produced in-house.

Recent Nonfiction Title(s): *The Legal Guide for Starting Running a Small Business*, by Fred S. Steingold; *Safe Homes, Safe Neighborhoods: Stopping Crime Where You Live*, by Stephanie Mann with M.C. Blakeman.

‡NOONDAY PRESS, Imprint of Farrar Straus Giroux, Inc., 19 Union Square W., New York NY 10003. (212)741-6900. Fax: (212)633-2427. **Acquisitions:** Judy Klein, executive editor. Noonday emphasizes literary nonfiction and fiction, as well as fiction and poetry reprints. Publishes trade paperback originals and reprints. Publishes 70 titles/year. Receives 1,500-2,000 queries/mss per year. Pays 6% royalty on retail price. Advance varies. Publishes book 1 year after acceptance of ms. Accepts simultaneous submissions. Reports in 2 months on queries and proposals. Book catalog and ms guidelines free.
Nonfiction: Biography. Subjects include child guidance/parenting, education, language/literature. Query with outline, 2-3 sample chapters, CV, cover letter discribing project and SASE. *No unsolicited mss.*
Recent Nonfiction Title(s): *Message from My Father*, by Calvin Trillin (memoir); *Fighting Terrorism*, by Benjamin Netanyahu; *Coyote V. Acme*, by Ian Frazier (humor/essays).
Fiction: Literary. Mostly reprints of classic authors.
Recent Fiction Title(s): *Annie John*, by Jamaica Kincaid; *Enemies: A Love Story*, by Isaac Bashevis Singer.
Recent Poetry Title(s): *The Spirit Level*, by Seamus Heaney.

NORTH LIGHT BOOKS, Imprint of F&W Publications, 1507 Dana Ave., Cincinnati OH 45207. Editorial Director: David Lewis. **Acquisitions:** Acquisitions Coordinator. North Light Books publishes craft and design books, including watercolor, drawing, colored pencil and decorative painting titles that emphasize how-to art instruction. Publishes hardcover and trade paperback how-to books. Publishes 40-45 titles/year. Pays 10-20% royalty on net receipts. Offers $4,000 advance. Accepts simultaneous submissions. Reports in 1 month. Book catalog for 9 × 12 SAE with 6 first-class stamps.
Nonfiction: Watercolor, drawing, colored pencil, decorative painting, craft and graphic design instruction books. Interested in books on watercolor painting, basic drawing, pen and ink, colored pencil, airbrush, crafts, decorative painting, basic design, computer graphics, layout and typography. Do not submit coffee table art books without how-to art instruction. Query or submit outline and examples of artwork (transparencies and photographs).
Recent Nonfiction Title(s): *Painting Sunlit Still Lifes in Watercolor*, by Liz Donovan; *Priscilla Hauser's Book of Decorative Painting*; *The Best of Wildlife Art*, edited by Rachel Rubin Wolf.

‡NORTH POINT PRESS, Imprint of Farrar Straus Giroux, Inc., 19 Union Square W., New York NY 10003. (212)741-6900. Fax: (212)633-2427. **Acquisitions:** Ethan Nosowsky, editor. Estab. 1980. "We are a broad-based literary trade publisher—high quality writing only." Hardcover and trade paperback originals. Publishes 25 titles/year. Receives hundreds of queries and hundreds of mss/year. 20% of books from first-time authors; 90% from unagented writers. Pays 6% royalty on retail price. Advance varies. Publishes book 18 months after acceptance of ms. Accepts simultaneous submissions. Reports in 2 months on queries and proposals, 3 months on mss. Manuscript guidelines for #10 SASE.
● North Point Press no longer publishes fiction.
Nonfiction: Biography. Subjects include cooking/foods/nutrition, history, nature/environment, religion (no New Age), sports, travel. "Be familiar with press's list. No genres." Query with outline, 1-2 sample chapters and SASE.
Recent Nonfiction Title(s): *But Beautiful: A Book About Jazz*, by Geoff Dyer; *Olives: Life & Love of a Noble Fruit*, by Mort Rosenblum.

‡NORTH STAR LINE, Imprint of Blue Moon Books, 61 Fourth Ave., New York NY 10003. (212)505-6880. Fax: (212)673-1039. **Acquisitions:** Barney Rosset, editor/publisher. "North Star Line is aesthetically oriented, publishing poetry and poetic prose." Publishes hardcover originals, trade paperback originals and reprints. Publishes 10-15 titles/year. Pays 7½-10% royalty on retail price. Offers $500 advance. Publishes book 1 year after acceptance of ms. Accepts simultaneous submissions. Reports in 2 months on queries.
Fiction: Literary, short story collections, anthologies. Query with synopsis and 1-2 sample chapters.
Recent Fiction Title(s): *Stirrings Still*, by Samuel Beckett (reprint).
Poetry: Query with 10 sample poems.
Recent Poetry Title(s): *New & Selected Poems 1930-1990*, by Richard Eberhart.

NORTHERN ILLINOIS UNIVERSITY PRESS, DeKalb IL 60115-2854. (815)753-1826/753-1075. Fax: (815)753-1845. **Acquisitions:** Mary L. Lincoln, director/editor-in-chief. Estab. 1965. "Our mission is to facilitate the advancement of knowledge and disseminate the results of scholarly inquiry. In carrying out its role, the press publishes both specialized scholarly work and books of general interest to the informed public." Publishes 18-20 titles/year. Pays 10-15% royalty on wholesale price. Book catalog free.
● Northern Illinois University Press has increased their number of books published from 3 to 18-20 titles/year.
Nonfiction: "The NIU Press publishes mainly history, political science, social sciences, philosophy, literary criticism and regional studies. We do not consider collections of previously published essays, nor do we consider unsolicited poetry." Accepts nonfiction translations. Query with outline and 1-3 sample chapters.
Recent Nonfiction Title(s): *Double Deception: Stalin, Hitler and the Invasion of Russia*, by James Barros and Richard Gregor (political science); *The Anti-Federalists and Early American Political Thought*, by Christopher M. Duncan (political science); *Freedom in Rousseau's Political Philosophy*, by Daniel E. Cullen (political philosophy).

‡NORTHFIELD PUBLISHING, Imprint of Moody Press, 820 N. LaSalle Dr., Chicago IL 60610. (312)329-2101. Fax: (312)329-2144. **Acquisitions:** Acquisitions Coordinator. "Northfield publishes a line of books for non-Christians or those exploring the Christian faith. While staying true to Biblical principles, we eliminate some of the Christian wording and scriptual references to avoid confusion." Publishes 5-10 titles/year. Less than 1% of books from first-time authors; 95% from unagented writers. Pays royalty on retail price. Offers $500-50,000 advance. Publishes books 6 months after acceptance of ms. Accepts simultaneous submissions, but prefers not to. Reports in 2 months on queries. Book catalog for 9×12 SAE with 2 first-class stamps. Manuscript guidelines for #10 SASE.

Nonfiction: Biographies (classic). Subjects include business/economics, child guidance/parenting, finance. Query with outline, 2-3 sample chapters, table of contents, author's market study of why this book will be successful and SASE.
Recent Nonfiction Title(s): *The Five Love Languages*, by Gary Chapman (religion).

NORTHLAND PUBLISHING CO., INC., P.O. Box 1389, Flagstaff AZ 86002-1389. (520)774-5251. Fax: (520)774-0592. E-mail: emurphy@northlandpub.com. Website: http://www.northlandpub.com. **Acquisitions:** Erin Murphy, editor-in-chief. Estab. 1958. "We seek authoritative manuscripts on our specialty subjects; no mainstream, general fiction or nonfiction." Publishes hardcover and trade paperback originals. Publishes 25 titles/year. Receives 4,000 submissions/year. 30% of books from first-time authors; 95% from unagented writers. Pays 8-12% royalty on net receipts, depending upon terms. Offers $1,000-3,000 average advance. Publishes book 2 years after acceptance. Accepts simultaneous submissions if so noted. No fax or e-mail submissions. Reports in 1 month on queries, 3 months on mss. Book catalog and ms guidelines for 9×12 SAE with $1.50 in postage.

  ● This publisher has received the following awards in the past year: National Cowboy Hall of Fame Western Heritage Award for Outstanding Juvenile Book (*The Night the Grandfathers Danced*); Colorado Book Awards—Best Children's Book (*Goose and the Mountain Lion*); Reading Rainbow Book (*It Rained on the Desert Today*).
Imprint(s): Rising Moon (books for young readers).
Nonfiction: Subjects include animals, anthropology/archaeology, art/architecture, cooking, history, nature/environment, photography. All titles are regional (American West/Southwest). "We are seeking authoritative, well-written manuscripts on natural history subjects. We do not want to see poetry, general fiction, mainstream, New Age or science fiction material." Query or submit outline/synopsis and sample chapters. Reviews manuscripts and artwork/photos separately.
Recent Nonfiction Title(s): *Following the Sun and Moon: Hopi Kachina Tradition*, by Alph H. Secakuku, in cooperation with the Heard Museum; *Pueblo and Mission: Cultural Roots of the Southwest*, by Susan Lamb, photographs by Chuck Place (Southwest culture).
Fiction: Unique children's picture book and middle reader chapter book stories, especially those with Southwest/West regional theme; Native American folktales (retold by Native Americans only, please). Picture book mss should be 350-1,500 words; chapter book mss should be approximately 20,000 words. Does not want to see "mainstream" stories. Northland does not publish general trade fiction.
Recent Fiction Title(s): *The Night the Grandfathers Danced*, by Linda Theresa Raczek, illustrated by Katalin Ohla Ehling; *My Name is York*, by Elizabeth Van Steenwyk, illustrated by Bill Farnsworth (children's book).
Tips: "Our audience is composed of general interest readers and those interested in specialty subjects such as Native American culture and crafts. It is not necessarily a scholarly market, but it is sophisticated."

‡NORTH-SOUTH BOOKS, affiliate of Nord-Sud Verlag AG, 1123 Broadway, Suite 800, New York NY 10010. (212)463-9736. **Acquisitions:** Julie Amper. Website: http://www.northsouth.com. Estab. 1985. "The aim of North-South is to build bridges—bridges between authors and artists from different countries and between readers of all ages. We believe children should be exposed to as wide a range of artistic styles as possible with universal themes." Publishes 100 titles/year. Receives 5,000 queries/year. 5% of books from first-time authors. Pays royalty on retail price. Publishes book 2 years after acceptance of ms. Returns submissions accompanied by SASE. "But is very low priority."

  ● This publisher accepts agented submissions only.
Fiction: Picture books, easy-to-read. "We are currently accepting only picture books; all other books are selected by our German office." Query. Does not respond unless interested. All unsolicited mss returned unopened.
Recent Fiction Title(s): *Wake Up, Santa Claus!*, by Marcus Pfister (picture); *The Other Side of the Bridge*, Wolfram Hänel (easy-to-read); *A Mouse in the House*, by G. Wagener.

  ● North-South Books is the publisher of the international bestseller, *The Rainbow Fish*.

NORTHWORD PRESS, INC., P.O. Box 1360, Minocqua WI 54548. (715)356-7644. Fax: (715)356-6066. E-mail: nwpedit@newnorth.net. Managing Editor: Barbara K. Harold. **Acquisitions:** Laura Evert. Publishes hardcover and trade paperback originals for adults, teens, and children. Publishes 30 titles/year. Estab. 1984. "We publish exclusively nature and wildlife titles." Receives 600 submissions/year. 50% of books are from first-time authors; 90% are from unagented writers. Pays 10-15% royalty on wholesale price. Offers $2,000-20,000 advance. Publishes book 1 year after acceptance. Accepts simultaneous submissions. Reports in 2 months on queries. Book catalog for 9×12 SAE with 7 first-class stamps. Manuscript guidelines for SASE.

MARKET CONDITIONS are constantly changing! If this is 1999 or later, buy the newest edition of *Writer's Market* at your favorite bookstore or order directly from Writer's Digest Books.

• Northword Press has published books by such authors as Schim Schimmel, Kennan Ward and Valerius Geist.
Nonfiction: Coffee table books, introductions to wildlife and natural history, guidebooks, children's illustrated books; nature and wildlife subjects exclusively. Query with outline, sample chapters and SASE.
Recent Nonfiction Title(s): *Superior: Journeys on an Inland Sea*, by Gary and Joanie McGuffin (pictoral/essay).
Tips: "We do not publish poetry, fiction or memoirs. We have expanded our wildlife/natural history topics to include exotic and non-North American species."

W.W. NORTON CO., INC., 500 Fifth Ave., New York NY 10110. Website: http://www.wwnorton.com. **Acquisitions:** Liz Malcolm. General trade publisher of fiction and nonfiction, educational and professional books. "W. W. Norton & Company strives to carry out the imperative of its founder to 'publish books not for a single season, but for the years' in the areas of fiction, nonfiction, and poetry." Publishes hardcover and paperback originals and reprints. Publishes 300 titles/year. Pays royalty.
Imprint(s): Backcountry Publishing, **Countryman Press**, **Foul Play Press**, W.W. Norton.
Nonfiction and Fiction: Subjects include antiques and collectibles, architecture, art/design, autobiography/memoir, biography, business, child care, cooking, current affairs, family, fiction, games, health, history, law, literature, music, mystery, nature, photography, poetry, politics/political science, reference, religion, sailing, science, self-help, transportation, travel. College Department: subjects include biological sciences, economics, psychology, political science, and computer science. Professional Books specializes in psychotherapy. "We are not interested in considering books from the following categories: juvenile or young adult, religious, occult or paranormal, genre fiction (formula romances, sci-fi or westerns), and arts and crafts. Please give a brief description of your submission, of your writing credentials, and of any experience, professional or otherwise, which is relevant to your submission. Submit 2 or 3 sample chapters, one of which should be the first chapter with SASE."
Recent Nonfiction Title(s): *Crystal Fire: The Birth of the Information Age*, by Michael Riordan and Lillian Hoddeson; *Warriors of the Rising Sun: A History of the Japanese Military*, by Robert Edgerton; *We Are Your Sisters: Black Women in the Nineteenth Century*, edited by Dorothy Sterling.
Recent Fiction Title(s): *The Hide*, by Barry Unsworth; *Allegro*, by Joseph Machlis.
Recent Poetry Title(s): *Glare*, by A.R. Ammons; *Odd Mercy*, by Gerald Stern; *Wordling*, by Elizabeth Spires.

NOVA PRESS, 11659 Mayfield Ave., Suite 1, Los Angeles CA 90049. (310)207-4078. Fax: (310)5751-0908. E-mail: novapress@aol.com. Website: http://www.majon.com/www/novapress.html. **Acquisitions:** Jeff Kolby, president. "All our books relate to academics—mainly test prep for college entrance exams." Publishes trade paperback originals. Publishes 10 titles/year. Pays 10-22½% royalty on net price. Publishes book 6 months after acceptance of ms. Book catalog free.
Nonfiction: How-to, self-help, technical. Subjects include education, software.
Recent Nonfiction Title(s): *The MCAT Physics Book*, by Garrett Biehle; *LSAT Prep Course Software*.

NOYES DATA CORP., 369 Fairview Ave., Westwood NJ 07675. Fax: (201)666-5111. **Acquisitions:** Editorial Department. Noyes publishes technical books primarily of interest to business executives, research scientists and research engineers. Estab. 1959. Publishes hardcover originals. Publishes 30 titles/year. Pays 12% royalty on net proceeds. Advance varies, depending on author's reputation and nature of book. Reports in 2 weeks. Book catalog free.
Nonfiction: Technical. Subjects include industrial processing, science, economic books pertaining to chemistry, chemical engineering, food, textiles, energy, electronics, pollution control, material science, semi-conductor material and process technology. Length: 50,000-250,000 words.

NTC/CONTEMPORARY PUBLISHING COMPANY, 4255 W. Touhy Ave., Lincolnwood IL 60646-1975. (847)679-5500. Fax: (847)679-2494. E-mail: ntcpub2@aol.com. Editorial Director: John T. Nolan. **Acquisitions:** Alina Cowden, editor. Estab. 1947. "We are midsize, niche-oriented, backlist-oriented publisher. We publish exclusively nonfiction in general interest trade categories plus travel, reference and quilting books." Publishes hardcover originals and trade paperback originals and reprints. Publishes 400 titles/year. Receives 9,000 submissions/year. 10% of books from first-time authors; 25% of books from unagented writers. Pays 6-15% royalty on retail price. Publishes book 10 months after acceptance. Accepts simultaneous submissions. Reports in 2 months. Manuscript guidelines for SASE.
• NTC/Contemporary has published such authors as Donna Corwin, Norman Kolpas, and Jinny Beyer.
Imprint(s): Contemporary Books, Passport Books, NTC Business Books, **VGM Career Horizons**, The Quilt Digest Press, **National Textbook Company**.
Nonfiction: Biography, cookbook, how-to, humor, reference, self-help. Subjects include business, careers, child guidance/parenting, crafts (especially quilting), finance, cooking, health/fitness, nutrition, popular culture, psychology, real estate, sports, travel, women's studies. Submit outline, sample chapters and SASE. Reviews artwork/photos.
Recent Nonfiction Title(s): *How to Make Anyone Fall in Love with You*, by Leil Lowndes (relationships/self-help); *The Cook's Dictionary and Culinary Reference*, by Jonathan Bartlett (cooking/reference).

OAK KNOLL PRESS, 414 Delaware St., New Castle DE 19720. (302)328-7232. Fax: (302)328-7274. E-mail: oakknoll @oakknoll.com. Website: http://www.oakknoll.com. **Acquisitions:** Editor. "We specialize in books about books— preserving the art and lore of the printed word." Publishes hardcover and trade paperback originals and reprints. Publishes 12 titles/year. Receives 25 queries and 5 mss/year. 5% of books from first-time authors; 100% from unagented writers. Pays 7-10% royalty on income. Publishes book 18 months after acceptance of ms. Accepts simultaneous submissions. Reports in 1 month on queries. *Writer's Market* recommends allowing 2 months for reply. Catalog free.

Nonfiction: Book arts. Subjects include printing, papermaking, bookbinding, book collecting, etc. Query. Reviews artwork/photos as part of ms package. Send photocopies.

Recent Nonfiction Title(s): *American Book Design and William Morris*, by Susan Otis Thompson; *History of English Craft Bookbinding Technique*, by Bernard C. Middleton; *Greek Letters*, edited by Michael S. Macrakis.

OASIS PRESS, Imprint of PSI Research, 300 N. Valley Dr. Grants Pass OR 97526, Grants Pass OR 97526. (503)479-9464. Fax: (503)476-1479. **Acquisitions:** Emmett Ramey, president. Estab. 1975. Oasis Press publishes books for small business or individuals who are entrepreneurs or owners or managers of small businesses (1-300 employees). Publishes hardcover, trade paperback and binder originals. Publishes 20-30 books/year. Receives 90 submissions/year. 60% of books from first-time authors; 90% from unagented writers. Pays 10% royalty on the net received, except wholesale sales. No advance. Publishes book 1 year after acceptance. Accepts simultaneous submissions. Reports in 2 months (initial feedback) on queries. Book catalog and ms guidelines for SASE.

Imprint(s): Hellgate Press.

Nonfiction: How-to, reference, textbook. Subjects include business/economics, computers, education, money/finance, retirement, exporting, franchise, finance, marketing and public relations, relocations, environment, taxes, business start up and operation. Needs information-heavy, readable mss written by professionals in their subject fields. Interactive where appropriate. Authorship credentials less important than hands-on experience qualifications. Query for unwritten material or to check current interest in topic and orientation. Submit outline/synopsis and sample chapters. Reviews artwork/photos as part of ms package.

Recent Nonfiction Title(s): *Location, Location, Location*, by Luigi Salvaneschi; *Which Business*, by Nancy Drescher (how to select a business); *Profit Power*, by Paul Peyton (ideas to increase profit).

Tips: "Best chance is with practical, step-by-step manuals for operating a business, with worksheets, checklists. The audience is made up of entrepreneurs of all types: small business owners and those who would like to be; attorneys, accountants and consultants who work with small businesses; college students; dreamers. Make sure your information is valid and timely for its audience, also that by virtue of either its content quality or viewpoint, it distinguishes itself from other books on the market."

OCTAMERON ASSOCIATES, 1900 Mt. Vernon Ave., Alexandria VA 22301. (703)836-5480. E-mail: octameron@aol.com. **Acquisitions:** Karen Stokstad, editorial director. Estab. 1976. Octameron publishes college and career reference books. They emphasize college admission and financial aid titles. Publishes trade paperback originals. Publishes 15 titles/year. Receives 100 submissions/year. 10% of books from first-time authors; 100% from unagented writers. Average print order for a first book is 8,000-10,000. Pays 7½% royalty on retail price. Publishes book 6 months after acceptance. Accepts simultaneous submissions. Reports in 2 months. Book catalog for #10 SAE with 2 first-class stamps.

Nonfiction: Reference, career, post-secondary education subjects. Especially interested in "paying-for-college and college admission guides." Query with outline and 2 sample chapters. Reviews artwork/photos as part of ms package.

Recent Nonfiction Title(s): *SAT Savvy: Last Minute Tips and Strategies*, by Marian and Sandra Martin; *Don't Miss Out: The Ambitious Student's Guide to Financial Aid*, by Anna and Robert Leider.

OHIO STATE UNIVERSITY PRESS, 1070 Carmack Rd., Columbus OH 43210. (614)292-6930. Fax: (614)292-2065. E-mail: bucy.4@osu.edu. **Acquisitions:** Charlotte Dihoff, assistant director/editor-in-chief; Barbara Hanrahan, director. Ohio State University Press publishes general scholarly nonfiction, fiction and poetry. Pays 7½-15% royalty on wholesale or retail price. Publishes 30 titles/year. Reports in 3 months; ms held longer with author's permission.

Imprint(s): Sandstone Books.

● Ohio State University Press has published such authors as James Miller and Cynthia Gillespie.

Nonfiction: Scholarly studies with special interests in African American studies, business and economic history, criminology, literary criticism, political science regional studies, teaching and higher education, Victorian studies, women's and gender studies, women's health. Query with outline and sample chapters.

Recent Nonfiction Title(s): *Murder in America*, by Roger Lane (history/criminology); *Punch*, by Richard Altick (literary criticism); *Cheap Seats*, by James Campbell (political science).

Recent Fiction Title(s): *Love Is the Crooked Thing*, by Lee K. Abbott (short fiction); *Strangers in Paradise*, by Lee K. Abbott (short fiction); *Hamlet's Planets*, by Lynda Sexson (short fiction).

Recent Poetry Title(s): *Broken Symmetry*, by David Citino; *Adventures in Ancient Egypt*, by Albert Goldbarth.

Tips: "Publishes some poetry and fiction. Query first."

OHIO UNIVERSITY PRESS, Scott Quadrangle, Athens OH 45701. (614)593-1155. **Acquisitions:** Gillian Berchowitz, senior editor. "Ohio University Press publishes and disseminates the fruits of research and creative endeavor, specifically in the areas of literary studies, regional works, philosophy, contemporary history, African studies and Western Americana. Its charge to produce books of value in service to the academic community and for the enrichment of the broader culture is in keeping with the university's mission of teaching, research and service to its constituents." Publishes hardcover and trade paperback originals and reprints. Publishes 40-45 titles/year. Receives 500 queries and 50 mss/year. 20% of books from first-time authors; 95% from unagented writers. Pays 7½-15% royalty on net sales. No advance. Publishes book 1 year after acceptance of ms. Reports in 1 month on queries and proposals, 2 months on mss. Book catalog free. Manuscript guidelines for #10 SASE.

Imprint(s): Swallow Press (David Sanders, director); Ohio University Monographs in International Studies (Gillian

Berchowitz).
Nonfiction: Biography, cookbook, how-to, illustrated book, reference, scholarly, self-help. Subjects include African studies, agriculture/horticulture, Americana, animals, anthropology/archaeology, art/architecture, business/economics, cooking/foods/nutrition, education, ethnic, gardening, government/politics, health/medicine, history, language/literature, military/war, music/dance, nature/environment, philosophy, psychology, recreation, regional, religion, sociology, translation, travel, women's issues/studies. Query with proposal package, including outline, sample chapter and SASE. "We prefer queries or detailed proposals rather than manuscripts pertaining to scholarly projects that might have a general interest. Proposals should explain the thesis and details of the subject matter, not just sell a title." Reviews artwork/photos as part of ms package. Send photocopies.
Recent Nonfiction Title(s): *Hired Press: Professional Writers in America's Golden Age of Print*, by Ronald Weber; *Frozen in Silver: The Life and Frontier Photography of P.E. Larson*, by Ronald T. Bailey; *Hands Across the Sea? U.S.-Japan Relations, 1961-1981*, by Timothy P. Maga.
Recent Fiction Titles: *Selected Short Stories of William Dean Howells*, edited by Ruth Bardon; *The Apple Falls from the Apple Tree*, by Helen Papanikolas (short stories); *The Imigrant Train and Other Stories*, by Natalie Petesch.
Recent Poetry Titles: *The Poems of J.V. Cunningham*, edited by Timothy Steele; *And Still Birds Sing: New and Collected Poems*, by Lucien Stry; *Infinite Morning*, by Meredith Carson (winner of the Hollis Summers Poetry Prize).
Tips: "Rather than trying to hook the editor on your work, let the material be compelling enough and well-presented enough to do it for you."

‡ONE WORLD, Imprint of Ballantine Publishing, 201 E. 50th St., New York NY 10022. (212)572-2620. Fax: (212)940-7539. Website: http://www.randomhouse.com. **Acquisitions:** Cheryl Woodruff, associate publisher; Gary Brozek, associate editor. Estab. 1992. "One World's list includes books written by and focused on African Americans, Native Americans, Asian Americans and Latino Americans. We concentrate on *American* multicultural experiences." Publishes hardcover and trade paperback originals, trade and mass market paperback reprints. Publishes 8-10 titles/year. Receives 1,200 queries and mss/year. 25% of books from first-time authors; 5% from unagented writers. Pays 8-12% royalty on retail price, varies from hardcover to mass market. Advance varies. Publishes book 2 years after acceptance of ms. Accepts simultaneous submissions, if so noted. Reports in 4 months. Catalog and ms guidelines for #10 SASE.
Nonfiction: Biography, cookbook, memoir, relationships. Subjects include business/economics, child guidance/parenting, cooking/foods/nutrition, ethnic, gay/lesbian, health/medicine, religion/inspirational, sociology, women's issues/studies. "We are dealing with American people of color." Query or submit proposal package including 200 pages with SASE. Reviews artwork/photos as part of ms package, where germane. Send photocopies.
Recent Nonfiction Title(s): *Native Wisdom for White Minds*, by Ann Wilson Shaef (inspirational); *Getting Good Loving*, by Audrey Chapman (relationships/self-help); *Keeping It Real: Post MTV Reflections on Race, Sex & Politics*, by Kevin Powell (essays).
Fiction: Historical. "We are looking for good contemporary fiction. In the past, topics have mostly been 'pre-Civil rights era and before.' " Query with synopsis, 3 sample chapters (100 pages) and SASE.
Recent Fiction Title(s): *Kinfolks*, by Kristin Hunter Lattany (novel).
Tips: "For first-time authors, have a completed manuscript. You won't be asked to write on speculation."

OPEN ROAD PUBLISHING, P.O. Box 20226, Columbus Circle Station, New York NY 10023. Fax: (212)974-2108. E-mail: jopenroad@aol.com. Website: http://www.openroadpub.com. Publisher: Jonathan Stein. **Acquisitions:** Betty Borden. "We will have more than 50 travel guides by the end of 1997; our goal is worldwide coverage." Publishes trade and mass market paperback originals. Publishes 17-20 titles/year. Receives 200 queries and 125 mss/year. 30% of books from first-time authors; 95% from unagented writers. Pays 5-6% royalty on retail price. Offers $500-4,000 advance. Publishes book 6 months after acceptance of ms. Accepts simultaneous submissions. Reports in 1 month on proposals. *Writer's Market* recommends allowing 2 months for reply. Book catalog free. Manuscript guidelines for #10 SASE.
• Open Road Publishing will be expanding to include health/fitness books.
Nonfiction: Travel guides. Subjects also include sports, especially running and fitness guides. "We're looking for opinionated, selective travel guides that appeal to mainstream travelers in their mid-20s to early 50s. Our guides are fun, literate and have a sense of adventure, offering readers solid cultural background and the opportunity to experience the country or city—not just visit it." Submit cover letter, outline and 2 sample chapters.
Recent Nonfiction Title(s): *Czech & Slovak Republics Guide*, by Ted Brewer; *San Francisco Guide*, by Stephanie Gold; *The Smart Runner's Handbook, 2nd edition*, by Matt Greenwald (how-to).

OPTIMA BOOKS, 2820 Eighth St., Berkeley CA 94710. (510)848-8708. **Acquisitions:** Dan Connell, editor. Publishes books for English as a second language. Publishes 4 titles/year. Receives 8 queries and 5 mss/year. 0% of books from first-time authors; 100% from unagented writers. Makes outright purchase. No advance. Publishes book 8 months after acceptance of ms. Accepts simultaneous submissions. Reports in 2 months on mss.
Nonfiction: Textbook, self teaching. Subjects include language/literature, ESL (English as a second language). "Books should be usable in the classroom or by the individual in a self-teaching capacity. Should be written for the non-native speaker desiring knowledge of American slang and jargon." Query with SASE. Reviews artwork/photos as part of ms package. Send photocopies.
Recent Nonfiction Title(s): *Street German-1*, by David Burke.

‡ORBIS BOOKS, P.O. Box 308, Maryknoll NY 10545-0308. (914)941-7590. **Acquisitions:** Robert Ellsberg, editor-in-chief. "We seeking books illuminating religious and social situations of Third World Christians, the lessons of the Third World for the North, global dimensions of Christian faith and the challenge of the world church." Publishes hardcover and trade paperback originals. Publishes 50-55 titles/year. Receives 1,500 queries and 700 mss/year. 2% of books from first-time authors; 99% from unagented writers. Pays 10-15% royalty on wholesale price net. Offers $500-3,000 advance. Publishes book 15 months after acceptance of ms. Reports in 2 months on proposals. Book catalog and ms guidelines free.
Nonfiction: Reference. Subjects include spirituality, theology, religion. Submit proposal package, including outline, summary, 10-20 page chapter of intro."
Recent Nonfiction Title(s): *Praying with Icons*, by Jim Forest.

‡ORCHARD BOOKS, Division of Grolier Publishing, 95 Madison Ave., New York NY 10016. (212)951-2650. **Acquisitions:** Sarah Caguiat, editor; Dominic Barth, associate editor. Orchard specializes in children's illustrated and picture books. Publishes hardcover and trade paperback originals. Publishes 60-70 titles/year. Receives 1,600 queries/year. 25% of books from first-time authors; 50% from unagented writers. Pays 7½-15% royalty on retail price. Advance varies. Publishes book 1 year after acceptance of ms. Reports in 3 months on queries.
Nonfiction: Children's/juvenile, illustrated book. Subjects include animals, history, nature/environment. Query with SASE. "No unsolicited ms at this time. Queries only! Be as specific and enlightening as possible about your book." Reviews artwork/photos as part of the ms package. Send photocopies.
Recent Nonfiction Title(s): *Extraordinary Life*, by Pringle and Marstall; *Tale of a Tadpole*, Porte and Cannon.
Fiction: Picture books, young adult, middle reader, board book, novelty. Query with SASE.
Recent Fiction Title(s): *Silver Packages*, by Rylant and Soentpiet; *Mysterious Thelonius*, by Raschka.
Tips: "Go to a bookstore and read several Orchard Books to get an idea of what we publish. Write what you feel and query us if you think it's 'right.' It's worth finding the right publishing match."

ORCHISES PRESS. P.O. Box 20602, Alexandria VA 22320-1602. (703)683-1243. E-mail: rlathbur@osfl.gmu.edu. Website: http://mason.gmu.edu/~rlathbur. **Acquisitions:** Roger Lathbury, editor-in-chief. Estab. 1983. Orchises Press publishes professional, literate and academic nonfiction and poetry based on literary and commercial merit. It prides itself on the attractiveness of its volumes. Publishes hardcover and trade paperback originals and reprints. Publishes 4-5 titles/year. Receives 600 queries and 200 mss/year. 1% of books from first-time authors; 95% from unagented writers. Pays 36% of receipts after Orchises has recouped its costs. Publishes book 1 year after acceptance. Accepts simultaneous submissions. Reports in 3 months. Book catalog for #10 SASE.
Nonfiction: Biography, how-to, humor, reference, technical, textbook. No real restrictions on subject matter. Query. Reviews artwork/photos as part of the ms package. Send photocopies.
Recent Nonfiction Title(s): *College*, by Stephen Akey (memoir).
Poetry: Poetry must have been published in respected literary journals. Although publishes free verse, but has strong formalist preferences. Query or submit 5 sample poems.
Recent Poetry Title(s): *North Star*, by L.S. Asekoff.
Tips: "Show some evidence of appealing to a wider audience than simply people you know."

OREGON STATE UNIVERSITY PRESS, 101 Waldo Hall, Corvallis OR 97331-6407. (541)737-3166. Fax: (541)737-3170. Managing Editor: Jo Alexander. **Acquisitions:** Acquisitions Editor. Estab. 1965. "Oregon State University Press publishes several scholarly and specialized books and books of particular importance to the Pacific Northwest. OSU Press plays an essential role by publishing books that may not have a large audience, but are important to scholars, students and librarians in the region." Publishes hardcover and paperback originals. Publishes 9 titles/year. Receives 100 submissions/year. 75% of books from first-time authors; 100% of books from unagented writers. Average print order for a first book is 1,500. Pays royalty on net receipts. No advance. Publishes book 1 year after acceptance. Reports in 3 months. Book catalog for 6×9 SAE with 2 first-class stamps.
● This publisher recently won the Oregon Book Award for their Oregon Literature series.
Nonfiction: Publishes scholarly books in history, biography, geography, literature, life sciences and natural resource management, with strong emphasis on Pacific or Northwestern topics. Submit outline and sample chapters.
Recent Nonfiction Title(s): *Planning a New West*, by Carl Abbott, Sy Adler and Margorie Post Abbott..
Tips: "Over the next few years we will increase the number of books we publish from approximately 9/year to 20. We have launched two new series: Culture & Environment in the Pacific West and Northwest Readers."

ORLOFF PRESS, P.O. Box 80774, Athens GA 30608. (706)548-0701. Fax: (706)548-0701. E-mail: orloffpress@aol.com. **Acquisitions:** John Spencer, editor. Publishes hardcover originals and reprints. Orloff specializes in literary and contemporary fiction and has begun a creative nonfiction line. Publishes 4-6 titles/year. Receives 100 queries and 200 mss/year. 50% of books from first-time authors; 50% from unagented writers. Pays 10% royalty on wholesale price. No advance. Publishes book 9 months after acceptance. Accepts simultaneous submissions. Reports in 1 month on queries, 2 months on mss. Book catalog free.
● In addition to fiction, Orloff Press recently began publishing (and actively seeking submissions of) creative nonfiction.
Recent Nonfiction Title(s): *The Education of a Poker Player*, by Herbert O. Yardley (creative nonfiction).
Fiction: Erotica, historical, humor, literary, mainstream/contemporary, mystery, short story collections. Submit synopsis,

3 sample chapters and SASE.
Recent Fiction Title(s): *Superstoe*, by William Borden (novel); *Larger Than Death*, by Lynne Murray (mystery).

ORTHO INFORMATION SERVICES, The Solaris Group/Monsanto, P.O. Box 5006, San Ramon CA 94583. **Acquisitions:** Christine Jordan, editorial director. Ortho publishes gardening and home improvement titles for building enthusiasts. Publishes 10 titles/year. Makes outright purchase.
Nonfiction: How-to. Subjects include gardening, home improvement, building. Query. All unsolicited mss returned unopened.

ORYX PRESS, 4041 N. Central Ave., Suite 700, Phoenix AZ 85012. (602)265-2651. Fax: (602)265-6250. E-mail: info@oryxpress.com. Website: http://www.oryxpress.com/. President: Phyllis B. Steckler. **Acquisitions:** Donna Sanzone, Henry Rasof, Jake Goldberg, acquisitions editors; Martha Wilke Montz (submission). Estab. 1975. Publishes print and/or electronic reference resources for public, college, K-12 school, business and medical libraries, and multicultural/literature-based/social studies resource materials for K-12 classroom use. Publishes 50 titles/year. Receives 500-1,000 submissions/year. 40% of books from first-time authors; 80% from unagented writers. Average print order for a first book is 1,500. Pays 10% royalty on net receipts. No advance. Publishes book 9 months after acceptance. Proposals via Internet welcomed. Reports in 3 months. Book catalog and author guidelines free.
Nonfiction: Directories, dictionaries, encyclopedias, multimedia (CD-ROM) other general reference works; special subjects: business, education, consumer health care, government information, gerontology, social sciences. Query or submit outline/rationale and samples. Queries/mss may be routed to other editors in the publishing group.
Recent Nonfiction Title(s): *Distinguished African American Scientists in the 20th Century*, by Morin, Kessler, Kidd, Kidd (reference); *Inside American History*, by Sperry, Bowman, Wehile, Guterman and Packer (multimedia); *Africa*, by Edward Bever (government/politics).
Tips: "We are accepting and promoting more titles over the Internet. We are also looking for up-to-date, relevant ideas to add to our established line of print and electronic works."

OSBORNE/MCGRAW-HILL, Subsidiary of The McGraw-Hill Companies, Dept. WM, 2600 10th St., Berkeley CA 94710. (510)548-2805. (800)227-0900. **Acquisitions:** Scott Rogers, executive editor. Estab. 1979. Osborne publishes technical computer books and software. Publishes trade paperback originals. Publishes 65 titles/year. Receives 120 submissions/year. 30% of books from first-time authors; 95% from unagented writers. Pays 8-15% royalty on wholesale price. Offers $5,000 average advance. Publishes book an average of 6 months after acceptance. Accepts simultaneous submissions. Reports in 2 months. Book catalog free.
Nonfiction: Software, technical. Subjects include computers. Query with outline and sample chapters. Reviews artwork/photos as part of ms package.
Recent Nonfiction Title(s): *Great American Websites: An Online Discovery of a Hidden America*, by Edward J. Renehan, Jr.; *WordPerfect for Windows for Busy People*, by Elden Nelson; *Microsoft Office 97: The Complete Reference*, by Stephen L. Nelson and Peter Weverka.

OUR SUNDAY VISITOR, INC., 200 Noll Plaza, Huntington IN 46750-4303. (219)356-8400. Fax: (219)359-9117. President/Publisher: Robert Lockwood. Editor-in-Chief: Greg Erlandson. **Acquistions:** James Manney or Jackie Lindsey, acquisitions editors. Estab. 1912. "We are a Catholic publishing company seeking to educate and deepen our readers in their faith." Publishes paperback and hardbound originals. Averages 20-30/year. Receives over 100 submissions/year. 10% of books from first-time authors; 90% from unagented writers. Pays variable royalty on net receipts. Offers $1,000 average advance. Publishes book 1 year after acceptance. Reports in 3 months on most queries and submissions. Author's guide and catalog for SASE.
Nonfiction: Catholic viewpoints on current issues, reference and guidance, family, prayer and devotional books, and Catholic heritage books. Prefers to see well-developed proposals as first submission with annotated outline and definition of intended market. Reviews artwork/photos as part of ms package.
Recent Nonfiction Title(s): *The Encyclicals of John Paul II* (reference); *Sisters in Crisis*, by Ann Carey (history).
Tips: "Solid devotional books that are not first person, well-researched church histories or lives of the saints and catechetical books have the best chance of selling to our firm. Make it solidly Catholic, unique, without pious platitudes."

‡**OUT THERE PRESS**, P.O. Box 1173, Asheville NC 28802. **Acquisitions:** Jim Bannon, publisher. "We specialize in outdoor guidebooks." Publishes trade paperback originals. Publishes 3-6 titles/year. Pays 5-7½% royalty on retail price. Publishes book 4 months after acceptance of ms. Accepts simultaneous submissions. Reports in 2 months on queries. Book catalog for #10 SASE.
Nonfiction: Reference. Subjects include recreation, regional, sports, travel. "We are looking for new titles in our 'Guide to Backcountry Travel & Adventure' series." Query with SASE.
Recent Nonfiction Title(s): *Virginia: A Guide to Backcountry Travel & Adventure*, by Bannon; *South Carolina: A Guide to Backcountry Travel & Adventure*, by Giffen; *Sea Kayaking the Carolinas*, by Bannon/Giffen; (guides).

RICHARD C. OWEN PUBLISHERS INC., P.O. Box 585, Katonah NY 10536. Fax: (914)232-3977. **Acquisitions:** Janice Boland, director of children's books; Amy Haggblom, project editor (professional books). "Our focus is literacy education with a meaning-centered perspective. We believe students become enthusiastic, independent, life-long learners when supported and guided by skillful teachers. The professional development work we do and the books we publish support these beliefs." Publishes hardcover and paperback originals. Publishes 23 titles/year. Receives 150 queries and 1,000 mss/year. 99% of books from first-time authors; 100% from unagented writers. Pays 5% royalty on wholesale price. Publishes book 3 years after acceptance of ms. Accepts simultaneous submissions, if so noted. Reports in 1 month on queries and proposals, 2 months and mss. Manuscript guidelines for SASE with 52¢ postage.

● "We are also seeking manuscripts for our new collection of short, snappy stories for 8-10-year-old children (3rd and 4th grades). Subjects include humor, careers, mysteries, science fiction, folktales, women, fashion trends, sports, music, myths, journalism, history, inventions, planets, architecture, plays, adventure, technology, vehicles."

Nonfiction: Children's/juvenile humor, illustrated book. Subjects include animals, nature/environment, gardening, music/dance, recreation, science, sports. "Our books are for 5-7-year-olds. The stories are very brief—under 100 words—yet well structured and crafted with memorable characters, language and plots." Send for ms guidelines, then submit complete ms with SASE.

Recent Nonfiction Title(s): *The Changing Caterpillar*, by Sherry Shahan (science/nature); *New York City Buildings*, by Anne Mace (architecture); *Chicken*, by Rhonda Cox (animals).

Fiction: Picture books. "Brief, strong story line, real characters, natural language, exciting—child-appealing stories with a twist. No lists, alphabet or counting books." Send for ms guidelines, then submit full ms with SASE.

Recent Fiction Title(s): *There Was a Mouse*, by Blanchard/Suhr; *Jump the Broom*, by Candy Helmso.

Poetry: Poems that excite children, fun, humorous, fresh. No jingles. Must rhyme without force or contrivance. Send for ms guidelines, then submit complete ms with SASE.

Tips: "We don't respond to queries. Because our books are so brief it is better to send entire ms."

‡**OWL BOOKS**, Imprint of Henry Holt & Co., Inc., 115 W. 18th St., New York NY 10011. (212)886-9200. **Acquisitions:** Theresa Burns, editor. Estab. 1996. "We are looking for original, great ideas that have commercial appeal, but that you can respect." Firm publishes 135-140 titles/year. 30% of books from first-time authors; 10% from unagented writers. Pays 6-7½% royalty on retail price. Advance varies. Publishes book 1 year after acceptance of ms. Accepts simultaneous submissions. Reports in 2 months on proposals.

Nonfiction: "Broad range." Subjects include art/architecture, biography, cooking/foods/nutrition, gardening, health/medicine, history, language/literature, nature/environment, regional, sociology, sports, travel. Query with outline, 1 sample chapter and SASE.

Recent Nonfiction Title(s): *Sex, Laws, and Cyberspace*, by Jonathan Wallace and Mark Mangan (law/Internet); *Yoga Journals, Yoga Basics: A Beginner's Yoga Instructional Guide*, by Mara Carrico (self-help/health).

Fiction: Query with synopsis, 1 sample chapter and SASE.

Recent Fiction Title(s): *White Boy Shuffle*, by Paul Beatty; *The Debt to Pleasure*, by John Lanchester.

OWL CREEK PRESS, 2693 SW Camaro Dr., Camaro Island WA 98292. **Acquisitions:** Rich Ives, editor. "We publish selections on artistic merit only." Publishes hardcover originals, trade paperback originals and reprints. Publishes 4-6 titles/year. 50% of books from first time authors; 95% from unagented writers. Pays 10-15% royalty, makes outright purchase or with a percentage of print run. Publishes book 2 years after acceptance. Reports in 3 months. Book catalog for #10 SASE.

● Owl Creek Press has published such authors as Sandra McPherson, Ellen Watson and E.G. Burrows.

Recent Nonfiction Title(s): *The Truth About the Territory*, edited by Rich Ives (Northwest creative nonfiction).

Fiction: Literary, short story collections. Submit 1 sample chapter.

Recent Fiction Title(s): *The Body of Martin Aguilera*, by Percival Everett; *Sailing to Corinth*, by Irene Wanner.

● Owl Creek Press holds two contests, the Owl Creek Poetry Prize and the Green Lake Chapbook Prize, and publishes the winners. See the Contests and Awards section for details.

Recent Poetry Title(s): *The Wedding Boat*, by Sue Ellen Thompson.

PACIFIC BOOKS, PUBLISHERS, P.O. Box 558, Palo Alto CA 94302-0558. (415)965-1980. **Acquisitions:** Henry Ponleithner, editor. "We publish general interest and scholarly nonfiction including professional and technical books, and college textbooks since 1945." Publishes 6-12 titles/year. Pays 7½-15% royalty. No advance. Reports in 1 month. *Writer's Market* recommends allowing 2 months for reply. Book catalog and guidelines for 9×12 SASE.

Nonfiction: General interest, professional, technical and scholarly nonfiction trade books. Specialties include western Americana and Hawaiiana. Looks for "well-written, documented material of interest to a significant audience." Also considers text and reference books for high school and college. Accepts artwork/photos and translations. Query with outline and SASE.

Recent Nonfiction Title(s): *How To Choose a Nursery School: A Parents' Guide to Preschool Education, 2nd edition*, by Ada Anbar (education/parenting); *Issei Women: Echoes From Another Frontier*, by Eileen Sunada Sarasohn (history/women's studies).

PACIFIC PRESS PUBLISHING ASSOCIATION, Book Division, P.O. Box 5353, Nampa ID 83653-5353. (208)465-2570. Fax: (208)465-2584. E-mail: kenwad@pacificpress.com. Website: http://www.pacificpress.com. **Acquisitions:** Jerry Thomas. Estab. 1874. "We are an exclusively religious publisher. We are looking for practical, how-to oriented manuscripts on religion, health, and family life that speak to human needs, interests and problems from a Biblical perspective." Publishes hardcover and trade paperback originals and reprints. Publishes 35 titles/year. Receives 600 submissions and proposals/year. Up to 35% of books from first-time authors; 100% from unagented writers. Pays

8-16% royalty on wholesale price. Offers $300-1,500 average advance depending on length. Publishes book 10 months after acceptance. Reports in 3 months. Manuscript guidelines for #10 SASE.
Nonfiction: Biography, cookbook (vegetarian), how-to, juvenile, self-help. Subjects include cooking and foods (vegetarian only), health, nature, religion, family living. "We can't use anything totally secular or written from other than a Christian perspective." Query or request information on how to submit a proposal. Reviews artwork/photos as part of ms package.
Recent Nonfiction Title(s): *The Miracle from the Streets*, by Cheri Peters; *How to Hug a Heart*, by Tamara Horst (practical Christianity); *Stand at the Cross*, by Lonnie Melashenko and John McClarty.
Recent Fiction Title(s): *Prayer Warriors*, by Celeste Perrino Walker; *Detective Zack #9; Trapped in Darkmoor Manor*, by Jerry D. Thomas (adventure, ages 8-12).
Tips: "Our primary audiences are members of our own denomination (Seventh-day Adventist), the general Christian reading market, and the secular or nonreligious reader. Books that are doing well for us are those that relate the Biblical message to practical human concerns and those that focus more on the experiential rather than theoretical aspects of Christianity. We are assigning more titles, using less unsolicited material—although we still publish manuscripts from freelance submissions and proposals."

PACIFIC VIEW PRESS, P.O. Box 2657, Berkeley CA 94702. **Acquisitions:** Pam Zumwalt, acquisitions editor. Pacific View Press publishes books for "persons professionally/personally aware of the growing importance of the Pacific Rim and/or the modern culture of these countries, especially China." Publishes hardcover and trade paperback originals. Publishes 4-6 titles/year. 50% of books from first-time authors; 100% from unagented writers. Pays 10% maximum royalty on retail price. Offers $1,000-5,000 advance. Publishes book 1 year after acceptance. Accepts simultaneous submissions. Reports in 2 months on queries and proposals. Book catalog free. Writer's guidelines for #10 SASE.
Nonfiction: Children's/juvenile (Asia/multicultural only), reference, textbook (Chinese medicine only), contemporary Pacific Rim affairs. Subjects include business/economics (Asia and Pacific Rim only), health/medicine (Chinese medicine), history (Asia), regional (Pacific Rim), travel (related to Pacific Rim). Query with proposal package including outline, 1-2 chapters, target audience and SASE.
Recent Nonfiction Title(s): *Made in China: Ideas and Inventions from Ancient China*, by Suzanne Williams (illustrated Chinese history for kids); *Tibet: Abode of the Gods, Pearl of the Motherland*, by Barbara Erickson.
Tips: "Audience is business people, academics, travelers, etc."

PALADIN PRESS, P.O. Box 1307, Boulder CO 80306-1307. (303)443-7250. Fax: (303)442-8741. E-mail: clubed@rmii.com. President/Publisher: Peder C. Lund. **Acquisitions:** Jon Ford, editorial director. Estab. 1970. Paladin Press publishes the "action library" of nonfiction in military science, police science, weapons, combat, personal freedom, self-defense, survival, "revenge humor." Publishes hardcover and paperback originals and paperback reprints. Publishes 50 titles/year. 50% of books from first-time authors; 100% from unagented writers. Pays 10-12-15% royalty on net sales. Publishes book 1 year after acceptance. Accepts simultaneous submissions. Reports in 2 months. Catalog free.
Nonfiction: "Paladin Press primarily publishes original manuscripts on military science, weaponry, self-defense, personal privacy, financial freedom, espionage, police science, action careers, guerrilla warfare, fieldcraft and 'creative revenge' humor. How-to manuscripts are given priority. If applicable, send sample photographs and line drawings with complete outline and sample chapters." Query with outline and sample chapters.
Recent Nonfiction Title(s): *Scams from the Great Beyond*, by Peter Huston; *The World's Most Dangerous Places*, by Robert Young Pelton and Coskun Aral; *The Professional Gambler's Handbook*, by Weasel Murphy.
Tips: "We need lucid, instructive material aimed at our market and accompanied by sharp, relevant illustrations and photos. As we are primarily a publisher of 'how-to' books, a manuscript that has step-by-step instructions, written in a clear and concise manner (but not strictly outline form) is desirable. No fiction, first-person accounts, children's, religious or joke books. We are also interested in serious, professional videos and video ideas (contact Michael Janich)."

PANTHEON BOOKS, Division of Random House, Inc., 201 E. 50th St., 25th Floor, New York NY 10022. (212)751-2600. Fax: (212)572-6030. Editorial Director: Dan Frank. **Acquisitions:** Adult Editorial Department. "Pantheon Books, which Kurt and Helen Wolff established in 1942 to introduce intellectual European writers to American readers, publishes both Western and non-Western authors of literary fiction and important nonfiction." Pays royalty. Offers advance. Query.
Nonfiction: History, politics, autobiography, biography, interior design.
Recent Nonfiction Title(s): *Bad Land*, by Jonathan Raban; *All Over But The Shoutin'*, by Rick Bragy; *Shattered Faith*, by Sheila Rauch Kennedy (current affairs).
Recent Fiction Title(s): *Crooked Little Heart*, by Anne Lamott; *Cosi Fan Tutti*, by Michael Dibdin (mystery).

PAPER CHASE PRESS, 5721 Magazine St., #152, New Orleans LA 70115. **Acquisitions:** Jennifer Osborn, editor. "Our audience is mainstream—people who read a lot and are open to all kinds of fiction, literary or otherwise." Publishes hardcover and trade paperback originals and reprints. Publishes 5 titles/year. 90% of books from first-time authors; 100% from unagented writers. Pays royalty on retail price; varies from hardcover to trade. Publishes book 18 months after acceptance of ms. Accepts simultaneous submissions. Responds only if interested.
Nonfiction: How-to, self-help. Subjects include business/economics, hobbies, psychology, recreation, sports, women's issues/studies. "We look for enthusiasm about subject matter, fresh ideas, willingness of author to be involved in promotion of book (good speaking ability, willing to travel, etc.)." Send 1-page query letter only.
Recent Nonfiction Title(s): *The Quickening: Today's Trends, Tomorrow's World*, by Art Bell (current events).

Fiction: Mainstream/contemporary. "We don't want to see someone's first draft. Stay in tune with current trends in fiction. The beginning of the story should be strong enough to *immediately* generate interest in the whole book—sympathetic characters with depth and variety." Query; submit synopsis and first 2 chapters only.
Tips: "Relationship issues are particularly interesting to us, i.e., family relationhips, personal relationships. Make your characters and your story believable!"

PAPIER-MACHE PRESS, 627 Walker St., Watsonville CA 95076. (408)763-1420. **Acquisitions:** Shirley Coe, acquisitions editor. "We publish books about women's lives—primarily midlife women—and the art of growing older." Publishes 8-10 titles/year. 50% of books from first-time authors; 75% from unagented writers. Pays royalty. Offers $500-1,000 advance. Publishes book 18 months after acceptance. Accepts simultaneous submissions. Reports in 2 months on queries, 4 months on mss. Book catalog and ms guidelines free.
  ● Papier-Mache Press is no longer accepting poetry mss.
Nonfiction: Women's self-help and personal development. Subjects include women's issues/studies, aging. Focus on women's issues; no technical or how-to books; some creative nonfiction. Query with proposal package, including outline, 3-4 sample chapters, target audience, author's qualifications, similar books in marketplace and SASE.
Recent Nonfiction Title(s): *Wise Choices Beyond Midlife: Women Mapping the Journey Ahead*, by Lucy Scott.
Fiction: Feminist, mainstream/contemporary (women), short story collections (women), aging. "We don't consider books with graphic sex or violence." Query with synopsis, 3-4 sample chapters, author bio and SASE.
Recent Fiction Title(s): *Creek Walk and Other Stories*, by Molly Giles (short stories); *Hunger's Table*, by Margaret Randall.
Tips: Audience is women, 35-55 years old. Always request submission guidelines before submitting a ms.

PARADIGM PUBLISHING INC., Subsidiary of EMC Corporation, 875 Montreal Way, St. Paul MN 55102. (612)290-2800. Fax: (612)290-2828. E-mail: publish@emcp.com. Website: http://www.emcp.com. **Acquisitions:** Mel Hecker, publisher. "We focus on textbooks for business, office and computer information systems education marketed to proprietary business schools and community colleges." Publishes 50 titles/year. Receives 60 queries and 35 mss/year. 20% of books from first-time authors; 100% from unagented writers. Pays 6-10% royalty on net. Offers $1,000-2,500 advance. Publishes book 1 year after acceptance of ms. Accepts simultaneous submissions. Reports in 2 months on proposals. Book catalog for 8 × 12 SAE with 4 first-class stamps. Manuscript guidelines free.
  ● Publishes "textbooks enhanced by technology for existing full semester courses." They publish such authors as Rosemary Fruehling, Nita Rutkosky and Bill Mitchell.
Nonfiction: Textbook, multimedia. Subjects include business and office, communications, computers, psychology and accounting. Publishes "textbooks enhanced by technology for existing full semester courses." Submit outline and 2 sample chapters.
Recent Nonfiction Title(s): *Paradigm College Accounting*, by Robert Dansby, et al. (textbook).
Tips: "With the cost of paper escalating, multimedia is a sure winner in educational publishing."

PARKWAY PUBLISHERS, INC., Box 3678, Boone NC 28607. Phone/fax: (704)265-3993. E-mail: aluri@netins.net. Website: http://www.netins.net/showcase/alurir. **Acquisitions:** Rao Aluri, president. Publishes marketable, scholarly works for academic and research libraries, scholars and researchers. Publishes hardcover and trade paperback originals. Publishes 4-6 titles/year. Receives 15-20 queries and 10 mss/year. 75% of books from first-time authors; 100% from unagented writers. Pays 10-15% royalty on retail price. No advance. Publishes book 8 months after acceptance. Reports in 1 month on queries, 2 months on mss. Book catalog on website.
  ● Parkway Publishers is no longer accepting poetry.
Nonfiction: Reference, technical. Subjects include agriculture/horticulture, computers/electronics, science, North Caroliniana. Prefers complete ms with SASE. *Writer's Market* recommends sending a query with SASE first.
Recent Nonfiction Title(s): *Living with Autism: The Parents' Stories*, by Kathleen Dillon (psychology); *Fungi on Rhodedendron: A World Reference*, by Farr, Esteban and Palm.
Tips: Audience is academic and research libraries, scholars and researchers.

PARNASSUS IMPRINTS, 30 Perseverance Way, Suite 7, Hyannis MA 02601. (508)790-1175. Fax: (508)790-1176. **Acquisitions:** Wallace Exman, publisher. "The primary focus of the Parnassus Imprints list is nonfiction for readers interested in subjects relating to New England, particularly Cape Cod." Publishes hardcover originals, trade paperback originals and reprints. Publishes 6-8 titles/year. Receives 25-35 queries and 15-20 mss/year. 25% of books from first-time authors; 50% from unagented writers. Pays 7½-15% royalty on retail price. Offers variable advance. Publishes book 1 year after acceptance of ms. Accepts simultaneous submissions. Reports in 1 month on queries, 2 months on proposals and mss. Book catalog for $1 postage.
Nonfiction: Subjects include regional Americana, anthropology/archaeology, art/architecture, cooking/food/nutrition, gardening, history, hobbies, nature/environment, recreation, sports, travel. "One or more books per list will be of national interest." Query with outline, proposal, 3 sample chapters and SASE. Reviews artwork/photos as part of ms package. Send photocopies.
Recent Nonfiction Title(s): *Before the Curse: The Glory Days of New England Baseball, 1858-1918*, by Troy Soos (sports); *Your Garden Shouldn't Make You Crazy!*, by C.L. Fornari (gardening/horticulture); *Secrets in the Sand*, by Fred Dunford and Greg O'Brien (archaeology of Cape Cod).
Tips: Audience is readers interested in Cape Cod/New England subjects.

‡PASSEGGIATA PRESS, (formerly Three Continents Press), P.O. Box 636, Pueblo CO 81002. (719)544-7889. **Acquisitions:** Donald E. Herdeck, publisher/editor-in-chief; Harold Ames, Jr., general editor. Estab. 1973. "We search for books that will make clear the complexity and value of non-Western literature and culture." Publishes hardcover and paperback originals and reprints. Publishes 20-30 titles/year. Receives 200 submissions/year. 15% of books from first-time authors; 99% from unagented writers. Average print order for a first book is 1,000. Length: 50,000-125,000 words. Nonauthor-subsidy publishes 5% of books. Pays 10% royalty. Offers advance "only on delivery of complete manuscript which is found acceptable; usually $300." Accepts simultaneous submissions. Reviews artwork/photos as part of ms package. State availability of photos/illustrations. Reports in 2 months.
Nonfiction: Specializes in African, Caribbean, Middle Eastern (Arabic and Persian) and Asian-Pacific literature, criticism and translation, Third World literature and history, fiction, poetry, criticism, history and translations of creative writing, including bilingual texts (Arabic language/English translations). Query with outline, table of contents.
Recent Nonfiction Title(s): *Child of Two Worlds: An Autobiography of a Filipino-American or Vice Versa*, by Norman Reyes (autobiography).
Fiction: Query with synopsis, plot summary (1-3 pages).
Recent Fiction Title(s): *Inspector Ali*, by Driss Chraibi (novel).
Poetry: Submit 5-10 sample poems.
Recent Poetry Title(s): *The Right to Err*, by Nina Istrenko (bilingual-English and Russian); *Journey of Barbarus*, by Otto Orbáu.
Tips: We are always interested in genuine contributions to understanding non-Western culture. We need a *polished* translation, or original prose or poetry by non-Western authors *only*. Critical and cross-cultural studies are accepted from any scholar from anywhere."

PASSPORT PRESS, P.O. Box 1346, Champlain NY 12919-1346. **Acquisitions:** Jack Levesque, publisher. Estab. 1975. Passport Press publishes practical travel guides on specific countries. Publishes trade paperback originals. Publishes 4 titles/year. 25% of books from first-time authors; 100% from unagented writers. Pays 6% royalty on retail price. Publishes book 9 months after acceptance. Send 1-page query only. Does not return submissions.
Imprint(s): Travel Line Press.
Nonfiction: Travel books only, not travelogues. Especially looking for mss on practical travel subjects and travel guides on specific countries. Query. Reviews artwork/photos as part of ms package.
Recent Nonfiction Title(s): *Nicaragua Guide*, by Paul Glassman.

PAULINE BOOKS & MEDIA, Daughters of St. Paul, 50 St. Paul's Ave., Jamaica Plain MA 02130-3491. (617)522-8911. Fax: (617)541-9805. Website: http://www.pauline.org. **Acquisitions:** Sister Mary Mark Vickenheiser, FSP, director, editorial department. Estab. 1948. "As a Catholic publishing house, Pauline Books & Media communicates the Gospel message through all available forms of media. We serve the Church by responding to the hopes and needs of all people with the Word of God, in the spirit of St. Paul." Publishes trade paperback originals and reprints. Publishes 25-35 titles/year. Receives approximately 1,300 proposals/year. Pays authors 8-12% royalty on net sales. Publishes ms 2-3 years after acceptance. Reports in 3 months. Book catalog for 9×12 SAE with 4 first-class stamps.
Nonfiction: Saints' biographies, juvenile, spiritual growth and development. Subjects include child guidance/parenting, psychology, religion. "No strictly secular manuscripts." Query only. No unsolicited mss without prior query.
Recent Nonfiction Title(s): *Living in Prayer: A Practical Guide*, by Sandra Grant; *Mary from Nazareth*, by Bruno Battistella (life of the Virgin Mary); *Minute Meditations*, by Father Carl F. Peltz.
Fiction: Juvenile. Query only. No unsolicited mss without prior query.
Recent Fiction Title(s): *The Mystery of Half Moon Cove*, by Dan Montgomery (teen mystery novel).
Tips: "We are interested in books concerning faith and moral values, as well as works on spiritual growth and development and religious instruction for young adults and adults. Always interested in books of Christian formation for families. No New Age books, poetry or autobiographies please—all manuscripts must be consonant with Catholic theology."

PAULIST PRESS, 997 Macarthur Blvd., Mahwah NJ 07430. (201)825-7300. Fax: (201)825-8345. **Acquisitions:** Rev. Kevin A. Lynch, editor. Managing Editor: Donald Brophy. Children's and Juvenile Books: Karen Schilabba. Estab. 1865. Paulist Press publishes Christian and Catholic theology, spirituality and religion titles. Publishes hardcover and paperback originals and paperback reprints. Publishes 90-100 titles/year. Receives 500 submissions/year. 5-8% of books from first-time authors; 95% from unagented writers. Nonauthor subsidy publishes 1-2% of books. Pays royalty on retail price. Usually offers advance. Publishes book 10 months after acceptance. Reports in 2 months.
Nonfiction: Philosophy, religion, self-help, textbooks (religious). Accepts nonfiction translations from German, French and Spanish. "We would like to see theology (Catholic and ecumenical Christian), popular spirituality, liturgy, and religious education texts." Submit outline and 2 sample chapters. Reviews artwork/photos as part of ms package.
Recent Nonfiction Title(s): *After 50: Spiritually Embracing Your Own Wisdom Years*, by Robert J. Wicks; *The Death Penalty: A Historical and Theological Survey*, by James Megivern; *Responses to 101 Questions on Death and Eternal Life*, by Peter C. Phan.

PBC INTERNATIONAL INC., 1 School St., Glen Cove NY 11542. (516)676-2727. Fax: (516)676-2738. Publisher: Mark Serchuck. **Acquisitions:** Lisa Maruca, acquisitions and marketing development manager. Estab. 1980. "PBC International is the publisher of full-color visual idea books for the design, marketing and graphic arts professional." Publishes hardcover and paperback originals. Publishes 18 titles/year. Receives 100-200 submissions/year. Most of books from first-time authors and unagented writers done on assignment. Pays royalty and/or flat fees. Accepts simultaneous submissions. Reports in 2 months. Book catalog for 9×12 SASE.

Imprint(s): Library of Applied Design, Architecture & Interior Design Library, Great Graphics Series, Design In Motion Series, Showcase Edition.

Nonfiction: Subjects include design, graphic art, architecture/interior design, packaging design, marketing design, product design. No submissions not covered in the above listed topics. Query with outline and sample chapters. Reviews artwork/photos as part of ms package.

Recent Nonfiction Title(s): *Empowered Gardens: Architects and Designers at Home*, by Carol Soucek King, Ph.D. (interior design); *Kitchens & Baths: Designs for Living*, by Wanda Jankowski.

PEACHPIT PRESS, Division of Addison-Wesley Longman, 2414 Sixth St., Berkeley CA 94710. (510)548-4393. Fax: (510)548-8192. E-mail: roslyn@peachpit.com. Website: http://www.peachpit.com. **Acquisitions:** Acquisitions Editor. Estab. 1986. "Peachpit Press publishes books about computers, digital publishing, online communications, and other topics of interest to people who work with DOS, Windows, or Macintosh computers." Publishes trade paperback originals. Publishes over 30 titles/year. Receives 250 queries and 6 mss/year. 10% of books from first-time authors; 80% from unagented writers. Pays 12-20% royalty on wholesale price. Offers $2,000-15,000 advance. Publishes book 6 months after acceptance of ms. Accepts simultaneous submissions. Reports in 3 months on proposals. Catalog free.

Nonfiction: How-to, reference, technical. Subjects include computers/electronics. "We prefer no phone calls. Complete our new proposal template available on our website."

Recent Nonfiction Title(s): *Beyond The Little Mac Book*, by Robin Williams and Steve Broback; *Kai's Power Tools 3 for Macintosh: Visual QuickStart guide*, by Sandee Cohen.

‡PEACHTREE CHILDREN'S BOOKS, Imprint of Peachtree Publishers, Ltd. 494 Armour Circle NE, Atlanta GA 30324. (404)876-8761. Fax: (404)875-2578. **Acquisitions:** Helen Harriss, managing editor. "We publish a broad range of subjects and perspectives, with emphasis on innovative plots and strong writing." Publishes hardcover and trade paperback originals. Publishes 5-7 titles/year. 25% of books from first-time authors; 25% from unagented writers. Pays royalty on retail price. Advance varies. Publishes book 18 months after acceptance of ms. Accepts simultaneous submissions. Reports in 3 months on queries, 4 months on mss. Book catalog free. Ms guidelines for #10 SASE.

Nonfiction: Children's/juvenile. Subjects include history, regional. Submit complete ms with SASE. *Writer's Market* recommends sending a query with SASE first.

Recent Nonfiction Title(s): *When You Were a Baby*, by Deborah Shaw Lewis (photos); *When Someone Dies*, by Sharon Greenlee (counseling).

Fiction: Juvenile, picture books, young adult. Submit ms with SASE.

Recent Fiction Title(s): *Under the Backyard Sky*, by Neil Shulman and Sibley Fleming (middle reader).

PEACHTREE PUBLISHERS, LTD., 494 Armour Circle NE, Atlanta GA 30324-4888. (404)876-8761. **Acquisitions:** Managing Editor. Estab. 1977. Peachtree Publishers prefers to work with Southern writers and professional storytellers. They specialize in children's books, juvenile chapter books, young adult, regional guidebooks, cookbooks, topical nonfiction and Southern culture. Publishes hardcover and trade paperback originals. Publishes 15-20 titles/year; 1 fiction book/year. Approximately 33% of Peachtree's list consists of children's books. Receives up to 18,000 submissions/year. 25% of books from first-time authors; 75% from unagented writers. Pays 7½-15% royalty. Average print order for a first book is 5,000-10,000. Publishes book 2 years after acceptance. Reports in 6 months on queries. Book catalog for 9×12 SAE with 3 first-class stamps.

Imprint(s): Peachtree Children's Books.

Nonfiction: General and humor. Subjects include children's titles and juvenile chapter books, cooking/foods, history, health, self-help, gardening, biography, general gift, recreation. No technical or reference. Submit outline and sample chapters. Reviews artwork/photos as part of ms package. No originals, please.

Recent Nonfiction Title(s): *Handcrafted in the Blue Ridge: Discovering the Crafts, Artisans, and Studios of Western North Carolina*, by Irv Green and Andrea Gross (travel/craft); *The Peachtree Garden Book*, by The Peachtree Garden Club (gardening); *Food Gifts for All Seasons*, by Anne Byrn (cooking/gift).

Fiction: Literary, juvenile, mainstream. No fantasy, science fiction, mystery or romance. Submit sample chapters.

Recent Fiction Title(s): *Over What Hill? (Notes from the Pasture)*, by Effie Leland Wilder; *Master Switch*, by William H. Stender; *Out to Pasture*, by Effie Leland Wilder.

Tips: "Peachtree Publishers prefers to work with previously published authors."

PELICAN PUBLISHING COMPANY, 1101 Monroe St., P.O. Box 3110, Gretna LA 70053. (504)368-1175. Website: http://www.pelicanpub.com. **Acquisitions:** Nina Kooij, editor-in-chief. Estab. 1926. "We seek writers on the cutting edge of ideas. We believe ideas have consequences. One of the consequences is that they lead to a bestselling book." Publishes hardcover, trade paperback and mass market paperback originals and reprints. Publishes 60 titles/year. Receives 5,000 submissions/year. 25% of books from first-time authors; 85% from unagented writers. Pays royalty on actual receipts. Publishes book 18 months after acceptance. Reports in 1 month on queries. *Writer's Market* recommends allowing 2 months for reply. Writer's guidelines for SASE.

● Pelican has published such authors as Justin Wilson, Zig Ziglar, James Rice, Tammy Wynetter, Lee Greenwood, Ron Paolillo and Weseley Eure.

Nonfiction: Biography, coffee table book (limited), humor, popular history, sports, architecture, illustrated book, juve-

nile, motivational, inspirational, Scottish. Subjects include Americana (especially Southern regional, Ozarks, Texas, Florida and Southwest); business (popular motivational, if author is a speaker); health; history; music (American artforms: jazz, blues, Cajun, R&B); politics (special interest in conservative viewpoint); recreation; religion (for popular audience mostly, but will consider others). *Travel*: Regional and international (especially areas in Pacific). *Motivational*: with business slant. *Inspirational*: author must be someone with potential for large audience. *Cookbooks*: "We look for authors with strong connection to restaurant industry or cooking circles, i.e. someone who can promote successfully." Query with SASE. "We require that a query be made first. This greatly expedites the review process and can save the writer additional postage expenses." No multiple queries or submissions. Reviews artwork/photos as part of ms package. Send photocopies only.
Recent Nonfiction Title(s): *The Potato Cookbook*, by Janet Reeves; *Florida Scams*, by Victor M. Knight (history of infamous Florida cons); *The Maverick Guide to the Great Barrier Reef*, by Len Rutledge (travel guide, Australia).
Fiction: Historical, humor, Southern, juvenile. "We publish maybe one novel a year, ususally by an author we already have. Almost all proposals are returned. We are most interested in historical Southern novels." No young adult, romance, science fiction, fantasy, gothic, mystery, erotica, confession, horror, sex or violence. Submit outline/synopsis and 2 sample chapters with SASE.
Recent Fiction Title(s): *Cajun Humor from the Heart*, by Tommy Joe Breaux; *A Leprechaun's St. Patrick's Day*, by Sarah Kiwan Blazek; *Jenny Giraffe's Mardi Gras Ride*, by Cecilia Casrill Dartez (children's stories).
Tips: "We do extremely well with cookbooks, travel and popular histories. We will continue to build in these areas. The writer must have a clear sense of the market and knowledge of the competition. A query letter should describe the project briefly, give the author's writing and professional credentials, and promotional ideas."

PENCIL POINT PRESS, INC., 277 Fairfield Rd., Fairfield NJ 07004. **Acquisitions:** Gene Garone, publisher. Publishes educational supplemental materials for teachers of all levels. Publishes 12 titles/year. Receives 4 queries and 4 mss/year. 100% of books from first-time authors. Pays 5-16% royalty on retail price or makes outright purchase of $25-50/page. No advance. Publishes book 6 months after acceptance. Accepts simultaneous submissions. Reports in 2 months on proposals. Book catalog free.
Nonfiction: Reference, technical, textbook. Subjects include education, music, science, mathematics, language arts, ESL and special needs. Prefers supplemental resource materials for teachers grades K-12 and college (especially mathematics). Submit proposal package, including outline, 2 sample chapters and memo stating rationale and markets.
Recent Nonfiction Title(s): *Literature Bridges: Across the Content Areas*, by Theresa Flynn-Nason; *The Algebra Skill Builder*, by David P. Lawrence; *Rhythm and Melody Concepts: A Sequential Approach for Children*, by Michon Rozmajzl and Rosalie Castleberry.
Tips: Audience is K-8 teachers, 9-12 teachers and college-level supplements. No children's trade books or poetry.

PENGUIN PUTNAM INC., 375 Hudson St., New York NY 10014. President: Phyllis Gramm. **Acquisitions:** Editorial Department. General interest publisher of both fiction and nonfiction.
Imprint(s): Viking, Penguin, **Penguin Studio**, New American Library, Obelisk, Onyx, Plume, Roc, Topaz, **DAW Books, Donald I Fine Books**, Dutton/Signet, **Berkley Publishing Group, G.P. Putnam's Sons, Grosset**, Perigee Books, **Price Stern Sloan, Riverhead Books, Jeremy P. Tarcher, ACE**, Berkley, Jove, **Boulevard Books**. *Children's division*: **Cobblehill Books, Dial Books for Young Readers, Dutton's Children's Books, Grosset & Dunlap**, Lady Bird Books, **Lodestar Books**, Looney Tunes, **Philomel Books**, Platt & Munk, **Puffin Books**, Sandcastle Books, **Viking Children's Books**.

PENGUIN STUDIO, (formerly Viking Studio Books), Imprint of Penguin Putnam Inc., 375 Hudson St., New York NY 10014. (212)366-2191. **Acquisitions:** Michael Fragnito, publisher (nonfiction general interest); Christopher Sweet, executive editor (art, music, history, photography, sports); Cyril Nelson, senior editor (arts & crafts, decorative arts); Marie Timell, senior editor (nonfiction general interest, astrology, New Age); Sarah Scheffel, editor (cooking, gardening, decorative arts, history, gay/lesbian). "We do not accept unsolicited material. We publish high-quality hardcover/trade books." Publishes hardcover originals. Publishes 35-40 titles/year. Receives 300 submissions/year. Less than 10% of books are from first-time authors; less than 5% from unagented writers. Publishes book 1 year after acceptance. Accepts simultaneous submissions. Reports in 2 months.
● This publisher accepts agented submissions only.
Nonfiction: Coffee table book, cookbook, gift book, illustrated book. Subjects include Americana, cooking/foods/nutrition, gardening, gay/lesbian, health/medicine, military/war, music/dance, photography, science, women's issues/studies, New Age/metaphysics. Query. Reviews artwork as part of ms package. Send photocopies.
Recent Nonfiction Title(s): *Mother*, by Judy Olausen; *Naked Babies*, photographs by Nick Kelsh and text by Anna Quindien; *The Secret Language of Birthdays*, by Gory Goldschneider and Joost Elffers.
Tips: "Often writers/agents misspell the publisher's name—be careful. It's hard to take someone seriously when those kinds of mistakes are the first thing the editor or publisher sees on a query letter or manuscript."

PENNSYLVANIA HISTORICAL AND MUSEUM COMMISSION, Imprint of the Commonwealth of Pennsylvania, P.O. Box 1026, Harrisburg PA 17108-1026. (717)787-8099. Fax: (717)787-8312. Website: http://www.state.pa.us. **Acquisitions:** Diane B. Reed, chief, publications and sales division. Estab. 1913. "We have a tradition of publishing scholarly and reference works, as well as more popularly styled books that reach an even broader audience interested in some aspect of Pennsylvania." Publishes hardcover and paperback originals and reprints. Publishes 6-8 titles/year.

Receives 25 submissions/year. Pays 5-10% royalty on retail price. Makes outright purchase or sometimes makes special assignments. Publishes book 18 months after acceptance. Accepts simultaneous submissions. Reports in 4 months. Prepare mss according to the *Chicago Manual of Style*. Manuscript guidelines free.

Nonfiction: All books must be related to Pennsylvania, its history or culture: biography, illustrated books, reference, technical and historic travel. "The Commission seeks manuscripts on Pennsylvania, specifically on archaeology, history, art (decorative and fine), politics and biography." Query or submit outline and sample chapters.

Recent Nonfiction Title(s): *Prehistoric Cultures of Eastern Pennsylvania*, by Jay Custer (archaeology).

Tips: "Our audience is diverse—students, specialists and generalists—all of them interested in one or more aspects of Pennsylvania's history and culture. Manuscripts must be well researched and documented (footnotes not necessarily required depending on the nature of the manuscript) and interestingly written. Manuscripts must be factually accurate, but in being so, writers must not sacrifice style."

PENNWELL BOOKS, PennWell Publishing, P.O. Box 1260, 1421 S. Sheridan Rd., Tulsa OK 74101-6619. Fax: (918)832-9319. **Acquisitions:** Marla Patterson (petroleum); Jim Ferrier (electric); Diane Feldman (fire); Joe Blaes (dental); Bryon Chessar (municipal water). Estab. 1910. "We publish practical, how-to, reference-type books only for the industries we serve." Publishes hardcover originals. Publishes 50 titles/year. Receives 200 queries and 75 mss/year. 25% of books from first-time authors; 99% from unagented writers. Pays 5-15% royalty on net receipts. Publishes book 9 months after acceptance of ms. Reports in 6 months on proposals. Book catalogs free on request; call 1-800-752-9764.

Nonfiction: Technical. Subjects include petroleum, dental, environmental, electric utility and municipal water. "Texts must have practical application for professionals in the markets we serve. Study our catalogs first before submitting anything. Your expertise as a practitioner within the specific industry is an essential component. We do *not* publish theory or philosophy, nor do we publish texts for the general public." Submit proposal package, including table of contents, chapter-by-chapter synopsis, résumé and sample chapter(s) with SASE, "but we expect all authors to keep their originals, and we cannot be held responsible for any submissions." Reviews artwork/photos as part of ms package. Send photocopies.

Recent Nonfiction Title(s): *Financing Energy Projects in Emerging Economics*, by Hossein Razair, Ph.D.

Tips: Audiences include: Petroleum—engineers, geologists, chemists, geophysicists, economists, managers. Environmental—petroleum industry people needing information on hazardous materials, safety and crisis management. Electric utility—managers and engineers in the power industry. Dental—practicing dentists and hygienists and their staffs. Water—municipal water practitioners in water and wastewater facilities. Fire—fire engineering principles.

THE PERMANENT PRESS/SECOND CHANCE PRESS, 4170 Noyac Rd., Sag Harbor NY 11963. (516)725-1101. **Acquisitions:** Judith Shepard, editor. Estab. 1978. "We endeavor to publish quality writing—primarily fiction—without regard to authors' reputations or track records." Permanent Press publishes literary fiction. Second Chance Press devotes itself exclusively to re-publishing fine books that are out of print and deserve continued recognition. Publishes hardcover originals. Publishes 12 titles/year. Receives 7,000 submissions/year. 60% of books from first-time authors; 60% from unagented writers. Average print order for a first book is 2,000. Pays 10-20% royalty on wholesale price. Offers $1,000 advance for Permanent Press books; royalty only on Second Chance Press titles. Publishes book 18 months after acceptance. Accepts simultaneous submissions. Reports in 6 months on queries. Book catalog for 8 × 10 SAE with 7 first-class stamps. Manuscript guidelines for #10 SASE.

• Permanent Press does not employ readers and the number of submissions it receives has grown. If the writer sends a query or manuscript that the press is not interested in, a reply may take two or three weeks. But if there is interest, it may take 3 to 6 months.

Nonfiction: Biography, autobiography, historical. No scientific and technical material, academic studies. Query.

Fiction: Literary, mainstream, mystery. Especially looking for high line literary fiction, "original and arresting." No genre fiction. Query with first 20 pages.

Recent Fiction Title(s): *Life Between Wars*, by Robert H. Patton; *The Deer Mouse*, by Ken Grant; *Home to India*, by Jacquelin Singh.

Tips: "We are interested in the writing more than anything and long outlines are a turn-off. The SASE is vital to keep track of things, as we are receiving ever more submissions. We aren't looking for genre fiction but a compelling, well-written story."

‡**PERSPECTIVES PRESS**, P.O. Box 90318, Indianapolis IN 46290-0318. (317)872-3055. E-mail: ppress@iquest.net. Website: http://www.perspectivespress.com. **Acquisitions:** Pat Johnston, publisher. Estab. 1982. "Our purpose is to promote understanding of infertility issues and alternatives, adoption and closely-related child welfare issues, and to educate and sensitize those personally experiencing these life situations, professionals who work with such clients, and the public at large." Publishes hardcover and trade paperback originals. Averages 4 titles/year. Receives 200 queries/year. 95% of books from first-time authors; 95% from unagented writers. Pays 5-15% royalty on net sales. Publishes book 1 year after acceptance. Reports in 1 month on queries to schedule a full reading. *Writer's Market* recommends allowing 2 months for reply. Book catalog and writer's guidelines for #10 SAE with 2 first-class stamps.

Nonfiction: How-to, juvenile and self-help books on health, psychology and sociology. Must be related to infertility, adoption, alternative routes to family building. Query with SASE.
Recent Nonfiction Title(s): *Launching a Baby's Adoption*, by Patricia Irwin Johnston; *Toddler Adoption: The Weaver's Craft*, by Mary Hopkins Best.
Fiction: "No adult fiction!"
Tips: "For adults, we are seeking infertility and adoption decision-making materials, books dealing with adoptive or foster parenting issues, books to use with children, books to share with others to help explain infertility, adoption, foster care, third party reproductive assistance, special programming or training manuals, etc. For children, we will consider adoption or foster care-related fiction manuscripts that are appropriate for preschoolers and early elementary school children. We do not consider YA. Nonfiction manuscripts are considered for all ages. No autobiography, memoir or adult fiction. While we would consider a manuscript from a writer who was not personally or professionally involved in these issues, we would be more inclined to accept a manuscript submitted by an infertile person, an adoptee, a birthparent, an adoptive parent or a professional working with any of these."

PETER PAUPER PRESS, INC., 202 Mamaroneck Ave., White Plains NY 10601-5376. Fax: (914)681-0389. E-mail: pauperp@aol.com. **Acquisitions:** Solomon M. Skolnick, creative director. Estab. 1928. PPP publishes only small format illustrated gift books. "We focus on single themes or relationships, e.g., love, friendships, mothers, daughters, or appropriate to special occasions, e.g., Christmas, Kwanzaa, Father's Day, birthday, etc." Publishes hardcover originals. Publishes 36-50 titles/year. Receives 700 queries and 300 mss/year. 10% of books from first-time authors; 100% from unagented writers. Makes outright purchase only. Publishes ms 9-15 months after acceptance. Reports in 1 month. Book catalog and guidelines for $1. Manuscript guidelines for #10 SASE.
Nonfiction: Subjects include gardening, friendship, illustrated small-format gift books for special events and occasions (Valentines Day, Mother's Day, Christmas, etc.). "We do not publish narrative works. We publish collections of brief, original quotes, aphorisms, and wise sayings. Please do not send us others people's quotes, prescriptive material or how-to." Submit outline with SASE. Reviews artwork as part of ms package. Send color photocopies or transparencies.
Recent Nonfiction Title(s): *Seeds from a Secret Garden* (with seedpack), by Gertrude Hyde; *Simple Gifts, Abundant Treasures*, by Beth Mende Conny (women's self-help); *Lullabies & Daydreams*, book with music CD.
Tips: "Our readers are primarily female, 35 and over, who are likely to buy a 'gift' book in a stationery, gift or boutique store. Writers should become familiar with our previously published work. We publish only small-format illustrated hardcover gift books of between 750-3,000 words."

‡A.K. PETERS, LTD., 289 Linden St., Wellesley MA 02181. (617)235-2210. Fax: (617)235-2404. E-mail: akpeters@tiac.net. Website: http://www.tiac.net/users/akpeters. **Acquisitions:** Alice Peters, publisher. "Founded by Klaus & Alice Peters with more than 30 years experience in the publishing industry, A.K. Peters aims to publish high-quality, well-produced nonfiction and textbooks in science and technology at a reasonable price." Publishes hardcover originals and reprints. Publishes 15 titles/year. Receives 50 queries and 30 mss/year. 75% of books from first-time authors; 100% from unagented writers. Pays 12½-20% royalty on wholesale price. No advance. Publishes book 6 months after acceptance of ms. Accepts simultaneous submissions. Reports in 2-3 months on mss. Book catalog and ms guidelines free.
● A.K. Peters has published such authors as Elwyn Berlekamp, J.P. Serre and Saunders MacLane.
Nonfiction: Biography, multimedia (format: CD-ROM), technical, textbook. Subjects include computers/electronics, health/medicine, science, software, mathematics. "We are predominantly a publisher of mathematics and computer science, but we are very interested in expanding our list in robotics and health/medicine as well. Stories of people behind the science are also of interest. Proposals for nonfiction should be well organized and well written, clearly noting its audience and purpose." Submit proposal package, including outline or table of contents with sample chapters or full ms. Description of target audience also helpful. Reviews artwork/photos as part of the ms package. Send photocopies.
Recent Nonfiction Title(s): *Computer Facial Animation*, by Parke/Waters (computer science); *Logical Dilemmas: The Life & Work of Kurt Gödel*, by Dawson (mathematical biography); *Calculus Lite*, by F. Morgan (mathematics).

PETERSON'S, P.O. Box 2123, Princeton NJ 08543-2123. (800)338-3282. Fax: (609)243-9150. Website: http://www.petersons.com. Chief Executive Officer: Peter W. Hegener. President, Publishing: Carole Cushmore. **Acquisitions:** Ellen Fiore, executive assistant, editorial. Estab. 1966. Peterson's strives "to be the premier provider—in all appropriate media and formats—of the best information on lifelong education and career opportunities." Publishes trade and reference books. Publishes 55-75 titles/year. Receives 250-300 submissions/year. 50% of books from first-time authors; 90% from unagented writers. Average print order for a first book is 10,000. Pays 7½-12% royalty on net sales. Offers advance. Publishes book 1 year after acceptance. Reports in 3 months. Book catalog free.
● Peterson's has published such authors as Dr. Ernest L. Boyer, Pam Dixon and Michael Feldman.
Nonfiction: Business, careers, education, as well as educational, adult adventure and career directories. Submit complete

---

 THE DOUBLE DAGGER before a listing indicates that the listing is new in this edition. New markets are often more receptive to freelance submissions.

ms or table of contents, introduction and 2 sample chapters with SASE. *Writer's Market* recommends query with SASE first. Looks for "appropriateness of contents to our markets, author's credentials, and writing style suitable for audience."
Recent Nonfiction Title(s): *Portfolio Power: The New Way to Showcase All Your Job Skills and Experiences*; *Writing a Winning College Application Essay*, by Susan McCloskey and Wilma Davidson; *Why Change Doesn't Work*, by Harvey Robbins and Michael Finley (business).

PHI DELTA KAPPA EDUCATIONAL FOUNDATION, P.O. Box 789, Bloomington IN 47402. (812)339-1156. Fax: (812)339-0018. E-mail: special.pubs@pdkintl.org. Website: http://www.pdkintl.org. **Acquisitions:** Donovan R. Walling, editor of special publications. "We publish books for educators—K-12 and higher education. Our professional books are often used in college courses but are never specifically designed as textbooks." Publishes hardcover and trade paperback originals. Publishes 24-30 titles/year. Receives 100 queries and 50-60 mss/year. 50% of books from first-time authors; 100% from unagented writers. Pays honorarium of $500-5,000. Publishes book 6-9 months after acceptance of ms. Reports in 3 months on proposals. Book catalog and ms guidelines free.
  • Phi Delta Kappa Educational Foundation has published such authors as John Goodlad, John F. Jennings and Donald Cruickshank.
Nonfiction: How-to, reference, essay collections. Subjects include child guidance/parenting, education, legal issues. Query with outline and 1 sample chapter. Reviews artwork/photos as part of ms package.
Recent Nonfiction Title(s): *Against the Tide*, edited by Karen Doyle Walton (autobiographical essay by women college heads); *Can Democracy Be Taught?*, by Andrew Oldenquist (essays).

PHILOMEL BOOKS, Imprint Penguin Putnam Inc., 200 Madison Ave., New York NY 10016. (212)951-8700. **Acquisitions:** Patricia Lee Gauch, editorial director; Michael Green, editor. Estab. 1980. "We look for beautifully written, engaging manuscripts for children and young adults." Publishes hardcover originals. Publishes 20-25 titles/year. Receives 2,600 submissions/year. 15% of books from first-time authors; 30% from unagented writers. Pays standard (7½-15%) royalty. Advance negotiable. Publishes book 2 years after acceptance. Reports in 2 months on queries, 3 months on unsolicited mss. Book catalog for 9×12 SAE with 4 first-class stamps. Request book catalog from marketing department of Putnam Publishing Group.
Fiction: Children's picture books (ages 3-8); middle-grade fiction and illustrated chapter books (ages 7-10); young adult novels (ages 10-15). Particularly interested in picture book mss with original stories and regional fiction with a distinct voice. Historical fiction OK. Unsolicited mss accepted for picture books only; query first for long fiction. Always include SASE. No series or activity books.
Recent Fiction Title(s): *Junk Pile*, by Lady Borton, illustrated by Kimberly Bucklen Root; *Mudaket Millie*, by Frances Ward Weller, illustrated by Marcia Sewall; *In Enzo's Splendid Gardens*, by Patricia Polacco.
Tips: "We prefer a very brief synopsis that states the basic premise of the story. This will help us determine whether or not the manuscript is suited to our list. If applicable, we'd be interested in knowing the author's writing experience or background knowledge. We try to be less influenced by the swings of the market than in the power, value, essence of the manuscript itself."

PHILOSOPHY DOCUMENTATION CENTER, Bowling Green State University, Bowling Green OH 43403-0189. (419)372-2419, (800)444-2419. Fax: (419)372-6987. E-mail: phildoc@opie.bgsu.edu. Website: http://www.bgsu.edu/pdc/. **Acquisitions:** Dr. George Leaman, director. The Philosophy Documentation Center "works in cooperation with publishers, database producers, software developers, journal editors, authors, librarians and philosophers to create an electronic clearinghouse for philosophical publishing." Publishes 4 titles/year. Receives 4-6 queries and 4-6 mss/year. 50% of books from first-time authors. Pays 2½-10% royalty. Publishes book 1 year after acceptance. Reports in 2 months. Book catalog free.
Nonfiction: Textbook, software, guidebooks, directories in the field of philosophy. "We want to increase our range of philosophical titles and are especially interested in electronic publishing." Query with outline.
Recent Nonfiction Title(s): *Guidebook For Publishing Philosophy*, edited by Eric Hoffman; *Analytic Philosophy of Religion: A Bibliography from 1940-1995*, edited by Robert Wolf.

‡PICADOR USA, Imprint of St. Martin's Press, 175 Fifth Ave., New York NY 10010. **Acquisitions:** George Witte. Estab. 1994. "We publish high-quality literary fiction and nonfiction. We are open to a broad range of subjects, well written by authoritative authors." Publishes hardcover originals and trade paperback originals and reprints. Publishes 40-50 titles/year. 30% of books from first-time authors. Publishes "few" unagented writers. Pays 7½-12½% royalty on retail price. Advance varies. Publishes book 18 months after acceptance of ms. Accepts simultaneous submissions. Reports in 2 months on queries. Book catalog for 9×12 SASE and $2.60 postage. Manuscript guidelines for #10 SASE.
Nonfiction: Subjects include language/literature, philosophy, biography/memoir, pop culture, literary/poetry criticism. "When submitting queries, be aware of things outside the book, including credentials, that may affect our decision." Query only with SASE. No phone queries.
Recent Nonfiction Title(s): *Blue Windows: A Christian Science Childhood*, by Barbara Wilson (religion/women's studies); *As If*, by Blake Morrison (current affairs).
Fiction: Literary. Query only with SASE.
Recent Fiction Title(s): *Human Croquet*, by Kate Atkinson; *The Jade Peony*, by Wayson Choy; *In The Deep Midwinter*, by Robert Clark.

PICCADILLY BOOKS, P.O. Box 25203, Colorado Springs CO 80936-5203. (719)548-1844. **Acquisitions:** Bruce Fife, publisher. Estab. 1985. "Experience has shown that those who order our books are either kooky or highly intelligent or both. If you like to laugh, have fun, enjoy games, or have a desire to act like a jolly buffoon, we've got the books for you." Publishes hardcover and trade paperback originals and trade paperback reprints. Publishes 3-8 titles/year. Receives 300 submissions/year. 70% of books from first-time authors; 95% from unagented writers. Pays 5-10% royalty on retail price. Publishes book 1 year after acceptance. Accepts simultaneous submissions. Responds only if interested.
  • Piccadilly Books has published work by David Ginn, author of over 50 books, who has appeared in over 100 television shows, and is a nationally known children's entertainer.
Nonfiction: How-to books on entertainment, humor and performing arts. "We have a strong interest in subjects on clowning, magic, puppetry and related arts, including comedy skits and dialogs." Query with sample chapters.
Recent Nonfiction Title(s): *The Gospel in Greasepaint*, by Mark Stucky.

PICTON PRESS, Imprint of Picton Corp., P.O. Box 250, Rockport ME 04856-0250. (207)236-6565. Fax: (207)236-6713. E-mail: picton@midcoast.com. Website: http://www.midcoast.com/~picton. **Acquisitions:** Candy McMahan, office manager. "Picton Press is one of America's oldest, largest and most respected publishers of genealogical and historical books specializing in research tools for the 17th, 18th and 19th centuries." Publishes hardcover and mass market paperback originals and reprints. Publishes 30 titles/year. Receives 30 queries and 15 mss/year. 50% of books from first-time authors; 100% from unagented writers. Pays 0-10% royalty on wholesale price or makes outright purchase. Publishes book 6 months after acceptance of ms. Reports in 2 months on queries and proposals, 3 months on mss. Book catalog free.
Imprint(s): Cricketfield Press, Penobscot Press, New England History Press.
Nonfiction: Reference, textbook. Subjects include Americana, genealogy, history, vital records. Query with outline.
Recent Nonfiction Title(s): *Francis Cooke of the Mayflower*, by Ralph Van Wood; *18th Century Emigrants from Baden and Württmberg*, by Brigitte Burkett (account of German ancestry and departure for America); *Maine Marriages*, CD-ROM, by Lewis B. Rohrbach (625,000 marriages in Maine, 1892-1966).
Recent Fiction Title(s): *Ice Country*, by Mary Morton Cowan (one boy's adventure in the Arctic).

PILOT BOOKS, 127 Sterling Ave., P.O. Box 2102, Greenport NY 11944. (516)477-1094. Fax: (516)477-0978. E-mail: pilotbooks@aol.com. Website: www.pilotbooks.com. **Acquisitions:** Robert Ungerleider, president; Ruth Gruen, editor. Estab. 1959. "Pilot Books publishes personal, business and career guides, travel information and new ideas and trends for adults." Publishes paperback originals. Publishes 20-30 titles/year. Receives 100-200 submissions/year. 20% of books from first-time authors; 90% from unagented writers. Average print order for a first book is 3,000. Offers standard royalty contract based on wholesale or retail price. Offers $250 usual advance, but this varies, depending on author's reputation and nature of book. Publishes book an average of 8 months after acceptance. Reports in 1 month. *Writer's Market* recommends allowing 2 months for reply. Book catalog and guidelines for #10 SASE.
Nonfiction: Publishers of "complete personal, business and career guides, budget travel information and books on new ideas and trends for today's older adult." Wants clear, concise treatment of subject matter." Length: 10,000-40,000 words. Send outline. Reviews artwork/photos as part of ms package.
Recent Nonfiction Title(s): *Bare-Bones Guides to Better Business Writing*, by Sally Williams; *Never Too Late To Understand And Enjoy Casino Gambling*, by Phil Philcox.

‡PIÑATA BOOKS, Imprint of Arte Publico Press, University of Houston, Houston TX 77204-2090. (713)743-2841. Fax: (713)743-2847. **Acquisitions:** Nicolas Kanellos, president. Estab. 1994. "We are dedicated to the publication of children's and young adult literature focusing on U.S. Hispanic culture." Publishes hardcover and trade paperback originals. Publishes 10-15 titles/year. 60% of books from first-time authors. Pays 10% royalty on wholesale price. Offers $1,000-3,000 advance. Publishes book 2 years after acceptance of ms. Accepts simultaneous submissions. Reports in 1 month on queries, 6 months on mss. Book catalog free. Manuscript guidelines for #10 SASE.
Nonfiction: Children's/juvenile. Ethnic subjects. "Pinata Books specializes in publication of children's and young adult literature that authentically portrays themes, characters and customs unique to U.S. Hispanic culture." Query with outline/synopsis, 2 sample chapters and SASE.
Recent Nonfiction Title(s): *Mi primer diccionario*, by Catalina Prilick (reference, ages 2-8); *Barrio Teacher*, by Arcadia Lopez (autobiography); *Silent Dancing: A Partial Remembrance of a Puerto Rican Childhood*, by Judith Ortiz-Cofer (memoir, ages 11-adult).
Fiction: Adventure, juvenile, picture books, young adult. Query with synopsis, 2 sample chapters and SASE.
Recent Fiction Title(s): *The Secret of Two Brothers*, by Irene Beltran Hernandez (ages 11-adult); *Pepita Talks Twice*, by Ofelia Dumas Lachtman (picture book, ages 3-7); *Jumping Off to Freedom*, by Anilu Bernardo (young adult).
Poetry: Appropriate to Hispanic theme. Submit 10 sample poems.
Recent Poetry Title(s): *Tun-ta-ca-tun*, edited by Sylvia Pena (children's, preschool to young adult).
Tips: "Include cover letter with submission explaining why your manuscript is unique and important, why we should publish it, who will buy it, etc."

PINEAPPLE PRESS, INC., P.O. Box 3899, Sarasota FL 34230. (941)953-2797. **Acquisitions:** June Cussen, editor. Estab. 1982. "We are seeking quality nonfiction on diverse topics for the library and book trade markets." Publishes hardcover and trade paperback originals. Publishes 20 titles/year. Receives 1,500 submissions/year. 20% of books from first-time authors; 80% from unagented writers. Pays 6½-15% royalty on retail price. Seldom offers advance. Publishes

book 18 months after acceptance. Accepts simultaneous submissions. Reports in 3 months. Book catalog for 9×12 SAE with $1.24 postage.
Nonfiction: Biography, how-to, reference, regional (Florida), nature. Subjects include animals, history, gardening, nature. "We will consider most nonfiction topics. Most, though not all, of our fiction and nonfiction deals with Florida." No pop psychology or autobiographies. Query or submit outline/brief synopsis, sample chapters and SASE.
Recent Nonfiction Title(s): *Historical Traveler's Guide to Florida*, by Eliot Kleinberg; *Guide to the Lake Okeechobee Area*, by Bill and Carol Gregware; *Visiting Small-Town Florida*, by Bruce Hunt.
Fiction: Literary, historical, mainstream, regional (Florida). No romance, science fiction, children's. Submit outline/brief synopsis and sample chapters.
Recent Fiction Title(s): *My Brother Michael*, by Janis Owens (literature); *The Thang That Ate My Grandaddy's Dog*, by John Calvin Rainey (literature); *Conflict of Interest*, by Terry Lewis (mystery).
Tips: "If I were trying to market a book today, I would learn everything I could about book publishing and publicity and agree to actively participate in promoting my book. A query on a novel without a brief sample seems useless."

PINNACLE BOOKS, Imprint of Kensington, 850 Third Ave., 16th Floor, New York NY 10022. (212)407-1500.
Acquisitions: Paul Dinas, editor. "Pinnacle features bestselling commercial fiction, and also humor." Publishes hardcover, trade paperback and mass market paperback originals and reprints. Publishes 60 titles/year. 3-5% of books from first-time authors; 30% from unagented writers. Pays royalty on retail price, varies by author and type of book. Advance varies, by author and type of book. Publishes book 18 months after acceptance of ms. Accepts simultaneous submissions. Reports in 1 month on queries, 3 months on ms. Book catalog for #10 SASE.
Nonfiction: Humor, male-oriented. Subjects include true crime. Query with outline and SASE. "No unsolicited submissions at this time." Reviews artwork/photos, if integral to project. Send photocopies.
Recent Nonfiction Title(s): *Cruel Sacrifice*, by Aphrodite Jones (true crime); *The Joy of Self Employment*, by Todd Leigh Mayo; *The Athlete in You*, by William Bennett, M.D.
Fiction: General, male-oriented. Query with synopsis and SASE. "No unsolicited submissions at this time."
Recent Fiction Title(s): *The Preacher* Series, by William W. Johnstone.

PIPPIN PRESS, 229 E. 85th St., P.O. Box 1347, Gracie Station, New York NY 10028. (212)288-4920. Fax: (908)225-1562. **Acquisitions:** Barbara Francis, president and editor-in-chief; Joyce Segal, senior editor. Estab. 1987. Pippin publishes general nonfiction and fiction for children ages 4-11. Publishes hardcover originals. Publishes 4-6 titles/year. Receives 4,500 queries/year. 80% of queries from unagented writers. Pays royalty. Publishes book 2 years after acceptance. Reports in 3 weeks on queries. *Writer's Market* recommends allowing 2 months for reply. Book catalog for 6×9 SASE. Manuscript guidelines for #10 SASE.
● Pippin Press has published such authors as David Updike, Lee Lorenz and Charles Keller.
Nonfiction: Children's books: biography, humor, picture books. Subjects include animals, history, language/literature, nature, science. General nonfiction for children ages 4-10. Query with SASE only. Do *not* send mss. Reviews artwork/photos as part of ms package. Send photocopies.
Recent Nonfiction Title(s): *James Madison and Dolly Madison and Their Times*, by Robert Quackenbush (biography).
Fiction: Adventure, fantasy, historical, humor, mystery, picture books, suspense. "We're especially looking for small chapter books with animal-fantasy themes, stories for 7- to 11-year olds, by people of many cultures." Wants humorous fiction for ages 7-11. Query with SASE only.
Recent Fiction Title(s): *Abigail's Drum*, by John A. Minahan, illustrated by Robert Quackenbush (historical fiction).
Tips: "Read as many of the best children's books published in the last five years as you can. We are looking for multi-ethnic fiction and nonfiction for ages 7-10, as well as general fiction for this age group. I would pay particular attention to children's books favorably reviewed in *School Library Journal*, *The Booklist*, *The New York Times Book Review*, and *Publishers Weekly*."

‡PLANET DEXTER, Imprint of Addison Wesley Longman, Inc., One Jacob Way, Reading MA 01867. (617)944-3700. Fax: (617)944-8243. **Acquisitions:** Beth Wolfensberger, editor; Kaesmene Harrison, assistant editor. Planet Dexter publishes books for 8- to 14-year olds that introduce kids to the world in a fun way. "We want fun, hip, irreverent, educational titles—books that kids can learn from without realizing it (we call it 'stealth learning.')." Publishes hardcover and trade paperback originals. Publishes 12 titles/year. Receives hundreds of queries and hundreds of mss/year. 90% of books from first-time authors; 100% from unagented writers. "We prefer to deal with authors directly." Pays royalty on retail price. Offers advance. Publishes book 6 months after acceptance of ms. Accepts simultaneous submissions. Reports in 2-6 months on queries; 2 months on proposals and mss. Book catalog for 9×12 SASE. Manuscript guidelines for #10 SASE.
Nonfiction: Children's/juvenile. Subjects include history, hobbies, how-to, nature/environment, science, math. No curriculum-oriented or textbook-style mss. No characters or narratives. No fiction, poetry or picture books. Query with outline/synopsis, 2 sample chapters and SASE. Average length: middle readers 15,000 words; young readers 10,000 words.
Recent Nonfiction Title(s): *Lefty: A Handbook for Left-Handed Kids*, by the Editors of Planet Dexter; *The Midnight Hour: Bright Ideas for After Dark*, by Geoff Edgers; *The Blue Book: A Bluetiful, Bluesy, Blue-Ribbon, Blue-to-the-nth, Bolt Out of the Blue . . from Blueberries to Blue Moons*, by Michael Hainey.

PLANNERS PRESS, Imprint of American Planning Association, 122 S. Michigan Ave., Chicago IL 60603. Fax: (312)431-9985. E-mail: slewis@planning.org. Website: http://www.planning.org. **Acquisitions:** Sylvia Lewis, director of publications. "Our books have a narrow audience of city planners and often focus on the tools of city planning." Publishes hardcover and trade paperback originals. Publishes 4-6 titles/year. Receives 20 queries and 6-8 mss/year. 50% of books from first-time authors; 100% from unagented writers. Pays 7½-12% royalty on retail price. Publishes book 1 year after acceptance. Reports in 1 month on queries, 2 months on proposals and mss. Book catalog and ms guidelines free.
Nonfiction: Technical (specialty-public policy and city planning). Subjects include government/politics. Submit 2 sample chapters and table of contents. Reviews artwork/photos as part of ms package. Send photocopies.
Recent Nonfiction Title(s): *Best Development Practices*, by Reid Ewing (land development); *Planning Made Easy*, William Toner (training manual); *Rural By Design*, by Randall Arendt (land development).

PLANNING/COMMUNICATIONS, 7215 Oak Ave., River Forest IL 60305. (708)366-5200. Website: http://jobfind ersonline.com. **Acquisitions:** Daniel Lauber, president; Robert Pruter, senior assiciate. Planning Communications seeks to help people find jobs and get hired, and to address national issues. Publishes hardcover, trade and mass market paperback originals, trade paperback reprints. Publishes 3-8 titles/year. Receives 10 queries and 3 mss/year. 50% of books from first-time authors; 100% from unagented writers. Pays 15-20% royalty on net sales. Publishes book 6 months after acceptance of ms. Accepts simultaneous submissions. Reports in 2 months on queries, 3 months on proposals and mss. Book catalog for $1.95. Manuscript guidelines for #10 SASE.
• Planning/Communications no longer seeks mysteries.
Nonfiction: Careers, self-help, résumés, cover letters, interviewing. Subjects include business/economics (careers), education, government/politics, money/finance, sociology, software. Submit outline and 3 sample chapters with SASE. Reviews artwork/photos as part of ms package. Send photocopies.
Recent Nonfiction Title(s): *Professional's Job Finder*; *Government Job Finder*; *Non-Profits and Education Job Finder*; all by Daniel Lauber (careers).

PLAYERS PRESS, INC., P.O. Box 1132, Studio City CA 91614-0132. (818)789-4980. **Acquisitions:** Robert W. Gordon, vice president, editorial. Estab. 1965. "We publish quality plays, musicals and performing arts books for theater, film and television." Publishes hardcover and trade paperback originals, and trade paperback reprints. Publishes 35-70 titles/year. Receives 200-1,000 submissions/year. 15% of books from first-time authors; 80% from unagented writers. Pays royalty on wholesale price. Publishes book on or before the 24th month after acceptance. Reports on queries in 1 month, up to 1 year on mss. Book catalog and guidelines for 9 × 12 SAE with 4 first-class stamps.
• Players Press has increased their number of books published from 25-35 to 35-70 titles/year.
Nonfiction: Juvenile and theatrical drama/entertainment industry. Subjects include the performing arts, costume, theater and film crafts. Needs quality plays and musicals, adult or juvenile. Query. Reviews artwork/photos as part of package.
Recent Nonfiction Title(s): *Assignments in Musical Theatre*, by J. Wheeler (theater); *Silly Soup*, by Carol Kerty (drama, young audiences); *History of Children's Theatre*, by Nellie McCaslin (dance).
Fiction: Subject matter of plays include adventure, confession, ethnic, experimental, fantasy, historical, horror, humor, mainstream, mystery, religious, romance, science fiction, suspense, western. Submit complete ms for theatrical plays only. "No novels or story books are accepted."
Tips: "Plays, entertainment industry texts, theater, film and TV books have the only chances of selling to our firm."

PLEASANT COMPANY PUBLICATIONS, Imprint of American Girls Collection®. 8400 Fairway Pl., Middleton WI 53562. Fax: (608)836-1999. Website: http://www.pleasantco.com. **Acquistions:** Jennifer Hirsch, submissions editor. "Pleasant Company publishes fiction and nonfiction for girls 7-12 under its two imprints. The American Girls Collection and American Girl Library. The company relies primarily on its own team of writers, editors, and designers to produce its books and print products." Publishes hardcover and trade paperback originals. Publishes 3-25 title/year. Receives 400 queries and 400 mss/year. 50% of books from unagented writers. "Payment varies extremely depending on the nature of the work." Advance varies. Accepts simultaneous submissions. Reports in 2 months. Book catalog free.
Imprint(s): The American Girls Collection, American Girl Library.
Nonfiction: Children's/juvenile for girls, ages 7-12. Subjects include Americana, history, contemporary lifestyle, activities, how-to. Query.
Recent Nonfiction Title(s): *The Care and Keeping of Friends*; *Jazz Up Your Jeans*, by Brooks Whitney; *Oops! The Manners Guide for Girls*, by Nancy Holyoke.
Fiction: Juvenile for girls, ages 7-12. Subjects include historical fiction, mysteries. "No romance, fantasy, picture books, rhyme or stories about talking animals." Query.
Recent Fiction Title(s): *Meet Josefina, An American Girl*; *Josefina Learns a Lesson*, both by Valerie Tripp.

PLENUM PUBLISHING, 233 Spring St., New York NY 10013-1578. (212)620-8000. **Acquisitions:** Linda Greenspan Regan, executive editor, trade books. Estab. 1946. "Plenum publishes expertly-written, marketable books oncontemporary topics in the sciences and social sciences for the scientifically curious reader." Publishes hardcover originals. Publishes 350 titles/year; Plenum Trade publishes 18 titles/year. Receives 1,000 submissions/year. 20% of books from first-time authors; 20% from unagented writers. Offers standard royalty contract. Publishes book 8-16 months after acceptance. Accepts simultaneous submissions. Reports in 6-8 months.
Nonfiction: Subjects include trade science, criminology, anthropology, mathematics, sociology, psychology, health.

"We are seeking high quality, popular books in the sciences and social sciences." Query only.

Recent Nonfiction Title(s): *Mechanisms in the Pathogenesis of Enteric Diseases*, edited by Prem S. Paul, David H. Francis and David A. Benfield; *Countable Boolean Algebras and Decidability*, by Sergei S. Goncharov; *Adaptive Radiations of Neotropical Pirmates*, edited by Marilyn A. Norconk, Alfred L. Rosenberger and Paul A. Garber.

Tips: "Our audience consists of intelligent laymen and professionals. You should be experts on subject matter of book. Compare your book with competitive works, explain how it differs, and define its market."

POCKET BOOKS, Division of Simon & Schuster, Dept. WM, 1230 Avenue of the Americas, New York NY 10020. **Acquisitions:** Patricia McDonald, editorial director. Pocket Books publishes general interest nonfiction and adult fiction. Publishes paperback originals and reprints, mass market and trade paperbacks and hardcovers. Publishes 250 titles/year. Receives 2,500 submissions/year. 25% of books from first-time authors; less than 25% from agented writers. Pays 6-8% royalty on retail price. Publishes book an average of 2 years after acceptance. Book catalog free. Manuscript guidelines for #10 SASE.

Nonfiction: History, biography, reference and general nonfiction, humor, calendars.

Recent Nonfiction Title(s): *The Big Show: Inside America's SportsCenter*, by Keith Olberman and Dan Patrick (television/sports); *The Complete Guide to Foreign Adoption*, by Barbara Bascom, M.D., and Carole McKlvey, M.A.; *All I Really Need to Know in Business I Learned at Microsoft*, by Julie Brick.

Fiction: Adult (mysteries, thriller, psychological suspense, Star Trek ® novels, romance, westerns).

Recent Fiction Title(s): *Heart Song*, by V.C. Andrews; *Star Trek Avenger*, by William Shatner; *Green Candles*, by Tom DeHaven, illustrated by Robin Smith (graphic novel/mystery).

POPULAR CULTURE INK, P.O. Box 1839, Ann Arbor MI 48106. (313)677-6351. **Acquisitions:** Tom Schultheiss, publisher. Popular Culture Ink publishes directories and reference books for radio, TV, music and dance. Publishes hardcover originals and reprints. Publishes 4-6 titles/year. Receives 50 queries and 20 mss/year. 100% of books from first-time authors; 100% from unagented writers. Pays variable royalty on wholesale price. Offers variable advance. Publishes book 2 years after acceptance. Accepts simultaneous submissions. Reports in 1 month. *Writer's Market* recommends allowing 2 months for reply. Book catalog and ms guidelines free.

Nonfiction: Reference. Subjects include music/dance, popular entertainment. Query.

Recent Nonfiction Title(s): *Surfin' Guitars*, by Robert Dalley (1960s surf music).

Tips: Audience is libraries, avid collectors. "Know your subject backwards. Make sure your book is unique."

‡PPI PUBLISHING, P.O. Box 292239, Kettering OH 45429. (937)294-5057. **Acquisitions:** Shary Price, managing editor. "PPI Publishing seeks to provide top-quality, well researched, up to the-minute information on the 'hot' issues for teens." Publishes age-specific paperback originals and distributes them mostly to schools and public libraries. Publishes 10-15 titles/year. Receives 200 queries and 50 mss/year. 90% of books from first-time authors; 100% from unagented writers. Pays 10% royalty on retail price. Publishes book 10 months after acceptance of ms. Accepts simultaneous submissions. Reports in 2 months on queries, 3 months on proposals, 2 months on mss, longer for unsolicited ms. Catalog and guidelines for 9×12 SASE and 2 first-class stamps. Manuscript guidelines for #10 SASE.

Nonfiction: Children/young adult, how-to, self-help. Subjects include career guidance; motivational; social issues such as AIDS, abortion, teenage drinking; environmental issues such as the Rainforest and the ozone layer; teen sexuality, "hot youth topics." Publishes books in the Fall. Submit fresh topics with logical thought and writing. Query or submit outline with 3 sample chapters with SASE. Reviews artwork/photos as part of the ms package. Send photocopies.

Recent Nonfiction Title(s): *Respect Between the Sexes*, by Michael Dumond, M.S. (gender conflict and resolution); *The Best & Brightest High School Student Guide*, by Al Stenzel (how to succeed in school and life); *AIDS: Facts, Issues, Choices*, by Faith H. Brynie, Ph.D.

Tips: Readers are students in grades 7-12 and their teachers. "We're looking for quality material on 'hot' topics that will appeal to middle school/high school students."

‡PRACTICE MANAGEMENT INFORMATION CORP. (PMIC), 4727 Wilshire Blvd., Los Angeles CA 90010. (213)954-0224. Fax: (213)954-0253. E-mail: pmiceditor@aol.com. Website: http://www.medicalbookstore.com. **Acquisitions:** Kathryn Swanson, managing editor. "We seek to help doctors with the business of medicine." Publishes hardcover originals. Publishes 21 titles/year. Receives 10 queries and 25 mss/year. 10% of books from first-time authors; 90% from unagented writers. Pays 10-15% royalty on net receipts. Offers $1,000-5,000 advance. Publishes book 18 months after acceptance of ms. Reports in 3 months on queries. Book catalog and ms guidelines for #10 SASE.

Imprint(s): PMIC, Health Information Press.

Nonfiction: Reference, technical, textbook, medical practice management, clinical, nonfiction. Subjects include business/economics, health/medicine, science. Submit outline and proposal package, including letter stating who is the intended audience, the need/market for such a book, as well as outline, 3-5 sample chapters and curriculum vitae/résumé.

Recent Nonfiction Title(s): *Hematology*, by Richert Goyette, M.D. (textbook); *Clinical Research Opportunities*, by Matthew Heller, M.D., and Tony Boyle, M.D.; *Medico Mnemonica*, by Evan Marlowe, M.D. (study guide).

Tips: Audience is doctors, medical office and hospital staff, medical managers, insurance coding/billing personnel.

PRAEGER PUBLISHERS, Imprint of the Greenwood Publishing Group, Inc., 88 Post Road W., Westport CT 06881. (203)226-3571. Fax: (203)226-1502. Website: http://www.greenwood.com. General Manager: Jim Dunton. **Acquisitions:** James Ice, editor (business); Alan Sturmer, editor (textbooks); Elizabeth Murphy, editor (women's studies, ethnic

studies); Daniel Eades, senior editor (political science, history). Estab. 1950. "Praeger publishes scholarly and advanced texts in the the social and behavioral sciences and trade titles in the humanities, business, communications, international relations and military studies." Publishes hardcover originals and reprints and trade paperback originals. Publishes 280 titles/year. Receives 1,200 submissions/year. 5% of books from first-time authors; 90% from unagented writers. Pays 6½-15% royalty on net sales. Rarely offers advance. Publishes book an average of 1 year after acceptance. Accepts simultaneous submissions. Reports in 1 month. *Writer's Market* recommends allowing 2 months for reply. Book catalog and manuscript guidelines available on website.
Nonfiction: "We are looking for women's studies, sociology, psychology, education, contemporary history, military studies, political science, business, economics, international relations, philosophy. No language and literature." Query with proposal package, including: scope, organization, length of project; whether a complete ms is available, or when it will be; cv or résumé with SASE. No unsolicited ms.
Recent Nonfiction Title(s): *An American Paradox: Censorship in a Nation of Free Speech*, by Patrick Garry; *Black and Right: The Bold New Voice of Black Conservatives in America*, edited by Stan Faryna, Brad Stetson and Joseph G. Conti; *Assault on the Left: The FBI and the Sixties Antiwar Movement*, by James Kirkpatrick Davis.

PRAIRIE OAK PRESS, 821 Prospect Place, Madison WI 53703. (608)255-2288. **Acquisitions:** Jerry Minnich, president; Kristin Visser, vice president. Estab. 1991. Prairie Oak publishes exclusively Upper Great Lakes regional nonfiction. Publishes hardcover originals, trade paperback originals and reprints. Publishes 6-8 titles/year. Pays royalty or makes outright purchase. Offers $500-1,000 advance. Reports in 3 months on proposals.
Imprint Prairie Classics.
Nonfiction: History, folklore, gardening, sports, travel, architecture, other general trade subjects. "Any work considered must have a strong tie to Wisconsin and/or the Upper Great Lakes region." Query or submit outline and 1 sample chapter with SASE.
Recent Nonfiction Title(s): *Wisconsin with Kids*, by Visser (family travel guide).
Tips: "When we say we publish regional works only, we mean this region (Wisconsin, Minnesota, Michigan, Illinois). Please do not submit books of national interest. We cannot consider them."

PRECEPT PRESS, Subsidiary of Bonus Books, 160 E. Illinois St., Chicago IL 60611. (312)467-0424. Fax: (312)467-9271. E-mail: mcclain@bonus-books.com. Website: http://www.bonus-books.com. **Acquisitions:** Rachel Drzewicki, managing editor. "Precept Press features a wide variety of books for the technical community." Publishes hardcover and trade paperback originals. Publishes 20 titles/year. Receives 300 queries and 100 mss/year. 25% of books from first-time authors; 90% from unagented writers. Pays royalty. Publishes book 8 months after acceptance. Accepts simultaneous submissions if so noted. Reports in 3 months on proposals. Manuscript guidelines for #10 SASE.
Nonfiction: Including reference, technical, clinical, textbook. Subjects include business, CD-ROM, medical and oncology texts. Query with SASE.
Recent Nonfiction Title(s): *Raising Big Bucks*, by Cindy Kaitcer (organizing fund-raising events); *Nutrition Manual for At-Risk Infants and Toddlers*, by Janice Hovasi Cox, M.S., R.N.

‡**PRENTICE-HALL, INC.**, Imprint of Simon & Schuster, 1 Lake St., Upper Saddle River NJ 07458. (201)236-7000. Website: http://www.prenhall.com. **Acquisitions:** Sandy Steiner, business and management. "Our mission is to develop, produce, market and distribute quality education materials for all business-related disciplines in the worldwide higher education markets." Publishes hardcover and trade paperback originals. Publishes 1,500 titles/year. 30% of books from first-time authors; 100% from unagented writers. Pays average royalty of 10%; varies with area and author. Advance varies. Publishes book 6 months after acceptance of ms. Accepts simultaneous submissions, if noted. Reports in 4 months on proposals. Book catalog free. Manuscript guidelines free, also available online.
Nonfiction: Reference, textbook. Subjects include agriculture/horticulture, Americana, anthropology/archaeology, art/architecture, business/economics, computers/electronics, education, government/politics, health/medicine, history, language/literature, money/finance, nature/environment, philosophy, psychology, religion, science, sociology. "We are an educational publisher for college and advanced texts, covering just about every area covered in college courses." Submit outline, 3 sample chapters, author's bio, analysis of market and competition with SASE. Reviews artwork/photos.
Recent Nonfiction Title(s): *Marketing Management*, by Philip Kottler (business); *Cost Accounting*, by Charles Horngren (accounting).

‡**PRESERVATION PRESS, INC.**, P.O. Box 612, 25 Russell Mill Rd., Swedesboro NJ 08085. (609)467-8902. Fax: (609)467-3183. Website: http://www.preservationpress.com. **Acquisitions:** Norma J. Del Viscio, president. Estab. 1994. "Preservation Press is steadfastly committed to helping restore traditional Orthodox Christian thinking and living to our churches and culture." Publishes hardcover and trade paperback originals and reprints. Publishes 16 titles/year. Receives 50 queries and 30 mss/year. 33% of books from first-time authors; 100% from unagented writers. Pays 15% royalty on wholesale price. No advance. Publishes book 1 year after acceptance of ms. Accepts simultaneous submissions. Reports in 1 month on queries, 3 months on mss. Catalog and ms guidelines free.
Nonfiction: Gift book, self-help, prayer books, Bibles. Subjects include education, religion. "We only consider books rooted in traditional Orthodox Christian theology. We are 'pre-Vatican II.' We do not consider 'modern theology' topics." Query, (phone queries OK) or submit 2-3 sample chapters with SASE.
Recent Nonfiction Title(s): *Yesterday, Today and Forever: Jesus Christ and the Holy Trinity in the Teaching of the Seven Ecumenical Councils*, by Peter Toon; *The Sunday Sermons of the Great Fathers*, by N.S. Toal (compilation of

sermons, 4-volume series); *Hidden Glory: Sacred Order or Secular Chaos*, by Charles Caldwell.
Tips: "We have a broad audience, from Orthodox conservative Roman Catholics and conservative evangelicals searching to return to the early Church and its doctrines. We serve them because people are searching for the truth about the Church's origins. The work must be sound and founded on traditional Orthodox Christian doctrine. No new wave, trendy, feel-good stuff."

‡**PRESIDIO PRESS**, 505B San Marin Dr., Suite 300, Novato CA 94945-1340. (415)898-1081 ext. 125. Fax: (415)898-0383. **Acquisitions:** E.J. McCarthy, executive editor. Estab. 1974. "We publish the finest and most accurate military history and military affairs nonfiction, plus entertaining and provocative fiction related to military affairs." Publishes hardcover originals and reprints. Averages 24 titles/year. Receives 1,600 submissions/year. 35% of books from first-time authors; 65% from unagented writers. Pays 15-20% royalty on net receipts. Advance varies. Publishes book 12-18 months after acceptance. Reports within 1 month on queries. Book catalog and ms guidelines for 7½×10½ SAE with 4 first-class stamps.
Imprint(s): Lyford Books.
● Presidio Press publishes such well-known authors as Shelby Stanton, James McDonough and Lyn Crost.
Nonfiction: Subjects include military history and military affairs. Query. Reviews artwork/photos as part of ms package. Send photocopies.
Recent Nonfiction Title(s): *The Biographical History of World War II*, by Mark M. Boatner III; *Easy Target*, by Tom Smith (memoir of Vietnam War); *Destroyer Skipper*, by Don Sheppard (memoir of command at sea).
Fiction: Men's action-adventure, thriller, mystery, military, historical. Query.
Recent Fiction Title(s): *A Murder of Crows*, by Steve Sheppard (foiled attack on US); *Blood Tells*, by Ray Saunders (Vietnam veteran runs amok).
Tips: "Our audience consists of readers interested in military history, military affairs and military-oriented fiction. If I were a writer trying to market a book today, I would study the market. Find out what publishers are publishing, what they say they want and so forth. Then write what the market seems to be asking for, but with some unique angle that differentiates the work from others on the same subject. We feel that readers of hardcover fiction are looking for works of no less than 80,000 words."

PRICE STERN SLOAN, INC., Imprint of Penguin Putnam Inc., 200 Madison Ave., New York NY 10016. (212)951-8700. Fax: (212)951-8694. **Acquisitions:** Submissions Editor (juvenile submissions); Lisa Rojany (adult calendar submissions). Estab. 1963. Price Stern Sloan publishes juvenile fiction and nonfiction as well as desk and wall calendars for adults. Publishes trade paperback originals. Publishes 80 titles/year (95% children's). Receives 3,000 submissions/year. 20% of books from first-time authors; 30% from unagented writers. Pays royalty on net retail or makes outright purchase. Offers advance. Publishes book 1 year after acceptance. Reports in 3 months. Catalog for 9×12 SAE with 5 first-class stamps. Manuscript guidelines for SASE.
● Price Stern Sloan currently has smaller print runs and fewer titles per list.
Imprint(s): Troubador Press, Wee Sing®, Doodle Art®, Mad Libs®, Mad Mysteries®, Serendipity®, Plugged In™, Games to Go, Graphic Readers™.
Nonfiction and Fiction: Subjects include humor, calendars and satire (limited). Juvenile fiction and nonfiction (all ages). Query *only*. Reviews artwork/photos as part of ms package. Do not send *original* artwork or ms. "Most of our titles are unique in concept as well as execution."
Recent Titles: The *Bang on the Door* series; *Fabric Painting*, by Melanie Williams, illustrated by Paula Turnbull; *Murphy's Law 1998 Desk Calendar*, by Arthur Bloch.
Tips: "We have been assigning a lot of work-for-hires for ongoing series. But writers must have a proven track record in those formats. As electronic technology flourishes, the lines between traditional publishing and new media blur. As our books tie in with movies, TV, games, cultural trends and more, I imagine our products will expand as the new media grows. We think our edginess and our 'tude' make us quite distinct in the children's publishing arena."

‡**PRIDE PUBLICATIONS**, P.O. Box 148, Radnor OH 43066. E-mail: pridepblsh@aol.com. **Acquisitions:** Cris Newport, senior editor. "We publish work that is revolutionary in content, sheds light on misconceptions and challenges stereotypes." Publishes trade paperback originals and reprints. Publishes 10 titles/year. Receives 75 queries and 100 mss/year. 50% of books from first-time authors; 50% from unagented writers. Pays 10-15% royalty on wholesale price. Publishes book 1 year after acceptance of ms. Accepts simultaneous submissions. Reports in 2 months on mss. Book catalog and ms guidelines for #10 SASE.
Imprint(s): Rampant Gaming, Little Blue Works and Keystone Agencies.
● Pride has published such authors as Jennifer DiMarco, Rudy Kikel and Lesleá Newman.
Nonfiction: Biography, children's/juvenile, cookbook, how-to, humor, illustrated book, reference, self-help. Subjects include business/economics, cooking/foods/nutrition, education, gay/lesbian, history, language/literature, money/finance, philosophy, psychology. Submit synopsis and first 50 pages with SASE. Reviews artwork/photos as part of the ms package. Send photocopies.
Recent Nonfiction Title(s): *Step-By-Step to the Job You Want*, by Edward F. Hood (how-to).
Fiction: Adventure, cyberfiction, erotica, ethnic, experimental, fantasy, feminist, future fiction, gay/lesbian, gothic, historical, horror, humor, juvenile, literary, mainstream/contemporary, mystery, occult, plays, romance, science fiction, suspense, young adult. "We look for work that challenges the way we see the world." Submit synopsis and first 50 pages with SASE.

Recent Fiction Title(s): *The White Bones of Truth*, by Cris Newport (future fiction); *The Redemption of Corporal Nolan Giles*, by Jeane Heimberger Candido (historical fiction); *1000 Reasons You Might Think Is She My Lover*, by Angela Costa (erotica).

Poetry: "We look for poetry that others might consider 'too wild, too risky, too truthful.' A collection must have at least 100 poems for us to consider it." Submit complete ms.

Recent Poetry Title(s): *talking drums*, by Jan Bevilacqua (prose-poetry exploring gender).

Tips: "We publish for almost every audience. Read one of our books before sending anything."

PRIMA PUBLISHING, P.O. Box 1260, Rocklin CA 95677-1260. (916)768-0426. Publisher: Ben Dominitz. **Acquisitions:** Jennifer Bayse-Sander, senior acquisitions editor (lifestyles division); Ian Sheeler, acquisitions editor (computer professional reference division); Dan Francisco, acquisitions editor (entertainment division); Jennifer Basye Sander, senior editor; Georgia Hughes, acquisitions editor; Steve Martin, acquisitions editor; Jamie Miller, associate acquisitions editor; Susan Silva, acquisitions editor; Paula Mumier Lee, associate publisher. "Books for the way we live, work and play." Publishes hardcover originals and trade paperback originals and reprints. Publishes 300 titles/year. Receives 750 queries/year. 10% of books from first-time authors; 30% from unagented writers. Pays 15-20% royalty on wholesale price. Advance varies. Publishes book 18 months after acceptance. Accepts simultaneous submissions. Reports in 3 months. Catalog for 9×12 SAE with 8 first-class stamps. Writer's guidelines for #10 SASE.

• Prima publishes such authors as Mary Kay Ash, Richard Poe and Jane Nelson, and also the *Writer's Guide*, *Small Business Toolkit*, *Positive Discipline*, and *Walt Disney World with the Kids* series.

Nonfiction: Business, parenting, education, health, entertainment, writing, biography, self-help. Subjects include economics, cooking/foods, health, music, politics, psychology. "We want books with originality, written by highly qualified individuals. No fiction at this time." Query with SASE.

Recent Nonfiction Title(s): *Marketing for the Self-Employed*, by Martin Edic (how-to); *Nine Glorious Months: Daily Meditations and Reflections for Your Pregnancy*, by Michelle Leclaire O'Neill; *Ritalin-free Kids*, by Judyth and Robert Ullman (health).

Tips: "Prima strives to reach the primary and secondary markets for each of its books. We are known for promoting our books aggressively. Books that genuinely solve problems for people will always do well if properly promoted. Try to picture the intended audience while writing the book. Too many books are written to an audience that doesn't exist."

‡**PRO/AM MUSIC RESOURCES, INC.**, 63 Prospect St., White Plains NY 10606. (914)448-9327. **Acquisitions:** Thomas P. Lewis, publisher. Pro/Am publishes only nonfiction music titles. Publishes hardcover and trade paperback originals. Publishes 5 titles/year. Receives 20 mss/year. 50% of books from first-time authors. Pays 10% royalty on retail price. No advance. Publishes book 1 year after acceptance of ms. Accepts simultaneous submissions. Book catalog for #10 SASE.

Nonfiction: Music only. Query with SASE.

Recent Nonfiction Title(s): *History Through the Opera Glass*, by George Jelliner; *Performing Bach's Keyboard Music*, by George Kochevitsky; *The Music of My Time*, by Joan Peyser.

PROFESSIONAL PUBLICATIONS, INC., 1250 Fifth Ave., Belmont CA 94002-3863. (415)593-9119. Fax: (415)592-4519. E-mail: ppi@ppi2pass.com. **Acquisitions:** Catie Barkenfield, acquisitions editor. Estab. 1975. "PPI publishes for engineering architecture, land surveying and interior design professionals preparing to take examinations for national licensing." Publishes hardcover and paperback originals. Publishes over 30 titles/year. Receives 100-200 submissions/year. Publishes book 18 months after acceptance. Accepts simultaneous submissions. Reports in 2 weeks on queries. *Writer's Market* recommends allowing 2 months for reply. Catalog and ms guidelines free.

• Professional Publications wants only professionals practicing in the field to submit material.

Nonfiction: Reference, technical, textbook. Subjects include engineering mathematics, engineering, land surveying, architecture, interior design. Especially needs "review books for all professional licensing examinations." Query or submit outline and sample chapters. Reviews artwork/photos as part of ms package.

Recent Nonfiction Title(s): *EIT Review Manual*, by Michael R. Lindeburg (engineering); *Timber Design for the Civil and Structural Professional Engineer Examination*, by Rober and Jei Kim; *Calculus Refresher for the Fundamentals of Engineering Exam*, by Peter Schiavone.

Tips: "We specialize in books for working professionals: engineers, architects, land surveyors, interior designers, etc. The more technically complex the manuscript is the happier we are. We love equations, tables of data, complex illustrations, mathematics, etc. In technical/professional book publishing, it isn't always obvious to us if a market exists. We can judge the quality of a manuscript, but the author should make some effort to convince us that a market exists. Facts, figures, and estimates about the market—and marketing ideas from the author—will help sell us on the work."

‡**PROMETHEUS BOOKS**, 59 John Glenn Dr., Buffalo NY 14228. (716)691-0133. Fax: (716)691-0137. E-mail: 6205@aol.com. **Acquisitions:** Steven Mitchell, editorial director. Estab. 1969. "We are a niche, or specialized, publisher that focuses in the area of *critiquing* the paranormal, religious extremism and right wing fundamentalism. We are one of the largest independent publishers of philosophy in the country. We focus on free thought, critical thinking and scientific method." Publishes hardcover originals, trade paperback originals and reprints. Publishes 75-80 titles/year. Receives 2,500 queries and mss/year. 10% of books from first-time authors; 60% from unagented writers. Pays 10-15% royalty on wholesale price; other for paper. Offers $1,000-3,000 advance; advance rare, if ever, for children's books. Publishes book 1 year after acceptance of ms. Accepts simultaneous submissions, if noted. Reports in 1 week on queries,

1 month on proposals, 4 months on mss. Book catalog free. Manuscript guidelines for #10 SASE.

Nonfiction: Biography, children's/juvenile, reference. Subjects include education, government/politics, health/medicine, history, language/literature, philosophy, psychology, religion (not religious, but critiquing), critiques of the paranormal and UFO sightings, etc. "Ask for a catalog, go to the library, look at our books and others like them to get an idea of what our focus is." Submit proposal package including outline, synopsis and a well-developed query letter with SASE. Reviews artwork/photos as part of ms package. Send photocopies.

Recent Nonfiction Title(s): *The Truth About Everything: An Irreverent History of Philosophy*, by Matthew Stewart; *Love Affairs, Marriage and Fidelity*, by Richard Taylor; *School Prayer: The Court, Congress, and the First Amendment*, by Robert S. Alley.

Tips: "Audience is highly literate with multiple degrees. An older, but not 'old' audience that is intellectually mature and knows what it wants. They are aware, and we try to provide them with new information on topics of interest to them in mainstream and cognate-related areas."

PROMPT PUBLICATIONS, Imprint of Howard W. Sams & Co., A Bell Atlantic Company, 2647 Waterfront Parkway E. Dr., Indianapolis IN 46214-2041. (317)298-5400. Fax: (317)298-5604. E-mail: cdrake@in.net. Website: http://www.hwsams.com. **Acquisitions:** Candace Drake Hall, managing editor. "Our mission is to produce quality and reliable electronics technology publications to meet the needs of the engineer, technician, hobbyist and average consumer." Publishes trade paperback originals and reprints. Publishes 30 titles/year. Receives 50-75 queries and 30 mss/year. 40% of books from first-time authors; 90% from unagented writers. Pays royalty on retail price based on author's experience. Advance varies. Publishes book 1 year after acceptance of ms. Reports in 2 months on queries, 4 months on proposals, 6 months or more on mss. Book catalog free.

● Prompt Publications has published such authors as James "J.J." Barbarello, Irving Gottlieb, Joe Carr and Joe Desposito (electronics writers). They have increased their number of books published from 20 to 30 titles/year.

Nonfiction: How-to, reference, technical, textbook. Subjects include audio/visual, computers/electronics, electronics repair, energy, science (electricity). "Books should be written for beginners *and* experts, hobbyists *and* professionals. We do not publish books about software. We like manuscripts about household electronics, professional electronics, troubleshooting and repair, component cross-references and how to create or assemble various electronic devices." Established authors query; new authors send complete ms with SASE. Reviews artwork/photos as part of ms package. Send photocopies or sketches ("we have technicians to produce illustrations if necessary").

Recent Nonfiction Title(s): *Alternative Energy*, by Mark Hazen (technical); *Component Identifier & Source Book*, by Victor Meeldijk; *Howard W. Sams Internet Guide to the Electronics Industry (electronics directory)*.

Tips: Audience is electronics/technical hobbyists, professionals needing reference books, and technical schools. "Please keep in mind that most technical books have a short shelf life, and write accordingly. Remember, also, that it takes a while for a book to be published, so keep notes on updating your material when the book is ready to print. When submitting, above all, *be patient*. It can take up to a year for a publisher to decide whether or not to publish your book."

PRUETT PUBLISHING, 2928 Pearl St., Boulder CO 80301. (303)449-4919. Fax: (303)443-9019. E-mail: pruettbles@aol.com. Website: http://beherenow.com/colorado. Publisher: Jim Pruett. **Acquisitions:** Marykay Scott, editor. Estab. 1959. Pruett publishes books of the American West that bring the region to life. Publishes hardcover paperback and trade paperback originals and reprints. Publishes 10-15 titles/year. 60% of books are from first-time authors; 100% from unagented writers. Pays 10-12% royalty on net income. Publishes book 18 months after acceptance. Accepts simultaneous submissions. Reports in 2 months on queries. Book catalog and ms guidelines free.

● Pruett has published such authors as John Holt (fly fishing titles) and Stephen Bodio (nature titles).

Nonfiction: Regional history, guidebooks, nature, biography. Subjects include Americana (Western), archaeology (Native American), history (Western), nature/environment, recreation (outdoor), regional/ethnic cooking/foods (Native American, Mexican, Spanish), regional travel, regional sports (cycling, hiking, fishing). "We are looking for nonfiction manuscripts and guides that focus on the Rocky Mountain West." Reviews artwork/photos and formal proposal as part of ms package.

Recent Nonfiction Title(s): *Stars of the First People*, by Dorcas Miller (Native American constellations and star myths); *Stories & Stone*, by Reuben Ellis (anthology on the Anasazi); *Southern Arizona Nature Almanac*, by Hanson and Hanson.

Tips: "There has been a movement away from large publisher's mass market books and towards small publisher's regional interest books, and in turn distributors and retail outlets are more interested in small publishers. Authors don't need to have a big-name to have a good publisher. Look for similar books that you feel are well produced—consider design, editing, overall quality and contact those publishers. Get to know several publishers, and find the one that feels right—trust your instincts."

PRUFROCK PRESS, P.O. Box 8813, Waco TX 76714. (817)756-3337. Fax: (817)756-3339. E-mail: prufrock@prufrock.com or joel_mcintosh@prufrock.com. Website: http://www.prufrock.com. **Acquisitions:** Joel McIntosh, publisher. "Prufrock Press provides exciting, innovative and current resources supporting the education of gifted and talented learners." Publishes trade paperback originals and reprints. Publishes 15 titles/year. Receives 150 queries and 50 mss/year. 50% of books from first-time authors; 100% from unagented writers. Pays 10% royalty on sale price. Publishes book 9 months after acceptance of ms. Reports in 2 months. Book catalog and manuscript guidelines free.

Nonfiction: Children's/juvenile, how-to, textbook. Subjects include child guidance/parenting, education. "We publish for the education market. Our readers are typically teachers or parents of gifted and talented children. Many authors

send us classroom activity books. Our product line is built around professional development books for teachers. While some of our books may include activities, many are included to illustrate a teaching concept on strategies, or strategy in use at an application level." Request query package from publisher.
Recent Nonfiction Title(s): *Coping for Capable Kids*, by Dr. Leonora M. Cohen and Dr. Erica Frydenberg.
Tips: "We are one of the larger independent education publishers; however, we have worked hard to offer authors a friendly, informal atmosphere. Authors should feel comfortable calling up and bouncing an idea off of us or writing us to get our opinion of a new project idea."

PUBLISHERS ASSOCIATES, P.O. Box 140361, Las Colinas TX 75014-0361. (972)686-5332. Senior Editor: Belinda Buxjom. **Acquisitions:** Mary Markal, manuscript coordinator. Estab. 1974. "Publishers Associates publishes liberal academic studies titles emphasizing gay/lesbian history, pro-choice/feminist studies and liberal politics." Publishes trade paperback originals. Publishes 20 titles/year. Receives 1,500 submissions/year. 60% of books from first-time authors; 100% from unagented writers. Pays 4% and up royalty on retail price. Publishes book 1 year after acceptance. Reports in 4 months. Catalog for 6×9 SAE with 4 first-class stamps. Ms guidelines for #10 SAE with 2 first-class stamps.
Imprint(s): Hercules Press, **The Liberal Press**, Liberal Arts Press, Minuteman Press, Monument Press, Nichole Graphics, Scholars Books, Tagelwüld.
Nonfiction: Textbook (scholarly). Subjects include gay/lesbian, government/politics (liberal), history, religion (liberation/liberal), women's issues/studies. "Quality researched gay/lesbian history will pay beginning royalty of 7% and up. Academics are encouraged to submit. No biographies, evangelical fundamentalism/Bible, conservative politics, New Age studies or homophobic. No fiction or poetry." Query. Reviews artwork/photos as part of ms package.
Recent Nonfiction Title(s): *Harvest of Contempt*, by Joe Armey (liberal politics).
Tips: "Writers have the best chance with gender-free/nonsexist, liberal academic studies. We sell primarily to libraries and scholars. Our audience is highly educated, politically and socially liberal, if religious they are liberational. If I were a writer trying to market a book today, I would compare my manuscript with books already published by the press I am seeking to submit to."

‡**PUFFIN BOOKS**, Imprint of Penguin Putnam Inc., 375 Hudson St., New York NY 10014-3657. (212)366-2000. Website: http://www.penguin.com/childrens. **Acquisitions:** Sharyn November, senior editor; Joy Peskin, editorial assistant. "Puffin Books publishes high-end trade paperbacks and paperback reprints for preschool children, beginning and middle readers, and young adults." Publishes trade paperback originals and reprints. Publishes 175-200 titles/year. Receives 300 queries and mss/year. 1% of books by first-time authors; 5% from unagented writers. Royalty and advance vary. Publishes book 1 year after acceptance of ms. Accepts simultaneous submissions, if so noted. Reports in 1 month on mss. Book catalog for 9×12 SASE with 7 first-class stamps; send request to Marketing Department.
Nonfiction: Biography, children's/juvenile, illustrated book, young children's concept books (counting, shapes, colors). Subjects include education (for teaching concepts and colors, not academic), women in history. "'Women in history' books interest us." Submit 5 pages of ms with SASE. Reviews artwork/photos. Send color photocopies.
Recent Nonfiction Title(s): *Rachel Carson: Pioneer of Ecology*, by "Fadlinski" (history); *Grandma Moses*, by O'neill Ruff (history).
Fiction: Picture books, young adult novels, middle grade and easy-to-read grades 1-3. "We publish mostly paperback reprints. We do few original titles." Submit picture book ms or 3 sample chapters with SASE.
Recent Fiction Title(s): *A Gift for Mama*, by Esther Hautzig (Puffin chapter book).
Tips: "Our audience ranges from little children 'first books' to young adult (ages 14-16). An original idea has the best luck."

‡**PURDUE UNIVERSITY PRESS**, 1532 South Campus Courts, Bldg. E, West Lafayette IN 47907-1532. (317)494-2038. **Acquisitions:** Thomas Bacher, director; Margaret Hunt, managing editor. Estab. 1960. "Dedicated to excellence in scholarship and the advancement of critical thought that continually expands the horizons of knowledge." Publishes hardcover and trade paperback originals and trade paperback reprints. Publishes 14-20 titles/year. Receives 600 submissions/year. Pays 7½-15% royalty. Publishes book 9 months after acceptance. Reports in 2 months. Book catalog and ms guidelines for 9×12 SASE.
● This publisher has received Chicago Book Clinic design awards, the Association of American University Presses design award and the Chicago Women in Publishing design award.
Nonfiction: "We publish work of quality scholarship and titles with regional (Midwest) flair. Especially interested in innovative contributions to the social sciences and humanities that break new barriers and provide unique views on current topics. Expanding into veterinary medicine, engineering and business topics. Always looking for new authors who show creativity and thoroughness of research." Print and electronic projects accepted. Query before submitting.
Recent Nonfiction Title(s): *Between Pets and People: The Importance of Animal Companionship*, by Alan Beck and Aaron Katcher; *Possum in the Pawpaw Tree: A Seasonal Guide to Midwestern Gardening*, by Lerner and Netzhammer; *A First Aid Guide for Dog Owners*, by Heath, et al.
Poetry: One book selected each year by competition. Send SASE for guidelines.
Recent Poetry Title(s): *No Moon*, by Nancy Eimers; *The Body Mutinies*, by Lucia Perillo.

‡**G.P. PUTNAM'S SONS**, (Adult Trade), Imprint of Penguin Putnam, Inc., 200 Madison Ave., New York NY 10016. (212)951-8405. Fax: (212)951-8694. Website: http://www.putnam.com. Managing Editor: David Briggs. **Acquisitions:** Maya Rao, editorial assistant. Publishes hardcover and trade paperback originals. 5% of books from first-time authors;

none from unagented writers. Pays variable advance on retail price. Advance varies. Accepts simultaneous submissions. Reports in 6 months on queries. Request book catalog through mail order department. Manuscript guidelines free.

Imprint(s): Grosset, Philomel, Price Stern Sloan, Putnam, Riverhead, Jeremy P. Tarcher.

Nonfiction: Biography, celebrity-related topics, cookbook, self-help. Subjects include animals, business/economics, child guidance/parenting, cooking/foods/nutrition, health/medicine, military/war, nature/environment, religion/inspirational, science, sports, travel, women's issues/studies. Query with SASE. *No unsolicited mss.*

Recent Nonfiction Title(s): *Audrey Hepburn*, by Barry Paris (biography); *Like Father, Like Son*, by Hunter S. Fulghum (essays), *Conversations with God*, by Neil Donald Walsh (inspirational).

Fiction: Adventure, mainstream/contemporary, mystery, science fiction, suspense. Query with synopsis, *brief* writing sample (the shorter the better) and SASE. Prefers agented submissions.

Recent Fiction Title(s): *Executive Orders*, by Tom Clancy (adventure); *Small Vices*, by Robert B. Parker (mystery/thriller); *Chromosome 6*, by Robin Cook (medical thriller).

‡QUE BOOKS, Imprint of Simon & Schuster, 201 W. 103rd St., Indianapolis IN 46290. (317)581-3500. Website: http://www.mcp.com/que/. Publisher: Ronald Elgey. **Acquisitions:** Meggo Barthlow, executive assistant. Publishes hardcover, trade paperback and mass market paperback originals and reprints. Publishes 200 titles/year. 85% of books from unagented writers. Pays variable royalty on wholesale price or makes work-for-hire arrangements. Advance varies. Accepts simultaneous submissions. Reports in 1 month on proposals. Catalog and ms guidelines free.

● Que's website contains an author information form for online queries.

Nonfiction: How-to, illustrated book, reference, technical. Subjects include computers/electronics, hardware, software. Query with outline and marketing analysis and SASE. Reviews artwork/photos as part of ms package. Reviews PCX files (uses Collage software).

Recent Nonfiction Title(s): *Protect Your Privacy on the Internet*, by Marcus Golcaves (computers); *Web Storefront Construction Kit*, by Raymond Novello (computers).

QUEST BOOKS, Theosophical Publishing House, P.O. Box 270, Wheaton IL 60189. (630)665-0130. Fax: (630)665-8791. E-mail: questbooks@aol.com. **Acquisitions:** Brenda Rosen, executive editor. "TPH seeks works compatible with the theosophical philosophy, or books that illustrate connections between spiritually-oriented philosophy or viewpoints and some field of current interest." Publishes hardcover originals and trade paperback originals and reprints. Publishes 12-15 titles/year. Receives 400 queries and 150 mss/year. 25% of books from first-time authors; 50% from unagented writers. Pays 10% royalty on net minimum or 12% royalty on gross maximum. Offers $2,000-10,000 advance. Publishes book 20 months after acceptance of ms. Accepts simultaneous submissions. Reports in 1 month on queries and proposals, 3 months on mss. Book catalog and ms guidelines free.

● Quest gives preference to writers with established reputations/successful publications. Manuscript required on disk if accepted for publication.

Nonfiction: Subjects include self-development, self-help, philosophy (holistic), psychology (transpersonal), Eastern and Western religions, theosophy, comparative religion, men's and women's spirituality, Native American spirituality, holistic implications in science, health and healing, yoga, meditation, astrology. "Our audience includes the 'New Age' community, seekers in all religions, general public, professors, and health professionals. No submissions that do not fit the needs outlined above." Accepts nonfiction translations. Query or submit outline and sample chapters. Reviews artwork/photos as part of ms package.

Recent Nonfiction Title(s): *Shambhala*, by Victoria LePage (mythology/spirituality); *Dialogues with the Living Earth*, by James and Roberta Swan (architecture/New Age).

‡QUESTAR PUBLISHERS, INC., P.O. Box 1720, Sisters OR 97759. (541)549-1144. Fax: (541)549-2044. **Acquisitions:** Dan Benson (Christian living, men's); Steve Halliday (theology, sports); Alice Gray (gift books, women's); Melody Carlson (children's); Rod Morris (genre, men's fiction); Karen Ball (romance and women's fiction). "Our purpose is to be a Christian publishing company that glorifies God by creating products that change lives." Publishes hardcover and trade paperback originals. Publishes 130 titles/year. Receives 1,800-2,000 queries and mss/year. Receives 5% of books from first-time authors; 50% from unagented writers. Pays royalty on wholesale price. Publishes book an average of 1 year after acceptance of ms. Accepts simultaneous submissions. Reports in 3 months. Manuscript guidelines for 8×10 SAE and with 4 first-class stamps. No fax submissions.

Imprint(s): Multnomah Books, Gold'n'Honey Books, Palisades.

● Questar has published such authors as Dr. David Jeremiah, Ron Mehl and Joni Eareckson-Tada.

Nonfiction: Children's, coffee table book, gift book, humor, illustrated book. Subjects include child guidance/parenting, religion. Submit outline, 3 sample chapters with SASE. Review artwork/photos as part of ms package. Send photocopies.

Recent Nonfiction Title(s): *New Every Morning*, by D. James Kennedy (devotional); *Jesus, Who Is He?*, by Tim LaHaye (theology); *A New Time and Place*, by Jack Hayford (The Book of Ruth).

Fiction: Adventure, humor, mystery, religious, romance, suspense, western, all Christian-oriented. Submit synopsis and 3 sample chapters with SASE.

Recent Fiction Title(s): *Dominion*, by Randy Alcorn (novel); *Wings of the Wind*, by Al Lacy; *Benjamin's Box*, by Melody Carlson (children's Easter story).

QUILL DRIVER BOOKS/WORD DANCER PRESS, 950 N. Van Ness, Fresno CA 93728. (209)497-0809. Fax: (209)497-9266. E-mail: sbm12@csufresno.edu. **Acquisitions:** Stephen Blake Mettee, publisher. "We publish a modest

number of books per year, each of which makes a worthwhile contribution to the human community, and we have a little fun along the way." Publishes hardcover and trade paperback originals and reprints. Publishes 10-12 titles/year. (Quill Driver Books: 4/year, Word Dancer Press: 6-8/year). 20% of books from first-time authors; 95% from unagented writers. Pays 6-10% royalty on retail price. Offers $500-10,000 advance. Publishes book 9 months after acceptance. Accepts simultaneous submissions. Reports in 1 month on queries and proposals, 3 months on mss. Book catalog and ms guidelines for #10 SASE.
Nonfiction: Biography, how-to, reference, general nonfiction. Subjects include Americana, regional, fund-raising, writing. Query with proposal package. Reviews artwork/photos as part of ms package. Send photocopies.
Recent Nonfiction Title(s): *The Pediatrician's New Baby Owner's Manual*, by Horst D. Weinberg, M.D. (parenting); *The American Directory of Writer's Guidelines*, compiled and edited by John C. Mutchler (writing/reference).

QUIXOTE PRESS, 3544 Blakeslee St., Wever IA 52658. (319)372-7480. Fax: (319)372-7480. **Acquisitions:** Bruce Carlson, president. Quixote Press specializes in humorous regional folklore and special interest cookbooks. Publishes trade paperback originals and reprints. Publishes 20 titles/year. Receives 50-75 queries and 25-50 mss/year. 90% of books from first-time authors; 100% from unagented writers. Pays 10% royalty on wholesale price. No advance. Publishes book 1 year after acceptance. Accepts simultaneous submissions. Reports in 2 months. Book catalog and manuscript guidelines for #10 SASE.
Imprint(s): Blackiron Cooking Co., Hearts & Tummies Cookbook Co.
Nonfiction: Children's/juvenile, cookbook, humor, self-help. Subjects include agriculture/horticulture, Americana, cooking/foods/nutrition, regional, travel, folklore. "We must be in on ground floor of the product design." Submit outline, 2 sample chapters and SASE. Reviews artwork/photos as part of ms package. Send photocopies.
Recent Nonfiction Title(s): *Peaches! Peaches! Peaches!*, by M. Mosley (cookbook); *The Body Shop*, by S. Wolff (cookbook); *Herbal Cookery*, B. Carlson (herbal cooking).
Fiction: Adventure, ethnic, experimental, humor, short story collections, children's. Query with synopsis and SASE.
Recent Fiction Title(s): *Out Behind the Barn*, by B. Carlson (rural folklore).
Tips: Carefully consider marketing considerations. Audience is women in gift shops, on farm site direct retail outlets.

‡QUORUM BOOKS, Imprint of Greenwood Publishing Group, 88 Post Rd. W., Westport CT 06881. (203)226-3571. Fax: (203)222-1502. Website: http://www.greenwood.com. **Acquisitions:** Eric Valentine, publisher. "Quorum Books publishes professional and academic books in all areas of business and business-related law." Publishes 75 titles/year. 50% of books from first-time authors. Pays 7½-15% royalty on net price. Rarely offers advances. Publishes book an average of 1 year after acceptance on ms. Accepts simultaneous submissions. Reports in 2 months on queries and proposals. Website offers a catalog, ms guidelines and editorial contacts.
Nonfiction: Subjects include business, economics, finance. Query with proposal package, including scope, organization, length of project, whether a complete ms is available or when it will be, c.v. or résumé and SASE. *No unsolicited mss.*
Recent Nonfiction Title(s): *The Practice of Multinational Banking: Macro-Policy Issues and Key International Concepts, 2nd edition*, by Dara Khambata.
Tips: "We are not a trade publisher. Our products are sold almost entirely by mail, in hardcover and at relatively high list prices."

RAGGED MOUNTAIN PRESS, Imprint of International Marine/The McGraw-Hill Companies, P.O. Box 220, Camden ME 04843-0220. (207)236-4837. Fax: (207)236-6314. **Acquisitions:** Jeffery Serena, acquisitions editor; Jonathan Eaton, editorial director. Estab. 1969. Ragged Mountain Press publishes "books that take you off the beaten path." Publishes hardcover and trade paperback originals and reprints. Publishes 40 titles/year; imprint publishes 15, remainder are International Marine. Receives 200 queries and 100 mss/year. 30% of books from first-time authors; 90% from unagented writers. Pays 10-15% royalty on net price. Offers advance. Publishes book 1 year after acceptance of ms. Accepts simultaneous submissions. Reports in 1 month on queries. *Writer's Market* recommends allowing 2 months for reply. Book catalog for 9×12 SAE with 10 first-class stamps. Manuscript guidelines for #10 SASE.
Nonfiction: Outdoor-related how-to, guidebooks, essays. Subjects include camping, fly fishing, snowshoeing, backpacking, canoeing, outdoor cookery, skiing, snowboarding, survival skills and wilderness know-how, birdwatching, natural history, climbing and kayaking. "Ragged Mountain publishes nonconsumptive outdoor and environmental issues books of literary merit or unique appeal. Be familiar with the existing literature. Find a subject that hasn't been done or has been done poorly, then explore it in detail and from all angles." Query with outline and 1 sample chapter. Reviews artwork/photos as part of ms package. Send photocopies.
Recent Nonfiction Title(s): *The Ragged Mountain Press Guide to Outdoor Sports*, by Jonathon and Roseann Hanson; *The Outdoor Dutch Oven Cookbook*, by Sheila Mills; *The Ragged Mountain Press Pocket Guide to Wilderness Medicine and First Aid*, by Paul G. Gill, Jr., M.D.

‡RAIN DANCER BOOKS, 3211 W. Wadley, Bldg. 3A, Suite 143, Midland TX 79705. **Acquisitions:** T.R. Wayne, acquisitions editor. "We are wide open to publishing the best literature that makes its way to our door. We envision an audience with a zest for life, a love of reading and a copy of our catalog." Publishes trade paperback originals and reprints. Publishes 16 titles/year. Receives 500 queries and 200 mss/year. 68% of books from first-time authors; 100% from unagented writers. Pays 2-20% royalty on wholesale price or makes outright purchase. No advance. Publishes book 18 months after acceptance of ms. Accepts simultaneous submissions. Catalog and ms guidelines for #10 SASE.

• Rain Dancer Books sponsors the International Cowboy/Cowgirl Poet Laureate contest.
Imprint(s): Desert Rose Greeting Cards (Contact: Pam Dusenberry).
Nonfiction: Biography, children's/juvenile, coffee table book, cookbook, gift book, how-to, humor, multimedia (format: CD-ROM), reference, self-help, adult literacy. Subjects include agriculture/horticulture, Americana, animals, anthropology/archaeology, art/architecture, computers/electronics, cooking/foods/nutrition, education, ethnic, gardening, government/politics, health/medicine, history, hobbies, language/literature, music/dance, nature/environment, philosophy, photography, psychology, recreation, science, sociology, software, translation. "Often writers submit when they should have submitted to editing one more time." Query or submit outline and sample chapter. Reviews artwork/photos as part of the ms package. Send photocopies.
Recent Nonfiction Title(s): *High Plains Low-Fat Cuisine* (cookbook); *Trail Dreams* (dream book); *My Friend the Wind*, by Amy Browning (children's picture book, ages 2-6).
Fiction: Adventure, ethnic, experimental, fantasy, historical, humor, juvenile, literary, mainstream/contemporary, mystery, occult, picture books, plays, religious, romance, science fiction, short story collections, suspense, western, young adult. "We are interested in books that lend themselves to serialization, especially mysteries." Query or submit synopsis and sample chapter.
Recent Fiction Title(s): *Mystery of the Oil Rig*; *Mystery of the Tumbleweed*; *Mystery of the Lasso*; all by Linda Lee (mysteries for adult literacy students).
Poetry: "We publish all forms of poetry (we love riddles, humor and limericks). Have enough for a complete book."
Recent Poetry Title(s): *Trailing Moon*, by Clementine Mathis (children's riddles and songs); *Stone Songs*, by Alex Roman (adult poetry); *More Butterfly Lullabies*, by G.G. Thomson (children's picture book).
Tips: "Write from solid research. Revise when necessary. Send out simultaneous submissions. We do not return submissions. This saves us time and the author postage."

‡RAINBOW BOOKS, INC., P.O. Box 430, Highland City FL 33846. (941)648-4420. Fax: (941)648-4420. E-mail: naip@aol.com. **Acquisitons:** Betsy A. Lampe, editorial director. "We want to provide answers to problems and issues that concern today's readers, both adults and children ages 8-14." Publishes hardcover and trade paperback originals. Publishes 12-15 titles/year. Receives 300 queries and 100 mss/year. 90% of books from first-time authors; 80% from unagented writers. Pays 6-12% royalty on retail price. Offers $500-1,000 advance. Publishes book 1 year after acceptance of ms. Accepts simultaneous submissions. Reports in 1 month on queries and proposals, 2 months on mss. Book catalog and ms guidelines for #10 SASE.
• Rainbow Books has published such authors as Martha Baldwin and Craig Tuttle.
Nonfiction: Biography, children's/juvenile, gift book, how-to, humor, self-help. Subjects include animals, business/economics, child guidance/parenting, education, gardening, hobbies, money/finance, nature/environment, philosophy, psychology, recreation, science, sociology, sports, women's issues/studies. "We want books that provide authoritative answers to questions in layman language. We have also begun a list of 3rd-to-8th grade titles for young people along the same lines as our adult general nonfiction. Writers must include background credentials for having written the book they propose." Query with SASE. Reviews artwork/photos as part of ms package. Send photocopies.
Recent Nonfiction Title(s): *Tao of Surfing*, by Michael A. Allen (philosophy); *Stop Hurtful Words & Harmful Habits*, by Kenneth L. Baldwin, M.S. (psychology); *The Insect Book*, by Connie Zakowski (children's/how-to).
Tips: "We are addressing an adult population interested in answers to questions, and also 8- to 14-year-olds of the same mindset. Be professional in presentation of queries and manuscripts, and always provide a return mailer with proper postage attached in the event the materials do not fit our list."

RAINBOW PUBLISHERS, P.O. Box 261129, San Diego CA 92196. (619)271-7600. **Acquisitions:** Christy Allen, editor. "Rainbow Publishers strives to publish Bible-based materials that contribute to and inspire spiritual growth and development in children and adults." Publishes 12 titles/year. Receives 250 queries and 100 mss/year. 50% of books from first-time authors. Pays royalty based on wholesale price. Publishes book 18 months after acceptance of ms. Accepts simultaneous submissions. Reports in 3 months on queries, proposals and mss. Book catalog for 9×12 SAE with 2 first-class stamps. Manuscript guidelines for #10 SASE.
Imprint(s): Daybreak.
Nonfiction: How-to, textbook. "We publish 64-page, reproducible activity books for Christian teachers to use in teaching the Bible to children ages 2-12." Query with outline, sample pages, age level, introduction. "We use freelance artists. Send a query and photocopies of art samples."
Recent Nonfiction Title(s): *Teaching Children to Pray*, by Mary Davis (teacher's book); *Proverbs for Promise Keeping*, by Bob Beasley (devotions for men).
Tips: "We are seeking manuscripts for *both* the children's and adult Christian book market, focusing on Christian education. We plan a much more aggressive publishing schedule than in the past."

RANDOM HOUSE, 201 E. 50th St., New York NY 10022. (212)751-2600.
Imprints: *Ballantine Publishing*: Ballantine, Columbine, Del Rey, Fawcett, House of Collectibles, Ivy Books, One World; *Crown Publishing Group*: Clarkson Potter, Crown Books, Harmony Books, Alfred A. Knopf, Pantheon, Schocken, Times Books, Times Business Books, Villard Books, Vintage (reprints); *Random House*: Random House, Knopf and Crown Books for Young Readers, Random House Books for Young Readers.

RANDOM HOUSE, ADULT BOOKS, Division of Random House, Inc., 201 E. 50th St., 11th Floor, New York NY 10022. (212)751-2600. **Acquisitions:** Sandy Fine, submissions coordinator. "Random House Inc., founded in 1925, is the world's largest English-language general trade book publisher. It includes an array of prestigious imprints that publish some of the foremost writers of our time—in hardcover, trade paperback, mass market paperback, electronic, multimedia and other formats." Random House Trade Division publishes 120 titles/year. Receives 3,000 submissions/year. Pays royalty on retail price. Accepts simultaneous submissions. Reports in 2 months. Book catalog free. Manuscript guidelines for #10 SASE.
 • Random House has published such authors as William Faulkner, Truman Capote, James Michener, Norman Mailer, Maya Angelou, Robert Massie, David Remnick, John Berendt and Richard Preston.
Imprint(s): Random House, **Alfred A. Knopf, Ballantine, Crown, Del Rey, Fawcett,** Harmony, Modern Library, **Pantheon, Clarkson N. Potter, Villard, Vintage (reprints).**
Nonfiction: Biography, cookbook, humor, illustrated book, self-help. Subjects include Americana, art, business/economics, classics, cooking and foods, health, history, music, nature, politics, psychology, religion, sociology and sports. No juveniles or textbooks (separate division). Query with outline, at least 3 sample chapters and SASE.
Recent Nonfiction Title(s): *Random House Encyclopedia of Classical Music*, by Helicon Publishing Ltd.; *Shattered Faith*, by Sheila Rauch Kennedy; *Sex On Campus*, by Leland Elliott and Cynthia Brantley.
Fiction: Adventure, confession, experimental, fantasy, historical, horror, humor, mainstream, mystery, and suspense. Submit outline/synopsis, at least 3 sample chapters and SASE.
Recent Fiction Title(s): *Ticktock*, by Dean Koontz; *The Gospel According to the Son*, by Norman Mailer; *The Kiss*, by Kathryn Harrison.

‡RANDOM HOUSE BOOKS FOR YOUNG READERS, Imprint of Random House, 201 E. 50th St., New York NY 10022. (212)751-2600. Fax: (212)940-7685. Website: http://www.randomhouse.com. Publishing Director: Kate Klimo. **Acquisitions:** Maria de Seville, assistant. Estab. 1935. Publishes hardcover, trade paperback, and mass market paperback originals and reprints. "Random House Books aim to create books that nurture the hearts and minds of children, providing and promoting quality books and a rich variety of media that entertain and educate readers from 6 months to 12 years." Publishes 200 titles/year. Receives 1,000 queries/year. Pays 1-6% royalty or makes outright purchase. Advance varies. Publishes book 1 year after acceptance of ms. Accepts simultaneous submissions. Reports in 3 weeks-6 months. Book catalog free.
 • Random House Books for Young Readers accepts agented submissions only.
Nonfiction: Children's/juvenile. Subjects include animal, history, nature/environment, popular culture, science, sports. Agented submissions only. *No unsolicited mss.*
Recent Nonfiction Title(s): *The Titanic Sinks*, by Thomas Conklin (history); *The Story of Thomas Alva Edison*, by Margaret Cousins; *Oksana: Her Own Story*, by Oksana Baiul (sports autobiography).
Fiction: Humor, juvenile, mystery, picture books, young adult. "Familiarize yourself with our list. We look for original, unique stories. Do something that hasn't been done." Agented submissions only. *No unsolicited mss.*
Recent Fiction Title(s): *The Wubbulous World of Dr. Seuss*, by Dr. Seuss; *Critters of the Night: No Flying in the Hall*, by Mercer Mayer.

RANDOM HOUSE, INC. JUVENILE BOOKS, 201 E. 50th St., New York NY 10022. (212)572-2600. Juvenile Division: Kate Klimo, publishing director, Random House. Simon Boughton, vice president/publishing director, Andrea Cascardi, associate publishing director, Crown/Knopf. Managing Editor (all imprints): Sue Malone Barber. Publishes hardcover, trade paperback and mass market paperback originals, mass market paperback reprints. Publishes 300 titles/year.
 • This publisher accepts agented submissions only.
Imprint(s): Random House Books for Young Readers, **Alfred A. Knopf and Crown Children's Books,** Dragonfly Paperbacks.
Nonfiction: Biography, humor, illustrated books, juvenile. Subjects include animals, nature/environment, recreation, science, sports.
Fiction: Adventure, confession (young adult), fantasy, historical, horror, humor, juvenile, mystery, picture books, science fiction (juvenile/young adult), suspense, young adult.

‡RAWSON ASSOCIATES, Imprint of Scribner, Division of Simon & Schuster, 1230 Avenue of the Americas, New York NY 10020. (212)698-7000. **Acquisitions:** Eleanor Rawson, publisher. Rawson Associates publishes self-help, popular psychology and health titles. "We are interested in original concepts that deal with issues of concern to many people." Publishes hardcover originals. Publishes 5 titles/year. Receives "hundreds" of queries/year. Less than 10% of books from first-time authors. Pays 7½-12½% royalty on retail price. Advance varies. Accepts simultaneous submissions. Reports in 1 month on queries. *Writer's Market* recommends waiting 2 months for a reply.
Nonfiction: Subjects include business, contemporary lifestyle concerns, health/medicine, psychology. "We are looking for author's with strong credentials and ability to assist in marketing work." Query or submit outline with 1 sample chapter and credentials with SASE. Reviews artwork/photos as part of the ms package. Send photocopies.
Recent Nonfiction Title(s): *12 Steps to Mastering the Winds of Winds of Change*, by Erik Olesen; *The Power of Hope*, by Maurice Lamm.

REFERENCE PRESS INTERNATIONAL, P.O. Box 812726, Boca Raton FL 33481-2726. (561)994-3499. Fax: (561)994-1255. E-mail: ml2626@aol.com. **Acquisitions:** Cheryl Lacoff, senior editor. Reference Press specializes in instructional, reference and how-to titles. Publishes hardcover and trade paperback originals. Publishes 6 titles/year. Receives 50 queries and 20 mss/year. 75% of books from first-time authors; 100% from unagented writers. Pays royalty or makes outright purchase. Advance determined by project. Publishes book 6 months after acceptance. Accepts simultaneous submissions. Reports in 3 months. Book catalog for #10 SASE.
Nonfiction: How-to, illustrated book, multimedia (audio, video, CD-ROM), reference, technical, educational, instructional. Subjects include Americana, art/architecture, business/economics, hobbies, money/finance, gardening, photography, anything related to the arts or crafts field. "Follow the guidelines as stated concerning subjects and types of books we're looking for." Query with outline, 1-3 sample chapters and SASE. Reviews artwork/photos as part of ms package. Send photocopies.
Recent Nonfiction Title(s): *New Age Sourcebook*; *Holistic Health Sourcebook* (holistic and alternative health); *Who's Who in the Peace Corps*, (alumni directory).
Tips: "We are interested in both first-time and published authors."

REFERENCE SERVICE PRESS, 5000 Windplay Dr., Suite 4, El Dorado Hills CA 95762. (916)839-9620. Fax: (916)939-9626. E-mail: rspstaff@aol.com. Website: http://www.rspfunding.com. **Acquisitions:** Stuart Hauser, acquisitions editor. Estab. 1977. "We are interested only in directories and monographs dealing with financial aid." Publishes hardcover originals. Publishes 5-10 titles/year. 100% of books from unagented writers. Pays 10% or higher royalty. Publishes book 6 months after acceptance. Accepts simultaneous submissions. Reports in 2 months. Book catalog for #10 SASE.
• This publisher maintains databases on America Online.
Nonfiction: Reference for financial aid seekers. Subjects include education, ethnic, military/war, women's issues/studies, disabled. Submit outline and sample chapters.
Recent Nonfiction Title(s): *College Students' Guide to Merit Funding and Other No-Need Scholarships*, by Gail Ann Schlachter and R. David Weber.
Tips: "Our audience consists of librarians, counselors, researchers, students, reentry women, scholars and other fund-seekers."

‡REGAN BOOKS, Imprint of HarperCollins, 10 E. 53rd St., New York NY 10022. (212)207-7400. Fax: (212)207-6951. Website: http://www.harpercollins.com. **Acquisitions:** Judith Regan, president/publisher. Estab. 1994. "Regan Books publishes general fiction and nonfiction: biography, self-help, style and gardening books." Regan Books is known for contemporary topics and often controversial authors and titles. Publishes hardcover and trade paperback originals. Publishes 30 titles/year. Receives 7,500 queries and 5,000 mss/year. Pays royalty on retail price. Advance varies. Publishes book 1 year after acceptance of ms. Accepts simultaneous submissions. Reports in 3 months.
• Regan Books accepts agented submissions only.
Nonfiction: Biography, coffee table book, cookbook, gift book, illustrated book, reference, self-help. All subjects. Agented submissions only. *No unsolicited mss.* Reviews artwork as part of ms package. Send photocopies.
Recent Nonfiction Title(s): *American Girl: The Tragic Life of Mariel Hemingway*, by Peter Manso and Ellen Hawks (biography); *Story: A Guide to Screenwriting*, by Robert McKee (how-to screenwriting guide); *Recapturing the Joys of Victorian Life*, by Linda S. Lichter (inspirational/women's studies).
Fiction: All categories. Agented submissions only. *No unsolicited mss.*
Recent Fiction Title(s): *Aaron, Approximately*, by Zachary Lazar (coming of age novel); *Girlfriend in a Coma*, by Douglas Coupland.

REGNERY PUBLISHING, INC., 422 First St. SE, Suite 300, Washington DC 20003. Fax: (202)546-8759. Publisher: Alfred S. Regnery. Executive Editor: Harry Crocker. Associate Publisher: Richard Vigilante. Managing Editor: Margaret Bonillo. **Acquisitions:** Submissions Editor. Estab. 1947. "Regnery publishes well-written, well-produced, sometimes controversial, but always provocative books." Publishes hardcover originals and paperback originals and reprints. Publishes 30 titles/year. Pays 8-15% royalty on retail price. Offers $0-50,000 advance. Publishes book 1 year after acceptance. Accepts simultaneous submissions. No fax submissions. Reports in 6 months on proposals.
Imprint(s): Gateway Editions.
• Regnery has published such authors as William F. Buckley, Jr., Russell Kirk and Whitaker Chambers.
Nonfiction: Biography, business/economics, current affairs, education, government/politics, health/medicine, history, military/war, nature/environment, philosophy, religion, science, sociology. Query with outline and 2-3 sample chapters. Reviews artwork/photos as part of ms package. Send photocopies.
Recent Nonfiction Title(s): *Unlimited Access*, by Gary Aldrich; *Next War*, by Caspar Weinberger and Peter Schweizer; *Murder in Brentwood*, by Mark Fuhrman.
Recent Fiction Title(s): *Hannibal: A Novel*, by Ross Leckie.

RELIGIOUS EDUCATION PRESS, 5316 Meadow Brook Rd., Birmingham AL 35242-3315. (205)991-1000. Fax: (205)991-9669. E-mail: releduc@ix.netcom.com. Website: http://www.bham.net/releduc/. **Acquisitions:** Dr. Nancy J. Vickers, vice president, operations. Estab. 1974. "Religious Education Press's mission is directed toward helping fulfill, in an interfaith and ecumenical way, The Great Commission given by Jesus to teach all persons to come closer to God (Matthew 28:19-20)." Publishes trade paperback and hardback originals. Publishes 5 titles/year. Receives 350 submis-

sions/year. 40% of books from first-time authors; 100% of books from unagented writers. Pays royalty on net price. No advance. Reports in 2 months. Book catalog free.
Imprint(s): Doxa Books.
Nonfiction: Technical and textbook. Scholarly subjects in religion and religious education. "We publish significant, scholarly books on religious education and pastoral ministry." Query with outline, 1 sample chapter and SASE.
Recent Nonfiction Title(s): *Handbook of Planning in Religious Education*, edited by Nancy T. Foltz; *Ministry with Youth in Crisis*, by Harley Atkinson; *Multicultural Religious Education*, edited by Barbara Wilkerson.
Tips: "Our books are written for an ecumenical audience, pastors, religious educators and persons interested in the field of religious education, on a serious, scholarly level. No fiction, short stories or poetry."

REPUBLIC OF TEXAS PRESS, Imprint of Wordware Publishing, Inc., 1506 Capitol Ave., Plano TX 75074. (972)423-0090. Fax: (972)881-9147. E-mail: sales@wordware.com. Website: http://www.wordware.com. **Acquisitions:** Mary Goldman, managing editor (regional); George Baxter, acquisitions editor (game books); James S. Hill, publisher (computer titles). "We publish books pertaining to Western history, outlaws and folklore, military history, ghost stories and humor." Publishes trade and mass market paperback originals. Publishes 25-30 titles/year. Receives 400 queries and 300 mss/year. 80% of books from unagented writers. Pays 8-12% royalty on wholesale price. Publishes book 9 months after acceptance of ms. Reports in 2 months. Book catalog and ms guidelines for SASE.
Nonfiction: History, Texana material, general interest. Subjects include Old West, Southwest, military, women of the West, ghost stories, humor and biography. Submit table of contents, 2 sample chapters, target audience and author experience.
Recent Nonfiction Title(s): *A Cowboy of the Pecos*, by Patrick Dearen (historical); *Red River Women*, by Sherrie McLeRoy (historical); *Letters Home, A Soldier's Story*, by Roger Shaffer (military history).

RESURRECTION PRESS, LTD., P.O. Box 248, Williston Park NY 11596. (516)742-5686. Fax: (516)746-6872. **Acquisitions:** Emilie Cerar, publisher. Resurrection Press publishes religious, devotional and inspirational titles. Publishes trade paperback originals and reprints. Publishes 6-8 titles/year; imprint publishes 4 titles/year. Receives 100 queries and 100 mss/year. 25% of books from first-time authors; 100% from unagented writers. Pays 5-10% royalty on retail price. Offers $250-2,000 advance. Publishes book 1 year after acceptance of ms. Accepts simultaneous submissions. Reports in 1 month on queries and proposals, 2 months on mss. Book catalog and ms guidelines free.
Imprint(s): Spirit Life Series.
Nonfiction: Self-help. Religious subjects. Wants mss of no more than 200 double-spaced typewritten pages. Query with outline and 2 sample chapters. Reviews artwork/photos as part of ms package. Send photocopies.
Recent Nonfiction Title(s): *To Heal as Jesus Healed*, by Matthew Linn, Dennis Linn and Barbara Shlemon Ryan; *Surprising Mary: Meditations and Prayers on the Mother of Jesus*, by Mitch Finely.

FLEMING H. REVELL PUBLISHING, Division of Baker Book House, P.O. Box 6287, Grand Rapids MI 49516. Fax: (616)676-2315. E-mail: lholland@bakerbooks.com or petersen@bakerbooks.com. Website: http://www.bakerbooks .com. **Acquisitions:** Linda Holland, editorial director; Bill Petersen, senior acquisitions editor; Jane Campbell, senior editor (Chosen Books). "Revell publishes to the heart (rather than to the head). For 125 years, Revell has been publishing evangelical books for the personal enrichment and spiritual growth of general Christian readers." Publishes hardcover, trade paperback and mass market paperback originals and reprints. Publishes 50 titles/year; imprint publishes 10 titles/year. Receives 750 queries and 1,000 mss/year. 10% of books from first-time authors; 75% from unagented writers. Pays 7½-15% royalty on wholesale price. Publishes book 1 year after acceptance of ms. Accepts simultaneous submissions. Reports in 3 months. Manuscript guidelines for #10 SASE.
Imprint(s): Spire Books, **Chosen Books**.
● Revell has published such authors as Chuck Colson, Corrie Ten Boom and Dave Wilkerson.
Nonfiction: Biography, coffee table book, how-to, self-help. Subjects include child guidance/parenting, Christian Living. Query with outline and 2 sample chapters.
Recent Nonfiction Title(s): *In Search of Morality*, by Robert A. Schuller; *Our Values: Stories and Wisdom*, by Dale Evans Rogers with Carole Carlson; *God's Guidance*, by Elisabeth Elliot.
Fiction: Religious. Submit synopsis and 2 sample chapters.
Recent Fiction Title(s): *Perilous Bargain*, by Jane Peart (gothic romance-suspense); *A Time of War*, by Gilbert Morris; *The Eagle Stirs Her Nest*, by Linda Rae Rao.

‡REVIEW AND HERALD PUBLISHING ASSOCIATION, 55 W. Oak Ridge Dr., Hagerstown MD 21740. (301)791-7000. **Acquisitions:** Jeannette R. Johnson, editor. "Through print and electronic media, the Review and Herald Publishing Association nurtures a growing relationship with God by providing products that teach and enrich people spiritually, mentally, physically and socially as we near Christ's soon second coming." Publishes hardcover, trade paperback and mass market paperback originals and reprints. Publishes 40-50 titles/year. Receives 200 queries and 350 mss/year. 50% of books from first-time authors; 95% from unagented writers. Pays 7-15% royalty. Offers $500-1,000 advance. Publishes book 18 months after acceptance of ms. Accepts simultaneous submissions. Reports in 1 month on queries and proposals, 2 months on mss. Book catalog for 10×13 SASE. Manuscript guidelines for #10 SASE.
Nonfiction: Biography, children's/juvenile, cookbook, gift book, humor, multimedia, reference, self-help, textbook. Subjects include animals, anthropology/archaeology, child guidance/parenting, cooking/foods/nutrition, education,

health/medicine, history, nature/environment, philosophy, religion, women's issues/studies. Submit 3 sample chapters or proposal package, including cover letter and complete ms with SASE.
Recent Nonfiction Title(s): *Handbook for Bible Study*, by Lee J. Gugliotto (awarded Gold Medallion by Evangelical Christian Publishers); *Incredible Answers to Prayer*, by Roger Morneau.
Fiction: Adventure, historical, humor, juvenile, mainstream/contemporary, religious, all Christian-living related. Submit synopsis and complete ms or 3 sample chapters.
Recent Fiction Title(s): *Shadow Creek Ranch*, by Charles Mills (10-book juvenile adventure series); *The Liberation of Allyson Brown*, by Helen Godfrey Pyke (inspirational); *The Appearing*, by Penny Estes Wheeler (inspirational).
Tips: "We publish for a wide audience, preschool through adult."

‡**MORGAN REYNOLDS PUBLISHING**, Imprint of Morgan Reynolds, Inc., 620 S. Elm St., Suite 384, Greensboro NC 27406. **Acquisitions**: John Riley. "We publish non-fiction for juvenile and young adult readers. We publish titles in our five series: Notable Americans, World Writers, Great Events, Champions of Freedom, Great Athletes—as well as high-quality non-series works." Publishes hardcover originals. Publishes 10-12 titles/year. Receives 200-250 queries and 75-100 mss/year. 50% of books from first-time authors; 100% from unagented writers. Pays 8-12% royalty on wholesale price. Offers $500-1,000 advance. Publishes book 8 months after acceptance of ms. Accepts simultaneous submissions. Reports in 2 months.
Nonfiction: Biography. Subjects include Americana, business/economics, government/politics, history, language/literature, military/war, money/finance, women's issues/studies, all young adult/juvenile oriented. No children's books. "We plan to expand our biography lines. We are interested in well-written books on prominent women from ancient and medieval times." Submit outline and 3 sample chapters with SASE. Reviews artwork/photos as part of ms package. Send photocopies.
Recent Nonfiction Title(s): *Tiger Woods*, by Aaron Boyd (young adult biography); *Spirit Like a Storm: The Story of Mary Shelley*, by Calvin Craig Miller (young adult biography); *The Great Iron Link: The Building of the Central Pacific Railroad*, by Rosemary Laughlin (young adult history).
Tips: "Research the markets before submitting. We spend too much time dealing with manuscripts that shouldn't have been submitted."

RICHBORO PRESS, P.O. Box 947, Southampton PA 18966-0947. (215)355-6084. Fax: (215)364-2212. **Acquisitions**: George Moore, editor. Estab. 1979. Publishes hardcover, trade paperback originals and software. Richboro specializes in cooking titles. Publishes 4 titles/year. Receives 500 submissions/year. 90% of books from unagented writers. Pays 10% royalty on retail price. Publishes book 1 year after acceptance. Electronic submissions preferred. Reports in 2 months on queries. Free book catalog. Manuscript guidelines for $1 and #10 SASE.
Nonfiction: Cookbook, how-to, gardening. Subjects include cooking/foods. Query.

‡**THE RIEHLE FOUNDATION**, P.O. Box 7, Milford OH 45150. **Acquisitions:** Mrs. B. Lewis, general manager. "We are only interested in materials which are written to draw the reader to a deeper love for God." Publishes trade paperback originals and reprints. Publishes 6-7 titles/year. Receives 100 queries and 30 mss/year. 50% of books from first-time authors; 100% from unagented writers. Pays royalty. Publishes book 6 months after acceptance of ms. Accepts simultaneous submissions. Reports in 3 months on mss. Book catalog and ms guidelines for #10 SASE.
Nonfiction: Biography, reference, devotional. Subjects include religion (Roman Catholic). Submit entire ms, curriculum vitae, a statement of your purpose and intentions for writing the book and your intended audience with SASE. Reviews artwork/photos as part of ms package. Send photocopies.
Recent Nonfiction Title(s): *Preparing for the Third Millennium*, by Rev. Albert J.M. Shamon (devotional).
Fiction: Religious, short story collections; all with Roman Catholic subjects. Submit entire ms with SASE.
Recent Fiction Title(s): *Six Short Stories on the Via Dolorosa*, by Ernesto V. Laguette (devotional short stories).

‡**RISING STAR PRESS**, P.O. Box BB, Los Altos CA 94023. (415)966-8920. Fax: (415)968-2658. E-mail: rising.star.pr ess@worldnet.ATT.NET. **Acquisitions:** Michole Nicholson, editorial director. Publishes hardcover originals and reprints, trade paperback originals and reprints. Publishes 4-8 titles/year. "Rising Star selects manuscripts based on benefit to the reader. We are interested in a wide variety of nonfiction topics." Pays 10-15% royalty on wholesale price. Offers $1,000-8,000 advance. Publishes book 3-6 months after acceptance of ms. Accepts simultaneous submissions. Reports in 1 month on proposals.
Nonfiction: Biography, gift book, how-to, humor, reference, self-help, technical. Subjects include business/economics, computers/electronics, education, health/medicine, language/literature, philosophy, regional, religion, social issues, sociology, spirituality, sports. "Authors need to be able to answer these questions: Who will benefit from reading this? Why? Mistakes writers often make are not identifying their target market early and shaping the work to address it, and a lack of clarity regarding the writer's role—participant or reporter? If a participant, does the writer's presence in the narrative truly add value (sometimes ego intrudes inappropriately)." Query with proposal package including outline, 2 sample chapters, target market, author's connection to market, and author's credentials, with SASE.
Recent Nonfiction Title(s): *Soul and Silicon*, by Carl A. Goldman (spiritual life versus high-tech culture).

RISING TIDE PRESS, 5 Kivy St., Huntington Station NY 11746-2020. (516)427-1289. E-mail: rtpress@aol.com. Editor/Publisher: Lee Boojamra. **Acquisitions:** Alice Frier, senior editor. Estab. 1991. "Our books are for, by and about lesbian lives. They change lives and help create a better society." Publishes trade paperback originals. Publishes 10-20

titles/year. Receives 500 queries and 150 mss/year. 75% of books from first-time authors; 100% from unagented writers. Pays 10-15% royalty on wholesale price. Publishes book 15 months after acceptance. Reports in 1 week on queries, 1 months on proposals, 2 months on mss. Book catalog for $1. Writer's guidelines for #10 SASE.
Nonfiction: Lesbian nonfiction. Query with outline, entire ms and *large* SASE. *Writer's Market* recommends sending a query with SASE first. Reviews artwork/photos as part of ms package. Send photocopies.
Recent Nonfiction Title(s): *Feathering Your Nest: An Interactive Guide to a Loving Lesbian Relationship*, by Gwen Leonhard and Jenny Mast (self-help).
Fiction: "Lesbian fiction only." Adventure, erotica, fantasy, historical, horror, humor, literary, mainstream/contemporary, mystery, occult, romance, science fiction, suspense, mixed genres. "Major characters must be lesbian. Primary plot must have lesbian focus and sensibility." Query with synopsis or entire ms and SASE. *Writer's Market* recommends sending a query with SASE first.
Recent Fiction Title(s): *Emerald City Blues*, by Jean Stewart (romance); *Rough Justice*, by Claire Youmans (mystery).
Tips: "We welcome unpublished authors. We do *not* consider agented authors."

‡**RIVERHEAD BOOKS**, Imprint of Penguin Putnam, Inc., 200 Madison Ave., New York NY 10016. (212)951-8400. Fax: (212)779-8236. Website: http://www.putnam.com/putnam. Senior Editors: Julie Grau, Amy Hertz. **Acquisitions:** Kathryn Crosby, editorial assistant. Estab. 1994. "Riverhead aims to help readers open up themselves to new ideas, helpful advice, or healing words. Our books are well-written and try to raise readers' consciousness, not only entertain. Many of our titles deal with spiritual material, especially contemporary, progressive ways to think, act and live. Religion is a specialty." Publishes hardcover originals and reprints, trade paperback originals and reprints. Publishes 80 titles/year. Receives 3,000 queries and 2,000 mss/year. 60% of books from first-time authors; 10% from unagented writers. Pays 6-15% royalty on retail price or makes outright purchase of $7,500-1 million. Publishes book 9 months after acceptance of ms. Reports in 2 months on queries; 3 months on proposals; 4 months on mss. Book catalog free.
Nonfiction: Biography, cookbook, gift book, humor, self-help, spirituality. Subjects include cooking/foods/nutrition, education, ethnic, gay/lesbian, government/politics, health/medicine, history, hobbies, language/literature, military/war, nature/environment, philosophy, psychology, recreation, regional, religion, sociology, travel, women's issues/studies. "We are a small imprint with limited spaces, but we're always looking for very literary, mainstream nonfiction, especially geared toward spirituality." Submit outline and 2-3 sample chapters with SASE. Prefers agented submissions.
Recent Nonfiction Title(s): *Living Buddha Living Christ*, by Thich Nhat Hant (spirituality/Buddhism); *Kitchen Table Wisdom*, by Rachel Remen (spirituality/health/self-help); *Omens of Millennium*, by Harold Bloom (religion/literature).
Fiction: Adventure, confession, ethnic, experimental, feminist, gay/lesbian, historical, humor, literary, mainstream/contemporary, plays, religious, short story collections, suspense. "We like first-time novelists with fresh voices or an interesting perspective. Quality writing is our #1 priority." Query with synopsis and sample chapters. Prefers agented submissions. "Many writers submit the entire manuscript, which is daunting to read when there are hundreds in the office. It's best to submit an outline of the story along with a few chapters to give a sample of the writing."
Recent Fiction Title(s): *Going Down*, by Jennifer Belle (mainstream/contemporary); *The Beach*, by Alex Garland (suspense/adventure); *Drown*, by Junot Diaz (short story/ethnic).
Poetry: "We don't really publish poetry, unless it's highly unusual or written by a well-known writer. We usually do collections or anthologies."
Recent Poetry Title(s): *Rilke's Book of Hours*, translated by Macy/Barrons (religious); *Catch the Fire*, edited by D-Knowledge (African-American/contemporary).
Tips: "We envision our audience to be very literate, curious people who enjoy fine writing and enriching stories or information. Our audience ranges from high-schoolers to the elderly, in all parts of the country. If you're submitting, do some research and find out which editor might be most interested in your work—call the office or look in one of our books that might have a similar style or theme and check the acknowledgments—often the editor is listed."

‡**ROC BOOKS**, Imprint of Penguin Putnam Inc., 375 Huron St., New York NY 10014. (212)366-2000. **Acquisitions:** Laura Gilman, executive editor. Publishes mass market paperback originals and reprints. "We're looking for books that are a good read, that people will want to pick up time and time again." Publishes 48 titles/year. Receives 500 queries/year. 25% of books from first-time authors; less than 10% from unagented writers. Pays 7½-12½% royalty on retail price (industry standard). Advance negotiable. Publishes book 1 year after acceptance of ms. Accepts simultaneous submissions. Report in 2-3 months on queries.
Fiction: Fantasy, horror, science fiction. "We are trying to strike a balance between fantasy and science fiction." Query with synopsis and 1-2 sample chapters. *"We discourage unsolicited submissions."*
Recent Fiction Title(s): *Giant Bones*, by peter beagle (short stories); *The Deathstalker Series*, by Simon Green (science fiction).

ROCKBRIDGE PUBLISHING CO., P.O. Box 351, Berryville VA 22611-0351. (540)955-3980. Fax: (540)955-4126. E-mail: cwpub@visuallink.com. **Acquisitions:** Katherine Tennery, publisher. Estab. 1989. "We publish nonfiction books about the Civil War, Virginia tour guides, Virginia/Southern folklore and ghost stories." Publishes hardcover original and reprints, trade paperback originals. Publishes 4-6 titles/year. Pays royalty on wholesale price. No advance. Reports in 3 months on proposals.
Nonfiction: "We are developing a series of travel guides to the country roads in various Virginia counties. The self-guided tours include local history, identify geographic features, etc. We are also looking for material about the Civil

War, especially biographies, and expanding interests from Virginia to other southern states, notably Georgia." Query with outline, 3 sample chapters, author credentials and SASE.
Recent Nonfiction Title(s): *Charlotte's Boys: Letters of the Branch Family of Savannah*, by Mauriel Joslyn (Civil War letters); *Battlefield Ghosts*, by Keith Toney (ghost sightings).

‡**RODALE BOOKS**, Rodale Press, Inc., 400 S. Tenth St., Emmaus PA 18098. Website: http://www.rodalepress.com. Publisher: Carolyn Gavett. **Acquisitions:** Sally Reith, assistant acquisitions editor. Estab. 1932. "Our mission is to show people how they can use the power of their bodies and minds to make their lives better." Publishes hardcover originals, trade paperback originals and reprints. Publishes 75-100 titles/year; imprint publishes 10-15 titles/year. Pays 6-15% royalty on retail price. Publishes book 18 months after acceptance of ms. Accepts simultaneous submissions. Reports in 1 month on queries, 2 months on proposals and mss. Book catalog and ms guidelines free.
Imprint(s): Daybreak Books (Karen Kelly, editorial director).
Nonfiction: Cookbook, how-to, self-help. Subjects include cooking/foods/nutrition, gardening, health/medicine (men's, women's, alternative, African-American, seniors), hobbies. "Our publications focus on the individual and what you can do to make life more natural, more self-reliant and more healthful." Query or submit proposal package including 1-2 sample chapters, author's resume and SASE.
Recent Nonfiction Title(s): *New Choices in Natural Healing*, edited by Bill Gottlieb (medicine); *Stress Blasters*, by Brian Chichester and Perry Garfinkel (self-help); *Natural Landscaping*, by Sally Roth (gardening).
Tips: "We're looking for authors who can dig deeply for facts and details, report accurately and write with flair."

‡**THE ROSEN PUBLISHING GROUP**, 29 E. 21st St., New York NY 10010. (212)777-3017. Fax: (212)777-0277. E-mail: rosenpub@tribeca.ios.com. **Acquisitions:** Patra McSharry Sevastiades, editorial director. "The Rosen Publishing Group publishes young adult titles for sale to schools and libraries. Each book is aimed at teenage readers and addresses them directly." Publishes hardcover and trade paperback originals. Publishes 300 titles/year. Receives 150 queries and 75 mss/year. 10% of books from first-time authors; 95% from unagented writers. Pays 6-10% royalty on retail price or makes outright purchase of $300-1,000. Offers $500-1,000 advance. Publishes books 9 months after acceptance of ms. Reports in 2 months on proposals. Book catalog and ms guidelines free.
● The Rosen Publishing Group's imprint, Power Kids Press, publishes nonfiction for grades K-4 that are supplementary to the curriculum. Topics include conflict resolution, character building, health, safety, drug abuse prevention, history, self-help, religion and multicultural titles. Contact: Gina Strazzabosco-Hayn or Helen Packard, acquisitions editors.
Nonfiction: Juvenile, self-help, young adult, reference. Submit outline and 1 sample chapter. Books should be written at 4-6th or 8th grade reading level. Areas of particular interest include multicultural ethnographic studies, careers; coping with social, medical and personal problems; values and ethical behavior, drug abuse prevention, self-esteem, social activism, religion.
Recent Nonfiction Title(s): *Coping: A Young Woman's Guide to Breast Cancer Prevention*, by Bettijane Eisenpreis; *Merina*, by Rebecca L. Green, Ph.D. (from the African Peoples series); *In Control: Learning to Say No to Sexual Pressure*, by Anna Kreiner.
Tips: "The writer has the best chance of selling our firm a book on vocational guidance or personal social adjustment, or high-interest, low reading-level material for teens."

‡**FRED B. ROTHMAN & CO.**, 10368 W. Centennial Rd., Littleton CO 80127. (303)979-5657. Fax: (303)978-1457. E-mail: sjarrett@rothman.com. **Acquisitions:** Sheila Jarrett, editorial/production manager. Fred B. Rothman & Co., publishes references books for law librarians, legal researchers and those interested in legal writing. Publishes hardcover and trade paperback originals. Publishes 12 titles/year. Receives 30 queries and 15 mss/year. 20% of books from first-time authors; 100% from unagented writers. Pays 10-20% royalty on net price. Publishes book 9 months after acceptance of ms. Accepts simultaneous submissions. Does not return submissions. Reports in 3 months. Book catalog free.
Nonfiction: Reference. Subjects include law and librarianship. Submit outline, 3 sample chapters and proposal package, including intended audience.
Recent Nonfiction Title(s): *Lawyer's Book of Rules for Effective Legal Writing*, by Haggard; *Foreign Law: Current Sources of Codes and Basic Legislation in Jurisdictions of the World*, by Thomas H. Reynolds and Arturo A. Flores.

ROXBURY PUBLISHING CO., P.O. Box 491044, Los Angeles CA 90049. (213)653-1068. **Acquisitions:** Claude Teweles, executive editor. Roxbury Publishing Co. publishes only college textbooks in the humanities and social sciences. Publishes hardcover and paperback originals and reprints. Publishes 10 titles/year. Pays royalty. Accepts simultaneous submissions. Reports in 2 months.
Nonfiction: College-level textbooks *only*. Subjects include humanities, speech, developmental studies, social sciences, sociology, criminology, criminal justice. Query, submit outline/synopsis and sample chapters, or submit complete ms. *Writer's Market* recommends sending a query with SASE first.
Recent Nonfiction Title(s): *Images of Color, Images of Crime*, by Mann and Zatz; *Health, Illness, and Healing: Social Context and Personal Experience, an Anthology*, by Charmaz and Peterniti.

ROYAL FIREWORKS PRESS, 1 First Ave., P.O. Box 399, Unionville NY 10988. (914)726-4444. Fax: (914)726-3824. E-mail: rfpress@ny.frontiercomm.net. **Acquisitions:** Charles Morgan, editor. "For nearly 20 years, we have pursued the purpose of enhancing the educational experience of gifted and talented children. Our goal has been to provide the materials that enable teachers, administrators and parents to enrich the experience and life opportunities of gifted children." Publishes hardcover originals and reprints, trade paperback originals. Publishes 125 titles/year. 75% of books from first-time authors; 90% from unagented writers. Pays royalty. Publishes book 6 months after acceptance. Reports in 2 months on mss. Book catalog for 9×12 SAE with 5 first-class stamps. Manuscript guidelines for #10 SASE.

Nonfiction: Biography, children's/juvenile, how-to, humor, illustrated book, self-help, technical, textbook. Subjects include Americana, child guidance/parenting, computers/electronics, education, ethnic, history, language/literature, software, women's issues/studies. Submit proposal package, including entire ms with SASE. *Writer's Market* recommends sending a query with SASE first. Reviews artwork/photos as part of ms package. Send photocopies.

Recent Nonfiction Title(s): *My Days With Albert Schweitzer*, by Fredrick Frank; *Essence of Albert Schweitzer*, by Albert Schweitzer; *The Word Within Word, Volume 3*, by Michael Clay Thompson.

Fiction: Ethnic, juvenile, mystery, science fiction. "Most of our concentration will be on novels for middle school and young adult readers." Submit entire ms with synopsis and SASE. *Writer's Market* recommends sending a query with SASE first.

Recent Fiction Title(s): *Kipton & The Android*, by Charles L. Fontenay (science fiction); *Dragon Charmer*, by Ruth Siburt (science fiction); *The Sipit Walker*, by Paul Sullivan (environment).

Recent Poetry Title(s): *The Poetry Pad*, by Sue Thomas.

‡**RUNNING PRESS BOOK PUBLISHERS**, 125 S. 22nd St., Philadelphia PA 19103. (215)567-5080. Fax: (215)568-2919. **Acquisitions:** Mary Ellen Lewis, assistant editorial director; Nancy Steele, director of acquisitions; Brian Perrin, editorial director; Mary McGuire Ruggiero, editor (cookbooks). Estab. 1972. Publishes hardcover originals, trade paperback originals and reprints. Publishes 150 titles/year. Receives 600 queries/year. 50% of books from first-time authors; 30% from unagented writers. Payment varies. Advances varies. Publishes book 6-18 months after acceptance of ms. Accepts simultaneous submissions. Reports in 1 month on queries. Book catalog free. Ms guidelines for #10 SASE.

Imprint(s): Courage Books.

● Running Press has published Marvin Shanken, British spirits expert Michael Jackson and Ron Van der Meer.

Nonfiction: Children's/juvenile, how-to, self-help. Subjects include art/architecture, cooking/foods/nutrition, recreation, science, craft, how-to. Query, outline, contents, synopsis and SASE. Reviews artwork/photos as part of the ms package. Send photocopies.

Recent Nonfiction Title(s): *The Fountain Pen: A Collector's Companion*, by Alexander Crum Ewing (reference); *Sisters*, by Carol Saline and Sharon J. Wohlmuth (relationships).

‡**RUSSIAN HILL PRESS**, 6410 Geary Blvd., San Francisco CA 94121. (415)387-0846. **Acquisitions:** Kit Cooley, assistant editor. "Russian Hill Press focuses on West coast writers and topics with cutting edge themes." Publishes hardcover originals. Publishes 6-10 titles/year. Receives 100 queries and 60 mss/year. 25% of books from first-time authors; 10% from unagented writers. Pays 10-15% royalty on retail price. Advance varies. Publishes book 8 months after acceptance of ms. Accepts simultaneous submissions. Reports in 2 months on queries. Book catalog for $2. Manuscript guidelines for #10 SASE.

Nonfiction: Biography (literary). Subjects include government/politics. Query. Prefers agented submissions. Reviews artwork as part of ms package. Send photocopies.

Recent Nonfiction Title(s): *Straight to the Heart*, by Angela Alioto (political).

Fiction: Erotica, ethnic, feminist, gay/lesbian, humor, literary, mainstream/contemporary, mystery, suspense. Focuses on West Coast authors. "We're looking for angry, young, lively fiction." Query with sample chapter. Prefers agented submissions.

Recent Fiction Title(s): *Swamp Cats*, by Jeff Love (humorous); *Tainted Million*, by Susan Trott (mystery); *Funerals for Horses*, by Catherine Ryan Hyoe (literary).

RUSSIAN INFORMATION SERVICES, 89 Main St., Suite 2, Montpelier VT 05602. (802)223-4955. **Acquisitions:** Stephanie Ratmeyer, vice president. "Audience is business people and independent travelers to Russia and the former Soviet Union, SE Asia, Latin America." Publishes trade paperback originals and reprints. Publishes 5-10 titles/year. Receives 20-30 queries and 10 mss/year. 50% of books from first-time authors; 100% from unagented writers. Pays 8-12% royalty on retail price. Publishes book 8 months after acceptance of ms. Accepts simultaneous submissions. Reports in 2 months on mss. Book catalog free.

Nonfiction: Reference, travel, business. Subjects include business/economics, language/literature, travel. "Our editorial focus is on (1) Russia and the former Soviet Union, and (2) newly emerging economies, ripe for foreign investment (China, Latin America, SE Asia). We currently are seeking authors for these latter regions." Submit proposal package, including ms, summary and cv. *Writer's Market* recommends sending a query with SASE first. Reviews artwork/photos as part of ms package. Send photocopies.

Recent Nonfiction Title(s): *Russia Survival Guide: Business & Travel*, by Richardson (travel/business); *Bilingual Map of Russia and the Republics*.

‡**RUTGERS UNIVERSITY PRESS**, Livingston Campus, Bldg. 4161, New Brunswick NJ 08903. (908)932-7762. Website: http://info.rutgers/edu/Library/Rutgers/unipress/. **Acquisitions:** Leslie Mitchner, editor-in-chief. "Our press aims to reach audiences beyond the academic community with accessible writing." Publishes hardcover originals and trade paperback originals and reprints. Publishes 70 titles/year. Receives up to 1,500 queries and up to 300 books/year.

Up to 30% of books from first-time authors; 70% from unagented writers. Pays 7½-15% royalty on retail or net price. Offers $1,000-10,000 advance. Publishes book 1 year after acceptance of ms. Accepts simultaneous submissions if so noted. Reports in 1 month on proposals. Book catalog free.

Nonfiction: Biography, textbook and books for use in undergraduate courses. Subjects include Americana, anthropology, African-American studies, education, gay/lesbian, government/politics, health/medicine, history, language/literature, multicultural studies, nature/environment, regional, religion, science, sociology, translation, women's issues/studies. Submit outline and 2-3 sample chapters. Reviews artwork/photos as part of the ms package. Send photocopies.

Recent Nonfiction Title(s): *Frauen: German Women Recall the Third Reich*, by Alison Owings; *Black Entrepreneurs in America: Stories of Struggle and Success*, by Michael D. Woodard (business/African American studies).

Tips: Both academic and general audiences. "Many of our books have potential for undergraduate course use. We are more trade-oriented than most university presses. We are looking for intelligent, well-written and accessible books. Avoid overly narrow topics."

RUTLEDGE HILL PRESS, 211 Seventh Ave. N., Nashville TN 37219-1823. (615)244-2700. Fax: (615)244-2978. **Acquisitions:** Mike Towle, executive editor. Estab. 1982. "We are a publisher of market-specific books, focusing on particular genres or regions." Publishes hardcover and trade paperback originals and reprints. Publishes 50 titles/year. Receives 1,000 submissions/year. 40% of books from first-time authors; 90% from unagented writers. Pays 10-20% royalty on net price. Publishes book 1 year after acceptance. Reports in 3 months. Book catalog for 9×12 SAE with 4 first-class stamps.

● Rutledge Hill has published such authors as Peter Jenkins, Webb Garrison, Dawn Wells and Gail Greco.

Nonfiction: Biography, cookbook, humor, reference, self-help, travel, Civil War history, quilt books, sports. "The book must have an identifiable market, preferably one that is geographically limited." Submit outline and sample chapters. Reviews artwork/photos as part of ms package.

Recent Nonfiction Title(s): *A Communion of the Spirits*, by Roland Freeman (quilt history); *America's Dumbest Criminals*, by Daniel Butler, Alan Ray, Leland Gregory (true stories); *Life's Little Instruction Book, Volume III*, by H. Jackson Brown, Jr. (gift book).

‡SAE INTERNATIONAL, Imprint of Society of Automotive Engineers, 400 Commonwealth Dr., Warrendale PA 15096. (412)776-4841. **Acquisitions:** Jeff Worsinger, product manager; Edward Manns, product manager. "Automotive means anything self-propelled. We are a professional society serving this area, which includes aircraft, spacecraft, marine, rail, automobiles, trucks and off-highway vehicles." Publishes hardcover and trade paperback originals. Publishes 15-20 titles/year. Receives 250 queries and 75 mss/year. 30-40% of books from first-time authors; 100% from unagented writers. Pays royalty with possible advance. Publishes book 1 year after acceptance of ms. Accepts simultaneous submissions. Reports in 1 month. Book catalog and ms guidelines free.

Imprint(s): STS Press.

Nonfiction: Biography, multimedia (CD-ROM), reference, self-help, technical, textbook. Subjects include automotive and aerospace. "Request submission guidelines. Clearly define your book's market or angle." Query with SASE. Reviews artwork/photos as part of ms package. Send photocopies.

Recent Nonfiction Title(s): *Battery Reference Book, 2nd edition*, by J.R. Crompton (reference); *Creating the Customer-Driven Car Company*, by Karl Ludvigsen (business/how-to).

Tips: "Audience is automotive engineers, technicians, car buffs."

‡SAFARI PRESS INC., 15621 Chemical Lane, Building B, Huntington Beach CA 92649-1506. (714)894-9080. Fax: (714)894-4949. E-mail: info@safaripress.com. Website: http://www.safaripress.com. **Acquisitions:** Jacqueline Neufeld, editor. "We publish only books on big-game hunting, firearms and wingshooting, also African, North American, European, Asian and South American hunting and wingshooting." Publishes hardcover originals and reprints and trade paperback reprints. Publishes 6-15 titles/year. 50% of books from first-time authors; 99% from unagented writers. Pays 8-15% royalty on wholesale price. Does not accept simultaneous submissions. Book catalog for $1.

● Safari Press has published such authors as Peter Capstick, Craig Boddington and Russell Annabel.

Nonfiction: Biography, how-to, adventure stories. Subjects include hunting, firearms, wingshooting—"nothing else. We discourage autobiographies, unless the life of the hunter or firearms maker has been exceptional. We routinely reject manuscripts along the lines of 'Me and my buddies went hunting for . . . and a good time was had by all!' No fishing." Query with outline and SASE. "Request our 'Notice to Prospective Authors.'"

Recent Nonfiction Title(s): *Baron in Africa: The Remarkable Adventures of Werner von Alvensleben*, by Brian Marsh; *My Last Kambaku*, by Leo Kröger; *A Man Called Lion*, by Peter Capstick.

SAFER SOCIETY PRESS, Safer Society Foundation, Inc., P.O. Box 340, Brandon VT 05733. (802)247-3132. Fax: (802)247-4233. Website: http://www.merrymac.com/safer/safesoc.html. **Acquisitions:** Rob Freeman-Longo, press director. "Our mission is the prevention and treatment of sexual abuse. We publish self-help books and books for mental health professionals." Publishes trade paperback originals. Publishes 6-8 titles/year. Receives 15-20 queries and 10-15 mss/year. 90% of books from first-time authors; 100% from unagented writers. Pays 5% maximum royalty on retail price. No advance. Publishes book 1 year after acceptance. Accepts simultaneous submissions. Reports in 1 month on queries, 2 months on proposals, 6 months on mss. Book catalog free.

● Safer Society Press has published such authors as Carolyn Cunningham, Kee MacFarlane and Robert Prentky.

Nonfiction: Self-help (sex abuse prevention and treatment). Subjects include psychology (sexual abuse). Query with

proposal package, including complete ms with SASE. *Writer's Market* recommends sending a query with SASE first. Reviews artwork/photos as part of ms package. Send photocopies. "We are a small, nonprofit, nitch press."
Recent Nonfiction Title(s): *Impact: Working with Sexual Abuses*, by Bird; *Last Secret: Mothers Who Sexually Abuse Their Daughters*, by Rosencrans.

ST. ANTHONY MESSENGER PRESS, 1615 Republic St., Cincinnati OH 45210-1298. (513)241-5615. Fax: (513)241-0399. E-mail: stanthony@americancatholic.org. Website: http://www.americancatholic.org. Publisher: The Rev. Jeremy Harrington, O.F.M. **Acquisitions:** Lisa Biedenbach, managing editor. Estab. 1970. "St. Anthony Messenger Press/Franciscan Communications seeks to communicate the word that is Jesus Christ in the styles of Saints Francis and Anthony. Through print and electronic media marketed in North America and worldwide, we endeavor to evangelize, inspire and inform those who search for God and seek a richer Catholic, Christian, human life. Our efforts help support the life, ministry and charities of the Franciscan Fathers of St. John the Baptist Province, who sponsor our work." Publishes trade paperback originals. Publishes 12-16 titles/year. Receives 200 queries and 50 mss/year. 5% of books from first-time authors; 100% from unagented writers. Pays 10-12% royalty on net receipts of sales. Offers $1,000 average advance. Publishes book 18 months after acceptance. Reports in 1 month on queries, 2 months on proposals and mss. Book catalog for 9×12 SAE with 4 first-class stamps. Manuscript guidelines free.
Nonfiction: History, religion, Catholic identity and teaching, prayer and spirituality resources, scripture study. Query with outline and SASE. Reviews artwork/photos as part of ms package.
 • St. Anthony Messenger Press especially seeks books which will sell in bulk quantities to parishes, teachers, pastoral ministers, etc. They expect to sell at least 5,000 to 7,000 copies of a book. They have published such authors as Richard Rohr, O.F.M.; Alfred McBride, O. Praem; and Gloria Hutchinson.
Recent Nonfiction Title(s): *A Retreat With Therese of Lisieux*, by Elizabeth Ruth Obbend, O.D.C. (prayer/spirituality); *Reading the Gospels With the Church: From Christmas Through Easter*, by Raymond E. Brown (scripture); *Jesus of the Gospels: Teacher, Storyteller, Friend, Messiah*, by Arthur E. Zannoni (scripture).
Tips: "Our readers are ordinary 'folks in the pews' and those who minister to and educate these folks. Writers need to know the audience and the kind of books we publish. Manuscripts should reflect best and current Catholic theology and doctrine."

ST. BEDE'S PUBLICATIONS, Subsidiary of St. Scholastica Priory, P.O. Box 545, Petersham MA 01366-0545. (508)724-3407. Fax: (508)724-3574. Website: http://www.stbedes.org. **Acquisitions:** Sr. Scholastica Crilly, OSB, editorial director. Estab. 1978. Publishes hardcover originals, trade paperback originals and reprints. Publishes 8-12 titles/year. Receives 100 submissions/year. 30-40% of books from first-time authors; 98% from unagented writers. Nonauthor subsidy publishes 10% of books. Pays 5-10% royalty on wholesale price or retail price. No advance. Publishes book 2 years after acceptance. Accepts simultaneous submissions. Unsolicited mss not returned unless accompanied by sufficient return postage. Reports in 2 months. Book catalog and ms guidelines for 9×12 SAE and 2 first-class stamps.
Nonfiction: Textbook (theology), religion, prayer, spirituality, hagiography, theology, philosophy, church history, related lives of saints. "We are always looking for excellent books on prayer, spirituality, liturgy, church or monastic history. Theology and philosophy are important also. We publish English translations of foreign works in these fields if we think they are excellent and worth translating." No submissions unrelated to religion, theology, spirituality, etc. Query or submit outline and sample chapters.
Recent Nonfiction Title(s): *The Spirit of Solesmes*, by by Sr. Mary David Totah; *How Far to Follow? The Martyrs of Atlas*, by Bernardo Olivera, O.C.S.O.; *Contemplation 2000*, by James Kinn.
Tips: "There seems to be a growing interest in monasticism among lay people and we will be publishing more books in this area. For our theology/philosophy titles our audience is scholars, colleges and universities, seminaries, etc. For our other titles (i.e. prayer, spirituality, lives of saints, etc.) the audience is above-average readers interested in furthering their knowledge in these areas."

ST. MARTIN'S PRESS, 175 Fifth Ave., New York NY 10010. Publishes hardcover, trade paperback and mass market originals. Publishes 1,500 titles/year. General interest publisher of both fiction and nonfiction.
Imprint(s): Dead Letter, Thomas Dunne Books, Forge, Picador USA, Stonewall Inn Editions, Tor Books, Wyatt Books for St. Martin's Press.
Nonfiction: General nonfiction, reference, scholarly, textbook. Biography, business/economics, contemporary culture, cookbooks, self-help, sports, true crime.
Recent Nonfiction Title(s): *Crossing the Jordan: Rabin's Road to Peace*, by Samuel Segev (current events); *Building for the Lawn and Garden*, by John Kelsey and Ian J. Kirby; *El Sid*, by David Dalton (music/biography).
Fiction: General fiction. Fantasy, historical, horror, literary, mainstream, mystery, science fiction, suspense, thriller, Western (contemporary).
Recent Fiction Title(s): *The Memoirs of Cleopatra*, by Margaret George; *The House of the Vestals*, by Steven Saylor (mystery); *Chocolate Star*, by Sheila Copeland.

‡ST. MARTIN'S PRESS, SCHOLARLY & REFERENCE DIVISION, Division of St. Martin's Press, 257 Park Ave. S., New York NY 10010. (212)982-3900. Fax: (212)777-6359. **Acquisitions:** Garrett Kiely, director; Michael Flamini, senior editor. "We remain true to our origin as a scholarly press . . . with the backing of St. Martin's Press we are able to make books more accessible." Publishes hardcover and trade paperback originals. Firm publishes 500 titles/year. Receives 500 queries and 600 mss/year. 25% of books from first-time authors; 75% from unagented writers. Pays

INSIDER REPORT

Recruiting cutting-edge authors

Classic literature may last forever, but computer guides have a pretty short shelf life, according to Kelli Spenser, Director of Marketing for Sams Publishing, an imprint of Macmillan's Computer Publishing Group. "Typically, who ever comes out with a title first, sells the most," she says. That, and the ever changing nature of computer technology, puts a premium on getting books written and printed and on bookstore shelves as quickly as possible. Spenser says computer publishers must be more aggressive, and more willing to gamble, than mainstream publishers.

"A software package could literally become obsolete in six to twelve months," Spenser says, "so the challenge is to get the books out as soon as new software is released, so it has the longest possible shelf life." Computer publishers can't afford to sit back and wait to see what comes over the transom or through literary agents. When time is of the essence, editors need to know their market, anticipate trends, and actively acquire both authors and subjects.

"Sams has traditionally written computer books to a higher level audience," Spenser says, intermediate to advanced programmers and database developers who use computer technology everyday. She says some of the best authors come from the computer industry itself. Many Sams authors are program developers, webpage designers and database specialists. "You have to have a real understanding of the technology to write about it well." Sams looks for new authors the same way baseball scouts look for new players. "We look for people who have a reputation in the field," she says, "people who participate in seminars or do a lot of speeches or write articles."

But technical expertise is only half the equation, and Spenser says it's difficult to find experts who both understand the technology, and can translate that experience.

Author Lora LaMay is one of Sams success stories, and Spenser says it's an example of a gamble on an unknown author that paid off well for Sams. Although LaMay had never published a book, Spenser says the newcomer showed "a real talent for writing, for putting technology in language that everyone can understand." Her strong writing and conversational tone quickly sent LaMay's first book to the top of the bestseller list, and she has written several more books for Sams, including a successful series called the Lora LaMay Web Workshop.

Not all promising authors are ready to write a book of their own, and sometimes there's a need for a broad-based manual beyond the scope of one single author. Rather than wait for the perfect author to come along, the company will often take the initiative, contracting with several different authors to write a chapter, or several chapters, for a larger work. Because the computer field is always changing and evolving, it's difficult to find authors who are outstanding in all aspects at once. Spenser says this piecemeal approach benefits readers by giving them the most up-to-date information on a range of topics.

Accuracy is just as important as timing in the computer publishing business, and Sams works with a large roster of technical editors, people who review manuscripts and portions

INSIDER REPORT, *Spenser*

of software code to check for accuracy. Because of parent company Macmillan's prominence in the computer publishing field, many software companies provide pre-release copies of software, or "betas," which she admits gives Sams a bit of an edge on the competition. "We have a chance to go through it and check for bugs," she says, "and we're able to start writing books from the betas, and finalize them when the software is released." Spenser says the technical editors are a crucial part of producing the final text, and many books "are doubly and triply edited, from a technical perspective, just to make sure we have everything right." Spenser says technical editing is another way for writers to gain experience and confidence, and many use it as a springboard to writing their own books, which gives Sams another source of up-and-coming authors.

Spenser says the combination of timeliness and accuracy are what sets Sams apart from other computer publishers. The company enjoys a very loyal base of readers, which is an asset for any publisher, but especially important in the volatile field of computers. "The technology is changing so quickly that we often have people asking for a book on software that hasn't even been released yet," she says. And readers' needs often guide the company into new areas. "Obviously, with the explosion of the Internet we are now writing a number of books on related topics," she says, "areas like webpage design and how to build a database on the web." Spenser says the language of computer manuals is changing too, as more and more people take up the challenge of programming. Although the bulk of Sams books are reference works, the company has launched several series of more tutorial-oriented titles, "books that really explain the problem or define the task, then show you how to proceed."

Although the company publishes several electronic books, and carries many CD-ROM tutorials, the majority of Sams titles come out in old-fashioned book form. Spenser sees no irony in cutting-edge computer users relying on the printed page. "What we're hearing is that people *like* the electronic books," she says, "but they don't want to read through a thousand pages of screen. They want to have the actual printed book." And because many readers use computers at work, they turn around and teach others, using the manuals as a reference guide. Spenser says it's not uncommon to see a computer specialist with a large library of print books they refer to on a continual basis.

Despite the rapidly changing nature of computer technology, Spenser says Sams has the same goal as any publisher. "We really just want to put out the best, most accurate, most helpful books possible," she says. And being first doesn't hurt, either.

—*Alison Holm*

royalty: trade, 7-10% list; other, 7-10% net. Advance varies. Publishes book 7 months after acceptance of ms. Accepts simultaneous submissions. Reports in 1 month on proposals. Book catalog and ms guidelines free.
Nonfiction: Reference, scholarly. Subjects include business/economics, government/politics, history, language/literature, philosophy, religion, sociology, women's issues/studies, humanities, social studies. "We are looking for good solid scholarship." Query with proposal package including outline, 3-4 sample chapters, prospectus, cv and SASE. "We like to see as much completed material as possible." Reviews artwork/photos as part of ms package.

‡**SAMS PUBLISHING/SAMS.NET**, Imprint of Macmillan Computer Publishing (Division of Simon & Schuster), 201 W. 103rd St., Indianapolis IN 46290. (317)581-3500. Website: http://www.mcp.com/sams/. Publisher: Richard Swadley. **Acquisitions:** Andi Richter, assistant editor. Estab. 1951. "Sams Publishing has made a major commitment to publishing books that meet the needs of computer users, programmers, administrative and support personnel, and managers. The sams.net imprint focuses on Internet topics." Publishes trade paperback originals. Publishes 160 titles/year. 30% of books from first-time authors; 95% from unagented writers. Pays royalty on wholesale price, negotiable.

Advance negotiable. Publishes book 1 year after acceptance of ms. Accepts simultaneous submissions if noted; "however, once contract is signed, Sams Publishing retains first option rights on future works on same subject." Reports in 6 weeks on queries. Manuscript guidelines free.

Nonfiction: Computer subjects. Also contracts with first-time authors for chapters, especially in series. Query.

Recent Nonfiction Title(s): *Teach Yourself Java in 21 Days*, by Laura Lemay (computers).

Tips: "*Teach Yourself Java in 21 Days* is one of the best selling computer books of all time, and the author's first book."

‡SAN FRANCISCO PRESS, INC., P.O. Box 426800, San Francisco CA 94142-6800. (510)524-1000. **Acquisitions:** Terry Gabriel, president. Founded 1959. San Francisco Press publishes primarily texts in the sciences and public health. "Our books are aimed at specialized audiences; we do not publish works intended for the general public." Publishes hardcover originals and trade paperback originals and reprints. Averages 5-10 titles/year. Receives over 50 submissions/year. 50% of books from first-time authors; 90% from unagented writers. Pays 10-15% on wholesale price. Publishes book 6 months after acceptance. Accepts simultaneous submissions. Reports in 1 week on queries. *Writer's Market* recommends allowing 2 weeks for reply.

• This press is particularly interested in books with a potential to be used as college texts.

Nonfiction: Technical, college textbook. Subjects include electronics, biotechnology, public health, history of science and technology, musicology, science. Submit outline and sample chapters.

‡J.S. SANDERS & COMPANY, INC., P.O. Box 50331, Nashville TN 37205. **Acquisitions:** John Sanders, publisher. "J.S. Sanders & Company publishes new books in Southern letters and history, as well as a reprint list of 19th and 20th century titles in its Southern Classic series." Publishes hardcover originals and trade paperback originals and reprints. Publishes 5 titles/year. Receives 100 queries and 25 mss/year. 25% of books from unagented writers. Pays 7½-15% royalty. Publishes book 9 months after acceptance of ms. Accepts simultaneous submissions. Reports in 1 month on queries. Book catalog free.

Imprint(s): Caliban Books.

Nonfiction: Biography, humor. Subjects include Americana, government/politics, history, language/literature, military/war, regional, travel. Query with SASE. Reviews artwork/photos as part of ms package. Send photocopies.

Recent Nonfiction Title(s): *The War the Women Lived*, by Walter Sullivan (Civil War history); *A Less Perfect Union*, by Joseph Sobran (politics/law).

Fiction: Historical, literary. Submit 1 sample chapter with SASE.

Recent Fiction Title(s): *Nashville 1864: A Novel*, by Madison Jones (literary/historical); *The Women on the Porch*, by Caroline Gordon (literary reprint).

Poetry: Not accepting new poetry.

SANDLAPPER PUBLISHING CO., INC., P.O. Box 730, Orangeburg SC 29116-0730. (803)531-1658. Fax: (803)534-5223. **Acquisitions:** Amanda Gallman, managing editor. Estab. 1982. "We are an independent, regional book publisher specializing in nonfiction relating to South Carolina." Publishes hardcover and trade paperback originals and reprints. Publishes 6 titles/year. Receives 200 submissions/year. 80% of books from first-time authors; 95% from unagented writers. Pays 15% maximum royalty on net receipts. Publishes book 20 months after acceptance. Accepts simultaneous submissions, if so noted. Reports in 3 months. Book catalog and ms guidelines for 9×12 SAE with 4 first-class stamps.

Nonfiction: History, biography, illustrated books, humor, cookbook, juvenile (ages 9-14), reference, textbook. Subjects are limited to history, culture and cuisine of the Southeast and especially South Carolina. "We are looking for manuscripts that reveal under-appreciated or undiscovered facets of the rich heritage of our region. If a manuscript doesn't deal with South Carolina or the Southeast, the work is probably not appropriate for us. We don't do self-help books, children's books about divorce, kidnapping, etc., and absolutely no religious manuscripts." Query or submit outline and sample chapters "if you're not sure it's what we're looking for, otherwise complete ms." *Writer's Market* recommends query with SASE first. Reviews artwork/photos as part of ms package.

Recent Nonfiction Title(s): *The Man Who Loved the Flag*; *South Carolina a Day at a Time*.

Fiction: "We do not need fiction submissions at present, and will not consider any horror, romance or religious fiction." Query or submit outline/synopsis and sample chapters. "Submit books dealing with regional nature, science and outdoor subjects on South Carolina."

Tips: "Our readers are South Carolinians, visitors to the region's tourist spots, and out-of-state friends and family. We want to be a leading regional publisher for South Carolina. We are looking for more history and biography."

‡SANTA MONICA PRESS, P.O. Box 1076, Santa Monica CA 90406. **Acquisitions:** Jeffrey Goldman, president. "Santa Monica Press Publishes two lines of books: general how-to books written in simple, easy-to-understand terms; and books which explore sports and arts and entertainment from an offbeat perspective." Publishes trade paperback originals. Publishes 6-10 titles/year. Receives 50-100 queries and mss/year. 75% of books from first-time authors; 100% from unagented writers. Pays 6-12% royalty on wholesale price. Offers $500-2,500 advance. Publishes book 6-12 months after acceptance of ms. Accepts simultaneous submissions. Reports in 2 months on proposals. Book catalog and ms guidelines for #10 SASE.

Nonfiction: Gift book, how-to, illustrated book reference. Subjects include Americana, health/medicine, music/dance, sports, theater, film, general how-to. Submit proposal package, including outline, 2-3 sample chapters, biography, marketing potential of book with SASE. All unsolicited mss returned unopened. Reviews artwork/photos as part of the ms package. Send photocopies.

Recent Nonfiction Title(s): *Offbeat Museums*, by Saul Rubin (illustrated); *Health Care Handbook*, by Mark Cromer (how-to); *Letter Writing Made Easy!*, by Margaret McCarthy (how-to).

Tips: "Our how-to books are for the masses; we don't write down to our readers, but information is presented in simple, easy-to-understand terms. Our off-beat books are written for intelligent readers with a wicked sense of humor."

SAS INSTITUTE INC., SAS Campus Dr., Cary NC 27513-2414. (919)677-8000. Fax: (919)677-4444. E-mail: sasbbu @unx.sas.com. Website: http://www.sas.com. **Acquisitions:** David D. Baggett, editor-in-chief. Estab. 1976. "Our readers are SAS software users, both new and experienced." Publishes hardcover and trade paperback originals. Publishes 40 titles/year. Receives 10 submissions/year. 50% of books from first-time authors; 100% from unagented writers. Payment negotiable. Offers negotiable advance. Reports in 2 weeks on queries. *Writer's Market* recommends allowing 2 months for reply. Book catalog and ms guidelines free.

Nonfiction: Software, technical, textbook, statistics. "SAS Institute's Publications Division publishes books developed and written inhouse. Through the Books by Users program, we also publish books by SAS users on a variety of topics relating to SAS software. We want to provide our users with additional titles to supplement our primary documentation and to enhance the users' ability to use the SAS System effectively. We're interested in publishing manuscripts that describe or illustrate using any of SAS Institute's software products. Books must be aimed at SAS software users, either new or experienced. Tutorials are particularly attractive, as are descriptions of user-written applications for solving real-life business, industry or academic problems. Books on programming techniques using the SAS language are also desirable. Manuscripts must reflect current or upcoming software releases, and the author's writing should indicate an understanding of the SAS System and the technical aspects covered in the manuscript." Query. Submit outline/synopsis and sample chapters. Reviews artwork/photos as part of ms package.

Recent Nonfiction Title(s): *The Little SAS Book: A Primer*, by Lora D. Delwiche and Susan J. Slaughter (computer software guide); *SAS Macro Language* (reference); *Getting Started with the SAS System in the CMS Environment*, version 6 (software guide).

Tips: "If I were a writer trying to market a book today, I would concentrate on developing a manuscript that teaches or illustrates a specific concept or application that SAS software users will find beneficial in their own environments or can adapt to their own needs."

SASQUATCH BOOKS, 615 Second Ave., Suite 260, Seattle WA 98104. (206)467-4300. Fax: (206)467-4301. E-mail: books@sasquatchbooks.com. **Acquisitions:** Gary Luke, editorial director; Kate Rogers, editor (travel, children's books). Estab. 1986. Sasquatch Books publishes children's picture books and adult nonfiction from the Northwest, specializing in travel, cooking, gardening, history and nature. Publishes regional hardcover and trade paperback originals. Publishes 30-40 titles/year. 20% of books from first-time authors; 85% from unagented writers. Pays authors royalty on cover price. Offers wide range of advances. Publishes ms 6 months after acceptance. Reports in 3 months. Book catalog for 9×12 SAE with 2 first-class stamps.

Nonfiction: Subjects include regional art/architecture, children's books, cooking, foods, gardening, history, nature/environment, recreation, sports, travel and outdoors. "We are seeking quality nonfiction works about the Pacific Northwest and West Coast regions (including Alaska to California). In this sense we are a regional publisher, but we do distribute our books nationally." Query first, then submit outline and sample chapters.

Recent Nonfiction Title(s): *Home Field*, edited by John Douglas Marshall; *Cascadia*, by Ann Lovejoy, photographs by Sandra Lee Reha (gardening); *Seattle Sidewalk: The Restaurant Finder*.

Tips: "We sell books through a range of channels in addition to the book trade. Our primary audience consists of active, literate residents of the West Coast."

SCARECROW PRESS, INC., Division of University Press of America, 4720 Boston Way, Lanham MD 20706. (301)459-3366. Fax: (301)459-2118. Website: http://www.scarecrowpress.com. **Acquisitions:** Shirley Lambert, editorial director; Amanda Irwin, assistant editor. Estab. 1950. "We consider any scholarly title likely to appeal to libraries. Emphasis is on reference material." Scarecrow Press publishes several series: The Historical Dictionary series, which includes countries, religious, international organizations; and Composers of North America. Publishes hardcover originals. Publishes 165 titles/year. Receives 600-700 submissions/year. 70% of books from first-time authors; 99% from unagented writers. Average print order for a first book is 1,000. Pays 10% royalty on net of first 1,000 copies; 15% of net price thereafter. 15% initial royalty on camera-ready copy. Offers no advance. Publishes book 18 months after receipt of ms. Reports in 2 months. Book catalog for 9×12 SAE and 4 first-class stamps.

Nonfiction: Reference books and meticulously prepared annotated bibliographies, indices and books on women's studies, ethnic studies, music, movies, stage. library and information science, parapsychology, fine arts and handicrafts, social sciences, religion, sports, literature and language. Query. Occasionally reviews artwork/photos.

Recent Nonfiction Title(s): *The Jules Verne Encyclopedia*, by Brian Taves and Stephen Mizhaluk, Jr.; *Baseball's Biggest Blunder: The Bonus Rule of 1953-1957*, by Brent Kelley.

‡SCHIFFER PUBLISHING LTD., 4880 Lower Valley Rd., Atglen PA 19310. (610)593-1777. Fax: (610)593-2002. **Acquisitions:** Peter Schiffer, president. Estab. 1972. "We want books on collecting, hobby carving, military, architecture, aeronautic history and natural history." Publishes hardcover and trade paperback originals and reprints. Firm averages 170 titles/year; imprint averages 2 titles/year. Receives 1,000 submissions/year. 90% of books from first-time authors;

95% from unagented writers. Pays royalty on wholesale price. Publishes book 1 year after acceptance. Reports in 1 month. Book catalog free.

Imprint(s): Whitford Press.

Nonfiction: Coffee table book, how-to, illustrated book, reference, textbook. Subjects include Americana, art/architecture, aviation, history, hobbies, military/war, regional. Query or submit outline and sample chapters with SASE. Reviews artwork/photos as part of ms package.

SCHIRMER BOOKS, Imprint of Simon & Schuster, 1633 Broadway, New York NY 10019-6785. (212)654-8464. Fax: (212)654-4745. **Acquisitions:** Richard Carlin, executive editor; Jonathan Wiener, editor. Schirmer publishes scholarly and reference books on the performing arts. Publishes hardcover and paperback originals, related CDs, CD-ROMs, audiocassettes. Publishes 50 books/year. Receives 250 submissions/year. 25% of books from first-time authors; 75% of books from unagented writers. Submit photos and/or illustrations only "if central to the book, not if decorative or tangential." Publishes book 1 year after acceptance. Reports in 4 months. Book catalog and ms guidelines for SASE.

● Schirmer Books reports more interest in popular music, including rock and jazz.

Nonfiction: Publishes college texts, biographies, scholarly, reference, and trade on the performing arts specializing in music, film and theatre. Submit outline/synopsis, sample chapters and current vita. Reviews artwork/photos.

Recent Nonfiction Title(s): *Richard Thompson: The Biography*, by Patrick Humphries; *The Master Musicians* series; *Billboard's American Rock and Roll in Review*, by Jay Warner.

Tips: "The writer has the best chance of selling our firm a music book with a clearly defined, reachable audience, either scholarly or trade. Must be an exceptionally well-written work of original scholarship prepared by an expert who has a thorough understanding of correct manuscript style and attention to detail (see the *Chicago Manual of Style*)."

‡**SCHOCKEN**, Imprint of Knopf Publishing Group, Division of Random House, 201 E. 50th St., New York NY 10020. (212)751-2600. Website: http://www.randomhouse.com/knopf. **Acquisitions:** Arthur Samuelson, editorial director. Estab. 1933. "Schocken publishes a broad nonfiction list of serious, solid books with commercial appeal, as well as reprints of classics." Publishes hardcover originals and reprints, trade paperback originals and reprints. Publishes 24 titles/year. A small percentage of books are from first-time writers; small percentage from unagented writers. Pays royalty on net price. Advance varies. Accepts simultaneous submissions. Book catalog free.

Nonfiction: Subjects include education, ethnic, government/politics, health/medicine, history, Judaica, nature/environment, philosophy, religion, women's issues/studies. Submit proposal package, including "whatever is necessary to make the case for your book."

Recent Nonfiction Title(s): *Madame Blavatsky's Baboon*, by Peter Washington (spiritualism); *Choosing a Jewish Life*, by Anita Diamant (religion); *The Five Books of Moses: The Schocken Bible, Vol. 1*, translation and commentary by Everett Fox.

Fiction: Reprints classics.

SCHOLASTIC INC., 555 Broadway, New York NY 10012. (212)343-6100. Scholastic Inc. Editorial Director: Craig Walker. Estab. 1920. Publishes trade paperback originals for children ages 4-young adult. "We are proud of the many fine, innovative materials we have created—such as classroom magazines, book clubs, book fairs, and our new literacy and technology programs. But we are most proud of our reputation as 'The Most Trusted Name in Learning.' " Publishes juvenile hardcover picture books, novels and nonfiction. All divisions: Pays advance and royalty on retail price. Reports in 6 months. Manuscript guidelines for #10 SASE.

Imprint(s): Blue Sky Press, Cartwheel Books, Arthur Levine Books, Mariposa, Scholastic Press, Scholastic Professional Books.

Nonfiction: Publishes nonfiction for children ages 4 to teen. Query.

Recent Nonfiction Title(s): *The Great Fire*, by Jim Murphy (Newbery Medal Book).

Fiction: Hardcover—open to all subjects suitable for children. Paperback—family stories, mysteries, school, friendships for ages 8-12, 35,000 words. YA fiction, romance, family and mystery for ages 12-15, 40,000-45,000 words for average to good readers. Queries welcome; unsolicited manuscripts discouraged.

Recent Fiction Title(s): *Her Stories: African American Folktales, Fairy Tales and True Tales*, by Virginia Hamilton, illustrated by Leo and Diane Dillon.

Tips: New writers for children should study the children's book field before submitting.

‡**SCHOLASTIC PRESS**, Imprint of Scholastic Inc., 555 Broadway, New York NY 10012. (212)343-6100. Website: http://www.scholastic.com. **Acquisitions:** Brenda Bowen, editor. Scholastic Press publishes a range of picture books, middle grade and young adult novels. Publishes hardcover originals. Publishes 60 titles/year. Receives 2,500 queries/year. 5% of books from first-time authors. Pays royalty on retail price. Royalty and advance vary. Publishes book 18 months after acceptance of ms. Reports in 6 months on queries.

● Scholastic Press accepts agented submissions only.

Nonfiction: Children's/juvenile, general interest. Agented submissions only.

Recent Nonfiction Title(s): *The Great Fire*, by Jim Murphy (history).

Fiction: Juvenile, picture books. Agented submissions only.

Recent Fiction Title(s): *Slam*, by Walter Dean Myers.

SCHOLASTIC PROFESSIONAL BOOKS, Division of Scholastic, Inc., 411 Lafayette, New York NY 10003. Publishing Director: Claudia Cohl. Editor-in-Chief: Terry Cooper. **Acquisitions**: Shawn Richardson, assistant managing editor. Publishes 45-50 books/year. "Writer should have background working in the classroom with elementary or middle school children teaching pre-service students and developing quality, appropriate, and innovative learning experiences and/or solid background in developing supplementary educational materials for these markets." Offers standard contract. Reports in 2 months. Book catalog for 9 × 12 SAE.

Nonfiction: Elementary and middle-school level enrichment—all subject areas, whole language, theme units, integrated materials, writing process, management techniques, teaching strategies based on personal/professional experience in the classroom. Production is limited to printed matter: resource and activity books, professional development materials, reference titles. Length: 6,000-12,000 words. Query with table of contents, outline and sample chapter.

‡**SCRIBNER**, Unit of Simon & Schuster, 1230 Avenue of the Americas, New York NY 10020. (212)698-7000. **Acquisitions:** Jillian Blake, associate editor. Publishes hardcover originals. Publishes 70-75 titles/year. Receives thousands of queries/year. 20% of books from first-time authors; 10% from unagented writers. Pays 7½-12½% royalty on wholesale price. Advance varies. Publishes book 9 months after acceptance of ms. Accepts simultaneous submissions. Reports in 3 months on queries.

Imprint(s): Rawson Associates (contact Eleanor Rawson); **Lisa Drew Books** (contact Lisa Drew); Scribner Classics (reprints only); Scribner Poetry (by invitation only).
  ● Scribner accepts agented submissions only.

Nonfiction: Subjects include education, ethnic, gay/lesbian, health/medicine, history, language/literature, nature/environment, philosophy, psychology, religion, science, biography, criticism. Agented submissions only.

Recent Nonfiction Title(s): *Angela's Ashes*, by Frank McCourt (memoir, National Book Award winner).
  ● *Angela's Ashes* was awarded a Pulitzer Prize.

Fiction: Literary, mystery, suspense. Agented submissions only.

Recent Fiction Title(s): *Accordion Crimes*, by E. Annie Proulx (novel, Pulitzer Prize winning author); *Underworld*, by Don Delillo; *Go Now*, by Richard Hell (novel).

Poetry: Publishes few titles; by invitation only.

‡**SEAL PRESS**, 3131 Western Ave., Suite 410, Seattle WA 98121. E-mail: sealpress@sealpress.seanet.com. Website: http://www.sealpress.com. **Acquisitions:** Faith Conlon, editor and publisher. "We publish original, lively, radical, empowering and culturally diverse nonfiction by women addressing contemporary issues from a feminist perspective or speak positive to the experience of being female." Publishes hardcover and trade paperback originals. Publishes 14 titles/year. Receives 500 queries and 250 mss/year. 25% of books from first-time authors; 80% from unagented writers. Pays 6-10% royalty on retail price. Offers $500-1,000 advance. Publishes book 18 months after acceptance of ms. Accepts simultaneous submissions. Reports in 2 months on queries. Book catalog and ms guidelines free.

Imprint(s): Adventura Books.

Nonfiction: Self-help, literary nonfiction essays. Subjects include child guidance/parenting, ethnic, gay/lesbian, health/medicine, nature/outdoor writing, travel, women's issues/studies, popular culture. "We are not accepting fiction and do not publish poetry." Query with SASE. Reviews artwork/photos as part of ms package. Send photocopies.

Recent Nonfiction Title(s): *Listen Up: Voices from the Next Feminist Generation*, edited by Barbara Findlen (anthology); *Solo: On Her Own Adventure*, edited by Susan Fox Rogers (anthology).

Fiction: Ethnic, feminist, gay/lesbian, literary. "We are interested in alternative voices that aren't often heard from." Query with synopsis and SASE.

Recent Fiction Title(s): *Where the Oceans Meet*, by Bhargavi Mandava; *Nowle's Passing*, by Edith Forbes.

Tips: "Our audience is generally composed of women interested in reading about contemporary issues addressed from a feminist perspective."

SEASIDE PRESS, Imprint of Wordware Publishing, Inc., 1506 Capitol Ave., Plano TX 75074. (972)423-0090. Fax: (972)881-9147. E-mail: sales@wordware.com. Website: www.wordware.com. President: Russell A. Stultz. **Acquisitions:** Mary Goldman, managing editor. "Seaside Press publishes in the areas of travel, travel/history, pet care, humor and general interest." Publishes trade paperback originals and reprints and mass market paperback originals. Publishes 50-70 titles/year. Receives 50-60 queries and 10-15 mss/year. 40% of books from first-time authors; 95% from unagented writers. Pays 8-12% royalty on wholesale price. Publishes book 9 months after acceptance of ms. Accepts simultaneous submissions. Reports in 2 months. Book catalog and ms guidelines with SASE.

Nonfiction: How-to, pet care, humor. Subjects include travel/history (Cities Uncovered series). Submit proposal package, including table of contents, 2 sample chapters, target audience summation, competing products.

Recent Nonfiction Title(s): *Jackson Hole Uncovered*, by Sierra Sterling Adare (travel/history); *San Francisco Uncovered*, by Larenda Roberts (travel/history); *Your Kitten's First Year*, by Shawn Messonnier (pet care).

Tips: "We are not currently taking submissions for children's books."

‡**SEAWORTHY PUBLICATIONS, INC.**, 17125-C W. Blue Mound Rd., Brookfield WI 53005. (414)646-3966. **Acquisitions:** Joseph F. Janson, publisher. "Seaworthy Publications is a nautical book publisher that primarily publishes books of interest to serious bluewater sailors and boaters." Publishes trade paperback originals and reprints. Publishes 6 titles/year. Receives 60 queries and 20 mss/year. 60% of books from first-time authors; 100% from unagented writers. Pays 15% royalty on wholesale price. Offers $1,000 advance. Publishes book 6 months after acceptance of ms. Reports in 1 month. *Writer's Market* recommends allowing 2 months for reply. Book catalog and ms guidelines for #10 SASE.

Nonfiction: Cookbook, illustrated book, reference, technical—all dealing with boating. Subjects include cooking/foods/

nutrition, nautical history, hobbies of sailing and boating, regional boating guide books, sport sail racing, world travel. Query with 3 sample chapters and SASE. Reviews artwork/photos. Send photocopies or color prints.
Recent Nonfiction Title(s): *The Panama Guide*, by Nancy Schwalbe Zydler and Tom Zydler (regional cruising guide); *Meatless Galley Cookbook*, by Anne Carlson (boaters' cookbook).
Fiction: Nautical adventure, historical. "Our focus is clearly nonfiction. However, we will consider high quality fiction with a nautical theme." Query with 3 sample chapters and SASE.
Poetry: "Our focus is clearly nonfiction. However, we will consider high quality poetry with a nautical theme." Query with 5 sample poems and SASE.
Tips: "Our audience is sailors, boaters, and those with an interest in the sea, sailing or long distance cruising and racing."

‡**SEEDLING PUBLICATIONS, INC.**, 4079 Overlook Dr. E, Columbus OH 43214-2931. Phone/fax: (614)451-2412 or (614)792-0796. E-mail: sales@seedlingpub.com. Website: http://www.seedlingpub.com. **Acquisitions:** Josie Stewart, vice president. Seedling publishes books for young children to "keep young readers growing." Publishes trade paperback originals. Publishes 8-10 titles/year. Receives 10 queries and 200 mss/year. 80% of books from first-time authors; 100% from unagented writers. Pays 5% royalty or makes outright purchase of $150-300. Publishes book 1 year after of acceptance of ms. Accepts simultaneous submissions. Reports in 4-6 months. Book catalog for #10 SAE and 2 first-class stamps. Manuscript guidelines for #10 SASE.
Nonfiction: Children's/juvenile. Subjects include animals. Submit outline with SASE. Reviews artwork/photos as part of ms package. Send photocopies.
Recent Nonfiction Title(s): *Free to Fly*, by Kathleen Gibson (nonfiction in a story setting).
Fiction: Juvenile. Submit outline with SASE. Reviews artwork/photos as part of ms package. Send photocopies.
Recent Fiction Title(s): *Howie Has a Stomachache*, by Johnny Ray Moore (a pig with a stomachache); *Play Ball, Sherman*, by Betty Erickson; *Dinosaurs Galore*, by Audrey Eaton and Jane Kennedy.
Tips: "Follow our guidelines. Do not submit full-length picture books or chapter books. Our books are for children, ages 5-7, who are just beginning to read independently. Try a manuscript with young readers. Listen for spots in the text that don't flow. Rewrite until the text sounds natural to beginning readers."

SERENDIPITY SYSTEMS, P.O. Box 140, San Simeon CA 93452. (805)927-5259. E-mail: bookware@thegrid.net. Website: http://www.thegrid.net/bookware/bookware.htm. **Acquisitions:** John Galuszka, publisher. "Since 1986 Serendipity Systems has promoted and supported electronic publishing with electronic books for IBM-PC compatible computers." Publishes 6-12 titles/year; each imprint publishes 0-6 titles/year. Receives 600 queries and 150 mss/year. 95% of books from unagented writers. Pays 25-33% royalty on wholesale price or on retail price, "depending on how the book goes out." Publishes book 2 months after acceptance of ms. Accepts simultaneous submissions. Electronic submissions required. Queries by e-mail; mss, summaries with sample chapters and long documents should be sent by postal mail. Reports in 1 month on mss. *Writer's Market* recommends allowing 2 months for reply. Book catalog available online. Manuscript guidelines for #10 SASE, or on the Internet.
Imprint(s): Books-on-Disks™, Bookware™.
Nonfiction: "We only publish reference books on literature, writing and electronic publishing." Submit entire ms on disk in ASCII or HTML files. Query first.
Recent Nonfiction Title(s): *Diskbook—An Introduction to Electronic Publishing for Writers*, by J. Galuszka (reference); *The Electronic Publishing Forum*.
Fiction: "We want to see *only* works which use (or have a high potential to use) hypertext, multimedia, interactivity or other computer-enhanced features. No romance, religious, occult, New Age, fantasy, or children's mss. Submit entire ms on disk in ASCII files (unless author has already added hypertext, HTML, etc.) Query first.
Recent Fiction Title(s): *Say Goodbye to Midnight*, by C.J. Newton (mystery); *Side Show*, by Marian Allen.

SERGEANT KIRKLAND'S PRESS, Imprint of Sergeant Kirkland's Museum and Historical Society, Inc., 912 Lafayette Blvd., Fredericksburg VA 22401-5617. (540)899-5565. Fax: (540)899-7643. E-mail: civil-war@msn.com. **Acquisitions:** Pia S. Seagrave, Ph.D., editor. Sergeant Kirkland's Press publishes works on America, especially Civil War-related books. Publishes hardcover originals and reprints. Publishes 12-14 titles/year. Receives 30 queries and 25 mss/year. 60% of books from first-time authors; 100% from unagented writers. Pays 10% royalty on wholesale price. Publishes book 3 months after acceptance. Accepts simultaneous submissions. Reports in 1 month. *Writer's Market* recommends allowing 2 months for reply. Book catalog and ms guidelines free.
Nonfiction: Subjects include Americana, archaeology, history, military/war (American Civil War). Mistake writers most often make is not including biography, index, footnotes and table of contents. Query with outline and 2-3 sample chapters. Reviews artwork as part of ms package. Send photocopies.
Recent Nonfiction Title(s): *Unusual Persons of The Civil War*, by Dr. Webb Garrison; *The History of The Irish Brigade*, edited by Pis S. Seagrave (Irish-American history); *A Boy Lieutenant: 30th U.S. Colored Troops*, by Freeman S. Bowley (African-American history).
Recent Fiction Title(s): *Stonewall Jackson at Gettysburg*, by Douglas Lee Gibboney (historical fiction)
Recent Poetry Title(s): *Plantation Songs*, introduction by Barbara Hardaway, Ph.D. (African-American folklore).

SERVANT PUBLICATIONS, P.O. Box 8617, Ann Arbor MI 48107. (313)677-6490. **Acquisitions:** Anne Bannan. Estab. 1972. "Servant is a communications company whose materials spread the Gospel of Jesus Christ, help Christians live in accordance with that Gospel, promote renewal in the church and bear witness to Christian unity." Publishes hardcover, trade and mass market paperback originals and trade paperback reprints. Publishes 50 titles/year. 5% of books from first-time authors; 90% from unagented writers. Offers standard royalty contract. Publishes book 1 year after acceptance. Reports in 2 months. Book catalog for 9 × 12 SASE.

Imprint(s): Vine Books (for evanglical Protestant readers); Charis Books (for Roman Catholic readers).

Nonfiction: "We're looking for practical Christian teaching, devotionals, scripture, current problems facing the Christian church, and inspiration." No heterodox or non-Christian approaches. Submit query letter only. All unsolicited mss returned unopened.

Recent Nonfiction Title(s): *Tea with Patsy Clairmont*; *Celebrate 2000!*, by Pope John Paul II (reflections of the Trinity); *God Thinks You're Positively Awesome*, by Andrea Stephens (teenage guide to inner beauty).

Fiction: Accepts unsolicited queries only, from published authors or their agents. All unsolicited mss returned unopened.

Recent Fiction Title(s): *Copper Hill*, by Stephen and Janet Bly; *To Heal the Heart's Eye*, by Patricia Harrison Easton; *The President's Mother*, by Gloria Whelan.

SEVEN STORIES PRESS, 632 Broadway, 7th Floor, New York NY 10012. (212)995-0908. **Acquisitions:** Daniel Simon. Seven Stories Press publishes general, contemporary fiction and nonfiction for a well-educated, progressive, mainstream audience. Publishes hardcover and trade paperback originals. Publishes 15 titles/year. 15% of books from first-time authors; 15% from unagented writers. Pays 7-15% royalty on retail price. Publishes book 1-3 years after acceptance. Accepts simultaneous submissions. Reports in 3 months. Book catalog and ms guidelines free.

Nonfiction: Biography. Subjects include general nonfiction. Query only. *No unsolicited ms.*

Recent Nonfiction Title(s): *Harnessing Anger: The Way of an American Fencer*, by Peter Westbrook with Tej Hazarika; *The More You Watch, The Less You Know*, by Danny Schechter (media studies); *Interview*, by Claudia Dreifus (journalism).

Fiction: Contemporary. Query only.

Recent Fiction Title(s): *Parable of the Sower*, by Octavia E. Butler (feminist fiction); *I Who Have Never Known Men*, by Jacqueline Harpman (translation).

Tips: Audience is well-educated, progressive and mainstream.

HAROLD SHAW PUBLISHERS, 388 Gundersen Dr., P.O. Box 567, Wheaton IL 60189. (630)665-6700. **Acquisitions:** Joan Guest, editorial director. Bible Study Editor: Mary Horner Collins. Literary Editor: Lil Copan. Estab. 1967. "We publish a wide range (full circle) of books from a Christian perspective for use by a broad range of readers." Publishes mostly trade paperback originals and reprints. Publishes 40 titles/year. Receives 1,000 submissions/year. 10-20% of books from first-time authors; 90% from unagented writers. Offers 5-10% royalty on retail price. Offers $500-1,000 advance. Makes outright purchase of $375-2,500 for Bible studies and compilations. Publishes book 18 months after acceptance. Reports in 6 months. Guidelines for #10 SASE. Catalog for 9 × 12 SAE with 5 first-class stamps.

● Harold Shaw has published such authors as James I. Packer, Calvin Miller and Lloyd Ogilvie.

Nonfiction: Subjects include marriage, family and parenting, self-help, mental health, spiritual growth, Bible study and literary topics. "We are looking for adult general nonfiction with different twists—self-help manuscripts with fresh insight and colorful, vibrant writing style. No autobiographies or biographies accepted. Must have a Christian perspective for us even to review the manuscript." Query.

Recent Nonfiction Title(s): *Mothers & Daughters*, by Madeleine L'Engle and Maria Rooney; *Child Sexual Abuse*, by Maxine Hanson and Karen Mains (self-help).

Recent Fiction Title(s): *The Tower, The Mask & The Grove*, by Betty Smartt Carter (mystery).

Recent Poetry Title(s): *Winter Song: Christmas Readings*, by Madeleine L'Engle and Luci Shaw.

Tips: "Get an editor who is not a friend or a spouse who will tell you honestly whether your book is marketable. It will save a lot of your time and money and effort. Then do an honest evaluation. Who would read the book other than yourself? If it won't sell 5,000 copies, it's not very marketable and most publishers wouldn't be interested."

SIBYL PUBLICATIONS, INC., 1007 SW Westwood Dr., Portland OR 97201. (503)293-8391. Fax: (503)293-8941. **Acquisitions:** Miriam Selby, publisher. "We publish positive nonfiction books by and about women." Publishes trade paperback originals. Publishes 4-6 titles/year. 75% of books from first-time authors; 100% from unagented writers. Pays 10-15% royalty on wholesale price. Publishes book 9 months after acceptance of ms. Accepts simultaneous submissions. Reports in 1 month on queries, 2 months on proposals and mss. Book catalog and ms guidelines for #10 SASE.

Nonfiction: Biography, gift book, self-help, textbook, book and card set. Subjects include psychology, women's issues/studies, women's spirituality. Query with outline, 3 sample chapters and SASE.

Recent Nonfiction Title(s): *Sacred Myths: Stories of World Religions*, by Marilyn McFarlane; *Inventing Ourselves Again: Women Face Middle Age*, by Janis Chan.

Fiction: *Journey in the Middle of the Road*, by Muriel Murch (midlife issues).

Tips: Audience is women in midlife, ages 36-60, who are interested in spirituality, mythology, psychology, women's studies, women's issues. "Make your writing unique and compelling. Give the reader a reason to buy your book; something new, different, better. Create characters who are positive women who can be role models."

THE SIDRAN PRESS, Imprint of The Sidran Foundation, 2328 W. Joppa Rd., Suite 15, Lutherville MD 21093. (410)825-8888. Fax: (410)337-0747. E-mail: sidran@access.digex.net. Website: http://www.access.digex.net/~sidran. **Acquisitions:** Esther Giller, president. "Sidran Press is a nonprofit organization devoted to advocacy, education and research in support of people with psychiatric disabilities." Publishes hardcover originals and trade paperback originals and reprints. Publishes 5-6 titles/year. Receives 75 queries and 40 mss/year. 20% of books from first-time authors; 95% from unagented writers. Pays 8-10% royalty on wholesale price. Publishes book 1 year after acceptance of ms. No simultaneous submissions. Reports in 1 month on queries, 3 months on proposals, 6 months on mss. Book catalog and ms guidelines free.

Nonfiction: Reference, self-help, textbook, professional. Subjects include psychiatry, expressive therapies, psychology. Specializes in trauma/abuse/domestic violence and mental health issues. Query with proposal package including outline, 2-3 sample chapters, introduction, competing titles, market information.

Recent Nonfiction Title(s): *Vietnam Wives*, by Matsakis (self-help, psychology); *Trauma Research Methodology*, edited by Eve Bernstein Carlson, Ph.D.

SIERRA CLUB BOOKS, Dept. WM, 85 Second, San Francisco CA 94105. (415)977-5500. Fax: (415)977-5793. **Acquisitions:** James Cohee, senior editor. Estab. 1962. "The Sierra Club was founded to help people to explore, enjoy and preserve the nation's forests, waters, wildlife and wilderness. The books program looks to publish quality trade books about the outdoors and the protection of natural resources." Publishes hardcover and paperback originals and reprints. Publishes 20 titles/year. Receives 1,000 submissions/year. 50% of books from unagented writers. Pays 7½-15% royalty. Offers $3,000-15,000 average advance. Publishes book 18 months after acceptance. Reports in 2 months. Book catalog free.

Imprint(s): Sierra Club Books for Children.

Nonfiction: A broad range of environmental subjects: outdoor adventure, descriptive and how-to, women in the outdoors; landscape and wildlife pictorials; literature, including travel and works on the spiritual aspects of the natural world; travel and trail guides; natural history and current environmental issues, including public health and uses of appropriate technology; gardening; general interest; and children's books. "Specifically, we are interested in literary natural history, environmental issues, conservation, politics, and juvenile books with an ecological theme." Does *not* want "proposals for large color photographic books without substantial text; how-to books on building things outdoors; books on motorized travel; or any but the most professional studies of animals." Query first, then submit outline and sample chapters. Reviews artwork/photos as part of ms package. Send photocopies.

Recent Nonfiction Title(s): *Adventure in Indonesia*, by Holly S. Smith (travel); *Bird Brains*, by Candace Savage (animals); *Still Wild, Always Wild*, by Ann Zwinger (nature).

Fiction: Adventure, historical, mainstream and ecological fiction. "We are not considering fiction at this time."

Recent Fiction Title(s): *The Condor Brings the Sun*.

Recent Poetry Title(s): *News of the Universe* (poetry anthology).

‡SIERRA CLUB BOOKS FOR CHILDREN, Imprint of Sierra Club Books, 85 Second St., San Francisco CA 94105. (415)977-5500. **Acquisitions:** Helen Sweetland, director. "Sierra Club Books for Children publishes books that offer responsible information about the environment to young readers, with attention to the poetry and magic in nature that so fascinated and inspired John Muir, the poet-philosopher who was the Sierra Club's founder." Publishes hardcover originals and trade paperback originals and reprints. Publishes 15 titles/year. Receives 100 queries/year. 2% of books from first-time authors; 10% from unagented writers. Pays 8-10% royalty on retail price. Advance varies. Publishes book an average of 2 years after acceptance of ms; works waiting for illustrators may take significantly longer. Reports in up to 1 year on queries. Book catalog for 9×12 SASE.

● Sierra Club Books for Children prefers agented submissions.

Nonfiction: Children's/juvenile. Subjects include nature/environment. Query. All unsolicited mss returned unopened.

Recent Nonfiction Title(s): *Squishy, Misty, Damp & Muddy: The In Between World of Wetlands*, by Molly Cone (science); *In the Heart of the Village: The World of the Indian Banyan Tree*, by Barbara Bash.

Fiction: Juvenile, nature/environment. Query. All unsolicited mss returned unopened.

Recent Fiction Title(s): *Desert Trip*, by Barbara A. Steiner; *The Empty Lot*, by Dale H. Fife; *The Snow Whale*, by Caroline Pitcher.

‡SIGNET, Imprint of Penguin Putnam Inc., 375 Huron St., New York NY 10014. (212)366-2000. **Acquisitions:** Michaela Hamilton, vice president, editor-in-chief. Publishes mass market paperback originals and reprints. Publishes 500 titles/year. Receives 20,000 queries and 10,000 mss/year. 30-40% of books from first-time authors; 5% from unagented writers. Advance and royalty negotiable. Publishes book 18 months after acceptance of ms. Accepts simultaneous submissions. Report in 6 months on queries and proposals.

● This publisher accepts agented submissions only.

Imprints: Menot, Onyx, **ROC**, Signet Classic, Topaz.

Nonfiction: Biography, how-to, reference, self-help. Subjects include animals, child guidance/parenting, cooking/foods/nutrition, ethnic, health/medicine, language/literature, military/war, money/finance, psychology, sports. "Looking for reference and annual books." Query with outline and 3 sample chapters.

Recent Nonfiction Title(s): *Leonard Maltin's Movie and Video Guide*, by Leonard Maltin; *Wiping Out Head Lice*, by Nickolas Bakalar (parenting); *Gloria Estefan*, by Anthony De Stefano (celebrity biography).

Fiction: Erotica, ethnic, fantasy, historical, horror, literary, mainstream/contemporary, mystery, occult, romance, science fiction, suspense, western. "Looking for writers who can deliver a book a year (or faster) of consistent quality. No unagented mss; agented submissions only."

Recent Fiction Title(s): *The Deep End of the Ocean*, by Jacqueline Mitchard; *The Green Mile*, by Stephen King.

SILHOUETTE BOOKS, 300 E. 42nd St., New York NY 10017. (212)682-6080. Fax: (212)682-4539. Website: http://www.romance.net. Editorial Director, Silhouette Books, Harlequin Historicals: Isabel Swift. **Acquisitions:** Melissa Senate, senior editor (Silhouette Romance); Tara Gavin, senior editor (Silhouette Special Editions); Lucia Macro, senior editor (Silhouette Desire); Leslie Wainger, senior editor and editorial coordinator (Silhouette Intimate Moments and Silhouette Yours Truly); Anne Canadeo, editor (Love Inspired); Tracy Farrell, senior editor (Harlequin Historicals). Estab. 1979. Silhouette publishes contemporary adult romances. Publishes mass market paperback originals. Publishes 350 titles/year. Receives 4,000 submissions/year. 10% of books from first-time authors; 50% from unagented writers. Pays royalty. Publishes book 3 years after acceptance. No unsolicited mss. Send query letter, 2 page synopsis and SASE to head of imprint. Manuscript guidelines for #10 SASE.
Imprint(s): Silhouette Romances (contemporary adult romances, 53,000-58,000 words, Melissa Senate, senior editor). Silhouette Special Editions (contemporary adult romances, 75,000-80,000 words, Tara Gavin, senior editor). Silhouette Desires (contemporary adult romances, 55,000-60,000 words, Lucia Macro, senior editor). Silhouette Intimate Moments (contemporary adult romances, 80,000-85,000 words) and Silhouette Yours Truly (contemporary adult romances with themes of meeting through written words, 53,000-58,000 words), Leslie Wainger, senior editor and editorial coordinator. Harlequin Historicals (adult historical romances, 95,000-105,000 words, Tracy Farrell, senior editor). Love Inspired (Christian romances, 75,000-80,000 words, Anne Canadeo, editor).
Fiction: Romance (contemporary and historical romance for adults). "We are interested in seeing submissions for all our lines. No manuscripts other than the types outlined. Manuscript should follow our general format, yet have an individuality and life of its own that will make it stand out in the readers' minds."
Recent Fiction Title(s): *Tallchief for Keeps*, by Cait London.
Tips: "The romance market is constantly changing, so when you read for research, read the latest books and those that have been recommended to you by people knowledgeable in the genre. We are actively seeking new authors for all our lines, contemporary and historical."

SILVER BURDETT PRESS, Imprint of Simon & Schuster, 255 Jefferson Rd, Parsippany NJ 07054. (201)739-8000. **Acquisitions:** David Vissoe, manager. "Silver Burdett Ginn is the nation's leading provider of textbooks and interactive multimedia for grades K through 6. These comprehensive offerings span the complete range of curricula, including core and supplementary materials that bring important classroom service to life." Publishes hardcover and paperback originals. Publishes 65-80 titles/year. No unsolicited mss. Publishes book 1 year after acceptance. Offers variable advance. Book catalog free.
Imprint(s): Julian Messner, Silver Press (preschool and primary fiction and nonfiction), **Crestwood House, Dillon Press,** New Discovery.
Nonfiction: Juvenile and young adult reference. Subjects include Americana, science, history, nature, and geography. "We're primarily interested in nonfiction on subjects which supplement the classroom curricula, but are graphically appealing and, in some instances, have commercial as well as institutional appeal." Query.
Recent Nonfiction Title(s): *In the Path of Lewis and Clark: Traveling the Missouri*, by Peter Lourie; *Seeing is Believing: Activities to Show You How People Think and See*, by Dr. Patrick Green (The Amazing Brain series); *Zenj, Buganda: East Africa*, by Kenny Mann (African Kingdoms of the Past series).
Recent Fiction Title(s): *Lost in Merlins Castle*, by P.J. Stray (Passport Mysteries Series).
Tips: "Our books are primarily bought by school and public librarians for use by students and young readers. Virtually all are nonfiction and done as part of a series."

SILVER PRESS, Imprint of Silver Burdett Press (Division of Simon & Schuster), 299 Jefferson Rd., Parsippany NJ 07054. **Acquisitions:** Dorothy Goeller, editor. Publishes hardcover originals. Publishes 20 titles/year. Pays 3-7½% royalty. Average advance $4,000. Publishes book 2-3 years after acceptance of ms. Accepts simultaneous submissions. Reports in 6 months on queries, 1 year on mss. Book catalog for 9×12 SASE with $2.60 postage.
   • Silver Press is not accepting any unsolicited submissions.
Nonfiction: Children's/juvenile K-3. Not accepting any unsolicited submissions. All unsolicited mss returned unopened.
Fiction: Picture books K-3. Not accepting any unsolicited submissions. All unsolicited mss returned unopened.

SIMON & SCHUSTER, 1230 Avenue of the Americas, New York NY 10020. *Education Division* imprints include: **Silver Burdett Ginn (Crestwood House, Dillon Press, Julian Messner, Silver Burdett Press, Silver Press), Prentice-Hall, Allyn & Bacon.** *Consumer Group Division* imprints include: Simon & Schuster Trade (Simon & Schuster, **Scribner [Lisa Drew, Rawson Associates, Scribner], The Free Press,** Touchstone, Fireside), Simon & Schuster Children's Publishing (Aladdin Paperbacks, Simon Spotlight [**Little Simon**], Rabbit Ears Book and Audio, **Simon & Schuster Books for Young Readers, Atheneum Books for Young Readers, Margaret K. McElderry Books**), Simon & Schuster New Media, **Pocket Books** (Star Trek, MTV Books, Washington Square Press, **Pocket Books for Young Adults [Archway Paperbacks, Minstrel Books, Pocket Books for Young Adults]**). *International and Business & Professional Division* imprints include: Bureau of Business Practice, **Jossey-Bass (Jossey-Bass, New Lexington, Jossey-Bass/Pfeiffer).** *Macmillan Publishing USA* imprints include: Macmillan Computer Publishing (Brady Games, Hayden Books, **Que Publishing, New Riders Publishing, Sams Publishing), Macmillan General Reference (Macmillan Books, Macmillan Travel, Macmillan Brands, Consumer Information Group, Howell Book House**).

‡SIMON & SCHUSTER BOOKS FOR YOUNG READERS, Imprint of Simon & Schuster Children's Publishing Division, 1230 Avenue of the Americas, New York NY 10020. (212)698-7200. Website: http://www.simonandschuster.c

om. Executive Editor: Virginia Duncan. Senior Editor: David Gale. **Acquisitions:** Acquisitions Editor. "We publish mainly for the bookstore market, and are looking for books that will appeal directly to kids." Publishes hardcover originals. Publishes 80-90 titles/year. Receives 2,500 queries and 10,000 mss/year. 5-10% of books from first-time authors; 40% from unagented writers. Pays 4-12% royalty on retail price. Advance varies. Publishes book 1-3 years after acceptance of ms. Accepts simultaneous submissions. Reports in 2 months on queries. Manuscript guidelines for #10 SASE.

Nonfiction: Children's/juvenile. Subjects include animals, ethnic, history, nature/environment. "We're looking for innovative, appealing nonfiction especially for younger readers. Please don't submit education or textbooks." Query only, include SASE. *All unsolicited mss returned unread.* Reviews artwork/photos as part of ms package; send photocopies or transparencies. "We're glad to look at artwork or photos but it isn't *necessary* to submit them with a manuscript."

Recent Nonfiction Title(s): *I Have Lived A Thousand Years*, by Livia-Bitton-Jackson (young adult); *Food Fight*, by Janet Bode (middle grade); *Funny Bones*, by Anita Ganeri (picture book).

Fiction: Fantasy, historical, humor, juvenile, mystery, picture books, science fiction, young adult. "Fiction needs to be fresh, unusual and compelling to stand out from the competition. We're not looking for problem novels, stories with a moral, or rhymed picture book texts." Query only, include SASE. All unsolicited mss returned unread.

Recent Fiction Title(s): *Rats Saw God*, by Rob Thomas (young adult); *Frindle*, by Andrew Clements (middle grade); *Ernestine and Amanda*, by Sandra Belton (middle grade).

Poetry: "Most of our poetry titles are anthologies; we publish very few stand-alone poets." No picture book ms in rhymed verse. Query.

Recent Poetry Title(s): *I Feel A Little Jumpy Around You*, by Naomi Shihab Nye (young adult); *Song and Dance*, by Lee Bennett Hopkins (picture book poetry).

Tips: "We're looking for fresh, original voices and unexplored topics. Don't do something because everyone else is doing it. Try to find what they're *not* doing."

SJL PUBLISHING COMPANY, P.O. Box 152, Hanna IN 46340. (219)324-9678. Publisher/Editor: Sandra J. Cassady. SJL publishes scientific fiction and nonfiction. Publishes hardcover and trade paperback originals. Publishes 8-10 titles/year. Receives 1,000 queries and 100 mss/year. 40% of books from first-time authors; 100% from unagented writers. Pays 10% royalty. Publishes book 1 year after acceptance of ms. Accepts simultaneous submissions. Reports in 1 month on queries and proposals, 2 months on mss. Manuscript guidelines for #10 SASE.

Nonfiction: Cookbook, children's/juvenile, reference, self-help, technical. Subjects include business/economics, computers/electronics, cooking/foods/nutrition, gardening, government/politics, science, sports. "Looking for good scientific publications." Query with synopsis and SASE. Reviews artwork/photos. Send photocopies.

Recent Nonfiction Title(s): *The World Before Man—In Search of the Circle*, by Wolf Brinsbury (science).

Fiction: Humor, juvenile, science fiction. Query with synopsis and SASE.

‡SKINNER HOUSE BOOKS, Imprint of The Unitarian Universalist Association, 25 Beacon St., Boston MA 02108. (617)742-2100, ext 601. Fax: (617)742-7025. E-mail: skinner_house@uua.org. Website: http://www.uua.org. **Acquisitions:** Kristen Holmstrand, assistant editor. Audience is Unitarian Universalists, ministers, lay leaders, religious educators, feminists, gay and lesbian activists and social activists. Publishes trade paperback originals and reprints. Publishes 8-10 titles/year. 50% of books from first-time authors; 100% from unagented writers. Pays 5-10% royalty on net sales. Offers $100 advance. Publishes book 1 year after acceptance of ms. Reports in 2 months on queries. Book catalog for 6×9 SAE with 3 first-class stamps. Manuscript guidelines for #10 SASE.

Nonfiction: Biography, children's/juvenile, self-help. Subjects include gay/lesbian, history, religion, women's issues/studies, inspirational. "We publish titles in Unitarian Universalist faith, history, biography, worship, and issues of social justice. We also publish a selected number of inspirational titles of poetic prose and at least one volume of meditations per year. Writers should know that Unitarian Universalism is a liberal religious denomination committed to progressive ideals." Query. Reviews artwork/photos as part of ms package. Send photocopies.

Recent Nonfiction Title(s): *This Very Moment*, by James Ishmael Ford (Zen Buddhism for Unitarian Universalists); *Alabaster Village*, by Christine Morgan (autobiography, Transylvania); *Green Mountain Spring*, by Gary Kowalski (meditation and inspiration).

Fiction: Juvenile. "The only fiction we publish is for children, usually in the form of parables or very short stories (500 words) on liberal religious principles or personal development. Fiction for adults is not accepted." Query.

Tips: "From outside our denomination, we are interested in manuscripts that will be of help or interest to liberal churches, Sunday School classes, ministers and volunteers. Inspirational/spiritual titles must reflect liberal Unitarian Universalist values."

SKY PUBLISHING CORP., P.O. Box 9111, Belmont MA 02178-9111. (617)864-7360. Fax: (617)864-6117. E-mail: postmaster@skypub.com. Website: http://www.skypub.com. President/Publisher: Richard Tresch Fienberg. **Acquisitions:** J. Kelley Beatty, senior editor; Carolyn Collins Petersen, editor, books and products; Sally MacGillivey, publications manager. Estab. 1941. "Sky Publishing Corporation will be an advocate of astronomy and space science through its products and services and will aggressively promote greater understanding of these disciplines among laypeople." Publishes 6 titles/year. Publishes hardcover and trade paperback originals on topics of interest to serious amateur astronomers as well as *Sky & Telescope: The Essential Magazine of Astronomy* and *Skywatch: Your Guide to Stargazing and Space Exploration*. Nonfiction only. Magazine articles: pays 20¢/word. Books: pays 10% royalty on net sales. Magazine author and book proposal guidelines available. Catalog free.

Recent Nonfiction Title(s): *Astrophotography*, by H.J.P. Arnold (observer's guide); *Summer Stargazing*, by Terence Dickson; *The Modern Amateur Astronomer*, edited by Patrick Moore.

‡**GIBBS SMITH, PUBLISHER**, P.O. Box 667, Layton UT 84041. (801)544-9800. Fax: (801)544-5582. Website: http://www.gibbs~smith.com. **Acquisitions:** Madge Baird, editorial director (humor, western, gardening); Gail Yngve, editor (fiction, interior decorating, poetry); Theresa Desmond, editor (children's); Paul VandenBerghe, editor (regional, sports). Estab. 1969. "We publish books that make a difference." Publishes hardcover and trade paperback originals. Publishes 50 titles/year. Receives 1,500-2,000 submissions/year. 5-10% of books from first-time authors; 50% from unagented writers. Pays 6-15% royalty on net receipts. Offers $2,000-3,000 advance. Publishes book 1-2 years after acceptance of ms. Accepts simultaneous submissions ("but let us know"). Reports in 1 month on queries, 2 months on proposals and mss. Book catalog for 9 × 12 SAE and $2.13 in postage. Manuscript guidelines free.
Imprint(s): Peregrine Smith Books.
Nonfiction: Children's/juvenile, illustrated book, textbook. Subjects include Americana, art/architecture, humor, interior design, nature/environment, regional. Query or submit outline, several completed sample chapters and author's C.V. Reviews artwork/photos as part of the ms package. Send sample illustrations if applicable.
Recent Nonfiction Title(s): *Rocky Mountain Home: Spirited Western Hideaways*, by Elizabeth Clair Flood, photographs by Peter Woloszynski; *The Beautiful Necessity: Decorating With Arts and Crafts*, by Bruce Smith and Yoshiko Yamamoto; *Headin' for the Sweet Heat: Fruit and Fire Spice Cooking*, by Jacqueline Landeen.
Fiction: Literary, mainstream/contemporary. "We publish fewer than 3 novels a year." Submit complete ms with sample illustration if applicable.
Recent Fiction Title(s): *I Know What You Do When I Go to School*, by Ann Edwards Cannon (juvenile); *You Don't Always Get What You Hope For*, by Rick Walton (juvenile).
Poetry: "Our annual poetry contest accepts entries only in April. Charges $15 fee. Prize: $500." Submit complete ms.
Recent Poetry Title(s): *How Late Desire Looks*, by Katrina Roberts.

THE SMITH, The Generalist Association, Inc., 69 Joralemon St., Brooklyn NY 11201-4003. (718)834-1212. **Acquisitions:** Harry Smith, publisher/editor; Michael McGrinder, associate editor. Estab. 1964. The Smith publishes literature of "outstanding artistic quality." Publishes hardcover and trade paperback originals. Publishes 3-5 titles/year. Receives 2,500 queries/year. 50% of books from first-time authors; more than 90% from unagented writers. Pays royalty. Offers $500-1,000 advance. Publishes book 9 months after acceptance. Accepts simultaneous submissions. Reports in 3 months. Book catalog and guidelines on request for SASE.
  ● The Smith has published such authors as James T. Farrell, Menke Katz and Alicia Ostriker.
Nonfiction: Literary essays, language and literature. "The 'how' is as important as the 'what' to us. Don't bother to send anything if the prose itself is not outstanding. We don't publish anything about how to fix your car or your soul." Query with outline and sample chapter. Reviews artwork/photos as part of ms package. Send photocopies.
Recent Nonfiction Title(s): *Crank Letters*, by Kirby Congdon (letters).
Fiction: Experimental, literary, short story collections. "Emphasis is always on artistic quality. A synopsis of almost any novel sounds stupid." Query with 1 sample chapter. Do not send complete ms. Irregular hours preclude acceptance of registered mail.
Recent Fiction Title(s): *Bodo*, by John Bennett (novel); *Blue Eden*, by Luke Salisbury (novellas); *A Visit to Pinky Ryder's*, by Marshall Brooks (humor/art).
Poetry: "No greeting card sentiments, no casual jottings." Do not send complete ms. Do not send registered mail. Submit 7-10 sample poems.
Recent Poetry Title(s): *Poems New & Selected*, by Lloyd Van Brunt; *Your Heart Will Fly Away*, by David Rigsbee; *Matriarch*, by Glenna Lucschel.

SOCIAL SCIENCE EDUCATION CONSORTIUM, P.O. Box 21270, Boulder CO 80308-4270. (303)492-8154. Fax: (303)449-3925. E-mail: singletl@ucsu.colorado.edu. **Acquisitions:** Laurel R. Singleton, managing editor. Estab. 1963. "The mission of the SSEC is threefold: (1) to provide leadership for social science education, (2) to promote a larger role for the social sciences in the curriculum, and (3) to close the gap between frontier thinking in the social sciences and the curriculum." Publishes trade paperback originals. Publishes 8 titles/year. 25% of books from first-time authors; 100% from unagented writers. Pays 8-12% royalty on net sales (retail price minus average discount). Publishes book 6 months after acceptance. Accepts simultaneous submissions. Reports in 1 month on proposals. *Writer's Market* recommends allowing 2 months for reply.
  ● Social Science Education Consortium has published such well-known authors in the field of social studies education as Murry Nelson, Lynn Parisi, Janet Vaillant and John Patrick.
Nonfiction: Teacher resources. Subjects include education, government/politics, history; must include teaching applications. "We publish titles of interest to social studies teachers particularly; we do not generally publish on such broad educational topics as discipline, unless there is a specific relationship to the social studies/social sciences." Submit outline and 1-2 sample chapters.
Recent Nonfiction Title(s): *Teaching About the History and Nature of Science and Technology*; *Service Learning in the Middle School Curriculum*, by Schukar et al.; *A New Look at the American West*, by Eastman & Miller.

SOHO PRESS, INC., 853 Broadway, New York NY 10003. (212)260-1900. **Acquisitions:** Juris Jurjevics, editor-in-chief. Estab. 1986. "Soho Press publishes discerning authors for discriminating readers." Publishes hardcover and trade paperback originals. Publishes 25 titles/year. Receives 5,000 submissions/year. 75% of books from first-time authors; 50% from unagented writers. Pays 7½-15% royalty on retail price. Offers advance. Publishes book within 1 year after acceptance. Accepts simultaneous submissions. Reports in 1 month. Book catalog for 6×9 SAE with 2 first-class stamps.

- Soho Press also publishes two book series: Hera (serious historical fiction) and Soho Crime (mysteries, noir, procedurals).

Nonfiction: Literary nonfiction: travel, autobiography, biography, etc. No self-help. Submit outline and sample chapters.
Recent Nonfiction Title(s): *A Woman in Amber: Healing the Trauma of War and Exile*, by Agate Nesaule (American Book Award Winner).
Fiction: Adventure, ethnic, feminist, historical, literary, mainstream/contemporary, mystery, suspense. Submit complete ms with SASE. *Writer's Market* recommends query with SASE first.
Recent Fiction Title(s): *Explanation for Chaos*, by Julie Schumacher (1995 Pen/Hemingway finalist); *The Gun Seller*, by Hugh Laurie.

SOUNDPRINTS, Division of Trudy Corporation, 165 Water St., Norwalk CT 06856. Fax: (203)844-1176. **Acquisitions**: Assistant Editor. "Soundprints takes you on an Odyssey of discovery, exploring an historical event or a moment in time that affects our every day lives. Each Odyssey is approved by a Smithsonian Institution curator, so readers experience the adventures as if they were really there." Publishes hardcover originals. Publishes 10-14 titles/year. Receives 200 queries/year. 20% of books from first-time authors; 90% of books from unagented writers. Makes outright purchase. No advance. Publishes book 2 years after acceptance. Accepts simultaneous submissions. Reports on queries in 3 months. Book catalog for 9×12 SAE with $1.05 postage. Manuscript guidelines for #10 SASE.

- This publisher creates multimedia sets for the Smithsonian Wild Heritage Collection, the Smithsonian Oceanic Collection and Smithsonian's Backyard. Sets include a book, read-a-long audiotape and realistic stuffed animal, combining facts about North American wildlife with stories about each animal's habits and habitats. They have received the Parent's Choice Award for 1993, 1994 and 1995.

Nonfiction: Children's/juvenile, animals. "We focus on North American wildlife and ecology. Subject animals must be portrayed realistically and must not be anthropomorphic. Meticulous research is required." Query with SASE. Does not review artwork/photos as part of ms package. (All books are now illustrated in full color.)
Recent Nonfiction Title(s): *Three River Junction*, by Saranne D. Burnham, illustrated by Tom Antonishak; *Undersea City*, by Dana Meachen Rau, illustrated by Katie Lee.
Fiction: Juvenile. "When we publish juvenile fiction, it will be about wildlife and all information in the book *must* be accurate." Query.
Tips: "Our books are written for children from ages 4-8. Our most successful authors can craft a wonderful story which is derived from authentic wildlife facts. First inquiry to us should ask about our interest in publishing a book about a specific animal or habitat. We launched a new series in fall of 1996. Stories are about historical events that are represented by exhibits in the Smithsonian Institution's museums."

SOURCEBOOKS, INC., P.O. Box 372, Naperville IL 60566. (630)961-3900. Fax: (630)961-2168. Publisher: Dominique Raccah. **Acquisitions:** Todd Stocke, editor; Mark Warden (Legal Survival Guides self-help/law series). Estab. 1987. "Our goal is to provide customers with terrific, innovative books at reasonable prices." Publishes hardcover and trade paperback originals. Publishes 50 titles/year. 50% of books from first-time authors; 75% from unagented writers. Pays 6-15% royalty on wholesale price. Publishes book 1 year after acceptance. Accepts simultaneous submissions. Reports in 3 months on queries. Book catalog and ms guidelines for 9×12 SASE.
Imprint(s): Casablanca Press Legal Survival Guides, Sphinx Publishing.
Nonfiction: *Small Business Sourcebooks:* books for small business owners, entrepreneurs and students. "A key to submitting books to us is to explain how your book helps the reader, why it is different from the books already out there (please do your homework) and the author's credentials for writing this book." *Sourcebooks Trade:* gift books, self-help, general business, and how to. "Books likely to succeed with us are self-help, art books, parenting and childcare, psychology, women's issues, how-to, house and home, gift books or books with strong artwork." Query or submit outline and 2-3 sample chapters (not the first). *No complete mss.* Reviews artwork/photos as part of ms package.
Recent Nonfiction Title(s): *The Complete Scholarship Book*, by Student Services (reference); *Vacations That Can Change Your Life*, by Ellen Lederman (travel); *The Essential Business Buyer's Guide* (business).

- Sourcebooks, Inc. has published such authors as Sheila Ellison, Joseph Mancuso and Gregory J.P. Godek.

Tips: "We love to develop books in new areas or develop strong titles in areas that are already well developed."

SOUTH END PRESS, 116 Saint Botolph St., Boston MA 02115. (617)266-0629. Fax: (617)266-1595. **Acquisitions:** Loie Hayes (feminist/gay/lesbian studies, education); Anthony Arnove (labor, history, political theory, economics); Lynn Lu (cultural studies, media, Latin American studies); Dionne Brooks (African-American studies, global politics); Sonia Shah (creative nonfiction, Asian-American studies). "We publish nonfiction political books with a new left/feminist/ multicultural perspective." Publishes hardcover and trade paperback originals and reprints. Publishes 15 titles/year. Receives 400 queries and 100 mss/year. 50% of books from first-time authors; 95% from unagented writers. Pays 11% royalty on wholesale price. Occasionally offers $500-2,500 advance. Publishes book 9 months after acceptance. Accepts simultaneous submissions. Reports in up to 3 months on queries and proposals. Book catalog and ms guidelines free.

Nonfiction: Subjects include economics, education, ethnic, gay/lesbian, government/politics, health/medicine, history, nature/environment, philosophy, science, sociology, women's issues/studies, political. Query with 2 sample chapters, including intro or conclusion and annotated table of contents. Reviews artwork/photos. Send photocopies.

Recent Nonfiction Title(s): *Powers and Prospects*, by Noam Chomsky (U.S. foreign policy/media studies); *From a Native Son*, by Ward Churchill (American Indian politics); *Black Liberation in Conservative America*, by Manning Marable (Black studies).

SOUTHERN METHODIST UNIVERSITY PRESS, P.O. Box 415, Dallas TX 75275. Fax: (214)768-1428. **Acquisitions:** Kathryn Lang, senior editor. Estab. 1937. Southern Methodist University publishes in the fields of literary fiction, American studies, anthropology, archaeology, composition and rhetoric, ethics and human values, fiction, film and theatre, regional studies and religious studies. Publishes hardcover and trade paperback originals and reprints. Publishes 10-15 titles/year. Receives 500 queries and 500 mss/year. 75% of books from first-time authors; 95% from unagented writers. Pays up to 10% royalty on wholesale price. Offers $500 advance. Publishes book 1 year after acceptance. Reports in 1 month on queries and proposals, 6-12 months on mss.
 • SMU Press has published such authors as Fred Busch, Rick Bass and Alan Cheuse.
Nonfiction: Subjects include medical ethics/human values and history (regional). "We are seeking works in the following areas: theology; film/theater; medical ethics/human values." Query with outline, 3 sample chapters, table of contents and author bio. Reviews artwork/photos as part of the ms package. Send photocopies.
Recent Nonfiction Title(s): *In a Tangled Wood: An Alzheimer's Journey*, by Joyce Dyer (Alzheimer's memoir); *JFK for a New Generation*, by Conover Hunt.
Fiction: Literary novels and short story collections. Query.
Recent Fiction Title(s): *Willy Slater's Lane*, by Mitch Wieland (novel); *Brother Frank's Gospel Hour*, by W.P. Kinsella; *Bitter Lake*, by Ann Harleman.
Tips: Audience is general educated readers of quality fiction and nonfiction.

SOUTHFARM PRESS, Haan Graphic Publishing Services, Ltd., P.O. Box 1296, Middletown CT 06457. (860)346-8798. Fax: (860)347-9931. E-mail: haan/southfarm@usa.net. **Acquisitions:** Walter J. Haan, publisher; Wanda P. Haan, editor-in-chief. Estab. 1983. Southfarm publishes primarily history and military/war nonfiction. Publishes trade hardcover and paperback originals. Publishes 5 titles/year. 90% from first-time authors; 100% from unagented writers. Pays 5-10% royalty on retail price. No advance. Publishes book 1 year after acceptance. Accepts simultaneous submissions. Reports in 1 month. *Writer's Market* recommends allowing 2 months for reply.
Nonfiction: Subjects include history, military/war and dog breeds. Submit outline/synopsis and sample chapters.
Recent Nonfiction Title(s): *In the Hands of My Enemy*, by Sigrid Heide (one women's story of World War II); *Shadow Over My Berlin*, by Heidi Scriba Vance (one woman's story of World War II); *Till War Do Us Part*, by Frank and Mary Bogart (husband and wife's story of World War II in Pacific).

‡SPECTRA, Imprint of Bantam Books, Division of Bantam Doubleday Dell, 1540 Broadway, New York NY 10036. (212)782-9418, 354-6500. Website: http://www.bdd.com. **Acquisitions:** Anne Groell, editor. Estab. 1984. "Spectra has a high-quality list, but we buy across the board. If we like something, we'll try it." Publishes hardcover, trade and mass market paperback originals and reprints. Receives hundreds of queries and 500 mss/year. 20% of books from first-time authors. Pays 8-10% royalty on wholesale price. Pays $5,000 and up advance. Publishes book 1 year after acceptance of ms. Accepts simultaneous submissions, if so noted. Reports in 6 months. Manuscript guidelines for #10 SASE.
Fiction: Fantasy, humor (fantasy, science fiction), science fiction. "We try to have a high-quality list. If we love and are passionate about what we're reading, we'll do what we can to work with it." Submit synopsis, 3 sample chapters with SASE.
Recent Fiction Title(s): *Game of Thrones*, by George R. Martin (medieval fantasy); *Assassin's Quest*, by Robin Hobb (coming of age fantasy); *Blue Mars*, by Stanley Robinson (science fiction).
Tips: "We publish books for an adult audience. Market does not rule our list. We like to bring new authors in."

THE SPEECH BIN, INC., 1965 25th Ave., Vero Beach FL 32960-3062. (561)770-0007. **Acquisitions:** Jan Binney, senior editor. Estab. 1984. Publishes "unique, research-based nonfiction and fiction for special educators, speech-language pathologists and audiologists, occupational and physical therapists, parents, caregivers, and teachers of children and adults with developmental and post-trauma disabilities." Publishes trade paperback originals. Publishes 10-20 titles/year. Receives 500 mss/year. 50% of books from first-time authors; 90% from unagented writers. Pays negotiable royalty on wholesale price. Publishes ms 6 months after acceptance. Reports in up to 3 months. Book catalog for 9×12 SASE and $1.48 postage.

FOR INFORMATION on book publishers' areas of interest, see the nonfiction and fiction sections in the Book Publishers Subject Index.

● The Speech Bin is increasing their number of books published per year and is especially interested in reviewing treatment materials for adults and adolescents.

Nonfiction: How-to, illustrated book, juvenile (preschool-teen), reference, textbook, educational material and games for both children and adults. Subjects include health, communication disorders and education for handicapped persons. Query with outline and sample chapters. Reviews artwork/photos as part of ms package. Send photocopies only.

Recent Nonfiction Title(s): *Techniques for Aphasia Rehabilitation*, by Mary Jo Santo Pietro and Robert Goldfarb.

Fiction: "Booklets or books for children and adults about handicapped persons, especially with communication disorders." Query or submit outline/synopsis and sample chapters. "This is a potentially new market for The Speech Bin."

Tips: "Books and materials must be clearly presented, well written and competently illustrated. We'll be adding books and materials for use by other allied health professionals. We are also looking for more materials for use in treating adults and very young children with communication disorders. Please do not fax manuscripts to us."

SPINSTERS INK, 32 E. First St., #330, Duluth, MN 55802. (218)727-3222. Fax: (218)727-3119. E-mail: spinsters@aol .com. Website: http://www.lesbian.org/spinsters-ink. **Acquisitions:** Nancy Walker. Estab. 1978. "We are interested in books that not only name the crucial issues in women's lives, but show and encourage change and growth from a feminine perspective." Publishes trade paperback originals and reprints. Publishes 6 titles/year. Receives 300 submissions/year. 50% of books from first-time authors; 95% from unagented writers. Pays 7-11% royalty on retail price. Publishes book 18 months after acceptance. Reports in 4 months. Book catalog free. Manuscript guidelines for SASE.

● Spinsters Ink has published such authors as Shelly Roberts and JoAnn Loulan.

Nonfiction: Feminist analysis for positive change. Subjects include women's issues. "We do not want to see work by men, or anything that is not specific to women's lives (humor, children's books, etc.)." Query. Reviews artwork/photos as part of ms package.

Recent Nonfiction Title(s): *Cancer In Two Voices*, by Sandra Butler, Barbara Rosenblum (women's health); *Mother Journeys: Feminists Write About Mothering*, edited by Maureen Reddy, Martha Roth, Amy Sheldon (anthology); *Look Me in the Eye: Old Women, Aging and Ageism*, by Barbara MacDonald and Cynthia Rich.

Fiction: Ethnic, women's, lesbian. "We do not publish poetry or short fiction. We are interested in fiction that challenges, women's language that is feminist, stories that treat lifestyles with the diversity and complexity they deserve. We are also interested in genre fiction, especially mysteries." Submit outline/synopsis and sample chapters.

Recent Fiction Title(s): *Goodness*, by Martha Roth; *The Activist's Daughter*, by Ellyn Bache; *Silent Words*, by Joan Drury (Edgar Award-nominated mystery).

STACKPOLE BOOKS, 5067 Ritter Rd., Mechanicsburg PA 17055. Fax: (717)796-0412. **Acquisitions:** William C. Davis, editor (history); Mark Allison, editor (sports); Judith Schnell, editor (fly fishing, carving, woodworking); Ed Skender, editor (military guides). Estab. 1935. "Stackpole maintains a growing, changing and vital publishing program by featuring authors who are experts in their fields, from outdoor activities to hobbies to Civil War history." Publishes hardcover and paperback originals and reprints. Publishes 75 titles/year. Pays industry standard royalty. Publishes book 1 year after acceptance. Reports in 1 month. *Writer's Market* recommends allowing 2 months for reply.

● Stackpole Books has published such authors as Dave Hughes, Don Troiani and Rick Butz.

Nonfiction: Outdoor-related subject areas—nature, wildlife, outdoor skills, outdoor sports, fly fishing, paddling, climbing, crafts and hobbies, gardening, decoy carving, woodworking, history especially Civil War and military guides. Query. Unsolicited mss and materials will not be returned. Reviews artwork/photos as part of ms package.

Recent Nonfiction Title(s): *Cook & Peary*, by Robert Bryce (history); *Sport Climbing with Robyn Erbesfield* (rock climbing how-to).

Recent Fiction Title(s): *Shupton's Fancy*, by Paul Schullery (fly fishing mystery).

Tips: "Stackpole seeks well-written, authoritative manuscripts for specialized and general trade markets. Proposals should include chapter outline, sample chapter and illustrations and author's credentials."

STANDARD PUBLISHING, Division of Standex International Corp., 8121 Hamilton Ave., Cincinnati OH 45231. (513)931-4050. Publisher/Vice President: Eugene H. Wigginton. **Acquisitions:** Acquisitions Coordinator. Estab. 1866. Publishes hardcover and paperback originals and reprints. Specializes in religious books for children and religious education. Publishes book 18 months after acceptance. Reports in 3 months. Manuscript guidelines for #10 SASE; send request to Jolene Barnes.

Nonfiction: Publishes crafts (to be used in Christian education), children's picture books, Christian education (teacher training, working with volunteers), quiz, puzzle. *Writer's Market* recommends sending a query with SASE first.

Recent Nonfiction Title(s): *Child-Sensitive Teaching*, by Karyn Henley.

STANFORD UNIVERSITY PRESS, Stanford CA 94305-2235. (415)723-9598. **Acquisitions:** Norris Pope, director. Estab. 1925. Stanford University Press publishes scholarly books in the humanities, social sciences and natural history, high-level textbooks and some books for a more general audience. Publishes 110 titles/year. Receives 1,500 submissions/ year. 40% of books from first-time authors; 95% from unagented writers. Pays up to 15% royalty ("typically 10%, often none"). Sometimes offers advance. Publishes book 14 months after receipt of final ms. Reports in 6 weeks.

Nonfiction: History and culture of China, Japan and Latin America; literature, criticism, and literary theory; political science and sociology; European history; anthropology, linguistics and psychology; archaeology and geology; medieval and classical studies. Query with prospectus and an outline. Reviews artwork/photos as part of ms package.

Tips: "The writer's best chance is a work of original scholarship with an argument of some importance."

‡**STARBURST PUBLISHERS**, P.O. Box 4123, Lancaster PA 17604. (717)293-0939. **Acquisitions:** Ellen Hake, editorial director. Estab. 1982. Publishes hardcover and trade paperback originals. Publishes 10-15 titles/year. Receives 1,000 queries and mss/year. 50% of books from first-time authors, 75% from unagented writers. Pays 6-16% royalty on wholesale price. Advance varies. Publishes book 1 year after acceptance of ms. Accepts simultaneous submissions. Reports in 1 month on queries. *Writer's Market* recommends allowing 2 months for reply. Book catalog for 9 × 12 SASE with 4 first-class stamps. Manuscript guidelines for #10 SASE.

Nonfiction: General nonfiction, cookbook, gift book, how-to, self-help, Christian. Subjects include business/economics, child guidance/parenting, cooking/foods/nutrition, counseling/career guidance, education, gardening, health/medicine, money/finance, nature/environment, psychology, real estate, recreation, religion. "We are looking for contemporary issues facing Christians and today's average American." Submit proposal package including outline, 3 sample chapters, author's biography and SASE. Reviews artwork/photos as part of ms package. Send photocopies.

Recent Nonfiction Title(s): *God's Vitamin "C" for the Spirit of Women* (self-help/inspiration); *Baby Steps to Success*, by Vince Lombardi, Jr. and Dr. John Baucom (self-help); *The Frazzled Working Woman's Guide to Practical Motherhood*, by Mary Lyon (parenting).

Fiction: Inspirational. "We are only looking for good wholesome fiction that inspires or fiction that teaches self-help principles." Submit outline/synopsis, 3 sample chapters, author's biography and SASE.

Recent Fiction Title(s): *The Miracle of the Sacred Scroll.* by Johan Christian (self-help/inspirational); *The Remnant*, by Gilbert Morris (historical/fantasy).

Tips: "Fifty percent of our line goes into the Christian marketplace, fifty percent into the general marketplace. We have direct sales representatives in both the Christian and general (bookstore, library, health and gift) marketplace. Write on an issue that slots you on talk shows and thus establishes your name as an expert and writer."

‡**STEEPLE HILL**, Subsidiary of Harlequin Enterprises, 300 E. 42nd St., New York NY 10017. **Acquisitions**: Anne Canadeo, editor. "This series of contemporary, inspirational love stories portrays Christian characters facing the many challenges of life, faith and love in today's world." Publishes mass market paperback originals. Pays royalty. Manuscript guidelines for #10 SASE.

Imprint(s): Love Inspired.

Fiction: Romance (75,000-80,000 words). Query or submit synopsis and 3 sample chapters with SASE.

Tips: "Drama, humor and even a touch of mystery all have a place in this series. Subplots are welcome and should further the story's main focus or intertwine in a meaningful way. Secondary characters (children, family, friends, neighbors, fellow church members, etc.) may all contribute to a substantial and satisfying story. These wholesome tales of romance include strong family values and high moral standards. While there is no premarital sex between characters, a vivid, exciting romance that is presented with a mature perspective, is essential. Although the element of faith must clearly be present, it should be well integrated into the characterizations and plot. The conflict between the main characters should be an emotional one, arising naturally from the well-developed personalities you've created. Suitable stories should also impart an important lesson about the powers of trust and faith."

‡**STENHOUSE PUBLISHERS**, Subsidiary of Highlights for Children, P.O. Box 360, York ME 03909. Fax: (207)363-9730. E-mail: philippa@stenhouse.com. **Acquisitions:** Philippa Stratton, editorial director. "Stenhouse publishes books that support teachers' professional growth by connecting theory and practice in an accessible manner." Publishes paperback originals. Publishes 15 titles/year. Receives 300 queries/year. 30% of books from first-time authors; 99% from unagented writers. Pays royalty on wholesale price. Offers "very modest" advance. Publishes book 6 months after delivery of final ms. Reports in 1 month on queries, 2 months on proposals, 3 months on mss. Book catalog and ms guidelines free.

• Stenhouse Publishers has published such authors as Harvey Daniels, Kathy Short and Denny Taylor.

Nonfiction: Exclusively education. "All our books are a combination of theory and practice." Query with outline. Reviews artwork/photos as part of ms package. Send photocopies.

Recent Nonfiction Title(s): *In the Company of Children*, by Joanne Hindley; *Taking Note: Improving Your Observational Notetaking*, by Brenda Power; *Peer Mediation*, by Judith Ferrara.

Tips: Audience is teachers and teacher educators. "Make yourself familiar with our list to ensure that we would be an appropriate publisher for your work."

STERLING PUBLISHING, 387 Park Ave. S., New York NY 10016. (212)532-7160. Fax: (212)213-2495. **Acquisitions:** Sheila Anne Barry, acquisitions manager. Estab. 1949. "Publishes highly illustrated, accessible, hands-on, practical books for adults and children." Publishes hardcover and paperback originals and reprints. Publishes 200 titles/year. Pays royalty. Offers advance. Publishes book 8 months after acceptance. Reports in 2 months. Guidelines for SASE.

Nonfiction: Alternative lifestyle, fiber arts, games and puzzles, health, how-to, hobbies, children's humor, children's science, nature and activities, pets, recreation, reference, sports, wine, gardening, art, home decorating, dolls and puppets, ghosts, UFOs, woodworking, crafts, history, medieval, Celtic subjects, alternative health and healing, new consciousness. Query or submit complete chapter list, detailed outline and 2 sample chapters with photos if applicable. Reviews artwork/photos as part of ms package.

Recent Nonfiction Title(s): *Critical Thinking Puzzles*, by Michael A. DiSpezio; *Indoor Bonsai for Beginners*, by Werner M. Busch (gardening); the *Easy Golf* series, by John Lister (sports/how-to).

‡**STILL WATERS POETRY PRESS**, 459 Willow Ave., Galloway Township NJ 08201. Website: http://www2.netcom
.com/~salake/stillwaterspoetry.html. **Acquisitions**: Shirley Warren, editor. "Dedicated to significant poetry for, by or
about women, we want contemporary themes and styles set on American soil. We don't want gay, patriarchal religion,
lesbian, simple rhyme or erotic themes." Publishes trade paperback originals and chapbooks. Publishes 4 titles/year.
Receives 50 queries and 500 mss/year. 80% of books from first-time authors; 100% from unagented writers. Pays in
copies for first press run; 10% royalty for additional press runs. No advance. Publishes book 4 months after acceptance
of ms. Accepts simultaneous submissions. Reports in 1 month on queries and proposals, 3 months on mss. Book catalog
and ms guidelines for #10 SASE.
 • Still Waters Poetry Press has published such authors as Madeline Tiger and Charles Rafferty.
Recent Nonfiction Title(s): *The End* (poetic closure); *Zeroes for Zorba* (feminist criticism of novel), both by Shirley
Lake Warren.
Fiction: Literary, women's interests. "We seldom publish fiction. Don't send the same old stuff." No long books. Short
stories only with SASE.
Recent Fiction Title(s): *Grain Pie*, by Anne Lawrence (chapbook).
Poetry: "We publish chapbooks only, 20-30 pages, one author at a time. Do not expect publication of a single poem.
Enclose SASE. Query then submit complete ms.
Recent Poetry Title(s): *Sisters in Rain*, by Cecily Markham; *The Marigold Poems*, by Margaret Renkl; *Junebug
Prophecy*, by Jesse Ryan (family).
Tips: "Audience is adults with literary awareness. Don't send mss via certified mail."

STILLPOINT PUBLISHING, Division of Stillpoint International, Inc., P.O. Box 640, Walpole NH 03608. (603)756-
9281. Fax: (603)756-9282. E-mail: stillpoint@top.monad.net. **Acquisitions**: Errol Sowers, co-director. Stillpoint Publishing "helps people heal their lives and their relationships in order to live full, joyful and loving lives that reflect their
highest purpose." Publishes hardcover originals and trade paperback originals and reprints that awaken the human spirit.
Publishes 8-10 titles/year. Receives 500 submissions/year. 50% of books from first-time authors; 90% from unagented
writers. Pays 8-15% royalty. Publishes book 15 months after acceptance. Accepts simultaneous submissions. Responds
in 10 weeks. Manuscript guidelines for SASE.
 • Stillpoint has published such authors as Caroline Myss, Meredith Young-Sowers and John Robbins.
Nonfiction: Topics include personal growth and spiritual development; holistic health and healing for individual and
global well-being; inspirational; psychology/self-help. Submit complete ms or query with table of contents and sample
chapters. *Writer's Market* recommends sending a query with SASE first.
Recent Nonfiction Title(s): *Souls of Animal*, by Gary Kowalski (animals/spirituality); *Listening to the Garden Grow*,
by Betty-Sue Eaton (nature/spirituality).
Tips: "We are looking for manuscripts with a unique, clearly-stated theme supported by persuasive evidence. We publish
nonfiction based on experience and/or research that illuminates an area of personal growth or spiritual development. The
work needs to be insightful and practical. We're now looking for books with mass-market appeal in the spiritual/new
thought/inspirational categories."

STIPES PUBLISHING CO., 10-12 Chester St., Champaign IL 61824-9933. (217)356-8391. Fax: (217)356-5753.
Acquisitions: Robert Watts. Estab. 1925. Stipes Publishing is "oriented towards the education market and educational
books with some emphasis in the college trade market." Publishes hardcover and paperback originals. Publishes 15-30
titles/year. Receives 150 submissions/year. 50% of books from first-time authors; 95% from unagented writers. Pays
15% maximum royalty on retail price. Publishes book 4 months after acceptance. Reports in 2 months.
Nonfiction: Technical (some areas), textbooks on business/economics, music, chemistry, CADD, AUTO-CADD, agri-
culture/horticulture, environmental education, and recreation and physical education. "All of our books in the trade area
are books that also have a college text market. No books unrelated to educational fields taught at the college level."
Submit outline and 1 sample chapter.
Recent Nonfiction Title(s): *The MicroStation Modeler Workbook*, by Michael Ward and Mike Arroyo (CADD);
Keyboard Fundamentals, by James Lyke, et al (CADD).

STOEGER PUBLISHING COMPANY, 5 Mansard Court, Wayne NJ 07470. (201)872-9500. Fax: (201)872-2230.
Acquisitions: David Perkins, vice president. Estab. 1925. "For hunting, shooting sports, fishing, cooking, nature and
wildlife, Stoeger books lead the industry in outstanding quality, content and unprecedented sales and profits, year
after year." Publishes trade paperback originals. Publishes 12-15 titles/year. Royalty varies, depending on ms. Accepts
simultaneous submissions. Reports in 1 month on queries. *Writer's Market* recommends allowing 2 months for reply.
Book catalog for #10 SAE with 2 first-class stamps.
Nonfiction: Specializing in reference and how-to books that pertain to hunting, fishing and appeal to gun enthusiasts.
Submit outline and sample chapters.
Recent Nonfiction Title(s): *Complete Guide to Compact Handguns*, by Gene Gangarosa Jr.; *Sporting Collectibles*,
by R. Stephen Irwin, M,D,; *Fish & Shellfish Care & Cookery*, by Kenn Oberrecht.

STONE BRIDGE PRESS, P.O. Box 8208, Berkeley CA 94707. (510)524-8732. Fax: (510)524-8711. E-mail: sbp@sto
nebridge.com. Website: http://www.stonebridge.com/. **Acquisitions:** Peter Goodman, publisher. Strives "to publish and
distribute high-quality informational tools about Japan." Publishes hardcover and trade paperback originals. Publishes
6 titles/year; imprint publishes 2 titles/year. Receives 100 queries and 75 mss/year. 15-20% of books from first-time

authors; 90% from unagented writers. Pays royalty on wholesale price. Advance varies. Publishes book 2 years after acceptance. Accepts simultaneous submissions. Reports in 1 month on queries and proposals, 4 months on mss. Book catalog free.

• Stone Bridge Press is no longer accepting fiction or poetry submissions.

Imprint(s): The Rock Spring Collection of Japanese Literature.

Nonfiction: How-to, reference. Subjects include art/architecture, business/economics, government/politics, language/literature, philosophy, translation, travel, women's issues/studies. "We publish Japan- (and some Asia-) related books only." Query with SASE. Reviews artwork/photos as part of ms package. Send photocopies.

Recent Nonfiction Title(s): *Suiseki*, by Felix Rivera (art of landscape stones); *The Big Book of Sumo*, by Mina Hall (Sumo wrestling); *The Japan Style Sheet: The SWET Guide for Writers, Editors and Translators*.

Recent Fiction Title(s): *Ravine and Other Stories*, by Yoshikichi Furui (translation); *The Broken Bridge*, by Susan Kamata (fiction from expatriates in Japan); *Milky Way Railroad*, by Kenji Miyazawa (modern-day fable).

Poetry: Translations from Japanese only. Query.

Tips: Audience is "intelligent, worldly readers with an interest in Japan based on personal need or experience. No children's books. No fiction. Realize that interest in Japan is a moving target. Please don't submit yesterday's trends or rely on a view of Japan that is outmoded. Stay current!"

‡**STONEWALL INN**, Imprint of St. Martin's Press, 175 Fifth Ave., New York NY 10010. (212)674-5151. Website: http://www.stonewallinn.com. **Acquisitions:** Keith Kahla, general editor. "Stonewall Inn is the only gay and lesbian focused imprint at a major house . . . and is more inclusive of gay men than most small presses." Publishes trade paperback originals and reprints. Publishes 20-23 titles/year. Receives 3,000 queries/year. 40% of books from first-time authors; 25% from unagented writers. Pays standard royalty on retail price. Pays $5,000 advance (for first-time authors). Publishes book 1 year after acceptance of ms. Accepts simultaneous submissions. Reports in 6 months on queries. Book catalog free.

Nonfiction: Subjects include gay/lesbian, philosophy, photography, sociology. "We are looking for well-researched sociological works; author's credentials count for a great deal." Query with SASE.

Recent Nonfiction Title(s): *A Girl's Guide to Taking Over the World: Writings from the Girl Zine Revolution*, edited by Karen Green and Tristan Taylor (essays); *Mrs. Keppel and Her Daughter*, by Diana Souham (biography).

Fiction: Gay/lesbian, literary, mystery. "Anybody who has any question about what a gay novel is should go out and read half a dozen. For example, there are hundreds of 'coming out' novels in print." Query with SASE.

Recent Fiction Title(s): *Love Alone*, by Paul Monette; *Buddies*, by Ethan Mordden.

‡**STONEYDALE PRESS**, 523 Main St., Stevensville MT 59870. (406)777-2729. Fax: (406)777-2521. **Acquisitions:** Dale A. Burk, publisher. Estab. 1976. "We seek to publish the best available source books on big game hunting, historical reminiscence and outdoor recreation in the Northern Rocky Mountain region." Publishes hardcover and trade paperback originals. Publishes 4-6 titles/year. Receives 40-50 queries and 6-8 mss/year. 90% of books from unagented writers. Pays 12-15% royalty. Publishes book 18 months after acceptance of ms. Reports in 2 months. Book catalog available.

Nonfiction: How-to hunting books. "We are interested only in hunting books." Query.

Recent Nonfiction Title(s): *Copenhaver Country*, by Howard Copenhauer (historical reminiscence); *High Pressure Elk Hunting*, by Mike Lapinski (elk hunting); *Camp Cookbook*, by Dale Burk (camp cooking).

STOREY PUBLISHING/GARDEN WAY PUBLISHING, (formerly Storey Communications/Garden Way Publishing), Schoolhouse Rd., Pownal VT 05261. (802)823-5200. Fax: (802)823-5819. **Acquisitions:** Gwen Steege, editorial director; Deborah Bremuth (crafts, herbs); Elizabeth McHale (animals, beer, building); Pamela Lappies (lifestyle, cooking); Charly Smith (gardening). Estab. 1983. "We publish practical information that encourages personal independence in harmony with the environment." Publishes hardcover and trade paperback originals and reprints. Publishes 45 titles/year. Receives 350 queries and 150 mss/year. 25% of books from first-time authors; 80% from unagented writers. Pays royalty or makes outright purchase. Publishes book within 2 years of acceptance. Accepts simultaneous submissions. Reports in 1 month on queries, 3 months on proposals and mss. Book catalog and ms guidelines free.

Nonfiction: Cookbook, how-to, children's/juvenile. Subjects include agriculture/horticulture, animals, building, beer, cooking/foods/nutrition, crafts, gardening, hobbies, nature/environment. Submit proposal package, including outline, sample chapter, competitive books, author résumé. Occasionally reviews artwork/photos as part of the ms package.

Recent Nonfiction Title(s): *Real Gardener's True Confessions*, by Pat Stone; *Horse Handling and Grooming*, by Cherry Hill; *Natural Baby Care*, by Colleen Dodt.

STORY LINE PRESS, Three Oaks Farm, Brownsville OR 97327. (541)466-5352. Fax: (541)466-3200. E-mail: slp@pt inet.com ("No manuscripts over the net!") Website: www.ptinet.com/~slp. **Acquisitions:** Robert McDowell, publisher/editor. "Our mission is to keep alive the stories of our time." Publishes hardcover and trade paperback originals. Publishes 12-16 titles/year. Receives 100 queries and 100 mss/year. 10% of books from first-time authors; most from unagented writers. Pays 10-15% royalty on retail price or makes outright purchase of $250-1,000. Offers $0-1,000 advance. Publishes book 2 years after acceptance of ms. Accepts simultaneous submissions. Reports in 1 month on queries, 2 months on mss. Book catalog free. Manuscript guidelines for #10 SASE.

• Story Line has published such authors as Donald Hall, Louis Simpson, Rita Dove and Liam Rector.

Nonfiction: Literary. Subjects include authors/literature. Query with SASE.

Recent Nonfiction Title(s): *The Night-Side*, by Floyd Skloot (literary essays on chronic fatigue syndrome); *The*

Reaper Essays, by Robert McDowell/Mark Jarman (reprinted essays about poetry and the state of poetry in America).
Fiction: Literary, no popular genres. "We currently have a backlist through the year 2000. Please send query letter first." Query with SASE.
Recent Fiction Title(s): *A Place In Mind*, by Sydney Lea (paperback reprint, friendship); *Dreams Like Thunder*, by Diane Simmons (girls coming of age).
Poetry: "Backlist for publication is through the year 2000. Please send query letter first. Consider our Nicholas Roerich Poetry Prize for previously unpublished poetry book authors of book-length manuscripts." Query.
Recent Poetry Title(s): *Rebel Angels: 25 Poets of the New Formalism*, by Mark Jarman/David Mason; *The Country I Remember*, by David Mason (narratives and new formalist).
Tips: Audience is "the interested literary reader who displays alignment with the principles of New Formalism and New Narrative poetry and with the story line in every book. Seventy-five percent of our list is poetry (generally formal, new formalist and narrative) and books about poetry, next is nonfiction and last is fiction. We strongly recommend that first-time poetry authors submit their manuscript in the Nicholas Roerich Poetry Contest. To view our list, visit our website. We have a long list to publish, and it keeps growing, so save postage and send a query first with a SASE."

LYLE STUART, Imprint of Carol Publishing Group, 120 Enterprise Ave., Secaucus NJ 07094. (201)866-0490. Fax: (201)866-8159. **Acquisitions:** Allen Wilson, executive editor. Publishes hardcover originals and reprints, trade paperback originals. Publishes 15-20 titles/year. 10% of books from first-time authors; 10% from unagented writers. Pays 5-15% on retail price. Offers $5,000-10,000 advance. Publishes book 1 year after acceptance of ms. Accepts simultaneous submissions. Reports in 2 months on proposals.
Nonfiction: How-to, humor. Hobbies, gaming, pop culture. Query with outline, 2-3 sample chapters and SASE. Reviews artwork/photos as part of ms package.
Recent Nonfiction Title(s): *Why Do We Need Another Baby?*, by Cynthia MacGregor (parenting); *Playing Roulette As a Business*, by R.J. Smart (recreation).

SUCCESS PUBLISHERS, (formerly Markowski International Publishers), One Oakglade Circle, Hummelstown PA 17036-9525. (717)566-0468. Fax: (717)566-6423. **Acquisitions:** Mike Markowski, president (Aviation Publishers); Marjorie L. Markowski, editor-in-chief (Success Publishers). Estab. 1981. "Our mission is to help the people of the world grow and become the best they can be, through the written and spoken word. We strive to make a difference in people's lives and make the world a better place to live. We help our authors share their messages and expand their careers." Publishes trade paperback originals. Publishes 12 titles/year. Receives 1,000 submissions/year. 90% of books from first-time authors; 100% from unagented writers. Average print order for a first book is 5,000-50,000. Royalty agreements vary according to book format and quantity sold or makes outright purchase. Publishes book 1 year or less after acceptance. Accepts simultaneous submissions. Reports in 2 months. Book catalog and ms guidelines for #10 SAE with 2 first-class stamps.
Imprint(s): Success Publishers, Aviation Publishers.
Nonfiction: Primary focus on personal development, self-help, personal growth, sales and marketing, leadership training, network marketing, motivation and success topics. "We are interested in how-to, motivational and instructional books of short to medium length that will serve recognized and emerging needs of society." Query or submit outline and entire ms. Reviews artwork/photos as part of ms package.
Recent Nonfiction Title(s): *Reject Me—I Love It!*, by John Furhman; *Fired Up!*, by Snowden McFall; *No Excuse!*, by Jay Rifenbary (motivational/self-help titles).
Tips: "We're intensifying our search for bestseller manuscripts. We're looking for authors who are dedicated to their message and want to make a difference in the world. We especially like to work with authors who speak and consult."

SUDBURY PRESS, Profitable Technology, Inc., 40 Maclean Dr., Sudbury MA 01776. Fax: (508)443-0734. E-mail: press@intertain.com. Website: http://www.intertain.com. **Acquisitions:** Susan Gray, publisher. Sudbury Press publishes only cozy mysteries and autobiographies and biographies of women. Publishes hardcover and mass market paperback originals. Publishes 8 titles/year. Receives 100 queries and 100 mss/year. 100% of books from first-time authors; 100% from unagented writers. Pays 10% royalty on wholesale price. Offers $0-3,000 advance. Publishes book 6 months after acceptance. Reports in 3 months. Book catalog on Internet.
Nonfiction: "We want biographies and autobiographies of ordinary women in extraordinary circumstances."
Recent Nonfiction Title(s): *To Auschwitz and Back: My Personal Journey*, by Ruth Bindefeld Neray.
Fiction: "We look for exclusively cozy mysteries in the style of Agatha Christie. We are not interested in thrillers, chillers, horror, legal mysteries or true crime." Submit synopsis, 2 sample chapters and SASE. Prefers complete ms.

SULZBURGER & GRAHAM PUBLISHING, LTD., 505 Eighth Ave., New York NY 10018. **Acquisitions:** Neil Blond, publisher. Publishes hardcover and trade paperback originals and reprints. Publishes 35 titles/year. Publishes 10-15 imprint titles/year. Receives 400 queries and 100 mss/year. 80% of books from first-time authors; 95% from unagented writers. Pays 0-15% royalty on wholesale price. Offers $100-2,000 advance. Publishes book 6 months after acceptance of ms. Accepts simultaneous submissions. Reports in 2 months on queries and proposals, 4 months on mss. Book catalog for 8×11 SAE with 4 first-class stamps. Manuscript guidelines for #10 SASE.
Imprint(s): Human Services Institute, Blond's Law Guides, Carroll Press.
Nonfiction: How-to, reference, self-help, technical, textbook. Subjects include business/economics, child guidance/parenting, computers/electronics, education, health/medicine, hobbies, money/finance, psychology, recreation, science,

software, travel, women's issues/studies. Query with outline and 1 sample chapter. Reviews artwork/photos as part of ms package. Send photocopies.
Recent Nonfiction Title(s): *Scoring High on Bar Exams*, by Mary Gallagher (test preparation).

SUMMERS PRESS, INC., also known as Business Publishing, 950 Westbank Dr., Suite 204, Austin TX 78746.
Acquisitions: Mark Summers, editor. Summers Press publishes reference books for businesses. Publishes hardcover originals. Publishes 5 titles/year. Some books from first-time authors. Pays 2-5% royalty on retail price or makes outright purchase. Offers $1,000-2,500 advance. Also purchases completed mss. Accepts simultaneous submissions.
Nonfiction: Reference, technical, legal references for businesses. Subjects include employment, health, and safety law. Includes software. "Manuscript should be easily accessible, use short sentences, and attempt to convey complex information on a 10-12th grade reading level." Query with outline, 1 chapter and SASE.
Recent Nonfiction Title(s): *OSHA Compliance Guide*, (reference book for businesses).

THE SUMMIT PUBLISHING GROUP, One Arlington Center, 1112 E. Copeland, 5th Floor, Arlington TX 76011.
Acquisitions: Len Oszustowicz, publisher; Bill Scott, editor. Summit Publishing Group seeks contemporary books with a nationwide appeal. Publishes hardcover originals, trade paperback originals and reprints. Publishes 35 titles/year. 40% of books from first-time authors; 80% from unagented writers. Pays 5-20% royalty on wholesale price. Offers $2,000 and up advance. Publishes book 6 months after acceptance of ms. Accepts simultaneous submissions. Reports in 1 month on queries and proposals, 3 months on mss.
Nonfiction: Biography, children's/juvenile, coffee table book, cookbook, gift book, how-to, humor, self-help. Subjects include art/architecture, business/economics, cooking, ethnic, gardening, government/politics, health/medicine, history, hobbies, military/war, money/finance, nature/environment, recreation, regional, religion, science, sociology, sports, women's issues/studies. "Books should have obvious national-distribution appeal, be of a contemporary nature and be marketing-driven: author's media experience and contacts a strong plus. Submit proposal package including outline, 2 sample chapters, table of contents, proposal marketing letter and résumé with SASE. Reviews artwork/photos as part of ms package. Send photocopies.
Recent Nonfiction Title(s): *On the Brink: The Life and Leadership of Norman Brinker*, by Norman Brinker and Donald T. Phillips (business biography); *Love and War: 250 Years of Wartime Love Letters*, by Susan Besze Wallace (history).
Fiction: Literary, religious. Submit synopsis, 2 sample chapters and SASE.
Recent Fiction Title(s): *The Gospel of Elvis*, by Louie Ludwig (humor).

SUNSTONE PRESS, Imprint of Sunstone Corp., P.O. Box 2321, Santa Fe NM 87504-2321. (505)988-4418. **Acquisitions:** James C. Smith, Jr., president. Estab. 1971. "Sunstone Press has traditionally focused on Southwestern themes, especially for nonfiction. However, in the past 18 months, general fiction titles have become very successful nationwide." Publishes paperback and hardcover originals. Publishes 25 titles/year. Receives 400 submissions/year. 70% of books from first-time authors; 100% from unagented writers. Average print order for a first book is 2,000-5,000. Pays 7½-15% royalty on wholesale price. Publishes book 18 months after acceptance. Reports in 1 month.
Imprint(s): Sundial Publications.
• The focus of this publisher is still the Southwestern U.S. but it receives many, many submissions outside this subject. It does not publish poetry.
Nonfiction: How-to series craft books. Books on the history, culture and architecture of the Southwest. "Looks for strong regional appeal (Southwestern)." Query with SASE. Reviews artwork/photos as part of ms package.
Recent Nonfiction Title(s): *Ernie Pyle in the American Southwest*, by Richard Melzer (biography); *Dinetah: An Early History of the Navajo*, by Dean Sundberg; *Silvio: Congressman for Everyone*, by Peter Lynch.
Fiction: Publishes material with Southwestern theme. Query with SASE.
Recent Fiction Title(s): *Hillcountry Warriors*, by Johnny Neil Smith; *Goldtown*, by Rita Cleary.

‡SURREY BOOKS, 230 E. Ohio St., Suite 120, Chicago IL 60611. Fax: (312)751-7334. E-mail: surreybks@aol.com. **Acquisitions:** Susan Schwartz, publisher. "Surrey publishes books for the way we live today." Publishes hardcover and trade paperback originals. Publishes 10-15 titles/year. Receives 150 queries and 20 mss/year. 5% of books from first-time authors; 80% from unagented writers. Pays 10-15% on wholesale price. Offers $500-5,000 advance. Publishes book 1 year after acceptance of ms. Accepts simultaneous submissions. Does not return submissions. Reports in 1 month on queries, 3 months on proposals if interested. Book catalog free.
Nonfiction: Cookbook, how-to, self-help. Subjects include business, child guidance/parenting, cooking/foods/nutrition, gardening, health/medicine, recreation, sports, travel. "Books must be marketable to a distinct audience—not everyone. Don't submit topics we don't publish." Query or proposal package, including sample chapters, outline and marketing ideas. All unsolicited mss returned unopened.
Recent Nonfiction Title(s): *1,001 Low-Fat Vegetarian Recipes*, edited by Sue Spitler with Linda Yoakum; *Undiscovered Museums of Paris*, by Eloise Danto (travel).
Tips: "Proposals should be well thought out and well developed. Be as professional as possible."

SWAN-RAVEN & CO., Imprint of Blue Water Publishing, Inc., P.O. Box 190, Mill Spring NC 28756. (704)894-8444. Fax: (704)894-8454. E-mail: bluewaterp@aol.com. Website: http://www.5thworld.com/bluewater. **Acquisitions:** Pamela Meyer, publisher. "Swan-Raven strives to preserve the Earth by publishing books that draw on the ancient wisdom of indigenous cultures to bring information from the otherworlds to our world." Publishes trade paperback originals. Publishes 6 titles/year. Receives 40 queries and 25 mss/month. 80% of books from first-time authors; 90% from unagented writers. Pays 5-12% royalty on wholesale price. Publishes book 16 months after acceptance of ms. Accepts simultaneous submissions. Reports in 2 months on mss. Book catalog and ms guidelines for SASE with 55¢ postage.

● Swan-Raven has published such authors as Christina Baldwin and Malidoma Somé.

Nonfiction: Subjects include health, philosophy, women's issues/studies, spiritual, future speculation. Query with outline. Reviews artwork/photos as part of ms package. Send photocopies.

Recent Nonfiction Title(s): *Angels & Archetypes*, by Carmen Boulter (feminine/astrology); *A Magical Universe*, by Langevin/Snider (New Age); *Plant Spirit Medicine*, by Eliot Cowan (natural health).

SWEDENBORG FOUNDATION, P.O. Box 549, West Chester PA 19381-0549. (610)430-3222. Fax: (610)430-7982. E-mail: info@swedenborg.com. **Acquisitions:** Dr. David Eller. "The Swedenborg Foundation publishes books by and about Emanuel Swedenborg (1688-1772), his ideas, how his ideas have influenced others, and related topics." Publishes hardcover and trade paperback originals and reprints. Publishes 6-10 titles/year; imprints publish 4 titles/year. Pays 5-10% royalty on net receipts or makes outright purchase. Offers $500 minimum advance. Reports in 3 months on queries, 6 months on proposals, 9 months on mss. Book catalog and ms guidelines free.

Imprint(s): Chrysalis Books, Swedenborg Foundation Press, Chrysalis Reader.

● See also *Chrysalis Reader* under Consumer Magazines/Religious.

Nonfiction: Biography, spiritual growth, self-transformation, writings of Emanuel Swedenborg. Subjects include philosophy, psychology, religion. Query with proposal package, including synopsis, outline, sample chapter and SASE. Reviews artwork/photos as part of ms package. Send photocopies.

Recent Nonfiction Title(s): *Return to the Promised Land: The Story of Our Spiritual Recovery*, by Grant Schnarr.

Tips: "Most readers of our books are thoughtful, well-read individuals seeking resources for their philosophical, spiritual or religious growth. Especially sought are nonfiction works that bridge contemporary issues to spiritual insights."

SYBEX, INC., 1151 Marina Village Pkwy., Alameda CA 94501. (510)523-8233. Fax: (510)523-2373. E-mail: kplachy @sybex.com. Website: http://www.sybex.com. Editorial Director: Bruce M. Spatz. **Acquisitions:** Kristine Plachy, acquisitions manager. Estab. 1976. Sybex publishes computer and software titles. Publishes paperback originals. Publishes 120 titles/year. Pays standard royalties. Offers competitive average advance. Publishes book 3 months after acceptance. Accepts simultaneous submissions. Reports in up to 6 months. Free book catalog.

Nonfiction: Computers, computer software. "Manuscripts most publishable in the field of database development, word processing, programming languages, suites, computer games, Internet/Web and networking." Submit outline and 2-3 sample chapters. Looks for "clear writing, logical presentation of material; and good selection of material such that the most important aspects of the subject matter are thoroughly covered; well-focused subject matter; clear understanding of target audience; and well-thought-out organization that helps the reader understand the material." Views artwork/photos, disk/CD as part of ms package.

Recent Nonfiction Title(s): *Mastering Windows 95*, by Robert Cowart; *The Complete PC Upgrade and Maintenance Guide, 7th edition*; *CNE-4 Study Guide for IntranetWare™*.

Tips: Queries/mss may be routed to other editors in the publishing group. Also seeking freelance writers for revising existing works and as contributors in multi-author projects.

SYSTEMS CO., INC., P.O. Box 339, Carlsborg WA 98324. (360)683-6860. **Acquisitions:** Richard H. Peetz, Ph.D., president. "We publish succinct and well-organized technical and how-to-do-it books with minimum filler." Publishes hardcover and trade paperback originals. Publishes 3-5 titles/year. 50% of books from first-time authors; 100% from unagented writers. Pays 20% royalty on wholesale price after costs. Publishes book 6 months after acceptance of ms. Accepts simultaneous submissions. Reports in 2 months. Book catalog free. Manuscript guidelines for $1.

Nonfiction: How-to, self-help, technical, textbook. Subjects include business/economics, automotive, health/medicine, money/finance, nature/environment, science/engineering. "In submitting nonfiction, writers often make the mistake of picking a common topic with lots of published books in print." Submit outline, 2 sample chapters and SASE. Reviews artwork/photos as part of ms package. Send photocopies.

Recent Nonfiction Title(s): *Basic Budgeting & Money Management*, by Peetz (personal finance); *Tell MacArthur To Wait*, by Hibbs (Japanese prison camp diary); *Existentialism & Folklore*, by Henscher (psychology).

Tips: "Our audience consists of people in technical occupations, people interested in doing things themselves."

‡**NAN A. TALESE**, Imprint of Doubleday, 1540 Broadway, New York NY 10036. (212)782-8918. Fax: (212)782-9261. Website: http://www.bdd.com. **Acquisitions:** Nan A. Talese, editorial director. "Nan A. Talese publishes nonfiction with a powerful guiding narrative and relevance to larger cultural trends and interests, and literary fiction of the highest quality." Publishes hardcover originals. Publishes 15 titles/year. Receives 400 queries and mss/year. Pays royalty on retail price, varies. Advance varies. Publishes book 8 months after acceptance of ms. Accepts simultaneous submissions. Reports in 1 week on queries, 1 month on proposals and mss.

● This publisher accepts agented submissions only.

Nonfiction: Biography, gift book, select. Subjects include art/architecture, health/medicine, history, philosophy, current trends. Agented submissions only.

Recent Nonfiction Title(s): *Dancing With Mr. D*, by Bert Keizer (health/medicine/philosophy); *Snakes and Ladders*,

by Gita Mehta (essays); *Worldly Goods*, by Lisa Jardin (renaissance art history).
Fiction: Literary. "We're interested in everything literary—we're not interested in genre fiction. No low-market stuff." Agented submissions only.
Recent Fiction Title(s): *The Dancer Upstairs*, by Nicholas Shakespeare (novel); *Alias Grace*, by Margaret Atwood (novel); *Into the Great Wide Open*, by Kevin Carty (first novel).
Tips: "Audience is highly literate people interested in literary books. We want well-written material."

‡**JEREMY P. TARCHER, INC.**, Imprint of Penguin Putnam, Inc., 200 Madison Ave., New York NY 10016. (212)951-8461. Publisher: Joel Fotinos. **Acquisitions:** Irene Prokop, editor-in-chief. "Although Tarcher is not a religion imprint per se, Jeremy Tarcher's vision was to publish ideas and works about human consciousness that were large enough to include matters of spirit and religion." Publishes hardcover and trade paperback originals and reprints. Publishes 20-30 titles/year. Receives 500 queries and 500 mss/year. 10% of books from first-time authors; 10% from unagented writers. Pays 5-8% royalty on retail price. Offers advance. Accepts simultaneous submissions. Reports in 1 month. Book catalog free.
Nonfiction: How-to, self-help. Subjects include business/economics, child guidance/parenting, gay/lesbian, health/medicine, nature/environment, philosophy, psychology, religion, women's issues/studies. "We do not publish 4-color books." Query with SASE.
Recent Nonfiction Title(s): *The Artist's Way*, by Julia Cameron (creativity); *The Wonder of Boys*, by Michael Gurian (parenting); *Secrets of Self-Employment*, by Paul and Sarah Edwards (business).
Tips: "Audience seeks personal growth through books. Understand the imprint's focus and categories. We stick with the tried and true."

TAYLOR PUBLISHING COMPANY, 1550 W. Mockingbird Lane, Dallas TX 75235. (214)819-8560. Fax: (214)819-8580. Website: http://www.taylorpub.com. **Acquisitions:** Editorial Department, Trade Books Division. Estab. 1981. "We publish solid, practical books that should backlist well. We look for authors who are expert authors in their field and already have some recognition, i.e., magazine articles, radio appearances or their own show, speaker or educator, etc." Publishes hardcover and softcover originals. Publishes 35 titles/year. Receives 1,500 submissions/year. 5% of books from first-time authors; 25% from unagented writers. Publishes book 1-2 years after acceptance. Accepts simultaneous submissions. Reports in 2 months. Book catalog and ms guidelines for 10×13 SASE.
Nonfiction: Gardening, sports, popular culture, parenting, health, home improvement, how-to, popular history, spiritual/inspiration, celebrity biography, miscellaneous nonfiction. Submit outline, sample chapter, an overview of the market and competition and an author bio as it pertains to proposed subject matter. Reviews artwork/photos.
• No longer seeking true crime, cookbooks, humor, self-help, trivia or business. Taylor has published such authors as Bill Hanna (of Hanna-Barbera), Dr. Lynn Weiss and Brother Victor-Antoine d'Avila-Latourrette.
Recent Nonfiction Title(s): *I Was That Masked Man*, by Clayton Moore (autobiography of Lone Ranger); *The Kennedys in Hollywood*, by Larry Quirk (film/biography); *Easy Garden Projects for All Seasons*, Barbara Pleasant.

TEACHERS COLLEGE PRESS, 1234 Amsterdam Ave., New York NY 10027. (212)678-3929. Fax: (212)678-4149. Website: http://www.tc.columbia.edu/tcpress. Director: Carole P. Saltz. **Acquisitions:** Faye Zucker, executive acquisitions editor. Estab. 1904. Teachers College Press publishes a wide range of educational titles for all levels of students: early childhood to higher education. "Publishing books that respond to, examine and confront issues pertaining to education, teacher training and school reform." Publishes hardcover and paperback originals and reprints. Publishes 40 titles/year. Pays standard industry royalty. Publishes book 1 year after acceptance. Reports in 2 months. Catalog free.
• Teachers College Press has published such authors as William Ayers, Frank Smith and James P. Comer.
Nonfiction: "This university press concentrates on books in the field of education in the broadest sense, from early childhood to higher education: good classroom practices, teacher training, special education, innovative trends and issues, administration and supervision, film, continuing and adult education, all areas of the curriculum, computers, guidance and counseling and the politics, economics, philosophy, sociology and history of education. We have recently added women's studies to our list. The Press also issues classroom materials for students at all levels, with a strong emphasis on reading and writing and social studies." Submit outline and sample chapters.
Recent Nonfiction Title(s): *Educating Citizens in a Multicultural Society*, by James A. Banks; "*The Having of Wonderful Ideas*" *and Other Essays*, by Eleanor Duckworth; *How Schools Might Be Governed and Why*, by Seymour Sarason.

TEMPLE UNIVERSITY PRESS, USB, 1601 N. Broad St., Philadelphia PA 19122-6099. (215)204-8787. Fax: (215)204-4719. E-mail: tempress@astro.ocis.temple.edu. Website: http://www.temple.edu. **Acquisitions:** Michael Ames, editor-in-chief; Janet Francendese, executive editor; Doris Braendel, senior acquisitions editor. "Temple University Press has been publishing useful books on Asian-Americans, law, gender issues, film, women's studies and other interesting areas for nearly 30 years for the goal of social change." Publishes 60 titles/year. Pays royalty of up to 10% on wholesale price. Publishes book 10 months after acceptance. Reports in 2 months. Book catalog free.
• Temple University Press has published such authors as Richard Delgado, Gary Fancione and Martine Rothblatt.
Nonfiction: American history, sociology, women's studies, health care, ethics, labor studies, photography, urban studies, law, Latin American studies, African-American studies, Asian-American studies, public policy and regional (Philadelphia area). "No memoirs, fiction or poetry." Uses *Chicago Manual of Style*. Reviews artwork/photos. Query.
Recent Nonfiction Title(s): *Journeys of Women in Science & Engineering*, by Ambrose, et al (profiles); *Swingin'*

at the Savoy: The Memoir of a Jazz Dancer, by Miller (African-American culture); *The Politics of Manhood*, by Kimmel.

TEN SPEED PRESS, P.O. Box 7123, Berkeley CA 94707. (510)559-1600. Fax: (510)524-1052. E-mail: info@ten speed.com. Publisher: Kirsty Melville. Address submissions to "Acquisitions Department." Estab. 1971. Ten Speed Press publishes authoritative books with a long shelf life for an audience interested in innovative, proven ideas. Publishes trade paperback originals and reprints. Firm publishes 60 titles/year; imprint averages 20 titles/year. 25% of books from first-time authors; 50% from unagented writers. Pays 8-12% royalty on retail price. Offers $2,500 average advance. Publishes book 1 year after acceptance. Accepts simultaneous submissions. Reports in 3 months on queries. Book catalog for 9×12 SAE with 6 first-class stamps. Manuscript guidelines for #10 SASE.
Imprints Celestial Arts, Tricycle Press.
Nonfiction: Cookbook, how-to, reference, self-help. Subjects include business and career, child guidance/parenting, cooking/foods/nutrition, gardening, health/medicine, money/finance, nature/environment, recreation, science. "We mainly publish innovative how-to books. We are always looking for cookbooks from proven, tested sources—successful restaurants, etc. *Not* 'Grandma's favorite recipes.' Books about the 'new science' interest us. No biographies or autobiographies, first-person travel narratives, fiction or humorous treatments of just about anything." Query or submit outline and sample chapters.
Recent Nonfiction Title(s): *The Joy of Not Working*, by Ernie Zelinski; *Why Cats Paint*, by Burton Silver (humor/cats/art history); *What Color is Your Parachute?*, by Richard Bolles (career/job-hunting).
Tips: "We like books from people who really know their subject, rather than people who think they've spotted a trend to capitalize on. We like books that will sell for a long time, rather than nine-day wonders. Our audience consists of a well-educated, slightly weird group of people who like food, the outdoors and take a light but serious approach to business and careers. If I were a writer trying to market a book today, I would study the backlist of each publisher I was submitting to and tailor my proposal to what I perceive as their needs. Nothing gets a publisher's attention like someone who knows what he or she is talking about, and nothing falls flat like someone who obviously has no idea who he or she is submitting to."

TEXAS A&M UNIVERSITY PRESS, Drawer C, College Station TX 77843-4354. (409)845-1436. Fax: (409)847-8752. E-mail: fdl@tampress.tamu.edu. Website: http://www.tamu.edu/upress. **Acquisitions:** Noel Parsons, editor-in-chief; Mary Lenn Dixon, managing editor (presidential studies, folklore); Dennis Lynch, associate editor (nautical archaeology). Estab. 1974. Texas A&M University Press publishes a wide range of nonfiction of regional and national interest. Publishes 40 titles/year. Nonauthor-subsidy publishes 25% of books. Pays in royalties. Publishes book 1 year after acceptance. Reports in 1 month on queries. *Writer's Market* recommends allowing 2 months for reply. Catalog free.
● Texas A&M University Press has published by Dr. Frank Vandiver, Liz Carpenter, Leon Hale.
Nonfiction: "Texas A&M University Press's editorial program consists of books on Texas and the Southwest, military studies, American and western history, Texas and western literature, Mexican-U.S. borderlands studies, nautical archaeology, women's studies, ethnic studies, natural history, the environment, presidential studies, economics, business history, architecture, Texas and western art and photography, and veterinary medicine." Query with SASE.
Recent Nonfiction Title(s): *Ships Bilge Pumps*, by Thomas Oertling (nautical archaeology); *The Caddos, the Wichitas, and the United States 1846-1901*, F. Todd Smith (American history); *Bigmamma Didn't Shop at Woolworth's*, by Sunny Nash (Texas history).
Tips: New publishing fields of Eastern European studies and U.S.-Mexican Borderlands studies.

TEXAS CHRISTIAN UNIVERSITY PRESS, P.O. Box 298300, TCU, Fort Worth TX 76129. (817)921-7822. Fax: (817)921-7333. Director: Judy Alter. **Acquisitions:** Tracy Row, editor. Estab. 1966. Texas Christian publishes "scholarly monographs, other serious scholarly work and regional titles of significance focusing on the history and literature of the American." Publishes hardcover originals, some reprints. Publishes 10 titles/year. Receives 100 submissions/year. 10% of books from first-time authors; 75% from unagented writers. Nonauthor-subsidy publishes 10% of books. Pays 10% royalty on net price. Publishes book 16 months after acceptance. Reports in 3 months.
Nonfiction: American studies, literature and criticism. Query. Reviews artwork/photos as part of ms package.
Recent Nonfiction Title(s): *Mexicans at Arms*, by Pedro Santoni; *Black Frontiersman*, edited and compiled by Theodore Harris (memoir).
Fiction: Regional fiction. Considers mss by invitation only. Please do not query.
Recent Fiction Title(s): *Hunter's Trap*, by C.W. Smith; *Tales from the Sunday House*, by Minetta Altgelt Goyne (history); *The Coldest Day in Texas*, by Peggy Pursy Freeman (juvenile).
Tips: "Regional and/or Texana nonfiction or fiction have best chance of breaking into our firm."

TEXAS STATE HISTORICAL ASSOCIATION, 2.306 Richardson Hall, University Station, Austin TX 78712. (512)471-1525. **Acquisitions:** George Ward, assistant director. "We are interested in scholarly historical articles and books." Publishes hardcover and trade paperback originals and reprints. Publishes 8 titles/year. Receives 50 queries and 50 mss/year. 10% of books from first-time authors; 95% from unagented writers. Pays 10% royalty on net cash proceeds. Publishes book 1 year after acceptance. Reports in 2 months on mss. Catalog and ms guidelines free.
Nonfiction: Biography, coffee table book, illustrated book, reference. Historical subjects. Query. Reviews artwork/photos as part of ms package. Send photocopies.
Recent Nonfiction Title(s): *Texas Oil, American Dreams*, by Lawrence Goodwyn (history); *A Nation Within a*

Nation, by Mark Nackman (history/politics); *Texas, Her Texas: The Life and Times of Frances Goff*, by Nancy Beck Young and Lewis Gould (history/politics).

TEXAS WESTERN PRESS, Imprint of The University of Texas at El Paso, El Paso TX 79968-0633. (915)747-5688. Fax: (915)747-7515. Director: John Bristol. **Acquisitions:** Marcia Daudistel, associate director. Estab. 1952. Texas Western Press specializes in the history and culture of the Southwest. Publishes hardcover and paperback originals. Publishes 7-8 titles/year. "This is a university press, 45 years old; we offer a standard 10% royalty contract on our hardcover books and paperbacks. We try to treat our authors professionally, produce handsome, long-lived books and aim for quality, rather than quantity of titles carrying our imprint." Reports in 2 months. Catalog and ms guidelines free.
Imprint(s): Southwestern Studies.
● This publisher has launched a new numbered series—*The Border/La Frontera*, which deals with current border related issues. Interdisciplinary in scope, it will include research from the fields of biology, public health, demography, applied environmental sciences, education, research in literature, history and social sciences, among others. Volumes will be published in English, Spanish or a bilingual format as warranted by the subject matter up to 300 book pages or 75,000 words.
Nonfiction: Scholarly books. Historic and cultural accounts of the Southwest (West Texas, New Mexico, northern Mexico and Arizona). Also art, photographic books, Native American and limited regional fiction reprints. Occasional technical titles. "Our *Southwestern Studies* use manuscripts of up to 30,000 words. Our hardback books range from 30,000 words up. The writer should use good exposition in his work. Most of our work requires documentation. We favor a scholarly, but not overly pedantic, style. We specialize in superior book design." Query with outline. Follow *Chicago Manual of Style*.
Recent Nonfiction Title(s): *Into a Far Wild Country*, by Jerry Thompson.
Recent Fiction Title(s): *Some Sweet Day*, by Wooley Bryan.
Tips: "Texas Western Press is interested in books relating to the history of Hispanics in the U.S., will experiment with photo-documentary books, and is interested in seeing more 'popular' history and books on Southwestern culture/life."

THIRD SIDE PRESS, INC., 2250 W. Farragut, Chicago IL 60625. **Acquisitions:** Midge Stocker, editor/publisher. Third Side Press publishes feminist and lesbian women's studies, nonfiction and fiction. Publishes 4-5 titles/year. 30% of books from first-time authors; 100% from unagented writers. Pays 6% royalty and up on wholesale price. Publishes book 18 months after acceptance of ms. Accepts simultaneous submissions (with nonfiction). Reports in 1 month on queries, 6 months on mss. Book catalog for 9×12 SAE with 2 first-class stamps. Manuscript guidelines for #10 SASE.
Nonfiction: Self-help. Subjects include health/medicine (women's only), lesbian, psychology, women's issues/studies. "We are looking for manuscripts that approach women's health issues from a feminist perspective." Query with SASE.
Recent Nonfiction Title(s): *Beyond Bedlam: Contemporary Women Psychiatric Surviors Speak Out*, edited by Jeanine Grobe; *Coming Full Circle*, by Nancy Van Arsdall (relationships).
Fiction: Contemporary, experimental, feminist, lesbian, literary. "We are not seeking collections of short stories by individual authors. We are seeking quality novels with lesbian main characters." Query with complete ms and SASE.
Recent Fiction Title(s): *Not So Much the Fall*, by Kerry Hart (lesbian first novel); *Aftershocks*, by Jess Wells.

THUNDER'S MOUTH PRESS, 632 Broadway, 7th Floor, New York NY 10012. (212)780-0380. Publisher: Neil Ortenberg. **Acquisitions:** Daniel O'Connor, managing editor. Estab. 1982. Publishes hardcover and trade paperback originals and reprints, almost exclusively nonfiction. Publishes 15-20 titles/year. Receives 1,000 submissions/year. 10% of books from unagented writers. Average print order for a first book is 7,500. Pays 5-10% royalty on retail price. Offers $15,000 average advance. Publishes book 8 months after acceptance. Reports in 3 months on queries.
Nonfiction: Biography, politics, popular culture. Query with SASE; no unsolicited mss.
Fiction: Query only.

TIARE PUBLICATIONS, P.O. Box 493, Lake Geneva WI 53147-0493. Fax: (414)248-8927. E-mail: info@tiare.com. Website: http://www.tiare.com. **Acquisitions:** Gerry L. Dexter, president. Estab. 1986. "Tiare Publications specializes in books for radio communications hobbyists." Publishes trade paperback originals. Publishes 6-12 titles/year. Receives 25 queries and 10 mss/year. 40% of books from first-time authors; 100% from unagented writers. Pays 15% royalty on retail/wholesale price. Publishes book 3 months after acceptance. Reports in 1 month on queries. *Writer's Market* recommends allowing 2 months for reply. Book catalog for $1.
Imprint(s): Limelight Books and Balboa Books.
Nonfiction: Technical, general nonfiction, mostly how-to, (Limelight); jazz/big bands (Balboa). Query.
Recent Nonfiction Title(s): *Cyber Crime*, by Laura Quarantiello (online crime prevention); *The Root Beer Book*, by Quarantiello (celebration of America's favorite soft drink); *Easy Calculator Math for Electronics*, by Larry Luchi.

‡TIDE-MARK PRESS, P.O. Box 280311, East Hartford CT 06128-0311. (860)289-0363. Fax: (860)289-3654. **Acquisitions:** Carol Berto, editor. "Focus is on illustrations and text about journeys of discovery into the natural world." Publishes hardcover originals. Publishes 4-6 titles/year. Receives 50-100 queries/year. 50% of books from first-time authors; most from unagented writers. Pays 10% on net sales. Advances vary with projects. Publishes book 1 year after acceptance of ms. Reports in 1 month. Call for proposal guidelines.
Nonfiction: Coffee table book, gift book. "The explorer/illustrator can be a scientist with a camera, a perceptive

traveler, or someone thoroughly grounded in a particular landscape or region." Reviews artwork/photos.
Recent Nonfiction Title(s): *Sea Changes*, by Beth Leonard; *Voices of the Great Smoky Mountains*, photography by Adam Jones, text by George Ellison; *Portrait of Rhode Island*, photography by Paul Rezendes, text by Lisa Beade.

TIDEWATER PUBLISHERS, Imprint of Cornell Maritime Press, Inc., P.O. Box 456, Centreville MD 21617-0456. (410)758-1075. Fax: (410)758-6849. **Acquisitions:** Charlotte Kurst, managing editor. Estab. 1938. "Tidewater Publishers issues adult nonfiction works related to the Chesapeake Bay area, Delmarva or Maryland in general. The only fiction we handle is juvenile and must have a regional focus." Publishes hardcover and paperback originals. Publishes 7-9 titles/year. Receives 150 submissions/year. 41% of books from first-time authors; 99% from unagented writers. Pays 7½-15% royalty on retail price. Publishes book 1 year after acceptance. Reports in 2 months. Book catalog for 10×13 SAE with 5 first-class stamps.
Nonfiction: Cookbook, history, illustrated book, juvenile, reference. Regional subjects only. Query or submit outline and sample chapters. Reviews artwork/photos as part of ms package.
Recent Nonfiction Title(s): *Lighting the Bay: Tales of Chesapeake Lighthouses*, by Pay Vojtech (history); *Maryland Loyalists*, by M. Christopher New (history); *Ghost Fleet of Mallows Bay*, by Donald Shomette (underwater archaeology).
Fiction: Regional juvenile fiction only. Query or submit outline/synopsis and sample chapters.
Recent Fiction Title(s): *Toulouse: The Story of a Canada Goose*, by Priscilla Cummings (picture book); *Oyster Moon*, by Margaret Meacham (adventure).
Tips: "Our audience is made up of readers interested in works that are specific to the Chesapeake Bay and Delmarva Peninsula area."

TIMES BOOKS, Imprint of Random House, Inc., 201 E. 50th St., New York NY 10022. (212)751-2600. Website: www.randomhouse.com. Vice President and Publisher: Peter Bernstein. Vice President and Associate Publisher: Carie Freimuth. **Acquisitions:** Elizabeth Rapoport (health, family, education); Karl Weber (business); John Mahaney (business); Geoffrey Shandler (current events, history); Stanley Newman (crossword puzzles); Tracy Smith (technology, business). "Times Books, acquired by Random House in 1984, is noted for its books on current affairs and political commentary, as well as a popular line of puzzles and games." Publishes hardcover and paperback originals and reprints. Publishes 50-60 titles/year. Pays royalty. Offers average advance. Publishes book 1 year after acceptance. *Writer's Market* recommends allowing 2 months for reply.
● Times Books has published such authors as Rosalyn Carter, Anatoly Dobrynin and Al Dunlap.
Nonfiction: Business/economics, science and medicine, history, biography, women's issues, the family, cookbooks, current affairs. Accepts only solicited mss. Reviews artwork/photos as part of ms package.
Recent Nonfiction Title(s): *Living Faith*, by Jimmy Carter (inspiration); *The Witch Doctors*, by Wooldridge & Micklethwait (business); *American Heart Association Around the World Cookbook* (cooking).

‡TIMES BUSINESS, Imprint of Random House, Inc., 201 E. 50th St., New York NY 10022. (212)572-8104, 751-2600. Fax: (212)572-4949. Website: http://www.randomhouse.com. **Acquisitions:** John Mahany, executive editor. Estab. 1995. Publishes hardcover and trade paperback originals. Publishes 20-25 titles/year. 50% of books from first-time authors; 15% from unagented writers. Pays negotiable royalty on list price; hardcover on invoice price. Advance negotiable. Publishes book 9 months after acceptance of ms. Accepts simultaneous submissions. Reports in 1 month on proposals. Book catalog free from Random House (same address). Manuscript guidelines for #10 SASE.
Nonfiction: Subjects include business/economic, money/finance, management, technology and business. Query with proposal package including outline, 1-2 sample chapters, market analysis and SASE.
Recent Nonfiction Title(s): *Profit Zone*, by Adrian Zlywotzky and David Morrison; *Apple: The Intrigue, Egomania and Business Blunders That Toppled An American Icon*, by Jim Carlton (business).

TODD PUBLICATIONS, P.O. Box 635. Nyack NY 10960. (914)358-6213. E-mail: toddpub@aol.com. **Acquisitions:** Barry Klein, president. Todd publishes and distributes reference books and directories of all types. Publishes hardcover and trade paperback originals. Publishes 5 titles/year. 1% of books from first-time authors. Pays 5-15% royalty on wholesale price. Publishes book 6 months after acceptance. Accepts simultaneous submissions. Reports in 2 months on proposals. Book catalog free. Manuscript guidelines for #10 SASE.
Nonfiction: How-to, reference, directories, self-help. Subjects include business/economics, ethnic, health/medicine, money/finance, travel. Submit 2 sample chapters.
Recent Nonfiction Title(s): *Directory Of Mastercard & Visa Credit Card Sources*; *Insider's Guide To Bank Cards With No Credit Check*; *Indian Country Address Book*.

TOR BOOKS, Subsidiary of Tom Doherty Associates, Inc., Imprint of St. Martin's Press, 175 Fifth Ave., New York NY 10010. **Acquisitions:** Patrick Nielsen Hayden, senior editor; Melissa Singer (Forge Books). "Tor Books publishes what is arguably the largest and most diverse line of science fiction and fantasy ever produced by a single English-language publisher." Publishes hardcover originals and trade and mass market paperback originals and reprints. Publishes 150-200 books/year. 2-3% of books from first-time authors; 3-5% from unagented writers. Pays royalty on retail price. Publishes book 1-2 years after acceptance. No simultaneous submissions. "No queries please." Reports in 2-6 months on proposals and mss. Book catalog for 9×12 SAE with 2 first-class stamps; ms guidelines for SASE.
Fiction: Adventure, fantasy, historical, horror, science fiction. Submit synopsis and 3 sample chapters.
Recent Fiction Title(s): *A Crown of Swords*, by Robert Jordan (fantasy); *Legacy*, by Greg Bear (science fiction); *The*

Fortune Fall, by Raphael Carter (science fiction).
Tips: "We're never short of good sci-fi or fantasy, but we're always open to solid, technologically knowledgeable hard science fiction or thrillers by writers with solid expertise."

TOTLINE PUBLICATIONS, (formerly Warren Publishing House, Inc.), a division of Frank Schaffer Publications, Inc., P.O. Box 2250, Everett WA 98203-0250. (206)353-3100. **Acquisitions:** Kathleen Cubley, managing editor (book manuscripts); Submissions Editor (single activity ideas). Estab. 1975. "All the products we publish must be educationally and developmentally appropriate for 2-year-olds, 3-5-year-olds, or 6-year-olds." Publishes educational activity books and parenting books for teachers and parents of 2-6-year-olds. Publishes 50-60 titles/year. Considers activity book and single activity submissions from early childhood education professionals. Considers parenting activity mss from parenting experts. 100% from unagented writers. Makes outright purchase plus copies of book/newsletter author's material appears in. Book catalog and ms guidelines free upon written request.
Nonfiction: Illustrated activity books for parents and teachers of 2-6-year-olds. Subjects include animals, art, child guidance/parenting, cooking with kids, foods and nutrition, education, ethnic, gardening, hobbies, language/literature, music, nature/environment, science. "We consider activity ideas submitted by early childhood professionals. Manuscripts and ideas must be appropriate for people (teachers/parents) who work with children two to six years old." Query. No children's storybooks, fiction or poetry.
Recent Nonfiction Title(s): *Songs and Games for Toddlers*, edited by Carol Gnojewski; *Ready to Learn Colors, Shapes and Numbers*, edited by Elizabeth McKinnon; *Multisensory Theme-A-Saurus*, edited by Gayle Bittinger.
Tips: "Our audience is teachers and parents who work with children ages 2-6. Write for submission requirements. We are especially interested in parent-child activities for 0- to 3-year-olds and teacher-child activities for toddler groups."

TOWER PUBLISHING, 588 Saco Rd., Standish ME 04084. (207)642-5400. Fax: (207)642-5463. E-mail: tower@mainelink.net. Website: http://www.mainelink.net/tower. **Acquisitions:** Michael Lyons, president. Estab. 1972. "Tower Publishing has proven itself to be one of the most comprehensive business information resources available." They specialize in business and professional directories. Publishes hardcover originals and reprints, trade paperback originals. Publishes 15 titles/year. Receives 60 queries and 30 mss/year. 10% of books from first-time authors; 90% from unagented writers. Pays royalty on net receipts. No advance. Publishes book 6 months after acceptance of ms. Accepts simultaneous submissions. Reports in 1 month on queries, 2 months on proposals and mss. Book catalog and guidelines free.
● Tower Publishing has increased their number of books published from 10 to 15 titles/year.
Nonfiction: Reference. Subjects include business/economics. Looking for legal books of a national stature. Query with outline.
Recent Nonfiction Title(s): *Maine Manufacturing Directory*; *The New England Legal Services Directory*.

TRAFALGAR SQUARE PUBLISHING, P.O. Box 257, N. Pomfret VT 05053-0257. (802)457-1911. Fax: (802)457-1913. E-mail: tsquare@sover.net. Publisher: Caroline Robbins. **Acquisitions:** Martha Cook, managing editor. "We publish high quality instructional books for horsemen and horsewomen, always with the horse's welfare in mind." Publishes hardcover and trade paperback originals and reprints. Publishes 8 titles/year. Pays royalty. No advance. Reports in 1 month on queries and proposals, 2 months on mss.
● Trafalgar Square has published such authors as Jane Savoie, Sally Swift and Mary Wanless.
Nonfiction: Books about horses. "We publish books for intermediate to advanced riders and horsemen. No stories, children's books or horse biographies." Query with proposal package, including outline, 1-2 sample chapters, letter of writer's qualifications and audience for book's subject.
Recent Nonfiction Title(s): *Reflections on Riding & Jumping*, by William Steinkraus; *My Horses, My Teachers*, by Alois Podhajsky; *Let's Ride! With Linda Tellington-Jones* , by L. Tellington-Jones and Andrea Pabel.

‡TRANSNATIONAL PUBLISHERS, INC., One Bridge St., Irvington NY 10533. (914)591-4288. Fax: (914)591-2688. E-mail: lawbooks@village.ios.com. Editor: Maria Angelini. **Acquisitions**: Adriana Maida, acquisitions editor. "We provide specialized publications for the teaching of law and law-related subjects in law school classroom, clinic and continuing legal education settings." Publishes hardcover and trade paperback originals. Publishes 15-20 titles/year. Receives 40-50 queries and 30 mss/year. 60% of books from first-time authors; 95% from unagented writers. Pays 15% royalty of net revenue. Offers no advance. Publishes book 8 months after acceptance of ms. Accepts simultaneous submissions. Reports in 1 month. Book catalog and ms guidelines free.
Imprint(s): Bridge Street Books.
● Transnational has published such authors as Louis Sohn, M.C. Bassiouni and Anthony D'Amato.
Nonfiction: Reference, technical, textbook. Subjects include business/economics, government/politics, women's issues/studies. Query or submit proposal package, including table of contents, introduction, sample chapter with SASE.
Recent Nonfiction Title(s): *Legal & Regulatory Issues in International Aviation*, by R.I.R. Abeyratne; *International Human Rights Litigation in U.S. Courts*, by Beth Stephens and Michael Rather; *Humanitarian Intervention, 2nd edition*, by Fernando Tesón.

‡TREASURE LEARNING SYSTEMS, Imprint of Treasure Publishing, MSC 1000, 829 S. Shields St., Fort Collins CO 80521. (970)484-8483. **Acquisitions**: Mark A. Steiner, senior editor. Treasure publishes Christian-oriented, educational, children's nonfiction and poetry. Publishes hardcover originals. Publishes 4 titles/year. Receives 150 queries and 150 mss/year. 50% of books from first-time authors; 80% from unagented writers. Pays royalty on retail price or makes outright purchase. Offers $5,000 advance. Publishes book 6 months after acceptance of ms. Accepts simultaneous submissions. Reports in 1 month on queries and mss, 2 months on proposals. Book catalog and ms guidelines free.

Nonfiction: Children's/juvenile, illustrated book. Subjects include education, Bible stories. All books are Christian oriented. "No novels or shallow content." Query with SASE. Reviews artwork/photos. Send photocopies.

Poetry: Must be Christian oriented.

Tips: Audience is children, schools, churches.

‡**TRIANGLE TITLES**, Imprint of Obelesk Books, P.O. Box 1118, Elkton MD 21922. E-mail: obelesk@netgsi.com. Website: www.netgsi.com/~obelesk. **Acquisitions:** Gary Bowen, editor. Publishes science fiction, fantasy and horror books featuring minority characters of all types and strong women characters. Publishes trade paperback originals and reprints. Publishes 4 titles/year. Receives 100 queries and 1,000 mss/year. 10% of books from first-time authors; 100% from unagented writers. Pays $10-20 for one-time rights. Accepts simultaneous submissions. Reports in 1 month on queries and mss. Book catalog and ms guidelines for #10 SASE.

• Publishes such well-known authors as Edward Lee and Shannah Jay.

Fiction: Fantasy, gothic, horror, science fiction, short story collections. "We publish gay/lesbian, bisexual and transgendered science fiction, fantasy and horror. We prefer minority characters: racial, ethnic, sexual, disabled and strong women. No stories about straight, white men. Length: 5,000 words maximum. No novel excerpts or poetry."

Recent Fiction Title(s): *Floating Worlds: Oriental Fantasies (short fiction); Icarus & Angels: Flights of Fantasy* (science fiction); *Cyber Magic: Lesbian Science Fiction.*

Tips: "Audience are mature, open-minded and multicultural. We are especially looking for minority authors; disabled, racial, ethnic and sexual minorities and women."

‡**TRICYCLE PRESS**, Imprint of Ten Speed Press, P.O. Box 7123, Berkeley CA 94707. (510)559-1600. Fax: (510)524-1052. **Acquisitions:** Nicole Geiger, acquisitions editor. "Tricycle Press looks for something outside the mainstream; books that encourage children to look at the world from a possibly alternative angle." Publishes hardcover trade paperback originals. Publishes 10-12 titles/year. 20% of books from first-time authors; 60% from unagented authors. Pays 15% royalty on wholesale price (lower if books is illustrated). Offers $0-9,000 advance. Publishes book 1 year after acceptance of ms. Accepts simultaneous submissions. Reports in 3 months on queries. Book catalog for 9×12 SAE and 3 first-class stamps; manuscript guidelines for #10 SASE; or one large envelope for both.

Nonfiction: Children's/juvenile, how-to, self-help, picture books, activity books. Subjects include art/architecture, gardening, health/medicine, nature/environment, science, geography, how-to, self-help. Submit complete ms for activity books; 2-3 chapters or 20 pages for others. Reviews artwork/photos as part of ms package. Send photocopies.

Recent Nonfiction Title(s): *Splash: A Penguin Counting Book*, by Jonathan Chester and Kirsty Melville (picture book); *Mousetracks*, by Peggy Steinhauser (computer activity); *Raptors, Fossils, Fins & Fangs*, by Ray Troll and Brad Matsen (science/natural history).

Fiction: Picture books. Submit complete ms for picture books. Query with synopsis and SASE for all others.

Recent Fiction Title(s): *Amelia Hits the Road*, by Marissa Moss; *Arm in Arm*, by Remy Charlip Peter; *Toes Are To Tickle*, by Shen Roddle and Katie McDonald-Denton.

TRILOGY BOOKS, 50 S. DeLacey Ave., Suite 201, Pasadena CA 91105. (818)440-0669. Fax: (818)585-9441. E-mail: 72274,44@compuserve.com. **Acquisitions:** Marge Wood, publisher. "We publish women's studies, self-help and psychology that have both mainstream and scholarly appeal." Publishes trade paperback originals. Publishes 4 titles/year. Pays 10% royalty on net revenues. Advance varies. Publishes book 1 year after acceptance of ms. Accepts simultaneous submissions. Reports in 1 month on queries. *Writer's Market* recommends allowing 2 months for reply. Book catalog and ms guidelines free.

Nonfiction: Subjects include women's history, women's issues/studies, self-help, psychology. Query.

Recent Nonfiction Title(s): *Sisters of the Wind: Voices of Early Women Aviators*, by Elizabeth S. Bell (women's history); *Becoming One*, by Sarah Olson; *Double Vision*, by Anna Richardson.

Tips: Audience is academic and well-educated mainstream women.

TSR, INC., P.O. Box 707, Renton WA 98057-0707. (425)226-6500. Estab. 1975. Executive Editor: Brian Thomsen. **Acquisitions:** Submissions Editor. TSR publishes science fiction and fantasy titles. Publishes hardcover and trade paperback originals and trade paperback reprints. Publishes 40-50 titles/year. Receives 600 queries and 300 mss/year. 10% of books from first-time authors; 20% from unagented authors. Pays 4-8% royalty on retail price. Offers $4,000-6,000 average advance. Publishes book 1 year after acceptance. Accepts simultaneous submissions. Reports in 2 months on queries.

• TSR was recently purchased by Wizards of the Coast, which plans to continue publishing under the name TSR. Editorial offices will gradually be moved to Washington.
Imprint(s): TSR™ Books, Dungeons & Dragons Books, Dragonlance® Books, Forgotten Realms™ Books, Ravenloft™ Books, Dark Sun™ Books, Planescape™ Books, Birthright™ Books.
Nonfiction: "All of our nonfiction books are generated inhouse."
Fiction: Fantasy, gothic, humor, science fiction short story collections, young adult. "We have a very small market for good science fiction and fantasy for the TSR Book line. We also need samples from writers willing to do work-for-hire for our other lines. No violent or gory fantasy or science fiction." Query with outline/synopsis and 3 sample chapters.
Recent Fiction Title(s): *Cormyr*, by Ed Greenwood and Jeff Grubb; *The Forgotten Realms* series.
Tips: "Our audience is comprised of highly imaginative 12-40 year-old males."

‡TURTLE POINT PRESS, 103 Hog Hill, Chappaqua NY 10514. (914)244-3840. **Acquisitions:** Jonathan Rabinowitz, president. Estab. 1991. "Even though we are a small press, we don't restrict ourselves. We look for diverse voices and style, the odd and uncatagorizable." Trade paperback originals and reprints. Publishes 8 titles/year. Receives 250 queries/year. 50% of books from first-time authors; 75% from unagented writers. Pays 5% royalty on net price. Offers $1,000 advance. Publishes book up to 1 year after acceptance of ms. Accepts simultaneous submissions. Reports in 1 month on queries. Book catalog free.
Nonfiction: Subjects include history and criticism, literary criticism. Query with SASE.
Recent Nonfiction Title(s): *Portrait of Zelide*, by Geoffrey Scott with new foreward by novelist Shirly Hazard.
Fiction: Literary, contemporary. Query with SASE.
Recent Fiction Title(s): *Hotel Sarajevo*, by Jack Kersh; *The Dead of the House*, by Hannah Green; *Lord of Dark Places*, by Hal Bennett.
Poetry: Query.
Recent Poetry Title(s): *100 Best Poems To Memorize*, edited by the Academy of American Poets.

TURTLE PRESS, Subsidiary of S.K. Productions Inc., P.O. Box 290206, Wethersfield CT 06129-0206. (860)529-7770. Fax: (860)529-7775. E-mail: editorial@turtlepress.com. Website: http://www.turtlepress.com. **Acquisitions:** Cynthia Kim, editor. Turtle Press publishes sports and martial arts nonfiction and juvenile fiction for a specialty niche audience. Publishes hardcover originals, trade paperback originals and reprints. Publishes 4-6 titles/year. Pays 8-10% royalty. Offers $500-1,000 advance. Reports in 1 month on queries.
Nonfiction: How-to, martial arts, philosophy, self-help, sports. "We prefer tightly targeted topics on which there is little or no information available in the market, particularly for our sports and martial arts titles." Query with SASE
Recent Nonfiction Title(s): *Neng Da: Super Punches*, by Hei Long (martial arts); *Herding the Ox*, by Dr. John Donahue (philosophy); *Martial Arts for Women*, by Jennifer Lawler (martial arts).
Fiction: "We have just begun a line of children's martial arts adventure stories and are very much interested in submissions to expand this line." Query with SASE.
Recent Fiction Title(s): *A Part of the Ribbon*, by Ruth Hunter and Debra Fritsch (children's chapter book).

CHARLES E. TUTTLE CO., 153 Milk St., 5th Floor, Boston MA 02109. **Acquisitions:** Michael Lewis, acquisitions editor. "Tuttle is America's leading publisher of books on Japan and Asia." Publishes hardcover and trade paperback originals and reprints. Publishes 60 titles/year. Receives 200 queries/year. 20% of books from first-time authors; 60% from unagented writers. Pays 5-8% royalty on retail price. Offers $1,000 average advance. Publishes book 18 months after acceptance of ms. Accepts simultaneous submissions. Reports in 6 weeks on proposals. Book catalog free.
Nonfiction: Self-help, Eastern philosophy, alternative health. Subjects include cooking/foods/nutrition (Asian related), philosophy, Buddhist, Taoist, religion (Eastern). Submit query, outline and SASE. Cannot guarantee return of ms.
Recent Nonfiction Title(s): *Zen Around the World*, by Alex and Annellen Simpkins; *The Stress Management Kit*, by Alix Needham; *Japanese Garden Design*, by Marc P. Keane.

‡TWAYNE PUBLISHERS, Imprint of Simon & Schuster, 866 Third Ave., New York NY 10022. (212)654-8476. **Acquisitions:** Mark Zadrozny, senior editor. Publishes concise, introductory, scholarly books and volumes in series for the general and academic reader. Publishes hardcover and paperback originals. Publishes 100 titles/year. Receives 1,000 submissions/year. 5% of books from first-time authors; 90% from unagented writers. Pays royalty. Reports in 4 months on queries.
Nonfiction: Literary criticism, biography, history, women's studies, film studies, current affairs, social science. Query.
Recent Nonfiction Title(s): *Jane Austen*, by John Lauber; *Garrison Keillor*, by Peter A. Scholl.
Tips: "Queries may be routed to other editors in the publishing group. Unsolicited manuscripts will not be read."

TWENTY-FIRST CENTURY BOOKS, A division of Henry Holt and Company, Inc., 115 W. 18th St., New York NY 10011. **Acquisitions:** Editorial Department. Twenty-First Century Books publishes only nonfiction current events or social issues titles for children and young adults. Publishes hardcover originals. Publishes 50 titles/year. Receives 200 queries and 50 mss/year. 20% of books from first-time writers; 75% from unagented writers. Pays 5-8% royalty on net price. Offers $2,000 advance. Publishes book 10-12 months after acceptance of ms. Accepts simultaneous submissions. Reports in 3 months on proposals.
Nonfiction: Children's and young adult nonfiction. Subjects include government/politics, health/medicine, history, military/war, nature/environment, science, current events and social issues. "We publish primarily in series of four or

more titles, for ages 10 and up, grades 5-8 (middle grade), and single titles for grades 7 and up. No picture books, fiction or adult books." Submit proposal package including outline, sample chapter and SASE. Does not review artwork.
Recent Nonfiction Title(s): The *Exploring Earth's Biomes* series; *Teens and Tobacco*; *Virtual Reality*.
Tips: "We are now accepting single titles for both middle grade and young adult readers."

‡TWO DOT, Imprint of Falcon Press Publishing Co. Inc., Box 1718, Helena MT 59624. (406)442-6597. Fax: (406)442-2995. E-mail: falcon@desktop.org. **Acquisitions:** Rick Newby, editorial director; Megan Hiller, series editor. "Two Dot looks for lively writing for a popular audience, well-researched, on western themes." Publishes hardcover and trade paperback originals. Publishes 6 titles/year. 30% of books from first-time authors; 100% from unagented writers. Pays 8-12½% on net. Offers minimal advance. Publishes book 1 year after acceptance of ms. Accepts simultaneous submissions. Reports in 4 months on queries. Book catalog for 9×12 SASE with 3 first-class stamps. Manuscript guidelines free.
Nonfiction: Subjects include Americana (western), cooking/foods/nutrition, history, regional. Two state by state series of interest: *More Than Petticoats*, on notable women; and *It Happened In . . .*, state history. Submit outline, 1 sample chapter and SASE. Reviews artwork/photos as part of the ms package. Send photocopies.
Recent Nonfiction Title(s): *More Than Petticoats: Remarkable Montana Women*, Gayle C. Shirley (history); *Charlie's Trail: The Life and Art of C.M. Russell*, by Gayle C. Shirley (biography); *Montana Campfire Tales: 14 Historical Narratives*, Dave Walter (history).

TYNDALE HOUSE PUBLISHERS, INC., 351 Executive Dr., P.O. Box 80, Wheaton IL 60189-0080. (630)668-8300. Vice President, Editorial: Ronald Beers. **Acquisitions:** Manuscript Review Committee. Estab. 1962. Tyndale House publishes "practical, user-friendly Christian books for the home and family." Publishes hardcover and trade paperback originals and mass paperback reprints. Publishes 100 titles/year. 5-10% of books from first-time authors. Average first print order for a first book is 5,000-10,000. Royalty and advance negotiable. Publishes book 18 months after acceptance. Send query and synopsis, not whole ms. Reviews solicited mss only. Reports in up to 2 months. Book catalog and ms guidelines for 9×12 SAE with 9 first-class stamps.
• This publisher has received Book of the Year Award (CBA) and the *Campus Life* Book of the Year Award.
Nonfiction: Christian growth/self-help, devotional/inspirational, theology/Bible doctrine, children's nonfiction, contemporary/critical issues." Query.
Recent Nonfiction Title(s): *Home with a Heart*, by Dr. James Dobson (home and family); *The Power of Personal Integrity*, by Charles Dyer; *7 Habits of a Healthy Home*, by Bill Carmichael.
Fiction: "Biblical, historical and other Christian themes. No short story collections. Youth books: character building stories with Christian perspective. Especially interested in ages 10-14." Query.
Recent Fiction Title(s): *Tribulation Force*, by Tim LaHaye and Jerry B. Jenkins; *The Atonement Child*, by Francine Rivers; *The Treasure of Zanzibar*, by Catherine Palmer (Christian romance).

‡ULI, THE URBAN LAND INSTITUTE, 1025 Thomas Jefferson St. N.W., Washington DC 20007-5201. (202)627-7040. Fax: (202)624-7140. **Acquisitions**: Frank H. Spink, Jr., vice president/publisher. Estab. 1936. ULI publishes technical books on real estate development and land planning. Publishes hardcover and trade paperback originals. Averages 15-20 titles/year. Receives 20 submissions/year. No books from first-time authors; 100% of books from unagented writers. Pays 10% royalty on gross sales. Offers $1,500-2,000 advance. Publishes book 6 months after acceptance. Book catalog and ms guidelines for 9×12 SAE.
Nonfiction: "The majority of manuscripts are created inhouse by research staff. We acquire two or three outside authors to fill schedule and subject areas where our list has gaps. We are not interested in real estate sales, brokerages, appraisal, making money in real estate, opinion, personal point of view, or manuscripts negative toward growth and development." Query. Reviews artwork/photos as part of ms package.
Recent Nonfiction Title(s): *Hotel Development*, by PKF Consulting; *Sports, Convention and Entertainment Facilities*, by David Petersen; *Moving Beyond Gridlock, Traffic and Development*, by Robert Dunphy.

UNITY BOOKS, Unity School of Christianity, 1901 NW Blue Parkway, Unity Village MO 64065-0001. (816)524-3550 ext. 3190. Fax: (816)251-3552. E-mail: sprice@unityworldhq.org. Website: http://www.unityworldhq.org. **Acquisitions**: Michael Maday, editor; Brenda Markle, associate editor. "We are a bridge between traditional Christianity and New Age spirituality. Unity School of Christianity is on Christian principles, spiritual values and the healing power of prayer as a resource for daily living. Publishes hardcover and trade paperback originals and reprints. Publishes 16 titles/year. Receives 100 queries and 300 mss/year. 30% of books from first-time authors; 95% from unagented writers. Pays 10-15% royalty on net receipts. Publishes book 13 months after acceptance of final ms. Reports in 1 month on queries and proposals, 2 months on mss. Book catalog and ms guidelines free.
• Unity Books has published such authors as Eric Butterworth and James Dillet Freeman.
Nonfiction: Inspirational, self-help, reference (spiritual/metaphysical). Subjects include health (holistic), philosophy (perennial/New Thought), psychology (transpersonal), religion (spiritual/metaphysical Bible interpretation/modern Biblical studies). "Writers should be familiar with principles of metaphysical Christianity but not feel bound by them. We are interested in works in the related fields of holistic health, spiritual psychology and the philosophy of other world religions." Book proposal and/or query with outline and sample chapter. Reviews artwork/photos as part of ms package. Send photocopies.
Recent Nonfiction Title(s): *Setting a Trap for God*, by Dr. Rocco Errico (interpretation of the Lord's Prayer using

Aramaic language and culture); *Torch-Bearer to Light the Way: The Life of Myrtle Fillmore*, by Neal Vahle.).
Fiction: Spiritual, inspirational, metaphysical. Query with synopsis and sample chapter.

UNIVELT, INC., P.O. Box 28130, San Diego CA 92198. (619)746-4005. Fax: (619)746-3139. **Acquisitions:** Robert H. Jacobs, publisher. Estab. 1970. Univelt publishes astronautics, spaceflight, aerospace technology and history titles. Publishes hardcover originals. Publishes 8 titles/year. Receives 20 submissions/year. 5% of books from first-time authors; 5% from unagented writers. Nonauthor-subsidy publishes 10% of books. Average print order for a first book is 400-1,500. Pays 10% royalty on actual sales. No advance. Publishes book 4 months after acceptance. Reports in 1 month. *Writer's Market* recommends allowing 2 months for reply. Book catalog and ms guidelines for SASE.
Imprint(s): American Astronautical Society, National Space Society.
Nonfiction: Publishes in the field of aerospace, especially astronautics, including application of aerospace technology to Earth's problems. Call and then submit outline and 1-2 chapters. Reviews artwork/photos.
Recent Nonfiction Title(s): *The Case for Mars V*, edited by Penelope J. Boston; *Mars Exploration*, edited by Robert M. Zubrin (reprinted articles from *The Journal of the British Interplanetary Society*); *Strategies for Mars: A Guide to Human Exploration, Volume 86*, edited by Carol Stoker and Carter Emmart.
Tips: "Writers have the best chance of selling manuscripts on the history of astronautics (we have a history series) and astronautics/spaceflight subjects. We publish for the American Astronautical Society."

‡THE UNIVERSITY OF AKRON PRESS, 374B Bierce Library, Akron OH 44325-1703. (330)972-5342. Fax: (330)972-6383. E-mail: press@uakron.edu. Website: http://www.uakron.edu/uapress. **Acquisitions:** Elton Glaser, director. Estab. 1988. "The University of Akron Press strives to be the University's ambassador for scholarship and creative writing at the national and international levels." Publishes hardcover and trade paperback originals. Publishes 4-5 titles/year. Receives 40-60 queries and over 500 mss/year (because of poetry contest). 20% of books from first-time authors; 100% from unagented writers. Pays 4-10% on wholesale price. Publishes book 14 months after acceptance of ms. Accepts simultaneous submissions (only for poetry contest.) Reports in 1 month on queries, 2 months on proposals, 5 months on mss. Book catalog free. Manuscript guidelines for #10 SASE.
Nonfiction: Scholarly, Ohio history. Subjects include regional, technology and environment. "We publish mostly in our two nonfiction series: Technology and the Environment; Ohio history and culture. Writers often do not submit material suitable to our series books." Query. Reviews artwork/photos as part of ms package. Send photocopies.
Recent Nonfiction Title(s): *Written on the Hills*, by Frances McGovern (Ohio history); *Energy and the Making of Modern California*, by James C. Williams (technology/environment); *The Search for the Ultimate Sink: Urban Pollution in Historical Perspective*, by Joel Tarr (technology/environment).
Poetry: Follow the guidelines and submit manuscripts only for the contest.
Recent Poetry Title(s): *Her Slender Dress*, by Susan Yuzna (literary poetry).
Tips: "We have mostly an audience of general educated readers, with a more specialized audience of public historians, sociologists and political scientists for the scholarly series."

UNIVERSITY OF ALASKA PRESS, P.O. Box 756240, 1st Floor Gruening Bldg., UAF, Fairbanks AK 99775-6240. (907)474-6389. Fax: (907)474-5502. E-mail: fypress@aurora.alaska.edu. Manager: Debbie Van Stone. **Acquisitions:** Pam Odom. Estab. 1967. "The University of Alaska Press aims to encourage, publish and disseminate works of scholarship that will enhance the store of knowledge about Alaska and the North Pacific Rim." Publishes hardcover originals, trade paperback originals and reprints. Publishes 5-10 titles/year. Receives 100 submissions/year. Pays 7½-10% royalty on net sales. Publishes book within 2 years after acceptance. Reports in 2 months. Book catalog free.
Imprint(s): Ramuson Library Historical Translation Series, LanternLight Library, Oral Biographies, and Classic Reprints.
• University of Alaska Press has published such authors as Brian Garfield.
Nonfiction: Biography, reference, technical, textbook, scholarly nonfiction relating to Alaska-circumpolar regions. Subjects include agriculture/horticulture, Americana (Alaskana), animals, anthropology/archaeology, art/architecture, education, ethnic, government/politics, health/medicine, history, language, military/war, nature/environment, regional, science, translation. Nothing that isn't northern or circumpolar. Query or submit outline. Reviews copies of artwork/photos as part of ms package.
Recent Nonfiction Title(s): *Bear Man of Admiralty Island: A Biography of Allen E. Hasselborg*, by John R. Howe (biography/history); *A Special Gift: The Kutchin Beadwork Tradition*, by Kate Duncan with Eunice Carney (history/crafts); *Alaskan Eskimo Life in the 1890s, As Sketched by Native Artists*, by George Phebus, Jr. (illustrated history).
Tips: "Writers have the best chance with scholarly nonfiction relating to Alaska, the circumpolar regions and North Pacific Rim. Our audience is made up of scholars, historians, students, libraries, universities, individuals."

UNIVERSITY OF ARIZONA PRESS, 1230 N. Park Ave., #102, Tucson AZ 85719-4140. (520)621-1441. Fax: (520)621-8899. E-mail: uapress@uapress.arizona.edu. Website: http://www.uapress.arizona.edu. **Acquisitions**: Stephen Cox, director (Western history, environmental history, nature essays), Joanne O'Hare, senior editor (Native American, Latin American, and Chicano studies and literatures); Martha Moutray (behavioral sciences, integrative medicine, space sciences); Christine Szuter (anthropology, natural history, environmental studies). Estab. 1959. "Great publishing rooted in the Southwest." Publishes hardcover and paperback originals and reprints. Publishes 50 titles/year. Receives 300-400 submissions/year. 30% of books from first-time authors; 95% from unagented writers. Average print order is 1,500. Royalty terms vary; usual starting point for scholarly monograph is after sale of first 1,000 copies. Publishes book 1

year after acceptance. Reports in 3 months. Book catalog for 9×12 SASE. Manuscript guidelines for #10 SASE.
• *Re-imaging the Modern American West: A Century of Fiction, History, and Art*, by Richard W. Etulain, was awarded the 1997 Western Heritage Award for nonfiction. University of Arizona Press has published such authors as N. Scott Momaday, Anna Roosevelt and Richard Shelton.
Nonfiction: Scholarly books about anthropology, Arizona, American West, archaeology, behavioral sciences, Chicano studies, environmental science, global change, Latin America, Native Americans, natural history, space sciences and women's studies. Query with outline, sample chapter and current curriculum vitae or résumé. Reviews artwork/photos as part of ms package.
Recent Nonfiction Title(s): *The Planet Mars: A History of Observation and Discover*, by William Sheehan.
Recent Fiction Title(s): *El Milagro and Other Stories*, by Patricia Preciado Martin (stories from the barrio).
Recent Poetry Title(s): *Breathing Between the Lines: Poems*, by Demetria Martínez.
Tips: "Perhaps the most common mistake a writer might make is to offer a book manuscript or proposal to a house whose list he or she has not studied carefully. Editors rejoice in receiving material that is clearly targeted to the house's list, 'I have approached your firm because my books complement your past publications in . . .,' presented in a straightforward, businesslike manner."

THE UNIVERSITY OF ARKANSAS PRESS, 201 Ozark Ave., Fayetteville AR 72701-1201. (501)575-3246. Fax: (501)575-6044. Director: Miller Williams. **Acquisitions:** Kevin Brock, acquisitions editor. Estab. 1980. "Regional awareness, national impact . . . through books." Publishes hardcover and trade paperback originals and reprints. Publishes 32 titles/year. Receives 4,000 submissions/year. 30% of books from first-time authors; 90% from unagented writers. Pays 10% royalty on net receipts from hardcover; 6% on paper. Publishes book 1 year after acceptance. Accepted mss must be submitted on disk. Reports in up to 3 months. Book catalog for 9×12 SAE with 5 first-class stamps. Manuscript guidelines for #10 SASE.
Nonfiction: Americana, history, humanities, nature, general politics and history of politics, sociology. "Our current needs include literary criticism, history and biography. We won't consider manuscripts for texts, juvenile or religious studies, or anything requiring a specialized or exotic vocabulary." Query or submit outline and sample chapters.
Recent Nonfiction Title(s): *Black Savannah, 1788-1864*, by Whittington B. Johnson; *Encyclopedia of the Blues*, by Gérand Herzhaft (music); *Faubus*, by Roy Reed (biography).
Poetry: Arkansas Poetry Award offered for publication of first book. Write for contest rules.

UNIVERSITY OF CALIFORNIA PRESS, 2120 Berkeley Way, Berkeley CA 94720. Director: James H. Clark. Associate Director: Lynne E. Withey. **Acquisitions**: Doug Abrams Arava, editor (religion); Doris Kretschmer, executive editor (natural history, biology); Deborah Kirshman, editor (art); Mary Lamprech, editor (classics); Sheila Levine, editorial director (Asian studies, history); Monica McCormick, editor (African studies, American history); Naomi Schneider, executive editor (sociology, politics, gender studies); Howard Boyer, executive editor (science); Linda Norton, editor (literature, poetry); Stephanie Fay, editor (art); Stan Holwitz, assistant director (anthropology, sociology); Ed Dimendberg, editor (film, philosophy); Lynne Withey, associate director (music, Middle Eastern studies). Estab. 1893. Los Angeles office: 405 Hilgard Ave., Los Angeles CA 90024-1373. UK office: University Presses of California, Columbia, and Princeton, 1 Oldlands Way, Bognor Regis, W. Sussex PO22 9SA England. "Most of our publications are hardcover nonfiction written by scholars." Publishes hardcover and paperback originals and reprints. "On books likely to do more than return their costs, a standard royalty contract beginning at 7% on net receipts is paid; on paperbacks it is less." Publishes 180 titles/year. Queries are always advisable, accompanied by outlines or sample material. Accepts nonfiction translations. Send to Berkeley address. Reports vary, depending on the subject. *Writer's Market* recommends allowing 2 months for reply. Enclose return postage.
Nonfiction: Publishes scholarly books including history, art, literary studies, social sciences, natural sciences and some high-level popularizations. No length preferences. *Writer's Market* recommends query with SASE first.
Recent Nonfiction Title(s): *Los Angeles A to Z*, by Leonard and Dale Pitt (reference); *The Transformation of the Roman World*, edited by Leslie Webster and Michelle Brown; *Schubert: The Music and the Man*, by Brian Newbould.
Fiction and Poetry: Publishes fiction and poetry only in translation.

‡**UNIVERSITY OF CHICAGO PRESS**, 5801 Ellis Ave., Chicago IL 60637. (773)702-7700. Fax: (773)702-9756. **Acquisitions**: Editorial Department. Estab. 1891. "We are a scholarly and academic press that also publishes books for a wider audience." Publishes hardcover originals, trade paperback originals and reprints. Publishes 260 titles/year. 10% of books from first-time authors; 85% from unagented writers. Pays 5-10% royalty on hardcover, 7½% for paperback on net receipts for first-time authors. Advance varies. Publishes book 1 year after acceptance of ms. Accepts simultaneous submissions. Reports in 3 weeks on proposals. Catalog and guidelines free; "call marketing department."
Imprint(s): Midway Reprints (reprints only), Phoenix Books (poetry and fiction by invitation only).
Nonfiction: Subjects include anthropology/archaeology, art/architecture, business/economics, education, ethnic, gay/lesbian, government/politics, history, language/literature, money/finance, music/dance, philosophy, psychology, religion, science, sociology, translation, women's issues/studies, law, physical sciences, linguistics. Prefers authors with established credentials. Query or submit proposal package, including: prospectus, table of contents, 2-3 sample chapters and author's c.v. with SASE. Reviews artwork/photos as part of the ms package. Send photocopies.
Recent Nonfiction Title(s): *The Fourth Great Awakening*, by Robet Fogel (history); *The Long Affair: Jefferson and the French Revolution*, by Conor Cruise O'Brien (history); *Scientific Revolution*, by Steven Shapin (history/technology).
Poetry: Publishes 4 titles/year by invitation. Does not accept any unsolicited submissions.

Recent Poetry Title(s): *Confession*, by Susan Han; *In the Belly*, by David Gewants; *The World at Large*, by James McMichael.

‡UNIVERSITY OF GEORGIA PRESS, 330 Research Dr., Athens GA 30602-4901. (706)369-6130. Fax: (706)369-6131. E-mail: ugapress@uga.edu. **Acquisitions:** David Dejardines, acquisition editor. Estab. 1938. University of Georgia Press is a midsized press "with attention to design and production. We can't cover all areas, but what we do, we do well. We are neither conservative nor edgy, but open-minded." Publishes hardcover originals, trade paperback originals and reprints. Publishes 85 titles/year; imprint publishes 10-15 titles/year. Receives 600 queries/year. 33% of books from first-time authors; 66% from unagented writers. Pays 7-10% royalty on net price. Rarely offers advance; amount varies. Publishes book 1 year after acceptance of ms. Reports in 2 months on queries. Book catalog free. Manuscript guidelines for #10 SASE.
Imprint(s): Brown Thrasher Books, David Dejardines, acquisition editor (paperback originals and reprints, Southern history, literature and culture).
Nonfiction: Subjects include Americana, anthropology/archaeology, art/architecture, government/politics, history, language/literature, nature/environment, philosophy, psychology, regional, religion, sociology. Query or submit outline with 1 sample chapter, author's bio with SASE. Reviews artwork/photos as part of ms package if essential to book.
Recent Nonfiction Title(s): *Knights of Spain, Warriors of the Sun: Hernando de Soto and the South's Ancient Chieftains*, by Charles Hudson (biography).
Fiction: Literary. Query with 1-2 sample chapters and SASE.
Recent Fiction Title(s): *The Quarry*, by Harvey Grossinger (novel); *Lost in Translation*, by Steven Harvey (essays).
Poetry: Query first for guidelines and submission periods; $10 submission fee required.
Recent Poetry Title(s): *Viridian*, by Paul Hoover; *The Secularist*, by Claudia Keelan.

UNIVERSITY OF IDAHO PRESS, 16 Brink Hall, Moscow ID 83844-1107. (208)885-5939. Fax: (208)885-9059. E-mail: uipress@raven.csrv.uidaho.edu. **Acquisitions:** Peggy Pace, director. Estab. 1972. The University of Idaho specializes in regional history and natural history, Native American studies, literature and literary criticism, and Northwest folklore. Publishes hardcover and trade paperback originals and reprints. Publishes 8-10 titles/year. Receives 150-250 queries and 25-50 mss/year. 100% of books from unagented writers. Pays up to 10% royalty on net sales. Publishes book 1 year after acceptance of ms. Reports in 6 months. Book catalog and ms guidelines free.
Imprint(s): Northwest Folklife; Idaho Yesterdays; Northwest Naturalist Books; Living the West.
Nonfiction: Biography, reference, technical, textbook. Subjects include agriculture/horticulture, Americana, anthropology/archaeology, ethnic, folklore, history, language/literature, nature/environment, recreation, regional, women's issues/studies. "Writers should contact us to discuss projects in advance and refer to our catalog to become familiar with the types of projects the press publishes. Avoid being unaware of the constraints of scholarly publishing, and avoid submitting queries and manuscripts in areas we don't publish in." Query or submit proposal package, including sample chapter, contents, vita. Reviews artwork/photos as part of ms package. Writers should send photocopies.
Recent Nonfiction Title(s): *Arams of Idaho*, by Kristi Youngdahl (history); *Fire, Faults and Floods: Exploring the Origins of the Columbia River Basin*, by Marge and Ted Mueller; *The Milwaukee Revisited*, by Stanley W. Johnson.
Tips: Audience is educated readers, scholars.

UNIVERSITY OF ILLINOIS PRESS, 1325 S. Oak St., Champaign IL 61820-6903. (217)333-0950. Fax: (217)244-8082. E-mail: uipress@uiuc.edu. Website: http://www.uiuc.edu/providers/uipress. **Acquisitions:** Richard Wentworth, director/editor-in-chief. Estab. 1918. University of Illinois Press publishes "scholarly books and serious nonfiction" with a wide range of study interests. Publishes hardcover and trade paperback originals and reprints. Publishes 100-110 titles/year. 50% of books from first-time authors; 95% from unagented writers. Nonauthor-subsidy publishes 10% of books. Pays 0-10% royalty on net sales; offers $1,000-1,500 average advance (rarely). Publishes book 1 year after acceptance. Reports in 1 month. *Writer's Market* recommends allowing 2 months for reply. Book catalog for 9×12 SAE with 2 first-class stamps.
   ● University of Illinois Press has published such authors as James McPherson, John Hope Franklin, Michael Harper, David Montgomery, Allen Guttmann and David Lewis.
Nonfiction: Biography, reference, scholarly books. Subjects include Americana, history (especially American history), music (especially American music), politics, sociology, philosophy, sports, literature. Always looking for "solid, scholarly books in American history, especially social history; books on American popular music, and books in the broad area of American studies." Query with outline.
Recent Nonfiction Title(s): *Woody, Cisco, and Me: Seamen Three in the Merchant Marine*, edited by Jim Longhi; *Atomic Spaces: Living on the Manhattan Project*, by Peter Bacon Hales; *Last Cavalier: The Life and Times of John A. Lomax, 1867-1948*, by Nolan Porterfield.
Fiction: Ethnic, experimental, mainstream. "We are not presently looking at unsolicited collections of stories. We do not publish novels." Query.
Recent Fiction Title(s): *Distant Friends and Intimate Strangers*, by Charles East; *Taking It Home: Stories from the Neighborhood*, by Tony Ardizzone; *Flights in the Heavenlies*, by Ernest J. Finney.
Recent Poetry Title(s): *The Ways We Touch*, by Miller Williams; *My Alexandria*, by Mark Doty; *Walt Whitman Bathing*, by David Wagoner.
Tips: "Serious scholarly books that are broad enough and well-written enough to appeal to non-specialists are doing well for us in today's market."

UNIVERSITY OF IOWA PRESS, 119 W. Park Rd., Iowa City IA 52242-1000. (319)335-2000. Fax: (319)335-2055. Website: http://www.uiowa.edu/~uipress. **Acquisitions:** Paul Zimmer, director. Estab. 1969. "We publish authoritative, original nonfiction that we market mostly by direct mail to groups with special interests in our titles and by advertising in trade and scholarly publications." Publishes hardcover and paperback originals. Publishes 35 titles/year. Receives 300-400 submissions/year. 30% of books from first-time authors; 95% from unagented writers. Average print order for a first book is 1,000-1,200. Pays 7-10% royalty on net price. Publishes book 1 year after acceptance. Reports within 4 months. Book catalog and ms guidelines free.
Nonfiction: Publishes anthropology, archaeology, British and American literary studies, history (Victorian, U.S., regional Latin American), jazz studies, history of photography and natural history. Looks for evidence of original research; reliable sources; clarity of organization; complete development of theme with documentation, supportive footnotes and/ or bibliography; and a substantive contribution to knowledge in the field treated. Query or submit outline. Use *Chicago Manual of Style*. Reviews artwork/photos as part of ms package.
Recent Nonfiction Title(s): *The Guide to Classic Recorded Jazz*, by Tom Piazza; *Snake's Daughter*, by Gail Hasking Gilberg (autobiography/military history); *Small-Town Heroes: Images of Minor League Baseball*, by Hank Davis.
Fiction and Poetry: Currently publishes the Iowa Short Fiction Award selections and winners of the Iowa Poetry Prize Competition. Query regarding poetry or fiction before sending ms.
Tips: "Developing a list of books on baseball history."

UNIVERSITY OF MASSACHUSETTS PRESS, P.O. Box 429, Amherst MA 01004-0429. (413)545-2217. Fax: (413)545-1226. Website: http://www.umass.edu/umpress. Director: Bruce Wilcox. **Acquisitions**: Clark Dougan, senior editor. Estab. 1963. "Our mission is to publish first-rate books, design them well and market them vigorously. In so doing, the Press enhances the visibility and stature of the university." Publishes hardcover and paperback originals, reprints and imports. Publishes 40 titles/year. Receives 600 submissions/year. 20% of books from first-time authors; 90% from unagented writers. Average print order for a first book is 2,000. Royalties generally begin at 10% of net income. Advance sometimes offered. Publishes book 1 year after acceptance. Preliminary report in 1 month. *Writer's Market* recommends allowing 2 months for reply. Book catalog free.
Nonfiction: Publishes African-American studies, art and architecture, biography, criticism, history, natural history, philosophy, poetry, public policy, sociology and women's studies in original and reprint editions. Accepts nonfiction translations. Submit outline and 1-2 sample chapters. Reviews artwork/photos as part of ms package.
Recent Nonfiction Title(s): *Dr. America: The Lives of Thomas A. Dooley, 1927-1961*, by James T. Fisher; *The Farm: Life Inside a Women's Prison*, by Andi Rierden (women's studies/criminology); *The Lesbian Menace: Ideology, Identity and the Representation of Lesbian Life*, by Sherrie A. Inness (gay/lesbian studies).

UNIVERSITY OF MISSOURI PRESS, 2910 LeMone Blvd., Columbia MO 65201. (573)882-7641. Website: http://www.system.missouri.edu/press. Director: Beverly Jarrett. **Acquisitions:** Mr. Clair Willcox, acquisitions editor. University of Missouri Press publishes primarily scholarly nonfiction in the social sciences and also some short fiction collections. Publishes hardcover and paperback originals and paperback reprints. Publishes 50 titles/year. Receives 500 submissions/year. 25-30% of books from first-time authors; 90% from unagented writers. Average print order for a first book is 1,000-1,500. Pays up to 10% royalty on net receipts. No advance. Publishes book 1 year after acceptance. Reports in 6 months. Book catalog free.
Nonfiction: Scholarly publisher interested in history, literary criticism, political science, journalism, social science, some art history. Also regional books about Missouri and the Midwest. No mathematics or hard sciences. Query or submit outline and sample chapters. Consult *Chicago Manual of Style*.
Recent Nonfiction Title(s): *Shades of Blue and Gray*, by Herman Hattaway (Civil War history); *Confessions of a Depression Muralist*, by Frank W. Long (autobiography); *Zion in the Valley*, by Walter Ehrlich (Jewish studies).
Fiction: "Collections of short fiction are considered throughout the year; the press does not publish novels. Inquiries should include sample story, a table of contents and a brief description of the manuscript that notes its length."
Recent Fiction Title(s): *Four Decades: New and Selected Stories*, by Gordon Weaver; *Quake*, by Nance Van Winckel.

UNIVERSITY OF NEBRASKA PRESS, 312 N. 14th St., P.O. Box 880484, Lincoln NE 68588-0484. (402)472-3581. Fax: (402)472-0308. E-mail: press@unlinfo.unl.edu. Website: http://www.unl.edu./UP/home.htm. **Acquisitions:** Douglas Clayton, editor-in-chief (fiction in translation, humanities); Dan Ross, director (military, sports); Gary Dunham, editor (Native American anthropology); Clark Whitehorn, editor (history, nature). Estab. 1941. "The University of Nebraska Press seeks to encourage, develop, publish and disseminate research, literature and the publishing arts. The Press maintains scholarly standards and fosters innovations guided by referred evaluations." Publishes hardcover and paperback originals and reprints. Publishes 75 new titles, 80 paperback reprints (*Bison Books*)/year. Receives more than 1,000 submissions/year. 25% of books from first-time authors; 95% from unagented writers. Average print order for a first book is 1,200. Pays graduated royalty from 7% on original books. Occasional advance. Reports in 4 months. Book catalog and guidelines for 9 × 12 SAE with 5 first-class stamps.
 ● University of Nebraska Press has published such authors as N. Scott Momaday, Rolena Adorna (Cabeza de Vaca) and Diane Glancy.
Imprint(s): Bison Books, Jay Fultz, editor (paperback reprints); Landmark Editions (hardcover reprints).
Nonfiction: Specializes in scholarly nonfiction, some regional books; reprints of Western Americana, American history and culture. Publishes Americana, biography, history, military, nature, photography, psychology, sports, literature, agriculture, American Indian, anthropology, ethnohistory, music, criticism, women's studies, Judaica, political science. "We

are particularly interested in good writing about Nebraska." Accepts nonfiction translations. Query with outline/synopsis, 1 sample chapter and introduction. Looks for "an indication that the author knows his/her subject thoroughly and interprets it intelligently." Reviews artwork/photos as part of ms package.
Recent Nonfiction Title(s): *Art for Art's Sake and Literary Life*, by Gene H. Bell-Villada (aesthetics, culture); *The Turn to the Native*, by Arnold Krupat (Native American culture and criticism); *The Machete & the Cross*, by Don Dumond (ethnic conflict in the Yucatan peninsula, 19th century).
Fiction: Accepts fiction translations but no original fiction.
Recent Fiction Title(s): *School Days*, by Patrick Chamoiseau (Caribbean childhood memoir); *Rue Ordener, Rue Labat*, Sarah Kofman (France-Judaism, 20th century); *Celebration in the Northwest*, by Ana Maria Matute (contemporary Spanish women's fiction).

UNIVERSITY OF NEVADA PRESS, MS 166, Reno NV 89557. (702)784-6573. Fax: (702)784-6200. E-mail: dalrympl@scs.unr.edu. Director: Ronald E. Latimer. Editor-in-Chief: Margaret F. Dalrymple. **Acquisitions:** Trudy McMurrin, acquisitions editor. Estab. 1961. "We are the first university press to sustain a sound series on Basque studies—New World and Old World." Publishes hardcover and paperback originals and reprints. Publishes 35 titles/year. 20% of books from first-time authors; 99% from unagented writers. Average print order for a first book is 2,000. Pays average of 10% royalty on net price. Publishes book 1 year after acceptance. Preliminary report in 2 months. Book catalog and ms guidelines free.
Nonfiction: Specifically needs regional history and natural history, literature, current affairs, ethnonationalism, gambling and gaming, anthropology, biographies, Basque studies. No juvenile books. Submit complete ms. *Writer's Market* recommends query with SASE first. Reviews photocopies of artwork/photos as part of ms package.
Recent Nonfiction Title(s): *Atlas of Nevada Conifers: A Phytogeographic Reference*, by David Alan Charlet; *The Archaeology of the Donner Party*, by Donald L. Hardesty (history); *Old Heart of Nevada*, by Shawn Hall.
Recent Fiction Title(s): *The Measurable World*, by Katharine Coles (novel); *Separations*, by Oakley Hall; *Breathe Something Nice*, by Emily Hammond.
Recent Poetry Title(s): *From the Still Empty Grave*, by A. Wilber Stevens (collected poems).

UNIVERSITY OF NEW MEXICO PRESS, 1720 Lomas Blvd. NE, Albuquerque NM 87131-1591. (505)277-2346. **Acquisitions:** Dana Asbury, editor. Estab. 1929. "The Press is well known as a scholarly publisher, especially in the fields of anthropology, archaeology, Latin American studies, photography, architecture and the history and culture of the American West." Publishes hardcover originals and trade paperback originals and reprints. Publishes 50 titles/year. Receives 600 submissions/year. 12% of books from first-time authors; 90% from unagented writers. Pays up to 15% royalty on wholesale price. Publishes book 1 year after acceptance. Reports in 2 weeks on queries. *Writer's Market* recommends allowing 2 months for reply. Book catalog free.
Nonfiction: Biography, illustrated book, scholarly books. Subjects include anthropology/archaeology, art/architecture, ethnic, history, photography. "No how-to, humor, juvenile, self-help, software, technical or textbooks." Query. Reviews artwork/photos as part of ms package. Prefers to see photocopies first.
Tips: "Most of our authors are academics. A scholarly monograph by an academic has a better chance than anything else. Our audience is a combination of academics and interested lay readers."

UNIVERSITY OF NORTH TEXAS PRESS, P.O. Box 13856, Denton TX 76203-3856. Fax: (817)565-4590. E-mail: vick@acad.admin.unt.edu or wright@acad.admin.unt.edu. Website: accessible through www.tamu.edu/upress. **Acquisitions**: Frances B. Vick, director. Charlotte Wright, editor. Estab. 1987. "We have series called War and the Southwest; Environmental Philosophy Series; Practical Guide Series; Texas Folklore Society Publications series; the Western Life Series; Literary Biographies of Texas Writers series." Publishes hardcover and trade paperback originals and reprints. Publishes 15-20 titles/year. Receives 400 queries and mss/year. 95% of books from unagented writers. Pays 7½-10% royalty of net. Publishes book 2 years after acceptance of ms. Reports in 3 months on queries. Book catalog for 8½×11 SASE.
 • University of North Texas Press has published such authors as A.C. Greene and John R. Erickson (the creator of "Hank the Cowdog").
Nonfiction: Biography, reference. Subjects include agriculture/horticulture, Americana, ethnic, government/politics, history, language/literature, military/war, nature/environment, regional. Query. Reviews artwork/photos as part of ms package. Send photocopies.
Recent Nonfiction Title(s): *A Sniper in the Tower: The Charles Whitman Murders*, by Gary Lavergne (Texas/American history/social sciences); *Cowboy Fiddler in Bob Wills' Band*, by Frankie McWhorter as told to John R. Erickson (music/ranching).
Recent Fiction Title(s): *Monday's Meal*, by Les Edgerton (short stories).
Poetry: Offers the Vassar Miller Prize in Poetry, an annual, national competition resulting in the publication of a winning manuscript each fall. Query first.
Tips: Books distributed by Texas A&M University Consortium.

UNIVERSITY OF OKLAHOMA PRESS, 1005 Asp Ave., Norman OK 73019-0445. (405)325-5111. Fax: (405)325-4000. E-mail: jdrayton@ou.edu. **Acquisitions:** John Drayton, editor-in-chief (western history); Ron Chrisman, acquisitions editor (paperbacks); Kimberly Wiar, acquisitions editor (Native American literature, political science, natural history, literary criticism, classics). Estab. 1928. University of Oklahoma Press strives "to publish books of use to both

a scholarly and general audience." Publishes hardcover and paperback originals and reprints. Publishes 90 titles/year. Pays royalty comparable to those paid by other publishers for comparable books. Publishes book 12-18 months after acceptance. Reports in 3 months. Book catalog for $1 and 9×12 SAE with 6 first-class stamps.
Imprint(s): Oklahoma Paperbacks.
● University of Oklahoma Press has published such authors as Gerald Vizenor, Louis Owens and John C. Ewers.
Nonfiction: Publishes Native American studies, Western U.S. history, political science, literary theory, natural history, women's studies, classical studies. No unsolicited poetry and fiction. Query with outline, 1-2 sample chapters and author résumé. Use *Chicago Manual of Style* for ms guidelines. Reviews artwork/photos as part of ms package.
Recent Nonfiction Title(s): *Encyclopedia of United States Army Insignia and Uniforms*, by William K. Emerson (military); *Alias Frank Canton*, by Robert K. DeArment (western biography); *The C-Span Revolution*, by Stephen Frantzich and John Sullivan (political science).
Recent Fiction Title(s): *From the Glittering World: A Navajo Story*, by Irvin Morris (Native American); *Ride the Lightning*, by Robert H. Mitchell (Oklahoma history).

UNIVERSITY OF SCRANTON PRESS, University of Scranton, Scranton PA 18510-4660. (717)941-4228. Fax: (717)941-4309. E-mail: rousseaur1@uofs.edu. Website: http://www.uofs.edu.uofspress/uofspress.html. **Acquisitions:** Richard Rousseau, director. Estab. 1981. The University of Scranton Press, a member of the Association of Jesuit University Presses, publishes primarily scholarly monographs in theology, philosophy and the culture of northeast Pennsylvania. Publishes hardcover paperbacks and originals. Publishes 5 titles/year. Receives 200 queries and 45 mss/year. 60% of books from first-time authors; 100% from unagented writers. Pays 10% royalty. Publishes book 1 year after acceptance. Reports in 1 month on queries. Book catalog and ms guidelines free.
Imprint(s): Ridge Row Press.
Nonfiction: Scholarly monographs. Subjects include art/architecture, language/literature, philosophy, religion, sociology. Looking for clear editorial focus: theology/religious studies; philosophy/philosophy of religion; scholarly treatments; the culture of northeast Pennsylvania. Query or submit outline and 2 sample chapters.
Recent Nonfiction Title(s): *The Christianity of Constantine the Great*, by T.G. Elliott; *No Higher Court*, by Germain Kopaczynski.
Poetry: Only poetry related to northeast Pennsylvania.
Recent Poetry Title(s): *Coalseam, 2nd edition*, edited by K. Blomain.

THE UNIVERSITY OF TENNESSEE PRESS, 293 Communications Bldg., Knoxville TN 37996-0325. Fax: (423)974-3724. E-mail: jsiler@utk.edu. Website: http://www.lib.utk.edu/UTKgophers/UT-PRESS. **Acquisitions:** Joyce Harrison, acquisitions editor; Jenifer Siler, director. Estab. 1940. "Our mission is to stimulate scientific and scholarly research in all fields; to channel such studies, either in scholarly or popular form, to a larger number of people; and to extend the regional leadership of the University of Tennessee by stimulating research projects within the South and by non-university authors." Publishes 30 titles/year. Receives 450 submissions/year. 35% of books from first-time authors; 99% from unagented writers. Average print order for a first book is 1,000. Nonauthor-subsidy publishes 10% of books. Pays negotiable royalty on net receipts. Publishes book 1 year after acceptance. Reports in 2 months. Book catalog for 12×16 SAE with 2 first-class stamps. Manuscript guidelines for SASE.
● The University of Tennessee Press now accepts submissions of *regional* fiction.
Nonfiction: American history, cultural studies, religious studies, vernacular architecture and material culture, literary criticism, African-American studies, women's studies, Caribbean, anthropology, folklore and regional studies. Prefers "scholarly treatment and a readable style. Authors usually have Ph.D.s." Submit outline, author vita and 2 sample chapters. No poetry or plays. Reviews artwork/photos as part of ms package.
Recent Nonfiction Title(s): *Echoes from the Holocaust*, by Mira Kimmelman (Judaica studies); *New Negroes and Their Music*, by Jon Michael Spencer (African-American studies); *Hiking Trails of the Great Smoky Mountains*, by Kenneth Wise (hiking guide).
Fiction: Regional. *Writer's Market* recommends sending a query with SASE first.
Recent Fiction Title(s): *Sharpshooter*, by David Madden (Civil War novel).
Tips: "Our market is in several groups: scholars; educated readers with special interests in given scholarly subjects; and the general educated public interested in Tennessee, Appalachia and the South. Not all our books appeal to all these groups, of course, but any given book must appeal to at least one of them."

UNIVERSITY OF TEXAS PRESS, P.O. Box 7819, Austin TX 78713-7819. Fax: (512)320-0668. E-mail: castiron@mail.utexas.edu. Website: http://www.utexas.edu/utpress/. **Acquisitions:** Theresa May, assistant director/executive editor (social sciences, Latin American studies); Joanna Hitchcock, director (humanities, classics); Shannon Davies, acquisitions editor (science). Estab. 1952. "The mission of the University of Texas Press is to advance and disseminate knowledge through the publication of books. In addition to publishing the results of advanced research for scholars worldwide, UT Press has a special obligation to the people of its state to publish authoritative books on Texas." Publishes 80 titles/year. Receives 1,000 submissions/year. 50% of books from first-time authors; 99% from unagented writers. Average print order for a first book is 1,000. Pays royalty usually based on net income. Offers advance occasionally. Publishes book 18 months after acceptance. Reports in up to 3 months. Book catalog and ms guidelines free.
Nonfiction: General scholarly subjects: natural history, American, Latin American, Native American, Chicano and Middle Eastern studies, classics and the ancient world, film, contemporary regional architecture, archaeology, anthropology, geography, ornithology, environmental studies, biology, linguistics, women's literature, literary biography (Modern-

ist period). Also uses specialty titles related to Texas and the Southwest, national trade titles and regional trade titles. Accepts nonfiction translations related to above areas. Query or submit outline and 2 sample chapters. Reviews artwork/photos as part of ms package.

Recent Nonfiction Title(s): *How Writing Came About*, by Denise Schmandt-Besserat (archaeology); *Surviving in Two Worlds*, by Lois Crozier-Hogle and Darryl Babe Wilson (Native American studies); *Contemporary Mexican Women Writers*, by Gabriella de Beer (Latin American studies).

Fiction: Latin American and Middle Eastern fiction only in translation.

Recent Fiction Title(s): *Satan's Stones*, by Moniru Ravanipur (short stories).

Recent Poetry Title(s): *Twentieth-Century Latin American Poetry: A Bilingual Anthology*, edited by Stephen Tapscott.

Tips: "It's difficult to make a manuscript over 400 double-spaced pages into a feasible book. Authors should take special care to edit out extraneous material. Looks for sharply focused, in-depth treatments of important topics."

UNIVERSITY PRESS OF COLORADO, 4699 Nautilus Court, Suite 403, Boulder CO 80301. (303)530-5337. Fax: (303)530-5306. Director: Luther Wilson. **Acquisitions:** Laura Furney, acquisitions editor. Estab. 1965. "We are a university press. Books should be solidly researched and from a reputable scholar." Publishes hardcover and paperback originals. Publishes 20 titles/year. Receives 1,000 submissions/year. 50% of books from first-time authors; 95% from unagented writers. Average print order for a first book is 1,500-2,000. Pays 7½-10-12½-15% royalty contract on net price. No advance. Publishes book 2 years after acceptance. Reports in 6 months. Book catalog free.

● University Press of Colorado has reduced their number of book published from 40 to 20 titles/year. They have published such authors as Max Evans and George McGovern.

Nonfiction: Scholarly, regional and environmental subjects. Length: 250-500 pages. Query first with table of contents, preface or opening chapter. Reviews artwork/photos as part of ms package.

Recent Nonfiction Title(s): *Colorado Byways*, by Thomas Huber (natural history); *Prehistory in Peril*, by Florence C. Lister (archaeology); *Apache Pilgrimage*, by Karen Hayes (Western history).

Fiction: Limited fiction series; works of fiction on the trans-Mississippi West, by authors residing in the region. Query.

Recent Fiction Title(s): *Roll On Columbia*, by Bill Gulick (historical fiction); *Mari*, by Jane Valentine Barker (historical fiction/Women's West series).

Tips: "We have series on the Women's West and on Mesoamerican worlds."

‡UNIVERSITY PRESS OF FLORIDA, 15 NW 15th St., Gainesville FL 32611. (352)392-1351. **Acquisitions:** Meredith Morris-Babb, editor-in-chief. "The Press seeks to maintain the professional excellence of American university presses in general and to present the finest national and international scholarship in those academic areas in which we publish. In recognition of the State University System's educational mission and public role, the Press also publishes books of interest and significance for our region and state." Publishes hardcover and trade paperback originals and reprints. Publishes 60-70 titles/year. Receives 400 queries and 75 mss/year. 30% of books from first-time quthors; 100% from unagented writers. Pays 5-10% royalty on wholesale price. No advance. Publishes book 1 year after acceptance of ms. Accepts simultaneous submissions. Reports in 2 weeks on queries, 1 month on proposals, 2 months on mss.

Nonfiction: Academic and regional interest. Subjects include Floridiana, archaeology, architecture, history, language/literature, photography, international relations: Latin America, Middle East.

Recent Nonfiction Title(s): *Indian Art of Ancient Florida*, by Barbara A. Purdy; *The Black Seminoles*, by Kenneth W. Porter (history); *Celebrating Florida: Works of Art from the Vickers Collection*, edited by Gary R. Libley.

Tips: "Our audience has a regional interest for our trade and academic titles."

UNIVERSITY PRESS OF KENTUCKY, 663 S. Limestone, Lexington KY 40508-4008. (606)257-2951. Fax: (606)257-2984. Website: http://www.uky.edu/UniversityPress/. **Acquisitions:** Nancy Grayson Holmes, editor-in-chief. Estab. 1951. "We are a scholarly publisher, publishing chiefly for an academic and professional audience." Publishes hardcover and paperback originals and reprints. Publishes 60 titles/year. Payment varies. No advance. Publishes ms 1 year after acceptance. Reports in 2 months on queries. Book catalog free.

Nonfiction: Biography, reference, monographs. "Strong areas are American history, literature, women's studies, American studies, folklore and ethnomusicology, Appalachian studies, Irish studies and military history film studies. No textbooks, genealogical material, lightweight popular treatments, how-to books or books unrelated to our major areas of interest." The Press does not consider original works of fiction or poetry. Query.

Recent Nonfiction Title(s): *Women Politicians and the Media*, by Maria Braden; *A New History of Kentucky*, by Lowell Harrison and James Klotter; *Life on the Ohio*, by Captain James Coomer.

Tips: "Most of our authors are drawn from our primary academic and professional audience. We are probably not a good market for the usual freelance writer."

UNIVERSITY PRESS OF MISSISSIPPI, 3825 Ridgewood Rd., Jackson MS 39211-6492. (601)982-6205. Fax: (601)982-6217. E-mail: press@ihl.state.ms.us. Director: Richard Abel. Associate Director and Editor-in-Chief: Seetha Srinivasan. **Acquisitions:** Acquisitions Editor. Estab. 1970. "University Press of Mississippi publishes scholarly and trade titles, as well as special series, including: American Made Music; Author and Artist; Comparative Diaspora Studies; Faulkner and Yoknapatawpha; Fiction Series; Folk Art and Artists; Folklife in the South; Literary Conversations; Natural History; Performance Studies in Culture; Studies in Popular Culture; Understanding Health and Sickness; Writers and Their Work." Publishes hardcover and paperback originals and reprints. Publishes 55 titles/year. Receives 750 submissions/year. 20% of books from first-time authors; 90% from unagented writers. "Competitive royalties and terms."

Publishes book 1 year after acceptance. Reports in 3 months. Catalog for 9×12 SAE with 3 first-class stamps.
Imprint(s): Muscadine Books (regional trade) and Banner Books (literary reprints).
Nonfiction: Americana, biography, history, politics, folklife, literary criticism, ethnic/minority studies, art, photography, music, health, popular culture with scholarly emphasis. Interested in southern regional studies and literary studies. Submit outline, sample chapters and curriculum vita. "We prefer a proposal that describes the significance of the work and a chapter outline." Reviews artwork/photos as part of ms package.
Recent Nonfiction Title(s): *The Several Lives of Chester Himes*, by Edward Margolies and Michel Fabre (biography); *Swamp Pop: Cajun and Creole Rhythm and Blues*, by Shane K. Bernard (Cajun and zydeco music); *After the Machine: Visual Arts and the Erasing of Cultural Boundaries*, by Miles Orvell.
Fiction: Commissioned trade editions by prominent writers.
Recent Fiction Title(s): *Skin Deep*, by Diana Wagman; *Me: A Book of Remembrance*, by Winnifred Eaton.

UNIVERSITY PRESS OF NEW ENGLAND, (includes Wesleyan University Press), 23 S. Main St., Hanover NH 03755-2048. (603)643-7100. Fax: (603)643-1540. E-mail: university.press@dartmouth.edu. Director: Peter Gilbert. **Acquisitions:** Phil Pochoda, editorial director. Editor: Phyliss Deutch. Estab. 1970. "University Press of New England is a consortium of university presses. Some books—those published for one of the consortium members—carry the joint imprint of New England and the member: Wesleyan, Dartmouth, Brandeis, Tufts, University of New Hampshire and Middlebury College. Associate member: Salzburg seminar." Publishes hardcover and trade paperback originals, trade paperback reprints. Publishes 70 titles/year. Nonauthor-subsidy publishes 80% of books. Pays standard royalty. Offers advance occasionally. Reports in 2 months. Book catalog and guidelines for 9×12 SAE with 5 first-class stamps.
Nonfiction: Americana (New England), art, biography, history, music, nature, politics, reference, sociology, regional (New England). No festschriften, memoirs, unrevised doctoral dissertations, or symposium collections. Submit outline, 1-2 sample chapters with SASE.
Recent Nonfiction Title(s): *Winter's Light*, by John Preston (memoir/gay studies); *The Measure of My Days*, by David Loxterkamp (medicine/memoir); *The Face of Glory*, by William Anderson (philosophy).
Fiction: Regional (New England) novels and reprints.
Recent Fiction Title(s): *Water Witches*, by Chris Bohjalian (novel); *A Great Place to Die*, by Sean Connolly; *Professor Romeo*, by Anne Bernays.

‡UPSTART PUBLISHING CO., Imprint of Dearborn Publishing Group, 155 N. Wacker Dr., Chicago IL 60606. (312)836-4400. Website: http://www.dearborn.com. **Acquisitions:** Danielle Egan-Miller, acquisitions editor. Estab. 1979. "Upstart Publishing Company works with colleges and universities to provide hands-on textbooks on business and management, and publishes detailed guides for entrepreneurs." Publishes trade paperback originals. Publishes 20 titles/year. 50% of books from first-time authors; 50% from unagented writers. Pays 1-15% royalty of wholesale price. Offers advance, $2,000 average. Publishes book 6 months after acceptance of ms. Accepts simultaneous submissions. Reports in 2 months on queries. Book catalog and ms guidelines free.
Nonfiction: Textbooks, multimedia (CD-ROM). Business subjects. Query with proposal package including 2 chapters, author information, "any unusual credentials, seminar experience, etc. is useful" and SASE.
Recent Nonfiction Title(s): *Anatomy of a Business Plan*, by Linda Pinson and Jerry Jinnett; *The Business Planning Guide*, by David Bang.

UTAH STATE UNIVERSITY PRESS, Logan UT 84322-7800. (801)797-1362. Fax: (801)797-0313. Website: http://www.usu/edu/~usupress. Director: Michael Spooner. **Acquisitions:** John Alley, editor. Estab. 1972. "Particularly interested in book-length scholarly manuscripts dealing with folklore, Western history, Western literature." Publishes hardcover and trade paperback originals and reprints. Publishes 15 titles/year. Receives 170 submissions/year. 8% of books from first-time authors. Pays royalty on net price. No advance. Publishes book 18 months after acceptance. Reports in 1 month on queries. Book catalog free. Manuscript guidelines for SASE.
  • Utah State University Press is especially interested in supporting Native American writers with scholarly or creative manuscripts.
Nonfiction: Biography, reference and textbook on folklore, Americana (history and politics). *Writer's Market* recommends query with SASE first. Reviews artwork/photos as part of ms package.
Recent Nonfiction Title(s): *Unfortunate Emigrants*, edited by Kristin Johnson; *Wolf Tourist: One Summer in the West*, by Jay Robert Elhard; *Worth Their Salt*, edited by Colleen Whitley.
Poetry: "Accepting very few creative works at present. Query before sending manuscript."
Tips: "Marketability of work is more important than ever."

VALLEY OF THE SUN PUBLISHING, P.O. Box 38, Malibu CA 90265. President: Richard Sutphen. **Acquisitions:** Laura King, editor. "Our purpose is to promote mental, physical and philosophical self-sufficiency. We are dedicated to communicating Master of Life concepts: a personal philosophy of becoming all you are capable of being, and a perspective of involved detachment in which you accept all the warmth and joy in life while mentally detaching from negativity." Publishes trade paperback originals and trade paperback reprints. Publishes 12 titles/year. 20% of books from first-time authors; 100% from unagented writers. Pays 8-10% royalty on net price. "We have a large-circulation magalog, and it's not unusual to sell half our books directly at full price. The 8-10% is based upon what we sell them for." Offers $1,500-2,000 advance. Publishes book 9 months after acceptance of ms. Accepts simultaneous submissions. Reports in 2 months. Book catalog free. Manuscript guidelines for #10 SASE.

Nonfiction: Self-help, New Age metaphysical. Submit outline with 2 sample chapters or complete ms. *Writer's Market* recommends sending a query with SASE first. Reviews artwork/photos as part of ms package. Send photocopies.
Recent Nonfiction Title(s): *Metaphysical Techniques That Really Work*, by Audrey Davis (New Age); *The Couple Who Became Each Other*, by David L. Calof (self-help); *Conversations With God*, by Neale Donald Walsch.

VANDAMERE PRESS, Imprint of AB Associates International, Inc., P.O. Box 5243, Arlington VA 22205. **Acquisitions:** Jerry Frank, editor. Vandamere publishes general fiction as well as nonfiction of historical, biographical or regional interest. Publishes hardcover and trade paperback originals and reprints. Publishes 8-15 titles/year. Receives 750 queries and 2,000 mss/year. 25% of books from first-time authors; 90% from unagented writers. Pays royalty on revenues generated. Publishes book 1-3 years after acceptance. Accepts simultaneous submissions. Reports in 6 months.
• Vandamere Press is looking for more history and biography manuscripts. They have published such authors as Hugh G. Gallagher and Dr. Richard Edlich.
Nonfiction: Subjects include Americana, biography, child guidance/parenting, education, history, military/war, regional (Washington D.C./Mid-Atlantic). Submit outline and 2-3 sample chapters. Reviews artwork/photos as part of ms package. Send photocopies.
Recent Nonfiction Title(s): *Simpler Times*, by J. George Butler (history); *Hostile Fire*, Philip Bigler (biography); *Midwest Computer Job Guide*, by Carol Covin (career guide).
Fiction: General fiction including adventure, erotica, humor, mystery, suspense. Submit synopsis and 5-10 sample chapters. *Writer's Market* recommends sending a query with SASE first.
Recent Fiction Title(s): *Hegemon*, by Alexander M. Grace (adventure/suspense).
Tips: "Authors who can provide endorsements from significant published writers, celebrities, etc., will *always* be given serious consideration. Clean, easy-to-read, *dark* copy is essential. Patience in waiting for replies is essential. All unsolicited work is looked at, but at certain times of the year our review schedule will stop." No response without SASE.

VANDERBILT UNIVERSITY PRESS, Box 1813, Station B, Nashville TN 37235. (615)322-3585. Fax: (615)343-8823. E-mail: vupress@vanderbilt.edu. Website: http://www.vanderbilt.edu/Publications/VUPress/welcome. **Acquisitions:** Charles Backus, director. Among other titles, publishes Vanderbilt Library of American Philosophy (Herman J. Saatkamp, editor). Also distributes for and co-publishes with the Country Music Foundation. "Vanderbilt University Press, the publishing arm of the nation's leading research university, has maintained a strong reputation as a publisher of distinguished titles in the humanities, social sciences, education, medicine and regional studies, for both academic and general audiences, responding to rapid technological and cultural changes, while upholding high standards of scholarly publishing excellence." Publishes hardcover originals and trade paperback originals and reprints. Publishes 15-20 titles/year. Receives 200-250 queries/year. 25% of books from first-time authors; 90% from unagented writers. Pays 15% maximum royalty on net income. Sometimes offers advance. Publishes book 10 months after acceptance. Accepts simultaneous submissions but prefers first option. Reports in 3 months on proposals. Book catalog and ms guidelines free.
• Vanderbilt University Press is not currently accepting poetry or fiction. They have published such authors as Charles K. Wolfe and Phillip Silver.
Nonfiction: Biography, illustrated book, reference, textbook, scholarly. Subjects include Americana, anthropology/archaeology, art/architecture, education, government/politics, health/medicine, history, language/literature, music and popular culture, nature/environment, philosophy, regional, religion, translation, women's issues/studies. Submit outline, 1 sample chapter and cv. Reviews artwork/photos as part of ms package. Send photocopies.
Recent Nonfiction Title(s): *Ramblin' Rose: The Life and Career of Rose Maddox*, by Jonny Whiteside (country music/biography); *Genuine Individuals and Genuine Communities: A Roycean Public Philosophy*, by Jacquelyn Ann K. Kegley (philosophy).
Tips: "Our audience consists of scholars and educated general readers."

‡VENTURE PUBLISHING, INC., 1999 Cato Ave., State College PA 16801. Fax: (814)234-1651. E-mail: vpublish@venturepublish.com. Website: http://www.venturepublish.com. **Acquisitions:** Geof Godbey, editor. Venture publishes textbooks for college academic and professional study. Publishes hardcover originals and reprints. Publishes 6-8 titles/year. Receives 50 queries and 20 mss/year. 40% of books from first-time authors; 100% from unagented writers. Pays royalty on wholesale price. Offers $1,000 advance. Publishes book 9 months after acceptance of ms. Reports in 1 month on queries; 2 months on proposals and mss. Book catalog and ms guidelines free.
Nonfiction: Textbook, college academic, professional. Subjects include nature/environment (outdoor recreation management and leadership texts), recreation, sociology (leisure studies), long-term care nursing homes, therapeutic recreation. "Textbooks and books for recreation activity leaders high priority." Submit outline and 1 sample chapter.
Recent Nonfiction Title(s): *Aerobics of the Mind: Keeping the Mind Active in Aging—A New Perspective on Programming for Older Adults*, by Marge Engelman; *File o' Fun: A Recreation Planner for Games & Activities, 3rd edition*, by Jane Harris Ericson.

VERSO, 180 Varick St., 10th Fl., New York NY 10014. Website: http://www.best.com/~verso. **Acquisitions:** Colin Robinson, managing director. "Our books cover politics, culture, and history (among other topics), but all come from a critical, Leftist viewpoint, on the border between trade and academic." Publishes hardcover and trade paperback originals. Publishes 40-60 titles/year. Receives 300 queries and 150 mss/year. 10% of mss from first-time authors, 95%

from unagented writers. Pays royalty. Publishes book 1 year after acceptance of ms. Accepts simultaneous submissions. Reports in 5 months. Book catalog free.

Nonfiction: Illustrated book. Subjects include economics, government/politics, history, philosophy, sociology and women's issues/studies. "We are loosely affiliated with *New Left Review* (London). We are not interested in academic monographs." Submit proposal package, including at least one sample chapter.

Recent Nonfiction Title(s): *The Making of New World Slavery*, by Robin Blackburn; *Red Dirt: Growing Up Okie*, by Roxanne Dunbar-Ortiz (American studies/biography); *Wall Street*, by Doug Henwood (politics/economics).

‡**THE VESTAL PRESS, LTD.**, 320 N. Jensen Rd., P.O. Box 97, Vestal NY 13851-0097. (607)797-4872. **Acquisitions:** Elaine Stuart, acquisitions editor. Vestal specializes in Americana, particularly history, film and musical instruments. Publishes hardcover and trade paperback originals. Publishes 6-8 titles/year. Receives 50 queries and 35 mss/year. 50% of books from first-time writers; 85% from unagented authors. Pays 10% royalty. No advance. Publishes books 18 months after acceptance of ms. Accepts simultaneous submissions. Reports in 2 months on queries, 3 months on proposals, 9 months on mss. Book catalog and ms guidelines free.

Nonfiction: Biography, gift book, how-to, illustrated book, reference, technical. Subjects include Americana, history, hobbies, musical instruments, film history, woodworking. "Submissions should be well researched, well documented and only involve our appropriate subject matter." Submit outline, 3 sample chapters and proposal package, including intended audience. Reviews artwork/photos as part of ms package. Send photocopies.

Recent Nonfiction Title(s): *A Thousand Faces*, by Michael F. Blake (film history); *Carving Miniature Carousel Animals*, by Jerry Reinhardt (woodworking); *The American Reed Organ and the Harmonium*, by Robert F. Wellerman.

Tips: "Make your proposal as interesting and well-written as possible. Make us want to see more."

VGM CAREER HORIZONS, Imprint of NTC/Contemporary Publishing Company, 4255 W. Touhy Ave., Lincolnwood IL 60646-1975. (708)679-5500. Fax: (708)679-2494. Editorial Group Director: John Nolan. **Acquisitions:** Betsy Lancefield, editor. Estab. 1963. Publishes career-focused titles for job seekers, career planners, job changers and students and adults in education and trade markets. Publishes hardcover and paperback originals. Publishes 85-95 titles/year. Receives 200-250 submissions/year. 15% of books from first-time authors; 95% from unagented writers. Pays royalty or makes outright purchase. Advance varies. Publishes book 1 year after acceptance. Accepts simultaneous submissions. Reports in 3 months. Book catalog and ms guidelines for 9×12 SAE with 5 first-class stamps.

● VGM also hires revision authors to handle rewrites and new editions of existing titles and has increased their number of books published from 70-75 to 85-95/year.

Nonfiction: Textbook and general trade on careers in medicine, business, environment, etc. Query or submit outline and sample chapters. Reviews artwork/photos as part of ms package.

Recent Nonfiction Title(s): *Joyce Lain Kennedy's Career Book*, (3rd Edition); *The Guide to Internet Job Searching*.

Tips: "Study our existing line of books before sending proposals."

‡**VICTOR BOOKS**, Adult imprint of Chariot Victor Publishing, 4050 Lee Vance View, Colorado Springs CO 80918. Fax: (719)536-3269. **Acquisitions:** Acquisitions Editor. Estab. 1934. "Victor is interested in both historical and contemporary fiction that is compelling and wholesome, but not preachy." Publishes hardcover and trade paperback originals, both fiction and nonfiction. Averages 40-50 titles/year. Receives 1,200 submissions/year. Pays royalty on all books. Sometimes offers advance. Accepts simultaneous submissions if specified. Reports in 1 month on queries. *Writer's Market* recommends allowing 2 months for reply. Manuscript guidelines for #10 SASE.

Recent Nonfiction Title(s): *Billy Graham: Personal Thoughts of a Public Man*; *The Heritage: How To Be Intentional About the Legacy You Leave*; *The Christian Dad's Answer Book*.

Recent Fiction Title(s): *The Victors*, by Jack Cavanaugh; *My Son, My Savior*, by Calvin Miller; *Shadows on Stoney Creek*, by Wanda Luttrell.

Tips: "All books must in some way be Bible-related by authors who themselves are evangelical Christians with a platform. Victor, therefore, is not a publisher for everybody. Only a small fraction of the manuscripts received can be seriously considered for publication. Most books result from contacts that acquisitions editors make with qualified authors, though from time to time an unsolicited proposal triggers enough excitement to result in a contract. A writer has the best chance of selling Victor a well-conceived and imaginative manuscript that helps the reader apply Christianity to his/her life in practical ways. Christians active in the local church and their children are our audience."

‡**VIKING**, Imprint of Penguin Putnam Inc., 375 Huron St., New York NY 10014. (212)366-2000. **Acquisitions:** Barbara Grossman, publisher. Publishes a mix of academic and popular fiction and nonfiction. Publishes hardcover and trade paperback originals. Pays 10-15% royalty on retail price. Advance negotiable. Publishes book 1 year after acceptance of ms. Accepts simultaneous submissions. Report in 4-6 months on queries.

Nonfiction: Subjects include biography, business/economics, child guidance/parenting, cooking/foods/nutrition, health/medicine, history, language/literature, music/dance, philosophy, women's issues/studies. Agented submissions only.

Recent Nonfiction Title(s): *Without a Doubt*, by Marcia Clark (popular culture).

Fiction: Literary, mainstream/contemporary, mystery, suspense. "Looking for writers who can deliver a book a year (or faster) of consistent quality. No unagented mss. Agented submissions only.

Recent Fiction Title(s): *Out to Canaan*, by John Karon (novel).

‡**VIKING CHILDREN'S BOOKS**, Imprint of Penguin Putnam Inc., 375 Huron St., New York NY 10014. (212)366-2000. **Acquisitions:** Elizabeth Law, editor-in-chief. "Viking Children's Books publishes the highest quality trade books

for children including fiction, nonfiction, and novelty books for pre-schoolers through young adults." Publishes hardcover originals. Publishes 80 books/year. Receives 7500 queries/year. 25% of books from first-time authors; 33% from unagented writers. Pays 10% royalty on retail price. Advance negotiable. Publishes book 1 year after acceptance of ms. Accepts simultaneous submissions. Report in 2 months on queries.
Nonfiction: Children's Books. Subject. Query with outline, one sample chapter and SASE.
Recent Nonfiction Title(s): *See Through History*, series by various authors (history); *Charlotte Bronte and Jane Eyre*, by Stewart Ross (biography).
Fiction: Juvenile, young adult. Query with synopsis, one sample chapter and SASE. Picture books submit entire ms.
Recent Fiction Title(s): *The Awful Aardvarks Go to School*, by Reeve Lindbergh (picture book); *Virtual World*, by Chris Westwood (young adult novel).
Tips: Mistakes often made is that "authors disguise nonfiction in a fictional format."

VILLARD BOOKS, Random House, 201 E. 50th St., New York NY 10022. (212)572-2878. Publisher: David Rosenthal. Director of Publicity: Adam Rothberg. **Acquisitions:** Acquisitions Editor. Estab. 1983. "Villard Books is the publisher of savvy and sometimes quirky bestseller hardcovers and trade paperbacks." Publishes hardcover and trade paperback originals. Publishes 55-60 titles/year. 95% of books are agented submissions. Pays varying advances and royalties; negotiated separately. Accepts simultaneous submissions. *Writer's Market* recommends allowing 2 months for reply.
• Villard has published such authors as Robert Fulghum and Michael Chabon. This publisher accepts agented submissions only.
Nonfiction and Fiction: Looks for commercial nonfiction and fiction. Submit outline/synopsis and up to 50 pages in sample chapters. No unsolicited submissions.
Recent Nonfiction Title(s): *Marriage Shock: The Emotional Transformation of Women Into Wives*, by Dalma Heyn (relationships); *Jacob's Ladder*, by Noah benShea (inspiration); *Into Thin Air*, by Jon Krakauer (biography/nature).

‡**VINTAGE**, Imprint of Knopf Publishing Group, Division of Random House, 201 E. 50th St., New York NY 10020. **Acquisitions:** Linda Rosenberg, managing editor. Publishes trade paperback originals and reprints. Imprint publishes 200 titles/year. Receives 600-700 mss/year. 5% of books from first time-authors; less than 1% from unagented writers. Pays 4-8% on retail price. Offers $2,500 and up advance. Publishes book 1 year after acceptance of ms. Accepts simultaneous submissions. Reports in 6 months.
Nonfiction: Subjects include anthropology/archaeology, biography, business/economics, child guidance/parenting, education, ethnic, gay/lesbian, government/politics, health/medicine, history, language/literature, military/war, nature/environment, philosophy, psychology, regional, science, sociology, translation, travel, women's issues/studies. Submit outline and 2-3 sample chapters. Reviews artwork as part of ms package. Send photocopies.
Recent Nonfiction Title(s): *A Civilization*, by Harr (current affairs); *Original Meanings*, by Rakon (history).
Fiction: Literary, mainstream/contemporary, short story collections. Submit synopsis with 2-3 sample chapters.
Recent Fiction Title(s): *Snow Falling on Cedars*, by Guterson (contemporary); *Martin Dressler*, by Milllhauser (literary).

‡**VISIONS COMMUNICATIONS**, 205 E. 10th St., 2D, New York NY 10003. **Acquisitions:** Beth Bay. Visions specializes in technical and reference titles. Publishes hardcover originals and trade paperback originals and reprints. Publishes 5 titles/year. Receives 20 queries and 10 mss/year. 50% of books from first-time authors; 75% from unagented writers. Pays 5-20% royalty on wholesale price. Offers $2,000 advance. Publishes book 6 months after acceptance of ms. Accepts simultaneous submissions. Reports in 1 month on queries, 2 months on proposals, 3 months on mss. Manuscript guidelines free.
Nonfiction: Children's/juvenile, how-to, self-help, reference, technical, textbook. Subjects include art/architecture, business/economics, health/medicine, psychology, religion, science, women's issues/studies. Submit outline, 3 sample chapters and proposal package.
Recent Nonfiction Title(s): *Illumination Engineering*, by Joseph Murdoch (engineering); *Lighting Listing*, by the Lighting Research Center (reference); *Restructuring Electricity Markets*, by Charles Cicchetti (economics/technical).

VOLCANO PRESS, INC., P.O. Box 270, Volcano CA 95689-0270. (209)296-3445. Fax: (209)296-4515. E-mail: sales@volcanopress.com. Website: http://www.volcanopress.com. **Acquisitions:** Ruth Gottstein, publisher. "We believe that the books we are producing today are of even greater value than the gold of yesteryear, and that the symbolism of the term 'Mother Lode' is still relevant to our work." Publishes trade paperback originals. Publishes 4-6 titles/year. Pays royalties based on monies received from sales. Offers $500-1,000 advance. Reports in 1 month on queries. "Please make submissions by mail only. No submissions by e-mail or fax."
Nonfiction: "We publish women's health and social issues, particularly in the field of domestic violence, and multicultural books for children that are non-racist and non-sexist." Query with brief outline and SASE.
Recent Nonfiction Title(s): *Walking on Eggshells: Practical Counseling for Women in or Leaving a Violent Relationship*, by Ogawa (domestic violence); *Menopause, Naturally*, by Sadja Greenwood, M.D. (health); *Family Violence and Religion*, edited by David Charlsen, et al.
Tips: "Obtain a free catalog from us, or look at our titles on the Web, and then submit materials that are consistent with what we already publish."

VOYAGEUR PRESS, 123 N. Second St., Stillwater MN 55082. (612)430-2210. Fax: (612)430-2211. **Acquisitions:** Michael Dregni, editorial director. "Voyageur Press is internationally known as a leading publisher of quality natural history, wildlife, sports/recreation, travel and regional books." Publishes hardcover and trade paperback originals. Publishes 30 titles/year. Receives 1,200 queries and 500 mss/year. 10% of books from first-time authors; 90% from unagented writers. Pays royalty. Publishes book 1 year after acceptance of ms. Accepts simultaneous submissions. Reports in 3 months. Book catalog and ms guidelines free.
Nonfiction: Coffee table book (and smaller format photographic essay books), cookbook. Subjects include natural history, nature/environment, Americana, collectibles, history, outdoor recreation, regional, travel. Query or submit outline and proposal package. Reviews artwork/photos. Send transparencies—duplicates only and tearsheets.
Recent Nonfiction Title(s): *The Arctic Wolf*, by L. David Mech.
Recent Fiction Title(s): *The Last Standing Woman*, by Wyona La Duke.
Tips: "We publish books for a sophisticated audience interested in natural history and cultural history of a variety of subjects. Please present as focused an idea as possible in a brief submission (one page cover letter; two page outline or proposal). Note your credentials for writing the book. Tell all you know about the market niche and marketing possibilities for proposed book."

WADSWORTH PUBLISHING COMPANY, Division of International Thomson Publishing, Inc., 10 Davis Dr., Belmont CA 94002. (415)595-2350. Fax: (415)637-7544. Website: http://www.thomson.com/wadsworth.html. **Acquisitions:** Rob Zwettler, editorial director. Estab. 1956. Other ITP Education Group divisions include Brooks/Cole Pub. Co., Heinle & Heinle Publishing Co., Delmar Publishing Company, South-Western Publishing Company, Course Technologies Inc. "We publish books and media products that use fresh teaching approaches to all courses taught at schools of higher education throughout the U.S. and Canada." Publishes hardcover and paperback originals and software. Publishes 240 titles/year. 35% of books from first-time authors; 99% of books from unagented writers. Pays 5-15% royalty on net price. Advances not automatic policy. Publishes ms 1 year after acceptance. Accepts simultaneous submissions. Book catalog (by subject area) and ms guidelines available.
Nonfiction: Textbooks and multimedia products: higher education only. Subjects include biology, astronomy, earth science, music, social sciences, philosophy, religious studies, speech and mass communications, broadcasting, TV and film productions, college success multimedia. "We specifically do not publish textbooks in art." Query or submit outline/synopsis and sample chapters.
Recent Nonfiction Title(s): *Everyday Encounters*, by Julia Wood (interpersonal communication); *Successful Public Speaking*, by Cheryl Hamilton; *Production and Operations Management*, 7th edition, by Norman Gaither.

WAKE FOREST UNIVERSITY PRESS, P.O. Box 7333, Winston-Salem NC 27109. (910)759-5448. **Acquisitions:** Dillon Johnston, director. Manager: Candide Jones. Estab. 1976. "We publish exclusively poetry and criticism of the poetry of Ireland and bilingual editions of contemporary French poetry." Publishes hardcover and trade paperback originals. Publishes 5 titles/year. Receives 80 submissions/year. Pays 10% on retail price. Offers $500 average advance. Publishes book 6 months after acceptance. Reports in 2 months on queries. Book catalog free.
Nonfiction: Subjects include language/literature. Query.
Recent Poetry Title(s): *Opera Et Cetera*, by Ciran Carson; *Edge*, by Claire Malroux.
Tips: "Readers of contemporary poetry and of books of Irish interest or French interest are our audience. We are no longer considering books on or about photography."

J. WESTON WALCH, PUBLISHER, P.O. Box 658, Portland ME 04104-0658. (207)772-2846. Fax: (207)774-7167. Editor-in-Chief: Joan E. Whitney. **Acquisitions:** Lisa French, editor-in-chief; Kate O'Halloran, editor; Julie Mazur, editor; Lisa Chmelecki, assistant editor. Estab. 1927. Publishes educational paperback originals and software for grades 6-12 in the U.S. and Canada. Publishes 75 titles/year. Receives 300 submissions/year. 10% of books from first-time authors; 95% from unagented writers. Average print order for a first book is 1,200. Offers 8-12% royalty on gross receipts. No advance. Publishes book 18 months after acceptance. Reports in 4 months. Book catalog for 9×12 SAE with 5 first-class stamps. Manuscript guidelines for #10 SASE.
Nonfiction: Subjects include art, business, computer education, economics, English, foreign language, geography, government, health, history, literacy, mathematics, middle school, music, psychology, science, social studies, sociology, special education. "We publish only supplementary educational material for grades six to twelve in the US and Canada. Formats include books, posters, blackline masters, card sets, cassettes, microcomputer courseware, video and mixed packages. Most titles are assigned by us, though we occasionally accept an author's unsolicited submission. We have a great need for author/artist teams and for authors who can write at third- to tenth-grade levels. We do *not* want basic texts, anthologies or industrial arts titles. Most of our authors—but not all—have secondary teaching experience. *Query first.* Looks for sense of organization, writing ability, knowledge of subject, skill of communicating with intended audience." Reviews artwork/photos as part of ms package.
Recent Nonfiction Title(s): *Ellis Island and Beyond*, by Wendy Wilson and Jack Papadonis (reproducible teaching book); *Using a Scientific Calculator*, by Susan Brendel and Eugene McDevitt; *Notefinders for String Instruments*, by Clark A. Chaffee.

WALKER AND CO., Division of Walker Publishing Co., 435 Hudson St., New York NY 10014. Fax: (212)727-0984. **Acquisitions:** Submissions Editor. Estab. 1959. Walker publishes general nonfiction on a variety of subjects as well as some adult and juvenile fiction. Publishes hardcover and trade paperback originals and a few reprints of British books. Publishes 100 titles/year. Receives 4,500 submissions/year. 30% of books from first-time authors; 30% from unagented writers. Pays royalty on retail price, 7½-12% on paperback, 10-15% on hardcover. Offers $1,000-3,000 average advance, "but could be higher or lower." Material without SASE will not be returned. Responds in 3 months. Book catalog and guidelines for 9 × 12 SAE with 3 first-class stamps.

Nonfiction: Biography, business, science and natural history, health, music, nature and environment, parenting, reference, popular science, sports/baseball, personal finance, some regional titles and self-help books. Query or submit outline and sample chapter. No phone calls. Reviews photos as part of ms package. Do not send originals.

Recent Nonfiction Title(s): *Cod: A Biography of the Fish That Changed the World*, by Mark Kurlansky (history); *Hamilton's Blessing*, by John Steele Gordon (history); *The Joy of Keeping Score*, by Paul Dickson (sports).

Fiction: Mystery/suspense, western, juvenile (ages 5 and up).

Recent Fiction Title(s): *Eater of Souls*, by Lynda S. Robinson (mystery); *The Bum's Rush*, by G.M. Ford (mystery); *A Wasteland of Strangers*, by Bill Pronzini (mystery).

Tips: "We also need preschool to young adult nonfiction, biographies and middle-grade novels. Query."

WARD HILL PRESS, P.O. Box 04-0424, Staten Island NY 10304-0008. **Acquisitions**: Elizabeth Davis, editorial director. Estab. 1989. Ward Hill Press publishes fiction and nonfiction for middle readers and young adults (ages 10 and up), with a special focus on American history since 1860, as well as multiculturalism. Publishes hardcover and paperback originals. Publishes 4-6 titles/year. Receives several hundred queries and mss/year. 75% of books from first-time authors; 90% from unagented writers. Pays 6-12% royalty on retail price. Offers advance. Publishes book 1 year after acceptance. Reports in 2 months on queries. Manuscript guidelines for #10 SASE.

Nonfiction and Fiction: "Looking for multiple biographies (biographies of six or more people in one manuscript), particularly those profiling minority women; first-person accounts of noteworthy events in history; and young adult fiction, set in a contemporary, urban environment, that deals with issues of race or culture." Query. Reviews artwork/photos as part of ms package. Send photocopies. "Query first. No phone calls please."

Recent Nonfiction Title(s): *Flatboating on the Yellowstone 1877*, by Fred G. Bond (historical narrative).

Recent Fiction Title(s): *My Best Defense*, by Bob Riggs (novel, ages 9-14).

WARNER ASPECT, 1271 Avenue of the Americas, New York NY 10020. Editor-in-Chief: Betsy Mitchell. Imprint of Warner Books. "We're looking for 'epic' stories in both fantasy and science fiction." Publishes hardcover, trade paperback, mass market paperback originals and mass market paperback reprints. Imprint publishes 30 titles/year. Receives 500 queries and 350 mss/year. 5-10% of books from first-time authors; 1% from unagented writers. Pays royalty on retail price. Offers $5,000-up advance. Publishes book 14 months after acceptance of ms. Reports in 10 weeks on mss.

● This publisher accepts agented submissions only.

Fiction: Fantasy, science fiction. "Sample our existing titles—we're a fairly new list and pretty strongly focused." Mistake writers often make is "hoping against hope that being unagented won't make a difference. We simply don't have the staff to look at unagented projects."

Recent Fiction Title(s): *Encounter with Tiber*, by Buzz Aldrin and John Barnes (science fiction); *Finity's End*, by C.S. Cheugh (science fiction).

Tips: "Think big."

WARNER BOOKS, Time & Life Building, 1271 Avenue of the Americas, New York NY 10020. (212)522-7200. Warner publishes general interest fiction and nonfiction. Publishes hardcover, trade paperback and mass market paperback originals and reprints. Publishes 350 titles/year.

Imprint(s): Mysterious Press, **Warner Aspect**, Warner Vision.

Nonfiction: Biography, business, cooking, current affairs, health, history, home, humor, popular culture, psychology, reference, self-help, sports.

Recent Nonfiction Title(s): *Simple Abundance*, by Sarah Ban Breathnach; *Just Give Me the Damn Ball!*, by Keyshawn Johnson with Shelley Smith (sports); *Brain Longevity*, by Dharma Singh Khalsa, M.D. (health).

Fiction: Fantasy, horror, mainsteam, mystery, romance, science fiction, suspense, thriller.

Recent Fiction Title(s): *The Celestine Prophecy*, by James Redfield; *Nocturne*, by Ed McBain (mystery); *Mail*, by Mameve Medwed.

WASHINGTON STATE UNIVERSITY PRESS, Pullman WA 99164-5910. (800)354-7360. Fax: (509)335-8568. Website: http://www.publications.wsu.edu/wsupress. Director: Thomas H. Sanders. Editor: Glen Lindeman. **Acquisitions**: Keith Petersen, editor. Estab. 1928. WSU Press publishes books on the history, pre-history, culture, and politics of the West, particularly the Pacific Northwest. Publishes hardcover originals, trade paperback originals and reprints. Publishes 10 titles/year. Receives 300-400 submissions/year. 50% of books from first-time writers; mostly unagented authors. Pays 5% minimum royalty, graduated according to sales. Publishes book 18 months after acceptance. Reports on queries in 2 months.

● Washington State University Press has published such authors as Jacqueline Williams and Murray Morgan.

Nonfiction: Subjects include Americana, art, biography, economics, environment, ethnic studies, history (especially of the American West and the Pacific Northwest), politics, essays. "We seek manuscripts that focus on the Pacific Northwest as a region. No romance novels, how-to books, gardening books or books used specifically as classroom texts. We welcome innovative and thought-provoking titles in a wide diversity of genres, from essays and memoirs to history, anthropology and political science." Submit outline and sample chapters. Reviews artwork/photos.

Recent Nonfiction Title(s): *Wandering and Feasting: A Washington Cookbook*, by Mary Caditz; *Very Close to Trouble: The Johnny Grant Memoir*, edited by Lyndel Miekle (memoir/biography); *Landscape of the Heart: Writings on Daughters and Journeys*, by Stephen J. Lyons (essays).

Tips: "Our audience consists of specialists and general readers who are interested in well-documented research presented in an attractive, well-written format. We have developed our marketing in the direction of regional and local history and have attempted to use this as the base upon which to expand our publishing program. In regional history, the secret is to write a good narrative—a good story—that is substantiated factually. It should be told in an imaginative, clever way. Have visuals (photos, maps, etc.) available to help the reader envision what has happened. Tell the regional history story in a way that ties it to larger, national, and even international events. Weave it into the large pattern of history. We have published our first books of essays and a regional cookbook and will do more in these and other fields if we get the right manuscript."

‡WATSON-GUPTILL PUBLICATIONS, Division of Billboard Publications, Inc., 1515 Broadway, New York NY 10036. (212)764-7300. Fax: (212)536-5359. **Acquisitions:** Candace Raney, senior acquisitions editor (art); Bob Nirkind, senior editor (Billboard-music); Ziva Freiman, senior editor (Whitney-architecture); Dale Ramsey, senior editor (Back Stage-theater); Robin Simmen, senior editor (Amphoto-photography). "We are an arts book publisher." Publishes hardcover and trade paperback originals and reprints. Receives 150 queries and 50 mss/year. 50% of books from first-time authors; 75% from unagented writers. Pays royalty on wholesale price. Publishes book 9 months after acceptance of ms. Accepts simultaneous submissions. Reports in 2 months on queries; 3 months on proposals. Book catalog and ms guidelines free.

Imprint(s): Watson-Guptill, Amphoto, Whitney Library of Design, Billboard Books, Back Stage Books.

Nonfiction: Coffee table book, gift book, how-to, illustrated book, reference, textbook. Subjects include art, photography, architecture, music, theater. "Writers should be aware of the kinds of books (crafts, graphic design, mostly instructional) Watson-Guptill publishes before submitting. Although we are growing and will consider new ideas and approaches, we will not consider a book if it is clearly outside of our publishing schedule." Query or submit outline, 1-2 sample chapters and proposal package, including non-original art samples. Reviews artwork/photos as part of the ms package. Send photocopies or transparencies.

Recent Nonfiction Title(s): *Christopher Hart's Portable Action Hero Comic Book Studio*, by Christopher Hart (how-to, art instruction); *The New American House: Innovations in Residential Design and Construction*, by Oscar Riera Ojeda; *This Business of Commercial Photography*, by Ira Wexler (how-to/reference).

Tips: Audience is all types of artists: student, professional, amateur, curious, all levels. "Request a catalog before submitting; understand what kind of book the house is interested in."

FRANKLIN WATTS, INC., Division of Grolier, Inc., Sherman Turnpike, Danbury CT 06816. (203)797-6802. Fax: (203)797-6986. E-mail: rprimm@grolier.com. Website: http://publishing.grolier.com/publishing.html. Publisher: John Selfridge. **Acquisitions:** E. Russell Primm, editorial director. Estab. 1942. Franklin Watts publishes curriculum materials and books and teacher's materials (K-12) to supplement textbooks. Publishes both hardcover and softcover originals for grades K-12. Publishes 400 titles/year. 5% of books from first-time authors; 95% from unagented writers. Pays royalty to established authors; makes outright purchase for first-time authors. Advance varies. Publishes book 18 months after acceptance of ms. Prefers to work with unagented authors. Accepts simultaneous submissions. No complete mss. Reports in 4 months on queries with SASE. Book catalog for $3 postage. Manuscript guidelines free.

● Franklin Watts is discouraging submissions for the next 18 months. Franklin Watts has published Elaine Landau, Milton Meltzer, Janet Bode, Larry Dane Brimner, Charran Simon, Hedda Garza and James Cockcroft.

Nonfiction: History, science, social issues, biography. Subjects include education, language/literature, American and world history, politics, natural and physical sciences, sociology. Multicultural, curriculum-based nonfiction lists published twice a year. Strong also in the area of contemporary problems and issues facing young people. No humor, coffee table books, fiction, poetry, cookbooks or gardening books. Query with outline and SASE. No calls or unsolicited mss.

Recent Nonfiction Title(s): *The Soaring 20s*, by Tom Gilbert (Babe Ruth and the Home Run Decade); *Physics Lab in a Hardware Store*, by Robert Friedhoffer; *Young Vegetarian's Companion*, by Jan Parr.

Tips: Most of this publisher's books are developed inhouse; less than 5% come from unsolicited submissions. However, they publish several series for which they always need new books. Study catalogs to discover possible needs.

‡WEATHERHILL, INC., 568 Broadway, Suite 705, New York NY 10012. **Acqusitions:** Raymond Furse, editorial director. Weatherhill publishes exclusively Asia-related nonfiction and Asian fiction and poetry in translation. Publishes hardcover and trade paperback originals and reprints. Publishes 36 titles/year. Receives 250 queries and 100 mss/year. 20% of books from first-time authors; 95% from unagented writers. Pays 12-18% royalty on wholesale price. Offers advances up to $10,000. Publishes books 8 months after acceptance of ms. Accepts simultaneous submissions. Reports in 1 month on proposals. Book catalog and ms guidelines free.

Imprint(s): Weatherhill, Tengu Books.

Nonfiction: Asia-related topics only. Biography, coffee table book, cookbook, gift book, how-to, humor, illustrated book, reference, self-help. Subjects include anthropology/archaeology, art/architecture, cooking/foods/nutrition, gardening, history, language/literature, music/dance, nature/environment, photography, regional, religion, sociology, translation, travel. Submit outline, 2 sample chapters and sample illustrations (if applicable). Reviews artwork/photos as part of ms package. Send photocopies.

Recent Nonfiction Title(s): *Holy Terror: Armageddon in Tokyo*, by D.W. Brackett (recent events); *A Haiku Garden*, by Stephen Addiss (Japanese prints and poetry); *A Kiie Journey Through India*, by Tal Streeter (crafts/travel).
Fiction: "We publish only important Asian writers in translation. Asian fiction is a hard sell. Authors should check funding possibilities from appropriate sources: Japan Foundation, Korea Foundation, etc." Query with synopsis.
Recent Fiction Title(s): *The Kobe Hotel*, by Saito Sanki (war memoirs); *The Fugu Plan*, by Marvin Tokayer and Mary Swarty (historical fiction).
Poetry: Only Asian poetry in translation. Query.

WEIDNER & SONS PUBLISHING, P.O. Box 2178, Riverton NJ 08077. (609)486-1755. Fax: (609)486-7583. E-mail: weidner@waterw.com. Website: http://www.waterw.com/~weidner. **Acquisitions:** James H. Weidner, president. Estab. 1967. "We publish primarily science, text and reference books for scholars, college students and researchers." Publishes hardcover and trade paperback originals and reprints. Publishes 10-20 titles/year; imprint publishes 10 titles/year. Receives hundreds of queries and 50 mss/year. 100% of books from first-time authors; 90% from unagented writers. Pays 10% maximum royalty on wholesale price. Average time between acceptance and publication varies with subject matter. Accepts simultaneous submissions. Reports in 1 month on queries. *Writer's Market* recommends allowing 2 months for reply. Book catalog for $1 (refundable with order).
Imprint(s): Hazlaw Books, Medlaw Books, Bird Sci Books, Delaware Estuary Press, Tycooly Publishing USA and Pulse Publications.
Nonfiction: Reference, technical, textbook. Subjects include agriculture/horticulture, animals, business/economics, child guidance/parenting, computers/electronics, education, gardening, health/medicine, hobbies (electronic), language/literature, nature/environment, psychology, science and ecology/environment. "We rarely publish fiction; never poetry. No topics in the 'pseudosciences': occult, astrology, New Age and metaphysics, etc." Query or submit outline and sample chapters. Reviews artwork/photos as part of ms package. Send photocopies. "Suggest 2 copies of ms, double spaced, along with PC disk in Word, Word Perfect, Write or Pagemaker."
Recent Nonfiction Title(s): *At Risk*; *Sexual Behavior Scale for Diagnosis*; *International Guide to Educational Standards*.

SAMUEL WEISER, INC., P.O. Box 612, York Beach ME 03910-0612. (207)363-4393. Fax: (207)363-5799. E-mail: weiserbooks@worldnet.att.net. **Acquisitions:** Eliot Stearns, editor. Estab. 1956. "We look for strong books in oriental philosophy, metaphysics, esoterica of all kinds (tarot, astrology, qabalah, magic, etc.) written by teachers and people who know the subject." Publishes hardcover originals and trade paperback originals and reprints. Publishes 18-20 titles/year. Receives 200 submissions/year. 50% of books from first-time authors; 98% from unagented writers. Pays 10% royalty on wholesale and retail price. Offers $500 average advance. Publishes book 18 months after acceptance. Reports in 3 months. Book catalog free.
● Samuel Weiser has published such authors as Liz Greene, D.T. Suzuki and Maurice Nicoll.
Nonfiction: How-to, self-help. Subjects include health, music, philosophy, psychology, religion. "We don't want a writer's rehash of all the astrology books in the library, only texts written by people with strong backgrounds in the field. No poetry or novels." Submit complete ms. *Writer's Market* recommends query with SASE first. Reviews artwork/photos as part of ms package.
Recent Nonfiction Title(s): *Ayurveda: A Way of Life*, by Dr. Vinod Verma; *Handbook of T'ai Chi Ch'uan Exercises*, by Zhang Fuxing; *Ethic for the Age of Space*, by Lawrence LeShan (health).
Tips: "Most new authors do not check permissions, nor do they provide proper footnotes. If they did, it would help. We look at all manuscripts submitted to us. We are interested in seeing freelance art for book covers."

WEKA PUBLISHING, INC., 1077 Bridgeport Ave., Shelton CT 06484. **Acquisitions:** Josephine Palmieri, product manager. Weka publishes how-to, reference and technical books for industries. Publishes 8 titles/year. Receives 5-10 queries and 2-5 mss/year. 100% of books from first-time authors. Publishes book 6 months after acceptance of ms. Accepts simultaneous submissions. Reports in 2 months on queries, 1 month on proposals and mss. *Writer's Market* recommends allowing 2 months for reply. Book catalog and ms guidelines free.
Nonfiction: How-to, reference, technical, OSHA, electronics, quality topics. Subjects include computers/electronics, hobbies. "We look for how-to articles. These articles go into our title. Can be a part of more than one title." Submit proposal package, including table of contents, target market, benefits of chapters, unique selling point. Reviews artwork/photos as part of ms package. Send photocopies.
Recent Nonfiction Title(s): *OSHA in the Construction Industry*.
Tips: "Our markets are manufacturing, health care, mining, transportation and construction. Prefer legal topics."

WESCOTT COVE PUBLISHING CO., P.O. Box 130, Stamford CT 06904. (203)322-0998. **Acquisitions:** Julius M. Wilensky, president. Estab. 1968. "We publish the most complete cruising guides, each one an authentic reference for the area covered." Publishes trade paperback originals and reprints. Publishes 4 new titles/year. Receives 15 queries and 10 mss/year. 25% of books from first-time authors; 95% from unagented writers. Pays 5-10% royalty on retail price. Offers $1,000-1,500 advance. Publishes book 1 year after acceptance of ms. Accepts simultaneous submissions. Reports in 1 month on queries. Book catalog free.
● Wescott Cove has published such authors as Earl Hinz, Don Johnson and Sue Moesly.
Nonfiction: How-to, humor, illustrated book, reference, nautical books. Subjects include history, hobbies, regional, travel. "All titles are nautical books; half of them are cruising guides. Mostly we seek out authors knowledgeable in

sailing, navigation, cartography and the area we want covered. Then we commission them to write the book." Query with outline, 1-2 sample chapters, author's credentials and SASE.
Recent Nonfiction Title(s): *Chesapeake Bay Cruising Guide—Volume I, Upper Bay*, by Tom Neale; *Cruising Guide to Belize and Mexico's Caribbean Coast Including Guatemala's Rio Dulce, Second Edition*, by Captain Freya Rauscher; *First Time Around*, by Jamie Bryson.

‡**WESLEYAN UNIVERSITY PRESS**, 110 Mount Vernon St., Middletown CT 06459. (860)685-2420. **Acquisitions:** Suzanna Tamminen, editor. "We are a scholarly press with a focus on cultural studies." Publishes hardcover originals. Publishes 20-25 titles/year. Receives 1,500 queries and 1,000 mss/year. 10% of books from first-time authors; 80% from unagented writers. Pays 10% royalty. Offers up to $3,000 advance. Publishes book 1 year after acceptance of ms. Accepts simultaneous submissions. Reports in 1 month on queries, 2 months on proposals, 3 months on mss. Book catalog free. Manuscript guidelines for #10 SASE.
Nonfiction: Biography, textbook, scholarly. Subjects include art/architecture, ethnic, gay/lesbian, history, language/literature, music/dance, philosophy, sociology, theater, film. Submit outline, proposal package, including: introductory letter, curriculum vitae, table of contents. Reviews artwork/photos as part of ms package. Send photocopies.
Recent Nonfiction Title(s): *Music-Society-Education*, by Christopher Small (scholarly); *Historiography of the Twentieth Century*, by Georg Iggers (scholarly).
Fiction: Science fiction. "We publish very little fiction, less than 3% of our entire list."
Recent Fiction Title(s): *Dhalgren*, by Samuel R. Delany.
Poetry: "Writers should request a catalog and guidelines." Submit 5-10 sample poems.
Recent Poetry Title(s): *The Spaces Between Birds*, by Sandra McPherson; *Millennium Hotel*, by Mark Rudman.
Tips: Audience is the informed general reader to specialized academic reader.

‡**WESTCLIFFE PUBLISHERS**, P.O. Box 1261, Englewood CO 80150. (303)935-0900. Fax: (303)935-0903. **Acquisitions:** Linda Doyle, director of marketing; Harlene Finn, production manager. "Westcliffe Publishers produces the highest quality in regional photography and essays for our coffee table-style books and calendars." Publishes hardcover originals, trade paperback originals and reprints. Publishes 15 titles/year. Receives 100 queries and 10 mss/year. 75% of books from first-time authors; 100% from unagented writers. Pays 3-15% royalty on retail price. Offers advance of 50% of the first year's royalties. Publishes book 18 months for acceptance ms. Accepts simultaneous submissions. Reports in 1 month. Book catalog and ms guidelines free.
• Westcliffe has published such authors as James Kilgo, Tom Blagden, Jr. and George Humphries.
Nonfiction: Coffee table book, gift book, illustrated book, reference. Subjects include Americana, animals, gardening, nature/environment, photography, regional, travel. "Writers need to do their market research to justify a need in the marketplace." Submit outline with proposal package, including photographs, slides, duplicates. Reviews artwork/photos as part of ms package.
Recent Nonfiction Title(s): *Colorado's Continental Divide Trail*, by John Fiedler (guidebook); *A North Carolina Christmas*, by Jan Kiefer (Americana); *The Blue Wall*, by C. Thomas Wyche (photography).
Tips: Audience are nature and outdoors enthusiasts and photographers. "Just call us!"

WESTERNLORE PRESS, P.O. Box 35305, Tucson AZ 85740. Fax: (520)297-1722. **Acquisitions:** Lynn R. Bailey, editor. Publishes Western Americana of a scholarly and semischolarly nature. Publishes 6-12 titles/year. Pays standard royalties on retail price "except in special cases." Reports in 2 months.
Nonfiction: Subjects include anthropology, history, biography, historic sites, restoration, and ethnohistory pertaining to the American West. Re-publication of rare and out-of-print books. Length: 25,000-100,000 words. Query with SASE.
Recent Nonfiction Title(s): *The Apache Kid*, by de la Gaza (western history).

‡**WESTVIEW PRESS**, Division of HarperCollins, 5500 Central Ave., Boulder CO 80301-2877. (303)444-3541. Fax: (303)449-3356. Website: http://www.hcacademic.com. **Acquisitions:** Marcus Boggs, publisher. Estab. 1975. "Westview Press publishes a wide range of general interest and scholarly nonfiction (including undergraduate and graduate-level textbooks) in the social sciences and humanities. Our mission is to publish 'books that matter.'" Publishes hardcover and trade paperback originals and reprints. Publishes 300 titles/year. Receives 1,000 queries and 500 mss/year. 25% of books from first-time authors; 90% from unagented writers. Pays 6-15% royalty on net receipts. Advance varies, $0-20,000 and up. Publishes book 1 year after acceptance of ms. Accepts simultaneous submissions, if so noted. Reports in 1 week on queries, 6 weeks on proposals and mss. Book catalog available on Website. Manuscript guidelines free.
Imprint(s): Icon Editions.
Nonfiction: Biography, reference, textbook, trade, monograph. Subjects include anthropology, art/architecture (criticism and history), education, ethnic (cultural studies), government/politics, history, military/war (history), psychology, religious studies, sociology, women's issues/studies. "Know our focus. We publish books of original scholarship. To gain our interest, write a book that is both original and interesting." Query or submit outline, 3 sample chapters, table of contents with SASE. Reviews artwork/photos as part of ms package, if germane. Send photocopies.
Recent Nonfiction Title(s): *American Wine Landscapes*, by Gary Peters (geography); *Faces of Feminism*, by Sheila Tobias (feminism); *The New Britain*, by Tony Blair (politics).
Tips: "Audience is academics, educated lay readers interested in serious books."

WHISPERING COYOTE PRESS, INC., 300 Crescent Court, Suite 860, Dallas TX 75201. Fax: (214)871-5577, (214)319-7298. **Acquisitions:** Mrs. Lou Alpert, publisher. Publishes picture books for children ages 3-10. Publishes 6

titles/year. 20% of books from first-time authors; 90% from unagented writers. Pays 8% royalty on retail price of first 10,000 copies, 10% after (combined author and illustrator). Offers $2,000-8,000 advance (combined author, illustrator). Publishes book 2 years after acceptance of ms. Accepts simultaneous submissions. Reports in 3 months. Book catalog and ms guidelines for #10 SASE.
Fiction: Adventure, fantasy, juvenile picture books. "We only do picture books." Submit complete ms. If author is illustrator also, submit sample art. Send photocopies, no original art.
Recent Fiction Title(s): *The Red Shoes*, retold and illustrated by Barbara Bazilian, adapted from a story by Hans Christian Anderson; *Cats on Judy*, by JoAnn Early Macken, illustrated by Judith DuFour Love; *Hush! A Gaelic Lullaby*, by Carole Gerber, illustrated by Mary Husted.
Poetry: "We like poetry—if it works in a picture book format. We are not looking for poetry collections."
Recent Poetry Title(s): *I'm A Little Teapot*, by Iza Trapani (extended rhyme picture book); *Hey Diddle Diddle*, by Kin Eagle (extended rhyme).

WHITE CLIFFS MEDIA, INC., P.O. Box 433, Tempe AZ 85280-0433. (602)834-1444. **Acquisitions:** Lawrence Aynesmith. Estab. 1985. White Cliffs publishes ethnic music titles for an academic and general audience. Publishes hardcover and trade paperback originals. Publishes 5-10 titles/year. 50% of books from first-time authors; 50% from unagented writers. Pays 5-12% royalty or makes outright purchase. Publishes book 1 year after acceptance. No simultaneous submissions. Reports in 2 months on queries, 4 months on proposals, 6 months on mss. Book catalog for #10 SASE.
Nonfiction: Biography, textbook. Subjects include anthropology, ethnic, music/dance. Query. Reviews artwork/photos as part of ms package. Send photocopies.
Recent Nonfiction Title(s): *Drum Damba: Talking Drum Lessons*, by Locke (musical instruction); *Mandiani Drum and Dance*, by Djimbe (performance and Black aesthetics).
Tips: "Distribution is more difficult due to the large number of publishers. Writers should send proposals that have potential for mass markets as well as college texts, and that will be submitted and completed on schedule. Our audience reads college texts, general interest trade publications. If I were a writer trying to market a book today, I would send a book on music comparable in quality and mass appeal to a book like Stephen Hawking's *A Brief History of Time*."

WHITE PINE PRESS, 10 Village Square, Fredonia NY 14063. (716)672-5743. Fax: (716)672-4724. E-mail: pine@net .blumoon.net. Website: www.bluemoon.net/~pine/. **Acquisitions:** Dennis Maloney, editor/publisher (nonfiction); Elaine LaMattina, managing director (fiction). "White Pine Press is your passport to a world of voices, emphasizing literature from around the world." Publishes hardcover and trade paperback originals. Publishes 10 titles/year. Receives 200 queries and 150 mss/year. 20% of books from first-time authors; 99% from unagented writers. Pays 5-10% royalty on wholesale price. Offers $250 and up advance. Publishes book 18 months after acceptance of ms. Accepts simultaneous submissions. Reports in 2 months on queries. Book catalog free.
Imprint(s): Springhouse Editions.
Nonfiction: Subjects include ethnic, language/literature, translation, women's issues/studies. Query.
Recent Nonfiction Title(s): *Ashes of Revolt*, by Marjorie Agosin.
Fiction: Ethnic, literary, short story collections. Interested in strong novels. Query with synopsis and 2 chapters.
Recent Fiction Title(s): *Black Flames*, by Daniel Pearlman; *Lost Chronicles of Terra Firma*, by Rosario Aguilar.
Poetry: "We do a large amount of poetry in translation. We award the White Pine Press Poetry Prize annually. Write for details. We read manuscripts of American poetry only as part of our annual competition." Query.
Recent Poetry Title(s): *Treehouse*, by William Kloefkorn; *Bodily Course*, by Deborah Gorlin.

‡ALBERT WHITMAN AND CO., 6340 Oakton St., Morton Grove IL 60053-2723. (847)581-0033. **Acquisitions**: Kathleen Tucker, editor-in-chief. Estab. 1919. Albert Whitman publishes "good books for children." Publishes hardcover originals and paperback reprints. Averages 30 titles/year. Receives 5,000 submissions/year. 20% of books from first-time authors; 70% from unagented writers. Pays 10% royalty. Publishes book an average of 18 months after acceptance. Accepts simultaneous submissions. Reports in 5 months. Book catalog for 8×10 SAE and 2 first-class stamps. Manuscript guidelines for #10 SASE.
Nonfiction: "All books are for ages 2-12." Concept books about special problems children have, easy science, social studies, math. Query.
Recent Nonfiction Title(s): *The Fragile Frog*, by William Mara (nature); *Small Steps: The Year I Got Polio*, by Peg Kehret (autobiography).
Fiction: "All books are for ages 2-12." Adventure, ethnic, fantasy, historical, humor, mystery, picture books and concept books (to help children deal with problems). "We need easy historical fiction and picture books. No young adult and adult books." Submit outline/synopsis and sample chapters (novels) and complete ms (picture books).
Recent Fiction Title(s): *Turkey Pox*, by Laurie Halse Anderson; *The Hand-Me-Down Horse*, by Pomeranc; *The Last Man's Reward*, by Patneaude.
Tips: "There is a trend toward highly visual books. The writer can most easily sell us strong picture book text that has good illustration possibilities. We sell mostly to libraries, but our bookstore sales are growing. If I were a writer trying to market a book today, I would study published picture books."

‡THE WHITSTON PUBLISHING CO., P.O. Box 958, Troy NY 12181-0958. Phone/fax: (518)283-4363. E-mail: whitson@capital.net. Website: http://www.capital.net/com/whitston. **Acquisitions:** Jean Goode, editorial director. Estab. 1969. "We are concentrating mostly on American literture." Publishes hardcover originals. Averages 15 titles/year.

Receives 100 submissions/year. 50% of books from first-time authors; 100% from unagented writers. Pays 10% royalty on price of book (wholesale or retail) after sale of 500 copies. Publishes book 30 months after acceptance. Reports in up to 6 months. Book catalog for $1.

Nonfiction: "We publish scholarly and critical books in the arts, humanities and some of the social sciences. We will consider author bibliographies. We are interested in scholarly monographs and collections of essays." Query. Reviews artwork/photos as part of ms package.

Recent Nonfiction Title(s): *Steinbeck's Typewriter*, by Robert DeMott (American literature); *Art and Architecture in the Poetry of Robert Browning*, by Charles Thomas (British poetry); *One Million Words of Book Notes*, by Richard Kostelantz (literary criticism).

Recent Poetry Title(s): *The Ghost Dance Anthology*, edited by Hugh Fox.

‡**MICHAEL WIESE PRODUCTIONS**, 11288 Ventura Blvd., Suite 821, Studio City CA 91604. (818)379-8799. **Acquisitions:** Ken Lee, vice president. Michael Wiese publishes how-to books for professional film or video makers, film schools and bookstores. Publishes trade paperback originals. Publishes 4-6 titles/year. Receives 10-15 queries/year. 90% of books from first-time authors. Pays 7-10% royalty on retail price. Offers $500-1,000 advance. Publishes book 10 months after acceptance of ms. Accepts simultaneous submissions. Reorts in 1 month on queries and proposals, 2 months on mss. Book catalog free.

Nonfiction: How-to. Subjects include professional film and videomaking. Writers should call before submitting nonfiction. Submit outline with 3 sample chapters.

Recent Nonfiction Title(s): *Fade In, 2nd Edition*; *The Director's Journey*; *Producer to Producer, 2nd Edition*.

Tips: Audience is professional filmmakers, writers, producers, directors, actors and university film students.

WILD FLOWER PRESS, Imprint of Blue Water Publishing, P.O. Box 190, Mill Spring NC 28756. (704)894-8444. Fax: (704)894-8454. E-mail: bluewaterp@aol.com. Website: http://www.5thworld.com/bluewater. President: Pam Meyer. **Acquisitions:** Brian Crissey. "Wild Flower Press strives to preserve the Earth by publishing books that develop new wisdom about our emerging planetary citizenship, bringing information from the outerworlds to our world." Publishes hardcover originals and trade paperback originals and reprints. Publishes 6 titles/year. Receives 50 queries and 25 mss/month. 80% of books from first-time authors; 90% from unagented writers. Pays 7½-15% royalty. Publishes book 16 months after acceptance of ms. Accepts simultaneous submissions. Reports in 2 months on mss. Book catalog and ms guidelines for SASE with 55¢ postage.

● Wild Flower Press has published Raymond E. Fowler, Michael Lindemann and Eduard 'Billy' Meier.

Nonfiction: Books about extraterrestrial research and experiences. Submit outline. Reviews artwork/photos as part of ms package. Send photocopies.

Recent Nonfiction Title(s): *The God Hypothesis*, by Joe Lewels, Ph.D.; *At the Threshold*, by Charles Emmons, Ph.D. (sociology/ufology); *Plant Spirit Medicine*, by Eliot Cowan.

WILDER PUBLISHING CENTER, 919 Lafond Ave., St. Paul MN 55104. (612)659-6013. **Acquisitions:** Vincent Hyman, editorial director. Wilder Publishing Center emphasizes community and nonprofit organization management and development. Publishes trade paperback originals. Publishes 4-6 titles/year. Receives 30 queries and 15 mss/year. 75% of books from first-time authors; 100% from unagented writers. Pays 10% royalty on net. Books are sold through direct mail; average discount is 15%. Offers $1,000-3,000 advance. Publishes book 1 year after acceptance of ms. Accepts simultaneous submissions, if so noted. Reports in 1 month on queries and proposals, 3 months on mss. Book catalog and ms guidelines free.

Nonfiction: Nonprofit management, organizational development, community organizing, violence prevention. Subjects include government/politics, sociology. "We are in a growth mode and welcome proposals in these areas. We are seeking manuscripts that report 'best practice' methods using handbook or workbook formats." Phone query OK before submitting proposal with detailed chapter ouline, 1 sample chapter and SASE.

Recent Nonfiction Title(s): *Foundations for Violence Free Living*, by Dave Mathews (sociology/domestic abuse treatment package); *Effective Strategies in Community Building*; *Marketing Workbook for Nonprofits, Volume II: Mobilize People for Marketing Success*.

Tips: "Writers must be practitioners with a passion for their work and experience presenting their techniques at conferences. Freelance writers with an interest in our niches could do well searching out and teaming up with such practitioners as our books sell very well to a tightly-targeted market."

WILDERNESS PRESS, 2440 Bancroft Way, Berkeley CA 94704-1676. (510)843-8080. Fax: (510)548-1355. E-mail: 74642.1147@compuserve.com. **Acquisitions:** Thomas Winnett, editorial director; Caroline Winnett, assistant publisher. Estab. 1967. "We seek to publish the most accurate, reliable and useful guidebooks for self-propelled outdoor activities." Publishes paperback originals. Publishes 10 titles/year. Receives 150 submissions/year. 20% of books from first-time authors; 95% from unagented writers. Average print order for a first book is 5,000. Pays 8-10% royalty on retail price. Offers $1,000 average advance. Publishes book 8 months after acceptance. Reports in 1 month. *Writer's Market* recommends allowing 2 months for reply. Book catalog free.

● Wilderness Press has published such authors as Galen Rowell and Amy Schad. They have increased their number of books published from 6 to 10 titles/year.

Nonfiction: "We publish books about the outdoors. Most are trail guides for hikers and backpackers, but we also publish how-to books about the outdoors. The manuscript must be accurate. The author must thoroughly research an

area in person. If he is writing a trail guide, he must walk all the trails in the area his book is about. The outlook must be strongly conservationist. The style must be appropriate for a highly literate audience." Request proposal guidelines.
Recent Nonfiction Title(s): *Hot Showers, Soft Beds, and Dayhikes in the Sierra*, by Kathy Morey; *How to Rent a Fire Lookout in the Pacific Northwest*, by Tom Foley and Tish Steinfeld.

JOHN WILEY & SONS, INC., 605 Third Ave., New York NY 10158. Associate Publisher/Editor-in-Chief of General Interest Publishing: Carole Hall. **Acquisitions**: Editorial Department. "We publish books, journals, and electronic products for the scientific, technical, educational, professional and consumer markets. We are committed to providing information in those formats most accessible to our readers and are taking advantage of the rapid advances in digital information technology to our print publications and develop a range of offerings in electronic formats." Publishes hardcover originals, trade paperback originals and reprints in Professional & Trade and College Divisions. Publishes 100 titles/year. Pays "competitive royalty rates." Publishes book 1 year after acceptance. Accepts simultaneous submissions. Book catalog free.
Nonfiction: Biography, how-to, children's/juvenile, reference, self-help. Subjects include accounting, architecture and engineering, business, child guidance/parenting, computers, current affairs, finance and investment, health/medicine, history, hospitality, law, military/war, psychology, real estate, science, women's issues/studies. Query.
Recent Nonfiction Title(s): *The Case of the Killer Robot: Stories About the Professional, Ethnical and Societal Dimensions of Computing*, by Richard G. Epstein; *The FASB Cases on Recognition and Measurement, 2nd edition*, by L. Todd Johnson and Kimberley R. Petrone.

WILLIAMSON PUBLISHING CO., P.O. Box 185, Church Hill Rd., Charlotte VT 05445. Website: http://www.williamsonbooks.com. **Acquisitions**: Susan Williamson, editorial director. Estab. 1983. "Our mission is to help every child fulfill his/her potential and experience personal growth." Publishes trade paperback originals. Publishes 15 titles/year. Receives 1,500 queries and 800 mss/year. 75% of books from first-time authors; 90% from unagented writers. Pays 7½-15% royalty on retail price. Advance negotiable. Publishes book 18 months after acceptance. Accepts simultaneous submissions, but prefers 6 weeks exclusivity. Reports in 4 months with SASE. Book catalog for 8½×11 SAE with 4 first-class stamps.
● Williamson's big success is its *Kids Can!®* series books like *Super Science Concoction. The Kids' Multicultural Art Book* won the Parents' Choice Gold Award; *Tales Alive* won Benjamin Franklin best juvenile fiction.
Nonfiction: Children's/juvenile, children's creative learning books on subjects ranging from science, art, to early learning skills. Adult books include psychology, cookbook, how-to, self-help. "Williamson has four very successful children's book series: *Kids Can!®* (ages 5-10), *Little Hands®* (ages 2-6), *Tales Alive®* (folktales plus activities, age 4-10) and *Kaleidoscope Kids®* (96-page, single subject, ages 7-12). They must incorporate learning through doing. *No picture books please!* Please don't call concerning your submission. It never helps your review, and it takes too much of our time. With an SASE, you'll hear from us." Submit outline, 2-3 sample chapters and SASE.
Recent Nonfiction Title(s): *Pyramids!*, by Hart and Mantell (*Kaleidoscope Kids®*); *Math Play!*, by Schrooten and McGowan (*Little Hands®*).
Tips: "Our children's books are used by kids, their parents, and educators. They encourage self-discovery, creativity and personal growth. Our books are based on the philosophy that children learn best by doing, by being involved. Our authors need to be excited about their subject area and equally important, excited about kids."

‡WILLOW CREEK PRESS, P.O. Box 147, 9931 Highway 70 W., Minocqua WI 54548. (715)358-7010. **Acquisitions:** Tom Petrie, editor-in-chief. Willow Creek specializes in nature, outdoor and animal books, calendars and videos with high-quality photography. Publishes hardcover and trade paperback originals and reprints. Publishes 25 titles/year. Receives 400 queries and 150 mss/year. 15% of books from first-time authors; 50% from unagented writers. Pays 6-15% royalty on wholesale price. Offers $2,000-5,000 advance. Publishes book 10 months after acceptance of ms. Accepts simultaneous submissions. Reports in 2 months. Book catalog for $1.
Nonfiction: Children's/juvenile, coffee table book, cookbook, how-to, humor, illustrated book. Subjects include animals, cooking/foods/nutrition, gardening, hobbies, nature/environment, photography, recreation, sports. Submit outline and 1 sample chapter. Reviews artwork/photos as part of ms package. Send photocopies.
Recent Nonfiction Title(s): *Garden Birds of America*, by George H. Harrison (coffee table/animals); *Just Goldens*, by Tom Davis (pets); *Build a Better Birdhouse*, by Malcolm Wells (how-to).
Fiction: Adventure, humor, picture books, short story collections. Submit synopsis and 2 sample chapters.
Recent Fiction Title(s): *Cold Noses and Warm Hearts*, edited by Laurie Morrow (short story collection); *Flashes in the River*, by Ed Gray (illustrated fiction); *Poetry for Guys*, by Kathy Schmook.

WILSHIRE BOOK CO., 12015 Sherman Rd., North Hollywood CA 91605-3781. (818)765-8579. **Acquisitions:** Melvin Powers, publisher and Marcia Grad, senior editor. Estab. 1947. "You are not only what you are today, but also what you choose to become tomorrow." Publishes trade paperback originals and reprints. Publishes 25 titles/year. Receives 3,000 submissions/year. 80% of books from first-time authors; 75% from unagented writers. Pays standard royalty. Publishes book 6 months after acceptance. Reports in 2 months.
Nonfiction: Self-help, motivation/inspiration/spirituality, psychology, recovery, how-to. Subjects include personal success, entrepreneurship, making money on the Internet, mail order, horsemanship. Minimum 60,000 words. Requires detailed chapter outline, 3 sample chapters and SASE. Accepts queries and complete mss. Welcomes telephone calls to discuss mss or book concepts. Reviews artwork/photos as part of ms package. Send photocopies.

Recent Nonfiction Title(s): *How to Get Rich in Mail Order*, by Melvin Powers; *The Magic of Thinking Big*, by Dr. David Schwartz.
Fiction: Allegories that teach principles of psychological/spiritual growth or offer guidance in living. Min. 30,000 words. Requires synopsis, 3 sample chapters and SASE. Accepts complete mss.
Recent Fiction Title(s): *The Princess Who Believed in Fairy Tales*, by Marcia Grad; *The Knight in Rusty Armor*, by Robert Fisher; *Greatest Salesman in the World*.
Tips: "We are vitally interested in all new material we receive. Just as you hopefully submit your manuscript for publication, we hopefully read every one submitted, searching for those that we believe will be successful in the marketplace. Writing and publishing must be a team effort. We need you to write what we can sell. We suggest that you read the successful books mentioned above or others that are similar to the manuscript you want to write. Analyze them to discover what elements make them winners. Duplicate those elements in your own style, using a creative new approach and fresh material, and you will have written a book we can catapult onto the bestseller list."

‡WINDSOR BOOKS, Subsidiary of Windsor Marketing Corp., P.O. Box 280, Brightwaters NY 11718-0280. (516)321-7830. **Acquisitions:** Jeff Schmidt, managing editor. Estab. 1968. "Our books are for serious investors." Publishes hardcover and trade paperback originals, reprints, and very specific software. Averages 8 titles/year. Receives approximately 40 submissions annually. 60% of books from first-time authors; 90% from unagented writers. Pays 10% royalty on retail price; 5% on wholesale price (50% of total cost). Offers variable advance. Publishes book an average of 6 months after acceptance. Accepts simultaneous submissions. Reports in 2 weeks on queries. *Writer's Market* recommends allowing 2 months for reply. Book catalog and ms guidelines free.
Nonfiction: How-to, technical. Subjects include business/economics (investing in stocks and commodities). Interested in books on strategies, methods for investing in the stock market options market and commodity markets. Query or submit outline and sample chapters. Reviews artwork/photos as part of ms package.
Tips: "We sell through direct mail to our mailing list and other financial lists. Writers must keep their work original; this market tends to have a great deal of information overlap among publications."

WINDWARD PUBLISHING, INC., P.O. Box 371005, Miami FL 33137-1005. (305)576-6232. **Acquisitions**: Jack Zinzow, vice president. Estab. 1973. Windward publishes illustrated natural history and recreation books for children. Publishes trade paperback originals. Publishes 6 titles/year. Receives 50 queries and 10 mss/year. 35% of books from first-time authors; 100% from unagented writers. Pays 10% royalty on wholesale price. Publishes book 14 months after acceptance of ms. Accepts simultaneous submissions. Reports in 2 weeks on queries. *Writer's Market* recommends allowing 2 months for reply.
Nonfiction: Illustrated books, children's/juvenile natural history, handbooks. Subjects include agriculture/horticulture, animals, gardening, nature/environment, recreation (fishing, boating, diving, camping), science. Query. Reviews artwork/photos as part of the ms package.
Recent Nonfiction Title(s): *Mammals of Florida* (children's).

WISDOM PUBLICATIONS, 361 Newbury St., 4th Floor, Boston MA 02115. (617)536-3358. Fax: (617)536-1897. **Acquisitions:** Editorial Project Manager. "Wisdom Publications is a nonprofit publisher for works on Buddhism, Tibet and East-West themes." Publishes hardcover originals, trade paperback originals and reprints. Publishes 12-15 titles/year. Receives 150 queries and 50 mss/year. 50% of books from first-time authors; 95% from unagented writers. Pays 4-8% royalty on wholesale price (net). Publishes book 2 years after acceptance. Book catalog and ms guidelines free.
Nonfiction: Subjects include philosophy (Buddhist or comparative Buddhist/Western), East-West, Buddhism, Buddhist texts and Tibet, meditation. Query with SASE. "Unsolicited manuscripts will not be read." Reviews artwork/photos as part of ms package. Send photocopies.
Recent Nonfiction Title(s): *Mindfulness with Breathing*, by Buddhadhasa Bhikku (meditation); *Meditation on Emptiness*, by Jeffrey Hopkins (meditation); *The Good Heart*, by The Dalai Lama (Buddhist/Christian dialogue).
Fiction: Children's books with Buddhist themes.
Recent Fiction Title(s): *Her Father's Garden*, by James Vollbracht; *The Gift*, by Isia Osuchowska.
Poetry: Buddhist, contemplative.
Recent Poetry Title(s): *Drinking the Mountain Stream*, by Lana Kinja and Brian Cutillo, translators (sacred Tibetan poetry by Milarepa).
Tips: "We are now publishing children's books with Buddhist themes and contemplative/Buddhist poetry."

WOODBINE HOUSE, 6510 Bells Mill Rd., Bethesda MD 20817. (301)897-3570. Fax: (301)897-5838. **Acquisitions**: Susan Stokes, editor. Estab. 1985. "We publish books for or about individuals with disabilities that will, in our judgment, help those individuals and their families live fulfilling and satisfying lives in their communities." Publishes hardcover and trade paperback originals and reprints. Publishes 8 titles/year. 90% of books from unagented writers. Pays 10-12% royalty. Publishes book 18 months after acceptance. Accepts simultaneous submissions. Reports in 2 months. Book catalog and ms guidelines for 6×9 SAE with 3 first-class stamps.
Nonfiction: Publishes books for and about children and adults with disabilities. No personal accounts or general parenting guides. Submit outline and 3 sample chapters with SASE. Reviews artwork/photos as part of ms package.
Recent Nonfiction Title(s): *Children with Facial Differences*, by Hope Charkins (parenting guide); *Gross Motor Skills for Children with Down Syndrome*, by Patricia C. Winders.
Fiction: Children's picture books. Submit outline and 3 sample chapters with SASE.

Recent Fiction Title(s): *Andy and His Yellow Frisbee*, by Mary Thompson (picture book); *Zipper, the Kid with ADHD*, by Caroline Janover.

Tips: "Do not send us a proposal on the basis of this description. Examine our catalog and a couple of our books to make sure you are on the right track. Put some thought into how your book could be marketed (aside from in bookstores). Keep cover letters concise and to the point; if it's a subject that interests us, we'll ask to see more."

WOODLAND PUBLISHING INC., P.O. Box 160, Pleasant Grove UT 84062. Fax: (801)785-8511. Publisher: Mark Lisonbee. Executive Vice President: Trent Tenney. **Acquisitions**: Cord Odall, editor. "Our readers are interested in herbs and other natural health topics. Most of our books are sold through health food stores." Publishes perfect bound and trade paperback originals. Publishes 20 titles/year. Receives 100 queries and 60 mss/year. 50% of books from first-time authors; 100% from unagented writers. Publishes book 6 months after acceptance of ms. Accepts simultaneous submissions. Reports in 1 month on proposals. *WM* recommends allowing 2 months for reply. Book catalog free.
Nonfiction: Health/alternative medicine subjects. Query.
Recent Nonfiction Title(s): *Today's Herbal Health for Children*, by Louise Tenney.

WORDWARE PUBLISHING, INC., 1506 Capitol Ave., Plano TX 75074. (214)423-0090. Fax: (214)881-9147. E-mail: jhill@wordware.com. Website: http://www.wordware.com. President: Russell A. Stultz. **Acquisitions:** Jim Hill, publisher. Wordware publishes computer/electronics books covering a broad range of technologies for professional programmers and developers. Publishes trade paperback and mass market paperback originals. Publishes 50-70 titles/year. Receives 100-150 queries and 50-75 mss/year. 40% of books from first-time authors; 95% from unagented writers. Pays 8-12% royalty on wholesale price. Offers $3,000-5,000 advance. Publishes book 6 months after acceptance of ms. Accepts simultaneous submissions. Reports in 2 months. Book catalog and ms guidelines free.
Imprint(s): Iron Castle Productions (George Baxter, acquisitions editor), **Republic of Texas Press**, Seaside Press.
● Wordware has published such authors as Nathan Wallace and David Campbell.
Nonfiction: Reference, technical, textbook. Subjects include computers, electronics. Submit proposal package, including table of contents, 2 sample chapters, target audience summation, competing books.
Recent Nonfiction Title(s): *The Practical Guide to SGML Filters*, by Norman Smith (reference); *Learn Internet Relay Chat*, by Kathryn Toyer; *Learn Microsoft Office 97*, by Russell A. Stelty (software).

‡WORKMAN PUBLISHING CO., 708 Broadway, New York NY 10003. (212)254-5900. Fax: (212)254-8098. E-mail: mged@workman.com. Website: http://www.workman.com. Editor-in-Chief: Sally Kovalchik. Estab. 1967. Publishes hardcover and trade paperback originals. Publishes 40 titles/year. Receives thousands of queries/year. Open to first-time authors. Pays variable royalty on retail price. Advance varies. Publishes book 1 year after acceptance of ms. Accepts simultaneous submissions. Reports in 4 months. Book catalog free.
Imprint(s): Artisan, **Algonquin Books of Chapel Hill**.
Nonfiction: Cookbook, gift book, how-to, humor. Subjects include child guidance/parenting, gardening, health/medicine, sports, travel. *Writer's Market* recommends sending query with SASE first. Reviews artwork/photos as part of ms package "if relevant to project. Don't send anything you can't afford to lose."

WORLD LEISURE, P.O. Box 160, Hampstead NH 03841. (617)569-1966. Fax: (617)561-7654. E-mail: wleisure@aol.com. **Acquisitions:** Charles Leocha, president. World Leisure specializes in travel books, activity guidebooks and self-help titles. Publishes trade paperback originals. Publishes 6-8 titles/year. Pays royalty or makes outright purchase. No advance. Reports in 2 months on proposals.
Nonfiction: "We will be publishing annual updates to *Ski Europe* and *Skiing America*. Writers planning any ski stories should contact us for possible add-on assignments at areas not covered by our staff. We also will publish general travel titles such as Travelers' Rights, Family travel guides, guidebooks about myths and legends, the *Cheap Dates* (affordable activity guidebooks) series and self/help books such as *Getting To Know You*, and *A Woman's ABCs of Life*." Submit outline, intro chapter and annotated table of contents with SASE.
Recent Nonfiction Title(s): *Travel Rights*, by Charles Leocha; *Seababies and Their Friends*, by Cathleen Arone.

WRITE WAY PUBLISHING, 10555 E. Dartmouth, Suite 210, Aurora CO 80014 **Acquisitions**: Dorrie O'Brien, owner/editor. "Write Way is a fiction-only small press concentrating on genre publications such as mysteries, soft science fiction, fairy tale/fantasy and horror/thrillers." Publishes hardcover and trade paperback originals. Publishes 10-15 titles/year. Receives 1,000 queries and 350 mss/year. 50% of books from first-time authors; 95% from unagented writers. Pays 8-10% royalty on wholesale price. No advance. Publishes book within 3 years after acceptance. Accepts simultaneous submissions. Reports in 1 month on queries and proposals; 6 months on mss. "We only consider completed works." Book brochure and ms guidelines free for SASE.
Fiction: Adventure, fantasy, historical, horror, mystery, occult, science fiction, suspense. Query with short synopsis, 1-2 sample chapters and postage with proper-sized box or envelope.
Recent Fiction Title(s): *Shards*, by Tom Piccirilli; *Just Bones*, by Jeffrey Denhart.
Tips: "We find that lengthy outlines and/or synopsis are unnecessary and much too time-consuming for our editors to read. We prefer a very short plot review and 1-2 chapters to get a feel for the writer's style. If we like what we read, then we'll ask for the whole manuscript."

WRITER'S DIGEST BOOKS, Imprint of F&W Publications, 1507 Dana Ave., Cincinnati OH 45207. Editor: Jack Heffron. **Acquisitions:** Acquisitions Coordinator. Estab. 1920. Writer's Digest Books is the premiere source for books about writing, publishing instructional and reference books for writers that concentrate on the creative technique and craft of writing rather than the marketing of writing. Publishes hardcover and paperback originals. Publishes 28 titles/year. Pays 10-20% royalty on net receipts. Accepts simultaneous submissions, if so noted. Publishes book 18 months after acceptance. Reports in 2 months. Book catalog for 9 × 12 SAE with 6 first-class stamps.

Nonfiction: Instructional and reference books for writers. "Our instruction books stress results and how specifically to achieve them. Should be well-researched, yet lively and readable. Our books concentrate on writing techniques over marketing techniques. We do *not* want to see books telling readers how to crack specific nonfiction markets: *Writing for the Computer Market* or *Writing for Trade Publications*, for instance. Concentrate on broader writing topics. In the offices here we refer to a manuscript's 4T value—manuscripts must have information writers can Take To The Typewriter. We are continuing to grow our line of reference books for writers, such as *Modus Operandi* and *Malicious Intent* in our Howdunit series, and *A Writer's Guide to Everyday Life in the Middle Ages*. References must be usable, accessible, and, of course, accurate." Query or submit outline and sample chapters with SASE. "Explain how your book differs from existing books on the subject." *No fiction or poetry.* "Writer's Digest Books also publishes instructional books for photographers and songwriters, but the main thrust is on writing books. The same philosophy applies to songwriting and photography books: they must instruct about the creative craft, as opposed to instructing about marketing."

Recent Nonfiction Title(s): *Ten Steps to Publishing Children's Books*, by Berthe Amoss and Eric Suben; *Writing the Private Eye Novel: A Handbook by the Private Eye Writers of America*, edited by Robert J. Randisi.

‡**WRITERS PRESS**, 5278 Chinden Blvd., Boise ID 83714. (208)327-0566. Fax: (208)327-3477. E-mail: writers@cyberhighway.net. Website: www.writerspress.com. **Acquisitions:** John Ybarra, editor. "Our philosophy is to show children how to help themselves and others. By publishing high-quality children's literature that is both fun and educational, we are striving to make a difference in today's educational world." Publishes hardcover and trade paperback originals. Publishes 6 titles/year. Receives 50 queries and 30 mss/year. 60% of books from first-time authors; 100% from unagented writers. Pays 4-12% royalty or makes outright purchase of up to $1,500. Publishes book 6 months after acceptance of ms. Reports in 1 month on queries, 2 months on proposals, 4 months on mss. Catalog and guidelines free.

Nonfiction: Children's/juvenile. Subjects include education, history, inclusion, special education. Query. Reviews artwork/photos as part of ms package. Send photocopies.

Fiction: Adventure, historical, juvenile, picture books, young adult, inclusion, special education. Query.

Recent Fiction Title(s): *Eagle Feather*, by Sonia Gardner, illustrated by James Spurlock (picture book).

Recent Poetry Title(s): *Hodgepodge*, by Kevin Boos.

‡**A WYATT BOOK FOR ST. MARTIN'S PRESS**, Imprint of St. Martin's Press, 175 Fifth St., New York NY 10010. (212)674-5151. **Acquisitions:** Robert Wyatt, publisher. "We have a literary list devoted to the novel as intelligent entertainment." Publishes hardcover originals and trade paperback originals and reprints. Publishes 16-17 titles/year. 60% of books from first-time authors; 10-15% from unagented writers. Royalty and advance vary. Publishes book 18 months after acceptance of ms. Accepts simultaneous submissions if noted. Reports in 2 months on queries. Book Catalog for #10 SASE.

Nonfiction: "We are concentrating primarily on fiction now." Query only on completed ms; no "works in progress."

Recent Nonfiction Title(s): *The Great Adventure: How The Mounties Conquered The West*, by David Cruise and Alison Griffiths (history).

Fiction: Literary. "No short story, no genre fiction." Query only on completed ms; no "works in progress." SASE.

Recent Fiction Title(s): *A Cab Called Reliable*, by Patti Kim; *Naming the New World*, by Calvin Baker.

‡**WYNDHAM HALL PRESS**, 52857 C.R. 21, Bristol IN 46507. (219)848-4834. **Acquisitions:** Milton L. Clayton, publisher. Estab. 1982. "Wyndham Hall was begun by a college professor, and the focus is on scholarly texts. Ninety percent of authors are affiliated with universities and education." Publishes hardcover and trade paperback originals and reprints. Publishes 20 titles/year. Receives 100 queries and 50 mss/year. 90% of books from first-time authors; 100% from unagented writers. Pays 10-15% on wholesale price. Publishes book 4 months after acceptance of ms. Accepts simultaneous submissions. Reports in 1 month. Book catalog and ms guidelines free.

Nonfiction: Reference, textbook. Subjects include education, ethnic, government/politics, health/medicine, philosophy, psychology, religion, science, sociology. "We publish serious scholarly work. Writers must include their credentials or qualifications for writing the book." Submit proposal package, including completed ms and qualifications. Reviews artwork/photos as part of ms package. Send photocopies.

Recent Nonfiction Title(s): *The Rise of the Islamic Empire and the Threat to the West*; *The Bosnia Files*.

‡**YALE UNIVERSITY PRESS**, 302 Temple St., New Haven CT 06520. (203)432-0960. Fax: (203)432-0948. Website: http://www.yale.edu/yup. **Acquisitions:** Charles Grench, editor-in-chief (anthropology, archaeology, history, Judaic studies, religion, women's studies); Jean E. Thomson Black, editor (science, medicine); Jonathan Brent, executive editor (classics, literature, philosophy, poetry); Judith Calvert, editor (editions and series, foreign languages); John S. Covell, senior editor (economics, law, political science); Harry Haskell, editor (music and performing arts); Fred Kameny, reference editor (reference books); Judy Metro, senior editor (art, art history, architecture, geography); Gladys Topkis, senior editor (education, psychiatry, psychology, sociology). Estab. 1908. "We publish scholarly and general interest books." Publishes hardcover and trade paperback originals. Publishes 200 titles/year. Receives 8,000 queries and 400 mss/year. 15% of books from first-time authors; 85% from unagented writers. Pays 0-15% royalty on net price. Offers $500-30,000 advance (based on expected sales). Publishes book 1 year after acceptance of ms. Accepts simultaneous

submissions, if so noted. Reports in 1 month on queries, 2 months on proposals, 3 months on mss. Book catalog and ms guidelines for #10 SASE.

Nonfiction: Biography, illustrated book, reference, textbook, scholarly works. Subjects include Americana, anthropology/archaeology, art/architecture, economics, education, history, language/literature, medicine, military/war, music/dance, philosophy, psychology, religion, science, sociology, women's issues/studies. "Our nonfiction has to be at a very high level. Most of our books are written by professors or journalists, with a high level of expertise." Query by letter with SASE. "We'll ask if we want to see more. No unsolicited manuscripts. We won't return them." Reviews artwork/photos as part of ms package. Send photocopies, not originals.

Recent Nonfiction Title(s): *Mary Through The Centuries*, by Charles Jaroslaupelikan (general interest); *The Elements of Teaching*, by James Banner and Harold Cannon (education); *Braque: The Late Works*, by John Golding (art history).

Poetry: Publishes 1 book each year. Submit ms to Yale Younger Poets Competition. Open to poets under 40 without a book published. Submit ms of 48-64 pages in February. Entry fee: $15. Send SASE for rules and guidelines.

ZEBRA BOOKS, Imprint of Kensington, 850 Third Ave., 16th Floor, New York NY 10022. (212)407-1500. Publisher: Lynn Brown. **Acquisitions:** Ann Lafarge, editor. "Zebra Books is dedicated to women's fiction, which includes, but is not limited to romance." Publishes hardcover originals, trade paperback and mass market paperback originals and reprints. Publishes 140-170 titles/year. 5% of books from first-time authors; 30% from unagented writers. Pays variable royalty and advance. Publishes book 18 months after acceptance of ms. Accepts simultaneous submissions. Reports in 1 month on queries, in 3 months on mss. Book catalog for #10 SASE.

Fiction: Romance, women's fiction. Query with synopsis and SASE. Not accepting unsolicited submissions.

Recent Fiction Title(s): *By Candelight*; *Love With a Stranger*, by Janell Taylor (romance).

ZOLAND BOOKS, INC., 384 Huron Ave., Cambridge MA 02138. (617)864-6252. Fax: (617)661-4998. **Acquisitions:** Roland Pease, Jr., publisher/editor: Estab. 1987. "Zoland Books is an independent publishing company producing fiction, poetry and art books of literary interest." Publishes hardcover and trade paperback originals. Publishes 8-12 titles/year. Receives 400 submissions/year. 15% of books from first-time authors; 60% from unagented writers. Pays 7½% royalty on retail price. Publishes book 18 months after acceptance. Reports in 4 months. Book catalog for 6½ × 9½ SAE with 2 first-class stamps.

● Zoland has published such authors as Sallie Bingham, James Laughlin and Myra Goldberg.

Nonfiction: Biography, art book. Subjects include art/architecture, language/literature, nature/environment, photography, regional, translation, travel, women's issues/studies. Query. Reviews artwork/photos as part of ms package.

Recent Nonfiction Title(s): *The United States of Jasper Johns*, by John Yau (art); *Furthering My Education*, by William Corbett (memoir).

Fiction: Literary, short story collections. Submit complete ms. *Writer's Market* recommends querying with SASE first.

Recent Fiction Title(s): *Gas Station*, by Joseph Torra; *Billy in Love*, by Norman Kotker (novel).

Recent Poetry Title(s): *Cross a Parted Sea*, by Sam Cornish (African-American).

Tips: "We are most likely to publish books which provide original, thought-provoking ideas, books which will captivate the reader, and are evocative."

ZONDERVAN PUBLISHING HOUSE, Division of HarperCollins Publishers, 5300 Patterson Ave. SE, Grand Rapids MI 49530-0002. (616)698-6900. **Acquisitions:** Manuscript Review Editor. Estab. 1931. "Our mission is to be the leading Christian communications company meeting the needs of people with resources that glorify Jesus Christ and promote biblical principles." Publishes hardcover and trade paperback originals and reprints. Publishes 120 titles/year. Receives 3,000 submissions/year. 20% of books from first-time authors; 80% from unagented writers. Average print order for a first book is 5,000. Pays 14% royalty on net amount received on sales of cloth and softcover trade editions; 12% royalty on net amount received on sales of mass market paperbacks. Offers variable advance. Reports in 3 months on proposals. SASE required. Guidelines for #10 SASE. Call (616)698-6900 for submissions policy.

Nonfiction and Fiction: Biography, autobiography, self-help, devotional, contemporary issues, Christian living, Bible study resources, references for lay audience; some adult fiction; youth and children's ministry; teens and children. Academic and Professional Books: college and seminary textbooks (biblical studies, theology, church history); preaching, counseling, discipleship, worship, and church renewal for pastors, professionals and lay leaders in ministry; theological and biblical reference books. All from religious perspective (evangelical). Submit outline/synopsis, 1 sample chapter, and SASE for return of materials.

Recent Nonfiction Title(s): *The Jesus I Never Knew*, by Philip Yancey; *Just As I Am*, by Billy Graham (autobiography); *What Does She Want From Me, Anyway?*, by Holly Faith Phillips with Gregg Lewis (Christian living).

Recent Fiction Title(s): *The Campaign*, by Marilyn Tucker Quayle and Nancy Tucker Northcott; *Presumption of Guilt*, by Terri Blackstock (suspense); *Caught in the Middle*, by Gayle Roper (mystery).

MARKETS THAT WERE listed in the 1997 edition of *Writer's Market* but do not appear this year are listed in the General Index with a notation explaining why they were omitted.

Canadian and International Book Publishers

Canadian book publishers share the same mission as their U.S. counterparts—publishing timely books on subjects of concern and interest to a targetable audience. Most of the publishers listed in this section, however, differ from U.S. publishers in that their needs tend toward subjects that are specifically Canadian or intended for a Canadian audience. Some are interested in submissions only from Canadian writers. There are many regional Canadian publishers that concentrate on region-specific subjects, and many Quebec publishers will consider only works in French.

U.S. writers hoping to do business with Canadian publishers should take pains to find out as much about their intended markets as possible. The listings will inform you about what kinds of books the companies publish and tell you whether they are open to receiving submissions from non-Canadians. To further target your markets and see very specific examples of the books they are publishing, send for catalogs from the publishers you are interested in.

There has always been more government subsidy of publishing in Canada than in the U.S. However, with continued cuts in such subsidies, government support appears to be on the decline. There are a few author-subsidy publishers in Canada and writers should proceed with caution when they are made this offer.

Publishers offering author subsidy arrangements (sometimes referred to as "joint venture," "co-publishing" or "cooperative publishing") are not listed in *Writer's Market*. If one of the publishers in this section offers you an author-subsidy arrangement or asks you to pay for all or part of the cost of any aspect of publishing (printing, marketing, etc.) or asks you to guarantee the purchase of a number of books yourself, please let us know about that company immediately.

Despite a healthy book publishing industry, Canada is still dominated by publishers from the United States. Two out of every three books found in Canadian bookstores are published in the U.S. These odds have made some Canadian publishers even more determined to concentrate on Canadian authors and subjects. Writers interested in additional Canadian book publishing markets should consult *Literary Market Place* (R.R. Bowker & Co.), *The Canadian Writer's Guide* (Fitzhenry & Whiteside) and *The Canadian Writer's Market* (McClelland & Stewart).

INTERNATIONAL MAIL

U.S. postage stamps are useless on mailings originating outside of the U.S. When enclosing a self-addressed envelope for return of your query or manuscript from a publisher outside the U.S., you must include International Reply Coupons (IRCs). IRCs are available at your local post office and can be redeemed for stamps of any country. You can cut a substantial portion of your international mailing expenses by sending disposable proposals and manuscripts (i.e., photocopies or computer printouts which the recipient can recycle if she is not interested), instead of paying postage for the return of rejected material. Please note that the cost for items such as catalogs is expressed in the currency of the country in which the publisher is located.

For a list of publishers according to their subjects of interest, see the nonfiction and fiction sections of the Book Publishers Subject Index. Information on book publishers and producers listed in the previous edition but not included in this edition of *Writer's Market* can be found in the General Index.

THE ALTHOUSE PRESS, U.W.O., Faculty of Education, 1137 Western Rd., London, Ontario N6G 1G7 Canada. (519)661-2096. Fax: (519)661-3833. E-mail: press@edu.uwo.ca. Website: http://www.uwo.ca./edu/press. **Acquisitions:** Katherine Butson, editorial assistant. Publishes trade paperback originals and reprints. Publishes 1-5 titles/year. Receives 30 queries and 19 mss/year. 100% of books from unagented writers. Pays 10% royalty on net price. Offers $300 advance. Accepts simultaneous submissions. Reports in 2 weeks on queries, 4 months on mss. Book catalog and manuscript guidelines free on request.
Nonfiction: Education subjects. Query. Reviews artwork/photos as part of ms package. Send photocopies.
Recent Nonfiction Title: *Crocus Hill Reunion*, by Garry Jones (education).
Tips: Audience is practicing teachers and graduate education students.

‡ANVIL PRESS, 204-A E. Broadway, Vancouver, British Columbia V5T 1W2 Canada. (604)876-8710. **Acquisitions:** Brian Kaufman. "Anvil Press publishes contemporary fiction, poetry and drama, giving voice to up-and-coming Canadian writers, exploring all literary genres, discovering, nurturing and promoting new Canadian literary talent." Publishes trade paperback originals. Publishes 4 titles/year. Receives 100 queries/year. 80% of books from first-time authors; 70% from unagented writers. Pays 10-15% on wholesale price. Offers $200-400 advance. Publishes ms 8 months after acceptance of ms. Reports in 2 months on queries and proposals, 6 months on mss. Book catalog for 9 × 12 SAE with 2 first-class stamps. Manuscript guidelines for #10 SASE.
• Anvil Press also publishes the literary magazine *sub-Terrain* and sponsors the 3-Day Novel Writing Contest.
Fiction: Literary, plays, short story collections. Contemporary, modern literature—no formulaic or genre. Query with 2 sample chapters and SASE.
Recent Fiction Titles: *Salvage King, Ya! (A Herky-Jerky Picaresque)*, by Mark Jarman; *Monday Night Man*, by Grant Buday (short stories); *Sub-Rosa & Other Fiction*, by Catherine Bennett (prose); *Shylock*, by Mark Leiren-Young (drama).
Poetry: "Get our catalog, look at our poetry, read *sub-Terrain* magazine (our quarterly literary magazine). We do very little poetry in book form—maybe 1 title per year." Query with 12 sample poems.
Recent Poetry Titles: *Lonesome Monsters*, by Bud Osborn; *Ivanhoe Station*, by Lyle Neff.
Tips: Audience is young, informed, educated, aware, with an opinion, culturally active (films, books, the performing arts). "No U.S. authors, unless selected as the winner of our 3-Day Novel Contest. Research the appropriate publisher for your work. If no luck, publish yourself in magazine or book form."

ARSENAL PULP PRESS, 103, 1014 Homer St., Vancouver, British Columbia V6B 2W9 Canada. (604)687-4233. **Acquisitions**: Linda Field, editor. Estab. 1980. Imprint is Tillacum Library. Publishes hardcover and trade paperback originals, trade paperback reprints. Publishes 12-15 titles/year. Receives 400 queries and 200 mss/year. 25% of books from first-time authors; 100% from unagented writers. Pays 15% royalty on wholesale price. Advance varies. Publishes book 1 year after acceptance of ms. Reports in 4 months on queries, with exceptions. Book catalog and ms guidelines free on request with 9 × 12 SASE. Publishes only Canadian writers.
Nonfiction: Humor. Subjects include ethnic (Canadian, aboriginal issues), gay/lesbian, popular music, history (cultural), literature, regional (British Columbia), sociology, women's issues/studies. Submit outline and 2-3 sample chapters.
Recent Nonfiction Titles: *Out Of This World*, by Chris Gudgeon (biography); *It Pays to Play*, by Peter White (art history); *Bringing It Home*, edited by Brenda Lea Brown (women's studies).
Fiction: Experimental, feminist, gay/lesbian, literary and short story collections. Submit synopsis and 2-3 sample chapters.
Recent Fiction Titles: *Everything But the Truth*, by Christopher McPherson (short fiction); *Hunting with Diana*, by David Watmough (short fiction); *Silence Descends*, by George Cage (novel).
Recent Poetry Title: *Kingsway*, by Michael Turner.

BALLANTINE BOOKS OF CANADA, Division of Random House of Canada, Ltd., 1265 Aerowood Dr., Mississauga, Ontario L4W 1B9, Canada. General interest publisher of nonfiction and fiction. Query before submitting. *No unsolicited mss.*

BANTAM BOOKS CANADA, INC., Subsidiary of Bantam Doubleday Dell Publishing Group, 105 Bond St., Toronto, Ontario M5B 1Y3, Canada. Query with proposal letter and résumé to Submissions Editor. *No unsolicited mss.* Reports in 3 months.

BEACH HOLME PUBLISHERS LTD., 226-2040 W. 12th Ave., Vancouver, British Columbia V6J 2G2 Canada. (604)773-4868. Fax: (604)733-4860. E-mail: bhp@beachholme.bc.ca. Website: http://www.beachholme.bc.ca. **Acquisitions:** Joy Gugeler, managing editor; Theresa Bubela, editor. Estab. 1971. Publishes trade paperback originals. Publishes 10 titles/year. Receives 1,000 submissions/year. "Accepting only Canadian submissions." 40% of books from first-time authors; 75% from unagented writers. Pays 10% royalty on retail price. Offers $500 average advance. Publishes ms 1 year after acceptance. Accepts simultaneous submissions, if so noted. Reports in 2 months. Manuscript guidelines free.
• Beach Holme no longer publishes nonfiction.

Fiction: Adult literary fiction and poetry from authors published in Canadian literary magazines. Young adult (Canada historical/regional). "Interested in excellent quality, imaginative writing."

Recent Fiction Title: *Inappropriate Behavior*, by Irene Mock (short fiction).

Tips: "Make sure the manuscript is well written. We see so many that only the unique and excellent can't be put down. Send cover letter, SASE, outline and two chapters. Prior publication is a must. This doesn't necessarily mean book length manuscripts, but a writer should try to publish his or her short fiction."

BOREALIS PRESS, LTD., 9 Ashburn Dr., Nepean, Ontario K2E 6N4 Canada. Fax: (613)829-7783. Editorial Director: Frank Tierney. **Acquisitions:** Glenn Clever, senior editor. Estab. 1972. Publishes hardcover and paperback originals. Publishes 10-12 titles/year. Receives 400-500 submissions/year. 80% of books from first-time authors; 95% from un-agented writers. Pays 10% royalty on list price. No advance. Publishes book 18 months after acceptance. Reports in 2 months. Book catalog for $3 and SASE.

Imprint: Tecumseh Press.

Nonfiction: "Only material Canadian in content." Biography, children's/juvenile, reference. Subjects include government/politics, history, language/literature. Query with outline, 2 sample chapters and SASE. No unsolicited mss. Reviews artwork/photos as part of ms package. Looks for "style in tone and language, reader interest, and maturity of outlook."

Recent Nonfiction Title: *All My Sisters*, by Clara Thomas (selected essays on Canadian women's writing); *The Community Doukhobors: A People in Transition*, by John Friesen and Michael Verigin.

Fiction: "Only material Canadian in content and dealing with significant aspects of the human situation." Adventure, ethnic, historical, juvenile, literary, romance, short story collections, young adult. Query with synopsis, 1-2 sample chapters and SASE. No unsolicited mss.

Recent Fiction Title: *Sunshine Sketches of a Little Town*, by Stephen Leacock (a critical edition); *The Imperialist*, by Sara Jeannette Duncan (critical edition).

Recent Poetry Title: *Fidelities*, by Liliane Welch; *The Trouble with Light*, by Fred Cogswell.

THE BOSTON MILLS PRESS, 132 Main St., Erin, Ontario N0B 1T0 Canada. (519)833-2407. Fax: (519)833-2195. E-mail: books@boston-mills.on.ca. Website: boston-mills.on.ca. President: John Denison. **Acquisitions**: Noel Hudson, managing editor. Estab. 1974. Boston Mills Press publishes specific market titles of Canadian and American interest including history, transportation and regional guidebooks. Publishes hardcover and trade paperback originals. Publishes 20 titles/year. Receives 200 submissions/year. 75% of books from first-time authors; 90% from unagented writers. Pays 10% royalty on retail price. Offers small advance. Publishes book 1 year after acceptance. Accepts simultaneous submissions. Reports in 2 months. Book catalog free.

Nonfiction: Illustrated book. Subjects include history, nature, guidebooks. "We're interested in anything to do with Canadian or American history—especially transportation." No autobiographies. Query. Reviews artwork/photos as part of ms package.

Recent Nonfiction Titles: *Wild Wings*, by Michael Runtz (birds); *Superior*, by Gary and Joan McGuffin (Lake Superior).

Tips: "We can't compete with the big boys so we stay with short-run specific market books that bigger firms can't handle. We've done well this way so we'll continue in the same vein."

BROADVIEW PRESS LTD., P.O. Box 1243, Peterborough, Ontario K9J 7H5 Canada. (705)743-8990. Fax: (705)743-8353. **Acquisitions**: Don LePan, president. Estab. 1985. "We specialize in university/college supplementary textbooks which often have both a trade and academic market." Publishes paperback originals. Publishes 20-25 titles/year. Receives 250 submissions/year. 5-10% of books from first-time authors; 95% from unagented writers. Pays 4-10% royalty on retail price. Publishes book 18 months after acceptance. Accepts simultaneous submissions but prefers not to. Reports in 4 months on proposals.

Nonfiction: Textbook, scholarly/academic, general nonfiction. Subjects include anthropology, art/architecture, ethnic and Native American studies, government/politics, history, language/literature, nature/environment, philosophy, sociology, women's issues/studies. "All titles must have some potential for university or college-level course use. Cross-over titles are acceptable." Query or submit outline and sample chapters and proposal package, including quick description of intended market, table of contents and cv. Sometimes reviews artwork/photos as part of ms package. Send photocopies.

Recent Nonfiction Title: *In Search of Authority: An Introduction to Literary Theory*, by Stephen Bunnycastle.

Tips: "We now consider *only* works aimed at least in *part* at a university textbook market in the Arts or Social Sciences."

BROWN BEAR PRESS, 122 Felbrigg Ave., Toronto, Ontario M5M 2M5 Canada. **Acquisitions**: Ruth Bradley-St-Cyr, publisher. Publishes trade paperback original nonfiction from Canadian authors only and reprints of Canadian

---

ALWAYS SUBMIT unsolicited manuscripts or queries with a self-addressed, stamped envelope (SASE) within your country or a self-addressed envelope with International Reply Coupons (IRC) purchased from the post office for other countries.

classics. "We do not publish new fiction." Publishes 4 titles/year. Pays 8-10% royalty on retail price. Offers $100-300 advance. Publishes books 1 year after acceptance of ms. Reports in 2 months on proposals. Submission guidelines free with Canadian SASE.

Nonfiction: Canadian social, political and family issues.

Fiction: Reprints only. Canadian literature for adults and children.

‡BUTTERWORTHS CANADA, 75 Clegg Rd., Markham, Ontario L6G 1A1 Canada. (905)479-2665. Fax: (905)479-2826. E-mail: info@butterworths.ca. Website: www.butterworths.ca. **Acquisitions:** Ruth Epstein, publishing director. Butterworths publishes professional reference material for the legal, business and accounting markets. Publishes 100 titles/year. Receives 100 queries and 10 mss/year. 50% of books from first-time authors; 100% from unagented writers. Pays 5-15% royalty on wholesale price; occasionally by fee. Offers $1,000-5,000 advance. Publishes book 6 months after acceptance of ms. Accepts simultaneous submissions. Reports in 1 month on proposals. Book catalog free.

Nonfiction: Multimedia (disk and CD-Rom), reference, looseleaf. Subjects include health/medicine (medical law), legal and business reference. Query with SASE.

Recent Nonfiction Titles: *The Law of Confidential Communication*, by Ronald Manes and Michael Silver; *Directors and Officers Duties and Liabilities in Canada*, law firm of McCarthy Tetrault; *The Law of Search and Seizure in Canada, 4th Edition*, by Judge Fontana (legal reference).

Tips: Audience is legal community, business, medical, accounting professions.

CAITLIN PRESS, INC., P.O. Box 2387 Station B, Prince George, British Columbia V2N 2S6 Canada. (604)964-4953. Fax: (604)964-4970. **Acquisitions**: Cynthia Wilson. Estab. 1978. "We publish books about the British Columbia interior or by people from the interior." Publishes trade paperback and soft cover originals. Publishes 6-7 titles/year. Receives 105-120 queries and 50 mss/year. 100% of books from unagented writers. Pays 15% royalty on wholesale price. Publishes book 18 months after acceptance of ms. Accepts simultaneous submissions. Reports in 3 months on queries.

Nonfiction: Biography, cookbook. Subjects include history, photography, regional. "We are not interested in manuscripts that do not reflect a British Columbia influence." Submit outline and proposal package. Reviews artwork/photos as part of ms package. Send photocopies.

Recent Nonfiction Title: *Atlin's Gold*, by Peter Steele (autobiography/history/adventures).

Fiction: Adventure, historical, humor, mainstream/contemporary, short story collections, young adult. *Writer's Market* recommends query with SASE first.

Poetry: Submit sample poems or complete ms.

Recent Poetry Title: *The Centre*, by Barry McKinnon.

Tips: "Our area of interest is BC and Northern Canada. Submitted manuscripts should reflect our interest area."

CANADIAN INSTITUTE OF UKRAINIAN STUDIES PRESS, CIUS Toronto Publications Office, University of Toronto, Dept. of Slavic Languages and Literatures, 21 Sussex Ave., Toronto, Ontario M5S 1A1 Canada. (416)978-8240. Fax: (416)978-2672. E-mail: cius@chass.utoronto.ca. Website: http://www.utoronto.ca/cius. **Acquisitions**: Maxim Tarnawsky, director. Estab. 1976. "We publish scholarship about Ukraine and about Ukrainians in Canada." Publishes hardcover and trade paperback originals and reprints. Publishes 5-10 titles/year. Receives 10 submissions/year. Nonauthor-subsidy publishes 20-30% of books. Pays 0-2% royalty on retail price. Publishes book 2 years after acceptance. Reports in 1 month on queries, 3 months on mss. Book catalog and ms guidelines free.

Nonfiction: Scholarly. Subjects include education, ethnic, government/politics, history, language/literature, religion, sociology, translation. "We publish scholarly works in the humanities and social sciences dealing with the Ukraine or Ukrainians in Canada." Query or submit complete ms. *Writer's Market* recommends sending a query with SASE first. Reviews artwork/photos as part of ms package.

Recent Nonfiction Title: *The Ukrainian Greek Catholic Church and the Soviet State (1939-1950)*, by Bohdan R. Bociurkiw.

Fiction: Ukrainian literary works. "We do not publish fiction except for use as college textbooks."

Recent Fiction Title: *Yellow Boots*, by Vera Lysenko.

Tips: "We are a scholarly press and do not normally pay our authors. Our audience consists of University students and teachers and the general public interested in Ukrainian and Ukrainian-Canadian affairs."

CANADIAN LIBRARY ASSOCIATION, 200 Elgin St., Suite 602, Ottawa, Ontario K2P 1L5 Canada. (613)232-9625. Fax: (613)563-9895. E-mail: bj491@freenet.carleton.ca. Website: www.cla.amlibs.ca. **Acquisitions:** Elizabeth Morton, monographs editor. "CLA publishes practical/professional/academic materials with a Canadian focus or direct Canadian application as a service to CLA members and to contribute to the professional development of library staff." Publishes trade paperback originals. Publishes 4 titles/year. Receives 10 queries and 5 mss/year. 50% of books from first-time authors; 100% from unagented writers. Pays 10% minimum royalty on wholesale price. No advance. Publishes book 6 months after acceptance of ms. Reports in 1 month on queries, 3 months on proposals and mss. Book catalog and manuscript guidelines free on request.

Nonfiction: Reference, professional, academic. Subjects include history, library science. Query with outline. Reviews artwork/photos as part of ms package. Send photocopies.

Recent Nonfiction Titles: *Photocopying in Public Libraries in Canada: Report of the 1996 Survey*, by Françoise Hébert; *The National Library of Canada and Canadian Libraries: Essays in Honour of Guy Sylvestre/La Bibliothèque* *nationale du Canada et les bibliothèques canadiennes: essais en l'honneur de Guy Sylvestre*, edited by Jean-Rémi Brault, Gwynneth Evans and Richard Paré (history of libraries); *Readings in Canadian Library History*, edited by Peter F. McNally (library history).

Tips: Audience is library and information scientists.

CANADIAN PLAINS RESEARCH CENTER, University of Regina, Regina, Saskatchewan S4S 0A2 Canada. (306)585-4795. Fax: (306)585-4699. **Acquisitions**: Brian Mlazgar, coordinator. Estab. 1973. Publishes scholarly paperback originals and some casebound originals. Publishes 5-6 titles/year. Receives 10-15 submissions/year. 35% of books from first-time authors. Nonauthor-subsidy publishes 80% of books. Publishes book 2 years after acceptance. Reports in 2 months. Book catalog and ms guidelines free. Also publishes *Prairie Forum*, a scholarly journal.

Nonfiction: Biography, illustrated book, technical, textbook, scholarly. Subjects include business and economics, history, nature, politics, sociology. "The Canadian Plains Research Center publishes the results of research on topics relating to the Canadian Plains region, although manuscripts relating to the Great Plains region will be considered. Material *must* be scholarly. Do not submit health, self-help, hobbies, music, sports, psychology, recreation or cookbooks unless they have a scholarly approach. For example, we would be interested in acquiring a pioneer manuscript cookbook, with modern ingredient equivalents, if the material relates to the Canadian Plains/Great Plains region." Submit complete ms. *Writer's Market* recommends query with SASE first. Reviews artwork/photos as part of ms package.

Recent Nonfiction Title: *The Records of the Department of the Interior and Research Concerning Canada's Western Frontier of Settlement*, by Irene M. Spry and Bennett McCardle.

Tips: "Pay great attention to ms preparation and accurate footnoting, according to the *Chicago Manual of Style*."

CARSWELL THOMSON PROFESSIONAL PUBLISHING, Imprint of the Thomson Corp., One Corporate Plaza, 2075 Kennedy Rd., Scarborough, Ontario M1T 3V4 Canada. (416)298-5024. Fax: (416)298-5094. E-mail: grodrigues@carswell.com. Website: http://www.carswell.com. **Acquisitions**: Robert Freeman, vice president, publishing. "Carswell Thomson is Canada's national resource of information and legal interpretations for law, accounting, tax and business professionals." Publishes hardcover originals. Publishes 150-200 titles/year. 30-50% of books from first-time authors. Pays 5-15% royalty on wholesale price. Offers $1,000-5,000 advance. Publishes book 6 months after acceptance. Accepts simultaneous submissions. Reports in 3 months. Book catalog and ms guidelines free.

Nonfiction: Legal, tax and business reference. "Canadian information of a regulatory nature is our mandate." Submit proposal package, including résumé and outline.

Recent Nonfiction Title: *The Dictionary of Canadian Law*, by Daphne Dukalow and Betsy Nase (dictionary).

Tips: Audience is Canada and persons interested in Canadian information; professionals in law, tax, accounting fields; business people interested in regulatory material.

CHARLTON PRESS, 2040 Yonge St., Suite 208, Toronto, Ontario M4S 1Z9 Canada. Fax: (416)488-4656. **Acquisitions**: Nicola Leedham, managing editor. Publishes trade paperback originals and reprints. Publishes 15 titles/year. Receives 30 queries and 5 mss/year. 10% of books from first-time authors; 100% from unagented writers. Pays 10% minimum royalty on wholesale price or makes variable outright purchase. Offers $1,000 advance. Publishes book 6 months after acceptance of ms. Accepts simultaneous submissions. Reports in 1 month on queries and proposals, 2 months on mss. Book catalog free on request.

Nonfiction: Reference (price guides on collectibles). Subjects include art/architecture, hobbies, military/war, money/finance, sports. Submit outline. Reviews artwork/photos as part of ms package. Send photocopies.

Recent Nonfiction Title: *Royal Doulton Figurines*, by J. Dale (reference guide).

CHEMTEC PUBLISHING, 38 Earswick Dr., Toronto-Scarborough, Ontario M1E 1C6 Canada. (416)265-2603. Fax: (416)265-1399. E-mail: chemtec@io.org. Website: http://www.io.org/~chemtec. **Acquisitions**: Anna Wypych, president. Publishes hardcover originals. Publishes 5 titles/year. Receives 10 queries and 7 mss/year. 20% of books from first-time authors. Pays 5-15% royalty on retail price. Publishes book 6 months after acceptance of ms. Accepts simultaneous submissions. Reports in 2 months on queries, 4 months on mss. Book catalog and ms guidelines free on request.

Nonfiction: Technical, textbook. Subjects include nature/environment, science, chemistry, polymers. Submit outline or sample chapter(s).

Recent Nonfiction Title: *Template Polymerization*, by Stefan Polowinski; *Polymer Blends Thermodynamics*, by Yuri Lipatov; *Concepts in Polymer Thermodynamics*, by M.A. van Dijk and K. Wakker.

Tips: Audience is industrial research and universities.

COTEAU BOOKS, 2206 Dewdney Ave., Suite 401, Regina, Saskatchewan S4R 1H3 Canada. (306)777-0170. Fax: (306)522-5152. E-mail: coteau@coteau.unibase.com. Website: http://coteau.unibase.com. **Acquisitions**: Geoffrey Ursell, publisher. Estab. 1975. "Coteau Books publishes the finest Canadian fiction, poetry, drama and children's literature, with an emphasis on western writers." Publishes fiction, poetry, drama, anthologies, young adult novels— only by Canadian writers. Publishes 12 titles/year. Receives approximately 1,000 queries and mss/year. 10% of books from first-time authors; 95% from unagented writers. Pays 10% royalty on retail price or makes outright purchase of $50-200 for anthology contributors. Publishes book 18 months after acceptance. Reports in 1 month on queries, 4 months on mss. Book catalog for SASE.

Nonfiction: Reference, desk calendars. Subjects include language/literature, regional studies. "We publish only Canadian authors." *Writer's Market* recommends sending a query with SASE first.

Recent Nonfiction Title: *Many Patrols: Reminiscences of a Game Officer*, by R.D. Symons; *Her Story: the Annual Canadian Women's Daybook*.
Fiction: Ethnic, feminist, humor, juvenile, literary, mainstream/contemporary, plays, short story collections. "No popular, mass market sort of stuff. We are a literary press." Submit complete ms. *Writer's Market* recommends sending a query with SASE first. "We publish fiction and poetry only from Canadian authors."
Recent Fiction Titles: *Banjo Lessons*, by David Carpenter; *Inspection of A Small Village*, by Connie Gault; *Long Distance Calls*, by Dave Margoshis.
Recent Poetry Titles: *Gray Owl: The Mystery of Archie Belaney*, by Armand Garret Ruffo; *White Crane Spreads Wings*, by Gary Hyland.
Tips: "We do not publish picture books, but are interested in juvenile and YA fiction from Canadian authors."

‡CULTURE CONCEPTS PUBLISHERS, INC., 69 Ashmount Crescent, Toronto, Ontario M9R 1C9 Canada. (416)231-1692. E-mail: cultureconcepts@sympatico.ca. Website: http://www3.sympatico.ca/cultureconcepts. **Acquisitions**: Thelma Barer-Stein, Ph.D., publisher. Publishes hardcover and trade paperback originals. Publishes 3-4 titles/year. Receives 40 queries and 10 mss/year. 50% of books from first-time authors; 95% from unagented writers. Pays 6-12% royalty. Offers $200-2,000 advance. Publishes book 2 years after acceptance of ms. Accepts simultaneous submissions. Reports in 1 month. Book catalog and ms guidelines free.
Nonfiction: Cookbook, how-to, humor, reference. Subjects include cooking, foods & nutrition, education (adult). "Contact us before sending any mss." Query with SASE.
Recent Nonfiction Title: *Making Sense of Adult Learning*, by Dorothy Mackeracher; *Workplace Education: The Changing Landscape*, edited by Maurice C Taylor; *Alpha 97—Basic Education & Institutional Environments*, edited by Jean-Paul Hautecoeur (a joint publication of UNESCO Institute for Education and Culture Concepts Publishers).
Tips: Audience is university-educated adults. "Culture Concepts publishes books that won't stay on the shelf."

ROBERT DAVIES PUBLISHING, #311, 4999 St. Catherine St. W, Montreal, Quebec H3Z 1T3 Canada. Fax: (514)481-9973. E-mail: rdppub@vir.com. Website: http://www.rdppub.com. Publishes trade paperback originals and reprints. Publishes 32 titles/year. Receives 2,000 queries and 800 mss/year. 20% of books from first-time authors; 80% from unagented writers. Pays 10-15% royalty on retail price. Offers $2,000 advance if warranted. Publishes book 1 year after acceptance of ms. Accepts simultaneous submissions. Reports in 9 months. Book catalog for 9×12 SAE with 2 first-class Canadian stamps.
Nonfiction: Biography, children's/juvenile, coffee table book, cookbook, gift book, how-to, humor, illustrated book, self-help. Subjects include art/architecture, business and economics, child guidance/parenting, cooking/foods/nutrition, gay/lesbian, health/medicine, history, hobbies, language/literature, money/finance, philosophy, psychology, religion, sociology, translation, women's issues/studies. Query with SASE.
Recent Nonfiction Title: *Manufacturing Victims*, by Dr. Tana Dineen (psychology).
Fiction: Adventure, fantasy, gay/lesbian, historical, juvenile, literary, mainstream/contemporary, mystery. Query with SASE.
Tips: Audience is general to university. "Don't oversell your idea. Present it rationally and neatly."

DETSELIG ENTERPRISES LTD., 1220 Kensington Rd. NW, 210, Calgary, Alberta T2N 3P5 Canada. Fax: (403)283-6947. E-mail: temeron@telusplanet.net. **Acquisitions**: T.E. Giles, president. Publishes hardcover and trade paperback originals. Publishes 20 titles/year. Receives 500 queries and 200 mss/year. 75% of books from first-time authors; 95% from unagented writers. Pays 8-13% royalty on wholesale price. No advance usually. Publishes book 10 months after acceptance of ms. Accepts simultaneous submissions. Reports in 3 months on queries, 4 months on proposals, 6 months on mss. Book catalog free on request.
Imprint: Temeron Books.
Nonfiction: Biography, coffee table book, gift book, how-to, humor, illustrated book, reference, self-help, textbook. Subjects include animals, art/architecture, business and economics, child guidance/parenting, education, ethnic, government/politics, health/medicine, history, military/war, money/finance, nature/environment, philosophy, psychology, recreation, religion, sociology, women's issues/studies. Submit outline and 2 sample chapters. Reviews artwork/photos as part of ms package. Send photocopies.
Recent Nonfiction Title: *Adolescent Vulnerability*, by J. Mitchell (psychology).

DOUBLEDAY CANADA LIMITED, 105 Bond St., Toronto, Ontario M5B 1Y3, Canada.
 • This publisher prefers not to receive unsolicited submissions.

DUNDURN PRESS LTD., 2181 Queen St. E., Suite 301, Toronto, Ontario M4E 1E5 Canada. (416)698-0454. Fax: (416)698-1102. Publisher: Kirk Howard. **Acquisitions**: Barry Jowett and Nigel Wood, senior editors. Estab. 1972. Publishes hardcover and trade paperback originals and reprints. Publishes 35 titles/year. Receives 500 submissions/year. 45% of books from first-time authors; 90% from unagented writers. Average print order for a first book is 2,000. Pays 10% royalty on retail price; 8% royalty on some paperback children's books. Publishes book 1 year after acceptance. Accepts simultaneous submissions. Reports in 3 months.
Imprints: Boardwalk Books, **Hounslow Press**, **Simon & Pierre Publishing**.
Nonfiction: Biography, coffee table books, illustrated book, juvenile (12 and up), literary, reference, self-help. Subjects include anthropology/archaeology, art/architecture, business and economics, Canadiana, education, government/politics,

health/medicine, history, Canadian history, language/literature, literary criticism, military/war, money/finance, nature/environment, philosophy, regional, religion, science, sociology, women's issues/studies; especially looking for Canadian biographies. Submit outline, 3 sample chapters and proposal package, including author biography with SASE. Reviews artwork/photos as part of ms package.

Recent Nonfiction Titles: *World Enough and Time*, by Andea Mudry (women's issues); *Lord Strathcona*, by Donna McDonald (history); *Our Genetic Destiny*, by Amil Shah (science/biology).

Fiction: Adventure, ethnic, fantasy, feminist, gothic, historical, horror, humor, juvenile, literary, mainstream/contemporary, mystery, occult, picture books, plays, short story collections, suspense, young adult. "Our fiction list is limited, therefore submissions should be of high quality. We discard submissions with an undersized SASE or incorrect postage." Submit synopsis, 3 sample chapters and author biography with SASE.

Recent Fiction Titles: *Bloody York*, edited by David Skene-Melvin (crime stories); *Love Minus One & other stories*, by Norma Harrs (short fiction); *Ear-Witness*, by Mary Ann Scott (mystery/young adult).

Poetry: "We publish very little poetry, so it should be of high quality." Query and submit 20 sample poems.

Recent Poetry Titles: *After Paradise*, by Janis Rapaport.

Tips: "If sending submissions from the U.S., remember we cannot use American stamps in Canada, so SASE should have Canadian postage. Also, there is a greater chance of acceptance if your book has a Canadian hook to it."

ECRITS DES FORGES, C.P. 335, 1497 Laviolette, Trois-Rivières, Quebec G9A 5G4 Canada. (819)379-9813. Fax: (819)376-0774. E-mail: ecrits.desforges@aiqnet.com. **Acquisitions:** Gaston Bellemare, president. Publishes hardcover originals. Publishes 40 titles/year. Receives 30 queries and 1,000 mss/year. 10% of books from first-time authors; 90% from unagented writers. Pays 10-30% royalty. Offers 50% advance. Publishes book 9 months after acceptance of ms. Accepts simultaneous submissions. Reports in 9 months. Book catalog free on request.
  ● Ecrits Des Forges has published such authors as Claude Beausoleil, Nicole Brossard and Jean-Marc Desgent.

Poetry: Poetry only and written in *French*. Submit 20 sample poems.

Recent Poetry Titles: *Poètes québécois*, by Louise Blouin/Bernard Pozier; *Poètes mexicains contemporains*, by Émile Martel; *Écrits profanes*, by Sor Juana Ines de la Cruz.

ECW PRESS, 2120 Queen St. E., Suite 200, Toronto, Ontario M4E 1E2 Canada. (416)694-3348. Fax: (416)698-9906. E-mail: ecw@sympatico.ca. President: Jack David. Estab. 1979. Publishes hardcover and trade paperback originals. Publishes 20 titles/year. Receives 120 submissions/year. 50% of books from first-time authors; 80% from unagented writers. Nonauthor-subsidy publishes up to 5% of books. Pays 10% royalty on retail price. Accepts simultaneous submissions. Reports in 2 months. Book catalog free.

Nonfiction: "ECW is particularly interested in popular biography sports books and general trade books." Query. Reviews artwork/photos as part of ms package.

Recent Nonfiction Title: *Paul Molitor*, by S. Broomer (biography).

Tips: "ECW does not accept unsolicited fiction or poetry manuscripts. We are looking for sports books and music biographies; please query first."

EDITIONS DU NOROÎT, 1835 Les Hauteurs, St. Hippolyte, Quebec J0R 1P0 Canada. Phone/fax: (514)563-1644. **Acquisitions:** Claude Prud-Homme, Helene Dorion, Paul Belanger, directors. Publishes trade paperback originals and reprints. Publishes 27 titles/year. Receives 500 queries and 500 mss/year. 50% of books from first-time authors; 95% from unagented writers. Pays 10% royalty on retail price. Publishes book 1 year after acceptance. Accepts simultaneous submissions. Reports in 3 months on mss. Book catalog for SASE.
  ● Editions du Noroît has increased their number of books published from 22 to 27 titles/year. They have published such poets as Héléne Dorion, Paul Belanger and Marie Uguay.

Poetry: Submit 40 sample poems.

Recent Poetry Title: *Au fond du jardin*, by Jacques Brault (poetry essay); *Anthologie du Noroît 1971-1996* .

ÉDITIONS LA LIBERTÉ INC., 3020 Chemin Ste-Foy, Ste-Foy, Quebec G1X 3V6 Canada. Phone/fax: (418)658-3763. Director of Operations: Nathalie Roy. Publishes trade paperback originals. Publishes 4-5 titles/year. Receives 125 queries and 100 mss/year. 75% of books from first-time authors; 90% from unagented writers. Pays 10% royalty on retail price. Accepts only mss written in French. Publishes book 4 months after acceptance of ms. Accepts simultaneous submissions. Book catalog free.

Nonfiction: Biography, children's/juvenile. Subjects include Americana, animals, anthropology/archaeology, child guidance/parenting, cooking/foods/nutrition, education, government/politics, history, hobbies, language/literature, music/dance, nature/environment, psychology, science, sociology. Submit proposal package, including complete ms. *Writer's Market* recommends sending a query with SASE first.

Recent Nonfiction Title: *Le Partage des Responsabilités Publique en Environnement*, by Paul Painchaud.

Fiction: Historical, juvenile, literary, mainstream/contemporary, short story collections, y/a. Query with synopsis.

Recent Fiction Title: *L'espace Montauban/Le Dernier Roman Scout*, by Jean Désy.

EDITIONS PHIDAL, 5740 Ferrier, Mont-Royal, Quebec H4P 1M7 Canada. (514) 738-0202. Chief Editor: Lionel Soussan. Publishes hardcover and mass market paperback originals. Publishes 50-70 titles/year. Receives 50 queries and 20 mss/year. 5% of books from first-time authors; 5% from unagented writers. Pays 10% royalty on retail price. Publishes book 6 months after acceptance. Accepts simultaneous submissions. Reports in 2 months on mss.

Fiction: Juvenile. "We specialize in children's books ages three and up. Illustrations are very helpful." Submit synopsis and 3-5 sample chapters.
Recent Fiction Title: *Les Voyelles*, by Nicole Sallenave (children's).
Tips: Audience is children, both in English and French languages. Ages 3 and up.

EKSTASIS EDITIONS, P.O. Box 8474, Main Post Office, Victoria, British Columbia V8W 3S1 Canada. Phone/fax: (604)385-3378. **Acquisitions**: Richard Olafson, publisher. Publishes hardcover and trade paperback originals and reprints. Publishes 8-12 titles/year. Receives 85 queries and 100 mss/year. 65% of books from first-time authors; 100% from unagented writers. Pays 10% royalty on wholesale price. Publishes book 6 months after acceptance of ms. Accepts simultaneous submissions. Reports in 5 months on mss. Book catalog free on request.
Nonfiction: Biography. Subjects include government/politics, nature/environment, psychology, translation. Query. Reviews artwork/photos as part of ms package. Send photocopies.
Recent Nonfiction Title: *Eternal Lake O'Hara*, by Carol Ann Sokoloff (history).
Fiction: Erotica, experimental, gothic, juvenile, literary, mainstream/contemporary, plays, science fiction, short story collections. Query with synopsis and 3 sample chapters.
Recent Fiction Title: *Cities of India*, by Steve Noyes (short stories).
Poetry: "Ekstasis is a literary press, and publishes the best of modern poetry and fiction." Submit 20 sample poems.
Recent Poetry Title: *From the Mouths of Angels*, by Richard Stevenson (lyric poetry).

EMPYREAL PRESS, P.O. Box 1746, Place Du Parc, Montreal, Quebec HZW 2R7 Canada. Website: www.generation. net/~talisher/empyreal. **Acquisitions**: Geof Isherwood, publisher. "Our mission is the publishing of Canadian and other literature which doesn't fit into any standard 'mold'—writing which is experimental yet grounded in discipline, imagination." Publishes trade paperback originals. Publishes 1-4 titles/year. 50% of books from first-time authors; 90% from unagented writers. Pays 10% royalty on wholesale price. Offers $300 (Canadian) advance. Book catalog for #10 SASE.
Recent Nonfiction Title: *1941 Diary*, by Louis Dudek (literary, Canadiana).
Fiction: Experimental, feminist, gay/lesbian, literary, short story collections. No unsolicited mss.
Recent Fiction Title: *Winter, Spring, Summer, Fall*, by Robert Sandiford (short stories).
Recent Poetry Title: *A Demolition Symphony*, by Sonja Skarstedt (the current era).

FITZHENRY & WHITESIDE, LTD., 195 Allstate Parkway, Markham, Ontario L3R 4T8 Canada. (905)477-9700. Fax: (905)477-9179. Estab. 1966. Publishes hardcover and paperback originals and reprints. Publishes 10 titles/year, text and trade. Royalty contract varies. Advance negotiable. Enclose return postage.
Nonfiction: "Interested only in topics of interest to Canadians, and by Canadians," history, nature, Native studies. Submit outline and 1 sample chapter. Length: open.
Recent Nonfiction Title: *Trees of Canada*.

GOOSE LANE EDITIONS, 469 King St., Fredericton, New Brunswick E3B 1E5 Canada. **Acquisitions**: Laurel Boone, acquisitions editor. Estab. 1956. Goose Lane publishes fiction and nonfiction from well-read authors with finely-crafted literary writing skills. Publishes 12-14 titles/year. Receives 500 submissions/year. 20% of books from first-time authors; 75-100% from unagented writers. Pays royalty on retail price. Reports in 6 months. Manuscript guidelines for SASE (Canadian stamps or IRCs).
Nonfiction: Biography, illustrated book, literary history (Canadian). Subjects include art/architecture, history, language/literature, nature/environment, translation, women's issues/studies. No crime, confessional, how-to, self-help, medical, legal or cookbooks. Query first.
Fiction: Experimental, feminist, historical, literary, short story collections. "Our needs in fiction never change: substantial, character-centred literary fiction. No children's, YA, mainstream, mass market, genre, mystery, thriller, confessional or sci-fi fiction." Query with SASE first.
Tips: "Writers should send us outlines and samples of books that show a very well-read author who has thought long and deeply about the art of writing and, in either fiction or nonfiction, has something of Canadian relevance to offer. We almost never publish books by non-Canadian authors, and we seldom consider submissions from outside the country. Our audience is literate, thoughtful and well-read. If I were a writer trying to market a book today, I would contact the targeted publisher with a query letter and synopsis, and request manuscript guidelines. Purchase a recent book from the publisher in a relevant area, if possible. Never send a complete manuscript blindly to a publisher. *Never* send a manuscript or sample without an SASE with IRC's or sufficient return postage in Canadian stamps."

GUERNICA EDITIONS, Box 117, Station P, Toronto, Ontario M5S 2S6 Canada. (416)658-9888. Fax: (416)657-8885. **Acquisitions**: Antonio D'Alfonso, editor/publisher. Estab. 1978. Publishes trade paperback originals, reprints and software. Publishes 20 titles/year. Receives 1,000 submissions/year. 5% of books from first-time authors. Average print order for a first book is 1,000. "Subvention in Canada is received only when the author is established, Canadian-born and active in the country's cultural world. The others we subsidize ourselves." Pays 3-10% royalty on retail price or makes outright purchase of $200-5,000. Offers 10¢/word advance for translators. IRCs required. "American stamps are of no use to us in Canada." Reports in 3 months. Book catalog for SASE.
Nonfiction: Biography, art, film, history, music, philosophy, politics, psychology, religion, literary criticism, ethnic history, multicultural comparative literature.
Fiction: Original works and translations. "We wish to open up into the fiction world and focus less on poetry. Also

specialize in European, especially Italian, translations." Query.

Poetry: "We wish to have writers in translation. Any writer who has translated Italian poetry is welcomed. Full books only. Not single poems by different authors, unless modern, and used as an anthology. First books will have no place in the next couple of years." Submit samples.

Recent Poetry Title: *Daughters For Sale*, by Gianna Patriarca.

Tips: "We are seeking less poetry, more prose, essays, novels, and translations into English."

GUTTER PRESS, 118 Peter St., Suite 1, Toronto, Ontario M5V 2G7 Canada. (416)593-7036. E-mail: gutter@io.org. Website: http://www.io.org/~gutter/. **Acquisitions**: Sam Hiyate, publisher. Publishes trade paperback originals and reprints. Publishes 6 titles/year. Each imprint publishes 2 titles/year. 50% of books from first-time authors; 100% from unagented writers. Pays 10-15% royalty on retail price. Offers $500-1,500 (Canadian) advance. Publishes book 2 years after acceptance of ms. Accepts simultaneous submissions. Reports in 6 months. Ms guidelines for SAE and IRC.

Imprints: Ken Sparling Books, Eye Press, Kaleyard.

Nonfiction: Biography, humor, literary theory. Subjects include art/architecture, education (theoretical), gay/lesbian, government/politics, history, language/literature, philosophy. Query.

Recent Nonfiction Title: *Fringe Film*, by Mike Hoolboom (pop. culture).

Fiction: Literary. "Ultimately, language is what has to be at issue, the issue you address with all your heart. Give us your heart and we'll give you ours back." Submit 3 sample chapters with SAE and IRC.

Recent Fiction Title: *Dark Rides*, by Derek McCormack.

Tips: "Our audience is people who care about language and what it can accomplish beyond what has already been accomplished."

HARCOURT BRACE CANADA, INC., Subsidiary of Harcourt Brace & Company Canada, Ltd., 55 Horner Ave., Toronto, Ontario M8Z 4X6 Canada. Editorial Directors (School Division): Hans Mills and Wendy Cochran. Publishes educational material K-12.

HARLEQUIN ENTERPRISES, LTD., Subsidiary of Torstar Corporation, Home Office: 225 Duncan Mill Rd., Don Mills, Ontario M3B 3K9 Canada. (416)445-5860. President and Chief Executive Officer: Brian E. Hickey. Editorial divisions: Harlequin Books (Randall Toye, editorial director); Silhouette Books (Isabel Swift, editorial director; for editorial requirements, see separate listing, under Silhouette Books); and Worldwide Library/Gold Eagle Books (Randall Toye, editorial director; see separate listing under Worldwide Library). Estab. 1949. Submissions for Harlequin Intrigue, Harlequin American Romance and Harlequin Historicals should be directed to the designated editor and sent to Harlequin Books, 300 E. 42nd St., New York NY 10017. (212)682-6080. Romance and Presents submissions should be sent to Harlequin Mills and Boon, Eton House, 18-24 Paradise Rd., Richmond Surey TW9 1SR United Kingdom. All other submissions should be directed to the Canadian address. Publishes mass market paperback originals. Publishes 780 titles/year; receives 10,000 submissions annually. 10% of books from first-time authors; 20% from unagented writers. Pays royalty. Offers advance. Publishes book 1 year after acceptance. Reports in 6 weeks on queries. *Writer's Market* recommends allowing 2 months for reply. Writer's guidelines free.

Imprints: Harlequin Books: Harlequin Romance and Harlequin Presents (Karin Stoecker, director UK); Harlequin Superromance (Paula Eykelhof, senior editor); Harlequin Temptation (Birgit Davis-Todd, senior editor); Harlequin Intrigue and Harlequin American Romance (Debra Matteucci, senior editor and editorial coordinator); Harlequin Historicals (Tracy Farrell, senior editor); **Silhouette Books**; **Worldwide Library**.

Fiction: Adult contemporary and historical romance, including novels of romantic suspense (Intrigue), short contemporary romance (Presents and Romance), long contemporary romance (Superromance), short contemporary sensuals (Temptation) and adult historical romance (Historicals). "We welcome submissions to all of our lines. Know our guidelines and be familiar with the style and format of the line you are submitting to. Stories should possess a life and vitality that makes them memorable for the reader." *Writer's Market* recommends sending a query with SASE first.

Tips: "Harlequin's readership comprises a wide variety of ages, backgrounds, income and education levels. The audience is predominantly female. Because of the high competition in women's fiction, readers are becoming very discriminating. They look for a quality read. Read as many recent romance books as possible in all series to get a feel for the scope, new trends, acceptable levels of sensuality, etc."

HARPERCOLLINS PUBLISHERS LTD., 55 Avenue Rd., Suite 2900, Toronto, Ontario M5R 3L2 Canada. (416) 975-9334. Publisher/Editor-in-Chief: Iris Tupholme. Publishes hardcover originals and reprints, trade paperback originals and reprints, mass market paperback reprints. Publishes 40-60 titles/year. Pays 5-15% royalty on retail price. Offers from $500 to over six figures advance. Publishes book 18 months after acceptance. Reports in 1 month on queries and proposals. *Writer's Market* recommends allowing 2 months for reply. "We do not accept unsolicited mss. Query first." Book catalog free on request.

Nonfiction: Biography, cookbook, children's/juvenile, self-help. Subjects include business and economics, cooking/foods/nutrition, gardening, gay/lesbian, government/politics, health/medicine, history, language/literature, money/finance, nature/environment, religion, travel, women's issues/studies. Query.

Recent Nonfiction Title: *The Gift of Death: Confronting Canada's Tainted Blood Tragedy*, by André Picard (exposé).

Fiction: Ethnic, experimental, feminist, juvenile, literary, mainstream/contemporary, picture books, religious, short story collections, young adult. Query.

Recent Fiction Title: *Let Me Be the One*, by Hanor (short stories).

HERITAGE HOUSE PUBLISHING CO. LTD., Box 115, R.R. #2, Outrigger Rd., Nanoose Bay, British Columbia V0R 2R0 Canada. Fax: (250)468-5318. E-mail: herhouse@island.net. Website: http://www.rapidexmall.com/bc/bc/heritage. **Acquisitions**: Rodger Touchie, publisher/president. Heritage House is primarily a regional publisher of Western Canadiana and the Pacific Northwest. "We aim to publish popular history, contemporary recreational literature and culturally appealing manuscripts." Publishes trade paperback originals. Publishes 10-12 titles/year. Receives 50 queries and 30 mss/year. 50% of books from first-time authors; 100% from unagented writers. Pays 10-12% royalty. Publishes book 1 year after acceptance. Reports in 2 months. Book catalog for SASE.
Nonfiction: Biography, cookbook, how-to, illustrated book. Subjects include animals, anthropology/archaeology, cooking/foods/nutrition, history, nature/environment, recreation, regional, sports, western Canadiana. "Writers should include a sample of their writing, an overview sample of photos or illustrations to support the text and a brief letter describing who they are writing for." Query with outline, 2-3 sample chapters and SASE. Reviews artwork/photos as part of ms package. Send photocopies.
Recent Nonfiction Title: *101 Dives in Washington & British Columbia*, by Betty Pratt Johnson (guidebook); *Totem Poles & Tea*, by Hughina Harold (autobiography/history); *Provincial & National Park Campgrounds in BC*, by Jayne Seagrave (recreational guidebook).
Fiction: Juvenile. Query with synopsis and SASE.
Recent Fiction Title: *Eagle's Reflection*, by Jim Challenger (children's); *Orca's Family & More Northwest Coast Stories*, by Jim Challenger (children's).
Tips: "Our books appeal to residents and visitors to the northwest quadrant of the continent. Present your material after you have done your best. Double space. Don't worry about getting an agent if yours is a one-shot book. Write for the love it. The rest will take care of itself."

HIPPOPOTAMUS PRESS, 22 Whitewell Rd., Frome, Somerset BA11 4EL United Kingdom. 0173-466653. Fax: 01373-466653. **Acquisitions**: R. John, editor. Hippopotamus Press publishes literary poetry and nonfiction. Publishes hardcover and trade paperback originals. Publishes 6-12 titles/year. 90% of books from first-time authors; 90% from unagented writers. Pays 7½-10% royalty on retail price. Rarely offers advance. Publishes book 10 months after acceptance of ms. Accepts simultaneous submissions. Reports in 1 month. *Writer's Market* recommends allowing 2 months for reply. Book catalog free on request.
Imprints: Hippopotamus Press, *Outposts* Poetry Quarterly; distributor for University of Salzburg Press.
• Hippopotamus Press has published such authors as Peter Dale and Peter Russell.
Nonfiction: Essays, literary criticism. Subjects include language/literature, translation. Submit ms. *Writer's Market* recommends sending a query with SASE first.
Recent Nonfiction Title: *Immigrants of Loss*, by G.S.Sharat Chandra (selected poems).
Poetry: "Read one of our authors! Poets often make the mistake of submitting poetry not knowing the type of verse we publish." Submit complete ms.
Recent Poetry Titles: *A Late Flowering*, by David Clarke; *Mystic Bridge*, by Edward Lowbury.
Tips: "We publish books for a literate audience. Read what we publish."

HORSDAL & SCHUBART PUBLISHERS LTD., 623-425 Simcoe St., Victoria, British Columbia V8V 4T3 Canada. (250)360-0829. **Acquisitions**: Marlyn Horsdal, editor. Publishes hardcover originals and trade paperback originals and reprints. Publishes 8-10 titles/year. 50% of books from first-time authors; 100% from unagented writers. Pays 15% royalty on wholesale price. Negotiates advance. Publishes books 6 months after acceptance of ms. Accepts simultaneous submissions. Reports in 1 month on queries. Book catalog free.
Nonfiction: Biography. Subjects include anthropology/archaeology, art/architecture, government/politics, history, nature/environment, recreation, regional. Query with outline, 2-3 sample chapters and SASE or SAE with IRCs. Reviews artwork/photos as part of ms package. Send photocopies.
Recent Nonfiction Title: *Moonraker*, by Beth Hill; *South Pole: 900 Miles On Foot*, by Gareth Wood with Eric Jamieson; *Spring Rain*, by Bet Oliver.

HOUNSLOW PRESS, Subsidiary of Dundurn Press Limited, 2181 Queen St., Suite 301, Toronto, Ontario M4E 1E5 Canada. Fax: (416)698-1102. **Acquisitions**: Tony Hawke, general manager. Estab. 1972. Publishes hardcover and trade paperback originals. Publishes 8 titles/year. Receives 250 submissions/year. 10% of books from first-time authors; 95% from unagented writers. Pays 10-12½% royalty on retail price. Offers $500 average advance. Publishes book 1 year after acceptance. Reports in 2 months on queries. Book catalog free.
Nonfiction: Biography, coffee-table book, cookbook, how-to, humor, illustrated book, self-help. Subjects include animals, art/architecture, business and economics, child guidance/parenting, cooking/foods/nutrition, health/medicine, history, money/finance, photography, translation, travel. "We are looking for controversial manuscripts and business books." Query.
Fiction: Literary and suspense. "We really don't need any fiction for the next year or so." Query.
Tips: "If I were a writer trying to market a book today, I would try to get a good literary agent to handle it."

‡HOUSE OF ANANSI PRESS, Subsidiary of Stoddart Publishing, 1800 Steeles Ave. West, Concord, Ontario L4K 2P3 Canada. (905)660-0611. E-mail: anansi@irwin-pub.com. Website: http://www.irwin-pub.com/irwin/anansi/. **Acquisitions:** Martha Sharpe, editor. "Our mission is to publish the best new literary writers in Canada and to continue to grow and adapt along with the Canadian literary community, while maintaining Anansi's rich history." Publishes

hardcover and trade paperback originals. Publishes 10-15 titles/year. Receives 750 queries/year. 5% of books from first-time authors; 99% from unagented writers. Pays 8-15% royalty on retail price. Offers $500-2,000 advance. Publishes book 9 months after acceptance of ms. Accepts simultaneous submissions. Reports in 2 months on queries, 3 months on proposals, 4 months on mss.
  • House of Anansi has published such authors as John Ralston Saul, Margaret Atwood, Michael Ondaatje, Charles Taylor, Northrop Frye, Noam Chomsky, Conor Cruise O'Brien and George Grant.
Nonfiction: Biography, critical thought, literary criticism. Subjects include anthropology, gay/lesbian, government/politics, history, language/literature, philosophy, science, sociology, women's issues/studies, only Canadian writers. "Our nonfiction list is literary, but not overly academic. Some writers submit academic work better suited for university presses or pop-psychology books, which we do not publish." Submit outline with 2 sample chapters and SASE. Send photocopies of artwork/photos.
Recent Nonfiction Titles: *The Admen Move on Lhasa*, by Steven Heighton (essays on "Writing in a Virtual World"); *Hard Core Roadshow*, by Noel S. Baker (diary of a screenwriter's experiences); *Lunar Perspectives*, by Michael Keefer (political/philosopht/literary criticism).
Fiction: "We publish literary fiction by Canadian authors." Experimental, feminist, gay/lesbian, literary, short story collections, only Canadian writers. "Authors must have been published in established literary magazines and/or journals. We only want to consider sample chapters." Submit synopsis, 2 sample chapters with SASE.
Recent Fiction Titles: *Taken*, by Daphne Marlatt (literary); *Affairs of Art*, by Lise Bissonnette; *Aurelien, Clara, Mademoiselle and the English Lieutenant*, by Anne Hébert (literary translated from French).
Poetry: "We only publish book-length works by Canadian authors. Poets must have a substantial résumé of published poems in literary magazines or journals. We only want samples from a ms." Submit 10-15 sample poems or 15 pages.
Recent Poetry Titles: *Pearl*, by Lynn Crosbie (literary); *Blues & True Concussions*, edited by Michael Redhill (anthology of 6 Toronto poets); *Search Procedures*, by Lynn Crosbie (narrative poetry).
Tips: "Submit often to magazines and journals. Read and buy other writers' work. Know and be a part of your writing community."

HUMANITAS, 990 Croissant Picard, Brossard, Quebec J4W 1S5 Canada. Phone/fax: (514)466-9737. **Acquisitions:** Constantin Stoiciu, president. Publishes hardcover originals. Publishes 20 titles/year. Receives 200 queries and 200 mss/year. 20% of books from first-time authors. Pays 10-12% royalty on wholesale price. Publishes book 2 months after acceptance of ms. Accepts simultaneous submissions. Book catalog and mss guidelines free on request.
Nonfiction: Biography. Subjects include history, language/literature, philosophy, photography, science. Query. Reviews artwork/photos as part of ms package. Send photocopies.
Recent Nonfiction Title: *Propos sur le Québec et la Francophonie*, by Axel Maugey (essai).
Fiction: Fantasy, romance, short story collections. Query.
Recent Fiction Title: *La ronde de jour*, by Jean-Louis Le Scouarnec (roman).
Poetry: Query.
Recent Poetry Title: *Territoire d'enfance*, by Saint-John Kauss.

‡**HUNT & THORPE**, Laurel House, Station Approach, Alresford, Hants SO24 9JH United Kingdom. **Acquisitions:** J. Hunt. Publishes hardcover and trade paperback originals. Publishes 30 titles/year. Receives 200 mss/year. 5% of books from first-time authors; 20% from unagented writers. Pay varies. Offers $100-10,000 advance. Publishes book 18 months after acceptance of ms. Reports in 1 month. Book catalog for SAE with IRCs.
Nonfiction: Children's/juvenile, illustrated book. Religious subjects, mostly Christian. "We only publish full-color illustrated books." Submit outline and 1 sample chapter. Reviews artwork/photos as part of ms package.
Recent Nonfiction Titles: *Treasury of Christmas Stories for Children* (children's story collection); *A Child's First Book of Prayers*, by Marjorie Newan, illustrated by Elvia Dadd (children's religious).

HYPERION PRESS, LTD., 300 Wales Ave., Winnipeg, Manitoba R2M 2S9 Canada. (204)256-9204. Fax: (204)255-7845. **Acquisitions:** Dr. Marvis Tutiah, president. "We are interested in a good story or well researched how-to material." Publishes hardcover and trade paperback originals and reprints of children's picture books and how-to craft books for all ages. Publishes 8 titles/year. Receives 500 queries and 1,000 mss/year. 30% of books from first-time authors; 100% from unagented writers. Pays royalty. Publishes book 1 year after acceptance of ms. Accepts simultaneous submissions. Reports in 6 months on mss. Book catalog free on request.
Nonfiction: How-to, children's/juvenile. Ethnic subjects. Reviews artwork/photos as part of ms package. Send photocopies.
Recent Nonfiction Titles: *Paper Birds That Fly*, by Norman Schmidt (how-to/crafts); *Candy Making for Beginners*, by Evelyn Howe Fryatt (cooking); *The Peacock's Pride*, by Melissa Kajpust (children's picture book).

SOME CANADIAN publishers will consider book proposals by Canadian authors only. Please check each listing carefully for this restriction.

INSTITUTE OF PSYCHOLOGICAL RESEARCH, INC./INSTITUT DE RECHERCHES PSYCHOLOGI-QUES, INC., 34 Fleury St. W., Montréal, Québec H3L 1S9 Canada. (514)382-3000. Fax: (514)382-3007. **Acquisitions**: Jean-Marc Chevrier, president/general director. Estab. 1958. Institute of Psychological Research publishes psychological tests and science textbooks for a varied professional audience. Publishes hardcover and trade paperback originals and reprints. Publishes 12 titles/year. Receives 15 submissions/year. 10% of books from first-time authors; 100% from unagented writers. Pays 10-12% royalty. Publishes book 6 months after acceptance. Reports in 2 months.
Nonfiction: Textbooks, psychological tests. Subjects include philosophy, psychology, science, translation. "We are looking for psychological tests in French or English." Submit complete ms. Query with SASE first.
Recent Nonfiction Title: *Épreuve individuelle d'habileté mentale*, by Jean-Marc Chevrier (intelligence test).
Tips: "Psychologists, guidance counsellors, professionals, schools, school boards, hospitals, teachers, government agencies and industries comprise our audience."

KEY PORTER BOOKS LTD., 70 The Esplanade, Toronto, Ontario M5E 1R2 Canada. (416)862-7777. President/Editor-in-Chief: Susan Renouf. **Acquisitions**: Michael Mailand, senior editor (nonfiction); Barbara Berson, senior editor (fiction). Publishes hardcover originals and trade paperback originals and reprints. Publishes 50-60 titles/year.
  • Key Porter has Margaret Atwood, Farley Mowat, Allan Fothingham, Ed Mirvish and Fred Bruemmer.
Imprint: Firefly Books.
Nonfiction: Biography, coffee table book, cookbook, humor, illustrated book, children's/juvenile, self-help. Subjects include agriculture/horticulture, animals, business and economics, cooking/foods/nutrition, government/politics, health/medicine, military/war, money/finance, nature/environment, photography, sports, women's issues/studies. Query with SASE. *No unsolicited mss.*
Recent Nonfiction Titles: *1997 RRSP Guide—how to build your wealth and retire in comfort*, by Garth Turner; *Rebel Daughter*, by Doris Anderson (autobiography); *Fighting for Canada*, by Diane Francis (politics).
Fiction: Humor, mainstream/contemporary, picture books. *No longer accepts unsolicited mss. Query with SASE.*
Recent Fiction Titles: *Angel Falls*, by Tim Wynveen; *Ancestral Suitcase*, by Sylvia Fraser.

KINDRED PRODUCTIONS, 4-169 Riverton Ave., Winnipeg, Manitoba R2L 2E5 Canada. (204)669-6575. Fax: (204)654-1865. E-mail: kindred@cdnmbconf.ca. Website: http://www.mbconf.org/mbc/kp/kindred.htm, **Acquisitions**: Marilyn Hudson, manager. "Kindred Productions publishes, promotes and markets print and nonprint resources that will shape our Christian faith and discipleship from a Mennonite Brethren perspective." Publishes trade paperback originals and reprints. Publishes 3 titles/year. 1% of books from first-time authors; 100% from unagented writers. Nonauthor subsidy publishes 20% of books. Pays 10-15% royalty on retail price. Publishes book 18 months after acceptance of ms. Accepts simultaneous submissions. Reports in 3 months on queries, 5 months on proposals. Book catalog and ms guidelines free on request.
Nonfiction: Biography (select) and Bible study. Religious subjects. "Our books cater primarily to our Mennonite Brethren denomination readers." Query with outline, 2-3 sample chapters and SASE.
Recent Nonfiction Titles: *Authentic Living*, by Herb Kopp (study of the Epistle of James); *All Are Witnesses*, edited by Delores Friesen (collection of sermons by women); *Curriculum Series*, by various authors (Core Values Studies).
Fiction: Historical (religious), juvenile, religious. "All our publications are of a religious nature with a high moral content." Submit synopsis, 2-3 sample chapters and SASE.
Tips: "Most of our books are sold to churches, religious bookstores and schools. We are concentrating on devotional and inspirational books. We are accepting *very* few children's manuscripts."

‡LAURIER BOOKS, LTD., P.O. Box 2694, Station D, Ottawa, Ontario K1P 5W6 Canada. (613)738-2163. **Acquisitions:** L. Marthe, manager. Publishes hardcover originals and reprints. Publishes 6 titles/year. 10% of books from first-time authors. Makes outright purchase. Book catalog and ms guidelines free.
Nonfiction: How-to, reference. Subjects include ethnic, language/literature. Query with proposal.
Recent Nonfiction Title: *Dictionary of Islam*, by Thomas Patrick Hughes (reference).

‡LE LOUP DE GOUTTIÈRE, 347 Rue Saint-Paul, Quebec, Quebec G1P 1N5 Canada. (418)694-2224. **Acquisitions**: France Gagné, adjointe a l'édition. Publishes 16 titles/year. Receives 150 queries/year. 15% of books from first-time authors. Pays 10% royalty. Offers no advance. Publishes book 1 year after acceptance of ms. Reports in 1 year on mss. Book catalog free.
Nonfiction: Subjects include art/architecture, literature, philosophy, psychology.
Recent Nonfiction Titles: *Les Aventures Mathématiques de Mathilde et David*, by Marie-France Daniel, Louise Lafortune, Richard Pallascio and Pierre Sykes.
Fiction: Literary, short story collections. Submit 3 sample chapters in French.
Recent Fiction Titles: *L'Amour Sauce Tomate*, by Sylvie Nicolas; *Docteur Wincet*, by Jean Désy.
Poetry: Submit complete ms in French.
Recent Poetry Title: *L'éclair*, by Elaine Audet.

‡LES ÉDITIONS DU VERMILLON, 305 St. Patrick St., Ottawa, Ontario K1N 5K4 Canada. (613)241-4032. **Acquisitions**: Monique Bertoli, general manager. Publishes trade paperback originals. Publishes 15 books/year. Receives 150 mss/year. 30% of books from first-time authors; 100% from unagented writers. Pays 10% royalty. Offers no advance. Publishes book 18 months after acceptance of ms. Reports in 1 year on mss. Book catalog free.

Nonfiction: Children's/juvenile. Subjects include education, language/literature, philosophy, sociology. Query with synopsis.
Recent Nonfiction Title: *Le Pari sur l'incertain:ou l'apologie de la religion chrétienne de Blaise Pascal*, by Edmond Robillard.
Fiction: Juvenile, literary, religious, short story collections, young adult. Query.
Recent Fiction Titles: *Beaurivage Tome I Les eaux chantentes Roman*, by Jean-Eudes Dubé; *Une affaire de famille*, by Jean-François Somain; *Lettres á deux mains*, by Jean-Louis Grosmaire.
Poetry: Submit complete ms.
Recent Poetry Titles: *Polyphonie*, by Yves Antoine; *Ô Sirènes, libèrez-moi*, by Nicole Champeau.

LONE PINE PUBLISHING, 10426 81st Ave., #206, Edmonton, Alberta T6E 1X5 Canada. (403)433-9333. Fax: (403)433-9646. **Acquisitions:** Nancy Foulds, senior editor. Estab. 1980. "We publish recreational and natural history titles, and some historical biographies." Publishes trade paperback originals and reprints. Publishes 12-20 titles/year. Receives 200 submissions/year. 45% of books from first-time authors; 95% from unagented writers. Pays royalty. Accepts simultaneous submissions. Reports in 2 months on queries. Book catalog free.
    • Lone Pine has published such authors as Lois Hole, Thom Henley and Linda Kershaw.
Imprints: Lone Pine, Home World, Pine Candle and Pine Cone.
Nonfiction: Nature/recreation guide books. Subjects include animals, anthropology/archaeology, botany/ethnobotany, gardening, history, nature/environment ("this is where most of our books fall"), travel ("another major category for us"). The list is set for the next year and a half, but we are interested in seeing new material. Submit outline and sample chapters. Reviews artwork/photos as part of ms package.
Recent Nonfiction Titles: *Lois Hole's Rose Favorites*, by Lois Hole (gardening); *Birds of Seattle and Puget Sound*, by Chris Fisher (birding); *Amphibians of British Columbia, Washington and Oregon*, by Char Corkran and Chris Thoms (amphibian guide).
Tips: "Writers have their best chance with recreational or nature guidebooks and popular history. Most of our books are strongly regional in nature. We are mostly interested in books for Western Canada, Ontario and the US Pacific Northwest."

JAMES LORIMER & CO., PUBLISHERS, 35 Britain St., Toronto, Ontario M5A 1R7 Canada. (416)362-4762. Fax: (416)362-3939. **Acquisitions:** Diane Young, senior editor. "James Lorimer & Co. publishes Canadian authors only, on Canadian issues/topics. For juvenile list, realistic themes only, especially mysteries and sports." Publishes trade paperback originals. Publishes 20 titles/year. Receives 150 queries and 50 mss/year. 10% of books from first-time authors; 100% from unagented writers. Pays 5-10% royalty on retail price. Offers negotiable advance. Publishes book 6 months after acceptance of ms. Reports in 4 months on proposals. Book catalog for #10 SASE.
Nonfiction: Children's/juvenile. Subjects include business and economics, government/politics, history, sociology, women's issues/studies. "We publish Canadian authors only and Canadian issues/topics only." Submit outline, 2 sample chapters and résumé.
Recent Nonfiction Titles: *Silent Coup*, by Tony Clark (business takeovers); *Canadian Family in Crises*, by John F. Conway (families); *Final Appeal*, by Greene, Baar, McCormick, Szablowski, Thomas (law).
Fiction: Juvenile, young adult. "No fantasy, science fiction, talking animals; realistic themes only. Currently seeking chapter books for ages 7-11 and sports novels for ages 9-13 (Canadian writers only)." Submit synopsis and 2 sample chapters.
Recent Fiction Titles: *Face Off*, by Chris Forsyth (sports); *Camp All-Star*, by Michael Coldwell (basketball).

‡LYNX IMAGES, INC., P.O. Box 5961, Station A, Toronto, Ontario M5W 1P4 Canada. (416)535-4553. **Acquisitions:** Russell Floren, president. Publishes hardcover and trade paperback originals. Publishes 4 titles/year. Receives 45 queries and 20 mss/year. 80% of books from first-time authors; 80% from unagented writers. Makes outright purchase of $10,000-20,000. Offers 40% advance. Publishes book 6 months after acceptance of ms. Accepts simultaneous submissions. Reports in 6 months on mss. Book catalog free.
Nonfiction: Coffee table book, gift book, multimedia (video). Subjects include history, nature/environment, travel. Submit proposal package, including sample chapter. Reviews artwork/photos as part of ms package. Send photocopies.
Recent Nonfiction Titles: *Ghost of the Bay*, by Floren (travel); *Alone in the Night*, by Gustche (history).

McGRAW-HILL RYERSON LIMITED, Trade & Professional division of The McGraw-Hill Companies, 300 Water St., Whitby, Ontario L1N 9B6 Canada. Fax: (416)430-5020. Website: http://www.mcgrawhill.ca. **Acquisitions:** Joan Homewood, publisher. McGraw-Hill Ryerson, Ltd., publishes books on Canadian small business and personal finance for the Canadian market. Publishes hardcover and trade paperback originals and reprints. Publishes 20 new titles/year. 75% of books are originals; 25% are reprints. 15% of books from first-time authors; 85% from unagented writers. Pays 7½-10% royalty on retail price. Offers $2,000 average advance. Publishes book 1 year after acceptance. Accepts simultaneous submissions. Reports in 6 months on queries.
Nonfiction: How-to, reference, professional. Subjects include business, management, personal finance, Canadian military history, sports, training for business skills. "No books and proposals that are American in focus. We publish primarily for the Canadian market, but work with McGraw-Hill U.S. on business, management and training titles." Query. Submit outline and sample chapters.
Recent Nonfiction Titles: *The Complete Canadian Home Business Guide to Taxes*, by Evelyn Jades; *Boards That*

Work: What Canadian Directors Must Do to Make Boards More Effective, by David Leighton/Don Thain.
Tips: "Writers have the best chance of selling us well-priced nonfiction, usually trade paper format. Proposal guidelines are available. Thorough market research on competitive titles increases chances of your proposal getting serious consideration, as does endorsement by or references from relevant professionals."

‡MARCUS BOOKS, P.O. Box 327, Queensville, Ontario L0G 1R0 Canada. (905)478-2201. Fax: (905)478-8338. **Acquisitions:** Tom Rieder, president. Publishes trade paperback originals and reprints. Publishes 3-4 titles/year. Receives 12 queries and 6 mss/year. 90% of books from first-time authors; 100% from unagented writers. Pays 10% royalty on retail price. Publishes book 6 months after acceptance of ms. No simultaneous submissions. Query for electronic submissions. Reports in 4 months on mss. Book catalog for $1.
Nonfiction: "Interested in alternative health and esoteric topics." Submit outline and 3 sample chapters.

MARITIMES ARTS PROJECTS PRODUCTIONS, (formerly M.A.P. Productions), Box 596, Station A, Fredericton, New Brunswick E3B 5A6 Canada. (506)454-5127. Fax: (506)454-5127. E-mail: jblades@nbnet.nb.ca. **Acquisitions:** Joe Blades, publisher. "We are a small literary and regional (Atlantic Canadian) publishing house." Publishes trade paperback originals and reprints. Publishes 8-12 titles/year. 50-75% of books from first-time authors; 100% from unagented writers. Pays 10% royalty on retail price or 10% of print run. Offers $0-100 advance. Publishes book 1 year after acceptance of ms. Reports in 6 months on mss. Book catalog for 6½×9½ SAE with 2 first-class Canadian stamps. Manuscript guidelines for #10 SASE (Canadian postage or IRC).
● Maritime Arts Projects Productions has published David Adams Richards, Robin Skelton and James Deshl.
Imprints: Broken Jaw Press, Book Rat, SpareTime Editions, Dead Sea Physh Products.
Nonfiction: Illustrated book. Subjects include history, language/literature, nature/environment, regional, women's issues/studies, criticism, culture. Query with SASE (Canadian postage or IRC). Reviews artwork/photos as part of ms package. Send photocopies, transparencies.
Recent Nonfiction Titles: *Memories of Sandy Point, St. George's Bay, Newfoundland*, by Phyllis Pieroway (local history); *A View from The Bucket*, by Jean Redekopp (memoir).
Fiction: Literary. Query with bio and SASE.
Recent Fiction Title: *Diary of a Broken Heart*, by Shane MacDonald.
Poetry: Submit complete ms for annual New Muse Award with $15 fee. Guidelines for SASE. Deadline: March 31.
Recent Poetry Title: *St. Valentine's Day*, by Jennifer Footman.

NATURAL HERITAGE/NATURAL HISTORY, P.O. Box 95, Station O, Toronto, Ontario M4A 2M8 Canada. (416)694-7907. **Acquisitions:** Jane Gibson, editor-in-chief. "We are a Canadian publisher in the natural heritage and history fields." Publishes hardcover and trade paperback originals. Publishes 10-12 titles/year. 50% of books from first-time authors; 85% from unagented writers. Pays 8-10% royalty on retail price. Publishes book 2 years after acceptance of ms. Reports in 4 months on queries; 6 months on proposals and mss. Book catalog free. Manuscript guidelines for #10 SAE and IRC.
Imprint: Natural Heritage.
Nonfiction: Subjects include anthropology/archaeology, art/architecture, ethnic, history, military/war, nature/environment, photography, recreation, regional. Submit outline with *details* of visuals.
Recent Nonfiction Title: *Travels in the Shining Island*, by Roger Burford Mason (Aboriginal language, missionary work, Canadian history).
Fiction: Historical, short story collections. Query.
Recent Poetry Title: *Spring Again and other Poems*, by Robert Nero (nature).

NEWEST PUBLISHERS LTD., Box 60632, U of A Postal Outlet, Edmonton, Alberta T6G 2S8 Canada. (403)492-4428. Fax: (403)492-4099. E-mail: newest@planet.eon.net. **Acquisitions:** Liz Grieve, managing editor. Estab. 1977. "We only publish Western Canadian authors. Our audience consists of people interested in the west and north of Canada; teachers, professors." Publishes trade paperback originals. Publishes 8 titles/year. Receives 200 submissions/year. 40% of books from first-time authors; 90% from unagented writers. Pays 10% royalty. Publishes book 2 years after acceptance. Accepts simultaneous submissions. Reports in 2 months on queries. Book catalog for 9×12 SAE with 4 first-class Canadian stamps or US postal forms.
● NeWest has published such authors as Rudy Wiebe, Robert Koetsch, Aritha van Herk and Thomas Wharton.
Nonfiction: Literary/essays (Western Canadian authors). Subjects include ethnic, government/politics (Western Canada), history (Western Canada), Canadiana. Query.
Fiction: Literary. Submit outline/synopsis and sample chapters.
Recent Fiction Title: *Diamond Grill*, by Fred Wah.
Tips: "Trend is towards more nonfiction submissions. Would like to see more full-length literary fiction."

NINE PINES PUBLISHING, Unity Arts Inc., 26 Concourse Gate, Nepean, Ontario K2E 7T7 Canada. (613)727-6200. Publishing Director: Barry Brown. Publishes hardcover originals, trade paperback originals and reprints. Publishes 4 titles/year. Receives 100 queries and 40 mss/year. 50% of books from first-time authors; 100% from unagented writers. Pays 5-9% royalty on retail price. Publishes book 1 year after acceptance of ms. Accepts simultaneous submissions. Reports in 2 months on queries and proposals, 4 months on mss. Book catalog for $4.
Nonfiction: Biography, children's/juvenile, self-help. Subjects include child guidance/parenting, psychology, Baháí

religion. Writers must be intimately familiar with the Bahá'í Faith. Query with outline, 1 sample chapter and SASE.
Recent Nonfiction Title: *The Great Adventure*, by Florence Mayberry (autobiography).

‡NORTHSTONE PUBLISHING INC., 330-1980 Cooper Rd., Kelowna, British Columbia V1Y 9G8 Canada. **Acquisitions:** Michael Schwartzentruber, editorial director. "Northstone publishes books that are rooted in everyday life and specific situations. No academia." Publishes hardcover and trade paperback originals. Publishes 14 titles/year. Receives 100 queries/year. 30% of boks from first-time writers; 100% from unagented writers. Pays 8% royalty on retail price. Publishes book 18 months after acceptance of ms. Accepts simultaneous submissions. Reports in 2 months on proposals. Book catalog for $2 (Canadian) and 9×12 SAE. Manuscript guidelines for #10 SASE.
Nonfiction: Self-help. Subjects include health/medicine (healing, holistic approach, spiritual), philosophy (voluntary simplicity/lifestyle), spirituality (grounded in everyday life), sociology (social issues). Submit outline with SASE; all unsolicited mss returned unopened. Reviews artwork/photos as part of ms package. Send photocopies.(
Recent Nonfiction Titles: *The Alternative Wedding Book* (simple lifestyle); *God for Beginners*, by Ralph Milton (spirituality); *Healing Times: A personal workbook*, by Louise Giroux (health/healing).
Tips: "Our audience is primarily women, baby boomers, spiritually interested though not necessarily connected to institutional religion; inner-directed with strong interests in social issues, ecology and justice."

‡ONEWORLD PUBLICATIONS, 185 Banbury Rd., Oxford OX2 7AR United Kingdom. Oneworld publishes college level, "academic texts" to accompany college courses. Publishes hardcover and trade paperback originals. Publishes 25 titles/year. 50% of books from first-time authors; 75-80% from unagented writers. Pays 7½% royalty on retail price. Offers advance. Reports in 2 months on queries. Book catalog and ms guidelines for #10 SASE.
Nonfiction: Reference. Subjects include philosophy, psychology, religion, social issues, comparative religion, Islamic studies. Query with proposal package, including outline, 2-3 sample chapters, contents, author's bio and SASE. Reviews artwork/photos as part of ms package. Send photocopies.
Recent Nonfiction Title: *Muhammed: A Short Biography*, by Martin Forward (world religion).

ORCA BOOK PUBLISHERS LTD., P.O. Box 5626 Station B, Victoria, British Columbia V8R 6S4 Canada. (250)380-1229. Fax: (250)380-1892. E-mail: orca@pinc.com. Website: http://www.swiftly.com/orca. Publisher: R. Tyrrell. **Acquisitions**: Ann Featherstone, children's book editor. Estab. 1984. Publishes hardcover and trade paperback originals. Publishes 20-25 titles/year. Receives 600-800 submissions/year. 50% of books from first-time authors; 80% from unagented writers. Pays 10-12½% royalty on retail price. Offers $1,000 average advance. Publishes book 1 year after acceptance. Reports in 2 months on queries. Book catalog for 9×12 SAE and $2 postage (Canadian). Manuscript guidelines for SASE or IRCs.
Nonfiction: Biography, illustrated book, travel guides, children's. Subjects include history, nature/environment, recreation, sports, travel. Needs history (*West Coast Canadian*) and young children's book. Query or submit outline and sample chapters. Reviews artwork/photos as part of ms package. *Publishes Canadian material only.*
Fiction: Juvenile, illustrated children's books, 4-8-year-old range older juvenile and YA. Query or submit outline/synopsis and sample chapters.
Recent Nonfiction Title: *S.O.S. Guide to Essay Writing*, by Steve Good and Bill Jensen (essay writing guide).
Recent Fiction Title: *Tuesday Cafe*, by Don Trembath (young adult).

PACIFIC EDUCATIONAL PRESS, Faculty of Education, University of British Columbia, Vancouver, British Columbia V6T 1Z4 Canada. Fax: (604)822-6603. E-mail: cedwards@interchange.ubc.ca. Director: Catherine Edwards. Publishes trade paperback originals. Publishes 6-8 titles/year. Receives 200 submissions/year. 15% of books from first-time authors; 100% from unagented writers. Accepts simultaneous submissions, if so noted. Reports in 6 months on mss. Book catalog and ms guidelines for 9×12 SAE with IRCs.
● Pacific Educational Press considers Canadian authors only for children's titles. Non-Canadian writers may submit educational titles.
Nonfiction: Children's/juvenile, reference for teacher, textbook. Subjects for children: animals, Canadiana, history, language/literature. Subjects for children and teachers: art/architecture, education, ethnic (for children or professional resources for teachers), music/dance, nature/environment, regional (Pacific Northwest), science. "Our books often straddle the trade/educational line, but we make our selections based on educational potential (in classrooms or school libraries)." Submit outline. Reviews artwork/photos as part of ms package. Send photocopies (color, if possible).
Recent Nonfiction Title: *In the Street of the Temple Cloth Printers*, by Dorothy Field (nonfiction picture book about traditional Hindu craftpeople for readers aged 11+).
Fiction: For children: ethnic, historical, juvenile, mystery, science fiction, young adult. For children or teachers: plays. "We select fiction based on its potential for use in language arts classes as well as its literary merit." Submit synopsis.
Recent Fiction Title: *The Reluctant Deckhand*, by Jan Padgett (juvenile novel about a young girl's summer aboard her mother's fishing boat).

PEGUIS PUBLISHERS LIMITED, 318 McDermot Ave., Winnipeg, Manitoba R3A OA2 Canada. (204)987-3500. Fax: (204)947-0080. E-mail: peguis@peguis.mb.ca. Website: http://www.magic.mb.ca/~peguis. **Acquisitions**: Mary Dixon. Estab. 1967. Educational paperback originals. Publishes 8 titles/year. Receives 150 submissions/year. 50% of books from first-time authors; 100% from unagented writers. Pays 10% average royalty on educational net (trade less 20%). Publishes book 2 years after acceptance. Accepts simultaneous submissions. Reports in 3 months on queries, 1

month on mss if quick rejection, up to 1 year if serious consideration. Book catalog free.
Nonfiction: Educational (focusing on teachers' resource material for primary education, integrated whole language). Submit outline/synopsis and sample chapters or complete ms.
Recent Nonfiction Title: *Helping Kids Deal with Conflict*, by Gerry Sheanh (peace and co-operation).
Tips: "Writers have the best chance selling us quality professional materials for teachers that help them turn new research and findings into classroom practice."

PENGUIN BOOKS CANADA LTD., Subsidiary of The Penguin Group, Suite 300, 10 Alcorn Ave., Toronto, Ontario M4V 3B2 Canada.
Nonfiction: Sports, true crime and any Canadian subject by Canadian authors. No unsolicited mss.
Recent Nonfiction Title: *The Canadian Revolution*, by Peter C. Newman (politics/history).
Recent Fiction Title: *The Saxon Shore*, by Jack Whyte.

PLAYWRIGHTS CANADA PRESS, Imprint of Playwrights Union of Canada, 54 Wolseley St., 2nd Floor, Toronto, Ontario M5T 1A5 Canada. (416)703-0201. Fax: (416)703-0059. E-mail: cdplays@interlog.com. Website: http://www.pu cc.ca. **Acquisitions**: Angela Rebeiro, publisher. Estab. 1972. Publishes paperback originals and reprints of plays by Canadian citizens or landed immigrants, whose plays have been professionally produced on stage. Receives 100 member submissions/year. 50% of plays from first-time authors; 50% from unagented authors. Pays 10% royalty on list price. Publishes 1 year after acceptance. Reports in up to 1 year. Play catalog for $5. Manuscript guidelines free. Non-members should query. Accepts children's plays.

PRENTICE-HALL CANADA INC., Trade Division, Subsidiary of Simon & Schuster, 1870 Birchmount Rd., Scarborough, Ontario M1P 2J7 Canada. (416)293-3621. Fax: (416)293-3625. **Acquisitions**: Jill Lambert, acquisitions editor. Estab. 1960. Publishes hardcover and trade paperback originals. Publishes 40 titles/year. Receives 750-900 submissions/year. 15% of books from first-time authors; 50% from unagented writers. Pays negotiable royalty. Offers advance. Publishes book 9 months after acceptance. Reports in 3 months. Manuscript guidelines for #10 SAE with 1 IRC.
Nonfiction: Subjects of Canadian and international interest: politics and current affairs, technology, self-help, pop culture, business, finance, health, food. Submit outline and sample chapters. Reviews artwork/photos as part of ms package.
Recent Nonfiction Title: *Get Wired, Your Hired: Canadian Guide to Job Hunting Online*, by Mark Swartz.
Tips: "Present a clear, concise thesis, well-argued with a thorough knowledge of existing works with strong Canadian orientation. Need general interest nonfiction books on topical subjects."

PRODUCTIVE PUBLICATIONS, P.O. Box 7200 Station A, Toronto, Ontario M5W 1X8 Canada. (416)483-0634. Fax: (416)322-7434. **Acquisitions**: Iain Williamson, owner. Estab. 1985. Productive Publications publishes books to help readers meet the challenges of the new economy. Publishes trade paperback originals. Publishes 24 titles/year. Receives 60 queries and 20 mss/year. 80% of books from first-time authors; 100% from unagented writers. Pays 10-15% royalty on wholesale price. Publishes book 3 months after acceptance of ms. Reports in 1 month on queries and proposals, 3 months on mss. Accepts simultaneous submissions. Book catalog free on request.
 • Productive Publications is also interested in books on business computer software, the Internet for business purposes, investment, stock market and mutual funds, etc.
Nonfiction: How-to, reference, self-help, technical. Subjects include business and economics, computers and electronics, health/medicine, hobbies, money/finance, software (business). "We are interested in small business/entrepreneurship/employment/self-help (business)/how-to/health and wellness—100 pages." Submit outline. Reviews artwork as part of ms package. Send photocopies.
Recent Nonfiction Title: *Meeting the Samurai*, by Jonathon King (business strategies); *The Net Effect*, by Iain Williamson (technology/computers); *Make It On Your Own*, by Barrie Jackson (business).
Tips: "We are looking for books written by *knowledgeable, experienced experts* who can express their ideas *clearly* and *simply*."

PURICH PUBLISHING, Box 23032, Market Mall Post Office, Saskatoon, Saskatchewan S7J 5H3 Canada. (306)373-5311. Fax: (306)373-5315. **Acquisitions**: Donald Purich, publisher. "We are a specialized publisher focusing on law, Aboriginal issues and western history for the education and professional trade reference market." Publishes trade paperback originals. Publishes 3-5 titles/year. 20% of books from first-time authors. Pays 8-12% royalty on retail price or makes outright purchase. Offers $100-1,500 advance. Publishes book 4 months after acceptance of ms. Accepts simultaneous submissions. Reports in 1 month on queries, 3 months on mss. Book catalog free on request.
Nonfiction: Reference, technical, textbook. Subjects include agriculture/horticulture, government/politics, history, law, Aboriginal issues. "We are a specialized publisher and only consider work in our subject areas." Query.
Recent Nonfiction Titles: *Municipalities and Canadian Law*, by Felix Hoehn; *Aboriginal Law*, by Thomas Isaac.

QUARRY PRESS, P.O. Box 1061, Kingston, Ontario K7L-4Y5 Canada. (613)548-8429. **Acquisitions**: Bob Hilderley, publisher. Publishes hardcover originals, trade paperback originals and reprints. Publishes 30-40 titles/year. 10% of books from first-time authors; 90% from unagented writers. Pays 10% royalty on retail price. Publishes book 1 year after acceptance. Reports in 7 months. Book catalog for 9 × 12 SAE. Manuscript guidelines for #10 SASE.
Nonfiction: Biography, children's/juvenile (only by Canadians), gift book, humor. Subjects include art/architecture,

education, gay/lesbian, history, language/literature, music/dance, photography, regional, religion, travel. "Our authors are generally Canadian." Query with SASE. Reviews artwork/photos as part of ms package. Send photocopies.

Recent Nonfiction Title: *Superman's Song: The Story of the Crash Test Dummies*, by Stephen Ostick (music/rock).

Fiction: Experimental, feminist, gay/lesbian, literary, mainstream/contemporary, science fiction, short story collections. Query with SASE.

Recent Fiction Title: *Under My Skin*, by Mary di Michele (fiction).

Poetry: "We publish Canadian poets only." Submit complete ms.

Recent Poetry Title: *Slow Reign of Calamity Jane*, by Gillian Robinson.

QUINTET PUBLISHING LIMITED, The Fitzpatrick Bldg., 188-195 York Way, London, England N7 9QR. Tel: 011.44.171.700.2001. Fax: 011.44.171.700.4985. **Acquisitions**: Stefanie Foster, new titles acquisitions editor. "We are a distinguished international illustrated book packager, and proposals must show the promise of broad appeal in many countries on all continents." Publishes hardcover and trade paperback originals and reprints. Publishes 70 titles/year. 50% of books from first-time authors; 100% from unagented writers. Makes outright purchase of $1,000-8,000 (US). Offers 33% advance. Publishes book 9 months after acceptance. Reports in 1 month.

Nonfiction: Coffee table book, cookbook, gift book, how-to, reference, technical. Subjects include: Americana, animals, anthropology/archaeology, art/architecture, child guidance/parenting, cooking/foods/nutrition, gardening, history, hobbies, military/war, music/dance, nature/environment, photography, recreation, sports. Writers should show a thorough awareness, reflected in their market analysis, of previously published titles in the subject area for which they are making a proposal. Query with proposal package including 1 sample chapter, marketing analysis and SASE. "Include a synopsis of all the elements of the book, so that we can consider how to make a flat-plan for an illustrated title." Reviews artwork/photos as part of ms package. Send transparencies.

Recent Nonfiction Titles: *The Cigar Companion*, by Simon Chase and Anwar Bati; *Barbie*, by Janine Fenwick; *Simple Tarts*, by Elizabeth Wolf Cohen.

• Quintet no longer accepts fiction mss.

RAINCOAST BOOK DISTRIBUTION LIMITED, 8680 Cambie St., Vancouver, British Columbia V6P 6M9 Canada. **Acquisitions**: Michael Carroll, managing editor. Publishes hardcover and trade paperback originals and reprints. Publishes 15-20 titles/year. Receives 800 queries and 500 mss/year. 1% of books from first-time authors; 80% from unagented writers. Pays 8-12% royalty on retail price. Offers $1,000-6,000 advance. Publishes book within 2 years after acceptance of ms. Reports in 1 month on queries, 2 months on proposals, 3 months on mss. Book catalog and ms guidelines for #10 SASE.

• Raincoast has published such authors as David Bouchard, Paul Grescoe, Daniel Wood and Dick North.

Imprint: Raincoast Books.

Nonfiction: Children's, coffee table book, cookbook, gift book, humor, illustrated book. Subjects include animals, art/architecture, cooking/foods/nutrition, history, nature/environment, photography, recreation, regional, sports, travel, business, Canadian subjects and native studies/issues. "We are expanding rapidly and plan on publishing a great deal more over the next two or three years, particularly nonfiction. Proposals should be focused and include background information on the author. Include a market study or examination of competition. We like to see proposals that cover all bases and offer a new approach to subjects we're interested in. Query first with SASE. *No unsolicited manuscripts*.

Recent Nonfiction Title: *The Merchants of Venus*, by Paul Grescoe (business); *Honour Song*, by Barbara Hager (Native Indian affairs).

Fiction: Children's picture books. "Our interest is high-quality children's picture books with Canadian themes. Query first with SASE. We do not accept unsolicited manuscripts."

Recent Fiction Titles: *Voices from the Wild*, by David Bouchard and Henry Ripplinger, illustrated by Ron Parker; *Rainbow Bay*, by Stephen Eaton Hume and Pascal Milelli (children's picture books).

Tips: "We have very high standards. Our books are extremely well designed and the texts reflect that quality. Be focused in your submission. Know what you are trying to do and be able to communicate it. Make sure the submission is well organized, thorough, and original. We like to see that the author has done some homework on markets and competition, particularly for nonfiction."

RANDOM HOUSE OF CANADA, Subsidiary of Random House, Inc., Suite 210, 33 Yonge St., Toronto, Ontario M5E 1G4 Canada. Imprint is Vintage Imprints. Publishes hardcover and trade paperback originals. Publishes 56 titles/year. No unsolicited mss. Agented submissions only. All unsolicited mss returned unopened. "We are NOT a mass market publisher."

RED DEER COLLEGE PRESS, Box 5005, 56th Ave. and 32nd St., Red Deer, Alberta T4N 5H5 Canada. (403)342-3321. Managing Editor: Dennis Johnson. Publishes trade paperback originals and occasionally reprints. Publishes 14-17 titles/year. Receives 1,700 queries and 2,000 mss/year. 20% of books from first-time authors; 90% from unagented writers. Pays 8-10% royalty on retail price. Publishes book 1 year after acceptance of ms. Accepts simultaneous submissions. Reports in 6 months. Book catalog free.

Imprints: Northern Lights Books for Children, Northern Lights Young Novels, Discovery Books, Roundup Books, Writing West.

Nonfiction: Children's/juvenile, cookbook, humor, illustrated book. Subjects include anthropology/archaeology/paleontology, cooking/foods/nutrition, gardening, history (local/regional), nature/environment (local/regional), regional,

travel. Nonfiction list focuses on regional history, paleontology, and some true crime, travel, gardening—much with a regional (Canadian) emphasis. "Writers should assess their competition in the marketplace and have a clear understanding of their potential readership." Query with SASE. Reviews artwork/photos as part of ms package. Send photocopies.
Recent Nonfiction Title: *Alaska and Yukon History Along the Highway*, by Ted Stone.
Fiction: Adventure, ethnic, experimental, fantasy, historical, humor, juvenile, literary, mainstream/contemporary, picture books, plays (occasionally), short story collections (occasionally), western, young adult. Adult fiction list includes well-established Canadian writers writing literary fiction, though the press is open to accepting other forms if tastefully and skillfully done. Query.
Recent Fiction Title: *The Rose Garden*, by Kristjana Gunnars.
Poetry: Query.
Recent Poetry Title: *Taking the Gate*, by Stephen Scobie.
Tips: Audience varies from imprint to imprint. "Know as much as you can about the potential market/readership for your book and indicate clearly how your book is different from or better than others in the same genre."

REIDMORE BOOKS INC., 1200 Energy Square, 10109-106 Street, Edmonton, Alberta T5J 3L7 Canada. (403)424-4420. Fax: (403)441-9919. E-mail: reidmore@compusmart.ab.ca. Website: http://www.reidmore.com. **Acquisitions**: Suzanne Moquin-Vani, director of marketing/sales. Estab. 1979. Publishes hardcover originals and modular materials for elementary mathematics (grades 4, 5, 6). Publishes 10-12 titles/year. Receives 18-20 submissions/year. 60% of books from first-time authors; 100% from unagented writers. Subsidy publishes 5% of books. Pays royalty. Offers $1,500 average advance. Publishes book 1 year after acceptance. Reports in 3 months on queries. Book catalog free.
Nonfiction: Textbook. Subjects include ethnic, government/politics, history, elementary mathematics and social studies. Query. Most manuscripts are solicited by publisher from specific authors.
Recent Nonfiction Title: *Canada: Its Land and People*, by Massey (educational).

ROCKY MOUNTAIN BOOKS, #4 Spruce Centre SW, Calgary, Alberta T3C 3B3 Canada. (403)249-9490. Fax: (403)249-2968. E-mail: tonyd@cadvision.com. Website: http://www.culturenet.ca/rmb/. **Acquisitions**: Tony Daffern, publisher. "We are focused on Western Canada and also mountaineering." Publishes trade paperback originals. Publishes 5 titles/year. Receives 30 queries/year. 75% of books from first-time authors; 100% from unagented writers. Pays 10% royalty. Offers $1,000-2,000 advance. Publishes book 1 year after acceptance. Reports in 1 month on queries. *Writer's Market* recommends allowing 2 months for reply. Book catalog and ms guidelines free.
Nonfiction: How-to. Subjects include nature/environment, recreation, travel. "Our main area of publishing is outdoor recreation guides to Western and Northern Canada." Query.
Recent Nonfiction Titles: *Planning a Wilderness Trip in Canada and Alaska*, by Keith Morton (recreation); *GPS Made Easy*, by Lawrence Letham (how-to).

RONSDALE PRESS, 3350 W. 21st Ave., Vancouver, British Columbia V6S 1G7 Canada. **Acquisitions:** Ronald B. Hatch, director (nonfiction). "We aim to publish the best Canadian writers. We are particularly interested in books that help Canadians know one another better." Publishes trade paperback originals. Publishes 8 titles/year. Receives 100 queries and 200 mss/year. 60% of books from first time authors; 95% from unagented writers. Pays 10% royalty on retail price. Publishes book 1 year after acceptance of ms. Accepts simultaneous submissions. Reports in 1 week on queries, 1 month on proposals, 3 months on mss. Book catalog for #10 SASE.
● Ronsdale has published such authors as Robin Shelton, Marya Fiamengo, Linda Rogers and Sue Ann Alderson.
Nonfiction: Biography, children's/juvenile. No picture books. Subjects include history, language/literature, nature/environment, regional. Writers *must* be Canadian citizens or landed immigrants.
Recent Nonfiction Titles: *Hamatsa-The Enigma of Cannibalism on the Pacific Northwest Coast*, by Jim McDowell (cannibalism); *Take My Words*, by Howard Richler (uses of language).
Fiction: Experimental, novels, short story collections, children's literature. Query with at least 80 pages.
Recent Fiction Title: *Danema Days*, by Terry Watada (Japanese Canadian WWII internment camp).
Poetry: "Poets should have published some poems in magazines/journals and should be well-read in some contemporary masters." Submit complete ms.
Recent Poetry Titles: *Rifts in The Visible*, by Inge Israel (life and work of painter Chaim Soutine); *Hong Kong Poems*, by A. Parkin and L. Wong (about Hong Kong in English and Chinese).

ROUSSAN PUBLISHERS INC., Roussan Editeur Inc., 2110 Decarie Blvd., Suite 100, Montreal, Quebec H4A 3J3 Canada. (514)481-2895. Fax: (514)487-2899. Website: http://www.magnet.ca/roussan. **Acquisitions:** Kathryn Rhoades, editor; Jane Frydenlund, editor-in-chief. Roussan Publishers Inc., specializes in reality-based fiction for young adults and pre-teens. Publishes trade paperback originals. Publishes 12 titles/year; each division publishes 6 titles/year. Receives 75 queries and 120 mss/year. 40% of books from first-time authors; 100% from unagented writers. Pays 8-10% royalty on retail price. Publishes book 1 year after acceptance of ms. Accepts simultaneous submissions. Reports in 3 months on proposals.
● Roussan Publishers Inc. has published such authors as George Bowering, Dayle Gaetz and Beth Goobie.
Fiction: Young adult and junior readers only—adventure, fantasy, feminist, historical, juvenile, mystery, science fiction. No picture books. Submit synopsis and 3 sample chapters.
Recent Fiction Titles: *Home Child*, by Barbara Haworth-Attard (historical); *The Vampire's Visit*, by David Poulsen; *Gone to Maui*, by Cherylyn Stacey (young adult).

SCHOLASTIC CANADA LTD., 123 Newkirk Rd., Richmond Hill, Ontario L4C 3G5 Canada. **Acquisitions**: Diane Kerner, Sandra Bogart Johnston, editors, children's books. Publishes hardcover and trade paperback originals. Publishes 30 titles/year; imprint publishes 4 titles/year. 3% of books from first-time authors; 50% from unagented writers. Pays 5-10% royalty on retail price. Offers $1,000-5,000 (Canadian) advance. Publishes book 1 year after acceptance of ms. Reports in 1 month on queries, 3 months on proposals. Book catalog for 8½×11 SAE with 2 first-class stamps (IRC or Canadian stamps only).
Imprints: North Winds Press (contact Joanne Richter); Les Éditions Scholastic (contact Sylvie Andrews, French editor).
Nonfiction: Children's/juvenile. Subjects include animals, history, hobbies, nature, recreation, science, sports. Query with outline, 1-2 sample chapters and SASE. No unsolicited mss. Reviews artwork/photos as part of ms package. Send photocopies.
Recent Nonfiction Title: *Take a Hike*, by Sharon Mackay and David Macleod (informal guide to hiking for kids).
Fiction: Children's/juvenile, young adult. Query with synopsis, 3 sample chapters and SASE.
Recent Fiction Title: *After the War*, by Carol Matas (juvenile novel).

SELF-COUNSEL PRESS, 1481 Charlotte Rd., North Vancouver, British Columbia V7J 1H1 Canada. (604)986-3366. Also 1704 N. State Street, Bellingham, WA 98225. (360)676-4530. **Acquisitions:** Ruth Wilson, managing editor. Estab. 1970. "We look for manuscripts full of useful information that will allow readers to take the solution to their needs or problems into their own hands and succeed. We do not want personal self-help accounts, however." Publishes trade paperback originals. Publishes 15-20 titles/year. Receives 1,000 submissions/year. 80% of books from first-time authors; 95% from unagented writers. Pays 10% royalty on net receipts. Publishes book 9 months after acceptance. Accepts simultaneous submissions. Reports in 2 months. Book catalog and ms guidelines for 9×12 SAE.
Nonfiction: How-to, self-help. Subjects include business, law, reference. Query or submit outline and sample chapters.
Recent Nonfiction Title: *Small Business Guide to Doing Big Business on the Internet*, by Brian Hurley and Peter Birkwood (business).
Tips: "The self-counsel author is an expert in his or her field and capable of conveying practical, specific information to those who are not."

‡SEVERN HOUSE PUBLISHERS, 9-15 High St., Sutton, Surrey SM1 1DF United Kingdom. (0181)770-3930. Fax: (0181)770-3850. **Acquisitions**: Yvette Taylor, editorial assistant. Publishes hardcover and trade paperback originals and reprints. Publishes 120 titles/year. Receives 250 queries and 50 mss/year. 0.5% of books from first-time authors; 0.5% from unagented writers. Pays 7½-15% royalty on retail price. Offers $750-2,500. Accepts simultaneous submissions. Reports in 3 months on proposals. Book catalog free.
• Severn House accepts agented submissions only.
Fiction: Adventure, fantasy, historical, horror, mainstream/contemporary, mystery, romance, science fiction, short story collections, suspense. Submit synopsis and 3 sample chapters. Agented submissions only.
Recent Fiction Titles: *Tender Warrior*, by Fern Michaels (historical romance); *The Geneva Rendezvous*, by Julie Ellis (romance); *Devil May Care*, by Elizabeth Peters (crime and mystery); *Blood and Honor*, by W.E.B. Griffin (war fiction).

SHORELINE, Ste.-Anne, Ste.-Anne-de-Bellevue 23, Quebec H9X 1L1 Canada. Phone/fax: (514)457-5733. **Acquisitions:** Judy Isherwood, editor. "Our mission is to support new authors by publishing literary works of considerable merit." Publishes trade paperback originals. Publishes 3 titles/year. Pays 10% royalty on retail price. Publishes book 1 year after acceptance. Reports in 1 month on queries, 4 months on ms. Book catalog for 50¢ postage.
Nonfiction: Biography, essays, humour, illustrated book, reference. Subjects include: America, art, Canada, education, ethnic, health/mental health, history, mediation, regional, religion, Mexico, Spain, travel, women's studies.
Recent Nonfiction Titles: *The Inside Story: Journey of a former Jesuit priest and talk show host towards self-discovery*, by Neil McKenty; *The Lights of Lancaster: Letters to Romé*, by Margaret Coza (journal of a stroke victim); *Looking Back*, by Best Rinett (memoir).
Tips: Audience is "adults and young adults who like their nonfiction personal, different and special. Beginning writers welcome, agents unnecessary. Send your best draft (not the first!), make sure your heart is in it."

‡SIMON & PIERRE PUBLISHING CO. LTD., A Subsidiary of Dundurn Press, Suite 301, 2181 Queen St. E., Toronto, Ontario M4E 1E5 Canada. (416)463-0313. **Acquisitions**: Carl Brand, director of operations. Estab. 1972. Simon & Pierre publishes "Canadian themes by Canadian authors," both fiction and nonfiction literary and contemporary subjects such as Sherlockian literature and drama. Publishes hardcover and trade paperback originals and reprints. Averages 6-8 titles/year. Receives 300 submissions/year. 50% of books are from first-time authors; 85% from unagented writers. Trade book royalty 10-15% on retail price. Education royalty 8% of net. Offers $500 average advance. Publishes book 1 year after acceptance. Accepts simultaneous submissions. Reports in 3 months. Ms guidelines free.
• Simon & Pierre no longer publishes children's or young adult books.
Nonfiction: *Canadian authors only*. Biography, reference, drama, language/literature, music/dance (drama), Sherlockian literature and criticism. "We are looking for Canadian drama and drama related books." Query or submit outline and sample chapters. Sometimes reviews artwork/photos as part of ms package.
Fiction: Adventure, literary, mainstream/contemporary, mystery, plays (Canadian, must have had professional production). "No romance, sci-fi or experimental." Query or submit outline/synopsis and sample chapters.
Recent Fiction Title: *Found: A Body*, by Betsy Struthers (novel).
Tips: "We are looking for Canadian themes by Canadian authors. Special interest in drama and drama related topics;

also Sherlockian. If I were a writer trying to market a book today, I would check carefully the types of books published by a publisher before submitting manuscript; books can be examined in bookstores, libraries, etc.; should look for a publisher publishing the type of book being marketed. Clean manuscripts essential; if work is on computer disk, give the publisher that information. Send information on markets for the book, and writer's résumé, or at least why the writer is an expert in the field. Covering letter is important first impression."

SNOWAPPLE PRESS, Box 66024, Heritage Postal Outlet, Edmonton, Alberta T6J 6T4 Canada. **Acquisitions**: Vanna Tessier, editor. "We focus on topics that are interesting, unusual and controversial." Publishes hardcover originals, trade paperback originals and reprints, mass market paperback originals and reprints. Publishes 5-6 titles/year. Receives 300 queries/year. 50% of books from first-time authors; 100% from unagented writers. Pays 10-50% royalty on retail price or makes outright purchase of $100 or pays in copies. Offers $100-200 advance. Publishes book 2 years after acceptance. Accepts simultaneous submissions. Reports in 1 month on queries, 3 months on proposals and mss.
• Snowapple Press has published such authors as John Chalmers, Gilberto Finzi and Doris Hillis.
Fiction: Adventure, ethnic, experimental, fantasy, feminist, historical, literary, mainstream/contemporary, mystery, picture books, short story collections, young adult. Query with SASE.
Recent Fiction Title: *Gypsy Drums*, by Vanna Tessier (relationships).
Poetry: Query with SASE.
Recent Poetry Title: *Nightchant*, by Paolo Valesio (alienation).
Tips: "We are a small press that will publish original, interesting and entertaining fiction and poetry."

SONO NIS PRESS, 1725 Blanshard St., Victoria, British Columbia V8W 2J8 Canada. (250)382-1024. Fax: (250)382-0775. E-mail: sono.nis@islandnet.com. Website: http://www.islandnet.com/~sononis/. **Acquisitions:** A. West, editor. Estab. 1968. Sono Nis Press specializes in transportation, history and Western Canadian historical biographies. Publishes hardcover and trade paperback originals and reprints. Publishes 9 titles/year. Receives hundreds of queries/year. 5-10% of books from first-time authors; 80% from unagented writers. Pays 10-12% royalty on retail price. Publishes book 14 months after acceptance. Accepts simultaneous submissions. Reports in 2 months on queries. Book catalog for 9×12 SAE with 3 IRCs.
• The press has published such authors as Linda Rogers and Rona Murray.
Nonfiction: Biography, reference. Subjects include history (British Columbia), hobbies (trains), regional (British Columbia), maritime (British Columbia), transportation (Western Canada). Query or submit outline and 3 sample chapters. Reviews artwork/photos as part of ms package. Send photocopies.
Recent Nonfiction Titles: *Helicopters in the High Country*, by P. Covley-Smith (aviation); *Steam on the Kettle Valley*, by Robert Turner (railway); *No Better Land*, by Roberta Bagshaw (history/biography, Colonial period).
Poetry: Query.
Recent Poetry Titles: *Climate & The Affections*, by Crispin Elsted; *Shadow Weather*, by Charles Lillard.

SOUND AND VISION PUBLISHING LIMITED, 359 Riverdale Ave., Toronto, Ontario M4J 1A4 Canada. (416)465-2828. Fax: (416)465-0755. **Acquisitions:** Geoff Savage. Publishes trade paperback originals. Publishes 2 titles/year. Reports in 3 months on proposals.
Nonfiction: Humor. Music/dance subjects. Submit outline and SASE.
Recent Nonfiction Titles: *How to Stay Awake, During Anybody's Second Movement*, by D. Walden; *Love Lives of the Great Composers*, by B. Howitz; *Tenors, Tantrums and Trills*, by D.W. Barber.

‡STODDART PUBLISHING CO., LTD., Subsidiary of General Publishing Co., Ltd., 34 Lesmill Rd., Toronto, Ontario M3B 2T6 Canada. **Acquisitions:** Donald G. Bastian, managing editor. Stoddart publishes "important Canadian books" for a general interest audience. Publishes hardcover, trade paperback and mass market paperback originals and trade paperback reprints. Publishes 100 titles/year. Receives 1,200 queries and mss/year. 10% of books from first-time authors; 50% from unagented writers. Pays 8-10% royalty on retail price. Publishes book 1 year after acceptance of ms. Accepts simultaneous submissions. Reports in 2 months. Book catalog and ms guidelines for #10 SASE.
Imprint(s): Stoddart Kids (Kathryn Cole, publisher).
Nonfiction: Biography, children's/juvenile, coffee table book, cookbook, gift book, how-to, humor, illustrated book, self-help. Subjects include art/architecture, business and economics, child guidance/parenting, computers and electronics, cooking/foods/nutrition, gardening, government/politics, health/medicine, history, language/literature, military/war, money/finance, nature/environment, psychology, science, sociology, sports. Submit outline, 2 sample chapters, outline, résumé, with SASE.
Recent Nonfiction Title(s): *Peter Munk*, by Donald Rumball (business biography); *The Japan We Never Knew*, by David Suzuki, Keibo Oiwa (travel); *The Pig and the Python*, by David Cork, Susan Lightstone (financial planning).

THISTLEDOWN PRESS, 633 Main St., Saskatoon, Saskatchewan S7H 0J8 Canada. (306)244-1722. Fax: (306)244-1762. Editor-in-Chief: Patrick O' Rourke. **Acquisitions**: Jesse Strothers. Estab. 1975. Publishes trade paperback originals by resident Canadian authors *only*. Publishes 10-12 titles/year. Receives 350 submissions/year. 10% of books from first-time authors; 90% from unagented writers. Average print order for a first poetry book is 500; fiction is 1,000. Pays standard royalty on retail price. Publishes book 2 years after acceptance. Reports in 2 months. Book catalog and guidelines for #10 SASE.
Fiction: Juvenile (ages 8 and up), literary. Interested in fiction mss from resident Canadian authors only. Minimum of

30,000 words. Accepts no unsolicited work. Query first.

Recent Fiction Title: *Under Newest Eyes*, edited by Paul Denhem and Gail Youngberg (anthology).

Poetry: "The author should make him/herself familiar with our publishing program before deciding whether or not his/her work is appropriate." No poetry by people *not* citizens and residents of Canada. Prefers poetry mss that have had some previous exposure in literary magazines. Accepts no unsolicited work. Query first.

Recent Poetry Title: *Overheard*, by Conifers Jon V. Hicks.

Tips: "We prefer to receive a query letter first before a submission. We're looking for quality, well-written literary fiction—for children and young adults and for our adult fiction list as well. Increased emphasis on fiction (short story collections and novels) for young adults, aged 12-18 years."

THOMPSON EDUCATIONAL PUBLISHING INC., 14 Ripley Ave., Suite 104, Toronto, Ontario M6S 3N9 Canada. (416)766-2763. Fax: (416)766-0398. E-mail: thompson@canadabooks.ingenia.com. Website: http://canadabook s.ingenia.com. **Acquisitions:** Keith Thompson, president. Thompson Educational Publishing Co. specializes in high-quality educational texts in the social sciences and humanities." Publishes textbooks. Publishes 10 titles/year. Receives 15 queries and 10 mss/year. 80% of books from first-time authors; 100% from unagented writers. Pays 10% royalty on net price. Publishes book 1 year after acceptance. Reports in 1 month on proposals. *Writer's Market* recommends allowing 2 months for reply. Book catalog free.

Nonfiction: Textbook. Subjects include business and economics, education, government/politics, sociology, women's issues/studies. Submit outline and 1 sample chapter and résumé.

Recent Nonfiction Titles: *Canadian Politics: An Introduction*, by Tom Chambers (politics); *Seeing Ourselves: Exploring Race, Ethnicity and Culture*, by Carl James (race and ethnicity).

TITAN BOOKS LTD., 42-44 Dolben St., London SE1 OUP England. Fax: (0171)620-0200. **Acquisitions**: D. Barraclough, senior editor. Publishes trade and mass market paperback originals and reprints. Publishes 60-90 titles/year. Receives 1,000 queries and 500 mss/year. Less than 1% of books from first-time authors; 50% from unagented writers. Pays royalty of 6-8% on retail price. Advance varies. Publishes books 1 year after acceptance of ms. Accepts simultaneous submissions. Reports in 1 month on queries, 3 months on proposals, 6 months on mss. Ms guidelines for SASE with IRC.

Nonfiction: Biography, how-to, humor, illustrated book. Subjects include music, film and TV. Query. Reviews artwork/photos as part of ms package. Send photocopies.

Recent Nonfiction Title: *Sacred Monsters*, by Doug Bradley (cinema).

Fiction: Erotica, comics. Query.

Recent Fiction Title: *The Safety of Unknown Cities*, by Lucy Taylor (erotica).

TURNSTONE PRESS, 607-100 Arthur St., Winnipeg, Manitoba R3B 1H3 Canada. (204)947-1555. Fax: (204)942-1555. E-mail: editor@turnstonepress.mb.ca. Managing Editor: Manuela Dias. Estab. 1971. "Turnstone Press is a literary press that publishes Canadian writers with an emphasis on writers from, and writing on, the Canadian west." Publishes trade paperback originals. Publishes 10-12 titles/year. Receives 1,000 mss/year. Publishes Canadians and permanent residents only. 25% of books from first-time authors; 75% from unagented writers. Pays 10% royalty on retail price. Offers $100-500 advance. Publishes book 1 year after acceptance of ms. Reports in 4 months. Book catalog free.

Nonfiction: Turnstone Press would like to see more nonfiction books, particularly travel, memoir.

Recent Nonfiction Titles: *Miss O: My Life in Dance*, by Betty Oliphant (autobiography); *Chinese Brushtrokes*, by Sandra Hutchison (travel writing); *Black Taxi: Shooting South Africa*, by Kendall Hunter (travel writing/photography).

Fiction: Adventure, ethnic, experimental, feminist, humor, literary, mainstream/contemporary, short story collections. Would like to see more novels. Query with SASE (Canadian postage) first.

Recent Fiction Titles: *Sam and Angie*, by Margaret Sweatman; *Summer of My Amazing Luck*, by Miriam Toewl; *Flying to Yellow*, by Linda Holeman.

Poetry: Submit complete ms.

Recent Poetry Titles: *circuitry of veins*, by Sylvia Legris; *Jerusalem, beloved*, by Di Brandt.

Tips: "We also publish one literary critical study per year and one general interest nonfiction book per year. Would like to see more ethnic writing, women's writing, gay and lesbian writing, as well as more travel, memoir, life-writing as well as eclectic novels. There is more than one way to tell a story."

‡UMBRELLA PRESS, 56 Rivercourt Blvd., Toronto, Ontario M4J 3A4 Canada. (416)696-6665. Fax: (416)696-9189. E-mail: umbpress@interlog.com. **Acquisitions:** Ken Pearson, publisher. "We focus on books for young people directed to schools and libraries as supplemental and reference. The emphasis is on issues of multiculturalism." Publishes hardcover and softbound originals. Publishes 6 titles/year. Receives 10 queries and 5 mss/year. 75% of books from first-time authors; 100% from unagented writers. Pays 10-15% royalty on wholesale price for education, on retail price for trade. Offers $250-500 advance. Publishes book 18 months after acceptance of ms. Accepts simultaneous submissions. Reports in 1 month on queries; 2 months on proposals; 3 months on mss. Book catalog and ms guidelines free.

Nonfiction: Biography, reference, library/education supplement. Subjects include multiculturalism, education, history, women's issues/studies. Submit outline with 2 sample chapters.

Recent Nonfiction Titles: *Tubman: Harriet Tubman and the Underground Railroad*, by Rosemary Sadlier (biography); *Towards Freedom: The African-Canadian Experience*, by Ken Alexander and Aris Glaze (history); *Deemed Unsuitable*, by R. Bruce Shepard (history).

UNFINISHED MONUMENT PRESS, Mekler & Deahl, Publishers, 237 Prospect St. S., Hamilton, Ontario L8M 2Z6 Canada. (905)312-1779. Fax: (905)312-8285. E-mail: ad507@freenet.hamilton.on.ca. **Acquisitions:** Gilda Mekler, editor (nonfiction); James Deahl, editor (fiction). Publishes trade paperback originals and reprints. Publishes 4-6 titles/ year. No books from first-time authors; 100% from unagented writers. Pays 10-12% royalty on retail price. Publishes book 10 months after acceptance. Accepts simultaneous submissions. Reports in 1 month on queries. *Writer's Market* recommends allowing 2 months for reply. Book catalog and ms guidelines free on request.
Imprints: Unfinished Monument Northland (James Deahl, manager); Unfinished Monument America (Michael Wurster, manager); Hamilton Haiku Press.
Nonfiction: Medical books, biography. Query with SASE.
Recent Nonfiction Title: *One Day She Will Fly* (a survivor's story of a traumatic brain injury); *Railing Against the Rush of Years*, by Claire Ridker and Patricia Savage (art therapy/aging).
Fiction: Plays. "We hope to get into short stories soon." Query with SASE.
Recent Fiction Title: *The Road to Charlottetown* (play).
Poetry: "We have a special interest in people's poetry." Query.
Recent Poetry Title: *Not To Rest In Silence*, edited by Ted Plantos (poetry anthology); *To Hear the Faint Bells*, by Milton Acorn (poetry and haiku).
Tips: American authors can use our US address: P.O. Box 4279, Pittsburgh PA 15203, %Michael Wurster, Manager.

THE UNITED CHURCH PUBLISHING HOUSE (UCPH), 3250 Bloor St. W., 4th Floor, Etobicoke, Ontario M8X 2Y4 Canada. (416)231-5931. Fax: (416)232-6004. E-mail: bookpub@uccan.org. Website: http://www.uccan.org. **Acquisitions:** Ruth Bradley-St-Cyr, managing editor. "We are committed to publishing books and resources that help people to engage in Christian ministry. We are further committed to engaging readers, regardless of denomination or faith, in consideration of the spiritual aspects of their lives." Publishes trade paperback originals from Canadian authors only. Publishes 12-16 titles/year. Receives 80 queries and 30 mss/year. 80% of books from first-time authors; 99% from unagented writers. Pays 10% royalty on retail price. Offers $100-300 advance. Publishes book 1 year after acceptance. Reports in 2-4 months on proposals. Proposal guidelines free with SASE.
   ● UCPH has published such authors as Michael McAteer, Christopher Levan and Dorothy MacNeill.
Nonfiction: Subjects relate to United Church of Canada interests only, in the following areas: history, religion, sociology, women's issues/studies, theology and biblical studies. Query first. *No unsolicited mss.*
Recent Nonfiction Titles: *The Wounds of Manuel Saquic*, by Jim Manly (biblical reflections); *God at the Corners*, by Robert A. Wallace (devotion/worship); *Ministry as an Art*, by Saunders and Woodbury (Christian leadership).

THE UNIVERSITY OF ALBERTA PRESS, 141 Athabasca Hall, Edmonton, Alberta T6G 2E8 Canada. (403)492-3662. Fax: (403)492-0719. E-mail: uap@gpu.srv.ualberta.ca. Website: www.quasar.ualberta.ca/press. **Acquisitions:** Glenn Rollans, director. Estab. 1969. "For more than a quarter-century, the University of Alberta Press has steadily built its reputation for publishing important scholarly works and fine books for broad audiences." Publishes hardcover and trade paperback originals and trade paperback reprints. Publishes 18-25 titles/year. Receives 200 submissions/year. 60% of books from first-time authors; majority from unagented writers. Average print order for a first book is 1,000. Pays 10% royalty on net price. Publishes book within 1 year after acceptance. Reports in 3 months. Book catalog and ms guidelines free.
   ● The University of Alberta Press has increased the number of books published from 10 titles/year to 18-25
   titles/year. They publish such authors as Olive P. Dickason, George Woodcock and David C. Jones.
Nonfiction: Submit table of contents, 1-2 chapters, sample illustrations and cv.
Tips: "Since 1969, the University of Alberta Press has earned recognition and awards from the Association of American University Presses, the Alcuin Society, the Book Publishers Association of Alberta and the Bibliographical Society of Canada, among others. Now we're growing—in the audiences we reach, the numbers of titles we publish, and our energy for new challenges. But we're still small enough to listen carefully, to work closely with our authors, to explore possibilities. Our list is strong in Canadian, western and northern topics, but it ranges widely. The University of Alberta Press opens important books to the world."

UNIVERSITY OF MANITOBA PRESS, 15 Gillson St., #244, University of Manitoba, Winnipeg, Manitoba R3T 5V6 Canada. **Acquisitions:** David Carr, director. Estab. 1967. "Western Canadian focus or content is important." Publishes nonfiction hardcover and trade paperback originals. Publishes 4-6 titles/year. Pays 5-15% royalty on wholesale price. Reports in 3 months.
Nonfiction: Scholarly. Subjects include Western Canadian history, women's issues/studies, Native history. Query.
Recent Nonfiction Title: *River Road: Essays on Manitoba and Prairie History* , by Gerald Friesen.

UNIVERSITY OF MONTREAL PRESS, P.O. Box 6128, Station Downtown, Montreal H3C 3J7 Canada. (514)343-6929. Fax: (514)343-2232. E-mail: pumedit@ere.umontreal.ca. Website: www.pum.umontreal.ca/pum/. **Acquisitions:** Marise Labrecque, editor-in-chief. Publishes hardcover and trade paperback originals. Publishes 20-25 titles/year. Nonauthor-subsidy publishes 25% of books. Pays 8-12 % royalty on net price. Publishes book 6 months after acceptance of ms. Reports in 1 month on queries and proposals, 3 months on mss. Book catalog and ms guidelines free on request.
Nonfiction: Reference, textbook. Subjects include anthropology, education, health/medicine, history, language/literature, philosophy, psychology, religion, sociology, translation. Submit outline and 2 sample chapters.

UNIVERSITY OF OTTAWA PRESS, 542 King Edward, Ottawa, Ontario K1N 6N5 Canada. (613)562-5246. Fax: (613)562-5247. E-mail: press@uottawa.ca. Website: http://www.uopress.uottawa.ca. Editor: Isabelle Bossé. Estab. 1936. The University Press publishes books for the scholarly and educated general audiences. They were "the first *officially* bilingual publishing house in Canada." Publishes 22 titles/year; 10 titles/year in English. Receives 140 submissions/year. 20% of books from first-time authors; 95% from unagented writers. Determines nonauthor subsidy by preliminary budget. Pays 5-10% royalty on net price. Publishes book 4 months after acceptance. Reports in 2 months on queries, 4 months on mss. Book catalog and author's guide free.
Nonfiction: Reference, textbook, scholarly. Subjects include criminology, education, Canadian government/politics, Canadian history, language/literature, nature/environment, philosophy, religion, sociology, translation, women's issues/studies. Submit outline/synopsis and sample chapters.
Recent Nonfiction Title: *When Science Becomes Culture: World Survey of Scientific Culture*, edited by Bernard Schiele.
Tips: "Envision audience of academic specialists and (for some books) educated public."

‡THE UNIVERSITY OF WESTERN ONTARIO, 1137 Western Rd., London, Ontario N6G 1G7 Canada. (519)661-2096. Fax: (519)661-3833. E-mail: press@edu.uwo.ca. Website: http://www.uwo.ca/edu/press. **Acquisitions:** Don Gutteridge, director. "We publish scholarly books for teachers and graduate students in education." Publishes trade paperback originals. Publishes 3 titles/year. Receives 12 queries and 12 mss/year. 50% of books from first-time authors; 100% from unagented writers. Pays 10% royalty on wholesale price. No advance. Publishes book 6 months after acceptance of ms. Reports in 1 month on queries and proposals, 3 months on mss. Manuscript guidelines free.
• University of Western Ontario has published Kieran Egan, Max van Manen and Robin Barrow.
Imprint: The Althouse Press.
Nonfiction: Education (scholarly) subjects. "Beware of sending incomplete manuscripts that are only marginally apt to our market and limited mandate." Query or submit outline or proposal package including completed ms. Reviews artwork/photos as part of ms package. Send photocopies.
Recent Nonfiction Titles: *Ring Some Alarm Bells in Ontario*, edited by G. Milburn (scholarly/education); *Exceptional Solutions*, edited by Sitko and Sitko (special education); *Crocus Hill Reunion*, by Jones (life in grade 6 classroom).

UPNEY EDITIONS, (formerly Escart Press), 19 Applachian Crescent, Kitchener, Ontario N2E 1A3 Canada. **Acquisitions:** Gary Brannon, managing editor. Publishes trade paperback originals. Publishes 3 titles/year. 33% of books from first-time authors; 100% from unagented writers. Pays 10-15% royalty on wholesale price. No advance. Publishes book 6 months after acceptance. Accepts simultaneous submissions. Reports in 1 month. *Writer's Market* recommends allowing 2 months for reply. Book catalog free on request.
Nonfiction: Biography, reference. Subjects include Americana, art/architecture, history, nature/environment, regional, travel. "We will consider travel books—Europe, North America. Our North American Heritage Series documents history that involves Canada and US—100-175 pages softcover." Query with outline, 2 sample chapters and SASE for Canada. "We prefer to see manuscripts well thought out chapter by chapter, not just a first chapter and a vague idea of the rest." Reviews artwork/photos as part of ms package. Send photocopies.
Recent Nonfiction Title: *The Journeys of Remarkable Women*, by Les Harding (biography/travel).
Tips: "Electronic, preformatted submissions on disk are preferred—we are a MAC environment."

VANWELL PUBLISHING LIMITED, 1 Northrup Crescent, P.O. Box 2131, St. Catharines, Ontario L2M 6P5 Canada. (905)937-3100. Fax: (905)937-1760. **Acquisitions:** Angela Dobler, general editor; Simon Kooter, editor (military). Estab. 1983. "Vanwell is considered Canada's leading naval heritage publisher. We also publish military aviation, biography, WWII and WWI histories. Recently publishing children's fiction and nonfiction, but not picture books." Publishes trade originals and reprints. Publishes 5-7 titles/year. Receives 100 submissions/year. Publishes Canadian authors only. 85% of books from first-time authors; 100% from unagented writers. Pays 8-15% royalty on wholesale price. Offers $200 average advance. Publishes book 1 year after acceptance. Reports in 3 months on queries. Book catalog free.
• Vanwell Publishing Ltd. has received awards from Education Children's Book Centre and Notable Education Libraries Association. It is seeing increased demand for biographical nonfiction for ages 10-14.
Nonfiction: Biography. Subjects include military/war. All military/history related. *Writer's Market* recommends query with SASE first. Reviews artwork/photos as part of ms package.
Recent Nonfiction Titles: *The Canadian Naval Chronicle*, by Fraser McKee and Bob Darlington (Canadian naval history); *Her Story II*, by Susan Merritt (women's history Canada).
Recent Fiction Titles: *The Stone Orchard*, by Susan Merritt (historical fiction); *The Wagner Whacker*, by Joseph Romain (baseball, historical fiction).
Tips: "The writer has the best chance of selling a manuscript to our firm which is in keeping with our publishing program, well written and organized. Our audience: older male, history buff, war veteran; regional tourist; students. *Canadian* only military/aviation, naval, military/history and children's nonfiction have the best chance with us."

VÉHICULE PRESS, Box 125, Place du Parc Station, Montreal, Quebec H2W 2M9 Canada. (514)844-6073. Fax: (514)844-7543. Website: http://www.cam.org/~vpress. **Acquisitions**: Simon Dardick, president/publisher. Estab. 1973. "Montreal's Véhicule Press has published the best of Canadian and Quebec literature—fiction, poetry, essays, translations and social history." Publishes trade paperback originals by Canadian authors *only*. Publishes 13 titles/year. Receives

250 submissions/year. 20% of books from first-time authors; 95% from unagented writers. Pays 10-15% royalty on retail price. Offers $200-500 advance. Publishes book 1 year after acceptance. Reports in 4 months on queries. Book catalog for 9×12 SAE with IRCs.

Imprints: Signal Editions (poetry), Dossier Quebec (history, memoirs).

Nonfiction: Biography, memoir. Subjects include Canadiana, feminism, history, politics, social history, literature. Especially looking for Canadian social history. Query. Reviews artwork/photos as part of ms package.

Recent Nonfiction Title: *Open Your Hearts: The Story of the Jewish War Orphans in Canada*, by Fraidie Mortz.

Poetry: Contact: Michael Harris. Canadian authors *only*. Not accepting new material before 1998.

Recent Poetry Title: *Visions Fugitive*, by Ralph Gustofson.

Tips: "We are only interested in Canadian authors."

VERSO, 6 Meard St., London WIV 3HR England. Fax: (171)734-0059. **Acquisitions:** Lucy Heller, commisioning editor. Estab. 1970. Publishes hardcover and tradepaper originals. Publishes 60 titles/year. Receives 500 submissions/year. 15% of books from first-time authors; 80% from unagented writers. Pays royalty and offers advance. Publishes book 15 months after acceptance. Reports in 2 months.

Nonfiction: Academic, general. Subjects include economics, education, government/politics/social sciences, language/literature, nature/environment, philosophy, science, cultural and media studies, sociology, travel, women's issues/studies. Submit outline and sample chapters. Unsolicited mss not accepted.

Recent Nonfiction Titles: *Wall Street*, by Doug Henwood; *The Invention of the White Race, Vol. II: The Origins of Racial Oppression in Anglo-America*, by Theodore W. Allen.

WALL & EMERSON, INC., 6 O'Connor Dr., Toronto, Ontario M4K 2K1 Canada. (416)467-8685. Fax: (416)696-2460. E-mail: wall@tor.hookup.net. President: Byron E. Wall. Vice President: Martha Wall. Estab. 1987. Publishes hardcover and trade paperback originals and reprints. Publishes 3 titles/year. 50% of books from first-time authors; 100% from unagented writers. Nonauthor-subsidy publishes 10% of books. (Only subsidies provided by external granting agencies accepted. Generally these are for scholarly books with a small market.) Pays royalty of 8-15% on wholesale price. Publishes book 1 year after acceptance. Accepts simultaneous submissions. Reports in 2 months on queries.

Nonfiction: Reference, textbook. Subjects include adult education, health/medicine, philosophy, science, mathematics. "We are looking for any undergraduate college text that meets the needs of a well-defined course in colleges in the US and Canada." Submit outline and sample chapters.

Recent Nonfiction Title: *Introduction to Industrial Ergonomics*, by T.M. Fraser.

Tips: "We are most interested in textbooks for college courses; books that meet well-defined needs and are targeted to their audiences are best. Our audience consists of college undergraduate students and college libraries. Our ideal writer is a college professor writing a text for a course he or she teaches regularly. If I were a writer trying to market a book today, I would identify the audience for the book and write directly to the audience throughout the book. I would then approach a publisher that publishes books specifically for that audience."

WHITECAP BOOKS LTD., 351 Lynn Ave., North Vancouver, British Columbia V7J 2C4 Canada. (604)980-9852. **Acquisitions**: Colleen MacMillan, publisher. Whitecap Books publishes a wide range of nonfiction with a general and regional (Canadian) focus. Publishes hardcover and trade paperback originals. Publishes 24 titles/year. Receives 150 queries and 200 mss/year. 20% of books from first-time authors; 90% from unagented writers. Royalty and advance negotiated for each project. Publishes book 12-18 months after acceptance. Accepts simultaneous submissions. Reports in 2 months on proposals.

Nonfiction: Biography, coffee table book, cookbook, children's/juvenile. Subjects include animals, gardening, history, nature/environment, recreation, regional, travel. "We require an annotated outline. Writers should also take the time to research our list." Submit outline, 1 sample chapter, table of contents and SASE. Send photocopies, not original material.

Recent Nonfiction Titles: *Clara and Me: The Story of an Unexpected Friendship*; *Adventures in Asian Tapas and Wild Sushi*, by Trevor Hooper (cookbook); the *Discover Canada* series (photography/regional guidebook).

Tips: "We want well-written, well-researched material that presents a fresh approach to a particular topic."

WORDSTORM PRODUCTIONS INC., Box 49132, 7740 18th St. SE, Calgary, Alberta T2C 3W5 Canada. Phone/fax: (403)236-1275. E-mail: wordstrm@cadvision.com. **Acquisitions:** Perry P. Rose, president; Eileen A. Rose, vice president. "We provide the highest possible quality of works by published and nonpublished authors." Publishes trade and mass market paperback originals. Publishes 5-7 titles/year. 90% of books from first-time authors; 95% from unagented writers. Pays 10-12% royalty on retail price. (Works released in USA paid 66% of above.) Publishes book 1 year after acceptance of ms. Reports in 2 months on queries, 4 months on proposals, 6 months on mss. Manuscript guidelines for #10 SASE.

Nonfiction: Humor. Query with outline, 3 sample chapters and SASE or SAE and IRCs. Reviews artwork/photos as part of ms package. Send photocopies.

Recent Nonfiction Title: *Nurse, Hear You, Hear Me*, by Lillian Tymchuk, R.N. (true nursing stories).

Fiction: Adventure, humor, mainstream/contemporary, mystery, suspense, children's books. Query with synopsis, 3 sample chapters and SASE or SAE and IRCs. All unsolicited mss returned unopened.

Recent Fiction Titles: *228*, by David E. Weischadle (adventure); *Kosha™ Tells: Orville the Orphan Tree*, by Perry P. Rose and Audrey Lazarus (children 5-9 years.)

Tips: When sending self-addressed return envelope, please remember to use an international postal coupon if mailing is originating outside Canada. U.S. stamps cannot be used to mail "from" Canada.

‡**WORLDWIDE LIBRARY**, Division of Harlequin Enterprises Ltd., 225 Duncan Mill Rd., Don Mills, Ontario M3B 3K9 Canada. (416)445-5860. Editorial Director: Randall Toye. **Acquisitions**: Feroze Mohammed, senior editor/editorial coordinator. Estab. 1949. Publishes 72 titles/year.
   ● Worldwide Library is not currently accepting new submissions.
Imprints: Gold Eagle and Worldwide Mystery. Mysteries are a reprint program.
Fiction: Paramilitary, law enforcement, action-adventure and near-future fiction.
Recent Fiction Title: *Skydark*, by James Axler.

‡**WUERZ PUBLISHING, LTD.**, 895 McMillan Ave., Winnipeg, Manitoba R3M 0T2 Canada. (204)453-7429. **Acquisitions:** Steve Wuerz. "We publish books on science and native languages." Publishes trade paperback originals and reprints. Publishes 12 titles/year. Receives 25 queries and 12 mss/year. 90% of books from first-time authors; 100% from unagented writers. Pays 10-15% royalty. on wholesale price. Publishes book 1-2 years after acceptance of ms. Reports in 1 month on queries and proposals, 2 months on mss.
Nonfiction: Multimedia, textbook. Subjects include language/literatuare, nature/environment, science. "Do not ask for our marketing plans before we've seen your manuscript." Query or submit outline with 3 sample chapters and proposal package. Reviews artwork/photos as part of ms package. Send photocopies.
Recent Nonfiction Titles: *Environmental Chemistry*, by Ondrus (college textbook); *General Relativity & Cosmology*, by Chow (college text); *Cree-English, English-Cree* (bilingual dictionary).

YORK PRESS LTD., 77 Carlton St., Suite 305, Toronto, Ontario M5B 2J7 Canada. (416)599-6652. Fax: (416)599-2675. **Acquisitions:** Dr. S. Elkhadem, general manager/editor. Estab. 1975. "We publish scholarly books and creative writing of an experimental nature." Publishes trade paperback originals. Publishes 10 titles/year. Receives 50 submissions/year. 10% of books from first-time authors; 100% from unagented writers. Pays 10-20% royalty on wholesale price. Publishes book 6 months after acceptance. Reports in 2 months.
Nonfiction and Fiction: Reference, textbook, scholarly. Especially needs literary criticism, comparative literature and linguistics and fiction of an experimental nature by well-established writers. Query.
Recent Nonfiction Title: *Herman Melville: Romantic & Prophet*, by C.S. Durer (scholarly literary criticism).
Recent Fiction Title: *The Moonhare*, by Kirk Hampton (experimental novel).
Tips: "If I were a writer trying to market a book today, I would spend a considerable amount of time examining the needs of a publisher *before* sending my manuscript to him. The writer must adhere to our style manual and follow our guidelines exactly."

MARKETS THAT WERE listed in the 1997 edition of *Writer's Market* but do not appear this year are listed in the General Index with a notation explaining why they were omitted.

Small Presses

"Small press" is a relative term. Compared to the dozen or so conglomerates, the rest of the book publishing world may seem to be comprised of small presses. A number of the publishers listed in the Book Publishers section consider themselves small presses and cultivate the image. For our purpose of classification, the publishers listed in this section are called small presses because they publish three or fewer books per year.

The publishing opportunities are slightly more limited with the companies listed here than with those in the Book Publishers section. Not only are they publishing fewer books, but small presses are usually not able to market their books as effectively as larger publishers. Their print runs and royalty arrangements are usually smaller. It boils down to money, what a publisher can afford, and in that area, small presses simply can't compete with conglomerates.

However, realistic small press publishers don't try to compete with Bantam or Random House. They realize everything about their efforts operates on a smaller scale. Most small press publishers get into book publishing for the love of it, not solely for the profit. Of course, every publisher, small or large, wants successful books. But small press publishers often measure success in different ways.

Many writers actually prefer to work with small presses. Since small publishing houses are usually based on the publisher's commitment to the subject matter, and since they necessarily work with far fewer authors than the conglomerates, small press authors and their books usually receive more personal attention than the larger publishers can afford to give them. Promotional dollars at the big houses tend to be siphoned toward a few books each season that they have decided are likely to succeed, leaving hundreds of "midlist" books underpromoted, and, more likely than not, destined for failure. Since small presses only commit to a very small number of books every year, they are vitally interested in the promotion and distribution of each title they publish.

Just because they publish three or fewer titles per year does not mean small press editors have the time to look at complete manuscripts. In fact, the editors with smaller staffs often have even less time for submissions. The procedure for contacting a small press with your book idea is exactly the same as it is for a larger publisher. Send a one-page query with SASE first. If the press is interested in your proposal, be ready to send an outline or synopsis, and/or a sample chapter or two. Be patient with their reporting times; small presses can be slower to respond than larger companies. You might consider simultaneous queries, as long as you note them, to compensate for the waiting game.

For more information on small presses, see *Novel & Short Story Writer's Market* and *Poet's Market* (Writer's Digest Books), and *Small Press Review* and *The International Directory of Little Magazines and Small Presses* (Dustbooks).

For a list of publishers according to their subjects of interest, see the nonfiction and fiction sections of the Book Publishers Subject Index. Information on book publishers and producers listed in the previous edition but not included in this edition of *Writer's Market* can be found in the General Index.

‡**aatec publications**, P.O. Box 7119, Ann Arbor MI 48107. Phone/fax: (313)995-1470. E-mail: aatecpub@aol.com. Publisher: Christina Bych. Publishes hardcover and trade paperback originals. Publishes 1-3 titles/year. Receives 20 queries and 10 mss/year. 75% of books from first-time authors; 100% from unagented writers. Pays 15% royalty. Offers no advance. Publishes book 1 year after acceptance of ms. Reports in 1 month. Book catalog free.

Nonfiction: How-to, technical. Subjects include environment, renewable energies. "We publish—and update—the best basic books on the theory and practical use of solar electricity. Future publications should supplement or advance on this in some way." Submit outline with 2-3 sample chapters, including introductory chapter, author biography, marketing prospects. Reviews artwork/photos as part of ms package. Send photocopies. Recent nonfiction title: *The New Solar Electric Home*, by Joel Davidson (how-to).
Tips: "Audience is nontechnical, potential users of renewable energies. Review existing publications (available at many libraries.) Create a book an actual (or potential) renewable energy user would want to read."

ACME PRESS, P.O. Box 1702, Westminster MD 21158-1702. (410)848-7577. Managing Editor: Ms. E.G. Johnston. Estab. 1991. Publishes hardcover and trade paperback originals. Publishes 1-2 titles/year. Pays 50% of profits. Offers small advance. Reports in 2 months on mss.
Fiction: Humor. "We accept submissions on any subject as long as the material is humorous; prefer full-length novels. No cartoons or art (text only). No pornography, poetry, short stories or children's material." Submit outline, first 50-75 pages and SASE. Recent fiction title: *Hearts of Gold*, by James Magorian (comic mystery).
Tips: "We are always looking for the great comic novel."

ADAMS-HALL PUBLISHING, 11661 San Vicente Blvd., Suite 210, Los Angeles CA 90049. (800)888-4452. Editorial Director: Sue Ann Bacon. Publishes hardcover and trade paperback originals and reprints. Publishes 3-4 titles/year. Pays 10% royalty on net receipts to publisher. Advance negotiable. Reports in 1 month on queries. *Writer's Market* recommends allowing 2 months for reply. Accepts simultaneous submissions, if so noted.
Nonfiction: Quality business and personal finance books. Small, successful house that aggressively promotes select titles. Only interested in business or personal finance titles with broad appeal. Query first with proposed book idea, a listing of current, competitive books, author qualifications, how book is unique and the market(s) for book. Then submit outline and 2 sample chapters with SASE. Recent nonfiction title: *Organized To Be The Best! New Timesaving Ways to Simplify and Improve How You Work* (third edition), by Susan Silver.

‡AHSAHTA PRESS, Boise State University, Dept. of English, 1910 University Dr., Boise ID 83725-1525. (208)385-1999. Fax: (208)385-4373. E-mail: rentrusk@idbsu.idbsu.edu. Co-Editor: Tom Trusky. Estab. 1974. Publishes Western American poetry in trade paperback. Reads SASE samplers annually, January-March. Not reading until 1998.

AMERICAN CATHOLIC PRESS, 16565 S. State St., South Holland IL 60473. (312)331-5845. Editorial Director: Rev. Michael Gilligan, Ph.D. Estab. 1967. Publishes hardcover originals and hardcover and paperback reprints. "Most of our sales are by direct mail, although we do work through retail outlets." Publishes 4 titles/year. Pays by outright purchase of $25-100. No advance.
Nonfiction: "We publish books on the Roman Catholic liturgy—for the most part, books on religious music and educational books and pamphlets. We also publish religious songs for church use, including Psalms, as well as choral and instrumental arrangements. We are interested in new music, meant for use in church services. Books, or even pamphlets, on the Roman Catholic Mass are especially welcome. We have no interest in secular topics and are not interested in religious poetry of any kind."

AMIGADGET PUBLISHING COMPANY, P.O. Box 1696, Lexington SC 29071. (803)957-1106. Fax: (803)957-7495. E-mail: jaygross@calweb.com. Website: http://www.calweb.com/~jaygross. Editor-in-chief: Jay Gross. Publishes trade paperback originals. Publishes 2 titles/year. Pays royalty or makes outright purchase. Advance negotiable. Reports in 6 months.
Nonfiction: "Do not send manuscript. Queries only. No books on Windows." Recent title: *How to Start Your Own Underground Newspaper*, by J. Gross (how-to).

ARIADNE PRESS, 4817 Tallahassee Ave., Rockville MD 20853-3144. (301)949-2514. President: Carol Hoover. Estab. 1976. "Our purpose is to promote the publication of emerging fiction writers." Publishes hardcover and trade paperback originals. Publishes 1 book/year. Pays 10% royalty on retail price. No advance. Reports in 1 month on queries, 3 months on mss.
Fiction: Adventure, feminist, historical, humor, literary, mainstream/contemporary. "We look for exciting and believable plots, strong themes, and non-stereotypical characters who develop in fascinating and often unpredictable directions." Query with 1-2 page plot summary, bio and SASE. Recent fiction title: *Steps of the Sun*, by Eva Thaddeus, winner of Ariadne Prize for best first novel, 1997.

‡ARTEMIS CREATIONS PUBLISHING, 3395 Nostrand Ave., 2-J, Brooklyn NY 11229. President: Shirley Oliveira. Imprints are Fem Suprem, Matriarch's Way. Publishes trade paperback originals and reprints. Publishes 3-4 titles/year. Pays 5-10% royalty on retail price or makes outright purchase of $300 minimum (30,000 words). No advance. Publishes book 18 months after acceptance of ms. Accepts simultaneous submissions. Reports in 1 month. Book catalog and ms guidelines for #10 SASE.
Nonfiction: Subjects include women's issues/studies. "Strong feminine archetypes, subjects only. Query or submit outline, 3 sample chapters, author bio and SASE. Reviews artwork/photos as part of the ms package. Send photocopies. Recent nonfiction title: *Gospel of Goddess*, by Bond and Suffield (metaphysical).
Fiction: Erotica, experimental, fantasy, feminist, gothic, horror, mystery, occult, religious, science fiction. Query or

submit synopsis and 3 sample chapters with SASE. Recent fiction title: *Welts*, by Gloria and Dave Wallace (erotica).
Tips: "Our readers are looking for strong, powerful feminie archetypes in fiction and nonfiction."

AUSTEN SHARP, P.O. Box 12, Newport RI 02840. (401)846-9884. President: Eleyne Austen Sharp. Estab. 1996. Children's imprint is Blue Villa. Publishes hardcover and trade paperback originals. Publishes 1-2 titles/year. Pays up to 40% royalty on wholesale price. Reports in 2 months on queries, 3 months on mss.
Nonfiction: Children's picture books, cookbooks, crafts, New Age, regional, seasonal, self-help and travel. "Currently, we have a special interest in New England travel books. Submissions should be well-researched and creative, not your run-of-the-mill history or guidebook. Not interested in family recipe cookbooks." Query only. Recent nonfiction title: *Haunted Newport*, by Eleyne Austen Sharp.
Tips: "Query with a one-page cover letter first. Phone queries are not accepted. If we are interested in seeing the manuscript, we will notify you. Book publishing is extremely competitive, so know the market! What you think is an original idea may be published already."

AUTO BOOK PRESS, P.O. Bin 711, San Marcos CA 92079-0711. (619)744-3582. Editorial Director: William Carroll. Estab. 1955. Publishes hardcover and paperback originals. Publishes 2-4 titles/year. Pays negotiated royalty on wholesale price. Advance varies. Reports in 1 month on queries. *Writer's Market* recommends allowing 2 months for reply.
Nonfiction: Automotive material only: technical or definitive how-to. Query with SASE. Recent nonfiction title: *Two Wheels to Panama*.

‡B. DAZZLE, INC., 500 Meyer Lane, Redondo Beach CA 90278. (310)374-3000. President & CEO: Kathie Gavin. "We publish unique gift books with intrinsic educational, sociological and ecological value." Publishes hardcover and trade paperback originals. Publishes 2 titles/year. Pays 3-5% royalty on wholesale price. Reports in 3 months on queries. Book catalog free.
Nonfiction: Children's/juvenile, gift book, how-to, humor, illustrated book. Query. Recent Nonfiction Title: *Kids On The Go*, by Jennifer Walsh McIntosh (travel activities for children).
Fiction: Adventure, experimental, fantasy, historical, humor, juvenile, picture books, short story collections. Query.
Poetry: Query.
Tips: "Our audience consists of intelligent, cultured, educated persons of all ages sensitive to humanity, nature and beauty. Do not expert immediate evaluation and response."

BALCONY PRESS, 2690 Locksley Place, Los Angeles CA 90039. (213)644-0741. Publisher: Ann Gray. Publishes hardcover and trade paperback originals. Publishes 2-4 titles/year. Pays 10% royalty on wholesale price. No advance. Reports in 1 month on queries and proposals; 3 months on mss. Book information free on request.
Nonfiction: Biography, coffee table books and illustrated books. Subjects include art/architecture, ethnic, gardening, history (relative to design, art and architecture) and regional. "We are interested in the human side of design as opposed to technical or how-to. We like to think our books will be interesting to the general public who might not otherwise select an architecture or design book." Query by telephone or letter. Submit outline and 2 sample chapters with introduction if applicable. Recent nonfiction title: *Vacant Eden*, by Jim Heimann (roadside motels).
Tips: Audience consists of architects, designers and the general public who enjoy those fields. "Our books typically cover California subjects but that is not a restriction. It's always a nice surprise when an author has strong ideas about the audience and how the book can be effectively marketed. We are not afraid of small niches if a good sales plan can be devised."

‡BAYLOR UNIVERSITY PRESS, P.O. Box 97363, Waco TX 76798. (817)755-3164. Acquisitions: Janet L. Burton. Imprint is Markham Press Fund. Publishes hardcover and trade paperback originals. Publishes 2 titles/year. Pays 10% royalty on wholesale price. Publishes book 6 months after acceptance of ms. Reports in 2 months on proposals. Book catalog free.
Nonfiction: Scholarly. Subjects include anthropology/archaeology, history, regional, religion, women's issues/studies. Submit outline and 1-3 sample chapters.
Tips: Audience is scholarly.

BLISS PUBLISHING CO., P.O. Box 920, Marlborough MA 01752. (508)779-2827. Publisher: Stephen H. Clouter. Publishes hardcover and trade paperback originals. Publishes 2-4 titles/year. Pays 10-15% royalty on wholesale price. No advance. Reports in 2 months.
Nonfiction: Biography, illustrated book, reference, textbook. Subjects include government/politics, history, music/dance, nature/environment, recreation, regional. Submit proposal package, including outline, table of contents, 3 sample chapters, brief author biography, table of contents, SASE. Recent nonfiction title: *Ninnuock, The Algonkian People of New England*, by Steven F. Johnson.

BLUE SKY MARKETING, INC., P.O. Box 21583, St. Paul MN 55121. (612)456-5602. President: Vic Spadaccini. Publishes hardcover and trade paperback originals. Publishes 3 titles/year. Pays royalty on wholesale price. Reports in 3 months. Manuscript guidelines for 6×9 SAE with 4 first-class stamps.
Nonfiction: Gift book, how-to. Subjects include gardening, hobbies, regional, travel, house and home. Submit proposal package, including outline, 1 sample chapter, author bio, intended market, analysis comparison to competing books with

SASE. Recent nonfiction title: *Twin Cities Family Fun Spots*, by Lisa Sabroski (regional).
• Blue Sky no longer accepts fiction.
Tips: "Our books are primarily 'giftbooks,' and are sold primarily to women in specialty stores and gift shops as well as bookstores."

BRETT BOOKS, INC., P.O. Box 290-637, Brooklyn NY 11229-0637. Publisher: Barbara J. Brett. Estab. 1993. Publishes hardcover originals. Publishes 2 titles/year. Pays 5-15% royalty on retail price. Offers advance beginning at $1,000. Reports in 2 months on queries.
Nonfiction: General interest nonfiction books on timely subjects. "We are looking for general-interest inspirational nonfiction. Minimum length is 40,000 words; maximum is 50,000. Query with SASE. Recent nonfiction title: *Friendships in the Dark: A Blind Woman's Story of the People and Pets Who Light Up Her World*, by Phyllis Campbell (inspirational).
Tips: "Send a query letter of no more than two pages in which you briefly state your professional background and summarize your book or book proposal in two to four paragraphs. Queries without SASE aren't answered or returned."

‡BRIDGE LEARNING SYSTEMS, INC., 351 Los Altos Place, American Canyon CA 94589. (510)228-3177. Publisher: Alfred J. Garrotto. Publishes trade paperback originals. Publishes 1-3 titles/year. Receives 5-10 queries and 1 mss/year. 5% of books from first-time authors; 100% from unagented writers. Pays 15% royalty on publisher's selling price. Offers no advance. Publishes book 6 months after acceptance of ms. Accepts simultaneous submissions. Reports in 1 month. Book catalog and ms guidelines free.
Nonfiction: How-to, technical. Subjects include computers and electronics (tutorials), religion, software. "We are looking for keystroke-by-keystroke tutorials of software and hardware products." Query. Reviews artwork/photos as part of ms package. Send photocopies. Recent nonfiction titles: *Jump Start*, by James Potter and Alfred Garrotto (tutorial).
Tips: Audience ranges from middle schools to university and vocational schools.

‡BRIDGE STREET BOOKS, Imprint of Transnational Publishers, Inc., One Bridge St., Irvington-on-Hudson NY 10533. Fax: (914)591-2688. E-mail: lawbooks@village.ios.com. Vice President: Heike Fenton. Publishes hardcover and trade paperback originals. Publishes 3-4 titles/year. Receives 10-20 queries/year. 85% of books from first-time authors; 85% from unagented writers. Pays 5-15% royalty on retail price. Offers no advance. Publishes book 10 months after acceptance of ms. Accepts simultaneous submissions. Reports in 1 month. Book catalog and ms guidelines free.
Nonfiction: How-to, reference, self-help, textbook. Subjects include government/politics, law, current affairs. "Writers should adhere to their topic area." Query or submit proposal package, including table of contents, introduction, sample chapter. Recent nonfiction title: *Swift and Sure*, by Judge William Cornelius (law).

BRIGHT MOUNTAIN BOOKS, INC., 138 Springside Rd., Asheville NC 28803. (704)684-8840. Editor: Cynthia F. Bright. Imprint is Historical Images. Publishes trade paperback originals and reprints. Publishes 3 titles/year. Pays 5-10% royalty on retail price. No advance. Reports in 1 month on queries; 3 months on mss.. *Writer's Market* recommends allowing 2 months for reply.
Nonfiction: "Our current emphasis is on regional titles set in the Southern Appalachians and Carolinas, which can include nonfiction by local writers." Query with SASE. Recent nonfiction title: *Mountain Fever*, by Tom Alexander (regional autobiography).

CADMUS EDITIONS, P.O. Box 126, Tiburon CA 94920. Director: Jeffrey Miller. Publishes hardcover and trade paperback originals. Publishes 3-4 titles/year. Pays negotiated royalty. No advance. Reports in 1 month. *Writer's Market* recommends allowing 2 months for reply.
Fiction: Literary fiction. "We publish only 3-4 titles per year and are thus seeking only truly distinguished work." Query with SASE. Recent fiction title: *The Pelcari Project*, by R. Rey Rusa (novel about Guatemalan abuse of human rights).
Poetry: Query with SASE. Recent poetry title: *Wandering into the Wind*, by Sāntoka, translated by Cid Corman (Haiku poetry of last wandering itinerant monk in Japan).
Tips: "Do not submit unless work is truly distinguished and will fit well in our short but carefully selected and produced title list."

CALYX BOOKS, P.O. Box B, Corvallis OR 97339-0539. (541)753-9384. Also publishes *Calyx, A Journal of Art & Literature by Women*. Managing Editor: Margarita Donnelly. Estab. 1986 for Calyx Books; 1976 for Calyx, Inc. Publishes fine literature by women, fiction, nonfiction and poetry. Publishes 3 titles/year. Pays 10% royalty on net price. Offers $200-$500 advance. Reports in 6 months on queries.
Nonfiction: Query with outline, 3 sample chapters and SASE. Recent nonfiction title: *Natalie on the Street*, by Ann Nietzke (story of author's friendship with elderly homeless woman living in her neighborhood).
Fiction: Query with SASE, Recent nonfiction title: *Into the Forest*, by Jean Hegland.
Poetry: "We only publish 1 poetry book a year." Query with SASE. Recent poetry title: *The Country of Women*, by Sandra Kohler.
Tips: "Please be familiar with our publications."

CAROLINA WREN PRESS, 120 Morris St., Durham NC 27701. (919)560-2738. "We publish poetry, fiction, nonfiction, biography, autobiography, literary nonfiction work by and/or about people of color, women, gay/lesbian issues." *Not currently accepting mss.*

CAROUSEL PRESS, P.O. Box 6061, Albany CA 94706-0061. (510)527-5849. Editor and Publisher: Carole T. Meyers. Estab. 1976. Publishes trade paperback originals and reprints. Publishes 1-2 titles/year. Pays 10-15% royalty on wholesale price. Offers $1,000 advance. Reports in 1 month on queries. *Writer's Market* recommends allowing 2 months for reply.
Nonfiction: Family-oriented travel and other travel books. Query with outline, 1 sample chapter and SASE. Recent nonfiction title: *The Zoo Book: A Guide to America's Best*, by A. Nyhius (guide).

CASSANDRA PRESS, P.O. Box 868, San Rafael CA 94915. (415)382-8507. President: Gurudas. Estab. 1985. Publishes trade paperback originals. Publishes 3 titles/year. Receives 200 submissions/year. 50% of books from first-time authors; 50% from unagented writers. Pays 6-8% maximum royalty on retail price. Advance rarely offered. Publishes book 1 year after acceptance. Accepts simultaneous submissions. Reports in 3 weeks on queries, 3 months on mss. Book catalog and ms guidelines free.
  • Cassandra Press has reduced their number of books published from 6 to 3 titles/year.
Nonfiction: New Age, how-to, self-help. Subjects include cooking/foods/nutrition, health/medicine (holistic health), philosophy, psychology, religion (New Age), metaphysical, political tyranny. "We like to do around 3 titles a year in the general New Age, metaphysical and holistic health fields so we continue to look for good material. No children's books or novels." Submit outline and sample chapters. Reviews artwork/photos as part of ms package. Recent nonfiction title: *Treason the New World Order*, by Gurudas (political).
Tips: "Not accepting fiction or children's book submissions."

CENTER FOR AFRICAN-AMERICAN STUDIES PUBLICATIONS, University of California at Los Angeles, 160 Haines Hall, 405 Hilgard Ave., Los Angeles CA 90095-1545. (310)206-6340. Managing Editor: Toyomi Igus. Publishes hardcover and trade paperback originals. "All manuscripts should be scholarly works about the African-American experience. Authors should be able to demonstrate a thorough knowledge of the subject matter. Not interested in autobiographies, poetry or fiction." Recent title: *Residential Apartheid: The American Legacy*, edited by Robert Bullard, J. Eugene Grigsby III and Charles Lee.

CLARITY PRESS INC., 3277 Roswell Rd. NE, #469, Atlanta GA 30305. (404)231-0649. Fax: (404)231-3899. E-mail: clarity@islandnet.com. Website: http://www.bookmasters.com/clarity. Editorial committee contact: Annette Gordon. Estab. 1984. Publishes mss on minorities, human rights in US, Middle East and Africa. No fiction. Responds *only* if interested, so do *not* enclose SASE.
Nonfiction: Human rights/minority issues. Query. Recent nonfiction title: *American Indians: Myths & Realities*, by Devon A. Mihesuah (trade/university level text).
Tips: "Check our titles on website."

CLEVELAND STATE UNIVERSITY POETRY CENTER, R.T. 1813, Cleveland State University, Cleveland OH 44115-2440. (216)687-3986. Fax: (216)687-6943. E-mail: poetrycenter@popmail.csuohio.edu. Editors: Leonard M. Trawick and Ted Lardner. Estab. 1962. Publishes trade paperback and hardcover originals. Publishes 4 titles/year. Receives 500 queries and 1,000 mss/year. 60% of books from first-time authors; 100% from unagented writers. 30% of titles subsidized by CSU, 20% by government subsidy. CSU Poetry Series pays one-time, lump-sum royalty of $200-400, plus 50 copies; Cleveland Poetry Series (Ohio poets only) pays 100 copies. $1,000 prize for best ms each year. No advance. Publishes book within 18 months of acceptance. Accepts simultaneous submissions. Reports in 1 month on queries, 8 months on mss. Book catalog for 6×9 SAE with 2 first-class stamps. Manuscript guidelines for SASE. Manuscripts are not returned.
Poetry: No light verse, inspirational, or greeting card verse. ("This does not mean that we do not consider poetry with humor or philosophical/religious import.") Query; ask for guidelines. Submit only December-February. $15 reading fee. Reviews artwork/photos if applicable (e.g., concrete poetry). Recent poetry title: *The Work of the Bow*, by Robert Hill Long.
Tips: "Our books are for serious readers of poetry, i.e. poets, critics, academics, students, people who read *Poetry, Field, American Poetry Review*, etc. Trends include movement away from 'confessional' poetry; greater attention to form and craftsmanship. Project an interesting, coherent personality; link poems so as to make coherent unity, not just a miscellaneous collection. Especially need poems with *mystery*, i.e., poems that suggest much, but do not tell all."

CORKSCREW PRESS, INC., 2300 W. Victory Blvd., Suite C-313, Burbank CA 91506. Editorial Director: J. Croker Norge. Estab. 1988. Reports in 6 months.
Nonfiction: Publishes trade humor and humorous how-to books.

‡DA CAPO PRESS, Plenum Publishing, 233 Spring St., New York NY 10013. Fax: (212)647-1898. **Acquisitions:** Yuval Taylor, senior editor (music, film, art); Michael Dorr, editor (history). Da Capo Press specializes in reissuing hard-to-find nonfiction books in inexpensive quality paperback format. Publishes trade paperback reprints. Publishes 60 titles/year. Pays 6% royalty on wholesale price. Offers $1,500-2,000 advance. Publishes book 6 months after acceptance of ms. Accepts simultaneous submissions. Reports in 3 months on queries. Book catalog free.

• Da Capo Press wishes to emphasize that it publishes only one or two paperback originals per year; the rest are reprints.

Nonfiction: Biography, history. Subjects include art/architecture, gay/lesbian, government/politics, military/war, music/ dance, psychology, science, sports. Query. Recent nonfiction title(s): *The Gershwin Years*, by Edward Jablonski and Lawrence D. Stewart (music); *Remembering Buddy*, by John Goldrasen and John Beeches (music).

‡**DAWBERT PRESS, INC.**, Box 2758, Duxbury MA 023331. (617)934-7202. Publishes mass market paperback originals. Publishes 3 titles/year. Pays 5-10% royalty on retail price. Publishes book 6 months after acceptance of ms. Accepts simultaneous submissions.

Nonfiction: Reference. Subjects include recreation, travel. "We only publish travel and recreation books." Submit outline. Reviews artwork/photos as part of ms package. Send photocopies. Recent nonfiction title: *On the Road Again with Man's Best Friend*, by Habgood (travel).

‡**DEPTH CHARGE**, P.O. Box 7037, Evanston IL 60201. (847)864-6258. Editor: Eckhard Gerdes. Publishes trade paperback originals. Publishes 2-4 titles/year. Pays 10% royalty on retail price. Book catalog for 9×12 SAE with 2 first-class stamps. Manuscript guidelines for #10 SASE.

Fiction: Experimental, literary fiction. "Familiarize yourselves with our publications and be aware that we publish 'subterficial' fiction. Be aware of what subterficial is." Recent fiction title: *Openings*, by Richard Kostelanetz (experimental fiction/interfaced with poetry).

Poetry: "The only poetry we publish is that which meets subterficial fiction at their interface area." Submit ms.

DICKENS PRESS, P.O. Box 4289, Irvine CA 92616. (714)725-0788. Editorial Director: Diane Dennis. Publishes hardcover and trade paperback originals. Publishes 2-3 titles/year. Pays 12-16% royalty on wholesale price or offers work-for-hire. Offers up to $7,500 advance. Reports in 1 week on queries and proposals; 1 month on mss. Manuscript guidelines free on request.

Nonfiction: Coffee table book, gift book, how-to, reference and self-help. Subjects include child guidance/parenting, education, government/politics, history and psychology. Query. Submit proposal package, including: outline, sample chapters, author bio, market analysis and SASE. Recent nonfiction title: *Ambush at Ruby Ridge*, by Alan Bock.

Fiction: Mainstream/contemporary, suspense. Query with one-page synopsis. All unsolicited mss returned unopened.

Tips: "Audience consists of people who want to have more control over their lives by being better informed."

DOWN THE SHORE PUBLISHING CORP., Imprint of Cormorant Books & Calendars, P.O. Box 3100, Harvey Cedars NJ 08008. Publisher: Raymond G. Fisk. Publishes hardcover originals and trade paperback originals and reprints. "As a small regional publisher, we must limit our efforts and resources to our established market: New Jersey shore and mid-Atlantic. We specialize in regional histories and pictorial, coffee table books." Query with synopsis.

EARTH-LOVE PUBLISHING HOUSE LTD., 3440 Youngfield St., Suite 353, Wheat Ridge CO 80033. (303)233-9660. Fax: (303)233-9354. Director: Laodeciae Augustine. Publishes trade paperback originals. Publishes 1-2 books/ year. Pays 6-10% royalty on wholesale price. Reports in 1 month on queries and proposals, 3 months on mss.

Nonfiction: Metaphysics and minerals. Query with SASE. Recent nonfiction title: *Love Is In The Earth—Kaleidoscope Pictorial Supplement*, by Melody (metaphysical reference).

EASTERN PRESS, P.O. Box 881, Bloomington IN 47402-0881. Publisher: Don Lee. Estab. 1981. Publishes hardcover originals and reprints. Publishes 3 titles/year. Pays by arrangement with author. No advance. Reports in 3 months.

Nonfiction: Academic books on Asian subjects and pedagogy on languages. Query with outline and SASE. Recent nonfiction title: *Autohaiku*, by Don Y. Lee (6×9 hardcover).

ECOPRESS, 1029 NE Kirsten Place, Corvallis OR 97330. (541)758-7545. Editor-in-Chief: Christopher Beatty. Publishes hardcover originals, trade paperback originals and reprints. Publishes 2-4 titles/year. Pays 6-15% royalty on publisher's receipts. Offers $0-5,000 advance. Reports in 1 month on queries and proposals, 3 months on mss. Manuscript guidelines for #10 SASE.

Nonfiction: How-to, multimedia (CD or electronic). Subjects include agriculture/horticulture, animals, education, gardening, nature/environment, recreation (outdoor, hiking), science, sports (outdoor, fishing). "The work must have some aspect that enhances environmental awareness. Do a competitive analysis and create a marketing plan for your book or proposal." Submit proposal package, including outline, 3 sample chapters and how the author would participate in marketing the work. Recent nonfiction title: *Two Wheels Around New Zealand*, by S. Bischke.

Fiction: Mainstream/contemporary. "There must be some aspect of the work that deals with nature or the environment." Query with synopsis. Recent fiction title: *Sapo*, by R. Beatty (novel).

Tips: Audience is "nature-oriented people and those who could be after reading our books!" Nonfiction: 1) Pick an issue you care about; 2) Make a proposal; 3) Do research; 4) Write and submit a manuscript.

‡**EMERALD WAVE**, Box 969, Fayetteville AR 72702. Contact: Joya Pope. Publishes trade paperback originals. Publishes 1-3 titles/year. Pays 7-10% royalty. No advance. Reports in 1 month on queries, 3 months on mss.

Nonfiction: Spiritual/metaphysical New Age. Subjects include health, environment, philosophy, psychology. "We publish thoughtful New Age books which relate to everyday life and/or the environment on this planet with enlightened attitudes. Nothing poorly written, tedious to read or too 'out there.' It's got to have style too." Submit outline and 3 sample chapters with SASE. Reviews artwork/photos as part of ms package. Send photocopies. Recent nonfiction title: *Spirit at Work*, by Lois Grant (angels/healing).

EMIS, INC., (formerly Essential Medical Information Systems, Inc.), P.O. Box 1607, Durant OK 74702. Vice President-Operations: Mark Gibson. Publishes trade paperback originals. Publishes 2 titles/year. Pays 12-25% royalty on retail price. Reports in 1 month. Book catalog and manuscript guidelines free on request.
Nonfiction: Reference. Subjects include health/medicine and psychology. Query. Recent nonfiction title: *Managing Contraceptive Pill Patients*, by Richard P. Dickey, M.D. (medical reference).
Tips: Audience is medical professionals and medical product manufacturers and distributors.

EVRAS PRESS, 1402 Tilman, Richmond TX 77469. Managing Editor: Tony Sakkis. Publishes trade and mass market paperback originals. Publishes 1-3 titles/year. Pays 10-25% royalty on wholesale price. Offers $1,000-10,000 advance. Reports in 1 month. Query with SASE.
Nonfiction: Reference, technical. Subjects include ethnic, sports, translation, travel. "We are looking for work that can fill out our universal guide series as well as automotive- and motorsports-related works. No 'personal awakening' travel or related writing. Concrete reference guides only." Query with SASE. Recent nonfiction title: *Encyclopedia of Drag Racing*, by Phillpson.

FALLEN LEAF PRESS, P.O. Box 10034, Berkeley CA 94709-5034. Phone/fax: (510)848-7805. E-mail: abasart@ix.ne tcom.com. Owner: Ann Basart. Estab. 1984. Publishes hardcover and trade paperback originals. Publishes reference books on music, books on contemporary composers, and scores of contemporary American chamber music. "We publish three series: Fallen Leaf Reference Books in Music; Fallen Leaf Monographs in Contemporary Composers; and a series of musical scores, Fallen Leaf Publications in Contemporary Music." Publishes 1-3 books/year. Pays 3.75-15% royalty on wholesale price. Offers $250-500 advance. Reports in 3 months.
Nonfiction: "Reference books are scholarly, aimed at music librarians and/or performers; authors/compilers should be experienced bibliographers, if possible. Monographs on 20th-century composers are aimed at general music-loving audiences, not for specialists." Submit proposal package, including outline, sample entries (for reference books) or outline and sample chapter for books on composers. Recent nonfiction title: *Collected Editions*, by Hill and Stephens.

THE FAMILY ALBUM, Rt. 1, Box 42, Glen Rock PA 17327. (717)235-2134. Fax: (717)235-8765. E-mail: ronbiblio@ delphi.com. Contact: Ron Lieberman. Estab. 1969. Publishes hardcover originals and reprints and software. Publishes 2 titles/year. Average print order for a first book is 1,000. Pays royalty on wholesale price. "Significant works in the field of (nonfiction) bibliography. Worthy submissions in the field of Pennsylvania history, folk art and lore. We are also seeking materials relating to books, literacy, and national development. Special emphasis on Third World countries, and the role of printing in international development." No religious material or personal memoirs. Submit outline and sample chapters.

FIESTA CITY PUBLISHERS, ASCAP, P.O. Box 5861, Santa Barbara CA 93150. (805)681-9199. President: Frank E. Cooke. Publishes hardcover and mass market paperback originals. Publishes 2-3 titles/year. Pays 5-20% royalty on wholesale price. No advance. Reports in 1 month on queries, 3 months on proposals. Book catalog and ms guidelines for #10 SASE.
Nonfiction: Children's/juvenile, cookbook, how-to, humor nonfiction and musical plays. "Prefers material appealing to young readers, especially related to music: composing, performing, etc." Query with outline and SASE. Recent nonfiction title: *Anything I Can Play, You Can Play Better* (self-teaching guitar method).
Fiction: Musical plays only. "Must be original, commercially viable, preferably short, with eye-catching titles." Query with SASE. Recent fiction title: *Carrie*, by Frank Cooke (musical based on life of Carry A. Nation).
Tips: "Looking for material which would appeal to young adolescents in the modern society. Prefer little or no violence with positive messages. Carefully-constructed musical plays always welcome for consideration."

FLOWER VALLEY PRESS, INC., 7851-C Beechcraft Ave., Gaithersburg MD 20879. (301)990-6405. Editor: Seymour Bress. Publishes hardcover and trade paperback originals. Publishes 3-5 titles/year. Pays 5.83-10% royalty on retail price. Offers $1,000 advance. Reports in 2 months on queries and proposals, 3 months on mss. Book catalog for #10 SASE.
Nonfiction: Coffee table book, how-to nonfiction. Subjects include art, crafts and jewelry made with Polymer clay. "We look particularly for new and unique work of high quality (all of our recent books have been completely illustrated in color) and where the market for the book is relatively easy to identify and reach. "For how-to books, make certain that directions are clear and complete so reader can actually finish a project by simply following them. If diagrams are necessary for clarity, they must be provided." Query. Reviews artwork/photos as part of ms package. Send transparencies. Recent nonfiction title: *The New Clay*, by Nan Roche (how-to).
Fiction: "We have no specific plans for fiction and have only accepted two fiction titles so far. The subject we are most likely to accept is one that would most appeal to a specific audience and one which can easily be reached." Submit synopsis with query letter.
Tips: "We look for niche markets. The author should be able to tell us the kinds of people who would be interested in the book and how we can reach them."

FRONT ROW EXPERIENCE, 540 Discovery Bay Blvd., Byron CA 94514-9454. Phone/fax: (510)634-5710. Contact: Frank Alexander. Estab. 1974. Imprint is Kokono. Publishes trade paperback originals and reprints. Publishes 1-2 titles/year. Pays 10% royalty on income received. No advance. Reports in 1 month. *Writer's Market* recommends allowing 2 months for reply.
Nonfiction: Teacher/educator edition paperback originals. Only wants submissions for "Movement Education," special education and related areas. Will accept submissions for parenting type books only from those people who are active in the field and can promote it through their activities. Query with SASE. Recent nonfiction title: *Joy of Sports: Star Program*, by Andrew Oser (lesson plans).

GAFF PRESS, P.O. Box 1024, Astoria OR 97103-3051. (503)325-8288. E-mail: gaffpres@pacifier.com. Publisher: Paul Barrett. Publishes hardcover and trade paperback originals, poetry chapbooks. Publishes 1-2 titles/year. Payment varies with individual. Reports in 2 months.
Nonfiction: "Particularly interested in extraordinary ocean tales for next (third) book of sea stories and wondrous irresistible poems." Query with sample chapter and SASE. Recent nonfiction title: *Crow: A Wild Creature*, by Barrett.
Poetry: "I want to see only the absolute best the poet can offer." Submit 10 sample poems or complete ms with SASE. Recent poetry title: *The Bearheart Chronicles*, by L.B. Doran-Maurer.

GAMBLING TIMES INCORPORATED, 16140 Valerio St., Suite B, Van Nuys CA 91406-2916. (818)781-9355. Fax: (818)781-3125. Publisher: Stanley R. Suudikoff. Publishes hardcover and trade paperback originals. Publishes 2-4 titles/year. Pays royalty. No advance. Reports in 2 months on queries, 3 months on proposals, 6 months on mss.
Nonfiction: How-to and reference books on gambling. Submit proposal package, including ms and SASE. *Writer's Market* recommends sending a query with SASE first. Recent nonfiction title: *Book of Tells*, by Caro (poker).

GOOD BOOK PUBLISHING COMPANY, P.O. Box 959, Kihei HI 96753-0959. Phone/fax: (808)874-4876. Publisher: Richard G. Burns. Publishes trade paperback originals and reprints. Publishes 3 titles/year. Pay 10% royalty. No advance. Reports in 1 month. *Writer's Market* recommends allowing 2 months for reply.
Nonfiction: Spiritual roots of Alcoholics Anonymous. Query with SASE. Recent nonfiction title: *Turning Point*, by Dick B. (history of AA's early spiritual roots).

HEMINGWAY WESTERN STUDIES SERIES, Boise State University, 1910 University Dr., Boise ID 83725. (208)385-1999. Fax: (208)385-4373. E-mail: rentrusk@idbsu.idbsu.edu. Editor: Tom Trusky. Publishes multiple edition artist's books which deal with Rocky Mountain political, social and environmental issues. Write for author's guidelines and catalog.

HERBAL STUDIES LIBRARY, 219 Carl St., San Francisco CA 94117. (415)564-6785. Fax: (415)564-6799. Owner: J. Rose. Publishes trade paperback originals. Publishes 3 titles/year. Pays 5-10% royalty on retail price. Offers $500 advance. Reports in 1 month on mss with SASE. *Writer's Market* recommends allowing 2 months for reply.
Nonfiction: How-to, reference, self-help. Subjects include gardening, health/medicine, herbs and aromatherapy. No New Age. Query with sample chapter and SASE. Recent nonfiction title: *Guide to Essential Oils*, by Jeanne Rose (scientific information about essential oils).

HI-TIME PUBLISHING CORP., 12040-L W. Feerick St., Milwaukee WI 53222-2136. (414)466-2420. Senior Editor: Lorraine M. Kukulski. Publishes 3 titles/year. Payment method may be outright purchase, royalty or down payment plus royalty. Book catalog and ms guidelines free on request.
Nonfiction: "We publish religious education material for Catholic junior high through adult programs. Most of our material is contracted in advance and written by persons with theology or religious education backgrounds. Query with SASE. Recent nonfiction title: *Pray To Love, Love To Pray/Prayers, Reflections, and Life Stories of 14 Great Pray-ers*, by Carol Graser; (biographical sketches/prayer selections).

W.D. HOARD & SONS CO., Imprint of Hoard's Dairyman, 28 Milwaukee Ave. W., Fort Atkinson WI 53538-0801. Editor: Elvira Kau. Estab. 1870. Publishes trade paperback originals. Publishes 3-4 titles/year. Pays 8-15% royalty on wholesale or retail price. No advance. Reports in 2½ weeks on queries and mss. *Writer's Market* recommends allowing 2 months for reply.
Nonfiction: "We primarily are a dairy publishing company, but we have had success with a veterinarian who authored two James Herriott-type humor books for us, and we would consider regional (Wisconsin) titles as well. We also have published and would like to see submissions for agricultural science texts." Query with SASE. Recent nonfiction title: *Dairy Cattle Fertility & Sterility*, by Hafs/Boyd (text).

THE HOFFMAN PRESS, P.O. Box 2996, Santa Rosa CA 95405. Publisher: R.P. Hoffman. Publishes mass market paperback originals. Publishes 2-4 titles/year. Pays 5-10% royalty on wholesale price. No advance. Publishes book 2 years after acceptance of ms. Reports in 2 months.
Nonfiction: "We publish cookbooks only." Query with 3 sample chapters and SASE. Reviews artwork/photos as part of ms package. Send photocopies. Recent nonfiction title: *The California Wine Country Herbs & Spices Cookbook*.

I.A.A.S. PUBLISHERS, 7676 New Hampshire Ave., Suite 306, Langley Park MD 20783. (301)499-6308. Acquisition Editor: A.G. Felix. I.A.A.S. specializes in classroom texts. Publishes hardcover, trade paperback and mass market paperback originals. Pays 10% royalty on wholesale price. Reports in 1 month on queries, 2 months on proposals, 4 months on mss. Manuscript guidelines free on request.

Nonfiction: Biography, children's/juvenile, how-to, illustrated book, textbook, Afro-America. Subjects include business and economics, child guidance/parenting, education, government/politics, health/medicine, history, military/war, money/ finance, philosophy, psychology, sociology, Afro-American/African issues. Request "Guidelines for Authors" in advance of submission. Submit proposal package. Recent nonfiction title: *Cultural and Demographic Aspects of Health Care in Contemporary Sub-Saharan Africa*, edited by Ezekiel Kalipeni and Philip Thiuri.

IN PRINT PUBLISHING, 6770 W. State Route 89A, 346, Sedona AZ 86336-9758. (520)282-4589. Fax: (520)282-4631. Publisher/Editor: Tomi Keitlen. Estab. 1991. Publishes trade paperback originals. Publishes 3-5 titles/year. Pays 6-8% royalty on retail price. Offers $250-500 advance. Reports in 2 months on queries and proposals, 3 months on mss.

Nonfiction: "We are interested in books that will leave a reader with hope. We are also interested in books that are metaphysical, books that give ideas and help for small business management and books that have impact in all general subjects. No violence, sex or poetry." Query with SASE. Recent nonfiction title: *Sacred History & Earth Prophecies*, by Dinalva (metaphysical/philosophy/current affairs).

Tips: "We are interested in books about Angels. We are also interested in short books that will be part of a Living Wisdom Series℠. These books must be no more than 18,000-20,000 words. We are not interested in any books that are over 300 pages—and are more likely interested in 75,000 words or less."

INDIANA HISTORICAL SOCIETY, 315 W. Ohio St., Indianapolis IN 46202-3299. (317)232-1882. Fax: (317)233-3109. Director of Publications: Thomas A. Mason. Estab. 1830. Publishes hardcover originals. Publishes 3 titles/year. Pays 6% royalty on retail price. Reports in 1 month on queries. *Writer's Market* recommends allowing 2 months for reply.

Nonfiction: "We seek book-length manuscripts that are solidly researched and engagingly written on topics related to the history of Indiana." Query with SASE. Recent nonfiction title: *Sherman Minton: New Deal Senator, Cold War Justice*, by Linda C. Gugin and James E. St. Clair.

INTERTEXT, 2633 E. 17th Ave., Anchorage AK 99508-3207. Editor: Sharon Ann Jaeger. Estab. 1982. Publishes trade paperback originals. Publishes 1-2 titles/year. Pays 10% after costs are met. No advance. Reports in 6 months on queries.

Nonfiction: "Only *solicited* nonfiction will be published, usually translations of essays by noted international authors or literary criticism or theory. (No immediate plans as we have a backlog of other titles.)" Query with SASE. "No response without it in most cases."

Poetry: "We look for poetry that is rich in imagery, is skillfully crafted, is powerful and compelling and avails itself of the varied resonance and melody of the language. Cannot use religious verse. We expect book manuscripts to run 48-96 pages. (Please do *not* send an entire manuscript unless we specifically ask to see it.)" Submit 3-5 sample poems by first-class mail with SASE. Recent poetry title: *Tibetan Tanka*, by Kyi May Kaung (poetry).

Tips: "Intertext is extremely selective; thus beginners should submit elsewhere. We regret that we cannot offer critiques of rejected work. Queries and samples lacking SASE cannot be returned. Poets we admire include William Stafford, Gary Snyder, W.S. Merwin, Sarah Kirsch, António Ramos Rosa, Rainer Maria Rilke, Louis Hammer, Tomas Tranströmer and Bob Perelman. We are moving toward electronic (and inventory-free) publishing."

IVY LEAGUE PRESS, INC., P.O. Box 3326, San Ramon CA 94583-8326. 1-(800)IVY-PRESS or (510)736-0601. Fax: (510)736-0602. E-mail: ivyleaguepress@worldnet.att.net. Editor: Maria Thomas. Publishes hardcover, trade paperback and mass market paperback originals. Reports in 3 months.

Nonfiction: Subjects include health/medicine, Judaica and self-help nonfiction. Query with SASE. Recent nonfiction title: *Jewish Divorce Ethics*, by Bulka.

Fiction: Medical suspense. Query with SASE. Recent fiction title: *Allergy Shots*, by Litman.

• Ivy League is focusing more on medical thrillers, although it still welcomes Judaica and other submissions.

‡JAMENAIR LTD., P.O. Box 241957, Los Angeles CA 90024-9757. (310)470-6688. Publisher: P.K. Studner. Estab. 1986. Publishes originals and reprints on business and economics, computers and electronics, education and career-advancement/job search.

JELMAR PUBLISHING CO., INC., P.O. Box 488, Plainview NY 11803. (516)822-6861. President: Joel J. Shulman. Publishes hardcover and trade paperback originals. Publishes 2-5 titles/year. Pays 25% royalty after initial production and promotion expenses of first printing. Reports in 1 week. *Writer's Market* recommends allowing 2 months for reply.

Nonfiction: How-to and technical subjects on the packaging, package printing and printing fields. "The writer must be a specialist and recognized expert in the field." Query with SASE. Recent nonfiction title: *Graphic Design for Corrugated Packaging*, by Donald G. McCaughey Jr. (graphic design).

JOHNSTON ASSOCIATES, INTERNATIONAL (JASI), P.O. Box 313, Medina WA 98039. (206)454-3490. Publisher: Ann Schuessler. Publishes trade paperback originals. Publishes 3-5 titles/year. Pays 10-15% royalty on wholesale price. Offers $500-1,500 advance. Reports in 1 month. *Writer's Market* recommends allowing 2 months for reply. Book catalog and ms guidelines for #10 SASE.

Nonfiction: Recreation, regional (any region), travel and other nonfiction. Query with proposal package, including outline, sample chapter, target market, competition, reason why the book is different and SASE. Recent nonfiction title: *Brewpub Explorer of the Pacific Northwest*, by Dodd, Latterell, MacCormack and Zucker (regional guidebook).
Tips: "We are interested in books that fit unique niches or look at a topic in a unique way."

KALI PRESS, P.O. Box 2169, Pagosa Springs CO 81147. (970)264-5200. E-mail: kalipres@rmi.net. Contact: Cynthia Olsen. Publishes trade paperback originals. Publishes 5 titles/year. Pays 8-12% royalty on retail price. No advance. Reports in 1 month on queries, 6 weeks on proposals, 2 months on mss.
Nonfiction: Children's/juvenile, natural health and spiritual nonfiction. Subjects include education (on natural health issues). Children's books with a lesson and natural health (international topics also). Query with 2 sample chapters and SASE. Reviews artwork/photos as part of ms package. Send photocopies. Recent nonfiction title: *Essiac: A Native Herbal Cancer Remedy*, by Cynthia Olsen (health/medicine).

LAHONTAN IMAGES, 210 S. Pine St., Susanville CA 96130. (916)257-6747. Fax: (916)251-4801. Owner: Tim I. Purdy. Estab. 1986. Publishes hardcover and trade paperback originals. Publishes 2 titles/year. Pays 10-15% royalty on wholesale or retail price. No advance. Reports in 2 months.
Nonfiction: Publishes nonfiction books pertaining to northeastern California and western Nevada. Query with outline and SASE. Recent nonfiction title: *Maggie Greeno*, by George McDow Jr. (biography).

LANDMINE BOOKS, P.O. Box 250702, Glendale CA 91225-0702. (213)860-9897. Editor: Jack Russell. Publishes trade paperback originals. Publishes 1-3 titles/year. Pays 5-7% royalty on retail price. Reports in 1 month on queries, 3 months on proposals and mss.
  • Landmine Books is no longer considering nonfiction.
Fiction: Adventure, gothic, horror, literary, mainstream/contemporary, mystery, science fiction, suspense. Query only with SASE. All unsolicited mss returned unopened. Recent fiction title: *Stripmall Bohemia*, by Jethro Paris (crime).

LAWCO LTD., P.O. Box 2009, Manteca CA 95336-1209. (209)239-6006. Imprints are Money Tree and Que House. Senior Editor: Bill Thompson. Publishes 3-6 titles/year. Pays 3-12% royalty on wholesale price or makes outright purchase of $500 minimum. No advance. Reports in 1 month on queries, 4 months on mss.
Nonfiction: Books on billiards industry. "We are looking for business books targeting the small business. We will also consider sports-related books." Query with SASE. Recent nonfiction title: *The Pool Player's Road Atlas*, by J.R. Lucas (sports).
Tips: "Know the market, what the sales potential is, why the book is needed, who will buy it and why."

LIBRARY OF VIRGINIA, 800 E. Broad St., Richmond VA 23219. (804)692-3999. Director of Publications: John Kneebone. **Acquisitions**: Gregg D. Kimball, assistant director. "We publish only in the field of Virginia history and culture." Publishes hardcover and trade paperback originals and hardcover reprints. Publishes 3 titles/year. Payment varies. Reports in 1 month on queries and proposals, 3 months on mss. Book catalog and ms guidelines free on request.
Nonfiction: Biography, illustrated book, reference and monographs (documentary editions). Subjects include history and regional (Virginia). Query. Recent nonfiction title: *The Fire of Liberty in Their Hearts: The Diary of Jacob E. Yoder of the Freedmen's Bureau School, Lynchburg, Virginia, 1866-1870*, edited by Samuel L. Horst (documentary edition).
Tips: Audience is the general public interested in Virginia, Southern and U.S. history, especially scholars and researchers.

LINCOLN SPRINGS PRESS, P.O. Box 269, Franklin Lakes NJ 07417. Contact: M. Gabrielle. Estab. 1987.
Nonfiction: Americana, ethnic, government/politics, history, language/literature, military/war, sociology, women's issues/studies. *Writer's Market* recommends sending a query with SASE first.
Fiction: Ethnic, feminist, gothic, historical, literary, mainstream/contemporary, mystery, romance, short story collections. *Writer's Market* recommends sending a query with SASE first.

‡LINTEL, 24 Blake Lane, Middletown NY 10940. (212)674-4901. Editorial Director: Walter James Miller. Estab. 1978. Publishes experimental fiction, art poetry and selected nonfiction.

LOLLIPOP POWER BOOKS, 120 Morris St., Durham NC 27701. (919)560-2738. Editor: Ruth A. Smullin. Children's imprint of Carolina Wren Press. Publishes trade paperback originals.
Fiction: "Current publishing pointers are 1) books with African-American, Latino or native American charcacters 2) bilingual books (English/Spanish) 3) books that show gay men or lesbian women as ordinary people who can raise children." *Not currently accepting mss.*

LORIEN HOUSE, P.O. Box 1112, Black Mountain NC 28711-1112. (704)669-6211. Owner/Editor: David A. Wilson. Estab. 1969. Publishes nonfiction. Subjects include Americana, history, nature/environment, philosophy, science. "Most of our problems concern photographs where the writer uses copyrighted photos in work (from magazines) and thinks it is proper to do so."

McBOOKS PRESS, 908 Steam Mill Rd., Ithaca NY 14850. (607)272-2114. Website: http://www.mcbooks.com. Editorial Director: Ms. S.K. List. Publisher: Alexander G. Skutt. "We are a growing publishing house interested in any

nonfiction of substance." Publishes trade paperback and hardcover originals and reprints. Pays 5-10% royalty on retail price. Offers $1,000-5,000 advance.
Nonfiction: Subjects include child guidance/parenting, cooking, regional, sports. "Of particular interest: sports, vegetarianism, parenting, regional books about New York State, reference, popular trends. Authors' ability to promote a plus." Query or submit outline and 2 sample chapters with SASE. Reports in 2 months. Recent nonfiction title: *The Ice Bowl*, by Ed Gruver (football).

MADWOMAN PRESS, P.O. Box 690, Northboro MA 01532-0690. (508)393-3447. E-mail: 76620.460@compuserve.com. Editor/Publisher: Diane Benison. Publishes trade paperback originals. Estab. 1991. Publishes 1-2 titles/year. Pays 15% royalty on revenues collected after production costs are recovered. No advance. Reports in 2 months on queries, 4 months on mss.
Nonfiction: Lesbian nonfiction. Query with outline and SASE. Recent nonfiction title: *Lesbians in the Military Speak Out*, by Winni S. Webber.
Fiction: Lesbian fiction. Primarily interested in mysteries. Query with synopsis (which must include an explanation of how the novel ends) and SASE. Recent fiction title: *The Grass Widow*, by Nanci Little (historical novel).
Tips: "We hold ourselves out as a press that publishes *only* works by lesbian women. Please don't query if you don't meet the qualification. We make no exceptions to that policy."
• Madwoman Press is looking for more mystery novels.

‡MAGICKAL CHILDE INC., 35 W. 19th St., New York NY 10011. (212)242-7182. Publishes nonfiction books on occult.

‡MANAGEMENT TECHNOLOGY INSTITUTE, 2919 E. Military Trail, Suite 155, West Palm Beach FL 33409. (561)791-1200. **Acquisitions:** Margaret E. Haase, editor. Publishes 2 titles/year. 100% of books from first-time authors; 100% from unagented writers. Pays 7½-25% royalty on wholesale price. No advance. Publishes book 18 months after acceptance of ms. Accepts simultaneous submissions. Reports in 6 months on mss.
Nonfiction: How-to, self-help, textbook. Subjects include business, education, psychology, women's issues/studies. Submit outline and 1 sample chapter with SASE. Reviews artwork/photos as part of ms package. Send photocopies.
Recent Nonfiction Title(s): *Throw Away the Textbook (T.A.T.T.)*, by Jordan (management); *Don't Buy the Lie (D.B.L.)*, by Jordan (management).
Poetry: Submit 3 sample poems.
Tips: Audience is college and university business students, business executives and managers, employees, supervisors, and lower management.

MANGAJIN, INC., P.O. Box 77188, Atlanta GA 30357-1188. Publisher: V.P. Simmons. Publishes mass market paperback originals and reprints. Publishes 2-3 titles/year. Pays 5-15% royalty on wholesale price. Reports in 2 months on queries.
Nonfiction: Reference, textbook. Subjects include business and economics, government/politics, language/literature, religion, sociology, translation, travel. Mangajin publishes books about Japanese language and culture. Query. Recent nonfiction title: *Mr. Benihana: The Rocky Aoki Story* (business/biography).
Tips: Audience is "people interested in Japanese language and culture."

‡MARADIA PRESS, 228 Evening Star Dr., Naugatuck CT 06770-3548. (203)723-0758. Vice President: Peter A. Ciullo. Estab. 1990. Interested in well-researched works dealing with the effect of technology on American culture, any era from Colonial times to the present.

‡MEGA MEDIA PRESS, 3838 Raymert Dr., #203, Las Vegas NV 89121. (702)433-5388. President: Lillian S. Payn. Publishes trade paperback originals. Publishes 3 titles/year. Pay varies.
Nonfiction: Subjects include business and economics, software. Query. Recent nonfiction title: *Consultant's Advanced Instruction Book*, Ray Payn (business).

MEYERBOOKS, PUBLISHER, P.O. Box 427, Glenwood IL 60425-0427. (708)757-4950. Publisher: David Meyer. Estab. 1976. Imprint is David Meyer Magic Books. Publishes hardcover and trade paperback originals and reprints. Publishes 5 titles/year. Pays 10-15% royalty on wholesale or retail price. No advance. Reports in 3 months on queries.
Nonfiction: History, reference and self-help works published on subjects of Americana, health and herbal studies, history of stage magic. Query with SASE. Recent nonfiction title: *Stage Flying: 431 B.C. to Modern Times*, by McKinven (theatrical history).

MIDDLE PASSAGE PRESS INC., 5517 Secrest Dr., Los Angeles CA 90043. (213)298-0266. Publisher: Barbara Bramwell. Estab. 1992. Publishes trade and mass market paperback and hardcover originals. Publishes 1 title/year. Pays 3-10% royalty on wholesale price. Offers $500-1,500 advance. Reports in 2 months.
Nonfiction: "The emphasis is on contemporary issues that deal directly with the African-American Experience. No fiction, no poetry." Query with SASE. Recent nonfiction title: *Beyond O.J.: Race, Sex & Class Lessons for America*, by Earl Ofari Hutchinson, Ph.D.
Tips: "Don't include scripts in place of manuscripts. I prefer query with 2 written chapters as opposed to a proposal.

I want to see how someone writes.''

MOSAIC PRESS MINIATURE BOOKS, 358 Oliver Rd., Cincinnati OH 45215-2615. (513)761-5977. Publisher: Miriam Irwin. Estab. 1977. Publishes 1 nonfiction book/year. "Subjects range widely. Please query.''

MOUNTAIN AUTOMATION CORPORATION, P.O. Box 6020, Woodland Park CO 80866-6020. (719)687-6647. President: Claude Wiatrowski. Estab. 1976. Publishes trade paperback originals. Publishes 1 title/year. Pays 10% royalty on wholesale price. No advance. Reports in 1 month. *Writer's Market* recommends allowing 2 months for reply.
Nonfiction: Illustrated souvenir books and videos for specific tourist attractions. Query with SASE. Recent nonfiction title: *German Village*, by Jean Conte (illustrated souvenir paperback).
Tips: "We are emphasizing videos more and books less.''

MOUNTAIN HOUSE PRESS, Box 353, Philo CA 95466. (707)895-3241. Publisher: J.D. Colfax. Estab. 1988. Publishes trade paperback originals and reprints. Publishes 3-5 titles/year. Pays 15% royalty on wholesale price. No advance. Reports in 1 month. *Writer's Market* recommends allowing 2 months for reply.
Nonfiction: Publishes books on education, politics, folklore and alternative agriculture. Query with 1 sample chapter and SASE. Recent nonfiction title: *Boontling*, by C. Adams (paperback, folklore/linguistics).

NEW ENGLAND CARTOGRAPHICS, INC., P.O. Box 9369, North Amherst MA 01059. (413)549-4124. Fax: (413)549-3621. President: Christopher Ryan. Publishes trade paperback originals and reprints. Publishes 3-5 titles/year. Pays 5-15% royalty on retail price. No advance. Reports in 1 month. *Writer's Market* recommends allowing 2 months for reply.
Nonfiction: Outdoor recreation nonfiction subjects include nature/environment, recreation, regional. "We are interested in specific "where to" in the area of outdoor recreation guidebooks of the northeast US. Topics of interest are hiking/backpacking, skiing, canoeing etc. Query with outline, sample chapters and SASE. Reviews artwork/photos as part of ms package. Send photocopies. Recent nonfiction title: *Skiing the Pioneer Valley*, by Ryan, Scofield and Prajing (outdoor recreation).

NEW YORK NICHE PRESS, 175 Fifth Ave., Suite 2646, New York NY 10010. (718)779-1754. Publisher: Michael Danowski. Publishes trade paperback originals and newsletters. Publishes 2 titles/year. Receives 4 queries/year. 50% of books from first-time authors; 100% from unagented writers. Accepts simultaneous submissions.
Nonfiction: Regional, travel. Subjects include New York City recreation and travel. "Timely information should be balanced with useful material that will not date the work. Should be street-smart in style." Submit outline with 1 sample chapter. Reviews artwork/photos as part of ms package. Send photocopies. Recent nonfiction title: *Dim Sum: How About Some? A Guide to NYC's Liveliest Chinese Dining & How To Make A Day of It*, by Wanda Chin and Michael P. Danowski (New York restaurant/travel guide).
Tips: "Our readers are New York residents and enthusiastic visitors to NYC. We use material with the 'New York attitude.' We are considering children's fiction about and for New York.''

NICOLAS-HAYS, Box 612, York Beach ME 03910. (207)363-4393. Publisher: B. Lundsted. Publishes hardcover originals and trade paperback originals and reprints. Publishes 2-4 titles/year. Pays 15% royalty on wholesale price. Offers $200-500 advance. Reports in 2 months on mss.
Nonfiction: Publishes self-help; nonfiction. Subjects include philosophy (oriental), psychology (Jungian), religion (alternative), women's issues/studies. Query with 3 sample chapters and SASE. Recent nonfiction title: *Relationships: Transforming Archetypes*, by Dr. Narina Valcarenghi, translated from Italian (Jungian psychology).
Tips: "We only publish books that are the lifework of authors—our editorial plans change based on what the author writes.''

OBERLIN COLLEGE PRESS, Rice Hall, Oberlin College, Oberlin OH 44074. (216)775-8407. Editors: Stuart Friebert, David Young, Alberta Turner, David Walker. Imprints are Field Magazine: Contemporary Poetry & Poetics, Field Translation Series, Field Poetry Series. Publishes hardcover and trade paperback originals. Publishes 2-3 titles/year. Pays 7½-10% royalty on retail price. Offers $500 advance. Reports in 1 month on queries and proposals, 2 months on mss.
Poetry: Query with SASE. Recent poetry title; *By Common Salt*, by Killarney Clary.
Tips: "Make it look fresh, as if we were first in the universe to lay eyes on it!''

C. OLSON & CO., P.O. Box 100-WM, Santa Cruz CA 95063-0100. (408)458-9004. E-mail: clayolson@aol.com. Owner: C. Olson. Estab. 1981. Publishes trade paperback originals. Publishes 1-2 titles/year. Royalty negotiable. Reports in 2 months on queries.
Nonfiction: "We are looking for nonfiction manuscripts or books that can be sold at natural food stores and small independent bookstores on health and on how to live a life which improves the earth's environment." Query first with SASE. Recent nonfiction title: *World Health, Carbon Dioxide & The Weather*, by J. Recklaw (ecology).

OMEGA PUBLICATIONS, 256 Darrow Rd., New Lebanon NY 12125-9801. (518)794-8181. Fax: (518)794-8187. E-mail: omegapub@wisdomschild.com. Contact: Abi'l-Khayr. Estab. 1977. Publishes hardcover and trade paperback

originals and reprints. Publishes 2-3 titles/year. Pays 6-12% royalty on wholesale price. Offers $500-1,000 advance. Reports in 3 months on mss.
Nonfiction: "We are interested in any material related to Sufism, and only that." Query with 2 sample chapters. Recent nonfiction title: *Creating the Person*, by Khan (spirituality).

PACIFIC VIEW PRESS, P.O. Box 2657, Berkeley CA 94702. (510)849-4213. President: Pam Zumwalt. Publishes hardcover and trade paperback originals. Publishes 3 titles/year. Pays 5-10% royalty on wholesale price. Offers $500-2,000 advance. Reports in 2 months. Book catalog free on request.
Nonfiction: Subjects include Asia-related business and economics, Asian current affairs, Chinese medicine, nonfiction Asian-American multicultural children's books. "We are only interested in Pacific Rim related issues." Query with proposal package, including outline, 1 sample chapter, author background, audience info and SASE. Recent nonfiction title: *Tibet: Abode of the Gods, Pearl of the Motherland*, by Barbara Erickson (reportage)

PAIDEIA PRESS, P.O. Box 121303, Arlington TX 76012. (817)294-8215. E-mail: pdpress@resourcegp.org. Website: http://www.resourcegp.org. Managing Editor: N.R. VanBoskirk. Publishes trade paperback originals. Publishes 3 titles/year. 80% of books from first-time authors; 100% from unagented writers. Pays 5-15% royalty on retail price or makes outright purchase of $500. No advance. Publishes book 8 months after acceptance of ms. Accepts simultaneous submissions. Reports in 1 month on queries and proposals, 2 months on mss. Manuscript guidelines for #10 SASE.
Nonfiction: Theory and practice, multimedia (CD-ROM, software), textbook. Subjects include education and supplementary texts for education market (grades 5-college), women's issues/studies. "We are currently interested in education works relating to math, reading comprehension, and social ecology." Query with SASE. Reviews artwork/photos as part of ms package. Send photocopies. Recent nonfiction title: *Discovering the Essay*, by F. Andrew Wolf, Jr. (education/developmental writing).
Tips: Audience is education/school market; retail and specialty store (e.g., teacher supply); library. "We are primarily interested in education hearing from writers regarding math and social ecology texts."

PARROT PRESS, 42307 Osgood Rd., Unit N, Fremont CA 94539. (510)659-1030. Editor: Jennifer Warshaw. Publishes 3 titles/year. Pays 10-15% royalty on gross sales (wholesale, retail price).
Nonfiction: How-to, reference, self-help. Pet birds only. "We publish nonfiction books written for pet bird owners. We are most interested in well-researched books on pet bird husbandry, health care, diet and species profiles. Good, clear, accessible writing is a requirement." Submit outline and 1-3 sample chapters with SASE.

PARTNERS IN PUBLISHING, P.O. Box 50374, Tulsa OK 74150-0374. Phone/fax: (918)835-8258. Editor: P.M. Fielding. Estab. 1976. Publishes trade paperback originals. Publishes 1-2 titles/year. Pays royalty on wholesale price. No advance. Reports in 2 months on queries.
Nonfiction: "Understand that we are only interested in older teen and young adults with learning disabilities." Biography, how-to, reference, self-help, technical and textbooks on learning disabilities, special education for youth and young adults. Query with SASE. Recent nonfiction title: *Enhancing Self-Esteem for Exceptional Learners*, by John R. Moss and Elizabeth Ragsdale (for parents and teachers who deal with exceptional youth and young adults).
• This press reports being deluged with submissions having nothing to do with learning disabilities.

‡PEEL PRODUCTIONS, INC., P.O. Box 546, Columbus NC 28722. Managing Editor: S. DuBosque. Estab. 1985. Publishes hardcover and trade paperback originals. Publishes 3-5 titles/year. Publishes how-to draw and picture books. Looking for how-to-draw books. Pays royalty on wholesale price. Offers $300-500 advance. Query first with outline/synopsis, sample chapters and SASE. Reports in 1 month. *Writer's Market* recommends allowing 2 months for reply.
Nonfiction: Recent nonfiction title: *Draw Desert Animals*, by Doug DuBosque.

‡PENDAYA PUBLICATIONS, INC., 510 Woodvine Ave., Metairie LA 70005. (504)834-8151. Manager: Earl J. Mathes. Estab. 1986. Publishes hardcover originals. Publishes 1-2 titles/year. Pays 4-8% royalty on retail price (varies). Offers $500-3,000 advance.
Nonfiction: Coffee table book, illustrated book. Subjects include anthropology/archaeology, art/architecture, photography, travel, design. Submit proposal package. Send sample transparencies.

‡PIONEER INSTITUTE, 85 Devonshire St., 8th Floor, Boston MA 02109. (617)723-2277. Research Director: Gabriela Mead. Publishes trade paperback originals. Publishes 2-3 titles/year. Makes outright purchase or provides foundation grant. No advance. Reports in 1 month. *Writer's Market* recommends allowing 2 months for reply. Book catalog free.
Nonfiction: Scholarly nonfiction. Subjects include business and economics, education, government/politics, health/medicine, sociology. "Pioneer Institute will generally make overtures to a chosen author. Queries and author introductions are preferred. Unsolicited manuscripts will probably not be read by our staff." Query.
Tips: Audience is public policy makers in Massachusetts and nationally college professors and students.

POGO PRESS, INCORPORATED, 4 Cardinal Lane, St. Paul MN 55127-6406. E-mail: pogopres@minn.net. Vice President: Leo J. Harris. Publishes trade paperback originals. Publishes 3 titles/year. Receives 20 queries and 20 mss/year. 100% of books from unagented writers. Pays royalty on wholesale price. Publishes book 6 months after acceptance. Reports in 2 months. Book catalog free on request.

Nonfiction: "We limit our publishing to Breweriana, history, art and popular culture. Our books are heavily illustrated." Query. Reviews artwork/photos as part of ms package. Send photocopies. Recent nonfiction title: *Songs of Life—The Meaning of Country Music*, by Jennifer Lawler.

THE POST-APOLLO PRESS, 35 Marie St., Sausalito CA 94965. Publisher: Simone Fattal. Editorial Assistant: Margaret Butterfield. Publishes trade paperback originals and reprints. Publishes 2-3 titles/year. Pays 5-7% royalty on wholesale price. No advance. Reports in 3 months. Book catalog and ms guidelines for #10 SASE.
Nonfiction: Essay, letters. Subjects include art/architecture, language/literature, translation, women's issues/studies. Query. Recent nonfiction title: *Rumi & Sufism*, Eva de Vitray-Meyerovitch (religion/philosophy).
Fiction: Ethnic, experimental, feminist, gay/lesbian, humor, literary, plays. Submit 1 sample chapter and SASE. Recent fiction title: *A Beggar At Damascus Gate*, by Yasmine Zahran (novel).
Poetry: Experimental/translations. Submit 1-5 sample poems and SASE. Recent poetry title: *A Descriptive Method*, by Claude Royet-Journoud (experimental/contemporary).
Tips: "We are interested in writers with a fresh and original vision. We often publish women who are well-known in their country, but new to the American reader."

‡POT SHARD PRESS, P.O. Box 215, Comptche CA 95427. (707)937-2058. **Acquisitions:** M.L. Harrison Mackie, publisher. Publishes hardcover originals and reprints, trade paperback originals and reprints. Publishes 2 titles/year. 50% of books from first-time authors; 100% from unagented writers. Pays negotiable royalty. No advance. Publishes book 6 months after acceptance of ms.
Nonfiction: Women's issues/studies. Query.
Poetry: Query.
Recent Poetry Title(s): *Calabash*, by Johanna M. Bedford, Jane Harris Austin, Mary Bradish O'Connor, M.L. Harrison Mackie (free verse/sonnets).

PRAKKEN PUBLICATIONS, INC., P.O. Box 8623, Ann Arbor MI 48107-8623. (313)769-1211. Fax: (313)769-8383. Publisher: George Kennedy. **Acquisitions:** Dudley Barlow, media reviewer. Estab. 1934. Publishes educational hardcover and paperback originals as well as educational magazines. Publishes 2 book titles/year. Receives 50 submissions/year. 20% of books from first-time authors; 95% from unagented writers. Pays 10% royalty on net sales (negotiable, with production costs). Publishes book 1 year after acceptance. Accepts simultaneous submissions. Reports in 2 months if reply requested and SASE furnished. Book catalog for #10 SASE.
Nonfiction: Industrial, vocational and technology education and related areas; general educational reference. "We are interested in manuscripts with broad appeal in any of the specific subject areas of industrial arts, vocational-technical education, and reference for the general education field." Submit outline and sample chapters. Reviews artwork/photos as part of ms package.
Recent Nonfiction Title(s): *The Winning Ways: Best Practices in Work-Based Learning*, by Albert J. Pantles Jr. and Deborah Buffananti.
Tips: "We have a continuing interest in magazine and book manuscripts which reflect emerging issues and trends in education, especially vocational, industrial and technological education."

PRIMER PUBLISHERS, 5738 N. Central Ave., Phoenix AZ 85012. (602)234-1574. Publishes trade paperback originals. Publishes 4-5 titles/year. Pays royalty. No advance. Reports in 1 month on queries. *Writer's Market* recommends allowing 2 months for reply.
Nonfiction: Mostly regional subjects; travel, outdoor recreation, history, etc. "We target Southwestern US parks, museum gift shops. We want to know how your book will sell in these retailers." Query first.

PUCKERBRUSH PRESS, 76 Main St., Orono ME 04473-1430. (207)581-3832 or 866-4808. Publisher/Editor: Constance Hunting. Estab. 1971. Publishes trade paperback originals and reprints of literary fiction and poetry. Publishes 3-4 titles/year. Pays 10-15% royalty on wholesale price or makes outright purchase. Reports in 2 months.
Nonfiction: Belles lettres, translations. Query with SASE. Recent nonfiction title: *Reminiscences of Tolstoi*, by Gorky (translation).
Fiction: Literary and short story collections. Recent fiction title: *An Old Pub Near the Angel*, by J. Relman (short stories of Glasgow).
Poetry: Highest literary quality. Submit complete ms with SASE. Recent poetry title: *The Movie Queen*, by F. Blair (poems on art and film).

‡RACE POINT PRESS, P.O. Box 770, Provincetown MA 02657. Vice President: Roselyn Callahan. Publishes trade paperback originals. Publishes 2 titles/year. Pays 7-12% royalty on wholesale price or makes outright purchase. Reports in 2 months on proposals.
Nonfiction: How-to, reference, self-help, technical. Subjects include art/architecture, health/medicine, aging. "Our focus is on books for the senior market which highlight available programs or practical advice on accessing needed services." Query or submit outline or proposal package, including 2 sample chapters and probable completion date; author biography. All unsolicited mss returned unopened. Recent nonfiction title: *The Medicare Answer Book* by Connacht Cash (technical).

RED EYE PRESS, INC., P.O. Box 65751, Los Angeles CA 90065. Vice President: L.P. Kallan. Publishes trade paperback originals. Publishes 2 titles/year. Pays 8-12% royalty on retail price. Offers $1-2,000 advance. Reports in 1 month on queries and proposals, 2 months on mss.
Nonfiction: How-to, gardening, reference books. Query with outline, 2 sample chapters and SASE. Recent nonfiction title: *Hashish!*, by Robert C. Clarke.

REDBRICK PRESS, P.O. Box 1895, Sonoma CA 95476-1895. (707)996-2774. E-mail: jeredbrick@aol.com. Publisher: Jack Erickson. Estab. 1987. "RedBrick Press currently is publishing only books on microbreweries and specialty beers."
Nonfiction: "We are not currently accepting queries on topics other than on craft brewing."

‡REVOLUTIONARY PRESS PUBLISHING, 546 SW 1st St., Suite 402, Miami FL 33130. (305)545-5474. COO: Douglas Labrozzi. Publishes mass market paperback originals. Publishes 3 titles/year. 95% of books from first-time authors. Pays 2-8% royalty on retail price. Offers no advance. Publishes book 5 months after acceptance of ms. Reports in 2 months on queries, 6 months on proposals, 8 months on mss. Manuscript guidelines for #10 SASE.
Nonfiction: Cookbook, gift book, how-to, humor, self-help, college studies. Subjects include education, language/literature, philosophy, psychology. "Beware of a lack of structure." Query. Reviews artwork/photos as part of ms package. Send photocopies. Recent nonfiction title: *The College Power Course*, by Blake Robinson (college studies).

SCOTTWALL ASSOCIATES, 95 Scott St., San Francisco CA 94117. (415)861-1956. Contact: James Heig. Publishes hardcover and trade paperback originals. Publishes 2-3 titles/year. Pays 6-10% royalty on retail price. No advance. Reports in 1 month on queries and proposals, 2 months on mss. Book catalog and ms guidelines free on request.
Nonfiction: Biography, illustrated book. Subjects include art/architecture, California history/biography. Submit 1-2 sample chapters and SASE. Reviews artwork/photos as part of the ms package. Send photocopies.

‡SOUND VIEW PRESS, 170 Boston Post Rd., Madison CT 06443. President: Peter Hastings Falk. Estab. 1985. Publishes hardcover and trade paperback originals, dictionaries, exhibition records, and price guides exclusively to fine art. All titles are related.

‡SPECTACLE LANE PRESS INC., P.O. Box 1237, Mt. Pleasant SC 29465-1237. Phone/fax: (803)851-1502. Editor: James A. Skardon. Publishes nonfiction hardcover and trade paperback originals. Publishes 2-4 titles/year. Pays 7-10% royalty on wholesale price. Offers $500-1,000 advance. Reports in 1 month. *Writer's Market* recommends allowing 2 months for reply. Will do occasional title on subjects of import and strong current interest, but concentration is on sports and family-related humor books. "Query first. Then send outline and 3 chapters with SASE if we are interested." Recent nonfiction title: *Sorry, No Turkeys This Year*, by Brian Eden (business management).

STA-KRIS, INC., 107 N. Center, Marshalltown IA 50158. (515)753-4139. President: Kathy Wagoner. Publishes hardcover and trade paperback originals. Publishes 4 titles/year. Pays negotiated royalty on wholesale price or makes outright purchase. Advance negotiable. Publishes book 1 year after acceptance. Accepts simultaneous submissions. Reports in 2 months on queries and proposals, 4 months on mss. Book catalog free.
Nonfiction: Coffee table book, gift book, illustrated book, self-help. "We publish nonfiction gift books that portray universal feelings, truths and values or have a special occasion theme, plus small format compilations of statements about professions, issues, attitudes, etc." Query with proposal package including synopsis, bio, published credits. Recent nonfiction title: *She Taught Me to Eat Artichokes*, by Mary Kay Shanley (illustrated gift book).
Tips: "Our audience tends to be women ages 20 and older. We are an independent publisher who supports the marketing of their books with great energy and knowledge."

STEEL BALLS PRESS, P.O. Box 1532, Kona HI 96745. Owner: R. Don Steele. "We publish only controversial nonfiction." Publishes hardcover and trade paperback originals. Publishes 2-3 titles/year. Pays 10% royalty on retail price after break-even. No advance. Reports in 1 month on queries. *Writer's Market* recommends allowing 2 months for reply. Book catalog for #10 SASE.
Nonfiction: How-to, self-help. Subjects include business and economics, money/finance, psychology, sociology, women's issues/studies. No humor, homeless, incest/molestation. Query (1 page) only with SASE. Recent nonfiction title: *Body Language: A Guide During Courtship & Dating*, by John J. White (self-help, men and women).
Tips: "Write a persuasive one-page query letter. Explain who will buy and why."

STORM PEAK PRESS, 157 Yesler Way, Suite 413, Seattle WA 98104. (206)223-0162. Publishes trade paperback originals and reprints. Publishes 3 books/year. Pays royalty on retail price or net revenues. Reports in 2 months.
Nonfiction: Memoirs. Subjects include Americana, health/medicine, history, travel. "We only consider high-quality, unique manuscripts." Query with SASE. Recent nonfiction title: *Catch A Falling Star*, by Betty Baker Spohr (autobiography).
Fiction: Juvenile adventure. Recent fiction title: *The Ballad of Big Ben's Boots & Other Tales for Telling*, by John Dashney.
Tips: "Get editorial help before sending a manuscript. Be confident the material is well-written."

STORMLINE PRESS, P.O. Box 593, Urbana IL 61801. Publisher: Raymond Bial. Estab. 1985. Publishes hardcover and trade paperback originals. Publishes 1-2 titles/year. Pays 10% royalty on retail price or "sometimes authors take a percentage of the print run in lieu of royalties." Reports in 1 month on queries, 3 months on mss. "Publishes fiction and nonfiction, generally with a Midwest connection. The Press considers queries (with SASE only) during November and December. We do not consider unsolicited manuscripts."

Nonfiction: Needs photography and regional works of the highest literary quality, especially those having to do with rural and small town themes. Stormline prefers works which are rooted in a specific place and time, such as *When the Waters Recede: Rescue and Recovery During the Great Flood*, by Dan Guillory. Query with SASE.

Fiction: "We only publish books with rural, midwestern themes and very little fiction." Query with SASE. Recent fiction title: *Silent Friends*, by Margaret Lacey (short story collection).

Poetry: "We publish very little poetry." Query with SASE. Recent poetry title: *The Alligatory Inventions*, by Dan Guillory.

STUDENT COLLEGE AID PUBLISHING DIVISION, 7950 N. Stadium Dr. #229, Houston TX 77030. Fax: (713)796-9963. Owner: Edward Rosenwasser. Publishes trade paperback originals. Publishes 2 titles/year. Pays 10-12½% royalty on wholesale price. Reports in 1 month on queries. *Writer's Market* recommends allowing 2 months for reply. "We publish books about college financial aid and careers. Any book that is informative and interesting will be considered."

Nonfiction: Query with SASE. Recent nonfiction title: *How To Achieve Quality of Life in a Nursing Home*, by Elizabeth Yeh.

STUDIO 4 PRODUCTIONS, P.O. Box 280400, Northridge CA 91328. (818)700-2522. Editor-in-Chief: Charlie Matthews. Publishes trade paperback originals. Publishes 2-5 titles/year. Pays 10% royalty on retail price. Offers $500-1,000 advance. Reports in 2 weeks on queries, 1 month on proposals and mss. *Writer's Market* recommends allowing 2 months for reply.

Nonfiction: Subjects include character education (values, ethics and morals), child guidance, parenting, self-help. "Writers should be familiar with the Character Education movement. We are taking the 'big picture,' publishing books which encourage participation by schools. We are not interested in curriculum materials." Query with SASE. Recent nonfiction title: *The Case for Character Education*, by Brooks & Goble (education).

THE SUGAR HILL PRESS, 216 Stoddard Rd., Hancock NH 03449-5102. Publisher: L. Bickford. Estab. 1990. Publishes trade paperback originals. Publishes 1 title/year. Pays 15-20% royalty on publisher's revenues. No advance. Reports in 2 months on proposals.

Nonfiction: "We publish technical manuals for users of school administrative software *only*. (These are supplemental materials, not the manuals which come in the box.) A successful writer will combine technical expertise with crystal-clear prose." Query with outline and 2 sample chapters. Recent nonfiction title: *A Report Cards Handbook*, by Geoffrey Hirsch (technical manual).

THE SYSTEMSWARE CORPORATION, 973C Russell Ave., Gaithersburg MD 20879. (301)948-4890. Fax: (301)926-4243. Editor: Pat White. Estab. 1987.

Nonfiction: "We specialize in innovative books and periodicals on Knowledge Engineering or Applied Artificial Intelligence and Knowledge Based Systems. We also develop intelligent procurement-related software packages for large procurement systems." *Writer's Market* recommends sending a query with SASE first.

TAMARACK BOOKS, INC., P.O. Box 190313, Boise ID 83719-0313. (800)962-6657. (208)387-2656. Fax: (208)387-2650. President/Owner: Kathy Gaudry. Publishes trade paperback originals and reprints. Publishes 4-5 titles/ year. Pays 10-15% royalty. Reports in 4 months on queries.

Nonfiction: History, travel, cookbooks and illustrated books on West for people living in or interested in the American West. "We are looking for manuscripts for popular audience, but based on solid research. Can be travel, history, cookbook, but based in West." Query with outline and SASE. Recent nonfiction title: *Eyewitness to American History*, by James Crutchfield (history).

Tips: "We look for authors who want to actively participate in the marketing of their books."

‡**TAMBRA PUBLISHING**, P.O. Box 4611, Las Vegas NV 89127-0611. E-mail: experts1@aol.com. Editor: Tambra Campbell. Publisher: Kate Stevens. Estab. 1985. Publishes how-to books on handwriting analysis; also accepts well-written screenplays and manuscripts with good storylines with some action that can be adapted into screenplays, as well as being published. Will consider works on psychology and on family relations, love stories. Include large SASE for return of ms or sp. *Writer's Market* recommends sending a query with SASE first. Reports in 4 months.

TECHNICAL BOOKS FOR THE LAYPERSON, INC., P.O. Box 391, Lake Grove NY 11755. (540)877-1477. Contact: Mary Lewis. Publishes trade paperback originals. Publishes 3 titles/year. Pays 10-40% royalty on actual earnings. No advance. Reports in 2 months on mss. Book catalog and ms guidelines free. *Absolutely no phone calls.*

Nonfiction: How-to, reference, self-help, technical, textbook. "Our primary goal is consumer-friendliness ('Books by consumers for consumers'). All topics are considered. There is a preference for completed work which equips an ordinary consumer to deal with a specialized or technical area." Submit 1 sample chapter. Recent nonfiction title: *Common Blood Tests*, by Gifford (medical reference).

Tips: "Our audience is the consumer who needs very explicit information to aid in making good purchasing decisions."

Format chapter for camera-ready copy, with text enclosed in 4½×7 area (including headers and footers).

THUNDER DOG PRESS, 1624 Williams Hwy., #33, Grants Pass OR 97527. (541)471-0658. Publisher: Kathleen Doyle. Publishes trade paperback originals. Publishes 3 titles/year. Pays 8-10% royalty on wholesale price. Reports in 3 months on queries and proposals. Ms guidelines for #10 SASE.
• Thunder Dog Press is no longer seeking fiction.
Nonfiction: How-to. Subjects include agriculture/horticulture, animals, gardening, nature/environment, women's is-sues/studies. "We welcome all queries on cutting edge environmental and social issues." Query with writing sample and SASE. Recent nonfiction title: *Give Me Shelter: An Action Guide for Abused Women*, by Kathleen Doyle (6×9 trade paperback).
Tips: "Research and prove that your proposed book is different from all similar books."

TIA CHUCHA PRESS, A Project of The Guild Complex, P.O. Box 476969, Chicago IL 60647. (773)252-5321. Fax: (773)252-5388. Director: Luis Rodriguez. Publishes trade paperback originals. Publishes 2-4 titles/year. Receives 25-30 queries and 150 mss/year. Pays 10% royalty on wholesale price. Reports in 1 month on queries and proposals, 9 months on mss. Publishes book 1 year after acceptance. Book catalog and ms guidelines free on request.
Poetry: "No restrictions as to style or content. We do cross-cultural, performance-oriented poetry. It has to work on the page, however." Submit complete ms with SASE. Recent poetry title: *Body of Life*, by Elizabeth Alexander.
Tips: Audience is "those interested in strong, multicultural, urban poetry—the best of bar-cafe poetry. Annual manuscript deadline is June 30. Send your best work. No fillers. We read in the summer; we decide in the fall what books to publish for the following year."

‡THE UNIVERSITY OF OKLAHOMA NATIONAL RESOURCE CENTER FOR YOUTH SERVICE, 202 W. Eighth St., Tulsa OK 74119. (918)585-2986. Fax: (918)592-1841. E-mail: klcharles@ou.edu. Program Supervisor: Kristi Charles. Publishes hardcover and trade paperback originals. "University of Oklahoma Press aims to enhance the services provided to the nation's at-risk youth by improving the effectiveness of human services." Publishes 2 titles/ year. Pays 15% royalty. Reports in 2 months on proposals, 4 months on mss. Book catalog and ms guidelines free.
Nonfiction: Children's/juvenile, reference. Subjects include child guidance/parenting, gay/lesbian. Query. Reviews artwork/photos as part of ms package. Recent nonfiction title: *Toward a Gang Solution: The Redirectional Method*, by Sidney M. Rosen, Pasimi V. Hingano, and L.K. Spencer.
Tips: Audience is public and private nonprofit child welfare, juvenile justice and youth services professionals.

VALIANT PRESS, INC., P.O. Box 330568, Miami FL 33233. (305)665-1889. President: Charity Johnson. Estab. 1991. Publishes hardcover and trade paperback originals. Publishes 1-3 titles/year. Pays royalty on net receipts. Offers minimal advance. Reports in 1 month on proposals. *Writer's Market* recommends allowing 2 months for reply.
Nonfiction: "We are interested in nonfiction books on Florida subjects." Submit proposal package, including outline, 2-3 sample chapters, author's background, marketing info with SASE. Recent nonfiction title: *Sharing the Sun, A Kid's Guide to South Florida*, by Debbie Fox and Marie Suarez.

‡VISIONS COMMUNICATIONS, 205 E. Tenth St., Suite 2D, New York NY 10003. Publisher: Beth Bay. Publishes hardcover originals and trade paperback originals and reprints. Publishes 3 titles/year. Pays 5-20% royalty on retail price. Reports in 2 months on queries, 3 months on proposals, 6 months on mss.
Nonfiction: Children's/juvenile, how-to, reference, self-help, technical, textbook. Subjects include art/architecture, business and economics, computers and electronics, nature/environment, religion, science. Submit résumé, outline, 2 sample chapters with SASE. Recent nonfiction title: *Restructuring Electricity Markets*, by Charles Cichetti.

WAYFINDER PRESS, P.O. Box 217, Ridgway CO 81432-0217. (970)626-5452. Owner: Marcus E. Wilson. Estab. 1980. Publishes trade paperback originals. Publishes 2 titles/year. Pays 8-12% royalty on retail price. Accepts simultane-ous submissions. Reports in 1 month on queries with SASE. *Writer's Market* recommends allowing 2 months for reply.
• Wayfinder Press no longer accepts fiction or children manuscripts.
Nonfiction: Illustrated book, reference. Subjects include Americana, government/politics, history, nature/environment, photography, recreation, regional, travel. "We are looking for books on western Colorado: history, nature, recreation, photo, and travel. No books on subjects outside our geographical area of specialization." Query or submit outline/ synopsis, sample chapters and SASE. Reviews artwork/photos as part of ms package. Recent nonfiction title: *Hiking the Gunnison Basin*, by Bloomquist (hiking guide).
Tips: "Writers have the best chance selling us tourist-oriented books. The local population and tourists comprise our audience."

‡WESTERN TANAGER PRESS, P.O. Box 2088, Santa Cruz CA 95063. (408)425-1112. Fax: (408)425-0171. Pub-lisher: Hal Morris. Estab. 1979. Publishes historical biography, hiking and biking guides and regional history hardcover and trade paperback originals and reprints.

WHITE-BOUCKE PUBLISHING, P.O. Box 400, Lafayette CO 80026. (303)604-0661. Partner: Laurie Boucke. Publishes trade paperback originals. Publishes 2-5 titles/year. Pays 0-10% royalty on retail price. Reports in 1 month on queries and proposals, 2 months on mss.

Nonfiction: Biography, humor, reference, self-help. Subjects include child guidance/parenting, music/dance, sports. "Topical, lively works, preferably containing a strong element of humor." Query with outline, 3 sample chapters and SASE. Recent nonfiction title: *The Stay-at-home Mom's Survival Guide*, by Anne Voelckers Palumbo (lifestyles/humor).

WHITEHORSE PRESS, P.O. Box 60, North Conway NH 03860-0060. (603)356-6556. Fax: (603)356-6590. Publisher: Dan Kennedy. Estab. 1988. Publishes trade paperback originals. Publishes 3-4 titles/year. Pays 10% maximum royalty on wholesale price. No advance. Reports in 1 month on queries. *Writer's Market* recommends allowing 2 months for reply.
Nonfiction: "We are actively seeking nonfiction books to aid motorcyclists in topics such as motorcycle safety, restoration, repair and touring. We are especially interested in technical subjects related to motorcycling." Query. Recent nonfiction title: *How to Set Up Your Motorcycle Workshop*, by Charlie Masi (trade paperback).
Tips: "We like to discuss project ideas at an early stage and work with authors to develop those ideas to fit our market."

WILDERNESS ADVENTURE BOOKS, P.O. Box 217, Davisburg MI 48350-0217. Fax: (810)634-0946. Editor: Erin Sims Howarth. Estab. 1983. Publishes hardcover and trade paperback originals and reprints. Publishes 6 titles/year. Receives 250 submissions/year. 90% of books from first-time authors; 90% from unagented writers. Pays 5-10% royalty on retail price. Offers $100 average advance. Publishes book 16 months after acceptance. Accepts simultaneous submissions. Reports in 2 months.
Nonfiction: How-to, illustrated book. Subjects include Americana, animals, history, nature/environment, regional, noncompetitive sports, travel. Query. Reviews artwork/photos as part of ms package. Recent nonfiction title(s): *Cadillac and the Dawn of Detroit*, by A. Hivert-Garthew (Michigan history).

‡WOMAN IN THE MOON, P.O. Box 2087, Cupertino CA 95015. (408)279-6626. Fax: (408)279-6636 (*). Contact: Dr. SDiane A. Bogus. Estab. 1979. Publishes hardcover and trade paperback originals and trade paperback reprints. Also publishes short stories and nonfiction. Reports on queries in 1 month. *Writer's Market* recommends allowing 2 months for reply. Catalog for $4 and $1.01 postage.
• Woman in the Moon has a subsidiary imprint, The Crow's Magic, and a newsletter, *The Spirit*.
Nonfiction: "We are very interested in New Age topics: angels, healing, ghosts, psychic phenomena, goddess worship, spiritual biography, etc." Recent nonfiction title: *Palm Reading for Fun and Profit*.

‡WOODBRIDGE PRESS, P.O. Box 209, Santa Barbara CA 93102. (805)965-7039. Fax: (805)963-0540. E-mail: woodpress@aol.com. Website: http://www.woodbridgepress.com. Editor: Howard Weeks. Estab. 1971. "We publish books by expert authors on special forms of gardening, vegetarian cooking, very limited self-help psychology and humor." Publishes hardcover and trade paperback originals. Publishes 2-3 titles/year. Pays 10-15% on wholesale price. Publishes book 8 months after acceptance. Accepts simultaneous submissions. Reports as expeditiously as possible with SASE. *Writer's Market* recommends allowing 2 months for reply. Book catalog free.
• Woodbridge Press has published such authors as Ashleigh Brilliant and Richard Armour.
Nonfiction: Cookbook (vegetarian), self-help. Subjects include agriculture/horticulture, cooking/foods/nutrition, gardening, health, psychology (popular). Query. Reviews artwork/photos as part of ms package. Recent nonfiction title: *Hydroponic Food Production*, by Howard Resh (hydroponic gardening).

YMAA PUBLICATION CENTER, 38 Hyde Park Ave., Jamaica Plain MA 02130. (800)669-8892. Fax: (617)524-4184. Editor: Andrew Murray. Estab. 1982. "We are a well-established publisher of books on Chinese Chi Kung (Qigong) and Chinese martial arts. We are expanding our focus to include books on healing, wellness, meditation and subjects related to Chinese culture and Chinese medicine." Publishes hardcover originals and trade paperback originals and reprints. Publishes 6 titles/year. Pays royalty on retail price. No advance. Reports in 2 months on proposals.
Nonfiction: "We publish Chinese philosophy, health, meditation, massage and martial arts. We no longer publish or solicit books for children. We also produce instructional videos to accompany our books on traditional Chinese martial arts, meditation, massage and Chi Kung." Send proposal with outline, 1 sample chapter and SASE. Recent nonfiction title: *Chinese Fitness*, by Qingshan Liu (Qigong exercise instruction book).
Fiction: No children's books. Must have Asian, particularly Chinese, focus or theme. This is a *new* focus. Submit outline, 1 sample chapter and SASE.

MARKETS THAT WERE listed in the 1997 edition of *Writer's Market* but do not appear this year are listed in the General Index with a notation explaining why they were omitted.

Book Producers

Book producers provide services for book publishers, ranging from hiring writers to editing and delivering finished books. Most book producers possess expertise in certain areas and will specialize in producing books related to those subjects. They provide books to publishers who don't have the time or expertise to produce the books themselves (many produced books are highly illustrated and require intensive design and color-separation work). Some work with on-staff writers, but most contract writers on a per-project basis.

Most often a book producer starts with a proposal; contacts writers, editors and illustrators; assembles the book; and sends it back to the publisher. The level of involvement and the amount of work to be done on a book by the producer is negotiated in individual cases. A book publisher may simply require the specialized skill of a particular writer or editor, or a producer could put together the entire book, depending on the terms of the agreement.

Writers have a similar working relationship with book producers. Their involvement depends on how much writing the producer has been asked to provide. Writers are typically paid by the hour, by the word, or in some manner other than on a royalty basis. Writers working for book producers usually earn flat fees. Writers may not receive credit (a byline in the book, for example) for their work, either. Most of the contracts require work for hire, and writers must realize they do not own the rights to writing published under this arrangement.

The opportunities are good, though, especially for writing-related work, such as fact checking, research and editing. Writers don't have to worry about good sales. Their pay is secured under contract. Finally, writing for a book producer is a good way to broaden experience in publishing. Every book to be produced is different, and the chance to work on a range of books in a number of capacities may be the most interesting aspect of all.

Book producers most often want to see a query detailing writing experience. They keep this information on file and occasionally even share it with other producers. When they are contracted to develop a book that requires a particular writer's experience, they contact the writer. There are well over 100 book producers, but most prefer to seek writers on their own. The book producers listed in this section have expressed interest in being contacted by writers. For a list of more producers, contact the American Book Producers Association, 160 Fifth Ave., Suite 625, New York NY 10010, or look in *Literary Market Place* (R.R. Bowker).

For a list of publishers according to their subjects of interest, see the nonfiction and fiction sections of the Book Publishers Subject Index. Information on book publishers and producers listed in the previous edition but not included in this edition of *Writer's Market* can be found in the General Index.

‡**A.G.S. INCORPORATED**, P.O. Box 460313, San Francisco CA 94146. Contact: Bill Yenne. Averages 10-12 titles/year. 15% of books from first-time authors; 100% from unagented writers. Makes outright purchase. Reports in 2 months.
Nonfiction: Coffee table book, illustrated book, reference. Subjects include Americana, animals, history, military/war, photography, transportation. Query.

AMERICAN & WORLD GEOGRAPHIC PUBLISHING, P.O. Box 5630, Helena MT 59604. (406)443-2842. General Manager: Brad Hurd. **Acquisitions:** Barbara Fifer, publications director. Publishes trade paperback originals. Publishes 6 titles/year. Receives 40 queries and 8 mss/year. 10% of books from first-time authors; 100% from unagented writers. Makes outright purchase of $7,000-8,000. No advance. Publishes book 18 months after acceptance of ms. Accepts simultaneous submissions. Reports in 4 months on proposals. Book catalog and ms guidelines free on request.
Nonfiction: Coffee table book, gift book, illustrated book. Subjects include recreation, regional. "Most of our titles

are commissioned. We are placing more emphasis on packaging and distribution for other publishers now." Query with proposal package, including outline, sample chapter, photography with SASE. Reviews artwork/photos as part of ms package. Send transparencies; dupes acceptable.
Recent Nonfiction Title: *Natchez Trace: Two Centuries of Travel*, text and photos by Bert Gildart.

B&B PUBLISHING, INC., P.O. Box 96, Walworth WI 53184-0096. (414)275-9474. Fax: (414)275-9530. President: William Turner. Managing Director: Katy O'Shea. Produces supplementary educational materials for grades K-12. Produces 5-10 titles/year. 10% of books from first-time authors, 90% from unagented writers. Payment varies, mostly "work-for-hire" contracts. Reports in 3 months. Book catalog and ms guidelines for SASE.
   • This company is also listed in Book Publishers.
Nonfiction: Query. Reviews artwork/photos as part of ms package.
Recent Nonfiction Title: *Awesome Almanac Georgia*, by Suzanna Martin (reference).

BLACKBIRCH GRAPHICS, INC., P.O. Box 3573, Woodbridge CT 06525. Fax: (203)389-1596. Senior Editor: Deborah Kops. Estab. 1979. Produces hardcover originals. Produces 70 titles/year. 20% of books from first-time authors; 85% from unagented writers. Pays 5-10% on net receipts. Makes outright purchase of $1,000-5,000. Offers $1,500 average advance. Does *not* return submissions, even those accompanied by SASE. Reports in 2 months. No phone calls, please.
Nonfiction: Only. Biography, how-to, illustrated books, juvenile, reference, self-help. Subjects include women, African-Americans, Native Americans, and nature/environment. Nonfiction only. Submit proposal. Reviews artwork/photos as part of ms package.
Tips: "Young adult publishing offers *series* work quite often. This means small advances and tight budgets on a *per book* basis, but can allow authors to get commitments on 4-8 titles at a time." Do not send fiction proposals or those not appropriate for young readers.

BOOK CREATIONS INC., Schillings Crossing Rd., Canaan NY 12029. (518)781-4171. Fax: (518)781-4170. Editorial Director: Elizabeth Tinsley. Estab. 1973. Produces trade paperback and mass market paperback originals, primarily historical fiction. Produces 10-15 titles/year. 75% of books from unagented writers. Pays royalty on net receipts or makes outright purchase. Advance varies with project. Reports in up to 8 months.
Fiction: Historicals, frontier, contemporary action/adventure, mystery. Submit proposal and 30 pages of the work in progress.
Recent Fiction Title: *Prairie*, by Greg Tobin.

‡THE BOOK ENHANCERS, 401 First Ave., Suite 13C, New York NY 10010-4005. (212)683-3963. Fax: (212)779-0151. Director: Paule Von Freihofer. "We publish quality works, market leading, rather then market directed." Produces hardcover and mass market paperback originals. Produces 3 titles/year. 50% of books from first-time authors. Pays royalty on net receipts. Reports in 3 weeks. *Writer's Market* recommends allowing 2 months for reply. Manuscript guidelines free.
Nonfiction: Self-help, technical. Subjects include business and economics, health, money/finance, women's studies. Query.
Recent Nonfiction Title: *Treasurer's & Controllers Desk Book, 2nd Edition*, by Gotthilf (guide to financial officer's duties vis-a-vis corporate restructuring and globalization).
Fiction: Erotica, mainstream, mystery, science fiction, western. Query.
Recent Fiction Title: *Innocent Bystander* (western).
Tips: "Provide a marketing memo naming three competitive products (or works in a genre) and why yours will sell."

‡BOOKWORKS, INC., P.O. Box 204, West Milton OH 45383. (937)698-3619. Fax: (937)698-3651. E-mail: bookwor ks@worldnet.att.net. President: Nick Engler. Produces hardcover originals. Produces 4 titles/year. 100% of books from unagented writers. Pays "on-staff salary." Reports in 1 month.
Nonfiction: How-to. Subjects include hobbies (woodworking). Query.
Recent Nonfiction Title: *Nick Engler's Woodworking Wisdom*.
Tips: "Query for short books, 128-320 pages in length."

‡BOOKWRIGHTS PRESS, 2522 Willard Dr., Suite 108, Charlottesville VA 22903. (804)296-0686. Fax: (804)296-0686. Publisher: Mayapriya Long. Produces hardcover and trade paperback originals. Averages 4 titles/year. 40% of books from first-time authors; 100% from unagented writers. Pays royalty. Reports in 2 months. Manuscript guidelines for #10 SASE.
Nonfiction: How-to, self-help, technical, textbook. Subjects include cooking, foods & nutrition, gardening, military/war, regional, religion. Query with résumé.
Recent Nonfiction Titles: *America's Adopted Son* (biography); *Pagan Resurrection Myths and the Resurrection of Christ* (religious/scholarly).
Fiction: Historical, mainstream. Query or submit proposal.
Recent Fiction Titles: *Greenbrier!* (Civil War fiction).
Tips: "Manuscript must be on disk with accompanying hard copy."

ALISON BROWN CERIER BOOK DEVELOPMENT, INC., 815 Brockton Lane N., Plymouth MN 55410. (612)449-9668. Fax: (612)449-9674. Produces hardcover and trade paperback originals. Produces 4 titles/year. 50% of books from first-time authors; 90% from unagented writers. Payment varies with the project. Reports in 3 weeks. *Writer's Market* recommends allowing 2 months for reply.
Nonfiction: Cookbook, how-to, reference, self-help. Subjects include child guidance/parenting, cooking/foods/nutrition, health, psychology, sports. Query.
Recent Nonfiction Title: *American Medical Association Complete Guide to Women's Health* (Random House).
Tips: "I often pair experts with writers and like to know about writers and journalists with co-writing experience."

COMPASS PRODUCTIONS, 211 E. Ocean Blvd., #360, Long Beach CA 90802. (562)432-7613. Fax: (562)495-0445. Vice President: Dick Dudley. Produces hardcover originals. Pays 2-8% royalty on wholesale price for total amount of books sold to publisher. Offers $2,000 advance for idea/text. Reports in 6 weeks. *Writer's Market* recommends allowing 2 months for reply.
Nonfiction: Humor, illustrated book, juvenile, ("all our books are pop-up and novelty books"). Subjects include Americana, animals, child guidance/parenting, education, recreation, regional, religion, sports, travel (concept-early age books). Query with SASE.
Recent Nonfiction Title: *Busy Beaver Pond*, by Silver (pop-up).
Fiction: Adventure, fantasy, horror, humor, juvenile, mystery, picture books, plays, religious, science fiction. Query with SASE.
Recent Fiction Title: *Counting On Angels*, by Ward (pop-up).
Tips: "Keep in mind our books are *pop-up*, *dimensional*, or novelty *only*! Short verse, couplets or short nonfiction text for 6-7 spreads per book."

COURSE CRAFTERS, INC., 33 Low St., 2nd Floor, Newburyport MA 01950. (508)465-2040. Fax: (508)465-5027. E-mail: ccrafters@aol.com. President: Lise B. Ragan. Produces textbooks and publishes packages for early childhood/family learning that feature storytelling and music. Makes outright purchase. Manuscript guidelines vary based upon project-specific requirements.
Nonfiction: Textbook. Subjects include language, education (preschool-adult), and early childhood. Submit résumé, publishing history and clips. Reviews artwork/photos as part of ms package.
Tips: "Mail (or fax) résumé with list of projects related to specific experience with ESL, bilingual and/or foreign language textbook development. Also interested in storytellers and musicians for our new audio/game packages."

THE CREATIVE SPARK, 26792 Calle Real, Capistrano Beach CA 92624. (714)496-0433. Fax: (714)496-0441. President: Mary Francis-Demarois. Contact: Elizabeth Sirimarco, editorial director. Produces hardcover originals. Produces 20-30 titles/year. Makes outright purchase. *Assigns writers to preconceived projects.*
  • The Creative Spark continues to receive unsolicited manuscripts, which they do not accept. Writers are contracted to produce a manuscript on a pre-arranged topic.
Nonfiction: Biography, juvenile, reference, self-help. Subjects include animals, child guidance/parenting, education, ethnic, government/politics, history, sociology, sports, women's studies. Submit résumé, publishing history and clips. *No unsolicited mss.*
Recent Nonfiction Title: *Enduring Issues in Criminology* (anthology).

J.K. ECKERT & CO., INC., 4370 S. Tamiami Tr., Suite 106, Sarasota FL 34231-3400. (941)925-0468. Fax: (941)925-0272. E-mail: jkeckert@packet.net. Website: http://www.webbooks.net. Acquisitions Editor: William Marshall. Produces hardcover originals. Produces 12-18 titles/year. 80% of books from first-time authors; 100% from unagented writers. Pays 10-50% royalty on net receipts. Reports usually in 6 weeks. *Writer's Market* recommends allowing 2 months for reply. Manuscript guidelines free on request.
Nonfiction: Reference, software, technical, textbook. Subjects include telecommunications, circuit design, computer science and electronic engineering. Submit proposal. Reviews artwork/photos as part of ms package. Professional-level books only.
Recent Nonfiction Title: *Handbook of Parallel and Distributed Processing*, by Zomaya (professional engineering).
Tips: "1) Keep art and text separate—do not use page layout software. 2) Save any artwork as EPS or TIFF; use a real art program like Adobe Illustrator—not something built into a word processor. 3) Don't get creative with fonts—stick to Times and Helvetica. Avoid True-Type if humanly possible. 4) Send synopsis, TOC, and sample chapter (preferably not Chapter 1). Include bio if you want, but if the book is good, we don't care who you are."

ERIAKO ASSOCIATES, 1380 Morningside Way, Venice CA 90291. (310)392-6537. Fax: (310)396-4307. Director: Erika Fabian. Produces hardcover and trade paperback originals. Produces 3-4 titles/year. 100% of books from unagented writers. Pays per contract agreement per individual artist. Reports in 6 weeks. *Writer's Market* recommends allowing 2 months for reply.
Nonfiction: Coffee table book, illustrated book, juvenile. Subjects include business and economics, ethnic, photography, travel. Query with résumé, publishing history and clips with SASE. Reviews artwork/photos as part of ms package.
Recent Nonfiction Title: *Maluku: Land of Bounty for Trade, Investment and Tourism.*
Fiction: Young adult (multi-ethnic, educational about a particular country and its culture, through the eyes of children). Submit résumé, publishing history and clips with SASE.

Recent Fiction Title: *Adventure in Splendid China* (juvenile, ages 9-12).
- Eriako Associates is not planning any fiction titles for the coming year.

Tips: "We're interested in travel writers/photographers with a proven track record in professional photojournalism, and ability to function in foreign countries under all types of circumstances."

‡**GENERAL LICENSING COMPANY**, 24 W. 25th St., 11th Floor, New York NY 10010. (212)645-9870. Fax: (212)645-9874. Katherine Raymond, assistant editor. Produces 10 titles/year. 50% of books from unagented writers. Payment and advance vary depending on the writer and project. Reports in 6 months.
Nonfiction: Juvenile, young adult, humor, illustrated book. Submit résumé, publishing history and clips.
Fiction: Adventure, fantasy, horror, humor, mainstream, mystery, romance, science fiction, short stories, all children's or young adult-oriented. Submit résumé, publishing history and clips.
Recent Fiction Title: *Phantom Rider: Ghost Vision*, by Scholastic (middle-grade fiction); *Sunset Holiday*, by Berkley (young adult romance).
Tips: "We look for writers who match up well with existing projects, not unsolicited manuscripts or series. Please submit samples."

THE K S GINIGER COMPANY INC., 250 W. 57th St., Suite 519, New York NY 10107-0599. (212)570-7499. President: Kenneth S. Giniger. Estab. 1964. Produces hardcover, trade paperback and mass paperback originals. Produces 8 titles/year. Receives 250 submissions/year. 25% of books from first-time authors; 75% from unagented writers. Pays 5-15% royalty on retail price. Offers $3,500 average advance. Publishes book 18 months after acceptance. Reports in 6 weeks on queries. *Writer's Market* recommends allowing 2 months for reply.
Nonfiction: Biography, coffee table book, illustrated book, reference, self-help. Subjects include business and economics, health, history, travel. "No religious books, poetry, cookbooks, personal histories or personal adventure." Query with SASE. All unsolicited mss returned unread (if postage is enclosed).
Recent Nonfiction Title: *The Complete Guide to Buying and Selling at Auction.*
Tips: "We look for a book whose subject interests us and which we think can achieve success in the marketplace. Most of our books are based on ideas originating with us by authors we commission, but we have commissioned books from queries submitted to us."

GRABER PRODUCTIONS INC., 60 W. 15th St., New York MI 10011. (212)929-0154. Fax: (212-929-9630. President: Eden Graber. Produces hardcover and trade paperback originals. Produces 2 books/year. 50% from agented writers. Pay varies by project or makes outright purchase.
Nonfiction: Juvenile, reference, self-help. Subjects include child guidance/parenting, gardening, health, science, sports, travel. Query.
Recent Nonfiction Titles: *Staying Healthy In A Risky Environment: The NYU Medical Center Family Guide.*

HILLER BOOK MANUFACTURING, 631 North 400 W., Salt Lake City UT 84103. (801)521-2411. Fax: (801)521-2420. President: Melvin Hiller. Produces hardcover originals. Produces 10 titles/year. 10% of books from first-time authors; 20% from unagented writers. Pays royalty on net receipts. Reports in 1 month. *Writer's Market* recommends allowing 2 months for reply. Book catalog free.
Nonfiction: Coffee table book, cookbook, illustrated book, juvenile, reference, journals, scrapbooks, seminar education materials. Subjects include cooking, education, religion. Submit proposal. Reviews artwork/photos as part of ms package.
Fiction: Historical, humor, juvenile, picture books, religious.

‡**IMAGE GRAFX**, (formerly Desktop Grafx), 410 Main St., Danville VA 24541. President: Hilary Levy. Designs hardcover, trade paperback and mass market paperback originals. Averages 1-2 titles/year. 90% of books from first-time authors; 10% from unagented writers. Pays 5-20% royalty. Query for electronic submissions.
Nonfiction: How-to, self-help, software, technical, textbook. Subjects include business and economics, computer/ electronics, regional, translation. Submit proposal. Reviews artwork/photos as part of ms package. Now working on travel/tourism magazines.
Tips: "I will edit, proofread and design the book or magazine—including the cover design. Please submit your manuscript on disk. Call ahead for computer requirements, etc. I specialize in graphic design."

JENKINS GROUP, 121 E. Front St., 4th Floor, Traverse City MI 49684. (616)933-0445. Fax: (616)933-0448. E-mail: mdressler@smallpress.com. Website: http://www.smallpress.com. Vice President/Publisher: Mark Dressler. Produces hardcover, trade paperback originals. Produces 20 titles/year. 50% of books from first-time authors; 75% from unagented writers. Makes outright purchase of $2,000-5,000. Reports in 1 month. *Writer's Market* recommends allowing 2 months for reply.
Imprint: Rhodes & Easton.
Nonfiction: Biography, coffee table book, cookbook, how-to, humor, illustrated book, juvenile, self-help, corporate and premium books. Subjects include Americana, business and economics, child guidance/parenting, cooking/foods/ nutrition, education, health, hobbies, money/finance, photography, recreation, regional, travel. Submit résumé, publishing history and clips. Reviews artwork/photos as part of ms package.
Recent Nonfiction Titles: *Inside the Bestsellers*, by Jerrold Jenkins (writing/inspiration/publishing); *Deer Camp Dictionary*, by Greg Nachazel (hunting/humor); *Muffin Maddness*, by Marilyn Taylor (food/recipes).

Tips: "We look for situation-specific experience."

JSA PUBLICATIONS, INC., 29205 Greening Blvd., Farmington Hills MI 48334-2945. (810)932-0090. Fax: (810)932-2659. E-mail: jsapub@aol.com. Director: Joseph S. Ajlouny. Editor: Gwen Foss. Imprints are Push/Pull/Press, producers of original illustrated humor books; Compositional Arts, producers of creative nonfiction; Scrivener Press, producers of history and travel. Packages trade paperback and mass market paperback originals. Produces 15-18 titles/year. Receives 400 queries and 100 mss/year. 75% of books from first-time authors; 100% from unagented writers. Negotiates percentage and advance. Accepts simultaneous submissions. Reports in 1 month. *Writer's Market* recommends allowing 2 months for reply.
  • Formerly publishers, JSA Publications has shifted its focus to book development and packaging.
Nonfiction: Popular culture, popular reference, humor, how-to, music, Americana, history, hobbies, sports. Submit proposal package including illustration samples (photocopies) and SASE.
Recent Nonfiction Titles: *The Universal Crossword Index*, by Diane Spino (Putnam); *The Seven Ancient Wonders of the World*, by Gwen Foss (Berkley); *Who Said That?*, by Joey West (Gramercy Books).
Tips: "Your submissions must be clever!"

‡LOUISE B. KETZ AGENCY, 1485 First Ave., Suite 4B, New York NY 10021. (212)535-9259. President: Louise B. Ketz. Produces and agents hardcover and paperback originals. Averages 1-3 titles/year. 90% of books from unagented writers. Pays flat fees and honoraria to writers. Reports in 6-8 weeks.
Nonfiction: Biography, reference. Subjects include Americana, business and economics, history, military/war, science, sports. Submit proposal.
Recent Nonfiction Title: *The Five Greatest Ideas in Science* (Wiley).
Tips: "It is important for authors to list their credentials relevant to the book they are proposing (i.e., why they are qualified to write that nonfiction work). Also helps if author defines the market (who will buy the book and why)."

GEORGE KURIAN REFERENCE BOOKS, Box 519, Baldwin Place NY 10505. Phone/fax: (914)962-3287. President: George Kurian. Produces hardcover originals. Produces 6 titles/year. 10% of books from first-time authors; 50% from unagented writers. Pays 10-15% royalty on net receipts. Reports in 3 months. Book catalog for 8½×11 SAE with 2 first-class stamps. Manuscript guidelines for #10 SASE.
Nonfiction: Biography, illustrated book, reference. Subjects include Americana, business and economics, education, ethnic, government/politics, history, military/war, philosophy, photography, science, religion, travel. Query or submit proposal.
Recent Nonfiction Title: *Encyclopedia of the Future* (2 vols., reference); *Historical Guide to American Government*.

LAING COMMUNICATIONS INC., 16250 NE 80th St., Redmond WA 98052-3821. (206)869-6313. Fax: (206)869-6318. Vice President/Editorial Director: Christine Laing. Estab. 1985. Imprint is Laing Research Services (industry monographs). Produces hardcover and trade paperback originals primarily for or in partnership with institutions and publishers. Produces 6-10 titles/year. 5% of books from first-time authors; 100% from unagented writers. Payment "varies dramatically since all work is sold to publishers as royalty-inclusive package." Reports in 1 month. *Writer's Market* recommends allowing 2 months for reply.
Nonfiction: How-to, illustrated book, juvenile, medical, museum, reference, software, technical, textbook. Subjects include Americana, business and economics, computers/electronics, history. Query. Reviews artwork/photos as part of ms package. The company also manages book divisions for 3 firms, producing 8-12 titles annually in regional, technical and health care fields.
Recent Nonfiction Title: *Beyond the Mississippi: Early Westward Expansion of the United States* (Lodestar Books).

‡LAMPPOST PRESS INC., 1172 Park Ave., New York NY 10128-1213. (212)876-9511. President: Roseann Hirsch. Estab. 1987. Produces hardcover, trade paperback and mass market paperback originals. Averages 25 titles/year. 50% of books from first-time authors; 85% from unagented writers. Pays 50% royalty or makes outright purchase.
Nonfiction: Biography, cookbook, how-to, humor, illustrated book, juvenile, self-help. Subjects include child guidance/parenting, cooking/foods/nutrition, gardening, health, money/finance, women's issues. Query or submit proposal. Reviews artwork/photos as part of ms package.

LAYLA PRODUCTIONS, INC., 340 E. 74th St., New York NY 10021. (212)879-6984. Fax: (212)879-6399. President: Lori Stein. Produces hardcover and trade paperback originals. Produces 6 titles/year. 50% of books from first-time authors; 50% from unagented writers. Pays 1-5% royalty or makes outright purchase, depending on contract with publisher. Offers $2,000-10,000 advance. Does not return submissions, even those accompanied by SASE. Reports in 6 months.
Nonfiction: Coffee table book, cookbook, how-to, humor, illustrated book, juvenile. Subjects include Americana, cooking/foods/nutrition, gardening, history, photography, recreation. Query. Reviews artwork/photos as part of ms package.
Recent Nonfiction Title: *The American Garden Guides* (Pantheon Books).

McCLANAHAN BOOK COMPANY INC., 23 W. 26th St., New York NY 10010. (212)725-1515. Acquisitions: Kathy Costello, editorial director. Produces 50-60 titles/year. 5% of books from first-time authors; 90% from unagented writers. Makes outright purchase. Reports within 3 months to submissions with SASE.

Nonfiction: Juvenile. Submit proposal. Reviews artwork/photos as part of ms package.

Recent Nonfiction Title: *Crabs Grab*, by Kees Moerbeck (pop-up).

Fiction: Juvenile, picture books. Submit complete ms, proposal, résumé, publishing history and clips. *Writer's Market* recommends sending a query with SASE first.

MEGA-BOOKS, INC., 240 E. 60th St., New York NY 10022. (212)355-6200. Fax: (212)355-6303. President: Pat Fortunato. Contact: Molly Walsh. Produces trade paperback and mass market paperback originals and fiction and nonfiction for the educational market. Produces 95 titles/year. Works with first-time authors, established authors and unagented writers. Makes outright purchase for $3,000 and up. Offers 50% average advance. *No unsolicited mss.*

Fiction: Juvenile, mystery, young adult. Submit résumé, publishing history and clips. *No unsolicited mss.*

Recent Fiction Titles: *Nancy Drew* and *Hardy Boys* series; *Pocahontas* and *The Lion King* (Disney).

Tips: "Please be sure to obtain a current copy of our writers' guidelines before writing."

MENASHA RIDGE PRESS, INC., P.O. Box 43059, Birmingham AL 35243. (205)322-0439. Fax: (205)326-1012. Publisher: R.W. Sehlinger. **Acquisitions:** Budd Zehmer, senior acquisitions editor (outdoors); Molly Burns (travel, reference). Estab. 1982. Produces hardcover and trade paperback originals. Produces 35 titles/year. Receives 600-800 submissions/year. 30% of books from first-time authors; 85% of books from unagented writers. Average print order for a first book is 4,000. Royalty and advances vary. Publishes book 1 year after acceptance. Accepts simultaneous submissions. Reports in 2 months. Book catalog for 9×12 SAE with 4 first-class stamps.

Nonfiction: How-to, humor, outdoor recreation, travel guides, small business. Subjects include business and economics, regional, recreation, adventure sports, travel. No fiction, biography or religious copies. Submit proposal, résumé and clips. Reviews artwork/photos.

Recent Nonfiction Titles: *Travelers Tool Kit*, by Rob Sangster (travel); *Fly Fishing Sourcebook*, by Mark Williams (fishing); *Season on the Trail*, by Lynn Setzer (hiking).

Tips: "Audience: age 25-60, 14-18 years' education, white collar and professional, $30,000 median income, 75% male, 55% east of Mississippi River."

NEW ENGLAND PUBLISHING ASSOCIATES, INC., P.O. Box 5, Chester CT 06412. (860)345-READ. Fax: (860)345-3660. E-mail: nepa@nepa.com. **Acquisitions:** Elizabeth Frost-Knappman, president; Edward W. Knappman, vice president/treasurer. Staff: Victoria Harlow, Rebecca Berardy, Ron Formica. Estab. 1983. "Our mission is to provide personalized service to a select list of clients." NEPA develops adult and young adult reference and information titles and series for the domestic and international markets. Produces hardcover and trade paperback originals. 25% of books from first-time authors. Reports in 2 months.

● Elizabeth Frost-Knappman's *Women's Progress in America* was selected by *Choice* as Outstanding Reference Book of the Year.

Recent Nonfiction Titles: *Where America Stands: 1996* (John Wiley); *Women's Rights on Trial* (Gale Research).

Tips: "We are looking for writers in the area of women's history and political science."

OTTENHEIMER PUBLISHERS, INC., 10 Church Lane, Baltimore MD 21208. (410)484-2100. Fax: (410)484-7591. Chairman of the Board: Allan T. Hirsh Jr. President: Allan T. Hirsh III. Publisher: Dan Wood. Contact: Laura Wallace. Estab. 1890. Produces hardcover and paperback originals and reprints. Produces 200 titles/year. Receives 500 submissions/year. 20% of books from first-time authors; 85% of books from unagented writers. Average print order for a first book is 15,000. Negotiates royalty and advance, sometimes makes outright purchase. Publishes book 9 months after acceptance. Reports in 2 months.

Nonfiction: Coffee table book, cookbooks, illustrated book, juvenile, reference, self-help, Subjects include animals, cooking/foods/nutrition, gardening, health, religion, alternative medicine, New Age. Submit proposal. Reviews artwork/photos as part of ms package.

Recent Nonfiction Title: *Pictorial Atlas of the World*.

Tips: "Ottenheimer Publishers is primarily a book packager. We tend to assign projects to writers based on their specialties and style, rather than accept manuscripts. We do occasionally purchase original materials. Check your proposal for accuracy and typos. We are always interested in adult health psychology and self-help books."

OWL BOOKS, P.O. Box 53, 370 King St W., Suite 300, Toronto, Ontario M5V 1J9 Canada. Website: http://www.owl.on.ca. Publishing Director: Sheba Meland. Estab. 1976. Produces hardcover and trade paperback originals. Produces 10 titles/year. Receives 100 queries and 500 mss/year. 15% of books from first-time authors; 80% from unagented writers. Pays royalty on retail price. Publishes book 18 months after acceptance of ms. Accepts simultaneous submissions. Reports in 3 months. Catalog and ms guidelines for #10 SAE with IRC. (No US stamps).

Nonfiction: Children's/juvenile. Subjects include animals, hobbies, nature/environment, science and science activities. "We are closely affiliated with the discovery-oriented children's magazines *Owl* and *Chickadee*, and concentrate on fresh, innovative nonfiction and picture books with nature/science themes, and quality children's craft/how-to titles." Submit proposal package, including outline, vita and 3 sample chapters. Reviews artwork/photos as part of ms package. Send photocopies or transparencies (not originals).

Recent Nonfiction Title: *CyberSurfer*, by Nyla Ahmad (kids' guide to the Internet).

Fiction: Picture books. Submit complete ms. *Writer's Market* recommends sending a query with SASE first.

Recent Fiction Title: *Wild in the City*, by Jan Thornhill (nature picture book).
Tips: "To get a feeling for our style of children's publishing, take a look at some of our recent books and at *Owl* and *Chickadee* magazines. We publish Canadian authors in the main, but will occasionally publish a work from outside Canada if it strikingly fits our list."

PUBLICOM, INC., 411 Massachusetts Ave., Acton MA 01720-3739. (508)263-5773. Fax: (508)263-7553. Vice President, Educational Materials: Patricia Moore. "We create and support superior publishing teams in service to educational publishers and publish exemplary nonfiction that promotes learning, compassion and self-reliance." Produces textbooks, and produces hardcover and trade paperback originals under the imprint VanderWyk & Burnham. Produces 1-3 titles/year. 50% of books from first-time authors; 50% from unagented writers. "Work for hire" for textbooks; pays 3-10% royalty or makes variable outright purchase. Offers up to $3,000 advance for trade publishing. Reports in 6 months.
Nonfiction: Biography, how-to, illustrated book, self-help, textbook. Subjects include business, child guidance/parenting, education, aging. Submit proposal, résumé, publishing history and clips.
Recent Nonfiction Title: *Life Worth Living: How Someone You Love Can Still Enjoy Life in a Nursing Home*, by William H. Thomas, M.D. (aging); *The Sacred Rules of Management*, by Stanley Smith (business).

PUBLISHERS RESOURCE GROUP, INC. (PRG), 307 Camp Craft Rd., Suite 100, Austin TX 78746. (512)328-7007. Fax: (512)328-9480. Editorial Directors: Claudia Capp and Lucia McKay. Pays per project/per page.
Nonfiction: Teacher editions, student materials—textbook and ancillary for all major educational publishing companies, all elementary and secondary subject areas. Submit résumé, publishing history and writing samples.
Recent Nonfiction Title: *Chemistry*, for Prentice-Hall (teacher's edition, teaching resources/student materials).
Tips: "If they have written classroom instructional materials before—have taught and/or worked for an educational publisher, they are usually the best prepared to work for PRG."

RESOURCE PUBLICATIONS, INC., 160 E. Virginia St., Suite #290, San Jose CA 95112-5876. (408)286-8505. Fax: (408)287-8748. E-mail: orders@rpinet.com. Website: http://www.rpinet.com/ml/ml.html. Editorial Director (religious books): Nick Wagner. Secular Books Editor: Kenneth Guentert. "We help liturgists and ministers make the imaginative connection between liturgy and life." Produces trade paperback originals. Produces 20 titles/year. 30% of books from first-time authors; 95% from unagented writers. Pays 8% royalty (for a first project). Rarely offers advance. Reports in 10 weeks. Catalog for 9×12 SAE with postage for 10 ozs. Manuscript guidelines for #10 SASE.
Nonfiction: How-to, self-help. Subjects include child guidance/parenting, education, music/dance, religion, professional ministry resources for worship, education, clergy and other leaders, for use in Roman Catholic and mainline Protestant churches. Submit proposal. Reviews artwork as part of freelance ms package.
Recent Nonfiction Title: *Heartwaves*, by Mary S. Burnett (meditations for children); *Velvet and Steel*, by John K. Ream (effective fathering); *Dreams That Help You Mourn*, by Lois Hendricks (dreams in grieving).
Fiction: Fables, anecdotes, faith sharing stories, any stories useful in preaching or teaching. Query.
Recent Fiction Title: *Nun Better* (short stories).
Tips: "We are publishers and secondarily we are book packagers. Pitch your project to us for publication first. If we can't take it on on that basis, we may be able to take it on as a packaging and production project."

SACHEM PUBLISHING ASSOCIATES, INC., P.O. Box 412, Guilford CT 06437-0412. (203)453-4328. Fax: (203)453-4320. E-mail: sachem@iconn.net. President: Stephen P. Elliott. Estab. 1974. Produces hardcover originals. Produces 3 titles/year. 25% of books from first-time authors; 100% from unagented writers. Pays royalty or makes outright purchase. Reports in 1 month. *Writer's Market* recommends allowing 2 months for reply.
Nonfiction: Reference. Subjects include Americana, government/politics, history, military/war. Submit résumé and publishing history.
Recent Nonfiction Title(s): *Reference Guide to U.S. Military History*, edited by Charles R. Shrader, 5 vols. (reference); *American Heritage Encyclopedia of American History*, by John Mack Faragher, general editor.

SILVER MOON PRESS, 160 Fifth Ave., New York NY 10010. (212)242-6499. Fax: (212)242-6799. E-mail: dskatz@aol.com. Publisher: David Katz. "We publish books of entertainment and educational value and develop books which fit neatly into curriculum for grades 4-6." Produces hardcover originals. Produces 2-4 books/year. 10% of books from first-time authors; 90% from unagented writers. Book catalog free.
Nonfiction: Juvenile. Subjects include education, history, science, sports. Submit proposal. Reviews artwork/photos as part of ms package.
Recent Nonfiction Title: *Beauty Lab*, Mildred Dawson (science).
Fiction: Historical, juvenile, mystery. Submit complete ms or proposal.
Recent Fiction Title: *The Hessian's Secret Diary*, by Lisa Banim (history).

SOMERVILLE HOUSE BOOKS LIMITED, 3080 Yonge St., Suite 5000, Toronto Ontario M4N 3N1 Canada. Contact: Acquisition Department. Produces literary paperback originals. Produces 6 titles/year. 5% of books from first-time authors; 0% from unagented writers. Reports in 4 months. Manuscript guidelines for #10 SASE with postage (Canadian or IRC).
Nonfiction: Subjects include technology and metaphysics. Query.
Recent Nonfiction Title: *The Skin of Culture* (media/technology).

Fiction: Literary novels and short story collections. Query.
Recent Fiction Title: *Mister Sandman*, by Barbara Gowdy.
Tips: "Remember that we publish very few adult fiction and nonfiction a year. And all those we have published have been agented, so far. Also, we do *not* accept manuscripts for children's books."

TENTH AVENUE EDITIONS, 625 Broadway, Suite 903, New York NY 10012. (212)529-8900. Fax: (212)529-7399. Managing Editor: Clive Giboire. **Acquisitions:** Suzanne Cobban,submissions editor. Matthew Moore. Estab. 1984. Produces hardcover, trade paperback and mass market paperback originals. Produces 6 titles/year. Pays advance paid by publisher less our commission. Reports in 2 months.
Nonfiction: Biography, how-to, crafts, illustrated book, juvenile, catalogs. Subjects include music/dance, photography, women's issues/studies, art, children's. *Queries only.* Reviews artwork/photos as part of ms package.
Recent Nonfiction Title: *Waiter, There's a Fly in My Soup*, by Leslie N. Lewis (BookMark).
Tips: "Send query with publishing background. Return postage a must."

2M COMMUNICATIONS LTD., 121 W. 27th St., New York NY 10001. (212)741-1509. Fax: (212)691-4460. Contact: Editorial Director: Madeleine Morel Produces hardcover, trade paperback and mass market paperback originals. Produces 15 titles/year. 50% of books from first-time authors. Reports in 2 weeks. *Writer's Market* recommends allowing 2 months for reply.
Nonfiction: Biography, cookbook, how-to, humor. Subjects include child guidance/parenting, cooking/foods/nutrition, ethnic, gay/lesbian, health, psychology, women's studies. Query or submit proposal with résumé and publishing history.

DANIEL WEISS ASSOCIATES, INC., 33 W. 17th St., 11th Floor, New York NY 10011. (212)645-3865. Fax: (212)633-1236. Editorial Assistant: Kieran Scott. Estab. 1987. Produces mass market paperback originals. Produces 135 titles/year. 10% of books from first-time authors; 40% from unagented writers. Pays 1-4% royalty on retail price or makes outright purchase of $1,500-6,500 "depending on author's experience." Offers $1,500-6,500 advance. Reports in 2 months. Guidelines for #10 SASE.
Fiction: Adventure, historical, horror, juvenile, romance, science-fiction, young adult. "Middle grade, young adult, adult romance and early reader. Mostly series fiction. Ask for guidelines prior to submission." Query with synopsis, 2 sample chapters and SASE.
Recent Fiction Title: Series: Love Stories, Bone Chillers, Extreme Zone.
Tips: "We need writers for Bone Chillers, Love Stories, Sweet Valley High and Sweet Valley University."

WIESER & WIESER, INC., 118 E. 25th St. New York NY 10010. (212)260-0860. Fax: (212)505-7186. Producer: George J. Wieser. Estab. 1976. Produces hardcover, trade paperback and mass market paperback originals. Produces 25 titles/year. 10% of books from first-time authors; 90% from unagented writers. Makes outright purchase of $5,000 or other arrangement. Offers $5,000 average advance. Reports in 2 weeks. *Writer's Market* recommends allowing 2 months for reply.
Nonfiction: Coffee table book. Subjects include Americana, cooking/foods/nutrition, gardening, health, history, hobbies, military/war, nature/environment, photography, recreation, sports, travel. Query. Reviews artwork/photos only as part of ms package.
Recent Nonfiction Title: *Civil War Guide*, by Cawliss.
Tips: "Have an original idea and develop it completely before contacting us."

MARKETS THAT WERE listed in the 1997 edition of *Writer's Market* but do not appear this year are listed in the General Index with a notation explaining why they were omitted.

Consumer Magazines

Selling your writing to consumer magazines is as much an exercise of your marketing skills as it is of your writing abilities. Editors of consumer magazines are looking not simply for good writing, but for good writing which communicates pertinent information to a specific audience—their readers. Why are editors so particular about the readers they appeal to? Because it is only by establishing a core of faithful readers with identifiable and quantifiable traits that magazines attract advertisers. And with many magazines earning up to half their income from advertising, it is in their own best interests to know their readers' tastes and provide them with articles and features that will keep their readers coming back.

APPROACHING THE CONSUMER MAGAZINE MARKET

Marketing skills will help you successfully discern a magazine's editorial slant and write queries and articles that prove your knowledge of the magazine's readership to the editor. The one complaint we hear from magazine editors more than any other is that many writers don't take the time to become familiar with their magazine before sending a query or manuscript. Thus, editors' desks become cluttered with inappropriate submissions—ideas or articles that simply will not be of much interest to the magazine's readers.

You can gather clues about a magazine's readership—and thus establish your credibility with the magazine's editor—in a number of ways:
• Start with a careful reading of the magazine's listing in this section of *Writer's Market*. Most listings offer very straightforward information about their magazine's slant and audience.
• Send for a magazine's writer's guidelines, if available. These are written by each particular magazine's editors and are usually quite specific about their needs and their readership.
• If possible, talk to an editor by phone. Many will not take phone queries, particularly those at the higher-profile magazines. But many editors of smaller publications will spend the time to help a writer over the phone.
• Perhaps most important, read several current issues of the target magazine. Only in this way will you see firsthand the kind of stories the magazine actually buys.

Writers who can correctly and consistently discern a publication's audience and deliver stories that speak to that target readership will win out every time over writers who simply write what they write and send it where they will.

AREAS OF CURRENT INTEREST

Today's consumer magazines reflect societal trends and interests. As baby boomers age and the so-called "Generation X" comes along behind, magazines arise to address their concerns, covering topics of interest to various subsets of both of those wide-ranging demographic groups. Some areas of special interest now popular among consumer magazines include gardening, health & fitness, family leisure, computers, travel, fashion and cooking.

As in the book publishing business, magazine publishers are experimenting with a variety of approaches to marketing their publications electronically, whether on the Internet, the World Wide Web or via CD-ROM. For more information about magazines in the electronic age, see Interactive Writing by Anthony Tedesco.

WHAT EDITORS WANT

In nonfiction, editors continue to look for short feature articles covering specialized topics. They want crisp writing and expertise. If you are not an expert in the area about which you are writing, make yourself one through research.

Always query by mail before sending your manuscript package, and do not e-mail or fax a query unless an editor specifically mentions an openness to this in the listing. Publishing, despite all the electronic advancements, is still a very paper-oriented industry. Once a piece has been accepted, however, many publishers now prefer to receive your submission via disk or modem so they can avoid re-keying the manuscript. Some magazines will even pay an additional amount for disk submission.

Fiction editors prefer to receive complete short story manuscripts. Writers must keep in mind that marketing fiction is competitive and editors receive far more material than they can publish. For this reason, they often do not respond to submissions unless they are interested in using the story. Before submitting material, check the market's listing for fiction requirements to ensure your story is appropriate for that market. More comprehensive information on fiction markets can be found in *Novel & Short Story Writer's Market* (Writer's Digest Books).

Many writers make their articles do double duty, selling first or one-time rights to one publisher and second serial or reprint rights to another noncompeting market. The heading, **Reprints**, offers details when a market indicates they accept previously published submissions, with submission form and payment information if available.

When considering magazine markets, be sure not to overlook opportunities with Canadian and international publications. Many such periodicals welcome submissions from U.S. writers and can offer writers an entirely new level of exposure for their work.

Regardless of the type of writing you do, keep current on trends and changes in the industry. Trade magazines such as *Folio*, *Advertising Age* and *Writer's Digest* will keep you abreast of start-ups and shutdowns and other writing/business trends.

PAYMENT

Writers make their living by developing a good eye for detail. When it comes to marketing material, the one detail of interest to almost every writer is the question of payment. Most magazines listed here have indicated pay rates; some give very specific payment-per-word rates while others state a range. Any agreement you come to with a magazine, whether verbal or written, should specify the payment you are to receive and when you are to receive it. Some magazines pay writers only after the piece in question has been published. Others pay as soon as they have accepted a piece and are sure they are going to use it.

In *Writer's Market*, those magazines that pay on acceptance have been highlighted with the phrase **pays on acceptance** set in bold type. Payment from these markets should reach you faster than from markets who pay on publication. There is, however, some variance in the industry as to what constitutes payment "on acceptance"—some writers have told us of two- and three-month waits for checks from markets that supposedly pay on acceptance. It is never out of line to ask an editor when you might expect to receive payment for an accepted article.

So what is a good pay rate? There are no standards; the principle of supply and demand operates at full throttle in the business of writing and publishing. As long as there are more writers than opportunities for publication, wages for freelancers will never skyrocket. Rates vary widely from one market to the next, however, and the news is not entirely bleak. One magazine industry source puts the average pay rate for consumer magazine feature writing at $1.25 a word, with "stories that require extensive reporting . . . more likely to be priced at $2.50 a word." In our opinion, those estimates are on the high side of current pay standards. Smaller circulation magazines and some departments of the larger magazines will pay a lower rate.

Editors know that the listings in *Writer's Market* are read and used by writers with a wide range of experience, from those as-yet unpublished writers just starting out, to those with a successful, profitable freelance career. As a result, many magazines publicly report pay rates in the lower end of their actual pay ranges. Experienced writers will be able to successfully negotiate higher pay rates for their material. Newer writers should be encouraged that as your reputation grows (along with your clip file), you will be able to command higher rates.

Information on publications listed in the previous edition but not included in this edition of *Writer's Market* may be found in the General Index.

ANIMAL

The publications in this section deal with pets, racing and show horses, and other domestic animals and wildlife. Magazines about animals bred and raised for the market are classified in the Farm category of Trade, Technical and Professional Journals. Publications about horse racing can be found in the Sports section.

‡AKC GAZETTE, American Kennel Club, 51 Madison Ave., New York NY 10010-1603. (212)696-8333. Fax: (212)696-8272. Website: http://www.akc.org/akc/. Editor-in-Chief: Diane Vasey. 50% freelance written. Monthly association publication on purebred dogs. "Material is slanted to interests of fanciers of purebred dogs as opposed to commercial interests or pet owners." Estab. 1889. Circ. 58,000. **Pays on acceptance of final ms.** Publishes ms an average of 6 months after acceptance. Byline given. Buys first North American serial rights. Submit seasonal material 6 months in advance. Reports in up to 2 months. Writer's guidelines for #10 SASE.
  ● *AKC Gazette* plans to publish more short fillers and "featurettes" in future issues.
Nonfiction: General interest, historical, how-to, humor, photo feature, profiles, dog art, travel. No poetry, tributes to individual dogs, or fiction. Buys about 75 mss/year. Query with or without published clips. Length: 1,000-2,000 words. Pays $200-350.
Photos: State availability of photos with submission. Reviews transparencies and prints. Offers $25-150/photo. Captions required. Buys one-time rights. Photo contest guidelines for #10 SASE.
Fiction: Annual short fiction contest only. Guidelines for #10 SASE.
Tips: "Contributors should be involved in the dog fancy or expert in area they write about (veterinary, showing, field trialing, obedience, training, dogs in legislation, dog art or history or literature). All submissions are welcome but the author must be a credible expert or be able to interview and quote the experts. Veterinary articles must be written by or with veterinarians. Humorous features are personal experiences relative to purebred dogs that have broader applications. For features generally, know the subject thoroughly and be conversant with jargon peculiar to the sport of dogs."

‡AMERICA'S CUTTER, Published by GoGo Communications, Inc., 201 W. Moore, Suite 200, Terrell TX 75160. (972)563-7001. Fax: (972)563-7004. Contact: Carroll Brown Arnold, publisher/editor. 25% freelance written. Works with small number of new/unpublished writers each year. Monthly magazine covering cutting horses, owners, trainers and riders. Estab. 1995. Circ. 6,500. Pays on publication. Publishes ms an average of 2 months after acceptance. Buys one-time, North American serial rights or second (reprint) rights. Byline given. Reports in 1 month. Sample copy $2.50.
Nonfiction: Informational and historical articles on cutting horse competition and equipment; new products; interviews/profiles. Length: 250-2,000 words. Pays $10-150.
Reprints: Send photocopy of article, typed ms with rights for sale noted and information about when and where the article previously appeared.
Photos: Send photo with submission. Reviews 35mm slide transparencies, 5×7 and 8×10 photos, color and b&w. Pays $5-15/photo.
Poetry: Accepts some poetry geared toward cutters and cutting horse owners and trainers. Pays $5-25.
Tips: "We are interested only in cutting horse-related subjects. Writing style should show a deep interest in horses coupled with knowledge of the world of cutting."

ANIMALS, Massachusetts Society for the Prevention of Cruelty to Animals, 350 S. Huntington Ave., Boston MA 02130. (617)522-7400. Fax: (617)522-4885. Editor: Joni Praded. Managing Editor: Paula Abend. 90% freelance written. Bimonthly magazine publishing "articles on wildlife (American and international), domestic animals, balanced treatments of controversies involving animals, conservation, animal welfare issues, pet health and pet care." Estab. 1868. Circ. 100,000. **Pays on acceptance.** Publishes ms an average of 5 months after acceptance. Byline given. Offers negotiable kill fee. Buys one-time rights or makes work-for-hire assignments. Submit seasonal material 6 months in advance. Reports in 6 weeks. Sample copy for $2.95 and 9×12 SAE with 4 first-class stamps. Writer's guidelines for #10 SASE.
Nonfiction: Exposé, general interest, how-to, opinion and photo feature on animal and environmental issues and controversies, plus practical pet-care topics. "*Animals* does not publish breed-specific domestic pet articles or 'favorite pet' stories. Poetry and fiction are also not used." Buys 50 mss/year. Query with published clips. Length: 2,200 words maximum. Sometimes pays the expenses of writers on assignment.

Photos: State availability of photos with submission, if applicable. Reviews contact sheets, 35mm transparencies and 5×7 or 8×10 prints. Payment depends on usage size and quality. Captions, model releases and identification of subjects required. Buys one-time rights.

Columns/Departments: Books (book reviews of books on animals and animal-related subjects). Buys 18 mss/year. Query with published clips. Length: 300 words maximum. Profile (women and men who've gone to extraordinary lengths to aid animals). Length: 800 words maximum. Buys 6 mss/year. Query with clips.

Tips: "Present a well-researched proposal. Be sure to include clips that demonstrate the quality of your writing. Stick to categories mentioned in *Animals'* editorial description. Combine well-researched facts with a lively, informative writing style. Feature stories are written almost exclusively by freelancers. We continue to seek proposals and articles that take a humane approach. Articles should concentrate on how issues affect animals, rather than humans."

‡**APPALOOSA JOURNAL**, Appaloosa Horse Club, 5070 Hwy. 8 West, P.O. Box 8403, Moscow ID 83843-0903. (208)882-5578. Fax: (208)882-8150. E-mail: journal@appaloosa.com. Contact: Robin Hirzel, editor. 20-40% freelance written. Monthly magazine covering Appaloosa horses. Estab. 1946. Circ. 30,000. Pays on publication. Publishes ms an average of 3 months after acceptance. Byline given. Buys first North American serial rights. Reports in 1 month on queries; 2 months on mss. Sample copy and writer's guidelines free.
• *Appaloosa Journal* no longer accepts material for columns.

Nonfiction: Historical, how-to, interview/profile, horse health, photo feature. Buys 15-20 mss/year. Query with or without published clips, or send complete ms. Length: 1,000-3,000 words. Pays $100-400. Sometimes pays expenses of writers on assignment.

Photos: Send photos with submission. Payment varies. Captions and identification of subjects required.

Tips: "Articles by writers with horse knowledge, news sense and photography skills are in great demand. If it's a solid article about an Appaloosa, the writer has a pretty good chance of publication. Historical breed features and 'how-to' training articles are needed. A good understanding of the breed and the industry is helpful. Avoid purely sentimental, nostalgic horse owner stories. Make sure there's some substance and a unique twist."

‡**BEARS MAGAZINE, The environmentalist publication about bears**, P.O. Box 88, Tremonton UT 84337. (801)257-3634. Fax: (801)257-7341. Website: http://www.bearsmag.com. Contact: Brad Garfield, publisher. 80% freelance written. Quarterly magazine on bears: grizzly, black, polar, etc. "We are looking for entertaining, informative and educational articles about bears, their lives and behaviors." Estab. 1995. Circ. 15,000. Pays on publication. Publishes ms an average of 6 months after acceptance. Byline sometimes given. Buys one-time rights. Editorial lead time 3 months. Submit seasonal material 6 months in advance. Accepts simultaneous and previously published submissions. Reports in 3 weeks on queries; 1 month on mss. Sample copy $2. Writer's guidelines for 4⅛×9½ SAE and 1 first-class stamp.

Nonfiction: Book excerpts, exposé, general interest, historical/nostalgic, how-to, humor, interview/profile, new product, personal experience, photo feature, technical, travel. No inspirational, religious or essays. Buys 30 mss/year. Query. Length: 500-3,500 words. Pays 10-20¢/word. Sometimes pays expenses of writers on assignment.

Reprints: Send tearsheet or photocopy of article and information about when and where the article previously appeared. Pays 50% of amount paid for an original article.

Photos: State availability of photos with submission. Reviews 35mm transparencies. Offers $25-100/photo. Captions, model releases and identification of subjects required. Buys one-time rights.

Columns/Departments: Most departments are assigned. Buys 10 mss/year. Query. Pays 10-20¢/word.

Tips: "Call me and inquire about upcoming wants and needs."

CAT FANCY, Fancy Publications, Inc., P.O. Box 6050, Mission Viejo CA 92690. (714)855-8822. Website: http://www.petchannel.com. Contact: Jane Calloway, editor. 80-90% freelance written. Monthly magazine mainly for women ages 25-54 interested in all phases of cat ownership. Estab. 1965. Circ. 303,000. Pays on publication. Publishes ms an average of 6 months after acceptance. Buys first North American serial rights. Byline given. Absolutely no simultaneous submissions. Submit seasonal material 4 months in advance. Reports in 3 months. Sample copy for $5.50. Writer's guidelines for SASE.

Nonfiction: Historical, medical, how-to, humor, informational, personal experience, photo feature, technical; must be cat oriented. Buys 5-7 mss/issue. *Query first with published clips.* Length: 500-3,000 words. Pays $35-400; special rates for photo/story packages.

Photos: Photos purchased with or without accompanying ms. Pays $35 minimum for 8×10 b&w glossy and $50 minimum for color prints; $50-200 for 35mm or 2¼×2¼ color transparencies; occasionally more for particularly outstanding or unusual work. Photo guidelines for SASE; then send prints and transparencies. Model release required.

Columns/Departments: Cat Newsline (news of national interest to cat lovers), 1,000 words max.; Kids for Cats (short stories, how-to, crafts, puzzles for 10-16 year olds); Feline Friends (once or twice/year, readers' special cats).

Poetry: Short, cat-related poems. Submit any number but always with SASE.

Fiction: Adventure, fantasy, historical, humorous. Nothing written with cats speaking or from cat's point of view. Buys 3-5 mss/year. *Query first.* Length: 500-3,000 words. Pays $50-400.

Fillers: Newsworthy or unusual; items with photos. Query first. Buys 5/year. Length: 500-1,000 words. Pays $35-100.

Tips: "Most of the articles we receive are profiles of the writers' own cats or profiles of cats that have recently died. We reject almost all of these stories. What we need are well-researched articles that will give our readers the information they need to better care for their cats or to help them fully enjoy cats. Please review past issues and notice the informative nature of articles before querying us with an idea. *Please query first."*

CATS MAGAZINE, P.O. Box 1790, Peoria IL 61656. (309)682-6626. Fax: (309)679-5454. E-mail: editor@catsmag.com. Website: http://www.catsmag.com. Contact: Annette Bailey, editor. 80% freelance written. Monthly magazine for owners and lovers of cats. Estab. 1945. Circ. 127,000. **Pays on acceptance.** Byline given. Buys all rights. Editorial works 6 months in advance. Sample copy and writer's guidelines for $3 and 9×12 SAE.
Nonfiction: General interest (concerning cats); how-to (care, etc. for cats); health-related; personal experience; travel. Special issues: Winter Happenings (January 1998); Research & Health (February 1998); Behavior—Training Trends (March 1998)); Spring Happenings (April 1998); Kittens (babies) (May 1998); The Business of Cats (careers/breeding/showing) (June 1998); Summer Happenings (July 1998); Cat Care (grooming, etc.) (August 1998). Query with outline. Length 1,500-2,500 words. Pays $50-500.
Photos: State availability of photos with submissions. Reviews color slides, 2¼×2¼ transparencies. Identification of subjects required. Buys all rights.
Columns/Departments: Cat Tales (true and fictional cat-theme short stories), 250-1,000 words. Pays $25-50.
Tips: "Writer must show an affinity for cats. Extremely well-written, thoroughly researched, carefully thought out articles have the best chance of being accepted. Innovative topics or a new twist on an old subject are always welcomed."

THE CHRONICLE OF THE HORSE, P.O. Box 46, Middleburg VA 20118. (540)687-6341. Fax: (540)687-3937. Editor: John Strassburger. Managing Editor: Nancy Comer. Contact: Patricia Booker, assistant editor. 80% freelance written. Weekly magazine about horses. "We cover English riding sports, including horse showing, grand prix jumping competitions, steeplechase racing, foxhunting, dressage, endurance riding, handicapped riding and combined training. We are the official publication for the national governing bodies of many of the above sports. We feature news, how-to articles on equitation and horse care and interviews with leaders in the various fields." Estab. 1937. Circ. 22,000. **Pays for features on acceptance;** other items on publication. Publishes ms an average of 4 months after acceptance. Byline given. Buys first North American rights and makes work-for-hire assignments. Submit seasonal material 3 months in advance. Reports in 6 weeks. Sample copy for $2 and 9×12 SAE. Guidelines for #10 SASE.
Nonfiction: General interest; historical/nostalgic (history of breeds, use of horses in other countries and times, art, etc.); how-to (trailer, train, design a course, save money, etc.); humor (centered on living with horses or horse people); interview/profile (of nationally known horsemen or the very unusual); technical (horse care, articles on feeding, injuries, care of foals, shoeing, etc.). Length: 6-7 pages. Pays $125-200. News of major competitions, "clear assignment with us first." Length: 1,500 words. Pays $100-150. Small local competitions, 800 words. Pays $50-75. Special issues: Steeplechase Racing (January); American Horse in Sport and Grand Prix Jumping (February); Horse Show (March); Junior and Pony (April); Combined Training (May); Dressage (June); Hunt Roster (September); Vaulting and Handicapped (November); Stallion (December). No Q&A interviews, clinic reports, Western riding articles, personal experience or wild horses. Buys 300 mss/year. Query or send complete ms. Length: 300-1,225 words. Pays $25-200.
Photos: State availability of photos. Accepts prints or color slides. Accepts color for b&w reproduction. Pays $25-30. Identification of subjects required. Buys one-time rights.
Columns/Departments: Dressage, Combined Training, Horse Show, Horse Care, Racing over Fences, Young Entry (about young riders, geared for youth), Horses and Humanities, Hunting. Query or send complete ms. Length: 300-1,225 words. Pays $25-200.
Poetry: Light verse, traditional. No free verse. Buys 30/year. Length: 5-25 lines. Pays $15.
Fillers: Anecdotes, short humor, newsbreaks, cartoons. Buys 300/year. Length: 50-175 lines. Pays $10-20.
Tips: "Get our guidelines. Our readers are sophisticated, competitive horsemen. Articles need to go beyond common knowledge. Freelancers often attempt too broad or too basic a subject. We welcome well-written news stories on major events, but clear the assignment with us."

‡DOG FANCY, Fancy Publications, Inc., P.O. Box 6050, Mission Viejo CA 92690-6050. (714)855-8822. Fax: (714)855-3045. E-mail: http://www.dogfancy.com. Editor: Betty Liddick. Contact: Julie Jordan, managing editor. 95% freelance written. Monthly magazine for men and women of all ages interested in all phases of dog ownership. Estab. 1970. Circ. 276,000. Pays on publication. Publishes ms an average of 1 year after acceptance. Byline given. Buys first North American serial and electronic rights. Submit seasonal material 6 months in advance. Accepts simultaneous submissions. Reports in 2 months. Writer's guidelines for #10 SASE.
Nonfiction: Essays, general interest, how-to, humor, informational, inspirational, interview/profile, personal experience, photo feature, travel. Buys 100 mss/year. Query. Length: 350-1,800 words. Pays $50-500. Sometimes pays expenses of writers on assignment.
Photos: Send photos with submission. Reviews transparencies. Offers no additional payment for photos accepted with ms. Model release, identification of subjects required. Buys one-time and electronic rights.
Columns/Departments: Dogs On the Go (travel with dogs), 900 words; Dogs that Make a Difference (heroic dogs), 900 words. Buys over 25 mss/year. Query. Pays $150-350.
Tips: "We're looking for the unique experience that communicates something about the dog/owner relationship—with the dog as the focus of the story, not the owner. Medical articles are assigned to veterinarians. Note that we write for a lay audience (non-technical), but we do assume a certain level of intelligence: no talking down to people. If you've never seen the type of article you're writing in *Dog Fancy*, don't expect to. No 'talking dog' articles."

‡DOGGONE, The Newsletter About Fun Places to Go And Cool Stuff to Do With Your Dog, P.O. Box 651155, Vero Beach FL 32965-1155. Fax: (561)569-1124. E-mail: doggonenl@aol.com. Contact: Wendy Ballard, publisher. "*DogGone* is a bimonthly travel and activity newsletter for dog owners. All destination pieces are written with a dog slant, including lodgings that accept pets, dog-allowed tourist attractions, parks, hiking trails, walking tours, even restaurants with outdoor seating that don't mind a pooch on the porch." Estab. 1993. Circ. 3,000. Pays on publication. Publishes ms an average of 4 months after acceptance. Buys first rights and electronic rights. Editorial lead time 4 months. Submit seasonal material 4 months in advance. Reports in 1 month. Sample copy for 9 × 12 SASE and 3 first-class stamps. Writer's guidelines for #10 SASE.
Nonfiction: Exposé, historical, how-to, personal experience, travel. "No poetry or 'My dog is the best because . . .' articles." Query with published clips or send complete ms. Length: 300-1,000 words. Pays $34-100. Writers may opt to accept subscription to *DogGone* as partial payment.
Photos: Send photos with submission. Reviews prints. Offers no additional payment for photos accepted with ms. Captions required. Buys rights with ms.
Columns/Departments: Beyond Fetch (creative activities to enjoy with dogs), 300-900 words; Parks Department (dogs-allowed national, state, regional parks), 300 words; Visiting Vet (travel-related), 300 words; Touring (walking or driving tours with pets-allowed stops), 600-900 words. Query with published clips or send complete ms. Pays $34-100.
Fillers: Facts, dogs-allowed events. Length: 50-200 words. Pays $15.

‡THE EQUINE IMAGE, Reflections of the Equestrian Lifestyle, Heartland Communications, P.O. Box 916, 1003 Central Ave., Ft. Dodge IA 50501. (800)247-2000. Fax: (515)574-2213. E-mail: hli1@dodgenet.com. Website: http://www.equineimages.com. Contact: Nancy Ann Thompson editor. 45% freelance written. Bimonthly magazine covering horses and the equestrian lifestyle. "*The Equine Image* is aimed at horse owners and enthusiasts, equine art lovers and equestrians with an appreciation for the horse in their lifestyle. Topics covered include celebrity and artist profiles, travel features, equestrian-styled clothing, accessories or home decor, equestrian literature and more." Estab. 1986. Circ. 12,500. Pays on publication. Publishes ms an average of 3 months after acceptance. Byline given. Buys first North American serial rights. Editorial lead time 3 months. Submit seasonal material 6 months in advance. Accepts simultaneous submissions. Reports in 6 weeks on queries; 2 months on mss. Sample copy for $6.95. Writer's guidelines free.
Nonfiction: Book excerpts, essays, general interest, historical/nostalgic, interview/profile, photo feature, travel, art; all articles must have an equestrian tie. Buys 25-40 mss/year. Query with published clips. Length: 500-2,000 words. Pays $100-500. Pays in contributor copies on individual arrangements.
Reprints: Send tearsheet or photocopy of article or short story. Pay varies.
Photos: State availability of photos with submissions. Reviews contact sheets, 4 × 5 transparencies, 3 × 5 prints. Offers no additional payment for photos. Identification of subjects required. Buys one-time rights.
Columns/Departments: Style Column (equestrian-styled fashion or home decor), 1,200 words. "Most columnists are regular contributors arranged on individual basis." Query with published clips. Pays $100-500.
Fiction: Mainstream, novel excerpts, slice-of-life vignettes, western; all must have an equestrian tie. "This new section will publish only equestrian or horse-related fiction; short, general interest pieces are best; no children's fiction." Send complete ms. Pays $0-300.
Poetry: Free verse, light verse, traditional; all must have an equestrian tie. Buys 6-18 poems/year. Submit maximum 5 poems at a time. Length: 5-40 lines. Pays $0-200.
Tips: "Send complete queries with details on headlines, interviews and available visuals. Direct specific questions on editorial submissions to the editor *in writing*. Notify the editorial department with as much advance notice as possible of any specific trips. Freelance assignments are often made on basis of events and locations."

THE GREYHOUND REVIEW, P.O. Box 543, Abilene KS 67410. (913)263-4660. Fax: (913)263-4689. E-mail: nga@jc.net. Website: http://www.jc.net/greyhd. Editor: Gary Guccione. Contact: Tim Horan, managing editor. 20% freelance written. Monthly magazine covering greyhound breeding, training and racing. Estab. 1911. Circ. 5,000. **Pays on acceptance.** Byline given. Buys first rights. Submit seasonal material 2 months in advance. Reports in 2 weeks on queries; 1 month on mss. Sample copy for $3. Writer's guidelines free.
Nonfiction: How-to, interview/profile, personal experience. "Articles must be targeted at the greyhound industry: from hard news, special events at racetracks to the latest medical discoveries. Do not submit gambling systems." Buys 24 mss/year. Query. Length: 1,000-10,000 words. Pays $85-150. Sometimes pays the expenses of writers on assignment.
Reprints: Send photocopy of article. Pays 100% of the amount paid for an original article.
Photos: State availability of photos with submission. Reviews 35mm transparencies and 8 × 10 prints. Offers $10-50/photo. Identification of subjects required. Buys one-time rights.

HORSE ILLUSTRATED, The Magazine for Responsible Horse Owners, Fancy Publications, Inc., P.O. Box 6050, Mission Viejo CA 92690-6050. (714)855-8822. Fax: (714)855-3045. E-mail: joltmann@fancypubs.com. Website: http://www.horseillustrated.com. Contact: Jennifer Oltman, associate editor. 90% freelance written. Prefers to work with published/established writers but will work with new/unpublished writers. Monthly magazine covering all aspects of horse ownership. "Our readers are adults, mostly women, between the ages of 18 and 40; stories should be geared to that age group and reflect responsible horse care." Estab. 1976. Circ. 190,000. Pays on publication. Publishes ms an average of 8 months after acceptance. Byline given. Buys one-time rights; requires first North American rights among equine publications. Submit seasonal material 6 months in advance. Reports in 3 months. Sample copy for $3.50. Writer's guidelines for #10 SASE.

Nonfiction: How-to (horse care, training, veterinary care), photo feature. No "little girl" horse stories, "cowboy and Indian" stories or anything not *directly* relating to horses. "We are looking for longer, more authoritative, in-depth features on trends and issues in the horse industry. Such articles must be queried first with a detailed outline of the article and clips. We rarely have a need for fiction." Buys 20 mss/year. Query or send complete ms. Length: 1,000-2,000 words. Pays $100-300 for assigned articles; $50-300 for unsolicited articles.

Photos: Send photos with submission. Reviews 35mm transparencies, medium format transparencies and 5×7 prints.

Tips: "Freelancers can break in at this publication with feature articles on Western and English training methods; veterinary and general care how-to articles; and horse sports articles. We rarely use personal experience articles. Submit photos with training and how-to articles whenever possible. We have a very good record of developing new freelancers into regular contributors/columnists. We always look for fresh talent, but enjoy working with established writers who 'know the ropes' as well. We are accepting less freelance work—much of our material is assigned and contracted."

‡THE HORSE, Your Guide To Equine Health Care, The Blood Horse, Inc. P.O. Box 4680, Lexington KY 40544-4680. (606)276-6771. Fax: (606)276-4450. E-mail: kherbert@thehorse.com. Website: http://www.thehorse.com. Contact: Kimberly S. Herbert, editor. 75% freelance written. Monthly magazine covering equine health and care. *The Horse* is "an educational/news magazine geared toward the professional, hands-on horse owner." Estab. 1983. Circ. 27,000. Pays on publication. Publishes ms an average of 2 months after acceptance. Byline given. Buys first rights and on-line rights. Reports in 2 months on queries. Sample copy for $2.95. Writer's guidelines free.

Nonfiction: How-to, technical, topical interviews. "No first-person experiences not from professionals; this is a technical magazine to inform horse owners." Buys 90 mss/year. Query with published clips. Length: 500-5,000 words. Pays $75-450. Sometimes pays expenses of writers on assignment.

Photos: Send photos with submission. Reviews transparencies. Offers $10-150/photo. Captions and identification of subjects required. Buys one-time rights.

Columns/Departments: Up Front (news on horse health), 100-500 words; Equinomics (economics of horse ownership), 2,500 words. Buys 40 mss/year. Query with published clips. Pays $50-250.

Tips: "We publish reliable horse health information from top industry professionals from around the world. Manuscript must be submitted electronically or on disk."

HORSES ALL, North Hill Publications, 4000-19 St. NE, Calgary, Alberta T2P 2G4 Canada. (403)250-6633. Fax: (403)291-0703. E-mail: nhpubs@netway.ab.ca. Contact: Vanessa Peterelli, editor. 70% freelance written. Eager to work with new/unpublished writers. Monthly tabloid for horse owners and the horse industry. "We prefer knowledgeable horsepeople as our writers. Estab. 1977. Circ. 9,000. Pays on publication. Publishes ms an average of 3 months after acceptance. Byline given. Offers 30% kill fee. Buys first North American serial rights. Submit seasonal material 3 months in advance. Accepts simultaneous submissions. Sample copy and writer's guidelines free.

Nonfiction: Book excerpts, essays, general interest, historical/nostalgic, how-to (training, horse care and maintenance), humor, inspirational, interview/profile, personal experience, photo feature. "We want more general stories, no specific local events or shows." Buys 3 mss/year. Query with published clips. Length: 800-1,400 words. Pays $50-75 (Canadian).

Reprints: Accepts previously published submissions.

Photos: Send photos with submission. Reviews prints 3×4 or larger. Negotiates payment individually. Captions, model releases, identification of subjects required. Buys one-time rights.

Fillers: Anecdotes, facts, newsbreaks, short humor. Buys 5 mss/year. Length: 300-1,000 words. Pays $20-50 Canadian.

Tips: "Our writers must be knowledgeable about horses and the horse industry, and be able to write features in a readable, conversational manner, but in third person only, please."

‡I LOVE CATS, I Love Cats Publishing, 450 Seventh Ave., Suite 1701, New York NY 10123. (212)244-2351. Fax: (212)244-2367. Editor: Lisa Sheets. 85% freelance written. Bimonthly magazine covering cats. "*I Love Cats* is a general interest cat magazine for the entire family. It caters to cat lovers of all ages. Stories in the magazine include fiction, nonfiction, how-to, humorous and columns for the cat lover." Estab. 1989. Circ. 200,000. Pays on publication. Publishes ms an average of 2 years after acceptance. Byline given. No kill fee. Buys all rights. Must sign copyright consent form. Submit seasonal material 9 months in advance. Reports in 2 months. Sample copy $4. Writer's guidelines for #10 SASE.

Nonfiction: Essays, how-to, humor, inspirational, interview/profile, opinion, personal experience, photo feature. No poetry. Buys 200 mss/year. Send complete ms. Length: 100-1,000 words. Pays $40-250, contributor copies or other premiums "if requested." Sometimes pays expenses of writers on assignment.

Photos: Send photos with submission. Offers no additional payment for photos accepted with ms. Identification of subjects required. Buys all rights.

Fiction: Adventure, fantasy, historical, humorous, mainstream, mystery, novel excerpts, slice-of-life vignettes, suspense. "This is a family magazine. No graphic violence, pornography or other inappropriate material. *I Love Cats* is strictly 'G-rated.' " Buys 50 mss/year. Send complete ms. Length: 500-1,200 words. Pays $40-250.

Fillers: Quizzes and short humor. Buys 20/year. Pays $10-35.

Tips: "Please keep stories short and concise. Send complete ms with photos, if possible. I buy lots of first-time authors. Nonfiction pieces w/color photos are always in short supply. With the exception of the standing columns, the rest of the magazine is open to freelancers. Be witty, humorous or take a different approach to writing."

‡PETS MAGAZINE, Moorshead Publications, Ltd., 10 Gateway Blvd., Suite 490, North York, Ontario M3C 3T4 Canada. (416)969-5488. Fax: (416)696-7395. E-mail: pets@moorshead.com. Editor: Edward Zapletal. 40% freelance written. Bimonthly magazine for "pet owners, primarily cat and dog owners, but we also cover rabbits, guinea pigs, hamsters, gerbils, birds and fish. Issues covered include: pet health care, nutrition, general interest, grooming, training humor, human-animal bond stories. No fiction! No poetry!" Estab. 1983. Circ. 51,000. Pays within 30 days of publication. Publishes ms an average of 2 months after acceptance. Byline given. Offers 50% kill fee. Buys first North American serial rights or other negotiable rights. Editorial lead time 3 months. Submit seasonal material 2 months in advance. Sample copy for #10 SAE with IRCs. Writer's guidelines for 9½×4 SAE with IRCs.

Nonfiction: General interest, humor, new product, personal experience, veterinary medicine, human interest (i.e., working animal), training and obedience. No fiction. Buys 10 mss/year. Query. Length: 500-1,500 words. Pays 12-18¢/word (Canadian funds).

Reprints: Considers reprints of previously published submissions. Pays 6-9¢/word.

Photos: Prefers color pictures, slides. Reviews photocopies. Identification of subjects required. Buys one-time rights.

Columns/Departments: Grooming Your Pet (mostly dogs and cats), 300-400 words. Buys 6-12 mss/year. Query.

Fillers: Facts. Buys 5/year. Length: 20-100 words. Pays $10-20.

Tips: "Always approach with a query letter first. E-mail is good if you've got it. We'll contact you if we like what we see. I like writing to be friendly, informative, well-balanced with pros and cons. Remember, we're catering to pet owners, and they are a discriminating audience."

‡PETS QUARTERLY MAGAZINE, Omnicom Publication, Inc., 2495 Main St., Box 15, Buffalo NY 14214. (416)955-1550. Fax: (416)955-1391. Contact: Richard Soren, managing editor. 50% freelance written. Quarterly magazine covering pet health care and nutrition (dogs, cats, fish, exotics). Estab. 1991. Circ. 62,000. Pays on publication. Publishes ms an average of 6 months after acceptance. Byline given. Buys one-time rights. Editorial lead time 1-3 months. Submit seasonal material 3 months in advance. Reports in 1 month on queries; 2 months on mss. Sample copy for $2. Writer's guidelines free.

Nonfiction: Humor, inspirational, opinion, personal experience. No personal stories about your pets. Query. Length: 500-1,200 words. Pays $25-50.

Photos: State availability of photos with submission or send photos with submission. Reviews 3×5 prints. Offers $25/photo. Captions required. Buys one-time rights.

Tips: "Scan our magazine for familiarization before submitting."

THE QUARTER HORSE JOURNAL, P.O. Box 32470, Amarillo TX 79120. (806)376-4811. Fax: (806)376-8364. E-mail: aqhajrnl@arnet. Website: http://www.aqha.com. Editor-in-Chief: Jim Jennings. Contact: Lesli Groves, editor. 20% freelance written. Prefers to work with published/established writers. Monthly official publication of the American Quarter Horse Association. Estab. 1948. Circ. 75,000. **Pays on acceptance.** Publishes ms an average of 6 months after acceptance. Buys first North American serial rights. Submit seasonal material 6 months in advance. Reports in 2 months. Sample copy and writer's guidelines free.

Nonfiction: How-to (fitting, grooming, showing, or anything that relates to owning, showing, or breeding); informational (educational clinics, current news); interview (feature-type stories—must be about established horses or people who have made a contribution to the business); personal opinion; and technical (equine updates, new surgery procedures, etc.). Buys 20 mss/year. Length: 800-1,800 words. Pays $150-300.

Photos: Purchased with accompanying ms. Captions required. Send prints or transparencies. Uses 4×6 color glossy prints, 2¼×2¼, 4×5 or 35mm color transparencies. Offers no additional payment for photos accepted with ms.

Tips: "Writers must have a knowledge of the horse business."

REPTILE & AMPHIBIAN MAGAZINE, 1168 Route 61 Hwy. S., Pottsville PA 17901-9219. (717)622-6050. Fax: (717)622-5858. E-mail: eramus@csrlink.net. Website: http://petstation.com/repamp.html. Editor: Erica Ramus. 80% freelance written. Full-color digest-size bimonthly magazine covering reptiles and amphibians. Devoted to the amateur herpetologist who enjoys articles on life cycles of various reptiles and amphibians; special behavioral characteristics of common species dealing with reproduction, feeding, adaptation to environmental changes, etc.; interrelationships with other species, including man; and captive care and breeding. "Many of our articles are written from an ecological perspective, but we do not actively promote any special causes." Estab. 1989. Circ. 15,000. **Pays on acceptance.** Publishes ms an average of 6 months after acceptance. Byline given. Buys first North American serial, one-time and (occasionally) second serial (reprint) rights. Reports in 2 weeks. Sample copy for $5. Writer's guidelines for #10 SASE.

Nonfiction: General interest, photo feature, technical. Publishes articles on life cycles of various reptiles and amphibians, natural history, captive care and breeding. No first-person narrative, "me-and-Joe" stories or articles by writers unfamiliar with the subject matter. "Readers are already familiar with the basics of herpetology and are usually advanced amateur hobbyists." Buys 50 mss/year. Query or send complete ms. Length: 1,500-2,500 words. Pays $100. Sometimes pays expenses of familiar or regular writer on assignment.

Reprints: Send tearsheet of article. Pays 50% of amount paid for an original article.

Photos: Send photos with submission whenever possible. Reviews 35mm slide transparencies, 4×6, 5×7 and 8×10 glossy prints. Offers $10 for b&w, $25 for color photos. Captions, model releases and identification of subjects required. Animals should be identified by common and/or scientific name. Buys one-time rights.

Columns/Departments: Photo Dept./Herp•Art Dept., 500-750 words; Book Review, 500-750 words. Buys 12 mss/year. Send complete ms. Pays $50-75.

Tips: "Note your personal qualifications, such as experience in the field or advanced education. Writers have the best chance selling us feature articles—know your subject and supply high quality color photos. Adopt a journalistic/textbook style and avoid first-person narratives."

‡**TROPICAL FISH HOBBYIST, "The World's Most Widely Read Aquarium Monthly,"** TFH Publications, Inc., 211 W. Sylvania Ave., Neptune City NJ 07753. (908)988-8400. Fax: (908)988-9635. E-mail: tfhfish@aol.com or tfhpub@aol.com. Contact: John Mallard, associate editor. Managing Editor: Neal Pronek. 90% freelance written. Monthly magazine covering the tropical fish hobby. "Our publication is directed at both beginner and expert aquarium and herptile hobbyists. Our readers enjoy articles on the captive care, feeding, behavior, and breeding of herps and both freshwater and marine fishes and invertebrates. Articles on technical aspects of the hobby (such as filtration, lighting, etc.) are also welcome. We favor articles well illustrated with good color slides and aimed at both the neophyte and veteran tropical fish hobbyist." Estab. 1952. Circ. 60,000. **Pays on acceptance.** Publishes ms an average of 15 months after acceptance. Byline given. Buys all rights. Submit seasonal material 4 months in advance. Accepts simultaneous submissions. Reports in 1 month. Sample copy for $3 and 9 × 12 SAE with 6 first-class stamps. Guidelines for #10 SASE.
Nonfiction: General interest, how-to, personal experience, photo feature, technical, and articles dealing with beginning and advanced aspects of the aquarium hobby. No "How I got started in the hobby" articles that impart little solid information. Buys 40-50 mss/year. Length: 1,200-2,500 words. Pays $50-250.
Reprints: Send photocopy of article or typed ms with rights for sale noted and information about when and where the article previously appeared. Pays 100% of the amount paid for an original article.
Photos: State availability of or send photos with ms. Reviews contact sheets, transparencies, color slides, prints. Offers $10-15/photo. Identification of subjects required. Buys all rights.
Columns/Departments: Freshwater, saltwater, reptile, and amphibian sections (from a keeping standpoint), 1,000-2,000 words. Buys 10-20 mss/year. Pays $80-200.
Fiction: Publishes novel excerpts.

‡**THE WESTERN HORSEMAN, World's Leading Horse Magazine Since 1936**, Western Horseman, Inc., P.O. Box 7980, Colorado Springs CO 80933-7980. (719)633-5524. Editor: Pat Close. 50% freelance written. Works with a small number of new/unpublished writers each year. Monthly magazine for horse owners covering horse care and training. Estab. 1936. Circ. 230,322. **Pays on acceptance.** Publishes ms an average of 5 months after acceptance. Buys one-time and North American serial rights. Byline given. Submit seasonal material 6 months in advance. Reports in 3 weeks. Sample copy for $5. Writer's guidelines for #10 SASE.
Nonfiction: How-to (horse training, care of horses, tips, ranch/farm management, etc.), informational (on rodeos, ranch life, historical articles of the West emphasizing horses). Buys 250 mss/year. Query; no fax material. Length: 500-2,500 words. Pays $35-500, "sometimes higher by special arrangement."
Photos: Send photos with ms. Offers no additional payment for photos. Uses 5 × 7 or 8 × 10 b&w glossy prints and 35mm transparencies. Captions required.
Tips: "Submit clean copy, double-spaced, with professional quality photos. Stay away from generalities. Writing style should show a deep interest in horses coupled with a wide knowledge of the subject."

ART AND ARCHITECTURE

Listed here are publications about art, art history, specific art forms and architecture written for art patrons, architects, artists and art enthusiasts. Publications addressing the business and management side of the art industry are listed in the Art, Design and Collectibles category of the Trade section. Trade publications for architecture can be found in Building Interiors, and Construction and Contracting sections.

AMERICAN INDIAN ART MAGAZINE, American Indian Art, Inc., 7314 E. Osborn Dr., Scottsdale AZ 85251-6417. (602)994-5445. Fax: (602)945-9533. Contact: Roanne P. Goldfein, editor. 97% freelance written. Works with a small number of new/unpublished writers each year. Quarterly magazine covering Native American art, historic and contemporary, including new research on any aspect of Native American art north of the US/Mexico border. Estab. 1975. Circ. 30,000. Pays on publication. Publishes ms an average of 3 months after acceptance. Byline given. Buys one-time and first rights. Reports in 3 weeks on queries; 3 months on mss. Writer's guidelines for #10 SASE.
Nonfiction: New research on any aspect of Native American art. No previously published work or personal interviews with artists. Buys 12-18 mss/year. Query. Length: 1,000-2,500 words. Pays $75-300.
Tips: "The magazine is devoted to all aspects of Native American art. Some of our readers are knowledgeable about the field and some know very little. We seek articles that offer something to both groups. Articles reflecting original research are preferred to those summarizing previously published information."

ARCHITECTURAL DIGEST, Conde Nast Publications, Inc., 350 Madison Ave., New York NY 10017. (212)880-8800. Publisher: Thomas P. Losee Jr. Monthly magazine covering architecture, interior design, art and antiques. "*Architectural Digest, The International Magazine of Fine Interior Design*, is a chronicle of aesthetic excellence. It showcases the work of some of today's most gifted interior designers and architects, with text by noted experts in the field of architecutre and interior design; and also encompasses topics such as art, travel and home electronics." Estab. 1920. Circ. 879,000. This magazine did not respond to our request for information. Query before submitting.

ART & ANTIQUES, Trans World Publishing, Inc., 2100 Powers Ferry Rd., Atlanta GA 30339. (770)955-5656. Fax: (770)952-0669. Publisher: Douglas C. Billian. Monthly magazine. "*Art & Antiques* is edited for people who enjoy fine art and antiques, art lovers and collectors. Editorial focuses on the art and antiques world, with articles by artists, writers and poets, investigative articles, and glimpses into the lives and works of important artists and collectors. Regular features include review of gallery shows, contemporary art openings, the domestic and international market, an expert's guide to distinguishing the value of antiques, analysis of important exhibits, and the inside story on a single personality or work of art." Estab. 1978. Circ. 24,371. This magazine did not respond to our request for information. Query before submitting.

ART PAPERS, Atlanta Art Papers, Inc., P.O. Box 77348, Atlanta GA 30357. (404)588-1837. Fax: (404)588-1836. E-mail: ruth@pd.org. Contact: Ruth Resnicow, editor-in-chief. 75% freelance written. Bimonthly magazine covering contemporary art and artists. "*Art Papers*, about regional and national contemporary art and artists, features a variety of perspectives on current art concerns. Each issue presents topical articles, interviews, reviews from across the US, and an extensive and informative artists' classified listings section. Our writers and the artists they cover represent the scope and diversity of the country's art scene." Estab. 1977. Circ. 5,000. Pays on publication. Publishes ms an average of 3 months after acceptance. Byline given. Buys all rights. Editorial lead time 2 months. Submit seasonal material 2 months in advance. Accepts simultaneous and previously published submissions. "Writers should contact us regarding manuscript status." Sample copy for $1.24 check. Writer's guidelines for #10 SASE.
Nonfiction: "Feature articles are thematic. See editorial schedule." Buys 300 mss/year. "We rely on our writers' initiative for exhibition review coverage." Pays $35-100 unless approved in advance, unsolicited articles are on spec.
Photos: Send photos with submission. Reviews color slides, b&w prints. Offers no additional payment for photos accepted with ms. Identification of subjects required.
Columns/Departments: Michael Pittari, associate editor. Newsbriefs (current art concerns and news—call for scope). Buys 18-24 mss/year. Query. Pays $35.
Tips: "Write for a copy of our writer's guidelines and request a sample copy of *Art Papers*. Interested writers should call Ruth Resnicow to discuss intents."

ART REVUE MAGAZINE, Innovative Artists, 302 W. 13th St., Loveland CO 80537. Phone/fax: (970)669-0625. Editor: Jan McNutt. 85% freelance written. Quarterly magazine covering fine art of sculpture and painting. "Articles are focused on fine art: how to, business of art, profiles of artists, museums, galleries, art businesses, art shows and exhibitions. Light and breezy articles on artists, their personalities and their work. We are not particularly interested in an artist's philosophy or their 'art statements.' " Estab. 1990. Circ. 8,000. Pays on publication. Publishes ms an average of 3 months after acceptance. Byline given. Offers 25% kill fee or $25. Buys first rights. Editorial lead time 3 months. Submit seasonal material 6 months in advance. Reports in 1 month on queries, 3 months on mss. Sample copy for $3. Writer's guidelines for #10 SASE.
Nonfiction: Essays, how-to, humor, interview/profile, new product, opinion, personal experience, photo feature, technical, travel. No crafts, pottery, doll-making, inspirational, religious, tie-dying. Special issues: Galleries and Gallery Owners (February); Artists in the: West, North, South, East (May). Buys 4-6 mss/year. Query or preferably send complete ms. Length: 500-2,000 words. Pays $100 and up.
Photos: State availability of photos with submission. Reviews prints. Offers no additional payment for photos accepted with ms. Identification of subjects required. Acquires one-time rights.
Columns/Departments: Art Matters (interesting art happenings), 100-200 words; Meet... (short q&a with artist), 100-300 words; Frivolous Art (interesting, eclectic, fun), 50-100 words. Buys 6 mss/year. Query. Pays $25-50.
Tips: "Write about unusual, fun, interesting artists or art happenings, galleries or museums. Don't try to be too serious. Put in your personality as well as what you're writing about. We're more interested in style than formula."

ART TIMES, A Literary Journal and Resource for All the Arts, P.O. Box 730, Mount Marion NY 12456-0730. Phone/fax: (914)246-6944. E-mail: arttimes@mhv.net. Website: http://www.rain.org/sculptura/arttimes/arttimes.html. Editor: Raymond J. Steiner. 10% freelance written. Prefers to work with published/established writers; works with a small number of new/unpublished writers each year. Monthly tabloid covering the arts (visual, theater, dance, etc.). "*Art Times* covers the art fields and is distributed in locations most frequented by those enjoying the arts. Our copies are sold at newsstands and are distributed throughout upstate New York counties as well as in most of the galleries in Soho, 57th Street and Madison Avenue in the metropolitan area; locations include theaters, galleries, museums, cultural centers and the like. Our readers are mostly over 40, affluent, art-conscious and sophisticated. Subscribers are located across U.S. and abroad (Italy, France, Germany, Greece, Russia, etc.)." Estab. 1984. Circ. 15,000. Pays on publication. Publishes ms an average of 2 years after acceptance. Byline given. Buys first serial rights. Submit seasonal material 8 months in advance. Accepts simultaneous submissions. Reports in 3 months on queries; 6 months on mss. Sample copy for 9×12 SAE with 6 first-class stamps. Writer's guidelines for #10 SASE.
Fiction: Raymond J. Steiner, fiction editor. "We're looking for short fiction that aspires to be *literary*. No excessive violence, sexist, off-beat, erotic, sports, or juvenile fiction." Buys 8-10 mss/year. Send complete ms. Length: 1,500 words maximum. Pays $25 maximum (honorarium) and 1 year's free subscription.
Poetry: Cheryl A. Rice, poetry editor. Poet's Niche. Avant-garde, free verse, haiku, light verse, traditional. "We prefer

well-crafted 'literary' poems. No excessively sentimental poetry." Buys 30-35 poems/year. Submit maximum 6 poems. Length: 20 lines maximum. Offers contributor copies and 1 year's free subscription.

Tips: "Be advised that we are presently on an approximate two-year lead. We are now receiving 300-400 poems and 40-50 short stories per month. We only publish two to three poems and one story each issue. Be familiar with *Art Times* and its special audience. *Art Times* has literary leanings with articles written by a staff of scholars knowledgeable in their respective fields. Although an 'arts' publication, we observe no restrictions (other than noted) in accepting fiction/ poetry other than a concern for quality writing—subjects can cover anything and not specifically arts."

THE ARTIST'S MAGAZINE, F&W Publications, Inc., 1507 Dana Ave., Cincinnati OH 45207-1005. (513)531-2690, ext. 467. Fax: (513)531-2902. Editor: Sandra Carpenter. Contact: Jennifer King, associate editor. 80% freelance written. Works with a small number of new/unpublished writers each year. Monthly magazine covering primarily two-dimensional art instruction for working artists. "Ours is a highly visual approach to teaching the serious amateur artist techniques that will help him improve his skills and market his work. The style should be crisp and immediately engaging." Circ. 250,000. **Pays on acceptance.** Publishes ms an average of 6 months after acceptance. Bionote given for feature material. Offers 20% kill fee. Buys first North American serial and second serial (reprint) rights. Reports in 3 months. Sample copy for $3 and 9×12 SAE with 3 first-class stamps. Writer's guidelines for #10 SASE.

  ● Writers must have working knowledge of art techniques. This magazine's most consistent need is for instructional feature articles written in the artist's voice.

Nonfiction: Instructional only—how an artist uses a particular technique, how he handles a particular subject or medium, or how he markets his work. "The emphasis must be on how the reader can learn some method of improving his artwork, or the marketing of it." No unillustrated articles; no seasonal material; no travel articles. Buys 60 mss/year. Query first; all queries must be accompanied by slides, transparencies, prints or tearsheets of the artist's work as well as the artist's bio, and the writer's bio and clips. Length: 1,200-2,200 words. Pays $200-350 and up. Sometimes pays the expenses of writers on assignment.

Photos: "Transparencies are required with every accepted article since these are essential for our instructional format. Full captions must accompany these." Buys one-time rights.

Columns/Departments: "Three departments are open to freelance writers." Swipe File is a collection of tips and suggestions, including photos and illustrations. No query required. Length: up to 100 words. Pays $10 and up. Spotlight is a brief profile of a working artist practicing an unusual art form, a creative marketing technique, etc. Query first, including 8-12 slides/transparencies. Length: 600-800 words. Pays $100. Drawing Board is a monthly column that covers basic art or drawing skills. Query first with illustrations. Length: 1,200 words. Pays $250 and up.

Tips: "Look at several current issues and read the author's guidelines carefully. Submissions must include artwork. Remember that our readers are fine and graphic artists."

ARTNEWS, ABC, 48 W. 38th St., New York NY 10018. (212)398-1690. Fax: (212)819-0394. Editor: Milton Esterow. Monthly. "*Artnews* reports on the art, personalities, issues, trends and events that shape the international art world. Investigative features focus on art ranging from old masters to contemporary, including painting, sculpture, prints and photography. Regular columns offer exhibition and book reviews, travel destinations, investment and appreciation advice, design insights and updates on major art world figures." Estab. 1902. Circ. 9,877. This magazine did not respond to our request for information. Query before submitting.

ART-TALK, Box 8508, Scottsdale AZ 85252. (602)948-1799. Fax: (602)994-9284. Editor: Bill Macomber. Contact: Thom Romeo. 30% freelance written. Newspaper published 9 times/year covering fine art. "*Art-Talk* deals strictly with fine art, the emphasis being on the Southwest. National and international news is also covered. All editorial is of current interest/activities and written for the art collector." Estab. 1981. Circ. 40,000. **Pays on acceptance.** Publishes ms an average of 2 months after acceptance. Byline given. Buys first North American serial rights and makes work-for-hire assignments. Editorial lead time 3 months. Submit seasonal material 4 months in advance. Accepts simultaneous submissions. Reports in 2 weeks on queries; 1 month on mss. Sample copy free.

Nonfiction: Exposé, general interest, humor, interview/profile, opinion, personal experience, photo feature. No articles on non-professional artists (e.g., Sunday Painters) or about a single commercial art gallery. Buys 12-15 mss/year. Query with published clips. Length: 500-4,000 words. Pays $75-800 for assigned articles; $50-750 for unsolicited articles. Sometimes pays expenses of writers on assignment.

Photos: State availability of photos with submission. Reviews transparencies, prints. Offers no additional payment for photos accepted with ms. Captions, identification of subjects required. Buys one-time rights.

Columns/Departments: Maintains 9 freelance columnists in different cities. Buys 38 mss/year. Query with published clips. Pays $100-175.

Tips: "Good working knowledge of the art gallery/auction/artist interconnections. Should be a part of the 'art scene' in an area known for art."

‡C, international contemporary art, C Arts Publishing and Production, Inc., P.O. Box 5, Station B, Toronto, Ontario M5T 2T2. (416)539-9495. E-mail: cmag@istar.ca. Contact: Joyce Mason, editor. Managing Editor: Lisa Gabrielle Mark. 80% freelance written. Quarterly magazine covering international contemporary art. "*C* is a magazine of contemporary art and criticism. It provides a vital and vibrant forum for the presentation of contemporary art and the discussion of issues surrounding art in our culture, including feature articles, dialogue, reviews and reports, as well as original artists' projects." Estab. 1983. Circ. 5,000. Pays on publication. Publishes ms an average of 4 months after acceptance. Byline given. Offers 50% kill fee. Editorial lead time 3 months. Accepts simultaneous submissions. Reports in 6 weeks on queries; 4 months on mss. Sample copy for $11 (US). Writer's guidelines free.

Nonfiction: Essays, general interest, opinion, personal experience. Buys 50 mss/year. Query. Length: 1,000-3,000 words. Pays $75-400.

Photos: State availability of photos with submission or send photos with submission. Reviews 4×5 transparencies or 8×10 prints. Offers no additional payment for photos accepted with ms. Captions required. Buys one-time rights.

Columns/Departments: Reviews (review of art exhibitions), 500 words. Buys 30 mss/year. Query. Pays $75-100.

‡**FUSE MAGAZINE, A magazine about issues of art & culture**, ARTONS Publishing, 401 Richmond St. W., #454, Toronto, Ontario M5V 3A8 Canada. (416)340-8026. Fax: (416)340-0494. E-mail: fuse@interlog.com. Contact: The Editorial Board. 100% freelance written. Quarterly magazine covering art and art criticism; analysis of cultural and political events as they impact on art production and exhibition. Estab. 1976. Circ. 2,500. Pays on publication. Publishes ms an average of 4 months after acceptance. Byline given. Offers 50% kill fee for commissioned pieces only. Buys first North American serial rights all languages. Editorial lead time 4 months. Submit seasonal material 2 months in advance. Accepts simultaneous submissions. Sample copy for $5 (US funds if outside Canada). Guidelines for #10 SAE with IRCs.

Nonfiction: Essays, interview/profile, opinion, art reviews. Buys 50 mss/year. Query with published clips and detailed proposal or send complete ms. Length: 800-6,000 words. Pays 10¢/word or $100 for reviews (Canadian funds).

Photos: State availability of photos with submission. Reviews 5×7 prints. Offers no additional payment for photos accepted with ms. Captions required.

Columns/Departments: Buys 10 mss/year. Pays 10¢/word.

Tips: Send detailed, but not lengthy, proposals or completed manuscripts for review by the editorial board.

METROPOLIS, The Magazine of Architecture and Design, Bellerophon Publications, 177 E. 87th St., New York NY 10128. (212)722-5050. Fax: (212)427-1938. E-mail: kira@metropolismag.com. Website: http://www.metropoli smag.com. Editor: Susan S. Szenasy. Contact: Kira Gould, managing editor. 75% freelance written. Monthly magazine (combined issues January/February and July/August) for consumers interested in architecture and design. Estab. 1981. Circ. 40,000. **Pays on acceptance.** Publishes ms an average of 3 months after acceptance. Byline given. Buys first rights or makes work-for-hire assignments. Submit calendar material 6 weeks in advance. Reports in 8 months. Sample copy for $4.95.

Nonfiction: Essays (design, architecture, urban planning issues and ideas), profiles (on multi-disciplinary designers/ architects). No profiles on individual architectural practices, information from public relations firms, or fine arts. Buys 30 mss/year. Direct feature queries with clips to Marisa Bartolucci, executive editor or Susan Szenasy, editor-in-chief. Length: 500-2,000 words. Pays $100-1,000.

Photos: State availability of or send photos with submission. Reviews contact sheets, 35mm or 4×5 transparencies, or 8×10 b&w prints. Payment offered for certain photos. Captions required. Buys one-time rights.

Columns/Departments: Insites (short takes on design and architecture), 100-600 words; pays $50-150. In Print (book review essays: focus on issues covered in a group of 2-4 books), 2,500-3,000 words; The Metropolis Observed (architecture and city planning news features and opinion), 750-1,500 words; pays $200-500. Visible City (historical aspects of cities), 1,500-2,500 words; pays $600-800; direct queries to Kira Gould, managing editor. By Design (product design), 1,000-2,000 words; pays $600-800; direct queries to Janet Rumble, senior editor;. Buys 40 mss/year. Query with published clips.

Tips: "We're looking for ideas, what's new, the obscure or the wonderful. Keep in mind that we are interested *only* in the consumer end of architecture and design. Send query with examples of photos explaining how you see illustrations working with article. Also, be patient and don't expect an immediate answer after submission of query."

"Avoid technical jargon. Keep in mind that at *Metropolis*, a firm's new work isn't a story—but the critical issues that their work brings to light might be a story. We do not cover conferences or seminars, though if such events offer new perspectives on contemporary issues in the world of art, architecture, design, graphics, urbanism, development, planning, or preservation, then an article could be framed that way."

‡**MIX, The Magazine of Artist-Run Culture**, Parallélogramme Artist-Run Culture and Publishing, Inc., 401 Richmond St. #446, Toronto, Ontario M5V 3A8 Canada. (416)506-1012. Fax: (416)340-8458. E-mail: mix@web.net. Contact: Kyo Maclear, editor. Managing Editor: Amy Gottlieb. 90% freelance written. Quarterly magazine covering artist-run gallery activities. "*Mix* represents and investigates contemporary artistic practices and issues, especially in the progressive Canadian artist-run scene." Estab. 1973. Circ. 3,500. Pays on publication. Publishes ms an average of 6 months after acceptance. Byline given. Offers 60% kill fee. Buys first North American serial rights. Editorial lead time 6 months. Submit seasonal material 4 months in advance. Reports in 2 months on queries; 3 months on mss. Sample copy for $6.50, 9×12 SASE and 6 first-class stamps. Writer's guidelines free.

Nonfiction: Essays, interview/profile. Buys 12-20 mss/year. Query with published clips. Length: 750-3,500 words. Pays $100-500. Sometimes pays expenses of writers on assignment.

Reprints: Accepts previously published submissions.

Photos: State availability of photos with submission. Offers $25/photo. Captions and identification of subjects required. Buys one-time rights.

Columns/Departments: Extracts, 1,000-2,500 words; Artist's Texts, 2,000-3,000 words; Interviews, 2,000-3,000 words. Query with published clips. Pays $100-300.

Tips: "Read the magazine and other contemporary art magazines. Understand the idea 'artist-run.' "

SOUTHWEST ART, CBH Publishing, 5444 Westheimer #1440, Houston TX 77056. (713)296-7900. Fax: (713)850-1314. Editor-in-Chief: Susan H. McGarry. 60% freelance written. Monthly fine arts magazine "directed to art collectors interested in artists, market trends and art history of the American West." Estab. 1971. Circ. 60,000. **Pays on acceptance.** Publishes ms an average of 1 year after acceptance. Byline given. Offers $125 kill fee. Submit seasonal material 8 months in advance. Reports in 6 months. Writer's guidelines free.
Nonfiction: Book excerpts, interview/profile, opinion. No fiction or poetry. Buys 70 mss/year. Query with published clips. Length 1,400-1,600 words. Pays $500. Send photos with submission.
Photos: Reviews 35mm, 2¼, 4×5 transparencies and 8×10 prints. Captions and identification of subjects required. Negotiates rights.

THEDAMU, The Black Arts Magazine, Detroit Black Arts Alliance, 13217 Livernois, Detroit MI 48238-3162. (313)931-3427. Editor: David Rambeau. Managing Editor: Titilaya Akane. Art Director: Charles Allen. 20% freelance written. Quarterly online literary magazine on the arts. "We publish Afro-American feature articles on local artists." Estab. 1965. Circ. 4,000. Pays on publication. Publishes 4 months after acceptance. Byline given. Buys one-time rights. Submit seasonal material 4 months in advance. Accepts simultaneous submissions. Reports in 1 month on queries; 3 months on mss. Sample copy for $2 in U.S. postage stamps (no checks or money orders) and 6×9 SAE with 4 first-class stamps. Writer's guidelines for #10 SASE.
Nonfiction: Essays, interview/profile. Buys 20 mss/year. Send complete ms. Length: 500-1,500 words. Pays $10-25 for unsolicited articles. Pays with contributor copies or other premiums if writer agrees.
Reprints: Accepts previously published submissions. Send photocopy of article and information about when and where the article previously appeared.
Photos: State availability of photos with submission. Reviews 5×7 prints. Offers no additional payment for photos accepted with ms. Captions, model releases and identification of subjects required. Buys one-time rights.
Tips: "Send a résumé and sample manuscript. Query for fiction, poetry, plays and film/video scenarios. Especially interested in Afro-centric cartoonists for special editions and exhibitions."

U.S. ART: All the News That Fits Prints, MSP Communications, 220 S. Sixth St., Suite 500, Minneapolis MN 55402. (612)339-7571. Fax: (612)339-5806. Editor/Publisher: Frank Sisser. Contact: Sara Gilbert, managing editor. 50% freelance written. Monthly magazine. Two artist profiles per issue; an average of 6 features per issue, 1,000-2,000 words each; service articles to inform limited-edition print collectors of trends and options in the market; round-up features spotlighting a particular genre (wildlife, western, fantasy art, etc.) All artists featured must be active in the market for limited-edition prints. Circ. 55,000. Distributed primarily through a network of 900 galleries as a free service to their customers. Writer byline given. Pays $400-550 for features. Offers 25% kill fee. Departments/columns are staff-written.
Photos: Color transparencies are preferred. Returns materials after 2 months.

WESTART, P.O. Box 6868, Auburn CA 95604. (916)885-0969. Contact: Martha Garcia, editor-in-chief. Semimonthly 12-page tabloid emphasizing art for practicing artists and artists/craftsmen; students of art and art patrons. Estab. 1961. Circ. 4,000. Pays on publication. Buys all rights. Byline given. Sample copy and writer's guidelines free.
Nonfiction: Informational, photo feature, profile. No hobbies. Buys 6-8 mss/year. Query or submit complete ms with SASE for reply or return. Phone queries OK. Length: 700-800 words. Pays 50¢/column inch.
Photos: Purchased with or without accompanying ms. Send b&w prints. Pays 50¢/column inch.
Tips: "We publish information which is current—that is, we will use a review of an exhibition only if exhibition is still open on the date of publication. Therefore, reviewer must be familiar with our printing and news deadlines."

WILDLIFE ART, The Art Journal of the Natural World, Pothole Publications, Inc. 4725 Hwy. 7, P.O. Box 16246, St. Louis Park MN 55416-0246. (612)927-9056. Fax: (612)927-9353. E-mail: pbarry@mail.winternet.com. Website: http://www.wildlifeart.mag.com. Editor-in-Chief: Robert Koenke. Editor: Rebecca Hakala Rowland. 80% freelance written. Bimonthly magazine of wildlife art and conservation. "*Wildlife Art* is the world's largest wildlife art magazine. Features cover interviews on living artists as well as wildlife art masters, illustrators and conservation organizations. Audience is publishers, collectors, galleries, museums, show promoters worldwide." Estab. 1982. Circ. 50,000. **Pays on acceptance.** Publishes ms an average of 6 months after acceptance. Byline given. Negotiable kill fee. Buys second serial (reprint) rights. Reports in 4-6 months. Sample copy for 9×12 SAE with 10 first-class stamps. Writer's guidelines for #10 SASE.
Nonfiction: Buys 40 mss/year. Query with published clips; include samples of artwork. Length: 800-5,000 words. Pays $150-900.
Columns/Departments: Buys up to 6 mss/year. Pays $100-300.

ASSOCIATIONS

Association publications allow writers to write for national audiences while covering local stories. If your town has a Kiwanis, Lions or Rotary Club chapter, one of its projects might merit a story in the club's magazine. If you are a member of the organization, find out before you write an article if the publication pays members for stories; some associations do not. In addition, some association publications gather their own club information and rely on freelancers solely for outside features. Be sure to find out what these policies are before you submit a manuscript. Club-financed magazines that carry material not directly related to the group's activities are classified by their subject matter in the Consumer and Trade sections.

‡THE ATA MAGAZINE, The Alberta Teachers' Association, 11010 142nd St., Edmonton, Alberta T5N 2R1 Canada. (403)453-2411. Fax: (403)455-6481. Website: http://www.teachers.ab.ca. Editor: Tim Johnston. Contact: Raymond Gariépy, managing editor. 10% freelance written. Quarterly magazine covering education. Estab. 1920. Circ. 39,500. Pays on publication. Publishes ms an average of 4 months after acceptance. Byline given. Buys negotiable rights or makes work-for-hire assignments. Editorial lead time 2 months. Sample copy and writer's guidelines free.
Nonfiction: Education. Buys 4 mss/year. Query with published clips. Length: 500-1,000 words. Pays $75-100.
Photos: State availability of photos with submission.
Fillers: Buys 2/year. Pays $75.

‡COMEDY WRITERS ASSOCIATION NEWSLETTER, P.O. Box 23304, Brooklyn NY 11202-0066. (718)855-5057. Contact: Robert Makinson, editor. 10% freelance written. Semiannual newsletter on comedy writing for association members. Estab. 1989. **Pays on acceptance.** Publishes ms an average of 3 months after acceptance. Byline given. Buys all rights. Reports in 2 weeks on queries; 1 month on mss. Sample copy for $6. Writer's guidelines for #10 SASE.
Nonfiction: How-to, humor, opinion, personal experience. "No exaggerations about the sales that you make and what you are paid. Be accurate." Query. Length: 250-500 words. "You may submit articles and byline will be given if used, but at present payment is only made for jokes. Emphasis should be on marketing, not general humor articles."
Tips: "The easiest way to be mentioned in the publication is to submit short jokes. (Payment is $1-3 per joke.) Jokes for professional speakers preferred. Include SASE when submitting jokes."

THE ELKS MAGAZINE, 425 W. Diversey, Chicago IL 60614-6196. E-mail: elksmag@aol.com. Website: http://www.elksmag.com. Editor: Fred D. Oakes. Managing Editor: Anne L. Idol. 50% freelance written. Prefers to work with published/established writers. Magazine published 10 times/year emphasizing general interest with family appeal. Estab. 1922. Circ. 1,5000,000. **Pays on acceptance.** Buys first North American serial rights. Reports within 1 month. Sample copy and writer's guidelines for 9×12 SAE with 4 first-class stamps.
Nonfiction: Information, business, contemporary life problems and situations, nostalgia, or just interesting topics, ranging from medicine, science and history to sports. "The articles should not just be a rehash of existing material. They must be fresh, thought-provoking, well-researched and documented." No fiction, political articles, 1st person, religion, travel, fillers or verse. Buys 2-3 mss/issue. Query; no phone queries. Length: 1,500-3,000 words. Pays from $150.
Tips: "Requirements are clearly stated in our guidelines. A submission, following a query letter go-ahead, should include several prints if the piece lends itself to illustration."

KIWANIS, 3636 Woodview Trace, Indianapolis IN 46268-3196. Fax: (317)879-0204. Website: http://www.kiwanis.org. Managing Editor: Chuck Jonak. 85% of feature articles freelance written. Buys about 40 mss/year. Magazine published 10 times/year for business and professional persons and their families. Estab. 1917. Circ. 276,500. **Pays on acceptance.** Buys first serial rights. Offers 40% kill fee. Publishes ms an average of 6 months after acceptance. Byline given. Reports within 2 months. Sample copy and writer's guidelines for 9×12 SAE with 5 first-class stamps.
Nonfiction: Articles about social and civic betterment, small-business concerns, science, education, religion, family, youth, health, recreation, etc. Emphasis on objectivity, intelligent analysis and thorough research of contemporary issues. Positive tone preferred. Concise, lively writing, absence of clichés, and impartial presentation of controversy required. When applicable, include information and quotations from international sources. Avoid writing strictly to a US audience. "We have a continuing need for articles of international interest. In addition, we are very interested in proposals that concern helping youth, particularly prenatal through age five: day care, developmentally appropriate education, early intervention for at-risk children, parent education, safety and health." Length: 2,000-2,500 words. Pays $600-1,000. "No fiction, personal essays, profiles, travel pieces, fillers or verse of any kind. A light or humorous approach is welcomed where the subject is appropriate and all other requirements are observed." Usually pays the expenses of writers on assignment. Query first. Must include SASE for response.
Photos: "We accept photos submitted with manuscripts. Our rate for a manuscript with good photos is higher than for one without." Model release and identification of subjects required. Buys one-time rights.
Tips: "We will work with any writer who presents a strong feature article idea applicable to our audience and who will prove he or she knows the craft of writing. First, obtain writer's guidelines and a sample copy. Study for general style and content. When querying, present detailed outline of proposed manuscript's focus, direction, and editorial intent. Indicate expert sources to be used for attribution, as well as article's tone and length. Present a well-researched, smoothly written manuscript that contains a 'human quality' with the use of anecdotes, practical examples, quotations, etc."

THE LION, 300 22nd St., Oak Brook IL 60521-8842. (630)571-5466. Fax: (630)571-8890. E-mail: lions@lionsclubs.org. Website: http://www.lionsclubs.org. Contact: Robert Kleinfelder, editor. 35% freelance written. Works with a small number of new/unpublished writers each year. Monthly magazine covering service club organization for Lions Club members and their families. Estab. 1918. Circ. 600,000. **Pays on acceptance.** Publishes ms an average of 5 months after acceptance. Buys all rights. Byline given. Reports in 6 weeks. Sample copy and writer's guidelines free.

Nonfiction: Informational (issues of interest to civic-minded individuals) and photo feature (must be of a Lions Club service project). No travel, biography or personal experiences. Welcomes humor, if sophisticated but clean; no sensationalism. Prefers anecdotes in articles. Buys 4 mss/issue. Query. Phone queries OK. Length: 500-2,200. Pays $100-750. Sometimes pays the expenses of writers on assignment.

Photos: Purchased with or without accompanying ms or on assignment. Captions required. Query for photos. Black and white and color glossies at least 5×7 or 35mm color slides. Total purchase price for ms includes payment for photos accepted with ms. "Be sure photos are clear and as candid as possible."

Tips: "Incomplete details on how the Lions involved actually carried out a project and poor quality photos are the most frequent mistakes made by writers in completing an article assignment for us. We are geared increasingly to an international audience. Writers who travel internationally could query for possible assignments, although only locally-related expenses could be paid."

THE OPTIMIST, Optimist International, 4494 Lindell Blvd., St. Louis MO 63108. (314)371-6000. Fax: (314)371-6006. E-mail: dlockol@aol.com. Website: http://www.optimist.org. Editor: Dennis R. Osterwisch. 10% freelance written. Bimonthly magazine about the work of Optimist clubs and members for members of the Optimist clubs in the United States and Canada. Circ. 154,000. **Pays on acceptance.** Publishes ms an average of 4 months after acceptance. Buys first North American serial rights. Submit seasonal material 3 months in advance. Reports in 1 week. Sample copy and writer's guidelines for 9×12 SAE with 4 first-class stamps.

Nonfiction: "We want articles about the activities of local Optimist clubs. These volunteer community-service clubs are constantly involved in projects, aimed primarily at helping young people. With over 4,000 Optimist clubs in the US and Canada, writers should have ample resources. Some large metropolitan areas boast several dozen clubs. We are also interested in feature articles on individual club members who have in some way distinguished themselves, either in their club work or their personal lives. Good photos for all articles are a plus and can mean a bigger check." Will also consider short (200-400 word) articles that deal with self-improvement or a philosophy of optimism. Buys 1-2 mss/issue. Query. "Submit a letter that conveys your ability to turn out a well-written article and tells exactly what the scope of the article will be." Length: up to 1,000 words. Pays $300 and up.

Reprints: Send photocopy of article and information about when and where the article previously appeared. Pays 50% of amount paid for an original article.

Photos: State availability of photos. Payment negotiated. Captions preferred. Buys all rights. "No mug shots or people lined up against the wall shaking hands."

Tips: "Find out what the Optimist clubs in your area are doing, then find out if we'd be interested in an article on a specific club project. All of our clubs are eager to talk about what they're doing. Just ask them and you'll probably have an article idea. We would like to see short pieces on the positive affect an optimistic outlook on life can have on an individual. Examples of famous people who overcame adversity because of their positive attitude are welcome."

PERSPECTIVE, Pioneer Clubs, P.O. Box 788, Wheaton IL 60189-0788. (630)293-1600. Fax: (630)293-3053. E-mail: pclubs@ix.netcom.com. Website: http://www.pioneerclubs.org. Contact: Rebecca Powell Parat, editor. 15% freelance written. Works with a number of new/unpublished writers each year. Triannual magazine for "volunteer leaders of clubs for girls and boys age 2-grade 12. Clubs are sponsored by local churches throughout North America." Estab. 1967. Circ. 24,000. **Pays on acceptance.** Publishes ms an average of 6 months after acceptance. Buys first rights for assigned articles, first North American serial rights for unsolicited mss, and second serial (reprint) rights. Submit seasonal material 9 months in advance. Reports in 2 months. Writer's guidelines and sample copy for $1.75 and 9×12 SAE with 6 first-class stamps.

Nonfiction: Informational (relationship skills, leadership skills); inspirational (stories of leaders and children in Pioneer Clubs); interview (Christian education leaders, club leaders); personal experience (of club leaders). Buys 2-3 mss/year. Byline given. Length: 1,000-1,500 words. Pays $50-90.

Reprints: Send photocopy of article or typed ms with rights for sale noted and information about when and where the article previously appeared.

Columns/Departments: Storehouse (game, activity, outdoor activity, service project suggestions—all related to club projects for age 2 through grade 12). Buys 2-3 mss/year. Submit complete ms. Length: 150-250 words. Pays $8-15.

Tips: "Submit articles directly related to club work, practical in nature, i.e., ideas for leader training in communication, discipline, teaching skills. However, most of our articles are assigned. Writers who have contact with a Pioneer Club program in their area and who are interested in working on assignment are welcome to contact us."

RECREATION NEWS, Official Publication of the League of Federal Recreation Associations, Inc., Icarus Publishers, Inc. and the Washington DC chapter of the National Employee Services and Recreation Association, P.O. Box 32335, Calvert Station, Washington DC 20007-0635. (202)965-6960. Fax: (202)965-6964. E-mail: recreation_news @mcimail.com. Contact: Rebecca Heaton, editor. 85% freelance written. Monthly guide to leisure-time activities for federal and private industry workers covering outdoor recreation, travel, fitness and indoor pastimes. Estab. 1979. Circ. 104,000. Pays on publication. Publishes ms an average of 8 months after acceptance. Byline given. Buys first rights and second serial (reprint) rights. Submit seasonal material 10 months in advance. Accepts simultaneous submissions. Reports in 2 months. Sample copy and writer's guidelines for 9×12 SAE with 4 first-class stamps.

Nonfiction: Articles Editor. Leisure travel (no international travel); sports; hobbies; historical/nostalgic (Washington-related); personal experience (with recreation, life in Washington). Special issues: skiing (December). Query with clips of published work. Length: 800-2,000 words. Pays from $50-300.

Reprints: Send photocopy of article or typed ms with rights for sale noted, with information about where and when it previously appeared. Pays $50.

Photos: Photo editor. State availability of photos with query letter or ms. Uses b&w prints. Pays $25. Uses color transparency on cover only. Pays $50-125 for transparency. Captions and identification of subjects required.

Tips: "Our writers generally have a few years of professional writing experience and their work runs to the lively and conversational. We like more manuscripts in a wide range of recreational topics, including the off-beat. The areas of our publication most open to freelancers are general articles on travel and sports, both participational and spectator, also historic in the DC area. In general, stories on sites visited need to include info on nearby places of interest and places to stop for lunch, to shop, etc."

THE ROTARIAN, Rotary International, 1560 Sherman Ave., Evanston IL 60201-1461. (847)866-3000. Fax: (847)866-9732. E-mail: 75457.3577@compuserve.com. Website: http://www.rotary.org. Editor-in-chief: Willmon L. White. Contact: Charles W. Pratt, managing editor. 40% freelance written. Monthly magazine for Rotarian business and professional men and women and their families, schools, libraries, hospitals, etc. "Articles should appeal to an international audience and in some way help Rotarians help other people. The organization's rationale is one of hope, encouragement and belief in the power of individuals talking and working together." Estab. 1911. Circ. 521,111. **Pays on acceptance**. Byline sometimes given. Kill fee negotiable. Buys one-time or all rights. Reports in 2 weeks. Sample copy for 9×12 SAE with 6 first-class stamps. Writer's guidelines for #10 SASE.
  ● Ranked as one of the best markets for freelance writers in *Writer's Yearbook* magazine's annual "Top 100 Markets," January 1997.

Nonfiction: Essays, general interest, humor, inspirational, photo feature, travel, business, environment. No fiction, religious or political articles. Query with published clips. Length: 1,500 words maximum. Negotiates payment.

Reprints: Send tearsheet or photocopy of article or typed ms with rights for sale noted and information about when and where the article previously appeared. Negotiates payment.

Photos: State availability of photos with submission. Reviews contact sheets, transparencies. Buys one-time rights.

Columns/Departments: Manager's Memo (business), Executive Health, Executive Lifestyle, Earth Diary, Travel Tips, Trends. Length: 800 words. Query.

Tips: "The chief aim of *The Rotarian* is to report Rotary International news. Most of this information comes through Rotary channels and is staff written or edited. The best field for freelance articles is in the general interest category. These run the gamut from humor pieces and 'how-to' stories to articles about such significant concerns as business management, world health and the environment."

‡THE SAMPLE CASE, The Order of United Commercial Travelers of America, 632 N. Park St., Box 159019, Columbus OH 43215-8619. (614)228-3276. Fax: (614)228-1898. Editor: Megan Woitovich. Contact: Linda Fisher, managing editor. Quarterly magazine covering news for members of the United Commercial Travelers emphasizing fraternalism for its officers and active membership. Estab. 1891. Circ. 150,000. Pays on publication. Buys one-time rights. Reports in 3 months. Submit seasonal material 6 months in advance. Accepts submissions.

Nonfiction: Articles on health/fitness/safety; family; hobbies/entertainment; fraternal/civic activities; business finance/insurance; travel in the US and Canada; food/cuisine. Length: 1,000-3,000 words. Pays $200-300.

Reprints: Send tearsheet of article, photocopy of article, or typed ms with rights for sale noted and information about when and where the article previously appeared. Pays 100% of amount paid for an original article.

Photos: David Knapp, art director. State availability of photos with ms. Prefers color prints. Pay negotiable. Captions required.

SCOUTING, Boy Scouts of America, 1325 W. Walnut Hill Lane, P.O. Box 152079, Irving TX 75015-2079. (972)580-2367. Fax: (972)580-2079. E-mail: 103064.3363@compuserve.com. Website: http://www.bsa.scouting.org. Contact: Jon C. Halter, editor. Executive Editor: Scott Daniels. 90% freelance written. Magazine published 6 times/year on Scouting activities for adult leaders of the Boy Scouts and Cub Scouts. Estab. 1913. Circ. 1,000,000. **Pays on acceptance**. Publishes ms an average of 6 months after acceptance. Byline given. Buys first North American serial rights. Submit seasonal material 9 months in advance. Reports in 2-3 weeks. Sample copy for $1 and #10 SAE with 4 first-class stamps. Writer's guidelines for #10 SASE.
  ● *Scouting* is looking for more articles about scouting families involved in interesting/unusual family-together activities/hobbies, i.e., caving, bicycle touring, (two that they've done) and profiles of urban/inner-city scout leaders and packs or troop with successful histories.

Nonfiction: Buys 60 mss/year. Query with published clips. Length: 1,000-1,500 words. Pays $500-800 for major articles; $200-500 for shorter features. Pays expenses of writers on assignment.

Reprints: Send photocopy and information about where and when the article previously appeared. "First-person accounts on Scouting experiences (previously published in local newspapers, etc.) are a popular subject for this category."

Photos: State availability of photos with submission. Reviews contact sheets and transparencies. Identification of subjects required. Buys one-time rights.

Columns/Departments: Way it Was (Scouting history), 1,000 words; Family Talk (family—raising kids, etc.), 1,000 words. Buys 6 mss/year. Query. Pays $200-400.

THE TOASTMASTER, Toastmasters International, 23182 Arroyo Vista, Rancho Santa Margarita CA 92688 or P.O. Box 9052, Mission Viejo, CA 92690-7052. (714)858-8255. Fax: (714)858-1207. Website: http://www.toastmasters.org. Contact: Suzanne Frey, editor. Associate Editor: Beth Curtis. 50% freelance written. Monthly magazine on public speaking, leadership and club concerns. "This magazine is sent to members of Toastmasters International, a nonprofit educational association of men and women throughout the world who are interested in developing their communication and leadership skills. Members range from novice speakers to professional orators and come from a wide variety of backgrounds." Estab. 1932. Circ. 170,000. **Pays on acceptance.** Publishes ms an average of 10 months after acceptance. Byline given. Buys second serial (reprint), first-time or all rights. Submit seasonal material 3 months in advance. Accepts simultaneous submissions. Reports in 6 weeks on queries; 1 month on mss. Sample copy for 9×12 SAE with 4 first-class stamps. Writer's guidelines for #10 SASE.
Nonfiction: Book excerpts, how-to (communications related), humor (only if informative; humor cannot be off-color or derogatory), interview/profile (only if of a very prominent member or former member of Toastmasters International or someone who has a valuable perspective on communication and leadership). Buys 50 mss/year. Query. Length: 1,000-2,500 words. Pays $75-250. Sometimes pays expenses of writers on assignment. "Toastmasters members are requested to view their submissions as contributions to the organization. Sometimes asks for book excerpts and reprints without payment, but original contribution from individuals outside Toastmasters will be paid for at stated rates."
Reprints: Send typed ms with rights for sale noted and information about when and where the article previously appeared. Pays 100% of amount paid for an original article.
Photos: Reviews b&w prints. No additional payment for photos accepted with ms. Captions required. Buys all rights.
Tips: "We are looking primarily for 'how-to' articles on subjects from the broad fields of communications and leadership which can be directly applied by our readers in their self-improvement and club programming efforts. Concrete examples are useful. Avoid sexist or nationalist language."

VFW MAGAZINE, Veterans of Foreign Wars of the United States, 406 W. 34th St., Kansas City MO 64111. (816)756-3390. Fax: (816)968-1169. Website: http://www.vfw.org. Contact: Rich Kolb, editor-in-chief. 40% freelance written. Monthly magazine on veterans' affairs, military history, patriotism, defense and current events. "*VFW Magazine* goes to its members worldwide, all having served honorably in the armed forces overseas from World War II through Bosnia." Circ. 2,000,000. **Pays on acceptance.** Offers 50% kill fee on commissioned articles. Buys first rights. Submit seasonal material 6 months in advance. Submit detailed query letter, résumé and sample clips. Reports in 2 months. Sample copy for 9×12 SAE with 5 first-class stamps.
● *VFW Magazine* is becoming more current-events oriented.
Nonfiction: Veterans' and defense affairs; recognition of veterans and military service; current foreign policy; American armed forces abroad and international events affecting U.S. national security are in demand. Resolutions passed each August at VFW national convention; effect of recent legislation on average veteran. Buys 25-30 mss/year. Query with 1-page outline and published clips. Length: 1,000 words. Pays up to $500 maximum unless otherwise negotiated.
Photos: Send photos with submission. Color transparencies (2¼×2¼) preferred; b&w prints (5×7, 8×10). Reviews contact sheets, negatives, transparencies and prints. Captions, model releases and identification of subjects required. Buys first North American rights.
Tips: "Absolute accuracy and quotes from relevant individuals are a must. Bibliographies useful if subject required extensive research and/or is open to dispute. Consult *The Associated Press Stylebook* for correct grammar and punctuation. Please enclose 3-sentence biography describing your military service in the field in which you are writing." Welcomes member and freelance submissions.

ASTROLOGY, METAPHYSICAL AND NEW AGE
Magazines in this section carry articles ranging from shamanism to extraterrestrial phenomena. With the coming millennium, there is increased interest in spirituality, angels, near death experiences, mind/body healing and other New Age concepts and figures. The following publications regard astrology, psychic phenomena, metaphysical experiences and related subjects as sciences or as objects of serious study. Each has an individual personality and approach to these phenomena. If you want to write for these publications, be sure to read them carefully before submitting.

‡ASTROLOGY YOUR DAILY HOROSCOPE, Popular Magazine Group, 7002 W. Butler Pike, Ambler PA 19002. Contact: Arthur Ofner, editor. 90% freelance written. Monthly magazine covering astrology and horoscopes. "*Astrology*

MARKET CONDITIONS are constantly changing! If this is 1999 or later, buy the newest edition of *Writer's Market* at your favorite bookstore or order directly from Writer's Digest Books.

Your Daily Horoscope is a monthly astrology magazine that covers all facets of astrology, including weekly and daily predictions, advice from astrologers, prophetic numerology, lunar forecasts, birthday horoscopes and forecasts about love, money and health issues. Feature articles relate to planetary transits, how astrology is used in individual lives and how-to articles. Publishes ms an average of 4 months after acceptance. Byline given. Buys all rights. Editorial lead time 4 months. Submit seasonal material 6 months in advance. Reports in 2 months. Sample copy for $2.95. Writer's guidelines for #10 SASE.

Nonfiction: Book excerpts, how-to (interpret a natal chart), chart analysis of celebrities. Buys 48 mss/year. Send complete ms. Length: 1,000-2,500 words. Pays $40-100.

Photos: State availability of photos with submission. Reviews 4×6 prints. Offers no additional payment for photos accepted with ms. Captions, identification of subjects required. Rights purchased are negotiable.

FATE, Llewellyn Worldwide, Ltd., P.O. Box 64383, St. Paul MN 55164-0383. Fax: (612)291-1908. E-mail: lwlpc@fate mag.com. Website: http://www.llewellyn.com. Contact: Craig Miller, associate editor. 70% freelance written. Estab. 1901. Circ. 59,000. Buys all rights. Byline given. Pays after publication. Sample copy and writer's guidelines for $3 and 9×12 SAE with 5 first-class stamps. Reports in 3 months.

Nonfiction and Fillers: Personal psychic and mystical experiences, 350-500 words. Pays $25. Articles on parapsychology, Fortean phenomena, cryptozoology, parapsychology, spiritual healing, flying saucers, new frontiers of science, and mystical aspects of ancient civilizations, 500-3,000 words. Must include complete authenticating details. Prefers interesting accounts of single events rather than roundups. "We very frequently accept manuscripts from new writers; the majority are individual's first-person accounts of their own psychic/mystical/spiritual experiences. We do need to have all details, where, when, why, who and what, included for complete documentation. We ask for a notarized statement attesting to truth of the article." Query or submit completed ms. Pays 10¢/word. Fillers are especially welcomed and must be be fully authenticated also, and on similar topics. Length: 50-300 words.

Photos: Buys slides or prints with mss. Pays $10.

Tips: "We would like more stories about *current* paranormal or unusual events."

GNOSIS, A Journal of the Western Inner Traditions, Lumen Foundation, P.O. Box 14217, San Francisco CA 94114. (415)974-0600. Fax: (415)974-0366. E-mail: smoley@well.com (queries); gnosis@well.com (unsolicited mss). Website: http://www.lumen.org. Contact: Richard Smoley, editor. 75% freelance written. Quarterly magazine covering esoteric spirituality. "*Gnosis* is a journal covering the esoteric, mystical, and occult traditions of Western civilization, including Judaism, Christianity, Islam, and Paganism." Estab. 1985. Circ. 16,000. Pays on publication. Publishes ms an average of 3 months after acceptance. Byline given. Buys first North American serial rights. Editorial lead time 5 months. Submit seasonal material 5 months in advance. Reports in 1 month on queries; 4 months on mss. Sample copy for $9. Writer's guidelines for #10 SASE.

Nonfiction: Book excerpts, essays, religious. Buys 32 mss/year. Query with published clips. Length: 1,000-5,000 words. Pays $100-300 for assigned articles; $50-200 for unsolicited articles. All contributors receive 4 contributor's copies plus a year's subscription in addition to payment.

Photos: State availability of photos with submissions. Reviews contact sheets, prints. Offers $50-125/photo. Captions, identification of subjects required. Buys one-time rights.

Columns/Departments: Theme issue articles, (esoteric traditions and practices, past and present), 1,000-5,000 words; News & Notes (items of current interest in esoteric spirituality), 1,000 words. Pays $100-250. Book Reviews (reviews of new books in the field), 250-1,000 words. Pays $50. Buys 45 mss/year. Query with published clips.

Tips: "We give strong preference to articles related to our issue themes (available with writer's guidelines)."

‡HOROSCOPE GUIDE, JBH Publishing Co., 7002 W. Butler Pike, Ambler PA 19002. Contact: Arthur Offner, editor. 90% freelance written. Monthly magazine covering personal horoscopes and daily forecasts for all sun signs. "*Horoscope Guide* is a monthly astrology magazine with comprehensive daily forecasts for all signs of the zodiac, monthly forecasts on love, yearly prophesies, astrology advice columns, and feature articles dealing with any facet of astrology, from the mundane to the esoteric. Audience is 90% female, ages 25-55, with high school or above education level." Pays on publication. Publishes ms an average of 4 months after acceptance. Byline given. Buys all rights. Editorial lead time 4 months. Submit seasonal material 6 months in advance. Reports in 2 months. Sample copy for $2.95. Writer's guidelines for #10 SASE.

Nonfiction: Book excerpts, how-to (interpret a natal chart), chart analysis of celebrities. Buys 60 mss/year. Send complete ms. Length: 1,000-2,500 words. Pays $40-100.

Photos: State availability of photos with submission. Reviews 4×6 prints. Offers no additional payment for photos accepted with ms. Captions, identification of subjects required. Rights purchased negotiable.

Columns/Departments: HealthScope (health predictions, trends for each sun sign) 1,200 words (100 words per zodiac sign). Query with published clips. Pays $48-60.

MAGICAL BLEND MAGAZINE, A Primer for the 21st Century, Magical Blend, P.O. Box 600, Chico CA 95927. (916)893-9037. E-mail: magical@crl.com. Website: http://www.magicalblend.com. Contact: Jerry Snider, managing editor. 50% freelance written. Bimonthly magazine covering social and mystical transformation. "*Magical Blend* endorses no one pathway to spiritual growth, but attempts to explore many alternative possibilities to help transform the planet." Estab. 1980. Circ. 65,000. Pays on publication. Publishes ms an average of 2 months after acceptance. Byline given. Reports in 2 months. Sample copy free. Writer's guidelines for #10 SASE.

Nonfiction: Book excerpts, essays, general interest, inspirational, interview/profile, religious. "Articles must reflect our standards: see our magazine. No poetry or fiction." Buys 24 mss/year. Send complete ms. Length: 1,000-5,000 words. Pay varies. Contributor copies.

Photos: State availability of photos with submission. Reviews transparencies. Negotiates payment individually. Model releases, identification of subjects required. Buys all rights.

Fillers: Newsbreaks. Buys 12-20/year. Length: 300-450 words. Pay varies.

‡**NEW AGE JOURNAL**, 42 Pleasant St., Watertown MA 02172. Fax: (617)926-5021. Fax: (617)926-5021. Website: http://www.newage.com. Executive Editor: Jody Kolodzey. Editor: Joan Duncan Oliver. Contact: Devra First, editorial assistant. 35% freelance written. Works with a small number of new/unpublished writers each year. Bimonthly magazine emphasizing "personal fulfillment and social change. The audience we reach is college-educated, social-service/hi-tech oriented, 25-55 years of age, concerned about social values, humanitarianism and balance in personal life." Estab. 1974. Cir. 197,000. Publishes ms an average of 5 months after acceptance. Byline given. Offers 25% kill fee. Buys first North American serial and reprint rights. Submit seasonal material 6 months in advance. Accepts simultaneous submissions. Reports in 3 months on queries. Sample copy for $5 and 9×12 SAE. Writer's guidelines for #10 SASE.

Nonfiction: Book excerpts, exposé, general interest, how-to (travel on business, select a computer, reclaim land, plant a garden), behavior, trend pieces, humor, inspirational, interview/profile, new product, food, sci-tech, nutrition, holistic health, education, personal experience. Buys 60-80 mss/year. Query with published clips. No phone calls. Length: 500-4,000 words. Pays $50-2,500. Pays the expenses of writers on assignment.

Reprints: Send tearsheet or photocopy of article.

Photos: State availability of photos. Model releases, identification of subjects required. Buys one-time rights.

Columns/Departments: Body/Mind; Reflections; First Person, Upfront. Buys 60-80 mss/year. Query with published clips. Length: 750-1,500 words. Pays $100-850.

Tips: "Submit short, specific news items to the Upfront department. Query first with clips. A query is one to two paragraphs—if you need more space than that to *present* the idea, then you don't have a clear grip on it. The next open area is columns: First Person and Reflections often take first-time contributors. Read the magazine and get a sense of type of writing run in these two columns. In particular we are interested in seeing inspirational, first-person pieces that highlight an engaging idea, experience or issue. We are also looking for new cutting edge thinking."

PARABOLA, The Magazine of Myth and Tradition, The Society for the Study of Myth and Tradition, 656 Broadway, New York NY 10012-2317. (212)505-9037. Fax: (212)979-7325. E-mail: parabola@panix.com. Website: http://www.parabola.org. Managing Editor: Natalie Baan. Quarterly magazine on mythology, tradition and comparative religion. "*Parabola* is devoted to the exploration of the quest for meaning as expressed in the myths, symbols, and tales of the religious traditions. Particular emphasis is on the relationship between this wisdom and contemporary life." Estab. 1976. Circ. 40,000. Pays on publication. Publishes ms 3 months after acceptance. Byline given. Offers kill fee for assigned articles only (usually $100). Buys first North American serial, first, one-time or second serial (reprint) rights. Editorial lead time 4 months. Accepts simultaneous submissions. Reports in 3 weeks on queries; on mss "variable—for articles directed to a particular theme, we usually respond the month of or the month after the deadline (so for an April 15 deadline, we are likely to respond in April or May). Articles not directed to themes may wait four months or more!" Sample copy for $6.95 current issue; $8.95 back issue. Writers guidelines and list of themes for SASE.

• *Parabola* no longer accepts submissions of poetry.

Nonfiction: Book excerpts, essays, photo feature. Send for current list of themes. No articles not related to specific themes. Special issues: Miracles (November 1997); Millenium (February 1998). Buys 4-8 mss/year. Query. Length: 2,000-4,000 words. Pays $100 minimum. Sometimes pays expenses of writers on assignment.

Reprints: Send photocopy of article or short story (must include copy of copyright page) and information about when and where the article previously appeared.

Photos: State availability of photos with submission. Reviews contact sheets, any transparencies and prints. Identification of subjects required. Buys one-time rights.

Columns/Departments: Tangents (reviews of film, exhibits, dance, theater, video, music relating to theme of issue), 2,000-4,000 words; Book Reviews (reviews of current books in religion, spirituality, mythology and tradition), 500 words; Epicycles (retellings of myths and folk tales of all cultures—no fiction or made-up mythology!), under 2,000 words. Buys 2-6 unsolicited mss/year. Query. Pays $75.

Fiction: "We *very* rarely publish fiction; must relate to upcoming theme." Query. Publishes novel excerpts.

‡**PSYCHIC WORLD**, Popular Magazine Group, Inc., 7002 W. Butler Pike, Ambler PA 19002. Contact: Arthur Ofner, editor. 90% freelance written. Quarterly magazine covering psychic phenomena, paranormal and New Age. "*Psychic World* is published quarterly and contains feature articles relating to psychic phenomena and the paranormal, including angels, past lives, channeling, psychometry, psychic powers, profiles of famous psychics, places of magic and mystery, miracles, etc. It serves a mixed audience, interested in all New Age topics." Pays on publication. Publishes ms an average of 4 months after acceptance. Byline given. Buys all rights. Editorial lead time 4 months. Submit seasonal material 6 months in advance. Reports in 2 months. Sample copy for $4.95. Writer's guidelines for #10 SASE.

Nonfiction: Book excerpts, general interest, historical, how-to (strengthen psychic powers, read a crystal ball, select a psychic reader), interview/profile (famous psychics), new product (New Age), personal experience, (psychic or paranormal), photo feature, religious. Special issue: Astrology Annual (Fall). Buys 48 mss/year. Send complete ms. Length: 1,000-2,500 words. Pays $40-100.

Photos: State availability of photos with submission. Reviews 4×6 prints. Offers no additional payment for photos accepted with ms. Captions, identification of subjects required. Rights purchased are negotiable.
Fillers: Facts. Buys 28/year. Length: 250-1,000 words. Pays $10-40.

THE SANTA FE SUN, Northern New Mexico's Progressive Paper, New Mexico Sun, Ltd. Co., 1807 2nd St. #29, Santa Fe NM 87505. (505)989-8381. Fax: (505)989-4767. E-mail: editor@santafesun.com. Contact: Alan Hutner, editor. 80% freelance written. Monthly newspaper covering alternative/New Age, with a preference to articles with a northern New Mexico slant. Estab. 1988. Circ. 23,000. Pays on publication. Publishes ms an average of 2 months after acceptance. Byline given. Not copyrighted. Buys first rights. Editorial lead time 2 months. Submit seasonal material 1 month in advance. Accepts simultaneous submissions. Reports in 1 month on queries. Sample copy for $3. Writer's guidelines for #10 SASE.
Nonfiction: Book excerpts, essays, inspirational, interview/profile, opinion, personal experience, photo feature, religious, travel. Buys 12 mss/year. Query with published clips. Length: 600-2,200 words. Pays $50-200 for assigned articles. Sometimes pays expenses of writers on assignment.
Reprints: Send photocopy and information about when and where the article previously appeared. Pay negotiable.
Photos: State availability of photos with submission. Reviews contact sheets. Negotiates payment individually. Identification of subjects required. Buys one-time rights.
Columns/Departments: Pays 7¢/word.
Poetry: Avant-garde, free verse, haiku, light verse, traditional.

SHAMAN'S DRUM, A Journal of Experiential Shamanism, Cross-Cultural Shamanism Network, P.O. Box 97, Ashland OR 97520. (541)552-0839. Website: http://www.shamans.net. Contact: Timothy White, editor. 75% freelance written. Quarterly educational magazine of cross-cultural shamanism. "*Shaman's Drum* seeks contributions directed toward a general but well-informed audience. Our intent is to expand, challenge, and refine our readers' and our understanding of shamanism in practice. Topics include indigenous medicineway practices, contemporary shamanic healing practices, ecstatic spiritual practices, and contemporary shamanic psychotherapies. Our overall focus is cross-cultural, but our editorial approach is culture-specific—we prefer that authors focus on specific ethnic traditions or personal practices about which they have significant firsthand experience. We are looking for examples of not only how shamanism has transformed individual lives but also practical ways it can help ensure survival of life on the planet. We want material that captures the heart and feeling of shamanism and that can inspire people to direct action and participation, and to explore shamanism in greater depth." Estab. 1985. Circ. 17,000. Publishes ms 6 months after acceptance. Buys first North American serial and first rights. Editorial lead time 1 year. Reports in 3 months. Sample copy for $5. Writer's guidelines for #10 SASE.
Nonfiction: Book excerpts, essays, interview/profile (please query), opinion, personal experience, photo feature. *No fiction, poetry or fillers.* Buys 16 mss/year. Send complete ms. Length: 5,000-8,000. "We pay 5-8¢/word, depending on how much we have to edit. We also send two copies and tearsheets in addition to cash payment."
Reprints: Accepts rarely. Send typed ms with rights for sale noted and information about when and where the article previously appeared. Pays 50% of amount paid for an original article.
Photos: Send photos with submission. Reviews contact sheets, transparencies and all size prints. Offers $40-50/photo. Identification of subjects required. Buys one-time rights.
Columns/Departments: Judy Wells, Earth Circles editor. Earth Circles (news format, concerned with issues, events, organizations related to shamanism, indigenous peoples and caretaking Earth. Relevant clippings also sought. Clippings paid with copies and credit line), 500-1,500 words. Buys 8 mss/year. Send complete ms. Pays 5-8¢/word. Reviews: Timothy White, editor (in-depth reviews of books about shamanism or closely related subjects such as indigenous lifestyles, ethnobotany, transpersonal healing and ecstatic spirituality), 500-1,500 words. "Please query us first and we will send *Reviewer's Guidelines*." Pays 5-8¢/word.
Tips: "All articles must have a clear relationship to shamanism, but may be on topics which have not traditionally been defined as shamanic. We prefer original material that is based on, or illustrated with, first-hand knowledge and personal experience. Articles should be well documented with descriptive examples and pertinent background information. Photographs and illustrations of high quality are always welcome and can help sell articles."

THE SPIRIT (OF WOMAN IN THE MOON), P.O. Box 2087, Cupertino CA 95015-2087. (408)279-6626. Fax: (408)279-6636. E-mail: womaninmoon@earthlink.net. Publicity & Editor-in-Chief: Dr. SDiane Adams-Bogus. 90% freelance written. Semiannual news magazine covering New Age, African American, feminist, gay/lesbian. "*The Spirit* wants work that heals and guides. It wants insight and joy, new views, uncommon ideas. It wants to hear from enlightened people who know it. New stories, new approaches. Dream a world." Estab. 1990. Circ. 3,000. Pays on publication. Publishes ms an average of 6 months after acceptance (depending on submission date). Byline given. Offers $10-25 kill fee. Buys first North American serial, first, one-time, second serial (reprint) rights, and makes work-for-hire assignments. Editorial lead time 3 months. Submit seasonal material 3 months in advance. Accepts simultaneous submissions, if so noted. Reports in 3 weeks on queries; 6 weeks on mss. "We write full editorial responses because we charge small fee to submit." Sample copy for $4 and SAE with $1.01 postage. Writer's guidelines for $2 and SAE with 78¢ postage.
Nonfiction: Book excerpts, essays, exposé, how-to, humor, inspirational, interview/profile, opinion, personal experience, religious, travel, book reviews. "We have prose prizes—The Audre Lorde Memorial Prize (fiction and nonfiction) and The Pat Parks Award. Write for guidelines." Health, healing, Angel encounters, past life connections, writing stories,

business ideas, narratives and biography. Buys 4-18 mss/year. Query with résumé, photo of self and complete ms. Length: 500-3,000 words. Pays $10-100.
Reprints: Accepts previously published submissions, if so noted with full biography.
Photos: Send photos with submission. Offers no additional payment for photos accepted with ms. Model releases, identification of subjects required. Buys one-time rights.
Columns/Departments: Omen (visions/dreams/prophesies), 50-500 words; Subject (essay feature on DCM topics), 500-3,000 words; Book Review (writers/New Age/gay/lesbian/black/business/women), 1,500 words. Query or send complete ms. Pays $10-100.
Fiction: Ethnic, experimental, historical, novel excerpts, religious, science fiction, slice-of-life vignettes, New Age. Does not want things slanted for only Anglo Saxon-European lineage audiences. Buys 4-18 mss/year. Send complete ms. Length: 500-3,000 words. Pays $10-100.
Poetry: Wants free verse, haiku, narrative. "No bitter bombastics, unkind, explicitly sexual, pieces that refer to the white race ("her skin like milk") specifically. Diversity is the key here." Length: 5-50 lines. "We have a poetry contest— T. Nelson Gilbert Award $100, $75, $50, $25 and certificate and publication."
Tips: "We like our writers and poets to feel connected to the moon. If they can communicate their spirit, we will feel it and generally respond."

WHOLE LIFE TIMES, P.O. Box 1187, Malibu CA 90265. (310)317-4200. Fax: (310)317-4206. E-mail: wholelifex@aol.com. Contact: Shila Alcantara, associate editor. Monthly consumer tabloid covering holistic thinking. Estab. 1979. Circ. 55,000. Pays on publication. Buys first North American serial rights. Sample copy for $3. Writer's guidelines for #10 SASE.
Nonfiction: Exposé, general interest, how-to, humor, inspirational, interview/profile, spiritual, technical, travel, leading-edge information, book excerpts. Special issues: Holistic Business/Vitamin & Supplement (September), Healing Arts (October), Relationships (February). Buys 25 mss/year. Query with published clips or send complete ms. Length: 1,600-2,000 words. Pays 5¢/word.
Reprints: Send typed ms with rights for sale noted with information about when and where the article previously appeared. Pays 50% of amount paid for an original article.
Tips: "Queries should show an awareness of current topics of interest in our subject area. We welcome investigative reporting and are happy to see queries that address topics in a political context. We are especially looking for articles on health and nutrition."

AUTOMOTIVE AND MOTORCYCLE

Publications in this section detail the maintenance, operation, performance, racing and judging of automobiles and recreational vehicles. Publications that treat vehicles as means of shelter instead of as a hobby or sport are classified in the Travel, Camping and Trailer category. Journals for service station operators and auto and motorcycle dealers are located in the Trade Auto and Truck section.

AMERICAN MOTORCYCLIST, American Motorcyclist Association, 33 Collegeview Rd, Westerville OH 43081-6114. (614)891-2425. Contact: Greg Harrison, executive editor. Monthly magazine for "enthusiastic motorcyclists, investing considerable time and money in the sport. We emphasize the motorcyclist, not the vehicle." Estab. 1942. Circ. 190,000. Pays on publication. Rights purchased vary with author and material. Pays 25-50% kill fee. Byline given. Submit seasonal material 4 months in advance. Reports in 1 month. Writer's guidelines for SASE.
Nonfiction: How-to (different and/or unusual ways to use a motorcycle or have fun on one); historical (the heritage of motorcycling, particularly as it relates to the AMA); interviews (with interesting personalities in the world of motorcycling); photo feature (quality work on any aspect of motorcycling); technical articles. No product evaluations or stories on motorcycling events not sanctioned by the AMA. Buys 20-25 mss/year. Query with SASE. Length: 500 words minimum. Pays minimum $7/published column inch.
Photos: Purchased with or without accompanying ms or on assignment. Captions required. Query. Pays $40/photo minimum.
Tips: "Accuracy and reliability are prime factors in our work with freelancers. We emphasize the rider, not the motorcycle itself. It's always best to query us first and the further in advance the better to allow for scheduling."

AMERICAN WOMAN MOTORSCENE, American Woman Motorscene, 1510 11th St., Suite 201B, Santa Monica CA 90401. (310)260-0192. Fax: (310)260-0175. Contact: Courtney Caldwell, editor-in-chief. Editor: BJ Kineen. 80% freelance written. Monthly magazine on women in automotive and recreational motorsports. "We are an automotive/adventure lifestyle magazine for women." Estab. 1988. Circ. 100,000. Pays on publication an average of 2 months after acceptance. Byline always given. Buys first rights and second serial (reprint) rights or makes work-for-hire assignments. Submit seasonal material 4 months in advance. Reports in 2 months. Free sample copy.
Nonfiction: Humor, inspirational, interview/profile, new product, photo feature, travel, lifestyle. No articles depicting women in motorsports or professions that are degrading, negative or not upscale. Buys 30 mss/year. Send complete ms.

Length 250-1,500 words. Pays 10¢/word for assigned articles; 7¢ for unsolicited articles. Sometimes pays expenses of writers on assignment.

Reprints: Send photocopy of article and information about when and where the article previously appeared.

Photos: Send photos with submission. Reviews contact sheets. Black and white or Kodachrome 64 preferred. Offers $10-50/photo. Captions, model releases and identification of subjects required. Buys all rights.

Columns/Departments: Lipservice (from readers); Tech Talk: (The Mall) new products; Tale End (News); 100-750 words. "Humor is best."

Fillers: Anecdotes, facts, gags to be illustrated by cartoonist, newsbreaks, short humor. Buys 12/year. Length: 25-100 words. Negotiable.

Tips: "It helps if the writer is into cars, trucks or motorcycles. It is a special sport. If he/she is not involved in motorsports, he/she should have a positive point of view of motorsports and be willing to learn more about the subject. We are a lifestyle type of publication more than a technical magazine. Positive attitudes wanted."

AUTOMOBILE QUARTERLY, The Connoisseur's Magazine of Motoring Today, Yesterday, and Tomorrow, Kutztown Publishing Co., P.O. Box 348, 15076 Kutztown Rd., Kutztown PA 19530-0348. (610)683-3169. Fax: (610)683-3287. Publishing Director: Jonathan Stein. Contact: Karla Rosenbusch, managing editor. Assistant Editor: Stuart Wells. 85% freelance written. Quarterly hardcover magazine covering "automotive history, with excellent photography." Estab. 1962. Circ. 13,000. **Pays on acceptance.** Publishes ms an average of 1 year after acceptance. Byline given. Buys first international serial rights. Editorial lead time 9 months. Reports in 2 weeks on queries; 2 months on mss. Sample copy for $19.95.

Nonfiction: Essays, historical/nostalgic, photo feature, technical. Buys 25 mss/year. Query. Length: typically 3,500-8,000 words. Pays approximately 30¢/word. Sometimes pays expenses of writers on assignment.

Photos: State availability of photos with submission. Reviews 4×5, 35mm and 120 transparencies and historical prints. Buys one-time rights.

Tips: "Study the publication, and stress original research."

‡BLVD MAGAZINE, Motorcycling with Style, Hansen Communications, 11435 N. Cave Creek Rd., Suite 101, Phoenix AZ 85020. (602)997-5887. Fax: (602)997-6567. E-mail: joshua@verdenet.com. Contact: Joshua Placa, editor. 50% freelance written. "Bimonthly coffee table magazine with national distribution for professional, affluent cruiser-style motorcycle enthusiasts. Crosses all brand lines in coverage. Query for events. Freestyle, technical, off-beat and humorous or travel (bike included) features." Estab. 1996. Circ. 150,000. Pays on publication. Publishes ms an average of 3 months after acceptance. Byline given. Offers 50% kill fee. Buys all rights. Editorial lead time 2 months. Submit seasonal material 6 months in advance. Accepts simultaneous submissions. Reports as soon as possible. Sample copy and writer's guidelines free.

Nonfiction: General interest, how-to, humor, interview/profile, new product, personal experience, photo feature, technical, travel. Buys 20-30 mss/year. Query with published clips. Length: 500-2,500 words. Pays $150-750. Sometimes pays expenses of writers on assignment.

Photos: Send photos with submission. Negotiates payment individually. Buys all rights.

Columns/Departments: Street Beat (industry, insurance, legal news), words vary; Where to Be Scene (events), 200 words; Fashion (motor clothes), 1,000 words; Staying Alive (riding safety), 1,000 words. Buys 12 mss/year. Query with published clips. Pays $50-300.

Fillers: Anecdotes, facts, gags to be illustrated by cartoonist, newsbreaks, short humor. Length: 50-200 words. Pays $50-150.

‡BRACKET RACING USA, 299 Market St., Saddle Brook NJ 07663. (201)712-9300. Fax: (770)410-9253. Contact: Dale Wilson, editor. Managing Editor: Nancy Cifune. Magazine published 8 times/year covering bracket cars and bracket racing. Estab. 1989. Circ. 45,000. Pays on publication. Publishes ms 6 months after acceptance. Byline given. Buys first North American serial rights. Sample copy for $3 and 9×12 SAE with 5 first-class stamps.

Nonfiction: Automotive how-to and technical. Buys 35 mss/year. Query. Length: 500-1,500 words. Pays $150/page for all articles. Sometimes pays expenses of writers on assignment.

Photos: Send photos with submission.

BRITISH CAR MAGAZINE, 343 Second St., Suite H, Los Altos CA 94022-3639. (415)949-9680. Fax: (415)949-9685. E-mail: britcarmag@aol.com. Contact: Gary G. Anderson, editor and publisher. 50% freelance written. Bimonthly magazine covering British cars. "We focus upon the cars built in Britain, the people who buy them, drive them, collect them, love them. Writers must be among the aforementioned. Written by enthusiasts for enthusiasts." Estab. 1985. Circ. 30,000. Pays on publication. Publishes ms an average of 3 months after acceptance. Byline given. Buys all rights, unless other arrangements made. Submit seasonal material 4 months in advance. Reports in 1 month. Sample copy for $5. Writer's guidelines for #10 SASE.

● The editor is looking for more technical and restoration articles by knowledgeable enthusiasts and professionals.

Nonfiction: Historical/nostalgic; how-to (repair or restoration of a specific model or range of models, new technique or process); humor (based upon a realistic nonfiction situation); interview/profile (famous racer, designer, engineer, etc.); photo feature; technical. Buys 30 mss/year. Send complete ms. "Include SASE if submission is to be returned." Length: 750-4,500 words. Pays $2-5/column inch for assigned articles; $2-3/column inch for unsolicited articles.

Photos: Send photos with submission. Reviews transparencies and prints. Offers $15-75/photo. Captions and identification of subjects required. Buys all rights, unless otherwise arranged.

Columns/Departments: Update (newsworthy briefs of interest, not too timely for bimonthly publication), approximately 50-175 words. Buys 20 mss/year. Send complete ms.

Tips: "Thorough familiarity of subject is essential. *British Car* is read by experts and enthusiasts who can see right through superficial research. Facts are important, and must be accurate. Writers should ask themselves 'I know I'm interested in this story, but will most of *British Car* readers appreciate it?' "

CAR AND DRIVER, Hachette Filipacchi Magazines, Inc., 2002 Hogback Rd., Ann Arbor MI 48105-9736. (313)971-3600. Fax: (313)971-9188. E-mail: editors@caranddriver.com. Website: http://www.caranddriver.com. Contact: Csaba Csere, editor-in-chief. Monthly magazine for auto enthusiasts; college-educated, professional, median 24-35 years of age. Estab. 1956. Circ. 1,100,000. **Pays on acceptance.** Byline given. Offers 25% kill fee. Rights purchased vary with author and material. Buys all rights or first North American serial rights. Reports in 2 months.

● Ranked as one of the best markets for freelance writers in *Writer's Yearbook* magazine's annual "Top 100 Markets," January 1997.

Nonfiction: Non-anecdotal articles about automobiles, new and old. Automotive road tests, informational articles on cars and equipment, some satire and humor and personalities, past and present, in the automotive industry and automotive sports. "Treat readers as intellectual equals. Emphasis on people as well as hardware." Informational, humor, historical, think articles and nostalgia. All road tests are staff-written. "Unsolicited manuscripts are not accepted. Query letters must be addressed to the Managing Editor. Rates are generous, but few manuscripts are purchased from outside." Pays maximum $3,000/feature; $750-1,500/short piece. Pays expenses of writers on assignment.

Photos: Color slides and b&w photos sometimes purchased with accompanying mss.

Tips: "It is best to start off with an interesting query and to stay away from nuts-and-bolts ideas because that will be handled in-house or by an acknowledged expert. Our goal is to be absolutely without flaw in our presentation of automotive facts, but we strive to be every bit as entertaining as we are informative."

CAR CRAFT, Petersen Publishing Co., 6420 Wilshire Blvd., Los Angeles CA 90048. (213)782-2320. Fax: (213)782-2263. Editor: Chuck Schifsky. Monthly magazine for men and women, 18-34, "enthusiastic owners of 1949 and newer muscle cars and street machines." Circ. 400,000. Pays generally on publication.

● *Car Craft* tells us they no longer accept freelance submissions.

CC MOTORCYCLE MAGAZINE, (formerly *Motomag*), Motomag Corp., P.O. Box 1046, Nyack NY 10960. (914)353-MOTO. Fax: (914)353-5240. E-mail: motomag@aol.com. Contact: Mark Kalan, editor. 90% freelance written. Monthly magazine covering motorcycles. "Positive coverage of motorcycling in America—riding, travel, racing and tech." Estab. 1989 (as *CC Motorcycle Magazine*). Circ. 30,000. Pays on publication. Publishes ms an average of 2 months after acceptance. Byline given. Buys one-time rights. Editorial lead time 3 months. Submit seasonal material 3 months in advance. Accepts simultaneous submissions. Reports in 1 month. Sample copy for $3. Writer's guidelines for #10 SASE.

Nonfiction: Essays, general interest, historical/nostalgic, how-to, humor, inspirational, interview/profile, new product, personal experience, photo feature, technical, travel. Special issues: Annual Edition. Buys 12 mss/year. Query with published clips. Length: 1,000-2,000 words. Pays $50-250 for assigned articles; $25-125 for unsolicited articles. Sometimes pays expenses of writers on assignment.

Reprints: Accepts previously published submissions.

Photos: State availability of photos with submission. Reviews contact sheets, transparencies. Negotiates payment individually. Captions, model releases, identification of subjects required. Buys one-time rights.

Fiction: Adventure, fantasy, historical, romance, slice-of-life vignettes. All fiction must be motorcycle related. Buys 6 mss/year. Query with published clips. Length: 1,500-2,500 words. Pays $50-250

Poetry: Avant-garde, free verse, haiku, light verse, traditional. Must be motorcycle related. Buys 6 poems/year. Submit 12 maximum poems. Length: open. Pays $10-50.

Fillers: Anecdotes, cartoons. Buys 12/year. Length: 100-200 words. Pays $10-50.

Tips: "Ride a motorcycle and be able to construct a readable sentence!"

CHEVY HIGH PERFORMANCE, Petersen Publishing Co., 6420 Wilshire Blvd., Los Angeles CA 90048. (213)782-2000. Editor: Mike Magda. Managing Editor: Karen Smart. 20% freelance written. Monthly magazine covering "all aspects of street, racing, restored high-performance Chevrolet vehicles with heavy emphasis on technical modifications and quality photography." Estab. 1985. Circ. 175,000. **Pays on acceptance.** Byline given. Buys all rights. Submit seasonal material 6 months in advance. Reports in 1 month. Sample copy for 9×12 SAE with 5 first-class stamps.

Nonfiction: How-to, new product, photo feature, technical. "We need well-researched and photographed technical articles. Tell us how to make horse-power on a budget." Buys 30 mss/year. Query. Length: 500-2,000 words. Pays $500-1,000. Sometimes pays expenses of writers on assignment.

Photos: Send photos with submission. Reviews contact sheets, any transparencies and any prints. Offers no additional payment for photos accepted with ms. Model releases required. Buys all rights.

Columns/Departments: Buys 24 mss/year. Query. Length: 100-1,500. Pays $150-500.

Tips: "Writers must be aware of the 'street scene.' Please read the magazine closely before query. We need well-photographed step-by-step how-to technical articles. No personality profiles, fluffy features and especially personal experiences. If you don't know the difference between Z/28 and Z28 Camaros, camel-hump and 18-degree heads or what COPO and RPO stand for, there's a good chance your background isn't what we're looking for."

CLASSIC AUTO RESTORER, Fancy Publishing, Inc., P.O. Box 6050, Mission Viejo CA 92690-6050. (714)855-8822. Fax: (714)855-3045. Editor: Dan Burger. Managing Editor: Ted Kade. 85% freelance written. Monthly magazine on auto restoration. "Our readers own old cars and they work on them. We help our readers by providing as much practical, how-to information as we can about restoration and old cars." Estab. 1989. Pays on publication. Publishes ms an average of 3 months after acceptance. Offers $50 kill fee. Buys first North American serial or one-time rights. Submit seasonal material 4 months in advance. Reports in 2 months. Sample copy for $5.50. Writer's guidelines free.
Nonfiction: How-to (auto restoration), new product, photo feature, technical, product evaluation. Buys 120 mss/year. Query with or without published clips. Length: 200-2,500 words. Pays $100-500 for assigned articles.
Photos: Send photos with submission. Reviews contact sheets, transparencies and 5×7 prints. Offers no additional payment for photos accepted with ms.
Tips: "Query first. Interview the owner of a restored car. Present advice to others on how to do a similar restoration. Seek advice from experts. Go light on history and non-specific details. Make it something that the magazine regularly uses. Do automotive how-tos."

FOUR WHEELER MAGAZINE, 3330 Ocean Park Blvd., Santa Monica CA 90405. (310)392-2998. Fax: (310)392-1171. Editor: John Stewart. 20% freelance written. Works with a small number of new/unpublished writers each year. Monthly magazine covering four-wheel-drive vehicles, back-country driving, competition and travel/adventure. Estab. 1963. Circ. 355,466. Pays on publication. Publishes ms an average of 4 months after acceptance. Buys all rights. Submit seasonal material at least 4 months in advance. Writer's guidelines for #10 SASE.
Nonfiction: 4WD competition and travel/adventure articles, technical, how-tos, and vehicle features about unique four-wheel drives. "We like the adventure stories that bring four wheeling to life in word and photo: mud-running deserted logging roads, exploring remote, isolated trails, or hunting/fishing where the 4×4 is a necessity for success." See features by Gary Wescott and Matt Conrad for examples. Query with photos before sending complete ms. Length: 1,200-2,000 words. Pays $200-300/feature vehicles; $350-600/travel and adventure; $100-800/technical articles.
Photos: Requires professional quality color slides and b&w prints for every article. Captions required. Prefers Kodachrome 64 or Fujichrome 50 in 35mm or 2¼ formats. "Action shots a must for all vehicle features and travel articles."
Tips: "Show us you know how to use a camera as well as the written word. The easiest way for a new writer/photographer to break in to our magazine is to read several issues of the magazine, then query with a short vehicle feature that will show his or her potential as a creative writer/photographer."

4-WHEEL DRIVE & SPORT UTILITY, McMullen-Argus, 774 S. Placentia Ave., Placentia CA 92670. (714)572-2255. Fax: (714)572-1864. Editor: Phil Howell. 40% freelance written. Monthly magazine covering outdoor automotive adventure travel for the enthusiast. Estab. 1985. Circ. 96,000. Pays on publication. Byline given. Buys all rights. Editorial lead time 4 months. Submit seasonal material 6 months in advance. Sample copy for $3.50. Writer's guidelines free.
Nonfiction: General interest, how-to, humor, new product, personal experience, photo feature, travel. No "How I Built My Truck," etc. Buys 40 mss/year. Query. Pays $100-600.
Photos: Send photos with submission. Reviews contact sheets, transparencies. Offers no additional payment for photos accepted with ms. Captions, model releases, identification of subjects required. Buys all rights.

HOT ROD, Petersen Publishing Co., 6420 Wilshire Blvd., Los Angeles CA 90048-5515. (310)854-2280. Fax: (310)854-2223. Editor: Drew Hardin. 5% freelance written. Monthly magazine. Estab. 1948. Pays on publication. This magazine did not respond to our request for information. Query before submitting.

IN THE WIND, Paisano Publications, P.O. Box 3000, Agoura Hills CA 91376-3000. (818)889-8740. Fax: (818)889-1252. Editor: Kim Peterson. Managing Editor: Lisa Pedicini. 50% freelance written. Bimonthly magazine covering Harley-Davidson motorcycle owners' lifestyle. "Aimed at Harley-Davidson motorcycle riders and motorcycling enthusiasts, *In the Wind* is mainly a pictorial—action photos of bikes being ridden, and events, with a monthly travel piece—Travelin' Trails." Estab. 1978. Circ. 90,000. Pays on publication. Publishes ms an average of 9 months after acceptance. Byline given. Buys all rights. Editorial lead time 6 months. Submit seasonal material 8 months in advance. Reports in 2 weeks on queries; 2 months on mss. Writer's guidelines free.
Nonfiction: Photo feature, travel. No long-winded tech articles. Buys 6 mss/year. Query. Length: 1,000-1,500 words. Pays $250-600. Sometimes pays expenses of writers on assignment.
Photos: Send photos with submission. Reviews transparencies. Offers $35-100/photo. Model releases, identification of subjects required. Buys all rights.
Columns/Departments: Travelin' Trails (good spots to ride to, places to stay, things to do, history), 1,200 words. Buys 6 mss/year. Query. Pays $250-600.
Poetry: Free verse. Does not want to see graphic violence. Buys 10 poems/year. Submit maximum 3 poems. Length: 10-100 lines. Pays $20-100.
Tips: "Know the subject. Looking for submissions from people who ride their own bikes."

MOTOR TREND, Petersen Publishing Co., 6420 Wilshire Blvd., Los Angeles CA 90048. (213)782-2220. Fax: (213)782-2355. Editor: C. Van Tune. 5-10% freelance written. Prefers to work with published/established writers. Monthly magazine for automotive enthusiasts and general interest consumers. Circ. 900,000. Publishes ms an average of 3 months after acceptance. Buys all rights. "Fact-filled query suggested for all freelancers." Reports in 1 month.

Nonfiction: "Automotive and related subjects that have national appeal. Emphasis on domestic and imported cars, road tests, driving impressions, auto classics, auto, travel, racing, and high-performance features for the enthusiast. Packed with facts. Freelancers should confine queries to photo-illustrated exotic drives and other feature material; road tests and related activity are handled inhouse."

Photos: Buys photos, particularly of prototype cars and assorted automotive matter. Pays $25-500 for transparencies.

‡MUSTANG MONTHLY, Dobbs Publishing Group, Inc., P.O. Box 7157, Lakeland FL 33807. (941)644-0449. Fax: (941)648-1187. E-mail: dobbs@gate.net. Website: http://www.D-P-G.com. Editor: Jeff Ford. Contact: Mary Jean Wesche, managing editor. 25% freelance written. Monthly magazine covering 1964½ through current Mustangs with an emphasis on restoration. Estab. 1977. Circ. 75,000. Pays on publication. Rarely publishes speculative materials. All freelance work assigned. Welcomes article proposals that include text and photography. Byline given. Buys first North American rights. Writer's guidelines for #10 SASE.

Nonfiction: How-to, technical. Color car features. No seasonal, holiday, humor, fiction or material. Buys approximately 25 mss with artwork/year. Query with or without published clips. Write for editorial guidelines first. No complete mss. Length: 2,500 words maximum. Pays $125-200/published page.

Photos: Always send photos with submission; photography is of the highest quality/importance. Reviews proofsheets with negatives and color transparency. No color prints. Offers $125-200/page color. Captions, technical description sheets and model releases (on our forms) are required.

Tips: "We are looking for passionate Mustang enthusiasts who can provide articles that fit our formats. The content includes b&w technical articles and color feature articles. Our format rarely varies."

NASCAR TRUCK RACING, (formerly *NASCAR SuperTruck Racing*), McMullen Argus Publishing Corp., 774 S. Placentia Ave., Placentia CA 92670. (714)572-2255. Fax: (714)572-1864. Editor: Steve Stillwell. Contact: Randall Jachmann, editor at large. 50% freelance written. Bimonthly magazing covering NASCAR Craftsman Truck Series. "The *NASCAR Truck Racing* magazine audience is largely race enthusiasts looking for a more personal glimpse of their 'heroes.' Articles should not be statistics, rather family-oriented slice-of-life type memoirs, personal histories." Estab. 1995. Circ. 127,000. Pays on publication. Publishes ms an average of 4 months after acceptance. Byline given. Offers 50% kill fee. Buys all rights. Editorial lead time 3 months. Accepts simultaneous submissions. Reports in 1 month. Writer's guidelines free.

Nonfiction: Interview/profile, photo feature, SuperTruck driver/team related articles. Technical articles must be approved by editors. Buys 35 mss/year. Query. Length: 500-2,000 words. Pays $75-150/page. Sometimes pays expenses of writers on assignment.

Reprints: Accepts previously published submissions.

Photos: Send photos with submission. Reviews contact sheets, transparencies, 3×5 prints. Negotiates payment individually. Captions, model releases, identification of subjects required.

Fillers: Newsbreaks. Buys 5-10/year. Length: 100-500 words. Pay negotiable.

Tips: "At *NASCAR Truck Racing* magazine, we prefer queries, as all information must meet the guidelines of NASCAR. The book is interview-heavy, with an emphasis placed on personal rather than professional backgrounds, information, etc., for each interviewee."

OFF-ROAD, McMullen & Yee Publishing, Inc., 774 S. Placentia Ave., Placentia CA 92670-6846. (714)572-2255. Fax: (714)572-1864. Editor: Duane Elliott. 40% freelance written. Monthly magazine covering off-road vehicles, racing, travel. "Written to hard-core off-road truck enthusiasts." Estab. 1969. Circ. 100,000. Pays on publication. Publishes ms an average of 6 after acceptance. Byline given. Buys first North American rights. Editorial lead time 4 months. Submit seasonal material 6 months in advance. Accepts simultaneous submissions. Reports in 2 weeks on queries.

Nonfiction: How-to, interview/profile, photo feature, technical, travel. Buys 36 mss/year. Send complete ms. Length: 550-650 words. Pays $150/published page. Sometimes pays expenses of writers on assignment.

Photos: Send photos with ms. Reviews contact sheets, negatives, transparencies, prints. No additional payment for photos accepted with ms. Captions, model releases, identification of subjects required. Buys one-time rights.

Fiction: Adventure, historical, humorous. Buys 1-2 mss/year. Send complete ms. Length: 500-2,000 words. Pays $150/page.

Fillers: Facts, newsbreaks. Buys 10/year. Length: 50-500 words. Pays $15/page.

Tips: "Study mag for style!"

‡OPEN WHEEL MAGAZINE, General Media, 65 Parker St., Newburyport MA 01950. (508)463-3789. Fax: (508)463-3250. Editor: Dick Berggren. 80% freelance written. Monthly magazine "covering sprint cars, midgets, super-modifieds and Indy cars. *OW* is an enthusiast's publication that speaks to those deeply involved in oval track automobile racing in the United States and Canada. *OW*'s primary audience is a group of men and women actively engaged in competition at the present time, those who have recently been in competition and those who plan competition soon. That audience includes drivers, car owners, sponsors and crew members who represent perhaps 50-70% of our readership. The rest who read the magazine are those in the racing trade (parts manufacturers, track operators and officials) and serious fans who see 30 or more races per year." Circ. 150,000. Pays on publication. Publishes ms an average of 6 months after acceptance. Byline given. Buys all rights. Submit seasonal material 2 months in advance. Reports in 3 weeks on queries. Sample copy for 9×12 SAE with 7 first-class stamps. Writer's guidelines for #10 SASE.

Nonfiction: General interest, historical/nostalgic, how-to, humor, interview/profile, new product, photo feature, technical. "We don't care for features that are a blow-by-blow chronology of events. The key word is interest. We want features which allow the reader to get to know the main figure very well. Our view of racing is positive. We don't think all is lost, that the sport is about to shut down and don't want stories that claim such to be the case, but we shoot straight and avoid whitewash." Buys 125 mss/year. Query with complete ms.

Photos: State availability of photos with submission. Reviews contact sheets, negatives, transparencies, prints. Buys one-time rights.

Fillers: Anecdotes, facts, short humor. Buys 100/year. Length: 1-3 pages, double-spaced. Pays $35.

Tips: "Virtually all our features are submitted without assignment. An author knows much better what's going on in his backyard than we do. We ask that you write to us before beginning a story theme. Judging of material is always a combination of a review of the story and its support illustrations. Therefore, we ask for photography to accompany the manuscript on first submission. We're especially in the market for tech."

RIDER, TL Enterprises, Inc., 2575 Vista Del Mar Dr., Ventura CA 93001. (805)667-4100. Managing Editor: Donya Carlson. Contact: Mark Tuttle, Jr., editor. 50% freelance written. Monthly magazine on motorcycling. "*Rider* serves owners and enthusiasts of road and street motorcycling, focusing on touring, commuting, camping and general sport street riding." Estab. 1974. Circ. 140,000. Pays on publication. Publishes ms an average of 6-12 months after acceptance. Byline given. Offers 25% kill fee. Buys first North American serial rights. Editorial lead time 4 months. Submit seasonal material 6 months in advance. Reports in 2 months. Sample copy for $2.95. Writer's guidelines for #10 SASE.

Nonfiction: General interest, historical/nostalgic, how-to (re: motorcycling), humor, interview/profile, personal experience. Does not want to see "fiction or articles on 'How I Began Motorcycling.' " Buys 30 mss/year. Query. Length: 500-1,500 words. Pays $100 minimum for unsolicited articles.

Photos: Send photos with submission. Reviews contact sheets, transparencies and 5×7 prints (b&w only). Offers no additional payment for photos accepted with ms. Captions required. Buys one-time rights.

Columns/Departments: Rides, Rallies & Clubs (favorite ride or rally), 800-1,000 words. Buys 15 mss/year. Query. Pays $150.

Tips: "We rarely accept manuscripts without photos (slides or b&w prints). Query first. Follow guidelines available on request. We are most open to feature stories (must include excellent photography) and material for 'Rides, Rallies and Clubs.' Include information on routes, local attractions, restaurants and scenery in favorite ride submissions."

ROAD & TRACK, Hachette Filipacchi Magazines Inc., 1499 Monrovia Ave., Newport Beach CA 92663. (714)720-5300. Fax: (714)631-2757. Editor: Thomas L. Bryant. Contact: Ellida Maki, managing editor. 25% freelance written. Monthly magazine covering automotive. Estab. 1947. Circ. 740,000. Pays on publication. Publishes ms an average of 6 months after acceptance. Kill fee varies. Buys first rights. Editorial lead time 3 months. Reports in 1 month on queries; 2 months on mss.

Nonfiction: Automotive interest. No how-to. Query. Length: 2,000 words. Pay varies. Pays expenses of writers on assignment.

Reprints: Send photocopy of article or short story or typed ms with rights for sale noted.

Photos: State availability of photos with submissions. Reviews transparencies, prints. Negotiates payment individually. Model releases required. Buys one-time rights.

Columns/Department: Reviews (automotive), 500 words. Query. Pay varies.

Fiction: Automotive. Query. Length: 2,000 words. Pay varies.

Tips: "Because mostly written by staff or assignment, we rarely purchase unsolicited manuscripts—but it can and does happen! Writers must be knowledgeable about enthusiast cars."

‡STOCK CAR RACING MAGAZINE, General Media, 65 Parker St., #2, Newburyport MA 01950. (508)463-3789. Fax: (508)463-3250. Editor: Dick Berggren. 80% freelance written. Eager to work with new/unpublished writers. Monthly magazine for stock car racing fans and competitors. Circ. 400,000. Pays on publication. Publishes ms an average of 3 months after acceptance. Buys all rights. Byline given. Reports in 6 weeks. Writer's guidelines free.

Nonfiction: General interest, historical/nostalgic, how-to, humor, interviews, new product, photo features, technical. "Uses nonfiction on stock car drivers, cars and races. We are interested in the story behind the story in stock car racing. We want interesting profiles and colorful, nationally interesting features. We are looking for more technical articles, particularly in the area of street stocks and limited sportsman." Query with or without published clips or submit complete ms. Buys 50-200 mss/year. Length: 100-6,000 words. Pays up to $450.

Photos: State availability of photos. Pays $20 for 8×10 b&w photos; up to $250 for 35mm or larger transparencies. Captions required.

Fillers: Anecdotes, short humor. Buys 100 each year. Pays $35.

Tips: "We get more queries than stories. We just don't get as much material as we want to buy. We have more room for stories than ever before. We are an excellent market with 12 issues per year. Virtually all our features are submitted without assignment. An author knows much better what's going on in his backyard than we do. We ask that you write to us before beginning a story theme. If nobody is working on the theme you wish to pursue, we'd be glad to assign it to you if it fits our needs and you are the best person for the job. Judging of material is always a combination of a review of the story and its support illustration. Photography should accompany manuscript on first submission."

TRUCKIN', World's Leading Sport Truck Publication, McMullen & Yee Publishing, 774 S. Placentia Ave., Placentia CA 92670. (714)572-2255. Fax: (714)572-1864. Editor: Steve Stillwell. 15% freelance written. Monthly magazine covering customized sport trucks. "We purchase events coverage, technical articles and truck features, all having to be associated with customized—½ ton pickups and mini-trucks." Estab. 1975. Circ. 200,000. Pays on publication. Buys all rights unless previously agreed upon. Editorial lead time 3 months. Submit seasonal material 6 months in advance. Reports in 2 weeks on queries; 1 month on mss. Sample copy for $4.50. Writer's guidelines free.

Nonfiction: How-to, new product, photo feature, technical, events coverage. Buys 50 mss/year. Query. Length: 1,000 words minimum. Pay negotiable. Sometimes pays expenses of writers on assignment.

Photos: Send photos with submission. Reviews contact sheets and transparencies. Captions, model releases, identification of subjects required. Buys all rights unless previously agreed upon.

Columns/Departments: Bill Blankenship. Insider (latest automotive/truck news), 2,000 words. Buys 70 mss/year. Send complete ms. Pays $25 minimum.

Fillers: Bill Blankenship. Anecdotes, facts, newsbreaks. Buys 50/year. Length: 600-1,000 words. Pay negotiable.

Tips: "Send all queries and submissions in envelopes larger than letter size to avoid being detained with a mass of reader mail. Send complete packages with transparencies and contact sheets (with negatives). Submit hard copy and a computer disc when possible. Editors purchase the materials that are the least complicated to turn into magazine pages! All materials have to be fresh/new and primarily outside of California."

AVIATION

Professional and private pilots and aviation enthusiasts read the publications in this section. Editors want material for audiences knowledgeable about commercial aviation. Magazines for passengers of commercial airlines are grouped in the Inflight category. Technical aviation and space journals and publications for airport operators, aircraft dealers and others in aviation businesses are listed under Aviation and Space in the Trade section.

AIR & SPACE/SMITHSONIAN MAGAZINE, 370 L'Enfant Promenade SW, 10th Floor, Washington DC 20024-2518. (202)287-3733. Fax: (202)287-3163. E-mail: airspacedt@aol.com. Website: http://www.airspacemag.com. Editor: George Larson. Contact: Linda Shiner, executive editor. 80% freelance written. Prefers to work with published/established writers. Bimonthly magazine covering aviation and aerospace for a non-technical audience. "The emphasis is on the human rather than the technological, on the ideas behind the events. Features are slanted to a technically curious, but not necessarily technically knowledgeable audience. We are looking for unique angles to aviation/aerospace stories, history, events, personalities, current and future technologies, that emphasize the human-interest aspect." Estab. 1985. Circ. 284,000. **Pays on acceptance.** Byline given. Offers kill fee. Buys first North American serial rights. Adapts from previously published or soon to be published books. Reports in 3 months. Sample copy for $5. Writer's guidelines free.

• Ranked as one of the best markets for freelance writers in *Writer's Yearbook* magazine's annual "Top 100 Markets," January 1997.

Nonfiction: Book excerpts, essays, general interest (on aviation/aerospace), historical/nostalgic, humor, photo feature, technical. Buys 50 mss/year. Query with published clips. Length: 1,500-3,000 words. Pays $1,000-2,500 average. Pays expenses of writers on assignment.

• The editors are actively seeking stories covering space and aviation during the Vietnam War.

Photos: State availability of illustrations with submission. Reviews 35mm transparencies. Refuses unsolicited material.

Columns/Departments: Above and Beyond (first person), 1,500-2,000 words; Flights and Fancy (whimsy), approximately 1,200 words; From the Field (science or engineering in the trenches), 1,200 words; Collections (profiles of unique museums), 1,200 words. Buys 25 mss/year. Query with published clips. Pays $1,000 maximum. Soundings (brief items, timely but not breaking news), 500-700 words. Pays $150-300.

Tips: "Soundings section most open to freelancers. We continue to be interested in stories about space exploration."

AIR LINE PILOT, Air Line Pilots Association, 535 Herndon Parkway, P.O. Box 1169, Herndon VA 20172. (703)481-4460. Fax: (703)689-4370. E-mail: 73741.14@compuserve.com. Website: http://www.alpa.org. Editor: Gary DiNunno. 10% freelance written. Prefers to work with published/established writers; works with a small number of new/unpublished writers each year. Monthly magazine for airline pilots covering commercial aviation industry information—economics, avionics, equipment, systems, safety—that affects a pilot's life in professional sense. Also includes information about management/labor relations trends, contract negotiations, etc. Estab. 1931. Circ. 72,000. **Pays on acceptance.** Publishes ms an average of 6 months after acceptance. Offers 50% kill fee. Buys all rights except book rights. Submit seasonal material 6 months in advance. Reports in 2 months. Sample copy for $2. Writer's guidelines for #10 SASE.

Nonfiction: Humor, inspirational, photo feature, technical. Buys 20 mss/year. Query with or without published clips, or send complete ms. Length: 700-3,000 words. Pays $200-600 for assigned articles; pays $50-600 for unsolicited articles.

Reprints: Send photocopy of article or typed ms with rights for sale noted and information about when and where the article previously appeared.

Photos: Send photos with submission. Reviews contact sheets, 35mm transparencies and 8×10 prints. Offers $10-35/

b&w photo, $20-50 for color used inside and $350 for color used as cover. For cover photography, shoot vertical rather than horizontal. Identification of subjects required.

Tips: "For our feature section, we seek aviation industry information that affects the life of a professional airline pilot from a career standpoint. We also seek material that affects a pilot's life from a job security and work environment standpoint. Any airline pilot featured in an article must be an Air Line Pilot Association member in good standing. Our readers are very experienced and require a high level of technical accuracy in both written material and photographs."

AOPA PILOT, Official Publication of: Aircraft Owners and Pilots Association, 421 Aviation Way, Frederick MD 21701. (301)695-2350. Fax: (301)695-2180. Editor-in-Chief: Thomas B. Haines. Monthly. "*AOPA Pilot* is published principally for general aviation pilots and aircraft owners who are members of the *Aircraft Owners and Pilots Association*. *AOPA Pilot* contains feature articles that report on both new and older aircraft, piloting techniques, safety issues and regulatory initiatives that affect Federal Aviation Regulations. Articles are tailored to address their special informational requirements." Circ. 8,178. This magazine did not respond to our request for information. Query before submitting.

BALLOON LIFE, Balloon Life Magazine, Inc., 2336 47th Ave. SW, Seattle WA 98116-2331. (206)935-3649. Fax: (206)935-3326. E-mail: blnlife@scn.org. Website: http://www.balloonlife.com. Contact: Tom Hamilton, editor-in-chief. 75% freelance written. Monthly magazine for sport of hot air ballooning. Estab. 1986. Circ. 4,000. Pays on publication. Byline given. Offers 50-100% kill fee. Buys non-exclusive all rights. Submit seasonal material 4 months in advance. Reports in 3 weeks on queries; 1 month on mss. Sample copy for 9 × 12 SAE with $2 postage. Writer's guidelines for #10 SASE.
Nonfiction: Book excerpts, general interest, events/rallies, safety seminars, balloon clubs/organizations, how-to (flying hot air balloons, equipment techniques), interview/profile, new product, letters to the editor, technical. Buys 150 mss/year. Query with or without published clips, or send complete ms. Length: 1,000-1,500 words. Pays $50-75 for assigned articles; $25-50 for unsolicited articles. Sometimes pays expenses of writers on assignment.
Reprints: Send photocopy of article or short story and information about when and where the article previously appeared. For reprints, pays 100% of amount paid for original article.
Photos: Send photos with submission. Reviews transparencies, prints. Offers $15/inside photo, $50/cover. Identification of subjects required. Buys non-exclusive all rights.
Columns/Departments: Hangar Flying (real life flying experience that others can learn from), 800-1,500 words; Crew Quarters (devoted to some aspect of crewing), 900 words; Preflight (a news and information column), 100-500 words; pays $50. Logbook (recent balloon events—events that have taken place in last 3-4 months), 300-500 words; pays $20. Buys 60 mss/year. Send complete ms.
Fiction: Humorous. Buys 3-5 mss/year. Send complete ms. Length: 800-1,500 words. Pays $50.
Tips: "This magazine slants toward the technical side of ballooning. We are interested in articles that help to educate and provide safety information. Also stories with manufacturers, important individuals and/or of historic events and technological advances important to ballooning. The magazine attempts to present articles that show 'how-to' (fly, business opportunities, weather, equipment). Both our Feature Stories section and Logbook section are where most manuscripts are purchased."

‡CESSNA OWNER MAGAZINE, Jones Publishing, Inc., N7450 Aanstad Rd., P.O. Box 5000, Iola WI 54945. (715)445-5000. Fax: (715)445-4053. E-mail: jonespub@gglbbs.com. Contact: Bruce Loppnow, editor. 50% freelance written. Monthly magazine covering Cessna single and twin engine aircraft. "*Cessna Owner Magazine* is the official publication of the Cessna Owner Organization (C.O.O.). Therefore, our readers are Cessna aircraft owners, renters, pilots, and enthusiasts. Articles should deal with buying/selling, flying, maintaining, or modifying Cessnas. The purpose of our magazine is to promote safe, fun, and affordable flying." Estab. 1975. Circ. 6,000. Pays on publication. Publishes ms an average of 3 months after acceptance. Byline given. Buys first, one-time or second serial (reprint) rights or makes work-for-hire assignment on occasion. Editorial lead time 1 month. Submit seasonal material 3 months in advance. Reports in 2 weeks on queries; 1 month on mss. Sample copy and writer's guidelines free.
Nonfiction: Historical/nostalgic (of specific Cessna models), how-to (aircraft repairs and maintenance), humor, interview/profile, new product, personal experience, photo feature, technical (aircraft engines and airframes), travel. "We are always looking for articles about Cessna aircraft modifications. We also need articles on Cessna twin-engine aircraft. April, July, and October are always big issues for us, because we attend various airshows during these months and distribute free magazines. Feature articles on unusual, highly-modified, or vintage Cessnas are especially welcome during these months. Good photos are also a must." Buys 24 mss/year. Query. Length: 1,500-3,500 words.
Reprints: Send typed ms with rights for sale noted. Pays 50% of amount paid for an original article.
Photos: Send photos with submission. Reviews 3 × 5 and larger prints. Offers no additional payment for photos accepted with ms. Captions and identification of subjects required.
Tips: "Always submit a hard copy or ASCII formatted computer disk. Color photos mean a lot to us, and manuscripts stand a much better chance of being published when accompanied by photos. Freelancers can best get published by submitting articles on aircraft modifications, vintage planes, restorations, flight reports, twin-engine Cessnas, etc."

FLYING, Hachette Filipacchi Magazines, Inc. Publication, 500 W. Putnam, Greenwich CT 06830. (203)622-2700. Fax: (203)622-2715. Publisher: Dick Koenig. Monthly. "*Flying Magazine* is a general aviation magazine, edited for active aviation-oriented individuals including pilots, aircraft owners, aircraft buyers, and people who make frequent use of general aviation aircraft in business and personal life. The magazine's editorial includes articles on aviation news and semi-technical, entertaining and informative features covering general and business aviation; evaluation reports on new or used single-engine, multi-engine, turboprop, pure jet and rotary wing aircraft; pilot proficiency, navigation, weather, safety, FAA regulations, travel and destinations, and new equipment." Estab. 1927. Circ. 13,163. This magazine did not respond to our request for information. Query before submitting.

GENERAL AVIATION NEWS & FLYER, N.W. Flyer, Inc., P.O. Box 39099, Tacoma WA 98439-0099. (206)471-9888. Fax: (206)471-9911. E-mail: comments@ganflyer.com. Website: http://www.ganflyer.com. Contact: Kirk Gormley, managing editor. 30% freelance written. Prefers to work with published/established writers. Biweekly tabloid covering general, regional, national and international aviation stories of interest to pilots, aircraft owners and aviation enthusiasts. Estab. 1949. Circ. 35,000. Pays 1 month after publication. Publishes ms an average of 3 months after acceptance. Byline given. Buys one-time and first North American serial rights; on occasion second serial (reprint) rights. Submit seasonal material 2 months in advance. Reports in 2 months. Sample copy for $3.50. Writer's and style guidelines for #10 SASE.
Nonfiction: "We stress news. A controversy over an airport, a first flight of a new design, storm or flood damage to an airport, a new business opening at your local airport—those are the sort of projects that may get a new writer onto our pages, if they arrive here soon after they happen. We are especially interested in reviews of aircraft." Personality pieces involving someone who is using his or her airplane in an unusual way, and stories about aviation safety are of interest. Query first on historical, nostalgic features and profiles/interviews. Many special sections throughout the year; send SASE for list. Buys 100 mss/year. Query or send complete ms. Length: 500-2,000 words. Pays up to $3/printed column inch maximum. Rarely pays the expenses of writers on assignment.
Reprints: Accepts previously published submissions from noncompetitive publications, if so noted. Payment varies.
Photos: Shoot clear, up-close photos, preferably color prints or slides. Send photos with ms. Captions and photographer's ID required. Pays $10/b&w photo and $50/cover photo 1 month after publication.
Fiction: Publishes novel excerpts.
Tips: "The longer the story, the less likely it is to be accepted. A 1,000-word story with good photos is the best way to see your name in print. If you are covering controversy, send us both sides of the story. Most of our features and news stories are assigned in response to a query."

‡**PIPERS MAGAZINE**, Jones Publishing, Inc., N7450 Aanstad Rd., P.O. Box 5000, Iola WI 54945. (715)445-5000. Fax: (715)445-4053. Contact: Bruce Loppnow, editor. 50% freelance written. Monthly magazine covering Piper single and twin engine aircraft. "*Pipers Magazine* is the official publication of the Piper Owner Society (P.O.S). Therefore, our readers are Piper aircraft owners, renters, pilots, mechanics and enthusiasts. Articles should deal with buying/selling, flying, maintaining or modifying Pipers. The purpose of our magazine is to promote safe, fun and affordable flying." Estab. 1988. Circ. 4,000. Pays on publication. Publishes ms an average of 3 months after acceptance. Buys first, one-time or second serial (reprint) rights or makes work-for-hire assignment on occasion. Editorial lead time 1 month. Submit seasonal material 3 months in advance. Reports in 2 weeks on queries; 1 month on mss. Sample copy and writer's guidelines free.
Nonfiction: Historical/nostalgic (of specific models of Pipers), how-to (aircraft repairs & maintenance), humor, interview/profile (industry leaders), new product, personal experience, photo feature, technical (aircraft engines and airframes), travel. "We are always looking for articles about Piper aircraft modifications. We also are in need of articles on Piper twin engine aircraft, and late-model Pipers. April, July, and October are always big issues for us, because we attend airshows during these months and distribute free magazines." Feature articles on unusual, highly-modified, vintage, late-model, or ski/float equipped Pipers are especially welcome. Good photos are a must. Buys 24 mss/year. Query. Length: 1,500-3,500 words.
Reprints: Send typed ms with rights for sale noted. Pays 50% of amount paid for an original article.
Photos: Send photos with submissions. Reviews transparencies, 3×5 and larger prints. Offers no additional payment for photos accepted. Captions, identification of subjects required.
Tips: "Always submit a hard copy or ASCII formatted computer disk. Color photos mean a lot to us, and manuscripts stand a much greater chance of being published when accompanied by photos. Freelancers can best get published by submitting articles on aircraft modifications, vintage planes, late-model planes, restorations, twin-engine Pipers, etc."

‡**PLANE AND PILOT**, Werner Publishing Corp., 12121 Wilshire Blvd., Suite 1220, Los Angeles CA 90025. (310)820-1500. Fax: (310)826-5008. Website: PandPmag@aol.com. Editor: Steve Werner. Contact: Jenny Shearer, assistant editor. 100% freelance written. Monthly magazine that covers general aviation. "We think a spirited, conversational writing style is most entertaining for our readers. We are read by private and corporate pilots, instructors, students, mechanics and technicians—everyone involved or interested in general aviation." Estab. 1964. Circ. 130,000. Pays on publication. Publishes ms an average of 3 months after acceptance. Byline given. Kill fee negotiable. Buys all rights. Submit seasonal material 4 months in advance. Reports in 2 months. Sample copy for $5.50. Writer's guidelines free.
Nonfiction: Book excerpts, essays, general interest, how-to, humor, inspirational, new product, personal experience, technical, travel, pilot proficiency and pilot reports on aircraft. Buys 150 mss/year. Submit query with idea, length and the type of photography you expect to provide. Length: 1,000-2,500 words. Pays $200-500. Rates vary depending on the value of the material as judged by the editors. Pays expenses of writers on assignment.
Reprints: Send photocopy of article or typed ms with rights for sale noted with information about when and where the article previously appeared. Pays 50% of amount paid for original article.
Photos: Submit suggested heads, decks and captions for all photos with each story. Submit b&w photos in proof sheet

form with negatives or 8×10 prints with glossy finish. Submit color photos in the form of 2¼×2¼ or 4×5 or 35mm transparencies in plastic sleeves. Offers $50-300/photo. Buys all rights.

Fiction: Publishes novel excerpts.

Columns/Departments: Readback (any newsworthy items on aircraft and/or people in aviation), 100-300 words; Flight To Remember (a particularly difficult or wonderful flight), 1,000-1,500 words; Jobs & Schools (a feature or an interesting school or program in aviation), 1,000-1,500 words; and Travel (any traveling done in piston-engine aircraft), 1,000-2,500 words. Buys 30 mss/year. Send complete ms. Length: 1,000-2,500 words. Pays $200-500. Rates vary depending on the value of the material as judged by the editors.

PROFESSIONAL PILOT, Queensmith Communications, 3014 Colvin St., Alexandria VA 22314. (703)370-0606. Fax: (703)370-7082. E-mail: propilot@flightdata.com. Website: http://www.flightdata.com/propilot. Contact: Chad Trautvetter, associate editor. 75% freelance written. Monthly magazine on regional airline, corporate and various other types of professional aviation. "The typical reader has a sophisticated grasp of piloting/aviation knowledge and is interested in articles that help him/her do the job better or more efficiently." Estab. 1967. Circ. 33,500. **Pays on acceptance.** Publishes ms an average of 3 months after acceptance. Byline given. Kill fee negotiable. Buys all rights.

Nonfiction: "Typical subjects include new aircraft design, new product reviews (especially avionics), pilot techniques, profiles of regional airlines, fixed base operations, profiles of corporate flight departments and technological advances." All issues have a theme such as regional airline operations, maintenance, jet aircraft, helicopters, etc. Special issues: Salary Study and Paris Show (June); FBO/Flight Support Directory and Contest Awards (July); Corporate Aircraft Product Support (August); NBAA Convention Issue (September); Outfitting and Overhaul and Hubs, Spokes & Catchment (October); Post NBAA Issue and Powerplant Product Support and Air Traffic Control (November); FBO Contest Ballot and Awards (December). Buys 40 mss/year. Query. Length: 750-2,000 words. Pays $200-1,000. A fee for the article will be established at the time of assignment. Sometimes pays expenses of writers on assignment.

Photos: Send photos with submission. Prefers transparencies or slides. Offers no additional payment for photos accepted with ms. Captions and identification of subjects required. Buys all rights.

Tips: Query first. "Freelancer should be a professional pilot or have background in aviation. Authors should indicate relevant aviation experience and pilot credentials (certificates, ratings and hours). We place a greater emphasis on corporate operations and pilot concerns."

WOMAN PILOT, Aviatrix Publishing, Inc., P.O. Box 485, Arlington Heights IL 60006-0485. Contact: Danielle Clarneaux, editor. 80% freelance written. Bimonthly magazine covering women who fly all types of aircraft. Personal profiles, history careers in all areas of aviation. Estab. 1993. Circ. 5,000. Pays on publication. Publishes ms an average of 10 months after acceptance. Byline given. Buys first North American serial rights. Editorial lead time 4 months. Sample copy for $3. Writer's guidelines for #10 SASE.

Nonfiction: Book excerpts, historical/nostalgic, humor, interview/profile, new product, personal experience, photo feature. Buys 35 mss/year. Query with published clips or send complete ms. Length: 500-3,000 words. Pays $ 20-55 for assigned articles; $20-40 for unsolicited articles; and contributor copies.

Reprints: Send tearsheet or photocopy of article or short story or typed ms with rights for sale noted and information about when and where the article previously appeared.

Photos: State availability of or send photos/photocopies with submission. Negotiates payment individually. Captions, model releases, identification of subjects required. Buys one-time rights.

Fiction: Adventure, historical, humorous, slice-of-life vignettes. Buys 4 mss/year. Query with or without published clips. Length: 500-2,000 words. Pays $20-35.

Poetry: Buys 4 poems/year. Submit maximum 3 poems. Length: short. Pays $10.

Fillers: Cartoons. Buys 6/year. Pays $10-20.

Tips: "If a writer is interested in writing articles from our leads, she/he should send writing samples and explanation of any aviation background. Include any writing background."

BUSINESS AND FINANCE

Business publications give executives and consumers a range of information from local business news and trends to national overviews and laws that affect them. National and regional publications are listed below in separate categories. Magazines that have a technical slant are in the Trade section under Business Management, Finance or Management and Supervision categories.

National

BLACK ENTERPRISE, ABC, 130 Fifth Ave., New York NY 10011. (212)242-8000. Executive Vice President: Earl G. Graves Jr. Monthly magazine. "*Black Enterprise* is a business service publication for African-American professionals, corporate executives and entrepreneurs. Feature articles include money management, career and management issues, investment strategies and business news and trends. *Black Enterprise* also provides regular departments which include personal finance, technology and profiles of successful black businesses and professionals. The magazine also offers a career marketplace and classified section." Estab. 1970. Circ. 22,730. This magazine did not respond to our request for information. Query before submitting.

BUSINESS FRONT, The Publisher's Group, P.O. Box 510366, Salt Lake City UT 84151-0366. Fax: (801)322-1098. E-mail: annee@thepublishers.com. Contact: Anne E. Zombro, vice president of publishing. 50% freelance written. Quarterly magazine covering business management. "Focuses on meeting the ever-changing needs of the businessperson. Offers company and entrepreneurial profiles, trends in finance, technology and the Internet." Estab. 1996. Circ. 10,000. Pays on publication. Publishes ms an average of 6 months after acceptance. Byline given. Buys first North American serial and second serial (reprint) rights. Editorial lead time 2 months. Submit seasonal material 4 months in advance. Accepts simultaneous submissions. Reports in 1 month on queries; 2 months on mss. Sample copy for $3 and 9×12 SASE. Writer's guidelines for #10 SASE.
Nonfiction: Book excerpts, interview/profile, new product, technical, quality control (TQM). Buys 6 mss/year. Query with published clips. Length: 1,000-1,300 words. Pays $125-800.
Reprints: Accepts previously published submissions. Pays 50% of amount paid for an original article.
Photos: Send photos with submission. Reviews 4×5 transparencies (preferred), any size prints. Negotiates payment individually. Captions, model releases, identification of subjects required. Buys one-time or all rights.

BUSINESS START-UPS, Entrepreneur Media, Inc., 2392 Morse Ave., Irvine CA 92614. (714)261-2083. Fax: (714)755-4211. E-mail: 76711,1724@compuserve.com. Website: http://www.entrepreneurmag.com. Contact: Donna Clapp, editor. 50-75% freelance written. Monthly magazine on small business. "Provides how-to information for starting a small business, running a small business during the 'early' years and profiles of entrepreneurs who have started successful small businesses." Estab. 1989. Circ. 220,000. **Pays on acceptance.** Byline given. Offers 20% kill fee. Buys first time international rights. Submit seasonal material 6 months in advance. Reports in 2 months on queries. Sample copy for $3. Writer's guidelines for SASE (please write: "Attn: Writer's Guidelines" on envelope).
Nonfiction: "Our readers want new business ideas. Hence our almost constant theme, 'A Bazillion New Businesses to Start.' We're also looking for how-to articles about starting a business that focus precisely on one element of the process: marketing, PR, business plan writing, taxes, financing, selling, low-cost advertising, etc." Interview/profiles on entrepreneurs. "Please read the magazine and writer's guidelines before querying." Query. Feature length: 1,800 words. Pays $400-600 for features, $200-400 for departments and $100 for briefs.
Reprints: Send photocopy of article or typed ms with rights for sale noted and information about when and where the article previously appeared. Payment negotiable.
Photos: Markas Platt, art director. State availability of photos with submission. Identification of subjects required.
Tips: "We're looking for articles that will appeal to two distinct groups: people who are eager to launch their own companies and people who run new or very small—but growing companies." Articles should be lessons-oriented, to-the-point, and concrete, using specific real-world examples that avoid management theory. Write with self reliance in mind. "Don't tell our readers how to hire someone to write their business plan. Tell them how they can do it themselves."

BUSINESS WEEK, The McGraw Hill Companies, 1221 Avenue of the Americas, New York NY 10020. Weekly publication covering news and trends in the worlds of business. "*Business Week* is edited to keep readers informed of important news that affects the business community in the U.S. and abroad, and to interpret, analyze and evaluate these news events for business management." Estab. 1929. Circ. 877,700.
● *Business Week* does not accept freelance submissions.

BUSINESS98, Success Strategies For Small Business, Group IV Communications, Inc., 125 Auburn Court, #100, Thousand Oaks CA 91362-3617. (805)496-6156. Editor: Daniel Kehrer. Contact: Maryann Hammers, managing editor. 75% freelance written. Bimonthly magazine for small and independent business. "We publish only practical articles of interest to small business owners all across America." Estab. 1993. Circ. 610,000. **Pays on acceptance.** Publishes ms an average of 4 months after acceptance. Byline given. Offers 25% kill fee. First and non-exclusive reprint rights. Reports in 3-6 months. Sample copy for $4. Writer's guidelines for #10 SASE.
● Submissions are also considered for *Independent Business*, also published by Group IV.
Nonfiction: How-to articles for operating a small business. No "generic" business articles, articles on big business, articles on how to start a business or general articles on economic theory. Buys 80-100 mss/year. Query with résumé and clips; do not send ms. Length: 1,000-2,000 words. Pays $500-1,500. Pays expenses of writers on assignment.
Columns/Departments: Tax Tactics, Small Business Computing, Marketing Moves, Ad-visor, Banking & Finance, Business Cost-Savers, all 1,000-2,000 words. Buys 40-50 mss/year. Query with résumé and published clips. Pays $500-1,500.
Tips: "Talk to small business owners anywhere in America about what they want to read, what concerns or interests them in running a business. All areas open, but we use primarily professional business writers with top credentials."

‡DIVIDENDS, Imagination Publishing, 820 W. Jackson Blvd., Suite 450, Chicago IL 60607. (312)627-1020. Fax: (312)627-1105. E-mail: dividends@aol.com. Contact: Molly Tschida, editor. Managing Editor: Rebecca Rolfes. 60% freelance written. Custom bimonthly publication for Staples covering small business management. "*Dividends* is a resource for small business owners. Articles should include general tips, specific contacts, resources, etc." Circ. 300,000. Pays within 60 days of invoice. Publishes ms an average of 3 months after acceptance. Byline given. Buys first North American serial rights.

Nonfiction: Interview/profile, sales, management, home/office, technology, finance, customer service, small business. Buys 25 mss/year. Query with published clips. Length: 400-1,800 words. Pays 50¢/word.
Photos: State availability of photos with submission.
Columns/Departments: Pays 50¢/word.

ENTREPRENEUR MAGAZINE, 2392 Morse Ave., Irvine CA 92614. Fax: (714)755-4211. E-mail: entmag@msn.com. Website: entrepreneurmag.com. Contact: Rieva Lesonsky, editor. 40% freelance written. "Readers are small business owners seeking information on running a better business. *Entrepreneur* readers already run their own businesses. They have been in business for several years and are seeking innovative methods and strategies to improve their business operations. They are also interested in new business ideas and opportunities, as well as current issues that affect their companies." Circ. 510,000. **Pays on acceptance.** Publishes ms an average of 5 months after acceptance. Buys first international rights. Byline given. Submit seasonal material 6 months in advance of issue date. Reports in 3 months. Sample copy for $3. Writer's guidelines for #10 SASE (please write "Attn: Writer's Guidelines" on envelope).
• *Entrepreneur* publishes the bimonthly *Entrepreneur International* which covers the latest in U.S. trends and franchising for an international audience. (This is not written for a U.S. audience.) They encourage writers with expertise in this area to please query with ideas.
Nonfiction: How-to (information on running a business, dealing with the psychological aspects of running a business, profiles of unique entrepreneurs). Buys 10-20 mss/year. Query with clips of published work and SASE or query by fax. Length: 2,000 words. Payment varies. Columns not open to freelancers.
Photos: "We use color transparencies to illustrate articles. Please state availability with query." Uses standard color transparencies. Buys first rights.
Tips: "Read several issues of the magazine! Study the feature articles versus the columns. Probably 75 percent of our freelance rejections are for article ideas covered in one of our regular columns. It's so exciting when a writer goes beyond the typical, flat 'business magazine query'—how to write a press release, how to negotiate with vendors, etc.— and instead investigates a current trend and then develops a story on how that trend affects small business."

EXECUTIVE FEMALE, NAFE, 30 Irving Place, 5th Floor, New York NY 10003. (212)477-2200. Fax: (212)477-8215. E-mail: nafe@nafe.com. Website: http://www.nafe.com. Contact: Gay Bryant, editor-in-chief. Executive Editor: Betsy Wiesendanger. 60% freelance written. Bimonthly magazine emphasizing "useful career, business and financial information for the upwardly mobile career woman." Prefers to work with published/established writers. Estab. 1975. Circ. 200,000. Byline given. **Pays on acceptance.** Publishes ms an average of 3 months after acceptance. Submit seasonal material 6 months in advance. Buys first rights, second serial (reprint) rights to material originally published elsewhere. Reports in 2 months. Sample copy for $2.50. Writer's guidelines for #10 SASE.
Nonfiction: Articles on any aspect of career advancement and financial planning. Needs how-tos for managers and articles about coping on the job, trends in the workplace, financial planning, trouble shooting, business communication, time and stress management, career goal-setting and get-ahead strategies. Written queries only. Submit photos with ms (b&w prints or transparencies) or include suggestions for artwork. Length: 800-2,000 words. Pays 50-75¢/word.
Reprints: Send photocopy of article or typed ms with rights for sale noted and information about when and where the article previously appeared. Pays 25% of amount paid for an original article.
Columns/Departments: Your Money (savings, financial advice, economic trends, interesting tips); Managing Smart (tips on managing people, getting ahead); Your Business (entrepreneurial stories); Careers (how to move ahead); Technology and Cyberspace (taking advantage of the latest workplace tools). Buys 20 mss/year. Query with published clips or send complete ms. Length: 250-1,000 words. Pays 50-75¢/word.
Tips: Plans more short book reviews, book summaries.

FORBES, 60 Fifth Ave., New York NY 10011. (212)620-2200. Publisher: Jeffrey M. Cunningham. Biweekly magazine covering business and finance. "*Forbes* is for top management and for those aspiring to positions of corporate leadership. With over 50 concise stories in each issue, *Forbes* covers companies and the people who run them, industries, marketing, law, taxes, technology, computers and communications and investments, management performance and global business trends. *Forbes* also produces two special editorial supplements: Forbes FYI covering executive, leisure and lifestyle pursuits; and Forbes ASAP covering computers and high technology for business managers. Estab. 1917. Circ. 777,000. This magazine did not respond to our request for information. Query before submitting.

FORTUNE, Time Inc. Magazine Co., Time & Life Bldg., Rockefeller Center, 15th Floor, New York NY 10020. (212)522-1212. Publisher: Jolene Sykes. Biweekly magazine. "*Fortune* is edited primarily for high-demographic business people. It reports in-depth on hard-to-access executives and personalities, offers foresight and forecasts, and provides business building solutions and ideas. It specializes in big stories about companies, business personalities, technology, managing, Wall Street, media, marketing, personal finance, politics, policy and important corporate trends." Estab. 1930. Circ. 59,244. This magazine did not respond to our request for information. Query before submitting.

HARVARD BUSINESS REVIEW, Harvard Business School Publishing, 60 Harvard Way-230 W., Boston MA 02163. (617)495-6800. Fax:(617)496-8145. Contact: Editor. Bimonthly magazine. "*Harvard Business Review* is a journal of management theory and practice edited for a broadly based audience of top executives in the U.S. and abroad. Each issue contains such regular editorial departments such as HBR Case Study, World View and Perspectives, along with in-depth articles on issues of current concern to corporate managers. The magazine identifies current business issues providing readers with the practical input they need to operate their companies more effectively. It stresses real life experience at the proper echelons of management." Estab. 1922. Circ. 16,552. This magazine did not respond to our request for information. Query before submitting.

‡**INDEPENDENT BUSINESS: America's Small Business Magazine**, Group IV Communications, Inc., 125 Auburn Ct., #100, Thousand Oaks CA 91362-3617. (805)496-6156. Website: http://www.yoursource.com. Contact: Maryann Hammers, managing editor. Editorial Director: Don Phillipson. 75% freelance written. Bimonthly magazine for small and independent business with practical articles of interest to small business owners all across America." Estab. 1989. Circ. 630,000. **Pays on acceptance.** Publishes ms an average of 4 months after acceptance. Byline given. Offers 25% kill fee. First and non-exclusive reprint rights. Reports in 6 months. Sample copy for $4. Writer's guidelines for #10 SASE.

• All submissions will also be considered for *Business98*, also published by Group IV.

Nonfiction: How-to articles for operating a small business. No "generic" business articles, articles on big business, how to start a business or general economic theory. Buys 80-100 mss/year. Query with résumé and published clips; do not send mss. Length: 1,000-2,000 words. Pays $500-1,500. Pays expenses of writers on assignment.

• Ranked as one of the best markets for freelance writers in *Writer's Yearbook* magazine's annual "Top 100 Markets," January 1997.

Columns/Departments: Tax Tactics, Small Business Computing, Marketing Moves, Ad-visor, Banking & Finance, Business Cost-Savers, all 1,000-2,000 words. Buys 40-50 mss/year. Query with résumé and published clips. Pays $500-1,500.

Tips: "Talk to small business owners anywhere in America about what they want to read, what concerns or interests them in running a business. All areas open, but we use primarily professional business writers with top credentials."

‡**INDIVIDUAL INVESTOR**, Individual Investor Group, 1633 Broadway, 38th Floor, New York NY 10019. (212)843-2777. Fax: (212)843-2794. E-mail: aweintraub@individualinvestor.com. Website: http://www.individualinvestor.com. Editor: Paul Libassi. Contact: Arlene Weintraub, senior editor. 40% freelance written. Monthly magazine covering stocks, mutual funds and personal finance. "Our readers range from novice to experienced investors. Our articles aim to be lively, informative, interesting, and to uncover 'undiscovered' investing opportunities." Circ. 400,000. **Pays on acceptance.** Publishes ms an average of 3 months after acceptance. Byline given. Buys all rights. Editorial lead time 2 months. Submit seasonal material 4 months in advance. Sample copy free.

Columns/Departments: Paul Libassi, editor. Personal P&L (investing basics and special topics), 1,500 words. Buys 12 mss/year. Query with published clips. Pays up to $1/word.

MONEY, Time & Life Bldg., Rockefeller Center, New York NY 10020. (212)522-3263. Managing Editor: Frank Lalli. Monthly publication covering all aspects of personal finance. "In addition to presenting solid stategies for intelligent investing and saving, *Money* offers advice relating to retirement, spending for maximum value, travel planning, consumer awareness, tax preparation and education." Estab. 1972. Circ. 1,923,000. Query before submitting.

Tips: "Know the magazine and its readers. *Money Magazine* provides services for its readers—know how to do this."

THE NETWORK JOURNAL, Black Professional and Small Business News, The Network Journal Communication, 333 Nostrand Ave., Brooklyn NY 11216. (718)857-8773. Fax: (718)399-9027. E-mail: aziz@tnj.com. Editor: Tania Padgett. Managing Editor: Njeru Waithaka. Contact: Akinshijn C. Ola, editor. 25% freelance written. Monthly tabloid covering business and career articles. *The Network Journal* caters to Black professionals and small-business owners, providing quality coverage on business, financial, technology and career news germane to the Black community. Estab. 1993. Circ. 11,000. Pays on publication. Byline given. Buys all rights. Editorial lead time 2 months. Submit seasonal material 3 months in advance. Accepts simultaneous submissions. Sample copy for $1. Writer's guidelines free.

Nonfiction: How-to, interview/profile. Send complete ms. Length: 1,200-1,500 words. Pays $40. Sometimes pays expenses of writers on assignment.

Reprints: Accepts previously published submissions.

Photos: Send photos with submission. Offers $20/photo. Identification of subjects required. Buys one-time rights.

Columns/Departments: Book reviews, 700-800 words; career management and small business development, 800 words. Pays $25.

Tips: "We are looking for vigorous writing and reporting for our cover stories and feature articles. Pieces should have gripping leads, quotes that actually say something and that come from several sources. Unless it is a column, please do not submit a one-source story. Always remember that your article must contain a nutgraph—that's usually the third paragraph telling the reader what the story is about and why you are telling it now. Editorializing should be kept to a minimum. If you're writing a column, make sure your opinions are well-supported."

 THE DOUBLE DAGGER before a listing indicates that the listing is new in this edition. New markets are often more receptive to freelance submissions.

‡**PROFIT**, Investor Portfolio, Profit Publications, Inc., 69-730 Highway 111, Suite 102, Rancho Mirage CA 92270. (619)202-1555. Fax: (619)202-1544. E-mail: profitpc@aol.com. Editor: Jayne Lanza. Managing Editor: Paula Carrick. Contact: Cynthia A. Rushton, staff writer. 25% freelance written. Bimonthly magazine covering financial issues/lifestyle. "*Profit* is an upscale magazine with financial and lifestyle subject matter. Our reader base is upper income individuals." Estab. 1995. Circ. 60,000. **Pays on acceptance.** Publishes ms an average of 4 months after acceptance. Byline sometimes given. Buys first rights or second serial (reprint) rights. Editorial lead time 2 months. Submit seasonal material 4 months in advance. Sample copy and writer's guidelines free.

Nonfiction: Book excerpts, essays, expose, general interest, historical/nostalgic, humor, inspirational, interview/profile, new product, technical, travel. No religion, personal experience or pornography. Buys 6-12 mss/year. Send complete ms. Length: 500-2,000 words. Pays $250-750. Sometimes pays expenses of writers on assignment.

Reprints: Accepts previously published submissions.

Photos: State availability of photos with submission. Negotiates payment individually. Captions, model releases and identification of subjects required. Rights purchased vary.

Columns/Departments: Travel Guide, 600-1,200 words; Health & Medicine, 600-1,800 words; Editorial 800-1,800 words. Buys 12 mss/year. Query. Pays $150-500.

Fiction: Novel excerpts. Buys 6 mss/year. No religion or pornography. Send complete ms. Length: 500-1,000 words. Pays $250-750.

Tips: "We're looking for a creative display of financial facts, new slants. We want to see variety and risky writing that is postitive overall. Submit query and manuscript or query and samples. We want to see your writing style."

PROFIT, The Magazine for Canadian Entrepreneurs, CB Media Limited, 777 Bay St., 5th Floor, Toronto, Ontario Canada M5W 1A7. (416)596-5999. Fax: (410)596-5111. Contact: Rick Spence, editor. 80% freelance written. Bimonthly magazine covering small and medium business. "We specialize in specific, useful information that helps our readers manage their businesses better. We want Canadian stories only." Estab. 1982. Circ. 110,000. **Pays on acceptance.** Publishes ms an average of 2 months after acceptance. Byline given. Kill fee varies. Buys first North American serial rights and database rights. Submit seasonal material 6 months in advance. Reports in 1 month on queries; 6 weeks on mss. Sample copy for 9 × 12 SAE with 84¢ postage (Canadian). Writer's guidelines free.

Nonfiction: How-to (business management tips), strategies and Canadian business profiles. Buys 50 mss/year. Query with published clips. Length: 800-2,000 words. Pays $500-2,000 (Canadian). Pays expenses of writers on assignment. State availability of photos with submission.

Columns/Departments: Finance (info on raising capital in Canada), 700 words; Marketing (marketing strategies for independent business), 700 words. Buys 80 mss/year. Query with published clips. Length: 200-800 words. Pays $150-600 (Canadian).

Tips: "We're wide open to freelancers with good ideas and some knowledge of business. Read the magazine and understand it before submitting your ideas."

SMART MONEY, Wall Street Journal Magazine of Personal Business, 1755 Broadway, 4th Floor, New York NY 10019. (212)492-1300. Fax:(212)245-7276. Publisher: Christopher L. Lambiase. Monthly magazine. "*Smart Money* is a personal business magazine edited for discriminating investors, featuring practical and imaginative ideas for investing, spending and saving. Articles and features provide action-oriented information on investment opportunities and pitfalls. Editorial asks tough questions about big names and big businesses that affect important personal business decisions." Estab. 1992. Circ. 30,209. This magazine did not respond to our request for information. Query before submitting.

TECHNICAL ANALYSIS OF STOCKS & COMMODITIES, The Trader's Magazine, Technical Analysis, Inc., 4757 California Ave. SW, Seattle WA 98116-4499. Fax: (206)938-1307. E-mail: editor@traders.com. Website: http://www.traders.com. Publisher: Jack K. Hutson. Editor: Thomas R. Hartle. 75% freelance written. Eager to work with new/unpublished writers. Magazine covers methods of investing and trading stocks, bonds and commodities (futures), options, mutual funds and precious metals. Estab. 1982. Circ. 53,000. Pays on publication. Publishes ms an average of 3 months after acceptance. Byline given. Buys all rights; however, second serial (reprint) rights revert to the author, provided copyright credit is given. Reports in 3 weeks on queries; 1 month on mss. Sample copy for $5. Writer's guidelines for #10 SASE or on website.

Nonfiction: Thomas R. Hartle, editor. Reviews (new software or hardware that can make a trader's life easier, comparative reviews of software books, services, etc.); how-to (trade); technical (trading and software aids to trading); utilities (charting or computer programs, surveys, statistics or information to help the trader study or interpret market movements); humor (unusual incidents of market occurrences, cartoons). "No newsletter-type, buy-sell recommendations. The article subject must relate to trading psychology, technical analysis, charting or a numerical technique used to trade securities or futures. Virtually requires graphics with every article." Buys 150 mss/year. Query with published clips if available or send complete ms. Length: 1,000-4,000 words. Pays $100-500. (Applies per inch base rate and premium rate—write for information). Sometimes pays expenses of writers on assignment.

Reprints: Send tearsheet or photocopy of article or typed ms with rights for sale noted and information about when and where the article appeared.

Photos: Christine M. Morrison, art director. State availability of art or photos. Pays $60-350 for b&w or color negatives with prints or positive slides. Captions, model releases and identification of subjects required. Buys one-time and reprint rights.

Columns/Departments: Buys 100 mss/year. Query. Length: 800-1,600 words. Pays $50-300.

Fillers: Karen Wasserman, fillers editor. Jokes and cartoons on investment humor. Must relate to trading stocks, bonds, options, mutual funds, commodities or precious metals. Buys 20/year. Length: 500 words. Pays $20-50.

Tips: "Describe how to use technical analysis, charting or computer work in day-to-day trading of stocks, bonds, commodities, options, mutual funds or precious metals. A blow-by-blow account of how a trade was made, including the trader's thought processes, is the very best received story by our subscribers. One of our primary considerations is to instruct in a manner that the layperson can comprehend. We are not hyper-critical of writing style."

YOUR MONEY, Consumers Digest Inc., 5705 N. Lincoln Ave., Chicago IL 60659. (773)275-3590. Contact: Dennis Fertig, editor. 75% freelance written. Bimonthly magazine on personal finance. "We cover the broad range of topics associated with personal finance—spending, saving, investing earning, etc." Estab. 1979. Circ. 500,000. **Pays on acceptance.** Publishes ms an average of 2 months after acceptance. Byline given. Offers 50% kill fee. Buys first rights and second serial (reprint) rights. Reports in 3 months (or longer) on queries. Do not send computer disks. Sample copy and writer's guidelines for 9×12 SAE with 4 first-class stamps. Writer's guidelines for #10 SASE.

• *Your Money* has been receiving more submissions and has less time to deal with them. Accordingly, they often need more than three months reporting time.

Nonfiction: How-to. "No first-person success stories or profiles of one company." Buys 25 mss/year. Send complete ms or query and clips. Include stamped, self-addressed postcard for more prompt response. Length: 1,500-2,500 words. Pays 50¢/word. Pays expenses of writers on assignment.

Tips: "Know the subject matter. Develop real sources in the investment community. Demonstrate a reader-friendly style that will help make the sometimes complicated subject of investing more accessible to the average person. Fill manuscripts with real-life examples of people who actually have done the kinds of things discussed—people we can later photograph."

Regional

THE ADCOM NET, P.O. Box 840, Sherborn MA 01170-1840. E-mail: publisher@adcom.net. Website: http://www.adcom.net. Editor: Carl Shedd. 10% freelance written. "*The Adcom Net* provides information and features on advertising, marketing, media, PR and related fields within New England. Primary freelance need: case studies and strategies. Readership: ad agencies, corporate advertising staff." Pays 30 days after publication. Publishes ms an average of 2 days after acceptance. Byline given. No kill fee. Reports in 1 month.

Nonfiction: How-to, opinion, strategies, case studies, industry overviews. Query with published clips. Length: 500-3,000 words. Pays $50 for assigned articles; $25 for unsolicited articles.

Reprints: E-mail copy of article and information about when and where the article previously appeared.

Photos: State availability of photos with submission. Reviews contact sheets, transparencies and 5×7 prints. Offers $10/photo. Captions, model releases and identification of subjects required. Buys one-time rights.

Columns/Departments: Case Study (case study of a company's advertising/marketing program; must be a New England company), 1,200-3,000 words; Strategies ("how-to" or explanatory articles that relate to advertising, PR, marketing, direct marketing or media), 400-700 words; Industry Overview (an overview of marketing/advertising within specific industries in New England), 700-2,500 words. Query with published clips. Length: 400-3,000 words. Pays $50.

Tips: "Our magazine is now all electronic on the Internet."

‡ALASKA BUSINESS MONTHLY, Alaska Business Publishing, 501 W. Northern Lights Blvd., Suite 100, Anchorage AK 99503. (907)276-4373. Fax: (907)279-2900. E-mail: editor@akbizmag.com. Contact: Ron Dalby, editor. 80% freelance written. Monthly magazine covering Alaska-oriented business and industry. "Our audience is Alaska business men and women who rely on us for timely features and up-to-date information about doing business in Alaska." Estab. 1985. Circ. 10,000. **Pays on acceptance.** Publishes ms an average of 2 months after acceptance. Byline given. Offers $50 kill fee. Buys first North American serial rights, first rights, one-time rights or makes work-for-hire assignments. Editorial lead time 2 months. Submit seasonal material 3 months in advance. Reports in 2 weeks on queries; 1 month on mss. Sample copy for 9×12 SAE and 6 first-class stamps. Writer's guidelines free.

Nonfiction: Humor, interview/profile, new product, opinion, technical, business. No fiction, poetry or anything not pertinent to Alaska. Buys 45 mss/year. Send complete ms. Length: 500-2,500 words. Pays $150-300. Sometimes pays expenses of writers on assignment.

Photos: Send photos with submission. Reviews 35mm or larger transparencies and 5×7 or larger prints. Offers $25-400/photo. Captions, model releases and identification of subjects required. Buys one-time rights.

Columns/Departments: Required Reading (business book reviews); Small Business Profile, 500 words. Buys 12 mss/year. Send complete ms. Pays $100-150.

Tips: "Send a well-written manuscript on a subject of importance to Alaska businesses. Include photos."

ARIZONA BUSINESS MAGAZINE, 3111 N. Central Ave., Suite 230, Phoenix AZ 85012. (602)277-6045. Fax: (602)650-0827. E-mail: editorial@azbusmag.com. Website: http://www.azbusmag.com. Contact: D.J. Burrough, editor. 35% freelance written. Bimonthly magazine covering business topics specific to Arizona: health care, banking, finance, legal issues, the environment, real estate and development, international, etc. "Our readers are primarily high-level executives and business owners. The magazine is recognized for its well-balanced articles and high-quality photography.

We strive to offer readers well-researched, objective articles on the business issues facing our state." Estab. 1984. Circ. 90,000. Pays on completion of final draft for publication. Publishes ms an average of 3 months after acceptance. Byline given. Offers 100% kill fee. Buys first rights and makes work-for-hire assignments. Editorial lead time 2 months. Submit seasonal material 1 year in advance. Reports in 2 months on queries; 4 months on mss. Sample copy for 9×12 SAE with 6 first-class stamps. Writer's guidelines for #10 SASE.
Nonfiction: General interest, historical/nostalgic, interview/profile, new product, opinion, photo feature. No how-to articles. Buys 20-24 mss/year. Query with published clips. Length: 1,500-2,200 words. Pays $100-250. All articles are assigned. Sometimes pays expenses of writers on assignment.
Reprints: Send photocopy of article and information about when and where the article previously appeared. Pays 50% of amount paid for an original article.
Photos: State availability of photos with submissions. Reviews transparencies or slides. Negotiates payment individually. Captions, identification of subjects required. Buys one-time rights.
Columns/Departments: HealthWatch, High Finance, Power of Attorney, Environomics, Real Estate, Arizona Entrepreneur (all are general interest stories focusing on the industries mentioned), 1,500-2,000 words. Query with published clips. Pays $100-250.
Fillers: Personality profiles. Buys 8-12/year. Length: 400-600 words. Pays $25-100.
Tips: "Always begin with a one-page query letter/outline of the story idea and include one or two samples of your work. We rarely accept manuscripts. More often, we are impressed with the writer's presentation and respect for our time than with the story proposal. Grab us with one powerful point, fact or idea and you'll have your foot in the door for future assignments. The most important key is to be brief and to the point."

BC BUSINESS, Canada Wide Magazines & Communications Ltd., 4th Floor, 4180 Lougheed Highway, Burnaby, British Columbia V5C 6A7 Canada. (604)299-7311. Fax: (604)299-9188. Editor: Bonnie Irving. 80% freelance written. Monthly magazine covering business. "*BC Business* reports on the significant issues and trends shaping the province's business environment. Stories are lively, topical and extensively researched." Circ. 26,000. Pays 2 weeks prior to publication. Publishes ms an average of 2 months after acceptance. Byline given. Kill fee varies. Buys first Canadian rights. Editorial lead time 4 months. Submit seasonal material 4 months in advance. Accepts simultaneous submissions. Reports in 6 weeks on queries. Writer's guidelines free.
Nonfiction: Query with published clips. Length: 800-3,000 words. Pays 40-60¢/word, depending on length of story (and complexity). Sometimes pays expenses of writers on assignment.
Photos: State availability of photos with submission.

BIRMINGHAM BUSINESS JOURNAL, 2101 Magnolia Ave. S., Birmingham AL 35205. (205)322-0000. Fax: (205)322-0040. E-mail: editor@bbj.com/. Website: http://www.bbj.com/. Contact: Dick Gentry, editor. 1-2% freelance written. Weekly tabloid covering health care, banking, commercial real estate, general business. "Writer should have expertise in subject covered." Estab. 1983. Circ. 9,000. Pays on publication. Byline given. Offers 10% kill fee. Buys all rights. Editorial lead time 2 weeks. Submit seasonal material 1 month in advance. Reports in 3 weeks on queries.
Nonfiction: Exposé, interview/profile, new product, technical. Special issue: Economic Forecast (January). Buys 5 mss/year. Query. Pays $80-500. Sometimes pays expenses of writers on assignment.
Photos: State availability of photos with submission. Reviews 5×7 prints. Negotiates payment individually. Identification of subjects required. Buys one-time rights.
Tips: "Writers should submit specific story ideas and explain their expertise in the subject matter. If the idea is worth consideration, we would also like to know if the writer is experienced enough to expedite it."

BOULDER COUNTY BUSINESS REPORT, 4865 Sterling Dr., Suite 200, Boulder CO 80301-2349. (303)440-4950. Fax: (303)440-8954. E-mail: jwlewis@bcbr.com. Website: http://www.bcbr.com. Editor: Jerry W. Lewis. 75% freelance written. Prefers to work with published/established writers; works with a small number of new/unpublished writers each year. Monthly newspaper covering Boulder County business issues. Offers "news tailored to a monthly theme and read primarily by Colorado businesspeople and by some investors nationwide. Philosophy: Descriptive, well-written articles that reach behind the scene to examine area's business activity." Estab. 1982. Circ. 18,000. Pays on publication. Publishes ms an average of 1 month after acceptance. Byline given. Buys one-time rights and second serial (reprint) rights. Reports in 1 month on queries; 2 weeks on mss. Sample copy for $1.44.
Nonfiction: Interview/profile, new product, examination of competition in a particular line of business. "All our issues are written around one or two monthly themes. No articles are accepted in which the subject has not been pursued in depth and both sides of an issue presented in a writing style with flair." Buys 120 mss/year. Query with published clips. Length: 250-2,000 words. Pays $50-300.
Photos: State availability of photos with query letter. Reviews b&w contact sheets. Pays $10 maximum for b&w contact sheet. Identification of subjects required. Buys one-time rights and reprint rights.
Tips: "Must be able to localize a subject. In-depth articles are written by assignment. The freelancer located in the Colorado area has an excellent chance here."

BUSINESS JOURNAL OF CENTRAL NY, CNY Business Review, Inc., 231 Wallton St., Syracuse NY 13202. (315)472-3104. Fax: (315)472-3644. E-mail: blrbmeistr@aol.com. Editor: Norm Poltenson. 35% freelance written. Biweekly newspaper covering business in Central New York. "*The Business Journal* covers business news in a 16-county area surrounding Syracuse for owners and managers of businesses." Estab. 1985. Circ. 8,500. Pays on publication.

Publishes ms an average of 2 months after acceptance. Byline given. Kill fee negotiable. Buys first rights. Editorial lead time 1 month. Accepts previously published submissions. Sample copy and writer's guidelines free.
Nonfiction: Humor, opinion. Buys 100 mss/year. Query. Length: 750-2,000 words. Pays $75-500. Sometimes pays in copies. Sometimes pays expenses of writers on assignment.
Photos: State availability of photos with submission. Reviews contact sheets. Negotiates payment individually. Captions, model releases, identification of subjects required.
Columns/Departments: Buys 20 mss/year. Query with published clips.
Fillers: Facts, newsbreaks, short humor. Buys 10/year. Length: 300-600 words. Pays $50-150.
Tips: "The audience is comprised of owners and managers. Focus on their needs. Call or send associate editor story ideas: be sure to have a Central New York 'hook.' "

BUSINESS NH MAGAZINE, 404 Chestnut St., Suite 201, Manchester NH 03101-1831. Fax: (603)626-6359. E-mail: businessnh@nh.interwebb.com. Contact: Janet Phelps, editor. 50% freelance written. Monthly magazine with focus on business, politics and people of New Hampshire. "Our audience consists of the owners and top managers of New Hampshire businesses." Estab. 1983. Circ. 13,000. Pays on publication. Publishes ms an average of 2 months after acceptance. Byline given.
Nonfiction: Features—how-to, interview/profile. Buys 24 mss/year. Query with published clips and résumé. "No unsolicited manuscripts; interested in local writers only." Length: 750-2,500 words. $75-275.
Photos: Both b&w and color photos used. Pays $40-80. Buys one-time rights.
Tips: "I *always* want clips and résumé with queries. Freelance stories are almost always assigned. Stories *must* be local to New Hampshire."

THE BUSINESS TIMES, Blackburn Magazine Group, 231 Dundas St., Suite 203, London, Ontario N6A 1H1 Canada. (519)679-4901. Fax: (519)434-7842. E-mail: editor@businesstimes.com. Editor: Pauline Braitwait. 75% freelance written. Monthly tabloid covering local business news, events and trends. "Local angle a must—aimed at business owners and executives." Estab. 1993. Circ. 11,000. **Pays on acceptance.** Byline given. Offers $25 kill fee. Buys all rights. Editorial lead time 1 month. Submit seasonal material 2 months in advance. Accepts simultaneous submissions. Reports in 1 month on queries; 2 months on mss. Sample copy and writer's guidelines free.
Nonfiction: Interview/profile, new product, technical. No advertorial, non-local news. Query with published clips. Length: 250-700 words. Pays $50-200. Sometimes pays expenses of writers on assignment.
Photos: State availability of photos with submission. Offers $25-75/photo. Negotiates payment individually. Identification of subjects required. Buys one-time rights.
Tips: "Need local industry contacts to break news; need to know local sources, trends, events. Query by letter with sample news clips."

COAST BUSINESS, Ship Island Holding Co., P.O. Box 1209, Gulfport MS 39502. Fax: (601)867-2986. E-mail: coastbusiness@nse.com. Contact: Lauren Thompson, editor. 10% freelance written. Biweekly tabloid covering business. "*Coast Business* covers local and national business news and issues. Our readers represent the business community of the Mississippi Gulf Coast." Estab. 1989. Circ. 8,000. Pays on publication. Publishes ms an average of 1 month after acceptance. Byline given. Buys first North American serial rights. Editorial lead time 3 months. Submit seasonal material 3 months in advance. Reports in 2 weeks on queries; 1 month on mss. Sample copy for $1.
Nonfiction: How-to, interview/profile, new product, opinion. All articles must be business related. Buys 26 mss/year. Query with published clips. Length: 700-1,500 words. Pays $50-150. Sometimes pays expenses of writers on assignment.
Photos: Send photos with submission. Reviews prints. Negotiates payment individually. Captions, identification of subjects required. Buys one-time rights.
Columns/Departments: Computers (product reviews, tips); Finance (personal or business); Travel (business); all 700-750 words. Query with published clips. Pays $50-75.
Tips: "Our audience is the business community of the Mississippi Gulf Coast. We cover local news as well as national issues that affect the way the Coast does business."

COLORADO BUSINESS, Wiesner Inc., 7009 S. Potomac St., Englewood CO 80112. (303)397-7600. Fax: (303)397-7619. E-mail: bgold@wins.usa.com. Website: http://www.cobizmag.com. Contact: Bruce Goldberg, editor. 75% freelance written. Monthly magazine covering Colorado-based businesses. "Our features focus on the big picture, on trends and overviews in Colorado business; we rarely write about only one company. We try to include businesses from around the state, not just the Front Range. Charts and graphs are welcome. Our readership is a high-end audience, with average salaries of $142,000. Many are CEOs, business owners, or high-ranking executives or managers. Our readership is 75 percent male, but also includes many successful women business owners and operators. They seek information on any business development that's new, interesting and useful to their business life or personal life as well as trends, and interesting individuals and businesses, in the state." Estab. 1973. Circ. 20,000. **Pays on acceptance.** Publishes ms an average of 3 months after acceptance. Byline given. Offers 50% kill fee. Buys first rights. Editorial lead time 4 months. Submit seasonal material 6 months in advance. Reports in 1 month on queries. Prefers Colorado writers.
Nonfiction: Business, health care, financials, telecommunications, how-to, interview/profile, new product, photo feature, technical. Buys 40 mss/year. Query with published clips. Length: 1,500 words, including sidebars. Pays $350. Sometimes pays expenses of writers on assignment.

Photos: State availability of photos with submission. Reviews contact sheets, transparencies. Negotiates payment individually. Captions, identification of subjects required. Buys one-time rights.

Columns/Departments: Turning Point (an individual who has made or is making changes in his/her life and business); On Target (advice column for business owners and entrepreneurs), 900 words. Buys 24 mss/year. Query with published clips. Pays $200.

Tips: "Know the magazine before you pitch me. Solid story ideas specifically geared to Colorado audience. No boring stories. No corporatese."

CRAIN'S DETROIT BUSINESS, Crain Communications Inc., 1400 Woodbridge Ave., Detroit MI 48207. (313)446-6000. Fax: (313)446-1687. E-mail: 75147.372@compuserve.com. Website: http://bizserve.com/crains/. Editor: Mary Kramer. Executive Editor: Cindy Goodaker. Contact: Philip Nussel, managing editor. 5% freelance written. Weekly tabloid covering business in the Detroit metropolitan area—specifically Wayne, Oakland, Macomb, Washtenaw and Livingston counties. Estab. 1985. Circ. 143,500. Pays on publication. Publishes ms an average of 1 month after acceptance. Byline given. Offers $150 kill fee. Buys all rights and all electronic rights. Sample copy for $1.
- *Crain's Detroit Business* uses only area writers and local topics.

Nonfiction: New product, technical, business. Buys 100 mss/year. Query with published clips. Length: 20-40 words/column inch. Pays $10/column inch. Pays expenses of writers on assignment.

Photos: State availability of photos with submissions.

Tips: "Contact special sections editor in writing with background and, if possible, specific story ideas relating to our type of coverage and coverage area."

‡DBA HOUSTON, The magazine for growing business, Impax Enterprises Inc., 13111 Westheimer, Suite 315, Houston TX 77077. (281)870-9933. Fax: (281)870-9996. E-mail: dbahouston.com. Contact: Cathy Schmermund, managing editor. 50% freelance written. Monthly business-to-business magazine with all articles by, about and for Houston people and business. "*DBA Houston* provides a superior-quality monthly business publication that enables Houston's growing and emerging companies to increase their business success. Articles are how-to, need-to-know oriented. Most freelance articles are assigned." Estab. 1990. Circ. 25,000. Pays on publication. Publishes ms an average of 2 months after acceptance. Byline given. Buys all rights. Editorial lead time 2 months. Sample copy and ms guidelines free.

Nonfiction: Book reviews (Houston authors), general interest, how-to (business), interview/profile. Buys 100 mss/year. Query. Length: 700-2,000 words. Pays $50-75. Pays some expenses of writers on assignment.

Columns/Departments: Managing Health (making informed decisions about employee health-care coverage) 1,000 words; Book Review (business books by Houston authors) 700 words; High-Tech Houston (business uses/successes) 1,000 words. Buys 12-20 mss/year. Query. Pays $50-75.

Tips: "Send résumé and samples; show knowledge of *DBA Houston*'s content and audience."

INGRAM'S, Show-Me Publishing, Inc., 306 E. 12th St., Suite 1014, Kansas City MO 64106. (816)842-9994. Fax: (816)474-1111. Contact: Toni Carderella, managing editor. 50% freelance written. Monthly magazine covering Kansas City business/executive lifestyle. "Upscale, affluent audience. Business executives and professionals. Looking for sophisticated writing with style and humor when appropriate. All articles must have a Kansas City angle." Estab. 1989. Circ. 24,000. **Pays on acceptance**. Publishes ms an average of 2 months after acceptance. Byline given. Offers 50% kill fee. Buys first rights. Editorial lead time 2 months. Submit seasonal material 3 months in advance. Reports in 6 weeks on queries. Sample copy for $3 current, $5 back. Writer's guidelines free.

Nonfiction: How-to (businesses and personal finance related), interview/profile (KC execs and politicians, celebrities), opinion. Buys 30 mss/year. Query with published clips. "We don't accept unsolicited manuscripts except for opinion column." Length: 500-3,000 words. Pays $175-1,500 maximum. Sometimes pays expenses of writers on assignment.

Columns/Departments: Say-So (opinion), 1,500 words. Buys 12 mss/year. Pays $175 maximum.

Tips: "Writers must understand the publication and the audience—knowing what appeals to a business executive, entrepreneur, or professional in Kansas City."

‡INLAND EMPIRE BUSINESS JOURNAL, Daily Planet Publishing, Inc., 8560 Vineyard Ave., Suite 306, Rancho Cucamonga CA 91730-4352. (909)484-9765. Fax: (909)391-3160. E-mail: busjournal@earthlink.net. Managing Editor: Ingrid Anthony. Contact: Gary Brodlur, editor. 80% freelance written. Monthly magazine covering business related news and features occuring in or pertinent to the "Inland Empire" of Southern California—Riverside and San Bernardino counties. "Audience: decision makers in the two-county area, including CEOs, CFOs, COOs, regional and branch managers, entrepreneurs, politicians and bureaucrats. Philosophy: politically conservative, caters to employer-entrepreneur-professional." Estab. 1988. Circ. 30,000. Pays 30 days after publication. Publishes ms an average of 1 month after acceptance. Byline sometimes given. Buys first North American serial rights or makes work-for-hire assignments. Editorial lead time 2 weeks. Submit seasonal material 1 month in advance. Reports in 3 weeks on queries. Sample copy for $2 plus $1.70 postage. Writer's guidelines free.

Nonfiction: Opinion. Buys 60 mss/year. Query with published clips. Length: 300-1,500 words. Pays 5¢/word. Sometimes pays expenses of writers on assignment.

Photos: State availability of photos with query or send photos with submission. Reviews negatives, transparencies or 4×6 prints. Offers $7.50-15/photo. Captions and identification of subjects required. Buys one-time rights.

Columns/Departments: Exporting (how-to); The Employers Group (employer issues); Corner on the Market (marketing info); Manager's Bookshelf (business book reviews); Mead on Wine (wine reviews); Executive Time Out (travel and photos); all 850 words. Query with published clips.

LONDON BUSINESS MAGAZINE, Bowes Publishers, Box 7400, London, Ontario N5Y 4X3 Canada. (519)472-7601. Editor: Janine Foster. 60% freelance written. Monthly magazine covering business stories in London and area. "Our audience is primarily small and medium businesses and entrepreneurs. Focus is on success stories and how to better operate your business." Estab. 1987. Circ. 13,000. Pays on publication. Publishes ms an average of 2 months after acceptance. Byline given. Offers 50% kill fee. Buys first rights. Editorial lead time 3 months. Reports in 10 weeks on queries. Sample copy for #10 SASE. Writer's guidelines free.
Nonfiction: How-to (business topics), humor, interview/profile, new product (local only), personal experience. Must have a London connection. Buys 24 mss/year. Query with published clips. Length: 250-1,500 words. Pays $25-800.
Photos: Send photos with submission. Reviews contact sheets, transparencies. Negotiates payment individually. Identification of subjects required. Buys one-time rights.
Tips: "Phone with a great idea. The most valuable thing a writer owns is ideas. We'll take a chance on an unknown if the idea is good enough."

‡LOS ANGELES BUSINESS JOURNAL, 5700 Wilshire Blvd., #170, Los Angeles CA 90036. (213)549-5225. Fax: (213)549-5255. Website: http://www.labiz.com. Contact: Mark Lacter, editor. 20% freelance written. Weekly Los Angeles business newspaper. "Our mission is to cover all aspects of Los Angeles business." Estab. 1978. Circ. 40,000. Pays 30 days after publication. Byline given. Offers $50 kill fee. Buys all rights. Reports in 2 weeks on queries.
Nonfiction: Essays, how-to, new product, opinion. "Freelancers are used mostly for our special reports on real estate, health care, banking, finance and investing. Beat-related news is handled by our staff reporters." Buys 100 mss/year. Query with published clips. Length: 1,000 words. Pays $265. Sometimes pays expenses of writers on assignment.
Tips: "We're looking for writers who have a good sense of business writing and a good feel for the L.A. business community."

MONEY SAVING IDEAS, The National Research Bureau, 320 Valley St., Burlington IA 52601. (319)752-5415. Fax: (319)752-3421. Contact: Nancy Heinzel, editor. 75% freelance written. Quarterly magazine that features money saving strategies. "We are interested in money saving tips on various subjects (insurance, travel, heating/cooling, buying a house, ways to cut costs and balance checkbooks). Our audience is mainly industrial and office workers." Estab. 1948. Circ. 1,000. Pays on publication. Publishes ms an average of 1 year after acceptance. Byline given. Buys all rights. Sample copy and writers guidelines for #10 SAE with 2 first-class stamps. Writer's guidelines for #10 SASE.
Nonfiction: How-to (save on grocery bills, heating/cooling bills, car expenses, insurance, travel). Query with or without published clips, or send complete ms. Length: 500-700 words. Pays 4¢/word.
Tips: "Follow our guidelines. Keep articles to stated length, double-spaced, neatly typed. If writer wishes rejected manuscript returned include SASE. Name, address and word length should appear on first page."

NEW MEXICO BUSINESS JOURNAL, Sierra Publishing Group, Inc., 420 Central SW, Albuquerque NM 87102. (505)243-3444. Fax: (505)243-4118. E-mail: sierrapq@ix.netcom.com. Editor: Bob Cochnar. Contact: Kathryn Matousek, assistant editor. 85% freelance written. Monthly magazine covering general business in New Mexico and Southwest. "*The Business Journal* tries to provide indepth analytical coverage of subjects that are of particular interest to people doing business in New Mexico and west Texas." Estab. 1976. Circ. 22,000. Pays on the 15th of the month of publication. Publishes ms 2-3 months after acceptance. Byline given. Offers 25% kill fee. Buys one-time rights. Editorial lead time 2 months. Submit seasonal material 3 months in advance. Accepts simultaneous submissions. Reports in 2 weeks on queries; 1 month on mss. Sample copy for 9×12 SAE with 3 first-class stamps. Writer's guidelines free.
Nonfiction: Book excerpts, interview/profile, business subjects. Buys 50-75 mss/year. Query. Length: 900-3,000 words. Pays $200-750, assigned articles; $150-400, unsolicited articles. Sometimes pays expenses of writers on assignment.
Photos: State availability of photos with submission. Reviews contact sheets, transparencies. Negotiates payment individually. Captions, identification of subjects required. Buys one-time rights.
Columns/Departments: Pays $100-250.

VERMONT BUSINESS MAGAZINE, Lake Iroquois Publications, 2 Church St., Burlington VT 05401. (802)863-8038. Fax: (802)863-8069. E-mail: vtbizmag@together.net. Editor: Timothy McQuiston. 80% freelance written. Monthly tabloid covering business in Vermont. Circ. 8,000. Pays on publication. Publishes ms an average of 1 month after acceptance. Byline given. Offers kill fee. Accepts simultaneous submissions. Not copyrighted. Buys one-time rights. Reports in 2 months. Sample copy for 11×14 SAE with 7 first-class stamps.
Nonfiction: Business trends and issues. Buys 200 mss/year. Query with published clips. Length: 800-1,800 words. Pays $100-200. Pays the expenses of writers on assignment.
Reprints: Send tearsheet of article and information about when and where the article previously appeared.
Photos: Send photos with submission. Reviews contact sheets. Offers $10-35/photo. Identification of subjects required.
Tips: "Read daily papers and look for business angles for a follow-up article. We look for issue and trend articles rather than company or businessman profiles. Note: Vermont-specific material *only*. The articles *must* be about Vermont."

CAREER, COLLEGE AND ALUMNI

Three types of magazines are listed in this section: university publications written for students, alumni and friends of a specific institution; publications about college life for students; and publications on career and job opportunities. Literary magazines published by colleges and universities are listed in the Literary and "Little" section.

AMERICAN CAREERS, Career Communications, Inc., 6701 W. 64th St., Overland Park KS 66202. Fax: (913)362-4864. Contact: Mary Pitchford, editor. 50% freelance written. Middle, junior and high school and vocational/technical school student publication published 3 times during school year covering careers, career statistics, skills needed to get jobs. Most stories are provided at no charge by authors in business, education and government. Estab. 1990. Circ. 500,000. Byline sometimes given. Buys all rights and makes work-for-hire assignments. Reports in 1 month. Sample copy for $2. Writer's guidelines free with SASE.
Nonfiction: Career and education features related to 6 basic career paths: arts and communication; business, management and related technology; health services; human services; industrial and engineering technology; and natural resources and agriculture. Buys 10 mss/year. Query with published clips. Length: 350-750 words. Negotiates payment. Pays expenses of writers on assignment.
Reprints: Send photocopy of article or typed ms with rights for sale noted and information about when and where the article previously appeared. Pays 25% of amount paid for an original article.
Photos: State availability of photos with submission. Reviews contact sheets. Negotiates payment individually. Captions, model releases and identification of subjects required.
Columns/Departments: Reality Check (brief career-related facts), 25-100 words; Career Profile, 250-300 words. Some reviewing of current related books. Buys 6 mss/year. Negotiates payment.
Tips: "Letters of introduction or query letters with samples are ways we get to know writers. Samples should include how-to articles and career-related articles. Articles written for teenagers also would make good samples. Short feature articles on careers, career-related how-to articles and self-assessment tools (10-20 point quizzes with scoring information) are primarily what we publish. We are interested in writers for children in early elementary grades K-4, and we are interested in writers who do classroom activity books and teacher's guides for this age group."

THE BLACK COLLEGIAN, The Career & Self Development Magazine for African American Students, Black Collegiate Services, Inc., 140 Carondelet St., New Orleans LA 70130. (504)523-0154. Fax: (504)523-0271. E-mail: jim@black-collegian.com. Website: http://www.black-collegian.com. Contact: Jim Perry, editor. 25% freelance written. Magazine published biannually (October and February) during school year for African-American college students and recent graduates with an interest in career and job information, African-American cultural awareness, personalities, history, trends and current events. Estab. 1970. Circ. 109,000. Buys one-time rights. Byline given. Pays on publication. Submit seasonal and special interest material 2 months in advance of issue date. Reports in 6 months. Sample copy for $4 and 9×12 SAE. Writer's guidelines for #10 SASE.
Nonfiction: Material on careers, sports, black history, news analysis. Articles on problems and opportunities confronting African-American college students and recent graduates. Book excerpts, exposé, general interest, historical/nostalgic, how-to (develop employability), opinion, personal experience, profile, inspirational. Buys 40 mss/year (6 unsolicited). Query with published clips or send complete ms. Length: 500-1,500 words. Pays $100-500.
Photos: State availability of or send photos with query or ms. Black and white photos or color transparencies purchased with or without ms. 8×10 prints preferred. Captions, model releases and identification of subjects required. Pays $35/b&w; $50/color.

CAMPUS CANADA, Canadian Controlled Media Communications, 287 MacPherson Ave., Toronto Ontario M4V 1A4 Canada. (416)928-2909. Managing Editor: Sarah Moore. 75% freelance written. Quarterly magazine. "*Campus Canada* is written for the Canadian university student. Stories range in topic from current issues (date rape, etc.) to entertainment to collegiate sports." Estab. 1984. Circ. 125,000. Pays on publication. Byline given. Offers 50% kill fee. Buys first North American serial rights. Editorial lead time 3 months. Submit seasonal material 2 months in advance. Accepts simultaneous submissions. Reports in 2 months on queries. Sample copy on request.
Nonfiction: General interest, humor, interview/profile, opinion, personal experience, travel. Buys 15 mss/year. Query with published clips. Length: 1,000 words maximum. Pays $50-300.
Photos: State availability of photos with submissions. Identification of subjects required. Buys one-time rights.
Columns/Departments: Movies (upcoming releases), 800 words; Sports (Canadian university), 800 words; Music (Canadian pop/alternative), 500 words.

CAREER FOCUS, For Today's Rising Professional, Communications Publishing Group, Inc., 3100 Broadway, Suite 660, Kansas City MO 64111. (816)960-1988. Fax: (816)960-1989. Editor: Neoshia Michelle Paige. Contact: Amy Schiska, assistant manager of editorial. 80% freelance written. Bimonthly magazine "devoted to providing positive insight, information, guidance and motivation to assist Blacks and Hispanics (ages 21-40) in their career development and attainment of goals." Estab. 1988. Circ. 250,000. Pays on publication. Byline often given. Buys second serial (reprint) rights and makes work-for-hire assignments. Submit seasonal material 6 months in advance. Accepts simultaneous submissions. Reports in 2 months. Sample copy for 9×12 SAE with 4 first-class stamps. Writer's guidelines for #10 SASE.

● The editor notes that if the writer can provide the manuscript on 3.25 disk, saved in generic ASCII, pay is $10 higher and chance of acceptance is greater.

Nonfiction: Book excerpts, general interest, historical, how-to, humor, inspirational, interview/profile, personal experience, photo feature, technical, travel. Length: 750-2,000 words. Pays $150-400 for assigned articles; 10¢/word for unsolicited articles. Sometimes pays expenses of writers on assignment.

Reprints: Send tearsheet of article or short story and information about when and where the article previously appeared. Pays 50% of amount paid for an original article.

Photos: State availability of photos with submission. Reviews transparencies. Pays $20-25/photo. Captions, model releases and identification of subjects required. Buys all rights.

Columns/Departments: Profiles (striving and successful Black and Hispanic young adult, ages 21-40). Buys 15 mss/year. Send complete ms. Length: 500-1,000 words. Pays $50-250.

Fiction: Adventure, ethnic, historical, humorous, mainstream, slice-of-life vignettes. Buys 3 mss/year. Send complete ms. Length: 500-2,000 words. Pay varies.

Fillers: Anecdotes, facts, gags to be illustrated by cartoonist, newsbreaks, short humor. Buys 10/year. Length: 25-250 words. Pays $25-100.

Tips: For new writers: Submit full ms that is double-spaced; clean copy only. If available, send clips of previously published works and résumé. Should state when available to write. Most open to freelancers are profiles of successful and striving persons including photos. Profile must be of a Black or Hispanic adult living in the US. Include on first page of ms name, address, phone number, Social Security number and number of words in article.

CAREERS & MAJORS (for College Students), Oxendine Publishing, Inc., P.O. Box 14081, Gainesville FL 32604-2081. (904)373-6907. E-mail: 75143.2043@compuserve.com. Editor: W.H. "Butch" Oxendine Jr. Managing Editor: Kay Quinn King. Assistant Editor: Teresa Beard. 35% freelance written. Quarterly magazine for college careers and job opportunities. Estab. 1983. Circ. 18,000. Pays on publication. Publishes ms an average of 3 months after acceptance. Byline given. Buys all rights. Submit seasonal material 4 months in advance. Accepts simultaneous submissions. Reports in 1 month on queries. Sample copy for 8×11 SAE with 3 first-class stamps. For query/response and/or writer's guidelines send SASE.

Nonfiction: How-to, humor, new product, opinion. "No lengthy individual profiles or articles without primary and secondary sources of attribution." Buys 10 mss/year. Query with published clips. Length: 800-900 words. Pays $35 maximum. Pays contributor copies to students or first-time writers.

Reprints: Send tearsheet or photocopy of article or typed ms with rights for sale noted and information about when and where the article previously appeared.

Photos: State availability of photos with submission. Reviews contact sheets, negatives and transparencies; size "doesn't matter." Offers $50/photo maximum. Captions, model releases and identification of subjects required. Buys all rights.

Fiction: Publishes novel excerpts.

Columns/Departments: College Living (various aspects of college life, general short humor oriented to high school or college students), 250-1,000 words. Buys 10 mss/year. Query. Length: 250-1,000 words. Pays $35 maximum.

Fillers: Tips, book reviews, facts, newsbreaks, short humor. Buys 10/year. Length: 100-500 words. No pay for fillers.

Tips: "Read other high school and college publications for current issues, interests. Send manuscripts or outlines for review. All sections open to freelance work. Always looking for lighter, humorous articles, as well as features on Florida colleges and universities, careers, jobs. Multi-sourced (5-10) articles best."

CARNEGIE MELLON MAGAZINE, Carnegie Mellon University, Bramer House, Pittsburgh PA 15213-3890. (412)268-2132. Fax: (412)268-6929. Editor: Ann Curran. Estab. 1914. Quarterly alumni publication covering university activities, alumni profiles, etc. Circ, 60,000. **Pays on acceptance.** Byline given. Reports in 1 month. Sample copy for $2 and 9×12 SAE.

Nonfiction: Book reviews (faculty alumni), general interest, humor, interview/profile, photo feature. "We use general interest stories linked to Carnegie Mellon activities and research." No unsolicited mss. Buys 5 features and 5-10 alumni profiles/year. Query with published clips. Length: 800-2,000 words. Pays $100-400 or negotiable rate.

Poetry: Avant-garde, traditional. No previously published poetry. No payment.

‡CAROLINA ALUMNI REVIEW, UNC General Alumni Association, P.O. Box 660, Chapel Hill NC 27514-0660. (919)962-1208. Fax: (919)962-0010. E-mail: alumni@unc.edu. Contact: Regina Oliver, editor. Managing Editor: Diana Palmer. Bimonthly University of North Carolina alumni magazine seeking understanding of issues and trends in higher education. Estab. 1912. Circ. 55,000. **Pays on acceptance.** Publishes ms an average of 4 months after acceptance. Byline given. Offers 50% kill fee. Buys first North American serial rights and second serial (reprint) rights (for electronic republishing). Editorial lead time 9 months. Submit seasonal material 6 months in advance. Reports in 2 months on mss, 1 month on queries. Sample copy free.

Nonfiction: Interview/profile, photo feature. Nothing unrelated to UNC or higher education. Buys 25 mss/year. Query with published clips. Length: 1,000-3,000 words. Pays $200-1,000. "We take very few unsolicited pieces." Pays the expenses of writers on assignment with limit agreed upon in advance.

Photos: State availability of photos with submission. Reviews contact sheets, negatives, transparencies or prints. Offers $25-700/photo. Identification of subjects required. Buys one-time and electronic republishing rights.

Tips: "Be familiar with *Chronicle of Higher Education* and other journals covering higher education, including other alumni magazines."

CIRCLE K MAGAZINE, 3636 Woodview Trace, Indianapolis IN 46268-3196. Fax: (317)879-0204. E-mail: circlek@i quest.net. Website: http://www.kiwanis.org/circlek.home.html. Contact: Nicholas K. Drake, executive editor. 60% freelance written. "Our readership consists almost entirely of above-average college students interested in voluntary community service and leadership development. They are politically and socially aware and have a wide range of interests." Published 5 times/year. Circ. 15,000. **Pays on acceptance.** Buys first North American serial rights. Byline given. Reports in 2 months. Sample copy and writer's guidelines for large SAE with 3 first-class stamps.
Nonfiction: Articles published in *Circle K* are of 2 types—serious and light nonfiction. "We are interested in general interest articles on topics concerning college students and their lifestyles, as well as articles dealing with careers, community concerns and leadership development. No first person confessions, family histories or travel pieces." Query. Length: 800-1,900 words. Pays $200-400.
Photos: Purchased with accompanying ms. Captions required. Total purchase price for ms includes payment for photos.
Tips: "Query should indicate author's familiarity with the field and sources. Subject treatment must be objective and in-depth, and articles should include illustrative examples and quotes from persons involved in the subject or qualified to speak on it. We are open to working with new writers who present a good article idea and demonstrate that they've done their homework concerning the article subject itself, as well as concerning our magazine's style. We're interested in college-oriented trends, for example: entrepreneur schooling, high-tech classrooms, music, leisure and health issues."

COLLEGE BOUND, The Magazine for High School Students By College Students, Ramholtz Publishing Inc., 2071 Clove Rd., Suite 206, Staten Island NY 10304. (718)273-5700. Fax: (718)273-2539. E-mail: editorial@cbnet.com. Website: http://www.cbnet.com/collegebound. Managing Editor: Roseann Blake. Contact: Gina LaGuardia, editor-in-chief. 85% freelance written. Bimonthly magazine covering the transition from high school to college. "*College Bound* is written by college students for high school students and is designed to provide a view of college life from the inside." Estab. 1987. Circ. 95,000. Pays on publication. Publishes ms an average of 4 months after acceptance. Byline given. Offers 100% kill fee or $100. Buys first and second rights. Editorial lead time 4 months. Submit seasonal material 4 months in advance. Accepts simultaneous submissions. Reports in 5 weeks on queries; 5 weeks on mss. Sample copy and writer's guidelines for 9×12 SASE.
Nonfiction: How-to (apply for college, prepare for the interview, etc.), personal experience (college experiences). Buys 30 mss/year. Query with published clips. Length: 1,200-1,500 words. Pays $50-75. Sometimes pays expenses of writers on assignment.
Reprints: Send photocopy of article. Pays 75% of amount paid for an original article.
Photos: Send photos with submission. Reviews negatives, prints. Offers no additional payment for photos accepted with ms. Buys one time rights.
Columns/Departments: Campus Traditions (unique traditions from different colleges), 100-150 words; Clip Notes (admissions facts and advice, as well as interesting tidbits on "happenings" related to junior and senior students' lifestyles); Books (reviews of books and guides to college life and preparation); Traditions (events on campus that are timeless or entertaining); Focus (indepth profile of a community organization, student-founded group or other group of interest); Campus Tours (walk the readers through a college campus); Applause! (schools that have won awards, big scholarship winners, etc.); Interview (a look at the college application process, presenting a profile of various college administrators, deans, teachers, career advisors, etc.); That's Life (issues outside the academic realm, i.e., money tips, current events, social commentary); all 500-800 words. Buys 30 mss/year. Query with published clips. Pays $15-50.
Fillers: Anecdotes, facts, gags to be illustrated, newsbreaks, short humor. Buys 10/year. Length: 50-200 words. Pays $15-25.
Tips: "College students from around the country are welcome to serve as correspondents to provide our teen readership with personal accounts on all aspects of college. Give us your expertise on everything from living with a roommate, choosing a major, and joining a fraternity or sorority, to college dating, interesting course offerings on your campus, how to beat the financial headache and other college application nightmares."

‡COLLEGE BOUND.NET, A Student's Interactive Guide to College Life, Ramholtz Publishing, Inc., 2071 Cove Rd., Staten Island NY 10304. (718)273-5700. Fax: (718)273-2539. E-mail: editorial@cbnet.com. Website: http://www.cbnet.com/collegebound. Contact: Gina LaGuardia, editor-in-chief. 60% freelance written. "Online magazine for students making the transition from high school to college." Estab. 1996. Pays on publication. Publishes ms an average of 4 months after acceptance. Byline given. Offers 100% kill fee. Buys first rights and second serial (reprint) rights. Editorial lead time 4 months. Submit seasonal material 4 months in advance. Reports in 2 months on queries. Writer's guidelines for #10 SASE.
Nonfiction: Essays, general interest, how-to, humor, inspirational, interview/profile, new product, personal experience, student travel. Query. Length: 300-700 words. Pays $25-75. Sometimes pays the expenses of writers on assignment.
Reprints: Send photocopy of article. Pays 75% of amount paid for an original article.
Photos: State availability of photos with submission. Reviews transparencies and prints. Offers no additional payment for photos accepted with ms. Captions and identification of subjects required.
Columns/Departments: Digital Details (technology), Money, Food, Sports, Music, Shout!, 300-500 words. Buys 30 mss/year. Query with published clips. Pays $15-40.
Fillers: Anecdotes, facts, gags to be illustrated by cartoonist, newsbreaks, short humor. Buys 10/year. Length: 50 words.

COLLEGE MONTHLY, The Student Point-of-View, 23 E. Tenth St., #706, New York NY 10003. Phone/fax: (212)529-1519. Editor: Sara Fiedelholtz. 85% freelance written. Bimonthly magazine covering college life. "*College*

Monthly is written by college students for college students." Estab. 1984. Circ. 375,000. Pays on publication. Publishes ms an average of 3 months after acceptance. Byline given. Offers 100% kill fee or $100. Buys all first rights. Editorial lead time 4 months. Submit seasonal material 4 months in advance. Accepts simultaneous submissions. Reports in 3 weeks on queries; 1 month on mss. Sample copy and writer's guidelines free.

Nonfiction: Interview/profile (college athletics, volunteers), personal experience, travel (spring break, study abroad). Buys 30 mss/year. Query with published clips. Length: 750-2,000 words. Pays $50-150.

Reprints: Accepts previously published submissions.

Photos: Send photos with submission. Reviews negatives, prints. Offers no additional payment for photos accepted with ms. Buys one-time rights.

Columns/Departments: Sports (profiles of college athletes), 1,000 words; Viewpoint (profiles of student volunteers), 1,000 words. Buys 10-12 mss/year. Query with pubished clips. Pays $50-150.

COLLEGE PREVIEW, A Guide for College-Bound Students, Communications Publishing Group, 3100 Broadway, Suite 660, Kansas City MO 64110. (816)960-1988. Fax: (816)960-1989. Editor: Neoshia Michelle Paige. Contact: Amy Schiska, assistant manager of editorial. 80% freelance written. Quarterly educational and career source guide. "Contemporary guide designed to inform and motivate Black and Hispanic young adults, ages 16-21 years old about college preparation, career planning and life survival skills." Estab. 1985. Circ. 600,000. Pays on publication. Byline often given. Buys first serial and second serial (reprint) rights or makes work-for-hire assignments. Submit seasonal material 6 months in advance. Accepts simultaneous submissions. Reports in 2 months. Sample copy for 9×12 SAE with 4 first-class stamps. Writer's guidelines for #10 SASE.
- The editor notes that if the writer can provide the manuscript on 3.25 disk, saved in generic ASCII, pay is $10 higher and chance of acceptance is greater.

Nonfiction: Book excerpts or reviews, general interest, how-to (dealing with careers or education), humor, inspirational, interview/profile (celebrity or "up and coming" young adult), new product (as it relates to young adult market), personal experience, photo feature, technical, travel. Send complete ms. Length: 750-2,000 words. Pays $150-400 for assigned articles; 10¢/word for unsolicited articles. Sometimes pays expenses of writers on assignment.

Reprints: Send photocopy of article or short story or typed ms with rights for sale noted and information about when and where the article previously appeared. Payment varies.

Photos: State availability of photos with submission. Reviews transparencies. Offers $20-$25/photo. Captions, model releases and identification of subjects required. Will return photos—send SASE.

Columns/Departments: Profiles of Achievement (striving and successful minority young adults ages 16-35 in various careers). Buys 30 mss/year. Send complete ms. Length: 500-1,500. Pays 10¢/word.

Fiction: Adventure, ethnic, historical, humorous, mainstream, slice-of-life vignettes. Buys 3 mss/year. Send complete ms. Length: 500-2,000 words. Pay varies.

Fillers: Anecdotes, facts, gags to be illustrated by cartoonist, newsbreaks, short humor. Buys 10/year. Length: 25-250 words. Pays $25-100.

Tips: For new writers—send complete ms that is double spaced; clean copy only. If available, send clips of previously published works and résumé. Should state when available to write. Include on first page of ms name, address, phone, Social Security number, word count and SASE.

DIRECT AIM, For Today's Career Strategies, Communications Publishing Group, 3100 Broadway, Suite 660, Kansas City MO 64110. (816)960-1988. Fax: (816)960-1989. Editor: Neoshia Michelle Paige. Contact: Amy Schiska, assistant manager of editorial. 80% freelance written. Quarterly educational and career source guide for Black and Hispanic college students at traditional, non-traditional, vocational and technical institutions. "This magazine informs students about college survival skills and planning for a future in the professional world." Buys second serial (reprint) rights or makes work-for-hire assignments. Submit seasonal material 6 months in advance. Accepts simultaneous submissions. Reports in 2 months. Sample copy for 9×12 SAE with 4 first-class stamps. Writer's guidelines for #10 SASE.
- The editor notes that if the writer can provide the manuscript on 3.25 disk, saved in generic ASCII, pay is $10 higher and chance of acceptance is greater.

Nonfiction: Book excerpts or reviews, general interest, how-to (dealing with careers or education), humor, inspirational, interview/profile (celebrity or "up and coming" young adult), new product (as it relates to young adult market), personal experience, photo feature, technical, travel. Query or send complete ms. Length: 750-2,000 words. Pays $150-400 for assigned articles; 10¢/word for unsolicited articles. Sometimes pays expenses of writers on assignment.

Reprints: Send photocopy of article or typed ms with rights for sale noted and information about when and where the article previously appeared. Payment varies.

Photos: State availability of photos with submission. Reviews transparencies. Offers $20-25/photo. Captions, model releases and identification of subjects required. Will return photos.

Columns/Departments: Profiles of Achievement (striving and successful minority young adult age 18-35 in various technical careers). Buys 25 mss/year. Send complete ms. Length: 500-1,500. Pays $50-250.

Fiction: Publishes novel excerpts. Adventure, ethnic, historical, humorous, mainstream, slice-of-life vignettes. Buys 3 mss/year. Send complete ms. Length: 500-2,000 words. Pay varies.

Fillers: Anecdotes, facts, gags to be illustrated by cartoonist, newsbreaks, short humor. Buys 30/year. Length: 25-250 words. Pays $25-100.

Tips: For new writers—send complete ms that is double spaced; clean copy only. If available, send clips of previously published works and résumé. Should state when available to write. Include on first page of ms name, address, phone, Social Security number and word count. Photo availability is important."

EEO BIMONTHLY, Equal Employment Opportunity Career Journal, CASS Communications, Inc., 1800 Sherman Ave., Suite 300, Evanston IL 60201-3769. (847)475-8800. Fax: (847)475-8807. E-mail: casspubs@casscom.com. Website: http://www.casscom.com. Contact: Robert Shannon, senior editor. 85% freelance written. Bimonthly magazine covering career management, specifically for women, minorities and persons with disabilities. "Although our audience is specifically female and minority, much of our content applies to all white-collar professionals—career management tips, industry overviews and trends, and job search techniques. Anything job- or career-related (interviewing, résumé writing, relocating, communicating, automating, etc.) fits our publication." Estab. 1969. Circ. 7,500. **Pays on acceptance.** Publishes ms an average of 4 months after acceptance. Byline given. Buys multiple rights for use in smaller publications. Editorial lead time 3 months. Accepts simultaneous submissions. Reports in 3 weeks on queries; 1 month on mss. Sample copy for 10×12 SAE with 6 first-class stamps.
Nonfiction: General interest (career/workplace related), how-to (career planning related), interview/profile. Buys 24-30 mss/year. Query with published clips. Length: 1,800-3,000 words. Pays $350-600 for assigned articles; $250-500 for unsolicited articles.
Reprints: Send photocopy of article and information about when and where the article previously appeared.
Photos: State availability of photos with submissions. Reviews contact sheets, transparencies, prints. Negotiates payment individually. Captions, model releases, identification of subjects required. Buys one-time rights.
Columns/Departments: Success Stories (profiles of successful individuals either female, minority or disabled—but not entrepreneurs; "we are looking for corporate types, especially in engineering and other technical fields"), 2,000 words. Buys 10-12 mss/year. Query with published clips. Pays $250-600.
Tips: "Your queries can be informal outlines; just show us that you can write and that you know your subject."

EQUAL OPPORTUNITY, The Nation's Only Multi-Ethnic Recruitment Magazine for Black, Hispanic, Native American & Asian American College Grads, Equal Opportunity Publications, Inc., 1160 E. Jericho Turnpike, Suite 200, Huntington NY 11743. (516)421-9421. Fax: (516)421-0359. E-mail: eopub@aol.com. Website: www.eop.com. Contact: James Schneider, editor. 50% freelance written. Prefers to work with published/established writers. Triannual magazine covering career guidance for minorities. "Our audience is 90% college juniors and seniors; 10% working graduates. An understanding of educational and career problems of minorities is essential." Estab. 1967. Circ. 10,000. Controlled circulation, distributed through college guidance and placement offices. Pays on publication. Publishes ms an average of 6 months after acceptance. Byline given. Buys first rights. Deadline dates: fall (June 10); winter (September 15); spring (January 1). Accepts simultaneous queries. Sample copy and writer's guidelines for 9×12 SAE with 5 first-class stamps.
Nonfiction: Book excerpts and articles (job search techniques, role models); general interest (specific minority concerns); how-to (job-hunting skills, personal finance, better living, coping with discrimination); humor (student or career related); interview/profile (minority role models); opinion (problems of minorities); personal experience (professional and student study and career experiences); technical (on career fields offering opportunities for minorities); travel (on overseas job opportunities); and coverage of Black, Hispanic, Native American and Asian American interests. Special issues include role model profiles and career guidance articles. Query or send complete ms. Length: 1,000-1,500 words. Sometimes pays expenses of writers on assignment. Pays 10¢/word.
Reprints: Send information about when and where the article previously appeared. Pays 10¢/word.
Photos: Prefers 35mm color slides and b&w. Captions and identification of subjects required. Buys all rights. Pays $15/photo use.
Tips: "Articles must be geared toward questions and answers faced by minority and women students."

FIRST OPPORTUNITY, Today's Career Options, Communications Publishing Group, 3100 Broadway, Suite 660, Kansas City MO 64111. (816)960-1988. Fax: (816)960-1989. Editor: Neoshia Michelle Paige. Contact: Amy Schiska, assistant manager of editorial. 80% freelance written. Resource publication focusing on advanced vocational/technical educational opportunities and career preparation for Black and Hispanic young adults, ages 16-21. Circ. 500,000. Pays on publication. Byline sometimes given. Buys second serial (reprint) rights or makes work-for-hire assignments. Submit seasonal material 6 months in advance. Accepts simultaneous submissions. Reports in 2 months. Sample copy for 9×12 SAE with 4 first-class stamps. Writer's guidelines for #10 SASE.
• The editor notes that if the writer can provide the manuscript on 3.25 disk, saved in generic ASCII, pay is $10 higher and chance of acceptance is greater.
Nonfiction: Book excerpts or reviews, general interest, how-to (dealing with careers or education), humor, inspirational, interview/profile (celebrity or "up and coming" young adult), new product (as it relates to young adult market), personal experience, photo feature, technical, travel. Length: 750-2,000 words. Pays $150-400 for assigned articles; 10¢/word for unsolicited articles. Sometimes pays expenses of writers on assignment.
Reprints: Send photocopy of article or typed ms with rights for sale noted and information about when and where the article previously appeared. Payment varies.
Photos: State availability of photos with submission. Prefers transparencies. Offers $20-25/photo. Captions, model releases, identification of subjects required. Buys all rights.
Columns/Departments: Profiles of Achievement (striving and successful minority young adult, age 16-35 in various vocational or technical careers). Buys 15 mss/year. Send complete ms. Length: 500-1,500. Pays $50-250.

Fiction: Adventure, ethnic, historical, humorous, mainstream, slice-of-life vignettes. Buys 3 mss/year. Send complete ms. Length: 500-5,000 words. Pay varies.

Fillers: Anecdotes, facts, gags to be illustrated by cartoonist, newsbreaks, short humor. Buys 10/year. Length: 25-250 words. Pays $25-100.

Tips: For new writers—send complete ms that is double spaced; clean copy only. If available, send clip of previously published works and résumé. Should state when available to write. Include on first page of ms name, address, phone, Social Security number and word count. Photo availability is important.

FLORIDA LEADER (for college students), P.O. Box 14081, Gainesville FL 32604. (904)373-6907. Fax: (904)373-8120. E-mail: 75143.2043@compuserve.com. Publisher: W.H. "Butch" Oxendine, Jr. Managing Editor: Kay Quinn King. Assistant Editor: Teresa Beard. 10% freelance written. Quarterly "college magazine, feature-oriented, especially activities, events, interests and issues pertaining to college students." Estab. 1981. Circ. 27,000. Publishes ms an average of 2 months after acceptance. Byline given. Submit seasonal material 6 months in advance. Reports in 2 months on queries. Sample copy and writer's guidelines for 9×12 SAE with 5 first-class stamps.

Nonfiction: How-to, humor, interview/profile, feature—all multi-sourced and Florida college related. Special issues: Careers and Majors (January, June); Florida Leader high school edition (August, January, May); Transfer (for community college transfers, November, July); Returning Student (for nontraditional-age students, July); Back to School (September); Student Leader (October, March—pays double). Query with SASE. Length: 800-900 words. Payment varies. Sometimes pays expenses of writers on assignment.

Reprints: Send tearsheet or photocopy of article or typed ms with rights for sale noted and information about when and where the article previously appeared.

Photos: State availability of photos with submission. Reviews negatives and transparencies. Captions, model releases, identification of subjects requested.

Fiction: Publishes novel excerpts.

THE JOB SOURCE SERIES, 2000 L St. NW, Suite 200, Washington DC 20036. (202)337-7800. Fax: (202)337-3121. Editor: Donna Caroline Hicks. Contact: Ben Psillas, managing editor. 50% freelance written. Annual career/job guide covering careers/where to live in major U.S. and international cities. "The JOB Source Series focuses on how and where to find internships, entry-level or middle management jobs in metropolitan areas across the country. Our job guides also help people find places to live, shop and dine in their respective metro area." Estab. 1992. Circ. 15,000. **Pays on acceptance.** Publishes ms an average of 9 months after acceptance. Byline given. Offers 50% kill fee. Buys all rights. Editorial lead time 3 months. Submit seasonal material 9 months in advance. Sample copy $7.50. Writer's guidelines free.

Nonfiction: How-to, careers/jobs. Future Books: New York, LA, Chicago, San Francisco, London, Montreal and Toronto job sources. April 1-December. Buys 5 mss/year. Query with published clips. Length: 500-2,000 words. Pays $350-750. Sometimes pays expenses of writers on assignment.

Reprints: Send photocopy of article or typed ms with rights for sale noted and information about when and where the article previously appeared.

LINK MAGAZINE, The College Magazine, Creative Media Generations, Inc., 110 Greene St., #407, New York NY 10012. (212)966-1100. Fax: (212)966-1380. Website: http://www.linkmag.com. Contact: Peter Kraft. 95% of mss are solicited. Rarely accepts unsolicited materials. Quarterly magazine covering college news, issues and lifestyle. Estab. 1993. Circ. 1,000,000. Pays on publication. Publishes ms an average of 6 months after acceptance. Byline given. Offers 25% kill fee. Buys first or one-time rights. Editorial lead time 4 months. Submit seasonal material 4 months in advance. Accepts simultaneous submissions. Reports in 2 months on queries, 3 months on mss. Writer's guidelines for #10 SASE.

Nonfiction: Book excerpts, essays, exposé, general interest, how-to (educational, financial, lifestyle, etc.), interview/profile, photo feature, travel. Special issues: Environmental, Job Hunting, Computers. Buys 5 mss/year. Query with published clips. Length: 400-3,000. Pays $150-500 for assigned articles; $100-200 for unsolicited articles. Pays expenses of writers on assignment.

Photos: Send photos with submission. Reviews contact sheets, transparencies, prints. Negotiates payment individually. Captions required. Buys one-time rights.

Columns/Departments: Get A Job (how-to job hunting), 700-800 words; It's Your Life (lifestyle), 700-800 words; Interview (national politicians, writers), 700-1,500 words. Buys 5 mss/year. Query with published clips. Pays $200-250.

Tips: "Research very informative, insightful or how-to articles and present completed ideas with clips in a query. Keep everything geared only to what college students would appreciate."

NATIONAL BUSINESS EMPLOYMENT WEEKLY, Dow Jones & Co., P.O. Box 300, Princeton NJ 08543. (609)520-4306. Website: www.nbew.com. Contact: Tony Lee, editor-in-chief. Managing Editor: Perri Capell. 60% freelance written. Weekly magazine covering career-guidance and job-search issues. Estab. 1981. Circ. 30,000. Pays on publication. Publishes ms an average of 2 months after acceptance. Byline given. Offers 50% kill fee. Buys first North American serial, second serial (reprint), all rights or makes work-for-hire assignments. Editorial lead time 3 months. Submit seasonal material 4 months in advance. Reports in 3 weeks on queries; 1 month on mss. Guidelines free.

Nonfiction: Book excerpts, how-to (job search), opinion, small business/entrepreneurial articles, conceptual, statistical analyses, trends. No generic job-search advice. Buys 50 mss/year. Query with published clips. Length: 1,200-1,800

words. Pays $100-250 for assigned articles; $50-200 for unsolicited articles. Sometimes pays expenses of writers on assignment.
Reprints: Accepts previously published submissions if author owns the rights. Send typed ms with rights for sale noted and information about when and where the article previously appeared.
Columns/Departments: From My Perspective (opinion/personal experience on job hunting/career advancement), 800-1,000 words. Buys 50 mss/year. Send complete ms. Pays $50.
Tips: "We are aimed at middle- to senior-level executives who are attempting to change jobs or advance their careers. All submissions must be targeted to that audience." When writing for the *NBEW*, please keep in mind that all feature-length articles should include case studies that can focus on real people who have experience with and can talk about the article's topic; and quotes gathered from experts in the field nationally who can validate the article's premise.

NOTRE DAME MAGAZINE, University of Notre Dame, Administration Bldg., Room 415, Notre Dame IN 46556-0775. (219)631-5335. Fax: (219)631-6767. E-mail: ndmag.1@nd.edu. Editor: Kerry Temple. Managing Editor: Carol Schaal. 75% freelance written. Quarterly magazine covering news of Notre Dame and education and issues affecting contemporary society. "We are interested in the moral, ethical and spiritual issues of the day and how Christians live in today's world. We are universal in scope, Catholic in viewpoint and serve Notre Dame alumni, friends and other constituencies." Estab. 1972. Circ. 135,000. **Pays on acceptance.** Publishes ms an average of 1 year after acceptance. Byline given. Kill fee negotiable. Buys first rights. Reports in 1 month. Free sample copy.
Nonfiction: Opinion, personal experience, religion. Buys 35 mss/year. Query with clips of published work. Length: 600-3,000 words. Pays $250-1,500. Sometimes pays expenses of writers on assignment.
Photos: State availability of photos. Reviews b&w contact sheets, transparencies and 8×10 prints. Model releases and identification of subjects required. Buys one-time rights.

OREGON QUARTERLY, The Magazine of the University of Oregon, 5228 University of Oregon, Eugene OR 97403-5228. (541)346-5048. Fax: (541)346-2220. E-mail: gmaynard@oregon.uoregon.edu. Website: http://www.uoregon.edu/~oqrtly/oq.html. Editor: Guy Maynard. Assistant Editor: Kathleen Holt. 50% freelance written. Quarterly university magazine of people and ideas at the University of Oregon and the Northwest. Estab. 1919. Circ. 95,000. Pays on publication. Publishes ms an average of 3 months after acceptance. Byline given. Offers 20% kill fee. Buys first North American serial rights. Reports in 2 months. Sample copy for 9×12 SAE with 4 first-class stamps.
Nonfiction: Northwest issues and culture from the perspective of UO alumni and faculty. Buys 30 mss/year. Query with published clips. Length: 250-2,500 words. Pays $50-500. Sometimes pays expenses of writers on assignment.
Reprints: Send photocopy of article and information about when and where the article previously appeared. Pays 50% of the amount paid for an original article.
Photos: State availability of photos with submission. Reviews 8×10 prints. Offers $10-25/photo. Identification of subjects required. Buys one-time rights.
Fiction: Publishes novel excerpts.
Tips: "Query with strong, colorful lead; clips."

THE PENN STATER, Penn State Alumni Association, 105 Old Main, University Park PA 16802. (814)865-2709. Fax: (814)863-5690. E-mail: penn-stater@psu.edu. Website: http://www.alumni.alu.psu.edu. Editor: Tina Hay. 75% freelance written. Bimonthly magazine covering Penn State and Penn Staters. "All of our readers are members of the Penn State Alumni Association. They are highly educated, but view our publication as 'easy reading' and a link back to their alma mater. There is a lot of pride in knowing that one out of every 750 Americans went to Penn State." Estab. 1910. Circ. 120,000. **Pays on acceptance.** Publishes ms an average of 4 months after acceptance. Byline given. Offers 50% kill fee. Buys first North American serial rights or second serial (reprint) rights. Editorial lead time 3 months. Submit seasonal material 4-5 months in advance. Accepts simultaneous and previously published submissions. Reports in 1 month on queries; 2 months on mss. Sample copy and writer's guidelines free.
Nonfiction: Book excerpts (by Penn Staters), general interest, historical/nostalgic, humor, interview/profile, personal experience (sometimes), photo feature, science/research. Buys 20 mss/year. Query with published clips. Length: 750-3,000 words. Pays $150-300. Sometimes pays expenses of writers on assignment.
Photos: Send photos with submission. Reviews transparencies and prints. Negotiates payment individually. Captions required. Buys one-time rights.
Tips: "We're always looking for stories from out of state. Stories that have some national slant, that consider a national view of an issue, and somehow involve a Penn Stater are desirable. Profiles of unusual or successful alumni are an 'easy in.' We accept freelance articles almost exclusively for our features section. Generally we run three to four features per issue, plus a photo feature and nostalgia/history piece."

THE PURDUE ALUMNUS, Purdue Alumni Association, Purdue Memorial Union 160, 101 N. Grant St., West Lafayette IN 47906-6212. (765)494-5184. Fax: (765)494-9179. Editor: Tim Newton. 50% freelance written. Prefers to work with published/established writers; works with small number of new/unpublished writers each year. Bimonthly magazine covering subjects of interest to Purdue University alumni. Estab. 1912. Circ. 65,000. Pays on publication. Publishes ms an average of 2 months after acceptance. Byline given. Buys first rights and makes work-for-hire assignments. Submit seasonal material 6 months in advance. Accepts simultaneous submissions. Reports in 2 weeks on queries; 1 month on mss. Sample copy for 9×12 SAE with 2 first-class stamps.
Nonfiction: Book excerpts, general interest, historical/nostalgic, humor, interview/profile, personal experience. Focus

is on alumni, campus news, issues and opinions of interest to 65,000 members of the Alumni Association. Feature style, primarily university-oriented. Issues relevant to education. Buys 12-20 mss/year. Length: 1,500-2,500 words. Pays $250-500. Pays expenses of writers on assignment.
Reprints: Accepts previously published submissions.
Photos: State availability of photos. Reviews b&w contact sheet or 5×7 prints.
Tips: "We have 300,000 living, breathing Purdue alumni. If you can find a good story about one of them, we're interested. We use local freelancers to do campus pieces."

RIPON COLLEGE MAGAZINE, P.O. Box 248, Ripon WI 54971-0248. (414)748-8364. Fax: (414)748-9262. E-mail: booneL@mac.ripon.edu. Website: http://www.ripon.edu. Editor: Loren J. Boone. 15% freelance written. Quarterly magazine that "contains information relating to Ripon College and is mailed to alumni and friends of the college." Estab. 1851. Circ. 14,000. Pays on publication. Publishes ms an average of 3 months after acceptance. Byline given. Not copyrighted. Makes work-for-hire assignments. Reports in 2 weeks.
Nonfiction: Historical/nostalgic, interview/profile. Buys 4 mss/year. Query with or without published clips, or send complete ms. Length: 250-1,000 words. Pays $25-350.
Photos: State availability of photos with submission. Reviews contact sheets. Offers additional payment for photos accepted with ms. Captions and model releases are required. Buys one-time rights.
Tips: "Story ideas must have a direct connection to Ripon College."

RUTGERS MAGAZINE, Rutgers University, Alexander Johnston Hall, New Brunswick NJ 08903. (908)932-7315. Fax: (908)932-8412. E-mail: lchambe@communications.rutgers.edu. Website: http://www.rutgers.edu/magazine. Contact: Lori Chambers, editor. 50% freelance written. Quarterly university magazine of "general interest, but articles must have a Rutgers University or alumni tie-in." Circ. 110,000. **Pays on acceptance.** Publishes ms an average of 4 months after acceptance. Byline given. Pays 30-35% kill fee. Buys first North American serial rights. Submit seasonal material 8 months in advance. Reports in 1 month. Sample copy for $3 and 9×12 SAE with 5 first-class stamps.
Nonfiction: Book excerpts, essays, general interest, historical/nostalgic, science/research, interview/profile, arts/humanities, and photo feature. No articles without a Rutgers connection. Buys 15-20 mss/year. Query with published clips. Length: 2,000-4,000 words. Pays competitively. Pays expenses of writers on assignment.
Fiction: Novel excerpts.
Photos: State availability of photos with submission. Payment varies. Identification of subjects required. Buys one-time rights.
Columns/Departments: Business, Opinion, Sports, Alumni Profiles (related to Rutgers), 1,200-1,800 words. Buys 6-8 mss/year. Query with published clips. Pays competitively.
Tips: "Send ideas. We'll evaluate clips and topic for most appropriate use."

STUDENT LEADER (for college students), Oxendine Publishing Inc., P.O. Box 14081, Gainesville FL 32604-2081. (904)373-6907. E-mail: 75143.2043@compuserve.com. Editor: W.H. "Butch" Oxendine Jr.. Managing Editor: Kay Quinn King. 30% freelance written. Semiannual magazine covering student government, leadership. Estab. 1993. Circ. 200,000. Pays on publication. Byline given. Buys all rights. Submit seasonal material 4 months in advance. Reports in 1 month on queries. Sample copy for #10 SAE with 3 first-class stamps. Writer's guidelines for #10 SASE.
Nonfiction: How-to, humor, new product, opinion. "No lengthy individual profiles or articles without primary or secondary sources of attribution." Buys 10 mss/year. Query with SASE. Length: 800-900 words. Pays $75 maximum. Pays contributor copies to students or first-time writers.
Photos: State availability of or send photos with submission. Reviews contact sheets, negatives, transparencies. Offers $50 photo/maximum. Captions, model releases, identification of subjects required. Buys all rights.
Columns/Departments: Buys 10 mss/year. Query. Length: 250-1,000 words. Pays $100 maximum.
Fillers: Facts, newsbreaks, tips. Buys 10/year. Length: 100 words minimum. No payment for fillers.
Tips: "Read other high school and college publications for current ideas, interests. Send outlines or manuscripts for review. All sections open to freelance work. Always looking for lighter, humorous articles, as well as features on colleges and universities, careers, jobs. Multi-sourced (5-10) articles are best."

SUCCEED, The Magazine for Continuing Education, Ramholtz Publishing Inc., 2071 Clove Rd., Staten Island NY 10304. (718)273-5700. Fax: (718)273-2539. E-mail: ramholtz@intercall.com. Managing Editor: Roseann Blake. Contact: Gina LaGuardia, editor-in-chief. 85% freelance written. Triannual magazine covering continuing education and career transitions. "*Succeed*'s readers are interested in continuing education, whether it be for changing careers or enhancing their current career." Estab. 1994. Circ. 155,000. Pays on publication. Publishes ms an average of 4 months after acceptance. Byline given. Offers 100% kill fee or $100. Buys first rights. Editorial lead time 4 months. Submit seasonal material 4 months in advance. Accepts simultaneous submissions. Reports in 2 months on queries; 5 weeks on mss. Sample copy for $1.50. Writer's guidelines for 9×12 SASE.
Nonfiction: Essays, exposé, general interest, how-to (change careers), interview/profile (interesting careers) new product, opinion, personal experience, photo feature, technical. Buys 15 mss/year. Query with published clips. Length: 700-1,500 words. Pays $50-125. Sometimes pays expenses of writers on assignment.
Reprints: Send photocopy of article. Pays 75% of amount paid for an original article.
Photos: Send photos with submission. Reviews negatives, prints. Offers no additional payment for photos accepted with ms. Captions and identification of subjects required. Buys one-time rights.

Columns/Departments: Tech Zone (new media/technology), 300-700 words; To Be... (personality/career profile), 600-800 words; Financial Fitness (finance, money management), 100-300 words. Buys 10 mss/year. Query with published clips. Pays $15-70.
Fillers: Facts, newsbreaks. Buys 5/year. Length: 50-200 words.

‡**U, The National College Magazine**, American Collegiate Network Inc., 1800 Century Park E., #820, Los Angeles CA 90067. (310)551-1831. Fax: (310)551-1659. E-mail: editor@umagazine.com. Website: http://www.umagazine.com. Contact: Frances Huffman, editor. 70% freelance written. Magazine published 9 times/year. "Is written for college students by college students. It covers news lifestyle and entertainment that relates to college students and college life." Estab. 1987. Circ. 1.5 million. **Pays on acceptance.** Publishes ms an average of 3 months after acceptance. Byline given. Buys all rights. Editorial lead time 3 months. Submit seasonal material 3 months in advance. Reports in 2 months. Sample copy and writer's guidelines free.
Nonfiction: Exposé, general interest, historical/nostalgic, humor, interview/profile, opinion, photo feature, travel. No articles that do not relate to college students or college life. Buys 150-200 mss/year. Query with published clips. Length: 250-1,000 words. Pays $25-100. Sometimes pays expenses of writers on assignment.
Photos: Reviews transparencies, prints. Negotiates payment individually. Buys all rights.
Columns/Departments: U. News (college news), 300 words; U. Life (college lifestyle/trends), 400 words; Byte Me (technology), 300 words; U. Lose (wrongdoings of administration, organization or student); R&R (entertainment, reviews). Buys 200 mss/year. Query with published clips. Pays $25-35.
Tips: Contributors must be enrolled as a college student. "*U* is written in 'college speak.' The tone is conversational, lively, engaging, smart, hip, and a little irreverent. Write articles as if you were talking to your friends at school. *U* is a magazine, not a newspaper—no inverted pyramid stories please! Magazine style requires a punchy lead that grabs the reader, a compelling main body and a witty walk-off."

WHAT MAKES PEOPLE SUCCESSFUL, The National Research Bureau, Inc., 320 Valley St., Burlington IA 52601. (319)752-5415. Fax: (319)752-3421. Contact: Nancy Heinzel, editor. 75% freelance written. Eager to work with new/unpublished writers and works with a small number each year. Quarterly magazine. Estab. 1948. Pays on publication. Publishes ms an average of 1 year after acceptance. Buys all rights. Submit seasonal material 8 months in advance of issue date. Sample copy and writer's guidelines for #10 SAE with 2 first-class stamps.
Nonfiction: How-to (be successful); general interest (personality, employee morale, guides to successful living, biographies of successful persons, etc.); experience; opinion. No material on health. Buys 3-4 mss/issue. Query with outline. Length: 500-700 words. Pays 4¢/word.
Tips: Short articles (rather than major features) have a better chance of acceptance because all articles are short.

CHILD CARE AND PARENTAL GUIDANCE

Magazines in this section address the needs and interests of families with children. Some publications are national in scope, others are geographically specific. Some offer general advice for parents, while magazines such as *Black Child* or *Catholic Parent* answer the concerns of smaller groups. Other markets that buy articles about child care and the family are included in the Religious and Women's sections and in the Trade Education and Counseling section. Publications for children can be found in the Juvenile and Teen sections.

AMERICAN BABY MAGAZINE, For Expectant and New Parents, K-III Communications, 249 W. 17th St., New York NY 10011. (212)462-3500. Fax: (212)367-8332. Website: http://www.enews.com.80/magazines/baby/. Contact: Judith Nolte, editor-in-chief. 90% freelance written. Prefers to work with published/established writers; works with a small number of new/unpublished writers each year. Monthly national publication dedicated to being a guide for pregnant couples and new parents, particularly those having their first child or those whose child is between the ages of birth and 2 years old. Mothers are the primary readers, but fathers' issues are equally important. "A simple, straightforward, clear approach is mandatory." Estab. 1938. Circ. 1,600,000. **Pays on acceptance.** Publishes ms an average of 6 months after acceptance. Byline given. Buys first North American serial rights. Submit seasonal holiday material 6 months in advance. Simultaneous submissions OK. Reports in 4 weeks on queries; 2 months on mss. Sample copy for 9 × 12 SAE with 6 first-class stamps. Writer's guidelines for #10 SASE.
● Ranked as one of the best markets for freelance writers in *Writer's Yearbook* magazine's annual "Top 100 Markets," January 1997.
Nonfiction: Book excerpts, how-to (some aspect of pregnancy or baby care), humor and personal experience. "No 'hearts and flowers' or fantasy pieces." Full-length articles should offer helpful expert information on some aspect of pregnancy or child care; should cover a common problem of child-raising, along with solutions; or should give expert advice on a psychological or practical subject. Articles about products, such as toys and nursery furniture, are not accepted, as these are covered by staff members. Buys 60 mss/year. Query with published clips or send complete ms. Length: 1,000-2,000 words. Pays $750-1,200 for assigned articles; $600-800 for unsolicited articles. Pays the expenses of writers on assignment.
Reprints: Send photocopy of article and information about when and where the article previously appeared. Pays 50%

of amount paid for an original article.

Photos: State availability of photos with submission. Reviews transparencies and prints. Model release and identification of subjects required. Buys one-time rights.

Columns/Departments: Personal Experience, 900-1,200 words, pays $500; Short Items, Crib Notes (news and feature items) and Medical Update, 50-250 words, pays $100.

Tips: "Our readers want to feel connected to other parents, both to share experiences and to learn from one another. They want reassurance that the problems they are facing are solvable and not uncommon. They want to keep up with the latest issues affecting their new family, particularly health and medical news, but they don't have a lot of spare time to read. We forgo the theoretical approach to offer quick-to-read, hands-on information that can be put to use immediately."

‡**AT-HOME MOTHERING**, At-Home Mothers' Resource Center, 406 E. Buchanan Ave., Fairfield IA 52556. (515)472-3202. Contact: Jeanette Lisefski, editor. 100% freelance written. Quarterly magazine covering at-home mothering. "*At-Home Mothering* provides support for at-home mothers and features up-beat articles that reinforce their choice to stay at home with their children, helping them to find maximum fulfillment in this most cherished profession. Through education and inspiration, we also help those mothers who want to stay at home find ways to make this goal a reality." **Pays on acceptance.** Publishes ms an average of 3-12 months after acceptance. Byline given. Buys first North American serial rights or second serial (reprint) rights. Editorial lead time 3 months. Accepts simultaneous submissions. Reports in 1 month on queries; 2 months on mss. Sample copy for $4. Writer's guidelines for #10 SASE.

Nonfiction: Essays, how-to, humor, inspirational, interview/profile, personal experience, photo feature. Features and departments focus on: Choosing Home, Earning at Home, Earning by Saving at Home, Mothers' Self-Esteem and Happiness at Home, Managing at Home, Celebrating Motherhood, Parenting Skills, Flexible Work Options, Teaching at Home, Learning at Home. Buys 120 mss/year. Query with or without published clips. Length: 1,200-2,500 words. Pays $25-150.

Reprints: Accepts previously published submissions.

Photos: Send photos with submission. Reviews prints. Offers $10-50. Model releases required. Buys one-time rights.

Columns/Departments: Book reviews, 300-400 words. Query with or without published clips. Pays $10-50.

Poetry: Free verse, light verse, traditional. Buys 8 poems/year. Length: 4-50 lines. Pays $10-50.

Fillers: Anecdotes, facts, short humor. Buys 20/year. Length: 20-500 words. Pays $10-50.

Tips: "Follow our writer's guidelines. Write specifically to at-home mothers."

ATLANTA PARENT/ATLANTA BABY, Suite 506, 4330 Georgetown Square II, Atlanta GA 30338-6217. (770)454-7599. Editor: Liz White. Managing Editor: Peggy Middendorf. 50% freelance written. *Atlanta Parent* is a monthly tabloid covering parenting of children from birth-16 years old. Offers "down-to-earth help for parents." Estab. 1983. Circ. 70,000. *Atlanta Baby* is a quarterly magazine for expectant and new parents. Circ. 30,000. Pays on publication. Publishes ms 3 months after acceptance. Byline given. Buys one-time rights. Submit seasonal material 6 months in advance. Reports in 4 months. Sample copy for $2.

Nonfiction: General interest, how-to, humor, interview/profile, travel. Special issues: Private school (January); Birthday parties (February); Camp (March/April); Maternity and Mothering (May); Child care (July); Back-to-school (August); Drugs (October); Holidays (November/December). No first-person accounts or philosophical discussions. Buys 60 mss/year. Query with or without published clips, or send complete ms. Length: 700-2,100 words. Pays $15-30. Sometimes pays expenses of writers on assignment.

Reprints: Send photocopy of article or typed ms with rights for sale noted and information about when and where the article previously appeared. Pays $15-30.

Photos: State availability of photos with submission and send photocopies. Reviews 3×5 photos "b&w preferably." Offers $10/photo. Buys one-time rights.

Tips: "Articles should be geared to problems or situations of families and parents. Should include down-to-earth tips and clearly written. No philosophical discussions or first person narratives."

BABY, Baby Publishing Group, 124 E. 40th St., Suite 1101, New York NY 10016. (212)986-1422. Fax: (212)338-9011. E-mail: thebabymag@aol.com. Contact: Jeanne Muchnick, editor. 20% freelance written. Bimonthly magazine covering birth, first year of baby's life. "*Baby* is distributed by diaper services, doctor's offices and retail outlets to national circulation of 750,000. The primary recipients are women in the last trimester of pregnancy and new parents." Estab. 1994. Circ. 750,000. **Pays on acceptance.** Publishes ms an average of 2 months after acceptance. Byline given. Buys first North American serial rights. Editorial lead time 4 months. Submit seasonal material 4 months in advance. Reports in 1 month. Sample copy for SAE with 3 first-class stamps.

Nonfiction: Essays (e.g. first-time dad), how-to (any topics of interest to new parents, e.g. baby care, photography, siblings, traveling, choosing doctor, breast feeding, etc.), personal experience, photo feature, professional or expert articles on baby care, family issues. "We do not include stories about toilet-training, preschool or anything related to children over age one." Buys 18 mss/year. Send complete ms. Length: 400-750 words.

Reprints: Send tearsheet of article and information about when and where the article previously appeared.

Columns/Departments: Ask Dr. Sears, BaBY's Best, Your Healthy Baby, Mom Knows Best, BaBY Album, Prenatal Preview, Excerpts from "The Pregnancy Cookbook," We Tried and Liked, Twin Tips, Adoption Notes, Tips for Single Moms, Parenting Online, Book and Video Reviews, News and Trends.

BABY TALK, Time Publishing Ventures, 1325 Ave. of the Americas, 27th Floor, New York NY 10019. (212)522-8989. Fax:(212)522-8750. Editor-in-Chief: Trishia Thompson. Magazine published 10 times a year. "*Baby Talk* offers an array of baby and child care experts who guide parents with up-to-date medical and developmental information and hands-on baby care articles. A panel of 18 doctors answers questions for new mothers, while regular features address nutrition, health baby products, maternity and baby fashion, toys and safety. The magazine also features first-hand experiences of parents facing the day-to-day dilemmas of new parenthood." Estab. 1935. Circ. 1,102,651. This magazine did not respond to our request for information. Query before submitting.

‡BABY'S WORLD MAGAZINE, America's Baby Magazine, Baby's World Publications Inc., 16 Peniston Ave. E., Hanover NJ 07936. (201)503-0700. Fax: (201)887-6801. E-mail: info@babysworld.com. Contact: Taylor Scott, managing editor. 75% freelance written. Quarterly magazine with "features, columns and stories for new and expectant parents of newborns-to-toddlers regarding health, medicine and nutrition for both baby and mother. Also includes safety, first aid and all-around fun reading." Estab. 1996. Circ. 100,000. Pays on publication. Publishes ms an average of 3 months after acceptance. Byline given. Buys first North American serial rights. Editorial lead time 2 months. Submit seasonal material 3 months in advance. Accepts simultaneous and previously published submissions. Reports in 6 weeks on queries; 2 months on mss. Sample copy for 9 × 12 SAE and 4 first-class stamps. Writer's guidelines for #10 SASE.
Nonfiction: General interest, how-to, humor, inspirational, interview/profile, new product, opinion, personal experience, photo feature. Buys 25 mss/year. Query with or without published clips. Length: 250-3,000 words. Pays $25-500 for assigned articles; $25-200 for unsolicited articles.
Photos: Send photos with submission. Reviews contact sheets, transparencies and prints. Offers $25-50/photo. Negotiates payment individually. Model releases and identification of subjects required. Buys one-time rights.
Columns/Departments: You Need To Know (bits and tips), 25 words; Celebrity Parenting, 250 words. Buys 10 mss/year. Query with or without published clips. Pays $10-250.
Fillers: Anecdotes, facts, gags to be illustrated by cartoonist, newsbreaks, short humor. Buys 10/year. Length: 25-50 words. Pays $10-25.
Tips: "We are looking for fresh, innovative writing on the latest in baby care, articles on the newest procedures, answers to new parents' most-asked questions, and fun reading for women expecting their new baby."

BAY AREA BABY, 401 Alberto Way, Suite A, Los Gatos CA 95032. (408)358-1414. Editor: Anne Chappell Belden. Contact: Mary Brence Martin, managing editor. Magazine published 3 times a year covering pregnancy and new parenthood (usually first-time). "*Bay Area Baby* targets pregnant couples and new (usually first-time) parents. We provide local, up-to-the minute information on pregnancy and babies." Estab. 1986. Circ. 60,000. Pays on publication. Publishes ms an average of 6 months after acceptance. Byline given. Buys first rights. Editorial lead time 4 months. Submit seasonal material 6 months in advance. Accepts simultaneous submissions. Reports in 2 months. Sample copy for 8½ × 11½ SAE with 5 first-class stamps. Writer's guidelines for #10 SASE.
Nonfiction: Book excerpts, essays, interview/profile, personal experience (must be related to pregnancy or new parenthood). Buys 9 mss/year. Send complete ms. Length: 600-1,400 words. Pays 6¢/word. Sometimes pays expenses of writers on assignment.
Reprints: Accepts previously published submissions.
Photos: State availability of photos with submission. Reviews contact sheets, transparencies, prints. Offers $10-15/photo. Buys one-time rights.

BAY AREA PARENT MAGAZINE, Bay Area Publishing Group Inc., 401 Alberto Way, Suite A, Los Gatos CA 95032-5404. Fax: (408)356-4903. Editor: Lynn Berardo. Contact: Mary Brence Martin, managing editor. 80% freelance written. Works with locally-based published/established writers and some non-local writers. Monthly tabloid of resource information for parents and teachers. Circ 77,000. Pays on publication. Publishes ms an average of 6 months after acceptance. Byline given. Buys one-time rights. Submit seasonal material 4 months in advance. Accepts simultaneous submissions. Sample copy for 9 × 12 SAE with 8 first-class stamps. Writer's guidelines for #10 SASE.
Nonfiction: Book excerpts (related to our interest group); exposé (health, psychology); how-to (related to kids/parenting); humor; interview/profile; photo feature; travel (with kids, family). Special issues: Music (March); Art and Kid's Birthdays (April); Summer Camps and Vacations (May); Family Fun and Health and Medicine (June); Working Parents (July); Fashion and Sports (August); Back-to-School (September). No opinion or religious articles. Buys 45-60 mss/year. Query or send complete ms. Length: 150-1,500 words. Pays 6-9¢/word. Sometimes pays expenses of writers on assignment.
Reprints: Send typed ms with rights for sale noted and information about when and where the article previously appeared.
Photos: State availability of photos. Prefers b&w contact sheets and/or 3 × 5 b&w prints. Pays $10-15. Model release

---

 A BULLET introduces comments by the editors of *Writer's Market* indicating special information about the listing.

required. Buys one-time rights.
Columns/Departments: Child Care, Family Travel, Birthday Party Ideas, Baby Page, Toddler Page, Adolescent Kids. Buys 36 mss/year. Send complete ms. Length: 400-1,200 words. Pays 6-9¢/word.
Tips: "Submit new, fresh information concisely written and accurately researched. We also produce *Bay Area Baby Magazine*, published three times a year; *Valley Parent* Magazine, which focuses on central Contra Costa County and southern Alameda County; and *Bay Area Parent of Teens*, a subscription-only publication for parents of adolescents."

BIG APPLE PARENTS' PAPER/QUEENS PARENTS' PAPER, Family Communications, Inc., 36 E. 12th St., New York NY 10003. (212)533-2277. Fax: (212)475-6186. Contact: Helen Freedman, managing editor. 99% freelance written. Monthly tabloids covering New York City family life. "BAPP readers live in high-rise Manhattan apartments; it is an educated, upscale audience. Often both parents are working full time in professional occupations. Child-care help tends to be one-on-one, in the home. Kids attend private schools for the most part. While not quite a suburban approach, some of our QPP readers do have backyards (though most live in high-rise apartments). It is a more middle-class audience in Queens. More kids are in day care centers; majority of kids are in public schools." Estab. 1985. Big Apple circ. 62,000, Queens circ. 40,000. Pays within month of publication. Byline given. Offers 50% kill fee. Buys first New York City rights. Reserves the right to publish an article in either or both the Manhattan and Queens editions and online. Submit seasonal material 3 months in advance. Accepts simultaneous submissions. Reports immediately; however, request no submissions during the summer months. Sample copy and writer's guidelines free.
Nonfiction: Essays, exposé, general interest, how-to, inspirational, interview/profile, opinion, photo feature, family health, education. Buys 60-70 mss/year. Query or send complete ms. Length: 600-1,000 words. Pays $35-50. Sometimes pays expenses of writers on assignment.
Reprints: Send tearsheet or photocopy of article or typed ms with rights for sale noted and information about when and where the article previously appeared. Pays 100% of amount paid for an original article.
Photos: State availability of or send photos with submission. Reviews contact sheets, prints. Offers $20/photo. Captions required. Buys one-time rights.
Columns/Departments: Dads; Education; Family Finance. Buys 50-60 mss/year. Send complete ms.
Tips: "We have a very local focus; our aim is to present articles our readers cannot find in national publications. To that end, news stories and human interest pieces must focus on New York and New Yorkers. Child-raising articles must include quotes from New York and Queens' experts and sources. We are always looking for news and newsy pieces; we keep on top of current events, frequently giving issues that may relate to parenting a local focus so that the idea will work for us as well."

BLACK CHILD MAGAZINE, Interrace Publications, P.O. Box 12048, Atlanta GA 30355. (404)364-9195. Fax: (404)364-9965. Contact: Candy Mills, editor. 80% freelance written. Bimonthly magazine covering parenting of black children. "Covers all concerns/issues relating to healthy parenting of African-American children from birth to early teens.!" Estab. 1995. Circ. 65,000. Pays on publication. Publishes ms an average of 3 months after acceptance. Byline given. Buys first, one- or second serial (reprint) rights. Submit seasonal material 4 months in advance. Reports in 1 month on queries; 2 months on mss. Sample copy for $2 and 9×12 SAE with 4 first-class stamps. Writer's guidelines for #10 SASE.
Nonfiction: Book excerpts, essays, exposé, general interest, historical/nostalgic, how-to, humor, inspirational, interview/profile, new product, opinion, personal experience, photo feature. Buys 30 mss/year. Send complete ms. No simultaneous submissions. Length: 800-2,000 words. Pays 4¢/word.
Reprints: Send photocopy and information about when and where the article previously appeared. Pays 4¢/word.
Photos: State availability of or send photos with submissions. Reviews contact sheets, negatives, transparencies, prints. Offers $25-50/photo. Model releases, identification of subjects required. Buys one-time rights.
Columns/Departments: Health/Fitness, Education, Discipline; all 700-1,400 words. Buys 10 mss/year. Query. Pays 4¢/word..
Tips: "Unique parental articles with hard hitting, no-nonsense approach always preferred. Empowering the parents to raise happy healthy African-American children is our goal! No fiction!"

CATHOLIC PARENT, Our Sunday Visitor, 200 Noll Plaza, Huntington IN 46750. (219)356-8400. Editor: Woodeene Koenig-Bricker. 95% freelance written. Bimonthly magazine covering parenting with a Catholic emphasis. "We look for practical, realistic parenting articles written with a primarily Roman Catholic audience. They key is practical, not pious." Estab. 1993. Circ. 32,000. **Pays on acceptance**. Publishes ms an average of 6 months after acceptance. Byline given. Kill fee varies. Buys first North American serial rights. Editorial lead time 6 months. Submit seasonal material 6 months in advance. Accepts simultaneous submissions. Reports in 2 months. Sample copy for $3.
  • *Catholic Parent* is extremely receptive to first-person accounts of personal experiences dealing with parenting issues that are moving, emotionally engaging and uplifting for the reader. Bear in mind the magazine's mission to provide practical information for parents.
Nonfiction: Essays, how-to, humor, inspirational, personal experience, religious. Buys 50 mss/year. Send complete ms. Length: 850-1,200 words. Pay varies. Sometimes pays expenses of writers on assignment.
Photos: State availability of photos with submissions.
Columns/Departments: This Works (tips), 200 words. Buys 50 mss/year. Send complete ms. Pays $15-25.

CHILD, Gruner + Jahr, 375 Lexington Ave., New York NY 10017-5514. (212)499-2000. Fax: (212)499-2038. E-mail: childmag@aol.com. Editor: Pamela Abrams. Executive Editor: Sylvia Barsotti. Contact: Susan Lapinski, articles editor. 95% freelance written. Monthly magazine for parenting. Estab. 1986. Circ. 875,000. **Pays on acceptance.** Byline given. Offers 25% kill fee. Buys first North American serial, first, one-time and second serial (reprint) rights. Editorial lead time 3 months. Submit seasonal material 6 months in advance. Reports in 2 months. Sample copy for $3.95. Writer's guidelines free.
  • Ranked as one of the best markets for freelance writers in *Writer's Yearbook* magazine's annual "Top 100 Markets," January 1997.
Nonfiction: Book excerpts, general interest, interview/profile, new product, photo feature. No poetry. Query with published clips. Length: 250-2,000 words. Payment negotiable. Pays expenses of writers on assignment.
Photos: State availability of photos with submission. Reviews transparencies. Negotiates payment individually. Buys one-time rights.
Columns/Departments: First Person (mother's or father's perspective); Lesson Learned (experience mother or father learned from). Query with published clips.

CHRISTIAN PARENTING TODAY, Good Family Magazines, 4050 Lee Vance View, Colorado Springs CO 80918. (719)531-7776. Fax: (719)535-0172. E-mail: cptmag@aol.com. Editor: Erin Healy. Contact: Kathy Davis, associate editor. 90% freelance written. Bimonthly magazine covering parenting today's children. "*CPT* encourages and informs parents of children ages birth to 12 who want to build strong families and raise their children from a positive, authoritative Christian perspective. *CPT* strives to give parents practical tools in four areas: 1) encouraging the spiritual and moral growth of their children; 2) guiding the physical, emotional, social and intellectual development of their children; 3) enriching the reader's marriage; and 4) strengthening the reader's family relationships." Estab. 1988. Circ. 250,000. Pays on acceptance or publication. Byline given. Buys first North American serial or second serial (reprint) rights. Submit seasonal material 8 months in advance. Reports in 2 months. Sample copy for 9×12 SAE with $3 postage. Writer's guidelines for #10 SASE.
Nonfiction: Book excerpts, how-to, humor, inspirational, religious. Feature topics of greatest interest: practical guidance in spiritual/moral development and values transfer; practical solutions to everyday parenting issues; tips on how to enrich readers' marriages; ideas for nurturing healthy family ties; family activities that focus on parent/child interaction; humorous pieces about everyday family life. Buys 50 mss/year. Query. Length: 750-2,000 words. Pays 15-25¢/word. Sometimes pays expenses of writers on assignment.
Reprints: Send photocopy of article and typed ms with rights for sale noted and information about when and where the article previously appeared. Pays $50.
Photos: State availability of photos with submission. Do not submit photos without permission. Reviews transparencies. Model release required. Buys one-time rights.
Columns/Departments: Parent Exchange (family-tested parenting ideas from our readers), 25-100 words (pays $40); Life In Our House (entertaining, true, humorous stories about your family), 25-100 words (pays $25); Your Child Today (specifics of emotional, physical, social and intellectual development of children in 5 age brackets: Babies, Toddlers, Preschoolers, Early Elementary and Late Elementary), 300-400 words (pays $50-75); Train Them Up (spiritual development topics from a Christian perspective), 300-400 words (pays $50-75); Healthy & Safe (practical how-to articles that speak to parents' desire to provide their children with an emotionally and physically safe environment both at home and away), 300-400 words (pays $50-75); Family Room ("go do something with your kids" activities), 600-700 words (pays $125); The Lighter Side (humorous everyday family life), 600-700 words (pays $125); The Homefront Store (parent-tested reviews of children's and parenting products), query Colin Miller, associate editor (pays $25-35). Buys 120 mss/year. Submissions become property of *CPT*. Submissions to *Life In Our House* and *Parent Exchange* are not acknowledged or returned.
Tips: "Tell it like it is. Readers have a 'get real' attitude that demands a down-to-earth, pragmatic take on topics. Don't sugar-coat things. Give direction without waffling. If you've 'been there,' tell us. The first-person, used appropriately, is OK. Don't distance yourself from readers. They trust people who have walked in their shoes. Get reader friendly. Fill your article with nuts and bolts: developmental information, age-specific angles, multiple resources, sound-bite sidebars, real-life people and anecdotes and realistic, vividly explained suggestions."

‡DPX, Divorced Parents X-Change, Inc., P.O. Box 1127, Athens OH 45701-1127. (614)664-3030. Contact: Terri Andrews, editor/founder. 75% freelance written. Monthly nonprofit newsletter covering divorced- and step-parenting. "The DPX is a national publication devoted to supporting, informing, educating and assisting divorced- and step-parenting. We emphasize co-parenting, communication and positive parenting." Estab. 1993. Circ. 250. Pays on publication. Publishes ms an average of 3 months after acceptance. Buys one-time rights. Editorial lead time 3 months. Submit seasonal material 4 months in advance. Accepts simultaneous submissions. Reports in 6 weeks on queries; 1 month on mss. Sample copy free. Manuscript guidelines for #10 SASE.
Nonfiction: Book excerpts, essays, general interest, how-to, humor, inspirational, interview/profile, personal experience, self-help. "No how-to-get-even-with-your-ex articles." Buys 40 mss/year. Send complete ms. Length: 200-1,000 words. Pays 1¢/word. Pays with contributor copies at writer's request.
Reprints: Send photocopy of article and information about when and where the article previously appeared. Pays 50% of amount paid for an original article.
Poetry: Avant-garde, free verse, haiku, light verse, traditional. Submit maximum 5 poems. Length: 6-20 lines. Pays 1¢/word.

Fillers: Facts, short humor. Length: 10-100 words. Pays 1¢/word.
Tips: "Read our newsletter first. We focus on the positive side of co-parenting. We inspire and motivate parents—not add fuel to their anger."

‡EXCEPTIONAL PARENT, Parenting Your Child or Young Adult with a Disability, 209 Harvard St., Suite 303, Brookline MA 02146. (617)730-5800. Editor-in-Chief: Dr. Stan Klein. 75% freelance written (mostly reader and professionally written). Monthly magazine covering children and young adults with disabilities. Estab. 1971. Circ. 70,000. Pays on publication. Byline given. Buys first North American serial rights. Submit seasonal material 6 months in advance. Accepts previously published submissions. Query for electronic submissions. Reports in 6 months. Sample copy and writer's guidelines free.
Nonfiction: Book excerpts, essays, humor, inspirational, opinion, personal experience, religious, travel. Buys 50 mss/ year. Query or send complete ms. Length varies. Pays $25 maximum and contributor copies.
Photos: Send photos with submission. Offers no additional payment for photos accepted with ms. Model releases and identification of subjects required. Buys all rights.
Columns/Departments: Fathers' Voices (fathers write about having child with disability), 600-1,000 words; Role Model (stories by and/or about role models who grew up with disability), 1,200 words; Children's Play (friends, siblings, children with disabilities write about their experiences), 300-500 words. Buys 40 mss/year. Send complete ms. Pays $25 maximum.
Tips: "Read back issues of magazine. Majority of the magazine is written by parents of children with disabilities and professionals. Pieces are usually advice from experience."

FAMILY LIFE, Hachette-Filipacchi Magazines, Inc., 1633 Broadway, New York NY 10019. Fax: (212)489-4561. E-mail: familylife@aol.com. Editor-in-Chief: Peter Herbst. Contact: Ziona Hochbaum. 90% freelance written. Bimonthly magazine for parents of children ages 3-12. Estab. 1993. Circ. 400,000. **Pays on acceptance.** Publishes ms an average of 4 months after acceptance. Byline given. Offers 25% kill fee. Buys first North American rights. Editorial lead time 5 months. Submit seasonal material 8 months in advance. Accepts simultaneous submissions. Reports in 6 weeks on queries. Sample copy for $3, call (908)367-2900. Writer's guidelines for #10 SASE.
Nonfiction: Parenting book excerpts, essays, general interest, new product, photo feature, travel. No articles about children under 3 or childbirth. Query with published clips. Pays $1/word. Pays expenses of writers on assignment.
Photos: State availability of photos with submission. Reviews transparencies. Negotiates payment individually. Buys one-time rights.

FAMILY TIMES, Family Times, Inc., 1900 Superfine Lane, Wilmington DE 19802. (302)575-0935. Fax: (302)575-0933. Contact: Denise Yearian, editor. 50% freelance written. Monthly tabloid for parenting. "Our targeted distribution is to parents via a controlled network of area schools, daycares, pediatricians and places where families congregate. We only want articles related to parenting, children's issues and enhancing family life." Estab. 1990. Circ. 35,000. Pays on publication. Publishes ms an average of 2 months after acceptance. Byline given. Buys one-time or second serial (reprint) rights. Editorial lead time 2 months. Submit seasonal material 2 months in advance. Accepts simultaneous submissions. Reports in 3 months on mss. Sample copy for 3 first-class stamps.
Nonfiction: Book excerpts, how-to parenting, inspirational, interview/profile, new product, opinion, personal experience, photo feature, travel, children, parenting. Special issues: Schools (October); Camps (February); Maternity (July); Holiday (December); Fitness (March); Birthday (May); Back to School (August). Buys 60 mss/year. Send complete ms. Length: 350-1,200 words. Pays $30 minimum for assigned articles; $25 for unsolicited articles. Sometimes pays expenses of writers on assignment.
Reprints: Accepts previously published submissions.
Photos: State availability of photos with submission. Negotiates payment individually. Identification of subjects required. Buys one-time rights.
Columns/Departments: Pays $25-50.
Tips: "Work with other members of PPA (Parenting Publications of America) since we all share our writers and watch others' work. We pay little but you can sell the same story to 30 other publications in different markets. Online use offers additional author credit and payment based on accesses. We are most open to general features."

FAMILYFUN, Disney Magazine Publishing Inc., 244 Main St., Northampton MA 01060. Fax: (413)586-5724. Website: http://www.familyfun.com. Contact: Susan Claire Ellis, editor. Magazine published 10 times/year covering activities for families with kids ages 3-12. "*Family Fun* is about all the great things families can do together. Our writers are either parents or professionals in education." Estab. 1991. Circ. 1,000,000. **Pays on acceptance.** Publishes ms an average of 4 months after acceptance. Byline sometimes given. Offers 25% kill fee. Buys simultaneous rights or makes work-for-hire assignments. Editorial lead time 4 months. Submit seasonal material 6 months in advance. Accepts simultaneous submissions. Reports in 2 months on queries. Sample copy and writer's guidelines for $3 (call (800)289-4849).
Nonfiction: Book excerpts, essays, general interest, how-to (crafts, cooking, educational activities), humor, interview/ profile, personal experience, photo feature, travel. Special issues: Crafts, Holidays, Back to School, Summer Vacations. Buys hundreds mss/year. Query with published clips. No unsolicited mss. Length: 850-3,000 words. Pays $1/word. Sometimes pays expenses of writers on assignment.
Photos: State availability of photos with submissions. Reviews contact sheets, negatives, transparencies. Offers $75-500/photo. Model releases, identification of subjects required. Buys all rights (simultaneous).

Columns/Departments: Family Ties (essay on family relationships and traditions), 1,500 words; My Great Idea (essay on a simple idea [usually a tradition] that is wonderful for families and is a proven hit with author's family), 600-800 words. Buys 20-25 mss/year. Query with published clips or send complete ms. Pays 50¢/word.
Tips: "Many of our writers break into *FF* by writing for either *Family Almanac* (front-of-book department with 75-300 word pieces on crafts, food, games, etc.) or *Family Traveler* (also a front-of-the-book department, but with 75-800 word pieces). We also pay $50-75 for ideas."

GROWING PARENT, Dunn & Hargitt, Inc., P.O. Box 620, Lafayette IN 47902-0620. (765)423-2624. Fax: (765)742-8514. Contact: Nancy Kleckner, editor. 40-50% freelance written. Works with a small number of new/unpublished writers each year. "We do receive a lot of unsolicited submissions but have had excellent results in working with some unpublished writers. So, we're always happy to look at material and hope to find one or two jewels each year." Monthly newsletter which focuses on parents—the issues, problems, and choices they face as their children grow. "We want to look at the parent as an adult and help encourage his or her growth not only as a parent but as an individual." Estab. 1973. Pays on publication. Publishes ms an average of 6 months after acceptance. Byline given. Buys first North American serial rights; maintains exclusive rights for three months. Submit seasonal material 6 months in advance. Reports in 2 weeks. Sample copy and writer's guidelines for 5×8 SAE with 2 first-class stamps.
Nonfiction: "We are looking for informational articles written in an easy-to-read, concise style. We would like to see articles that help parents deal with the stresses they face in everyday life—positive, upbeat, how-to-cope suggestions. We rarely use humorous pieces, fiction or personal experience articles. Writers should keep in mind that most of our readers have children under two years of age." Buys 15-20 mss/year. Query. Length: 1,000-1,500 words; will look at shorter pieces. Pays 10-15¢/word (depends on article).
Reprints: Send tearsheet of article and information about when and where it previously appeared.
Tips: "Submit a very specific query letter with samples."

HEALTHY KIDS, K-III Publishing, 249 W. 17th St., New York NY 10011. (212)462-3300. Fax: (212)367-8332. Managing Editor: Laura Broadwell. Contact: Keri Klein, assistant editor. 90% freelance written. Bimonthly magazine that addresses all elements that go into the raising of a healthy, happy child, from basic health care information to an analysis of a child's growing mind and behavior patterns. Extends the wisdom of the pediatrician into the home, and informs parents of young children (ages birth to 10 years) about proper health care. The only magazine produced for parents in association with the American Academy of Pediatrics, the nonprofit organization of more than 49,000 pediatricians dedicated to the betterment of children's health. Distributed free to parents through participating CAP members' offices. To ensure accuracy, all articles are reviewed by an editorial advisory board comprised of distinguished pediatricians. Estab. 1989. Circ. 1.5 million. **Pays on acceptance.** Byline given. Buys first rights. Submit seasonal material at least 6 months in advance. Reports in 1 month on queries. Writer's guidelines for #10 SASE.
• Ranked as one of the best markets for freelance writers in *Writer's Yearbook* magazine's annual "Top 100 Markets," January 1997.
Nonfiction: How-to help your child develop as a person, keep safe, keep healthy. No poetry, fiction, travel or product endorsement. Special issues: Good Eating!—A complete guide to feeding your family (February/March); School Days—A back-to-school guide for preschoolers and the early grades, including tips on kids and computers, working with your child's teacher, school bus safety, school lunches and more (August/September). Buys 30 mss/year. Query. No unsolicited mss. Length: 1,500-2,000 words. Pays $750-1,200. Pays expenses of writers on assignment.
Columns/Departments: Focus On . . . (an informal conversation with a pediatrician, in a question-and-answer format, about a timely health issue); Let's Eat (advice on how to keep mealtimes fun and nutritious, along with some child-friendly recipes); Behavior Basics (a helpful article on how to deal with some aspect of a child's behavior—from first friendships to temper tantrums). Buys 30 mss/year. Query. Length: 1,500-2,000 words. Pays $750-1,200.
Tips: A simple, straightforward, clear approach is mandatory. Articles should speak with the voice of medical authority in children's health issues, while being helpful and encouraging, cautionary but not critical, and responsible but not preachy. All articles should include interviews with appropriate Academy-member pediatricians and other health care professionals. A bibliography or list of sources and contacts is required with submission of a researched article.

HOME EDUCATION MAGAZINE, P.O. Box 1083, Tonasket WA 98855-1083. Fax: (509)486-2628. E-mail: homedmag@aol.com. Website: http://www.home-ed-press.com. Contact: Helen E. Hegener, managing editor. 80% freelance written. Eager to work with new/unpublished writers each year. Bimonthly magazine covering home-based education. "We feature articles which address the concerns of parents who want to take a direct involvement in the education of their children—concerns such as socialization, how to find curriculums and materials, testing and evaluation, how to tell when your child is ready to begin reading, what to do when homeschooling is difficult, teaching advanced subjects, etc." Estab. 1983. Circ. 25,000. **Pays on acceptance.** Publishes ms an average of 4 months after acceptance. Byline given. ("Please include a 30-50 word credit with your article.") Buys first North American electronic, serial, first, one-time rights. Submit seasonal material 6 months in advance. Reports in 2 months. Sample copy for $4.50. Writer's guidelines for #10 SASE or via e-mail.
Nonfiction: Essays, how-to (related to home schooling), humor, interview/profile, personal experience, photo features, technical. Buys 40-50 mss/year. Query with or without published clips, or send complete ms. Length: 750-2,500 words. Pays $25-50. Sometimes pays expenses of writers on assignment.
Photos: Send photos with submission. Reviews enlargements, 35mm prints, b&w snapshots, CD-ROMs. Color transparencies for covers $50 each; inside b&w $10 each. Identification of subjects preferred. Buys one-time rights.

Tips: SASE. "We would like to see how-to articles (that don't preach, just present options); articles on testing, account-ability, working with the public schools, socialization, learning disabilities, resources, support groups, legislation and humor. We need answers to the questions that homeschoolers ask."

INDY'S CHILD, 836 E. 64, Indianapolis IN 46220. Fax: (317)722-8510. E-mail: indychild@family.com. Contact: Vonda Lutz, managing editor. 100% freelance written. Monthly magazine covering parenting. "*Indy's Child* is a parenting magazine circulated throughout Central Indiana. We cover topics ranging from maternity, camps, birthday parties, mental health, enrichment, education and discipline to finances and computers. Ninety-five percent of our readers are college-educated, middle to upperclass women ages 25-45." Estab. 1984. Circ. 70,000. Pays on publication. Publishes ms an average of 3 months after acceptance. Byline given. Buys first rights or second serial (reprint) rights. Editorial lead time 3 months. Submit seasonal material 3 months in advance. Reports in 2 months. Sample copy for 9×12 SAE with 4 first-class stamps. Writer's guidelines for #10 SASE.
Nonfiction: Essays, general interest, how-to (anything that deals with parenting. humor, inspirational, personal experi-ence, travel. Nothing political or one sided. Special issue: Baby Guide. Buys 36 mss/year. Send complte ms. Length: 1,000-2,500 words. Pays $50-175 for assigned articles; $25-135 for unsolicited articles. Sometimes pays expenses of writers on assignment.
Reprints: Send tearsheet of article or short story or typed ms with rights for sale noted and information about when and where the article previously appeared.
Photos: State availability of photos with submission. Reviews 3×5 prints. Negotiates payment individually. Identifica-tion of subjects required. Negotiates rights purchased.
Fiction: Humorous, life lesson. Buys 2 mss/year. Send complete ms. Length: 1,000-1,500 words. Pays $50-150.
Tips: "We tend to accept articles that are not only serious issues to parents but that also have great solutions or specific places to turn to for help. Everything needs a local slant."

L.A. PARENT, The Magazine for Parents in Southern California, P.O. Box 3204, Burbank CA 91504. (818)846-0400. Fax: (818)841-4964. E-mail: laparent@compuserve.com. Editor: Jack Bierman. Contact: David Jamieson, manag-ing editor. 80% freelance written. Prefers to work with published/established writers, but works with a small number of new/unpublished writers each year. Monthly tabloid covering parenting. Estab. 1980. Circ. 200,000. **Pays on acceptance**. Publishes ms an average of 4 months after acceptance. Byline given. Buys first and reprint rights. Submit seasonal material 3 months in advance. Accepts simultaneous queries. Reports in 3 months. Sample copy and writer's guidelines for $2 and 11×14 SAE with 5 first-class stamps.
    • *L.A. Parent* is looking for more articles pertaining to infants and early childhood.
Nonfiction: General interest, how-to. Special issues: High Potential Parenting and Nutrition of the Young Child. "We focus on generic parenting for ages 0-10 and Southern California activities for families, and do round-up pieces, i.e., a guide to private schools, art opportunities." Buys 60-75 mss/year. Query with clips of published work. Length: 700-1,200 words. Pays $250-350 plus expenses.
Reprints: Send photocopy of article or typed ms with rights for sale noted and information about when and where the article previously appeared. Pays 50% of amount paid for an original article.
Tips: "We will be using more contemporary articles on parenting's challenges. If you can write for a 'city magazine' in tone and accuracy, you may write for us. The 'Baby Boom' has created a need for more generic parenting material. We look for a sophisticated tone in covering the joys and demands of being a mom or dad in the 90s."

LONG ISLAND PARENTING NEWS, RDM Publishing, P.O. Box 214, Island Park NY 11558. (516)889-5510. Fax: (516)889-5513. E-mail: liparent@family.com. Website: family.com. Contact: Pat Simms-Elias, editorial director. Director: Andrew Elias. 70% freelance written. Free community newspaper published monthly covering parenting, children and family issues. "For concerned parents with active families and young children. Our slogan is: 'For parents who care to know.' " Estab. 1989. Circ. 54,500. Pays on publication. Publishes ms an average of 3 months after acceptance. Byline given (also 1-3 line bio, if appropriate). Buys one-time rights. Accepts simultaneous submissions. Reports in 3 months. Sample copy for $3 and 9×12 SAE with 5 first-class stamps. Writer's guidelines free.
Nonfiction: Essays, general interest, humor, interview/profile, travel. Needs articles covering childcare, childbirth/maternity, schools, camps and back-to-school. Special issues: Schools, Sleepaway Camps and Family Safety (January); Camps, Family Health and Kids' Rooms (February); Sports and Fitness Programs (March); Swing Sets, Party Planning, Sports and Camping, Pets (April); Summer Programs and Camps, Summer Vacations (May); Maternity & Birthing (June); Schools and Fall Programs, Continuing Education and Special Needs (August); Dance, Music and Arts Programs, Party Planning, Children's Health (September); Women's Health, Halloween (October); Winter Vacations, Special Needs (November); Winter and Spring Programs, Home Entertainment, Continuing Education (December). Buys 30-50 mss/year. Query with or without published clips, or send complete ms. Length: 350-2,000 words. Pays $25-150. "Sometimes trade article for advertising space." Sometimes pays expenses of writers on assignment.
Reprints: Send photocopy of article or typed ms with rights for sale noted and information about when and where the article previously appeared. Negotiates fee.
Photos: Send photos, preferably b&w, with submission. Reviews 4×5 prints. Offers $5-50/photo. Captions required. Buys one-time rights.
Columns/Departments: On the Island (local, national and international news of interest to parents); Off The Shelf (book reviews); Fun & Games (toy and game reviews); KidVid (reviews of kids' video); The Beat (reviews of kids' music); Monitor (reviews of computer hardware and software for kids); The Big Picture (reviews of kids' films); Soon

Come (for expectant parents); Educaring (parenting info and advice); Something Special (for parents of kids with special needs); Growing Up (family health issues); On the Ball (sports for kids); Family Matters (essays on family life); Words Worth (storytelling); Getaway (family travel); Teen Time (for parents of teenagers). Buys 20-30 mss/year. Send complete ms. Length: 500-1,000 words. Pays $25-150.

Fillers: Facts and newsbreaks. Buys 1-10/year. Length: 200-500. Pays $10-25.

METRO PARENT MAGAZINE, All Kids Considered, Ltd., 24567 Northwestern Hwy., Suite 150, Southfield MI 48075. (810)352-0990. Fax: (810)352-5066. E-mail: metparent@aol.com. Website: http://family.com. Contact: Susan Feightner, editor. 100% freelance written. Monthly tabloid covering parenting/family issues. *"Metro Parent* is a local parenting publication geared toward parents with children under the age of 12. We look for sound, pertinent information for our readers, preferably using local experts as sources." Estab. 1986. Distributed throughout Oakland, Macomb and Wayne Counties and the city of Ann Arbor. Circ. 70,000. Pays on publication. Publishes ms an average of 2 months after acceptance. Byline given. Buys one-time rights. Editorial lead time 3 months. Submit seasonal material 4 months in advance. Accepts simultaneous submissions. Sample copy and writer's guidelines free.

Nonfiction: Book excerpts, general interest, how-to, humor, inspirational, interview/profile, new product, travel. Special issues: Metro Baby Magazine (geared for expectant parents, August, January); Camps (January-May); Birthdays (March); Back to School (August/September); and Holiday issues (October, November, December, February). Buys 25 mss/year. Query with published clips. Length: 600-2,000 words. Pays $75-150 for assigned articles.

Reprints: Accepts previously published submissions. Send photocopy of article or short story and information about when and where the article previously appeared. Pays $35 for reprints.

Photos: State availability of photos with submission. Reviews 4×6 prints. Negotiates payment individually. Captions, model releases, identification of subjects required. Buys one-time rights.

Columns/Departments: Bits'n' Pieces (new products) 100 words; Multi Media (video, movie, books, audio, software), 700 (total) words; Boredom Busters (craft ideas, games & activities), 700 words; Let's Party! (fun, unique ideas for parties and other celebrations), 700 words. Buys 35 mss/year. Query with published clips. Pays $30-50.

METROKIDS MAGAZINE, The Resource for Delaware Valley Families, Kidstuff Publications, Inc., 1080 N. Delaware Ave., #702, Philadelphia PA 19125-4330. (215)291-5560. Fax: (215)291-5563. E-mail: metrokid@family.com. Contact: Nancy Lisagor, editor-in-chief. 70% freelance written. Monthly tabloid providing information for parents and kids in Philadelphia and surrounding counties. Estab. 1990. Circ. 75,000. Pays on publication. Byline given. Buys one-time rights. Submit seasonal material 4 months in advance. Reports in up to 8 months on queries. Sample copy for $2 and 9×12 SAE. Writer's guidelines for #10 SASE.

● *MetroKids* welcomes query letters or faxes. They especially want to hear from writers in their area.

Nonfiction: General interest, how-to, humor, new product, travel. Special issues: Baby First editions (March and September); Camps (January-May); Special Kids edition (October); Vacations and Theme Parks (May, June); Holidays (November-December). Buys 40 mss/year. Query with or without published clips. Length: 800-1,200 words maximum. Pays $1-50. Sometimes pays expenses of writers on assignment.

Reprints: Send photocopy of article and information about when and where the article previously appeared. Pays 75-80% of amount paid for an original article.

Photos: State availability of photos with submission. Captions required. Buys one-time rights.

Columns/Departments: Away We Go (travel); On Call (medical); Book Beat (book reviews); Bytesize, 500-800 words. *"MetroKids* also features monthly health columns on topics like breast cancer, the insurance quagmire, women's health issues, children's health; travel columns to local destinations like the Poconos, the Shore & points in between." Buys 25 mss/year. Query. Pays $1-50.

Tips: "Query several months before a scheduled topical issue; then follow-up with a telephone call. We are interested in receiving feature articles (on specified topics) or material for our regular columns (which should have a regional/seasonal base). Editorial calendar available on request. We are also interested in finding local writers for assignments."

‡MOTHERING, P.O. Box 1690, Santa Fe NM 87504. (505)984-8116. Fax: (505)986-8335. Contact: Ashisha, senior editor. Quarterly magazine covering natural family living for mothers and fathers, as well as grandparents, educators and health care workers. Estab. 1975. Circ. 70,250. Pays on publication. Publishes ms 6-12 months after acceptance. Byline given. Buys one-time rights. Reports in 2 weeks. Sample copy $3. Writer's guidelines for #10 SASE.

Nonfiction: Essays, general interest, how-to, inspirational, interview/profile, personal experience. *"Mothering* has 6 regular features: 'The Art of Mothering' (inspirational and spiritual side of nurturing); 'Health' (new approaches to health care for the whole family—we encourage articles on unconventional approaches to common childhood health questions); 'A Child's World' (reflecting the world as a child sees it. We especially like to feature activities, crafts, arts, music and stories for children); 'Pregnancy, Birth & Midwifery' (all aspects of pregnancy and birth as well as actual experiences and stories of childbirth. This section encompasses all types of noninterventionist birth attendance of use to midwinves and of interest to parents, largely in an inspirational rather than a technical vein.); 'Ways of Learning' (innovative, multidimensional, people-centered approaches to education. This section focuses on how people learn rather than where they learn, and includes learning about traditional subjects as well as subjects usually thought of as outside the realm of education: responsibility, ethics, adventure, travel, intuition, spirituality. We want to know about new ways of learning and rediscovered old ways.); 'Family Living' (information sharing, general interest stories, helpful hints, practical suggestions and insights into the daily realities of parenting)." Buys 100 mss/year. Query. Length: 1,000-1,500 words. Pays $175-500.

Reprints: Accepts previously published submissions.
Columns/Departments: Breastfeeding, Work & Family Life, Your Letters, Good News, Reflections, For the Children.
Photos: State availability of photos with submission. Reviews 5×7 or 8×10 b&w prints. Negotiates payment individually. Buys one-time rights. Photographer's/artist's guidelines available for #10 SASE.
Tips: "Be familiar with our magazine before submitting articles. We are more likely to publish your article if you are a *Mothering* reader and are familiar with the issues we discuss. Think about the subjects you know well and areas in which little information exists. The 'Your Letters' section of the magazine is a good place to find topics of interest to our readers. Our main goal is to be truly helpful, to provide information that empowers our readers to make changes or simply to get what they want from their lives. We like articles that have a strong point of view and come from the heart. We like articles that are moving or challenging. We publish articles in relation to other articles we have published on the subject, how new the topic is to us, and how unique the presentation is."

NEW JERSEY FAMILY MAGAZINE, 210 W. State St., Trenton NJ 08608. (609)695-5646. Fax: (609)695-5612. Website: http://www.njfamily.com. Editor: Barbara M. Gaeta. 90% freelance written. Monthly newspaper covering family oriented topics for parents and kids. "We publish an information-based newsmagazine where articles should provide information specifically for New Jersey families." Estab. 1993. Circ. 30,000. Pays 30 days after publication. Publishes ms an average of 6 months after acceptance. Byline given. Buys first, one-time, second serial (reprint) rights or makes work-for-hire assignments. Editorial lead time 6 months. Submit seasonal material 3 months in advance. Accepts simultaneous submissions. Only responds when interested. Sample copy and writer's guidelines free.
Nonfiction: Books excerpts, essays, general interest, historical/nostalgic, how-to, interview/profile, new product, photo feature, travel. No first person narratives about potty-training litty Johnny or other "cute" stories. Buys 40-60 mss/year. Send complete ms. Length: 500-1,500 words. Pays $30-75 for assigned articles; $10-75 for unsolicited articles. Sometimes pays expenses of writers on assignment.
Reprints: Accepts previously published submissions.
Photos: Send photos with submission. Reviews prints. Offers no additional payment for photos accepted with ms. Identification of subjects required. Buys one-time rights.
Columns/Departments: "We expect to include reviews (books, video, movie and software) within the year." Query with published clips. Pays $10-35.
Poetry: Free verse, light verse, traditional. Buys 1-2 poems/year. Length: open. Pays $10.
Fillers: Anecdotes, facts, gags to be illustrated by cartoonist, newsbreaks, short humor. Length: 75-200 words. Pays $5-10.
Tips: "Send well written, informational articles with facts or resources documented, on any topics relevant to today's family environment."

NEW MOON NETWORK: FOR ADULTS WHO CARE ABOUT GIRLS, New Moon Publishing, Inc., P.O. Box 3620, Duluth MN 55803. (218)728-5507. Fax: (218)728-0314. E-mail: newmoon@cp.duluth.mn.us. Website: www.newmoon.org. Contact: Joe Kelly, editor. 10% freelance written. Bimonthly magazine covering adults (parents, teachers, others) who work with girls age 8-14. "*New Moon Network* is the companion publication to *New Moon: The Magazine For Girls and Their Dreams*. It is written by and for adults—parents, teachers, counselors and others—who are working to raise healthy, confident girls. Its goal is to celebrate girls and support their efforts to hang onto their voices, strengths and dreams as they move from being girls to becoming women." Estab. 1992. Circ. 3,000. Pays on publication. Publishes ms an average of 2 months after acceptance. Byline given. Buys first rights and second serial (reprint) rights. Editorial lead time 3 months. Submit seasonal material 4 months in advance. Accepts simultaneous submissions. Reports in 1 month on queries; 2 months on mss. Sample copy for $6.50. Writer's guidelines free.
Nonfiction: Essays, general interest, historical/nostalgic, humor, inspirational, interview/profile, opinion, personal experience, photo feature, religious, technical, book reviews. Editorial calendar available. Buys 6 mss/year. Query. Length: 750-1,500 words. Pays 4-8¢/word.
Reprints: Send photocopy and information about when and where the piece previously appeared.
Photos: State availability of photos with submissions (prefers b&w). Reviews 4×5 prints. Negotiates payment individually. Captions, model releases, identification of subjects required. Buys one-time rights.
Columns/Departments: Mothering (personal experience), 900 words; Fathering (personal experience), 900 words; Current Research (girl-related), 900-1,800 words; Book Reviews, 900 words. Buys 3 mss/year. Query. Pays 4-8¢/word.
Fiction: Humorous, slice-of-life vignettes, multicultural/girl centered. Buys 1 mss/year. Query. Length: 900-1,800 words. Pays 4-8¢/word.
Tips: "Writers and artists who comprehend our goals have the best chance of publication. Refer to our guidelines and upcoming themes. We are not looking for advice columns or 'twelve tips for being a successful parent' formula articles. Write for clarity and ease of understanding, rather than in an 'academic' style."

PARENTING MAGAZINE, 1325 Avenue of the Americas, 27th Floor, New York NY 10019. (212)522-8989. Fax: (212)522-8699. Editor-in-Chief: Janet Chan. Executive Editor: Lisa Bain. Contact: Articles Editor. Magazine published 10 times/year "for parents of children from birth to twelve years old, with the most emphasis put on the under-sixes, and covering both the psychological and practical aspects of parenting." Estab. 1987. **Pays on acceptance.** Byline given. Offers 25% kill fee. Buys first rights. Reports in 2 months. Sample copy for $1.95 and 9×12 SAE with 5 first-class stamps. Writer's guidelines for #10 SASE.

• Ranked as one of the best markets for freelance writers in *Writer's Yearbook* magazine's annual "Top 100 Markets," January 1997.

Nonfiction: Articles editor. Book excerpts, humor, investigative reports, personal experience, photo feature. Buys 20-30 features/year. Query with or without published clips. Length: 1,000-3,000 words. Pays $500-2,000. Sometimes pays expenses of writers on assignment.

Columns/Departments: Family Reporter (news items relating to children/family), 100-400 words; Ages and Stages (health, nutrition, new products and service stories), 100-500 words. Buys 50-60 mss/year. Query to the specific departmental editor. Pays $50-500.

PARENTLIFE, Lifeway Press, 127 Ninth Ave. N., Nashville TN 37234. (615)251-2229. Fax: (615)251-5008. E-mail: parentlife@bssb.com. Contact: Michelle Hicks, managing editor. 30% freelance written. Works with a small number of new/unpublished writers each year. Monthly magazine covering parenting issues for parents of infants through 12-year-olds, "written and designed from a Christian perspective." Estab. 1994. Circ. 120,000. **Pays on acceptance.** Byline given. Buys all or first rights. Submit seasonal material 1 year in advance. Résumés and queries only. Reports in 1 month on queries; 2 months on mss. Sample copy for 9×12 SASE. Writer's guidelines free.

PARENTS MAGAZINE, Gruner + Jahr, 375 Lexington Ave., New York NY 10017-5514. Fax: (212)499-2000. Editor-in-Chief: Ann Pleshette Murphy. 25% freelance written. Monthly. Estab. 1926. Circ. 1,825,000. **Pays on acceptance.** Publishes ms an average of 8 months after acceptance. Usually buys first serial or first North American serial rights; sometimes buys all rights. Offers 25% kill fee. Reports in approximately 4 months. Sample copy for $2. Writer's guidelines for #10 SASE.

Nonfiction: "We are interested in well-documented articles on the development and behavior of infants, preschool, school-age and pre-teen children and their parents; good, practical guides to the routines of baby care; articles that offer professional insights into family and marriage relationships; reports of new trends and significant research findings in education and in mental and physical health; articles encouraging informed citizen action on matters of social concern; and first-person true stories on aspects of parenthood. Especially need articles on women's issues, pregnancy, birth, baby care and early childhood. We're also interested in opinion essays on topics of interest to our readers such as education, interpersonal relationships. We prefer a warm, colloquial style of writing, one that avoids the extremes of either slang or technical jargon. Anecdotes and examples should be used to illustrate points which can then be summed up by straight exposition." Query. Length: 2,500 words maximum. Pays 75¢-$1/word. Pays the expenses of writers on assignment up to an agreed-upon limit.

PARENTS' PRESS, The Monthly Newspaper for Bay Area Parents, 1454 Sixth St., Berkeley CA 94710. (510)524-1602. Editor: Dixie M. Jordan. Contact: Patrick Totty, managing editor. 50% freelance written. Monthly tabloid for parents. Estab. 1980. Circ. 75,000. Pays within 60 days of publication. Publishes ms an average of 4 months after acceptance. Kill fee varies (individually negotiated). Buys first rights, second serial (reprint) and almost always Northern California Exclusive rights. Submit seasonal material 6 months in advance. Reports in 2 months. Sample copy for $3. Writer's guidelines and editorial calendar for #10 SASE. Rarely considers simultaneous submissions.

Nonfiction: Book excerpts (family, children), how-to (parent, raise children, nutrition, health, etc.), humor (family life, children), interview/profile (of Bay Area residents, focus on their roles as parents), travel (family), family resources and activities. "Annual issues include Pregnancy and Birth, Travel, Back-to-School, Children's Health. Write for planned topic or suggest one. We require a strong Bay Area focus where appropriate. Please don't send 'generic' stories. While we publish researched articles which spring from personal experience, we do not publish strictly personal essays. Please, no birth stories." Buys 30-50 mss/year. Query with or without published clips, or send complete ms. Length: 300-3,000 words; 1,500-2,000 average. Pays $50-500 for assigned articles; $25-250 for unsolicited articles. Will pay more if photos accompany article. Negotiable. Will negotiate fees for special projects written by Bay Area journalists.

Reprints: Send photocopy of article with rights for sale noted and information about when and where the article previously appeared. For reprints pays up to $50.

Photos: State availability of photos with submission. Reviews prints, any size, b&w only. Offers $10-15/photo. Model release and identification of subject required. Buys one-time rights.

Columns/Departments: "In My Life" column pays $150 for first-person essays or reminiscences relating to parenthood." Sole criterion for acceptance: The manuscript must be superlatively written. 'Cute' doesn't make it."

Tips: "All sections of *Parents' Press* are open to freelancers, but we ask writers to query whether a topic has been addressed in the last three years. Best bets to break in are family activities, including "Places To Go/Things To Do" articles, education, nutrition, family dynamics and issues. While we prefer articles written by experts, we welcome well-researched journalism with quotes from experts and 'real life' parents."

‡PARENT.TEEN, The Magazine for Bay Area Families with Teens, Parents' Press, 1454 Sixth St., Berkeley CA 94710. (510)524-1602. Editor: Dixie M. Jordan. Contact: Patrick Totty, managing editor. 75% freelance written. Bimonthly magazine for parents of teens. Estab. 1997. Circ. 50,000. Pays within 60 days of publication. Publishes ms an average of 3 months after acceptance. Kill fee varies (individually negotiated). Buys all rights, first rights, second serial (reprint) and almost always Northern California Exclusive rights. Submit seasonal material 6 months in advance. Reports in 2 months. Sample copy for $3. Writer's guidelines and editorial calendar for #10 SASE.

Nonfiction: Regular features, open to all, cover adolescent medicine, teen psychology, youth culture and trends, education, college preparation, work, sports, sex, gender roles, family relationships, legal topics, financial issues and profiles of interesting teens, colleges and programs. "We require a strong Bay Area focus in most articles. Use quotes from experts and Bay Area teens." Buys 60 mss/year. Query with clips or send complete ms on spec. "We pay for lively, information-packed content, not length." Length: 500-1,200 words. Pays $150-500.

Reprints: Send a photocopy of article with rights for sale noted and information about when and where the article previously appeared. Pays up to $50.

Photos: State availability of photos with submission. Payment rates higher for mss with photos. Photos only: $15-50 for one-time rights (b&w). Reviews color slides for cover; contact art director Renee Benoit before sending. Photos returned only if accompanied by SASE. Model releases and subject identification required.

Columns/Departments: Pays $5-10 for "grab bag" items, ranging from one sentence to one paragraph on "weird facts about teens" or teen-related Bay Area news item. Submissions must cite sources of information.

Tips: "We do not commission stories by writers who are unknown to us, so your best bet is to send us original articles on spec or already published articles offered for reprint rights. We are looking for writers who can pack a lot of information in as few words as possible in lively prose. No first-person 'How I Got My Kid Through Teenhood' articles."

SAN DIEGO FAMILY MAGAZINE, San Diego County's Leading Resource for Parents & Educators Who Care!, P.O. Box 23960, San Diego CA 92193-3960. E-mail: sandyofm@family.com. Website: http://sandiegofamily.c om. Contact: Sharon Bay, editor. 75% freelance written. Monthly magazine for parenting and family issues. "*SDFM* strives to provide informative, educational articles emphasizing positive parenting for our typical readership of educated mothers, ages 25-45, with an upper-level income. Most articles are factual and practical, some are humor and personal experience. Editorial emphasis is uplifting and positive." Estab. 1982. Circ. 76,000. Pays on publication. Byline given. Buys first, one-time or second serial (reprint) rights. Editorial lead time 2 months. Submit seasonal material 3 months in advance. Reports in 2 months on queries; 3 months on mss. Sample copy and writer's guidelines for $3.50 with 9×12 SAE.

Nonfiction: How-to, parenting, new baby help, enhancing education, family activities, interview/profile (influential or noted persons or experts included in parenting or the welfare of children) and articles of specific interest to or regarding San Diego (for California) families/children/parents/educators. "No rambling, personal experience pieces." Buys 75 mss/year. Send complete ms. Length: 1,000 maximum words. Pays $1.25/column inch. "Byline and contributor copies if writer prefers."

Reprints: Send typed ms with rights for sale noted and information about when and where the article previously appeared.

Photos: State availability of photos with submission. Reviews contact sheets and 3½×5 or 5×7 prints. Negotiates payment individually. Identification of subjects preferred. Buys one-time rights.

Columns/Departments: Kids' Books (topical book reviews), 800 words. Buys 12 mss/year. Query with published clips. Pays $1.25/column inch minimum.

Fillers: Facts and newsbreaks (specific to the family market). Buys 10/year. Length: 50-200 words. Pays $1.25/column inch minimum.

SAN FRANCISCO PENINSULA PARENT, Peninsula Parent Newspaper Inc., 1480 Rollins Rd., Burlingame CA 94010. (415)342-9203. Fax: (415)342-9276. E-mail: sfpp@aol.com. Website: http://www.family.com. Contact: Lisa Rosenthal, editor. 25% freelance written. Monthly magazine geared to parents of children from birth to age 12. "We provide articles that empower parents with the essential parenting skills they need and offer local resource information." Estab. 1984. Circ. 65,000. Pays on publication. Publishes ms 3 months after acceptance. Byline given. Offers 50% kill fee. Buys first and second serial (reprint) rights. Editorial lead time 5 months. Submit seasonal material 4 months in advance. Reports in 2 months on queries; 3 months on mss. Sample copy and writer's guidelines free.

Nonfiction: Humor, interview/profile, travel (family-related). No articles that preach to parents, no first-person memories. Buys 8 mss/year. Query with or without published clips. Length: 800-1,200 words. Pays $100-200 for assigned articles; $25-100 for unsolicited articles. Sometimes pays expenses of writers on assignment.

Reprints: Accepts previously published submissions. Send typed ms with rights for sale noted and information about when and where the article previously appeared. Pays $25-50.

Photos: State availability of photos with submission. Offers $25-$50/photo; negotiates payment individually. Captions and model releases required. Buys one-time rights.

Columns/Departments: Upclose (profile), 1,000 words; Healthbeat (health news for families), 1,000 words. Buys 2 mss/year. Query with or without published clips. Pays $25-100.

SESAME STREET PARENTS, Children's Television Workshop, 1 Lincoln Plaza, New York NY 10023. (212)595-3456. Fax: (212)875-6105. Editor-in-Chief: Ira Wolfman. Contact: Aileen Love, assistant editor. 80% freelance written. Magazine published 10 times/year for parents of preschoolers that accompanies every issue of Sesame Street Magazine. Circ. 1,000,000. **Pays on acceptance.** Byline given. Offers 33% kill fee. Buys varying rights. Submit seasonal material 7 months in advance. Reports in 1 month on queries. Sample copy for 9×12 SAE with 6 first-class stamps. Writer's guidelines for #10 SASE.

● Ranked as one of the best markets for freelance writers in *Writer's Yearbook* magazine's annual "Top 100 Markets," January 1997.

Nonfiction: Child development/parenting, how-to (practical tips for parents of preschoolers), interview/profile, personal experience, book excerpts, essays, photo feature, travel (with children). Buys 100 mss/year. Query with published clips or send complete ms. Length: 500-2,000 words. Pays $300-2,000 for articles.

Reprints: Send typed ms with rights for sale noted and information about when and where the article previously appeared. Negotiates payment.

Photos: State availability of photos with submission. Model releases, identification of subjects required. Buys one-time or all rights.

‡**SINGLE WITH KIDS**, Wharton Publishing Inc., 35111-F Newark Blvd., #265, Newark CA 94560. (510)494-8514. Fax: (510)494-1852. Contact: Cheryl Fabroth, editor. Managing editor: Cecil Berkley. 85% freelance written. Monthly tabloid covering child care and parental guidance for single parents. "We are a magazine that provides down-to-earth articles that are informative and supportive for today's single parents. Articles dealing with family law, child care, budgeting time and money and all the issues, problems, and choices single parents deal with every day. We want to encourage our readers to grow not only as a parent, but also as an individual." Estab. 1996. Circ. 20,000. Pays on publication. Publishes ms an average of 4 months after acceptance. Byline given. Kill fee varies. Buys first rights, second serial (reprint) rights or makes work-for-hire assignments. Editorial lead time 3 months. Submit seasonal material 3 months in advance. Accepts simultaneous submissions. Reports in 2 weeks on queries; 2 months on mss. Sample copy for $3. Writer's guidelines for SASE.

Nonfiction: Book excerpts, general interest, historical/nostalgic, how-to (budget time and money), humor, interview/profile, new product, personal experience, photo feature, travel. Buys 70-100 mss/year. Query or send complete ms. Length: 200-2,000 words. Pays $50-150 for assigned articles; $20-140 for unsolicited articles. Sometimes pays expenses of writers on assignment.

Reprints: Accepts previously published submissions.

Photos: State availability of photos with submission. Reviews any size prints. Offers $5-25/photo. Captions, model releases required. Buys one-time rights.

Columns/Departments: Family Law (everything from child support to domestic violence), 500-1,500 words; See, Read and Play (review of parenting and children's books, videos and toys), 200-500 words. Buys 30-50 mss/year. Send complete ms. Pays $20-40.

Poetry: Open to all styles. Buys 20-50 poems/year. Submit maximum 5 poems. Open length. Pays $5-20.

Fillers: Anecdotes, facts, gags to be illustrated by cartoonist, newsbreaks, short humor. Buys 20-40/year. Open length. Pays $5-40.

Tips: "The single parent market is wide open. Our readers and editors are looking for articles that are supportive, informative, concisely written and accurately researched. Don't talk down to our readers. They are well-read and they need informative material that will help with the daily grind of being a single parent. We would like to thank all writers who submit work to Wharton Publishing Inc. Good luck."

SOUTH FLORIDA PARENTING, 8323 NW 12th St., Suite 212, Miami FL 33126. (305)599-5318. Fax: (305)599-5304. E-mail: kbochi@tribune.com. Website: http://www.sfparenting.com. Managing Editor: KiKi Bochi. 90% freelance written. Monthly magazine covering parenting, family. Estab. 1989. Circ. 100,000. Pays on publication. Publishes ms an average of 3 months after acceptance. Byline given. Buys one-time rights or second serial (reprint) rights. Editorial lead time 4 months. Submit seasonal material 4 months in advance. Accepts simultaneous submissions. Prefers submission of actual ms. Response to queries only if SASE enclosed. Will rarely contract with a writer without sample of work. Writer's guidelines for SASE.

Nonfiction: General interest, how-to, humor, interview/profile, new product, personal experience. Special issues: Education Issue/Winter Health Issue (January); Birthday Party Issue (February); Spring Catalog/Summer Camp Issue (March); Maternity Issue (April); Florida/Vacation Guide (May); Sports and Your Child (June); Healthy, from Head to Toe (July); Back to School Catalog (August); Getting To Know You (September); Kid Crown Awards (October); Family Restaurant Guide, All About Kids Show (November); Holiday Catalog (December); Annual Survival Guide. Buys 30-40 mss/year. Send complete ms. Length: 600-1,800 words. Pays $75-350 for articles; $25 for reprints. Sometimes pays expenses of writers on assignment.

Reprints: Accepts previously published submissions "if not published in our circulation area." Send photocopy of article and information about when and where the article appeared. Pays $25-100.

Photos: State availability of photos with submission. Sometimes offers additional payment for ms with photos.

Tips: "A unique approach to a universal parenting concern will be considered for publication, also profiles or interviews of courageous parents. Opinion pieces on child rearing should be supported by experts and research should be listed. First person stories should be fresh and insightful. All writing should be clear and concise. Submissions can be typewritten, double-spaced, but the preferred format is on diskette."

‡**TODAY'S PARENT, Canada's Parenting Magazine**, Professional Publishing Associates Ltd., 269 Richmond St. West, Toronto, Ontario M5V 1X1 Canada. (416)596-8680. Fax: (416)596-1991. E-mail: todaysparent.com. Editor-in-Chief: Fran Fearnley. Contact: Linda Lewis, managing editor. 99% freelance written; *Canadian writers only*. Magazine published 10 times/year. *"Today's Parent* is a magazine for parents of children aged 0-12." Circ. 160,000. **Pays on acceptance**. Publishes ms an average of 5 months after acceptance. Byline given. Buys first North American serial rights. Reports in 6 weeks on queries. Sample copy for $5 (Canadian). Writer's guidelines for #10 SASE.

Nonfiction: Features: Exposé, general interest, how-to. Query with published clips by mail only; include SASE. Length: 1,000-3,000 words. Pays $750-1,800 for assigned articles. Sometimes pays expenses of writers on assignment.

Columns/Departments: Health, Behavior, Education, all 1,200-1,500 words. Pays $750-900. Slice of Life (humor), 750 words. Pays $500. Query with published clips.

TOLEDO AREA PARENT NEWS, Toledo Area Parent News, Inc., 1120 Adams St., Toledo OH 43624. (419)244-9859. Fax: (419)244-9871. E-mail: tolparnt@family.com. Editor: Veronica Hughes. 50% freelance written. Monthly tabloid covering parenting issues. "We are a publication for Northwest Ohio/Southeast Michigan parents. We accept queries and opinion pieces only, from local writers only. Send cover letter and clips to be considered for assignments." Estab. 1992. Circ. 50,000. Pays on publication. Publishes ms an average of 1 month after acceptance. Byline given. Makes work-for-hire assignments. Editorial lead time 6 months. Reports in 1 month. Sample copy for $1.50. "We use only local writers, by assignment only."
Nonfiction: General interest, interview/profile, opinion. Buys 30 mss/year. Query with published clips. Length: 1,000-2,500 words. Pays $75-125.
Photos: State availability of photos with submission. Negotiates payment individually. Identification of subjects required. Buys all rights.

TWINS, The Magazine for Parents of Multiples, 5350 S. Roslyn St., Suite 400, Englewood CO 80121. (303)290-8500. Fax: (303)290-9025. Website: http://www.twinsmagazine.com. Editor-in-Chief: Susan J. Alt. Contact: Heather White, assistant editor. 90% freelance written. Eager to work with new/unpublished writers. Bimonthly national magazine designed to give professional guidance to help multiples, their parents and those professionals who care for them learn about twin facts and research. Estab. 1984. Circ. 50,000. Pays on publication. Publishes ms an average of 6 months after acceptance. Byline given. Buys all rights. Submit seasonal material 10 months in advance. Reports in 6 weeks on queries; 2 months on mss. Sample copy for $5. Writer's guidelines for #10 SASE.
Nonfiction: General interest, how-to, humor, interview/profile, personal experience, photo feature. "No articles that substitute the word 'twin' for 'child'—those that simply apply the same research to twins that applies to singletons without any facts backing up the reason to do so." Special issues: cooking with multiples; traveling with multiples (camping, outing ideas); caring for multiples (nannies, child care, etc.); issues surrounding dressing multiples alike; family finances; equipment; playtime ideas/tips; healthy ideas for multiples; reading with multiples. Buys 70 mss/year. Query with or without published clips, or send complete ms. Length: 750-2,000 words. Payment varies.
Photos: Send photos with submission. Reviews contact sheets, 4×5 transparencies, all size prints. Captions, model releases, identification of subjects required. Buys all rights.
Columns/Departments: Supertwins, Triplets and Higher, Family Health, Twice as Funny, Double Focus (series from pregnancy through adolescence), Personal Perspective (first-person accounts of beliefs about a certain aspect of parenting multiples), Over the Back Fence (specific tips that have worked for the writer in raising multiples), On Being Twins (first-person accounts of growing up as a twin), On Being Parents of Twins (first-person accounts of the experience of parenting twins), Double Takes (fun photographs of twins), Education Matters, Special Miracles (first-person accounts of life with physically, mentally or emotionally challenged twins). Buys 40 mss/year. Query with published clips. Length: 750-1,500 words. Payment varies.
Tips: "Features and columns are both open to freelancers. Columnists write for *Twins* on a continuous basis, so the column becomes their own. We are looking for a wide variety of the latest, well-researched practical information. There is no other magazine of this type directed to this market. We are interested in personal interviews with celebrity twins or celebrity parents of twins, tips on rearing twins from experienced parents and/or twins themselves and reports on national and international research studies involving twins."

VALLEY PARENT MAGAZINE, Bay Area Publishing Group, Inc., 401 Alberto Way, Suite A, Los Gatos CA 95032. (408)358-1414. Editor: Lynn Berardo. Contact: Mary Brence Martin, managing editor. 43% freelance written. Monthly magazine covering parenting children ages birth through early teens. "The information we are most likely to use is local, well-researched and geared to our readers, who are primarily parents of children ages birth to early teens." Estab. 1992. Circ. 55,000. Pays on publication. Publishes ms an average of 6 months after acceptance. Byline given. Buys first rights. Editorial lead time 4 months. Submit seasonal material 4 months in advance. Accepts simultaneous submissions. Reports in 2 months on queries; 2 months on mss. Sample copy for 8½×12 SAE with 5 first-class stamps. Writer's guidelines for #10 SASE.
Nonfiction: Book excerpts, interview/profile, opinion, personal experience (all must be parenting-related). Buys 22 mss/year. Length: 900-2,000 words. Pays 6-9¢/word. Sometimes pays expenses of writers on assignment.
Reprints: Send tearsheet or photocopy of article or typed ms with rights for sale noted and information about when and where the article previously appeared. Pays 100% of amount paid for an original article.
Photos: State availability of photos with submission. Reviews contact sheets, negatives, transparencies, prints. Offers $10-15/photo. Buys one-time rights.
Columns/Departments: Way to Go! (local and state outings); Little Kids (children ages 2-5) 950-1,000 words. Query with published clips or send complete ms. Pays 6-9¢/word.

‡VISITATION, The Source for Non-Traditional Families, Take Charge Productions, P.O. Box 91345, Austin TX 78709-1345. (512)338-1125. Fax: (512)338-0564. E-mail: takechg@worldnet.att.net. Contact: Mary Roland, editor. Managing Editor: Stephanie Mosher. 30% freelance written. Bimonthly magazine covering the positive resolution of parenting issues, re: single parents, step-parents, adoptive, non-custodial, grandparents, blended families. "Writers should focus on positive resolutions to parenting issues. These may be in the form of interviews/stories of persons or ways and programs of innovative therapists, educators, and others. Stories from young adult or grown children of non-traditional families are also beneficial to the readers. Readers are parents, all over the country, from professional to agency-supported." Estab. 1996. Circ. 20,000. Pays on publication. Publishes ms an average of 2 months after acceptance. Byline given. Buys one-time rights and makes work-for-hire assignments. Editorial lead time 1 month. Submit seasonal material 3 months in advance. Reports in 1 month on queries. Sample copy for $5 and SAE. Writer's guidelines free (included with sample copy).

Nonfiction: Essays, how-to (get kids to eat, co-parent effectively, find time for self), humor (family oriented), inspirational, interview/profile, opinion, personal experience, photo feature, travel, financial tips. No negative, agenda-rich articles, political, religious. "This magazine is for all types of people—no one is excluded." Buys 8-15 mss/year. Query. Length: 600-850 words. Pays $45 for assigned articles, $25 for unsolicited articles. Sometimes pays expenses of writers on assignment.

Photos: State availability of photos with submission. Reviews contact sheets. Offers no additional payment for photos accepted with ms. Captions, model releases, identification of subjects required. Buys one-time rights.

Columns/Departments: Travel Tips (family friendly travel, contact Cynthia Leitich-Smith), 650-850 words; Money Matters (financial helps, contact Stephanie Mosher), 650-850 words. Buys 6 mss/year. Query. Pays $45.

Fiction: Children's short story. Buys 6 mss/year. Query. Length: 400-600 words. Pays $25-45.

Fillers: Anecdotes, facts, gags to be illustrated by cartoonist, short humor. Buys 6-12 mss/year. Length: 50-250 words. Pays $10-20.

Tips: "Writers may submit article ideas via e-mail or regular mail, but should read the magazine to understand our goals and focus. We are always looking for a new approach which positively resolves these parenting issues."

WORKING MOTHER MAGAZINE, MacDonald Communications, 135 W. 50th St., New York NY 10020. (212)445-6100. Fax: (212)445-6174. E-mail: jculbreth@womweb.com. Contact: Judsen Culbreth, editor-in-chief. 90% freelance written. Prefers to work with published/established writers; works with a small number of new/unpublished writers each year. Monthly magazine for women who balance a career with the concerns of parenting. Circ. 925,000. Publishes ms an average of 4 months after acceptance. Byline given. Buys all rights. Pays 20% kill fee. Submit seasonal material 6 months in advance. Sample copy for $4. Writer's guidelines for SASE.

Nonfiction: Service, humor, child development, material pertinent to the working mother's predicament. Query to *Working Mother Magazine.* Buys 9-10 mss/issue. Length: 750-2,000 words. Pays expenses of writers on assignment.

Tips: "We are looking for pieces that help the reader. In other words, we don't simply report on a trend without discussing how it specifically affects our readers' lives and how they can handle the effects. Where can they look for help if necessary?"

COMIC BOOKS

Comic books aren't just for kids. Today, this medium also attracts a reader who is older and wants stories presented visually on a wide variety of topics. In addition, some instruction manuals, classics and other stories are being produced in a comic book format.

This doesn't mean you have to be an artist to write for comic books. Most of these publishers want to see a synopsis of one to two double-spaced pages. Be concise. Comics use few words and rely on graphics as well as words to forward the plot.

Once your synopsis is accepted, either an artist will draw the story from your plot, returning these pages to you for dialogue and captions, or you will be expected to write a script. Scripts run approximately 23 typewritten pages and include suggestions for artwork as well as dialogue. Try to imagine your story on actual comic book pages and divide your script accordingly. The average comic has six panels per page, with a maximum of 35 words per panel.

If you're submitting a proposal to Marvel, your story should center on an already established character. If you're dealing with an independent publisher, characters are often the property of their creators. Your proposal should be for a new series. Include a background sheet for main characters who will appear regularly, listing origins, weaknesses, powers or other information that will make your character unique. Indicate an overall theme or direction for your series. Submit story ideas for the first three issues. If you're really ambitious, you may also include a script for your first issue. As with all markets, read a sample copy before making a submission. The best markets may be those you currently read, so consider submitting to them even if they aren't listed in this section.

‡**CARTOON WORLD**, P.O. Box 1164, Kent WA 98035. E-mail: cartoonworld@usa.net. Editor: Vic Stredicke. (206)854-6649. Monthly newsletter for professional and serious amateur cartoonists who want to find new cartoon

markets. Circ. 300. **Pays on acceptance.** Byline given. Offers counsel to new writers. Submit seasonal material 3 months in advance. Reports in 1 month. Sample copy free.
Nonfiction: "Want articles about the business of cartooning. Most features should be first-person accounts of cartoon editing, creating ideas, work habits." All cartoons run must have been published elsewhere. Length: 1,000 words. Pays $5/page/feature.
Reprints: Accepts previously published submissions. Note where previously appeared. Pays $5/page.

MARVEL COMICS, 387 Park Ave. S., New York NY 10016. (212)696-0808. Art Director/New Talent Manager: Darren Auck. 80% freelance written. Publishes 75 comics and magazines/month, specials, paperbacks and industrials. Over 9 million copies sold/month. Pays a flat fee for most projects, plus a royalty type incentive based upon sales. Also works on advance/royalty basis on certain projects. **Pays on acceptance.** Publishes ms an average of 4 months after acceptance. Byline given. Offers variable kill fee. Rights purchased depend upon format and material. Submit seasonal material 1 year in advance. Accepts simultaneous submissions. Reports in 6 months. Writer's guidelines for #10 SASE. Additional guidelines on request.
   ● Since Marvel has been cutting their line of books, there are more professional writers looking for work, making it a much tougher market for a newcomer to break in.
Fiction: Super hero, action-adventure, science fiction, fantasy and other material. Only comics. Buys 600-800 mss/year. Query with brief plot synopses only. Do not send scripts, short stories or long outlines. A plot synopsis should be one typed page; send two synopses at most. Pays expenses of writers on assignment.
Tips: "The market is still tight. It's very difficult for newcomers."

CONSUMER SERVICE AND BUSINESS OPPORTUNITY

Some of these magazines are geared to investing earnings or starting a new business; others show how to make economical purchases. Publications for business executives and consumers interested in business topics are listed under Business and Finance. Those on how to run specific businesses are classified by category in the Trade section.

‡JERRY BUCHANAN'S INFO MARKETING REPORT, TOWERS Club Press, Inc., P.O. Box 2038, Vancouver WA 98668-2038. (360)574-3084. Fax: (360)576-8969. Editor: Jerry Buchanan. 5-10% freelance written. Works with a small number of unpublished writers each year. Monthly of 10 or more pages on entrepreneurial enterprises, reporting especially on self-publishing of how-to reports, books, audio and video tapes, seminars, etc. "By-passing big trade publishers and marketing your own work directly to consumer (mail order predominantly)." Estab. 1974. Circ. 10,000. Pays on publication. Publishes ms an average of 2 months after acceptance. Byline given. Buys one-time rights. Reports in 2 weeks. Sample copy for $15 and 6×9 SASE.
Nonfiction: Exposé (of mail order fraud); how-to (personal experience in self-publishing and marketing); book reviews of new self-published nonfiction how-to-do-it books (must include name and address of author). "Welcomes well-written articles of successful self-publishing/marketing ventures. Must be current, and preferably written by the person who actually did the work and reaped the rewards. There's very little we will not consider, *if* it pertains to unique money-making enterprises that can be operated from the home." Buys 10 mss/year. Send complete ms. Fax submissions accepted of no more than 3 pages. Length: 500-1,500 words. Pays $150-250. Pays extra for b&w photo and bonus for excellence in longer ms.
Reprints: Send tearsheet or photocopy of article or typed ms with rights for sale noted and information about when and where the article previously appeared. Pays 25% of the amount paid for an original article.
Tips: "The most frequent mistake made by writers in completing an article for us is that they think they can simply rewrite a newspaper article and be accepted. That is only the start. We want them to find the article about a successful self-publishing enterprise, and then go out and interview the principal for a more detailed how-to article, including names and addresses. We prefer that writer actually interview a successful self-publisher. Articles should include how idea first came to subject; how they implemented and financed and promoted the project; how long it took to show a profit and some of the stumbling blocks they overcame; how many persons participated in the production and promotion; and how much money was invested (approximately) and other pertinent how-to elements of the story. Glossy photos (b&w) of principals at work in their offices will help sell article."

‡CONSUMERS DIGEST MAGAZINE, For People who Demand Value, Consumers Digest, Inc., 8001 N. Lincoln Ave., Skokie IL 60077. (847)763-9200. Contact: Elliott H. McCleary, executive editor. 70% freelance written. Bimonthly magazine offering "practical advice on subjects of interest to consumers: products and services, automobiles, health, fitness, consumer legal affairs, personal money management, etc." Estab. 1959. Circ. 1,300,000. **Pays on acceptance.** Publishes ms an average of 3 months after acceptance. Byline given. Offers 50% kill fee. Buys all rights. Submit seasonal material 6 months in advance. Accepts simultaneous submissions. Reports in 6 weeks on queries; 3 months on mss. Sample copy for 9×12 SAE with 6 first-class stamps. Writer's guidelines free.
Nonfiction: Elliott H. McCleary, articles editor. Exposé, general interest, how-to (financial, purchasing), new product, travel, health, fitness. Buys 80 mss/year. Query with published clips. Length: 1,000-3,000 words. Pays $1,000-3,500 for assigned articles; $400-1,700 for unsolicited articles. Sometimes pays expenses of writers on assignment.

Photos: State availability of photos with submission. Reviews transparencies. Pays $100-500/photo. Captions, model releases and identification of subjects required. Buys all rights.

Columns/Departments: Mary S. Butler, column editor. Consumerscope (brief items of general interest to consumers—auto news, travel tips, the environment, smart shopping, news you can use). Buys 10 mss/year. Query. Length: 200-500 words. Pays $200-500.

Tips: "Keep the queries brief and tightly focused. Read our writer's guidelines first and request an index of past articles for trends and to avoid repeating subjects. Focus on subjects of broad national appeal. Stress personal expertise in proposed subject area. We need expert advice to help consumers save money on all spending for products and services, from computer software to health care, or food processors to legal and investment advice. Our advice is always very specific—which model of any product offers the best value. Generalities are not useful without specific, hand-holding recommendations."

ECONOMIC FACTS, The National Research Bureau, Inc., 320 Valley St., Burlington IA 52601. (319)752-5415. Fax: (319)752-3421. Contact: Nancy Heinzel, editor. 75% freelance written. Eager to work with new/unpublished writers; works with a small number of new/unpublished writers each year. Quarterly magazine. Estab. 1948. Pays on publication. Publishes ms an average of 1 year after acceptance. Buys all rights. Byline given. Sample copy and writer's guidelines for #10 SAE with 2 first-class stamps.

Nonfiction: General interest (private enterprise, government data, graphs, taxes and health care). Buys 10 mss/year. Query with outline of article. Length: 500-700 words. Pays 4¢/word.

‡INCOME OPPORTUNITIES, IO Publications, 1500 Broadway, New York NY 10036-4015. (212)642-0600. Fax: (212)302-8269. E-mail: incomeed@aol.com. Editor-in-Chief: Linda Molnar. Managing Editor: Penelope Patsuris. 90% freelance written. Monthly magazine covering small and home-based business for 40 years, focusing on companies with 5 employees and under. Estab. 1956. Circ. 425,000. Pays 30 days after acceptance. Publishes ms an average of 5 months after acceptance. Byline given. Offers 15% kill fee. Buys all rights and makes work-for-hire assignments. Submit seasonal material 6 months in advance. Reports in 2 months. Sample copy free. Writer's guidelines for #10 SASE.

• "We won the 1996 National Press Club Consumer Journalism Award for magazines and are looking for more award-winning stories."

Nonfiction: "We need insightful, practical articles that help people starting or running a small or home-based business, interested in investigative journalism, how-to pieces on managing, financing and marketing a small business, and profiles of well-known entrepreneurs who started on a shoestring." No purely inspirational articles. Buys 60 mss/year. Query with published clips. Length: 600-2,500 words. Pay varies. Pays expenses of writers on assignment.

Photos: Send photos with submission. Offers no additional payment for photos accepted with ms. Identification of subjects required. Buys all rights.

Columns/Departments: Length: 1,000 words. Buys 130 mss/year. Query with published clips. Pay varies.

Tips: Areas most open to freelancers are "profiles of successful small-business operators. Details of how they started, start-up costs, how they operate, advertising methods, tools, materials, equipment needed, projected or actual earnings, advice to readers for success."

KIPLINGER'S PERSONAL FINANCE, 1729 H St. NW, Washington DC 20006. (202)887-6400. Fax: (202)331-1206. Website: http://www.kiplinger.com. Editor: Ted Miller. Contact: Atilla Akgun, editorial assistant. Less than 10% freelance written. Prefers to work with published/established writers. Monthly magazine for general, adult audience interested in personal finance and consumer information. "*Kiplinger's* is a highly trustworthy source of information on saving and investing, taxes, credit, home ownership, paying for college, retirement planning, automobile buying and many other personal finance topics." Estab. 1947. Circ. 1,000,000. **Pays on acceptance.** Publishes ms an average of 2 months after acceptance. Buys all rights. Reports in 1 month.

Nonfiction: "Most material is staff-written, but we accept some freelance. Thorough documentation is required for fact-checking." Query with clips of published work. Pays expenses of writers on assignment.

Tips: "We are looking for a heavy emphasis on personal finance topics."

LIVING SAFETY, A Canada Safety Council publication for safety in the home, traffic and recreational environments, 1020 Thomas Spratt Place, Ottawa, Ontario K1G 5L5 Canada. (613)739-1535. Fax (613)739-1566. E-mail: csc@safety-council.org. Website: http://www.safety-council.org. Editor: Jack Smith. 65% freelance written. Quarterly magazine covering off-the-job safety. "Off-the job health and safety magazine covering topics in the home, traffic and recreational environments. Audience is the Canadian employee and his/her family." Estab. 1983. Circ. 100,000. **Pays on acceptance.** Publishes ms an average of 2 months after acceptance. Byline given. Buys all rights. Editorial lead time 4 months. Submit seasonal material 6 months in advance. Accepts simultaneous submissions. Reports in 1 month on queries. Sample copy and writer's guidelines free.

Nonfiction: General interest, how-to (safety tips, health tips), personal experience. Buys 24 mss/year. Query with published clips. "Send intro letter, query, résumé and published clips (magazine preferable). Editor will call if interested." Length: 1,000-2,500 words. Pays $500 maximum. Sometimes pays expenses of writers on assignment.

Reprints: Send tearsheet of article or short story.

Photos: State availability of photos with submission. Reviews contact sheet, negatives, transparencies, prints. Offers no additional payment for photos accepted with ms. Identification of subjects required.

‡**SPARE TIME MAGAZINE, The Magazine of Money Making Opportunities**, Kipen Publishing Corp., 5810 W. Oklahoma Ave., Milwaukee WI 53219. (414)543-8110. Fax: (414)543-9767. E-mail: editor@spare-time.com. Contact: Peter Abbott, editor. 75% freelance written. Monthly magazine published 9 times/year covering affordable money-making opportunities. "We publish information the average person can use to begin and operate a spare-time business or extra income venture, with the possible goal of making it fulltime. This is not the place for an expensive franchise opportunity." Estab. 1955. Circ. 300,000. Pays on publication. Publishes ms an average of 3 months after acceptance. Byline given. Buys first North American serial rights. Editorial lead time 3 months. Submit seasonal material 4 months in advance. Accepts simultaneous submissions, query first. Reports in 1 month on queries; 2 months on mss. Sample copy for $2.50. Writer's guidelines and editorial calendar for #10 SASE.
Nonfiction: Book excerpts and reviews (small business related), how-to (market, keep records, stay motivated, choose opportunity), interview/profile and personal experience (small business related). Special issues: Starting a new business (January); Hobby businesses (February); Taxes (March); Low cost franchising (April); Sales and marketing (May/June); Education and training (August). Buys 24-54 mss/year. Query. Length: up to 1,100 words (cover story: 1,500-2,000 words; installment series; three parts up to 1,100 words each). Pays 15¢/word upon publication. Sometimes pays expenses of writers on assignment.
Reprints: Send photocopy of story with information about when and where the article previously appeared. Pays 50% of amount paid for an original article.
Photos: State availability of photos with submission. Reviews contact sheets, 3×5 or larger prints. Pays $15/published photo. Captions, identification of subjects required. Buys one-time rights.
Tips: "It is always best to query. At all times keep in mind that the audience is the average person, not over-educated in terms of business techniques. The best pieces are written in lay language and relate to that type of person."

CONTEMPORARY CULTURE

These magazines often combine politics, current events and cultural elements such as art, literature, film and music, to examine contemporary society. Their approach to institutions is typically irreverent and investigative. Some, like *Strength* or *Swing Magazine*, report on alternative culture and appeal to a young adult "Generation X" audience. Others, such as *Mother Jones* or *Rolling Stone*, treat mainstream culture for a baby boomer generation audience.

‡**A&U AMERICA'S AIDS MAGAZINE**, Art & Understanding, Inc., 25 Monroe St., Albany NY 12210. (518)426-9010. Fax: (518)436-5354. E-mail: mailbox@aumag.org. Contact: David Waggoner, editor. 50% freelance written. Monthly magazine covering cultural responses to AIDS/HIV. Estab. 1991. Circ. 240,000. Pays on publication. Publishes ms an average of 3 months after acceptance. Byline given. Offers 20% kill fee. Buys first North American serial rights. Editorial lead time 6 months. Accepts simultaneous submissions. Reports in 1 month on queries; 2 months on mss. Sample copy for $5. Writer's guidelines free.
Nonfiction: Book excerpts, essays, general interest, how-to, humor, interview/profile, new product, opinion, personal experience, photo feature, travel, medical news. Buys 120 mss/year. Query with published clips. Length: 800-4,800 words. Pays $80-2,000 for assigned articles; $50-500 for unsolicited articles. Sometimes pays expenses of writers on assignment.
Photos: State availability of photos with submission. Reviews contact sheets, transparencies, prints. Offers $25-100/photo. Captions, model releases, identification of subjects required. Buys one-time rights.
Columns/Departments: The Culture of AIDS (reviews of books, music, film), 800 words; Viewpoint (personal opinion), 800-1,200 words; MediaWatch (mass media opinion), 800-1,200 words. Buys 100 mss/year. Send complete ms. Pays $75-150.

BOSTON REVIEW, E53-407, M.I.T., Cambridge MA 02139. (617)253-3642. Fax: (617)252-1549. E-mail: bostonreview@mit.edu. Website: http://www-polisci.mit.edu/BostonReview. Editor: Josh Cohen. Contact: Matthew Howard, managing editor. 100% freelance written. Works with a small number of new/unpublished writers each year. Bimonthly magazine of cultural and political analysis, reviews, fiction and poetry. "The editors are committed to a society and culture that foster human diversity and a democracy in which we seek common grounds of principle amidst our many differences. In the hope of advancing these ideals, the *Review* acts as a forum that seeks to enrich the language of public debate." Estab. 1975. Circ. 20,000. **Pays on acceptance.** Publishes ms an average of 3 months after acceptance. Buys first American serial rights. Byline given. Reports in 6 months. Sample copy $4.50. Writer's guidelines for #10 SASE.
Nonfiction: Critical essays and reviews, natural and social sciences, literature, music, film and photography. Query with clips. "We do not accept unsolicited book reviews: if you would like to be considered for review assignments, please send your résumé along with several published clips." Buys 20 unsolicited mss/year. Length: 1,500-4,000 words. Pays $100 average.
Fiction: Jodi Daynard, fiction editor. "I'm looking for stories that are emotionally and intellectually substantive and also interesting on the level of language. Things that are shocking, dark, lewd, comic, or even insane are fine so long as the fiction is controlled and purposeful in a masterly way. Subtlety, delicacy and lyricism are attractive too." Length: 1,200-5,000 words. Publishes novel excerpts.
Poetry: Mary Jo Bang and Timothy Donnelly, poetry editors. Pays $40 average.

Tips: "We look for in-depth knowledge of an area, an original view of the material, and a presentation which makes these accessible to a sophisticated reader who will be looking for more and better articles that anticipate ideas and trends on the intellectual and cultural frontier."

BRUTARIAN, The Magazine That Dares To Be Lame, Box 25222, Arlington VA 22202. E-mail: brutarian@juno. com. Editor: Dominick Salemi. 100% freelance written. Quarterly magazine covering popular and unpopular culture. "A healthy knowledge of the great works of antiquity and an equally healthy contempt for most of what passes today as culture." Estab. 1991. Circ. 3,000. Pays on publication. Publishes ms an average of 3 months after acceptance. Byline given. Buys first or one-time rights. Editorial lead time 2 months. Submit seasonal material 6 months in advance. Reports in 1 week on queries; 2 months on mss. Sample copy for $6.

Nonfiction: Book excerpts, essays, exposé, general interest, humor, interview/profile, reviews of books, film and music. Buys 10-20 feature articles/year. Send complete ms. Length: 1,000-10,000 words. Pays $100-400. Sometimes pays expenses of writers on assignment.

Reprints: Send typed ms with rights for sale noted and information about when and where the article previously appeared. Pays 50% of amount paid for an original article.

Photos: State availability of photos with submission. Reviews contact sheets. Offers no additional payment for photos accepted with ms. Caption, model releases, identification of subjects required. Buys one-time rights.

Columns/Departments: Celluloid Void (critiques of cult and obscure films), 500-1,000 words; Brut Library (critiques of books), 500-1,000 words; Audio Depravation (short critiques of odd, R&B, jazz and R&R music), 50-100 words. Buys "hundreds" of mss/year. Send complete ms. Pays $5-25.

Fiction: Adventure, confession, erotica, experimental, fantasy, horror, humorous, mystery, novel excerpts, suspense. Buys 8-10 mss/year. Send complete ms. Length: 1,000-10,000 words. Pays $100-500, 10¢/word for established writers. Publishes novel excerpts.

Poetry: Avant-garde, free verse, traditional. Buys 10-15 poems/year. Submit maximum 3 poems. Length: 25-1,000. Pays $20-200.

Tips: "Send résumé with completed manuscript. Avoid dry tone and excessive scholasticism. Do not cover topics or issues which have been done to death unless you have a fresh approach or new insights on the subject."

‡BUILD MAGAZINE A Magazine About Young People Building Communities, Do Something, 423 W. 55th St., New York NY 10019. (212)523-1175. Fax: (212)582-1307. E-mail: daramay@aol.com. Contact: Dara Mayers, editor. 100% freelance written. Quarterly magazine covering activism, youth leadership, social justice and entertainment. "The goal of *Build* is to inspire young people to take action in their communities. We also seek to provide issue-oriented information which may not otherwise be accessible to a young audience. *Build* also entertains while it educates." Estab. 1996. Circ. 100,000. Pays on publication. Byline given. Offers 15% kill fee. Makes work-for-hire assignments. Editorial lead time 6 weeks. Submit seasonal material 2 months in advance. Accepts simultaneous submissions. Sample copy and writer's guidelines for SASE.

Nonfiction: Essays, general interest, historical/nostalgic, how-to, inspirational, interview/profile, opinion, personal experience, photo feature, religious. "We are always looking for socially active celebrities and charismatic grass roots leaders. Buys 20 mss/year. Query with published clips. Length: 250-3,000 words. Pays $100-400. Sometimes pays expenses of writers on assignment.

Reprints: Accepts previously published material.

Photos: Send photos with submission. Reviews negatives. Negotiates payment individually. Captions, identification of subjects required. Buys one-time rights.

Columns/Departments: Kelly Chase, editorial assistant. Recommended Consumption (socially relevant reviews of movies, books and films), 100-150 words; Action Shots (actions taking place locally), 100-150 words; Protius (young activists personal histories), 1,500-2,000 words. Buys 50 mss/year. Query with published clips. Pays $25-150.

Tips: "Information should be presented in a way which appeals to 16- to 25-year-olds; hip, but not cynical."

‡CANADIAN DIMENSION, Dimension Publications Inc., 91 Albert St., Room 2-B, Winnipeg, Manitoba, R3B 1G5 Canada. Fax: (204)943-4617. E-mail: info@canadiandimension.mb.ca. Website: http://www.canadiandimension.mb.ca/cd/index.htm. 80% freelance written. Manager: Michelle Torres. Bimonthly magazine "that makes sense of the world. We bring a socialist perspective to bear on events across Canada and around the world. Our contributors provide in-depth coverage on popular movements, peace, labour, women, aboriginal justice, environment, third world and eastern Europe." Estab. 1963. Circ. 4,000. Pays on publication. Publishes ms an average of 6 months after acceptance. Copyrighted by *CD* after publication. Accepts simultaneous and previously published submissions. Reports in 6 weeks on queries. Sample copy for $2. Writer's guidelines for #10 SAE with IRC.

Nonfiction: Interview/profile, opinion, reviews, political commentary and analysis, journalistic style. Buys 8 mss/year. Length: 500-2,000 words. Pays $25-100.

Reprints: Sometimes accepts previously published submissions. Send typed ms with rights for sale noted (electronic copies when possible) and information about when and where the article previously appeared.

‡CANNABIS CANADA, The Magazine of Canada's Cannabis Culture, Hemp BC, #504-21 Water St., Vancouver, British Columbia V6B 1A1 Canada. (604)669-9069. Fax: (604)669-9038. E-mail: muggles@hempbc.com. Website: http://www.hempbc.com. Contact: Dana Larsen, editor. 25% freelance written. Quarterly magazine covering marijuana and hemp. "Marijuana is good—prohibition is wrong." Estab. 1994. Circ. 25,000. Pays on publication. Publishes ms an average of 6 months after acceptance. Byline given. Offers 50% kill fee. Not copyrighted. Buys first rights or one-time rights and rights for website use. Editorial lead time 2 months. Submit seasonal material 6 months in advance. Accepts simultaneous submissions. Reports in 1 month. Sample copy for $5.

Nonfiction: Current events, historical/nostalgic, how-to (grow marijuana), interview/profile, legal and cultural issues, new product, personal experience, travel. "No articles on why pot is good/illegal. We know." Buys 3-6 mss/year. Send complete ms. Length: 1,000-4,000 words. Pays 4¢/word. Sometimes pays expenses of writers on assignment.

Photos: Send photos with submission. Reviews prints. Offers $30 minimum, negotiates payment individually. Caption, identification of subjects required. Buys one-time rights.

Fillers: Newsbreaks. Length: 50-1,000 words. Pays 4¢/word.

Tips: "Be obsessed with all things marijuana and hemp."

‡FRANCE TODAY, FrancePress Inc., 1051 Divisadero St., San Francisco CA 94115. (415)921-5100. Fax: (415)921-0213. E-mail: fpress@hookednet. Editor: Anne Prah-Perochon. Executive Editor: Jean-Sebastien Stehl. Contact: Jeanenne Ray, publication coordinator. 90% freelance written. Tabloid published 10 times/year covering contemporary France. "*France Today* is a feature publication on contemporary France including sociocultural analysis, business, trends, current events and travel." Estab. 1989. Circ. 30,000. Pays on publication. Publishes ms an average of 3-5 months after acceptance. Byline given. Buys first North American and second serial (reprint) rights. Submit seasonal material 4 months in advance. Reports in 3 months. Sample copy and writer's guidelines for 10×13 SAE with 3 first-class stamps.

Nonfiction: Essays, exposé, general interest, historical, humor, interview/profile, personal experience, travel. "No travel pieces about well-known tourist attractions." Buys 50% mss/year. Query with or without published clips, or send complete ms. Length: 500-1,500 words. Pays $150-250. Pays expenses of writers on assignment.

Photos: Offers $25/photo. Identification of subjects required. Buys one-time rights.

HIGH TIMES, Trans High Corp., 235 Park Ave. S., 5th Floor, New York NY 10003-1405. (212)387-0500. Fax: (212)475-7684. E-mail: hteditor@hightimes.com. Website: http://www.hightimes.com. Contact: Steve Hager, editor. News Editor: Dean Latimer. 30% freelance written. Monthly magazine covering marijuana and the counterculture. Estab. 1974. Circ. 250,000. Pays on publication. Byline given. Offers 20% kill fee. Buys one-time or all rights or makes work-for-hire assignments. Submit seasonal material 6 months in advance. Reports in 1 month on queries; 4 months on mss. Sample copy for $5 and #10 SASE. Writer's guidelines for SASE.

• No longer accepts fiction or poetry. Staff now writes more for each issue than freelancers.

Nonfiction: Book excerpts, exposé, humor, interview/profile, new product, personal experience, photo feature, travel. Buys 30 mss/year. Send complete ms. Length: 2,000-7,000 words. Pays $300-1,000. Sometimes pays in trade for advertisements. Sometimes pays expenses of writers on assignment.

Reprints: Send tearsheet of article or typed ms with rights for sale noted. Pays in ad trade.

Photos: Chris Eudaley, photo editor. Send photos with submission. Pays $25-400, $400 for cover photos, $350 for centerfold. Captions, model release, identification of subjects required. Buys all rights or one-time use.

Columns/Departments: Steve Bloom, music editor. Chris Simunek, cultivation editor. Peter Gorman, views editor. Drug related books, news. Buys 10 mss/year. Query with published clips. Length: 100-2,000 words. Pays $25-300.

Fillers: Gags to be illustrated by cartoonist, newsbreaks, short humor. Buys 10 mss/year. Length: 100-500 words. Pays $10-50. Frank Max, cartoon editor.

Tips: "Although promoting the legalization and cultivation of medicinal plants, primarily cannabis, is central to our mission. *High Times* does not promote the indiscriminate use of such plants. We are most interested in articles on cannabis cultivation, the history of hemp, the rise of the modern hemp industry, the history of the counterculture and countercultural trends and events. The best way for new writers to break in is through our news section. We are always looking for regional stories involving the Drug War that have national significance. This includes coverage of local legal battles, political controversies, drug testing updates and legalization rally reports. All sections are open to good, professional writers."

‡INSIDER MAGAZINE, Careers, Issues & Entertainment for the Next Generation, 4124 W. Oakton, Skokie IL 60201. Fax: (847)329-0358. E-mail: insideread@aol.com. Website: insidermag.com. Contact: David M. Glines, editorial director. 50% freelance written. Bimonthly magazine covering outdoor/adventure, winter sports, computer/software, travel, automotive. Estab. 1982. Circ. 200,000. Pays on publication. Publishes ms an average of 3 months after acceptance. Byline given. Rights purchased vary. Editorial lead time 2 months. Submit seasonal material 2 months in advance. Accepts simultaneous submissions. Reports in 2 months. Sample copy and writer's guidelines free.

Nonfiction: General interest, humor, inspirational, interview/profile, new product, personal experience, technical, travel. No articles mentioning or written for students. Buys 5-10 mss/year. Send complete ms. Length: 800-2,100 words. Pays 3¢/word maximum.

Reprints: Send tearsheet of article and information on when and where the article previously appeared. Pay varies.

Photos: Send photos with submission. Offers no additional payment for photos accepted with ms. Captions, model releases and identification of subjects required. Buys all rights.

Columns/Departments: Pays 5¢/word maximum.

Tips: "*INsider* targets college students, but wants to make no reference to them within the copy. To appeal to college students you must write above them."

MOTHER JONES, Foundation for National Progress, 731 Market St., Suite 600, San Francisco CA 94103. (415)665-6637. Fax: (415)665-6696. E-mail: query@motherjones.com. Website: http://www.motherjones.com. Editor: Jeffrey Klein. Contact: Kerry Lauerman, investigative editor; John Cook, editorial assistant. 80% freelance written. Bimonthly national magazine covering politics, investigative reporting, social issues and pop culture. "*Mother Jones* is a 'progressive' magazine—but the core of its editorial well is reporting (i.e., fact-based). No slant required." Estab. 1976. Circ. 140,000. Pays on publication. Publishes ms an average of 4 months after acceptance. Byline given. Offers 33% kill fee. Buys first North American serial rights, first rights, one-time rights or online rights (limited). Editorial lead time 4 months. Submit seasonal material 6 months in advance. Reports in 2 months. Sample copy for 9×12 SAE with 4 first-class stamps. Writer's guidelines for #10 SASE.
Nonfiction: Book excerpts, essays, exposé, humor, interview/profile, opinion, personal experience, photo feature, current issues, policy. Buys 70-100 mss/year. Query with 2-3 published clips and SASE. Length: 2,000-5,000 words. Pays 80¢/word. Sometimes pays expenses of writers on assignment.
Columns/Departments: Colleen Quinn. Outfront (short, newsy and/or outrageous and/or humorous items), 200-500 words; Profiles of "Hellraisers," "Visionaries" (short interviews), 250 words. Pays 80¢/word.
Fiction: Publishes novel excerpts.
Tips: "We're looking for hard-hitting, investigative reports exposing government cover-ups, corporate malfeasance, scientific myopia, institutional fraud or hypocrisy; thoughtful, provocative articles which challenge the conventional wisdom (on the right or the left) concerning issues of national importance; and timely, people-oriented stories on issues such as the environment, labor, the media, health care, consumer protection, and cultural trends. Send a great, short query and establish your credibility as a reporter. Explain what you plan to cover and how you will proceed with the reporting. The query should convey your approach, tone and style, and should answer the following: What are your specific qualifications to write on this topic? What 'ins' do you have with your sources? Can you provide full documentation so that your story can be fact-checked?"

NEW HAVEN ADVOCATE, News & Arts Weekly, New Mass Media Inc., 1 Long Wharf Dr., New Haven CT 06511-5991. (203)789-0010. Fax: (203)787-1418. E-mail: newhadvo@pcnet.com. Website: www.newhavenadvocate.com. Contact: Joshua Mamis, editor. 10% freelance written. Alternative weekly tabloid. "Alternative, investigative, cultural reporting with a strong voice. We like to shake things up." Estab. 1975. Circ. 55,000. Pays on publication. Byline given. Buys on speculation. Buys one-time rights. Editorial lead time 1 month. Submit seasonal material 2 months in advance. Accepts simultaneous submissions. Reports in 1 month on queries.
Nonfiction: Book excerpts, essays, exposé, general interest, humor, interview/profile. Buys 15-20 mss/year. Query with published clips. Length: 750-2,000 words. Pays $50-150. Sometimes pays expenses of writers on assignment.
Photos: Freelancers should state availability of photos with submission. Captions, model releases, identification of subjects required. Buys one-time rights.
Tips: "Strong local focus; strong literary voice, controversial, easy-reading, contemporary, etc."

‡ON THE ISSUES, The Progressive Woman's Quarterly, Choices Women's Medical Center, Inc., 97-77 Queens Blvd., Suite 1120, Forest Hills NY 33174. Fax: (718)997-1206. E-mail: onissues@echonyc.com. Website: http://www.igc.apc.org/onissues. Contact: Ronni Sandroff. 90% freelance written. "*On The Issues* is a quarterly magazine for 'thinking feminists'—women and men interested in progressive social change, advances in feminist thought, and coverage of politics, society, economics, medicine, relationships, the media and the arts from a range of feminist viewpoints." Estab. 1983. Circ. 15,285. **Pays on acceptance.** Publishes ms an average of 5 months after acceptance. Byline given. Offers 20% kill fee. Buys first North American serial rights or all rights. Editorial lead time 3 months. Accepts simultaneous and previously published submissions, if so notified. Reports in 2 months. Sample copy and writer's guidelines free.
Nonfiction: Book excerpts, essays, exposé, general interest, historical/nostalgic, humor, interview/profile, opinion, personal experience, photo feature. Buys 40 mss/year. Query with published clips. Length: 75-2,500 words. Pays $25-400. Sometimes pays expenses of writers on assignment.
Photos: State availability of photos with submissions. Negotiates payment individually. Captions, identification of subjects required. Buys all rights.
Columns/Departments: Talking Feminist (personal experience), 1,500 words; Win Some Lose Some (briefs/news/humor), 200-500 words; Cutting Some Slack (Humor), 600 words; Book Reviews (query Nina Mehta, book review editor), 500 words. Buys 15 mss/year. Query with published clips. Pays $25-150.
Tips: "Always looking for investigative, newsworthy pieces. Query first. Our columns are also a good place to start. "Cutting Some Slack," on our last page, features a 600 word essay: humor or political satire with a feminist edge."

FOR EXPLANATION of symbols, see the Key to Symbols and Abbreviations. For unfamiliar words, see the Glossary.

"Talking Feminist" can be on any subject: a personal experience or editorial style essay. We're particularly interested in recruiting more writers for this column."

ROLLING STONE, Wenner Media Inc., 1290 Avenue of the Americas, New York NY 10104. (212)484-1616. Fax: (212)767-8205. Editor: Jann S. Wenner. Magazine published 24 times/year covering popular culture. "*Rolling Stone* is a magazine edited for young adults who have a special interest in popular culture, particularly music, film and politics." Estab. 1967. Circ. 1,176,000. This magazine did not respond to our request for information. Query before submitting.

SHEPHERD EXPRESS, Alternative Publications, Inc., 1123 N. Water St., Milwaukee WI 53202. (414)276-2222. Fax: (414)276-3312. Website: http://www.shepherd-express.com. Contact: Joel McNally, editor. 50% freelance written. Weekly tabloid covering "news and arts with a progressive news edge and a hip entertainment perspective." Estab. 1982. Circ. 55,000. Pays on publication. Publishes ms an average of 2 weeks after acceptance. Byline given. No kill fee. Buys first, one-time or all rights or makes work-for-hire assignments. Editorial lead time 2 weeks. Submit seasonal material 1 month in advance. Accepts simultaneous submissions. Reports in 2 weeks on queries; 1 month on mss. Sample copy for $3.
Nonfiction: Book excerpts, essays, exposé, opinion. Buys 300 mss/year. Query with published clips or send complete ms. Length: 600-3,500 words. Pays $25-350 for assigned articles; $10-200 for unsolicited articles. Sometimes pays expenses of writers on assignment.
Reprints: Accepts previously published submissions.
Photos: State availability of photos with submissions. Reviews prints. Negotiates payment individually. Captions, model releases, identification of subjects required. Buys one-time rights.
Columns/Departments: Opinions (social trends, politics, from progressive slant), 800-1,200 words; Books Reviewed (new books only: Social trends, environment, politics), 600-1,200 words. Buys 10 mss/year. Send complete ms.
Tips: "Include solid analysis with point of view in tight but lively writing. Nothing cute. Do not tell us that something is important, tell us why."

STRENGTH MAGAZINE, Quality Boards and Noize since 1995, Delinquent Publishing, 5050 Section Ave., Cincinnati OH 45212. (513)531-0202. Fax: (513)531-1421. E-mail: mattd@nucodist.com. Website: http://www.strength mag.com. Editor: Christian Strike. Contact: Matt Deak, managing editor. 50% freelance written. Bimonthly magazine covering music, snowboarding, skating. "*Strength* is a core music and board sports magazine." Estab. 1995. Circ. 40,000. **Pays on acceptance**. Publishes ms an average of 2 months after acceptance. Byline given. Offers 20% kill fee. Buys all rights. Editorial lead time 2 months. Submit seasonal material 3 months in advance. Accepts simultaneous submissions. Reports in 2 weeks on queries; 2 months on mss. Sample copy for $5. Writer's guidelines free.
Nonfiction: General interest, humor, interview/profile, new product, opinion, personal experience, photo feature, travel. Query. Length: 200-1,500 words. Pays $300-600 for assigned articles; $100-400 for unsolicited articles. Pays expenses of writers on assignment.
Reprints: Send tearsheet of article or short story. Pays 50% of amount paid for an original article.
Photos: State availability of photos with submission. Reviews contact sheets, transparencies. Negotiates payment individually. Identification of subjects required. Buys one-time rights.
Columns/Departments: Music Interviews, Board Sports Location Stories and Board Sports Interviews (no holds barred, in your face), 500-2,000 words. Buys over 50 mss/year. Query. Pays $500-1,000.
Fiction: Adventure, humorous. Buys 5-10 mss/year. Query. Length: 500-2,000 words. Pays $300-500.
Poetry: Free verse, haiku. Length: 10-100 lines. Pays $20-100.
Fillers: Anecdotes, facts, gags to be illustrated by cartoonist, newsbreaks, short humor. Buys 500/year. Length: 20-500 words. Pays $20-200.
Tips: "We're very accessible. Just give us a call."

‡SWING MAGAZINE, The Swing Corporation, 342 Madison Ave., Suite 1402, New York NY 10017. (212)490-0525. Fax: (212)490-8073. E-mail: swingmag1@aol.com. Editor: David Lauren. Managing Editor: Lynne Sanford. Contact: Megan Liberman, executive editor. 70% freelance written. Magazine published 10 times/year covering twenty-something life styles. "The reader of our magazine is usually 18- to 34-years-old and looking for pertinent, newsworthy information and features on politics, sports, entertainment and technology that can guide twentysomethings in making decisions." Estab. 1994. Circ. 100,000. **Pays on acceptance**. Publishes ms an average of 3 months after acceptance. Byline given. Offers 25% kill fee. Makes work-for-hire assignments. Editorial lead time 3 months. Submit seasonal material 4 months in advance. Accepts simultaneous submissions. Reports in 3 weeks on queries; 2 months on mss. Writer's guidelines free.
Nonfiction: General interest, interview/profile, personal experience, service pieces on personal finance, careers, health, travel, relationships, technology. Special issues: The Most Powerful Twentysomethings in America (December/January); Love & Relationships (February); Jobs (June); Best Places to Live (July/August). Buys 40-50 mss/year. Query with published clips. Length: 1,500-3,500 words. Pays 50¢-$1/word. Pays expenses of writers on assignment.
Reprints: Accepts previously published submissions.
Photos: State availability of photos with submission. Reviews contact sheets, transparencies. Negotiates payment individually. Model releases, identification of subjects required. Buys one-time rights.
Columns/Departments: Health, Finance, Travel; all 800 words. Buys 50 mss/year. Query with published clips. Pays 50-75¢/word.

Tips: "Send specific queries with concrete names and ideas. The more general, the less chance."

UTNE READER, 1624 Harmon Place, Suite 330, Minneapolis MN 55403. Fax: (612)338-6043. E-mail: editor@utne. com. Website: http://www.utne.com. Managing Editor: Craig Cox. No unsolicited mss.
Reprints: Accepts previously published submissions only. Send tearsheet or photocopy of article or typed ms with rights for sale noted and information about when and where the article previously appeared.
   • The *Utne Reader* has been a finalist three times for the National Magazine Award for general excellence.

XSeSS LIVING, CDZeene, ComEnt Media Group, Inc., 3932 Wilshire Blvd., #212, Los Angeles CA 90010. Fax: (213)383-1093. E-mail: xsesscdzne@aol.com. Website: www.allmediadist.com. Editor: Sean Perkin. 80% freelance written. Bimonthly lifestyles publication covering fashion, business, politics, music, entertainment, etc. Estab. 1992. Circ. 30,000. Pays within 2 weeks after publication. Publishes ms an average of 1 month after acceptance. Byline given. Buys one-time rights and makes work-for-hire assignments. Editorial lead time 3 months. Submit seasonal material 4 months in advance. Accepts simultaneous submissions. Sample copy $12.50. Writer's guidelines on hiring.
Nonfiction: Exposé, interview/profile, new product, travel. Query. Payment varies.
Reprints: Send photocopy and information about when and where the article previously appeared. Payment varies.

‡**YES! A Journal of Positive Futures**, Positive Futures Network, P.O. Box 10818, Bainbridge Island WA 98110. (206)842-0216. Fax: (206)842-5208. E-mail: yes@futurenet.org. Editor: Sarah van Gelder. Contact: Jane Engel, assistant editor. Quarterly magazine emphasizing sustainability and community. "Interested in stories on building a positive future: sustainability, overcoming divisiveness, ethical business practices, etc." Estab. 1996. Circ. 11,000. Pays on publication. Byline given. Buys various rights. Editorial lead time 4 months. Accepts simultaneous submissions. Reports in 2 months on mss; 1 month on queries. Sample copy for $8. Writer's guidelines for #10 SASE.
Nonfiction: Book excerpts, essays, how-to, humor, interview/profile, personal experience, photo feature, technical, environmental. "No negativity or blanket prescriptions for changing the world." Query with published clips. Length: 200-3,500 words. Pays $20-60. Pays writers with contributor copies or other premiums at writers option only. Sometimes pays expenses of writers on assignment.
Reprints: Send photocopy of article or short story or typed ms with rights for sale noted and information about when and where the article previously appeared. Pays 100% of amount paid for an original article.
Photos: State availability of photos with submission. Reviews contact sheets, negatives, transparencies and prints. Offers $20-75/photo. Identification of subjects required. Buys one-time rights.
Columns/Departments: Query with published clips. Pays $20-60.
Fiction: Experimental, historical, slice-of-life vignettes, novel excerpts. "No downers. We want fiction that explores human possibility." Query with published clips.
Poetry: Avant-garde, free verse, haiku, light verse, traditional. Buys 2-3 poems/year. Submit maximum 10 poems.
Tips: "Read and become familiar with the publication's purpose, tone and quality. We are about facilitating the creation of a better world. We are looking for writers who want to participate in that process. *Yes!* is less interested in bemoaning the state of our problems and more interested in highlighting promising solutions."

DETECTIVE AND CRIME

Fans of detective stories want to read accounts of actual criminal cases, detective work and espionage. Markets specializing in crime fiction are listed under Mystery publications.

‡**DETECTIVE CASES**, Detective Files Group, 1350 Sherbrooke St. West, Suite 600, Montreal, Quebec H3G 2T4. (514)849-7733. Editor-in-Chief: Dominick A. Merle. Bimonthly magazine. See *Detective Files*.

‡**DETECTIVE DRAGNET**, Detective Files Group, 1350 Sherbrooke St. West, Suite 600, Montreal, Quebec H3G 2T4. (514)849-7733. Editor-in-Chief: Dominick A. Merle. Bimonthly, 72-page magazine. See *Detective Files*.

‡**DETECTIVE FILES**, Detective Files Group, Globe Communication Corp., 1350 Sherbrooke St. West, Suite 600, Montreal, Quebec H3G 2T4. (514)849-7733. Editor: Dominick A. Merle. 100% freelance written. Bimonthly magazine featuring "narrative accounts of true murder mysteries leading to arrests and convictions." **Pays on acceptance.** Publishes ms an average of 6 months after acceptance. Byline given. Buys all rights. Reports in 2 weeks on queries; 2 months on mss. Sample copy and writer's guidelines for SASE.
Nonfiction: True crime cases only; no fiction. Query. Length: 3,000-6,000 words. Pays $250-350.
Photos: Send photos with submission. Offers no additional payment for photos accepted with ms. Captions, identification of subjects required. Buys all rights.
Tips: "Build suspense and police investigation leading to arrest. No smoking gun or open and shut cases. Do a thorough job; don't double-sell (sell the same article to more than one market); deliver, and you can have a steady market. Neatness, clarity and pace will help you make the sale."

‡**HEADQUARTERS DETECTIVE**, Detective Files Group, 1350 Sherbrooke St. West, Suite 600, Montreal, Quebec H3G 2T4. (514)849-7733. Editor-in-Chief: Dominick A. Merle. Bimonthly magazine; 72 pages. See *Detective Files*.

P. I. MAGAZINE, America's Private Investigation Journal, 755 Bronx, Toledo OH 43609. (419)382-0967. Fax: (419)382-0967. E-mail: pimag@aol.com. Website: http://www.PIMALL.com. Contact: Bob Mackowiak, editor/publisher. 75% freelance written. "Audience includes professional investigators and mystery/private eye fans. Estab. 1988. Circ. 4,000. Pays on publication. Publishes ms an average of 3 months after acceptance. Buys one-time rights. Submit seasonal material 3 months in advance. Accepts simultaneous submissions. Reports in 3 months on queries; 4 months on mss. Sample copy for $6.75.

Nonfiction: Interview/profile, personal experience and accounts of real cases. Special issue: 10th anniversary issue (Spring 1998), has a special section of profiles and cases and always needs these articles. Buys 4-10 mss/year. Send complete ms. Length: 1,000 words. Pays $25 minimum for unsolicited articles.

Photos: Send photos with submission. May offer additional payment for photos accepted with ms. Model releases, identification of subjects required. Buys one-time rights.

Tips: "The best way to get published in *P.I.* is to write a detailed story about a professional P.I.'s true-life case."

‡**STARTLING DETECTIVE**, Detective Files Group, 1350 Sherbrooke St. West, Suite 600, Montreal, Quebec H3G 2T4. (514)849-7733. Editor-in-Chief: Dominick A. Merle. Bimonthly 72-page magazine. See *Detective Files*.

‡**TRUE POLICE CASES**, Detective Files Group, 1350 Sherbrooke St. West, Suite 600, Montreal, Quebec H3G 2T4. (514)849-7733. Editor-in-Chief: Dominick A. Merle. Bimonthly, 72-page magazine. Buys all rights. See *Detective Files*.

DISABILITIES

These magazines are geared toward disabled persons and those who care for or teach them. A knowledge of disabilities and lifestyles is important for writers trying to break in to this field; editors regularly discard material that does not have a realistic focus. Some of these magazines will accept manuscripts only from disabled persons or those with a background in caring for disabled persons.

ACCENT ON LIVING, P.O. Box 700, Bloomington IL 61702-0700. (309)378-2961. Fax: (309)378-4420. E-mail: acntlvg@aol.com. Website: http://www.blvd.com/accent. Contact: Betty Garee, editor. 75% freelance written. Eager to work with new/unpublished writers. Quarterly magazine for physically disabled persons and rehabilitation professionals. Estab. 1956. Circ. 20,000. Buys first and second (reprint) rights. Byline usually given. Pays on publication. Publishes ms an average of 6 months after acceptance. Reports in 1 month. Sample copy and writer's guidelines $3.50 for #10 SAE with 7 first-class stamps. Writer's guidelines for #10 SASE.

Nonfiction: Articles about new devices that would make a disabled person with limited physical mobility more independent; should include description, availability and photos. Medical breakthroughs for disabled people. Intelligent discussion articles on acceptance of physically disabled persons in normal living situations; topics may be architectural barriers, housing, transportation, educational or job opportunities, organizations, or other areas. How-to articles concerning everyday living, giving specific, helpful information so the reader can carry out the idea himself/herself. News articles about active disabled persons or groups. Good strong interviews. Vacations, accessible places to go, sports, organizations, humorous incidents, self improvement and sexual or personal adjustment—all related to physically handicapped persons. "We are looking for upbeat material." Buys 50-60 unsolicited mss/year. Query. Length: 250-1,000 words. Pays 10¢/word for published articles (after editing and/or condensing by staff).

Reprints: Send tearsheet and information about when and where the article previously appeared. Pays 10¢/word.

Photos: Pays $10 minimum for b&w photos purchased with accompanying captions. Amount will depend on quality of photos and subject matter. Pays $50 and up for four-color cover photos. "We need good-quality color or b&w photos (or slides and transparencies)."

Tips: "Ask a friend who is disabled to read your article before sending it to *Accent*. Make sure that he/she understands your major points and the sequence or procedure."

ACTIVE LIVING, (formerly *Disability Today*), Disability Today Publishing Group, Inc., 627 Lyons Lane, Suite 203, Oakville, Ontario L6J 5Z7 Canada. (905)338-6894. Fax: (905)338-1836. Editor: Hilda Hoch. Contact: Amanda Cleghorn, managing editor. 70% freelance written. Bimonthly magazine covering health, fitness and recreation for people with disability. Estab. 1990. Circ. 45,000. Pays on publication. Publishes ms an average of 3 months after acceptance. Byline given. Offers 75% kill fee. Buys one-time or second serial (reprint) rights. Editorial lead time 3 months. Submit seasonal material 6 months in advance. Sample copy $5.50. Writer's guidelines for #10 SAE and IRC.

Nonfiction: Book excerpts, health and fitness, humor, inspirational, interview/profile, new product, opinion, personal experience, photo feature, recreation, travel. Annual features: Acquired Brain Injury (August); Kids & Disability (October). Buys 12 mss/year. Query. Length: 1,000-2,500 words. Pays $100-400. Sometimes pays expenses of writers on assignment.

Reprints: Send photocopy of article.

Photos: Send photos with submission. Reviews 4×6 prints. Offers no additional payment for photos accepted with ms. Model releases and identification of subjects required. Buys one-time rights.

Columns/Departments: Injury Prevention, 800 words; Newspage ("what's new"), 400 words; Sports (disabled

sports), 800 words; Alternative Therapies, 600 words; Destinations (travel), 600 words; Nutrition, 600 words. Buys 24 mss/year. Query. Pays $50-200.
Tips: "Provide outline for a series of contributions; identify experience in field of disability."

ARTHRITIS TODAY, Arthritis Foundation. 1330 W. Peachtree St., Atlanta GA 30309. (404)872-7100. Fax: (404)872-9559. E-mail: smorrow@arthritis.org. Website: http://www.arthritis.org. Editor: Cindy T. McDaniel. Managing Editor: Susan Percy. Executive Editor: Marcy O'Koon. Contact: Shelly Morrow, associate editor. 70% freelance written. Bi-monthly magazine about living with arthritis; latest in research/treatment. "*Arthritis Today* is written for the nearly 40 million Americans who have arthritis and for the millions of others whose lives are touched by an arthritis-related disease. The editorial content is designed to help the person with arthritis live a more productive, independent and painfree life. The articles are upbeat and provide practical advice, information and inspiration." Estab. 1987. Circ. 500,000. **Pays on acceptance.** Offers 25% kill fee. Buys first North American serial rights but requires unlimited reprint rights in any Arthritis Foundation-affiliated endeavor. Submit seasonal material 6 months in advance. Considers simultaneous submissions. Reports in 1 month on queries; 2 months on mss. Sample copy for 9×11 SAE with 4 first-class stamps. Writer's guidelines for #10 SASE.
  • Ranked as one of the best markets for freelance writers in *Writer's Yearbook* magazine's annual "Top 100 Markets," January 1997.
Nonfiction: General interest, how-to (tips on any aspect of living with arthritis), service, inspirational, opinion, personal experience, photo feature, technical, nutrition, general health and lifestyle. Buys 45 mss/year. Query with published clips or send complete ms. Length: 750-3,500. Pays $450-1,800. Pays expenses of writers on assignment.
Reprints: Send photocopy of article with rights for sale noted and information about when and where the article previously appeared. Pays 25-50% of amount paid for an original article.
Photos: Submit slides, tearsheets or prints for consideration. Reprints $50. Captions, model releases, identification of subjects required. Buy one-time North American serial rights.
Columns/Departments: Quick Takes (arthritis-specific and medical news); Research Spotlight (research news about arthritis); Lifestyle (travel, leisure); Well Being (general health, nutrition, exercise), 200-600 words. Buys 16-20 mss/year. Query with published clips. Pays $150-400.
Tips: "In addition to articles specifically about living with arthritis, we look for articles to appeal to an older audience on subjects such as hobbies, general health, lifestyle, etc."

‡ASTHMA MAGAZINE, Strategies For Taking Control, Lifelong Publications, 55 Chapel St., Newton MA 02158. (617)964-4910. Fax: (617)964-8095. E-mail: asthmamag@aol.com. Contact: Rachel Butler, editor-in-chief. 50% freelance written. Bimonthly magazine covering information about asthma and how to manage it. "*Asthma Magazine* offers unbiased education for people with asthma. We are an independent publication (not sponsored by any drug company) and we provide indepth education to help the asthmatic manage his/her disease and live an active and healthy life." Estab. 1995. Circ. 30,000. Pays on publication. Publishes ms an average of 1 month after acceptance. Byline given. Offers 25% kill fee. Buys all rights. Editorial lead time 6 weeks. Submit seasonal material 3 months in advance. Sample copy and writer's guidelines free.
Nonfiction: How-to, humor, inspirational, interview/profile, new product (usually a news blurb, not a full article), personal experience, technical, travel—all related to the subject matter. Buys 12-15 mss/year. Query with published clips. Length: 800-1,200 words. Pays $200-500.
Photos: State availability of photos with submission. Reviews prints. Offers no additional payment for photos accepted with ms. Buys all rights.
Columns/Departments: Hear My Story (personal experience of a person with asthma); Spotlight (interview or article about someone who has accomplished something significant despite their asthma, or someone in the asthma/medical field); all 450 words. Query with published clips. Pays $250.
Tips: "We look for writers who have had experience writing for the medical community for either clinicians or patients. Writing must be clear, concise and easy to understand (7th-9th grade reading level), as well as thoroughly researched and medically accurate."

‡CAREERS & the disABLED, Equal Opportunity Publications, 1160 E. Jericho Turnpike, Suite 200, Huntington NY 11743. (516)421-9421. Fax: (516)421-0359. E-mail: eopub@aol.com. Website: http://www.eop.com. Contact: James Schneider, editor. 60% freelance written. Quarterly career guidance magazine that is distributed through college campuses for disabled college students and professionals. "The magazine offers role-model profiles and career guidance articles geared toward disabled college students and professionals and promotes personal and professional growth." Pays on publication. Publishes ms an average of 6 months after acceptance. Estab. 1967. Circ. 10,000. Byline given. Buys first North American serial rights. Editorial lead time 6 months. Submit seasonal material 6 months in advance. Accepts simultaneous submissions. Reports in 3 weeks. Sample copy and writer's guidelines for 9×12 SAE with 5 first-class stamps.
Nonfiction: Essays, general interest, how-to, interview/profile, new product, opinion, personal experience. Buys 30 mss/year. Query. Length: 1,000-2,500 words. Pays 15¢/word, $350 maximum. Sometimes pays the expenses of writers on assignment.
Reprints: Send information about when and where the article previously appeared. Pays 10% of amount paid for an original article.
Photos: State availability of or send photos with submission. Reviews transparencies, prints. Offers $15-50/photo.

Captions, identification of subjects required.. Buys one-time rights.
Tips: "Be as targeted as possible. Role model profiles and specific career guidance strategies that offer advice to disabled college students are most needed."

‡DIABETES INTERVIEW, Kings Publishing, 3715 Balboa St., San Francisco CA 94121. (415)387-4002. Fax: (415)387-3604. E-mail: diabetesest.com. Contact: Ben Eastman, editor. Managing Editor: Melissa Settlay. 40% freelance written. Monthly tabloid covering diabetes care. *"Diabetes Interview* covers the latest in diabetes care, medications and patient advocacy. Personal accounts are welcome as well as medical-oriented articles by MDs, RNs and CDEs (certified diabetes educators)." Estab. 1991. Circ. 40,000. Pays on publication. Publishes ms 2 months after acceptance. Byline given. Buys all rights. Editorial lead time 2 months. Submit seasonal material 2 months in advance. Sample copy and writer's guidelines free.
Nonfiction: Essays, how-to, inspirational, interview/profile, new product, opinion, personal experience. Buys 25 mss/year. Pays $50 for smaller articles, $150 for features.
Reprints: Accepts previously published submissions.
Photos: State availability or send photos with submission. Negotiates payment individually.
Tips: "Be actively involved in the diabetes community or have diabetes. However, writers need not have diabetes to write an article, but it must be diabetes-related."

DIABETES SELF-MANAGEMENT, R.A. Rapaport Publishing, Inc., 150 W. 22nd St., Suite 800, New York NY 10011-2421. (212)989-0200. Fax: (212)989-4786. Editor-in-Chief: James Hazlett. 20% freelance written. Bimonthly magazine about diabetes. "We publish how-to health care articles for motivated, intelligent readers who have diabetes and who are actively involved in their own health care management. All articles must have immediate application to their daily living." Estab. 1983. Circ. 285,000. Pays on publication. Publishes ms an average of 3 months after acceptance. Byline given. Offers 20% kill fee. Buys all rights. Submit seasonal material 6 months in advance. Reports in 1 month. Sample copy for $3.50 and 9×12 SAE with 6 first-class stamps. Writer's guidelines for #10 SASE.
Nonfiction: How-to (exercise, nutrition, diabetes self-care, product surveys), technical (reviews of products available, foods sold by brand name), travel (considerations and prep for people with diabetes). Buys 10-12 mss/year. Query with published clips. Length: 1,500-2,500 words. Pays $400-600 for assigned articles; $200-600 for unsolicited articles.
Tips: "The rule of thumb for any article we publish is that it must be clear, concise, useful and instructive, and it must have immediate application to the lives of our readers."

DIALOGUE, Blindskills, Inc., P.O. Box 5181, Salem OR 97301-0181. (800)860-4224; (503)581-4224. Fax: (503)581-0178. E-mail: blindskl@teleport.com. Website: www.teleport.com/blindskl. Contact: Carol M. McCarl, editor. 85% freelance written. Quarterly journal covering the visually impaired. Estab. 1961. Circ. 1,100. Pays on publication. Publishes ms an average of 8 months after acceptance. Byline given. Buys first rights. Editorial lead time 3 months. Submit seasonal material 3 months in advance. Sample copy $6. Writer's guidelines free.
Nonfiction: Essays, general interest, historical/nostalgic, how-to, humor, interview/profile, new product, personal experience. Prefer material by visually impaired writers. No controversial, explicit sex or religious or political topics. Buys 20 mss/year. Send complete ms. Length: 500-1,200 words. Pays $10-35 for assigned articles; $10-25 for unsolicited articles.
Reprints: Send tearsheet or photocopy of article or short story or typed ms with rights for sale noted and information about when and where the article previously appeared.
Columns/Departments: All material should be relative to blind and visually impaired readers. Careers, 1,000 words; What's New & Where to Get It (resources, new product), 2,500 words; What Do You Do When . . . ? (dealing with sight loss), 1,000 words. Buys 40 mss/year. Send complete ms. Pays $10-25.
Fiction: Adventure, humorous, science fiction, slice-of-life vignettes, first person experiences. Prefer material by visually impaired writers. No controversial, explicit sex. No religious or political. Buys 6-8 mss/year. Query with complete ms. Length: 800-1,200 words. Pays $15-25.
Poetry: Free verse, light verse, traditional. Prefer material by visually impaired writers. No controversial, explicit sex or religious or political topics. Buys 15-20 poems/year. Submit maximum 5 poems. Length: 20 lines maximum. Pays $10-15.
Fillers: Anecdotes, facts, newsbreaks, short humor. Length: 50-150 words. No payment.
Tips: Send SASE for free writers guidelines, $6 for sample in Braille, cassette or large print.

HEARING HEALTH, Voice International Publications, Inc., P.O. Drawer V, Ingleside TX 78362-0500. Fax: (512)776-3278. Editor: Paula Bonillas. 20% freelance written. Bimonthly magazine covering issues and concerns pertaining to hearing and hearing loss. Estab. 1984. Circ. 20,000. Pays on publication. Byline given. Buys one-time rights. Editorial lead time 2 months. Submit seasonal material 4 months in advance. Accepts simultaneous submissions. Reports in 6 weeks on queries; 2 months on mss. Sample copy for $2. Writer's guidelines for #10 SASE.
Nonfiction: Books excerpts, essays, exposé, general interest, historical/nostalgic, humor, inspirational, interview/profile, new product, opinion, personal experience, photo feature, technical, travel. No self-pitying over loss of hearing. Query with published clips. Length: 500-2,000 words. Sometimes pays expenses of writers on assignment.
Reprints: Accepts previously published submissions, if so noted.
Photos: State availability of photos with submission. Reviews contact sheets. Negotiates payment individually. Captions, model releases, identification of subjects required. Buys one-time rights.

Columns/Departments: Kidink (written by kids with hearing loss), 300 words; People (shares stories of successful, everyday people who have loss of hearing), 300-400 words. Buys 2 mss/year. Query with published clips.

Fiction: Fantasy, historical, humorous, novel excerpts, science fiction. Nothing inappropriate for children 10 or younger. Buys 2 mss/year. Query with published clips. Length: 400-1,500 words.

Poetry: Avant-garde, free verse, light verse, traditional. Buys 2 poems/year. Submit maximum 2 poems. Length: 4-50 lines.

Fillers: Anecdotes, facts, gags to be illustrated, newsbreaks, short humor. Buys 6/year. Length: 25-1,500 words.

Tips: "We look for fresh stories, usually factual but occasionally fictitious, about coping with hearing loss. A positive attitude is a must for *Hearing Health*. Unless one has some experience with deafness or hearing loss—whether their own or a loved one's—it's very difficult to 'break in' to our publication. Experience brings about the empathy and understanding—the sensitivity—and the freedom to write humorously about any handicap or disability."

KALEIDOSCOPE: International Magazine of Literature, Fine Arts, and Disability, Kaleidoscope Press, 326 Locust St., Akron OH 44302-1876. (330)762-9755. Fax: (330)762-0912. Contact: Dr. Darshan Perusek, editor-in-chief. Subscribers include individuals, agencies and organizations that assist people with disabilities and many university and public libraries. Estab. 1979. Circ. 1,500. 75% freelance written. Byline given. Rights return to author upon publication. Eager to work with new/unpublished writers; appreciates work by established writers as well. Especially interested in work by writers with a disability, but features writers both with and without disabilities. "Writers without a disability must limit themselves to our focus, while those with a disability may explore any topic (although we prefer original perspectives about experiences with disability)." Reports in 3 weeks, acceptance or rejection may take 6 months. Sample copy for $4 prepaid. Guidelines free for SASE.

Nonfiction: Personal experience essays, book reviews and articles related to disability. Special issues: Disability: The Lighter Side (January, deadline August); Disability and Alternate Healing (July, deadline March). Submit photocopies with SASE for return of work. Please type submissions. All submissions should be accompanied by an autobiographical sketch. May include art or photos that enhance works, prefer b&w with high contrast. Publishes 8-14 mss/year. Maximum 5,000 words. Pays $10-125 plus 2 copies.

Reprints: Send typed ms with rights for sale noted and information about when and where the article previously appeared. Publishes novel excerpts.

Fiction: Short stories, novel excerpts. Traditional and experimental styles. Works should explore experiences with disability. Use people-first language.

Poetry: Limit 5 poems/submission. Publishes 12-20 poems/year. Do not get caught up in rhyme scheme. High quality with strong imagery and evocative language. Reviews any style.

Tips: "Inquire about future themes of upcoming issues. Sample copy very helpful. Works should not use stereotyping, patronizing or offending language about disability. We seek fresh imagery and thought-provoking language."

MAINSTREAM, Magazine of the Able-Disabled, Exploding Myths, Inc., 2973 Beech St., San Diego CA 92102. (619)234-3138. Fax: (619)234-3155. E-mail: editor@mainstream-mag.com. Website: http://www.mainstream-mag.com. Publisher: Cyndi Jones. Contact: William Stothers, editor. 100% freelance written. Eager to develop writers who have a disability. Magazine published 10 times/year (monthly except January and June) covering disability-related topics, written for active and upscale disabled consumers. Estab. 1975. Circ. 19,400. Pays on publication. Publishes ms an average of 3 months after acceptance. Byline given. Buys all rights. Submit seasonal material 4 months in advance. Reports in 4 months. Sample copy for $5, or 9 × 12 SAE and $4 with 6 first-class stamps. Guidelines for #10 SASE.

Nonfiction: Book excerpts, exposé, how-to (daily independent living tips), humor, interview/profile, personal experience (dealing with problems/solutions), photo feature, technology, computers, travel, politics and legislation. "All must be disability-related, directed to disabled consumers." No articles on " 'my favorite disabled character,' 'my most inspirational disabled person,' 'poster child stories.' " Buys 65 mss/year. Query with or without published clips or send complete ms. Length: 8-12 pages. Pays $100-150. May pay subscription if writer requests.

Photos: State availability of photos with submission. Reviews contact sheets, 1½ × ¾ transparencies and 5 × 7 or larger prints. Offers $20-25/b&w photo. Captions, identification of subjects required. Buys all rights.

Columns/Departments: Creative Solutions (unusual solutions to common aggravating problems); Personal Page (deals with personal relations: dating, meeting people). Buys 10 mss/year. Send complete ms. Length: 500-800 words. Pays $75. "We also are looking for disability rights cartoons."

Tips: "It seems that politics and disability are becoming more important. Please include your phone number on cover page. We accept 5.25 or 3.5 floppy disks—ASCII, Wordperfect, IBM."

NEW MOBILITY, P.O. Box 8987, Malibu CA 90265-8987. (310)317-4522. Fax: (303)526-2879. E-mail: bcorbet@ix.n etcom.com. Website: http://www.newmobility.com. Contact: Barry Corbet, editor. 60% freelance written. Monthly full color magazine for people who use wheelchairs. "*New Mobility* covers the lifestyles of *active* wheelchair users with articles on health and medicine; sports, recreation and travel; equipment and technology; relationships, family and sexual issues; personalities; civil rights and legal issues. Writers should address topics with solid reporting and strong voice." Estab. 1989. Circ. 30,000. Pays 30 days after publication. Publishes ms an average of 6 months after acceptance. Byline given. Offers 50% kill fee. Buys first North American serial rights. Editorial lead time 6 months. Accepts simultaneous submissions. Reports in 3 months. Sample copy $5. Writer's guidelines for #10 SASE.

Nonfiction: Essays, exposé, humor, interview/profile, new product, opinion, photo feature, travel, medical feature.

"No inspirational tear-jerkers." Buys 30 mss/year. Query with 1-2 published clips. Length: 700-2,000 words. Pays up to $600/article. Sometimes pays expenses of writers on assignment.

Reprints: Accepts previously published submissions only if material does not appear in other disability publications and is rewritten. Send photocopy of article with rights for sale noted and information about when and where the article previously appeared. Pays 100% of amount paid for an original article, "because we require additional work."

Photos: State availability of photos with submission. Reviews contact sheets, transparencies, prints. Considers photo submissions made separately from any story, particularly in the areas of current events or lifestyle. Negotiates payment individually. Identification of subjects required. Buys one-time rights.

Columns/Departments: My Spin (opinion piece on disability-related topic), 700 words; Media (reviews of books, videos on disability), 300-400 words; People (personality profiles of people w/disabilities), 300-700 words. Buys 20 mss/year. Query with published clips. Send complete ms.

Tips: "Avoid 'courageous' or 'inspiring' tales of people who 'overcome' their disability. Writers don't have to be disabled to write for this magazine, but they should be familiar with the issues people with disabilities face. Most of our readers have disabilities, so write for this audience. We are most open to personality profiles, either for our short People department or as feature articles. In all of our departments, we like to see adventurous people, irreverent opinions and lively writing. Don't be afraid to let your *voice* come through."

RAGGED EDGE MAGAZINE, (formerly *The Disability Rag & Resource*), The Advocado Press, P.O. Box 145, Louisville KY 40201. E-mail: rgarr@iglou.com. Website: http://www.iglou.com/why/edge. Contact: Mary Johnson, editor. Bimonthly magazine covering disability-related rights issues. "*The Rag* is a forum for discussion of issues related to living with a disability in American society today. It is interested in exploring and exposing the roots of discrimination, supporting positive change and developing disability community and culture. Its readers tend to be active, involved and informed, and want to be better informed." Estab. 1980. Circ. 3,200. Pays on publication. Publishes ms an average of 8 months after acceptance. Byline given. Buys first North American serial rights. Editorial lead time 2 months. Submit seasonal material 6 months in advance. Accepts electronic submissions by disk. Reports in 1 month on queries; 3 months on mss. Sample copy for $4 (put toward your subscription if desired). Writer's guidelines for #10 SASE.

Nonfiction: Book excerpts, essays, exposé, humor, opinion, reportage, analysis. Does not want to see inspirational, profile, personal experience except as part of or sidebar to broader piece. Prefers journalistic approach, appealing to a broad audience that includes non-disabled readers as well. Buys 20 mss/year. Query. Length: 500-2,000 words. Pays $25-150 ($25 per printed page). Sometimes pays expenses of writers on assignment.

Photos: State availability of photos with submissions. Reviews contact sheets, prints. Offers $25/photo. Model releases, identification of subjects required. Buys one-time rights.

Columns/Departments: Reading (book reviews on disability, rights issues); Myth and Media (film, TV, other media images of disability); Views of Ourselves (disability identity). Length: 500-1,000 words. Buys 6 mss/year. Query with published clips. Pays $25-75.

Fiction: Anne Finger, fiction editor. Erotica, ethnic, experimental, humorous, mainstream, novel excerpts, science fiction, slice-of-life vignettes, interested in work by writers with disabilities or treating disability themes. "We'd love to see work from writers exploring the intersections of ethnicity and disability, sexual identity and disability, writing that's experimental; work in which it's clear that the writer has thought about disability culture and aesthetic practice." Short poems and short pieces of fiction have a better shot at getting published. Buys 2 mss/year (but would like to use more). Send complete ms. Length: 500-3,500 words. Pays $25-150 ($25 for printed page).

Poetry: Anne Finger, poetry editor. Any contemporary form, by writers with disabilities or dealing with aspects of the disability experience. Buys 18 poems/year. Submit maximum 5 poems. Pays $25/poem (unless exceptionally long, multi-part poems).

Tips: "Be familiar with the disability rights movement and the issues that concern it."

‡SILENT NEWS, World's Most Popular Newspaper of the Deaf and Hard of Hearing People, Silent News, Inc., 133 Gaither Dr., Suite E, Mt. Laurel NJ 08054-1710. (609)802-1977 (voice) or (609)802-1978 (TTY). Fax: (609)802-1979. E-mail: silentnews@aol.com. Contact: Betty Broecker, editor-in-chief. 50% freelance written. Monthly newspaper covering news of deaf, hard of hearing and deaf-blind concerns, the "World's Most Popular Newspaper of the Deaf and Hard of Hearing." Estab. 1969. Circ. 15,000. **Pays on acceptance**. Publishes ms an average of 2 months after acceptance. Byline given. Editorial lead time 2 months. Submit seasonal material 3 months in advance. Accepts simultaneous submissions. Reports in 2 weeks on queries; 2 months on mss.

Nonfiction: General interest, historical/nostalgic, humor, inspirational, interview/profile, new product, opinion, personal experience, photo feature, religious, technical, travel. All articles must concern deaf and hard of hearing or deaf-blind people. Special issues: Deaf Awareness (September); Holiday Shoppers Guide (November); Assistive Technology (March); Hard of Hearing Issues (May). Buys 60 mss/year. Query with published clips. Length: 100-500 words. Pays $40-200. Sometimes pays expenses of writers on assignment.

Reprints: Accepts previously published submissions.

Photos: Send photos with submission. Reviews negatives, 5×7 transparencies and prints. Negotiates payment individually. Identification of subjects required. Buys all rights.

Columns/Departments: National News, International News (both regarding hard of hearing and deaf); Sports (for the blind); all 500 words. Buys 60 mss/year. Query with published clips.

Fiction: "Presently we don't use fiction, but we would be interested in reviewing subject-appropriate material." Query.

Poetry: Light verse. "Nothing too deep!" Buys 12 poems/year. Submit maximum 2 poems. Length: 10-20 lines.

Fillers: Anecdotes, facts, gags to be illustrated, newsbreaks, short humor. Buys 100/year. Length: 50-100 words.
Tips: "Writers must have understanding of issues confronting deaf, hard of hearing, and deaf-blind people."

ENTERTAINMENT

This category's publications cover live, filmed or videotaped entertainment, including home video, TV, dance, theater and adult entertainment. In addition to celebrity interviews, most publications want solid reporting on trends and upcoming productions. Magazines in the Contemporary Culture and General Interest sections also use articles on entertainment. For those publications with an emphasis on music and musicians, see the Music section.

‡CINEASTE, America's Leading Magazine on the Art and Politics of the Cinema, Cineaste Publishers, Inc., 200 Park Ave. S., #1601, New York NY 10003. Phone/fax: (212)982-1241. E-mail: cineaste@cineaste.com. Contact: Gary Crowdus, editor. 30% freelance written. Quarterly magazine covering motion pictures with emphasis on social and political perspective on cinema. Estab. 1967. Circ. 10,000. Pays on publication. Publishes ms an average of 4 months after acceptance. Byline given. Offers 50% kill fee. Buys first North American serial rights. Editorial lead time 3 months. Submit seasonal material 4 months in advance. Reports in 1 month. Sample copy $5. Guidelines for #10 SASE.
Nonfiction: Essays, historical/nostalgic, humor, interview/profile, opinion. Buys 20-30 mss/year. Query with published clips. Length: 2,000-5,000 words. Pays $30-50. Pays in contributor copies at author's request.
Photos: State availability of photos with submission. Reviews transparencies, 8×10 prints. Offers no additional payment for photos accepted with ms. Identification of subjects required. Buys one-time rights.

CINEFANTASTIQUE MAGAZINE, The Review of Horror, Fantasy and Science Fiction Films, P.O. Box 270, Oak Park IL 60303. (708)366-5566. Fax: (708)366-1441. Editor: Frederick S. Clarke. 100% freelance written. Willing to work with new/unpublished writers. Bimonthly magazine covering horror, fantasy and science fiction films. Estab. 1970. Circ. 60,000. Pays on publication. Publishes ms an average of 6 months after acceptance. Byline given. Buys all magazine rights. Reports in 2 months or longer. Sample copy for $7 and 9×12 SAE.
Nonfiction: Historical/nostalgic (retrospects of film classics); interview/profile (film personalities); new product (new film projects); opinion (film reviews, critical essays); technical (how films are made). Buys 100-125 mss/year. Query with published clips and SASE. "Enclose SASE if you want your manuscript back." Length: 1,000-10,000 words. Pays expenses of writers on assignment.
Photos: State availability of photos with query letter or ms.
Tips: "Study the magazine to see the kinds of stories we publish. Develop original story suggestions; develop access to film industry personnel; submit reviews that show a perceptive point of view."

COUNTRY AMERICA, Meredith Corporation, 1716 Locust, Des Moines IA 50309-3023. (515)284-3787. Fax: (515)284-3035. Editor: Richard Krumme. Contact: Bill Eftink, managing editor. Bimonthly magazine covering country entertainment/lifestyle. Estab. 1989. Circ. 900,000. **Pays on acceptance.** Buys all rights (lifetime). Submit seasonal material 8 months or more in advance. Reports in 3 months. Guidelines for #10 SASE.
Nonfiction: Food, general interest, historical/nostalgic, how-to, interview/profile (country music entertainers), photo feature, travel. Special issues: Christmas, travel, country music. Buys 130 mss/year. Query. Pays $100-1,000. Sometimes pays expenses of writers on assignment.
Photos: State availability of photos with submission. Reviews contact sheets, negatives, 35mm transparencies. Offers $50-500/photo. Captions, identification of subjects required. Buys all rights.
Fillers: Country curiosities that deal with animals, people, etc.
Tips: "Think visually. Our publication will be light on text and heavy on photos. Be general; this is a general interest publication meant to be read by every member of the family. We are a service-oriented publication; please stress how-to sidebars and include addresses and phone numbers to help readers find out more."

DANCE INTERNATIONAL, Vancouver Ballet Society, 1415 Barclay St., Vancouver, British Columbia V6G 1J6 Canada. (604)681-1525. Fax: (604)681-7732. Editor: Maureen Riches. Contact: Deborah Meyers, contributing editor. 100% freelance written. Quarterly magazine covering dance arts. "Articles and reviews on current activities in world dance, with occasional historical essays (generally on Canadian issues); reviews of dance films, video and books." Estab. 1973. Circ. 850. Pays on publication. Publishes ms an average of 3 months after acceptance. Byline given. Offers 50% kill fee. Buys one-time rights. Editorial lead time 3 months. Submit seasonal material 2 months in advance. Reports in 2 weeks on queries; 1 month on mss. Sample copy and writer's guidelines free.
Nonfiction: Book excerpts, essays, historical/nostalgic, interview/profile, personal experience, photo feature. Buys 100 mss/year. Query. Length: 1,200-2,200 words. Pays $40-150.
Reprints: Accepts previously published submissions.
Photos: Send photos with submission. Reviews prints. Offers no additional payment for photos accepted with ms. Identification of subjects required.
Columns/Departments: Leland Windreich, copy editor. Dance Bookshelf (recent books reviewed), 1,200 words;

Regional Reports (events in each region), 1,200-2,000 words. Buys 100 mss/year. Query. Pays $60-70.
Tips: "Send résumé and samples of recent writings."

DRAMATICS MAGAZINE, Educational Theatre Association, 3368 Central Pkwy., Cincinnati OH 45225-2392. (513)559-1996. Fax: (513)559-0012. E-mail: pubs@one.net. Website: http://www.etassoc.org. Editor-in-Chief: Donald Corathers. 70% freelance written. Works with small number of new/unpublished writers. For theater arts students, teachers and others interested in theater arts education. Magazine published monthly, September-May. Estab. 1929. Circ. 35,000. **Pays on acceptance.** Publishes ms an average of 3 months after acceptance. Buys first North American serial rights. Byline given. Submit seasonal material 3 months in advance. Accepts simultaneous submissions. Reports in 3 months; longer on unsolicited mss. Sample copy for 9×12 SAE with 5 first-class stamps. Writer's guidelines free.
Nonfiction: How-to (technical theater, directing, acting, etc.), informational, interview, photo feature, humorous, profile, technical. Buys 30 mss/year. Submit complete ms. Length: 750-3,000 words. Pays $50-300. Rarely pays expenses of writers on assignment.
Reprints: Send tearsheet or photocopy of article or play, or typed ms with rights for sale noted and information about when and where the article previously appeared. Pays 75% of amount paid for an original article.
Photos: Purchased with accompanying ms. Uses b&w photos and transparencies. Query. Total purchase price for ms usually includes payment for photos.
Fiction: Drama (one-act and full-length plays). "No plays for children, Christmas plays or plays written with no attention paid to the conventions of theater." Prefers unpublished scripts that have been produced at least once. Buys 5-9 mss/year. Send complete ms. Pays $100-400.
Tips: "The best way to break in is to know our audience—drama students, teachers and others interested in theater—and to write for them. Writers who have some practical experience in theater, especially in technical areas, have a leg-up here, but we'll work with anybody who has a good idea. Some freelancers have become regular contributors. Others ignore style suggestions included in our writer's guidelines."

EAST END LIGHTS, The Quarterly Magazine for Elton John Fans ,Voice Communications Corp., P.O. Box 760, New Baltimore MI 48047. (810)949-7900. Fax: (810)949-2217. Contact: Tom Stanton, editor. 90% freelance written. Quarterly magazine covering British rock star Elton John. "In one way or another, a story must relate to Elton John, his activities or associates (past and present). We appeal to discriminating Elton fans. No gushing fanzine material. No current concert reviews." Estab. 1990. Circ. 1,400. Pays 3 weeks after publication. Publishes ms an average of 3 months after acceptance. Byline given. Offers 100% kill fee. Buys first rights and second serial (reprint) rights. Submit seasonal material 3 months in advance. Reports in 2 months. Sample copy for $2.
Nonfiction: Book excerpts, essays, exposé, general interest, historical/nostalgic, humor and interview/profile. Buys 20 mss/year. Query with or without published clips or send complete ms. Length: 400-1,000 words. Pays $50-200 for assigned articles; $40-150 for unsolicited articles. Pays with contributor copies only if the writer requests.
Reprints: Send tearsheet or photocopy of article or typed ms with rights for sale noted and information about when and where the article previously appeared. Pays 50% of amount paid for an original article.
Photos: State availability of photos with submission. Reviews negatives and 5×7 prints. Offers $40-75/photo. Buys one-time rights and all rights.
Columns/Departments: Clippings (non-wire references to Elton John in other publications), maximum 200 words. Buys 12 mss/year. Send complete ms. Length: 50-200 words. Pays $10-20.
Tips: "Approach with a well-thought-out story idea. We'll provide direction. All areas equally open. We prefer interviews with Elton-related personalities—past or present. We are particularly interested in music/memorabilia collecting of Elton material."

EMMY MAGAZINE, Academy of Television Arts & Sciences, 5220 Lankershim Blvd., North Hollywood CA 91601-3109. (818)754-2800. Fax: (818)761-2827. E-mail: emmymag@emmys.org. Website: http://www.emmys.org/. Editor/Publisher: Hank Rieger. Contact: Gail Polevoi, managing editor. 90% freelance written. Prefers to work with published established writers. Bimonthly magazine on television for TV professionals and enthusiasts. Circ. 12,000. Pays on publication or within 6 months. Publishes ms an average of 4 months after acceptance. Byline given. Offers 25% kill fee. Buys first North American serial rights. Reports in 1 month. Sample copy for 9×12 SAE with 6 first-class stamps.
Nonfiction: Articles on issues, trends, and VIPs (especially those behind the scenes) in broadcast and cable TV; programming and new technology. "We require TV industry expertise and clear, lively writing." Query with published clips. Length: 2,000 words. Pays $800-1,000. Pays some expenses of writers on assignment.
Columns/Departments: Most written by regulars, but newcomers can break into CloseUps or The Industry. Query with published clips. Length: 500-1,500 words, depending on department. Pays $250-750.
Tips: "Study our publication. No fanzine, academic or nostalgic approaches, please."

‡ENTERTAINMENT WEEKLY, Time Inc. Magazine Co., 1675 Broadway, New York NY 10016. (212)522-5600. Fax: (212)522-0074. Publisher: Michael J. Klingensmith. Contact: Jeannie Park, assistant managing editor. Weekly magazine covering popular entertainment. "*Entertainment Weekly* provides both a critical guide to popular culture and an informative inside look at the people, motives and ideas that shape the increasingly influential world of entertainment." Estab. 1990. Circ. 1,201,000. Pays on publication. Byline usually given. Offers 50% kill fee. Buys all rights. Accepts simultaneous submissions.
Nonfiction: Buys fewer than 5 mss/year. Query with published clips. Length: 1,500-3,000 words. Pays $1-2/word.

Columns/Departments: Length: 500-1,000 words. Buys 10 mss/year. Query with published clips. Pays $1-2/word.
Tips: "*EW* editors welcome story suggestions covering almost any aspect of entertainment news, with emphasis on the word 'news.' While most of our coverage focuses on popular culture on a national level, our monthly section, Metro, covers the local entertainment scene in major cities. We are interested in news scoops about entertainment people and products; inside stories about the making of movies, TV, albums, etc.; entertainment trends; and entertainment-related or celebrity anecdotes (with quotes). We are generally not interested in ideas for celebrity profiles or other obvious entertainment-related stories. An *EW* editor's 'dream' article would be one that breaks news and makes news; is thoroughly researched and reported, with quotes from significant industry insiders; is written in a lively and accessible manner; and would never have been thought of by one of our own staffers. Writers wishing to work for *EW* must grasp our 'style'—of approach, reporting, and writing. The best preparation for querying *EW* is to read it closely."

ET AL., The Publisher's Group, P.O. Box 510366, Salt Lake City UT 84151-0366. Fax: (801)322-1098. E-mail: annee@thepublishers.com. Contact: Anne E. Zombro, vice president of publishing. 50% freelance written. Quarterly magazine covering entertainment. "Entertainment and fine arts are the major thrusts of *Et Al*. Includes articles on celebrities, Q&As and stories of everyday folks who have made a difference." Estab. 1996. Circ. 15,000. Pays on publication. Publishes ms an average of 4 months after acceptance. Byline given. Buys first North American serial and second serial (reprint) rights. Editorial lead time 2 months. Submit seasonal material 4 months in advance. Accepts simultaneous submissions. Reports in 1 month on queries; 2 months on mss. Sample copy for $3 and 9×12 SASE. Writer's guidelines for #10 SASE.
Nonfiction: General interest, inspirational, interview/profile. Nothing controversial. Buys 6-8 mss/year. Query with published clips. Length: 1,000-1,300 words. Pays $125-800.
Reprints: Accepts previously published submissions. Send tearsheet or photocopy of article or typed ms with rights for sale noted and information about when and where the article previously appeared. Pays 50% of amount paid for an original article.
Photos: Send photos with submission. Reviews 4×5 transparencies (preferred), any size prints. Negotiates payment individually. Captions, model releases, identification of subjects required. Buys one-time or all rights.

FANGORIA: Horror in Entertainment, Starlog Communications, Inc., 475 Park Ave. S., 8th Floor, New York NY 10016. (212)689-2830. Fax: (212)889-7933. Contact: Anthony Timpone, editor. 95% freelance written. Works with a small number of new/unpublished writers each year. Magazine published 10 times/year covering horror films, TV projects, comics, videos and literature and those who create them. "We emphasize the personalities and behind-the-scenes angles of horror filmmaking." Estab. 1979. Pays on publication. Publishes ms an average of 3 months after acceptance. Byline given. Buys all rights. Submit seasonal material 6 months in advance. Reports in 6 weeks. "We provide an assignment sheet (deadlines, info) to writers, thus authorizing queried stories that we're buying." Sample copy for $3.50 and 10×13 SAE with 4 first-class stamps. Writer's guidelines for #10 SASE.
  • *Fangoria* is looking for more articles on independent filmmakers and video game companies.
Nonfiction: Book excerpts; interview/profile of movie directors, makeup FX artists, screenwriters, producers, actors, noted horror/thriller novelists and others—with genre credits; special FX and special makeup FX how-it-was-dones (on filmmaking only). No "think" pieces, opinion pieces, reviews (excluding books), or sub-theme overviews (i.e., vampire in the cinema). Buys 100 mss/year. Query by letter (never by phone) with ideas and published clips. Length: 1,000-3,500 words. Pays $100-225. Rarely pays expenses of writers on assignment. Avoids articles on science fiction films—see listing for sister magazine *Starlog* in *Writer's Market* Science Fiction consumer magazine section.
Reprints: Send photocopy of article and information about when and where the article previously appeared. Pays 25% of amount paid for an original article.
Photos: State availability of photos. Reviews b&w and color prints and transparencies. "No separate payment for photos provided by film studios." Captions, identification of subjects required. Photo credit given. Buys all rights.
Columns/Departments: Monster Invasion (news about new film productions; must be exclusive, early information; also mini-interviews with filmmakers and novelists). Query with published clips. Length: 300-500 words. Pays $45-75.
  • *Fangoria* emphasizes that it does not publish fiction or poetry.
Tips: "Other than recommending that you study one or several copies of *Fangoria*, we can only describe it as a horror film magazine consisting primarily of interviews with technicians and filmmakers in the field. Be sure to stress the interview subjects' words—not your own opinions as much. We're very interested in small, independent filmmakers working outside of Hollywood. These people are usually more accessible to writers, and more cooperative. *Fangoria* is also sort of a *de facto* bible for youngsters interested in movie makeup careers and for young filmmakers. We are devoted only to *reel* horrors—the fakery of films, the imagery of the horror fiction of a Stephen King or a Clive Barker—*we do not* want nor would we *ever* publish articles on real-life horrors, murders, etc. A writer must *like* and *enjoy* horror films and horror fiction to work for us. If the photos in *Fangoria* disgust you, if the sight of (*stage*) blood repels you, if you feel 'superior' to horror (and its fans), you aren't a writer for us and we certainly aren't the market for you. We love giving new writers their *first* chance to break into print in a national magazine."

FILM COMMENT, Film Society of Lincoln Center, 70 Lincoln Center Plaza, New York NY 10023. (212)875-5610. Fax: (212)875-5636. E-mail: rtjfc@aol.com. Editor: Richard T. Jameson. 100% freelance written. Bimonthly magazine covering film criticism and film history. "*FC* publishes authoritative, personal writing (not journalism) reflecting experience of and involvement with film as an art form." Estab. 1962. Circ. 30,000. Pays on publication. Publishes ms an average of 2 months after acceptance. Byline given. Offers 50% kill fee (assigned articles only). Editorial lead time 6 weeks. Accepts simultaneous submissions. Reports in 2 weeks on queries. Writer's guidelines free.

Nonfiction: Essays, historical/nostalgic, interview/profile, opinion, personal experience. Buys 100 mss/year. Send complete ms. "We respond to queries, but rarely *assign* a writer we don't know." Length: 800-8,000 words. "We don't use a separate pay scale for solicited or unsolicited. There is no fixed rate, but roughly based on 3 words/$1."

Reprints: Rarely accepts previously published submissions. Send typed ms with information about when and where the article previously appeared. Pays 50% of amount paid for an original article.

Photos: State availability of photos with submission. Offers no additional payment for photos accepted with ms. Buys one-time rights.

Columns/Departments: Life With Video (impact of video on availability and experience of films; video as new imaginative dimension), 1,000-2,000 words. Pays $250 and up.

Tips: "Demonstrate ability and inclination to write *FC*-worthy articles. We read and consider everything we get, and we do print unknowns and first-timers. Probably the writer with a shorter submission (1,000-2,000 words) has a better chance than with an epic article that would fill half the issue."

GLOBE, A Globe Communications Corp. Publication, 5401 NW Broken Sound Blvd., Boca Raton FL 33487. (561)997-7733. Publisher: James Fraguela. Weekly. "*Globe* is edited for an audience interested in a wide range of human-interest stories, with particular emphasis on celebrities, health, medicine, science and news of the great and near-great in the world of entertainment, politics and business. Topics related to human success and suffering, poverty and riches, and how men and women strive to overcome obstacles and meet day-to-day contemporary challenges are featured, with strong emphasis on success and achievement in many areas of human endeavor." Circ. 1,615. This magazine did not respond to our request for information. Query before submitting.

HOME THEATER, Curt Co./Freedom Group, 29160 Heathecliff Rd., Malibu CA 90265. (310)589-3100. Fax: (212)333-5560. E-mail: peterb@curtco.com. Website: www.hometheatermag.com. Contact: Peter Barry, editorial director. Managing Editor: Christy Grosz. 30% freelance written. Monthly magazine covering audio/video hardware and software. Estab. 1994. Circ. 100,000. Pays on publication. Publishes ms an average of 1 month after acceptance. Byline given. Buys first North American serial, second serial and electronic rights. Editorial lead time 3 months. Reports in 2 months. Sample copy for $4.95.

Nonfiction: Interview/profile, new product, technical. Publishes quarterly buyer's guides. No general interest, non-technical articles. Buys 50 mss/year. Query with published clips. Length: 150-2,500 words. Pays $100-1,000. Sometimes pays expenses of writers on assignment.

Photos: State availability of photos with submission. Reviews contact sheets, negatives, transparencies, prints. Negotiates payment individually. Captions required. Buys all rights.

Columns/Departments: Dish Head (satellite TV), 1,500 words; Tech Talk, 1,000 words. Buys 20 mss/year. Query. Pays $500-1,000.

Tips: "You must be highly experienced with audio and/or video gear or particularly knowledgeable about relevant new technologies, and preferably a published writer."

KPBS ON AIR MAGAZINE, San Diego's Guide to Public Broadcasting, KPBS Radio/TV, 5200 Campanile Dr., San Diego CA 92182-5400. (619)594-3766. Fax: (619)265-6417. Contact: Michael Good, editor. 15% freelance written. Monthly magazine on public broadcasting programming and San Diego arts. "Our readers are very intelligent, sophisticated and rather mature. Your writing should be, too." Estab. 1970. Circ. 63,000. Pays on publication. Publishes ms an average of 1 month after acceptance. Byline given. Offers 50% kill fee. Not copyrighted. Buys first North American serial rights. Submit seasonal material 3 months in advance. Reports in 3 months. Sample copy for 9×12 SAE with 4 first-class stamps.

Nonfiction: Interview/profile of PBS personalities and/or artists performing in San Diego, opinion, profiles of public TV and radio personalities, backgrounds on upcoming programs. Nothing over 1,500 words. Buys 60 mss/year. Query with published clips. Length: 300-1,500 words. Pays 20¢/word, 25¢/word if the article is received via modem or computer disk. Sometimes pays expenses of writers on assignment.

Reprints: Rarely accepts reprints of previously published submissions. Send tearsheet or typed ms with rights for sale noted and information about when and where the article previously appeared. Pays 25¢/word.

Photos: State availability of photos with submission. Reviews transparencies, 5×7 prints. Offers $30-300/photo. Identification of subjects required. Buys one-time rights.

Columns/Departments: On the Town (upcoming arts events in San Diego), 800 words; Short Takes (backgrounds on public TV shows), 500 words; Radio Notes (backgrounders on public radio shows), 500 words. Buys 35 mss/year. Query with or without published clips. Length: 300-800 words. Pays 20¢/word; 25¢/word if the article is received via modem or computer disk.

Tips: "Feature stories for national writers are most open to freelancers. Arts stories for San Diego writers are most open. Read the magazine, then talk to me."

LONG ISLAND UPDATE, 990 Motor Pkwy., Central Islip NY 11722. (516)435-8890. Fax: (516)435-8925. Contact: Cheryl Ann Meglio, editor. Managing Editor: Michael Coffino. 50% freelance written. Monthly magazine covering "regional entertainment interests as well as national interests." Estab. 1980. Circ. 60,000. Pays on publication. Publishes ms an average of 4 months after acceptance. Byline given. Buys all rights. Submit seasonal material 3 months in advance. Reports in 5 weeks on queries.

Nonfiction: General interest, humor, interview/profile, new product, travel. Query with published clips. Length: 250-1,500 words. Pays $25-125.

Reprints: Send photocopy of article and information about when and where the article previously appeared. Pays 100% of amount paid for an original article.

Columns/Departments: Nightcap (humor piece), 700 words. Query with published clips. Pays $50.

THE NEWFOUNDLAND HERALD, Sunday Herald Ltd., Box 2015, St. John's, Newfoundland A1C 5R7 Canada. (709)726-7060. Fax: (709)726-8227/6971. E-mail: herald@voyager.newcomm.net. Editor-in-Chief: Greg Stirling. Contact: Karen Dawe, managing editor. 25% freelance written. Weekly entertainment magazine. "We prefer Newfoundland and Labrador-related items." Estab. 1946. Circ. 45,000. Pays on publication. Publishes ms an average of 2 months after acceptance. Byline given. Buys first North American serial, one-time or all rights. Editorial lead time 4 months. Submit seasonal material 3 months in advance. Sample copy for $5. Writer's guidelines free via fax ($1 by mail).

Nonfiction: General interest, how-to, interview/profile, travel. No opinion, humor, poetry, fiction, satire. Buys 500 mss/year. Query with published clips. Length: 700-2,500 words. Pays $30 minimum. Sometimes pays expenses of writers on assignment.

Reprints: Send typed ms with rights for sale noted (disk or e-mail attachment of text preferred).

Photos: Send photos with submission. Offers $7.50-25/photo. Captions required. Buys one-time rights.

Columns/Departments: Music (current artists), Video/Movies (recent releases/themes), TV shows (Top 20); all 1,500-2,500 words. Buys 500 mss/year. Query with published clips.

Tips: "Know something about Newfoundlanders and Labradorians—for example, travel writers should know where we like to travel. No opinion pieces, satire, humor or poetry is purchased; fiction is not accepted. Original cartoons which focus on local politics will be considered. Photos should be submitted with all articles. Please use color 35mm print or slide film. No b&w photos unless otherwise requested. Please read several issues before submitting any material. Query first. If the story is breaking, phone. If you can't afford it, leave a message and we will call you back."

PEOPLE, Time Inc. Magazine Co., Time & Life Bldg., Rockefeller Center, New York NY 10020. (212)522-1212. Fax: (212)522-0536. Publisher: Nora McAniff. Weekly magazine covering celebrities and other interesting people. "*People* is a guide to who and what is hot in the arts, science, business, politics, television, movies, books, records and sports." Estab. 1984. Circ. 2,284,000. This magazine did not respond to our request for information. Query before submitting.

‡PERFORMING ARTS MAGAZINE, 3539 Motor Ave., Los Angeles CA 90034. (310)839-8000. Editor: Dana Kitaj. 100% freelance written. Monthly magazine covering theater, music, dance, visual art. "We publish general pieces on the arts of a historical or 'current-events' nature." Estab. 1965. Circ. 700,000. Pays on publication. Publishes ms an average of 2 months after acceptance. Offers $150 kill fee. Buys one-time rights. Submit seasonal material 3 months in advance. Sample copy for 9×12 SASE.

Nonfiction: Book excerpts (on the Arts), general interest (theater, dance, opera), historical/nostalgic, interview/profile (performers, artists), travel. No critical texts, religious, political essays or reviews. Buys 60 mss/year. Query with published clips. Length: 1,500-3,000 words. Pays $500-1,000. Sometimes pays expenses of writers on assignment.

Reprints: Accepts previously published submissions.

Photos: State availability of photos with submission. Reviews transparencies. Offers no additional payment for photos accepted with ms. Buys one-time rights.

Tips: "Theater, dance and music on the West Coast are our main interests. Write broad information pieces or interviews."

‡PREMIERE, Hachette Filipacchi Magazines, 1633 Broadway, New York NY 10019. (212)767-5400. Fax: (212)767-5444. E-mail: frcohn@aol.com. Website: http://www.premieremag.com. Editor-in-Chief: James Meigs. Contact: Katherine Heintzellman, executive editor. Monthly magazine covering movies. "*Premiere* is a magazine for young adults that goes behind the scenes of movies in release and production. Feature articles include interviews, profiles plus film commentary and analysis. Monthly departments provide coverage of the movie business, video technology and hardware, home video, film and video reviews/releases, movie music/scoring and books." Estab. 1987. Circ. 617,000. **Pays on acceptance.** Byline given. Offers 25-33% kill fee. Buys all rights. Reports in 1 month. Writer's guidelines for #10 SASE.

Nonfiction: "Deeply reported, well-written pieces that focus on how movies are made." Query with published clips by mail or e-mail. Length: 2,000-4,000 words. Pays $1-2/word. Pays the expenses of writers on assignment.

Columns/Departments: Length: 750-2,000 words. Query with published clips by mail or e-mail. Pays $1/word.

Tips: "We are not interested in queries that simply list the names of actors a writer would like to interview. Writers without specialized experience covering the film industry are generally not considered for freelance assignments."

PRE-VUE ENTERTAINMENT MAGAZINE, National Pre-Vue Network, 7825 Fay Ave., La Jolla CA 92037. (619)456-5577. Fax: (619)542-0114. E-mail: prevuemag@aol.com. Website: Pre-VueMagazine.com. Contact: Penny Langford, publisher. 100% freelance written. Bimonthly magazine covering movies, music celebrities. Estab. 1990. Circ. 200,000. Sometimes pays on acceptance, sometimes up to 30 days after publication. Byline given. Offers 10% kill fee. Buys one-time rights. Editorial lead time 1 month. Submit seasonal material 2 months in advance. Accepts simultaneous submissions. Reports in 2 weeks on queries. Sample copy for 6×9 SAE with 55¢ postage. Writer's guidelines free.

Nonfiction: General interest, interview/profile, photo feature. Special issues: travel, fashion, vacations of film and music celebrities. Buys 30 mss/year. Query with published clips. Length: 225-1,200 words. Pays $100-300 for assigned articles; $75-200 for unsolicited articles. Sometimes pays expenses of writers on assignment.

Photos: State availability of photos with submission. Reviews transparencies. Negotiates payment individually. Captions, model releases, identification of subjects required. Buys one-time rights.

Columns/Departments: Interviews (personal lifestyles), 225-1,200 words. Buys 6-12 mss/year. Query with published clips. Pays $25-75.

Fillers: Facts, gags to be illustrated, newsbreaks, short humor. Buys 6/year. Length: 25-75 words. Pays $25-50.

Tips: "Writers who have an appealing writing style which shows personality as well as well-thought-out and well researched text, tend to get more assignments."

‡**THE READERS SHOWCASE**, Suggitt Publishing, Ltd., 10608-172 St., Edmonton, Alberta T5S 1H8 Canada. (403)486-5802. Fax: (403)481-9276. E-mail: suggitt@planet.eon.net. Contact: Tanis Nessler, editor. 100% freelance written. Monthly magazine covering books available at SmithBooks and Coles bookstores. "*The Readers Showcase* consists of author interviews, book reviews, book excerpts, industry news, contests, book-related editorials, etc." Estab. 1993. Circ. 300,000 (1,000,000 in November). Pays on publication. Publishes ms an average of 1 month after acceptance. Byline given. Offers 50% kill fee. Editorial lead time 2 months. Submit seasonal material 2 months in advance. Accepts simultaneous submissions. Sample copy and writer's guidelines free.

Nonfiction: Book excerpts, interview/profile, book reviews. Buys 300 mss/year. Query with published clips. Length: 400-2,000 words. Pays 15¢/word. Sometimes pays expenses of writers on assignment.

Reprints: Accepts previously published submissions.

RIGHT ON!, Sterling's Magazines, 233 Park Ave. S., New York NY 10003. (212)780-3519. Contact: Cynthia Horner, editorial director. 10% freelance written. Monthly black entertainment magazine for teenagers and young adults. Circ. 250,000. Pays on publication. Publishes ms an average of 3 months after acceptance. Byline given. Buys all rights. Submit seasonal material 4 months in advance. Reports in 1 month on queries.

Nonfiction: Interview/profile. "We only publish entertainment-oriented stories or celebrity interviews." Buys 15-20 mss/year. Query with or without published clips, or send ms. Length: 500-4,000 words. Pays $50-200. Sometimes pays expenses of writers on assignment.

Photos: State availability of photos with submission. Reviews transparencies, 8 × 10 b&w prints. Offers no additional payment for photos accepted with ms. Identification of subjects required. Buys one-time or all rights.

‡**SATELLITE ORBIT**, Commtek Communications Corp., Suite 600, 8330 Boone Blvd., Vienna VA 22182. (703)827-0511. Fax: (703)827-0159. E-mail: satorbit@aol.com. Publisher: John Misrasi. Editor: Linda Casey. 25% freelance written. Monthly magazine on television available to owners of large satellite dishes. Estab. 1979. **Pays on acceptance.** Publishes an average of 2 months after acceptance. Kill fee varies. Reports in 1 month.

Nonfiction: "Wants to see articles on satellite programming, equipment, television trends, sports and celebrity interviews." Query with published clips. Length: 700 words. Pay varies.

Reprints: Pays 20% of amount paid for an original article.

SOAP OPERA DIGEST, K-III Magazines, 45 W. 25th St., New York NY 10010. Contact: Lynn Leahey, editor. Managing Editor: Carolyn Hinsey. 5% freelance written. Bimonthly magazine covering soap operas. "Extensive knowledge of daytime and prime time soap operas is required." Estab. 1975. Circ. 1,400,000. **Pays on acceptance.** Publishes ms an average of 3 months after acceptance. Byline given. Offers 30% kill fee. Buys first North American serial and second serial (reprint) rights. Submit seasonal material 4 months in advance. Reports in 1 month.

Nonfiction: Interview/profile. No essays. Buys 10 mss/year. Query with published clips. Length: 1,000-2,000 words. Pays $250-500 for assigned articles; $150-250 for unsolicited articles. Pays meal expenses of writers on assignment.

Photos: Offers no additional payment for photos accepted with ms. Buys all rights.

‡**SOAP OPERA MAGAZINE**, American Media, Inc., 660 White Plains Rd., Tarrytown NY 10591. (914)332-5021. Fax: (800)331-4936. Editor: Garrett A. Foster. Contact: Lynne Dorsey, executive editor. 15% freelance written. Weekly magazine covering daytime soap operas. "We cover TV soap operas from a storyline and off-camera standpoint." Estab. 1991. Circ. 350,000. Pays on publication. Publishes ms an average of 2 weeks after acceptance. Byline given. Buys first North American serial rights. Editorial lead time 2 weeks. Submit seasonal material 2 months in advance.

Nonfiction: No articles not pertaining to the field of soap opera. Buys 100 mss/year. Query with published clips. Length: 1,000-2,000 words. Pays $250-750. Sometimes pays expenses of writers on assignment.

Photos: State availability of photos with submission. Negotiates payment individually. Captions, identification of subjects required. Buys one-time rights.

Columns/Departments: Buzz in the Biz (soap news), 100 words. Buys 100 mss/year. Query. Pays $50-100.

Tips: "You have to be interested in soap operas and be able to develop story ideas that will appeal to other soap fans. It's that simple."

‡**SOAP OPERA UPDATE**, Bauer Publishing, 270 Sylvan Ave., Englewood Cliffs NJ 07632. (201)569-6699. Fax: (201)569-2510. Editor-in-Chief: Richard Spencer. 25% freelance written. Biweekly magazine on daytime serials. "We cover the world of daytime and prime time soap operas with preview information, in-depth interviews and exclusive photos, feature interviews, history, character sketches, events where soap stars are seen and participate." Estab. 1988.

Circ. 288,000. Pays on publication. Byline given. Buys first North American serial rights. Submit seasonal material 3 months in advance. Reports in 1 month.

Nonfiction: Humor, interview/profile. "Only articles directly about actors, shows or history of a show." Buys 100 mss/year. Query with published clips. Length: 750-2,200 words. Pays $200. Sometimes pays expenses of writers on assignment.

Photos: State availability of photos with submission. Reviews transparencies. Offers $25. Captions and identification of subjects required. Buys all rights.

Tips: "Come up with fresh, new approaches to stories about soap operas and their people. Submit ideas and clips. Take a serious approach; don't talk down to the reader. All articles must be well written and the writer knowledgeable about his subject matter."

SOAP OPERA WEEKLY, K-3 Magazines Publication, 1775 Broadway, Suite 720, New York NY 10019. (212)641-5240. Fax:(212)641-5260. Publisher: Linda Vaughan. Weekly magazine. "*Soap Opera Weekly* is a pictorial newsmagazine devoted to the plots and personalities that enliven the TV soaps. Stories cover the stars who make the headlines; features on food, fashion, fitness and personal style." Estab. 1989. Circ. 5,084. This magazine did not respond to our request for information. Query before submitting.

‡STAR MAGAZINE, 600 S. East Coast Ave., Lantana FL 33462. (916)332-5000. Editor-in-Chief: Phil Bunton. Contact: Dick Belsky. Weekly magazine covering celebrity news. Estab. 1973. Circ. 2,220,700. Pays on publication. Publishes ms 10 days after acceptance. Buys all rights. Responds in 1 day. Sample copy for $1.49. No writer's guidelines.

Nonfiction: Expose, general interest, interview/profile, photo feature—all celebrity news-related. Buys 2,000 mss/year. Query with published clips. Length: 1,000 words. Pays $300-1,000.

TDR; The Drama Review: The Journal of Performance Studies, New York University, 721 Broadway, 6th Floor, New York NY 10003. (212)998-1626. Fax: (212)995-4571. E-mail: tdr@nyu.edu. Managing Editor: Julia Whitworth. Editor: Richard Schechner. Contact: Mariellen R. Sandford, associate editor. 95% freelance written. Works with a small number of new/unpublished writers each year. Quarterly magazine "with emphasis not only on theater but also dance, ritual, musical performance, performance art and other facets of performative behavior. For the theater and art community, students and professors of performance studies, anthropology and related fields. Political material is welcome." Estab. 1955. Circ. 5,000. Pays on publication. Submit material 1 year in advance. Reports in 3 months. Publishes ms an average of 6 months after acceptance. Sample copy for $10 (from MIT Press). Writer's guidelines free.

Nonfiction: Buys 10 mss/issue. Query by letter only. Pay determined by page count. Submit both hard copy and disk (Word or WordPerfect).

Reprints: Accepts previously published submissions if published in another language. Send information about when and where the article previously appeared.

Photos: State availability of photos and artwork with submission. Captions required.

Tips: "*TDR* is a place where contrasting ideas and opinions meet. A forum for writing about performances and the social, economic and political contexts in which performances happen. The editors want interdisciplinary, intercultural, multivocal, eclectic submissions."

‡THEATREFORUM, International Theatre Journal, UCSD Department of Theatre, 9500 Gilman Dr., La Jolla CA 92093-0344. (619)534-6598. Fax: (619)534-1080. E-mail: theatreforum@ucsd.edu./ Editor: Jim Carmody. 75% freelance written. Semiannual magazine covering performance, theatrical and otherwise. "*TheatreForum* is an international journal of theater and performance art and dance theater and music theater and forms yet to be devised. We publish performance texts, interviews with artists on their creative process, and articles about innovative productions and groups. Written by and for members of both the academic and artistic community, we represent a wide variety of aesthetic and cultural interests." Estab. 1992. Circ. 2,000. Pays on publication. Byline given. Buys one-time rights or anthology rights for scripts. Editorial lead time 4 months. Query for electronic submissions. Reports in 1 month on queries; 2 months on mss. Sample copy for $5. Writer's guidelines for #10 SASE.

Nonfiction: Essays, interview/profile, photo feature, performance criticism. Buys 10-12 mss/year. Query with published clips. Length: 1,000-5,000 words. Pays 5¢/word.

Photos: State availability of photos with submission. Negotiates payment individually. Identification of subjects required. Buys one-time rights.

Scripts: Previously published plays are not considered. Buys 4-6 mss/year. Query with published clips. Pays $200.

Tips: "We are interested in documenting, discussing, and disseminating innovative and provocative theaterworks. Nontraditional and inventive texts (plays) are welcome. We also publish in-depth analyses of innovative theatrical productions. We are interested in finding artists who want to write about other artists."

TV GUIDE, 1211 Avenue of the Americas, New York NY 10036. Contact: Editor (National Section). 50% freelance written. Prefers to work with published/established writers but works with a small number of new/unpublished writers each year. Weekly. Estab. 1953. Circ. 13,000,000.

Nonfiction: "The national editorial section looks at the shows, the stars and covers the medium's impact on news, sports, politics, literature, the arts, science and social issues through reports, profiles, features and commentaries."

US, Wenner Media Inc., 1290 Avenue of the Americas, 2nd Floor, New York NY 10104. (212)767-8205. Publisher: Andy Amill. Monthly magazine. "*US* covers films, video, television, and contemporary music, providing in-depth editorial on top personalities, events and developments that are current in the world of entertainment." Estab. 1977. Circ. 29,708. This magazine did not respond to our request for information. Query before submitting.

ETHNIC/MINORITY

Ideas and concerns of interest to specific nationalities and religions are covered by publications in this category. General interest lifestyle magazines for these groups are also included. Many ethnic publications are locally-oriented or highly specialized and do not wish to be listed in a national publication such as *Writer's Market*. Query the editor of an ethnic publication with which you're familiar before submitting a manuscript, but do not consider these markets closed because they are not listed in this section. Additional markets for writing with an ethnic orientation are located in the following sections: Career, College and Alumni; Juvenile; Literary and "Little"; Men's; Women's; and Teen and Young Adult.

AIM MAGAZINE, AIM Publishing Company, 7308 S. Eberhart Ave., Chicago IL 60620-0554. (773)874-6184. Managing Editor: Dr. Myron Apilado. Contact: Ruth Apilado, associate editor. Estab. 1975. 75% freelance written. Works with a small number of new/unpublished writers each year. Quarterly magazine on social betterment that promotes racial harmony and peace for high school, college and general audience. Circ. 10,000. Pays on publication. Publishes ms an average of 3 months after acceptance. Offers 60% kill fee. Not copyrighted. Buys one-time rights. Submit seasonal material 6 months in advance. Accepts simultaneous submissions. Reports in 2 months on queries. Sample copy and writer's guidelines for $4 and 9×12 SAE with $1.70 postage.
Nonfiction: Exposé (education); general interest (social significance); historical/nostalgic (Black or Indian); how-to (create a more equitable society); profile (one who is making social contributions to community); book reviews and reviews of plays "that reflect our ethnic/minority orientation." No religious material. Buys 16 mss/year. Send complete ms. Length: 500-800 words. Pays $25-35.
Photos: Reviews b&w prints. Captions, identification of subjects required.
Fiction: Ethnic, historical, mainstream, suspense. "Fiction that teaches the brotherhood of man." Buys 20 mss/year. Send complete ms. Length: 1,000-1,500 words. Pays $25-35.
Poetry: Avant-garde, free verse, light verse. No "preachy" poetry. Buys 20 poems/year. Submit maximum 5 poems. Length: 15-30 lines. Pays $3-5.
Fillers: Jokes, anecdotes, newsbreaks. Buys 30/year. Length: 50-100 words. Pays $5.
Tips: "Interview anyone of any age who unselfishly is making an unusual contribution to the lives of less fortunate individuals. Include photo and background of person. We look at the nations of the world as part of one family. Short stories and historical pieces about Blacks and Indians are the areas most open to freelancers. Subject matter of submission is of paramount concern for us rather than writing style. Articles and stories showing the similarity in the lives of people with different racial backgrounds are desired."

ALBERTA SWEETGRASS, Aboriginal Multi-Media Society of Alberta, 15001 112th Ave., Edmonton, Alberta T5M 2V6 Canada. (403)455-2945. Fax: (403)455-7639. E-mail: edsweet@ammsa.com. Contact: R. John Hayes, editor. Monthly tabloid newspaper. 50% freelance written. "*Alberta Sweetgrass* is a community paper which focuses on people, especially successful people, from within Alberta's first nations, métis and non-status aboriginal communities." Estab. 1993. Circ. 7,500. Pays 10th of month following publication. Publishes ms an average of 1 month after acceptance. Byline given. Offers 50% kill fee. Buys first, one-time or second serial rights. Editorial lead time 2 months. Reports in 2 weeks on queries; 1 month on mss. Sample copy free. Writer's guidelines and production schedule for #10 SASE.
Nonfiction: Essays, features, general interest, interview/profile, opinion, photo feature, travel, community-based stories, all with an Alberta angle (no exceptions). Usually runs 2-3 focus sections/month. Buys 120 mss/year. Query with published clips and SASE. Length: 300-1,000 words (most often 500-800 words). Pays $3/published inch for one-source stories; $3.60 for multiple sources (reduced rate for excess editorial work). Pays expenses of writers by prior arrangement.
Reprints: Send typed ms with rights for sale noted. Pays 50% of amount paid for an original article.
Photos: State availability of photos with submission. Captions, model releases, identification of subjects required. Reviews contact sheets, negatives, transparencies, prints. Offers $15/b&w photo; $50/color cover; $25/inside color.
Columns/Departments: Book/Film/Art Reviews (Alberta Aboriginal), 450-500 words; Briefs (community news shorts), 150-200 words. Buys 40-60 mss/year. Query with published clips or send complete ms. Pays $3/published inch for single-source stories, $3.60/published inch for multiple-source stories.
Tips: "We are moving from profiles to more news-hook-oriented items. Don't let our Alberta angle requirement scare you off. We've had stories from Alaska, Minnesota, the Vatican and all across Canada in the last year."

‡**AMERICAN JEWISH WORLD**, AJW Publishing Inc., 4509 Minnetonka Blvd., Minneapolis MN 55416. (612)920-7000. Fax: (612)920-6205. E-mail: 6803375@mcimail.com. Contact: Marshall Hoffman, editor. 1-5% freelance written. Weekly Jewish newspaper covering local, national and international stories. Estab. 1912. Circ. 6,500. Pays on publication. Publishes ms an average of 4 months after acceptance. Byline given. Publication copyrighted. Makes work-for-hire assignments. Submit seasonal material 3 months in advance. Accepts simultaneous submissions. Sample copy and editorial calendar free.

• *American Jewish World* is focusing more on Midwest and Minnesota angles.

Nonfiction: Essays, exposé, general interest, historical/nostalgic, humor, inspirational, interview/profile, opinion, personal experience, photo feature, religious, travel. Buys 12-15 mss/year. Query with or without published clips. No unsolicited mss. Length: 750 words maximum. Pays $10-75. Sometimes pays expenses of writers on assignment.

Reprints: Send typed ms with rights for sale noted.

Photos: State availability of photos with submission. Reviews prints. Pays $5/photo. Identification of subjects required. Buys one-time rights.

AMERICAN VISIONS, The Magazine of Afro-American Culture, 1156 15th St. NW, Suite 615, Washington DC 20005. (202)496-9593. Fax: (202)496-9851. E-mail: articles@avs.americanvisions.com. Website: http://www.americanv isions.com. Editor: Joanne Harris. Contact: Eric T. Vinson, Jr., managing editor. 75% freelance written. Bimonthly magazine on African-American art, culture and history. "Editorial is reportorial, current, objective, 'pop-scholarly'. Audience is ages 25-54, mostly black, college educated. The scope of the magazine includes the arts, history, literature, cuisine, genealogy and travel—all filtered through the prism of the African-American experience." Estab. 1986. Circ. 125,000. Pays 30 days after publication. Publishes ms an average of 2 months after acceptance. Byline given. Offers 25% kill fee. Buys all and second serial (reprint) rights. Submit seasonal material 5 months in advance. Accepts simultaneous submissions. Reports in 3 months. Free sample copy and writer's guidelines with SASE.

Nonfiction: Book excerpts, general interest, historical, interview/profile literature, photo feature, travel. Publishes travel supplements—domestic, Africa, Europe, Canada, Mexico. No fiction, poetry, personal experience or opinion. Buys about 60-70 mss/year. Query with or without published clips, or send complete ms. Length: 500-2,500 words. Pays $100-600 for assigned articles; $100-400 for unsolicited articles. Sometimes pays expenses of writers on assignment.

Reprints: Send tearsheet of article or typed ms with rights for sale noted and information about when and where the article previously appeared.

Photos: State availability of photos with submission. Reviews contact sheets, 3×5 transparencies, and 3×5 or 8×10 prints. Offers $15 minimum. Identification of subjects required. Buys one-time rights.

Columns/Departments: Books, Cuisine, Film, Music, Profile, Genealogy, Computers & Technology, Travel, 750-1,750 words. Buys about 40 mss/year. Query or send complete ms. Pays $100-400.

Fiction: Publishes novel excerpts.

Tips: "Little-known but terribly interesting information about black history and culture is desired. Aim at an upscale audience. Send ms with credentials." Looking for writers who are enthusiastic about their topics.

ARMENIAN INTERNATIONAL MAGAZINE, 207 S. Brand Blvd., Suite 205, Glendale CA 91204. (818)246-7979. Fax: (818)246-0088. E-mail: aimagazine@aol.com. Contact: Salpi H. Ghazarian, editor/publisher. 50% freelance written. Monthly magazine about the Causasus and the global Armenian diaspora. "Special reports and features about politics, business, education, culture, interviews and profiles. Each month, *AIM* is filled with essential news, situation analysis, and indepth articles with local and international coverage of events that effect Armenian life." Estab. 1989. Circ. 10,000. Pays on publication. Publishes ms an average of 3 months after acceptance. Byline given. Buys all rights. Reports in 2 weeks on queries; 6 weeks on mss.

Nonfiction: General interest, historical, interview/profile, photo feature and travel. Special issue: Armenian restaurants around the world. Buys 60 mss/year. Query with published clips. Length: 600-1,200 words. Pays $50-400 for assigned articles; $50-200 for unsolicited articles. Sometimes pays expenses of writers on assignment.

Reprints: Send photocopy of article.

Photos: State availability of photos with submission. Reviews negatives, transparencies and prints. Offers $10-50/photo. Captions and identification of subjects required.

BLACK DIASPORA MAGAZINE, Black Diaspora Communications Ltd., 298 Fifth Ave., 7th Floor, New York NY 10001. (212)268-8348. Fax: (212)268-8370. Executive Editors: Michelle Phipps and Jerry King. Contact: Michelle Phipps, executive editor. 25% freelance written. Monthly "general interest publication geared toward the entire Black Diaspora between ages 18-49." Estab. 1979. Circ. 250,000. Pays 30 days after acceptance. Byline given. Buys first North American serial and second serial (reprint) rights. Submit seasonal material 2 months in advance. Reports in 6 weeks. Sample copy for 9×12 SAE with 4 first-class stamps. Writer's guidelines for #10 SASE.

Nonfiction: Exposé, general interest, historical/nostalgic, interview/profile, religious, sports, travel, international, In Focus. Query with published clips. Length: 500-1,300 words. Pays 10¢/word maximum. Sometimes pays expenses of writers on assignment.

Photos: Send photos with submission. Offers no additional payment for photos accepted with ms. Captions, model releases, identification of subjects required. Buys all rights.

Columns/Departments: Length: 500-1,300 words. Pays 10¢/word maximum.

Poetry: Buys 10-20 poems/year. Submit maximum 5 poems. Pays $15 maximum.

THE B'NAI B'RITH INTERNATIONAL JEWISH MONTHLY, 1640 Rhode Island Ave. NW, Washington DC 20036. (202)857-6645. Fax: (202)296-1092. E-mail: ijm@bnaibrith.org. Website: http://bnaibrith.org/ijm. Editor: Glenn Garelik. 50% freelance written. Bimonthly magazine covering Jewish affairs. Estab. 1886. Circ. 200,000. **Pays on acceptance.** Publishes ms an average of 3 months after acceptance. Byline given. Kill fee depends on rate of payment. Buys first North American serial rights. Submit seasonal material 6 months in advance. Reports in 1 month. Sample copy for $2 and 9×13 SAE with 2 first-class stamps. Writer's guidelines free.

Nonfiction: General interest pieces of relevance to the Jewish community of U.S. and abroad; interview/profile, photo feature. Buys 15-25 mss/year. Query with published clips. Length: 750-3,000 words. Pays $300-750 for assigned articles; $300-500 for unsolicited articles. Sometimes pays expenses of writers on assignment.
Photos: State availability of photos with submission. Reviews contact sheets, 2×3 transparencies and prints. Pays $150/page for color, $100/page for b&w. Identification of subjects required. Buys one-time rights.
Tips: "Writers should submit clips with their queries. The best way to break in to the *Jewish Monthly* is to submit a range of good story ideas accompanied by clips. We aim to establish relationships with writers and we tend to be loyal. All sections are equally open."

CONGRESS MONTHLY, American Jewish Congress, 15 E. 84th St., New York NY 10028. (212)879-4500. Editor: Maier Deshell. 90% freelance written. Bimonthly magazine covering topics of concern to the American Jewish community representing a wide range of views. Distributed mainly to the members of the American Jewish Congress. "*Congress Monthly*'s readership is popular, but well-informed; the magazine covers political, social, economic and cultural issues of concern to the Jewish community in general and to the American Jewish Congress in particular." Estab. 1933. Circ. 35,000. Pays on publication. No simultaneous submissions. Responds to queries in 1 month. Publishes ms an average of 3 months after acceptance. Byline given. Buys one-time rights. Submit seasonal material 2 months in advance. Reports in 2 months.
Nonfiction: General interest ("current topical issues geared toward our audience"). No technical material. Query only. *No unsolicited mss*. Length: 1,200-1,500 words. Book reviews, 750-1,000 words; author profiles, film and theater reviews, travel. Payment amount determined by author experience and article length.
Photos: State availability of photos. Reviews b&w prints. "Photos are paid for with payment for ms."

‡DIMENSIONS, the Magazine of Jewish Lifestyle in South Florida, Skarco Press Inc., 10400 Griffin Rd., #204, Cooper City FL 33328. (954)252-9393. Contact: Helen Hill, editor. Quarterly magazine covering Jewish lifestyle in Southern Florida, geared toward 30-50-year-olds. Estab. 1995. Circ. 40,000. **Pays on acceptance**. Byline given. Buys first North American and second serial rights. Editorial lead time 4 months. Submit seasonal material 4 months in advance. Accepts simultaneous submissions. Reports in 2 months. Sample copy for $3 plus $1.24 postage.
Nonfiction: Book excerpts, general interest, humor, interview/profile (with celebrity or well-known person), religious (Jewish). Buys 16-20 mss/year. Query with published clips. Length: 800-2,000 words. Pays $100-300. Sometimes pays expenses of writers on assignment.
Photos: State availability of photos with submission. Negotiates payment individually. Captions, model releases, identification of subjects required. Buys one-time rights.
Columns/Departments: Kidimensions (hands-on parenting), 800 words; Body Works (medical for 30-50-year-olds), 800-1,000 words. Buys 4-6 mss/year. Query. Pays $100.
Tips: "Writers should understand our market and readers' lifestyle: Jewish professionals, families and singles aged 30s-50s, affluent, upscale, living in South Florida. Very cosmopolitan."

EBONY MAGAZINE, 820 S. Michigan Ave., Chicago IL 60605. (312)322-9200. Publisher: John H. Johnson. Executive Editor: Lerone Bennett, Jr. Monthly magazine. "*Ebony* is a black-oriented, general, picture magazine dealing primarily with contemporary topics." Estab. 1945. Circ. 1,928,000.
• *Ebony* is completely staff-written and does not accept freelance writing.

EMERGE, Black America's Newsmagazine, Emerge Communications, Inc., 1 BET Plaza, 1900 W Place NE, Washington DC 20018. (202)608-2093. Fax: (202)608-2598. Editor: George E. Curry. Managing Editor: Florestine Purnell. 80% freelance written. African-American news monthly. "*Emerge* is a general interest publication reporting on a wide variety of issues from health to sports to politics, almost anything that affects Black Americans. Our audience is comprised primarily of African-Americans 25-49, individual income of $35,000, professional and college educated." Estab. 1989. Circ. 200,000. **Pays on acceptance.** Publishes ms an average of three months after acceptance. Byline given. Offers 25% kill fee. Buys first North American serial rights. Submit seasonal material 6 months in advance. Reports in 5 weeks. Sample copy for $3 and 9×12 SAE. Writer's guidelines for #10 SAE with 2 first-class stamps.
• Ranked as one of the best markets for freelance writers in *Writer's Yearbook* magazine's annual "Top 100 Markets," January 1997.
Nonfiction: Essays, exposé, general interest, historical/nostalgic, humor, interview/profile, technical, travel. "We are not interested in standard celebrity pieces that lack indepth reporting as well as analysis, or pieces dealing with interpersonal relationships." Query with published clips. Length: 600-2,000 words. Pays 60-75¢/word.
Photos: State availability of photos with submission. Reviews contact sheets. Negotiated payment. Captions, model releases, indentification of subjects required. Buys one-time rights.
Columns/Departments: Query.
Tips: "If a writer doesn't have a completed manuscript, then he should mail a query letter with clips. No phone calls. First-time authors should be extremely sensitive to the *Emerge* style and fit within these guidelines as closely as possible. We do not like to re-write or re-edit pieces. We are a news monthly so articles must be written with a 3-month lead time in mind. If an assignment is given and another one is desired, writers must assist our research department during fact checking process and closing. Read at least six issues of the publication before submitting ideas."

‡ESTYLO MAGAZINE, Latina Lifestyle, Mandalay Publishing, 3660 Wilshire Blvd., Suite 530, Los Angeles CA 90010. (213)383-6300. Fax: (213)383-6499. Editor: Juana I. Gallegos. Contact: Brian Thompson, managing editor. 75%

freelance written. Quarterly magazine for Latinas 18- to 44-year-olds. "*Estylo* is a fashion, beauty and entertainment magazine for the affluent and mobile Latina. It contains a wide variety of features and departments devoted to all areas of interest to Latinas: career, cuisine, travel, health, fitness, beauty, fashion and entertainment topics. Estab. 1997. Circ. 50,000. Pays on publication. Publishes ms an average of 2 months after acceptance. Byline given. Buys first rights. Editorial lead time 3 months. Submit seasonal material 3 months in advance. Accepts simultaneous submissions. Reports in 2 weeks on queries; 1 month on mss. Writer's guidelines free.

Nonfiction: Expose, general interest, how-to (career, fitness, health), humor, inspirational, interview/profile, new product, opinion, personal experience, photo feature, religious, technical, travel. Buys 15-20 mss/year. Query with published clips. Length: 1,200-2,000 words. Pays $100 minimum. Sometimes pays expenses of writers on assignment.

Photos: State availability of photos with submission. Reviews contact sheets. Negotiates payment individually. Captions, model releases, identificiation of subjects required. Buys all rights.

Columns/Departments: Buys 15-20 mss/year. Query with published clips. Pays $100 minimum.

Fillers: Anecdotes, facts, gags to be illustrated by cartoonist, newsbreaks, short humor. Buys 5-10/year. Length: open. Pays $100 minimum.

FILIPINAS, A magazine for all Filipinos, Filipinas Publishing, Inc., 655 Sutter St., Suite 333, San Francisco CA 94102. (415)563-5878. Fax: (415)292-5993. E-mail: filmagazin@aol.com. Website: http://www.filipinas.com. Editor: Rene Ciria-Cruz. Monthly magazine focused on Filipino American affairs. "*Filipinas* answers the lack of mainstream media coverage of Filipinos in America. It targets both Filipino immigrants and American-born Filipinos, gives in-depth coverage of political, social, cultural events in The Philippines and in the Filipino American community. Features role models, history, travel, food and leisure, issues and controversies." Estab. 1992. Circ. 40,000. Pays on publication. Publishes ms an average of 3 months after acceptance. Byline given. Offers $10 kill fee. Buys first rights or all rights. Editorial lead time 2 months. Submit seasonal material 4 months in advance. Reports in 5 weeks on queries; 18 months on mss. Sample copy for $5. Writer's guidelines for 9½×4 SASE.

Nonfiction: Exposé, general interest, historical/nostalgic, how-to, humor, interview/profile, personal experience, travel. No academic papers. Buys 80-100 mss/year. Query with published clips. Length: 800-1,500 words. Pays $50-100. Sometimes pays writers other than cash payment "per specific agreement with writer."

Photos: State availability of photos with submission. Reviews 2¼×2¼ and 4×5 transparencies. Offers $15-35/photo. Captions and model releases required. Buys one-time rights.

Columns/Departments: Entree (reviews of Filipino restaurants), 1,200 words; Cultural Currents (Filipino traditions, beliefs), 1,500 words. Query with published clips. Pays $50-75.

GERMAN LIFE, Zeitgeist Publishing, 1 Corporate Dr., Grantsville MD 21536. (301)895-3859. Fax: (301)895-5029. E-mail: gwwc14a@prodigy.com. Website: http://langlab.uta.edu/germ/German_Life/. Contact: Heidi L. Whitesell, editor. 50% freelance written. Bimonthly magazine covering Germany. "*German Life* is for all interested in the diversity of German culture, past and present, and in the various ways that the United States (and North America in general) has been shaped by its German immigrants. The magazine is dedicated to solid reporting on cultural, historical, social and political events." Estab. 1994. Circ. 50,000. Pays on publication. Publishes ms an average of 6 months after acceptance. Byline given. Buys first North American serial rights. Editorial lead time 4 months. Submit seasonal material 4 months in advance. Reports in 1 month on queries; 3 months on mss. Sample copy for $4.95 and SAE with 4 first-class stamps. Writer's guidelines free.

Nonfiction: Exposé, general interest, historical/nostalgic, how-to (German crafts, recipes, gardening), interview/profile, opinion (only for final column), photo feature, travel. Special issues: Oktoberfest-related (October); seasonal relative to Germany, Switzerland or Australia (December); travel to German-speaking Europe (April); education or politics in Germany (August). Buys 60 mss/year. Query with published clips. Length: 1,000-2,000 words. Pays $200-500 for assigned articles; $200-350 for unsolicited articles. Sometimes pays expenses of writers on assignment.

Photos: State availability of photos with submission. Reviews color transparencies, 5×7 color or b&w prints. Offers no additional payment for photos accepted with ms. Identification of subjects required. Buys one-time rights.

Columns/Departments: German-Americana (regards specific German-American communities, organizations and/or events past or present), 1,500 words; Profile (portrays prominent Germans, Americans, or German-Americans), 800 words; At Home (cuisine, home design, gardening, crafts, etc. relating to Germany), 800 words; Library (reviews of books, videos, CDs, etc.), 300 words. Buys 30 mss/year. Query with published clips. Pays $130-300.

Fillers: Anecdotes, facts, newsbreaks, short humor. Length: 100-300 words. Pays $50-150.

Tips: "The best queries include several informative proposals. Ideally, clips show a background in a German-related topic, but more importantly, a flair for 'telling stories.' Majority of articles present a human interest angle. Even though *German Life* is a special interest magazine, writers should avoid overemphasizing autobiographical experiences/stories."

ALWAYS SUBMIT unsolicited manuscripts or queries with a self-addressed, stamped envelope (SASE) within your country or a self-addressed envelope with International Reply Coupons (IRC) purchased from the post office for other countries.

HADASSAH MAGAZINE, 50 W. 58th St., New York NY 10019. Executive Editor: Alan M. Tigay. 90% freelance written. Works with small number of new/unpublished writers each year. Monthly (except combined issues June/July and August/September). "*Hadassah* is a general interest, Jewish feature and literary magazine. We speak to our readers on a vast array of subjects ranging from politics to parenting, to midlife crisis to Mideast crisis. Our readers want coverage on social and economic issues, the arts, travel and health." Circ. 334,000. Buys first rights (with travel and family articles, buys all rights). Sample copy and writer's guidelines for SASE.

Nonfiction: Primarily concerned with Israel, Jewish communities around the world and American civic affairs as relates to the Jewish community. "We are also open to art stories that explore trends in Jewish art, literature, theater, etc. Will not assign/commission a story to a first-time writer for Hadassah." Buys 10 unsolicited mss/year. Send query and writing samples. No phone queries. Length: 1,500-2,000 words. Pays $350 minimum, $75 for reviews. Sometimes pays expenses of writers on assignment.

Photos: "We buy photos only to illustrate articles, with the exception of outstanding color photos from Israel which we use on our covers. We pay $175 and up for a suitable cover photo." Offers $50 for first photo; $35 for each additional. "Always interested in striking cover (color) photos, especially of Israel and Jerusalem."

Columns/Departments: "We have a Family column and a Travel column, but a query for topic or destination should be submitted first to make sure the area is of interest and the story follows our format."

Fiction: Joan Michel, fiction editor. Short stories with strong plots and positive Jewish values. No personal memoirs, "schmaltzy" or women's magazine fiction. "We continue to buy very little fiction because of a backlog." Length: 3,000 words maximum. Pays $300 minimum. "Require proper size SASE."

Tips: "We are interested in reading articles that offer an American perspective on Jewish affairs (1,500 words). For example, a look at the presidential candidates from a Jewish perspective. Send query of topic first."

‡HERITAGE FLORIDA JEWISH NEWS, P.O. Box 300742, Fern Park FL 32730-0742. (407)834-8787. Fax: (407)831-0507. E-mail: heritagefl@aol.com. Publisher/Editor: Jeffrey Gaeser. Contact: Chris Allen, associate editor. 20% freelance written. Weekly tabloid on Jewish subjects of local, national and international scope, except for special issues. "Covers news of local, national and international scope of interest to Jewish readers and not likely to be found in other publications." Estab. 1976. Circ. 3,500. Pays on publication. Publishes ms an average of 2 months after acceptance. Byline given. Buys first North American serial, first, one-time, second serial (reprint) or simultaneous rights. Submit seasonal material 3 months in advance. Reports in 1 month. Sample copy for $1 and 9×12 SASE.

Nonfiction: General interest, interview/profile, opinion, photo feature, religious, travel. "Especially needs articles for these annual issues: Rosh Hashanah, Financial, Chanukah, Celebration (wedding and bar mitzvah), Passover, Health and Fitness, Education, Travel. No fiction, poems, first-person experiences." Buys 50 mss/year. Send complete ms. Length: 500-1,000 words. Pays 50¢/column inch.

Reprints: Send typed ms with rights for sale noted.

Photos: State availability of photos with submission. Reviews b&w prints up to 8×10. Offers $5/photo. Captions, identification of subjects required. Buys one-time rights.

THE HIGHLANDER, Angus J. Ray Associates, Inc., P.O. Box 22307, Kansas City MO 64113. Fax: (816)523-7474. Editor: David K. Ray. 50% freelance written. Works with a number of new/unpublished writers each year. Bimonthly magazine covering Scottish history, clans, genealogy, travel/history, and Scottish/American activities. Estab. 1961. Circ. 35,000. **Pays on acceptance.** Publishes ms an average of 6 months after acceptance. Byline given. Buys first North American serial and second serial (reprint) rights. Submit seasonal material 6 months in advance. Reports in 1 month. Sample copy for $5. Writer's guidelines free.

Nonfiction: Historical/nostalgic. "No fiction; no articles unrelated to Scotland." Buys 100 mss/year. Query. Length: 750-2,000 words. Pays $75-150.

Reprints: Send tearsheet or photocopy of article or typed ms with information about when and where the article previously appeared. Pays 50% of amount paid for an original article.

Photos: State availability. Reviews b&w contact sheets. Identification of subjects required. Buys one-time rights.

Tips: "Submit something that has appeared elsewhere."

HISPANIC, 98 San Jacinto Blvd., Suite 1150, Austin TX 78701. (512)476-5599. Fax: (512)320-1943. E-mail: mcole@hisp.com. Website: http://www.hisp.com. Publisher: Alfredo J. Estrada. Contact: Melanie Cole, managing editor. 80% freelance written. Monthly English-language magazine for the U.S. Hispanic community. "*Hispanic* is a general interest publication emphasizing political issues, business news, and cultural affairs." Estab. 1987. Circ. 250,000. Pays on publication. Publishes ms an average of 4 months after acceptance. Byline given. Offers 25% kill fee. Buys all rights, puts some features on the Internet (*Hispanic Online*). Editorial lead time 3 months.

Nonfiction: General interest, business news, career strategies, politics, investigative pieces, culture features, opinion, personal essays. Buys 200 mss/year. Query in writing or submit ms on spec. Length: 1,400-3,500 words. Pays $200-450. Pays phone expenses, "but these must be cleared with editors first."

Photos: State availability of photos with submission. Reviews transparencies. Offers $25-500/photo. Captions, model releases, identification of subjects required.

Columns/Departments: Forum (op-ed), portfolio (product coverage, travel destinations, book, film and music reviews, money tips, cars). Pays $75.

Tips: "We prefer a tone that doesn't overexplain the Hispanic perspective (such as not explaining Hispanic symbolism or translating Spanish words to English). Generally, the point of view should in inclusive: 'we' rather than 'they.' "

INSIDE, The Jewish Exponent Magazine, Jewish Federation of Greater Philadelphia, 226 S. 16th St., Philadelphia PA 19102. (215)893-5700. Fax: (215)546-3957. E-mail: expent@netaxs.com. Contact: Jane Biberman, editor. Managing Editor: Martha Ledger. 95% freelance written (by assignment). Works with published/established writers and a small number of new/unpublished writers each year. Quarterly Jewish regional magazine for a sophisticated and upscale Jewish readership 25 years of age and older. Estab. 1979. Circ. 75,000. Pays on publication. Offers 20% kill fee. Publishes ms an average of 2 months after acceptance. Byline given. Buys first rights. Submit seasonal material 3 months in advance. Reports in 2 weeks on queries; 1 month on mss. Sample copy for $5 and 9×12 SAE. Writer's guidelines for #10 SASE.
Nonfiction: Book excerpts, general interest, historical/nostalgic, humor, interview/profile, personal experience, religious. Philadelphia angle desirable. Buys 12 unsolicited mss/year. Query. Length: 1,000-3,500 words. Pays $100-1,000.
Reprints: Send photocopy of article or short story. Pays $50-100.
Photos: State availability of photos with submission. Identification of subjects required. Buys first rights.
Fiction: Short stories. Publishes novel excerpts.
Tips: "Personalities—very well known—and serious issues of concern to Jewish community needed."

‡INTERNATIONAL EXAMINER, 622 S. Washington, Seattle WA 98104. (206)624-3925. Fax: (206)624-3046. Contact: Holly S. Smith, managing editor. 75% freelance written. Biweekly newspaper covering Asian-American issues and stories. "We write about Asian-American issues and things of interest to *Asian-Americans*. We do not want stuff about *Asian* things (stories on your trip to China, Japanese Tea Ceremony, etc. will be rejected). Yes, we are in English." Estab. 1974. Circ. 12,000. Pays on publication. Publishes ms an average of 1 month after acceptance. Buys one-time rights. Editorial lead time 1 month. Submit seasonal material 2 months in advance. Accepts simultaneous submissions. Sample copy, writer's guidelines and editorial calendar for #10 SASE.
Nonfiction: Essays, exposé, general interest, historical/nostalgic, humor, interview/profile, opinion, personal experience, photo feature. Buys 100 mss/year. Query with published clips. Length: 750-5,000 words, depending on subject. Pays $25-100. Sometimes pays expenses of writers on assignment.
Reprints: Accepts previously published submissions (as long as not published in same area). Send typed ms with rights for sale noted and information about when and where the article previously appeared. Pay negotiable.
Photos: State availability of photos with submission. Reviews contact sheets. Negotiates payment individually. Captions, identification of subjects required. Buys one-time rights.
Fiction: Asian-American authored fiction. Buys 1-2 mss/year. Query.
Tips: "Write decent, suitable material on a subject of interest to Asian-American community. All submissions are reviewed; all good ones are contacted. Also helps to call and run idea by editor before or after sending submissions."

ISRAEL HORIZONS, Progressive Zionist Quarterly, Hashomer Hatzair, 114 W. 26th St., Suite 1001, New York NY 10001. (212)868-0377. Fax: (212)989-9842. Editor: Don Goldstein. 15% freelance written. Quarterly magazine covering Israel and the American Jewish community. "We have an educated and intellectual readership. We cover political, social and economic issues concerning Israel and the American Jewish community from a progressive viewpoint. Our major concern is the peace process. We are also very interested in the Kibbutz movement." Estab. 1952. Circ. 3,000. Pays on publication. Publishes ms an average of 3 months after acceptance. Byline given. Buys one-time or second serial (reprint) rights. Editorial lead time 2 months. Submit seasonal material 3 months in advance. Reports in 3 weeks on queries; 1 month on mss.
Nonfiction: Essays, historical/nostalgic, interview/profile, opinion, personal experience. Buys 8 mss/year. Send complete ms. Length: 800-3,000 words. Pays $25-50.
Reprints: Accepts previously published submissions.
Photos: State availability of photos with submission. Offers no additional payment for photos accepted with ms. Identification of subjects required.
Columns/Departments: Book, Film Reviews (Jewish, Israeli, progressive political), 1,000 words. Buys 3 mss/year. Pays $25-50.
Poetry: Rochelle Ratner, Jonathan Shevin, poetry consultants. Free verse, light verse, traditional. Buys 6 poems/year. Submit maximum 2 poems. Length: 12-50 lines. Pays $10-20.

‡ITALIAN AMERICA, Official Publication of the Order Sons of Italy in America, Order Sons of Italy in America, 219 E. St. NE, Washington DC 20002. E-mail: markeditor@aol.com. Contact: Anthony Mark Dalessandro, editor. 25% freelance written. Quarterly magazine covering Italian Americans and Italian culture in America. "*Italian America* strives to provide timely information about OSIA, while reporting on individuals, institutions, issues and events of current or historical significance in the Italian-American community." Estab. 1996. Circ. 75,000. Pays on publication. Publishes ms an average of 3 months after acceptance. Byline given. Offers 50% kill fee. Buys first North American serial rights. Editorial lead time 3 months. Accepts simultaneous submissions. Sample copy and guidelines free.
Nonfiction: Essays, expose, historical, nostalgic, interview/profile, opinion, personal experience, travel. Buys 10 mss/year. Query with published clips. Length: 500-2,500 words. Pays $150-1,000. Sometimes pays expenses of writers on assignment.
Photos: State availability of photos with submission. Reviews contact sheets. Negotiates payment individually. Identification of subjects required. Buys one-time rights.
Columns/Departments: Community Notebook (Italian American life), 500 words; Postcard from Italy (life in Italy

today), 750 words; Reviews (books, films by or about Italian Americans), 500 words. Buys 5 mss/year. Send complete ms. Pays $100-500.

JEWISH ACTION, Union of Orthodox Jewish Congregations of America, 333 Seventh Ave., 18th Floor, New York NY 10001-5072. (212)563-4000, ext. 146, 147. Fax: (212)564-9058. Editor: Charlotte Friedland. Contact: Elissa Epstein, assistant editor. 80% freelance written. "Quarterly magazine offering a vibrant approach to Jewish issues, Orthodox lifestyle and values." Circ. 30,000. Pays 4-6 weeks after publication. Byline given. Submit seasonal material 4 months in advance. Reports in 3 months. Sample copy and guidelines for 9×12 SAE with 5 first-class stamps.
Nonfiction: Current Jewish issues, history, biography, art, inspirational, humor, music and book reviews. Query with published clips. Length: 1,000-3,000 words, including footnotes. Pays $100-300 for assigned articles; $75-150 for unsolicited articles. Buys 30-40 mss/year.
Fiction: Must have relevance to Orthodox reader. Length: 1,000-2,000 words.
Poetry: Limited number accepted. Pays $25-75.
Columns/Departments: Student Voice (about Jewish life on campus), 1,000 words. Buys 4 mss/year. Just Between Us (personal opinion on current Jewish life and issues), 1,000 words. Buys 4 mss/year. Jewish Living (section pertaining to holidays, contemporary Jewish practices), 1,000-1,500 words. Buys 10 mss/year.
Photos: Send photos with submission. Identification of subjects required.
Tips: "Remember that your reader is well-educated and has a strong commitment to Orthodox Judaism. Articles on the Holocaust, holidays, Israel and other common topics should offer a fresh insight. Because the magazine is a quarterly, we do not generally publish articles which concern specific timely events."

MANGAJIN, Japanese Pop Culture and Language Learning, Mangajin, Inc., P.O. Box 77188, Atlanta GA 30357-1188. Fax: (404)724-0897. E-mail: virginia@mangajin.com. Website: http://www.mangajin.com. Contact: Virginia Murray, editor. 10-20% freelance written. Magazine published 10 times/year. "Japanese pop culture provides a window on Japanese society and language. We look at contemporary Japanese culture as accessible, understandable, and entertaining. All issues deal with modern Japan. No inscrutable Orient here." Estab. 1990. Circ. 28,000. Pays on publication. Byline given. Offers $50-100 kill fee. Buys all rights or makes work-for-hire assignments. Editorial lead time 3 months. Submit seasonal material 3 months in advance. Reports in 2 weeks on queries; 1 month on mss. Write for editorial calendar.
Nonfiction: General interest, humor, interview/profile, new product. No "My experience in Japan" articles. Buys 15 mss/year. Query. Length: 500-2,000 words. Pays $150-850 for assigned articles; $150-500 for unsolicited articles. Sometimes pays expenses of writers on assignment.
Photos: State availability of photos with submission. Netotiates payment individually. Buys all rights.
Columns/Departments: Book Reviews (Japan-related books), 750 words; Computer Corner (Japan-oriented software), 750 words. Buys 15 mss/year. Query. Pays $125-250.

‡MIDSTREAM, A Monthly Jewish Review, 110 E. 59 St., New York NY 10022-1373. Editor: Joel Carmichael. 90% freelance written. Works with a small number of new/unpublished writers each year. Bimonthly magazine. "*Midstream* magazine is the Zionist periodical of record; in fact, there is no other journal of its kind which publishes Zionist historiography on a monthly basis in the world." Estab. 1954. Circ. 10,000. Buys first North American serial rights. Byline given. Pays after publication. Publishes ms an average of 6 months after acceptance. Reports in 3 months. Fiction guidelines for #10 SASE.
 • *Midstream* has gone from monthly to bimonthly in frequency.
Nonfiction: "Articles offering a critical interpretation of the past, searching examination of the present, and affording a medium for independent opinion and creative cultural expression. Articles on the political and social scene in Israel, on Jews in Russia, the US and elsewhere. Pays 5¢/word.
Fiction: Primarily of Jewish and related content. Pays 5¢/word.
Tips: "A book review is a good way to start. Send us a sample review or a clip, let us know your area of interest, suggest books you would like to review. For longer articles, give a brief account of your background or credentials in this field. Send query describing article or ms with cover letter. Since we are a bimonthly, we look for critical analysis rather than a 'journalistic' approach."

‡MINORITY ADVANCEMENT PROFILE, 30 N. Raymond, Suite 211, Pasadena CA 91103. (818)577-1984. Fax: (818)755-1953. E-mail: map@pacificnet.net. Website: www.pacificnet.net/~map. Publisher: Darrell R. Dansby. Senior Editor: Jeanetta M. Standefor. Contact: editorial staff. 40% freelance written. Bimonthly newsletter written for African-American entrepreneurs and career professionals covering all aspects of business and careers. "We provide how-to information for starting and growing small businesses, profiles of entrepreneurs, career advancement advice and profiles of successful career professionals." Estab. 1996. Pays on publication. Byline given. Buys first rights and second serial (reprint) rights. Submit seasonal material 2 months in advance. Reports in 2 months. Sample copy for $3. Writer's guidelines for #10 SASE with "Attn: Writer's Guidelines" on envelope.
Nonfiction: "We are especially seeking 'how-to-do-it-better' articles for starting a small business or any aspect of career advancement. Please read the newsletter and writer's guidelines before querying. Articles covering up-to-date practical business and career information and interviews or profiles of successful entrepreneurs and career professionals are welcome." Query. Length: 300-1,000 words. Pays $100-500.
Reprints: Accepts previously published submissions.
Photos: State availability of photos with submission. Captions, model releases, identification of subjects required. Pays

$5-20/photo. Buys one-time rights.

Columns/Departments: Entrepreneur/Career Profiles; MAP Hall of Shame (humorous personal, business or work experiences); Entrepreneur Report (timely, professional, practical information for entrepreneurs); Career Management (how-to advice and opportunities for career advancement); Keeping You in the Know (personal career, business advice and information); Product Review and Recommendation (books, product, service reviews); Just Ask Us . . . Q&A (business and career issues).

Tips: "MAP addresses the specific needs of African-American entrepreneurs and career professionals. Each issue combines dual information, issues and events about and from the African-American perspective. Departments and columns are most open to freelancers."

‡**MODERNA MAGAZINE**, The Latina Magazine, Hispanic Publishing Corp., 98 San Jacinto Blvd., Suite 1150, Austin TX 78701. (512)476-5599. E-mail: moderna@hisp.com. Contact: Christine Granados, editor. 60% freelance written. Quarterly magazine covering fashion, beauty and health for 18- 44-year-old college-educated Latinas, published bilingually. Estab. 1996. Circ. 150,000. Pays on publication. Byline given. Offers 25% kill fee. Buys all rights. Editorial lead time 2 months. Submit seasonal material 6 months in advance. Accepts simultaneous submissions. Reports in 3 months on queries. Sample copy for $3. Writer's guidelines free.

Nonfiction: General interest, how-to, humor, interview/profile, new product, opinion, personal experience, travel. Query with published clips. Length: 1,200-3,000 words. Pays $200-300. Sometimes pays expenses of writers on assignment.

Photos: Send photos with submission. Reviews contact sheets, negatives. Negotiates payment individually. Model releases, identification of subjects required. Buys one-time rights.

Columns/Departments: Que Pasa, 50-100 words; Sabor (food), 750-1,000 words; Travel, 75-1,000 words; Mi Vida, 750 words; Punto de Vista, 750 words; Working It Out, 750 words; Hotline, 50-100 words. Query with published clips. Pays $50-100.

Fillers: Facts, gags to be illustrated by cartoonist, newsbreaks. Length: 25-100 words. Pays $25-50.

Tips: "*Moderna* is bilingual, and publishes newsworthy, fashion-related stories, profiles of Latina personalties, and entertaining stories about health and fitness, relationships, parenting, food and recipes, travel, film and book reviews, and any other aspect of US society that affects Latinas. Moderna is a bilingual magazine with 1/3 of its articles published in Spanish. There are English translations of all Spanish articles published in the back section."

MOMENT, The Magazine of Jewish Culture & Opinion, Jewish Educational Ventures & Biblical Archaeology Society, 4710 41st St. NW, Washington DC 20016. (202)364-3300. Fax: (202)364-2636. E-mail: basmom@clark.net. Publisher/Editor: Hershel Shanks. Managing Editor: Suzanne Singer. Contact: Stacey Freed, assistant editor. 90% freelance written. "*Moment* is an independent Jewish bimonthly general interest magazine that specializes in cultural, political, historical, religious and 'lifestyle' articles relating chiefly to the North American Jewish community and Israel." Estab. 1975. Circ. 70,000. Pays on publication. Publishes ms an average of 6 months after acceptance. Byline given. Buys first North American serial rights. Editorial lead time 3 months. Submit seasonal material 6 months in advance. Accepts simultaneous submissions. Reports in 1 month on queries; 2 months on mss. Sample copy for $4.50 and SAE. Writer's guidelines free.

Nonfiction: Book excerpts, essays, interview/profile, opinion, religious. Buys 60-80 mss/year. Query with published clips. Writers of potentially lengthy articles are urged to send a detailed query letter first, either by regular mail or e-mail. Length: 2,500-4,000 words. Pays $40-1,100 for assigned articles; $40-500 for unsolicited articles. Sometimes pays expenses of writers on assignment.

Photos: State availability of photos with submission. Negotiates payment individually. Identification of subjects required. Buys one-time rights.

Columns/Departments: Guest Column (personal/opinion), including "Why I Became Jewish" and "Why I am Jewish," 750-1,000 words; Holiday (seasonal celebrations), 750-1,500 words; Responsa (rabbinic response to contemporary dilemmas), 800-1,200 words; book reviews (fiction and nonfiction) are occasionally accepted but mostly assigned, 400-800 words. Buys 15 mss/year. Query with published clips. Pays $150-250.

Tips: "Stories for *Moment* are mostly assigned, but unsolicited manuscripts are occasionally selected for publication. Successful features offer readers an in-depth journalistic treatment of an issue, phenomenon, institution, or individual. The more the writer can follow the principle of 'show, don't tell,' the better."

NA'AMAT WOMAN, Magazine of NA'AMAT USA, the Women's Labor Zionist Organization of America, NA'AMAT USA, 200 Madison Ave., New York NY 10016. (212)725-8010. Contact: Judith A. Sokoloff, editor. 80% freelance written. Magazine published 5 times/year covering Jewish themes and issues; Israel; women's issues; and social and political issues. Estab. 1926. Circ. 25,000. Pays on publication. Byline given. Not copyrighted. Buys first North American serial, one-time, first serial and second serial (reprint) rights to book excerpts and makes work-for-hire assignments. Reports in 3 months. Writer's guidelines for SASE.

Nonfiction: Exposé, general interest (Jewish), historical/nostalgic, interview/profile, opinion, personal experience, photo feature, travel, art and music. "All articles must be of particular interest to the Jewish community." Buys 35 mss/year. Query with clips of published work or send complete ms. Pays 10¢/word.

Photos: State availability of photos. Pays $25-45 for 4×5 or 5×7 prints. Captions, identification of subjects required. Buys one-time rights.

Columns/Departments: Film and book reviews with Jewish themes. Buys 20-25 mss/year. Query with clips of published work or send complete ms. Pays 10¢/word.

Fiction: Historical/nostalgic, humorous, women-oriented and novel excerpts. "Intelligent fiction with Jewish slant. No maudlin nostalgia or trite humor." Buys 3 mss/year. Send complete ms. Length: 1,200-3,000 words. Pays 10¢/word.

NATIVE PEOPLES MAGAZINE, The Arts and Lifeways, 5333 N. Seventh St., Suite C-224, Phoenix AZ 85014-2804. (602)252-2236. Fax: (602)265-3113. E-mail: native_peoples@amcolor.com. Website: http://www.atiin.com/native_peoples/. Contact: Rebecca Withers, managing editor. Editor: Gary Avey. Quarterly full-color magazine on Native Americans. "The primary purpose of this magazine is to offer a sensitive portrayal of the arts and lifeways of native peoples of the Americas." Estab. 1987. Circ. 120,000. Pays on publication. Byline given. Buys one-time rights. Reports in 1 month on queries; 2 months on mss. Sample copy for 9×12 SAE with 7 first-class stamps. Writer's guidelines and sample copy free. "Extremely high quality reproduction with full-color throughout."
Nonfiction: Book excerpts (pre-publication only), historical/nostalgic, interview/profile, personal experience, photo feature. Buys 45 mss/year. Query with published clips. Length: 1,800-2,800 words. Pays 25¢/word.
Photos: State availability of photos with submission. Reviews transparencies (all formats). Offers $45-150/page rates. Identification of subjects required. Buys one-time rights.

‡SCANDINAVIAN REVIEW, The American-Scandinavian Foundation, 725 Park Ave., New York NY 10021. (212)879-9779. Fax: (212)249-3444. Contact: Adrienne Gyongy, editor. 75% freelance written. Triannual magazine for contemporary Scandinavia. Audience: members, embassies, consulates, libraries. Slant: popular coverage of contemporary affairs in Scandinavia. Estab. 1913. Circ. 4,000. Pays on publication. Publishes ms 2 months after acceptance. Byline given. Buys first North American serial and second serial (reprint) rights. Editorial lead time 3 months. Submit seasonal material 3 months in advance. Reports in 6 weeks on queries. Sample copy and writer's guidelines free.
Nonfiction: General interest, interview/profile, photo feature, travel (must have Scandinavia as topic focus). Special issue on Scandinavian travel. *No pornography*. Buys 30 mss/year. Query with published clips. Length: 1,500-2,000 words. Pays $300 maximum. Pays contributor's copies at writer's request.
Reprints: Accepts previously published submissions.
Photos: State availability or send photos with submission. Reviews 3×5 transparencies or prints. Pays $25-50/photo; negotiates payment individually. Captions required. Buys one-time rights.

THIRD FORCE MAGAZINE, Issues & Actions in Communities of Color, Center for Third World Organizing, 1218 E. 21st St., Oakland CA 94606. (510)533-7583. Fax: (510)533-0923. E-mail: ctwo@igc.apc.org. Website: http://www.ctwo.org. Contact: John Anner, editor/publisher. 65% freelance written. Bimonthly magazine covering communities of color, grassroots organizing, low-income communities. "Must reflect knowledge and understanding of issues in various communities of color. Writers of color are especially encouraged to submit queries. Approximately 70% of articles are written by authors of color." Estab. 1984. Circ. 5,000. Pays on publication. Publishes ms an average of 3 months after acceptance. Byline given. Offers 40% kill fee. Buys first North American serial rights. Editorial lead time 3 months. Submit seasonal material 4 months in advance. Reports in 6 weeks on queries; 2 months on mss. Sample copy and writer's guidelines free.
Nonfiction: Essays, exposé, general interest, historical, interview/profile, opinion, photo feature. Special issues: 2 each year. Buys 40 mss/year. Query with published clips or writing samples. Length: 700-3,500 words. Pays $150 minimum plus 1 year subscription. Sometimes pays expenses of writers on assignment.
Reprints: Send information about when and where the article previously appeared. Pays 50% of amount paid for an original article.
Photos: State availability of photos with submissions. Negotiates payment individually. Captions, identification of subjects required. Buys one-time rights.
Columns/Departments: Editorial/Commentary (political, cultural, social), 800 words; Historical (histories of organizing or other issues in communities of color), 1,000 words. Buys 6 mss/year. Query with published clips or send complete ms. Pay negotiable.
Fillers: Timely political/social cartoons (strip or single panel) or illustrations. Buys 6/year. Pay negotiable.
Tips: "The best way for writers to break in is to write or propose a short feature about a particular political struggle or grassroots campaign that the writer is familiar with. Authors of short features are often assigned longer features. Queries should be concise and clear and should include information on the writer's experience and expertise."

THE UKRAINIAN WEEKLY, Ukrainian National Association, 30 Montgomery St., Jersey City NJ 07302-3821. (201)434-0237. Website: http://world.std.com/~sabre/UKRAINE.html in "Current Events" section. Contact: Roma Hadzewycz, editor-in-chief. 30% freelance written (mostly by a corps of regular contributors). Weekly tabloid covering news and issues of concern to Ukrainian community, primarily in North America but also around the world, and events in Ukraine. "We have news bureaus in Kyiv, capital of Ukraine, and in Toronto." Estab. 1933. Circ. 10,000. Pays on publication. Publishes ms an average of 2 months after acceptance. Byline given. Buys first North American serial and second serial (reprint) rights or makes work-for-hire assignments. Submit seasonal material 1 month in advance. Reports in 1 month. Sample copy for 9×12 SAE with 3 first-class stamps.
Nonfiction: Book excerpts, essays, exposé, general interest, historical/nostalgic, interview/profile, opinion, personal experience, photo feature, news events. Special issues: Easter, Christmas, anniversary of Ukraine's independence proclamation (August 24, 1991), student scholarships, anniversary of Chornobyl nuclear accident and year-end review of news. Buys 80 mss/year. Query with published clips. Length: 500-2,000 words. Pays $45-100 for assigned articles; $25-100 for unsolicited articles. Sometimes pays expenses of writers on assignment.

Reprints: Send typed ms with rights for sale noted and information about when and where the article previously appeared. Pays 25-50% of amount paid for an original article.

Photos: Send photos with submission. Reviews contact sheets, negatives and 3×5, 5×7 or 8×10 prints. Offers no additional payment for photos accepted with ms.

Columns/Departments: News & Views (commentary on news events), 500-1,000 words. Buys 10 mss/year. Query. Pays $25-50.

Tips: "Become acquainted with the Ukrainian community in the US and Canada. The area of our publication most open to freelancers is community news—coverage of local events. We put more emphasis on events in Ukraine now that it has re-established its independence."

UPSCALE MAGAZINE, The Successful Black Magazine, Upscale Communications, Inc., 600 Bronner Brothers Way SW, Atlanta, GA 30310. (404)758-7467. Fax: (404)755-9892. Editor-in-Chief: Sheila Bronner. Contact: Paula M. White, associate editor. 75-80% freelance written. Monthly magazine covering topics that inspire, inform or entertain African-Americans. "*Upscale* is a general interest publication featuring a variety of topics—beauty, health and fitness, business news, travel, arts, relationships, entertainment and other issues that affect day to day lives of African-Americans." Estab. 1989. Circ. 242,000. Byline given. Offers 25% kill fee. Buys all rights in published form. Editorial lead time 3 months. Submit seasonal material 4 months in advance. Accepts simultaneous submissions. Sample copy for $2. Writer's guidelines free.

Nonfiction: Book excerpts/reviews, general interest, historical/nostalgic, inspirational, interview/profile, personal experience, religious, travel. Buys 135 mss/year. Query. Pays $150 minimum. Sometimes pays expenses of writers.

Photos: State availability of photos with submission. Reviews contact sheets, transparencies, prints. Negotiates payment individually. Captions, model releases, identification of subjects required. Buys one-time or reprint rights.

Columns/Departments: Lee Bliss, senior editor. Positively You, Viewpoint, Perspective (personal inspiration/perspective). Buys 50 mss/year. Query. Pays $75.

Fiction: Publishes novel excerpts.

Tips: "*Upscale* does not accept unsolicited fiction, poetry or essays. Unsolicited nonfiction is accepted for our Perspective, Positively You, and Viewpoint sections. Query letters for exciting and informative nonfiction story ideas are welcomed."

WINDSPEAKER, Aboriginal Multi-Media Society of Alberta, 15001-112 Ave., Edmonton Alberta T5M 2V6 Canada. (403)455-2700. Editor: Debora Lockyer. 75% freelance written. Monthly tabloid covering native issues. "Focus on events and issues that affect and interest native peoples." Estab. 1983. Circ. 12,500. Pays on publication. Publishes ms an average of 1 month after acceptance. Byline given. Offers $25 kill fee. Buys first rights. Editorial lead time 1 month. Submit seasonal material 2 months in advance. Accepts simultaneous submissions. Sample copy and guidelines free.

Nonfiction: Humor, interview/profile, opinion, personal experience, photo feature, travel, reviews: books, music, movies. Special issues: Powwow (June); Travel (May). Buys 200 mss/year. Query with published clips or by phone with story ideas. Length: 300-1,000 words. Pays $3-3.60/published inch. Sometimes pays expenses of writers on assignment.

Photos: Send photos with submission. Reviews negatives, prints. Offers $15-50/photo. Identification of subjects required. Buys one-time rights.

Columns/Departments: Arts reviews (Aboriginal artists), 500-800 words. Buys 25 mss/year. Query with published clips. Pays $3-3.60/inch.

FOOD AND DRINK

Magazines appealing to gourmets, health-conscious consumers and vegetarians are classified here. Publications such as *Bon Appetit, Fine Cooking* and *Food & Wine* emphasize "the art and craft" of cooking for food enthusiasts who enjoy developing these skills as a leisure activity. Another popular trend stresses healthy eating and food choices, and is represented by such magazines as *Eating Well, Fast and Healthy* and *Delicious*! Many magazines in the Health and Fitness category present a holistic approach to well-being through nutrition and fitness for healthful living. Magazines in General Interest and Women's categories also buy articles on food topics. Journals aimed at food processing, manufacturing and retailing are in the Trade section.

ALL ABOUT BEER MAGAZINE, Chautauqua, Inc., 1627 Marion Ave., Durham NC 27705. (919)490-0589. Fax: (919)490-0865. E-mail: allabtbeer@aol.com. Editor: Daniel Bradford. Managing Editor: Julie Johnson Bradford. 15% freelance written. Bimonthly magazine covering specialty beer. Estab. 1979. Circ. 40,000. Pays on publication. Byline given. Offers 50% kill fee. Buys first North American serial rights. Editorial lead time 4 months. Submit seasonal material 4 months in advance. Reports in 6 weeks on queries; 2 months on mss. Sample copy for $3.50. Writer's guidelines for #10 SASE.

Nonfiction: Essays, historical/nostalgic, humor, interview/profile, new product, travel. Buys 7-10 mss/year. Query with published clips. Length: 500-3,000 words. Pays $100-350 for assigned articles; $50-250 for unsolicited articles.

Photos: State availability of photos with submissions. Reviews contact sheets, transparencies. Offers $25-50/photo. Captions, identification of subjects required. Buys one-time rights.
Columns/Departments: Stylistically Speaking (a look at a specific beer style) 700-900 words; Small Beers (news items) 200-500 words. Buys 28 mss/year. Query with published clips. Pays $100-250.
Fillers: Anecdotes, facts, newsbreaks. Buys 14/year. Length: 50-150 words. Pays $25.

‡**BEER CONNOISSEUR, The Guide to Beer and the Good Life**, Adams Media, Inc., 1180 Sixth Ave., 11th Floor, New York NY 10036, (212)827-4732. Fax: (212)827-4720. E-mail: agiglio3@aol.com. Contact: Anthony Giglio, editor. Managing editor: Beth Sherman. 75% freelance written. Magazine published 9 times/year. "*Beer Connoisseur* targets a young, affluent and mostly male audience (21 to 34 years old with incomes of $50,000+). It's about beer— and so much more. Lifestyle issues include topics today's young urban professionals have come to associate with the rewards of hard work. From style to sex, travel to tax tips, music to menus, *Beer Connoisseur* is a veritiable handbook on how to live." Estab. 1996. Circ. 100,000. Pays on publication. Publishes ms an average of 3 months after acceptance. Byline given. Offers 25% kill fee. Buys first rights. Editorial lead time 3 months. Submit seasonal material 6 months in advance. Reports in 1 month on queries, 2 months on mss. Sample copy and writer's guidelines free.
Nonfiction: General interest, how-to, interview/profile, new product, personal experience, photo feature, travel. Buys 30 mss/year. Query with published clips. Length: 1,500-3,000 words. Pays $1,000-3,000. Sometimes pays expenses of writers on assignment.
Photos: State availability of photos with submission. Reviews transparencies. Offers $250-1,000/photo. Captions, identification of subjects required. Buys one-time rights.
Columns/Departments: Pub Crawl (best brewpubs around the world); Interview (celebrities); Savoir Bier (interesting brewers around the world); Traveling Man (places with a cool attitude toward beer and the good life); Tastings, Ratings & Reviews (distinguished panel of connoisseurs taste, rate and recommend the latest brews); Zymurgist (latest in home-brewing with "how-to" information, recipes and advice); Imbibing (beyond brews: distinctive liquors, fine wines and alternative beverages); Cigars; Connectivity (the latest in technology and gadgets); The Good Life (style picks; sex, health and fitness advice; food; music; money talk); all 750-1,200 words. Buys 180 mss/year. Query with published clips. Pays $750-1,500.
Tips: "A great query includes anecdotes, a brief description of how the article will be executed, and potential photography leads."

BON APPETIT, America's Food and Entertaining Magazine, Condé Nast Publications, Inc., 6300 Wilshire Blvd., Los Angeles CA 90048. (213)965-3600. Fax: (213)937-1206. Executive Editor: Barbara Fairchild. Editor-in-Chief: William J. Garry. 10% freelance written. Monthly magazine that covers fine food, restaurants and home entertaining. "*Bon Appetit* readers are upscale food enthusiasts and sophisticated travelers. They eat out often and entertain four to six times a month." Estab. 1975. Circ. 1,331,853. **Pays on acceptance**. Byline given. Negotiates rights. Submit seasonal material 1 year in advance. Reports in 6 weeks on queries. Writer's guidelines for #10 SASE.
Nonfiction: Travel (restaurant or food-related), food feature, dessert feature. "No cartoons, quizzes, poetry, historic food features or obscure food subjects." Buys 45 mss/year. Query with published clips; include list of 6-8 recipes with 2-3 sentence descriptions detailing ingredients, seasoning, garnish, size, shape, color. Length: 750-2,000 words. Pays $500-1,800. Pays expenses of writers on assignment.
Photos: Never send photos.
Tips: "We are most interested in receiving travel stories from freelancers. They must have a good knowledge of food (as shown in accompanying clips) and a light, lively style with humor. Nothing long and pedantic please."

CHILE PEPPER, The Magazine of Spicy Foods, Magnolia Media Group, 1227 W. Magnolia Ave., Ft. Worth TX 76104. Editor: Eric O'Keefe, editor. Publisher: Joel Gregory. 70-80% freelance written. Bimonthly magazine on spicy foods. "The magazine is devoted to spicy foods, and most articles include recipes. We have a very devoted readership who love their food hot!" Estab. 1986. Circ. 85,000. Pays on publication. Buys first and second rights and first electronic rights. Submit seasonal material 6 months in advance. Sample copy for 9×12 SAE with 5 first-class stamps. Writer's guidelines for #10 SASE.
  ● *Chile Pepper* also publishes a new trade journal, *Hot Times*, which debuted in April, 1997.
Nonfiction: Book excerpts (cookbooks), how-to (cooking and gardening with spicy foods), humor (having to do with spicy foods), new product (hot products), travel (having to do with spicy foods). Buys 50 mss/year. Query. Length: 1,000-3,000 words. Pays $300 minimum for feature article.
Reprints: Send tearsheet or photocopy of article and information about when and where the article previously appeared. Pays 25% of amount paid for an original article.
Photos: State availability of photos with submission. Reviews contact sheets, negatives, transparencies, prints. Offers $25/photo minimum. Captions, identification of subjects required. Buys one-time rights.
Tips: "We're always interested in queries from *food* writers. Articles about spicy foods with six to eight recipes are just right. No fillers. Need location travel/food pieces from inside the U.S. and Mexico."

‡**CIGAR AFICIONADO**, M. Shanken Community, Inc., 387 Park Ave. S., New York NY 10016. (212)684-4224. Fax: (212)684-5424. Website: cigaraficionado.com. Editor: Marvin Shanken. Contact: Gordon Mott, managing editor. 75% freelance written. Bimonthly magazine covering cigars. Estab. 1992. Circ. 400,000. **Pays on acceptance.** Publishes ms an average of 9 months after acceptance. Byline given. Offers 25% kill fee. Buys all rights. Editorial lead time 3

months. Submit seasonal material 3 months in advance. Sample copy and writer's guidelines free.
Nonfiction: Query. Length: 2,000 words. Sometimes pays expenses of writers on assignment.

COOKING LIGHT, The Magazine of Food and Fitness, P.O. Box 1748, Birmingham AL 35201-1681. (205)877-6000. Fax: (205)877-6600. Website: http://cookinglight.com. Editor: Douglas Crichton. Executive Editor: Nathalie Dearing. Contact: Jill Nelton, senior food editor (food); Lisa Delaney, senior health and fitness editor (fitness). 75% freelance written. Magazine published 10 times/year on healthy recipes and fitness information. "*Cooking Light* is a positive approach to a healthier lifestyle. It's written for healthy people on regular diets who are counting calories or trying to make calories count toward better nutrition. Moderation, balance and variety are emphasized. The writing style is fresh, upbeat and encouraging, emphasizing that eating a balanced, varied, lower-calorie diet and exercising regularly do not have to be boring." Estab. 1987. Circ. 1,300,000. **Pays on acceptance.** Publishes ms 1 year after acceptance. Byline sometimes given. Offers 33% kill fee. Submit seasonal material 1 year in advance. Reports in 1 year.
● Ranked as one of the best markets for freelance writers in *Writer's Yearbook* magazine's annual "Top 100 Markets," January 1997.
Nonfiction: Personal experience on nutrition, healthy recipes, fitness/exercise. Back up material a must. Buys 150 mss/year. Query with published clips. Length: 400-2,000 words. Pays $250-2,000. Pays expenses of writers on assignment.
Columns/Departments: Try On a Sport (introducing readers to new sports as well as new ways to view old sports), 1,000 words; Health Watch (focuses on wide range of health issues), 1,000 words; Food for Thought (collection of food-related articles on the following topics—mini profile on a chef, restaurant and eating-out trends, food products and equipment, cooking tips and diet concerns) 250-350 words, short, 400-500 words, long. Buys 30 mss/year. Query. Pays $50-2,000.
Tips: "Emphasis should be on achieving a healthier lifestyle through food, nutrition, fitness, exercise information. In submitting queries, include information on professional background. Food writers should include examples of healthy recipes which meet the guidelines of *Cooking Light*."

DELICIOUS!, Your Magazine of Natural Living, New Hope Communications, 1301 Spruce St., Boulder CO 80302. E-mail: delicious@newhope.com. Website: http://www.newhope.com/delicious. Editor: Kathryn Arnold. Contact: Laurel Kallenbach, senior editor. 65% freelance written. Monthly magazine covering natural products, nutrition, herbal medicines. "*Delicious!* magazine empowers natural foods store shoppers to make health-conscious choices in their lives. Our goal is to improve consumers' perception of the value of natural methods in achieving health. To do this, we educate consumers on nutrition, disease prevention, botanical medicines and natural personal care products." Estab. 1985. Circ. 375,000. **Pays on acceptance.** Publishes ms an average of 6 months after acceptance. Byline given. Offers 10% kill fee. Buys first North American serial rights. Editorial lead time 4 months. Submit seasonal material 6 months in advance. Accepts simultaneous submissions. Reports in 6 weeks on queries; 2 months on mss. Sample copy and guidelines free.
Nonfiction: Book excerpts, how-to, personal experience (regarding natural or alternative health), health nutrition, herbal medicines, alternative medicine. Buys 150 mss/year. Query with published clips. Length: 700-1,500 words. Pays $50-350 for assigned articles; $25-100 for unsolicited articles.
Photos: State availability of photos with submission. Reviews 3×5 prints. Offers no additional payment for photos accepted with ms. Identification of subjects required. Buys one-time rights.
Columns/Departments: Herbal Kingdom (scientific evidence supporting herbal medicines) 1,200 words; Nutrition (new research on diet for good health) 1,000 words; Dietary Supplements (new research on vitamins/minerals, etc.) 1,000 words. Query with published clips. Pays $50-250.
Tips: "Highlight any previous health/nutrition/medical writing experience. Demonstrate a knowledge of natural medicine, nutrition, or natural products. Health practitioners who demonstrate writing ability are ideal freelancers."

DRINK MAGAZINE, (formerly *Beer Across America*), GulfStream Communications, P.O. Box 1794, Mt. Pleasant SC 29465. (803)971-9811. E-mail: drink@gulfstreamcom.com. Website: http://www.drinkonline.com. Editor: Kathleen W. Kranking. 90% freelance written. Quarterly magazine covering beer and spirits. "*Drink Magazine* is a lifestyle magazine for educated, affluent readers who have an appreciation for beer, spirits and life. *Drink* covers travel, music, food and other topics of interest to beer and spirits connoisseurs." Estab. 1995. Circ. 150,000. Pays 30 days after publication. Publishes ms an average of 6 months after acceptance. Byline given. Offers 25% kill fee. Buys first North American serial rights. Editorial lead time 3 months. Submit seasonal material 3 months in advance. Reports in 6 weeks. Sample copy for $2 and 9×12 SAE with 5 first-class stamps. Writer's guidelines for #10 SASE.
Nonfiction: General interest, historical/nostalgic, humor, interview/profile, travel, music (all with a beer or spirits tie-in). Buys 10 mss/year. Query with published clips. Length: 750-2,000 words. Pays $100-500 for assigned articles; $100-450 for unsolicited articles. Sometimes pays expenses of writers on assignment.
Photos: State availability of photos with submission. Reviews transparencies. Negotiates payment individually. Identification of subjects required. Buys one-time rights.
Columns/Departments: Beer Nuts (people with an out of the ordinary dedication to beer, i.e., a brew pub poet's society); Affordable Luxuries (any indulgence that would appeal, i.e., steins, gourmet coffee); both 1,000-1,200 words. Buys fewer than 10 mss/year. Query with published clips. Pays $100-350.
Tips: "Query first with published clips. We're looking for light, clever writing covering fresh angles. No beer-party stories or beer festival reviews. Look for original ways to cover beer or spirits; for example, we recently did an article called 'America's Best 19th Holes.'"

EATING WELL, The Magazine of Food and Health, 823 A Ferry Rd., Charlotte VT 05445. (802)425-3961. Fax: (802)425-3675. Editor: Marcelle DiFalco. Food Editor: Patsy Jamieson. 90% freelance written. Magazine published 8 times/year. Estab. 1989. Circ. 640,000. Pays 45 days after acceptance. Publishes ms an average of 6 months after acceptance. Byline given. Buys first North American serial rights. Submit seasonal material 1 year in advance. Reports in 2 months.

Nonfiction: Nutrition, cooking, interview/profile, food, travel. Query with published clips. Length: 2,000-4,000 words. Pays $1,500-3,500. Pays expenses of writers on assignment.

Columns/Departments: Eating Well in America (current news in the food world), 150-400 words. Buys 60 mss/ year. Query. Pays $200-500.

Tips: "We invite experienced, published science writers to do a broad range of in-depth, innovative food-health-nutrition features. Read the magazine first."

FAST AND HEALTHY MAGAZINE, Pillsbury Co., 200 S. Sixth St., M.S. 28M7, Minneapolis MN 55402. Fax: (612)330-4875. Contact: Betsy Wray, editor. 50% freelance written. "*Fast and Healthy* is a family-oriented bimonthly food magazine with healthful recipes for active people. All recipes can be prepared in 30 minutes or less and meet the U.S. Dietary guidelines for healthful eating. The magazine's emphasis is on Monday through Friday cooking. Our readers are busy people who are looking for information and recipes that help them prepare healthy meals quickly." Estab. 1992. Circ. 200,000. **Pays on acceptance.** Publishes ms an average of 8 months after acceptance. Byline given. Offers 20% kill fee. Buys all rights. Editorial lead time 1 year. Submit seasonal material 18 months in advance. Reports in 6 weeks on queries. Sample copy for $3. Writer's guidelines for #10 SASE.

Nonfiction: Food topics related to health, nutrition, convenience. Buys 6 mss/year. Query with résumé and published clips. Length: 100-1,500 words. Pays $50-500.

Columns/Departments: Living Better (health, nutrition, healthy lifestyle news), 25-200 words. Buys 25 mss/year. Query with published clips. Pays $25-200.

FOOD & WINE, American Express Publishing Corp., 1120 Avenue of the Americas, New York NY 10036. (212)382-5618. Editor-in-Chief: Dana Cowin. Managing Editor: Mary Ellen Ward. Executive Editor: Denise Martin. Food Editor: Tina Ujlaki. Monthly magazine for "active people for whom eating, drinking, entertaining, dining out and travel are central to their lifestyle." Estab. 1978. Circ. 750,000. **Pays on acceptance.** Byline given. Offers 25% kill fee. Buys first world rights. Submit seasonal material 9 months in advance. Reports in 3 weeks on queries; 2 weeks on mss. Sample copy for $5. Writer's guidelines for #10 SASE.

• *Food & Wine* notes that they are very selective in choosing outside freelance writers.

Nonfiction: Food trends and news, how-to, kitchen and dining room design, travel. Query with published clips. Buys 125 mss/year. Length: 1,000-3,000 words. Pays $800-2,000. Pays expenses of writers on assignment.

Photos: State availability of photos with submission. No unsolicited photos or art. Offers $100-450/photo. Model releases and identification of subjects required. Buys one-time rights.

Columns/Departments: Restaurants, Travel, Style, Selects-Food, Selects-Design, Health, Low-fat Cooking, Dinner in Under an Hour, Experts. Buys 120 mss/year. Query with published clips. Length: 800-3,000 words. Pays $800-2,000.

Tips: "Good service, good writing, up-to-date information, interesting article approach and appropriate point of view for *F&W*'s audience are important elements to keep in mind. Look over several recent issues before writing query."

KASHRUS MAGAZINE, The Bimonthly for the Kosher Consumer and the Trade, Yeshiva Birkas Reuven, P.O. Box 204, Parkville Station, Brooklyn NY 11204. (718)336-8544. Contact: Rabbi Yosef Wikler, editor. 25% freelance written. Prefers to work with published/established writers, but will work with new/unpublished writers. Bimonthly magazine covering kosher food industry and food production. Estab. 1980. Circ. 10,000. Pays on publication. Publishes ms an average of 2 months after acceptance. Byline given. Offers 50% kill fee. Buys first or second serial (reprint) rights. Submit seasonal material 2 months in advance. Accepts simultaneous submissions. Reports in 1 week on queries, 2 weeks on mss. *Writer's Market* recommends allowing 2 months for reply. Sample copy for $3. Professional discount on subscription: $18/10 issues (regularly $33).

Nonfiction: General interest, interview/profile, new product, personal experience, photo feature, religious, technical and travel. Special issues feature: International Kosher Travel (October); Passover (March). Buys 8-12 mss/year. Query with published clips. Length: 1,000-1,500 words. Pays $100-250 for assigned articles; up to $100 for unsolicited articles. Sometimes pays expenses of writers on assignment.

Reprints: Send tearsheets or photocopy of article and information about when and where the article previously appeared. Pays 25-50% of amount paid for an original article.

Photos: State availability of photos with submission. Offers no additional payment for photos accepted with ms. Acquires one-time rights.

Columns/Departments: Book Review (cook books, food technology, kosher food), 250-500 words; People in the News (interviews with kosher personalities), 1,000-1,500 words; Regional Kosher Supervision (report on kosher supervision in a city or community), 1,000-1,500 words; Food Technology (new technology or current technology with accompanying pictures), 1,000-1,500 words; Travel (international, national), must include Kosher information and Jewish communities, 1,000-1,500 words; Regional Kosher Cooking, 1,000-1,500 words. Buys 8-12 mss/year. Query with published clips. Pays $50-250.

Tips: "*Kashrus Magazine* will do more writing on general food technology, production, and merchandising as well as human interest travelogs and regional writing in 1998 than we have done in the past. Areas most open to freelancers are interviews, food technology, cooking and food preparation, dining, regional reporting and travel. We welcome stories on the availability and quality of Kosher foods and services in communities across the U.S. and throughout the world. Some of our best stories have been by non-Jewish writers about kosher observance in their region. We also enjoy humorous articles. Just send a query with clips and we'll try to find a storyline that's right for you."

‡**ON THE GRILL**, On The Grill, Inc., 11063 Topeka Pl., Cooper City FL 33026. (954)430-0282. Fax: (954)43-3430. E-mail: onthegrill@aol.com. Contact: Scott M. Fine, editor-in-chief. 80% freelance written. Bimonthly magazine, "the first and only magazine dedicated to outdoor grilling and BBQing." Estab. 1996. Circ. 40,000. Pays on publication. Publishes ms an average of 3 months after acceptance. Byline given. Buys first rights. Editorial lead time 10 weeks. Submit seasonal material 3 months in advance. Reports in 1 month. Sample copy free.
Nonfiction: General interest, how-to, travel. Buys 18 mss/year. Query with published clips. Length: 1,500-2,500 words. Pays $350-600 for assigned articles; $350-500 for unsolicited articles. Pays expenses of writers on assignment.
Photos: State availability of photos with submission. Reviews 2¼×2¼ transparencies. Offers no additional payment for photos accepted with ms. Captions required. Buys one-time rights.
Columns/Departments: Buys 18 mss/year. Query.

RISTORANTE, Foley Publishing, P.O. Box 73, Liberty Corner NJ 07938. (908)766-6006. Fax: (908)766-6607. E-mail: barmag@aol.com. Website: http://www.bartender.com. Contact: Raymond Foley, publisher. Editor: Jaclyn Foley. 75% freelance written. Bimonthly magazine covering "Italian anything! *Ristorante—The magazine for the Italian Connoisseur.* For Italian restaurants and those who love Italian food, travel, wine and all things Italian!" Estab. 1994. Circ. 40,000. Pays on publication. Publishes ms an average of 3 months after acceptance. Byline sometimes given. Buys first North American and one-time rights. Editorial lead time 3 months. Submit seasonal material 3 months in advance. Reports in 1 month on queries; 2 months on mss. Sample copy and guidelines for 9×12 SAE and 4 first-class stamps.
Nonfiction: Book excerpts, general interest, historical/nostalgic, how-to (prepare Italian foods), humor, new product, opinion, personal experience, travel. Buys 25 mss/year. Send complete ms. Length: 100-1,000 words. Pays $100-350 for assigned articles; $75-300 for unsolicited articles. Sometimes pays expenses of writers on assignment.
Reprints: Send tearsheet of article and information about when and where the article previously appeared. Pays 25% of amount paid for an original article.
Photos: Send photos with submission. Reviews 3×5 prints. Negotiates payment individually. Captions, model releases required. Buys one-time rights.
Columns/Departments: Send complete ms. Pays $50-200.
Fillers: Anecdotes, facts, short humor. Buys 10/year. Pays $10-50.

SAVEUR, Mether Communications, 100 Avenue of the Americas, New York NY 10013. (212)334-2400. Fax: (212)334-1257. Publisher: Joe Armstrong. Bimonthly magazine covering fine dining. "*Saveur* is for people who are interested in the subject of food. It covers the world of food to make the cooking, the eating, the reading about food more satisfying. Special features include '*Saveur* Fare,' with informative news about the food world and an agenda of culinary events, and 'The *Saveur* Kitchen,' with tips, techniques and discoveries from the food editor." Estab. 1994. Circ. 114,000. This magazine did not respond to our request for information. Query before submitting.

‡**SHAPE COOKS, The Guide to Healthy Eating**, Weider Publications, 21100 Erwin St., Woodland Hills CA 91367. E-mail: shapette@aol.com. Editor: Katherine M. Tomlinson. Managing Editor: Elizabeth Turner. Contact: Maureen Healy, assistant editor. 80% freelance written. Quarterly magazine covering healthful low-fat cooking and eating. "*Shape Cooks* provides cutting-edge, hands-on information for active people who want healthful eating to taste great." Estab. 1996. Circ. 300,000. **Pays on acceptance.** Publishes ms an average of 3 months after acceptance. Offers 30% kill fee. Editorial lead time 6 months. Submit seasonal material 8 months in advance. Reports in 6 weeks on queries. Sample copy not available. Writer's guidelines for #10 SASE.
Nonfiction: Book excerpts, general interest, how-to, humor, new product, travel. Buys 35 mss/year. Query with published clips. *No unsolicited manuscripts.* Length: 600-2,500 words. Pays 70¢-$1.20/word.
Columns/Departments: Nutrition (hands-on tips and info); Fitness (reports on how food and nutrition affect physical performance); Traveling Light (vacations/adventures with a healthy-eating slant); all 600-1,200 words. Buys 25 mss/year. Query with published clips. Pays 70¢-$1.20/word

VEGETARIAN TIMES, 4 High Ridge Park, Stamford CT 06905. (203)321-1758. Fax: (203)322-1966. Editorial Director: Toni Apgar. 50% freelance written. Prefers to work with published/established writers; works with small number of new/unpublished writers each year. Monthly magazine. Circ. 320,000. Buys first serial or all rights. Byline given unless extensive revisions are required or material is incorporated into a larger article. **Pays on acceptance.** Publishes ms an average of 4 months after acceptance. Submit seasonal material 6 months in advance. Reports in 3 months. Query. Writer's guidelines for #10 SASE.
Nonfiction: Features articles that inform readers about how vegetarianism relates to diet, cooking, lifestyle, health, consumer choices, natural foods, environmental concerns and animal welfare. "All material should be well-documented and researched, and written in a sophisticated and lively style." Informational, how-to, personal experience, interview, profile, investigative. Query with published clips. Length: average 2,000 words. Pays flat rate of $100-1,000, sometimes higher, depending on length and difficulty of piece. Also uses 200-500-word items for news department. Sometimes pays expenses of writers on assignment.

Photos: Payment negotiated/photo.
Tips: "You don't have to be a vegetarian to write for *Vegetarian Times*, but it is vital that your article have a vegetarian perspective. The best way to pick up that slant is to read several issues of the magazine (no doubt a tip you've heard over and over). We are looking for stories that go beyond the obvious 'Why I Became a Vegetarian.' A well-written provocative query plus samples of your best writing will increase your chances of publication."

VEGGIE LIFE, Growing Green, Cooking Lean, Feeling Good, EGW Publishing, 1041 Shary Circle, Concord CA 94518. (510)671-9852. Fax: (510)671-0692. E-mail: veggieed@aol.com. Website: http://www.veggielife.com. Contact: Sharon Barcla, editor. 90% freelance written. Bimonthly magazine covering vegetarian cooking, natural health, herbal healing and organic gardening. Estab. 1992. Circ. 380,000. **Pays on acceptance**, half on publication. Publishes ms an average of 4 months after acceptance. Byline given. Offers 25% kill fee. Buys simultaneous rights or makes work-for-hire assignments. Editorial lead time 4-6 months. Submit seasonal material 4-6 months in advance. Reports in 2-4 months, no phone calls, please. E-mail OK. Writer's guidelines for #10 SASE.
Nonfiction: Vegetarian cooking/recipes, gardening how-to, natural health, herbal healing, nutrition, fitness. No animal rights issues/advocacy, religious/philosophical, personal opinion or product/company bashing. Buys 30-50 mss/year. Query with published clips. Length: 1,500-2,000 words. Pays 25-35¢/word. More for credentialed professionals.
Photos: State availability of photos with submission. Negotiates payment individually. Captions, model releases and identification of subjects required. Buys one-time rights or makes work-for-hire assignments.
Columns/Departments: Meal in Minutes, 100-150 words followed by three quick and easy 60 minute recipes; Cooking with Soy, 150-200 word introduction followed by 3-4 eggless, dairy-free recipes made with a soy product. Remakes of old favorites encouraged. Pays 25-30¢/published word plus $25-35/published recipe.
Tips: "Research back issues; be authoritative; no 'Why I Became a Vegetarian . . .' or negative investigative stories. Please state why you are qualified to write particular subject matter—a *must* on health/herbal mss. No article will be considered without sufficient fact verification information. Gender specific and age specific (i.e., children, adolescents, seniors) topics are encouraged. Photographs are a strong plus in considering gardening submissions."

WINE SPECTATOR, M. Shanken Communications, Inc., 387 Park Ave. S., New York NY 10016. (212)684-4224. Fax: (212)684-5424. Website: winespectator.com. Contact: Jim Gordon, managing editor. 20% freelance written. Prefers to work with published/established writers. Biweekly consumer newsmagazine. Estab. 1976. Circ. 200,000. Pays within 30 days of publication. Publishes ms an average of 2 months after acceptance. Byline given. Buys all rights and makes work-for-hire assignments. Submit seasonal material 4 months in advance. Reports in 3 months. Sample copy for $5. Writer's guidelines free.
Nonfiction: General interest (news about wine or wine events); interview/profile (of wine, vintners, wineries); opinion; travel, dining and other lifestyle pieces; photo feature. No "winery promotional pieces or articles by writers who lack sufficient knowledge to write below just surface data." Query. Length: 100-2,000 words average. Pays $50-500.
Photos: Send photos with ms. Pays $75 minimum for color transparencies. Captions, model releases, identification of subjects required. Buys all rights.
Tips: "A solid knowledge of wine is a must. Query letters essential, detailing the story idea. New, refreshing ideas which have not been covered before stand a good chance of acceptance. *Wine Spectator* is a consumer-oriented *news magazine*, but we are interested in some trade stories; brevity is essential."

GAMES AND PUZZLES

These publications are written by and for game enthusiasts interested in both traditional games and word puzzles and newer role-playing adventure, computer and video games. Other puzzle markets may be found in the Juvenile section.

CHESS LIFE, United States Chess Federation, 3054 NYS Route 9W, New Windsor NY 12553-7698. (914)562-8350. Fax: (914)561-2437 or (914)236-4852. Contact: Glenn Petersen, editor. 15% freelance written. Works with a small number of new/unpublished writers each year. Monthly magazine covering the chess world. Estab. 1939. Circ. 70,000. Pays variable fee. Publishes ms an average of 5 months after acceptance. Byline given. Offers 50% kill fee. Buys first or negotiable rights. Submit seasonal material 8 months in advance. Accepts simultaneous submissions. Reports in 3 months. Sample copy and writer's guidelines for 9×11 SAE with 5 first-class stamps.
Nonfiction: General interest, historical, interview/profile, technical—all must have some relation to chess. No "stories about personal experiences with chess." Buys 30-40 mss/year. Query with samples "if new to publication." Length: 3,000 words maximum. Pays $100/page (per 800-1,000 words). Sometimes pays the expenses of writers on assignment.
Reprints: Send tearsheet or photocopy of article or short story with typed ms with rights for sale noted and information about when and where the article previously appeared.
Photos: Reviews b&w contact sheets and prints, and color prints and slides. Captions, model releases and identification of subjects required. Buys all or negotiable rights. Pays $25-35 inside; $100-300 for covers.
Columns/Departments: Chess Review (brief articles on unknown chess personalities and "Chess in Everyday Life."
Fiction: "Chess-related, high quality." Buys 2-3 mss/year. Pays variable fee.
Fillers: Cartoons, poems, puzzles. Submit with samples and clips. Buys first or negotiable rights. Pays $25 upon

acceptance.

Tips: "Articles must be written from an informed point of view—not from view of the curious amateur. Most of our writers are specialized in that they have sound credentials as chessplayers. Freelancers in major population areas (except New York and Los Angeles, which we already have covered) who are interested in short personality profiles and perhaps news reporting have the best opportunities. We're looking for more personality pieces on chessplayers around the country; not just the stars, but local masters, talented youths, and dedicated volunteers. Freelancers interested in such pieces might let us know of their interest and their range. Could be we know of an interesting story in their territory that needs covering. Recent examples are articles on a locally produced chess television program, a meeting of chess set collectors from around the world, chess in our prisons, and chess in the works of several famous writers."

‡COMPUTER GAMING WORLD, The #1 Computer Game Magazine, Ziff Davis Consumer Media Group, 135 Main St., 14th Floor, San Francisco CA 94105. (415)357-4900. Fax: (415)357-4977. E-mail: 76703.622@compuserve.com. Website: http://www.computergaming.com. Contact: Denny Atkin, features editor. 75% freelance written. Works with a small number of new/unpublished writers each year. Monthly magazine covering computer games. "*Computer Gaming World* is now in its 15th year of publication and reaches approximately 200,000 readers, which is the largest circulation of any magazine in the field. The magazine's editorial philosophy is based on the ideals of journalistic integrity, impartiality, and thoughtful critical analysis. The magazine's focus is primarily new game coverage, but the scope also includes technology and new hardware (including computer systems, processors, CD-ROM drives, graphic accelerators, sound cards, game controllers) and other peripherals." Estab. 1981. Pays on publication. Publishes ms an average of 3 months after acceptance. Byline given. Buys all rights. Submit seasonal material 4 months in advance. Electronic submissions preferred, but not required. Query first. Reports in 4 months. Sample copy for $3.50. Writer's guidelines free.

Nonfiction: Reviews, strategy tips, industry insights. Buys 60 mss/year. Query. Length: 750-2,000 words. Pays 15-20¢/word. Sometimes pays the expenses of writers on assignment.

DRAGON MAGAZINE, TSR, Inc., P.O. Box 707, Renton WA 98057-0707. (425)226-6500. Fax: (425)204-5928. Website: http://tsrinc.com. Contact: Dave Gross, editor. Monthly magazine of fantasy and science-fiction role-playing games. 90% freelance written. Eager to work with published/established writers as well as new/unpublished writers. Estab. 1976. Circ. 100,000, primarily across the US, Canada and Great Britain. Byline given. Offers kill fee. Submit seasonal material 8 months in advance. Pays on publication for articles to which all rights are purchased; pays on acceptance for articles to which first/worldwide rights in English are purchased. Publishing dates vary from 1-24 months after acceptance. Reports in 3 months. Sample copy $5.50. Writer's guidelines for #10 SAE with 1 first-class stamp.

● TSR was purchased by Wizards of the Coast. Editorial offices were moved to Washington.

Nonfiction: Articles on the hobby of science fiction and fantasy role-playing. No general articles on gaming hobby. "Our article needs are *very* specialized. Writers should be experienced in gaming hobby and role-playing. No strong sexual overtones or graphic depictions of violence." Buys 120 mss/year. Query. Length: 1,000-8,000 words. Pays $50-500 for assigned articles; $5-400 for unsolicited articles.

Fiction: Michelle Vuckovich, fiction editor. Fantasy only. "No strong sexual overtones or graphic depictions of violence." Buys 6-12 mss/year. Send complete ms. Length: 2,000-8,000 words. Pays 6-8¢/word.

Tips: "*Dragon Magazine* is *not* a periodical that the 'average reader' appreciates or understands. A writer must *be* a reader and must share the serious interest in gaming our readers possess."

FANTASY BASEBALL INDEX, DFL Publishing, 18247 66th Ave. NE Seattle WA 98155. (206)487-9000. Fax: (206)485-3699. E-mail: ffmag@netcom.com. Editor: Bruce Taylor. 5-10% freelance written. Annual magazine covering fantasy sports games. "*Fantasy Baseball Index* and its sister publications are study guides for participants in fantasy sports leagues. All articles are written from a fantasy perspective. We are not interested in articles on handicapping." Estab. 1987. Circ. 210,000. Pays on publication. Publishes ms an average of 2 months after acceptance. Byline given. Buys all rights. Editorial lead time 2 months. Submit seasonal material 2 months in advance. Sample copy $3. Writer's guidelines free.

Nonfiction: How-to (general interest to fantasy coaches), opinion, technical. Special issues: Football (March); Baseball (November); Basketball (June). Nothing pertaining to handicapping or gambling. Buys 2 mss/year. Query. Length: 1,000-4,000 words. Pays $100-300.

Photos: State availability of photos with submission. Reviews 35mm transparencies, 5×7 prints. Negotiates payment individually. Identification of subjects required.

Columns/Departments: Pays $100-300

Tips: "Please contact us several months in advance if you have an idea for a story. We will want to see a brief outline along with samples of your work. We want only articles focusing on fantasy sports—please, no general interest."

FANTASY FOOTBALL INDEX, DFL Publishing, 18247 66th Ave. NE Seattle WA 98155. (206)487-9000. Fax: (206)485-3699. E-mail: ffmag@netcom.com. Website: http://www.fantasyindex.com. Contact: Bruce Taylor, editor. 5-10% freelance written. Annual magazine covering fantasy sports games. "*Fantasy Football Index* and its sister publications are study guides for participants in fantasy sports leagues. All articles are written from a fantasy perspective. We are not interested in articles on handicapping." Estab. 1987. Circ. 210,000. Pays on publication. Publishes ms an average of 2 months after acceptance. Byline given. Buys all rights. Editorial lead time 2 months. Submit seasonal material 2 months in advance. Sample copy $3. Writer's guidelines free.

Nonfiction: How-to (general interest to fantasy coaches), opinion, technical. Special issues: Football (March); Baseball (November); Basketball (June). Nothing pertaining to handicapping or gambling. Buys 2 mss/year. Query. Length: 1,000-4,000 words. Pays $100-300.
Photos: State availability of photos with submission. Reviews 35mm transparencies, 5×7 prints. Negotiates payment individually. Identification of subjects required.
Columns/Departments: Pays $100-300
Tips: "Please contact us several months in advance if you have an idea for a story. We will want to see a brief outline along with samples of your work. We want only articles focusing on fantasy sports—please no general interest."

GAMEPRO, International Data Group, 951 Mariner's Island Blvd. Suite 700, San Mateo CA 94404. (415)349-4300. Fax:(415)349-7482. Publisher: Wes Nihei. Monthly magazine. "*GamePro* is a multi-platform interactive gaming magazine covering the electronic game market. It is edited for the avid online, video and PC game enthusiast. The editorial includes a mix of news, reviews, strategy and specific topical sections such as Fighter's Edge, Role Player's Realm and the Sports Pages." Estab.1988. Circ. 3,932. This magazine did not respond to our request for information. Query before submitting.

‡GAMES MAGAZINE, Games Publications, Inc., 7002 W. Butler Pike, Suite 210, Ambler PA 19002. (215)643-6385. Fax: (215)628-3571. E-mail: gamespub@aol.com. Contact: R. Wayne Schmittberger, editor-in-chief. 50% freelance written. Bimonthly magazine covering puzzles and games. "*Games* is a magazine of puzzles, contests, and features pertaining to games and ingenuity. It is aimed primarily at adults and has an emphasis on pop culture." Estab. 1977. Circ. 225,000. Pays on publication. Publishes ms an average of 4 months after acceptance. Byline given. Offers 25% kill fee. Buys first North American serial rights, first rights, one-time rights, second serial (reprint) rights, all rights or makes work-for-hire assignments. Editorial lead time 3 months. Submit seasonal material 6 months in advance. Accepts simultaneous submissions. Reports in 6 weeks on queries; 3 months on mss. Sample copy for $5. Writer's guidelines for #10 SASE.
Nonfiction: Photo features, puzzles, games. Buys 3 mss/year; 100 puzzles/year. Query. Length: 1,500-2,500 words. Pays $1,000-1,750. Sometimes pays expenses of writers on assignment.
Reprints: Accepts previously published submissions.
Photos: State availability of photos with submission. Reviews contact sheets, negatives, transparencies, prints. Negotiates payment individually. Captions, model releases, identification of subjects required. Buys one-time rights.
Columns/Departments: Gamebits (game/puzzle news), 250 words; Games & Books (product reviews), 350 words; Wild Cards (short text puzzles), 100 words. Buys 50 mss/year. Query. Pays $25-250.
Fiction: Interactive adventure and mystery stories. Buys 1-2 mss/year. Query. Length: 1,500-2,500 words. Pays $1,000-1,750.
Tips: "Look for real-life people, places, or things that might in some way be the basis for a puzzle."

GIANT CROSSWORDS, Scrambl-Gram, Inc., Puzzle Buffs International, 1772 State Rd., Cuyahoga Falls OH 44223-1200. (216)923-2397. Contact: C.R. Elum, editor. Submissions Editor: S. Bowers. 40% freelance written. Eager to work with new/unpublished writers. Quarterly crossword puzzle and word game magazine. Estab. 1970. **Pays on acceptance.** Publishes ms an average of 1 month after acceptance. No byline given. Buys all rights. Reports in 1 month. "We offer constructors' kits, master grids, clue sheets and a 'how-to-make-crosswords' book for $37.50 postpaid." Send #10 SASE for details.
Nonfiction: Crosswords and word games only. Query. Pays according to size of puzzle and/or clues.
Reprints: Send information about when and where the article previously appeared.
Tips: "We are expanding our syndication of original crosswords and our publishing schedule to include new titles and extra issues of current puzzle books."

‡INQUEST, 151 Wells Ave., Congers NY 10920-2036. (914)268-2000. Contact: Tom Slizewski, managing editor. Monthly magazine covering all of adventure gaming, particularly collectible card games (i.e., Magic) but also roleplaying and fantasy, sci fi and board games. Pays on publication. Publishes ms an average of 2 months after acceptance. Byline given. Buys one-time and all rights. Reports in 6 weeks. Sample copy for $5. Writer's guidelines for #10 SASE.
Nonfiction: Interview/profile (Q&As with big-name personalities in sci-fi and fantasy field, special access stories like set visits to popular TV shows or films). No advertorials or stories on older, non-current games. Buys 60 mss/year. Query with published clips. Length: 2,000-4,000 words. Pays $350-1,000.
Columns/Departments: On Deck (mini game reviews), technical columns on how to play currently popular games. Buys 100 mss/year. Query with published clips. Pays $50-250.
Tips: "*InQuest* is always looking for good freelance news and feature writers who are interested in card, roleplaying or electronic games. A love of fantasy or science fiction books, movies, or art is desirable. Experience is preferred; sense of humor a plus; a flair for writing mandatory. Above all you must be able to find interesting new angles to a story, work hard and meet deadlines."

PC GAMES, The Complete Guide to Computer Gaming, IDG Communications, 951 Mariners Island Blvd., #700, San Mateo CA 94404. (415)349-4300. Fax: (415)349-7482. E-mail: cgrech@iftw.com. Editor-in-chief: Steve Klett. 40% freelance written. Monthly magazine covering PC and Mac games, virtual reality, interactive TV, entertainment. Estab. 1993. Circ. 150,000. **Pays on acceptance.** Publishes ms an average of 3 months after acceptance. Byline given. Buys all rights. Editorial lead time 3-4 months. Submit seasonal material 6 months in advance.

Nonfiction: Exposé, how-to, humor, interview/profile, new product, opinion, personal experience, photo feature, technical (games or gaming experiences). Query with published clips. Length: 100-4,000 words. Pays $50-1,000.

Photos: Send photos with submission. Reviews negatives, transparencies or computer files. Offers no additional payment for photos accepted with ms. Captions required. Buys all rights.

Columns/Departments: Game reviews, 400-600 words. Buys 12 mss/year. Query with clips. Pays $50-150.

Fillers: Anecdotes, facts, short humor. Length: 25-100 words. Pays $25.

Tips: "Read the magazine, know about the field, have proven writing skills, and propose ideas with fresh angles."

‡**POPULAR CROSSWORDS**, Hachette Filipacchi Magazines, Inc., 1633 Broadway, New York NY 10019. Contact: Florence Bierman, editor. 100% freelance written. Monthly magazine composed of crossword puzzles. "Would like some easy (15×15) puzzles." Estab. 1930. Circ. over 30 million. Pays on publication. Publishes ms an average of 6 months after acceptance. Buys all rights. Editorial lead time 6 months. Submit seasonal material 6 months in advance. Reports in 2 weeks on queries; 2 months on mss. Writer's guidelines for #10 SASE.

Nonfiction: Pays $17.50/puzzle minimum.

‡**PREMIUM CROSSWORD PUZZLES**, Hachette Filipacchi Magazines, Inc., 1633 Broadway, New York NY 10019. Editor: Florence Bierman. 100% freelance written. Monthly magazine composed of crossword puzzles. "Would like themed crosswords of any size, as well as medium to difficult puzzles." Estab. 1994. Circ. 30 million. Pays on publication. Publishes ms an average of 6 months after acceptance. Byline sometimes given. Buys all rights. Submit seasonal material 6 months in advance. Reports in 2 weeks on queries; 2 months on mss. Writer's guidelines for #10 SASE.

Nonfiction: Pays $30/puzzle minimum.

SCHOOL MATES, United States Chess Federation, 186 Route 9W, New Windsor NY 12553-5794. (914)562-8350 ext. 152. Fax: (914)561-CHES (2437). E-mail: uscf@delphi.com. Publication Director: Jay Hastings. Editor: Beatriz Marinello. 10% freelance written. Bimonthly magazine of chess for the beginning (some intermediate) player. Includes instruction, player profiles, chess tournament coverage, listings. Estab. 1987. Circ. 30,000. Pays on publication. Publishes ms an average of 6 months after acceptance. Byline given. Publication copyrighted "but not filed with Library of Congress." Buys first rights. Editorial lead time 2 months. Submit seasonal material 3 months in advance. Accepts simultaneous submissions. Reports in 6 months. Sample copy and writer's guidelines free.

Nonfiction: How-to, humor, personal experience (chess, but not "my first tournament"), photo feature, technical, travel and any other chess related item. Poetry. Fiction. Buys 10-20 mss/year. Query. Length: 250-1,000 words. Pays $50/1,000 words, $20 minimum). "We are not-for-profit; we try to make up for low $ rate with complimentary copies." Sometimes pays expenses of writers on assignment.

Reprints: Send tearsheet, photocopy of article or typed ms with rights for sale noted and information about when and where the article previously appeared. Pays 100% of amount paid for an original article.

Photos: Send photos with submission. Reviews prints. Offers $25/photo for first time rights. Captions, identification of subjects required. Buys one-time rights, pays $15 for subsequent use.

Columns/Departments: Test Your Tactics/Winning Chess Tactics (explanation, with diagrams, of chess tactics; 8 diagrammed chess problems, e.g., "white to play and win in 2 moves"); Basic Chess (chess instruction for beginners). Query with published clips. Pays $50/1,000 words ($20 minimum).

Tips: "Know your subject; chess is a technical subject, and you can't fake it. Human interest stories on famous chess players or young chess players can be 'softer,' but always remember you are writing for children, and make it lively. We use the Frye readability scale (3rd-6th grade reading level), and items written on the appropriate reading level do stand out immediately! We are most open to human interest stories, puzzles, cartoons, photos. We are always looking for an unusual angle, e.g., (wild example) a kid who plays chess while surfing, or (more likely) a blind kid and how she plays chess with her specially-made chess pieces and board, etc."

‡**VIDEOGAMES FOR VIRGINS**, Com Ent Media Group, Inc., 3932 Wilshire Blvd., #212, Los Angeles CA 90010. Fax: (213)383-1093. Website: http://www.allmediadist.com. Contact: Sean Perkin, editor. 80% freelance written. Biannual publication. "Designed as not only a reference guide on technological change, *VideoGames For Virgins* explores the impact and implications of technology on all of us. The CDZeene also includes a special section on cyberculture as well as a promotional CD-ROM containing game demos, interviews and product profiles. From the very best CD-ROM adventures to the latest in hardware, Internet information, and emerging techno trends, *VideoGames For Virgins* is the comprehensive guide to understanding the technological world." Estab. 1992. Circ. 25,000. Pays within 2 weeks after publication. Publishes ms an average of 1 month after acceptance. Byline given. Buys one-time rights, makes work-for-hire assignments. Editorial lead time 3 months. Submit seasonal material 4 months in advance. Accepts simultaneous submissions. Sample copy for $12.50. Writer's guidelines provided upon hiring.

Nonfiction: Exposé, interview/profile, new product, travel.

Reprints: Send photocopy of article and information about when and where the article previously appeared. Payment varies.

GAY AND LESBIAN INTEREST

The magazines listed here cover a wide range of politics, culture, news, art, literature and issues of general interest to gay and lesbian communities. Magazines of a strictly sexual content are listed in the new Sex section.

‡THE ADVOCATE, Liberation Publications, Inc., 6922 Hollywood Blvd., 10th Floor, Suite 1000, Los Angeles CA 90028-6148. (213)871-1225. Fax: (213)467-6805. E-mail: newsroom@advocate.com. Contact: Judy Wieder, editor-in-chief. Biweekly magazine covering national news events with a gay and lesbian perspective on the issues. Estab. 1967. Circ. 76,228. Pays on publication. Byline given. Buys first North American serial rights. Responds in 1 month. Sample copy for $3.95. Writer's guidelines for #10 SASE.

Nonfiction: Essays, exposé, interview/profile, personal experience. "Here are elements we look for in all articles: *Angling*: An angle is the one editorial tool we have to attract a reader's attention. An *Advocate* editor won't make an assignment unless he or she has worked out a very specific angle with you. Once you've worked out the angle with an editor, don't deviate from it without letting the editor know. Some of the elements we look for in angles are: a news hook; an open question or controversy; a 'why' or 'how' element or novel twist; national appeal; and tight focus. *Content*: There is a series of specific elements we look for in a completed story: a strong lead and billboard graf close to the top; a big finish; conflict; attribution; thoroughness; mainstream sourcing; specifics; quotes; logical structure; and clear, economical and understandable language. *Tone*: Tone is the element that makes an emotional connection. Some characteristics we look for: toughness; edginess; fairness and evenhandedness; multiple perspectives." Query. Length: 1,200 words. Pays $550.

Columns/Departments: Arts & Media (news and profiles of well-knwon gay or lesbians in entertainment) is most open to freelancers. Query. Length: 750 words. Pays $1-500.

Tips: "*The Advocate* is a unique newsmagazine. While we report on gay and lesbian issues and are published by one of the country's oldest and most established gay-owned companies, we also play by the rules of mainstream-not gay-community-journalism."

BAY WINDOWS, New England's Largest Gay and Lesbian Newspaper, Bay Windows, Inc., 1523 Washington St., Boston MA 02118-2034. (617)266-6670. Fax: (617)266-5973. E-mail: news@baywindows.com. Editor: Jeff Epperly. Arts Editor: Rudy Kikel. Contact: Loren King, assistant editor. 30-40% freelance written. Weekly newspaper of gay news and concerns. "*Bay Windows* covers predominantly news of New England, but will print non-local news and features depending on the newsworthiness of the story. We feature hard news, opinion, news analysis, arts reviews and interviews." Estab. 1983. Publishes ms within 2 months of acceptance, pays within 2 months of publication. Byline given. Offers 50% kill fee. Rights obtained varies, usually first serial rights. Simultaneous submissions accepted if other submissions are outside of New England. Submit seasonal material 3 months in advance. Reports in 3 months. Sample copy for $5. Writer's guidelines for #10 SASE.

Nonfiction: Hard news, general interest with a gay slant, interview/profile, opinion, photo features. Publishes 200 mss/year. Query with clips or send complete ms. Length: 500-1,500 words. Pay varies: $25-100 news; $10-60 arts.

Reprints: Send tearsheet or photocopy of article and information about when and where the article previously appeared. Pays 75% of amount paid for an original article.

Photos: Pays $25/published photo. Model releases and identification of subjects required.

Columns/Departments: Film, music, dance, books, art. Length: 500-1,500 words. Buys 200 mss/year. Pays $25-100. Letters, opinion to Jeff Epperly, editor; news, features to Loren King, assistant editor; arts, reviews to Rudy Kikel, arts editor.

Poetry: All varieties. Publishes 50 poems/year. Length: 10-30 lines. No payment.

Tips: "Too much gay-oriented writing is laden with the clichés and catch phrases of the movement. Writers must have intimate knowledge of gay community; however, this doesn't mean that standard English usage isn't required. We look for writers with new, even controversial perspectives on the lives of gay men and lesbians. While we assume gay is good, we'll print stories which examine problems within the community and movement. No pornography or erotica."

‡CURVE MAGAZINE, Outspoken Enterprises, Inc., 1 Haight St., #B, San Francisco CA 94102. Fax: (415)863-1609. E-mail: curvemag@aol.com. Editor-in-chief: Frances Stevens. Contact: Rebecca Alber, managing editor. 40% freelance written. Bimonthly magazine covering lesbian general interest categories. "We want dynamic and provocative articles written by, about and for lesbians." Estab. 1991. Circ. 65,000. Pays on publication. Byline given. Offers 30% kill fee. Buys first North American serial rights. Editorial lead time 3 months. Submit seasonal material 3 months in advance. Sample copy for $3.95 with $2 postage. Writer's guidelines free.

Nonfiction: Book excerpts, essays, exposé, general interest, how-to, humor, interview/profile, opinion, photo feature, travel. No fiction or poetry. Buys 25 mss/year. Query. Length: 200-2,500 words. Pays $40-300. Sometimes pays expenses of writers on assignment.

Photos: Send photos with submission. Offers $50-100/photo; negotiates payment individually. Captions, model releases, identification of subjects required. Buys one-time rights.

Columns/Departments: Buys 72 mss/year. Query. Pays $75-300.

EVERGREEN CHRONICLES, A Journal of Gay, Lesbian, Bisexual, and Transgender Arts and Cultures, P.O. Box 8939, Minneapolis MN 55408. (612)823-6638. Editor: Jim Berg. Contact: Louisa Castner, managing editor. 75% freelance written. Triannual magazine covering gay, lesbian, bisexual, and transgender communities. "We are interested in work that challenges and explores the meaning of 'gay,' 'lesbian,' 'bisexual,' or 'transgender,' especially as related to race, class, sexuality, and gender." Estab. 1984. Circ. 2,000. Pays on publication. Publishes ms an average of 3 months after acceptance. Byline given. Buys first rights. Submit seasonal material 2 months in advance. Reports in 2 weeks on queries; 3 months on mss. Sample copy for $8. Writer's guidelines for #10 SASE.

Nonfiction: Book excerpts, essays, historical/nostalgic, interview/profile, opinion, personal experience. Buys 6 mss/ year. Query or send complete ms. Length: up to 4,000 words. Pays $50.

Photos: State availability of photos with submissions. Reviews contact sheets. Captions required. Buys one-time rights. Pays $50.

Fiction: Erotica, ethnic, experimental, fantasy, historical, novel excerpts. Buys 20 mss/year. Send 4 copies of ms. Length: up to 4,000 words. Pays $50.

Poetry: All types. Buys 40 poems/year. Submit maximum 4 poems. Pays $50.

‡**50-50 MAGAZINE**, Wendy Jill York Productions, 2336 Market St., #20, San Francisco CA 94114. (415)861-8210. Fax: (415)621-1703. E-mail: fift50mag@aol.com. Editor: Wendy Jill York. 80% freelance written. Quarterly magazine covering gay and lesbian interests, art and entertainment. "We publish high-quality articles of interest to our target audience, reviews and profiles of artists and entertainers. No sexually explicit material." Estab. 1994. Circ. 20,000. Pays on publication. Publishes ms an average of 3 months after acceptance. Byline given. Offers 20% kill fee. Buys one-time rights. Editorial lead time 3 months. Submit seasonal material 4 months in advance. Reports in 3 weeks on queries; 1 month on mss. Sample copy for $6. Writer's guidelines for $1.

Nonfiction: Interview/profile, photo feature, travel, entertainment, music, movie reviews. No sexually explicit material. Buys 20-28 mss/year. Query with published clips or send complete ms. Length: 400-2,000 words. Pays $15-50 for assigned articles; $10-30 for unsolicited articles. "Other forms of payment negotiated on an individual basis at the writer's request." Sometimes pays expenses of writers on assignment.

Photos: State availability of photos with submission. Reviews contact sheets and prints. Offers $10-25 or negotiates payment individually. Model releases and identification of subjects required. Buys one-time rights.

Columns/Departments: Taste (food/restaurants), 600-800 words; Music (reviews/profiles), reviews: 400 words, profiles: 1,200 words; Body (information/sports), 600-1,000 words. Buys 12 mss/year. Send complete ms. Pays $10-25.

Fiction: Stephanie Mazow, fiction contest manager. "Nothing in poor taste. We are very artistic—not graphic." Send complete ms. Length: 2,000 words. "We have an annual fiction contest. October is the deadline. First prize: $300 plus the winner gets published in the magazine."

Tips: "Submissions should be printed double-spaced. Include a Macintosh disk in Microsoft Word 5.0 or above."

GENRE, Genre Publishing, 7080 Hollywood Blvd., #1104, Hollywood CA 90028. (213)896-9778. Fax: (213)467-8365. E-mail: genre@aol.com. Website: http://www.genremagazine.com. Editor: Ronald Mark Kraft. Contact: John Polly, senior editor. 90% freelance written. Magazine published 10 times/year. "*Genre*, America's best-selling gay men's lifestyle magazine, covers entertainment, fashion, travel and relationships in a hip, upbeat, upscale voice. The award-winning publication's mission is best summarized by its tagline—'How We Live.' " Estab. 1991. Circ. 50,000. Pays on publication. Publishes ms an average of 3 months after acceptance. Byline given. Offers 25% kill fee. Buys first North American serial rights and all rights. Editorial lead time 3 months. Submit seasonal material 3 months in advance. Sample copy for $7.95 ($5 plus $2.95 postage). Writer's guidelines for #10 SASE.

Nonfiction: Book excerpts, exposé, general interest, interview/profile, photo feature, travel, relationships, fashion. Query with published clips. Length: 1,500-3,500 words. Pays 10-50¢/word. Pays writer with contributor copies or other premiums rather than a cash payment if so negotiated.

Photos: State availability of photos with submission. Negotiates payment individually. Model releases and identification of subjects required.

Columns/Departments: Tweaked (short, punchy, celeb Q&As), 500 words. Buys 20 mss/year. Query with published clips. Pays $25-150.

Fiction: Adventure, experimental, horror, humorous, mainstream, mystery, novel excerpts, religious, romance, science fiction, slice-of-life vignettes, suspense. Buys 10 mss/year. Send complete ms. Length: 2,000-4,000 words.

GIRLFRIENDS MAGAZINE, America's fastest-growing lesbian magazine, 3415 Cesar Chavez, Suite 101, San Francisco CA 94110. (415)648-9464. Fax: (415)648-4705. E-mail: staff@gfriends.com. Website: http://www.gfriends.com. Editor: Heather Findlay. Contact: Diane Anderson, managing editor. Bimonthly lesbian magazine. *Girlfriends* provides its readers with intelligent, entertaining and visually-pleasing coverage of culture, politics and sexuality—all from an informed and critical lesbian perspective. Estab. 1994. Circ. 60,000. Pays on publication. Publishes ms an average of 6 months after acceptance. Byline given. Offers 25% kill fee. Buys first rights, use for advertising/promoting *Girlfriends*. Editorial lead time 3 months. Submit seasonal material 6 months in advance. Accepts simultaneous submissions. Reports in 3 weeks on queries; 2 months on mss. Sample copy for $4.95 plus $1.50 shipping and handling. Writer's guidelines for #10 SASE.

Nonfiction: Book excerpts, essays, exposé, humor, interview/profile, personal experience, photo feature, travel. Special features: lesbians related to famous historical figures; best lesbian restaurants in the US; exposé on Scientology and its followers. Buys 20-25 mss/year. Query with published clips. Length: 1,000-3,500 words. Pays 10¢/word.

● This magazine was recently redesigned and has expanded its editorial pages. It is doing more profiles (celebrities, political leaders) and more investigative features. It is planning on becoming a monthly title in 1998.

Reprints: Send photocopy and information about when and where the article or story previously appeared.

Photos: Send photos with submissions. Reviews contact sheets, 4×5 or 2¼×2¼ transparencies, prints. Offers $30-

250/photo. Captions, model releases, identification of subjects required. Buys one-time rights, use for advertising/ promoting *GF*.

Columns/Departments: Lesbian Parenting, 600 words; Sports, 800 words; Travel, 800 words; Health, 600 words; Spirituality, 600 words. Buys 50 mss/year. Query with published clips. Pays 10¢/word.

Fiction: Erotica, ethnic, experimental, fantasy, historical, humorous, mystery, novel concepts, science fiction, novel excerpts. Buys 6-10 mss/year. Query with complete ms. Length: 800-2,500 words. Pays 10¢/word.

Poetry: Avant-garde, free verse, Haiku, light verse, traditional. Buys 6-10 poems/year. Submit maximum 5 poems. Length: 3-75 lines. Pays $50.

Fillers: Gags to be illustrated by cartoonist, short humor. Buys 6-10/year. Length: 500-800 words. Pays $50.

Tips: "Be unafraid of controversy—articles should focus on problems and debates raised around lesbian culture, politics, and sexuality. Fiction should be innovative and eyebrow-raising. Avoid being 'politically correct.' Photographers should aim for the suggestive, not the explicit. We don't want just to know what's happening in the lesbian world, we want to know how what's happening in the world affects lesbians."

THE GUIDE, To Gay Travel, Entertainment, Politics and Sex, Fidelity Publishing, P.O. Box 990593, Boston MA 02199-0593. (617)266-8557. Fax: (617)266-1125. E-mail: theguide@guidemag.com. Website: http://www.guidema g.com. Contact: French Wall, editor. 25% freelance written. Monthly magazine on the gay and lesbian community. Estab. 1981. Circ. 31,000. **Pays on acceptance.** Publishes ms an average of 2 months after acceptance. Kill fee negotiable. Buys first-time rights. Submit seasonal material 2 months in advance. Accepts simultaneous submissions. Reports in 3 months. Sample copy for 9×12 SAE with 8 first-class stamps. Writer's guidelines for #10 SASE.

Nonfiction: Book excerpts (if yet unpublished), essays, exposé, general interest, historical/nostalgic, humor, interview/ profile, opinion, personal experience, photo feature, religious. Buys 24 mss/year. Query with or without published clips or send complete ms. Length: 500-5,000 words. Pays $60-200.

Photos: Send photos with submission. Reviews contact sheets. Offers no additional payment for photos accepted with ms (although sometimes negotiable). Captions, model releases, identification of subjects prefered; releases required sometimes. Buys one-time rights.

Tips: "Brevity, humor and militancy appreciated."

HX MAGAZINE, Two Queens, Inc., 19 W. 21 St., #504, New York NY 10010. (212)627-0747. Fax: (212)627-5280. E-mail: editor@hx.com. Website: http://www.hx.com. Contact: Joseph Manghise, editor. 25% freelance written. Weekly magazine covering gay New York City nightlife and entertainment. "We publish a magazine for gay men who are interested in New York City nightlife and entertainment." Estab. 1991. Circ. 32,000. Pays on publication. Publishes ms an average of 1 month after acceptance. Byline given. Buys first North American serial, second serial (reprint) and electronic reprint rights. Editorial lead time 2 months. Submit seasonal material 2 months in advance. "We must be exclusive East Coast publisher to accept." Only responds if interested.

Nonfiction: General interest, arts and entertainment, celebrity profiles, reviews. Buys 50 mss/year. Query with published clips. Length: 500-2,000 words. Pays $50-150 for assigned articles; $25-100 for unsolicited articles.

Reprints: Send tearsheet or photocopy of article or typed ms with rights for sale noted and information about when and where the article previously appeared. Pays 50% of amount paid for an original article.

Photos: State availability of photos with submission. Reviews contact sheets, negatives, 8×10 prints. Negotiates payment individually. Captions, model releases, identification of subjects required. Buys one-time, reprint and electronic reprint rights.

Columns/Departments: Buys 200 mss/year. Query with published clips. Pays $25-125.

LAMBDA BOOK REPORT, A Review of Contemporary Gay and Lesbian Literature, Lambda Rising, Inc., P.O. Box 73910, Washington DC 20056-3910. (202)462-7924. Fax: (202)462-5264. E-mail: lbreditor@aol.com. Contact: Kanani Kauka, senior editor. Assistant Editor: Charles Mitchess-Diago. 90% freelance written. Monthly magazine that covers gay/lesbian literature. "*Lambda Book Report* devotes its entire contents to the discussion of gay and lesbian books and authors. Any other submissions would be inappropriate." Estab. 1987. Circ. 11,000. Pays 30 days after publication. Byline given. Buys first rights. Reports in 2 months. Sample copy for $4.95 and 9×12 SAE with 5 first-class stamps. Writer's guidelines free.

● This editor sees an increasing need for writers familiar with economic and science/medical-related topics.

Nonfiction: Book excerpts, essays (on gay literature), interview/profile (of authors), book reviews. "No historical essays, fiction or poetry." Query with published clips. Length: 200-2,000 words. Pays $15-125 for assigned articles; $5-25 for unsolicited articles.

Photos: Send photos with submission. Reviews contact sheets. Offers $10-25/photo. Model releases required. Buys one-time rights.

Tips: "Assignments go to writers who query with 2-3 published book reviews and/or interviews. It is helpful if the writer is familiar with gay and lesbian literature and can write intelligently and objectively on the field. Review section is most open. Clips should demonstrate writers' knowledge, ability and interest in reviewing gay books."

MOM GUESS WHAT NEWSPAPER, 1725 L St., Sacramento CA 95814. (916)441-6397. E-mail: info@mgwnew.c om. Website: www.mgwnews.com. Editor: Linda Birner. 80% freelance written. Works with small number of new/ unpublished writers each year. Biweekly tabloid covering gay rights and gay lifestyles. A newspaper for gay men, lesbians and their straight friends in the State Capitol and the Sacramento Valley area. First and oldest gay newspaper in Sacramento. Estab. 1977. Circ. 21,000. Publishes ms an average of 3 months after acceptance. Byline given. Buys all rights. Submit seasonal material 3 months in advance. Reports in 2 months. Sample copy for $1. Writer's guidelines for 10×13 SAE with 4 first-class stamps.

Nonfiction: Interview/profile and photo feature of international, national or local scope. Buys 8 mss/year. Query. Length: 200-1,500 words. Payment depends on article. Pays expenses of writers on special assignment.

Reprints: Send photocopy of article and information about when and where the article previously appeared. Pay varies.

Photos: Send photos with submission. Reviews 5×7 prints. Offers no additional payment for photos accepted with ms. Captions and identification of subjects required. Buys one-time rights.

Columns/Departments: News, Restaurants, Political, Health, Film, Video, Book Reviews. Buys 12 mss/year. Query. Payment depends on article.

Tips: "*MGW* is published primarily from volunteers. With some freelancers payment is made. Put requirements in your cover letter. Byline appears with each published article; photos credited. Editors reserve right to edit, crop, touchup, revise, or otherwise alter manuscripts, and photos, but not to change theme or intent of the work. Enclose SASE postcard for acceptance or rejection. We will not assume responsibility for returning unsolicited material lacking sufficient return postage or lost in the mail."

OUT, 110 Greene St., Suite 600, New York NY 10012. (212)334-9119. Editor: Sarah Pettit. Contact: department editor. 80% freelance written. Monthly national gay and lesbian general-interest magazine. "Our subjects range from current affairs to culture, from fitness to finance." Estab. 1992. Circ. 120,000. Pays on publication. Publishes ms an average of 3 months after acceptance. Byline given. Offers 25% kill fee. Buys first North American serial rights, second serial (reprint) rights for anthologies (additional fee paid) and 30-day reprint rights (additional fee paid if applicable). Editorial lead time 3 months. Submit seasonal material 5 months in advance. Accepts simultaneous submissions. Reports in 6 weeks on queries; 2 months on mss. Sample copy for $6. Writer's guidelines for #10 SASE.

Nonfiction: Book excerpts, essays, exposé, general interest, historical/nostalgic, humor, interview/profile, new product, opinion, personal experience, photo feature, travel, fashion/lifestyle. Buys 200 mss/year. Query with published clips. Length: 50-10,000 words. Pays 50¢/word. Sometimes pays expenses of writers on assignment.

Photos: State availability of photos with submission. Reviews contact sheets, transparencies, prints. Negotiates payment individually. Captions, model releases, identification of subjects required. Buys one-time rights.

Tips: "*Out's* contributors include editors and writers from the country's top consumer titles: skilled reporters, columnists, and writers with distinctive voices and specific expertise in the fields they cover. But while published clips and relevant experience are a must, the magazine also seeks out fresh, young voices. The best guide to the kind of stories we publish is to review our recent issues—is there a place for the story you have in mind? Be aware of our long lead time."

OUTSMART, Up & Out Communications, 3406 Audubon Place, Houston TX 77006. (713)520-7237. Fax: (713)522-3275. Editor: Eric Roland. Contact: Greg Jeu, publisher. 70% freelance written. Monthly magazine covering gay and lesbian issues. "*OutSmart* provides positive information to gay men, lesbians and their associates to enhance and improve the quality of our lives." Estab. 1994. Circ. 15,000. Pays on publication. Publishes ms an average of 2 months after acceptance. Byline given. Buys one-time rights and simultaneous rights. Editorial lead time 2 months. Submit seasonal material 2 months in advance. Accepts simultaneous submissions. Reports in 6 weeks on queries; 2 months on mss. Sample copy and writer's guidelines for SASE.

Nonfiction: Historical/nostalgic, interview/profile, opinion, personal experience, photo feature, travel. Special issues: Communicating Through Computers (September 1996); Arts & Entertainment (October 1996); Mental Health (November 1996). Buys 10 mss/year. Send complete ms. Length: 700-4,000 words. Pays $20-60.

Reprints: Accepts previously published submissions.

Photos: State availability of photos with submission. Reviews 4×6 prints. Negotiates payment individually. Identification of subjects required. Buys one-time rights.

Tips: Using fewer personal experience stories, more hard-hitting feature articles.

‡Q SAN FRANCISCO, Q Communications Inc., 584 Castro St., Suite 521, San Francisco CA 94114. (415)764-0324. Fax: (415)626-5744. E-mail: qsf1@aol.com. Website: www.qsanfrancisco.com. Contact: Robert Adams, editor. Managing Editor: Robin Dorman. 50% freelance written. Bimonthly magazine covering gay and lesbian travel and entertainment with "positive images of gay men, lesbians, bisexuals and transgenders." Estab. 1994. Circ. 47,000. Pays on publication. Publishes ms an average of 1 month after acceptance. Buys first North American serial rights and second serial (reprint) rights. Editorial lead time 2 months. Submit seasonal material 2 months in advance. Accepts simultaneous submissions. Reports in 2 months. Writer's guidelines for #10 SASE.

Nonfiction: Robin Dorman, senior editor. Book excerpts, essays, exposé, general interest, humor, inspirational, interview/profile, photo feature, travel. Buys 6 mss/year. Query with published clips. Length: 500-3,000 words. Pays $50-200. Sometimes pays expenses of writers on assignment.

Photos: State availability of photos with submission. Reviews contact sheets and transparencies. Negotiates payment individually. Model releases required. Negotiable rights are purchased on photos.

Columns/Departments: Music (contemporary/gay and lesbian), 900 words; Wellness (holistic medicine), 900 words. Buys 6 mss/year. Query with published clips. Pays $50-100.

Fiction: Robin Dorman, senior editor. Adventure, fantasy, historical, humorous, mystery, romance, science fiction, slice-of-life vignette, suspense. Buys 4 mss/year. Query with published clips. Length: 700-2,000 words. Pays $75-125.

Poetry: Robin Dorman. Avant-garde, free verse, haiku, light verse, traditional. Buys 4 poems/year. Submit maximum

6 poems. Length: 5-50 lines. Pays $25-100.
Tips: "Perseverance is the key; send a follow-up letter after two weeks, and e-mail or fax after 3 weeks. Commitment to gay and lesbian civil rights is important."

‡**THE WASHINGTON BLADE**, Washington Blade, Inc., 1408 U St., NW, Washington DC 20009-3916. (202)797-7000. Fax: (202)797-7040. E-mail: sul@washblade.com. Contact: Mark Sullivan, managing editor. 20% freelance written. Nation's oldest and largest weekly news tabloid covering the gay/lesbian community. "Articles (subjects) should be written from or directed to a gay perspective." Estab. 1969. Circ. 50,000. Pays in 1 month. Publishes ms an average of 1 month after acceptance. Byline given. Offers kill fee. Buys first North American serial rights. Submit seasonal material 1 month in advance. Reports in 2 months. Sample copy and writer's guidelines for 9×12 SAE with 6 first-class stamps.
Nonfiction: Most news stories are staff-generated; writers with news or news feature ideas should query first.
Reprints: Send typed ms with rights for sale noted and information about when and where the article previously appeared.
Photos: "A photo or graphic with feature/lifestyle articles is particularly important. Photos with news stories are appreciated." Send photos. Pays $25 minimum. Captions preferred. On assignment, photographer paid mutually agreed upon fee, with expenses reimbursed. Publication retains all rights.
Columns/Departments: Arts (books, travel and profiles of gay figures in the arts), pays 10-12¢/word. Send submissions to Sheila Walsh. Opinion columns 2-3 times/week (reactions to political developments, cultural observations, and moving or funny personal stories), 900-950 words. Pays $25. Send submissions to Kristine Campbell. No sexually explicit material.
Tips: "Send a résumé, good examples of your writing and know the paper before you submit a manuscript for publication. We get a lot of submissions which are entirely inappropriate. We're looking for more features, but fewer AIDS-related features. Greatest opportunity for freelancers resides in current events, features, interviews and book reviews."

GENERAL INTEREST

General interest magazines need writers who can appeal to a broad audience—teens and senior citizens, wealthy readers and the unemployed. Each magazine still has a personality that suits its audience—one that a writer should study before sending material to an editor. Other markets for general interest material are in these Consumer categories: Contemporary Culture, Ethnic/Minority, Inflight, Men's, Regional and Women's.

THE AMERICAN LEGION MAGAZINE, P.O. Box 1055, Indianapolis IN 46206-1055. (317)630-1200. Editorial Administrator: Joan L. Berzins. Contact: Joe Stuteville, editor. Monthly magazine. "Working through 15,000 community-level posts, the honorably discharged wartime veterans of The American Legion dedicate themselves to God, country and traditional American values. They believe in a strong defense; adequate and compassionate care for veterans and their families; community service; and the wholesome development of our nation's youth. We publish articles that reflect these values. We inform our readers and their families of significant trends and issues affecting our nation, the world and the way we live. Our major features focus on national security, foreign affairs, business trends, social issues, health, education, ethics and the arts. We also publish selected general feature articles, articles of special interest to veterans, and question-and-answer interviews with prominent national and world figures." 70% freelance written. Prefers to work with published/established writers, but works with a small number of new/unpublished writers each year. Estab. 1919. Circ. 2,850,000. Buys first North American serial rights. Reports in 4-6 weeks on submissions "promptly." **Pays on acceptance.** Publishes ms an average of 6 months after acceptance. Byline given. Reports in 2 months. Sample copy for 9×12 SAE with 6 first-class stamps. Writer's guidelines for #10 SASE.
Nonfiction: Query first, considers unsolicited mss only from veterans concerning their wartime experiences. Query should explain the subject or issue, article's angle and organization, writer's qualifications and experts to be interviewed. Well-reported articles or expert commentaries cover issues/trends in world/national affairs, contemporary problems, general interest, sharply-focused feature subjects. Monthly Q&A with national figures/experts. Few personality profiles. No regional topics. Buys 50-60 mss/year. Length: 1,000-2,000 words. Pays 30¢/word and up. Pays phone expenses of writers on assignment.
Photos: On assignment.
Tips: "Queries by new writers should include clips/background/expertise; no longer than 1½ pages. Submit suitable material showing you have read several issues. *The American Legion Magazine* considers itself 'the magazine for a strong America.' Reflect this theme (which includes economy, educational system, moral fiber, social issues, infrastruc-

FOR INFORMATION on setting your freelance fees, see How Much Should I Charge?

ture, technology and national defense/security). We are a general interest, national magazine, not a strictly military magazine. No unsolicited jokes."

THE AMERICAN SCHOLAR, The Phi Beta Kappa Society, 1811 Q Street NW, Washington DC 20009-9974. (202)265-3808. Editor: Joseph Epstein. Contact: Jean Stipicevic, managing editor. 100% freelance written. Intellectual quarterly. "Our writers are specialists writing for the college-educated public." Estab. 1932. Circ. 25,000. Pays after author has seen edited piece in galleys. Byline given. Offers 50% kill fee. Buys first rights. Submit seasonal material 6 months in advance. Reports in 2 weeks on queries; 2 months on ms. Sample copy for $6.95. Writer's guidelines for #10 SASE.

Nonfiction: Book excerpts (prior to publication only), essays, historical/nostalgic, humor. Buys 40 mss/year. Query. Length: 3,000-5,000 words. Pays $500.

Columns/Departments: Buys 16 mss/year. Query. Length: 3,000-5,000 words. Pays $500.

Poetry: Sandra Costich, poetry editor. Buys 20/year. Submit maximum 3 poems. Length: 34-75 lines. Pays $50. "Write for guidelines."

Tips: "The section most open to freelancers is the book review section. Query and send samples of reviews written."

‡**THE ATLANTIC MONTHLY**, 745 Boylston St., Boston MA 02116. (617)536-9500. Editor: William Whitworth. Managing Editor: Cullen Murphy. Contact: Michael Curtis, senior editor. Monthly magazine of arts and public affairs. "Seeks fiction that is clear, tightly written with strong sense of 'story' and well-defined characters." Circ. 500,000. Pays on acceptance. Byline given. Buys first North American serial rights. Simultaneous submissions discouraged. Reporting time varies. All unsolicited mss must be accompanied by SASE.

● Writers should be aware that this is not a market for beginner's work (nonfiction and fiction), nor is it truly for intermediate work. Study this magazine before sending only your best, most professional work.

Nonfiction: Book excerpts, essays, general interest, humor, personal experience, religious, travel. Query with or without published clips or send complete ms. Length: 1,000-6,000 words. Payment varies. Sometimes pays expenses of writers on assignment.

Fiction: Literary and contemporary fiction. Buys 12-15 mss/year. Send complete ms. Length: 2,000-6,000 words preferred. Payment $2,500.

● Ranked as one of the best markets for fiction writers in the last *Writer's Digest* magazine's annual "Fiction 50."

Poetry: Peter Davison, poetry editor. Buys 40-60 poems/year.

Tips: When making first contact, "cover letters are sometimes helpful, particularly if they cite prior publications or involvement in writing programs. Common mistakes: melodrama, inconclusiveness, lack of development, unpersuasive characters and/or dialogue."

CAPPER'S, Ogden Publications, Inc., 1503 SW 42nd St., Topeka KS 66609-1265. (913)274-4346. Fax: (913)274-4305. E-mail: npeavler@kspress.com. Contact: Nancy Peavler, editor. Associate Editors: Cheryl Ptacek, Ann Crahan, Rosemary Rebek. 25% freelance written. Works with a small number of new/unpublished writers each year. Biweekly tabloid emphasizing home and family for readers who live in small towns and on farms. Estab. 1879. Circ. 325,000. **Pays for poetry and fiction on acceptance;** articles on publication. Publishes ms an average of 3-6 months after acceptance. Buys one-time serial rights only. Submit seasonal material at least 3 months in advance. Reports in 4 months; 10 months for serialized novels. Sample copy for $1.50. Writer's guidelines for #10 SASE.

Nonfiction: Historical (local museums, etc.), inspirational, nostalgia, budget travel (Midwest slants), people stories (accomplishments, collections, etc.). Special issues: Health and Fitness, also Grandparenting Charms and Challenges (September); Crafts and Fall Festivals, also Winterizing (October); Winter Travel, also Welcoming the Holidays (November); Winter Projects-Crafts, also Quilting, Needlework, Home Decorating, Christmas Joy and Salute to Volunteers (December). Buys 50 mss/year. Submit complete ms. Length: 700 words maximum. Pays $2/inch.

Reprints: Send tearsheet, photocopy or typed ms with rights for sale noted and information about when and where the article previously appeared. Pays $1.50/column inch as printed.

Photos: Purchased with accompanying ms. Submit prints. Pays $10-15 for 8×10 or 5×7 b&w glossy prints. Purchase price for ms includes payment for photos. Limited market for color photos (35mm color slides); pays $30-40.

Columns/Departments: Heart of the Home (homemakers' letters, recipes, hints); Community Heartbeat (volunteerism). Submit complete ms. Length: 300 words maximum. Pays $1 gift certificate-$20.

Fiction: "We buy very few fiction pieces—longer than short stories, shorter than novels." Adventure and romance mss. No explicit sex, violence or profanity. Buys 4-5 mss/year. Query. Pays $75-400 for 7,500-40,000 words.

Poetry: Free verse, haiku, light verse, traditional, nature, inspiration. "The poems that appear in *Capper's* are not too difficult to read. They're easy to grasp. We're looking for everyday events and down-to-earth themes." Buys 5-6/issue. Limit submissions to batches of 5-6. Length: 4-16 lines. Pays $10-15.

Tips: "Study a few issues of our publication. Most rejections are for material that is too long, unsuitable or out of character for our magazine (too sexy, too much profanity, wrong kind of topic, etc.). On occasion, we must cut material to fit column space."

THE CHRISTIAN SCIENCE MONITOR, 1 Norway St., Boston MA 02115. (617)450-2000. Contact: Submissions. International newspaper issued daily except Saturdays, Sundays and holidays in North America; weekly international edition. Estab. 1908. Circ. 95,000. Buys all newspaper rights worldwide for 3 months following publication. Buys limited number of mss, "top quality only." Publishes original (exclusive) material only. Pays on publication. Reports in 1 month. Submit complete original ms or letter of inquiry. Writer's guidelines for #10 SASE.

Nonfiction: Jane Lampmann, feature editor. In-depth features and essays. "Style should be bright but not cute, concise but thoroughly researched. Try to humanize news or feature writing so reader identifies with it. Avoid sensationalism, crime and disaster. Accent constructive, solution-oriented treatment of subjects." Home Forum page buys essays of 400-900 words. Pays $150 average. Education, arts, environment, food, science and technology pages will consider articles not usually more than 800 words appropriate to respective subjects. No medical stories." *Writer's Market* recommends sending a query with SASE first. Pays $150-200.

Poetry: Traditional, blank and free verse. Seeks non-religious poetry of high quality and of all lengths up to 75 lines. Pays $35-75 average.

Tips: "We prefer neatly typed originals. No handwritten copy. Enclosing an SAE and postage with ms is a must."

‡CIVILIZATION, 666 Pennsylvania Ave. SE, Washington DC 20003. Publisher: Quentin Walz. Contact: Sara Sklaroff, senior editor. Bimonthly magazine. "*Civilization* is the membership magazine of the Library of Congress covering contemporary culture. Well-known writers contribute articles on the arts, travel, government, history, education, biography and social issues." Estab. 1994. Circ. 200,000.

Nonfiction: *Civilization*'s departments and columns are staff written, but virtually all features come from freelancers. Pays up to $5,000, ⅓ on acceptance, ⅔ on publication, for exclusive 90-day rights to features. (Pay depends on subject matter, quality and the amount of time a writer has put into a piece.)

Tips: "*Civilization* is not a history magazine. We are a magazine of American culture. The key thing for us is that when we do look into the past, we connect it to the present." The magazine is now giving more emphasis to contemporary subjects. "We take relatively few over-the-transom pieces. But we do look at everything that comes in, and sometimes we pick up something that looks really impressive. We put an enormous stress on good writing. Subject is important, but unless a writer can show us a sheaf of clips, we won't get started with them. There is a *Civilization* sensibility that we try to maintain. If you don't know the magazine well, you won't really understand what we're trying to do." To break in, look to contemporary subjects and the arts—including fine arts, the lively arts and book reviews.

DIVERSION, Hearst Business Publishing, 1790 Broadway, New York NY 10019. (212)969-7500. Fax: (212)969-7557. Contact: Tom Passavant, editor-in-chief. Monthly magazine covering travel and lifestyle, edited for physicians. "*Diversion* offers an eclectic mix of interests beyond medicine. Regular features include stories on domestic and foreign travel destinations, discussions of food and wine, sports columns, guidance on gardening and photography, and information on investments and finance. The editorial reflects its readers' affluent lifestyles and diverse personal interests. Although *Diversion* doesn't cover health subjects, it does feature profiles of doctors who excel at nonmedical pursuits." Estab. 1973. Circ. 176,000. Pays 3 months after acceptance. Offers 25% kill fee. Editorial lead time 4 months.

• Ranked as one of the best markets for freelance writers in *Writer's Yearbook* magazine's annual "Top 100 Markets," January 1997.

Nonfiction: Length: 2,200 words. Pays $800. Query with proposal, published clips and author's credentials.

Columns/Departments: Travel, food & wine, photography, gardening, finance. Length: 1,200 words. Pays $500-750. Query with proposal, published clips and author's credentials.

EQUINOX: Canada's Magazine of Discovery, Malcolm Publishing, 120 Eglinton Ave. East, Suite 1100, Toronto, Ontario M2N 6S7 Canada. (416)481-2657. Fax: (514)327-0514. E-mail: amorantz@limestone.kosone.com. Contact: Alan Morantz, editor. Bimonthly magazine "encompassing the worlds of human cultures and communities, the natural world and science and technology." Estab. 1982. Circ. 175,000. **Pays on acceptance.** Byline given. Offers 50% kill fee. Buys first North American serial rights only. Submit seasonal queries 1 year in advance. Reports in 2 months. Sample copy for $5. Writer's guidelines for #10 SASE (U.S. writers must send IRCs, not American stamps).

Nonfiction: Book excerpts (occasionally). No travel articles. Should have Canadian focus. Query. Length: 1,500-5,000 words. Pays $1,750-3,000 negotiated.

Photos: Send photos with ms. Reviews color transparencies—must be of professional quality; no prints or negatives. Captions and identification of subjects required.

Columns/Departments: Nexus (current science that isn't covered by daily media); Scope (reviews). Query with clips of published work. Length: 200-800 words. Pays $250-500.

Tips: "Submit ideas for short photo essays as well as longer features."

FRIENDLY EXCHANGE, The Aegis Group: Publishers, Friendly Exchange Business Office, P.O. Box 2120, Warren MI 48090-2120. Publication Office: (810)558-7026. Editor: Dan Grantham. 80% freelance written. Works with a small number of new/unpublished writers each year. Quarterly magazine for policyholders of Farmers Insurance Group of Companies exploring travel, lifestyle and leisure topics of interest to active families. "These are traditional families (median adult age 39) who live primarily in the area bounded by Ohio on the east and the Pacific Ocean on the west, along with Tennessee, Alabama, and Virginia." Estab. 1981. Circ. 5,700,000. **Pays on acceptance.** Publishes ms an average of 5 months after acceptance. Offers 25% kill fee. Buys all rights. Submit seasonal material 1 year in advance. Accepts simultaneous queries. Reports in 2 months. Sample copy for 9×12 SAE with 5 first-class stamps. Writer's guidelines for #10 SASE.

Nonfiction: "We provide readers with 'news they can use' through articles that help them make smart choices about lifestyle issues. We focus on home, auto, health, personal finance, travel and other lifestyle/consumer issues of interest to today's families. Readers should get a sense of the issues involved, and information that could help them make those decisions. Style is warm and colorful, making liberal use of anecdotes and quotes." Buys 8 mss/issue. Query. Length: 200-1,200 words. Pays $300-$1,200/article including expenses.

Photos: Art director. Pays $150-250 for 35mm color transparencies; $50 for b&w prints. Cover photo payment negotiable. Pays on publication.

Columns/Departments: Consumer issues, health and leisure are topics of regular columns.

Tips: "We concentrate on providing readers information relating to current trends. Don't focus on destination-based travel, but on travel trends. We prefer tightly targeted stories that provide new information to help readers make decisions about their lives."

‡**THE FUTURIST, A magazine of forecasts, trends and ideas about the future**, World Future Society, 7910 Woodmont Ave., Suite 450, Bethesda MD 20814. (301)656-8274. Fax: (301)951-0394. E-mail: wfsinfo@wfs.org. Editor: Edward Cornish. Contact: Cynthia G. Wagner, managing editor. Less than 5% freelance written. Bimonthly magazine covering futures research; general trends in all subjects. "*The Futurist* serves as a neutral clearinghouse for ideas about the future. Subscribers are members of the World Future Society, an association of people interested in the technological, social and other trends shaping the future." Estab. 1966. Circ. 30,000. **Pays on acceptance.** Publishes ms an average of 4 months after acceptance. Byline sometimes given. Kill fee negotiated. Buys first rights or second serial rights or makes work-for-hire assignments. Editorial lead time 4 months. Accepts simultaneous submissions, if so noted. Reports in 1 week on queries; 1-6 months on mss. Sample copy for $7. Writer's guidelines free.

Nonfiction: Book excerpts, general interest, interview/profile, new product, opinion, photo feature. Freelancers are used by assignment only and for short departmental items. Query. Length: 75-1,000 words. Pays $25-50. Sometimes pays with contributors copies for feature articles.

Photos: Send photos with submission. Reviews transparencies, prints. Negotiates payment individually.

Columns/Departments: World Trends & Forecasts (future trends), 75-1,000 words. Buys 10-12 mss/year. Query. Pays $25-50.

Tips: "*The Futurist* is not a good market for professional writers since we only work with freelancers for a limited number of assignments. We *are* a good market for scholars in our field—experts who wish to share their insights about the future with the members but who are not necessarily professional writers."

GRIT: American Life and Traditions, Ogden Publications, 1503 SW 42nd St., Topeka KS 66609-1265. (913)274-4300. Fax: (913)274-4305. E-mail: ddoyle@kspress.com. Contact: Donna Doyle, editor-in-chief. 60% freelance written. Open to new writers. "*Grit* is Good News. As a wholesome, family-oriented magazine published for more than a century and distributed nationally, *Grit* features articles about family lifestyles, traditions, values and pastimes. *Grit* accents the best of American life and traditions—past and present. Our readers cherish family values and appreciate practical and innovative ideas. Many of them live in small towns and rural areas across the country; others live in cities but share many of the values typical of small-town America." Estab. 1882. Circ. 200,000. Pays on publication. Byline given. Buys all and first rights. Submit seasonal material 8 months in advance. Sample copy and writer's guidelines for $4 and 11 × 14 SAE with 4 first-class stamps.

Nonfiction: Need of features (timely, newsworthy, touching but with a *Grit* angle), profiles, humor, readers' true stories, outdoor hobbies, collectibles. Also articles on gardening, crafts, hobbies, leisure pastimes. The best way to sell work is by reading each issue cover to cover. Special issues: Gardening (January-October); Health (twice a year). Pays 15-22¢/word for articles plus $25-200 each for photos depending on finality and placement. Main features run 1,200 to 1,500 words. Department features average 800-1,000 words.

Fiction: Short stories, 1,500-2,000 words; may also purchase accompanying art if of high quality and appropriate. Need serials (romance, westerns, mysteries) of at least 3,500 words. Send ms with SASE to Fiction Dept.

Photos: Professional quality photos (b&w prints or color slides) increase acceptability of articles. Photos: $25-200 each according to quality, placement and color/b&w.

Tips: "Articles should be directed to a national audience. Sources identified fully. Our readers are warm and loving. They want to read about others with heart. Send us something that will make us cry with joy."

HARPER'S MAGAZINE, 666 Broadway, 11th Floor, New York NY 10012. (212)614-6500. Fax: (212)228-5889. Editor: Lewis H. Lapham. 90% freelance written. Monthly magazine for well-educated, socially concerned, widely read men and women who value ideas and good writing. "*Harper's Magazine* aims to provide its readers with a window on our world, in a format that features highly personal voices; that encourages national discussion on current and significant issues; that offers arresting facts and intelligent opinions. Through original journalistic forms—Harper's Index, Readings, Forum, and Annotation—and through its acclaimed essays, fiction, and reporting, *Harper's* continues the tradition begun with its first issue in 1850: to inform readers across the whole spectrum of political, literary, cultural, and scientific affairs." Estab. 1850. Circ. 205,000. Rights purchased vary with author and material. Pays negotiable kill fee. **Pays on acceptance.** Reports in 2 weeks. Publishes ms an average of 3 months after acceptance. Sample copy for $3.95.

Nonfiction: "For writers working with agents or who will query first only, our requirements are: public affairs, literary, international and local reporting and humor." No interviews; no profiles. Complete ms and query must include SASE. No unsolicited poems will be accepted. Publishes one major report per issue. Length: 4,000-6,000 words. Publishes one major essay/issue. Length: 4,000-6,000 words. "These should be construed as topical essays on all manner of subjects (politics, the arts, crime, business, etc.) to which the author can bring the force of passionately informed statement."

• *Harper's Magazine* is the first national magazine to announce a policy of splitting past and future revenues from new-media and online sources with the material's original writers.
Reprints: Accepts previously published submissions for its "Readings" section. Send tearsheet or photocopy of article, or typed ms with rights for sale noted and information about when and where the article previously appeared.
Fiction: Publishes one short story/month. Generally pays 50¢-$1/word.
Photos: Contact: Angela Riechers, art director. Occasionally purchased with mss; others by assignment. Pays $50-500.
Tips: "Some readers expect their magazines to clothe them with opinions in the way that Halston or Bloomingdale's dresses them for the opera. The readers of *Harper's Magazine*, I suspect, always belonged to a different crowd. They strike me as the kind of people who would rather have the tools to work the American grain into a knowledge of their own making."

HOPE MAGAZINE, Humanity Making A Difference, Hope Publishing, Inc., P.O. Box 160, Brooklin ME 04616. (207)359-4651. Fax: (207)359-8920. E-mail: editor@hopemag.com. Editor: Jon Wilson. Contact: Kimberly Ridley, senior editor. 90% freelance written. Bimonthly magazine covering humanity at its best and worst. "We strive to evoke empathy among readers." Estab. 1996. Circ. 50,000. **Pays on acceptance.** Publishes ms an average of 6 months after acceptance. Byline given. Offers 20% kill fee. Buys first, one-time or second serial (reprint) rights. Editorial lead time 4 months. Submit seasonal material 6 months in advance. Accepts simultaneous submissions. Reports in 3 months. Sample copy for $5. Writer's guidelines for #10 SASE.
• Ranked as one of the best markets for freelance editors in *Writer's Yearbook* magazine's annual "Top 100 Markets," January 1997.
Nonfiction: Book excerpts, essays, general interest, inspirational, interview/profile, personal experience, photo feature. Nothing explicitly religious, political or New Age. Buys 50-75 mss/year. Query with published clips. Length: 250-6,000 words. Pays $50-3,000. Sometimes pays expenses of writers on assignment.
Reprints: Accepts previously published submissions.
Photos: State availability of or send photos with submission. Reviews contact sheets and 5×7 prints. Negotiates payment individually. Captions and identification of subjects required. Buys one-time rights.
Columns/Departments: Signs of Hope (inspiring dispatches/news) 250-1,000 words. Buys 50-60 mss/year. Query with published clips. Send complete ms. Pays $50-300.
Tips: "Write very personally, and very deeply. We're not looking for shallow 'feel-good' pieces. Approach uncommon subjects. Cover the ordinary in extraordinary ways. Go to the heart."

IDEALS MAGAZINE, Ideals Publications Inc., P.O. Box 305300, Nashville TN 37230. (615)333-0478. Publisher: Patricia Pingry. Editor: Lisa Ragan. Contact: Michelle Burke, copy editor. 95% freelance written. Seasonal magazine. "Our readers are generally conservative, educated women over 50. The magazine is mainly light poetry and short articles with a nostalgic theme. Issues are seasonally oriented and thematic." Circ. 180,000. Pays on publication. Publishes ms an average of 1 year after acceptance. Byline given. Buys one-time, worldwide serial and subsidiary rights. Submit seasonal material 8 months in advance. Accepts simultaneous submissions. Reports in 3 months. Sample copy for $4. Writer's guidelines for #10 SASE.
Nonfiction: Essays, historical/nostalgic, humor, inspirational, personal experience. "No depressing articles." Buys 20 mss/year. Send complete ms. Length: 800-1,000 words. Pays 10¢/word.
Reprints: Send tearsheet or photocopy of article or short story and information about when and where the article previously appeared.
Photos: Guidelines for SASE. Reviews tearsheets. Offers no additional payment for photos accepted with ms. Captions, model releases, identification of subjects required. Buys one-time rights. Payment varies.
Fiction: Slice-of-life vignettes. Buys 10 mss/year. Length: 800-1,000 words. Pays 10¢/word.
Poetry: Light verse, traditional. "No erotica or depressing poetry." Buys 250 poems/year. Submit maximum 15 poems, 20-30 lines. Pays $10/poem.
Tips: "Poetry is the area of our publication most open to freelancers. It must be oriented around a season or theme. Nostalgia is an underlying theme of every issue. Poetry must be optimistic."

LEFTHANDER MAGAZINE, Lefthander International, P.O. Box 8249, Topeka KS 66608-0249. (913)234-2177. Contact: Kim Kipers, managing editor. 80% freelance written. Eager to work with new/unpublished writers. Bimonthly magazine for "lefthanded people of all ages and interests in 50 US states and 12 foreign countries. The one thing they have in common is an interest in lefthandedness." Estab. 1975. Circ. 26,000. Pays on publication. Publishes ms an average of 4 months after acceptance. Byline usually given. Offers 25% kill fee. Rights negotiable. Reports on queries in 2 months. Sample copy for $2 and 9×12 SAE. Writer's guidelines for #10 SASE.
Nonfiction: Interviews with famous lefthanders; features about lefthanders with interesting talents and occupations; how-to features (sports, crafts, hobbies for lefties); research on handedness and brain dominance; exposé on discrimination against lefthanders in the work world; features on occupations and careers attracting lefties; education features relating to ambidextrous right brain teaching methods. Buys 50-60 mss/year. Length: 1,500-2,000 words for features. Pays $85-100. Buys 6 personal experience shorts/year. Pays $25. Pays expenses of writer on assignment. Query with SASE.
Photos: State availability of photos for features. Pays $10-15 for good contrast color glossies, slides, transparencies. Rights negotiable.
Tips: "All material must have a lefthanded hook. We prefer practical, self-help and self-awareness types of editorial

content of general interest."

LIFE, Time & Life Bldg., Rockefeller Center, New York NY 10020. (212)522-1212. Managing Editor: Daniel Okrent. Articles: Jay D. Lovinger, executive editor: 10% freelance written. Prefers to work with published/established writers; rarely works with new/unpublished writers. Monthly general interest picture magazine for people of all ages, backgrounds and interests. "*Life* shows the world through the power of pictures. It explores domestic and international news, business, the arts, lifestyle and human interest stories." Estab. 1936. Circ. 1,500,000. **Pays on acceptance.** Publishes ms an average of 3 months after acceptance. Byline given. Buys first North American serial rights. Submit seasonal material 4 months in advance. Accepts simultaneous submissions. Reports in 2 months.
Nonfiction: "We've done articles on anything in the world of interest to the general reader and on people of importance. It's extremely difficult to break in since we buy so few articles. Most of the magazine is pictures. We're looking for very high quality writing. We select writers whom we think match the subject they are writing about." Query with clips of previously published work. Length: 1,000-4,000 words.

NATIONAL GEOGRAPHIC MAGAZINE, 1145 17th St. NW, Washington DC 20036. (202)857-7000. Fax: (202)828-6667. Website: http://www.nationalgeographic.com. Editor: William Allen. Contact: Robert M. Poole, associate editor. 60% freelance written. Prefers to work with published/established writers. Monthly magazine for members of the National Geographic Society. "Timely articles written in a compelling, 'eyewitness' style. Arresting photographs that speak to us of the beauty, mystery, and harsh realities of life on earth. Maps of unprecedented detail and accuracy. These are the hallmarks of *National Geographic* magazine. Since 1888, the *Geographic* has been educating readers about the world—uncovering its past, illuminating its distant corners, and chronicling its sweeping changes. Its uncompromising quality, creativity, and innovation have made a permanent mark on American journalism." Estab. 1888. Circ. 9,200,000.
Nonfiction: *National Geographic* publishes general interest, illustrated articles on science, natural history, exploration, cultures and geographical regions. Of the freelance writers assigned, a few are experts in their fields; the remainder are established professionals. Fewer than 1% of unsolicited queries result in assignments. Query (500 words) by letter, not by phone, to Associate Editor Robert Poole. Do not send mss. Before querying, study recent issues and check a *Geographic Index* at a library since the magazine seldom returns to regions or subjects covered within the past 10 years. Length: 2,000-8,000 words. Pays expenses of writers on assignment.
Photos: Photographers should query in care of the Photographic Division.
Tips: "State the theme(s) clearly, let the narrative flow, and build the story around strong characters and a vivid sense of place. Give us rounded episodes, logically arranged."

‡THE NEW YORK TIMES MAGAZINE, 229 W. 43rd St., New York NY 10036. (212)556-1234. Fax: (212)556-3830. *The New York Times Magazine* appears in *The New York Times* on Sunday.
Nonfiction: Most articles are assigned but some unsolicited material is published, especially in the "Lives" column, a weekly 900-word personal-essay feature. Other articles may vary in length from 500-10,000 words. Views should be fresh, lively and provocative on national and international news developments, science, education, family life, social trends and problems, arts and entertainment, personalities, sports and the changing American scene. Address unsolicited articles to the Articles Editor, and "Lives" essays to the "Lives" Editor. Pays $1,000 for "Lives" essays; payment for other articles varies. Enclose SASE for reply. *Arts and Leisure* section of *The New York Times* appears on Sunday. Wants "to encourage imaginativeness in terms of form and approach—stressing ideas, issues, trends, investigations, symbolic reporting and stories delving deeply into the creative achievements and processes of artists and entertainers—and seeks to break away from old-fashioned gushy, fan magazine stuff." Length: 1,500-2,000 words. Pays $100-350, depending on length. *Arts and Leisure* Editor: Diane Cardwell.
Photos: Send to Photo Editor. Pays $75 minimum for b&w photos.
Tips: "The Op Ed page is always looking for new material and publishes many people who have never been published before. We want material of universal relevance which people can talk about in a personal way. When writing for the Op Ed page, there is no formula, but the writing itself should have some polish. Don't make the mistake of pontificating on the news. We're not looking for more political columnists. Op Ed length runs about 750 words, and pays about $150."

THE NEW YORKER, 20 W. 43rd St., New York NY 10036-7441. (212)536-5400. Editor: Tina Brown. Weekly. Estab. 1925. Circ. 750,000. "*The New Yorker* is a national magazine edited to address current issues, ideas and events. The magazine blends domestic and international news analysis with in-depth features, critiques and humorous observations on politics and business, culture and the arts, education, style, sports and literature." *The New Yorker* is one of today's premier markets for top-notch nonfiction, fiction and poetry. Query before submitting. To submit material, please direct your ms to the appropriate editor, (i.e. fact, fiction, poetry or humor) and enclose SASE. The editors deal with a tremendous number of submissions every week; writers hoping to crack this market should be prepared to wait at least 2 or 3 months for a reply. **Pays on acceptance.**
Tips: "We are always happy to welcome new contributors to our pages, but our editors generally find it impossible to make judgments on the basis of descriptions of or excerpts from stories; they prefer to read the stories themselves. If you plan to submit a long Fact piece, however, you may send a query letter, with a detailed proposal, to the Fact Editor. We have no guidelines as such. If you feel that your work might be right for us, please send your submission (prose

typed double-spaced; poetry single-spaced, and no more than six poems at a time) to the appropriate editors—Fact, Fiction, Talk of the Town, or Poetry. Please include SASE with any submission."

NEWSWEEK, 251 W. 57th St., New York NY 10019. (212)445-4000. Circ. 3,180,000. Contact: My Turn Editor. "*Newsweek* is edited to report the week's developments on the newsfront of the world and the nation through news, commentary and analysis. News is divided into National Affairs, International, Business, Lifestyle, Society, and the Arts. Relevant charts, maps, cartoons and photographs accompany most of the articles. Opinion columns deal with views on national and international trends in politics, the economy, personal business, the Washington scene, current affairs, lifestyles, the arts, society, health, science, and technology." Accepts unsolicited mss for My Turn, a column of personal opinion. The 1,000- to 1,100-word essays for the column must be original, not published elsewhere and contain verifiable facts. Payment is $1,000, on publication. Buys non-exclusive world-wide rights. Reports in 2 months only on submissions with SASE.

THE NORTHERN CENTINEL, The Centinel Company, 30 Reservoir Rd., Hanover NH 03755-1310. Managing Editor: Peter J. Gardner. 75% freelance written. Bimonthly tabloid. Estab. 1788. Circ. 20,000. Pays on publication. Publishes ms an average of 4 months after acceptance. Byline given. Buys first rights. Editorial lead time 3 months. Submit seasonal material 4 months in advance. Accepts simultaneous submissions. Reports in 1 month on queries; 3 months on mss. Writer's guidelines for #10 SASE.
Nonfiction: Essays, exposé, general interest, humor, interview/profile, opinion (does not mean letters to the editor), photo feature, travel, political. Buys 40 mss/year. Send complete ms. Length: 800-1,200 words. Pays $20 minimum.
Photos: State availability of photos with submission. Offers $10/photo. Captions, identification of subjects required. Buys one-time rights.
Columns/Departments: Buys 60-70 mss/year. Send complete ms. Pays $20 minimum.
Poetry: Ellen, Rachlin, Lucie Aidinoff, poetry editors. Avant-garde, free verse, haiku, light verse, traditional. Buys 12-18 poems/year. Length: 50 lines. Pays $20 minimum.

‡THE OXFORD AMERICAN, A Magazine From the South, The Oxford American, Inc., P.O. Drawer 1156, Oxford MS 38655. Editor: Marc Smirnoff. 30-50% freelance written. Bimonthly magazine covering the South. "*The Oxford American* is a general-interest literary magazine about the South." Estab. 1992. Circ. 4,000. Pays 30 days after publication. Publishes ms an average of 6 months after acceptance. Byline given. Offers 25% kill fee. Buys first North American serial rights and one-time rights. Editorial lead time 2 months. Submit seasonal material 4 months in advance. Reports in 3 weeks on queries; 3 months on mss. Sample copy for $6.50. Writer's guidelines for #10 SASE.
Nonfiction: Essays, general interest, humor, personal experience, reporting, profiles, memoirs concerning the South. Buys 6 mss/year. Query with published clips or send complete ms. Pay varies. Sometimes pays expenses of writers on assignment.
Photos: Negotiates payment individually. Captions required. Buys one-time rights.
Columns/Departments: Send complete ms. Pay varies.
Fiction: Buys 10 mss/year. Send complete ms. Pay varies.
Tips: "Like other editors, I stress the importance of being familiar with the magazine. Those submitters who know the magazine always send in better work because they know what we're looking for. To those who don't bother to at least flip through the magazine, let me point out we only publish articles with some sort of Southern connection."

PARADE, Parade Publications, Inc., 711 Third Ave., New York NY 10017. (212)450-7000. Fax: (212)450-7284. Editor: Walter Anderson. Contact: Articles Editor. Weekly magazine for a general interest audience. 90% freelance written. Circ. 37,000,000. **Pays on acceptance.** Publishes ms an average of 3 months after acceptance. Kill fee varies in amount. Buys first North American serial rights. Reports in 6 weeks on queries. Writer's guidelines for #10 SASE.
Nonfiction: General interest (on health, trends, social issues or anything of interest to a broad general audience); interview/profile (of news figures, celebrities and people of national significance); and "provocative topical pieces of news value." Spot news events are not accepted, as *Parade* has a 6-week lead time. No fiction, fashion, travel, poetry, cartoons, nostalgia, regular columns, quizzes or fillers. Unsolicited queries concerning celebrities, politicians, sports figures, or technical are rarely assigned. Address single-page queries to Articles Editor; include SASE. Length of published articles: 800-1,500 words. Pays $2,500 minimum. Pays expenses of writers on assignment.
Tips: "Send a well-researched, well-written 3-paragraph query targeted to our national market. No phone or fax queries. Keep subject tightly focused—you should be able to state the point or theme in three or four sentences."

PRIME TIMES, Grote Publishing, 634 W. Main St., Suite 207, Madison WI 53703-2634. Managing Editor: Barbara Walsh. 75% freelance written. Quarterly membership magazine for the National Association for Retired Credit Union People (NARCUP). "*Prime Times* is a topical magazine of broad appeal to a general adult audience, emphasizing issues relevant to people over age 50. It offers timely articles on health, fitness, finance, travel, outdoor sports, consumer issues, lifestyle, home arts and family relationships. Estab. 1979. Circ. 76,000. May share a core of editorial material with sister magazine *American Times* (est. 1993), sent to financial institutions' older adult customers. Pays on publication. Publishes ms an average of 9 months after acceptance. Byline given. Buys first North American serial rights, one-time rights and second serial (reprint) rights. Editorial lead time 7 months. Submit seasonal material 8 months in advance. Reports in 6 weeks on queries; 2 months on mss. Sample copy for $3 and 9 × 12 SAE with 4 first-class stamps. Writer's guidelines for #10 SASE.

Nonfiction: Book excerpts, general interest, health/fitness, travel, historical, humor, recipes, photo features. "No nostalgia pieces, medical or financial pieces based solely on personal anecdotes, personal opinion essays, fiction or poetry." Buys 4-8 mss/year, 8-16 reprints. Prefers to see complete ms. Length: 1,000-2,000 words. Pays $250 minimum for full-length assigned articles; $100 minimum for unsolicited full-length articles; $50 for "American Short Tales."
Reprints: Send photocopy of article or typed ms with rights for sale noted and information about when and where the article previously appeared. Pays $50-125, depending on length, quality and number of times published.
Photos: Needs professional-quality photos. State availability of or send photos with submission. Welcomes text-photo packages. Reviews contact sheets, transparencies and prints. Negotiates payment individually. Model releases and identification of subjects required. Buys one-time rights.
Tips: "Articles that contain useful, well-documented, up-to-date information have the best chance of publication. Don't send personal essays, or articles that repeat information readily available in mainstream media. Articles on health and medical issues *must* be founded in sound scientific method and include current data. You must be able to document your research. Make it easy for us to make a decision on your submission. If the article is written, submit the entire thing—manuscript with professional-quality photos. If you query, be specific. Write part of it in the style in which you would write the article. Be sure to enclose clips. With every article we publish, something about the story must lend itself to strong graphic representation."

RANDOM LENGTHS, Harbor Independent News, P.O. Box 731, San Pedro CA 90733-0731. (310)519-1016. Editor: James Elmendorf. 30% freelance written. Biweekly tabloid covering alternative news/features. "*Random Lengths* follows Twain's dictum of printing news 'to make people mad enough to do something about it.' Our writers do exposés, scientific, environmental, political reporting and fun, goofy, insightful, arts and entertainment coverage, for a lefty, labor-oriented, youngish crowd." Estab. 1979. Circ. 30,000. Pays in 60 days. Byline given. Offers 50% kill fee. Buys all rights. Editorial lead time 1 month. Submit seasonal material 2 months in advance. Accepts simultaneous submissions. Reports in 6 weeks on queries. Sample copy for 9×13 SAE with 3 first-class stamps. Writer's guidelines free.
Nonfiction: Exposé, general interest, historical/nostalgic, interview/profile, opinion. Special issues: Labor Day, triannual book edition; women and black history months. Buys 150 mss/year. Query. Length: 300-2,000 words. Pays 5¢/word. Sometimes pays expenses of writers on assignment.
Reprints: Accepts previously published submissions.
Photos: State availability of photos with submissions. Reviews prints. Offers $10/photo. Captions, identification of subjects required. Buys all rights.
Columns/Departments: Community News (local angle), 300-600 words; Commentary (national/world/opinion), 600-800 words; Feature (books/music/local events), 300-600 words. Buys 75 mss/year. Query. Pays 5¢/word.
Tips: "We use mostly local material and local writers, but we are open to current-event, boffo entertaining writing. Read other alternative weeklies for reference. We need local news most. Next, entertainment stuff with a local pitch."

READER'S DIGEST, Reader's Digest Rd., Pleasantville NY 10570-7000. E-mail: readersdigest@notes.compuserve. com. Contact: Diana Arfine, associate editor. Monthly general interest magazine. "We are looking for contemporary stories of lasting interest that give the magazine variety, freshness and originality." Estab. 1922. Circ. 15,000,000. **Pays on acceptance.** Byline given. Buys exclusive world periodical rights, electronic rights, among others. Editorial lead time 3 months. Submit seasonal material 6 months in advance. Does not read or return unsolicited mss. Address article queries and tearsheets of published articles to the editors.
● Ranked as one of the best markets for freelance writers in *Writer's Yearbook* magazine's annual "Top 100 Markets," January 1997.
Nonfiction: Book excerpts, essays, exposé, general interest, historical/nostalgic, humor, inspirational, interview/profile, opinion, personal experience. Buys 100 mss/year. Query with published clips. Length: 2,500-4,000 words. Original article rates begin at $5,000.
Reprints: Send tearsheet of article with rights for sale noted and information about where and when the article appeared. Pays $1,200/*Reader's Digest* page for World Digest rights (usually split 50/50 between original publisher and writer).
Columns/Departments: "Original contributions become the property of *Reader's Digest* upon acceptance and payment. Life-in-These-United States contributions must be true, unpublished stories from one's own experience, revealing adult human nature, and providing appealing or humorous sidelights on the American scene." Length: 300 words maximum. Pays $400 on publication. True, unpublished stories are also solicited for Humor in Uniform, Campus Comedy, Tales Out of School and All in a Day's Work. Length: 300 words maximum. Pays $400 on publication. Towards More Picturesque Speech—the first contributor of each item used in this department is paid $50 for original material, $35 for reprints. For items used in Laughter, the Best Medicine, Personal Glimpses, Quotable Quotes, Notes From All Over, Points to Ponder and elsewhere in the magazine payment is as follows; to the *first* contributor of each from a published source, $35. For original material, $30/*Reader's Digest* two-column line. Previously published material must have source's name, date and page number. Contributions cannot be acknowledged or returned. Send complete anecdotes to *Reader's Digest*, Box LL, Pleasantville NY 10570, or fax to (914)238-6390. CompuServe address is notes:readersdigest or use readersdigest@notes.compuserve.com from other online services and the Internet."
　　　"Roughly half the 30-odd articles we publish every month are reprinted from magazines, newspapers, books and other sources. The remaining 15 or so articles are original—most of them assigned, some submitted on speculation. While many of these are written by regular contributors—on salary or on contract—we're always looking for new talent and for offbeat subjects that help give our magazine variety, freshness and originality. Above all, in the writing we publish, *The Digest* demands accuracy—down to the smallest detail.

Our worldwide team of 60 researchers scrutinizes every line of type, checking every fact and examining every opinion. For an average issue, they will check some 3500 facts with 1300 sources. So watch your accuracy. There's nothing worse than having an article fall apart in our research checking because an author was a little careless with his reporting. We make this commitment routinely, as it guarantees that the millions of readers who believe something simply because they saw it in *Reader's Digest* have not misplaced their trust."

READERS REVIEW, The National Research Bureau, Inc., 320 Valley St., Burlington IA 52601. (319)752-5415. Fax: (319)752-3421. Contact: Nancy Heinzel, editor. 75% freelance written. Works with a small number of new/unpublished writers each year, and is eager to work with new/unpublished writers. Quarterly magazine. Estab. 1948. Pays on publication. Publishes ms an average of 1 year after acceptance. Buys all rights. Submit seasonal material 7 months in advance of issue date. Sample copy and writers guidelines for #10 SAE with 2 first-class stamps.
Nonfiction: General interest (steps to better health, attitudes on the job); how-to (perform better on the job, do home repairs, car maintenance); travel. Buys 10-12 mss/year. Query with outline or submit complete ms. Length: 500-700 words. Pays 4¢/word.
Tips: "Writers have a better chance of breaking in at our publication with short articles."

REAL PEOPLE, The Magazine of Celebrities and Interesting People, Main Street Publishing Co., Inc., 450 Seventh Ave., Suite 1701, New York NY 10123. (212)244-2351. Fax: (212)244-2367. Contact: Alex Polner, editor. 75% freelance written. Bimonthly magazine for ages 35 and up focusing on celebs and show business, but also interesting people who might appeal to a national audience. Estab. 1988. Circ. 100,000. Pays on publication. Byline given. Pays 33% kill fee. Buys all rights. Submit seasonal material 6 months in advance. Reports within 1 month. Sample copy for $4 and 8×11 SAE with 3 first-class stamps. Writer's guidelines for #10 SASE.
Nonfiction: Interview/profile. "We do a fall preview of TV and film in September. Material must be in by June. Other seasonal stories are 3-6 months in advance." Buys 80 mss/year. Query with published clips and SAE. Length: 500-2,000 words. Pays $200-500 for assigned articles; $100-250 for unsolicited articles.
Columns/Departments: Newsworthy shorts—up to 200 words. "We are doing more shorter (75-250 word) pieces for our 'Real Shorts' column." Pays $25-50. Submit to Brad Hamilton, editor.
Photos: State availability of photos with submissions. Reviews 5×7 prints and/or slides. Offers no additional payment for photos accepted with ms. Captions, model releases and identification of subjects required. Buys one-time rights.
Tips: "We are mainly interested in articles/interviews with celebrities of national prominence (Hollywood, music, authors, politicians, businesspeople in the media). Profiles must be based on personal interviews. As a rule, profiles should be tough, revealing, exciting and entertaining."

REUNIONS MAGAZINE, P.O. Box 11727, Milwaukee WI 53211-0727. (414)263-4567. Fax: (414)263-6331. E-mail: reunions@execpc.com. Website: http://www.execpc.com/~reunions. Publisher: Edith Wagner. 75% freelance written. Quarterly magazine covering reunions—all aspects, all types. "*Reunions Magazine* is primarily for people actively involved with class, family and military reunions or ongoing adoptive or genealogical searchers. We want easy, practical ideas about organizing, planning, researching/searching, attending or promoting reunions." Estab. 1990. Circ. 18,000. Pays on publication. Publishes ms an average of 1 year after acceptance. Byline given. Buys one-time rights. Editorial lead time minimum 6 months. Submit seasonal material 1 year in advance. Appreciates e-mail submissions. Reports in 6 months on queries. Sample copy free. Writer's guidelines for #10 SASE.
Nonfiction: Historical/nostalgic, how-to, humor, interview/profile, new product, personal experience, photo feature, travel, reunion recipes with reunion anecdote—all must be reunion-related. Needs reviewers for books, videos, software (include your requirements). Special issues: African-American family reunions (December); Kids Stuff (March); Golf at Reunions (June); reunions in various sections of the US; ethnic reunions. Buys 25 mss/year. Query with published clips. Length: 500-3,000 words. Pays $25. Often rewards with generous copies.
Reprints: Send tearsheet or photocopy of article or typed ms with rights for sale noted and information about when and where the article previously appeared.
Photos: State availability of photos with submission. Reviews contact sheets, negatives, 35mm transparencies and prints. Offers no additional payment for photos accepted with ms. Captions, model releases and identification of subjects required. Buys one-time rights. Always looking for cover photos.
Fillers: Anecdotes, facts, newsbreaks, short humor—must be reunion-related. Buys 20/year. Length: 50-250 words. Pays $5.
Tips: "Write a lively account of an interesting or unusual reunion, either upcoming or soon afterward while it's hot. Tell readers why reunion is special, what went into planning it and how attendees reacted. Our *Masterplan* section is a great place for a freelancer to start. Send us how-tos or tips on any aspect of reunion organizing. Open your minds to different types of reunions—they're all around!"

ROBB REPORT, The Magazine for the Affluent Lifestyle, 1 Acton Place, Acton MA 01720. (508)263-7749. Fax: (508)263-0722. Contact: Steven Castle, senior editor. Managing Editor: Janice Stillman. 60% freelance written. Monthly magazine. "We are a lifestyle magazine geared toward active, affluent readers. Addresses upscale autos, luxury travel, boating, technology, lifestyles, watches, fashion, sports, investments, collectibles." Estab. 1976. Circ. 88,000. Pays on publication. Byline given. Offers 50% kill fee. Buys all rights or first North American serial rights. Submit seasonal material 5 months in advance. Reports in 2 months on queries; 1 month on mss. Sample copy for $10.95 plus shipping and handling. Writer's guidelines for #10 SASE.

Nonfiction: General interest (autos, lifestyle, etc.), interview/profile (business owners/entrepreneurs), new product (autos, boats, consumer electronics), travel (international and domestic). No essays, bargain travel. Special issues: Home issue (September); Watch issue (November). Buys 60 mss/year. Query with published clips if available. Length: 500-3,500 words. Pays $150-1,500. Sometimes pays expenses of writers on assignment.

Photos: State availability of photos with submission. Payment depends on article. Buys one-time rights.

Tips: "We want to put the reader there, whether the article is about test driving a car, fishing for marlin, touring a luxury home or profiling a celebrity. The best articles will be those that tell stories, with all the details about products or whatever else you may be writing about placed in that context. Anecdotes should be used liberally, especially for leads, and the fun should show up in your writing."

THE SATURDAY EVENING POST, The Saturday Evening Post Society, 1100 Waterway Blvd., Indianapolis IN 46202. (317)636-8881. Editor: Cory SerVaas, M.D. Managing Editor: Ted Kreiter. Travel Editor: Holly Miller. 30% freelance written. Bimonthly general interest, family-oriented magazine focusing on physical fitness, preventive medicine. "Ask almost any American if he or she has heard of *The Saturday Evening Post*, and you will find that many have fond recollections of the magazine from their childhood days. Many readers recall sitting with their families on Saturdays awaiting delivery of their *Post* subscription in the mail. *The Saturday Evening Post* has forged a tradition of "forefront journalism." The *Post*'s legacy of being the first forum for new ideas has earned the loyalty and trust of millions of readers. *The Saturday Evening Post* continues to stand at the journalistic forefront with its coverage of health, nutrition, and preventive medicine." Estab. 1728. Circ. 500,000. Pays on publication. Publishes ms an average of 3 months after acceptance. Byline given. Buys second serial (reprint) and all rights. Submit seasonal material 4 months in advance. Accepts simultaneous submissions. Reports in 1 month on queries; 6 weeks on mss. Writer's guidelines for #10 SASE.

Nonfiction: Book excerpts, general interest, how-to (gardening, home improvement), humor, interview/profile, travel. "No political articles or articles containing sexual innuendo or hypersophistication." Buys 50 mss/year. Query with or without published clips, or send complete ms. Length: 750-2,500 words. Pays $200 minimum, negotiable maximum for assigned articles. Sometimes pays expenses of writers on assignment.

Photos: State availability of photos with submission. Reviews negatives and transparencies. Offers $50 minimum, negotiable maxmium per photo. Model release, identification required. Buys one-time or all rights.

Columns/Departments: Travel (destinations); Post Scripts (well-known humorists); Post People (activities of celebrities). Buys 16 mss/year. Query with published clips or send complete ms. Length: 750-1,500 words. Pays $200 minimum, negotiable maximum.

Fiction: Jack Gramling, fiction editor. Historical, humorous, mainstream, mystery, science fiction, western. "No sexual innuendo or profane expletives." Send complete ms. Length: 1,000-2,500 words. Pays $150 min., negotiable max.

Poetry: Light verse.

Fillers: Post Scripts Editor: Steve Pettinga. Anecdotes, short humor. Buys 200/year. Length: 300 words. Pays $15.

Tips: "Areas most open to freelancers are Health, Post Scripts and Travel. For travel we like text-photo packages, pragmatic tips, side bars and safe rather than exotic destinations. Query by mail, not phone. Send clips."

SATURDAY NIGHT, Saturday Night Magazine Ltd., 184 Front St. E, Suite 400, Toronto, Ontario M5A 4N3 Canada. Phone: (416)368-7237. Fax: (416)368-5112. E-mail: editorial@saturdaynight.ca. Editor: Kenneth Whyte. Contact: Gillian Burnett, assistant to the editor. 95% freelance written. Monthly magazine. Readership is urban concentrated. Well-educated, with a high disposable income. Average age is 43. Estab. 1887. Circ. 410,000. Pays on receipt of a publishable ms. Byline sometimes given. Offer 50% kill fee. Buys first North American serial rights. Editorial lead time 3-4 months. Submit seasonal material 3-4 months in advance. Accepts simultaneous submissions. Sample copy for $3.50. Writer's guidelines free.

Nonfiction: Book excerpts, essays, general interest, interview/profile, opinion, personal experience, photo feature. Buys 100 mss/year. Query. Length: 200-5,000 words. Pays $1/word.

Photos: State availability of photos with submission. Negotiates payment individually. Model releases and identification of subjects required. Buys one-time rights.

Columns/Departments: Findings (short, interesting stories), Flavor of the Month, both 200-500 words. Query. Pays $1/word.

Fiction: Publishes novel excerpts.

SMITHSONIAN MAGAZINE, 900 Jefferson Dr., Washington DC 20560. E-mail: siarticles@aol.com. Website: http://www.smithsonianmag.si.edu. Contact: Marlane A. Liddell, articles editor. 90% freelance written. Prefers to work with published/established writers. Monthly magazine for associate members of the Smithsonian Institution; 85% with college education. "*Smithsonian Magazine*'s mission is to inspire fascination with all the world has to offer by featuring unexpected and entertaining editorial that explores different lifestyles, cultures and peoples, the arts, the wonders of nature and technology, and much more. The highly educated, innovative readers of *Smithsonian* share a unique desire to celebrate life, seeking out the timely as well as the timeless, the artistic as well as the academic and the thought-provoking as well as the humorous." Circ. 2,300,000. Buys first North American serial rights. "Payment for each article to be negotiated depending on our needs and the article's length and excellence." **Pays on acceptance.** Publishes ms an average of 3-6 months after acceptance. Submit seasonal material 3 months in advance. Reports in 2 months. Sample copy for $3, % Judy Smith. Writer's guidelines for #10 SASE.

• Ranked as one of the best markets for freelance writers in *Writer's Yearbook* magazine's annual "Top 100 Markets," January 1997.

Nonfiction: "Our mandate from the Smithsonian Institution says we are to be interested in the same things which now interest or should interest the Institution: cultural and fine arts, history, natural sciences, hard sciences, etc." Query. Back Page humor: 1,000 words; full length article 3,500-4,500 words. Pays various rates per feature, $1,000 per department article, and various rates per short piece. Pays expenses of writers on assignment.

Photos: Purchased with or without ms and on assignment. Captions required. Pays $400/full color page.

Tips: "We prefer a written proposal of one or two pages as a preliminary query. The proposal should convince us that we should cover the subject, offer descriptive information on how you, the writer, would treat the subject and offer us an opportunity to judge your writing ability. Background information and writing credentials and samples are helpful. All unsolicited proposals are sent to us on speculation and you should receive a reply within eight weeks. Please include a self-addressed stamped envelope. We also accept proposals via electronic mail at siarticles@aol.com. If we decide to commission an article, the writer receives full payment on acceptance of the manuscript. If the article is found unsuitable, one-third of the payment serves as a kill fee."

"We consider focused subjects that fall within the general range of Smithsonian Institution interests, such as: culturall history, physical science, art and natural history. We are always looking for offbeat subjects and profiles. We do not consider fiction, poetry, travel features, political and news events, or previously published articles. We have a two-month lead time. Illustrations are not the responsibility of authors, but if you do have photographs or illustration materials, please include a selection of them with your submission. In general, 35mm color transparencies or black-and-white prints are perfectly acceptable. Photographs published in the magazine are usually obtained through assignments, stock agencies or specialized sources. No photo library is maintained and photographs should be submitted only to accompany a specific article proposal. We publish only 12 issues a year, so it is difficult to place an article in *Smithsonian*, but please be assured that all proposals are considered."

THE STAR, 660 White Plains Rd., Tarrytown NY 10591. (914)332-5000. Fax: (914)332-5043. Editor: Richard Kaplan. Executive Editor: Steve LeGrice. 40% freelance written. Prefers to work with published/established writers. Weekly magazine "for every family; all the family—kids, teenagers, young parents and grandparents." Estab. 1974. Circ. 2,277,263. Publishes ms an average of 1 month after acceptance. Buys first North American serial, occasionally second serial book rights. Reports in 2 months. Pays expenses of writers on assignment.

Nonfiction: Exposé (government waste, consumer, education, anything affecting family); general interest (human interest, consumerism, informational, family and women's interest); how-to (psychological, practical on all subjects affecting readers); interview (celebrity or human interest); new product; photo feature; profile (celebrity or national figure); health; medical; diet. No first-person articles. Query or submit complete ms. Length: 500-1,000 words. Pays $50-1,500.

Photos: Contact: Alistair Duncan, photo editor. State availability of photos with query or ms. Pays $25-100 for 8 × 10 b&w glossy prints, contact sheets or negatives; $150-1,000 for 35mm color transparencies. Captions required. Buys one-time or all rights.

THE SUN, A Magazine of Ideas, The Sun Publishing Company, 107 N. Roberson St., Chapel Hill NC 27516. (919)942-5282. Editor: Sy Safransky. 90% freelance written. Monthly general interest magazine. "We are open to all kinds of writing, though we favor work of a personal nature." Estab. 1974. Circ. 29,000. Pays on publication. Publishes ms an average of 6 months after acceptance. Byline given. Buys first or one-time rights. Reports in 1 month on queries; 3 months on mss. Sample copy for $3.50. Send SASE for writer's guidelines.

• *The Sun* no longer accepts simultaneous submissions.

Nonfiction: Book excerpts, essays, general interest, interview, opinion, personal experience, spiritual. Buys 24 mss/year. Send complete ms. Length: 7,000 words maximum. Pays $300-750. "Complimentary subscription is given in addition to payment (applies to payment for *all* works, not just nonfiction)."

Reprints: Send photocopy of article or short story and information about when and where the article previously appeared. Pays 50% of amount paid for an original article.

Photos: Send b&w photos with submission. Offers $50-200/photo. Model releases preferred. Buys one-time rights.

Fiction: Experimental, literary. "We avoid stereotypical genre pieces like sci-fi, romance, western and horror. Read an issue before submitting." Buys 30 mss/year. Send complete ms. Length: 7,000 words maximum. Pays $300-500.

• Ranked as one of the best markets for fiction writers in the last *Writer's Digest*'s annual "Fiction 50."

Poetry: Free verse, prose poems, short and long poems. Buys 24 poems/year. Submit 6 poems max. Pays $50-200.

TIME, Time Inc. Magazine, Time & Life Bldg., 1271 Avenue of the Americas, New York NY 10020. (212)522-1212. Fax: (212)522-0536. Contact: Jim Gaines. Weekly magazine. "*Time* covers the full range of information that is important to people today—breaking news, national and world afairs, business news, societal and lifestyle issues, culture and entertainment news and reviews." Estab. 1923. Circ. 4,096,000. This magazine did not respond to our request for information. Query before submitting.

TOWN & COUNTRY, The Hearst Corp., 1700 Broadway, New York NY 10019. (212)903-5000. Fax: (212)765-8308. Deputy Editor: John Cantrell. 40% freelance written. Monthly lifestyle magazine. "*Town & Country* is a lifestyle guide for the affluent market. Features focus on fashion, beauty, travel, design and architecture, as well as individuals' accomplishments and contributions to society." Estab. 1846. Circ. 488,000. **Pays on acceptance.** Offers 25% kill fee. Buys first North American serial and electronic rights. Reports in 2 months on queries.

• Ranked as one of the best markets for freelance writers in *Writer's Yearbook* magazine's annual "Top 100 Markets," January 1997.

Nonfiction: "We're looking for engaging service articles for a high income, well-educated audience, in numerous categories: travel, personalities, design, fashion, beauty, jewelry, health, city news, country life news, philanthropy." Length: 1,500-2,000 words. Buys shorter pieces of 1,000 words. Pays $1-2/word. Query with clips before submitting.

Tips: "We have served the affluent market for 150 years, and our writers need to be an expert in the needs and interests of that market."

TROIKA, Wit, Wisdom & Wherewithal, Lone Tout Publications, Inc., 125 Main St., Suite 360, Westport CT 06880. (203)227-5377. Editor: Celia Meadow. 80% freelance written. Quarterly magazine covering general interest, lifestyle. "A new magazine for men and women seeking a balanced, three-dimensional lifestyle: personal achievement, family commitment, community involvement. Readers are upscale, educated, 30-50 age bracket. The *Troika* generation is a mix of what is called the X generation and the baby boomers. We are that generation. We grew up with sex, drugs and rock 'n roll, but now it really is our turn to make a difference, if we so choose." Estab. 1993. Circ. 100,000. Pays on publication. Publishes ms an average of 6 months after acceptance. Byline given. Buys first North American serial rights. Editorial lead time 3 months. Submit seasonal material 6 months in advance. Accepts simultaneous submissions. Reports in 2 months. Sample copy for $5. Writer's guidelines for #10 SASE.

Nonfiction: Essays, exposé, general interest, historical/nostalgic, how-to (leisure activities, pro bono, finance), humor, inspirational, interview/profile (non-celebrity), opinion, personal experience. No celebrity profiles. Buys 60-80 mss/year. Query or send complete ms. Length:1,800-3,000 words. Pays $250-1,000 for assigned articles; $250-400 for first appearance of unsolicited articles.

Reprints: Accepts previously published submissions (depending on locale and circulation).

Photos: State availability of photos with submission. Reviews negatives, transparencies. Offers no additional payment for photos accepted with ms. Captions, model releases, identification of subjects required.

Columns/Departments: Literati; Pub Performances (literary, theater, arts, culture); Blueprints (architecture, interior design, fashion); Body of Facts (science); Hippocratic Horizons (health); Home Technology; Capital Commitments (personal finance); all 750-1,200 words. Buys 40-60 mss/year. Query or send complete ms. Pays $250 maximum.

Fiction: Lawrence Crowe. Adventure, confession, experimental, fantasy, historical, mainstream, mystery, novel excerpts, slice-of-life vignettes, suspense. Buys 4-8 mss/year. Send complete ms. Length: 3,000 words maximum. Pays $250 maximum.

USA WEEKEND, Gannett Co., Inc., 1000 Wilson Blvd., Arlington VA 22229. Editor: Marcia Bullard. Contact: Amy Eisman, executive editor. 70% freelance written. Weekly Friday-Sunday newspaper magazine. Estab. 1985. Circ. 17,500,000. **Pays on acceptance.** Publishes ms an average of 3 months after acceptance. Byline given. Offers 25% kill fee. Buys first worldwide serial rights. Submit seasonal material 5 months in advance. Reports in 5 weeks.

Nonfiction: Food and Family Issues; Trends and Entertainment (contact: Gayle Carter); Recreation; Cover Stories (contact: Dan Olmsted). Also looking for book excerpts, general interest articles, how-to, interview/profile, travel, food, recreation. No first-person essays, historic pieces or retrospective pieces. Buys 200 mss/year. Query with published clips. No unsolicited mss accepted. Length: 50-2,000 words. Pays $75-2,000. Sometimes pays expenses of writers on assignment.

Photos: State availability of photos with submission.

Columns/Departments: Food, Travel, Entertainment, Books, Recreation. "All stories must be pegged to an upcoming event, must report new and refreshing trends in the field and must include high profile people." Length: 50-1,000 words. Query with published clips. Pays $250-500.

Tips: "We are looking for authoritative, lively articles that blend the author's expertise with our style. All articles must have a broad, timely appeal. One-page query should include peg or timeliness of the subject matter. We generally look for sidebar material to accompany each article."

VANITY FAIR, Condé Nast Publications, Inc., 350 Madison Ave., New York NY 10017. (212)880-8800. Publisher: Mitchell B. Fox. Monthly magazine. "*Vanity Fair* presents the issues, events and people that define our times. This chronicle of contemporary culture features art, entertainment, politics, business, and the media." Estab. 1983. Circ. 1,200,000. This magazine did not respond to our request for information. Query before submitting.

‡WESTCOAST REFLECTIONS, Rand Communications, 2604 Quadra St., Victoria, British Columbia U8T 4E4 Canada. (250)383-1149. Fax: (250)388-4479. Editor: Jane A. Kesar. 30% freelance written. Monthly magazine covering lifestyle issues for baby boomers. Estab. 1990. Circ. 15,000. Pays on publication. Byline sometimes given. Buys first rights and second serial (reprint) rights. Editorial lead time 3 months. Accepts simultaneous submissions. Reports in 2 months. Sample copy for $2. Writer's guidelines free.

Nonfiction: General interest, how-to, interview/profile, travel. No fiction, first person, religious or political articles. Buys 6 mss/year. Query with published clips. Length: 750 words. Pays 10¢/word. Sometimes pays expenses of writers on assignment.

Photos: State availability of photos with submission. Reviews contact sheets. Negotiates payment individually. Captions, model releases, identification of subjects required.

Columns/Departments: Health, 300-400 words; Travel, 400-700 words; Sexuality (non-graphic), 400-700 words. Buys 12 mss/year. Query with published clips. Pays 10¢/word.
Fillers: Facts, newsbreaks. Buys 4-6/year. Length: 50-100 words. Pays 10¢/word.
Tips: "Be in touch with baby boomer lifestyle issues."

THE WORLD & I, A Chronicle of Our Changing Era, News World Communications, Inc., 3600 New York Ave. NE, Washington DC 20002. (202)635-4000. Fax: (202)269-9353. E-mail: theworldandi@mermail.com. Editor: Morton A. Kaplan. Executive Editor: Michael Marshall. Contact: Gary Rowe, editorial office coordinator. 90% freelance written. Publishing more than 40 articles each month, this is a broad interest magazine for the thinking person. Estab. 1986. Circ. 30,000. Pays on publication. Publishes ms an average of 6 months after acceptance. Byline given. Offers 20% kill fee. Buys all rights. Submit seasonal material 5 months in advance. Reports in 6 weeks on queries; 10 weeks on mss. Sample copy for $5 and 9×12 SASE. Writer's guidelines for #10 SASE.
Nonfiction: "Description of Sections: Current Issues: Politics, economics and strategic trends covered in a variety of approaches, including special report, analysis, commentary and photo essay. The Arts: International coverage of music, dance, theater, film, television, craft, design, architecture, photography, poetry, painting and sculpture—through reviews, features, essays, opinion pieces and a 6-page Gallery of full-color reproductions. Life: Surveys all aspects of life in 22 rotating subsections which include: Travel and Adventure (first person reflections, preference given to authors who provide photographic images), Profile (people or organizations that are "making a difference"), Food and Garden (must be accompanied by photos), Education, Humor, Hobby, Family, Consumer, Trends, and Health. Send SASE for complete list of subsections. Natural Science: Covers the latest in science and technology, relating it to the social and historical context, under these headings: At the Edge, Impacts, Nature Walk, Science and Spirit, Science and Values, Scientists: Past and Present, Crucibles of Science and Science Essay. Book World: Excerpts from important, timely books (followed by commentaries) and 10-12 scholarly reviews of significant new books each month, including untranslated works from abroad. Covers current affairs, intellectual issues, contemporary fiction, history, moral/religious issues and the social sciences. Currents in Modern Thought: Examines scholarly research and theoretical debate across the wide range of disciplines in the humanities and social sciences. Featured themes are explored by several contributors. Investigates theoretical issues raised by certain current events, and offers contemporary reflection on issues drawn from the whole history of human thought. Culture: Surveys the world's people in these subsections: Peoples (their unique characteristics and cultural symbols), Crossroads (changes brought by the meeting of cultures), Patterns (photo essay depicting the daily life of a distinct culture), Folk Wisdom (folklore and practical wisdom and their present forms), and Heritage (multicultural backgrounds of the American people and how they are bound to the world). Photo Essay: Patterns, a 6- or 8-page photo essay, appears monthly in the Culture section. Emphasis is placed on comprehensive photographic coverage of a people or group, their private or public lifestyle, in a given situation or context. Accompanying word count: 300-500 words. Photos must be from existing stock, no travel subsidy. Life & Ideals, a 6- or 8-page photo essay, occasionally appears in the Life section. First priority is given to those focused on individuals or organizations that are "making a difference." Accompanying word count: 700-1,000 words. 'No *National Enquirer*-type articles.' " Buys 1,200 mss/year. Query with published clips. Length: 1,000-5,000 words. Pays 10-20¢/word. Seldom pays expenses of writers on assignment.
Reprints: Send tearsheet or photocopy of article, typed ms with rights for sale noted and information about when and where the article previously appeared.
Poetry: Contact: Arts Editor. Avant-garde, free verse, haiku, light verse, traditional. Buys 4-6 poems/year. Query with maximum 5 poems. Pays $30-75.
Photos: State availability of photos with submission. Reviews contact sheets, transparencies and prints. Payment negotiable. Model releases and identification of subjects required. Buys one-time rights.
Tips: "Send a short query letter with a viable story idea (no unsolicited manuscripts, please!) for a specific section and/or subsection."

HEALTH AND FITNESS

The magazines listed here specialize in covering health and fitness topics for a general audience. Health and fitness magazines have experienced a real boom lately. Most emphasize developing healthy lifestyle choices in exercise, nutrition and general fitness. Many magazines offer alternative healing and therapies that are becoming more mainstream, such as medicinal herbs, health foods and a holistic mind/body approach to well-being. As wellness is a concern to all demographic groups, publishers have developed editorial geared to specific audiences. *Men's Fitness* is aimed at men's concerns. *Shape* addresses women's issues, while *Heart & Soul* presents information expressly for African-American women. Older readers find their needs dealt with in titles such as *Remedy* and *New Choices*. Also see the Sports/Miscellaneous section where publications dealing with health and particular sports may be listed. For magazines that cover healthy eating, refer to the Food and Drink section. Many general interest publications are also potential markets for health or fitness articles. Magazines covering health topics from a medical perspective are listed in the Medical category of Trade.

AMERICAN FITNESS, 15250 Ventura Blvd., Suite 200, Sherman Oaks CA 91403. (818)905-0040. Fax: (818)990-5468. Editor-at-Large: Peg Jordan, R.N. Managing Editor: Rhonda J. Wilson. 75% freelance written. Eager to work with new/unpublished writers. Bimonthly magazine covering exercise and fitness, health and nutrition. "We need timely, in-depth, informative articles on health, fitness, aerobic exercise, sports nutrition, age-specific fitness and outdoor activity." Circ. 36,000. Pays 6 weeks after publication. Publishes ms an average of 6 months after acceptance. Byline given. Buys all rights. Submit seasonal material 4 months in advance. Accepts simultaneous submissions. Reports in 6 weeks. Sample copy for $3 and SAE with 6 first-class stamps. Writer's guidelines for SAE.
Nonfiction: Women's health and fitness issues (pregnancy, family, pre- and post-natal, menopause and eating disorders); exposé (on nutritional gimmickry); historical/nostalgic (history of various athletic events); inspirational (sports leader's motivational pieces); interview/profile (fitness figures); new product (plus equipment review); personal experience (successful fitness story); photo feature (on exercise, fitness, new sport); youth and senior fitness; travel (activity adventures). No articles on unsound nutritional practices, popular trends or unsafe exercise gimmicks. Buys 18-25 mss/year. Query. Length: 800-1,500 words. Pays $140-180. Sometimes pays expenses of writers on assignment.
Reprints: Accepts previously published submissions.
Photos: Sports, action, fitness, aquatic aerobics, aerobics competitions and exercise classes. "We are especially interested in photos of high-adrenalin sports like rock climbing and mountain biking." Pays $15 for b&w prints; $50 for transparencies. Captions, model release and identification of subjects required. Usually buys all rights; other rights purchased depend on use of photo.
Columns/Departments: Alternative paths (non-mainstream approaches to health, wellness and fitness); strength (latest breakthroughs in weight training); research (latest exercise and fitness findings); clubscene (profiles and highlights of fitness club industry). Query with published clips or send complete ms. Length: 800-1,000 words. Pays $120-140.
Tips: "Cover a unique aerobics or fitness angle, provide accurate and interesting findings, and write in a lively, intelligent manner. We are looking for new health and fitness reporters and writers. *AF* is a good place for first-time authors or regularly published authors who want to sell spin-offs or reprints."

AMERICAN HEALTH FOR WOMEN, (formerly *American Health Magazine, Fitness of Body and Mind*), Reader's Digest Corp., 28 W. 23rd St., New York NY 10010. (212)366-8900. Fax: (212)624-3833. Editor: Freddi Greenberg. Executive Editor: Miriam Arond. 70% freelance written. Women's health magazine published 10 times/year covering both scientific and "lifestyle" aspects of women's health at mid-life, including medicine, fitness, nutrition and psychology. Estab. 1982. Circ. 900,000. **Pays on acceptance.** Publishes ms an average of 6 months after acceptance. Byline or tagline given. Offers 25% kill fee. Buys first North American serial rights. Reports in 6 weeks. Sample copy for $3. Writer's guidelines for #10 SASE.
  ● Ranked as one of the best markets for freelance writers in *Writer's Yearbook* magazine's annual "Top 100 Markets," January 1997.
Features: Mail to Editorial. News-based articles usually with a service angle; well-written pieces with an investigative or unusual slant; profiles (health or fitness related). No mechanical research reports, unproven treatments. "Stories should be written clearly, without jargon. Information should be new, authoritative and helpful to readers." Buys 60-70 mss/year (plus many more news items). Query with 2 clips of published work. Length: 1,000-2,500 words. Payment varies. Pays expenses of writers on assignment.
Reprints: Send information about when and where the article previously appeared.
Columns/Departments: Mail to Editorial: Medicine, Fitness, Nutrition, Pulse, Medical Diary, Lifestyle, Mental Health, Healthscope, Family, Dental. Other news sections included from time to time. Buys about 300 mss/year. Query with clips of published work. Pays $150-250 upon acceptance.
Tips: "*American Health For Women* has no full-time staff writers; we rely on outside contributors for most of our articles. The magazine needs good ideas and good articles from experienced journalists and writers. Feature queries should be short (no longer than a page) and to the point. Give us a good angle and a paragraph of background. Queries only. We are not responsible for material not accompanied by a SASE."

BETTER HEALTH, Better Health Press, 1450 Chapel St., New Haven CT 06511-4440. (203)789-3972. Fax: (203)789-4053. Publishing Director: Magaly Olivero. 90% freelance written. Prefers to work with published/established writers; will consider new/unpublished writers. Bimonthly magazine devoted to health, wellness and medical issues. Estab. 1979. Circ. 450,000. **Pays on acceptance.** Byline given. Offers $75 kill fee. Buys first rights. Query first; do not send article. Sample copy for $2.50. Writer's guidelines for #10 SASE.
Nonfiction: Wellness/prevention issues are of prime interest. New medical techniques or nonmainstream practices are not considered. No fillers, poems, quizzes, seasonal, heavy humor, inspirational or personal experience. Length: 2,500-3,000 words. Pays $500.

‡BETTER NUTRITION, Intertec/K-III, 5 Penn Plaza, 13th Floor, New York NY 1001. (212)613-9757. Fax: (212)563-3028. E-mail: 103422.1531@compuserve.com. Contact: James J. Gormley, editor. 57% freelance written. Monthly magazine covering nutritional news and approaches to optimal health. "Since 1938, *Better Nutrition*'s mission has been to inform our readers about the latest breakthroughs in nutritional approaches to optimal health and ongoing research into supplementation with vitamins, botanicals, minerals and other natural products." Estab. 1938. Circ. 475,000. Pays on publication. Publishes ms an average of 2 months after acceptance. Byline given. Offers 100% kill fee. Rights purchased vary. Editorial lead time 3 months. Sample copy free.

Nonfiction: Clinical research boiled down to accessible articles, nutrition, health, alternative medicine, disease prevention, FDA exposés. No unsolicited articles. Special issues: Colds & Flu (October); Digestion Aids (November); Stress (December). Buys 120-180 mss/year. Length: 700-2,000 words. Pays $150-300. Sometimes pays expenses of writers on assignment.

Photos: State availability of photos with query. Reviews 4×5 transparencies and 3×5 prints. Negotiates payment individually. Captions, model releases, identification of subjects required if applicable. Buys one-time rights or non-exclusive reprint rights.

Columns/Departments: Nutrition Hotline, Health Watch, Nutrition News, Women's Health, Veggie Corner, Lifestyle, Vitamin Update, Natural Energy, Children's Health, Sports Nutrition, Earth Watch, Homeopathy, Botanical Medicine, Meatless Meals, Trim Time, Earth Medicine, Liquid Nutrition, Healthier Pets, Ayurvedic Medicine, Chinese Herbs, Longevity, Healing Herbs, Natural Beauty, Tea Time.

Fillers: Anecdotes, facts and newsbreaks. All related to nutrition and alternative medicine.

Tips: "Be on top of what's newsbreaking in nutrition and alternative medicine. Be pro-supplementation-oriented (although not blatantly so). Be available for one-week-assignment/in-our-hands turnarounds. Fact-check, fact-check, fact-check. Find out what distinguishes us from other consumer-directed industry publications. Send in a résumé (including Social Security/IRS number) and a list of article possibilities."

COMMON GROUND MAGAZINE, Ontario's Quarterly Guide to Natural Foods & Lifestyles, New Age Times Ink, 356 Dupont St., Toronto, Ontario M5R 1V9 Canada. Contact: Julia Woodford, editor. 50% freelance written. Quarterly magazine covering holistic health, nutritional medicine. "We give top priority to well-researched articles on nutritional medicine, healing properties of foods and herbs, environmental health issues, natural lifestyles, alternative healing for cancer, arthritis, heart disease, etc. Organic foods and issues. Estab. 1985. Circ. 50,000. Pays on publication. Publishes ms 3 months after acceptance. Byline given. Buys first rights, one-time rights or second serial (reprint) rights. Editorial lead time 3 months. Submit seasonal material 3 months in advance. Accepts simultaneous submissions. Reports "when we have time." Sample copy for $2 (cash only).

Nonfiction: Book excerpts, exposé, how-to (on self-health care), inspirational, personal experience. "Nothing endorsing drugs, surgery, pharmaceuticals. No submissions from public relations firms." Buys 8-12 mss/year. Send complete ms. Length 1,000-1,800 words. Pays 10¢ (Canadian)/word.

Reprints: Send typed ms with rights for sale noted and information about when and where the article previously appeared. Pays 100% of amount paid for an original article.

Photos: Send photos with ms. Offers $25-30 (Canadian)/photo. Must identify subjects. Buys one-time rights.

Fiction: Publishes novel excerpts to a maximum of 2,000 words.

Fillers: Facts, newsbreaks.

Tips: "Must have a good working knowledge of subject area and be patient if not responded to immediately. Features are most open to freelancers. Write well, give me the facts, but do it in layman's terms. A sense of humor doesn't hurt. All material must be relevant to our *Canadian* readership audience. If you're doing a critical piece on products in the marketplace, give me brand names."

‡COUNTRY LIVING'S HEALTHY LIVING, Hearst Magazines, 224 W. 57th St., New York NY 10019. Fax: (212)586-5430. Executive Editor: Vicky Carlisle. Editor: Rachel Newman. Contact: Nancy Bilyeau, managing editor. 80% freelance written. Bimonthly magazine. "*Country Living's Healthy Living* covers alternative health for a mainstream audience. Subjects include nutrition, fitness, beauty, profiles, news, recipes. Most readers are baby boomer women." Estab. 1996. Circ. 350,000. **Pays on acceptance.** Byline given. Offers 15% kill fee. Editorial lead time 3 months. Submit seasonal material 6 months in advance. Accepts simultaneous submissions. Reports in 1 month.

Nonfiction: Book excerpts, essays, general interest, humor, inspirational, interview/profile, new product, opinion, personal experience, photo feature, travel. Buys 60 mss/year. Query with published clips or send complete ms on spec. Length: 200-1,500 words. Pays $75-1,000 for assigned articles; $75-500 for unsolicited articles. Sometimes pays expenses of writers on assignment.

Reprints: Accepts previously published submissions.

Photos: State availability of photos with submission. Reviews transparencies. Negotiates payment individually. Identification of subjects required. Buys all rights.

Columns/Departments: "Our columnists are already chosen, and departments make up most of the magazine. See the nonfiction list of topics." Pays $75-800.

Tips: "Have some knowledge of the world of alternative health. We love it if a writer is reading the journals and attending the conferences, so the ideas are timely."

ENERGY TIMES, Enhancing Your Life Through Proper Nutrition, 548 Broadhollow Rd., Melville NY 11747. (516)777-7773. E-mail: kristine@natplus.com. Editor: Gerard McIntee. Contact: Kristine Garland, associate editor. 70% freelance written. Magazine published 10 times/year covering nutrition, health and beauty aids, alternative medicinal, herbs (medicinal and culinary), natural foods. Estab. 1991. Circ. 650,000. **Pays on acceptance.** Publishes ms an average of 2 months after acceptance. Byline given. Offers 10% kill fee. Buys all rights. Editorial lead time 2 months. Submit seasonal material 6 months in advance. Reports in 1 month on queries, 2 months on mss. Sample copy for $2.50. Writer's guidelines for #10 SASE.

Nonfiction: Book excerpts, how-to (food, natural beauty aids), interview/profile, new product, photo feature, technical (science related to nutrition and alternative medicines), travel. Buys 36 mss/year. Query. Length: 1,500-2,500 words. Pays $300. Sometimes pays expenses of writers on assignment.

Photos: State availability of photos with submissions. Reviews negatives, transparencies, prints. Negotiates payment individually. Model releases, identification of subjects required. Buys one-time rights.

Columns/Departments: Nutritional news (current information on nutrition foods/supplements/vitamins), 850 words; university update (current research on nutrition, health related topics, herbs, vitamins), 850 words. Send complete ms. Pays $50.

Tips: "Although we hire lay freelancers and professional journalists, we prefer to maintain an active group of professional medical/healthcare practitioners with accredited degrees. Queries should be brief (one page) and to the point. Show us why your article needs to be in our magazine."

FDA CONSUMER, 5600 Fishers Lane, Rockville MD 20857. (301)443-3220. Fax: (301)443-9057. Website: http://www.fda.gov. Contact: FDA Consumer Editor. 10% freelance written. Prefers to work with experienced health and medical writers. Bimonthly magazine for general public interested in health issues. A federal government publication (Food and Drug Administration). Circ. 20,000. Pays after acceptance. Publishes ms an average of 3 months after acceptance. Byline given. Not copyrighted. Pays 50% kill fee. "All rights must be assigned to the USA so that the articles may be reprinted without permission." Query with résumé and clips only. Buys 5-10 freelance mss/year. "We cannot be responsible for any work by writer not agreed upon by prior contract."

Nonfiction: "Upbeat feature articles of an educational nature about FDA regulated products and specific FDA programs and actions to protect the consumer's health and pocketbook. Articles based on health topics connected to food, drugs, medical devices, and other products regulated by FDA. All articles subject to clearance by the appropriate FDA experts as well as acceptance by the editor. All articles based on prior arrangement by contract." Length: 2,000-2,500 words. Pays $800-950 for "first-timers," $1,200 for those who have previously published in *FDA Consumer*. Pays phone and mailing expenses.

Photos: Black and white photos are purchased on assignment only.

Tips: "Besides reading the feature articles in *FDA Consumer*, a writer can best determine whether his/her style and expertise suit our needs by submitting a résumé and clips; story suggestions are unnecessary as most are internally generated."

FIT, GCR Publishing Group, Inc., 1700 Broadway, 34th Floor, New York NY 10019. (212)541-7100. Editor: Lisa Klugman. Managing Editor: Sandra Kosherick. 50% freelance written. Works with a small number of new/unpublished writers each year. Bimonthly magazine covering fitness and health for active young, middle-class women. Circ. 125,000. Pays on publication. Publishes ms an average of 5 months after acceptance. Byline given. Offers 20% kill fee. Buys all rights. Submit seasonal material 6 months in advance. Reports in 1 month if rejecting ms, longer if considering for publication.

Nonfiction: Health, fitness, sports, beauty, psychology, relationships, athletes and nutrition. Buys 60 mss/year. Query with published clips. No phone queries. Length: variable. Pays $300-400 for assigned articles; $200 for unsolicited articles.

Photos: Reviews contact sheets, transparencies, prints. Model releases, subject identification required. Buys all rights.

Columns/Departments: Finally Fit! Contest. Readers can submit "before and after" success stories along with color slides or photos. Pays $100.

Tips: "We strive to provide the latest health and fitness news in an entertaining way—that means coverage of real people (athletes, regular women, etc.) and/or events (fitness shows, marathons, etc.), combined with factual information. First-person is okay. Looking for stories that are fun to read, revealing, motivational and informative."

‡FITNESS MAGAZINE, 375 Lexington Ave., New York NY 10017-5514. (212)499-2000. Executive Editor: Jennifer Cook. Published 10 times/year for women in their twenties and thirties who are interested in fitness and living a healthy life. **Pays on acceptance**. Byline given. Offers 20% kill fee. Buys first North American serial rights. Reports in 2 months on queries. Writer's guidelines for #10 SASE.

Nonfiction: "We need timely, well-written nonfiction articles on exercise and fitness, beauty, health, diet/nutrition, and psychology. We always include boxes and sidebars in our stories." Buys 40 mss/year. Query. Length: 1,500-2,500 words. Pays $1,500-2,500. Pays expenses of writers on assignment.

Reprints: Accepts previously published submissions.

Columns/Departments: Buys 60 mss/year. Query. Pays $600-1,200. Length: 600-1,200 words.

Tips: "Our pieces must get inside the mind of the reader and address her needs, hopes, fears and desires. *Fitness* acknowledges that getting and staying fit is difficult in an era when we are all time-pressured."

FLEX, Weider Publications, Inc., 21100 Erwin St., Woodland Hills CA 91367. (818)884-6800. Fax:(818)716-5626. Publisher: Joseph Weider. Monthly magazine. "*Flex* is devoted to covering the sport of bodybuilding for the purist, whether it be the competitor or the hardcore fan. *Flex* examines the various facets of both men's and women's bodybuilding. Covered are workout routines and nutritional discoveries and backstage bodybuilding events." Estab. 1983. Circ. 1,749. This magazine did not respond to our request for information. Query before submitting.

HEALTH, Time Publishing Ventures, 301 Howard St., 18th Floor, San Francisco CA 94105. (415)512-9100. Editor: Barbara Paulsen. Send submissions to: Amanda Uhry, editorial assistant. Magazine published 7 times/year on health, fitness and nutrition. "Our readers are predominantly college-educated women in their 30s and 40s. Edited to focus not on illness, but on events, ideas and people." Estab. 1987. Circ. 900,000. **Pays on acceptance**. Byline given. Offers 25% kill fee. Buys first North American serial rights. Accepts simultaneous submissions. Reports in 2 months on queries. Sample copy for $5 to "Back Issues." Writer's guidelines for #10 SASE. "No phone calls, please."

  ● *Health* stresses that writers must send for guidelines before sending a query, and that only queries that closely follow the guidelines get passed on to editors.

Nonfiction: Buys 25 mss/year. No unsolicited mss. Query with published clips and SASE. Length: 1,200 words. Pays $1,800. Pays the expenses of writers on assignment.

  ● Ranked as one of the best markets for freelance writers in *Writer's Yearbook* magazine's annual "Top 100 Markets," January 1997.

Columns/Departments: Food, Mind, Vanities, Fitness, Family, Money.

Tips: "We look for well-articulated ideas with a narrow focus and broad appeal. A query that starts with an unusual local event and hooks it legitimately to some national trend or concern is bound to get our attention. Use quotes, examples and statistics to show why the topic is important and why the approach is workable. We need to see clear evidence of credible research findings pointing to meaningful options for our readers. Stories should offer practical advice and give clear explanations."

‡HEALTH, MONEY & TRAVEL, A Guide to Good Living, Grass Roots Publishing, 450 Seventh Ave., Suite 1701, New York NY 10123. Contact: Marcia Vickers, editor. 90% freelance written. Bimonthly magazine covering health, money and travel. "We are a national consumer magazine for men and women ages 25 and up. We cover health topics that are mainstream such as 'Is Your Multi-Vitamin Right For You?,' etc." Estab. 1997. Circ. 50,000. Pays on publication. Publishes ms an average of 6 months after acceptance. Byline given. Buys all rights. Editorial lead time 8 months. Submit seasonal material 8 months in advance. Accepts simultaneous submissions occasionally. Reports in 2 months. Sample copy for $5. Writer's guidelines for #10 SASE.

Nonfiction: Book excerpts, how-to, inspirational, interview/profile, travel, health, personal finance. No essays, editorials, memoirs, fiction. Buys 60 mss/year. Query with published clips or send complete ms. Length: 1,000-2,000 words. Pays $250 minimum.

Photos: State availability of photos with submissions. Offers $25/photo maximum.

HEALTH STYLES, The Publisher's Group, P.O. Box 510366, Salt Lake City UT 84151-0366. Fax: (801)322-1098. E-mail: annee@thepublishers.com. Contact: Anne E. Zombro, vice president of publishing. 50% freelance written. Quarterly magazine covering health and fitness. "The slant is towards fitness, mental wellness and nutrition. Also features inspirational profiles and people in the health-care profession." Estab. 1996. Circ. 15,000. Pays on publication. Publishes ms an average of 6 months after acceptance. Byline given. Buys first North American serial and second serial (reprint) rights. Editorial lead time 2 months. Submit seasonal material 4 months in advance. Accepts simultaneous submissions. Reports in 1 month on queries; 2 months on mss. Sample copy for $3 and 9×12 SASE. Writer's guidelines for #10 SASE.

Nonfiction: Book excerpts, inspirational, interview/profile, new product, personal experience, fitness. No medical treatments or diseases. Buys 6-8 mss/year. Query with published clips. Length: 1,000-1,300 words. Pays $125-800.

Reprints: Pays 50% of amount paid for original article.

Photos: Send photos with submission. Reviews 4×5 transparencies (preferred), any size prints. Negotiates payment individually. Captions, model releases, identification of subjects required. Buys one-time or all rights.

HEART & SOUL, Health and Fitness for African-American Women, Rodale Press, 733 Third Ave., New York NY 10017. Editor-in-Chief: Stephanie Stokes Oliver. Managing Editor: Teresa L. Ridley. Contact: Claire McIntosh, senior editor. Bimonthly magazine covering how-to health, fitness, nutrition, beauty, healthy travel, weight loss, parenting, relationships; information researched and edited specifically for African-Americans. Estab. 1993. Circ. 255,000. **Pays on acceptance**. Publishes ms an average of 4 months after acceptance. Byline given. Offers 25% kill fee. Buys all rights or first North American serial rights. Editorial lead time 6-9 months. Submit seasonal material 6 months in advance. Reports in 6 weeks. Sample copy for 9×12 SAE with $1.93 postage. Writer's guidelines for #10 SASE.

Nonfiction: Book excerpts, how-to (health, fitness), relationships, interview/profile (champions of the community), humor, spiritual health. Buys 5-10 mss/year. Query with published clips. Length: 1,200-2,000 words. Pays 75¢-$1/word for assigned articles; 75¢/word for unsolicited articles. Pays itemized expenses of writers on assignment.

Reprints: Accepts previously published submissions.

Columns/Departments: My Body (personal experience, makeovers); Healthy Smile (dental health); Health Front (health news); Weight Loss (how-to); Mind and Spirit (inspiration); Body (illness prevention); Healthy Vacations; Healthy Kids. Length: 1,000-1,500 words. Buys 60 mss/year. Query with published clips. Pays 75¢-$1.

Tips: "Writers should be experienced in health and service writing and knowledgeable about issues important to African-American women. We do not accept unsolicited manuscripts; queries only."

LET'S LIVE MAGAZINE, Franklin Publications, Inc., 320 N. Larchmont Blvd., P.O. Box 74908, Los Angeles CA 90004-3030. (213)469-3901. Fax: (213)469-9597. E-mail: letslive@caprica.com. Editor-in-Chief: Beth Salmon. Contact: Elizabeth Coombs, managing editor. Monthly magazine emphasizing health and preventive medicine. "We are interested in articles about alternative medicine, vitamins, herbs, natural foods and recipes, and exercise." 75% freelance written. Works with a small number of new/unpublished writers each year; expertise in health field helpful. Estab. 1933. Circ.

1,700,000. Pays on publication. Publishes ms an average of 4 months after acceptance. Buys all rights. Byline given. Submit seasonal material 6 months in advance. Reports in 2 months on queries; 3 months on mss. Sample copy for $5 for 10×13 SAE with 6 first-class stamps. Writer's guidelines for #10 SASE.
• The editors are looking for more cutting-edge, well-researched natural health information that is substantiated by experts and well-respected scientific research literature.

Nonfiction: General interest (effects of vitamins, minerals and nutrients in improvement of health or afflictions); historical (documentation of experiments or treatment establishing value of nutrients as boon to health); how-to (enhance natural beauty, exercise/bodybuilding, acquire strength and vitality, improve health of adults and/or children and prepare tasty, healthy meals); interview (benefits of research in establishing prevention as key to good health); personal opinion (views of orthomolecular doctors or their patients on value of health foods toward maintaining good health); profile (background and/or medical history of preventive medicine, M.D.s or Ph.D.s, in advancement of nutrition). Manuscripts must be well-researched, reliably documented and written in a clear, readable style. Buys 2-4 mss/issue. Query with published clips. Length: 1,600-1,400 words. Pays $500. Sometimes pays expenses of writers on assignment.

Photos: Send photos with ms. Pays $50 for 8×10 color prints and 35mm transparencies. Captions and model releases required.

Tips: "We want writers with experience in researching nonsurgical medical subjects and interviewing experts with the ability to simplify technical and clinical information for the layman. A captivating lead and structural flow are essential. The most frequent mistakes made by writers are in writing articles that are too technical; in poor style; written for the wrong audience (publication not thoroughly studied), or have unreliable documentation or overzealous faith in the topic reflected by flimsy research and inappropriate tone."

MASSAGE MAGAZINE, Keeping Those Who Touch—In Touch, 200 Seventh Ave. #240, Santa Cruz CA 95062. (408)477-1176. Fax: (408)477-2918. E-mail: edit@massagemag.com. Website: http://www.massagemag.com. Contact: Karen Menehan, managing editor. Senior Editor: Melissa B. Mower. 80% freelance written. Prefers to work with published/established writers, but works with a number of new/unpublished writers each year. Bimonthly magazine on massage-bodywork and related healing arts. Estab. 1985. Circ. 25,000. Pays 30 days after publication. Publishes ms an average of 6 months after acceptance. Byline given. Buys first North American rights. Reports in 1 month on queries; 2 months on mss. Sample copy and writer's guidelines free.

Nonfiction: General interest, historical/nostalgic, how-to, experiential, inspirational, interview/profile, new product, photo feature, technical, travel. Length: 600-2,000 words. Pays $25-250 for articles.

Reprints: Send tearsheet of article and typed ms with rights for sale noted and information about when and where the article previously appeared. Pays 50-75% of amount paid for an original article.

Photos: Send photos with submission. Offers $10-25/photo. Identification of subjects required. Buys one-time rights.

Columns/Departments: Touching Tales (experiential); Profiles, Insurance; Table Talk (news briefs); Practice Building (business); In Touch with Associations (convention highlights); In Review/On Video (product, book, and video reviews); Technique; Body/mind; Convention Calendar (association convention listings). Length: 800-1,200 words. Pays $60-150 for most of these columns.

Fillers: Facts, news briefs. Length: 100 words. Pays $25 maximum.

Tips: "In-depth profiles of innovative and exceptional bodywork professionals are a high priority."

MEN'S FITNESS, Men's Fitness, Inc., 21100 Erwin St., Woodland Hills CA 91367-3712. (818)884-6800. Fax: (818)704-5734. Editor-in-Chief: Peter Sikowitz. Editorial Assistant: Bobby Lee. 95% freelance written. Works with small number of new/unpublished writers each year. Monthly magazine for health-conscious men ages 18-45. Provides reliable, entertaining guidance for the active male in all areas of lifestyle. Estab. 1984. Circ. 315,000. Pays 1 month after acceptance. Publishes ms an average of 4 months after acceptance. Offers 33% kill fee. Buys all rights. Submit seasonal material 4 months in advance. Reports in 2 months. Writer's guidelines for 9×12 SAE.

Nonfiction: Service, informative, inspirational and scientific studies written for men. Few interviews or regional news unless extraordinary. Query with published clips. Length: 1,200-1,800 words. Pays $500-1,000.

Columns/Departments: Nutrition, Mind, Appearance, Sexuality, Health. Length: 1,200-1,500 words. Pays $400-500.

Tips: "Be sure to know the magazine before sending in queries."

‡MEN'S HEALTH, Rodale Press, Inc., 33 E. Minor St., Emmaus PA18098. (610)967-5171. Fax: (610)967-8963. Editor: Michael Lafavore. Contact: Steve Perrine, articles editor. 10% freelance written. Magazine published 10 times/year covering men's health and fitness. "*Men's Health* is a lifestyle magazine showing men the practical and positive actions that make their lives better, with articles covering fitness, nutrition, relationships, travel, careers, grooming and health issues." Estab. 1986. Circ. 1,326,000. Buys all rights. Responds in 1 week. Pays 75¢/word. Query before submitting. Writer's guidelines for SASE.

Nonfiction: Freelancers have the best chance with the front-of-the-book piece, Malegram. Query.

Tips: "We have a wide definition of health. We believe that being successful in every area of your life is being healthy." The magazine focuses on all aspects of health, from stress issues to nutrition to exercise to sex. It is mostly staff written, but about 10% of the final product comes from freelancers. The best way to break in is not by covering a particular subject, but by covering it within the magazine's style. "There is a very particular tone and voice to the magazine. A writer has to be a good humor writer as well as a good service writer."

MUSCLE & FITNESS, The Science of Living Super-Fit, Weider Health & Fitness, 21100 Erwin St., Woodland Hills, CA 91367. (818)884-6800. Fax: (818)595-0463. Website: http://www.muscle-fitness.com. Editor: Bill Geiger. Contact: Vincent Scalisi, editor. 50% freelance written. Monthly magazine covering fitness, health, injury prevention and treatment, bodybuilding. Estab. 1950. Circ. 500,000. **Pays on acceptance.** Publishes ms an average of 2 months after acceptance. Offers 25-40% kill fee. Buys all rights and second serial (reprint) rights. Editorial lead time 3 months. Submit seasonal material 3 months in advance. Accepts simultaneous submissions. Reports in 2 weeks on queries; 1 month on mss. Sample copy per request.

 • Ranked as one of the best markets for freelance writers in *Writer's Yearbook* magazine's annual "Top 100 Markets," January 1997.

Nonfiction: Bill Geiger. Book excerpts, how-to (training), humor, interview/profile, photo feature. Buys 120 mss/year. "All features and departments are written on assignment." Query with published clips. Length: 800-1,800 words. Pays $250-800. Pays expenses of writers on assignment.

Reprints: Send photocopy of article or short story or typed ms with rights for sale noted and information about when and where the article previously appeared.

Photos: State availability of photos with submission.

Tips: "Have a knowledge of weight-training (especially in gyms); know the 'culture'; know applied-nutrition."

MUSCLE MAG INTERNATIONAL, 6465 Airport Rd., Mississauga, Ontario L4V 1E4 Canada. Fax: (905)678-9236. Editor: Johnny Fitness. 80% freelance written. "We do not care if a writer is known or unknown; published or unpublished. We simply want good instructional articles on bodybuilding." Monthly magazine for 16- to 60-year-old men and women interested in physical fitness and overall body improvement. Estab. 1972. Circ. 300,000. Buys all rights. **Pays on acceptance.** Publishes ms an average of 4 months after acceptance. Byline given. Buys 200 mss/year. Sample copy for $5 and 9×12 SAE. Reports in 2 months. Submit complete ms with IRCs.

Nonfiction: Articles on ideal physical proportions and importance of supplements in the diet, training for muscle size. Should be helpful and instructional and appeal to young men and women who want to live life in a vigorous and healthy style. "We would like to see articles for the physical culturist on new muscle building techniques or an article on fitness testing." Informational, how-to, personal experience, interview, profile, inspirational, humor, historical, expose, nostalgia, personal opinion, photo, spot news, new product, merchandising technique. "Also now actively looking for good instructional articles on Hardcore Fitness." Length: 1,200-1,600 words. Pays 20¢/word. Sometimes pays the expenses of writers on assignment.

Columns/Departments: Nutrition Talk (eating for top results) Shaping Up (improving fitness and stamina). Length: 1,300 words. Pays 20¢/word.

Photos: Color and b&w photos are purchased with or without ms. Pays $30 for 8×10 glossy exercise photos; $30 for 8×10 b&w posing shots. Pays $200-500 for color cover and $35 for color used inside magazine (transparencies). More for "special" or "outstanding" work.

Fillers: Newsbreaks, puzzles, quotes of the champs. Length: open. Pays $10 minimum.

Tips: "The best way to break in is to seek out the muscle-building 'stars' and do in-depth interviews with biography in mind. Color training picture support essential. Writers have to make their articles informative in that readers can apply them to help gain bodybuilding success. Specific fitness articles should quote experts and/or use scientific studies to strengthen their theories."

‡**NATURAL HEALTH**, Boston Common Press, 17 Station St., P.O. Box 1200, Brookline Village MA 02147. Fax: (617)232-1572. Editor: Anne Alexander. Contact: Elizabeth Cameron. 50% freelance written. Bimonthly magazine covering alternative health and natural living. "We are an authoritative guide to the best in mind, body and spirit self-care." Estab. 1971. Circ. 350,000. **Pays on acceptance.** Publishes ms an average of 3 months after acceptance. Byline given. Offers 25% kill fee. Buys first rights and reprint rights. Editorial lead time 8 months. Submit seasonal material 8 months in advance. Accepts simultaneous submissions. Reports in 4 months on queries. Writer's guidelines free.

Nonfiction: Book excerpts, exposé, how-to, inspirational, personal experience. No fiction, reprints from other publications or event/personality coverage. Buys 15 mss/year. Query with published clips. Length: 150-3,000 words. Pays $75-2,000. Sometimes pays the expenses of writers on assignment.

Photos: State availability of photos with submission. Buys one-time rights.

Columns/Departments: My Story (personal account of illness or condition treated naturally), 1,500 words. Buys 6 mss/year. Query. Pays $100-200.

Tips: "Read the magazine. The recipes are always vegan. The products are non-chemical. Read books written by the columnists: Andrew Weil, Christiane Northrup, Joseph Pizzorno, Susan Lark, etc.)"

‡**NATURAL REMEDIES, A Practical Guide to Alternative Medicine**, Cowles Enthusiast Media, 4 High Ridge Park, Stamford CT 06905. (203)321-1777. Fax: (203)322-1966. Contact: Carol Wiley Lorente. Managing Editor: Karin Horgan Sullivan. 25% freelance written. Quarterly magazine covering alternative medicine. "*Natural Remedies* is consumery, friendly with a focus on practicality—how the reader can use alternative medicine to improve his life." Estab. 1996. **Pays on acceptance.** Publishes ms an average of 2 months after acceptance. Byline given. Offers $50 kill fee. Makes work-for-hire assignments. Editorial lead time 4 months. Submit seasonal material 5 months in advance. Accepts simultaneous submissions. Sample copy for $3.99.

Nonfiction: Book excerpts, how-to, inspirational, interview/profile, new product, personal experience. No New Age, "crystal," "out-there" therapies. Query with published clips. Length: 2,000-2,500 words. Pays $500-1,000. Sometimes pays expenses of writers on assignment.

Photos: State availability of photos with submission. Reviews transparencies. Negotiates payment individually. Model releases and identification of subjects required. Rights purchased vary.

Columns/Departments: Family Practice (family health); Health Habitat (healthy home and office environment); Herbal Healing (herbs for health); all 1,500 words. Buys 12-24 mss/year. Query with published clips. Pays $500-750.

Tips: "We are looking for consumer friendly articles about how the traditional modalities of alternative medicine— homeopathy, herbs, acupuncture, etc.— can help people live better. Articles should quote experts in the field about common problems and illnesses and should give the reader practical advice about those problems or illnesses. Query first, and send samples and information about your expertise in the subject."

‡**THE NATURAL WAY**, Natural Way Publications, 566 Westchester Ave., Rye Brook NY 10573. (914)939-2111. Fax: (914)939-5138. E-mail: natway@aol.com. Editor/Contact: Norine Dworkin. 80% freelance written. Bimonthly magazine covering alternative health. *The Natural Way* publishes previously published articles on a range of alternative healthcare topics, including vegetarianism, natural remedies, fitness and longevity. Estab. 1994. Circ. 125,000. Pays on publication. Publishes ms an average of 8 months after acceptance. Byline given. Buys one-time and second serial (reprint) rights. Editorial lead time 8 months. Submit seasonal material 8 months in advance. Accepts previously published submissions. Reports in 3 months on queries. Sample copy and writer's guidelines free.

Nonfiction: How-to (pertaining to healthy living). No magical cures, wild or unsubstantiated claims or healing, personal stories or food articles. Query with published clips. Length: 1,500-2,500 words. Pays $50-500.

Tips: "Query with previously published clips. Know the alternative health field. Back articles up with scientific data."

NEW CHOICES, Living Even Better After 50, RD. Publications, Inc., 28 W. 23rd St., New York NY 10010. (212)366-8600. Fax: (212)366-8786. Contact: JoAnn Tomback, editorial administrative assistant. Magazine published 10 times/year covering retirement lifestyle. "*New Choices, Living Even Better After 50* is a lifestyle magazine for adults 50 and over. Editorial focuses on travel, health, fitness, investments, food and home." Estab. 1960. Circ. 604,000.

Nonfiction: Planning for retirement, personal health and fitness, financial strategies, housing options, travel, profiles/ interviews (celebrities and newsmakers), relationships, leisure pursuits, various lifestyle/service subjects. Buys 60 mss/ year. Length: 750-2,000 words. Pay varies. Query with 2-3 published clips.

Columns/Departments: Personal essays, humor, manners/etiquette, news of interest to over-50s, single lifestyle, travel, style. Buys 84 mss/year. Pay varies. Query with 2-3 published clips.

‡**NEW LIVING**, New Living, Inc., P.O. Box 1519, Stony Brook NY 11790. (516)981-7232. E-mail: newliving@aol.c om. Editor: Christine Harvey. 20% freelance written. Monthly news magazine covering health and fitness and sports. "We feature exercise tips, body building, nutrition, holistic and preventive medicine, chiropractic, adventure, mental health, family and relationship advice and leisure sports (running, cycling, great outdoors). Estab. 1991. Circ. 100,000. Pays on publication. Publishes ms an average of 3 months after acceptance. Byline given. Offers $25 kill fee. Buys all rights. Editorial lead time 2 months. Submit seasonal material 3 months in advance. Accepts simultaneous submissions. "*New Living* will only reply if writer sends SASE with proper postage." Sample copy for $1.25 plus SASE with 9 × 12 envelope.

Nonfiction: General interest, how-to, inspirational, new product, celebrity interviews. Only health and fitness-related. No humor or anything that does not pertain to health and fitness. Buys 10 mss/year. Query with published clips. Length: 500-1,000 words. Pays $25-100. Pays writers with contributor copies for travel articles.

Photos: State availability of photos with ms. Offers $5-10/photo. Identification of subjects required. Buys all rights.

Columns/Departments: Buys 10 mss/year. Query with published clips. Pays $25-100.

Fillers: Facts. Buys 25/year. Length: 150-250 words. Pays $25-50.

Tips: "Please don't send more than 2 clips. Send a sample article (500 words) only on health and fitness. We are not interested in anything other than that topic."

‡**OXYGEN!, Serious Fitness for Serious Women**, Muscle Mag International, 6465 Airport Rd., Mississauga, Ontario L4V 1E4 Canada. (905)678-7311. Fax: (905)678-9236. Contact: Pamela Cottrell, editor. 70% freelance written. Bimonthly magazine covering women's health and fitness. "*Oxygen* encourages various exercise, good nutrition to shape and condition the body." Estab. 1997. Circ. 180,000. **Pays on acceptance**. Publishes ms an average of 4 months after acceptance. Byline given. Offers 25% kill fee. Buys all rights. Editorial lead time 3 months. Submit seasonal material 6 months in advance. Reports in 5 weeks on queries; 2 months on mss. Sample copy for $5.

Nonfiction: Exposé, how-to (training and nutrition), humor, inspirational, interview/profile, new product, personal experience, photo feature. No "poorly researched articles that do not genuinely help the readers towards physical fitness,

---

ALWAYS CHECK the most recent copy of a magazine for the address and editor's name before you send in a query or manuscript.

health and physique." Buys 100 mss/year. Send complete ms. Length: 1,400-1,800 words. Pays $250-1,000. Sometimes pays expenses of writers on assignment.

Photos: State availability of or send photos with submission. Reviews contact sheets, 35mm transparencies, prints. Offers $35-500. Identification of subjects required. Buys all rights.

Columns/Departments: Nutrition (low fat recipes), 1,700 words; Weight Training (routines and techniques), 1,800 words; Aerobics (how-tos), 1,700 words. Buys 50 mss/year. Send complete ms. Pays $150-500.

Tips: "Every editor of every magazine is looking, waiting, hoping and praying for the magic article. The beauty of the writing has to spring from the page; the edge imparted has to excite the reader because of its unbelievable information.

PREVENTION, Rodale Press, Inc., 33 E. Minor St., Emmaus, PA 18098. (610)967-5171. Fax: (610)967-7723. Editor: Mark Bricklin. Assistant Managing Editor: Marty Munson. Monthly magazine covering health and fitness. "*Prevention* is for readers who take an active role in achieving and maintaining good health and fitness for themselves and their families. Stressing health promotion and disease prevention, *Prevention* features practical guidance on nutrition, diet and food preparation, medical care, exercise, weight control, skin care and personal psychology." Estab. 1950. Circ. 3,519,000.

Tips: *Prevention*, "America's Leading Health Magazine," is a market only for the most-experienced freelancers. "We are not a good market for somebody who's interested in breaking into the health market. However, once they're established, then we can talk," says assistant managing editor Marty Munson. The monthly aims to inform readers about current developments in health. Because this information is medically and scientifically specialized, expertise and research are primary requirements. Only experienced health writers should query the magazine.

REMEDY MAGAZINE, Prescriptions for a Healthy Life, Remedy, Inc., 120 Post Rd. West, Westport CT 06880. Editor-in-chief: Valorie G. Weaver. Contact: Shari Miller Sims, consulting editor. 95% freelance written. Bimonthly magazine covering health for people age 55 and over. "REMEDY covers everything that affects and improves the health of people 55 and up—nutrition and exercise, medicine and medications, mainstream and alternative approaches, hormones and hair loss, you name it—and does it in an in-depth but reader-friendly way." Estab. 1992. Circ. 2,000,000 households. **Pays on acceptance**. Publishes ms an average of 4 months after acceptance. Byline given. Offers 20% kill fee. Buys first North American serial rights. Editorial lead time 3 months. Submit seasonal material 6 months in advance. Accepts simultaneous submissions. Reports in 6 weeks on queries; 2 months on mss. Samples for $3 and SAE with 4 first-class stamps. Writer's guidelines free.

• Ranked as one of the best markets for freelance writers in *Writer's Yearbook* magazine's annual "Top 100 Markets," January 1997.

Nonfiction: Book excerpts, exposé (medical), how-to (exercise and nutrition for people age 55 and over), interview/profile (health); medical journalism/reporting for lay readers. Buys 30 mss/year. Query with published clips. Length: 600-2,500 words. Pays $1-1.25/word for assigned articles; 75¢-$1.25/word for unsolicited articles. Pays pre-approved expenses of writers on assignment.

Photos: State availability of photos with submission. Negotiates payment individually. Model releases, identification of subjects required. Buys one-time rights.

Columns/Departments: The Nutrition Prescription (how-to research), The Fitness Prescription (how-to research), Housecall (interviews with top specialists), Mediview (overviews of topical subjects, e.g., "endless" menopause, see-better surgery), all 600-900 words. Buys 15 mss/year. Query. Pays $1-1.25/word.

Tips: "Query should include specific doctors/practitioners likely to be interviewed for piece, and at least one clip showing writing/reporting familiarity with topic of query. Also, an ability to write in a casual, friendly way about often complex material is essential."

SHAPE MAGAZINE, Weider Health & Fitness, 21100 Erwin St., Woodland Hills CA 91367. (818)595-0593. Fax: (818)704-7620. Editor-in-Chief: Barbara Harris. Contact: Peg Moline, editorial director. 70% freelance written. Prefers to work with published/established writers. Monthly magazine covering women's health and fitness. *Shape*, reaches women who are committed to the healthful, active lifestyles. Our readers are participating in a variety of sports and fitness related activities, in the gym, at home and outdoors, and they are also proactive about their health and are nutrition conscious." Estab. 1981. Circ. 900,000. **Pays on acceptance**. Offers 33% kill fee. Buys all rights and reprint rights. Submit seasonal material 8 months in advance. Reports in 2 months. Sample copy for 9×12 SAE and 4 first-class stamps.

• Weider Health Fitness also publishes *Living Fit*, covering women's health and fitness for women over 35.

Nonfiction: Book excerpts; exposé (health, fitness, nutrition related); how-to (get fit); interview/profile (of fit women); health/fitness, recipes. "We use some health and fitness articles written by professionals in their specific fields. No articles that haven't been queried first." Special issues: every September is an anniversary issue. Query with clips of published work. Length: 500-2,000 words. Pays negotiable fee.

Photos: Submit slides or photos with photographer's name or institution to be credited. Provide necessary captions and all model releases.

Tips: Provide source verification materials and sources for items readers may buy, including 800 numbers.

VIBRANT LIFE, A Magazine for Healthful Living, Review and Herald Publishing Assn., 55 W. Oak Ridge Dr., Hagerstown MD 21740-7390. (301)791-7000. Fax: (301)790-9734. E-mail: lbecker@vibrantlife.com. Website: http://www.vibrantlife.com. Contact: Larry Becker, editor. 80% freelance written. Enjoys working with published/established

writers; works with a small number of new/unpublished writers each year. Bimonthly magazine covering health articles (especially from a prevention angle and with a Christian slant). Estab. 1845. Circ. 50,000. **Pays on acceptance.** "The average length of time between acceptance of a freelance-written manuscript and publication of the material depends upon the topics: some immediately used; others up to 2 years." Byline always given. Buys first serial, first world serial, or sometimes second serial (reprint) rights. Submit seasonal material 9 months in advance. Reports in 2 months. Sample copy for $1. Writer's guidelines for #10 SASE.
  • Ranked as one of the best markets for freelance writers in *Writer's Yearbook* magazine's annual "Top 100 Markets," January 1997.
Nonfiction: Interview/profile (with personalities on health). "We seek practical articles promoting better health and a more fulfilled life. We especially like features on breakthroughs in medicine, and most aspects of health. We need articles on how to integrate a person's spiritual life with their health. We'd like more in the areas of exercise, nutrition, water, avoiding addictions of all types and rest—all done from a wellness perspective." Buys 50-60 mss/year. Send complete ms. Length: 500-1,500 words. Pays $75-250.
Reprints: Send tearsheet of article and information about when and where the article previously appeared. Pays 50% of amount paid for an original article.
Photos: Send photos with ms. Needs 35mm transparencies. Not interested in b&w photos.
Tips: "*Vibrant Life* is published for baby boomers, particularly young professionals, age 35-50. Articles must be written in an interesting, easy-to-read style. Information must be reliable; no faddism. We are more conservative than other magazines in our field. Request a sample copy, and study the magazine and writer's guidelines."

VIM & VIGOR, America's Family Health Magazine, 1010 E. Missouri Ave., Phoenix AZ 85014-2601. (602)395-5850. Fax: (602)395-5853. E-mail: jakep@mcpub.com. Contact: Jake Poinier, associate publisher/editor. 75% freelance written. Quarterly magazine covering health and healthcare. Estab. 1985. Circ. 900,000. **Pays on acceptance.** Publishes ms an average of 3 months after acceptance. Byline given. Buys all rights. Reports in 2 weeks on queries. Sample copy for 9×12 SAE with 8 first-class stamps. Writer's guidelines for #10 SASE.
Nonfiction: Health, diseases, medical breakthroughs, exercise/fitness trends, wellness, and healthcare. "Absolutely no complete manuscripts will be accepted. All articles are assigned to freelance writers. Send samples of your style. Any queries regarding story ideas will be placed on the following year's conference agenda and will be addressed on a topic-by-topic basis. Consideration for actual article assignment will be given to those individuals who have submitted story ideas; however, the magazine welcomes anyone with feature- or news-writing ability to submit qualifications for assignment." Buys 4 mss/year. Query with published clips. Length: 2,000 words. Pays $500. Pays expenses of writers on assignment.
Photos: Send photos with submission. Reviews contact sheets and any size transparencies. Offers no additional payment for photos accepted with ms. Captions, model releases, identification of subjects required. Buys one-time rights.
Tips: "The magazine does not accept unsolicited articles or article queries."

‡**THE WALKING MAGAZINE,** Walking Inc., 9-11 Harcourt St., Boston MA 02116. (617)266-3322. Fax: (617)266-7373. Editor: Seth Bauer. 60% freelance written. Bimonthly magazine covering health and fitness. "*The Walking Magazine* is written for healthy, active adults who are committed to fitness walking as an integral part of their lifestyle. Each issue offers advice on exercise techniques, diet, nutrition, personal care and contemporary health issues. It also covers information on gear and equipment, competition and travel, including foreign and domestic destinations for walkers." Estab. 1986. Circ. 510,200. **Pays on acceptance.** Offers 25% kill fee. Editorial lead time 2 months. Accepts simultaneous submissions. Responds in 2 months. Sample copy for $3.95. Writer's guidelines for SASE.
Nonfiction: Walks for travel and adventure, fitness, health, nutrition, fashion, equipment, famous walkers, and other walking-related topics. Buys 35-42 mss/year. Query with published clips (no more than 3). Length: 1,500-2,500 words. Pays $750-2,500.
Columns/Departments: Walking Shorts, Health, Nutrition, Fundamentals, Only In America, Events, In Gear (gear and equipment), Portfolio (photo), Ramblings (back page essay), 300-1,200 words. Query with clips. Pays $150-600.

WEIGHT WATCHERS MAGAZINE, Healthy Living, Inc., P.O. Box 12847, Birmingham AL 35202-2847. (205)877-6000. Fax: (205)877-5790. E-mail: wwmag@mindspring.com. Editor-in-Chief: Kate Greer. Editorial Assistant: Chris O'Connell. Contact: Melissa Chessher Aspell, senior editor. Food Editor: Alyson Haynes. Beauty & Fitness Editor: Mary Martin Niepold. Approximately 80% freelance written. Monthly magazine mostly for women interested in healthy lifestyle/behavior information/advice, including news on health, nutrition, fitness, psychology and food/recipes. Success and before-and-after stories also welcome. Estab. 1968. Circ. 1,000,000. **Pays on acceptance.** Buys first North American rights. Editorial lead time 3-12 months. Sample copy and guidelines $1.95 for 9×12 SASE.
  • Ranked as one of the best markets for freelance writers in *Writer's Yearbook* magazine's annual "Top 100 Markets," January 1997.
Nonfiction: Covers fitness, nutrition, psychology, health clubs, spas, beauty, fashion, style, travel and products for both the kitchen and an active lifestyle. "We are interested in general health, nutrition and behavioral/psychological articles (stories with a strong weight loss angle always a plus). Some fitness—everything from beginner to advanced ideas—freelanced out. Personal triumph/success stories of individuals who lost weight also of interest. Back page a humorous look at some aspect of getting/staying in shape or achieving better health. Our articles have an authoritative yet friendly tone. How-to and service information crucial for all stories. To expedite fact-checking, we require a second, annotated manuscript including names, phone numbers, journal/newsletter citations of sources." Send detailed queries

with published clips and SASE. Average article length: 700-1,200 words. Pay: $350-800.

Reprints: Pays 33% of amount paid for an original article.

Tips: "Well developed, tightly written queries always a plus, as are ideas that have a strong news peg. Trend pieces welcome and we're always on the lookout for a fresh angle on an old topic. Sources must be reputable; we prefer subjects to be medical professionals with university affiliations who are published in their field of expertise. Lead times require stories to be seasonal, long-range and forward-looking. Keep in mind that a trend today may be old news in six months. We're looking for fresh, innovative stories that yield worthwhile information for our readers—the latest exercise alternatives, a suggestion of how they can reduce stress, nutritional information that may not be common knowledge, suggestions from experts on skin care, reassurance about their lifestyle or health concerns, etc."

THE YOGA JOURNAL, California Yoga Teachers Association, 2054 University Ave., Berkeley CA 94704. (510)841-9200. Contact: Rick Fields, editor. 75% freelance written. Bimonthly magazine covering yoga, holistic health, conscious living, spiritual practices, ecology and nutrition. "We reach a middle-class, educated audience interested in self-improvement and higher consciousness." Estab. 1975. Circ. 90,000. Pays on publication. Publishes ms an average of 10 months after acceptance. Byline given. Offers $50 kill fee. Buys first North American serial rights only. Submit seasonal material 4 months in advance. Reports in 3 months. Sample copy for $3.50. Writer's guidelines free.

Nonfiction: Book excerpts; how-to (exercise, yoga, massage, etc.); inspirational (yoga or related); interview/profile; opinion; photo feature; and travel (if about yoga). "Yoga is our main concern, but our principal features in each issue highlight other New Age personalities and endeavors. Nothing too far-out and mystical. Prefer stories about Americans incorporating yoga, meditation, etc., into their normal lives." Buys 40 mss/year. Query. Length: 750-5,000 words. Pays $150-500.

Reprints: Submit tearsheet or photocopy and information about when and where the article previously appeared.

Photos: Jonathan Wieder, art director. Send photos with ms. Pays $200-600 for cover transparencies; $25-100 for 8×10 b&w prints. Model release (for cover only) and identification of subjects required. Buys one-time rights.

Columns/Departments: Forum; Cooking; Nutrition; Natural Body Care; Bodywork; Meditation; Well-Being; Psychology; Profiles; and Book Reviews. Buys 12-15 mss/year. Pays $150-400 for columns; $50-100 for book reviews.

Tips: "We always read submissions. We are very open to freelance material and want to encourage writers to submit to our magazine. We're looking for out-of-state contributors, particularly in the Midwest and East Coast."

YOUR HEALTH, Globe Communications Corp., 5401 NW Broken Sound Blvd., Boca Raton FL 33487. (561)997-7733. Fax: (561)997-9210. E-mail: yhealth@aol.com. Contact: Susan Gregg, editor. Associate Editor: Lisa Rappa. 70% freelance written. Semimonthly magazine on health and fitness. "*Your Health* is a lay-person magazine covering the entire gamut of health, fitness and medicine." Estab. 1962. Circ. 50,000. Pays on publication. Byline given. Buys first North American serial and second serial (reprint) rights. Submit seasonal material 3 months in advance. Reports in 1 month on queries; 6 weeks on mss. Sample copy and writer's guidelines free.

Nonfiction: Book excerpts, general interest, how-to (on general health and fitness topics), inspirational, interview/profile, medical breakthroughs, natural healing and alternative medicine, new products. "Give us something new and different." Buys 75-100 mss/year. Query with clips or send complete ms. Length: 300-2,000 words. Pays $25-200.

Reprints: Send tearsheet of article and information about when and where the article previously appeared. Pays 75% of amount paid for original article.

Photos: Send photos with submission. Reviews contact sheets, negatives, transparencies, prints. Offers $50-100/photo. Captions, model releases, identification of subjects required. Buys one-time rights.

Tips: "Freelancers can best break in by offering us stories of national interest that we won't find through other channels, such as wire services. Well-written self-help articles, especially ones that focus on natural prevention and cures are always welcome. We're looking for more natural health and alternative therapy stories."

YOUR HEALTH & FITNESS, General Learning Communications, 60 Revere Dr., Northbrook IL 60062-1574. (847)205-3000. Fax: (847)564-8197. Executive Editor: Carol Lezak. 90-95% freelance written. Prefers to work with published/established writers. Quarterly magazine covering health and fitness. Needs "general, educational material on health, fitness and safety that can be read and understood easily by the layman." Estab. 1969. Circ. 1,000,000. Pays after publication. Publishes ms an average of 6 months after acceptance. No byline given (contributing editor status given in masthead). Offers 50% kill fee. Buys all rights. Reports in 1 year.

Nonfiction: General interest. "All article topics assigned. No queries; if you're interested in writing for the magazine, send a cover letter, résumé, curriculum vitae and writing samples. All topics are determined a year in advance of publication by editors. No unsolicited manuscripts." Buys approximately 65 mss/year. Length: 350-850 words. Pays $100-400.

Tips: "Write to a general audience that has only a surface knowledge of health and fitness topics. Possible subjects include exercise and fitness, psychology, nutrition, safety, disease, drug data, and health concerns."

HISTORY

There has been an increasing interest in history in recent years. The popularity of historical documentaries, such as "The Civil War" and "Baseball," The History Channel debut in 1995, and the approach of the year 2000 may all play a part in this trend. Listed here are magazines

and other periodicals written for historical collectors, genealogy enthusiasts, historic preserva-
tionists and researchers. Editors of history magazines look for fresh accounts of past events in
a readable style. Some publications cover an era, such as the Civil War, or a region, while others
specialize in historic preservation.

‡AMERICAN HERITAGE, 60 Fifth Ave., New York NY 10011. (212)206-5500. Fax: (212)620-2332. Editor: Richard
Snow. 70% freelance written. Magazine published 8 times/year. "*American Heritage* writes from a historical point of
view on politics, business, art, current and international affairs, and our changing lifestyles. The articles are written with
the intent to enrich the reader's appreciation of the sometimes nostalgic, sometimes funny, always stirring panorama of
the American experience." Circ. 300,000. Usually buys first North American rights or all rights. Byline given. **Pays
on acceptance.** Publishes ms an average of 6-12 months after acceptance. Before submitting material, "check our index
to see whether we have already treated the subject." Submit seasonal material 1 year in advance. Reports in 1 month.
Writer's guidelines for #10 SASE.
Nonfiction: Wants "historical articles by scholars or journalists intended for intelligent lay readers rather than for
professional historians." Emphasis is on authenticity, accuracy and verve. "Interesting documents, photographs and
drawings are always welcome. Query. Style should stress readability and accuracy." Buys 30 unsolicited mss/year.
Length: 1,500-5,000 words. Sometimes pays the expenses of writers on assignment.
Tips: "We have over the years published quite a few 'firsts' from young writers whose historical knowledge, research
methods and writing skills met our standards. The scope and ambition of a new writer tell us a lot about his or her
future usefulness to us. A major article gives us a better idea of the writer's value. Everything depends on the quality
of the material. We don't really care whether the author is 20 and unknown, or 80 and famous, or vice versa."

AMERICAN HISTORY, P.O. Box 8200, Harrisburg PA 17105-8200. (717)657-9555. Fax: (717)657-9526. Editor:
Peggy Fortier. 60% freelance written. Bimonthly magazine of cultural, social, military and political history published
for a general audience. Estab. 1966. Circ. 120,000. **Pays on acceptance.** Byline given. Buys all rights. Reports in 10
weeks on queries. Writer's guidelines for #10 SASE. Sample copy and guidelines for $4.50 (includes 3rd class postage)
or $4 and 9×12 SAE with 4 first-class stamps.
Nonfiction: Features biographies of noteworthy historical figures and accounts of important events in American history.
Also includes pictorial features on artists, photographers and graphic subjects. "Material is presented on a popular rather
than a scholarly level." Query. "Query letters should be limited to a concise 1-2 page proposal defining your article
with an emphasis on its unique qualities." Buys 10-15 mss/year. Length: 1,000-5,000 words depending on type of
article. Pays $200-1,000.
Photos: Welcomes suggestions for illustrations.
Tips: "Key prerequisites for publication are thorough research and accurate presentation, precise English usage and
sound organization, a lively style, and a high level of human interest. Submissions received without return postage will
not be considered or returned. Inappropriate materials include: fiction, book reviews, travelogues, personal/family
narratives not of national significance, articles about collectibles/antiques, living artists, local/individual historic build-
ings/landmarks and articles of a current editorial nature. Currently seeking articles on significant Civil War subjects."

AMERICA'S CIVIL WAR, Cowles History Group, 741 Miller Dr., SE, Suite D-2, Leesburg VA 20175-8920. (703)771-
9400. Fax: (703)779-8345. E-mail: cheryls@cowles.com. Website: www.thehistorynet.com. Contact: Roy Morris, Jr.,
editor. Managing Editor: Carl Von Wodtke. 95% freelance written. Bimonthly magazine of "popular history and straight
historical narrative for both the general reader and the Civil War buff covering strategy, tactics, personalities, arms and
equipment." Estab. 1988. Circ. 125,000. Pays on publication. Publishes ms up to 2 years after acceptance. Byline given.
Buys all rights. Reports in 3 months on queries; 6 months on mss. Sample copy for $5. Guidelines for #10 SASE.
Nonfiction: Book excerpts, historical, travel. No fiction or poetry. Buys 24 mss/year. Query. Length: 3,500-4,000
words maximum and should include a 500-word sidebar. Pays $300 maximum.
Photos: Send photos with submission or cite sources. "We'll order." Captions and identification of subjects required.
Columns/Departments: Personality (probes); Ordnance (about weapons used); Commands (about units); Travel
(about appropriate historical sites). Buys 24 mss/year. Query. Length: 2,000 words. Pays up to $150.
Tips: "Include suggested readings in a standard format at the end of your piece. Manuscript must be typed, double-
spaced on one side of standard white 8½×11, 16 to 30 pound paper—no onion skin paper or dot matrix printouts.
All submissions are on speculation. Prefer subjects to be on disk (floppy or hard). Choose stories with strong art
possibilities."

THE ARTILLERYMAN, Historical Publications, Inc., RR 1 Box 36, Tunbridge VT 05077. (802)889-3500. Fax:
(802)889-5627. E-mail: firetec@firetec.com ("attention: the Artilleryman"). Website: firetec@tecfiretec.com. Editor:
C. Peter Jorgensen. 60% freelance written. Quarterly magazine covering antique artillery, fortifications and crew-served
weapons 1750-1900 for competition shooters, collectors and living history reenactors using artillery. "Emphasis on
Revolutionary War and Civil War but includes everyone interested in pre-1900 artillery and fortifications, preservation,
construction of replicas, etc." Estab. 1979. Circ. 2,200. Pays on publication. Publishes ms an average of 6 months after
acceptance. Byline given. Not copyrighted. Buys one-time rights. Accepts simultaneous submissions. Reports in 3
weeks. Sample copy and writer's guidelines for 9×12 SAE with 4 first-class stamps.
Nonfiction: Historical; how-to (reproduce ordnance equipment/sights/implements/tools/accessories, etc.); interview/

profile; new product; opinion (must be accompanied by detailed background of writer and include references); personal experience; photo feature; technical (must have footnotes); travel (where to find interesting antique cannon). Interested in "artillery *only*, for sophisticated readers. Not interested in other weapons, battles in general." Buys 24-30 mss/year. Send complete ms. Length: 300 words minimum. Pays $20-60. Sometimes pays the expenses of writers on assignment.
Reprints: Send tearsheet or photocopy of article and information about when and where the article previously appeared.
Photos: Send photos with ms. Pays $5 for 5×7 and larger b&w prints. Captions, identification of subjects required.
Tips: "We regularly use freelance contributions for Places-to-Visit, Cannon Safety, The Workshop and Unit Profiles departments. Also need pieces on unusual cannon or cannon with a known and unique history. To judge whether writing style and/or expertise will suit our needs, writers should ask themselves if they could knowledgeably talk *artillery* with an expert. Subject matter is of more concern than writer's background."

AVIATION HISTORY, Cowles History Group, 741 Miller Dr., SE, Suite D-2, Leesburg VA 20175-8920. (703)771-9400. Fax: (703)779-8345. E-mail: cheryls@cowles.com. Website: www.thehistorynet.com. Contact: Arthur Sanfelici, editor. Managing Editor: Carl von Wodtke. 95% freelance written. Bimonthly magazine covering military and civilian aviation from first flight to the jet age. It aims to make aeronautical history not only factually accurate and complete, but also enjoyable to varied subscriber and newsstand audience. Estab. 1990. Circ. 80,000. Pays on publication. Publishes ms up to 2 years after acceptance. Byline given. Buys all rights. Editorial lead time 6 months. Submit seasonal material 1 year in advance. Accepts simultaneous submissions. Reports in 3 months on queries; 6 months on mss. Sample copy for $5. Writers guidelines for #10 SASE.
Nonfiction: Book excerpts, historical/nostalgic, interview/profile, personal experience, travel. Buys 24 mss/year. Query. Length: Feature articles should be 3,500-4,000 words, each with a 500-word sidebar, author's biography and book suggestions for further reading. Pays $300.
Photos: State availability of art and photos with submission, cite sources. "We'll order." Reviews contact sheets, negatives, transparencies. Identification of subjects required. Buys one-time rights.
Columns/Departments: People and Planes, Enduring Heritage, Aerial Oddities, Art of Flight; all 2,000 words. Pays $150. Book reviews, 300-750 words; payment by the word.
Tips: "Choose stories with strong art possibilities."

CHICAGO HISTORY, The Magazine of the Chicago Historical Society, Chicago Historical Society, Clark St. at North Ave., Chicago IL 60614-6099. (312)642-4600. Fax: (312)266-2077. E-mail: adams@chicagohs.org. Website: http://www.chicagohs.org. Contact: Rosemary Adams, editor. 100% freelance written. Works with a small number of new/unpublished writers each year. Triannual magazine covering Chicago history: cultural, political, economic, social and architectural. Estab. 1945. Circ. 9,500. Pays on publication. Publishes ms an average of 1 year after acceptance. Byline given. Buys all rights. Submit seasonal material 9 months in advance. Reports in 4 months. Sample copy for $3.50 and 9×12 SAE with 3 first-class stamps. Writer's guidelines free.
 ● Writer's guidelines for *Chicago History* are also available on its website.
Nonfiction: Book excerpts, essays, historical, photo feature. Articles should be "analytical, informative, and directed at a popular audience with a special interest in history." No "cute" articles, no biographies. Buys 8-12 mss/year. Query or send complete ms. Length: approximately 4,500 words. Pays $150-250.
Photos: Send photocopies with submission. Would prefer no originals. Offers no additional payment for photos accepted with ms. Identification of subjects required.
Tips: "A freelancer can best break in by 1) calling to discuss an article idea with editor; and 2) submitting a detailed outline of proposed article. All sections of *Chicago History* are open to freelancers, but we suggest that authors do not undertake to write articles for the magazine unless they have considerable knowledge of the subject and are willing to research it in some detail. We require a footnoted manuscript, although we do not publish the notes."

GATEWAY HERITAGE, Missouri Historical Society, P.O. Box 11940, St. Louis MO 63112-0040. (314)746-4557. Fax: (314)746-4548. Contact: Tim Fox, editor. 75% freelance written. Quarterly magazine covering Missouri history. "*Gateway Heritage* is a popular history magazine which is sent to members of the Missouri Historical Society. Thus, we have a general audience with an interest in history." Estab. 1980. Circ. 6,200. Pays on publication. Publishes ms an average of 6 months after acceptance. Byline given. Offers $75 kill fee. Buys first North American serial rights. Editorial lead time 6 months. Submit seasonal material 1 year in advance. Reports in 2 weeks on queries; 2 months on mss. Sample copy for 9×12 SAE with 7 first-class stamps. Writer's guidelines for #10 SASE.
Nonfiction: Book excerpts, historical/nostalgic, interview/profile, personal experience, photo feature. No genealogies. Buys 12-15 mss/year. Query with published clips. Length: 3,500-5,000 words. Pays $200.
Photos: State availability of photos with submission.
Columns/Departments: Literary Landmarks (biographical sketches and interviews of famous Missouri literary figures) 1,500-2,500 words; Missouri Biographies (biographical sketches of famous and interesting Missourians) 1,500-2,500 words; Gateway Album (excerpts from diaries and journals) 1,500-2,500 words. Buys 6-8 mss/year. Query with published clips. Pays $100.
Tips: "Ideas for submissions to our departments are a good way to break into *Gateway Heritage*."

GOOD OLD DAYS, America's Premier Nostalgia Magazine, House of White Birches, 306 E. Parr Rd., Berne IN 46711. (219)589-8741. Contact: Ken Tate, editor. 75% freelance written. Monthly magazine of first person nostalgia, 1900-1955. "We look for strong narratives showing life as it was in the first half of this century. Our readership is comprised of nostalgia buffs, history enthusiasts and the people who actually lived and grew up in this era." Pays on publication. Publishes ms an average of 8 months after acceptance. Byline given. Buys all, first North American serial or one-time rights. Submit seasonal material 10 months in advance. Reports in 2 months. Sample copy for $2. Writer's guidelines for #10 SASE.

Nonfiction: Historical/nostalgic, humor, interview/profile, personal experience, favorite food/recipes and photo features, year-round seasonal material, biography, memorable events, fads, fashion, sports, music, literature, entertainment. Regular features: Good Old Days on Wheels (transportation auto, plane, horse-drawn, tram, bicycle, trolley, etc.); Good Old Days In the Kitchen (favorite foods, appliances, ways of cooking, recipes); Home Remedies (herbs and poultries, hometown doctors, harrowing kitchen table operations). Buys 350 mss/year. Query or send complete ms. Preferred. length: 500-1,200 words. Pays $15-75, depending on quality and photos. No fiction accepted.

Photos: Send photos or photocopies of photos alone or with submission. Offers $5/photo. Identification of subjects required. Buys one-time or all rights.

Tips: "Most of our writers are not professionals. We prefer the author's individual voice, warmth, humor and honesty over technical ability."

MILITARY HISTORY, Cowles History Group, 741 Miller Dr., SE, Suite D-2, Leesburg VA 20175-8920. (703)771-9400. Fax: (703)779-8345. E-mail: cheryls@cowles.com. Website: www.thehistorynet.com. Contact: Jon Guttman, editor. Managing Editor: Carl Von Wodtke. 95% freelance written. Circ. 150,000. "We'll work with anyone, established or not, who can provide the goods and convince us as to its accuracy." Bimonthly magazine covering all military history of the world. "We strive to give the general reader accurate, highly readable, often narrative popular history, richly accompanied by period art." Pays on publication. Publishes ms 2 years after acceptance. Byline given. Buys all rights. Submit anniversary material at least 1 year in advance. Reports in 3 months on queries; 6 months on mss. Sample copy for $5. Writer's guidelines for #10 SASE.

Nonfiction: Historical; interview (military figures of commanding interest); personal experience (only occasionally). Buys 18 mss, plus 6 interviews/year. Query with published clips. "To propose an article, submit a short, self-explanatory query summarizing the story proposed, its highlights and/or significance. State also your own expertise, access to sources or proposed means of developing the pertinent information." Length: 4,000 words and should include a 500-word sidebar. Pays $400.

Columns/Departments: Intrigue, Weaponry, Perspectives, Personality and review of books, video, CD-ROMs, software—all relating to military history. Buys 24 mss/year. Query with published clips. Length: 2,000 words. Pays $200.

Tips: "We would like journalistically 'pure' submissions that adhere to basics, such as full name at first reference, same with rank, and definition of prior or related events, issues cited as context or obscure military 'hardware.' Read the magazine, discover our style, and avoid subjects already covered. Pick stories with strong art possibilities (*real* art and photos), send photocopies, tell us where to order the art. Avoid historical overview, focus upon an event with appropriate and accurate context. Provide bibliography. Tell the story in popular but elegant style."

PERSIMMON HILL, 1700 NE 63rd St., Oklahoma City OK 73111. Fax: (405)478-4714. E-mail: nchf@aol.com. Website: http://www.horseworld.com. Editor: M.J. Van Deventer. 70% freelance written. Prefers to work with published/established writers; works with a small number of new/unpublished writers each year. Quarterly magazine for an audience interested in Western art, Western history, ranching and rodeo, including historians, artists, ranchers, art galleries, schools, and libraries. Publication of the National Cowboy Hall of Fame and Western Heritage Center. Estab. 1970. Circ. 15,000. Buys first rights. Byline given. Pays on publication. Publishes ms an average of 6-24 months after acceptance. Reports in 3 months. Sample copy for $9 and 12 first-class stamps. Writer's guidelines for #10 SASE.

Nonfiction: Historical and contemporary articles on famous Western figures connected with pioneering the American West, Western art, rodeo, cowboys, etc. (or biographies of such people), stories of Western flora and animal life and environmental subjects. "We want thoroughly researched and historically authentic material written in a popular style. May have a humorous approach to subject. No broad, sweeping, superficial pieces; i.e., the California Gold Rush or rehashed pieces on Billy the Kid, etc." Length: 1,500 words. Buys 35-50 mss/year. Query with clips. Pays $150-250.

Photos: Glossy b&w prints or color transparencies purchased with ms, or on assignment. Pays according to quality and importance for b&w and color photos. Suggested captions required.

Tips: "Send us a story that captures the spirit of adventure and individualism that typifies the Old West or reveals a facet of the Western lifestyle in contemporary society. Excellent illustrations for articles are essential!"

TIMELINE, Ohio Historical Society, 1982 Velma Ave., Columbus OH 43211-2497. (614)297-2360. Fax: (614)297-2367. Editor: Christopher S. Duckworth. 90% freelance written. Works with a small number of new/unpublished writers each year. Bimonthly magazine covering history, natural history, archaeology and fine and decorative arts. Estab. 1885. Circ. 19,000. **Pays on acceptance.** Publishes ms an average of 1 year after acceptance. Byline given. Offers $75 minimum kill fee. Buys first North American serial or all rights. Submit seasonal material 6 months in advance. Reports in 3 weeks on queries; 6 weeks on mss. Sample copy for $6 and 9×12 SAE. Writer's guidelines for #10 SASE.

Nonfiction: Book excerpts, essays, historical, profile (of individuals), photo feature. Buys 22 mss/year. Query. Length: 500-6,000 words. Pays $100-900.

Photos: Send photos with submission. Submissions must include ideas for illustration. Reviews contact sheets, transparencies, 8×10 prints. Captions, model releases, identification of subjects required. Buys one-time rights.

Tips: "We want crisply written, authoritative narratives for the intelligent lay reader. An Ohio slant may strengthen a submission, but it is not indispensable. Contributors must know enough about their subject to explain it clearly and in an interesting fashion. We use high-quality illustration with all features. If appropriate illustration is unavailable, we can't use the feature. The writer who sends illustration ideas with a manuscript has an advantage, but an often-published illustration won't attract us."

TRACES OF INDIANA AND MIDWESTERN HISTORY, Indiana Historical Society, 315 W Ohio St., Indianapolis IN 46202-3299. (317)233-6073. Fax: (317)233-3109. E-mail: mmckee@statelib.lib.in.us. Website: http://www.ihs1830.org/traces.htm. Executive Editor: Thomas A. Mason. Managing Editor: J. Kent Calder. Contact: Megan McKee, editor. 80% freelance written. Quarterly magazine on Indiana and Midwestern history. "Conceived as a vehicle to bring to the public good narrative and analytical history about Indiana in its broader contexts of region and nation, *Traces* explores the lives of artists, writers, performers, soldiers, politicians, entrepreneurs, homemakers, reformers, and naturalists. It has traced the impact of Hoosiers on the nation and the world. In this vein, the editors seek nonfiction articles that are solidly researched, attractively written, and amenable to illustration, and they encourage scholars, journalists, and freelance writers to contribute to the magazine." Estab. 1989. Circ. 11,000. **Pays on acceptance.** Publishes ms an average of 6 months after acceptance. Byline given. Buys one-time rights. Submit seasonal material 1 year in advance. Reports in 3 months on mss. Sample copy $5 and 9×12 SAE with 6 first-class stamps. Writer's guidelines for #10 SASE.
Nonfiction: Book excerpts, historical essays, historical photographic features. Buys 20 mss/year. Send complete ms. Length: 2,000-4,000 words. Pays $100-500.
Photos: Send photos with submission. Reviews contact sheets, photocopies, transparencies and prints. Pays "reasonable photographic expenses." Captions, permissions and identification of subjects required. Buys one-time rights.
Tips: "Freelancers should be aware of prerequisites for writing history for a broad audience. Should have some awareness of this magazine and other magazines of this type published by midwestern and western historical societies. Preference is given to subjects with an Indiana connection and authors who are familiar with *Traces*. Quality of potential illustration is also important."

TRUE WEST and OLD WEST, Western Periodicals, Inc., P.O. Box 2107, Stillwater OK 74076-2107. (405)743-3370. Fax: (405)743-3374. E-mail: western@cowboy.net. Website: http://www.cowboy.net/western. Contact: Marcus Huff, editor. 100% freelance written. Works with a small number of new/unpublished writers each year. *True West* (monthly), and *Old West* (quarterly) are magazines on Western American history from prehistory to 1930. "We want reliable research on significant historical topics written in lively prose for an informed general audience. More recent topics may be used if they have a historical angle or retain the Old West flavor of trail dust and saddle leather." Estab. 1953. Circ. 40,000. **Pays on acceptance.** Sends galleys. Publishes ms an average of 4 months after acceptance. Byline given. Buys first North American serial rights. Editorial lead time 3 months. Submit seasonal material 6 months in advance. Accepts simultaneous submissions. Reports in 1 month on queries; 2 months on mss. Sample copy for $2 and 9×12 SAE. Writer's guidelines for #10 SASE.
Nonfiction: Historical/nostalgic, how-to, humor, photo feature, travel, Native Americans, trappers, miners, cowboys, ranchers, pioneers, military ghost towns, lost mines, women and minorities. "We do not want rehashes of worn-out stories, historical fiction or history written in a fictional style." Special issue: ghost stories published every October (deadline June 5.) Buys 150 mss/year. Query. Ideal length: 2,000 words, maximum length 4,000 words; shorter pieces, especially humor, 300-1,500 words. Pays 3-6¢/word.
Photos: "We usually need from four to eight photos for each story, and we rely on writers to provide them." Send photos with accompanying query or ms. "Appropriate maps enhance our articles, and we appreciate receiving sketches for our artists to work from." Pays $10 for b&w prints. Identification of subjects required. Buys one-time rights.
Columns/Departments: Western Roundup—200-300-word short articles on historically oriented places to go and things to do in the West. Should include one b&w print. Buys 24 mss/year. Send complete ms. Pays $25-75.
Fillers: Short humor. Buys 12/year. Length: 500-1,000 words. Pays 3-6¢/word.
Tips: "Do original research on fresh topics. Stay away from controversial subjects unless you are truly knowledgable in the field. Read our magazines and follow our guidelines. A freelancer is most likely to break in with us by submitting thoroughly researched, lively prose on relatively obscure topics. First person accounts rarely fill our needs. Historical accuracy and strict adherence to the facts are essential. We much prefer material based on primary sources (archives, court records, documents, contemporary newspapers and first person accounts) to those that rely mainly on secondary sources (published books, magazines, and journals). Note: We are currently trying to take *True West* and *Old West* back to their 'roots' by publishing shorter pieces. Ideal length is between 1,500-3,000 words."

VIETNAM, Cowles History Group, 741 Miller Dr. SE, #D-2, Leesburg VA 20175-8920. (703)771-9400. Fax: (703)779-8345. E-mail: cheryls@cowles.com. Website: www.thehistorynet.com. Contact: Colonel Harry G. Summers, Jr., editor. Managing Editor: Carl Von Wodtke. 80-90% freelance written. Bimonthly magazine that "provides in-depth and authoritative accounts of the many complexities that made the war in Vietnam unique, including the people, battles, strategies, perspectives, analysis and weaponry." Estab. 1988. Circ. 115,000. Pays on publication. Publishes ms up to 2 years after acceptance. Byline given. Buys all rights. Reports in 3 months on queries; 6 months on mss. Sample copy for $5. Writer's guidelines for #10 SASE.
Nonfiction: Book excerpts (if original), historical, interview, personal/experience, military history. "Absolutely no fiction or poetry; we want straight history, as much personal narrative as possible, but not the gung-ho, shoot-em-up variety, either." Buys 24 mss/year. Query. Length: 4,000 words maximum. Pays $300 for features, sidebar 500 words.
Photos: Send photos with submission or state availability and cite sources. Identification of subjects required.

Columns/Departments: Arsenal (about weapons used, all sides); Personality (profiles of the players, all sides); Fighting Forces (about various units or types of units: air, sea, rescue); Perspectives. Query. Length: 2,000 words. Pays $150.

Tips: Choose stories with strong art possibilities.

WESTERN TALES, P.O. Box 33842, Granada Hills CA 91394. Contact: Mariann Kumke, editor. Publisher: Dorman Nelson. 100% freelance written. Quarterly magazine covering "Western fiction genre—prose and poetry—westward expansion, Native Americans, pioneers, cowboys, wildlife, romance, adventure, mystery, intrigue. Primarily historical fiction and tales, but modern and future western subjects considered." Estab. 1993. Circ. 3,000. **Pays on acceptance**. Publishes ms an average of 4 months after acceptance. Byline given. Buys first North American serial rights. Editorial lead time 4 months. Submit seasonal material 4 months in advance. Accepts simultaneous submissions. Reports in 1 month on queries; 4 months on mss. Sample copy for $6. Writer's guidelines for #10 SASE.

Nonfiction: Book excerpts, essays, general interest (western fiction), how-to (western-oriented), humor, inspirational, new product (for advertising and information section), opinion, personal experience (fictionalized). Special issues: Edgar Rice Burroughs edition (he did write western genre fiction as well as his Tarzan and Carter of Mars.) Also—a women's edition created and written by women authors. Send complete ms. Pays $100 for unsolicited articles and 1 copy.

Reprints: Send typed ms with rights for sale noted and information about when and where the article previously appeared. Pays $100/story; $25/poetry; $10/cartoons.

Photos: Send photos with submission. Negotiates payment individually. Buys one-time rights.

Columns/Departments: Book review (Western fiction genre), 1,200-2,000 words. Buys 4-10 mss/year. Send complete ms. Pay negotiable.

Fiction: Adventure, historical, horror, humorous, mainstream, mystery, novel excerpts, romance, slice-of-life vignettes, suspense, western. Buys 80-100 mss/year. Send complete ms. Pays $100 maximum.

Poetry: Avant-garde, free verse, haiku, light verse, traditional (all Western oriented). Buys 60 poems/year. Submit maximum 4 poems. Pays $25.

Fillers: Mariann Kumke, editor. Anecdotes, facts, gags to be illustrated by cartoonist, short humor. Buys 25/year. Length: 50 words maximum. Pays $5-25.

Tips: "Send in a good tale!"

WILD WEST, Cowles History Group, 741 Miller Dr., SE, Suite D-2, Leesburg VA 20175-8920. (703)771-9400. Fax: (703)779-8345. E-mail: cheryls@cowles.com. Website: www.thehistorynet.com. Contact: Gregory Lalire, editor. Managing Editor: Carl Von Wodtke. 95% freelance written. Bimonthly magazine on history of the American West. "*Wild West* covers the popular (narrative) history of the American West—events, trends, personalities, anything of general interest." Estab. 1988. Circ. 275,000. Pays on publication. Byline given. Buys all rights. Submit seasonal material 1 year in advance. Sample copy for $5. Writer's guidelines for #10 SASE.

Nonfiction: Historical/nostalgic, humor, travel. No fiction or poetry—nothing current. Buys 24 mss/year. Query. Length: 4,000 words with a 500-word sidebar. Pays $300.

Photos: Send photos with submission; cite sources. "We'll order." Captions, identification of subjects required.

Columns/Departments: Travel; Gun Fighters & Lawmen; Personalities; Warriors & Chiefs; Artist West; Books Reviews. Buys 16 mss/year. Length: 2,000. Pays $150 for departments, by the word for book reviews.

Tips: "Manuscripts must be typed, double-spaced on one side of standard white 8½×11, 16 to 30 pound paper—no onion skin paper or dot matrix printouts. All submissions are on speculation. Prefer subjects to include disk (floppy or hard). Submit a query letter. Choose stories with strong art possibilities."

WORLD WAR II, Cowles History Group, 741 Miller Dr., SE, Suite D-2, Leesburg VA 20175-8920. (703)771-9400. Fax: (703)779-8345. E-mail: cheryls@cowles.com. Website: www.thehistorynet.com. Contact: Michael Haskew, editor. Managing Editor: Carl Von Wodtke. 95% freelance written. Prefers to work with published/established writers. Bimonthly magazine covering "military operations in World War II—events, personalities, strategy, national policy, etc." Estab. 1986. Circ. 200,000. Pays on publication. Publishes ms an average of 2 years after acceptance. Byline given. Buys all rights. Submit anniversary-related material 1 year in advance. Reports in 3 months on queries; 6 months or more on mss. Sample copy for $4. Writer's guidelines for #10 SASE.

Nonfiction: World War II military history. No fiction. Buys 24 mss/year. Query. Length: 4,000 words with a 500-word sidebar. Pays $200.

Photos: State availability of art and photos with submission. For photos and other art, send photocopies and cite sources. "We'll order." Captions and identification of subjects required.

Columns/Department: Undercover (espionage, resistance, sabotage, intelligence gathering, behind the lines, etc.); Personalities (WW II personalities of interest); Armaments (weapons, their use and development), all 2,000 words. Pays $100. Book reviews, 300-750 words. Buys 18 mss/year (plus book reviews). Query with SASE.

Tips: "List your sources and suggest further readings in standard format at the end of your piece—as a bibliography for our files in case of factual challenge or dispute. All submissions are on speculation."

HOBBY AND CRAFT

Magazines in this category range from home video to cross-stitch. Craftspeople and hobbyists who read these magazines want new ideas while collectors need to know what is most valuable and why. Collectors, do-it-yourselfers and craftspeople look to these magazines for inspiration and information. Publications covering antiques and miniatures are also listed here. Publications covering the business side of antiques and collectibles are listed in the Trade Art, Design and Collectibles section.

THE AMERICAN MATCHCOVER COLLECTORS CLUB, The Retskin Report, P.O. Box 18481, Asheville NC 28814-0481. (704)254-4487. Fax: (704)254-1066. E-mail: club@circle.net. Editor: Bill Retskin. 25% freelance written. Quarterly newsletter for matchcover collectors and historical enthusiasts. Estab. 1986. Circ. 700. Pays on publication. Publishes ms an average of 3 months after acceptance. Byline given. Offers 20% kill fee. Buys first North American serial rights. Submit seasonal material 6 months in advance. Sample copy for 9×12 SAE with 2 first-class stamps. Writer's guidelines for #10 SASE.
Nonfiction: General interest, historical/nostalgic, how-to (collecting techniques), humor, personal experience, photo feature; all relating to match industry, matchcover collecting hobby or ephemera. Buys 2 mss/year. Query with published clips. Length: 200-1,200 words. Pays $25-50 for assigned articles; $10-25 for unsolicited articles.
Photos: Send photos with submission. Reviews b&w contact sheets and 5×7 prints. Offers $2-5/photo. Captions and identification of subjects required.
Fiction: Historical (matchcover related only). Buys 2 mss/year. Query with published clips. Length: 200-1,200 words. Pays $25-50.
Tips: "We are interested in clean, direct style with the collector audience in mind."

AMERICAN WOODWORKER, Rodale Press, Inc., 33 E. Minor St., Emmaus PA 18098-0099. (610)967-5171. Fax: (610)967-7692. Fax: (610)967-7692. E-mail: www.awtims@aol.com. Editor/Publisher: David Sloan. Executive Editor: Ellis Wallentine. Contact: Tim Snyder, managing editor. 70% freelance written. Magazine published 7 times/year. "*American Woodworker* is a how-to magazine edited for the woodworking enthusiast who wants to improve his/her skills. We strive to motivate, challenge and entertain." Estab. 1985. Circ. 300,000. Pays on publication. Publishes ms an average of 6 months after acceptance. Byline given. Buys one-time and second serial (reprint) rights. Submit seasonal material 8 months in advance. Reports in 1 month. Sample copy and writer's guidelines free.
Nonfiction: Essays, historical/nostalgic, how-to (woodworking projects and techniques), humor, inspirational, interview/profile, new product, personal experience, photo feature, technical. ("All articles must have woodworking theme.") Buys 30 mss/year. Query. Length: up to 2,500 words. Pays new authors base rate of $150/published page. Sometimes pays expenses of writers on assignment.
Reprints: Send photocopy of article or typed ms with rights for sale noted. Payment varies.
Photos: Send photos with submission. Reviews 35mm or larger transparencies. Offers no additional payment for photos accepted with ms. Model releases required. Buys one-time rights.
Columns/Departments: Offcuts (woodworking news and nonsense, 1,000 word max). Buys 10 mss/year. Send complete ms. Pays $100-300.
Poetry: Avant-garde, free verse, Haiku, light verse, traditional. "All poetry must have woodworking or craftsmanship theme." Buys 1 poem/year. Submit maximum 5 poems. Pays $50-100.
Tips: "Reading the publication is the only real way to get a feel for the niche market *American Woodworker* represents and the needs and interests of our readers. Magazine editorial targets the serious woodworking enthusiast who wishes to improve his/her skills. Feature stories and articles most accessible for freelancers. Articles should be technically accurate, well organized and reflect the needs and interests of the amateur and small-shop professional."

ANTIQUE REVIEW, P.O. Box 538, Worthington OH 43085-0538. Contact: Charles Muller, editor. (614)885-9757. Fax: (614)885-9762. 60% freelance written. Eager to work with new/unpublished writers. Monthly tabloid for an antique-oriented readership, "generally well-educated, interested in Early American furniture and decorative arts, as well as folk art." Estab. 1975. Circ. 10,000. Pays on publication date assigned at time of purchase. Publishes ms an average of 2 months after acceptance. Buys first North American serial and second (reprint) rights to material originally published in dissimilar publications. Byline given. Phone queries OK. Reports in 3 months. Free sample copy and writer's guidelines for #10 SASE.
Nonfiction: "The articles we desire concern history and production of furniture, pottery, china, and other quality Americana. In some cases, contemporary folk art items are acceptable. We are also interested in reporting on antiques shows and auctions with statements on conditions and prices. We do not want articles on contemporary collectibles." Buys 5-8 mss/issue. Query with clips of published work. Query should show "author's familiarity with antiques, an interest in the historical development of artifacts relating to early America and an awareness of antiques market." Length: 200-2,000 words. Pays $100-200. Sometimes pays the expenses of writers on assignment.
Reprints: Accepts previously published submissions if not first printed in competitive publications. Send tearsheet or photocopy of article or typed ms with rights for sale noted and information about when and where the article previously appeared. Pays 100% of amount paid for an original article.
Photos: Send photos with query. Payment included in ms price. Uses 3×5 or larger glossy b&w or color prints. Captions required. Articles with photographs receive preference.
Tips: "Give us a call and let us know of specific interests. We are more concerned with the background in antiques than in writing abilities. The writing can be edited, but the knowledge imparted is of primary interest. A frequent mistake

is being too general, not becoming deeply involved in the topic and its research. We are interested in primary research into America's historic material culture."

THE ANTIQUE TRADER WEEKLY, P.O. Box 1050, Dubuque IA 52004-1050. (800)531-0880. Fax: (319)588-0888. E-mail: traderpubs@aol.com. Contact: Juli Hoppensteadt, associate editor. 50% freelance written. Works with a small number of new/unpublished writers each year. Weekly newspaper for collectors and dealers in antiques and collectibles. Estab. 1957. Circ. 60,000. Publishes ms an average of 1 year after acceptance. Buys all rights. Payment at beginning of month following publication. Accepts simultaneous submissions. Submit seasonal material 4 months in advance. Sample copy for $1 and #10 SASE. Writer's guidelines free.
Nonfiction: "We invite authoritative and well-researched articles on all types of antiques and collectors' items and in-depth stories on specific types of antiques and collectibles. No human interest stories. We do not pay for brief information on new shops opening or other material printed as a service to the antiques hobby." Buys about 60 mss/year. Query or submit complete ms. Pays $25-100 for feature articles; $100-250 for feature cover stories.
Photos: Submit a liberal number of good b&w photos to accompany article. Uses 35mm slides for cover. Offers no additional payment for photos accompanying mss.
Tips: "Send concise, polite letter stating the topic to be covered in the story and the writer's qualifications. No 'cute' letters rambling on about some 'imaginative' story idea. Writers who have a concise yet readable style and know their topic are always appreciated. I am most interested in those who have personal collecting experience or can put together a knowledgable and informative feature after interviewing a serious collector/authority."

‡AUTOGRAPH COLLECTING, Odyssey Publications, 510-A South Corona Mall, Corona CA 91719. (909)734-9636. Fax: (909)371-7139 E-mail: DBTOGI@aol.com. Website: http://www.AutographCollecting.com. Contact: Ev Phillips, editor. 80% freelance written. Monthly magazine covering the autograph collecting hobby. "The focus of *Autograph Collecting* is on documents, photographs or any collectible item that has been signed by a famous person, whether a current celebrity or historical figure. Articles stress how and where to locate celebrities and autograph material, authenticity of signatures and what they are worth." Byline given. Negotiable kill fee. Buys all rights. Editorial lead time 2 months. Submit seasonal material 3 months in advance. Reports in 2 weeks on queries; 1 month on mss. Sample copy and writer's guidelines free.
Nonfiction: Historical/nostalgic, how-to, interview/profile, personal experience. "Articles must address subjects that appeal to autograph collectors and should answer six basic questions: Who is this celebrity/famous person? How do I go about collecting this person's autograph? Where can I find it? How scarce or available is it? How can I tell if it's real? What is it worth?" Buys 25-35 mss/year. Query. Length: 1,750-2,250 words. Pays 5¢/word. Sometimes pays expenses of writers on assignment.
Photos: State availability of photos with submission. Reviews transparencies, prints. Offers $3/photo. Captions, identification of subjects required. Buys one-time rights.
Columns/Departments: "*Autograph Collecting* buys 8-10 columns per month written by regular contributors. Send query for more information." Buys 90-100 mss/year. Query. Pays $50 or as determined on a per case basis.
Fillers: Anecdotes, facts. Buys 20-25/year. Length: 200-300 words. Pays $15.
Tips: "Ideally writers should be autograph collectors themselves and know their topics thoroughly. Articles must be well-researched and clearly written. Writers should remember that *Autograph Collector* is a celebrity-driven magazine and name recognition of the subject is important."

BECKETT BASEBALL CARD MONTHLY, Statabase, Inc., 15850 Dallas Pkwy., Dallas TX 75248. (214)991-6657. Fax: (214)991-8930. Website: http://www.beckett.com. Editor: Dr. James Beckett. Editorial Director: Pepper Hastings. Contact: Mike Pagel, assistant editor. 85% freelance written. Monthly magazine on baseball card and sports memorabilia collecting. "Our readers expect our publication to be entertaining and informative. Our slant is that hobbies are fun and rewarding. Especially wanted are how-to-collect articles." Estab. 1984. Circ. 620,341. **Pays on acceptance.** Publishes ms an average of 4 months after acceptance. Byline given. Pays $50 kill fee. Buys all rights. Submit seasonal material 6 months in advance. Reports in 1 month. Sample copy for $2.95. Writer's guidelines free.
Nonfiction: Book excerpts, historical/nostalgic, how-to, humor, interview/profile, new product, opinion, personal experience, photo feature, technical. Special issues: Spring training (February); season preview (April); All-Star game (July); stay in school (August); World Series (October). No articles that emphasize speculative prices and investments. Buys 145 mss/year. Send complete ms. Length: 300-1,500 words. Pays $100-400 for assigned articles; $50-200 for unsolicited articles. Sometimes pays expenses of writers on assignment.
Photos: Send photos with submission. Reviews 35mm transparencies, 5×7 or larger prints. Offers $10-300/photo. Captions, model releases and identification of subjects required. Buys one-time rights.
Fiction: Humorous only.
Tips: "A writer for *Beckett Baseball Card Monthly* should be an avid sports fan and/or a collector with an enthusiasm for sharing his/her interests with others. Articles must be factual, but not overly statistic-laden. First person (not research) articles presenting the writer's personal experiences told with wit and humor, and emphasizing the stars of the game, are *always* wanted. Acceptable articles must be of interest to our two basic reader segments: teenaged boys and their middle-aged fathers who are re-experiencing a nostalgic renaissance of their own childhoods. Prospective writers should write down to neither group!"

BECKETT BASKETBALL MONTHLY, Statabase, Inc., 15850 Dallas Pkwy., Dallas TX 75248. (214)991-6657. Fax: (214)991-8930. Website: http://www.beckett.com. Publisher: Dr. James Beckett. Editorial Director: Pepper Hastings. Contact: Mike Payne, managing editor. 85% freelance written. Monthly magazine on basketball card and sports memorabilia collecting. "Our readers expect our publication to be entertaining and informative. Our slant is that hobbies are fun and rewarding. Especially wanted are articles dealing directly with the hobby of basketball card collecting." Estab. 1990. Circ. 392,854. **Pays on acceptance.** Publishes ms an average of 4 months after acceptance. Byline given. Pays $50 kill fee. Buys first North American serial rights. Submit seasonal material 6 months in advance. Reports in 1 month. Sample copy for $2.95. Writer's guidelines free.

Nonfiction: Book excerpts, historical/nostalgic, how-to, humor, interview/profile, new product, opinion, personal experience, photo feature, technical. Special issues: All Star game, stay in school (February); playoffs (June); new card sets (September). No articles that emphasize speculative prices and investments. Buys 145 mss/year. Send complete ms. Length: 300-1,500 words. Pays $100-400 for assigned articles; $100-200 for unsolicited articles. Sometimes pays expenses of writers on assignment.

Photos: Send photos with submission. Reviews 35mm transparencies, 5×7 or larger prints. Offers $10-300/photo. Captions, model releases and identification of subjects required. Buys one-time rights.

Fiction: Humorous only.

Tips: "A writer for *Beckett Basketball Monthly* should be an avid sports fan and/or a collector with an enthusiasm for sharing his/her interests with others. Articles must be factual, but not overly statistic-laden. First person (not research) articles presenting the writer's personal experiences told with wit and humor, and emphasizing the stars of the game, are *always* wanted. Acceptable articles must be of interest to our two basic reader segments: late teenaged boys and their fathers who are re-experiencing a nostalgic renaissance of their own childhoods. Prospective writers should write down to neither group!"

BECKETT FOCUS ON FUTURE STARS AND SPORTS COLLECTIBLES, Statabase, Inc., 15850 Dallas Pkwy., Dallas TX 75248. (214)991-6657. Fax: (214)991-8930. Website: http://www.beckett.com. Editor: Dr. James Beckett. Editorial Director: Pepper Hastings. Contact: Mike Pagel, assistant editor. 85% freelance written. Monthly magazine offering superstar coverage of young, outstanding players in baseball (major-league rookies, minor league stars and college), basketball (college), football (college) and hockey (juniors and college), with an emphasis on collecting sports cards and memorabilia. "Our readers expect our publication to be entertaining and informative. Our slant is that hobbies are fun and rewarding. Especially wanted are how-to-collect articles." Estab. 1991. Circ. 73,128. **Pays on acceptance.** Publishes ms an average of 4 months after acceptance. Byline given. Pays $50 kill fee. Buys all rights. Submit seasonal material 8 months in advance. Reports in 1 month. Sample copy for $2.95. Guidelines free.

Nonfiction: Book excerpts, historical/nostalgic, how-to, humor, interview/profile, new product, opinion, personal experience, photo feature, technical. Special issues: card sets in review (January); stay in school (February); draft special (June). No articles that emphasize speculative prices and investments on cards. Buys 145 mss/year. Send complete ms. Length: 300-1,500 words. Pays $100-400 for assigned articles; $50-200 for unsolicited articles. Sometimes pays expenses of writers on assignment.

Photos: Send photos with submission. Reviews 35mm transparencies, 5×7 or larger prints. Offers $25-300/photo. Captions, model releases and identification of subjects required. Buys one-time rights.

Fiction: Humorous only

Tips: "A writer for *Beckett Focus on Future Stars and Sports Collectibles* should be an avid sports fan and/or a collector with an enthusiasm for sharing his/her interests with others. Articles must be factual, but not overly statistic-laden. First person (not research) articles presenting the writer's personal experiences told with wit and humor, and emphasizing the stars of the game, are *always* wanted. Acceptable articles must be of interest to our two basic reader segments: teenaged boys and their middle-aged fathers who are re-experiencing a nostalgic renaissance of their own childhoods. Prospective writers should write down to neither group!"

BECKETT FOOTBALL CARD MONTHLY, Statabase, Inc., 15850 Dallas Pkwy., Dallas TX 75248. (214)991-6657. Fax: (214)991-8930. Website: http://www.beckett.com. Editor: Dr. James Beckett. Editorial Director: Pepper Hastings. Contact: Mike Pagel, assistant editor. 85% freelance written. Monthly magazine on football card and sports memorabilia collecting. "Our readers expect our publication to be entertaining and informative. Our slant is that hobbies are fun and rewarding. Especially wanted are how-to-collect articles." Estab. 1989. Circ. 206,194. **Pays on acceptance.** Publishes ms an average of 4 months after acceptance. Byline given. Pays $50 kill fee. Buys all rights. Submit seasonal material 6 months in advance. Reports in 1 month. Sample copy for $2.95. Writer's guidelines free.

Nonfiction: Book excerpts, historical/nostalgic, how-to, humor, interview/profile, new product, opinion, personal experience, photo feature, technical. Special issues: Super Bowl (January); Pro Bowl (February); NFL draft (April); stay in school (August) preview (September). No articles that emphasize speculative prices and investments. Buys 145 mss/year. Send complete ms. Length: 300-1,500 words. Pays $100-400 for assigned articles; $50-200 for unsolicited articles. Sometimes pays expenses of writers on assignment.

Photos: Send photos with submission. Reviews 35mm transparencies, 5×7 or larger prints. Offers $10-300/photo. Captions, model releases, identification of subjects required. Buys one-time rights.

Fiction: Humorous only.

Tips: "A writer for *Beckett Football Card Monthly* should be an avid sports fan and/or a collector with an enthusiasm for sharing his/her interests with others. Articles must be factual, but not overly statistic-laden. Acceptable articles must be of interest to our two basic reader segments: teenaged boys and their middle-aged fathers who are re-experiencing a nostalgic renaissance of their own childhoods. Prospective writers should write down to neither group!"

BECKETT HOCKEY MONTHLY, Statabase, Inc., 15850 Dallas Pkwy., Dallas TX 75248. (214)991-6657. Fax: (214)991-8930. Website: http://www.beckett.com. Editor: Dr. James Beckett. Editorial Director: Pepper Hastings. Contact: Mike Pagel, assistant editor. 85% freelance written. Monthly magazine on hockey, hockey card and memorabilia collecting. "Our readers expect our publication to be entertaining and informative. Our slant is that hobbies are for fun and rewarding. Especially wanted are how-to-collect articles." Estab. 1990. Circ. 159,346. **Pays on acceptance.** Publishes ms an average of 3 months after acceptance. Byline given. Pays $50 kill fee. Buys all rights. Submit seasonal material 6 months in advance. Reports in 1 month. Sample copy for $2.95. Writer's guidelines free.
Nonfiction: Book excerpts, historical/nostalgic, how-to, humor, interview/profile, new product, opinion, personal experience, photo feature, technical. Special issues: All-Star game (February); Stanley Cup preview (April); draft (June); season preview (October). No articles that emphasize speculative prices and investments. Buys 145 mss/year. Send complete ms. Length: 300-1,500 words. Pays $100-400 for assigned articles; $50-200 for unsolicited articles. Sometimes pays expenses of writers on assignment.
Photos: Send photos with submission. Reviews 35mm transparencies, 5×7 or larger prints. Offers $10-300/photo. Captions, model releases and identification of subjects required. Buys one-time rights.
Fiction: Humorous only.
Tips: "A writer for *Beckett Hockey Monthly* should be an avid sports fan and/or a collector with an enthusiasm for sharing his/her interests with others. Articles must be factual, but not overly statistic-laden. Acceptable articles must be of interest to our two basic reader segments: teenaged boys and their middle-aged fathers who are re-experiencing a nostalgic renaissance of their own childhoods. Prospective writers should write down to neither group!"

BECKETT RACING MONTHLY, Statabase, Inc., 15850 Dallas Pkwy., Dallas TX 75248. (972)991-6657. Fax: (972)991-8930. E-mail: markzeske@beckett.com. Website: http://www.beckett.com. Editor: Dr. James Beckett. Editorial Director: Pepper Hastings. Contact: Mark Zeske, senior editor. 85% freelance written. Monthly magazine on racing card, die cast and sports memorabilia collecting. "Our readers expect our publication to be entertaining and informative. Our slant is that hobbies are fun and rewarding. Especially wanted are articles dealing directly with the hobby of card collecting." Estab. 1994. Circ. 100,000 **Pays on acceptance.** Publishes ms an average of 4 months after acceptance. Byline given. Pays $50 kill fee. Buys all rights. Submit seasonal material 6 months in advance. Reports in 1 month Sample copy for $3.95. Writer's guidelines free.
Nonfiction: Book excerpts, historical/nostalgic, how-to, humor, interview/profile, new product, opinion, personal experience, photo feature, technical. No articles that emphasize speculative prices and investments. Send complete ms. Length: 300-1,500 words. Pays $100-400 for assigned articles; $100-200 for unsolicited articles. Sometimes pays expenses of writer on assignment.
Photos: Send photos with submission. Reviews 35mm transparencies, 5×7 or larger prints. Offers $10-300/photo. Captions, model releases and identification of subjects required. Buys one-time rights.
Fiction: Humorous only.
Tips: "A writer for *Beckett Racing Monthly* should be an avid sports fan and/or a collector with an enthusiasm for sharing his/her interests with others. Articles must be factual, but not overly statistic-laden. First person (not research) articles presenting the writer's personal experiences told with wit and humor, and emphasizing the stars of the sport, are always wanted."

‡BECKETT VINTAGE SPORTS, Beckett Publications, 15850 Dallas Pkwy., Dallas TX 75248. (972)991-6657. Fax: (972)991-8930. E-mail: vinview.com. Editor: Pepper Hastings. Contact: Mark Zeske, senior editor. 80% freelance written. Monthly magazine covering the collecting of vintage (pre-1970) sports memorabilia and cards. Estab. 1996. **Pays on acceptance**. Publishes ms an average of 2 months after acceptance. Byline given. Offers 100% kill fee. Buys first North American serial rights. Editorial lead time 3 months. Submit seasonal material 3 months in advance. Sample copy for $3.95. Writer's guidelines free.
Nonfiction: Book excerpts, general interest, historical/nostalgic, how-to, interview/profile, personal experience, photo feature. Buys 80 mss/year. Query. Length: 800-1,500 words. Pays $150-250. Sometimes pays expenses of writers on assignment.
Photos: State availability of photos with submission. Reviews contact sheets. Negotiates payment individually. Captions required. Buys one-time rights.
Columns/Departments: Big Finds; Game (used equipment); Autographs. Buys 24 mss/year. Query. Pays $150-250.

THE BLADE MAGAZINE, Krause Publications, 700 E. State St., Iola WI 54945. (715)445-2214. Fax: (715)445-4087. Editor: Steve Shackleford. 90% freelance written. Monthly magazine for knife enthusiasts who want to know as much as possible about quality knives and edged weapons. Estab. 1973. Circ. 25,400. Pays on publication. Publishes ms an average of 6 months after acceptance. Buys all rights. Submit seasonal material 6 months in advance. Reports in 2 months. Sample copy for $3.25. Writer's guidelines for #10 SASE.
  ● *Blade Magazine* is putting more emphasis on new products, knife accessories, knife steels, knife handles, knives and celebrities, knives in the movies.
Nonfiction: How-to; historical (on knives); adventure on a knife theme; celebrities who own knives; knives featured in movies with shots from the movie, etc.; new product; nostalgia; personal experience; photo feature; technical. "We would also like to receive articles on knives in adventuresome life-saving situations." No poetry. Buys 75 unsolicited

mss/year. "We evaluate complete manuscripts and make our decision on that basis." Length: 500-1,000 words, longer if content warrants it. Pays $200/story minimum; more for "better" writers. "We will pay top dollar in the knife market." Sometimes pays the expenses of writers on assignment.

Reprints: Accepts previously published submissions if not run in other knife publications. Send photocopy of article or typed ms with rights for sale noted and information about when and where the article previously appeared. Pays 90% of the amount paid for an original article.

Photos: Send photos with ms. Offers no additional payment for photos accepted with ms. Captions required. "Photos are critical for story acceptance."

Fiction: Publishes novel excerpts.

Tips: "We are always willing to read submissions from anyone who has read a few copies and studied the market. The ideal article for us is a piece bringing out the romance, legend, and love of man's oldest tool—the knife. We like articles that place knives in peoples' hands—in life saving situations, adventure modes, etc. (Nothing gory or with the knife as the villain.) People and knives are good copy. We are getting more and better written articles from writers who are reading the publication beforehand. That makes for a harder sell for the quickie writer not willing to do his homework."

‡**CAR MODELER**, Kalmbach Publishing Co., 21027 Crossroads Circle, P.O. Box 1612, Waukesha WI 53187-1612. (414)796-8776. Fax: (414)796-0126. Contact: Kirk Bell, senior editor. Managing editor: Mark Thompson. 100% free-lance written. Bimonthly magazine covering model car building indepth. "Freelancers should have a strong knowledge of how to build models, with lots of experience." Estab. 1990, Circ. 50,000. **Pays on acceptance.** Publishes ms an average of 6 months after acceptance. Byline given. Buys all rights. Editorial lead time 3 months. Submit seasonal material 2 months in advance. Reports in 1 month on queries; 3 months on mss. Sample copy and guidelines free.

Nonfiction: Book excerpts, historical/nostalgic, how-to, interview/profile, personal experience, photo feature, technical. Query or send complete ms. Length: 200-4,000 words. Pays $75-100/published page.

Photos: Send photos with submission. Reviews negatives, prints. Negotiates payment individually. Captions, model releases, identification of subjects required. Buys all rights.

Columns/Departments: Buys 30 mss/year. Query. Pays $75-100/published page.

Fillers: Gags to be illustrated by cartoonist. Buys 5/year. Pays percentage of $75/page rate.

Tips: "Ask for writer's guidelines; then send queries or call with ideas. We are always interested in seeing material from new writers. Although we do not 'assign' or commission articles, we do review those sent to us and, if suitable, they are eventually used in either *Car Modeler* or *Scale Auto Enthusiast* magazine. We don't expect our writers to be Pulitzer Prize-winning journalists. We are looking for model builders, collectors, and enthusiasts who feel their models and/or modeling techniques and experiences would be of interst and benefit to our readership. When we evaluate articles we look at the quality of accompanying photos and illustrations (diagrams, drawings, etc.), content of the how-to material, and finally, the writing style. If the photos and content are good, the article can be worked on by our staff, if necessary, to improve its readability."

CLASSIC TOY TRAINS, Kalmbach Publishing Co., 21027 Crossroads Circle, Waukesha WI 53187. (414)796-8776. Contact: Neil Besougloff, editor. 75-80% freelance written. Magazine published 8 times/year covering collectible toy trains (O, S, Standard, G scale, etc.) like Lionel, American Flyer, Marx, Dorfan, etc. "For the collector and operator of toy trains, *CTT* offers full-color photos of layouts and collections of toy trains, restoration tips, operating information, new product reviews and information, and insights into the history of toy trains." Estab. 1987. Circ. 77,000. **Pays on acceptance.** Publishes ms an average of 1 year after acceptance. Byline given. Buys all rights. Editorial lead time 2 months. Submit seasonal material 6 months in advance. Reports in 2 weeks on queries; 3 months on mss. Sample copy for $3.95 plus s&h. Writer's guidelines for #10 SASE.

Nonfiction: General interest, historical/nostalgic, how-to (restore toy trains; designing a layout; build accessories; fix broken toy trains), interview/profile, personal experience, photo feature, technical. Buys 90 mss/year. Query. Length: 500-5,000 words. Pays $75-500. Sometimes pays expenses of writers on assignment.

Photos: Send photos with submission. Reviews 4×5 transparencies; 5×7 prints preferred. Offers no additional payment for photos accepted with ms or $15-75/photo. Captions required. Buys all rights.

Fillers: Uses cartoons. Buys 6 fillers/year. Pays $30.

Tips: "It's important to have a thorough understanding of the toy train hobby; most of our freelancers are hobbyists themselves. One-half to two-thirds of *CTT*'s editorial space is devoted to photographs; superior photography is critical."

‡**COLLECTING TOYS, History●Nostalgia●Values**, Kalmbach Publishing Co., 21027 Crossroads Circle, Waukesha WI 53187. (414)796-8776. Fax: (414)796-1142. E-mail: thammel@toysmag.com. Website: www.toysmag.com. Contact: Tom Hammel, editor. 80% freelance written. Bimonthly magazine covering toy collecting. "We are the premiere collecting magazine of post-war boys' toys. We don't cover Barbie dolls, dolls of any type or teddy bears." Estab. 1993. Circ. 48,000. **Pays on acceptance.** Publishes ms an average of 9 months after acceptance. Byline given. Submit seasonal material 6 months in advance. Writer's guidelines for #10 SASE.

Nonfiction: Historical/nostalgic, interview/profile (toy companies, etc.), new product (toys, diecast model kits, etc.), personal experience ("my favorite toy"). No dolls, teddy bears, craft items, Barbies. Buys 25-30 mss/year. Query or send complete ms. Length: 100-900 words. Pays $50-700 for assigned articles; $50-500 for unsolicited articles. Published "My favorite toy" articles receive one-year subscription and 6 copies of that issue. Sometimes pays expenses of writers on assignment.

Photos: Send photos with submission. Reviews transparencies and 5×7 prints. Identification of subjects required.

Buys all rights.

Columns/Departments: Diecast (new products/reviews), 800 words; Figures (new products/reviews), 800 words; Grafitti (names and news in the toy business), 600 words. Buys 15 mss/year. Query. Pays $50-400.

Tips: "Try to include clear photos with any manuscript submission. Mark the envelope clearly "Manuscript enclosed." Visit our home page to get a flavor of what areas we cover and our writing style—http://www.toysmag.com.

‡**COLLECTOR EDITIONS**, Collector Communications Corp., 170 Fifth Ave., New York NY 10010-5911. (212)989-8700. Fax: (212)645-8976. Contact: Joan Muyskens Pursley, editor. 40% freelance written. Works with a small number of new/unpublished writers each year. Published 7 times/year, it covers porcelain and glass collectibles and limited-edition prints. "We specialize in contemporary (post-war ceramic and glass) collectibles, including reproductions, but also publish articles about antiques, if they are being reproduced today and are generally available." Estab. 1973. Circ. 96,000. Buys first North American serial rights. "First assignments are always done on a speculative basis." Pays within 30 days of acceptance. Publishes ms an average of 6 months after acceptance. Reports in 2 months. Sample copy for $2. Writer's guidelines for #10 SASE.

Nonfiction: "Short features about collecting, written in tight, newsy style. We specialize in contemporary (postwar) collectibles. Values for pieces being written about should be included." Informational, interview, profile, exposé, nostalgia. Special issues: New Plates, Figurines, Cottages & Buildings (September/October); Auto Art (November); Christmas Collectibles (December). Buys 15-20 mss/year. Query with sample photos. Length: 800-1,500 words. Pays $200-350. Sometimes pays expenses of writers on assignment.

Columns/Departments: Staff written; not interested in freelance columns.

Photos: B&w and color photos purchased with accompanying ms with no additional payment. Captions are required. "We want clear, distinct, full-frame images that say something."

Tips: "Unfamiliarity with the field is the most frequent mistake made by writers in completing an article for us."

‡**COLLECTOR'S MART, Contemporary Collectibles**, Limited Edition Art & Gifts, Krause Publications, 700 E. State St., Iola WI 54990. (715)445-2214. Fax: (715)445-4087. Website: http://www.krause.com. Contact: Steve Ellinboe, editor. 50% freelance written. Monthly magazine covering antiques and collectibles, for serious collectors of all types. Estab. 1993. Circ. 85,000. Pays on publication. Publishes ms an average of 6 months after acceptance. Byline given. Offers $25-50 kill fee. Buys perpetual but non-exclusive rights. Editorial lead time 2 months. Submit seasonal material 4 months in advance. Accepts simultaneous submissions. Reports in 1 month on mss. Sample copy free. Writer's guidelines not available.

Nonfiction: How-to about antiques and collectibles. Buys 60-75 mss/year. Send complete ms. Length: 500-3,000 words. Pays $50-200.

Reprints: Accepts previously published submissions.

Photos: Send photos with submission. Reviews transparencies, prints. Offers no additional payment for photos accepted with ms. Captions required. Buys one-time rights.

Tips: "I want detailed articles about specific collecting areas—nothing too broad or general. I need lots of information about pricing and values, along with a brief history and background."

COLLECTORS NEWS & THE ANTIQUE REPORTER, P.O. Box 156, Grundy Center IA 50638-0156. (319)824-6981. Fax: (319)824-3414. E-mail: collect@collectors-news.com. Website: http://collectors-news.com. Contact: Linda Kruger, managing editor. 20% freelance written. Estab. 1959. Works with a small number of new/unpublished writers each year. Monthly magazine-size publication on newsprint covering antiques, collectibles and nostalgic memorabilia. Circ. 13,000. Byline given. Pays on publication. Publishes ms an average of 1 year after acceptance. Buys first rights and makes work-for-hire assignments. Submit seasonal material 3 months in advance. Reports in 2 weeks on queries; 6 weeks on mss. Sample copy for $4 for 9×12 SAE. Writer's guidelines free.

Nonfiction: General interest (any subject re: collectibles, antique to modern); historical/nostalgic (relating to collections or collectors); how-to (display your collection, care for, restore, appraise, locate, add to, etc.); interview/profile (covering individual collectors and their hobbies, unique or extensive); celebrity collectors, and limited edition artists); technical (in-depth analysis of a particular antique, collectible or collecting field); and travel (coverage of special interest or regional shows, seminars, conventions—or major antique shows, flea markets; places collectors can visit, tours they can take, museums, etc.). Special issues: 12-month listing of antique and collectible shows, flea markets and conventions, (January includes events January-December 1998; June includes events June 1998-May 1999); international contemporary collectibles expo (September); holidays (October-December). Buys 70 mss/year. Query with sample of writing. Length: 800-1,000 words. Pays $1/column inch.

Photos: "Articles accompanied by photographs are given first consideration." A selection of 2-8 prints is suggested. "Articles are eligible for full-color front page consideration when accompanied by quality color prints, color slides, and/or color transparencies. Only one article is highlighted on the cover per month. Any article providing a color photo selected for front page use receives an additional $25." Reviews color or b&w prints. Payment for photos included in payment for ms. Captions required. Buys first rights.

Tips: Articles most open to freelancers are on farm/country/rural collectibles; celebrity collectors; collectors with unique and/or extensive collections; music collectibles; transportation collectibles; advertising collectibles; bottles; glass, china and silver; primitives; furniture; jewelry; lamps; western; textiles; toys; black memorabilia; political collectibles; movie memorabilia and any 20th century and timely subjects.

‡**CRAFTS MAGAZINE**, 2 News Plaza, Peoria IL 61657. Contact: Judith Brossart, editor. Monthly magazine covering crafts and needlecrafts, mostly how-to projects using products found in a craft, needlework or fabric store. **Pays on acceptance**. Byline given. Buys all rights. Reports in 1 month on queries. Writer's guidelines for #10 SASE.
Nonfiction: All how-to articles. Buys 400 mss/year. Query with sketch of how-to project. Pays $150-400.
Tips: "Project should use readily-available supplies. Project needs to be easily duplicated by reader. Most projects are made for gifts, home decorating accents, wearable, holidays, especially Christmas. Must know likes, dislikes and needs of today's crafter and have in-depth knowledge of craft products. *Crafts* is a mix of traditional techniques plus all the latest trends and fads."

CRAFTS 'N' THINGS, Clapper Communications Companies, 2400 Deven, Suite 375, Des Plaines IL 60018-4618. (847)635-5800. Fax: (847)635-6311. Editor: Julie Stephani. 80% freelance written. How-to and craft project magazine published 10 times/year. "We publish instruction for craft projects for beginners to intermediate level hobbyists." Estab. 1975. Circ. 300,000. Pays on publication. Publishes ms an average of 4 months after acceptance. Byline given. Offers $50 kill fee. Buys first, second serial (reprint) or all rights. Submit seasonal material 6 months in advance. Sample copy and writer's guidelines free.
Nonfiction: How-to (craft projects), new product (for product review column). Send SASE for list of issue themes. Buys 240 mss/year. Send complete ms with photos and instructions. Pays $50-250. Offers listing exchange as a product source instead of payment in some cases.
Reprints: Send photocopy of article and information about when and where the article previously appeared.
Columns/Departments: Bright Ideas (original ideas for working better with crafts—hints and tips). Buys 30 mss/year. Send complete ms. Length: 25-50 words. Pays $20.
Tips: "Query for guidelines and list of themes and deadlines. How-to articles are the best bet for freelancers."

‡**CROCHET DIGEST**, House of White Birches, 306 E. Parr Rd., Berne IN 46711. (219)589-8741. Fax: (219)589-8093. Contact: Laura Scott, editor. Editorial Assistant: Marla Freeman. 100% freelance written. Quarterly magazine covering crochet designs. "The magazine is for all ages offering a variety of crochet designs. The 48-page digest includes patterns for sweaters, home dec, accessories, afghans, doilies, toys." Estab. 1993. Circ. 74,692. Pays within 2 months of acceptance. Publishes ms an average of 1 year after acceptance. Byline given. Offers 100% kill fee. Buys all rights. Editorial lead time 9 months. Submit seasonal material 9 months in advance. Accepts simultaneous submissions. Reports in 2 months on queries; 6 months on mss. Writer's guidelines free.
Nonfiction: How-to (crochet skills), humor, technical (crochet field). Buys 6-8 mss/year. Send complete ms. Length: 500 words. Pays $50-250.
Photos: Send photos with submission.

CROCHET WORLD, House of White Birches, P.O. Box 776, Henniker NH 03242. Fax: (603)428-7289. Contact: Susan Hankins, editor. 100% freelance written. Bimonthly magazine covering crochet patterns. "*Crochet World* is a pattern magazine devoted to the art of crochet. We also feature a Q&A column, letters (swap shop) column and occasionally non-pattern manuscripts, but it must be devoted to crochet." Estab. 1978. Circ. 75,000. Pays on publication. Byline given. Buys all rights. Editorial lead time 4 months. Submit seasonal material 6 months in advance. Reports in 1 month. Sample copy for $2. Writer's guidelines free.
Nonfiction: How-to (crochet). Buys 0-2 mss/year. Send complete ms. Length: 500-1,500 words. Pays $50.
Columns/Departments: Touch of Style (crocheted clothing); It's a Snap! (quick one-night simple patterns); Pattern of the Month, first and second prize each issue. Buys dozens of mss/year. Send complete pattern. Pays $40-300.
Poetry: Strictly crochet-related. Buys 0-10 poems/year. Submit maximum 2 poems. Length: 6-20 lines. Pays $10-20.
Fillers: Anecdotes, facts, gags to be illustrated, short humor. Buys 0-10/year. Length: 25-200 words. Pays $5-30.
Tips: "Be aware that this is a pattern generated magazine for crochet designs. I prefer the actual item sent along with complete directions/graphs etc. over queries. In some cases a photo submission or good sketch will do. Crocheted designs must be well-made and original and directions must be complete. Write for Designer's Guidelines which detail how to submit designs. Non-crochet items, such as fillers, poetry *must* be crochet-related, not knit, not sewing, etc."

DECORATIVE ARTIST'S WORKBOOK, F&W Publications, Inc., 1507 Dana Ave., Cincinnati OH 45207-1005. (513)531-2690, ext. 461. Fax: (513)531-2902. E-mail: dawedit@aol.com. Editor: Anne Hevener. Estab. 1987. 50% freelance written. Bimonthly magazine covering decorative painting projects and products of all sorts. Offers "straight-forward, personal instruction in the techniques of decorative painting." Circ. 90,000. **Pays on acceptance.** Byline given. Offers 25% kill fee. Buys first North American serial rights. Submit seasonal material 8 months in advance. Reports in 1 month. Sample copy for $4.65 and 9×12 SAE with 5 first-class stamps.
Nonfiction: How-to (related to decorative painting projects), new products, techniques, artist profiles. Buys 30 mss/year. Query with slides or photos. Length: 1,200-1,800 words. Pays 10-25¢/word.
Photos: State availability of or send photos with submission. Reviews 35mm, 4×5 transparencies and quality photos. Offers no additional payment for photos accepted with ms. Captions required. Buys one-time rights.
Tips: "The more you know—and can prove you know—about decorative painting the better your chances. I'm looking for experts in the field who, through their own experience, can artfully describe the techniques involved. How-to articles are most open to freelancers. Be sure to query with photo slides, and show that you understand the extensive graphic requirements for these pieces and can provide painted progressives—slides or illustrations that show works in progress."

‡DOLL COLLECTOR'S PRICE GUIDE, House of White Birches, 306 E. Parr Rd., Berne IN 46711. (219)589-8741. Contact: Cary Raesher, editor. Quarterly magazine covering doll collecting. Audience is interested in informative articles about collecting and investing in dolls, museum exhibits, doll history, etc. Estab. 1991. Circ. 43,985. Pays pre-publication. Byline given. Buys first, one-time or all rights. Editorial lead time 6 months. Accepts previously published submissions. Reports in 3 months. Sample copy for $2. Writer's guidelines for #10 SASE.
Nonfiction: Historical/nostalgic. Buys 20 mss/year. Send complete ms. Pays $50.
Photos: Send photos with submission. Captions and identification of subjects required.

‡DOLL WORLD The Magazine for Doll Lovers, House of White Birches, 306 E. Parr Rd., Berne IN 46711. (219)589-8741. Fax: (219)589-8093. Contact: Cary Raesner, editor. 90% freelance written. Bimonthly magazine covering doll collecting, restoration. "Interested in informative articles about doll history and costumes, interviews with doll artists and collectors, and how-to articles." Estab. 1978. Circ. 54,000. Pays pre-publication. Byline given. Buys all rights. Submit seasonal material 6 months in advance. Accepts previously published submissions. Reports in 2 months on queries; 4 months on mss. Sample copy for $2.95. Writer's guidelines for SASE.
Nonfiction: How-to, interview/profile. Buys 100 mss/year. Send complete ms. Pays $50.
Photos: Send photos with submission. Captions and identification of subjects required. Buys one-time or all rights.
Tips: "Choose a specific manufacturer and talk about his dolls or a specific doll—modern or antique—and explore its history and styles made."

‡ELECTRONICS NOW, Gernsback Publications, Inc., 500 Bi-County Blvd., Farmingdale NY 11735. (516)293-3000. Contact: Carl Laron, editor. 75% freelance written. Monthly magazine on electronics technology and electronics construction, such as communications, computers, test equipment, components, video and audio. Estab. 1929. Circ. 104,000. **Pays on acceptance.** Publishes ms an average of 6 months after acceptance. Byline given. Buys all rights. Submit seasonal material 5-6 months in advance. Reports in 2 months on queries; 4 months on mss. Sample copy and writer's guidelines free.
Nonfiction: How-to (electronic project construction), humor (cartoons), new product. Buys 150-200 mss/year. Send complete ms. Length: 1,000-10,000 words. Pays $200-800 for assigned articles; $100-800 for unsolicited articles.
Photos: Send photos with submission. Offers no additional payment for photos accepted with ms. Captions, model releases and identification of subjects required. Buys all rights.

FIBERARTS, The Magazine of Textiles, Altamont Press, 50 College St., Asheville NC 28801. (704)253-0467. Fax: (704)253-7952. E-mail: larkmail@larkbooks.com. Website: http://www.larkbooks.com. Contact: Ann Batchelder, editor. 100% freelance written. Eager to work with new writers. Magazine published 5 times/year covering textiles as art and craft (contemporary trends in fiber sculpture, weaving, quilting, surface design, stitchery, papermaking, basketry, felting, wearable art, knitting, fashion, crochet, mixed textile techniques, ethnic dying, fashion, eccentric tidbits, etc.) for textile artists, craftspeople, hobbyists, teachers, museum and gallery staffs, collectors and enthusiasts. Estab. 1975. Circ. 25,250. Pays 30 days after publication. Publishes ms an average of 4 months after acceptance. Byline given. Buys first rights. Editorial guidelines and style sheet available. Sample copy for $4.95 and 10×12 SAE with 2 first-class stamps. Writer's guidelines for #10 SAE with 2 first-class stamps.
Nonfiction: Historical, artist interview/profile, opinion, photo feature, technical, education, trends, exhibition reviews, textile news. Query with brief outline prose synopsis and SASE. No phone queries. "Please be very specific about your proposal. Also an important consideration in accepting an article is the kind of photos—35mm slides and/or b&w glossies—that you can provide as illustration. We like to see photos in advance." Length: 250-2,000 words plus 4-5 photos. Pays $200-350, depending on article. Rarely pays the expenses of writers on assignment or for photos.
Photos: Visuals must accompany every article. The more photos to choose from, the better. Full photo captions are essential. Please include a separate, number-keyed caption sheet. The names and addresses of those mentioned in the article or to whom the visuals are to be returned are necessary.
Columns/Departments: Swatches (new ideas for fiber, unusual or offbeat subjects, work spaces, resources and marketing, techniques, materials, equipment, design and trends), 250-350 words, pays $75-100; Profile (focuses on one artist), 350-400 words and one photo, pays $100. Reviews (exhibits and shows; summarize quality, significance, focus and atmosphere, then evaluate selected pieces), 350-400 words and 3-5 photos. Pays $100. (Do not cite works for which visuals are unavailable; you are not eligible to review a show in which you have participated as an artist, organizer, curator or juror.)
Tips: "Our writers are very familiar with the textile field, and this is what we look for in a new writer. Familiarity with textile techniques, history or events determines clarity of an article more than a particular style of writing. The writer should also be familiar with *Fiberarts*, the magazine. While the professional is essential to the editorial depth of *Fiberarts*, and must find timely information in the pages of the magazine, this is not our greatest audience. Our editorial philosophy is that the magazine must provide the non-professional textile enthusiast with the inspiration, support, useful information, and direction to keep him or her excited, interested, and committed."

‡FINE TOOL JOURNAL, Antique & Collectible Tools, Inc., 27 Fickett Rd., Pownal ME 04069. (207)688-4962. Fax: (207)688-4152. E-mail: ftjceb@aol.com. Contact: Clarence Blanchard, editor. 90% freelance written. Quarterly magazine covering user and antique hand tools. "The *Fine Tool Journal* is a quarterly magazine specializing in older or antique hand tools from all traditional trades. Readers are primarily interested in woodworking tools, but some subscribers have interests in such areas as leatherworking, wrenches, kitchen tools and machinist tools. Readers range from beginners just getting into the hobby to advanced collectors and organizations." Estab. 1927. Circ. 2,000. Pays on publication. Publishes ms an average of 6 months after acceptance. Byline given. Offers $50 kill fee. Buys first and second serial (reprint) rights. Editorial lead time 6 months. Submit seasonal material 6 months in advance. Reports in 2 months on queries; 3 months on mss. Sample copy for $5. Writer's guidelines for SASE.

Nonfiction: General interest, historical/nostalgic, how-to (make, use, fix and tune tools), interview/profile, personal experience, photo feature, technical. "We're looking for articles about tools from all trades. Interests include collecting, preservation, history, values and price trends, traditional methods and uses, interviews with collectors/users/makers, etc. Most articles published will deal with vintage, pre-1950, hand tools. Also seeking articles on how to use specific tools or how a specific trade was carried out. However, how to articles must be detailed and not just of general interest. We do on occasion run articles on modern toolmakers who produce traditional hand tools." Buys 24 mss/year. Send complete ms. Length: 400-2,000 words. Pays $50-200. Sometimes pays expenses of writers on assignment.

Reprints: Accepts previously published submissions.

Photos: Send photos with submisison. Reviews 4×5 prints. Negotiates payment individually. Model releases, identification of subjects required. Buys all rights.

Columns/Departments: Stanley Tools (new finds and odd types), 300-400 words; Tips of the Trade (how to use tools), 100-200 words. Buys 12 mss/year. Send complete ms. Pays $30-60.

Tips: "The easiest way to get published in the *Journal* is to have personal experience or know someone who can supply the detailed information. We are seeking articles that go deeper than general interest and that knowledge requires experience and/or research. Short of personal experience find a subject that fits our needs and that interests you. Spend some time learning the ins and outs of the subject and with hard work and a little luck you will earn the right to write about it."

FINE WOODWORKING, The Taunton Press, P.O. Box 5506, Newtown CT 06470-5506. (203)426-8171. Fax: (203)270-6751. E-mail: fw@taunton.com. Website: http://www.taunton.com. Editor: Scott Gibson. Bimonthly magazine on woodworking in the small shop. "All writers are also skilled woodworkers. It's more important that a contributor be a woodworker than a writer. Our editors (also woodworkers) will fix the words." Estab. 1975. Circ. 270,000. **Pays on acceptance.** Byline given. Kill fee varies; "editorial discretion." Buys first rights and rights to republish in anthologies and use in promo pieces. Submit seasonal material 6 months in advance. Accepts simultaneous submissions. Reports in 2 months. Writer's guidelines free.

Nonfiction: How-to (woodworking). Buys 120 mss/year. Query with proposal letter. "No specs—our editors would rather see more than less." Pays $150/magazine page. Sometimes pays expenses of writers on assignment.

Photos: Send photos with submission. Reviews contact sheets, negatives, transparencies, prints. Captions, model releases, identification of subjects required. Buys one-time rights.

Columns/Departments: Notes & Comment (topics of interest to woodworkers); Question & Answer (woodworking Q & A); Follow-Up (information on past articles/readers' comments); Methods of Work (shop tips); Tool Forum (short reviews of new tools). Buys 400 items/year. Length varies. Pays $10-150/published page.

Tips: "Send for authors guidelines and follow them. Stories about woodworking reported by non-woodworkers are *not* used. Our magazine is essentially reader-written by woodworkers."

"We're looking for good articles on almost all aspects of woodworking from the basics of tool use, stock preparation and joinery to specialized techniques and finishing. We're especially keen on articles about shop-built tools, jigs and fixtures or any stage of design, construction, finishing and installation of cabinetry and furniture. Whether the subject involves fundamental methods or advanced techniques, we look for high-quality workmanship, thoughtful designs, safe and proper procedures."

‡FINESCALE MODELER, Kalmbach Publishing Co., 21027 Crossroads Circle, P.O. Box 1612, Waukesha WI 53187. (414)796-8776. Fax: (414)796-1383. E-mail: rmcnally@finescale.com. Website: http://www.finescale.html. Editor: Bob Hayden. Contact: Dick McNally, managing editor. 80% freelance written. Eager to work with new/unpublished writers. Magazine published 10 times/year "devoted to how-to-do-it modeling information for scale model builders who build non-operating aircraft, tanks, boats, automobiles, figures, dioramas, and science fiction and fantasy models." Circ. 80,000. **Pays on acceptance.** Publishes ms an average of 14 months after acceptance. Byline given. Buys all rights. Reports in 6 weeks on queries; 3 months on mss. Sample copy for 9×12 SAE with 3 first-class stamps. Writer's guidelines free.

Nonfiction: How-to (build scale models); technical (research information for building models). Query or send complete ms. Length: 750-3,000 words. Pays $45/published page minimum.

• This magazine is especially looking for how-to articles for car modelers.

Photos: Send color photos with ms. Pays $7.50 minimum for transparencies and $5 minimum for color prints. Captions and identification of subjects required. Buys one-time rights.

Columns/Departments: *FSM* Showcase (photos plus description of model); *FSM* Tips and Techniques (model building hints and tips). Buys 25-50 Tips and Techniques/year. Query or send complete ms. Length: 100-1,000 words. Pays $10-20.

Tips: "A freelancer can best break in first through hints and tips, then through feature articles. Most people who write for *FSM* are modelers first, writers second. This is a specialty magazine for a special, quite expert audience. Essentially, 99% of our writers will come from that audience."

GOLD AND TREASURE HUNTER, 27 Davis Rd., P.O. Box 47, Happy Camp CA 96039-0047. (916)493-2062. Fax: (916)493-2095. E-mail: goldgold@snowcrest.net. Editor: Dave McCracken. Contact: Marcie Stumpf, managing editor. Bimonthly magazine on small-scale gold mining and treasure hunting. "We want interesting fact and fiction stories and articles about small-scale mining, treasure hunting, camping and the great outdoors." Estab. 1987. Circ. 50,000. Pays on publication. Buys all rights. Submit seasonal material 4 months in advance. Reports in 1 month. Sample copy for 9 × 12 SAE with 5 first-class stamps. Writer's guidelines free.

Nonfiction: How-to, humor, inspirational, interview/profile, new product, personal experience, photo feature, travel, legal rights, politics and issues. "No promotional articles concerning industry products." Buys 125 mss/year. Send complete ms. Length: 1,500-2,000 words. Pays 3¢/word.

Reprints: Send tearsheet, photocopy of article or typed ms with rights for sale noted and information about when and where the article previously appeared. Pays 50% of amount paid for an original article.

Photos: Good quality photographs a must. Send photos with submission. Reviews any size transparencies and prints. Pays $10-50/photo. Captions are required. Buys all rights. Please do not write on the front or back of photos.

Fiction: Adventure, experimental, historical, horror, humorous, mystery, suspense, western—all related to gold mining/treasure hunting. Publishes novel excerpts.

Tips: "Our general readership is comprised mostly of individuals who are actively involved in gold mining and treasure hunting, or people who are interested in reading about others who are active and successful in the field. True stories of actual discoveries, along with good color photos—particularly of gold—are preferred. Also, valuable how-to information on new and workable field techniques, preferably accompanied by supporting illustrations and/or photos. Important: We do not print stories or articles which are primarily oriented toward the promotion of a product or service. However, we do not object to the author mentioning the type of equipment used during a gold find or treasure discovery or who to contact for more information about locations to visit or other services written about in an article."

THE HOME SHOP MACHINIST, 2779 Aero Park Dr., P.O. Box 1810, Traverse City MI 49685. (616)946-3712. Fax: (616)946-3289. E-mail: vpshop@aol.com. Website: http://members.aol.com/vpshop/hsm.htm. Contact: Joe D. Rice, editor. 95% freelance written. Bimonthly magazine covering machining and metalworking for the hobbyist. Circ. 29,400. Pays on publication. Publishes ms an average of 2 years after acceptance. Byline given. Buys first North American serial rights only. Reports in 2 months. Free sample copy and writer's guidelines for 9 × 12 SASE.

Nonfiction: How-to (projects designed to upgrade present shop equipment or hobby model projects that require machining), technical (should pertain to metalworking, machining, drafting, layout, welding or foundry work for the hobbyist). No fiction or "people" features. Buys 40 mss/year. Query or send complete ms. Length: open—"whatever it takes to do a thorough job." Pays $40/published page, plus $9/published photo.

Photos: Send photos with ms. Pays $9-40 for 5 × 7 b&w prints; $70/page for camera-ready art; $40 for b&w cover photo. Captions and identification of subjects required.

Columns/Departments: Book Reviews; New Product Reviews; Micro-Machining; Foundry. "Become familiar with our magazine before submitting." Query first. Buys 25-30 mss/year. Length: 600-1,500 words. Pays $40-70/page.

Fillers: Machining tips/shortcuts. No news clippings. Buys 12-15/year. Length: 100-300 words. Pays $30-48.

Tips: "The writer should be experienced in the area of metalworking and machining; should be extremely thorough in explanations of methods, processes—always with an eye to safety; and should provide good quality b&w photos and/or clear dimensioned drawings to aid in description. Visuals are of increasing importance to our readers. Carefully planned photos, drawings and charts will carry a submission to our magazine much farther along the path to publication."

‡IN THE FLESH, Art & Ink Enterprises, 5 Marine View Plaza, Suite 207, Hoboken NJ 07030. (201)653-2700. Fax: (201)653-7892. Contact: Jean-Chris Miller, editorial director. Managing editor: Amy Becker. 33% freelance written. Quarterly magazine covering all aspects of body modification. "Our subjects and audience are extremely diverse. Subjects include tatooing, piercing, branding, corsetry, scarification, implants, as well as historical accounts of these practices." Estab. 1995. Pays on publication. Publishes ms an average of 3 months after acceptance. Byline sometimes given. Buys first rights. Editorial lead time 3 months. Submit seasonal material 4 months in advance. Accepts simultaneous submissions. Sample copy $7. Writer's guidelines for #10 SASE.

Nonfiction: Essays, historical/nostalgic, humor, inspirational, interview/profile, new product, opinion, personal experience, photo feature, religious (pertaining to body modification rituals)." Buys 4 mss/year. Query. Length: 500-4,000 words. Pays $10-50.

Photos: Send photos with submission. Reviews transparencies, prints. Negotiates payment individually. Model releases, identification of subjects required. Buys one-time rights.

Fiction: "We accept all types of fiction pertaining to body modification, as long as it isn't too long." Buys 4 mss/year. Query with published clips. Length: 500-3,000 words. Pays up to $50.

Fillers: Anecdotes, facts, gags to be illustrated by cartoonist, newsbreaks, short humor. Buys 2/year. Length: 500 words maximum. Pays up to $50.

Tips: "We encourage people to send in a duplicate rather than their only copy of a manuscript. If they'd like materials returned, make sure to enclose SASE with adequate postage."

KITPLANES, For designers, builders and pilots of experimental aircraft, Cowles Enthusiast Media, Inc., 1000 Quail St., Suite 190, Newport Beach CA 92660. (714)477-2295. Fax: (714)477-3484. Editor: Dave Martin. Managing Editor: Keith Beveridge. 70% freelance written. Eager to work with new/unpublished writers. Monthly magazine covering self-construction of private aircraft for pilots and builders. Estab. 1972. Circ. 85,000. Pays on publication. Publishes ms an average of 3 months after acceptance. Byline given. Offers negotiable kill fee. Buys first North American serial rights. Submit seasonal material 6 months in advance. Reports in 2 weeks on queries; 6 weeks on mss. Sample copy for $3. Writer's guidelines free.

Nonfiction: How-to, interview/profile, new product, personal experience, photo feature, technical, general interest. "We are looking for articles on specific construction techniques, the use of tools, both hand and power, in aircraft building, the relative merits of various materials, conversions of engines from automobiles for aviation use, installation of instruments and electronics." No general-interest aviation articles, or "My First Solo" type of articles. Buys 80 mss/year. Query. Length: 500-5,000 words. Pays $100-400, including story photos.

Photos: State availability of or send photos with query or ms. Pays $250 for cover photos. Captions and identification of subjects required. Buys one-time rights.

Tips: "*Kitplanes* contains very specific information—a writer must be extremely knowledgeable in the field. Major features are entrusted only to known writers. I cannot emphasize enough that articles must be directed at the individual aircraft builder. We need more 'how-to' photo features in all areas of homebuilt aircraft."

KNITTING DIGEST, House of White Birches, 306 E. Parr Rd., Berne IN 46711. Fax: (219)589-8093. Contact: Jeanne Stauffer, editor. Managing Editor: Vicki Steensma. 100% freelance written. Bimonthly magazine covering knitting designs and patterns. "We print only occasional articles, but are always open to knitting designs and proposals." Estab. 1993. Circ. 50,000. Pays within 2 months of acceptance. Publishes ms an average of 6 months after acceptance. Byline given. Offers 100% kill fee. Buys all rights. Accepts simultaneous submissions. Reports in 2 months on queries; 6 months on mss. Writer's guidelines free. Send SASE.

Nonfiction: How-to (knitting skills); humor, technical (knitting field). Buys 4-6 mss/year. Send complete ms. Length: 500 words maximum. Pay varies. Also pays in contributor copies.

Fillers: Anecdotes, facts, gags to be illustrated, short humor. Buys 24-36/year. Length: 50 words max. Pays $15-25.

Tips: "Clear concise writing. Humor is appreciated in this field, as much as technical tips. The magazine is a digest, so space is limited. All submissions must be typed and double-spaced."

KNIVES ILLUSTRATED, The Premier Cutlery Magazine, 265 S. Anita Dr., Suite 120, Orange CA 92868-3310. (714)939-9991. Fax: (714)939-9909. E-mail: budlang.pacbell.net. Contact: Bud Lang, editor. 40-50% freelance written. Bimonthly magazine covering high-quality factory and custom knives. "We publish articles on different types of factory and custom knives, how-to-make knives, technical articles, shop tours, articles on knife makers and artists. Must have knowledge about knives and the people who use and make them. We feature the full range of custom and high tech production knives, from miniatures to swords, leaving nothing untouched. We're also known for our outstanding how-to articles and technical features on equipment, materials and knife making supplies. We do not feature knife maker profiles as such, although we do spotlight some makers by featuring a variety of their knives and insight into their background and philosophy." Estab. 1987. Circ. 35,000. Pays on publication. Byline given. Editorial lead time 3 months. Reports in 2 weeks on queries. Sample copy and writer's guidelines for #10 SASE.

Nonfiction: How-to, interview/profile, photo features, technical. Buys 35-40 mss/year. Query first. Length: 400-2,000 words. Pays $100-500 minimum. Sometimes pays expenses of writers on assignment.

Photos: Send photos with submission. Reviews 35mm, 2¼×2¼, 4×5 transparencies, 5×7 prints. Negotiates payment individually. Captions, model releases, identification of subjects required.

Tips: "Most of our contributors are involved with knives, either as collectors, makers, engravers, etc. To write about this subject requires knowledge. A 'good' writer can do OK if they study some recent issues. If you are interested in submitting work to *Knives Illustrated* magazine, it is suggested you analyze at least two or three different editions to get a feel for the magazine. It is also recommended that you call or mail in your query to determine if we are interested in the topic you have in mind. While verbal or written approval may be given, all articles are still received on a speculation basis. We cannot approve any article until we have it in hand, whereupon we will make a final decision as to its suitability for our use. Bear in mind we do not suggest you go to the trouble to write an article if there is doubt we can use it promptly."

LAPIDARY JOURNAL, 60 Chestnut Ave., Suite 201, Devon PA 19333-1312. (610)293-1112. Fax: (610)293-1717. E-mail: ljmagazine@aol.com. Editor: Merle White. Contact: Hazel Wheaton, managing editor. 70% freelance written. Monthly magazine covering gem, mineral and jewelry arts. "Our audience is hobbyists who usually know something about the subject before they start reading. Our style is conversational and informative. There are how-to projects and profiles of artists and materials." Estab. 1947. Circ. 59,800. Pays on publication. Publishes ms an average of 4 months after acceptance. Byline given. Buys one-time and worldwide rights. Editorial lead time 3 months.

Nonfiction: How-to jewelry/craft, interview/profile, new product, personal experience, technical, travel. Buys 50-100 mss/year. Query. Sometimes pays expenses of writers on assignment.

Reprints: Accepts previously published submissions. Send photocopy of article. Pay varies.

THE LEATHER CRAFTERS & SADDLERS JOURNAL, 331 Annette Court, Rhinelander WI 54501-2902. (715)362-5393. Fax: (715)362-5391. Contact: William R. Reis, editor-in-chief. Managing Editor: Dorothea Reis. 100% freelance written. Bimonthly magazine. "A leather-working publication with how-to, step-by-step instructional articles using full-size patterns for leathercraft, leather art, custom saddle, boot and harness making, etc. A complete resource for leather, tools machinery and allied materials plus leather industry news." Estab. 1990. Circ. 8,000. Pays on publication. Publishes ms an average of 2 months after acceptance. Byline given. "All assigned articles subject to review for acceptance by editor." Buys first North American serial and second serial (reprint) rights. Submit seasonal material 6 months in advance. Accepts simultaneous submissions. Reports in 1 month. Sample copy for $5. Writer's guidelines for #10 SASE.

Nonfiction: How-to (crafts and arts and any other projects using leather). "I want only articles that include hands-on, step-by-step, how-to information." Buys 75 mss/year. Send complete ms. Length: 500-2,500 words. Pays $20-250 for assigned articles; $20-150 for unsolicited articles. Send good contrast color print photos and full size patterns and/or full-size photo-carve patterns with submission. Lack of these reduces payment amount. Captions required.

Reprints: Send tearsheet or photocopy of article. Pays 50% of amount paid for original article.

Columns/Departments: Beginners, Intermediate, Artists, Western Design, Saddlemakers, International Design and Letters (the open exchange of information between all peoples). Length: 500-2,500 on all. Buys 75 mss/year. Send complete ms. Pays 5¢/word.

Fillers: Anecdotes, facts, gags illustrated by cartoonist, newsbreaks. Length: 25-200 words. Pays $5-20.

Tips: "We want to work with people who understand and know leathercraft and are interested in passing on their knowledge to others. We would prefer to interview people who have achieved a high level in leathercraft skill."

LINN'S STAMP NEWS, Amos Press, 911 Vandemark Rd., P.O. Box 29, Sidney OH 45365. (937)498-0801. Fax: (800)340-9501. E-mail: linns@bright.net. Website: http://www.best.com/~linns. Editor: Michael Laurence. Contact: Elaine Boughner, managing editor. 50% freelance written. Weekly tabloid on the stamp collecting hobby. "All articles must be about philatelic collectibles. Our goal at *Linn's* is to create a weekly publication that is indispensable to stamp collectors." Estab. 1928. Circ. 70,000. Pays within one month of publication. Publishes ms an average of 1 month after acceptance. Byline given. Buys first North American serial rights. Submit seasonal material 2 months in advance. Reports in 2 weeks on mss. Free sample copy. Writer's guidelines for #10 SAE with 2 first-class stamps.

Nonfiction: General interest, historical/nostalgic, how-to, interview/profile, technical, club and show news, current issues, auction realization and recent discoveries. "No articles merely giving information on background of stamp subject. Must have philatelic information included." Buys 300 mss/year. Send complete ms. Length: 500 words maximum. Pays $20-50. Rarely pays expenses of writers on assignment.

Photos: Good illustrations a must. Send photos with submission. Provide captions on separate sheet of paper. Prefers crisp, sharp focus, high-contrast glossy b&w prints. Offers no additional payment for photos accepted with ms. Captions required. Buys all rights.

Tips: "Check and double check all facts. Footnotes and bibliographies are not appropriate to our newspaper style. Work citation into the text. Even though your subject might be specialized, write understandably. Explain terms. *Linn's* features are aimed at a broad audience of relatively novice collectors. Keep this audience in mind. Do not write down to the reader but provide information in such a way to make stamp collecting more interesting to more people. Embrace readers without condescending to them."

LOST TREASURE, INC., P.O. Box 451589, Grove OK 74345. Fax: (918)786-2192. E-mail: managingeditor@losttreasure.com. Website: http://www.losttreasure.com. Contact: Patsy Beyerl, managing editor. 75% freelance written. Monthly and annual magazines covering lost treasure. Estab. 1966. Circ. 55,000. Buys all rights. Byline given. Buys 225 mss/year. Pays on publication. Reports in 2 months on ms, 2-4 weeks on queries. Writers guidelines for #10 SASE. Sample copies (2 magazines) and guidelines for 10×13 SAE with $1.47 postage each magazine. Editorial calendar for *Lost Treasure* available on request. Send SASE with 32¢ postage.

Nonfiction: 1) *Lost Treasure*, a monthly publication, is composed of lost treasure stories, legends, folklore, and how-to articles, 500-1,500 words. 2) *Treasure Facts*, a monthly publication, consists of how-to information for treasure hunters, treasure hunting club news, who's who in treasure hunting, tips, 500-1,500 words. 3) *Treasure Cache*, an annual publication, contains stories about documented treasure caches with a sidebar from the author telling the reader how to search for the cache highlighted in the story. Length: 1,000-2,000 words. Query on *Treasure Cache* only. Fax OK. Pays 4¢/word.

Photos: Black and white or color prints, hand-drawn or copied maps, art with source credit with mss will help sell your story. Pays $5/published photo. We are always looking for cover photos with or without accompanying ms. Pays $100/published photo. Must be 35mm color slides, vertical. Captions required.

Tips: "We are only interested in treasures that can be found with metal detectors. Queries welcome but not required. If you write about famous treasures and lost mines, be sure we haven't used your selected topic recently and story must have a new slant or new information. Source documentation required (for *Treasure Facts*). How-tos should cover some aspect of treasure hunting and how-to steps should be clearly defined. If you have a *Treasure Cache* story we will, if necessary, help the author with the sidebar telling how to search for the cache in the story. *Lost Treasure* articles should coordinate with theme issues when possible."

MINIATURE QUILTS, Chitra Publications, 2 Public Ave., Montrose PA 18801. (717)278-1984. Fax: (717)278-2223. Contact: Editorial Team. 40% freelance written. Bimonthly magazine on miniature quilts. "We seek articles of an instructional nature (all techniques), profiles of talented quiltmakers and informational articles on all aspects of miniature quilts. Article should be written by quilters or quilting professionals. Miniature is defined as quilts made up of blocks smaller than five inches." Estab. 1990. Circ. 50,000. Pays on publication. Publishes ms an average of 6 months after acceptance. Byline given. Buys second serial (reprint) rights. Submit seasonal material 8 months in advance. Reports in 2 months on queries and mss. Writer's guidelines for SASE.

Photos: Send photos with submission. Reviews 35mm slides and larger transparencies. Offers $20/photo. Captions,

model releases and identification of subjects required. Buys all rights, unless rented from a museum.
Tips: "Publication hinges on good photo quality. Query with ideas; send samples of prior work."

MODEL RAILROADER, P.O. Box 1612, Waukesha WI 53187. Fax: (414)796-1142. E-mail: mrmag@mrmag.com. Website: http://www.modelrailroader.com/. Contact: Andy Sperandeo, editor. Monthly for hobbyists interested in scale model railroading. "We publish articles on all aspects of model-railroading and on prototype (real) railroading as a subject for modeling." Buys exclusive rights. Reports on submissions within 60 days.
Nonfiction: Wants construction articles on specific model railroad projects (structures, cars, locomotives, scenery, benchwork, etc.). Also photo stories showing model railroads. Query. "Study publication before submitting material." First-hand knowledge of subject almost always necessary for acceptable slant. Pays base rate of $90/page.
Photos: Buys photos with detailed descriptive captions only. Pays $10 and up, depending on size and use. Pays double b&w rate for color; full color cover earns $200.
Tips: "Before you prepare and submit any article, you should write us a short letter of inquiry describing what you want to do. We can then tell you if it fits our needs and save you from working on something we don't want."

MONITORING TIMES, Grove Enterprises Inc., P.O. Box 98, Brasstown NC 28902-0098. (704)837-9200. Fax: (704)837-2216. E-mail: mteditor@grove.net. Website: http://www.grove.net/hmpgmt.html. Managing Editor: Rachel Baughn. Publisher: Robert Grove. 20% freelance written. Monthly magazine for radio hobbyists. Estab. 1982. Circ. 30,000. Pays 30-60 days before date of publication. Publishes ms an average of 4 months after acceptance. Byline given. Buys first North American serial rights and limited reprint rights. Submit seasonal material 4 months in advance. Reports in 1 month. Sample copy and writer's guidelines for 9×12 SAE and 9 first-class stamps.
Nonfiction: General interest, how-to, humor, interview/profile, personal experience, photo feature, technical. Buys 72 mss/year. Query. Length: 1,000-2,500 words. Pays $150-200.
Reprints: Send photocopy of article and information about when and where the article previously appeared. Pays 25% of amount paid for an original article.
Photos: Send photos with submission. Captions required. Buys one-time rights.
Columns/Departments: "Query managing editor."
Tips: "Need articles explaining new wireless technology and trunked systems; are accepting more technical projects."

‡NUTSHELL NEWS, For creators and collectors of scale miniatures, Kalmbach Publishing Co., 21027 Crossroads Circle, Waukesha WI 53187-9951. (414)798-6618. Fax: (414)796-1383. E-mail: cpaul@nutshell.com. Website: http://www.nutshell.com. Editor: Kay Melchiasedech Olsen. Contact: Christine Paul, managing editor. 50% freelance written. Monthly magazine covering dollhouse scale miniatures. "*Nutshell News* is aimed at passionate miniatures hobbyists. Our readers take their miniatures seriously and do not regard them as toys. We avoid 'cutesiness' and treat our subject as a serious art form and/or an engaging leisure interest." Estab. 1971. Circ. 40,000. Pays advance fee on acceptance and balance on publication. Byline given. Buys all rights but will revert rights by agreement. Submit seasonal material 1 year in advance. Reports in 3 weeks on queries; 2 months on mss. Sample copy for $3.50. Writer's guidelines for #10 SASE.
Nonfiction: How-to miniature projects in 1″, ½″, ¼″ scales, interview/profile (artisans or collectors), photo feature (dollhouses, collections, museums). Special issues: hobbies, games and pastimes; Saints & Sinners/Mardi Gras; All Creatures Great and Small; Water, Water Everywhere; The Great Outdoors; Down On The Farm; Vintage Television Shows; Miniatures As Teaching Tools. No articles on miniature shops or essays. Buys 120 mss/year. Query with few sample photos. Length: 1,000-1,500 words for features, how-to's may be longer. "Payment varies, but averages $150 for features, more for long how-to's."
Photos: Send photos with submission. Requires 35mm slides and larger, 3×5 prints. "Photos are paid for with manuscript. Seldom buy individual photos." Captions preferred; identification of subjects required. Buys all rights.
Tips: "It is essential that writers for *Nutshell News* be active miniaturists, or at least very knowledgeable about the hobby. Our readership is intensely interested in miniatures and will discern lack of knowledge or enthusiasm on the part of an author. A writer can best break in to *Nutshell News* by sending photos of work, credentials and a story outline. Photographs must be sharp and properly exposed to reveal details. Photos showing scale are especially appreciated. For articles about subjects in the Chicago/Milwaukee area, we can usually send our staff photographer."

PACK-O-FUN, Projects For Kids & Families, Clapper Communications, 2400 Devon Ave., Des Plaines IL 60018-4618. (847)635-5800. Fax: (847)635-6311. E-mail: 72567.1066@compuserve.com. Editor: Bill Stephani. Contact: Janice Brandon, associate editor. 85% freelance written. Bimonthly magazine covering crafts and activities for kids and those working with kids. Estab. 1951. Circ. 102,000. Pays 30 days after signed contract. Byline given. Buys all rights. Editorial lead time 8 months. Submit seasonal material 8 months in advance. Accepts simultaneous submissions. Reports in 1 month. Sample copy for $2.95.
Nonfiction: "We request quick and easy, inexpensive crafts and activities. Projects must be original, and complete instructions are required upon acceptance." Pay is negotiable.
Photos: Photos of project may be submitted in place of project at query stage.
Fillers: Facts, gags to be illustrated by cartoonist. Buys 20/year. Length: 25-50 words.
Tips: "*Pack-O-Fun* is looking for original how-to projects for kids and those working with kids. We're looking for recyclable ideas for throwaways. It would be helpful to check out our magazine before submitting."

PAPERWEIGHT NEWS, 761 Chestnut St., Santa Cruz CA 95060. (408)427-0111. E-mail: lselman@got.net. Editor: Lawrence Selman. Managing Editor: Ron Rosenberg. Contact: Ron Rosenberg. 80% freelance written. Quarterly magazine covering glass paperweights. "We accept fiction, technical and inspriational stories that revolve around glass paperweights. Contributors range from museum curators to housewives." Estab. 1975. Circ. 10,000. Pays on publication. Publishes ms an average of 6 months after acceptance. Byline given. Buys first North American serial rights. Editorial lead time 6 months. Submit seasonal material 6 months in advance. Accepts simultaneous submissions. Reports in 10 weeks on queries; 2 months on mss. Sample copy for $15.
Nonfiction: Book excerpts, essays, exposé, general interest, historical/nostalgic, how-to, humor, inspirational, interview/profile, new paperweight, personal experience, photo feature, technical, travel, puzzles/cartoons. "All stories must focus on paperweights." Buys 18 mss/year. Query. Length: 1,000-5,000 words. Pays $25-200 for assigned articles; $25-100 for unsolicited articles.
Photos: State availability of photos with submission. Send photos with submission. Reviews negatives, 4×5 transparencies, 4×6 prints. Offers no additional payment for photos accepted with ms. Negotiates payment individually. Captions, model releases, identification of subjects required.
Columns/Departments: Technically Speaking . . . (paperweight legends). Query.
Fiction: Adventure, condensed novels, confessions, ethnic, experimental, fantasy, historical, horror, humorous, mainstream, mystery, novel excerpts, romance, science fiction, serialized novels, slice-of-life vignettes, suspense, western. Length: 1,000-5,000 words. Pays $25-200.
Poetry: Avant-garde, free verse, haiku, light verse, traditional, limericks. Buys 5-10 poems/year. Pays $25-100.
Fillers: Anecdotes, facts, gags to be illustrated by cartoonist, newsbreaks, short humor. Buys 20/year. Length: 80-500 words. Pays $25-100.
Tips: "Do not send a submission that shows ignorance about the art form."

‡PLASTIC CANVAS CRAFTS, House of White Birches, 306 E. Parr Rd., Berne IN 46711. (219)589-8741. Fax: (219)589-8093. Managing Editor: June Sprunger. Contact: Laura Scott, editor. 100% freelance written. Bimonthly magazine covering plastic canvas patterns. "Our 32-page issues feature creative plastic canvas designs worked in a variety of styles on 7-, 10-, 14- and 5-count plastic canvas." Estab. 1993. Circ. 45,000. Pays within 2 months of acceptance. Publishes ms an average of 8 months after acceptance. Byline given. Offers 100% kill fee. Buys all rights. Editorial lead time 9 months. Submit seasonal material 9 months in advance. Accepts simultaneous submissions. Reports in 2 months on queries; 3-6 months on mss. Writer's guidelines free.
Nonfiction: How-to (plastic canvas skills), humor, technical (plastic canvas field). No fiction. Buys 2-4 mss/year. Send complete ms. Length: 500 words. Pays $50-250.

‡POPULAR COMMUNICATIONS, CQ Communications, Inc., 76 N. Broadway, Hicksville NY 11801. (516)681-2922. Fax: (516)681-2926. E-mail: popularcom.@aol.com. Contact: Harold Ort, editor. 25% freelance written. Monthly magazine covering the radio communications hobby. Estab. 1982. Circ. 65,000. Pays on publication. Publishes ms an average of 6 months after acceptance. Buys first North American serial rights. Editorial lead time 3 months. Submit seasonal material 6 months in advance. Reports in 1 month on queries; 2 months on mss. Sample copy free. Writer's guidelines for #10 SASE.
Nonfiction: General interest, how-to, new product, photo feature, technical. Buys 6-10 mss/year. Query. Length: 1,800-3,000 words. Pays $35/printed page.
Photos: State availability of photos with submission. Negotiates payment individually. Captions, model releases, identification of subjects required.
Tips: "Be a radio enthusiast and/or ham radio enthusiast with a keen interest in shortwave, amateur, scanning or CB radio."

POPULAR ELECTRONICS, Gernsback Publications, Inc., 500 Bi-County Blvd., Farmingdale NY 11735-3931. (516)293-3000. Fax: (516)293-3115. E-mail: peeditor@gernsback.com. Website: http://www.gernsback.com. Editor: Julian Martin. 80% freelance written. Monthly magazine covering hobby electronics—"features, projects, ideas related to audio, radio, experimenting, test equipment, computers, antique radio, communications, consumer electronics, state-of-the-art, etc." Circ. 78,000. **Pays on acceptance.** Byline given. Buys all rights. Submit seasonal material 9 months in advance. Reports in 1 month. Free sample copy, "include mailing label." Writer's guidelines for #10 SASE.
Nonfiction: General interest, how-to, photo feature, technical. Buys 200 mss/year. Query or send complete ms. Length: 1,000-3,500 words. Pays $100-500.
Photos: Send photos with submission. Wants b&w glossy photos. Offers no additional payment for photos accepted with ms. Captions required. Buys all rights.
Tips: "All areas are open to freelancers. Project-type articles and other 'how-to' articles have best success."

POPULAR MECHANICS, Hearst Corp., 224 W. 57th St., 3rd Floor, New York NY 10019. (212)649-2000. Fax: (212)586-5562. E-mail: popularmechanics@hearst.com. Website: http://www.popularmechanics.com. Contact: Joe Oldham, editor-in-chief. Managing Editor: Deborah Frank. 10% freelance written. Monthly magazine on automotive, home improvement, science, boating, outdoors, electronics. "We are a men's service magazine that tries to address the diverse interests of today's male, providing him with information to improve the way he lives. We cover stories from do-it-yourself projects to technological advances in aerospace, military, automotive and so on." Estab. 1902. Circ. 1,400,000. **Pays on acceptance.** Publishes ms an average of 6 months after acceptance. Byline given. Offers 25% kill fee. Buys all rights. Submit seasonal material 6 months in advance. Query. Reports in 3 weeks on queries; 1 month on mss. Writer's guidelines for SASE.

Nonfiction: General interest, how-to (shop projects, car fix-its), new product, technical. Special issues: Boating Guide (February); Home Improvement Guide (April); Consumer Electronics Guide (May); New Cars Guide (October); Woodworking Guide (November). No historical, editorial or critique pieces. Buys 2 mss/year. Query with or without published clips or send complete ms. Length: 500-1,500 words. Pays $500-1,500 for assigned articles; $300-1,000 for unsolicited articles. Sometimes pays expenses of writers on assignment.

Photos: Send photos with submission. Reviews slides and prints. Offers no additional payment for photos accepted with ms. Captions, model releases and identification of subjects required. Buys all rights.

Columns/Departments: New Cars (latest and hottest cars out of Detroit and Europe), Car Care (Maintenance basics, How It Works, Fix-Its and New products: send to Don Chaikin. Electronics, Audio, Home Video, Computers, Photography: send to Joe Oldham. Boating (new equipment, how-tos, fishing tips), Outdoors (gear, vehicles, outdoor adventures): send to James Gorant. Home & Shop Journal: send to Steve Willson. Science (latest developments), Tech Update (breakthroughs) and Aviation (sport aviation, homebuilt aircraft, new commercial aircraft, civil aeronautics): send to Jim Wilson. All columns are about 800 words.

POPULAR WOODWORKING, F&W Publications, 1507 Dana Ave., Cincinnati OH 45207. (513)531-2690, ext 238. Fax: (513)531-7107. E-mail: wudworker@aol.com. Editor: Steve Shanesy. Contact: Christopher Schwarz, managing editor. 10% freelance written. *"Popular Woodworking* is a bimonthly magazine that invites woodworkers of all levels into a community of experts who share their hard-won shop experience through in-depth projects and technique articles, which helps the readers hone their existing skills and develop new ones. Related stories increase the readers' understanding and enjoyment of their craft. Any project submitted must be aesthetically pleasing, of sound construction and offer a challenge to readers. On the average, we use six to nine features per issue. Our primary needs are 'how-to' articles on woodworking projects and instructional features dealing with woodworking tools and techniques. Our secondary need is for articles that will inspire discussion concerning woodworking. Tone of articles should be conversational and informal, as if the writer is speaking directly to the reader. Our readers are the woodworking hobbyist and small woodshop owner. Writers should have a knowledge of woodworking, or be able to communicate information gained from woodworkers." Estab. 1981. Circ. 284,000. **Pays on acceptance.** Publishes ms an average of 10 months after acceptance. Byline given. Buys first North American serial rights. Submit seasonal material 6 months in advance. Reports in 2 months. Sample copy and writer's guidelines for $4.50 and 9×12 SAE with 6 first-class stamps.

Nonfiction: How-to (on woodworking projects, with plans); humor (woodworking anecdotes); technical (woodworking techniques). Special issues: Shop Journal, Finishing issue, "Cutting Edge" issue (on sharpening tools); Hand Tools issue, Alternative Materials issue and Holiday Projects issue. Buys 10 mss/year. Query with or without published clips or send complete ms. Pays up to $125/published page. "The project must be well-designed, well constructed, well built and well finished. Technique pieces must have practical application."

Reprints: Send photocopy of article or typed ms with rights for sale noted and information about when and where the article previously appeared. Pays 100% of amount paid for an original article.

Photos: Send photos with submission. Reviews color only, slides and transparencies, 3×5 glossies acceptable. Offers no additional payment for photos accepted with ms. Photographic quality may affect acceptance. Need sharp close-up color photos of step-by-step construction process. Captions and identification of subjects required.

Columns/Departments: Tricks of the Trade (helpful techniques), Out of the Woodwook (thoughts on woodworking as a profession or hobby, can be humorous or serious), 500-1,500 words. Buys 6 mss/year. Query.

Fillers: Anecdotes, facts, short humor, shop tips. Buys 15/year. Length: 50-500 words.

Tips: "Submissions should include materials list, complete diagrams (blue prints not necessary), and discussion of the step-by-step process. We have become more selective on accepting only practical, attractive projects with quality construction. We are also looking for more original topics for our other articles."

QST, American Radio Relay League, Inc., 225 Main St., Newington CT 06111-1494. (869)594-0200. Fax: (860)594-0259. E-mail: qst@arrl.org. Website: http://www.arrl.org. Editor: Mark Wilson. Contact: Steve Ford, managing editor. 40% freelance written. Monthly magazine covering amateur radio interests and technology. "Ours are topics of interest to radio amateurs and persons in the electronics and communications fields." Estab. 1914. Circ. 175,000. Pays on publication. Publishes ms an average of 4 months after acceptance. Byline given. Usually buys all rights. Submit seasonal material 5 months in advance. Reports in 3 weeks on queries. Free sample copy and writer's guidelines for 10×13 SAE with 5 first-class stamps.

Nonfiction: General interest, how-to, humor, new products, personal experience, photo feature, technical (anything to do with amateur radio). Buys 50 mss/year. Query with or without published clips, or send complete ms. Length: open. Pays $65/published page. Sometimes pays expenses of writers on assignment.

Photos: Send photos with submission. Sometimes offers additional payment for photos accepted with ms or for cover. Captions, model releases and identification of subjects required. Usually buys all rights.

Columns/Departments: Hints and Kinks (hints/time saving procedures/circuits/associated with amateur radio), 50-200 words. Buys 100 mss/year. Send complete ms. Pays $20.

Tips: "Write with an idea, ask for sample copy and writer's guide. Technical and general interest to amateur operators, communications and electronics are most open."

‡QUILT WORLD, House of White Birches, 306 E. Parr Rd., Berne IN 46711. (219)589-8741. Fax: (207)794-3290. Contact: Sandra L. Hatch, editor. 100% freelance written. Works with a small number of new/unpublished writers each year. Bimonthly magazine covering quilting. "We publish articles on quilting techniques, profiles of quilters and coverage of quilt shows. Reader is 30-70 years old, midwestern." Circ. 130,000. Pays on publication. Publishes ms an average of 6 months after acceptance. Byline given. Buys all, first, one-time and second serial (reprint) rights. Submit seasonal material 9 months in advance. Reports in 1 month. Sample copy for $3. Writer's guidelines for #10 SASE.
Nonfiction: How-to, interview/profile (quilters), technical, new product (quilt products), photo feature. Buys 18-24 mss/year. Query. Length: open. Pays $35-100.
Reprints: Send photocopy of article and information about when and where it previously appeared.
Photos: Send photos with submission. Reviews transparencies and prints. Offers $15/photo (except covers). Identification of subjects required. Buys all or one-time rights.
Tips: "Send list of published articles with résumé and SASE. List ideas on which you plan to base your articles."

QUILTER'S NEWSLETTER MAGAZINE, 741 Corporate Circle, Suite A, Golden CO 80401-5622. Fax: (303)277-0370. Editor: Mary Leman Austin. Senior Features Editor: Jeannie Spears. Magazine published 10 times/year. Estab. 1969. Circ. 200,000. Buys first North American serial rights or second rights. Buys about 25 mss/year. Pays on publication, sometimes on acceptance. Reports in 2 months. Free sample copy.
Nonfiction: "We are interested in articles on the subject of quilts and quiltmakers *only*. We are not interested in anything relating to 'Grandma's Scrap Quilts' but could use fresh material." Submit complete ms. Pays 10¢/word minimum, usually more.
Reprints: Send tearsheet of article or typed ms with rights for sale noted and information about when and where the article previously appeared.
Photos: Additional payment for photos depends on quality.
Fillers: Related to quilts and quiltmakers only.
Tips: "Be specific, brief, and professional in tone. Study our magazine to learn the kind of thing we like. Send us material which fits into our format but which is different enough to be interesting. Realize that we think we're the best quilt magazine on the market and that we're aspiring to be even better, then send us the cream off the top of your quilt material."

QUILTING TODAY MAGAZINE, Chitra Publications, 2 Public Ave., Montrose PA 18801. (717)278-1984. Fax: (717)278-2223. Contact: Editorial Team. 80% freelance written. Bimonthly magazine on quilting, traditional and contemporary. "We seek articles that will cover one or two full pages (800 words each); informative to the general quilting public, present new ideas, interviews, instructional, etc." Estab. 1986. Circ. 90,000. Pays on publication. Publishes ms an average of 6 months after acceptance. Byline given. Buys second serial (reprint) rights. Submit seasonal material 8 months in advance. Reports in 1 month on queries; 2 months on mss. Writer's guidelines for SASE.
  • *Quilting Today Magazine* has a department appearing occasionally—"History Lessons," featuring a particular historical style or period in quiltmaking history.
Nonfiction: Book excerpts, essays, how-to (for various quilting techniques), humor, interview/profile, new product, opinion, personal experience, photo feature. "No articles about family history related to a quilt or quilts unless the quilt is a masterpiece of color and design, impeccable workmanship." Buys 20-30 mss/year. Query with or without published clips, or send complete ms. Length: 800-1,600 words. Pays $50-75/page.
Reprints: Occasionally accepts previously published submissions. Send photocopy of article or typed ms with rights for sale noted and information about when and where the article previously appeared. Pays $75/published page.
Photos: Send photos with submission. Reviews 35mm slides and larger transparencies. Offers $20/photo. Captions, identification of subjects required. Buys all rights unless rented from a museum.
Columns/Departments: Quilters Lesson Book (instructional), 800-1,600 words. Buys 10-12 mss/year. Send complete ms. Pays up to $75/column.
Tips: "Query with ideas; send samples of prior work so that we can assess and suggest assignment. Our publications appeal to traditional quilters (generally middle-aged) who use the patterns in each issue. Must have excellent photos."

‡RECREATING HISTORY, Historic Crafts, Cooking and Clothing for Reenactors, Recreating History, P.O. Box 4277, Santa Clara CA 95056. (888)733-6228. E-mail: info@recreating~history.com. Website: http://www.recreating-history.com. Contact: Willow Polson, editor. 80% freelance written. Published bimonthly, "*Recreating History* inspires and instructs living history enthusiasts from pre-medieval to Victorian times, and those thinking about getting started. Our primary focus is to provide how-to articles on historic arts and skills." Pays half on acceptance, half on publication. Publishes ms an average of 6 months after acceptance. Byline given. Offers 50% kill fee. Buys all rights to edited ms only and makes work-for-hire assignments. Editorial lead time 3 months. Submit seasonal material 3 months in advance. Reports in 3 weeks on queries; 2 months on mss. Sample copy for $3.95 and $1 postage. Writer's guidelines free.
Nonfiction: Book excerpts, how-to (historically accurate craft projects, documented skills), interview/profile, new product, technical. No poetry, puzzles, religion, politics or historical trivia. Buys 30 mss/year. Query with published clips. Length: 1,000-2,500 words. Pays $50-300.
Reprints: Send photocopy of article or typed ms with rights for sale noted and information about when and where the article previously appeared. Pays 100% of amount paid for an original article.
Photos: Send photos with submission. Reviews prints. Offers no additional payment for photos accepted with ms.

Captions, model releases, identification of subjects required. Buys all rights.

Columns/Departments: Provender (period recipes and menus), 1,500-2,000 words; Silhouette (artisan/personality profile), 1,500-2,000 words; Weekend Workshop (easy craft projects), 1,000-1,500 words; History Today (news of living history, not events), 100-200 words; The Library (book reviews), 50-150 words. Buys 10 mss/year. Query with published clips. Pays $10-250.

Fillers: Facts, newsbreaks, finished cartoons. Buys 5/year. Length: 25-200 words. Pays $10-100.

Tips: "We need very specific types of articles, so always query first. The editor can then guide you toward just what we need and how it should be written. We're always interested in new article ideas, so even if it doesn't quite fit into one of the categories listed here, but it relates to living history, query anyway and we'll talk."

RUG HOOKING MAGAZINE, Stackpole Magazines, 500 Vaughn St., Harrisburg PA 17110-2220. Fax: (717)234-1359. Website: http://www.rughookingonline.com. Editor: Patrice Crowley. Contact: Brenda Wilt, editorial assistant. 75% freelance written. Magazine published 5 times/year covering the craft of rug hooking. "This is the only magazine in the world devoted exclusively to rug hooking. Our readers are both novices and experts. They seek how-to pieces, features on fellow artisans and stories on beautiful rugs new and old." Estab. 1989. Circ. 10,000. **Pays on acceptance.** Publishes ms an average of 1 year after acceptance. Byline given. Buys all rights. Editorial lead time 6 months. Submit seasonal material 6 months in advance. Reports in 2 months. Sample copy for $5.

Nonfiction: How-to (hook a rug or a specific aspect of hooking), personal experience. Buys 30 mss/year. Query with published clips. Length: 825-2,475 words. Pays $74.25-222.75. Sometimes pays expenses of writers on assignment.

Reprints: Send photocopy of article and information about when and where the article previously appeared.

Photos: Send photos with submission. Reviews 2×2 transparencies, 3×5 prints. Negotiates payment individually. Identification of subjects required. Buys all rights.

‡SCALE AUTO ENTHUSIAST, Kalmbach Publishing Co., 21027 Crossroads Circle, P.O. Box 1612, Waukesha WI 53187-1612. (414)796-8776. Fax: (414)796-0126. Contact: Kirk Bell, senior editor. Managing editor: Mark Thompson. 95% freelance written. Bimonthly magazine covering model car building. "We are looking for model builders, collectors and enthusiasts who feel their models and/or modeling techniques and experiences would be of interest and benefit to our readership." Estab. 1979. Circ. 75,000. **Pays on acceptance.** Publishes ms an average of 6 months after acceptance. Byline given. Buys all rights. Editorial lead time 3 months. Submit seasonal material 2 months in advance. Reports in 1 month on queries; 3 months on mss. Sample copy and writer's guidelines free.

Nonfiction: Book excerpts, historical/nostalgic, how-to (build models, do different techniques), interview/profile, personal experience, photo feature, technical. Query or send complete ms. Length: 200-4,000 words. Pays $75-100/published page.

Photos: Send photos with submission. Reviews prints. Negotiates payment individually. Captions, model releases, identification of subjects required. Buys all rights.

Columns/Departments: Buys 50 mss/year. Query. Pays $75-100/published page.

Fillers: Gags to be illustrated by cartoonist. Buys 5/year. Pays percentage of $75/published page rate.

SEW NEWS, The Fashion Magazine for People Who Sew, PJS Publications, Inc., News Plaza, P.O. Box 1790, Peoria IL 61656. (309)682-6626. Fax: (309)682-7394. E-mail: sewnews@aol.com. Contact: Linda Turner Griepentrog, editor. 90% freelance written. Works with a small number of new/unpublished writers each year. 12 issues/year covering fashion-sewing. "Our magazine is for the beginning home sewer to the professional dressmaker. It expresses the fun, creativity and excitement of sewing." Estab. 1980. Circ. 261,000. **Pays on acceptance.** Publishes ms an average of 6 months after acceptance. Byline given. Buys all rights. Submit seasonal material 6 months in advance. Reports in 2 months. Sample copy for $4.50. Writer's guidelines for #10 SAE with 2 first-class stamps.

● All stories submitted to *Sew News* must be on disk.

Nonfiction: How-to (sewing techniques), interview/profile (interesting personalities in home-sewing field). Special issue: Holidays (fall, 1997). Buys 200-240 ms/year. Query with published clips if available. Length: 500-2,000 words. Pays $25-500. Rarely pays expenses of writers on assignment.

Photos: Send photos. Prefers color photographs or slides. Payment included in ms price. Identification of subjects required. Buys all rights.

Tips: "Query first with writing sample and outline of proposed story. Areas most open to freelancers are how-to and sewing techniques; give explicit, step-by-step instructions plus rough art. We're using more home decorating editorial content."

SPORTS COLLECTORS DIGEST, Krause Publications, 700 E. State St., Iola WI 54990. (715)445-2214. Fax: (715)445-4087. E-mail: kpsports@aol.com. Contact: Tom Mortenson, editor. Estab. 1952. 50% freelance written. Works with a small number of new/unpublished writers each year. Weekly sports memorabilia magazine. "We serve collectors of sports memorabilia—baseball cards, yearbooks, programs, autographs, jerseys, bats, balls, books, magazines, ticket stubs, etc." Circ. 52,000. Pays after publication. Publishes ms an average of 3 months after acceptance. Byline given. Buys first North American serial rights only. Submit seasonal material 3 months in advance. Reports in 5 weeks on queries; 2 months on mss. Free sample copy. Writer's guidelines for #10 SASE.

Nonfiction: General interest (new card issues, research on older sets); historical/nostalgic (old stadiums, old collectibles, etc.); how-to (buy cards, sell cards and other collectibles, display collectibles, ways to get autographs, jerseys and other memorabilia); interview/profile (well-known collectors, ball players—but must focus on collectibles); new product (new

card sets); personal experience ("what I collect and why"-type stories). No sports stories. "We are not competing with *The Sporting News*, *Sports Illustrated* or your daily paper. Sports collectibles only." Buys 100-200 mss/year. Query. Length: 300-3,000 words; prefers 1,000 words. Pays $50-125.
Reprints: Send tearsheet of article. Pays 100% of amount paid for an original article.
Photos: Unusual collectibles. Send photos. Pays $5-15 for b&w prints. Must identify of subjects. Buys all rights.
Columns/Departments: "We have all the columnists we need but welcome ideas for new columns." Buys 100-150 mss/year. Query. Length: 600-3,000 words. Pays $90-125.
Tips: "If you are a collector, you know what collectors are interested in. Write about it. No shallow, puff pieces; our readers are too smart for that. Only well-researched articles about sports memorabilia and collecting. Some sports nostalgia pieces are OK. Write only about the areas you know about."

SUNSHINE ARTIST, America's Premier Show & Festival Publication, Palm House Publishing Inc., 2600 Temple Dr., Winter Park FL 32789. (407)539-1399. Fax: (407)539-1499. E-mail: sunart@margicnet.net. Website: http://www.aartvark.com/au/sunshine. Publisher: David F. Cook. Editor: Amy Detwiler. Monthly magazine covering art shows in the United States. "We are the premier-marketing/reference magazine for artists and crafts professionals who earn their living through art shows nationwide. We list more than 4,000 shows annually, critique many of them and publish articles on marketing, selling and other issues of concern to professional show circuit artists." Estab. 1972. Circ. 12,000. Pays on publication. Publishes ms an average of 3 months after acceptance. Byline given. Buys first North American serial rights. Reports within 2 months. Sample copy for $5.
Nonfiction: "We publish articles of interest to artists and crafts professionals who travel the art show circuit. Current topics include marketing, computers and RV living." No how-to. Buys 5-10 freelance mss/year. Query or ms. Length: 1,000-2,000 words. Pays $50-150 for accepted articles.
Reprints: Send photocopy of article and information about when and where the article previously appeared.
Photos: Send photos with submission. Offers no additional payment for photos accepted with ms. Captions, model releases and identification of subjects required.

‡TEDDY BEAR REVIEW, Collector Communications Corp., 170 Fifth Ave., New York NY 10010. (212)989-8700. Contact: Stephen L. Cronk, editor. 75% freelance written. Works with a small number of new/unpublished writers each year. Bimonthly magazine on teddy bears for collectors, enthusiasts and bearmakers. Estab. 1985. Pays 30 days after acceptance. Byline given. Buys first North American serial rights. Submit seasonal material 6 months in advance. Sample copy and writer's guidelines for $2 and 9×12 SAE.
Nonfiction: Book excerpts, historical, how-to, interview/profile. No nostalgia on childhood teddy bears. Buys 30-40 mss/year. Query with photos and published clips. Length: 900-1,800 words. Pays $100-350. Sometimes pays the expenses of writers on assignment "if approved ahead of time."
Photos: Send photos with submission. Reviews transparencies and b&w prints. Offers no additional payment for photos accepted with ms. Captions required. Buys one-time rights.
Tips: "We are interested in good, professional writers around the country with a strong knowledge of teddy bears. Historical profile of bear companies, profiles of contemporary artists and knowledgeable reports on museum collections are of interest."

‡TODAY'S COLLECTOR, The Nation's Antiques and Collectibles Marketplace, Krause Publications, 700 E. State St., Iola WI 54990. (715)445-2214. Fax: (715)445-4087. Website: http://www.krause.com. Contact: Steve Ellingbee, editor. 50% freelance written. Monthly magazine covering antiques and collectibles. "*Today's Collector* is for serious collectors of all types of antiques and collectibles." Estab. 1993. Circ. 85,000. Pays on publication. Publishes ms an average of 6 months after acceptance. Byline given. Offers $25-50 kill fee. Buys perpetual but non-exclusive rights. Editorial lead time 2 months. Submit seasonal material 4 months in advance. Accepts simultaneous submissions. Reports in 1 month on mss. Sample copy free.
Nonfiction: How-to (antiques and collectibles). No articles that are too general—specific collecting areas only. Buys 60-75 mss/year. Send complete ms. Length: 500-3,000 words. Pays $50-200.
Reprints: Accepts previously published submissions.
Photos: Send photos with submission. Reviews transparencies, prints. Offers no additional payment for photos accepted with ms. Captions required. Buys one-time rights.
Tips: "I want detailed articles about specific collecting areas—nothing too broad or general. I need lots of information about pricing and values, along with brief history and background."

‡TODAY'S WOODWORKER, Rockler Companies, Inc., 4365 Willow Dr., Medina MN 55340. (612)478-8255. Fax: (612)478-8396. E-mail: editor@todayswoodworker.com. Contact: Stan Schmidt, editor. 50% freelance written. Bimonthly magazine on woodworking. "Projects, tips and techniques for the beginner and the serious woodworking hobbyist." Estab. 1989. Circ. 130,000. **Pays on acceptance.** Publishes ms an average of 1 year after acceptance. Byline given. Buys first North American serial rights. Editorial lead time 1 year. Submit seasonal material 1 year in advance. Sample copy and writer's guidelines free.
Nonfiction: How-to (woodworking). Buys 12 mss/year. Query. Length: 200-2,000 words. Pays $40-1,500.
Photos: State availability of photos with submission. Reviews transparencies. Negotiates payment individually. Identification of subjects required. Buys one-time rights.
Columns/Departments: Techniques; Today's Shop (operating specific tools); Finishing Thoughts (applying specific

finishes). Length: 500 words. Buys 6 mss/year. Query. Pays $100-500.
Tips: "Study past issues of magazine to get the style."

‡**TOY SHOP**, Krause Publications, 700 E. State St., Iola WI 54990. (715)445-2214. Fax: (715)445-4087. Website: http://www.krause.com. Editor: Sharon Korbeck. 95% freelance written. Biweekly tabloid covering toy collecting. "We cover primarily vintage collectible toys from the 1930s-1960s. Stories focus on historical toy companies, the collectibility of toys and features on prominent collections." Estab. 1986. Circ. 70,000. Pays on publication. Publishes ms an average of 4 months after acceptance. Byline given. Buys "perpetual, nonexclusive rights." Editorial lead time 6 months. Accepts simultaneous submissions. Reports in 1 month. Sample copy for $1. Writer's guidelines free.
Nonfiction: Essays, general interest, historical/nostalgic (toys, toy companies), interview/profile (toy collectors), new product (toys), personal experience, photo feature (toys), features on old toys. No opinion, broad topics or poorly researched pieces. Buys 100 mss/year. Query. Length: 1,000-3,000 words. Pays $50-200. Contributor's copies included with payment. Sometimes pays expenses of writers on assignment.
Reprints: Accepts previously published submissions.
Photos: State availability of or send photos with submission. Reviews negatives, transparencies, 3×5 prints. Negotiates payment individually. Captions, model releases, identification of subjects required. Rights purchased with ms rights.
Columns/Departments: Collector Profile (profile of toy collectors), 1,000 words; Toys I Loved (essay on favorite toys), 250-500 words. Buys 25 mss/year. Query. Pays $50-150.
Tips: "Articles must be specific. Include historical info, quotes, photos with story. Talk with toy dealers and get to know how big the market is."

TRADITIONAL QUILTER, The Leading Teaching Magazine for Creative Quilters, All American Crafts, Inc., 243 Newton-Sparta Rd., Newton NJ 07860. (201)383-8080. Fax: (201)383-8133. E-mail: tqphyllis@aol.com. Contact: Phyllis Barbieri, editor. 45% freelance written. Bimonthly magazine on quilting. Estab. 1988. Pays on publication. Byline given. Buys first or all rights. Submit seasonal 6 months in advance. Reports in 2 months. Sample copy for 9×12 SAE with 4 first-class stamps. Writer's guidelines for #10 SASE.
Nonfiction: Quilts and quilt patterns with instructions, quilt-related projects, historical/nostalgic, humor, interview/profile, opinion, personal experience, photo feature, travel—all quilt related. Query with published clips. Length: 350-1,000 words. Pays 10¢/word.
Photos: Send photos with submission. Reviews all size transparencies and prints. Offers $10-15/photo. Captions and identification of subjects required. Buys one-time or all rights.
Columns/Departments: Feature Teacher (qualified quilt teachers with teaching involved—with slides); Remnants (reports on conventions, history—humor); Profile (award-winning and interesting quilters); The Guilded Newsletter (reports on quilting guild activities, shows, workshops, and retreats). Length: 1,000 words maximum. Pays 10¢/word.

TRADITIONAL QUILTWORKS, The Pattern Magazine for Traditional Quilters, Chitra Publications, 2 Public Ave., Montrose PA 18801. (717)278-1984. Fax: (717)278-2223. Contact: Editorial Team. 50% freelance written. Bimonthly magazine on quilting. "We seek articles of an instructional nature, profiles of talented teachers, articles on the history of specific areas of quiltmaking (patterns, fiber, regional, etc.)." Estab. 1988. Circ. 90,000. Pays on publication. Publishes ms an average of 6 months after acceptance. Byline given. Buys second serial (reprint) rights. Submit seasonal material 8 months in advance. Reports in 2 months. Writer's guidelines for SASE.
Nonfiction: Historical, instructional, quilting education. "No light-hearted entertainment." Buys 12-18 mss/year. Query with photos, with or without published clips, or send complete ms. "Publication hinges on photo quality." Length: 1,500 words maximum. Pays $75/page.
Photos: Send photos with submission. Reviews 35mm slides and larger transparencies (color). Offers $20/photo. Captions, model releases and identification of subjects required. Buys all rights.
Tips: "Our publications appeal to traditional quilters, generally middle-aged and mostly who use the patterns in the magazine. Publication hinges on good photo quality."

TREASURE CHEST, The Information Source & Marketplace for Collectors and Dealers of Antiques and Collectibles, Treasure Chest Publishing Inc., Box 245, N. Scituate RI 02857. (401)647-0050. Contact: David F. Donnelly, owner. 100% freelance written. Monthly newspaper on antiques and collectibles. Estab. 1988. Circ. 50,000. Pays on publication. Publishes ms an average of 3 months after acceptance. Byline given. Buys first and second serial (reprint) rights. Reports in 2 months on mss. Sample copy for 9×12 SAE with $2. Writer's guidelines for #10 SASE.
Nonfiction: Primarily interested in feature articles on a specific field of antiques or collectibles. Buys 40 mss/year. Send complete ms. Articles on diskette preferred. Length: 1,000 words. Pays $30 with photos.
Reprints: Send tearsheet or photocopy of article and information about when and where the article previously appeared. Pays 60% of amount paid for original article.
Fillers: Anecdotes, facts, gags to be illustrated, short humor. Buys 12/year. Length: 100-350 words. Pays $10.
Tips: "Learn about your subject by interviewing experts—appraisers, curators, dealers."

VIDEOMAKER, Camcorders, Computers, Tools & Techniques for Creating Video, Videomaker Inc., P.O. Box 4591, Chico CA 95927. (916)891-8410. Fax: (916)891-8443. E-mail: editor@videomaker.com. Website: http://www.videomaker.com. Editor: Stephen Muratore. Managing Editor: Karen Director. 75% freelance written. Monthly magazine on video production. "Our audience encompasses video camera users ranging from broadcast and cable TV producers to special-event videographers to video hobbyists . . . labeled professional, industrial, 'prosumer' and consumer. Editorial emphasis is on video*making* (production and exposure), *not* reviews of commercial videos. Personal video phenomenon is a young 'movement'; readership is encouraged to participate—get in on the act, join the fun." Estab. 1986. Circ. 90,000. Pays on publication. Publishes ms an average of 4-6 months after acceptance. Byline given. Buys all rights. Submit seasonal material 6 months in advance. Accepts simultaneous submissions. Reports in 3 months. Sample copy for 9×12 SAE with 9 first-class stamps. Writer's guidelines free.

Nonfiction: How-to (tools, tips, techniques for better videomaking); interview/profile (notable videomakers); product probe (review of latest and greatest or innovative); personal experience (lessons to benefit other videomakers); technical (state-of-the-art audio/video). Articles with comprehensive coverage of product line or aspect of videomaking preferred. Buys 70 mss/year. Query with or without published clips, or send complete ms. Length: open. Pays 10¢/word.

Reprints: Send tearsheet or information about when and where the article previously appeared. Payment negotiable.

Photos: Send photos and/or other artwork with submissions. Reviews contact sheets, transparencies and prints. Captions required. Payment for photos accepted with ms included as package compensation. Buys one-time rights.

Columns/Departments: Sound Track (audio information); Getting Started (beginner's column); Quick Focus (brief reviews of current works pertaining to video production); Profitmaker (money-making opportunities); Edit Points (tools and techniques for successful video editions). Buys 40 mss/year. Pays 10¢/word.

Tips: "Comprehensiveness a must. Article on shooting tips covers *all* angles. Buyer's guide to special-effect generators cites *all* models available. Magazine strives for an 'all-or-none' approach. Most topics covered once (twice tops) per year, so we must be thorough. Manuscript/photo package submissions helpful. *Videomaker* wants videomaking to be fulfilling and fun."

VOGUE KNITTING, Butterick Company, 161 Sixth Ave., New York NY 10013-1205. Fax: (212)620-2731. Editor: Trisha Malcolm. Managing Editor: Daryl Brower. Quarterly magazine that covers knitting. "High fashion magazine with projects for knitters of all levels. In-depth features on techniques, knitting around the world, interviews, bios and other articles of interest to well-informed readers." Estab. 1982. Circ. 200,000. **Pays on acceptance**. Publishes ms an average of 4 months after acceptance. Buys all rights. Editorial lead time 6 months. Submit seasonal material 6 months in advance. Accepts simultaneous submissions. Writer's guidelines free.

Nonfiction: Essays, general interest, historical/nostalgic, how-to, interview/profile, personal experience, photo feature, technical, travel. Buys 25 mss/year. Query. Length: 600-1,200 words. Pays $250 minimum.

Photos: Send photos with submission. Reviews 3×5 transparencies. Negotiates payment individually. Captions, model releases and identification of subjects required. Buys all rights.

WOODSHOP NEWS, Soundings Publications Inc., 35 Pratt St., Essex CT 06426-1185. (860)767-8227. Fax: (860)767-1048. E-mail: woodshop@ix.netcom.com. Website: http://www.woodshopnews.com. Editor: Ian C. Bowen. Contact: Thomas Clark, senior editor. 20% freelance written. Monthly tabloid "covering woodworking for professionals and hobbyists. Solid business news and features about woodworking companies. Feature stories about interesting amateur woodworkers. Some how-to articles." Estab. 1986. Circ. 100,000. Pays on publication. Publishes ms an average of 3 months after acceptance. Byline given. Offers 25% kill fee. Buys first North American serial rights. Submit seasonal material 4 months in advance. Reports in 3 weeks on queries; 1 month on mss. Sample copy and writer's guidelines free.

  • *Woodshop News* needs writers in major cities in all regions except the Northeast. Also looking for more editorial opinion pieces.

Nonfiction: How-to (query first), interview/profile, new product, opinion, personal experience, photo feature. Key word is "newsworthy." No general interest profiles of "folksy" woodworkers. Buys 50-75 mss/year. Query with published clips or submit ms. Length: 100-1,200 words. Pays $50-400 for assigned articles; $40-250 for unsolicited articles; $40-100 for workshop tips. Pays expenses of writers on assignment.

Photos: Send photos with submission. Reviews contact sheets and prints. Offers $20-35/photo. Captions and identification of subjects required. Buys one-time rights.

Columns/Departments: Pro Shop (business advice, marketing, employee relations, taxes etc. for the professional written by an established professional). Length: 1,200-1,500 words. Buys 12 mss/year. Query. Pays $250-350.

Tips: "The best way to start is a profile of a business or hobbyist woodworker in your area. Find a unique angle about the person or business and stress this as the theme of your article. Avoid a broad, general-interest theme that would be more appropriate to a daily newspaper. Our readers are woodworkers who want more depth and more specifics than would a general readership. If you are profiling a business, we need standard business information such as gross annual earnings/sales, customer base, product line and prices, marketing strategy, etc. Black and white 35 mm photos are a must. We need more freelance writers from the Mid-Atlantic, Midwest and West Coast."

WOODWORK, A Magazine For All Woodworkers, Ross Periodicals, P.O. Box 1529, Ross CA 94957-1529. (415)382-0580. Fax: (415)382-0587. Editor: John McDonald. Publisher: Tom Toldrian. 90% freelance written. Bimonthly magazine covering woodworking. "We are aiming at a broad audience of woodworkers, from the home enthusiast/hobbyist to more advanced." Estab. 1986. Circ. 80,000. Pays on publication. Byline given. Buys first North American serial and second serial (reprint) rights. Sample copy for $3 and 9×12 SAE with 6 first-class stamps. Writer's guidelines for #10 SASE.

Nonfiction: How-to (simple or complex, making attractive furniture), interview/profile (of established woodworkers that make attractive furniture), photo feature (of interest to woodworkers), technical (tools, techniques). "Do not send a how-to unless you are a woodworker." Query first. Length: 1,500-2,000 words. Pays $150/published page.

Photos: Send photos with submission. Reviews 35mm slides. Offers no additional payment for photos accepted with ms. Captions and identification of subjects required. Buys one-time rights.

Columns/Departments: Feature articles 1,500-3,000 words. From non-woodworking freelancers, we use interview/ profiles of established woodworkers. Bring out woodworker's philosophy about the craft, opinions about what is happening currently. Good photos of attractive furniture a must. Section on how-to desirable. Query with published clips. Pays $150/published page.

Tips: "If you are not a woodworker, the interview/profile is your best, really only chance. Good writing is essential as are good photos. The interview must be entertaining, but informative and pertinent to woodworkers' interests."

WORKBENCH, 700 W. 47th St., Suite 310, Kansas City MO 64112. (816)531-5730. Fax: (816)531-3873. Executive Editor: A. Robert Gould. 75% freelance written. Prefers to work with published/established writers; but works with a small number of new/unpublished writers each year. For woodworkers and home improvement do-it-yourselfers. "*Workbench* focuses on woodworking throughout the home: from weekend projects and furniture, to built-in cabinets and shelves, to decks, windows, doors and remodeling. Every issue is filled with detailed illustrations, color photographs, and step-by-step descriptions, In addition to all the project how-to information, each issue includes articles on woodworking and home improvement skills, features on tools and tool use, and information on the products and materials used in home improvement and woodworking. Shop Tips and Q&A are also standard." Estab. 1957. Circ. 750,000. **Pays on acceptance.** Publishes ms an average of 1 year after acceptance. Byline given. Buys all rights. Reports in 3 months. Sample copy for 9×12 SAE with 6 first-class stamps. Writer's guidelines free.

Nonfiction: "We have continued emphasis on do-it-yourself woodworking, home improvement and home maintenance projects. We provide in-progress photos, technical drawings and how-to text for all projects. We are very strong in woodworking, cabinetmaking and classic furniture construction. Projects range from simple toys to reproductions of furniture now in museums. We would like to receive woodworking projects that can be duplicated by both beginning do-it-yourselfers and advanced woodworkers." Query. Pays $175/published page or more depending on quality of submission. Additional payment for good color photos. "If you can consistently provide good material, including photos, your rates will go up and you will get assignments."

Columns/Departments: Shop Tips bring $25 with a line drawing and/or b&w photo.

Tips: "Our magazine focuses on woodworking, covering all levels of ability, and home improvement projects from the do-it-yourselfer's viewpoint, emphasizing the most up-to-date materials and procedures. We would like to receive articles on home improvements and remodeling, and/or simple contemporary furniture. Projects should be both functional and classic in design. We can photograph projects worthy for publication, so feel free to send snapshots."

HOME AND GARDEN

The baby boomers' turn inward, or "cocooning," has caused an explosion of publications in this category. Gardening magazines in particular have blossomed, as more people are developing leisure interests at home. Some magazines here concentrate on gardens; others on the how-to of interior design. Still others focus on homes and gardens in specific regions of the country. Be sure to read the publication to determine its focus before submitting a manuscript or query.

THE ALMANAC FOR FARMERS & CITY FOLK, Greentree Publishing, Inc., 850 S. Rancho, #2319, Las Vegas NV 89106. (702)387-6777. Editor: Lucas McFadden. Managing Editor: Thomas Alexander. 40% freelance written. Annual almanac of "down-home, folksy material pertaining to farming, gardening, animals, etc." Estab. 1983. Circ. 800,000. Pays on publication. Publishes ms 6 months after acceptance. Byline given. Buys first North American serial rights. Deadline: January 31. Reports in 2 weeks on queries; 1 month on mss. Sample copy for $3.95.

Nonfiction: Essays, general interest, how-to, humor. No fiction or controversial topics. Buys 30 mss/year. Send complete ms. Length: 350-1,400 words. Pays $45/page.

Poetry: Buys 1 poem/year. Pays $45 for full page, otherwise proportionate share thereof.

Fillers: Anecdotes, facts, short humor, gardening hints. Buys 60/year. Length 125 words maximum. Pays $10-45.

Tips: "Typed submissions essential as we scan in manuscript. Short, succinct material is preferred. Material should appeal to a wide range of people and should be on the 'folksy' side, with a thread of humor woven in."

THE AMERICAN GARDENER, Publication of the American Horticultural Society, 7931 E. Blvd. Dr., Alexandria VA 22308-1300. (703)768-5700. E-mail: editorahs@aol.com. Website: http://eMall.com. Contact: Kathleen Fisher, editor. 90% freelance written. Bimonthly magazine "*The American Gardener* is the official publication of the American Horticultural Society (AHS), a national, nonprofit, membership organization for gardeners founded in 1922. AHS is dedicated to promoting the art and science of horticulture in America through its publication and programs. Readers of *The American Gardener* include the approximately 20,000 members of the American Horticultural Society. Another 6,000 are sold on newsstands." Estab. 1922. Circ. 25,000. Pays on publication. Publishes ms an average of 6 months after acceptance. Byline given. Buys first North American serial rights. Reports in 3 months on queries if SASE included. Sample copy for $3. Writer's guidelines for SASE.

Nonfiction: Book excerpts, historical, children and nature, plants and health, city gardening, humor, interview/profile, personal experience, technical (explain science of horticulture to lay audience). Buys 30-40 mss/year. Query with published clips. Length: 1,000-2,500 words. Pays $100-400. Pays with contributor copies or other premiums when other horticultural organizations contribute articles.

Photos: Send photos with query. Pays $50-75/photo. Captions required. Buys one-time rights.

Columns/Departments: Offshoots (humorous, sentimental or expresses an unusual viewpoint), 1,200 words; Conservationist's Notebook (articles about individuals or organizations attempting to save endangered species or protect natural areas), 750 words; Natural Connections (explains a natural phenonmenon—plant and pollinator relationships, plant and fungus relationships, parasites—that may be observed in nature or in the garden), 750 words; Urban Gardener (looks at a successful small space garden—indoor, patio, less than a quarter-acre; a program that successfully brings plants to city streets or public spaces; or a problem of particular concern to city dwellers), 750-1,500 words; Planting the Future (children and youth gardening programs), 750 words; Plants and Your Health (all aspects of gardening and health, from sunburn, poison ivy and strained backs to herbal medicines), 750 words; Regional Happenings (events that directly affect gardeners only in 1 area, but are of interest to others: an expansion of a botanical garden, a serious new garden pest, the launching of a regional flower show, a hot new gardening trend), 250-500 words.

Tips: "We run very few how-to articles. Our readers are advanced, sophisticated amateur gardeners; about 20 percent are horticultural professionals. Our articles are intended to bring this knowledgeable group new information, ranging from the latest scientific findings that affect plants, to the history of gardening and gardens in America."

AMERICAN HOMESTYLE & GARDENING MAGAZINE, Gruner & Jahr USA Publishing, 110 Fifth Ave., New York NY 10011. (212)463-1633. Fax: (212)463-1646. Editor-in-Chief: Karen Saks. Bimonthly magazine. "*American Homestyle & Gardening* is a guide to complete home design. It is edited for buyers of decorating, building and remodeling products. It focuses on an actionable approach to home design." Estab. 1986. Circ. 875,000. **Pays on acceptance.** Byline given. Offers 20% kill fee. Buys first North American serial rights with additional fee for electronic rights. Reports in 1 month on queries. Sample copy and writer's guidelines for #10 SASE.
 • Ranked as one of the best markets for freelance writers in *Writer's Yearbook* magazine's annual "Top 100 Markets," January 1997.

Nonfiction: Writers with expertise in design, decorating, building or gardening. Buys 60 mss/year. Query. Length: 750-1,250 words. Pays $750-1,500. Pays expenses of writers on assignment.

Tips: "Writers should have knowledge of design, building and gardening, and the ability to entertain."

ATLANTA HOMES AND LIFESTYLES, 1100 Johnson Ferry Rd., Suite 595, Atlanta GA 30342. (404)252-6670. Fax: (404)252-6673. Editor: Barbara S. Tapp. 65% freelance written. Bimonthly magazine. "*Atlanta Homes and Lifestyles* is designed for the action-oriented, well-educated reader who enjoys his/her shelter, its design and construction, its environment, and living and entertaining in it." Estab. 1983. Circ. 33,091. Pays on publication. Byline given. Publishes ms an average of 6 months after acceptance. 25% kill fee. Buys all rights. Reports in 3 months. Sample copy $2.95.

Nonfiction: Historical, interview/profile, new products, well-designed homes, antiques (then and now), photo features, gardens, local art, remodeling, food, preservation, entertaining. "We do not want articles outside respective market area, not written for magazine format, or that are excessively controversial, investigative or that cannot be appropriately illustrated with attractive photography." Buys 35 mss/year. Query with published clips. Length: 500-750 words. Pays $350 for features. Sometimes pays expenses of writers on assignment "if agreed upon in advance of assignment."

Reprints: Send tearsheet or photocopy of article and information about where and when it previously appeared. Pays 50% of amount paid for original article.

Photos: Send photos with submission; most photography is assigned. Reviews transparencies. Offers $40-50/photo. Captions, model releases and identification of subjects required. Buys one-time rights.

Columns/Departments: Short Takes (newsy items on home and garden topics); Quick Fix (simple remodeling ideas); Cheap Chic (stylish decorating that is easy on the wallet); Digging In (outdoor solutions from Atlanta's gardeners); Big Fix (more extensive remodeling projects); Real Estate News; Interior Elements (hot new furnishings on the market); Weekender (long or short weekend getaway subjects). Query with published clips. Buys 25-30 mss/year. Length: 350-500 words. Pays $50-200.

BACKHOME: Your Hands-On Guide to Sustainable Living., Wordsworth Communications, Inc., P.O. Box 70, Hendersonville NC 28793. (704)696-3838. Fax: (704)696-0700. E-mail: backhome@mailbox.ioa.com. Website: http://www.magamall.com. Contact: Lorna K. Loveless, editor. 80% freelance written. Bimonthly magazine. "*BackHome* encourages readers to take more control over their lives by doing more for themselves: productive organic gardening; building and repairing their homes; utilizing alternative energy systems; raising crops and livestock; building furniture; toys and games and other projects; creative cooking. *BackHome* promotes respect for family activities, community programs and the environment." Estab. 1990. Circ. 23,000. Pays on publication. Publishes ms 3-12 months after acceptance. Byline given. Offers $25 kill fee at publisher's discretion. Buys first North American serial rights. Editorial lead time 3 months. Submit seasonal material 3-6 months in advance. Reports in 6 weeks on queries; 2 months on mss. Sample copy for $5. Writer's guidelines with SASE.
 • *The Millennium Whole Earth Catalog*, 1995, stated that *BackHome* contains "the most effective, practical, and appropriate tools and ideas for thinking and acting independently for the 21st century."

Nonfiction: How-to (gardening, construction, energy, home business), interview/profile, personal experience, technical, self-sufficiency. Buys 80 mss/year. Query. Length: 750-5,000 words. Pays $25 (approximately) for printed page.

Reprints: Send tearsheet or photocopy of article or typed ms with rights for sale noted and information about when and where the article previously appeared. Pays 100% of amount paid for an original article.

Photos: Send photos with submission: 35mm slides and color prints. Offers additional payment for photos published. Identification of subjects required. Buys one-time rights.

Tips: "Very specific in relating personal experiences in the areas of gardening, energy, and homebuilding how-to. Third-person approaches to others' experiences are also acceptable but somewhat less desireable. Clear color photo prints, especially those in which people are prominent, help immensely when deciding upon what is accepted."

BETTER HOMES AND GARDENS, 1716 Locust St., Des Moines IA 50309-3023. Fax: (515)284-3684. Website: http://www.bhglive.com. Editor-in-Chief: Jean LemMon. Editor (Building): Joan McCloskey. Editor (Food & Nutrition): Nancy Byal. Editor (Garden/Outdoor Living): Mark Kane. Editor (Health): Martha Miller. Editor (Education & Parenting): Barbara Hall Palar. Editor (Money Management, Automotive, Electronics): Lamont Olson. Editor (Features & Travel): Martha Long. Editor (Interior Design): Sandy Soria. 10-15% freelance written. *"Better Homes and Gardens* provides home service information for people who have a serious interest in their homes." Estab. 1922. Circ. 7,605,000. **Pays on acceptance.** Buys all rights. "We read all freelance articles, but much prefer to see a letter of query rather than a finished manuscript."

Nonfiction: Travel, education, gardening, health, cars, money management, home entertainment. "We do not deal with political subjects or with areas not connected with the home, community, and family." Pays rates "based on estimate of length, quality and importance." No poetry.

● Most stories published by this magazine go through a lengthy process of development involving both editor and writer. Some editors will consider *only* query letters, not unsolicited manuscripts.

Tips: Direct queries to the department that best suits your story line.

‡BIRDS & BLOOMS, Reiman Publications, 5925 Country Lane, Greendale WI 53129. Editor: Tom Curl. Contact: Jeff Nowak, managing editor. 15% freelance written. Bimonthly magazine focusing on the "beauty in your own backyard. *Birds & Blooms* is a sharing magazine that lets backyard enthusiasts chat with each other by exchanging personal experiences. This makes *Birds & Blooms* more like a conversation than a magazine, as readers share tips and tricks on producing beautiful blooms and attracting feathered friends to their backyards." Estab. 1995. Circ. 1.1 million. Pays on publication. Publishes ms an average of 7 months after acceptance. Byline given. Buys all rights. Editorial lead time 2 months. Submit seasonal material 4 months in advance. Accepts simultaneous submissions. Reports in 1 month on queries; 2 months on mss. Sample copy for $2, 9×12 SAE and $1.95 postage. Writer's guidelines free.

Nonfiction: Essays, how-to, humor, inspirational, personal experience, photo feature, natural crafting and "plan" items for building backyard accents. No bird rescue or captive bird pieces. Buys 12-20 mss/year. Send complete ms. Length: 250-1,000 words. Pays $100-400.

Photos: Trudi Bellin, photo coordinator. Send photos with submission. Reviews transparencies and prints. Identification of subjects required. Buys one-time rights.

Columns/Departments: Backyard Banter (odds, ends and unique things); Bird Tales (backyard bird stories); Local Lookouts (community-backyard happenings); all 200 words. Buys 12-20 mss/year. Send complete ms. Pays $50-75.

Fillers: Anecdotes, facts, gags to be illustrated by cartoonist. Buys 25/year. Length: 10-250 words. Pays $10-75.

Tips: "Focus on conversational writing—like you're chatting with a neighbor over your fence. Manuscripts full of tips and ideas that people can use in backyards across the country have the best chance of being used. Photos that illustrate these points also increase chances of being used."

CANADIAN GARDENING, Camar Communications, 130 Spy Court, Markham, Ontario L3R 0W5 Canada. (905)475-8440. Fax: (905)475-9246. Editor: Liz Primeau. Contact: Rebecca Fox, managing editor. 99% freelance written. Magazine published 7 times/year covering home gardening. "We cover garden design, growing, projects for the garden, products, regional information (pests, growing, etc.) for the Canadian gardener. Fundamental plants are the focus, but each issue contains at least one vegetable piece, usually with recipes." Estab. 1990. Circ. 140,000. **Pays on acceptance.** Publishes ms 18 months after acceptance. Byline given. Offers 25-50% kill fee. Buys first North American serial rights. Editorial lead time 3 months. Submit seasonal material 5 months in advance. Reports in 3 months. Sample copy and writer's guidelines free.

Nonfiction: Book excerpts, how-to (gardening, garden projects, pruning, pest control, etc.), personal experience and photo feature (as they relate to gardening). No U.S. gardens or growing; no *public* gardens. Buys about 70 mss/year. Query with published clips. Length: 300-2,000 words. Pays $50-700. Sometimes pays expenses of writers on assignment.

Photos: State availability of photos with ms. Offers $50-250/photo. Must identify subjects. Buys one-time rights.

Reprints: Rarely accepts previously published submissions.

Columns/Departments: Gardeners' Journal (garden facts, how-tos—homemade pest sprays, e.g.—and personal experience), 300-500 words; Techniques (gardening techniques), 500-800 words. Buys 50 mss/year. Query. Pays $50-200.

Tips: "We prefer to use untried (to us) writers on small items for Gardeners' Journal, the upfront section. Short outlines that are already well-focused receive the most attention."

‡CANADIAN WORKSHOP, The Do-It-Yourself Magazine, Camar Publications (1984) Inc., 130 Spy Court, Markham, Ontario L3R 0W5 Canada. (416)475-8440. Fax: (905)475-4856. E-mail: letters@canadianworkshop.ca. Website: http://www.canadianworkshop.ca. Contact: Doug Bennet, editor. 90% freelance written; half of these are assigned. Monthly magazine covering the "do-it-yourself" market including woodworking projects, renovation, restoration and maintenance. Circ. 130,000. Payment in two installments: half when received, half the month following. Byline given.

Offers 50% kill fee. Rights are negotiated with the author. Submit seasonal material 6 months in advance. Reports in 4-6 weeks. Sample copy for 9×12 SASE. Writer's guidelines for #10 SASE.

Nonfiction: How-to (home maintenance, renovation projects, woodworking projects and features). Buys 40-60 mss/year. Query with clips of published work. Length: 1,500-2,500 words. Pays $800-1,200. Pays expenses of writers on assignment.

Photos: Send photos with ms. Payment for photos, transparencies negotiated with the author. Captions, model releases, identification of subjects required.

Tips: "Freelancers must be aware of our magazine format. Products used in how-to articles must be readily available across Canada. Deadlines for articles are four months in advance of cover date. How-tos should be detailed enough for the amateur but appealing to the experienced."

COLONIAL HOMES, Hearst Magazines, 1790 Broadway, 14th Floor, New York NY 10019. Fax: (212)586-3455. E-mail: ashanley@hearst.com. Editor: Annette Stramesi. Contact: Audra Shanley, chief copy editor. 20% freelance written. Bimonthly magazine. "*Colonial Homes* is a shelter book that celebrates 17th-, 18th- and 19th-century design, architecture, decorative arts and decorating." Estab. 1975. Circ. 500,000. Pays on publication. Byline given. Buys all rights. Editorial lead time 5 months. Submit seasonal material 6 months in advance. Reports in 2 weeks on queries. Sample copy for #10 SASE. Writer's guidelines free.

Nonfiction: Contact individual department editors. General interest, historical/nostalgic, new product, travel. Buys 2 mss/year. Query with published clips. Length: 500-1,500 words. Pays $500-750. Pays expenses of writers on assignment.

Photos: Send photos with ms. Negotiates payment individually. Identification of subjects required. Buys all rights.

Columns/Departments: Masterworks (craftsperson), 750 words. Buys 2 mss/year. Query. Pays $500-700.

Tips: "We accept few unsolicited story ideas, so the best way to propose an idea is with a detailed outline and snapshots."

COLORADO HOMES & LIFESTYLES, 7009 S. Potomac St., Englewood CO 80112-4029. (303)397-7600. Fax: (303)397-7619. E-mail: emcgraw@winc.usa.com. Contact: Evalyn McGraw, editor. Associate Editor: Heather Prouty. Publisher: Pat Cooley. 50% freelance written. Bimonthly magazine covering Colorado homes and lifestyles for upper-middle-class and high income households as well as designers, decorators and architects. Circ. 35,000. **Pays on acceptance.** Publishes ms an average of 3 months after acceptance. Byline given. Buys all rights. Submit seasonal material 6 months in advance. Reports in 3 months.

● The editor reports that *Colorado Homes & Lifestyles* is doing many more lifestyle articles and needs more unusual and interesting worldwide travel and upbeat health stories in 1998. A recent addition has been profiles of Colorado artisans and craftspeople.

Nonfiction: Fine homes and furnishings, regional interior design trends, interesting personalities and lifestyles, gardening and plants—all with a Colorado slant. Special issues: Rustic Mountain Homes and Lifestyles (people, etc.) (January/February); Great Bathrooms (March/April); Great Kitchens (September/October). Buys 40 mss/year. Send complete ms. Length: 1,000-1,500 words. "For unique, well-researched feature stories, pay is $150-300. For regular departments, $125-175." Sometimes pays the expenses of writers on assignment. Provide sources with phone numbers.

Reprints: Send tearsheet or photocopy of article or typed ms with rights for sale noted and information about when and where the article previously appeared. Pays 35-50% of amount paid for an original article.

Photos: Send photos with ms. Reviews 35mm, 4×5 and 2¼ color transparencies and b&w glossy prints. Identification of subjects required. Title and caption suggestions appreciated. Please include photographic credits.

Fiction: Occasionally publishes novel excerpts.

Tips: "The more interesting and unique the subject the better. A frequent mistake made by writers is failure to provide material with a style and slant appropriate for the magazine, due to poor understanding of the focus of the magazine."

COTTAGE LIFE, Quarto Communications, 111 Queen St. E., Suite 408, Toronto, Ontario M5C 1S2 Canada. (416)360-6880. Fax: (416)360-6814. E-mail: clmag@cottagelife.com. Contact: Ann Vanderhoof, editor. Managing Editor: David Zimmer. 80% freelance written. Bimonthly magazine. "*Cottage Life* is written and designed for the people who own and spend time at waterfront cottages throughout Canada and bordering U.S. states." Estab. 1988. Circ. 70,000. **Pays on acceptance.** Publishes ms 2 months after acceptance. Byline given. Buys first North American serial rights.

Nonfiction: Book excerpts, exposé, historical/nostalgic, how-to, humor, interview/profile, personal experience, photo feature, technical. Buys 90 mss/year. Query with published clips. Length: 150-3,500 words. Pays $100-2,200. Pays $50-1,000 for unsolicited articles. Sometimes pays expenses of writers on assignment. Query first.

Columns/Departments: Cooking, Real Estate, Fishing, Nature, Watersports, Personal Experience and Issues. Length: 150-1,200 words. Query with published clips. Pays $100-750.

‡COUNTRY FOLK ART MAGAZINE, Long Publications, 8393 E. Holly Rd., Holly MI 48442. Editor: Cheryl Anderson. Contact: Managing Editor. Bimonthly magazine "catering to those who have an interest in country decorating, how-to crafts, gardening, recipes, artist profiles." Estab. 1988. Circ. 173,000. **Pays on acceptance**; photography paid on publication. Publishes ms 1 year after acceptance. Byline given. Buys first North American serial rights. Editorial lead time 6 months. Submit seasonal material 1 year in advance. Reports in 2 months. Sample copy and writer's guidelines for 9×12 SASE.

Nonfiction: Historical/nostalgic, how-to craft, interview/profile, photo feature, home decorating. Buys 50-75 mss/year. Query with published clips. Length: 1,200 words. Pays $250. Pays expenses of writers on assignment.

Photos: State availability of photos or send photos with submission. Reviews (2¼×2¼, 4×5, 35mm) transparencies.

Offer $25/photo. Captions, identification of subjects required. Buys one-time rights.
Tips: "Solid writing background is preferred. Be prepared to work with editor for clean, concise copy."

COUNTRY JOURNAL, Cowles Enthusiast Media, 4 High Ridge Park, Stamford CT 06905. (203) 321-1778. Fax: (203) 322-1966. Bimonthly magazine. "*Country Journal* covers homes, tools, and projects, emphasizing craftsmanship, quality, value and usefuness." Estab. 1974. Circ. 154,344.
Nonfiction: "Features also cover gardening, food, health, the natural world, small-scale farming, land conservation, the environment, energy and other issues affecting country life."
Columns/Departments: "Regular departments include Housesmith, Cook's Tour, Perennial Landscape, Vegetable Garden, The Pet Doctor, Portable Workshop." *Writer's Market* recommends sending query with SASE.

COUNTRY LIVING, The Hearst Corp., 224 W. 57th St., New York NY 10019. (212)649-3509. Contact: Marjorie Gage, features editor. Monthly magazine covering home design and interior decorating with an emphasis on 'country' style. "*Country Living* is a lifestyle magazine for readers who appreciate the warmth and traditions associated with American home and family life. Each monthly issue embraces American country decorating and includes features on furniture, antiques, gardening, home building, real estate, cooking, entertaining and travel." Estab. 1978. Circ. 1,816,000.
Nonfiction: Most open to freelancers: antiques articles from authorities, personal essay. Buys 20-30 mss/year. Pay varies. Send complete ms.
Columns/Departments: Most open to freelancers: Kids in the Country, Readers Corner. Pay varies. Send complete ms.

COUNTRY SAMPLER, Sampler Publications, Inc., 707 Kautz Rd., St. Charles IL 60174. (630)377-8000. Fax: (630) 377-8194. Bimonthly magazine. Publisher: Margaret B. Kernan. Bimonthly magazine. "*Country Sampler* is a country decorating magazine and a country product catalog." Estab. 1984. Circ. 525,160.
Nonfiction: "Furniture, accessories and decorative accents created by artisans throughout the country are displayed and offered for purchase directly from the maker. Fully decorated room settings show the readers how to use the items in their homes to achieve the warmth and charm of the country look." Query with SASE.

EARLY AMERICAN HOMES, Enthusiast Media, 6405 Flank Dr., Harrisburg PA 17112. Fax: (717)657-9552. Editor: Mimi Handler. 20% freelance written. Bimonthly magazine for "people who are interested in capturing the warmth and beauty of the 1600 to 1840 period and using it in their homes and lives today. They are interested in antiques, traditional crafts, travel, restoration and collecting." Estab. 1970. Circ. 150,000. Buys worldwide rights. Buys 40 mss/year. **Pays on acceptance.** Publishes ms an average of 1 year after acceptance. Reports in 3 months. Sample copy and writer's guidelines for 9×12 SAE with 4 first-class stamps. Query or submit complete ms with SASE.
  • The editor of this publication is looking for more on architecture, gardens and antiques.
Nonfiction: "Social history (the story of the people, not epic heroes and battles), travel to historic sites, country inns, antiques and reproductions, refinishing and restoration, architecture and decorating. We try to entertain as we inform. While we're always on the lookout for good pieces on any of our subjects. Would like to see more on how real people did something great to their homes." Buys 40 mss/year. Query or submit complete ms. Length: 750-3,000 words. Pays $100-600. Pays expenses of writers on assignment.
Photos: Pays $10 for 5×7 (and up) b&w photos used with mss, minimum of $25 for color. Prefers $2\frac{1}{4} \times 2\frac{1}{4}$ and up, but can work from 35mm.
Tips: "Our readers are eager for ideas on how to bring early America into their lives. Conceive a new approach to satisfy their related interests in arts, crafts, travel to historic sites, and especially in houses decorated in the early American style. Write to entertain and inform at the same time. Be prepared to help us with sources for illustrations."

ELLE DECOR, Hachette Filipacchi, 1633 Broadway, 44th Floor, New York NY 10019. (212)767-5921. (212) 767-5608. Publisher: John Miller. Editor-in-Chief: Marian McEvoy. Bimonthly magazine. "*Elle Decor* showcases the most fashion-forward international designers and their innovative ideas in architecture, home designs and the decorative arts." Estab. 1989. Circ. 432,769.
Nonfiction: "*Elle Decor* provides the latest information on the world's top architects and interior designers, and then follows up with retail resource shopping information." *Writer's Market* recommends sending query with SASE.

FAMILY HANDYMAN, Home Service Publications, Inc., 28 W. 23rd St., New York NY 10010. (212) 366-8686. Publisher: Thomas Witschi. Published 10 times/year. "*Family Handyman* is edited for the homeowner with an active interest in home improvement and remodeling." Estab. 1951. Circ. 1,045,289.
Nonfiction: "Major editorial categories include home remodeling, repair and maintenance, energy efficiency, home furnishings and decorating, yard and garden care. Additional themes include woodworking, auto maintenance, new products and housing. The graphic emphasis is on step-by-step photos and illustrations as well as detailed plans and diagrams." Query with SASE.
Columns/Departments: "Editorial departments include Handy Hints, Ask Handyman, How a House Works, How to Repair, New Products, Workshop Tips, Using Tools, Woodworks, Wordless Workshop." *Writer's Market* recommends sending query with SASE.

FINE GARDENING, Taunton Press, 63 S. Main St., P.O. Box 5506, Newtown CT 06470-5506. (203)426-8171. Fax: (203)426-3434. E-mail: lwhite@taunton.com. Contact: LeeAnne White, editor. Bimonthly "high-value technical magazine on landscape and ornamental gardening. Articles written by avid gardeners—first person, hands-on-gardening experiences." Estab. 1988. Circ. 200,000. **Pays on acceptance.** Publishes ms an average of 6 months after acceptance. Byline given. Buys all rights. Editorial lead time 1 year. Submit seasonal material 1 year in advance. Guidelines free.

Nonfiction: Book review, essays, how-to, opinion, personal experience, photo feature. Buys 60 mss/year. Query. Length: 1,000-3,000 words. Pays $300-1,000. Sometimes pays expenses of writers on assignment.

Photos: Send photos with submission. Reviews 35mm transparencies. Buys serial rights.

Columns/Department: Book, video and software reviews (on gardening); Last Word (essays/serious, humorous, fact or fiction). Query. Length: 250-1,000 words. Buys 30 mss/year. Pays $50-200.

Tips: "It's most important to have solid first-hand experience as a gardener. Tell us what you've done with your own landscape and plants."

‡FINE HOMEBUILDING, The Taunton Press, 63 S. Main St., P.O. Box 5506, Newtown CT 06470-5506. (800) 283-7252. Fax: (203) 270-6751. Contact: Kevin Ireton, editor. "*Fine Homebuilding* is a bimonthly magazine for builders, architects, contractors, owner/builders and others who are seriously involved in building new houses or reviving old ones." Estab. 1981. Circ. 247,712. Pays half on acceptance, half on publication. Publishes ms 1 year after acceptance. Byline given. Offers on acceptance payment as kill fee. Buys first and reprint rights. Reports in 1 month. Writer's guidelines for SASE.

Nonfiction: "We're interested in almost all aspects of home building, from laying out foundations to capping cupolas." Query with outline, description, photographs, sketches and SASE. Pays $150/published page with "a possible bonus on publication for an unusually good manuscript."

Photos: "Take lots of work-in-progress photos. Color print film, ASA 400, from either Kodak or Fuji works best. If you prefer to use slide film, use ASA 100. Keep track of the negatives; we will need them for publication. If you're not sure what to use or how to go about it, feel free to call for advice."

Columns/Departments: Tools & Materials, Reviews, Questions & Answers, Tips & Techniques, Cross Section, What's the Difference?, Finishing Touches, Great Moments. Query with outline, description, photographs, sketches and SASE. Pays $150/published page.

Tips: "Our chief contributors are home builders, architects and other professionals. We're more interested in your point of view and technical expertise than your prose style. Adopt an easy, conversational style and define any obscure terms for non-specialists. We try to visit all our contributors and rarely publish building projects we haven't seen, or authors we haven't met."

FLOWER AND GARDEN MAGAZINE, 700 W. 47th St., Suite 310, Kansas City MO 64112. (816)531-5730. Fax: (816)531-3873. Contact: Doug Hall, editor. 80% freelance written. Works with a small number of new/unpublished writers each year. Bimonthly picture magazine. "*Flower & Garden* focuses on ideas that can be applied to the home garden and outdoor environs, primarily how-to, but also historical and background articles are considered if a specific adaptation can be obviously related to home gardening." Estab. 1957. Circ. 600,000. Buys first-time nonexclusive reprint rights. Byline given. **Pays on acceptance.** Publishes ms an average of 1 year after acceptance. Reports in 2 months. Sample copy for $4.50. Writer's guidelines for #10 SASE.

● The editor tells us good quality photos accompanying articles are more important than ever.

Nonfiction: Interested in illustrated articles on how to do certain types of gardening and descriptive articles about individual plants. Flower arranging, landscape design, house plants and patio gardening are other aspects covered. "The approach we stress is practical (how-to-do-it, what-to-do-it-with). We emphasize plain talk, clarity and economy of words. An article should be tailored for a national audience." Buys 20-30 mss/year. Query. Length: 500-1,000 words. Rates vary depending on quality and kind of material and author's credentials, $200-500.

Reprints: Sometimes accepts previously published articles. Send typed ms with rights for sale noted, including information about when and where the article previously appeared.

Photos: Color slides and transparencies preferred, 35mm and larger but 35mm slides or prints not suitable for cover. Submit cover photos as 2¼ × 2¼ or larger transparencies. An accurate packing list with appropriately labeled photographs and numbered slides with description sheet (including Latin botanical and common names) must accompany submissions. In plant or flower shots, indicate which end is up on each photo. Photos are paid for on publication, $100-200 inside, $300-500 for covers.

Tips: "The prospective author needs good grounding in gardening practice and literature. Offer well-researched and well-written material appropriate to the experience level of our audience. Photographs help sell the story. Describe special qualifications for writing the particular proposed subject."

GARDEN DESIGN, 100 Avenue of the Americas, New York NY 10013. (212)334-1212. E-mail: grdndsgn@aol.com. Executive Editor: Deborah Papier. Contact: Sarah Gray Miller, associate editor. Magazine published 8 times/year devoted to the fine art of garden design. Circ. 325,000. Pays 2 months after acceptance. Byline given. Buys first North American rights. Submit seasonal material 6 months in advance. Sample copy for $5. Writer's guidelines for #10 SASE.

Nonfiction: "We look for literate writing on a wide variety of garden-related topics—art, architecture, food, furniture, decorating, travel, shopping, personalities." Query with outline, published clips and SASE. Length: 800-2,000 words. Sometimes pays expenses of writer or photographer on assignment.

Photos: Submit scouting photos when proposing article on a specific garden.

Tips: "Our greatest need is for extraordinary private gardens. Scouting locations is a valuable service freelancers can perform, by contacting designers and garden clubs in the area, visiting gardens and taking snapshots for our review. All departments of the magazine are open to freelancers. Familiarize yourself with our departments and pitch stories accordingly. Writing should be as stylish as the gardens we feature."

THE HERB COMPANION, Interweave Press, 201 E. Fourth St., Loveland CO 80537-5655. (970)669-7672. Fax: (970)667-8317. E-mail: hc@iwp.ccmail.compuserve.com. Contact: Kathleen Halloran, editor. 80% freelance written. Bimonthly magazine about herbs: culture, history, culinary, crafts and some medicinal use for both experienced and novice herb enthusiasts. Circ. 110,000. Pays on publication. Byline given. Buys first North American serial rights. Editorial lead time 4 months. Reports in 2 months. Query in writing. Sample copy for $4. Guidelines for #10 SASE.
Nonfiction: Practical horticultural, original recipes, historical, how-to, herbal crafts, profiles, helpful hints and book reviews. Submit detailed query or ms. Length: 4 pages or 1,000 words. Typical payment $125/published page.
Photos: Send photos with submission. Transparencies preferred. Returns photos and artwork.
Tips: "New approaches to familiar topics are especially welcome. If you aren't already familiar with the content, style and tone of the magazine, we suggest you read a few issues. Technical accuracy is essential. Please use scientific as well as popular names for plants and cover the subject in depth while avoiding overly academic presentation. Information should be made accessible to the reader, and we find this is best accomplished by writing from direct personal experience where possible and always in an informal style."

HERB QUARTERLY, P.O. Box 689, San Anselmo CA 94960-0689. Fax: (415)455-9541. E-mail: herbquart@aol.com. Publisher: James Keough. Contact: Associate Editor. 80% freelance written. Quarterly magazine for herb enthusiasts. Estab. 1979. Circ. 35,000. Pays on publication. Publishes ms an average of 6 months after acceptance. Buys first North American serial and second (reprint) rights. Query letters recommended. Reports in 2 months. Sample copy for $5 and 9×12 SASE. Writer's guidelines for #10 SASE.
Nonfiction: Gardening (landscaping, herb garden design, propagation, harvesting); medicinal and cosmetic use of herbs; crafts; cooking; historical (folklore, focused piece on particular period—*not* general survey); interview of a famous person involved with herbs or folksy herbalist; personal experience; photo essay ("cover quality" 8×10 b&w or color prints). "We are particularly interested in herb garden design, contemporary or historical." No fiction. Query. Length: 1,000-3,500 words. Pays $75-250.
Tips: "Our best submissions are narrowly focused on herbs with much practical information on cultivation and use for the experienced gardener."

HOME FRONT, The Publisher's Group, P.O. Box 510366, Salt Lake City UT 84151-0366. Fax: (801)322-1098. E-mail: annee@thepublishers.com. Contact: Anne E. Zombro, vice president of publishing. 30% freelance written. Quarterly magazine. "*Home Front* features mid-income approaches to home decorating, building products, gardening, remodeling and cooking." Estab. 1996. Circ. 15,000. Pays on publication. Publishes ms an average of 4 months after acceptance. Byline given. Buys first North American serial and second serial (reprint) rights. Editorial lead time 2 months. Accepts simultaneous submissions. Reports in 1 month on queries; 2 months on mss. Sample copy for $3 and 9×12 SASE. Writer's guidelines for #10 SASE.
Nonfiction: Decorating, new products, remodeling. Buys 8 mss/year. Query with published clips. Length: 1,000-1,300 words. Pays $125-800.
Reprints: Accepts previously published submissions. Pays 50% of amount paid for an original article.
Photos: Send photos with submission. Reviews 4×5 transparencies (preferred), any size prints. Negotiates payment individually. Captions, model releases, identification of subjects required. Buys one-time or all rights.
Columns/Departments: Gardening, Remodeling, Decorating; all 500 words. Buys 6-10 mss/year. Query with published clips. Pays $50-125.

HOMES & COTTAGES, The In-Home Show Ltd., 6557 Mississauga Rd., Suite D, Mississauga, Ontario L5N 1A6 Canada. (905)567-1440. Fax: (905)567-1442. E-mail: jimhc@pathcom.com. Website: http://www.homesandcottages.c om. Editor: Janice Naisby. Contact: Jim Adair, managing editor. 50% freelance written. Magazine published 8 times/ year covering building and renovating; "technically comprehensible articles." Estab. 1987. Circ. 64,000. Pays on publication. Publishes mss average of 2 months after acceptance. Byline given. Offers 10% kill fee. Buys first North American serial rights. Editorial lead time 3 months. Submit seasonal material 3 months in advance. Sample copy for SAE. Writer's guidelines free.
Nonfiction: Humor (building and renovation related), new product, technical. Buys 32 mss/year. Query. Length: 1,000-2,000 words. Pays $300-750. Sometimes pays expenses of writers on assignment.
Photos: Send photos with submission. Reviews transparencies and prints. Negotiates payment individually. Captions and identification of subjects required. Buys one-time rights.

‡HORTICULTURE, The Magazine of American Gardening, 98 N. Washington St., Boston MA 02114. (617)742-5600. Fax: (617) 367-6364. Contact: Thomas Fischer, executive editor. Magazine published 10 times/year. "*Horticulture*, the country's oldest gardening magazine, is designed for active amateur gardeners. Our goal is to offer a blend of text, photographs and illustrations that will both instruct and inspire readers." Circ. 340,000. Byline given. Offers kill fee. Buys one-time or first North American serial rights. Submit seasonal material 10 months in advance. Reports in 3 months. Writer's guidelines for SASE.
Nonfiction: "We look for an encouraging personal experience, anecdote and opinion. At the same time, a thorough article should to some degree place its subject in the broader context of horticulture." Buys 15 mss/year. Query with

published clips, subject background material and SASE. Include disk where possible. Length: 1,500-3,500 words. Pays $600-1,000. Pays expenses of writers on assignment if previously arranged with editor.

Columns/Departments: Query with published clips, subject background material and SASE. Include disk where possible. Length: 1,000-1,500 words. Pays $50-600.

Tips: "We believe every article must offer ideas or illustrate principles that our readers might apply on their own gardens. No matter what the subject, we want our readers to become better, more creative gardeners."

HOUSE BEAUTIFUL, The Hearst Corp., 1700 Broadway, New York NY 10019-5905. (212)903-5100. Fax: (212)586-3439. Publisher: Jeffrey I. Burch. Editor: Margaret Kennedy. Monthly magazine covering home design and interior decorating. "*House Beautiful*'s editorial encompasses the world of decorating and design. Editorial includes home furnishing, design, architecture, remodeling, travel, food, entertaining and gardening features." Estab. 1896. Circ. 973,000. This magazine did not respond to our request for information. Query with SASE before submitting.

IN STYLE, Celebrity + Lifestyle + Beauty + Fashion, Time Inc., Rockefeller Center, New York NY 10020. (212)522-1212. Fax:(212)522-3684. Publisher: Ann W. Jackson. Monthly. "*In Style* is a guide to the lives and lifestyles of the world's fascinating people. The magazine covers the private side of public faces and the expression of personal style—the choices people make about their homes, their clothes, their pastimes and passions. With photos and features, it opens the door to celebrities' homes, families, parties, weddings, and charity events, offering ideas about beauty and fashion, fitness and entertaining." Estab. 1994. Circ. 950,680. This magazine did not respond to our request for information. Query before submitting.

ISLAND HOME MAGAZINE, The Showcase of Island Architecture, Design & Lifestyle, Island Productions, Inc., 6490 S. McCarran Blvd., Suite 30, Reno NV 89509. (702)826-2044. Fax: (702)826-1971. Contact: Editorial Department. 30% freelance written. Bimonthly magazine. "We have lavishly illustrated articles about architecture and interior design of island homes around the world from Hawaii and the South Pacific to Caribbean, Mediterranean, etc. Also travel features about international world-class destinations, island dining around the world, art and culture (both islands and other places), plus designer fashions, fine wines, expensive yachts, automobiles, planes, etc. Our readership is decidedly upscale, with about half of our readership in Hawaii, a large share on the West Coast of the U.S. mainland and the rest scattered across the U.S. and in several foreign countries." Estab. 1990. Circ. 30,000. Pays within 30 days after publication. Byline given. Kill fee negotiable. Buys one-time rights. Editorial lead time 4 months. Submit seasonal material 6 months in advance. Reports in 2 months. Sample copy for 10 × 13 SAE with 10 first-class stamps. Writer's guidelines for #10 SASE.

Nonfiction: Travel, island dining features, island home features (focus on architecture and design as well as location), island artist features. "Our annual golf issue is every June, in which we feature homes, restaurants and travel destinations with a golf or golf course focus. No articles that do not fall into our categories, which are Private Places, Interiors, Dining, Travel and Art & Culture. Nothing else will be considered as our categories do not change." Buys 3-4 mss/year from new freelancers; the rest are from existing pool of freelance writers. Query with published clips. Length: 1,200-1,500 words. Pays 20¢/word.

Reprints: Accepts previously published submissions.

Photos: State availability of photos or send photos with submission—preferable. No additional payment for photos with articles. Reviews contact sheets, 2¼ × 2¼ and 4 × 5 transparencies and 8 × 10 prints. Captions required—after acceptance only. Buys one-time rights.

KITCHEN GARDEN: Growing and Cooking Great Food, The Taunton Press, 63 S. Main St., Newtown CT 06470. (203)426-8171. Fax: (203)426-3434. E-mail: kg@taunton.com. Website: http://www.taunton.com. Contact: Mary Morgan, editor. 90% freelance written. Bimonthly magazine covering vegetable gardening for both expert and novice home gardeners and cooks. Estab. 1996. Circ. 100,000. **Pays on acceptance.** Publishes ms an average of 6 months after acceptance. Byline given. Kill fee negotiated. Buys all rights. Editorial lead time 1 year. Submit seasonal material 1 year in advance. Reports in 1 month. Writer's guidelines free.

Nonfiction: How-to. Regular features include Plant Profiles (in-depth coverage of vegetable, fruit or herb); Kitchen Talk (1-3 sidebar recipes featuring profiled plant); Garden Profiles (tours of beautiful, striking or unusual kitchen gardens); basic and advanced Techniques; Design; Projects (things to build and do); and Cooking (as distinct from Kitchen Talk, focuses entirely on cooking). Buys 60 mss/year. Query by letter, phone or e-mail. Length: 1,000-3,000 words. Pays $300-1,000. Sometimes pays expenses of writer on assignment.

Photos: Send photos with submission. Reviews contact sheets, negatives, transparencies, prints. Negotiates payment individually. Identification of subjects required. Buys all rights.

Columns/Departments: Reviews (books, software), 500 words. Buys 30 mss/year. Query with published clips. Pays $50-200.

Tips: "Our articles are written in the first-person by people with first-hand experience who have something of substance to say. While we are happy to find accomplished writers who also have significant gardening or cooking expertise, the expertise is more important than the writing skills. Our editors work very closely with authors throughout the process of generating a story, and they are very good at working with words, as well as with gardeners, so first-time authors should not be deterred."

"In most cases, an editor visits the author before an article is definitely assigned. This is so scouting photographs can be taken and the editor can get to know the author, which facilitates developing an outline and then the story. It is important that our authors grow the plants about which they write, and that their gardens be suitable for photographing for the magazine."

LOG HOME LIVING, Home Buyer Publications Inc., 4200-T Lafayette Center Dr., Chantilly VA 20151. (703)222-9411. Fax: (703)222-3209. Website: http://www.loghomeliving.com. Editor: John Kupferer. Contact: Janice Brewster, executive editor. 50% freelance written. Monthly magazine for enthusiasts who are dreaming of, planning for, or actively building a log home. Estab. 1989. Circ. 132,000. **Pays on acceptance.** Publishes ms about 6 months after acceptance. Byline given. $100 kill fee. Buys first or second serial (reprint) rights. Editorial lead time 6 months. Submit seasonal material 6 months in advance. Reports in 6 weeks. Sample copy $3.50. Guidelines for #10 SASE.
Nonfiction: Book excerpts, how-to (build or maintain log home), interview/profile (log home owners), personal experience, photo feature (log homes), technical (design/decor topics), travel. "We do not want historical/nostalgic material." Buys 6 mss/year. Query. Length: 1,000-2,000 words. Pays $250-500. Pays expenses of writers on assignment.
Reprints: Send tearsheet of article and information about when and where the article previously appeared. Pays 50% of amount paid for an original article.
Photos: State availability of photos with submission. Reviews contact sheets, 4×5 transparencies and 4×6 prints. Negotiates payment individually. Buys one-time rights.

METROPOLITAN HOME, Hachette Filipacchi Inc., 1633 Broadway, New York NY 10019. (212)767-5522. Fax: (212)767-5636. E-mail: metedit1@aol.com. Articles Director: Michael Lassell. Bimonthly magazine covering "home design, home furnishings, fashion, food, wines and spirits, entertaining and electronics with an editorial focus on the art of living well. It is edited for quality-conscious young adults and contains news and guidance toward achieving personal style." Estab. 1969. Circ. 632,000. **Pays on acceptance.** Byline given. Offers 25% kill fee. Buy first North American serial rights with (negotiable) additional fee for electronic rights. Reports in 1-2 months on queries.
• Ranked as one of the best markets for freelance writers in *Writer's Yearbook*'s annual "Top 100 Markets," January 1997.
Nonfiction: Needs home-related lifestyle stories for sophisticated audience; full of accessible ideas; written from expert view. No how-to stories. Buys 8-12 mss/year. Query with published clips. Length: 1,000-2,000 words. Pays $1,000-2,000. Pays expenses of writers on assignment.
Columns/Departments: 800-1,500 words. Buys 10-20 mss/year. Query with published clips. Pays $750-1,800.
Tips: "We use only experienced writers or experts who know their subject—interior design and home style. We're on the cutting edge of home style."

MIDWEST LIVING, A Meredith Corporation Publication, 1716 Locust St., Des Moines IA 50309-3023. (515)284-2912. Fax:(515)284-2877. Publisher: Matt Petersen. Bimonthly magazine. "*Midwest Living* is a regional service magazine that celebrates the interests, values, and lifestyles of Midwestern families. It provides region-specific information on travel and events, food and dining, and home and garden." Estab. 1986. Circ. 24,349. This magazine did not respond to our request for information. Query before submitting.

‡MOUNTAIN LIVING, Wiesner Publishing, 7009 S. Potomac St., Englewood CO 80112. (303)397-7600. Fax: (303)397-7619. E-mail: rgriggs@winc.usa.com. Contact: Robyn Griggs, editor. 90% freelance written. Bimonthly magazine covering "shelter and lifestyle issues for people who live in, visit or hope to live in the mountains." Estab. 1994. Circ. 35,000. **Pays on acceptance.** Publishes ms an average of 4 months after acceptance. Byline given. Offers 15% kill fee. Buys first North American serial or second serial (reprint) rights. Editorial lead time 6 months. Submit seasonal material 6 months in advance. Accepts simultaneous submissions. Reports in 6 weeks on queries; 2 months on mss. Sample copy for $3.95. Writer's guidelines for #10 SASE.
Nonfiction: Book excerpts, essays, historical/nostalgic, interview/profile, personal experience, photo feature, travel, home features. Buys 30 mss/year. Query with published clips. Length: 1,200-2,000 words. Pays $75-400. Sometimes pays expenses of writers on assignment.
Reprints: Send photocopy of article or typed ms with rights for sale noted. Payment varies.
Photos: State availability of photos with submission. Negotiates payment individually. Buys one-time rights.
Columns/Departments: Architecture, Gardening, Sporting Life, Travel, History, Health, Cuisine. Buys 35 mss/year. Query with published clips. Length: 300-1,500 words. Pays $75-300.
Tips: "A deep understanding of and respect for the mountain environment is essential. Think out of the box. We love to be surprised. And always send clips."

NATIONAL GARDENING, National Gardening Association, 180 Flynn Ave., Burlington VT 05401. (802)863-1308. Fax: (802)863-5962. Contact: Michael MacCaskey, editor. Managing Editor: Eileen Murray. 80% freelance written. Willing to work with new/unpublished writers. Bimonthly magazine covering all aspects of food gardening and ornamentals. "We publish not only how-to garden techniques, but also news that affects home gardeners, like breeding advancements and new variety releases. Detailed, experienced-based articles with carefully worked-out techniques for planting, growing, harvesting and using garden fruits and vegetables sought as well as profiles of expert gardeners in this country's many growing regions. Our material is for both experienced and beginning gardeners." Estab. 1979. Circ. 250,000. **Pays on acceptance.** Publishes ms an average of 9 months after acceptance. Byline given. Buys first serial and occasionally second (reprint) rights. Reports in 2 months. Sample copy for $3. Writer's guidelines for #10 SASE.
Nonfiction: How-to, humor, interview/profile, pest profiles, opinion, personal experience, recipes. Buys 50-60 mss/

year. Query first. Length: 500-2,500 words. Pays 25¢/word. Sometimes pays expenses of writers on assignment with prior approval.
Photos: Dan Hickey, managing editor. Send photos with ms. Pays $20-40 for b&w photos; $50 for color slides. Captions, model releases and identification of subjects required.
Tips: "Take the time to study the style of the magazine—the focus of the features and the various departments. Keep in mind that you'll be addressing a national audience."

ORGANIC GARDENING, Rodale Press, 33 E. Minor, Emmaus PA 18098. (610)967-5171. Managing Editor: Vicki Mattern. 30% freelance written. Magazine published 9 times/year. "*Organic Gardening* is for gardeners who garden, who enjoy gardening as an integral part of a healthy lifestyle. Editorial shows readers how to grow anything they choose without chemicals. Editorial details how to grow vegetables, flowers, herbs and fruit, and provides information on soil building, pest control, regional tips and outdoor power equipment use." Circ. 800,879. Pays between acceptance and publication. Buys all rights. Reports in 2 months on queries; 1 month on mss.
Nonfiction: "Our title says it all." Query with published clips and outline. Pays up to 50¢/word.

PLANT & GARDEN, Canada's Practical Gardening Magazine, Helpard Publishing, Inc., 1200 Markham Rd., Suite 300, Scarborough, Ontario M1H 3C3 Canada. (416)438-7777. Fax: (416)438-5333. Contact: Mr. Lynn Helpard. 95% freelance written. Magazine published 5 times/year covering gardening in Canada. "*Plant & Garden* is a *practical* gardening magazine focusing on how-to, step-by-step type articles on all aspects of garden and houseplant care. Readers are both novice and experienced Canadian gardeners." Estab. 1988. Circ. 36,000. Pays on publication. Publishes ms 4 months after acceptance. Byline given. Offers 50% kill fee. Buys first North American serial rights. Editorial lead time 4 months. Submit seasonal material 4 months in advance. Accepts simultaneous submissions. Reports in 2 months. Sample copy for $4 and 9 × 12 SAE. Writer's guidelines for SAE and IRC or, preferably, SAE with sufficient Canadian postage affixed.
Nonfiction: Historical/nostalgic, how-to, humor, interview/profile, new product, personal experience—garden-related topics only. Buys 60 mss/year. Query with published clips. Length: 600-1,800 words. Pays $75 minimum (600 words). Sometimes pays expenses of writers on assignment.
Photos: Send photos with submission. Reviews negatives and 4 × 5 transparencies. Offers no additional payment for photos accepted with ms. Captions required. Buys one-time rights. Illustrations are usually commissioned.
Columns/Departments: Profile (profiles of gardens and/or gardeners); Hydroponics (how-to for home gardener); Environment; Down to Earth (humor/essay on gardening); Herb Garden (herb profiles). Length: 600-800 words. Buys 16 mss/year. Query with published clips. Pays $75-150.
Tips: "Please be knowledgeable about gardening—not just a freelance writer. Be accurate and focus on plants/techniques that are appropriate to Canada. Be as down to earth as possible. We want good quality writing and interesting subject matter. Areas most open to freelancers are Down to Earth, Profile and Environment. We are especially looking for garden profiles from outside Ontario and Quebec. All submitted materials must be accompanied by a SAE with sufficient Canadian postage affixed to ensure return."

SAN DIEGO HOME/GARDEN LIFESTYLES, Mckinnon Enterprises, Box 719001, San Diego CA 92171-9001. (714)233-4567. Fax: (619)571-1889. Contact: Wayne Carlson, editor. Senior Editor: Phyllis Van Doren. 50% freelance written. Monthly magazine covering homes, gardens, food, intriguing people, real estate, art, culture, and local travel for residents of San Diego city and county. Estab. 1979. Circ. 45,000. Pays on publication. Publishes ms an average of 3 months after acceptance. Byline given. Buys first North American serial rights only. Submit seasonal material 3 months in advance. Reports in 3 months. Sample copy for $4.
Nonfiction: Residential architecture and interior design (San Diego-area homes only); remodeling (must be well-designed—little do-it-yourself); residential landscape design; furniture; other features oriented towards upscale readers interested in living the cultured good life in San Diego. Articles must have local angle. Query with published clips. Length: 700-2,000 words. Pays $50-350.
Tips: "No out-of-town, out-of-state subject material. Most freelance work is accepted from local writers. Gear stories to the unique quality of San Diego. We try to offer only information unique to San Diego—people, places, shops, resources, etc. We plan more food and entertaining-at-home articles and more articles on garden products. We also need more in-depth reports on major architecture, environmental, and social aspects of life in San Diego and the border area."

‡SNOW COUNTRY, 5520 Park Ave., Trumbull CT 06611-0395. E-mail: sceditors@aol.com. Editor: Roger Toll. Published 8 times/year for people who love the mountains, whether they live or visit there. Circ. 481,251. **Pays on acceptance**. Byline given. Offers 40-60% kill fee. Buys first rights. Accepts simultaneous submissions. Reports in 2 months. Sample copy for $3 plus SASE. Writer's guidelines for #10 SASE.
Nonfiction: "We need articles that educate, inform or entertain. Whether in a first-person feature or a straightforward service article, we're interested in colorful quotes, unexpected anecdotes and engaging material that not only imparts information but also paints a colorful picture for readers." Buys 20 mss/year. Query with clips. Length: 2,500-3,500 words. Pays 80¢-$1/word.
Columns/Departments: Buys 50 mss/year. Query with published clips. Pays 80¢-$1/word. Length: 1,000-1,800 words.
Fillers: Length: 800 words. Pays 80¢-$1/word.
Tips: "It's critical that an article be carefully researched and accurate. We don't have a fact-checker to catch mistakes,

so we insist that writers verify their own work."

SOUTHERN ACCENTS, Southern Progress Corp., 2100 Lakeshore Dr., Birmingham AL 35209. (205) 877-6000. Contact: Kathleen Pearson, editor. "*Southern Accents* celebrates the best of the South." Estab. 1977. Circ. 318,657. **Nonfiction:** "Each issue features the finest homes and gardens along with a balance of features that reflect the affluent lifestyles of its readers, including architecture, antiques, entertaining, collecting and travel." *Writer's Market* recommends sending query with SASE.

TEXAS GARDENER, The Magazine for Texas Gardeners, by Texas Gardeners, Suntex Communications, Inc., P.O. Box 9005, Waco TX 76714-9005. (817)772-1270. E-mail: suntex@calph.com. Editor: Chris S. Corby. Contact: Vivian Whatley, managing editor. 80% freelance written. Works with a small number of new/unpublished writers each year. Bimonthly magazine covering vegetable and fruit production, ornamentals and home landscape information for home gardeners in Texas. Estab. 1981. Circ. 30,000. Pays on publication. Publishes ms an average of 4 months after acceptance. Byline given. Buys first North American serial and all rights. Submit seasonal material 6 months in advance. Reports in 2 months. Sample copy for $2.75 and SAE with 5 first-class stamps. Guidelines for #10 SASE.
Nonfiction: How-to, humor, interview/profile, photo feature. "We use feature articles that relate to Texas gardeners. We also like personality profiles on hobby gardeners and professional horticulturists who are doing something unique." Buys 50-100 mss/year. Query with clips of published work. Length: 800-2,400 words. Pays $50-200.
Photos: "We prefer superb color and b&w photos; 90% of photos used are color." Send photos. Pays negotiable rates for 2¼ or 35mm color transparencies and 8×10 b&w prints and contact sheets. Model release and identification of subjects required.
Tips: "First, be a Texan. Then come up with a good idea of interest to home gardeners in this state. Be specific. Stick to feature topics like 'How Alley Gardening Became a Texas Tradition.' Leave topics like 'How to Control Fire Blight' to the experts. High quality photos could make the difference. We would like to add several writers to our group of regular contributors and would make assignments on a regular basis. Fillers are easy to come up with in-house. We want good writers who can produce accurate and interesting copy. Frequent mistakes made by writers in completing an article assignment for us are that articles are not slanted toward Texas gardening, show inaccurate or too little gardening information or lack good writing style. We will be doing more 'people' features and articles on ornamentals."

TODAY'S HOMEOWNER, (formerly *Home Mechanix*), 2 Park Ave., New York NY 10016. (212)779-5000. Fax: (212)725-3281. Website: http://www.homideas.com. Editor: Michael Chotiner. Contact: Alan Kearney. 50% freelance written. Prefers to work with published/established writers. "If it's good, and it fits the type of material we're currently publishing, we're interested, whether writer is new or experienced." Magazine published 10 times/year for the active home and car owner. "Articles emphasize an active, home-oriented lifestyle. Includes information useful for maintenance, repair and renovation to the home and family car. Information on how to buy, how to select products useful to homeowners/car owners. Emphasis in home-oriented articles is on good design, inventive solutions to styling and space problems, useful home-workshop projects." Estab. 1928. Circ. 1,000,000. **Pays on acceptance.** Publishes ms an average of 6 months after acceptance. Byline given. Buys first North American serial rights. Reports in 3 months. Query.
Nonfiction: Feature articles relating to homeowner/car owner, 1,500-2,500 words. "This may include personal home-renovation projects, professional advice on interior design, reports on different or unusual construction methods, energy-related subjects, outdoor/backyard projects, etc. No high-tech subjects such as aerospace, electronics, photography or military hardware. Most of our automotive features are written by experts in the field, but fillers, tips, how-to repair, or modification articles on the family car are welcome. Articles on construction, tool use, refinishing techniques, etc., are also sought. Pays $300 minimum for features; fees based on number of printed pages, photos accompanying mss., etc." Query only; *no unsolicited mss*. Pays expenses of writers on assignment.
Photos: Photos should accompany mss. Pays $600 and up for transparencies for cover. Inside color: $300/1 page, $500/2, $700/3, etc. Captions and model releases required.
Tips: "The most frequent mistake made by writers in completing an article assignment for *Home Mechanix* is not taking the time to understand its editorial focus and special needs."

HUMOR

Publications listed here specialize in gaglines or prose humor, some for readers and others for performers or speakers. Other publications that use humor can be found in nearly every category in this book. Some have special needs for major humor pieces; some use humor as fillers; many others are interested in material that meets their ordinary fiction or nonfiction requirements but also has a humorous slant. The majority of humor articles must be submitted as complete manuscripts on speculation because editors usually can't know from a query whether or not the piece will be right for them.

FUNNY TIMES, A Monthly Humor Review, Funny Times, Inc., P.O. Box 18530, Cleveland Heights OH 44118. (216)371-8600. Fax: (216)371-8696. E-mail: ft@funnytimes.com. Website: http://www.funnytimes.com. Editors: Raymond Lesser, Susan Wolpert. 10% freelance written. Monthly tabloid for humor. "*Funny Times* is a monthly review of America's funniest cartoonists and writers. We are the *Reader's Digest* of modern American humor with a progressive/ peace-oriented/environmental/politically activist slant." Estab. 1985. Circ. 50,000. Pays on publication. Publishes ms an average of 3 months after acceptance. Byline given. Buys one-time or second serial (reprint) rights. Editorial lead time 2 months. Accepts simultaneous submissions. Reports in 3 months on mss. Sample copy for $3 or 9×12 SAE with 4 first-class stamps. Writer's guidelines for #10 SASE.

Nonfiction: Essays (funny), humor, interview/profile, opinion (humorous), personal experience (absolutely funny). "We only publish humor or interviews with funny people (comedians, comic actors, cartoonists, etc.). Everything we publish is very funny. If your piece isn't extremely funny then don't bother to send it. Don't send us anything that's not outrageously funny. Don't send anything other people haven't read and told you they laughed so hard they peed their pants." Buys 36 mss/year. Send complete ms. Length: 1,000 words. Pays $50 minimum for unsolicited articles.

Reprints: Accepts previously published submissions.

Fiction: Humorous. Buys 6 mss/year. Query with published clips. Length: 500 words. Pays $50-150.

Fillers: Short humor. Buys 6/year. Pays $20.

Tips: "Send us a small packet (1-3 items) of only your very funniest stuff. If this makes us laugh we'll be glad to ask for more. We particularly welcome previously published material that has been well-received elsewhere."

LATEST JOKES, P.O. Box 23304, Brooklyn NY 11202-0066. (718)855-5057. Contact: Robert Makinson, editor. Estab. 1974. 20% freelance written. Bimonthly newsletter of humor for TV and radio personalities, comedians and professional speakers. **Pays on acceptance.** Byline given. Buys all rights. Submit seasonal material 3 months in advance. Reports in 2 months. Sample copy for $3 and SASE.

• The editor says jokes for public speakers are most needed.

Nonfiction: Humor (short jokes). "No way-out, vulgar humor. Jokes about human tragedy also unwelcome." Send up to 20 jokes with SASE. Pays $1-3/joke.

Tips: "No famous personality jokes. Clever statements are not enough. Be original and surprising. Our emphasis is on jokes for professional speakers."

MAD MAGAZINE, 1700 Broadway, New York NY 10019. (212)506-4850. Contact: Nick Meglin, John Ficarra, editors. 100% freelance written. Monthly magazine "always on the lookout for new ways to spoof and to poke fun at hot trends." Estab. 1952. Circ. 1,000,000. **Pays on acceptance.** Publishes ms an average of 6 months after acceptance. Byline given. Buys all rights. Submit seasonal material 6 months in advance. Reports in 10 weeks. Writer's guidelines for #10 SASE.

Nonfiction: Satire, parody. "We're *not* interested in formats we're already doing or have done to death like 'what they say and what they really mean.'" Buys 400 mss/year. "Submit a premise with three or four examples of how you intend to carry it through, describing the action and visual content. Rough sketches not necessary. One-page gags: two to eight panel cartoon continuities at minimum very funny, maximum hilarious!" Pays minimum of $400/*MAD* page. "*Don't* send previously published submissions, riddles, advice columns, TV or movie satires, book manuscripts, top ten lists, articles about Alfred E. Neuman, poetry, essays, short stories or other text pieces."

Tips: "Have fun! Remember to think visually! Surprise us! Freelancers can best break in with nontopical material. Include SASE with each submission. Originality is prized. We like outrageous, silly and/or satirical humor."

NEW HUMOR MAGAZINE, Savaria Jr./Tschanz Publishers, P.O. Box 216, Lafayette Hill PA 19444. Fax: (215)487-2640. E-mail: newhumor@aol.com. Contact: Edward Savaria Jr., editor-in-chief. Managing Editor: Suzanne Tschanz. 90% freelance written. Bimonthly magazine covering humor. "Tasteful, intelligent and funny. Looking for clean humor in a sense that funny stories, jokes, poems and cartoons do not have to sink to sexist, bathroom or ethnic subjects to be humorous." Estab. 1994. Circ. 9,500. Pays on publication. Publishes ms an average of 4 months after acceptance. Byline given. Buys first North American serial, second serial (reprint) or simultaneous rights. Editorial lead time 4 months. Submit seasonal material 4 months in advance. Accepts simultaneous submissions. Reports in 1 month on queries. Sample copy for $3.50. Writer's guidelines for #10 SASE.

Nonfiction: Book excerpts, essays, humor, interview/profile, new product (humorous), travel. Buys 12 mss/year. Send complete ms. Length: 250-1,000 words. Pays $25-100.

Reprints: Send photocopy of article or short story or typed ms with rights for sale noted. Pays same amount paid for an original article.

Columns/Departments: Open to Column Ideas, 250-750 words. Pays $25-100.

Fiction: Humorous. Buys 40 mss/year. Send complete ms. Length: 25-1,500 words. Pays $25-100.

Poetry: Avant-garde, free verse, haiku, light verse. Buys 30 poems/year. Submit maximum 10 poems. Length: 1-50 lines. Pays $7-30.

Fillers: Anecdotes, short humor. Buys 20/year. Length: 25-300 words. Pays $15-65.

Tips: "If you think it's funny—it might be. Test stories on friends, see if they laugh. Don't be afraid to send odd humor—something completely different."

INFLIGHT

Most major inflight magazines cater to business travelers and vacationers who will be reading, during the flight, about the airline's destinations and other items of general interest.

ABOARD MAGAZINE, 100 Almeria, Suite 220, Coral Gables FL 33134. Fax: (305)441-9739. Editor: Robert Casin. Contact: Lillian Calderón, traffic coordinator. 40% freelance written. Bimonthly bilingual inflight magazine designed to reach travelers to and from Latin America, carried on 11 major Latin-American airlines. Estab. 1976. Circ. 180,000. Pays on publication. Byline given. Buys one-time or simultaneous rights. Accepts simultaneous submissions. Reports in 2 months.
Nonfiction: General interest, new product, business, science, art, fashion, photo feature, technical, travel. "No controversial or political material." Query with SASE. Buys 50 mss/year. Length: 1,200-1,500 words. Pays $100-150.
Reprints: Send photocopy of article or typed ms with rights for sale noted and information about when and where the article previously appeared. Pays 50% of amount paid for an original article.
Photos: Send photos with submission. Reviews 35mm slides or transparencies only. Offers no additional payment for photos accepted with ms. Offers $20/photo minimum. Identification of subjects required. Buys one-time rights.
Fillers: Facts. Buys 6/year. Length: 800-1,200 words. Pays $100.
Tips: "Send article with photos. We need lots of travel material on Chile, Ecuador, Bolivia, El Salvador, Honduras, Guatemala, Uruguay, Nicaragua, Paraguay, Brazil."

‡ABOVE & BEYOND, The Magazine of the North, Above & Beyond Ltd., Box 2348, Yellowknife, Northwest Territory X1A 2P7 Canada. (403)873-2299. Fax: (403)873-2295. E-mail: abeyond@internorth.com. Contact: Annelies Pool, editor. 100% freelance written. Quarterly inflight magazine for First Air, Canada's 3rd largest airline serving Northern Canada. Estab. 1988. Circ. 30,000. Pays on publication. Publishes ms an average of 4 months after acceptance. Byline given. Offers 50% kill fee. Buys first North American serial rights. Editorial lead time 8 months. Submit seasonal material 1 year in advance. Sample copy and writer's guidelines free.
Nonfiction: General interest, historical/nostalgic, humor, interview/profile, personal experience, photo feature, travel. "We are interested in feature articles pertaining to: political, social and economic activities from a northern perspective; outdoor and recreational activities; profile pieces on northern individuals, communities and destinations; wildlife, fishing and hunting; travel features. We don't want articles about new products being used in the North or any articles that don't concern the North." Buys 20 mss/year. Send complete ms. Length: 1,000-1,500 words. Pays $300. Sometimes pays expenses of writers on assignment.
Photos: Send photos with submission. Reviews color transparencies and prints. Pays $25/photo. Captions, identification of subjects required. Buys one-time rights.
Tips: "Submit clean, insightful articles about life in the North within our length requirements. Much of our readership is in Northern Canada so we don't want any 'Gee, whiz, aren't things different in the North' articles."

AMERICA WEST AIRLINES MAGAZINE, Skyword Marketing, Inc., 4636 E. Elwood St., Suite 5, Phoenix AZ 85040-1963. (602)997-7200. Contact: Michael Derr, editor. 60% freelance written. Works with small number of new/unpublished writers each year. Monthly general interest inflight magazine covering destinations served by the airline. "We look for unconventional, newsworthy, compelling subject matter." Estab. 1986. Pays on publication. Publishes ms an average of 4 months after acceptance. Byline given. Offers 15% kill fee. Buys first North American rights. Submit seasonal material 8 months in advance. Accepts simultaneous submissions, if so noted. Reports in 1 month on queries; 5 weeks on mss. Sample copy for $3. Writer's guidelines for 9×12 SAE with 3 first-class stamps.
   ● *America West* is not accepting unsolicited queries or manuscripts at this time.
Nonfiction: General interest, adventure, profile, photo feature, science, sports, business, entrepreneurs, nature, arts, travel, trends. Also considers essays and humor. No puzzles, reviews or highly controversial features. Buys 130-140 mss/year. Length: 300-2,200. Pays $150-900. Pays some expenses.
Photos: State availability of original photography. Offers $50-250/photo. Captions, model releases and identification of subjects required. Buys one-time rights.

AMERICAN WAY, P.O. Box 619640, Dallas/Fort Worth Airport TX 75261-9640. (817)967-1804. Fax: (817)967-1571. Editor-in-Chief: John H. Ostdick. Managing Editor: Elaine Srnka. 98% freelance written. Works exclusively with published/established writers. Biweekly inflight magazine for passengers flying with American Airlines. Estab. 1966. **Pays on acceptance.** Publishes ms an average of 4 months after acceptance. Buys first serial rights. Reports in 5 months.
   ● *American Way* is only accepting fiction queries now.
Fiction: Chuck Thompson, senior editor. Length: 2,500 words maximum. Pays $1,100.

‡THE AUSTRALIAN WAY, Qantas Inflight Magazine, BRW Media, G.P.O. Box 55A, Melbourne, Victoria 3000 Australia. Fax: (03)96420852. E-mail: brwmedia@brw.com.an. (attn: Mike Dobbie). Editor: Mike Dobbie. 80% freelance written. Monthly magazine catering to Qantas Airways passengers travelling on both internal Australian routes and overseas. It provides articles on international events, travel, the arts, science and technology, sport, natural history and humor. The focus is on elegant writing and high-quality photography. There is a heavy emphasis on Australian personalities, culture and lifestyle." Estab. 1993. Circ. 1,600,000. Pays on publication. Publishes ms an average of 3 months after acceptance. Byline given. Buys first rights. Editorial lead time 3 months. Submit seasonal material 4 months in advance.
Nonfiction: General interest, historical/nostalgic, interview/profile, photo feature, travel. Query with published clips. Buys 200 mss/year. Length: 800-1,500 words. Pays $500 (Australian) assigned articles.

Fiction: Publishes novel excerpts (Australian authors only).

Photos: State availability of photos with submission. Reviews transparencies and prints. Negotiates payment individually. Captions, identification of subjects required. Buys all rights if commissioned; one-time rights if unsolicited.

Tips: "Guidelines for writers available on request. Writers should entertain as well as inform both an Australian and international readership. Features can be of general interest, about personalities, or on cultural, business or sporting interests. The magazine tends to avoid travel 'destination' pieces *per se*, though it carries appropriate stories that use these locations as backdrops."

‡CONTINENTAL, The Magazine of Continental Airlines, (formerly *Profiles*), Cadmus Custom Publishing, 101 Huntington Ave., 13th Floor, Boston MA 02199. (617)424-7700. Fax: (617)424-8905. Website: http://www.cadmuscustom.com. Editor: Anne Studabaker. Managing Editor: Heather Sargent. Contact: Tony Bogar, executive editor. 80% freelance written. Monthly magazine "for a business traveler audience. We look for the person behind the company." Estab. 1986. Circ. 350,000. Pays 30 days from invoice. Publishes ms 3 months after acceptance. Byline given. Offers 25% kill fee. Buys first rights. Editorial lead time 6 months. Submit seasonal material 6 months in advance. Reports in 1 month on queries. Sample copy and writer's guidelines free.

Nonfiction: Business executives, destinations, entertainers and athletes, luxuries, social and political leaders. Buys 45 mss/year. Query with published clips. Length: 300-1,500 words. Pays $1/word, but occasionally varies. Pays expenses of writers on assignment.

Reprints: Send photocopy of article and information about when and where the article previously appeared. Pays 25% of amount paid for an original article.

Photos: State availability of photos with submission. Reviews transparencies. Negotiates payment individually.

Columns/Departments: Gusto (food and culture); Golf; Executive Edge (products and services for the regular traveler); Personal Business (human side of business); Mind of the Manager (issues); Reviews in Brief (books, software and websites); Fun (crosswords, games and cartoons). Buys 60 mss/year.

FANTASTIC FLYER MAGAZINE, Two Roads Publishing for Delta Air Line, 3060 Peachtree St. NW, Suite 500, Atlanta GA 30305. (404)364-8684. Fax: (404)262-0300. Editor: Vicky Favorite. 50% freelance written. Quarterly magazine covering travel for children. "Children want to read about children. We educate and entertain interactively." Estab. 1990. Circ. 1,200,000.

● *Fantastic Flyer* is almost completely staff written and no longer accepts freelance submissions.

HEMISPHERES, Pace Communications for United Airlines, 1301 Carolina St., Greensboro NC 27401. (910)378-6065. Contact: Randy Johnson, editor. 95% freelance written. Monthly magazine for the educated, sophisticated business and recreational frequent traveler on an airline that spans the globe. Estab. 1992. Circ. 500,000. **Pays on acceptance**. Publishes ms 3 months after acceptance. Byline given. Offers 20% kill fee. Buys first, worldwide rights. Editorial lead time 8 months. Submit seasonal material 8 months in advance. Reports in 10 weeks on queries; 4 months on mss. Sample copy for $5. Writer's guidelines for #10 SASE.

● Ranked as one of the best markets for freelance writers in *Writer's Yearbook* magazine's annual "Top 100 Markets," January 1997.

Nonfiction: General interest, humor, personal experience. "Keeping 'global' in mind, we look for general interest, humor, personal experience, travel, and other topics that reflect a modern appreciation of the world's cultures and environment. No "What I did (or am going to do) on a trip to . . .". Query with published clips. Length: 500-3,000 words. Pays 50¢/word and up.

Photo: State availability of photos with submission. Reviews transparencies "only when we request them." Negotiates payment individually. Captions, model releases, identification of subjects required. Buys one-time rights.

Columns/Departments: Making a Difference (Q&A format interview with world leaders, movers, and shakers. A 500-600 word introduction anchors the interview. We want to profile an international mix of men and women representing a variety of topics or issues, but all must truly be making a difference. No puffy celebrity profiles.); On Location (A snappy selection of one or two sentences, "25 Fascinating Facts" that are obscure, intriguing, or travel-service-oriented items that the reader never knew about a city, state, country or destination.); Executive Secrets (Things that top executives know); Case Study (Business strategies of international companies or organizations. No lionizations of CEOs. Strategies should be the emphasis. "We want international candidates."); Weekend Breakway (Takes us just outside a major city after a week of business for a physically active, action-packed weekend. This isn't a sedentary "getaway" at a "property."); Roving Gourmet (Insider's guide to interesting eating in major city, resort area, or region. The slant can be anything from ethnic to expensive; not just "best." The four featured eateries span a spectrum from "hole in the wall," to "expense account lunch" and on to "big deal dining."); Collecting (Photo with lengthy caption or occasional 800-word story on collections and collecting with emphasis on travel); Eye on Sports (Global look at anything of interest in sports); Vintage Traveler (Options for mature, experienced travelers); Savvy Shopper (Insider's tour of best places in the world to shop. *Savvy Shopper* steps beyond all those stories that just mention the great shopping at a particular destination. A shop-by-shop, gallery-by-gallery tour of the best places in the world."); Science and Technology alternates with Computers (Substantive, insightful story. Not just another column on audio components or software. No gift guides!"); Aviation Journal (For those fascinated with aviation. *Aviation Journal* is an opportunity to enthrall all of those fliers who are fascinated with aviation. Topics range widely. Stories have covered the history of the classic DC-3, the next generation of airplanes, airport identifiers, LAX, etc., computer flight simulators, airport traffic lights, and pilots' shades.); Of Grape And Grain (Wine and spirits with emphasis on education, not one-upmanship); Show Business (Films, music and entertainment); Musings (Humor or just curious musings); Quick Quiz (Tests to amuse and educate); Travel News (Brief, practical, invaluable, trend-oriented tips); Book Beat (Tackles topics like the Wodehouse Society, the birth of a book, the competition between local bookshops and national chains. Please, no review proposals. Slant—what the world's reading—residents explore how current best sellers tell us what their country is thinking.). Length: 1,400 words. Query with published clips. Pays 50¢/word and up.

Fiction: Adventure, humorous, mainstream, slice-of-life vignettes. Buys 4 mss/year. Query. Length: 500-2,000 words. Pays 50¢/word and up.

Tips: "We increasingly require writers of 'destination' pieces or departments to 'live whereof they write.' Increasingly want to hear from U.S., U.K. or other English speaking/writing journalists (business & travel) who reside outside the U.S. in Europe, South America, Central America and the Pacific Rim—all areas that United flies."

"We're not looking for writers who aim at the inflight market. *Hemispheres* broke the fluffy mold of that tired domestic genre. Our monthly readers are a global mix on the cutting edge of the global economy and culture. They don't need to have the world filtered by US writers. We want a Hong Kong restaurant writer to speak for that city's eateries, so we need English speaking writers around the globe. That's the 'insider' story our reader's respect. We use resident writers for departments such as Roving Gourmet, Savvy Shopper, On Location, 3 Perfect Days and Weekend Breakaway, but authoritative writers can roam in features. Sure we cover the US, but with a global view: No 'in this country' phraseology. 'Too American' is a frequent complaint for queries. We use UK English spellings in articles that speak from that tradition and we specify costs in local currency first before US dollars. Basically, all of above serves the realization that today, 'global' begins with respect for 'local.' That approach permits a wealth of ways to present culture, travel and business for a wide readership. We anchor that with a reader service mission that grounds everything in 'how to do it.' "

LATITUDES, 8403 Colesville Rd., Suite 830, Silver Spring MD 20910. (301)588-2300. Fax: (301)588-2256. E-mail: affcarib@aol.com. Editor: Mike Harms. Contact: Natalie Aristy, assistant editor. 50% freelance written. Quarterly magazine covering American Eagle travel locations in Florida, the Caribbean, Northeast US and Canada. Estab. 1991. Circ. 80,000. Pays on publication. Publishes ms 6-12 months after acceptance. Byline given. Buys first North American serial rights. Submit seasonal material 9 months in advance. Accepts simultaneous submissions. Reports in 1 month on queries; 2 months on mss. Sample copy for 9×12 SAE with 5 first-class stamps. Writer's guidelines for #10 SASE.

• *Latitudes* is published in English and Spanish.

Nonfiction: Travel. Query with published clips. Length: 2,000-3,000. Pays $250 minimum. Sometimes pays expenses of writers on assignment.

Reprints: Send photocopy or typed ms with rights for sale noted. Pays 50% of amount paid for an original article.

Photos: State availability of photos with submission. Reviews slides. Offers $75-250/photo. Buys one-time rights.

Columns/Departments: Tropical Pantry (food/dining in the Caribbean and Florida, i.e., "St. Thomas Dining"); Island Buys (i.e., "Palm Beach Shopping"); all 1,000-1,500 words. Taking Off (short destination pieces focusing on attractions/events), 400-750 words, pays $75; Business Brief (latest Caribbean business trends), 800-1,000 words, pays $150. Buys 1-2 mss/year. Query.

Fillers: Brief descriptions of new or interesting attractions and festivals in Florida, the Caribbean, Northeast US and Canada. Buys 10-12/year. Length 300-800 words. Pays $75 minimum.

Tips: "We've expanded our coverage to include those destinations served by American Eagle's New York City (JFK) hub. Whereas we used to cover the Caribbean and Florida only, we now also cover the Northeastern U.S. and Canada."

‡**SKY**, Pace Communications for Delta Air Lines, 1301 Carolina St., Greensboro NC 27401. E-mail: skymag@aol.com. Managing Editor: Mickey McLean. Published monthly for business and leisure travelers aboard Delta Air Lines. **Pays on acceptance.** Byline given. Offers 25% kill fee. Buys first worldwide serial rights. Reports in 6 months on queries. Sample copy for $5.

Nonfiction: "Needs timely, interesting and informative articles on business, technology, travel, sports and humor." Buys 48 mss/year. Query with published clips. Length: 1,500-3,000 words. Pays $1,500-3,000. Pays the expenses of writers on assignment.

Columns/Departments: Buys 180 mss/year. Query with clips. Pays $1,200-1,500. Length: 1,200-1,500 words.

Fillers: Length: 100-400 words. Pays $75-300.

Tips: "*USA Today* said *Sky* is 'redefining inflight magazines . . .' We don't want run-of-the-mill inflight articles; we want fresh—sometimes humorous—takes on business, technology, travel and sports."

‡**SOUTHWEST AIRLINES SPIRIT**, 4333 Amon Carter Blvd., Fort Worth TX 76155-9616. (817)967-1804. Editor: John Clark. Monthly magazine for passengers on Southwest Airlines. Estab. 1992. Circ. 250,000. **Pays on acceptance.** Byline given. Buys first North American serial and electronic rights. Reports in 1 month on queries. Sample copy free.

Nonfiction: "Seeking accessible, entertaining, relevant and timely glimpses of people, places, products and trends in the regions Southwest Airlines serves. Newsworthy/noteworthy topics; well-researched and multiple source only. Business, travel, technology, sports and lifestyle (food, fitness and culture) are some of the topics covered in *Spirit*." Buys 48 mss/year. Query with published clips. Length: 2,500 words. Pays $2,000. Pays expenses of writers on assignment.

Columns/Departments: Buys 21 mss/year. Query with published clips. Pays $1,000. Length: 1,200 words.

Fillers: Buys 12/year. Length: 250 words. Pay varies.

‡**TWA AMBASSADOR**, 4636 E. Elwood St., Suite 5, Phoenix AZ 85040-1963. Contact: Ellen Alperstein, consulting editor. Monthly magazine for foreign and domestic TWA passengers. Estab. 1968. Circ. 223,000. **Pays on acceptance**. Byline given. Offers 25% kill fee. Buys first rights. Reports in 6 weeks on queries. Sample copy for SASE plus $1.93 postage. Writer's guidelines for #10 SASE.
Nonfiction: "We need stories that address the accommodations people make to their circumstances, individually and collectively. Stories cover a range of general interest topics—business, sports, entertainment, food, media, money, family and more. No traditional travel stories." Buys 40-45 mss/year. Query with published clips. Length: 700-2,500 words. Pays 75¢-$1/word. Pays expenses of writers on assignment.
Columns/Departments: Buys 45-50 mss/year. Query with published clips. Pays 75¢-$1/word. Length: 500-1,200 words.
Fiction: "We accept fiction but buy very little."

U.S. AIRWAYS ATTACHÉ, (formerly *USAir Magazine*), Pace Communications, 1301 Carolina St., Greensboro NC 27401. (910)378-6065. Editor: Jay Heinrichs. Contact: Kendra Gemma, assistant editor. 90% freelance written. Monthly magazine covering travel/lifestyle for travelers on USAir. Estab. 1979. Circ. 441,000. **Pays on acceptance**. Publishes ms an average of 4 months after acceptance. Byline given. Offers 25% kill fee. Editorial lead time 3 months. No simultaneous submissions. Reports in 1 month on queries. Sample copy for $5. Writer's guidelines for #10 SASE.
Nonfiction: Essays, food, general interest, interview/profile, lifestyle, sports, travel. Buys 120-150 mss/year. Query with published clips. Length: 500-2,500 words. Pay varies with freelancers' degree of experience and expertise. Sometimes pays expenses of writers on assignment.
Photos: State availability of photos with submission. Reviews contact sheets, negatives, transparencies. Negotiates payment individually. Model releases, identification of subjects required. Buys one-time rights.
Columns/Departments: Buys 50-75 mss/year. Query with published clips. Pay varies with freelancers' degree of experience and expertise.
Tips: "Study the magazine for content, style and tone. Queries for story ideas should be to the point and presented clearly. Any correspondence should include SASE."

‡**WASHINGTON FLYER MAGAZINE**, #111, 1707 L St., NW, Washington DC 20036. Fax: (202)331-7311. Associate Editor: Melanie McLeod. 80% freelance written. Bimonthly inflight magazine for business and pleasure travelers at Washington National and Washington Dulles International airports INSI. "Primarily affluent, well-educated audience that flies frequently in and out of Washington, DC." Estab. 1989. Circ. 180,000. **Pays on acceptance.** Byline given. Buys first North American rights. Submit seasonal material 4 months in advance. Reports in approximately 10 weeks. Sample copy and writer's guidelines for 9×12 SAE with 9 first-class stamps.
Nonfiction: General interest, interview/profile, travel, business. Buys 20-30 mss/year. Query with published clips. Length: 300-1,200 words. Pays $100-600.
Photos: State availability of photos with ms. Reviews negatives and transparencies (almost always color). Considers additional payment for top-quality photos accepted with ms. Must identify subjects. Buys one-time rights.
Tips: "Know the Washington market and issues relating to frequent business/pleasure travelers as we move toward a global economy."

JUVENILE

Just as children change and grow, so do juvenile magazines. Children's magazine editors stress that writers must read recent issues. A wide variety of issues are addressed in the numerous magazines for the baby boom echo. Respecting nature, developing girls' self-esteem and establishing good healthy habits all find an editorial niche. This section lists publications for children up to age 12; *Babybug* is for infants as young as 6 months. Magazines for young people 13-19 appear in the Teen and Young Adult category. Many of the following publications are produced by religious groups and, where possible, the specific denomination is given. A directory for juvenile markets, *Children's Writer's and Illustrator's Market*, is available from Writer's Digest Books.

AMERICAN GIRL, Pleasant Company Publications, 8400 Fairway Place, Middleton WI 53562. E-mail: readermail@ ag.pleasantco.com. Website: http://www.pleasantco.com. Editor: Judith Woodburn. Managing Editor: Julie Finlay. Contact: Magazine Department Assistant. 5% freelance written. Bimonthly magazine covering hobbies, crafts, profiles and history of interest to girls ages 8-12. "*American Girl* is a bimonthly 4-color magazine for girls. Our mission is to celebrate girls yesterday and today." Estab. 1992. Circ. 700,000. **Pays on acceptance**. Byline given for larger features, not departments. Offers 50% kill fee. Buys all rights, occasionally first North American serial rights. Editorial lead time 6 months. Submit seasonal material 6 months in advance. Accepts simultaneous submissions. Reports in 3 months on queries. Sample copy for 9×12 SAE with $1.93 postage. Writer's guidelines for #10 SASE.

• Best opportunity for freelancers is the Girls Express section.

Nonfiction: General contemporary interest, how-to. No historical profiles about obvious female heroines—Annie Oakley, Amelia Earhart; no romance or dating. Buys 1 ms/year. Query with published clips. Length: 100-800 words, depending on whether its a feature or for a specific department. Pay varies. Pays expenses of writers on assignment.
Reprints: Accepts reprints of previously published fiction.
Photos: State availability of photos with submission. "We prefer to shoot." Buys all rights.
Fiction: Adventure, condensed novels, ethnic, historical, humorous, slice-of-life vignettes. No romance, science fiction, fantasy. Buys 1 ms/year. Query with published clips. Length: 2,300 words maximum. Pay varies.
Columns/Departments: Girls Express (short profiles of girl "stars"), 175 words, query; Giggle Gang (puzzles, games, etc—especially looking for seasonal).

BABYBUG, Carus Corporation, P.O. Box 300, Peru IL 61354. (815)224-6656. Editor-in-Chief: Marianne Carus. Contact: Paula Morrow, editor. 50% freelance written. Board-book magazine published every 6 weeks. "*Babybug* is 'the listening and looking magazine for infants and toddlers,' intended to be read aloud by a loving adult to foster a love of books and reading in young children ages 6 months-2 years." Estab. 1994. Circ. 45,000. Pays on publication. Publishes ms an average of 18 months after acceptance. Byline given. Buys first, second serial (reprint) or all rights. Editorial lead time 8-10 months. Submit seasonal material 1 year in advance. Accepts simultaneous submissions, if so noted. Sample copy for $5. Writer's guidelines for #10 SASE.
Nonfiction: General interest and "World Around You" for infants and toddlers. Buys 5-10 mss/year. Send complete ms. Length: 1-10 words. Pays $25.
Fiction: Adventure, humorous and anything for infants and toddlers. Buys 5-10 mss/year. Send complete ms. Length: 2-8 short sentences. Pays $25.
Poetry: Buys 8-10 poems/year. Submit maximum 5 poems. Length: 2-8 lines. Pays $25.
Tips: "Imagine having to read your story or poem—out loud—fifty times or more! That's what parents will have to do. Babies and toddlers demand, 'Read it again!' Your material must hold up under repetition."

BOYS' LIFE, Boy Scouts of America, P.O. Box 152079, Irving TX 75015-2079. Contact: J.D. Owen, managing editor. 75% freelance written. Prefers to work with published/established writers; works with small number of new/unpublished writers each year. Monthly magazine covering activities of interest to all boys ages 8-18. Most readers are Scouts or Cub Scouts. Estab. 1911. Circ. 1,300,000. **Pays on acceptance.** Publishes ms an average of 1 year after acceptance. Buys one-time rights. Reports in 2 months. Sample copy for $2.50 and 9 × 12 SAE. Writer's guidelines for #10 SASE.
• Ranked as one of the best markets for freelance writers in *Writer's Yearbook* magazine's annual "Top 100 Markets," January 1997.

Nonfiction: Subject matter is broad, everything from professional sports to American history to how to pack a canoe. Look at a current list of the BSAs more than 100 merit badge pamphlets for an idea of the wide range of subjects possible. Major articles run 500-1,500 words; preferred length is about 1,000 words including sidebars and boxes. Pays $400-1,500. Uses strong photo features with about 500 words of text. Separate payment or assignment for photos. Buys 60 major articles/year. Also needs how-to features and hobby and crafts ideas. Query in writing with SASE. No phone queries. Pays expenses of writers on assignment.
Columns: Rachel Buchholz, special features editor. "Column headings are science, nature, earth, health, sports, space and aviation, cars, computers, entertainment, pets, history, music are some of the columns for which we use 300-750 words of text. This is a good place to show us what you can do." Query first in writing. Pays $250-300. Buys 75-80 columns/year.
Fiction: Shannon Lowry, associate editor. Humor, mystery, science fiction and adventure. Short stories 1,000-1,500 words; rarely longer. Send complete ms with SASE. Pays $750 minimum. Buys 12-15 short stories/year.
Fillers: Also buys freelance comics pages and scripts.
Tips: "We strongly recommend reading at least 12 issues of the magazine before you submit queries. We are a good market for any writer willing to do the necessary homework."

BOYS QUEST, Bluffton News Publishing, 103 N. Main, P.O. Box 227, Bluffton OH 45817. (419)358-4610. Editor: Marilyn Edwards. Contact: Becky Jackman, editorial assistant. 70% freelance written. Bimonthly magazine covering boys ages 6-12, with a mission to inspire boys to read, maintain traditional family values, and emphasize wholesome, innocent childhood interests. Estab. 1995. Circ. 4,000. Pays on publication. Byline given. Buys first North American serial rights. Editorial lead time 1 year. Submit seasonal material 1 year in advance. Accepts simultaneous submissions. Reports in 1 month on queries; 2 months on mss. Sample copy for $3. Writer's guidelines for #10 SASE.
Nonfiction: General interest, historical/nostalgic, how-to (building), humor, interview/profile, personal experience. Send complete ms. Length: 300-700 words with photos. Pays 5¢/word.
Reprints: Send photocopy of article or short story or typed ms with rights for sale noted. Pays 5¢/word.
Photos: State availability of photos or send with submission. Offers $10/photo. Model releases required. Buys one-time rights.
Columns/Departments: Send complete ms. Pays 5¢/word.
Fiction: Adventure, historical, humorous. Send complete ms. Length: 300-700 words. Pays 5¢/word.
Poetry: Traditional. Buys 25-30 poems/year. Length: 10-30 lines. Pays $10-15.

CALLIOPE: The World History Magazine for Young People, Cobblestone Publishing, Inc., 7 School St., Peterborough NH 03458-1454. (603)924-7209. Fax: (603)999-4217. E-mail: editorial@cobblestone.mv.com. Website: http://www.cobblestonepub.com. Editors: Rosalie and Charles Baker. Contact: Rosalie F. Baker. 50% freelance written. Prefers to work with published/established writers. Magazine published 9 times/year covering world history through 1800 AD for 8- to 14-year-olds. Articles must relate to the issue's theme. Pays on publication. Byline given. Buys all rights. Accepts simultaneous submissions. Sample copy for $4.50 and 7½×10½ SASE with 4 first-class stamps. Writer's guidelines for SASE.

Nonfiction: Essays, general interest, historical/nostalgic, how-to (activities), recipes, humor, interview/profile, personal experience, photo feature, technical, travel. Articles must relate to the theme. No religious, pornographic, biased or sophisticated submissions. Buys approximately 30-40 mss/year. Query with published clips. Length: feature articles 700-800 words. Pays 20-25¢/printed word. Supplemental nonfiction 300-600 words. Pays 20-25¢/printed word.

Photos: State availability of photos with submission. Reviews contact sheets, color slides and b&w prints. Buys one-time rights. Pays $15-100 for b&w (color cover negotiated).

Fiction: All fiction must be theme-related. Buys 10 mss/year. Query with published clips. Length: up to 800 words. Pays 20-25¢/word.

• Ranked as one of the best markets for fiction writers in the last *Writer's Digest* magazine's "Fiction 50."

Poetry: Light verse, traditional. No religious or pornographic poetry or poetry not related to the theme. Submit maximum 1 poem. Pays on individual basis. Length: up to 100 lines.

Columns/Departments: Puzzles and Games (no word finds); crossword and other word puzzles using the vocabulary of the issue's themes; mazes and picture puzzles relating to the theme. Activities (crafts, recipes, projects); up to 700 words. Pays on an individual basis.

Tips: "Writers must have an appreciation and understanding of world history. Writers must not condescend to our readers."

CHICKADEE MAGAZINE, For Young Children from *OWL*, Owl Communications, 370 King St. W., Suite 300, Toronto, Ontario M5V 1J8 Canada. (416)971-5275. Fax: (416)971-5294. E-mail: susie.berg@combinedmedia.com. Website: http://www.owl.on.ca. Contact: Susie Berg, editor. 25% freelance written. Magazine published 9 times/year for 6- to 9-year-olds. "We aim to interest young children in the world around them in an entertaining and lively way." Estab. 1979. Circ. 110,000 Canada and US. Pays on publication. Byline given. Buys all rights. Reports in 2 months. Sample copy for $4 and SAE ($2 money order or IRCs). Writer's guidelines for SAE.

Nonfiction: How-to (easy and unusual arts and crafts); personal experience (real children in real situations). No articles for older children; no religious or moralistic features.

Reprints: Send tearsheet of article or short story and information about when and where the piece previously appeared. Pays 20% of amount paid for an original article.

Photos: Send photos with ms. Reviews 35mm transparencies. Identification of subjects required.

Fiction: Adventure (relating to the 6-9-year-old), humor. No talking animal stories or religious articles. Send complete ms with $1 money order for handling and return postage. Pays $210 (US).

Tips: "A frequent mistake made by writers is trying to teach too much—not enough entertainment and fun."

CHILD LIFE, Children's Better Health Institute, P.O. Box 567, Indianapolis IN 46206-0567. (317)636-8881. Fax: (317)684-8094. Editor: Lise Hoffman. Magazine (published 8 times/year) covering "general topics of interest to children with emphasis on health." At this time, *Child Life* is not accepting manuscripts for publication. Content consists largely of reprinted stories and artwork accompanied by children's submissions and other features that reflect the Children's Better Health Institute's health and fitness mission. The latter will be handled in-house or assigned. This applies to *Child Life* only. Continue to submit material to CBHI's other children's magazines."

CHILDREN'S PLAYMATE, Children's Better Health Institute, P.O. Box 567, Indianapolis IN 46206-0567. (317)636-8881. Fax: (317)684-8094. Contact: (Ms.) Terry Harshman, editor. 75% freelance written. Eager to work with new/unpublished writers. Magazine published 8 times/year for children ages 6-8. "We are looking for articles, stories, poems, and activities with a health, sports, fitness or nutritionally oriented theme. We also publish general interest fiction and nonfiction. We try to present our material in a positive light, and we try to incorporate humor and a light approach wherever possible without minimizing the seriousness of what we are saying." Estab. 1929. Buys all rights. Byline given. Pays on publication. Submit seasonal material 8 months in advance. Reports in 3 months; sometimes may hold mss for up to 1 year, with author's permission. Sample copy for $1.25. Writer's guidelines for #10 SASE.

Nonfiction: "A feature may be an interesting presentation on good health, exercise, proper nutrition and safety." Include word count. Length: 500 words maximum. Buys 40 mss/year. "We would very much like to see more nonfiction features on nature and gardening. Material will not be returned unless accompanied by a SASE." Submit complete ms; no queries. Pays up to 17¢/word.

Fiction: Short stories for beginning readers, not over 700 words. Seasonal stories with holiday themes. Humorous stories, unusual plots. "We are interested in stories about children in different cultures and stories about lesser-known holidays (not just Christmas, Thanksgiving, Halloween, Hanukkah)." Vocabulary suitable for ages 6-8. Submit complete ms. Include word count with stories. Pays up to 17¢/word.

Fillers: Recipes, crafts, puzzles, dot-to-dots, color-ins, hidden pictures, mazes. Buys 30 fillers/year. Payment varies. Prefers camera-ready activities. Activity guidelines for #10 SASE.

Tips: "We're especially interested in features, stories, poems and articles about health, nutrition, fitness, and fun."

‡**CLUBHOUSE MAGAZINE**, Focus on the Family, 8605 Explorer Dr., Colorado Springs CO 80920. Editor: Lisa Brock. Contact: Annette Brashler, assistant editor. 40% freelance written. Monthly magazine geared for Christian kids ages 8-12. Estab. 1987. Circ. 100,000. **Pays on acceptance.** Byline given. Offers negotiable kill fee. Buys first rights. Editorial lead time 5 months. Submit seasonal material 5 months in advance. Accepts simultaneous submissions. Reports in 8 months on mss. Sample copy for $1.50. Writer's guidelines for #10 SASE.
Nonfiction: General interest, historical/nostalgic, how-to, humor, inspirational, interview/profile, religious. "We don't publish anything that doesn't have a Christian slant." Buys 20 mss/year. Send complete ms. Length: 400-1,500 words. Sometimes pays expenses of writers on assignment.
Photos: State availability of photos with submission. Reviews contact sheets. Negotiates payment individually. Captions, model releases, identification of subjects required. Buys negotiable rights.
Fiction: Adventure, ethnic, historical, religious (Christian), western, children's literature (Christian). Buys 40 mss/year. Send complete ms. Length: 400-1,500 words. Pays $75-500.

COBBLESTONE: The History Magazine for Young People, Cobblestone Publishing, Inc., 7 School St., Peterborough NH 03458-1457. (603)924-7209. Fax: (603)924-7380. Editor: Meg Chorlian. 100% (except letters and departments) freelance written (approximately 1 issue/year is by assignment only). Prefers to work with published/established writers. Monthly magazine (September-May) covering American history for children ages 8-14. "Each issue presents a particular theme, from different angles, making it exciting as well as informative. Half of all subscriptions are for schools." Circ. 36,000. Pays on publication. Publishes ms an average of 4 months after acceptance. Byline given. Offers 50% kill fee. Buys all rights. All material must relate to monthly theme. Editorial lead time 9 months. Accepts simultaneous submissions. Reports in 4 months. Sample copy for $4.50 and 7½×10½ SAE with 4 first-class stamps. Writer's guidelines and query deadlines for SASE.
Nonfiction: Historical, interview, plays, biography, recipes, activities, personal experience. "Request a copy of the writer's guidelines to find out specific issue themes in upcoming months." No material that editorializes rather than reports. Buys 80 mss/year. Query with published clips, outline and bibliography. Length: Feature articles 600-800 words. Supplemental nonfiction 300-500 words.
Reprints: Accepts previously published submissions.
Photos: State availability of photos with submission. Reviews contact sheets, transparencies, prints. Offers $15 for non-professional quality, $100 for professional quality. Captions, identification of subjects required. Buys one-time rights. Photos must relate to theme.
Fiction: Adventure, ethnic, historical, biographical fiction. "Has to be very strong and accurate." Buys 5 mss/year. Length: 500-800 words. Query with published clips. Pays 20-25¢/printed word.
Poetry: Free verse, light verse, traditional. Buys 5 poems/year. Length: up to 100 lines. Pays on an individual basis. Must relate to theme.
Columns/Departments: Puzzles and Games (no word finds); crossword and other word puzzles using the vocabulary of the issue's theme.
Tips: "All material is considered on the basis of merit and appropriateness to theme. Query should state idea for material simply, with rationale for why material is applicable to theme. Request writer's guidelines (includes themes and query deadlines) before submitting a query. Include SASE. In general, please keep in mind that we are a magazine for children ages 8-14. We want the subject to be interesting and historically accurate, but not condescending to our readers. We are looking for articles from social science teachers and educators in the middle school grades. Queries should include a detailed outline and a bibliography."

COUNSELOR, Scripture Press Publications, 4050 Lee Vance View, Cold Springs CO 80918. Fax: (719)536-0100. Contact: Janice K. Burton, editor. 60% freelance written. Quarterly Sunday School take-home paper with 13 weekly parts. "Our readers are 8-11 years old. All materials attempt to show God's working in the lives of children. Must have a true Christian slant, not just a moral implication." **Pays on acceptance.** Publishes ms an average of 1-2 years after acceptance. Byline given. Buys all or one-time rights with permission to reprint. Editorial lead time 1 year. Submit seasonal material 1 year in advance. Reports in 2 months on mss. Sample copy and writer's guidelines for #10 SASE.
Nonfiction: Inspirational (stories), Interview/profile, personal experience, religious. All stories must have a spiritual perspective. Show God at work in a child's life. Buys 10-20 mss/year. Send complete ms. Length: 900-1,000 words. Pays 8-10¢/word.
Reprints: Send typed ms with rights for sale noted and information about when and where the article previously appeared. Pays 8¢/word.
Columns/Departments: God's Wonders (seeing God through creation and the wonders of science), Kids in Action (kids doing unusual activities to benefit others), World Series (missions stories from child's perspective), all 300-500 words. Send complete ms. Pays 8-10¢/word.
Fiction: Adventure, ethnic, religious. Buys 10-15 mss/year. Send complete ms. Length: 900-1,000 words. Pays 8-10¢/word.
Fillers: Buys 8-12 puzzles, games, fun activities/year. Length: 150 words maximum. Pays 8-10¢/word.
Tips: "Show a real feel for the age level. Know your readers and what is age appropriate in terms of concepts and vocabulary. Submit only best quality manuscripts."

CRAYOLA KIDS MAGAZINE, Co-published by Meredith Corporation and Binney & Smith Properties, Inc., 1912 Grand Ave., Des Moines IA 50309-3379. (515)284-2390. Fax: (515)284-2064. Editor: Mary L. Heaton. 25% freelance written. Bimonthly magazine covering children (ages 3-8). "Our mission is to excite families with young children about the magic of reading and the wonder of creativity. We do that by reprinting a children's trade book (in its entirety) and by presenting open-ended crafts and fun puzzles and activities related to a particular theme." Estab. 1994. Circ. 400,000 subscribers plus newsstand. **Pays on acceptance**. Publishes ms an average of 4 months after acceptance. Byline sometimes given. Buys second serial (reprint) and all rights, makes work-for-hire assignments. Editorial lead time 8 months. Submit seasonal material anytime. Accepts simultaneous submissions, if so noted. Reports in 3 weeks on queries; 4 months on mss. Sample copy for $2.95 and writer's guidelines for #10 SASE.

Nonfiction: How-to/kids' crafts—seasonal and theme-related, puzzles. Buys 30-40 mss/year. Query. Length: 250 words maximum. Pays $50-300 for assigned articles; $30-150 for unsolicited articles.

Photos: "It would be very rare for us to buy a photo. We usually assign a freelance photographer for off-site shoots."

Fiction: "We buy only prepublished fiction from major publishing houses."

Fillers: For fillers we want ideas for visual puzzles that are fresh and fun. Do not send art except as a rough indicator of how the puzzle works."

Tips: "Send a sample with crafts—they should be made from easy-to-find materials, be fun to make and then play with and should be kid-tested. Send for list of themes before submitting crafts or puzzles or activities that are not seasonal."

CRICKET, Carus Publishing Co., P.O. Box 300, Peru IL 61354-0300. (815)224-6656. Editor-in-Chief: Marianne Carus. Monthly general interest literary magazine for children ages 9-14. Estab. 1973. Circ. 77,000. Pays on publication. Byline given. Buys first publication rights in the English language. Submit seasonal material 1 year in advance. Reports in 3 months. Sample copy and writer's guidelines for $4 and 9×12 SAE. Writer's guidelines only for #10 SASE.

● *Cricket* is looking for more fiction and nonfiction for the older end of its 9-14 age range. It also seeks humorous stories.

Nonfiction: Adventure, biography, foreign culture, geography, history, natural science, science, social science, sports, technology, travel. (A short bibliography is required for *all* nonfiction articles.) Send complete ms. Length: 200-1,500 words. Pays up to 25¢/word.

Reprints: Send typed ms with rights for sale noted and information about when and where the article previously appeared. Pays 50% of amount paid for an original article.

Fiction: Adventure, ethnic, fairy tales, fantasy, historical, humorous, mystery, novel excerpts, science fiction, suspense, western. No didactic, sex, religious or horror stories. Buys 75-100 mss/year. Send complete ms. Length: 200-2,000 words. Pays up to 25¢/word.

● Ranked as one of the best markets for fiction writers in the last *Writer's Digest* magazine's "Fiction 50."

Poetry: Buys 20-30 poems/year. Length: 50 lines maximum. Pays up to $3/line on publication.

CRUSADER MAGAZINE, P.O. Box 7259, Grand Rapids MI 49510-7259. Fax: (616)241-5558. E-mail: cadets@aol.com. Website: http://www.gospelcom.net/cadets/. Contact: G. Richard Broene, editor. 40% freelance written. Works with a small number of new/unpublished writers each year. Magazine published 7 times/year. "*Crusader Magazine* shows boys 9-14 how God is at work in their lives and in the world around them." Estab. 1958. Circ. 14,000. **Pays on acceptance**. Byline given. Publishes ms an average of 8 months after acceptance. Rights purchased vary with author and material; buys first serial, one-time, second serial (reprint) and simultaneous rights. Submit seasonal material (Christmas, Easter) at least 5 months in advance. Accepts simultaneous submissions. Reports in 2 months. Sample copy and writer's guidelines for 9×12 SAE with 3 first-class stamps.

Nonfiction: Articles about young boys' interests: sports, outdoor activities, bike riding, science, crafts, etc., and problems. Emphasis is on a Christian multi-racial perspective, but no simplistic moralisms. Informational, how-to, personal experience, interview, profile, inspirational, humor. Buys 20-25 mss/year. Submit complete ms. Length: 500-1,500 words. Pays 2-5¢/word.

Reprints: Send typed ms with rights for sale noted. Pay varies.

Photos: Pays $4-25 for b&w photos purchased with mss.

Columns/Departments: Building to the Lord's Code (September/October); Learning the Hard Way (November); Character and Reputation (December); Prejudice (January); Sportsmanship (February); Be Prepared (March); Careers (April/May).

Fiction: "Considerable fiction is used. Fast-moving stories that appeal to a boy's sense of adventure or sense of humor are welcome. Avoid preachiness. Avoid simplistic answers to complicated problems. Avoid long dialogue and little action." Length: 900-1,500 words. Pays 2¢/word minimum.

Fillers: Uses short humor and any type of puzzles as fillers.

CURIOCITY FOR KIDS, Thomson Newspapers, 730 N. Franklin, Suite 706, Chicago IL 60610. Fax: (312)573-3810. E-mail: curioed@ttmedia.com. Website: http://www.freezone.com. Contact: Jessica Solomon, editor. 85% freelance written. Monthly magazine. "*curiocity* is a kid-driven magazine that uses humor and a light-hearted, inquisitive approach to inform and entertain kids 7-12 about people, places and things around the country and around the town." Estab. 1994. Circ. 85,000. Pays on publication. Publishes ms an average of 2 months after acceptance. Offers 50% kill fee. Buys all rights. Editorial lead time 2 months. Submit seasonal material 5 months in advance. Reports in 1 month.

Nonfiction: General interest, how-to, humor, interview/profile, travel, kid sports. Regular features include: Cover story (talk to at least two kids), 750 words including sidebar; Good Sports (sports for kids that not everyone plays; should include a "Stumper" question about the subject), 500 words; Pop Culture (current kids' movies, TV, music, books, trends), 300 words; Profile (of adults and sometimes kids with interesting jobs, including a related "Do It" project),

300 words; Center Spread (in-depth look at interesting subject), 450-700 words; Tech-know (kid reviews of software or technology-related topic), 500-600 words; Hands-On (something to do), 300-400 words; Grub Club (easy kid recipes), 300 words. Buys 60 mss/year. Pays $100-450. Only queries accepted; no mss will be reviewed.
  • Ranked as one of the best markets for freelance writers in *Writer's Yearbook* magazine's annual "Top 100 Markets," January 1997.
Photos: State availability of photos with submission. Offers no additional payment for photos accepted with ms. Identification of subjects required.
Columns/Departments: Pack Rats (collections and hobbies, include one kid quote), 400 words; Best of the Bunch (rates products on scale of 1-4 bananas), 400 words; Spotlight (extraordinary kids), 400 words; Short Takes (2-3 brief items of interest to kids. Query with published clips. Pays $100-450.
Fiction: Adventure, fantasy, humorous, mystery, science fiction, suspense, western. Buys 12 mss/year. Query with published clips. Length: 600 words. Pays $150-300.
Tips: "Don't talk down to kids; language should be lively and humorous, but don't go overboard; take care not to overuse trendy sland words; try to talk to at least one kid for each story, make sure to get their age; try to talk to kids from different parts of the country; include at least one curio at the bottom of all stories except Fiction. Curios are interesting/weird facts that are somewhat related to the subject of the story. Stories must have elements of humor and be fun."

‡CURRENT HEALTH I, The Beginning Guide to Health Education, General Learning Communications, 900 Skokie Blvd., Suite 200, Northbrook IL 60062-4028. (847)205-3000. Fax: (847)564-8197. Senior Editor: Carole Rubenstein. 95% freelance written. An educational health periodical published monthly, September-May. "Our audience is 4th-7th grade health education students. Articles should be written at a 5th grade reading level. As a curriculum supplementary publication, info should be accurate, timely, accessible and highly readable." Estab. 1976. Circ. 200,000. Pays on publication. Publishes ms an average of 9 months after acceptance. Buys all rights.
Nonfiction: Health curriculum. Buys 70 mss/year. Query with introductory letter, résumé and clips. *No unsolicited mss. Articles are on assignment only.* Length: 800-2,000 words. Pays $100-400.
Tips: "We are looking for good writers with preferably an education and/or health background, who can write for the age group in a scientifically accurate way. Ideally, the writer should be an expert in the area in which he or she is writing. All topics are open to freelancers: disease, drugs, fitness and exercise, psychology, nutrition, first aid and safety, environment, and personal health."

FACES, The Magazine About People, Cobblestone Publishing Company, 7 School St., Peterborough NH 03458. (603)924-7209. Contact: Lynn L. Slonecker, editor. 90-100% freelance written. Monthly magazine published during school year. "*Faces* stands apart from other children's magazines by offering a solid look at one subject and stressing strong editorial content, color photographs throughout and original illustrations. *Faces* offers an equal balance of feature articles and activities, as well as folktales and legends." Estab. 1984. Circ. 15,000. Pays on publication. Publishes ms an average of 4 months after acceptance. Byline given. Offers 50% kill fee. Buys all rights. Editorial lead time 1 year. Accepts simultaneous submissions. Sample copy for $4.50 and 7½×10½ SAE with 4 first-class stamps. Writer's guidelines for #10 SASE.
Nonfiction: Historical/nostalgic, humor, interview/profile, personal experience, photo feature, travel, recipes, activities (puzzles, mazes). All must relate to theme. Buys 45-50 mss/year. Query with published clips. Length: 300-1,000. Pays 20-25¢/word.
Photos: State availability of photos with submission or send copies of related images for photo researcher. Reviews contact sheets, transparencies, prints. Offers $15-100 (for professional). Negotiates payment individually (for non-professional). Captions, model releases, identification of subjects required. Buys one-time rights.
Fiction: Ethnic, historical, retold legends or folktales. Depends on theme. Query with published clips. Length: 500-1,000 words. Pays 20-25¢/word.
Poetry: Avant-garde, free verse, haiku, light verse, traditional. Length: 100 words maximum. Pays on individual basis.
Tips: "Freelancers should send for a sample copy of magazine and a list of upcoming themes and writer's guidelines. The magazine is based on a monthly theme (upcoming themes include Vietnam, The Dominican Republic, the Rain Forest People of Peru). We appreciate professional queries that follow our detailed writer's guidelines."

THE FRIEND, 50 E. North Temple, Salt Lake City UT 84150. Managing Editor: Vivian Paulsen. 50% freelance written. Eager to work with new/unpublished writers as well as established writers. Monthly publication of The Church of Jesus Christ of Latter-Day Saints for children ages 3-11. Circ. 350,000. **Pays on acceptance.** Buys all rights. Submit seasonal material 8 months in advance. Sample copy and guidelines for $1.50 and 9×12 SAE with 4 first-class stamps.
Nonfiction: Subjects of current interest, science, nature, pets, sports, foreign countries, things to make and do. Special issues: Christmas, Easter. "Submit only complete manuscript—no queries, please." Length: 1,000 words maximum. Pays 9¢/word minimum.
Fiction: Seasonal and holiday stories, stories about other countries and their children. Wholesome and optimistic; high motive, plot and action. Character-building stories preferred. Length: 1,200 words maximum. Stories for younger children should not exceed 250 words. Submit complete ms. Pays 9¢/word minimum.
Poetry: Serious, humorous, holiday. Any form with child appeal. Pays $25.
Tips: "Do you remember how it feels to be a child? Can you write stories that appeal to children ages 3-11 in today's world? We're interested in stories with an international flavor and those that focus on present-day problems. Send

material of high literary quality slanted to our editorial requirements. Let the child solve the problem—not some helpful, all-wise adult. No overt moralizing. Nonfiction should be creatively presented—not an array of facts strung together. Beware of being cutesy."

GIRL'S LIFE, Monarch Publishing, 4517 Harford Rd., Baltimore MD 21214. Fax: (410)254-0991. Editor: Karen Bokram. Contact: Kelly A. White, senior editor. Bimonthly magazine covering girls ages 7-14. Estab. 1994. Circ. 980,000. Pays on publication. Publishes ms an average of 3 months after acceptance. Byline given. Buys first North American serial rights. Editorial lead time 5 months. Submit seasonal material 6 months in advance. Reports in 3 months. Sample copy for $5. Writer's guidelines for #10 SASE.
Nonfiction: Book excerpts, essays, general interest, how-to, humor, inspirational, interview/profile, new product, personal experience, travel. Buys 20 mss/year. Query with published clips. Submit complete mss on spec only. Length: 700-2,000 words. Pays $150-800.
Photos: State availability of photos with submission. Reviews contact sheets, negatives, transparencies. Negotiates payment individually. Captions, model releases, identification of subjects required.
Columns/Departments: Outta Here! (travel information); Sports (interesting); It Happened to Me (personal accounts); Huh? (explain something like Watergate or Woodstock, at anniversary of an event); Try It! (new stuff to try); all 1,200 words. Buys 12 mss/year. Query with published clips. Pays $150-450.
Fiction: Publishes novel excerpts.
Fillers: Gags to be illustrated by cartoonist, short humor. Buys 12/year. Pays $25-100.
Tips: Send queries with published writing samples and detailed résumé.

GUIDEPOSTS FOR KIDS, P.O. Box 638, Chesterton IN 46304. Fax: (219)926-3839. Website: http://www.guideposts. org. Contact: Mary Lou Carney, editor. 30% freelance written. Bimonthly magazine for kids. "*Guideposts for Kids* is a value-centered, fun-to-read kids magazine for 7-12-year-olds (with an emphasis on the upper end of this age bracket). Issue-oriented, thought-provoking. No preachy stories." *Guideposts For Kids* is very interested in seasonal stories, especially Thanksgiving and Christmas. Estab. 1990. Circ. 200,000. **Pays on acceptance.** Byline given. Offers 25% kill fee. Buys all rights. Editorial lead time 6 months. Submit seasonal material 6 months in advance. Reports in 6 weeks. Sample copy for $3.25. Writer's guidelines for #10 SASE.
Nonfiction: Issue-oriented features, general interest, humor, inspirational, interview/profile, technical (technology). No articles with adult voice/frame of reference or Sunday-School-type articles. Buys 20 mss/year. Query. (Send complete ms if under 300 words.) Length: 300-1,500 words. Pays $100-500. Sometimes pays expenses of writers on assignment.
Photos: State availability of or send photos with submission. Negotiates payment individually. Identification of subjects required. Buys one-time rights.
Columns/Departments: Tips from the Top (Christian celebrities), 650 words; Featuring Kids (profiles of interesting kids), 100-300 words. Buys 15 mss/year. Query. Send complete ms. Pays $100-400.
Fiction: Adventure, fantasy, historical, humorous, mystery, suspense, western. Buys 8 mss/year. Send complete ms. Length: 700-1,300 words. Pays $200-500.
Fillers: Facts, newsbreaks, short humor. Buys 8-10/year. Length: 250 words maximum. Pays $25-175.
Tips: "Before you submit to one of our departments, study the magazine. In most of our pieces, we look for a strong kid voice/viewpoint. We do not want preachy or overtly religious material. Looking for value-driven stories and profiles. In the fiction arena, we are very interested in historical and mysteries. In nonfiction, we welcome tough themes and current issues."

HIGHLIGHTS FOR CHILDREN, 803 Church St., Honesdale PA 18431-1824. Managing Editor: Christine French Clark. Contact: Beth Troop, manuscript coordinator. 80% freelance written. Monthly magazine for children ages 2-12. Estab. 1946. Circ. 3,000,000. **Pays on acceptance.** Buys all rights. Reports in about 2 months. Sample copy free. Writer's guidelines for #10 SASE.
Nonfiction: "We need articles on science, technology and nature written by persons with strong backgrounds in those fields. Contributions always welcomed from new writers, especially engineers, scientists, historians, teachers, etc., who can make useful, interesting facts accessible to children. Also writers who have lived abroad and can interpret the ways of life, especially of children, in other countries in ways that will foster world brotherhood. Sports material, biographies and articles of general interest to children. Direct, original approach, simple style, interesting content, not rewritten from encyclopedias. State background and qualifications for writing factual articles submitted. Include references or sources of information." Length: 900 words maximum. Pays $100 minimum. Articles geared toward our younger readers (3-7) especially welcome, up to 400 words. Also buys original party plans for children ages 4-12, clearly described in 300-600 words, including drawings or samples of items to be illustrated. Also, novel but tested ideas in crafts, with clear directions and made-up models. Projects must require only free or inexpensive, easy-to-obtain materials. Especially desirable if easy enough for early primary grades. Also, fingerplays with lots of action, easy for very young children to grasp and to dramatize. Avoid wordiness. We need creative-thinking puzzles that can be illustrated, optical illusions, brain teasers, games of physical agility and other 'fun' activities." Pays minimum $35 for party plans; $20 for crafts ideas; $25 for fingerplays.
• Ranked as one of the best markets for freelance writers in *Writer's Yearbook* magazine's annual "Top 100 Markets," January 1997.
Photos: Color 35mm slides, photos or art reference materials are helpful and sometimes crucial in evaluating ms.
Fiction: Unusual, meaningful stories appealing to both girls and boys, ages 2-12. "Vivid, full of action. Engaging plot,

strong characterization, lively language." Prefers stories in which a child protagonist solves a dilemma through his or her own resources. Seeks stories that the child ages 8-12 will eagerly read, and the child ages 2-7 will begin to read and/or will like to hear when read aloud (400-900 words). "We publish stories in the suspense/adventure/mystery, fantasy and humor category, all requiring interesting plot and a number of illustration possiblities. Also need rebuses (picture stories 125 words or under), stories with urban settings, stories for beginning readers (100-400 words), sports and horse stories and retold folk tales. We also would like to see more material of 1-page length (300-500 words), both fiction and factual. War, crime and violence are taboo." Pays $120 minimum.

● Ranked as one of the best markets for fiction writers in the last *Writer's Digest* magazine's "Fiction 50."

Tips: "We are pleased that many authors of children's literature report that their first published work was in the pages of *Highlights*. It is not our policy to consider fiction on the strength of the reputation of the author. We judge each submission on its own merits. With factual material, however, we do prefer that writers be authorities in their field or people with first-hand experience. In this manner we can avoid the encyclopedic article that merely restates information readily available elsewhere. We don't make assignments. Query with simple letter to establish whether the nonfiction subject is likely to be of interest. A beginning writer should first become familiar with the type of material that *Highlights* publishes. Include special qualifications, if any, of author. Write for the child, not the editor."

HOPSCOTCH, The Magazine for Girls, Bluffton News Publishing & Printing Co., P.O. Box 164, Bluffton OH 45817-0164. (419)358-4610. Fax: (419)358-5027. Editor: Marilyn B. Edwards. Contact: Becky Jackman, editorial assistant. 90% freelance written. Bimonthly magazine on basic subjects of interest to young girls. "*Hopscotch* is a digest-size magazine with a four-color cover and two-color format inside. It is designed for girls ages 6-12 and features pets, crafts, hobbies, games, science, fiction, history, puzzles, careers, etc." Estab. 1989. Pays on publication. Byline given. Buys first or second rights. Submit seasonal material 8 months in advance. Accepts simultaneous submissions. Reports in 3 weeks on queries; 2 months on mss. Sample copy for $3. Writer's guidelines, current theme list and needs for #10 SASE.

● *Hopscotch* has a sibling magazine, *Boys' Quest*, for ages 6-13, with the same old-fashioned principles that *Hopscotch* has and is a good market for freelance writers. See the listing for *Boys' Quest* earlier in this section.

Nonfiction: Book excerpts, general interest, historical/nostalgic, how-to (crafts), humor, inspirational, interview/profile, personal experience, pets, games, fiction, careers, sports, cooking. "No fashion, hairstyles, sex or dating articles." Buys 60 mss/year. Send complete ms. Length: 400-1,000 words. Pays 5¢/word.

Reprints: Send tearsheet or photocopy of article or typed ms with rights for sale noted. Pays 100% of amount paid for original article.

Photos: Send photos with submission. Prefers b&w photos, but color photos accepted. Offers $5-10/photo. Captions, model releases and identification of subjects required. Buys one-time rights.

Columns/Departments: Science—nature, crafts, pets, cooking (basic), 400-700 words. Send complete ms. Pays $10-35/column.

Fiction: Adventure, historical, humorous, mainstream, mystery, suspense. Buys 15 mss/year. Send complete ms. Length: 600-900 words. Pays 5¢/word.

Poetry: Free and light verse, traditional. "No experimental or obscure poetry." Submit 6 poems max. Pays $10-30.

Tips: "Almost all sections are open to freelancers. Freelancers should remember that *Hopscotch* is a bit old-fashioned, appealing to *young* girls (6-12). We cherish nonfiction pieces that have a young girl or young girls directly involved in unusual and/or worthwhile activities. Any piece accompanied by decent photos stands an even better chance of being accepted."

HUMPTY DUMPTY'S MAGAZINE, Children's Better Health Institute, P.O. Box 567, Indianapolis IN 46206-0567. (317)636-8881. Fax: (317)684-8094. Contact: Sandy Grieshop, editor. 90% freelance written. "We try not to be overly influenced by an author's credits, preferring instead to judge each submission on its own merit." Bimonthly magazine (monthly March, June, September, December) covering health, nutrition, hygiene, exercise and safety for children ages 4-6. Pays on publication. Publishes ms at least 8 months after acceptance. Buys all rights (but will return one-time book rights if author has name of interested publisher and tentative date of publication). Submit seasonal material 8 months in advance. Reports in 3 months. Sample copy for $1.25. Writer's guidelines for #10 SASE.

Nonfiction: "We are open to nonfiction on almost any age-appropriate subject, but we especially need material with a health theme—nutrition, safety, exercise, hygiene. We're looking for articles that encourage readers to develop better health habits without preaching. Very simple factual articles that creatively teach readers about their bodies. We use simple crafts, some with holiday themes. We also use several puzzles and activities in each issue—dot-to-dot, hidden pictures and other activities that promote following instructions, developing finger dexterity and working with numbers and letters." Submit complete ms with word count. Length: 500 words maximum. Pays up to 22¢/word.

Fiction: "We use some stories in rhyme and a few easy-to-read stories for the beginning reader. All stories should work well as read alouds. Currently we need sports/fitness stories and seasonal stories with holiday themes. We use contemporary stories and fantasy, some employing a health theme. We try to present our health material in a positive light, incorporating humor and a light approach wherever possible. Avoid stereotyping. Characters in contemporary stories should be realistic and up-to-date. Remember, many of our readers have working mothers and/or come from single-parent homes. We need more stories that reflect these changing times but at the same time communicate good, wholesome values." Submit complete ms with word count. Length: 500 words maximum. Pays up to 22¢/word.

Poetry: Short, simple poems. Pays $20 minimum.

Tips: "Writing for *Humpty Dumpty* is similar to writing picture book manuscripts. There must be a great economy of words. We strive for at least 50% art per page (in stories and articles), so space for text is limited. Because the illustrations are so important, stories should lend themselves well to visual imagery. We are always looking for cute, funny stories that lend well to illustration, especially those with a health theme. We are also looking for nonfiction articles, particularly those about nature, animals, the environment—those things kids find outside their back doors."

JACK AND JILL, Children's Better Health Institute, P.O. Box 567, Indianapolis IN 46206-0567. (317)636-8881. Fax: (317)684-8094. Contact: Daniel Lee, editor. 70% freelance written. Magazine published 8 times/year for children ages 7-10. Pays on publication. Publishes ms an average of 8 months after acceptance. Buys all rights. Byline given. Submit seasonal material 8 months in advance. Reports in 10 weeks. May hold material being seriously considered for up to 1 year. "Material will not be returned unless accompanied by SASE with sufficient postage." Sample copy for $1.25. Writer's guidelines for #10 SASE.

Nonfiction: "Because we want to encourage youngsters to read for pleasure and for information, we are interested in material that will challenge a young child's intelligence *and* be enjoyable reading. Our emphasis is on good health, and we are in particular need of articles, stories, and activities with health, safety, exercise and nutrition themes. We try to present our health material in a positive light—incorporating humor and a light approach wherever possible without minimizing the seriousness of what we are saying." Straight factual articles are OK if they are short and interestingly written. "We would rather see, however, more creative alternatives to the straight factual article. We'd like to see articles about interesting kids involved in out-of-the-ordinary activities. We're also interested in articles about people with unusual hobbies for our Hobby Shop department." Buys 10-15 nonfiction mss/year. Length: 500-800 words. Pays a minimum of 15¢/word.

Photos: When appropriate, photos should accompany ms. Reviews sharp, contrasting b&w glossy prints. Sometimes uses color slides, transparencies or good color prints. Pays $20 for b&w, $35 for color, minimum of $50 for cover. Buys one-time rights.

Fiction: May include, but is not limited to, realistic stories, fantasy adventure—set in past, present or future. "All stories need a well-developed plot, action and incident. Humor is highly desirable. Stories that deal with a health theme need not have health as the primary subject." Length: 500-800 words (short stories). Pays 15¢/word minimum. Buys 20-25 mss/year.

Fillers: Puzzles (including various kinds of word and crossword puzzles), poems, games, science projects, and creative craft projects. We get a lot of these. To be selected, an item needs a little extra spark and originality. Instructions for activities should be clearly and simply written and accompanied by models or diagram sketches. "We also have a need for recipes. Ingredients should be healthful; avoid sugar, salt, chocolate, red meat and fats as much as possible. In all material, avoid references to eating sugary foods, such as candy, cakes, cookies and soft drinks."

Tips: "We are constantly looking for new writers who can tell good stories with interesting slants—stories that are not full of out-dated and time-worn expressions. We like to see stories about kids who are smart and capable, but not sarcastic or smug. Problem-solving skills, personal responsibility and integrity are good topics for us. Obtain *current* issues of the magazines and *study* them to determine our present needs and editorial style."

LADYBUG, the Magazine for Young Children, Carus Publishing Co., P.O. Box 300, Peru IL 61354-0300. (815)224-6656. Editor-in-Chief: Marianne Carus. Editor: Paula Morrow. Monthly general interest magazine for children ages 2-6. "We look for quality writing—quality literature, no matter the subject." Estab. 1990. Circ. 139,000. Pays on publication. Byline given. All accepted mss are published. Buys first publication rights in the English language. Submit seasonal material 1 year in advance. Reports in 3 months. Sample copy and guidelines for $4 and 9×12 SAE. Guidelines only for #10 SASE.

• *Ladybug* needs even more activities based on concepts (size, color, sequence, comparison, etc.) and interesting, appropriate nonfiction. Also needs articles and parent-child activities for its parents' section. See sample issues for what they like.

Nonfiction: Can You Do This?, 1-2 pages; The World Around You, 2-4 pages; activities based on concepts (size, color, sequence, comparison, etc.), 1-2 pages. Buys 35 mss/year. Send complete ms; no queries. "Most *Ladybug* nonfiction is in the form of illustration. We'd like more simple science, how-things-work and behind-the-scenes on a preschool level." Length: 250-300 words maximum. Pays up to 25¢/word.

Fiction: Adventure, ethnic, fantasy, folklore, humorous, mainstream, mystery. Buys 30 mss/year. Send complete ms. Length: 850 words maximum. Pays up to 25¢/word.

• Ranked as one of the best markets for fiction writers in the last *Writer's Digest* magazine's "Fiction 50."

Poetry: Light verse, traditional, humorous. Buys 20 poems/year. Submit *maximum* 5 poems. Length: 20 lines maximum. Pays up to $3/line.

Fillers: Anecdotes, facts, short humor. Buys 10/year. Length: about 250 words max. Pays up to 25¢/word. "We welcome interactive activities: rebuses, up to 100 words; *original* fingerplays and action rhymes (up to 8 lines)."

Tips: "Reread manuscript *before* sending in. Keep within specified word limits. Study back issues before submitting to learn about the types of material we're looking for. Writing style is paramount. We look for rich, evocative language and a sense of joy or wonder. Remember that you're writing for preschoolers—be age-appropriate but not condescending. A story must hold enjoyment for both parent and child through repeated read-aloud sessions. Remember that we live in a multicultural world. People come in all colors, sizes, physical conditions and have special needs. Be inclusive!"

‡MUSE, Carus Publishing, 332 S. Michigan, #2000, Chicago IL 60604. (312)939-1500. Fax: (312)939-8150. E-mail: caruspub@aol.com. Editor: André W. Carus. Associate Editor: Laurence Schorsch. Editorial Contact: Submissions

Editor. 100% freelance written. Bimonthly nonfiction magazine for children. Estab. 1996. Pays 60 days after acceptance or upon acceptance. Offers 50% kill fee. Buys all rights. Reports in 3 months on queries. Sample copy for $5. Writer's guidelines for #10 SASE.

Nonfiction: Children's. "The goal of *Muse* is to give as many children as possible access to the most important ideas and concepts underlying the principle areas of human knowledge. It will take children seriously as developing intellects by assuming that, if explained clearly, the ideas and concepts of an article will be of interest to them. Articles should meet the highest possible standard of clarity and transparency aided, wherever possible, by a tone of skepticism, humor and irreverence." Query with published clips, résumé and possible topics. Length: 1,000-2,500 words. Pays 50¢/word for assigned articles; 25¢/word for unsolicited articles; plus 3 free copies of issue in which article appears.

Tips: "Unsolicited manuscripts should be sent to *Muse* Submissions Editor, The Cricket Magazine Group, P.O. Box 300, Peru IL 61354."

MY FRIEND, The Catholic Magazine for Kids, Pauline Books & Media/Daughters of St. Paul, 50 St. Paul's Ave., Jamaica Plain, Boston MA 02130-3491. (617)522-8911. Website: http://www.pauline.org. (click on Kidstuff). Editor-in-Chief: Sister Rose Pacatte, fsp. Contact: Sister Kathryn James Hermes, fsp, managing editor. Over 60% staff written. Magazine published 10 times/year for children ages 6-12. Circ. 12,000. "*My Friend* is a 32-page monthly Catholic magazine for boys and girls. Its goal is to celebrate the Catholic Faith—as it is lived by today's children and as it has been lived for centuries." Pays on editorial completion of the issue (five months ahead of publication date). Buys serial rights. Reports in 2 months. Sample copy for $2.95. Writer's guidelines for #10 SASE. No theme lists.

Nonfiction: How-to, religious, technical, crafts, media-related articles, real-life features. "This year we are emphasizing cultural and ecumenical themes. We prefer authors who have a rich background and mastery in these areas. We would be interested in hearing from authors who have lived abroad and can share the lives of children in other countries and how the Catholic Faith is lived in culturally different perspectives. Nevertheless contributions are welcomed from new writers who can make useful, interesting, authentic faith and facts accessible to children. We are looking for fresh perspectives into a child's world that are imaginative, unique, challenging, informative, current and fun. We prefer articles that are visual, not necessarily text-based—articles written in 'windows' style with multiple points of entry." Send complete ms. Length: 150-800 words. Pays $35-100. Pays in contributor copies by prior agreement with an author "who wishes to write as a form of sharing our ministry."

Photos: Send photos with submission.

Fiction: "We are looking for stories that immediately grab the imagination of the reader. Good dialogue, realistic character development, current lingo are necessary. A child protagonist must resolve a dilemma through his or her own resources. We prefer seeing a sample or submission of a story. Often we may not be able to use a particular story but the author will be asked to write another for a specific issue based on his or her experience, writing ability, etc. At this time we are especially analyzing submissions for the following: intercultural relations, periodic appearance of a child living with a disability or a sibling of a child or adult with a disability, realistic and current issues kids face today and computer literacy."

Fillers: Puzzles and jokes. "We need new creative ideas, small-size puzzles, picture puzzles, clean jokes." Jokes pay $7. Puzzles pay $10-15.

Tips: "We have a strong commitment to working with our authors to produce material that is factual, contemporary and inspiring. We prefer those authors who write well and are able to work as a team with us."

NEW MOON: THE MAGAZINE FOR GIRLS & THEIR DREAMS, New Moon Publishing, Inc., P.O. Box 3620, Duluth MN 55803. Fax: (218)728-0314. E-mail: newmoon@newmoon.duluth.mn.us. Website: http://www.newmoon.org. Contact: Barbara Stretchberry or Tya Ward, managing editors. 10% freelance written. Bimonthly magazine covering girls ages 8-14, edited by girls aged 8-14. "In general, all material should be pro-girl and feature girls and women as the primary focus. *New Moon* is for every girl who wants her voice heard and her dreams taken seriously." Estab. 1992. Circ. 30,000. Pays on publication. Publishes ms 6 months after acceptance. Byline given. Buys first rights and second serial (reprint) rights. Editorial lead time 6 months. Submit seasonal material 10 months in advance. Accepts simultaneous submissions. Reports in 3 months on queries; 3 months on mss. Sample copy for $6.50. Writer's guidelines for SASE.

Nonfiction: General interest, humor, inspirational, interview/profile, opinion, personal experience, photo feature, religious, technical, travel, multicultural/girls from other countries. Special issues: Music and Entertainment (March/April 1998, deadline October 1, 1997); Religion and Spirituality (May/June 1998, deadline December 1, 1997); Astronomy, Astrology and Mythology (July/August 1998, deadline February 1, 1998); Adventures and Mysteries (September/October 1998, deadline April 1, 1998); and Animals (November/December 1998, deadline June 1, 1998). Buys 10 mss/year. Query. Length: 300-900 words. Pays 4-8¢/word.

Reprints: Send typed ms with rights for sale noted and information about when and where the article previously appeared. Negotiates fee.

Photos: State availability of photos with submission. Reviews 4×5 prints. Negotiates payment individually. Captions, model releases, identification of subjects required. Buys one-time rights.

Columns/Departments: Global Village (girl's life in another country), 900 words; Women's Work (profile of a woman's career), 600-900 words; She Did It (real girls doing real things), 300-600 words. Buys 10 mss/year. Query. Pays 4-8¢/word.

Fiction: Adventure, experimental, fantasy, historical, humorous, mystery, religious, romance, science fiction, serialized novels (on occasion), slice-of-life vignettes, suspense, all girl-centered. Buys 4 mss/year. Query. Send complete ms. Length: 300-1,200 words. Pays 4-8¢/word.

Poetry: Does not publish poetry by adults.
Tips: "Writers and artists who comprehend our goals have the best chance of publication. Refer to our guidelines and upcoming themes."

ON THE LINE, Mennonite Publishing House, 616 Walnut Ave., Scottdale PA 15683-1999. (412)887-8500. Fax: (412)887-3111. E-mail: mary%mph@mcimail.com. Contact: Mary Clemens Meyer, editor. 90% freelance written. Works with a small number of new/unpublished writers each year. Monthly Christian magazine for children ages 9-14. "*On the Line* helps upper elementary and junior high children understand and appreciate God, the created world, themselves and others." Estab. 1908. Circ. 6,500. **Pays on acceptance.** Publishes ms an average of 1 year after acceptance. Byline given. Buys one-time rights. Submit seasonal material 6 months in advance. Accepts simultaneous submissions. Reports in 1 month. Sample copy for 9 × 12 SAE with 2 first-class stamps.
Nonfiction: How-to (things to make with easy-to-get materials including food recipes); informational (300-500 word articles on wonders of nature, people who have made outstanding contributions). Buys 95 unsolicited mss/year. Send complete ms. Pays $10-30.
Reprints: Send typed ms with rights for sale noted and information about when and where the article previously appeared. Pays 65% of amount paid for an original article.
Photos: Limited number of photos purchased with or without ms. Pays $25-50 for 8 × 10 b&w photos. Total purchase price for ms includes payment for photos.
Fiction: Adventure, humorous, religious. Buys 50 mss/year. Send complete ms. Length: 1,000-1,500 words. Pays 2-5¢/word.
Poetry: Light verse, religious. Length: 3-12 lines. Pays $5-15.
Fillers: Appropriate puzzles, cartoons, quizzes.
Tips: "Study the publication first. We need short well-written how-to and craft articles. Don't send query; we prefer to see the complete manuscript."

OWL MAGAZINE, The Discovery Magazine for Children, Owl Communications, 370 King St. W., Suite 300, Toronto, Ontario M5V 1J8 Canada. (416)971-5275. Fax: (416)971-5294. E-mail: owl@owlkids.com. Website: http://www.owl.on.ca. Editor: Nyla Ahmad. Contact: Keltie Thomas, managing editor. 25% freelance written. Works with small number of new writers each year. Magazine published 10 times/year (no July or August issues) covering science and nature. Aims to interest children in their environment through accurate, factual information about the world presented in an easy, lively style. Estab. 1976. Circ. 160,000. Pays on publication. Publishes ms an average of 3 months after acceptance. Byline given. Buys all rights. Submit seasonal material 1 year in advance. Reports in 10 weeks. Sample copy for $4.28. Writer's guidelines for SAE (large envelope if requesting sample copy) and money order for $1 postage (no stamps please).
Nonfiction: Personal experience (real life children in real situations); photo feature (natural science, international wildlife, and outdoor features); science and environmental features. No problem stories with drugs, sex or moralistic views, or talking animal stories. Query with clips of published work.
Photos: State availability of photos. Reviews 35mm transparencies. Identification of subjects required. Send for photo package before submitting material.
Tips: "Write for editorial guidelines first. Review back issues of the magazine for content and style. Know your topic and approach it from an unusual perspective. Our magazine never talks down to children. We would like to see more articles about science and technology that aren't too academic."

POCKETS, The Upper Room, P.O. Box 189, Nashville TN 37202-0189. (615)340-7333. Fax: (615)340-7006. E-mail: pockets@upperroom.org. Website: http://www.upperroom.org. Editor: Janet R. Knight. Contact: Lynn Gilliam, associate editor. 60% freelance written. Eager to work with new/unpublished writers. Monthly magazine (except January/February) covering children's and families' spiritual formation. "We are a Christian, non-denominational publication for children 6-11 years of age." Estab. 1981. Circ. 99,000. **Pays on acceptance.** Byline given. Offers 4¢/word kill fee. Buys first North American serial rights. Submit seasonal material 1 year in advance. Reports in 10 weeks on mss. Sample copy for 7½ × 10½ SAE with 4 first-class stamps. Writer's guidelines and themes for #10 SASE.
  ● *Pockets* has expanded to 48 pages and needs more fiction and poetry, as well as short, short stories (500-750 words) for children 4-7. They publish one of these stories per issue.
Nonfiction: Interview/profile, religious (retold scripture stories), personal experience. Each issue is built around a specific theme; list of themes for special issues available with SASE. No violence or romance. Buys 5 mss/year. Send complete ms. Length: 400-1,000 words. Pays 12¢/word.
Reprints: Accepts one-time previously published submissions. Send typed ms with rights for sale noted and information about when and where the article previously appeared. Pays 100% of amount paid for an original article.
Photos: Send photos with submission. Prefer no photos unless they accompany an article. Reviews contact sheets, transparencies and prints. Offers $25-50/photo. Buys one-time rights.
Columns/Departments: Refrigerator Door (poetry and prayer related to themes), 25 lines; Pocketsful of Love (family communications activities), 300 words; Activities/Games ($25 and up); Peacemakers at Work (profiles of people, particularly children, working for peace, justice and ecological concerns), 300-800 words. Buys 20 mss/year. Send complete ms. Pays 12¢/word; recipes $25.
Fiction: Adventure, ethnic, slice-of-life. "Stories should reflect the child's everyday experiences through a Christian

approach. This is often more acceptable when stories are not preachy or overtly Christian." Buys 44 mss/year. Send complete ms. Length: 600-1,500 words. Pays 12¢/word and up.

Poetry: Buys 22 poems/year. Length: 4-24 lines. Pays $2/line.

Tips: "Theme stories, role models and retold scripture stories are most open to freelancers. We are also looking for nonfiction stories about children involved in peace/justic/ecology efforts. Poetry is also open. It's very helpful if writers send for our themes. These are *not* the same as writer's guidelines. We also have an annual $1,000 Fiction Writing Contest. Guidelines available with SASE."

POWER AND LIGHT, 6401 The Paseo, Kansas City MO 64131. Fax: (816)333-4439. E-mail: mhammer@nazarene.org. Editor: Beula Postlewait. Associate Editor: Melissa Hammer. Mostly freelance written. Weekly magazine for boys and girls ages 11-12 using WordAction Sunday School curriculum. Estab. 1992. Publishes ms an average of 1 year after acceptance. Buys multiple use rights. Reports in 3 months. "Minimal comments on pre-printed form are made on rejected material." Sample copy and guidelines for SASE.

Fiction: Stories with Christian emphasis on high ideals, wholesome social relationships and activities and right choices. Informal style. Submit complete ms. Length: 500-700 words. Pays 5¢/word.

Reprints: Send tearsheet or photocopy of article or typed ms with rights for sale noted and information about when and where article previously appeared. Pays 3½¢/word.

Tips: "All themes and outcomes should conform to the theology and practices of the Church of the Nazarene."

R-A-D-A-R, 8121 Hamilton Ave., Cincinnati OH 45231. (513)931-4050. Fax: (513)931-0950. Contact: Elaina Meyers, editor. 75% freelance written. Weekly for children in grades 3 and 4 in Christian Sunday schools. Estab. 1866 (publishing house). Rights purchased varies with material; prefers buying first serial rights, but will buy second (reprint) rights. Occasionally overstocked. **Pays on acceptance.** Publishes ms an average of 1 year after acceptance. Reports in 2 months. Sample copy and writer's guidelines and theme list for #10 SASE.

Nonfiction: Articles on hobbies and handicrafts, nature, famous people, seasonal subjects, etc., written from a Christian viewpoint. No articles about historical figures with an absence of religious implication. Length: 400-500 words. Pays 3-7¢/word.

Reprints: Send tearsheet or photocopy of article or short story or typed ms with rights for sale noted and information about when and where the piece previously appeared. Pays 4-5¢/word.

Fiction: Short stories of heroism, adventure, involving mystery, animals, sports, travel, relationships (with parents, friends and others), biography. "True or possible plots stressing clean, wholesome, Christian character-building ideas, but not preachy. Make prayer, church attendance and Christian living a natural part of the story. We correlate our fiction and other features with a definite Bible lesson. Writers who want to meet our needs should send a #10 SASE for a theme list." No talking animal stories, science fiction, Halloween stories or first-person stories from an adult's viewpoint. Length: 900-1,000 words. Pays 3-7¢/word.

Poetry: Biblical, or about nature. Pays 50¢/line.

● Ranked as one of the best markets for fiction writers in the last *Writer's Digest* magazine's "Fiction 50."

Fillers: Puzzles. "Our puzzles correlate with the quarterly theme list or with holidays and special occasions. Some types of puzzles we use are word searches, acrostics, crosswords, fill in the blank, matching. Our official translation for puzzles is the *New International Version* of the Bible. Puzzles should be challenging, but not too difficult." Length: No more than one page in length with answers included, pays $15-17.50; Cartoons (appeal to children 8-12), pays $15-20.

Tips: "Keep in mind that children today are different from the way they were when you were a child. Get to know children before you begin to write for them. Many manuscripts are returned simply because the plot or vocabulary is outdated for modern children."

RANGER RICK, National Wildlife Federation, 8925 Leesburg Pike, Vienna VA 22184. (703)790-4274. Editor: Gerald Bishop. 40% freelance written. Works with a small number of new/unpublished writers each year. Monthly magazine for children from ages 6-12, with the greatest concentration in the 7-10 age bracket. Buys all world rights unless other arrangements made. Byline given "but occasionally, for very brief pieces, we will identify author by name at the end. Contributions to regular columns usually are not bylined." Estab. 1967. **Pays on acceptance.** Publishes ms an average of 18 months after acceptance. Reports in 6 weeks. "Anything written with a specific month in mind should be in our hands at least 10 months before that issue date." Writer's guidelines for #10 SASE.

Nonfiction: "Articles may be written on anything related to nature, conservation, the outdoors, environmental problems or natural science. Please avoid articles about animal rehabilitation, unless the species are endangered." Buys 25-35 unsolicited mss/year. Query with SASE. Pays $50-75, depending on length, quality and content (maximum length, 900 words). Unless you are an expert in the field or are writing from direct personal experience, all factual information must be footnoted and backed up with current, reliable references.

Fiction: "Same categories as nonfiction plus fantasy and science fiction. The attributing of human qualities to animals is limited to our regular feature, 'The Adventures of Ranger Rick,' so please do not humanize wildlife. We discourage keeping wildlife as pets."

Photos: "Photographs, when used, are paid for separately. It is not necessary that illustrations accompany material."

Tips: "In your query letter, include details of what the manuscript will cover; sample lead; evidence that you can write playfully and with great enthusiasm, conviction and excitement (formal, serious, dull queries indicate otherwise). Think of an exciting subject we haven't done recently, sell it effectively with query, and produce a manuscript of highest quality. Read past issues to learn successful styles and unique approaches to subjects.

SHOFAR MAGAZINE, 43 Northcote Dr., Melville NY 11747-3924. (516)643-4598. Fax: (516)643-4598. Managing Editor: Gerald H. Grayson. 80-90% freelance written. Children's magazine on Jewish subjects published monthly from October to May, double issues December/January and April/May. Estab. 1984. Circ. 17,000. Pays on publication. Byline given. Buys one-time rights. Submit seasonal material 6 months in advance. Accepts simultaneous submissions. Reports in 2 months. Sample copy and writer's guidelines for 9×12 SAE and $1.01 postage.
Nonfiction: Historical/nostalgic, humor, inspirational, interview/profile, personal experience, photo feature, religious, travel. Buys 15 mss/year. Send complete ms. Length: 750-1,000 words. Pays 7-10¢/word. Sometimes pays the expenses of writers on assignment.
Photos: State availability of or send photos with submission. Offers $10-50/photo. Identification of subjects required. Buys one-time rights.
Fiction: Adventure, historical, humorous, religious. Buys 15 mss/year. Send complete ms. Length: 750-1,000 words. Pays 7-10¢/word.
Poetry: Free verse, light verse, traditional. Buys 4-5 poems/year. Length: 8-50 words. Pays 7-10¢/word.
Tips: "Submissions *must* be on a Jewish theme and should be geared to readers who are 8- to 12-years-old."

SPIDER, The Magazine for Children, The Cricket Magazine Group, P.O. Box 300, Peru IL 61354. (815)224-6656. Fax: (815)224-6615. Editor-in-Chief: Marianne Carus. Editor: Christine Walske. Contact: Submissions Editor. 80% freelance written. Monthly magazine covering literary, general interest. "*Spider* introduces 6- to 9-year-old children to the highest quality stories, poems, illustrations, articles and activities. It was created to foster in beginning readers a love of reading and discovery that will last a lifetime. We're looking for writers who respect children's intelligence." Estab. 1994. Circ. 92,000. Pays on publication. Publishes ms an average of 1 year after acceptance. Byline given. Buys first North American serial rights (for stories, poems, articles), second serial (reprint) rights or all rights (for crafts, recipes, puzzles). Editorial lead time 9 months. Submit seasonal material 1 year in advance. Accepts simultaneous submissions. Reports in 4 months on mss. Sample copy for $4. Writer's guidelines for #10 SASE.
Nonfiction: Adventure, biography, geography, history, science, social science, sports, technology, travel. A bibliography is required with all nonfiction mss. Buys 12-15 mss/year. Send complete ms. Length: 300-800 words. Pays 25¢/word.
Reprints: Note rights for sale and information about when and where article previously appeared.
Photos: Send photos with submission (prints or slide dupes OK). Reviews contact sheets, 35mm to 4×4 transparencies, 8×10 maximum prints. Offers $50-200/photo. Captions, model releases, identification of subjects required. Buys one-time rights.
Fiction: Adventure, ethnic, fantasy, historical, humorous, mystery, science fiction, suspense, realistic fiction, folk tales, fairy tales. No romance, horror, religious. Buys 30-40 mss/year. Send complete ms. Length: 300-1,000 words. Pays 25¢/word.
Poetry: Free verse, traditional, nonsense, humorous, serious. No forced rhymes, didactic. Buys 20-30 poems/year. Submit maximum 5 poems. Length: 20 lines maximum. Pays $3/line maximum.
Fillers: Puzzles, mazes, hidden pictures, games, brainteasers, math and word activities. Buys 15-20/year. Payment depends on type of filler.
Tips: "Most importantly, do not write down to children. We'd like to see more of the following: multicultural fiction and nonfiction, strong female protagonists, stories about people who are physically or mentally challenged, fantasy, science fiction, environmental articles, hard science (e.g., physics, chemistry, cosmology, microbiology, science biography and history)."

SPORTS ILLUSTRATED FOR KIDS, Time-Warner, Time & Life Building, 1271 Sixth Ave., New York NY 10020. (212)522-5437. Fax: (212)522-0120. Managing Editor: Neil Cohen. Contact: Erin Egan, associate editor. 20% freelance written. Monthly magazine on sports for children 8 years old and up. Content is divided 50/50 between sports as played by kids, and sports as played by professionals. Estab. 1989. **Pays on acceptance.** Publishes ms an average of 3 months after acceptance. Byline given. Offers 25% kill fee. Buys all rights. For sample copy call (800)992-0196. Writer's guidelines for #10 SASE.
Nonfiction: Games, general interest, how-to, humor, inspirational, interview/profile, photo feature, puzzles. Buys 15 mss/year. Query with published clips. Length: 100-1,500 words. Pays $75-1,000 for assigned articles; $75-800 for unsolicited articles. Pays expenses of writers on assignment.
Photos: State availability of photos with submission. Buys one-time rights.
Columns/Departments: The Worst Day I Ever Had (tells about day in pro athlete's life when all seemed hopeless), 500-600 words; Sports Shorts (short, fresh news about kids doing awaiting things, on and off the field), 100-250 words. Buys 10-15 mss/year. Query with published clips. Pays $75-600.

STONE SOUP, The Magazine by Young Writers and Artists, Children's Art Foundation, P.O. Box 83, Santa Cruz CA 95063-0083. (408)426-5557. Fax: (408)426-1161. E-mail: editor@stonesoup.com. Website: http://www.stonesoup.com. Contact: Ms. Gerry Mandel, editor. 100% freelance written. Bimonthly magazine of writing and art by children, including fiction, poetry, book reviews, and art by children through age 13. Estab. 1973. Audience is children, teachers, parents, writers, artists. "We have a preference for writing and art based on real-life experiences; no formula stories or poems." Pays on publication. Publishes ms an average of 3 months after acceptance. Buys all rights. Submit seasonal material 6 months in advance. Reports in 1 month. Sample copy for $4. Writer's guidelines with SASE.

Nonfiction: Book reviews. Buys 10 mss/year. Query. Pays $15.
Reprints: Send photocopy of article or story and information about when and where the piece previously appeared. Pays 100% of amount paid for an original article.
Fiction: Adventure, ethnic, experimental, fantasy, historical, humorous, mystery, science fiction, slice-of-life vignettes, suspense. "We do not like assignments or formula stories of any kind." Accepts 55 mss/year. Send complete ms. Pays $10 for stories. Authors also receive 2 copies and discounts on additional copies and on subscriptions.
Poetry: Avant-garde, free verse. Accepts 20 poems/year. Pays $10/poem. (Same discounts apply.)
Tips: "All writing we publish is by young people ages 13 and under. We do not publish any writing by adults. We can't emphasize enough how important it is to read a couple of issues of the magazine. We have a strong preference for writing on subjects that mean a lot to the author. If you feel strongly about something that happened to you or something you observed, use that feeling as the basis for your story or poem. Stories should have good descriptions, realistic dialogue and a point to make. In a poem, each word must be chosen carefully. Your poem should present a view of your subject and a way of using words that are special and all your own."

STORY FRIENDS, Mennonite Publishing House, 616 Walnut Ave., Scottdale PA 15683-1999. (412)887-8500. Fax: (412)887-3111. Contact: Rose Mary Stutzman, editor. 80% freelance written. Monthly story paper in weekly parts for children ages 4-9. "*Story Friends* is planned to provide wholesome Christian reading for the 4-9-year-old. Practical life stories are included to teach moral values and remind the children that God is at work today. Activities introduce children to the Bible and its message for them." Estab. 1905. Circ. 7,000. **Pays on acceptance.** Publishes ms an average of 1 year after acceptance. Byline given. Publication not copyrighted. Buys one-time and second serial (reprint) rights. Submit seasonal material 6 months in advance. Accepts simultaneous submissions. Reports in 1 month. Sample copy for 9×12 SAE with 2 first-class stamps. Writer's guidelines for #10 SASE.
Nonfiction: How-to (craft ideas for young children), photo feature. Buys 20 mss/year. Send complete ms. Length: 300-500 words. Pays 3-5¢/word.
Reprints: Send photocopy or typed ms with rights for sale noted and information about when and where the article previously appeared. Pays 50% of amount paid for an original article.
Photos: Send photos with submission. Reviews 8½×11 b&w prints. Offers $20-25/photo. Model releases required. Buys one-time rights.
Fiction: See guidelines for *Story Friends*. Buys 50 mss/year. Send complete ms. Length: 300-800 words. Pays 3-5¢/word.
Poetry: Traditional. Buys 20 poems/year. Length: 4-16 lines. Pays $5-10/poem.
Tips: "Send stories that children from a variety of ethnic backgrounds can relate to; stories that deal with experiences similar to all children. For example, all children have fears but their fears may vary depending on where they live. I want to include more humor. I hope to choose stories with a humorous twist."

TOUCH, P.O. Box 7259, Grand Rapids MI 49510. Fax: (616)241-5558. Editor: Jan Boone. Contact: Carol Smith, publications coordinator. 80% freelance written. Works with new published/established writers. Monthly magazine "to show girls ages 9-14 how God is at work in their lives and in the world around them. The May/June issue annually features material written by our readers." Estab. 1972. Circ. 15,500. **Pays on acceptance.** Publishes ms an average of 1 year after acceptance. Byline given. Buys second serial (reprint) and first North American serial rights. Submit seasonal material 9 months in advance. Accepts simultaneous submissions. Reports in 2 months. Sample copy and writer's guidelines for 9×12 SAE with 3 first-class stamps.
Nonfiction: Biographies and autobiographies of "heroes of the faith." How-to (crafts girls can make easily and inexpensively); informational (write for issue themes); humor (need much more); inspirational (seasonal and holiday); interview; multicultural materials; travel; personal experience (avoid the testimony approach); photo feature (query first). "Because our magazine is published around a monthly theme, requesting the letter we send out twice a year to our established freelancers would be most helpful. We do not want easy solutions or quick character changes from bad to good. No pietistic characters. Constant mention of God is not necessary if the moral tone of the story is positive. We do not want stories that always have a happy ending." Buys 36-45 unsolicited mss/year. Submit complete ms. Length: 100-1,000 words. Pays 2½-5¢/word, depending on the amount of editing.
Reprints: Send typed ms with rights for sale noted and when and where the article previously appeared.
Photos: Purchased with or without ms. Reviews 5×7 or 8×10 clear color glossy prints. Appreciate multicultural subjects. Pays $20-50 on publication.
Fiction: Adventure (that girls could experience in their hometowns or places they might realistically visit); humorous; mystery (believable only); romance (stories that deal with awakening awareness of boys are appreciated); suspense (can be serialized); religious (nothing preachy). Buys 30 mss/year. Submit complete ms. Length: 300-1,000 words. Pays 2½-5¢/word.
Poetry: Free verse, haiku, light verse, traditional. Buys 10/year. Length: 30 lines maximum. Pays $5-15 minimum.
Fillers: Puzzles, short humor, cartoons, factual tidbits. Buys 3/issue. Pays $7-15.
Tips: "Prefers not to see anything on the adult level, secular material or violence. Writers frequently over-simplify the articles and often write with a Pollyanna attitude. An author should be able to see his/her writing style as exciting and appealing to girls ages 9-14. The style can be fun, but also teach a truth. The subject should be current and important to *Touch* readers. We would like to receive material that features a multi-cultural slant."

TOY FARMER, Toy Farmer Publications, 7496-106 A Ave. SE, LaMoune ND 58458. (701)883-5206. Fax: (701)883-5209. Editor: Claire D. Scheibe. Contact: Cathy Scheibe, assistant editor. 65% freelance written. Monthly magazine covering farm toys. Must slant toward youth involvement. Estab. 1978. Circ. 27,000. Pays on publication. Publishes ms an average of 1 month after acceptance. Byline given. Buys first North American serial rights. Editorial lead time 3 months. Submit seasonal material 3 months in advance. Accepts previously published submissions. Reports in 1 month on queries; 2 months on mss. Sample copy for $4. Writer's guidelines free.
Nonfiction: General interest, historical/nostalgic, humor, new product, technical. Buys 100 mss/year. Query with published clips. 800-1,500 words. Pays $50-150. Sometimes pays expenses of writers on assignment.
Photos: State availability of photos with submission. Reviews transparencies. Offers no additional payment for photos accepted with ms. Buys one-time rights.
Columns/Departments: Buys 36 mss/year. Query with published clips. Pays $50-150.

TURTLE MAGAZINE FOR PRESCHOOL KIDS, Children's Better Health Institute, P.O. Box 567, Indianapolis IN 46206-0567. (317)636-8881. Fax: (317)684-8094. Contact: Sandy Grieshop, editor. 90% freelance written. Bimonthly magazine (monthly March, June, September, December). General interest, interactive magazine with the purpose of helping preschoolers develop healthy minds and bodies. Pays on publication. May hold mss for up to 1 year before acceptance/publication. Byline given. Buys all rights. Submit seasonal material 8 months in advance. Reports in 3 months. Sample copy for $1.25. Writer's guidelines for #10 SASE.
Nonfiction: "Uses very simple science experiments. These should be pretested. Also publish simple, healthful recipes."
Fiction: All should have single-focus story lines and work well as read-alouds. "Most of the stories we use have a character-building bent, but are not preachy or overly moralistic. We are in constant need of stories to help a preschooler appreciate his/her body and what it can do; stories encouraging active, vigorous play; stories about good health. We no longer buy stories about 'generic' turtles because we now have PokeyToes, our own trade-marked turtle character. All should 'move along' and lend themselves well to illustration. Writing should be energetic, enthusiastic and creative—like preschoolers themselves."
Poetry: "We're especially looking for action rhymes to foster creative movement in preschoolers. We also use short verse on our back cover."
Tips: "We are trying to include more material for our youngest readers. Stories must be age-appropriate for two- to five-year-olds, entertaining and written from a healthy lifestyle perspective. We are especially interested in material concerning sports and fitness, including profiles of famous amateur and professional athletes; 'average' athletes (especially children) who have overcome obstacles to excel in their areas; and new or unusual sports, particularly those in which children can participate."

‡U.S. KIDS, A Weekly Reader Magazine, Children's Better Health Institute, P.O. Box 567, Indianapolis IN 46206-0567. (317)636-8881. Editor: Jeff Ayers. 50% freelance written. Published 8 times/year featuring "kids doing extraordinary things, especially activities related to heatlh, sports, the arts, interesting hobbies, the environment, computers, etc." Reading level appropriate for 3rd/4th grade readers. Estab. 1987. Circ. 250,000. Pays on publication. Publishes ms an average of 6 months after acceptance. Byline given. Buys all rights. Editorial lead time 8 months. Submit seasonal material 6 months in advance. Reports in 3 months on mss. Sample copy for $2.50. Writer's guidelines for #10 SASE.
Nonfiction: General interest, how-to, humor, interview/profile, personal experience, fitness, health, world cultures, kids using computers. Buys 12-18 mss/year. Send complete ms. Length: 400-800 words. Pays up to 20¢/word.
Photos: State availability of photos with ms. Reviews contact sheets or color photocopies, negatives, transparencies, prints. Negotiates payment individually. Captions, model releases, subject identification required. Buys one-time rights.
Columns/Departments: Real Kids (kids doing interesting things); Fit Kids (sports, healthy activities); Computer Zone. Length: 300-400 words. Send complete ms. Pays up to 20¢/word.
Fiction: Adventure, ethnic, historical, humorous, mainstream, slice-of-life vignettes, suspense. Buys 8 mss/year. Send complete ms. Length: 400-800 words. Pays up to 20¢/word.
Poetry: Light verse, traditional, kid's humorous. Buys 4 poems/year. Submit maximum 3 poems. Length: 8-24 lines. Pays $25-50.
Fillers: Facts, newsbreaks (related to kids, especially kids' health), short humor. Length: 200-500 words. Pays 20¢/word.
Tips: "Looking for fun and informative articles on activities, hobbies, accomplishments of real kids, especially those related to fitness, sports and health. Should appeal to readers in a broad age range. Availability of good photos a plus."

‡WILD OUTDOOR WORLD (W.O.W.), Rocky Mountain Elk Foundation, P.O. Box 1249, Helena MT 59624. (406)449-1335. Fax: (406)449-9197. E-mail: wowmag@MT.net. Contact: Carolyn Zieg Cunningham, editorial director. 75% freelance written. Bimonthly magazine covering North American wildlife for children ages 8-12. "W.O.W. emphasizes the conservation of North American wildlife and habitat. Articles reflect sound principles of ecology and environmental education. It stresses the 'web of life,' nature's balance and the importance of habitat." Estab. 1993. Circ. 100,000. **Pays on acceptance.** Publishes ms an average of 12-18 months after acceptance. Byline given. Buys first North American and electronic rights. Editorial lead time 4 months. Submit seasonal material 8 months in advance. Accepts simultaneous submissions. Reports in 2 months. Sample copy and writer's guidelines free.
Nonfiction: How-to (children's outdoor-related projects, camping, hiking, other healthy outdoor pursuits), interview/profile, personal experience, photo feature, life histories and habitat needs of wild animals. No anthropomorphism, no domestic animal stories. Buys 24-30 mss/year. Query. Length: 600-850 words. Pays $100-500.

Photos: State availability of photos with submission. Reviews 35mm transparencies. Offers $50-250/photo. Captions, model releases, identification of subjects required. Buys one-time rights.

Columns/Departments: Making a Difference (kids' projects that improve their environment and surrounding habitat), 500 words; Short Stuff (short items, puzzles, games, interesting facts about nature), 300 words. Buys 25 mss/year. Send complete ms. Pays $50-100.

Fiction: Adventure (outdoor, nature and exploring, ethical, 'hunting' stories that reflect good sportsmanship and behavior). "We haven't used fiction, but are willing to consider stories that reflect oudoors and environmental ethics, caring for the land and animals." Query. Length: 600-850 words. Pays $100-500.

Poetry: Haiku, light verse, traditional. No poetry that is not nature-related. No religious tone, please. Buys 4 poems/year. Pays $50.

Fillers: Facts. Buys 15-20/year. Length: 300 words maximum. Pays $50-100.

Tips: "Because our publisher is a nonprofit whose mission is to conserve habitat for wildlife, we look for a gentle conservation/habitat/environmental ethics message. Stories should be scientifically accurate because the magazine is used in many classrooms. We also look for a hopeful, light-hearted, *fun* style."

WONDER TIME, 6401 The Paseo, Kansas City MO 64131. (816)333-7000. Fax: (816)333-4439. E-mail: lperrigo@nazarene.org. or ssmith@nazarene.org. Contact: Lois Perrigo, editor. 75% freelance written. "Willing to read and consider appropriate freelance submissions." Published weekly by WordAction for children ages 6-8. Correlates to the Bible Truth in the weekly Sunday School lesson. Pays on publication. Publishes ms an average of 1 year after acceptance. Byline given. Buys rights to reuse and all rights for curriculum assignments. Reports in 1 month. Sample copy and writer's guidelines for 9×12 SAE with 2 first-class stamps.

Fiction: Buys stories portraying Christian attitudes without being preachy. Uses stories for special days—stories teaching honesty, truthfulness, kindness, helpfulness or other important spiritual truths, and avoiding symbolism. Also, stories about real life problems children face today. "God should be spoken of as our Father who loves and cares for us; Jesus, as our Lord and Savior." Buys 52 mss/year. Length: 250-350 words. Pays $25 on publication.

Tips: "Any stories that allude to church doctrine must be in keeping with Wesleyan beliefs. Any type of fantasy must be in good taste and easily recognizable."

LITERARY AND "LITTLE"

Fiction, poetry, essays, book reviews and scholarly criticism comprise the content of the magazines listed in this section. Some are published by colleges and universities, and many are regional in focus.

Everything about "little" literary magazines is different than other consumer magazines. Most carry few or no ads, and many do not seek them. Circulations under 1,000 are common. And sales often come more from the purchase of sample copies than from the newsstand.

The magazines listed in this section cannot compete with the pay rates and exposure of the high-circulation general interest magazines also publishing fiction and poetry. But most "little" literary magazines don't try. They are more apt to specialize in publishing certain kinds of fiction or poetry: traditional, experimental, works with a regional sensibility, or the fiction and poetry of new and younger writers. For that reason, and because fiction and poetry vary so widely in style, writers should *always* invest in the most recent copies of the magazines they aspire to publish in.

Many "little" literary magazines pay contributors only in copies of the issues in which their works appear. *Writer's Market* lists only those that pay their contributors in cash. However, *Novel & Short Story Writer's Market* includes nonpaying fiction markets, and has in-depth information about fiction techniques and markets. The same is true of *Poet's Market* for nonpaying poetry markets (both books are published by Writer's Digest Books). Many literary agents and book editors regularly read these magazines in search of literary voices not found in mainstream writing. There are also more literary opportunities listed in the Contests and Awards section.

‡ACM (Another Chicago Magazine), Left Field Press, 3709 N. Kenmore, Chicago IL 60613. Contact: Barry Silesky, editor. 98% freelance written. Open to new/unpublished writers. Biannual literary journal. Estab. 1977. Circ. 2,500. Pays on publication. Publishes ms an average of 6 months after acceptance. Byline given. Buys first serial rights. Accepts simultaneous queries and submissions. Reports in 3 months. Sample copy for $8. Writer's guidelines for #10 SASE.

Nonfiction: S.L. Wisenberg, nonfiction editor. Interview (contemporary poets and fiction writers), essays (contemporary literature), reviews of small press publications. Buys 5-6 mss/year. Query. Length: 1,000-20,000 words. Pays $5-25.

Fiction: Sharon Solwitz, fiction editor. Serious ethnic and experimental fiction, novel excerpts. Buys 10-20 mss/year.

Send complete ms. Length: 50-10,000 words. Pays $5-25.
Poetry: Serious poetry. No light verse or inspirational. Buys 50 poems/year. Length: 1-1,000 lines. Pays $5-25.

AFRICAN AMERICAN REVIEW, Indiana State University, Department of English, ISU, Terre Haute IN 47809. (812)237-2968. Fax: (812)237-4382. E-mail: wsmalloy@amber.indstate.edu. Website: http://web.indstate.edu:80/Artsci/ AAR. Contact: Joe Weixlmann, editor. Managing Editor: Connie LeComte. 65% freelance written. Quarterly magazine covering African-American literature and culture. "Essays on African-American literature, theater, film, art and culture generally; interviews; poetry and fiction by African-American authors; book reviews." Estab. 1967. Circ. 4,500. Pays on publication. Publishes ms an average of 1 year after acceptance. Byline given. Buys first North American serial rights. Editorial lead time 1 year. Reports in 1 month on queries; 3 months on mss. Sample copy for $5. Writer's guidelines for #10 SASE.
Nonfiction: Essays, interview/profile. Buys 30 mss/year. Query. Length: 3,500-6,000 words. Pays $50-150. Pays in contributor copies upon request.
Photos: State availability of photos with submission. Offers no additional payment for photos accepted with ms. Captions required.
Fiction: Ethnic. Buys 4 mss/year. Send complete ms. Length: 2,500-5,000 words. Pays $50-150.
Poetry: Avant-garde, free verse, haiku, traditional. No light verse. Buys 20 poems/year. Submit maximum 6 poems. Pays $25-75.

‡AGNI, Dept. WM, Boston University, 236 Bay State Rd., Boston, MA 02215. (617)353-5389. Fax: (617)353-7136. E-mail: agni@acs.bu.edu. Website: http://www.cais.net/aesir/fiction/AGNI. Contact: Askold Melnyczuk, editor; Valerie Duff, managing editor. Book Review Editor: Joe Osterhaus. Biannual literary magazine. "*AGNI* publishes poetry, fiction and essays. Also regularly publishes translations and is committed to featuring the work of emerging writers. We have published Derek Walcott, Joyce Carol Oates, Sharon Olds, John Updike, and many others, including then unknown writers: Sven Birkerts, Carolyn Chute, Tom Sleigh and Mary Morris." Estab. 1972. Circ. 2,000. Pays on publication. Publishes ms an average of 6 months after acceptance. Byline given. Buys first North American serial rights and rights to reprint in *AGNI* anthology (with author's consent). Editorial lead time 6 months. Accepts simultaneous submissions. Reports in 2 weeks on queries; 4 months on mss. Sample copy for $7. Writer's guidelines for #10 SASE.
● The $1 reading fee has been abolished! Send only a SASE with submission.
Fiction: Short stories. Buys 6-12 mss/year. Send complete ms. Pays $20-150.
Poetry: Buys more than 140/year. Submit maximum 5 poems. Pays $20-150.
Tips: "We suggest writers read *AGNI* first, and if they feel their work is compatible, send story or 1-5 poems for consideration. We read from October 1 through April 30. Manuscripts sent at other times will be returned unread."

ALASKA QUARTERLY REVIEW, College of Arts & Sciences, University of Alaska-Anchorage, 3211 Providence Dr., Anchorage AK 99508. (907)786-6916. Contact: Ronald Spatz, executive editor. 95% freelance written. Prefers to work with published/established writers; eager to work with new/unpublished writers. Semiannual magazine publishing fiction, poetry, literary nonfiction and short plays in traditional and experimental styles. Estab. 1982. Circ. 1,500. Pays honorariums on publication when funding permits. Publishes ms an average of 6 months after acceptance. Byline given. Buys first North American serial rights. Upon request, rights will be transferred back to author after publication. Reports in 4 months. Sample copy for $5. Writer's guidelines for SASE.
● *Alaska Quarterly* reports they are always looking for freelance material and new writers.
Nonfiction: Literary nonfiction: essays and memoirs. Buys 0-5 mss/year. Query. Length: 1,000-20,000 words. Pays $50-200 subject to funding; pays in copies and subscriptions when funding is limited.
Reprints: Accepts previously published submissions under special circumstances (special anthologies or translations). Send photocopy of article or short story or typed ms with rights for sale noted and information about when and where the piece previously appeared.
Fiction: Experimental and traditional literary forms. No romance, children's or inspirational/religious. Publishes novel excerpts. Buys 20-26 mss/year. Send complete ms. Length: Up to 20,000 words. Pays $50-200 subject to funding; pays in contributor's copies and subscriptions when funding is limited.
Drama: Experimental and traditional one-act plays. Buys 0-2 mss/year. Query. Length: Up to 20,000 words but prefers short plays. Pays $50-200 subject to funding; contributor's copies and subscriptions when funding is limited.
Poetry: Avant-garde, free verse, traditional. No light verse. Buys 10-30 poems/year. Submit maximum 10 poems. Pays $10-50 subject to availability of funds; pays in contributor's copies and subscriptions when funding is limited.
Tips: "All sections are open to freelancers. We rely almost exclusively on unsolicited manuscripts. *AQR* is a nonprofit literary magazine and does not always have funds to pay authors."

AMELIA MAGAZINE, Amelia Press, 329 E St., Bakersfield CA 93304. (805)323-4064. Contact: Frederick A. Raborg, Jr., editor. Estab. 1983. 100% freelance written. Eager to work with new/unpublished writers. "*Amelia* is a quarterly international magazine publishing the finest poetry and fiction available, along with expert criticism and reviews intended for all interested in contemporary literature. *Amelia* also publishes three supplements each year: *Cicada*, which publishes only high quality traditional or experimental haiku and senryu plus fiction, essays and cartoons pertaining to Japan; *SPSM&H*, which publishes the highest quality traditional and experimental sonnets available plus romantic fiction and essays pertaining to the sonnet; and the annual winner of the Charles William Duke long poem contest." Circ. 1,750. **Pays on acceptance.** Publishes ms an average of 6 months after acceptance. Byline given. Offers 50% kill fee. Buys first North American serial rights. Submit seasonal material 2 months in advance. Reports in 3 months on mss. Sample copy for $9.95 (includes postage). Sample copy of any supplement for $4.95. Writer's guidelines for #10 SASE.

● An eclectic magazine, open to greater variety of styles—especially genre and mainstream stories unsuitable for other literary magazines. Receptive to new writers.

Nonfiction: Historical/nostalgic (in the form of belles lettres); humor (in fiction or belles lettres); interview/profile (poets and fiction writers); opinion (on poetry and fiction only); personal experience (as it pertains to poetry or fiction in the form of belles lettres); travel (in the form of belles lettres only); criticism and book reviews of poetry and small press fiction titles. "Nothing overtly slick in approach. Criticism pieces must have depth; belles lettres must offer important insights into the human scene." Buys 8 mss/year. Send complete ms. Length: 1,000-2,000 words. Pays $25 or by arrangement. Sometimes pays the expenses of writers on assignment.

Fiction: Adventure, book excerpts (original novel excerpts only), erotica (of a quality seen in Anais Nin or Henry Miller only), ethnic, experimental, fantasy, historical, horror, humorous, mainstream, mystery, novel excerpts, science fiction, suspense, western. "We would consider slick fiction of the quality seen in *Esquire* or *Vanity Fair* and more excellent submissions in the genres—science fiction, wit, Gothic horror, traditional romance, stories with complex *raisons d'être*; avant-garde ought to be truly avant-garde." No pornography ("good erotica is not the same thing"). Buys 24-36 mss/year. Send complete ms. Length: 1,000-5,000 words. Pays $35 or by arrangement for exceptional work.

● Ranked as one of the best markets for fiction writers in the last *Writer's Digest* magazine's annual "Fiction 50."

Poetry: Avant-garde, free verse, haiku, light verse, traditional. "No patently religious or stereotypical newspaper poetry." Buys 100-160 poems/year depending on lengths. Prefers submission of at least 3 poems. Length: 3-100 lines. Pays $2-25; additional payment for exceptional work, usually by established professionals. *Cicada* pays $10 each to 3 "best of issue" poets; *SPSM&H* pays $14 to 2 "best of issue" sonnets; winner of the long poem contest receives $100 plus copies and publication.

Tips: "*Have something to say* and say it well. If you insist on waving flags or pushing your religion, then do it with subtlety and class. We enjoy a good cry from time to time, too, but sentimentality does not mean we want to see mush. Read our fiction carefully for depth of plot and characterization, then try very hard to improve on it. With the growth of quality in short fiction, we expect to find stories of lasting merit. I also hope to begin seeing more critical essays which, without sacrificing research, demonstrate a more entertaining obliqueness to the style sheets, more 'new journalism' than MLA. In poetry, we also often look for a good 'storyline' so to speak. Above all we want to feel a sense of honesty and value in every piece."

AMERICAN SHORT FICTION, Parlin 108, Dept. of English, University of Texas at Austin, Austin TX 78712-1164. (512)471-1772. Contact: Joseph Kruppa, editor. 90% freelance written. Quarterly fiction magazine. "*American Short Fiction* carries fiction of all lengths up to and including the novella, and is aimed at a general readership." Estab. 1990. **Pays on acceptance.** Publishes ms an average of 9 months after acceptance. Buys first serial rights. Accepts simultaneous submissions if notified. Reports in 4 months. Sample copy for $9.95 and $2 for foreign postage if necessary.

Fiction: "Stories are selected for their originality and craftsmanship. No condensed novels or slice-of-life vignettes, please." Buys 20-30 mss/year. Send complete ms and SASE. Pays $400.

● *American Short Fiction* sponsors an annual fiction contest. Send SASE for details.

Tips: "Manuscripts are only accepted September 1-May 31."

ANTIETAM REVIEW, 7 W. Franklin St., Hagerstown MD 21740-4804. (301)791-3132. Contact: Susanne Kass, editor. 100% freelance written. Annual magazine of fiction (short stories), poetry and b&w photography. Estab. 1982. Circ. 1,500. Pays on publication. Byline given. Reports in 2 months. Sample copy for $3.15 (back issue), $5.25 (current issue). Writer's guidelines for SASE.

Fiction: Novel excerpts (if work as independent pieces), short stories of a literary quality. No religious, romance, erotica, confession, horror or condensed novels. Buys 9 mss/year. Query or send complete ms. Length: 5,000 words. Pays $50-100.

Poetry: Crystal Brown. Avant-garde, free verse, traditional. Does not want to see haiku, religious and most rhyme. Buys 15-20 poems/year. Submit 5 poems maximum. Pays $20.

Tips: "Spring 98 annual issue will need fiction, poetry and b&w photography not previously published. Still seeking high quality work from both published and emerging writers. Writers must live in or be native of, Maryland, Pennsylvania, Delaware, Virginia, West Virginia or District of Columbia. Also we now have a summer Literary Contest. We consider materials from September 1-February 1."

‡THE ANTIGONISH REVIEW, St. Francis Xavier University, P.O. Box 5000, Antigonish, Nova Scotia B2G 2W5 Canada. (902)867-3962. Fax: (902)867-2389. E-mail: tar@stfx.ca. Managing Editor: Gertrude Sanderson. Contact: George Sanderson, editor. 100% freelance written. Quarterly literary magazine. Estab. 1970. Circ. 850. Pays on publication. Publishes ms an average of 2-4 months after acceptance. Byline given. Offers variable kill fee. Rights retained by author. Editorial lead time 4 months. Submit seasonal material 4 months in advance. Reports in 4 months on mss; 1 month on queries. Sample copy for $4. Writer's guidelines free.

Nonfiction: Essays, interview/profile, book reviews/articles. No academic pieces. Buys 15-20 mss/year. Query. Length: 1,500-5,000 words. Pays $50-200.

Fiction: Literary. No erotica. Buys 35-40 mss/year. Send complete ms. Length: 500-5,000 words. Pays in copies.

Poetry: Buys 100-125 poems/year. Submit maximum 5 poems. Pays in copies.

Tips: "Send for guidelines and/or sample copy. Send ms with cover letter and SASE with submission."

ANTIOCH REVIEW, P.O. Box 148, Yellow Springs OH 45387-0148. Contact: Robert S. Fogarty, editor. Quarterly magazine for general, literary and academic audience. Estab. 1941. Copyright held by *Antioch Review*; reverts to author upon publication. Byline given. Pays on publication. Publishes ms an average of 10 months after acceptance. Reports in 2 months. Sample copy for $6. Writer's guidelines for #10 SASE.

Nonfiction: "Contemporary articles in the humanities and social sciences, politics, economics, literature and all areas of broad intellectual concern. Somewhat scholarly, but never pedantic in style, eschewing all professional jargon. Lively, distinctive prose insisted upon." Length: 2,000-8,000 words. Pays $10/published page.

Fiction: "Quality fiction only, distinctive in style with fresh insights into the human condition." No science fiction, fantasy or confessions. Pays $10/published page.

Poetry: No light or inspirational verse. Contributors should be familiar with the magazine before submitting. "We do not read poetry May 1-September 1."

‡ARC, Canada's National Poetry Magazine, Arc Poetry Society, Box 7368, Ottawa, Ontario K1L 8E4 Canada. Contact: John Barton and Rita Donovan, co-editors. Semiannual literary magazine featuring poetry, poetry-related articles and criticism. "Our focus is poetry, and Canadian poetry in general, although we do publish writers from elsewhere. We are looking for the best poetry from new and established writers. We often have special issues. SASE for upcoming special issues and contests." Estab. 1978. Circ. 750. Pays on publication. Publishes ms an average of 6 months after acceptance. Byline given. Buys one-time rights. Reports in 4 months on queries. Sample copy for $4 with 10 first-class stamps.

Nonfiction: Essays, interview/profile, photo feature. Query. Length: 1,000 words. Pays $25 plus 2 copies.

Photos: Query with samples. Pays $25. Buys one-time rights.

Poetry: Avant-garde, free verse, haiku. Buys 40/year. Submit max. 6 poems. Pays $25 (Canadian)/printed page.

Tips: "SASE for guidelines. We prefer brief or no cover letters."

AUTHORS, 501 Cambridge St. SE, Medicine Hat, Alberta T1A 0T3 Canada. Fax: (403)526-8020. E-mail: authmag @aol.com. Website: http://members.aol.com/authmag/authors.htm. Contact: Philip Murphy, editor. 100% freelance written. Monthly magazine providing a competitive platform that will both enhance professional skills as well as develop the novice. Estab. 1992. Circ. 300. "We no longer issue assignments." Buys one-time rights. Editorial lead time 2 months. Submit seasonal material 3 months in advance. Accepts simultaneous submissions. Reports in 2 weeks on queries; 1 month on mss. Sample copy and writer's guidelines available online.

Nonfiction: Book excerpts, essays, general interet, historical/nostalgic, humor, inspirational, interview/profile, opinion, personal experience, religious, travel. Buys 6 mss/year. Query. Length: 1,500-10,000 words. Pays $100 for unsolicited articles. "We no longer issue assignments."

Reprints: Accepts previously published submissions. Send photocopy of article or short story.

Fiction: Adventure, condensed novel, confession, ethnic, experimental, fantasy, historical, horror, humorous, mainstream, mystery, novel excerpts, religious, romance, science fiction, serialized novels, slice-of-life vignettes, suspense, western. Buys 12 mss/year. Query. Length: 300-10,000 words. Pays $100.

Poetry: Avant-garde, free verse, haiku, light verse, traditional. Buys 12 poems/year. Length: 1-1,000 lines. Pays $100.

Fillers: Anecdotes, facts, short humor. Pays free copy.

Tips: "*Authors* is reluctant to send out rejection slips. Since its purpose is to provide a platform for both novice and professional writers, it will endeavour to publish all serious noncontroversial inquiries, either on a nonmonetary or monetary basis, affording them both exposure and feedback, limited only by the subscriber base."

‡B&A NEW FICTION, P.O. Box 702, Station P, Toronto, Ontario M5S 2Y4 Canada. (416)535-1233. E-mail: blood@ io.org. Contact: Dennis Bock and Michelle Alfano, fiction editors. 100% freelance written. Quarterly magazine. Estab. 1990. Circ. 2,000. Pays on publication. Publishes ms an average of 6 months after acceptance. Byline given. Buys first North American serial rights, electronic and anthology rights. Editorial lead time 2 months. Accepts simultaneous submissions. Reports in 2 weeks on queries; 2 months on mss. Sample for $6 (U.S. funds). Guidelines for #10 SASE with IRCs.

Fiction: Experimental, historical, humorous, novel excerpts. No confession, sci-fi, poetry. Buys 20-30 mss/year. Send complete ms. Length: 500-7,000 words. Pays $35/printed page.

‡BANGTALE INTERNATIONAL, P.O. Box 83984, Phoenix AZ 85071-3984. E-mail: bangtale@mailhost.primenet. com. Contact: William Edward Dudley, editor. 75% freelance written. Semiannual magazine. "We actively seek poetry that is telling and doesn't complicate itself through evasive word salad but seeks understanding and gives emotion. We want short stories and essays that in their own way have a poetic underpinning. We lean toward works that explore how different cultures enrich our lives and increase our sense of the world's people. Above all we encourage writing as an instrument that disentangles your thought process. (We would rather see your ideas than set up restrictions.) We encourage humor and irony." Publishes ms 10 months after acceptance. Byline given. Buys one-time rights. Editorial lead time 4 months. Reports in 2-4 weeks. Sample copy for $5.

Nonfiction: Cultural interest, book excerpts, essays, humor, interview/profile, personal experience. Buys 5 mss/year. Send complete ms hard copy and if available disk with indication of the program in which it was written. Length: 300-1,000 words. Pays $25-50.

Photos: Reviews artistic 3×5 prints (b&w). Negotiates payment individually.

Fiction: Experimental, character studies, humor, novel excerpts, slice-of-life, vignettes. Publishes novel excerpts. Send complete ms hard copy and if available disk with indication of the program in which it was written. Length: 300-3,000 words. Pays $25-50.

Poetry: Anything poetic, free verse, light verse. Submit maximum 15 poems. Pays in contributor's copy.

Tips: "Use quality in language that is humane, humorous, passionate, delightfully understandable, culturally forward, and unexpected."

BLACK WARRIOR REVIEW, P.O. Box 2936, Tuscaloosa AL 35486-2936. (205)348-4518. Website: http://www.sa.ua.edu/osm/bwr. Contact: Ning Cabiles, managing editor. Editor: Christopher Chambers. 95% freelance written. Semiannual magazine of fiction, poetry, essays and reviews. Estab. 1974. Circ. 2,000. Pays on publication. Publishes ms an average of 6 months after acceptance. Byline given. Buys first rights. Reports in 2 weeks on queries; 3 months on mss. Sample copy for $8. Writer's guidelines for #10 SASE.

• Consistently excellent magazine. Placed stories and poems in recent *Best American Short Stories*, *Best American Poetry* and *Pushcart Prize* anthologies.

Nonfiction: Interview/profile, book reviews and literary/personal essays. Buys 5 mss/year. Query or send complete ms. No limit on length. Payment varies.

Photos: State availability of photos with submission. Offers no additional payment for photos accepted with ms. Identification of subjects required. Buys one-time rights.

Fiction: Ariana-Sophia Kartsois, fiction editor. Buys 10 mss/year. Publishes novel excerpts if under contract to be published. One story/chapter per envelope, please.

Poetry: Alan May, poetry editor. Submit 3-6 poems. Long poems encouraged. Buys 50 poems/year.

Tips: "Read the *BWR* before submitting; editor changes each year. Send us your best work. Submissions of photos and/or artwork is encouraged. We sometimes choose unsolicited photos/artwork for the cover. Address all submissions to the appropriate genre editor."

‡BOMB MAGAZINE, 594 Broadway, #905, New York NY 10012. (212) 431-3943. Contact: Jennifer Berman, senior editor. Quarterly literary magazine covering art, literature, film, theater and music. Estab. 1981. Circ. 12,000. Pays on publication. Publishes ms an average of 6 months after acceptance. Byline given. Buys one-time rights. Reports in 4 months. Sample copy for $4 and 10 first-class stamps.

Nonfiction: Book excerpts. "Literature only" Query. Length: 250-5,000 words. Pays $100 minimum.

Photos: Pays $100 minimum. Captions required. Buys one-time rights.

Fiction: Experimental, novel excerpts. "No commercial fiction." Buys 28 mss/year. Send complete ms. Length: 250-5,000 words. Pays $100 minimum.

Poetry: Avant-garde. Buys 10/year. Submit maximum 5 poems. Pays $50.

BOULEVARD, Opojaz, Inc., 4579 Laclede Ave., #332, St. Louis MO 63108-2103. Contact: Richard Burgin, editor. 100% freelance written. Triannual literary magazine covering fiction, poetry and essays. "*Boulevard* is a diverse literary magazine presenting original creative work by well-known authors, as well as by writers of exciting promise." Estab. 1985. Circ. 3,000. Pays on publication. Publishes ms an average of 1 year after acceptance. Byline given. No kill fee. Buys first North American serial rights. Accepts simultaneous submissions. Reports in 2 weeks on queries; 2 months on mss. Sample copy for $7. Writer's guidelines for #10 SASE.

Nonfiction: Book excerpts, essays, interview/profile. "No pornography, science fiction, children's stories or westerns." Buys 8 mss/year. Send complete ms. Length: 8,000 words maximum. Pays $50-150 (sometimes higher).

Fiction: Confession, experimental, mainstream, novel excerpts. "We do not want erotica, science fiction, romance, western or children's stories." Buys 20 mss/year. Send complete ms. Length: 8,000 words maximum. Pays $50-150 (sometimes higher).

Poetry: Avant-garde, free verse, haiku, traditional. "Do not send us light verse." Buys 80 poems/year. Submit maximum 5 poems. Length: up to 200 lines. Pays $25-150 (sometimes higher).

Tips: "Read the magazine first. The work *Boulevard* publishes is generally recognized as among the finest in the country. We continue to seek more good literary or cultural essays. Send only your best work."

‡CANADIAN LITERATURE, #225-2029 West Mall, University of British Columbia, Vancouver, British Columbia V6T 1Z2 Canada. (604)822-2780. Fax: (604)822-5504. E-mail: emk@cdn-lit.ubc.ca. Website: http://www.swifty.com/cdn_lit/. Contact: Eva-Marie Kröller, editor. 70% freelance written. Works with "both new and established writers depending on quality." Quarterly. Estab. 1959. Circ. 1,200. Not copyrighted. Buys first Canadian rights only. Pays on publication. Publishes ms an average of 2 years after acceptance. Reports in 3 months. Sample copy and writer's guidelines for $15 (Canadian) plus postage (include SASE).

Nonfiction: Articles of high quality only on Canadian books and writers written in French or English. Articles should be scholarly and readable. Query "with a clear description of the project." Length: 2,000-5,500 words.

THE CAPILANO REVIEW, The Capilano Press Society, 2055 Purcell Way, North Vancouver, British Columbia V7J 3H5 Canada. Fax: (604)983-7520. E-mail: rsherrin@capcollege.bc.ca. Website: http://www.capcollege.bc.ca. Editor: Robert Sherrin. 100% freelance written. "Triannual visual and literary arts magazine that publishes only what the editors consider to be the very best fiction, poetry, or visual art being produced. *TCR* editors are interested in fresh, original work that stimulates and challenges readers. Over the years, the magazine has developed a reputation for pushing beyond the boundaries of traditional art and writing. We are interested in work that is new in concept and in execution." Estab. 1972. Circ. 1,000. Pays on publication. Publishes ms 3 months after acceptance. Byline given. Buys first North American serial rights. Reports in 1 month on queries; 5 months on mss. Sample copy for $9. Writer's guidelines for #10 SASE with IRC or Canadian stamps.

- *The Capilano Review* is seeking more stories focusing on experiences in British Columbia or other areas of Canada, and more stories that reflect multiculturalism.

Nonfiction: Essays, interview/profile, personal experience, creative nonfiction. Buys 1-2 mss/year. Query. Pays $50-200, plus 2 copies and 1 year subscription. "Most nonfiction is assigned to writers we have worked with before. If we know you, you may send a query. If we don't, send complete ms."

Fiction: Literary. Buys 10-15 mss/year. Send complete ms. Pays $50-200. Publishes novel excerpts.

Poetry: Avant-garde, free verse. Buys 40 poems/year. Submit 5-10 poems. Pays $50-200.

THE CHARITON REVIEW, Truman State University, Kirksville MO 63501-9915. (816)785-4499. Fax: (816)785-7486. Contact: Jim Barnes, editor. 100% freelance written. Semiannual (fall and spring) magazine covering contemporary fiction, poetry, translation and book reviews. Circ. 600. Pays on publication. Publishes ms an average of 6 months after acceptance. Byline given. Buys first North American serial rights. Reports in 1 week on queries; 1 month on mss. Sample copy for $5 and 7×10 SAE with 4 first-class stamps.

Nonfiction: Essays, essay reviews of books. Buys 2-5 mss/year. Send complete ms. Length: 1,000-5,000. Pays $15.

Reprints: Send typed ms with rights for sale noted and when and where the article previously appeared.

Fiction: Ethnic, experimental, mainstream, novel excerpts, traditional. Publishes novel excerpts if they can stand alone. "Not interested in slick material." Buys 6-10 mss/year. Send complete ms. Length: 1,000-6,000 words. Pays $5/page.

Poetry: Avant-garde, traditional. Buys 50-55 poems/year. Submit maximum 5 poems. Length: open. Pays $5/page.

Tips: "Read *Chariton*. Know the difference between good literature and bad. Know what magazine might be interested in your work. We are not trendy. We publish only the best. All sections open to freelancers. Know your market or you're wasting your time—and mine. Do *not* write for guidelines; the only guideline is excellence in all matters."

CHELSEA, Chelsea Associates, P.O. Box 773, Cooper Station, New York NY 10276. Contact: Richard Foerster, editor. 70% freelance written. Semiannual literary magazine. "We stress style, variety, originality. No special biases or requirements. Flexible attitudes, eclectic material. We take an active interest, as always, in cross-cultural exchanges, superior translations, and are leaning toward cosmopolitan, interdisciplinary techniques, but maintain no strictures against traditional modes." Estab. 1958. Circ. 1,800. Pays on publication. Publishes ms an average of 6 months after acceptance. Byline given. Buys first North American serial rights. Reports in 3 months on mss. Include SASE. Sample copy for $6.

- *Chelsea* also sponsors fiction and poetry contests. Send SASE for guidelines.

Nonfiction: Essays, book reviews (query first with sample). Buys 6 mss/year. Send complete ms. Length: 6,000 words. Pays $15/page.

Fiction: Mainstream, literary, novel excerpts. Buys 12 mss/year. Send complete ms. Length: 5-6,000 words. Pays $15/page.

Poetry: Avant-garde, free verse, traditional. Buys 60-75 poems/year. Pays $15/page.

Tips: "We only accept written queries. We are looking for more super translations, first-rate fiction and work by writers of color."

CICADA, *Amelia Magazine*, 329 E St., Bakersfield CA 93304. (805)323-4064. Contact: Frederick A. Raborg, Jr., editor. 100% freelance written. Quarterly magazine covering Oriental fiction and poetry (haiku, etc.). "Our readers expect the best haiku and related poetry forms we can find. Our readers circle the globe and know their subjects. We include fiction, book reviews and articles related to the forms or to the Orient." Estab. 1984. Circ. 600. Pays on publication. Publishes ms an average of 6 months after acceptance. Byline given. Offers 50% kill fee. Buys first North American serial rights. Editorial lead time 2 months. Submit seasonal material 3 months in advance. Accepts simultaneous submissions. Reports in 2 weeks on queries, 3 months on mss. Sample copy for $4.95. Guidelines for #10 SASE.

Nonfiction: Essays, general interest, historical/nostalgic, humor, interview/profile, opinion, personal experience, travel. Buys 1-3 mss/year. Send complete ms. Length: 500-2,500 words. Pays $10.

Photos: Send photos with submission. Reviews 5×7 or 8×10 prints. Offers $10-25/photo. Model releases required. Buys one-time rights.

Fiction: Adventure, erotica, ethnic, experimental, fantasy, historical, horror, humorous, mainstream, mystery, romance,

---

ALWAYS SUBMIT unsolicited manuscripts or queries with a self-addressed, stamped envelope (SASE) within your country or a self-addressed envelope with International Reply Coupons (IRC) purchased from the post office for other countries.

science fiction, slice-of-life vignettes, suspense. Buys 4 mss/year. Send complete ms. Length: 500-2,500 words. Pays $10-20.
Poetry: Buys 400 poems/year. Submit maximum 12 poems. Length: 1-50 lines. Pays 3 "best of issue" poets $10.
Fillers: Anecdotes, short humor. Buys 1-4/year. Length: 25-500 words. No payment for fillers.
Tips: "Writers should understand the limitations of contemporary Japanese forms particularly. We also use poetry based on other Asian ethnicities and on the South Seas ethnicities. Don't be afraid to experiment within the forms. Be professional in approach and presentation."

CIMARRON REVIEW, Oklahoma State University, 205 Morrill Hall, OSU, Stillwater OK 74078-0135. (405)744-9476. Contact: E.P. Walkiewicz, editor. 85% freelance written. Quarterly literary magazine. "We publish short fiction, poetry, and essays of serious literary quality by writers often published, seldom published and previously unpublished. We have no bias with respect to subject matter, form (traditional or experimental) or theme. Though we appeal to a general audience, many of our readers are writers themselves or members of a university community." Estab. 1967. Circ. 500. Pays on publication. Published ms an average of 1 year after acceptance. Byline given. Buys all rights (reprint permission freely granted on request). Reports in 1 week on queries; 3 months on mss. Sample copy for $3 and 7×10 SASE. Writer's guidelines for #10 SASE.
Nonfiction: Essays, general interest, historical, interview/profile, opinion, personal experience, travel, literature and arts. "We are not interested in highly subjective personal reminiscences, obscure or arcane articles, or short, light 'human interest' pieces." Special issues: flash fiction; Native American writers; Irish writers. Buys 9-12 mss/year. Send complete ms. Length: 1,000-7,500 words. Pays $50 plus 1 year's subscription.
Fiction: Mainstream, literary, novel excerpts. No juvenile or genre fiction. Buys 12-17 mss/year. Send complete ms. Length: 1,250-7,000 words. Pays $50.
Poetry: Free verse, traditional. No haiku, light verse or experimental poems. Buys 55-70 poems/year. Submit maximum 6 poems. Pays $15/poem.
Tips: "For prose, submit legible, double-spaced typescript with name and address on manuscript. Enclose SASE and brief cover letter. For poetry, same standards apply, but single-spaced is conventional. Be familiar with high quality, contemporary mainstream writing. Evaluate your own work carefully."

CLOCKWATCH REVIEW, (a journal of the arts), Dept. of English, Illinois Wesleyan University, Bloomington IL 61702-2900. (309)556-3352. Fax: (309)556-3411. E-mail: jplath@titan.iwu.edu. Website: http://titan.iwu.edu/~jplath/. Contact: James Plath and Zarina Mullan Plath, editors. 85% freelance written. Semiannual literary magazine. Estab. 1983. Circ. 1,500. **Pays on acceptance.** Byline given. Buys first North American serial rights. Submit seasonal material 6 months in advance. Reports in 6 months. Sample copy for $4. Writer's guidelines for #10 SASE.
Nonfiction: Literary essays, criticism (MLA style), interviews with writers, musicians, artists. Special issue: Sex and Gender in American Culture. Buys 4-8 mss/year. Query with or without published clips. Length: 1,500-4,000 words. Pays up to $25 for creative nonfiction and interviews. No payment for criticism except copies.
Photos: State availability of photos with submission. Reviews contact sheets, negatives, transparencies. Offers no additional payment for photos accepted with ms. Buys one-time rights.
Fiction: Experimental, humorous, mainstream, novel excerpts. "Also literary quality genre stories that break the mold. No straight mystery, fantasy, science fiction, romance or western." Buys 8-10 mss/year. Send complete ms. Length: 1,500-4,000 words. Pays up to $25 for creative nonfiction and interviews. No payment for criticism except copies.
Poetry: Avant-garde, free verse, light verse, traditional. Buys 30-40 poems/year. Submit maximum 6 poems. Length: 32 lines maximum. Pays $5.

CONFRONTATION, A Literary Journal, Long Island University, Brookville NY 11548. (516)299-2391. Fax: (516)299-2735. Editor: Martin Tucker. Assistant to Editor: Emily Berkowitz. 75% freelance written. Semiannual literary magazine. "We are eclectic in our taste. Excellence of style is our dominant concern." Estab. 1968. Circ. 2,000. Pays on publication. Publishes ms an average of 1 year after acceptance. Byline given. "We rarely offer kill fee." Buys first North American serial, first, one-time or all rights. Accepts simultaneous submissions. Reports in 3 weeks on queries; 2 months on mss. Sample copy for $3.
Nonfiction: Essays, personal experience. Buys 15 mss/year. Send complete ms. Length: 1,500-5,000 words. Pays $100-300 for assigned articles; $15-300 for unsolicited articles.
Photos: State availability of photos with ms. No additional payment for photos accepted with ms. Buys one-time rights.
Fiction: Jonna Semeiks. Experimental, mainstream, science fiction, slice-of-life vignettes, novel excerpts (if they are self-contained stories). "We judge on quality, so genre is open." Buys 60-75 mss/year. Send complete ms. Length 6,000 words maximum. Pays $25-250.
Poetry: Katherine Hill-Miller. Avant-garde, free verse, haiku, light verse, traditional. Buys 60-75 poems/year. Submit maximum 6 poems. Length open. Pays $10-100.
Tips: "Most open to fiction and poetry."

CRAZYHORSE, Crazyhorse Association at UALR, English Dept., University of Arkansas, Little Rock AR 72204. (501)569-3161. Contact: Ralph Burns, editor. 100% freelance written. Semiannual magazine of poetry and critical prose. "*Crazyhorse* publishes quality poetry; no special slant." Estab. 1960. Circ. 1,000. Pays on publication. Publishes ms 1 year after acceptance. Buys first North American serial rights. Editorial lead time 18 months. Reports in 6 months on mss. Sample copy for $5 and #10 SASE.

Nonfiction: Dennis Vannatta, criticism editor. Interview/profile, reviews of contemporary poetry and short fiction. Buys 3 mss/year. Send complete ms. Length 1,000-6,000 words. Pays $10/printed page and 2 contributor's copies.
Poetry: Ralph Burns, poetry editor. Traditional. Buys 50-60 poems/year. Submit maximum 6 poems. Pays $10/printed page and 2 contributor's copies.
Tips: "Buy a sample copy to see the kind of work we publish. We do not have any guidelines."

CURRICULUM VITAE, Grove City Factory Stores, P.O. Box 1309, Grove City PA 16127. E-mail: mdittman@owl.eng l.sru.edu. Editor: Michael Dittman. Managing Editor: Mark McClusky. 90% freelance written. Quarterly magazine covering pop culture with a Generation-X intellectual edge. "We cater to an audience of highly-educated with young readers who are concerned with social and philosophical issues." Estab. 1995. Circ. 2,500. Pays on publication. Publishes ms an average of 3 months after acceptance. Byline given. Offers 10% kill fee. Editorial lead time 3 months. Submit seasonal material 3 months in advance. Accepts simultaneous submissions. Reports in 3 weeks on queries; 1 month on mss. Sample copy for $4. Writer's guidelines for #10 SASE.
Nonfiction: Book excerpts, essays, exposé, general interest, interview/profile, new product, opinion (does not mean letters to the editor), personal experience, photo feature, travel. No overly sentimental articles. Buys 6 mss/year. Pays $15-100. Sometimes pays writers with contributor's copies. Sometimes pays expenses of writers on assignment.
Reprints: Include information about when and where the article previously appeared. Pay negotiable.
Photos: Send photos with submission. Reviews contact sheets. Offers no additional payment for photos accepted with ms. Captions, model releases and identification of subjects required.
Columns/Departments: Reviews (film, book, product) 100 words. Buys 12 mss/year. Query. Send complete ms. Pays $5-25.
Fiction: Erotica, ethnic, experimental, novel excerpts, serialized novels. "Must be top-notch cutting edge, no sentimentality." Buys 3 mss/year. Query. Send complete ms. Pays $5-100.
Poetry: Avant-garde, free verse, haiku, traditional. "Moon, June, croon stuff is a big no." Buys 2 poems/year. Submit maximum 5 poems. Pays $5-25.
Tips: "*Curriculum Vitae* is committed to giving breaks to new writers. We want edgy work. We want new writing. We want to reshape American culture. We especially want to work with hungry new artists. All of our issues have themes. Artists should query ahead of time for the theme. We make exceptions for great work."

DANDELION, Dandelion Magazine Society, 922 Ninth Ave. SE, Calgary, Alberta T2G 0S4 Canada. (403)265-0524. E-mail: esalon@conuck.com. Managing Editor: Bonnie Bennoit. 90% freelance written. Semiannual magazine. "*Dandelion* is a literary and visual arts journal with an international audience. There is no restriction on subject matter or form, be it poetry, fiction, visual art or review." Reviews Canadian book authors—showcases Canadian visual artists. Estab. 1975. Circ. 1,000. Pays on publication. Publishes ms an average of 3 months after acceptance. Byline given. Buys one-time rights. Editorial lead time 3 months. Reports in 3 weeks on queries; 4 months on mss. Sample copy for $5. Writer's guidelines for #10 SAE and IRC.
Nonfiction: Margo Laing, reviews editor. Buys 4-6 mss/year. Query with published clips. Length: 750 words.
Photos: Alice Simmons. Send photos with submission. Reviews contact sheets. Negotiates payment individually. Captions required. Buys one-time rights.
Fiction: Elizabeth Haynes and Adele Megann, fiction editors. Adventure, ethnic, experimental, historical, humorous, mainstream, novel excerpts. Buys 6-8 mss/year. Send complete ms. Length: approx. 3,500 words maximum. Pays $125.
Poetry: Gordon Pengilly, Bob Stallworthy, poetry editors. Avant-garde, free verse, haiku, traditional, long poem. Buys 50 poems/year. Submit maximum 10 poems. Pays $25/poem; payment negotiated for long poems.
Tips: "The mandate is so large and general, only a familiarity with literary journals and reviews will help. Almost all our material comes unsolicited; thus, find out what we publish and you'll have a means of 'breaking in.' "

DESCANT, Descant Arts & Letters Foundation, P.O. Box 314, Station P, Toronto, Ontario M5S 2S8. (416)593-2557. Editor: Karen Mulhallen. Managing Editor: Tracy Jenkins. Quarterly literary journal. Estab. 1970. Circ. 1,200. Pays on publication. Publishes ms 16 months after acceptance. Editorial lead time 4 months. Submit seasonal material 4 months in advance. Sample copy for $8. Writer's guidelines for SASE.
Nonfiction: Book excerpts, essays, historical/nostalgic, interview/profile, personal experience, photo feature, travel. Special issue: Romantic Love (spring 1998). Query or send complete ms. Pays $100 honorarium and 1 yr. subscription.
Photos: State availability of photos with submission. Reviews contact sheets and prints. Offers no additional payment for photos accepted with ms. Buys one-time rights.
Fiction: Send complete ms. Pays $100.
Poetry: Free verse, light verse, traditional. Submit maximum 10 poems. Pays $100.
Tips: "Familiarize yourself with our magazine before submitting."

‡DOGWOOD TALES MAGAZINE, P.O. Box 172068, Memphis TN 38187. Contact: P. Carman, editor. **Pays on acceptance.** Buys first and reprint rights. Accepts simultaneous submissions and previously published submissions. Reports in 1 month on mss. Sample copy for $3.50. Writer's guidelines for #10 SASE.
Fiction: Buys 48-60 mss/year. Send complete ms with cover letter. Length: 3,000 words. Pays ¼-½¢/word plus copy.
Tips: "We publish any genre suitable for a family environment. No religious, pornography, nonfiction, poorly developed plots, cardboard characters or weak endings."

‡**DOUBLE TAKE**, 1317 W. Pettigrew St., Durham NC 27705. Contact: Fiction Editor. **Pays on acceptance.** Byline given. Buys first North American serial rights. Accepts simultaneous submissions. Reports in 3 months on mss. Sample copy for $12. Writer's guidelines for #10 SASE.
Fiction: "Realistic fiction in all of its variety; its very unlikely we'd ever publish science fiction or gothic horror, for example." Buys 12 mss/year. Send complete ms with cover letter. Length: 3,000-8,000 words. Pays "competitively."
Tips: "Use a strong, developed narrative voice. Don't attempt too much or be overly melodramatic, lacking in subtlety, nuance and insight."

‡**DREAMS OF DECADENCE**, P.O. Box 13, Greenfield MA 01302-0013. (413)772-0725. Contact: Angela Kessler, editor. Quarterly literary magazine featuring vampire fiction and poetry. Pays on publication. Publishes ms an average of 6 months after acceptance. Buys first North American serial rights. Accepts simultaneous submissions. Reports in 1 month. Sample copy for $5. Writer's guidelines for #10 SASE.
Fiction: "I like elegant prose with a Gothic feel. The emphasis is on dark fantasy rather than horror. No vampire feeds, vampire has sex, someone becomes a vampire pieces." Buys 30-40 mss/year. Send complete ms. Length: 1,000-5,000 words. Pays 1-5¢/word.
Poetry: "Looking for all forms; however, the less horrific and the more explicitly vampiric a poem is, the more likely it is to be accepted." Pays in copies.
Tips: "We look for atmospheric, well-written stories with original ideas, not rehashes."

‡**EVENT**, Douglas College, P.O. Box 2503, New Westminster, British Columbia V3L 5B2 Canada. (604)527-5293. Fax: (604)527-5095. Editor: Calvin Wharton. Contact: Bonnie Bauder, assistant editor. 100% freelance written. Literary magazine published 3 times/year containing fiction, poetry and reviews. "We are eclectic and always open to content that invites involvement. Generally, we like strong narrative." Estab. 1971. Circ. 1,000. Pays on publication. Publishes ms an average of 8 months after acceptance. Byline given. Buys first North American serial rights. Accepts simultaneous submissions. Reports in 1 month on queries; 4 months on mss. Sample copy for $5. Writer's guidelines for #10 SASE.
● *Event* does not read manuscripts in July.
Fiction: Christine Dewar, fiction editor. "In fiction we're looking for readability, style and a lusty point of view (although not necessarily all in the same story)." Buys 20-25 mss/year. Send complete ms. Length: 5,000 words. Submit maximum 2 stories. Pays $22/page to $500.
Poetry: Gillian Garding-Russell, poetry editor. Free verse and prose poems. No light verse. "In poetry, we tend to appreciate the narrative and sometimes the confessional modes." Buys 30-40 poems/year. Submit maximum 10 poems. Pays $25-500.

‡**THE FIDDLEHEAD**, Campus House, University of New Brunswick, P.O. Box 4400, Fredericton, New Brunswick E3B 5A3 Canada. (506)453-3501. Fax: (506)453-4599. Contact: Bill Gaston, editor. 90% freelance written. Eager to work with new/unpublished writers. Quarterly magazine covering poetry, short fiction and book reviews. Estab. 1945. Circ. 1,000. Pays on publication. Publishes ms an average of 1 year after acceptance. Not copyrighted. Buys first North American serial rights. Submit seasonal material 6 months in advance. Reports in 4 months. Sample copy $9.
Fiction: Banny Belyea, Ted Colson, fiction editors. "Stories may be on any subject—acceptance is based on quality alone." Buys 30 mss/year. Send complete ms. Length: 50-3,000 words. Pays $10/page.
Poetry: Robert Gibbs, Robert Hawkes, Eric Hill, Demetres Tryphonopoulos, poetry editors. Avant-garde, free verse, light verse. "Poetry may be on any subject—acceptance is based on quality alone." Buys 100 poems/year. Submit maximum 10 poems. Pays $12/page; $100 maximum. Offers annual poetry and short fiction contest with different themes. Deadline is always December 15th.
Tips: "Quality alone is the criterion for publication. *Canadian return postage or IRCs* should accompany all mss."

FIELD MAGAZINE, Contemporary Poetry & Poetics, Rice Hall, Oberlin College, Oberlin OH 44074-1095. (216)775-8407/8. Fax: (216)775-8124. Editors: Stuart Friebert, David Young, David Walker, Alberta Turner. Managing Editor: Dolorus Nevels. 60% freelance written. Semiannual magazine of poetry, poetry in translation, and essays on contemporary poetry by poets. Estab. 1969. Circ. 2,300. Pays on publication. Byline given. Buys first rights. Editorial lead time 4 months. Reports in 1 month on mss. Sample copy for $7.
Poetry: Buys 100 poems/year. Submit maximum 10 poems. Pays $15-25 minimum/page.

FIRST WORD BULLETIN, Amick Associates Magazines, Calle Domingo Fernandez 5, Box 500, 28036 Madrid Spain. (34)1-359-64-18. Fax: (34)1-320-8961. E-mail: gw8@correo.interlink.es. Website: http://www.interlink.es/per aso/first. Contact: G.W. Amick, editor. 60-80% freelance written. Quarterly magazine. "Our audience is the general public, but the magazine is specifically aimed at writers who wish to get published for credits. We welcome unpublished writers; since our audience is mainly writers we expect high-quality work. We like writers who have enough self-confidence to be willing to pay the postage to get to us. They should write for guidelines first and then follow them to the letter." Estab. 1995. Pays on publication. Publishes ms an average of 6 months after acceptance. Byline given. Offers 10% kill fee or $5. Buys first world or second serial (reprint) rights. Editorial lead time 3 months. Submit seasonal material 5 months in advance. Accepts simultaneous submissions. Reports in 3 weeks on queries; 2 months on mss. Sample copy $3.50 and SAE with $3 postage or 3 IRCs. Writer's guidelines for SAE with $2 postage or 2 IRCs.
Nonfiction: General interest, how-to, humor, personal experience, environment, self-help, preventive medicine, literary,

experimental. Buys 40 mss/year. Send complete ms. Length: 500-4,000 words. Pays 2½¢/word up to $50. Pays in contributor copies for fillers, bullets, pieces less than 50 words.

Reprints: Send tearsheet of article or short story and information about when and where the piece previously appeared. Pays 2½¢/word up to $50.

Fiction: Adventure, environment, experiment, humorous, mainstream, self-help. No smut, pornography, science fiction, romance/love stories or horror. Buys 10-30 mss/year. Send complete ms. Length: 500-4,000 words. Pays 2½¢/word up to $50.

Poetry: Free verse, light verse. "We are not interested in poetry per se, but will accept poetry as sidebar or filler." Buys 4-8 poems/year. Submit max. 1 poem. Length: 14 lines for filler; 24 lines for sidebar. Pays 2½¢/word to $50.

Fillers: Anecdotes, facts, gags to be illustrated by cartoonist, short humor. Buys 32/year. Length: 10-80 words. Pays 2½¢/word up to $50.

Tips: "Write for guidelines. Pay close attention to the market study. Follow directions to the letter. Get the editor's name correct. Don't request return of manuscript, ask for the first page only to save postage. If you submit a self-help article, don't let God do all the work. For an environmental article, study the subject carefully and get your facts correct. Use positive thinking at all times. Last year was heavy on ecology and I still feel strong about it but this year I would like to see something on alternative medicine, homeopathy, perhaps some exotic stories on medicines from herbs in Brazil and Venezuela. I need crossword puzzles also. We now have an office in the United States for accepting submissions from the U.S., Canada and all American possessions. Also accepting submissions from Jamaica. The U.S. office address: The First Word Bulletin, PDS Margaret H. Swain, 2046 Lothbury Dr., Fayetteville NC 28304-5666 USA."

FRANK, An International Journal of Contemporary Writing & Art, Association Frank, 32 rue Edouard Vaillant, Montreuil France. (33)(1)48596658. E-mail: david@paris-anglo.com. Website: http://www.paris-anglo.com/frank. Contact: David Applefield, editor. 80% freelance written. Bilingual magazine covering contemporary writing of all genres. "Writing that takes risks and isn't ethnocentric is looked upon favorably." Estab. 1983. Circ. 4,000. Pays on publication. Publishes ms an average of 1 year after acceptance. Byline given. Buys one-time rights. Editorial lead time 6 months. Reports in 1 month on queries; 2 months on mss. Sample copy for $10. Writer's guidelines free.

Nonfiction: Interview/profile, travel. Buys 2 mss/year. Query. Pays $100. Pays in contributor copies by agreement.

Photos: State availability of photos with submission. Negotiates payment individually. Buys one-time rights.

Fiction: Experimental, international, novel excerpts. Buys 8 mss/year. Send complete ms. Length: 1-3,000 words. Pays $100.

Poetry: Avant-garde, translations. Buys 20 poems/year. Submit maximum 10 poems. Pays $20.

Tips: "Suggest what you do or know best. Avoid query form letters—we won't read the ms. Looking for excellent literary/cultural interviews with leading American writers or cultural figures."

THE GETTYSBURG REVIEW, Gettysburg College, Gettysburg PA 17325. (717)337-6770. Contact: Peter Stitt, editor. Managing Editor: Emily Ruark Clarke. Quarterly literary magazine. "Our concern is quality. Manuscripts submitted here should be extremely well-written." Estab. 1988. Circ. 4,000. Pays on publication. Byline given. Buys first North American serial rights. Editorial lead time 1 year. Submit seasonal material 9 months in advance. Reports in 1 month on queries; 3 months on mss. Sample copy for $7. Writer's guidelines for #10 SASE. Reading period September-May. No simultaneous submissions.

Nonfiction: Essays. Buys 20/year. Send complete ms. Length: 3,000-7,000. Pays $25/page.

Fiction: High quality, literary. Publishes novel excerpts. Buys 20 ms/year. Send complete ms. Length: 2,000-7,000, Pays $25/page.

Poetry: Buys 50 poems/year. Submit maximum 3 poems. Pays $2/line.

GLIMMER TRAIN STORIES, Glimmer Train Press, Inc., 710 SW Madison St., #504, Portland OR 97205. (503)221-0836. Fax: (503)221-0837. Website: http://www.GlimmerTrainPress.com. Contact: Linda Davies, co-editor. Co-editor: Susan Burmeister-Brown. 90% freelance written. Quarterly magazine covering short fiction. "We are interested in well-written, emotionally-moving short stories published by unknown, as well as known, writers." Estab. 1991. Circ. 16,000. **Pays on acceptance.** Byline given. Buys first rights. Accepts simultaneous submissions. Reports in 3 months on mss. Sample copy for $9. Writer's guidelines for #10 SASE.

Fiction: "We are not restricted to any types." Publishes novel excerpts. Buys 32 mss/year. Send complete ms. Length: 1,200-8,000 words. Pays $500.

● Ranked as one of the best markets for fiction writers in the last *Writer's Digest* magazine's "Fiction 50."

Tips: "Manuscripts should be sent to us in the months of January, April, July and October. Be sure to include a sufficiently-stamped SASE. We are particularly interested in receiving work from new writers." See *Glimmer Train*'s Short Story Award for New Writers listing in Contest and Awards section.

GRAIN LITERARY MAGAZINE, Saskatchewan Writers Guild, P.O. Box 1154, Regina, Saskatchewan S4P 3B4 Canada. Fax: (306)244-0255. E-mail: grain.mag@sk.sympatico.ca. Website: http://www.sasknet.com/corporate/skwriter. Contact: J. Jill Robinson, editor. Business Manager: Steven Smith. 100% freelance written. Quarterly literary magazine covering poetry, fiction, creative nonfiction, drama. "*Grain* publishes writing of the highest quality, both traditional and nontraditional in nature. *The Grain* editors' aim: To publish work that challenges its readers; to encourage promising new writers; and to produce a well-designed, visually exciting magazine." Estab. 1971. Circ. 1,700. Pays on publication. Publishes ms an average of 11 months after acceptance. Byline given. Buys first, Canadian, serial rights. Editorial lead time 6 months. Reports in 1 month on queries; 3 months on mss. Sample copy for $6.95. Writer's guidelines free. Does not accept e-mail submissions.

Nonfiction: Interested in creative nonfiction.

Fiction: Literary fiction of all types. "No romance, confession, science fiction, vignettes, mystery." Buys 40 mss/year. Query or send complete ms. Pays $30-100.

Poetry: Avant-garde, free verse, haiku, traditional. "High quality, imaginative, well-crafted poetry. No sentimental, end-line rhyme, mundane." Buys 78 poems/year. Submit maximum 10 poems. Pays $30-100.

Tips: "Submit your best unpublished work."

‡**GRAND STREET**, 131 Varick St., Suite 906, New York NY 10013. Pays on publication. Byline given. Buys one-time rights. Accepts simultaneous and previously published submissions. Reports in 2 months on mss. Sample copy for $15. Writer's guidelines for #10 SASE.

• *Grand Street* accepts agented submissions only.

Fiction: Novel excerpts, serialized novels, short stories and novellas. "We accept all types of fiction and welcome experimental work. The only criterion for acceptance is quality." Buys 25 mss/year. Length: 2,000-10,000 words. Pays $200-1,000.

‡**HAPPY**, 240 E. 35th St., Suite 11A, New York NY 10016. Contact: Bayard, editor. Pays on publication. Byline given. Buys one-time rights. Accepts simultaneous and previously published submissions. Reports in 1 month on mss. Sample copy for $9. Writer's guidelines for #10 SASE.

Fiction: Novel excerpts, short stories. "We accept anything that's beautifully written. Genre isn't important. It just has to be incredible writing." Buys 100-130 mss/year. Send complete ms with cover letter. Length: 250-5,000 words. Pays $5/1,000 words.

Tips: "If you imagine yourself Ernest Hemingway, you and your work have been dead for 30 years and are of no interest to us."

HIGH PLAINS LITERARY REVIEW, 180 Adams St., Suite 250, Denver CO 80206. (303)320-6828. Fax: (303)320-0463. Contact: Robert O. Greer, Jr., editor-in-chief. Managing Editor: Phyllis A. Harwell. 80% freelance written. Triannual literary magazine. "The *High Plains Literary Review* publishes short stories, essays, poetry, reviews and interviews, bridging the gap between commercial quarterlies and academic reviews." Estab. 1986. Circ. 1,200. Pays on publication. Byline given. Buys first North American serial rights. Accepts simultaneous submissions. Reports in 3 months. Sample copy for $4. Writer's guidelines for #10 SASE.

• Its unique editorial format—between commercial and academic—makes for lively reading. Could be good market for that "in between" story.

Nonfiction: Essays, reviews. Buys 20 mss/year. Send complete ms. Length: 10,000 words maximum. Pays $5/page.

Fiction: Ethnic, historical, humorous, mainstream. Buys 12 mss/year. Send complete ms. Length: 10,000 words maximum. Pays $5/page.

Poetry: Buys 45 poems/year. Pays $10/page.

THE HOLLINS CRITIC, P.O. Box 9538, Hollins College, Roanoke VA 24020. E-mail: acockrell@hollins.edu. Contact: Amanda Cockrell, managing editor. 18% freelance written. "Non-specialist periodical published 5 times/year with artist's cover sketch and an essay on work of a contemporary poet, fiction writer or dramatist. Brief book review section and poetry." Estab. 1964. Circ. 488. Buys first rights. Sample copy for $1.50. Guidelines for #10 SASE.

Nonfiction: Feature essays on contemporary authors are by prearrangement with contributors, and unsolicited mss are not accepted. Rarely accepts unsolicited book reviews.

Poetry: Cathryn Hankla, poetry editor. Pays $25 on publication.

INDIANA REVIEW, Indiana University, 465 Ballantine Hall, Bloomington IN 47405. (812)855-3439. Contact: Geoffry Pollock, editor. Associate Editor: Bob King. 100% freelance written. Semiannual magazine. "*Indiana Review*, a non-profit organization run by IU graduate students, is a journal of previously unpublished poetry and fiction. Literary interviews and essays also considered. We publish innovative fiction and poetry. We're interested in energy, originality and careful attention to craft. While we publish many well-known writers, we also welcome new and emerging poets and fiction writers." Estab. 1982. **Pays on acceptance.** Byline given. Buys first North American serial rights. Reports within 4 months. Sample copy for $7. Writer's guidelines free.

Nonfiction: Essays. No strictly academic articles dealing with the traditional canon. Buys 8 mss/year. Query. Length: 7,500 maximum. Pays $25-200.

Fiction: Experimental, mainstream, novel excerpts. Buys 18 mss/year. Send complete ms. Length: 250-15,000. Pays $5/page.

Poetry: Avant-garde, free verse. Looks for inventive and skillful writing. Buys 80 mss/year. Submit up to 5 poems at one time only. Length: 5 lines minimum. Pays $5/page.

Tips: "Read us before you submit. Often reading is slower in summer months."

THE IOWA REVIEW, 369 EPB, The University of Iowa, Iowa City IA 52242. (319)335-0462. Fax: (319)335-2535. E-mail: iareview@blue.weeg.uiowa.edu. Website: http://www.uiowa.edu/~english/iareview.html. Editor: David Hamilton. Contact: Mary Hussmann, editor. Triannual magazine. Estab. 1970. Buys first North American and non-

exclusive anthology, classroom and online serial rights. Reports in 3 months. Sample copy for $6.
Nonfiction, Fiction and Poetry: "We publish essays, reviews, novel excerpts, stories and poems and would like for our essays not always to be works of academic criticism. We have no set guidelines as to content or length." Buys 65-85 unsolicited mss/year. Submit complete ms with SASE. Pays $1/line for verse; $10/page for prose.
 • This magazine uses the help of colleagues and graduate assistants. Its reading period is September-April.

JAPANOPHILE, P.O. Box 223, Okemos MI 48864-0223. E-mail: japanlove@aol.com. Website: http://www.voyager. net/japanophile. Editor: Earl Snodgrass. 80% freelance written. Works with a small number of new/unpublished writers each year. Quarterly magazine for literate people interested in Japanese culture anywhere in the world. Estab. 1974. Pays on publication. Publishes ms an average of 3 months after acceptance. Buys first North American serial rights. Reports in 3 months. Sample copy for $4, postpaid. Writer's guidelines for #10 SASE.
 • *Japanophile* would like to receive more haiku and more humorous articles and fillers. It needs more book reviews. It would also like to find one or more columnists to cover California, Hawaii and New York. This column would probably be like "Tokyo Topics."
Nonfiction: "We want material on Japanese culture in *North America or anywhere in the world*, even Japan. We want articles, preferably with pictures, about persons engaged in arts of Japanese origin: a Virginia naturalist who is a haiku poet, a potter who learned raku in Japan, a vivid 'I was there' account of a Go tournament in California. We would like to hear more about what it's like to be a Japanese in the U.S. Our particular slant is a certain kind of culture wherever it is in the world: Canada, the U.S., Europe, Japan. The culture includes flower arranging, haiku, sports, religion, travel, art, photography, fiction, etc. It is important to study the magazine." Buys 8 mss/issue. Query preferred but not required. Length: 1,800 words maximum. Pays $8-20.
Reprints: Send information about when and where the article was previously published. Pays up to 100% of amount paid for original article.
Photos: Pays $10-20 for glossy prints. "We prefer b&w people pictures."
Fiction: Experimental, mainstream, mystery, adventure, humorous, romance, historical. Themes should relate to Japan or Japanese culture. Length: 1,000-4,000 words. Annual contest pays $100 to best short story (contest reading fee $5). Should include 1 or more Japanese and non-Japanese characters in each story.
Columns/Departments: Regular columns and features are Tokyo Topics and Japan in North America. "We also need columns about Japanese culture in various American cities." Query. Length: 1,000 words. Pays $20 maximum.
Poetry: Traditional, avant-garde and light verse related to Japanese culture or any subject in a Japanese form such as haiku. Length: 3-50 lines. Pays $1-20.
Fillers: Newsbreaks, clippings and short humor of up to 200 words. Pays $1-5.
Tips: "We want to see more articles about Japanese culture in the U.S., Canada and Europe. Lack of convincing fact and detail is a frequent mistake."

THE JOURNAL, Ohio State University, 421 Denney Hall, 164 W. 17th Ave., Columbus OH 43210. (614)292-4076. Fax: (614)292-7816. E-mail: thejournal05@postbox.acs.ohio-state.edu. Website: http://www.cohums.ohio-state.edu/engl ish/journals/the_journal/homepage.htm. Contact: Kathy Fagan, Michelle Herman, editors. 100% freelance written. Semi-annual literary magazine. "We're open to all forms; we tend to favor work that gives evidence of a mature and sophisticated sense of the language." Estab. 1972. Circ. 1,500. Pays on publication. Byline given. Buys first North American serial rights. Reports in 2 weeks on queries; 2 months on mss. Sample copy for $5. Guidelines for #10 SASE.
Nonfiction: Essays, interview/profile. Buys 2 mss/year. Query. Length: 2,000-4,000 words. Pays $25 maximum and contributor's copies.
Columns/Departments: Reviews of contemporary poetry, 2,000-4,000 words. Buys 2 mss/year. Query. Pays $25.
Fiction: Novel excerpts, literary short stories. Pays $25 minimum.
Poetry: Avant-garde, free verse, traditional. Buys 100 poems/year. Submit maximum 5 poems/year. Pays $25.

KALLIOPE, a journal of women's art, Florida Community College at Jacksonville, 3939 Roosevelt Blvd., Jacksonville FL 32205. (904)381-3511. Contact: Mary Sue Koeppel, editor. 100% freelance written. Triannual magazine. "*Kalliope* publishes poetry, short fiction, reviews, and b&w art, usually by women artists. We look for artistic excellence." Estab. 1978. Circ. 1,600. Pays on publication. Publishes ms an average of 3 months after acceptance. Buys first rights. Reports in 1 week on queries. Sample copy for $7 (recent issue) or $4 (back copy). Writer's guidelines for #10 SASE.
Nonfiction: Interview/profile, reviews of new works of poetry and fiction. Buys 6 mss/year. Send complete ms. Length: 500-2,000 words. Pays $10 honorarium.
Fiction: Ethnic, experimental, fantasy, humorous, mainstream, slice-of-life vignettes, suspense. Buys 12 mss/year or more. Send complete ms. Length: 100-2,000 words. Pays $10 honorarium.
Poetry: Avant-garde, free verse, haiku, light verse, traditional. Buys 75 poems/year. Submit 3-5 poems. Length 2-120 lines. Pays $10 honorarium.
Tips: "We publish the best of the material submitted to us each issue. (We don't build a huge backlog and then publish from that backlog for years.) Although we look for new writers and usually publish several with each issue alongside already established writers, we love it when established writers send us their work. We've recently published Tess Gallagher, Enid Shomer and works of Colette published in English for the first time. Send a bio with all submissions."

THE KENYON REVIEW, Kenyon College, Gambier OH 43022. (614)427-5208. Fax: (614)427-5417. E-mail: kenyon review@kenyon.edu. Contact: David H. Lynn, editor. 100% freelance written. Triannual magazine covering contemporary literature and criticism. "An international journal of literature, culture and the arts dedicated to an inclusive representation of the best in new writing, interviews and criticism from established and emerging writers." Estab. 1939. Circ. 4,500. Pays on publication. Publishes ms 1 year after acceptance. Byline given. Buys first, one-time rights. Editorial lead time 1 year. Submit seasonal material 1 year in advance. Reports in 2 weeks on queries; 3 months on mss. Sample copy for $8. Writer's guidelines for 4×9 SASE.

• *The Kenyon Review* does not read unsolicited submissions during April through August, December and January. Submissions from subscribers who so identify themselves are read year-round.

Nonfiction: Book excerpts (before publication), essays, interview/profile (query first), translations. Buys 12 mss/year. Query. Length: 7,500 words maximum. Pays $10/published page.

Fiction: Experimental, humorous, mainstream, novel excerpts (before publication), science fiction, slice-of-life vignettes. Buys 30 mss/year. Send complete ms. Length: 7,500 words maximum. Pays $10/published page.

Poetry: Avant-garde, free verse, haiku, light verse, traditional. Buys 60 poems/year. Submit maximum 6 poems. Pays $15/published page.

‡**LEGIONS OF LIGHT**, Box 874, Margaretville, NY 12455. (914)586-2759. E-mail: beth@stepahead.net. Contact: Elizabeth Mami, editor. 100% freelance written. Bimonthly magazine. "*Legions of Light* accepts all material except graphic. All ages read the magazine, all subjects welcomed. Estab. 1990. Circ. 2,000. Pays on publication. Publishes ms an average of 1 year after acceptance. Byline sometimes given. Buys one-time rights. Editorial lead time 4 months. Submit seasonal material 6 months in advance. Accepts simultaneous submissions. Reports in 6 weeks on queries. Sample copy for $3. Writer's guidelines free.

Nonfiction: Historical/nostalgic, humor, inspirational, humor/profile, personal experience, religious. No graphic violence or adult material. Buys 10-20 mss/year. Send complete ms. Length: 500-1,500 words. Pays $5-10.

Reprints: Accepts previously published submissions.

Photos: State availability of photos with submission. Reviews 3×5 prints. Offers no additional payment for photos accepted with ms. Identification of subjects required. Buys one-time rights.

Fiction: Adventure, ethnic, experimental, fantasy, historical, horror, humorous, mainstream, mystery, religious, romance, science fiction, slice-of-life vignettes, suspense, western. No adult or graphic violence. Buys 20-30 mss/year. Query or send complete ms. Length: 1,500 words maximum. Pays $5-10.

Poetry: Avant-garde, free verse, haiku, light verse, traditional. No erotica. Buys 15-20 poems/year. Length: open. Pays $5-10.

Fillers: Anecdotes, facts, newsbreaks, short humor. Buys 5-15/year. Pays $5-10.

Tips: "*Legions of Light* caters to unpublished talent, especially children. Subscribers are used first, but subscribing is *not* a requirement to be accepted for publication."

‡**LITERARY MAGAZINE REVIEW**, Department of English Language and Literature, University of Northern Iowa, Cedar Falls IA 50614-0502. (319)273-2821. Fax: (319)273-5807. E-mail: grant.tracey@uni.edu. Editor: Grant Tracey. 98% freelance written. Quarterly magazine devoted almost exclusively to reviews of the current contents of small circulation serials publishing some fiction or poetry. "Most of our reviewers are recommended to us by third parties." Estab. 1981. Circ. 500. Pays on publication. Publishes ms an average of 1 month after acceptance. Byline given. Buys first rights. Reports in 2 weeks. *Writer's Market* recommends allowing 2 months for reply. Sample copy for $5.

Nonfiction: Buys 60 mss/year. Query. Length: 1,500 words. Pays $25 maximum and 2 contributor's copies for assigned articles. Sometimes pays expenses of writers on assignment.

Photos: State availability of photos with submission. Identification of subjects required.

Tips: "Interested in omnibus reviews of magazines sharing some quality, editorial philosophy, or place of origin and in articles about literary magazine editing and the literary magazine scene."

MAGIC REALISM, Pyx Press, P.O. Box 922648, Sylmar CA 91392-2648. Contact: C. Darren Butler, editor. 85% freelance written. Quarterly literary magazine of magic realism, literary fantasy, and related fiction. Estab. 1990. Circ. 1,200. **Pays on acceptance**. Publishes ms an average of 6-18 months after acceptance. Buys first North American serial or one-time rights, non-exclusive (reprint) rights, or Spanish language rights (optional). Editorial lead time 4 months. Accepts simultaneous submissions. Reports in 1 month on queries, 6 months on mss. Sample copy for $4.95 (back issue); $5.95 (current issue). Writer's guidelines for #10 SASE.

• *Magic Realism* also offers a short fiction contest. See the Contest and Awards section.

Nonfiction: Book excerpts, essays, interview/profile, translations. Buys 2 mss/year. Query. Length: 8,000 words maximum. Pays ¼¢ word.

Reprints: Accepts previously published submissions. Include description(s) of previous venue(s) and approximate circulation.

Photos: State availability of photos with submission. Reviews contact sheets, prints. Offers $2-100/photo. Model releases preferred. Buys one-time rights.

Fiction: Experimental, fantasy, magic realism. Buys 70-80 mss/year. Send complete ms. Length: up to 8,000 words. Pays ¼¢ word.

• Ranked as one of the best markets for fiction writers in the last *Writer's Digest* magazine's "Fiction 50."

Poetry: All styles considered. Buys 25 poems/year. Prefers shorter poems of 3-30 lines. Submit maximum 8 poems. Pays $3/magazine page.

Tips: "We prefer a short cover letter with bio and/or credits. We especially need short-short fiction of 200-2,000 words.

No wizards/witches, dragons, occult/parapsychology, fortune telling, sword and sorcery, vampires, werewolves, elves/ little people, or sleight-of-hand magicians. No God/Heaven, Devil/Hell, Adam & Eve, or before-life/after-death stories. We rarely accept stories with children or youth protagonists, ghosts or hauntings, visit(s) to psychoanalyst(s), science fiction, explicit sex or language, or wherein anything is labeled as 'magic.' "

THE MALAHAT REVIEW, The University of Victoria, P.O. Box 1700, Victoria, British Columbia V8W 2Y2 Canada. Fax: (250)477-2297. E-mail: malahat@uuic.ca. Contact: Derk Wynand, editor. 100% freelance written. Eager to work with new/unpublished writers. Quarterly covering poetry, fiction, drama and reviews. Estab. 1967. Circ. 1,700. **Pays on acceptance.** Publishes ms up to 1 year after acceptance. Byline given. Offers 100% kill fee. Buys first serial rights. Reports in 2 weeks on queries; 3 months on mss. Sample copy for $8.
Photos: Pays $25 for b&w prints. Captions required. Pays $100 for color print used as cover.
Fiction: Buys 20 mss/year. Send complete ms up to 20 pages. Pays $25/magazine page.
  ● Ranked as one of the best markets for fiction writers in the last *Writer's Digest* magazine's "Fiction 50."
Poetry: Avant-garde, free verse, traditional. Length: 5-10 pages. Buys 100/year. Pays $25/magazine page.
Tips: "Please do not send more than one manuscript (the one you consider your best) at a time. Query first about review articles or critical essays, interviews, and visual art, which we generally solicit."

MANOA, A Pacific Journal of International Writing, University of Hawaii Press, 1733 Donaghho Rd., Honolulu HI 96822. (808)956-3070. Fax: (808)956-3083. E-mail: fstewart@hawaii.edu. Website: http://www2.hawaii.edu/mjourn al. Contact: Frank Stewart, editor. Associate Editor: Charlene Gilmore. Managing Editor: Patricia Matsueda. Semiannual literary magazine. "No special slant. Just high quality literary fiction, poetry, essays, personal narrative, reviews. About half of each issue devoted to U.S. writing, and half new work from Pacific and Asian nations. Our audience is primarily in the U.S., although expanding in Pacific countries. U.S. writing need not be confined to Pacific settings or subjects." Estab. 1989. Circ. 2,500. Pays on publication. Byline given. Buys first North American serial or non-exclusive, one-time reprint rights. Editorial lead time 6 months. Submit seasonal material 8 months in advance. Reports in 3 weeks on queries; 2 months on poetry mss, 4 months on fiction. Sample copy for $10. Writer's guidelines free.
Nonfiction: Frank Stewart, editor. Book excerpts, essays, interview/profile, creative nonfiction or personal narrative related to literature or nature. No Pacific exotica. Charlene Gilmore, reviews editor. Buys 3-4 mss/year, excluding reviews. Query or send complete ms. Length: 1,000-5,000 words. Pays $25/printed page, plus contributor copies.
Fiction: Ian MacMillan, fiction editor. "We're potentially open to anything of literary quality, though usually not genre fiction as such." Publishes novel excerpts. No Pacific exotica. Buys 12-18 mss/year in the US (excluding translation). Send complete ms. Length: 1,000-7,500. Pays $100-500 normally ($25/printed page).
Poetry: Frank Stewart, editor. No light verse. Buys 40-50 poems/year. Pays $25.
Tips: "Although we are a Pacific journal, we are a general interest U.S. literary journal, not limited to Pacific settings or subjects."

THE MASSACHUSETTS REVIEW, Memorial Hall, University of Massachusetts, Amherst MA 01003-9934. (413)545-2689. Editors: Mary Heath, Jules Chametzky, Paul Jenkins. Quarterly magazine. Estab. 1959. Pays on publication. Publishes ms 6-18 months after acceptance. Buys first North American serial rights. Reports in 3 months. Does not return mss without SASE. Sample copy for $6 with 3 first-class stamps.
Nonfiction: Articles on literary criticism, women, public affairs, art, philosophy, music and dance. Length: 6,500 words average. Pays $50.
Fiction: Short stories. Length: 25-30 pages maximum. Pays $50.
Poetry: Pays 35¢/line or $10 minimum.
Tips: "No manuscripts are considered June-October."

MICHIGAN QUARTERLY REVIEW, 3032 Rackham Bldg., University of Michigan, Ann Arbor MI 48109-1070. Contact: Laurence Goldstein, editor. 75% freelance written. Prefers to work with published/established writers. Quarterly. Estab. 1962. Circ. 1,500. Publishes ms an average of 1 year after acceptance. Pays on publication. Buys first serial rights. Reports in 2 months. Sample copy for $2.50 with 2 first-class stamps.
Nonfiction: "*MQR* is open to general articles directed at an intellectual audience. Essays ought to have a personal voice and engage a significant subject. Scholarship must be present as a foundation, but we are not interested in specialized essays directed only at professionals in the field. We prefer ruminative essays, written in a fresh style and which reach interesting conclusions. We also like memoirs and interviews with significant historical or cultural resonance." Length: 2,000-5,000 words. Pays $100-150.
Fiction and Poetry: No restrictions on subject matter or language. "We publish about ten stories a year and are very selective. We like stories which are unusual in tone and structure, and innovative in language." Send complete ms. Pays $10/published page.
Tips: "Read the journal and assess the range of contents and the level of writing. We have no guidelines to offer or set expectations; every manuscript is judged on its unique qualities. On essays—query with a very thorough description of the argument and a copy of the first page. Watch for announcements of special issues, which are usually expanded issues and draw upon a lot of freelance writing. Be aware that this is a university quarterly that publishes a limited amount of fiction and poetry; that it is directed at an educated audience, one that has done a great deal of reading in all types of literature."

MID-AMERICAN REVIEW, Dept. of English, Bowling Green State University, Bowling Green OH 43403. (419)372-2725. Editor-in-Chief: George Looney. Willing to work with new/unpublished writers. Semiannual literary magazine of "the highest quality fiction, poetry and translations of contemporary poetry and fiction." Also publishes critical articles and book reviews of contemporary literature. Estab. 1972. Pays on publication. Publishes ms less than 6 months after acceptance. Byline given. Buys one-time rights. Reports in 4 months. Sample copy for $7 (current issue), $5 (back issue); rare back issues $10.
   • *Mid-American Review* only reads manuscripts September through May.
Nonfiction: George Looney, nonfiction editor. Essays and articles focusing on contemporary authors and topics of current literary interest. Length: 15-20 pages; also short (500-1,000 words) book reviews.
Fiction: Rebecca Meachem, fiction editor. Character-oriented, literary. Buys 12 mss/year. Send complete ms; do not query. Pays $10/page up to $50, pending funding.
Poetry: Tony Gardner, poetry editor. Strong imagery and sense of vision. Buys 60 poems/yr. Pays $10/page up to $50.
Tips: "We are seeking translations of contemporary authors from all languages into English; submissions must include the original."

THE MISSOURI REVIEW, 1507 Hillcrest Hall, University of Missouri, Columbia MO 65211. (573)882-4474. Website: http://www.missouri.edu/~moreview. Editor: Speer Morgan. Managing Editor: Greg Michalson. 100% freelance written. Triannual literary magazine. "We publish contemporary fiction, poetry, interviews, personal essays, cartoons, special features—such as 'History as Literature' series and 'Found Text' series—for the literary and the general reader interested in a wide range of subjects." Estab. 1978. Circ. 6,500. Pays on signed contract. Byline given. Buys first rights or one-time rights. Editorial lead time 6 months. Reports in 2 weeks on queries; 3 months on mss. Sample copy for $7. Writer's guidelines for #10 SASE.
Nonfiction: Evelyn Somers, associate editor. Book excerpts, essays. No literary criticism. Buys 10 mss/year. Send complete ms. Pays approximately $15-20/printed page up to $750.
Fiction: Mainstream, literary. Buys 25 mss/year. Send complete ms. Pays $15-20 per printed page up to $750.
   • Ranked as one of the best markets for fiction writers in the last *Writer's Digest* magazine's "Fiction 50."
Poetry: Greg Michalson, poetry editor. Publishes 3-5 poetry features of 6-12 pages each per issue. "Please familiarize yourself with the magazine before submitting poetry." Buys 50 poems/year. Pays $125-250.

NEW ENGLAND REVIEW, Middlebury College, Middlebury VT 05753. (802)443-5075. E-mail: nereview@middlebury.edu. Editor: Stephen Donadio. Managing Editor: Jodee Stanley. Contact on envelope: Poetry, Fiction, or Nonfiction Editor; on letter: Stephen Donadio. Literary quarterly magazine. Serious literary only. Estab. 1978. Circ. 3,200. Pays on publication. Publishes ms an average of 6 months after acceptance. Byline given. Buys first North American serial rights. Accepts simultaneous submissions. Reads September 31 to May 31 (postmark dates). Reports in 2 weeks on queries; 3 months on mss. Sample copy for $7. Writer's guidelines for #10 SASE.
Nonfiction: Serious literary only. Buys 20-25 mss/year. Send complete ms. Length: 7,500 words maximum, though exceptions may be made. Pays $20 minimum; $10/page; plus 2 copies.
Reprints: Rarely accepts previously published submissions, (only if out of print or previously published abroad only.)
Fiction: Serious literary only. Buys 25 mss/year. Send complete ms. Send 1 story at a time. Pays $10/page, minimum $20, plus 2 copies.
Poetry: Serious literary only. Buys 75-90 poems/year. Submit maximum 6 poems. Pays $10/page or $20 plus 2 copies.
Tips: "We consider short fiction, including shorts, short-shorts, novellas, and self-contained extracts from novels. We consider a variety of general and literary, but not narrowly scholarly, nonfiction: long and short poems; speculative, interpretive, and personal essays; book reviews; screenplays; graphics; translations; critical reassessments; statements by artists working in various media; interviews; testimonies; and letters from abroad. We are committed to exploration of all forms of contemporary cultural expression in the United States and abroad. With few exceptions, we print only work not published previously elsewhere."

NEW LETTERS, University of Missouri-Kansas City, University House, 5101 Rockhill Rd., Kansas City MO 64110-2499. (816)235-1168. Fax: (816)235-2611. Contact: James McKinley, editor. Managing Editor: Robert Stewart. 100% freelance written. Quarterly magazine. "*New Letters* is intended for the general literate reader. We publish literary fiction, nonfiction, essays, poetry. We also publish art." Estab. 1934. Circ. 1,800. Pays on publication. Publishes ms an average of 5 months after acceptance. Byline given. Buys first North American serial rights. Editorial lead time 6 months. Submit seasonal material 6 months in advance. Accepts simultaneous submissions. Reports in 1 month on queries; 3 months on mss. Sample copy for $2.50. Writer's guidelines free.
Nonfiction: Essays. No self-help, how-to or non-literary work. Buys 6-8 mss/year. Send complete ms. Length: 5,000 words maximum. Pays $40-100.
Photos: Send photos with submission. Reviews contact sheets, 2×4 transparencies, prints. Offers $10-40/photo. Buys one-time rights.
Fiction: No genre fiction. Buys 12 mss/year. Send complete ms. Length: 5,000 words maximum. Pays $30-75.
Poetry: Avant-garde, free verse, haiku, traditional. No light verse. Buys 40 poems/year. Submit maximum 3 poems. Length: open. Pays $10-25.

‡NEW THOUGHT JOURNAL, the beat of a thousand drummers, 2520 Evelyn Dr., Dayton OH 45409. (937)293-9717. Fax: (937)866-9603. E-mail: ntjmag@aol.com. Contact: Jeffrey M. Ohl, editor. 100% freelance written.

Quarterly literary magazine covering "psychology, philosophy, ecology, spirituality, art, literature, poetry and music. *New Thought Journal* reflects the creative and inspirational intent of authors, artists, musicians, poets and philosophers as they mirror a quiet, intuitive consensus that is building naturally in our world." Estab. 1994. Circ. 5,000. Pays on publication. Publishes ms an average of 3 months after acceptance. Byline given. Buys one-time rights. Editorial lead time 6 months. Submit seasonal material 6 months in advance. Accepts simultaneous and previously published submission. Reports in 3 months on queries; 6 months on mss. Sample copy for $5. Writer's guidelines for #10 SASE.

Nonfiction: Book excerpts, inspirational, interview/profile, opinion, personal experience, photo feature. Buys 20-30 mss/year. Send complete ms. Length: 250-2,500 words. Pays writers with contributor copies or up to $20/printed published page as negotiated.

Reprints: Send photocopy of article or short story and information about when and where the piece previously appeared.

Photos: State availability of photos with submission or send photos with submission. Reviews contact sheets, transparencies and prints. Negotiates payment individually. Buys one-time rights.

Columns/Departments: Reviews, 100-500 words. Buys 18 mss/year. Send complete ms.

Fiction: Experimental, fantasy, novel excerpts, slice-of-life vignettes, spiritual, tranformational. Buys 18 mss/year. Send complete ms. Pays writers with contributor copies or up to $20/printed published page as negotiated.

Poetry: Avant-garde, free verse, haiku, light verse, traditional. Buys 40-50 poems/year. Submit maximum 5 poems.

NORTH CAROLINA LITERARY REVIEW: A Magazine of Literature, Culture, and History, English Dept., East Carolina University, Greenville NC 27858-4353. (919)328-4876. Fax: (919)328-4889. Editor: Tom Douglass. 80% freelance written. Annual literary magazine published in spring covering North Carolina/Southern writers, literature, culture, history. "Articles should have North Carolina/Southern slant; essays by writers associated with North Carolina may address any subject. First consideration is always for quality of work. Although we treat academic and scholarly subjects, we do not wish to see jargon-laden prose; our readers, we hope, are found as often in bookstores and libraries as in academia. We seek to combine best elements of magazine for serious readers with best of scholarly journal." Estab. 1992. Circ. 1,500. Pays on publication. Publishes ms 9 months after acceptance. Byline given. Offers 25% kill fee. Buys first North American serial rights. (Rights returned to writer on request.) Editorial lead time 6 months. Reports in 10 weeks on queries, 2 months on mss, 8 months on unsolicited mss. Sample copy for $10. Writer's guidelines free.

Nonfiction: Book excerpts, essays, exposé, general interest, historical/nostalgic, humor, interview/profile, opinion, personal experience, photo feature, travel, reviews, short narratives; surveys of archives. "No reviews that treat single books by contemporary authors or jargon-laden academic articles." Buys 25-35 mss/year. Query with published clips. Length: 500-5,000 words. Pays $50 minimum. (Usually Pays $100-300, sometimes higher, depending on article.)

Photos: State availability of photos with query. Reviews 5×7 or 8×10 prints; snapshot size or photocopy OK. Negotiates payment individually. Captions and identification of subjects required. (Releases when appropriate.) Buys one-time rights.

Columns/Departments: Archives (survey of North Carolina-writer archives), 500-1,500 words; Thomas Wolfe (Wolfe-related articles/essays), 1,000-2,000 words; Readers/Writers Places (bookstores or libraries, or other places readers and writers gather), 500-1,500; Black Mountain College, 1,000-2,000 words; Reviews (essay reviews of North Carolina-related literature (fiction, creative nonfiction, poetry). Buys 10 mss/year. Send complete ms. Pays $50-150.

Fiction: "No unsolicited mss; fiction and poetry are published in thematic sections or by invitation." Adventure, ethnic, experimental, fantasy, historical, horror, humorous, mainstream, mystery, novel excerpts, romance, science fiction, slice-of-life vignettes, suspense, western. Buys 3-4 mss/year. Query. Length: 5,000 words max. Pays $100-300.

Poetry: Solicited by editor only; *no unsolicited submissions, please.* Buys 8-10 poems/year. Length: 30-150 lines. Pays $30-150.

Fillers: Buys 2-10/year. Length: 50-300 words. Pays $10-25.

Tips: "By far the easiest way to break in is with departments; we are especially interested in reports on conferences, readings, meetings that involve North Carolina writers; and personal essays or short narratives with strong sense of place to use in loosely defined Readers/Writers Places department. We are more interested in essays that use creative nonfiction approaches than in straight articles of informational nature. See back issues for other departments. These are the only areas in which we encourage unsolicited manuscripts; but we welcome queries and proposals for all others. Interviews are probably the other easiest place to break in; no discussions of poetics/theory, etc., except in reader-friendly (accessible) language; interviews should be personal, more like conversations, that explore connections between a writer's life and his/her work."

NOSTALGIA, A Sentimental State of Mind, Nostalgia Publications, P.O. Box 2224, Orangeburg SC 29116. Contact: Connie L. Martin, editor. 100% freelance written. Semiannual magazine for "true, personal experiences that relate faith, struggle, hope, success, failure and rising above problems common to all." Estab. 1986. Circ. 1,000. Pays on publication. Publishes ms an average of 1 year after acceptance. Byline given. Buys one-time rights. Submit seasonal material 6 months in advance. Reports in 6 weeks on queries. Sample copy for $5. Writer's guidelines for #10 SASE.

Nonfiction: General interest, historical/nostalgic, humor, inspirational, opinion, personal experience, photo feature, religious and travel. Does not want to see anything with profanity or sexual references. Buys 10 or more stories/year. Send complete ms. Length: 1,500 words. Pays $25 minimum. Pays contributor copies "if copies are preferred." Short Story Award $150 plus publication.

Reprints: Send photocopy of article or short story and information about when and where the piece previously appeared. Payment varies.

Photos: State availability of photos with submission. Offers no additional payment for photos with ms.

Poetry: Free verse, haiku, light verse, traditional and modern prose. "No ballads; no profanity; no sexual references." Submit 3 poems max. Length: no longer than 45-50 lines preferably. Pays $150 (/semiannual Nostalgia Poetry Award).
Tips: Write for guidelines before entering contests. Short Story Award (deadlines March 31 and August 31); Poetry Award (deadlines June 30 and December 31). Entry fees reserve future edition.

THE OHIO REVIEW, 209C Ellis Hall, Ohio University, Athens OH 45701-2979. (614)593-1900. Editor: Wayne Dodd. Contact: Robert Kinsley, assistant editor. 40% freelance written. Semiannual magazine. "A balanced, informed engagement of contemporary American letters, with special emphasis on poetics." Circ. 3,500. Publishes ms an average of 8 months after acceptance. Rights acquired vary with author and material; usually buys first serial or first North American serial rights. Unsolicited material will be read September-May only. Reports in 10 weeks.
Nonfiction, Fiction and Poetry: Buys essays of general intellectual and special literary appeal. Not interested in narrowly focused scholarly articles. Seeks writing that is marked by clarity, liveliness and perspective. Interested in the best fiction and poetry. Submit complete ms. Buys 75 unsolicited mss/year. Pays minimum $5/page, plus copies.
Tips: "Make your query very brief, not gabby—one that describes some publishing history, but no extensive bibliographies. We publish mostly poetry—essays, short fiction, some book reviews."

THE PARIS REVIEW, 45-39 171st Place, Flushing NY 11358. Submit mss to 541 E. 72nd St., New York NY 10021. (212)861-0016. Fax: (212)861-4504. Contact: George A. Plimpton, editor. Quarterly magazine. Buys all rights. Pays on publication. Reporting time varies. Address submissions to proper department. Sample copy for $10. Writer's guidelines for #10 SASE (from Flushing Office). Reporting time often 6 months or longer.
Fiction: Study the publication. No length limit. Pays up to $600. Annual Aga Khan Fiction Contest award of $1,000.
Poetry: Richard Howard, poetry editor. Study the publication. Pay varies according to length, $35 minimum. Awards $1,000 in Bernard F. Conners Poetry Prize contest.

PARNASSUS, Poetry in Review, Poetry in Review Foundation, 205 W. 89th St., #8-F, New York NY 10024. (212)362-3492. Fax: (212)875-0148. E-mail: parnew@aol.com. Contact: Herbert Leibowitz, editor. Managing Editor: Ben Downing. Semiannual trade paperback-size magazine covering poetry and criticism. Estab. 1972. Circ. 1,500. Pays on publication. Publishes ms an average of 5 months after acceptance. Byline given. Buys one-time rights. Sample copy for $15.
Nonfiction: Essays. Buys 30 mss/year. Query with published clips. Length: 1,500-7,500 words. Pays $50-300. Sometimes pays writers in contributor copies or other premiums rather than a cash payment upon request.
Poetry: Accepts most types of poetry including avant-garde, free verse, traditional. Buys 3-4 unsolicited poems/year.

PIG IRON SERIES, Pig Iron Press, P.O. Box 237, Youngstown OH 44501-0237. (330)747-6932. Fax: (330)747-0599. Website: http://WebScribe.com/Scribe.pig.htm. Contact: Jim Villani, publisher. 95% freelance written. Annual magazine emphasizing literature/art for writers, artists and intelligent lay audience interested in popular culture. Circ. 1,000. Buys one-time rights. Pays on publication. Publishes ms an average of 18 months after acceptance. Byline given. Reports in 3 months. Sample copy $5. Writer's guidelines and current theme list for #10 SASE.
Nonfiction: General interest, personal opinion, criticism, new journalism and lifestyle. Special issues: Years of Rage: 1960s; deadline December 1997. Theme for 1999: Religion in Modernity; deadline December 1998. Buys 5-10 mss/year. Query. Length: 6,000 words maximum. Pays $5/page minimum.
Reprints: Accepts previously published mss. Send information about when and where the article previously appeared.
Photos: Submit photos with query. Pays $5 minimum for 5×7 or 8×10 b&w glossy prints. Buys one-time rights.
Fiction: Narrative fiction, living history, novel excerpts, psychological fiction, environment, avant-garde, experimental, metafiction, satire, parody. Buys 4-12 mss/issue. Submit complete ms. Length: 6,000 words max. Pays $5 minimum.
Poetry: Avant-garde and free verse. Buys 25-50/issue. Submit in batches of 5 or less. Length: open. Pays $5 minimum.
Tips: "Looking for fiction and poetry that is sophisticated, elegant, mature and polished. Interested in literary works that are consistent with the fundamental characteristics of modern and contemporary literature, including works that address alienation, the unconscious, the individual, tradition, vision, new age, loss, despair and historical continuity and discontinuity."

‡PLEIADES, Poems and Prose, Pleiades Press, Dept. of English & Philosophy, Central Missouri State University, Warrensburg MO 64093. (816)543-4425. Fax: (816)543-8544. E-mail: rmk8708@cmsu2.cmsu.edu. Contact: R.M. Kinder, editor. Managing Editor: Kevin Prufer. 100% freelance written. Semiannual journal (5½×8½ perfect bound). "We publish contemporary fiction, poetry, interviews, literary essays, special-interest personal essays, reviews. We're especially interested in cross genre pieces and ethnic explorations. General and literary audience." Estab. 1991. Circ. 400. Pays on publication. Publishes ms an average of 9 months after acceptance. Byline given. Buys first North American and second serial (reprint) rights (occasionally requests rights for WordBeat, TV, radio reading). Editorial lead time 9 months. Submit seasonal material 9 months in advance. Accepts simultaneous submissions. Reports in 3 weeks. Sample copy for $3.50 back issue/$5 current. Writer's guidelines for #10 SASE.
Nonfiction: Book excerpts, essays, interview/profile, reviews. "Nothing pedantic, slick or shallow." Buys 4-6 mss/year. Send complete ms. Length: 2,000-4,000 words. Pays $10.
Fiction: Ethnic, experimental, humorous, mainstream, novel excerpts, magic realism. No science fiction, fantasy, confession, erotica. Buys 16-20 mss/year. Send complete ms. Length: 2,000-6,000 words. Pays $10.
Poetry: Kevin Prufer, managing editor. Avant-garde, free verse, haiku, light verse, traditional. "Nothing didactic,

pretentious, or overly sentimental." Buys 40-50 poems/year. Submit maximum 6 poems. Pays $3/poem.
Tips: "Show care for your material and your readers—submit quality work in a professional format. Include cover letter with brief bio and list of publications. Include SASE."

PLOUGHSHARES, Emerson College, Dept. M, 100 Beacon St., Boston MA 02116. Website: http://www.emerson.edu/ploughshares/. Contact: Don Lee, editor. Triquarterly magazine for "readers of serious contemporary literature." Circ. 6,000. Pays on publication, $50 minimum/title, $250/author maximum, with 2 copies and 1-year subscription. Publishes ms an average of 6 months after acceptance. Buys first North American serial rights. Accepts simultaneous submissions if notified. Reports in 5 months. Sample copy for $8 (back issue). Writer's guidelines for SASE. Reading period: August 1-March 31.
 • A competitive and highly prestigious market. Rotating and guest editors make cracking the line-up even tougher, since it's difficult to know what is appropriate to send.
Nonfiction: Personal and literary essays (accepted only occasionally). Length: 5,000 words maximum. Pays $25/printed page, $50-$250. Reviews (assigned). Length: 500 words maximum. Pays $50.
Fiction: Literary and mainstream. Buys 25-35 unsolicited mss/year. Length: 300-6,000 words. Pays $25/printed page, $50 minimum, $250 maximum.
 • Ranked as one of the best markets for fiction writers in the last *Writer's Digest* magazine's "Fiction 50."
Poetry: Traditional forms, blank verse, free verse and avant-garde. Length: open. Pays $25/printed page, $50 minimum, $250 maximum.
Tips: "We no longer structure issues around preconceived themes. If you believe your work is in keeping with our general standards of literary quality and value, submit at any time during our reading period."

THE PRAIRIE JOURNAL of Canadian Literature, P.O. Box 61203, Brentwood Postal Services, 217K-3630 Brentwood Rd. NW, Calgary, Alberta T2L 2K6 Canada. Contact: A. Burke, editor. 100% freelance written. Semiannual magazine of Canadian literature. Estab. 1983. Circ. 600. Pays on publication; "honorarium depends on grant." Byline given. Buys first North American serial rights. Reports 6 months. Sample copy for $6 and IRC (Canadian stamps) or 50¢ payment for postage.
Nonfiction: Interview/profile, scholarly, literary. Buys 5 mss/year. Query first. Include IRCs. Pays $25-100 depending on length. Pays contributor copies or honoraria for literary work.
Photos: Send photocopies of photos with submission. Offers additional payment for photos accepted with ms. Identification of subjects required. Buys first North American rights.
Fiction: Literary. Buys 10 mss/year. Send complete ms.
Poetry: Avant-garde, free verse. Buys 10 poems/year. Submit maximum 6-10 poems.
Tips: "Commercial writers are advised to submit elsewhere. Art needed, b&w pen and ink drawings or good-quality photocopy. Do not send originals. We are strictly small press editors interested in highly talented, serious artists. We are oversupplied with fiction but seek more high-quality poetry, especially the contemporary long poem or sequences from longer works."

PRISM INTERNATIONAL, Department of Creative Writing, Buch E462, 1866 Main Mall, University of British Columbia, Vancouver, British Columbia V6T 1Z1 Canada. (604)822-2211. Fax: (604)822-3616. E-mail: prism@unixg.ubc.ca. Website: http://www.arts.ubc.ca/crwr/prism/prism.html. Contact: Meloney Little or Sioux Browning, editors. Executive Editor: Shannon McFerran. 100% freelance written. Eager to work with new/unpublished writers. Quarterly magazine emphasizing contemporary literature, including translations, for university and public libraries, and private subscribers. Estab. 1959. Circ. 1,200. Pays on publication. Publishes ms an average of 4 months after acceptance. Buys first North American serial rights. Reports in 3 months. Sample copy for $5. Writer's guidelines for #10 SAE with 1 first-class Canadian stamp (Canadian entries) or 1 IRC (US entries).
Nonfiction: "*Creative* nonfiction that reads like fiction." No reviews, tracts or scholarly essays.
Fiction: Rick Maddocks, fiction editor. Experimental, traditional, novel excerpts. Buys 3-5 mss/issue. Send complete ms. Length: 5,000 words maximum. Pays $20/printed page and 1-year subscription. Publishes novel excerpts, maximum length: 25 double-spaced pages.
Poetry: Regina Weaver, poetry editor. Avant-garde, traditional. Buys 20 poems/issue. Submit maximum 6 poems. Pays $20/printed page and 1-year subscription.
Drama: One-acts preferred. Pays $20/printed page and 1-year subscription.
Tips: "We are looking for new and exciting fiction. Excellence is still our number one criterion. As well as poetry, imaginative nonfiction and fiction, we are especially open to translations of all kinds, very short fiction pieces and drama which work well on the page. Translations must come with a copy of the original language work. Work may be submitted through e-mail or our website. We pay an additional $10/printed page to selected authors whose work we place on our on-line version of *Prism*."

‡QUARTERLY WEST, University of Utah Publications Council, 317 Olpin Union, University of Utah, Salt Lake City UT 84112. (801)581-3938. Contact: Lawrence Coates and Margot Schilp, co-editors. Semiannual magazine. "We publish fiction, poetry, and nonfiction in long and short formats, and will consider experimental as well as traditional works." Estab. 1976. Circ. 1,900. Pays on publication. Publishes ms an average of 6 months after acceptance. Buys first North American serial and all rights. Accepts simultaneous submissions if so noted. Reports in 2-6 months on mss. Sample copy for $7.50. Writer's guidelines for #10 SASE.

Nonfiction: Essays, interview/profile, book reviews. Buys 2-3 mss/year. Send complete ms. Length: 10,000 words maximum. Pays $25.

Fiction: Heather Hirschi. Ethnic, experimental, humorous, mainstream, novel excerpts, short shorts, slice-of-life vignettes, translations. Buys 20-30 mss/year. Send complete ms. Pays $25-500. No preferred lengths; interested in longer, fuller short stories, as well as short shorts.

Poetry: Jennifer Tonge. Avant-garde, free verse, traditional. Buys 30-50 poems/year. Submit 5 poems max. Pays $15-100.

Tips: "We publish a special section or short shorts every issue, and we also sponsor a biennial novella contest. We are open to experimental work—potential contributors should read the magazine! We solicit quite frequently, but tend more toward the surprises—unsolicited. Don't send more than one story per submission, but submit as often as you like."

QUEEN'S QUARTERLY, A Canadian Review, Queen's University, Kingston, Ontario K7L 3N6 Canada. (613)545-2667. Fax: (613)545-6822. E-mail: qquartly@post.queensu.ca. Website: http://info.queensu.ca/quarterly. Contact: Boris Castel, editor. Estab. 1893. Quarterly magazine covering a wide variety of subjects, including science, humanities, arts and letters, politics and history for the educated reader. 15% freelance written. Circ. 3,000. Pays on publication. Publishes ms an average of 3 months after acceptance. Byline given. Buys first North American serial rights. Requires 1 double-spaced hard copy and 1 copy on disk in WordPerfect. Reports in 1 month on mss. *Writer's Market* recommends allowing 2 months for reply. Sample copy $6.50.
  • No longer accepting fantasy fiction.

Fiction: Historical, humorous, mainstream and science fiction. Publishes novel excerpts. Buys 8-12 mss/year. Send complete ms. Length: 4,000 words maximum. Pays $150-250.

Poetry: Avant-garde, free verse, haiku, light verse, traditional. No "sentimental, religious, or first efforts by unpublished writers." Buys 25/year. Submit maximum 6 poems. Length: open. Pays $100-200.

Tips: "Poetry and fiction are most open to freelancers. Don't send less than the best. No multiple submissions. No more than six poems or two stories per submission. We buy very few freelance submissions."

‡RARITAN A Quarterly Review, 31 Mine St., New Brunswick NJ 08903. (908)932-7887. Fax: (908)932-7855. Editor: Richard Poirier. Contact: Suzanne Katz Hyman, managing editor. Quarterly magazine covering literature, general culture. Estab. 1981. Circ. 3,500. Pays on publication. Publishes ms 1 year after acceptance. Byline given. Buys first North American serial rights. Editorial lead time 5 months. Accepts simultaneous submissions.

Nonfiction: Book excerpts, essays. Buys 50 mss/year. Send complete ms. Length 15-30 pages. Pays $100.

‡RIVER STYX, Big River Association, 3207 Washington St., Louis MO 63103. (314)533-4541. Fax: (314)531-2787. Contact: Richard Newman, editor. Senior Editors: Quincy Troupe and Michael Castro. Triannual literary magazine. *"River Styx* publishes the highest quality fiction, poetry, interviews, essays and visual art. We are an internationally distributed multicultural literary magazine." Estab. 1975. Pays on publication. Manuscripts read May-November. Publishes ms an average of 6-12 months after acceptance. Byline given. Buys one-time rights. Accepts simultaneous submissions, if so noted. Reports in 4 months on mss. Sample copy for $7. Writer's guidelines for #10 SASE.

Nonfiction: Essays, interview. Special issue: A Vision Takes Form (issue dedicated to formal poetry). Buys 2-5 mss/year. Send complete ms. Pays 2 contributor copies, plus one-year subscription; $8/page if funds are available.

Photos/Art: Send with submission. Reviews 5×7 or 8×10 b&w prints or color. Also slides. Pays 2 contributor copies, plus one-year subscription; $8/page if funds are available. Buys one-time rights.

Fiction: Literary, novel excerpts. Buys 6 mss/year. Send complete ms. Pays 2 contributor copies, plus one-year subscription; $8/page if funds are available.

Poetry: Traditional, free verse, avant-garde. No religious. Buys 40-50 poems/year. Submit maximum 6 poems. Pays 2 contributor copies, plus one-year subscription. $8/page if funds are available.

ROSEBUD, The Magazine For People Who Enjoy Good Writing, Rosebud, Inc., P.O. Box 459, Cambridge WI 53523. (608)423-9609. Editor: Rod Clark. 100% freelance written. Quarterly magazine "for people who love to read and write. Our readers like good storytelling, real emotion, a sense of place and authentic voice." Estab. 1993. Circ. 9,000. Pays on publication. Publishes ms an average of 2 months after acceptance. Byline given. Buys one-time or second serial (reprint) rights. Editorial lead time 3 months. Submit seasonal material 3 months in advance. Accepts simultaneous submissions. Reports in 2 months. Sample copy for $5.95. Writer's guidelines for SASE.

Nonfiction: Book excerpt, essays, general interest, historical/nostalgic, humor, interview/profile, personal experience, travel. "No editorializing." Buys 6 mss/year. Send complete ms. Length: 1,200-1,800 words. Pays $45-195 and 2 contributor's copies.

Reprints: Send tearsheet or photocopy of article or short story and typed ms with rights for sale noted. Pays 100% of amount paid for an original piece.

Photos: State availability of photos with submission. Offers no additional payment for photos accepted with ms. Captions, model releases and identification of subjects required. Buys one-time rights.

Fiction: Ethnic, experimental, historical, humorous, mainstream, novel excerpts, slice-of-life vignettes, suspense. "No contrived formula pieces." Buys 80 mss/year. Send complete ms. Length: 1,200-1,800 words. Pays $45-195.

Poetry: Avant-garde, free verse, traditional. No inspirational poetry. Buys 36 poems/year. Submit maximum 5 poems. Length: open. Pays $45-195.

Tips: "Something has to 'happen' in the pieces we choose, but what happens inside characters is much more interesting to us than plot manipulation."

SAN FRANCISCO REVIEW, Santa Fe Ventures, 582 Market St., San Francisco CA 94104. Fax: (415)575-1459. E-mail: sfreview@aol.com. Editor: Matthew T. Humphrey. Contact: Emily E. Lundberg, assistant editor or Matthew T. Humphrey, editor. 100% freelance written. Bimonthly magazine covering books. "We publish book reviews, interviews with authors, commentary on the book publishing industry, short fiction, and pieces concerning the process of writing. Circ. 10,000. Pays on publication. Publishes ms an average of 6 weeks after acceptance. Byline given. Buys first rights. Editorial lead time 2 months. Submit seasonal material 2 months in advance. Reports in 2 months. Sample copy for $2.95. Writer's guidelines for #10 SASE.
Nonfiction: Essays, exposé, humor, inspirational, interview/profile, opinion, book reviews (prefer short). Buys 400 mss/year. Query with published clips. Length: 200-1,900 words. Pays 5¢/word.
Columns/Departments: Short Cuts (short book reviews), 300-600 words.
Fiction: Curtis Bonney, fiction editor. Publishes novel excerpts. Buys 12 mss/year. Send complete ms up to 1,000 words. *Writer's Market* recommends sending a query letter first.
Tips: "We are most concerned with the quality of writing we publish. Please send published clips. We review books right when they are pubilshed. Reviewers must receive galleys from publishers. Interviews can take place directly after publication of the book."

SHENANDOAH, The Washington and Lee University Review, Washington and Lee University, Troubadour Theater, 2nd Floor, Lexington VA 24450. (540)463-8765. Contact: R.T. Smith, editor. Managing Editor: Lynn Leech. Literary quarterly magazine. Estab. 1950. Circ. 2,000. Pays on publication. Publishes ms an average of 10 months after acceptance. Byline given. Buys first North American serial and one-time rights. Reports in 2 months on mss. Sample copy for $3.50.
Nonfiction: Book excerpts, essays. Buys 6 mss/year. Send complete ms. Pays $25/page.
Fiction: Mainstream, novel excerpts. No sloppy, hasty, slight fiction. Buys 15 mss/year. Send complete ms. Pays $25/page.
Poetry: No inspirational, confessional poetry. Buys 70 poems/year. Submit maximum 6 poems. Length open. Pays $2.50/line.

SHORT STUFF, for Grown-ups, Bowman Publications, P.O. Box 7057, Loveland CO 80537. (970)669-9139. Contact: Donna Bowman, editor. 98% freelance written. Bimonthly magazine. "We are perhaps an enigma in that we publish only clean stories in any genre. We'll tackle any subject, but don't allow obscene language or pornographic description. Our magazine is for grown-ups, *not* X-rated 'adult' fare." Estab. 1989. Circ. 5,400. Payment and contract on publication. Byline given. Buys first North American serial rights. Editorial lead time 3 months. Submit seasonal material 3 months in advance. Reports in 6 months on mss. Sample copy for $1.50 and 11×14 SAE with 5 first-class stamps. Writer's guidelines for #10 SASE.
Nonfiction: Humor. Special issues: "We are holiday oriented and each issue reflects the appropriate holidays." Buys 20 mss/year. Most nonfiction is staff written. Send complete ms. Length: 500-1,800 words. Pays $10-50.
Reprints: Send typed ms with rights for sale noted.
Photos: Send photos with submission. Offers no additional payment for photos accepted with ms. Identification of subjects required. Buys one-time rights.
Fiction: Adventure, historical, humorous, mainstream, mystery, romance, science fiction (seldom), suspense, western. Buys 144 mss/year. Send complete ms. Length: 500-1,800 words. Pays $10-50.
Fillers: Anecdotes, short humor. Buys 200/year. Length: 20-500 words. Pays $1-5.
Tips: "Don't send floppy disks or cartridges. Do include cover letter about the author, not a synopsis of the story. We are holiday oriented; mark on *outside* of envelope if story is for Easter, Mother's Day, etc. We receive 500 manuscripts each month. This is up about 200%. Because of this, I implore writers to send one manuscript at a time. I would not use stories from the same author more than once an issue and this means I might keep the others too long."

SING HEAVENLY MUSE!, Women's Poetry and Prose, Sing Heavenly Muse! Inc., Box 13320, Minneapolis MN 55414. Contact: Editorial Circle. 100% freelance written. Annual journal of women's literature. Circ. 1,000. Pays on publication. Publishes ms an average of 1 year after acceptance. Byline given. Buys first North American serial rights. Reports in 3 months. Sample copy for $4. Writer's guidelines for #10 SASE.
● Manuscripts that pass the first screening may be held longer.
Fiction: Women's literature, journal pieces, memoir and novel excerpts. Buys 15-20 mss/year. Length: 10,000 words maximum. Pays $15-25; contributors receive 2 free copies. Publishes novel excerpts.
Poetry: Avant-garde, free verse, haiku, light verse, traditional. Accepts 75-100 poems/year. No limit on length. Pays $15-25.
Tips: "To meet our needs, writing must be feminist and women-centered. Reading periods vary. Issues are often related to a specific theme; writers should always query for guidelines and upcoming themes and reading periods before submitting manuscripts."

THE SOUTHERN REVIEW, 43 Allen Hall, Louisiana State University, Baton Rouge LA 70803-5001. (504)388-5108. Fax: (504)388-5098. Contact: James Olney and Dave Smith, editors. 100% freelance written. Works with a moderate number of new/unpublished writers each year. Quarterly magazine "with emphasis on contemporary literature in the United States and abroad, and with special interest in Southern culture and history." Estab. 1935. Circ. 3,100. Buys first serial rights only. Byline given. Pays on publication. Publishes ms an average of 6 months after acceptance. No queries. Reports in 2 months. Sample copy for $6. Writer's guidelines for #10 SASE. Reading period: September through May.

Nonfiction: Essays with careful attention to craftsmanship, technique and seriousness of subject matter. "Willing to publish experimental writing if it has a valid artistic purpose. Avoid extremism and sensationalism. Essays should exhibit thoughtful and sometimes severe awareness of the necessity of literary standards in our time." Emphasis on contemporary literature, especially southern culture and history. No footnotes. Buys 25 mss/year. Length: 4,000-10,000 words. Pays $12/page for prose.

Fiction and Poetry: Short stories of lasting literary merit, with emphasis on style and technique, also novel excerpts. Length: 4,000-8,000 words; 1-4 pages, poetry. Pays $12/page for prose; $20/page for poetry.

SPARROW, Sparrow Press, 103 Waldron St., West Lafayette IN 47906. Contact: Felix Stefanile, editor. 60% freelance written. Annual magazine covering poetry, the sonnet, articles on craft, criticism. "Writers who admire and are loyal to the lyric tradition of the English language enjoy our magazine. We are not affiliated with any group or ideology, and encourage poetry that uses meter, rhyme and structured verse, mainly the sonnet. We are not a 'school of resentment' publication." Estab. 1954. Circ. 1,000. Pays on publication. Publishes ms 8 months after acceptance. Byline given. Offers 100% kill fee. Buys first North American serial rights and second serial (reprint) rights. Editorial lead time up to 6 months. Reports in 6 weeks. Sample copy for $5, back issue; $6, current issue. Writer's guidelines for #10 SASE.

• *Sparrow* does not read manuscripts from October-December.

Reprints: Accepts previously published submissions. But "we usually seek this material out. 90% of our work is original." Pays 100% of amount paid for an original article.

Poetry: Traditional, 90% sonnets. No free verse. Submit maximum 5 poems. Length: 14 lines. Pays $3/poem; $25 prize, best of the issue.

Tips: "We are interested in seeing material from poets and critics with a serious commitment to the lyric tradition of the English language, with emphasis on the formal sonnet of a contemporary accent. Our yearbook is used in classes, an audience we aim for. We are not for 'poets' who think the sonnet is passé. Neither do we consider ourselves part of any creative writing program network."

‡THE SPIRIT THAT MOVES US, The Spirit That Moves Us Press, Inc., P.O. Box 720820WM, Jackson Heights NY 11372-0820. (718)426-8788. Editor: Morty Sklar. Annual book of literary works. "We don't push any 'schools'; we're open to many styles and almost any subject matter. We favor work that expresses feeling, whether subtle or passionate. Irregularly we publish *Editor's Choice: Fiction, Poetry & Art from the U.S. Small Press*, which consists of selections from nominations made by other small literary publishers. When writers see our open call for nominations for this anthology, they should encourage their publishers to nominate their and other people's work." Estab. 1975. Pays on publication. Publishes ms an average of 3 months after acceptance. Byline given. Buys first North American serial and/or second serial (reprint) rights. Accepts simultaneous submissions, if so noted. Reports in 2 weeks on queries; 3 months after deadline date on mss (nothing is accepted until everything is read). Sample copy for $5.75 for *15th Anniversary Issue*, $10.75 for *Editor's Choice* to readers of *Writer's Market*.

Nonfiction: Book excerpts, essays, interview/profile, personal experience. Upcoming special issue: *Phoenix (stories, poems and essays from former drug addicts)*. Buys 20-30 mss for special issues. Query; "or if you've seen our call for mss and know the theme, send the ms." Length: 8,500 words maximum. Pays $15-25 plus a free copy and offers extra copies at 40% discount. Pays in contributor copies if so requested by author. "Royalty set-up for single-author books, with a cash advance."

Reprints: Accepts previously published submissions ("only for those collections that we specify"). Send tearsheet or photocopy of article or short story and information about when and where piece previously appeared. Pays 100% of amount paid for original piece.

Photos: Reviews contact sheets and 8×10 prints. Offers $15/photo; $100 for cover photos plus a free copy and 40% off additional copies. Buys one-time rights. "Photos are considered for artistic merit, and not just illustrative function. All art that we use has to stand on its own."

Fiction: "Nothing slick or commercial." Buys 15-30 mss/year. Query; "or if you know our theme and time frame, send complete ms." Length: 8,500 words maximum. Pays $15-25 plus a free copy and 40% off additional copies.

Poetry: "Not interested in work that just tries to be smart, flashy, sensational; if it's technically skilled but conveys no feeling, we don't care about it for publication. We were the first U.S. publisher to bring out a collection by the Czech poet Nobel Laureate of 1984—and before he won the Nobel prize." Buys 50-100 poems/year. Pays $15 (depending on length and funding/sales obtained) plus a free copy and 40% off additional copies.

Tips: "Writers and visual artists should query first to see what we're working on if they haven't seen our latest call for manuscripts in *Poets & Writers* magazine or elsewhere. Send #10 SASE for themes and time frames."

SPSM&H, *Amelia Magazine*, 329 E St., Bakersfield CA 93304. (805)323-4064. Editor: Frederick A. Raborg, Jr., 100% freelance written. Quarterly magazine featuring fiction and poetry with Romantic or Gothic theme. "SPSM&H (Shakespeare, Petrarch, Sidney, Milton and Hopkins) uses one short story in each issue and 20-36 sonnets, plus reviews of books and anthologies containing the sonnet forms and occasional articles about the sonnet form or about some romantic or Gothic figure or movement. We look for contemporary aspects of the sonnet form." Estab. 1984. Circ. 600. Pays on publication. Publishes ms an average of 6 months after acceptance. Byline given. Offers 50% kill fee. Buys first North American serial rights. Editorial lead time 2 months. Submit seasonal material 3 months in advance. Accepts simultaneous submissions. Reports in 2 weeks on queries; 3 months on mss. Sample copy for $4.95. Writer's guidelines for #10 SASE.

Nonfiction: Essays, general interest, historical/nostalgic, humor, interview/profile, opinion and anything related to sonnets or to romance. Buys 1-4 mss/year. Send complete ms. Length: 500-2,000 words. Pays $10.

Photos: Send photos with submission. Reviews 8×10 or 5×7 prints. Offers $10-25/photo. Model releases required. Buys one-time rights.

Fiction: Confession, erotica, experimental, fantasy, historical, humor, humorous, mainstream, mystery, romance, slice-of-life vignettes. Buys 4 mss/year. Send complete ms. Length: 500-2,500 words. Pays $10-20.

Poetry: Sonnets, sonnet sequences. Buys 140 poems/year. Submit maximum 10 poems. Length: 14 lines. Two "best of issue" poets each receive $14.

Fillers: Anecdotes, short humor. Buys 2-4/year. Length: 25-500 words. No payment for fillers.

Tips: "Read a copy certainly. Understand the limitations of the sonnet form and, in the case of fiction, the requirements of the romantic or Gothic genres. Be professional in presentation, and realize that neatness does count. Be contemporary and avoid Victorian verse forms and techniques. Avoid convolution and forced rhyme. Idiomatics ought to be contemporary. Don't be afraid to experiment. We consider John Updike's 'Love Sonnet' to be the extreme to which poets may experiment."

STAND MAGAZINE, 179 Wingrove Rd., Newcastle Upon Tyne NE4 9DA United Kingdom. Phone/fax: (091)273-3280. E-mail: dlatane@vcu.edu. Editors: Jon Silkin, Lorna Tracy, Rodney Pybus, Peter Bennet. Managing Editor: Philip Bomford. Contact: David Latané, U.S. editor, Dept. of English, VCU, Richmond VA 23284-2005. 99% freelance written. Quarterly magazine covering short fiction, poetry, criticism and reviews. "*Stand Magazine* was given this name because it was begun as a stand against apathy towards new writing and in social relations." Estab. 1952. Circ. 4,500 worldwide. Pays on publication. Publishes ms an average of 2 years after acceptance. Byline given. Buys first world rights. Editorial lead time 2 months. Reports in 1 week on queries, 2 months on mss. Sample copy for $7. Writer's guidelines for sufficient number of IRCs.

Nonfiction: Essays, interview/profile, reviews of poetry/fiction. "Reviews are commissioned from known freelancers." Buys 8 mss/year. Query. Length: 200-5,000 words. Pays $30/1,000 words.

Fiction: "No genre fiction." Buys 8-10 mss/year. Send complete ms. Length: 8,000 words maximum. Pays $37.50/1,000 words.

Poetry: Avant-garde, free verse, traditional. Buys 30-40 poems/year. Submit maximum 6 poems. Pays $37.50/poem.

Tips: "Poetry/fiction areas are most open to freelancers. Buy a sample copy first (suggestion)." Submissions to England should be accompanied by U.K. SAE or sufficient IRCs.

‡STONEFLOWER LITERARY JOURNAL, Stoneflower Press, 1824 Nacogdoches, Suite 191, San Antonio TX 78209. E-mail: stonflower@aol.com. Contact: Brenda Davidson-Shaddox, editor. 100% freelance written. Annual magazine. "Readers are educated, lovers of literature. Only requirement is top quality writing." Estab. 1995. Circ. 1,000. Pays on publication. Publishes ms an average of 1 year after acceptance. Byline given. Buys one-time rights. Editorial lead time 2 months. Accepts simultaneous submissions. Reports in 6 weeks on queries; 3 months on mss. Sample copy for $4 plus 6×9 SAE with $1.25 postage for U.S. or $2 foreign delivery. Writer's guidelines for #10 SASE.

Nonfiction: Interview/profile only. Buys 1 mss/year. Query. Length: 2,500 words. Pays $10.

Photos and Artwork: Black and white photos and ink drawings. Unfolded, up to 9×14. Any subject. Pays $8. State availability of photos with submission. Offers no additional payment for photos accepted with ms.

Fiction: Ethnic, experimental, historical, humorous, mainstream. "No children's stories. No horror, erotica, no 'causes.' " Buys 6-10 mss/year. Send complete ms. Length: 2,500 words. Pays $10.

Poetry: Avant-garde, free verse, haiku, traditional. "No 'God is Great' poems. No sappy, sentimental. No egocentric." Buys 12-20 poems/year. Submit maximum 6 poems. Length: 40 lines, including line breaks. Pays $5.

Tips: "Don't give up. We often read several submissions from the same contributor before accepting one. Don't send cover letter explaining how wonderful the story/poem is. We determine quality from the work, not from the cover letter. Section devoted to works by children."

STORY, F&W Publications, Inc., 1507 Dana Ave., Cincinnati OH 45207-1005. (513)531-2222. Fax: (513)531-1843. Contact: Lois Rosenthal, editor. 100% freelance written. Quarterly literary magazine of short fiction. "We want short stories and self-inclusive novel excerpts that are extremely well written. Our audience is sophisticated and accustomed to the finest imaginative writing by new and established writers." Estab. 1931. Circ. 40,000. **Pays on acceptance.** Byline given. Buys first North American serial rights. Reports in 1 month. Sample copy for $6.95 and $7\frac{1}{2} \times 10\frac{1}{2}$ SAE with 5 first-class stamps. Writer's guidelines for #10 SASE.

● *Story* won the National Magazine Award for Fiction in 1992 and 1995, was nominated in 1994 and 1996.

Fiction: No genre fiction. Buys 50-60 mss/year. Send complete ms. Length: up to 8,000 words. Pays $1,000 for short stories and $750 for short shorts.

Tips: "No replies without SASE."

‡THE STRAIN, Interactive Arts Magazine, 1307 Diablo, Houston TX 77532-3004. Editor: Norman Clark Stewart Jr. 80% freelance written. Monthly literary compilation. Estab. 1987. Circ. 200-1,000. Pays on publication. Publishes ms an average of 3 years after acceptance. Byline given. Buys first, one-time or second serial rights. Makes work-for-hire assignments. Reports in up to 2 years.

● The primary purpose for this magazine is the exchange of ideas and criticism among its contributors and to develop or find material suitable for collections and anthologies.

Nonfiction: Alicia Alder, articles editor. Essays, exposé, how-to, humor, photo feature, technical. Buys 2-20 mss/year. Send complete ms. Pays $5 minimum.

Reprints: Send typed ms with rights for sale noted and information about when and where article previously appeared.

Photos: Send photos with submissions. Reviews transparencies and prints. Model releases and identification of subjects required. Buys one-time rights.

Columns/Departments: Charlie Mainze, editor. Multi-media performance art. Send complete ms. Pays $5 minimum.

Fiction: Michael Bond, editor. Buys 1-35 mss/year. Send complete ms. Pays $5 minimum. Rarely publishes novel excerpts.

Poetry: Annas Kinder, editor. Avant-garde, free verse, light verse, traditional. Buys 100. Submit maximum 5 poems. Pays $5 minimum.

‡TALE SPINNER, P.O. Box 336, Bedford IN 47421. (812)279-8863. 100% freelance written. Bimonthly magazine. Byline given. Buys one-time first North American serial rights. Reports in 6 weeks. Sample copy for $3.95. Writer's guidelines for #10 SASE.

Nonfiction: Interview/profile withfiction writers. Length: 3,000 words. Pays $15-25. Query.

Reprints: Accepts previously published mterial. Pays $10-20.

Fiction: Commercial fiction. Buys 50-60 mss/year. Length: 800-4,000 words. Pays up to 3¢/word.

Poetry: Pays $5-10.

TAMPA REVIEW, University of Tampa Press, 401 W. Kennedy Blvd., Tampa FL 33606. (813)253-3333. Editor: Richard B. Mathews. Semiannual literary magazine. An international literary journal publishing art and literature from Florida and Tampa Bay as well as new work and translations from throughout the world. Estab. 1988. Circ. 500. Pays on publication. Publishes ms an average of 10 months after acceptance. Byline given. Buys first North American serial rights. Editorial lead time 6-18 months. Reports in 5 months on mss. Sample copy for $5. Writer's guidelines free.

Nonfiction: Paul Linnehan, nonfiction editor. Essays, general interest, interview/profile, personal experience. No "how-to" articles; fads; journalistic reprise etc. Buys 6 mss/year. Send complete ms. Length: 250-7,500 words. Pays $10/printed page upon publication.

Photos: State availability of photos with submission. Reviews contact sheets, negatives, transparencies, prints. Offers $10/photo. Caption identification of subjects required. Buys one-time rights.

Fiction: Lisa Birnbaum, fiction editor. Ethnic, experimental, fantasy, horror, humorous, mainstream, science fiction, literary fiction. Buys 6 mss/year. Send complete ms. Length: 200-10,000 words. Pays $10/printed page upon publication.

Poetry: Don Morrill, Kathryn Van Spanckeven, poetry editors. Avant-garde, free verse, haiku, light verse, traditional, visual/experimental. No greeting card verse; hackneyed, sing-song, rhyme-for-the-sake-of-rhyme. Buys 45 poems/year. Submit up to 10 poems at one time. Length: 2-225 lines.

Tips: "Send a clear cover letter stating previous experience or background."

THEATER MAGAZINE, Yale School of Drama, Yale University, 222 York St., New Haven CT 06511. (203)432-8336. E-mail: theater.magazine@yale.edu. Website: http://www.yale.edu/drama/publications/theater. Editor: Erika Munk. Contact: Shawn Garret, associate editor. Managing Editor: Scott Hamlin. University journal published 3 times/year covering theater—US and Abroad. Estab. 1968. Circ. 3,000. Pays on publication. Publishes ms an average of 4 months after acceptance. Byline given. Editorial lead time 4 months. Writer's guidelines free.

Nonfiction: Essays, general interest, interview/profile, reviews. Buys 3 mss/year. Query. Pays $75-200. Sometimes pays expenses of writers on assignment.

Photos: Send photos with ms. Negotiates payment individually. Captions required. Photographer retains photo rights.

Columns/Departments: Book Reviews, Performance Reviews, Symposia. Buys 3 mss/year. Query.

Fiction: Buys 2 mss/year. Query. Pays $150 minimum.

Tips: "We want critical writing and polemics on modern and contemporary theater in the U.S. and abroad; new plays, translations, adaptations; book and production reviews."

THEMA, Box 74109, Metairie LA 70033-4109. (504)887-1263. Contact: Virginia Howard, editor. 100% freelance written. Triannual literary magazine covering a different theme for each issue. "*Thema* is designed to stimulate creative thinking by challenging writers with unusual themes, such as 'laughter on the steps' and 'jogging on ice.' Appeals to writers, teachers of creative writing and general reading audience." Estab. 1988. Circ. 350. **Pays on acceptance.** Byline given. Buys one-time rights. Reports in 5 months on mss (after deadline for particular issue). Sample copy for $8. Writer's guidelines for #10 SASE. Query with SASE for upcoming themes.

Fiction: Adventure, ethnic, experimental, fantasy, historical, humorous, mainstream, mystery, religious, science fiction, slice-of-life vignettes, suspense, western, novel excerpts. "No alternate lifestyle or erotica." Special issues: Don't call me Thelma! (March 1, 1998); Magnolia's in My Briefcase (July 1, 1998). Buys 33 mss/year. Send complete ms and *specify theme* for which it is intended. Pays $10-25.

● Ranked as one of the best markets for fiction writers in the last *Writer's Digest* magazine's "Fiction 50."

Reprints: Send typed ms with rights for sale noted and when and where the article previously appeared.

Poetry: Avant-garde, free verse, haiku, light verse, traditional. No erotica. Buys 27 poems/year. Submit maximum 3 poems. Length: 4-50 lines. Pays $10.

Tips: "Be familiar with the themes. *Don't submit* unless you have an upcoming theme in mind. Specify the target theme on the first page of your manuscript or in a cover letter. Put your name on *first* page of manuscript only. (All submissions are judged in blind review after the deadline for a specified issue.) Most open to fiction and poetry. Don't be hasty when you consider a theme—mull it over and let it ferment in your mind. We appreciate interpretations that are carefully constructed, clever, subtle, well thought out."

THE THREEPENNY REVIEW, P.O. Box 9131, Berkeley CA 94709. (510)849-4545. Contact: Wendy Lesser, editor. 100% freelance written. Works with small number of new/unpublished writers each year. Quarterly literary tabloid. "We are a general interest, national literary magazine with coverage of politics, the visual arts and the performing arts as well." Estab. 1980. Circ. 9,000. **Pays on acceptance.** Publishes ms an average of 1 year after acceptance. Byline given. Buys first North American serial rights. Reports in 1 month on queries; 2 months on mss. Does *not* read mss in summer months. Sample copy for $6 and 10×13 SAE with 5 first-class stamps. Writer's guidelines for SASE.

Nonfiction: Essays, exposé, historical, personal experience, book, film, theater, dance, music and art reviews. Buys 40 mss/year. Query with or without published clips, or send complete ms. Length: 1,500-4,000 words. Pays $200.

Fiction: No fragmentary, sentimental fiction. Buys 10 mss/year. Send complete ms. Length: 800-4,000 words. Pays $200.

● Ranked as one of the best markets for fiction writers in the last *Writer's Digest* magazine's "Fiction 50."

Poetry: Free verse, traditional. No poems "without capital letters or poems without a discernible subject." Buys 30 poems/year. Submit maximum 5 poems. Pays $100.

Tips: "Nonfiction (political articles, memoirs, reviews) is most open to freelancers."

‡**THE TRICKSTER REVIEW: ART, LITERATURE, COMMUNICATIONS**, The International Citizen's Corps., 122 E. Texas Ave. #1016, Baytown TX 77520. Editor: Yvonne McCall. Semiannual literary magazine. Publishes ms an average of 1 year after acceptance. Buys first North American serial rights. Accepts simultaneous submissions. Reports in 2 months on queries; 6 months on mss. Sample copy for $7. Writer's guidelines for #10 SASE and $1.

Nonfiction: Book excerpts, essays, exposé, general interest, historical/nostalgic, humor, interview/profile, opinion, personal experience, photo feature, politics, art, literature, communication. Send complete ms. Pays $10 plus 3 copies.

Fiction: Larry Jacob, fiction editor. Ethnic, experimental, fantasy, historical, humorous, mainstream, novel excerpts, literary, suspense, censorship issues, "serious but not morose" fiction. "Don't be more interested in a grandiose plan for a ten-book series than your 2,000 word essay." Buys 10-15 mss/year. Send complete ms. Length: approximately 2,000 words.

Poetry: Richard Wayne, poetry editor. Avant-garde, free verse, traditional. Buys 10 poems/year. Submit 5 poems max.

Tips: "Our readers have read extensively. Many are writer's themselves. We are open to new and established writers. We publish lucid writers representing the best of the material submitted each issue. We are interested in translations into English of contemporary authors."

TRIQUARTERLY, 2020 Ridge Ave., Northwestern University, Evanston IL 60208-4302. (847)491-3490. Contact: Susan Hahn, editor. 70% freelance written. Eager to work with new/unpublished writers. Triannual magazine of fiction, poetry and essays, as well as artwork. Estab. 1964. Pays on publication. Publishes ms an average of 1 year after acceptance. Buys first serial and nonexclusive reprint rights. Reports in 3 months. Study magazine before submitting. Sample copy for $5. Writer's guidelines for #10 SASE.

● *TriQuarterly* has had several stories published in the *O. Henry Prize* anthology and *Best American Short Stories* as well as poetry in *Best American Poetry.*

Nonfiction: Query before sending essays (no scholarly or critical essays except in special issues).

Fiction and Poetry: No prejudice against style or length of work; only seriousness and excellence are required. Buys 20-50 unsolicited mss/year. Payment varies depending on grant support.

‡**THE VINCENT BROTHERS REVIEW**, 4566 Northern Circle, Riverside OH 45424-5733. Contact: Kimberly Willardson, editor. **Pays on acceptance.** Byline given. Buys first rights. Reports in 3 months on mss. Sample copy for $6.50.

Nonfiction: Query with SASE.

Fiction: Condensed novels, novel excerpts, serialized novels, short stories and novellas. Buys 18-30 mss/year. Query with SASE; for short stories, send complete ms. Length: 250-10,000 words. Pays $10-110.

Poetry: Query with SASE.

Tips: "We publish a variety of genres and subject matters, but always haunting stories. We want to be hooked immediately by a story and rendered unable to put it down until we've read the last word of it. We like to offer our readers stories they'll want to go back to read again. Common submission flaws: boring beginnings; tacked-on endings; flat, stereotyped characters; trite or mundane plot lines; pedestrian prose; and unimaginative or inconcise language."

VIRGINIA QUARTERLY REVIEW, University of Virginia, One West Range, Charlottesville VA 22903. (804)924-3124. Fax: (804)924-1397. E-mail: jco7e@virginia.edu. Contact: Staige D. Blackford, editor. Quarterly magazine. "A national journal of literature and thought." Estab. 1925. Circ. 4,000. Pays on publication. Publishes ms an average of 1 year after acceptance. Byline given. Buys first rights. Editorial lead time 6 months. Submit seasonal material 6 months

in advance. Reports in 2 weeks on queries; 2 months on mss. Sample copy $5. Writer's guidelines for #10 SASE.
Nonfiction: Book excerpts, essays, general interest, historical/nostalgic, humor, inspirational, personal experience, travel. Send complete ms. Length: 2,000-4,000 words. Pays $10/page maximum.
Fiction: Adventure, ethnic, historical, humorous, mainstream, mystery, novel excerpts, romance. Send complete ms. Length: 2,000-4,000 words. Pays $10/page maximum.
Poetry: Gregory Orr, poetry editor. All types. Submit maximum 5 poems. Pays $1/line.

WASCANA REVIEW OF CONTEMPORARY POETRY AND SHORT FICTION, University of Regina, Department of English, Regina, Saskatchewan S4T 1V9 Canada. Editor: Kathleen Wall. 100% freelance written. Semiannual magazine covering contemporary poetry and short fiction. "We seek poetry and short fiction that combines craft with risks, pressure with grace. Critical articles should articulate a theoretical approach and also explore either poetry or short fiction. While we frequently publish established writers, we also welcome—and seek to foster—new voices." Estab. 1966. Circ. 200. Pays on publication. Publishes ms an average of 4 months after acceptance. Buys first North American rights. Editorial lead time 4 months. Reports in 1 week on queries; 2 months on mss. Writer's guidelines free.
Columns/Departments: Reviews of contemporary poetry and short fiction (ask for guidelines), 1,000-1,500 words. Buys 8 mss/year. Query. Pays $3/printed page.
Fiction: No genre-bound fiction, or stories with sentimental or predictable endings. Buys 8-10 mss/year. Send complete ms. Pays $3/printed page plus 2 contributor's copies.
Poetry: Troni Grande. Avant-garde, free verse. No sentimental, fee-good verse, no predictable rhyme and meter. Buys 40 poems/year. Submit maximum 5 poems. Pays $10/printed page plus contributor's copies.
Tips: "The best advice I can give is to read back issues."

WEST COAST LINE, A Journal of Contemporary Writing & Criticism, West Coast Review Publishing Society, 2027 EAA. Simon Fraser University, Burnaby, British Columbia V5A 1S6 Canada. (604)291-4287. Fax: (604)291-5737. E-mail: jlarson@sfu.ca. Website: http://www.sfu.ca/west-coast-line/WCL.html. Managing Editor: Jacqueline Larson. Triannual magazine of contemporary literature and criticism. Estab. 1990. Circ. 500. Pays on publication. Buys one-time rights. Editorial lead time 4 months. Submit seasonal material 4 months in advance. Reports in 2 weeks on queries; 3 months on mss. Sample copy for $10. Writer's guidelines free, only with SASE (U.S. must include IRC).
Nonfiction: Essays (literary/scholarly), experimental prose. "No journalistic articles or articles dealing with nonliterary material." Buys 8-10 mss/year. Send complete ms. Length: 1,000-5,000 words. Pays $8/page, 2 contributor's copies, and a year's free subscription.
Fiction: Experimental, novel excerpts. Buys 3-6 mss/yr. Send complete ms. Length: 1,000-7,000 words. Pays $8/pg.
Poetry: Avant-garde. "No light verse, traditional." Buys 10-15 poems/yr. Length: 5-6 pages max. Pays $8/pg.
Tips: "Submissions must be either scholarly or formally innovative. Contributors should be familiar with current literary trends in Canada and the U.S. Scholars should be aware of current schools of theory. All submissions should be accompanied by a brief cover letter; essays should be formatted according to the MLA guide. The publication is not divided into departments. We accept innovative poetry, fiction, experimental prose and scholarly essays."

‡WESTERN HUMANITIES REVIEW, University of Utah, Salt Lake City UT 84112-1107. (801)581-6070. Contact: Tom Hawks, managing editor. Quarterly magazine for educated readers. Estab. 1947. Circ. 1,200. **Pays on acceptance.** Publishes ms an average of 3-12 months after acceptance. Buys all rights. Accepts simultaneous submissions. Reports in 3-5 months.
Nonfiction: Barry Weller, editor-in-chief. Authoritative, readable articles on literature, art, philosophy, current events, history, religion and anything in the humanities. Interdisciplinary articles encouraged. Departments on film and books. Buys 4-5 unsolicited mss/year. Pays $50-150.
Fiction: David Kranes, fiction editor. Any type, including experimental. Recent contributors include Robert Coover, Deborah Eisenberg, Chuck Rosenthal, Stephen Dixon, James McManus, Alan Singer, Cris Mazza, Norman Lavers and Francine Prose. Buys 8-12 mss/year. Send complete ms. Average payment $150.
Poetry: Richard Howard, poetry editor. Recent contributors include Allen Grossman, Joseph Brodsky, Daniel Halpern, Albert Goldbarth, Debora Greger, Jane Flanders, Lucie Brock-Broido and Jacqueline Osherow.
Tips: "Because of changes in our editorial staff, we urge familiarity with *recent* issues of the magazine. Inappropriate material will be returned without comment."

‡WHETSTONE, Barrington Area Arts Council, Box 1266, Barrington IL 60011. Co-Editors: S. Berris, J. Fleenor. M. Portnoy. Contact: Jean Tolle, co-editor. 100% freelance written. Annual literary magazine featuring fiction, creative nonfiction and poetry. "We publish work by emerging and established authors for readers hungry for poetry and prose of substance." Estab. 1982. Circ. 700. Pays on publication. Publishes ms an average 1-14 months after acceptance. Byline given. Not copyrighted. Buys first North American serial rights. Accepts simultaneous submissions. Reports in 3-5 months on mss. "No queries." Sample copy and writer's guidelines for $3.25.
Nonfiction: Creative essay. "No articles." Buys 0-3 mss/year. Send complete ms. Length: 500-5,000 words. Pays with 2 copies and variable cash payment.
Fiction: Novel excerpts (literary) and short stories. Buys 10-12 mss/year. Send complete ms. Length: 500-5,000 words. Pay varies.
Poetry: Free verse, traditional. No light verse, for children, political poems." Buys 10-20 poems/year. Submit maximum 7 poems. Pay varies.

INSIDER REPORT

A Matter of the Right Story

Adrienne Brodeur

When Adrienne Brodeur heard from a variety of sources that film director Francis Ford Coppola was interested in short fiction, possibly even in beginning a fiction magazine, she realized it might just be "publishing gossip." But she found the rumors intriguing enough to write a letter basically saying, "Dear Mr. Coppola, I love short fiction, too."

That was the spring of 1995 and Brodeur really didn't expect a response from Coppola. "But about six months later, I got a call late one night from a man asking, 'Is this Adrienne Brodeur?' I said, 'Yes,' and he said, 'This is Francis.' My response was, "Francis who?' "

For several months, Brodeur in New York and Coppola in California engaged in an e-mail relationship over "our philosophy of short fiction and what we each like in a short story. It was kind of a meeting of the minds, and from that we gave birth to the concept of a magazine."

Named after Coppola's film studio, *Zoetrope: Short Stories* was launched early in 1997. Unlike most literary journals, *Zoetrope*'s $10\frac{1}{2} \times 14$ size and newsprint-quality paper would be quite at home with magazines vying for attention in grocery checkout lines. The premier issue had a print run of 50,000, many times more than most literary magazines. Those copies were distributed in Starbucks coffee shops, high schools and colleges—free for the taking and reading. All this is in keeping with Coppola's two-fold goal of providing a no-frills place for fine, new short fiction and making that fiction accessible to as many readers as possible.

Editor-in-chief Brodeur says *Zoetrope* will be published quarterly in 1998. She and Coppola also plan to continue including approximately 90 percent new fiction and one story commissioned by Coppola in each edition. Stories are optioned as film ideas for two years. Writers of commissioned stories are paid $5,000. Authors of noncommissioned stories receive $1,000. Each issue will also run an essay about the short story form, a reprint of a classic short story that later became a play or movie, and a one-act play.

The philosophy of short fiction Brodeur and Coppola share is that a story should tell a story. "My understanding, having now worked for Francis for a while, is that he really loves the short story genre. He particularly loves a good story in the classic sense of the word 'story.' We both like literary stories, but he's not one to want anything too experimental. The critical elements to him are characters you can get involved with, whether you love them or hate them. He also likes a story that takes you somewhere—you're not the same squeeze of toothpaste coming out that you were going in.

"This all sounds very basic, but there are some wonderful literary magazines that focus on really magnificent writing and lovely descriptions, but that isn't exactly what we look for. We're looking more for the classic narrative arc."

Although they work thousands of miles apart, Brodeur maintains that Coppola stays

INSIDER REPORT, *Brodeur*

very involved in the *Zoetrope* operation. "Francis is an e-mail king; everything we do is on a Lotus Notes computer system. I always let him know what I'm doing. I post stories I'm interested in and he comments. Most often, I buy the stories in advance of when he reads them. It's a big relief, then, when he likes something I bought weeks before."

Brodeur also finds authors for the stories Coppola commissions. "He gives me a general idea of something he'd be interested in reading a story about. Then, because I read all the literary journals and go to readings and that sort of thing, I'll recommend three or four writers I think have the voice for the story. It's a very different process than someone writing a work and handing it to you as a done piece. But it's worked out very well." Sara Powers's "The Baker's Wife," Coppola's first commissioned piece, was being developed by Coppola's film company soon after its appearance in the premier edition of *Zoetrope*. But Brodeur insists that finding movie material is only an added benefit, not the primary purpose, of the magazine. "If Francis only wanted to find movie scripts, he wouldn't have hired me; he would have found someone with a film background. He could buy stories for potential movies; he wouldn't need to do a magazine—a magazine is an expensive beast. I think he's an artist who's made it and wants to put something back into new writers and new talent, and that's really a large part of his goal. It's certainly a large part of my goal, too."

Currently, all the manuscripts received in the *Zoetrope* office are read with the help of a group of "great first readers," says Brodeur. "We have a first-tier reading and ranking system, then one of the three other fulltime editors and myself look at everything. Some manuscripts float to the surface and we look at them more carefully. Then every other week we have a dinner meeting with our editorial board where we look at three to six stories again to see how the board feels about them and make our decisions that way. We also try hard, although it's becoming harder, to write a few comments when we send back a manuscript."

Brodeur says the influx of manuscripts has quadrupled since she first put out her word-of-mouth call for stories, but the number of publishable manuscripts has not. "We're getting many more manuscripts, but there are not necessarily that many more stories we would be interested in publishing. In the beginning, since it was all word of mouth, we were hitting very targeted audiences of writers and we found fine manuscripts."

A publishable story to Brodeur is one she will remember the next day or next week. "When you read hundreds of stories, few actually stand out in your mind. But there are some stories you can remember pieces of, that have touched some rod inside you. It's a visceral response that's hard for me to break down, but I think it's characters you can really get involved with, whether you like or don't like them. And it's a story that really takes you somewhere. It's hard to walk away loving a story, even though it might be beautifully written, if it doesn't affect you on some level. Some people assume their writing is so lovely that anyone is going to want to read about them watching the bird walk down the sidewalk for five pages. With us, that just is not so."

As hard as it seems for an unknown to get published today, Brodeur says, "It really is a matter of the right story. It seems a lot of stories by unpublished writers are making it to our editorial board. Just last week we found an interesting and promising story in our slush pile from a writer who learned about us from who knows where. I know it's easy to get discouraged, but if you have faith in your work and you know it's good, you just have to keep sending it out until it gets published."

—*Barbara Kuroff*

Tips: "We look for fresh approaches to original material. We appreciate careful work. Send us your best. We welcome unpublished authors. Though we pay in copies and small monetary amounts that depend on the generosity of our patrons and subscribers, we offer prizes for work published in *Whetstone*. For the last 3 years these prizes have totaled $750, and were given to two or three writers. The editors make their decisions at the time of publication. This is not a contest. In addition, we nominate authors for Pushcart, Best American Short Story, Poetry and Essays, Best of the South, Illinois Arts Council Awards, and other prizes and anthologies as they come to our attention. Though our press run is moderate, we work for our authors and offer a prestigious vehicle for their work."

‡WILLOW SPRINGS, 526 Fifth St., MS-1, Eastern Washington University, Cheney WA 99004. (509)458-6429. Contact: Christopher Howell, editor. 100% freelance written. Semiannual literary magazine. "We publish quality contemporary poetry, fiction, nonfiction and works in translation." Estab. 1977. Circ. 1,500. Publishes ms an average of 10 months after acceptance. Byline given. Acquires first publication rights. Editorial lead time 2 months. Reports in 2 months. Sample copy for $5. Writer's guidelines for #10 SASE.
  ● A magazine of growing reputation. Takes part in the AWP Intro Award program.
Nonfiction: Essays. Accepts 4 mss/year. Send complete ms.
Fiction: Literary fiction only. "No genre fiction, please." Accepts 5-8 mss/year. Send complete ms.
Poetry: Avant-garde, free verse. "No haiku, light verse or religious." Accepts 50-80 poems/year. Submit maximum 6 poems. Length: 12 pages maximum.
Tips: "We do not read manuscripts in June, July and August."

WINDSOR REVIEW, Department of English, University of Windsor, Windsor, Ontario N9B 3P4 Canada. (519)253-4232. ext. 2332. Fax: (519)973-7050. Website: http://www.CS.uwindsor.ca/units/english/pub.htm. Contact: Alistair Mac-Leod (fiction); John Ditsky (poetry). Biannual comprising original poetry, fiction and art. Estab. 1965. Circ. 300. Buys first North American serial rights. Reports in 2 months. Sample copy for $5 and postage. Enclose SAE with Canadian postage or IRCs only.
Fiction: Alistair MacLeod. Mainstream prose with open attitude toward themes. Length: 2,000-6,000 words. Pays $50.
Poetry: John Ditsky. Accepts traditional forms, blank verse, free verse, avant-garde. No epics. Pays $15.

WITNESS, Oakland Community College, 27055 Orchard Lake Rd., Farmington Hills MI 48334. (313)471-7740. Contact: Peter Stine, editor. 100% freelance written. Semiannual literary magazine. "*Witness* highlights the role of writer as witness." Estab. 1987. Circ. 2,800. Pays on publication. Publishes ms an average of 1 year after acceptance. Byline given. Buys first North American serial rights. Editorial lead time 6 months. Accepts simultaneous submissions. Reports in 3 months. Sample copy for $7. Writer's guidelines for #10 SASE.
  ● A rising and energetic magazine. The frequent theme issues require more work from the writer in studying this market.
Nonfiction: Essays, interview/profile. Buys 10 mss/yr. Send complete ms. Length: 1,000-10,000 words. Pays $6/pg.
Fiction: Ethnic, experimental, mainstream, literary. Buys 20 mss/year. Send complete ms. Length: 1,000-6,000 words. Pays $6/page.
Poetry: Avant-garde, free verse, traditional. Buys 20 poems/year. Submit maximum 4 poems. Pays $10/page.
Tips: "One story or essay per submission at a time, please."

THE YALE REVIEW, Yale University, P.O. Box 208243, New Haven CT 06520-8243. (203)432-0499. Editor: J.D. McClatchy. Managing Editor: Susan Bianconi. 20% freelance written. Buys first North American serial rights. Estab. 1911. Pays prior to publication. Responds in 2 months. Publishes in 5-12 months. "No writer's guidelines available. Consult back issues."
  ● *The Yale Review* has published work chosen for the Pushcart anthology, *The Best American Poetry*, and the O. Henry Award.
Nonfiction and Fiction: Authoritative discussions of politics, literature and the arts. Buys quality fiction. Does not accept previously published submissions. Length: 3,000-5,000 words. Pays $100-500.

YELLOW SILK: Journal of Erotic Arts, verygraphics, Box 6374, Albany CA 94706. (510)644-4188. E-mail: shebert@well.com. Contact: Lily Pond, editor. 90% freelance written. Prefers to work with published/established writers. Annual international journal of erotic literature and visual arts. "Editorial policy: All persuasions; no brutality. Our publication is artistic and literary, not pornographic or pandering. Humans are involved: heads, hearts and bodies—not just bodies alone; and the quality of the literature is as important as the erotic content though erotic content is important too." Pays on publication. Byline given. Buys all publication rights for 1 year following publication, at which time they revert to author, non-active and reprint electronic and anthology rights for duration of copyright. Reports in 3 months on mss. Sample copy for $7.50.
Nonfiction: Book excerpts, essays, humor, reviews. "We often have theme issues, but non-regularly and usually not announced in advance. No pornography, romance-novel type writing, sex fantasies. No first-person accounts or blow-by-blow descriptions. No articles. No novels." Buys 5-10 mss/year. Send complete ms. All mss should be typed, double-spaced, with name, address and phone number on each page; always enclose SASE. No length requirements.
Photos: Photos may be submitted independently, not as illustration for submission. Reviews photocopies, contact sheets, transparencies and prints. "We accept 4-color and b&w artwork." Offers varying payment for series of 8-20 used, plus copies. Buys one-time rights and reprint rights.

Columns/Departments: Reviews (book, movie, art, dance, food, music, anything). "Erotic content and how it's handled is focus of importance. Old or new does not matter. We want to bring readers information of what's out there." Buys 8-10 mss/year. Send complete ms or query.

Fiction: Erotic literature, including ethnic, experimental, fantasy, humorous, mainstream, novel excerpts, science fiction. See "Nonfiction." Buys 12-16 mss/year. Send complete ms.

Poetry: Avant-garde, free verse, haiku, light verse, traditional. "No greeting-card poetry." Buys 40-60 poems/year. No limit on number of poems submitted, "but don't send book-length manuscripts."

Tips: "The best way to get into *Yellow Silk* is produce excellent, well-crafted work that includes eros freshly, with strength of voice, beauty of language, and insight into character. I'll tell you what I'm sick of and have, unfortunately, been seeing more of lately: the products of 'How to Write Erotica' classes. This is not brilliant fiction; it is poorly written fantasy and not what I'm looking for."

‡ZOETROPE, Azx Publications, 126 5th Ave. #300, New York NY 10011. (212)675-0064. Fax: (212)675-0274. Contact: Adrienne Brodeur, editor. Quarterly literary magazine specializing in high caliber short fiction. "*Zoetrope* seeks to provide a new forum for short fiction and to make short fiction more accessible to the public at large." Open to outstanding work by beginning and established writers. Estab. 1997. Circ. 50,000. Publishes ms 2-6 months after acceptance. Byline given. Buys first serial rights. Accepts simultaneous submissions. Reports in 3 months. Query with SASE and complete ms (2 stories maximum). Sample copy and writer's guidelines for 9×12 SAE with 7 first-class stamps. Guidelines only for SASE.

Fiction: Literary, mainstream/contemporary, one act plays. 7,000 words maximum. No short shorts or reprints. Receives 6,000 submissions/year. Buys 32-40 ms/year. Query with SASE and complete ms.

Tips: "*Zoetrope* considers unsolicited submissions of short stories no longer than 7,000 words. Excerpts from larger works, screenplays, treatments and poetry will be returned unread. Submissions accompanied by an SASE will receive a response within three months. We regret we are unable to respond to submissions without SASE."

ZYZZYVA, The Last Word: West Coast Writers & Artists, 41 Sutter St., Suite 1400, San Francisco CA 94104-4987. (415)752-4393. Fax: (415)752-4391. E-mail: zyzzyvainc@aol.com. Editor: Howard Junker. 100% freelance written. Works with a small number of new/unpublished writers each year. "We feature work by West Coast writers only. We are essentially a literary magazine, but of wide-ranging interests and a strong commitment to nonfiction." Estab. 1985. Circ. 3,500. **Pays on acceptance.** Publishes ms an average of 3 months after acceptance. Byline given. Buys first North American serial rights and one-time anthology rights. Reports in 1 week on queries; 1 month on mss. Sample copy for $5.

Nonfiction: Book excerpts, general interest, historical/nostalgic, humor, personal experience. Buys 15 mss/year. Query. Length: open. Pays $50.

Fiction: Ethnic, experimental, humorous, mainstream. Buys 20 mss/year. Send complete ms. Length: open. Pays $50-250.

• Ranked as one of the best markets for fiction writers in the last *Writer's Digest* magazine's "Fiction 50."

Poetry: Buys 20 poems/year. Submit maximum 5 poems. Length: 3-200 lines. Pays $50.

MEN'S

Magazines in this section offer features on topics of general interest primarily to men. Magazines that also use material slanted toward men can be found in Business and Finance, Child Care and Parental Guidance, Ethnic/Minority, Gay & Lesbian Interest, General Interest, Health and Fitness, Military, Relationships and Sports sections. Magazines featuring pictorial layouts accompanied by stories and articles of a sexual nature, both gay and straight, appear in the Sex section.

DETAILS, Condé Nast Publications, Inc., 632 Broadway, New York NY 10012. Monthly magazine for men ages 18-34 interested in style, sex, pop cultures, new and sports. "*Details* is edited as a lifestyle magazine for today's generation of young adults who are rapidly assuming their places as leaders in American society. Articles are written from the standpoint of a peer—in contemporary language that readers can relate to, within an intelligent, sophisticated perspective on the world. From culture to sports to entertaining to relationships—fashion, careers, music, clubs and technology, *Details* covers the various aspects of its readers' lives." Estab. 1982. Circ. 473,000. **Pays on acceptance.** Byline given. Offers 25-50% kill fee. Accepts simultaneous submissions. Reports in 2 months on queries.

• Ranked as one of the best markets for freelance writers in *Writer's Yearbook* magazine's annual "Top 100 Markets," January 1997.

Nonfiction: News stories of interest to young men; personal essays and service features on lifestyle topics from shops to booze, sports, travel, relationships, courtship, automotive. Buys 60 mss/year. Query with published clips. Length: 3,000-5,000 words. Pays 75¢-$1/word.

Columns/Departments: 800-1,500 words. Buys 120 mss/year. Query with published clips. Pays 75-$1/word.

Fillers: Buys 60/year. Length: 500-800 words. Pays 75¢-$1/word.

Tips: "Topical news stories that affect or interest men in their 20s. Timely subject, stylishly written that makes people laugh and cry. *Details* maintains a high standard of modern journalism and encourages a creative, stylish, confessional, personal emotional writing style. We include all kinds of people with all kinds of interest and beliefs. We speak to our readers in a contemporary manner, with a unique tone that touches the heart and mind and tickles that funny bone."

ESQUIRE, 250 W. 55th St., New York NY 10019. (212)649-4020. Editor-in-Chief: Edward Kosner. Articles Editor: Bill Tonelli. Monthly magazine for smart, well-off men. Estab. 1933. General readership is college educated and sophisticated, between ages 30 and 45. Written mostly by contributing editors on contract. Rarely accepts unsolicited mss. **Pays on acceptance**. Offers 20% kill fee. Publishes ms an average of 2 months after acceptance. Retains first worldwide periodical publication rights for 90 days from cover date.
  • Ranked as one of the best markets for freelance writers in *Writer's Yearbook* magazine's annual "Top 100 Markets," January 1997.
Nonfiction: Columns average 1,500 words; features average 5,000 words; short front-of-book pieces average 200-400 words. Focus is on the ever-changing trends in American culture. Topics include current events and politics, social criticism, sports, celebrity profiles, the media, art and music, men's fashion. Queries must be sent by letter. Buys 4 features and 12 short pieces. Pays $1/word.
Photos: Marianne Butler, photo editor. Uses mostly commissioned photography. Payment depends on size and number of photos.
Fiction: Contact: literary editor. "Literary excellence is our only criterion." Accepts work chiefly from literary agencies. Publishes short stories, some poetry, and excerpts from novels, memoirs and plays.
Tips: "A writer has the best chance of breaking in at *Esquire* by querying with a specific idea that requires special contacts and expertise. Ideas must be timely and national in scope."

GENTLEMEN'S QUARTERLY, Condé Nast, 350 Madison Ave., New York NY 10017. (212)880-8800. Editor-in-Chief: Arthur Cooper. Contact: Martin Beiser, managing editor. 60% freelance written. Circ. 650,000. Monthly magazine emphasizing fashion, general interest and service features for men ages 25-45 with a large discretionary income. **Pays on acceptance.** Byline given. Pays 25% kill fee. Submit seasonal material 6 months in advance. Reports in 1 month.
Nonfiction: Politics, personality profiles, lifestyles, trends, grooming, nutrition, health/fitness, sports, travel, money, investment and business matters. Buys 4-6 mss/issue. Query with published clips. Length: 1,500-4,000 words. Pay varies.
Columns/Departments: Query with published clips. Length: 1,000-2,500 words. Pay varies.
Tips: "Major features are usually assigned to well-established, known writers. Pieces are almost always solicited. The best way to break in is through the columns, especially Contraria, Enthusiasms or First Person."

HEARTLAND USA, UST Publishing, 1 Sound Shore Dr., Suite 3, Greenwich CT 06830-7251. (203)622-3456. Fax: (203)863-5393. E-mail: husaedit@aol.com. Contact: Brad Pearson, editor. 10% freelance written. Bimonthly magazine for working people. "*Heartland USA* is a general interest, lifestyle magazine for working people 18 to 53. It covers spectator sports (primarily motor sports, football, baseball and basketball, hunting, fishing, how-to, travel, music, gardening, the environment, human interest, etc.), emphasizing the upbeat or humorous." Estab. 1991. Circ. 750,000. **Pays on acceptance**. Byline given. Offers 20% kill fee. Buys first North American serial and second serial (reprint) rights. Submit seasonal material 1 year in advance. Accepts simultaneous submissions. Reports in 1 month on queries. Sample copy on request. Writer's guidelines free.
Nonfiction: Book excerpts, general interest, historical/nostalgic, how-to, humor, inspirational, interview/profile, new product, personal experience, photo feature, technical, travel. "No fiction or dry expository pieces." Buys 6 mss/year. Query with or without published clips or send complete ms. Length: 350-1,200 words. Pays 50-80¢/word for assigned articles; 25-80¢/word for unsolicited articles. Sometimes pays expenses of writers on assignment.
Reprints: Send photocopy of article and information about when and where the article previously appeared. Pays $200.
Photos: Send photos with submission. Reviews transparencies. Identification of subjects required. Buys one-time rights.
Tips: "Features with the possibility of strong photographic support are open to freelancers, as are our shorter departments. We look for a relaxed, jocular, easy-to-read style, and look favorably on the liberal use of anecdote or interesting quotations."

‡ICONTHOUGHTSTYLE, Magazine for Men, Icon, L.P., 595 Broadway, 4th Floor, New York NY 10012. (212)219-2654. Fax: (212)219-4045. Contact: Robin Dolch, editor. Bimonthly magazine covering general interest issues for young men, ages 18-34. "*ICONThoughtstyle*'s mission is to confront the concept of success carefully and objectively, and to explore its many meanings and manifestations boundlessly, so that young men are better able to define the concept for themselves. Editorial focuses on comprehensive profile/interviews of men who have achieved large-scale successes in their respective fields. *Icon* will aim to educate and civilize, to inspire and encourage." Estab. 1997. Circ. 100,000. Pays within 30 days after acceptance. Byline given. Buys all rights. Reports in 2 weeks. Writer's guidelines for #10 SASE.
Nonfiction: Interview/profile. "*Icon* Profiles examine the world's most successful, interesting men, providing blueprints for success. These pieces could cover a CEO, a physicist or a choreographer. We hold no preconceived definitions of what exactly *success* is. Our role is to find people who are working to fulfill their own vision of it and then report on their efforts." Feature articles also focus on organizations, places, ideas, etc. "Whereas the *Icon* Profiles start with an individual and work inward, features start with one or more people and work outward, looking at their lives' work, the

effort in which they are presently or were previously involved. The stories are personality based, with a heavy stress on reporting, observation and interviews. Recurrent themes are business ventures, failures and comebacks, off-the-beaten path characters and families, and generally provocative characters." Query with published clips. Length: 5,000 words. Pays $1/word.

Columns/Departments: Observations (first-person account of an extreme experience or a personal exploration), 2,000 words. ICONnoisseur (mini-mag of 5 departments within *Icon* that 'celebrates and examines the tools and rituals of a man's life'): Clothing (i.e., the 3-piece suit or the white T-shirt), Accessories, Elixirs (smokes, drinks and drugs), Ego (nutrition, health, fitness and protocol), Form & Function (consumer technology and design), 2,000 words. Re:Views (3 departments covering the realm of artistic expression): Vision (examining the artist), Creation (dealing with the artistic process), and Effect (reactions or responses elicited by the artist and his work), 2,000 words. Pays $1/word.

MEN'S JOURNAL, Wenner Media Inc., 1290 Avenue of the Americas, New York NY 10104-0298. (212)484-1616. Fax: (212)767-8205. Editor: John Rasmus. Monthly magazine covering general lifestyle for men, ages 25-49. *"Men's Journal* is for active men with an interest in participatory sports, travel, fitness and adventure. It provides practical, informative articles on how to spend quality leisure time." Estab. 1992. Circ. 344,000.
Nonfiction: Features and profiles. 2,000-7,000 words; shorter features of 400-1,200 words; equipment and fitness stories 400-1,800 words. Query with SASE. Pay varies.

NEW MAN, Strang Communications Co., 600 Rinehart Rd., Lake Mary FL 32746. (407)333-0600. Fax: (407)333-7133. E-mail: peterson@strang.com. Website: http://www.strang.com. Contact: Brian Peterson, editorial director. 70% freelance written. Magazine published 8 times a year covering Christian men with Christ-centered lives. *"New Man* appeals to men of all denominations and ethnic groups. It is bold and straightforward in its editorial content, but it avoids topics that act as barriers between Christian men. It aims to inform and equip men with Christ-centered perspectives in every aspect of their lives and to be a godly influence in their worlds." Estab. 1994. Circ. 320,000. Pays on publication. Publishes ms an average of 4 months after acceptance. Byline given. Offers $50 kill fee. Buys first or all rights. Editorial lead time 4 months. Submit seasonal material 8 months in advance. Accepts simultaneous submissions. Reports in 4 months. Sample copy for $3. Writer's guidelines free.
Nonfiction: Book excerpts, humor, interview/profile, personal experience, photo feature. Buys 50 mss/year. Prefers query with or without published clips, or send complete ms. Length: 2,000 words maximum. Pays 10-35¢/word. Pays expenses of writers on assignment.
Reprints: Send typed ms with rights for sale noted and information about when and where the article previously appeared. Payment varies.
Photos State availability of photos with submission. Reviews any size prints. Negotiates payment individually. Identification of subjects required. Buys one-time rights.
Columns/Departments: Women (written to men about women by women); Health (men's health concerns); Finances; all 1,000 words. Buys 15 mss/year. Send complete ms. Pays $100-300.
Fillers: Anecdotes, facts, newsbreaks. Length: 250 words maximum. Pays 10-35¢/word.

"New Man magazine addresses every aspect of a man's world: spiritual, physical, emotional, social. The articles cover topics of interest to singles, husbands and fathers. Most of our readers are married and between the ages of 20 and 60. Examples of key topics: career, children, church, conflicts, current events, entertainment, evangelism, fathering, finances, fitness and nutrition, prejudice and racism, relationships, sex, sports, thrill and adventure, and women. Freelance articles that are most likely to be published: *Unsung heros*: We're looking for articles on everyday men who are doing something extraordinary in their area, from all parts of the world. *Clips*: short items of interest for men (50 to 250 words), including unusual facts, motivational quotes, perspectives on current news and events; *Thrill and adventure*: action-packed stories, outdoor family adventures; *Trends* indepth look at issues confronting today's man."

‡P.O.V. Guy's Survival Guide, BYOB Ventures/Freedom Communications, 38 The Fenway, Boston MA 02118. (617)247-3200. Editor: Randall Lane. Contact: Michael Callahan, managing editor. 80% freelance written. Published 10 times/year. "Our motto is cash, careers and living large. Our audience is up-and-coming guys in their twenties and early thirties. If it's not of interest to them, it's not of interest to us." Estab. 1995. Circ. 150,000. Pays 30 days after acceptance. Publishes ms an average of 3 months after acceptance. Byline given. Offers 20% kill fee. Buys first North American serial and electronic rights. Editorial lead time 4 months. Submit seasonal material 6 months in advance. Reports in 2 months on queries. Sample copy for $3 plus postage.
Nonfiction: Book excerpts, essays, how-to (business), interview, travel, personal finance. "No 'memory' essays or personal experience (unless it relates specifically to our audience)." Buys 150 mss/year. Query with published clips. Length: 400-3,000 words. Pays 50¢/word. Sometimes pays expenses of writers on assignment.
Photos: State availability of photos with submission. Negotiates payment individually. Captions, identification of subjects required. Buys one-time rights.
Tips: "Numerous story ideas that show a strong familiarity with the editorial content of the magazine are critical. Solid writing experience for national magazines is preferred."

‡PRIME HEALTH & FITNESS, Weidner Publication, Inc., 21100 Erwin St., Woodland Hills CA 91367. (818)595-0442. Fax: (818)595-0463. E-mail: primefit1@aol.com. Contact: Bill Bush, editor. 75% freelance written. Quarterly magazine covering health & fitness for the baby boomer or over-40 male. *Prime Health & Fitness* is for the man who refuses to grow old as he grows up. We offer straight talk on parenthood, careers, diseases, stress and success with cutting-edge information for men of experience who know what they like and are confident enough to try something new." Estab. 1995. Circ. 100,000. **Pays on acceptance.** Publishes ms an average of 2 months after acceptance. Byline given. Offers 30% kill fee. Buys all rights. Editorial lead time 3 months. Submit seasonal material 5 months in advance. Reports in 1 month on queries; 2 months on mss. Sample copy and writer's guidelines free.

Nonfiction: General interest, how-to, humor, inspirational, interview/profile, new product, technical, travel, health, fitness, disease, boomer lifestyle. No women's issues or under-40 male interests. Buys 40 mss/year. Query with published clips. Length: 300-1,800 words plus sidebars. Pays 60-80¢/word for assigned articles; 60-70¢/word for unsolicited articles. Sometimes pays expenses of writers on assignment.

Photos: State availability of photos with submission. Reviews transparencies. Offers no additional payment for photos accepted with ms or negotiates payment individually. Captions, model releases, identification of subjects required. Buys all rights or offers negotiable rights.

Columns/Departments: Research & Development (new products, health & fitness oriented), 150-200 words; Success Stories (before and after with pictures), Antiaging/Longevity, Nutrition, Work-outs, Sex, 400-800 words. Buys 60 mss/year. Query with published clips. Pays 60-80¢/word.

Tips: "We write to the over-40 male audience in guy language so twist your topics accordingly. Back your research with references. Be accurate on word count."

‡RAGE MAGAZINE, 8484 Wilshire Blvd., Beverly Hills CA 90211. E-mail: edwyer@lfp.com. Contact: John Newlin, managing editor. Monthly magazine for men ages 25-35. Pays on production of issue. Byline given. Offers 20% kill fee. Buys first and second serial rights. Accepts simultaneous submissions. Reports in 1 month on queries. Writer's guidelines for #10 SASE.

Nonfiction: Needs "unique, cutting-edge journalism geared to the 20-something generation, music, politics, radio, extreme sports. No sex and no clichés." Buys 60-72 mss/year. Query with published credits. Length: 3,000 words. Pays $800. Pays the expenses of writers on assignment.

Columns/Departments: Buys 60 mss/year. Query with published credits. Pays $400-750. Length: 650-1,200 words.

Fiction: Query with published clips.

Fillers: Buys 20/year. Length: 650 words. Pays $200.

MILITARY

These publications emphasize military or paramilitary subjects or other aspects of military life. Technical and semitechnical publications for military commanders, personnel and planners, as well as those for military families and civilians interested in Armed Forces activities are listed here. Publications covering military history can be found in the History section.

AMERICAN SURVIVAL GUIDE, Y-Visionary Publishing, 265 S. Anita Dr., Suite 120, Orange CA 92868-3310. Fax: (714)939-9909. E-mail: jim4asg@aol.com. Contact: Jim Benson, editor. Managing Editor: Scott Stoddard. 50% freelance written. Monthly magazine covering "self-reliance, defense, meeting day-to-day and possible future threats— survivalism for survivalists." Circ. 60,000. Pays on publication. Publishes ms up to 1 year after acceptance. Byline given. Submit seasonal material 5 months in advance. Sample copy for $3.50. Writer's guidelines for SASE.

- *American Survival Guide* recently changed hands, and circulation and pay rates have both increased. The staff notes they are always looking for more good material with quality artwork (photos). They want articles on recent events and new techniques, etc. giving the latest available information to their readers.

Nonfiction: Exposé (political); how-to; interview/profile; personal experience (how I survived); photo feature (equipment and techniques related to survival in all possible situations); emergency medical; health and fitness; communications; transportation; food preservation; water purification; self-defense; terrorism; nuclear dangers; nutrition; tools; shelter; etc. "No general articles about how to survive. We want specifics and single subjects." Buys 60-100 mss/year. Query or send complete ms. Length: 1,500-2,000 words. Pays $160-400. Sometimes pays some expenses of writers on assignment.

Photos: Send photos with ms. "One of the most frequent mistakes made by writers in completing an article assignment for us is sending photo submissions that are inadequate." Captions, model releases and identification of subjects mandatory. Buys exclusive one-time rights.

Tips: "We need hard copy with computer disk and photos or other artwork. Prepare material of value to individuals who wish to sustain human life no matter what the circumstance. This magazine is a text and reference."

ARMY MAGAZINE, Box 1560, Arlington VA 22210. (703)841-4300. Fax: (703)525-9039. E-mail: ausaarmag@aol.com. Website: http://www.ausa. Contact: Mary Blake French, editor. 70% freelance written. Prefers to work with published/established writers. Monthly magazine emphasizing military interests. Estab. 1904. Circ. 130,000. Pays on publication. Publishes ms an average of 5 months after acceptance. Buys all rights. Byline given except for back-up research. Submit seasonal material 3 months in advance. Sample copy and writer's guidelines for 9×12 SAE with $1 postage.

- *Army Magazine* looks for shorter articles.

Nonfiction: Historical (military and original); humor (military feature-length articles and anecdotes); interview; new

product; nostalgia; personal experience dealing especially with the most recent conflicts in which the US Army has been involved (Desert Storm, Panama, Grenada); photo feature; profile; technical. No rehashed history. "We would like to see more pieces about little-known episodes involving interesting military personalities. We especially want material lending itself to heavy, contributor-supplied photographic treatment. The first thing a contributor should recognize is that our readership is very savvy militarily. 'Gee-whiz' personal reminiscences get short shrift, unless they hold their own in a company in which long military service, heroism and unusual experiences are commonplace. At the same time, Army readers like a well-written story with a fresh slant, whether it is about an experience in a foxhole or the fortunes of a corps in battle." Buys 8 mss/issue. Submit complete ms. Length: 1,500 words, but shorter items, especially in 1,000 to 1,500 range, often have better chance of getting published. Pays 12-18¢/word. No unsolicited book reviews.
Photos: Submit photo material with accompanying ms. Pays $25-50 for 8×10 b&w glossy prints; $50-350 for 8×10 color glossy prints or $2\frac{1}{4} \times 2\frac{1}{4}$ transparencies; will also accept 35mm. Captions preferred. Buys all rights. Pays $35-50 for cartoon with strong military slant.
Columns/Departments: Military news, books, comment (*New Yorker*-type "Talk of the Town" items). Buys 8/issue. Submit complete ms. Length: 1,000 words. Pays $40-150.

ARMY/NAVY/AIR FORCE TIMES, Army Times Publishing Co., 6883 Commerce Dr., Springfield VA 22159. (703)750-9000. Fax: (703)750-8622. Weeklies edited separately for Army, Navy, Marine, Coast Guard, and Air Force military personnel and their families. They contain career information such as pay raises, promotions, news of legislation affecting the military, housing, base activities and features of interest to military families. Estab. 1940. Circ. 286,800. **Pays on acceptance.** Byline given. Offers kill fee. Buys first rights. Accepts simultaneous submissions. Reports in 1 month on queries. Sample copy and writer's guidelines free.
 • Ranked as one of the best markets for freelance writers in *Writer's Yearbook* magazine's annual "Top 100 Markets," January 1997.
Nonfiction: Features of interest to career military personnel and their families. No advice pieces. Query. Buys 150-175 mss/year. Length: 750-2,000 words. Pays $100-250.
Columns/Departments: Length: 500-900 words. Buys 75 mss/year. Pays $100-150.
Fillers: Buys 5-10/year. Length: 250-500 words. Pays $25-75.
Tips: Looking for "travel pieces with a military connection. Stories on successful civilian careers after military service, and about military authors. Understand the special demands of military life."

FAMILY MAGAZINE, The Magazine for Military Wives, PABCO, P.O. Box 21177, Catonville MD 21228. (410)719-6968. E-mail: soleprop@aol.com. Editor: Stacy P. Brassington. 90% freelance written. Monthly magazine covering military family lifestyle. "*Family* contains features on military family life: relocating, decorating, cooking, travel, education, children, careers, marriage and family health." Estab. 1973. Circ. 500,000. Pays on publication. Byline given. Buys one-time rights. Editorial lead time 3 months. Submit seasonal material 6 months in advance. Accepts simultaneous submissions. Reports in 2 months on queries only if interested. Sample copy for $1.25. Writer's guidelines for #10 SASE.
Nonfiction: General interest, how-to, travel, food/recipe. Buys 100 mss/year. Send complete ms by e-mail. Length: 1,000-1,500 words. Pays $50-200.
Photos: State availability of photos with submission. Offers $25-50/photo. Buys one-time rights.
Columns/Departments: Send complete ms. Pays $75-150.

NAVY TIMES, 6883 Commercial Dr., Springfield VA 22159. (703)750-8636. Fax: (703)750-8622. E-mail: navydesk@aol.com. Editor: Tobias Naegele. Contact: Jean Reid Norman, managing editor. Weekly newspaper covering sea services. News and features of men and women in the Navy, Coast Guard and Marine Corps. Estab. 1950. Circ. 90,000. **Pays on acceptance.** Byline given. Buys first North American serial or second serial (reprint) rights. Submit seasonal material 2 months in advance. Reports in 2 months. Writer's guidelines free.
Nonfiction: Historical/nostalgic, opinion. No poetry. Buys 100 mss/year. Query. Length: 500-1,000 words. Pays $50-500. Sometimes pays expenses of writers on assignment.
Reprints: Send tearsheet of article or short story.
Photos: Send photos with submission. Offers $20-100/photo. Captions and identification of subjects required. Buys one-time rights.

OFF DUTY MAGAZINE, 3303 Harbor Blvd., Suite C-2, Costa Mesa CA 92626-1500. (714)549-7172. Fax: (714)549-4222. E-mail: odutyedit@aol.com. Contact: Gary Burch, executive editor. 30% freelance written. Bimonthly magazine covering the leisure-time activities and interests of the military community. "Our audience is solely military members and their families; many of our articles could appear in other consumer magazines, but we always slant them toward the military; i.e. where to get a military discount when traveling." Estab. 1970. Circ. 507,000. **Pays on acceptance.** Publishes ms an average of 3 months after acceptance. Byline given. Buys one-time rights. Submit seasonal material at least 4 months in advance. Accepts simultaneous submissions. Reports in 2 months on queries. Sample copy for 9×12 SAE with 6 first class stamps. Writer's guidelines for SASE.
Nonfiction: Travel, finance, lifestyle (with a military angle), interview/profile (music and entertainment). "Must be familiar with *Off Duty* and its needs." Buys 30-40 mss/year. Query. Length: 800-2,100 words. Pays $160-420.
 • Editor is not interested in seeing World War II reminiscences. He reports they are buying fewer articles due to slimmer issues and fewer magazines per year.

Reprints: Send photocopy of article and information about when and where the article previously appeared. Pays 50% of amount paid for an original article.

Photos: State availability of photos with submission. Reviews contact sheets. Offers $50-300/photo (cover). Captions and identification of subjects required. Buys one-time rights. Unsolicited photos not returned without SASE.

Tips: "Get to know the military community and its interests beyond the stereotypes. Query with the idea of getting on our next year's editorial calendar. We choose our primary topics at least six months in advance."

PARAMETERS: U.S. Army War College Quarterly, U.S. Army War College, Carlisle Barracks PA 17013-5050. (717)245-4943. E-mail: awca-parameters@carlisle-emh2.army.mil. Website: http://carlisle-www.army.mil/usawc/Parameters/. Contact: Col. John J. Madigan, U.S. Army Retired, editor. 100% freelance written. Prefers to work with published/established writers or experts in the field. Readership consists of senior leadership of US defense establishment, both uniformed and civilian, plus members of the media, government, industry and academia interested in national and international security affairs, military strategy, military leadership and management, art and science of warfare, and military history (provided it has contemporary relevance). Most readers possess a graduate degree. Estab. 1971. Circ. 13,500. Not copyrighted; unless copyrighted by author, articles may be reprinted with appropriate credits. Buys first serial rights. Byline given. Pays on publication. Publishes ms an average of 6 months after acceptance. Reports in 6 weeks. Sample copy and writer's guidelines free.

 • *Parameters* has an online edition at http://carlisle-www.army.mil/usawc/Parameters/.

Nonfiction: Articles are preferred that deal with current security issues, employ critical analysis and provide solutions or recommendations. Liveliness and verve, consistent with scholarly integrity, appreciated. Theses, studies and academic course papers should be adapted to article form prior to submission. Documentation in complete endnotes. Submit complete ms. Length: 4,500 words average, preferably less. Pays $150 average (including visuals).

Tips: "Make it short; keep it interesting; get criticism and revise accordingly. Tackle a subject only if you are an authority."

THE RETIRED OFFICER MAGAZINE, 201 N. Washington St., Alexandria VA 22314-2539. (800)245-8762. Fax: (703)838-8179. E-mail: editor@troa.org. Website: http://www.troa.org. Editor: Col. Warren S. Lacy, USA-Ret. Executive Editor: Julia Leigh. Contact: Heather Lyons, associate editor. 60% freelance written. Prefers to work with published/established writers. Monthly magazine for officers of the 7 uniformed services and their families. "*The Retired Officer Magazine* covers topics such as current military/political affairs; recent military history, especially Vietnam and Korea; travel; money; hobbies; health and fitness; second career job opportunities; and military family and retirement lifestyles." Estab. 1945. Circ. 395,000. **Pays on acceptance.** Publishes ms an average of 9-12 months after acceptance. Byline given. Buys first serial rights. Submit seasonal material (holiday stories with a military theme) at least 9-12 months in advance. Reports on material accepted for publication within 3 months. Sample copy and writer's guidelines for 9 × 12 SAE with 6 first-class stamps.

 • Ranked as one of the best markets for freelance writers in *Writer's Yearbook* magazine's annual "Top 100 Markets," January 1997.

Nonfiction: Current military/political affairs, health and wellness, recent military history, travel, second-career job opportunities, military family lifestyle. Emphasis now on current military and defense issues. "We rarely accept unsolicited manuscripts. We look for detailed query letters with résumé and sample clips attached. We do not publish poetry or fillers." Buys 48 mss/year. Length: 800-2,000 words. Pays up to $1,200.

Photos: Query with list of stock photo subjects. Reviews 8 × 10 b&w photos (normal halftone). Original slides or transparencies must be suitable for color separation. Pays up to $200 for inside color; up to $300 for cover.

SOLDIER OF FORTUNE, The Journal of Professional Adventurers, Omega Group, Ltd., P.O. Box 693, Boulder CO 80306-0693. (303)449-3750. Fax: (303)444-5617. E-mail: editor@sofmag.com. Website: http://wwwsofmag.com. Managing Editor: Dwight Swift. Deputy Editor: Tom Reisinger. Contact: Marty Kufus, assistant editor. 50% freelance written. Monthly magazine covering military, paramilitary, police, combat subjects and action/adventure. "We are an action-oriented magazine; we cover combat hot spots around the world such as Afghanistan, El Salvador, Angola, etc. We also provide timely features on state-of-the-art weapons and equipment; elite military and police units; and historical military operations. Readership is primarily active-duty military, veterans and law enforcement." Estab. 1975. Circ. 175,000. Byline given. Offers 25% kill fee. Buys all rights; will negotiate. Submit seasonal material 5 months in advance. Reports in 3 weeks on queries; 1 month on mss. Sample copy for $5. Writer's guidelines for #10 SASE.

Nonfiction: Exposé; general interest; historical/nostalgic; how-to (on weapons and their skilled use); humor; profile; new product; personal experience; novel excerpts; photo feature ("number one on our list"); technical; travel; combat reports; military unit reports and solid Vietnam and Operation Desert Storm articles. "No 'How I won the war' pieces; no op-ed pieces *unless* they are fully and factually backgrounded; no knife articles (staff assignments only). *All* submitted articles should have good art; art will sell us on an article." Buys 75 mss/year. Query with or without published clips or send complete ms. Send mss to articles editor; queries to managing editor. Length: 2,000-3,000 words. Pays $150-250/page. Sometimes pays the expenses of writers on assignment.

Reprints: Send disk copy and photocopy of article and information about when and where the article previously appeared. Pays 25% of amount paid for an original article.

Photos: Send photos with submission (copies only, no originals). Reviews contact sheets and transparencies. Offers no additional payment for photos accepted with ms. Pays $500 for cover photo. Captions, identification of subjects required. Buys one-time rights.

Columns/Departments: Combat craft (how-to military and police survival skills); I Was There (first-person accounts of the arcane or unusual based in a combat or law-enforcement environment), both 600-800 words. Buys 16 mss/year. Send complete ms. Length: 600-800 words. Pays $150.

Fillers: Bulletin Board editor. Newsbreaks; military/paramilitary related, "*has* to be documented." Length: 100-250 words. Pays $50.

Tips: "Submit a professionally prepared, complete package. All artwork with cutlines, double-spaced typed manuscript with 5.25 or 3.5 IBM-compatible disc, if available, cover letter including synopsis of article, supporting documentation where applicable, etc. Manuscript must be factual; writers have to do their homework and get all their facts straight. One error means rejection. We will work with authors over the phone or by letter, tell them if their ideas have merit for an acceptable article, and help them fine-tune their work. I Was There is a good place for freelancers to start. Vietnam features, if carefully researched and art heavy, will always get a careful look. Combat reports, again, with good art, are number one in our book and stand the best chance of being accepted. Military unit reports from around the world are well received as are law-enforcement articles (units, police in action). If you write for us, be complete and factual; pros read *Soldier of Fortune*, and are *very* quick to let us know if we (and the author) err. Read a current issue to see where we're taking the magazine in the 1990s."

TIMES NEWS SERVICE, Army Times Publishing Co., 6883 Springfield Dr., Springfield VA 22159-0200. (703)750-8125. Fax: (703)750-8781. E-mail: mconews@aol.com. Website: http://www.armytimes.com. Special Sections Editor: Margaret Roth. Features Editor: Maureen Rhea. 15% freelance written. Willing to work with new/unpublished writers. Manages weekly lifestyle section of Army, Navy and Air Force Times covering current lifestyles and problems of career military families around the world. Circ. 300,000. **Pays on acceptance.** Publishes ms an average of 2 months after acceptance. Byline given. Buys first worldwide rights. Submit seasonal material 3 months in advance. Reports in about 1 month. Writer's guidelines for #10 SASE.
- *Times News Service* accepts few exposé-type articles from freelancers but it is always interested in seeing queries. If you have news, they will accept it from a freelancer, but staff writers generally get the news before any freelancers can.

Nonfiction: Exposé (current military); interview/profile (military); personal experience (military only); travel (of military interest). Buys about 200 mss/year. Query with published clips. Length: 500-2,000 words. Pays $75-300. Sometimes pays the expenses of writers on assignment.

Photos: Send photos or send photos with ms. Reviews 35mm color contact sheets and prints. Captions, model releases and identification of subjects required.

Tips: "In your query write a detailed description of story and how it will be told. A tentative lead is nice. A military angle is crucial. Just one good story 'breaks in' a freelancer. Follow the outline you propose in your query letter and humanize articles with quotes and examples."

MUSIC

Music fans follow the latest industry news in these publications that range from opera to hip hop. Types of music and musicians or specific instruments are the sole focus of some magazines. Publications geared to the music industry and professionals can be found in the Trade Music section. Additional music and dance markets are found in the Contemporary Culture and Entertainment section.

‡**AMERICAN SONGWRITER**, 121 17th Ave. S., Nashville TN 37203-2707. (615)244-6065. Fax: (615)742-1123. E-mail: asongmag@aol.com. Website: http://www.nol.com/~nol/asongmag.html. Contact: Vernell Hackett, editor. 30% freelance written. Bimonthly magazine about songwriters and the craft of songwriting for many types of music, including pop, country, rock, metal, jazz, gospel, and r&b. Estab. 1984. Circ. 5,000. Pays on publication. Publishes ms an average of 2 months after acceptance. Offers 25% kill fee. Buys first North American serial rights. Reports in 2 months. Sample copy for $3. Writer's guidelines for SASE.

Nonfiction: General interest, interview/profile, new product, technical, home demo studios, movie and TV scores, performance rights organizations. No fiction. Buys 20 mss/year. Query with published clips. Length: 300-1,200 words. Pays $25-60.

Reprints: Send photocopy of article and note when and where the article previously appeared. Pay negotiable.

Photos: Send photos with submission. Reviews 3×5 prints. Offers no additional payment for photos accepted with ms. Identification of subjects required. Buys one-time rights.

Tips: "*American Songwriter* strives to present articles which can be read a year or two after they were written and still be pertinent to the songwriter reading them."

‡**BBC MUSIC MAGAZINE, Complete Guide to Classical Music**, BBC Magazines, 80 Wood Lane, London W12 0TT England. (181)576-3283. Fax: (181)576-3292. Contact: Fiona Maddocks, editor. Managing Editor: Jessica Gibson. 90% freelance written. Monthly magazine covering all aspects of classical music, including CDs, composers etc., for all levels of interest and knowledge. Estab. 1992. Circ. 250,000. Pays on publication. Publishes ms 3-4 months after acceptance. Byline given. Buys all rights. Editorial lead time 3 months. Submit seasonal material 1 year in advance.

Nonfiction: Essays, exposé, how-to (understand aspects of music better), interview/profile, opinion. Buys 300 mss/year. Query. Length: 500-2,500 words. Pays $150-1,500. Sometimes pays expenses of writers on assignments.
Photos: State availability of photos with submissions. Negotiates payment individually.
Fillers: Newsbreaks. Buys 100/year. Length: 100-200 words. Pays $50.
Tips: Send brief letter outlining idea(s) to editor.

BLUEGRASS UNLIMITED, Bluegrass Unlimited, Inc., P.O. Box 111, Broad Run VA 20137-0111. (540)349-8181 or (800)BLU-GRAS. Fax: (540)341-0011. Editor: Peter V. Kuykendall. Contact: Sharon Watts, managing editor. 80% freelance written. Prefers to work with published/established writers. Monthly magazine on bluegrass and old-time country music. Estab. 1966. Circ. 24,500. Pays on publication. Publishes ms an average of 4 months after acceptance. Byline given. Kill fee negotiated. Buys first North American serial, one-time, all rights and second serial (reprint) rights. Submit seasonal material 4 months in advance. Reports in 2 weeks on queries; 2 months on mss. Sample copy free. Writer's guidelines for #10 SASE.
Nonfiction: General interest, historical/nostalgic, how-to, interview/profile, personal experience, photo feature, travel. No "fan"-style articles. Buys 75-80 mss/year. Query with or without published clips. Length: open. Pays 8-10¢/word.
Reprints: Send photocopy or typed ms with rights for sale noted and information about when and where the article previously appeared. Payment is negotiable.
Photos: State availability of or send photos with query. Reviews 35mm transparencies and 3×5, 5×7 and 8×10 b&w and color prints. Pays $50-150 for transparencies; $25-50 for b&w prints; $50-250 for color prints. Identification of subjects required. Buys one-time and all rights.
Fiction: Ethnic, humorous. Buys 3-5 mss/year. Query. No set word length. Pays 8-10¢/word.
Tips: "We would prefer that articles be informational, based on personal experience or an interview with lots of quotes from subject, profile, humor, etc."

CHAMBER MUSIC, Chamber Music America, 305 Seventh Ave., New York NY 10001-6008. (212)242-2022. Fax: (212)242-7955. E-mail: 103132@compuserve.com. Editor: Gwendolyn Freed. Bimonthly magazine covering chamber music. Estab. 1977. Circ. 13,000. Pays on publication. Publishes ms an average of 8 months after acceptance. Byline given. Offers kill fee. Buys all rights. Editorial lead time 4 months.
Nonfiction: Issue-oriented stories of relevance to the chamber music field. Buys 50 mss/year. Query. Length: 2,500-3,500 words. Pays $500 minimum. Sometimes pays expenses of writers on assignment.
Photos: State availability of photos with submission. Offers no additional payment for photos accepted with ms.

‡GUITAR PLAYER MAGAZINE, Miller Freeman, Inc., 411 Borel Ave., Suite 100, San Mateo CA 94402. (415)358-9500. Fax: (415)358-9216. E-mail: guitplyr@mfi.com. Contact: Richard Johnston, editor. 70% freelance written. Monthly magazine for persons "interested in guitars, guitarists, manufacturers, guitar builders, equipment, careers, etc." Circ. 150,000. Buys first serial and all reprint rights. **Pays on acceptance.** Publishes ms an average of 3 months after acceptance. Byline given. Reports in 6 weeks. Writer's guidelines for #10 SASE.
Nonfiction: Publishes "wide variety of articles pertaining to guitars and guitarists: interviews, guitar craftsmen profiles, how-to features—anything amateur and professional guitarists would find fascinating and/or helpful. On interviews with 'name' performers, be as technical as possible regarding strings, guitars, techniques, etc. We're not a pop culture magazine, but a magazine for musicians. The essential question: What can the reader take away from a story to become a better player?" Buys 30-40 mss/year. Query. Length: open. Pays $250-450. Sometimes pays expenses of writers on assignment.
Photos: Reviews b&w glossy prints. Buys 35mm color transparencies. Payment varies. Buys one time rights.

HIT PARADER, 210 Route 4 E., Suite 401, Paramus NJ 07652. (201)843-4004. Editor: Andy Secher. Managing Editor: Mary Anne Cassata. 5% freelance written. Monthly magazine covering heavy metal music. "We look for writers who have access to the biggest names in hard rock/heavy metal music." Estab. 1943. Circ. 200,000. Pays on publication. Publishes ms an average of 4 months after acceptance. Byline given. Buys all rights. Submit seasonal material 5 months in advance. Sample copy for 9×12 SAE with 6 first-class stamps.
Nonfiction: General interest, interview/profile. Buys 3-5 mss/year. Query with published clips. Length: 600-800 words. Pays $75-140. Lifestyle-oriented and hardball pieces. "Study and really know the bands to get new angles on story ideas."
Photos: Reviews transparencies, 5×7 and 8×10 b&w prints, Kodachrome 64 slides. Offers $25-200/photo. Buys one-time rights. "We don't work with new photographers."
Tips: "Interview big names in hard rock/metal, get published in other publications. We don't take chances on new writers."

‡HOW TO PLAY GUITAR, Miller Freeman Inc., 411 Borel, #100, San Mateo CA 94402. Contact: Greg Hofmann, editor. 75% freelance written. Bimonthly magazine emphasizing guitar lessons and musicianship. "The audience is intermediate guitar players who want to refine their skills in rock, blues, jazz, country and folk." Estab. 1994. Circ. 45,000. Pays on publication. Byline given. Buys all rights. Editorial lead time 2 months. Accepts simultaneous submissions. Reports in 2 weeks on queries; 1 month on mss. Writer's guidelines free.
Nonfiction: How-to. No opinion or profiles. Buys 20 mss/year. Query. Length: 600-1,500 words. Pays $300-600. Sometimes pays expenses of writers on assignment.

Photos: State availability of photos with submission. Offers $25-100/photo. Captions required. Buys one-time rights.
Tips: "Submit a clear query with details of proposed lesson."

‡INTERNATIONAL MUSICIAN, American Federation of Musicians, Paramount Building, 1501 Broadway, Suite 600, New York NY 10036. (212)869-1330. Fax: (212)302-4374. E-mail: intlmus@afm.org. Editor: Stephen R. Sprague. Contact: Jessica Roe, managing editor. 10% freelance written. Prefers to work with published/established writers. Monthly magazine for professional musicians. Estab. 1900. Pays on publication. Publishes ms an average of 3 months after acceptance. Byline given. Reports in 3 months.
Nonfiction: Articles on prominent instrumentalists (classical, jazz, rock or country) who are members of the American Federation of Musicians. Send complete ms. Length: 1,500 words maximum.
Reprints: Send typed ms with rights for sale noted. Payment varies.

JAM MAGAZINE, P.O. Box 151720, Altamonte Springs FL 32715. (407)767-8377. Fax: (407)767-0533. E-mail: jamnorth@digital.net. Contact: Curtis Hayes, editor. 95% freelance written. Biweekly free magazine about music and musicians. "Intelligent news, reviews and interviews about music and the people who make it." Estab. 1988. Circ. 90,000. Pays on publication. Byline given. Buys one-time, second serial (reprint) rights (not within market), simultaneous rights (not within market) or other rights (exclusive within market only). Submit seasonal material 6 weeks in advance. Accepts simultaneous submissions. Sample copy for $4. Call for writer's guidelines.
Nonfiction: Exposé, interview/profile and music. Special issues: Guitar Month (April). Buys 150 mss/year. Query with published clips or send complete ms. Length: 200-2,500 words. Pays $20-50. Sometimes pays expenses of writers on assignment.
Reprints: Send tearsheet or photocopy of article.
Photos: Send photos with submission. Reviews prints. Captions and identification of subjects required. Buys one-time rights (exclusive within market only). Credit given.

MODERN DRUMMER, 12 Old Bridge Rd., Cedar Grove NJ 07009. (201)239-4140. Fax: (201)239-7139. Editor-in-Chief: Ronald Spagnardi. Features Editor: William F. Miller. Managing Editor: Rick Van Horn. Monthly magazine for "student, semi-pro and professional drummers at all ages and levels of playing ability, with varied specialized interests within the field." 60% freelance written. Circ. 98,000. Pays on publication. Publishes ms an average of 3 months after acceptance. Buys all rights. Reports in 2 weeks. Sample copy for $4.95. Writer's guidelines free.
Nonfiction: How-to, informational, interview, new product, personal experience, technical. "All submissions must appeal to the specialized interests of drummers." Buys 20-30 mss/year. Query or submit complete ms. Length: 5,000-8,000 words. Pays $200-500.
Reprints: Accepts previously published submissions.
Photos: Purchased with accompanying ms. Reviews 8×10 b&w prints and color transparencies.
Columns/Departments: Jazz Drummers Workshop, Rock Perspectives, In The Studio, Show Drummers Seminar, Teachers Forum, Drum Soloist, The Jobbing Drummer, Strictly Technique, Book Reviews, Record Reviews, Video Reviews, Shop Talk. "Technical knowledge of area required for most columns." Buys 40-50 mss/year. Query or submit complete ms. Length: 500-1,000 words. Pays $25-150.

MUSICIAN, Billboard Publications, 11th Floor, 1515 Broadway, New York NY 10036. (212)536-5208. Editor: Robert Doerschuk. Senior Editors: Mark Rowland, Mac Randall. 85% freelance written. Monthly magazine covering contemporary music, especially rock, pop and jazz. Estab. 1976. Circ. 170,000. Pays on publication. Byline given. Offers 25-33% kill fee. Buys first world serial rights. Submit seasonal material 3 months in advance.
Nonfiction: All music-related: book excerpts, exposé, historical, how-to (recording and performing), humor, interview/profile, new product, technical. Buys 150 mss/year. Query with published clips. Length: 300-10,000 words. Payment negotiable. Pays expenses of writers on assignment.
Photos: Assigns photo shoots. Uses some stock. Offers $50-300/photo.
Columns/Departments: Jazz (jazz artists or works), 1,000-5,000 words; Reviews (record reviews), 300-500 words; Rough Mix (short, newsy stories), 300 words; Fast Forward (technical "trade" angles on musicians), 1,000-3,000 words. Query with published clips. Length 300-1,500 words. Payment negotiable.
Tips: "Be aware of special music writers' style; don't gush, be somewhat skeptical; get the best quotes you can and save the arcane criticism for reviews; know and apply Strunk and White; be interesting. Please send *published* clips; we don't want to be anyone's first publication. Our writing is considered excellent (in all modesty), even though we don't pay as much as we'd like. We recognize National Writers Union."

‡MUSICWORKS, Explorations in Sound, 179 Richmond St. W, Toronto, Ontario M5V 1V3 Canada. (416)977-3546. Fax: (416)204-1084. E-mail: sound@musicworks.web.net/sound. Editor: G. Young. Triannual magazine with a full-length compact disc. Estab. 1978. Byline given. Editorial lead time 10 months. Sample copy for $5 (without CD). Writer's guidelines free.
Nonfiction: Interview/profile, music, reviews. Buys 9 mss/year. Query. Length varies. Pays honorarium.
Photos: State availability of photos with submission. Reviews 4×5 prints. Offers no additional payment for photos accepted with ms. Captions, identification of subjects required. Buys one-time rights.

OPERA NEWS, Metropolitan Opera Guild, Inc., 70 Lincoln Center Plaza, New York NY 10023-6593. (212)769-7080. Fax: (212)769-7007. Editor: Patrick J. Smith. Managing Editor: Brian Kellow. Contact: Kitty Marsh. 75% freelance written. Monthly magazine (May-November) and biweekly (December-April), for people interested in opera; the opera professional as well as the opera audience. Estab. 1936. Circ. 130,778. Pays on publication. Publishes ms an average of 4 months after acceptance. Byline given. Buys first serial rights only. Sample copy for $4.

Nonfiction: Most articles are commissioned in advance. Monthly issues feature articles on various aspects of opera worldwide; biweekly issues contain articles related to the broadcasts from the Metropolitan Opera. Emphasis is on high quality writing and an intellectual interest to the opera-oriented public. Informational, personal experience, interview, profile, historical, think pieces, personal opinion, opera reviews. "Also willing to consider quality fiction and poetry on opera-related themes though acceptance is rare." Query by mail. Length: 1,500-2,800 words. Pays $450-1,000. Sometimes pays expenses of writers on assignment.

Photos: State availability of photos with submission. Buys one-time rights.

Columns/Departments: Buys 24 mss/year.

RAP SHEET, James Communications, Inc., 2270 Centinela Ave., Box B-40, Los Angeles CA 90064. Fax: (310)670-6236. E-mail: sheetrap@aol.com. Editor: Darryl James. Contact: Billy Johnson, Jr., managing editor. Monthly newspaper covering hip hop artists, music and culture. Estab. 1992. Circ. 100,000. Pays on publication. Byline given. Editorial lead time 2 months.

Nonfiction: Exposé, general interest, historical/nostalgic, interview/profile, photo feature, technical. Query with published clips. Length: 500-3,500. Pays $50-300. Sometimes pays expenses of writers on assignment.

Photos: Send photos with submission. Negotiates payment individually.

Columns/Departments: Check the Wax, Trax (album and single reviews), albums (200-300 words) singles (100 words); Back in the Day (profile on old school hip hop artist) 500-800 words; On the set (hip hop related film news) 1,000 words. Buys 50 mss/year. Query with published clips. Pays $50-300.

Tips: "Submit writing samples consistent with our style and format. Explain specifically how you would like to contribute and offer ideas. Articles must be well organized, containing a powerful lead, thesis statement, body and conclusion. Writing the traditional, biography styled profile is discouraged. The biography only works with extremely interesting life stories, which are rare. Instead, we prefer the writer to familiarize his/herself with the artist's background through research, finding the most intriguing things about the artist. Then, the story should be shaped around that information. Again, the articles must be tightly focused, avoiding rambling, and drifting off to unrelated subjects."

RELIX MAGAZINE, Music for the Mind, P.O. Box 94, Brooklyn NY 11229. Fax: (718)692-4345. E-mail: relixedit@aol.com. Website: www.relix.com. Contact: Toni A. Brown, editor. 60% freelance written. Eager to work with new/unpublished writers. Bimonthly magazine covering classic rock 'n' roll music and specializing in Grateful Dead and other San Francisco and 60s-related groups, but also offering new music alternatives. Estab. 1974. Circ. 70,000. Pays on publication. Publishes ms an average of 6 months after acceptance. Byline given. Buys all rights. Reports in 1 year. Sample copy for $4.

Nonfiction: Historical/nostalgic, interview/profile, new product, personal experience, photo feature, technical. Feature topics include blues, bluegrass, rock, jazz and world music; also deals with environmental and cultural issues. Special issue: year-end special. Query with published clips if available or send complete ms. Length: 1,200-3,000 words. Pays $1.75/column inch.

Reprints: Send photocopy of article and information about when and where the article previously appeared.

Photos: "Whenever possible, submit promotional photos with articles."

Fiction: Publishes novel excerpts.

Columns/Departments: Query with published clips, if available, or send complete ms. Pays variable rates.

Tips: "The most rewarding aspects of working with freelance writers are fresh writing and new outlooks."

‡RHYTHM MUSIC, Global Sounds and Ideas, World Marketing Corporation, 872 Massachusetts Ave., Suite 2-2, Cambridge MA 02139. E-mail: rhymusedit@aol.com. Editor: Howard Mandel. Reviews Editor: Mark Schwartz. 80% freelance written. Monthly magazine covering world music and culture. "We want vivid writing and informed substance dealing with music interacting with and/or reflecting greater culture from anywhere in the world. Our audience is literate and broad in age and interests." Estab. 1992. Pays on publication. Publishes ms an average of 2 months after acceptance. Byline given. Offers 15% kill fee. Buys first North American serial and second serial (reprint) rights. Editorial lead time 3 months. Submit seasonal material 4 months in advance. Accepts simultaneous submissions. Reports 1 month on queries; 2 months on mss. Sample copy for 9×12 SASE. Writer's guidelines free.

Nonfiction: Book excerpts, essays, exposé, general interest, historical/nostalgic, how-to, humor, interview/profile, new product, opinion, photo feature, travel. No "My First Trip to Where Everyone Else Has Been" articles. Buys 30 mss/year. Query with published clips. Length: 200-4,000 words. Pays $50-350. Sometimes pays expenses of writers on assignment.

Reprints: Accepts previously published submissions.

FOR INFORMATION on setting your freelance fees, see How Much Should I Charge?

Photos: State availability of photos with submission. Negotiates payment individually. Captions required. Buys one-time rights.

Columns/Departments: Mark Schwartz, reviews editor. Talk of the Globe (news items), 200-500 words; Live Reviews (world music performance), 300-750 words; Endnote (oddities, lifestyle, world music; informative essay with a critical slant), 500-800 words; Theater, Film, Art, Fashion reviews, all 500-1,000 words. Buys 30 mss/year. Query with published clips. Pays $50-150.

Tips: "Give us a call or e-mail with specific ideas, but know us and your subject."

SOUNDTRACK, The Journal of the Independent Music Association, SoundTrack Publishing, 76 N. Maple Ave., Suite 371, Ridgewood NJ 07450. (201)818-6789. Fax: (201)818-6996. Website: http://www.imamusic.com. Editor: Don Kulak. 60% freelance written. Bimonthly music and business magazine. Estab. 1988. Circ. 10,000. Pays on publication. Publishes ms an average of 3 months after acceptance. Byline sometimes given. Buys first rights and second serial (reprint) rights. Submit seasonal material 4 months in advance. Accepts simultaneous submissions. Reports in 1 week on queries; 3 weeks on mss. Sample copy free. Writer's guidelines for 9 × 12 SAE with $2 postage.

• *Soundtrack* now has an investigative reporting section on political, social, economic and environmental topics.

Nonfiction: Book excerpts, exposé, how-to, interview/profile, opinion, technical. Buys 36 mss/year. Query with published clips. *No unsolicited mss.* Length: 1,000-2,000 words. Pays $50-200. Sometimes pays with contributor copies by "mutually beneficial agreement." Sometimes pays expenses of writers on assignment.

Reprints: Send photocopy of article. Pays 50% of amount paid for an original article.

Photos: Send photos with submissions. Offers $10-20/photo. Buys all rights.

Columns/Departments: The Business of Music (promotion, distribution, forming a record label; alternative markets—film scores, jingles, etc.; how-to's on generating more income from own music). Buys 24 mss/year. Query with published clips. Length: 1,000-2,000 words.

Tips: "Write a letter explaining background, interests, and areas of special study and what you hope to get out of writing for our publication. All sections are open to freelancers. Writing should be fluid and direct. We especially need more how-to information on record marketing and distribution."

SPIN, 6 W. 18th St., 8th Floor, New York NY 10011-4608. (212)633-8200. Fax: (212)633-2668. Publisher: Bob Guccione, Jr. Contact: Craig Marks, executive editor. Monthly magazine covering music and popular culture. "*Spin* covers progressive rock as well as investigative reporting on issues from politics, to pop culture. Editorial includes reviews, essays, profiles and interviews on a wide range of music from rock to jazz. It also covers sports, movies, politics, humor, fashion and issues—from AIDS research to the environment. The editorial focuses on the progressive new music scene and young adult culture more from an 'alternative' perspective as opposed to mainstream pop music. The magazine discovers new bands as well as angles for the familiar stars." Estab. 1985. Circ. 413,000.

Nonfiction: Cultural, political or social issues. New writers: submit complete ms with SASE. Established writers: query specific editor with published clips. Features are not assigned to writers who have not established a prior relationship with *Spin.*

Columns/Departments: Most open to freelancers: Exposure (short articles on music and popular culture), 300-600 words, query Lee Smith, associate editor; Spins (record reviews), 150 or 400 words, queries/mss to Eric Weisbard, senior editor. Query before submitting.

Tips: "The best way to break into the magazine is the Exposure and Spins sections. We primarily work with seasoned, professional writers who have extensive national magazine experience and very rarely make assignments based on unsolicited queries."

‡STEREO REVIEW, Hachette Filipacchi Magazines, Inc., 1633 Broadway, New York NY 10019. (212)767-6000. Editor-in-Chief: Louise Boundas. Executive Editor: Bob Ankosko. Classical Music Editor: Robert Ripps. Popular Music Editor: Ken Richardson. 65% freelance written, almost entirely by established contributing editors, and on assignment. Monthly magazine. Estab. 1958. Circ. 500,000. **Pays on acceptance.** Publishes ms an average of 5 months after acceptance. Byline given. Buys first North American serial or all rights. Reports in 5 months. Sample copy for 9 × 12 SAE with 11 first-class stamps.

Nonfiction: Equipment and music reviews, how-to-buy, how-to-use, stereo, interview/profile. Buys approximately 25 mss/year. Query with published clips. Length: 1,500-3,000 words. Pays $600-2,000.

Tips: "Send proposals or outlines, rather than completed articles, along with published clips to establish writing ability. Publisher assumes no responsibility for return or safety of unsolicited art, photos or manuscripts."

‡VIBE, 205 Lexington Ave., 3rd Floor, New York NY 10019. (212)522-7092. Fax: (212)522-4578. Managing Editor: Jesse Washington. Contact: individual editors as noted below. Magazine published 10 times/year covering urban music and culture. "*Vibe* chronicles and celebrates urban music and the youth culture that inspires and consumes it." Estab. 1993. Circ. 458,670. Pays on publication. Buys all rights. Editorial lead time 3 months. Reports in 2 months. Sample copy available on newsstands. Writer's guidelines for #10 SASE.

Nonfiction: Rob Kenner, features editor. Cultural, political or social issues. Contact Sheena Lester, music editor, for music features. Query with published clips, resume and SASE. Length: 800-3,000 words. Pays $1/word.

Columns/Departments: Start (introductory news-based section), 75-400 words, contact Carter Harris, senior editor; Revolutions (music reviews), 100-800 words, contact Karen Good, assistant editor; Book reviews, contact Omoronke Idowu, assistant editor. Pays $1/word. Query with published clips, résumé and SASE.

Tips: "A writer's best chance to be published in *Vibe* is through the Start or Revolutions sections. Keep in mind that *Vibe* is a national magazine, so ideas should have a national scope. People in Cali should care as much about the story as people in NYC. Also, *Vibe* has a three-month lead time. What we work on today will appear in the magazine three or more months later. Stories must be timely with respect to this fact."

‡**XSeSS MUSIC**, ComEnt Media Group, Inc., 3932 Wilshire Blvd., #212, Los Angeles CA 90010. Fax: (213)383-1093. E-mail: xsesscdzne@aol.com. Website: http://www.allmediadist.com. Contact: Sean Perkin, editor. 80% freelance written. Quarterly publication covering music and entertainment. "Focusing on both the national and international music scenes, every issue explores the relationship of music and its influence on pop culture, fashion, art, politics, and sex. It also examines the ever changing music universe with editorial, photography and a full-length music CD sampler." Estab. 1992. Circ. 25,000. Pays within 2 weeks after publication. Publishes ms an average of 1 month after acceptance. Byline given. Buys one-time rights, makes work-for-hire assignments. Editorial lead time 3 months. Submit seasonal material 4 months in advance. Accepts simultaneous submissions. Sample copy for $12.50. Writer's guidelines provided only upon assignment.
Nonfiction: Exposé, interview/profile, new product, travel.
Reprints: Send photocopy of article and information about when and where the article appeared. Payment varies.

MYSTERY

These magazines buy fictional accounts of crime, detective work, mystery and suspense. Skim through other sections to identify markets for fiction; some will consider mysteries. Markets for true crime accounts are listed under Detective and Crime. Also see the second edition of *Mystery Writer's Sourcebook* (Writer's Digest Books).

HARDBOILED, Gryphon Publications, P.O. Box 209, Brooklyn NY 11228. Editor: Gary Lovisi. 100% freelance written. Quarterly magazine covering crime/mystery fiction and nonfiction. "Hard-hitting crime fiction and columns/ articles and reviews on hardboiled crime writing and private-eye stories—the newest and most cutting-edge work and classic reprints." Estab. 1988. Circ. 1,000. Pays on publication. Publishes ms an average of 6-18 months after acceptance. Byline given. Offers 100% kill fee. Buys one-time rights. Editorial lead time 2 months. Submit seasonal material 6 months in advance. Accepts simultaneous submissions. Reports in 2 weeks on queries; 2 months on mss. Sample copy for $7. Writer's guidelines for #10 SASE.
Nonfiction: Book excerpts, essays, exposé. Query first. Buys 8-10 mss/year. Length: 500-3,000 words. Pays 1 copy for nonfiction.
Reprints: Query first.
Photos: State availability of photos with submission.
Columns/Departments: "Various review columns/articles on hardboiled writers—query first." Buys 16-24 mss/ year. Query.
Fiction: Mystery, hardboiled crime and private-eye stories *all* on the cutting-edge. Buys 60 mss/year. Send complete ms. Length: 500-3,000 words. Pays $5-50, depending on length and quality.

ALFRED HITCHCOCK MYSTERY MAGAZINE, Dell Magazines Fiction Group, 1270 Avenue of Americas, New York NY 10022. Editor: Cathleen Jordan. Monthly magazine featuring new mystery short stories. Circ. 215,000 paid; 615,000 readers. **Pays on acceptance.** Byline given. Buys first and foreign rights. Submit seasonal material 7 months in advance. Reports in 2 months. Writer's guidelines for SASE.
Fiction: Original and well-written mystery and crime fiction. Length: up to 14,000 words. Send complete ms with SASE. Pays 8¢/word.
  • Ranked as one of the best markets for fiction writers in the last *Writer's Digest* magazine's "Fiction 50."

MURDEROUS INTENT, A Magazine of Mystery & Suspense, Madison Publishing Co., P.O. Box 5947, Vancouver WA 98668-5947. E-mail: madison@teleport.com. Website: http://www.teleport.com/~madison. Contact: Margo Power, editor. 90% freelance written. Quarterly magazine covering mystery. "Everything in *Murderous Intent* is mystery/ suspense related. We bring you quality nonfiction articles, columns, interviews and 10-12 (or more) pieces of short mystery fiction per issue. You'll find stories and interviews by Carolyn Hart, Ed Gorman, Barbara Paul, Jerimiah Healy and many more excellent authors." Estab. 1994. Circ. 5,000. **Pays on acceptance.** Publishes ms an average of 12-18 months after acceptance. Byline given. Offers 100% kill fee or $10. Buys first North American serial rights. Submit seasonal material 6 months in advance. Accepts simultaneous submissions, if so noted. Reports in 1 month on queries; 4 months on mss. Sample copy for $5, 9 × 12 SAE and 4 first-class stamps. Writer's guidelines for #10 SASE.
Nonfiction: Humor (mystery), interview/profile (mystery authors), mystery-related nonfiction. Buys 8-12 mss/year. Query with published clips. Length: 2,000-4,000 words. Pays $10. Sometimes pays expenses of writers on assignment.
Photos: State availability of photos and artwork with ms. No additional payment for photos accepted with ms or negotiates payment individually. Captions, model releases, identification of subjects required. Buys one-time rights.
Fiction: Humorous (mystery), mystery. "Please don't send anything that is not mystery/suspense-related in some way." Buys 48-52 mss/year. Send complete ms. Length: 200-5,000 words. Pays $10.

● Ranked as one of the best markets for fiction writers in the last *Writer's Digest* magazine's "Fiction 50."

Poetry Free verse, haiku, light verse, traditional. Nothing that is not mystery/suspense-related. Buys 12-36 poems/year. Length: 4-16 lines. Pays $2-5.

Fillers: Anecdotes, facts. All fillers must be mystery related. Length: 25-200 words. Pays $2-5.

Tips: "Mail all submissions flat in 9×12 envelopes. Follow the guidelines. Submit only one story or article at a time. Do include a typed cover letter. Be prepared to submit accepted material on 3½″ floppy. We don't publish material that is not on disk. We also seek permission to include select stories and articles on the Website. There is no additional payment at this time."

THE MYSTERY REVIEW, A Quarterly Publication for Mystery Readers, C. von Hessert & Associates, P.O. Box 233, Colborne, Ontario K0K 1S0 Canada. (613)475-4440. Fax: (613)475-3400. E-mail: 71554.551@compuserve.com. Website: http://www.inline-online.com/mystery/. Contact: Barbara Davey, editor. 80% freelance written. Quarterly magazine covering mystery and suspense. "Our readers are interested in mystery and suspense books, films. All topics related to mystery—including real life unsolved mysteries." Estab. 1992. Circ. 4,500 (70% of distribution is in US). Pays on publication. Publishes ms an average of 6 months after acceptance. Byline given. Buys first North American serial rights. Editorial lead time 6 months. Submit seasonal material 6 months in advance. Reports in 6 weeks on queries; 1 month on mss. Sample copy for $5. Writer's guidelines free.

Nonfiction: Interview/profile. Query. Length: 2,000-5,000 words. Pays $30 maximum.

Photos: Send photos with submission. Reviews 5×7 b&w prints. Offers no additional payment for photos accepted with ms. Model releases, identification of subjects required. Buys all rights.

Columns/Departments: Book reviews (mystery/suspense titles only), 500-700 words; Truly Mysterious ("unsolved," less generally known cases), 2,000-5,000 words; Book Shop Beat (bookstore profiles), 500 words. Buys 50 mss/year. Query with published clips. Pays $10-30.

Poetry: Only poems with a mystery theme. Buys 3 poems/year. Submit maximum 2 poems. Pays $10-20.

Fillers: Puzzles (particularly crosswords), trivia, shorts (items related to mystery/suspense). Buys 4/year. Length: 100-500 words. Pays $10-20.

‡**NEW MYSTERY, The World's Best Mystery**, Crime and Suspense Stories, 175 Fifth Ave., 2001 The Flatiron Bldg., New York NY 10010. E-mail: newmyst@aol. Website: mysterynew.com. Editor: Charles Raisch III. Contact: Editorial Committee. 100% freelance written. Quarterly magazine featuring mystery short stories and book reviews. Estab. 1989. Circ. 80,000. **Pays on acceptance.** Publishes ms an average of 6 months after acceptance. Byline given. Does not return mss. Buys first North American serial or all rights. Editorial lead time 6 months. Submit seasonal material 1 year in advance. Accepts simultaneous submissions. Reports in 2 months on mss. Sample copy for $5 and 9×12 SAE with 4 first-class stamps.

Nonfiction: New product, short book reviews. Buys 40 mss/year. Send complete ms. 250-2,000 words. Pays $20-50.

Fiction: Mystery, crime, noire, police procedural, hardboiled, child-in-jeopardy, suspense. Buys 50 mss/year. Send complete ms. Length: 2,000-6,000 words. Pays $50-500.

Fillers: Acrostic or crossword puzzles. Pays $25-50.

ELLERY QUEEN'S MYSTERY MAGAZINE, Dell Magazine Fiction Group, 1270 Avenue of the Americas, New York NY 10020. (212)698-1313. Fax: (212)698-1198. Contact: Janet Hutchings, editor. 100% freelance written. Magazine published 11 times/year featuring mystery fiction. Estab. 1941. Circ. 500,000 readers. **Pays on acceptance.** Publishes ms an average of 6 months after acceptance. Byline given. Buys first serial or second serial (reprint) rights. Accepts simultaneous submissions. Reports in 3 months. Writer's guidelines for #10 SASE.

Fiction: Special consideration given to "anything timely and original. We publish every type of mystery: the suspense story, the psychological study, the private-eye story, the deductive puzzle—the gamut of crime and detection from the realistic (including stories of police procedure) to the more imaginative (including 'locked rooms' and impossible crimes). We always need detective stories. No sex, sadism or sensationalism-for-the-sake-of-sensationalism, no gore or horror. Seldom publishes parodies or pastiches. Buys up to 13 mss/issue. Length: 10,000 words maximum; occasionally higher but not often. Also buys 2-3 short novels/year of up to 20,000 words, by established authors and minute mysteries of 250 words. Short shorts of 1,500 words welcome. Pays 3-8¢/word, occasionally higher for established authors. Send complete ms with SASE.

● Ranked as one of the best markets for fiction writers in the last *Writer's Digest* magazine's "Fiction 50."

Poetry: Short mystery verses, limericks. Length: 1 page, double-spaced maximum.

Tips: "We have a Department of First Stories to encourage writers whose fiction has never before been in print. We publish an average of 11 first stories every year."

‡**RED HERRING MYSTERY MAGAZINE**, Potpourri Publications, P.O. Box 8278, Prairie Village KS 66208. (913)642-1503. Fax: (913)642-3128. E-mail: rhmmag@aol.com. Editors: Tom Gray. Juliet Kincaid, Kitty Mendehall, Donna Trombla. 100% freelance written. Quarterly magazine featuring mysteries. "Our only criteria are excellence in writing and a compelling mystery." Estab. 1994. Pays on publication. Publishes ms an average of 9 months after acceptance. Byline given. Buys first North American serial rights. Submit seasonal material 6 months in advance. Accepts simultaneous submissions. Reports in 1 week on queries; 3 months on mss. Sample copy for $4.95 and a 9×12 SAE. Writer's guidelines free.

Fiction: No gratuitous sex or violence. No true crime. Send complete ms. Length: 6,000 words maximum. Pays $10.

Poetry: "Any type is acceptable, but must be a mystery."
Tips: "Submit neat, typewritten material of mystery or suspense with well developed characters and original plot."

‡**WHISPERING WILLOW'S MYSTERY MAGAZINE**, Whispering Willow's Ltd., Co., 2517 S. Central, Oklahoma City OK 73129. (405)239-2531. Fax: (405)232-3848. E-mail: wwillows@telepath.com. Editor: Peggy D. Farris. Contact: Darlene Hoffman, acquisitions editor. 80% freelance written. Quarterly magazine featuring "mystery stories, poems, cartoons and illustrations. Written by writers from all over the U.S. for men and women, young and old. It's new. It's different. It's just what you need when you want to read mystery." Estab. 1996. Circ. 2,000. Pays on publication. Publishes ms an average of 8 months after acceptance. Byline given. Offers 10% kill fee. Buys first North American serial or second serial (reprint) rights. Editorial lead time 3 months. Submit seasonal material 6 months in advance. Accepts simultaneous submissions. Reports in 1 month on queries; 2 months on mss. Sample copy for $7. Writer's guidelines for #10 SASE.
• *Whispering Willow's* also holds several contests. Send SASE for more information.
Nonfiction: Interview/profile, personal experience of the mysterious or the unexplained, photo feature, all mystery-oriented. "No explicit sex, gore, extreme violence." Buys 4 mss/year. Send complete ms. Length: 500-1,200 words. Pays $40-80 for assigned articles; $20-48 for unsolicited articles.
Reprints: Accepts previously published submissions.
Photos: Send photos with submission. Reviews 5×7 prints. Offers $5-25/photo. Captions, model releases, identification of subjects required. Buys one-time rights.
Fiction: Mystery, romance (combined with mystery), suspense, mysteries unexplained. Nothing other than mystery. "I do not want any explicit sex, gore or extreme violence." Buys 60 mss/year. Send complete ms. Length: 1,000-5,000 words. Pays $40-200.
Poetry: Haiku, light verse, traditional. Nothing that does not pertain to mystery. Buys 4 poems/year. Submit maximum 3 poems. Length: 16-36 lines. Pays $15-35.
Fillers: Anecdotes, facts, gags to be illustrated by cartoonist, short humor. Buys 10/year. 20-100 words. Pays $5-20.
Tips: "I want to be surprised with the ending. Have a good hook in the first paragraph. Write the mystery with the ability to make us try to guess the ending. Then build the story so it leaves a lasting memory. Send a brief bio with credits."

NATURE, CONSERVATION AND ECOLOGY

These publications promote reader awareness of the natural environment, wildlife, nature preserves and ecosystems. Many of these "green magazines" also concentrate on recycling and related issues, and a few focus on environmentally-conscious sustainable living. They do not publish recreation or travel articles except as they relate to conservation or nature. Other markets for this kind of material can be found in the Regional; Sports (Hiking and Backpacking in particular); and Travel, Camping and Trailer categories, although magazines listed there require that nature or conservation articles be slanted to their specialized subject matter and audience. Some publications listed in Juvenile and Teen, such as *Ranger Rick* or *Owl*, focus on nature-related material for young audiences, while others occasionally purchase such material. For more information on recycling publications, turn to the Resources and Waste Reduction section in Trade.

AMC OUTDOORS, The Magazine of the Appalachian Mountain Club, Appalachian Mountain Club, 5 Joy St., Boston MA 02108. (617)523-0655 ext. 312. Fax: (617)523-0722. E-mail: amcoutdoors@mcimail.com. Editor/Publisher: Catherine K. Buni. 90% freelance written. Monthly magazine covering outdoor recreation and conservation issues in the Northeast. Estab. 1907. Circ. 66,000. Pays on publication. Publishes ms an average of 3 months after acceptance. Byline given. Offers 25% kill fee. Buys all rights. Editorial lead time 3 months. Submit seasonal material 4 months in advance. Reports in 1 month on queries; 2 months on mss. Sample copy for 9×12 SASE. Guidelines free.
Nonfiction: Book excerpts, essays, exposé, general interest, historical/nostalgic, how-to, interview/profile, opinion, personal experience, photo feature, technical, travel. Special issues: Northern Forest Report (April) featuring the northern areas of New York, New Hampshire, Vermont, and Maine, and protection efforts for these areas. Buys 10 mss/year. Query with or without published clips. Length: 500-3,000 words. Sometimes pays expenses of writers on assignment.
Photos: State availability of photos with submission. Reviews contact sheets, transparencies and prints. Model releases and identification of subjects required.
Columns/Departments: Jane Bambery. News (environmental/outdoor recreation coverage of Northeast), 1,300 words. Buys 20 mss/year. Query. Pays $50-500.

AMERICAN FORESTS, American Forests, P.O. Box 2000, Washington DC 20003. (202)667-3300. E-mail: mrobbins @amfor.org. Website: http://www.amfor.org. Contact: Michelle Robbins, editor. 80% freelance written (most of that assigned articles). Quarterly magazine "of trees and forests, published by a nonprofit citizens' organization for the advancement of intelligent management and use of our forests, soil, water, wildlife and all other natural resources necessary for an environment of high quality." Estab. 1895. Circ. 30,000. **Pays on acceptance.** Publishes ms an average of 8 months after acceptance. Byline given. Buys one-time rights. Written queries required. Send résumé and clips to be considered for assignment. Submit seasonal material 5 months in advance. Reports in 2 months. Sample copy for $2. Writer's guidelines for SASE.

• This magazine is looking for more urban and suburban-oriented pieces.

Nonfiction: General interest, historical, how-to, humor, inspirational. All articles should emphasize trees, forests, forestry and related issues. Buys 2-3 mss/issue. Query. Length: 1,200-2,000 words. Pays $250-800.

Reprints: Send tearsheet of article or typed ms with rights for sale noted and information about when and where the article previously appeared. Pays 50% of amount paid for an original article.

Photos: Send photos. Offers no additional payment for photos accompanying ms. Uses 8×10 b&w glossy prints; 35mm or larger transparencies, originals only. Captions required. Buys one-time rights.

Tips: "Query should have honesty and information on photo support."

THE AMICUS JOURNAL, Natural Resources Defense Council, 40 W. 20th St., New York NY 10011. (212)727-2700. Fax: (212)727-1773. E-mail: amicus@nrdc.org. Website: http:///www.nrdc.org/nrdc. Contact: Kathrin Day Lassila, editor. 80% freelance written. Quarterly magazine covering national and international environmental issues. "*The Amicus Journal* is intended to provide the general public with a journal of thought and opinion on environmental affairs, particularly those relating to policies of national and international significance." Estab. 1979. Estab. 175,000. Pays on publication. Publishes ms an average of 6 months after acceptance. Offers 25% kill fee. Buys first North American serial rights (and print/electronic reprint rights). Submit seasonal material 6 months in advance. Reports in 3 months on queries. Sample copy for $4 with 9×12 SAE. Writer's guidelines for SASE.

• This publication is now accepting occasional literary (personal) essays on environmental issues or with environmental themes. The editor stresses that submissions must be of the highest quality only and must be grounded in thorough knowledge of subject.

Nonfiction: Exposé, interview/profile, essays, reviews. Query with published clips. Length: 200-3,500 words. Pay negotiable. Sometimes pays expenses of writers on assignment. Buys 35 mss/year.

Photos: State availability of photos with submission. Reviews contact sheets, color transparencies, 8×10 b&w prints. Negotiates payment individually. Captions, model releases, identification of subjects required. Buys one-time rights.

Columns/Departments: News & Comment (summary reporting of environmental issues, usually tied to topical items), 700-2,000 words; International Notebook (new or unusual international environmental stories), 700-2,000 words; People, 2,000 words; Reviews (in-depth reporting on issues and personalities, well-informed essays on books of interest to environmentalists interested in policy and history), 500-1,000 words. Query with published clips. Pay negotiable.

Poetry: Brian Swann. Avant-garde, free verse, haiku, others. All poetry should be rooted in nature. Must submit with SASE. Buys 16 poems/year. Pays $50 plus a year's subscription.

Tips: "Please stay up to date on environmental issues, and review *The Amicus Journal* before submitting queries. Except for editorials all departments are open to freelance writers. Queries should precede manuscripts, and manuscripts should conform to the Chicago Manual of Style."

APPALACHIAN TRAILWAY NEWS, Appalachian Trail Conference, P.O. Box 807, Harpers Ferry WV 25425-0807. (304)535-6331. Fax: (304)876-6918. Editor: Judith Jenner. Contact: Brian King. 50% freelance written. Bimonthly magazine. Estab. 1925. Circ. 26,000. **Pays on acceptance.** Byline given. Buys first North American serial or second serial (reprint) rights. Reports in 2 months. Sample copy, guidelines for $2.50. Writer's guidelines only for SASE.

• Articles must relate to Appalachian Trail.

Nonfiction: Essays, general interest, historical/nostalgic, how-to, humor, inspirational, interview/profile, photo feature, technical, travel. No poetry or religious materials. Buys 15-20 mss/year. Query with or without published clips, or send complete ms. Length: 250-3,000 words. Pays $25-300. Pays expenses of writers on assignment. Publishes, but does not pay for "hiking reflections."

Reprints: Send photocopy of article or typed ms with rights for sale noted and information about when and where the article previously appeared.

Photos: State availability of b&w photos with submission. Reviews contact sheets, negatives, 5×7 prints. Offers $25-125/photo. Identification of subjects required. Negotiates future use by Appalachian Trail Conference.

Tips: "Contributors should display an obvious knowledge of or interest in the Appalachian Trail. Those who live in the vicinity of the Trail may opt for an assigned story and should present credentials and subject of interest to the editor."

AUDUBON, The Magazine of the National Audubon Society, National Audubon Society, 700 Broadway, New York NY 10003-9501. Fax: (212)477-9069. Website: http://audubon/.org/audubon. Contact: Michael W. Robbins, editor. 85% freelance written. Bimonthly magazine "reflecting nature with joy and reverence and reporting the issues that affect and endanger the delicate balance and life on this planet." Estab. 1887. Circ. 430,000. **Pays on acceptance.** Byline given. Buys first North American serial rights, second serial (reprint) rights on occasion. Reports in 3 months. Sample copy for $4 and 9×12 SAE with 10 first-class stamps or $5 for magazine and postage. Guidelines for #10 SASE.

• Ranked as one of the best markets for freelance writers in *Writer's Yearbook* magazine's annual "Top 100 Markets," January 1997.

Nonfiction: Essays, investigative, historical, humor, interview/profile, opinion, photo feature, book excerpts (well in advance of publication). Query before submission. Length: 250-4,000 words. Pays $250-4,000. Pays expenses of writers on assignment.

Photos: Query with photographic idea before submitting slides. Reviews 35mm transparencies. Offers page rates per photo on publication. Captions and identification of subjects required. Write for photo guidelines.

"*Audubon* articles deal with the natural and human environment. They cover the remote as well as the familiar. What they all have in common, however, is that they have a story to tell, one that will not only interest *Audubon* readers, but that will interest everyone with a concern for the affairs of humans and nature. We want good solid journalism. We want stories of people and places, good news and bad: humans and nature in conflict, humans and nature working together, humans attempting to comprehend, restore and renew the natural world. We are looking for new voices and fresh ideas. Among the types of stories we seek: profiles of individuals whose life and work illuminate some issues relating to natural history, the environment, conservation, etc.; balanced reporting on environmental issues and events here in North America and abroad; analyses of events, policies, and issues from fresh points of view. We do not publish fiction or poetry. We're not seeking first person meditations on 'nature,' accounts of wild animals rescue or taming, or birdwatching articles."

BIRD WATCHER'S DIGEST, Pardson Corp., P.O. Box 110, Marietta OH 45750. Editor: William H. Thompson III. 60% freelance written. Works with a small number of new/unpublished writers each year. Bimonthly magazine covering natural history—birds and bird watching. "*BWD* is a nontechnical magazine interpreting ornithological material for amateur observers, including the knowledgeable birder, the serious novice and the backyard bird watcher; we strive to provide good reading and good ornithology." Estab. 1978. Circ. 85,000. Pays on publication. Publishes ms an average of 1 year after acceptance. Byline given. Buys one-time, first serial and second serial (reprint) rights. Submit seasonal material 6 months in advance. Reports in 2 months. Sample copy for $3.50. Writer's guidelines for #10 SASE.

Nonfiction: Book excerpts, how-to (relating to birds, feeding and attracting, etc.), humor, personal experience, travel (limited—we get many). "We are especially interested in fresh, lively accounts of closely observed bird behavior and displays and of bird watching experiences and expeditions. We often need material on less common species or on unusual or previously unreported behavior of common species." No articles on pet or caged birds; none on raising a baby bird. Buys 75-90 mss/year. Send complete ms. All submissions must be accompanied by SASE. Length: 600-3,500 words. Pays from $50.

Reprints: Accepts previously published submissions.

Photos: Send photos with ms. Pays $10 min. for b&w prints; $50 min. for transparencies. Buys one-time rights.

Tips: "We are aimed at an audience ranging from the backyard bird watcher to the very knowledgeable birder; we include in each issue material that will appeal at various levels. We always strive for a good geographical spread, with material from every section of the country. We leave very technical matters to others, but we want facts and accuracy, depth and quality, directed at the veteran bird watcher and at the enthusiastic novice. We stress the joys and pleasures of bird watching, its environmental contribution, and its value for the individual and society."

E THE ENVIRONMENTAL MAGAZINE, Earth Action Network, P.O. Box 5098, Westport CT 06881-5098. (203)854-5559. Fax: (203)866-0602. E-mail: emagazine@prodigy.com. Website: http://www.emagazine.com. Editor: Jim Motavalli. Contact: Tracey C. Rembert, managing editor. 80% freelance written. Bimonthly magazine. "*E Magazine* was formed for the purpose of acting as a clearinghouse of information, news and commentary on environmental issues." Estab. 1990. Circ. 50,000. Pays on publication. Byline given. Buys first North American serial rights. Editorial lead time 3 months. Submit seasonal material 6 months in advance. Accepts simultaneous submissions. Query for all submissions. Sample copy for $5. Writer's guidelines for #10 SASE.

Nonfiction: Exposé (environmental), how-to (the "Green Living" section), interview/profile, new product, opinion. No fiction or poetry. Buys 100 mss/year. Query with published clips. Length: 100-5,000 words. Pays 20¢/word, negotiable. On spec or free contributions welcome. Sometimes pays telephone expenses of writers on assignment.

Photos: Mention photo availability, but send only when requested. Reviews printed samples, e.g., magazine tearsheet, postcards, etc. to be kept on file. Negotiates payment individually. Must identify subjects. Buys one-time rights.

Columns/Departments: In Brief/Currents (environmental news stories/trends), 400-1,000 words; Interviews (environmental leaders), 2,000 words; Green Living; Your Health; Going Green (travel); Eco-home; Green Business; Consumer News; New & Different Products (each 700-1,200 words). Query with published clips. Pays 20¢/word, negotiable. On spec or free contributions welcome.

Tips: "Contact us to obtain writer's guidelines and back issues of our magazine. Tailor your query according to the department/section you feel it would be best suited for. Articles must be lively, well-researched, and relevant to a mainstream, national readership."

ENVIRONMENT, Heldref Publications, 1319 18th St. NW, Washington DC 20036-1802. Managing Editor: Barbara T. Richman. 2% freelance written. Magazine published 10 times/year for high school and college students and teachers, scientists, business and government executives, citizens interested in environment or effects of technology and science in public affairs. Estab. 1958. Circ. 12,500. Buys all rights. Byline given. Pays on publication to professional writers. Publishes ms an average of 4 months after acceptance. Reports in 3 months. Sample copy for $7.

Nonfiction: Scientific and environmental material, effects of technology on society. Preferred length: 4,000 words for full-length article. Pays $100-300, depending on material. Query or submit 3 double-spaced copies of complete ms.

"All full-length articles must offer readers authoritative analyses of key environmental problems. Articles must be annotated (referenced), and all conclusions must follow logically from the facts and arguments presented." Prefers articles centering around policy-oriented, public decision-making, scientific and technological issues.
Columns/Departments: 1,000-1,700/words. Pays $100.

HIGH COUNTRY NEWS, High Country Foundation, P.O. Box 1090, Paonia CO 81428-1090. (303)527-4898. E-mail: bestym@HCN.org. Website: http://www.infosphere.comHCN. Contact: Betsy Marston, editor. 80% freelance written. Works with a small number of new/unpublished writers each year. Biweekly tabloid covering Rocky Mountain West, the Great Basin and Pacific Northwest environment, rural communities and natural resource issues in 10 western states for environmentalists, politicians, companies, college classes, government agencies, grass roots activists, public land managers, etc. Estab. 1970. Circ. 19,000. Pays on publication. Publishes ms an average of 2 months after acceptance. Byline given. Buys one-time rights. Reports in 1 month. Sample copy and writer's guidelines free.
Nonfiction: Reporting (local issues with regional importance); exposé (government, corporate); interview/profile; personal experience; centerspread photo feature. Length: up to 3,000 words. Buys 100 mss/year. Query. Pays 20¢/word minimum. Sometimes pays expenses of writers on assignment for lead stories.
Reprints: Send tearsheet of article, information about when and where article previously appeared. Pays 15¢/word.
Photos: Send photos with ms. Prefers b&w prints. Captions and identification of subjects required.
Columns/Departments: Roundups (topical stories), 800 words; opinion pieces, 1,500 words.
Tips: "We use a lot of freelance material, though very little from outside the Rockies. Familiarity with the newspaper is a must. Start by writing a query letter. We define 'resources' broadly to include people, culture and aesthetic values, not just coal, oil and timber."

INTERNATIONAL WILDLIFE, National Wildlife Federation, 8925 Leesburg Pike, Vienna VA 22184-0001. (703)790-4000. Fax: (703)827-2585. E-mail: pubs@nwf.org. Website: http://www.nwf.org/nwf. Contact: Jonathan Fisher, editor. 85% freelance written. Prefers to work with published/established writers. Bimonthly magazine for persons interested in natural history and the environment in countries outside the US. Estab. 1971. Circ. 325,000. **Pays on acceptance.** Publishes ms an average of 4 months after acceptance. Usually buys all rights. "We are now assigning most articles but will consider detailed proposals for quality feature material of interest to a broad audience." Reports in 6 weeks. Writer's guidelines for #10 SASE.
• Ranked as one of the best markets for freelance writers in *Writer's Yearbook* magazine's annual "Top 100 Markets," January 1997.
Nonfiction: Focuses on world wildlife, environmental problems and peoples' relationship to the natural world as reflected in such issues as population control, pollution, resource utilization, food production, etc. Stories deal with non-US subjects. Especially interested in articles on animal behavior and other natural history, first-person experiences by scientists in the field, well-reported coverage of wildlife-status case studies which also raise broader themes about international conservation and timely issues. Query. Length: 2,000 words. Examine past issues for style and subject matter. Pays $2,000 minimum for long features. Sometimes pays expenses of writers on assignment.
Photos: Purchases top-quality color photos; prefers packages of related photos and text, but single shots of exceptional interest and sequences also considered. Prefers Kodachrome or Fujichrome transparencies. Buys one-time rights.

NATIONAL PARKS, 1776 Massachusetts Ave. NW, Washington DC 20036. (202)223-6722. Fax: (202)659-0650. E-mail: editornp@aol.com. Website: http://www.npca.org/. Editor-in-Chief: Leslie Happ. Contact: Linda Rancourt, managing editor. 85% freelance written. Prefers to work with published/established writers. Bimonthly magazine for a largely unscientific but highly educated audience interested in preservation of National Park System units, natural areas and protection of wildlife habitat. Estab. 1919. Circ. 500,000. **Pays on acceptance.** Publishes ms an average of 2 months after acceptance. Offers 33% kill fee. Sends author galleys. Buys first North American serial and second serial (reprint) rights. Reports in 3-5 months. Sample copy for $3 and 9×12 SAE. Writer's guidelines for #10 SASE.
• Ranked as one of the best markets for freelance writers in *Writer's Yearbook* magazine's annual "Top 100 Markets," January 1996.
Nonfiction: Exposé (on threats, wildlife problems in national parks); descriptive articles about new or proposed national parks and wilderness parks; natural history pieces describing park geology wildlife or plants; new trends in park use; legislative issues. All material must relate to national parks. No poetry, philosophical essays or first person narratives. "Queries are welcome, but unsolicited manuscripts are not accepted." Length: 2,000-2,500 words. Pays $1,000 for full-length features; $400 for service articles.
Photos: Send photos with submission. No color prints or negatives. Prefers color slides and transparencies. Pays $100-200 inside; $500 for covers. Captions required. Buys first North American serial rights.
Tips: "Articles should have an original slant or news hook and cover a limited subject, rather than attempt to treat a broad subject superficially. Specific examples, descriptive details and quotes are always preferable to generalized information. The writer must be able to document factual claims, and statements should be clearly substantiated with evidence within the article. *National Parks* does not publish fiction, poetry, personal essays or 'My trip to . . .' stories."

NATIONAL WILDLIFE, National Wildlife Federation, 8925 Leesburg Pike, Vienna VA 22184-0001. (703)790-4524. Fax: (703)827-2585. Contact: Bob Strohm, editor-in-chief; Mark Wexler, editor. 75% freelance written, "but assigns almost all material based on staff ideas. Assigns few unsolicited queries." Bimonthly magazine. "Our purpose is to promote wise use of the nation's natural resources and to conserve and protect wildlife and its habitat. We reach a broad audience that is largely interested in wildlife conservation and nature photography." Estab. 1963. Circ. 660,000. **Pays on acceptance.** Publishes ms an average of 1 year after acceptance. Offers 25% kill fee. Buys all rights. Submit seasonal material 8 months in advance. Reports in 6 weeks. Writer's guidelines for #10 SASE.

 • Ranked as one of the best markets for freelance writers in *Writer's Yearbook* magazine's annual "Top 100 Markets," January 1996.

Nonfiction: General interest (2,500-word features on wildlife, new discoveries, behavior, or the environment); how-to (an outdoor or nature related activity); personal experience (outdoor adventure); photo feature (wildlife); short 700-word features on an unusual individual or new scientific discovery relating to nature. "Avoid too much scientific detail. We prefer anecdotal, natural history material." Buys 50 mss/year. Query with or without published clips. Length: 750-2,500 words. Pays $500-2,000. Sometimes pays expenses of writers on assignment.

Photos: John Nuhn, photo editor. Send photos or send photos with query. Prefers Kodachrome or Fujichrome transparencies. Buys one-time rights.

Tips: "Writers can break in with us more readily by proposing subjects (initially) that will take only one or two pages in the magazine (short features)."

NATURAL HISTORY, Natural History Magazine, Central Park W. at 79th St., New York NY 10024. (212)769-5500. Fax: (212)769-5511. E-mail: nhmag@amnh.org. Contact: Bruce Stutz, editor-in-chief. 15% freelance written. Monthly magazine for well-educated, ecologically aware audience: professional people, scientists and scholars. Circ. 500,000. Pays on publication. Publishes ms an average of 3 months after acceptance. Byline given. Buys first serial rights and becomes agent for second serial (reprint) rights. Submit seasonal material at least 6 months in advance.

Nonfiction: Uses all types of scientific articles except chemistry and physics—emphasis is on the biological sciences and anthropology. "We always want to see new research findings in almost all branches of the natural sciences—anthropology, archeology, zoology and ornithology. We find it is particularly difficult to get something new in herpetology (amphibians and reptiles) or entomology (insects), and would like to see material in those fields." Buys 60 mss/year. Query or submit complete ms. Length: 1,500-3,000 words. Pays $500-2,500, additional payment for photos used.

Photos: Rarely uses 8×10 b&w glossy prints; pays $125/page maximum. Much color is used; pays $300 for inside and up to $600 for cover. Buys one-time rights.

Columns/Departments: Journal (reporting from the field); Findings (summary of new or ongoing research); Naturalist At Large; The Living Museum (relates to the American Museum of Natural History); Discovery (natural or cultural history of a specific place).

Tips: "We expect high standards of writing and research. We favor an ecological slant in most of our pieces, but do not generally lobby for causes, environmental or other. The writer should have a deep knowledge of his subject, then submit original ideas either in query or by manuscript. Acceptance is more likely if article is accompanied by high-quality photographs."

NATURAL LIFE, The Alternate Press, RR1, St. George, Ontario N0E 1N0 Canada. Fax: (519)448-4411. E-mail: natlife@netroute.net. Website: http://www.netroute.net/~altpress. Editor: Wendy Priesnitz. 25% freelance written. Bimonthly tabloid covering "news about self-reliance and sustainability. How-to and inspiration for people living an environmentally aware lifestyle. Includes gardening, natural foods, health, home business, renewal energy." Estb. 1976. Circ. 25,000. Pays on publication. Publishes ms an average of 3 months after acceptance. Byline given. Offers 50% kill fee. Buys first North American serial and electronic rights. Editorial lead time 4 months. Submit seasonal material 4 months in advance. Reports in 3 weeks on queries. Sample copy for $3.50. Writer's guidelines for #10 SASE (Canadian stamps please).

Nonfiction: How-to. Buys 20 mss/year. Query with published clips. Length: 800-1,000 words. Pays 10¢/word to $100 maximum.

Photos: State availability of photos with query. Reviews prints. Offers no additional payment for photos accepted with ms. Captions, identification of subjects required. Buys all rights.

NATURE CANADA, Canadian Nature Federation, 1 Nicholas St., Suite 606, Ottawa, Ontario KIN 7B7 Canada. Fax: (613)562-3371. E-mail: cnf@web.net. Website: http://www.web.apc.org/~CNF. Editor: Barbara Stevenson. Quarterly membership magazine covering conservation, natural history and environmental/naturalist community. "*Nature Canada* is written for an audience interested in nature. Its content supports the Canadian Nature Federation's philosophy that all species have a right to exist regardless of their usefulness to humans. We promote the awareness, understanding and enjoyment of nature." Estab. 1971. Circ. 20,000. Pays on publication. Publishes ms an average of 3 months after acceptance. Byline given. Offers $100 kill fee. Buys one-time rights. Editorial lead time 3 months. Submit seasonal material 6 months in advance. Reports in 3 months on mss. Sample copy for $5. Writer's guidelines free.

Nonfiction: Canadian environmental issues and natural history. Buys 20 mss/year. Query with published clips. Length: 2,000-4,000 words. Pays 25¢/word (Canadian).

Photos: State availability of photos with submission. Offers $40-100/photo (Canadian). Identification of subjects required. Buys one-time rights.

Columns/Departments: The Green Gardener (naturalizing your backyard), 1,200 words; Small Wonder (on less well-known species such as invertebrates, nonvascular plants, etc.), 800-1,500 words; Connections (Canadians making a difference for the environment), 1,000-1,500 words. Buys 16 mss/year. Query with published clips. Pays 25¢/word (Canadian).

Tips: "Our readers are knowledgeable about nature and the environment so contributors should have a good understanding of the subject. We also deal exclusively with Canadian issues and species."

‡**PACIFIC DISCOVERY**, California Academy of Sciences, Golden Gate Park, San Francisco CA 94118-4599. (415)750-7116. Fax: (415)221-4853. Website: www.calacademy.org/pacdis/. Contact: Keith Howell, editor. 100% freelance written. Prefers to work with published/established writers. "Quarterly journal of nature and culture in California, the West and the Pacific read by scientists, naturalists, teachers, students and others having a keen interest in knowing the natural world more thoroughly." Estab. 1948. Circ. 30,000. Buys first North American serial rights. Pays prior to publication. Reports within 2 months. Sample copy for 9×12 SAE with 6 first-class stamps. Guidelines for #10 SASE.
Nonfiction: "Subjects of articles include behavior and natural history of animals and plants, ecology, evolution, anthropology, indigenous cultures, geology, paleontology, biogeography, taxonomy and related topics in the natural sciences. Occasional articles are published on the history of natural science, exploration, astronomy and archaeology. Emphasis is on current research findings. Authors need not be scientists; however, all articles should be based, at least in part, on firsthand experience. Accuracy is crucial." Query with 100-word summary of projected article for review before preparing finished ms. Length: 1,000-4,000 words. Pays 25¢/word.
Reprints: Rarely accepts reprints of previously published submissions. Send typed ms with right for sale noted and information about when and where the article previously appeared.
Photos: Send photos with submission "even if an author judges that his own photos should not be reproduced. Referrals to professional photographers with coverage of the subject will be greatly appreciated." Reviews 35mm, 4×5 or other transparencies or 8×10 b&w glossy prints. Offers $75-175 and $200 for the cover. Buys one-time rights.
Columns/Departments: Skywatcher (research in astronomy), 2,000-3,000 words; Featured Creature/Greenery Gallery (unusual behavior in a particular species or genus), 1,000 words plus excellent photos.

SEASONS, Ontario's Nature and Environment Magazine, Federation of Ontario Naturalists, 355 Lesmill Rd., Don Mills, Ontario M3B 2W8 Canada. (416)652-6556. E-mail: seasons@web.net. Website: http://www.web.net.fon. Contact: Margaret Webb, editor. 75% freelance written. Quarterly magazine. "*Seasons* focuses on Ontario natural history, parks and environmental issues, with appeal for general readers as well as naturalists." Estab. 1963 (published as *Ontario Naturalist* 1963-1980). Circ. 16,000. Pays on publication. Publishes ms an average of 6 months after acceptance. Byline given. Offers 50% kill fee. Buys first Canadian serial rights. Editorial lead time 6 months. Submit seasonal material 1 year in advance. Reports in 2-3 months. Sample copy for $7.20. Writer's guidelines for #10 SASE.
Nonfiction: Essays, general interest, how-to (identify species, be a better birder, etc.), opinion, personal experience, photo feature, travel. No cute articles about cute animals or biology articles cribbed from reference books. Buys 16-20 mss/year. Query with published clips. Length: 1,500-3,000 words. Pays $350-1,000. Sometimes pays expenses of writers on assignment.
Photos: State availability of photos with submission. Reviews 35mm transparencies. Negotiates payment individually. Model releases, identification of subjects required. Buys one-time rights.
Columns/Departments: Naturalist's Notebook (tips on birding, improving naturalist's skills), 700 words. Buys 4 mss/year. Query with published clips. Pays $200-400.

SIERRA, 85 Second St., 2nd Floor, San Francisco CA 94105-3441. (415)977-5500. Fax: (415)977-5794. E-mail: sierra.letters@sierraclub.org. Website: http://www.sierraclub.org. Editor-in-Chief: Joan Hamilton. Senior Editors: Reed McManus, Paul Rauber. Contact: Robert Schildgen, managing editor. Works with a small number of new/unpublished writers each year. Bimonthly magazine emphasizing conservation and environmental politics for people who are well educated, activist, outdoor-oriented and politically well informed with a dedication to conservation. Estab. 1893. Circ. 550,000. **Pays on acceptance.** Publishes ms an average of 4 months after acceptance. Byline given. Buys first North American serial rights. Reports in 2 months.
• Ranked as one of the best markets for freelance writers in *Writer's Yearbook* magazine's annual "Top 100 Markets," January 1997.
Nonfiction: Exposé (well-documented articles on environmental issues of national importance such as energy, wilderness, forests, etc.); general interest (well-researched nontechnical pieces on areas of particular environmental concern); photo feature (photo essays on threatened or scenic areas); journalistic treatments of semi-technical topics (energy sources, wildlife management, land use, waste management, etc.). No "My trip to . . ." or "why we must save wildlife/nature" articles; no poetry or general superficial essays on environmentalism; no reporting on purely local environmental issues. Special issues: Children (November/December 1997); Travel (March/April 1998). Buys 5-6 mss/issue. Query with published clips. Length: 800-3,000 words. Pays $450-2,000. Pays limited expenses of writers on assignment.
Reprints: Send photocopy of article with typed ms with rights for sale noted and information about when and where the article previously appeared. Pay negotiable.
Photos: Naomi Williams, art and production manager. Send photos. Pays $300 maximum for transparencies; more for cover photos. Buys one-time rights.
Tips: "Queries should include an outline of how the topic would be covered and a mention of the political appropriateness and timeliness of the article. Statements of the writer's qualifications should be included."

WATERFOWL & WETLANDS, South Carolina Waterfowl Association, 434 King St., Charleston SC 29403. (803)722-0942. Contact: Doug Gardner, editor. 35% freelance written. Quarterly company publication of South Carolina Waterfowl Association covering waterfowl and wetland issues. "We are a 5,000+ member nonprofit association. Our quarterly magazine includes feature articles on waterfowl and current issues affecting duck and goose populations, hunting and behavior." Estab. 1987. Circ. 6,500. **Pays on acceptance**. Publishes ms an average of 6 months after acceptance. Byline given. Not copyrighted. Buys one-time or second serial (reprint) rights. Editorial lead time 4 months. Submit seasonal material 4 months in advance. Accepts simultaneous and previously published submissions. Reports in 3 weeks on queries. Sample copy and writer's guidelines free.

Nonfiction: Book excerpts, general interest, historical/nostalgic, how-to, humor, interview/profile, new product, opinion, personal experience, photo feature, travel. Buys 6 mss/year. Query. Length: 1,000-3,000 words. Pays $75-300 for unsolicited articles. Offer work barter arrangements with different groups.

Photos: State availability of photos with submission. Reviews 3×5 prints. Pays $50-125. Captions, identification of subjects required. Buys one-time rights.

Columns/Departments: Going Places (hunting/fishing trips) 1,200 words. Buys 2 mss/year. Query. Pays $50-200.

Poetry: Avant-garde, free verse, traditional.

Tips: "We are interested in national waterfowl issues and also articles which address the waterfowler and waterfowling tradition. A query letter to the editor will be responded to in a timely fashion."

WILDLIFE CONSERVATION MAGAZINE, Wildlife Conservation Society, 185th St. and Southern Blvd., Bronx NY 10460-1068. (212)220-5121. Contact: Joan Downs, editor. 50% freelance written. Bimonthly magazine. "*Wildlife Conservation* is edited for the reader interested in conservation through first-hand accounts by wildlife researchers." Estab. 1895. Circ. 157,000. **Pays on acceptance.** Publishes ms an average of 1 year or more after acceptance. Byline given. Buys first North American serial rights. Submit seasonal material 1 year in advance. Accepts simultaneous submissions. Reports in 2 months on queries; 3 months on mss. Sample copy for $3.95 and 9×12 SAE with 7 first-class stamps. Writer's guidelines for SASE.

● Ranked as one of the best markets for freelance writers in *Writer's Yearbook* magazine's annual "Top 100 Markets," January 1997.

Nonfiction: Nancy Simmons, senior editor. Essays, personal experience, wildlife articles. No pet or domestic animal stories. Buys 12 mss/year. Query. Length: 1,500 words. Pays $500-1,500 for assigned articles; $500-750 for unsolicited articles.

Photos: Send photos with submission. Reviews transparencies. Buys one-time rights.

Tips: "Articles for *Wildlife Conservation* should be lively and entertaining, as well as informative. We feature articles from an author's own research and experience. We like them to be first-person, but we don't want the author to intrude. Avoid textbookish or encyclopedic articles. Pin the article to an underlying theme, point or reason and weave in atmosphere—sights, smells, sounds, colors, weather. Let the reader see through your eyes and help them become involved."

PERSONAL COMPUTERS

Personal computer magazines continue to evolve. The most successful have a strong focus on a particular family of computers or widely-used applications and carefully target a specific type of computer use, although as technology evolves, some computers and applications fall by the wayside. Be sure you see the most recent issue of a magazine before submitting material.

BYTE MAGAZINE, 1 Phoenix Mill Lane, Peterborough NH 03458-0809. (603)924-9281. Fax: (603)924-2550. E-mail: jmontgomery@bix.com. Website: http://www.byte.com. Editor: Rafe Needleman. Contact: John Montgomery, features editor. Monthly magazine. "*Byte* provides information systems professionals with technology solutions to real world business problems. *Byte* readers are the decision makers who determine the technology direction for their corporations. They solve business problems using technology solutions including enterprise networking and intranet/Internet applications, software applications and development, operating systems, database management and computing systems." 50% freelance written. Estab. 1975. Circ. 515,000. **Pays on acceptance.** Byline given. Buys all rights. Reports on rejections in 6 weeks; 3 months if accepted. Writer's guidelines for #10 SASE.

Nonfiction: News, reviews, in-depth discussions of topics related to microcomputers or technology. Buys 160 mss/year. Query. Length: 1,500-5,000 words. Pays $350-1,000 for assigned articles; $500-750 for unassigned.

Tips: "Always interested in hearing from freelancers who are technically astute users of personal computers. Especially interested in stories on new computing technologies, from anywhere in the world. Read several issues of *Byte* to see what we cover, and how we cover it. Read technical journals to stay on the cutting edge of new technology and trends. Send us a proposal with a short outline of an article explaining some new technology, software trend, and the relevance to advanced business users of personal computers. Our readers want accurate, useful, technical information; not fluff and not meaningless data presented without insight or analysis."

COMPUTER CURRENTS, Computing in the Real World, Computer Currents Publishing, 5720 Hollis St., Emeryville CA 94608. (510)547-6800. Fax: (510)547-4613. E-mail: rluhn@aol.com. Website: www.currents.net. Contact: Robert Luhn, editor-in-chief. 90% freelance written. Biweekly magazine "for fairly experienced PC and Mac users. We provide where to buy, how to buy and how to use information. That includes buyers guides, reviews, tutorials and more." Estab. 1983. Circ. 662,000. **Pays on acceptance**. Byline given. Offers 20% kill fee. Buys all rights. Editorial lead time 2 months. Submit seasonal material 2 months in advance. Reports in 2 weeks on queries; 2 months on mss. Sample copy for 10×12 SAE with $3 postage. Writer's guidelines for #10 SASE.

Nonfiction: Book excerpts, exposé, how-to (using PC or Mac products), new product, opinion, technical. Special issues: CD-ROM Buyers Guide (October); Holiday Gift Guide (November). "No fiction, poetry or 'I just discovered PCs' essays." Buys 40 mss/year. Query with published clips. Length: 300-2,500 words. Pays $50-2,000. Sometimes pays expenses of writers on assignment.

Photos: State availability of photos with submission. Reviews 35mm transparencies, 8 × 10 prints. Offers no additional payment for photos accepted with ms. Buys first North American and nonexclusive reprint rights.

Columns/Departments: Cheryl Massé, managing editor. Multimedia in Review (new multimedia CDs and hardware; web sites; books), 300 words; Features (PC, Mac, hardware, software, investigative pieces), 1,000-2,500 words. Buys 60 mss/year. Query with published clips. Pays $50-500.

Tips: "Writers must know PC or Mac technology and major software and peripherals. Know how to write, evaluate products critically, and make a case for or against a product under review. *Computer Currents* is the magazine for the rest of us. We don't torture test 500 printers or devote space to industry chit-chat. Instead, we provide PC and Mac users with real-world editorial they can use every day when determining what to buy, where to buy it, and how to use it. Along with supplying this kind of nitty-gritty advice to both small and large business users alike, we also demystify the latest technologies and act as a consumer advocate. We're also not afraid to poke fun at the industry, as our annual 'Editor's Choice' issue and biweekly 'Gigglebytes' column demonstrate."

COMPUTER LIFE, Ziff-Davis Publishing, 135 Main St., San Francisco CA 94105. (415)357-5200. Fax: (415)357-5216. E-mail: ceditors@zd.com. Website: www.zdnet.com/complife. Contact: John Dickinson, editor; Michael Penwarden, executive editor. "Distinctly human in voice, *Computer Life* meets the information needs of enthusiasts who have made computing a significant part of their personal lives. Speaking in an experienced-based tone, *Computer Life* presents products, ideas and techniques that enable enthusiasts to further enrich their personal computing experience and better fulfill their aspirations." 80% freelance written. Monthly magazine covering personal computers. "*Computer Life* is aimed at computer enthusiasts who are looking for new and interesting ways to use PCs in their personal (nonwork) lives." Estab. 1994. Circ. 500,000. **Pays on acceptance**. Publishes ms an average of 3 months after acceptance. Byline given. Offers 25% kill fee. Buys all rights. Editorial lead time 3 months. Submit seasonal material 5 months in advance. Reports in 6 weeks on queries. Writer's guidelines free.

Nonfiction: "*Computer Life* contains features, reviews and step-by-step visual guides to help readers use their computers in new and exciting ways." How-to, new product, technical. Buys 50-100 mss/year. Query with published clips. Length: 500-3,000 words. Pays $100 minimum. Sometimes pays expenses of writers on assignment.

Photos: State availability of photos with submissions. Negotiates payment individually. Captions, model releases, identification of subjects required. Buys one-time rights.

COMPUTOREDGE, San Diego's Computer Magazine, The Byte Buyer, Inc., P.O. Box 83086, San Diego CA 92138. (619)573-0315. Fax: (619)573-0205. E-mail: patricia@computoredge.com. Website: http://www.computoredge.com. Executive Editor: Leah Steward. Editor: John San Filippo. Contact: Patricia Smith, senior editor. 90% freelance written. "We are the nation's largest regional computer weekly, providing San Diego County with non-technical, entertaining articles on all aspects of computers. We cater to the novice/beginner/first-time computer buyer. Humor is welcome." Estab. 1983. Circ. 80,000. Pays on publication. Net 30 day payment after publication. Byline given. Offers $15 kill fee. Buys first North American serial rights. Submit seasonal material 2 months in advance. Reports in 2 months. Writer's guidelines and an editorial calendar for #10 SASE "or call (619)573-1675 with your modem and download writer's guidelines. Read sample issue on-line." Sample issue for SAE with 7 first-class stamps.

• *ComputorEdge* has added another regional publication in the Denver area.

Nonfiction: General interest (computer), how-to, humor, personal experience. Buys 80 mss/year. Send complete ms. Length: 900-1,200 words. Pays $100-150.

Columns/Departments: Beyond Personal Computing (a reader's personal experience). Buys 80 mss/year. Send complete ms. Length: 500-1,000 words. Pays $50-75.

Fiction: Confession, fantasy, slice-of-life vignettes. No poetry. Buys 20 mss/year. Send complete ms. Length: 900-1,200 words. Pays $100-150.

Tips: "Be relentless. Convey technical information in an understandable, interesting way. We like light material, but not fluff. Write as if you're speaking with a friend. Avoid the typical 'Love at First Byte' article. Avoid the 'How My Grandmother Loves Her New Computer' article. We do not accept poetry. Avoid sexual innuendoes/metaphors. Reading a sample issue is advised."

HOME OFFICE COMPUTING/SMALL BUSINESS COMPUTING, Scholastic Inc., 411 Layfayette, New York NY 10003. (212)505-4220. Fax: (212)505-4260. E-mail: 76703.2025@compuserve.com. Contact: Bernadette Gray, editorial director; Dennis Eskow, editor-in-chief; Cathy Grayson Bowen, executive editor. Managing Editor: Gail Gabriel. 75% freelance written. Monthly magazine on computing, home/small businesses with 5 or fewer employers. Estab. 1983. Circ. 440,000. **Pays on acceptance.** Publishes ms an average of 3 months after acceptance. Byline given. Offers 25% kill fee. Buys all rights or makes work-for-hire assignments. Submit seasonal material 6 months in advance. Accepts simultaneous submissions. Sample copy and writer's guidelines for 9 × 12 SAE.

Nonfiction: How-to, interview/profile, new product, technical, reviews. "No fiction, humor, opinion." Buys 30 mss/year. Query with published clips. Length: 200-4,000 words. Pays $100-2,000. Sometimes pays the expenses of writers on assignment.

Photos: Send photos with submission.

Columns/Departments: Sales & Marketing, Desktop Publishing, Office Design, Communications, Legal Matters, Money, Hardware/Software Reviews. Length: 800-1,200 words. Pays $100-2,000.
Tips: "Submission must be on disk or telecommunicated."

‡**HOME PC**, 600 Community Dr., Manhasset NY 11030. E-mail: homepc@aol.com. Contact: Amy Lipton, executive editor. Monthly magazine covering "entertainment, education and personal productivity products for home computer users." Estab. 1994. Circ. 426,246. **Pays on acceptance.** Byline given. Offers 50% kill fee. Buys all rights. Reports in 1 month on queries. Sample copy free. Writer's guidelines for #10 SASE.
Nonfiction: "Designed in an easy-to-read format, the magazine features new products, reviews, how-to, photo essays, advice and ratings for home PC users of various skill levels. We need writers who can combine technical information with conversational style to help make computing easier for home and home-business users." Buys 50 mss/year. Query with published clips. Length: 1,500-2,000 words. Pays 75¢/word. Pays expenses of writers on assignment.
Columns/Departments: Buys 50 mss/year. Query with published clips. Pays 75¢/word. Length: 1,200-1,500 words.
Fillers: Buys 25/year. Length: 250-500 words. Pays 75¢/word.
Tips: "Writers must have a solid understanding of home computing technology and trends and be able to communicate that information in a cohesive, clear and intriguing way."

‡**INTERNET WORLD**, Mecklermedia Corporation, 20 Ketchum St., Westport CT 06990. (203)226-6967. Fax: (203)454-5840. Editor-in-Chief: Gus Venditto. "*Internet World* is the authoritative resource for users to gain professional and personal productivity from the Internet. For the professional and advanced user, *Internet World* brings the Net into focus." Estab. 1990. Circ. 319,068.
Nonfiction: "*Internet World* provides information and analysis about products, trends and technologies shaping the Internet as well as key issues of fundamental importance to the Internet community." *Writer's Market* recommends sending a query with SASE.

‡**MACADDICT**, Imagine Publishing, 150 North Hill Dr., Suite 40, Brisbane CA 94005. (415)468-4684. Fax: (415)468-4686. E-mail: cengland@macaddict.com. Contact: Cheryl England, editor-in-chief. Managing Editor: Judy Lewenthal. 25% freelance written. Monthly magazine covering Macintosh computers. "*MacAddict* is a magazine for Macintosh computer enthusiasts of all levels. Writers must know, love and own Macintosh computers." Estab. 1996. Circ. 127,000. Pays on publication. Publishes ms an average of 3 months after acceptance. Byline given. Buys all rights. Editorial lead time 3 months. Submit seasonal material 5 months in advance. Accepts simultaneous submissions. Reports in 1 month.
Nonfiction: General interest, how-to, new product, photo feature, technical. No humor, case studies, personal experiences, essays. Buys 30 mss/year. Query with or without published clips. Length: 750-5,000 words. Pays $50-2,500. Sometimes pays expenses of writers on asssignment.
Photos: State availability of photos with submission. Negotiates payment individually. Captions, model releases, identification of subjects required. Buys one-time rights.
Columns/Departments: Reviews (always assigned), 300-750 words; How-to's (detailed, step-by-step), 500-4,000 words; features, 1,000-4,000 words. Buys 30 mss/year. Query with or without published clips. Pays $50-2,500.
Fillers: Kathy Tofel, associate editor. Newsbreaks. Buys 20/year. Length: 50-500 words. Pays $25-200.
Tips: "Send us an idea for a short 1-2 page how-to and/or send us a letter outlining your publishing experience and areas of Mac expertise so we can assign a review to you (reviews editor is Dan Turner)."

MACWEEK, Ziff-Davis, 301 Howard St., 15th Floor, San Francisco CA 94105. (415)243-3500. Fax: (415)243-3651. E-mail: catherine_lacroix@zd.com. Website: www.macweek.com. Contact: Catherine LaCroux, executive editor/features. 35% freelance written. Weekly tabloid "reaching sophisticated buyers of Macintosh-related products for large organizations." Estab. 1986. Circ. 100,000. **Pays on acceptance.** Publishes ms an average of 1 month after acceptance. Byline given. Offers 25% kill fee. Buys all worldwide rights. Editorial lead time: news, 10 days; reviews, 2 months; features, 1 month. Submit seasonal material 2 months in advance. Reports in 1 month on mss. Writer's guidelines free.
● Ranked as one of the best markets for freelance writers in *Writer's Yearbook* magazine's annual "Top 100 Markets," January 1996.
Columns/Departments: Andrew Gore (news); Stephen Howard (reviews). Reviews (new product testing), 500-1,200 words; Solutions (case histories), 1,000 words. Buys 30 mss/year. Query with published clips. Pays 65 cents-$1/word.
Tips: "We do not accept unsolicited material. If a writer would like to pitch a story to me by e-mail, I'm open to that. Knowledge of the Macintosh market is essential. Know which section you would like to write for and submit to the appropriate editor."

‡**PC PORTABLES MAGAZINE**, (formerly *PC Laptop*), LFP, Inc., 8484 Wilshire Blvd., Beverly Hills CA 90211. (213)651-5400. E-mail: tnozick@lfp.com. Editor: Mark Kellner. Contact: Theresa Barry Nozick, managing editor. 40% freelance written. "We are a monthly, comprehensive, reader-friendly portable computer magazine with a focus on portable computer users in the workplace and mobile situations." Estab. 1989. Circ. 60,000. **Pays on acceptance.** Publishes ms an average of 3 months after acceptance. Byline given. Offers 20% kill fee. Buys all rights and makes work for hire assignments. Editorial lead time 4 months. Sample copy for $5. Writer's guidelines for #10 SASE.
Nonfiction: New product reviews, technical. Query with published clips. Length: 300-1,500 words. Pays $400-1,500 (negotiable). Does not accept unsolicited articles. Sometimes pays the expenses of writers on assignment.
Photos: State availability of photos with submission. Reviews contact sheets, negatives, transparencies and prints.

Negotiates payment individually. Captions, model releases, identification of subjects required. Buys all rights.
Tips: "This is a portable computer and mobile technology magazine targeting the laptop computer user. Focus is on hardware and software that applies to portable computing and mobile situations. *PC Portables* is a 'reader friendly' publication for both new and experienced laptop computer users. Therefore, all information is presented in a clear, concise format. All technical information should be defined in simple, easy to understand terms."

PC/COMPUTING, Ziff-Davis Publishing Co., 50 Beale St., 13th Floor, San Francisco CA 94105. (415)578-8000. Fax: (415)578-8029. Contact: Paul Somerson, vice president/editor-in-chief. Monthly magazine for business users of desktop computers. Estab. 1988. Circ. 1,000,000. **Pays on acceptance.** Byline given. Offers negotiable kill fee. Makes work-for-hire assignments. Reports in 1 month. Sample copy for $2.95. Writer's guidelines for #10 SASE.
• Ziff-Davis Publishing Company has created an electronic information service called the Interchange Online Network that draws on the contents of its various computer magazines. It includes *PC Magazine, PC Computing, PC Week, Mac User, Mac Week, Computer Shopper* and *Computer Gaming World*.
Nonfiction: Book excerpts, how-to, new product, technical. Query with published clips. Payment negotiable. Sometimes pays expenses of writers on assignment.
Tips: "We're looking for helpful, specific information that appeals to advanced users of PCs. No novice material. Writers must be knowledgeable about personal computers."

‡PORTABLE COMPUTING, Direct Shopper, Curtco Freedom Group, 29160 Heathercliff Rd., Suite 200, Malibu CA 90265. (310) 579-3400. Fax: (310) 579-3300. E-mail: pcds@curtco.com. Editor: Elliot Borin. Managing Editor: Susan Borden. Contact: Michelle Delio, executive editor. 80% freelance written. Monthly magazine "attracting the information seeking buyer of portable computing products. We list and review state of the art portable technology." Estab. 1997. Circ. 130,000. Pays on publication. Publishes ms 3 months after acceptance. Byline given. Buys negotiable rights. Editorial lead time 3 months. Submit seasonal material 1 month in advance. Reports in 1 week on queries, 1 month on mss.
Nonfiction: How-to (computer-related), humor, interview/profile, new product, personal experience, technical. Buys 200 mss/year. Query with published clips or send complete ms. Length: 750-2,000 words. Pays $300-1,000. Pays expenses of writers on assignment.
Photos: Send photos with submission. Reviews transparencies (4×5), slides, or prints (8×11). Offers no additional payment for photos accepted with ms. Photos are usually provided by manufacturers, or photographers are assigned.
Fillers: Anecdotes, facts, gags to be illustrated by cartoonist, newsbreaks, short humor. Length: 350 words maximum. Pays $50-100.
Tips: "Writers need a fresh, even humorous approach, excellent writing skills and a background of knowledge in computers. They need to demonstrate these abilities via clips or article submission. Timeliness and the ability to turn around copy in a short time are major pluses too."

PUBLISH, The Magazine for Electronic Publishing, 501 Second St., San Francisco CA 94107. (415)243-0600. Fax: (415)975-2613. E-mail: mnaman@publish.com Website: http://www.publish.com. Editor: Jake Widman. Contact: M. Naman. 50% freelance written. Monthly magazine on desktop publishing and presentations. Estab. 1986. Circ. 97,000. Pays on publication. Publishes ms an average of 4-5 months after acceptance. Byline given. Buys first international rights. Reports in 3 weeks. Writer's guidelines for #10 SASE.
Nonfiction: Book excerpts, product reviews, how-to (publishing topics), news, new products, technical tips. Buys 120 mss/year. Query with published clips. Length: 400-2,300 words. No unsolicited mss.
Photos: Send photos with submission. Reviews contact sheets. Captions and identification of subjects required.

WINDOWS MAGAZINE, CMP Publications, Inc., 1 Jericho Plaza, Jericho NY 10465. (516)733-8300. Website: http://www.winmag.com. Senior Editor: Donna Tapellini. Monthly magazine for business users of Windows hardware and software. "*Windows* contains information on how to evaluate, select, acquire, implement, use, and master Windows-related software and hardware." Estab. 1990. Circ. 570,000. **Pays on acceptance.** Byline given. 25% kill fee. Buys first worldwide and electronic rights. Reports in 1-2 months on queries. Sample copy and guidelines available.
• Ranked as one of the best markets for freelance writers in *Writer's Yearbook* magazine's annual "Top 100 Markets," January 1996.
Nonfiction: How-to, technical. Buys 30 mss/year. Query with published clips. Length: 1,500-4,000 words. Pays $1,200-3,000.
Columns/Departments: 1,500 words. Buys 12 mss/year. Query with published clips. Pays $1,000-1,500.
Tips: Needs "clear, entertaining, technical features on Windows hardware and software." Wants to see "how-to and how-to-buy articles, and insider's look at new products." Should be well-written, entertaining and technically accurate. "We concentrate on hands-on tips and how-to information."

WIRED MAGAZINE, 520 Third St., 4th Floor, San Francisco CA 94107-1815. (415)276-5000. E-mail: submissions@wired.com. Website: http://www.wired.com. Editor/Publisher: Louis Rossetto. Contact: Ted Roberts, editorial assistant. 95% freelance written. Monthly magazine covering technology and digital culture. "We cover the digital revolution and related advances in computers, communications and lifestyles." Estab. 1993. Circ. 350,000. Pays on publication. Publishes ms an average of 3 months after acceptance. Byline given. Offers 25% kill fee. Buys first North American serial rights, global rights with 25% payment. Editorial lead time 3 months. Query for electronic submissions. Reports

in 3 weeks on queries. Sample copy for $4.95. Writer's guidelines for #10 SASE or e-mail to guidelines@wired.com.
Nonfiction: Essays, interview/profile, opinion. "No poetry or trade articles." Buys 85 features, 130 short pieces, 200 reviews, 36 essays and 50 other mss/year. Query. Pays expenses of writers on assignment.

WORDPERFECT FOR WINDOWS MAGAZINE, Ivy International Communications, 270 W. Center St., Orem UT 84057-4683. (801)226-5555. Fax: (801)226-8804. Contact: Terry Bruning, editor-in-chief. 60% freelance written. Monthly magazine of "how-to" articles for users of WordPerfect for Windows and compatible software. Estab. 1991. Circ. 200,000. **Pays on acceptance.** Publishes ms an average of 8 months after acceptance. Byline given. Pays negotiable kill fee. Buys first and secondary world rights. Submit seasonal material 8 months in advance. Reports in 2 months. Sample copy for 9×12 SAE with 7 first-class stamps. Free writers guidelines.
Nonfiction: How-to, step-by-step applications (with keystrokes and screenshots in PCX format), interview/company profile, new product, technical. "Easy-to-understand articles written with *minimum* jargon. Articles should provide readers good, useful information about word processing and other computer functions." Buys 120-160 mss/year. Query with or without published clips. Length: 800-1,800 words.
Columns/Departments: Desktop Publishing, Printing; Basics (tips for beginners); Advanced Macros, Help, all 1,000-1,400 words. Buys 90-120 mss/year. Query with published clips. Pays $400-700.
Tips: "Studying publication provides best information. We're looking for writers who can both inform *and* entertain our specialized group of readers."

PHOTOGRAPHY

Readers of these magazines use their cameras as a hobby and for weekend assignments. To write for these publications, you should have expertise in photography. Magazines geared to the professional photographer can be found in the Professional Photography section.

CLUB MODÈLE, Aquino International, P.O. Box 125, Rochester VT 05767. (802)767-9341. Fax: (802)767-4526. E-mail: aaquino@together.net. Website: http://www.aaquino/modele.htm. Contact: Andres Aquino, publisher. 40% freelance written. Free monthly magazine on the Internet. "*Club Modèle* covers the business of modeling entertainment and fashion, including: performers, entertainers, dancers, actors, models, celebrities, agents, producers and managers, photographers; casting, TV, film, video, theater and show productions; fashion industries, trade shows and exhibits." Estab. 1991. Publishes ms an average of 2 months after acceptance. Byline given sometimes. Buys first North American serial or all rights. Editorial lead time 2 months. Submit seasonal material 2 months in advance. Accepts simultaneous submissions. Reports in 3 weeks on queries; 1 month on mss. Sample copy free on the web. Writer's guidelines for 9×12 SAE with 6 first-class stamps, or free at www.aaquino.com/writers.htm.
Nonfiction: General interest, how-to, interview/profile, photo feature and travel. Send complete ms. Length: 250-1,500 words. Pays for articles with credit line.
Photos: Send photos with submission. Reviews 35 mm slides, 2×2 transparencies, 8×10 prints and digital photos. Captions, model release and identification of subjects required. Buys one-time or all rights.
Tips: "Covers how-to articles: how to succeed in film, video, modeling. How to break into any aspect of the fashion and entertainment industries. Be specific. Send $4 for a sample of 2 past articles and specific guidelines. Know the content of *Club Modèle*. We are most open to interviews with celebrities (with photos) and how-to articles. Visit us on the Internet."

NATURE PHOTOGRAPHER, Nature Photographer Publishing Co., Inc., P.O. Box 2019, Quincy MA 02269. (617)847-0095. Fax: (617)847-0952. E-mail: mjsquincy@pipeline.com. Editor: Evamarie Mathaey. Contact: Helen Longest-Slaughter, photo editor. 65% freelance written. Bimonthly magazine "emphasizing nature photography that uses low-impact and local less-known locations, techniques and ethics. Articles include how-to, travel to world-wide wilderness locations and how nature photography can be used to benefit the environment and environmental education of the public." Estab. 1990. Circ. 20,000. Pays on publication. Buys one-time rights. Submit seasonal material 8 months in advance. Accepts simultaneous submissions. Reports in 2 months. Sample copy for 9×12 SAE with 6 first-class stamps. Writer's guidelines for #10 SASE.
Nonfiction: How-to (underwater, exposure, creative techniques, techniques to make photography easier, low-impact techniques, macro photography, large-format, wildlife), photo feature, technical, travel. No articles about photographing in zoos or on game farms. Buys 12-18 mss/year. Query with published clips or writing samples. Length: 750-2,500 words. Pays $75-150.

ALWAYS CHECK the most recent copy of a magazine for the address and editor's name before you send in a query or manuscript.

Reprints: Send photocopy of article and information about when and where the article previously appeared. Pays 75% of amount paid for an original article.

Photos: Send photos upon request. Do not send with submission. Reviews 35mm, 2¼×2¼ and 4×5 transparencies. Offers no additional payment for photos accepted with ms. Identification of subjects required. Buys one-time rights.

Tips: "Query with original, well-thought-out ideas and good writing samples. Make sure you send SASE. Areas most open to freelancers are travel, how-to and conservation. Must have good, solid research and knowledge of subject. Be sure to obtain guidelines by sending SASE with request before submitting query. If you have not requested guidelines within the last year, request an updated version of guidelines."

‡OUTDOOR PHOTOGRAPHER, Werner Publishing, 12121 Wilshire Blvd., Suite 1200, Los Angeles CA 90025. (310)820-1500. Fax: (310)826-5008. Contact: Editor. Published 10 times/year. "*Outdoor Photographer* looks at our modern photographic world by encouraging photography as part of a lifestyle." Estab. 1985. Circ. 205,230. *Writer's Market* recommends sending query with SASE.

Nonfiction: "*Outdoor Photographer* emphasizes the practical use of the camera in the field, highlighting technique rather than the technical. The editorial is written to stimulate outdoor, sporting, nature and travel enthusiasts to expand their recreational and travel enjoyment through photography and satisfy the needs of amateur photographers with special interests in the outdoors. *Outdoor Photographer* motivates readers to make use of equipment and their talents in conjunction with recreational activities. Articles are intended to inspire readers to seek new equipment, try new techniques and travel to new destinations." *Writer's Market* recommends sending query with SASE.

PHOTO TECHNIQUES, Preston Publications, Inc., P.O. Box 48312, Niles IL 60714. (847)647-2900. Fax: (847)647-1155. Publisher: S. Tinsley Preston III. Contact: Mike Johnston, editor. 50% freelance written. Bimonthly publication covering photochemistry, lighting, optics, processing and printing, Zone System, special effects, sensitometry, etc. Aimed at advanced workers. Prefers to work with experienced photographer-writers; happy to work with excellent photographers whose writing skills are lacking. "Article conclusions often require experimental support." Estab. 1979. Circ. 35,000. Pays within 2 weeks of publication. Publishes ms an average of 8 months after acceptance. Byline given. Buys one-time rights. Sample copy for $5. Writer's guidelines with #10 SASE.

Nonfiction: Special interest articles within above listed topics; how-to, technical product reviews, photo features. Query or send complete ms. Length open, but most features run approximately 2,500 words or 3-4 magazine pages. Pays $100/published page for well-researched technical articles.

Photos: Photographers have a much better chance of having their photos published if the photos accompany a written article. Manuscript payment includes payment for photos. Prefers transparencies and 8×10 b&w prints. Captions, model releases (where appropriate) and technical information required. Buys one-time rights.

Tips: "Study the magazine! Virtually all writers we publish are readers of the magazine. We are now more receptive than ever to articles about photographers, history, aesthetics and informative backgrounders about specific areas of the photo industry or specific techniques. Successful writers for our magazine are doing what they write about."

PICTURE PERFECT, Aquino International, P.O. Box 125, Rochester VT 05767. (802)767-9341. Fax: (802)767-4526. E-mail: aaquino@together.net. Website: http://www.aaquino.com/writers.htm or www.aaquino.com/pperfect. Contact: Elaine Hallgren, editor. Managing Editor: Andres Aquino. 50% freelance written. Free bimonthly magazine on the Internet covering photography in all its facets: fashion, commercial, travel, stock, creative, beauty. Estab. 1989. Pays on publication with credit line and tearsheets only. Publishes ms an average of 3 months after acceptance. Buys first North American serial rights or all rights. Submit seasonal material 3 months in advance. Accepts simultaneous submissions. Reports in 3 weeks on queries; 6 weeks on mss. Sample copies of articles from past issues for $4. Writer's guidelines for SAE and 2 first-class stamps; free guidelines on website.

Nonfiction: Book excerpts, how-to, interview/profile, new product, personal experience, photo feature, travel. Buys 36-48 mss/year. Send complete ms. Length 250-1,500 words.

Photos: Send photos with submission. Reviews b&w prints, 35mm slides, 2¼×2¼ transparencies. Captions, model releases, identification of subjects required. Buys one-time rights or first North American rights.

POPULAR PHOTOGRAPHY, 1633 Broadway, New York NY 10019. Editor: Jason Schneider. "*Popular Photography*, the world's largest-circulation photo magazine, is written by photo enthusiasts for everyone who enjoys taking pictures, from amateurs trying to choose their very first good camera—and learning how to use it—to well-established professionals keeping up on the latest techniques and equipment."

Nonfiction: Query with SASE. All articles must include photographs. Looking for specialty; different, unusual photos. Do not send originals—dupes or prints. Most articles are written by staff.

SHUTTERBUG MAGAZINE, Patch Communications, 5211 S. Washington Ave., Titusville FL 32780. (407)268-5010. Fax: (407)267-1894. Editor: Bob Shell. Editorial Director: Bonnie Paulk. Contact: Bob Shell. 100% freelance written. Monthly magazine "providing how-to articles for advanced amateur to professional photographers." Estab. 1970. Circ. 100,000. Byline given. Buys first rights and second serial (reprint) rights. Editorial lead time 6 months. Reports in 6-8 weeks on queries. Sample copy free. No outside solicitations. Query letters only.

Nonfiction: Historical/nostalgic (photography), how-to (photography), humor, interview/profile, new product, photo feature, technical. "All photo related." *No unsolicited articles.* Buys 60 mss/year. Query. Pays $300 minimum for assigned articles; $200 minimum for unsolicited articles. Pays expenses of writers on assignment.

Photos: Send photos with submission. Reviews any transparencies, 8×10 prints. Offers no additional payment for photos accepted with ms. Captions and model releases required. Buys one-time rights.

Tips: "Submit only material similar in style to that in our magazine. All sections are open to freelancers."

‡**TODAY'S PHOTOGRAPHER INTERNATIONAL, The Make Money With Your Camera Magazine**, P.O. Box 777, Lewisville NC 27023. (910)945-9867. Fax: (901)945-3711. Website: http://www.aipress.com. Editor: Vonda H. Blackburn. Contact: Sarah Hinshaw, associate editor. 100% freelance written. Bimonthly magazine addressing "how to make money—no matter where you live—with the equipment that you currently own." Estab. 1986. Circ. 85,000. Editor's sweepstakes pays $500 for the best story in each issue. Publishes ms an average of 6 months after acceptance.. Byline given. Buys one-time rights. Editorial lead time 6 months. Submit seasonal material 6 months in advance. Accepts simultaneous submissions. Reports in 3 weeks on queries; 3 months on mss. Sample copy for $2, 9×12 SAE and 4 first-class stamps or for $3. Writer's guidelines free.

Nonfiction: How-to, new product, opinion, personal experience, photo feature, technical, travel. No "What I did on my summer vacation" stories.

Reprints: Accepts previously published submissions.

Photos: Reviews transparencies and prints. Offers no additional payment for photos accepted with ms. Captions, model releases, identification of subjects required.

Columns/Departments: Vonda Blackburn, editor. Books (how-to photography), 200-400 words; Sports (how-to photograph sports), 1,000 words. Buys 40 mss/year. Query. Pay negotiable.

Tips: Present a complete submission package containing: your manuscript, photos (with captions, model releases and technical data) and an inventory list of the submission package.

POLITICS AND WORLD AFFAIRS

These publications cover politics for the reader interested in current events. Other publications that will consider articles about politics and world affairs are listed under Business and Finance, Contemporary Culture, Regional and General Interest. For listings of publications geared toward the professional, see Government and Public Service in the Trade section.

‡**AMERICAN SPECTATOR**, 2020 N. 14th St., #750, Arlington VA 22201. (703)243-3733. Fax: (703)243-6814. Editor-in-Chief: R. Emmett Tyrell. Monthly magazine. "For many years, one ideological viewpoint dominated American print and broadcast journalism. Today, that viewpoint still controls the entertainment and news divisions of the television networks, the mass-circulation news magazines, and the daily newspapers. *American Spectator* has attempted to balance the Left's domination of the media by debunking its perceived wisdom and advancing alternative ideas through spirited writing, insightful essays, humor and, most recently, through well-researched investigative articles that have themselves become news." Estab. 1967. Circ. 200,011. Send queries and mss to Attn: Manuscripts.

Nonfiction: "Topics include politics, the press, foreign relations, the economy, culture. Stories most suited for publication are timely articles on previously unreported topics with national appeal. Articles should be thoroughly researched with a heavy emphasis on interviewing and reporting, and the facts of the article should be verifiable. We prefer articles in which the facts speak for themselves and shy away from editorial and first person commentary. No unsolicited poetry, fiction, satire or crossword puzzles." Query with resume, clips and SASE.

Columns/Departments: The Continuing Crisis and Current Wisdom (humor); On the Prowl ("Washington insider news"). Query with resume, clips and SASE.

CALIFORNIA JOURNAL, 2101 K St., Sacramento CA 95816. (916)444-2840. Fax: (916)444-2339. E-mail: agb@sta tenet.com. Contact: Steve Scott, managing editor. 20% freelance written. Prefers to work with published/established writers. Monthly magazine "with non-partisan coverage aimed at a literate, well-informed, well-educated readership with strong involvement in issues, politics or government." Estab. 1970. Circ. 17,000. Pays on publication. Publishes ms an average of 3 months after acceptance. Byline given. Buys all rights. Reports in 2 weeks on queries, 2 months on mss. Writer's guidelines and sample copy for #10 SASE.

Nonfiction: Profiles of state and local government officials and political analysis. No outright advocacy pieces, fiction, poetry, product pieces. Buys 25 unsolicited mss/year. Query. Length: 900-3,000 words. Pays $300-1,000. Sometimes pays the expenses of writers on assignment.

Photos: State availability of photos with submission. Reviews contact sheets. Negotiates payment individually. Identification of subjects required. Buys all rights.

Columns/Departments: Soapbox (opinion on current affairs), 800 words. Does not pay.

Tips: "Be well versed in political and environmental affairs as they relate to California."

‡**CHURCH & STATE, Americans United for Separation of Church and State**, 1816 Jefferson Place, NW, Washington DC 20036. (202)466-3234. Fax: (202)466-2587. Contact: Joseph Conn, editor. 10% freelance written. Prefers to work with published/established writers. Monthly magazine emphasizing religious liberty and church/state relations matters. Strongly advocates separation of church and state. Readership is well-educated. Estab. 1947. Circ. 33,000. **Pays on acceptance.** Publishes ms an average of 2 months after acceptance. Buys all rights. Accepts simultane-

ous submissions. Reports in 2 months. Sample copy and writer's guidelines for 9×12 SAE with 3 first-class stamps.
Nonfiction: Exposé, general interest, historical, interview. Buys 11 mss/year. Query. Length: 3,000 words maximum. Pays negotiable fee.
Reprints: Send tearsheet of article, photocopy of article or typed ms with rights for sale noted and information about when and where the article previously appeared.
Photos: Send photos with query. Pays negotiable fee for b&w prints. Captions preferred. Buys one-time rights.
Tips: "We're looking for feature articles on underreported local church-state controversies. We also consider 'viewpoint' essays that offer a unique or personal take on church-state issues."

COMMONWEAL, A Review of Public Affairs, Religion, Literature and the Arts, Commonweal Foundation, 15 Dutch St., New York NY 10038. (212)732-0800. Contact: Patrick Jordan, managing editor. Editor: Margaret O'Brien Steinfels. Biweekly magazine. Estab. 1924. Circ. 19,000. **Pays on acceptance** or publication. Byline given. Buys all rights. Submit seasonal material 2 months in advance. Reports in 2 months. Free sample copy.
Nonfiction: Essays, general interest, interview/profile, personal experience, religious. Buys 20 mss/year. Query with published clips. Length: 1,200-3,000 words. Pays $75-100.
Poetry: Rosemary Deen, poetry editor. Free verse, traditional. Buys 25-30 poems/year. Pays 75¢/line.

‡COUNTRY CONNECTIONS, Seeking the Good Life—For the Common Good, Earth Alert, Inc., P.O. Box 6748, Pine Mountain CA 93222-6748. (805)242-1047. Fax: (805)242-5704. E-mail: country@frazmtn.com. Editor: Catherine Roberts Leach. Contact: Britt Leach, associate editor. 25% freelance written. Bimonthly magazine with "outspoken, literate and from-the-heart essays and articles on progressive politics, social activism, ecological protection, ethics, animal rights, civil liberties and economic democracy." Estab. 1995. Circ. 3,000. Pays on publication. Publishes ms an average of 4 months after acceptance. Byline given. Offers 100% kill fee. Buys first North American serial rights. Editorial lead time 2 months. Submit seasonal material 4 months in advance. Accepts simultaneous submissions. Reports in 2 months. Sample copy for $4. Writer's guidelines for #10 SASE.
Nonfiction: Essays, humor/satire, interview/profile, opinion, political, environmental. "We have a specific audience. Read the magazine first." Buys 30 mss/year. Send complete ms. Length: 1,000-2,500 words. Pays $25. Sometimes pays the expenses of writers on assignment.
Photos: State availability of photos with submission. Reviews prints. Offers $10/photo. Identification of subjects required. Buys one-time rights.
Columns/Departments: Guest Room (opinion), 900-1,200 words; Book Reviews, 1,000 words. Buys 12 mss/year. Query with published clips for book reviews. Send complete ms for column. Pays $25.
Fiction: "No erotica, horror, mystery, religious, romance, western. Read the magazine first." Buys 12 mss/year. Send complete ms. Length: 900-2,500 words. Pays $25.
Poetry: "Send anything but very long poems." Buys 24 poems/year. Submit maximum 4 poems. Pays $15.
Tips: "Please include address and phone number. Cover letter not required; we read work and decide on that rather than what the writer has published in the past. Our title is deceptive. We are not a country magazine, but rather an alternative/progressive journal for those reconsidering the status quo. Clear, honest writing is appreciated, also satire and humor."

EMPIRE STATE REPORT, The Magazine of Politics and Public Policy in New York State, 4 Central Ave., 3rd Floor, Albany NY 12210. (518)465-5502. Fax: (518)465-9822. Editor: Victor Schaffner. 50% freelance written. Monthly magazine providing "timely political and public policy features for local and statewide public officials in New York State. Anything that would be of interest to them is of interest to us." Estab. 1983. Circ. 10,000. Pays 2 months after publication. Byline given. Buys first North American serial rights. Reports in 1 month on queries; 2 months on mss. Sample copy for $3.95 with 9×12 SASE.
Nonfiction: Essays, exposé, interview/profile and opinion. "Writers should send for our editorial calendar." Buys 48 mss/year. Query with published clips. Length: 500-4,500 words. Pays $50-500. Sometimes pays expenses of writers on assignment.
Photos: Send photos with submission. Reviews any size prints. Offers $50-100/photo. Identification of subjects required. Buys one-time rights.
Columns/Departments: New York Digest (short news stories about state politics), 300-900 words; Perspective (opinion pieces), 900-950 words. Perspectives do not carry remuneration.
Tips: "Send us a query. If we are not already working on the idea, and if the query is well written, we might work something out with the writer."

EUROPE, Delegation of the European Commission, 2300 M St. NW, 3rd Floor, Washington DC 20037. (202)862-9555. Fax: (202)429-1766. Editor: Robert Guttman. Managing Editor: Peter Gwin. 50% freelance written. Monthly magazine for anyone with a professional or personal interest in Europe and European/US relations. Estab. 1963. Circ. 75,000. Pays on publication. Publishes ms an average of 3 months after acceptance. Byline given. Offers 50% kill fee. Buys first serial and all rights. Editorial lead time 2 months. Submit seasonal material 4 months in advance. Reports in 6 months.
Nonfiction: General interest, historical/nostalgic, interview/profile. Interested in current affairs (with emphasis on economics, business and politics), the Single Market and Europe's relations with the rest of the world. Publishes monthly cultural travel pieces, with European angle. "High quality writing a must. We publish articles that might be useful to

people (primarily American readers) with a professional interest in Europe." Query or submit complete ms or article outline. Include résumé of author's background and qualifications. Buys 20 mss/year. Length: 600-1,500 words. Pays $50-500 for assigned articles; $50-400 for unsolicited articles.

Columns/Departments: Arts & Leisure (book, art, movie reviews, etc.), 200-800 words. Pays $50-250.

Photos: Photos purchased with or without accompanying mss. Buys b&w and color. Pays $25-35 for b&w print, any size; $100 for inside use of transparencies; $450 for color used on cover; per job negotiable.

Tips: "We are always interested in stories that connect Europe to the U.S.—especially business stories. Company profiles, a U.S. company having success or vice versa, are a good bet."

THE FREEMAN, 30 S. Broadway, Irvington-on-Hudson NY 10533. (914)591-7230. Fax: (914)591-8910. Contact: Beth Hoffman, managing editor. 85% freelance written. Eager to work with new/unpublished writers. Monthly for "the layman and fairly advanced students of liberty." Buys all rights, including reprint rights. Estab. 1946. Pays on publication. Byline given. Publishes ms an average of 5 months after acceptance. Sample copy for 7½ × 10½ SASE with 4 first-class stamps.

Nonfiction: "We want nonfiction clearly analyzing and explaining various aspects of the free market, private enterprise, limited government philosophy. Though a necessary part of the literature of freedom is the exposure of collectivistic cliches and fallacies, our aim is to emphasize and explain the positive case for individual responsibility and choice in a free economy. Especially important, we believe, is the methodology of freedom—self-improvement, offered to others who are interested. We try to avoid name-calling and personality clashes and find satire of little use as an educational device. Ours is a scholarly analysis of the principles underlying a free market economy. No political strategy or tactics." Buys 100 mss/year. Length: 3,500 words maximum. Pays 10¢/word. Sometimes pays expenses of writers on assignment.

Reprints: Send tearsheet or photocopy of article and information about when and where the article previously appeared. Pays 50% of amount paid for an original article.

Tips: "It's most rewarding to find freelancers with new insights, fresh points of view. Facts, figures and quotations cited should be fully documented, to their original source, if possible."

GEORGE, Hachette Filippacchi Magazines, 1633 Broadway, 41st Floor, New York NY 10019. (212)767-6100. Publisher: Elinor Carmody. Contact: Matthew Cowen. "*George* is edited to spotlight the personalities who shape public issues; from elected officials to media moguls to Hollywood stars. It contains insightful reporting, commentary, cartoons, photos and charts. It covers the points where politics and popular culture converge. *George* demystifies the political process and shows readers how to get the most from their government while staying abreast of the issues that matter." Estab. 1995. This magazine did not respond to our request for information. Query before submitting.

Nonfiction: "We are primarily a political magazine publishing profiles, process stories, reviews, news items and interviews." Query with published clips and SASE. "The rate of payment depends upon the importance and quality of the feature, and our presentation of it."

THE NATION, 72 Fifth Ave., New York NY 10011-8046. (212)242-8400. Fax: (212)463-9712. Editor: Katrina Vanden Heuvel. Contact: Peggy Suttle, assistant to editor. 75% freelance written. Works with a small number of new/unpublished writers each year. Weekly magazine "firmly committed to reporting on the issues of labor, national politics, business, consumer affairs, environmental politics, civil liberties, foreign affairs and the role and future of the Democratic Party." Buys first serial rights. Free sample copy and writer's guidelines for 6 × 9 SASE.

Nonfiction: "We welcome all articles dealing with the social scene, from an independent perspective." Queries encouraged. Buys 100 mss/year. Length: 2,000 words maximum. Pays $225-300. Sometimes pays expenses of writers on assignment.

Columns/Departments: Editorial, 500-700 words. Pays $75.

Poetry: *The Nation* publishes poetry of outstanding aesthetic quality. Pays $1/poem. Contact: Grace Schulman, poetry editor. Send poems with SASE.

‡NATIONAL REVIEW, 150 E. 35th St., New York NY 10016. E-mail: 4744326@mcimail.com. Articles Editor: Drew Oliver. Biweekly magazine featuring political commentary from a conservative viewpoint. Pays on publication. Byline given. Kill fee varies. Buys all rights. Reports in 2 months.

Nonfiction: Send complete ms. Length: 2,000-3,000 words. Pays $250/printed page. Sometimes pays expenses of writers on assignment.

Columns/Departments: Length: 900 words. Pays $250/printed page.

Fillers: Length: 1,000 words. Pays $250/printed page.

Tips: *National Review*'s audience is political.

NEW JERSEY REPORTER, A Journal of Public Issues, The Center for Analysis of Public Issues, 16 Vandeventer Ave., Princeton NJ 08542. (609)924-9750. Fax: (609)924-0363. E-mail: njreporter@aol.com. Website: http://njreporter. org. Contact: Michele Ruess, managing editor. 90% freelance written. Prefers to work with published/established writers but will consider proposals from others. Bimonthly magazine covering New Jersey politics, public affairs and public issues. "*New Jersey Reporter* is a hard-hitting and highly respected magazine published for people who take an active interest in New Jersey politics and public affairs, and who want to know more about what's going on than what newspapers and television newscasts are able to tell them. We publish a great variety of stories ranging from analysis to exposé." Estab. 1970. Circ. 2,200. Pays on publication. Byline given. Buys all rights. Reports in 1 month. Sample copy available on request.

• This magazine continues to increase its use of freelance writing.

Nonfiction: Book excerpts, exposé, interview/profile, opinion. "We like articles from specialists (in planning, politics, economics, corruption, etc.)—particularly if written by professional journalists—but we reject stories that do not read well because of jargon or too little attention to the actual writing of the piece. Our magazine is interesting as well as informative." Buys 18-25 mss/year. Query with published clips. Length: 1,000-4,000 words. Pays $100-600.

Tips: "Queries should be specific about how the prospective story is an issue that affects or will affect the people of New Jersey and its government. The writer's résumé should be included. Stories—unless they are specifically meant to be opinion—should come to a conclusion but avoid a 'holier than thou' or preachy tone. Allegations should be scrupulously substantiated. Our magazine represents a good opportunity for freelancers to acquire great clips. Our publication specializes in longer, more detailed, analytical features. The most frequent mistake made by writers in completing an article for us is too much personal opinion versus reasoned advocacy. We are less interested in opinion than in analysis based on sound reasoning and fact. *New Jersey Reporter* is a well-respected publication, and many of our writers go on to nationally respected newspapers and magazines."

THE NEW REPUBLIC, 1220 19th St. NW, Washington DC 20036. (202)331-7494. Fax: (202)331-0275. Editor-in-Chief: Martin Peretz. Weekly newsmagazine. "*The New Republic* is a journal of opinion with an emphasis on politics and domestic and international affairs. It carries feature articles by staff and contributing editors. The second half of each issue is devoted to books and the arts." Estab. 1914. Circ. 101,200. This magazine did not respond to our request for information. Query before submitting.

Tips: "All of the opinions expressed in *The New Republic* are sharp, informed and urgent. We pride ourselves on our pugnacity. The editors and writers often take issue with each other in the same pages. *The New Republic* affords the unique opportunity to communicate with the most important and elusive people in America in an authoritative setting. Our readers are the recognized leaders in their fields who have pronounced intellectual curiosity and little time for nonsense. They value the variety and the insight that *The New Republic* gives them. Though a relatively small group in number, they are among the most influential people in the country."

POLICY REVIEW: The Journal of American Citizenship, The Heritage Foundation, 214 Massachusetts Ave. NE, Washington DC 20002. (202)546-4400. Editor: Adam Meyerson. Managing Editor: D.W. Miller. Deputy Editor: Joe Loconte. Bimonthly magazine. "We have been described as 'the most thoughtful, the most influential and the most provocative publication of the intellectual right.' *Policy Review* illuminates the families, communities, voluntary associations, churches and other religious organizations, business enterprises, public and private schools, and local governments that are solving problems more effectively than large, centralized, bureaucratic government." Estab. 1977. Circ. 30,000. Pays on publication. Byline given.

Nonfiction: "We are looking especially for articles on private and local institutions that are putting the family back together, cutting crime, improving education and repairing the bankruptcy of government." Buys 4 mss/year. Send complete ms. Length: 2,000-6,000 words. Pays average $500 per article.

‡POLITICALLY CORRECT MAGAZINE, P.O. Box 750, Athens OH 45701-0750. (614)664-3030. Contact: Terri J. Andrews, editor. 50% freelance written. Monthly educational magazine. "*Politically Correct* breaks down legal, current political and basic government issues and information, U.S. history and law, so that teens/college students will be educated, informed, empowered and inspired to vote, meet with officials and fight for their rights." Estab. 1997. Pays on publication. Publishes ms an average of 4 months after acceptance. Byline given. Offers 50% kill fee. Buys one-time rights. Editorial lead time 3 months. Submit seasonal material 4 months in advance. Reports in 6 weeks. Sample copy for $3. Writer's guidelines for #10 SASE.

Nonfiction: Book excerpts, essays, exposé, general interest, historical/nostalgic, how-to, humor, inspirational, interview/profile, opinion, personal experience. Buys 12 mss/year. Query or send complete ms. Length: 100-3,000 words. Pays 1¢/word. Sometimes pays writers with contributor copies or other premiums rather than a cash payment when writer agrees.

Photos: Send photos alone or with submission. Reviews contact sheets. Negotiates payment individually. Captions, model releases, identification of subjects required. Buys one-time rights.

Fillers: Anecdotes, facts, gags to be illustrated by cartoonist, newsbreaks, poetry, short humor. Buys 24/year. Length: 20-200 words. Pays 1¢/word.

Tips: "Teens and college age students have the best chance of getting published in P.C. The shorter the piece, the better! We are interested in any topic that would pertain to young adults—from teen pregnancy and alcohol advertising to women in history and today's political systems. If young people are talking about it, we want to publish it!"

THE PROGRESSIVE, 409 E. Main St., Madison WI 53703-2899. (608)257-4626. Fax: (608)257-3373. E-mail: progressive@peacenet.org. Contact: Matthew Rothschild, editor. 75% freelance written. Monthly. Estab. 1909. Pays on publication. Publishes ms an average of 6 weeks after acceptance. Byline given. Buys all rights. Reports in 1 month. Sample copy for 9×12 SAE with 4 first-class stamps. Writer's guidelines for #10 SASE.

Nonfiction: Primarily interested in articles which interpret, from a progressive point of view, domestic and world affairs. Occasional lighter features. "*The Progressive* is a *political* publication. General-interest material is inappropriate." Query. Length: 3,000 words maximum. Pays $100-300.

Tips: "*The Progressive* is always looking for writers who can describe and explain political, social and economic developments in a way that will interest non-specialists. We like articles that recount specific experiences of real people to illustrate larger points. We're looking for writing that is thoughtful, clear and graceful, conversational and non-academic. Display some familiarity with our magazine, its interests and concerns, its format and style. We want query letters that fully describe the proposed article without attempting to sell it—and that give an indication of the writer's competence to deal with the subject."

TOWARD FREEDOM, A progressive perspective on world events, Toward Freedom Inc., 209 College St., Burlington VT 05401. (802)658-2523. Fax: (802)658-3738. Editor: Greg Guma. 75% freelance written. Political magazine published 8 times/year covering politics/culture, focus on Third World, Europe and global trends. "*Toward Freedom* is an internationalist journal with a progressive perspective on political, cultural, human rights and environmental issues around the world. Also covers the United Nations, the post-nationalist movements and U.S. foreign policy." Estab. 1952. Byline given. Circ. 3,500. Pays on publication. Kill fee "rare–negotiable." Buys first North American serial and one-time rights. Editorial lead time 1 month. Reports in 1-3 months on queries and mss. Sample copy for $3. Writer's guidelines free.
Nonfiction: Features, essays, book reviews, interview/profile, opinion, personal experience, travel, foreign, political analysis. Special issues: Women's Visions (March); Global Media (December/January). No how-to, fiction. Buys 80-100 mss/year. Query. Length: 700-2,500 words. Pays up to 10¢/word.
Photos: Send photos with submission, if available. Reviews any prints. Offers $35 maximum/photo. Identification of subjects required. Buys one-time rights.
Columns/Departments: *TF* Reports (from foreign correspondents), UN, Population, Art and Book Reviews, 800-1,200 words. Buys 20-30 mss/year. Query. Pays up to 10¢/word. Last Word (creative commentary), 900 words. Buys 8/year. Pays $100.
Tips: "Except for book or other reviews, writers should have first-hand knowledge of country, political situation, foreign policy, etc., on which they are writing. Occasional cultural 'travelogues' accepted, especially those that would enlighten our readers about a different way of life. Writing must be professional."

WORLD POLICY JOURNAL, World Policy Institute, Suite 413, 65 Fifth Ave., New York NY 10003. (212)229-5808. Fax: (212)229-5579. Fax: (206)815-3445. E-mail: @mary.wvus.org. Editor: James Chace. Estab. 1983. 10% freelance written. "We are eager to work with new or unpublished writers as well as more established writers." A quarterly journal covering international politics, economics, and security issues, as well as historical and cultural essays, book reviews, profiles, and first-person reporting from regions not covered in the general media. "We hope to bring a new sense of imagination, principle and proportion, as well as a restored sense of reality and direction to America's discussion of its role in the world." Circ. 8,000. Pays on publication. Publishes ms an average of 3 months after acceptance. Byline given. Offers variable kill fee. Buys all rights. Reports in 2 months. Sample copy for $7.50 and 9×12 SAE with 10 first-class stamps.
Nonfiction: Articles that "define policies that reflect the shared needs and interests of all nations of the world." Query. Length: 20-30 pages (8,000 words maximum). Pays variable commission rate.
Reprints: Accepts previously published submissions. Query.
Tips: "By providing a forum for many younger or previously unheard voices, including those from Europe, Asia, Africa and Latin America, we hope to replace lingering illusions and fears with new priorities and aspirations. Articles submitted on speculation very rarely suit our particular needs."

WORLD VISION, World Vision, Inc., P.O. Box 5716, Federal Way WA 98063-9716. Fax: (206)815-3445. E-mail: @mary.wvus.org. Editor: Terry Madison. Contact: Bruce Brander, managing editor. Up to 50% freelance written. Bi-monthly magazine covering world humanitarian issues for opinion leaders. "*World Vision*, a Christian humanitarian relief and development agency working in 100 countries." Estab. 1955. Circ. 84,000. **Pays on acceptance**. Byline given. Kill fee varies. Buys multiple-use international and electronic rights and makes work-for-hire assignments. Editorial lead time 6 months. Submit seasonal material 6 months in advance. Reports in 3 weeks on queries; 2 weeks on mss. Sample copy and writer's guidelines free.
Nonfiction: Essays, general interest, inspirational, interview/profile, photo feature, religious, global issues. Buys 8 mss/year. Query with published clips. Send complete ms. Length: 700-3,000. Pays $1,500 maximum for assigned articles; $850 maximum for unsolicited articles. Sometimes pays expenses of writers on assignment.
Photos: State availability of photos with submissions. Reviews contact sheets, transparencies, 3×5 prints. Offers no additional payment for photos accepted with ms. Captions, identification of subjects required. Negotiable rights bought.
Tips: "As a nonprofit humanitarian agency aiding the poor worldwide, we give assignments to accomplished journalistic writers and photographers who travel the globe. We cover world issues with a humanitarian slant, such as: 'Are We

Trashing Our Third-World Neighbors?,' 'Homeless With Children,' and 'The Human Cost of the Small Arms Trade.' We invite traveling journalists to check with us for assignments."

PSYCHOLOGY AND SELF-IMPROVEMENT

These publications focus on psychological topics, how and why readers can improve their own outlooks, and how to understand people in general. Many General Interest, Men's and Women's publications also publish articles in these areas. Magazines treating spiritual development appear in the Astrology, Metaphysical and New Age section, as well as in Religion, while markets for holistic mind/body healing strategies are listed in Health and Fitness.

THE HEALING WOMAN, The Monthly Newsletter for Women Survivors of Childhood Sexual Abuse, P.O. Box 28040, San Jose CA 95159. (408)246-1788. Fax: (408)247-4309. E-mail: healingw@aol.com. Website: http://members.aol.com/healingw/healingw.htm. Contact: Molly Fisk, editor. Publisher/Editorial Director: Margot Silk Forrest. 70% freelance written. Bimonthly newsletter covering recovery from childhood sexual abuse. "Submissions accepted only from writers with personal or professional experience with childhood sexual abuse. We are looking for intelligent, honest and compassionate articles on topics of interest to survivors. We also publish first-person stories, poetry, interviews and book reviews." Estab. 1992. Circ. 11,000. **Pays on acceptance**. Publishes ms an average of 3 months after acceptance. Byline given. Offers 50% kill fee. Buys first North American serial rights and one-time electronic rights. Submit seasonal material 4 months in advance. Submit no more than 3 pieces at a time. Reports in 1 month on queries. Writer's guidelines for #10 SASE. "No fax or e-mail submissions please."
Nonfiction: Book excerpts, essays, general interest, interview/profile, opinion, personal experience. "No articles on topics with which the writer has not had first-hand experience. If you've been there, you can write about it for us. If not, don't write about it." Buys 30 mss/year. Query with published clips. Length: 300-2,500 words. Pays $25-50. "Pays in copies for poems, short first-person pieces."
Reprints: Send photocopy of article or typed ms with rights for sale noted and information about when and where the article previously appeared. Pay negotiable.
Photos: Send photos with submission. Negotiates payment for photos individually. Identification of subjects required. Buys one-time rights.
Columns/Departments: Book Reviews (books or accounts of incest survivors, therapy for incest survivors), 500-600 words; and Survivors Speak Out (first-person stories of recovery), 200-400 words.
Tips: "Although our subject matter is painful, *The Healing Woman* is not about suffering—it's about healing. Our department called 'Survivors Speak Out' features short, honest, insightful first-person essays with a conversational tone. We are happy to work with unpublished writers in this department. Articles should be more storytelling than lecture. In other words, articles should include your own—or your clients'—first-hand experiences in struggling and coping with the issues you are writing about. Use specific examples to illustrate your points, and the more the better. This is extremely important to us."

‡PSYCHOLOGY TODAY, Sussex Publishers, Inc., 49 E. 21st St., 11th Floor, New York NY 10010. (212)260-7210, ext. 134. Fax: (212)260-7445. Contact: Peter Doskoch, executive editor. Bimonthly magazine. "*Psychology Today* explores every aspect of human behavior, from the cultural trends that shape the way we think and feel to the intricacies of modern neuroscience. We're sort of a hybrid of a science magazine, a health magazine and a self-help magazine. While we're read by many psychologists, therapists and social workers, most of our readers are simply intelligent and curious people interested in the psyche and the self." Estab. 1967. Circ. 331,400. Pays on publication. Publishes ms an average of 3 months after acceptance. Byline given. Buys first North American serial rights. Editorial lead time 5 months. Reports in 1 month. Sample copy for $3.50. Writer's guidelines for #10 SASE.
Nonfiction: "Nearly any subject related to psychology is fair game. We value originality, insight, and good reporting; we're not interested in stories or topics that have already been covered *ad nauseum* by other magazines unless you can provide a fresh new twist and much more depth. We're not interested in simple-minded 'pop psychology.' " No fiction, poetry or first-person essays on "How I Conquered Mental Disorder X." Buys 20-25 mss/year. Query with published clips. Length: 1,500-5,000 words. Pays $1,000-2,500.
Columns/Departments: Contact: News Editor. News & Trends (short pieces, mostly written by staff, occasionally by freelancers), 150-300 words; Style (looks at trends in style from a psychological point of view), 600 words. Query with published clips to news editor. Pays $150-500.

‡ROSICRUCIAN DIGEST, Rosicrucian Order, AMORC, 1342 Naglee Ave., San Jose CA 95191-0001. (408)947-3600. Website: www.rosicrucian.org. Contact: Robin M. Thompson, editor-in-chief. 50% freelance written. Works with a small number of new/unpublished writers each year. Quarterly magazine emphasizing mysticism, science and the arts for educated men and women of all ages seeking alternative answers to life's questions. **Pays on acceptance.** Publishes ms an average of 6 months after acceptance. Buys first serial and second serial (reprint) rights. Byline given. Submit seasonal material 5 months in advance. Accepts previously published submissions. Reports in 2 months. Free sample copy. Writer's guidelines for #10 SASE.
Nonfiction: How to deal with life—and all it brings us—in a positive and constructive way. Informational articles—

new ideas and developments in science, the arts, philosophy and thought. Historical sketches, biographies, human interest, psychology, philosophical and inspirational articles. "We are always looking for good articles on the contributions of ancient civilizations to today's civilizations, the environment, ecology, inspirational (non-religious) subjects." No religious, astrological or political material or articles promoting a particular group or system of thought. Buys variable amount of mss/year. Query. Length: 1,000-1,500 words. Pays 6¢/word.

Reprints: Send typed ms with rights for sale noted. Pays 50% of amount paid for an original article; 100% "if article is really good and author has rights."

Photos: Purchased with accompanying ms. Send prints. Pays $10/8 × 10 b&w glossy print.

Fillers: Short inspirational or uplifting (not religious) anecdotes or experiences. Buys 6/year. Query. Length: 22-250 words. Pays 2¢/word.

Tips: "We are looking for well-written articles with a positive, constructive approach to life in these trying times. This seems to be a time of indecision and apathy in many areas, and we are encouraged when we find an article that lets the reader know that he/she can get involved, take positive action, make a change in his/her life. We are also looking for articles about how other cultures outside our own deal with the big questions, problems and changes in life, i.e., the questions of 'Who am I?', 'Where do I fit in?', 'How can I direct my own life and learn how to experience inner peace?', the role of elders in passing on culture to new generations, philosophical aspects of other cultures that can help us grow today."

REGIONAL

Many regional publications rely on staff-written material, but others accept work from freelance writers who live in or know the region. The best regional publication to target with your submissions is usually the one in your hometown, whether it's a city or state magazine or a Sunday supplement in a newspaper. Since you are familiar with the region, it is easier to propose suitable story ideas.

Listed first are general interest magazines slanted toward residents of and visitors to a particular region. Next, regional publications are categorized alphabetically by state, followed by Canada. Publications that report on the business climate of a region are grouped in the regional division of the Business and Finance category. Recreation and travel publications specific to a geographical area are listed in the Travel, Camping and Trailer section. Keep in mind also that many regional publications specialize in specific areas, and are listed according to those sections. Regional publications are not listed if they only accept material from a select group of freelancers in their area or if they did not want to receive the number of queries and manuscripts a national listing would attract. If you know of a regional magazine that is not listed, approach it by asking for writer's guidelines before you send unsolicited material.

General

BLUE RIDGE COUNTRY, Leisure Publishing, P.O. Box 21535, Roanoke VA 24018-9900. (703)989-6138. Fax: (703)989-7603. E-mail: leisure@infi.net. Contact: Kurt Rheinheimer, editor-in-chief. 75% freelance written. Bimonthly magazine. "The magazine is designed to celebrate the history, heritage and beauty of the Blue Ridge region. It is aimed at the adult, upscale readers who enjoy living or traveling in the mountain regions of Virginia, North Carolina, West Virginia, Maryland, Kentucky, Tennessee, South Carolina and Georgia." Estab. 1988. Circ. 75,000. Pays on publication. Publishes ms an average of 8 months after acceptance. Byline given. Offers $50 kill fee for commissioned pieces only. Buys first and second serial (reprint) rights. Submit seasonal material 6 months in advance. Reports in 2 months. Sample copy for 9 × 12 SAE with 6 first-class stamps. Writer's guidelines for #10 SASE.

Nonfiction: General interest, historical/nostalgic, personal experience, photo feature, travel, history. Buys 25-30 mss/year. Query with or without published clips or send complete ms. Length: 500-1,800 words. Pays $50-250 for assigned articles; $25-250 for unsolicited articles.

• This magazine is looking for more backroads travel, history and legend/lore pieces.

Photos: Send photos with submission. Prefers transparencies. Offers $10-25/photo and $100 for cover photo. Identification of subjects required. Buys all rights.

Columns/Departments: Country Roads (shorts on people, events, travel, ecology, history, antiques, books). Buys 12-24 mss/year. Query. Pays $10-40.

Tips: "Freelancers needed for regional departmental shorts and 'macro' issues affecting whole region. Need field reporters from all areas of Blue Ridge region. Also, we need updates on the Blue Ridge Parkway, Appalachian Trail, national forests, ecological issues, preservation movements."

‡EXPLORE NEW ENGLAND, New England Outdoors Publishing, LLC, 88 Elm St., Camden ME 04843. (207)236-3908. Fax: (207)236-7049. E-mail: explore@midcoast.com. Contact: Lafe Low, editor. 80% freelance written. Bimonthly magazine. "*Explore New England* covers outdoor activities in New England. Our features describe where to go and what to do in the six-state region—from skiing in Vermont, hiking in New Hampshire and rafting in Maine to mountain biking in Connecticut, camping in Massachusetts or just relaxing on the beach in Rhode Island. We focus on human powered activities—no motorsports or hunting." Estab. 1995. Circ. 30,000. Pays on publication. Publishes ms an average of 3 months after acceptance. Byline given. Offers 33% kill fee. Buys all rights and makes work-for-hire assignments for photographers. Editorial lead time 3 months. Submit seasonal material 8 months in advance. Reports in 3 weeks on queries; 1 month on mss. Sample copy and writer's guidelines free.

Nonfiction: Book excerpts (occasionally), general interest, historical/nostalgic, how-to (techniques for specific activities), interview/profile (query first), personal experience (Live and Learn column), photo feature (query first), technical (relating to outdoor equipment), travel. No generic "this is what I did on my vacation" articles. We cover specific activities and specific destinations." Buys 30 features/year. Query with published clips. Length: 1,500-1,800 words. Pays $150-700. Sometimes pays expenses of writers on assignment (generally restricted to phone expenses for interview intensive assignments).

Photos: State availability of photos with submissions or send photos with submission. Reviews transparencies (slides preferred) and prints. Offers $75-600/photo or negotiates payment individually. Model releases, identification of subjects required. Buys one-time rights.

Columns/Departments: Techniques (how-to articles relating to specific activity—i.e., how to ski bumps, mastering a bracing stroke for kayaking, how to pack a backpack. Also equipment related pieces such as rotating the wheels on your in-line skates), 700-800 words. Buys 18-24 mss/year. Query with published clips. Pays $150-200.

Tips: "Please query with ideas and send clips as a first strike. Don't be bashful about following up with a call. If I say I'm keeping you in mind, I really am. I'm not just blowing you off. We have limited editorial real estate, so I have to be selective. Be sure to check out the magazine first. That will definitely help. I have a solid stable of contributors, but I am always interested in hearing new voices."

MYSTIC TRAVELER, Traveler Publications Inc., Suite 205, 174 Bellevue Ave., Newport RI 02840. (401)847-0226. Fax: (401)847-5267. Contact: Joseph Albano, Karen Laughlin, editors. Contact: Jeff Hall, publisher. 30% freelance written. Monthly tabloid covering places of interest strictly in New England. "Stories that get the reader to "do, see, or act upon." Estab. 1992. Circ. 120,000 winter, 240,000 summer. Pays on publication. Byline given. Buys all rights. Editorial lead time 2 months. Submit seasonal material 2 months in advance. Accepts simultaneous submissions. Reports in 2 months on mss. Sample copy and writer's guidelines for 9×12 SAE with $1.50 postage.

Nonfiction: Essays, general interest, historical/nostalgic, how-to, photo feature (travel). Buys 40 mss/year. Send complete ms. Length: 500-800 words. Pays 5¢/word. Sometimes pays expenses of writers on assignment.

Reprints: Send photocopy of article and information about when and where the article previously appared. Pays 90% of amount paid for an original article.

Photos: Send photos with submission. Reviews prints. Negotiates payment individually. Buys one-time rights.

Columns/Departments: Dining Reviews, Kids's Page, Galleries, outdoors, From a New England Kitchen, Club Review, Vineyards, Antiques.

Fillers: Facts. Buys 30/year. Length: 50-200 words. Pays 5¢/word.

Tips: "We are very interested in tours that cover an entire area. It could be a tour of wineries, a certain kind of shop, golf courses, etc. Our publication is monthly, so articles should be of interest throughout the month. Always include address, phone, hours, admission prices. Only articles about Southern New England will be considered."

NORTHWEST TRAVEL, Northwest Regional Magazines, 1525 12th St., P.O. Box 18000, Florence OR 97439. (541)997-8401. (800)348-8401. Fax: (541)997-1124. Contact: Judy Fleagle,co-editor. Co-editor: Jim Forst. 60% freelance written. Bimonthly magazine. "We like energetic writing about popular activities and destinations in the Pacific Northwest. *Northwest Travel* aims to give readers practical ideas on where to go in the region. Magazine covers Oregon, Washington, Idaho and British Columbia; occasionally Alaska and Western Montana." Estab. 1991. Circ. 50,000. Pays after publication. Publishes ms an average of 8 months after acceptance. Offers 33% kill fee. Buys first North American serial rights. Submit seasonal material 6 months in advance. Reports in 1 month on queries; 3 months on mss. Sample copy for $4.50. Writer's guidelines for #10 SASE.

• *Northwest Travel* now emphasizes day trips or loop drives in the Pacific Northwest area.

Nonfiction: Book excerpts, general interest, historical/nostalgic, interview/profile (rarely), photo feature, travel (only in Northwest region). "No cliché-ridden pieces on places that everyone covers." Buys 40 mss/year. Query with or without published clips. Length: 1,250-2,000 words. Pays $100-350 for feature articles and 2-5 contributor copies.

Reprints: Rarely accepts reprints of previously published submissions. Send photocopy of article and information about when and where the article appeared. Pays 60% of amount paid for an original article.

Photos: State availability of photos with submission. Reviews transparencies (prefers dupes) and prints ("for good color we need reproduction negatives with prints"). Captions, model releases (cover photos), credits and identification of subjects required. Buys one-time rights.

Columns/Departments: Restaurant Features, 1,000 words. Pays $125. Worth a Stop (brief items describing places "worth a stop"), 300-500 words. Buys 25-30 mss/year. Send complete ms. Pays $50. Back Page (photo and text package keyed to a specific activity, season or festival with some technical photo info), 80-100 words and 1 photo. Pays $75.

Tips: "Write fresh, lively copy (avoid clichés) and cover exciting travel topics in the region that haven't been covered in other magazines. A story with stunning photos will get serious consideration. Areas most open to freelancers are Worth a Stop and the Restaurant Feature. Take us to fascinating and interesting places we might not otherwise discover."

‡**NOW AND THEN, The Appalachian Magazine**, Center for Appalachian Studies and Services, P.O. Box 70556-ETSU, Johnson City TN 37614-0556. (423)439-6173. Fax: (423)439-6340. E-mail: woodsidj@etsu-tn.edu. Managing Editor: Nancy Fischman. Contact: Jane Harris Woodside, editor. 80% freelance written. Magazine published 3 times/year covering Appalachian region from Southern New York to Northern Mississippi. *"Now & Then* accepts a variety of writing genres: fiction, poetry, nonfiction, essays, interviews, memoirs and book reviews. All submissions must relate to Appalachia and to the issue's specific theme. Our readership is educated and interested in the region." Estab. 1984. Circ. 1,000. Pays on publication. Publishes ms an average of 4 months after acceptance. Byline given. Buys all rights. Editorial lead time 5 months. Accepts simultaneous submissions. Reports in 5 months. Sample copy for $4.50. Writer's guidelines for #10 SASE.

Nonfiction: Book excerpts, essays, general interest, historical/nostalgic, humor, interview/profile, opinion, personal experience, photo feature, book reviews of books from and about Appalachia. "No articles which have nothing to do with Appalachia; articles which blindly accept and employ regional stereotypes (dumb hillbillies, poor and downtrodden hillfolk and miners)." Special issues: Food (November 1 deadline); Poetry (March 1 deadline); Transportation (July 1 deadline). Query with published clips. Length: 1,000-2,500 words. Pays $15-250 for assigned articles; $15-100 for unsolicited articles. Sometimes pays expenses of writers on assignment.

Reprints: Send typed ms with rights for sale noted and information about when and where the article previously appeared. Pays 100% of amount paid for an original article. Typically $15-60.

Photos: State availability of photos with submission. Offers no additional payment for photos accepted with ms. Captions and identification of subjects required. Buys one-time rights.

Fiction: Adventure, ethnic, experimental, fantasy, historical, humorous, mainstream, slice-of-life vignettes. "Fiction has to relate to Appalachia and to the issue's theme in some way." Buys 3-4 mss/year. Send complete ms. Length: 750-2,500 words. Pays $15-100.

Poetry: Free verse, haiku, light verse, traditional. "No stereotypical work about the region. I want to be both surprised and embraced by the language, the ideas, even the form." Buys 25-30 poems/year. Submit 5 poems max. Pays $10.

Tips: "Get the Writers' Guidelines and read them carefully. Show in your cover letter that you know what the theme of the upcoming issue is and how your submission fits the theme."

‡**ROCKY MOUNTAIN RIDER, The Magazine About Horses, People & the West**, Rocky Mountain Rider Magazine, P.O. Box 1011, Hamilton MT 59840. (406)363-4085. Fax: (406)363-1056. Contact: Natalie Riehl, editor. 90% freelance written. Monthly magazine "aiming to satisfy the interests of a wide range of readers involved in a horse and Western lifestyle. Our readers are authentic Westerners, not dudes. They appreciate the values of honesty, generosity and hard work. We carry informative articles, personality profiles, book excerpts, cowboy poetry and humor." Estab. 1993. Circ. 12,500. Pays on publication. Publishes ms an average of 6 months after acceptance. Byline given. Buys one-time rights. Submit seasonal material 6 months in advance. Accepts simultaneous submissions. Reports in 1 month on queries; 2 months on mss. Sample copy free. Writer's guidelines for #10 SASE.

Nonfiction: Book excerpts, essays, general interest, historical/nostalgic, humor, interview/profile, new product, personal experience, photo feature, travel, cowboy poetry. Buys 100 mss/year. Send complete ms. Length: 500-2,000 words. Pays $15-90 for unsolicited articles. Pays writers with trade advertising.

Photos: Send photos with submission. Reviews 3×5 prints. Offers no additional payment for photos accepted with ms or $5/photo. Captions, identification of subjects required. Buys one-time rights.

Poetry: Light verse, traditional. Buys 25 poems/year. Submit maximum 10 poems. Length: 6-36 lines. Pays $10.

Fillers: Anecdotes, facts, gags to be illustrated by cartoonist, short humor. Length: 200-750 words. Pays $15.

Tips: *"RMR* is looking for positive, human interest stories that appeal to an audience of horsepeople, ranchers, seniors, sportsmen and folks who love living in the West. Pieces may include profiles of unusual people or animals, history, humor, anecdotes, coverage of regional events and new products. We aren't looking for many 'how to' or training articles, and are not currently looking at any fiction."

SOUTHERN EXPOSURE, A Journal of Politics and Culture, Institute for Southern Studies, P.O. Box 531, Durham NC 27702. (919)419-8311. Editor: Pronita Gupta. 80% freelance written. Quarterly magazine covering Southern politics and culture. "With special focus sections, investigative journalism, features, fiction, interviews and news, *Southern Exposure* covers the wide range of Southern life today—and puts events and trends in perspective. Our goal is to provide information, ideas and historical understanding of Southern social struggles that will help bring about progressive change." Estab. 1973. Circ. 4,000. Pays on publication. Publishes ms an average of 6 months after acceptance. Byline given. Buys first rights, one-time rights, second serial (reprint) rights or all rights. Editorial lead time 6 months. Accepts simultaneous submissions. Reports in 3 months on queries; 6 months on mss. Sample copy for $5. Writer's guidelines for #10 SASE.

Nonfiction: Book excerpts, essays, exposé, how-to (build a grass roots organization, conduct a citizen's campaign), humor, interview/profile, personal experience, photo feature. "Everything we publish has to have something to do with the South." Special issues: Women & Health, Timber, building community—community breakdown. Buys 50 mss/year. Query with published clips. Length: 250-3,500 words. Pays $50-250. Sometimes pays expenses of writers on assignment.

Photos: Send photos with submission. Reviews contact sheets, transparencies, prints. Offers $50 maximum/photo. Negotiates payment individually. Captions, identification of subjects required. Buys one-time rights.

Columns/Departments: Blueprint (how to change the South—from a person or organization's experience), 1,400 words; Voices (stories by or about people who have developed a point of view, strong feelings, actions), 2,100 words; Roundup (anecdotes and news from the region), 250-700 words; Still the South (information and statistics on some aspect of Southern life), 650 words; Reviews (essay on one or more related books and/or other media), 2,100 words. Buys 15 mss/year. Query with published clips or send complete ms. Pays $50-100.

Fiction: Erotica, ethnic, experimental, historical, horror, humorous, novel excerpts. Buys 4 mss/year. Send complete ms. Length: 3,500 words maximum. Pays $100-250.

Tips: "Lively writing and original thinking are what we're after, new ways to look at events, people, places. Give a new perspective on arts, politics, local struggles, corruption, movements. We like in-depth reporting, plenty of specific information—quotes!—and everything we publish must pertain to the South in some way."

SOUTHERN LIVING, Southern Progress Corp., 2100 Lakeshore Dr., Birmingham AL 35209. (205)877-6000. Fax: (205)877-6700. Editor: John A. Floyd, Jr. Managing Editor: Clay Nordan. Contact: Dianne Young. Monthly magazine. "*Southern Living* highlights the tastes and interests of contemporary Southerners. The magazine regularly traces developments in the areas of travel and recreation, homes and building, gardening and landscaping, and dining and entertaining." Estab. 1966. Circ. 2,461,416. **Pays on acceptance.** Publishes ms an average of 1 year after acceptance. 25% kill fee. Buys all rights or other negotiated rights. Editorial lead time 6 months. Submit seasonal material 1 year in advance. Reports in 1 month on queries, 2 months on mss. Writer's guidelines free.

Nonfiction: Essays, humor. Accepts unsolicited freelance only for personal, nonfiction essays about Southern life. Buys 45-50 mss/year. Query with or without published clips, but prefers completed mss. Length: 700 words minimum. Payment negotiated individually. Sometimes pays expenses of writers on assignment.

Photos: State availability of photos with submissions. Reviews 4×5 transparencies. Negotiates payment individually. Captions, model releases, identification of subjects required. Buys one-time rights.

Columns/Departments: Southern Journal (Southern lifestyle and subjects), 700 words. Buys 12 mss/year. Query with published clips.

‡SUNSET MAGAZINE, Sunset Publishing Corp., 80 Willow Rd., Menlo Park CA 94025-3691. (415)321-3600. Fax: (415)327-7537. Executive Editor: Melissa Houtte. Contact: Editorial Services. Monthly magazine covering the lifestyle of the Western states. "*Sunset* is a Western lifestyle publication for educated, active consumers. Editorial provides localized information on gardening and travel, food and entertainment, home building and remodeling." Freelance articles should be timely and only about the 13 Western states. Pays on acceptance. Byline given. Guidelines for freelance travel items for #10 SASE addressed to Editorial Services.

Nonfiction: "Travel items account for the vast majority of *Sunset*'s freelance assignments, although we also contract out some short garden items. However, *Sunset* is largely staff-written." Travel in the West. Buys 50-75 mss/year. Length: 550-750 words. Pays $1/word. Query before submitting.

Columns/Departments: Departments open to freelancers are: Building & Crafts, Food, Garden, Travel. *Travel Guide* length: 300-350 words. Direct queries to the specific editorial department.

Tips: "Here are some subjects regularly treated in *Sunset*'s stories and Travel Guide items: outdoor recreation (i.e., bike tours, bird-watching spots, walking or driving tours of historic districts); indoor adventures (i.e., new museums and displays, hands-on science programs at aquariums or planetariums, specialty shopping); special events (i.e., festivals that celebrate a region's unique social, cultural, or agricultural heritage. Also looking for great weekend getaways, backroad drives, urban adventures and culinary discoveries such as ethnic dining enclaves. Planning and assigning begins a year before publication date."

YANKEE, Yankee Publishing Inc., P.O. Box 520, Dublin NH 03444-0520. (603)563-8111. Fax: (603)563-8252. E-mail: queries@yankeepub.com. Editor: Judson D. Hale, Sr. Managing Editor: Tim Clark. Contact: Don Weafer, assistant editor. 50% freelance written. Monthly magazine that features articles on New England. "Our mission is to express and perhaps, indirectly, preserve the New England culture—and to do so in an entertaining way. Our audience is national and has one thing in common—they love New England." Estab. 1935. Circ. 700,000. Pays within 30 days of acceptance. Byline given. Offers 33% kill fee. Buys first rights. Submit seasonal material 5 months in advance. Accepts simultaneous submissions. Reports in 2 months on queries. Writer's guidelines for #10 SASE.

  • *Yankee* won two White Awards from the City & Regional Magazine Association in 1994, four in 1995 and seven in 1996. In addition, it was a finalist for General Excellence in the National Magazine Awards in 1995 and 1996.

Nonfiction: Essays, general interest, historical/nostalgic, humor, interview/profile, personal experience. "No 'good old days' pieces, no dialect humor and nothing outside New England!" Buys 30 mss/year. Query with published clips. Length: 250-2,500 words. Pays $50-2,000 for assigned articles; $50-500 for unsolicited articles. Sometimes pays expenses of writers on assignment.

Reprints: Send tearsheet, photocopy of article or short story, typed ms with rights for sale noted and information about when and where the material previously appeared. Pays 100% of the amount paid for an original piece.

Photos: Send photos with submission. Reviews contact sheets and transparencies. Offers $50-150/photo. Identification of subjects required. Buys one-time rights.

Columns/Departments: New England Sampler (short bits on interesting people, anecdotes, lost and found), 100-400 words; Recipe with a History (family favorites that have a story behind them), 100-200 words plus recipe; I Remember (nostalgia focused on specific incidents), 400-500 words. Buys 80 mss/year. Query with published clips. Pays $50-400.

Fiction: Edie Clark, fiction editor. "We publish high-quality literary fiction that explores human issues and concerns in a specific place—New England." Publishes novel excerpts. Buys 6 mss/year. Send complete ms. Length: 500-2,500 words. Pays $1,000.

• Ranked as one of the best markets for fiction writers in the last *Writer's Digest* magazine's "Fiction 50."

Poetry: Jean Burden, poetry editor. "We don't choose poetry by type. We look for the best. No inspirational, holiday-oriented, epic, limericks, etc." Buys 40 poems/year. Submit maximum 3 poems. Length: 2-20 lines. Pays $50.

Tips: "Submit lots of ideas. Don't censor yourself—let *us* decide whether an idea is good or bad. We might surprise you. Remember we've been publishing for 60 years, so chances are we've already done every 'classic' New England subject. Try to surprise us—it isn't easy. These departments are most open to freelancers: New England Sampler; I Remember; Recipe with a History. Study the ones we publish—the format should be apparent. Surprise us!"

Alabama

‡ALABAMA HERITAGE, University of Alabama, Box 870342, Tuscaloosa AL 35487-0342. (205)348-7467. Fax: (205)348-7434. Editor: Suzanne Wolfe. 50% freelance written. "*Alabama Heritage* is a nonprofit historical quarterly published by the University of Alabama and the University of Alabama at Birmingham for the intelligent lay reader. We are interested in lively, well written and thoroughly researched articles on Alabama/Southern history and culture. Readability and accuracy are essential." Estab. 1986. Pays on publication. Byline given. Buys first rights and second serial (reprint) rights. Reports in 1 month. *Writer's Market* recommends allowing 2 months for reply. Sample copy for $5. Writer's guidelines for #10 SASE.

Nonfiction: Historical. "We do not want fiction, poetry, book reviews, articles on current events or living artists and personal/family reminiscences." Buys 10 mss/year. Query. Length: 1,500-5,000 words. Pays $100 minimum. Also sends 10 copies to each author plus 1-year subscription.

Photos: Reviews contact sheets. Identification of subjects required. Buys one-time rights.

Tips: "Authors need to remember that we regard history as a fascinating subject, not as a dry recounting of dates and facts. Articles that are lively and engaging, in addition to being well researched, will find interested readers among our editors. No term papers, please. All areas of our magazine are open to freelance writers. Best approach is a written query."

‡ALABAMA LIVING, Alabama Rural Electric Assn., P.O. Box 244014, Montgomery AL 36124. (334)215-2732. Fax: (334)215-2733. E-mail: area@mindspring.com. Website: www.gobox.com/area. Contact: Darryl Gates, editor. 10% freelance written. Monthly magazine covering rural electric consumers. "Our magazine is an editorially balanced, informational and educational service to members of rural electric cooperatives. Our mix regularly includes Alabama history, nostalgia, gardening, outdoor and consumer pieces." Estab. 1948. Circ. 311,572. Pays on publication. Publishes ms an average of 3 months after acceptance. Byline given. Publication is not copyrighted. Buys second serial (reprint) rights. Editorial lead time 3 months. Submit seasonal material 4 months in advance. Accepts simultaneous submissions. Reports in 1 month on queries. Sample copy free.

Nonfiction: Historical/nostalgic, rural-oriented. Special issues: Gardening (November); Holiday Recipes (December). Buys 6 mss/year. Send complete ms (copy). Length: 300-750 words. Pays $100 minimum for assigned articles; $40 minimum for unsolicited articles.

Reprints: Send tearsheet or photocopy of article or typed ms with rights for sale noted. Pays 100% of the amount paid for an original article.

Tips: "The best way to break into *Alabama Living* is to give us a bit of history or nostalgia about Alabama or the Southeast."

‡MOBILE BAY MONTHLY, PMT Publishing, P.O. Box 66200, Mobile AL 36660. (334)473-6269. Fax: (334)479-8822. Contact: Michelle Roberts, editor. 50% freelance written. "*Mobile Bay Monthly* is a monthly lifestyle magazine for the South Alabama/Gulf Coast region focusing on the people, ideas, issues, arts, homes, food, culture and businesses that make Mobile an interesting place." Estab. 1990. Circ. 10,000. Pays on publication. Publishes ms an average of 4 months after acceptance. Byline given. Buys first rights. Editorial lead time 4 months. Submit seasonal material 6 months in advance. Sample copy for $2.

Nonfiction: Historical/nostalgic, interview/profile, personal experience, photo feature, travel. Buys 10 mss/year. Query with published clips. Length: 1,200-3,000 words. Pays $100-300.

Photos: State availability of photos with submission. Negotiates payment individually. Identification of subjects required. Buys one-time rights.

Tips: "We use mostly local writers. Strong familiarity with the Mobile area is a must. No phone calls; please send query letters with writing samples."

Alaska

ALASKA, The Magazine of Life on the Last Frontier, 4220 B St., Suite 210, Anchorage AK 99503. (907)561-4772. Fax: (907)561-5669. General Manager: David C. Foster. Contact: Ken Marsh, editor. Editorial Assistant: Donna

Rae Thompson. 80% freelance written. Eager to work with new/unpublished writers. Monthly magazine covering topics "uniquely Alaskan." Estab. 1935. Circ. 205,000. Pays on publication. Publishes ms an average of 6 months after acceptance. Byline given. Buys first or one-time rights. Submit seasonal material 1 year in advance. Reports in 2 months. Sample copy for $3 and 9×12 SAE with 7 first-class stamps. Writer's guidelines for #10 SASE.

Nonfiction: Historical/nostalgic, adventure, how-to (on anything Alaskan), outdoor recreation (including hunting, fishing), humor, interview/profile, personal experience, photo feature. Also travel articles and Alaska destination stories. No fiction or poetry. Buys 60 mss/year. Query. Length: 100-2,500 words. Pays $100-1,250 depending upon length. Pays expenses of writers on assignment.

Photos: Send photos with submission. Reviews 35mm or larger transparencies. Captions and identification of subjects required.

Tips: "We're looking for top-notch writing—original, well-researched, lively. Subjects must be distinctly Alaskan. A story on a mall in Alaska, for example, won't work for us; every state has malls. If you've got a story about a Juneau mall run by someone who is also a bush pilot and part-time trapper, maybe we'd be interested. The point is *Alaska* stories need to be vivid, focused and unique. Alaska is like nowhere else—we need our stories to be the same way."

Arizona

ARIZONA HIGHWAYS, 2039 W. Lewis Ave., Phoenix AZ 85009-9988. (602)271-5900. Fax: (602)254-4505. Website: http://www.arizonahighways.com. Contact: Richard G. Stahl, senior editor. 90% freelance written. Prefers to work with published/established writers. State-owned magazine designed to help attract tourists into and through Arizona. Estab. 1925. Circ. 425,000. **Pays on acceptance.** Reports in up to 3 months. Writer's guidelines for SASE.

• Ranked as one of the best markets for freelance writers in *Writer's Yearbook* magazine's annual "Top 100 Markets," January 1997.

Nonfiction: Feature subjects include narratives and exposition dealing with history, anthropology, nature, wildlife, armchair travel, out of the way places, small towns, Old West history, Indian arts and crafts, travel, etc. Travel articles are experience-based. All must be oriented toward Arizona. Buys 6 mss/issue. Buys first serial rights. Query with a lead paragraph and brief outline of story. "We deal with professionals only, so include list of current credits." Length: 600-2,000 words. Pays 35-55¢/word. Pays expenses of writers on assignment.

Photos: "We will use transparencies of 2¼×2¼, 4×5 or larger, and 35mm when they display exceptional quality or content. We prefer 35mm Kodachrome. Each transparency *must* be accompanied by information attached to each photograph: where, when, what. No photography will be reviewed by the editors unless the photographer's name appears on *each* and *every* transparency." Pays $80-350 for "selected" transparencies. Buys one-time rights.

Columns/Departments: Departments include Focus on Nature, Along the Way, Back-Road Adventure, Legends of the Lost, Hike of the Month and Arizona Humor. "Back Road and Hikes also must be experience-based."

Tips: "Writing must be of professional quality, warm, sincere, in-depth, well-peopled and accurate. Avoid themes that describe first trips to Arizona, the Grand Canyon, the desert, Colorado River running, etc. Emphasis is to be on Arizona adventure and romance as well as flora and fauna, when appropriate, and themes that can be photographed. Double check your manuscript for accuracy."

‡**PHOENIX**, Media America Corporation, 5555 N. Seventh Ave., #B-200, Phoenix AZ 85013-1755. (602)207-3750. Fax: (602)207-3777. Editor/Publisher: Richard S. Vonier. Contact: Robert Stieve, managing editor. 70% freelance written. Monthly magazine covering regional issues, personalities, events, customs and history of the Southwest, state of Arizona and metro Phoenix. Estab. 1966. Circ. 50,000. **Pays on acceptance.** Publishes ms an average of 5 months after acceptance. Byline given. Offers 10% kill fee. Buys first North American serial rights and one-time rights. Submit seasonal material 4 months in advance. Accepts simultaneous submissions. Reports in 2 months. Sample copy for $3 and 9×12 SAE with 5 first-class stamps. Writer's guidelines for #10 SASE.

Nonfiction: Book excerpts, essays, investigative, general interest, historical/nostalgic, how-to, humor, inspirational, interview/profile, opinion, personal experience, photo feature, religious, technical, travel. "No material dealing with travel outside the region or other subjects that don't have an effect on the area." Buys 50 mss/year. Query with published clips. Lenght: 5,000 words. Pays $750-1,500. Sometimes pays expenses of writers on assignment.

Reprints: Send tearsheet or photocopy of article and/or typed ms with rights for sale noted and information about when and where the article previously appeared. Pays 50% of their fee for an original article.

Photos: Send photos with submissions. Reviews contact sheets, negatives, transparencies, prints. Offers $25-100/photo. Captions, model releases and identification of subjects required. Buys one-time rights.

Fiction: Query with published clips.

Fillers: Buys 6/year. Length: 1,000 words. Pays $400.

Tips: "Our audience is well-educated, upper middle-class Phoenicians. We have no published guidelines. Articles should be of local or regional interest with vivid descriptions that put the reader in the story and present new information or a new way of looking at things. We are not afraid of opinion."

TUCSON LIFESTYLE, Citizen Publishing Company of Wisconsin, Inc., dba Old Pueblo Press, Suite 12, 7000 E. Tanque Verde Rd., Tucson AZ 85715-5318. (602)721-2929. Fax: (602)721-8665. Contact: Sue Giles, editor-in-chief. 90% freelance written. Prefers to work with published/established writers. Monthly magazine covering Tucson-related

events and topics. Estab. 1982. Circ. 27,000. **Pays on acceptance.** Publishes ms an average of 6 months after acceptance. Byline given. Buys first rights and second serial (reprint) rights. Submit seasonal material 1 year in advance. Reports in 2 months on queries; 3 months on mss. Sample copy for $2.50 plus $3 postage. Writer's guidelines free.
Nonfiction: All stories need a Tucson angle. Historical/nostalgic, humor, interview/profile, personal experience, travel, local stories. Special issues: Remodeling & Redecorating (October); In Health (November); New Homes (December). "We do not accept *anything* that does not pertain to Tucson or Arizona." Buys 100 mss/year. Query. Pays $50-500. Sometimes pays expenses of writers on assignment.
Reprints: Send typed ms with rights for sale noted and information about when and where the article previously appeared. Pays 25-50% of amount paid for an original article.
Photos: Reviews contact sheets, 2¼×2¼ transparencies and 5×7 prints. Offers $25-100/photo. Identification of subjects required. Buys one-time rights.
Columns/Departments: In Business (articles on Tucson businesses and business people); Lifestylers (profiles of interesting Tucsonans); Travel (Southwest, Baja and Mexico). Buys 36 mss/year. Query. Pays $100-200.
Tips: Features are most open to freelancers. "Style is not of paramount importance; good, clean copy with interesting lead is a must."

California

THE EAST BAY MONTHLY, The Berkeley Monthly, Inc., 1301 59th St., Emeryville CA 94608. (510)658-9811. Fax: (510)658-9902. E-mail: themonthly@aol.com. Contact: Tim Devaney, editor. 95% freelance written. Monthly tabloid. "We like stories about local people and issues, but we also accept ideas for articles about topics that range beyond the East Bay's borders or have little or nothing to do with the region." Estab. 1970. Circ. 75,000. Pays on publication. Byline given. Offers 25% kill fee. Buys first rights or second serial (reprint) rights. Editorial lead time 2 months. Submit seasonal material 2 months in advance. Accepts simultaneous submissions. Reports in 1 month. Sample copy for $1. Writer's guidelines for #10 SASE.
Nonfiction: Essays, exposé, general interest, historical/nostalgic, humor, interview/profile, opinion, personal experience, photo feature, travel. Buys 55 mss/year. Query with published clips. Length: 1,500-3,000 words. Pays 10¢/word.
Reprints: Send tearsheet of article and information about when and where the article previously appeared.
Photos: State availability of photos with submission. Reviews contact sheets, 4×5 transparencies, 8×10 prints. Negotiates payment individually. Identification of subjects required. Buys one-time rights.
Fiction: Publishes novel excerpts.
Columns/Departments: Shopping Around (local retail news), 2,000 words; Food for Thought (local food news), 2,000 words; First Person, 2,000 words. Buys 15 mss/year. Query with published clips. Pays 10¢/word.

LOS ANGELES MAGAZINE, ABC, 11100 Santa Monica Blvd., 7th Floor, Los Angeles CA 90025. (310)477-1181. Fax: (310)996-6885. Contact: Bob Roe, executive editor; Michael Caruso, editor. 98% freelance written. Monthly magazine about southern California. "Our editorial mission is to provide an authentic, compelling voice that engages and entertains one of the most media-savvy audiences in the world. Showcasing the diversity and vitality of the city, *Los Angeles*' quest is to deliver a timely, vibrant, must-read magazine that is witty, funny, sophisticated and skeptical but not cynical—a book that has regional resonance and national import." Estab. 1963. Circ. 174,000. Pays on publication. Publishes ms an average of 4 months after acceptance. Byline given. 30% kill fee. Buys first North American serial rights. Submit seasonal material 6 months in advance. Reports in 3 months. Sample copy for $5. Guidelines for #10 SASE.
   • *Los Angeles Magazine* continues to do stories with local angles, but it is expanding its coverage to include topics of interest on a national level.
Nonfiction: "Coverage includes both high and low culture—people, places, politics, the Industry and lifestyle trends." Book excerpts (about L.A. or by famous L.A. author); exposé (any local issue); general interest; historical/nostalgic (about L.A. or Hollywood); interview/profile (about L.A. person). Buys up to 100 mss/year. Query with published clips. Length: 250-3,500 words. Pays $50-2,000. Sometimes pays expenses of writers on assignment.
Photos: Amy Osburn, photo editor. Send photos.
Columns/Departments: Buys 170 mss/year. Query with published clips. Length: 250-1,200 words. Pays $50-600.
Tips: "*Los Angeles* magazine seeks a stimulating mix of timely journalism, eye-catching design and useful service pieces that will appeal to the broadest possible audience."

LOS ANGELES TIMES MAGAZINE, *Los Angeles Times*, Times Mirror Sq., Los Angeles CA 90053. (213)237-7000. Fax: (213)237-7386. Contact: Alice Short, editor. 50% freelance written. Weekly magazine of regional general interest. Circ. 1,164,388. Payment schedule varies. Publishes ms an average of 2 months after acceptance. Byline given. Buys first North American serial rights. Submit seasonal material 3 months in advance. Accepts simultaneous submissions. Reports in 2 months. Sample copy and writer's guidelines free.
Nonfiction: General interest, investigative and narrative journalism, interview/profiles and reported essays. Covers California, the West, the nation and the world. Query with published clips only. Length: 2,500-4,500 words. Pays agreed upon expenses.
Photos: Query first; prefers to assign photos. Reviews color transparencies and b&w prints. Payment varies. Captions,

model releases and identification of subjects required. Buys one-time rights.

Tips: "Prospective contributors should know their subject well and be able to explain why a story merits publication. Previous national magazine writing experience preferred."

METRO, Metro Newspapers, 550 S. 1st St., San Jose CA 95113-2806. (408)298-8000. Website: http://www.metroactive. com. Editor: Dan Pulcrano. Managing Editor: Corinne Asturias. 20-30% freelance written. Weekly alternative newspaper. "*Metro* is for a sophisticated urban audience—stories must be more in-depth with an unusual slant not covered in daily newspapers." Estab. 1985. Circ. 212,000. Pays on publication from one week to two months. Publishes ms after acceptance. Byline given. Offers kill fee only with assignment memorandum signed by editor. Buys first North American serial and second serial (reprint) rights—non-exclusive. Submit seasonal material 3 months in advance. Reports in 2 months on queries; 4 months on mss. Sample copy for $4. Writer's guidelines for #10 SASE.

Nonfiction: Book excerpt, exposé and interview/profile (particularly entertainment oriented), personal essay. Some sort of local angle needed. Buys 75 mss/year. Query with published clips. Length: 500-4,000 words. Pays $50-500 for articles. Sometimes pays expenses of writers on assignment.

Reprints: Send photocopy of article including information about when and where the article previously appeared. Pays $25-200 (50% of amount paid for an original article).

Photos: Send photos with submission. Reviews contact sheets, negatives, any size transparencies and prints. Offers $25-50/photo, more if used on cover. Captions, model releases, identification of subjects required. Buys one-time rights.

Columns/Departments: MetroMenu (food, dining out), 500-1,000 words; MetroGuide (entertainment features, interviews), 500-1,500 words. Buys 75 mss/year. Query with published clips. Pays $25-200.

Tips: "Seasonal features are most likely to be published, but we take only the best stuff. Local stories or national news events with a local angle will also be considered. Preferred submission format is Macintosh disk with printout. We are enthusiastic about receiving freelance inquiries. What impresses us most is newsworthy writing, compellingly presented. We define news broadly and consider it to include new information about old subjects as well as a new interpretation of old information. We like stories which illustrate broad trends by focusing in detail on specific examples."

‡METRO SANTA CRUZ, Metro Newspapers, 111 Union St., Santa Cruz CA 95060. (408)457-9000. E-mail: buzz@sj metro.com. Website: http://www.metroactive.com. Contact: Buzz Bezore, editor. 20-30% freelance written. Weekly alternative newspaper. "*Metro* is for a sophisticated coastal university town audience—stories must be more in-depth with an unusual slant not covered in daily newspapers." Estab. 1994. Circ. 50,000. Pays on publication from 2-3 weeks. Publishes ms after acceptance. Byline given. Offers kill fee only with assignment memorandum signed by editor. Buys first North American serial and second serial (reprint) rights—non-exclusive. Submit seasonal material 3 months in advance. Reports in 2 months on queries; 4 months on mss. Sample copy for $4. Writer's guidelines for #10 SASE.

Nonfiction: Features include a cover story of 3,000-3,500 words and a hometown story of 1,000-1,200 words about an interesting character. Book excerpt, exposé and interview/profile (particularly entertainment oriented), personal essay. Some sort of local angle needed. Buys 75 mss/year. Query with published clips. Length: 500-4,000 words. Pays $50-500 for articles. Sometimes pays expenses of writers on assignment.

Reprints: Send photocopy of article including information about when and where the article previously appeared. Pays $25-200 (50% of amount paid for an original article).

Photos: Send photos with submission. Reviews contact sheets, negatives, any size transparencies and prints. Offers $25-50/photo, more if used on cover. Captions, model releases, subject identification required. Buys one-time rights.

Columns/Departments: MetroMenu (food, dining out), 500-1,000 words; MetroGuide (entertainment features, interviews), 500-1,500 words; Taste (quarterly), 3,000 words. Buys 75 mss/year. Query with published clips. Pays $25-200.

Tips: "Seasonal features are most likely to be published, but we take only the best stuff. Local stories or national news events with a local angle will also be considered. Preferred submission format is Macintosh disk with printout. We are enthusiastic about receiving freelance inquiries. What impresses us most is newsworthy writing, compellingly presented. We define news broadly and consider it to include new information about old subjects as well as a new interpretation of old information. We like stories which illustrate broad trends by focusing in detail on specific examples."

NEW TIMES LOS ANGELES, (formerly *Los Angeles Reader*), 1950 Sawtelle Blvd., Suite 200, Los Angeles CA 90025. (310)477-0403. Fax: (310)478-9873. E-mail: editor@newtimesla.com Contact: Rick Barrs, editor. 85% freelance written. Weekly magazine of features and reviews for "intelligent young Los Angelenos interested in politics, the arts and popular culture." Estab. 1996. Circ. 100,000. Pays on publication. Publishes ms an average of 60 days after acceptance. Byline given. Buys first North American serial rights. Accepts simultaneous submissions.

Nonfiction: General interest, journalism, interview/profile, personal experience, photo features—all with strong local slant. Buys "scores" of mss/year. Query, send complete ms. Length: 200-5,000 words. Pays $25-2,500.

Tips: "Break in with submissions for our Cityside pages which use short (400-800 words) news items on Los Angeles happenings, personalities and trends. Try to have some conflict in submissions: 'x exists' is not as good a story as 'x is struggling with y over z.' Stories must have Los Angeles angle. We much prefer submissions in electronic form."

ORANGE COAST MAGAZINE, The Magazine of Orange County, Orange Coast Kommunications Inc., 245-D Fischer Ave., Suite 8, Costa Mesa CA 92626-4514. (714)545-1900. Fax: (714)545-1932. E-mail: ocmag@aol.com. Website: http://orangecoast.com. Contact: Martin J. Smith, editor. Managing Editor: Allison Joyce. 95% freelance written. Monthly magazine "designed to inform and enlighten the educated, upscale residents of Orange County, California; highly graphic and well-researched." Estab. 1974. Circ. 40,000. **Pays on acceptance.** Publishes ms an average of 4 months after acceptance. Byline given. Buys one-time rights. Submit seasonal material at least 6 months in advance. Accepts simultaneous submissions. Reports in 2 months. Sample copy for $2.95 and 10×12 SAE with 8 first-class stamps. Writer's guidelines for SASE.

Nonfiction: Exposé (Orange County government, politics, business, crime), general interest (with Orange County focus); historical/nostalgic, guides to activities and services, interview/profile (prominent Orange County citizens), local sports, travel. Special issues: Dining and Entertainment (March); Health and Fitness (January); Resort Guide (November); Home and Garden (June); Holiday (December). Buys 100 mss/year. Query or send complete ms. Absolutely no phone queries. Length: 2,000-3,000 words. Pays $400-800.

Reprints: Send tearsheet or photocopy of article or typed ms with rights for sale noted and information about when and where the article previously appeared.

Columns/Departments: Business statistics. Most departments are not open to freelancers. Buys 200 mss/year. Query or send complete ms. Length: 1,000-2,000 words. Pays $200 maximum.

Fiction: Buys only under rare circumstances. Send complete ms. Length: 1,000-5,000 words. Pays $250.

Tips: "Most features are assigned to writers we've worked with before. Don't try to sell us 'generic' journalism. *Orange Coast* prefers articles with specific and unusual angles focused on Orange County. A lot of freelance writers ignore our Orange County focus. We get far too many generalized manuscripts."

PALM SPRINGS LIFE, The Town & Club Magazine, Desert Publications, Inc., 303 N. Indian Canyon, Palm Springs CA 92262. (619)325-2333. Fax: (619)325-7008. Editor: Stewart Weiner. Contact: Sarah Hagerty, senior editor. 100% freelance written. Monthly magazine covering "affluent resort/southern California/Palm Springs desert resorts. *Palm Springs Life* is a luxurious magazine aimed at the affluent market." Estab. 1958. Circ. 16,000. Pays on publication. Publishes ms an average of 3 months after acceptance. Byline given. Offers 25% kill fee. Buys all rights (negotiable). Submit seasonal material 6 months in advance. Reports in 3 weeks on queries. Sample copy for $3.95.

Nonfiction: Book excerpts, essays, interview/profile. Query with published clips. Length: 500-2,500 words. Pays $50-750 for assigned articles; $25-500 for unsolicited articles. Sometimes pays the expenses of writers on assignment.
● Increased focus on desert region and business writing opportunities.

Photos: State availability of photos with submissions. Reviews contact sheets. Offers $5-125/photo. Captions, model releases, identification of subjects required. Buys all rights.

Columns/Departments: Around Town (local news), 50-250 words. Buys 12 mss/year. Query with or without published clips. Pays $5-200.

‡SACRAMENTO MAGAZINE, 4471 D St., Sacramento CA 95819. Fax: (916)452-6061. Contact: Krista Minard, editor. Managing Editor: Darlena Belushin McKay. 100% freelance written. Works with a small number of new/unpublished writers each year. Monthly magazine emphasizing a strong local angle on politics, local issues, human interest and consumer items for readers in the middle to high income brackets. Estab. 1975. Circ. 19,610. Pays on publication. Publishes ms an average of 3 months after acceptance. Rights vary; generally buys first North American serial rights, rarely second serial (reprint) rights. Reports in 2 months. Sample copy for $4.50. Writer's guidelines for #10 SASE.

Nonfiction: Local issues vital to Sacramento quality of life. Buys 5 unsolicited feature mss/year. Query first in writing. Length: 1,500-3,000 words, depending on author, subject matter and treatment. Pays minimum $250. Sometimes pays expenses of writers on assignment.

Photos: Send photos. Payment varies depending on photographer, subject matter and treatment. Captions (including IDs, location and date) required. Buys one-time rights.

Columns/Departments: Business, home and garden, media, parenting, first person essays, regional travel, gourmet, profile, sports, city arts (1,000-1,800 words); City Lights (250-400 words). Pays $50-400.

SAN FRANCISCO BAY GUARDIAN, 520 Hampshire St., San Francisco CA 94110-1417. (415)255-3100. Fax: (415)255-8762. E-mail: mandy@sflag.com. Website: http://www.sfbayguardian.com. Editor/Publisher: Bruce Brugmann. Contact: Mandy Weltman, editorial coordinator. 40% freelance written. Works with a small number of new/unpublished writers each year. Weekly news magazine specializing in investigative, consumer and lifestyle reporting for a sophisticated, urban audience. Estab. 1966. Circ. 140,000. Pays 2 weeks after publication. Publishes ms an average of 1 month after acceptance. Byline given. Buys 200 mss/year. Buys first rights. No simultaneous or multiple submissions. Reports in 2 months.

Nonfiction: Ron Curran, news editor; J.H. Tompkins, arts & entertainment editor; Miriam Wolf, features editor. Publishes "incisive local news stories, investigative reports, features, analysis and interpretation, how-to, consumer and entertainment reviews. Most stories have a Bay Area angle." Freelance material should have a "public interest advocacy journalism approach." Query with 3 clips. Sometimes pays the expenses of writers on assignment.

Reprints: Send tearsheet or photocopy of article and when and where the article previously appeared. Payment varies.

Photos: Ondine Kilker, art director. Purchased with or without mss.

Tips: "Work with our volunteer and intern projects in investigative, political and consumer reporting. We teach the techniques and send interns out to do investigative research. We like to talk to writers in our office before they begin doing a story."

SAN FRANCISCO FOCUS, The City Magazine for the San Francisco Bay Area, 2601 Mariposa St., San Francisco CA 94110-1400. (415)398-6777. Fax: (415)398-6777. Contact: Melanie Haiken, managing editor. 80% freelance written. Prefers to work with published/established writers. Monthly city/regional magazine. Estab. 1968. Circ.

180,000. Pays on publication. Publishes ms an average of 2 months after acceptance. Byline given. Offers 25% kill fee. Submit seasonal material 5 months in advance. Reports in 2 months. Sample copy for $2.50. Writer's guidelines for SASE.

Nonfiction: Exposé, interview/profile, the arts, politics, public issues, sports, consumer affairs and travel. All stories should relate in some way to the San Francisco Bay Area (travel excepted). Query with published clips. Length: 750-4,000 words. Pays $75-2,000 plus some expenses.

VENTURA COUNTY & COAST REPORTER, VCR Inc., 1567 Spinnaker Dr., Suite 202, Ventura CA 93001. (805)658-2244. Fax: (805)658-7803. Editor: Nancy Cloutier. 12% freelance written. Works with a small number of new/unpublished writers each year. Weekly tabloid covering local news. Circ. 35,000. Pays on publication. Publishes ms an average of 2 weeks after acceptance. Byline given. Buys first North American serial rights. Reports in 3 weeks.

Nonfiction: General interest (local slant), humor, interview/profile, travel (local—within 500 miles). Ventura County slant predominates. Length: 2-5 double-spaced typewritten pages. Pays $10-25.

Photos: Send photos with ms. Reviews b&w contact sheet.

Columns/Departments: Entertainment, Sports, Dining News, Real Estate, Boating Experience (Southern California). Send complete ms. Pays $10-25.

Tips: "As long as topics are up-beat with local slant, we'll consider them."

Colorado

ASPEN MAGAZINE, Ridge Publications, P.O. Box G-3, Aspen CO 81612. (970)920-4040. Fax: (970)920-4044. Contact: Melissa Coleman, managing editor; Janet C. O'Grady, editor. 85% freelance written. "We rarely accept submissions by new freelance writers." Bimonthly magazine covering Aspen and the Roaring Fork Valley. Estab. 1974. Circ. 16,000. Pays within 30 days of publication. Byline given. Kill fee varies. Buys first North American serial rights. Reports in 6 months. Sample copy for 9×12 SAE with 10 first-class stamps. Writer's guidelines for #10 SASE.

Nonfiction: Essay, historical, interview/profile, photo feature, enrivonmental and local issues, architecture and design, sports and outdoors, arts. "We do not publish general interest articles without a strong Aspen hook. We do not publish 'theme' (skiing in Aspen) or anniversary (40th year of Aspen Music Festival)." Buys 30-60 mss/year. Query with published clips. Length: 50-4,000 words. Pays $50-1,000.

Photos: Send photos with submission. Reviews contact sheets, negatives, transparencies, prints. Model release and identification of subjects required.

Columns/Departments: Town and mountain news, sports, business, travel, health, beauty, fitness, art news. "We rarely accept freelance travel stories. Virtually all travel is written inhouse." Query with published clips. Length: 200-1,500. Pays $50-150.

STEAMBOAT MAGAZINE, Mac Media LLC, 2955 Village Dr., P.O. Box 4328, Steamboat Springs CO 80477. (303)879-5250 ext. 12. Fax: (970)879-4650. E-mail: rollywahl@m&nmags.com. Website: http://www.steamboatweb.com. Contact: Rolly Wahl, editor. 80% freelance written. Semiannual magazine "showcases the history, people, lifestyles and interests of Northwest Colorado. Our readers are generally well-educated, well-traveled, active people visiting our region to ski in winter and recreate in summer. They come from all 50 states and many foreign countries. Writing should be fresh, entertaining and informative." Estab. 1978. Circ. 20,000. Pays on publication. Publishes ms an average of 6 months after acceptance. Byline given. Offers 100% kill fee. Buys one-time and electronic reprint rights. Editorial lead time 1 year. Submit seasonal material 1 year in advance. Accepts simultaneous submissions. Reports in 1 month on queries; 2 months on mss. Sample copy for $5.95 and SAE with 10 first-class stamps. Writer's guidelines free.

Nonfiction: Essays, general interest, historical/nostalgic, humor, interview/profile, personal experience, photo feature. Buys 10-15 mss/year. Query with published clips. Length: 500-3,000 words. Pays $100-500 for assigned articles; $50-300 for unsolicited articles. Sometimes pays expenses of writers on assignment.

Reprints: Send tearsheet of article. Pays 50% of the amount paid for an original article.

Photos: State availability of photos with submission. Reviews transparencies. Offers $50-250/photo. Captions, model releases, identification of subjects required. Buys one-time rights.

Tips: "Western lifestyles, regional history, nature (including environmental subjects) sports and recreation are very popular topics for our readers. Please query first with ideas to make sure subjects are fresh and appropriate. We try to make subjects and treatments 'timeless' in nature, because our magazine is a 'keeper' with a multi-year shelf life."

VAIL/BEAVER CREEK MAGAZINE, Flatirons/Vail L.L.C., P.O. Box 4328, Steamboat Springs CO 80477. (970)476-6600. Contact: Don Berger, editor. 80% freelance written. Semiannual magazine "showcases the lifestyles and history of the Vail Valley. We are particularly interested in personality profiles, home and design features, the arts, winter and summer recreation and adventure stories, and environmental articles." Estab. 1975. Circ. 30,000. Pays on publication. Publishes ms an average of 6 months after acceptance. Byline given. Offers 100% kill fee. Buys one-time rights. Editorial lead time 1 year. Submit seasonal material 1 year in advance. Accepts simultaneous submissions. Reports in 1 month on queries; 2 months on mss. Sample copy for $5.95 and SAE with 10 first-class stamps. Writer's guidelines free.

Nonfiction: Essays, general interest, historical/nostalgic, humor, interview/profile, personal experience, photo feature. Buys 20-25 mss/year. Query with published clips. Length: 500-3,000 words. Pays $100-500 for assigned articles; $50-300 for unsolicited articles. Sometimes pays expenses of writers on assignment.

Photos: State availability of photos with submission. Reviews transparencies. Offers $50-250/photo. Captions, model releases and identification of subjects required. Buys one-time rights.
Tips: "Be familiar with the Vail Valley and its 'personality.' Approach a story that will be relevant for several years to come. We produce a magazine that is a 'keeper.' "

Connecticut

‡**CONNECTICUT MAGAZINE**, Communications International, 789 Reservoir Ave., Bridgeport CT 06606. (203)374-3388. Fax: (203)371-0318. Editor: Charles Monagan. Contact: Managing Editor. 80% freelance written. Prefers to work with published/established writers who know the state and live/have lived here. Monthly magazine "for an affluent, sophisticated, suburban audience. We want only articles that pertain to living in Connecticut." Estab. 1971. Circ. 93,000. Pays on publication. Publishes ms an average of 4 months after acceptance. Byline given. Offers 20% kill fee. Buys first North American serial rights. Submit seasonal material 4 months in advance. Reports in 6 weeks on queries. Writer's guidelines for #10 SASE.
Nonfiction: Book excerpts, exposé, general interest, interview/profile, other topics of service to Connecticut readers. No personal essays. Buys 50 mss/year. Query with published clips. Length: 3,000 words maximum. Pays $600-1,200. Sometimes pays the expenses of writers on assignment.
Photos: Send photos with submission. Reviews contact sheets and transparencies. Offers $50 minimum/photo. Model releases and identification of subjects required. Buys one-time rights.
Columns/Departments: Business, Health, Politics, Connecticut Guide, Arts, Gardening, Environment, Education, People, Sports, Media. Buys 50 mss/year. Query with published clips. Length: 1,500-2,500 words. Pays $300-600.
Fillers: Short pieces about Connecticut trends, curiosities, interesting short subjects, etc. Buys 50/year. Length: 150-400 words. Pays $75.
Tips: "Make certain your idea has not been covered to death by the local press and can withstand a time lag of a few months. Freelancers can best break in with Around and About; find a story that is offbeat and write it in a lighthearted, interesting manner. Again, we don't want something that has already received a lot of press."

NORTHEAST MAGAZINE, *The Hartford Courant*, 285 Broad St., Hartford CT 06115-2510. (860)241-3700. Website: http://www.courant.com. Contact: Donna Prindle, editorial assistant. Editor: Lary Bloom. 5% freelance written. Eager to work with new/unpublished writers. Weekly magazine for a Connecticut audience. Estab. 1982. Circ. 316,000. **Pays on acceptance.** Publishes ms an average of 5 months after acceptance. Byline given. Buys one-time rights. Reports in 3 months.
Nonfiction: General interest (has to have strong Connecticut tie-in); in-depth investigation of stories behind news (has to have strong Connecticut tie-in); historical/nostalgic; personal essays (humorous or anecdotal). No poetry. Buys 10 mss/year. Length: 750-2,500 words. Pays $200-1,500.
Photos: Most assigned; state availability of photos. "Do not send originals."
Fiction: Well-written, original short stories and (rarely) novel excerpts. Length: 750-1,500 words.
• Ranked as one of the best markets for fiction writers in the last *Writer's Digest* magazine's annual "Fiction 50."
Tips: "Less space available for all types of writing means our standards for acceptance will be much higher. We can only print three to four short stories a year."

District of Columbia

WASHINGTON CITY PAPER, 2390 Champlain St., Washington DC 20009. (202)232-2100. Fax: (202)462-8323. E-mail: aripley@washcp.com. Website: http://www.washingtoncitypaper.com. Editor: David Carr. 50% freelance written. "Relentlessly local alternative weekly in nation's capital covering city politics, media and arts. No national stories." Estab. 1981. Circ. 90,000. Pays on publication. Publishes ms an average of 1 month after acceptance. Byline given. Offers 10% kill fee. Buys first rights. Editorial lead time 1 week. Reports in 1 month. Writer's guidelines for #10 SASE.
Nonfiction: "The paper's greatest single need is for well-reported stories about the city, which includes (but is not limited to) profiles, investigative pieces, 'Talk of the Town'-type articles and stories about local institutions. We're not interested in op-ed material, fiction, poetry, stories about news conferences or demonstrations, or service journalism. Nor are we much interested in celebrity-worshipping journalism." No national politics. Buys 100 mss/year. Length: 2,500-10,000 words, feature stories; 200-2,000 words, shorter stories. Pays 10-20¢/word. Query with published clips or submit complete ms. Sometimes pays expenses of writers on assignment.
Photos: Pays minimum of $75. Make appointment to show portfolio to Sandos Rothstein, art director.
Columns/Departments: Glenn Dixon. Music Writing (eclectic), 1,200 words. Buys 30 mss/year. Query with published clips or submit complete ms. Pays 10-20¢/word.
Tips: "Send local stories that describe the city in new ways. A great idea is the best leverage. We will work with anyone who has a strong idea, regardless of vita."

THE WASHINGTON POST, 1150 15th St. NW, Washington DC 20071. (202)334-7750. Fax: (202)334-1069. Contact: Linda L. Halsey, travel editor. 60% freelance written. Prefers to work with published/established writers.

Weekly newspaper travel section (Sunday). Pays on publication. Publishes ms an average of 6 months after acceptance. Byline given. "We are now emphasizing staff-written articles as well as quality writing from other sources. Stories are rarely assigned; all material comes in on speculation; there is no fixed kill fee." Buys only first North American serial rights. Travel must not be subsidized in any way. Usually reports in 1 month.
Nonfiction: Emphasis is on travel writing with a strong sense of place, color, anecdote and history. Query with published clips. Length: 1,500-2,500 words, plus sidebar for practical information.
Photos: State availability of photos with ms.

Florida

BOCA RATON MAGAZINE, JES Publishing, 6413 Congress Ave., Suite 100, Boca Raton FL 33487. (561)997-8683. Fax: (561)997-8909. E-mail: bocamag@aol.com. Editor: Marie Speed. Associate Editor: Carole Bodger. 70% freelance written. Bimonthly lifestyle magazine "devoted to the residents of South Florida, featuring fashion, interior design, food, people, places and issues that shape the affluent South Florida market." Estab. 1981. Circ. 20,000. **Pays on acceptance.** Publishes ms an average of 3 months after acceptance. Byline given. Buys second serial (reprint) rights. Submit seasonal material 7 months in advance. Accepts simultaneous submissions. Reports in 1 month. Sample copy for $3.95 for 10×13 SAE with 10 first-class stamps. Writer's guidelines for #10 SASE.
Nonfiction: General interest, historical/nostalgic, humor, interview/profile, photo feature, travel. Special issues: Interior Design (September-October); Bridal (January-February); Health (July-August). Query with or without published clips, or send complete ms. Length: 800-2,500 words. Pays $50-600 for assigned articles; $50-300 for unsolicited articles.
Reprints: Send tearsheet of article. Pays 50% of amount paid for an original article.
Photos: Send photos with submission.
Columns/Departments: Body & Soul (health, fitness and beauty column, general interest), 1,000 words; Hitting Home (family and social interactions), 1,000 words. Buys 6 mss/year. Query with published clips or send complete ms. Pays $50-250.
Tips: "We prefer shorter manuscripts, highly localized articles, excellent art/photography."

FLORIDA KEYS MAGAZINE, Gibbons Publishing, Inc., P.O. Box 6524, Key West FL 33041-6524. (800)273-1026. Fax: (305)296-7414. Contact: Tara Valdez, editorial assistant. Editor: Gibbons D. Cline. 75% freelance written. Bimonthly magazine for "full-time residents of the Florida Keys. These are people with a unique lifestyle and a rich, colorful history." Estab. 1978. Circ. 10,000. Pays on publication. Publishes ms an average of 4-6 months after acceptance. Byline given. Buys first North American serial, first or all rights. Editorial lead time 4-6 months. Submit seasonal material at least 6 months in advance. Reports in 1 month on queries; 2 months on mss. Sample copy for $2.50. Writer's guidelines free.
Nonfiction: General interest, historical/nostalgic, humor, interview/profile (Keys residents *only*), travel. Special issues: Gourmet (January); Home & Garden (March); Weddings and Travel (May); Fantasy Fest-Key West (September); The Holidays (November). "No erotica or personal experiences in the Keys . . . please do not send Hemingway-related stories or stories regarding your Keys vacation!" Buys 20-30 mss/year. Query with published clips. Length: 500-1,500 words. Pays $2/column inch, $50 maximum per story.
Photos: Send photos with submissions. Reviews transparencies (any size), prints, slides. Offers no additional payment for photos accepted with ms. Model releases and identification of subjects required. Buys all rights.
Columns/Departments: Dining Guide (Keys recipes, restaurant reviews), 1,200 words; Keys Travel (short getaways); FKM Highlights (profiles of interesting residents); Conch Republic Update (current goings-on of this tiny island nation); Keys Currents (tidbits of interesting information); Nature of the Keys (environmental issues); Fact or Fishin'? (fishing tales, tips, tournaments and recipes); History of the Keys.
Fiction: Publishes novel excerpts.
Tips: "It is difficult to write about Keys unless the writer is a resident of Monroe County, Florida, or frequent visitor. Must be familiar with unique atmosphere and lifestyle of Florida Keys. Submit résumé with query and/or manuscript. If author is unfamiliar with Keys, massive research is suggested (strongly). We are most open to new and unusual angles on fishing, boating, diving, snorkeling, sailing, shelling, sunbathing and Keys special events."

GULFSHORE LIFE, 2975 S. Horseshoe Dr., Suite 100, Naples FL 34104. (941)643-3933. Fax: (941)643-5017. E-mail: gsleditor@aol.com. Contact: Amy Bennett, editor. 75% freelance written. Magazine published 11 times/year for "southwest Florida, the workings of its natural systems, its history, personalities, culture and lifestyle." Estab. 1970. Circ. 26,000. Pays on publication. Publishes ms an average of 4 months after acceptance. Byline given. Offers 25% kill fee. Buys first North American serial rights. Submit seasonal material 8 months in advance. Accepts simultaneous submissions. Sample copy for 9×12 SAE with 10 first-class stamps.
Nonfiction: Historical/nostalgic, interview/profile, issue/trend. All articles must be related to Southwest Florida. Buys 100 mss/year. Query with published clips. Length: 500-3,000 words. Pays $100-1,000.
Photos: Send photos with submission, if available. Reviews 35mm transparencies and 5×7 prints. Pays $25-50. Model releases and identification of subjects required. Buys one-time rights.
Tips: "We buy superbly written stories that illuminate southwest Florida personalities, places and issues. Surprise us!"

JACKSONVILLE, White Publishing Co., 1032 Hendricks Ave., Jacksonville FL 32207. (904)396-8666. Fax: (904)396-0926. Contact: Joseph White, managing editor. 80% freelance written. Monthly magazine covering life and business in northeast Florida "for upwardly mobile residents of Jacksonville and the Beaches, Orange Park, St. Augustine and Amelia Island, Florida." Estab. 1985. Circ. 25,000. Pays on publication. Byline given. Offers 25-33% kill fee to writers on assignment. Buys first North American serial rights or second serial (reprint) rights. Editorial lead time 3 months. Submit seasonal 4 months in advance. Reports in 6 weeks on queries; 1 month on mss. Sample copy for $5 (includes postage). Writer's guidelines free.

Nonfiction: Book excerpts, exposé, general interest, historical, how-to (service articles), humor, interview/profile, personal experience, commentary, photo feature, travel, local business successes, trends, personalities, community issues, how institutions work. All articles *must* have relevance to Jacksonville and Florida's First Coast (Duval, Clay, St. Johns, Nassau, Baker counties). Buys 50 mss/year. Query with published clips. Length: 1,200-3,000 words. Pays $50-500 for feature-length pieces. Sometimes pays expenses of writers on assignment.

Reprints: Accepts reprints of previously published submissions. Send photocopy of article. Pay varies.

Photos: State availability of photos with submission. Reviews contact sheets, transparencies. Negotiates payment individually. Captions, model releases required. Buys one-time rights.

Columns/Departments: Business (trends, success stories, personalities), 1,000-1,200 words; Health (trends, emphasis on people, hopeful outlooks), 1,000-1,200 words; Smart Money (practical personal financial/advice using local people, anecdotes and examples), 1,000-1,200 words; Real Estate/Home (service, trends, home photo features), 1,000-1,200 words; Technology (local people and trends concerning electronics and computers), 1,000-1,200 words; Travel (weekends; daytrips; excursions locally, regionally and internationally), 1,000-1,200 words; occasional departments and columns covering local history, sports, family issues, etc; Last Word (commentary on local topic or issue), 600-750 words. Buys 40 mss/year. Pays $150-250.

Tips: "We are a writer's magazine and demand writing that tells a story with flair. While the whole magazine is open to freelancers, new writers can break in via 'The Insider'—50-300 word stories about trends, phenomena, products, services, trivia, events, significant historical anniversaries, gossip and people in the First Coast area."

SENIOR VOICE OF FLORIDA, Florida's Leading Newspaper for Active Mature Adults, Suncoast Publishing Group, 18860 US Hwy. 19N, Suite 151, Clearwater FL 34624-3106. Publisher: Loree Russell. Contact: Nancy Yost, editor. 25% freelance written. Prefers to work with published/established writers. Monthly newspaper serving the needs of mature adults 50 years of age and over in the Florida Gulf Coast. Estab. 1981. Circ. 70,000. Pays on publication. Publishes ms an average of 3 months after acceptance. Byline given. Buys one-time rights. Submit seasonal material 6 months in advance. Accepts simultaneous submissions. Reports in 2 months. Sample copy for $1 and 10×13 SAE with 6 first-class stamps. Writer's guidelines for SAE with 1 first-class stamp.

Nonfiction: General interest, historical, how-to, humor, inspirational, interview/profile, opinion, photo feature, travel, health, finance, all slanted to a senior audience. Buys 10 mss/year. Send complete ms; 300-600 words. Pays $5-15.

Reprints: Send typed ms with rights for sale noted. Pays flat fee.

Photos: Send photos with submission. Reviews 4×6 color and 5×7 b&w prints. Identification of subjects required.

Columns/Departments: Travel (senior slant) and V.I.P. Profiles (mature adults). Buys 3 mss/year. Send complete ms. Length: 300-600 words. Pays $5-15.

Fillers: Anecdotes, facts, cartoons, short humor. Buys 3/year. Length: 150-250 words. Pays $5.

Tips: "Our service area is the Florida Gulf Coast, an area with a high population of resident retirees and repeat visitors who are 50 plus. In writing for that readership, keep their interests in mind; what they are interested in, we are interested in. We like a clean, concise writing style. Photos are important."

‡SOUTH FLORIDA, Florida Media Affiliates, 800 Douglas Rd., Suite 500, Coral Gables FL 33134. (305)445-4500. Fax: (305)445-4600. Website: www.sfm.com. Contact: Leslie Sternlieb, executive editor. 50% freelance written. Monthly general interest magazine for Miami, Fort Lauderdale, the Florida Keys and Palm Beach County. Estab. 1975. Circ. 70,000. Pays 30-45 days after acceptance. Publishes ms an average of 3 months after acceptance. Byline given. Buys all North American serial rights. Submit seasonal material 4 months in advance. Reports in 2 months on queries. Sample copy for $3 plus 5 first-class stamps. Florida residents add 6% sales tax. Writer's guidelines for #10 SASE.

• Editor's note: This magazine has a new editorial focus—more topical, newsy, harder edged; fewer soft articles.

Nonfiction: Exposé, general interest, interview/profile, lifestyle. Buys 60 mss/year. Query with published clips. Length: 3,500 words maximum. Pays $100-750. Sometimes pays expenses of writers on assignment.

Photos: Send photos with submission. Identification of subjects required. Buys one-time rights.

Fiction: Publishes novel excerpts.

SUNSHINE: THE MAGAZINE OF SOUTH FLORIDA, The Sun-Sentinel Co., 200 E. Las Olas Blvd., Fort Lauderdale FL 33301-2293. (305)356-4685. 60% freelance written. Prefers to work with published/established writers, but works with a small number of new/unpublished writers each year. General interest Sunday magazine for the *Sun-Sentinel*'s 800,000 readers in south Florida. Pays within 1 month of acceptance. Publishes ms an average of 2 months after acceptance. Byline given. Offers 25% kill fee for assigned material. Buys first serial rights or one-time rights in the state of Florida. Submit seasonal material 2 months in advance. Accepts simultaneous submissions. Reports in 1 month on queries; 2 months on mss. Sample copy and writer's guidelines free.

Nonfiction: General interest, interview/profile, travel. "Articles must be relevant to the interests of adults living in south Florida." Buys about 150 mss/year. Query with published clips. Length: 1,000-3,000 words; preferred length 2,000-2,500 words. Pays 30-35¢/word to $1,200 maximum.

Reprints: Send tearsheet or photocopy of article or typed ms with rights for sale noted and information about when and where the article previously appeared.

Photos: Send photos. Pays negotiable rate for 35mm and 2¼×2¼ color slides. Captions and identification of subjects required; model releases required for sensitive material. Buys one-time rights for the state of Florida.

Tips: "Do not phone, but do include your phone number on query letter. Keep your writing tight and concise—south Florida readers don't have the time to wade through masses of prose. We are always in the market for first-rate profiles, human-interest stories, travel stories and contributions to our regular 1,000-word features, 'First Person,' 'Weekenders' and 'Unsolved Mysteries.' "

TROPIC MAGAZINE, Sunday Magazine of the Miami Herald, Knight Ridder, 1 Herald Plaza, Miami FL 33132-1693. (305)376-3432. Editor: Bill Rose. Executive Editor: Tom Shroder. 20% freelance written. Works with small number of new/unpublished writers each year. Weekly magazine covering general interest, locally oriented topics for south Florida readers. Circ. 500,000. Pays on publication. Publishes ms an average of 2 months after acceptance. Byline given. Buys first serial rights. Submit seasonal material 2 months in advance. Reports in 3 months. Sample copy for 11×14 SAE.

Nonfiction: General interest, interview/profile (first person), personal experience. No poetry. Buys 20 mss/year. Query with published clips or send complete ms with SASE. Length: 1,500-3,000 words. Pays $200-1,000/article.

Reprints: Send typed ms and information about when and where the article previously appeared. Pay negotiable.

Photos: Janet Santelices, art director. Do not send original photos.

Fiction: Short fiction, novel excerpts. Length: up to 900 words. Query with SASE.

Columns/Departments: Relationships. Length: 900 words. Query with SASE.

WATERFRONT NEWS, Ziegler Publishing Co., Inc., 1523 S. Andrews Ave., Ft. Lauderdale FL 33316-2507. (954)524-9450. Fax: (954)524-9464. E-mail: h2o@aol.com. Contact: Jennifer Heit, editor. 40% freelance written. Monthly tabloid covering marine and boating topics for the Greater Ft. Lauderdale waterfront community. Estab. 1984. Circ. 36,000. Pays on publication. Publishes ms an average of 2 months after acceptance. Byline given. Buys first serial, second serial (reprint) rights or simultaneous rights in certain circumstances. Submit seasonal material 3 months in advance. Reports in 1 month on queries. Sample copy for 9×12 SAE with 4 first-class stamps.

Nonfiction: Regional articles on south Florida's waterfront issues; marine communities; profiles on people important in boating, i.e., racers, boat builders, designers, etc. (does not have to be from south Florida); trends in boating and waterfront lifestyle; some how-to (how-to find a good marina, boat mechanic, teach kids about sailing); humor with an eye toward boating topics. Buys 50 mss/year. Query with published clips. Length: 500-1,000 words. Pays $50-125 for assigned articles; $25-125 for unsolicited articles. Sometimes pays the expenses of established writers on assignment.

Photos: Send photos or send photos with submission. Reviews contact sheets and 3×5 or larger prints. Offers $15/photo. Buys one-time rights. Photos may be submitted digitally.

Columns/Departments: Query with published clips. Length 500 words. Pays $25-100.

Fillers: Anecdotes, facts, nautical one-liners to be illustrated by cartoonist, newsbriefs, short humor. Buys 12/year. Length 100-500 words. Pays $10-200.

Tips: "Nonfiction marine, nautical or south Florida stories only. No fiction or poetry. Keep it under 1,000 words. Photos or illustrations help. Send for a sample copy of *Waterfront News* so you can acquaint yourself with our publication and our unique audience. Although we're not necessarily looking for technical articles, it helps if the writer has sailing or powerboating experience. Writers should be familiar with the region and specific when dealing with local topics."

Georgia

‡ATLANTA, 1360 Peachtree St., Suite 1800, Atlanta GA 30309. Contact: Lee Walburn, editor. Monthly magazine devoted to Atlanta. It explores government, education, the arts, urban affairs, politics, regional happenings, restaurants, shopping, etc. for a general adult audience. Circ. 51,142. **Pays on acceptance.** Byline given. Offers 20% kill fee. Buys first North American serial rights. Reports in 1 month on queries.

Nonfiction: Buys 36-40 mss/year. Query with published clips. Length: 1,500-5,000 words. Pays $300-2,000. Pays expenses of writer on assignment.

Columns/Departments: Buys 48 mss/year. Query with published clips. Pays $500. Length: 1,000-1,500 words.

Fillers: Buys 120/year. Length: 75-175 words. Pays $50-100.

Tips: "Writers must know what makes their piece a story rather than just a subject."

GEORGIA JOURNAL, The Indispensable Atlanta Co., Inc., P.O. Box 1604, Decatur GA 30031-1604. (404)377-4275. Fax: (404)377-1820. E-mail: 74467.1243@compuserve.com. Website: http://www.georgiajournal.com. Contact: David R. Osier, editor. 90% freelance written. Works with a small number of new/unpublished writers each year. Bimonthly magazine primarily interested in "*authoritative* nonfiction articles with a *well-defined point of view* on any aspect of Georgia's human and natural history." Estab. 1980. Circ. 25,000. Please query first. Pays on publication. Publishes ms an average of 1 year after acceptance. Byline given. Buys first serial rights. Submit seasonal material 6 months in advance. Reports in 6 months. Sample copy for $5. Writer's guidelines for #10 SASE.

Nonfiction: "*Georgia Journal* has published articles on the roles historic personalities played in shaping our state, important yet sometimes overlooked historical/political events, archaeological discoveries, unsolved mysteries (natural and human), flora and fauna, and historic preservation. Sidebars are encouraged, such as interesting marginalia and bibliographies. We also are looking for adventures that explore the Georgia landscape from weekend antique hunting, camping, walking tours, arts & crafts festivals, and auto trips to more strenuous activities such as biking, boating, rafting, back-packing, rock climbing and caving. Adventures should also have a well-defined point of view, and be told through the author's personal experience. Articles should be accompanied by detailed map data and other pertinent location information, such as tips on access, lodging and camping. *Georgia Journal* has a place for authoritative topical articles as well—Georgia's environment, mysteries and trends in living or profiles of Georgia authors, adventurers, artisans, artists, sports figures and other personalities." Buys 30-40 mss/year. Query. Length: 200-5,000 words. Pays 10¢/word.

Reprints: Accepts previously published submissions. Send photocopy of article or short story.

Columns/Departments: Books and writers; interesting or historic houses/buildings for sale; Commentary section; Pure Georgia—uses shorter pieces; Calendar of events; reviews of restaurants, B&Bs and historic inns.

Fiction: See submission guidelines. *Georgia Journal* publishes a limited amount of fiction, but while it encourages promising new writers, it is not looking for first-time or unpublished authors. Publishes novel excerpts. Optimum length is 4,000 words. Stories must have a Georgia theme or Georgia setting. Payment varies, depending on publishing history. Unless mss are submitted with a return envelope with sufficient postage, they will not be returned.

Poetry: Contact: Janice Moore. Free verse, haiku, light verse, traditional. Uses poetry from or dealing with Georgia suitable for a general audience. Uses 20 poems/year. Submit maximum 4 poems. Length: 25 lines. Pays in copies.

GEORGIA MAGAZINE, Georgia Electric Membership Corp., P.O. Box 1707, Tucker GA 30085. (770)270-6950. Fax: (770)270-6995. E-mail: ann.elstad@opc.com. Website: http://www.Georgiamag.com. Editor: Ann Elstad. 50% freelance written. "We are a monthly magazine for and about Georgians, with a friendly, conversational tone and human interest topics." Estab. 1945. Circ. 280,000. Pays on publication. Publishes ms an average of 4 months after acceptance. Byline given. Buys first North American serial rights and website rights. Editorial lead time 2 months. Submit seasonal material 6 months in advance. Accepts simultaneous submissions. Reports in 1 month on subjects of interest. Sample copy for $2 each. Writer's guidelines free.

Nonfiction: General interest, historical/nostalgic, how-to (in the home and garden), humor, inspirational, interview/profile, photo feature, travel. Buys 8 mss/year. Query with published clips. Length: 800 words; 500 words for smaller features and departments. Pays $200-300. Pays contributor copies upon negotiation. Sometimes pays expenses of writers on assignment.

Photos: State availability of photos with submission. Reviews contact sheets, transparencies, prints. Negotiates payment individually. Model releases, identification of subjects required. Buy one-time rights.

NORTH GEORGIA JOURNAL, Legacy Communications, Inc., P.O. Box 127, Roswell GA 30077. Editor: Olin Jackson. 70% freelance written. Quarterly magazine "for readers interested in travel, history, and mountain lifestyles of north Georgia." Estab. 1984. Circ. 17,461. Pays on publication. Publishes ms an average of 5 months after acceptance. Byline given. Offers 25% kill fee. Buys first and all rights. Editorial lead time 6 months. Submit seasonal material 6 months in advance. Sample copy for 9×12 SAE and 8 first-class stamps. Writer's guidelines for #10 SASE.

Nonfiction: Historical/nostalgic, how-to (survival techniques; mountain living; do-it-yourself home construction and repairs, etc.), interview/profile (celebrity), personal experience (anything unique or unusual pertaining to north Georgia mountains), photo feature (any subject of a historic nature which can be photographed in a seasonal context, i.e.—old mill with brilliant yellow jonquils in foreground), travel (subjects highlighting travel opportunities in North Georgia). Query with published clips. Pays $75-350.

Photos: Send photos with submission. Reviews contact sheets, transparencies. Negotiates payment individually. Captions, model releases, identification of subjects required. Buys all rights.

Tips: "Good photography is crucial to the acceptance of all articles. Send written queries then *wait* for a response. *No telephone calls please*. The most useful material involves a first person experience of an individual who has explored a historic site or scenic locale and *interviewed* a person or persons who were involved with or have first-hand knowledge of a historic site/event. Interviews and quotations are crucial to acceptance. Articles should be told in the writer's own words."

Hawaii

ALOHA, THE MAGAZINE OF HAWAII AND THE PACIFIC, Davick Publications, P.O. Box 3260, Honolulu HI 96801. (808)593-1191. Fax: (808)593-1327. E-mail: alohamag@aol.com. Contact: Cheryl Tsutsumi, editorial director. 50% freelance written. Bimonthly regional magazine of international interest. "Most of our readers do not live in Hawaii, although most readers have been to the Islands at least once. The magazine is directed primarily to residents of Hawaii in the belief that presenting material to an immediate critical audience will result in a true and accurate presentation that can be appreciated by everyone. Travelers to Hawaii will find *Aloha* shares vignettes of the real Hawaii." Estab. 1977. Circ. 95,000. Pays on publication. Publishes ms an average of 6 months after acceptance;

unsolicited mss can take a year or more. Byline given. Offers variable kill fee. Buys first rights. Submit seasonal material 1 yr. in advance. Reports in 2 months. Sample copy for $2.95, SAE and 10 first-class stamps. Writer's guidelines free.
Nonfiction: Book excerpts, historical/nostalgic (historical articles must be researched with bibliography), interview/profile, photo features. Subjects include the arts, business, flora and fauna, people, sports, destinations, food, interiors, history of Hawaii. "We don't want stories of a tourist's experiences in Waikiki or odes to beautiful scenery." Buys 24 mss/year. Query with published clips. Length: 2,000-3,000 words average. Pay ranges from $150-400. Sometimes pays expenses of writers on assignment.
Photos: Send photos with query. Pays $25 for b&w prints; prefers negatives and contact sheets. Pays $75 for 35mm (minimum size) color transparencies used inside; $100 for full page; $125 for double-page bleeds; $250 for color transparencies used as cover art. "*ALOHA* features Beautiful Hawaii, a collection of photographs illustrating that theme, in every issue. A second photo essay by a sole photographer on a theme of his/her own choosing is also published occasionally. Queries are essential for the sole photographer essay." Model releases, identification of subjects are required. Buys one-time rights.
Fiction: Ethnic, historical. "Fiction depicting a tourist's adventures in Waikiki is not what we're looking for. As a general statement, we welcome material reflecting the true Hawaiian experience." Buys 2 mss/year. Send complete ms. Length: 1,000-2,500 words. Pays $300.
Poetry: Haiku, light verse, traditional. No seasonal poetry or poetry related to other areas of the world. Buys 6 poems/year. Submit maximum 6 poems. Prefers "shorter poetry"—20 lines or less. Pays $30.
Tips: "Read *Aloha*. Research meticulously and have good illustrative material to accompany your text."

HAWAII MAGAZINE, Fancy Publications, Inc., 1400 Kapiolani Blvd., A-25, Honolulu HI 96814. (808)942-2556. Fax: (808)947-0924. E-mail: hawaiiedit@lava.net. Contact: Jim Borg, editor. Managing Editor: Julie Applebaum. 60% freelance written. Bimonthly magazine "written for residents and frequent visitors who enjoy the culture, people and places of the Hawaiian Islands." Estab. 1984. Circ. 71,000. Pays on publication. Byline given. Buys first North American serial rights. Submit seasonal material 6 months in advance. Reports in 1 month on queries; 6 weeks on mss. Sample copy for $3.95. Writer's guidelines free.
Nonfiction: General interest, historical/nostalgic, how-to, interview/profile, personal experience, photo feature, travel. "No articles on the following: first trip to Hawaii, how I discovered the Islands, the Hula, Poi, or Luaus." Buys 66 mss/year. Query with or without published clips, or send complete ms. Length: 4,000 words maximum. Pays $100-500.
Photos: Send photos with submission. Reviews contact sheets and transparencies. Prefers color transparencies. Offers $35/photo. Identification of subjects preferred. Buys one-time rights.
Columns/Departments: Backdoor Hawaii (a light or nostalgic look at culture or history), 800-1,200 words; Hopping the Islands (news, general interest items), 100-200 words. Buys 6-12 mss/year. Query. Length: 800-1,500 words. Pays $100-200. New department, WeatherWatch, focuses on Hawaii weather phenomena (450 words). Pays $50.
Tips: "Freelancers must be knowledgeable about Island subjects, virtual authorities on them. We see far too many first-person, wonderful-experience types of gushing articles. We buy articles only from people who are thoroughly grounded in the subject on which they are writing."

HONOLULU, Honolulu Publishing Co., Ltd., 36 Merchant St., Honolulu HI 96813. (808)524-7400. Fax: (808)531-2306. E-mail: honmag@pixi.com. Publisher: John Alves. Contact: John Heckathorn, editor. Managing Editor: Janice Otaguro. 50% freelance written. Prefers to work with published/established writers. Monthly magazine covering general interest topics relating to Hawaii residents. Estab. 1888. Circ. 30,000. **Pays on acceptance.** Publishes ms an average of 4 months after acceptance. Byline given. Buys first-time rights. Submit seasonal material 5 months in advance. Accepts simultaneous submissions. Reports in 2 months. Sample copy for $2 and 9×12 SAE with 8 first-class stamps. Writer's guidelines free.
Nonfiction: Exposé, general interest, historical/nostalgic, photo feature—all Hawaii-related. "We write for Hawaii residents, so travel articles about Hawaii are not appropriate." Buys 30 mss/year. Query with published clips if available. Length: 2,000-3,000 words. Pays $100-700. Sometimes pays expenses of writers on assignment.
Photos: Teresa Black, art director. Send photos. Pays $75-175 for single image inside; $500 maximum for cover. Captions and identification of subjects required as well as model release. Buys one-time rights.
Columns/Departments: Calabash ("newsy," timely, humorous department on any Hawaii-related subject). Buys 15 mss/year. Query with published clips or send complete ms. Length: 50-750 words. Pays $35-100. First Person (personal experience or humor). Buys 10 mss/year. Length: 1,500 words. Pays $200-300.

Idaho

SUN VALLEY MAGAZINE, Wood River Publishing, Drawer 697, Hailey ID 83333. (208)788-0770. Fax: (208)788-3881. E-mail: 103057.201@compuserve.com. Contact: Colleen Daly, editor. 95% freelance written. Triannual magazine covering lifestyle of Sun Valley area (recreation, history, profiles). Estab. 1973. Circ. 15,000. Pays on publication. Publishes ms an average of 4 months after acceptance. Byline given. Buys first North American serial rights. Editorial lead time 1 year. Submit seasonal material 14 months in advance. Accepts simultaneous submissions. Reports in 1 month on queries; 6 weeks on mss. Sample copy for $3.95 and $3 postage.
Nonfiction: All articles are focused specifically on Sun Valley, the Wood River Valley and immediate surrounding areas.

Special issues: Sun Valley Home Design (fall). Query with published clips. Length varies. Pays $40-450. Sometimes pays expenses of writers on assignment.

Reprints: Occasionally accepts previously published submissions.

Photos: State availability of photos with submission. Reviews transparencies. Offers $60-250/photo. Model releases, identification of subjects required. Buys one-time rights.

Columns/Departments: Conservation issues, winter/summer sports, mountain-related activities and subjects, home (interior design), garden. All must have local slant. Query with published clips. Pays $40-250.

Fiction: We use local writers exclusively.

Tips: "Most of our writers are locally based. Also, we rarely take submissions that are not specifically assigned, with the exception of fiction. However, we always appreciate queries."

Illinois

CHICAGO LIFE, P.O. Box 11311, Chicago IL 60611-0311. (773)880-1360. E-mail: chgolife@mcs.com. Publisher: Pam Berns. Contact: Joan Blade, editor. 95% freelance written. Bimonthly magazine on Chicago life. Estab. 1984. Circ. 60,000. Pays on publication. Byline given. Kill fee varies. Submit seasonal material 8 months in advance. Accepts simultaneous submissions. Reports in 3 months. Sample copy for 9 × 12 SAE with 7 first-class stamps.

Nonfiction: Book excerpts, essays, exposé, how-to, photo feature, travel. Buys 50 mss/year. Send complete ms. Length: 400-1,200 words. Pays $30 for unsolicited articles. Sometimes pays the expenses of writers on assignment.

Reprints: Send photocopy of article and information about when and where the article previously appeared. Pays 100% of amount paid for an original article.

Photos: Send photos with submission. Reviews contact sheets, negatives, transparencies, prints. Offers $15-30/photo. Buys one-time rights.

Columns/Departments: Law, Book Reviews, Travel. Send complete ms. Length: 500 words. Pays $30.

Fillers: Facts. Pays $15-30.

Tips: "Please send finished work with visuals (photos, if possible). Topics open include travel, self improvement, how-to-do almost anything, entrepreneurs, how to get rich, beautiful, more well-informed."

CHICAGO MAGAZINE, 500 N. Dearborn, Suite 1200, Chicago IL 60610-4901. Fax: (312)222-0699. Managing Editor: Shane Tritsch. 40% freelance written. Prefers to work with published/established writers. Monthly magazine for an audience which is "95% from Chicago area; 90% college educated; upper income, overriding interests in the arts, politics, dining, good life in the city and suburbs. Most are in 25-50 age bracket, well-read and articulate." Estab. 1968. Circ. 165,000. Buys first serial rights. **Pays on acceptance.** Publishes ms an average of 6 months after acceptance. Submit seasonal material 4 months in advance. Reports in 1 month. For sample copy, send $3 to Circulation Dept. Writer's guidelines for #10 SASE.

Nonfiction: "On themes relating to the quality of life in Chicago: past, present, and future." Writers should have "a general awareness that the readers will be concerned, influential, longtime Chicagoans. We generally publish material too comprehensive for daily newspapers." Personal experience and think pieces, profiles, humor, spot news, historical articles, exposés. Buys 50 mss/year. Query; indicate "specifics, knowledge of city and market, and demonstrable access to sources." Length: 500-6,000 words. Pays $100-$2,500. Pays expenses of writers on assignment.

Photos: Reviews b&w glossy prints, 35mm color transparencies or color prints. Usually assigned separately, not acquired from writers.

Tips: "Submit detailed queries, be business-like and avoid clichéd ideas."

‡CHICAGO READER, Chicago's Free Weekly, Chicago Reader, Inc., 11 E. Illinois, Chicago IL 60611. (312)828-0350. Fax: (312)828-9926. Editor: Alison True. Managing Editor: Patrick Arden. 50% freelance written. Alternative weekly tabloid for Chicago. Estab. 1971. Circ. 136,000. Pays on publication. Publishes ms an average of 3 months after acceptance. Byline given. No kill fee. Buys one-time rights. Editorial lead time up to 6 months. Accepts simultaneous submissions. Responds if interested. Sample copy and writer's guidelines free.

Nonfiction: Book excerpts, essays, exposé, general interest, historical/nostalgic, humor, interview/profile, opinion, personal experience, photo feature. No celebrity interviews, national news or issues. Buys 500 mss/year. Send complete ms. Length: 4,000-50,000 words. Pays $100-2,000. Sometimes pays expenses of writers on assignment.

Reprints: Accepts previously published submissions.

Columns/Departments: Reading, First Person, Cityscape, Neighborhood News, all 1,500-2,500 words; arts and entertainment reviews, up to 1,200 words; calendar item, 400-1,000 words. Pays $100-2,000.

Tips: "Our greatest need is for full-length magazine-style feature stories on Chicago topics. We're *not* looking for: hard news (What the Mayor Said About the Schools Yesterday); commentary and opinion (What I Think About What the Mayor Said About the Schools Yesterday); fiction; poetry. We are not particularly interested in stories of national (as opposed to local) scope, or in celebrity for celebrity's sake (a la *Rolling Stone*, *Interview*, etc.). More than half the articles published in the *Reader* each week come from freelancers, and once or twice a month we publish one that's come in 'over the transom'—from a writer we've never heard of and may never hear from again. We think that keeping the *Reader* open to the greatest possible number of contributors makes a fresher, less predictable, more interesting paper. So we not only publish unsolicited freelance writing, we depend on it."

THE CHICAGO TRIBUNE MAGAZINE, Chicago Tribune Newspaper, 435 N. Michigan Ave., Chicago IL 60611. (312)222-3573. Website: http://www.trib mag@aol.com. Editor: Denis Gosselin. Managing Editor: Douglas Balz. 50% freelance written. Weekly Sunday magazine. "We look for unique, compelling, all-researched, elequently written articles on subjects of general interest." Circ. 1,300,000. Pays on publication. Publishes ms an average of 2 months after acceptance. Offers $250 kill fee. Buys one-time rights. Submit seasonal material 6 months in advance. Reports in 1 month on queries; 6 weeks on mss.
Nonfiction: Book excerpts, exposé, general interest, interview/profile, photo feature, technical, travel. Buys 35 mss/year. Query or send complete ms. Length: 2,500-5,000 words. Pays $750-1,000. Sometimes pays the expenses of writers on assignment.
Reprints: Send typed ms and information on when and where the article previously appeared. Pay negotiable.
Photos: Send photos with submission. Payment varies for photos. Captions and identification of subjects required. Buys one-time rights.
Columns/Departments: First Person (Chicago area subjects only, talking about their occupations), 1,000 words; Chicago Voices (present or former high-profile Chicago area residents with their observations on or reminiscences of the city of Chicago), 1,000 words. Buys 40 mss/year. Query. pays $250. Buys 52 mss/year. Query. Pays $250.
Fiction: Length: 1,500-2,000 words. Pays $750-1,000.

‡ILLINOIS ENTERTAINER, Chicago's Music Monthly, Roberts Publishing, Inc., 124 W. Polk, #103, Chicago IL 60605. (312)922-9333. E-mail: ieeditors@aol.com. Contact: Michael C. Harris, editor. 80% freelance written. Free monthly magazine covering "popular and alternative music, as well as other entertainment: film, theater, media. We're more interested in new, unknown artists than the usual Madonna/Prince fare. Also, we cover lots of Chicago-area artists." Estab. 1974. Circ. 75,000. Pays on publication. Publishes ms an average of 2 months after acceptance. Byline given. Offers 50% kill fee. Buys first North American serial rights. Editorial lead time 2 months. Submit seasonal material 2 months in advance. Accepts simultaneous submissions. Reports in 2 months. Sample copy for $5.
Nonfiction: Exposé, how-to, humor, interview/profile, new product, reviews. No personal, confessional, inspirational articles. Buys 75 mss/year. Query with published clips. Length: 600-2,600 words. Pays $10-125. Sometimes pays expenses of writers on assignment.
Reprints: Send typed ms with rights for sale noted and information about when and where the article previously appeared. Pays 100% of amount paid for an original article.
Photos: Send photos with submission. Reviews contact sheets, transparencies and 5×7 prints. Offers $20-200/photo. Captions, model releases, identification of subjects required. Buys one-time rights.
Columns/Departments: Spins (LP reviews), 250-300 words. Buys 200-300 mss/year. Query with published clips. Pays $10-20.
Tips: "Send clips, résumé, etc. and be patient. Also, sending queries that show you've seen our magazine and have a feel for it greatly increases your publication chances."

NEW CITY, Chicago's News and Arts Weekly, New City Communications, Inc., 770 N. Halsted, Suite 208, Chicago IL 60622. (312)243-8786. Fax: (312)243-8802. E-mail: frank@newcitynet.com. Website: http://www.newcityne t.com. Contact: Frank Sennett, managing editor. Editor: Brian Hieggelke. 50% freelance written. Weekly magazine. Estab. 1986. Circ. 65,000. Pays 30 days after publication. Publishes ms an average of 1 month after acceptance. Byline given. Offers 20% kill fee in certain cases. Buys first rights and non-exclusive electronic rights. Editorial lead time 2 months. Submit seasonal material 2 months in advance. Reports in 1 month. Sample copy for $3. Writer's guidelines for #10 SASE.
Nonfiction: Essays, exposé, general interest, interview/profile, personal experience, service. Buys 100 mss/year. Query via e-mail, if possible. Length: 100-4,000 words. Pays $15-450. Rarely pays expenses of writers on assignment.
Photos: State availability of photos with submissions. Reviews contact sheets. Captions, model releases, identification of subjects required. Buys one-time rights.
Columns/Departments: Lit (literary supplement), 300-2,000 words; Music, Film, Arts (arts criticism), 150-800 words; Chow (food writing), 300-2,000 words. Buys 50 mss/year. Query via e-mail, if possible. Pays $15-300.

NORTH SHORE, The Magazine of Chicago's North and Northwest Suburbs, PB Communications, 874 Green Bay Rd., Winnetka IL 60093. (847)441-7892. Publisher: Asher Birnbaum. Contact: Jon Birnbaum, managing editor. Senior Editor: Barry Hochfelder. 75% freelance written. Monthly magazine. "Our readers are diverse, from middle-class communities to some of the country's wealthiest zip codes. But they all have one thing in common— proximity to Chicago." Circ. 57,092. Pays on publication. Publishes ms an average of 1-3 months after acceptance. Byline given. Offers 50% kill fee. Buys first North American serial rights. Submit seasonal material 5 months in advance. Reports in 3 months. Writer's guidelines for #10 SASE.
Nonfiction: Book excerpts, exposé, general interest, how-to, interview/profile, photo feature, travel. Special issues: Weddings (January, July); Fitness (February); Homes/Gardens (March, June, September, December); Weekend Travel (May); Nursing/Retirement Homes (August); Dining and Nightlife (October). Buys 50 mss/year. Query with published clips. Length: 500-4,000 words. Pays $100-800. Sometimes pays expenses of writers on assignment.
Reprints: Accepts previously published submissions.
Photos: Send photos with submission. Reviews contact sheets, negatives, transparencies, prints. Identification of subjects required. Buys one-time rights.
Fiction: Publishes novel excerpts.

Columns/Departments: "Prelude" (shorter items of local interest), 250 words. Buys 12 mss/year. Query with published clips. Pays $50.
Tips: "We're always looking for something of local interest that's fresh and hasn't been reported elsewhere. Look for local angle. Offer us a story that's exclusive in the crowded Chicago-area media marketplace. Well-written feature stories have the best chance of being published. We cover all of Chicago's north and northwest suburbs together with some Chicago material, not just the North Shore."

WINDY CITY SPORTS MAGAZINE, Chicago Sports Resources, 1450 W. Randolph, Chicago IL 60607. (312)421-1551. Fax: (312)421-2060. E-mail: wcpublish@aol.com. Contact: Jeff Banowetz, editor. 75% freelance written. *"Windy City Sports Magazine* is a 70-130 page monthly magazine covering amateur, participatory, endurance sports in the Chicago metropolitan area. We cover running, cycling, in-line skating, outdoor sports; we do not cover professional football, basketball, etc." Estab. 1987. Circ. 100,000. Pays on publication. Byline given. Offers 25% kill fee. Buys one-time rights. Editorial lead time 2 months. Submit seasonal material at least 2 months in advance. Accepts simultaneous submissions. Reports in 1 month. Sample copy for $2 or SAE (manila) with $2 postage. Writer's guidelines free.
Nonfiction: Book excerpts, essays, general interest, historical/nostalgic, how-to, humor, inspirational, interview/profile, new product, opinion, personal experience, technical, travel. "No articles on professional sports." Query with published clips. Length: 700-1,200 words. Pays $75-150. Sometimes pays expenses of writers on assignment.
Reprints: Send photocopy of article or typed ms with rights for sale noted and information about when and where the article previously appeared. Payment varies.
Photos: Freelancers should state availability of photos with submission. Send photos with submission. Reviews b&w photos. Negotiates payment individually. Captions, identification of subject required. Buys one-time rights.
Columns/Departments: Running, women's, nutrition, cycling, road trip, sports medicine, fitness centers. 800-1,000 words for all columns. Buys 70 mss/year. Query with published clips. Send complete ms. Pays $75-125.
Poetry: Anything. "Must be sports related."
Fillers: Anecdotes, facts, cartoons, short humor. Buys 25/year. Length: 50-250 words. Pays $25-100.
Tips: "It helps to be active in the sport you choose to write about. Being a runner when writing a running article gives extra credentials. The columns/departments are most open to freelancers. I must fill these columns every month, 11 times per year. Also, be aware of the season when pitching ideas."

Indiana

ARTS INDIANA, Arts Indiana, Inc. 47 S. Pennsylvania, Suite 701, Indianapolis IN 46204-3622. (317)632-7894. Fax: (312)632-7966. E-mail: artsmag@iquest.net. Website: http://www.cinergy.com/artsmag. Contact: Julie Pratt McQuiston, editor. 90% freelance written. Monthly (September-June) magazine on artists, writers, performers and arts organizations working in Indiana—literary, visual and performing. Estab. 1978. Circ. 11,000. **Pays on acceptance.** Publishes ms an average of 3 months after acceptance. Byline given. Offers 10% kill fee. Buys first North American serial rights. Submit seasonal material 5 months in advance. Reports in 5 weeks. Sample copy available for $3.50 plus postage
Nonfiction: Indiana-linked essays, historical/nostalgic, interview/profile, opinion, photo feature, interviews. Query with published clips. Length: up to 3,000 words. Pays $50-300 for articles. Sometimes pays expenses of writer on assignment.
Reprints: Send typed ms or photocopy of article and information on when and where the article previously appeared. Pay negotiable.
Photos: Send b&w photos with submission. Reviews 5×7 or larger prints. Sometimes offers additional payment for photos accepted with ms. Captions and identification of subjects required. Buys one-time rights.
Tips: "We are looking for interesting, insightful features that go beyond the press release and open doors to the arts for our readers. We also publish short stories, poetry and novel excerpts from *established*, published writers as part of our 'Writer's Block' column. Best to read a recent copy of the magazine."

INDIANAPOLIS MONTHLY, Emmis Publishing Corp., 950 N. Meridian St., Suite 1200, Indianapolis IN 46204. (317)237-9288. Fax: (317)237-9496. E-mail: im-input@iquest.net. Website: http://www.iquest.net/indymonthly. Editor-in-Chief: Deborah Paul. Contact: Sam Stall, editor. 50% freelance written. Prefers to work with published/established writers. Monthly magazine of "upbeat material reflecting current trends. Heavy on lifestyle, homes and fashion. Material must be regional (Indianapolis and/or Indiana) in appeal." Estab. 1977. Circ. 45,000. Pays on publication. Publishes ms an average of 2 months after acceptance. Byline given. Offers 50% kill fee in some cases. Buys first North American serial rights and one-time rights. Submit seasonal material 3 months in advance. Reports in 2 months. Sample copy for $6.10. Writers' guidelines for #10 SASE.
Nonfiction: General interest, interview/profile, photo feature. Must have a strong Indianapolis or Indiana angle. No poetry, fiction or domestic humor; no "How Indy Has Changed Since I Left Town" or "An Outsider's View of the 500" stories. Buys 50 mss/year. Query with published clips or send complete ms (200-3,000 words). Pays $50-600.
   ● This magazine is using more first-person essays, but they must have a strong Indianapolis or Indiana tie. It will consider nonfiction book excerpts of material relevant to its readers.
Reprints: Accepts reprints only from non-competing markets. Send typed ms with rights for sale noted and information about when and where the article previously appeared. Pays 100% of the amount paid for an original article.

Columns/Departments: Around the Circle; 9 to 5 (profile of person with intriguing job); Sport (star athletes and trendy activities); Health (new technology; local sources); Controversy; Hoosiers at Large; Coping (overcoming adversity). "Again, a local angle is the key." Query with published clips or send complete mss. Pays $150-300.
Tips: "Tell us something we didn't know about Indianapolis. Find a trendy subject with a strong Indianapolis (or Indiana) angle and sell it with a punchy query and a few of your best clips. Don't confuse 'general interest' with 'generic interest'—all material must focus sharply on Indianapolis and/or Indiana. Topics, however, can vary from serious to wacky: Recent issues have included everything from a feature story about Indianapolis Colts quarterback Jim Harbaugh to a two-paragraph piece on an Indiana gardening supply house that sells insects by mail. Another good bet is to pitch us an inside piece on a national celeb with Hoosier ties; a recent hot-selling cover story was titled 'Oprah's Indiana home.' Best breaking-in topics for freelancers are Around the Circle (short takes on trendy local topics); Hoosiers at Large (Indiana natives relate first-person experiences); and First Person (self-explanatory, relating to Indiana). Fax and e-mail queries OK; no phone queries please."

Kansas

KANSAS!, Kansas Department of Commerce and Housing, 700 SW Harrison, Suite 1300, Topeka KS 66603-3957. (913)296-3479. Editor: Andrea Glenn. 90% freelance written. Quarterly magazine emphasizing Kansas travel attractions and events. Estab. 1945. Circ. 52,000. **Pays on acceptance.** Publishes ms an average of 1 year after acceptance. Byline given. Buys one-time rights. Submit seasonal material 8 months in advance. Reports in 2 months. Sample copy and writer's guidelines available.
Nonfiction: General interest, photo feature, travel. "Material must be Kansas-oriented and have good potential for color photographs. The focus is on travel with articles about places and events that can be enjoyed by the general public. In other words, events must be open to the public, places also. Query letter should clearly outline story. I'm especially interested in Kansas freelancers who can supply their own photos." Length: 750-1,250 words. Pays $200-300.
Photos: "We are a full-color photo/manuscript publication." Send photos (original transparencies only) with query. Pays $50-75 (generally included in ms rate) for 35mm or larger format transparencies. Captions required.
Tips: "History and nostalgia stories do not fit into our format because they can't be illustrated well with color photos."

KANSAS CITY MAGAZINE, 7101 College Blvd., Suite 600, Overland Park KS 66210. (913)338-0900. Fax: (913)338-1148. Contact: Zim Loy, editorial director. 75% freelance written. Bimonthly magazine. "Our mission is to celebrate living in Kansas City. We are a consumer lifestyle/general interest magazine focused on Kansas City, its people and places." Estab. 1994. Circ. 31,000. **Pays on acceptance.** Publishes ms an average of 3 months after acceptance. Byline given. Offers 10% kill fee. Buys first North American serial rights. Editorial lead time 4 months. Submit seasonal material 6 months in advance. Accepts simultaneous submissions. Sample copy for #10 SASE.
Nonfiction: Exposé, general interest, interview/profile, photo feature. Buys 30-50 mss/year. Query with published clips. Length: 250-2,500 words. Pays 50¢/word minimum. Sometimes pays expenses of writers on assignment.
Photos: Negotiates payment individually. Buys one-time rights.
Columns/Departments: Entertainment (Kansas City only), 1,000 words; Food (Kansas City food and restaurants only), 1,000 words. Buys 10 mss/year. Query with published clips. Pays $200-500.

Kentucky

BACK HOME IN KENTUCKY, Greysmith Publishing Inc., P.O. Box 681629, Franklin TN 37068-1629. (615)794-4338. Fax: (615)790-6188. Contact: Nanci P. Gregg, managing editor. 50% freelance written. "Bimonthly magazine covering Kentucky heritage, people, places, events. We reach Kentuckians and 'displaced' Kentuckians living outside the state." Estab. 1977. Circ. 8,163. Pays on publication. Publishes ms an average of 6 months after acceptance. Byline given. Buys first North American serial rights. Submit seasonal material 8 months in advance. Reports in 2 months. Sample copy for $3 and 9×12 SAE with 5 first-class stamps. Writer's guidelines for #10 SASE.
• This magazine is increasing its emphasis on the "Back Home." It is interested in profiles of Kentucky gardeners, Kentucky cooks, Kentucky craftspeople.
Nonfiction: Historical (Kentucky-related eras or profiles), profiles (Kentucky cooks, gardeners and craftspersons), memories (Kentucky related), photo feature (Kentucky places and events), travel (unusual/little known Kentucky places). No inspirational or religion. Buys 25 mss/year. Query with or without published clips, or send complete ms. Length: 500-2,000 words. Pays $50-150 for assigned articles; $15-75 for unsolicited articles. "In addition to normal payment, writers receive 4 copies of issue containing their article." Sometimes pays expenses of writers on assignment.
Reprints: Occasionally accepts previously published submissions. Send tearsheet of article and information about when and where the article previously appeared. Pays 50% of amount paid for an original article.
Photos: Send photos with submission. Reviews transparencies and 4×6 prints. Offers no additional payment for photos accepted with ms. Model releases and identification of subjects required. Rights purchased depends on situation. Also looking for color transparencies for covers. Vertical format. Pays $50-150.
Columns/Departments: Kentucky travel, Kentucky crafts, Kentucky gardeners. Buys 10-12 mss/year. Query with

published clips. Length: 500-750 words. Pays $15-40.
Tips: "We work mostly with unpublished writers who have a feel for Kentucky's people, places and events. Areas most open are little known places in Kentucky, unusual history and profiles of interesting, unusual Kentuckians."

‡**LOUISVILLE MAGAZINE**, 137 W. Muhammad Ali Blvd., Louisville KY 40202-1438. (502)625-0100. Fax: (502)625-0109. E-mail: loumag@louisville.com. Website: http://www.louisville.com. Contact: Ronni Lundy, editor. 67% freelance written. Monthly magazine "for and generally about people of the Louisville Metro area. Routinely covers arts, entertainment, business, sports, dining and fashion. Features range from news analysis/exposé to silly/funny commentary. We like lean, clean prose, crisp leads." Estab. 1950. Circ. 20,000. Publishes ms an average of 2-3 months after acceptance. Byline given. Offers 50% kill fee. Buys first North American serial rights. Editorial lead time 6 weeks. Submit seasonal material 6 months in advance. Reports in 3 months. Sample copy for $2.
Nonfiction: Book excerpts, essays, exposé, general interest, historical, interview/profile, photo feature. Special issues: City Guide (January); Kentucky Derby (May). Buys 75 mss/year. Query. Length: 500-3,500 words. Pays $100-500 for assigned articles; $100-400 for unsolicited articles.
Photos: State availability of photos with submissions. Reviews transparencies. Offers $25-50/photo. Identification of subjects required. Buys one-time rights.
Columns/Departments: End Insight (essays), 850 words. Buys 10 mss/year. Send complete ms. Pays $100-150.

Louisiana

SUNDAY ADVOCATE MAGAZINE, P.O. Box 588, Baton Rouge LA 70821-0588. (504)383-1111, ext. 350. Fax: (504)388-0351. Website: HTTP://www.TheAdvocate.com. Contact: Freda Yarbrough, news/features editor. 5% freelance written. "We are backlogged but still welcome submissions." Byline given. Estab. 1925. Pays on publication. Publishes ms up to 3 months after acceptance.
Nonfiction and Photos: Well-illustrated, short articles; must have local, area or Louisiana angle, in that order of preference. Also interested in travel pieces. Photos purchased with mss. Pays $100-200, $30/published photo.
Reprints: Send tearsheet or typed ms with rights for sale noted and information about when and where the article previously appeared. Pays $100-200.
Tips: "Style and subject matter vary. Local interest is most important. No more than 4-5 typed, double-spaced pages."

Maine

‡**ISLESBORO ISLAND NEWS**, HC60 Box 227, Islesboro ME 04848. (207)734-6745. Fax: (207)734-6519. Publisher: Agatha Cabaniss. 10% freelance written. Monthly tabloid on island of Islesboro and people. Estab. 1985. **Pays on acceptance.** Byline given. Buys one-time rights. Sample copy for $2. Writer's guidelines for #10 SASE.
Nonfiction: Articles about contemporary issues on the islands, historical pieces, personality profiles, arts, lifestyles and businesses on the islands. Any story must have a definite Maine island connection. No travel pieces. Query or send complete ms. Pays $20-50.
Reprints: Accepts previously published submissions. Send typed ms with rights for sale noted. Payment varies.
Photos: Send photos with submission.
Tips: "Writers must know the Penobscot Bay Islands. We are not interested in pieces of a generic island nature unless they relate to development problems or the viability of the islands as year round communities. We do not want 'vacation on a romantic island,' but we are interested in island historical pieces."

Maryland

BALTIMORE MAGAZINE, Inner Harbor East, 1000 Lancaster St., Suite 1000, Baltimore MD 21202. (410)752-4200. Fax: (410)625-0280. E-mail: bmag@abs.net. Website: http://www.baltimoremag.com. Editor: Ramsey Flynn. Contact: Ken Iglehart, managing editor. 10-20% freelance written. Monthly magazine. "Pieces must address an educated, active, affluent reader and must have a very strong Baltimore angle." Estab. 1907. Circ. 57,000. Pays within 60 days of acceptance. Byline given. Offers 30% kill fee. Buys first rights. Submit seasonal material 4 months in advance. Reports in 2 months on queries; 2 weeks on assigned mss; 3 months on unsolicited mss. Sample copy for $2.95 and 9×12 SAE with 10 first-class stamps. Writer's guidelines for a business-sized SASE.
Nonfiction: Book excerpt (Baltimore subject or author), essays, exposé, humor, interview/profile (w/Baltimorean), personal experience, photo feature, travel (local and regional to Maryland *only*). "Nothing that lacks a strong Baltimore focus or angle." Special issues: Education (October); Top Doctors (November); Holiday Events (December). Query with published clips or send complete ms. Length: 2,000-4,500 words. Pays $25-2,500 for assigned articles; $25-500 for unsolicited articles. Sometimes pays expenses of writers on assignment.
Columns/Departments: Hot Shot, Body & Soul. Length: 1,000-1,500 words. Query with published clips. "These shorter pieces are the best places to break into the magazine."

Tips: "Writers who live in the Baltimore area can send résumé and published clips to be considered for first assignment. Must show an understanding of writing that is suitable to an educated magazine reader and show ability to write with authority, describe scenes, help reader experience the subject. Too many writers send us newspaper-style articles. We are seeking: 1) *Human interest features*—strong, even dramatic profiles of Baltimoreans of interest to our readers. 2) *First-person accounts* of experience in Baltimore, or experiences of a Baltimore resident. 3) *Consumer*—according to our editorial needs, and with Baltimore sources. Writers new to us have most success with small humorous stories and 1,000-word personal essays that exhibit risky, original thought."

Massachusetts

BOSTON GLOBE MAGAZINE, *Boston Globe*, P.O. Box 2378, Boston MA 02107. (617)929-2955. Contact: Evelynne Kramer, editor-in-chief. Assistant Editors: Paul Hemp, Louise Kennedy. 50% freelance written. Weekly magazine. Circ. 805,099. **Pays on acceptance**. Publishes ms an average of 2 months after acceptance. Buys first serial rights. Editorial lead time 2 months. Submit seasonal material 3 months in advance. Reports in 2 months. Sample copy for 9×12 SAE with 2 first-class stamps.
Nonfiction: Exposé (variety of issues including political, economic, scientific, medical and the arts), interview (not Q&A), profile, book excerpts (first serial rights only). No travelogs or poetry. Buys up to 100 mss/year. Query; SASE must be included with ms or queries for return. Length: 2,500-5,000 words. Payment negotiable.
Photos: Purchased with accompanying ms or on assignment. Reviews contact sheets. Pays standard rates according to size used. Captions required.

BOSTON MAGAZINE, Metrocorp, 300 Massachusetts Ave., Boston MA 02115. (617)262-9700. Fax: (617)267-1774. E-mail: bosmag@aol.com. Website: http://www.bostonmagazine.com. Contact: Kerry Nugent-Wells. Editor: Craig Unger. 15% freelance written. Monthly magazine covering the city of Boston. Estab. 1972. Circ. 114,476. Pays on publication. Publishes ms an average of 3 months after acceptance. Byline given. Offers 20% kill fee. Buys first North American serial rights. Editorial lead time 2 months. Submit seasonal material 4 months in advance. Reports in 2 weeks on queries; 1 month on mss. Writer's guidelines free with SASE.
Nonfiction: Book excerpts, exposé, general interest, how-to, interview/profile, new product. Buys 20 mss/year. Query. Length: 1,200-5,000 words. Pays $400-5,000. Sometimes pays expenses of writers on assignment.
Photos: State availability of photos with submissions. Negotiates payment individually. Buys one-time rights.
Columns/Departments: Sports, Dining, Finance, City Life, Personal Style, Politics. Query. Pays $400-1,200.

CAPE COD LIFE, Including Martha's Vineyard and Nantucket, Cape Cod Life, Inc., P.O. Box 1385, Pocasset MA 02559-1385. (508)564-4466. Fax: (508)564-4470. E-mail: capelife@capecodlife.com. Website: http://www.capecod life.com. Editor: Brian F. Shortsleeve. Contact: Laura Reckford, managing editor. 80% freelance written. Bimonthly magazine focusing on "area lifestyle, history and culture, people and places, business and industry, and issues and answers for year-round and summer residents of Cape Cod, Nantucket and Martha's Vineyard as well as non-residents who spend their leisure time here." Circ. 39,500. Pays 30 days after publication. Byline given. Offers 20% kill fee. Buys first North American serial rights or makes work-for-hire assignments. Submit seasonal material 6 months in advance. Reports in 6 months on queries and ms. Sample copy for $5. Writer's guidelines for #10 SASE.
Nonfiction: General interest, historical, gardening, interview/profile, photo feature, travel, marine, nautical, nature, arts, antiques. Buys 20 mss/year. Query with or without published clips. Length: 1,000-3,000 words. Pays $100-400.
Photos: Pays $25-225 for photos. Captions and identification of subjects required. Buys first rights with right to reprint. Photo guidelines for #10 SASE.
Tips: "Freelancers submitting *quality* spec articles with a Cape Cod and Islands angle have a good chance at publication. We like to see a wide selection of writer's clips before giving assignments. We accept more spec work written about Cape and Islands history than any other subject. We also publish *Cape Cod Home: Living and Gardening on the Cape and Islands* covering architecture, landscape design and interior design with a Cape and Islands focus."

PROVINCETOWN ARTS, Provincetown Arts, Inc., 650 Commercial St., Provincetown MA 02657. (508)487-3167. Fax: (508)487-8634. Website: http://www.capecodaccess.com. Contact: Christopher Busa, editor. 90% freelance written. Annual magazine for contemporary art and writing. "*Provincetown Arts* focuses broadly on the artists and writers who inhabit or visit the Lower Cape, and seeks to stimulate creative activity and enhance public awareness of the cultural life of the nation's oldest continuous art colony. Drawing upon a 75-year tradition rich in visual art, literature, and theater, *Provincetown Arts* offers a unique blend of interviews, fiction, visual features, reviews, reporting, and poetry." Estab. 1985. Circ. 8,000. Pays on publication. Publishes ms an average of 4 months after acceptance. Offers 50% kill fee. Buys one-time and second serial (reprint) rights. Editorial lead time 6 months. Submit seasonal material 6 months in advance. Reports in 3 weeks on queries; 2 months on mss. Sample copy for $10. Writer's guidelines for #10 SASE.
Nonfiction: Book excerpts, essays, humor, interview/profile. Buys 40 mss/year. Send complete ms. Length: 1,500-4,000 words. Pays $150 minimum for assigned articles; $125 minimum for unsolicited articles. Sometimes pays expenses of writers on assignment.
Photos: Send photos with submission. Reviews 8×10 prints. Offers $20-100/photo. Identification of subjects required. Buys one-time rights.

Fiction: Mainstream. Also publishes novel excerpts. Buys 7 mss/year. Send complete ms. Length: 500-5,000 words. Pays $75-300.
Poetry: Buys 25 poems/year. Submit maximum 3 poems. Pays $25-150.

WORCESTER MAGAZINE, 172 Shrewsbury St., Worcester MA 01604-4636. (508)755-8004. Fax: (508)755-8860. E-mail: 75662.1176@compuserve.com. Contact: Martha M. Akstin, managing editor. 10% freelance written. Weekly tabloid emphasizing the central Massachusetts region. Estab. 1976. Circ. 40,000. Pays on publication. Publishes ms an average of 3 weeks after acceptance. Byline given. Buys all rights. Submit seasonal material 2 months in advance. Does not report on unsolicited material.
Nonfiction: Exposé (area government, corporate), how-to (concerning the area, homes, vacations), interview (local), personal experience, opinion (local), photo feature. "We are interested in any piece with a local angle." Buys 75 mss/ year. Length: 500-1,500 words. Pays $35-250.
Photos: Send photos with query. Pays $10 for b&w photos. Captions preferred; model release required. Buys all rights.

Michigan

ABOVE THE BRIDGE MAGAZINE, P.O. Box 41, Marquette MI 49855. Website: http://www.portup.com/above. Contact: Mikel B. Classen, editor. 75% freelance written. Bimonthly magazine. "All material, including fiction, has an Upper Peninsula of Michigan slant. Our readership is past and present UP residents." Circ. 3,500. Pays on publication. Publishes ms an average of 1 year after acceptance. Byline given. Buys one-time rights. Submit seasonal material 6 months in advance. Reports in 1 year. Sample copy for $4.50. Writer's guidelines for #10 SASE.
Nonfiction: Book excerpts (books on Upper Peninsula or UP writer), essays, historical/nostalgic (UP), interview/profile (UP personality or business), personal experience, photo feature (UP). Travel by assignment only. "This is a family magazine. No material in poor taste." Buys 90 mss/year. Send complete ms. Length: 500-2,000 words. Pays 2¢/word.
Reprints: Send typed ms with rights for sale noted and information about when and where the article previously appeared.
Photos: Send photos with submission. Reviews prints (5×7 or larger). Offers $5. Captions, model releases, identification of subjects required. Buys one-time rights.
Fiction: Ethnic (UP heritage), humorous, mainstream, mystery. No horror or erotica. "Material set in UP is required for publication." Buys 18 mss/year. Send complete ms. Length: 1,000-2,000 words. Pays 2¢/word.
Poetry: Free verse, haiku, light verse, traditional. No erotica. Buys 30 poems/year. Shorter poetry preferred. Pays $5.
Fillers: Anecdotes, short humor. Buys 25/year. Length: 100-500 words. Pays 2¢/word maximum.
Tips: "Material on the shorter end of our requirements has a better chance for publication. We're very well-stocked at the moment. We can't use material by out-of-state writers with content not tied to Upper Peninsula of Michigan. Know the area and people, read the magazine. Most material received is too long or not UP related. Stick to our guidelines. We love to publish well written material by previously unpublished writers."

ANN ARBOR OBSERVER, Ann Arbor Observer Company, 201 E. Catherine, Ann Arbor MI 48104. Fax: (313)769-3375. E-mail: hilton@aaobserver.com. Website: http://www.arborweb.com. Editor: John Hilton. 50% freelance written. Works with a small number of new/unpublished writers each year. Monthly magazine featuring the people and events in Ann Arbor. "We depend heavily on freelancers and we're always glad to talk to new ones. We look for the intelligence and judgment to fully explore complex people and situations, and the ability to convey what makes them interesting. We've found that professional writing experience is not a good predictor of success in writing for the *Observer*. So don't let lack of experience deter you. Writing for the *Observer* is, however, a demanding job. Our readers range from U-M faculty members to hourly workers at GT Products. That means articles have to be both accurate and accessible." Estab. 1976. Circ. 60,000. Pays on publication. Publishes ms an average of 2 months after acceptance. Byline given. Reports in 3 weeks on queries; several months on mss. Sample copy for 12½×15 SAE with $3 postage. Writer's guidelines free.
Nonfiction: Historical, investigative features, profiles, brief vignettes. Must pertain to Ann Arbor. Buys 75 mss/year. Length: 100-7,000 words. Pays up to $1,000/article. Sometimes pays expenses of writers on assignment.
Columns/Departments: Inside Ann Arbor (short, interesting tidbits), 200-500 words. Pays $75. Around Town (unusual, compelling ancedotes), 750-1,500 words. Pays $150-200.
Tips: "If you have an idea for a story, write a 100-200-word description telling us why the story is interesting. We are most open to intelligent, insightful features of up to 5,000 words about interesting aspects of life in Ann Arbor."

‡ON-THE-TOWN, The Arts & Entertainment Magazine of West Michigan, On-the-Town Publications, Inc., 705 Bagley SE, East Grand Rapids MI 49506. (616)451-0361. Fax: (616)454-4666. E-mail: townmag@mail.iserv.net. Contact: Christopher Scapelliti, editor. 80% freelance written. Monthly tabloid covering arts, entertainment, dining in west Michigan and literary offerings (fiction, essay). "Our readers share an interest in the arts. They are open-minded and quite accustomed to our frequent anti-establishment stance on social issues." Estab. 1982. Circ. 35,000. Pays on publication. Byline given. Offers 100% kill fee. Buys first rights and makes work-for-hire assignments. Editorial lead time 2 months. Submit seasonal material 2 months in advance. Accepts simultaneous submissions. Reports in 2 weeks on queries; 1 month on mss. Sample copy and writer's guidelines free.

Nonfiction: Book excerpts, interview/profile, personal experience, photo feature. Buys 60 mss/year. Send complete ms. Length: 600-1,000 words. Pays $50-75. Sometimes pays expenses of writers on assignment.
Reprints: Send photocopy of article or short story and information about when and where the piece previously appeared.
Photos: State availability of photos with submission. Reviews 4×6 prints. Offers $25/published photo. Identification of subjects required. Buys one-time rights.
Columns/Departments: In Session (new music on CD/tape/vinyl), 600 words; Pressing Issues (new books), 300-750 words; Cine-Matic (new alternative films), 600 words. Buys 100 mss/year. Send complete ms. Pays $25-75.
Fiction: Condensed novels, erotica, ethnic, experimental, fantasy, humorous, novel excerpts, slice-of-life vignettes. No "subjective morality masquerading as social dilemma i.e. inspirational pro-life stories and anti-drug anecdotes." Buys 3-6 mss/year. Send complete ms. Length: 1,000-2,500 words. Pays $100.
Poetry: Avant-garde, free verse, haiku, light verse, traditional. Buys 3-6 poems/year. Submit maximum 3 poems. Maximum length 60 lines. Pays $25-100.
Tips: "Make your cover letter a pitch letter. Tell me why I should be interested in what you're sending me. Also, no typos. They are an instant turn-off."

TRAVERSE, Northern Michigan's Magazine, Prism Publications, Inc., 121 S. Union St., Traverse City MI 49684. (616)941-8174. Fax: (616)941-8391. E-mail: traverse@freshwater.com or traversemag@aol.com. Contact: Carolyn Faught, managing editor. Editor: Deborah W. Fellows. 40% freelance written. Monthly magazine covering "the lifestyle, natural beauty and current events, including scenic and environmental points of interest, history, culture, art, homes, dining, shopping, activities and the people and places of Northern Michigan." Estab. 1981. Circ. 15,000. Pays on publication. Publishes ms an average of 6 months after acceptance. Offers 25% kill fee. Buys first North American serial rights. Editorial lead time 6 months. Submit seasonal material 1 year in advance. Accepts simultaneous submissions. Reports in 3 weeks on queries; 1 month on mss. Sample copy for $3.50 and SAE. Writer's guidelines for #10 SASE.
Nonfiction: Book excerpts, essays, exposé, general interest, historical/nostalgic, how-to, humor, interview/profile, personal experience. Buys 25-35 mss/year. Query with published clips or send complete ms. Length: 700-3,500 words. Pays $75-500 for assigned articles; $50-400 for unsolicited articles. Sometimes pays expenses of writers on assignment.
Reprints: Send tearsheet of article or short story and information about when and where the piece previously appeared.
Columns/Departments: Up in Michigan (profiles or first person accounts of elements of life in Northern Michigan), 750 words; Your Environment (what *you* can do to help the Northern environment—i.e., from land use to nature preservation, etc. Also, detail a hike or other natural experience as a destination.), 750 words. Buys 9-12 mss/year. Query with published clips or send complete ms. Pays $50-175. Great Northern Discovery (off-the-beaten-path short features—i.e., a shop, restaurant, hike, product, place to stay unique to Northern Michigan), 500-700 words. Buys 4-6 mss/year. Pays $50-100.
Fiction: Publishes very little fiction and only that which is rooted in or about Northern Michigan. Query with published clips or send complete ms. Length: 1,000-3,500 words. Pays $150-350.
Tips: "We're very writer-friendly! We encourage submissions on spec. We will review and accept, or return with comments/suggestions where applicable."

Minnesota

LAKE SUPERIOR MAGAZINE, Lake Superior Port Cities, Inc., P.O. Box 16417, Duluth MN 55816-0417. (218)722-5002. Fax: (218)722-4096. E-mail: edit@lakesuperior.com. Website: http://www.lakesuperior.com. Editor: Paul L. Hayden. Contact: Hugh Bishop, managing editor. 60% freelance written. Works with a small number of new/unpublished writers each year. Bimonthly regional magazine covering contemporary and historic people, places and current events around Lake Superior. Estab. 1979. Circ. 20,000. Pays on publication. Publishes ms an average of 10 months after acceptance. Byline given. Offers $25 kill fee. Buys first North American serial and some second rights. Submit seasonal material 1 year in advance. Reports in 2 months. Sample copy for $3.95 and 5 first-class stamps. Writer's guidelines for #10 SASE.
Nonfiction: Book excerpts, general interest, historic/nostalgic, humor, interview/profile (local), personal experience, photo feature (local), travel (local), city profiles, regional business, some investigative. Buys 45 mss/year. Query with published clips. Length 300-2,200 words. Pays $80-600. Sometimes pays the expenses of writers on assignment.
Photos: Quality photography is our hallmark. Send photos with submission. Reviews contact sheets, 2×2 and larger transparencies, 4×5 prints. Offers $20 for b&w and $40 for color. $75 for covers. Captions, model releases, identification of subjects required.
Columns/Departments: Current events and things to do (for Events Calendar section), less than 300 words; Around The Circle (media reviews; short pieces on Lake Superior; Great Lakes environmental issues; themes, letters and short pieces on events and highlights of the Lake Superior Region); I Remember (nostalgic lake-specific pieces), up to 1,100 words; Life Lines (single personality profile with photography), up to 900 words. Other headings include Destinations, Nature, Wilderness Living, Heritage, Shipwreck, Chronicle, Lake Superior's Own, House for Sale. Buys 20 mss/year. Query with published clips. Pays $90.
Fiction: Ethnic, historic, humorous, mainstream, novel excerpts, slice-of-life vignettes, ghost stories. Must be targeted regionally. Buys only 2-3 mss/year. Query with published clips. Length: 300-2,500 words. Pays $1-125.

Tips: "Well-researched queries are attended to. We actively seek queries from writers in Lake Superior communities. We prefer manuscripts to queries. Provide enough information on why the subject is important to the region and our readers, or why and how something is unique. We want details. The writer must have a thorough knowledge of the subject and how it relates to our region. We prefer a fresh, unused approach to the subject which provides the reader with an emotional involvement. Almost all of our articles feature quality photography, color or black and white. It is a prerequisite of all nonfiction. All submissions should include a *short* biography of author/photographer; mug shot sometimes used. Blanket submissions need not apply."

‡**MINNESOTA MONTHLY**, 10 S. Fifth St., Suite 1000, Minneapolis MN 55402. Contact: David Mahoney, editor. 50% freelance written. "*Minnesota Monthly* is a regional lifestyle publication written for a sophisticated, well-educated audience living primarily in the Twin Cities area." Estab. 1967. Circ. 80,000. **Pays on acceptance.** Guidelines for SASE.
Nonfiction: Regional news and events, issues, services, places, people. "We are looking for fresh ideas and concise, compelling, well-crafted writing." Query with résumé, published clips and SASE. Length: 1,000-4,000 words. Pay negotiable.
Columns/Departments: Insider (Minnesota news and slice-of-life stories), fewer than 400 words; Portrait (photo-driven profile), 360 words; People (three short profiles), 250 words each; Just Asking (interview), 900 words; Arts & Entertainment, 450 words; Midwest Traveler, 950-2,000 words; History; Back Page (essay), 500-600 words. Query with résumé, published clips and SASE. Pay negotiable.
Tips: "Our readers like to travel, eat out, attend arts events and read. With that in mind, our goal is to provide readers with the information they need to enrich their active lives."

MPLS. ST. PAUL MAGAZINE, 220 S. Sixth St., Suite 500, Pillsbury Center-South Tower, Minneapolis MN 55402-4507. (612)339-7571. Fax: (612)339-5806. Editor: Brian Anderson. Contact: Bonnie Blodgett, executive editor. Managing Editor: Allison Campbell. 70% freelance written. Monthly general interest magazine covering the metropolitan area of Minneapolis/St. Paul and aimed at college-educated professionals who enjoy living in the area and taking advantage of the cultural, entertainment and dining out opportunities. Reports on people and issues of importance to the community. Estab. 1978. Circ. 64,335. **Pays on acceptance.** Publishes ms an average of 3 months after acceptance. Byline given. Offers 25% kill fee. Buys first North American serial rights. Submit seasonal material 5 months in advance. Reports in 1 month. Sample copy for $4.18.
Nonfiction: Book excerpts, general interest, historical/nostalgic, interview/profile (local), new product, photo feature (local), travel (regional). Buys 200 mss/year. Query with published clips. Length: 1,000-4,000 words. Pays $100-1,500. Sometimes pays expenses of writers on assignment.
Photos: Jim Nelson, photo editor.
Columns/Departments: Nostalgia (Minnesota historical); Home (interior design, local). Query with published clips. Length: 750-2,000 words. Pays $100-500.

Mississippi

COAST MAGAZINE, Ship Island Holding Co., P.O. Box 1209, Gulfport MS 39502. (601)868-1182. Fax: (601)867-2986. Contact: Carla Arsaga, editor. 30% freelance written. Bimonthly magazine. "We describe ourselves as a lifestyle magazine. Our slant is positive and upbeat, but we aren't afraid to tackle tough or sensitive issues." Estab. 1993. Circ. 25,000. Pays on publication. Publishes ms an average of 4 months after acceptance. Byline given. Offers $25 kill fee. Buys first North American serial rights. Editorial lead time 4 months. Submit seasonal material 4 months in advance. Reports in 1 month on queries. Sample copy for $3. Writer's guidelines for #10 SASE.
Nonfiction: General interest, historical/nostalgic, humor, inspirational, interview/profile, new product, photo feature, travel. Buys 6 mss/year. Query with published clips. Pays $25-500. Sometimes pays expenses of writers on assignment.
Photos: Send photos with submission. Reviews 3×5 transparencies. Negotiates payment individually. Captions, model releases, identification of subjects required. Buys all rights.
Columns/Departments: Kathy O'Brien, assistant editor. Hot Shots (interesting people), 400 words; Art Scene (local artists), 1,000 words; Reflections (historical), 2,000 words. Buys 6 mss/year. Query with published clips. Pays $25-150.
Fiction: Buys 1 ms/year. Query with published clips. Length: 3,000 words maximum.
Tips: "Being familiar with *Coast Magazine* and its readership is a must. Freelancers should send the editor a cover letter that is indicative of his or her writing style along with strong writing samples."

Missouri

PITCH WEEKLY, Pitch Publishing, Inc., 3535 Broadway, Suite 400, Kansas City MO 64111-2826. (816)561-6061. Fax: (816)756-0502. E-mail: pitch@pitch.com. Website: http://www.pitch.com. Contact: Bruce Rodgers, editor. 75% freelance written. Weekly alternative newspaper that covers arts, entertainment, politics and social and cultural awareness in the Kansas City metro region. Estab. 1980. Circ. 85,000. Pays 1 month from publication. Buys first or one-time rights or makes work-for-hire assignments. Editorial lead time 1 month. Submit seasonal material 2 months in advance. *Query first!* Reports in 2 months on queries.

Nonfiction: Exposé, humor, interview/profile, opinion, news, photo feature. Special issues: all holidays; Best of Music; Best of Film; Education Guide. Buys 40-50 mss/year. Query with published clips. Length: 500-5,000 words. Pays $25-300. Sometimes pays expenses of writers on assignment. Prefers nonfiction with local hook.

Reprints: Send tearsheet or photocopy of article or short story or typed ms with rights for sale noted and information about when and where the piece previously appeared. Pays 50% of amount paid for an original piece.

Photos: Send photos with submission. Reviews contact sheets. Pays for photos with ms: $25-75. Captions and identification of subjects required. Buys one-time rights.

Fiction: Holiday-theme fiction published on Christmas, Thanksgiving, Valentine's Day, Halloween, April Fool's (humor/satire). "Must be slightly off-beat and good." Length: 1,500-2,500 words. Payment $75-125.

Tips: "Approach us with unusual angles on current political/social topics. Send well-written, clear, concise query with identifiable direction of proposed piece and SASE for reply or return. Previous publication in AAN paper a plus. We're looking for features and secondary features: current events in visual and performing arts (include new trends, etc.); social issues (OK to have an opinion as long as facts are well-documented); liberal politics."

RIVER HILLS TRAVELER, Todd Publishing, Route 4, Box 4396, Piedmont MO 63957. (314)223-7143. Contact: Bob Todd, editor. 60% freelance written. Monthly consumer tabloid covering "outdoor sports and nature in the southeast quarter of Missouri, the east and central Ozarks. Topics like those in *Field & Stream* and *National Geographic*." Estab. 1973. Circ. 7,500. Pays on publication. Publishes an average of 2 months after acceptance. Byline given. Buys one-time rights. Editorial lead time 2 months. Submit seasonal material 1 year in advance. Accepts simultaneous submissions. Reports in 1 month. Sample copy and writer's guidelines free.

Nonfiction: Historical/nostalgic, how-to, humor, opinion, personal experience ("Me and Joe"), photo feature, technical, travel. "No stories about other geographic areas." Buys 80 mss/year. Query with writing samples. Length: 1,500 maximum words. Pays $15-50. Sometimes pays expenses of writers on assignment.

Reprints: Send typed ms with rights for sale noted and information about when and where the article previously appeared. Pays 100% of amount paid for original article.

Photos: Send photos with submission. Reviews contact sheets and prints. Negotiates payment individually. Pays $25 for covers. Identification of subjects required. Buys one-time rights.

Fillers: Gags. Pays $10.

Tips: "We are a 'poor man's' *Field & Stream* and *National Geographic*—about the eastern Missouri Ozarks. We prefer stories relate an adventure that causes a reader to relive an adventure of his own or consider embarking on a similar adventure. By adventure, we mean active and new. Think of an adventure in camping or cooking, not just fishing and hunting. How-to is great, but not simple instructions. We encourage good first-person reporting."

SPRINGFIELD! MAGAZINE, Springfield Communications Inc., P.O. Box 4749, Springfield MO 65808-4749. (417)882-4917. Contact: Robert C. Glazier, editor. 85% freelance written. Eager to work with a small number of new/unpublished writers each year. "This is an extremely local and provincial monthly magazine. No *general* interest articles." Estab. 1979. Circ. 10,000. Pays on publication. Publishes ms an average of 6 months after acceptance. Byline given. Buys first serial rights. Submit seasonal material 1 year in advance. Reports in 3 months on queries; 6 months on mss. Sample copy for $5.30 and 9½ × 12½ SAE.

Nonfiction: Book excerpts (Springfield authors only), exposé (local topics only), historical/nostalgic (top priority but must be local history), how-to, humor, interview/profile (needs more on females than males), personal experience, photo feature, travel (1 page/month). Local interest *only*; no material that could appeal to other magazine elsewhere. Buys 150 mss/year. Query with published clips or send complete ms with SASE. Length: 500-5,000 words. Pays $35-250.

Photos: Send photos or send photos with query or ms. Reviews b&w and color contact sheets, 4 × 5 color transparencies, 5 × 7 b&w prints. Pays $5-35 for b&w, $10-50 for color. Captions, model releases, identification of subjects required. Buys one-time rights.

● *Springfield! Magazine* needs more photo features of a nostalgic bent.

Columns/Departments: Buys 250 mss/year. Query or send complete ms. Length varies, usually 500-2,500 words.

Tips: "We prefer writers read eight or ten copies of our magazine prior to submitting any material for our consideration. The magazine's greatest need is for features which comment on these times in Springfield. We are overstocked with nostalgic pieces right now. We also need profiles about young women and men of distinction."

Montana

MONTANA MAGAZINE, American Geographic Publishing, P.O. Box 5630, Helena MT 59604-5630. (406)443-2842. Fax: (406)443-5480. Editor: Beverly R. Magley. 90% freelance written. Bimonthly "strictly Montana-oriented magazine that features community and personality profiles, contemporary issues, travel pieces." Estab. 1970. Circ. 40,000. Publishes ms an average of 1 year after acceptance. Byline given. Offers $50-100 kill fee on assigned stories only. Buys one-time rights. Submit seasonal material at least 6 months in advance. Accepts simultaneous submissions. Reports in 3 months. Sample copy for $3.95. Writer's guidelines for #10 SASE.

Nonfiction: Essays, general interest, interview/profile, photo feature, travel. Special features on summer and winter destination points. Query by September for summer material; March for winter material. No 'me and Joe' hiking and hunting tales; no blood-and-guts hunting stories; no poetry; no fiction; no sentimental essays. Buys 30 mss/year. Query. Length: 300-3,000 words. Pays 15¢/word for articles. Sometimes pays the expenses of writers on assignment.

Reprints: Note when and where the article previously appeared. Pays 50% of amount paid for an original article.

Photos: Send photos with ms. Reviews contact sheets, 35mm or larger format transparencies, 5×7 prints. Additional payment for photos accepted with ms. Captions, model releases, subject identification required. Buys one-time rights.

Columns/Departments: Memories (reminisces of early-day Montana life), 800-1,000 words; Small Towns (profiles of communities), 1,500-2,000 words; Made in MT (successful cottage industries), 700-1,000 words plus b&w or color photo. Humor, 800-1,000 words. Query.

Tips: "We avoid commonly-known topics so Montanans won't ho-hum through more of what they already know. If it's time to revisit a topic, we look for a unique slant."

Nevada

NEVADA MAGAZINE, 1800 E. Hwy. 50, Carson City NV 89710-0005. (702)687-5416. Fax: (702)687-6159. E-mail: nevmag@aol.com. Website: http://www.travelnevada.com. Editor: David Moore. Contact: Carolyn Graham, associate editor. 50% freelance written. Works with a small number of new/unpublished writers each year. Bimonthly magazine published by the state of Nevada to promote tourism. Estab. 1936. Circ. 90,000. Pays on publication. Publishes ms an average of 6 months after acceptance. Byline given. Buys first North American serial rights. Submit seasonal material at least 6 months in advance. Reports in 1 month. Sample copy for $1. Writer's guidelines free.

Nonfiction: Nevada topics only. Historical, nostalgia, photo feature, people profile, recreational, travel, think pieces. "We welcome stories and photos on speculation." Publishes nonfiction book excerpts. Buys 40 unsolicited mss/year. Submit complete ms or query. Accepts phone queries. Length: 500-1,800 words. Pays $50-300.

Reprints: Rarely accepts reprints of previously published submissions. Send photocopy of article or typed ms with rights for sale noted and information about when and where the article previously appeared.

Photos: Denise Barr, art director. Send photo material with accompanying ms. Pays $10-75 for color transparencies and glossy prints. Name, address and caption should appear on each photo or slide. Buys one-time rights.

Tips: "Keep in mind the magazine's purpose is to promote Nevada tourism. Keys to higher payments are quality and editing effort (more than length). Send cover letter; no photocopies. We look for a light, enthusiastic tone of voice without being too cute; articles bolstered by facts and thorough research; and unique angles on Nevada subjects."

New Hampshire

‡**NEW HAMPSHIRE EDITIONS**, Connections Network, Inc., 100 Main St., Nashua NH 03060. Fax: (603)889-5557. E-mail: editor@nh.com. Website: http://www.nheditions.nh.com. Contact: Rick Broussard, editor. Managing Editor: Jennifer Breton. 50% freelance written. Monthly magazine devoted to New Hampshire people, issues, places, business. "We want stories written for, by and about the people of New Hampshire with emphasis on qualities that set us apart from other states. We promote business and economic development." Estab. 1986. Circ. 24,000. Pays on publication. Byline given. Offers 50% kill fee. Buys all rights. Editorial lead time 3 months. Submit seasonal material 3 months in advance. Accepts simultaneous submissions. Reports in 2 months on queries; 3 months on mss.

Nonfiction: Essays, general interest, historical/nostalgic, photo feature, travel, business. Buys 30 mss/year. Query with published clips. Length: 800-2,000 words. Pays $25-175. "We sometimes barter with advertisers and offer their products and services to writers." Sometimes pays expenses of writers on assignment.

Photos: State availability of photos with submission. Offers no additional payment for photos accepted with ms. Captions, model releases, identification of subjects required. Right purchased vary.

New Jersey

ATLANTIC CITY MAGAZINE, P.O. Box 2100, Pleasantville NJ 08232-1924. (609)272-7912. Fax: (609)272-7910. E-mail: epifanio@acy.digex.net. Contact: Editor. 80% freelance written. Works with small number of new/unpublished writers each year. Monthly regional magazine covering issues pertinent to the Jersey Shore area. Estab. 1978. Circ. 50,000. Pays on publication. Publishes ms an average of 4 months after acceptance. Byline given. Buys one-time rights. Offers variable kill fee. Submit seasonal material 6 months in advance. Reports in 6 weeks. Sample copy for $3 and 9×12 SAE with 6 first-class stamps. Writer's guidelines for SASE.

Nonfiction: Entertainment, general interest, recreation, history, lifestyle, interview/profile, photo feature, trends. "No hard news or investigative pieces. No travel pieces or any article without a south Jersey shore area/Atlantic City slant." Query. Length: 100-3,000 words. Pays $50-600 for assigned articles; $50-450 for unsolicited articles. Sometimes pays the expenses of writers on assignment.

Photos: Send photos. Reviews contact sheets, negatives, 2¼×2¼ transparencies, 8×10 prints. Pay varies. Captions,

model releases, identification of subjects required. Buys one-time rights.
Columns/Departments: Art, Business, Entertainment, Sports, Dining, History, Style, Real Estate. Query with published clips. Length: 500-2,000 words. Pays $150-400.
Tips: "Our readers are a broad base of local residents and visiting tourists. We need stories that appeal to both."

NEW JERSEY MONTHLY, P.O. Box 920, Morristown NJ 07963-0920. (201)539-8230. Contact: Jenny De Monte, editor. 50% freelance written. Monthly magazine covering "almost anything that's New Jersey-related." Estab. 1976. Circ. 94,000. Pays on completion of fact-checking. Byline given. Offers 10-30% kill fee. Buys first rights. Submit seasonal material 6 months in advance. Reports in 3 months. Sample copy for $5.95 (% Back Issue Dept.); writer's guidelines for #10 SASE.
  • This magazine continues to look for strong investigative reporters with novelistic style and solid knowledge of New Jersey issues.
Nonfiction: Book excerpts, essays, exposé, general interest, historical, humor, interview/profile, opinion, personal experience, travel. Special issues: Dining Out (February, August); Real Estate (March); Home & Garden (April); Great Weekends (May); Shore Guide (June); Fall Getaways (October); Holiday Shopping & Entertaining (November). "No experience pieces from people who used to live in New Jersey or general pieces that have no New Jersey angle." Buys 96 mss/year. Query with published magazine clips and SASE. Length: 200-3,000 words. Pays 30¢/word and up. Pays reasonable expenses of writers on assignment with prior approval.
  • Ranked as one of the best markets for freelance writers in *Writer's Yearbook* magazine's annual "Top 100 Markets," January 1996.
Photos: Send photos with submission. Payment negotiated. Identification of subjects and return postage required. "Submit dupes only. Drop off for portfolios on Wednesdays only. The magazine accepts no responsibility for unsolicited photography, artwork or cartoons." Buys exclusive first serial or one-time rights.
Columns/Departments: Business (company profile, trends, individual profiles); Health & Fitness (trends, personal experience, service); Home & Garden (homes, gardens, trends, profiles, etc.); Travel (in and out-of-state). Buys 36 mss/year. Query with published clips. Length: 750-1,500 words. Pays 30¢ and up/word.
Tips: "To break in, we suggest contributing briefs to our front-of-the-book section, 'Garden Variety' (light, off-beat items, trends, people, things; short service items, such as the 10 best NJ-made ice creams; short issue-oriented items; gossip; media notes). We pay a flat fee, from $50-150."

NEW JERSEY OUTDOORS, New Jersey Department of Environmental Protection, CN 402, Trenton NJ 08625. (609)633-7946. Fax: (609)984-0583. E-mail: njo@dep.state.nj.us. Website: http://www.state.nj.us/dep/njo. Editor: Beth Kuhles. 50% freelance written. Quarterly magazine highlighting New Jersey's natural and historic resources and activities related to them. Estab. 1950. Circ. 17,000. Pays on publication. Byline given. Buys one-time rights. Editorial lead time 1 year. Submit seasonal material 1 year in advance. Reports in 3 months on queries. Sample copy for $4.25. Writer's guidelines for #10 SASE.
Nonfiction: How-to, personal experience and general interest articles and photo features about the conservation and enjoyment of natural and historic resources (e.g., fishing, hunting, hiking, camping, skiing, boating, gardening, trips to/activities in specific New Jersey locations). "*New Jersey Outdoors* is not interested in articles showing disregard for the environment or in items demonstrating unskilled people taking extraordinary risks." Buys 30-40 mss/year. Query with published clips. Length: 600-2,000 words. Pays $100-500. Sometimes pays expenses of writers on assignment.
Reprints: Occasionally accepts previously published submissions. Send photocopy of article and information about when and where the article previously appeared. Pays 25-50% of amount paid for the original article.
Photos: State availability of photos with submission. Reviews transparencies and prints. Offers $20-125/photo. Buys one-time rights.
Columns/Departments: Afield (first person outdoor activities); Cityscape (environmental activities in cities or suburbs); Gardens (gardens or gardening tips); Outings (trips to specific N.J. locations); Profile (people who make a difference in environment); Volunteers (volunteers for environment). Buys 25 mss/year. Query with published clips. Pays $100-500.
Tips: "*New Jersey Outdoors* generally publishes season-specific articles, planned a year in advance. Topics should be fresh, and stories should be accompanied by *great* photography. Articles and photos *must* relate to New Jersey."

THE SANDPAPER, Newsmagazine of the Jersey Shore, The SandPaper, Inc., 1816 Long Beach Blvd., Surf City NJ 08008-5461. (609)494-2034. Fax: (609)494-1437. Contact: Jay Mann, managing editor. 10% freelance written. Weekly tabloid covering subjects of interest to Jersey shore residents and visitors. "*The SandPaper* publishes two editions covering many of the Jersey Shore's finest resort communities including Long Beach Island and Ocean City, New Jersey. Each issue includes a mix of news, human interest features, opinion columns and entertainment/calendar listings." Estab. 1976. Circ. 60,000. Pays on publication. Publishes ms an average of 1 month after acceptance. Byline given. Offers 100% kill fee. Buys first or all rights. Submit seasonal material 3 months in advance. Accepts simultaneous submissions. Reports in 1 month. Sample copy for 9×12 SAE with 8 first-class stamps.
Nonfiction: Essays, general interest, historical/nostalgic, humor, opinion, environmental submissions relating to the ocean, wetlands and pinelands. Must pertain to New Jersey shore locale. Also, arts, entertainment news, reviews if they have a Jersey Shore angle. Buys 10 mss/year. Send complete ms. Length: 200-2,000 words. Pays $25-200. Sometimes pays the expenses of writers on assignment.
Reprints: Send photocopy of article and information about when and where the article previously appeared. Pays 25-

50% of amount paid for an original article.

Photos: Send photos with submission. Offers $8-25/photo. Buys one-time or all rights.

Columns/Departments: SpeakEasy (opinion and slice-of-life, often humorous); Commentary (forum for social science perspectives); both 1,000-1,500 words, preferably with local or Jersey Shore angle. Buys 50 mss/year. Send complete ms. Pays $30.

Tips: "Anything of interest to sun worshippers, beach walkers, nature watchers and water sports lovers is of potential interest to us. There is an increasing coverage of environmental issues. The opinion page and columns are most open to freelancers. We are steadily increasing the amount of entertainment-related material in our publication. Articles on history of the shore area are always in demand."

New Mexico

NEW MEXICO MAGAZINE, Lew Wallace Bldg., 495 Old Santa Fe Trail, Santa Fe NM 87503. (505)827-7447. Editor-in-Chief: Emily Drabanski. Editor: Jon Bowman. Associate Editor: Walter K. Lopez. 70% freelance written. Monthly magazine emphasizing New Mexico for a college-educated readership with above average income and interest in the Southwest. Estab. 1922. Circ. 125,000. **Pays on acceptance.** Publishes ms an average of 6 months to a year after acceptance. Buys first North American serial rights. Submit seasonal material 1 year in advance. Reports in 2 months. Sample copy for $2.95. Writer's guidelines free.

● Ranked as one of the best markets for freelance writers in *Writer's Yearbook* magazine's annual "Top 100 Markets," January 1997.

Nonfiction: New Mexico subjects of interest to travelers. Historical, cultural, informational articles. "We are looking for more short, light and bright stories for the 'Asi Es Nuevo Mexico' section. However, we are publishing a 75th anniversary series from July '97-June '98. These are classic stories from past issues, so we will be buying fewer freelance pieces." No columns, cartoons, poetry or non-New Mexico subjects. Buys 7-10 mss/issue. Query with 3 published writing samples. No phone or fax queries. Length: 250-1,500 words. Pays $100-600.

Reprints: Rarely publishes reprints but sometimes publishes excerpts from novels and nonfiction books.

Photos: John Vaughan, art director. Purchased with accompanying ms or on assignment. Query or send contact sheet or transparencies. Pays $50-80 for 8×10 b&w glossy prints; $50-150 for 35mm—prefers Kodachrome. Photos should be in plastic-pocketed viewing sheets. Captions and model releases required. Buys one-time rights.

Tips: "Send a superb short (300 words) manuscript on a little-known person, event, aspect of history or place to see in New Mexico. Faulty research will ruin a writer's chances for the future. Good style, good grammar. No generalized odes to the state or the Southwest. No sentimentalized, paternalistic views of Indians or Hispanics. No glib, gimmicky 'travel brochure' writing. No first-person vacation stories. We're always looking for well-researched pieces on unusual aspects of New Mexico history and lively writing."

New York

ADIRONDACK LIFE, P.O. Box 97, Jay NY 12941-0097. Fax: (518)946-7461. E-mail: eimedia@aol.com. Contact: Elizabeth Folwell, editor. 70% freelance written. Prefers to work with published/established writers. Emphasizes the Adirondack region and the North Country of New York State in articles concerning outdoor activities, history and natural history directly related to the Adirondacks. Publishes 7 issues/year, including special Annual Outdoor Guide. Estab. 1970. Circ. 50,000. Pays 45 days after acceptance. Publishes ms an average of 6 months after acceptance. Buys first North American serial rights. Byline given. Submit seasonal material 1 year in advance. Reports in 1 month. Sample copy for $3 and 9×12 SAE. Writer's guidelines for #10 SASE.

Nonfiction: "*Adirondack Life* attempts to capture the unique flavor and ethos of the Adirondack mountains and North Country region through feature articles directly pertaining to the qualities of the area and through department articles examining specific aspects. Example: Barkeater (personal essay); Special Places (unique spots in the Adirondack Park); Working (careers in the Adirondacks); Wilderness (environmental issues); personal experiences." Special issues: Outdoors (May); Adirondack Photography (September). Buys 20-25 unsolicited mss/year. Query. Length: for features, 2,500-5,000 words; for departments, 1,200-2,400 words. Pays 25¢/word. Sometimes pays expenses of writers on assignment.

● Also considers first-serial novel excerpts in its subject matter and region.

Photos: All photos must have been taken in the Adirondacks. Each issue contains a photo feature. Purchased with or without ms or on assignment. All photos must be individually identified as to subject or locale and must bear photographer's name. Submit color transparencies or b&w prints. Pays $100 for full page, b&w or color; $300 for cover (color only, vertical in format). Credit line given.

Columns/Departments: Special Places; Watercraft; Barkeater (personal to political); Wilderness; Working; Home; Yesteryears; Kitchen; Profile; Historic Preservation; Sporting Scene.

Tips: "We are looking for clear, concise, well-organized manuscripts that are strictly Adirondack in subject. Check back issues to be sure we haven't already covered your topic."

AVENUE, 950 Third Ave., New York NY 10022. Fax: (212)758-7395. Editor-in-Chief: Sandra Bass. Managing Editor: Veronika Ullmer. Contact: Lisa Singer, assistant editor. 50% freelance written. Monthly magazine covering New York art, fashion, restaurants; business, design travel. "As *Avenue* is intended for readers on Manhattan's Upper East Side our subject matter is generally high end, and most pieces focus on a New York personality." Estab. 1976. Circ. 85,000. Pays on publication. Publishes ms an average of 2 months after acceptance. Byline given. Offers 15% kill fee. Buys all rights. Editorial lead time 3 months. Submit seasonal material 3 months in advance. Sample copy free.

Nonfiction: Essays, general interest, historical/nostalgic, humor, interview/profile, new product, opinion, personal experience, travel. No pieces lacking a strong upcoming New York news peg. Buys 30 mss/year. Query with published clips. Length: 150-1,800 words. Pays $150-1,500. Sometimes pays expenses of writers on assignment.

Photos: State availability of photos with submission. Reviews prints. Negotiates payment individually. Model releases, identification of subjects required. Buys one-time rights.

Columns/Departments: Columns (personal essay) 650 words; The A List (short profile tied to New York event) 150 words. Buys 30 mss/year. Query with published clips. Pays $150.

Tips: "Send submission by mail or fax after looking over a recent issue to familiarize yourself with our format."

‡BUFFALO SPREE MAGAZINE, Spree Publishing Co., Inc., 4511 Harlem Rd., Buffalo NY 14226-3859. (716)839-3405. Fax: (716)839-4384. Editor: Johanna Hall Van De Mark. Contact: Kerry Maguire, associate editor. 90% freelance written. Quarterly literary, consumer-oriented, city magazine. Estab. 1967. Circ. 21,000. Pays on publication. Publishes ms an average of 6-12 months after acceptance. Byline given. Buys first North American serial rights. Submit seasonal material 1 year in advance. Reports in 6 months on mss. Sample copy for $2 and 9 × 12 SAE with 9 first-class stamps.

Nonfiction: Essays, interview/profile, historical/nostalgic, humor, personal experience, regional, travel. Buys 50 mss/year. Send complete ms. Length: 1,000-2,000 words. Pays $100-150 for unsolicited articles.

Fiction: Original pieces with a strong sense of story. Literary humorous, mainstream and occasionally experimental. No pornographic or religious mss. Buys 60 mss/year. Send complete ms. Ideal length: 2,000 words. Pays $100-150.

Poetry: Janet Goldenberg, poetry editor. Buys 24 poems/year. Submit 4 poems max. Length: 50 lines maximum. Pays $25.

CITY LIMITS, City Limits Community Information Service, Inc., 40 Prince St., New York NY 10012. (212)925-9820. Fax: (212)996-3407. E-mail: citlim@aol.com. Website: http://www.citylimits.org. Contact: Kim Nauer, senior editor. Senior Editors: Kierna Mayo and Glenn Thrush. 50% freelance written. Works with a number of new/unpublished writers each year. Monthly magazine covering "news and issues in New York City as they relate to the city's poor, moderate and middle-income residents." Estab. 1976. Circ. 5,000. Pays on publication. Publishes ms an average of 2 months after acceptance. Byline given. Buys first North American serial, one-time or second serial (reprint) rights. Reports in 3 weeks. Sample copy for $4.

Nonfiction: Exposé, interview/profile, opinion, hard news, community profile. "No fluff, no propaganda." Length: 1,500-4,500 words. Pays $125-850. Sometimes pays expenses of writers on assignment.

Photos: Reviews contact sheets and 5 × 7 prints. Offers $20-40/photo. Identification of subjects required. Also interested in photo essays if they tell a compelling story about a particular issue. Buys one-time rights. By assignment only.

Columns/Departments: Briefs (brief news items on programs, policies, events, etc.), 250-400 words; Book Reviews (housing, urban development, planning, environment, criminal justice, etc.), 950 words; Pipeline (covers community organizations, new programs, government policies, etc.), 1,200-1,700 words; Profile (organizations, community groups, etc.), 1,200-1,700 words; PlanWatch (analysis of a particular urban or economic planning proposal); CityView (op-ed piece on current political affairs, city policy or other community-related issues); Spare Change (humor or satire on New York City issues). Buys 50-75 mss/year. Query with published clips. Pays $25-200.

Tips: "We are open to a wide range of story ideas in the community development field. If you don't have particular expertise in housing, urban planning, etc., start with a community profile or pertinent book or film review. The Briefs section is also good for anyone with reporting skills. We're looking for writing that is serious and informed but not academic or heavy handed."

LONG ISLAND UPDATE, MM&B Publishers, 990 Motor Pkwy., Central Islip NY 11722. (516)435-8890. Fax: (516)435-8925. Editor: Cheryl Ann Meglio. Managing Editor: Michael Coffino. Contact: Editorial Department. 50% freelance written. Monthly magazine. "*Update* features stories on topics concerning Long Islanders, from local events to new products. We also cover entertainment on both the local level and Hollywood." Estab. 1990. Circ. 56,000. Pays on publication. Publishes ms an average of 3 months after acceptance. Byline given. Buys first rights. Editorial lead time 2 months. Submit seasonal material 3 months in advance. Reports in 2 weeks on queries. Sample copy for 11 × 14 SAE with 8 first-class stamps. Writer's guidelines free.

Nonfiction: General interest, how-to (home remodeling, decorating, etc.), humor, interview/profile, new product, travel. Special issues: Bridal Guide (February 1997). Buys 100-120 mss/year. Query with published clips. Length: 200-1,700 words. Pays $25-125.

 THE DOUBLE DAGGER before a listing indicates that the listing is new in this edition. New markets are often more receptive to freelance submissions.

Photos: State availability of photos with submission. Reviews 3×5 transparencies, 5×7 prints. Offers no additional payment for photos accepted with ms. Buys one-time rights.
Columns/Departments: Business (money matters, personal finance); Gourmet (recipes, new products); Health (medical news, exercise, etc.; all 600-750 words. Query with published clips. Pays $25-50.
Fiction: Humorous. Buys 8-10 mss/year. Query with published clips. Length: 600-750 words. Pays $50.
Tips: "Queries are happily reviewed and responded to. Feel free to follow up with a phone call 2-3 weeks later."

NEW YORK MAGAZINE, K-III Magazine Corp., 755 Second Ave., New York NY 10017-5998. (212)880-0700. Editor: Caroline Miller. Managing Editor: Sarah Jewler. 25% freelance written. Weekly magazine focusing on current events in the New York metropolitan area. Circ. 433,813. **Pays on acceptance.** Offers 25% kill fee. Buys first world serial and electronic rights. Submit seasonal material 2 months in advance. Reports in 1 month. Sample copy for $3.50. Writer's guidelines for SASE.
Nonfiction: Exposé, general interest, profile, new product, personal experience, travel. Query. Pays $1/word. Pays expenses of writers on assignment.
Tips: "Submit a detailed query to Sarah Jewler, *New York*'s managing editor. If there is sufficient interest in the proposed piece, the article will be assigned."

NEW YORK SPORTSCENE, Sportscene Enterprises, Inc., 990 Motor Pkwy., Central Islip NY 11722. (516)435-8890. Fax: (516)435-8925. E-mail: mmbpub@pb.net. Editor in Chief: Anthony Stoeckert. Editor: Chris Ferraro. 80% freelance written. Monthly magazine "covering professional and major college teams in New York State, along with other notable events in the region (i.e.—Belmont Stakes, U.S. Open, NYC Marathon, etc.). Features include Interviews, Fan-in-the-street questions, trivia, calendar of upcoming games, etc." Estab. 1995. Circ. 125,000. Pays on publication. Publishes ms an average of 3 months after acceptance. Byline given. Makes work-for-hire assignments. Editorial lead time 3 months. Submit seasonal material 3 months in advance. Accepts simultaneous submissions. Sample copy free.
Nonfiction: Book excerpts, general interest, humor, interview/profile, new product, photo feature. Buys 90 mss/year. Query with published clips. Length: 500-1,500 words. Pays $25-75. Sometimes pays expenses of writers on assignment.
Reprints: Send typed ms or photcopy of article and when and where the article previously appeared. Pays $30-40.
Photos: State availability of photos with submission. Reviews transparencies. Negotiates payment individually. Captions, identification of subjects required.
Columns/Departments: Sports Cap (humorous take on NY sports), 750 words; Goat/Month/Penalty Box (those who ruin sports/give it a bad image), 750 words; Health/Fitness, 750 words. Buys 25 mss/year. Query with published clips. Pays $25-75.
Fiction: "As a new publication, we are looking for writers with solid contacts and creative story ideas. Obviously, a sports background is beneficial. We are especially interested in writers who can cover the lesser-covered sports—horse racing, tennis, golf, bowling, skiing, etc. Send résumé and clips for consideration."

NEWSDAY, Melville NY 11747-4250. Website: http://www.newsday.com. Contact: Noel Rubinton, viewpoints editor. Opinion section of daily newspaper. Byline given. Estab. 1940. Circ. 555,203.
Nonfiction: Seeks "opinion on current events, trends, issues—whether national or local, government or lifestyle. Must be timely, pertinent, articulate and opinionated. Preference for authors within the circulation area including New York City." Length: 700-800 words. Pays $150-200.
Tips: "It helps for prospective authors to be familiar with our paper and section."

SPOTLIGHT MAGAZINE, Meadow Publications Inc., 126 Library Lane, Mamaroneck NY 10543. (914)381-4740. Fax: (914)381-4641. Contact: Dana B. Asher, editor-in-chief. 50% freelance written. Monthly lifestyle magazine for the "upscale, educated, adult audience in the New York-New Jersey-Connecticut tri-state area. We try to appeal to a broad audience throughout our publication area." Estab. 1977. Circ. 73,000. Pays on publication. Byline given. Editorial lead time 3 months. Submit seasonal material 5 months in advance. Reports in 1 month. Sample copy for $3.
  ● *Spotlight* is looking for human interest articles and issue-related features woven around New York, New Jersey and Connecticut.
Nonfiction: Book excerpts, essays, exposé, general human interest, historical/nostalgic, how-to, humor, inspirational, interview/profile, new product, photo feature, travel, illustrations. Annual special-interest guides: Wedding (February, June, September); Dining (December); Home Design (March, April, October); Health (July, January); Education (January, August); Holiday Gifts (November); Corporate (March, October). No fiction or poetry. Buys 40 mss/year. Query. Pays $150 minimum.
Photos: State availability of or send photos with submission. Reviews transparencies and prints. Negotiates payment individually. Captions, model releases, identification of subjects required (when appropriate). Buys one-time rights.

SYRACUSE NEW TIMES, A. Zimmer, Ltd., 1415 W. Genesee St., Syracuse NY 13204. Fax: (315)422-1721. E-mail: newtimes@ras.com. Website: http://www.rway.com/newtimes/. Contact: Mike Greenstein, editor-in-chief. 50% freelance written. Weekly tabloid covering news, sports, arts and entertainment. "*Syracuse New Times* is an alternative weekly that can be topical, provocative, irreverent and intensely local." Estab. 1969. Circ. 43,000. Pays on publication. Publishes ms an average of 1 month after acceptance. Byline given. Buys one-time rights. Editorial lead time 3 months. Submit seasonal material 3 months in advance. Accepts simultaneous submissions. Reports in 2 weeks on queries; 1 month on mss. Sample copy for 9×11 SAE with 2 first-class stamps. Writer's guidelines for #10 SASE.

Nonfiction: Essays, general interest. Buys 200 mss/year. Query with published clips. Length: 250-2,500 words. Pays $25-200.
Reprints: Accepts previously published submissions.
Photos: State availability of photos or send photos with submission. Reviews 8×10 prints and color slides. Offers $10-25/photo or negotiates payment individually. Identification of subjects required. Buys one-time rights.
Tips: "Move to Syracuse and query with strong idea."

‡**TIME OUT NEW YORK**, Time Out New York Partners, LP, 627 Broadway, 7th Floor, New York NY 10012. (212)539-4444. Fax: (212)673-8382. Editor: Cyndi Stivers. Contact: Chris Bagley, features editor. 20% freelance written. Weekly magazine covering entertainment in New York City. "Those who want to contribute to *Time Out New York* must be intimate with New York City and its environs." Estab. 1995. Circ. 51,500. **Pays on acceptance.** Publishes ms an average of 1 month after acceptance. Byline sometimes given. Offers 25% kill fee. Makes work-for-hire assignments. Reports in 2 months.
Nonfiction: General interest, interview/profile, travel (within NYC area), reviews of various entertainment topics. No essays, articles about trends, unpegged articles. Query with published clips. Length: 250-1,500 words. Pays 20¢/word for b&w features and $300/page for color features.
Tips: "We're always looking for quirky, less-known news about what's going on in New York City."

North Carolina

CAROLINA COUNTRY, North Carolina Association of Electric Cooperatives, 3400 Sumner Blvd,, Raleigh NC 27604. E-mail: carolina.country@ncemcs.com. Editor: Michael E.C. Gery. 30% freelance written. Monthly magazine for members of North Carolina's electric cooperatives. General interest material concerning North Carolina's culture, business, history, people. Estab. 1952. Circ. 340,000. **Pays on acceptance.** Publishes ms an average of 3 months after acceptance. Byline given. Offers 50% kill fee. Buys all rights. Editorial lead time 3 months. Submit seasonal material 3 months in advance. Accepts simultaneous and previously published submissions (if outside North Carolina). Reports in 1 month on queries; 2 months on mss. All submissions must be made via e-mail.
Nonfiction: General interest, historical/nostalgic, humor, photo feature. Buys 12 mss/year. Send complete ms electronically. Length: 600-1,500 words. Pays $100-400.
Reprints: Send submission via e-mail. Pay negotiable.
Photos: State availability of photos with submission. Reviews transparencies, prints. Negotiates payment individually. Captions, identification of subjects required. Buys one-time rights.
Columns/Departments: Focus (useful resource news in North Carolina), 100 words. Buys 10 mss/year. Send complete ms electronically. Pays $20-100.
Tips: "Interested in North Carolina information that would not likely appear in local newspapers. Our readers are rural and suburban residents."

RALEIGH MAGAZINE, 5 West Hargett St., Suite 809, Raleigh NC 27601. (919)755-9200. Fax: (919)755-9201. E-mail: raleighmag@raleigh.vcn.com. Publisher: Bob Dill. 90% freelance written. Bimonthly magazine for Raleigh and regional lifestyles. "Though expanding, our current readership is largely female, 25-50. Our audience is urban, upscale, well-educated, and a mixture of native North Carolinians and young, mobile professionals making a warmer life in the sunbelt." *Raleigh* also publishes *Destination North Carolina*; published 3-4 times/year. Estab. 1978. Circ. 20,000. Pays on publication. Publishes ms an average of 2 months after acceptance. Byline given. Buys first North American serial rights. Editorial lead time 2 months. Submit seasonal material 4 months in advance. Accepts simultaneous submissions. Reports in 2 weeks on queries. Sample copy for $3 with 9×12 SASE. Writer's guidelines for #10 SASE.
Nonfiction: Essays, exposé, general interest, historical/nostalgic, how-to, humor, interview/profile, personal experience, photo feature, travel. "No generic how-to, pieces with no Raleigh or regional connection, humor with no Raleigh connection or syndicated (self or otherwise) material." Buys 30 mss/year. Query with published clips. Length: 750-2,500 words. Pays 12¢/word. Sometimes pays expenses of writers on assignment.
Reprints: Accepts previously published submissions.
Photos: Send photos with submission. Reviews transparencies and prints. Negotiates payment individually. Model releases and identification of subjects required. Buys one-time rights.
Columns/Departments: Essays (well written, humorous short essays on topics of interest to people who live in Raleigh), 750-1,000 words. Pays 12¢/word minimum; negotiable.
Fiction: "We run fiction once a year in our summer reading issue." Buys 1-2 mss/year. Query.
Tips: "For us, a strong feature idea is the best way to break in. New or interesting Raleigh or North Carolina slants on travel, fashion, personalities, are sought constantly here."

THE STATE: Down Home in North Carolina, P.O. Box 4552, Greensboro NC 27404. Fax: (910)286-0600. Contact: Mary Ellis, editor. "A monthly magazine, *Our State* has been the most comprehensive source of information on the people, places, events, attractions, history and folklore of North Carolina. Our readers are astute, with a keen eye for detail, and expect only the most factual material. We expect top-quality writing on subjects of interest to those who live in, visit or simply love the Tar Heel State." Estab. 1933. Circ. 25,000. Publishes ms an average of 1 year after acceptance. Byline given. No kill fee. Buys first serial rights. Pays on publication. Submit seasonal material 1 year in advance. Reports in 2 months. Sample copy for $2.75.

Nonfiction: General articles about places, people, events, history, nostalgia, general interest in North Carolina. Emphasis on travel in North Carolina. Will use humor if related to region. Length: 700-1,500 words average. Pays $150-250 for assigned articles; $75-125 for unsolicited articles.

Photos: Send photos with submission if possible. Reviews contact sheets and transparencies. Offers additional payment for photos. Captions and identification of subjects required. Buys one-time rights.

Columns/Departments: Tar Heel History ($125); Tar Heel Memories ($75); Tar Heel Profile (profiles of newsworthy North Carolinians).

‡**WILMINGTON MAGAZINE**, City Publishing USA, Inc., 201 N. Front St., Wilmington NC 28401. (910)815-0600. E-mail: dbetz@wilmington.net. Contact: Don Betz, publisher. Managing Editor: Kristin Gibson. 100% freelance written. Bimonthly magazine. "*Wilmington Magazine* appeals to residents, businesses and visitors alike. Our award-winning photography captures the faces and places of our community, complemented by articles that explore an indepth look at events and people. Estab. 1994. Circ. 8,000. Pays on publication. Publishes ms an average of 1 month after acceptance. Byline given. Buys first rights and one-time rights. Editorial lead time 6 weeks. Submit seasonal material 3 months in advance. Accepts simultaneous submissions. Reports in 1 month.

Nonfiction: Essays, general interest, historical/nostalgic, humor, interview/profile, photo feature, travel. No negative exposés or self-promotion. Buys 4 mss/year. Query with published clips. Length: 900-2,000 words. Pays 10-12.5¢/word. Sometimes pays expenses of writers on assignment.

Photos: Send photos with submission. Reviews transparencies. Offers $25-50/photo. Captions, model releases, identification of subjects required. Buys one-time rights.

Columns/Departments: Arts & Entertainment, Restaurant Spotlight, both 1,500-1,800 words. Buys 12 mss/year. Query with published clips. Pays 10-12.5¢/word.

Tips: "Be familiar with southeastern North Carolina."

Ohio

CINCINNATI MAGAZINE, 409 Broadway, Cincinnati OH 45202-3340. (513)421-4300. Fax: (513)562-2746. Contact: Emily Foster, editor. Homes Editor: Linda Vaccariello. Food Editor: Lilia F. Brady. Monthly magazine emphasizing Cincinnati living. Circ. 32,000. Pays on publication. Byline given. Buys all rights.

Nonfiction: Articles on personalities, business, sports, lifestyles, history relating to Cincinnati. Query. Feature length: 2,500-3,500 words. Pays $250-500.

Columns/Departments: Cincinnati dining, media, arts and entertainment, people, homes, politics, sports. Buys 2-4 mss/issue. Query. Length: 400-2,500 words. Pays $50-250.

Reprints: Rarely accepts reprints of previously published submissions. Send photocopy of article. Pays 50% of amount paid for an original article.

Tips: "Freelancers may find a market in quarterly Homes section (January, April, July, September), special sections on varying topics from golf to cardiac care. Always query in writing, with clips. All articles have a Cincinnati base. No generics, please. Also: no movie, book, theater reviews, poetry or fiction."

CLEVELAND MAGAZINE, City Magazines, Inc., 1422 Euclid Ave., #730Q, Cleveland OH 44115. Editor: Liz Ludlow. 70% freelance written, mostly by assignment. Monthly magazine with a strong Cleveland/northeast Ohio angle. Estab. 1972. Circ. 45,000. Pays on publication. Publishes ms an average of 3 months after acceptance. Byline given. Offers 50% kill fee. Buys first rights and second serial (reprint) rights. Editorial lead time 6 months. Submit seasonal material 8 months in advance. Accepts simultaneous submissions. Reports in 2 months.

Nonfiction: Book excerpts, general interest, historical/nostalgic, humor, interview/profile. Buys 1 ms/year. Query with published clips. Length: 800-5,000 words. Pays $200-800. Sometimes pays expenses of writers on assignment.

Columns/Departments: City Life (Cleveland trivia/humor/info briefs), 200 words. Buys 2 mss/year. Query with published clips. Pays $50.

COLUMBUS MONTHLY, P.O. Box 29913, Columbus OH 43229-7513. (614)888-4567. Editor: Lenore E. Brown. 20-40% freelance written. Prefers to work with published/established writers. Monthly magazine emphasizing subjects specifically related to Columbus and central Ohio. Pays on publication. Publishes ms an average of 2 months after acceptance. Byline given. Buys all rights. Reports in 1 month. Sample copy for $4.89.

Nonfiction: No humor, essays or first person material. "I like query letters which are well-written, indicate the author has some familiarity with *Columbus Monthly*, give me enough detail to make a decision and include at least a basic biography of the writer." Buys 4-5 unsolicited mss/year. Query. Length: 400-4,500 words. Pays $50-400. Sometimes pays the expenses of writers on assignment.

Photos: Send photos. Pay varies for b&w or color prints. Model release required.

Columns/Departments: Art, business, food and drink, politics, sports and theatre. Buys 2-3 columns/issue. Query. Length: 1,000-2,000 words. Pays $100-175.

Tips: "It makes sense to start small—something for our City Journal section, perhaps. Stories for that section run between 400-1,000 words."

‡**THE LIVING MAGAZINES**, Community Publications, Inc., 179 Fairfield Ave., Bellevue KY 41073. (606)291-1412. Fax: (606)291-1417. E-mail: livingreat@aol.com. Contact: Sean Halloran, managing editor. 53% freelance written. Group of monthly neighborhood magazines covering the people, places and events of Hyde Park, Oakwood, Wyoming, Orange Village, Moreland Hills, Pepper Pike, Indian Hill, and Blue Ash, Ohio; and Fort Mitchell and Fort Thomas, Kentucky. "We will not even entertain submissions without a direct tie to one of our communities." Circ. 1,100-5,500/magazine. Pays on publication. Publishes ms an average of 6 months after acceptance. Byline given, except for press releases. Buys one-time rights. Editorial lead time 3 months. Submit seasonal material 3 months in advance. Sample copy for $1.50 plus postage.
Nonfiction: Book excerpts (sometimes), general interest, historical/nostalgic, humor, inspirational, interview/profile, photo feature. No editorial opinions, political columns, new product reviews and travel articles. Buys 5 mss/year. Query with published clips. Length: 100-1,000 words. Pays $40 maximum. Does not pay for unsolicited articles. Sometimes pays the expenses of writers on assignment.
Photos: Send photos with ms. Negotiates payment individually. Subject identification required. Buys one-time rights.
Fiction: Historical, humorous, mainstream, slice-of-life vignettes. No unsolicited fiction. Buys 5 mss/year. Query with published clips. Length: 100-1,000 words. Pays $40 maximum.
Tips: "Write feature stories specific to one of our coverage areas, and find undiscovered stories among our readers. Keep the stories positive and be courteous and friendly when researching the story."

NORTHERN OHIO LIVE, LIVE Publishing Co., 11320 Juniper Rd., Cleveland OH 44106. (216)721-1800. Fax: (216)721-2525. E-mail: live@apki.net. Contact: Anton Zuiker, editor. Managing Editor: Kate Maloney. 70% freelance written. Monthly magazine covering Northern Ohio's arts, entertainment, education and dining. "*LIVE*'s reader demographic is mid-30s to 50s, though we're working to bring in the late 20s. Our readers are well-educated, many with advanced degrees. They're interested in Northern Ohio's cultural scene and support it." Estab. 1980. Circ. 32,000. Pays 20th of publication month. Publishes ms an average of 1 month after acceptance. Byline given. Offers 50% kill fee. Buys first North American serial rights. Editorial lead time 2 months. Submit seasonal material 4 months in advance. Reports in 3 weeks on queries; 2 months on mss. Sample copy for $3.
Nonfiction: Essays, exposé, general interest, humor, interview/profile, photo feature, travel. All should have a Northern Ohio slant and preferably an arts focus. Special issues: Gourmet Guide (restaurants) (May); Gallery Tour (May, October); After 5 (nightlife) (November). "No business/corporate articles." Buys 100 mss/year. Query with published clips. Length: 1,000-3,500 words. Pays $100-350. Sometimes pays expenses of writers on assignment.
Photos: State availability of photos with submission. Reviews contact sheets, 4×5 transparencies and 3×5 prints. Negotiates payment individually. Identification of subjects required. Buys one-time rights.
Columns/Departments: News & Reviews (arts previews, personality profiles, general interest), 800-1,800 words. Buys 60-70 mss/year. Query with published clips. Pays $100-150.

OHIO MAGAZINE, Ohio Magazine, Inc., Subsidiary of Dispatch Printing Co., 62 E. Broad St., Columbus OH 43215-3522. (614)461-5083. Website: http://www.ohiomagazine.com. Editor: Jean P. Kelly. 70% freelance written. Works with a small number of new/unpublished writers each year. Magazine published 10 times/year emphasizing news and feature material of Ohio for an educated, urban and urbane readership. Estab. 1978. Circ. 100,000. **Pays on acceptance.** Publishes ms an average of 6 months after acceptance. Buys all, second serial (reprint), one-time, first North American serial or first serial rights. Byline given except on short articles appearing in sections. Submit seasonal material minimum 6 months in advance. Reports in 3 months. Sample copy for $3 and 9×12 SAE. Writer's guidelines for #10 SASE.
Nonfiction: Features: 1,500-3,000 words. Pays $800-1,400. Sometimes pays expenses of writers on assignment.
Columns/Departments: Buys minimum 20 unsolicited mss/year.
Reprints: Accepts previously published submissions. Send tearsheet or photocopy of article and information about when and where article previously appeared. Pays 50% of amount paid for an original article.
Photos: Brooke Wenstrup, art director. Rate negotiable.
Tips: "Freelancers should send all queries in writing, not by telephone or fax. Successful queries demonstrate an intimate knowledge of the publication. Subject matter should be global enough to appeal to readers outside of Ohio, but regional enough to call our own. Ohio has diverse geography and people. A piece affecting a certain part of the state must also have statewide ramifications."

OVER THE BACK FENCE, Southern Ohio's Own Magazine, Back Fence Publishing, Inc., P.O. Box 756, Chillicothe OH 45601. (614)772-2165. Fax: (614)773-9273. E-mail: backfencpb@aol.com. Website: http://www.backfence.com. Contact: Ann Zalek, editor-in-chief. Quarterly magazine. "We are a regional magazine serving 18 counties in Southern Ohio. *Over The Back Fence* has a wholesome, neighborly style. It appeals to readers from young adults to seniors, often encouraging reader participation through replies." Estab. 1994. Circ. 15,000. Pays on publication. Byline given. Buys one-time North American print publication rights, making some work-for-hire assignments. Editorial lead time 6-12 months. Submit seasonal material 6-12 months in advance. Accepts simultaneous submissions, if so noted. Reports in 3 months. Sample copy for $4. Writer's guidelines for #10 SASE.
Nonfiction: General interest, historical/nostalgic, humor, inspirational, interview/profile, personal exprience, photo feature, travel. Buys 9-12 mss/year. Query with or without published clips or send complete ms. Length: 750-2,000 words. Pays 10¢/word minimum, negotiable depending on experience.

Reprints: Send photocopy of article or short story and typed ms with rights for sale noted and information about when and where the piece previously appeared. Pay negotiable.

Photos: State availability of photos with submission or send photos with submission. Reviews color transparencies (35mm or larger), 3⅕×5 prints. Offers $25-100/photo. Captions, model releases and identification of subjects required. Buys one-time usage rights. "If photos are to be sent as part of a text/photo package, please request our photo guidelines and submit color transparencies."

Columns/Departments: The Arts, 750-2,000 words; History (relevant to a designated county), 750-2,000 words; Inspirational (poetry or short story), minimum for poetry 4 lines, short story 600-850 words; Recipes, 750-2,000 words; Profiles From Our Past, 300-600 words; Sport & Hobby, 750-2,000 words; Our Neighbors (i.e., people helping others), 750-2,000 words. All must be relevant to Southern Ohio. Buys 24 mss/year. Query with or without published clips or send complete ms. Pays 10¢/word minimum, negotiable depending on experience; 10¢/word or minimum $25 whichever is greater for poetry.

Fiction: Humorous. Buys 4 mss/year. Query with published clips. Length: 300-850 words. Pays 10¢/word minimum, negotiable depending on experience.

Poetry: Wholesome, traditional free verse, light verse and rhyming. Buys 4 poems/year. Submit maximum 4 poems. Length: 4-32 lines preferred. Pays 10¢/word or $25 minimum.

Fillers: Anecdotes, short humor. Buys 0-8/year. Length: 100 words maximum. Pays 10¢/word or $25 minimum.

Tips: "Our approach can be equated to a friendly and informative conversation with a neighbor about interesting people, places and events in Southern Ohio (counties: Adams, Athens, Clinton, Fayette, Fairfield, Gallia, Greene, Highland, Hocking, Jackson, Lawrence, Meigs, Pickaway, Pike, Ross, Scioto, Vinton and Washington)."

PLAIN DEALER SUNDAY MAGAZINE, Plain Dealer Publishing Co., 1801 Superior Ave., Cleveland OH 44114. (216)344-4546. Fax: (216)999-6354. Contact: Anne Gordon, editor. 30% freelance written. Sunday weekly/general interest newspaper magazine focusing on Cleveland and northeastern Ohio. Circ. 550,000. Pays on publication. Publishes ms an average of 3 months after acceptance. Byline given. Buys first or one-time rights. Submit seasonal material 3 months in advance. Reports in 1 month on queries; 2 months on mss. Sample copy for $1.

Nonfiction: Profiles, in-depth features, essays, exposé, historical/nostalgic, humor, personal experience. Must focus on northeast Ohio people, places and issues. Buys 20 mss/year. Query with published clips or send complete ms. Mss must be double-spaced and should include a daytime telephone number. Length: 800-3,000 words. Pays $150-500.

Reprints: Occasionally accepts previously published submissions. Send typed ms with rights for sale noted and information about when and where the article previously appeared.

Photos: Send photos with submission. Buys one-time rights.

Columns/Departments: I Say (serious or humorous personal experience), 800 words. Pays $150.

Tips: "We're always looking for good writers and good stories."

Oklahoma

OKLAHOMA TODAY, P.O. Box 53384, Oklahoma City OK 73152-9971. Fax: (405)521-3992. E-mail: okteditor@mail.otrd.state.ok.us. Contact: Jeanne M. Devlin, editor. 80% freelance written. Works with a small number of new/unpublished writers each year. Bimonthly magazine covering people, places and things Oklahoman. "We are interested in showing off the best Oklahoma has to offer; we're pretty serious about our travel slant but regularly run history, nature and personality profiles." Estab. 1956. Circ. 45,000. **Pays on final acceptance.** Publishes ms an average of 6 months after acceptance. Byline given. Buys first serial rights. Submit seasonal material 1 year in advance "depending on photographic requirements." Reports in 4 months. Sample copy $2.50 and 9×12 SASE. Guidelines for #10 SASE.

● *Oklahoma Today* has won Magazine of the Year, awarded by the International Regional Magazine Association, four out of the last six years.

Nonfiction: Book excerpts (on Oklahoma topics); photo feature and travel (in Oklahoma). Special issues: Oklahoma Oil (Fall 1997); Native America (Spring 1998). Buys 40-60 mss/year. Query with published clips; no phone queries. Length: 1,000-3,000 words. Pays $25-750.

Reprints: Send photocopy of article and information about when and where the article previously appeared. Pay varies.

Photos: High-quality transparencies, b&w prints. "We are especially interested in developing contacts with photographers who live in Oklahoma or have shot here. Send samples and price range." Photo guidelines for SASE. Pays $50-100 for b&w and $50-750 for color; reviews 2¼ and 35mm color transparencies. Model releases, identification of subjects, other information for captions required. Buys one-time rights plus right to use photos for promotional purposes.

Tips: "The best way to become a regular contributor to *Oklahoma Today* is to query us with one or more story ideas, each developed to give us an idea of your proposed slant. We're looking for *lively*, concise, well-researched and reported stories, stories that don't need to be heavily edited and are not newspaper style. We have a two-person editorial staff, and freelancers who can write and have done their homework get called again and again."

Oregon

CASCADES EAST, P.O. Box 5784, Bend OR 97708-5784. (541)382-0127. Fax: (541)382-7057. E-mail: sunpub@sun-pub.com. Website: http://www.sunpub.com. Publisher: Geoff Hill. Associate Publisher/Editor: Kim Hogue, 90% freelance written. Prefers to work with published/established writers. Quarterly magazine for "all ages as long as they are interested in outdoor recreation in central Oregon: fishing, hunting, sight-seeing, golf, tennis, hiking, bicycling, mountain climbing, backpacking, rockhounding, skiing, snowmobiling, etc." Estab. 1972. Circ. 10,000 (distributed throughout area resorts and motels and to subscribers). Pays on publication. Publishes ms an average of 6 months after acceptance. Buys all rights. Byline given. Submit seasonal material at least 6 months in advance. Reports in 3 months. Sample copy and writer's guidelines for $5 and 9×12 SAE.

• *Cascades East* now accepts and prefers manuscripts along with a 3.5 disk. They can translate most word processing programs. You can also send electronic submissions.

Nonfiction: General interest (first person experiences in outdoor central Oregon—with photos, can be dramatic, humorous or factual), historical (for feature, "Little Known Tales from Oregon History," with b&w photos), personal experience (needed on outdoor subjects: dramatic, humorous or factual). "No articles that are too general, sight-seeing articles that come from a travel folder, or outdoor articles without the first-person approach." Buys 20-30 unsolicited mss/year. Query. Length: 1,000-2,000 words. Pays 5-10¢/word.

Reprints: Send information about when and where the article previously appeared.

Photos: "Old photos will greatly enhance chances of selling a historical feature. First-person articles need b&w photos also." Pays $10-25 for b&w; $15-100 for transparencies. Captions preferred. Buys one-time rights.

Tips: "Submit stories a year or so in advance of publication. We are seasonal and must plan editorials for summer '98 in the spring of '97, etc., in case seasonal photos are needed."

OREGON COAST, P.O. Box 18000, 1525 12st St., Florence OR 97439-0130. (541)997-8401 or (800)348-8401. Fax: (541)997-1124. Editors: Judy Fleagle and Jim Forst. 65% freelance written. Bimonthly regional magazine covering the Oregon Coast. Estab. 1982. Circ. 70,000. Pays after publication. Publishes ms an average of 1 year after acceptance. Byline given. Offers 33% kill fee. Buys first North American serial rights. Submit seasonal material 6 months in advance. Reports in 1 month on queries; 3 months on mss. Sample copy for $4.50. Writer's guidelines for #10 SASE.

• This magazine is using fewer freelancers because its staff is doing more writing inhouse. This company also publishes *Northwest Travel* and *Oregon Outside*.

Nonfiction: "A true regional with general interest, historical/nostalgic, humor, interview/profile, personal experience, photo feature, travel and nature as pertains to Oregon Coast." Buys 55 mss/year. Query with published clips. Length: 500-2,000 words. Pays $75-350 plus 2-5 contributor copies.

Reprints: Sometimes accepts previously published submissions. Enclose clips. Send tearsheet or photocopy of article and information about when and where the article previously appeared. Pays an average of 75% of the amount paid for an original article.

Photos: Send photos with submission. Reviews 35mm or larger transparencies and 3×5 or larger prints (with negatives for color). Photo submissions with no ms or stand alone or cover photos. Captions, model releases (for covers), photo credits, identification of subjects required. Buys one-time rights.

Fillers: Newsbreaks (no-fee basis).

Tips: "Slant article for readers who do not live at the Oregon Coast. At least one historical article is used in each issue. Manuscript/photo packages are preferred over mss with no photos. List photo credits and captions for each print or slide. Check all facts, proper names and numbers carefully in photo/ms packages. Need stories with great color photos— could be photo essays. Must pertain to Oregon Coast somehow."

‡**OREGON OUTSIDE**, Educational Publications Foundation, P.O. Box 18000, 1525 12th St., Suite C, Florence OR 97439-0130. (800)348-8401. Fax: (541)997-1124. Contact: Judy Fleagle, editor. 70% freelance written. Quarterly magazine covering "outdoor activities for experts as well as for families and older folks, from easy hikes to extreme skiing. We like first person, lively accounts with quotes, anecdotes, compelling leads and satisfying endings. Nitty-gritty info can be in sidebars. Send a rough map if needed." Estab. 1993. Circ. 20,000. Publishes ms an average of 1 year after acceptance. Byline given. 33% kill fee. Buys first North American serial (stories and story/photo packages) and one-time rights (stand alone photos, covers and calendars). Editorial lead time 4 months. Submit seasonal material 6 months in advance. Reports in 2 months on queries; 3 months on mss. Sample copy $4.50. Guidelines for #10 SASE.

Nonfiction: Book excerpts, how-to, interview/profile, new product, personal experience, photo feature. "Nothing overdone. We like understatement." Query with published clips. Length: 800-1,750 words. Pays $100-350.

Reprints: Send photocopy of article and information about when and where the story previously appeared. Pays 60% of amount paid for an original article.

Photos: Send photos with submission. Reviews 35mm up to 4×5 transparencies and prints (color with negatives). Offers $25-75 with story, $350/cover photo, $75/stand alone, $100/calendar. Captions, model releases, identification of subjects required for cover consideration. Buys one-time rights.

Columns/Departments: Back Page (unusual outdoor photo with technical information), 80-100 words. Contact: Judy Fleagle. Query with photo. Pays $75. Product Roundup, 800-1,000 words. Contact: Jim Forst. Query with published clips. Pays $100-150. Buys 12 mss/year.

Fillers: Newsbreaks, events. Uses 10/year. Length: 200-400 words. Does not pay for fillers.

Tips: "A short piece with a couple super photos for a 1- or 2-page article" is a freelancer's best chance for publication.

WILLAMETTE WEEK, Portland's Newsweekly, City of Roses Co., 822 SW Tenth Ave., Portland OR 97205. (503)243-2122. Fax: (503)243-1115. E-mail: rrana@wweek.com. Website: http://www.wweek.com. Editor: Mark Zusman. 50% freelance written. Weekly alternative newsweekly focusing on local news. Estab. 1974. Circ. 75,000. Pays on publication. Byline given. Offers 25% kill fee. Buys first North American serial rights. Editorial lead time 2 months. Submit seasonal material 2 months in advance. Accepts simultaneous submissions. Reports in 1 month. Sample copy and writer's guidelines for #10 SASE.

Nonfiction: Exposé, interview/profile. Special issues: Summer Guide, Best of Portland, Fall Arts, 21st Anniversary. Buys 30 mss/year. Query. Length: 400-3,000 words. Pays 10-30¢/word. Sometimes pays on-assignment expenses.

Reprints: Accepts previously published submissions. Pay negotiable.

Photos: State availability of photos with submission. Reviews contact sheets. Negotiates payment individually. Model releases, identification of subjects required. Buys one-time rights.

Fiction: Rarely accepts novel excerpts.

Pennsylvania

PENNSYLVANIA, Pennsylvania Magazine Co., P.O. Box 576, Camp Hill PA 17001-0576. (717)697-4660. Publisher: Albert E. Holliday. Contact: Matt Holliday, editor. 90% freelance written. Bimonthly magazine. Estab. 1981. Circ. 40,000. **Pays on acceptance** except for articles (by authors unknown to us) sent on speculation. Publishes ms an average of 1 year after acceptance. Byline given. Offers 25% kill fee for assigned articles. Buys first North American serial or one-time rights. Submit seasonal queries 6-9 months in advance. Reports in 1 month. Sample copy for $2.95. Writer's guidelines for #10 SASE.

Nonfiction: Features include general interest, historical/nostalgic, photo feature, vacations and travel, people/family success stories, consumer-related inventions, serious statewide issues—all dealing with or related to Pennsylvania. Nothing on Amish topics, hunting or skiing. Buys 75-120 mss/year. Query. Length: 750-2,500 words. Pays $50-400. *Will not consider without illustrations*; send photocopies of possible illustrations with query or mss.

Reprints: Send photocopy of article, typed ms with rights for sale noted and information about when and where the article previously appeared. Pays 5¢/word.

Photos: Reviews 35mm and 2¼ color transparencies (no originals) and 5×7 to 8×10 color and b&w prints. Do not send original slides. Pays $15-25 for inside photos; up to $100 for covers. Captions required. Buys one-time rights.

Columns/Departments: Panorama (short items about people, unusual events, family and individually owned consumer-related businesses), 250-500 words; Almanac (short historical items), 1,000-2,500 words; Museums, 400-500 words. All must be illustrated.

Tips: "Our publication depends upon freelance work—send queries."

PENNSYLVANIA HERITAGE, Pennsylvania Historical and Museum Commission and the Pennsylvania Historical Society, P.O. Box 1026, Harrisburg PA 17108-1026. (717)787-7522. Fax: (717)787-8312. Website: http://www.state.pa. us. Editor: Michael J. O'Malley III. 90% freelance written. Prefers to work with published/established writers. Quarterly magazine. "*Pennsylvania Heritage* introduces readers to Pennsylvania's rich culture and historic legacy, educates and sensitizes them to the value of preserving that heritage and entertains and involves them in such a way as to ensure that Pennsylvania's past has a future. The magazine is intended for intelligent lay readers." Estab. 1974. Circ. 13,000. **Pays on acceptance.** Publishes ms an average of 1 year after acceptance. Byline given. Buys all rights. Accepts simultaneous queries and submissions. Reports in 6 weeks on queries; 6 months on mss. Sample copy for $5 and 9×12 SAE; writer's guidelines for #10 SASE.

- *Pennsylvania Heritage* is now considering freelance submissions that are shorter in length (2,000 to 3,000 words), pictorial/photographic essays, biographies of famous (and not-so-famous Pennsylvanians) and interviews with individuals who have helped shape, make, preserve the Keystone State's history and heritage.

Nonfiction: Art, science, biographies, industry, business, politics, transportation, military, historic preservation, archaeology, photography, etc. No articles which in no way relate to Pennsylvania history or culture. "Our format requires feature-length articles. Manuscripts with illustrations are especially sought for publication. We are now looking for shorter (2,000 words) manuscripts that are heavily illustrated with *publication-quality* photographs or artwork. We are eager to work with experienced travel writers for destination pieces on historical sites and museums that make 'The Pennsylvania Trail of History.' " Buys 20-24 mss/year. Prefers to see mss with suggested illustrations. Length: 2,000-3,500 words. Pays $100-500.

Photos: State availability of, or send photos with ms. Pays $25-100 for transparencies; $5-25 for b&w photos. Captions and identification of subjects required. Buys one-time rights.

Tips: "We are looking for well-written, interesting material that pertains to any aspect of Pennsylvania history or culture. Potential contributors should realize that, although our articles are popularly styled, they are not light, puffy or breezy; in fact they demand strident documentation and substantiation (sans footnotes). The most frequent mistake made by writers in completing articles for us is making them either too scholarly or too sentimental or nostalgic. We want material which educates, but also entertains. Authors should make history readable and enjoyable. Our goal is to make the Keystone State's history come to life in a meaningful, memorable way."

‡PHILADELPHIA MAGAZINE, Curtco Freedom Group, 1818 Market St., 36th Floor, Philadelphia PA 19103. (215)564-7700. Fax: (215)656-3500. President/Publisher: David R. Lipson. Monthly magazine. "*Philadelphia* is edited for the area's community leaders and their families. It provides in-depth reports on crucial and controversial issues confronting the region—business trends, political analysis, metropolitan planning, sociological trends—plus critical

reviews of the cultural sports and entertainment scene." Estab. 1908. Circ. 133,083.
Nonfiction: "Articles range from law enforcement to fashion, voting trends to travel, transportation to theater, also includes background studies of the area newsmakers." *Writer's Market* recommends sending query with SASE.
Tips: "*Philadelphia Magazine* readers are an affluent, interested and influential group who can afford the best the region has to offer. They're the greater Philadelphia area residents who care about the city and its politics, lifestyles, business and culture."

PITTSBURGH MAGAZINE, WQED Pittsburgh, 4802 5th Ave., Pittsburgh PA 15213. (412)622-1360. Fax: (412)622-7066. E-mail: editor@wqed.org. Website: http://www.wqed.org/. Contact: Michelle Pilecki, managing editor. "*Pittsburgh* presents issues, analyzes problems and strives to encourage a better understanding of the community." 60% freelance written. Prefers to work with published/established writers. The monthly magazine is purchased on newsstands and by subscription and is given to those who contribute $40 or more/year to public TV in western Pennsylvania. Estab. 1970. Circ. 75,000. Pays on publication. Publishes ms an average of 2 months after acceptance. Buys first North American serial rights and second serial (reprint) rights. Offers kill fee. Byline given. Submit seasonal material 6 months in advance. Reports in 2 months. Sample copy for $2 (old back issues).
● Editor reports a need for more hard news and stories targeting readers in their 30s and 40s, especially those with young families.
Nonfiction: "Without exception—whether the topic is business, travel, the arts or lifestyle—each story is clearly oriented to Pittsburghers or the greater Pittsburgh region of today. We have minimal interest in historical articles and do not publish fiction, poetry, advocacy or personal reminiscence pieces." Exposé, lifestyle, sports, informational, service, business, medical, profile. Must have greater Pittsburgh angle. Query in writing with outline and clips. Length: 3,500 words or less. Pays $100-1,200.
Photos: Query for photos. Model releases required. Pays pre-negotiated expenses of writers on assignment.
Tips: "Less need for soft stories, e.g. feature profiles and historical pieces. Expanded need for service pieces geared to our region. More hard news."

SEVEN ARTS, Penn Communications Group, 260 S. Broad St., 3rd Floor, Philadelphia PA 19102. E-mail: editorial@sevenarts.voicenet.com. Website: http://sevenarts.voicenet.com. Editor: Virginia Moles. Executive Editor: Judith West. 25% freelance written. Monthly magazine. "*Seven Arts* aims to stimulate interest in the arts in the Philadelphia region." Estab. 1993. Circ. 50,000. Pays on publication. Publishes ms an average of 3 months after acceptance. Byline given. Offers 20% kill fee. Buys first North American serial rights. Editorial lead time 2 months. Submit seasonal material 6 months in advance. Accepts simultaneous submissions. Reports in 3 months. Sample copy free.
Nonfiction: Book excerpts, interview/profile, events-related. No non-arts related material. Buys 25 mss/year. Query with published clips. Length: 500-2,000 words. Pays $200-700. Sometimes pays expenses of writers on assignment.
Reprints: Accepts previously published submissions.
Photos: State availability of photos with submission. Reviews contact sheets. Negotiates payment individually. Captions, model releases and identification of subjects required. Buys one-time rights.
Columns/Departments: Theater, Music, Dance, Art, Film, Literature; 500 words. Buys 25 mss/year. Query with published clips. Pays $200.
Tips: "Consider breaking in with small, front-of-the-book pieces; pitch ideas for specific sections of the magazine; hook to specific cultural events."

‡WHERE & WHEN, Pennsylvania Travel Group, The Barash Group, 403 S. Allen St., State College PA 16801. (800)326-9584. Fax: (814)238-3415. E-mail: barash77@aol,com. Contact: Erik Kopp, editor. 50% freelance written. Bimonthly magazine covering travel and tourism in Pennsylvania. "*Where & When* presents things to see and do in Pennsylvania." Circ. 100,000. Pays on publication. Byline given. Offers 50% kill fee. Buys first North American serial rights. Editorial lead time 6 months. Submit seasonal material 6 months in advance. Reports in 1 month. Sample copy and writer's guidelines free.
Nonfiction: Travel. Buys 10-20 mss/year. Query. Length: 600-2,000 words. Pays $100-400.
Photos: State availability of photos with submission. Reviews 3×5 transparencies and prints. Negotiates payment individually. Captions, identification of subjects required. Buys one-time rights.
Columns/Departments: Bring the Kids (children's attractions); Budget Traveler (saving money while traveling); Small Town PA (villages and hamlets in Pennsylvania); all 700-1,000 words. Buys 10 mss/year. Query. Pays $100-250.

Rhode Island

NEWPORT LIFE, 174 Bellevue Ave., Suite 207, Newport RI 02840. Fax: (401)847-4460. Contact: Lynne Tungett, publisher. 90% freelance written. Quarterly magazine. "*Newport Life* is a community magazine focusing on the people, issues, history and events that make Newport County unique." Estab. 1993. Circ. 10,000. Pays on publication. Publishes ms an average of 3 months after acceptance. Byline given. Offers 20% kill fee. Buys one-time rights. Editorial lead time 1 year. Submit seasonal material 6 months in advance. Accepts simultaneous submissions. Reports in 1 month. Writer's guidelines for #10 SASE.
Nonfiction: General interest, historical/nostalgic, interview/profile, opinion, photo feature. Buys 20 mss/year. Query

with published clips. Length: 650-3,000 words. Pays $65-300. Sometimes pays expenses of writers on assignment.
Reprints: Send photocopy of article and information about when and where the article previously appeared.
Photos: State availability of photos with submission. Reviews 3×5 prints. Negotiates payment individually. Captions, model releases, identification of subjects required. Buys one-time rights.
Columns/Departments: Historical Newport (person or aspect of Newport County's history), 750-1,000 words; In Our Midst (local individuals who've contributed to the community), 650 words; At The Helm (significant person in the boating industry), 500 words; Arts Marquee (local artisans), 650 words. Buys 24 mss/year. Query with published clips. Pays $65-100.
Tips: "Articles should be specific, informative and thoroughly researched. Historical information and quotes are encouraged. New/unpublished writers welcome. Query with lead paragraph and outline of story."

South Carolina

CHARLESTON MAGAZINE, P.O. Box 1794, Mt. Pleasant SC 29465-1794. (803)971-9811. Fax: (803)971-0121. E-mail: gulfstream@awod.com. Editor: Louise Chase Dettman. Associate Editors: Dawn Chipman and Patrick Sharbaugh. 80% freelance written. Bimonthly magazine covering current issues, events, arts and culture, leisure pursuits, personalities as they pertain to the city of Charleston. "Each issue reflects an essential element of Charleston life and Lowcountry living." Estab. 1986. Circ. 20,000. Pays 30 days after publication. Publishes ms an average of 3 months after acceptance. Byline given. Buys one-time rights. Submit seasonal material 4 months in advance. Reports in 1 month. Sample copies for 9×12 SAE with 5 first-class stamps. Writer's guidelines free.
Nonfiction: General interest, humor, food, architecture, sports, interview/profile, opinion, photo feature, travel, current events/issues, art. "Not interested in 'Southern nostalgia' articles or gratuitous history pieces. Must pertain to the Charleston area and its present culture." Buys 50 mss/year. Query with published clips. Length: 150-1,500 words. Pays 15¢/published word. Sometimes pays expenses of writers on assignment.
Reprints: Rarely accepts previously published submissions. Send tearsheets. Pay negotiable.
Photos: Send photos with submission if available. Reviews contact sheets, transparencies, slides. Offers $35/photo maximum. Identification of subjects required. Buys one-time rights.
Columns/Departments: Channel Markers (general local interest), 200-400 words; Spotlight (profile of local interest), 300-400 words; The Home Front (interiors, renovations and gardens), 1,000 words; Sporting Life (humorous, adventurous tales of life outdoors), 1,000-1,200 words; Dining (restaurants and culinary trends in the city), 1,000-1,200 words; On the Road (travel opportunities near Charleston), 1,000-1,200 words.
Tips: "Charleston, although a city with a 300-year history, is a vibrant, modern community with a tremendous dedication to the arts and no shortage of newsworthy subjects. Don't bother submitting coffee-table magazine-style pieces. Areas most open to freelancers are Columns/Departments and features. Should be of local interest. We're looking for the freshest stories about Charleston—and those don't always come from insiders, but outsiders who are keenly observant."

SANDLAPPER, The Magazine of South Carolina, The Sandlapper Society, Inc., P.O. Box 1108, Lexington SC 29071-1108. (803)359-9954. Fax: (803)957-8226. Website: http://www.sandlapper.org. Executive Director: Dolly Patton. Editor: Robert P. Wilkins. Contact: Daniel E. Harmon, managing editor. 35% freelance written. Quarterly feature magazine focusing on the positive aspects of South Carolina. Estab. 1989. Circ. 5,000. Pays during the dateline period. Publishes ms an average of 4 months after acceptance. Byline given. Buys first North American serial rights and the right to reprint. Submit seasonal material 6 months in advance. Writer's guidelines free.
Nonfiction: Feature articles and photo essays about South Carolina's interesting people, places, cuisine, things to do. Occasional history articles. Query. Length: 600-5,000 words. Pays $50-500. Sometimes pays the expenses of writers on assignment.
Photos: "*Sandlapper* buys black-and-white prints, color transparencies and art. Photographers should submit working cutlines for each photograph." Pays $25-75, $100 for cover or centerspread photo.
Tips: "We're not interested in articles about topical issues, politics, crime or commercial ventures. Avoid first-person nostalgia and remembrances of places that no longer exist. We look for top-quality literature. Humor is encouraged. Good taste is a standard. unique angles are critical for acceptance. Dare to be bold, but not too bold."

South Dakota

DAKOTA OUTDOORS, South Dakota, Hipple Publishing Co., P.O. Box 669, 333 W. Dakota Ave., Pierre SD 57501-0669. (605)224-7301. Fax: (605)224-9210. E-mail: 73613.3456. Editor: Kevin Hipple. Contact: Rachel Engbrecht, managing editor. 50% freelance written. Monthly magazine on Dakota outdoor life. Estab. 1975. Circ. 6,500. Pays on publication. Publishes ms an average of 2 months after acceptance. Byline given. Submit seasonal material 3 months in advance. Accepts simultaneous submissions. Reports in 3 months. Sample copy for 9×12 SAE with 3 first-class stamps.
Nonfiction: General interest, how-to, humor, interview/profile, new product, opinion, personal experience, photo feature, technical (all on outdoor topics—prefer in Dakotas). Buys 50 mss/year. Query with or without published clips, or

send complete ms. Length: 200-1,000 words. Pays $5-50 for assigned articles; $40 maximum for unsolicited articles. Sometimes pays in contributor copies or other premiums (inquire).

Reprints: Send typed ms with rights for sale noted and information about when and where the article previously appeared. Pays 50% of amount paid for an original article.

Photos: Send photos with submission. Reviews 5×7 prints. Offers no additional payment for photos accepted with ms. Identification of subjects preferred. Buys one-time rights.

Fiction: Occasionally publishes novel excerpts.

Fillers: Anecdotes, facts, gags to be illustrated by cartoonist, newsbreaks, short humor. Buys 10/year. Also publishes line drawings of fish and game. Prefers 5×7 prints.

Tips: "Submit samples of manuscript or previous works for consideration; including photos or illustrations is helpful."

Tennessee

MEMPHIS, Contemporary Media, P.O. Box 256, Memphis TN 38101-0256. (901)521-9000. Fax: (901)521-0129. Editor: Tim Sampson. Contact: Michael Finger, senior editor. 60% freelance written. Works with a small number of new/unpublished writers. Estab. 1976. Circ. 21,917. Pays on publication. Publishes ms an average of 3 months after acceptance. Byline given. Buys first North American serial rights. Offers 20% kill fee. Accepts simultaneous submissions. Reports in 2 months. Sample copy for 9×12 SAE with 8 first-class stamps. Writer's guidelines for SASE.

Nonfiction: Exposé, general interest, historical, how-to, humor, interview, profile. "Virtually all of our material has strong Memphis area connections." Buys 25 freelance mss/year. Query or submit complete ms or published clips. Length: 500-5,000 words. Pays $50-500. Sometimes pays expenses of writers on assignment.

Tips: "The kinds of manuscripts we need most have a sense of story (i.e., plot, suspense, character), an abundance of evocative images to bring that story alive and a sensitivity to issues at work in Memphis. The most frequent mistakes made by writers in completing an article for us are lack of focus, lack of organization, factual gaps and failure to capture the magazine's style. Tough investigative pieces would be especially welcomed."

Texas

‡TEXAS HIGHWAYS, The Travel Magazine of Texas, Box 141009, Austin TX 78714-1009. (512)483-3675. Fax: (512) 483-3672. E-mail: jlawles@ailgw.dot.state.tx.us. Contact: Jack Lowry, editor. 80% freelance written. Monthly magazine "encourages travel within the state and tells the Texas story to readers around the world." Estab. 1974. Circ. 375,000. Publishes ms 1 year after acceptance. Buys first North American serial and electronic rights. Reports in 2 months. Writer's guidelines for SASE.

Nonfiction: "Subjects should focus on things to do or places to see in Texas. Include historical, cultural and geographic aspects if appropriate. Text should be meticulously researched. Include anecdotes, historical references, quotations and, where relevant, geologic, botanical and zoological information." Query with description, published clips, additional background materials (charts, maps, etc.) and SASE. Include disk copy if available. Length: 1,200-2,000 words. Pays 40-50¢/word. Send for copy of writer's guidelines.

Columns/Departments: Contact: Ann Gallaway. Speaking of Texas (history, folklore, facts), 50-200 words. Prints 3-5 items/month. Send complete ms with reference sources. Pays 40¢/word.

Tips: "We like strong leads that draw in the reader immediately and clear, concise writing. Specify and avoid superlatives. Avoid overused words. Don't forget the basics—who, what, where, why and how."

‡TEXAS MONTHLY, P.O. Box 1569, Austin TX 78767-1569. Website: http://www.texasmonthly.com. Contact: Gregory Curtis, editor. Monthly magazine appealing to an educated, urban Texas audience. Estab. 1973. Circ. 307,663. **Pays on acceptance.** Byline given. Reports in 2 months. Writer's guidelines for SASE.

Nonfiction: Texas politics, sports, business, culture, lifestyles, reviews, entertainment. "We like solidly researched reporting that uncovers issues of public concern, reveals offbeat and previously unreported topics or uses a novel approach to familiar topics. No fiction, poetry or cartoons." Query with outline and a description of the direction of the article and SASE. Length: 2,000-5,000 words. Pay negotiable.

Columns/Departments: Query with SASE. Length: 750-1,000 words. Pay negotiable.

TEXAS PARKS & WILDLIFE, 3000 South I.H. 35, Suite 120, Austin TX 78704. (512)912-7000. Fax: (512)707-1913. E-mail: jim.cox@tpwd.state.tx.us. Website: http://www.state.tx.us. Editor: David Baxter. Managing Editor: Mary-Love Bigony. Contact: Jim Cox, senior editor. 80% freelance written. Monthly magazine featuring articles about Texas hunting, fishing, outdoor recreation, game and nongame wildlife, state parks, environmental issues. All articles must be about Texas. Estab. 1942. Circ. 180,000. **Pays on acceptance.** Publishes ms an average of 6 months after acceptance. Byline given. Kill fee determined by editor, usually $200-250. Buys first rights. Submit seasonal material 6 months in advance. Reports in 1 month on queries; 3 months on mss. Sample copy and writer's guidelines free.

● *Texas Parks & Wildlife* needs more hunting and fishing material.

Nonfiction: Jim Cox, articles editor. General interest (Texas only), how-to (outdoor activities), photo feature, travel (state parks). Buys 60 mss/year. Query with published clips. Length: 250-2,500 words. Pays $600 maximum.

Photos: Send photos with submission. Reviews transparencies. Offers $65-350/photo. Captions and identification of subjects required. Buys one-time rights.

Columns/Departments: Buys 6 mss/year. Query with published clips. Pays $100-300. Monthly departments: hunting and fishing, the environment, photo column, places to go. Maximum 1,000 words.

Tips: "Read outdoor pages of statewide newspapers to keep abreast of news items that can lead to story ideas. Feel free to include more than one story idea in one query letter. All areas are open to freelancers. All articles must have a Texas focus."

Utah

SALT LAKE CITY, 1270 West 2320 S., Suite A, Salt Lake City UT 84119-1449. (801)975-1927. Fax: (801)975-1982. E-mail: slmagazine@aol.com. Contact: Barry Scholl, editor. Art Director: Scott Perry. 60% freelance written. Bimonthly. "Ours is a lifestyle magazine, focusing on the people, issues and places that make Utah and the Intermountain West unique. Our audience is mainly educated, affluent, ages 25-55. Again, we focus heavily on people." Estab. 1989. Circ. 18,000. Pays on publication. Publishes ms an average of 6 months after acceptance. Byline given. $25 kill fee. Buys first North American serial or second serial (reprint) rights. Submit seasonal material 6 months in advance. Accepts simultaneous submissions. Reports in 3 months on mss. Guidelines free.

Nonfiction: Essays (health, family matters, financial), general interest, historical/nostalgic (pertaining to Utah and Intermountain West), humor, interview/profile (famous or powerful people associated with Utah business, politics, media), personal experience, photo feature, travel. "No movie reviews or current news subjects, please. Even essays need a tight local angle." Buys 5 mss/year. Query with published clips or send complete ms. Follows Chicago style. Length: 800-2,000 words. Pays $75-400 for assigned articles; $75-250 for unsolicited articles. "Payment for a major feature is negotiable."

Reprints: Send photocopy or typed ms with rights for sale noted when and where the article previously appeared.

Photos: Send photos with submission. Reviews transparencies (size not important). Captions, model releases, identification of subjects required. Payment and rights negotiable. Don't send original negs/transparencies unless requested.

Columns/Departments: Up Close (standard personality profile), 1,200-1,500 words; Q & A of famous person, 1,200-1,500 words; Executive Signature (profile, business slant of major Utah entrepeneur); and Food (recipes must be included), 1,000-1,500 words. Buys 5-10 mss/year. Query with published clips or send complete ms. Pays $75-250.

• No longer accepting fiction and poetry. Also, more articles are being produced in-house. They are overstocked on general travel pieces and are focusing on travel pieces on the intermountain West.

Tips: "We are looking for well-written, well-researched, complete manuscripts. Writers are advised to refer to a sample issue before submitting work. *Salt Lake City* magazine is most interested in unique, people-oriented profiles, historical pieces and stories of local interest. For instance, the magazine has covered local recreation, child abuse, education, air pollution, health care issues, wilderness, militias and local personalities. The majority of our stories are focused on Utah and the West. Please write for a free sample issue if you have never read our magazine."

Vermont

VERMONT LIFE MAGAZINE, 6 Baldwin St., Montpelier VT 05602-2109. (802)828-3241. E-mail: vtlife@lif.state. vt.us. Website: http://www.state.vt.us/vtlife. Editor-in-Chief: Thomas K. Slayton. 90% freelance written. Prefers to work with published/established writers. Quarterly magazine. "*Vermont Life* is interested in any article, query, story idea, photograph or photo essay that has to do with Vermont. As the state magazine, we are most favorably impressed with pieces that present positive aspects of life within the state's borders." Estab. 1946. Circ. 90,000. Publishes ms an average of 9 months after acceptance. Byline given. Offers kill fee. Buys first serial rights. Submit seasonal material 1 year in advance. Reports in 1 month. Writer's guidelines for #10 SASE.

• Ranked as one of the best markets for freelance writers in *Writer's Yearbook* magazine's annual "Top 100 Markets," January 1996.

Nonfiction: Wants articles on today's Vermont, those which portray a typical or, if possible, unique aspect of the state or its people. Style should be literate, clear and concise. Subtle humor favored. No "Vermont clichés"—maple syrup, town meetings or stereotyped natives. Buys 60 mss/year. Query by letter essential. Length: 1,500 words average. Pays 20¢/word. Seldom pays expenses of writers on assignment.

Photos: Buys photographs with mss; buys seasonal photographs alone. Prefers b&w contact sheets to look at first on assigned material. Color submissions must be 4×5 or 35mm transparencies. Pays $75-250 inside color; $500 for cover. Gives assignments but only with experienced photographers. Query in writing. Captions, model releases, identification of subjects required. Buys one-time rights, but often negotiates for re-use rights.

Fiction: Publishes novel excerpts.

Tips: "Writers who read our magazine are given more consideration because they understand that we want authentic articles about Vermont. If a writer has a genuine working knowledge of Vermont, his or her work usually shows it. Vermont is changing and there is much concern here about what this state will be like in years ahead. It is a beautiful, environmentally sound place now and the vast majority of residents want to keep it so. Articles reflecting such concerns in an intelligent, authoritative, non-hysterical way will be given very careful consideration. The growth of tourism makes us interested in intelligent articles about specific places in Vermont, their history and attractions to the traveling public."

VERMONT MAGAZINE, 2 Maple St., Suite 400, Middlebury VT 05753. (802)388-8480. Fax: (802)388-8485. E-mail: vtmag@sover.net. Editor/publisher: David Sleeper. Managing Editor: Julie Kirgo. Bimonthly magazine about Vermont. Estab. 1989. Circ. 41,000. Buys first North American serial rights. Editorial lead time 6 months. Reports in 2 weeks. Writer's guidelines for #10 SASE.
Nonfiction: Journalism and reporting, book excerpts (pre- or post-book publication), essays, exposé, general interest, how-to, humor, interview/profile, photo feature, calendar. All material must be about contemporary Vermont. Buys 30 mss/year but most are assigned by the editor. Query with published clips. Length: 900-3,500 words. Pays $200-800. Sometimes pays expenses of writers on assignment. Rarely publishes reprints.
Photos: Vermont subjects a must. Send photos and illustrations to Carolyn Brown, art director. Reviews contact sheets, 35mm transparencies, 8×10 b&w prints. Captions, model releases (if possible), identification of subjects required. Buys one-time rights.
Fiction: Publishes novel excerpts and stories about Vermont (1-2/year, maximum).
Tips: "Our readers *know* their state; they know the 'real' Vermont can't be slipped inside a glib and glossy brochure. We're interested in serious journalism on major issues, plus coverage of arts, outdoors, living, nature, architecture."

Virginia

THE ROANOKER, Leisure Publishing Co., 3424 Brambleton Ave., P.O. Box 21535, Roanoke VA 24018-9900. (540)989-6138. Fax: (540)989-7603. E-mail: leisure@infi.net. Contact: Kurt Rheinheimer, editor. 75% freelance written. Works with a small number of new/unpublished writers each year. Magazine published 10 times/year. "*The Roanoker* is a general interest city magazine for the people of Roanoke, Virginia and the surrounding area. Our readers are primarily upper-income, well-educated professionals between the ages of 35 and 60. Coverage ranges from hard news and consumer information to restaurant reviews and local history." Estab. 1974. Circ. 14,000. Pays on publication. Publishes ms an average of 4 months after acceptance. Byline given. Buys all rights; makes work-for-hire assignments. Submit seasonal material 4 months in advance. Reports in 2 months. Sample copy for $2 and 9×12 SAE with 5 first-class stamps.
Nonfiction: Exposé, historical/nostalgic, how-to (live better in western Virginia), interview/profile (of well-known area personalities), photo feature, travel (Virginia and surrounding states). "Were looking for more photo feature stories based in western Virginia. We place special emphasis on investigative and exposé articles." Periodic special sections on fashion, real estate, media, banking, investing. Buys 60 mss/year. Query with published clips or send complete ms. Length: 1,400 words maximum. Pays $35-200.
Photos: Send photos with ms. Reviews color transparencies. Pays $5-10 for 5×7 or 8×10 b&w prints; $10 maximum for 5×7 or 8×10 color prints. Captions and model releases required. Rights purchased vary.
Tips: "It helps if freelancer lives in the area. The most frequent mistake made by writers in completing an article for us is not having enough Roanoke-area focus: use of area experts, sources, slants, etc."

Washington

SEATTLE, The Magazine for the Pacific Northwest, Adams Publishing of the Pacific Northwest, 701 Dexter Ave. N, Suite 101, Seattle WA 98109. (206)284-1750. Fax: (206)284-2550. E-mail: editor@seattlemag.com. Website: http://www.seattlemag.com Editor: Giselle Smith. 90% freelance written. "Monthly magazine serving the Seattle area and the Pacific Northwest. Articles should be written with our readers in mind. They are interested in the arts, social issues, their homes, gardens, travel and in maintaining the region's high quality of life." Estab. 1992. Circ. 70,000. Pays on publication. Publishes ms an average of 4 months after acceptance. Byline given. Offers 33% kill fee. Buys first rights or second serial (reprint) rights. Editorial lead time 3 months. Submit seasonal material 6 months in advance. Reports in 2 months. Sample copy and writer's guidelines for SASE.
Nonfiction: Book excerpts, general interest, interview/profile, photo feature, local interest. Buys 60-75 mss/year. Query with published clips. Length: 200-2,500 words. Pays $75 minimum for assigned articles; $50 minimum for unsolicited articles. Sometimes pays expenses of writers on assignment.
Reprints: Rarely accepts previously published submissions. Send photocopy of article and information about when and where the article previously appeared. Pay varies.
Photos: State availability of photos with submission. Negotiates payment individually. Buys one-time rights.
Columns/Departments: Northwest Portrait, At Issue, Weekends, Nightlife, Dining, Style, Neighborhood, Private Eye. Query with published clips. Pays $100-400.
Tips: "Good queries generally suggest how and when the proposed article will best fit into the magazine, and compelling reasons why the story is right for *Seattle*. In addition, they should show that the writer has read the magazine and understands its content and readership."

SEATTLE WEEKLY, Sasquatch Publishing, 1008 Western Ave., Suite 300, Seattle WA 98104. (206)623-0500. Fax: (206)467-4377. E-mail: editorial@seattleweekly.com. Editor: David Brewster. 20% freelance written. Eager to work with writers in the region. Weekly tabloid covering arts, politics, food, business and books with local and regional emphasis. Estab. 1976. Circ. 70,000. Pays 1 week after publication. Publishes ms an average of 1 month after acceptance. Byline given. Offers variable kill fee. Buys first North American serial rights. Submit seasonal material minimum 2 months in advance. Reports in 1 month. *Writer's Market* recommends allowing 2 months for reply. Sample copy for $3. Writer's guidelines for #10 SASE.

Nonfiction: Book excerpts, exposé, general interest, historical/nostalgic (Northwest), humor, interview/profile, opinion, arts-related essays. Buys 6-8 cover stories/year. Query with résumé and published clips. Length: 700-4,000 words. Pays $75-800. Sometimes pays the expenses of writers on assignment.

Reprints: Send tearsheet of article. Pay varies.

Tips: "The *Seattle Weekly* publishes stories on Northwest politics and art, usually written by regional and local writers, for a mostly upscale, urban audience; writing is high-quality magazine style."

Wisconsin

MILWAUKEE MAGAZINE, 312 E. Buffalo St., Milwaukee WI 53202. (414)273-1101. Fax: (414)273-0016. E-mail: milmag@qgraph.com@inet#. Contact: John Fennell, editor. 40% freelance written. Monthly magazine. "We publish stories about Milwaukee, of service to Milwaukee-area residents and exploring the area's changing lifestyle, business, arts, politics and dining." Circ. 42,000. Pays on publication. Publishes ms an average of 2 months after acceptance. Byline given. Offers 20% kill fee. Buys first rights. Submit seasonal material 6 months in advance. Reports in 6 weeks on queries. Sample copy for $4.

Nonfiction: Essays, exposé, general interest, historical, interview/profile, photo feature, travel, food and dining and other services. "No articles without a strong Milwaukee or Wisconsin angle." Buys 30-50 mss/year. Query with published clips and SASE. Full-length features: 2,500-6,000 words. Pays $400-1,000. Two-page "breaker" features (short on copy, long on visuals), 1,800 words. Query. Pays $150-400. Sometimes pays expenses of writers on assignment.

Photos: Send photos with submission. Reviews contact sheets, negatives, any transparencies and any prints. Offers no set rate per photo. Identification of subjects required. Buys one-time rights.

Columns/Departments: Steve Filmanowicz, departments editor. Insider (inside information on Milwaukee, exposé, slice-of-life, unconventional angles on current scene), up to 500 words; Mini reviews for Insider, 125 words; Endgame column (commentary), 850 words. Buys 60 mss/year. Query with published clips. Pays $25-125.

Tips: "Pitch something for the Insider, or suggest a compelling profile we haven't already done. Submit clips that prove you can do the job. The department most open is Insider. Think short, lively, offbeat, fresh, people-oriented. We are actively seeking freelance writers who can deliver lively, readable copy that helps our readers make the most out of the Milwaukee area. Because we're only human, we'd like writers who can deliver copy on deadline that fits the specifications of our assignment. If you fit this description, we'd love to work with you."

‡**WISCONSIN OUTDOOR JOURNAL**, Krause Publications, 700 E. State St., Iola WI 54990-0001. (715)445-2214. Fax: (715)445-4087. Website: http://www.krause.com/outdoors. Contact: Brian Lovett, editor. 95% freelance written. Magazine published 8 times/year. "*Wisconsin Outdoor Journal* is more than a straight hook-and-bullet magazine. Though *WOJ* carries how-to and where-to information, it also prints narratives, nature features and state history pieces to give our readers a better appreciation of Wisconsin's outdoors." Estab. 1987. Circ. 48,000. **Pays on acceptance.** Byline given. Buys first North American serial rights. Submit seasonal material 1 year in advance. Reports in 6 weeks. *Writer's Market* recommends allowing 2 months for reply. Sample copy for 9×12 SAE with 7 first-class stamps. Writer's guidelines for #10 SASE.

Nonfiction: Book excerpts, essays, historical/nostalgic, how-to, humor, interview/profile, personal experience, photo feature. No articles outside of the geographic boundaries of Wisconsin. Buys 80 mss/year. Query. Send complete ms. "Established writers may query, send the complete ms." Length: 1,500-2,000 words. Pays $100-250.

Photos: Send photos with submission. Reviews 35mm transparencies. Offers no additional payment. Captions required. Buys one-time rights. Photos without mss pay from $10-150. Credit line given.

Fiction: Adventure, historical, humorous, novel excerpts. "No eulogies of a good hunting dog." Buys 10 mss/year. Send complete ms. Length: 1,500-2,000 words. Pays $100-250.

Tips: "Writers need to know Wisconsin intimately—stories that appear as regionals in other magazines probably won't be printed within *WOJ*'s pages."

WISCONSIN TRAILS, P.O. Box 5650, Madison WI 53705-1056. (608)231-2444. Fax: (608)231-1557. E-mail: wistrail@mailbag.com. Contact: Kate Bast, managing editor. 40% freelance written. Prefers to work with published/ established writers. Bimonthly magazine for readers interested in Wisconsin and its contemporary issues, personalities, recreation, history, natural beauty and arts. Estab. 1959. Circ. 55,000. Buys first serial rights, one-time rights occasionally. Pays on publication. Submit seasonal material at least 1 year in advance. Publishes ms an average of 6 months after acceptance. Byline given. Reports in 2 months. Sample copy for 9×12 SAE with 10 first-class stamps. Writer's guidelines for #10 SASE.

Nonfiction: "Our articles focus on some aspect of Wisconsin life: an interesting town or event, a person or industry, history or the arts, and especially outdoor recreation. We do not use first-person essays or biographies about people who were born in Wisconsin but made their fortunes elsewhere. No poetry. No articles that are too local for our regional audience, or articles about obvious places to visit in Wisconsin. We need more articles about the new and little-known." Buys 3 unsolicited mss/year. Query or send outline. Length: 1,000-3,000 words. Pays $150-500 (negotiable), depending on assignment length and quality. Sometimes pays expenses of writers on assignment.

Reprints: Rarely accepts reprints. Send photocopy of article or typed ms with rights for sale noted and information about when and where the article previously appeared.

Photos: Purchased with or without mss or on assignment. Uses 35mm transparencies; larger format OK. Color photos usually illustrate an activity, event, region or striking scenery. Prefer photos with people in scenery. Black and white photos usually illustrate a given article. Pays $50 each for b&w on publication. Pays $50-75 for inside color; $100-200 for covers. Caption information required.

Tips: "We're looking for active articles about people, places, events and outdoor adventures in Wisconsin. We want to publish one in-depth article of state-wide interest or concern per issue, and several short (600-1,500 words) articles about short trips, recreational opportunities, personalities, restaurants, inns and cultural activities. We're looking for more articles about out-of-the-way Wisconsin places that are exceptional in some way."

Canada

‡ATLANTIC BOOKS TODAY, Atlantic Provinces Book Review Society, 1657 Barrington St., #502, Halifax, Nova Scotia B3J 2A1 Canada. Fax: (902)429-4454. E-mail: booksatl@istar.ca. Website: www.atlanticonline.nsca/index. Managing Editor: Elizabeth Eve. 50% freelance written. Quarterly tabloid covering books and writers in Atlantic Canada. "We only accept written inquiries for stories pertaining to promoting interest in the culture of the Atlantic region." Estab. 1992. Circ. 20 million. Pays on publication. Byline given. Offers $25 kill fee. Buys one-time rights. Editorial lead time 6 months. Submit seasonal material 3 months in advance. Accepts simultaneous submissions. Reports in 1 month on queries. Sample copy and writer's guidelines free.

Nonfiction: Book excerpts, general interest. Query with published clips. Length: 1,000 words maximum. Pays $120 maximum. Sometimes pays expenses of writers on assignment.

CANADIAN GEOGRAPHIC, 39 McArthur Ave., Ottawa, Ontario K1L 8L7 Canada. (613)745-4629. Fax: (613)744-0947. E-mail: editorial@cangeo.ca. Website: http://www.cangeo.ca/. Contact: Rick Boychuk, editor. Managing Editor: Eric Harris. 90% freelance written. Works with a small number of new/unpublished writers each year. Estab. 1930. Circ. 246,000. Bimonthly magazine. "*Canadian Geographic*'s colorful portraits of our ever-changing population show readers just how important the relationship between the people and the land really is." **Pays on acceptance.** Publishes ms an average of 3 months after acceptance. Buys first Canadian rights; interested only in first-time publication. Reports in 1 month. Sample copy for $4.25 (Canada.) and 9×12 SAE. Writer's guidelines free.

Nonfiction: Buys authoritative geographical articles, in the broad geographical sense, written for the average person, not for a scientific audience. Predominantly Canadian subjects by Canadian authors. Buys 30-45 mss/year. *Always query first in writing and enclose SASE.* Cannot reply personally to all unsolicited proposals. Length: 1,500-3,000 words. Pays 80¢/word minimum. Usual payment for articles ranges between $1,000-3,000. Higher fees reserved for commissioned articles. Sometimes pays the expenses of writers on assignment.

● They need articles on earth sciences.

Photos: Pays $75-400 for color photos, depending on published size.

THE COTTAGE MAGAZINE, Country Living in B.C. and Alberta, Harrison House Publishing, 4611 William Head Rd., Victoria, British Columbia V9B 5T7 Canada. (604)478-9209. Contact: Peter Chetteburgh, editor. 60% freelance written. Bimonthly magazine covering recreational property in British Columbia and Alberta. Estab. 1992. Circ. 10,000. Pays on publication. Publishes ms an average of 1 month after publication. Byline given. Offers 50% kill fee. Not copyrighted. Buys first North American serial rights. Editorial lead time 2 months. Submit seasonal material 3 months in advance. Accepts simultaneous submissions. Reports in 1 month on queries; 2 months on mss. Sample copy for $2. Writer's guidelines free.

Nonfiction: General interest, historical/nostalgic, how-to, humor, interview/profile, new product, personal experience, technical. Buys 30 mss/year. Query. Length: 200-2,000 words. Pays $50-500. Sometimes pays expenses of writers on assignment (telephone expenses mostly).

Photos: State availability of photos with submission. Reviews contact sheets, transparencies and prints. Offers no additional payment for photos accepted with ms. Buys one-time rights.

Columns/Departments: Utilities (solar and/or wind power), 650-700 words; Cabin Wit (humor), 650 words. Buys 10 mss/year. Query. Pays $100-200.

Fillers: Anecdotes, facts, gags to be illustrated by cartoonist, newsbreaks; 50-200 words. Buys 12/year. Pays 20¢/word.

OUTDOOR CANADA MAGAZINE, 703 Evans Ave., Suite 202, Toronto, Ontario M9C 5E9 Canada. (416)695-0311. Fax: (416)695-0381. Contact: James Little, editor-in-chief. 90% freelance written. Works with a small number of new/unpublished writers each year. Magazine published 8 times/year emphasizing noncompetitive outdoor recreation in Canada *only*. Estab. 1972. Circ. 95,000. Pays on publication. Publishes ms an average of 8 months after acceptance.

Buys first rights. Submit seasonal material 1 year in advance of issue date. Byline given. *Enclose SASE or IRCs or material will not be returned.* Reports in 1 month. *Writer's Market* recommends allowing 2 months for reply. Mention *Writer's Market* in request for editorial guidelines.

Nonfiction: Fishing, hiking, canoeing, hunting, adventure, outdoor issues, exploring, outdoor destinations in Canada, some how-to. Buys 35-40 mss/year, usually with photos. Length: 1,000-2,500 words. Pays $100 and up.

Photos: Emphasize people in the outdoors. Pays $35-225 for 35mm transparencies; and $400/cover. Captions and model releases required.

Fillers: Short news pieces. Buys 70-80/year. Length: 200-500 words. Pays $6/printed inch.

REGINA MAGAZINE, Concept Media, Ltd., 3030 Victoria Ave., Regina, Saskatchewan S4T 1K9 Canada. Fax: (306)522-5988. Contact: Pat Rediger, editor. 50% freelance written. Monthly magazine "profiles the people, places and events of the city. It is intended to showcase all the things that are good within the city. We place a special emphasis on the downtown." Estab. 1992. Circ. 35,000. Pays on publication. Publishes ms an average of 3 months after acceptance. Byline given. Offers 10% kill fee. Buys first rights. Editorial lead time 3 months. Submit seasonal material 3 months in advance. Reports in 2 weeks on queries. Sample copy and writer's guidelines for #10 SASE.

Nonfiction: General interest, historical/nostalgic, how-to, humor, interview/profile, personal experience, photo feature. Special issues: The Financial Times of Regina (February), Fiction (September). Buys 15-20 mss/year. Query with published clips. Length: 1,000-2,500 words. Pays $125-150 for assigned articles; $75-100 for unsolicited articles. Pays expenses of writers on assignment.

Photos: Send photos with submission. Reviews contact sheets. Negotiates payment individually. Identification of subjects required. Buys one-time rights.

Columns/Departments: Upfront (off-beat stories), 300 words; After Five (entertainment), 300 words. Buys 10 mss/year. Query with published clips. Pays $50-75.

Fillers: Anecdotes, gags to be illustrated by cartoonist, short humor. Buys 25/year. Length: 50-200 words. Pays $5-10.

Tips: "The magazine mainly profiles people and issues that pertain specifically to Regina. Very little freelance material from outside the city is required. However, we do purchase fillers, cartoons and jokes. We're also open to new ideas. If you think you've got a good one, let us know."

TORONTO LIFE, 59 Front St. E., Toronto, Ontario M5E 1B3 Canada. (416)364-3333. Fax: (416)861-1169. Website: http://www.tor-lifeline.com. Contact: John Macfarlane, editor. 95% freelance written. Prefers to work with published/established writers. Monthly magazine emphasizing local issues and social trends, short humor/satire, and service features for upper income, well educated and, for the most part, young Torontonians. Circ. 97,624. **Pays on acceptance.** Publishes ms an average of 4 months after acceptance. Byline given. Buys first North American serial rights. Pays 50% kill fee for commissioned articles only. Reports in 3 weeks. Sample copy for $3.50 with SAE and IRCs.

Nonfiction: Uses most types of articles. Buys 17 mss/issue. Query with published clips. Phone queries OK. Buys about 40 unsolicited mss/year. Length: 1,000-5,000 words. Pays $800-3,000.

Photos: Send photos with query. Uses good color transparencies and clear, crisp b&w prints. Seldom uses submitted photos. Captions and model release required.

Columns/Departments: "We run about five columns an issue. They are all freelanced, though most are from regular contributors. They are mostly local in concern and cover politics, money, fine art, performing arts, movies and sports." Length: 1,800 words. Pays $1,500.

UP HERE, Life in Canada's North, OUTCROP: The Northern Publishers, Box 1350, Yellowknife, Northwest Territories X1A 2N9 Canada. (403)920-4652. Fax: (403)873-2844. E-mail: outcrop@internorth.com. Editor: Rosemary Allerston. Contact: Liz Crompton, editorial assistant. 70% freelance written. Bimonthly magazine covering general interest about Canada's North. "We publish features, columns and shorts about people, wildlife, native cultures, travel and adventure in Northern Canada, with an occasional swing into Alaska. Be informative, but entertaining." Estab. 1984. Circ. 35,000. Pays on publication. Publishes ms an average of 6 months after acceptance. Byline given. Offers 50% kill fee. Buys first North American serial rights. Editorial lead time 6 months. Submit seasonal material 1 year in advance. Reports in 4 months. Sample copy for $3.50 (Canadian) and 9×12 SASE with $1.45 Canadian postage. Writer's guidelines for legal-sized SASE and 45¢ Canadian postage.

• This publication was a finalist for Best Editorial Package, National Magazine Awards.

Nonfiction: Book excerpts, essays, general interest, historical/nostalgic, how-to, humor, interview/profile, new product, personal experience, photo feature, technical, travel. No poetry or fiction. Buys 30 mss/year. Query. Length: 1,500-3,000 words. Pays $250-750 or 15-25¢/word. Pays with advertising space where appropriate.

Photos: Send photos with submission. Reviews transparencies and prints. Offers $25-350/photo (Canadian). Captions and identification of subjects required. Buys one-time rights.

Columns/Departments: Natural North (natural oddities of Northern landscape, animals, vegetation, etc.), 750-1,200 words; Outside (for outdoor enthusiasts), 750-1,500 words; Arctic Gourmet (where to find and how to eat Northern food), 750-1,200 words. Buys 20 mss/year. Query with published clips. Pays $150-250 or 15-25¢/word.

Tips: "You must have lived in or visited Canada's North (the Northwest Territories, Yukon, the extreme north of British Columbia, Alberta, etc.). We like well-researched, concrete adventure pieces, insights about Northern people and lifestyles, readable natural history. Features are most open to freelancers—travel, adventure and so on. Outer Edge (a shorter, newsy, gee-whiz section) is a good place to break in with a 50-500 word piece. We don't want a 'How I spent my summer vacation' hour-by-hour account. We want stories with angles, articles that look at the North through a different set of glasses. Photos are very important, and will increase your chances greatly with top-notch images."

WESTCOAST REFLECTIONS, RAND Communications, 2604 Quadra St., Victoria, British Columbia V8T 4E4 Canada. (250)383-1149. Website: http://www.islandnet.com/~magazine. Contact: Sharon Doherty, editor. 30% freelance written. Monthly magazine covering Westcoast lifestyle. "We publish upbeat, humorous, positive articles on travel, recreation, health & fitness, hobbies, home & garden, cooking, finance and continuing education. While the majority of the articles we publish are light-hearted in nature, periodically, we do accept material dealing with important societal concerns as it relates to housing and health." Estab. 1993. Circ. 30,000. Byline given. Buys all rights. Editorial lead time 2 months. Submit seasonal material 4 months in advance. Accepts simultaneous submissions. Reports in 1 month on queries; 2 months on mss. Sample copy and writer's guidelines for SAE with IRCs.
Nonfiction: General interest, historical/nostalgic, how-to, interview/profile, photo feature, travel. Buys 10 mss/year. Length: 700-950 words. Pays 10¢/word.
Reprints: Accepts previously published submissions.
Photos: Reviews contact sheets, negatives. Negotiates payment individually. Buys one-time rights.

WESTERN PEOPLE, Supplement to the Western Producer, Western Producer Publications, Box 2500, Saskatoon, Saskatchewan S7K 2C4 Canada. (306)665-3500. E-mail: people@producer.com. Website: http://www.producer.com. Contact: Michael Gillgannon, managing editor. Weekly farm newspaper supplement "reflecting the life and people of rural Western Canada both in the present and historically." Estab. 1978. Circ. 100,000. **Pays on acceptance.** Publishes ms an average of 6 months after acceptance. Byline given. Buys first rights. Submit seasonal material 3 months in advance. Reports in 3 weeks. Sample copy for 9×12 SAE and 3 IRCs. Writer's guidelines for #10 SAE and 2 IRCs.
Nonfiction: General interest, historical/nostalgic, humor, interview/profile, personal experience, photo feature. Buys 225 mss/year. Send complete ms. Length: 500-2,500 words. Pays $100-300.
Photos: Send photos with submission. Reviews transparencies and prints. Captions and identification of subjects required. No stand-alone photos.
Fiction: Adventure, historical, humorous, mainstream, mystery, romance, suspense, western stories reflecting life in rural Western Canada. Buys 25 mss/year. Send complete ms. Length: 1,000-2,000 words. Pays $150-250.
Poetry: Free verse, traditional, haiku, light verse. Buys 75 poems/year. Submit maximum 3 poems. Length: 4-50 lines. Pays $15-50.
Tips: "Western Canada is geographically very large. The approach for writing about an interesting individual is to introduce that person *neighbor-to-neighbor* to our readers."

WESTWORLD MAGAZINE, Canada Wide Magazines and Communications, 4180 Lougheed Hwy., 4th floor, Burnaby, British Columbia V5C 6A7 Canada. Fax: (604)299-9188. E-mail: wworld@canadawide.com. Contact: (Ms.) Robin Roberts, editor. 30% freelance written. Quarterly association "magazine distributed to members of The Canadian Automobile Association, so we require automotive and travel-related topics of interest to members." Estab. 1983. Circ. 500,000. Pays on publication. Byline given. 50% kill fee. Buys first North American serial rights; second serial (reprint) rights at reduced rate. Editorial lead time 6 months. Submit seasonal material 1 year in advance. Accepts simultaneous submissions. Reports in 1 month on queries; 4 months on mss. Guidelines for #10 SASE.
Nonfiction: Automotive. "No purple prose." Buys 6 mss/year. Query with published clips. Length: 1,000-1,500 words. Pays 35-50¢/word.
Reprints: Submit photocopy of article and information about when and where the article previously appeared. Pays 50% of amount paid for an original article.
Photos: State availability of photos with submission. Reviews transparencies and prints. Offers $35-75/photo. Captions, model releases and identification of subjects required. Buys one-time rights.
Columns/Departments: Buys 6 mss/year. Query with published clips. Pays 35-50¢/word.
Tips: "Don't send gushy, travelogue articles. We prefer stories that are informative with practical, useful tips that are well written and researched. Approach an old topic/destination in a fresh/original way."

International

‡BRAZZIL, Brazzil, P.O. Box 42536, Los Angeles CA 90050. (213)255-8062. Fax: (213)257-3487. E-mail: brazzil@brazzil.com. Website: http://www.brazzil.com. Contact: Rodney Mello, editor. 60% freelance written. Monthly magazine covering Brazilian culture. Estab. 1989. Circ. 12,000. Pays on publication. Publishes ms an average of 2 months after acceptance. Byline given. Offers 10% kill fee. Buys one-time rights. Editorial lead time 2 months. Submit seasonal material 2 months in advance. Accepts simultaneous submissions. Reports in 2 weeks on queries. Sample copy free.
Nonfiction: Book excerpts, essays, exposé, general interest, historical/nostalgic, interview/profile, personal experience, travel. "All subjects have to deal in some way with Brazil and its culture. We assume our readers know very little or nothing about Brazil, so we explain everything." Buys 15 mss/year. Query. Length: 800-5,000 words. Pays $20-50. Pays writers with contributor copies or other premiums by mutual agreement.
Reprints: Accepts reprints of previously published submissions. Pays 50% of amount paid for an original article.
Photos: State availability of photos with submission. Reviews prints. Offers no additional payment for photos accepted with ms. Identification of subjects required. Buys one-time rights.

Tips: "We are interested in anything related to Brazil: politics, economy, music, behavior, profiles. Please document material with interviews and statistical data if applicable. Controversial pieces are welcome."

RELATIONSHIPS

These publications focus on lifestyles and relationships of single adults. Other markets for this type of material can be found in the Women's category. Magazines of a primarily sexual nature, gay or straight, are listed under the Sex category. Gay and Lesbian Interest contains general interest editorial targeted to that audience.

ATLANTA SINGLES MAGAZINE, Hudson Brooke Publishing, Inc., 180 Allen Rd., Suite 304N, Atlanta GA 30328. (404)256-9411. Fax: (404)256-9719. Contact: Shannon V. McClintock, editor. 10% freelance written. Works with a small number of new/unpublished writers each year. A bimonthly for single, widowed or divorced adults, medium to high income level, many business and professionally oriented; single parents, ages 25-55. Estab. 1977. Circ. 15,000. Pays on publication. Publishes ms an average of 6 months after acceptance. Byline given. Buys one-time, second serial (reprint) and simultaneous rights. Submit seasonal material 6 months in advance. Accepts simultaneous submissions. Reports in 1 month. Sample copy for $2 and 8×10 SAE with 7 first-class stamps. Guidelines for #10 SASE.
Nonfiction: General interest, humor, personal experience, photo feature, travel. No fiction or pornography. Buys 5 mss/year. Send complete ms. Length: 600-1,200 words. Pays $50-150 for unsolicited articles; sometimes trades for personal ad.
Reprints: Send tearsheet or photocopy of article and information about when and where the article previously appeared. Pays 50% of amount paid for an original article.
Photos: Send photos with submission. Cover photos also considered. Reviews prints. Offers no additional payment for photos accepted with ms. Model releases and identification of subjects required. Buys one-time rights.
Columns/Departments: Will consider ideas. Query. Length: 600-800 words. Pays $25-150/column or department.
Tips: "We are open to articles on *any* subject that would be of interest to singles. For example, travel, autos, movies, love stories, fashion, investments, real estate, etc. Although singles are interested in topics like self-awareness, being single again and dating, they are also interested in many of the subjects married people are, such as those listed."

CHRISTIAN SINGLE, Baptist Sunday School Board, 127 9th Ave. N., Nashville TN 37234-0140. (615)251-5721. Fax: (615)251-5008. E-mail: christiansingle@bssb.com. Contact: Stephen Felts, editor-in-chief. 30% freelance written. Prefers to work with published/established writers. Monthly "current events magazine that addresses day-to-day issues from a Christian perspective. Seeks to be constructive and creative in approach." Estab. 1979. Circ. 73,000. **Pays on acceptance.** Byline given. Buys first rights or makes work-for-hire assignments. Submit seasonal material 6 months in advance. Reports in 2 months. Sample copy and writer's guidelines for 9×12 SAE with 4 first-class stamps.
 • *Christian Single* reports they want more humor and articles dealing with current news events.
Nonfiction: Humor (good, clean humor that applies to Christian singles), how-to (specific subjects which apply to singles), inspirational (of the personal experience type), high adventure personal experience (of single adults), photo feature (on outstanding Christian singles), financial articles targeted to single adults. Buys 60-75 unsolicited mss/year. Query with published clips. Length: 600-1,200 words. Payment negotiable.
Reprints: Send photocopy of article and typed ms and disk with rights for sale noted and information about when and where article previously appeared. Pays 75% of amount paid for an original article.
Fiction: "We are also looking for fiction suitable for our target audience." Publishes novel excerpts.
Tips: "We are looking for people who experience single living from a positive, Christian perspective."

ON THE SCENE MAGAZINE, 3507 Wyoming NE, Albuquerque NM 87111-4427. (505)299-4401. Fax: (505)299-4403. Contact: Gail Skinner, editor. 60% freelance written. Eager to work with new/unpublished writers. Monthly magazine covering lifestyles for all ages. Estab. 1979. Circ. 30,000. Pays on publication. Publishes ms within 12 months after acceptance. Byline given. Submit seasonal material 3 months in advance. Reports in 3 months. Sample copy for $3 postage and handling or send 9×12 SAE with $1.01 postage. Writer's guidelines for #10 SASE.
Nonfiction: General interest, how-to, humor, inspirational, opinion, personal experience, relationships, consumer guide, travel, finance, real estate, parenting, astrology. No suggestive or pornographic material. Buys 60 mss/year. Send complete ms. Manuscripts returned only if adequate SASE included. Also publishes some fiction. Length: 600-1,200 words. Pays $5-35.
Reprints: Send typed ms with rights for sale noted. Pays 100% of amount paid for original article.
Photos: Send photos with ms. Captions, model releases, identification of subjects required. Photo returned only if adequate SASE is included.
Tips: "We are looking for articles that deal with every aspect of living—whether on a local or national level. Our readers are of above-average intelligence, income and education. The majority of our articles are relationships, humor and seasonal submissions."

‡**SINGLE LIVING, Everything for a Better Single Lifestyle**, Passi Publications, 380 Lexington Ave., New York NY 10168. (212)551-1089. Fax: (212)878-6091. Contact: Laurie Sue Brockway, editor. 50% freelance written. Bi-

monthly magazine covering the single lifestyle. Estab. 1995. Circ. 300,000. Pays on publication. Publishes ms an average of 2 months after acceptance. Byline given. Offers 20% kill fee. Buys first North American serial rights. Editorial lead time 4 months. Submit seasonal material 5 months in advance. Accepts simultaneous submissions. Reports in 6 weeks. Sample copy for $3. Writer's guidelines free.
Nonfiction: Book excerpts, essays, general interest, how-to, humor, inspirational, interview/profile, new product, opinion, personal experience, travel—related to the single life. Buys 10 mss/year. Query with published clips. Length: 1,000-2,000 words. Pay varies.
Photos: State availability or send photos with submission. Reviews transparencies, prints.
Fiction: Fantasy, humorous, romance—with a single slant. Buys 5 mss/year. Send complete ms. Pay varies.

‡SINGLES LIFESTYLE & ENTERTAINMENT MAGAZINE, Single Lifestyle Publishing Group, 7611 S. Orange Blossom Trail, #330, Orlando FL 32809. Editor: Carol Orsino. 50% freelance written. Bimonthly tabloid "for single, divorced and widowed persons ages 25-50." Estab. 1997. Circ. 20,000. **Pays on acceptance.** Publishes ms 1 month after acceptance. Byline given. Offers 100% kill fee. Buys one-time rights. Editorial lead time 2 months. Submit seasonal material 2 months in advance. Reports in 3 weeks on queries. Sample copy and writer's guidelines free.
Nonfiction: General interest, humor, interview/profile, travel, single life, lifestyles, relationships, single parenting, trends, health, fitness. Buys 20 mss/year. Query with published clips. Length: 500-1,500 words. Pays 10¢/word. Sometimes pays expenses of writers on assignment (limit agreed upon in advance).
Photos: State availability of photos with submission. Reviews contact sheets. Negotiates payment individually. Model releases required. Buys one-time rights.
Columns/Departments: Single Lifestyles; Single Parenting; Coping with Divorce. Length: 250-1,000 words. Buys 25 mss/year. Query with published clips. Pays 10¢/word.
Fiction: Humor, romance. Buys 12 mss/year. Query with published clips. Length: 1,000-2,000 words. Pays 10¢/word.
Reprints: Accepts previously published mss.
Fillers: Anecdotes, facts, gags to be illustrated by cartoonist, newsbreaks, short humor. Buys 50/year. Length: 50-150 words. Pays 10¢/word.
Tips: "Freelance writers must review our writer's guidelines in depth, plus thoroughly read our issues for a true feel for what we look for in articles and features. Query first with past published clips (any subject). Be creative in your query. Think Single Lifestyle!"

RELIGIOUS

Religious magazines focus on a variety of subjects, styles and beliefs. Most are sectarian, but a number approach topics such as public policy, international affairs and contemporary society from a non-denominational perspective. Fewer religious publications are considering poems and personal experience articles, but many emphasize special ministries to singles, seniors or other special interest groups. Such diversity makes reading each magazine essential for the writer hoping to break in. Educational and inspirational material of interest to church members, workers and leaders within a denomination or religion is needed by the publications in this category. Religious magazines for children and teenagers can be found in the Juvenile and Teen and Young Adult classifications. Other religious publications can be found in the Contemporary Culture and Ethnic/Minority sections as well. Spiritual topics are also addressed in Astrology, Metaphysical and New Age as well as Health and Fitness. Publications intended to assist professional religious workers in teaching and managing church affairs are classified in Church Administration and Ministry in the Trade section.

AMERICA, 106 W. 56th St., New York NY 10019. (212)581-4640. Editor: Rev. George W. Hunt. Published weekly for adult, educated, largely Roman Catholic audience. Estab. 1909. **Pays on acceptance.** Byline given. Usually buys all rights. Reports in 3 weeks. Free writer's guidelines.
Nonfiction: "We publish a wide variety of material on politics, economics, ecology, and so forth. We are not a parochial publication, but almost all pieces make some moral or religious point. We are not interested in purely informational pieces or personal narratives which are self-contained and have no larger moral interest." Articles on literature, current political, social events. Length: 1,500-2,000 words. Pays $50-200.
Poetry: Patrick Samway, S.J., poetry editor. Length: 15-30 lines.

‡THE ANNALS OF SAINT ANNE DE BEAUPRÉ, Redemptorist Fathers, P.O. Box 1000, St. Anne De Beaupré, Quebec, Quebec G0A 3C0 Canada. (418)827-4538. Fax: (418)827-4530. Editor: Father Bernard Mercier, CSs.R. Contact: Father Roch Archard, managing editor. 80% freelance written. Monthly religious magazine. "Our mission statement includes a dedication to Christian family values and a devotion to St. Anne." Estab. 1885.. Circ. 45,000. **Pays on acceptance.** Buys first North American rights. Editorial lead time 6 months. Submit seasonal material 4 months in advance. Reports in 3 weeks. Sample copy and writer's guidelines for 8½×11 SAE and IRCs.

Nonfiction: Inspirational, religious. Buys 250 mss/year. Send complete ms. Length: 500-1,500 words. Pays 3-4/word, plus 3 copies.

Photos: Send photos with ms. Negotiates payment individually. Subject identification required. Buys one-time rights.

Fiction: Religious, inspirational. "No senseless, mockery." Buys 200 mss/year. Send complete ms. Length: 500-1,500 words. Pays 3-4¢/word.

Tips: "Write something inspirational with spiritual thrust. Reporting rather than analysis is simply not remarkable. Each article must have a spiritual theme. Please only submit first North American rights mss with the rights clearly stated. We maintain an article bank and pick from it for each month's needs which loosely follow the religious themes for each month. Right now, our needs lean towards nonfiction of approximately 1,100 words."

AREOPAGUS, A Living Encounter with Today's Religious World, Tao Fong Shan Christian Centre, P.O. Box 33, Shatin, New Territories, Hong Kong. (852)691-1904. Fax: (852)265-9885. E-mail: areopagus@imail.com. Website: http://www.areopagus.com. Managing Editor: Eric Bosell. Contact: John G. Lemond, editor. 75% freelance written. "*Areopagus* is a quarterly Christian periodical that seeks to engage its readers in a living encounter with today's religious world. Respecting the integrity of religious communities, *Areopagus* provides a forum for dialog between the good news of Jesus Christ and people of faith both in major world religious and new religious movements." Estab. 1987. Circ. 1,000. Pays on publication. Publishes ms an average of 6 months after acceptance. Offers 50% kill fee. Buys first-time rights. Editorial lead time 6 months. Submit seasonal material 6 months in advance. Accepts simultaneous submissions. Reports in 6 weeks on queries; 3 months on mss. Sample copy for $4. Writer's guidelines free.

• *Areopagus* no longer solicits poetry.

Nonfiction: Book excerpts, essays and exposé (all on religious themes), humor (of a religious nature), inspirational (interreligious encounter), interview/profile (w/religious figures), opinion (on religious subjects), personal experience (of spiritual journey), photo feature and religious. Issue themes under consideration: birth rites, death, family, sex, aging, suffering, war, hope, healing. "We are not interested in articles that seek to prove the superiority or inferiority of a particular religious tradition." Buys 40 mss/year. Send complete ms. Length: 1,000-5,000 words. Pays $100 minimum.

Reprints: Send typed ms with rights for sale noted and when and where the article previously appeared.

Photos: Send photos with submission. Offers $50-100/photo. Identification of subjects required. Buys one-time rights.

Columns/Departments: Getting to Know (objective description of major world religions), 4,000 words; Pilgrimage (stories of personal faith journies), 3,000 words; and People and Communities (description of faith communities), 3,000 words. Buys 10 mss/year. Send complete ms. Pays $50-100.

Fillers: Facts, newsbreaks. Buys 5/year. Length: 100-400 words. Pays $10-25.

Tips: "Articles that reflect a balanced approach to interreligious dialogue are the most likely candidates. Followers of all faiths are encouraged to write about personal experience. Articles about religious conspiracy and arcane religious conjecture are of little interest. Virtually all of our departments are open to freelancers. In general, we look for compassionate, direct and unself-conscious prose that reflects a writer firmly rooted in his or her own tradition but unafraid to encounter other traditions."

‡THE ASSOCIATE REFORMED PRESBYTERIAN, Associate Reformed Presbyterian General Synod, 1 Cleveland St., Suite 110, Greenville SC 29601-3696. (803)232-8297. Fax: (864)271-3729. E-mail: aprmaged@sprynet.com. Website: http://www.arpsynod.org. Contact: Ben Johnston, editor. 5% freelance written. Works with a small number of new/unpublished writers each year. Christian magazine serving a conservative, evangelical and Reformed denomination. Estab. 1976. Circ. 6,000. **Pays on acceptance.** Publishes ms an average of 4 months after acceptance. Byline given. Not copyrighted. Buys first, one-time, or second serial (reprint) rights. Submit seasonal material 4 months in advance. Accepts simultaneous submissions. Reports in 1 month. Sample copy for $1.50. Writer's guidelines for #10 SASE.

Nonfiction: Book excerpts, essays, inspirational, opinion, personal experience, religious. Buys 10-15 mss/year. Query. Length: 400-2,000 words. Pays $70 maximum.

Reprints: Send information about when and where the article previously appeared. Pays 100% of amount paid for an original article.

Photos: State availability of photos with submission. Offers $25 maximum/photo. Captions and identification of subjects required. Buys one-time rights.

Fiction: Religious and children's. Pays $50 maximum.

Tips: "Feature articles are the area of our publication most open to freelancers. Focus on a contemporary problem and offer Bible-based solutions to it. Provide information that would help a Christian struggling in his daily walk. Writers should understand that we are denominational, conservative, evangelical, Reformed and Presbyterian. A writer who appreciates these nuances would stand a much better chance of being published here than one who does not."

‡BRIGADE LEADER, Christian Service Brigade, P.O. Box 150, Wheaton IL 60189. (630)665-0630. Contact: Deborah Christiensen, editor. Quarterly magazine covering leadership issues for Christian Service Brigade leaders. "We're looking for male writers who are familiar with Christian Service Brigade and can address leadership issues." Estab. 1960. Circ. 6,000. Pays on publication. Publishes ms an average of 3 months after acceptance. Byline given. Offers $35 kill fee. Buys first rights or second serial (reprint) rights. Editorial lead time 3 months. Reports in 1 week on queries. Sample copy for $1.50 and 10×13 SAE with 4 first-class stamps. Writer's guidelines for #10 SASE.

Nonfiction: Religious leadership. Buys 8 mss/year. Query only. Length: 500-1,500 words. Pays 5-10¢/word. Sometimes pays expenses of writers on assignment.

Photos: State availability of photos. Reviews prints. Negotiates payment individually. Buys one-time rights.

Tips: "Know Brigade and be able to offer practical and creative ideas for men to be better leaders."

‡THE CANADIAN CATHOLIC REVIEW, Canadian Catholic Review Corporation, 1437 College Dr., Saskatoon Saskatchewan S7N 0W6 Canada. (306)966-8959. Fax: (306)966-8904. E-mail: callam@duke.usask.ca. Website: http://ccr.nethosting.com/rev/. Editor: Rev. Daniel Callam, CSB. 75% freelance written. Published 11 times/year. "Our purposes are to be faithful to the Magisterium and to maintain a solid spiritual aspect by professing the Gospel of Jesus Christ through saints, writers, founders and social activists, and through the Church's historical tradition." Estab. 1983. Circ. 1,000. Pays on publication. Publishes ms an average of 6 months after acceptance. Byline given. Buys first North American serial rights. Editorial lead time 2 months. Submit seasonal material 3 months in advance. Reports in 2 weeks on queries; 1 month on mss. Sample copy $3 and 9×12 SAE, 4 first-class stamps (IRCs).
Nonfiction: Book excerpt, exposé, general interest, historical/nostalgic, interview/profile, opinion, personal experience, religious, travel, devotional, reviews (books, films/videos, television). Buys 10 mss/year. Query. Length: 1,000-6,000 words. Pays $50-300.
Columns/Departments: Liturgy; Scripture; American Notes; The Church in Quebec. Buys 10 mss/yr. Query. Pays $50.
Tips: "We want writers to be lucid, articulate and faithful. The *CCR* is aimed at intelligent, though not scholarly, Catholics. It aims to enliven the faith of the laity and clergy."

CATHOLIC DIGEST, University of St. Thomas, P.O. Box 64090, St. Paul MN 55164. (612)962-6739. Fax: (612)962-6755. E-mail: cdigest@stthomas.edu. Website: http://www.CatholicDigest.org. Editor: Richard J. Reece. Managing Editor: Kathleen Stauffer. Contact: Marge France, assistant to the editors. 15% freelance written. Monthly magazine "publishes features and advice on topics ranging from health, psychology, humor, adventure and family, to ethics, spirituality and Catholics, from modern-day heroes to saints through the ages. Helpful and relevant reading culled from secular and religious periodicals." Estab. 1936. Circ. 509,385. **Pays on acceptance** for articles. Publishes ms an average of 4 months after acceptance. Byline given. Buys first rights, one-time rights or second serial (reprint) rights. Editorial lead time 4 months. Submit seasonal material 5 months in advance. Reports in 2 months on mss. Sample copy and writer's guidelines free.
Nonfiction: Book excerpts, essays, general interest, historical/nostalgic, how-to, humor, inspirational, interview/profile, personal experience, religious, travel. Buys 60 mss/year. Send complete ms; 1,000-5,000 words. Pays $200-400.
Reprints: "Most articles we use are reprinted." Send tearsheet of article or typed ms with rights for sale noted and information about when and where the article previously appeared. Pays $100.
Photos: State availability of photos with submission. Reviews contact sheets, transparencies, prints. Negotiates payment individually. Captions, model releases, identification of subjects required.
Columns/Departments: Buys 75 mss/year. Send complete ms. Pays $4-50.
Fillers: Contact: Filler Editor. Anecdotes, short humor. Buys 200/year. Length: 1 line minimum, 500 words maximum. Pays $2/per published line upon publication.
Tips: "We're a lot more aggressive with inspirational/pop psychology/how-to articles these days. Spiritual and all other wellness self-help is a good bet for us."

CATHOLIC HERITAGE, Our Sunday Visitor, Inc., 200 Noll Plaza, Huntington IN 46750. (219)356-8400. Fax: (219)359-9117. E-mail: 76440.3571@compuserve.com. Contact: Bill Dodds, editor. 75% freelance written. Bimonthly magazine "explores the history and heritage of the Catholic faith with special emphasis on its impact on culture." Estab. 1991. Circ. 25,000. **Pays on acceptance.** Publishes ms an average of 1 year after acceptance. Byline given. Buys first North American serial rights. Editorial lead time 8-12 months. Submit seasonal material 6 months in advance. Reports in 3 weeks on queries; 1 month on mss. Send SASE for guidelines.
● This editor prefers manuscript on computer disks or submitted through CompuServe.
Nonfiction: Feature topics include scripture, U.S. heritage, saints and personalities, religious art and culture, catechtics and apologetics, liturgy, universal Church heritage, seasonal celebrations and the history of prayers and devotions. Also book excerpts, general interest, interview/profile, photo feature, travel. "No nostalgia pieces about what it was like growing up Catholic or about life in the Church prior to Vatican II." Buys 30 mss/year. Query. Length: 1,000-1,200 words. Pays $200. Sometimes pays expenses of writers on assignment.
Columns/Departments: Book, tape and software reviews related to the above feature topics. Length: 150-175 words.
Photos: State availability of photos with submission. Reviews prints. Negotiates payment individually. Captions required. Buys one-time rights.
Tips: "Write solid queries that take an aspect of the Catholic heritage and apply it to developments today. Show a good knowledge of the Church and a flair for historical writing. General features are most open to freelancers. Use a non-academic style and remember our readers are: Catholics who enjoy articles about the Church; recent converts who want to learn more about the Church; and 30-somethings who want to supplement their Church education."

CATHOLIC NEAR EAST MAGAZINE, Catholic Near East Welfare Association, 1011 First Ave., New York NY 10022-4195. (212)826-1480. Fax: (212)826-8979. Editor: Michael La Cività. 50% freelance written. Bimonthly magazine for a Catholic audience with interest in the Near East, particularly its current religious, cultural and political aspects. Estab. 1974. Circ. 110,000. Pays on publication. Publishes ms an average of 6 months after acceptance. Byline given. Buys all rights. Reports in 2 months. Sample copy and writer's guidelines for 7½×10½ SAE with 2 first-class stamps.

Nonfiction: "Cultural, devotional, political, historical material on the Near East, with an emphasis on the Eastern Christian churches. Style should be simple, factual, concise. Articles must stem from personal acquaintance with subject matter, or thorough up-to-date research." Length: 1,200-1,800 words. Pays 20¢/edited word.

Photos: "Photographs to accompany manuscript are welcome; they should illustrate the people, places, ceremonies, etc. which are described in the article. We prefer color transparencies but occasionally use b&w. Pay varies depending on use—scale from $50-300."

Tips: "We are interested in current events in the regions listed above as they affect the cultural, political and religious lives of the people."

THE CHRISTIAN CENTURY, 407 S. Dearborn St., Chicago IL 60605-1150. (312)427-5380. Fax: (312)427-1302. E-mail: ccentury@aol.com. Editor: James M. Wall. Senior Editors: Martin E. Marty and Dean Peerman. Managing Editor: David Heim. 50% freelance written. Eager to work with new/unpublished writers. Weekly magazine for ecumenically-minded, progressive church people, both clergy and lay. Circ. 30,000. Pays on publication. Publishes ms an average of 2 months after acceptance. Usually buys all rights. Reports in 2 months. Sample copy available for $2. All queries, mss should be accompanied by 9 × 12 SASE.

Nonfiction: "We use articles dealing with social problems, ethical dilemmas, political issues, international affairs and the arts, as well as with theological and ecclesiastical matters. We focus on concerns that arise at the juncture between church and society, or church and culture." Query appreciated, but not essential. Length: 2,500 words maximum. Payment varies, but averages $50/page.

CHRISTIAN COURIER, Calvinist Contact Publishing, 4-261 Martindale Rd., St. Catharines, Ontario L2W 1A1 Canada. (905)682-8311. Fax: (905)682-8313. E-mail: cceditor@aol.com. Contact: Bert Witvoet, editor. 20% freelance written. Weekly newspaper covering news of importance to Christians, comments and features. "We assume a Christian perspective which acknowledges that this world belongs to God and that human beings are invited to serve God in every area of society." Estab. 1945. Circ. 5,000. Pays 30 days after publication. Publishes ms an average of 2 months after acceptance. Byline given. Offers 50% kill fee. Editorial lead time 1 month. Submit seasonal material 6 months in advance. Accepts simultaneous submissions. Reports back only if material accepted.

Nonfiction: Interview/profile, opinion. Buys 40 mss/year. Send complete ms. Length: 500-1,200 words. Pays $35-60 for assigned articles; $25-50 for unsolicited articles. Sometimes pays expenses of writers on assignment.

Reprints: Accepts previously published submissions.

Photos: State availability of photos with submission.

‡CHRISTIAN EDUCATION COUNSELOR, General Council of the Assemblies of God, 1445 Boonville, Springfield MO 65802-1894. (417)862-2781. Fax: (417)862-0503. E-mail: ceeditor@ag.org. Editor: Sylvia Lee. 60% freelance written. Works with small number of new/unpublished writers each year. Bimonthly magazine on religious education in the local church—the official Sunday school voice of the Assemblies of God channeling programs and help to local, primarily lay, leadership. Estab. 1994. Circ. 20,000. **Pays on acceptance.** Publishes ms an average of 9 months after acceptance. Byline given. Offers variable kill fee. Buys first North American serial, one-time, all, simultaneous, first serial or second serial (reprint) rights or makes work-for-hire assignments. Submit seasonal material 7 months in advance. Accepts simultaneous submissions. Reports in 1 month. Sample copy and writer's guidelines for SASE.

Nonfiction: How-to, inspirational, interview/profile, personal experience, photo feature. All related to religious education in the local church. Buys 100 mss/year. Send complete ms. Length: 300-1,800 words. Pays $25-150.

Reprints: Send tearsheet of article or typed ms with rights for sale noted and information about when and where the article previously appeared. Pays 50% of amount paid for an original article.

Photos: Send photos with ms. Reviews b&w and color prints. Model releases and identification of subjects required. Buys one-time rights.

  ● Looking for more photo-illustrated mss.

CHRISTIAN HOME & SCHOOL, Christian Schools International, 3350 East Paris Ave. SE, Grand Rapids MI 49512. (616)957-1070, ext. 234. Website: http://www.gospelcom.net/csi. Executive Editor: Gordon L. Bordewyk. Contact: Roger Schmurr, senior editor. 30% freelance written. Circ. 58,000. Works with a small number of new/unpublished writers each year. Bimonthly magazine covering family life and Christian education. "For parents who support Christian education. We feature material on a wide range of topics of interest to parents." Estab. 1922. Pays on publication. Publishes ms an average of 4 months after acceptance. Byline given. Buys first North American serial rights. Submit seasonal material 4 months in advance. Reports in 1 month. Sample copy and writer's guidelines for 9 × 12 SAE with 4 first-class stamps. Writer's guidelines only for #10 SASE.

Nonfiction: Book excerpts, interview/profile, opinion, personal experience, articles on parenting and school life. "We

 THE DOUBLE DAGGER before a listing indicates that the listing is new in this edition. New markets are often more receptive to freelance submissions.

publish features on issues that affect the home and school and profiles on interesting individuals, providing that the profile appeals to our readers and is not a tribute or eulogy of that person." Buys 40 mss/year. Send complete ms. Length: 750-2,000 words. Pays $75-150. Sometimes pays the expenses of writers on assignment.

Photos: "If you have any color photos appropriate for your article, send them along."

Tips: "Features are the area most open to freelancers. We are publishing articles that deal with contemporary issues that affect parents. Use an informal easy-to-read style rather than a philosophical, academic tone. Try to incorporate vivid imagery and concrete, practical examples from real life."

CHRISTIAN READER, A Digest of the Best in Christian Reading, Christianity Today, 465 Gundersen Dr., Carol Stream IL 60188. (630)260-6200. Fax: (630)260-0114. E-mail: creditoria@aol.com. Website: http://www.Christian ity.net. Contact: Bonne Steffen, editor. 35% freelance written. Bimonthly magazine for adult evangelical Christian audience. Estab. 1963. Circ. 225,000. **Pays on acceptance for first rights**; on publication for reprints. Byline given. Editorial lead time 6 months. Submit seasonal material 9 months in advance. Reports in 3 weeks. Sample copy for 5×8 SAE with 4 first-class stamps. Writer's guidelines for #10 SASE.

Nonfiction: Humor, inspirational, personal experience, religious. Buys 50 mss/year. Query or article on spec. Length: 500-1,200 words. Pays $100-250 depending on length. Pays expenses of writers on assignment.

Reprints: Send tearsheet or photocopy of article or typed manuscript with rights for sale noted and information about when and where the article previously appeared. Pays 35-50% of amount paid for original article on publication.

Photos: State availability of photos with submission. Negotiates payment individually. Buys one-time rights.

Columns/Departments: Contact: Cynthia Thomas, editorial coordinator. Lite Fare (adult church humor), 50-200 words; Kids of the Kingdom (kids say and do funny things), 50-200 words; Rolling Down the Aisle (humorous wedding tales), 50-200 words. Buys 150 mss/year. Send complete ms. Pays $25-35.

Fillers: End-of-article vignettes, 100-250 words. Send complete ms.

Tips: "Most of our articles are reprints or staff-written. Freelance competition is keen, so tailor submissions to meet our needs by observing the following: *The Christian Reader* audience is truly a general interest one, including men and women, urban professionals and rural homemakers, adults of every age and marital status, and Christians of every church affiliation. We seek to publish a magazine that people from the variety of ethnic groups in North America will find interesting and relevant."

CHRISTIAN SOCIAL ACTION, 100 Maryland Ave. NE, Washington DC 20002. (202)488-5621. Fax: (202)488-1617. E-mail: lranck@igc.org. Editor: Lee Ranck. 2% freelance written. Works with a small number of new/unpublished writers each year. Monthly for "United Methodist clergy and lay people interested in in-depth analysis of social issues, with emphasis on the church's role or involvement in these issues." Circ. 2,500. May buy all rights. Pays on publication. Publishes ms an average of 2 months after acceptance. Rights purchased vary with author and material. Returns rejected material in 5 weeks. Reports on accepted material in a month. Sample copy and writer's guidelines for #10 SASE.

Nonfiction: "This is the social action publication of The United Methodist Church published by the denomination's General Board of Church and Society. Our publication tries to relate social issues to the church—what the church can do, is doing; why the church should be involved. We only accept articles relating to social issues, e.g., war, draft, peace, race relations, welfare, police/community relations, labor, population problems, drug and alcohol problems. No devotional, 'religious,' superficial material, highly technical articles, personal experiences or poetry." Buys 25-30 mss/year. "Query to show that writer has expertise on a particular social issue, give credentials, and reflect a readable writing style." Length: 2,000 words maximum. Pays $75-125. Sometimes pays the expenses of writers on assignment.

Reprints: Send tearsheet of article and note where and when the article previously appeared. Payment negotiable.

Tips: "Write on social issues, but not superficially; we're more interested in finding an expert who can write (e.g., on human rights, alcohol problems, peace issues) than a writer who attempts to research a complex issue."

CHRISTIANITY TODAY, 465 Gundersen Dr., Carol Stream IL 60188-2498. Fax: (630)260-0114. E-mail: ctedit@aol. com. Website: http://www.christianity.net/ct. Contact: Carol Thiessen, administrative editor. 80% freelance written. Works with a small number of new/unpublished writers each year. Semimonthly magazine emphasizing orthodox, evangelical religion "covers Christian doctrine, issues, trends and current events and news from a Christian perspective. It provides a forum for the expression of evangelical conviction in theology, evangelism, church life, cultural life, and society. Special features include issues of the day, books, films, missions, schools, music and services aailable to the Christian market." Estab. 1956. Circ. 180,000. Publishes ms an average of 6 months after acceptance. Usually buys first serial rights. Submit seasonal material at least 8 months in advance. Reports in 3 months. Sample copy and writer's guidelines for 9×12 SAE with 3 first-class stamps.

Nonfiction: Theological, ethical, historical, informational (not merely inspirational). Buys 4 mss/issue. *Query only.* Unsolicited mss not accepted and not returned. Length: 1,000-4,000 words. Pays negotiable rates. Sometimes pays the expenses of writers on assignment.

Reprints: Send typed ms with rights for sale noted and information about when and where the article previously appeared. Pays 25% of amount paid for an original article.

Columns/Departments: Church in Action (profiles of not-so-well-known Christians involved in significant or offbeat services). Buys 7 mss/year. Query only. Length: 900-1,000 words.

Tips: "We are developing more of our own manuscripts and requiring a much more professional quality from others. Queries without SASE will not be answered and manuscripts not containing SASE will not be returned."

CHRYSALIS READER, P.O. Box 549, West Chester PA 19381-0549. Fax: (804)983-1074. E-mail: lawson@aba.org. Send inquiries and mss directly to the editorial office: Route 1, Box 184, Dillwyn VA 23936-9616. Contact: Carol S. Lawson, editor. Managing Editor: Susanna van Rensselaer. 60% freelance written. Biannual literary magazine on spiritually related topics. "*It is very important to send for writer's guidelines and sample copies before submitting.* Content of fiction, articles, reviews, poetry, etc., should be directly focused on that issue's theme and directed to the educated, intellectually curious reader." Estab. 1985. Circ. 3,000. Pays at page-proof stage. Publishes ms an average of 9 months after acceptance. Byline given. Buys first rights and makes work-for-hire assignments. Reports in 1 month on queries; 3 months on mss. Sample copy for $10 and 9×12 SAE. Writer's guidelines and copy deadlines for SASE.

Nonfiction: Essays and interview/profile. Upcoming themes: Play (Autumn 1996); The Good Life (Spring 1997); Symbols (Autumn 1997). Buys 30 mss/year. Query. Length: 2,500-3,500 words. Pays $50-250 for assigned articles; $50-150 for unsolicited articles.

Photos and Illustrations: Send suggestions for illustrations with submission. Offers no additional payment for photos accepted with ms. Captions and identification of subjects required. Buys original artwork for cover and inside copy; b&w illustrations related to theme; pays $25-150. Buys one-time rights.

Fiction: Patte Levan, fiction editor. Adventure, experimental, historical, mainstream, mystery, science fiction, related to theme of issue. Buys 6 mss/year. Query. Length: 2,500-3,500 words. Short fiction more likely to be published. Pays $50-150.

Poetry: Rob Lawson, senior editor. Avant-garde and traditional *but not religious*. Buys 15 poems/year. Pays $25. Submit maximum 6.

COLUMBIA, 1 Columbus Plaza, New Haven CT 06510. (203)772-2130. Editor: Richard McMunn. Monthly magazine for Catholic families. Caters particularly to members of the Knights of Columbus. Estab. 1921. Circ. 1,500,000. **Pays on acceptance.** Buys first serial rights. Free sample copy and writer's guidelines.

Nonfiction and Photos: Fact articles directed to the Catholic layman and his family dealing with current events, social problems, Catholic apostolic activities, education, ecumenism, rearing a family, literature, science, arts, sports and leisure. Color glossy prints, transparencies or contact prints with negatives are required for illustration. Articles without ample illustrative material are not given consideration. Pays up to $500, including photos. Buys 30 mss/year. Query. Length: 1,000-1,500 words.

CONSCIENCE, A Newsjournal of Prochoice Catholic Opinion, Catholics for a Free Choice, 1436 U St. NW, Suite 301, Washington DC 20009-3997. (202)986-6093. E-mail: cffc@ige.apc.org. Contact: Maggie Hume, editor. 80% freelance written. Sometimes works with new/unpublished writers. Quarterly newsjournal covering reproductive health and rights, including but not limited to abortion rights in the church, and church-state issues in US and worldwide. "A feminist, pro-choice perspective is a must, and knowledge of Christianity and specifically Catholicism is helpful." Estab. 1980. Circ. 12,000. Pays on publication. Publishes ms an average of 4 months after acceptance. Byline given. Buys first North American serial rights or makes work-for-hire assignments. Reports in 4 months. Sample copy for 9×12 SAE with 4 first-class stamps. Writer's guidelines for #10 SASE.

Nonfiction: Book excerpts, interview/profile, opinion, issue anaylsis, a small amount of personal experience. Especially needs material that recognizes the complexity of reproductive issues and decisions, and offers original, honest insight. Buys 8-12 mss/year. Query with published clips or send complete ms. Length: 1,000-3,500 words. Pays $25-150. "Writers should be aware that we are a nonprofit organization."

Reprints: Sometimes accepts previously published submissions. Send typed ms with rights for sale noted and information about when and where the article previously appeared. Pays 20-30% of amount paid for an original article.

Photos: State availability of photos with query or ms. Prefers b&w prints. Identification of subjects required.

Columns/Departments: Book reviews. Buys 6-10 mss/year. Length: 600-1,200 words. Pays $25-50.

Fillers: Newsbreaks. Uses 6/year. Length: 100-300 words. $25-35.

Tips: "Say something new on the issue of abortion, or sexuality, or the role of religion or the Catholic church, or women's status in the church. Thoughtful, well-researched and well-argued articles needed. The most frequent mistakes made by writers in submitting an article to us are lack of originality and wordiness."

CORNERSTONE, Cornerstone Communications, Inc., 939 W. Wilson, Chicago IL 60640-5718. (773)989-2080. Fax: (773)989-2076. Editor: Dawn Mortimer. Submissions Editor: Joyce Paskewich. 10% freelance written. Eager to work with new/unpublished writers. Quarterly magazine covering contemporary issues in the light of Evangelical Christianity. Estab. 1972. Pays after publication. Byline given. Buys first serial rights. Submit seasonal material 6 months in advance. Accepts simultaneous submissions. Does not return mss. "We will contact you *only* if your work is accepted for possible publication. We *encourage* simultaneous submissions because we take so long to get back to people! We prefer actual manuscripts to queries." Sample copy and writer's guidelines for 8½×11 envelope with 5 first-class stamps.

Nonfiction: Essays, personal experience, religious. Buys 1-2 mss/year. Query with SASE or send complete ms. 2,700 words maximum. Pays 8-10¢/word. Sometimes pays expenses of writers on assignment.

Reprints: Accepts previously published submissions. Pays 8-10¢/word.

Columns/Departments: Music (interview with artists, mainly rock, focusing on artist's world view and value system as expressed in his/her music), Current Events, Personalities, Film and Book Reviews (focuses on meaning as compared and contrasted to biblical values). Buys 1-4 mss/year. Query. Length: 100-2,500 words (negotiable). Pays 8-10¢/word.

Fiction: "Articles may express Christian world view but should not be unrealistic or 'syrupy.' Other than porn, the sky's the limit. We want fiction as creative as the Creator." Buys 1-4 mss/year. Send complete ms. Length: 250-2,500 words (negotiable). Pays negotiable rate, 8-10¢/word.

Poetry: Tammy Perlmutter, poetry editor. Avant-garde, free verse, haiku, light verse, traditional. No limits *except* for epic poetry ("We've not the room!"). Buys 10-50 poems/year. Submit maximum 5 poems. Payment negotiated. 1-15 lines: $10. Over 15 lines: $25.

Tips: "A display of creativity which expresses a biblical world view without clichés or cheap shots at non-Christians is the ideal. We are known as one of the most avant-garde magazines in the Christian market, yet attempt to express orthodox beliefs in language of the '90s. *Any* writer who does this may well be published by *Cornerstone*. Creative fiction is begging for more Christian participation. We anticipate such contributions gladly. Interviews where well-known personalities respond to the gospel are also strong publication possibilities."

THE COVENANT COMPANION, Covenant Publications of the Evangelical Covenant Church, 5101 N. Francisco Ave., Chicago IL 60625. (773)784-3000. Fax: (773)784-1540. E-mail: 73430.3316@compuserve.com. Contact: Jane K. Swanson-Nystrom, editor. 10-15% freelance written. "As the official monthly organ of The Evangelical Covenant Church, we seek to inform the denomination we serve and encourage dialogue on issues within the church and in our society." Circ. 20,000. Publishes ms an average of 2 months after acceptance. Byline given. Submit seasonal material 4 months in advance. Simultaneous submissions OK. Sample copy for $2.50 and 9 × 12 SASE. Guidelines for #10 SASE.

Nonfiction: Humor, contemporary issues, inspirational, religious. Buys 20-25 mss/year. Send complete ms. Unused mss returned only if accompanied by SASE. Length: 500-2,000 words. Pays $25-75 for assigned articles; pays $25-50 for unsolicited articles.

Reprints: Send tearsheet, photocopy of article or typed ms with rights for sale noted and information about when and where the article previously appeared.

Photos: Send photos with submissions. Reviews prints. Offers no additonal payment for photos accepted with ms. Identification of subjects required. Buys one-time rights.

Poetry: Traditional. Buys 5-10 poems/year. Submit maximum 10 poems. Pays $15-25.

Tips: "Seasonal articles related to church year and on national holidays are welcome."

‡COVENSTEAD, A Journal of the East Coast Pagan Community, Sapphire Press, 113 N. Washington St., #304, Rockville MD 20850. E-mail: saphrpress@aol.com. Editor: Sabrah n'haRaven. 75% freelance written. Quarterly magazine covering the Pagan religious community in the Eastern US. "Our audience is intelligent, active and aware. Material need not be written from a pagan perspective but should have an awareness of the pagan values of personal responsibility, love of diversity and respect for the Web of Life. Our outlook is optimistic, not 'fluffy-bunny.' " Estab. 1996. Pays on publication. Publishes ms an average of 2 months after acceptance. Byline given. Buys first North American serial and electronic rights for 3 months. Submit seasonal material 3 months in advance. Accepts simultaneous submissions. Reports in 1 months on queries; 2 months on mss. Sample copy for $4.95. Writer's guidelines for #10 SASE.

Nonfiction: Book excerpts, essays, general interest, historical/nostalgic, how-to (traditional or outdoor skills, magic), humor, inspirational, interview/profile, opinion, personal experience, photo feature, religious. Buys 20-30 mss/year. Send complete ms. Length: 500-5,000 words. Pays $5-50 for assigned articles; $5-25 for unsolicited articles. Pays writers with contributor copies or other premiums for simultaneous or previously published pieces, poetry and anything under 500 words. Sometimes pays the expenses of writers on assignment.

Photos: Send photos with submission. Reviews prints. Negotiates payment individually. Model releases, identification of subjects required. Buys one-time rights.

Columns/Departments: Parenting 1,500-2,500 words; Heartbeat (drum and dance as a spiritual practice), 750-1,500 words; Reviews (books, movies and music with pagan relevance), 700-800 words. Buys 10-12 mss/year. Send complete ms. Pays $5-25.

Poetry: Free verse, haiku, light verse, traditional. No prose poetry. Submit maximum 10 poems.

Tips: "Non-pagans should try nature or environmental pieces, articles on Eastern U.S. flora or fauna, outdoor skills, traditional crafts, homesteading or intentional communities. Pagan and magical material should be accessible to newbies but directed at readers who are experienced, comfortable with and committed to neo-paganism as a way of life."

DECISION, Billy Graham Evangelistic Association, 1300 Harmon Place, Minneapolis MN 55403-1988. (612)338-0500. Fax: (612)335-1299. E-mail: decision@graham-assn.org. Website: http://www.graham-assn.org/decision. Editor: Roger C. Palms. 25-40% freelance written. Works each year with small number of new/unpublished writers, as well as a solid stable of experienced writers. Monthly magazine with a mission "to set forth to every reader the Good News of salvation in Jesus Christ with such vividness and clarity that he or she will be drawn to make a commitment to Christ; to encourage, teach and strengthen Christians." Estab. 1960. Circ. 1,700,000. Pays on publication. Byline given. Buys first rights and assigns work-for-hire manuscripts, articles, projects. Include telephone number with submission. Submit seasonal material 10 months in advance; other mss published up to 18 months after acceptance. Reports in 3 months on mss. Sample copy for 9 × 12 SAE with 4 first-class stamps. Writer's guidelines for #10 SASE.

Nonfiction: How-to, motivational, personal experience and religious. "No personality-centered articles or articles that are issue-oriented or critical of denominations." Buys approximately 75 mss/year. Send complete ms. Length: 400-1,500 words. Pays $30-250. Pays expenses of writers on assignment.

Photos: State availability of photos with submission. Reviews prints. Captions, model releases and identification of subjects required. Buys one-time rights.

Poetry: Accepting submissions. No queries.

Tips: "We are seeking personal conversion testimonies and personal experience articles that show how God intervened in a person's daily life and the way in which Scripture was applied to the experience in helping to solve the problem. The conversion testimonies describe in first person what author's life was like before he/she became a Christian, how he/she committed his/her life to Christ and what difference He has made since that decision. We also are looking for vignettes on various aspects of personal evangelism. SASE required with submissions."

‡DISCIPLESHIP JOURNAL, NavPress, a division of The Navigators, P.O. Box 35004, Colorado Springs CO 80935-0004. (719)531-3529. Fax: (719)598-7128. E-mail: smaycini@navigato.mms.compuserve.com. Website: http://www.navigators.org/djhome.html. Contact: Susan Maycinik, editor. 90% freelance written. Works with a small number of new/unpublished writers each year. Bimonthly magazine. "The mission of *Discipleship Journal* is to help believers develop a deeper relationship with Jesus Christ, and to provide practical help in understanding the scriptures and applying them to daily life and ministry. We prefer those who have not written for us before begin with nontheme articles, about almost any aspect of Christian living. We'd like more articles that explain a Bible passage and show how to apply it to everyday life, as well as articles about developing a relationship with Jesus; reaching the world; or specific issues related to leadership and helping other believers grow." Estab. 1981. Circ. 95,000. **Pays on acceptance.** Publishes ms an average of 6 months after acceptance. Byline given. Buys first North American serial rights and second serial (reprint) rights. Submit seasonal material 6 months in advance. Reports in 6 weeks. Sample copy and writer's guidelines for $2.24 and 9×12 SAE.

● Ranked as one of the best markets for freelance writers in *Writer's Yearbook* magazine's annual "Top 100 Markets," January 1997.

Nonfiction: Book excerpts (rarely); how-to (grow in Christian faith and disciplines; help others grow as Christians; serve people in need; understand and apply the Bible); inspirational; interview/profile (focusing on one aspect of discipleship); and interpretation/application of the Bible. No personal testimony; humor; anything not directly related to Christian life and faith; politically partisan articles. Buys 80 mss/year. Query with published clips only. Length: 500-3,000 words. Pays 5¢/word for reprint; 20¢/word for first rights. Sometimes pays the expenses of writers on assignment.

Reprints: Send tearsheet of article and information about when and where the article previously appeared. Pays 25% of amount paid for an original article.

Tips: "Our articles are meaty, not fluffy. Study writer's guidelines and back issues and try to use similar approaches. Don't preach. Polish before submitting. About half of the articles in each issue are related to one theme. Freelancers should write to request theme list. We are looking for more practical articles on ministering to others and more articles dealing with world missions."

THE DOOR, P.O. Box 1444, Waco TX 76703-1444. E-mail: 103361.23@compuserve.com. Contact: Robert Darden. 50% freelance written. Works with a small number of new/unpublished writers each year. Bimonthly magazine. "*The Door* is the world's only, oldest and largest religious humor and satire magazine." Estab. 1969. Circ. 14,000. Pays on publication. Publishes ms an average of 1 year after acceptance. Buys first rights. Reports in 3 months. Sample copy for $4.50. Writer's guidelines for SASE.

Nonfiction: Humorous/satirical articles on church renewal, Christianity and organized religion. No book reviews. Buys about 30 mss/year. Submit complete ms. Length: 1,500 words maximum, 750-1,000 preferred. Pays $60-200. Sometimes pays expenses of writers on assignments.

Reprints: Send typed ms with rights for sale noted and information about when and where the article previously appeared. Pays 100% of amount paid for an original article.

Tips: "We look for someone who is clever, on our wave length, and has some savvy about the evangelical church. We are very picky and highly selective. The writer has a better chance of breaking in with our publication with short articles since we are a bimonthly publication with numerous regular features and the magazine is only 52 pages. The most frequent mistake made by writers is that they do not understand satire. They see we are a humor magazine and consequently come off funny/cute (like *Reader's Digest*) rather than funny/satirical (like *National Lampoon*)." *No* poetry.

EVANGEL, Free Methodist Publishing House, P.O. Box 535002, Indianapolis IN 46253-5002. (317)244-3660. Contact: Julie Innes, editor. 100% freelance written. Weekly take-home paper for adults. Estab. 1897. Circ. 22,000. Pays on publication. Publishes ms an average of 1 year after acceptance. Buys simultaneous, second serial (reprint) or one-time rights. Submit seasonal material 9 months in advance. Reports in 1 month. Sample copy and guidelines for #10 SASE.

Nonfiction: Interview (with ordinary person who is doing something extraordinary in his community, in service to others), profile (of missionary or one from similar service profession who is contributing significantly to society), personal experience (finding a solution to a problem common to young adults; coping with handicapped child, for instance, or with a neighborhood problem. Story of how God-given strength or insight saved a situation). Buys 100 mss/year. Submit complete ms. Length: 300-1,000 words. Pays 4¢/word.

Reprints: Send ms and information about when and where the article previously appeared.

Photos: Purchased with accompanying ms. Captions required.

Fiction: Religious themes dealing with contemporary issues dealt with from a Christian frame of reference. Story must "go somewhere." Buys 50 mss/year. Submit complete ms.

Poetry: Free verse, light verse, traditional, religious. Buys 20 poems/year. Submit maximum 6 poems. Length: 4-24 lines. Pays $10.

Tips: "Seasonal material will get a second look. Write an attention grabbing lead followed by an article that says something worthwhile. Relate the lead to some of the universal needs of the reader—promise in that lead to help the reader in some way. Lack of SASE brands author as a nonprofessional; I seldom even bother to read the script."

EVANGELIZING TODAY'S CHILD, Child Evangelism Fellowship Inc., Box 348, Warrenton MO 63383-0348. (314)456-4321. Contact: Elsie Lippy, editor. 50% freelance written. Prefers to work with published/established writers. Bimonthly magazine. "Our purpose is to equip Christians to win the world's children to Christ and disciple them. Our readership is Sunday school teachers, Christian education leaders and children's workers in every phase of Christian ministry to children up to 12 years old." Estab. 1942. Circ. 20,000. Pays within 90 days of acceptance. Publishes ms an average of 6 months after acceptance. Byline given. Offers kill fee if assigned. Buys first serial rights. Submit seasonal material 6 months in advance. Reports in 2 months. Sample copy for $2. Writer's guidelines for SASE.
Nonfiction: Unsolicited articles welcomed from writers with Christian education training or current experience in working with children. Buys 35 mss/year. Query. Length: 1,200. Pays 10-12¢/word.
Reprints: Send photocopy of article and information about when and where the article previously appeared. Pays 35% of amount paid for an original article.

FAITH TODAY, Canada's Evangelical News/Feature Magazine, Evangelical Fellowship of Canada, MIP Box 3745, Markham, Ontario L3R 0Y4 Canada. (905)479-5885. Fax: (905)479-4742. E-mail: ft@efc-canada.com. Contact: Marianne Meed Ward, managing editor. "*FT* is a bimonthly interdenominational, evangelical news/feature magazine that informs Canadian Christians on issues facing church and society, and on events within the church community. It focuses on corporate faith interacting with society rather than on personal spiritual life. Writers should have a thorough understanding of the *Canadian evangelical* community." Estab. 1983. Circ. 18,000. Pays on publication. Publishes ms an average of 6 months after acceptance. Byline given. Offers 30-50% kill fee. Buys first rights. Editorial lead time 4 months. Reports in 6 weeks. Sample copy and writer's guidelines free.
Nonfiction: Religious, news feature. Buys 75 mss/year. Query. Length: 400-2,000 words. Pays $250-600. Sometimes pays expenses of writers on assignment.
Reprints: Send photocopy of article. Pays 50% of amount paid for an original article.
Photos: State availability of photos with submission. Reviews contact sheets, prints. Identification of subjects required. Buys one-time rights.
Tips: "Query should include brief outline and names of the sources you plan to interview in your research. Use Canadian postage on SASE."

THE FAMILY DIGEST, P.O. Box 40137, Fort Wayne IN 46804. Editor: Corine B. Erlandson. 95% freelance written. Bimonthly digest-sized magazine. "*The Family Digest* is dedicated to the joy and fulfillment of the Catholic family, and its relationship to the Catholic parish." Estab. 1945. Circ. 150,000. Pays within 1-2 months of acceptance. Publishes ms usually within 1 year after acceptance. Byline given. Buys first North American rights. Submit seasonal material 7 months in advance. Reports in 2 months. Sample copy and writer's guidelines for 6×9 SAE with 2 first-class stamps.
Nonfiction: Family life, parish life, how-to, seasonal, inspirational, prayer life, Catholic traditions. Send ms with SASE. No poetry or fiction. Buys 60 unsolicited mss/year. Length: 750-1,200 words. Pays $40-60/article.
Reprints: Prefers to publish previously unpublished articles. Send typed ms with rights for sale noted and information about when and where the article previously appeared. Pays 5¢/word.
Fillers: Anecdotes, tasteful humor based on personal experience. Buys 3/issue. Length: 25-125 words maximum. Pays $10-20, on acceptance. Cartoons: Publishes 5 cartoons/issue, related to family and Catholic parish life. Pays $25/cartoon, on acceptance.
Tips: "Prospective freelance contributors should be familiar with the publication, and the types of articles we accept and publish. We are especially looking for upbeat articles which affirm the simple ways in which the Catholic faith is expressed in daily life. Articles on family and parish life, including seasonal articles, how-to pieces, inspirational, prayer, spiritual life and Church traditions, will be gladly reviewed for possible acceptance and publication."

‡FOURSQUARE WORLD ADVANCE, International Church of the Foursquare Gospel, 1910 W. Sunset Blvd., Suite 200, P.O. Box 26902, Los Angeles CA 90026-0176. Editor: Ronald D. Williams. 5% freelance written. Bimonthly magazine covering Devotional/Religious material, denominational news. "The official publication of the International Church of the Foursquare Gospel is distributed without charge to members and friends of the Foursquare Church." Estab. 1917. Circ. 98,000. Pays on publication. Publishes ms an average of 2 months after acceptance. Byline given. Buys first rights, one-time rights, second serial (reprint) rights and simultaneous rights. Editorial lead time 6 months. Submit seasonal material 6 months in advance. Reports in 2 weeks on queries. Sample copy and writer's guidelines free.
Nonfiction: Inspirational, interview/profile, personal experience, religious. Buys 2-3 mss/year. Send complete ms. Length: 800-1,200 words. Pays $75.
Reprints: Accepts previously published submissions.
Photos: State availability of photos with submission. Reviews 4×6 prints. Offers no additional payment for photos accepted with ms. Captions, model releases, identification of subjects required. Buys one-time rights.

GROUP MAGAZINE, Group Publishing Inc., P.O. Box 481, Loveland CO 80538. (303)669-3836. Fax: (303)669-3269. E-mail: rick_lawrence@ministrynet.usa.net. Contact: Rick Lawrence, editor. Publisher: Rocky Gilmore. Departments Editor: Barbara Beach. 60% freelance written. Bimonthly magazine covering youth ministry. "Writers must be actively involved in youth ministry. Articles we accept are practical, not theoretical, and focused for local church youth workers." Estab. 1974. Circ. 57,000. **Pays on acceptance.** Publishes ms an average of 6 months after acceptance. Byline given. Offers $20 kill fee. Buys all rights. Submit seasonal material 7 months in advance. Reports in 2 months. Sample copy for $2 and 9×12 SAE. Writer's guidelines for SASE.

Nonfiction: How-to (youth ministry issues). No personal testimony, theological or lecture-style articles. Buys 50-60 mss/year. Query. Length: 250-2,200 words. Pays $35-250. Sometimes pays for phone calls on agreement.

Photos: State availability of photos with ms. Model releases and identification of subjects required. Buys all rights.

Tips: "Need more 'mini-articles' of 250 words or less in the following areas: youth outreach ideas; working with parents; working with youth; working with adult volunteers; tips on managing your personal life."

GUIDEPOSTS MAGAZINE, 16 E. 34th St., New York NY 10016-4397. Website: http://www.guideposts.org. Contact: Fulton Oursler, Jr., editor. 30% freelance written. "Works with a small number of new/unpublished writers each year. *Guideposts* is an inspirational monthly magazine for people of all faiths, in which men and women from all walks of life tell in first-person narrative how they overcame obstacles, rose above failures, handled sorrow, learned to master themselves and became more effective people through faith in God." Estab. 1945. Publishes ms an "indefinite" number of months after acceptance. Pays 25% kill fee for assigned articles. "Most of our stories are ghosted articles, so the writer would not get a byline unless it was his/her own story." Buys all rights and second serial (reprint) rights. Reports in 2 months.

Nonfiction and Fillers: Articles and features should be written in simple, anecdotal style with an emphasis on human interest. Short mss of approximately 250-750 words (pays $100-250) considered for such features as "Angels Among Us," "The Divine Touch" and general one-page stories. Address short items to Celeste McCauley. For full-length mss, 750-1,500 words, pays $250-500. All mss should be typed, double-spaced and accompanied by SASE. Annually awards scholarships to high school juniors and seniors in writing contest. Buys 40-60 unsolicited mss/year. Pays expenses of writers on assignment.

Tips: "Study the magazine before you try to write for it. Each story must make a single spiritual point. The freelancer would have the best chance of breaking in by aiming for a one- or two-page article. Sensitively written anecdotes are extremely useful. And it is much easier to just sit down and write them than to have to go through the process of preparing a query. They should be warm, well written, intelligent and upbeat. We like personal narratives that are true and have some universal relevance, but the religious element does not have to be driven home with a sledge hammer. A writer succeeds with us if he or she can write a true article in short-story form with scenes, drama, tension and a resolution of the problem presented. We are especially in need of stories in which faith in God helps people succeed in business or with other life challenges."

HOME TIMES, A Good Little Newspaper, Neighbor News, Inc., 3676 Collin Dr., #12, West Palm Beach FL 33406. (407)439-3509. E-mail: 74157.363@compuserve.com. Contact: Dennis Lombard, publisher/editor. 80% freelance written. Monthly tabloid of conservative, pro-Christian news and views. "*Home Times* is a conservative newspaper written for the general public but with a pro-Christian, family-values slant. It is not religious or preachy. We went on the Internet in February 1997. We want to place our best articles on there too. We will **pay on acceptance** if we select your article and pay double." Estab. 1988. Circ. 5,000. Pays on publication. Publishes ms an average of 3 months after acceptance. Byline given. No kill fee. Buys one-time rights or makes work-for-hire assignments. Editorial lead time 1 month. Submit seasonal material 1 month in advance. Accepts simultaneous submissions. Reports in 1 month. Sample copy for $3. Writer's guidelines for #10 SASE.

● *Home Times* wants material for Human Heroes, Fatherhood, Light a Candle, Miracles, and People Features with photos. The editor notes the magazine became a weekly by year-end 1997, tripling freelance needs.

Nonfiction: Current events, essays, general interest, historical/nostalgic, how-to, humor, inspirational, interview/profile, opinion, personal experience, photo feature, religious, travel. "Nothing preachy, moralistic or with churchy slant." Buys 50 mss/year. Send complete ms. Length: 800 maximum words. Pays $5 minimum. Pays contributor's copies on mutual agreement. Sometimes pays expenses of writers on assignment.

Reprints: Send tearsheet or photocopy of article or short story and information about when and where the material previously appeared. Pays $5 minimum.

Photos: Send photos with submission. Reviews any size prints. Offers $5/photo used. Captions, model releases (when legally needed), identification of subjects required. Buys one-time rights.

Columns/Departments: Buys 50 mss/year. Send complete ms. Pays $5-25.

Fiction: Historical, humorous, mainstream, religious, issue-oriented contemporary. "Nothing preachy, moralistic." Buys 10 mss/year. Send complete ms. Length: 500-900 words. Pays $5-25.

Poetry: Free verse, light verse, traditional. Buys 12 poems/year. Submit max. 3 poems. Lines: 2-24 lines. Pays $5.

Fillers: Anecdotes, facts, good quotes, short humor. Uses 25/year. Length: to 100 words. Pays 6 issues.

Tips: "We encourage new writers. We are different from ordinary news or religious publications. We strongly suggest you read guidelines and sample issues. (Writer's subscription 12 issues for $9.) We are most open to material for new columns; journalists covering hard news in major news centers—with conservative slant. Also, lots of letters and op-eds though we don't always pay for them."

THE JEWISH NEWS, Or V'Shalom, Inc., P.O. Box 269, Northampton MA 01061. (413)582-9870. Fax: (413)582-9847. E-mail: jwnews18@aol.com. Contact: Kenneth G. White, editor. 25% freelance written. Jewish biweekly publication of news and features, secular and non-secular; World Judaism; arts (New England based). Estab. 1945. Circ. 5,000. Pays on publication. Publishes ms an average of 2 months after acceptance. Byline given. Not copyrighted. Buys first North American serial rights and second serial (reprint) rights. Submit seasonal material 2 months in advance. Accepts simultaneous submissions. Reports in 3 months. Sample copy for 9×12 SAE with 5 first-class stamps.

Nonfiction: Interview/profile, religious, travel. Special issues: Jewish New Year (September); Chanukah (December); Bridal (Winter/Fall); Bar/Bat Mitzvahs (May). Buys 20 mss/year. Send complete ms. Length: 500-1,000 words. Pays $15-35/article.

Reprints: Send photocopy of article and information about when and where the article previously appeared. Pays 100% of amount paid for an original article.

Photos: Send photos with submission. Reviews 5×7 prints. Pays $5. Identification of subjects required.

Columns/Departments: Jewish Kitchen (Kosher recipes), 300-500 words. Buys 10 mss/year. Query with published clips. Length: 300-1,000 words. Pays $15-25/article.

‡LIGUORIAN, Liguori MO 63057-9999. Fax: (314)464-8449. E-mail: 104626.1547@compuserve.com. Website: http://www.liguori.org. Editor: Rev. Allan Weinert. Managing Editor: Cheryl Plass. 25% freelance written. Prefers to work with published/established writers. General interest monthly magazine for Catholics. Estab. 1913. Circ. 300,000. **Pays on acceptance.** Buys all rights but will reassign rights to author *after* publication upon written request. Submit seasonal material 6 months in advance. Reports in up to 6 months. Sample copy and writer's guidelines for 6×9 SAE with 3 first-class stamps.

Nonfiction: "Pastoral, practical and personal approach to the problems and challenges of people today. No travelogue approach or unresearched ventures into controversial areas. Also, no material found in secular publications—fad subjects that already get enough press, pop psychology, negative or put-down articles." Buys 60 unsolicited mss/year. Buys 12 fiction mss/year. Length: 400-2,000 words. Pays 10-12¢/word. Sometimes pays expenses of writers on assignment.

Photos: Photographs on assignment only unless submitted with and specific to article.

THE LIVING CHURCH, Living Church Foundation, 816 E. Juneau Ave., P.O. Box 92936, Milwaukee WI 53202. (414)276-5420. Fax: (414)276-7483. E-mail: livngchrch@aol.com. Editor: David Kalvelage. Managing Editor: John Schuessler. 50% freelance written. Weekly religious magazine on the Episcopal church. News or articles of interest to members of the Episcopal church. Estab. 1878. Circ. 9,000. Does not pay unless article is requested. Publishes ms an average of 3 months after acceptance. Byline given. Buys one-time rights. Editorial lead time 3 weeks. Submit seasonal material 1 month in advance. Reports in 2 weeks on queries; 1 month on mss. Sample copy free.

Nonfiction: Opinion, personal experience, photo feature, religious. Buys 10 mss/year. Send complete ms. Length: 1,000 words. Pays $25-100. Sometimes pays expenses of writers on assignment.

Photos: Send photos with submission. Reviews any size prints. Offers $15-50/photo. Buys one-time rights.

Columns/Departments: Benediction (devotional) 250 words; Viewpoint (opinion) under 1,000 words. Send complete ms. Pays $50 maximum.

Poetry: Light verse, traditional.

LIVING WITH TEENAGERS, Lifeway Press, 127 Ninth Ave. N., Nashville TN 37234. (615)251-2229. Fax: (615)251-5008. E-mail: lwt@bssb.com. Contact: Michelle Hicks, managing editor. 30% freelance written. Works with a small number of new/unpublished writers each year. Monthly magazine about teenagers for parents of teenagers. Estab. 1978. Circ. 50,000. Pays within 2 months of acceptance. Publishes ms an average of 10 months after acceptance. Buys all or first rights. Submit seasonal material 1 year in advance. Reports in 2 months. Sample copy for 9×12 SAE with 4 first-class stamps. Writer's guidelines for #10 SASE. Résumés and queries only.

THE LOOKOUT, 8121 Hamilton Ave., Cincinnati OH 45231-9981. (513)931-4050. Fax: (513)931-0950. Contact: Andrea C. Ritze, managing editor. 40-50% freelance written. Weekly magazine for Christian adults, with emphasis on spiritual growth, family life, and topical issues. Audience is mainly conservative Christians. Estab. 1894. **Pays on acceptance.** Publishes ms an average of 6 months after acceptance. Byline given. Buys first serial, one-time, second serial (reprint) or simultaneous rights. Accepts simultaneous submissions. Reports in 4 months, sometimes longer. Sample copy and writer's guidelines for 75¢. "We now work from a theme list, which is available on request with our guidelines." Guidelines only for #10 SASE.

Nonfiction: "Seeks stories about real people; items that are helpful in practical Christian living (how-to's) or shed Biblical light on matters of contemporary controversy; and items that motivate, that lead the reader to ask, 'Why shouldn't I try that?' Articles should tell how real people are involved for Christ. In choosing topics, *The Lookout* considers timeliness, the church and national calendar, and the ability of the material to fit the above guidelines. Aim at laymen." Submit complete ms. Length: 400-1,800 words. Pays 5-12¢/word. We also use inspirational short pieces. "About 400-700 words is a good length for these. Relate an incident that illustrates a point without preaching."

Reprints: Send typed ms with rights for sale noted and information about when and where the article previously appeared. Pays 60% of amount paid for an original article.

Tips: "We have tightened the focus of *The Lookout*, to concentrate on three areas: (1) personal Christian growth; (2) home and family life; (3) social issues from a Christian perspective."

THE LUTHERAN, Magazine of the Evangelical Lutheran Church in America, Evangelical Lutheran Church in America, 8765 W. Higgins Rd., Chicago IL 60631-4183. (773)380-2540. Fax: (773)380-2751. E-mail: lutheran@elca.

org. Editor: Edgar R. Trexler. Managing Editor: Roger R. Kahle. 30% freelance written. Monthly magazine for "lay people in church. News and activities of the Evangelical Lutheran Church in America, news of the world of religion, ethical reflections on issues in society, personal Christian experience." Estab. 1988. Circ. 800,000. **Pays on acceptance.** Publishes ms an average of 3 months after acceptance. Byline given. Offers 50% kill fee. Buys first rights. Submit seasonal material 4 months in advance. Reports in 3 weeks. Free sample copy and writer's guidelines.
Nonfiction: David L. Miller. Inspirational, interview/profile, personal experience, photo feature, religious. "No articles unrelated to the world of religion." Buys 40 mss/year. Query with published clips. Length: 1,000-1,500 words. Pays $400-1,000 for assigned articles; $100-500 for unsolicited articles. Pays expenses of writers on assignment.
Photos: Send photos with submission. Reviews contact sheets, transparencies, prints. Offers $50-175/photo. Captions and identification of subjects required. Buys one-time rights.
Columns/Departments: Lite Side (humor—church, religious), In Focus, Living the Faith, Values & Society, In Our Churches, Our Church at Work, 25-100 words. Send complete ms. Length: 25-100 words. Pays $10.
Tips: "Writers have the best chance selling us feature articles."

THE LUTHERAN JOURNAL, 7317 Cahill Rd., Edina MN 55439-2081. Fax: (612)941-3010. Publisher: Michael L. Beard. Editor: Rev. Armin U. Deye. Contact: Stephani Kargas, editorial assistant. Quarterly family magazine for Lutheran Church members, middle age and older. Estab. 1938. Circ. 125,000. Pays on publication. Byline given. Accepts simultaneous submissions. Reports in 4 months. Sample copy for 9×12 SAE with 2 first-class stamps.
Nonfiction: Inspirational, religious, human interest, historical articles. Interesting or unusual church projects. Informational, how-to, personal experience, interview, humor, think articles. Buys 25-30 mss/year. Submit complete ms. Length: 1,500 words maximum; occasionally 2,000 words. Pays 1-4¢/word.
Reprints: Send tearsheet or photocopy of article or typed ms with rights for sale noted and information about when and where the article previously appeared. Pays up to 50% of amount paid for an original article.
Photos: Send photocopies of b&w and color photos with accompanying ms. Please do not send original photos.
Fiction: Mainstream, religious, historical. Must be suitable for church distribution. Length: 2,000 words maximum. Pays 1-2¢/word.

THE LUTHERAN WITNESS, The Lutheran Church—Missouri Synod, 1333 S. Kirkwood Rd., St. Louis MO 63122. (314)965-9000. Fax: (314)965-3396. E-mail: ic_mahsmadl@lcms.org. Editor: Rev. David Mahsman. Contact: David Strand, managing editor. 50% freelance written. Monthly magazine. "*The Lutheran Witness* provides Missouri Synod laypeople with stories and information that complement congregational life, foster personal growth in faith, and help interpret the contemporary world from a Christian perspective." Estab. 1882. Circ. 325,000. **Pays on acceptance.** Publishes ms an average of 6 months after acceptance. Byline given. Offers 50% kill fee. Buys first rights. Editorial lead time 4 months. Submit seasonal material 6 months in advance. Accepts simultaneous submissions. Reports in 2 months. Sample copy and writer's guidelines free.
Nonfiction: General interest, humor, inspirational, interview/profile, opinion, personal experience, religious. Buys 40-50 mss/year. Send complete ms. Length: 250-1,600. Pays $100-300. Pays expenses of writers on assignment.
Reprints: Accepts previously published submissions.
Photos: Send photos with submission. Offers $50-200/photo. Captions required. Buys one-time rights.
Columns/Departments: Humor, Opinion, Bible Studies. Buys 60 mss/year. Send complete ms. Pays $50-100.

‡MENNONITE BRETHREN HERALD, 3-169 Riverton Ave., Winnipeg, Manitoba R2L 2E5 Canada. (204)669-6575. Fax: (204)654-1865. E-mail: mbherald@cdnmbconf.ca. Website: www.cdnmbconf.ca/mb/mbherald.htm. Contact: Jim Coggins, editor or Susan Brandt, managing editor. 25% freelance written. Biweekly family publication "read mainly by people of the Mennonite faith, reaching a wide cross section of professional and occupational groups, including many homemakers. Readership includes people from both urban and rural communities. It is intended to inform members of events in the church and the world, serve personal and corporate spiritual needs, serve as a vehicle of communication within the church, serve conference agencies and reflect the history and theology of the Mennonite Brethren Church." Estab. 1962. Circ. 15,500. Pays on publication. Publishes ms an average of 6 months after acceptance. Not copyrighted. Byline given. Buys one-time rights. Sample copy for $1 and 9×12 SAE with 2 IRCs. Reports in 6 months.
Nonfiction: Articles with a Christian family orientation; youth directed, Christian faith and life, and current issues. Wants articles critiquing the values of a secular society, attempting to relate Christian living to the practical situations of daily living; showing how people have related their faith to their vocations. Send complete ms. Length: 250-1,500 words. Pays $30-40. Pays the expenses of writers on assignment.
Reprints: Send tearsheet of article. Pays 75% of amount paid for an original article.
Photos: Photos purchased with ms.
Columns/Departments: Viewpoint (Christian opinion on current topics), 850 words. Crosscurrent (Christian opinion on music, books, art, TV, movies), 350 words.
Poetry: Length: 25 lines maximum.
Tips: "We like simple style, contemporary language and fresh ideas. Writers should take care to avoid religious clichés."

‡MESSAGE MAGAZINE, Review and Herald Publishing, 55 West Oak Ridge Dr., Hagerstown MD 21740. (301)791-7000 ext. 2565. Fax: (301)714-1753. E-mail: 74617.3047@compuserve.com. Editor: Stephen P. Ruff. Assistant Editor: Lee Anna A. Jackson. Contact: Editorial Secretary. 10-20% freelance written. Bimonthly magazine. "*Message* is the oldest religious journal addressing ethnic issues in the country. Our audience is predominantly black and Seventh-day

Adventist; however, *Message* is an outreach magazine geared to the unchurched." Estab. 1798. Circ. 80,000. **Pays on acceptance**. Publishes ms an average of 6-12 months after acceptance. Byline given. Buys first North American serial rights; "the exception to this rule is for supplemental issues, for which we usually purchase all rights." Editorial lead time 6 months. Submit seasonal material 6 months in advance. Send complete ms. Reports in 6-9 months. Sample copy and writer's guidelines free.

Nonfiction: General interest to a Christian audience, how-to (overcome depression; overcome defeat; get closer to God; learn from failure, etc.), inspirational, interview/profile (profiles of famous African-Americans), personal experience (testimonies), religious. Buys 10 mss/year. Send complete ms. Length: 800-1,300 words. Pays $50-300.

Photos: State availability of photos with submission. Identification of subjects preferred. Buys one-time rights.

Columns/Departments: Voices in the Wind (community involvement/service/events/health info); Message, Jr. (stories for children with a moral, explain a biblical or moral principle); Recipes (no meat or dairy products—averages 12-15 recipes along with an intro); Healthspan (health issues); all 500 words. Buys 12-15 mss/year. Send complete ms for Message, Jr. and Healthspan. Query assistant editor with published clips for Voices in the Wind and Recipes. Pays $50-300.

Fiction: "We do not generally accept fiction, but when we do it's for Message, Jr. and/or has a religious theme. We buy about 3 (if that many) fictional manuscripts a year." Send complete ms. Length: 500-700 words. Pays $50-125.

Fillers: Anecdotes, facts, newsbreaks. Buys 1-5 fillers/year. Length: 200-500 words. Pays $50-125.

Tips: "Please look at the magazine before submitting manuscripts. *Message* publishes a variety of writing styles as long as the writing style is easy to read and flows—please avoid highly technical writing styles."

THE MESSENGER OF THE SACRED HEART, Apostleship of Prayer, 661 Greenwood Ave., Toronto, Ontario M4J 4B3 Canada. (416)466-1195. Editor: Rev. F.J. Power, S.J. Monthly magazine for "Canadian and U.S. Catholics interested in developing a life of prayer and spirituality; stresses the great value of our ordinary actions and lives." 20% freelance written. Estab. 1891. Circ. 16,000. Buys first rights only. Byline given. **Pays on acceptance.** Submit seasonal material 5 months in advance. Reports in 1 month. Sample copy for $1, 7½×10½ SAE. Writer's guidelines for SASE.

Fiction: Religious/inspirational. Stories about people, adventure, heroism, humor, drama. Buys 12 mss/year. Send complete ms with SAE and IRCs. Does not return mss without SASE. Length: 750-1,500 words. Pays 4¢/word.

Tips: "Develop a story that sustains interest to the end. Do not preach, but use plot and characters to convey the message or theme. Aim to move the heart as well as the mind. Before sending, cut out unnecessary or unrelated words or sentences. If you can, add a light touch or a sense of humor to the story. Your ending should have impact, leaving a moral or faith message for the reader."

THE MIRACULOUS MEDAL, 475 E. Chelten Ave., Philadelphia PA 19144-5785. (215)848-1010. Fax: (215)848-1014. Editorial Director: Rev. William J. O'Brien, C.M. Contact: Mr. Charles Kelly, office manager. 40% freelance written. Quarterly. Estab. 1915. **Pays on acceptance.** Publishes ms an average of 2 years after acceptance. Buys first North American serial rights. Buys articles only on special assignment. Reports in 3 months. Sample copy for 6×9 SAE with 2 first-class stamps.

Fiction: Should not be pious or sermon-like. Wants good general fiction—not necessarily religious, but if religion is basic to the story, the writer should be sure of his facts. Only restriction is that subject matter and treatment must not conflict with Catholic teaching and practice. Can use seasonal material, Christmas stories. Length: 2,000 words maximum. Occasionally uses short-shorts from 750-1,250 words. Pays 2¢/word minimum.

Poetry: Maximum of 20 lines, preferably about the Virgin Mary or at least with religious slant. Pays 50¢/line minimum.

THE MONTANA CATHOLIC, Diocese of Helena, P.O. Box 1729, Helena MT 59624. (406)442-5820. Fax: (406)442-5191. Contact: Gerald M. Korson, editor. 3% freelance written. Tabloid published 16 times/year. "We publish news and features from a Catholic perspective, particularly as they pertain to the church in western Montana." Estab. 1932. Circ. 9,100. **Pays on acceptance.** Publishes ms an average of 1 year after acceptance. Byline given. Buys first, one-time, second serial (reprint) or simultaneous rights. Editorial lead time 1 month. Submit seasonal material 3 months in advance. Accepts simultaneous submissions. Reports in 1 month on queries; 2 months on mss. Send SASE for reply and/or return of mss. Sample copy for $2. Writer's guidelines for #10 SASE.

Nonfiction: Special issues: Marriage (February); Vocations (Spring and Fall); Easter, Lent, Christmas, Advent; Health; Older Persons; Death and Dying (Fall). Buys 10 mss/year. Send complete ms. Length: 400-1,200 words. Pays $10-100 for assigned articles; $10-50 for unsolicited articles. Sometimes pays expenses of writers on assignment.

Reprints: Accepts previously published submissions. Send tearsheet, photocopy or typed ms with rights for sale noted and information about when and where article previously appeared.

Photos: Reviews contact sheets, 5×7 prints. Offers $5-20/photo. Must identify subjects. Buys one time rights.

Tips: "Best bet is seasonal pieces, topics related to our special supplements and features with a tie-in to western Montana—always with a Catholic angle."

MOODY MAGAZINE, Moody Bible Institute, 820 N. LaSalle Blvd., Chicago IL 60610. (312)329-2164. Fax: (312)329-2149. E-mail: moodyedit@aol.com. Website: http://moody.edu. Contact: Andrew Scheer, managing editor. 62% freelance written. Bimonthly magazine for evangelical Christianity (6 issues/year). "Our readers are conservative, evangelical Christians highly active in their churches and concerned about applying their faith in daily living." Estab. 1900. Circ. 115,000. **Pays on acceptance.** Publishes ms an average of 9 months after acceptance. Byline given. Buys first North American serial rights. Submit seasonal material 9 months in advance. Query first for all submissions, but

not by fax or phone. Unsolicited mss will be returned unread. Reports in 2 months. Sample copy for 9×12 SASE with $2 first-class postage. Writer's guidelines for #10 SASE.
* Ranked as one of the best markets for freelance writers in *Writer's Yearbook* magazine's annual "Top 100 Markets," January 1997.

Nonfiction: Personal narratives (on living the Christian life), a few reporting articles. Buys 55 mss/year. "No biographies, historical articles, or studies of Bible figures." Query. Length: 1,200-2,200 words. Pays 15¢/word for queried articles; 20¢/word for assigned articles. Sometimes pays the expenses of writers on assignment.

Columns/Departments: First Person (the only article written for non-Christians; a personal conversion testimony written by the author [will accept 'as told to's']; the objective is to tell a person's testimony in such a way that the reader will understand the gospel and want to receive Christ as Savior), 800-1,000 words; Just for Parents (provides practical anecdotal guidance for parents, solidly based on biblical principles), 1,500 words; News Focus (in-depth, researched account of current news or trend), 1,000-1,400 words. Buys 12 mss/year. May query by phone or fax for News Focus only. Pays 15¢/word.

Tips: "We have moved to bimonthly publication, with a larger editorial well in each issue. We want articles that cover a broad range of topics, but with one common goal: to foster application by a broad readership of specific biblical principles. By publishing accounts of people's spiritual struggles, growth and discipleship, our aim is to encourage readers in their own obedience to Christ. While *Moody* continues to look for many authors to use a personal narrative style, we're also looking for some pieces that use an anecdotal reporting approach."

MY DAILY VISITOR, Our Sunday Visitor, Inc., 200 Noll Plaza, Huntington IN 46750. (219)356-8400. Contact: Catherine and William Odell, editors. 99% freelance written. Bimonthly magazine of Scripture meditations based on the day's Catholic mass readings. Circ. 30,000. **Pays on acceptance.** Publishes ms an average of 6 months after acceptance. Byline given. Not copyrighted. Buys one-time rights. Reports in 2 months. Sample copy and writer's guidelines for #10 SAE with 2 first-class stamps. "Guest editors write on assignment basis only."

Nonfiction: Inspirational, personal experience, religious. Buys 12 mss/year. Query with published clips. Length: 150-160 words times number of days in month. Pays $500 for 1 month (28-31) of meditations. Pays writers 25 gratis copies.

NEW WORLD OUTLOOK, The Mission Magazine of The United Methodist Church, General Board of Global Ministries, 475 Riverside Dr., Room 1470, New York NY 10115. (212)870-3600. Fax: (212)870-3940. E-mail: nwo@gbgm-umc.org. Website: http://www.gbgm-umc.org. Editor: Alma Graham. Contact: Christie R. House. 20% freelance written. Bimonthly magazine covering United Methodist mission programs, projects, and personnel. "As the mission magazine of The United Methodist Church, we publish articles on or related to the mission programs, projects, institutions, and personnel of the General Board of Global Ministries, both in the United States and around the world." Estab. 1911. Circ. 30,000. Pays on publication. Publishes ms an average of 4 months after acceptance. Byline given. Offers 50% kill fee or $100. Buys all rights. Editorial lead time 4 months. Submit seasonal material 4 months in advance. No simultaneous or previously published submissions. Sample copy for $2.50.

Nonfiction: Photo features, mission reports, mission studies. Special issues: Indonesia; Refugees and Global Migration. Buys 24 mss/year. Query. Length: 500-2,000 words. Pays $50-300. Sometimes pays expenses of writers on assignment.

Photos: State availability of photos with submission. Reviews transparencies, prints. Offers $25-150/photo. Captions, identification of subjects required.

Tips: "Write for a list of United Methodist mission institutions, projects, or personnel in the writer's geographic area or in an area of the country or the world to which the writer plans to travel (at writer's own expense). Photojournalists have a decided advantage."

OBLATES, Missionary Association of Mary Immaculate, 9480 N. De Mazenod Dr., Belleville IL 62223-1160. (618)398-4848. Managing Editor: Christine Portell. Contact: Mary Mohrman, manuscripts editor. 30-50% freelance written. Prefers to work with published writers. Bimonthly inspirational magazine for Christians; audience mainly older Catholic adults. Circ. 500,000. **Pays on acceptance.** Usually publishes ms within 2 years after acceptance. Byline given. Buys first North American serial rights. Submit seasonal material 6 months in advance. Reports in 2 months. Sample copy and writer's guidelines for 6×9 or larger SAE with 2 first-class stamps.

Nonfiction: Inspirational and personal experience with positive spiritual insights. No preachy, theological or research articles. Avoid current events and controversial topics. Send complete ms; 500-600 words. "No queries." Pays $80.

Poetry: Light verse—reverent, well written, perceptive, with traditional rhythm and rhyme. "Emphasis should be on inspiration, insight and relationship with God." Submit maximum 2 poems. Length: 8-16 lines. Pays $30.

Tips: "Our readership is made up mostly of mature Americans who are looking for comfort, encouragement, and a positive sense of applicable Christian direction to their lives. Focus on sharing of personal insight to problem (i.e. death or change), but must be positive, uplifting. We have well-defined needs for an established market, but are always on the lookout for exceptional work."

ORTHODOX MISSION, AXIOS Publishing, Inc., 30-32 Macaw Ave., P.O. Box 279, Belmopan, Belize. (011)501-823284. Fax: (011)501-823633. E-mail: danielg@btl.net. Contact: Father Daniel, editor. 20% freelance written. Quarterly newsletter. "We cover the mission activities of the Orthodox Church in Belize, as well as cover all items of interest concerning Belize so the world in general may get to know the country better." Estab. 1990. Circ. 15,487. **Pays on acceptance.** Publishes ms an average of 4 months after acceptance. Byline given. Buys first rights. Editorial lead time 4 months. Submit seasonal material 5 months in advance. Accepts simultaneous submissions. Reports in 1 month on queries; 4 months on mss. Sample copy for $2. No American stamps please. Belize has its own post office.

Nonfiction: Book excerpts, essays, general interest, historical/nostalgic, interview/profile, religious, travel. Buys 10-20 mss/year. Query. Length: open. Pays $50-1,000.

Reprints: Send typed ms with rights for sale noted and information about when and where the article previously appeared. Pays 60% of amount paid for an original article.

Fillers: Anecdotes, facts, gags to be illustrated by cartoonist, short humor. Buys 10-15/year. Pays $10-100.

‡THE OTHER SIDE, 300 W. Apsley St., Philadelphia PA 19144-4285. (215)849-2178. Coeditors: Dee Dee Risher and Doug Davidson. 25% freelance written. Prefers to work with published/established writers. Bimonthly magazine emphasizing "spiritual nurture, prophetic reflection, forgotten voices and artistic visions from a radical Christian perspective." Estab. 1965. Circ. 14,000. **Pays on acceptance.** Publishes ms an average of 6 months after acceptance. Byline given. Buys all or first serial rights. Reports in 3 months. Sample copy for $4.50. Writer's guidelines for #10 SASE.

Nonfiction: Doug Davidson, coeditor. Current social, political and economic issues in the US and around the world: personality profiles, interpretative essays, interviews, how-to's, personal experiences, spiritual reflections, biblical interpretation and investigative reporting. "Articles must be lively, vivid and down-to-earth, with a radical faith-based Christian perspective." Length: 500-3,500 words. Pays $25-300.

Photos: Cathleen Benberg, art director. Photos or photo essays illustrating current social, political, or economic reality in the US and Third World. Especially interested in creative original art offering spiritual insight and/or fresh perspectives on contemporary issues. Pays $15-75 for b&w and $50-300 for color.

Fiction: Robert Finegan, fiction editor. "Short stories, humor and satire conveying insights and situations that will be helpful to Christians with a radical commitment to peace and justice." Length: 300-4,000 words. Pays $25-250.

Poetry: Rod Jellema, poetry editor. "Short, creative poetry that will be thought-provoking and appealing to radical Christians who have a strong commitment to spirituality, peace and justice." Length: 3-50 lines. No more than 4 poems may be submitted at one time by any one author. Pays $15-20.

Tips: "We're looking for tightly written pieces (1,000-1,500 words) on interesting and unusual Christians (or Christian groups) who are putting their commitment to peace and social justice into action in creative and useful ways. We're also looking for provocative analytical and reflective pieces (1,000-4,000 words) dealing with contemporary social issues in the U.S. and abroad."

OUR FAMILY, Oblate Fathers of St. Mary's Province, P.O. Box 249, Battleford, Saskatchewan S0M 0E0 Canada. (306)937-7771. Fax: (306)937-7644. Editor: Nestor Gregoire. 60% freelance written. Prefers to work with published/established writers. Monthly magazine for average family men and women with high school and early college education. Estab. 1949. Circ. 14,265. **Pays on acceptance.** Publishes ms an average of 6 months after acceptance. Byline given. Offers 100% kill fee. Generally purchases first North American serial rights; also buys all, simultaneous, second serial (reprint) or one-time rights. Submit seasonal material 4 months in advance. Accepts simultaneous submissions. Reports in 1 month. *Writer's Market* recommends allowing 2 months for reply. Sample copy for 9 × 12 SAE with $2.50 postage. Only Canadian postage or IRC useful in Canada. Writer's guidelines.

Nonfiction: Humor (related to family life or husband/wife relations), inspirational (anything that depicts people responding to adverse conditions with courage, hope and love), personal experience (with religious dimensions), photo feature (particularly in search of photo essays on human/religious themes and on persons whose lives are an inspiration to others). Accepts phone queries. Buys 72-88 unsolicited mss/year. Pays expenses of writers on assignment.

Reprints: Send tearsheet or photocopy of article or typed ms with rights for sale noted and information about when and where the article previously appeared.

Photos: Photos purchased with or without accompanying ms. Pays $35 for 5 × 7 or larger b&w glossy prints and color photos (which are converted into b&w). Offers additional payment for photos accepted with ms (payment for these photos varies according to their quality). Free photo spec sheet for SASE.

Poetry: Avant-garde, free verse, haiku, light verse, traditional. Buys 4-10 poems/issue. Length: 3-30 lines. Pays 75¢-$1/line. Must have a religious dimension.

Fillers: Jokes, gags, anecdotes, short humor. Buys 2-10/issue.

Tips: "Writers should ask themselves whether this is the kind of an article, poem, etc. that a busy housewife would pick up and read when she has a few moments of leisure. We are particularly looking for articles on the spirituality of marriage. We will be concentrating more on recent movements and developments in the church to help make people aware of the new church of which they are a part."

PENTECOSTAL EVANGEL, The General Council of the Assemblies of God, 1445 Boonville, Springfield MO 65802-1894. (417)862-2781. Fax: (417)862-0416. E-mail: pevangel@ag.org. Editor: Hal Donaldson. Contact: Ann Floyd, technical editor. 20% freelance written. Works with a small number of new/unpublished writers each year. Weekly magazine emphasizing news of the Assemblies of God for members of the Assemblies and other Pentecostal and charismatic Christians. Estab. 1913. Circ. 245,000. **Pays on acceptance.** Publishes ms an average of 6 months after acceptance. Byline given. Buys first serial rights, a few second serial (reprint) or one-time rights. Submit seasonal material 6 months in advance. Reports in 3 months. Sample copy and writer's guidelines available for $1.

Nonfiction: Informational (articles on homelife that convey Christian teachings), inspirational, personal experience, news, human interest, evangelical, current issues. Buys 3 mss/issue. Send complete ms. Length: 500-1,200 words. Pays $25-100. Pays expenses of writers on assignment.

Reprints: Send typed ms with rights for sale noted and information about when and where the article previously appeared. Pays 30% of amount paid for original article.

Photos: Photos purchased without accompanying ms. Pays $30 for 8×10 b&w glossy prints; $50 for 35mm or larger color transparencies. Total purchase price for ms includes payment for photos.

Tips: "We publish first-person articles concerning spiritual experiences; that is, answers to prayer for help in a particular situation, of unusual conversions or healings through faith in Christ. All articles submitted to us should be related to religious life. We are Protestant, evangelical, Pentecostal, and any doctrines or practices portrayed should be in harmony with the official position of our denomination (Assemblies of God)."

PIME WORLD, 17330 Quincy St., Detroit MI 48221-2765. (313)342-4066. E-mail: pwitte@rc.net. Website: http://www.rc.net/pime. Contact: Paul W. Witte, managing editor. 10% freelance written. Monthly (except July and August) magazine emphasizing foreign missionary activities of the Catholic Church in Burma, India, Bangladesh, the Philippines, Hong Kong, Africa, etc., for an adult audience, interested in current issues in the missions. Audience is largely high school educated, conservative in both religion and politics." Estab. 1954. Circ. 30,000. Pays on publication. Publishes ms an average of 3 months after acceptance. Buys all rights. Byline given. Submit seasonal material 4 months in advance. Accepts simultaneous submissions. Reports in 2 months.

Nonfiction: Informational and inspirational foreign missionary activities of the Catholic Church. Buys 5-10 unsolicited mss/year. Query or send complete ms. Length: 800-1,200 words. Pays 6¢/word.

Photos: Pays $10/color photo.

Tips: "Submit articles dealing with current issues of social justice, evangelization and pastoral work in Third World countries. Interviews of missionaries accepted. Good quality color photos greatly appreciated."

POWER FOR LIVING, Scripture Press Publications Inc., P.O. Box 36640, Colorado Springs CO 80936. Fax: (719)536-3243. Editor: Donald H. Alban, Jr. 50% freelance written. Quarterly Sunday School take-home paper with 13 weekly parts. "*Power*'s mission is twofold: to show Christian adults how the Lord can work in their lives, and to convince non-Christians of their need to receive Christ as Saviour." **Pays on acceptance.** Publishes ms an average of 1 year after acceptance. Byline given. Buys one-time rights and second serial (reprint) rights. Editorial lead time 1 year. Submit seasonal material 1 year in advance. Simultaneous submissions OK. Sample and guidelines for #10 SASE.

Nonfiction: Inspirational profiles of prominent Christians or ministries (Evangelical). Buys 50 mss/year. Send complete ms. Length: 1,500 words. Pays to 15¢/word.

Reprints: Send photocopy of article or typed ms with rights for sale noted and information about when and where the article previously appeared. Pays 66% of amount paid for an original article.

Photos: State availability of photos with submission. Negotiates payment individually. Model releases, identification of subjects required. Buys one-time rights.

PRAIRIE MESSENGER, Catholic Journal, Benedictine Monks of St. Peter's Abbey, P.O. Box 190, Muenster, Saskatchewan S0K 2Y0 Canada. (306)682-1772. Fax: (306)682-5285. E-mail: pmessenger@sk.sympatico.ca. Editor: Rev. Andrew Britz, OSB. Contact: Marian Noll, associate editor. 10% freelance written. Weekly Catholic journal with strong emphasis on social justice, Third World and ecumenism. Estab. 1904. Circ. 7,800. Pays on publication. Publishes ms an average of 4 months after acceptance. Byline given. Not copyrighted. Buys first North American serial, first, one-time, second serial (reprint) or simultaneous rights. Submit seasonal material 3 months in advance. Reports in 2 months. Sample and guidelines for 9×12 SAE with $1 Canadian postage or IRCs.

Nonfiction: Interview/profile, opinion, religious. "No articles on abortion or homosexuality." Buys 15 mss/year. Send complete ms. Length: 250-600 words. Pays $40-60. Sometimes pays expenses of writers on assignment.

Photos: Send photos with submission. Reviews 3×5 prints. Offers $15/photo. Captions required. Buys all rights.

PRESBYTERIAN RECORD, 50 Wynford Dr., North York, Ontario M3C 1J7 Canada. (416)444-1111. Fax: (416)441-2825. E-mail: pcrecord@presbyterian.ca. Website: http://www.presbycan.ca/. Contact: Rev. John Congram, editor. 50% freelance written. Eager to work with new/unpublished writers. Monthly magazine for a church-oriented, family audience. Circ. 55,000. Pays on publication. Publishes ms an average of 4 months after acceptance. Buys first serial, one-time or simultaneous rights. Submit seasonal material 3 months in advance. Reports on accepted ms in 2 months. Returns rejected material in 3 months. Sample copy and writer's guidelines for 9×12 SAE with $1 Canadian postage or IRCs.

Nonfiction: Material on religious themes. Check a copy of the magazine for style. Also personal experience, interview, inspirational material. No material solely or mainly American in context. No sermons, accounts of ordinations, inductions, baptisms, receptions, church anniversaries or term papers. When possible, photos should accompany manuscript; e.g., current events, historical events and biographies. Special upcoming themes: small groups in the church; conflict in the Church; lay leadership. Buys 15-20 unsolicited mss/year. Query. Length: 600-1,500 words. Pays $50 (Canadian). Sometimes pays expenses of writers on assignment.

Reprints: Send tearsheet, photocopy of article or typed ms with rights for sale noted and information about when and where the article previously appeared. Pays 80% of amount paid for an original article.

Photos: Pays $15-20 for b&w glossy photos. Uses positive transparencies for cover. Pays $50 plus. Captions required.

Columns/Departments: Vox Populi (items of contemporary and often controversial nature), 700 words; Mission Knocks (new ideas for congregational mission and service), 700 words.

Tips: "There is a trend away from maudlin, first-person pieces redolent with tragedy and dripping with simplistic, pietistic conclusions. Writers often leave out those parts which would likely attract readers, such as anecdotes and direct quotes. Using active rather than passive verbs also helps most manuscripts."

PURPOSE, 616 Walnut Ave., Scottdale PA 15683-1999. (412)887-8500. Editor: James E. Horsch. 95% freelance written. Weekly magazine "for adults, young and old, general audience with varied interests. My readership is interested in seeing how Christianity works in difficult situations." Estab. 1968. Circ. 13,000. **Pays on acceptance.** Publishes ms an average of 8 months after acceptance. Byline given, including city, state/province. Buys one-time rights. Submit seasonal material 6 months in advance. Accepts simultaneous submissions. Reports in 3 months. Sample copy and writer's guidelines for 6×9 SAE with 2 first-class stamps.

Nonfiction: Inspirational stories from a Christian perspective. "I want upbeat stories that go to the core of human problems in family, business, politics, religion, gender and any other areas—and show how the Christian faith resolves them. *Purpose* conveys truth through quality fiction or through articles that use the best story techniques. Our magazine accents Christian discipleship. Christianity affects all of life, and we expect our material to demonstrate this. I would like story-type articles about individuals, groups and organizations who are intelligently and effectively working at such problems as hunger, poverty, international understanding, peace, justice, etc., because of their faith." Buys 130 mss/year. Submit complete ms. Length: 900 words maximum. Pays 5¢/word maximum. Buys one-time rights only.

Reprints: Send tearsheet or photocopy of article or short story or typed ms with rights for sale noted and information about when and where the material previously appeared.

Photos: Photos purchased with ms. Pays $5-15 for b&w (less for color), depending on quality. Must be sharp enough for reproduction; requires prints in all cases. Captions desired.

Fiction: Humorous, religious, historical fiction related to discipleship theme. "Produce the story with specificity so that it appears to take place somewhere and with real people. Essays and how-to-do-it pieces must include a lot of anecdotal, life exposure examples."

● Ranked as one of the best markets for fiction writers in the last *Writer's Digest* magazine's annual "Fiction 50."

Poetry: Traditional poetry, blank verse, free verse, light verse. Buys 130 poems/year. Length: 12 lines maximum. Pays $7.50-20/poem depending on length and quality. Buys one-time rights only.

Fillers: Anecdotal items up to 599 words. Pays 4¢/word maximum.

Tips: "We are looking for articles which show the Christian faith working at issues where people hurt; stories need to be told and presented professionally. Good photographs help place material with us."

QUEEN OF ALL HEARTS, Montfort Missionaries, 26 S. Saxon Ave., Bay Shore NY 11706-8993. (516)665-0726. Fax: (516)665-4349. Managing Editor: Roger Charest, S.M.M. 50% freelance written. Bimonthly magazine. "Subject: Mary, Mother of Jesus, as seen in the sacred scriptures, tradition, history of the church, the early Christian writers, lives of the saints, poetry, art, music, spiritual writers, apparitions, shrines, ecumenism, etc." Estab. 1950. Circ. 3,000. **Pays on acceptance.** Publishes ms an average of 6 months after acceptance. Byline given. Not copyrighted. Submit seasonal material 6 months in advance. Reports in 2 months. Sample for $2.50.

Nonfiction: Essays, inspirational, personal experience, religious. Buys 25 ms/year. Send complete ms. Length: 750-2,500 words. Pays $40-60. Sometimes pays writers in contributor copies or other premiums "by mutual agreement."

Photos: Send photos with submission. Reviews transparencies, prints. Pay varies. Buys one-time rights.

Fiction: Religious. Buys 6 mss/year. Send complete ms. Length: 1,500-2,500 words. Pays $40-60.

Poetry: Joseph Tusiani, poetry editor. Free verse. Buys approximately 10 poems/year. Submit maximum of 2 poems at one time. Pays in contributor copies.

‡REFORM JUDAISM, Union of American Hebrew Congregations, 838 5th Ave., New York NY 10021. (212)650-4240. Editor: Aron Hirt-Manheimer. Managing Editor: Joy Weinberg. 30% freelance written. Quarterly magazine of Reform Jewish issues. "*Reform Judaism* is the official voice of the Union of American Hebrew Congregations, linking the institutions and affiliates of Reform Judaism with every Reform Jew. RJ covers developments within the Movement while interpreting events and Jewish tradition from a Reform perspective." Pays on publication. Publishes ms an average of 3 months after acceptance. Byline given. Offers kill fee for commissioned articles. Buys first North American serial rights. Submit seasonal material 6 months in advance. All submissions should be accompanied by an SASE. Reports in 1 month on queries and mss. Sample copy for $3.50.

Nonfiction: Book excerpt (reviews), exposé, general interest, historical/nostalgic, inspirational, interview/profile, opinion, personal experience, photo feature, travel. Buys 50 mss/year. Submit complete ms. Length: 600-2,000 words. Pays 30¢/word. Sometimes pays expenses of writers on assignment.

Reprints: Send tearsheet or photocopy of article or short story or typed ms with rights for sale noted and information about when and where the material previously appeared.

Photos: Send photos with ms. Prefers 8×10/color or slides and b&w prints. Pays $25-75. Identification of subjects required. Buys one-time rights.

Fiction: Sophisticated, cutting-edge, superb writing. Buys 4 mss/year. Send complete ms. Length: 600-2,500 words. Pays 30¢/word. Publishes novel excerpts.

THE REPORTER, Women's American ORT, Inc., 315 Park Ave. S., New York NY 10010. (212)505-7700. Fax: (212)674-3057. Contact: Aviva Patz, editor. 85% freelance written. Quarterly nonprofit journal published by Jewish women's organization covering "Jewish topics, social issues, education, Mideast and women." Estab. 1966. Circ. 80,000. Payment time varies. Publishes ms ASAP after acceptance. Byline given. Buys first North American serial rights. Submit seasonal material 6 months in advance. Reports in 3 months. Free sample copy for 9×12 SAE with 3 first-class stamps. Writer's guidelines for SASE.

Nonfiction: Book excerpts, essays, general interest. Cover feature profiles a dynamic Jewish woman (or man) making a difference in Judaism, women's issues, education, profiles, business, journalism, sports or the arts. Buys approximately 30 mss/year. Send complete ms. Length varies. No more than 1,800 words. Pays $425.

Photos: Send photos with submission. Identification of subjects required.

Columns/Departments: Education Update (trends in teaching methods, standards, censorship, etc.); Q&A (one-page interview); Last Impression (personal essay). Length: 800-1,000 words; pays $150-300. Up Front (short news item from Jewish world), 50-200 words; pays $50 each. Book reviews, 200-500 words; pays $150. ORT Matters, (length and pay varies); Face Off (two opposing opinions), 850 words; pays $150. Buys 4-10 mss/year. Send complete ms.

Fiction: Publishes novel excerpts and short stories as past of "Last Impressions." Buys 4-10 ms/year. Length: 800-1,000 words. Pays $150-300.

Tips: "Simply send manuscript or query; do not call. Looking for well-written, well-researched and lively stories on relevant topics that evoke a response from the reader."

REVIEW FOR RELIGIOUS, 3601 Lindell Blvd., Room 428, St. Louis MO 63108-3393. (314)977-7363. Fax: (314)977-7362. E-mail: foppema@sluvca.slu.edu. Contact: David L. Fleming, S.J., editor. 100% freelance written. Bimonthly magazine for Roman Catholic priests, brothers and sisters. Estab. 1942. Pays on publication. Publishes ms an average of 9 months after acceptance. Byline given. Buys first North American serial rights; rarely buys second serial (reprint) rights. Reports in 2 months.

Nonfiction: Articles on spiritual, liturgical, canonical matters only; not for general audience. Length: 1,500-5,000 words. Pays $6/page.

Tips: "The writer must know about religious life in the Catholic Church and be familiar with prayer, vows, community life and ministry."

ST. ANTHONY MESSENGER, 1615 Republic St., Cincinnati OH 45210-1298. Fax: (513)241-0399. E-mail: stantho ny@americancatholicorg. Website: http://www.AmericanCatholic.org. Contact: Norman Perry, editor. 55% freelance written. "Willing to work with new/unpublished writers if their writing is of a professional caliber." Monthly general interest magazine for a national readership of Catholic families, most of which have children or grandchildren in grade school, high school or college. Circ. 350,000. **Pays on acceptance.** Publishes ms an average of 9 months after acceptance. Byline given. Buys first serial and all electronic rights. Submit seasonal material 6 months in advance. Reports in 2 months. Sample copy and writer's guidelines for 9×12 SAE with 4 first-class stamps.

● The editor says he is short on seasonal, special occasion pieces. He also informs us that *St. Anthony Messenger* won four first place, including an award for general excellence, two second place, two third place and two honorable mention awards in Catholic Press Association competition in 1996.

Nonfiction: How-to (on psychological and spiritual growth, problems of parenting/better parenting, marriage problems/marriage enrichment), humor, informational, inspirational, interview, personal experience (if pertinent to our purpose), social issues, personal opinion (limited use; writer must have special qualifications for topic), profile. Buys 35-50 mss/year. Length: 1,500-3,000 words. Pays 15¢/word. Sometimes pays the expenses of writers on assignment.

Fiction: Mainstream, religious. Buys 12 mss/year. Submit complete ms. Length: 2,500-3,000 words. Pays 15¢/word.

Poetry: "*Our poetry needs are very limited.*" Submit 4-5 poems maximum. Up to 20-25 lines, "the shorter, the better." Pays $2/line.

Tips: "The freelancer should ask why his or her proposed article would be appropriate for us, rather than for *Redbook* or *Saturday Review*. We treat human problems of all kinds, but from a religious perspective. Articles should reflect Catholic theology, spirituality and employ a Catholic terminology and vocabulary. We need more articles on prayer, scripture, Catholic worship. Get authoritative information (not merely library research); we want interviews with experts. Write in popular style; use lots of examples, stories and personal quotes. Word length is an important consideration."

ST. JOSEPH'S MESSENGER & ADVOCATE OF THE BLIND, Sisters of St. Joseph of Peace, St. Joseph's Home, P.O. Box 288, Jersey City NJ 07303-0288. Contact: Sister Ursula Maphet, editor. 30% freelance written. Eager to work with new/unpublished writers. Semi annual magazine. Estab. 1898. Circ. 15,500. **Pays on acceptance.** Publishes ms an average of 3 months after acceptance. Buys first serial and second serial (reprint) rights; reassigns rights back to author after publication in return for credit line in next publication. Submit seasonal material 3 months in advance (no Christmas issue). Accepts simultaneous submissions. Reports in 1 month. Sample copy and writer's guidelines for 9×12 SAE with 2 first-class stamps.

Nonfiction: Humor, inspirational, nostalgia, personal opinion, personal experience. Buys 24 mss/year. Submit complete ms. Length: 300-1,500 words. Pays $3-15.

Reprints: Send typed ms with rights for sale noted and information about when and where the article previously appeared. Pays 100% of amount paid for an original article.

Fiction: Romance, suspense, mainstream, religious. Buys 30 mss/year. Submit complete ms. Length: 600-1,600 words. Pays $6-25.

Poetry: Light verse, traditional. Buys 25 poems/year. Submit max. 10 poems. Length: 50-300 words. Pays $5-20.

Tips: "It's rewarding to know that someone is waiting to see freelancers' efforts rewarded by 'print'. It's annoying, however, to receive poor copy, shallow material or inane submissions. Human interest fiction, touching on current happenings, is what is most needed. We look for social issues woven into story form. We also seek non-preaching articles that carry a message that is positive."

SCP JOURNAL and SCP NEWSLETTER, Spiritual Counterfeits Project, P.O. Box 4308, Berkeley CA 94704-4308. (510)540-0300. Fax: (510)540-1107. E-mail: scp@dnai.com. Website: www.scp-inc.org/. Contact: Tal Brooke, editor. Co-editor: Brooks Alexander. 5-10% freelance written. Prefers to work with published/established writers. "The *SCP Journal* and *SCP Newsletter* are quarterly publications geared to reach demanding non-believers while giving Christians authentic insight into the very latest spiritual and cultural trends." Their targeted audience is the educated lay reader. Estab. 1975. Circ. 18,000. Pays on publication. Publishes ms an average of 6 months after acceptance. Byline given. Rights negotiable. Accepts simultaneous submissions. Reports in 3 months. Sample copy for $8.75. Writer's guidelines for SASE.

Nonfiction: Book excerpts, essays, exposé, interview/profile, opinion, personal experience, religious. Query by telephone. Length: 2,500-3,500 words. Pay negotiated by phone.
  ● Less emphasis on book reviews and more focus on specialized "single issue" topics.

Reprints: Call for telephone inquiry first. Send photocopy of article or typed ms with rights for sale noted and information about when and where the article previously appeared. Payment is negotiated.

Photos: State available photos. Reviews contact sheets and prints or slides. Offers no additional payment for photos accepted with ms. Captions, model releases, identification of subjects required. Buys one-time rights.

Tips: "The area of our publication most open to freelancers is specialized topics covered by *SCP*. Do not send unsolicited samples of your work until you have checked with us by phone to see it it fits *SCP*'s area of interest and publication schedule. The usual profile of contributors is that they are published within the field, have advanced degrees from top ranked universities, as well as experience that makes their work uniquely credible."

‡SEEK, Standard Publishing, 8121 Hamilton Ave., Cincinnati OH 45231. (513)931-4050, ext. 365. Editor: Eileen H. Wilmoth. 98% freelance written. Prefers to work with published/established writers. Quarterly Sunday school paper, in weekly issues for young and middle-aged adults who attend church and Bible classes. Circ. 45,000. **Pays on acceptance.** Publishes ms an average of 1 year after acceptance. Byline given. Buys first serial and second serial (reprint) rights. Submit seasonal material 1 year in advance. Accepts previously published submissions. Send tearsheet of article or typed ms with rights for sale noted. For reprints, pays 50% of amount paid for an original article. Reports in 3 months. Sample copy and writer's guidelines for 6×9 SAE with 2 first-class stamps.

Nonfiction: "We look for articles that are warm, inspirational, devotional, of personal or human interest; that deal with controversial matters, timely issues of religious, ethical or moral nature, or first-person testimonies, true-to-life happenings, vignettes, emotional situations or problems; communication problems and examples of answered prayers. Article must deliver its point in a convincing manner but not be patronizing or preachy. It must appeal to either men or women, must be alive, vibrant, sparkling and have a title that demands the article be read. We always need stories about families, marriages, problems on campus and life testimonies." Buys 150-200 mss/year. Submit complete ms. Length: 400-1,200 words. Pays 5¢/word.

Photos: B&w photos purchased with or without mss. Pays $20 minimum for good 8×10 glossy prints.

Fiction: Religious fiction and religiously slanted historical and humorous fiction. No poetry. Length: 400-1,200 words. Pays 5¢/word.

Tips: "Submit mss which tell of faith in action or victorious Christian living as central theme. We select manuscripts as far as one year in advance of publication. Complimentary copies are sent to our published writers immediately following printing."

‡SHARING THE VICTORY, Fellowship of Christian Athletes, 8701 Leeds Rd., Kansas City MO 64129. (816)921-0909. Fax: (816)921-8755. Fax: stu@fca.org. E-mail: http://www.fea/org. Contact: John Dodderidge, managing editor. Assistant Editor: Will Greer. 50% freelance written. Prefers to work with published/established writers, but works with a growing number of new/unpublished writers each year. Monthly (September-May) magazine. "We seek to encourage and enable athletes and coaches at all levels to take their faith seriously on and off the 'field'." Estab. 1959. Circ. 60,000. Pays on publication. Publishes ms an average of 4 months after acceptance. Byline given. Buys first rights. Submit seasonal material 3 months in advance. Reports in 2 months on queries; 2 months on mss. *Writer's Market* recommends allowing 2 months for reply. Sample copy for $1 and 9×12 SAE with 3 first-class stamps. Free writer's guidelines for #10 SASE.

Nonfiction: Humor, inspirational, interview/profile (with "name" athletes and coaches solid in their faith), personal experience, photo feature. No "sappy articles on 'I became a Christian and now I'm a winner.'" Buys 5-20 mss/year. Query. Length: 500-1,000 words. Pays $100-200 for unsolicited articles, more for the exceptional profile.

Reprints: Send typed ms with rights for sale noted. Pays 50% of amount paid for an original article.

Photos: State availability of photos with submission. Reviews contact sheets. Pay depends on quality of photo but usually a minimum $50. Model releases required for "name" individuals. Buys one-time rights.

Poetry: Free verse. Buys 9 poems/year. Pays $25.

Tips: "Profiles and interviews of particular interest to coed athlete, primarily high school and college age. Our graphics and editorial content appeal to youth. The area most open to freelancers is profiles on or interviews with well-known athletes or coaches (male, female, minorities) and offbeat but interscholastic team sports."

SIGNS OF THE TIMES, Pacific Press Publishing Association, P.O. Box 5353, Nampa ID 83653-5353. (208)465-2500. Fax: (208)465-2531. E-mail: mmoore@pacificpress.com. Contact: Marvin Moore, editor. 40% freelance written. Works with a small number of new/unpublished writers each year. "We are a monthly Seventh-day Adventist magazine encouraging the general public to practice the principles of the Bible." Estab. 1874. Circ. 245,000. Pays on publication.

Publishes ms an average of 8 months after acceptance. Byline given. Offers kill fee. Buys first North American serial rights. Submit seasonal material 8 months in advance. Reports in 1 month on queries; 2 months on mss. *Writer's Market* recommends allowing 2 months for reply. Sample copy and writer's guidelines for 9×12 SAE with 3 first-class stamps.
Nonfiction: General interest, how-to, inspirational, interview/profile. "We want writers with a desire to share the good news of reconciliation with God. Articles should be people-oriented, well-researched and should have a sharp focus." Buys 75 mss/year. Query with or without published clips or send complete ms. Length: 650-2,500 words. Pays $100-400. Sometimes pays the expenses of writers on assignment.
Reprints: Send tearsheet or photocopy of article or typed ms with rights for sale noted and information about when and where the article previously appeared. Pays 50% of amount paid for an original article.
Photos: Merwin Stewart, photo editor. Send photos with query or ms. Reviews b&w contact sheets, 35mm color transparencies, 5×7 or 8×10 b&w prints. Pays $35-300 for transparencies; $20-50 for prints. Model releases and identification of subjects required (captions helpful). Buys one-time rights.
Tips: "Don't write for us unless you've read us and are familiar with Adventist beliefs."

SISTERS TODAY, The Liturgical Press, St. John's Abbey, Collegeville MN 56321-2099. Fax: (320)363-7130. E-mail: mwagner@csbsju.edu. Website: http://www.csbsju/osb.sisters/public.html. Contact: Sister Mary Anthony Wagner, O.S.B., editor-in-chief. Associate Editor: Sister Mary Elizabeth Mason, O.S.B. Reviews Editor: Sister Stefanie Weisgram, O.S.B. Poetry Editor: Sister Mary Virginia Micka, C.S.J. 80% freelance written. Prefers to work with published/established writers. Bimonthly magazine exploring the role of women and the Church, primarily. Circ. 3,500. Pays on publication. Publishes ms several months after acceptance probably. Byline given. Buys first rights. Submit seasonal material 4 months in advance. Sample copy for $4.50.
Nonfiction: How-to (pray, live in a religious community, exercise faith, hope, charity etc.), informational, inspirational. Also articles concerning religious renewal, community life, worship, the role of women in the Church and in the world today. Buys 50-60 unsolicited mss/year. Query. Length: 500-2,500 words. Pays $5/printed page.
Poetry: Free verse, haiku, light verse, traditional. Buys 5-6 poems/issue. Submit maximum 4 poems. Pays $10.
Tips: "Some of the freelance material evidences the lack of familiarity with *Sisters Today*. We would prefer submitted articles not to exceed eight or nine pages."

SOCIAL JUSTICE REVIEW, 3835 Westminster Place, St. Louis MO 63108-3472. (314)371-1653. Contact: Rev. John H. Miller, C.S.C. 25% freelance written. Works with a small number of new/unpublished writers each year. Bimonthly. Estab. 1908. Publishes ms an average of 1 year after acceptance. Not copyrighted; "however special articles within the magazine may be copyrighted, or an occasional special issue has been copyrighted due to author's request." Buys first serial rights. Sample copy for 9×12 SAE with 3 first-class stamps.
Nonfiction: Scholarly articles on society's economic, religious, social, intellectual, political problems with the aim of bringing Catholic social thinking to bear upon these problems. Query with SASE. Length: 2,500-3,000 words. Pays about 2¢/word.
Reprints: Send typed ms with rights for sale noted and when and where the article previously appeared.

SPIRITUAL LIFE, 2131 Lincoln Rd. NE, Washington DC 20002-1199. (202)832-8489. Fax: (202)832-8967. E-mail: edodonnell@aol.com. Website: http://www.ocd.or.at/. Contact: Br. Edward O'Donnell, O.C.D., editor. 80% freelance written. Prefers to work with published/established writers. Quarterly magazine for "largely Catholic, well-educated, serious readers. A few are non-Catholic or non-Christian." Circ. 12,000. **Pays on acceptance.** Publishes ms an average of 1 year after acceptance. Buys first North American serial rights. Reports in 2 months. Sample copy and writer's guidelines for 7×10 or larger SASE with 5 first-class stamps.
Nonfiction: Serious articles of contemporary spirituality and its pastoral application to everyday life. High quality articles about our encounter with God in the present day world. Language of articles should be college level. Technical terminology, if used, should be clearly explained. Material should be presented in a positive manner. Sentimental articles or those dealing with specific devotional practices not accepted. Buys inspirational and think pieces. "Brief autobiographical information (present occupation, past occupations, books and articles published, etc.) should accompany article." No fiction or poetry. Buys 20 mss/year. Length: 3,000-5,000 words. Pays $50 minimum and 6 contributor's copies. Book reviews should be sent to Br. Edward O'Donnell, O.C.D.

STANDARD, Nazarene International Headquarters, 6401 The Paseo, Kansas City MO 64131. (816)333-7000. Contact: Everett Leadingham, editor. 100% freelance written. Works with a small number of new/unpublished writers each year. Weekly inspirational paper with Christian reading for adults. Estab. 1936. Circ. 160,000. **Pays on acceptance.** Publishes ms an average of 15-18 months after acceptance. Byline given. Buys one-time rights and second serial (reprint) rights. Submit seasonal material 6 months in advance. Reports in 10 weeks. Free sample copy. Writer's guidelines for SAE with 2 first-class stamps.
  • *Standard* no longer publishes nonfiction but prefers fiction or fiction-type stories. Does not want how-to, inspiration/devotionals or social issues pieces.
Reprints: Send tearsheet of short story.
Fiction: Prefers fiction-type stories *showing* Christianity in action. Send complete ms; no queries. Length: 500-1,500 words. Pays 3½¢/word for first rights; 2¢/word for reprint rights.
Poetry: Free verse, haiku, light verse, traditional. Buys 50 poems/year. Submit maximum 5 poems. Length: 50 lines maximum. Pays 25¢/line.

Tips: "Stories should express Christian principles without being preachy. Setting, plot and characterization must be realistic."

‡SURSUM CORDA!, The Catholic Revival, Foundation for Catholic Reform, P.O. Box 993, Ridgefield CT 06877. Fax: (203)438-1305. E-mail: roger.mccaffrey@internetmci.com. Editor: Roger McCaffrey. Contact: Tom Woods, managing editor. "*Sursum Corda* is a quarterly magazine that covers the good things happening in the Catholic Church. It also runs a 16-page homeschooling section for Catholics who teach their children at home." Estab. 1995. Circ. 16,000. Pays on publication. Publishes ms an average of 6 months after acceptance. Byline given. Buys second serial (reprint) rights. Editorial lead time 2 months. Accepts simultaneous submissions. Reports in 1 month on queries; 2 months on mss. Sample copy free.
Nonfiction: Book excerpts, inspirational (Catholic), interview/profile, personal experience, religious, children's. No news reports or opinion pieces. Buys 2 mss/year. Send complete ms. Length: 2,000-5,000 words. Pays $150-500. Sometimes pays expenses of writers on assignment.
Photos: Send photos with submission. Reviews contact sheets. Offers $25/photo. Captions and identification of subjects required. Buys one-time rights.
Fiction: Religious. Send complete ms. Pay is negotiable.
Tips: "Fax a one-page cover letter to the editor or managing editor. Please bear in mind the theme of the magazine: we do features on the orthodox Catholic Revival. The magazine is conservative."

TEACHERS INTERACTION, Concordia Publishing House, 3558 S. Jefferson Ave., St. Louis MO 63118-3968. Fax: (314)268-1329. Editor: Jane Haas. Contact: Jean Muser, editorial associate. 20% freelance written. Quarterly magazine of practical, inspirational, theological articles for volunteer church school teachers. Material must be true to the doctrines of the Lutheran Church—Missouri Synod. Estab. 1960. Circ. 20,400. Pays on publication. Publishes ms an average of 1 year after acceptance. Byline given. Buys all rights. Submit seasonal material 1 year in advance. Reports in 3 months on mss. Sample copy for $2.75. Writer's guidelines for #10 SASE.
Nonfiction: How-to (practical help/ideas used successfully in own classroom), inspirational (to the church school worker—must be in accordance with LCMS doctrine), personal experience (of a Sunday school classroom nature—growth). No theological articles. Buys 6 mss/year. Send complete ms. Length: 750-1,500 words.
Fillers: "*Teachers Interaction* buys short Interchange items—activities and ideas planned and used successfully in a church school classroom." Buys 48/year. Length: 200 words maximum. Pays $20.
Tips: "Practical, or 'it happened to me' experiences articles would have the best chance. Also short items—ideas used in classrooms; seasonal and in conjunction with our Sunday school material, Our Life in Christ. Our format includes *all* volunteer church school teachers, Sunday school teachers, Vacation Bible School, and midweek teachers, as well as teachers of adult Bible studies."

‡THIS PEOPLE MAGAZINE, Exploring LDS issues and personalities, Utah Alliance Publishing Co., P.O. Box 50748, Provo UT 84605-0748. (801)375-1700 ext 19. Fax: (801)375-1703. E-mail: jimbell@byu.edu. Contact: Jim Bell, editor. 75% freelance written. Quarterly magazine "aimed at Mormon readers and examines Mormon issues and people in an upbeat, problem-solving way." Estab. 1979. Circ. 20,000. Pays on publication. Publishes ms an average of 6 months after acceptance. Byline given. Offers 15% kill fee. Buys first rights. Submit seasonal material 6 months in advance. Reports in 2 months. Sample copy for 9 × 12 SAE with 4 first-class stamps. Writer's guidelines for #10 SASE.
Nonfiction: Essays, historical/nostalgic, humor, inspirational, interview/profile, personal experience, photo feature, travel—all Mormon oriented. No poetry, cartoons, fiction. Buys 15-20 mss/year. Query with or without published clips, or send complete ms. Length: 1,000-3,500 words. Pays $150-400 for assigned articles; $100-400 for unsolicited articles. Sometimes pays expenses of writers on assignment.
Reprints: Accepts reprints of previously published submissions.
Photos: State availability of photos with ms. Model releases and identification of subjects required. Buys all rights.
Fiction: Publishes novel excerpts.
Tips: "I prefer query letters that include the first 6-8 paragraphs of an article plus an outline of the article. Clips and credits of previous publications are helpful."

THE UNITED CHURCH OBSERVER, 478 Huron St., Toronto, Ontario M5R 2R3 Canada. (416)960-8500. Fax: (416)960-8477. E-mail: general@ucobserver.org. Editor: Muriel Duncan. 20% freelance written. Prefers to work with published/established writers. Monthly newsmagazine for people associated with The United Church of Canada. Deals primarily with events, trends and policies having religious significance. Most coverage is Canadian, but reports on international or world concerns will be considered. Pays on publication. Publishes ms an average of 4 months after acceptance. Byline usually given. Buys first serial rights and occasionally all rights.

ALWAYS CHECK the most recent copy of a magazine for the address and editor's name before you send in a query or manuscript.

Nonfiction: Occasional opinion features only. Extended coverage of major issues usually assigned to known writers. No opinion pieces or poetry. Submissions should be written as news, no more than 1,200 words length, accurate and well-researched. Queries preferred. Rates depend on subject, author and work involved. Pays expenses of writers on assignment "as negotiated."

Photos: Buys photos with mss. Black & white, 5×7 minimum; color 35mm or larger format. Payment varies.

Tips: "The writer has a better chance of breaking in at our publication with short articles; this also allows us to try more freelancers. Include samples of previous *news* writing with query. Indicate ability and willingness to do research, and to evaluate that research. The most frequent mistakes made by writers in completing an article for us are organizational problems, lack of polished style, short on research, and a lack of inclusive language."

UNITY MAGAZINE, Unity School of Christianity, 1901 NW Blue Parkway, Unity Village MO 64065. Editor: Philip White. Contact: Janet McNamara, associate editor. 25% freelance written. Interested in working with authors who are skilled at writing in the metaphysical Christian/New Thought/spiritual development persuasion. Estab. 1889. Circ. 120,000. **Pays on acceptance.** Publishes ms an average of 6-12 months after acceptance. Byline given. Buys first North American serial rights. Submit seasonal material 7 months in advance. Reports in 3 months on mss. Sample copy and writer's guidelines free.

Nonfiction: *Spiritual* self-help and personal experience, holistic health, prosperity, biblical interpretation, religious, inspirational. Buys 200 mss/year. Send complete ms. No queries, please. Length: 1,000-1,800 words. Pays 20¢/word.

Reprints: Sometimes publishes reprints of previously published articles. Send photocopy of article and information about when and where the article previously appeared.

Photos: State availability of photos with submission. Reviews transparencies and prints. Offers $65-220/photo. Model releases and identification of subjects required. Buys one-time rights.

Poetry: Inspirational, religious and seasonal. Buys 25 poems/year. Submit maximum 5 poems. Length: 30 lines maximum. Pays $50 minimum.

THE UPPER ROOM, Daily Devotional Guide, P.O. Box 189, Nashville TN 37202-0189. (615)340-7252. Fax: (615)340-7006. E-mail: istafford@upperroom.org. Website: http://www.upperroom.org. Editor and Publisher: Janice T. Grana. Contact: Mary Lou Redding, managing editor. 95% freelance written. Eager to work with new/unpublished writers. Bimonthly magazine "offering a daily inspirational message which includes a Bible reading, text, prayer, 'Thought for the Day,' and suggestion for further prayer. Each day's meditation is written by a different person and is usually a personal witness about discovering meaning and power for Christian living through scripture study which illuminates daily life." Circ. 2.2 million (US); 385,000 outside US Pays on publication. Publishes ms an average of 1 year after acceptance. Byline given. Buys first North American serial rights and translation rights. Submit seasonal material 14 months in advance. Manuscripts are not returned. If writers include a stamped, self addressed postcard, we will notify them that their writing has reached us. This does not imply acceptance or interest in purchase. Sample copy and writer's guidelines with a 4× SAE and 2 first-class stamps. For guidelines only send #10 envelope.

• This market does not respond unless material is accepted for publication.

Nonfiction: Inspirational, personal experience, Bible-study insights. No poetry, lengthy "spiritual journey" stories. Buys 365 unsolicited mss/year. Send complete ms. Length: 250 words maximum. Pays $20.

Tips: "The best way to break into our magazine is to send a well-written manuscript that looks at the Christian faith in a fresh way. Standard stories and sermon illustrations are immediately rejected. We very much want to find new writers and welcome good material. We are particularly interested in meditations based on Old Testament characters and stories. Good repeat meditations can lead to work on longer assignments for our other publications, which pay more. A writer who can deal concretely with everyday situations, relate them to the Bible and spiritual truths, and write clear, direct prose should be able to write for *The Upper Room*. We want material that provides for more interaction on the part of the reader—meditation suggestions, journaling suggestions, space to reflect and link personal experience with the meditation for the day."

VIRTUE, Helping women build Christ-like character, 4050 Lee Vance View, Colorado Springs CO 80918-7102. (719)531-7776. Fax: (719)535-0172. E-mail: virtuemag@aol.com. Editor-at-Large: Nancie Carmichael. Contact: Laura J. Barker, editor. 75% freelance written. Works with small number of new/unpublished writers each year. Bimonthly magazine that "shows through features and columns the depth and variety of expression that can be given to women and faith." Estab. 1978. Circ. 111,000. Pays on acceptance or publication. Publishes ms an average of 4 months after acceptance. Byline given. Buys first North American serial rights. Submit seasonal material 9 months in advance. Reports in 2 months. Sample copy for 9×12 SAE with 7 first-class stamps. Writer's guidelines for #10 SASE.

Nonfiction: Book excerpts, health, how-to, humor, inspirational, interview/profile, opinion, personal experience, enhancing relationships, religious. Buys 60 mss/year. Query. Length: 1,000-1,300 words. Pays 15-25¢/word.

Reprints: Accepts previously published submissions from a non-competing market. Send photocopy of article or short story and information about when and where the piece previously appeared.

Photos: State availability of photos with submission.

Columns/Departments: Virtue in Action (Christianity in our culture and time); One Woman's Journal (personal experience); Family Matters (practical ideas and advice for baby-boomer women). Buys 25 mss/year. Query. Length: 200-1,000. Pays 15-25¢/word.

Fiction: Humorous, religious. Buys 4-6 mss/year. Send complete ms. Length: 1,500-1,800 words. Pays 15-25¢/word.

Poetry: Free verse, traditional. Buys 2-3 poems/year. Submit maximum 3 poems. Length: 3-30 lines. Pays $15-50.

THE WAR CRY, The Salvation Army, 615 Slaters Lane, Alexandria VA 22313. Fax: (703)684-5539. E-mail: uswarcry @aol.com. Contact: Lt. Colonel Marlene Chase, editor. Managing Editor: Jeff McDonald. 10% freelance written. Bi-weekly magazine covering army news and Christian devotional writing. Estab. 1881. Circ. 500,000. **Pays on acceptance.** Publishes ms an average of 3-12 months after acceptance. Byline given. Buys one-time rights. Editorial lead time 6 weeks. Submit seasonal material 1 year in advance. Reports in 1 month. Sample copy and writer's guidelines free.
Nonfiction: Humor, inspirational, interview/profile, personal experience, religious. No missionary stories, confessions. Buys 40 mss/year. Send complete ms. Pays up to 20¢/word for assigned articles; 10-20¢/word for unsolicited articles. Sometimes pays expenses of writers on assignment.
Reprints: Send information about when and where the article previously appeared. Pays 15¢/word.
Photos: Offers $35-200/photo. Identification of subjects required. Buys one-time rights.
Fiction: Religious. Buys 2-4 mss/year. Send complete ms. Length: 1,200-1,500 words maximum. Pays 20¢/word.
Poetry: Free verse. Inspirational only. Buys 10-20 poems/year. Submit maximum 5 poems. Length: 16 lines maximum. Pays $20-50.
Fillers: Anecdotes (inspirational). Buys 10-20/year. Length: 200-500 words. Pays 15-20¢/word.
Tips: "We are soliciting more short fiction, inspirational articles and poetry, interviews with Christian athletes, evangelical leaders and celebrities, and theme-focused articles."

‡THE WESLEYAN ADVOCATE, The Wesleyan Publishing House, P.O. Box 50434, Indianapolis IN 46250-0434. (317)576-8156. Fax: (317)842-1649. E-mail: weslyandoc@aol.com. Executive Editor: Dr. Norman G. Wilson. Contact: Jerry Brecheisen, managing editor. 50% freelance written. Monthly magazine of The Wesleyan Church. Estab. 1842. Circ. 20,000. Pays on publication. Publishes ms an average of 1 year after acceptance. Byline given. Buys first rights or simultaneous rights (prefers first rights). Submit seasonal material 6 months in advance. Accepts simultaneous submissions. Reports in 2 weeks. Sample copy for $2. Writer's guidelines for #10 SASE.
Nonfiction: Humor, inspirational, religious. Buys 50 mss/year. Send complete ms. Length: 250-650 words. Pays $10-40 for assigned articles; $5-25 for unsolicited articles.
Reprints: Send photocopy of article and typed ms with rights for sale noted and information about when and where the article previously appeared. Pays 50% of amount paid for an original article.
Photos: Send photos with submission. Reviews transparencies. Buys one-time rights.
Tips: "Write for a guide."

WHEREVER, In The World For Jesus' Sake, The Evangelical Alliance Mission, P.O. Box 969, Wheaton IL 60189. Fax: (630)653-1826. E-mail: dfelmly@teamworld.org. Contact: Dana Felmly, managing editor. 70% freelance written. "*Wherever* is a triannual thematic magazine which helps people decide if overseas missions is for them. Our audience is mostly college students, grad and seminary students, young professionals." Estab. 1976. Circ. 27,000. Pays on publication. Publishes ms an average of 8 months after acceptance. Byline given. Buys all rights unless other arrangements are made. Editorial lead time 9 months. No simultaneous submissions. Sample copy for 9 × 12 SAE with 3 first-class stamps. Writer's guidelines for #10 SASE.
Nonfiction: Book excerpts, humor, inspirational, interview/profile, personal experience. Buys 13 mss/year. Write for guidelines. Length: 500-1,000 words. Pays $75-125. Sometimes pays expenses of writers on assignment.
Reprints: Send tearsheet or photocopy of article or short story and information about when and where the piece previously appeared. Pay negotiable.
Fiction: *Only* if piece addresses the theme of a particular issue. Buys 1 mss/year. Write for guidelines. Length: 500-1,000 words. Pays $75-125.
Tips: "Last year, *Wherever* changed its focus to better relate to our Generation X readers. We are looking for writers who write in a style similar to that of popular Gen X magazines like *Wired* or *Details*. If you believe you are a writer in this category, please submit a résumé and writing samples to Dana Felmly."

THE WITNESS, Episcopal Church Publishing Co., 1249 Washington Blvd., #3115, Detroit MI 48226. (313)962-2650. Fax: (313)962-1012. E-mail: thewitness@ecunet.org. Editor: Jeanie Wylie-Kellermann. Managing Editor: Julie A. Wortman. Contact: Marietta Jaeger. 20% freelance written. Monthly magazine covering religion and politics from a left perspective. "Our readers are people of faith who are interested in wrestling with scripture and current events with the goal of serving God and effecting change that diminishes the privilege of the rich." Estab. 1917. Circ. 4,000. Pays on publication. Publishes ms an average of 3 months after acceptance. Byline given. Offers 50% kill fee. Buys first rights. Editorial lead time 6 weeks. Submit seasonal material 3 months in advance. Responds only to material accepted for publication. Sample copy and writer's guidelines free.
Nonfiction: Exposé, general interest, historical/nostalgic, humor, interview/profile, personal experience, photo feature, religious. Buys 10 mss/year. Query with or without published clips, or send complete ms. Length: 250-1,800 words. Pays $50-250 for assigned articles; $50-100 for unsolicited articles; and 1-year subscription. Sometimes pays expenses of writers on assignment.
Photos: State availability of photos with submissions. Reviews prints. Offers $0-30/photo. Captions, identification of subjects required. Buys one-time rights.
Poetry: Buys 10 poems/year. Submit maximum 5 poems. Pays $0-30.
Tips: "We're eager for *short* news pieces that relate to racial-, gender- and eco-justice. Our issues are thematic which makes queries advisable. We don't publish material written in a dry academic style, we like stories that allow marginalized people to speak in their own words."

WOMAN'S TOUCH, Assemblies of God Women's Ministries Department (GPH), 1445 Boonville Ave., Springfield MO 65802-1894. (417)862-2781. Fax: (417)862-0503. E-mail: womanstouch@ag.org. Contact: Peggy Musgrove, managing editor. Associate Editor: Aleda Swartzendruber. 50% freelance written. Willing to work with new/unpublished writers. Bimonthly inspirational magazine for women. "Articles and contents of the magazine should be compatible with Christian teachings as well as human interests. The audience is women, both homemakers and those who are career-oriented." Estab. 1977. Circ. 21,000. Pays on publication. Byline given. Buys one-time rights. Submit seasonal material 8 months in advance. Reports in 3 months. Sample copy for 9½×11 SAE with 3 first-class stamps. Writer's guidelines for #10 SASE.
Nonfiction: General interest, how-to, inspirational, personal experience, religious, health. Buys 30 mss/year. Send complete ms. Length: 500-800 words. Pays $10-35 for unsolicited articles.
Reprints: Send photocopy of article and information about when and where the article previously appeared. Pays 50-75% of amount paid for an original article.
Photos: State availability of photos with submission. Reviews negatives, transparencies, 4×6 prints. Offers no additional payment for photos accepted with ms. Identification of subjects required. Buys one-time rights.
Columns/Departments: 'A Final Touch' for short human interest articles—home and family or career-oriented." Length: 80-500 words. Pays $20-35. "A Better You" (health, wellness, beauty). Length: 200-500 words. Pays $15-25. "A Lighter Touch" (true, unpublished anecdotes). Length: 100 words. Pays $10.
Fillers: Facts. Buys 5/year. Length: 50-200. Pays $5-15.

THE WORLD, Unitarian Universalist Association, 25 Beacon St., Boston MA 02108-2800. (617)742-2100. Fax: (617)367-3237. E-mail: worldmag@uua.org. Editor-in-Chief: Tom Stites. 50% freelance written. Bimonthly magazine "to promote and inspire denominational self-reflection; to inform readers about the wide range of UU values, purposes, activities, aesthetics, and spiritual attitudes, and to educate readers about the history, personalities, and congregations that comprise UUism; to enhance its dual role of leadership and service to member congregations." Estab. 1987. Circ. 115,000. **Pays on acceptance.** Publishes ms an average of 1 year after acceptance. Byline given. Buys one-time rights. Editorial lead time 3 months. Submit seasonal material 3 months in advance. Pay varies. Reports in 2 months on queries; 3 months on mss. Sample copy and writer's guidelines for 9×12 SASE.
Nonfiction: All articles must have a UU angle. Essays, historical/nostalgic (Unitarian or Universalist focus), inspirational, interview/profile (with UU individual or congregation), commentary, photo feature (of UU congregation or project), religious. No unsolicited poetry or fiction. Buys 5 mss/year. Query with published clips. Length: 1,500-3,500 words. Pays $400 minimum for assigned feature articles. Sometimes pays expenses of writers on assignment.
Photos: State availability of photos with submission. Reviews contact sheets. Offers no additional payment for photos accepted with ms. Captions, model releases and identification of subjects required. Buys one-time rights.
Columns/Departments: Focus On (profiles); Community Projects (social service project profiles); Book Reviews (liberal religion, social issues, politics), 600-800 words. Query (profiles, book reviews). Pays $75-250 for assigned articles and book reviews.

RETIREMENT

January 1, 1996 the first baby boomer turned 50. With peak earning power and increased leisure time, this generation is able to pursue varied interests while maintaining active lives. More people are retiring in their 50s, while others are starting a business or traveling and pursuing hobbies. These publications give readers specialized information on health and fitness, medical research, finances and other topics of interest, as well as general articles on travel destinations and recreational activities.

ACTIVE TIMES MAGAZINE, 417 Main St., Carbondale CO 81623. Fax: (970)963-8252. E-mail: active@rof.net. Contact: Chris Kelly, editor. 80% freelance written. Quarterly magazine covering over-50 market. "We target active, adults over-50. We emphasize the positive, enjoyable aspects of aging." Estab. 1992. Circ. 7 million. Pays on publication. Publishes ms an average of 4 months after acceptance. Byline given. Offers 50% kill fee. Buys first North American serial rights. Editorial lead time 3 months. Submit seasonal material 6-9 months in advance. Reports in 5 weeks on queries. Sample copy for 9×12 SAE and 4 first-class stamps. Writer's guidelines for #10 SASE.
Nonfiction: General interest, interview/profile, travel round-ups (not destination stories), sports/recreation. Buys 50 mss/year. Query with published clips. Length: 500-800 words. Pays $75-500 for assigned articles; $50-250 for unsolicited articles. Sometimes pays expenses of writers on assignment.
Photos: State availability of photos with submission. Reviews contact sheets, 35mm transparencies, prints. Negotiates payment individually. Identification of subjects required.
Columns/Departments: Profile (interesting over-50), 700 words. Buys 4 mss/year. Query with published clips. Pays $150-400. Never-Evers (over-50 doing something never, ever did), 100 words. Send ms on spec. Pays $35.
Tips: "Write a detailed query, with substantiating clips. Show how story will appeal to active over-50 reader."

ALIVE! A Magazine for Christian Senior Adults, Christian Seniors Fellowship, P.O. Box 46464, Cincinnati OH 45246-0464. (513)825-3681. Editor: J. David Lang. Contact: A. June Lang, office editor. 60% freelance written. Bimonthly magazine for senior adults ages 55 and older. "We need timely articles about Christian seniors in vital, productive lifestyles, travels or ministries." Estab. 1988. Pays on publication. Byline given. Buys first or second serial (reprint) rights. Submit seasonal material 6 months in advance. Reports in 6-8 weeks. Membership $15/year. Sample copy for 9×12 SAE with 3 first-class stamps. Writer's guidelines for #10 SASE.

Nonfiction: General interest, humor, inspirational, interview/profile, photo feature, religious, travel. Buys 25-50 mss/year. Send complete ms. Length: 600-1,200 words. Pays $18-75. Organization membership may be deducted from payment at writer's request.

Reprints: Send photocopy of article, typed ms with rights for sale noted and information about when and where the article previously appeared. Pays 60-75% of amount paid for an original article.

Photos: State availability of photos with submission. Offers $10-25. Model releases and identification of subjects required. Buys one-time rights.

Columns/Departments: Heart Medicine (humorous personal anecdotes; prefer grandparent/grandchild stories or anecdotes re: over 55 persons), 10-100 words; Games n' Stuff (word games, puzzles, word search), 200-500 words. Buys 50 mss/year. Send complete ms. Pays $2-25.

Fiction: Adventure, humorous, religious, romance (if it fits age group), slice-of-life vignettes, motivational/inspirational. Buys 12 mss/year. Send complete ms. Length: 600-1,500 words. Pays $20-60.

Fillers: Anecdotes, facts, gags to be illustrated by cartoonist, short humor; 50-500 words. Buys 15/year. Pays $2-15.

Tips: "Include SASE and whether manuscript is to be returned or tossed."

50 AND FORWARD MAGAZINE, D&D Communications, Inc., 160 Mayo Rd., Suite 100, Edgewater MD 21037. Editor: Debra Asberry. 85% freelance written. Monthly magazine "informs, educates and entertains the active adult over 50. The editorial is diverse, ranging from funny to serious subjects." Estab. 1993. Circ. 60,000. **Pays on acceptance**. Publishes ms an average of 6 months after acceptance. Byline given. Not copyrighted. Buys first rights. Editorial lead time 3 months. Submit seasonal material 6 months in advance. Accepts simultaneous submissions. Reports in 6 weeks on queries; 2 months on mss. Sample copy for 9×13 SAE and 4 first-class stamps.

• At press time it was learned that *50 and Forward* has ceased publication.

Nonfiction: General interest, historical/nostalgic, interview/profile, photo feature, technical, travel. No opinion, religious or controversial. Buys 24-50 mss/year. Query or send complete ms. Length: 1,000-2,000 words. Pays $50-300.

Photos: Send photos with submission. Reviews 3×5 prints. Offers no additional payment for photos accepted with ms. Captions required. Buys one-time rights.

Columns/Departments: Caregiver (issues for caring for others), 800-1,200 words; Book Reviews (interest to 50+ reader), 800-1,200. Buys 10 mss/year. Query or send complete ms. Pays $25-100.

Tips: "Include a cover letter which summarizes your submission and suggest other topics you could write on."

‡FIFTY-FIVE PLUS, Promoting An Active Mature Lifestyle, Valley Publishers Inc., 95 Abbeyhill Dr., Kanata, Ontario K2L 2M8 Canada. (613)592-3578. Fax: (613)592-9033. Editor: Pat den Boer. 95% freelance written. Bimonthly magazine. "We focus on the health, financial, nutrition and travel interests of active retirees." Circ. 40,000. Pays on publication. Publishes ms an average of 1 year after acceptance. Byline given. Offers 50% kill fee. Buys first North American serial rights. Editorial lead time 3 months. Submit seasonal material 6 months in advance. Sample copy for 9×12 SAE and 3 first-class stamps. Writer's guidelines for #10 SASE.

Nonfiction: How-to, inspirational, travel. Buys 70 mss/year. Send complete ms. Length: 500-1,000 words. Pays $60-300. Pays writers with contributor copies or other premiums for travel promotional pieces. Sometimes pays expenses of writer on assignment.

Photos: Send photos with submission. Reviews 2×3 and 4×5 transparencies. Offers no additional payment for photos accepted with ms or negotiates payment individually. Buys one-time rights.

Columns/Departments: Health; Backyard Heroes (people giving back to community); Personal Finance; Nutrition; Great Mature Getaways. Length: 600 words. Buys 6 mss/year. Send complete ms. Pays $60.

FLORIDA RETIREMENT LIFESTYLES, Housing • Travel • Leisure, BC Holding Ltd., 3650 N. Federal Hwy., Suite 202, Lighthouse Point FL 33064. (954)946-0149. Fax: (954)946-0150. E-mail: retireinfl@aol.com. Editor: Kerry Smith. 20% freelance written. Monthly magazine directed toward Florida or Florida-bound retirees in an upbeat manner—unusual as well as typical Florida places, people, etc. Estab. 1946. Circ. 70,000. Pays on publication. Publishes ms an average of 3 months after acceptance. Buys first North American serial, first, one-time, second serial (reprint), simultaneous rights, all rights and/or makes work-for-hire assignments. Submit seasonal material 3 months in advance. Reports in 3 weeks on queries. Writer's guidelines free. Sample copy for $2.

• *Florida Retirement Lifestyles* has a new owner, circulation has doubled and the number of manuscripts purchased has increased.

Nonfiction: Hobbies, new careers, transition how to's, how-to (learn new skill as senior), humor, inspirational, interview/profile, new product, personal experience, photo feature, travel. Editorial calendar available on request. Only occasionally runs health-related articles. Buys 40 mss/year. Query with or without published clips or send complete ms. Length: 800-1,500 words. Pays 10¢/word. Sometimes pays expenses of writers on assignment.

Reprints: Send tearsheet or photocopy of article and information about when and where the article previously appeared. Pays 50% of amount paid for an original article.

Photos: Send photos with submissions. Reviews transparencies and prints. Offers $5-25/photo, higher for cover photos. Model releases and identification of subjects required. Buys one-time rights or all rights.

Tips: "Look for the unusual, little known but interesting aspects of Florida living that seniors want or need to know about. Housing, finance and real estate are of primary interest."

GRAND TIMES, Exclusively for Active Retirees, 403 Village Dr., El Cerrito CA 94530. (510)527-4337. Website: http://www.grandtimes.com. Contact: Kira Albin, managing editor. 10% freelance written. Bimonthly magazine "for active retirees in the San Francisco Bay Area. *Grand Times* also publishes an online edition for active retirees worldwide (see website). Controversial, entertaining and informative, *Grand Times* celebrates life's opportunities and examines life's challenges." Estab. 1992. Circ. 45,000. **Pays on acceptance.** Publishes ms an average of 3 months after acceptance. Byline given. Buys one-time rights. Editorial lead time 3 months. Accepts simultaneous submissions. Reports in 3 months on mss. Sample copy for $2 or 9×12 SAE and 4 first-class stamps (or $1.24 in postage stamps). Writer's guidelines for #10 SASE.
Nonfiction: General interest, historical/nostalgic, health, humor, inspirational, personal experience, travel. Buys 6-10 mss/year. Send complete ms. Length: 600-1,700 words. Pays $10-35 for unsolicited articles.
Reprints: Send photocopy of article or story with information about when and where the piece previously appeared.
Photos: State availability of photos with submission. Negotiates payment individually. Buys one-time rights.
Columns/Departments: Grand Travel (travel for older adults), 1,500 words; Making Sense (alternates between legal issues and finance), 800-900 words. Buys 4-6 mss/year. Send complete ms. Pays $10-35.
Fiction: Adventure, ethnic, historical, humorous, mainstream, mystery, romance, slice-of-life vignettes. Buys 4-6 mss/year. Send complete ms. Length: 600-1,700 words. Pays $10-35.
Tips: "Writers should first read guidelines then submit manuscripts with a cohesive theme that meet those guidelines. We are not interested in meandering 'I remember when . . .' articles. Do not stereotype characters as weak, forgetful, rigid, etc. It's okay to discuss disabilities and acknowledge issues of aging if done with humor or compassion."

‡MATURE LIFESTYLES, Florida's Largest 50-Plus News Magazine, News One Inc., 15951 McGregor Blvd. #2-D, Fort Myers FL 33908. Contact: Linda Heffley, editor. 50% freelance written. Monthly magazine covers "all types of features that appeal to the 50-plus reader, preferably with a Florida connection." Estab. 1986. Circ. 200,000. Pays on publication. Publishes ms an average of 6 months to 1 year after acceptance. Byline given. Offers 30% kill fee. Buys one-time or second serial (reprint) rights. Editorial lead time 2 months. Submit seasonal material 4 months in advance. Accepts simultaneous submissions. Reports in 6 weeks on queries; 2 months on mss. Sample copy and writer's guidelines free.
Nonfiction: Historical/nostalgic, opinion, holiday tie-in. Buys 30-50 mss/year. Send complete ms. Length: 500-1,000 words. Pays $35-75 for unsolicited articles. Sometimes pays expenses of writers on assignment.
Photos: State availability of photos with submission. Offers no additional payment for photos accepted with ms. Identification of subjects required. Buys one-time rights.
Columns/Departments: Pays $35-75.

MATURE LIVING, A Christian Magazine for Senior Adults, Sunday School Board of the Southern Baptist Convention, 127 Ninth Ave. N., Nashville TN 37234. (615)251-2274. Fax: (615)251-5008. Editor: Al Shackleford. Contact: Judy Pregel, managing editor. 70% freelance written. Monthly leisure reading magazine for senior adults 50 and older. Estab. 1977. Circ. 350,000. **Pays on acceptance.** Byline given. Prefers to purchase all rights if writer agrees. Submit seasonal material 1 year in advance. Reports in 3 months. Sample copy for 9×12 SAE with 4 first-class stamps. Writer's guidelines for #10 SASE.
Nonfiction: General interest, historical/nostalgic, how-to, humor, inspirational, interview/profile, personal experience, photo feature, crafts, travel. No pornography, profanity, occult, liquor, dancing, drugs, gambling. Buys 100 mss/year. Send complete ms. Length: 600-1,000 words maximum; prefers 950 words. Pays 5½¢/word (accepted); $75 minimum.
Photos: State availability of photos with submission. Offers $10-25/photo. Pays on publication. Buys one-time rights.
Columns/Departments: Cracker Barrel (brief, humorous, original quips and verses), pays $15; Grandparents' Brag Board (something humorous or insightful said or done by your grandchild or great-grandchild), pays $15; Inspirational (devotional items), pays $25; Food (introduction and 4-6 recipes), pays $50; Over the Garden Fence (vegetable or flower gardening), pays $40; Crafts (step-by-step procedures), pays $40; Game Page (crossword or word-search puzzles and quizzes), pays $40.
Fiction: Humorous, mainstream, slice-of-life vignettes. No reference to liquor, dancing, drugs, gambling; no pornography, profanity or occult. Buys 12 mss/year. Send complete ms. Length: 900-1,200 words. Pays 5½¢/word; $75 minimum.
Poetry: Light verse, traditional. Buys 30 poems/year. Submit maximum 5 poems. Length: open. Pays $13-20.

MATURE OUTLOOK, Meredith Corp., 1912 Grand Ave., Des Moines IA 50309-3379. Contact: Peggy Person, editor. 80% freelance written. Bimonthly magazine on travel, health, nutrition, money and people for over-50 audience. They may or may *not* be retired. "*Mature Outlook* is for the 50+ reder who is discovering new possibilities for a new time of life. It provides information for establishing a secure base of health and financial well-being, as well as stories of travel, hobbies, volunteerism and more." Circ. 725,000. **Pays on acceptance.** Publishes ms an average 7 months after acceptance. Byline given. Offers 20% kill fee. Buys all rights or makes work-for-hire assignments. Submit all material 9 months in advance. Reports in 2 weeks. Sample copy for $1. Writer's guidelines for #10 SASE.
Nonfiction: How-to, travel, health, fitness, financial, people profiles. No poetry. Buys 50-60 mss/year. Query with published clips. Length: 150-1,500 words. Pays $100-1,000. Pays telephone expenses of writers on assignment.
Photos: State availability of photos with submission.

Tips: "Please query. Please don't call."

MATURE YEARS, The United Methodist Publishing House, 201 Eighth Ave. S., Nashville TN 37202-0801. Fax: (615)749-6512. Contact: Marvin W. Cropsey, editor. 50% freelance written. Prefers to work with published/established writers. Quarterly magazine "designed to help persons in and nearing the retirement years understand and appropriate the resources of the Christian faith in dealing with specific problems and opportunities related to aging. Estab. 1954. Circ. 70,000. **Pays on acceptance.** Publishes ms an average of 1 year after acceptance. Buys one-time North American serial rights. Submit seasonal material 14 months in advance. Reports in 2 weeks on queries; 2 months for mss. Sample copy for $4.25 and 9×12 SAE. Writer's guidelines for #10 SASE.
Nonfiction: How-to (hobbies), inspirational, religious, travel (special guidelines), older adult health, finance. Especially important are opportunities for older adults to read about service, adventure, fulfillment and fun. Buys 75-80 mss/year. Send complete ms. Length: 900-2,000 words. Pays $45-125. Sometimes pays expenses of writers on assignments.
Reprints: Send photocopy or typed ms with rights for sale noted and information about when and where the article previously appeared. Pays 100% of amount paid for an original article.
Photos: Send photos with ms. Negotiates each payment. Captions, model releases required. Buys one-time rights.
Columns/Departments: Health Hints (retirement, health), 900-1,200 words; Going Places (travel, pilgrimmage), 1,000-1,500 words; Fragments of Life (personal inspiration), 250-600 words; Modern Revelations (religious/inspirational), 900-1,100 words; Money Matters (personal finance), 1,200-1,800 words; Merry-Go-Round (cartoons, jokes, 4-6 line humorous verse); Puzzle Time (religioius puzzles, crosswords). Buys 4 mss/year each. Send complete ms. Pays $45-125.
Fiction: Religious, slice-of-life vignettes, retirement years. Buys 4 mss/year. Send complete ms. Length: 1,000-2,000 words. Pays $60-125.
Poetry: Free verse, haiku, light verse, traditional. Buys 24 poems/year. Submit 6 poems maximum. Length: 3-16 lines. Pays $5-20.

MODERN MATURITY, American Association of Retired Persons, 601 E St., NW, Washington DC 20049. (310)496-2277. Contact: J. Henry Fenwick, editor. 50% freelance written. Prefers to work with published/established writers. Bimonthly magazine. "*Modern Maturity* is devoted to the varied needs and active life interests of AARP members, age 50 and over, covering such topics as financial planning, travel, health, careers, retirement, relationships and social and cultural change. Its editorial content serves the mission of AARP seeking through education, advocacy and service to enhance the quality of life for all by promoting independence, dignity and purpose." Circ. 20,500,000. **Pays on acceptance.** Publishes ms an average of 6 months after acceptance. Byline given. Buys first North American serial rights. Submit seasonal material 6 months in advance. Reports in 3 months. Free sample copy and writer's guidelines.
Nonfiction: Careers, workplace, practical information in living, financial and legal matters, personal relationships, consumerism. Query first. *No unsolicited mss.* Length: up to 2,000 words. Pays up to $3,000. Sometimes pays expenses of writers on assignment.
Photos: Photos purchased with or without accompanying ms. Pays $250 and up for color; $150 and up for b&w.
Fiction: Very occasional short fiction.
Tips: "The most frequent mistake made by writers in completing an article for us is poor follow-through with basic research. The outline is often more interesting than the finished piece. We do not accept unsolicited manuscripts."

‡SENIOR HIGHLIGHTS, Senior Highlights, Inc., 26081 Merit Circle, Suite 101, Laguna Hills CA 92653. (714)367-0776. Fax: (714)367-1006. Publisher/Editor: Lee McCamon. Contact: Cindy Werelius, assistant editor. 30% freelance written. "*Senior Highlights* is a monthly magazine designed to enrich the lifestyle for persons 50 and older. It features interesting and inspiring stories relative to this age group. Our objective is 'Making Your Next Years Your Best Years.' *Senior Highlights* informs readers throughout Central and Southern California. Five separate editions reach Greater Los Angeles, Orange and San Diego counties as well as the Inland Empire (Riverside and San Bernardino counties) and the San Fernando Valley (including Ventura county)." Estab. 1983. Circ. 444,000. Pays on publication. Publishes ms an average of 3 months after acceptance. Byline given. Buys first, second serial (reprint) rights and simultaneous rights. Editorial lead time 2 months. Submit seasonal material 3 months in advance. Accepts simultaneous submissions. Reports in 3 months. Sample copy for $3 and 9×12 SAE with 4 first-class stamps. Writer's guidelines for #10 SASE.
Nonfiction: General interest, historical/nostalgic, humor, inspirational, interview/profile, opinion/commentary, personal experience, travel (domestic and international), breakthroughs in science and medicine, health, exercise and nutrition, arts and entertainment (film, stage, art, music, literature, restaurants), hobbies, gardening and sports, retirement living/housing, personal finance, consumer protection & information. Special issues: editorial calendar available. "Do not send articles that discuss how to 'cure' old age. Do not send articles that talk 'about' seniors rather than 'to' seniors. Recognize who you are talking to: active, talented and intelligent older people." Buys 60 mss/year. Query or send

ALWAYS ENCLOSE a self-addressed, stamped envelope (SASE) with all your queries and correspondence.

complete ms. Length: 300-800 words. Pays $0-100 for assigned articles; $0-25 for unsolicited articles.

Reprints: Send information about when and where the article previously appeared. Does not pay for reprints.

Photos: State availability of or send photos with submission. Reviews color slides or transparencies, b&w prints. Offers no additional payment for photos accepted with ms. Captions are required.

Columns/Departments: Celebrity Feature (high profile, easily recognizable celebrities that are still actively involved), 800 words; Letters to the Editor (publish one per month; must be clearly written), 300 words; Health (nutrition/fitness; medical breakthroughs), 800 words; Lifestyles (housing, food/recipes, restaurants, gardening, hobbies, sports and legislation), 800 words; Moneywise (consumer issues, personal finance and investing), 800 words; Travel (domestic and international), 800 words; Who's to Say (outstanding, extraordinary seniors), 800 words. Buys 120 mss/year. Query or send complete ms. Pays $0-50.

Tips: "We are looking for articles that tie in to our editorial calendar topics in exciting and innovative ways. We have a special need for upbeat health articles that avoid stereotyping our readers as sickly and emphasize prevention. Talk directly to our readers and stick with subjects that directly impact their lives. Keep in mind our readers' needs and interests differ dramatically from 50 to over 100 years old. No telephone queries. Unorganized thoughts and materials are tossed."

SENIOR MAGAZINE, 3565 S. Higuera St., San Luis Obispo CA 93401. (805)544-8711. Fax: (805)544-4450. Editor/Publisher: Gary D. Suggs. Contact: George Brano, managing editor. 90% freelance written. Monthly magazine covering seniors to inform and entertain the "over-50" but young-at-heart audience. Estab. 1981. Circ. 240,000. Pays on publication. Byline given. Publishes ms an average of 1 month after acceptance. Not copyrighted. Buys first or second rights. Accepts simultaneous submissions. Submit seasonal material 2 months in advance. Reports in 1 month. Sample copy for 9 × 12 SAE with 6 first-class stamps. Writer's guidelines for SASE.

• *Senior Magazine* is currently running articles on maintaining physical fitness/training.

Nonfiction: Health, historical/nostalgic, humor, inspirational, personal experience, personality profiles of actors, sports figures, travel, writers. Special issues: Second Careers; Going Back to School; Christmas (December); Travel (October, March). Buys 30-75 mss/year. Query. Length: 600-900 words. Pays $1.50/inch.

Reprints: Send typed ms with rights for sale noted and information about when and where the article previously appeared. Pays 100% of amount paid for an original article.

Photos: Send photos with submission. Reviews 8 × 10 b&w prints only. Offers $10-25/photo. Captions and identification of subjects required. Buys one-time rights. Uses mostly well known personalities.

Columns/Departments: Finance (investment), Taxes, Auto, Health. Length: 300-900 words. Pays $1.50/inch.

SENIOR WORLD NEWSMAGAZINE, Kendell Communications, Inc., 500 Fesler St., Suite 207, P.O. Box 13560, El Cajon CA 92020-1565. (619)593-2910. Fax: (619)442-4043. Contact: Laura Impastato, executive editor. Travel Editor: Jerry Goodrum. Entertainment Editor: Holly Tani. Health Editor: Carolyn Pantier. Feature Editor: Carolyn Pantier. 5% freelance written. Prefers to work with published/established writers. Monthly tabloid newspaper for active older adults living in San Diego, Orange, Los Angeles, Riverside and San Bernardino counties. Estab. 1973. Circ. 475,000. Pays on publication. Buys first serial rights. Accepts simultaneous submissions. Reports in 2 months. Sample copy for $4. Writer's guidelines free.

Nonfiction: "We are looking for stories on health, stressing wellness and prevention; travel—international, domestic and how-to; profiles of senior celebrities and remarkable seniors; finance and investment tips for seniors; and interesting hobbies." Send query or complete ms. Length: 700-1,100 words. Pays $25-75.

Photos: State availability of photos with submission. Needs b&w with model release.

Columns/Departments: Most of our columns are local or staff-written. We will consider a query on a column idea accompanied by a sample column.

Tips: "No 'pity the poor seniors' material. We are primarily a news publication, and our content and style reflect that. Our readers are active, vital adults 55 years of age and older." No telephone calls, faxed queries or manuscripts.

ROMANCE AND CONFESSION

Listed here are publications that need stories of romance ranging from ethnic and adventure to romantic intrigue and confession. Each magazine has a particular slant; some are written for young adults, others to family-oriented women. Some magazines also are interested in general interest nonfiction on related subjects.

AFFAIRE DE COEUR,, 3976 Oak Hill Rd., Oakland CA 94605. Fax: (510)632-8868. E-mail: sseven@msn.com. Website: http://www.affairedecoeur.com. Contact: Louise Snead, publisher. 56% freelance written. Monthly magazine of book reviews, articles and information on publishing for romance readers and writers. Circ. 115,000. Pays on publication. Publishes ms an average of 1 year after acceptance. Byline given. Buys one-time rights. Submit seasonal material 3 months in advance. Accepts simultaneous submissions. Reports in 4 months. Sample copy for $5.

Nonfiction: Book excerpts, essays, general interest, historical/nostalgic, how-to, interview/profile, personal experience, photo feature. Buys 2 mss/year. Query. Length: 500-2,200 words. Pays $25-35. Sometimes pays writers with contributor copies or other premiums.

Reprints: Accepts previously published submissions.

Photos: State availability of photos with submission. Review prints. Identification of subjects required. Buys one-time rights.

Columns/Departments: Reviews (book reviews), bios, articles, 2,000 word or less.

Fiction: Historical, mainstream, romance. Pays $25.

Fillers: Newsbreaks. Buys 2/year. Length: 50-100 words. Does not pay.

Tips: "Please send clean copy. Do not send material without SASE. Do not expect a return for 2-3 months. Type all information. Send some sample of your work."

BLACK SECRETS, Sterling/McFadden Partnership, 233 Park Ave. S., 7th Floor, New York NY 10003. (212)780-3500. Fax: (212)979-7342. Editor: Marcia Mahan. See *Intimacy/Black Romance*.

Fiction: "This is our most romantic magazine of the five. We use one longer story between 20-24 pages for this book, and sometimes we feature it on the cover. Save your harsh, sleazy stories for another magazine. Give us your softest, dreamiest, most imaginative, most amorous story with a male love interest we can't help but fall in love with. Make sure your story has body and not just bodies. Our readers love romance, but they also require substance." Pays $100.

Tips: "Please request a sample and guidelines before submitting. Enclose a 9×12 SASE with 5 first-class stamps."

INTIMACY/BLACK ROMANCE, Sterling/McFadden Partnership, 233 Park Ave. S., 7th Floor, New York NY 10003. (212)780-3500. Fax: (212)979-7342. Editor: Marcia Mahan. 100% freelance written. Eager to work with new/unpublished writers. Bimonthly magazine of romance and love. Estab. 1982. Circ. 100,000. Pays on publication. Publishes ms an average of 2 months after acceptance. Byline given on articles only. Buys all rights. Submit seasonal material 6 months in advance. Reports in 2 months. Sample copy for 9×12 SAE with 5 first-class stamps. Writer's guidelines for #10 SASE.

Nonfiction: How-to (relating to romance and love) and feature articles on any aspect of relationships. Buys 100 mss/year. Query with published clips or send complete ms. Length: 3-5 pages. Pays $100.

Photos: Send photos with submission. Reviews contact sheets, negatives, transparencies.

Fiction: Confession and romance. "Stories that are too graphic in content and lack romance are unacceptable." Buys 300 mss/year. Accepts stories which are a bit more romantic than those written for *Jive*, *Black Confessions* or *Bronze Thrills*. Send complete ms (4,000-5,000 words). Pays $75-100.

Tips: "I still get excited when I read a ms by an unpublished writer whose use of language is magical and fresh. I'm always looking for that diamond in the fire. Send us your *best* shot. Writers who are careless, sloppy and ungrammatical are an immediate turn-off for me. Please do your homework first. Is it the type of story we buy? Is it written in ms format? Does it make one want to read it?"

INTIMACY/BRONZE THRILLS, Sterling/McFadden, 233 Park Ave. S., 5th Floor, New York NY 10003. (212)780-3500. Fax: (212)979-7342. Editor: Marcia Mahan. Estab. 1982. See *Intimacy/Black Romance*.

Fiction: "Stories can be a bit more extraordinary and uninhibited than in the other magazines but still they have to be romantic. For example, we might buy a story about a woman who finds out her husband is a transsexual in *Bronze Thrills*, but not for *Jive* (our younger magazine). The stories for this magazine tend to have a harder, more adult edge of reality than the others."

JIVE, Sterling/McFadden Partnership, 233 Park Ave. S., 7th Floor, New York NY 10003. (212)780-3500. Fax: (212)979-7342. Editor: Marcia Mahan. 100% freelance written. Eager to work with new/unpublished writers. Bimonthly magazine of romance and love. Estab. 1982. Circ. 100,000. Pays on publication. Publishes ms an average of 2 months after acceptance. Byline given on articles only. Buys all rights. Submit seasonal material 6 months in advance. Reports in 2 months on queries; 6 months on mss. Sample copy for 9×12 SASE with 5 first-class stamps. Free writer's guidelines.

Nonfiction: How-to (relating to romance and love) and feature articles on any aspect of relationships. "We like our articles to have a down-to-earth flavor. They should be written in the spirit of sisterhood, fun and creativity. Come up with an original idea our readers may not have thought of but will be dying to try out." Buys 100 mss/year. Query with published clips or send complete ms. Length: 3-5 typed pages. Pays $100.

Columns/Departments: Fashion, health, beauty articles accepted. Length: 3-5 pages.

Fiction: Confession and romance. "Stories that are too graphic and lack romance are unacceptable. However, all stories must contain one or two love scenes. Love scenes should allude to sex—romantic, not lewd." Buys 300 mss/year. Send complete ms (4,000-5,000 words). Pays $75-100.

Tips: "We are leaning toward more romantic writing styles as opposed to the more graphic stories of the past. Our audience is largely black teenagers. The stories should reinforce Black pride and should be geared toward teenage issues. Our philosophy is to show our experiences in as positive a light as possible without promoting any of the common stereotypes that are associated with Black men, lovemaking prowess, penile size, etc. Stereotypes of any kind are totally unacceptable. The fiction section which accepts romance stories and confession stories is most open to freelancers. Also, our special features section is very open. We would also like to see stories that are set outside the US (perhaps they could be set in the Caribbean, Europe, Africa, etc.) and themes that are reflective of things happening around us in the 90s—abortion, AIDS, alienation, surrogate mothers, etc. But we also like to see stories that transcend our contemporary problems and can give us a moment of pleasure, warmth, joy and relief. The characters should be anywhere from teenage to 30s but not the typical 'country bumpkin girl who was turned out by a big city pimp' type story. Please, writers who are not Black, research your story to be sure that it depicts Black people in a positive manner. Do not make a Black character a caricature of a non-Black character. Read contemporary Black fiction to ensure that your dialogue and speech idioms are natural to the Black vernacular."

MODERN ROMANCES, Sterling/Macfadden Partnership, 233 Park Ave. S., New York NY 10003. (212)979-4800. Fax: (212)979-7342. Editor: Colleen M. Murphy. 100% freelance written. Monthly magazine for family-oriented working women, ages 18-65 years old. Circ. 200,000. Pays the last week of the month of issue. Buys all rights. Submit seasonal material at least 6 months in advance. Reports in 11 months. Writer's guidelines for #10 SASE.
 • This editor is especially in need of short, well-written stories (approximately 3,000-7,000 words).
Nonfiction: Confession stories with reader identification and a strong emotional tone; a strong emphasis on character-ization and well-defined plots. Should be realistic and compelling. No third-person material. Buys 10 mss/issue. No query letters; submit complete ms. Length: 2,500-10,000 words. Pays 5¢/word. Buys all rights.
Poetry: Light, romantic poetry and seasonal subjects. Length: 24 lines maximum. Pays $2/line. Look at poetry published in previous issues before submitting.

TRUE CONFESSIONS, Macfadden Women's Group, 233 Park Ave. S., New York NY 10003. (212)979-4800. Fax: (212)979-7342. Contact: Pat Byrdsong, editor. 100% freelance written. Eager to work with new/unpublished writers. Monthly magazine for high-school-educated, blue-collar women, teens through maturity. Circ. 280,000. Buys all rights. Byline given on featured columns: My Man, Woman to Woman, Incredible But True, My Moment With God, and Family Zoo. Pays during the last week of month of issue. Publishes ms an average of 4 months after acceptance. Submit seasonal material 6 months in advance. Reports in 6-9 months.
Nonfiction: Timely, exciting, true emotional first-person stories on the problems that face today's women. The narrators should be sympathetic, and the situations they find themselves in should be intriguing, yet realistic. Many stories may have a strong romantic interest and a high moral tone; however, personal accounts or "confessions," no matter how controversial the topic, are encouraged and accepted. Careful study of a current issue is suggested. Length: 4,000-7,000 words; also book lengths of 8,000-10,000 words. Pays 5¢/word. Also publishes humor, poetry and mini-stories (1,500 words maximum). Submit complete ms. No simultaneous submissions. SASE required. Buys all rights.
 • Asian- Latina- and African-American stories are encouraged.
Tips: "Our magazine is almost 100% freelance. We purchase all stories that appear in our magazine."

TRUE EXPERIENCE, The Sterling/MacFadden Partnership, 233 Park Ave. S., New York NY 10003. (212)979-4800. Fax: (212)979-7342. Editor: Rose Bernstein. Associate Editor: Heather Young. 100% freelance written. Monthly magazine covering women's confession stories. *"True Experience* is a women's confession magazine which publishes first-person short stories on actual occurrences. Our stories cover such topics as love, romance, crime, family problems and social issues. The magazine's primary audience consists of working-class women in the South, Midwest and rural West. Our stories aim to portray the lives and problems of 'real women.' " Estab. 1928. Circ. 100,000. Pays on publication. Publishes ms an average of 4 months after acceptance. No byline. Buys all rights. Editorial lead time 4 months. Submit seasonal material 6 months in advance. Reports in 2 weeks on queries; 4 months on mss. Sample copy for $1.69. Writer's guidelines for #10 SASE.
Nonfiction: Confession, humorous, mystery, romance, slice-of-life vignettes. Buys 125 mss/year. Send complete ms. Length: 1,000-10,000 words. Pays 3¢/word.
Columns/Departments: Woman Talk (rites of passage in women's lives), 500-1,500 words; How We Met (anecdotes describing a couple's first meeting), 300-1,000 words. Buys 24 mss/year. Send complete ms. Pays $50-75.
Poetry: Light verse, traditional. Buys 5 poems/year. Submit maximum 10 poems. Length: 4-50 lines. Pays $2/line.
Tips: "The best way to break into our publication is to send us a well-written, interesting story with sympathetic characters. Stories focusing on topical subjects like sexual harassment, crime, AIDS, or natural disasters are most likely to receive serious considerations. No special submission methods. All stories must be written in first person."

TRUE LOVE, Macfadden Women's Group, 233 Park Ave. S., New York NY 10003. (212)979-4800. Fax: (212)979-7342. Contact: Alison Way, editor. 100% freelance written. Monthly magazine for young, blue-collar women, 22-55. Confession stories based on true happenings, with reader identification and a strong emotional tone. Circ. 200,000. Pays the last week of the month of the issue. Buys all rights. Submit seasonal material 6 months in advance. Reports in 9 months. Sample copy for $2 and 9×12 SAE. Writer's guidelines for #10 SASE.
 • *True Love* needs more romance stories.
Nonfiction: Confessions, true love stories, problems and solutions, health problems, marital and child-rearing difficult-ies. Avoid graphic sex. Stories dealing with reality, current problems, everyday events, with emphasis on emotional impact. No stories written in third person. Buys 10 stories/issue. Buy all rights. No query letters; submit complete ms; returned only with SAE and sufficient postage. Length: 2,000-10,000 words. Pays 3¢/word.
Columns/Departments: The Life I Live, $100; How I Know I'm In Love, 700 words or less; $75; Pet Shop, $50; Kids Will Be Kids, $50; Here Comes The Bride, $50.
Poetry: Light romantic poetry or holiday-related poems. Length: 24 lines maximum. Pay $2/line.
Tips: "The story must appeal to the average blue-collar woman. It must deal with her problems and interests. Charac-ters—especially the narrator—must be sympathetic. Focus is especially on young working women."

TRUE ROMANCE, Sterling/Macfadden Partnership, 233 Park Ave. S., New York NY 10003. (212)979-4800. Fax: (212)979-7342. Contact: Pat Vitucci, editor. 100% freelance written. Monthly magazine for women, teens through retired, offering compelling confession stories based on true happenings, with reader identification and strong emotional tone. No third-person material. Estab. 1923. Circ. 225,000. Pays 1 month after publication. Buys all rights. Submit seasonal material at least 6 months in advance. Reports within 8 months.

Nonfiction: Confessions, true love stories; mini-adventures: problems and solutions; dating and marital and child-rearing difficulties. Realistic yet unique stories dealing with current problems, everyday events; strong emotional appeal. Buys 12 stories/issue. Submit complete ms; 3,000-8,000 words. Pays 3¢/word; slightly higher rates for short-shorts.

Columns/Departments: That's My Child (photo and 50 words); Loving Pets (photo and 50 words), both pay $50; Cupid's Corner (photo and 500 words about you and spouse), pays $100; That Precious Moment (1,000 words about a unique experience), pays $50.

Poetry: Light romantic poetry. Length: 24 lines maximum. Pays $10-30.

Tips: "A timely, well-written story that is told by a sympathetic narrator who sees the central problem through to a satisfying resolution is *all* important to break into *True Romance*. We are always looking for interesting, emotional, identifiable stories."

TRUE STORY, Sterling/Macfadden Partnership, 233 Park Ave. S., New York NY 10003. (212)979-4800. Fax: (212)979-7342. Contact: Kristina M. Pappalardo, editor. 80% freelance written. Monthly magazine for young married, blue-collar women, 20-35; high school education; increasingly broad interests; home-oriented, but looking beyond the home for personal fulfillment. Circ. 1,700,000. Buys all rights. Byline given "on articles only." Pays 1 month after publication. Submit seasonal material 1 year in advance. Reports in 1 year.

Nonfiction: "First-person stories covering all aspects of women's interests: love, marriage, family life, careers, social problems, etc. The best direction a new writer can be given is to carefully study several issues of the magazine; then submit a fresh, exciting, well-written true story. We have no taboos. It's the handling and believability that make the difference between a rejection and an acceptance." Buys about 125 full-length mss/year. Submit only complete mss for stories. Length: 1,500-10,000 words. Pays 5¢/word; $150 minimum. Pays a flat rate for columns or departments, as announced in the magazine. Query for fact articles.

RURAL

These publications draw readers interested in rural lifestyles. Surprisingly, many readers are from urban centers who dream of or plan to build a house in the country. Magazines featuring design, construction, log homes and "country" style interior decorating appear in Home and Garden.

ALBERTA FARM AND RANCH, Alberta's Foremost Rural Magazine, North Hill Publications, 4000 19th St. NE, Calgary, Alberta T2E 6P8 Canada. (403)250-6633. Fax: (403)291-0502. Editor: Michael Dumont. 10-30% freelance written. Monthly magazine covering rural and agricultural issues in Alberta. Estab. 1983. Circ. 80,288. Pays on publication. Publishes ms an average of 4 months after acceptance. Byline given. Buys First Canadian Rights. Submit seasonal material 6 months in advance. Reports in 2 months. Sample copy for 8×10 SAE with 2 first class Canadian stamps or 2 IRCs. Writer's guidelines for #10 SASE with Canadian postage or #10 SAE with 1 IRC.

Nonfiction: General interest, historical/nostalgic, politics, interview/profile, technical. "September's issue always features Women in Agriculture and related issues. No non-relevant articles or articles not of interest to rural Albertans." Buys 20-30 mss/year. Query with published clips. Length: 1,000-2,000 words. Pays $50-200 for assigned articles; $50-100 for unsolicited articles.

Photos: Reviews 4×6 prints. Offers $5-10/photo. Captions and identification of subjects required.

Columns/Departments: "Columnists work on annual contracts only."

Tips: "While *AF&R* seldom accepts unsolicited manuscripts, we always encourage writers to send in queries before going to the time and expense of completing a story. The best way to break into our magazine is with a unique story idea with specific interest to rural Albertans. Stories looking at unique personalities, insightful material on age-related issues and stories of issues concerning the family tend to fill most pages. For new writers trying to solicit their material with little publishing experience, I suggest the submission of typed mss in lieu of tearsheets. Caution: the fastest way to get a rejection is to spell words incorrectly or glaring grammatical errors. Also, superficial stories that do not entice reading or leave extensive informational gaps tend to be overlooked. I would rather see penned-in corrections than errors left unchecked."

THE COUNTRY CONNECTION, The Magazine for Country Folk, Pinecone Publishing, P.O. Box 100, Boulter, Ontario K0L 1G0 Canada. Fax: (613)332-3651. Website: http://www.cyberus.ca/~queenswood/pinecone/. Contact: Gus Zylstra, editor. 75% freelance written. Semiannual magazine covering country life and tourism. "*The Country Connection* is a magazine for country folk and those who wish they were. Building on our commitment to heritage, cultural, artistic, and outdoor themes, we continually add new topics to illuminate the country experience of people living within nature. Our goal is to chronicle rural life in its many aspects, giving 'voice' to the countryside." Estab. 1989. Circ. 15,000. Pays on publication. Publishes ms an average of 6 months after acceptance. Byline given. Buys first rights. Editorial lead time 4 months. Submit seasonal material 4 months in advance. Sample copy $4.55. Writer's guidelines for #10 SAE and IRC.

Nonfiction: General interest, historical/nostalgic, humor, personal experience, photo feature, lifestyle, leisure, art and culture, travel, vegetarian recipes only. No hunting and fishing or animal husbandry articles. Buys 20 mss/year. Send complete ms. Length: 500-2,000 words. Pays 7-10¢/word. Sometimes pays expenses of writers on assignment.
Photos: Send photos with submission. Reviews transparencies and prints. Offers $10-50/photo. Captions required. Buys one-time rights.
Columns/Departments: Pays 7-10¢/word.
Fiction: Adventure, fantasy, historical, humorous, slice-of-life vignettes, country living. Buys 4 mss/year. Send complete ms. Length: 500-1,500 words. Pays 7-10¢/word.
Tips: "Send (original content) manuscript with appropriate support material such as photos, illustrations, maps, etc. We are getting a lot of SASE from the US with US stamps which are unusable here in Canada."

‡COUNTRY HEART MAGAZINE, The Alliance Press, Inc., 1320 N. Stewart, Springfield MO 65802. Fax: (417)831-8184. E-mail: timmcd@dialnet.net. Editor: Tim McDonald. Contact: Voletta Anderson, associate editor. 50% freelance written. Quarterly magazine "targeted to women ages 25-54. *Country Heart* presents material reflecting traditional midwestern values in a manner appropriate to a modern world. We want each article we publish to carry ideas or information a reader can put to use." Estab. 1995. Circ. 50,000. **Pays $100 on acceptance** and 5¢/word in edited version after publication. Byline given. Offers $100 kill fee. Buys first and second serial (reprint) rights. Editorial lead time 3 months. Submit seasonal material 4 months in advance. Accepts simultaneous submissions. Reports in 2 months on mss. Sample copy for 9 × 12 SAE and 5 first-class stamps. Writer's guidelines free.
Nonfiction: Essays, how-to, humor, personal experience, photo feature, travel, home/home decor features. No fiction. Buys 40 mss/year. Query with published clips or send complete ms. Length: 500-1,500 words. Pays $100-200. Pays writers with contributor copies or other premiums based on prior agreement.
Photos: State availability of photos with submission. Reviews contact sheets, transparencies and 4 × or larger prints. Offers $25/photo. Captions, model releases and identification of subjects required. Buys one-time rights.
Columns/Departments: Our Back Porch (collectibles), 750 words; Travel (unique travel destinations), 750 words.
Poetry: Light verse or traditional. Buys 4-5 poems/year. Submit maximum 6 poems. Length: 4-24 lines. Pays $50-100.
Tips: "Present a fully-outlined query or manuscript with care taken to show how the article can enrich a reader's life in an active way. Concentrate on positive approaches to dealing with modern life, and tie the best of yesterday's rural values to today's world."

‡COUNTRY JOURNAL, 4 High Ridge Park, Standford CT 06905. (203)321-1778. Fax: (203)322-1966. Group Publishing Director: Toni Apgar. Associate Editor: Cristin Marandino. 90% freelance written. Works with a small number of new/unpublished writers each year. Bimonthly magazine "that is the authoritative resource on rural life, providing practical advise for the country dweller. Readership aimed to middle and upper income levels." Estab. 1974. Circ. 150,000. Average issue includes 6-8 feature articles and 10 departments. **Pays on acceptance.** Rates range from 20-40¢/word. Byline given. Buys first North American serial rights. Submit seasonal material 1 year in advance. Accepts previously published submissions. Send photocopy of article. For reprints, pays 10% of the amount paid for an original article. Reports in 4 months. Sample copy for $4. Writer's guidelines for SASE.
Nonfiction: Conservation, gardening, nature, projects, small-scale farming, how-to, issues affecting rural areas. Query with published clips and SASE. Length: 1,500-2,000 words. Pays 20-40¢/word.
Photos: Art director. State availability of photos. Reviews b&w contact sheets, 5 × 7 and 8 × 10 b&w glossy prints and 35mm or larger transparencies with SASE. Captions, model release, identification of subjects required. Buys one-time rights.
Columns/Departments: Sentinel (brief articles on country topics, how-tos, current events and updates). Buys 5 mss/issue. Query with published clips and SASE. Length: 200-500 words. Pays approximately $75.
Tips: "Be as specific in your query as possible and explain why you are qualified to write the piece (especially for how-to's and controversial subjects). The writer has a better chance of breaking in at our publication with short articles."

FARM & RANCH LIVING, Reiman Publications, 5400 S. 60th St., Greendale WI 53129. (414)423-0100. Fax: (414)423-8463. E-mail: 76150.162@compuserve.com. Editor: Nick Pabst. 80% freelance written. Eager to work with new/unpublished writers. Bimonthly lifestyle magazine aimed at families that farm or ranch full time. "*F&RL* is *not a* 'how-to' magazine—it focuses on people rather than products and profits." Estab. 1968. Circ. 380,000. **Pays on acceptance.** Publishes ms an average of 6 months after acceptance. Byline given. Buys first serial rights and one-time rights. Submit seasonal material 6 months in advance. Reports in 6 weeks. Sample copy for $2. Writer's guidelines for #10 SASE.
Nonfiction: Interview/profile, photo feature, nostalgia, humor, inspirational, personal experience. No how-to articles or stories about "hobby farmers" (doctors or lawyers with weekend farms); no issue-oriented stories (pollution, animal rights, etc.). Buys 30 mss/year. Submit query or finished ms. Length: 600-1,200 words. Pays $150-300 for text-and-photos package.
Reprints: Send tearsheet of article or typed ms with rights for sale noted. Payment negotiable.
Photos: Scenic. State availability of photos with query. Pays $75-200 for 35mm color slides. Buys one-time rights.
Fillers: Jokes, anecdotes, short humor with farm or ranch slant. Buys 50/year. Length: 50-150 words. Pays $20.
Tips: "Our readers enjoy stories and features that are upbeat and positive. A freelancer must see *F&RL* to fully appreciate how different it is from other farm publications—ordering a sample is strongly advised (not available on

newsstands). Photo features (about interesting farm or ranch families) and personality profiles are most open to freelancers. We can make separate arrangements for photography if writer is unable to provide photos."

FARM FAMILY AMERICA, Fieldhagen Publishing, Inc., 190 Fifth St. E., Suite 121, St. Paul MN 55101. (612)292-1747. Contact: George Ashfield, editor. 75% freelance written. Five issues per year. Published by American Cyanamid and written to the non-farm related lifestyle, activities and travel interests of American farm families. Circ. 300,000. **Pays on acceptance.** Publishes ms an average of 2 months after acceptance. Byline given. Offers 25% kill fee. Buys first rights or second serial (reprint) rights. Submit seasonal material 6 months in advance. Accepts simultaneous submissions. Reports in 6 weeks. Writer's guidelines for #10 SASE.
Nonfiction: General interest and travel. Buys 30 mss/year. Query with published clips. Length: 1,000-1,800 words. Pays $400-650.
Photos: State availability of photos with submission. Reviews 35mm transparencies and prints. Offers $160-700/photo. Model releases and identification of subjects required. Buys one-time rights.

FARM TIMES, 504 Sixth St., Rupert ID 83350. (208)436-1111. Fax: (208)436-9455. E-mail: farmpub@cyberhighway.n et. Website: www.farmtimes.com. Contact: Eric Goodell, editor. 50% freelance written. Monthly regional tabloid for agriculture-farming/ranching. "*Farm Times* is 'dedicated to rural living.' Stories related to farming and ranching in the states of Idaho, Nevada, Utah, Wyoming and Oregon are our mainstay, but farmers and ranchers do more than just work. Human interest articles that appeal to rural readers are used on occasion." Estab. 1987. Pays on publication. Byline given. Editorial lead time 1 month. Submit seasonal material 3 months in advance. Reports in 2 months on queries. Writer's guidelines free on request. Send $1 for sample copy.
Nonfiction: Farm or ranch issues, exposé, general interest, how-to, interview/profile, new product (few), opinion, late breaking ag news. Always runs one feature article of interest to women. No humor, essay, first person, personal experience or book excerpts. Special issues: Irrigation, Chemical/Fertilizer, Potato Production. Buys 200 mss/year. Query with published clips. Send complete ms. Length: 700-800 words. Pays $1.50/column inch.
Reprints: Send information about when and where the article previously appeared. Pays 100% of amount paid for an original article.
Photos: Send photocopy of article and photos with submission. Reviews contact sheets with negatives, 35mm or larger transparencies and 3×5 or larger prints. Offers $7/b&w inside, $35/color cover. Captions, model releases, identification of subjects required. Buys one-time rights.
Column/Departments: Horse (horse care/technical), 500-600 words; Rural Religion (interesting churches/missions/religious activities) 600-800 words; Dairy (articles of interest to dairy farmers) 600-800 words. Buys 12 mss/year. Query. Send complete ms. Pays $1.50/column inch.
Tips: "Query with a well-thought-out idea that will appeal to rural readers. Of special interest is how environmental issues will affect farmers/ranchers, Endangered Species Act, EPA, etc. We are always looking for well-written articles on subjects that affect western farmers and ranchers."

MOTHER EARTH NEWS, 49 E. 21st St., 11th Floor, New York NY 10010. (212)260-7210. Fax: (212)260-7445. E-mail: mearthnews@aol.com. Contact: Molly Miller, senior editor. Editor: Matthew Scanlon. Managing Editor: Christine Cauchon Summer. Mostly freelance written. Bimonthly magazine emphasizing "country living and country skills, for both long-time and would-be ruralites. *Mother Earth News* is dedicated to presenting information which will help readers become more self-sufficient, financially independent, and environmentally aware." Circ. 450,000. Pays on publication. Byline given. Submit seasonal material 5 months in advance. No handwritten mss. Reports within 3 months. Publishes ms an average of 6 months after acceptance. Sample copy for $5. Writer's guidelines for #10 SASE with 2 first-class stamps.
Nonfiction: How-to, home business, alternative energy systems, home building, home retrofit and home maintenance, energy-efficient structures, seasonal cooking, gardening, crafts. Buys 100-150 mss/year. Query. "A short, to-the-point paragraph is often enough. If it's a subject we don't need at all, we can answer immediately. If it tickles our imagination, we'll ask to take a look at the whole piece. No phone queries, please." Length: 300-3,000 words. Publishes nonfiction book excerpts.
Reprints: Rarely accepts previously published submissions. Send information about when and where the article previously appeared.
Photos: Purchased with accompanying ms. Send prints or transparencies. Uses 8×10 b&w glossies or any size color transparencies. Include type of film, speed and lighting used. Total purchase price for ms includes payment for photos. Captions and credits required.
Columns/Departments: Country Love (down-home solutions to everyday problems); Bits & Pieces (snippets of news, events and silly happenings); Herbs & Remedies (home healing, natural medicine); Energy Tips (ways to conserve energy while saving money).
Tips: "Probably the best way to break in is to study our magazine, digest our writer's guidelines, and send us a concise article illustrated with color transparencies that we can't resist. When folks query and we give a go-ahead on speculation, we often offer some suggestions. Failure to follow those suggestions can lose the sale for the author. We want articles that tell what real people are doing to take charge of their own lives. Articles should be well-documented and tightly written treatments of topics we haven't already covered. The critical thing is length, and our payment is by space, not word count. *No phone queries.*"

RURAL HERITAGE, 281 Dean Ridge Lane, Gainesboro TN 38562-5039. (615)268-0655. Editor: Gail Damerow. Publisher: Allan Damerow. 98% freelance written. Willing to work with a small number of new/unpublished writers. Bimonthly magazine devoted to preserving a way of life such as the training and care of draft animals, and other traditional country skills. Estab. 1975. Circ. 3,000. Pays on publication. Publishes ms an average of 6 months after acceptance. Byline given. Buys first English language rights. Submit seasonal material 6 months in advance. Reports in 3 months. Sample copy for $6. Writer's guidelines #10 SASE.

Nonfiction: How-to (crafting and farming); interview/profile (people using draft animals); photo feature. No articles on *mechanized* farming. Buys 100 mss/year. Query or send complete ms. Length: 1,200-1,500 words. Pays 5¢/word.

Reprints: Accepts previously published submissions, but only if previous publication had limited or regional circulation. Send tearsheet or photocopy of article, typed ms with rights for sale noted and information about when and where the article previously appeared. Pays 100% of amount paid for an original article.

Photos: Send photos with ms. Pays $10. Captions and identification of subjects required. Buys one-time rights. Six covers/year (color transparency or 5×7 horizontal print), animals in harness $50; back covers, humorous rural scene (same size, format) $25. Photo guidelines for #10 SASE.

Columns/Departments: Self-sufficiency (modern people preserving traditional American lifestyle), 750-1,500 words; Drafter's Features (draft animals used for farming, shows and pulls—their care), 750-1,500 words; Crafting (implement designs and patterns), 750-1,500 words; Humor, 750-900 words. Pays 5¢/word.

Poetry: Traditional. Pays $5-25.

Tips: "Always welcome are: 1) Detailed descriptions and photos of horse-drawn implements 2) Prices and other details of draft animal and implement auctions and sales."

RURALITE, P.O. Box 558, Forest Grove OR 97116-0558. (503)357-2105. Fax: (503)357-8615. E-mail: ruralite@europa.com. Website: http://www.europa.com/~ruralite/. Contact: Curtis Condon, editor-in-chief. Associate Editor: Walt Wentz. 80% freelance written. Works with new, unpublished writers "who have mastered the basics of good writing." Monthly magazine aimed at members of consumer-owned electric utilities throughout 9 western states, including Alaska. Publishes 50 regional editions. Estab. 1954. Circ. 265,000. Buys first rights, sometimes reprint rights. Byline given. **Pays on acceptance.** Query first; unsolicited manuscripts submitted without request rarely read by editors. Reports in 1 month. Sample copy and writer's guidelines for 10×13 SAE with 4 first-class stamps.

Nonfiction: Looking for well-written nonfiction, dealing primarily with human interest topics. Must have strong Northwest perspective and be sensitive to Northwest issues and attitudes. Wide range of topics possible, from energy-related subjects to little-known travel destinations to unusual businesses located in areas served by consumer-owned electric utilities. "About half of our readers are rural and small town residents; others are urban and suburban. Topics with an obvious 'big-city' focus not accepted. Family-related issues, Northwest history (no encyclopedia rewrites), people and events, unusual tidbits that tell the Northwest experience are best chances for a sale. Special issues: Home Improvement (September 1997); Gardening (February 1998). Buys 50-60 mss/yr. Length 300-2,000 words. Pays $75-400.

Reprints: Send tearsheet of article or typed ms with rights for sale noted and information about when and where the article previously appeared. For reprints, pays 50% of "*our* regular freelance rates."

Photos: "Illustrated stories are the key to a sale. Stories without art rarely make it, with the exception of humor pieces. Black and white prints, color slides, all formats, accepted with 'razor-sharp' focus. Fuzzy, low-contrast photos may lose the sale."

Tips: "Study recent issues. Follow directions when given an assignment. Be able to deliver a complete package (story and photos). We're looking for regular contributors to whom we can assign topics from our story list after they've proven their ability to deliver quality mss."

SCIENCE

These publications are published for laymen interested in technical and scientific developments and discoveries, applied science and technical or scientific hobbies. Publications of interest to the personal computer owner/user are listed in the Personal Computers section. Journals for scientists and engineers are listed in Trade in various sections.

AD ASTRA, 600 Pennsylvania Ave. SE, Suite 201, Washington DC 20003-4316. (202)543-1900. Fax: (202)546-4189. E-mail: adastra@nss.org. Website: http://www.nss.org. Editor-in-Chief: Pat Dasch. 80% freelance written. Bimonthly magazine covering the space program. "We publish non-technical, lively articles about all aspects of international space programs, from shuttle missions to planetary probes to plans for the future." Estab. 1989. Circ. 25,000. Pays on publication. Byline given. Buys first North American serial rights. Reports on queries when interested. Sample copy for 9×12 SASE. Writer's guidelines for #10 SASE.

Nonfiction: Book excerpts, essays, expose, general interest, interview/profile, opinion, photo feature, technical. No science fiction or UFO stories. Query with published clips. Length: 1,200-3,000 words. Pays $100-250 for features.

Photos: State availability of photos with submission. Reviews 35mm slides, 3×5 color transparencies and b&w prints. Negotiates payment. Identification of subjects required. Buys one-time rights.

Columns/Departments: Touchdown (opinion pieces). Query.

Tips: "Require manuscripts to be accompanied by ASCII or Word or Word Perfect 6.0 floppy disk."

ARCHAEOLOGY, Archaeological Institute of America, 135 William St., New York NY 10038. (212)732-5154. Fax: (212)732-5707. Editor-in-Chief: Peter A. Young. 5% freelance written. "*Archaeology* combines worldwide archaeological findings with photography, specially rendered maps, drawings, and charts. Articles cover current excavations, recent discoveries, and special studies of ancient cultures. Regular features: Timelines, Newsbriefs, film and book reviews, current museum exhibits, The Forum. Two annual Travel Guides give trip planning information. We generally commission articles from professional archaeologists. The only magazine of its kind to bring worldwide archaeology to the attention of the general public." Estab. 1948. Circ. 200,000. Pays on publication. Byline given. Offers 25% kill fee. Buys first North American serial rights. Submit seasonal material 6 months in advance. Accepts simultaneous submissions. Query preferred. Free sample copy and writer's guidelines.
Nonfiction: Essays, general interest. Buys 6 mss/year. Length: 1,000-3,000 words. Pays $750 maximum. Sometimes pays expenses of writers on assignment.
• Ranked as one of the best markets for freelance writers in *Writer's Yearbook* magazine's annual "Top 100 Markets," January 1997.
Photos: Send photos with submission.
Tips: "We reach nonspecialist readers interested in art, science, history, and culture. Our reports, regional commentaries, and feature-length articles introduce readers to recent developments in archaeology worldwide."

ASTRONOMY, Kalmbach Publishing, P.O. Box 1612, Waukesha WI 53187-1612. (414)796-8776. Fax: (414)796-1142. E-mail: 72000.2704@compuserve.com. Editor: Robert Burnham. Managing Editor: Rhoda I. Sherwood. 75% freelance written. Monthly magazine covering astronomy—the science and hobby of. "Half of our magazine is for hobbyists (who may have little interest in the heavens in a scientific way); the other half is directed toward armchair astronomers who may be intrigued by the science." Estab. 1973. Circ. 170,000. **Pays on acceptance.** "We are governed by what is happening in the space program and the heavens. It can be up to a year before we publish a manuscript." Byline given. Buys first North American serial, one-time and all rights. Query for electronic submissions. Reports in 1 month on queries; 2 months on mss. Writer's guidelines for SASE.
Nonfiction: Book excerpts, space and astronomy, how-to for astro hobbyists, humor (in the viewpoints column and about astro), new product, photo feature, technical. Buys 100-200 mss/year. Query. Length: 500-4,500 words. Pays $50-500.
Photos: Send photos with submission. Reviews transparencies and prints. Pays $25/photo. Captions, model releases and identification of subjects required.
Tips: "Submitting to *Astronomy* could be tough. (Take a look at how technical astronomy is.) But if someone is a physics teacher (or math or astronomy), he or she might want to study the magazine for a year to see the sorts of subjects and approaches we use and then submit a proposal."

DISCOVER, Walt Disney Magazine Publishing Group, 114 Fifth Ave., New York NY 10011. (212)633-4400. Fax: (212)633-4809. "As the only truly accessible general-interest science and technology magazine on the market, *Discover* allows its audience of forward-thinking non-scientists to read today what will affect their lives tomorrow. *Discover's* editorial mission is based on empowering its readers with keen insight—and giving them the opportunity to be proactive in response to the innovations, concepts, thought processes, and systems that will shape our tomorrow. Much more than science, *Discover* defines the future—and chronicles the evolution of ideas that will take us there." Circ. 1,321,000. This magazine did not respond to our request for information. Query before submitting.

THE ELECTRON, CIE Publishing, 1776 E. 17th St., Cleveland OH 44114-3679. (216)781-9400. Fax: (216)781-0331. Website: http://www.cie.wc.edu. Managing Editor: Michael Manning. Contact: Ted Sheroke, advertising manager. 80% freelance written. Quarterly tabloid on development and trends electronics and high technology. Estab. 1934. Circ. 25,000. Pays on publication. Publishes ms an average of 2 months after acceptance. Byline given. Buys all rights. Reports as soon as possible. Sample copy and writer's guidelines for 8½×11 SASE.
Nonfiction: Technical (tutorial and how-to), technology news and feature, photo feature, career/educational. All submissions must be electronics/technology-related. Special issue: Electronics into the Year 2001 (October, November, December). Query with letter/proposal and published clips. Length: 800 words. Pays $50-500.
Reprints: Send photocopy of article or short story or typed ms with rights for sale noted and information about when and where the article previously appeared. Does not pay for reprints.
Photos: State availability of photos. Reviews 8×10 and 5×7 b&w prints. Captions and identification of subjects required.
Tips: "We would like to receive educational electronics/technical articles. They must be written in a manner understandable to the beginning-intermediate electronics student. We are also seeking news/feature-type articles covering timely developments in high technology."

FINAL FRONTIER, 1017 S. Mountain Ave., Monrovia CA 91016. Fax: (818)932-1036. E-mail: ffmagazine@aol.com. Editor: George Hague. Bimonthly magazine covering space exploration. "*Final Frontier* is about space technology, commerce and exploration. The missions and machines. People and politics. The pure adventures of space travel and astronomical discovery. Plus behind-the-scenes coverage of the international arena of space, commerce and exploration."

Estab. 1988. Circ. 100,200. **Pays on acceptance**. Byline given. Buys first North American serial rights. Offers 30% kill fee. Reports in 1-2 months on queries. Sample copy free on request.

• Ranked as one of the best markets for freelance writers in *Writer's Yearbook*'s annual "Top 100 Markets," January 1997.

Nonfiction: Interview/profile, human interest. Buys 20 mss/year. Query with published clips. Length:1,240-2,400 words. Pays 40¢/word. Sometimes pays expenses of writers on assignment.

Reprints: Accepts previously published submissions from non-competing markets. Pays 30¢/word.

Columns/Departments: Buys 30 mss/year (620 words) and 30 short pieces (150-450 words). Pays 40¢/word.

Fiction: Accepts excerpts from published novels.

Fillers: Buys 30/year. Length: 150-450 words. Pays 40¢/word.

Tips: Needs "strong reporting on all aspects of space. Short science fiction pieces, about 2,200 words, are in short supply."

‡**POPULAR SCIENCE**, 2 Park Ave., New York NY 10016. (212)779-5000. Fax: (212)481-8062. Website: http://www.popsci.com. Editor-in-Chief: Fred Abatemarco. Contact: Cecelia Wessner, executive editor. 50% freelance written. Prefers to work with published/established writers. Monthly magazine for the well-educated adult, interested in science, technology, new products. "*Popular Science* is devoted to exploring (and explaining) to a nontechnical but knowledge-able readership the technical world around us. We cover all of the sciences, engineering and technology, and above all, products. We are largely a 'thing'-oriented publication: things that fly or travel down a turnpike, or go on or under the sea, or cut wood, or reproduce music, or build buildings, or make pictures. We are especially focused on the new, the ingenious and the useful. Contributors should be as alert to the possibility of selling us pictures and short features as they are to major articles. Freelancers should study the magazine to see what we want and avoid irrelevant submissions." Estab. 1872. Circ. 1.55 million. **Pays on acceptance.** Publishes ms an average of 4 months after acceptance. Byline given. Buys first North American serial rights only. Pays negotiable kill fee. Reports in 4 weeks. Query. Writer's guidelines for #10 SASE.

Nonfiction: Buys several hundred mss/year. Uses only color photos. Pays expenses of writers on assignment.

Tips: "Probably the easiest way to break in here is by covering a news story in science and technology that we haven't heard about yet. We need people to be acting as scouts for us out there and we are willing to give the most leeway on these performances. We are interested in good, sharply focused ideas in all areas we cover. We prefer a vivid, journalistic style of writing, with the writer taking the reader along with him, showing the reader what he saw, through words. Please query first."

SCIENCE SPECTRA, The International Magazine of Contemporary Scientific Thought, Magazines Unlim-ited Ltd., P.O. Box 430, Collegeville PA 19426. Editor: Gerhart Friedlander. Contact: Heather Wagner, managing editor. 25% freelance written. Quarterly magazine covering science. "Our magazine's audience is composed primarily of scientists and the 'scientifically literate.' Writers must have experience writing for a scientific audience." Estab. 1995. Circ. 10,000. Pays on publication. Byline given. Buys all rights. Editorial lead time 3 months. Reports in 1 month on queries. Writer's guidelines for SAE and 1 first-class stamp.

Nonfiction: Interview/profile, science and technology. Buys 10-15 mss/year. Length: approximately 2,000 words. Pays 25¢/word for assigned articles.

Photos: Offers no additional payment for photos accepted with ms. Captions required. Buys all time rights.

Columns/Departments: From the Front Lines (cutting edge research/technology) 2,000 words; Portrait (profile of leading scientific figure) 2,000 words; Controversy Corner (presents both sides of current scientific debate) 2,000 words. Buys 5-10 mss/year. Query with published clips. Pays 25¢/word.

Tips: "Writers should include clips that demonstrate their knowledge of and/or experience in the scientific area about which they are writing. Do not send complete manuscripts; query letter with clips only."

‡**THE SCIENCES**, 655 Madison Ave., 16th Floor, New York NY 10021. Contact: Peter Brown, editor-in-chief. 50% freelance written. Bimonthly magazine. "The Sciences is the cultural magazine of science. This is the kind of magazine that scientists would come to after work, that they can talk about to a friend, a spouse, a colleague in another discipline." Pays on publication. Byline given. Query with SASE.

Nonfiction: Profiles, opinion, book or product reviews, features. Every piece must have "lots of science in it. It's important for writers to remember that many of our readers are members of the New York Academy of Science." Length: 3,000 words. Pays $750. Query with SASE.

Columns/Departments: Opinion, sciences news. Length: 1,000 words. Opinion pieces are always worth trying but that absolutely must include "significant scientific content." Query with SASE.

‡**SCIENTIFIC AMERICAN**, 415 Madison Ave., New York NY 10017. Fax: (212)755-1976. Website: http://www.sciam.com. Contact: Philip Yam, news editor. Monthly publication covering developments and topics of interest in the world of science. "*Scientific American* brings its readers directly to the wellspring of exploration and technological innovation. The magazine specializes in first-hand accounts by the people who actually do the work. Their personal experience provides an authoritative perspective on future growth. Over 100 of our authors have won Nobel Prizes. Complementing those articles are regular departments written by *Scientific American*'s staff of professional journalists, all specialists in their fields. . . . *Scientific American* is the authoritative source of advance information. Authors are the first to report on important breakthroughs, because they're the people who make them. . . . It all goes back to *Scientific American*'s

corporate mission: to link those who use knowledge with those who create it." Estab. 1845. Circ. 666,630. Query before submitting.
Nonfiction: Freelance opportunities limited to news and analysis section. Pays $1/word average.

‡**SKEPTIC**, Millennium Press, 2761 N. Marengo Ave., Altadena CA 91001. (818)794-3119. Fax: (818)794-1301. E-mail: skepticmag@aol.com. Editor: Michael Shermer. 75% freelance written. Quarterly magazine "promoting science and critical thinking, and disseminating information on scientific controversies, scientific revolutions, proto-science, pseudoscience, pseudohistory, the paranormal, magic, superstition, fringe claims and groups, and the history of science and pseudoscience, in articles, essays, reviews and letters. Estab. 1992. Circ. 25,000. Pays on acceptance or publication (negotiable). Publishes ms an average of 6 months after acceptance. Byline given. Buys first North American serial rights. Editorial lead time 3 months. Submit seasonal material 6 months in advance. Accepts simultaneous submissions. Reports in 2 weeks on queries; 3 months on mss. Sample copy for 9×12 SAE and 4 first-class stamps. Writer's guidelines for #10 SASE.
Nonfiction: Book excerpts, essays, exposé, general interest, historical/nostalgic, interview/profile, science. "Every issue of skeptic has a special theme, such as conspiracies, ethics, cults, religion plus other articles." Buys 6 mss/year. Send complete ms with bio and published clips. Length: 800-5,000 words. Pay varies. Payment with contributor copies or other premiums is negotiable.
Photos: State availability of photos with submission. Reviews transparencies and 8×10 transparencies. Offers no additional payment for photos accepted with ms. Captions, model releases and identification of subjects required. Buys one-time rights.
Tips: "*Skeptic* is always searching for cutting-edge controversies and ideas worthy of further exploration. It is not the purpose of *Skeptic* to debunk a claim; *Skeptic* is just a magazine title. We are a science magazine, and therefore we are evidence driven, not position driven."

WEATHERWISE, The Magazine About the Weather, Heldref Publications, 1319 18th St. NW, Washington DC 20036. (202)296-6267. E-mail: ww@heldref.org. Website: http://www.heldref.org. Contact: Doyle Rice, managing editor. Assistant Editor: Kimbra Cutlie. 75% freelance written. Bimonthly magazine covering weather and meteorology. "*Weatherwise* is America's only popular magazine about the weather. Our readers' range from professional weathercasters and scientists to basement-bound hobbyists, but all share a common craving for information about weather as it relates to technology, history, culture, society, art, etc." Estab. 1948. Circ. 12,500. Pays on publication. Publishes ms an average of 6 months after acceptance. Byline given. Offers 25% kill fee. Buys all rights or first North American serial or second (reprint) serial rights. Editorial lead time 6 months. Submit seasonal material 6 months in advance. Reports in 2 months on queries. Sample copy free on request. Writer's guidelines for #10 SASE.
Nonfiction: Book excerpts, essays, general interest, historical/nostalgic, how-to, humor, interview/profile, new product, opinion, personal experience, photo feature, technical, travel. Special issue: Photo Contest (August/September deadline May 31). Special issue: 1996 Weather in Review (February/March 97). "No blow-by-blow accounts of the biggest storm to ever hit your backyard." Buys 15-18 mss/year. Query with published clips. Length: 1,500-2,500 words. Pays $200-500 for assigned articles; $0-200 for unsolicited articles. Sometimes pays expenses of writers on assignment.
Reprints: Send photocopy of article and information about when and where the article previously appeared.
Photos: State availability of or send photos with submission. Reviews contact sheets, negatives, transparencies, prints. Negotiates payment individually. Captions, identification of subjects required. Buys one-time rights.
Columns/Departments: Front & Center (news, trends, opinion), 300-400 words; Weather Talk (folklore and humor), 1,000 words; The Lee Word (first person accounts of adventures with weather), 1,000 words. Buys 12-15 mss/year. Query with published clips. Pays $0-200.
Tips: "Don't query us wanting to write about broad types like the Greenhouse Effect, the Ozone Hole, El Niño, etc. If it's capitalized, you can bet you won't be able to cover it all in 2,000 words. With these topics and all others, find the story within the story. And whether you're writing about a historical storm or new technology, be sure to focus on the human element—the struggles, triumphs, and other anecdotes of individuals."

SCIENCE FICTION, FANTASY AND HORROR

These publications often publish experimental fiction and many are open to new writers. More information on these markets can be found in the Contests and Awards section under the Fiction heading.

ABERRATIONS, Sirius Fiction, P.O. Box 460430, San Francisco CA 94146-0430. (415) 777-3909. Editor: Richard Blair. Monthly magazine of science fiction, fantasy, and horror. "We're looking for speculative stories that run the gamut from the pulp-era SF/F/H of the 30s and 40s to the experimental and literary work of today." Estab. 1991. Circ. 1,500. Pays on publication. Publishes ms an average of 1 year after acceptance. Byline given. Buys first English language serial and one-time rights. Submit seasonal material 8 months in advance. Reports in 4 months. Sample copy for $4.50 postpaid. Writer's guidelines for #10 SASE.
Nonfiction: Anything with a SF/F/H tie-in. "However, please keep in mind that we're not interested in the paranormal, UFOs, nor are we looking for 'how to write science fiction' pieces." Send complete ms. Length: 3,000 words (query for longer). Pays ½¢/word.

Fiction: Science fiction, fantasy, and horror. "We use a variety of 'types' of stories within the speculative genres. Whether it's humorous horror or cerebral sci-fi, we want character-driven, plot intensive storylines. From sword-&-sorcery to space opera to psychological horror, however and whatever your muse is trying to beat out of you send it our way." Buys 120 mss/year. Send complete ms. Length: 8,000 words max. Pays ½¢/word.

Tips: "While there are still no restrictions on language and subject matter, we're seeking to expand the scope of stories within the magazine, and are therefore no longer looking exclusively for shock or splatter SF/F/H fiction. Stories that do possess graphically violent/sexual scenes should have these aspects be crucial to the plot. Under *no* circumstances are we interested in stories dealing with the violent/sexual abuse of children. All that said, we're very open to stories that take chances (whether this be through characterization, plotting, or structuring) as well as those that take more traditional approaches to science fiction, fantasy and horror. Both fiction and nonfiction are wide open."

ABSOLUTE MAGNITUDE, Science Fiction Adventures, DNA Publications, P.O. Box 13, Greenfield MA 01302. E-mail: absmag@shaysnet.com. Contact: Warren Lapine, editor-in-chief. 95% freelance written. Quarterly science fiction magazine covering science fiction short stories. "We specialize in action/adventure science fiction with an emphasis on hard science. Interested in tightly-plotted, character-driven stories." Estab. 1993. Circ. 6,000. Pays on publication. Publishes ms an average of 6 months after acceptance. Byline given. Buys first English language serial rights, first rights and second serial (reprint) rights. Editorial lead time 6 months. Accepts simultaneous submissions. Reports in 2 weeks on queries; 1 month on mss. Sample copy for $5. Writer's guidelines for #10 SASE.
  • This editor is still looking for tightly plotted stories that are character driven. He is now purchasing more short stories than before.

Reprints: Send typed ms with rights for sale noted and information about when and where the article previously appeared. Pays 33% of amount paid for an original article.

Fiction: Science fiction. Buys 40 mss/year. Send complete ms. Length: 1,000-25,000 words. Pays 3-5¢/word.
  • Ranked as one of the best markets for fiction writers in *Writer's Digest*'s last annual "Fiction 50."

Poetry: Any form. Buys 4 poems/issue. Submit maximum 5 poems. Length: up to 25,000 words. Pays 10¢/line. Best chance with light verse.

Tips: "We are very interested in working with new writers but we are not interested in 'drawer-cleaning' exercises. There is no point in sending less than your best effort if you are interested in a career in writing. We do not use fantasy, horror, satire, or funny science fiction. We're looking for character-driven action/adventure based Technical Science Fiction. We want tightly plotted stories with memorable characters. Characters should be the driving force behind the action of the story; they should not be thrown in as an afterthought. We need to see both plot development and character growth. Stories which are resolved without action on the protagonist's part do not work for us; characters should not be spectators in situations completely beyond their control or immune to their influence. Some of our favorite writers are Roger Zelazny, Frank Herbert, Robert Silverberg, and Fred Saberhagen."

‡ADVENTURES OF SWORD & SORCERY, Box 285, Xenia OH 45385. Editor: Randy Dannenfelser. **Pays on acceptance.** Byline given. Buys first North American serial rights. Reports in 2 months on mss. Sample copy for $5.50. Writer's guidelines for #10 SASE.

Fiction: Fantasy. Buys 40 mss/year. Send complete ms with cover letter. Length: 1,000-8,000 words. Pays 3-6¢/word.

Tips: "We want sword-and-sorcery, high fantasy and heroic fantasy that entertains and involves the reader. Some problems I see often are story beginnings just aren't enough to pull readers into the story. Also, endings are either obvious or inappropriate. A great ending is a surprise, but at the same time such a natural extension of the story that readers can't imagine a better way that it could have ended."

ANALOG SCIENCE FICTION & FACT, Dell Magazine Fiction Group, 1270 Avenue of the Americas, New York NY 10020. (212)698-1313. E-mail: 71154.662@compuserve.com. Editor: Dr. Stanley Schmidt. 100% freelance written. Eager to work with new/unpublished writers. For general future-minded audience. Monthly. Estab. 1930. Buys first North American serial and nonexclusive foreign serial rights. **Pays on acceptance.** Publishes ms an average of 10 months after acceptance. Byline given. Reports in 1 month. Sample copy for $3 and 6×9 SASE with 5 first-class stamps. Writer's guidelines for #10 SASE.
  • *Analog* was recently sold to Penny Marketing.

Nonfiction: Illustrated technical articles dealing with subjects of not only current but future interest, i.e., topics at the present frontiers of research whose likely future developments have implications of wide interest. Buys about 12 mss/year. Query; no e-mail queries or submissions. Length: 5,000 words. Pays 6¢/word.

Fiction: "Basically, we publish science fiction stories. That is, stories in which some aspect of future science or technology is so integral to the plot that, if that aspect were removed, the story would collapse. The science can be physical, sociological or psychological. The technology can be anything from electronic engineering to biogenetic engineering. But the stories must be strong and realistic, with believable people doing believable things—no matter how fantastic the background might be." Buys 60-100 unsolicited mss/year. Send complete ms of short fiction; query about serials. "We don't publish novel excerpts as such, though we occasionally do one that can stand on its own as an independent story." Length: 2,000-80,000 words. Pays 4¢/word for novels; 5-6¢/word for novelettes; 6-8¢/word for shorts under 7,500 words; $450-600 for intermediate lengths.
  • Ranked as one of the best markets for fiction writers in the last *Writer's Digest* magazine's annual "Fiction 50."

Tips: "In query give clear indication of central ideas and themes and general nature of story line—and what is distinctive or unusual about it. We have no hard-and-fast editorial guidelines, because science fiction is such a broad field that I don't want to inhibit a new writer's thinking by imposing 'Thou Shalt Not's.' Besides, a really good story can make an editor swallow his preconceived taboos. I want the best work I can get, regardless of who wrote it—and I need new writers. So I work closely with new writers who show definite promise, but of course it's impossible to do this with *every* new writer. No occult or fantasy."

ASIMOV'S SCIENCE FICTION, Dell Magazine Fiction Group, 1270 Avenue of the Americas, New York NY 10020. (212)698-1313. Fax: (212)698-1198 (for correspondence only, no submissions). E-mail: 71154.662@compuserve.com. Contact: Gardner Dozois, editor. Executive Editor: Sheila Williams. 98% freelance written. Works with a small number of new/unpublished writers each year. Published 11 times a year, including 1 double issue. Estab. 1977. Circ. 70,000. **Pays on acceptance.** Buys first North American serial and nonexclusive foreign serial rights; reprint rights occasionally. No simultaneous submissions. Reports in 2 months. Sample copy for $5 and 6½×9½ SAE. Writer's guidelines for #10 SASE.
  • *Asimov's* was recently sold to Penny Marketing.
Reprints: Send typed ms with rights for sale noted and information about when and where the article previously appeared.
Fiction: Science fiction primarily. Some fantasy and humor but no "Sword and Sorcery." No explicit sex or violence. Publishes novel excerpts; doesn't serialize novels. "It's best to read a great deal of material in the genre to avoid the use of some *very* old ideas." Buys 10 mss/issue. Submit complete ms and SASE with *all* submissions. Length: 750-15,000 words. Pays 5-8¢/word.
Poetry: Length should not exceed 40 lines; pays $1/line.
  • Ranked as one of the best markets for fiction writers in the last *Writer's Digest*'s annual "Fiction 50."
Tips: "In general, we're looking for 'character oriented' stories, those in which the characters, rather than the science, provide the main focus for the reader's interest. Serious, thoughtful, yet accessible fiction will constitute the majority of our purchases, but there's always room for the humorous as well. Borderline fantasy is fine, but no Sword & Sorcery, please. Neither are we interested in explicit sex or violence. A good overview would be to consider that all fiction is written to examine or illuminate some aspect of human existence, but that in science fiction the backdrop you work against is the size of the Universe. Please do not send us submissions on disk. We've bought some of our best stories from people who have never sold a story before."

MARION ZIMMER BRADLEY'S FANTASY MAGAZINE, P.O. Box 249, Berkeley CA 94701-0249. Fax: (510)644-9222. Website: http://www.well/com/user/mzbfm. Contact: Mrs. Marion Z. Bradley, editor. 100% freelance written. Quarterly magazine of fantasy fiction. Estab. 1988. **Pays on acceptance.** Publishes ms an average of 1 year after acceptance. Byline given. Buys first North American serial rights. Reports in 3 months. Sample copy for $4 and 9″×12″ SAE.
Fiction: Fantasy. No science fiction, no horror. Buys 55-60 mss/year. Send complete ms. Length: 300-5,500 words. Pays 3-10¢/word.
  • Ranked as one of the best markets for fiction writers in *Writer's Digest*'s last annual "Fiction 50."
Tips: "Do not submit without first reading guidelines."
  "We buy original fantasy (*not* sex fantasies) with no particular objection to modern settings, but we do want action and adventure. The primary purpose of your story should should be to entertain the reader; and although any good story has a central point behind the plot, the reader should be able to deduce it rather than having it thrust upon him. Fantasy content should start on the first page and must appear within the first three pages. We prefer strong female characters, and we will reject stories in which we find objectionable sexism. We also reject stories with bad grammar or spelling. We do not favor strong language because, although we ARE NOT a magazine aimed at children or young adults, we do have many young readers. Non-fiction should be queried; it is done on commission only. *Please read a few issues before submitting so that you can see the kind of thing we do buy.* Please *do not* submit: Poetry, serials, novel excerpts, children's stories, shared world stories, science fiction, hard technology, occult, horror, re-written fairy tales, radical feminism, romances (in which love, romance and marriage are the main motivations), surrealism, or avant-garde stories, stories written in the present tense, or stories about God, the Devil, of hearth-witches. Beware of: 'dime-a-dozen' subjects such as dragons, elves, unicorns, wizards, vampires, writers, sea creatures, brute warriors, ghosts, adventuring sorcerers/ sorceresses, thieves/assassins, or final exams for wizards. We get dozens of these kings of stories every week, and we reject all but the *truly* unusual and well-written ones."

CENTURY, Century Publishing, Inc., P.O. Box 150510, Brooklyn NY 11215. E-mail: robkill@aol.com. Website: http:// www.supranet.com/century/. Editor: Robert K.J. Killheffer. 100% freelance written. Bimonthly 6×9 magazine covering speculative fiction (science fiction, fantasy, horror). "We're looking for speculative fiction with a high degree of literary accomplishment—ambitious work which can appeal not only to the genre's regular audience but to readers outside the genre as well." Estab. 1994. Circ. 5,000. **Pays on acceptance.** Publishes ms an average of 6 months after acceptance. Byline given. Buys first world English rights, non-exclusive reprint rights. Reports in 3 months on mss. Sample copy for $5.95. Writer's guidelines for #10 SASE.
Fiction: Experimental, fantasy, horror, science fiction. Buys 65 mss/year. Send complete ms. Length: 1,000-20,000 words. Pays 4-6¢/word.

‡**THE CRYSTAL BALL**, The Starwind Press, P.O. Box 98, Ripley OH 45167. Contact: Marlene Powell, editor. 90% freelance written. Quarterly magazine covering science fiction and fantasy for young adult readers. "We are especially targeting readers of middle school age." Estab. 1997. **Pays on acceptance**. Publishes ms an average of 1 year after acceptance. Byline given. Offers 100% kill fee. Buys first or second serial (reprint) rights. Editorial lead time 4 months. Sample copy for 9×12 SASE and $3. Writer's guidelines for #10 SASE.
Nonfiction: How-to (science), interview/profile, personal experience, book reviews, science information. Buys 4-6 mss/year. Query. Length: 900-3,000 words. Pays ½-1¢/word.
Photos: Send photos with submission. Negotiates payment individually. Captions and identification of subjects required.
Columns/Departments: Book reviews (science fiction and fantasy), 100-200 words or less; museum reviews (science & technology, museums & centers, children's museums), 900 words. Buys 10-15 mss/year. Query. Pays ¼¢/word.
Fiction: Fantasy, science fiction. Buys 10-12 mss/year. Send complete ms. Length: 1,000-5,000 words. Pays ¼¢/word.
Tips: "Have a good feel for writing for kids. Don't 'write down' to your audience because they're kids. We look for articles of scientific and technological interest."

FANTASTIC WORLDS, Science Fiction ● Fantasy ● Horror, 1644 s. 11th West, Missoula MT 59801. Editor: Scott Becker. 90% freelance written. Science fiction, fantasy, horror magazine published 4-6 times a year. Estab. 1995. Circ. 1,000. Pays on publication. Publishes ms an average of 1 year after acceptance. Byline given. Offers 50% kill fee. Buys first North American serial rights and option to reprint story if it is subsequently chosen for a *Fantastic Worlds* "Best of" Anthology. Editorial lead time 3 months. Submit seasonal material 3 months in advance. Accepts simultaneous submissions. Reports in 2 months on queries; 3 months on mss. Sample copy for $5 (add $1 for foreign orders). Writer's guidelines for #10 SASE.
Nonfiction: Book excerpts, essays, exposé, general interest, humor, interview/profile, opinion. Buys 8-12 mss/year. Query with published clips. Length: 1,000-2,500 words. Pays 1¢/word ($25-100) and contributor copy.
Photos: State availability of photos with submission. Reviews contact sheets, up to 8×10 prints. Offers $5-30/photo. Negotiates payment individually. Buys one-time rights.
Columns/Departments: Interviews, Unique Features. Buys 6-18 mss/year. Query with published clips. Pays 1¢/word ($25-100) and contributor copy.
Fiction: Adventure, erotica, fantasy, horror, mystery, science fiction, serialized novels, suspense. No pornography or work that depicts children being brutalized. Buys 40-60 mss/year. Send complete ms. Pays 1¢/word ($25-100) and contributor copy.
Poetry: Avant-garde, free verse, haiku, light verse, traditional. Buys 40-60 poems/year. Submit maximum 3 poems. Pays $5-15 and contributor copy.

HOBSON'S CHOICE, The Starwind Press, P.O. Box 98, Ripley OH 45167-0098. (513)392-4549. Editors: David F. Powell and Susannah C. West. Contact: Susannah C. West. 75% freelance written. Eager to work with new/unpublished writers. Quarterly magazine "for older teenagers and adults who have an interest in science and technology, and who also enjoy reading well-crafted science fiction and fantasy." Estab. 1974. Circ. 2,500. Pays on publication. Publishes ms an average of 1 year after acceptance. Byline given. Rights vary with author and material; negotiated with author. Usually first serial rights and second serial reprint rights (nonfiction). "We encourage disposable submissions; easier for us and easier for the author. Just enclose SASE for our response." Prefers non-simultaneous submissions. Reports in 3 months. Sample copy for $2.25 and 9×12 SAE. Writer's guidelines for #10 SASE. "Tipsheet package for $1.50; contains all guidelines, tipsheets on science fiction writing, nonfiction science writing and submission etiquette."
● *Hobson's Choice* is often overstocked with fiction; their needs for nonfiction are greater than for fiction.
Nonfiction: How-to (technological interest, e.g., how to build a robot eye, building your own radio receiver, etc.), interview/profile (of leaders in science and technology fields), technical ("did you know" articles dealing with development of current technology). "No speculative articles, dealing with topics such as the Abominable Snowman, Bermuda Triangle, etc." Query. Length: 1,000-7,000 words. Pays 1-4¢/word.
Reprints: Send photocopy of article or short story and information about when and where material previously appeared. Pays 30% of amount paid for an original article.
Photos: Send photos with accompanying query or ms. Reviews b&w contact sheets and prints. Model releases and identification of subjects required. "If photos are available, we prefer to purchase them as part of the written piece." Buys negotiable rights.
Fiction: Fantasy, science fiction. "No stories whose characters were created by others (e.g., Lovecraft, *Star Trek*, *Star Wars* characters, etc.)." Buys 15-20 mss/year. Send complete ms. Length: 2,000-10,000 words. Pays 1-4¢/word. "We prefer previously unpublished fiction. No query necessary. We don't publish horror, poetry, novel excerpts or serialized novels."
Tips: "Almost all our fiction and nonfiction is unsolicited. We rarely ask for rewrites, because we've found that rewrites are often disappointing; although the writer may have rewritten it to fix problems, he/she frequently changes parts we liked, too."

THE MAGAZINE OF FANTASY & SCIENCE FICTION, Mercury Press, P.O. Box 1806, New York NY 10159. Fax: (212)982-2676. E-mail: gordonfsf@aol.com. Website: http://www.enews.com/magazines/fsf. Contact: Gordon Van Gelder, editor. 100% freelance written. Monthly fantasy fiction and science fiction magazine. "*The Magazine of Fantasy and Science Fiction* publishes various types of science fiction and fantasy short stories and novellas, making up about 80% of each issue. The balance of each issue is devoted to articles about science fiction, a science column by Gregory

Benford, book and film reviews, cartoons and competitions." Estab. 1949. Circ. 80,000. **Pays on acceptance.** Byline given. Buys first North American and foreign serial rights. Submit seasonal material 8 months in advance. Reports in 2 months. Sample copy for $5. Writer's guidelines for #10 SASE.
Fiction: Fantasy, horror, science fiction. Prefers character-oriented stories. Send complete ms. Length: 2,000-20,000 words. Pays 5-8¢/word.
   • Ranked as one of the best markets for fiction writers in the last *Writer's Digest*'s annual "Fiction 50."
Tips: "We need more hard science fiction and humor."

NIGHTCRY, Illustrated Magazine of Horror, CFD Productions, 360-A W. Merrick Rd., Suite 350, Valley Stream NY 11580. E-mail: cfdprod@aol.com. Website: http://www.loginet.com/cfd. Contact: Pamela Hazelton, editor. Managing Editor and Publisher: Joseph M. Monks. 100% freelance written. Illustrated magazine of horror. "Our readers like twisted, horrific stories. No 'things that go bump in the night.' Psychological horror also is enjoyed." Estab. 1994. Circ. 15,000. Pays one month after publication. Publishes ms an average of 8 months after acceptance. Byline given. Buys first North American serial rights. Editorial lead time 4 months. Accepts simultaneous submissions. Reports in 2 months. Copy for $3.50. Writer's guidelines for #10 SASE.
Fiction: Horror, mystery, science fiction. Publishes novel excerpts. Buys 10-30 mss/year. Send complete ms, comic script and/or panel to panel art. Pays $20-100.
Reprints: Send information about when and where the article previously appeared (no "buying of second rights").
Tips: "Follow comic script format guidelines—they are different from standard scripts. Many writers adapt their short stories to comics fairly well."

ON SPEC, The Canadian Magazine of Speculative Writing, The Copper Pig Writers Society, P.O. Box 4727, Edmonton, Alberta T6E 5G6 Canada. Fax: (403)413-0215. E-mail: onspec@freenet.edmonton.ab.ca. Website: http://www.greenwoods.com/onspec/. Editorial Collective: Barry Hammond, Susan MacGregor, Jena Snyder, Diane L. Walton. 95% freelance written. Quarterly literary magazine covering Canadian science fiction and fantasy. "*On Spec* is Canada's premier speculative fiction magazine. We publish Canadian writers only." Estab. 1989. Circ. 2,000. **Pays on acceptance.** Publishes ms an average of 1 year after acceptance. Byline given. Buys first North American serial rights. Editorial lead time 6 months. Reports in 5 months on queries. Sample copy for $6. Writer's guidelines for #10 SASE with Canadian stamp or IRC.
   • *On Spec* is a 3-time Aurora winner.
Nonfiction: Commissioned only. Yearly theme issue. 1998 theme is "Music"; all stories should contain reference to music. "Each year we offer $100 prize to best story by a young and upcoming author published in *On Spec*."
Fiction: Science fiction, fantasy, horror. No media tie-in or shaggy-alien stories. Buys 35 mss/year. Send complete ms only. Length: 6,000 words maximum. Pays $25-150 (Canadian) 2½¢/word.
Poetry: Barry Hammond, poetry editor. Avant-garde, free verse. "We rarely buy rhyming or religious material." Buys 6 poems/year. Submit maximum 6 poems. Length: 2-100 lines. Pays $15.
Tips: "Send for guidelines! We have specific (i.e. competition) format requirements. Please note that we accept submissions from Canadian writers only."

‡REALMS OF FANTASY, Sovereign Media, P.O. Box 527, Rumson NJ 07760. Editor: Shawna McCarthy. 100% freelance written. Bimonthly magazine covering heroic, contemporary, traditional, feminist, dark, light and unclassifiable fantasy. Estab. 1994. Circ. 53,000. **Pays on acceptance,** 30 days after contract. Publishes ms an average of 3 months after acceptance. Byline given. Offers 20% kill fee. Buys first world rights. Editorial lead time 2 months. Submit seasonal material 3 months in advance. Accepts simultaneous submissions. Reports in 2 months. Sample copy for $4.50. Writer's guidelines for #10 SASE.
Nonfiction: Interview/profile, new product (games), book reviews. Buys 24 mss/year. Query with published clips. Length: 2,500. Pays $150-300. Sometimes pays expenses of writers on assignment.
Reprints: Accepts previously published submissions.
Photos: State availability of photos with submission. Reviews contact sheets. Offers no additional payment for photos accepted with ms. Identification of subjects required. Buys one-time rights.
Columns/Departments: Book Reviews (newest fantasy book review), 200-2,500 words; Games (newest fantasy games), 200-2,500 words. Buys 12 mss/year. Query with published clips. Pays $50-200.
Fiction: Adventure, fantasy. Buys 36 mss/year. Send complete ms. Length: 600-10,000 words. Pays 3-5¢/word.

SCIENCE FICTION AGE, Sovereign Media, 441 Carlisle Dr., Herndon VA 22070. (703)471-1556. Fax: (703)471-1559. E-mail: sovmedia@erols.com. Editor: Scott Edelman. 100% freelance written. Bimonthly magazine of hard, soft science fiction, new wave, old guard, magic, cyberpunk, literary science fiction. "*Science Fiction Age* pledges allegiance to no one wing, partisan school or '-ism' of science fiction. Hard SF, soft SF, New Wave SF, Old Guard SF, magic, realism, cyberpunk, literary SF and so on, each, when done well, would find a home in *Science Fiction Age*. You will find writers rubbing shoulders in *Science Fiction Age* not seen together in any other science fiction magazine—running the gamut from Jerry Pournelle to Thomas M. Disch, Barry Malzberg to Ben Bova. We hope that *Science Fiction Age* is a medley of the finest flavors, so much so that you'll be unable to pin us down to any one '-ism.' " Estab. 1992. Circ. 64,000. **Pays on acceptance.** Publishes ms an average of 4 months after acceptance. Byline given. Offers 10% kill fee. Buys first North American serial rights, with an option on first world rights. Editorial lead time 3 months.

Submit seasonal material 3 months in advance. Reports in 2 months. Sample copy for $5. Writer's guidelines for #10 SASE.

Nonfiction: Essays, interview/profile, new product, opinion. Buys 24 mss/year. Query with published clips. Length: 200-2,500 words. Pays 10¢/word. Sometimes pays expenses of writers on assignment.

Photos: State availability of photos with submission. Reviews contact sheets. Offers no additional payment for photos accepted with ms. Identification of subjects required. Buys one-time rights.

Columns/Departments: Book Reviews, 800-1,200 words; Game Reviews, 1,750 words; Comics Review, 300 words; Essay, 2,000 words. Science, 2,500 words. Buys 30 mss/year. Query with published clips. Pays 10¢/word.

Fiction: Fantasy, science fiction. Buys 42 mss/year. Send complete ms. Length: 1,000-21,000 words. Pays 10¢/word.

   ● Ranked as one of the best markets for fiction writers in the last *Writer's Digest*'s annual "Fiction 50."

Tips: "Please keep in mind, however, that we are not looking for stories of straight horror or fantasy, though elements of horror or fantasy are allowed as long as there are science fictional themes. Our tastes and philosophy call for a story to work on all cylinders. We are looking for works that are literate, innovative, and ambitious, stories that take both writer and reader to new worlds, to new places of the heart. In depicting the world of his or her story, the writer must not fail to correctly depict both the story's scientific premises *and* the intricacies of the human spirit. The best indicator of a magazine's tastes, as always, is what is actually published. We have featured fiction by James Morrow, Paul Di Filippo, Robert Silverberg, Martha Soukup, Stephen Baxter, Ray Aldridge, Brian Stableford, Lawrence Watt-Evans, Allen Steele and many others. Please read *Science Fiction Age* to determine what we like. But at the same time, don't try to imitate what you see. The story you are most likely to sell is one told in your own unique voice, and not one written when you are trying to mimic someone else's. All writers, both unpublished beginners and old time vets, are encouraged to submit, because we are looking for powerful voices, not just names."

SHILLELAGH, Pyx Press, P.O. Box 922648, Sylmar CA 91392-2648. Editor: C. Darren Butler. Associate Editor: Lisa S. Laurencot. 50% freelance written. *Shillelagh* is published 2 times/year and is looking for dreamy, horrific, surreal or decadent short-shorts and poetry. "We try to publish intelligent horror and dark fantasy." Estab. 1990. Circ. 500. Pays on publication. Publishes ms an average of 18 months after acceptance. Byline given. Buys limited-edition first rights. Editorial lead time 6 months. Accepts simultaneous submissions. Reports in 1 month on queries; 3-6 months on mss (occasionally larger). Sample copy for $6.50. Writer's guidelines available for #10 SASE.

Nonfiction: Interviews, essays. Buys 0-4/year. Query first. Length: up to 4,000 words. Pays $2-10.

Fiction: Dreamy, surreal, imaginative short-shorts. Buys 10-20 mss/year. Send complete ms. Length: 2,500-20,000 words (query for works over 8,000 words). Pays $2-30. Length: up to 2,000 words.

Poetry: Uses 20 poems/issue.

THE SILVER WEB, A Magazine of the Surreal, Buzzcity Press, P.O. Box 38190, Tallahassee FL 32315. (904)385-8948. Fax: (904)385-4063. E-mail: annk19@mail.idt.net. Contact: Ann Kennedy, publisher/editor. 100% freelance written. Semiannual literary magazine that features science fiction, dark fantasy and horror. "*The Silver Web* is a semi-annual publication featuring fiction, poetry, art, and thought provoking articles. The editor is looking for works ranging from speculative fiction to dark tales and all weirdness in between; specifically works of the surreal." Estab. 1988. Circ. 2,000. **Pays on acceptance.** Byline given. Buys first North American serial, or one-time or second serial (reprint) rights. Accepts simultaneous submissions. Reports in 2 months. Sample copy for $7.20; subscription: $12. Writer's guidelines for #10 SASE.

Nonfiction: Essays, interview/profile, opinion. Buys 4-8 mss/year. Query. Length: 500-8,000 words. Pays 2-3¢/word.

Reprints: Send information before submitting ms about when and where material previously appeared. Pays 100% of amount paid for an original article.

Photos: State availability of photos with submission. Reviews prints. Offers no additional payment for photos accepted with ms. Identification of subjects required. Buys one-time rights.

Fiction: Experimental, horror, science fiction, dark fantasy, surreal. "We do not want to see typical storylines, endings or predictable revenge stories." Buys 20-25 mss/year. Send complete ms. Length: 500-8,000 words. Pays 2-3¢/word. Publishes novel excerpts but query first. Open to submissions January 1 to September 30.

Poetry: Avant-garde, free verse, haiku. Buys 10-15/year. Submit maximum 5 poems. Pays $10-50.

Fillers: Art fillers. Buys 10/year. Pays $5-10.

Tips: "Give us an unusual unpredictable story with strong, believable characters we care about. Surprise us with something unique. We do look for interviews with people in the field (writers, artists, filmmakers)."

SPACE AND TIME, 138 W. 70th St., 4B, New York NY 10023-4468. Website: http://www.bway.net/~cburns/space&time.html. Contact: Gordon Linzner, editor-in-chief. 100% freelance written. Biannual magazine of science fiction and fantasy. "We feature a mix of fiction and poetry in all aspects of the fantasy genre—science fiction, supernatural horror, sword & sorcery, mixed genre, unclassifiable. Its variety makes it stand out from more narrowly focused magazines. Our readers enjoy quality material that surprises and provokes." Estab. 1966. Circ. 2,000. **Pays on acceptance.** Publishes ms an average of 6 months after acceptance. Byline given. Buys first North American serial rights. Editorial lead time 6 months. Reports in 1 month on mss. Sample copy $5 plus $1.25 handling charge. Writer's guidelines for #10 SASE.

Nonfiction: Essays on fantasy, science fiction, science, etc. "No so-called 'true' paranormal." Buys 1-2 mss/year. Send complete ms. Length: 1,000 words maximum. Pays 1¢/word plus 2 contributor copies.

Photos/Artwork: Charles Burns, art director. Artwork (could include photos). Send nonreturnable photocopies. Reviews prints. Pays $10 for interior illustration, $25 for cover, plus 2 contributor copies. Model releases required. Buys one-time rights.

Fiction: Tom Piccirilli, fiction editor. Fantasy, horror, science fiction, mixed genre (i.e., science-fiction-mystery, western-horror, etc.) and unclassifiable; "Do not want anything that falls outside of fantasy/science fiction (but that leaves a lot)." Buys 15-20 mss/year. Send complete ms. Length: 10,000 words maximum. Pays 1¢/word plus 2 contributor copies.

Poetry: Lawrence Greenberg, poetry editor. Avant-garde, free verse, haiku, light verse, traditional; "anything that cannot conceivably fit into fantasy/science fiction/horror." Buys 10-15 poems/year. Submit maximum 3 poems. Length: no limits. Pays 1¢/word ($5 minimum) plus 2 contributor copies.

Tips: "Avoid clichés and standard plots unless you have something new to add."

STARLOG MAGAZINE, The Science Fiction Universe, Starlog Group, 475 Park Ave. S., 8th Floor, New York NY 10016-1689. Fax: (212)889-7933. E-mail: communications@starloggroup.com. Editor: David McDonnell. 90% freelance written. Willing to work with new/unpublished writers. Monthly magazine covering "the science fiction-fantasy genre: its films, TV, books, art and personalities." Estab. 1976. "We concentrate on interviews with actors, directors, writers, producers, special effects technicians and others. Be aware that 'sci-fi' and 'Trekkie' are seen as derogatory terms by our readers and by us." Pays on publication. Publishes ms an average of 4 months after acceptance. Byline given. Offers kill fee "only to manuscripts *written* or interviews *done for us*." Buys all rights. No simultaneous submissions. Reports in 6 weeks or less. "We provide an assignment sheet to *all* writers with deadline and other info, authorizing a queried piece." Sample copy for $5. Writer's guidelines for #10 SASE.

Nonfiction: Interview/profile (actors, directors, screenwriters who've made science fiction films and science fiction novelists); retrospectives of famous science fiction films and TV series; coverage of science fiction fandom, etc. "We also sometimes cover science fiction/fantasy animation and comics." No personal opinion think pieces/essays. *No* first person. Avoids articles on horror films/creators. "We prefer article format as opposed to Q&A interviews." Buys 175 mss/year. Query first with published clips. "We accept queries by mail *only*, by fax if there's a critical time factor. No phone calls. Ever! Unsolicited phone calls *cannot* be returned." Length: 500-3,000 words. Pays $35 (500-word or less items); $50-75 (sidebars); $150-275 (1,000-4,000 word pieces).

Reprints: Pays $50 for *each* reprint in online magazine version, foreign edition or such.

Photos: State availability of photos. Pays $10-25 for slide transparencies and $8 × 10$ b&w prints depending on quality. "No separate payment for photos provided by film studios." Captions, model releases, identification of subjects and credit line on photos required. Photo credit given. Buys all rights.

Columns/Departments: Loglines (mini interviews or stray quotes from celebrities, 25-200 words each, $25-35); Booklog (book reviews, $15 each, by assignment only). Buys 150 reviews/year. Query with published clips. Book review, 150 words maximum. No kill fee.

Tips: "Absolutely *no fiction*. We do *not* publish it and we throw away fiction manuscripts from writers who *can't* be bothered to include SASE. Nonfiction only please! A writer can best break into *Starlog* by getting an unusual interview or by *out-thinking* us and coming up with something *new* on a current film or book. We are always looking for *new* angles on the various *Star Trek* shows, *Star Wars*, *Doctor Who*, *Starman*, *Beauty & the Beast*, *Lost in Space*, *Space: 1999*, *Battlestar Galactica*, *The Twilight Zone*, *The Outer Limits*. Know your subject before you try us. Most full-length major assignments go to freelancers with whom we're already dealing. But if we like your clips and ideas, we'll be happy to give *you* a chance. We are looking for new freelancers who act professional—and they are *harder* to find. No calls! If a letter isn't good enough to pitch your story, we don't *need* that story. I'd rather see how you write (in a letter), than listen to your chit-chatty powers of persuasion on the phone."

STARSHIP EARTH, Black Moon Publishing, P.O. Box 484, Bellaire OH 43906. Phone/fax: (614)671-3253. Contact: Silver Shadowhorse, fiction editor. Managing Editor: Kirin Lee. 30% freelance nonfiction; 100% freelance fiction written. Bimonthly magazine featuring science fiction. "*Starship Earth* is geared toward science fiction fans of all ages. We do mostly nonfiction, but do print short stories. Our nonfiction focus: profiles of actors and industry people, conventions, behind the scenes articles on films and TV shows. We do cover action/adventure films and TV as well. Heavy Star Trek focus. We cover classic science fiction, too." Estab. 1996. Pays on publication. Publishes ms an average of 1 year after acceptance. Byline sometimes given. Buys first or one-time rights. Editorial lead time 9-12 months. Submit seasonal material 6 months in advance. Accepts simultaneous submissions. Reports in 3 weeks on queries; 2 months on mss. Writer's guidelines for #10 SASE.

Nonfiction: General interest, how-to (relating to science fiction, writing, model building, crafts, etc.), humor (cartoons), interview/profile, new product (relating to science of science fiction), nostalgia, personal experience, photo feature, travel (relating to attending conventions), behind the scenes of film/TV science fiction). Buys variable number of mss/year. Query. Length: up to 3,000 words. Pays ½-3¢/word. Pays in copies for book or film reviews. Sometimes pays expenses of writers on assignment.

Photos: State availability of photos with submission. Reviews transparencies, prints. Negotiates payment individually. Captions, model releases, identification of subjects required. Buys one-time rights.

Columns/Departments: Jenna Dawson, assistant editor. Costumes, conventions/events, science fiction music, upcoming book, film, TV releases, film reviews, book reviews, new products; all up to 700 words. Buys variable number of mss/year. Query. Pays ½-3¢/word.

Fiction: Silver Shadowhorse, editor. Fantasy, historical (with a science fiction twist), science fiction. No erotic content, horror, "Sword & Sorcery" violence or explicit language. Buys variable number of mss/year, 12 short stories/year. Query. Length: 500-3,000 words. Pays ½-3¢/word.

Fillers: Contact: Jenna Dawson, assistant editor. Anecdotes, facts, newsbreaks, short humor. Buys variable number of mss/year. Length: 50-250 words. Pays ½-3¢/word.

Tips: "We are willing to work with new and unpublished writers in most areas. All manuscripts must be in standard format. We are always looking for new or unusual angles on old science fiction shows/films, conventions, costumes, fx and people in the business. Articles from interviews must have sparkle and be interesting to a variety of readers. Absolutely no gossip or fluff."

A THEATER OF BLOOD, Pyx Press, P.O. Box 922648, Sylmar CA 91392-2648. Editor: C. Darren Butler. Associate Editor: Lisa S. Laurencot. 50% freelance written. Annual serial anthology of dark fantasy and literary horror. "We try to publish intelligent horror and dark fantasy." Estab. 1990. Circ. 500. Pays on publication. Publishes ms an average of 18 months after acceptance. Byline given. Buys limited-edition first rights. Editorial lead time 6 months. Accepts simultaneous submissions. Reports in 1 month on queries; 3-6 months on mss (occasionally larger). Sample copy for $6.50. Writer's guidelines available for #10 SASE.

• Open to unsolicited submissions from September 1-November 30 only.

Fiction: Horror: cosmic, supernatural, quiet, experimental, or dark fantasy. Buys 10-20 mss/year. Send complete ms. Length: 2,500-20,000 words (query for works over 8,000 words). Pays $2-30.

Tips: "*A Theater of Blood* has been published for several years as a little magazine of horrific short-short fiction and poetry. Since 1997 it is published as a serial book-anthology of fiction. All types of literary horror and dark fantasy are needed. All stories should contain a fantasy element. We no longer consider poetry. We have a strong bias against gratuity or excessive gore."

THE URBANITE, Surreal & Lively & Bizarre, Urban Legend Press, P.O. Box 4737, Davenport IA 52808. Contact: Mark McLaughlin, editor. 95% freelance written. Triannual magazine covering surreal fiction and poetry. "We look for quality fiction in an urban setting with a surrealistic tone... We prefer character-driven storylines. Our audience is urbane, culture-oriented, and hard to please!" Estab. 1991. Circ. 1,000. **Pays on acceptance.** Contributors to recent issues include Thomas Ligotti, Caitlin Kiernan, Hertzan Chimera, Joel Lane and Pamela Briggs. Fiction from the magazine has been reprinted in *The Year's Best Fantasy and Horror* and England's *Best New Horror,* and is forthcoming in *The Year's Best Fantastic Fiction.* Publishes ms an average of 6 months after acceptance. Byline given. Offers 100% kill fee. Buys first North American serial rights and non-exclusive rights for public readings (we hold readings of the magazine at various venues—like libraries). Reports in 1 month on queries; 3 months on mss. Sample copy for $5. Writer's guidelines for #10 SASE.

Fiction: Experimental, fantasy (contemporary), slipstream/cross genre, horror, humorous, science fiction (but not "high-tech"), surrealism of all sorts. Recent or upcoming themes: No. 8: Fabulous Creatures, No. 9: Strange Places, No. 10: Strange Love, No. 11: Strange Nourishment, and No. 12: The Zodiac. Buys 45 mss/year. Send complete ms. Length: 500-3,000 words. Pays $10-90 (2-3¢/word).

• Ranked as one of the best markets for fiction writers in the last *Writer's Digest*'s annual "Fiction 50."

Reprints: Accepts previously published submissions (but query first). Send typed ms with rights for sale noted and information about when and where the article previously appeared. Pays 100% of amount paid for an original article.

Poetry: Avant-garde, free verse, traditional, narrative poetry. Buys 15 poems/year. Submit maximum 3 poems. No length limits. Pays $10/poem.

Tips: "Writers should familiarize themselves with surrealism in literature: too often, we receive stories filled with genre clichés. Also: we prefer character-driven stories.We're looking to add nonfiction (at the same pay rate—2-3¢/word—as fiction). Reviews, articles, cultural commentary . . . the more unusual, the better."

SEX

Magazines featuring pictorial layouts accompanied by stories and articles of a sexual nature, both gay and straight, are listed in this section. Dating and single lifestyle magazines appear in the Relationships section. Other markets for articles relating to sex can be found in the Men's and Women's sections.

‡**BLISS, Journal of Spiritual Sexuality**, New Frontier Education Society, P.O. Box 17397, Asheville NC 28806. (704)252-0100. Editor: Swami Virato. 80% freelance written. Quarterly magazine covering sex. "We publish materials dealing with sexuality and sensuality as it relates to spirituality and metaphysics. Not pornographic, yet explicit. Estab. 1993. Circ. 10,000. Pays on publication. Publishes ms an average of 6 months after acceptance. Byline given. Offers 15% kill fee. Buys first North American serial rights, first rights, one-time rights and second serial (reprint) rights. Editorial lead time 3 months. Submit seasonal material 6 months in advance. Accepts simultaneous and previously published submissions. Reports in 2 months on queries; 3 months on mss. Sample copy for $3. Writer's guidelines for #10 SASE.

Nonfiction: Book excerpts, essays, exposé, general interest, humor, inspirational, interview/profile, opinion, personal experience, photo feature, religious. Buys 10 mss/year. Send complete ms. Length: 1,500-4,000 words. Pays $50-250 for assigned articles; $50-150 for unsolicited articles. Pays expenses of writers on assignment.

Photos: Send photos with submission. Reviews contact sheets, transparencies and 8 × 10 prints. Offers $10-100/photo. Captions, model releases, identification of subjects required. Buys all rights.

Columns/Departments: Getting Personal (personal sexual experiences); What's Hot (current spiritual/sexual), both 1,500-2,000 words. Buys 6 mss/year. Send complete ms. Pays $50-100.

Fiction: Confession, erotica, experimental, fantasy, religious. Buys 6 mss/year. Send complete ms. Length: 1,500-4,000 words. Pays $50-150.

Tips: "We regard human sexuality as sacred and want a writer to see it the same way. However, we are not prudes and seek explicit material."

‡**BOUDOIR NOIR**, P.O. Box 5, Station F, Toronto, Ontario M4Y 2L4 Canada. Fax: (416)591-1572. E-mail: boudoir@ boudoir~noir.com. Website: http://www.boudoir-noir.com. Contact: Diane Wilputte, editor. 70% freelance written. Quarterly magazine covering the S&M and fetish lifestyles in North America. "We publish only nonfiction articles that seek to explain S&M sexuality to our readers." Estab. 1992. Circ. 7,000. Publishes ms an average of 3 months after acceptance. Byline given. Buys second serial (reprint) rights. Submit seasonal material 3 months in advance. Reports in 2 weeks on queries; 1 month on mss. Sample copy for $10. Writer's guidelines free.

Nonfiction: Reviews, feature articles. Length: 500-1,000 words. No simultaneous submissions please.

Tips: "We like to get stories by e-mail or on disk, but we accept typed mss from a few writers (one writer in Russia sends handwritten copy). We like to know if someone has a particular fetish or area of expertise which gives them extra credentials to write a particular story. We prefer stories that focus on people, rather than abstract fetishes or issues. No fiction or poetry."

DRUMMER, Desmodus, Inc., P.O. Box 410390, San Francisco CA 94141-0390. (415)252-1195. Fax: (415)252-9574. E-mail: drummhq@slip.net. Managing Editor: Wickie Stamps. 50% freelance written. Gay male leather and related fetish erotica/news. Monthly magazine of "erotic aspects of leather and other masculine fetishes for gay men." Estab. 1976. Circ. 45,000. Pays 90 days after publication. Publishes ms an average of 3 months after acceptance. Byline given. Buys first North American serial rights or makes work-for-hire assignments. Written queries only. No response on unsolicited submissions. Sample copy for $6. Writer's guidelines for #10 SASE.

Nonfiction: Book excerpts, essays, historical/nostalgic, how-to, humor, interview/profile, new product, opinion, personal experience, photo feature, technical, travel. No feminine-slanted or heterosexual pieces. Buys 25 mss/year. Query with or without published clips, or send complete ms. Length: 1,000-15,000 words. Pays $50-100 for assigned articles; $50-100 for unsolicited articles.

Reprints: Send typed ms with rights for sale noted and information about when and where the article previously appeared. Pays 75% of amount paid for an original article.

Photos: Send photocopies with submission. Reviews contact sheets and transparencies. Offers $25-50/photo. Model releases, identification of subjects required. Buys one-time rights on all rights.

Fiction: Adventure, erotica, ethnic, fantasy, historical, horror, humorous, mystery, novel excerpts, science fiction, slice-of-life vignettes, suspense, western. Must have gay "macho" erotic elements. Buys 60-75 mss/year. Send complete ms. Length: 1,000-7,000 words. Occasionally serializes stories. Pays $100.

Fillers: Anecdotes, facts, gags, cartoons, newsbreaks. Manuscript must be scannable. Buys 50/year. Length: 10-100 words. Pays $10-50.

Tips: "*Drummer* is a hardcore raunch magazine for gay men. Keep that in mind and you're in the ballpark."

‡**EXOTIC MAGAZINE**, X Publishing, 625 SW 10th Ave. #324, Portland OR 97205. Fax: (503)241-7239. E-mail: xmag@teleport.com. Contact: Theresa Reed, editor. Monthly magazine covering adult entertainment, sexuality. "*Exotic* is pro-sex, informative, amusing, mature, intelligent. Our readers rent and/or buy adult videos, visit strip clubs and are interested in topics related to the adult entertainment industry and sexuality/culture. Don't talk down to them or fire too far over their heads. Many readers are computer literate and well-traveled. We're also interested in insightful fetish material. We are not a 'hard core' publication." Estab. 1993. Circ. 35,000. Pays on publication. Publishes ms an average of 6 months after acceptance. Byline given. Buys first North American serial rights; and on-line rights; may negotiate second serial (reprint) rights. Accepts simultaneous submissions. Reports in 2 weeks on queries; 2 months on mss. Sample copy for 9 × 12 SASE and 5 first-class stamps. Writer's guidelines for #10 SASE.

Nonfiction: Exposé, general interest, historical/nostalgic, how-to, humor, interview/profile, travel, news. No "men writing as women, articles about being a horny guy, opinion pieces pretending to be fact pieces." Buys 36 mss/year. Send complete ms. Length: 1,000-1,800 words. Pays 10¢/word up to $150.

Reprints: Accepts previously published submissions.

Photos: Rarely buys photos. Most provided by staff. Reviews prints. Negotiates payment individually. Model releases required.

Fiction: Erotica, slice-of-life vignettes. (Must present either erotic element or some "vice" of modern culture, such as gambling, music, dancing). Send complete ms. Length: 1,000-1,800 words. Pays 10¢/word up to $150.

Tips: "Read adult publications, spend time in the clubs doing more than just tipping and drinking. Look for new insights in adult topics. For the industry to continue to improve, those who cover it must also be educated consumers and affiliates. Please type, spell-check and be realistic about how much time the editor can take 'fixing' your manuscript."

FIRST HAND, Experiences For Loving Men, Firsthand, Ltd., 310 Cedar Lane, Teaneck NJ 07666. (201)836-9177. Fax: (201)836-5055. E-mail: firsthand3@aol.com. Contact: Bob Harris, editor. Publisher: Jackie Lewis. 75% freelance written. Eager to work with new/unpublished writers. Monthly magazine of homosexual erotica. Estab. 1980. Circ. 70,000. Pays on publication. Publishes ms an average of 8 months after acceptance. Byline given. Buys all rights (exceptions made) and second serial (reprint) rights. Submit seasonal material 10 months in advance. Reports in 4 months. Sample copy for $5. Writer's guidelines for #10 SASE.

Reprints: Send photocopy of previously published article. Pays 50% of amount paid for original articles.

Columns/Departments: Survival Kit (short nonfiction articles, up to 1,000 words, featuring practical information on safe sex practices, health, travel, psychology, law, fashion, and other advice/consumer/lifestyle topics of interest to gay or single men). "For this section, we sometimes also buy reprint rights to appropriate articles previously published in local gay newspapers around the country." Infotainment (short reviews up to 1,000 words on books, film, TV, video, theater, performance art, museums, etc.). Reviews must have a gay slant. Query. Pays $35-70, depending on length.

Fiction: Erotic fiction up to 5,000 words, average 2,000-3,000 words. "We prefer fiction in the first person which is believable—stories based on the writer's actual experience have the best chance. We're not interested in stories which involve underage characters in sexual situations. Other taboos include bestiality, rape—except in prison stories, as rape is an unavoidable reality in prison—and heavy drug use. Writers with questions about what we can and cannot depict should write for our guidelines, which go into this in more detail. We print mostly self-contained stories; we will look at novel excerpts, but only if they stand on their own."

Tips: "*First Hand* is a very reader-oriented publication for gay men. Half of each issue is made up of letters from our readers describing their personal experiences, fantasies and feelings. Our readers are from all walks of life, all races and ethnic backgrounds, all classes, all religious and political affiliations, and so on. They are very diverse, and many live in far-flung rural areas or small towns; for some of them, our magazines are the primary source of contact with gay life, in some cases the only support for their gay identity. Our readers are very loyal and save every issue. We return that loyalty by trying to reflect their interests—for instance, by striving to avoid the exclusively big-city bias so common to national gay publications. So bear in mind the diversity of the audience when you write."

‡FOX MAGAZINE, Montcalm Publishing, 401 Park Ave. S., New York NY 10016-8802. (212)779-8900. Fax: (212)725-7215. Website: http://www.gallerymagazine.com. Editorial Director: Marc Medoff. Managing Editor: Rich Friedman. 50% freelance written. Prefers to work with published/established writers. Monthly magazine "focusing on features of interest to the young American man." Estab. 1972. Circ. 500,000. Pays on publication. Byline given. Offers 25% kill fee. Buys first North American serial rights or makes work-for-hire assignments. Submit seasonal material 6 months in advance. Reports in 1 month on queries; 2 months on mss. Sample copy for $7.95 (add $2 for Canadian and foreign orders). Writers' guidelines for #10 SASE.

Nonfiction: Investigative pieces, general interest, how-to, humor, interview, new products, profile. Buys 4-5 mss/year. Query or send complete ms. Length: 1,500-5,000 words. Pays $300-1,500. "Special prices negotiated." Sometimes pays expenses of writers on assignment.

Reprints: Send tearsheet or photocopy of article or short story or typed ms with rights for sale noted and information about when and where the article previously appeared. Pays 25% of amount paid for an original article.

Photos: Send photos with accompanying ms. Pay varies. Reviews b&w or color contact sheets and negatives. Buys one-time rights. Captions preferred; model releases and photo IDs required.

Fiction: Adventure, erotica (special guidelines available), experimental, humorous, mainstream, mystery, suspense. Buys 1 ms/issue. Send complete ms. Length: 1,000-3,000 words. Pays $350-500.

GALLERY MAGAZINE, Montcalm Publishing Corp., 401 Park Ave. S., New York NY 10016-8802. (212)779-8900. Fax: (212)725-7215. Contact: Marc Medoff, editorial director. Managing Editor: Rich Friedman. 50% freelance written. Prefers to work with published/established writers. Monthly magazine "focusing on features of interest to the young American man. *Gallery* is a magazine aimed at entertaining and educating the contemporary man. *Gallery* covers political, cultural, and social trends on a national and global level through serious and provocative investigative reports, candid interviews, human-interest features, service-oriented articles, fiction, humor and photographic portfolios of beautiful women. Each issue of *Gallery* contains our 'Heroes' feature, a first-person account of the effects of the Vietnam War, 'Toys for Men' service feature; and columns dealing with travel, entertainment news, automotives, men's fashion, health and fitness, and outdoor leisure activities." Estab. 1972. Circ. 500,000. Pays on publication. Byline given. Pays 25% kill fee. Buys first North American serial rights or makes work-for-hire assignments. Submit seasonal material 6 months in advance. Reports in 1 month on queries; 2 months on mss. Sample copy for $7.95 (add $2 for Canadian and foreign orders). Writer's guidelines for SASE.

• *Gallery* works on Macintosh, so it accepts material on Mac or compatible disks if accompanied by hard copy.

Nonfiction: Investigative pieces, general interest, how-to, humor, interview, new products, profile. Buys 4-5 mss/issue. Query or send complete mss. Length: 1,500-5,000 words. Pays $1,500-3,000. "Special prices negotiated." Sometimes pays expenses of writers on assignment.

Reprints: Send tearsheet, photocopy or typed ms of article or story with rights for sale noted and information about when and where the article previously appeared. Pays 25% of amount paid for an original article.

Photos: Send photos with accompanying mss. Pay varies for b&w or color contact sheets and negatives. Buys one-time rights. Captions preferred; model release, photo ID required.

Fiction: Adventure, erotica (special guidelines available), experimental, humorous, mainstream, mystery, suspense. Buys 1 ms/issue. Send complete ms. Length: 1,000-3,000 words. Pays $350-500.

GENT, "Home of the D-Cups," Dugent Publishing Corp., 14411 Commerce Way, Suite 420, Miami Lakes FL 33016. Managing Editor: Steve Dorfman. 80% freelance written. Monthly men's sophisticate magazine with emphasis on big breasts. Estab. 1960. Circ. 150,000. Pays on publication. Byline given. Buys first North American serial or second serial (reprint) rights. Editorial lead time 4 months. Submit seasonal material 6 months in advance. Reports in 2 weeks on queries; 3 months on mss. Sample copy for $7. Writer's guidelines for #10 SASE.

Nonfiction: How-to ("anything sexually related"), personal experience ("any and all sexually related matters"). Buys 13-26 mss/year. Query. Length: 2,000-3,000 words. Pays $300.

Reprints: Accepts previously published submissions.

Photos: Send photos with submission. Reviews 35mm transparencies. Negotiates payment individually. Model releases and identification of subjects required. Buys first North American with reprint rights.

Fiction: Erotica, fantasy. Buys 26 mss/year. Send complete ms. Length: 2,000-3,000 words. Pays $200-250.

GUYS, First Hand Ltd., P.O. Box 1314, Teaneck NJ 07666-3441. (201)836-9177. Fax: (201)836-5055. E-mail: firsthand 3@aol.com. Editor: William Spencer. 80% freelance written. Monthly magazine of erotica for gay men. "A positive, romantic approach to gay sex." Estab. 1988. Circ. 100,000. Pays on publication. Publishes ms an average of 1 year after acceptance. Byline given. Buys first North American serial or all rights. Reports in 6 months. Sample copy for $5.50. Writer's guidelines for #10 SASE.

Fiction: Erotica. Buys 72 mss/year. Send complete ms. Length: 1,000-10,000 words. Pays $75-250.

HIGH SOCIETY MAGAZINE, Crescent Publishers, 801 Second Ave., New York NY 10017. (212)661-7878. Fax: (212)692-9297. Website: http://www.highsociety.mag. Editor: Vincent Stevens. Contact: Jody Schwartz, managing editor. Associate Editor: Richard Morgantown. 50% freelance written. Men's sophisticate magazine emphasizing men's entertainment. "Everything of interest to the American male." Estab. 1976. Circ. 400,000. **Pays on acceptance.** Byline given. Offers 20% kill fee. Buys first North American serial rights. Submit seasonal material 6 months in advance. Accepts simultaneous submissions. Reports in 2 weeks on queries. Sample copy for $2 and 9×12 SAE.

Nonfiction: Exposé, general interest, interview/profile, photo feature. Buys 12 mss/year. Query with or without published clips, or send complete ms. Length: 1,500-3,000 words. Pays $300-800 for assigned articles; $200-500 for unsolicited articles. Sometimes pays expenses of writers on assignment.

Photos: Send photos with submission. Reviews 35mm slides, 2¼×2¼ transparencies, 8×10 prints. Offers $100-200/ photo. Captions, model releases and photo identification of proof of age of subjects required. Buys one-time rights. Any photos of celebrity nudes entertained. Negotiates payment individually.

Columns/Departments: Private Passions (first person sexual accounts), 3,000 words; Bad Guys (crime-related exposes), 1,800 words; Sex & Music (biographies of female celebs in music business), 1,000 words. Buys 30 mss/year. Query with published clips. Pays $150-800.

HUSTLER, HG Inc., 8484 Wilshire Blvd., Suite 900, Beverly Hills CA 90211. Fax: (213)651-2741. Editor: Allan MacDonell. Contact: Dylan Ford, articles editor. 60% freelance written. Magazine published 13 times/year. "*Hustler* is the no-nonsense men's magazine. Our audience does not need to be told whether to wear their trousers cuffed or plain. The *Hustler* reader expects honest, unflinching looks at hard topics—sexual, social, political, personality profile, true crime." Estab. 1974. Circ. 750,000. Pays as boards ship to printer. Publishes ms an average of 3 months after acceptance. Byline given. Offers 20% kill fee. Buys all rights. Editorial lead time 4 months. Submit seasonal material 6 months in advance. Reports in 2 weeks on queries; 1 month on mss. Writer's guidelines for #10 SASE.

- *Hustler* is most interested in profiles of dynamic ground-breaking, indomitable individuals who don't mind "flipping a bird" at the world in general.

Nonfiction: Book excerpts, exposé, general interest, how-to, interview/profile, personal experience, trends. Buys 30 mss/yer. Query. Length: 3,500-4,000 words. Pays $1,500. Sometimes pays expenses of writers on assignment.

Columns/Departments: Sex Play (some aspect of sex that can be encapsulated in a limited space), 2,500 words. Buys 13 mss/year. Send complete ms. Pays $750.

Fiction: "Difficult fiction market. Must have two sex scenes; yet not be rote or boring." Buys 2 mss/year. Send complete ms. Length: 3,000-3,500. Pays $1,000.

Fillers: Pays $50-100. Jokes and "Graffilthy," bathroom-wall humor.

Tips: "Don't try and mimic the *Hustler* style. If a writer needs to be molded into our voice, we'll do a better job of it than he or she will."

IN TOUCH/INDULGE FOR MEN, In Touch International, Inc., 13122 Saticoy St., North Hollywood CA 91605-3402. (818)764-2288. Fax: (818)764-2307. E-mail: alan@intouchformen.com. Website: http://www.intouchformen.com. Contact: Alan W. Mills, editor. 80% freelance written. Works with a small number of new/unpublished writers each

---

 THE DOUBLE DAGGER before a listing indicates that the listing is new in this edition. New markets are often more receptive to freelance submissions.

year. Monthly magazine covering the gay male lifestyle, gay male humor and erotica. Estab. 1973. Circ. 70,000. Pays on publication. Byline given, pseudonym OK. Buys one-time rights. Accepts simultaneous submissions. Reports in 2 months. Sample copy for $5.95. Writer's guidelines for #10 SASE.

Nonfiction: Rarely buys nonfiction. Send complete ms. Length: 3,000-3,500 words. Pays $25-75.

Photos: Send photos with submission. Reviews contact sheets, transparencies, prints. Offers $25/photo. Captions, model releases, identification of subjects required. Buys one-time rights.

Fiction: Gay male erotica. Buys 82 mss/year. Send complete ms. Length: 3,000-3,500 words. Pays $75 maximum.

Fillers: Short humor. Buys 12/year. Length: 1,500-2,500 words. Pays $25-50.

Tips: "Our publications feature male nude photos plus three fiction pieces, several articles, cartoons, humorous comments on items from the media, photo features. We try to present positive aspects of the gay lifestyle, with an emphasis on humor. Humorous pieces may be erotic in nature. We are open to all submissions that fit our gay male format; the emphasis, however, is on humor and the upbeat. We receive many fiction manuscripts but not nearly enough unique, innovative, or even experimental material."

‡INTERACTIVE QUARTERLY, Interactive Entertainment For Men, Interactive Publications, 7 Oak Place, Montclair NJ 07042. Fax: (201)783-3686. E-mail: iqmag@aol.com. Managing Editor: Evan Robb. 80% freelance written. Quarterly CD-ROM magazine covering adult entertainment software and online material with "Honest, informed articles, short takes and reviews of adult software and Internet services. Writing should be witty and informed without being smug." Estab. 1995. Circ. 55,000. **Pays on acceptance.** Publishes ms an average of 2 months on acceptance. Byline given. Offers 40% kill fee. Buys first and all rights. Editorial lead time 4 months. Submit seasonal material 2 months in advance. Accepts simultaneous submissions. Sample copy for $5 to writers only.

Nonfiction: Humor, interview/profile, new product, personal experience, photo feature, technical. Buys 160 mss/year. Query with published clips. Length: 1,000 words maximum. Pays $25-375 for assigned articles. Sometimes pays expenses of writers on assignment.

Photos: State availability of photos with submission. Negotiates payment individually. Captions and model releases required. Buys all rights. Buys 16 mss/eyar. Query. Pays $50-150.

Tips: "As a Digizine (on CD-ROM), we are looking for writers who can direct a video crew and/or do in-camera interviews and commentary."

LIBIDO, The Journal of Sex & Sensibility, Libido, Inc., 5318 N. Paulina St., Chicago IL 60640, Fax: (773)275-0752. E-mail: rune@mcs.com. Website: http://www.indra.com\libido. Co-editors: Marianna Beck and Jack Hafferkamp. Submissions Editor: J.L. Beck. 50% freelance written. Quarterly magazine covering literate erotica. "*Libido* is about sexuality. Orientation is not an issue, writing ability is. The aim is to enlighten as often as it is to arouse. Humor—sharp and smart—is important, so are safer sex contexts." Estab. 1988. Circ. 10,000. Pays on publication. Byline given. Kill fee "rare, but negotiable." Buys one-time or second serial (reprint) rights. Editorial lead time 3 months. Submit seasonal material 4 months in advance. Payment negotiable. Reports in 6 months. Sample copy for $8. Writer's guidelines for #10 SASE.

Nonfiction: Book excerpts, essays, historical/nostalgic, humor, photo feature, travel. "No violence, sexism or misty memoirs." Buys 10-20 mss/year. Send complete ms. Length: 300-2,500 words. Pays $50 minimum for assigned articles; $15 minimum for unsolicited articles. Pays contributor copies "when money isn't an issue and copies or other considerations have equal or higher value." Sometimes pays expenses of writers on assignment.

Reprints: Send photocopy of article or short story and information about when and where the material previously appeared. Pays 100% of amount paid for an original article.

Photos: Reviews contact sheets and 5×7 and 8×10 prints. Negotiates payment individually. Model releases required. Buys one-time rights.

Fiction: Erotica. Buys 20 mss/year. Send complete ms. Length: 800-2,500 words. Pays $20-50.

Poetry: Uses humorous short erotic poetry. No limericks. Buys 10 poems/year. Submit maximum 3 poems. Pays $15.

Tips: "Send us a manuscript—make it short, sharp and with a lead that makes us want to read. If we're not hooked by paragraph three, we reject the manuscript."

NUGGET, Firestone Publishing Corp., 14411 Commerce Way, Suite 420, Miami Lakes FL 33016-1598. Fax: (305)557-6005. E-mail: editor-nugget@dugent.com. Website: http://www.dugent.com/nug/. Managing Editor: Nye Willden. Contact: Christopher James, editor-in-chief. 100% freelance written. Men's/adult magazine published 12 times a year covering fetish and kink. "*Nugget* is a one-of-a-kind publication which appeals to daring, open-minded adults who enjoy all forms of both kinky, alternative sex (catfighting, transvestism, fetishism, bi-sexuality, etc.) and conventional sex." Estab. 1960. Circ. 100,000. Pays on publication. Publishes ms an average of 1 year after acceptance. Byline given. Buys first North American serial rights. Editorial lead time 5 months. Submit seasonal material 1 year in advance. Accepts simultaneous submissions. Reports in 2 weeks on queries; 2 months on mss. Sample copy for $5. Writer's guidelines free on request.

Nonfiction: Interview/profile, sexual matters/trends (fetish and kink angle). Buys 8 mss/year. Query. Length: 2,000-3,000 words. Pays $200 minimum.

Photos: Send photos with submission. Reviews transparencies. Offers no additional payment for photos accepted with ms. Model releases required. Buys one-time second rights.

Fiction: Erotica, fantasy. Buys 20 mss/year. Send complete ms. Length: 2,000-3,000 words. Pays $200-250.

Tips: Most open to fiction submissions. (Follow readers guidelines for suitable topics.)

OPTIONS, AJA Publishing, P.O. Box 470, Port Chester NY 10573. (914)939-2111. E-mail: dianaeditr@aol.com. Editor: Don Stone. Contact: Diana Sheridan, associate editor. Mostly freelance written. Sexually explicit magazine for and about bisexuals and to a lesser extent homosexuals, published 10 times/year. "Articles, stories and letters about bisexuality. Positive approach. Safe-sex encounters unless the story clearly pre-dates the AIDS situation." Estab. 1977. Circ. 100,000. Pays on publication. Publishes mss an average of 10 months after acceptance. Byline given, usually pseudonymous. Buys all rights. Buys almost no seasonal material. Reports in 3 weeks. Sample copy for $2.95 and 6×9 SAE with 5 first-class stamps. Writer's guidelines for SASE.

Nonfiction: Essays (occasional), how-to, humor, interview/profile, opinion, personal experience (especially). All must be bisexually or gay related. Does not want "anything not bisexually/gay related, anything negative, anything opposed to safe sex, anything dry/boring/ponderous/pedantic. Write even serious topics informally if not lightly." Buys 10 nonfiction mss/year. Send complete ms. Length: 2,000-3,000. Pays $100.

Photos: Reviews transparencies and prints. Pays $20 for b&w photos; $200 for full color. Color or b&w sets $150. Previously published photos acceptable.

Fiction: "We don't usually get enough true first-person stories and need to buy some from writers. They must be bisexual, usually man/man, hot and believable. They must not read like fiction." Buys 70 fiction mss/year. Send complete ms. Length: 2,000-3,000. Pays $100.

Tips: "We use many more male/male pieces than female/female. Use only one serious article per issue. A serious/humorous approach is good here, but only if it's natural to you; don't make an effort for it. No longer buying 'letters'. We get enough real ones."

PENTHOUSE, General Media, 277 Park Ave., 4th Floor, New York NY 10172-0033. (212)702-6000. Fax: (212)702-6279. Website: http://www./penthousemag.com. Editor: Peter Bloch. Monthly magazine. "*Penthouse* is for the sophisticated male. Its editorial scope ranges from outspoken contemporary comment to photography essays of beautiful women. *Penthouse* features interviews with personalities, sociological studies, humor, travel, food and wines, and fashion and grooming for men." Estab. 1969. Circ. 1,100,000. **Pays 2 months after acceptance.** Byline given. Offers 25% kill fee. Buys all rights. Editorial lead time 2-3 months. Accepts simultaneous submissions. Writer's guidelines for #10 SASE.

Nonfiction: Exposé, general interest (to men), interview/profile. Buys 50 mss/year. Query, query with published clips or send complete ms. Length: 4,000-6,000. Pays $3,000.

Columns/Departments: Length: 1,000 words. Buys 25 mss/year. Query, query with published clips or send complete ms. Pays $500.

Fiction: L. Nahon, fiction editor. Erotica (written by women only).

Fillers: Buys 25/year. Length: 1,000. Pays $500.

Tips: "Because of our long lead time, writers should think at least 6 months ahead. We take chances. Go against the grain; we like writers who look under rocks and see what hides there."

PLAYBOY, 680 N. Lakeshore Dr., Chicago, IL 60611. Contact: Articles Editor or Fiction Editor. Monthly magazine. "As the world's largest general-interest lifestyle magazine for men, *Playboy* spans the spectrum of contemporary men's passions. From hard-hitting investigative journalism to light-hearted humor, the latest in fashion and personal technology to the cutting edge of the popular culture, *Playboy* is and always has been both guidebook and dream book for generations of American men . . . the definitive source of information and ideas for over 10 million readers each month. In addition, *Playboy*'s 'Interview' and '20 Questions' present profiles of politicians, athletes and today's hottest personalities." Estab. 1953. Circ. 3,283,000. Writer's guidelines for SASE. This magazine did not respond to our request for information. Query before submitting.

‡PLAYERS MAGAZINE, Players International Publications, 8060 Melrose Ave., Los Angeles CA 90046. (213)653-8060. Fax: (213)655-9452. E-mail: psi@loop.com. Contact: David Jamison, editor-in-chief. 85% freelance written. Monthly magazine with "issues, stories and celebrities of interest to the African-American community." Estab. 1973. Circ. 50,000. Pays on publication. Byline given. Offers 50% kill fee. Buys first North American serial rights, second serial (reprint) rights or all rights. Editorial lead time 5 months. Submit seasonal material 5 months in advance. Accepts simultaneous and previously published submissions. Reports in 1 week on queries; 1 month on mss. Sample copy for 8×10 SAE and 4 first-class stamps. Writer's guidelines for #10 SASE.

Nonfiction: Book excerpts, essays, exposé, general interest, historical/nostalgic, humor, inspirational, interview/profile, opinion, personal experience, photo feature, religious, travel. Buys 60 mss/year. Query with published clips. Length: 2,500-3,500 words. Pays 10-15¢/word. Pays expenses of writers on assignment.

Reprints: Send typed ms with rights for sale noted and information about when and where the article previously appeared. Payment negotiable.

Photos: Send photos with submission. Reviews 2¼×2¼ transparencies. Offers $50-100/photo. Captions, model releases and identification of subjects required. Buys one-time rights.

Columns/Departments: Did You Know (African-American history); Eyes on the Prize (pillars in community); Sign Off (first-person narratives). Length: 750-1,000 words. Buys 180 mss/year. Query with published clips. Pays 10¢/word minimum.

Fiction: Adventure, condensed novels, confession, erotica, ethnic, experimental, fantasy, historical, humorous, mainstream, mystery, novel excerpts, religious, romance, science fiction, serialized novels, slice-of-life vignettes, suspense. Buys 12 mss/year. Query with published clips. Length: 2,500-3,500 words. Pays 10-15¢/word.

Tips: "Be professional about submissions, open to rewrites and be patient about response time. Review a copy of magazine and know what section your submission would be appropriate for."

SCORE, Score Publishing Group, 13360 SW 128 St., Miami FL 33186. Fax: (305)238-6716. E-mail: quad@netrunner.n et. Editor: John C. Fox. Contact: Lisa Gable, editorial assistant. Men's magazine, published 13 times/year, specializing in big bust, slim-n-stacked women. Estab. 1991. Circ. 191,000. Pays on publication. Publishes ms an average of 3 months after acceptance. Byline given. Buys first rights. Editorial lead time 4 months. Submit seasonal material 6-8 months in advance. Reports in 2 weeks on queries; 1 month on mss. Sample copy for $7 (includes shipping and handling; no SASE required). Writer's guidelines for #10 SASE.

Nonfiction: Buys 15-20 mss/year. Traditional male subject matter about sexual interests such as male sexual health subjects or male entertainment (i.e., gambling). On-location reports including porn shoots, reviews of strip clubs (major international cities only please), etc. Send photos with submissions. Negotiates payment individually. Model releases required. Buys one-time rights. Please query first, but unsolicited mss are accepted.

Reprints: Send photocopy of article or story with information about when and where the article previously appeared. Pays 35% of amount paid for an original article.

Fiction: Buys 15-20 mss/year. Send complete ms. Provide SASE. The main female character should have huge breasts, and the story should focus on detailed descriptions of her breasts with lots of breast play. The readers should be able to easily identify with the main male character. The story should be written in first or third person and should contain at least two sex scenes, the first beginning within the first four pages. Publishes novel excerpts. Length: 2,500-4,000 words. Pays $350-500.

Tips: Send for writer's guidelines. Study sample copies of the publication for insights into our editorial needs. "Because 90% of the unsolicited manuscripts we receive are fiction, new writers have a better chance of being published if they submit nonfiction. I suggest querying with a list of nonfiction subjects, and we'll advise the author which ones we'll consider," John C. Fox advises.

SWANK, Swank Publications, 210 Route 4 E., Suite 401, Paramus NJ 07652. (201)843-4004. Fax: (201)843-8636. Editor: Paul Gambino. Contact: Chuck Keats, assistant editor. 75% freelance written. Works with new/unpublished writers. Monthly magazine on "sex and sensationalism, lurid. High quality adult erotic entertainment." Audience of men ages 18-38, high school and some college education, medium income, skilled blue-collar professionals, union men, some white-collar. Estab. 1954. Circ. 400,000. Pays on publication. Publishes ms an average of 4 months after acceptance. Byline given, pseudonym if wanted. Buys first North American serial rights. Submit seasonal material 6 months in advance. Reports in 3 weeks on queries; 1 month on mss. Sample copy for $6.95. Writer's guidelines for SASE.

• *Swank* reports a need for more nonfiction, non-sex-related articles.

Nonfiction: Exposé (researched), adventure must be accompanied by color photographs. "We buy articles on sex-related topics, which don't need to be accompanied by photos." Interested in unusual lifestyle pieces. Buys photo pieces on autos, action, adventure. Buys 34 mss/year. Query with or without published clips. Pays $350-500. Sometimes pays the expenses of writers on assignment. "It is strongly recommended that a sample copy is reviewed before submitting material."

Photos: Bruce Perez, photo editor. Send photos. "If you have good photographs of an interesting adventure/lifestyle subject, the writing that accompanies is bought almost automatically." Model releases required.

SPORTS

A variety of sports magazines, from general interest to sports medicine, are covered in this section. For the convenience of writers who specialize in one or two areas of sport and outdoor writing, the publications are subcategorized by the sport or subject matter they emphasize. Publications in related categories (for example, Hunting and Fishing; Archery and Bowhunting) often buy similar material. Writers should read through this entire section to become familiar with the subcategories. Publications on horse breeding and hunting dogs are classified in the Animal section, while horse racing is listed here. Publications dealing with automobile or motorcycle racing can be found in the Automotive and Motorcycle category. Markets interested in articles on exercise and fitness are listed in the Health and Fitness section. Outdoor publications that promote the preservation of nature, placing only secondary emphasis on nature as a setting for sport, are in the Nature, Conservation and Ecology category. Regional magazines are frequently interested in sports material with a local angle. Camping publications are classified in the Travel, Camping and Trailer category.

Archery and Bowhunting

BOWHUNTER, The Number One Bowhunting Magazine, Cowles Enthusiast Media, 6405 Flank Dr., Harrisburg PA 17112-8200. (717)657-9555. Fax: (717)657-9552. E-mail: bowhunter@cowles.com. Website: www.bowhuntermag.c

om. Contact: Richard Cochran, editorial director. Editor/Founder: M.R. James. 50% freelance written. Bimonthly magazine (with three special issues) on hunting big and small game with bow and arrow. "We are a special interest publication, produced by bowhunters for bowhunters, covering all aspects of the sport. Material included in each issue is designed to entertain and inform readers, making them better bowhunters." Estab. 1971. Circ. 180,000. **Pays on acceptance.** Publishes ms an average of 1 year after acceptance. Byline given. Kill fee varies. Buys first North American serial and one-time rights. Submit seasonal material 8 months in advance. Reports in 1 month on queries; 5 weeks on mss. Sample copy for $2. Free writer's guidelines.

Nonfiction: General interest, how-to, interview/profile, opinion, personal experience, photo feature. "We publish a special 'Big Game' issue each Fall (September) but need all material by mid-March. Another annual publication, *Whitetail Bowhunter*, is staff written or by assignment only. Our latest special issue is the *Gear Guide*, which highlights the latest in equipment. We don't want articles that graphically deal with an animal's death. And, please, no articles written from the animal's viewpoint." Buys 60 plus mss/year. Query. Length: 250-2,000 words. Pays $500 maximum for assigned articles; $100-400 for unsolicited articles. Sometimes pays expenses of writers on assignment.

Photos: Send photos with submission. Reviews 35mm and 2¼×2¼ transparencies and 5×7 and 8×10 prints. Offers $75-250/photo. Captions required. Buys one-time rights.

Tips: "A writer must know bowhunting and be willing to share that knowledge. Writers should anticipate *all* questions a reader might ask, then answer them in the article itself or in an appropriate sidebar. Articles should be written with the reader foremost in mind; we won't be impressed by writers seeking to prove how good they are—either as writers or bowhunters. We care about the reader and don't need writers with 'I' trouble. Features are a good bet because most of our material comes from freelancers. The best advice is: Be yourself. Tell your story the same as if sharing the experience around a campfire. Don't try to write like you think a writer writes."

BOWHUNTING WORLD, Ehlert Publishing Group, Suite 600, 601 Lakeshore Parkway, Minnetonka MN 55305-5215. (612)476-2200. Fax: (612)476-8065. Contact: Mike Strandlund, editor. 70% freelance written. Monthly magazine for bowhunting and archery enthusiasts who participate in the sport year-round. Estab. 1951. Circ. 130,000. **Pays on acceptance.** Publishes ms an average of 5 months after acceptance. Byline given. Buys first rights and reprint rights. Reports in 3 weeks on queries, 6 weeks on mss. Sample copy for $3 and 9×12 SAE with 10 first-class stamps. Writer's and photographers guidelines for SASE.

Nonfiction: How-to articles with creative slants on knowledgeable selection and use of bowhunting equipment and bowhunting methods. Articles must emphasize knowledgeable use of archery or hunting equipment, and/or specific bowhunting techniques. Straight hunting adventure narratives and other types of articles now appear only in special issues. Equipment-oriented articles must demonstrate wise and insightful selection and use of archery equipment and other gear related to the archery sports. Some product-review, field-test, equipment how-to and technical pieces will be purchased. We are not interested in articles whose equipment focuses on random mentioning of brands. Technique-oriented articles most sought are those that briefly cover fundamentals and delve into leading-edge bowhunting or recreational archery methods. "We are also looking for professional-quality articles and photos for our *Archery Business* and *3-D & Target Archery* titles. Primarily focusing on retail archery and tournament coverage." Buys 60 mss/year. Query or send complete ms. Length: 1,500-3,000 words. Pays $350 to over $500.

Photos: "We are seeking cover photos that depict specific behavioral traits of the more common big game animals (scraping whitetails, bugling elk, etc.) and well-equipped bowhunters in action. Must include return postage."

Tips: "Writers are strongly advised to adhere to guidelines and become familiar with our format, as our needs are very specific. Writers are urged to query before sending packages. We prefer detailed outlines of six or so article ideas per query. Assignments are made for the next 18 months."

PETERSEN'S BOWHUNTING, Petersen Publishing Company, L.L.C., 6420 Wilshire Blvd., Los Angeles CA 90048-5515. (213)782-2179. Editor: Greg Tinsley. 70% freelance written. Magazine published 8 times/year covering bowhunting. "Very equipment oriented. Our readers are 'superenthusiasts,' therefore our writers must have an advanced knowledge of hunting archery." Circ. 155,000. **Pays on acceptance.** Byline given. Buys all rights. Editorial lead time 6 months. Submit seasonal material 6 months in advance. Reports in 1 month. Sample copy for #10 SASE. Writer's guidelines free on request.

Nonfiction: How-to, humor, interview/profile, new product, opinion, personal experience, photo feature. Buys 40 mss/year. Send complete ms. Length: 2,000 words. Pays $300.

Photos: Send photos with submission. Reviews contact sheets, 35mm transparencies, 5×7 prints. Offers $35-250/photo. Captions and model releases required. Buys one-time rights.

Columns/Departments: Query. Pays $200-300.

Fillers: Facts, newsbreaks. Buys 12/year. Length: 150-400 words. Pays $25-75.

Tips: Feature articles must be supplied to *Petersen's Bowhunting* in either 5.25 IBM (or compatible) or 3.50 MacIntosh floppy disks.

Baseball

USA TODAY BASEBALL WEEKLY, 1000 Wilson Blvd., Arlington VA 22229. (703)558-5630. Fax:(703)558-4646. Publisher: Keith Cutler. Weekly magazine. "*USA Today Baseball Weekly* covers the major and the minor leagues, fantasy leagues, collectibles, nostalgia and much more. It includes every major league box score for every game, team-by-team notes, a special page for young baseball fans and complete college coverage including the weeekly Top 25 Coaches' Poll. *Baseball Weekly* also includes the nation's best minor league report with complete stats and organization reports." Estab. 1991. Circ. 2,293. This magazine did not respond to our request for information. Query before submitting.

Bicycling

ADVENTURE CYCLIST, Adventure Cycling Assn., Box 8308, Missoula MT 59807. (406)721-1776. Fax: (406)721-8754. E-mail: acaeditor@aol.com. Website: http://www.adv-cycling.org. Contact: Daniel D'Ambrosio, editor. 75% freelance written. Bicycle touring magazine for Adventure Cycling Association members published 9 times/year. Circ. 30,000. Pays on publication. Byline given. Buys first serial rights. Submit seasonal material 3 months in advance. Sample copy and guidelines for 9×12 SAE with 4 first-class stamps.
Nonfiction: Features include: U.S. or foreign tour accounts; special focus (on tour experience); how-to; humor; interview/profile; photo feature; technical; travel. Buys 20-25 mss/year. Query with published clips or send complete ms; include short bio with ms. Length: 800-2,500 words. Pay negotiable.
Reprints: Accepts previously published submissions. Send photocopy of article.
Photos: Color transparencies should accompany tour accounts and profiles. Bicycle, scenery, portraits. State availability of photos. Model releases, identification of subjects required.

BICYCLING, Rodale Press, Inc., 33 E. Minor St., Emmaus PA 18098. (610)967-5171. Fax: (610)967-8960. E-mail: bicmag@aol.com. Publisher: Mike Greehan. Executive Editor: Lisa Gosselin. Contact: Chris Engleman, editorial assistant. 20-25% freelance written. Prefers to work with published/established writers. Magazine published 10 times/year covering topics of interest to committed cyclists. "*Bicycling* features articles about fitness, training, nutrition, touring, racing, equipment, clothing, maintenance, new technology, industry developments, and other topics of interest to committed bicycle riders. Editorially, we advocate for the sport, industry, and the cycling consumer." Estab. 1961. Circ. 280,000. **Pays on acceptance.** Byline given. Buys all rights. Submit seasonal material 6 months in advance. Reports in 2 months. Sample copy for $2.50. Writer's guidelines for #10 SASE.
Nonfiction: How-to (on all phases of bicycle touring, repair, maintenance, commuting, new products, clothing, riding technique, nutrition for cyclists, conditioning); fitness is more important than ever; also travel (bicycling must be central here); photo feature (on cycling events of national significance); and technical (component review—query). "We are strictly a bicycling magazine. We seek readable, clear, well-informed pieces. We sometimes run articles that are pure humor or inspiration and some of each might flavor even our most technical pieces. No poetry or fiction." Buys 1-2 unsolicited mss/issue. Send complete ms. Length: 1,500 words average. Pays $25-1,200. Sometimes pays expenses of writers on assignment.
Reprints: Occasionally accepts previously published submissions.
Photos: State availability of photos with query letter or send photo material with ms. Pays $15-50 for b&w prints and $35-250 for transparencies. Captions preferred; model release required.
Fillers: Anecdotes and news items for Bike Shorts section.
Tips: "We're alway seeking interesting accounts of cycling as a lifestyle."

CRANKMAIL, Cycling in Northern Ohio, P.O. Box 45346, Cleveland OH 44145-0346. Fax: (216)281-9933. E-mail: crankmail@compuserve.com. Website: http://ourworld.compuserve.com/homepages/crankmail. Contact: James Guilford, editor. Monthly magazine covering bicycling in all aspects. "Our publication serves the interests of bicycle enthusiasts . . . established, accomplished adult cyclists. These individuals are interested in reading about the sport of cycling, bicycles as transportation, ecological tie-ins, sports nutrition, the history and future of bicycles and bicycling." Estab. 1977. Circ. 1,000. Pays on publication. Byline given. Not copyrighted. Buys one-time or second serial (reprint) rights. Editorial lead time 1 month. Submit seasonal material 3 months in advance. Sample copy for $1. Writer's guidelines for #10 SASE.
Reprints: Send typed ms with rights for sale noted and information about when and where the article previously appeared.
Nonfiction: Essays, historical/nostalgic, how-to, humor, interview/profile, personal experience, technical. "No articles encouraging folks to start or get involved in bicycling—our readers are already cyclists." Send complete ms; No queries." Length: 1,200-2,000 words. Pays $10 minimum for unsolicited articles.
Fillers: Cartoons. Pays $5-10.

CYCLING USA, The Official Publication of the U.S. Cycling Federation, One Olympic Plaza, Colorado Springs CO 80909. (719)578-4581. Fax: (719)578-4596. E-mail: usacycling@aol.com. Website: www.usacycling.org. Editor: Frank Stanley. 25% freelance written. Monthly magazine covering reportage and commentary on American bicycle racing, personalities and sports physiology, for USCF licensed cyclists. Circ. 35,000. Pays on publication. Publishes ms an average of 2 months after acceptance. Byline given. Reports in 2 weeks. Sample copy for 10×12 SAE with 2 first-class stamps.
 ● *Cycling USA* is looking for longer, more in-depth features (1,000-1,500 words).
Nonfiction: How-to (train, prepare for a bike race), interview/profile, opinion, personal experience, photo feature,

technical and race commentary on major cycling events. No comparative product evaluations. Buys 15 mss/year. Query with published clips. Length: 800-1,200 words. Pays 10¢/word.

Reprints: Send photocopy of article. Pays 100% of amount paid for an original article.

Photos: State availability of photos. Pays $15-50 for 5×7 b&w prints; $100 for transparencies used as cover. Captions required. Buys one-time rights.

Tips: "A background in bicycle racing is important because the sport is somewhat insular, technical and complex. Most major articles are generated inhouse. Race reports are most open to freelancers. Be concise, informative and anecdotal. Our format is more compatible with 800-1,200 word articles than longer features."

DIRT RAG, A.K.A. Productions, 181 Saxonburg Rd., Pittsburgh PA 15238. (412)767-9910. Fax: (412)767-9920. E-mail: dirtrag1@aol.com. Website: http://www.cyclery.com/dirt_rag/. Publisher: Maurice Tierney. Contact: Elaine Tierney, editor. 75% freelance written. Mountain biking magazine published 7 times/year. "*Dirt Rag*'s style is much looser, fun and down to earth than mainstream (glossy) magazines on the same subject. We appeal to hard-core (serious) mountain bikers, and these people make our finest contributions. Avant-garde, humorous, off-beat, alternative." Estab. 1989. Circ. 25,000. Pays on publication. Byline given. No kill fee. Buys one-time rights. Accepts simultaneous submissions. Sample copy for 5 first-class stamps. Writer's guidelines for SASE.

Nonfiction: Book excerpts, essays, exposé, general interest, historical/nostalgic, how-to (bike maintenance, bike technique), humor, interview/profile, opinion, personal experience, photo feature, technical, travel (places to ride). Anything with mountain biking. Buys 24 mss/year. Query. Pays $25-200.

Reprints: Send typed ms with rights for sale noted and information about when and where the material previously appeared. Pays 75% of amount paid for original material.

Photos: Send art or photos with or without submission. Reviews contact sheets and/or prints. Offers additional payment for photos accepted with ms. $200 for color cover. $25 inside (b&w preferred, color OK). Captions preferred. Buys one-time rights. Always looking for good photography and art regardless of subject.

Columns/Departments: Place to Ride, 500-2,000 words; Trialsin (coverage of the sport), 50-500 words; Race Reports (coverage of race events), 50-250 words. Buys 14 mss/year. Query. Pays $10-50.

Fiction: Adventure, fantasy, historical, humorous, mainstream, slice-of-life vignettes. Buys 1-10 mss/year. Query. Pays $25-100.

Poetry: Avant-garde, free verse, light verse, traditional. Pays $20-100.

Fillers: Anecdotes, facts, gags, newsbreaks, short humor. Buys 20/year. Pays $0-50.

VELONEWS, The Journal of Competitive Cycling, 1830 55th St., Boulder CO 80301-2700. (303)440-0601. Fax: (303)444-6788. E-mail: velonews@aol.com. Website: http://www.VeloNews.com/VeloNews. Contact: John Rezell, senior editor. 60% freelance written. Monthly tabloid September-February, biweekly March-August covering bicycle racing. Estab. 1972. Circ. 48,000. Pays on publication. Publishes ms an average of 1 month after acceptance. Byline given. Buys one-time rights. Accepts simultaneous submissions. Reports in 3 weeks. Sample copy for 9×12 SAE with 7 first-class stamps.

Nonfiction: Freelance opportunities include race coverage, reviews (book and videos), health-and-fitness departments. Buys 100 mss/year. Query. Length: 300-1,200 words.

Reprints: Send typed ms with rights for sale noted and information about when and where the article previously appeared.

Photos: State availability of photos. Pays $16.50-50 for b&w prints. Pays $150 for color used on cover. Captions and identification of subjects required. Buys one-time rights.

Boating

‡BOATING, Hachette Filipacchi Magazines, 1633 Broadway, New York NY 10019. Contact: Richard Stepler, editor-in-chief. (212)767-5585. Fax: (212)767-5618. Monthly magazine covering boating. "*Boating*'s readers are well educated and financed. The average reader owns at least 3 boats, has been on the water for 22 years, and considers himself an advanced boater. The most common activity is day cruising, followed by entertaining, then fishing, and weekend cruising. But he dreams of doing more." Estab. 1956. Circ. 200,830. **Pays on acceptance.** Publishes ms 3-6 months after acceptance. Buys first North American serial and electronic rights. Reports in 1 month. Sample copy for $4. Writer's guidelines for #10 SASE.

Nonfiction: How-to, travel. "Typically we feature things the reader can do with his boat that will elicit a 'Hey, I could do that' response. The reader must be able to put himself in the situation, whether it is a how-to (How to Live Aboard) or an adventure story (Cruising Through the Bermuda Triangle). Don't give us 'One Man's Story.' Give Us 'Here's How You Can Do It Too.' Buys 50 mss/year. Query. Length: 2,000-2,500 words. Pay varies.

Columns/Departments: Shorter features. "There's a lot of odd and humorous things that go on in and around the world of boating. Best are those that the reader might see himself doing, although he most likely won't. We are always looking for 300-word stories about the average boater in unusual situations, technical tips or practical advice. To get to know us, and for us to get to know you—start small. It is best, and less frustrating, to start with short pieces in Intelligencer (editor Pam Ruderman) or Short Casts (editor Lenny Rudow). If the idea sounds good, the editor will work with you to develop an outline." Buys 150 mss/year. Length: 200-400 words. Pay varies.

Tips: "Think of *Boating* magazine as a person who would be the ideal companion on a long cruise or car trip. While he may speak of many things—technical, nonsensical or serious—he is always entertaining and informative. *Boating*'s style is different from other magazines that cover the same subject. It is a very specific style and not always easy to grasp on your first try. Writing a piece and then submitting it is a sure way of getting rejected. Always begin with a query."

‡**CRUISING WORLD,** Cruising World Publications, Inc., Box 3400, Newport RI 02840-0992. (401)847-1588. Editor: Bernadette Bernon. 70% freelance written. Monthly magazine for all those who cruise under sail. Circ. 146,000. **Pays on acceptance.** Publishes ms an average of 8 months after acceptance. Offers variable kill fee, $50-150. Buys first North American periodical rights or first world periodical rights. Reports in about 2 months. Writer's guidelines free.
Nonfiction: Book excerpts, how-to, humor, inspirational, opinion, personal experience. "We are interested in seeing informative articles on the technical and enjoyable aspects of cruising under sail, especially seamanship, navigation and how-to." Buys 135-140 unsolicited mss/year. Submit complete ms. Length: 500-3,500 words. Pays $150-800.
Photos: 35mm slides purchased with accompanying ms. Captions and identification of subjects required. Buys one-time rights.
Columns/Departments: People & Food (recipes for preparation aboard sailboats); Shoreline (sailing news, vignettes); Workbench (projects for upgrading your boat). Send complete ms. Length: 150-500 words. Pays $25-150.
Tips: "Cruising stories should be first-person narratives. In general, authors must be sailors who read the magazine. Color slides always improve a ms's chances of acceptance. Technical articles should be well-illustrated."

CURRENTS, Voice of the National Organization for Rivers, 212 W. Cheyenne Mountain Blvd., Colorado Springs CO 80906. (719)579-8759. Fax: (719)576-6238. Editors: Greg Moore, Eric Leaper. 25% freelance written. Quarterly magazine covering river running (kayaking, rafting, river canoeing). Estab. 1979. Circ. 5,000. Pays on publication. Publishes ms an average of 6 months after acceptance. Byline given. Offers 25% kill fee. Buys first North American serial, first and one-time rights. Submit seasonal material 4 months in advance. Reports in 2 weeks on queries; 1 month on mss. Sample copy for $1 and 9 × 12 SAE with 3 first-class stamps. Writer's guidelines for #10 SASE.
Nonfiction: How-to (run rivers and fix equipment), in-depth reporting on river conservation and access issues and problems, humor (related to rivers), interview/profile (any interesting river runner), opinion, personal experience, technical, travel (rivers in other countries). "We tell river runners about river conservation, river access, river equipment, how to do it, when, where, etc." No trip accounts without originality; no stories about "my first river trip." Buys 20 mss/year. Query with or without clips. Length: 500-2,500 words. Pays $35-150.
Reprints: Accepts previously published submissions, if so noted.
Photos: State availability of photos. Pays $35-50. Reviews b&w or color prints or slides; b&w preferred. Captions and identification of subjects (if racing) required. Buys one-time rights. Captions must include names of the river and rapid.
Columns/Departments: Book and film reviews (river-related). Buys 5 mss/year. Query with or without clips, or send complete ms. Length: 100-500 words. Pays $25.
Fiction: Adventure (river). Buys 2 mss/year. Query. Length: 1,000-2,500 words. Pays $35-75. "Must be well-written, on well-known river and beyond the realm of possibility."
Fillers: Clippings, jokes, gags, anecdotes, short humor, newsbreaks. Must be related to river running. Buys 5/year. Length: 25-100 words. Pays $5-10.
Tips: "We need more material on river news—proposed dams, wild and scenic river studies, accidents, etc. If you can provide brief (300-500 words) on these subjects, you will have a good chance of being published. Material must be on rivers. Go to a famous river and investigate it; find out something we don't know—especially about rivers that are *not* in Colorado or adjacent states—we already know about those."

48° NORTH, Boundless Enterprises, 6327 Seaview Ave. NW, Seattle WA 98107. Website: http://www.48north.com. Editor: Richard Hazelton. Contact: C. Streatch, R. Hazelton, publishers. Monthly magazine covering sailing. "Must be sailing (as in boats with sails). No faking it. Our readers are pros. Would like fiction or humor with a hook." Estab. 1981. Circ. 27,000. Pays on publication. Publishes ms an average of 5 months after acceptance. Byline given. Not copyrighted. Buys one-time rights. Editorial lead time 1 month minimum.
Nonfiction: Exposé, general interest, how-to, humor, personal experience, photo feature, technical, travel. All must deal with sailing. Buys 50 mss/year. Send complete ms. Length: 2-3 pages. Payment negotiable.
Reprints: Occasionally accepts previously published submissions. Send typed ms with rights for sale noted. Payment varies with length and content.
Photos: Send photos with submission. Negotiates payment individually. Identification of subjects required. Buys one-time rights.
Columns/Departments: Pays $75-150.
Fiction: Adventure, erotica (mild), fantasy, historical, horror, humorous, mystery, science fiction, slice-of-life vignettes, suspense. Buys 25-35 mss/year. Send complete ms. Length: 2-3 pages. Payment negotiable.
Tips: Send SASE with manuscripts.

‡**GO BOATING MAGAZINE, The Family-Boat Authority,** Duncan McIntosh Co., 17782 Cowan, Suite C, Irvine CA 92614. (714)660-6150. Fax: (714)660-6172. Editor: Jim Youngs. Contact: Erin McNiff, managing editor. 60% freelance written. Published 5 times/year covering family power boating. Typical reader "owns a power boat between 14-25 feet long and has for 3-9 years." Estab. 1997. Circ. 100,000. Pays on publication. Publishes ms an average of 3

months after acceptance. Byline given. Buys first North American serial rights. Editorial lead time 3 months. Submit seasonal material 4 months in advance. Accepts simultaneous submissions. Reports in 1 month on queries; 2 months on mss. Sample copy free. Writer's guidelines for #10 SASE.

Nonfiction: General interest, how-to, humor, new product, personal experience, travel. Buys 10-15 mss/year. Query. Length: 1,200-1,500 words. Pays $150-400. Sometimes pays expenses of writers on assignment.

Photos: State availability of photos with submission. Reviews transparencies and prints. Offers $50-250/photo. Model releases and identification of subjects required. Buys one-time rights.

Columns/Departments: Buys 10 mss/year. Query. Pays $150-350.

Fillers: Anecdotes, facts and newsbreaks. Buys 10/year. Length: 250-500 words. Pays $50-100.

HEARTLAND BOATING, Inland Publications, Inc., P.O. Box 1067, Martin TN 38237-1067. (901)587-6791. Fax: (901)587-6893. Website: http://www.iwol.com/iww/customers/onlinemagazines/heartland/home.html. Contact: Molly Lightfoot Blom, editor. Estab. 1988. 50% freelance written. Magazine published 7 times/year during boating season. "*Heartland Boating* is the official magazine for the boater who isn't going around the world. The content is both informative and humorous—describing boating life as the heartland boater knows it. We aren't pretentious. But, we are boating and enjoying the outdoor, water oriented way of life. The content reflects the challenge, joy and excitement of our way of life afloat. We are devoted to both power and sail boating enthusiasts throughout middle America; houseboats are included. The focus is on the freshwater inland rivers and lakes of the Heartland; primarily the Tennessee, Cumberland, Ohio and Mississippi rivers and the Tennessee-Tombigbee Waterway. No Great Lakes or saltwater material will be considered unless it applies to our area." Circ. 20,000. Pays on publication. Publishes ms an average of 3 months after acceptance. Byline given. Buys first North American serial and sometimes second serial (reprint) rights. Submit seasonal material 6 months in advance. Accepts simultaneous submissions. Reports in 4 months. Sample copy for $5. Free writer's guidelines.

Nonfiction: General interest, historical/nostalgic, how-to, humor, interview/profile, new product, personal experience, photo feature, technical, travel. Special issue: Houseboats (May). Buys 20-40 mss/year. Prefers queries to unsolicited mss with or without published clips. Length: 800-2,000 words. Negotiates payment.

Reprints: Send tearsheet or photocopy of article and information about where and when it previously appeared. Pays 50% of amount paid for an original article.

Photos: Send photos with query. Reviews contact sheets, transparencies. Buys one-time rights.

Columns/Departments: Buys 50 mss/year. Query. Negotiates payment.

HOT BOAT, LFP Publishing, 8484 Wilshire Blvd., Suite 900, Beverly Hills CA 90211. (213)651-5400. Fax: (310)274-7985. Contact: Kevin Spaise, executive editor. Senior Editor: Brett Bayne. 50% freelance written. Monthly magazine on performance boating (16-35 feet), water skiing and water sports in general. "We're looking for concise, technically oriented 'how-to' articles on performance modifications; personality features on interesting boating-oriented personalities, and occasional event coverage." Circ. 90,000. Pays upon publication. Publishes ms an average of 2 months after acceptance. Byline given. Offers 40% kill fee. Buys all rights; also reprint rights occasionally. Submit seasonal material 3 months in advance. Reports in 3 weeks on queries; 1 month on mss. Sample copy for $3 and 9×12 SAE with $1.35 postage.

Nonfiction: How-to (increase horsepower, perform simple boat related maintenance), humor, interview/profile (racers and manufacturers), new product, personal experience, photo feature, technical. "Absolutely no sailing—we deal strictly in powerboating." Buys 30 mss/year. Query with published clips. Length: 500-2,000 words. Pays $75-450. Sometimes pays expenses of writers on assignment.

Reprints: Accepts previously published submissions. Pays $150-200/printed page.

Photos: Send photos with submission. Reviews transparencies. Captions, model releases, identification of subjects required. Buys all rights.

Tips: "We're always open to new writers. If you query with published clips and we like your writing, we can keep you on file even if we reject the particular query. It may be more important to simply establish contact. Once we work together there will be much more work to follow."

LAKELAND BOATING, The Magazine for Great Lakes Boaters, O'Meara-Brown Publications, 500 Davis St., Suite 1000, Evanston IL 60201-4802. (847)869-5400. Fax: (847)869-5989. E-mail: lbonline@aol.com. Contact: Randy Hess, editor. Associate Editor: Chad Schegel. 50% freelance written. Monthly magazine covering Great Lakes boating. Estab. 1946. Circ. 60,000. Pays on publication. Byline given. Buys first North American serial rights. Reports in 4 months. Sample copy for $5.50 and 9×12 SAE with 6 first-class stamps. Writer's guidelines for #10 SASE.

Nonfiction: Book excerpts, historical/nostalgic, how-to, interview/profile, personal experience, photo feature, technical, travel. No inspirational, religious, expose or poetry. Must relate to boating in Great Lakes. Buys 20-30 mss/year. Query. Length: 800-3,500 words. Pays $100-600.

Photos: State availability of photos. Reviews transparencies; prefers 35mm. Captions required. Buys one-time rights.

Columns/Departments: Bosun's Locker (technical or how-to pieces on boating), 100-1,000 words. Buys 40 mss/year. Query. Pays $30-100.

MOTOR BOATING & SAILING, 250 W. 55th St., New York NY 10019. (212)649-4099. Fax: (212)489-9258. Editor and Publisher: Peter A. Janssen. Monthly magazine covering powerboats and sailboats for people who own their own boats and are active in a yachting lifestyle. Estab. 1907. Circ. 135,056. **Pays on acceptance.** Byline given. Buys one-time rights. Reports in 2 months.

Nonfiction: General interest (navigation, adventure, cruising), how-to (maintenance). Buys 5-6 mss/issue. Average issue includes 8-10 feature articles. Query. Length: 2,000 words. Pays $750 average.

Photos: Reviews 5×7 b&w glossy prints and 35mm or larger color transparencies. Offers no additional payment for photos accepted with ms. Captions and model releases required.

NOR'WESTING, Nor'westing Publications, Inc., 6044 Seaview Ave. NW, Seattle WA 98107. (206)783-8939. Fax: (206)783-9011. Contact: Gloria Kruzner, editor. 75% freelance written. Monthly magazine covering Pacific Northwest boating, cruising destinations. "We want to pack our pages with cruising articles, special Northwest destinations, local boating personalities, practical boat maintenance tips." Estab. 1965. Circ. 9,000. Pays 1 month after publication. Publishes timely ms an average of 2 months after acceptance. Byline given. Buys first North American serial rights. Editorial lead time 3 months. Submit seasonal material 3 months in advance. Accepts simultaneous submissions; note where else it's being submitted. Reports in 2 months. Sample copy and writer's guidelines for large SASE.

Nonfiction: History, how-to (boat outfitting, electronics, fish, galley), interview/profile (boater personalities), new product, personal experience (cruising), photo feature, technical, travel (local destinations). Buys 35-40 mss/year. Send complete ms or query. Length: 1,500-3,000 words. Pays $100-150.

Reprints: Accepts previously published submissions if "reworked, timely and pertain to our cruising area." Send tearsheet or photocopy of article or typed ms with rights for sale noted and information about when and where the article previously appeared. Payment varies.

Photos: Send photos with submission. Reviews transparencies, 3×5 prints. Negotiates payment individually. Identification of subjects required. Normally buys one-time rights.

Columns/Departments: Trailerboating (small craft boating—tech/destination), 700-900 words; Galley Ideas (cooking afloat—recipes/ideas), 700-900 words; Hardwired (Boating Electronics), 1,000 words; Cruising Fisherman (Fishing tips, destinations), 700-900 words. Buys 36-40 mss/year. Query with published clips. Pays $50-75.

Fiction: Novel excerpts.

Tips: "Include specific information on destination—how many moorage buoys, cost for showers, best time to visit. Any hazards to watch for while approaching? Why bother going if excitement for area/boating doesn't shine through in piece?"

‡OFFSHORE, Boating Magazine of the Northeast, Offshore Communications, Inc., 220-9 Reservoir St., Needham MA 02194. (617)449-6204. Fax: (617)449-9702. E-mail: oshore@aol.com. Contact: Peter Serratore, editor. Estab. 1976. 80% freelance written. Monthly magazine covering power and sail boating and the coast from Maine to New Jersey. Circ. 35,000. **Pays on acceptance.** Publishes ms an average of 3-5 months after acceptance. Byline given. Offers negotiable kill fee. Buys first North American serial rights. Submit seasonal material 6 months in advance. Accepts simultaneous submissions. Pays $100 for reprints. Reports in 2 weeks. *Writer's Market* recommends allowing 2 months for reply. Sample copy for 10×13 SAE with 8 first-class stamps. Writer's guidelines for #10 SASE.

Nonfiction: Articles on boats, boating, New York, New Jersey and New England coastal places and people. Coastal history of NJ, NY, CT, RI, MA, NH and ME. Thumbnail and/or outline of topic will elicit immediate response. Buys 90 mss/year. Query with writing sample or send complete ms. Length: 1,800-2,500 words. Pays $200-400 for features; $500 and expenses for boat tests.

Reprints: Accepts reprints of previously published submissions in any format. Send information about when and where the article previously appeared. Pays $100.

Fiction: Boat-related fiction.

Photos: Reviews 35mm slides only. For covers, pays $300. Pays $125-150 for last-page photos—humorous or whimsical nautical subjects. Identification of subjects required. Buys one-time rights.

Tips: "Demonstrate familiarity with boats or region and ability to recognize subjects of interest to regional boat owners. Those subjects need not be boats. *Offshore* is serious but does not take itself as seriously as most national boating magazines. We prefer to work with an established 'family' of writers, but are always open to new people, the best of whom may gradually work their way in. Important to ask for (and follow) our writer's guidelines if you're not familiar with our magazine."

‡PACIFIC YACHTING, Power & Sail in British Columbia, OP Publishing Ltd., 780 Beatty St., Suite 300, Vancouver, British Columbia V6B 2M1 Canada. (604)606-4644. Fax: (604)687-1925. E-mail: op@mindlink.bc.ca. Editor: Duart Snow. 90% freelance written. Monthly magazine covering all aspects of recreational boating on British Columbia coast. Circ. 14,598. Pays on publication. Publishes ms an average of 6 months after acceptance. Byline given. Offers negotiable kill fee. Buys first North American serial and simultaneous rights. Editorial lead time 4 months. Submit seasonal material 6 months in advance. "We prefer electronic submissions by disk or modem." Sample copy for $2 plus postage charged to VISA credit card. Writer's guidelines free on request.

Nonfiction: Historical/nostalgic, how-to, humor, interview/profile, personal experience, travel, cruising and destinations on the B.C. coast. "We do not want articles from writers who are obviously not boaters!" Pays $150-500. Pays expenses of writers on assignment if arranged in advance.

Photos: Send sample photos with query. Reviews transparencies, 4×6 prints and slides. Offers no additional payment for photos accepted with ms and $25-300/photo not accepted with ms. Identification of subjects required. Buys one-time rights. Covers: (transparencies): $300.

Fillers: Tonnae Hennigan, editorial assistant. Facts, newsbreaks. Buys 24/year. Length: 50-150 words. Pays $25-75.

POWER BOATING CANADA, 2585 Skymark Ave., Unit 306, Mississauga, Ontario L4W 4L5 Canada. (905)624-8218. Fax: (905)624-6764. Editor: Peter Tasler. 70% freelance written. Bimonthly magazine covering recreational power boating. "*Power Boating Canada* offers boating destinations, how-to features, boat tests (usually staff written), lifestyle pieces—with a Canadian slant—and appeal to recreational power boaters across the country." Estab. 1984. Circ. 50,000. Pays on publication. Publishes ms an average of 3 months after acceptance. Byline given. Offers 20% kill fee. Buys first North American serial rights. Editorial lead time 2 months. Submit seasonal material 3 months in advance. Reports in 1 month on queries, 2 months on mss. Sample copy free.
Nonfiction: "Any articles related to the sport of power boating, especially boat tests." Historical/nostalgic, how-to, interview/profile, personal experience, travel (boating destinations). No general boating articles or personal anecdotes. Buys 40-50 mss/year. Query. Length: 1,200-2,500 words. Pays $150-300. Sometimes pays expenses of writers on assignment.
Reprints: Send photocopy of article or typed ms with rights for sale noted and information about when and where the article previously appeared.
Photos: Payment negotiable. Send photos with submission. Reviews contact sheets, negatives, transparencies, prints. Offers no additional payment for photos accepted with ms. Captions, identification of subjects required. Buys one-time rights.

SAIL, 84 State St., Boston MA 02109-2262. (617)720-8600. Fax: (617)723-0912. Editor: Patience Wales. Contact: Amy Ullrich, managing editor. 50% freelance written. Works with a small number of new/unpublished writers each year. Monthly magazine for audience that is "strictly sailors, average age 42, above average education." Focuses on techniques, joys and rewards of sailing in a practical and instructive way. "The only sailing publication that devotes the majority of its editorial to teaching." Estab. 1970. Circ. 180,000. **Pays on acceptance.** Publishes ms an average of 10 months after acceptance. Buys first North American rights. Submit seasonal or special material at least 6 months in advance. Reports in 10 weeks. Writer's guidelines for 1 first-class stamp.
Nonfiction: Amy Ullrich, managing editor. Wants "articles on sailing: technical, techniques and feature stories." Interested in how-to, personal experience, distance cruising, destinations, technical aspects of boat construction, systems. "Generally emphasize the excitement of sail and the human, personal aspect. No logs." Examples of shorter features (1,000-1,500 words) are: vignettes of day sailing, cruising and racing life (at home or abroad, straight or humorous); maritime history; astronomy; marine life; cooking; nautical love; fishing; boat owning, boat building and outfitting; regatta reports. Special issues: "Cruising, chartering, fitting-out, special race (e.g., America's Cup), boat show." Buys 100 mss/year (freelance and commissioned). Length: 1,500-3,500 words. Pays $200-800. Sometimes pays the expenses of writers on assignment.
Reprints: Send tearsheet or photocopy of article or typed ms with rights for sale noed and information about when and where the article previously appeared. Pays 33-50% of amount paid for an original article.
Photos: Offers additional payment for photos. Uses 50-100 ASA transparencies. Pays $600 if photo is used on the cover.
Tips: "Request an articles specification sheet."
"We look for unique ways of viewing sailing. Skim old issues of *Sail* for ideas about the types of articles we publish. Always remember that *Sail* is a sailing magazine. Stay away from gloomy articles detailing all the things that went wrong on your boat. Think constructively and write about how to avoid certain problems. You should focus on a theme or choose some aspect of sailing and discuss a personal attitude or new philosophical approach to the subject. Notice that we have certain issues devoted to special themes—for example, chartering, electronics, commissioning, and the like. Stay away from pieces that chronicle your journey in the day-by-day style of a logbook. These are generally dull and uninteresting. Select specific actions or events (preferably sailing events, not shorebound activities), and build your articles around them. Emphasize the sailing."

SAILING MAGAZINE, 125 E. Main St., Port Washington WI 53074-0249. (414)284-3494. Fax: (414)284-7764. E-mail: 75553.3666@compuserv.com. Website: http://www.sailnet.com. Contact: Micca Leffingwell Hutchins, editor. Publisher: William F. Schanen, III. Monthly magazine for the experienced sailor. Estab. 1966. Circ. 52,000. Pays on publication. Buys one-time rights. Reports in 2 months.
Nonfiction: "Experiences of sailing—cruising, racing or learning." Must be written to AP Stylebook. Buys 8 mss/year. Length: 750-1,500 words. Must be accompanied by photos, and maps if applicable. Pays $75-300.
Photos: Color photos (transparencies) purchased with or without accompanying text. Captions are required. Pays $15-100.
Tips: Prefers text in Word on disk for Mac or to e-mail address.

SAILING WORLD, N.Y. Times Magazine Group, 5 John Clarke Rd., Box 3400, Newport RI 02840-0992. Fax: (401)848-5048. E-mail: 70672.2725@compuserve.com. Editor: John Burnham. Contact: Kristan McClintock, managing editor. 40% freelance written. Monthly magazine emphasizing performance sailing. Estab. 1962. Circ. 68,089. Pays on publication. Publishes ms an average of 4 months after acceptance. Buys first North American and world serial rights. Byline given. Reports in 3 months. Sample copy for $5.
Nonfiction: How-to for racing and performance-oriented sailors, photo feature, profile, regatta reports and charter. No travelogs. Buys 5-10 unsolicited mss/year. Query. Length: 500-1,500 words. Pays $150-200/page text.

Tips: "Send query with outline and include your experience. The writer may have a better chance of breaking in with short articles and fillers such as regatta news reports from his or her own area."

SEA KAYAKER, Sea Kayaker, Inc., P.O. Box 17170, Seattle WA 98107-0870. (206)789-1326. Fax: (206)781-1141. E-mail: seakayak@eskimo.com. Website: http://eskimo.com/~seakayak. Managing Editor: Christopher Cunningham. Contact: Karen Matthee, editor. 80% freelance written. Works frequently with new/unpublished writers each year. Bimonthly magazine on the sport of sea kayaking. Estab. 1984. Circ. 20,000. Pays on publication. Publishes ms an average of 6 months after acceptance. Byline given. Offers 10% kill fee. Buys first North American serial or second serial (reprint) rights. Submit seasonal material 6 months in advance. Reports in 2 months. Sample copy for $5.30. Writer's guidelines for SASE.
Nonfiction: Essays, historical, how-to (on making equipment), humor, profile, opinion, personal experience, technical, travel. Buys 40 mss/year. Query with or without published clips, or send complete ms. Length: 750-4,000 words. Pays about 12¢/word. Sometimes pays the expenses of writers on assignment.
Photos: Send photos with submission. Reviews contact sheets. Offers $25-100/photo. Captions requested. Buys one-time rights.
Columns/Departments: History, Safety, Environment, Journey. Length: 750-4,000 words. Pays 10¢/word, minimum.
Fiction: Kayak related adventure, fantasy, historical, humorous, mainstream, slice-of-life vignettes. Send complete ms. Length: 750-4,000 words. Pays about 12¢/word.
Tips: "We consider unsolicited manuscripts that include a SASE, but we give greater priority to brief descriptions (several paragraphs) of proposed articles accompanied by at least two samples—published or unpublished—of your writing. Enclose a statement as to why you're qualified to write the piece and indicate whether photographs or illustrations are available to accompany the piece."

TRAILER BOATS MAGAZINE, Poole Publications, Inc., 20700 Belshaw Ave., Carson CA 90746-3510. (310)537-6322. Fax: (310)537-8735. Editor: Randy Scott. Contact: Mike Blake, managing editor. 30-40% freelance written. Works with a small number of new/unpublished writers each year. Monthly magazine (November/December issue combined) covering legally trailerable power boats and related powerboating activities. Circ. 85,000. **Pays on acceptance.** Publishes ms 6 months after acceptance. Byline given. Buys all rights. Submit seasonal material 5 months in advance. Reports in 1 month. Sample copy $1.25; writer's guidelines for #10 SASE.
Nonfiction: General interest (trailer boating activities); historical (places, events, boats); how-to (repair boats, installation, etc.); humor (almost any power boating-related subject); nostalgia (same as historical); personal experience; photo feature; profile; technical; and travel (boating travel on water or highways), product evaluations. No "How I Spent My Summer Vacation" stories, or stories not even remotely connected to trailerable boats and related activities. Buys 18-30 unsolicited mss/year. Query or send complete ms. Length: 500-2,000 words. Pays $300-700 for features, $100 for short fill pieces. Pays expenses of writers on assignment.
Photos: Send photos with ms. Pays $10-75 for 8×10 b&w prints; $25-350 for color transparencies. Captions required.
Columns/Departments: Boaters Bookshelf (boating book reviews); Over the Transom (funny or strange boating photos). Buys 2/issue. Query. Length: 100-500 words. Watersports (boat-related), 750-1,000 words; Seamanship (experienced boaters' tips on navigation, survival, safety etc.), 750-1,000 words. Pays $350. Open to suggestions for new columns/departments.
Tips: "Query should contain short general outline of the intended material; what kind of photos; how the photos illustrate the piece. Write with authority, covering the subject like an expert. Frequent mistakes are not knowing the subject matter or the audience. Use basic information rather than prose, particularly in travel stories. The writer may have a better chance of breaking in at our publication with short articles and fillers if they are typically hard to find articles. We do most major features inhouse."

WATERWAY GUIDE, Intertec Publishing Corp., a K-III Media Co., 6151 Powers Ferry Rd. NW, Atlanta GA 30339-2941. (770)618-0313. Fax: (770)618-0349. Associate Publisher: Judith Powers. 90% freelance written. Quarterly magazine on intracoastal waterway travel for recreational boats. "Writer must be knowledgeable about navigation and the areas covered by the guide." Estab. 1947. Circ. 45,000. Pays on publication. Publishes ms an average of 3 months after acceptance. Byline given sometimes. Kill fee varies. Buys all rights. Reports in 3 months on queries; 4 months on mss. Sample copy for $33.95 with $3 postage.
Nonfiction: Historical/nostalgic, how-to, photo feature, technical, travel. "No personal boating experiences." Buys 25 mss/year. Query with or without published clips, or send complete ms. Length: 200 words minimum. Pays $50-3,000. Pays in contributor copies or other premiums for helpful tips and useful information.
Photos: Send photos with submission. Reviews 3×5 prints. Offers $50/color photo, $600/color photos used on the cover. Identification of subjects required. Buys one-time rights.
Fillers: Facts. Buys 6/year. Length: 250-1,000 words. Pays $50-150.
Tips: "Must have on-the-water experience and be able to provide new and accurate information on geographic areas covered by *Waterway Guide*."

‡WAVE-LENGTH PADDLING MAGAZINE, Wave-Length Communications, R.R. 1, Site 17, C-49, Gabriola Island, British Columbia V0R 1X0 Canada. (250)247-9789. E-mail: awilson@island.net. Managing Editor: Alan Wilson. 75% freelance written. Bimonthly magazine covering sea kayaking. "We promote safe paddling, guide paddlers to useful products and services and explore marine and coastal environmental issues." Estab. 1991. Circ. 20,000. Pays on publication. Publishes ms an average of 4 months after acceptance. Byline given. Offers 10% kill fee. Buys first North American serial and electronic reprint rights. Editorial lead time 2 months. Submit seasonal material 2 months in advance. Reports in 2 months. Sample copy for $2.

Nonfiction: Book excerpts, essays, how-to (paddle, travel), humor, interview/profile, new product, opinion, personal experience, technical, travel. Buys 25 mss/year. Query. Length: 700-2,000 words. Pays $50-100. Pays businesses with advertising.

Photos: State availability of photos with submission. Reviews 4×6 prints. Offers $25-50/photo. Captions, model releases and identification of subjects required. Buys first and electronic rights. Query.

Columns/Departments: Environmental (marine issues), 1,000 words; Gear/Accessories, 1,000 words; Trips/Destinations (experience-based pieces), 1,500 words. Buys 12 mss/year. Query. Pays $50-100.

Fiction: Adventure, humorous. "Unless it has strong paddling aspect, don't bother." Query. Length: 700-1,500 words. Pays $50-75.

Poetry: Free verse, light verse. "Has to be paddling focused." Submit maximum 4 poems. Length: 10-25 words. Pays $10-25.

Fillers: Anecdotes, facts, gags to be illustrated by cartoonist, newsbreaks and short humor. Buys 8-10/year. Length: 25-250 words. Pays $10-25.

Tips: "You must know paddling—although novice paddlers are welcome. A strong environmental or wilderness appreciation component is advisable. We are willing to help refine work with flexible people. E-mail queries preferred."

WOODENBOAT MAGAZINE, The Magazine for Wooden Boat Owners, Builders, and Designers, WoodenBoat Publications, Inc., P.O. Box 78, Brooklin ME 04616. (207)359-4651. Fax: (207)359-8920. E-mail: wbeditor@woodenboat.com. Editor-in-Chief: Jonathan A. Wilson. Contact: Matthew P. Murphy, editor. Senior Editor: Mike O'Brien. Managing Editor: Jenny Bennett. 50% freelance written. Works with a small number of new/unpublished writers each year. Bimonthly magazine for wooden boat owners, builders and designers. "We are devoted exclusively to the design, building, care, preservation, and use of wooden boats, both commercial and pleasure, old and new, sail and power. We work to convey quality, integrity and involvement in the creation and care of these craft, to entertain, inform, inspire, and to provide our varied readers with access to individuals who are deeply experienced in the world of wooden boats." Estab. 1974. Circ. 106,000. Pays on publication. Publishes ms an average of 1 year after acceptance. Byline given. Offers variable kill fee. Buys first North American serial rights. Accepts simultaneous submissions. Reports in 3 weeks on queries; 2 months on mss. Sample copy for $4.50. Writer's guidelines for SASE.

Nonfiction: Technical (repair, restoration, maintenance, use, design and building wooden boats). No poetry, fiction. Buys 50 mss/year. Query with published clips. Length: 1,500-5,000 words. Pays $150-200/1,000 words. Sometimes pays expenses of writers on assignment.

Reprints: Send tearsheet or photocopy of article or typed ms with rights for sale noted with information about when and where the article previously appeared.

Photos: Send photos with query. Negatives must be available. Pays $15-75 for b&w; $25-350 for color. Identification of subjects required. Buys one-time rights.

Columns/Departments: On the Waterfront pays for information on wooden boat-related events, projects, boatshop activities, etc. Buys 25/year. "We use the same columnists for each issue." Send complete information. Length: 250-1,000 words. Pays $5-50 for information.

Tips: "We appreciate a detailed, articulate query letter, accompanied by photos, that will give us a clear idea of what the author is proposing. We appreciate samples of previously published work. It is important for a prospective author to become familiar with our magazine first. It is extremely rare for us to make an assignment with a writer with whom we have not worked before. Most work is submitted on speculation. The most common failure is not exploring the subject material in enough depth."

YACHTING, Times Mirror Magazines Inc., 20 E. Elm St., Greenwich CT 06830. (203)625-4480. Fax: (203)625-4481. Publisher: Linda Lindquist. Editor-in-Chief: Charles Barthold. 50% freelance written. "The magazine is written and edited for experienced, knowledgeable yachtsmen." Estab. 1907. Circ. 130,000. Pays on publication. Byline given. Buys first rights. Submit seasonal material 6 months in advance. Reports in 1 month.

Nonfiction: Book excerpts, personal experience, photo feature, travel. No cartoons, fiction, poetry. Query with published clips. Length: 250-2,000 words. Pays $250-1,000. Pays expenses of writers on assignment.

Photos: Send photos with submission. Reviews 35mm transparencies. Offers some additional payment for photos accepted with ms. Captions, model releases and identification of subjects required.

Columns/Departments: Cruising Yachtsman (stories on cruising; contact Dennis Caprio, senior editor); Yacht Yard (how-to and technical pieces on yachts and their systems; contact Dennis Caprio, senior editor). Buys 30 mss/year. Send complete ms. Length: 750 words maximum. Pays $250-500.

Tips: "We require considerable expertise in our writing because our audience is experienced and knowledgeable. Vivid descriptions of quaint anchorages and quainter natives are fine, but our readers want to know how the yachtsmen got there, too. They also want to know how their boats work."

"*Yachting* is edited for experienced, affluent boatowners—power and sail—who don't have the time nor the inclination to read sub-standard stories. They love carefully crafted stories about places they've never been or a different spin on places they have, meticulously reported pieces on issues that affect their yachting lives, personal accounts of yachting experiences from which they can learn, engaging profiles of people who share their passion for boats, insightful essays that evoke the history and traditions of the sport and compelling photographs of others enjoying the game as much as they do. They love to know what to buy and how things work. They love to be surprised. They don't mind getting their hands dirty or saving a buck here and there, but they're not interested in learning how to make a masthead light out of a mayonnaise jar. If you love what they love and can communicate like a pro (that means meeting deadlines, writing tight, being obsessively accurate and never misspelling a proper name), we'd love to hear from you."

Bowling

BOWLING, Dept. WM, 5301 S. 76th St., Greendale WI 53129. (414)423-3232. Fax: (414)421-7977. Contact: Bill Vint, editor. 15% freelance written. Bimonthly, official publication of the American Bowling Congress. Estab. 1934. Circ. 135,000. **Pays on acceptance.** Publishes ms an average of 2 months after acceptance. Byline given. Rights purchased vary with author and material; usually buys all rights. Reports in 1 month. Sample copy for $2.50.
Nonfiction: "This is a specialized field and the average writer attempting the subject of bowling should be well-informed. However, anyone is free to submit material for approval." Wants articles about unusual ABC sanctioned leagues and tournaments, personalities, etc., featuring male bowlers. Nostalgia articles also considered. No first-person articles or material on history of bowling. Length: 500-1,200 words. Pays $100-300. No poems, songs or fiction.
Photos: Pays $10-15/photo.
Tips: "Submit feature material on bowlers, generally amateurs competing in local leagues, or special events involving the game of bowling. Should have connection with ABC membership. Queries should be as detailed as possible so that we may get a clear idea of what the proposed story would be all about. It saves us time and the writer time. Samples of previously published material in the bowling or general sports field would help. Once we find a talented writer in a given area, we're likely to go back to him in the future. We're looking for good writers who can handle assignments professionally and promptly." No articles on professionals.

Gambling

BLACKJACK FORUM, RGE Publishing, 414 Santa Clara Ave., Oakland CA 94610. (510)465-6452. Fax: (510)465-4330. E-mail: asnyder@rge21.com. Website: http://www.rge21.com. Editor: Arnold Synder. 40% freelance written. Quarterly magazine covering casino blackjack. "For sophisticated and knowledgeable casino gamblers interested in legal issues, mathematical analyses, computer simulations, commonplace techniques. This is *not* a get-rich-quick type mag." Estab. 1981. Circ. 2,500. Pays on publication. Publishes ms an average of 6 months after acceptance. Byline given. Buys first and second serial (reprint) rights. Editorial lead time 6 months. Submit seasonal material 6 months in advance. Reports in 4 months on queries. Sample copy for $12.50.
Nonfiction: Exposé, how-to, personal experience, technical, travel. Buys 10-12 mss/year. Query or send complete ms. Length: 200-3,000 words. Pays $35/page. Sometimes pays expenses of writers on assignment.
Reprints: Send tearsheet or photocopy of article or typed ms with rights for sale noted and information about when and where the article previously appeared. Payment negotiable.
Photos: State availability of or send photos with submission. Reviews contact sheets, prints. Negotiates payment individually. Buys one-time rights.
Columns/Departments: Around The States (reports on blackjack conditions in US casinos); Around The World (ditto for foreign casinos); both 200-1,500 words. Buys 25 mss/year. Query or send complete ms. Pays in contributor's copies—$35.
Fiction: Publishes novel excerpts.
Tips: "Be very knowledgeable about casino blackjack, especially familiar with all noted authors—Thorp, Revere, Uston, Wong, Griffin, Carlson, etc."

CASINO REVIEW, Hyde Park Media, 635 Chicago Ave., #250, Evanston IL 60202. Contact: Articles Editor. 80% freelance written. Bimonthly covering casino and other legal gambling. Estab. 1994. Circ. 50,000. Pays on publication. Publishes ms an average of 4 months after acceptance. Byline given. Buys first rights, one-time rights, second serial (reprint) rights, simultaneous rights and all rights. Editorial lead time 4 months. Accepts simultaneous submissions. Reports in 1 month on queries; 2 months on mss. Sample copy for $4 and 10×13 SAE.
Nonfiction: Book excerpts, historical/nostalgic, how-to, humor, inspirational, interview/profile, opinion, personal experience, photo feature, travel (all with a gambling hook). Buys 100-150 mss/year. Query or send complete ms. Length: 800-2,000 words. Pays $50-250 for assigned articles; $25-100 for unsolicited articles.
Reprints: Send typed ms with rights for sale noted.
Photos: State availability of photos with submission. Reviews 5×7 prints. Negotiates payment individually. Captions, model releases, identification of subjects required. Buys all rights.
Tips: "Detailed queries and having quality art to go along with any proposed articles. We're always looking for highly stylized, quality art, i.e., photos and line art."

LOTTOWORLD MAGAZINE, Dynamic World Distributors, Inc., 2150 Goodlette Rd., Suite 200, Naples FL 34102. (813)643-1677. Fax: (941)263-0809. E-mail: ringle29@aol.com or vpyn24b@prodigy.com. Website: http://www.lottow

orldmagazine.com. Editor-in-Chief: Rich Holman. Managing Editor: Barry Miller. Contact: Lynne Groth, assistant editor. 60% freelance written. Monthly magazine covering lottery-related news. "LottoWorld Magazine is a national lottery news magazine targeted to the 100 million U.S. lottery players. Each issue is devoted to systems, tips, strategies, techniques and research 40%; human interest stories 30%; winning pick forecasting 20%; software, astrology, miscellaneous 10%." Estab. 1993. Pays 30 days after publication. Buys exclusive serial rights. Editorial lead time 2 months. Sample copy or writers guidelines for 8×11 SAE with 87¢ postage.

Nonfiction: General interest, how-to, humor, interview/profile, photo feature. Buys 36-72 mss/year. Query. Length: 400-1,200 words. Pay negotiated. Sometimes pays expenses of writers on assignment.

Photos: Freelancers should send photos with submission. Reviews prints. Additional payment for photos accepted with ms.

General Interest

‡**ALL-STATER SPORTS, America's High School Sports Almanac**, All-Stater Publishing, Inc., 315 Falmouth Dr., P.O. Box 16100, Rocky River OH 44116. (216)356-5682. Fax: (216)356-9485. E-mail: assports@aol.com. Contact: Nancy Petro, editor. 80% freelance written. Tabloid published 5 times/year covering high school sports. "The mission of *All-Stater Sports* is to inform, inspire and recognize today's high school student-athlete. Our audience consists of student-athletes, coaches and athletic directors, but our intention is to speak primarily to student-athletes." Estab. 1995. Circ. 25,000. Pays on publication. Publishes ms an average of 1 month after acceptance. Byline given. Editorial lead time 2 months. Submit seasonal material 1 month in advance. Accepts simultaneous and previously published submissions. Reports in 2 weeks on queries. Sample copy $5.50 for writers only.

Nonfiction: How-to (training, cross-training, strength building, etc.), humor inspirational, interview/profile, new product, opinion, personal experience, photo feature, technical (sports issues, skill building). Pays $50-100. "Profiles writers in our contributor's column, provides extra copies of issue, plugs product, institution, company, etc. Sometimes pays expenses of writers on assignment.

Photos: State availability of photos with submission. Reviews 5×7 minimum prints. Negotiates payment individually. Model release (if deemed necessary) and identification of subjects required. Buys one-time rights.

Columns-Departments: Getting The Edge (sports training/skill building), 1,200 words; Next Step articles about sports in (college sports), 1,200 words; Winning with Heart (overcoming odds to play sports), 1,000 words; In Recognition of Sportsmanship (specific act of sportsmanship in high school sports—real incidents), 1,000 words. Buys 10-15 mss/year. Query. Pays $50-100.

Fillers: Anecdotes, facts, gags to be illustrated by cartoonist, newsbreaks, short humor. Length: 50-300 words. Pays $15-30.

Tips: "We are happy to consider any material that would be of interest to high school athletes—even something that is not already included in our issues printed to date. We profile outstanding achievers, but would also like to have human interest stories of accomplishment, satisfaction, team bonding, unusually fine coaches, etc., from non-blue chipper's perspective as well."

‡**CABLE SPORTS NETWORK**, CSN-Sports, Probasketball Electronic Services, Inc., 27 Fletcher Ave., Sarasota FL 34237. (941)365-HOOP. E-mail: csn-sportsrobasketball.com. Website: http://www.probasketball.com. Contact: Mike Mullen, president. 75% freelance written. Weekly online magazines, each covering a different sport providing sports content for online services. "Cable Sports Network (CSN), a division of ProBasketball Electronic Services, Inc., provides sports content to online services (including Prodigy) and to thousands of computer bulletin board systems." Estab. 1988. Circ. 3,000,000. **Pays on acceptance.** Publishes ms an average of 1 month after acceptance. Byline given. Buys electronic media rights. Editorial lead time 1 month. Submit seasonal material 1 month in advance. Accepts simultaneous submissions. Reports in 3 weeks on mss; reports on e-mail submissions more quickly. Sample copies and writer's guidelines on website.

Nonfiction: Expose, general interest, how-to, humor, interview/profile, new product, personal experience, religious (player testimony). "If you can read about it in the newspaper, we don't want it, our readers already know about it. Companies pay us to provide them with original content, or at least reprint material that is of special interest. Sports fans have their own strong opinions, so unless you are famous, no opinions." Buys 300 mss/year. Send complete ms. Length: 250-1,000 words. Pays 10¢/word.

Reprints: Accepts previously published submissions.

Photos: State availability of photos with submission. "Note: photos of major sports would infringe on league copyrights." Reviews prints, snapshots. Negotiates payment individually. Identification of subjects required. Buys electronic media rights.

Columns/Departments: Basketball, baseball, football, hockey, motor sports, the great outdoors (fishing, hunting, biking, camping, etc.), soccer, water sports (boating, swimming, diving, sailing), and Christian testimony from professional or high-profile college athletes.

Fillers: Anecdotes, facts, newsbreaks, short humor. Length: 50-250 words. Pays 10¢/word.

Tips: "Help! I already have major advertisers for biking, skating, volleyball, fishing and other 'great outdoors' stories and everyone who contacts me wants to interview Michael Jordan. Send me a good short article about a 'minor' sport and I'll write you a check as soon as I read it. I don't want a query . . . . I want a finished manuscript. I love SLUSH!

Anything funny will get you another assignment. Minor league athletes LOVE to give interviews. Also any expose of a local team doing a no-no."

    "Until this year we have done only basketball. CSN was established to cover ALL sports. We need every well-written, short sports story we can get our hands on! We are also the largest sports-related commercial e-mailer in the world, sending one newsletter weekly for each sport we cover to a subscription list of more than 2 million readers. The important thing to realize is that our company consists of people who actually work for professional sports teams, so we want material from someone who really understands that particular sport. Also our readers want stories to be short so they don't have to 'page down' several times. We need stories almost on a daily basis. We have a stockpile of staff-written articles, but they go quickly. We need writers and more writers. I am a grad of *Writer's Digest* fiction and nonfiction schools, so I would love to see completed manuscripts from *Writer's Market* readers. 'Break-in' with us."

‡CONDÉ NAST SPORTS FOR WOMEN, Condé Nast Publications, Inc., 342 Madison Ave., 21st Floor, New York NY 10017. (212)880-8800. Fax: (212)880-4656. Contact: Stacy Morrison, managing editor. Monthly magazine covering sports from a women's perspective. "*Condé Nast Sports for Women* is a magazine all about participatory sports and spectator sports. We focus on women's involvement and roles in these everchanging fields." Estab. 1997. Circ. 350,000. **Pays on acceptance.** Byline given. Buys first North American serial and nonexclusive syndication rights. Reports in 2 months. Sample copy and writer's guidelines not yet available.
Nonfiction: "We're interested in emerging sport trends, athletes and attitudes, as well as breaking health and nutrition news. Buys 90 mss/year. Query with published clips. Length: 1,000-3,000 words. Pays $1/word.
Columns/Departments: FOB Score (gossip, culture, news). Pays $1/word. Other departments written by regular columnists.
Tips: "The best way to break in is to know something we don't: what's the new sport, the new hybrid sport, the new face in emerging sport trends.

THE FRONT ROW, The Publisher's Group, P.O. Box 510366, Salt Lake City UT 84151-0366. Fax: (801)322-1098. E-mail: annee@thepublishers.com. Contact: Anne E. Zombro, vice president of publishing. 50% freelance written. Quarterly magazine covering sports. "*The Front Row* covers the biggest names, the best games and everything in between. Emphasis is on professional sports. Also includes trivia, nostalgia, new equipment and outdoor sports." Estab. 1996. Circ. 20,000. Pays on publication. Publishes ms an average of 4 months after acceptance. Byline given. Buys first North American serial and second serial (reprint) rights. Editorial lead time 2 months. Submit seasonal material 4 months in advance. Accepts simultaneous submissions. Reports in 1 month on queries; 2 months on mss. Sample copy for $3 and 9×12 SASE. Writer's guidelines for #10 SASE.
Nonfiction: Book excerpts, humor, inspirational, interview/profile (of pro athletes). Buys 6 mss/year. Query with published clips. Length: 1,000-1,300 words. Pays $125-800.
Reprints: Accepts previously published submissions.Pays 50% of amount paid for an original article.
Photos: Send photos with submission. Reviews 4×5 transparencies, any size prints. Negotiates payment individually. Captions, model releases, identification of subjects required. Buys one-time or all rights.
Columns/Departments: Famous Moments (nostalgia), Rules (updates), Personal Experiences (outdoor adventures) all 500 words. Buys 6-8 mss/year. Query with published clips. Pays $50-125.

INSIDE SPORTS, Century Publishing Co., 990 Grove St., Evanston IL 60201. (847)491-6440. Contact: Ken Leiker, editor. 90% freelance written. Monthly magazine. "*Inside Sports*' contributors Mike Ditka, John Feinstein, Chuck Daly, Stedman Graham, Bob Trumpy and others provide sports enthusiasts of all kinds with previews and predictions, profiles, and insights that go beyond scores and statistics. The publication focuses solely on the big six sports of football, basketball, baseball, hockey, motor sports, and boxing." Circ. 675,000. Pays on publication. Publishes ms an average of 2-3 months after acceptance. Byline given. Offers 50% kill fee. Rights are negotiated individually. Reports on queries and mss in 6 weeks.
Nonfiction: Query with or without published clips, or send complete ms. Length of article and payment vary with each article and writer. Most run 2,000-3,500 words. Pays 10¢-$1/word. "Please include a SASE with query/article."
Columns/Departments: The Insider, Media, Pro & Con, Inside Interview, Numbers, The Fan. All 300-700 words.
Tips: "Please do not query us on obvious ideas; please limit submissions and queries to exclusive (not mass-mailed to other publications) and unique ideas."

NEW YORK OUTDOORS, 51 Atlantic Ave., Floral Park NY 11001. Fax: (516)437-6841. Fax: (516)487-6841. E-mail: nyomag@aol.com. Contact: Scott Shane, editor. 100% freelance written. Estab. 1992. Buys first North American serial rights. Publishes ms an average of 6 months after acceptance. Reports in 1 month on queries. Writer's guidelines for #10 SASE.
Nonfiction: "*New York Outdoors* is dedicated to providing information to its readers about all outdoor participatory activities in New York and its surrounding states. Paddlesports, camping, fishing, boating, skiing, travel, hiking, cycling, 'adventure' sports, etc." Query. Length: 1,500-2,000 words. A good selection of transparencies must accompany mss. Pays $250. Lead time 4 months. "Aside from accurate and interesting writing, provide source material for our readers who may wish to try the activity. We also use shorter pieces (to 500 words) on the same type of topics, but focusing on a single event, person, place or occurrence. Query. Pays up to $100."
Reprints: Send photocopy of article and information about where and when article previously appeared. Pays 35% of

amount paid for an original article.

Tips: Would like to see more queries on camping, hiking, in line, climbing, fishing, boating, skiing adventure, mountain biking topic areas with destination focus.

OUTDOOR ACTION MAGAZINE, Eagle Outdoor Publishing, P.O. Box 1431, Eagle ID 83616. (208)939-4500. Fax: (208)939-4600. Contact: Aaron Bible, editor. 75% freelance written. Monthly magazine covering outdoor-adventure sports. Estab. 1995. Circ. 40,000. Pays on publication. Publishes ms an average of 4 months after acceptance. Byline given. Buys first North American serial and one-time rights. Editorial lead time 4 months. Submit seasonal material 4 months in advance. Accepts simultaneous submissions. Writer's guidelines for SASE.

Nonfiction: How-to, humor, personal experience, photo feature. Query. Pays $250-750 for assigned articles; $350 maximum for unsolicited articles. Sometimes pays expenses of writers on assignment.

Reprints: Send tearsheets or photocopy of article or typed ms with rights for sale noted and information about when and where the article previously appeared. Payment negotiable.

Photos: State availability of photos with submission. Reviews contact sheets, transparencies. Negotiates payment individually. Captions, identification of subjects required. Buys one-time rights.

Columns/Departments: Query.

Fillers: Buys 10-15/year. Length: 200-500 words. Pays $350.

Tips: "Best way to break in are '50 tips' articles, trivia articles, locations of where to go mountain biking, rockclimbing, kayaking, hiking in U.S."

ROCKY MOUNTAIN SPORTS MAGAZINE, Rocky Mountain Sports, Inc., 428 E. 11th Ave, Suite 104, Denver CO 80203. (303)861-9229. Fax: (303)861-9209. Website: http://www.diveindenver.com. Publisher: Mary Thorne. Editor: Don Silver. 50% freelance written. Monthly magazine of sports in the Rocky Mountain States and Canada. "*Rocky* is a magazine for sports-related lifestyles and activities. Our mission is to reflect and inspire the active lifestyle of Rocky Mountain residents." Estab. 1987. Circ. 45,000. Pays on publication. Publishes ms an average of 2 months after acceptance. Byline given. Offers 25% kill fee. Buys second serial (reprint) rights. Editorial lead time 1½ months. Submit seasonal material 2 months in advance. Reports in 3 weeks on queries; 2 months on mss. Sample copy and writer's guidelines for #10 SASE.

• The editor of this publication says he wants to see mountain outdoor sports writing **only**. No ball sports, no hunting, no fishing.

Nonfiction: Book excerpts, essays, exposé, how-to: (no specific sports, trips, adventures), humor, inspirational, interview/profile, new product, opinion, personal experience, photo feature, travel. Special issues: Snowboarding (December); Alpine and Nordic (January and February); Mountain Biking (April). No articles on football, baseball, basketball or other sports covered in-depth by newspapers. Buys 24 mss/year. Query with published clips. Length: 2,500 words maximum. Pays $150 minimum. Also publishes short articles on active outdoor sports, catchall topics that are seasonably targeted. Query with idea first. Pays 10-15¢/word. Sometimes pays expenses of writers on assignment.

Reprints: Send photocopy of article or short story. Pays 20-50% of amount paid for an original article.

Photos: State availability of photos with submission. Reviews transparencies and prints. Offers $25-250/photo. Captions and identification of subjects required. Buys one-time rights.

Columns/Departments: Scree (short newsy items), 50-800 words; High Altitude (essay on quirky topics related to Rockies). Buys 20 mss/year. Query. Pays $25-200.

Tips: "Submit stories for the Scree section first."

SILENT SPORTS, Waupaca Publishing Co., P.O. Box 152, Waupaca WI 54981-9990. (715)258-5546. Fax: (715)258-8162. Contact: Greg Marr, editor. 75% freelance written. Eager to work with new/unpublished writers. Monthly magazine on running, cycling, cross-country skiing, canoeing, in-line skating, camping, backpacking and hiking aimed at people in Wisconsin, Minnesota, northern Illinois and portions of Michigan and Iowa. "Not a coffee table magazine. Our readers are participants from rank amateur weekend athletes to highly competitive racers." Estab. 1984. Circ. 10,000. Pays on publication. Publishes ms an average of 3 months after acceptance. Byline given. Offers 20% kill fee. Buys one-time rights. Submit seasonal material 4 months in advance. Reports in 3 months. Sample copy and writer's guidelines for 10×13 SAE with 6 first-class stamps.

• The editor needs local angles on in-line skating, recreation bicycling and snowshoeing.

Nonfiction: General interest, how-to, interview/profile, opinion, technical, travel. All stories/articles must focus on the Upper Midwest. First-person articles discouraged. Buys 25 mss/year. Query. Length: 2,500 words maximum. Pays $15-100. Sometimes pays expenses of writers on assignment.

Reprints: Send typed ms with rights for sale noted and information about when and where the article previously appeared. Pay negotiated.

Tips: "Where-to-go and personality profiles are areas most open to freelancers. Writers should keep in mind that this is a regional, Midwest-based publication. We want only stories/articles with a focus on our region."

SPORT, Petersen Publishing Co., 6420 Wilshire Blvd., Los Angeles CA 90048-5515. (213)782-2828. Fax: (213)782-2835. E-mail: sport@petersonpub.com. Editor: Cam Benty. 80% freelance written. Monthly magazine "for the active adult sports fan. *Sport* offers profiles of the players and the people behind the scenes in the world of sports. *Sport* magazine is the oldest, largest, monthly sports feature publication reaching over 4.3 million young, active, sports-minded enthusiasts each issue. Not a recap of what happened last week, but previews and predictions of what will happen this

month, next month, next year. In-depth profiles, investigative reporting, lively features about the action on and off the field! *Sport* magazine is the complete sports magazine written and edited for the ultimate sports fan!" Estab. 1946. Circ. 792,000. **Pays on acceptance**. Publishes ms an average of 3 months after acceptance. Offers 25% kill fee. Buys first North American serial or all rights. Reports in 2 months.
Nonfiction: "Prefers to see articles on professional, big-time sports: basketball, football, baseball, with some boxing. The articles we buy must be contemporary pieces, not a history of sports or a particular sport." Query with published clips. Length: News briefs, 200-300 words; Departments, 1,400 words; Features, 1,500-3,000 words. Averages 50¢/word for articles.

THE SPORTING NEWS, 10176 Corporate Square Dr., Suite 200, St. Louis MO 63132. E-mail: tsnsjm@aol.com. Executive Editor: Steve Meyerhoff. Published weekly for men with intense sports interests. **Pays on acceptance.** Byline given. Offers variable. Buys first North American serial rights and electronic rights. Accepts simultaneous and previously published submissions. Reports in 1 month. Writer's guidelines for #10 SASE.
Nonfiction: "Needs pieces for avid sports fans with in-depth knowledge of sports." Buys 5 mss/year. Query. Query with published clips or send complete ms. Length: 2,000-5,000 words. Pay varies. Pays the expenses of writers on assignment.
Columns/Departments: Buys 5 mss/year. Query, query with published clips or send complete ms. Length: 750-1,000 words. Pay varies.
Fillers: Buys 5/year. Length: 750 words. Pay varies.

SPORTS ILLUSTRATED, Time Inc. Magazine Co., Time & Life Bldg., Rockefeller Center, New York NY 10020. (212)522-1212. Contact: Myra Gelband. Weekly magazine covering sports. "*Sports Illustrated* reports and interprets the world of sport, recreation and active leisure. It previews, analyzes and comments upon major games and events, as well as those noteworthy for character and spirit alone. It features individuals connected to sport and evaluates trends concerning the part sport plays in contemporary life. In addition, the magazine has articles on such subjects as fashion, physical fitness and conservation. Special departments deal with sports equipment, books and statistics." Estab. 1954. Circ. 3,339,000. Query by mail only before submitting.

‡SPORTS SPECTRUM, Discovery House Publishers, Box 3566, Grand Rapids MI 49501. (616)954-1276. Fax: (616)957-5741. E-mail: ssmag@sport.org. Website: http://www.sport.org/. Contact: Dave Branon, managing editor. *Sports Spectrum* is produced monthly as a way of presenting the Christian faith through the lives of Christian athletes. Writers should share our interest in telling readers about Jesus Christ. Estab. 1987. Circ. 50,000. Pays on publication. Publishes ms an average of 2 months after acceptance. Byline given. Offers 40% kill fee. Not copyrighted. Buys first North American print rights. Editorial lead time 4 months. Reports in 1 month on queries. Sample copy for 8½×11 SAE and 4 first-class stamps. Writer's guidelines free.
Nonfiction: Interview/profile. No poems, reprints, fiction, profiles of sports ministries or unsolicited mss. Buys 60 mss/year. Query with published clips. Length: 725-2,000 words. Pays $110-340. Sometimes pays expenses of writers on assignment.
Photos: State availability of photos with submission. Reviews transparencies and prints. Negotiates payment individually.
Columns/Departments: Leaderboard (athletes in service to others), 725 words; Front Row (sports scene), 800 words. Buys 15 mss/year. Query with published clips. Pays $110-125.
Tips: "Make sure you understand our unique purpose and can write articles that contribute to the purpose. Send a query letter and clips. Tell why your story idea fits and how you propose to research the article."

WINDY CITY SPORTS MAGAZINE, Windy City Publishing, 1450 W. Randolph, Chicago IL 60607. (312)421-1551. Fax: (312)421-1454. E-mail: wcpublish@aol.com. Contact: Jeff Banowetz, editor. 75% freelance written. Monthly magazine covering amateur, participatory sports. Estab. 1987. Circ. 100,000 (Chicago and suburbs). Pays on publication. Offers 25% kill fee. Buys one-time rights. Editorial lead time 2 months. Submit seasonal material 2-12 months in advance. Accepts simultaneous submissions. Reports in 1 month on queries. Sample copy for $3 or 11½×14 SAE with $2 in postage. Writer's guidelines free on request.
Nonfiction: Essays (re: sports controversial issues), how-to (do sports), inspirational (profiles of accomplished athletes), interview/profile, new product, opinion, personal experience, photo feature (in Chicago), travel. No articles on professional sports. Special issues: Chicago Marathon (October); Skiing and Snowboarding (November); Winter Sports (December). Buys 120 mss/year. Query with clips. Length: 500-1,200 words. Pays 10¢/word. Sometimes pays expenses of writers on assignment.
Reprints: Send information about when and where the article previously appeared.
Photos: State availability or send photos with submission. Reviews contact sheets and prints. Negotiates payment individually. Captions and identification of subjects required. Buys one-time rights.
Columns/Departments: "We run the following columns every month: running, cycling, fitness centers, nutrition, sports medicine, women's, road trip (adventure travel) and in-line skating, all 1,000-1,200 words." Buys 70 mss/year. Query with published clips. Pays $125.
Fillers: Anecdotes, facts, gags to be illustrated by cartoonist, short humor. Buys 10/year. Length: 20-500 words. Pays $25-100.

Tips: "Best way to get assignment: ask for writer's guidelines, editor's schedule and sample copy ($3). *Read magazine!* Query me with story ideas for a column or query on features using editorial schedule. Always try to target Chicago looking Midwest."

WOMEN'S SPORTS + FITNESS MAGAZINE, Women's Sports & Fitness, Inc., 2025 Pearl St., Boulder CO 80302-5323. (303)440-5111. Fax: (303)440-3313. E-mail: dagnywsf@aol.com. Website: http://www.women.com. Senior Editor: Jean Weiss. Editor: Dagny Scott. Contact: Heather Prouty, assistant editor. 90% freelance written. Works with a small number of new/unpublished writers each year. Magazine published 9 times/year emphasizing women's sports, fitness and health. Estab. 1974. Circ. 210,000. **Pays on acceptance.** Publishes ms an average of 3 months after acceptance. Buys first North American serial rights. Submit seasonal material 3 months in advance. Sample copy for $5 and 9×12 SAE. Writer's guidelines for #10 SASE.

Nonfiction: Profile, service piece, interview, how-to, historical, personal experience, new product. "All articles should have the latest information from knowledgeable sources. All must be of national interest to athletic women." Buys 4 mss/issue. Length: 500-1,500 words. Query with published clips. Pays $500-2,000 for features, including expenses.

Reprints: Sometimes accepts previously published submissions. Send photocopy of article or typed ms with rights for sale noted and information about when and where the article previously appeared. Payment varies.

Photos: State availability of photos. Pays about $125-300 for b&w prints; $125-300 for 35mm color transparencies or prints. Buys one-time rights.

Columns/Departments: News + Views (The latest buzz on what's happening with people, events and products inside the world of sports and fitness); Winning Ways (Profiles of inspiring non-professionals who compete at a high level in their sport. These are working moms and students—our readers—who manage to train and compete with the best.); Being There (First-person accounts of exciting or unusual sports and adventures.); Leveling the Field (The Women's Sports Foundation reports on issues involving women in sport.); Training (The latest techniques on how to make the most of your workouts.); Nutrition (How to stay fueled for your optimal performance.); Body and Soul (Alternative and holistic approaches to health and fitness.); Great Gear (Roundups and reviews of the latest in sports equipment fit for a woman.); Wild Women (Spectacular and inspiring images of women in sport.); Observations (From the humorous to the sublime, first-person musings on what we do as women athletes and why we do it.). All 200-750 words. Buys 5-8/issue. Query with published clips. Pays $100-400.

Tips: "If the writer doesn't have published clips, best advice for breaking in is to concentrate on columns and departments (News & Views and Health & Fitness) first. Query letters should tell why our readers—active women (with an average age in the mid-thirties) who partake in sports or fitness activities six times a week—would want to read the article. We're especially attracted to articles with a new angle, fresh or difficult-to-get information. We go after the latest in health, nutrition and fitness research, or reports about lesser-known women in sports who are on the threshold of greatness. We also present profiles of the best athletes and teams. We want the profiles to give insight into the person as well as the athlete. We have a cadre of writers whom we've worked with regularly, but we are always looking for new writers."

Golf

GOLF DIGEST, New York Times Magazine Co., Dept. WM, 5520 Park Ave., Trumbull CT 06611. (203)373-7000. Editor: Jerry Tarde. 30% freelance written. Monthly magazine covering golf. Circ. 1.45 million. **Pays on acceptance.** Publishes ms an average of 6 weeks after acceptance. Buys all rights. Byline given. Submit seasonal material 4 months in advance. Reports in 6 weeks.

Nonfiction: Melissa Lausten, editorial assistant. How-to, informational, historical, humor, inspirational, interview, nostalgia, opinion, profile, travel, new product, personal experience, photo feature, technical; "all on playing and otherwise enjoying the game of golf." Query. Length: 1,000-2,500 words. Pays $3,500 and up.

Photos: Nick DiDio, art director. Purchased without accompanying ms. Pays $75-150 for 5×7 or 8×10 b&w prints; $100-300/35mm transparency. Model release required.

Poetry: Lois Hains, assistant editor. Light verse. Buys 1-2/issue. Length: 4-8 lines. Pays $50.

Fillers: Lois Hains, assistant editor. Jokes, gags, anecdotes, cutlines for cartoons. Buys 1-2/issue. Length: 2-6 lines. Pays $25-50.

GOLF GEORGIA, Moorhead Publications, 121 Village Pkwy., Bldg. 3, Marietta GA 30067. (770)988-8864. Fax: (770)955-1156. Editor: Bill Gregory. 25% freelance written. Bimonthly magazine covering "golf-related stories or features with some connection to the state of Georgia or members of the state association." Estab. 1986. Circ. 72,500. Pays on publication. Publishes ms an average of 3 months after acceptance. Byline given. Not copyrighted. Buys first North American serial rights. Editorial lead time 6 months. Submit seasonal material 3 months in advance.

Nonfiction: Historical/nostalgic, inspirational, interview/profile, new product, personal experience, photo feature, travel. Buys 6-9 mss/year. Query with published clips. Length: 800-2,500 words. Pays $200-600 for assigned articles; $100-250 for unsolicited articles. Sometimes pays expenses of writers on assignment.

Fiction: Publishes novel excerpts.

Photos: State availability of photos with submission. Reviews contact sheets. Negotiates payment individually. Model releases, identification of subjects required. Buys all rights.

GOLF ILLUSTRATED, Kachina Publications, Suite 250, 5050 N. 40th St., Phoenix AZ 85018. (918)491-6100. Fax: (918)491-9424. Editor-in-Chief: Mark Chestnut. Contact: Jason Sowards, managing editor. 15% freelance written. Monthly magazine for golf. "We cover everything and anything to do with golf, but we're not into the *politics* of the game. Humor, history, profiles of influential figures in golf, are the primary focus." Estab. 1983. Circ. 500,000. **Pays 30 days after acceptance.** Publishes ms an average of 3 months after acceptance. Byline given. Offers 20% kill fee. Buys first North American serial rights. Editorial lead time 10 weeks. Submit seasonal material 6 months in advance. Reports in 2 months on queries. Writer's guidelines free on request.
Nonfiction: Historical/nostalgic, how-to (golf instruction), humor, interview/profile (golf figures), technical, travel (focus on golf) and golf equipment. "No opinion or politics." Buys 20 mss/year. Query. Length: 1,500-2,000 words. Pays $1/word minimum. Sometimes pays expenses of writers on assignment.
Photos: Negotiates payment individually. Identification of subjects required. Buys one-time rights.
Columns/Departments: Gallery Shots (humorous short pieces), 200-400 words. Buys 40 mss/year. Query. Pays $50-400.
Fiction: Humorous and slice-of-life vignettes. Publishes novel excerpts. Buys 10 mss/year. Query. Length: 1,000-1,500 words. Pays $1/word minimum.
Poetry: Light verse. Buys 8 poems/year. Submit maximum 5 poems. Length: 10-20 lines. Pays $50-100.
Fillers: Anecdotes and short humor. Buys 20/year. Length: 50-200 words. Pays $50-200.
Tips: "Offer a unique perspective; short and sweet queries with SASE are appreciated. *Don't* call up every two weeks to find out when your story is going to be published. Be patient, we get lots of submissions and try our best to respond promptly. We are most open to humorous pieces—anything genuinely well-written."

‡**GOLF TIPS, The Game's Most In-Depth Instruction & Equipment Magazine**, Werner Publishing Corp., 12121 Wilshire Blvd., Suite 1200, Los Angeles CA 90025. (310)820-1500. Fax: (310)820-2793. Editor: Tom Dellner. Associate Editor: David DeNunzio. Contact: John Ledesma, managing editor. 95% freelance written. Magazine published 9 times/year covering golf instruction and equipment. "We provide mostly concise, very clear golf instruction pieces for the serious golfer." Estab. 1986. Circ. 275,000. Pays on publication. Publishes ms an average of 2 months after acceptance. Byline given. Offers 33% kill fee. Buys first rights and second serial (reprint) rights. Editorial lead time 3 months. Submit seasonal material 4 months in advance. Accepts previously published submissions. Reports in 1 month. Sample copy and writer's guidelines free.
Nonfiction: Book excerpts, how-to, interview/profile, new product, photo feature, technical, travel: all golf related. "General golf essays rarely make it." Buys 125 mss/year. Send complete ms. Length: 250-2,000 words. Pays $300-750 for assigned articles; $300-800 unsolicited articles. Occasionally negotiates other forms of payment. Sometimes pays expenses of writers on assignment.
Photos: State availability of photos with submission. Reviews 2×2 transparencies. Negotiates payment individually. Captions and identification of subjects required. Buys all rights.
Columns/Departments: Stroke Saver (very clear, concise instruction), 350 words; Fore Women (specific instruction for women), 750 words; Travel Tips (formated golf travel), 2,500 words. Buys 40 mss/year. Query with published clips or send complete ms. Pays $300-850.
Tips: "Contact a respected PGA Professional and find out if they're interested in being published. A good writer can turn an interview into a decent instruction piece."

‡**GOLF TRAVELER, Official Publication of Golf Card International**, Affinity Group, Inc., 2575 Vista del Mar, Ventura CA 93001. Fax: (805)667-4217. E-mail: vlaw@affinity.com. Website: www.tl.com. Contact: Valerie Law, editor. 90% freelance written. Bimonthly magazine "is the membership magazine for the Golf Card an organization that offers its 130,000 members reduced or waived greens fees at 3,000 affiliated golf courses in North America." Estab. 1976. Circ. 130,000. **Pays on acceptance.** Byline given. Offers 33% kill fee. Buys first North American serial rights. Editorial lead time 4 months. Submit seasonal material 4 months in advance. Accepts simultaneous and previously published submissions. Reports in 1 month. Sample copy for $2.50. Writer's guidelines free with SASE.
Nonfiction: Book excerpts, essays, how-to, interview/profile, new product, personal experience, photo feature, technical. PGA Orlando Merchandise Show (January-February). No poetry or cartoons. Buys 25 mss/year. Query with published clips or send complete ms. Length: 500-2,500 words. Pays $75-500. Sometimes pays expenses of writers on assignment.
Photos: Send photos with submission. Reviews transparencies. Negotiates payment individually. Model releases and identification of subjects required. Buys one-time rights.
Tips: "We're always looking for golf writers who can put together destination features revolving around our affiliated golf courses."

ALWAYS ENCLOSE a self-addressed, stamped envelope (SASE) with all your queries and correspondence.

‡GULF COAST GOLFER, Golfer Magazines, Inc., 9182 Old Katy Rd., Houston TX 77055. (713)464-0308. Fax: (713)464-0129. Editor: Bob Gray. Contact: Carl Mickelson, associate editor. 30% freelance written. Monthly tabloid covering golf in Texas. Estab. 1984. Circ. 35,000. Pays on publication. Publishes ms an average of 2 months after acceptance. Byline given. Buys first, one-time or second serial (reprint) rights. Editorial lead time 2 months. Submit seasonal material 3 months in advance. Reports in 2 weeks on queries; 1 month on mss. Sample copy free. Prefers direct phone discussion for writer's guidelines.

Nonfiction: Book excerpts, humor, personal experience all golf-related. No stories about golf outside of Texas. Buys 40 mss/year. Query. Pays $50-425.

Photos: State availability of photos with submission. Reviews contact sheets and prints. Offers no additional payment for photos accepted with ms, but offers $125 for cover photo. Captions and identification of subjects required. Buys one-time rights.

Tips: Most of the our purchases are in how-to area, so writers must know golf quite well and play the game."

THE LEADER BOARD, The Publisher's Group, P.O. Box 510366, Salt Lake City UT 84151-0366. Fax: (801)322-1098. E-mail: annee@thepublishers.com. Contact: Anne E. Zombro, vice president of publishing. 50% freelance written. Quarterly magazine. "Drive the fairway with Nicklaus, putt the green with Faldo, visit Pebble Beach. This magazine brings you all of this and more—tips from the pros, new equipment, rule and tour updates." Estab. 1996. Circ. 15,000. Pays on publication. Publishes ms an average of 6 months after acceptance. Byline given. Buys first North American serial and second serial (reprint) rights. Editorial lead time 2 months. Submit seasonal material 4 months in advance. Accepts simultaneous submissions. Reports in 1 month on queries; 2 months on mss. Sample copy for $3 and 9×12 SASE. Writer's guidelines for #10 SASE.

Nonfiction: Historical/nostalgic, interview/profile, personal experience, technical, golf. Buys 8-10 mss/year. Query with published clips. Length: 1,000-1,300 words. Pays $125-800.

Reprints: Accepts previously published submissions. Pays 50% of amount paid for an original article.

Photos: Send photos with submission. Reviews 4×5 transparencies (preferred), any size prints. Negotiates payment individually. Captions, model releases, identification of subjects required. Buys one-time or all rights.

Columns/Departments: Golf Tips (for the weekend golfer), Personal Experiences/Nostalgia (for the average golfer), both 500 words. Buys 8-10 mss/year. Query with published clips. Pays $50-125.

LINKS MAGAZINE, Southern Links Magazine Publishing Assoc., Box 7628, Hilton Head SC 29938. Editor: Matt Sullivan. Magazine published 7 times/year for avid, affluent golfers. "*Links Magazine* is edited for club-level golfers interested in travel and real estate opportunities. Other areas of editorial focus include history and traditions of golf, golf equipment updates, and interviews with golf's leaders and legends." Pays within 60 days of acceptance. Byline given. Offers 50% kill fee. Buys all rights. Accepts simultaneous submissions. Reports in 2 months on queries. Sample copy for $3. Writer's guidelines available.

Nonfiction: Historical/nostalgic, interview/profile, travel. "No instruction; we're 'where-to' not 'how-to.' " Buys 10-15 mss/year. Query with published clips. Length: 1,500 words minimum. Pays $800-1,200. Sometimes pays expenses of writers on assignment.

Reprints: Accepts previously published submissions.

Columns/Departments: Buys 15-20 mss/year. Query with published clips. Pays $800-1,200.

Fillers: Buys 10-15/year. Length: 300-1,000 words. Pays $300-500.

‡METROLINA GOLF MAGAZINE, Tayside Publishing Co. Inc., P.O. Box 9122, Hickory NC 28603-9122. (704)327-4332. E-mail: tayside@aol.com. Contact: Gil Capps, editor. 20% freelance written. Tabloid published 8 times/year. "*Metrolina Golf Magazine* is edited for golfers in the Charlotte metropolitan area of North and South Carolina. It features profiles of local players; coverage of regional tournaments; and reviews of courses, travel destinations and equipment." Estab. 1992. Circ. 24,000. Pays on publication. Publishes ms an average of 3 months after acceptance. Byline given. Offers $25 kill fee. Buys all rights. Editorial lead time 3 months. Submit seasonal material 6 months in advance. Sample copy for 9×12 SAE and 3 first-class stamps. Writer's guidelines for #10 SASE.

Nonfiction: Essays, exposé, general interest, historical/nostalgic, how-to, humor, interview/profile, new product, opinion, personal experience, photo feature, technical, travel (all pertaining to golf). Buys 15 mss/year. Query with published clips. Length: 400-1,200 words. Pays $25-100 for assigned articles; $0-75 for unsolicited articles. Sometimes pays expenses of writers on assignment.

Photos: State availability of photos with submission. Reviews 5×7 prints. Negotiates payment individually. Identification of subjects required. Buys one-time rights.

Fillers: Anecdotes, facts, gags to be illustrated by cartoonist, newsbreaks, short humor. Buys 2/year. Length: 1-300 words. Pays $5-50.

NORTH TEXAS GOLFER, Golfer Magazines, Inc., 9182 Old Katy Rd., Houston TX 77055. (713)464-0308. Fax: (713)464-0129. Editor: Bob Gray. Contact: Carl Mickelson, associate editor. 30% freelance written. Monthly tabloid covering golf in Texas. Estab. 1984. Circ. 31,000. Pays on publication. Publishes ms an average of 2 months after acceptance. Byline given. Buys first rights or second serial (reprint) rights. Editorial lead time 2 months. Submit seasonal material 3 months in advance. Reports in 2 weeks on queries; 1 month on mss. Sample copy free. Prefers direct phone discussion for writer's guidelines.

Nonfiction: Book excerpts, humor, personal experience, all golf related. Buys 40 mss/year. Query. Pays $50-425.

Photos: State availability of photos with submission. Reviews contact sheets and prints. Offers no additional payment for photos accepted with ms, but offers $125 for cover photo. Captions and identification of subjects required. Buys one-time rights.

Tips: "Most of our purchases are in how-to area, so writers must know golf quite well and play the game."

SCORE, Canada's Golf Magazine, Canadian Controlled Media Communications, 287 MacPherson Ave., Toronto, Ontario M4V 1A4 Canada. (416)928-2909. Fax: (416)928-1357. E-mail: weeksy@idirect.com. Website: http://www.scor egolf.com. Publisher: (Mr.) Kim Locke. Managing Editor: Bob Weeks. 70% freelance written. Works with a small number of new/unpublished writers each year. Magazine published 7 times/year covering golf. "*Score* magazine provides seasonal coverage of the Canadian golf scene, professional, amateur, senior and junior golf for men and women golfers in Canada, the US and Europe through profiles, history, travel, editorial comment and instruction." Estab. 1982. Circ. 130,000 audited. **Pays on acceptance.** Byline given. Offers negotiable kill fee. Buys all rights and second serial (reprint) rights. Submit seasonal material 8 months in advance. Reports in 8 months. Sample copy for $2.50 (Canadian) and 9 × 12 SAE with IRCs. Writer's guidelines for #10 SAE and IRC.

Nonfiction: Book excerpts (golf); historical/nostalgic (golf and golf characters); interview/profile (prominent golf professionals); photo feature (golf); travel (golf destinations only). The yearly April/May issue includes tournament results from Canada, the US, Europe, Asia, Australia, etc., history, profile, and regular features. No personal experience, technical, opinion or general-interest material. Most articles are by assignment only. Buys 25-30 mss/year. Query with published clips. Length: 700-3,500 words. Pays $200-1,500.

Photos: Send photos with query or ms. Pays $50-100 for 35mm color transparencies (positives) or $30 for 8 × 10 or 5 × 7 b&w prints. Captions, model release (if necessary), identification of subjects required. Buys all rights.

Columns/Departments: Profile (historical or current golf personalities or characters); Great Moments ("Great Moments in Canadian Golf"—description of great single moments, usually game triumphs); New Equipment (Canadian availability only); Travel (golf destinations, including "hard" information such as greens fees, hotel accommodations, etc.); Instruction (by special assignment only; usually from teaching golf professionals); The Mental Game (psychology of the game, by special assignment only); History (golf equipment collections and collectors, development of the game, legendary figures and events). Buys 17-20 mss/year. Query with published clips or send complete ms. Length: 700-1,700 words. Pays $140-400.

Tips: "Only writers with an extensive knowledge of golf and familiarity with the Canadian golf scene should query or submit in-depth work to *Score*. Many of our features are written by professional people who play the game for a living or work in the industry. All areas mentioned under Columns/Departments are open to freelancers. Most of our *major* features are done on assignment only."

‡SENIOR GOLFER MAGAZINE, Weidier Publications, 35 Corporate Dr., Trumbull CT 06611. (203)459-5190. Fax: (203)459-5199. Editor-in-Chief: Larry Dennis. Executive Editor: David Chmiel. Contact: Kevin Morris, managing editor. 33% freelance written. Magazine published 10 times/year covering golf in the 50+ market (Senior PGA Tour, travel, instruction, equipment). "We appeal to a market of those who're close to 50, have turned 50 and some who are well past 50. It's a market that knows and loves golf—from instruction to the Senior Tour to travel and finances. It's an upscale market of good players, average players and bad players who have the time and disposable income to chase and—hopefully—capture their golf dreams." Estab. 1993. Circ. 275,000. **Pays on acceptance.** Publishes ms an average of 6 months after acceptance. Byline given. Buys all rights. Editorial lead time 2 months. Submit seasonal material 4 months in advance. Sample copy free.

Nonfiction: David Chmiel, executive editor. Book excerpts, exposé, general interest, historical/nostalgic, humor, interview/profile, new product, opinion, photo feature, travel. "No cliched rehashes of players who've been in the spotlight for more than 30 years; stories with no regard for our demographic." Query with published clips or send complete ms. Sometimes pays expenses of writers on assignment.

Photos: State availability of photos with submission. Reviews contact sheets and transparencies. Negotiates payment individually. Captions and identification of subjects required.

Columns/Departments: Short Shots (interesting events in golf), 150-200 words. Query with published clips or send complete ms.

Fiction: David Chmiel, executive editor. Adventure, condensed novels, historical, humorous, mainstream, novel excerpts. Buys few mss/year. Query with published clips or send complete ms.

Fillers: Anecdotes, facts, newsbreaks, short humor.

Tips: "To get your works printed in *Senior Golfer*, it's imperative that you exhibit your knowledge, understanding and love of the game. Our readers are a sophisticated and fickle lot and know if someone's pretending to be golf literate."

Guns

‡AMERICAN RIFLEMAN, National Rifle Association of America, 11250 Waples Mill Rd., Fairfax VA 22030. (703)267-1336. Fax: (703)267-3971. Editor: E.G. Bell, Jr. Contact: Mark A. Keefe, IV, managing editor. 25% freelance written. Monthly magazine covering firearms and related topics for members of the NRA. "We are a member magazine devoted to the history, use, manufacturing, development and care of all types of portable small arms. We have a relatively sophisticated audience and international readership in this subject area." Estab. 1871. Circ. 1.8 million. **Pays**

on acceptance. Publishes ms an average of 3-5 months after acceptance. Byline given. No kill fee. Buys first North American serial rights. Submit seasonal material 3 months in advance. Accepts simultaneous submissions. Reports in 1 week on queries; 3 weeks on mss. Sample copy and writer's guidelines free on request.

Nonfiction: Historical/nostalgic (firearms), how-to (firearms making/repair), technical (firearms related). "No fiction, poetry, essays, pure hunting tales or anything unrelated to firearms." Buys 30-35 mss/year. Query. Length: 1,500-2,000 words maximum. Pays $300-$600. Sometimes pays expenses of writers on assignment.

Photos: Send photos with submission. Offers no additional payment for photos accepted with ms. Captions and identification of subjects required. Buys one-time rights.

Columns/Departments: From The Bench (articles on reloading ammunition or how-to firearms-related pieces), 800-1,200 words. Buys 12 mss/year. Query. Pays $250-400 maximum.

Tips: "For starters, it is unlikely that any of our potential authors are unfamiliar with this magazine. Well illustrated, high-quality gunsmithing articles are needed, as well as innovative material on reloading, any of the shooting sports, historical topics, etc. We have an abundance of scholarly material on the gun control issue, but we have bought the occasional thoughtful piece. Aside from our 'From The Bench' column we purchase only feature articles. We do accept unpaid submissions called 'In My Experience' that might introduce authors to us, but most are from long-time readers."

GUN DIGEST, DBI Books, Inc., Division of Krause Communications, 935 Lakeview Pkwy., Suite 101, Vernon Hills IL 60061. (800)767-6310. Editor-in-Chief: Ken Warner. 50% freelance written. Prefers to work with published/established writers but works with a small number of new/unpublished writers each year. Annual journal covering guns and shooting. Estab. 1944. **Pays on acceptance.** Publishes ms an average of 20 months after acceptance. Byline given. Buys all rights. Reports in 1 month.

Nonfiction: Buys 50 mss/issue. Query. Length: 500-5,000 words. Pays $100-600; includes photos or illustration package from author.

Photos: State availability of photos with query letter. Reviews 8×10 b&w prints. Payment for photos included in payment for ms. Captions required.

Tips: Award of $1,000 to author of best article (juried) in each issue.

‡GUNGAMES MAGAZINES, Wallyworld Publishing Incorporated, P.O. Box 516, Moreno Valley CA 92556. (909)485-7986. Fax: (909)485-6628. E-mail: ggamesed@aol.com. Website: http://www.gungames.com. Contact: Roni Toldanes, editor. 80% freelance written. Bimonthly magazine covering shooting sports. "This is the only gun magazine that doesn't talk about what type of bullet you should use to kill Bambi or what's the best gun to defend yourself in a dark alley." It talks only about the fun side of guns. All of its writers are World Champions in various shooting disciplines. Estab. 1995. Circ. 300,000. Pays on publication. Publishes ms an average of 2 months after acceptance. Byline given. Buys first rights. Editorial lead time 3 months. Submit seasonal material 3 months in advance. Accepts simultaneous submissions. Reports in 2 weeks on queries. Sample copy for $3.50.

Reprints: Send tearsheet of article or short story and information about when and where the article previously appeared. Pays 50% of amount paid for an original article.

Nonfiction: General interest, historical/nostalgic, how-to, humor, interview/profile, new product, personal experience, technical. Special issues: Shot Show (February-March) and Christmas issues. No articles on hunting or self-defense. Buys 24 mss/year. Send complete ms. Length: 1,200-2,000 words. Pays $150-300. Pays expenses or writers on assignment.

Photos: Send photos with submission. Reviews negatives, transparencies and prints. Negotiates payment individually. Captions and identification of subjects required. Buys one-time rights.

Columns/Departments: Shooting/Action Shooting (the fun side); GunGames Women's Issue, Shooters Guide to Cowboy Action and Guns (October/November 1997); GunGames Christmas Issue, Shooters Guide to Ear and Eye Protection (December 1996/January 1997); GunGames Shot Show issue (February/March 1998). All columns 1,500 words. Buys 24 mss/year. Send complete ms. Pays $150-300.

Fiction: Fantasy, humorous. "Not too serious or too boring." Buys 24 mss/year. Send complete ms. Length: 1,200-1,500 words. Pays $150-300.

GUNS & AMMO, Petersen Publishing Co., 6420 Wilshire Blvd., Los Angeles CA 90048. (213)782-2160. Fax: (213)782-2477. Editor: Kevin E. Steele. Managing Editor: Terry Thiel. 10% freelance written. Monthly magazine covering firearms. "*Guns & Ammo* is written for the firearms enthusiast. It contains articles about the history of guns, their application in hunting and target shooting, and the ammunition used by them, plus field tests of selected examples. Rifles, shotguns, handguns, black powder arms, and airguns are covered editorially as well as in a catalog section devoted to currently manufactured firearms. Tables of ballistic characteristics of commercial ammunition are also included. Contains articles on other outdoor-related subjects such as knives, leather goods, vehicles, reloading equipment, and personality profiles." Circ. 600,000. **Pays on acceptance.** Publishes ms 6 months after acceptance. Byline given. Buys all rights. Submit seasonal material 6 months in advance. Writer's guidelines for #10 SASE.

Nonfiction: Opinion. Buys 24 mss/year. Send complete ms. Length: 800-2,500 words. Pays $125-500.

Reprints: Send typed ms with rights for sale noted along with information about when and where the article previously appeared.

Photos: Send photos with submissions. Review 7×9 prints. Offers no additional payment for photos accepted with ms. Captions, model releases, identification of subjects required. Buys all rights.

Columns/Departments: RKBA (opinion column on right to keep and bear arms). Send complete ms. Length: 800-1,200 words. Pays $300.

‡**GUNS MAGAZINE**, Suite 200, 591 Camino de la Reina, San Diego CA 92108. (619)297-5352. Fax: (619)297-5353.Contact: Scott Ferrell, editor. Managing Editor: Lisa Parsons. 100% freelance written. Monthly magazine for firearms enthusiasts covering firearms, reviews, tactics and related products. Circ. 200,000. Pays on publication. Publishes manuscripts 4-6 months after acceptance. Buys all world rights. Offers $50 kill fee. Reports in 2 weeks. Writer's guidelines for SASE.
Nonfiction: Test reports on new firearms; round-up articles on firearms types; guns for specific purposes (hunting, target shooting, self-defense); custom gunmakers; and history of modern guns. Buys approximately 10 ms/year. Query. Length: 1,000-2,500 words. Pays $300-500.
Photos: Major emphasis on quality photography. Additional payment of $50-200 for color, 4×5 or 2¼×2¼ preferred.
Columns/Departments: Buys 5-10 columns. Query. Length: 1,000 words. Pays $400.

HANDGUNS, Petersen Publishing Co., 6420 Wilshire Blvd., Los Angeles CA 90048. (213)782-2153. Fax: (213)782-2477. Contact: (Mr.) Jan M. Libourel, editor. 60% freelance written. Monthly magazine covering handguns and handgun accessories. Estab. 1986. Circ. 150,000. **Pays on acceptance.** Byline given. No kill fee. Buys all rights. Reporting time varies. Free sample copy and writer's guidelines.
Nonfiction: General interest, historical, how-to, profile, new product and technical. "No articles not germane to established topics of magazine." Buys 50 mss/year. Send complete ms. Pays $300-500.
Photos: Send photos with submission. Reviews contact sheets, color transparencies, 5×7 prints. No additional payment for photos. Captions, model releases and identification of subjects required. Buys all rights.
Tips: "Send manuscript after querying editor by telephone and establishing acceptability. We are most open to feature stories. Be guided by published examples appearing in the magazine."

Hiking/Backpacking

AMERICAN HIKER, American Hiking Society, P.O. Box 20160, Washington DC 20041-2160. (301)565-6704. Fax: (301)565-6714. Website: http://www.orca.org/ahs/. Contact: Laura Loftus, editor. 25% freelance written. Bimonthly magazine. "*American Hiker* covers the recreation opportunities on America's trails and focuses on the people who work to protect them." Estab. 1988. Circ. 10,000. Pays on publication. Publishes ms 3 months after acceptance. Byline given. Buys first rights. Editorial lead time 3 months. Submit seasonal material 6 months in advance. Accepts simultaneous submissions. Reports in 2 weeks on queries; 2 months on mss. Sample copy for $1. Writer's guidelines for #10 SASE.
Nonfiction: Book excerpts, essays, interview/profile, travel. Especially interested in trail programs, hiking clubs and how-to stories on trail work. Buys 18 mss/year. Query with published clips. Length: 1,500-2,000 words. Pays $25-150 for assigned articles; $25-75 for unsolicited articles.
Reprints: Send tearsheet or photocopy of article and information about when and where the article previously appeared.
Photos: State availability of photos with submission. Reviews transparencies. Offers $25/photo. Buys one-time rights.
Columns/Departments: Hiking Family (family tips); Club Profile on AHS affiliate club; Soft Wear (low-impact camping); Hiker's Access (book reviews); all 800 words. Buys 12 mss/year. Query with published clips. Pays $75-125.
Tips: "Focus on people who are building and protecting trails—not accounts of travel."

BACKPACKER, Rodale Press, Inc., 33 E. Minor St., Emmaus PA 18098-0099. (610)967-8296. Fax: (610)967-8181. E-mail: bpeditor@aol.com. Editor: John Viehman. Managing Editor: Tom Shealey. Contact: Jim Gorman, Michele Morris, senior editors. 50% freelance written. Magazine published 9 times/year covering wilderness travel for backpackers 35-45 years old. Estab. 1973. Circ. 250,000. **Pays on acceptance.** Byline given. Offers 25% kill fee. Buys one-time rights or all rights. Reports in 2 months. Writer's guidelines for #10 SASE.
  ● *Backpacker* editors tell us they are receiving too many inappropriate queries and submissions.
Nonfiction: Essays, exposé, historical/nostalgic, how-to (expedition planner), humor, inspirational, interview/profile, new product, opinion, personal experience, technical, travel. No step-by-step accounts of what you did on your summer vacation—stories that chronicle every rest stop and gulp of water. Query with published clips and SASE. Length: 750-3,000 words. Pays $400-2,000. Sometimes pays (pre-determined) expenses of writers on assignment. "What we want are features that let us and the readers 'feel' the place, and experience your wonderment, excitement, disappointment or other emotions encountered 'out there.' If we feel like we've been there after reading your story, you've succeeded."
Photos: State availability of photos with submission. Amount varies—depends on size of photo used. Buys one-time rights.
Columns/Departments: Signpost, "News From All Over" (adventure, environment, wildlife, trails, techniques, organizations, special interests—well-written, entertaining, short, newsy item), 50-500 words; Body Language (in-the-field column), 750-1,200 words; Moveable Feast (food-related aspects of wilderness: nutrition, cooking techniques, recipes, products and gear), 500-750 words; Weekend Wilderness (brief but detailed guides to wilderness areas, providing thorough trip-planning information, only enough anecdote to give a hint, then the where/when/hows), 500-750 words; Technique (ranging from beginner to expert focus, written by people with solid expertise, details ways to improve performance, how-to-do-it instructions, information on equipment manufacturers and places readers can go), 750-1,500 words; and Backcountry (personal perspectives, quirky and idiosyncratic, humorous critiques, manifestos and misadventures, interesting angle, lesson, revelation or moral), 750-1,200 words. Buys 50-75 mss/year. Query with published clips. Pays $200-600. No phone calls regarding story ideas. Written queries only.

Tips: "Our best advice is to read the publication—most freelancers don't know the magazine at all. The best way to break in is with an article for the Backcountry, Weekend Wilderness or Signpost Department."

‡**OUTSIDE**, Mariah Media Inc., Outside Plaza, 400 Market St., Santa Fe NM 87501. (505)989-7100. Editor: Mark Bryant. Contact: Jon Tayman, executive editor. 90% freelance written. Monthly magazine on outdoor recreation and travel. "*Outside* is a monthly national magazine for active, educated, upscale adults who love the outdoors and are concerned about its preservation." Estab. 1977. Circ. 500,000. **Pays on acceptance.** Publishes ms an average of 3 months after acceptance. Byline given. Offers 25% kill fee. Buys first North American serial rights. Submit seasonal material 4-5 months in advance. Electronic submission OK for solicited materials; not for unsolicited. Reports in 6 weeks on queries; 2 months on mss. Sample copy for $5 and 9×12 SAE with 9 first-class stamps. Writer's guidelines for SASE.

Nonfiction: Book excerpts; essays; reports on the environment; outdoor sports and expeditions; general interest; how-to; humor; inspirational; interview/profile (major figures associated with sports, travel, environment, outdoor); opinion, personal experience (expeditions; trying out new sports); photo feature (outdoor photography); technical (reviews of equipment, how-to); travel (adventure, sports-oriented travel). All should pertain to the outdoors: Bike section; Downhill Skiing; Cross-country Skiing; Adventure Travel. Do not want to see articles about sports that we don't cover (basketball, tennis, golf, etc.). Buys 40 mss/year. Query with published clips and SASE. Length: 1,500-4,000 words. Pays $1/word. Pays expenses of writers on assignment.

Photos: "Do not send photos; if we decide to use a freelancer's story, we may request to see the writer's photos." Reviews transparencies. Offers $180/photo minimum. Captions and identification of subjects required. Buys one-time rights.

Columns/Departments: Dispatches, contact Adam Horowitz (news, events, short profiles relevant to outdoors), 200-1,000 words; Destinations, contact Stephanie Gregory (places to explore, news, and tips for adventure travelers), 250-400 words; Review, contact Eric Hagerman (evaluations of products), 200-1,500 words. Buys 180 mss/year. Query with published clips. Length: 200-2,000 words. Pays $1/word.

Tips: "Prospective writers should study the magazine before querying. Look at the magazine for our style, subject matter and standards." The departments are the best areas for freelancers to break in.

Outside magazine "is kind of unique," says executive editor Greg Clyburn. "We're not a straight environmental magazine. We're more of a general interest magazine about the outdoors." That means freelancers can publish articles on sports, the environment, adventure and travel, people and places, politics, art and science; just about anything, as long as it relates to the outdoor world. Yet *Outside* doesn't take just anything, Clyburn emphasizes. The magazine has a style that successful freelancers become familiar with. "There's a lot about our writing that's not immediately obvious from the outside," he says. "My advice to writers is to get recent back issues and really get familiar with them." In addition, some experience in magazine writing is a strong plus in Clyburn's eyes. "We expect a well-developed query letter with clips of published magazine pieces," he explains. "The people with the most success are journalists with experience in magazines." The best places for new writers to break in are the regular departments. Destinations uses short pieces on travel; Bodywork is about personal fitness and health; Review is a collection of equipment, book, and other consumer item evaluations; Dispatch is a section on news relating to the magazine's focus.

SIGNPOST FOR NORTHWEST TRAILS MAGAZINE, 1305 Fourth Ave., Suite 512, Seattle WA 98101-2401. E-mail: dnelson024@aol.com. Website: http://www.wta.org/wta/. Publisher: Washington Trails Association. Executive Editor: Dan A. Nelson. 30% freelance written. "We will consider working with both previously published and unpublished freelancers." Monthly magazine about hiking, backpacking and similar trail-related activities, strictly from a Pacific Northwest viewpoint. Estab. 1966. Will consider any rights offered by author. Publishes ms an average of 6 months after acceptance. Reports in 2 months. Query or submit complete ms. Writer's guidelines for #10 SASE.

Nonfiction: "Most material is donated by subscribers or is staff-written. Payment for purchased material is low, but a good way to break in to print and share your outdoor experiences."

Reprints: Include information about when and where the article previously appeared.

Tips: "We cover only *self-propelled* backcountry sports and won't consider manuscripts about trail bikes, snowmobiles or power boats. We *are* interested in articles about modified and customized equipment, food and nutrition, and personal experiences in the Pacific Northwest backcountry."

Hockey

HOCKEY PLAYER MAGAZINE, Hockey Player L.P., P.O. Box 1007, Okemos MI 48805-1007. Fax: (517)347-0686. E-mail: hockeymag@aol.com. Website: http://www.hockeyplayer.com. Contact: Quint Randle, editor. 90% freelance written. Monthly tabloid covering hockey for recreational players. "*Hockey Player* is written for players of recreational ice, roller and street hockey. It is not just a pro hockey fan magazine." Estab. 1991. Circ. 18,000. Pays on publication. Publishes ms an average of 2 months after acceptance. Byline given. Buys first North American serial and electronic rights. Editorial lead time 3 months. Submit seasonal material 4 months in advance. Accepts simultaneous submissions. Reports in 1 month. Sample copy and writer's guidelines free on request.

Nonfiction: How-to, interview/profile, new product, personal experience, photo feature. technical. Buys 50 mss/year.

Query with published clips. Length: 1,500-2,500 words. Pays $75-100.
Reprints: Send photocopy of article or short story. Pays 50% of amount paid for an original article.
Tips: "Writing 'how-to' article about playing the game is the easiest way to break in. We don't need a profile on some minor league player."

‡ROLLER HOCKEY MAGAZINE, Straight Line Communications, 12327 Santa Monica Blvd. #202, Los Angeles CA 90025. (310)442-6660. Fax: (310)442-6663. E-mail: info@rhockey.com. Editor: Greg Guss. 70% freelance written. Monthly magazine covering roller hockey. "We cover everything from the beginning/recreational roller hockey player to the pros, offering instruction, new product information and anything else of interest to this audience." Estab. 1992. Circ. 17,000. Pays on publication. Publishes ms an average of 2 months after acceptance. Byline given. Buys first North American serial rights. Editorial lead time 2 months. Submit seasonal material 3 months in advance. Reports in 3 weeks on queries; 1 month on mss. Sample copy and writer's guidelines not available.
Nonfiction: General interest, how-to, interview/profile, new product, personal experience, photo feature, technical. Buys 24 mss/year. Query with published clips. Length: 1,000-1,500 words. Pays 10-20¢/word for assigned articles. Sometimes pays expenses of writers on assignment.
Photos: State availability of photos with submission. Negotiates payment individually.
Columns/Departments: Pays $100-200.

Horse Racing

THE BACKSTRETCH, United Thoroughbred Trainers of America, Inc., P.O. Box 7065, Louisville KY 40257-0065. (502)893-0025. Fax: (502)893-0026. E-mail: uttainc@aol.com. Editor: Barrett Shaw. 90% freelance written. Estab. 1962. Circ. 10,000. Uses mostly established turf writers, but works with a few less experienced writers each year. Bimonthly magazine directed chiefly to Thoroughbred trainers but also to owners, fans and others working in or involved with the racing industry. Publishes ms 3 months after acceptance, often longer. Sample copy on request.
Nonfiction: Profiles of trainers, owners, jockeys, horses and other personalities who make up the world of racing; analysis of industry issues; articles on particular tracks or races, veterinary topics; information on legal or business aspects of owning, training or racing horses; and historical perspectives. Opinions should be informed by expertise on the subject treated. Non-commissioned articles are accepted on a speculation basis. Pays on publication. If not suitable, articles are returned only if a SASE is included. Length: 1,500-2,500 words.
Reprints: Occasionally accepts previously published material, especially if it has appeared only in a regional or specialized publication. Accepts either tearsheet or photocopy of article and information about when and where the article previously appeared. Pays about 50% of amount paid for an original article.
Photos: It is advisable to include photo illustrations when possible, or these can be arranged for separately.
Tips: "If an article is a simultaneous submission, this must be stated and we must be advised if it is accepted elsewhere. Articles should be double spaced and may be submitted by mail, fax or e-mail on 3½-inch disk saved in text or in program compatible with Quark XPress for Macintosh."

HOOF BEATS, United States Trotting Association, 750 Michigan Ave., Columbus OH 43215. (614)224-2291. Fax: (614)228-1385. Editor: Dean A. Hoffman. 35% freelance written. Works with a small number of new/unpublished writers each year. Monthly magazine covering harness racing for the participants of the sport of harness racing. "We cover all aspects of the sport—racing, breeding, selling, etc." Estab. 1933. Circ. 16,000. Pays on publication. Publishes ms an average of 3 months after acceptance. Byline given. Buys negotiable rights. Submit seasonal material 3 months in advance. Reports in 1 month. Free sample copy, postpaid.
Nonfiction: General interest, historical/nostalgic, humor, inspirational, interview/profile, new product, personal experience, photo feature. Buys 15-20 mss/year. Query. Length: open. Pays $100-400. Pays the expenses of writers on assignment with approval.
Reprints: Send photocopy of article or short story. Pay is negotiable.
Photos: State availability of photos. Pays variable rates for 35mm transparencies and prints. Identification of subjects required. Buys one-time rights.
Fiction: Historical, humorous, novel excerpts, interesting fiction with a harness racing theme. Buys 2-3 mss/year. Query. Length: open. Pays $100-400.

THE MARYLAND HORSE, Mid-Atlantic Thoroughbred, Maryland Horse Breeders Association., Box 427, Timonium MD 21094. (410)252-2100. Editor: Timothy T. Capps. Contact: Lucy Acton. 50% freelance written. Bimonthly magazine covering thoroughbred racing/racing and other horse sports in Maryland. **Pays on acceptance.** Publishes ms an average of 2 months after acceptance. Byline given. Buys all rights. Editorial lead time 2 months. No simultaneous or previously published submissions. Reports in 1 week on queries. Sample copy free on request.
Nonfiction: Book excerpts, essays, general interest, historical/nostalgic, how-to, humor, inspirational, interview/profile, new product, opinion, personal experience, photo feature—topics must all be related to horses. Buys 24 mss/year. Query. Length: 1,000-3,000 words. Pays $100-500. Sometimes pays expenses of writers on assignment.
Photos: State availability of photos with submission. Reviews contact sheets, prints. Offers $15/photo.
Columns/Departments: Pays $100-350.

THE QUARTER RACING JOURNAL, American Quarter Horse Association, P.O. Box 32470, Amarillo TX 79120. (806)376-4888. Fax: (806)349-6400. E-mail: aghajrnl@arn.net. Website: http://www.aqha.com. Contact: Amy Owens, editor. Executive Editor: Jim Jennings. 10% freelance written. Monthly magazine. "The official racing voice of the American Quarter Horse Association. We promote quarter horse racing. Articles include training, breeding, nutrition, sports medicine, health, history, etc." Estab. 1988. Circ. 10,000. **Pays on acceptance.** Publishes ms an average of 3 months after acceptance. Buys first North American serial rights. Submit seasonal material 3 months in advance. Reports in 1 month on queries. Free sample copy and writer's guidelines.

Nonfiction: Historical (must be on quarter horses or people associated with them), how-to (training), nutrition, health, breeding and opinion. "We welcome submissions year-round." Special issues: Stallion and Broad Mare Care (January-March 1998). Query. Length: 700-2,500 words. Pays $150-300.

Photos: Send photos with submission. Additional payment for photos accepted with ms might be offered. Captions and identification of subjects required.

Fiction: Publishes novel excerpts.

Tips: "Query first—must be familiar with quarter horse racing and the sport. If writing on nutrition, it must be applicable. Most open to features covering training, nutrition, health care. Use a knowledgeable source with credentials."

Hunting and Fishing

ALABAMA GAME & FISH, Game & Fish Publications, Inc., P.O. Box 741, Marietta GA 30061. Editor: Jimmy Jacobs. See *Game & Fish Publications*.

‡**AMERICAN ANGLER, the Magazine of Fly Fishing & Fly Tying**, Abenaki Publishers, Inc., 160 Benmont Ave., Bennington VT 05201. Fax: (802)447-2471. E-mail: garys@sover.net. Contact: Gary Soucie, editor. 95% freelance written. Bimonthly magazine covering fly fishing. "*American Angler* is dedicated to giving fly fishers information they can use—wherever they fish, whatever they fish for. The *practical* dimension looms large." Estab. 1976. Circ. 50,000. Pays on publication. Publishes ms an average of 6 months after acceptance. Byline given. Buys first North American serial rights or one-time rights. Editorial lead time over 3 months. Submit seasonal material 5 months in advance. Accepts simultaneous submissions, if so noted. Reports in 6 weeks on queries; 2 months on mss. Sample copy for $5. Writer's guidelines for SASE.

Nonfiction: Book excerpts (well in advance of publication), essays (a few), how-to (most important), humor, interview/profile, opinion (query first), personal experience ("but tired of the 'me 'n' Joe' stories"), photo feature (seldom), technical, travel ("but no 'come hither' pieces"). No promotional flack to pay back free trips or freebies or superficial coverage of subjects. Buys 45-60 mss/year. Query with published clips. Length: 500-2,500 words. Pays $250-400.

Photos: Send photos with submission. Reviews contact sheets, transparencies. Offers no additional payment for photos accepted with ms. Captions, identification of subjects required. Acquires one-time rights. "Photographs are important. Some articles can stand on the strength of the writing, but most need to be illustrated. Naturally, anecdotal and place-oriented stories must be illustrated with scenics, fishing shots, and other pictures that help flesh out the story and paint the local color. Technical pieces—those that deal with casting, rigging, fly tying and the like-must be accompanied by appropriate photography or rough sketches for our illustrator. A fly-tying submission should always include samples of flies to send to our staff photographer."

Columns/Departments: Sound advice (health and safety issues), 700-1,500 words. Buys 4-6 mss/year. Query with published clips. Pays $300-400.

Fiction: Humorous, mainstream, slice-of-life vignettes. No stories unrelated to fly fishing or aimed at novice fly fishers. Buys 1-2 mss/year. Send complete ms. Length: 500-2,000 words. Pays $200-350.

Poetry: Free verse, haiku, light verse, traditional. Buys 0-2 poems/year. Submit maximum 4 poems at one time. Length: 2-50 lines. Pays $50-200.

Fillers: Anecdotes, facts, short humor. Length: 25-150 words. Pays $0-25.

Tips: "If you are new to this editor, please submit complete queries. They needn't be long, but they should give what I need to decide to give you a go-ahead. Besides briefly outlining the subject, tell me *how* you will treat the material. As straightforward how-to? As first-person experiential narrative? As third-person piece of journalistic reporting? As writerly essay? Does the subject have seasonal or other *timeliness*? Some stories need to be run in a certain season; others can be run any time. Keep in mind that we work four months ahead of the issue date on the cover. *How few or many words will you need*? Most of our articles run 1,500 to 2,000 words. Some are too long or too short at that length. Write too long, and I'll cut the article. Write too short, and I'll reject it or ask for a rewrite. We need some articles that are less than 1,500 words and a few that are longer than 2,000. What are the *sidebar opportunities*? (Sources of further info, area contacts, tackle and pattern suggestions, fishing techniques in more detail than you can gracefully include in the article. Anything else about the subject that you found and think the reader will find interesting)? What sorts of *photos*, and how many of them, do you plan to submit? What *other sorts of illustrations* may be necessary or possible? Maps, Process drawings? Historical photos or art? Your rough sketches for our artist to finish? Do you plan to submit *patterns or dressings for flies*? (If so, we'd appreciate receiving a photo or photos, and a sample fly—in case we decide to use artwork or a specific setup photo instead of your snap.) Very important: Plan and write your query as carefully as you plan to write the article you are suggesting. I can only judge your ability by the organization and the writing in the query. Don't think I will believe you can write better than you've done in your query; I won't."

AMERICAN HUNTER, 11250 Waples Mill Rd., Fairfax VA 22030-9400. Fax: (703)267-3971. Editor: Tom Fulgham. Contact: Linda J. Faulk, editorial assistant. For hunters who are members of the National Rifle Association. "*The American Hunter* contains articles dealing with various sport hunting and related activities both at home and abroad. With the encouragment of the sport as a prime game management tool, emphasis is on technique, sportsmanship and safety. In each issue hunting equipment and firearms are evaluated, legislative happenings affecting the sport are reported, lore and legend are retold and the business of the Association is recorded in the Official Journal section." Circ. 1,300,000. Buys first North American serial rights. Byline given. Reports in 1 month. Writer's guidelines for #10 SASE.

Nonfiction: Factual material on all phases of hunting. Not interested in material on fishing or camping. Prefers queries. Length: 1,800-2,000 words. Pays $250-500.

Reprints: Send typed ms with rights for sale noted and information about when and where the article previously appeared.

Photos: No additional payment made for photos used with mss. Pays $25 for b&w photos purchased without accompanying mss. Pays $50-175 for color.

Tips: "Although unsolicited manuscripts are welcomed, detailed query letters outlining the proposed topic and approach are appreciated and will save both writers and editors a considerable amount of time. If we like your story idea, you will be contacted by mail or phone and given direction on how we'd like the topic covered. NRA Publications accept all manuscripts and photographs for consideration on a specualtion basis only. Subject matter for feature articles falls into five general categories that run in each issue: deer, upland birds, waterfowl, big game and varmints/small game. Features may be written in a number of prose styles, including expository how-to, where-to, and general interest pieces; humor; personal narratives; and semi-technical articles on firearms, wildlife management, or hunting. *American Hunter* does not buy poetry or articles on firearms legislation. Story angles should be narrow, but coverage must have depth. How-to articles are popular with readers and might range from methods for hunting to techniques on making gear used on successful hunts. Where-to articles should contain contacts and information needed to arrange a similar hunt. All submissions are judged on three criteria: story angle (it should be fresh, interesting, and informative); quality of writing (clear and lively—capable of holding the readers' attention throughout); and quality and quantity of accompanying photos (sharpness, reproduceability, and connection to text are most important.) *American Hunter* receives more than a thousand queries and manuscripts a year, and although the editors try to respond within three weeks, it may take a month or more for an author to receive a reply. The editors are not responsible for unsolicited manuscripts or photos."

ARKANSAS SPORTSMAN, Game & Fish Publications, Inc., P.O. Box 741, Marietta GA 30061. (770)953-9222. Editor: Bob Borgwat. See *Game & Fish Publications.*

BASSMASTER MAGAZINE, B.A.S.S. Publications, 5845 Carmichael Pkwy., Montgomery AL 36141-0900. (205)272-9530. Fax: (205)279-9530. Contact: Dave Precht, editor. 80% freelance written. Prefers to work with published/ established writers. Magazine published 10 issues/year about largemouth, smallmouth and spotted bass for dedicated beginning and advanced bass fishermen. Circ. 550,000. **Pays on acceptance.** Publication date of ms after acceptance "varies—seasonal material could take years"; average time is 8 months. Byline given. Buys all rights. Submit seasonal material 6 months in advance. Reports in 2 months. Sample copy for $2. Writer's guidelines for #10 SASE.

Nonfiction: Historical, interview (of knowledgeable people in the sport), profile (outstanding fishermen), travel (where to go to fish for bass), how-to (catch bass and enjoy the outdoors), new product (reels, rods and bass boats), conservation related to bass fishing. "No 'Me and Joe go fishing' type articles." Query. Length: 400-2,100 words. Pays 25¢/word.

  ● Needs destination stories (how to fish a certain area) for the Northwest and Northeast.

Columns/Departments: Short Cast/News & Views (upfront regular feature covering news-related events such as new state bass records, unusual bass fishing happenings, conservation, new products and editorial viewpoints); 250-400 words.

Photos: "We want only color photos." Pays $600 for color cover transparencies. Captions required; model releases preferred. Buys all rights.

Fillers: Anecdotes, newsbreaks. Buys 4-5 mss/issue. Length: 250-500 words. Pays $50-100.

Tips: "Editorial direction continues in the short, more direct how-to article. Compact, easy-to-read information is our objective. Shorter articles with good graphics, such as how-to diagrams, step-by-step instruction, etc., will enhance a writer's articles submitted to *Bassmaster Magazine*. The most frequent mistakes made by writers in completing an article for us are poor grammar, poor writing, poor organization and superficial research."

BC OUTDOORS, OP Publishing, 780 Beatty St., Suite 300, Vancouver, British Columbia V6B 2M1 Canada. (604)606-4644. Fax: (604)687-1925. E-mail: oppubl@istar.ca. Editor: Karl Bruhn. 80% freelance written. Works with a small number of new/unpublished writers each year. Magazine published 8 times/year covering fishing, camping, hunting and the environment of outdoor recreation. Estab. 1946. Circ. 42,000. Pays on publication. Publishes ms an average of 3 months after acceptance. Byline given. Offers negotiable kill fee. Buys first North American serial rights.

FOR INFORMATION on setting your freelance fees, see How Much Should I Charge?

Reports in 1 month. Sample copy and writer's guidelines for 8×10 SAE with 7 first-class stamps.

Nonfiction: How-to (new or innovative articles on outdoor subjects), personal experience (outdoor adventure), outdoor topics specific to British Columbia. "We would like to receive how-to, where-to features dealing with hunting and fishing in British Columbia." Buys 80-90 mss/year. Query. Length: 1,500-2,000 words. Pays $300-500. Sometimes pays the expenses of writers on assignment.

● Wants in-depth, informative, professional writing only.

Photos: State availability of photos with query. Pays $25-75 on publication for 5×7 b&w prints; $35-150 for color contact sheets and 35mm transparencies. Captions and identification of subjects required. Buys one-time rights.

Tips: "Emphasis on environmental issues. Those pieces with a conservation component have a better chance of being published. Subject must be specific to British Columbia. We receive many manuscripts written by people who obviously do not know the magazine or market. The writer has a better chance of breaking in at our publication with short, lesser-paying articles and fillers, because we have a stable of regular writers in constant touch who produce most main features."

BUGLE, Journal of Elk and the Hunt, Rocky Mountain Elk Foundation, 2291 W. Broadway, Missoula MT 59802. (406)523-4568. E-mail: rmef@rmef.org. Website: http://www.rmef.org. Editor: Dan Crockett. Contact: Jan Brocci, managing editor; David Stalling, conservation editor; Don Burgess, hunting editor. 50% freelance written. Quarterly magazine covering conservation and hunting. "*Bugle* is the membership publication of the Rocky Mountain Elk Foundation, a nonprofit wildlife conservation group; it also sells on newsstands. Our readers are predominantly hunters, many of them naturalists who care deeply about protecting wildlife habitat. Hunting stories and essays should celebrate the hunting experience, demonstrating respect for wildlife, the land and the hunt. Articles on elk behavior or elk habitat should include personal observations and entertain as well as educate." Estab. 1984. Circ. 150,000. **Pays on acceptance**. Publishes ms 9 months after acceptance. Byline given. Offers variable kill fee. Buys one-time rights. Editorial lead time 6 months. Submit seasonal material 6 months in advance. Reports in 1 month on queries; 2 months on mss. Sample copy $5. Writer's guidelines for #10 SASE.

Nonfiction: Book excerpts, essays, general interest (elk related), historical/nostalgic, humor, opinion, personal experience, photo feature. No how-to, where-to. Buys 20 mss/year. Query with or without published clips, or send complete ms. Length: 1,500-4,500 words. Pays 20¢/word and 3 contributor copies; more issues at cost.

Reprints: Send typed ms with rights for sale noted. Pays 15¢/word.

Columns/Departments: Situation Ethics, 1,000-2,000 words; Thoughts & Theories, 1,500-4,000 words; Women in the Outdoors, 1,000-3,000 words. Buys 12 mss/year. Query with or without published clips or send complete ms. Pays 20¢/word.

Fiction: Adventure, historical, humorous, slice-of-life vignettes, western. No fiction that doesn't pertain to elk or elk hunting. Buys 4 mss/year. Query with or without published clips or send complete ms. Length: 1,500-4,500 words. Pays 20¢/word.

Poetry: Free verse, haiku, light verse, traditional. Buys 1-2 poems/year. Submit maximum 6 poems.

Tips: "Creative queries (250-500 words) that showcase your concept and your style remain the most effective approach. We're hungry for submissions for two specific columns: Situation Ethics and Women in the Outdoors. Send a SASE for guidelines. We also welcome strong well-reasoned opinion pieces on topics pertinent to hunting and wildlife conservation, and humorous pieces about elk behavior or encounters with elk (hunting or otherwise)."

CALIFORNIA GAME & FISH, Game & Fish Publications, Inc., Box 741, Marietta GA 30061. Editor: Burt Carey. See *Game & Fish Publications*.

‡CANADIAN SPORTFISHING MAGAZINE, Canada's Fishing Authority, Canadian Sportfishing Productions, 937 Centre Rd., Dept. 2020, Waterdown, Ontario L0R 2H0 Canada. Editor: Kerry Knudsen. 70% freelance written. Bimonthly magazine covering sport fishing. Estab. 1988. Circ. 30,000. Pays on publication. Publishes ms an average of 3 months after acceptance. Byline given. Offers 50% kill fee. Buys all rights. Editorial lead time 6 months. Submit seasonal material 8 months in advance. Reports in 2 months on queries; 6 months on mss. Sample copy for $4. Writer's guidelines for #10 SASE.

Nonfiction: How-to, humor, new product. Buys 40 mss/year. Query. Length: 1,500-4,000 words. Pays 15¢/word minimum (Canadian funds). Sometimes pays expenses of writers on assignment.

Photos: Send photos with submission. Reviews contact sheets, transparencies and prints. Offers no additional payment for photos accepted with ms. Captions, model releases and identification of subjects required. Buys all rights.

‡DEER & DEER HUNTING, Krause Publications, 700 E. State St., Iola WI 54990-0001. Fax: (715)445-4087. Editor: Patrick Durkin. Contact: Dan Schmidt, associate editor. 95% freelance written. Published 8 times/year covering white-tailed deer and deer hunting, billed with practical and comprehensive information for white-tailed deer hunters. "Readers include a cross section of the deer hunting population—individuals who hunt with bow, gun or camera. The editorial content of the magazine focuses on white-tailed deer biology and behavior, management principle and practices, habitat requirements, natural history of deer, hunting techniques, and hunting ethics. We also publish a wide range of 'how-to' articles designed to help hunters locate and get close to deer at all times of the year. The majority of our readership consists of two-season hunters (bow and gun) and approximately one-third camera hunt." Estab. 1977. Circ. 140,000. **Pays on acceptance**. Byline given. Editorial lead time 6 months. Submit seasonal material 6 months in advance. Reports in 3 months. Sample copy for 9×12 SASE. Writer's guidelines free.

Nonfiction: General interest, how-to, inspirational, photo feature. No "Me and Joe" articles. Buys 30-50 mss/year. Query. Length: 750-3,000 words. Pays $150-525 for assigned articles; $150-325 for unsolicited articles. Sometimes pays expenses of writers on assignment.

Photos: Send photos with submission. Reviews transparencies. Negotiates payment individually. Captions, model releases and identification of subjects required.

Fiction: "Mood" deer hunting pieces. Buys 8 mss/year. Send complete ms.

Fillers: Facts, newsbreaks. Buys 40-50/year. Length: 100-500 words. Pays $15-150.

Tips: "Feature articles dealing with deer biology or behavior should be documented by scientific research (the author or that of others) as opposed to a limited number of personal observations."

DISCOVERING AND EXPLORING NEW JERSEY'S FISHING STREAMS AND THE DELAWARE

RIVER, New Jersey Sportsmen's Guides, P.O. Box 100, Somerdale NJ 08083. (609)783-1271. (609)665-8350. Fax: (609)665-8656. Editor: Steve Perrone. 60-70% freelance written. Annual magazine covering freshwater stream and river fishing. Estab. 1993. Circ. 4,500. **Pays on acceptance.** Publishes ms an average of 6 months after acceptance. Byline given. Buys first rights and makes work-for-hire assignments. Editorial lead time 6 months. Sample copy for $12.50 postage paid.

Nonfiction: How-to fishing and freshwater fishing. Buys 6-8 mss/year. Query with published clips. Length: 500-2,000 words. Pays $75-250.

Photos: State availability of photos with submission. Reviews 4×5 transparencies and prints. Negotiates payment individually. Captions, model releases, identification of subjects required. Buys one-time rights.

Tips: "We want queries with published clips of articles describing fishing experiences on New Jersey streams and the Delaware River."

FIELD & STREAM, 2 Park Ave., New York NY 10016-5695. Editor: Duncan Barnes. Contact: David E. Petzal,

executive editor. 50% freelance written. Eager to work with new/unpublished writers. Monthly. "Broad-based service magazine for the hunter and fisherman. Editorial content ranges from very basic how-to stories detailing a useful technique or a device that sportsmen can make, to articles of penetrating depth about national hunting, fishing, and related activities. Also humor and personal essays, nostalgia and 'mood pieces' on the hunting or fishing experience and profiles on outdoor people." Estab. 1895. Circ. 1,790,400. **Pays on acceptance.** Buys first rights. Byline given. Reports in 2 months. Query. Writer's guidelines for #10 SASE.

• Ranked as one of the best markets for freelance writers in *Writer's Yearbook* magazine's annual "Top 100 Markets," January 1997.

Nonfiction: Length: 1,000 words for features. Payment varies depending on the quality of work, importance of the article. Pays $800 and up to $1,500 and more on a sliding scale for major features. *Field & Stream* also publishes regional sections with feature articles on hunting and fishing in specific areas of the country. The sections are geographically divided into East, Midwest, West and South, and appear 12 months/year.

Reprints: Occasionally accepts previously published submissions if suitable. Send photocopy of article and information about when and where it previously appeared.

Photos: Prefers color slides to b&w. Query first with photos. When photos purchased separately, pays $450 minimum for color. Buys first rights to photos.

Fillers: Buys short "how it's done" fillers, 75 to 150 words, on unusual or helpful subjects. Also buys short (up to 500 words) pieces on tactics or techniques for specific hunting or fishing situations; short "Field Guide" pieces on natural phenomena as related to hunting and fishing; "Myths and Misconceptions," short pieces debunking a commonly held belief about hunting and fishing, and short "Outdoor Basics" and "Sportsman's Project" articles. In addition, welcomes queries on "Health and Safety" categories likely to affect outdoor sportsmen; hunting, fishing and natural history items of interest to young sportsmen; and odd or noteworthy items with hunting or fishing themes. Pays $75-400.

Tips: "Writers are encouraged to submit queries on article ideas. These should be no more than a page, and should include a summary of the idea, including the angle you will hang the story on, and a sense of what makes this piece different from all others on the same or a similar subject. Many queries are turned down because we have no idea what the writer is getting at. Be sure that your letter is absolutely clear. We've found that if you can't sum up the point of the article in a sentence or two, the article doesn't have a point. Pieces that depend on writing style, such as humor, mood, and nostalgia or essays often can't be queried and may be submitted in manuscript form. The same is true of short tips. All submissions to *Field & Stream* are on an on-spec basis. Before submitting anything, however, we encourage you to *study*, not simply read, the magazine. Many pieces are rejected because they do not fit the tone or style of the magazine, or fail to match the subject of the article with the overall subject matter of *Field & Stream*. Above all, study the magazine before submitting anything."

‡THE FISHERMAN, LIF Publishing Corp., 14 Ramsey Rd., Shirley NY 11967-4704. (516)345-5200. Fax: (516)345-

5304. Publisher: Fred Golofaro. Senior Editor: Tim Coleman. 4 regional editions: *Long Island*, *Metropolitan New York*, Tom Melton, editor; *New England*, Tim Coleman, editor; *New Jersey*, Pete Barrett, editor; *Delaware-Maryland-Virginia*, Keith Kaufman, editor; and *Florida*, Andy Dear, editor. 75% freelance written. A weekly magazine covering fishing with an emphasis on saltwater. Combined circ. 100,000. Pays on publication. Byline given. Offers variable kill fee. Buys all rights. Articles may be run in one or more regional editions by choice of the editors. Submit seasonal material 2 months in advance. Reports in 4-6 weeks. Free sample copy and writer's guidelines.

Nonfiction: Send submission to editor of regional edition. General interest, historical/nostalgic, how-to, interview/

profile, personal experience, photo feature, technical, travel. Special issues: Trout Fishing (April); Bass Fishing (June); Offshore Fishing (July); Surf Fishing (September); Tackle (October); Electronics (November). "No 'me and Joe' tales. We stress how, where, when, why." Buys approx. 300 mss/year, each edition. Length: 1,000-1,500 words. Pays $110-150 for unsolicited feature articles.

Photos: Send photos with submission; also buys single color photos for cover use (Pays $50-$100). Offers no additional payment for photos accepted with ms. Identification of subjects required.

Tips: "Focus on specific how-to and where-to subjects within each region."

FLORIDA GAME & FISH, Game & Fish Publications, Inc., Box 741, Marietta GA 30061. (770)953-9222. Editor: Jimmy Jacobs. See *Game & Fish Publications*.

FLORIDA SPORTSMAN, Wickstrom Publishers Inc., 5901 SW 74 St., Miami FL 33143. (305)661-4222. Fax: (305)284-0277. E-mail: editor@flsportsman.com. Website: http://www.flsportsman.com. Editor: Glenn Law. 70% freelance written. Works with new/unpublished writers. Monthly magazine covering fishing, boating and related sports—Florida and Caribbean only. "*Florida Sportsman* is edited for the boatowner and offshore, coastal and fresh water fisherman. It provides a how, when and where approach in its articles, which also include occasional camping, diving and hunting stories—plus ecology; in-depth articles and editorials attempting to protect Florida's wilderness, wetlands and natural beauty." Circ. 110,000. **Pays on acceptance**. Publishes ms an average of 6 months after acceptance. Byline given. Offers 50% kill fee. Buys first North American serial rights. Submit seasonal material 6 months in advance. Reports in 2 months on queries; 1 month on mss. Sample copy free. Writer's guidelines for #10 SASE.

Nonfiction: Essays (environment or nature), how-to (fishing, hunting, boating), humor (outdoors angle), personal experience (in fishing, etc.), technical (boats, tackle, etc., as particularly suitable for Florida specialties). "We use reader service pieces almost entirely—how-to, where-to, etc. One or two environmental pieces per issue as well. Writers *must* be Florida based, or have lengthy experience in Florida outdoors. All articles must have strong Florida emphasis. We do not want to see general how-to-fish-or-boat pieces which might well appear in a national or wide-regional magazine." Buys 40-60 mss/year. Query; no e-mail queries. Length: 2,000-3,000 words. Pays $300-400. Sometimes pays expenses of writers on assignment.

Photos: Send photos with submission. Reviews 35mm transparencies and 4×5 and larger prints. Offers no additional payment for photos accepted with ms. Pays up to $1,000 for cover photos. Buys one-time rights.

Tips: "Feature articles are most open to freelancers; however there is little chance of acceptance unless contributor is an accomplished and avid outdoorsman *and* a competent writer-photographer with considerable experience in Florida."

FLORIDA WILDLIFE, Florida Game & Fresh Water Fish Commission, 620 S. Meridian St., Tallahassee FL 32399-1600. (904)488-5563. Fax: (904)488-6988. E-mail: subletd@mail.state.fl.us. Website: http://www.state.fl.us/gfc/. Contact: Dick Sublette, editor. About 40% freelance written. Noncommercial state bimonthly magazine covering hunting, natural history, fishing, endangered species and wildlife conservation. "In outdoor sporting articles we seek themes of wholesome recreation. In nature articles we seek accuracy and conservation purpose." Estab. 1947. Circ. 26,000. Pays on publication. Byline given. Buys first North American serial and occasionally second serial (reprint) rights. Submit seasonal material 6 months in advance. Accepts simultaneous submissions. Reports in 2 months (acknowledgement of receipt of materials); up to 2 years for acceptance, usually less for rejections. Prefers photo/ms packages. Sample copy for $2.95. Writer's/photographer's guidelines for SASE.

Nonfiction: General interest (bird watching, hiking, camping, boating), how-to (hunting and fishing), humor (wildlife related; no anthropomorphism), inspirational (conservation oriented), personal experience (wildlife, hunting, fishing, outdoors), photo feature (Florida species: game, nongame, botany), technical (rarely purchased, but open to experts), nature appreciation and outdoor ethics. "We buy general interest hunting, fishing and nature stories. No stories that humanize animals, or opinionated stories not based on confirmable facts." Special issues: Annual Florida Fresh Water Fishing edition (March/April 1998); Hunting season (September/October 1997, November/December 1997). Buys 30-40 mss/year. Send slides/ms. Length: 500-1,500 words. Generally pays $50/published page plus a per-photo disbursement.

Reprints: Rarely accepts previously published submissions. Send tearsheet of article or typed ms with rights for sale noted and information about when and where the article previously appeared..

Photos: State availability of photos with story query. Accepts transparencies only (slides) of hunting, fishing, and natural science series of Florida wildlife species. Pays $25-75 for inside photos; $100 for front cover photos, $75 for back cover. "We like short, specific captions." Buys one-time rights.

Fiction: "We rarely buy fiction, and then only if it is true to life and directly related to good sportsmanship and conservation. No fairy tales, erotica, profanity or obscenity." Buys 2-3 mss/year. Send complete mss and label "fiction." Length: 500-1,200 words. Generally pays $50/published page.

Tips: "Read and study recent issues for subject matter, style and examples of our viewpoint, philosophy and treatment. We look for wholesome recreation, ethics, safety, and good outdoor experience more than bagging the game in our stories. We usually need well-written hunting and freshwater fishing articles that are entertaining and informative and that describe places to hunt and fish in Florida. We do not publish articles that feature a commercial interest or a specific brand name product. Use the active rather than the passive voice. Our readership varies from schoolchildren to senior citizens, and a large number of subscribers reside in urban areas and in all 50 states."

FLY FISHING IN SALT WATERS, Hook and Release Publications, Inc., 2001 Western Ave., Suite 210, Seattle WA 98121. (206)443-3273. Fax: (206)443-3293. E-mail: flyfishinsalt@flyfishers.com. Website: http://www.flyfishinsalt

.com/ffsw. Contact: R.P. Van Gytenbeek, managing editor. 90% freelance written. Bimonthly magazine covering fly fishing in salt waters anywhere in the world. Estab. 1994. Circ. 44,000. Pays on publication. Publishes ms an average of 1 year after acceptance. Byline given. Buys first North American serial rights and electronic rights. Editorial lead time 3 months. Submit seasonal material at least 2 months in advance. Reports in 1 month on queries; 2 months on mss. Sample copy for $6. Writer's guidelines for #10 SASE.

Nonfiction: Book excerpts, essays, historical/nostalgic, how-to, interview/profile, new product, personal experience, photo feature, technical, travel, resource issues (conservation); all on flyfishing. Buys 40-50 mss/year. Query with or without published clips. Length: 1,500-2,500 words. Pays $400-500.

Photos: Send photos with submission. Reviews transparencies (35mm color only). Negotiates payment individually: offers no additional payment for photos accepted with ms; pays $80-300/photo if purchased separately. Captions, identification of subjects required. Buys one-time rights.

Columns/Departments: Legends/Reminiscences (history-profiles-nostalgia), 2,000-2,500 words; Resource (conservation issues), 1,000-1,500 words; Fly Tier's Bench (how to tie saltwater flies), 1,000-1,200 words, photos critical; Tackle & Technique (technical how-to), 1,000-1,500 words, photos or illustrations critical; Boating (technical how-to), 2,000-2,500 words. (Other departments are mostly staff written or by assignment only.) Buys 25-30 mss/year. Query. Pays $400-500.

Fiction: Adventure, humorous, mainstream; all dealing with flyfishing. Buys 2-3 mss/year. Send complete ms. Length: 2,000-3,000 words. Pays $500.

Fillers: Most fillers are staff-written.

Tips: "Follow up on your inquiry with a phone call."

‡FLY FISHING QUARTERLY, Aqua-Field Publishing, 39 Avenue-At-The-Common, Shrewsbury NJ 07702. (908)935-1222. Fax: (908)935-9846. Editor & Publisher: Stephen C. Ferber. Contact: Bob Illes, managing editor. 90% freelance written. Quarterly magazine directed to the intermediate-to-expert fly fisherman. Estab. 1989. Circ. 54,000. **Usually pays on acceptance,** sometimes on publication. Publishes ms an average of 6 months after acceptance. Byline given. Offers $100 kill fee. Buys first North American serial rights. Editorial lead time 9 months. Submit seasonal material 6 months in advance. Reports in 3 weeks on queries; 2 months on mss. Sample copy and writer's guidelines free.

Nonfiction: How-to, interview/profile, new product, photo feature, travel. Special issues: Fly Fishing Made Easy, Fly Fishing For Trout, Saltwater Flyfishing. No worn out ideas. Buys 250 mss/year. Query. Length; 1,000-2,500 words. Pays $200-350 for assigned articles; $150-300 for unsolicited articles.

Photos: Send photos with submission. Reviews transparencies and 4×5 prints. Offers no additional payment for photos accepted with ms. Captions and identification of subjects required. Buys one-time rights.

Columns/Departments: Fly Tying (how-to), 500 words; Travel, 1,000 words; New Products, 500 words. All with pictures. Buys 50 mss/year. Query or send complete ms. Pays $100.

Tips: "Send clear queries, good pictures and original material."

FUR-FISH-GAME, 2878 E. Main, Columbus OH 43209-9947. Contact: Mitch Cox, editor. 65% freelance written. Works with a small number of new/unpublished writers each year. Monthly magazine for outdoorsmen of all ages who are interested in hunting, fishing, trapping, dogs, camping, conservation and related topics. Estab. 1900. Circ. 108,000. **Pays on acceptance.** Publishes ms an average of 7 months after acceptance. Byline given. Buys first serial rights or all rights. Reports in 2 months. Query. Sample copy for $1 and 9×12 with SAE. Writer's guidelines for #10 SASE.

Nonfiction: "We are looking for informative, down-to-earth stories about hunting, fishing, trapping, dogs, camping, boating, conservation and related subjects. Nostalgic articles are also used. Many of our stories are 'how-to' and should appeal to small-town and rural readers who are true outdoorsmen. Some recent articles have told how to train a gun dog, catch big-water catfish, outfit a bowhunter and trap late-season muskrat. We also use personal experience stories and an occasional profile, such as an article about an old-time trapper. 'Where-to' stories are used occasionally if they have broad appeal." Length: 500-3,000 words. Pays $75-150 depending upon quality, photo support, and importance to magazine. Short filler stories pay $35-80.

Photos: Send photos with ms. Photos are part of ms package and receive no additional payment. Prefers color prints or transparencies. Prints can be 5×7 or 8×10. Captions required.

Tips: "We are always looking for quality articles that tell how to hunt or fish for game animals or birds that are popular with everyday outdoorsmen but often overlooked in other publications, such as catfish, bluegill, crappie, squirrel, rabbit, crows, etc. We also use articles on standard seasonal subjects such as deer and pheasant, but like to see a fresh approach or new technique. Trapping articles, especially instructional ones based on personal experience, are useful all year. Articles on gun dogs, ginseng and do-it-yourself projects are also popular with our readers. An assortment of photos and/or sketches greatly enhances any manuscript, and sidebars, where applicable, can also help."

GAME & FISH PUBLICATIONS, INC., 2250 Newmarket Pkwy., Suite 110, Marietta GA 30067. (770)953-9222. Fax: (770)933-9510. Contact: Ken Dunwoody, editorial director. Publishes 30 different monthly outdoor magazines, each one covering the fishing and hunting opportunities in a particular state or region (see individual titles and editors). 90% freelance written. Estab. 1975. Circ. 540,000. Pays 75 days prior to cover date of issue. Publishes ms an average of 7 months after acceptance. Byline given. Offers negotiable kill fee. Buys first North American serial rights. Submit seasonal material at least 8 months in advance. Editors prefer to hold queries until that season's material is assigned. Reports in 3 months on mss. Sample copy for $2.50 and 9×12 SASE. Writer's guidelines for #10 SASE.

Nonfiction: Prefer queries over unsolicited ms. Article lengths either 1,500 or 2,500 words. Pays separately for articles and accompanying photos. Manuscripts pay $125-300, cover photos $250, inside color $75 and b&w $25. Reviews transparencies and b&w prints. Prefers captions and identification of species/subjects. Buys one-time rights to photos.
Fiction: Buys some humor and nostalgia stories pertaining to hunting and fishing. Pays $125-250. Length 1,500-2,500 words.
Tips: "Our readers are experienced anglers and hunters, and we try to provide them with useful, entertaining articles about where, when and how to enjoy the best hunting and fishing in their state or region. We also cover topics concerning game and fish management. Most articles should be aimed at outdoorsmen in one particular state. After familiarizing themselves with our magazine(s), writers should query the appropriate state editor (see individual listings) or send to Ken Dunwoody."

GEORGIA SPORTSMAN, Game & Fish Publications, Box 741, Marietta GA 30061. (770)953-9222. Editor: Jimmy Jacobs. See *Game & Fish Publications*.

GREAT PLAINS GAME & FISH, Game & Fish Publications, Box 741, Marietta GA 30061. (770)953-9222. Editor: Nick Gilmore. See *Game & Fish Publications*.

‡**GULF COAST FISHERMAN**, Harold Wells Gulf Coast Fisherman, Inc., P.O. Drawer P, 401 W. Main St., Port Lavaca TX 77979. Fax: (512)552-8864. Contact: Gary M. Ralston, publisher/editor. 95% freelance written. Quarterly magazine covering Gulf Coast saltwater fishing. "All editorial material is designed to expand the knowledge of the Gulf Coast angler and promote saltwater fishing in general." Estab. 1979. Circ 15,000. Pays on publication. Publishes ms an average of 2 months after acceptance. Byline given. Buys first North American serial rights. Submit seasonal queries 4-5 months in advance. Reports in 1 month. *Writer's Market* recommends allowing 2 months for reply. Sample copy and writer's guidelines for 9 × 12 SAE with 5 first-class stamps.
Nonfiction: How-to (any aspect relating to saltwater fishing that provides the reader specifics on use of tackle, boats, finding fish, etc.), interview/profile, new product, personal experience, technical. Buys 25 mss/year. Query with or without published clips or send complete ms. Length: 1,200-1,800 words. Pays $150-225.
Photos: State availability of photos with submission. Prefers b&w prints. Offers no additional payment for photos accepted with ms. Captions and identification of subjects required. Pays $125 for cover photos. Buys one-time rights.
Tips: "Features are the area of our publication most open to freelancers. Subject matter should concern some aspect of or be in relation to saltwater fishing in coastal bays or offshore. Prefers electronic submissions—3.5 Mac-compatible, 3.5 Mac or PC. Articles may be as broad as a review of the different technique used in pursuing redfish or trout by Gulf fishermen, to one on a particular bay, person or fish. From offshore to pier fishing, the reader should know enough about the subject after reading the article to repeat the writer's experience."

ILLINOIS GAME & FISH, Game & Fish Publications, Inc., Box 741, Marietta GA 30061. (770)953-9222. Editor: Bill Hartlage. See *Game & Fish Publications*.

INDIANA GAME & FISH, Game & Fish Publications, Inc., Box 741, Marietta GA 30061. (770)953-9222. Editor: Ken Freel. See *Game & Fish Publications*.

IN-FISHERMAN, 2 In-Fisherman Dr., Brainerd MN 56401. (218)829-1648. Fax: (218)829-2371Editor-in-Chief: Doug Stange. Magazine published 7 times/year for "freshwater anglers from beginners to professionals. Most articles focus on bass, walleyes, catfish, panfish, pike, muskies, trout and salmon. Maps, charts, photos, graphs illustrations and cartoons accompany each article. Regular features, include trip tips to fishing hot spots; peak daily and monthly fishing times; a Master Angler award program; editorial commentary; fishery science, industry issues; alternative fish species; reader feedback, a tested recipe; a time for reflection and a humorous offering." Estab. 1975. Circ. 334,000. **Pays on acceptance**. Byline given. Offers 50% kill fee. Buys first rights. Accepts simultaneous submissions. Reports in 2 months on queries.
Nonfiction: How-to, personal experience. Buys 20 mss/year. Query with published clips. Length: 1,500-4,500 words. Pay varies.
Columns/Departments: Length 1,000-1,500 words. Buys 14 mss/year. Query with published clips. Pay varies.
Tips: Need "new information on freshwater fishing techniques. Species-specific presentations that haven't appeared elsewhere." Would like to see "well-written, informative and entertaining treatment of a breakthrough presentation."

IOWA GAME & FISH, Game & Fish Publications, Inc., Box 741, Marietta GA 30061. (770)953-9222. Editor: Bill Hartlage. See *Game & Fish Publications*.

KENTUCKY GAME & FISH, Game & Fish Publications, Inc., Box 741, Marietta GA 30061. (770)953-9222. Editor: Bill Hartlage. See *Game & Fish Publications*.

LOUISIANA GAME & FISH, Game & Fish Publications, Inc., Box 741, Marietta GA 30061. (404)953-9222. Editor: Bob Borgwat. See *Game & Fish Publications*.

THE MAINE SPORTSMAN, P.O. Box 365, Augusta ME 04330. Editor: Harry Vanderweide. 80% freelance written. "Eager to work with new/unpublished writers, but because we run over 30 regular columns, it's hard to get into *The*

Maine Sportsman as a beginner." Monthly tabloid. Estab. 1972. Circ. 30,000. Pays during month of publication. Buys first rights. Publishes ms an average of 3 months after acceptance. Byline given. Reports in 2 weeks.
Nonfiction: "We publish only articles about Maine hunting and fishing activities. Any well-written, researched, knowledgeable article about that subject area is likely to be accepted by us." Mostly wants Maine-specific where-to-go articles. Buys 25-40 mss/issue. Submit complete ms. Length: 200-2,000 words. Pays $20-300. Sometimes pays the expenses of writers on assignment.
Reprints: Send typed ms with rights for sale. Pays 100% of amount paid for an original article.
Photos: "We can have illustrations drawn, but prefer 1-3 b&w photos." Submit photos with accompanying ms. Pays $5-50 for b&w print.
Tips: "It's rewarding finding a writer who has a fresh way of looking at ordinary events. Specific where-to-go about Maine is needed."

‡MARLIN, The International Sportfishing Magazine, Marlin Magazine, a division of World Publications, Inc., P.O. Box 2456, Winter Park FL 32790. (407)628-4802. Fax: (407)628-7061. E-mail: dr1@worldzine.com. Contact: David Ritchie, editor. 90% freelance written. Bimonthly magazine on big game fishing. "*Marlin* covers the sport of big game fishing (billfish, tuna, sharks, dorado and wahoo). Our readers are sophisticated, affluent and serious about their sport—they expect a high-class, well-written magazine that provides information and practical advice." Estab. 1982. Circ. 30,000. **Pays on acceptance for text**, on publication for photos. Publishes ms an average of 3 months after acceptance. Byline given. Buys first North American serial rights. Submit seasonal material 2-3 months in advance. Query for electronic submissions. Sample copy and writer's guidelines for $3.20 and SAE.
Nonfiction: General interest, how-to (bait-rigging, tackle maintenance, etc.), new product, personal experience, photo feature, technical, travel. "No freshwater fishing stories. No 'me & Joe went fishing' stories." Buys 30-50 mss/year. Query with published clips. Length: 800-3,000 words. Pays $250-500.
Photos: State availability of photos with submission. Original slides, please. Offers $25-300/photo. $750 for a cover. Buys one-time rights.
Columns/Departments: Tournament Reports (reports on winners of major big game fishing tournaments), 200-400 words; Blue Water Currents (news features), 100-400 words. Buys 25 mss/year. Query. Pays $100-250. Accepts previously published articles in news section only. Send photocopy of article, including information about when and where the article previously appeared. For reprints, pays 50-75% of the amount paid for an original article.
Tips: "Tournament reports are a good way to break in to *Marlin*. Make them short but accurate, and provide photos of fishing action or winners' award shots (*not* dead fish hanging up at the docks!). We always need how-tos and news items. Our destination pieces (travel stories) emphasize where and when to fish, but include information on where to stay also. For features: crisp, high action stories with emphasis on exotic nature, adventure, personality, etc.—nothing flowery or academic. Technical/how-to: concise and informational—specific details. News: Again, concise with good details—watch for legislation affecting big game fishing, outstanding catches, new clubs and organizations, new trends and conservation issues."

MICHIGAN OUT-OF-DOORS, P.O. Box 30235, Lansing MI 48909. (517)371-1041. Fax: (517)371-1505. E-mail: mucc@mucc.org. Website: http://www.mucc.org. Contact: Dennis C. Knickerbocker, editor. 50% freelance written. Works with a small number of new/unpublished writers each year. Monthly magazine emphasizing Michigan outdoor recreation, especially hunting and fishing, conservation and environmental affairs. Estab. 1947. Circ. 120,000. **Pays on acceptance.** Publishes ms an average of 6 months after acceptance. Byline given. Buys first North American serial rights. Phone queries OK. Submit seasonal material 6 months in advance. Reports in 1 month. Sample copy for $2.50. Free writer's guidelines.
Nonfiction: Exposé, historical, how-to, informational, interview, nostalgia, personal experience, personal opinion, photo feature, profile. No humor or poetry. "Stories *must* have a Michigan slant unless they treat a subject of universal interest to our readers." Special issues: Archery Deer Hunting (October); Firearm Deer Hunting (November); Cross-country Skiing and Early-ice Lake Fishing (December). Buys 8 mss/issue. Send complete ms. Length: 1,000-2,000 words. Pays $90 minimum for feature stories. Pays expenses of writers on assignment.
Photos: Purchased with or without accompanying ms. Pays $20 minimum for any size b&w glossy prints; $175 maximum for color (for cover). Offers no additional payment for photos accepted with accompanying ms. Buys one-time rights. Captions preferred.
Tips: "Top priority is placed on true accounts of personal adventures in the out-of-doors—well-written tales of very unusual incidents encountered while hunting, fishing, camping, hiking, etc. The most rewarding aspect of working with freelancers is realizing we had a part in their development. But it's annoying to respond to queries that never produce a manuscript."

MICHIGAN SPORTSMAN, Game & Fish Publications, Inc., Box 741, Marietta GA 30061. (770)953-9222. Editor: Dennis Schmidt. See *Game & Fish Publications*.

MID WEST OUTDOORS, Mid West Outdoors, Ltd., 111 Shore Drive, Hinsdale (Burr Ridge) IL 60521-5885. (630)887-7722. Fax: (630)887-1958. E-mail: mwdmagtv30@aol.com. Editor: Gene Laulunen. Monthly tabloid emphasizing fishing, hunting, camping and boating. 100% freelance written. Estab. 1967. Circ. 50,000. Pays on publication. Buys simultaneous rights. Byline given. Submit seasonal material 2 months in advance. Accepts simultaneous submissions. Reports in 3 weeks. Publishes ms an average of 3 months after acceptance. Sample copy for $1. Writer's guidelines for #10 SASE.

Nonfiction: How-to (fishing, hunting, camping in the Midwest) and where-to-go (fishing, hunting, camping within 500 miles of Chicago). "We do not want to see any articles on 'my first fishing, hunting or camping experiences,' 'cleaning my tackle box,' 'tackle tune-up,' or 'catch and release.' " Buys 1,800 unsolicited mss/year. Send complete ms and 1 or 2 photos on 3.5 diskette with ms included. Length: 1,000-1,500 words. Pays $15-30.

Reprints: Send tearsheet of article.

Photos: Offers no additional payment for photos accompanying ms unless used as covers; uses slides and b&w prints. Buys all rights. Captions required.

Columns/Departments: Fishing, Hunting. Open to suggestions for columns/departments. Send complete ms. Pays $25.

Tips: "Break in with a great unknown fishing hole or new technique within 500 miles of Chicago. Where, how, when and why. Know the type of publication you are sending material to."

MID-ATLANTIC GAME & FISH, Game & Fish Publications, Inc., Box 741, Marietta GA 30061. (770)953-9222. Editor: Ken Freel. See *Game & Fish Publications.*

MINNESOTA SPORTSMAN, Game & Fish Publications, Inc., Box 741, Marietta GA 30061. (770)953-9222. Editor: Dennis Schmidt. See *Game & Fish Publications.*

MISSISSIPPI GAME & FISH, Game & Fish Publications, Inc., Box 741, Marietta GA 30061. (770)953-9222. Editor: Bob Borgwat. See *Game & Fish Publications.*

MISSOURI GAME & FISH, Game & Fish Publications, Inc., Box 741, Marietta GA 30061. (404)953-9222. Editor: Bob Borgwat. See *Game & Fish Publications.*

MUSKY HUNTER MAGAZINE, Willow Creek Press, P.O. Box 147, Minocqua WI 54548. (715)356-6301. Fax: (715)358-2807. Editor: Jim Saric. 90% freelance written. Bimonthly magazine on musky fishing. "Serves the vertical market of musky fishing enthusiasts. We're interested in how-to where-to articles." Estab. 1988. Circ. 31,000. Pays on publication. Publishes ms an average of 4 months after acceptance. Byline given. Buys first or one-time rights. Submit seasonal material 4 months in advance. Reports in 2 months. Sample copy for 9×12 SAE with $1.93 postage. Writer's guidelines for #10 SASE.

Nonfiction: Historical/nostalgic (related only to musky fishing), how-to (modify lures, boats and tackle for musky fishing), personal experience (must be musky fishing experience), technical (fishing equipment), travel (to lakes and areas for musky fishing). Buys 50 mss/year. Send complete ms. Length: 1,000-2,000 words. Pays $100-200 for assigned articles; $50-200 for unsolicited articles. Payment of contributor copies or other premiums negotiable.

Photos: Send photos with submission. Reviews 35mm transparencies and 3×5 prints. Offers no additional payment for photos accepted with ms. Identification of subjects required. Buys one-time rights.

NEW ENGLAND GAME & FISH, Game & Fish Publications, Inc., Box 741, Marietta GA 30061. (770)953-9222. Editor: Steve Carpenteri. See *Game & Fish Publications.*

NEW JERSEY LAKE SURVEY FISHING MAPS GUIDE, New Jersey Sportsmen's Guides, P.O. Box 100, Somerdale NJ 08083. (609)783-1271. (609)665-8350. Fax: (609)665-8656. Editor: Steve Perrone. 30-40% freelance written. Annual magazine covering freshwater lake fishing. *"New Jersey Survey Fishing Maps Guide* is edited for freshwater fishing for trout, bass, perch, catfish and other species. It contains 128 pages and approximately 112 full-page maps of the surveyed lakes that illustrate contours, depths, bottom characteristics, shorelines and vegetation present at each location. The guide includes a 10-page chart which describes over 250 fishing lakes in New Jersey. It also covers trout stocked lakes, fishing tips and 'Bass'n Notes.' " Estab. 1989. Circ. 4,500. **Pays on acceptance.** Publishes ms an average of 6 months after acceptance. Byline given. Buys first rights and makes work-for-hire assignments. Editorial lead time 6 months. Sample copy for $12.50 postage paid.

Nonfiction: How-to fishing, freshwater fishing. Length: 500-2,000 words. Pays $75-250.

Photos: State availability of photos with submission. Reviews transparencies 4×5 slides or 4×6 prints. Captions, model releases, identification of subjects required. Buys one-time rights.

Tips: "We want queries with published clips of articles describing fishing experiences on New Jersey lakes and ponds."

NEW YORK GAME & FISH, Game & Fish Publications, Inc., Box 741, Marietta GA 30061. (770)953-9222. Editor: Steve Carpenteri. See *Game & Fish Publications.*

NORTH AMERICAN FISHERMAN, Official Publication of North American Fishing Club, 12301 Whitewater Dr., Suite 260, Minnetonka MN 55343. (612)936-9333. Fax: (612)936-9755. E-mail: fishingclub@pclink.com. Website: http://www.nafc.com. Publisher: Greg Carey. Editor: Steve Pennaz. 75% freelance written. Magazine published 7 times a year on fresh and saltwater fishing across North America. Estab. 1987. Circ. 500,000. **Pays on acceptance.** Publishes ms an average of 4 months after acceptance. Offers $150 kill fee. Buys first North American serial, one-time and all rights. Reports in 1 month. Sample copy for $5 and 9×12 SAE with 6 first-class stamps.

Nonfiction: How-to (species-specific information on how-to catch fish), news briefs on fishing from various state agencies, travel (where to information on first class fishing lodges). Buys 35-40 mss/year. Query by mail. Length: 700-2,100. Pays $100-500.

Photos: Send photos with submission. Additional payment made for photos accepted with ms. Captions and identification of subjects required. Buys one-time rights. Pays up to $200 for inside art, $500 for cover.

Fillers: Facts, newsbreaks. Buys 60/year. Length: 50-100. Pays $35-50.

Tips: "We are looking for news briefs on important law changes, new lakes, etc. Areas most open for freelancers are: full-length features, cover photos and news briefs. Know what subject you are writing about. Our audience of avid fresh and saltwater anglers knows how to fish and will see through weak or dated fishing information. Must be on cutting edge for material to be considered."

NORTH AMERICAN WHITETAIL, The Magazine Devoted to the Serious Trophy Deer Hunter, Game & Fish Publications, Inc., 2250 Newmarket Pkwy., Suite 110, Marietta GA 30067. (770)953-9222. Fax: (770)933-9510. Editor: Gordon Whittington. 70% freelance written. Magazine published 8 times/year about hunting trophy-class white-tailed deer in North America, primarily the US. "We provide the serious hunter with highly sophisticated information about trophy-class whitetails and how, when and where to hunt them. We are not a general hunting magazine or a magazine for the very occasional deer hunter." Estab. 1982. Circ. 170,000. Pays 75 days prior to cover date of issue. Publishes ms an average of 6 months after acceptance. Byline given. Offers negotiable kill fee. Buys first North American serial rights. Submit seasonal material 10 months in advance. Reports in 3 months on mss. Editor prefers to keep queries on file, without notification, until the article can be assigned or author informs of prior sale. Sample copy for $3 and 9 × 12 SAE with 7 first-class stamps. Writer's guidelines for #10 SASE.

Nonfiction: How-to interview/profile. Buys 50 mss/year. Query. Length: 1,000-3,000 words. Pays $150-400.

Photos: Send photos with submission. Reviews 2 × 2 transparencies and 8 × 10 prints. Offers no additional payment for photos accepted with ms. Captions and identification of subjects required. Buys one-time rights.

Columns/Departments: Trails and Tails (nostalgic, humorous or other entertaining styles of deer-hunting material, fictional or nonfictional), 1,400 words. Buys 8 mss/year. Send complete ms. Pays $150.

Tips: "Our articles are written by persons who are deer hunters first, writers second. Our hard-core hunting audience can see through material produced by non-hunters or those with only marginal deer-hunting expertise. We have a continual need for expert profiles/interviews. Study the magazine to see what type of hunting expert it takes to qualify for our use, and look at how those articles have been directed by the writers. Good photography of the interviewee and his hunting results must accompany such pieces."

NORTH CAROLINA GAME & FISH, Game & Fish Publications, Inc., Box 741, Marietta GA 30061. (770)953-9222. Fax: (770)933-9510. Editor: Bryan Hendricks. See *Game & Fish Publications*.

OHIO GAME & FISH, Game & Fish Publications, Inc., Box 741, Marietta GA 30061. (770)953-9222. Editor: Steve Carpenteri. See *Game & Fish Publications*.

OKLAHOMA GAME & FISH, Game & Fish Publications, Box 741, Marietta GA 30061. (770)953-9222. Fax: (770)933-9510. Editor: Nick Gilmore. See *Game & Fish Publications*.

‡ONTARIO OUT OF DOORS, Maclean Hunter Publishing Ltd., 777 Boy St., 6th Floor, Toronto, Ontario M5W 1A7 Canada. (416)596-5908. Fax: (416)596-2517. E-mail: 102677.1125@compuserv.com. Contact: Burt Myers, managing editor. Associate Editor: John Kerr. 90% freelance written. Magazine published 10 times/year cover the outdoors (hunting, fishing, camping). Estab. 1968. **Pays on acceptance.** Circ. 93,000. Publishes ms an average of 6 months after acceptance. Byline given. Offers 100% kill fee. Buys first and electronic rights. Editorial lead time 6 months. Submit seasonal material 6 months in advance. Reports in 3 months on queries. Sample copy and writer's guidelines free.

Nonfiction: Book excerpts, essays, exposé, how-to (fishing and hunting), humor, inspirational, interview/profile, new product, opinion, personal experience, photo feature, technical, travel. "No Me and Joe features or articles written from a women's point of view on how to catch a bass." Buys 100 mss/year. Query. Length: 1,500 words maximum. Pays $750 maximum for assigned articles; $700 maximum for unsolicited articles. Sometimes pays expenses of writers on assignment.

Photos: Send photos with submission. Reviews transparencies. Offers no additonal payment for photos accepted with ms except for cover and contents use. Captions required. Buys one-time rights.

Columns/Departments: Trips & Tips (travel pieces), 250 words. Buys 30-40 mss/year. Query. Pays $250 maximum.

Fiction: Humorous. Buys 6 mss/year. Send complete ms. Length: 1,000 words maximum. Pays $500 maximum.

Fillers: Facts, newsbreaks. Buys 40/year. Length: 25-100 words. Pays $15-50.

‡OUTDOOR EDGE, Keywest Marketing, 5829 97th St., Edmonton, Alberta T6E 3J2 Canada. (403)448-0381. Fax: (403)438-3244. Editor: Kevin Rolfe. Contact: Mark Yelic, associate editor. 100% freelance written. Bimonthly hunting and fishing magazine. Estab. 1990. Circ. 57,000. Pays on publication. Publishes ms an average of 6 months after acceptance. Byline given. Buys first North American serial rights and first rights. Editorial lead time 4 months. Submit seasonal material 4 months in advance. Accepts simultaneous submissions. Reports in 2 months. Sample copy for 8 × 12 SAE. Writer's guidelines free.

Nonfiction: How-to (hunting/fishing). Query or query with published clips. Length: 1,000-1,800 words. Pay negotiable.

Sometimes pays expenses of writers on assignment.
Reprints: Send tearsheet of article and information about when and where the article previously appeared. Payment negotiated.
Photos: Send photos with submission (duplicates only). Negotiates payment individually. Buys one-time rights.
Columns/Departments: Pays $100-200.

OUTDOOR LIFE, Times Mirror Magazines, Inc., 2 Park Ave., New York NY 10016. (212)779-5000. Fax: (212)686-6877. E-mail: olmagazine@aol.com. Editor: Todd W. Smith. Executive Editor: Bob Brown. Contact: Ed Scheff senior editor. 95% freelance written. Monthly magazine covering hunting and fishing. "*Outdoor Life* is an information source for the active outdoor enthusiast. The editorial provides the fishing and hunting enthusiast (and his family) with the 'how to', 'where-to-go' and what to bring on an outdoor adventure. It covers national and regional interests with wide range of subjects including: conservation, sportsmen's issues, photography, cooking, travel and nostalgia/history." Estab. 1890. Circ. 1,500,000. **Pays on acceptance.** Publishes ms an average of 1 year after acceptance. Byline given. Buys first North American serial rights. Submit seasonal material 1 year in advance. Reports in 1 month on queries; 2 months on mss. Writer's guidelines for #10 SASE.
Nonfiction: Book excerpts, essays, how-to (must cover hunting, fishing or related outdoor activities), interview/profile, new product, personal experience, photo feature, technical, travel. No articles that are too general in scope—need to write specifically. Buys 400 mss/year. "Query first; photos are *very important*." Length: 800-3,000 words. Pays $500-750 for 1,000-word features, national or regional; $1,200-2,000 for 2,000-word or longer features.
Photos: Send photos with submission. Reviews 35mm transparencies and 8×10 b&w prints. Offers variable payment. Captions and identification of subjects required. Buys one-time rights. "May offer to buy photos after first use if considered good and have potential to be used with other articles in the future (file photos)." Pays $250 for ¼ page color to $850 for 2-page spread in color; $1,000 for covers. All photos must be stamped with name and address.
Fillers: National and International newsbreaks (200 words maximum). Newsbreaks and do-it-yourself for hunters and fishermen. Buys unlimited number/year. Length: 1,000 words maximum. Payment varies.
Tips: "It is best for freelancers to break in by writing features for one of the regional sections—East, Midwest, South, West. These are where-to-go oriented and run from 800-1,500 words. Writers must send one-page query with photos."

PENNSYLVANIA ANGLER & BOATER, Pennsylvania Fish and Boat Commission, P.O. Box 67000, Harrisburg PA 17106-7000. (717)657-4518. E-mail: 76247.624@compuserve.com. Website: http://www.state.pa.us/fish. Editor: Art Michaels. 80% freelance written. Prefers to work with published/established writers but works with a few unpublished writers every year. Bimonthly magazine covering fishing and related conservation topics in Pennsylvania. Circ. 40,000. Pays 2 months after acceptance. Publishes ms an average of 8 months after acceptance. Byline given. Rights purchased vary. Submit seasonal material 8 months in advance. Query. Reports in 1 month on queries; 2 months on mss. Sample copy for 9×12 SAE with 9 first-class stamps. Writer's guidelines for #10 SASE.
Nonfiction: How-to, where-to, technical. No saltwater or hunting material. Buys 100 mss/year. Query. Length: 500-3,500 words. Pays $25-300.
Photos: Send photos with submission. Reviews 35mm and larger transparencies and 8×10 b&w prints. Offers no additional payment for photos accepted with ms. Captions, model releases and identification of subjects required. Also reviews photos separately. Rights purchased and rates vary.
Tips: "Our mainstays are how-tos, where-tos and conservation pieces."

PENNSYLVANIA GAME & FISH, Game & Fish Publications, Inc., Box 741, Marietta GA 30061. (770)953-9222. Editor: Steve Carpenteri. See *Game & Fish Publications.*

PETERSEN'S HUNTING, Petersen Publishing Co., 6420 Wilshire Blvd., Los Angeles CA 90048. (213)782-2184. Fax: (213)782-2477. Editor: Greg Tinsley. Managing Editor: Jennifer Tanabe. 40% freelance written. Works with a small number of new/unpublished writers each year. Monthly magazine covering sport hunting. "We are a 'how-to' magazine devoted to all facets of sport hunting, with the intent to make our readers more knowledgeable, more successful and safer hunters." Circ. 325,000. **Pays on acceptance.** Publishes ms an average of 9 months after acceptance. Byline given. Offers $50 kill fee. Buys all rights. Submit seasonal queries 9 months in advance. Reports in 2 weeks. Free sample copy and writer's guidelines covering format, sidebars and computer disks available on request.
Nonfiction: General interest, historical/nostalgic, how-to (on hunting techniques), travel. Special issues: Hunting Annual (August). Buys 30 mss/year. Query. Length: 2,000 words. Pays $350 minimum.
Photos: Send photos with submission. Reviews 35mm transparencies and 8×10 b&w prints. Offers no additional payment for b&w photos accepted with ms; offers $50-250/color photo. Captions, model releases, identification of subjects required. Buys one-time rights.

ROCKY MOUNTAIN GAME & FISH, Game & Fish Publications, Inc., Box 741, Marietta GA 30061. Fax: (770)933-9510. Contact: Burt Carey, editor. See *Game & Fish Publications.*

SAFARI MAGAZINE, The Journal of Big Game Hunting, Safari Club International, 4800 W. Gates Pass Rd., Tucson AZ 85745. (520)620-1220. Fax: (520)617-0233. Director of Publications/Editor: William R. Quimby. Contact: Elaine Cummings, manuscripts editor. 90% freelance written. Bimonthly club journal covering international big game hunting and wildlife conservation. Circ. 30,000. Pays on publication. Publishes ms an average of 18 months after

acceptance. Byline given. Offers $100 kill fee. Buys all rights on story; first rights on photos. Submit seasonal material 1 year in advance. Reports in 2 weeks on queries; 6 weeks on mss. Sample copy for $4. Writer's guidelines for SASE.
Nonfiction: Photo feature (wildlife), technical (firearms, hunting techniques, etc.). Buys 72 mss/year. Query or send complete ms. Length: 2,000-2,500 words. Pays $200 for professional writers, lower rates if not professional.
Photos: State availability of photos with query; or send photos with ms. Payment depends on size in magazine. Pays $45 for b&w; $100 color. Captions, model releases, identification of subjects required. Buys first rights.
Tips: "Study the magazine. Send complete manuscript and photo package. Make it appeal to knowledgeable, world-traveled big game hunters. Features on conservation contributions from big game hunters around the world are open to freelancers. We have enough stories on first-time African safaris and North American hunting. We need South American and Asian hunting stories, plus stories dealing with hunting and conservation, especially as it applies to our organization and members."

SALT WATER SPORTSMAN MAGAZINE, 77 Franklin St., Boston MA 02110. (617)338-2300. Fax: (617)338-2309. E-mail: 76424.1525@compuserve.com. Website: http://www.SWSFish.com. Contact: Barry Gibson, editor. Emphasizes saltwater fishing. 85% freelance written. Works with a small number of new/unpublished writers each year. Monthly magazine. "*Salt Water Sportsman* is edited for serious marine sport fishermen whose lifestyle includes the pursuit of game fish in US waters and around the world. It provides information on fishing trends, techniques and destinations, both local and international. Each issue reviews offshore and inshore fishing boats, high-tech electronics, innovative tackle, engines, vehicles and other new products. Coverage also focuses on sound fisheries management and conservation." Circ. 150,000. **Pays on acceptance.** Publishes ms an average of 5 months after acceptance. Byline given. Buys first North American serial rights. Offers 100% kill fee. Submit seasonal material 8 months in advance. Reports in 1 month. Sample copy and writer's guidelines for 9×12 SAE with 10 first-class stamps.
• Ranked as one of the best markets for freelance writers in *Writer's Yearbook*'s annual "Top 100 Markets," January 1997.
Nonfiction: How-to, personal experience, technical, travel (to fishing areas). "Readers want solid how-to, where-to information written in an enjoyable, easy-to-read style. Personal anecdotes help the reader identify with the writer." Prefers new slants and specific information. Query. "It is helpful if the writer states experience in salt water fishing and any previous related articles. We want one, possibly two well-explained ideas per query letter—not merely a listing. Good pictures with query often help sell the idea." Buys 100 mss/year. Length: 1,200-1,500 words. Pays $350 and up. Sometimes pays the expenses of writers on assignment.
Photos: Purchased with or without accompanying ms. Captions required. Uses color slides. Pays $1,000 minimum for 35mm, 2¼×2¼ or 8×10 transparencies for cover. Offers additional payment for photos accepted with accompanying ms.
Columns/Departments: Sportsman's Workbench (short, how-to tips and techniques on salt water fishing), 100 or more words.
Tips: "There are a lot of knowledgeable fishermen/budding writers out there who could be valuable to us with a little coaching. Many don't think they can write a story for us, but they'd be surprised. We work with writers. Shorter articles that get to the point which are accompanied by good, sharp photos are hard for us to turn down. Having to delete unnecessary wordage—conversation, clichés, etc.—that writers feel is mandatory is annoying. Often they don't devote enough attention to specific fishing information."

SOUTH CAROLINA GAME & FISH, Game & Fish Publications, Inc., Box 741, Marietta GA 30061. (770)953-9222. Editor: Bryan Hendricks. See *Game & Fish Publications*.

SOUTH CAROLINA WILDLIFE, P.O. Box 167, Rembert Dennis Bldg., Columbia SC 29202-0167. (803)734-3972. E-mail: scwmed@scdnr.state.sc.us. Editor: John Davis. Contact: Linda Renshaw, managing editor. Bimonthly magazine for South Carolinians interested in wildlife and outdoor activities. 75% freelance written. Estab. 1954. Circ. 60,000. Byline given. **Pays on acceptance.** Publishes ms an average of 6 months after acceptance. Buys first rights. Free sample copy. Reports in 2 months.
Nonfiction: Articles on outdoor South Carolina with an emphasis on preserving and protecting our natural resources. "Realize that the topic must be of interest to South Carolinians and that we must be able to justify using it in a publication published by the state department of natural resources—so if it isn't directly about outdoor recreation, a certain plant or animal, it must be somehow related to the environment and conservation. Readers prefer a broad mix of outdoor related topics (articles that illustrate the beauty of South Carolina's outdoors and those that help the reader get more for his/her time, effort, and money spent in outdoor recreation). These two general areas are the ones we most need. Subjects vary a great deal in topic, area and style, but must all have a common ground in the outdoor resources and heritage of South Carolina. Review back issues and query with a one-page outline citing sources, giving ideas for photographs, explaining justification and giving an example of the first two paragraphs." Does not need any column material. Generally does not seek photographs. The publisher assumes no responsibility for unsolicited material. Buys 25-30 mss/year. Length: 1,000-3,000 words. Pays an average of $200-400/article depending upon length and subject matter.
Tips: "We need more writers in the outdoor field who take pride in the craft of writing and put a real effort toward originality and preciseness in their work. Query on a topic we haven't recently done. Frequent mistakes made by writers in completing an article are failure to check details and go in-depth on a subject."

‡**SOUTHERN OUTDOORS MAGAZINE**, B.A.S.S. Publications, 5845 Carmichael Rd., Montgomery AL 36117. (205)277-3940. Editor: Larry Teague. Magazine published 9 times/year covering Southern outdoor activities, including hunting, fishing, boating, shooting and camping. 90% freelance written. Prefers to work with published/established writers. Estab. 1952. Circ. 257,000. **Pays on acceptance.** Publishes ms an average of 6 months to 1 year after acceptance. Buys all rights. Reports in 2 months. Sample copy for $3 and 9×12 SAE with 5 first-class stamps.

Nonfiction: Articles should be service-oriented, helping the reader excel in outdoor sports. Emphasis is on how-to, techniques, trends and conservation. Some "where-to" features purchased on Southern hunting and fishing destinations. Query. Buys 120 mss/year. Length: 2,000 words. Sidebars are a selling point. Pays 15-20¢/word.

Photos: Usually purchased with mss. Pays $75 for 35mm transparencies without ms, $400 for covers.

Fillers: Humorous or thought-provoking pieces (1,500 words) appear in each issue's S.O. Essay department.

Tips: "It's easiest to break in with short articles. We buy very little first-person. Stories most likely to sell: outdoor medicine, bass fishing, deer hunting, other freshwater fishing, inshore saltwater fishing, bird and small-game hunting, shooting, camping and boating."

SPORT FISHING, The Magazine of Saltwater Fishing, 330 W. Canton Ave., Winter Park FL 32789-7061. (407)628-4802. Fax: (407)628-7061. E-mail: sportfish@worldzine.com. Contact: Doug Olander, editor-in-chief. Managing Editor: Dave Ferrell. 60% freelance written. Magazine covering offshore sport fishing. Estab. 1986. Circ. 150,000. Pays within 6 weeks of acceptance. Byline given. Offers $100 kill fee. Buys first North American serial or one-time rights. Submit seasonal material 4-5 months in advance. Accepts simultaneous submission. Reports in 2 weeks. Sample copy and writer's guidelines for SASE.

Nonfiction: How-to (rigging & techniques tips), technical, travel (all on sport fishing). Buys 32-40 mss/year. Query with or without clips, e-mail preferred; fax, letter acceptable. Length: 1,500-2,500 words. Pays $150-600.

Photos: Send photos with submission. Reviews transparencies and returns within 1 weeks. Pays $50-300 inside; $1,000 cover. Identification of subjects required. Buys one-time rights.

Columns/Departments: Fish Tales (humorous sport fishing anecdotes), 800-1,500 words; Rigging (how-to rigging for sport fishing), 600-1,200 words; Technique (how-to technique for sport fishing), 800-1,500 words. Buys 8-24 mss/year. Send complete ms. Pays $200.

Tips: Do not query unless you are familiar with the magazine.

‡**SPORTING CLAYS MAGAZINE**, Patch Communications, 5211 S. Washington Ave., Titusville FL 32780. (407)268-5010. Fax: (407)267-1894. E-mail: dpsrun@aol.com. Website: http://www.sportingclays.net. Editor: George Conrad. Contact: Dan Sage, managing editor. Monthly magazine covering sporting clays. "*Sporting Clays* reports on shooting activities with instructional columns, equipment reviews and range listings, and is the official publication of the National Sporting Clays Association." Estab. 1987. Circ. 30,000. Pays on publication. Publishes ms an average of 6 months after acceptance. Byline given. Buys first North American serial rights. Editorial lead time 4 months. Submit seasonal material 6 months in advance. No simultaneous or previously published submissions. Reports in 1 month on queries.

Nonfiction: Historical/nostalgic, how-to (technique), interview/profile, new product, personal experience, photo feature, technical, travel. Buys 5 mss/year. Query with published clips and SASE. Length: 700-1,000 words.

Photos: Send photos with submission. Reviews transparencies, prints. Negotiates payment individually. Captions, identification of subjects required. Buys one-time rights.

SPORTS AFIELD, 250 W. 55th St., New York NY 10019-5201. (212)649-4000. Editor-in-Chief: Terry McDonell. Executive Editor: Fred Kesting. 20% freelance written. Magazine for the outdoor enthusiast with special interest in fishing and hunting. Covers a wide range of outdoor interests such as: boating, off-road, archery, survival, conservation, tackle, new gear, shooting sports, camping. Published 10 times/year. Estab. 1887. Circ. 450,000. Buys first North American serial rights for features. **Pays on acceptance.** Publishes ms an average of 6 months after acceptance. Byline given. "Our magazine is seasonal and material submitted should be in accordance. Fishing in spring and summer; hunting in the fall." Submit seasonal material 9 months in advance. Reports in 2 months. Query or submit complete ms. SASE for reply or writer's guidelines.

Nonfiction: "Informative how-to articles with emphasis on product and service and personal experiences with good photos on hunting, fishing, camping, conservation, and environmental issues (limited where-to-go) related to hunting and fishing. We want first-class writing and reporting." Buys 15-17 unsolicited mss/year. Length: 500-2,000 words.

Columns/Departments: Backcountry, 1,500 words maximum; Almanac (outdoor tips specifically for hunters, fishermen and campers, unusual, how-to and nature items), 200-300 words.

Photos: "For photos without ms, duplicates of 35mm color transparencies preferred."

Fiction: Adventure, humor, nostalgia (if related to hunting and fishing).

Tips: "Read a recent copy of *Sports Afield* so you know the market you're writing for. Manuscript *must* be available on disk."

"We are interested in where-to-go and how-to articles. Features based on outdoor products are welcome if they have a fresh slant. We also publish fiction, humor and cartoons, but no poetry. We prefer detailed queries first. This saves time and effort on your part as well as ours. If you are sending a finished manuscript, it should be double-spaced and a computer disk should be available if the story is accepted. If you are submitting photos, send only duplicates because there is always the chance that originals could be lost. Should we want original photos for publication, we will contact the photographer. *Sports Afield* is not responsible for any unsolicited photos or manuscripts."

TENNESSEE SPORTSMAN, Game & Fish Publications, Box 741, Marietta GA 30061. (770)953-9222. Editor: Bryan Hendricks. See *Game & Fish Publications*.

TEXAS SPORTSMAN, Game & Fish Publications, Inc., Box 741, Marietta GA 30061. (770)953-9222. Editor: Nick Gilmore. See *Game & Fish Publications*.

TIDE MAGAZINE, Coastal Conservation Association, 220W, 4801 Woodway, Houston TX 77056. (713)626-4222. Fax: (713)961-3801. Contact: Doug Pike, editor. Bimonthly magazine on saltwater fishing and conservation of marine resources. Estab. 1977. Circ. 52,000. Pays on publication. Byline given. Buys one-time rights. Submit seasonal material 6 months in advance. Reports in 1 month.
Nonfiction: Essays, exposé, general interest, historical/nostalgic, humor, opinion, personal experience and travel, related to saltwater fishing and gulf/Atlantic coastal habits. Buys 30 mss/year. Query with published clips. Length: 1,200-1,500 words. Pays $300 for ms/photo package.
Photos: Reviews 35mm transparencies and 8×10 b&w prints. Offers no additional payment for photos accepted with ms. Captions required. Buys one-time rights. Pays $25 for b&w, $50 for color inside.

TRAPPER & PREDATOR CALLER, Krause Publications Inc., 700 E. State St., Iola WI 54990. (715)445-2214. Fax: (715)445-4087. E-mail: gkrahn@add-inc.com. Website: http://www.Krause.com. Contact: Gordy Krahn, editor. 90% freelance written. Monthly tabloid covers trapping, predator calling and muzzleloading. "Our editorial goal is to entertain and educate our readers with national and regional articles that promote trapping." Estab. 1975. Circ. 35,000. Pays on publication. Offers $50 kill fee. Buys first North American serial rights. Submit seasonal material 6 months in advance. Reports in 2 weeks. *Writer's Market* recommends allowing 2 months for reply. Free sample copy and writer's guidelines.
Nonfiction: How-to, humor, interview/profile, new product, opinion and personal experience. Buys 60 mss/year. Query with or without published clips, or send complete ms. Length: 1,200-2,500 words. Pays $80-250 for assigned articles; $40-200 for unsolicited articles.
Photos: Send photos with submission. Reviews prints. Offers no additional payment for photos accepted with ms. Captions and identification of subjects required. Buys one-time rights.
Fillers: Facts, gags to be illustrated by cartoonist, newsbreaks and short humor. Buys 60/year. Length: 200-800 words. Pays $25-80.
Tips: "We are always looking for new ideas and fresh material on trapping, predator calling and black powder hunting."

‡TURKEY & TURKEY HUNTING, Krause Publications, 700 E. State St., Iola WI 54990-0001. (715)445-2214, ext. 484. Fax: (715)445-4087. Website: http://www.krause.com/outdoors. Contact: Brian Lovett, editor. 90% freelance written. Magazine published 6 times/year (4 spring, 1 fall, 1 winter) covering turkey hunting and turkey biology. "*Turkey & Turkey Hunting* is for serious, experienced turkey hunters." Estab. 1983. Circ. 28,000. *Pays on acceptance.* Publishes ms an average of 1 year after acceptance. Byline given. Offers 50% kill fee. Buys first North American serial rights. Editorial lead time 1 year. Submit seasonal material 1 year in advance. Reports in 2 months. Sample copy and writer's guidelines free.
Nonfiction: How-to, personal experience. Buys 45 mss/year. Query with published clips. Length: 2,000 words. Pays $275-300. Sometimes pays expenses of writers on assignment.
Photos: Send photos with submission. Reviews transparencies. Offers $75-300/photo, depending on size. Pays on publication for photos. Buys one-time rights.
Tips: "Have a thorough knowledge of turkey hunting and the hunting industry. Send fresh, informative queries, and indicate topics you'd feel comfortable covering on assignment."

TURKEY CALL, Wild Turkey Center, P.O. Box 530, Edgefield SC 29824-0530. (803)637-3106. Fax: (803)637-0034. E-mail: nwtf@gab.net. Editor: Jay Langston. Contact: Camille Roberegé-Myers, publishing assistant. 50-60% freelance written. Eager to work with new/unpublished writers and photographers. Bimonthly educational magazine for members of the National Wild Turkey Federation. Estab. 1973. Circ. 120,000. Buys one-time rights. Byline given. **Pays on acceptance.** Publishes ms an average of 6 months after acceptance. Reports in 1 month. Queries required. Submit complete package. Wants original mss only. Sample copy for $3 and 9×12 SAE. Writer's guidelines for #10 SASE.
Nonfiction: Feature articles dealing with the hunting and management of the American wild turkey. Must be accurate information and must appeal to national readership of turkey hunters and wildlife management experts. No poetry or first-person accounts of unremarkable hunting trips. May use some fiction that educates or entertains in a special way. Length: up 2,500 words. Pays $100 for short fillers of 600-700 words, $200-500 for illustrated features.
Reprints: Send photocopy of article and information about when and where the article previously appeared. Pays 50% of amount paid for an original article.
Photos: "We want quality photos submitted with features." Art illustrations also acceptable. "We are using more and more inside color illustrations." For b&w, prefer 8×10 glossies, but 5×7 OK. Transparencies of any size are acceptable. No typical hunter-holding-dead-turkey photos or setups using mounted birds or domestic turkeys. Photos with how-to stories must make the techniques clear (example: how to make a turkey call; how to sculpt or carve a bird in wood).

Pays $35 minimum for one-time rights on b&w photos and simple art illustrations; up to $100 for inside color, reproduced any size; $200-400 for covers.

Tips: "The writer should simply keep in mind that the audience is 'expert' on wild turkey management, hunting, life history and restoration/conservation history. He/she *must know the subject*. We are buying more third-person, more fiction, more humor—in an attempt to avoid the 'predictability trap' of a single subject magazine."

VIRGINIA GAME & FISH, Game & Fish Publications, Inc., Box 741, Marietta GA 30061. (770)953-9222. Editor: Bryan Hendricks. See *Game & Fish Publications*.

‡WARMWATER FLY FISHING, Abenaki Publishers, 160 Benmont Ave., P.O. Box 4100, Bennington VT 05201. (802)447-1518. Contact: John M. Likakis, editor. 95% freelance written. Bimonthly magazine covering fly fishing for bass, panfish, and other warmwater fish. "*Warmwater Fly Fishing* specializes in how-to, where-to, and when-to stories about fly fishing for warmwater species of fish. The emphasis is on nuts-and-bolts articles that tell the reader about specific techniques, places, equipment, etc." Estab. 1997. Circ. 10,000. Pays on publication. Publishes ms an average of 6 months after acceptance. Byline given. Buys first North American and one-time rights. Editorial lead time 6 months. Submit seasonal material 6 months in advance. Reports in 6 weeks on queries; 3 months on mss. Sample copy for $4.95. Writer's guidelines for $3 and #10 SASE.
Nonfiction: Historical/nostalgic, how-to, technical. No 'Me and Joe' fishing stories, exotic destinations, product reviews or puff pieces. Buys 70 mss/year. Query. Length: 1,000-2,500 words. Pays $250-350.
Photos: Send photos with submission. Reviews transparencies. Offers no additional payment for photos accepted with ms. "Unless otherwise specified, photos are considered part of the submission." Captions, model releases, identification of subjects reqired. Buys one-time rights.
Columns/Departments: Tech Tackle (innovative rigging); The Deep (fly fishing in deep water); The Tier (tying warmwater flies); all 1,500 words. Buys 54 mss/year. Query. Pays $250-350.
Tips: "Brief but complete query letters detailing what the article intends to cover. Neatness counts! Check your letter carefully for typos, misspellings, proper address and so forth."

WASHINGTON-OREGON GAME & FISH, Game & Fish Publications, Inc., Box 741, Marietta GA 30061. Editor: Burt Carey. See *Game & Fish Publications*.

WEST VIRGINIA GAME & FISH, Game & Fish Publications, Inc., Box 741, Marietta GA 30061. (770)953-9222. Editor: Ken Freel. See *Game & Fish Publications*.

WESTERN OUTDOORS, 3197-E Airport Loop, Costa Mesa CA 92626. (714)546-4370. E-mail: woutdoors@aol.com. Contact: Jack Brown, editor. 60% freelance written. Works with a small number of new/unpublished writers each year. Emphasizes fishing, boating for California, Oregon, Washington, Baja California, and Alaska. Publishes 9 issues/year. Estab. 1961. Circ. 100,000. **Pays on acceptance.** Publishes ms an average of 6 months after acceptance. Buys first North American serial rights. Submit seasonal material 6 months in advance. Reports in 2 weeks. Sample copy for $2, OWAA members, $1. Writer's guidelines for #10 SASE.
● *Western Outdoors* now emphasizes freshwater and saltwater fishing and boating exclusively. Area of coverage is limited to far west states and Baja California.
Nonfiction: Where-to (catch more fish, improve equipment, etc.), how-to informational, photo feature. "We do not accept fiction, poetry." Buys 45-55 assigned mss/year. Query in writing. Length: 1,000-1,500 words. Pays average $450.
Photos: Purchased with accompanying ms. Captions required. Prefers professional quality 35mm slides. Offers no additional payment for photos accepted with accompanying ms. Pays $250 for covers.
Tips: "Provide a complete package of photos, map, trip facts and manuscript written according to our news feature format. Excellence of color photo selections make a sale more likely. Include sketches of fishing patterns and techniques to guide our illustrators. Graphics are important. The most frequent mistake made by writers in completing an article for us is that they don't follow our style. Our guidelines are quite clear."

WESTERN SPORTSMAN, 140 Avenue F North, Saskatoon, Saskatchewan S7L 1V8 Canada. (306)665-6302. Fax: (306)244-8859. E-mail: copi@sk.sympatico.ca. Editor: George Gruenefeld. 90% freelance written. Bimonthly magazine for fishermen, hunters, campers and others interested in outdoor recreation. "Note that our coverage area is Alberta, Saskatchewan and Manitoba." Estab. 1968. Circ. 29,000. Rights purchased vary with author and material. Usually buys first North American serial or second serial (reprint) rights. Byline given. Pays on publication. "We try to include as much information as possible on all subjects in each edition. Therefore, we often publish fishing articles in our winter issues along with a variety of winter stories." Reports in 1 month. Sample copy for $4 and 9×12 SAE with 4 IRCs (US). Free writer's guidelines with SASE.
● *Western Sportsman* now accepts articles and news items relating to British Columbia, Yukon and Northwest Territories hunting and fishing.
Nonfiction: "It is necessary that all articles can identify with our coverage area. We are interested in manuscripts from writers who have experienced an interesting fishing or hunting experience. We also publish other informational pieces as long as they relate to our coverage area. We are more interested in articles which tell about the average guy living on beans, guiding his own boat, stalking his game and generally doing his own thing in our part of Western Canada

than a story describing a well-to-do outdoorsman traveling by motorhome, staying at an expensive lodge with guides doing everything for him except catching the fish or shooting the big game animal. The articles that are submitted to us need to be prepared in a knowledgeable way and include more information than the actual fish catch or animal or bird kill. Discuss the terrain, the people involved on the trip, the water or weather conditions, the costs, the planning that went into the trip, the equipment and other data closely associated with the particular event. We're always looking for new writers." Buys 60 mss/year. Submit complete ms and SASE or IRCs. Length: 1,500-2,000 words.

Reprints: Send typed ms with rights for sale noted and information about when and where the article previously appeared.

Photos: Photos purchased with ms with no additional payment. Also purchased without ms. Pays $150 for 35mm or larger transparency for front cover.

‡**WISCONSIN OUTDOOR JOURNAL**, Krause Publications, 700 E. State St., Iola WI 54990. (715)445-2214, ext. 484. Fax: (715)445-4087. Website: http://www.krause.com/outdoors. Contact: Brian Lovett, editor. 90% freelance written. Magazine published 8 times/year covering Wisconsin hunting, fishing, trapping, wildlife and related issues. "*Wisconsin Outdoor Journal* is for people interested in state-specific hunting, fishing, trapping and wildlife. We mix how-to features with area profiles and state outdoor issues." Estab. 1987. Circ. 26,000. **Pays on acceptance.** Publishes ms an average of 8-12 months after acceptance. Byline given. Offers 50% kill fee. Buys first North American serial rights. Editorial lead time 1 year. Submit seasonal material 1 year in advance. Reports in 2 months. Sample copy and writer's guidelines for SASE.

Nonfiction: General interest, historical/nostalgic, how-to. No stories focusing on out-of-state topics; no general recreation (hiking, biking, skiing) features. Buys 65 mss/year. Query with published clips. Length: 1,600-2,000 words. Pays $150-250. Sometimes pays expenses of writers on assignment.

Photos: Send photos with submission. Reviews transparencies. Offers $75-275/photo, depending on size. Buys one-time rights.

Columns/Departments: Wisconsin Field Notes (anecdotes, outdoor news items not extensively covered by newspapers, interesting outdoor occurrences, all relevant to Wisconsin; may include photos), 50-750 words. Pays $5-75 on publication. "Include SASE with photos only. Submissions other than photos for Field Notes will not be returned.

Tips: "Don't submit personal hunting and fishing stories. Seek fresh, new topics, such as an analysis of long-term outdoor issues."

WISCONSIN SPORTSMAN, Game & Fish Publications, Inc., Box 741, Marietta GA 30061. (770)953-9222. Editor: Dennis Schmidt. See *Game & Fish Publications*.

Martial Arts

BLACK BELT, Rainbow Publications, Inc., 24715 Ave. Rockefeller, Valencia CA 91355. (805)257-4066. Fax: (805)257-3028. E-mail: rainbow@cygnus.rsabbs.com. Website: http://www.blackbeltmag.com. Contact: Jim Coleman, executive editor. 80-90% freelance written. Works with a small number of new/unpublished writers each year. Monthly magazine emphasizing martial arts for both practitioner and layman. Estab. 1961. Circ. 100,000. Pays on publication. Publishes ms an average of 5 months after acceptance. Buys first North American serial rights, retains right to republish. Submit seasonal material 6 months in advance. Accepts simultaneous submissions if notified. Reports in 3 weeks.

Nonfiction: Exposé, how-to, informational, health/fitness, interview, new product, personal experience, technical, training, travel. "We never use personality profiles." Buys 8-9 mss/issue. Query with outline. Length: 1,200 words minimum. Pays $100-300.

Photos: Very seldom buys photos without accompanying mss. Captions required. Total purchase price for ms includes payment for photos. Model releases required.

Fiction: Historical, modern day, occasionally novel excerpts. Buys 1-2 mss/year. Query. Pays $100-150.

Tips: "We also publish an annual yearbook and special issues periodically. The yearbook includes our annual 'Black Belt Hall of Fame' inductees."

INSIDE KUNG-FU, The Ultimate In Martial Arts Coverage!, CFW Enterprises, 4201 Vanowen Place, Burbank CA 91505. (818)845-2656. Fax: (818)845-7761. Contact: Dave Cater, editor. 90% freelance written. Monthly magazine covering martial arts for those with "traditional, modern, athletic and intellectual tastes. The magazine slants toward little-known martial arts, and little-known aspects of established martial arts." Estab. 1973. Circ. 125,000. Pays on publication date on magazine cover. Publishes ms an average of 6 months after acceptance. Byline given. Offers 20% kill fee. Buys first North American serial rights. Editorial lead time 6 months. Submit seasonal material 6 months in advance. Accepts simultaneous submissions. Reports in 1 month on queries; 2 months on mss. Sample copy for $2.95 and 9×12 SAE with 5 first-class stamps. Writer's guidelines for #10 SASE.

● *Inside Kung-Fu* is looking for external-type articles (fighting, weapons, multiple hackers).

Nonfiction: Book excerpts, essays, exposé (topics relating to the martial arts), general interest, historical/nostalgic, how-to (primarily technical materials), cultural/philosophical, inspirational, interview/profile, new product, personal experience, photo feature, technical, travel. "Articles must be technically or historically accurate." No "sports coverage, first-person articles or articles which constitute personal aggrandizement." Buys 120 mss/year. Query or send complete ms. Length: 1,500-3,000 words (8-10 pages, typewritten and double-spaced). Pays $125-175.

Reprints: Send tearsheet of article or short story or typed ms with rights for sale noted and information about when and where the article previously appeared. No payment.

Photos: State availability or send photos with accompanying ms. Reviews contact sheets, negatives, 5×7 or 8×10 color prints. Offers no additional payment for photos. Captions, model release and identification of subjects required. Buys all rights.

Fiction: Adventure, historical, humorous, mystery, novel excerpts, suspense. "Fiction must be short (1,000-2,000 words) and relate to the martial arts. We buy very few fiction pieces." Publishes novel excerpts. Buys 2-3 mss/year.

Tips: "See what interests the writer. May have a better chance of breaking in at our publication with short articles and fillers since smaller pieces allow us to gauge individual ability, but we're flexible—quality writers get published, period. The most frequent mistakes made by writers in completing an article for us are ignoring photo requirements and model releases (always number one—and who knows why? All requirements are spelled out in writer's guidelines)."

JOURNAL OF ASIAN MARTIAL ARTS, Via Media Publishing Co., 821 W. 24th St., Erie PA 16502-2523. (814)455-9517. Fax: (814)838-7811. E-mail: viamedia@ncinter.net. Website: http://www.ncinter.net/~viamedia. Contact: Michael A. DeMarco, editor. 90% freelance written. Quarterly magazine covering "all historical and cultural aspects related to Asian martial arts, offering a mature, well-rounded view of this uniquely fascinating subject. Although the journal treats the subject with academic accuracy (references at end), writing need not lose the reader!" Estab. 1991. Pays on publication. Publishes ms an average of 1 year after acceptance. Byline given. Buys first world rights and second serial (reprint) rights. Submit seasonal material 6 months in advance. Reports in 1 month on queries; 2 months on mss. Sample copy for $10. Writer's guidelines for #10 SASE.

Nonfiction: Essays, exposé, historical/nostalgic, how-to (martial art techniques and materials, e.g., weapons, symbols), interview/profile, personal experience, photo feature (place or person), religious, technical, travel. "All articles should be backed with solid, reliable reference material. No articles overburdened with technical/foreign/scholarly vocabulary, or material slanted as indirect advertising or for personal aggrandizement." Buys 30 mss/year. Query with short background and martial arts experience. Length: 2,000-10,000 words. Pays $150-500 for unsolicited articles.

Reprints: Send information about when and where the article previously appeared.

Photos: State availability of photos with submission. Reviews contact sheets, negatives, transparencies, prints. Offers no additional payment for photos accepted with ms. Model releases and identification of subjects required. Buys one-time and reprint rights.

Columns/Departments: Location (city, area, specific site, Asian or Non-Asian, showing value for martial arts, researchers, history); Media Review (film, book, video, museum for aspects of academic and artistic interest). Buys 16 mss/year. Query. Length: 1,000-2,500 words. Pays $50-200.

Fiction: Adventure, historical, humorous, slice-of-life vignettes, translation. "We are not interested in material that does not focus on martial arts culture." Buys 1 mss/year. Query. Length: 1,000-10,000 words. Pays $50-500 or in copies.

Poetry: Avant-garde, free verse, haiku, light verse, traditional, translation. "No poetry that does not focus on martial art culture." Buys 2 poems/year. Submit maximum 10 poems. Pays $10-100 or in copies.

Fillers: Anecdotes, facts, gags to be illustrated by cartoonist, newsbreaks, short humor. Buys 2/year. Length: 25-500 words. Pays $1-50 in copies.

Tips: "Always query before sending a manuscript. We are open to varied types of articles; most however require a strong academic grasp of Asian culture. For those not having this background, we suggest trying a museum review, or interview, where authorities can be questioned, quoted and provide supportive illustrations. We especially desire articles/reports from Asia, with photo illustrations, particularly of a martial art style, so readers can visually understand the unique attributes of that style, its applications, evolution, etc. 'Location' and media reports are special areas that writers may consider, especially if they live in a location of martial art significance."

KARATE/KUNG FU ILLUSTRATED, Rainbow Publications, Inc., P.O. Box 918, Santa Clarita CA 91380. (805)257-4066. Fax: (805)257-3028. Website: http://www.blackbeltmag.com. Contact: Robert Young, executive editor. 70% freelance written. Bimonthly consumer magazine covering martial arts. "KKI presents factual historical accounts of the development of the martial arts, along with technical pieces on self-defense. We use only material from which readers can learn." Estab. 1969. Circ. 35,000. Pays on publication. Publishes ms an average of 8 months after acceptance. Byline given. Buys all rights. Editorial lead time 3 months. Submit seasonal material 4 months in advance. Accepts simultaneous submissions. Reports in 2 weeks on queries; 1 month on mss. Sample copy for 9×12 SAE and 5 first-class stamps. Writer's guidelines free.

• *Karate/Kung Fu Illustrated* now publishes "Black Belt for Kids," a separate section currently attached to the main magazine. Query with article ideas for young martial artists.

Nonfiction: Book excerpts, general interest (martial arts), historical/nostalgic (martial arts development), how-to (technical articles on specific kicks, punches, etc.), interview/profile (only with *major* martial artist), new products (for annual product review), travel (to Asian countries for martial arts training/research), comparisons of various styles and techniques. "No fiction or self-promotional pieces." Buys 30 mss/year. Query. Length: 1,000-3,000 words. Pays $100-200.

Photos: Freelancers should send photos with submission. Reviews contact sheets, negatives and 5×7 prints. Offers no additional payment for photos accepted with ms. Captions, model releases and identification of subjects required.

Columns/Departments: Bushido (essays explaining martial arts philosophy), 1,000-1,500 words; Counterkicks (letters to the editor). Buys 12 mss/year. Query. Pays $0-100.

Tips: "You need not be an expert in a specific martial art to write about it. But if you are not an expert, find one and use his knowledge to support your statements. Also, references to well-known books can help lend credence to the work of unknown writers. Inexperienced writers should begin by writing about a subject they know well. For example, if you study karate, start by writing about karate. Don't study karate for one year, then try to break in to a martial arts magazine by writing about Kung fu, because we already have Kung fu practitioners who write about that."

MARTIAL ARTS TRAINING, Rainbow Publications, P.O. Box 918, Santa Clarita CA 91380-9018. (805)257-4066. Fax: (805)257-3028. E-mail: rainbow@rsabbs.com. Website: http://www.blackbeltmag.com. Contact: Douglas Jeffrey, executive editor. 75% freelance written. Works with many new/unpublished writers each year. Bimonthly magazine about martial arts training. Estab. 1973. Circ. 35,000. Pays on publication. Publishes ms an average of 6 months after acceptance. Buys all rights. Submit seasonal material 4 months in advance. Reports in 1 month. Writer's guidelines for #10 SASE.

Nonfiction: How-to (training related features). Buys 30-40 unsolicited mss/year. Query. Length: 1,500-2,500 words. Pays $125-200.

Reprints: Accepts reprints of previously published submissions. Send tearsheet of article and information about when and where the article previously appeared.

Photos: "We prefer color prints. Please include the negatives." Model releases required. Buys all rights.

Tips: "I'm looking for how-to, nuts-and-bolts training stories that are martial arts related. Weight training, plyometrics, speed drills, cardiovascular workouts, agility drills, etc. Our magazine covers fitness and conditioning, not the martial arts techniques themselves."

T'AI CHI, Leading International Magazine of T'ai Chi Ch'uan, Wayfarer Publications, P.O. Box 26156, Los Angeles CA 90026. (213)665-7773. Fax: (213)665-1627. E-mail: taichi@tai-chi.com. Website: http://www.tai-chi.com. Contact: Marvin Smalheiser, editor. 90% freelance written. Bimonthly consumer magazine covering T'ai Chi Ch'uan as a martial art and for Health & Fitness. "Covers T'ai Chi Ch'uan and other internal martial arts, plus qigong and Chinese health, nutrition and philosophical disciplines. Readers are practitioners or laymen interested in developing skills and insight for self-defense, health and self-improvement." Estab. 1977. Circ. 30,000. Pays on publication. Publishes ms an average of 3 months after acceptance. Byline given. Buys first North American serial rights. Editorial lead time 3 months. Submit seasonal material 6 months in advance. Reports in 3 weeks on queries; 3 months on mss. Sample copy for $3.50. Writer's guidelines for #10 SASE.

● This publication needs more material but it must be related to the needs of its readers.

Nonfiction: Book excerpts, essays, how-to (on T'ai Chi Ch'uan, qigong and related Chinese disciplines), interview, personal experience. "Do not want articles promoting an individual, system or school." Buys 50-60 mss/year. Query or send complete ms. Length: 1,200-4,500 words. Pays $75-500. Sometimes pays expenses of writers on assignment.

Photos: Send photos with submission. Reviews color transparencies and color or b&w 3×5 prints. Offers no additional payment for photos accepted with mss but overall payment takes into consideration the number and quality of photos. Captions, model releases and identification of subjects required. Buys one-time and reprint rights.

Poetry: Free verse, light verse, traditional. "No poetry unrelated to our content." Buys 6 poems/year. Submit maximum 3 poems. Length: 12-30 lines. Pays $25-50.

Tips: "Think and write for practitioners and laymen who want information and insight and who are trying to work through problems to improve skills and their health. No promotional material."

Miscellaneous

‡BIG BROTHER, Pickhouse Publishing Group, Inc., 1330 E. Franklin St., El Segundo CA 90245. Contact: Marc McKee, editor. Managing Editor: Jeff Tremaine. 75% freelance written. Bimonthly magazine covering skateboarding. "*Big Brother* is a skateboard magazine with a wacky streak. While the typical *Big Brother* reader is a skateboarder in his teens and early twenties, readers also include moms and grandpas and any other relatives or the happy-go-lucky skateboard fanatic. The editorial tone of *Big Brother*, if it can be characterized at all, is irreverent with a strong tendency towards stupidity." Estab. 1992. Circ. 70,000. Pays on publication. Publishes ms an average of 2 months after acceptance. Byline given. Offers 5% kill fee. Buys all rights. Editorial lead time 3 months. Submit seasonal material 3 months in advance. Sample copy $3.95 with SAE and 6 first-class stamps.

Nonfiction: Humor, interview/profile, opinion, photo feature. "We do not want to see any articles with sad endings." Send complete ms. Length: 35-2,400 words. Pays 20-35¢/word. Sometimes pays expenses of writers on assignment.

Photos: Send photos with submission. Negotiates payment individually. Identification of subjects required. Buys all rights.

Columns/Departments: Who Fucking Cares (this column is set aside for thorough discussions of the most pointless topics, i.e., moist towelette package graphic design).

Fiction: Erotic, fantasy, horror, romance, science fiction. "We do not want to see any fiction that deals with animals." Buys 6 mss/year. Send complete ms. Length: 100-1,600 words. Pays 20-35¢/word.

Poetry: Traditional, limericks. "We don't want any poetry that doesn't deal exclusively with skateboarding." Buys 12 poems/year. Submit maximum 4 poems. Pays 20-35¢/word.

Fillers: Gags to be illustrated by cartoonist, short humor. Buys 24/year. Length 20-400 words. Pays 25-35¢/word.

Tips: "Submit all contributions on floppy disks (Mac only) with an accompanying hard copy. All contributions should be written with the intent that they be illustrated with either photographs (color slides) or illustrations (or both). All stories must begin with a brief synopsis of ten words or less summarizing their basic plot, their main theme and a complete description of their major characters."

‡**CANADIAN RODEO NEWS**, Canadian Rodeo News, Ltd., #223 NE, 2116 27th Ave., Calgary, Alberta T2E 7A6 Canada. (403)250-7292. Fax: (403)250-6926. E-mail: rodeonews@iul-ccs.com. Website: http://www.rodeocanada.com. Contact: Kirby Meston, editor. 60% freelance written. Monthly tabloid covering "Canada's professional rodeo (CPRA) personalities and livestock. Read by rodeo participants and fans." Estab. 1964. Circ. 48,000. Pays on publication. Publishes ms an average of 1 month after acceptance. Byline given. Buys first and second serial (reprint) rights. Editorial lead time 1 month. Submit seasonal material 1 month in advance. Accepts simultaneous submissions. Reports in 1 month on queries; 2 months on mss. Sample copy and writer's guidelines free.

Nonfiction: General interest, historical/nostalgic, interview/profile. Buys 70-80 mss/year. Query. Length: 500-1,200 words. Pays $25-50.

Reprints: Send tearsheet of article or short story.

Photos: Send photos with submission. Reviews 4×6 prints. Offers $10-15 maximum per cover photo. Buys one-time rights.

Tips: "Best to call first with the story idea to inquire if it is suitable for publication. Readers are very knowledgeable of the sport, so writers need to be as well."

‡**EXTREME SPORTS**, MVP Media, 1920 Higlhand Ave., Suite 220, Lombard IL 60148. Editor: Dan Butler. 30% freelance written. Annual magazine covering "skateboarding, hang gliding, roller blading, parasailing, motorcycling, etc. *Extreme Sports* is a graphics-heavy look at the new sports interests of the younger generation. It's aimed at readers aged 15-30. We're looking for profiles of the major figures, analysis and how-to features." Estab. 1996. **Pays on acceptance** depending on assignment and proximity to publication. Publishes ms an average of 3 months after acceptance. Byline given. Offers 10-25% kill fee. Buys various rights or makes work-for-hire assignments. Editorial lead time 4 months. Submit seasonal material 2 months in advance. Reports in 3 weeks on queries; 2 months on mss. Sample copy for 10×13 SAE and $2.25 in postage.

Nonfiction: Interview/profile, photo feature. Extreme Sports: Stories on skate boarding, roller blading, biking, etc. Extreme racing: Stories on cycle racing, snowmobiling, formula one, boat racing, etc. No first-person features without attribution. We prefer prospective freelancers to contact us first." Buys 20-50 mss/year. Query with published clips. Length: 1,000-4,000 words. Pays $100-500.

Photos: Send photos with submission. Reviews transparencies and prints. Negotiates payment individually. Captions and identification of subjects required. Buys all rights.

Tips: "Send samples, writing history, clips and SASE to the editor. We generally create assignment lists in-house and farm them out to freelancers. We're looking for writers who have good contacts. Know their subject matter and aren't afraid to adopt an irreverent style."

‡**LACROSSE MAGAZINE**, The Lacrosse Foundation, 113 W. University Pkwy., Baltimore MD 21210. (410)235-6882. Fax: (410)366-6735. E-mail: mbouchard@lacrosse.org. Website: http://www.lacrosse.org. Editor: Marc Bouchard. 75% freelance written. Magazine published 8 times/year during lacrosse season, bimonthly off-season, by the Lacrosse Foundation for its members. *Lacrosse Magazine* is the only national feature publication devoted to the sport of lacrosse. It is a benefit of membership in The Lacrosse Foundation, a nonprofit organization devoted to promoting the growth of lacrosse and preserving its history. Estab. 1978. Circ. 15,000. Pays on publication. Publishes ms 2 months after acceptance. Byline given. Buys one-time rights. Editorial lead time 2 months. Submit seasonal material 2 months in advance. Sample copy and writer's guidelines free.

Nonfiction: Book excerpts, general interest, historical/nostalgic, how-to (drills, conditioning, x's and o's, etc.), interview/profile, new product, opinion, personal experience, photo feature, technical. Buys 30-40 mss/year. Send complete ms. Length: 500-1,750 words. Pays $50-150 for assigned articles; $0-100 for unsolicited articles. Sometimes pays expenses of writers on assignment.

Reprints: Accepts reprints of previously published submissions. Publishes novel excerpts.

Photos: State availability of photos with submission. Reviews contact sheets and 4×6 prints. Negotiates payment individually. Captions and identification of subjects required. Buys one-time rights.

Columns/Departments: First Person (personal experience), 1,000 words; Fitness (conditioning/strength/exercise), 500-1,000 words. Buys 10-15 mss/year. Send complete ms. Pays $0-50.

Tips: "As the national development center of lacrosse, we are particularly interested in stories about the growth of the sport in non-traditional areas of the U.S. and abroad."

POLO, Polo Publications, Inc., 3500 Fairlane Farms Rd., Suite 9, Wellington FL 33414. (561)793-9524. Fax: (561)793-9576. E-mail: polomag@aol.com. Editor: Peter Rizzo. Contact: Gwen Rizzo, managing editor. Magazine published 10 times/year on polo—the sport and lifestyle. "Our readers are an affluent group. Most are well-educated, well-read and highly sophisticated." Circ. 6,500. **Pays on acceptance.** Publishes ms an average 4 months after acceptance. Kill fee varies. Buys first North American serial rights and makes work-for-hire assignments. Submit seasonal material 3 months in advance. Accepts simultaneous submissions. Reports in 3 months. Writer's guidelines for #10 SAE with 2 first-class stamps.

Nonfiction: Gwen Rizzo, senior editor. Historical/nostalgic, interview/profile, personal experience, photo feature, technical, travel. Buys 20 mss/year. Query with published clips or send complete ms. Length: 800-3,000 words. Pays $150-400 for assigned articles; $100-300 for unsolicited articles. Sometimes pays expenses of writers on assignment.

Reprints: Send tearsheet of article and information about when and where the article previously appeared. Pays 50% of amount paid for an original article.

Fiction: Publishes novel excerpts.

Photos: State availability of photos or send photos with submission. Reviews contact sheets, transparencies, prints. Offers $20-150/photo. Captions required. Buys one-time rights.

Columns/Departments: Yesteryears (historical pieces), 500 words; Profiles (clubs and players), 800-1,000 words. Buys 15 mss/year. Query with published clips. Pays $100-300.

Tips: "Query us on a personality or club profile or historic piece or, if you know the game, state availability to cover a tournament. Keep in mind that ours is a sophisticated, well-educated audience."

RACQUETBALL MAGAZINE, United States Racquetball Association, 1685 W. Uintah, Colorado Springs CO 80904. (719)635-5396. Fax: (719)635-0685. Director of Communications: Linda Mojer. 20-30% freelance written. Bimonthly magazine "geared toward a readership of informed, active enthusiasts who seek entertainment, instruction and accurate reporting of events." Estab. 1990. Circ. 45,000. Pays on publication. Publishes ms an average of 2 months after acceptance. Buys one-time rights. Editorial lead time 3 months. Submit seasonal material 3 months in advance. Accepts simultaneous submissions. Reports in 2 months. Sample copy for $4. Writer's guidelines free.

Nonfiction: How-to (instructional racquetball tips), humor, interview/profile (personalities who play racquetball). Buys 2-3 mss/year. Send complete ms. Length: 1,500-3,000 words. Pays $100. Sometimes pays expenses of writers on assignment.

Reprints: Send typed ms with rights for sale noted and information about when and where the article previously appeared.

Photos: Send photos with submission. Reviews 3×5 prints. Negotiates payment individually. Model releases, identification of subjects required. Buys one-time rights.

Fiction: Humorous (racquetball related). Buys 1-2 mss/year. Send complete ms. Length: 1,500-3,000 words. Pays $100-250.

REFEREE, Referee Enterprises, Inc., P.O. Box 161, Franksville WI 53126-9987. (414)632-8855. Fax: (414)632-5460. E-mail: refmag@execpc.com. Editor: Scott Ehret. Contact: Andrew Greene, associate editor. 30-40% freelance written. Works with a number of new/unpublished writers each year. Monthly magazine for well-educated, mostly 26- to 50-year-old male sports officials of all levels and all sports. Estab. 1975. Circ. 35,000. **Pays on acceptance** of completed ms. Publishes ms an average of 4 months after acceptance. Rights purchased varies. Submit seasonal material 6 months in advance. Reports in 2 weeks. Sample copy for 10×13 SAE with 7 first-class stamps. Writer's guidelines for #10 SASE.

Nonfiction: How-to, informational, humor, interview, profile, personal experience, photo feature, technical. Buys 54 mss/year. Query. Length: 700-3,000 words. Pays 10¢/word. "No general sports articles."

Reprints: Send photocopy of article or typed ms with rights for sale noted and information about when and where it previously appeared. Pays 50% of amount paid for an original article.

Photos: Purchased with or without accompanying ms or on assignment. Captions preferred. Send contact sheet, prints, negatives or transparencies. Pays $20 for each b&w used; $35 for each color used; $100 for color cover; $75 for b&w cover.

Columns/Departments: Law (legal aspects); Between the Lines (anecdotes); Heads Up (psychology). Buys 24 mss/year. Query. Length: 200-700 words. Pays 4¢/word up to $100 maximum for regular columns.

Fillers: Jokes, gags, anecdotes, puzzles, referee shorts. Query. Length: 50-200 words. Pays 4¢/word in some cases; others offer only author credit lines.

Tips: "Queries with a specific idea appeal most to readers. Generally, we are looking more for feature writers, as we usually do our own shorter/filler-type material. It is helpful to obtain suitable photos to augment a story. Don't send fluff—we need hard-hitting, incisive material tailored just for our audience. Anything smacking of public relations is a no sale. Don't gloss over the material too lightly or fail to go in-depth looking for a quick sale (taking the avenue of least resistance)."

‡RUGBY MAGAZINE, Rugby Press Limited, 2350 Broadway, New York NY 10024. (212)787-1160. Fax: (212)595-0934. E-mail: rugby@inch.com or rugbymag@aol.com. Website: http://www.inch.com/~rugby. Editor: Ed Hagerty. Contact: Michael Malone, managing editor. 75% freelance written. Monthly tabloid on the sport of rugby. "*Rugby Magazine* is the journal of record for the sport of rugby in the U.S. Our demographics are among the best in the country." Estab. 1975. Circ. 10,000. Pays on publication. Publishes ms an average of 2 months after acceptance. Byline given. Buys all rights. Editorial lead time 1 month. Submit seasonal material 2 months in advance. Accepts simultaneous and previously published submissions. Reports in 2 weeks on queries; 1 months on mss. Sample copy for $3. Writer's guidelines free.

Nonfiction: Book excerpts, essays, general interest, historical/nostalgic, how-to, humor, interview/profile, new product, opinion, personal experience, photo feature, technical, travel. Buys 15 mss/year. Send complete ms. Length: 600-2,000 words. Pays $50 minimum. Pays expenses of writers on assignment.

Reprints: Send tearsheet of article or short story or typed ms with rights for sale noted and information about when and where the article previously appeared. Pay varies.

Photos: Send photos with submission. Reviews negatives, transparencies and prints. Offers no additional payment for photos accepted with ms. Buys all rights.

Columns/Departments: Nutrition, athletic nutrition, 900 words; Referees' Corner, 1,200 words; The Zen Rugger (Rugby as Zen), 650 words. Buys 2-3 mss/year. Query with published clips. Pays $50 maximum.

Fiction: Condensed novels, humorous, novel excerpts, slice-of-life vignettes. Buys 1-3 mss/year. Query with published. Length: 1,000-2,500 words. Pays $50.

Tips: "Give us a call. Send along your stories or photos; we're happy to take a look. Tournament stories are a good way to get yourself published in *Rugby Magazine.*

SKYDIVING, 1725 N. Lexington Ave., DeLand FL 32724. (904)736-4793. Fax: (904)736-9786. Editor: Michael Truffer. 25% freelance written. Works with a small number of new/unpublished writers each year. Monthly tabloid featuring skydiving for sport parachutists, worldwide dealers and equipment manufacturers. Circ. 14,200. Average issue includes 3 feature articles and 3 columns of technical information. Pays on publication. Publishes ms an average of 3 months after acceptance. Byline given. Buys one-time rights. Accepts simultaneous submissions, if so noted. Reports in 1 month. Sample copy for $2. Writer's guidelines for 9 × 12 SAE with 4 first-class stamps.

Nonfiction: "Send us news and information on equipment, techniques, events and outstanding personalities who skydive. We want articles written by people who have a solid knowledge of parachuting." No personal experience or human-interest articles. Query. Length: 500-1,000 words. Pays $25-100. Sometimes pays the expenses of writers on assignment.

Reprints: Accepts previously published submissions.

Photos: State availability of photos. Reviews 5 × 7 and larger b&w glossy prints. Offers no additional payment for photos accepted with ms. Captions required.

Fillers: Newsbreaks. Length: 100-200 words. Pays $25 minimum.

Tips: "The most frequent mistake made by writers in completing articles for us is that the writer isn't knowledgeable about the sport of parachuting."

VOLLEYBALL MAGAZINE, Avcom Publishing, Ltd., 164 Avenida Granada, San Clemente CA 92672. (714)366-5910. Fax: (714)366-5975. E-mail: vballmag@aol.com. Contact: Rick Hazeltine, editor. Executive Editor: Don Patterson. 50% freelance written. Monthly magazine covering the sport of volleyball. Estab. 1990. Circ. 85,000. Pays on publication. Publishes ms an average of 3 months after acceptance. Byline given. Offers 50% kill fee. Buys first North American serial rights. Editorial lead time 3 months. Submit seasonal material 3 months in advance.

• The editor notes that he is particularly interested in short features (600-900 words) on individuals who are doing exceptional things in volleyball—such as a player overcoming tragedy or illness; someone who works to build the sport locally; special people; doing special things for the game. Pays $100-150.

Nonfiction: Historical/nostalgic, how-to (skills instruction, nutrition strategy, fitness), humor, interview/profile, technical. No event coverage. Buys 72 mss/year. Query with published clips. Length: 250-3,000 words. Pays $100-750. Pays expenses of writers on assignment.

Reprints: Send typed ms with rights for sale noted and information about when and where the article previously appeared. Payment negotiable.

Photos: Send photos with submission. Reviews transparencies—no duplicates. Offers $40-225/photo. Captions, model releases and identification of subjects requried. Buys one-time rights.

Columns/Departments: Fitness (must relate specifically to volleyball); Nutrition (for athletes); both 1,000-1,200 words. Buys 36 mss/year. Query with published clips. Pays $200-250.

Olympic Sports

INTERNATIONAL OLYMPIC LIFTER, IOL Publications, 3602 Eagle Rock, P.O. Box 65855, Los Angeles CA 90065. (213)257-8762. Fax: (213)344-9865. Editor: Bob Hise. 20% freelance written. Bimonthly magazine covering the Olympic sport of weightlifting. Estab. 1973. Circ. 10,000. Pays on publication. Publishes ms an average of 3 months after acceptance. Byline given. Offers $25 kill fee. Buys one-time rights or negotiable rights. Submit seasonal material 5 months in advance. Reports in 3 months. Sample copy for $4. Writer's guidelines for 9 × 12 SAE with 5 first-class stamps.

• *International Olympic Lifter* needs more biographies and training routines on the *Olympic* weightlifting top names.

Nonfiction: Training articles, contest reports, diet—all related to Olympic weightlifting. Buys 4 mss/year. Query. Length: 250-2,000 words. Pays $25-100.

Reprints: Send photocopy of article and information about when and where the article previously appeared. Payment is negotiated.

Photos: Action (competition and training). State availability of photos. Pays $1-5 for 5 × 7 b&w prints. Identification of subjects required.

Poetry: Dale Rhoades, poetry editor. Light verse, traditional—related to Olympic lifting. Buys 6-10 poems/year. Submit maximum 3 poems. Length: 12-24 lines. Pays $10-20.

Tips: "A writer must be acquainted with Olympic-style weightlifting. Since we are an international publication we do not tolerate ethnic, cultural, religious or political inclusions. Articles relating to AWA are readily accepted."

OLYMPIAN MAGAZINE, US Olympic Committee, One Olympic Plaza, Colorado Springs CO 80909. (719)578-4529. Fax: (719)578-4677. E-mail: fxzeng@aol.com. Managing Editor: Frank Zang. 50% freelance written. Bimonthly magazine covering olympic sports and athletes. Estab. 1974. Circ. 120,000. Pays on publication. Byline given. Offers 100% kill fee. Free writer's guidelines.
 • *Olympian Magazine* will have 2 special preview issues for the 1998 Olympic Winter Games. Part I (November/December '97); Part II (January/February '98).

Nonfiction: Photo feature, feature/profiles of athletes in Olympic sports. Query. Length: 1,200-2,000 words. Pays $300.

Reprints: Send photocopy of article. Pay 50% of amount paid for an original article.

Photos: State availability of photos with submission. Reviews transparencies and prints. Offers $50-250/photo. Captions, model releases and identification of subjects required. Buys one-time rights.

‡USA GYMNASTICS, 201 S. Capitol Ave., Suite 300, Pan American Plaza, Indianapolis IN 46225. (317)237-5050. Fax: (317)237-5069. Editor: Luan Peszek. 20% freelance written. Bimonthly magazine covering gymnastics—national and international competitions. Designed to educate readers on fitness, health, safety, technique, current topics, trends and personalities related to the gymnastics/fitness field. Readers are ages of 7-18, parents and coaches. Estab. 1981. Circ. 63,000. Pays on publication. Publishes ms an average of 4 months after acceptance. Byline given. Buys all rights. Submit seasonal material 4 months in advance. Accepts simultaneous and previously published submissions. Reports in 2 months. Sample copy for $5.

Nonfiction: General interest, how-to (related to fitness, health, gymnastics), inspirational, interview/profile, new product, opinion (Open Floor section), photo feature. Buys 3 mss/year. Query. Length: 1,500 words maximum. Payment negotiated.

Photos: Send photos with submission. Offers no additional payment for photos accepted with ms. Identification of subjects required. Buys all rights.

Tips: "Any articles of interest to gymnasts (men, women and rhythmic gymnastics) coaches, judges and parents, are what we're looking for. This includes nutrition, toning, health, safety, current trends, gymnastics techniques, timing techniques etc."

Running

‡INSIDE TEXAS RUNNING, 9514 Bristlebrook Dr., Houston TX 77083. (281)498-3208. Fax: (281)879-9980. E-mail: texasrun@ix.netcom.com. Website: http://www.RunningNetwork.com/TexasRunning. Editor: Joanne Schmidt. 70% freelance written. Monthly (except June and August) tabloid covering running and running-related events. "Our audience is made up of Texas runners who may also be interested in cross training with biking and swimming." Estab. 1977. Circ. 10,000. **Pays on acceptance.** Publishes ms an average of 1-2 months after acceptance. Byline given. Buys first rights, one-time rights, second serial (reprint) rights, exclusive Texas and all rights. Submit seasonal material 2 months in advance. Accepts previously published submissions. Send photocopy of article. Pays 100% of their fee for an original article. Reports in 1 month on mss. Sample copy for $1.50. Writer's guidelines for #10 SASE.

Nonfiction: Various topics of interest to runners. No personal experience such as 'Why I Love to Run,' 'How I Ran My First Marathon.' Buys 20 mss/year. Send complete ms. Length: 500-1,500 words. Pays $100 maximum for assigned articles; $50 maximum for unsolicited articles.

Reprints: Send tearsheet, photocopy or typed ms with rights for sale noted and information about when and where the article previously appeared. Pays 100% of amount paid for an original article.

Photos: Send photos with submission. Offers $25 maximum/photo. Captions required. Buys one-time rights.

Tips: "Writers should be familiar with the sport and the publication. The best way to break in to our publication is to submit brief (three or four paragraphs) fillers for our 'Texas Roundup' section."

NEW YORK RUNNING NEWS, New York Road Runners Club, 9 E. 89th St., New York NY 10128. (212)860-2280. Fax: (212)860-9754. Contact: Don Mogelefsky, editor. Associate Editor: Sarah Lorge. Bimonthly regional sports

---

ALWAYS SUBMIT unsolicited manuscripts or queries with a self-addressed, stamped envelope (SASE) within your country or a self-addressed envelope with International Reply Coupons (IRC) purchased from the post office for other countries.

magazine covering running, racewalking, nutrition and fitness. Material should be of interest to members of the New York Road Runners Club. Estab. 1958. Circ. 45,000. Pays on publication. Time to publication varies. Byline given. Offers 33% kill fee. Buys first North American serial rights. Submit seasonal material 4 months in advance. Accepts simultaneous submissions. Reports in 2 months. Sample copy for $3. Writer's guidelines for #10 SASE.

Nonfiction: Running and marathon articles. Special issues: N.Y.C. Marathon (submissions in by August 1). No non-running stories. Buys 25 mss/year. Query. Length: 750-1,000 words. Pays $50-250.

Reprints: Send photocopy of article with information about when and where it previously appeared. Pays 25-50% of amount paid for an original article.

Photos: Send photos with submission. Reviews 8×10 b&w prints. Offers $35-300/photo. Captions, model releases, identification of subjects required. Buys one-time rights.

Tips: "Be knowledgeable about the sport of running. Write like a runner."

RUNNER'S WORLD, Rodale Press, 33 E. Minor St., Emmaus PA 18098. (610)967-5171. Senior Editor: Bob Wischnia. Contact: Claire Kowalchik, managing editor. 5% freelance written. Monthly magazine on running, mainly long-distance running. "The magazine for and about distance running, training, health and fitness, injury precaution, race coverage, personalties of the sport." Estab. 1966. Circ. 435,000. Pays on publication. Publishes ms an average of 6 months after acceptance. Byline given. Buys all rights. Submit seasonal material 6 months in advance. Reports in 2 months. Writer's guidelines for #10 SASE.

Nonfiction: How-to (train, prevent injuries), interview/profile, personal experience. No "my first marathon" stories. No poetry. Buys 10 mss/year. Query. Pays $1,500-2,000. Pays expenses of writers on assignment.

Photos: State availability of photos with submission. Identification of subjects required. Buys one-time rights.

Columns/Departments: Christina Negron. Finish Line (personal experience—humor); Training Log (training of well-known runner); Women's Running. Buys 15 mss/year. Query. Pays $50 for departments, $300 for essays.

Skiing and Snow Sports

AMERICAN SKATING WORLD, Independent Newsmonthly of American Ice Skating, Business Communications Inc., 1816 Brownsville Rd., Pittsburgh PA 15210-3908. (412)885-7600. Fax: (412)885-7617. Editor: Robert A. Mock. Contact: H. Kermit Jackson, managing editor. 70% freelance written. Eager to work with new/unpublished writers. Monthly magtab on figure skating. Estab. 1979. Circ. 15,000. Pays following publication. Publishes ms an average of 3 months after acceptance. Byline given. Buys first North American serial rights and occasionally second serial (reprint) rights. Submit seasonal material 3 months in advance. Reports in 3 months. Sample copy and writer's guidelines for $3.50.

● The increased activity and interest in figure skating have increased demands on *American Skating World*'s contributor network. New writers from nontraditional areas (i.e., outside of East Coast, Upper Midwest, California) are particularly welcome.

Nonfiction: Competition coverage, exposé, historical/nostalgic, how-to (technique in figure skating), humor, inspirational, interview/profile, new product, opinion, performance coverage, personal experience, photo feature, technical, travel. Special issues: annual fashion issue (September); Skate Stuff (October 1997); The Industry (May 1998). Rarely accepts fiction. AP Style Guidelines are the basic style source, but we are not bound by that convention. Short, snappy paragraphs desired. Buys 150 mss/year. Send complete ms. "Include phone number; response time longer without it." Length: 600-1,000 words. Pays $25-100.

Reprints: Occasionally accepts previously published submissions. Send tearsheet of article and information about when and where the article previously appeared. Payment is negotiated.

Photos: Send photos with query or ms. Reviews transparencies and b&w prints. Pays $5 for b&w; $10 for color. Identification of subjects required. Buys all rights for b&w; one-time rights for color.

Columns/Departments: Buys 30 mss/year. Send complete ms. Length: 500-750 words. Pays $25-50.

Fillers: Clippings, anecdotes. No payment for fillers.

Tips: "Event coverage is most open to freelancers; confirm with managing editor to ensure event has not been assigned. We are drawing more extensively from non-U.S. based writers. Questions are welcome; call managing editor EST, 10-4, Monday-Friday."

‡AMERICAN SNOWMOBILER, The Enthusiast Magazine, Recreation Publications, Inc., 7582 Currell Blvd., #212, St. Paul MN 55125. (612)738-1953. Fax: (612)738-2302. E-mail: editor@amsnow.com. Website: http://www.amsnow.com. Contact: Jerry Bassett, editor. 30% freelance written. Magazine published 6 times seasonally covering snowmobiling. Estab. 1985. Circ. 80,000. **Pays on acceptance.** Publishes ms an average of 4 months after acceptance. Byline given. Offers 15% kill fee. Buys all rights including electronic. Editorial lead time 4 months. Submit seasonal material 6 months in advance. Reports in 1 month on queries; 2 months on mss. Writer's guidelines for #10 SASE.

Nonfiction: General interest, historical/nostalgic, how-to, interview/profile, new product, personal experience, photo feature, travel. Buys 10 mss/year. Query with published clips. Length: 1,000-2,000 words. Pay varies for assigned articles; $100 minimum for unsolicited articles.

Photos: State availability of photos with submission. Offers no additional payment for photos accepted with ms. Captions, model releases and identification of subjects required. Buys all rights.

‡**BLUNT SNOWBOARD MAGAZINE**, Dickhouse Publishing Group, Inc., 1330 E. Franklin St., El Segundo CA 90245. Contact: Marc McKee, editor. 75% freelance written. Magazine published 5 times/year covering snowboarding. *"Blunt* is dedicated to providing detailed, often sexually explicit, uncensored coverage of the savage, yet fascinating, world of the modern snowboarder. *Blunt*'s readership consists mainly of snowboarders ranging in age from their early teens to late twenties, and to appeal to their refined tastes we seek to offer only the most sensational and ridiculous reading." Estab. 1994. Circ. 75,000. Pays on publication. Publishes ms an average of 2 months after acceptance. Byline given. Offers 5% kill fee. Buys all rights. Editorial lead time 3 months. Submit seasonal material 3 months in advance. Sample copy for $3.95 with 9×12 SAE and 6 first-class stamps.
Nonfiction: Exposé, humor, inspirational, interview/profile, photo feature, religious, travel. "We do not want any articles on skiing." Buys 20 mss/year. Send complete ms. Length: 12-2,500 words. Pays 20-35¢/word. Sometimes pays expenses of writers on assignment.
Photos: Send photos with submission. Reviews color slides. Negotiates payment individually. Identification of subjects required. Buys all rights.
Columns/Departments: CD review section, 250 words. Buys 30 mss/year. Send complete ms. Pays 20-35¢/word.
Fiction: Adventure, confession, erotica, horror, humorous, religious, slice-of-life vignettes. "We do not want to see any fiction that is not hilarious." Buys 4 mss/year. Send complete ms.
Poetry: Avant-garde, haiku, traditional. "We do not want any poetry that doesn't rhyme, and we are not interested in sonnets." Buys 6 poems/year. Submit maximum 4 poems. Length: 4-12 syllables. Pays 20-35¢/word.
Fillers: Gags to be illustrated by cartoonist, short humor. Buys 20/year. Length: 17-500 words. Pays 20-35¢/word.
Tips: "Avoid submitting any long, rambling dissertations. The ideal *Blunt* story is short and to the point, but with a surprise ending. The best submission method is by floppy disk (Mac only), with an accompanying hard copy. All CD reviews must come with either a photo (color slide) or hard copy of the CD artwork."

SKATING, United States Figure Skating Association, 20 First St., Colorado Springs CO 80906-3697. (719)635-5200. Fax: (719)635-9548. E-mail: skatemag@aol.com. Editor: Jay Miller. Contact: Blain Fowler, assistant editor. Official publication of the USFSA, published 10 times/year. Estab. 1923. Circ. 40,000. Pays on publication. Publishes ms an average of 3 months after acceptance. Buys all rights. Byline given.
Nonfiction: Historical, informational, interview, photo feature, historical biographies, profile (background and interests of national-caliber amateur skaters), technical and competition reports. Special issues: 75th Anniversary of Skating (January 1998); 1998 Olympic Preview (February 1998). Buys 4 mss/issue. All work by assignment. Length: 400-800 words. Pay varies.
Reprints: Send photocopy of article and information about when and where the article previously appeared. Pay varies.
Photos: Photos purchased with or without accompanying ms. Pays $15 for 8×10 or 5×7 b&w glossy prints and $35 for color prints or transparencies. Query.
Columns/Departments: Ice Breaker (news briefs), Foreign National Reports, Center Ice (guest), Letters to Editor, People. Buys 4 mss/issue. All work by assignment. Length: 500-2,000 words.
Tips: "We want writing by experienced persons knowledgeable in the technical and artistic aspects of figure skating with a new outlook on the development of the sport. Knowledge and background in technical aspects of figure skating are essential to the quality of writing expected. We would also like to receive articles on former competitive skaters. No professional skater material."

SKI MAGAZINE, Times Mirror Magazines, 929 Pearl St., Suite 200, Boulder CO 80302. (303)440-3636. Website: http://www.skinet.com. Editor-in-Chief: Andy Bigford. Contact: Natalie Kurylko, managing editor. 15% freelance written. Monthly magazine on snow skiing. *"Ski* is a ski-lifestyle publication written and edited for recreational skiers. Its content is intended to help them ski better (technique), buy better (equipment and skiwear), and introduce them to new experiences, people and adventures." Estab. 1936. Circ. 430,000. **Pays on acceptance.** Publishes ms an average of 3 months after acceptance. Byline given. Offers 15% kill fee. Buys first North American serial rights. Submit seasonal material 8 months in advance. Reports in 1 month. Sample copy for 9×12 SAE with 5 first-class stamps.
Nonfiction: Essays, historical/nostalgic, how-to, humor, interview/profile and personal experience. Buys 5-10 mss/year. Send complete ms. Length: 1,000-3,500 words. Pays $500-1,000 for assigned articles; $300-700 for unsolicited articles. Pays the expenses of writers on assignment.
Photos: Send photos with submission. Offers $75-300/photo. Captions, model releases and identification of subjects required. Buys one-time rights.
Columns/Departments: Ski Life (interesting people, events, oddities in skiing), 150-300 words; Going Places (items on new or unique places, deals or services available to skiers); and Take It From Us (special products or services available to skiers that are real values or out of the ordinary), 25-50 words.
Fillers: Facts and short humor. Buys 10/year. Length: 60-75 words. Pays $50-75.
Tips: "Writers must have an extensive familiarity with the sport and know what concerns, interests and amuses skiers. Columns are most open to freelancers."

SKI TRIPPER, P.O. Box 20305, Roanoke VA 24018. (540)772-2225. Contact: Tom Gibson, editor. 60% freelance written. Newsletter published monthly November-March covering snow skiing in mid-Atlantic and southeast regions. *"Ski Tripper* brings inside information on downhill skiing to readers from Florida to southern Pennsylvania. Much of this is accomplished with trip reports on resorts within this region as well as destinations outside it. We also use features on skiing issues and trends that have a bearing on the region—topics have included discount ski cards, ski clubs, rental

cars, slope condition reports, and skiing information by computer. Need reports on trips taken to regional ski resorts and to long-distance resorts (western U.S./Canada, Europe, New Zealand, South America) from the region. Trip reports are written from an unbiased viewpoint and tell good and bad things about resorts and travel services. Also need informational pieces on skiing-related activities." Estab. 1993. Circ. 1,000. **Pays on acceptance**. Publishes ms an average of 3 months after acceptance. Buys first North American serial, simultaneous and reprint rights. Editorial lead time 1 month. Submit seasonal material 2 months in advance. Reports in 3 weeks on queries and mss. Sample copy and writer's guidelines free.
Nonfiction: Personal experience, travel. "No articles on ski shops and ski equipment." Buys 12 mss/year. Query. Length: 500-1,700 words. Pays $75-225.
Reprints: Send photocopy of article or short story or typed ms with rights for sale noted and information about when and where the article previously appeared.
Tips: "If you're going on a ski trip, let us know—it may be one we'd like to cover. We especially like to see stories with a unique twist—heli skiing, backcountry skiing, taking a train to a resort, skiing at a Club Med resort, etc."

SKIING, Times Mirror Magazines, Inc., 929 Pearl St., Boulder CO 80302. (303)448-7600. Fax: (303)448-7638. E-mail: rkahljr@aol.com. Website: http://www.skinet.com. Editor-in-Chief: Rick Kahl. Contact: Bill Grout, senior editor. Magazine published 7 times/year for the active skier who is interested in learning about skiing, travel, adventure, instruction, equipment, fashion and news. "*Skiing* is edited for the active skier—the beginning as well as the experienced skier who is interested in learning about the sport, its equipment, and its technique. Regular articles cover the latest in ski fashion, new and improved equipment, competition analyses, skiing personalities, and general news of people and places. Reports on the world's great ski areas are featured, with particular emphasis on unique photographic exposition. Ski technique is explained by professional ski instructors." Estab. 1948. Circ. 400,000. Byline given. Offers 40% kill fee. Query. No personal stories, previously published articles or poetry.
Nonfiction: Buys 10-15 features (1,500-2,000 words) and 12-24 short pieces (100-700 words). Pays $1,000-2,500/feature; 475-500/short piece.
Columns/Departments: Buys 2-3 articles/year. Length: 1,000-1,500 words. Pays $700-1,200.

‡SNOW COUNTRY, The Year-Round Magazine of Mountain Sports & Living, New York Times Magazine Group, 5520 Park Ave., Trumbull CT 06611. (203)323-7038. Fax: (203)373-7111. E-mail: editor@snowcountry.com. Website: http://www.snowcountry.com. Editor: Roger Toll. Managing Editor: Cathy Cusmano. Contact: Lynn Prowitt, associate editor. 85% freelance written. Monthly (September-February) and Spring, and Summer issues. Focuses on mountain lifestyles and recreation at and around ski resorts. "Because we publish year-round, we cover a broader range of subjects than ski-only publications. Besides skiing, topics include scenic drives, mountain biking, hiking, rollerblading, real estate, etc." Estab. 1988. Circ. 465,000. **Pays on acceptance**. Publishes ms an average of 6 months after acceptance. Byline given. Kill fee varies. Buys first North American serial rights and foreign affiliates. Submit seasonal material 6 months in advance. Reports in 1 month. Free writer's guidelines.
Nonfiction: General interest, historical/nostalgic, how-to, humor, interview/profile, new product, photo feature, technical and travel. Buys 45 mss/year. Query with published clips. Length: 250-1,200 words. Pays $200-1,000. Pays expenses of writers on assignment.
Photos: State availability of photos with submission. Reviews transparencies. Identification of subjects required. Buys one-time rights.
Columns/Departments: Follow Me (instructional items on skiing, mountain biking, photography, hiking), 200 words; Snow Country Store (items on mountain artisans, craftsmen and their products), 250 words. Buys 35 mss/year. Query with published clips. Pays $200-300.
Tips: "Area most open to freelancers: short articles on people who've moved to snow country and are making a living there."

‡SNOWBOARDER, The Magazine, For Better Living Communications, P.O. Box 1028, Dana Point CA 92629. (714)496-5922. Fax: (714)496-7849. E-mail: snwbrdrmag@aol.com. Contact: Steve Hawk, editor. Managing Editor: Rob Campbell. 50% freelance written. Magazine published monthly September-February covering snowboarding. Estab. 1987. Circ. 120,000. Pays on publication. Publishes ms an average of 4 months after acceptance. Byline given. 20% kill fee. Buys first North American serial rights. Query for electronic submissions. Reports in 1 month on queries. Sample copy for $1 with 1 first class stamp. Writer's guidelines for SASE.
Nonfiction: How-to, personal experience, photo feature, technical, travel, fiction. Buys 7-10 mss/year. Query with published clips. Length: 100-1,200 words. Pays $50-750. Sometimes pays expenses of writers on assignment.
Photos: State availability of photos with submissions. Reviews transparencies. Offers $50-600. Identification of subjects required. Buys one-time rights.

‡SNOWEST MAGAZINE, Harris Publishing, 520 Park Ave., Idaho Falls ID 83402. (208)524-7000. Fax: (208)522-5241. Editor: Lane Lindstrom. Managing Editor: Steve Janes. Monthly magazine covering snowmobiles. "*SnoWest* covers the sport of snowmobiling, the products and personalities therein. *SnoWest* slants towards the western states, mountain riding and deep powder, as well as trail riding." Estab. 1974. Circ. 172,000. Pays on publication. Byline given. Buys first North American serial rights. Editorial lead time 2 months. Submit seasonal material 2 months in advance.
Nonfiction: New product, technical, travel. Buys 3-5 mss/year. Query. Pays $150-300.

Photos: Send photos with submission. Negotiates payment individually. Identification of subjects required. Buys one-time rights.

‡**THE SNOWSHOER**, Comm-Strat Publishing, P.O. Box 458, Washburn WI 54891. (715)373-5556. Fax: (715)373-5003. E-mail: snoshu@win.bright.net. Contact: Jim Radtke, editor. 100% freelance written. Tabloid published 5 times/year during winter months on snowshoeing with "a broad demographic from recreational to competitive snowshoers and young families to older, more adventuresome adults. We are the only publication catering to snowshoers." Estab. 1995. Circ. 25,000. Pays on publication. Publishes ms an average of 2 months after acceptance. Byline given. Buys first rights. Editorial lead time 2 months. Submit seasonal material 4 months in advance. Sample copy for $1.50 with 9×12 SAE and 3 first-class stamps. Writer's guidelines for #10 SASE.
Nonfiction: General interest (snowshoe), how-to, humor, interview/profile, new product, personal experience, technical, destinations. Buys 40 mss/year. Query with published clips. Length: 1,000-1,500 words. Pays 5-7¢/word. Sometimes pays expenses of writers on assignment.
Reprints: Send photocopy of article or short story and information about when and where the article previously appeared.
Photos: State availability of photos with submission. Reviews 35mm transparencies and 3×5 prints. Offers $5 minimum/photo. Identification of subjects required. Buys one-time rights.
Fiction: Adventure, humorous. Query. Length: 1,000-1,200 words. Pays 5¢/word.
Tips: "Have some familiarity with snowshoeing. Love the outdoors in winter. Be environmentally aware."

Soccer

‡**SOCCER MAGAZINE**, Patch Communications, 5211 S. Washington Ave., Titusville FL 32780. (407)268-5010. Fax: (407)267-1894. E-mail: dpsrun@aol.com. Editor: Michael Lewis. Contact: Dan Sage, managing editor. Magazine published 6 times/year covering "the sport at every level for players, coaches, referees and parents, offering tournament and league coverage as well as player profiles and coaching, nutrition, youth/women's development and training tips columns." Estab. 1993. Circ. 20,000. Pays on publication. Publishes ms an average of 6 months after acceptance. Byline given. Buys first North American serial rights. Editorial lead time 4 months. Submit seasonal material 6 months in advance. No simultaneous or previously published submissions. Query for electronic submissions. Reports in 1 month on queries. Writer's guidelines for #10 SASE.
Nonfiction: How-to (coaching), interview/profile, new product, personal experience, photo feature, technical (nutrition). Buys 6 mss/year. Query with published clips and SASE. Length: 600-1,200 words.
Photos: Send photos with submission. Reviews transparencies, prints. Negotiates payment individually. Captions, identification of subjects required. Buys one-time rights.
Fiction: Novel excerpts.

Tennis

RACQUET, Heather & Pine, Inc., 21 E. 40th St., 13th Floor, New York NY 10016. (212)768-8360. Fax: (212)696-1678. Contact: Allison Roarty, managing editor. 30% freelance written. Bimonthly tennis/lifestyle magazine. "*Racquet* celebrates the lifestyle of tennis." Estab. 1978. Circ. 145,000. Pays on publication. Publishes ms an average of 3 months after acceptance. Byline given. Offers negotiable kill fee. Rights purchased negotiable. Submit seasonal material 5 months in advance. Accepts simultaneous submissions. Reports in 1 month. Sample copy for $4.
Nonfiction: Essays, exposé, historical/nostalgic, humor, interview/profile, opinion, personal experience, travel. "No instruction or poetry." Buys 15-20 mss/year. Query. Length: 1,000-4,000 words. Pays $200-750 for assigned articles; $100-300 for unsolicited articles. Pays in contributor copies or other negotiable premiums. Sometime pays expenses of writers on assignment.
Reprints: Send tearsheet or photocopy of article and information about when and where the article previously appeared.
Photos: State availability of photos with submission. Offers no additional payment for photos accepted with ms. Rights negotiable.
Columns/Departments: "Courtside" (personal experience—fun facts), 500-2,000 words. Buys 5-10 mss/year. Query. Pays $100-300.
Fiction: Publishes novel excerpts.
Fillers: Anecdotes, short humor. Buys 5/year. Length: 250-750 words. Pays $50-150.
Tips: "Get a copy, understand how we approach tennis, submit article written to style and follow-up. We are always looking for innovative or humorous ideas."

TENNIS WEEK, Tennis News, Inc., 341 Madison Ave., 6th Floor, New York NY 10017. (212)808-4750. Fax: (212)983-6302. Managing Editors: Heather H. Holland, Kim Kodl. 10% freelance written. Biweekly magazine covering tennis. "For readers who are either tennis fanatics or involved in the business of tennis." Estab. 1974. Circ. 80,000. Pays on publication. Byline given. Buys all rights. Editorial lead time 1 month. Submit seasonal material 1 month in advance. Reports in 1 month on queries. Sample copy for $3.

Nonfiction: Buys 15 mss/year. Query with or without published clips. Length: 1,000-2,000 words. Pays $300.

Water Sports

DIVER, Seagraphic Publications, Ltd., 11780 Hammersmith Way, Richmond, British Columbia V7A 5E3 Canada. (604)274-4333. Fax: (604)274-4366. E-mail: divermag@axionnet.com. Website: http://medianetcom.com/divermag/. Editor/Publisher: Peter Vassilopoulos. Contact: Stephanie Bold, editor. Magazine published 9 times/year emphasizing scuba diving, ocean science and technology (commercial and military diving) for a well-educated, outdoor-oriented readership. Circ. 17,500. Payment "follows publication." Buys first North American serial rights. Byline given. Submit seasonal material July-September for consideration for following year. Send SAE with IRCs. Reports in up to 3 months. Publishes ms up to 1 year after acceptance. "Articles are subject to being accepted for use in supplement issues on tabloid."
Nonfiction: How-to (underwater activities such as photography, etc.), general interest (underwater oriented), humor, historical (shipwrecks, treasure artifacts, archeological), interview (underwater personalities in all spheres—military, sports, scientific or commercial), personal experience (related to diving), photo feature (marine life), technical (related to oceanography, commercial/military diving, etc.), travel (dive resorts). No subjective product reports. Buys 25 mss/ year. Travel features considered only in September/October for use following year. Buys only 6 freelance travel items a year. Submit complete ms. Length: 800-1,500 words. Pays $2.50/column inch.
Photos: "Features are mostly those describing dive sites, experiences, etc. Photo features are reserved more as specials, while almost all articles must be well illustrated with color or b&w prints supplemented by color transparencies." Submit original photo material with accompanying ms. Pays $7 minimum for 5×7 or 8×10 b&w glossy prints; $15 minimum for 35mm color transparencies. Captions and model releases required. Buys one-time rights.
Columns/Departments: Book reviews. Submit complete ms. Length: 200 words maximum. No payment.
Fillers: Anecdotes, newsbreaks, short humor. Buys 8-10/year. Length: 50-150 words. No payment for news items.
Tips: "No phone calls inquiring about status of manuscript. Write if no response within reasonable time. Only brief, to-the-point correspondence will be answered. Lengthy communications will probably result in return of work unused. Publisher assumes no liability to use material even after lengthy waiting period. Acceptances only subject to final and actual use."

THE DIVER, 6772 Colony Dr., S., Saint Petersburg FL 33705-5905. (813)866-9856. Fax: (813)866-9740. Contact: Bob Taylor, publisher/editor. 50% freelance written. Magazine published 6 times/year for divers, coaches and officials. Estab. 1978. Circ. 1,500. Pays on publication. Byline given. Submit material at least 2 months in advance. Accepts simultaneous submissions. Reports in 2 weeks on queries; 1 month on mss. Sample copy for 9×12 SAE with 3 first-class stamps.
Nonfiction: Interview/profile (of divers, coaches, officials), results, tournament coverage, any stories connected with platform and springboard diving, photo features, technical. Buys 35 mss/year. Query. Length: 500-2,500 words. Pays $25-50.
Reprints: Send tearsheet of article. Pays 50% of amount paid for original article.
Photos: Pays $5-10 for b&w prints. Captions and identification of subjects required. Buys one-time rights.
Tips: "We're very receptive to new writers."

HOT WATER, Taylor Publishing Group, 2585 Skymark Ave., Unit 306, Mississauga, Ontario L4W 4L5 Canada. (905)624-8218. Fax: (905)624-6764. Contact: Peter Tasler, editorial director. 50% freelance written. Quarterly magazine covering personal watercraft market (jet skis sea-doo's). "Focused on fun-loving watersports enthusiasts, *Hot Water* contains features on new personal watercraft and accessories, places to ride, racing, and profiles on people in the industry. Technical and handling tips are also included." Estab. 1993. Circ. 18,000. Pays on publication. Publishes ms an average of 2 months after acceptance. Byline given. Offers 100% kill fee. Buys first North American serial rights. Editorial lead time 2 months. Submit seasonal material 3 months in advance. Sample copy and writer's guidelines free.
Nonfiction: Historical/nostalgic, how-to (anything technical or handling etc.), humor, interview/profile, personal experience, photo feature, technical, travel. Send complete ms. Length: 1,000-3,000 words. Pays $300 maximum. Sometimes pays expenses of writers on assignment.
Reprints: Send photocopy of article or typed ms with rights for sale noted and information about when and where the article previously appeared. Pay negotiable.
Photos: Send photos with submission. Reviews transparencies, 4×6 prints. Offers no additional payment for photos accepted with ms. Captions, model releases, identification of subjects required.
Columns/Departments: Klipboard (a racer's viewpoint); Workbench (technical tips); Hot Waterways (riding adventures); all 1,000 words. Buys 6 mss/year. Send complete ms. Pays $200 maximum.
Fillers: Facts, newsbreaks. Length: 500-1,000 words. Pays $150 maximum.
Tips: "If you have a story idea you feel is appropriate, feel free to contact the editor to discuss. Or, if you're familiar with watercraft but need some direction, call the editor who will gladly assign a feature."

‡RODALE'S SCUBA DIVING, 6600 Abercorn St., Suite 208, Savannah GA 31405. E-mail: rsdmgzn@aol.com. Executive Editor: David Taylor. Published 9 times/year for recreational scuba divers and underwater photographers.

Pays on acceptance. Byline given. Offers 25% kill fee. Buys first North American serial rights or all rights. Accepts simultaneous submissions. Reports in 2 weeks. Sample copy for $3.50. Writer's guidelines for #10 SASE.

Nonfiction: Buys 12 mss/year. Query with published clips. Length: 1,500-2,500 words. Pays 50¢-$2/word. Pays expenses of writers on assignment.

Reprints: Accepts previously published submissions.

Columns/Departments: Length: 1,000 words. Buys 36 mss/year. Query with published clips. Pays 50¢-$2/word.

Fillers: Buys 45/year. Length: 250-500 words. Pays 50¢-$2/word.

Tips: "We need articles in these areas: adventure dive travel, diving health and fitness, local diving, marine environmental news and features. Our major travel articles are staff written. We are most interested in local dive stories (500 words plus photos) for our Dive USA section, marine environment stories (150-500 words) for our Seaviews section and adventure dive stories. No articles on individual dive resorts or operators."

SCUBA TIMES, The Active Diver's Magazine, GBP, Inc., 14110 Perdido Key Dr., Pensacola FL 32507. (904)492-7805. Fax: (904)492-7805. Website: http://www.scubatimes.com. Managing Editor: Fred D. Garth. Contact: Christopher Grant, editor. 90% freelance written. Bimonthly magazine on scuba diving. Estab. 1979. Circ. 43,000. Pays on publication. Publishes ms an average of 6 months after acceptance. Byline given. Buys first North American serial rights. Submit seasonal material 1 year in advance. Reports in 6 weeks. Sample copy for $3. Writer's guidelines for #10 SASE.

Nonfiction: How-to (advanced diving techniques such as technical, very deep, mixed gases, cave diving, wreck diving); humor; interview/profile (colorful characters in diving); personal experience (only if it is astounding); photo feature (creatures, places to dive); technical (physics, biology, medicine as it relates to diving); travel (dive destinations). No beginner-level dive material. Buys 75 mss/year. Query with published clips or send complete ms. Length: 1,500 for major destination features, 150 words for sidebars. Pays $75/published page. Sometimes pays expenses of writers on assignment.

Reprints: Send information about when and where the article previously appeared. Pays 100% of amount paid for an original article.

Photos: Send photos with submission. Reviews transparencies. Offers $25-75/page; $150/ cover photo. Captions, identification of subjects required. Buys one-time rights.

Columns/Departments: What a Wreck (informative guide to any wreck, old or new), 750 words; Creature Feature (one knock-out photo of a mysterious sea creature plus story of life cycle and circumstances that led to photo), 500 words; Last Watering Hole, (great photos, usually topside, and story about a dive site so remote most divers will never go), 500 words; Dive America (informative article on local, fresh water dive sites, with photo), 300 words; Advanced Diving (how-to and advanced techniques for expanding dive adventure), 750 words. Buys 60 mss/year. Query with published clips. Length; 500-1,000 words. Pays $25-75/page.

Fillers: " 'Free Flowing' sections allows writers to be creative, thought provoking as they contemplate diver's relationship to the marine world." Anecdotes, short humor. Buys 10/year. Length: 300-900 words. Pays $25-75/page.

Tips: "Be a diver. Everyone tries for the glamorous destination assignments, but it is easier to break into the columns, especially, 'Last Watering Hole,' 'What a Wreck,' 'Dive America' and 'Creature Feature.' Outstanding photos are a must. We will coax a good article out of a great photographer whose writing skills are not developed. Very little is written inhouse. Diving freelancers are the heart and soul of *STM*. Unknowns receive as much consideration as the big names. Know what you are talking about and present it with a creative flair. Divers are often technical or scientific by profession or disposition and their writing lacks flow, power and grace. Make us *feel* those currents and *smell* the diesel from the yacht."

‡SEA MAGAZINE, America's Western Boating Magazine, Duncan McIntosh Co., 17782 Cowan, Suite C, Irvine CA 92614. (714)660-6150. Fax: (714)660-6172. E-mail: http://www.iwol.com/show.me/sea. Editor: Eston Ellis. 70% freelance written. Monthly magazine covering West Coast power boating. Estab. 1908. Circ. 60,000. Pays on publication. Publishes ms an average of 3 months after acceptance. Byline given. Buys first North American serial rights. Editorial lead time 3 months. Submit seasonal material 5 months in advance. Accepts simultaneous submissions. Reports in 6 weeks on queries.

Nonfiction: Exposé, how-to, new product, personal experience, technical, travel. Buys 36 mss/year. Query or send complete ms. Length: 300-1,200 words. Pay varies. Sometimes pays expenses of writers on assignment.

Photos: State availability of photos with submission. Reviews transparencies. Offers $50-250/photo. Captions, model releases and identification of subjects required. Buys one-time rights.

SPLASH MAGAZINE, The Complete Personal Watercraft Magazine, McMullen/Argus Publishing, 774 S. Placentia Ave., Placentia CA 92670. (714)572-2255. Fax: (714)572-1864. E-mail: splashmag@aol.com. Editor: Jeff Ames. 20% freelance written. Monthly magazine covering personal watercraft, riding spots, technical and racing. "From month to month, *Splash Magazine* provides extensive coverage of personal watercraft, equipment, accessories and personalities. Stunning color photography highlights all makes and models and showcases the best in custom craft, watersport events and races." Estab. 1987. Circ. 55,000. Pays on publication. Byline given. Buys first North American serial rights. Editorial lead time 3 months. Submit seasonal material 5 months in advance. Reports in 1 month. Sample copy free. Writer's guidelines for #10 SASE.

Nonfiction: General interest, how-to, humor, inspirational, interview/profile, new product, opinion, photo feature, technical, travel, race and new product test features. Buys 15-20 mss/year. Query with published clips. Length varies. Pays $100-150/page. Sometimes pays expenses of writers on assignment.

Photos: Send photos with submission. Reviews 35mm transparencies. Negotiates payment individually. Captions, model releases, identification of subjects required.
Columns/Departments: Free Ridin' (recreational and racer experiences), 250 words; Races Report (PWC racers articles), 1,000-2,000 words. Buys 60 mss/year. Pays $75-150/page.
Tips: "Submit query or completed editorial/photography with cover letter. Editorial may be submitted on disk. Photography should be captioned and numbered. Be knowledgeable of the sport."

‡**SPORT DIVER**, World Publications, 330 W. Canton Ave., Winter Park FL 32789. (407)628-4802. Fax: (407)628-7061. E-mail: sportdiver@worldzine.com. Editor: Pierce Hoover. Contact: Gary P. Joyce, managing editor. 75% freelance written. Bimonthly magazine covering scuba diving. "We portray the adventure and fun of diving—the reasons we all started diving in the first place." Estab. 1993. Circ. 120,000. Pays on publication, sometimes on acceptance. Byline given. Offers 50% kill fee. Buys first North American serial rights. Editorial lead time 3 months. Submit seasonal material 4 months in advance. Accepts simultaneous submissions. Reports in 2 weeks on queries; 3 months on mss. Writer's guidelines for #10 SASE.
Nonfiction: Personal experience, travel, diving. No non-diving related articles. Buys 150 mss/year. Query. Length: 800-2,000 words. Pays $400-500. Sometimes pays expenses of writers on assignment.
Photos: State availability of photos with submission. Reviews transparencies. Offers $50-500/photo. Captions required. Buys one-time rights.
Columns/Departments: Photo Op (underwater photography), 1,000 words; Dive Briefs (shorts), 150-450 words; Destinations (travel), 500-1,000 words. Buys 90-100 mss/year. Query. Pays $50-250.
Tips: "Know diving, and even more importantly, know how to write. Destinations is probably the best place to break in with a new look at any of the traditional tropical dive islands."

SURFER, Surfer Publications, P.O. Box 1028, Dana Point CA 92629. (714)496-5922. Fax: (714)496-7849. E-mail: surferedit@aol.com. Website: http://www.surfermag.com. Editor: Steve Hawk. Assistant Editor: Lisa Eilertson. Contact: Evan Slater, associate editor. 75% freelance written. Monthly magazine "aimed at experts and beginners with strong emphasis on action surf photography." Estab. 1960. Circ. 110,000. Pays on publication. Byline given. Buys first North American serial rights. Submit seasonal material 6 months in advance. Accepts simultaneous submissions. Reports in 2 months. Sample copy for $3.99 with 9×12 SASE. Writer's guidelines for #10 SASE.
Nonfiction: How-to (technique in surfing), humor, inspirational, interview/profile, opinion, personal experience (all surf-related), photo feature (action surf and surf travel), technical (surfboard design), travel (surf exploration and discovery—photos required). Buys 30-50 mss/year. Query with or without published clips, or send complete ms. Length: 500-2,500 words. Pays 20-25¢/word. Sometimes pays the expenses of writers on assignment.
Reprints: Send typed ms with rights for sale noted and information about when and where the article previously appeared. Pays 100% of amount paid for an original article.
Photos: Send photos with submission. Reviews 35mm negatives and transparencies. Buys 12-24 illustrations/year. Prices vary. Used for columns: Environment, Surf Docs and sometimes features. Send samples with SASE to Art Director. Offers $25-250/photo. Identification of subjects required. Buys one-time and reprint rights.
Columns/Departments: Environment (environmental concerns to surfers), 1,000-1,500 words; Surf Stories (personal experiences of surfing), 1,000-1,500 words; Reviews (surf-related movies, books), 500-1,000 words; Sections (humorous surf-related items with b&w photos), 100-500 words. Buys 25-50 mss/year. Send complete ms. Pays 20-25¢/word.
Fiction: Surf-related adventure, fantasy, horror, humorous, science fiction. Buys 10 mss/year. Send complete ms. Length: 750-2,000 words. Pays 15-20¢/word.
Tips: "All sections are open to freelancers but interview/profiles are usually assigned. 'People Who Surf' is a good way to get a foot in the door. Stories must be authoritative, oriented to the hard-core surfer."

‡**THE SURFWRITER'S QUARTERLY**, Pacific Trades, P.O. Box 700, Ventura CA 93002. (805)652-1914. Editor: Philip S. Wikel. Managing Editor: Larry Manson. 90% freelance written. Quarterly magazine covering all subjects related to the ocean. "*TSQ* is a publication for the passionate ocean enthusiast." Estab. 1994. Circ. 40,000. Byline sometimes given. Buys one-time rights. Editorial lead time 3 months. Submit seasonal material 3 months in advance. Accepts simultaneous submissions. Reports in 2 months. Sample copy for $3.50. Writer's guidelines for #10 SASE.
Nonfiction: Book excerpts, essays, exposé, general interest, historical/nostalgic, how-to, humor, inspirational, interview/profile, new product, opinion, personal experience, photo feature, technical, travel. No melodrama or pornography. Buys 15 mss/year. Query with published clips. Length: 1,000-4,000 words. Pays $50-400. Sometimes pays expenses of writers on assignment.
Reprints: Accepts previously published submissions.
Photos: Send photos with submission. Reviews transparencies. Captions and identification of subjects required. Buys one-time rights.
Columns/Departments: Fiction, 1,500-4,000 words; Travel, 1,500-4,000 words; Poetry, 50-1,000 words. All related to surfing, sailing or ocean sports. Buys 40 mss/year. Send complete ms. Pays $50-1,500.
Fiction: Adventure, ethnic, historical, humorous, mainstream, novel excerpts, slice-of-life vignettes. No melodrama, science fiction or pornography. Buys 16 mss/year. Send complete ms. Length: 1,000-4,000 words. Pays $50-400.
Poetry: Avant-garde, free verse, haiku, traditional. No melodrama. Buys 16 poems/year. Submit maximum 4 poems. Length: 75 line maximum. Pays $20-100.
Fillers: Anecdotes, facts, newsbreaks. Buys 8/year. Length: 50-300 words. Pays $25-100.

Tips: "Please be sure to know your subject matter as thoroughly as possible."

SWIM MAGAZINE, Sports Publications, Inc., P.O. Box 2025, Sedona AZ 86339-2025. (520)282-4799. Fax: (520)282-4697. E-mail: swimworld@aol.com. Website: http://www.swiminfo.com Editor: Dr. Phillip Whitten. 50% freelance written. Prefers to work with published/selected writers. Bimonthly magazine for adults interested in swimming for fun, fitness and competition. Readers are fitness-oriented adults from varied social and professional backgrounds who share swimming as part of their lifestyle. Readers are well-educated, affluent and range in age from 20-100 with most in the 30-49 age group; about 50% female, 50% male." Estab. 1984. Circ. 44,600. Pays approximately 1 month after publication. Publishes ms an average of 4 months after acceptance. Byline given. Submit seasonal material 4 months in advance. Reports in 1 month on queries; 3 months on mss. Sample copy for $3 (prepaid) and 9×12 SAE with 5 first-class stamps. Writer's guidelines free.

Nonfiction: How-to (training plans and techniques), interview/profile (people associated with fitness and competitive swimming), inspirational, general health, new product (articles describing new products for fitness and competitive training). "Articles need to be informative as well as interesting. In addition to fitness and health articles, we are interested in exploring fascinating topics dealing with swimming for the adult reader." Send complete ms. Length: 500-3,000 words. Pays 12¢/word minimum.

Reprints: Occasionally accepts previously published submissions. Send tearsheet, photocopy of article or typed ms with rights for sale noted with information about when and where the article previously appeared.

Photos: Send photos with ms. Offers no additional payment for photos accepted with ms. Captions, model releases, identification of subjects required.

Tips: "Our how-to and profile articles best typify *Swim Magazine*'s style for fitness and competitive swimmers. *Swim Magazine* accepts medical guidelines and exercise physiology articles primarily by M.D.s and Ph.Ds."

‡WAHINE MAGAZINE, Wahine, 5520 E. Second St., Suite K, Long Beach CA 90803. E-mail: wahinemag@aol.com. Editor: Elizabeth A. Glazner. 50% freelance written. Quarterly magazine covering water sports and beach culture for women. "*Wahine* is for athletic, intelligent, adventurous women who pursue all the beach lifestyle has to offer, including surfing, bodyboarding, windsurfing, sailing, swimming, diving, kayaking, canoeing, or just standing in appreciation of the water's edge. *Wahine* offers insightful travel, challenging tutorials, contemplative profiles, wearable fashions, enlightening environmental notes and informative food and fitness for both body and mind. Our readers are primarily female from 18-45." Byline given. Buys first rights. Editorial lead time 3 months. Submit seasonal material 6 months in advance. Reports in 2 months. Sample copy for 9×12 SAE and $5 check or money order.

Nonfiction: Book excerpts (relevant to water sports), essays, historical/nostalgic (old surf lifestyle), how-to (water sports technique), inspriational (personal stories of overcoming obstacles), interview/profile (athletes, filmmakers, other females of interest to wahines), new product, personal experience, photo feature, technical (board buyer's guides, other equipment, repair, etc.), travel (water destinations). Holiday shopping guide (November), wetsuits (July), swimsuits (April). "We receive numerous manuscripts intent on bemoaning sexism in surfing. We do not wish to be sexist ourselves by publishing them. Please, no more!" Query with published clips or send complete ms. Length: 500-3,000 words. Pays 10¢/word. Pays previously unpublished writers with contributor copies or other premiums.

Photos: Send photos with submission if possible. Reviews transparencies. Negotiates payment individually. Captions, model releases and identification of subjects required.

Columns/Departments: Offshore (beach culture), 50-500 words; Body (fitness), 800-1,200 words; Soul (personal stories relating to mind/spirit), 800-1,200 words; Food (whole foods explored in all their glory), 800-1,200 words; Planet (environmental success stories), 800-1,200 words. Buys 20 mss/year. Send complete ms. Pays 10¢/word.

Tips: "We appreciate positive, fresh, well-focused ideas. A good way to break in is by sending ideas for our Offshore section, along with good art. If you write well and understand the tone of *Wahine*, we'll encourage more. Also, we will read unsolicited manuscripts, but must SASE for return."

THE WATER SKIER, American Water Ski Association, 799 Overlook Dr., Winter Haven FL 33884. (941)324-4341. E-mail: usawsmagazine@worldnet.att.net. Website: http://usawaterski.org. Publisher and Editor-in-Chief: Don Cullimore. Contact: Jonathan W. Cullimore, managing editor. 10-20% freelance written. Magazine published 7 times/year for water skiing—all aspects of the sport. "*The Water Skier* is the official publication of the American Water Ski Association (AWSA), the national governing body for organized water skiing in the United States. The magazine has a controlled circulation and is available only to AWSA's membership, which is made up of 20,000 active competitive water skiers and 10,000 members who are supporting the sport. These supporting members may participate in the sport but they don't compete. The editorial content of the magazine features distinctive and informative writing about the sport of water skiing only." Estab. 1951. Circ. 30,000. Byline given. Offers 30% kill fee. Buys all rights (no exceptions). Editorial lead time 4 months. Submit seasonal material 6 months in advance. Reports in 2 weeks on queries. Sample copy for $1.25. Writer's guidelines for #10 SASE.

Nonfiction: Historical/nostalgic (has to pertain to water skiing), interview/profile (call for assignment), new product (boating and water ski equipment), travel (water ski vacation destinations). Buys 10-15 mss/year. Query. Length: 1,500-3,000 words. Pays $100-150 for assigned feature articles.

Reprints: Send photocopy of article. Pay negotiable.

Photos: State availability of photos with submission. Reviews contact sheets. Negotiates payment individually. Captions and identification of subjects required. Buys all rights.

Columns/Departments: Sports Science/Medicine (athlete conditioning, physical/mental training), 500-1,000 words;

The Water Skier News (small news items about people and events in the sport), 400-500 words; Waterways Issues (water skier's rights of access to waterways, environmental issues), 500-1,000 words. Other topics include safety, training (3-event, barefoot, disabled, show ski, ski race, kneeboard and wakeboard); champions on their way; new products. Query. Pays $50-100. Pay for columns negotiated individually with each writer.

Tips: "Contact the editor through a query letter (please no phone calls) with an idea. Avoid instruction, these articles are written by professionals. Concentrate on articles about the people of the sport. We are always looking for the interesting storys about people in the sport. Also, short news features which will make a reader say to himself, 'Hey, I didn't know that.' Keep in mind that the publication is highly specialized about the sport of water skiing." Most open to material for: feature articles (query editor with your idea), Sports/Science Medicine columns (query editor with ideas, looking for unique training or conditioning and method or sports rehabilitation), and The Starting Dock (interesting and unique news slants that are about the people and events in sport of water skiing).

WATERSKI MAGAZINE, The World's Leading Water Skiing Magazine, World Publications, 330 W. Canton Ave., Winter Park FL 32789. (407)628-4082. Fax: (407)628-7061. E-mail: waterski@worldzine.com. Contact: Rob May, editor. Managing Editor: Sue Whitney. 25% freelance written. Magazine published 10 times/year for water skiing and related watersports. "*WaterSki* instructs, advises, enlightens, informs *and* creates an open forum for skiers around the world. It provides definitive information on instruction, products, people and travel destinations." Estab. 1978. Circ. 105,000. **Pays on acceptance**. Publishes ms an average of 4 months after acceptance. Offers 25% kill fee. Buys first North American serial and second serial (reprint) rights. Editorial lead time 2 months. Submit seasonal material 2 months in advance. Query for electronic submissions. Reports in 1 month on queries; 2 months on mss. Sample copy for 8½ × 11 SAE with 4 first-class stamps. Writer's guidelines for #10 SASE.

Nonfiction: General interest, historical/nostalgic, how-to (water ski instruction boating-related), interview/profile, new product, photo feature, technical, travel. Does not want to see anything not directly related to the sport of water skiing. Buys 10 mss/year. Query with published clips. Length: 1,750-3,000 words. Pays $200 minimum. Pays other upon inability to meet author's pay request. Sometimes pays expenses of writers on assignment.

  • Continues to accept more stories that are not necessarily hard-core water skiing, especially travel.

Photos: Send photos with submission. Reviews 2¼ × 2¼ transparencies, all slides. Negotiates payment individually. Identification of subjects required. Buys one-time rights on color, all rights on b&w.

Columns/Departments: Shortline (interesting news of the sport), 300 words; Quick Tips (short instruction on water skiing and 500 words. Buys 10 mss/year. Query with published clips. Pays $75-125.

Fiction: Adventure, experimental, historical, humorous. Does not want to see anything not directly related to water skiing. Buys 10 mss/year. Query with published clips. Length: 1,750-4,000 words. Pays $200-500.

Fillers: Anecdotes, facts, gags to be illustrated by cartoonist, newsbreaks, short humor. Buys 15/year. Length: 200-500 words. Pays $75-125.

Tips: "I recommend a query call to see if there are any immediate openings in the calendar. Follow-up with a published submission (if applicable). Writers should have some interest in the sport, and understand its people, products and lifestyle. The features sections offer the most opportunity for freelancers. One requirement: It must have a positive, strong water skiing slant, whether it be personality, human interest, or travel."

Wrestling

‡**WRESTLING WORLD**, Sterling/MacFadden, 233 Park Ave. S., New York NY 10003. Phone/fax: (212)780-3500. Contact: Stephen Ciacciarelli, editor. 100% freelance written. Bimonthly magazine for professional wrestling fans. We run profiles of top wrestlers and managers and articles on current topics of interest on the mat scene." Circ. 100,000. **Pays on acceptance.** Byline given. Buys first North American serial rights. Reports in 2 weeks. Sample copy $3 for SAE with 3 first-class stamps.

Nonfiction: Interview/profile and photo feature. "No general think pieces." Buys 100 mss/year. Query with or without published clips or send complete ms. Length: 1,500-2,500 words. Pays $75-125.

Photos: State availability of photos with submission. Reviews 35mm transparencies and prints. Offers $25-50/photo package. Pays $50-150 for transparencies. Identification of subjects required. Buys one-time rights.

Tips: "Anything topical has the best chance of acceptance. Articles on those hard-to-reach wrestlers stand an excellent chance of acceptance."

TEEN AND YOUNG ADULT

Publications in this category are for teens (13-19). Publications for college students are listed in Career, College and Alumni. Those for younger children are in Juvenile.

‡**BRIO MAGAZINE**, Focus on the Family, 8605 Explorer Dr., Colorado Springs CO 80920. Editor: Susie Shellenberger. Contact: Susan Stevens, associate editor. 60% freelance written. "*Brio* is a monthly 4-color magazine geared to helping teen girls establish a strong relationship with God, a healthy self-concept and solid friendships with other girls and boys." Estab. 1990. Circ. 170,000. **Pays on acceptance.** Publishes ms an average of 1 year after acceptance. Offers

$100 kill fee. Buys first rights. Editorial lead time 5 months. Submit seasonal material 5 months in advance. Reports in 2 months on queries; 1 month on mss. Sample copy for $1.50.

Nonfiction: Susie Shellenberger, editor. General interest, how-to, humor, inspirational, interview/profile, new product, personal experience, photo feature, religious. Buys 10 mss/year. Send complete ms. Length: 800-1,000 words. Pays 8-15¢/word. Sometimes pays expenses of writers on assignment.

Photos: Send photos with submission. Reviews 5×7 transparencies, 3×5 prints. Negotiates payment individually. Identification of subjects required. Buys one-time rights.

Fiction: Susan Stevens, associate editor. Adventure, ethnic, humorous, mainstream, mystery, religious, slice-of-life vignettes. Buys 10 mss/year. Send complete ms. Length: 1,200-2,000 words. Pays 8-15¢/word.

Fillers: Facts, short humor. Buys 15/year. Length: 50-200 words. Pays $75-100.

Tips: "Know about teen girls before submitting anything!"

CAMPUS LIFE, Christianity Today, Inc., 465 Gundersen Dr., Carol Stream IL 60188. (630)260-6200. Fax: (630)260-0114. E-mail: cledit@aol.com. Website: http://www.christianity.net/campuslife. Editor: Harold Smith. Contact: Christopher Lutes, managing editor. 35% freelance written. Magazine published 9 times/year for the Christian life as it relates to today's teen. "*Campus Life* is a magazine for high-school and early college-age teenagers. Our editorial slant is not overtly religious. The indirect style is intended to create a safety zone with our readers and to reflect our philosophy that God is interested in all of life. Therefore, we publish 'message stories' side by side with general interest, humor, etc." Estab. 1942. Circ. 100,000. **Pays on acceptance.** Publishes ms an average of 5 months after acceptance. Byline given. Offers 50% kill fee. Buys first and one-time rights. Editorial lead time 4 months. Accepts simultaneous submissions. Reports in 5 weeks on queries; 2 months on mss. Sample copy for $3 and 8×10 SAE with 3 first-class stamps. Writer's guidelines for #10 SASE.

Nonfiction: Humor, personal experience, photo feature. Buys 5-10 mss/year. Query with published clips. Length: 750-1,500 words. Pays 15-20¢ minimum.

Reprints: Send tearsheet or photocopy of article or short story or typed ms with rights for sale noted and information about when and where the article previously appeared. Pays $50.

Photos: State availability of photos with submission. Reviews contact sheets, transparencies, 5×7 prints. Negotiates payment individually. Model release required. Buys one-time rights.

Fiction: Buys 1-5 mss/year. Query. Length: 1,000-2,000 words. Pays 15-20¢/word.

Tips: "The best way to break in to *Campus Life* is through writing first-person or as-told-to first-person stories. We want stories that capture a teen's everyday 'life lesson' experience. But query first with theme information telling the way this story would work for our audience."

CHALLENGE, Baptist Brotherhood Commission, 1548 Poplar Ave., Memphis TN 38104-2493. (901)272-2461. Editor: Joe Conway. 5% freelance written. Monthly magazine for "boys age 12-18 who are members of a missions organization in Southern Baptist churches." Circ. 28,500. Byline given. Pays on publication. Publishes ms an average of 8 months after acceptance. Buys simultaneous rights. Submit seasonal material 8 months in advance. Accepts simultaneous submissions. Reports in 1 month. Sample copy and writer's guidelines for 9×12 SAE with 3 first-class stamps. Writer's guidelines only for #10 SASE.

Nonfiction: How-to (crafts, hobbies), informational (youth), inspirational (sports/entertainment personalities); photo feature (sports, teen subjects). No "preachy" articles, fiction or excessive dialogue. Submit complete ms. Length: 500-800 words. Pays $20-50.

Reprints: Accepts previously published submissions. Send tearsheet or photocopy of article and information about where and when the article previously appeared. Pays 90% of the amount paid for an original article.

Photos: Purchased with ms or on assignment. Captions required. Query. Pays $10 for 8×10 b&w glossy prints.

Tips: "The writer has a better chance of breaking in at our publication with youth related articles (youth issues, and sports figures). Most topics are set years in advance. The most frequent mistake made by writers is sending us preachy articles. Aim for the mid- to older-teen instead of younger teen."

‡EDGE, The High Performance Magazine for Students, Journalistic Inc., 4905 Pine Cone Dr., Suite 2, Durham NC 27707. Fax: (919)489-4767. E-mail: gsanders@jayi.com. Website: http://www.jayi.com/so/Edge. Contact: Greg M. Sanders, editor. 60% freelance written. Bimonthly online magazine covering the teen market. "*Edge*'s readers are bright, sophisticated teenagers. In *Edge* we show them what's going on in the world around them, with the idea that they can learn from that. Think of it as 'industry coverage' for teenagers." Estab. 1993. Circ. 5,000. Pays within 30 days of acceptance. Publishes ms an average of 2 months after acceptance. Byline given. Offers 25% kill fee. Buys all rights. Editorial lead time 3 months. Submit seasonal material 6 months in advance. Reports in 6 weeks on queries; 2 months on mss. Sample copy and writer's guidelines for #10 SASE.

Nonfiction: Book excerpts, expose, general interest, how-to, personal experience (teenagers only), travel, literary nonfiction. "We'll consider any topic that's relevant to our readers. Examples include travel, summer programs, cars and driving, summer jobs, sports, college admissions, and technology. No 'Good Grades Aren't Enough' or 'How to Succeed in College'—these topics are way too general." Buys 15 mss/year. Query with published clips. Length: 1,200-2,000 words. Pays $300-500 for assigned articles, $200-275 for unsolicited articles.

Photos: Send photos with submission. Reviews transparencies, prints. Negotiates payment individually. Identification of subjects required. Rights purchased negotiable.

Columns/Departments: Performance (fine-tuning body and mind), 700-800 words; News to Use (what's up with teenagers around the world), 400-650 words; What's Hot Now (new products), 200-400 words; Mindstuff (reviews of vintage books), 400-600 words. Buys 30 mss/year. Query with clips or send complete ms. Pays $25-300.

Tips: "For our features we're keen on story—that is, a structure of complication, development and resolution. If you can do that well, you'll endear yourself to us forever. (I'd love to require all our writers to read Jon Franklin's excellent book, *Writing for Story*.) For shorter pieces, a firm grasp of the material and its relevance to teenagers is key."

EXPLORING MAGAZINE, Boy Scouts of America, P.O. Box 152079, Irving TX 75015-2079. (972)580-2365. Fax: (972)580-2079. Website: http://www.bsa.scouting.org. Contact: Scott Daniels, executive editor. 85% freelance written. Prefers to work with published/established writers. Quarterly magazine covering the co-ed teen-age Exploring program of the BSA. Estab. 1970. Circ. 350,000. **Pays on acceptance.** Publishes ms an average of 8 months after acceptance. Byline given. Buys first rights. Submit seasonal material 6 months in advance. Reports in 1 month. Sample copy for 9×12 SAE with 5 first-class stamps. Writer's guidelines and "What is Exploring?" fact sheet for #10 SASE.

Nonfiction: General interest: teenage popular culture, music, films, health, fitness, fashion, cars, computers, how-to (organize trips, meetings, etc.); interview/profile (of outstanding Explorer), travel (backpacking or canoeing with Explorers). Buys 15-20 mss/year. Query with clips. Length: 800-1,500 words. Pays $350-1,000. Pays expenses of writers on assignment.

Photos: Stephen Seeger, photo editor. State availability of photos. Reviews b&w contact sheets and 35mm transparencies. Captions required. Buys one-time rights.

Tips: "Contact the local Exploring Director in your area (listed in phone book white pages under Boy Scouts of America). Find out if there are some outstanding post activities going on and then query magazine editor in Irving, Texas. Strive for shorter texts, faster starts and stories that lend themselves to dramatic photographs."

FLORIDA LEADER (for high school students), Oxendine Publishing, Inc., P.O. Box 14081, Gainesville FL 32604-2081. (904)373-6907. E-mail: 75143.2043@compuserve.com. Editor: W.H. "Butch" Oxendine Jr. Managing Editor: Kay Quinn King. Contact: Sarah Beavers, assistant editor. Quarterly magazine covering high school and pre-college youth. Estab. 1983. Circ. 50,000. Pays on publication. Publishes ms an average of 3 months after acceptance. Buys all rights. Submit seasonal material 4 months in advance. Accepts simultaneous submissions. Reports in 2 months on queries. Sample copy for 8×11 with 3 first-class stamps. For query response and/or writer's guidelines send #10 SASE.

Nonfiction: How-to, humor, new product, opinion. "No lengthy individual profiles or articles without primary and secondary sources of attribution." Length: 250-1,000 words. Payment varies. Pays students or first-time writers with contributor's copies.

Reprints: Accepts previously published submissions.

Photos: Send photos with submission. Reviews contact sheets, negatives, transparencies. Offers $50/photo maximum. Captions, model releases, identification of subjects required. Buys all rights.

Columns/Departments: College Living (various aspects of college life, general short humor oriented to high school or college students), 250-1,000 words. Buys 10 mss/year. Query. Length: 250-1,000 words. Pays $35 maximum.

Fillers: Facts, newsbreaks, tips, book reviews. Buys 10/year. Length: 100-500 words. No payment.

Tips: "Read other high school and college publications for current issues, interests. Send manuscripts or outlines for review. All sections open to freelance work. Always looking for lighter, humorous articles as well as features on Florida colleges and universities, careers, jobs. Multi-sourced (5-10) articles are best."

GUIDE, 55 W. Oak Ridge Dr., Hagerstown MD 21740. Fax: (301)790-9734. Editor: Carolyn Rathbun. 50% freelance written. Works with a small number of new/unpublished writers each year. Weekly magazine journal for junior youth and early teens. "Its content reflects Christian Seventh-Day Adventist beliefs and standards." Estab. 1953. Circ. 34,000. Buys first serial, simultaneous and second serial (reprint) rights. **Pays on acceptance.** Publishes ms an average of 9 months after acceptance. Byline given. Submit seasonal material 6 months in advance. Reports in 3 weeks. Sample copy for SAE with 2 first-class stamps.

Nonfiction: We are especially interested in *true* stories that show God's involvement in 10- to 14-year-olds' lives. True adventure that illustrates a spiritual principle is high priority.

Reprints: Send typed ms with rights for sale noted and information about when and where the material previously appeared. Pays 50% of amount paid for an original article.

Fiction: Wants stories of character-building and spiritual value. Should emphasize the positive aspects of living, obedience to parents, perseverance, kindness, etc. "*We can always use Christian humor* and 'drama in real life' stories that show God's protection, and seasonal stories—Christmas, Thanksgiving, special holidays. We do not use stories of hunting, fishing, trapping or spiritualism. Many authors miss the mark by not setting forth a *clear application* of Biblical principles to everyday situations." Buys about 300 mss/year. Send complete ms (include word count and Social Security number). Length: up to 1,200 words. Pays 3-6¢/word. Length: 1,200 words maximum.

• *Guide* is still looking for sparkling humor and adventure stories, filled with mystery, action, discovery, dialogue.

Tips: "Typical topics we cover in a yearly cycle include choices (music, clothes, friends, diet); friend-making skills; school problems (cheating, peer pressure, new school); self-esteem; changes; sibling relationships; divorce; step-families; drugs; and communication. We often buy short fillers, and an author who does not fully understand our needs is more likely to sell with a short-short. Our target age is 10-14. Our most successful writers are those who present stories from the viewpoint of a young teen-ager, written in the active voice. Stories that sound like an adult's sentiments passing through a young person's lips are *not* what we're looking for. Use believable dialogue."

‡H.S. SPORTS, Sports + Fitness Publishing, Inc. 2025 Pearl St., Boulder CO 80302. (303)440-5111. Fax: (303)440-3313. Contact: Dagny Scott, editor. Semiannual magazine covering high school women's sports. *"h.s. sports* is for high school female athletes. It features role models for young girls, and focuses on staying involved in sports." Estab. 1994. Circ. 200,000.

Nonfiction: How-to (health, sports, nutrition), interview/profile, "It's important that writers have a solid knowledge of athletics for high school age girls." Length: 1,000-1,500 words. Buys 3-5 mss/year. Pays 50¢/word.

Columns/Departments: News + Views (short, news articles on health, fitness, sports and nutrition), 50-500 words; Health + Fitness training, health, nutrition and sports medicine topics), 600-900 words; Training (expert coaching on recommended training regimens), 600-900 words; Nutrition (current nutrition news and recommendations for maximizing benefits of exercise through diet), 600-900 words. Buys 3-5 mss/year. Pays 50¢/word.

INSIGHT, A Spiritual Lift for Teens, The Review and Herald Publishing Association, 55 W. Oak Ridge Dr., Hagerstown MD 21740. (301)791-7000. E-mail: lpeckham@rhpa.org or insight@rhpa.org. Website: http://www.rhpa.org. Editor: Lori Peckham. 80% freelance written. Weekly magazine covering spiritual life of teenagers. *"INSIGHT* publishes true dramatic stories, interviews, and community and mission service features that relate directly to the lives of Christian teenagers, particularly those with a Seventh-day Adventist background." Estab. 1970. Circ. 20,000. Pays on publication. Publishes ms an average of 4 months after acceptance. Byline given. Offers 50% kill fee. Buys first rights and second serial (reprint) rights. Editorial lead time 3 months. Submit seasonal material 6 months in advance. Reports in 1 month. Sample copy for $2 and #10 SASE. Writer's guidelines free.

Nonfiction: How-to (teen relationships and experiences), humor, interview/profile, personal experience, photo feature, religious. Buys 120 mss/year. Send complete ms. Length: 500-2,000 words. Pays $25-150 for assigned articles; $25-125 for unsolicited articles.

Reprints: Send typed ms with rights for sale noted and information about when and where the article previously appeared. Pays $50 of amount paid for an original article.

Photos: State availability of photos with submission. Reviews contact sheets, negatives, transparencies, prints. Negotiates payment individually. Model releases required. Buys one-time rights.

Columns/Departments: Interviews (Christian culture figures, esp. musicians), 2,000 words; Service With a Smile (teens contributing to community or church), 1,000 words; On the Edge (dramatic true stories about Christians), 2,000 words. Accepting reviews of contemporary Christian music and Christian books for teens. Buys 80 mss/year. Send complete ms. Pays $40-125.

Tips: "Skim two months of *INSIGHT*. Write about your teen experiences. Use informed, contemporary style and vocabulary. Become a Christian if you haven't already."

LISTEN MAGAZINE, Review & Herald Publishing Association, 55 W. Oak Ridge Dr., Hagerstown MD 21740. (301)745-3888. Fax: (301)790-9734. E-mail: 74617.3102@compuserve.com. Contact: Lincoln Steed, editor. Editorial Assistant: Anita Jacobs. 75% freelance written. Works with a small number of new/unpublished writers each year. Monthly magazine specializing in drug and alcohol prevention, presenting positive alternatives to various drug and alcohol dependencies. *"Listen* is used in many high school classes and by professionals: medical personnel, counselors, law enforcement officers, educators, youth workers, etc." Circ. 65,000. Buys first rights for use in *Listen,* reprints and associated material. Byline given. **Pays on acceptance.** Publishes ms an average of 6 months after acceptance. Accepts simultaneous submissions if notified. Reports in 2 months. Sample copy for $1 and 9 × 12 SASE. Free writer's guidelines.

Nonfiction: Seeks articles that deal with causes of drug use such as poor self-concept, family relations, social skills or peer pressure. Especially interested in youth-slanted articles or personality interviews encouraging non-alcoholic and non-drug ways of life and showing positive alternatives. Teenage point of view is essential. Popularized medical, legal and educational articles. Also seeks narratives which portray teens dealing with youth conflicts, especially those related to the use of or temptation to use harmful substances. Growth of the main character should be shown. "We don't want typical alcoholic story/skid-row bum, AA stories. We are also being inundated with drunk-driving accident stories. Unless yours is unique, consider another topic." Buys 30-50 unsolicited mss/year. Query. Length: 1,000-1,200 words. Pays 5-10¢/word. Sometimes pays the expenses of writers on assignment.

Reprints: Send photocopy of article or typed ms with rights for sale noted and information about when and where it previously appeared. Pays their regular rates.

Photos: Purchased with accompanying ms. Captions required. Color photos preferred, but b&w acceptable.

Fillers: Word square/general puzzles are also considered. Pays $15.

Tips: "True stories are good, especially if they have a unique angle. Other authoritative articles need a fresh approach. In query, briefly summarize article idea and logic of why you feel it's good. Make sure you've read the magazine to understand our approach."

THE NEW ERA, 50 E. North Temple, Salt Lake City UT 84150. (801)240-2951. Fax: (801)240-5997. Managing Editor: Richard M. Romney. 60% freelance written. "We work with both established writers and newcomers." Monthly magazine for young people of the Church of Jesus Christ of Latter-day Saints (Mormon), their church leaders and teachers. Estab. 1971. Circ. 230,000. **Pays on acceptance.** Publishes ms an average of 1 year after acceptance. Byline given. Buys all rights. Rights reassigned upon written request. Submit seasonal material 1 year in advance. Reports in 2 months. Sample copy for $1.50 and 9 × 12 SAE with 2 first-class stamps. Writer's guidelines for SASE.

Nonfiction: Material that shows how the Church of Jesus Christ of Latter-day Saints is relevant in the lives of young people today. Must capture the excitement of being a young Latter-day Saint. Special interest in the experiences of young Mormons in other countries. Special issues: Mormon Pioneers in Utah (July 97); Mormon Temples (February 97). No general library research or formula pieces without the *New Era* slant and feel. Uses informational, how-to, personal experience, interview, profile, inspirational, humor, historical, think pieces, travel, spot news. Query preferred. Length: 150-2,000 words. Pays 3-12¢/word. *For Your Information* (news of young Mormons around the world). Pays expenses of writers on assignment.

Photos: Uses b&w photos and transparencies with mss. Payment depends on use, $10-125 per photo. Individual photos used for *Photo of the Month.*

Fiction: Adventure, science fiction, humorous. Must relate to young Mormon audience. Pays minimum 3¢/word.

Poetry: Traditional forms, blank verse, free verse, light verse, all other forms. Must relate to editorial viewpoint. Pays minimum 25¢/line.

Tips: "The writer must to write from a Mormon point of view. We're looking for stories about successful family relationships. We anticipate using more staff-produced material. This means freelance quality will have to improve."

‡REACT, The Magazine That Raises Voices, Parade Publications, 711 Third Ave., New York NY 10017. (212)450-0900. E-mail: srgarvey@react.com. Website: http://www.react.com. Editor: Lee Kravitz. Contact: Susan Garvey, managing editor. 98% freelance written. "React is a weekly news, sports and entertainment magazine for teens." Estab. 1995. Circ. 3.3 million. **Pays on acceptance.** Publishes ms an average of 2 months after acceptance. Editorial lead time 2 months. Submit seasonal material 4 months in advance. Sample copy for 10½×12 SAE and 80¢ postage. Writer's guidelines for #10 SASE.

Nonfiction: No fiction or articles written for adults from adult points of view. Query with published clips. Pays $50-1,500. Sometimes pays expenses of writers on assignment.

Photos: All photos by assignment only; others purchased from stock houses. Model releases and identification of subjects required. Buys all rights.

Columns/Departments: Query with published clips.

Fiction: Publishes novel excerpts.

Tips: "We are interested in established writers with experience in writing for and about teenagers."

‡REAL, The magazine for growing minds, Elbert/Alan Publishing Co., Inc., 4747 Troost Ave., Kansas City MO 64110. (816)931-8336. Fax: (816)756-1530. E-mail: realeditor@aol.com. Editor: Susan Campbell. 20% freelance written. Bimonthly magazine covering teen issues and lifestyle. "Features should cover social issues faced by teens in a hip and positive way. Partnerships between adult freelancers and teen writers are encouraged. Departments cover lifestyle subjects, including but not limited to fashion, music, movies, sports, technology, advice, editorials, events and holidays." Estab. 1995. Circ. 100,000. Pays on publication. Publishes ms an average of 6 months after acceptance. Byline sometimes given. Editorial lead time 4 months. Submit seasonal material 4 months in advance. Accepts simultaneous and previously published submissions. Reports in 1 month on queries; 2 months on mss. Sample copy for $2.95 and a SAE and 6 first-class stamps. Writer's guidelines free.

Nonfiction: Book excerpts, humor, interview/profile, new product, personal experience. Buys 6 mss/year. Query with published clips. Length: 1,000-4,000 words. Pays $20-100. Sometimes pays teen writers with contributor copies or other premiums rathern than a cash payment.

Photos: State availability of photos with submission. Reviews prints. Negotiates payment individually. Model releases and identification of subjects required.

Columns/Departments: Advice (answers teen questions), 600 words. Buys 6 mss/year. Query. Pays $50.

Fiction: Humorous, slice-of-life vignettes. Nothing that's not applicable to teen-oriented issues. Query. Length: 600-2,000 words. Pays $20-100.

Fillers: Quirky facts. Buys 10/year. Length: 10-50 words. Pays $5.

SEVENTEEN, 850 Third Ave., New York NY 10022. Fax: (212)407-9899. Editor-in-Chief: Meredith Berlin. Contact: Robert Rorke, features editor. 80% freelance written. Works with a small number of new/unpublished writers each year. Monthly. "*Seventeen* is a young women's first fashion and beauty magazine. Tailored for young women in their teens and early twenties, seventeen covers fashion, beauty, health, fitness, food, cars, college, careers, talent, entertainment, fiction, plus crucial personal and global issues." Circ. 1,900,000. Buys one-time rights for nonfiction and fiction by adult writers and work by teenagers. Pays 25% kill fee. **Pays on acceptance.** Publishes ms an average of 6 months after acceptance. Byline given. Reports in up to 3 months.

Nonfiction: Articles and features of general interest to young women who are concerned with intimate relationships and how to realize their potential in the world; strong emphasis on topicality and helpfulness. Send brief outline and query, including a typical lead paragraph, summing up basic idea of article. Length: 1,200-2,000 words. Articles are commissioned after outlines are submitted and approved. Sometimes pays the expenses of writers on assignment. Pays $1/word, occasionally more.

Photos: Margaret Kemp, art director. Photos usually by assignment only.

Fiction: Ben Schrank, fiction editor. Thoughtful, well-written stories on subjects of interest to young women between the ages of 13 and 21. Avoid formula stories—"My sainted Granny," "My crush on Brad," etc.—no heavy moralizing or condescension of any sort. Length: 1,000-3,000 words. Pays $500-1,500.

Tips: "Writers have to ask themselves whether or not they feel they can find the right tone for a *Seventeen* article—a tone which is empathetic yet never patronizing; lively yet not superficial. Not all writers feel comfortable with, understand or like teenagers. If you don't like them, *Seventeen* is the wrong market for you. An excellent way to break in to the magazine is by contributing ideas for quizzes or the Voice (personal essay) column."

SPIRIT, Lectionary-based Weekly for Catholic Teens, Editorial Development Associates, 1884 Randolph Ave., St. Paul MN 55105-1700. (612)690-7005. Fax: (612)690-7039. Editor: Joan Mitchell, CSJ. Managing Editor: Therese Sherlock, CSJ. 50% freelance written. Weekly newsletter for religious education of high schoolers. "We want realistic fiction and nonfiction that raises current ethical and religious questions and conflicts in multi-racial contexts." Estab. 1988. Circ. 26,000. Pays on publication. Publishes ms an average of 6 months after acceptance. Byline given. Buys all rights. Submit seasonal material 6 months in advance. Accepts simultaneous submissions. Reports in 3 months on queries; 6 weeks on mss. Sample copy and writer's guidelines free.
Nonfiction: Interview/profile, personal experience, photo feature (homelessness, illiteracy), religious, Roman Catholic leaders, human interest features, social justice leaders, projects, humanitarians. "No Christian confessional pieces." Buys 12 mss/year. Query. Length: 1,100-1,200 words. Pays $150 for articles; $75 for one-page articles.
Photos: State availability of photos with submission. Reviews contact sheets, transparencies, prints. Offers $25-40/photo. Identification of subjects required. Buys one-time rights.
Fiction: Conflict vignettes. "We want realistic pieces for and about teens—non-pedantic, non-pious." We need good Christmas stories that show spirit of the season, and stories about teen relationship conflicts (boy/girl, parent/teen). Buys 12 mss/year. Query. Length: 1,100-1,200 words. Pays $150.
Tips: "Query to receive call for stories, spec sheet, sample issues."

STRAIGHT, Standard Publishing Co., 8121 Hamilton Ave., Cincinnati OH 45231-2323. (513)931-4050. Fax: (513)931-0950. Editor: Heather E. Wallace. 90% freelance written. Estab. 1950. Weekly magazine (published quarterly) for "teens, age 13-19, from Christian backgrounds who generally receive this publication in their Sunday School classes or through subscriptions." **Pays on acceptance.** Publishes ms an average of 1 year after acceptance. Buys first rights, second serial (reprint) rights or simultaneous rights. Byline given. Submit seasonal material 9-12 months in advance. Reports in 2 months. Sample copy and writer's guidelines for #10 SAE with 2 first-class stamps. "We use freelance material in every issue. Our theme list is available on a quarterly basis. Writers need only give us their name and address in order to be added to our mailing list."
Nonfiction: Religious-oriented topics, teen interest (school, church, family, dating, sports, part-time jobs), humor, inspirational, personal experience. "We want articles that promote Christian values and ideals." No puzzles. Query or submit complete ms. Include Social Security number on ms. "We're buying more short pieces these days; 12 pages fill up much too quickly." Length: 800-1,500 words.
Reprints: Send tearsheet of article or story or typed ms. Pays 5¢/word.
Fiction: Adventure, humorous, religious, suspense. "All fiction should have some message for the modern Christian teen. Fiction should deal with all subjects in a forthright manner, without being preachy and without talking down to teens. No tasteless manuscripts that promote anything adverse to the Bible's teachings." Submit complete ms. Length: 1,000-1,500 words. Pays 5-7¢/word.
  • Ranked as one of the best markets for fiction writers in the last *Writer's Digest* magazine's "Fiction 50."
Photos: Submit photos with ms. Pays $75-125 for color slides. Model releases available. Buys one-time rights.
Tips: "Don't be trite. Use unusual settings or problems. Use a lot of illustrations, a good balance of conversation, narration, and action. Style must be clear, fresh—no sermonettes or sickly-sweet fiction. Take a realistic approach to problems. Be willing to submit to editorial policies on doctrine; knowledge of the *Bible* a must. Also, be aware of teens today, and what they do. Language, clothing, and activities included in manuscripts should be contemporary. We are also looking for articles for a monthly feature entitled 'Straight Spotlight,' about real teens who are making a difference in their school, community or church. Articles for this feature should be approx. 900 words in length. We would also like a picture of the teen or group of teens to run with the article."

‡TEEN LIFE, Gospel Publishing House, 1445 Boonville Ave., Springfield MO 65802-1894. (417)862-2781, ext. 4357. Editor: Tammy Bicket. Mostly freelance written. Eager to work with new/unpublished writers. Quarterly magazine of Assemblies of God denomination of Christian fiction and articles for church-oriented teenagers, ages 12-17. Circ. 50,000. **Pays on acceptance.** Publishes ms an average of 15 months after acceptance. Byline given. Buys first North American serial, one-time, simultaneous and second serial (reprint) rights. Submit seasonal material 18 months in advance. Accepts simultaneous and previously published submissions. Send tearsheet or photocopy of article or typed ms with rights for sale noted and information about when and where the article previously appeared. Response time varies. Sample copy for 9×12 SAE with 2 first-class stamps. Writer's guidelines for #10 SASE.
Nonfiction: Interviews with Christian athletes, musicians, missionaries, authors, or others with notable and helpful Christian testimonies or helpful experiences; transcriptions of discussion sessions where a group of teens talk about a particular issue; information on a topic or issue of interest gathered from experts in those fields (i.e., a doctor talks about teens' sexuality, a psychologist talks about dysfunctional families, a police officer talks about the dangers of gangs, etc.). Book excerpts, church history, general interest, how-to (deal with various life problems), humor, inspirational, personal experience, world issues, apologetics, prayer, devotional life, the occult, angels, church. Buys 80-100 mss/year. Send complete ms. Length: 500-1,200 words. Pays 3-5¢/word.
Photos: Photos purchased with accompanying ms. Pays $35 for 8×10 b&w glossy print; $50 for 35mm slide.
Fiction: Adventure, humorous, mystery, romance, suspense. Buys 80-100 mss/year. Send complete ms. Length: 500-1,200 words. Pays 2-3¢/word.
Tips: "We need more male-oriented stories or articles and more about life in the city and about people of diverse races.

Avoid stereotypes. Avoid clichéd or trite situations with pat Christian answers and easy solutions. Avoid stories or articles without a Christian slant or emphasis, or those with a moral just tacked on at the end."

'TEEN, Petersen Publishing Co., 6420 Wilshire Blvd., Los Angeles CA 90048. (213)782-2950. (213)782-2660. Editor: Roxanne Camron. 40% freelance written. Monthly magazine covering teenage girls ages 12-19. " *'Teen* is edited for high school girls. We include all topics that are of interest to females aged 12-19. Our readers want articles on heavy hitting subjects like drugs, sex, teen pregnancy, etc., and we also devote a significant number of pages each month to health, beauty and fashion." Estab. 1957. Circ. 1,143,653. **Pays on acceptance.** Byline sometimes given. Buys all rights. Editorial lead time 6 months. Submit seasonal material 6 months in advance. Accepts simultaneous submissions. Reports in 10 weeks. Sample copy for $2.50. Writer's guidelines for #10 SASE.
Nonfiction: General interest, how-to (geared for teen market), humor, inspirational, personal experience. Buys 35 mss/ year. Query. Length: 250-750 words. Payment varies depending on length of research required.
Fiction: Adventure, condensed novels, fantasy, horror, mainstream, mystery, romance. Buys 12 mss/year. Send complete ms. Length: 2,500-3,500 words. Pays $250.

WHAT! A MAGAZINE, What! Publishers Inc., 108-93 Lombard Ave., Winnipeg, Manitoba R3B 3B1 Canada. Fax: (204)943-8991. E-mail: what@fox.nstn.ca. Contact: Stu Slayen, editor. 60% freelance written. Magazine covering teen issues published 5 times during the school year. "*What! A Magazine* is distributed to high school students across Canada. We produce a mag that is empowering, interactive and entertaining. We respect the reader—today's teens are smart and creative (and critical)." Estab. 1987. Circ. 200,000. Pays 30 days after publication. Publishes ms an average of 3 months after acceptance. Byline given. Offers negotiable kill fee. Buys first North American serial rights. Editorial lead time 5 months. Submit seasonal material 5 months in advance. Reports in 2 months on queries; 1 month on mss. Sample copy for 9 × 12 SASE with Canadian postage. Writer's guidelines for #10 SASE with Canadian postage.
Nonfiction: General interest, humor, interview/profile, issue-oriented features. No cliché teen material. Buys 6-10 mss/ year. Query with published clips. Length: 700-1,900 words. Pays $100-500 (Canadian). Sometimes pays expenses of writers on assignment.
Photos: Send photos with submission. Reviews transparencies, 4 × 6 prints. Negotiates payment individually. Identification of subjects required.
Tips: "Because *What! A Magazine* is distributed through schools (with the consent of school officials), it's important that each issue find the delicate balance between very cool and very responsible. We target very motivated young women and men. Pitches should stray from cliché and stories should challenge readers with depth, insight and color. All stories must be meaningful to a Canadian readership."

WITH, The Magazine for Radical Christian Youth, Faith and Life Press, 722 Main St., P.O. Box 347, Newton KS 67114-0347. (316)283-5100. Coeditors: Eddy Hall, Carol Duerksen. 60% freelance written. Magazine for teenagers published 8 times/year. "We are the magazine for Mennonite, Brethren, and Mennonite Brethren youth. Our purpose is to disciple youth within congregations." Circ. 6,100. **Pays on acceptance.** Byline given. Buys one-time rights. Submit seasonal material 6 months in advance. Accepts simultaneous submissions. Reports in 1 month on queries; 2 months on mss. Sample copy for 9 × 12 SAE with 4 first-class stamps. Writer's guidelines and theme list for #10 SASE. Additional detailed guidelines for first person stories, how-to articles and/or fiction available for #10 SASE.
Nonfiction: Humor, personal experience, religious, how-to, youth. Buys 15 mss/year. Send complete ms. Length: 400-1,800 words. Pays 5¢/word for simultaneous rights; 3¢/word for reprint rights for unsolicited articles. Higher rates for first-person stories and how-to articles written on assignment. (Query on these.)
Reprints: Send typed ms with rights for sale noted, including information about when and where the material previously appeared. Pays 60% of amount paid for an original article.
Photos: Sometimes pays the expenses of writers on assignment. Send photos with submission. Reviews 8 × 10 b&w prints. Offers $10-50/photo. Identification of subjects required. Buys one-time rights.
Columns/Departments: Service Missions (October/November 1997); Christmas (December 1997); Temptation (January/February 1998); Play (March 1998); Guilt and Grace (Easter) (April/May 1998); Conflict Resolution (June 1998); Sex and Dating (July/August 1998).
Fiction: Humorous, religious, youth, parables. Buys 15 mss/year. Send complete ms. Length: 500-2,000 words. Payment same as nonfiction.
Poetry: Avant-garde, free verse, haiku, light verse, traditional. Buys 0-2 poems. Pays $10-25.
Tips: "We're looking for more wholesome humor, not necessarily religious—fiction, nonfiction, cartoons, light verse. Christmas and Easter material has a good chance with us because we receive so little of it."

YM, Gruner & Jahr, 375 Lexington Ave, New York NY 10017-5514. (212)499-2000. Editor: Lesley Seymour. Contact: Christina Boyle, senior editor. 25% freelance written. Magazine covering teenage girls/dating. "We are a national magazine for young women ages 15-24. They're bright, enthusiastic and inquisitive. Our goal is to guide them—in effect, to be a 'best friend' and help them through the many exciting, yet often challenging, experiences of young adulthood." Estab. 1940s. Circ. 2,000,000. **Pays on acceptance.** Byline given. Offers 25% kill fee. Buys all rights. Editorial lead time 4 months. Submit seasonal material 5 months in advance. Accepts simultaneous submissions. Reports in 1 month. Sample copy for $2.50. Writer's guidelines free.
Nonfiction: How-to, interview/profile, personal experience, first-person stories. "*YM* publishes two special issues a year. One is a self-discovery issue, the other is a love issue filled with articles on relationships." Buys 20 mss/year.

Query with published clips (mark "Query" on the envelope). Length: 2,000 words maximum. Pays 75¢/word for assigned articles; 50-75¢/word for unsolicited articles. Pays expenses of writers on assignment.

Tips: "Our relationship articles are loaded with advice from psychologists and real teenagers. Areas most open to freelancers are: 2,000 word first-person stories covering a personal triumph over adversity—incorporating a topical social/political problem; 2,000 word relationship stories; 1,200 word relationship articles. All articles should be lively and informative, but not academic in tone, and any 'expert' opinions (psychologists, authors and teachers) should be included as a supplement to the feelings and experiences of young women."

YOUNG SALVATIONIST, The Salvation Army, P.O. Box 269, Alexandria VA 22313-0269. (703)684-5500. Fax: (703)684-5539. E-mail: uswarcry@aol.com. Contact: Lesa Davis, production manager. 80% freelance written. Works with a small number of new/unpublished writers each year. Monthly magazine for high school teens. "Only material with a definite Christian emphasis or from a Christian perspective will be considered." Circ. 50,000. **Pays on acceptance.** Publishes ms an average of 10 months after acceptance. Byline given. Buys first North American serial, first, one-time or second serial (reprint) rights. Submit seasonal material 6 months in advance. Reports in 2 months. Sample copy for 9 × 12 SAE with 3 first-class stamps. Writer's guidelines and theme list for #10 SASE.

Nonfiction: Inspirational, how-to, humor, interview/profile, personal experience, photo feature, religious. "Articles should deal with issues of relevance to teens (high school students) today; avoid 'preachiness' or moralizing." Buys 60 mss/year. Send complete ms. Length: 1,000-1,500 words. Pays 15¢/word for first rights.

Reprints: Send tearsheet, photocopy of article or typed ms with rights for sale noted and information about when and where the article previously appeared. Pays 10¢/word for reprints.

Fiction: Adventure, fantasy, humorous, religious, romance, science fiction—all from a Christian perspective. Length: 500-1,200 words. Pays 15¢/word.

Tips: "Study magazine, familiarize yourself with the unique 'Salvationist' perspective of *Young Salvationist*; learn a little about the Salvation Army; media, sports, sex and dating are strongest appeal."

YOUTH UPDATE, St. Anthony Messenger Press, 1615 Republic St., Cincinnati OH 45210-1298. (513)241-5615. Contact: Carol Ann Morrow, editor. 90% freelance written. Monthly 4-page newsletter of faith life for teenagers, "designed to attract, instruct, guide and challenge Catholics of high school age by applying the Gospel to modern problems/situations." Circ. 20,000. **Pays on acceptance.** Publishes ms an average of 6 months after acceptance. Byline given. Reports in 3 months. Sample copy and writer's guidelines for #10 SASE.

Nonfiction: Inspirational, practical self-help, spiritual. "Adults who pay for teen subs want more church-related and curriculum-related topics." Buys 12 mss/year. Query or send outline. Length: 2,200-2,300 words. Pays $350-400. Sometimes pays expenses of writers on assignment.

Tips: "Write for a 15-year-old with a C+ average."

TRAVEL, CAMPING AND TRAILER

Travel magazines give travelers indepth information about destinations, detailing the best places to go, attractions in the area and sites to see—but they also keep them up-to-date about potential negative aspects of these destinations. Publications in this category tell tourists and campers the where-tos and how-tos of travel. This category is extremely competitive, demanding quality writing, background information and professional photography. Each has its own slant. *Eco Traveler*, for example, covers "adventure travel with an environmental conscience," while *Trailer Life* presents articles on the recreational vehicle lifestyle. Sample copies should be studied carefully before sending submissions.

ADVENTURE WEST, America's Guide to Discovering the West, Adventure Media, Inc., P.O. Box 3210, Incline Village NV 89450. (702)832-1641. Fax: (702)832-1640. E-mail: editors@adv-media.com. Website: http://www.a dventurewest.com. Contact: Michael Oliver, associate editor. Managing Editor: Kristina Schreck. 40% freelance written. Bimonthly magazine covering adventure travel in the West. Estab. 1992. Circ. 155,000. Pays on publication. Publishes ms an average of 6 months after acceptance. Byline given. Offers 15% kill fee. Buys first North American serial rights. Editorial lead time 4 months. Submit seasonal material 6 months in advance. Accepts simultaneous submissions. Reports in 2 months. Sample copy for $3.50 and 10 × 13 SASE with 9 first-class stamps. Writer's guidelines for SASE.

Nonfiction: Historical/nostalgic, humor, interview/profile, personal experience, photo feature, travel. "We only publish adventure travel done in the West, including Alaska, Hawaii, western Canada and western Mexico." Buys 40 mss/year. Query with published clips. Length: 800-3,000 words. Pays 30¢/word. Sometimes pays expenses of writers on assignment.

Reprints: Occasionally accepts previously published submissions. Send tearsheet of article or short story and information about when and where the article previously appeared.

Photos: Send photos with submission. Reviews transparencies and slides. Negotiates payment individually. Captions and identification of subjects required. "We need itemized list of photos submitted." Buys one-time rights.

Columns/Departments: Buys 80 mss/year. Query with published clips. Pays $150-450.

Tips: "We like exciting, inspirational first-person stories on adventure. If the query or the unsolicited ms grabs us, we will use it. Our writer's guidelines are comprehensive. Follow them."

‡**AQUA, The Padi Diving Society Magazine**, Islands Publishing Co., P.O. Box 4728, Santa Barbara CA 93140-4728. Fax: (805)569-0349. E-mail: aqua@slandsmag.com. Contact: Bob Morris, executive editor. Managing Editor: Angela Tripp. 90% freelance written. Bimonthly magazine covering international travel for scuba diving, snorkeling, kayaking and other water sports enthusiasts. "*Aqua* puts its highest premium on lively storytelling. We avoid the 'been there, done that' treatment by sending our favorite writers to places they've never before visited. We want our readers to discover new destinations and share in water-borne adventures with a sense of awe and wonder that can only be conveyed by facile writers who craft stylish reportage." Estab. 1997. Circ. 125,000. **Pays on acceptance.** Publishes ms an average of 8 months in advance. Byline given. Offers 25% kill fee. Buys all rights. Editorial lead time 6 months. Submit seasonal material 6 months in advance. Reports in 2 months. Sample copy $6. Guidelines for #10 SASE.
Nonfiction: General interest, historical/nostalgic, humor, interview/profile, photo feature, travel. No technical articles or gear reviews; no 'my family dive vacation' articles. Buys 90 mss/year. Query with published clips or send complete ms; feature articles are commissioned. Length: 500-4,000 words. Pays $800-4,000. Pays expenses of writers on assignment.
Photos: State availability or send photos with submission. Reviews high-quality photocopies or 4×5 or 35mm transparencies. Offers $75-350/photo. Model releases, identification of subjects required. Buys one-time rights.
Columns/Departments: Local Dive (humorous profile of seedy or colorful watering hole or restaurant on the water), 500 words; Sea of Love (humorous look at the sex life of aquatic creatures), 1,200-1,500 words; Amphibian at Large (short feature piece on a water-related destination), 1,200-1,500 words; Aqua Culture (an aspect of the water enthusiast lifestyle, i.e., 'A Field Guide to Divers,' a humorous look at different species, or 'The Evolution of Aquaman,' a glimpse at the history and development of the DC Comics superhero), 1,200 words; Getaways (service pieces on diving, snorkeling, kayaking, whitewater rafting, etc., destinations in the US and Canada; basic nuts and bolts information on places that are good for day trips), 500 words. Buys 24 mss/year. Query with published clips or send complete ms. Pays $800-1,500.

ARUBA NIGHTS, Nights Publications, 1831 Rene Levesque Blvd. West, Montreal, Quebec H3H 1R4 Canada. Fax: (514)931-6273. E-mail: nights@odyssee.net. Contact: Stephen Trotter, editor. Managing Editor: Zelly Zuskin. 90% freelance written. Annual magazine covering the Aruban vacation lifestyle experience with an upscale, upbeat touch. Estab. 1988. Circ. 225,000. **Pays on acceptance.** Publishes ms an average of 9 months after acceptance. Offers 15% kill fee. Buys first North American serial and first Caribbean rights. Editorial lead time 1 month. Reports in 2 weeks on queries; 1 months on mss. Sample copy for $5. Writer's guidelines free.
Nonfiction: General interest, historical/nostalgic, how-to features relative to Aruba vacationers, humor, inspirational, interview/profile, eco-tourism, opinion, personal experience, photo feature, travel, Aruban culture, art, activities, entertainment, topics relative to vacationers in Aruba. "No negative pieces or stale rewrites." Buys 5-10 mss/year. Query with published clips. Length: 250-750 words. Pays $125-300 for assigned articles; $100-250 for unsolicited articles.
Photos: State availability with submission. Offers $50/photo. Captions, model releases, identification of subjects required. Buys one-time rights.
Tips: "Demonstrate your voice in your query letter. Be descriptive, employ vivid metaphors. Focus on individual aspects of the Aruban lifestyle and vacation experience (e.g., art, gambling tips, windsurfing, a colorful local character, a personal experience, etc.), rather than generalized overviews. Provide an angle that will be entertaining to both vacationers and Arubans."

ASU TRAVEL GUIDE, ASU Travel Guide, Inc., 1525 Francisco Blvd. E., San Rafael CA 94901. (415)459-0300. Fax: (415)459-0494. E-mail: chris@asuguide.com. Website: http://www.ASUguide.com. Contact: Christopher Gil, managing editor. 80% freelance written. Quarterly guidebook covering international travel features and travel discounts for well-traveled airline employees. Estab. 1970. Circ. 60,000. Publishes ms an average of 4 months after acceptance. Byline given. Buys first North American serial rights, first and second rights to the same material, and second serial (reprint) rights to material originally published elsewhere; also makes work-for-hire assignments. Submit seasonal material 6 months in advance. Accepts simultaneous submissions. Reports in 1 year. Sample copy available for 6×9 SAE with 5 first-class stamps. Writer's guidelines for #10 SASE.
Nonfiction: International travel articles "similar to those run in consumer magazines. Not interested in amateur efforts from inexperienced travelers or personal experience articles that don't give useful information to other travelers." Buys 16 ms/year. Destination pieces only; no "Tips On Luggage" articles. Unsolicited mss or queries without SASE will not be acknowledged. No telephone queries. Length: 1,800 words. Pays $200.
Reprints: Send tearsheet of article with information about when and where the article previously appeared. Pays 100% of amount paid for an original article.

ALWAYS CHECK the most recent copy of a magazine for the address and editor's name before you send in a query or manuscript.

Photos: "Interested in clear, high-contrast photos." Reviews 5×7 and 8×10 b&w or color prints. "Payment for photos is included in article price; photos from tourist offices are acceptable."

Tips: "Query with samples of travel writing and a list of places you've recently visited. We appreciate clean and simple style. Keep verbs in the active tense and involve the reader in what you write. Avoid 'cute' writing, coined words and stale cliches. The most frequent mistakes made by writers in completing an article for us are: 1) Lazy writing—using words to describe a place that could describe any destination such as 'there is so much to do in (fill in destination) that whole guidebooks have been written about it'; 2) Including fare and tour package information—our readers make arrangements through their own airline."

‡**AVENUES**, Automobile Club of Southern California, 2601 S. Figueroa St., Los Angeles CA 90007. (213)741-4760. Editor: Gail Harrington. Managine Editor: John Lehrer. 95% freelance written. Bimonthly magazine "published for the members of the Automobile Club of Southern California. *Avenues* takes a strong service approach to local issues, travel and automotive topics." Estab. 1993. Circ. 2.9 million. **Pays on acceptance.** Publishes ms an average of 6 months after acceptance. Byline given. Buys first North American serial rights. Editorial lead time 6 months. Sample copy and writer's guidelines free.

Nonfiction: Buys 20 mss/year. Query with published clips. Length: 1,500-3,200 words. Pays $1/word. Pays expenses of writers on assignment with limit agreed upon in advance.

Photos: Photos assigned by art director. Rarely use stock. Negotiates payment individually. Buys one-time rights.

Columns/Departments: John Lehrer, managing editor. Crack-Ups (humorous, automotive or driving), 350 words; Did You Know?, 450 words.

Tips: "Study the magazine and query with ideas that show an understanding of content and style. Include published clips. We discourage unsolicited manuscripts."

BEST WESTERN'S COMPASS MAGAZINE, HP Compass Magazine LLC, 1536 E. Maryland Ave., Phoenix AZ 85014. (602)277-4780. Contact: Jessica McCann, editor. 80% freelance written. Quarterly magazine covering travel. "*Compass* is the official in-room magazine for Best Western hotels throughout North America." Estab. 1997. Circ. 1,000,000. **Pays on acceptance.** Byline given. Offers 100% kill fee. Buys first North American serial rights. Editorial lead time 3 months. Submit seasonal material 1 year in advance. Accepts simultaneous submissions. Reports in 2 months. Sample copy for 9×12 SAE with 3 first-class stamps. Writer's guidelines for #10 SASE.

Nonfiction: Book excerpts, essays, general interest, historical/nostalgic, personal experience, photo feature, travel. "No generic travel pieces: Disneyland, Grand Canyon, etc. Articles are brief, light and easy to read. The goal is to capture a sense of place with visual and robust writing. Observations, anecdotes, penetrating quotes and storytelling are critical. A sense of humor is welcome when appropriate and a literary flair is never out of place." Buys 12-20 mss/year. Query with published clips. Length: 1,000-1,500 words. Pays $500-1,000.

Photos: State availability of photos with submission. Reviews transparencies, prints. Negotiates payment individually. Identification of subjects required.

Columns/Departments: Legend Has It . . . (local folklore and legend), 600 words; Rare & Well Done (restaurants, festivals and food), 600 words; Traveler's Journal (news, facts, services, etc.), 100-200 words. Query with published clips. Pays $100-500.

Fillers: Buys 5-10/year. Length: 100-200 words. Pays $100.

Tips: "*Compass* is an eclectic travel magazine that points readers to distinctive places and rewarding experiences. The content, supported by ample photography and practical information, is driven by stories offering personal insight and perspective—not all-you-ever-wanted-to-know about a place or experience, but rather an intimate view of travel, including the romantic and ironic, the comical and quirky, the poignant and pungent, the good and the for goodness-sake. *Compass* is a companion on the road less traveled."

BIG WORLD, Big World Publishing, P.O. Box 8743, Lancaster PA 17604. E-mail: bigworld@bigfoot.com. Website: http://www.paonline.com/bigworld. Contact: Jim Fortney, editor. 85% freelance written. Bimonthly magazine covering independent travel. "We're looking for casual, first-person narratives that take into account the cultural/sociological/political side of travel." Estab. 1995. Circ. 3,500. Pays on publication. Publishes ms an average of 3 months after acceptance. Byline given. Buys one-time rights. Editorial lead time 2 months. Submit seasonal material 4 months in advance. Reports in 1 months on queries; 2 months on mss. Sample copy for $3. Writer's guidelines for #10 SASE.

Nonfiction: New product, opinion, personal experience, photo feature, travel, how-to, tips on transportation bargains and adventuring, overseas work study advice. Buys 45 mss/year. Length: 500-4,000 words. Query. Pays $10-30.

Reprints: Accepts reprints of previously published submissions. Pay varies.

Photos: Reviews prints. Negotiates payment individually. Captions required. Buys one-time rights.

Columns/Departments: Readers Writes (book reviews by subscribers) 400-500 words. Hostel Intentions, My Town. Pay varies.

Tips: "Take a look at the glossy, fluffy travel mags in the bookstore. They're *not* what we're about. We're *not* looking for romantic getaway pieces or lap-of-luxury bits. Our readers are decidedly downbeat and are looking for similarly-minded on-the-cheap and down-to-earth, first-person articles. Be breezy. Be yourself. First-time writers especially encouraged."

BONAIRE NIGHTS, Nights Publications, 1831 René Lévesque Blvd. W., Montreal, Quebec H3H 1R4 Canada. Fax: (514)931-6273. E-mail: nights@odyssee.net. Contact: Stephen Trotter, editor. 90% freelance written. Annual magazine covering Bonaire vacation experience. "Upbeat entertaining lifestyle articles: colorful profiles of locals, eco-tourism; lively features on culture, activities (particularly scuba and snorkeling), special events, historical attractions, how-to features. Audience is North American tourist." Estab. 1993. Circ. 60,000. **Pays on acceptance.** Publishes ms an average of 9 months after acceptance. Byline given. Offers 15% kill fee on assigned mss only. Buys first North American serial rights and first Caribbean rights. Editorial lead time 1 month. Reports in 2 weeks on queries; 1 month on mss. Sample copy for $5. Writer's guidelines for #10 SASE.

Nonfiction: Lifestyle, general interest, historical/nostalgic, how-to, humor, inspirational, interview/profile, opinion, personal experience, photo feature, travel, local culture, art, activities, especially scuba diving, snorkeling, eco-tourism. Buys 6-9 mss/year. Query with published clips. Length: 250-750 words. Pays $125-350 for assigned articles; $100-250 for unsolicited articles.

Photos: State availability of photos with submission. Reviews transparencies. Offers $50/slide. Captions, model releases, identification of subjects required. Buys one-time or first rights.

Tips: "Demonstrate your voice in your query letter. Focus on the Bonaire lifestyle, what sets it apart from other islands. We want personal experience, not generalized overviews. Be positive and provide an angle that will appeal to residents as well as visitors."

BUON GIORNO, The Port Magazine of Costa Cruises, Onboard Media, 960 Alton Rd., Miami Beach FL 33139. (305)673-0400. Fax: (305)674-9396. Contact: Lynn Santa Lucia, managing editor. 95% freelance written. "This annual trilingual (English/French/Italian) in-cabin magazine reaches French, Italian and American cruise passengers traveling to various Caribbean port destinations. Stories must appeal to a multi-national readership." Estab. 1992. Circ. 69,950. Pays half on execution of agreement, half on acceptance of material. Publishes ms an average of 4 months after acceptance. Byline given. Offers 50% kill fee. Buys first or second serial (reprint) rights. Editorial lead time 6 months. Reports in 1 month. Sample copy for 11 × 14 SASE with $4 postage. Writer's guidelines for #10 SASE.

Nonfiction: Book excerpts, essays, general interest, humor, interview/profile, new product, photo feature, travel. Does not want politics, sex, religion, general history, shopping information or advertorials. No personal experience. Buys 12 features/year, plus assigned editorial covering ports-of-call and numerous fillers. Query with published clips. Length: 800-2,000 words. Pays $400-1,000 and contributor's copies. Sometimes pays expenses of writers on assignment.

Reprints: Accepts previously published submissions, if so noted.

Photos: State availability of photos with submission. Negotiates payment individually. Captions, model releases, identification of subjects required. Buys one-time and seasonal reprint rights. Photo credit and contributor copies given.

Fillers: Anecdotes, facts, newsbreaks, short humor. Buys 50/year. Length: 50-300 words. Pays $25-100 and copies.

Tips: "Know the port destinations we cover. Know our magazine. Demonstrate your voice in your query letter. Send a selection of published writing samples that reveals your range. The three essential things we look for are: 1) an authoritative voice; 2) intimate knowledge of the subject matter; and 3) original material. Having a clear-cut article in mind is a must. Do not query 'with an idea for an article on San Juan.' Outline your proposal and indicate your angle."

CAMPERS MONTHLY, Northeast Edition–Maine to New York; Mid Atlantic Edition—New York to Virginia, P.O. Box 260, Quakertown PA 18951. (215)536-6420. Fax: (215)536-6509. E-mail: werv2@aol.com. Website: http://www.RVGuide.com/campers. Editor: Paula Finkbeiner. 50% freelance written. Monthly (except December) tabloid. "With the above emphasis, we want to encourage our readers to explore all forms of outdoor recreation using a tent or recreational vehicle as a 'home away from home.' Travel-places to go, things to do and see." Estab. 1991 (Mid-Atlantic), 1993 (Northeast). Circ. 35,000 (Mid-Atlantic), 25,000 (Northeast). Pays on publication. Publishes ms an average of 2 months after acceptance. Byline given. Buys simultaneous rights. Editorial lead time 2 months. Submit seasonal material 4 months in advance. Accepts simultaneous submissions. Reports in 2 months. Sample copy and writer's guidelines free.

Nonfiction: Historical/nostalgic (tied into a camping trip), how-to (selection, care, maintenance of RV's, tents, accessories, etc.) humor, personal experience, travel (camping in the Mid-Atlantic or Northeast region). Special issue: Snowbird Issue (October)—geared towards campers heading South. This is generally the only time we accept articles on areas outside our coverage area. Buys 20-40 mss/year. Send complete ms. Length: 800-2,000 words. Pays $90-150 for assigned articles; $50 or more for unsolicited articles. Sometimes pays expenses of writers on assignment.

Reprints: Send photocopy of article or typed ms with rights for sale noted and information about when and where the article previously appeared. Pays 50% of amount paid for an original article.

Photos: Send photos with submission. Reviews 5 × 7 or 8 × 10 glossy b&w prints. Offers $3-5/photo. Don't send snapshots or polaroids. Avoid slides.

Columns/Departments: Campground Cook (Ideas for cooking in RV's, tents and over campfires, should include recipes), 500-1,000 words; Tales From The Road (humorous stories of "on-the-road" travel), 350-800 words; Tech Tips (technical pieces on maintenance and enhanced usage of RV-related equipment), 350-1,800 words. Buys 15 mss/year. Send complete ms. Pays $40-60. Cybersite (info on websites of interest to RVer's), 500-1,000 words. Buys 10 mss/year.

Fiction: Humorous, slice-of-life vignettes. Buys 10 mss/year. Query. Length: 300-1,000 words. Pays $60-75.

Fillers: Facts, short humor (must be RV-oriented). Buys 8/year. Length: 30-350. Pays $20-35.

Tips: Most open to freelancers are "destination pieces focusing on a single attraction or activity or closely clustered attractions are always needed. General interest material, technical or safety ideas (for RVs) is an area we're always looking for pieces on. Off the beaten track destinations always get priority. We're always looking for submissions for destination pieces for our Northeast and Mid-Atlantic edition."

‡CAMPING CANADA'S RV LIFESTYLES, 2585 Skymark Ave., Unit 306, Mississauga, Ontario L4W 4L5 Canada. (905)624-8218. Fax: (905)624-6764. Editor: Howard Elmer. Contact: Peter Tasler, editorial director. 50% freelance written. Magazine published 7 times/year (monthly January-June and November). "*Camping Canada's RV Lifestyles* is geared to readers who enjoy travel/camping. Upbeat pieces only. Readers vary from owners of towable campers or motorhomes to young families and entry-level campers (RV only)." Estab. 1971. Circ. 45,000. Pays on publication. Byline given. Buys first North American serial rights. Editorial lead time 2 months. Reports in 1 month on queries; 2 months on mss. Sample copy free.
Nonfiction: How-to, personal experience, travel. No inexperienced, unresearched or too general pieces. Buys 20-30 mss/year. Query. Length: 1,200-2,000 words. Pay varies. Sometimes pays expenses of writers on assignment.
Reprints: Occasionally accepts previously published submissions, if so noted.
Photos: Send photos with submission. Offers no additional payment for photos accepted with ms. Buys one-time rights.
Tips: "Pieces should be slanted toward RV living. All articles must have an RV slant."

CAMPING TODAY, Official Publication of the Family Campers & RVers, 126 Hermitage Rd., Butler PA 16001-8509. (412)283-7401. Editors: DeWayne Johnston and June Johnston. 30% freelance written. Prefers to work with published/established writers. Monthly official membership publication of the FCRV, "the largest nonprofit family camping and RV organization in the United States and Canada. Members are heavily oriented toward RV travel, both weekend and extended vacations. Concentration is on member activities in chapters. Group is also interested in conservation and wildlife. The majority of members are retired." Estab. 1983. Circ. 25,000. Pays on publication. Publishes ms an average of 6 months after acceptance. Byline given. Buys one-time rights. Submit seasonal material 3 months in advance. Accepts simultaneous submissions. Reports in 2 months. Sample copy and guidelines for 4 first-class stamps. Writer's guidelines only for #10 SASE.
Nonfiction: Travel (interesting places to visit by RV, camping), humor (camping or travel related, please, no "our first campout stories"), interview/profile (interesting campers), new products, technical (RVs related). Buys 10-15 mss/year. Send complete ms with photos. Length: 750-2,000 words. Pays $50-150.
Reprints: Send typed ms with rights for sale noted and information about when and where the article previously appeared. Pays 35-50% of amount paid for an original article.
Photos: Send photos with ms. Need b&w or sharp color prints inside (we can make prints from slides) and vertical transparencies for cover. Captions required.
Tips: "Freelance material on RV travel, RV maintenance/safety, and items of general camping interest throughout the United States and Canada will receive special attention."

CANCÚN NIGHTS, Nights Publications, 1831 Rene Levesque Blvd. West, Montreal, Quebec H3H 1R4 Canada. Fax: (514)931-6273. E-mail: night@odyssee.net. Contact: Stephen Trotter, editor. Managing Editor: Zelly Zuskin. 80% freelance written. Semiannual destination lifestyle magazine covering the Cancún vacation experience. Seeking "upbeat, entertaining lifestyle articles: colorful profiles of locals; lively features on culture, activities, night life, special events, historical attractions, Mayan achievements; how-to features; humor. Our audience is the North American vacationer." Estab. 1991. Circ. 650,000. **Pays on acceptance.** Publishes ms an average of 5 months after acceptance. Offers 15% kill fee on assigned mss only. Buys first North American serial rights and first Mexican rights. Editorial lead time 1 month. Reports 2 weeks on queries; 1 month on mss. Sample copy for $5. Writer's guidelines free on request.
Nonfiction: General interest, historical/nostalgic, how-to let vacationers get the most from their holiday, humor, inspirational, eco-tourism, interview/profile, lifestyle, opinion, personal experience, photo feature, travel, local culture, art, activities, night life, topics relative to vacationers in Cancún. No negative pieces, stale rewrites or cliché copy. Buys 8-12 mss/year. Query with published clips. Length: 250-750 words. Pays $125-300 for assigned articles; $100-250 for unsolicited articles.
Photos: State availability of photos with submission. Reviews transparencies. Offers $50/photo. Captions, model releases, identification of subjects required. Buys one-time rights.
Tips: "Demonstrate your voice in your query letter. Focus on individual aspects of the Cancún lifestyle and vacation experience (e.g., art, history, snorkeling, fishing, a colorful local character, a personal experience, etc.), entertaining to both vacationers and residents."

CAR & TRAVEL, American Automobile Association, 1000 AAA Dr., Heathrow Fl 32746-5063. (407)444-8544. Editor-in-Chief: Doug Damerst. Contact: Marianne Camas, senior editor. 20% freelance written. Magazine for AAA members—50+, college-educated, over $45,000 annual income. "*Car & Travel* contains features on buying, driving, and caring for cars, domestic and international travel destinations, and how to travel. Geographic editions supplement this with editorial pertaining to local and regional travel and car care." Estab. 1995. Circ. 5,000,000. Pays on publication. Byline given. Offers 25% kill fee. Buys first North American serial rights. Editorial lead time 4 months. Submit seasonal material 6 months in advance. Reports in 2 months. Sample copy and writer's guidelines free on request.
Nonfiction: Travel (automotive). No first-person travel. Buys 25 mss/year. Query with published clips. Length: 750-1,300 words. Pays $350-800. Sometimes pays expenses of writers on assignment.
Photos: State availability of photos with query. Reviews tearsheets (cannot return samples). Negotiates payment individually. Captions, model releases, identification of subjects required. Buys one-time rights.
Columns/Departments: Short-form features and departments on automotive and travel subjects. Cars (products, maintenance); Destination News (upcoming events); both 150-200 words. Buys 6 mss/year. Query with published clips. Pays $75-150.

Tips: "We're looking for tightly focused, reportorial style on caring for/buying cars and travel tips. Very few destination queries are considered."

CARIBBEAN TRAVEL AND LIFE, 8403 Colesville Rd., Suite 830, Silver Spring MD 20910. (301)588-2300. Editor-in-Chief: Veronica Gould Stoddart. 90% freelance written. Prefers to work with published/established writers. Bimonthly magazine covering travel to the Caribbean, Bahamas and Bermuda for sophisticated upscale audience. Estab. 1985. Circ. 130,000. **Pays on acceptance.** Publishes ms an average of 3 months after acceptance. Byline given. Offers 25% kill fee. Buys first North American serial rights. Submit seasonal material 6 months in advance. Reports in 2 months. Sample copy for 9×12 SAE with 9 first-class stamps. Writer's guidelines for #10 SASE.
Nonfiction: General interest, how-to, interview/profile, culture, personal experience, travel. No guidebook rehashing, superficial destination pieces or critical exposes. Buys 30 mss/year. Query with published clips. Length: 2,000-2,500 words. Pays $550.
Photos: Send photos with submission. Reviews 35mm transparencies. Offers $100-600/photo. Captions and identification of subjects required. Buys one-time rights.
Columns/Departments: Resort Spotlight (in-depth review of luxury resort); Tradewinds (focus on one particular kind of water sport or sailing/cruising); Island Buys (best shopping for luxury goods, crafts, duty-free); Island Spice (best cuisine and/or restaurant reviews with recipes); Money Matters (dollar-wise travel, bargain destinations, how to save money); EcoWatch (conservation efforts and projects); all 1,000-1,250 words; Just Back (newsy update on 1 individual island); Postcards from Paradise (short items on great finds in travel, culture, and special attractions), 500 words. Buys 36 mss/year. Query with published clips or send complete ms. Length: 500-1,250 words. Pays $75-300.
Tips: "We are especially looking for stories with a personal touch and lively, entertaining anecdotes, as well as strong insight into people and places being covered. Writer should demonstrate why he/she is the best person to do that story based on extensive knowledge of the subject, frequent visits to destination, residence in destination, specialty in field."

CHICAGO TRIBUNE, Travel Section, 435 N. Michigan Ave., Chicago IL 60611. (312)222-3999. Travel Contact: Randy Curwen, editor. Weekly Sunday newspaper leisure travel section averaging 22 pages aimed at vacation travelers. Circ. 1,100,000. Pays on publication. Publishes ms an average of 6 weeks after acceptance. Byline given. Buys one-time rights (which includes microfilm, online and CD/ROM usage). Submit seasonal material 2 months in advance. Accepts simultaneous submissions. Reports in 1 month. Sample copy for large SAE with $1.50 postage. Writer's guidelines for #10 SASE.
Nonfiction: Essays, general interest, historical/nostalgic, how-to (travel, pack), humor, opinion, personal experience, photo feature, travel. "There will be 16 special issues in the next 18 months." Buys 250 mss/year. Send complete ms. Length: 500-2,000 words. Pays $100-400.
Photos: State availability of photos with submission. Reviews 35mm transparencies, 8×10 or 5×7 prints. Offers $100/color photo; $25/b&w; $100 for cover. Captions required. Buys one-time rights.
Tips: "Be professional. Use a word processor. Make the reader want to go to the area being written about. Only 1% of manuscripts make it."

CLUBMEX, 660 Bay Blvd., Suite 214, Chula Vista CA 91910-5200. (619)585-3033. Fax: (619)420-8133. Contact: Roger Garay, publisher/editor. 75% freelance written. Bimonthly newsletter. "Our readers are travelers to Baja California and Mexico, and are interested in retirement, RV news, fishing and tours. They are knowledgeable but are always looking for new places to see." Estab. 1975. Circ. 5,000. Pays on publication. Publishes an average of 2 months after acceptance. Byline given. Buys first North American serial rights. Submit seasonal material at least 3 months in advance. Reports in 1 month. Writer's guidelines and free sample for 9×12 SAE with 2 first-class stamps.
• *Clubmex* accepts articles dealing with all of Mexico. They want upbeat, positive articles about Mexico which motivate readers to travel there by car.
Nonfiction: Historical, humor, interview, personal experience, travel. Buys 36-50 mss/year. Send complete ms. Length: 900-1,500 words. Pays $65 for the cover story, $50 for other articles used, and $25 for informative short pieces in Letter to the Editor format.
Reprints: Send photocopy or tearsheet of article or typed ms with rights for sale noted and information about when and where the article previously appeared, what rights were sold and what releases are needed. Pays 100% of amount paid for an original article.
Photos: State availability of photos with submission. Reviews 3×5 prints. Offers no additional payment for photos accepted with ms. Captions required. Buys one-time rights.

COAST TO COAST MAGAZINE, Affinity Group, Inc., 2575 Vista Del Mar Dr., Ventura CA 93001-3920. Fax: (805)667-4217. E-mail: wlaw@affinity.com. Website: http://www.tl.com. Contact: Valerie Law, editor. 80% freelance written. Club magazine published 8 times/year for members of Coast to Coast Resorts. "*Coast to Coast* focuses on travel, recreation and good times, with some stories targeted to recreational vehicle owners." Estab. 1982. Circ. 300,000. **Pays on acceptance.** Publishes ms an average of 5 months after acceptance. Byline given. Offers 33% kill fee. Buys first North American serial and electronic rights. Submit seasonal material 5 months in advance. Reports in 1 month on queries; 2 months on mss. Sample copy for $2 and 9×12 SASE.
Nonfiction: Book excerpts, essays, general interest, historical/nostalgic, how-to, humor, inspirational, interview/profile, new product, opinion, personal experience, photo feature, technical, travel. No poetry, cartoons. Buys 50 mss/year. Query with published clips. Length: 500-2,500 words. Pays $75-600.

Reprints: Send photocopy of article, information about when and where the article previously appeared. Pays approximately 50% of the amount paid for an original article.

Photos: Send photos with submission. Reviews transparencies. Offers $50-600/photo. Identification of subjects required. Buys one-time rights.

Tips: "Send published clips with queries, or story ideas will not be considered."

CONDÉ NAST TRAVELER, The Condé Nast Publications, 360 Madison Ave., New York NY 10017. (212)880-8800. Editor: Thomas J. Wallace. Managing Editor: Dee Aldrich. 75% freelance written. Monthly magazine covering travel. "Our motto, Truth in Travel, sums up our editorial philosophy: to present travel destinations, news and features in a candid, journalistic style. Our writers do not accept complimentary tickets, hotel rooms, gifts, or the like. While our departments present service information in a tipsheet or newsletter manner, our destination stories are literary in tone. Our readers are affluent, well-educated, and sophisticated about travel." Estab. 1987. Circ. 850,000. "Please keep in mind that we very rarely assign stories based on unsolicited queries because (1) our inventory of unused stories (features and departments) is very large, and (2) most story ideas are generated inhouse by the editors, as it is very difficult for outsiders to anticipate the needs of our inventory. To submit story ideas, send a brief (one paragraph) description of the idea(s) to the appropriate editor. Please do not send clips, resumes, photographs, itineraries, or abridged or full-length manuscripts. Due to our editorial policy, we *do not* purchase completed manuscripts. Telephone calls are not accepted."

● *Conde Nast Traveler* tells us that they are no longer accepting unsolicited submissions. Research this market carefully before submitting your best work.

CROWN & ANCHOR, The Port Magazine of Royal Caribbean Cruise Line, Onboard Media. 960 Alton Rd., Miami Beach FL 33137. (305)673-0400. Fax: (305)674-9396. Managing Editor: Lynn Santa Lucia. 95% freelance written. "This annual publication reaches cruise vacationers on board RCCL ships on 3-11 night Caribbean, Bahamas, Mexican Riviera, Alaska and Far East itineraries. Culture, art, architecutre, natural wonders, food, folklore, legends, lingo/idioms, festivals, literature, eco-systems, local wares of these regions. Current themes such as celebrity retreats, hit recordings and hot artists and writers are welcomed." Estab. 1992. Circ. 792,184. Pays half on execution of agreement, half on acceptance of material. Publishes ms an average of 4 months after acceptance. Offers 50% kill fee. Buys first or second serial (reprint) rights. Editorial lead time 6 months. Reports in 1 month. Sample copy for 11×14 SAE with 10 first-class stamps. Writer's guidelines for #10 SASE.

Nonfiction: Book excerpts, essays, general interest, humor, interview/profile, new product, photo feature, travel. Does not want politics, sex, religion, general history, shopping information or advertorials, no personal experience. Buys 25 features/year, plus assigned editorial covering ports-of-call and numerous fillers. Query with published clips. Length: 800-2,000 words. Pays $400-1,000, negotiable per assignment. Sometimes pays expenses of writers on assignment. Byline and bionote given. Contributor copies given.

Reprints: Accepts previously published submissions, if so noted.

Photos: State availability of photos with submission. Negotiates payment individually. Captions, model releases, identification of subjects required. Buys one-time and seasonal reprint rights.

Fillers: Anecdotes, facts, newsbreaks, short humor. Buys 50/year. Length: 50-200 words. Pays $25-100 or copies.

Tips: "Know the port destinations we cover. Know our magazine. Demonstrate your voice in your query letter. Send a selection of published writing samples that reveals your range. The three essential things we look for are: 1) an authoritative voice; 2) intimate knowledge of the subject matter; and 3) original material. Having a clear-cut article in mind is a must. Do not query 'with an idea for an article on San Juan.' Outline your proposal and indicate your angle."

CRUISE TRAVEL MAGAZINE, World Publishing Co., 990 Grove St., Evanston IL 60201-4370. (708)491-6440. Editor: Robert Meyers. Contact: Charles Doherty, managing editor. 95% freelance written. Bimonthly magazine. "This is a consumer-oriented travel publication covering the world of pleasure cruising on large cruise ships (with some coverage of smaller ships), including ports, travel tips, roundups." Estab. 1979. **Pays on acceptance.** Publishes ms an average of 6 months after acceptance. Byline given. Offers 50% kill fee. Buys first North American serial, one-time or second serial (reprint) rights. Accepts simultaneous submissions. Reports in 1 month. Sample copy for $5 postpaid. Writer's guidelines for #10 SASE.

Nonfiction: General interest, historical/nostalgic, interview/profile, personal experience, photo feature, travel. "No daily cruise 'diary', My First Cruise, etc." Buys 72 mss/year. Query with or without published clips, or send complete ms. Length: 500-1,500 words. Pays $100-400.

Reprints: Send tearsheet or photocopy of article and typed ms with rights for sale noted.

Photos: Send photos with submission. Reviews transparencies and prints. "Must be color, 35m preferred (other format OK); color prints second choice." Offers no additional payment for photos accepted with ms "but pay more for well-illustrated ms." Captions and identification of subjects required. Buys one-time rights.

Fillers: Anecdotes, facts. Buys 3 mss/year. Length: 300-700 words. Pays $75-200.

Tips: "Do your homework. Know what we do and what sorts of things we publish. Know the cruise industry—we can't use novices. Good, sharp, bright color photography opens the door fast. We still need good pictures—we are not interested in developing any new contributors who cannot provide color support to manuscripts."

CRUISING IN STYLE, The Port Magazine of Crystal Cruises, Onboard Media, Inc., 960 Alton Rd., Miami Beach FL 33137. (305)673-0400. Fax: (305)674-9396. Managing Editor: Lynn Santa Lucia. 95% freelance written.

Annual magazine covering Caribbean, Panama Canal, Mexican Riviera. "This in-cabin magazine reaches sophisticated cruise passengers seeking a vacation/learning experience. We are looking,for well-researched original material on interesting aspects of the port destination." Estab. 1992. Circ. 792,184. **Pays half on execution of agreement, half on acceptance of material.** Publishes ms an average of 4 months after acceptance. Byline given. Offers 50% kill fee. Buys first or second serial (reprint) rights. Editorial lead time 6 months. Reports in 1 month. Sample copy for 11×14 SAE with $4 postage. Writer's guidelines for #10 SASE.

Nonfiction: Book excerpts, essays, general interest, humor, interview/profile, new product, photo feature, travel. Does not want politics, sex, religion, general history, shopping information or advertorials. No personal experience. Buys 12 features/year, plus assigned editorial covering ports-of-call and numerous fillers. Query with published clips. Length: 800-2,000 words. Pays $400-1,000, negotiable per assignment. Sometimes pays expenses of writers on assignment.

Reprints: Accepts previously published submissions, if so noted.

Photos: State availability of photos with submission. Negotiates payment individually. Captions, model releases, identification of subjects required. Buys one-time and seasonal reprint rights. Photo credit and contributor copies given.

Fillers: Anecdotes, facts, newsbreaks, short humor. Buys 50/year. Length: 50-300 words. Pays $25-100 and contributor copies.

Tips: "Know the port destinations we cover. Know our magazine. Demonstrate your voice in your query letter. Send a selection of published writing samples that reveals your range. The three essential things we look for are: 1) an authoritative voice; 2) intimate knowledge of the subject matter; and 3) original material. Having a clear-cut article in mind is a must. Do not query 'with an idea for an article on San Juan.' Outline your proposal and indicate your angle."

CURAÇAO NIGHTS, Nights Publications, 1831 Rene Levesque Blvd. West, Montreal, Quebec H3H 1R4 Canada. (514)931-1987. Fax: (514)931-6273. E-mail: nights@odyssee.net. Contact: Stephen Trotter, editor. Managing Editor: Zelly Zuskin. 90% freelance written. Annual magazine covering the Curaçao vacation experience. "We are seeking upbeat, entertaining lifestyle articles; colorful profiles of locals; lively features on culture, activities, night life, eco-tourism, special events, gambling; how-to features; humor. Our audience is the North American vacationer." Estab. 1989. Circ. 155,000. **Pays on acceptance.** Publishes ms an average of 10 months after acceptance. Byline given. Offers 15% kill fee. Buys first North American serial and first Caribbean rights. Editorial lead time 1 month. Reports in 2 weeks on queries; 1 month on mss. Sample copy for $5. Writer's guidelines free.

Nonfiction: General interest, historical/nostalgic, how-to help a vacationer get the most from their vacation, eco-tourism, humor, inspirational, interview/profile, lifestyle, opinion, personal experience, photo feature, travel, local culture, art, activities, night life, topics relative to vacationers in Curaçao. "No negative pieces, generic copy or stale rewrites." Buys 5-10 mss/year. Query with published clips. Length: 250-750 words. Pays $125-$300 for assigned articles; $100-$250 for unsolicited articles.

Photos: State availability of photos with submission. Reviews transparencies. Offers $150/photo. Captions, model releases, identification of subjects required. Buys one-time rights.

Tips: "Demonstrate your voice in your query letter. Focus on individual aspects of the island lifestyle and vacation experience (e.g., art, gambling tips, windsurfing, a colorful local character, a personal experience, etc.), rather than generalized overviews. Provide an angle that will be entertaining to both vacationers and Curaçaoans."

DESTINATIONS, The Port Magazine of Celebrity Cruises, Onboard Media, 960 Alton Rd., Miami Beach FL 33139. (305)673-0400. Fax: (305)674-9396. Contact: Lynn Santa Lucia, managing editor. 95% freelance written. Annual magazine covering Caribbean, Mexican Riviera, Costa Rica, Panama Canal, The Bahamas. "This in-cabin magazine reaches cruise passengers traveling to various ports of call. We are looking for original material on interesting aspects of these Caribbean, Mexican and Central American destinations. We are also interested in articles on the cruising experience." Estab. 1992. Circ. 792,184. **Pays half on execution of agreement, half on acceptance of material**. Publishes ms an average of 4 months after acceptance. Offers 50% kill fee. Buys first or second serial (reprint) rights. Editorial lead time 6 months. Reports in 1 month. Sample copy free on written request and 11×14 SASE with $4 postage. Writer's guidelines for #10 SASE.

Nonfiction: Book excerpts, essays, general interest, humor, interview/profile, new product, photo feature, travel. Does not want politics, sex, religion, general history, shopping information or advertorials. No personal experience. Buys 12 features/year, plus assigned editorial covering ports-of-call and numerous fillers. Query with published clips. Length: 800-2,000 words. Pays $400-1,000 and contributors copies. Sometimes pays expenses of writers on assignment.

Reprints: Accepts previously published submissions, if so noted. Send photocopy of article and information about when and where the article previously appeared.

Photos: State availability of photos with submission. Negotiates payment individually. Captions, model releases, identification of subjects required. Buys one-time and seasonal reprint rights. Photo credit and contributor copies given. Request photographer's guidelines from Jessica Thomas, photo editor; include #10 SASE.

Fillers: Anecdotes, facts, newsbreaks, short humor. Buys 50/year. Length: 50-300 words. Pays $25-100 and copies.

Tips: "Know the port destinations we cover. Know our magazine. Demonstrate your voice in your query letter. Send a selection of published writing samples that reveal your range. The three essential things we look for are 1) an authoritative voice, 2) intimate knowledge of the subject matter, and 3) original material. Having a clear-cut article in mind is a must. Do not query with 'an idea for an article on San Juan.' Outline your proposal and indicate your angle."

ECOTRAVELER, EcoTraveler, Inc., 2601 NW Thurman, Portland OR 97210. (503)224-9080. Fax: (503)224-4266. E-mail: ecotrav@aol.com. Editor: Lisa Tabb. 90% freelance written. Bimonthly magazine covering adventure travel with an environmental conscience. "Our readers are educated, affluent, conscientious adventure seekers. They are left-leaning and active. The median age is 42 years old." Estab. 1990. Circ. 100,000. Pays 30 days after date of publication. Publishes ms an average of 4 months after acceptance. Byline given. Offers 25% kill fee or $150. Buys first North American serial and one-time rights. Editorial lead time 6 months. Submit seasonal material 4 months in advance. Responds in 3 months to queries with SASE. Accepts simultaneous submissions. Sample copy for $5..

Nonfiction: Book excerpts, general interest, historical/nostalgic, how-to, humor, inspirational, interview/profile, new product, opinion, personal experience, photo feature, travel. Special issues: Adventure cruises, Eco-hotels in the Caribbean. Buys 100 mss/year. Send complete ms. Pays $50-1,000 for assigned articles; $50-600 for unsolicited articles. Sometimes pays expenses of writers on assignment.

Reprints: Accepts previously published submissions.

Photos: State availability of or send photos with submission. Negotiates payment individually. Captions, identification of subjects required. Buys one-time and CD rights.

Columns/Departments: Heatlh, General, Travel Tips, Explorations, Photo, Historical, Profiles. Buys lots of mss/year. Send complete ms. Pays $50-300.

ENDLESS VACATION, Endless Vacation, P.O. 80260, Indianapolis IN 46280-0260. (317)871-9504. Fax: (317)871-9507. Contact: Jami Stall, senior editor. Prefers to work with published/established writers. Bimonthly magazine. "*Endless Vacation* is the vacation-idea magazine edited for people who love to travel. Each issue offers articles for America's dedicated and frequent leisure travelers—time-share owners. Articles and features explore the world through a variety of vacation opportunities and options for travelers who average 4 weeks of leisure travel each year." Estab. 1974. Circ. 1,024,287. **Pays on acceptance.** Publishes ms an average of 6 months after acceptance. Byline given. Buys first North American serial rights. Accepts simultaneous submissions. Reports in 2 months. Sample copy for $5 and 9×12 SAE with 3 first-class stamps. Writer's guidelines for #10 SASE.

• Ranked as one of the best markets for freelance writers in *Writer's Yearbook*'s annual "Top 100 Markets," January 1997.

Nonfiction: Contact: Senior Editor. Buys 24 mss/year (approximately). Most are from established writers already published in *Endless Vacation. Accepts very few unsolicited pieces.* Query with published clips. Length: 1,000-2,000 words. Pays $500-1,000 for assigned articles; $250-800 for unsolicited articles. Sometimes pays the expenses of writers on assignment.

Photos: Reviews 4×5 transparencies and 35mm slides. Offers $100-500/photo. Model releases and identification of subjects required. Buys one-time rights.

Columns/Departments: Complete Traveler (on travel news and service-related information); Weekender (on domestic weekend vacation travel). Query with published clips. Length: 800-1,000 words. Pays $150-600. Sometimes pays the expenses of writers on assignment. Also news items for Facts, Fads and Fun Stuff column on travel news, products or problems. Length: 100-200 words. Pays $100/item.

Tips: "We will continue to focus on travel trends and timeshare resort destinations. Articles must be packed with pertinent facts and applicable how-tos. Information—addresses, phone numbers, dates of events, costs—must be current and accurate. We like to see a variety of stylistic approaches, but in all cases the lead must be strong. A writer should realize that we require first-hand knowledge of the subject and plenty of practical information. For further understanding of *Endless Vacation*'s direction, the writer should study the magazine and guidelines for writers."

FAMILY MOTOR COACHING, Official Publication of the Family Motor Coach Association, 8291 Clough Pike, Cincinnati OH 45244-2796. (513)474-3622. Fax: (513)388-5286. Publishing Director: Pamela Wisby Kay. Contact: Robbin Gould, editor. 80% freelance written. "We prefer that writers be experienced RVers." Monthly magazine emphasizing travel by motorhome, motorhome mechanics, maintenance and other technical information. "*Family Motor Coaching* magazine is edited for the members and prospective members of the Family Motor Coach Association who own or about to purchase recreational vehicles of the motor coach style and use them exclusively for pleasure. Featured are articles on travel and recreations, association news; meetings, activities, and conventions plus articles on new products. Approximately ⅓ of editorial content is devoted to travel and entertainment, ⅓ to Association news, and ⅓ to new products and industry news." Estab. 1963. Circ. 110,000. **Pays on acceptance.** Publishes ms an average of 8 months after acceptance. Buys first North American serial rights. Byline given. Submit seasonal material 4 months in advance. Reports in 2 months. Sample copy for $2.50. Writer's guidelines for #10 SASE.

Nonfiction: Motorhome travel (various areas of country accessible by motor coach), how-to (do it yourself motor home projects and modifications), bus conversions, humor, interview/profile, new product, technical, nostalgia. Buys 8-10 mss/issue. Query with published clips . Length: 1,000-2,000 words. Pays $100-500.

Photos: State availability of photos with query. Offers no additional payment for b&w contact sheets, 35mm or 2¼×2¼ color transparencies. Captions, model releases required. Prefers first North American serial rights but will consider one-time rights on photos only.

Tips: "The greatest number of contributions we receive are travel; therefore, that area is the most competitive. However, it also represents the easiest way to break in to our publication. Articles should be written for those traveling by self-contained motor home. The destinations must be accessible to motor home travelers and any peculiar road conditions should be mentioned."

GIBBONS-HUMMS GUIDE, Florida Keys-Key West, Gibbons Publishing, Inc., P.O. Box 6524, Key West FL 33041-6524. (305)296-7300. Fax: (305)296-7414. Editor: Gibbons D. Cline. Contact: Tara Valdez, editorial assistant.

15% freelance written. Quarterly magazine targeted to tourists and frequent visitors to Florida Keys (Monroe County, FL, from Key Largo to Key West). Estab. 1972. Circ. 220,000. Pays on publication. Publishes ms an average of 6 months after acceptance. Byline given. Buys all rights. Editorial lead time 6 months. Submit seasonal material at least 6 months in advance. Reports in 6 months on queries; 3 months on mss. Sample copy free on request. Writer's guidelines free.

Nonfiction: General interest, historical/nostalgic, how-to (water sports), humor, new product (marine related), technical (water sports), travel. Special issues: Reefs and wrecks—highlighting artificial and natural reefs offshore for fishing, diving and snorkeling enthusiasts; Vacation accommodations—condos, bed and breakfast inns, resorts, hotels, hostels, etc. "We need accurate tourist tips—tell us about the best attractions and dining spots. No more vacation stories, quizzes, trivia. Would like to see more fishing, diving and boating. No religious or erotic material." Buys 5-10 mss/year. Query with published clips. Length: 500-1,500 words. Pays $2/column inch.

Reprints: Send typed manuscript with rights for sale noted and information about when and where the article previously appeared. Pays $50 maximum.

Photos: State availability of photos with submission. No additional payment offered for photos with ms. Reviews any size transparencies, prints, slides. Model releases and identification of subjects required. Buys all rights.

Columns/Departments: Fishing Digest (fishing hotspots, how-to, new equipment), 1,000 words; Keys Under the Seas (diving how-to, new equipment), 1,000 words; Touring Highlights (attractions: Key West, Lower Keys, Marathon, Islamorada, Key Largo), 1,000 words. Buys 5 mss/year. Query with published clips. Pays $2/column inch to $100.

Fiction: Publishes novel excerpts.

Fillers: Facts, trivia, puzzles—crossword or otherwise. Buys 3-5/year. Length: 100-800 words. Pays $2/column inch to $100.

Tips: "Please send résumé with query and/or manuscripts. It is helpful to visit Keys before trying to write about them. Get a feel for unique attitude, atmosphere and lifestyle in the Keys. Focus on things to do, like water sports. Try it, then write about it—but not from a personal experience angle. Find unique angles: strange characters, humorous anecdotes, etc. What makes *your* experience in the Keys different from everyone else's? Find a special bargain? Use new, state-of-the-art equipment? Meet a 90-year-old grandmother who windsurfs? We're looking for the unusual."

‡GO MAGAZINE, AAA Carolinas, P.O. Box 30008, Charlotte NC 28230. (704)377-7733. Fax: (704)358-1585. Contact: Tom Crosby, editor. 10% freelance written. Bimonthly newspaper covering travel, automotive, safety (traffic) and insurance. "Consumer oriented membership publication providing information on complex or expensive subjects—car buying, vacations, traffic safety problems, etc." Estab. 1928. Circ. 506,800. **Pays on acceptance.** Publishes ms an average of 2 months after acceptance. Buys second serial (reprint) rights, simultaneous rights or makes work-for-hire assignments. Editorial lead time 6 weeks. Submit seasonal material 6 weeks in advance. Reports in 2 weeks on queries; 2 months on mss. Sample copy for SAE with 4 first-class stamps. Writer's guidelines for #10 SASE.

Nonfiction: How-to (fix auto, travel safety, etc.), travel, automotive insurance, traffic safety. Buys 12-14 mss/year. Query with published clips. Length: 600-900 words. Pays 15¢/word.

Photos: Send photos with submission. Offers no additional payment for photos accepted with ms. Buys one-time rights.

‡GOLF & TRAVEL, Turnstile Publishing Co., 157 57th St., Suite 1400, Columbus Circle Station, NY 10019. Fax: (212)397-6069. E-mail: golfntravl@aol.com. Contact: Cindi Crain, editor. 50% freelance written. Quarterly magazine. *Golf & Travel* wants "solid travel writing with a critical eye. No fluff. No common tourist stops unless they're deserving. Destination stories with golf as one of the elements, but not the only element." Estab. 1997. Circ. 150,000. **Pays on acceptance.** Publishes ms an average of 3 months after acceptance. Byline given. Buys first rights or all rights. Editorial lead time 4 months. Submit seasonal material 18 months in advance. "We only reply to queries we're interested in. Too small a staff to answer every letter. Sorry." Sample copy for $3.95 plus postage; (800)678-9717. Writer's guidelines for #10 SASE.

Nonfiction: Interview/profile, new product, travel. "No articles about golf courses only; no articles on common golf destinations; no articles written in 'fluff' language." Buys 20 mss/year. Query with published clips. Length: 100-3,000 words. Pays $50-2,500. Sometimes pays expenses of writers on assignment.

Columns/Departments: Starter (golf packages, golf events, golf destination news), 100-150 words; Road & Driver (great road trips with golf along the way), 1,500-2,000 words; Urban Outings (places to golf within city limits), 1,000-1,500 words; Fairway Living (destination stories about places to live that offer good golf environment), 1,200-1,500 words. Query with published clips. Pays $50-1,500.

Tips: "Must be established travel writers with great destination stories in their clips file. Clips must demonstrate unusual angles—off the beaten path. Knowledge of golf extremely helpful. Straight golf writers are not encouraged to query."

‡GREECE TRAVEL MAGAZINE, Greece Travel Magazine, Inc., 830 Eyrie Dr., Suite 1, Oviedo FL 32765. (407)365-0663. Fax: (407)365-8180. E-mail: greecemag.aol.com. Editor: Candice Ricketts. Contact: Michelle Tirado, managing editor. 80% freelance written. Bimonthly magazine. "Features mainland and island destinations, cruises, yacht charters, art, history and archaeology." Estab. 1996. Circ. 25,000. Pays within 30 days of publication. Byline given. Buys one-time rights. Editorial lead time 3 months. Submit seasonal material 6 months in advance. Accepts simultaneous submissions. Reports in 6 weeks on queries; 2 months on mss. Sample copy for $4.95. Writer's guidelines for #10 SASE.

Nonfiction: Book excerpts, general interest, historical/nostalgic, humor, interview/profile, personal experience, photo feature, travel. Query with published clips. Length: 500-3,000 words. Pays $50-500 for assigned articles; $50-350 for unsolicited articles.

Reprints: Send photocopy of article or short story.
Photos: Send photos with submission. Reviews contact sheets, transparencies and prints. Captions, model releases and identification of subjects required. Buys one-time rights.
Columns/Departments: On The Menu (restaurant review), 500-1,000 words; Cultural Adventures (personal narrative involving traveler's cultural discoveries in Greece), 750-1,500 words; Anchors Away (traveler's experience on board a chartered yacht), 500-1,000 words. Buys 18 mss/year. Query with published clips. Pays $150-350.
Poetry: Query with published clips.
Fillers: Facts, tips, newsbreaks. Length: 50-200 words. Pays $10-50.

HIGHWAYS, The Official Publication of the Good Sam Club, TL Enterprises Inc., 2575 Vista Del Mar, Ventura CA 93001. (805)667-4100. Fax: (805)667-4454. E-mail: goodsam@tl.com. Website: http://www.tl.com. Editor: Ronald H. Epstein. 40% freelance written. Monthly magazine (November/December issues combined) covering recreational vehicle lifestyle. "All of our readers—since we're a membership publication—own or have a motorhome, trailer, camper or van conversion. Thus, our stories include road-travel conditions and terms and information about campgrounds and locations. Estab. 1966. Circ. 912,214. **Pays on acceptance**. Publishes ms an average of 6 months after acceptance. Byline given. Offers 50% kill fee. Buys first North American serial and electronic rights. Editorial lead time 15 weeks. Submit seasonal material 5 months in advance. Accepts simultaneous submissions. Reports in 3 weeks on queries; 1 month on mss. Sample copy and writer's guidelines free.
Nonfiction: How-to (repair/replace something on an RV); humor; technical; travel; (all RV related). Buys 15-25 mss/year. Query or send complete ms. Length: 1,800-2,500 words. Pays $150-500 for unsolicited articles.
Photos: Send photos with submission. Reviews contact sheets, negatives, transparencies, prints. Offers no additional payment for photos accepted with ms. Captions, model releases, identification of subjects required. Buys one-time rights.
Columns/Departments: Beginners (people buying an RV for the first time), 1,200 words; View Points (issue-related), 750 words. Query. Pays $200-250.
Tips: "Understand RVs and RVing. It's a unique lifestyle and different than typical traveling. Aside from that, we welcome good writers!"

‡HISTORIC TRAVELER, The Guide to Great Historic Destinations, Cowles Magazines, Inc. 6405 Flank Dr., Harrisburg PA 17112. (717)657-9555. Fax: (717)657-9552. E-mail: 102430.410@compuserve.com. Contact: Tom Huntington, editor. 80% freelance written. Bimonthly magazine covering "historic destinations for upscale reders with a strong interest in history and historic sites." Estab. 1994. Circ. 90,000. **Pays on acceptance.** Publishes ms an average of 4 months after acceptance. Byline given. Offers 25% kill fee. Buys first North American serial rights or all rights. Editorial lead time 6 months. Submit seasonal material 6 months in advance. Reports in 2 months. Sample copy for $5. Writer's guidelines for #10 SASE.
Nonfiction: Historical, travel. "Nothing without a strong historic destination(s) as the focus." Buys 42 mss/year. Query with published clips. Length: 1,500-3,000 words. Pays $300-1,000.
Photos: State availability of photos with submission. Negotiates payment individually. Identification of subjects required. Buys one-time rights.
Columns/Departments: All-American Towns (small towns); Museum Watch (unusual museums); Grand Tour (early travel experiences); all 1,500 words. Buys 20 mss/year. Query with published clips. Pays $300-500.
Tips: "A good query is always a strong start. Don't offer to write about something unless it interests you personally."

‡INTERNATIONAL LIVING, Agora, Inc., 105 W. Monument St., Baltimore MD 21201. Fax: (410)223-2669. E-mail: 103114.2472@compuserve.com. Editor: Vivian Lewis. Contact: Michael Palmer, assistant editor. 50% freelance written. Monthly newsletter covering retirement, travel, investment and real estate overseas. "We do not want descriptions of how beautiful places are. We want specifics, recommendations, contacts, prices, names, addresses, phone numbers, etc. We want offbeat locations and off-the-beaten-track spots." Estab. 1981. Circ. 110,000. Pays on publication. Publishes ms an average of 3 months after acceptance. Byline given. Offers 25-50% kill fee. Buys all rights. Editorial lead time 2 months. Submit seasonal material 3 months in advance. Accepts simultaneous submissions. Reports in 2 months. Sample copy for #10 SASE. Writer's guidelines free.
Nonfiction: How-to (get a job, buy real estate, get cheap airfares overseas, etc.), interview/profile (entrepreneur abroad), new product (travel), personal experience, travel, shopping, cruises, etc. No descriptive, run-of-the-mill travel articles. Buys 100 mss/year. Send complete ms. Length: 500-2,000 words. Pays $200-500 for assigned articles; $100-400 for unsolicited articles.
Reprints: Rarely publishes reprints of previously published submissions. Send information about when and where the article previously appeared.
Photos: State availability of photos with submission. Reviews contact sheets, negatives, transparencies or prints. Offers $50/photo. Identification of subjects required. Buys all rights.
Fillers: Facts. Buys 20/year. Length: 50-250 words. Pays $25-100.
Tips: "Make recommendations in your articles. We want first-hand accounts. Tell us how to do things: how to catch a cab, order a meal, buy a souvenir, buy property, start a business, etc. *International Living*'s philosophy is that the world is full of opportunities to do whatever you want, whenever you want. We will show you how."

‡THE INTERNATIONAL RAILWAY TRAVELER, Hardy Publishing Co., Inc., Editorial offices: P.O. Box 3747, San Diego CA 92163. (619)260-1332. Fax: (619)296-4220. E-mail: irt.trs@worldnet.att.net. 100% freelance written. Newsletter published 10 times/year covering rail travel. Estab. 1983. Circ. 3,500. Pays on publication. Byline given. Offers 25% kill fee. Buys first North American serial rights and all electronic rights. Editorial lead time 4 months. Submit seasonal material 6 months in advance. Query for electronic submissions. Reports in 1 month on queries; 2 months on mss. Sample copy for $6. Writer's guidelines for #10 SASE.
Nonfiction: Book reviews, general interest, how-to, interview/profile, new product, opinion, personal experience, travel. Buys 24-30 mss/year. Query with published clips or send complete ms. Include SASE for return of ms. Length: 800-1,200 words. Pays 4¢/word.
Photos: Send photos with submission. Include SASE for return of photos. Reviews contact sheets, negatives, transparencies, prints (8×10 preferred; will accept 5×7). Offers $10 b&w; $20 cover photo. Costs of converting slides and negatives to prints are deducted from payment. Captions and identification of subjects required. Buys one-time rights.
Tips: "We want factual articles concerning world rail travel which would not appear in the mass-market travel magazines. IRT readers and editors love stories and photos on off-beat train trips as well as more conventional train trips covered in unconventional ways. With IRT, the focus is on the train travel experience, not a blow-by-blow description of the view from the train window. Be sure to include details (prices, passes, schedule info, etc.) for readers who might want to take the trip."

ISLANDS, An International Magazine, Islands Publishing Company, 3886 State St., Santa Barbara CA 93105-3112. Fax: (805)569-0349. E-mail: islands@islandsmag.com. Editor: Joan Tapper. Contact: Denise Iest, copy/production editor. 95% freelance written. Works with established writers. Bimonthly magazine covering "accessible and once-in-a-lifetime islands from many different perspectives: travel, culture, lifestyle. We ask our authors to give us the essence of the island and do it with literary flair." Estab. 1981. Circ. 200,000. **Pays on acceptance.** Publishes ms an average of 8 months after acceptance. Byline given. Buys all rights. Reports in 2 months on queries; 6 weeks on ms. Sample copy for $6. Writer's guidelines for #10 SASE.
• Ranked as one of the best markets for freelance writers in *Writer's Yearbook* magazine's annual "Top 100 Markets," January 1997.
Nonfiction: General interest, personal experience, photo feature, any island-related material. No service stories. "Each issue contains 4-5 feature articles and 5-6 departments. Any authors who wish to be commissioned should send a detailed proposal for an article, an estimate of costs (if applicable) and samples of previously published work." Buys 25 feature mss/year. "The majority of our feature manuscripts are commissioned." Query with published clips or send complete ms. Feature length: 2,000-4,000 words. Pays $1,000-4,000. Pays expenses of writers on assignment.
Photos: State availability of or send photos with query or ms. Pays $75-300 for 35mm transparencies. "Fine color photography is a special attraction of *Islands*, and we look for superb composition, technical quality and editorial applicability." Label slides with name and address, include captions, and submit in protective plastic sleeves. Identification of subjects required. Buys one-time rights.
Columns/Departments: "Arts, Profiles, Nature, Sports, Lifestyle, Encounters, Island Hopping featurettes—all island related. Brief Logbook items should be highly focused on some specific aspect of islands." Buys 50 mss/year. Query with published clips. Length: 750-1,500 words. Pays $100-700.
Tips: "A freelancer can best break in to our publication with short (500-1,000 word) departments or Logbooks that are highly focused on some aspect of island life, history, people, etc. Stay away from general, sweeping articles. We are always looking for topics for our Islanders and Logbook pieces. We will be using big name writers for major features; will continue to use newcomers and regulars for columns and departments."

JOURNAL OF CHRISTIAN CAMPING, Christian Camping International, P.O. Box 62189, Colorado Springs CO 80962-2189. (719)260-9400. Fax: (719)260-6398. E-mail: editor@cciusa.org. Website: http://www.cciusa.org. Contact: Dean Ridings, editor. 75% freelance written. Prefers to work with published/established writers. Bimonthly magazine emphasizing the broad scope of organized camping with emphasis on Christian camping. "Leaders of youth camps and adult conferences read our magazine to get practical help in ways to run their operations." Estab. 1963. Circ. 7,000. Pays on publication. Publishes ms an average of 4 months after acceptance. Rights negotiable. Byline given. Reports in 1 month. Sample copy for $2.25 plus 9×12 SASE. Writer's guidelines for #10 SASE.
Nonfiction: General interest (trends in organized camping in general and Christian camping in particular); how-to (anything involved with organized camping from motivating staff, to programming, to record keeping, to camper follow-up); inspirational (limited use, but might be interested in practical applications of Scriptural principles to everyday situations in camping, no preaching); interview (with movers and shakers in camping and Christian camping in particular; submit a list of basic questions first); and opinion (write a letter to the editor). Buys 20-30 mss/year. Query required. Length: 600-1,200 words. Pays 6¢/word.
Reprints: Send photocopy of article and information about when and where the article previously appeared. Pays 50% of amount paid for an original article.
Photos: Send photos with ms. Pays $25-200 for 5×7 b&w contact sheet or print; price negotiable for 35mm color transparencies. Rights negotiable.
Poetry: Considers free verse.
Tips: "The most frequent mistake made by writers is that they send articles unrelated to our readers. Ask for our publication guidelines first. Profiles/interviews are the best bet for freelancers."

LEISURE WORLD, Ontario Motorist Publishing Company, 1253 Ouellette Ave., Box 580, Windsor, Ontario N8X 1J3 Canada. (519)971-3208. Fax: (519)977-1197. E-mail: ompc@mns.net. Contact: Douglas O'Neil, editor. 20% freelance written. Bimonthly magazine distributed to members of the Canadian Automobile Association in southwestern and midwestern Ontario, the Niagara Peninsula and the maritime provinces. Editorial content is focused on travel, entertainment and leisure time pursuits of interest to CAA members." Estab. 1988. Circ. 345,000. Pays on publication. Publishes ms an average of 2 months after acceptance. Buys first rights only. Submit seasonal material 4 months in advance. Reports in 2 months. Sample copy for $2. Free writer's guidelines with SASE.
Nonfiction: Lifestyle, humor, travel. Buys 20 mss/year. Send complete ms. Length: 800-1,200 words. Pays $50-200.
Photos: Reviews slides only. Offers $60/photo. Captions, model releases required. Buys one-time rights.
Tips: "We are most interested in travel destination articles that offer a personal, subjective and positive point of view on international (including U.S.) destinations. Good quality color slides are a must."

‡LEISUREWAYS, Canada Wide Magazines & Communications, Ltd., 2 Carlton St., Suite 801, Toronto, Ontario M5B 1J3 Canada. Fax: (416)924-6308. Editor: Deborah Milton. 80% freelance written. Bimonthly magazine. "*Leisureways* is the publication of two Canadian Automobile Association clubs offering readers superior local and international travel stories and information. *Leisureways* also features automotive columns as well as club information and detailed stories on products and services available to CAA members." Circ. 660,000. **Pays on acceptance**. Publishes ms an average of 2 months after acceptance. Byline given. Offers 50% kill fee. Buys first North American serial rights. Editorial lead time 6 months. Submit seasonal material 1 year in advance. Reports in 2 months on queries; 6 months on mss. Writer's guidelines free.
Nonfiction: Travel. Buys 20 mss/year. Query with published clips or send complete ms. Length: 800-1,500 words. Pays $400-750 (Canadian funds).
Photos: State availability of photos with submission. Reviews transparencies. Offers no additional payment for photos accepted with ms or negotiates payment individually if photos are offered without mss. Buys one-time rights.
Columns/Departments: Travel (Canada and int'l), 1,500 words. Query with published clips. Pays $400-750.
Tips: "All manuscripts and queries receive for consideration. We do not usually buy from U.S. writers since our needs can easily be met in Canada."

THE MATURE TRAVELER, Travel Bonanzas for 49ers-Plus, GEM Publishing Group, Box 50400, Reno NV 89513-0400. (702)786-7419. Editor: Gene E. Malott. 20% freelance written. Monthly newsletter on senior citizen travel. Estab. 1984. Circ. 2,500. **Pays on acceptance.** Publishes ms an average of 3 months after acceptance. Byline given. Offers 25% kill fee. Buys one-time rights. Submit seasonal material 3 months in advance. Accepts simultaneous submissions. Reports in 1 month. Sample copy and guidelines for $1 and #10 SAE with 2 first-class stamps. Writer's guidelines only for #10 SASE.
Nonfiction: Travel for seniors. "General travel and destination pieces should be senior-specific, aimed at 49ers and older." Query. Length: 600-1,200 words. Pays $50-100.
Reprints: Send tearsheet or photocopy of article and information about when and where the article previously appeared. Pays 50% of amount paid for an original article.
Photos: State availability of photos with submission. Reviews contact sheets and b&w (only) prints. Captions required. Buys one-time rights.
Tips: "Read the guidelines and write stories to our readers' needs—not to the general public. Most articles we reject are not senior-specific."

MICHIGAN LIVING, AAA Michigan, 1 Auto Club Dr., Dearborn MI 48126-2963. (313)336-1211. (313)336-1506. Fax: (313)336-1344. E-mail: michliving@aol.com Editor: Ron Garbinski. 50% freelance written. Monthly magazine. "*Michigan Living* is edited for the residents of Michigan and contains information about travel and lifestyle activities in Michigan, the U.S. and around the world. Articles also cover automotive developments, highway safety. Regular features include a car care column, a calendar of coming events, restaurant and overnight accomodations reviews and news of special interest to Auto Club members." Estab. 1922. Circ. 1,000,000. Pays on publication. Publishes ms an average of 6 months after acceptance. Buys first North American serial rights. Offers 20% kill fee. Byline given. Submit seasonal material 3 months in advance. Reports in 6 weeks. Free sample copy and writer's guidelines.
Nonfiction: Travel articles on US and Canadian topics. Buys few unsolicited mss/year. Query. Length: 200-1,000 words. Pays $75-600.
Photos: Photos purchased with accompanying ms. Captions required. Pays $400 for cover photos; $50-400 for color transparencies.
Tips: "In addition to descriptions of things to see and do, articles should contain accurate, current information on costs the traveler would encounter on his trip. Items such as lodging, meal and entertainment expenses should be included, not in the form of a balance sheet but as an integral part of the piece. We want the sounds, sights, tastes, smells of a place or experience so one will feel he has been there and knows if he wants to go back."

THE MIDWEST MOTORIST, AAA Auto Club of Missouri, 12901 N. 40 Dr., St. Louis MO 63141. (314)523-7350. Fax: (314)523-6982. Editor: Michael J. Right. Managing Editor: Deborah M. Klein. 80% freelance written. Bimonthly magazine. "We feature articles on regional and world travel, area history, auto safety, highway and transportation news." Estab. 1971. Circ. 398,173. **Pays on acceptance.** Byline given. Not copyrighted. Buys first North American serial rights, second serial (reprint) rights. Accepts simultaneous submissions. Reports in 1 month with SASE enclosed.

Sample copy for 12½×9½ SAE with 3 first-class stamps. Writer's guidelines for #10 SASE.
Nonfiction: Buys 40 mss/year. Query. Length: 2,000 words maximum. Pays $350 (maximum).
Reprints: Send typed ms with rights for sale noted and information about when and where the article previously appeared. Pays $150-250.
Photos: State availability of photos with submission. Reviews transparencies. Offers no additional payment for photos accepted with ms. Captions required. Buys one-time rights.
Tips: "Editorial schedule set 18 months in advance. Request a copy. Serious writers ask for media kit to help them target their piece. Some stories available throughout the year. Travel destinations and tips are most open to freelancers; auto-related topics handled by staff. Make the story bright and quick to read. We see too many 'Here's a recount of our family vacation' manuscripts. Go easy on first-person accounts."

MOTORHOME, Affinity Group, Inc., 2575 Vista Del Mar Dr., Ventura CA 93001. (805)667-4100. Fax: (805)667-4484. E-mail: http://www.tl.com. Managing Editor: Jim Brightly. Contact: Barbara Leonard, editorial director. 70% freelance written. "*Motorhome* is a monthly magazine edited for owners and prospective buyers of self-propelled vacation vehicles. Editorial material is both technical and non-technical in nature. Regular features include tests and descriptions of various models of motorhomes and mini-motorhomes, travel adventures on such vehicles, and objective analysis of equipment and supplies for such self-propelled recreational vehicles. Guides and directories within the magazine provide listings of manufacturers, rentals and other sources of equipment and accessories of interest to enthusiasts. Articles must have an RV slant and excellent transparencies accompanying text. Write for guidelines." Estab. 1968. Circ. 180,000. **Pays on acceptance.** Publishes ms an average of 6 months after acceptance. Byline given. Buys first North American serial and electronic rights. Editorial lead time 4 months. Submit seasonal material 6 months in advance. Reports in 3 weeks on queries; 2 months on mss. Sample copy free. Writer's guidelines for #10 SASE.
Nonfiction: How-to, humor, new product, personal experience, photo feature, technical, travel, all RV related. Buys 100-120 mss/year. Query with published clips. Length: 100-2,000 words. Pays varies. Sometimes pays expenses of writers on assignment.
Photos: Send photos with submission. Reviews transparencies. Offers no additional payment for photos accepted with ms. Captions, model releases and identification of subjects required. Buys one-time and electronic rights.
Columns/Departments: Jim Brightly, managing editor; Millie Evans, associate editor. Crossroads (people, places); Keepers (tips, recipes); MH News (RV, automotive, public lands). Query or send complete ms. Pays $50-150.
Fillers: Millie Evans, associate editor. Anecdotes, facts, short humor. Buys 100-120/year. Length: 25-150 words. Pay varies.
Tips: "If a freelancer has an idea for a good article it's best to send a query and include possible photo locations to illustrate the article. We prefer to assign articles and work with the author in developing a piece suitable to our audience. We are in a specialized field with very enthusiastic readers who appreciate articles by authors who actually enjoy motorhomes. The following areas are most open: Travel—places to go with a motorhome, where to stay, what to see etc.; we prefer not to use travel articles where the motorhome is secondary; and How-to—personal projects on author's motorhomes to make travel easier, etc., unique projects, accessories. Also articles on unique personalities, motorhomes, humorous experiences."

NATIONAL GEOGRAPHIC TRAVELER, National Geographic Society, 17th & M Sts. NW, Washington DC 20036. (202)775-6700. Fax: (202)828-5658. Vice President/Operations Director: Sarita L. Moffat. Bimonthly magazine. "*National Geographic Traveler* is filled with practical information and detailed maps that are designed to encourage readers to explore and travel the globe. Features on both domestic and foreign destinations, photography, the economics of travel, scenic drives, and weekend getaways help readers plan a variety of excursions. The Travel Wise section that accompanies each feature recommends places to stay and eat as well as things to see and do. Regional highlights list upcoming cultural events." Estab. 1984. Circ. 732,000. This magazine did not respond to our request for information. Query before submitting.

NEW YORK DAILY NEWS, Travel Section, 450 W. 33rd St., New York NY 10001. (212)210-1699. Fax: (212)210-2203. Contact: Linda Perney, travel editor. 30% freelance written. Prefers to work with published/established writers. Circ. 1.8 million. "We are the largest circulating newspaper travel section in the country and take all types of articles ranging from experiences to service oriented pieces that tell readers how to make a certain trip." Pays on publication. Publishes ms an average of 3 months after acceptance. Byline given. Submit seasonal material 4 months in advance. Reports "as soon as possible." Writer's guidelines for #10 SASE.
Nonfiction: General interest, historical/nostalgic, humor, personal experience, travel. "Most of our articles involve practical trips that the average family can afford—even if it's one you can't afford every year. We rarely run stories for the Armchair Traveler, an exotic and usually expensive trip. We are looking for professional quality work from professional writers who know what they are doing. The pieces have to give information and be entertaining at the same time. No 'How I Spent My Summer Vacation' type articles. No PR hype." Buys 60 mss/year. Query with SASE. Length: 1,000 words maximum. Pays $75-200.
Photos: "Good pictures always help sell good stories." State availability of photos with ms. Reviews contact sheets and negatives. Captions and identification of subjects required. Buys all rights.

NEWSDAY, 235 Pinelawn Rd., Melville NY 11747. (516)843-2980. Fax: (516)843-2065. E-mail: travel@newsday.com. Travel Editor: Marjorie Robins. Contact: Francine Brown, editorial assistant. 30% freelance written. General readership of Sunday newspaper travel section. Estab. 1940. Circ. 650,000. Buys all rights for New York area only. Buys 75 mss/year. Pays on publication. Simultaneous submissions considered if outside the New York area.

Nonfiction: No assignments to freelancers. No query letters. Only completed mss accepted on spec. Prefers typewritten mss. All trips must be paid for in full by writer. Proof required. Service stories preferred. Destination pieces must be for the current year. Length: 1,200 words maximum. Pays $75-350, depending on space allotment.

Photos: Color slides and b&w photos accepted: $50-250, depending on size of photo used.

NORTHEAST OUTDOORS, Woodall Publications, 13975 W. Polo Trail Dr., Lake Forest IL 60045. (800)323-9078. Fax: (847)362-6844. E-mail: Speterson@woodallpub.com. Website: http://www.woodalls.com. Contact: Brent Peterson, editor. 50% freelance written. Works with a small number of new/unpublished writers each year. Monthly tabloid covering family camping in the Northeastern US. Estab. 1968. Circ. 10,000. Pays on publication. Publishes ms an average of 4 months after acceptance. Byline given. Offers 50% kill fee. Buys first rights and regional rights. Submit seasonal material 5 months in advance. Reports in 2 weeks. Sample copy for 9 × 12 SAE with 4 first-class stamps. Writer's guidelines for #10 SASE.

• *Northeast Outdoors* has changed owners and location, and circulation has doubled.

Nonfiction: How-to (camping), new product (company and RV releases only), recreation vehicle and camping experiences in the Northeast, features about private (only) campgrounds and places to visit in the Northeast while RVing, personal experience, photo feature, travel. "No diaries of trips, dog or fishing-only stories, or anything not camping and RV related." Query. Length: 300-1,500 words. Pays 10¢/word.

Reprints: Send typed ms with rights for sale noted and information about when and where the article previously appeared.

Photos: Send photos with submission. Reviews contact sheets and 5 × 7 prints or larger. Captions and identification of subjects required. Pays $5/photo. Buys one-time rights.

Columns/Departments: Mealtime (campground cooking), 300-900 words. Buys 12 mss/year. Query or send complete ms. Length: 750-1,000 words. Pays $25-50.

Tips: "We most often need material on private campgrounds and attractions in New England. We are looking for upbeat, first-person stories about where to camp, what to do or see, and how to enjoy camping."

‡PORTHOLE MAGAZINE, A View of the Sea and Beyond, Panoff Publishing, 7100 W. Commercial Blvd., Suite 106, Ft. Lauderdale FL 33319. (954)746-5554. Fax: (954)746-5244. E-mail: cruiseed@aol.com. Contact: Leslie Caney, editor. 90% freelance written. Bimonthly magazine. "*Porthole* is a first-of-its-kind, internationally distributed glossy consumer cruise and travel magazine, distributed by Time Warner." Estab. 1994. Circ. 50,000. **Pays on acceptance.** Publishes ms an average of 6 months after acceptance. Byline given. Offers 35% kill fee. Buys first international serial rights and second serial (reprint) rights and makes work-for-hire assignments. Editorial lead time 3 months. Submit seasonal material 4 months in advance. Accepts simultaneous submissions. Reports in 1 month. Sample copy for 8 × 11 SAE with $3 postage. Writer's guidelines for #10 SASE.

Nonfiction: Essays (your cruise experience), general interest (cruise-related), historical/nostalgic, how-to (i.e., pick a cruise, not get seasick, travel tips), humor, interview/profile (crew on board or industry executives), new product, personal experience, photo features, travel (off-the-beaten path, adventure, ports, destinations, cruises), onboard fashion, spa articles, duty-free shopping, port shopping, ship reviews. No articles on destinations that can't be reached by ship. "Please don't write asking for a cruise so that you can do an article! You must be an experienced cruise writer to do a ship review." Buys 75 mss/year. Query with published clips or send letter with complete ms. Length: 400-2,000 words, average 1,100. Pays 25¢/word average. Sometimes pays expenses of writers on assignment

Reprints: Accepts previously published submissions.

Photos: Linda Douthat, photo editor. State availability of photos with submission. Reviews transparencies. Negotiates payment individually. Captions, model releases, identification of subjects required. Buys one-time rights.

Columns/Departments: Port Postcard (destination port cities), 1,200 words; Spa Spot (spa service on board), 700 words; Two If By Sea (travel tips, short bits), 400 words; Fashion File (onboard fashion), 400 words. Also humor, shopping, photo essays. Buys 50 mss/year. Query with published clips or send letter with complete ms. Pays 25¢/word.

Fillers: Facts, gags to be illustrated by cartoonist, newsbreaks, short humor. Buys 30/year. Length: 25-200 words. Pays 25¢/word.

Tips: "The best way to break in is to send a letter introducing yourself and stating your credits and include a manuscript—under 2,000 words—with a SASE. Solid queries along with clips are good to, but a manuscript is better. I do not take calls from writers who haven't written for me yet."

‡ROADS TO ADVENTURE, The Magazine of Family Camping, Affinity Group, Inc., 2575 Vista Del Mar Dr., Ventura CA 93001. (805)667-4100. Fax: (805)667-4484. E-mail: http://www.tl.com. Senior Editors: Jim Brightly and Sherry McBride. Contact: Barbara Leonard, editorial director. 80% freelance written. Quarterly magazine. "Articles must be slanted toward campers and their families, either with an RV or tents. Adventure is the primary focus of this publication, which is aimed at ages 35-50." Estab. 1996. **Pays on acceptance.** Publishes ms an average of 1 year after acceptance. Byline given. Buys first North American serial and electronic rights. Editorial lead time 6 months. Submit seasonal material 1 year in advance. Reports in 3 weeks on queries; 3 months on mss.

Nonfiction: Essays, humor, inspirational, interview/profile, opinion, personal experience, photo feature, travel, family reunions, health and children on the road. All camping related. Buys 50 mss/year. Query with published clips. Length:

750-2,000 words. Pays $300-500 for assigned articles; $200-400 for unsolicited articles. Sometimes pays the expenses of writers on assignment.
Photos: Send photos with submission. Reviews transparencies. Offers no additional payment for photos accepted with ms. Captions, model releases and identification of subjects required. Buys one-time and electronic rights.
Tips: "Have first-hand outdoor recreational experience. Enjoy adventure on the road."

RV WEST MAGAZINE, Vernon Publications Inc., 3000 Northup Way, Suite 200, Bellevue WA 98004. (800)700-6962. Fax: (206)822-9372. Publisher: Geoffrey P. Vernon. Contact: Michelle Arab, editor. 85% freelance written. Monthly magazine for those who own or are about to purchase an RV. The magazine provides comprehensive information on where to go and what to do in the West. Estab. 1976. Circ. 40,000. Pays 1 month following publication. Byline given. Buys one-time rights and electronic/digital rights. Submit seasonal material at least 3 months in advance of best month for publication. Accepts simultaneous submissions. Submit complete ms. Send SASE for writer's guidelines.
Nonfiction: Travel (Western destinations for RVs), historical/nostalgic (if RV-related), new product, personal experience (if RV-related), events of interest to RVers. No non-RV travel articles. Query with or without published clips. Length: 750-1,750 words. Pays $1.50/inch.
Photos: Send photos with submissions. Color slides and b&w prints preferred. Offers $5 for each published photo. Identification of subjects required.
Tips: "Include all information of value to RVers, and reasons why they would want to visit the location (13 Western states). Short items of interest may also be submitted, including tips, humorous anecdotes and jokes related to RVing. Indicate best time frame for publication."

ST. MAARTEN NIGHTS, Nights Publications, 1831 Rene Levesque Blvd. West, Montreal, Quebec H3H 1R4 Canada. Fax: (514)931-6273. E-mail: nights@odyssee.net. Contact: Stephen Trotter, editor. Managing Editor: Zelly Zuskin. 90% freelance written. Annual magazine covering the St. Maarten/St. Martin vacation experience seeking "upbeat entertaining lifestyle articles. Our audience is the North American vacationer." Estab. 1981. Circ. 225,000. **Pays on acceptance.** Publishes ms an average of 9 months after acceptance. Byline given. Offers 15% kill fee. Buys first North American serial and first Caribbean rights. Editorial lead time 1 month. Reports in 2 weeks on queries; 1 month on mss. *Writer's Market* recommends allowing 2 months for reply. Sample copy for $5. Writer's guidelines free.
Nonfiction: Lifestyle with a lively upscale touch. General interest, colorful profiles of islanders, historical/nostalgia, how-to (gamble), sailing, etc., humor, inspirational, interview/profile, opinion, ecological (eco-tourism), personal experience, photo feature, travel, local culture, art, activities, entertainment, night life, special events, topics relative to vacationers in St. Maarten/St. Martin. "No negative pieces or stale rewrites or cliché copy." Buys 8-10 mss/year. Query with published clips. Length: 250-750 words. Pays $125-300 for assigned articles; $100-250 for unsolicited articles.
Photos: State availability of photos with submission. Reviews transparencies. Offers $50/photo. Captions, model releases, identification of subjects required. Buys one-time rights.

‡SCOTTISH LIFE, 36 Highland Ave., Hull MA 02045. (617)925-2100. Fax: (610)925-1439. Contact: Neill Kennedy Ray, editor. 80% freelance written. Quarterly magazine. "*Scottish Life* covers the whole spectrum of Scottish experiences: Scotland's treasures and traditions, special events and public celebrations, tours of great houses and interesting places, historic sites, lore and legends. Stories should go beyond a step-by-step recounting of "we did this and then did that. They should be evocative, allowing readers to *experience* as they read, to feel like they are there." Estab. 1996. Circ. 10,000. **Pays on acceptance.** Publishes ms an average of 6 months after acceptance. Byline given. Buys first North American serial rights or second serial (reprint) rights. Editorial lead time 6 months. Submit seasonal material 6 months in advance. Accepts simultaneous submissions. Reports in 2 months on queries; 3 months on mss. Sample copy for $6. Writer's guidelines for #10 SASE.
Nonfiction: Historical/nostalgic, interview/profile, personal experience, photo feature, travel. Buys 30-50 mss/year. Query with published clips. Length: 1,200-1,800 words. Pays $350-500 for assigned articles; $250-300 for unsolicited articles.
Reprints: Accepts previously published submissions.
Photos: State availability of photos with submission. Reviews transparencies, prints. Negotiates payment individually. Identification of subjects required. Buys one-time rights.
Fillers: Facts, newsbreaks. Buys 30/year. Length: 50-100 words. Pays $25.

SPA, Travel, Well-Being and Renewal, Waterfront Press Co., 5305 Shilshole Ave. NW, #200, Seattle WA 98107. (206)789-6506. Fax: (206)789-9193. E-mail: editor@spamagazine.com. Website: http://www.spamagazine.com. Contact: Janet Thomas, editor. Quarterly magazine covering spa resorts, lifestyle issues, well-being and travel. "Our readership is sophisticated, well-educated and discerning. We want reporting of real substance and writing that is clear and bright. We also want to encourage a variety of voices." Estab. 1996. Circ. 75,000. **Pays on acceptance**. Publishes ms an average of 3 months after acceptance. Byline sometimes given. Buys first North American serial, one-time, second serial (reprint) rights and makes work-for-hire assignments. Editorial lead time 6 months. Reports in 1 month on queries. Sample copy for $9 × 12 and 8 first-class stamps. Writer's guidelines for #10 SASE.
Nonfiction: Essays, how-to, interview/profile, personal experience, photo feature, travel, health and fitness. Buys 30 mss/year. Query with published clips. Length: 300-3,000 words. Pays $100-2,000.
Reprints: Send tearsheet or photocopy of article or typed ms with rights for sale noted and information about where and when an article previously appeared. Payment negotiable.

Photos: State availability of photos with submission. Reviews transparencies (any format). Negotiates payment individually. Captions, identification of subjects required. Buys one-time rights.

Columns/Departments: Destinations (very short travel pieces involving resort spas and day spas) 300-400 words; pays $100-500. Cuisine (spa food) 600-1,000 words; Personal Space (add a spa touch at home), 800-1,000 words; Wild At Heart (a celebration of the adventurous spirit, portraits of people who take risks), 1,000-2,000 words; pays $600-800. Buys 20 mss/year. Query with published clips.

STAR SERVICE, Reed Travel Group, 500 Plaza Dr., Secaucus NJ 07096-3602. (201)902-2000. Fax: (201)319-1797. E-mail: sgordon@oag.com. Contact: Steven R. Gordon, publisher. "Eager to work with new/unpublished writers as well as those working from a home base abroad, planning trips that would allow time for hotel reporting, or living in major ports for cruise ships." Worldwide guide to accommodations and cruise ships founded in 1960 (as *Sloane Travel Agency Reports*) and sold to travel agencies on subscription basis. Pays 15 days after publication. Buys all rights. Query should include details on writer's experience in travel and writing, clips, specific forthcoming travel plans, and how much time would be available for hotel or ship inspections. Buys 6,000 reports/year. Pays $20/report used. Sponsored trips are acceptable. Reports in 3 months. Writer's guidelines and list of available assignments for #10 SASE.

Nonfiction: Objective, critical evaluations of hotels and cruise ships suitable for international travelers, based on personal inspections. Freelance correspondents ordinarily are assigned to update an entire state or country. "Assignment involves on-site inspections of all hotels and cruise ships we review; revising and updating published reports; and reviewing new properties. Qualities needed are thoroughness, precision, perseverance and keen judgment. Solid research skills and powers of observation are crucial. Travel and travel writing experience are highly desirable. Reviews must be colorful, clear, and documented with hotel's brochure, rate sheet, etc. We accept no advertising or payment for listings, so reviews should dispense praise and criticism where deserved." Now accepting queries for destination assignments with deadlines in March, June and September 1998.

Tips: "We may require sample hotel or cruise reports on facilities near freelancer's hometown before giving the first assignment. No byline because of sensitive nature of reviews."

‡STUDENT TRAVELS MAGAZINE, The Campus Agency, 132 E. 28th St., #400, New York NY 10016-8156. Fax: (212)252-8427. E-mail: stm@interport.net. Publisher: Michael T. Fuller. 40% freelance written. Semiannual magazine covering student travel. "Audience is 18- to 24-year-old college students. Youthful irreverent style is of interest." Circ. 475,000. Pays on publication. Publishes ms an average of 2 years after acceptance. Byline sometimes given. Offers $25 kill fee. Buys all rights. Editorial lead time 6 months. Submit seasonal material 6 months in advance. Accepts simultaneous submissions. Sample copy free. Writer's guidelines for #10 SASE.

Nonfiction: Travel. Buys 4 mss/year. Send complete ms. Length: 400-1,000 words. Pays 10¢/word. Sometimes pays expenses of writers on assignments.

Reprints: Accepts previously published submissions.

Photos: Send photos with submission. Offers $25/photo. Captions required. Buys all rights.

Columns/Departments: Hanging Out, 200 words. Send complete ms. Pays 10¢/word.

‡TIMES OF THE ISLANDS, The International Magazine of the Turks & Caicos Islands, Times Publications Ltd., P.O. Box 234, Caribbean Place, Providenciales Turks & Caicos Islands, British West Indies. (649)946-4788. Fax: (649)946-4703. E-mail: timespub@caribsurf.com. Website: http://www.turkscai.com. Contact: Kathy Borsuk, editor. 80% freelance written. Quarterly magazine covering The Turks & Caicos Islands. "*Times of the Islands* is used by the public and private sector to attract visitors and potential investors/developers to the Islands. It strives to portray the advantages of the Islands and their friendly people. It is also used by tourists, once on-island, to learn about services, activities and accommodations available." Estab. 1988. Circ. 5,500-8,000. Pays on publication. Publishes ms an average of 6 months after acceptance. Byline given. Buys second serial (reprint) rights and publication rights for 6 months with respect to other publications distributed in Caribbean. Editorial lead time 4 months. Submit seasonal material 4 months in advance. Accepts simultaneous submissions. Reports in 6 weeks on queries; 2 months on mss. "Keep in mind, mail to Islands is SLOW. Faxing can speed response time." Sample copy for $4 and postage between Miami and your destination. Writer's guidelines for #10 SASE.

Nonfiction: Book excerpts or reviews, essays, general interest (Caribbean art, culture, cooking, crafts), historical/nostalgic, humor, interview/profile (locals), personal experience (trips to the Islands), photo feature, technical (island businesses), travel, nature, ecology, business (offshore finance), watersports. Buys 30 mss/year. Query. Length: 500-3,000 words. Pays $100-350.

Reprints: Send photocopy of article along with information about when and where it previously appeared. Send information about when and where the article previously appeared. Pay varies.

Photos: Send photos with submission—slides preferred. Reviews 3×5 prints. Offers no additional payment for photos accepted with ms. Pays $15-100/photo. Identification of subjects required.

Columns/Departments: Profiles from Abroad (profiles of T&C Islanders who are doing something outstanding internationally), 500 words. Buys 4 mss/year. Query. Pays $75-150. On Holiday (unique experiences of visitors to Turks & Caicos), 500-1,500 words. Buys 4 mss/year. Query. Pays $100-250.

Fiction: Adventure (sailing, diving), ethnic (Caribbean), historical (Caribbean), humorous (travel-related), mystery, novel excerpts. Buys 1 ms/year. "Would buy 3-4 if available." Query. Length: 1,000-2,000 words. Pays $100-200.

Tips: "Make sure that the query/article specifically relates to the Turks and Caicos Islands. The theme can be general (ecotourism, for instance), but the manuscript should contain specific and current references to the Islands. We're a high-quality magazine, with a small budget and staff and are very open-minded to ideas (and manuscripts). Writers who have visited the Islands at least once would probably have a better perspective from which to write."

TRAILER LIFE, RVing At Its Best, Affinity Group, Inc., 2575 Vista Del Mar Dr., Ventura CA 93001. (805)667-4100. Fax: (805)667-4100. Website: http://www.tl.com. Contact: Barbara Leonard, editorial director. Managing Editor: Sherry McBride. 60% freelance written. Monthly magazine. "*Trailer Life* magazine is written specifically for active people whose overall lifestyle is based on travel and recreation in their RV. Every issue includes product tests, travel articles, and other features—ranging from cooking tips to vehicle maintenance." Estab. 1941. Circ. 290,000. **Pays on acceptance**. Publishes ms an average of 6 months after acceptance. Byline given. Offers 33% kill fee. Buys first North American rights and non-exclusive rights for other media. Editorial lead time 4 months. Submit seasonal material 6 months in advance. Reports in 2 months. Sample copy free. Writer's guidelines for #10 SASE.

• Ranked as one of the best markets for freelance writers in *Writer's Yearbook* magazine's annual "Top 100 Markets," January 1997.

Nonfiction: Historical/nostalgic, how-to (technical), new product, opinion, humor, personal experience, travel. No vehicle tests, product evaluations or road tests; tech material is strictly assigned. No diaries or trip logs, no non-RV trips; nothing without an RV-hook. Buys 75 mss/year. Query with or without published clips. Length: 250-2,500 words. Pays $150-600. Sometimes pays expenses of writers on assignment.

Photos: Send photos with submission. Reviews b&w contact sheets, transparencies. Offers no additional payment for photos accepted with ms. Model releases, identification of subjects required. Buys one-time and electronic rights.

Columns/Departments: Campground Spotlight (report with 1 photo of campground recommended for RVers) 250 words; Bulletin Board (news, trends of interest to RVers) 100 words; Etcetera (useful tips and information affecting RVers), 240 words. Buys 70 mss/year. Query or send complete ms. Pays $75-250.

Tips: "Prerequisite: must have RV focus. Photos must be magazine quality. These are the two biggest reasons why manuscripts are rejected. Our readers are travel enthusiasts who own all types of RVs (travel trailers, truck campers, van conversions, motorhomes, tent trailers, fifth-wheels) in which they explore North and South America, embrace the great outdoors in national, state and private parks as well as scenic roads, city sights, etc. They're very active although mature."

TRANSITIONS ABROAD, P.O. Box 1300, Amherst MA 01004-1300. E-mail: http://www.trabroad@aol.com. Website: transabroad.com. Editor/Publisher: Clay Hubbs. Contact: Jason Whitmarsh, managing editor. 80-90% freelance written. Eager to work with new/unpublished writers. Magazine resource for low-budget international travel, often with an educational or work component. Focus is on the alternatives to mass tourism. Estab. 1977. Circ. 29,000. Pays on publication. Buys first rights and second (reprint) rights. Byline given. Written or e-mail queries only. Reports in 1 month. Sample copy for $6.25. Writer's guidelines and topics schedule for #10 SASE.

Nonfiction: Lead articles (up to 1,500 words) provide first-hand practical information on independent travel to featured country or region (see topics schedule). Pays $75-150. Also, how-to find educational and specialty travel opportunities, practical information (evaluation of courses, special interest and study tours, economy travel), travel (new learning and cultural travel ideas). Foreign travel only. Few destination ("tourist") pieces. *Transitions Abroad* is a resource magazine for independent, educated, and adventurous travelers, not for armchair travelers or those addicted to packaged tours or cruises. Emphasis on information—which must be usable by readers—and on interaction with people in host country. Buys 20 unsolicited mss/issue. Query with credentials and SASE. Length: 500-1,500 words. Pays $25-150. Include author's bio with submissions.

Photos: Send photos with ms. Pays $10-45 for prints (color acceptable, b&w preferred), $125 for covers (b&w only). Photos increase likelihood of acceptance. Buys one-time rights. Captions and ID on photos required.

Columns/Departments: Worldwide Travel Bargains (destinations, activities and accomodations for budget travelers—featured in every issue); Tour and Program Notes (new courses or travel programs); Travel Resources (new information and ideas for independent travel); Working Traveler (how to find jobs and what to expect); Activity Vacations (travel opportunities that involve action and learning, usually by direct involvement in host culture); Responsible Travel (information on community-organized tours). Buys 10/issue. Send complete ms. Length: 1,000 words maximum. Pays $20-50.

Fillers: Info Exchange (information, preferably first-hand—having to do with travel, particularly offbeat educational travel and work or study abroad). Buys 10/issue. Length: 750 words maximum. Pays $20.

Tips: "We like nuts and bolts stuff, practical information, especially on how to work, live and cut costs abroad. Our readers want usable information on planning a travel itinerary. Be specific: names, addresses, current costs. We are very interested in educational and long-stay travel and study abroad for adults and senior citizens. *Overseas Travel Planner* published each year in July provides best information sources on work, study, and independent travel abroad. Each bimonthly issue contains a worldwide directory of educational and specialty travel programs. (Topics schedule included with writers' guidelines.)"

‡TRAVEL AMERICA, The U.S. Vacation Magazine, World Publishing Co., 990 Grove St., Evanston IL 60201-4370. (847)491-6440. Editor-in-Chief/Associate Publisher: Bob Meyers. Contact: Randy Mink, managing editor. 80% freelance written. Estab. 1985. Bimonthly magazine covering US vacation travel. Circ. 350,000. Byline given. Buys first North American serial rights. Submit seasonal material 6 months in advance. Reports in 1 month on queries; 6 weeks on ms. Sample copy for $5 and 9×12 SASE with 6 first-class stamps.

Nonfiction: Primarily destination-oriented travel articles and resort/hotel profiles and roundups, but will consider essays, how-to, humor, nostalgia, Americana. "It is best to study current contents and query first." Buys 60 mss/year. Average length: 1,000 words. Pays $125-300.

● Could use more stories on Americana and nostalgia—collectibles, old movie palaces, diners, etc.

Reprints: Send typed ms with rights for sale noted. Pay varies.

Photos: Top-quality original color slides preferred. Captions required. Buys one-time rights. Prefers photo feature package (ms plus slides), but will purchase slides only to support a work in progress.

Tips: "Because we are heavily photo-oriented, superb slides are our foremost concern. The most successful approach is to send 2-3 sheets of slides with the query or complete ms. Include a list of other subjects you can provide as a photo feature package."

TRAVEL & LEISURE, American Express Publishing Corp., 1120 Avenue of the Americas, New York NY 10036. (212)382-5600. E-mail: tlquery@amexpub.com. Website: http://www.amexpub.com. Editor-in-Chief: Nancy Novogrod. Executive Editor: Barbara Peck. Managing Editor: Mark Orwoll. 80% freelance written. *"Travel & Leisure* is a monthly magazine edited for affluent travelers. It explores the latest resorts, hotels, fashions, foods and drinks." Circ. 960,000. **Pays on acceptance.** Byline given. Offers 25% kill fee. Buys first world rights. Reports in 6 weeks. Sample copy for $5 from (800)888-8728 or P.O. Box 2094, Harlan IA 51537-4094. Writer's guidelines for #10 SASE.

● There is no single editorial contact for *Travel & Leisure.* It is best to find the name of the editor of each section, as appropriate for your submission.

Nonfiction: Travel. Buys 40-50 features (3,000-5,000 words) and 200 short pieces (125-500 words). Query by e-mail preferred. Pays $4,000-6,000/feature; $100-500/short piece. Pays the expenses of writers on assignment.

● Ranked as one of the best markets for freelance writers in *Writer's Yearbook* magazine's annual "Top 100 Markets," January 1997.

Columns/Departments: Buys 125-150 mss. Length: 1,200-2,500 words. Pays $1,000-2,500.

Photos: Discourages submission of unsolicited transparencies. Payment varies. Captions required. Buys one-time rights.

Tips: "Read the magazine. There are 2 regional editions: East and West. Regional sections are best places to start."

TRAVEL HOLIDAY, A Hachette Filipacchi Magazines, Inc. Publication, 1633 Broadway, 43rd Floor, New York NY 10019. (212)767-5100. Fax: (212)767-5111. Editor: John Owens. Published 10 times a year. *"Travel Holiday* is edited for sophisticated experienced travelers and contains relevant and accessible information about destinations around the globe. Each issue's features include: Arthur Frommer's Hot Sheet, an insider's guide to the world's best travel deals; Born to Shop, which highlights unique shopping destinations and shopping finds; and Globetrotter's Index, which offers a chart full of quirky information about nine destinations each month." Estab. 1901. Circ. 35,463.

● *Travel Holiday* informs us it no longer accepts freelance submissions.

‡TRAVEL IMPULSE, (formerly *Travel & Courier News*), Sun Tracker Enterprises Ltd., Suite 319, 7231 120th St., Delta, British Columbia V4C 6P5 Canada. (604)951-3238. Fax: (604)951-8732. Contact: Susan M. Boyce, editor/publisher. 95% freelance written. *"Travel Impulse* is a quarterly magazine for people who love to travel—in fact, they find travel irresistible. Appeal to their sense of adventure and the playfulness of travel. Many of our readers like to 'pick up and go' at short notice and are looking for inexpensive, unique ways to accomplish that." Estab. 1984. Circ. 1,000. Pays on publication. Publishes ms an average of 6-8 months after acceptance. Byline given. Buys first North American serial rights and second serial (reprint) rights. Editorial lead time 6-8 months. Submit seasonal material 8 months in advance. Reports in 2 months on queries; 4 months on mss. Sample copy for $5. Writer's guidelines for #10 SASE.

Nonfiction: Humor, interview/profile, new product (travel gadgets and gear), personal experience, photo feature. No political commentary. Buys 20-25 mss/year. Query or send complete ms. Length: 500-1,500 words. Pays $10-75 for assigned articles; $10-50 for unsolicited articles.

Reprints: Accepts previously published submissions.

Photos: State availability of photos with submission or send photocopies. Do not send originals until requested. Reviews 4×6 prints (preferred size). Offers no additional payment for photos accepted with ms. (However, photos greatly enhance your chances of acceptance). Captions, model releases, identification of subjects required. Buys rights with ms.

Columns/Departments: "Travel Tips" (unusual destination tips to travel inexpensively), 50-200 words; "Readers Rate" (the best & worst in travel & travel related items, i.e., airports, eateries, clothing); Medical. Send complete ms. Columns receive either a premium or an entry in a quarterly draw for travel-related accessories.

Fillers: Anecdotes, facts, newsbreaks. Use 100-150/year. Length: 50-200 words. ("Currently we do not pay for fillers. All names are entered in a draw for a travel related prize.")

Tips: "Our readers find travel irresistible. Entice them with unusual destinations and unique ways to travel inexpensively. Show us the playful side of travel."

TRAVEL NEWS, Travel Agents International, Inc., P.O. Box 42008, St. Petersburg FL 33742-4008. Fax: (813)579-0529. Editor: Matthew Wiseman. 40% freelance written. Monthly travel tabloid. "Travel stories written to praise a particular trip. We want readers to consider taking a trip themselves." Estab. 1982. Circ. 200,000. Pays on publication. Publishes ms an average of 2 months after acceptance. Byline given. Not copyrighted. Buys simultaneous rights. Submit seasonal material 6 months in advance. Accepts simultaneous submissions. Reports in 2 months. Sample copy and writer's guidelines for 9×12 SAE with 4 first-class stamps. No phone calls, please.

Nonfiction: General interest, new product, photo feature, travel. "Each issue focuses on one travel category. We will accept submissions anytime but prefer SASE for publication calendar. No negative articles that would discourage travel. Make sure stories you submit are geared toward the traveler using a travel agent." Buys 75 mss/year. Query with or without published clips or send complete ms. Length: 1,000-1,500 words. Pays $20-200 for assigned articles; $10-125 for unsolicited articles.

Reprints: Send photocopy of article or typed ms with rights for sale noted. Pays 100% of the amount paid for an original article.

Photos: State availability of photos with submission. Buys one-time rights.

Tips: "Send SASE for publication calendar, sample copy and submission requirements. Query well in advance of a trip to see what angle we would like the story to take. We will also review outlines."

TRAVEL SMART, Communications House, Inc., Dobbs Ferry NY 10522. (914)693-4208. Contact: H.J. Teison, editor. Managing Editor: Nancy Dunnan. Covers information on "good-value travel." Monthly newsletter. Estab. 1976. Pays on publication. Buys all rights. Reports in 6 weeks. Sample copy and writer's guidelines for 9×12 SAE with 3 first-class stamps.

Nonfiction: "Interested primarily in bargains or little-known deals on transportation, lodging, food, unusual destinations that are really good values. No destination stories on major Caribbean islands, London, New York, no travelogs, 'my vacation,' poetry, fillers. No photos or illustrations other than maps. Just hard facts. We are not part of 'Rosy fingers of dawn . . .' school." Write for guidelines, then query. Length: 100-1,500 words. Pays $150 maximum."

Tips: "When you travel, check out small hotels offering good prices, good restaurants, and send us brief rundown (with prices, phone numbers, addresses). Information must be current. Include your phone number with submission, because we sometimes make immediate assignments."

TRAVELER PUBLICATIONS, Publishers of *Sea Mass Traveler, Mystic Traveler* and *Newport Traveler*, 174 Bellevue Ave., Suite 207, Newport RI 02840. (401)847-0226. Fax: (401)847-5267. Editor: Joe Albano. Contact: Kara Laughlin, editor. 40% freelance written. Monthly regional tabloid covering places of interest in southern Massachusetts, southern Connecticut and all of Rhode Island. "Stories that get the reader to do, see, or act upon." Estab. 1992. Circ. 120,000 winter 240,000 summer. Pays on publication. Byline given. Buys all rights. Editorial lead time 2 months. Submit seasonal material 2 months in advance. Accepts simultaneous submissions. Reports in 2 months on mss. Sample copy and writer's guidelines free with 9×12 SASE and 5 first-class stamps.

> • Three magazines (above) are published by one editorial office. Send only one manuscript and it will be circulated among magazines.

Nonfiction: Essays, general interest, historical/nostalgic, photo feature (travel). All must be related to southern New England. Buys 40 mss/year. Send complete ms or query. Length: 500-800 words. Pays 5¢/word. Sometimes pays expenses of writers on assignment.

Reprints: Send photocopy of article or typed ms with rights for sale noted and information about when and where the article previously appeared. Pays 100% of amount paid for an original article.

Photos: Send photos with submission. Reviews prints. Negotiates payment individually. Buys one-time rights.

Columns/Departments: Dining reviews, Kids' Page, Galleries, Outdoors, From a New England Kitchen, Club Review, Vineyards, Antiques.

Fillers: Facts. Buys 30/year. Length: 50-200 words. Pays 5¢/word.

Tips: "We are very interested in tours that cover an entire area. It could be a tour of wineries, a certain kind of shop, golf courses, etc. Always include address, phone, hours, admissions prices."

TREKS & JOURNEYS, The Student International Travel Journal, Treks & Journeys Press, 715 Canyon Rd., Tuscaloosa AL 35406. (205)348-8247. Fax: (205)366-9866. E-mail: GFrangou@sa.ua.edu. Editor: George Frangoulis. 85% freelance written. Quarterly magazine. "*Treks & Journeys* is for a different kind of traveller. Directed towards students and young adults ages 20-35, it is for a person who is independent, adventurous, interested in spreading their wings and discovering new places of cultural interest and enrichment. It encompasses all aspects of travel, as well as study and working abroad." Estab. 1995. Circ. 127,000. **Pays on acceptance.** Byline given. Offers 50% kill fee. Editorial lead time 6 months. Submit seasonal material 6 months in advance. Reports in 2 weeks on queries; 3 months on mss. Sample copy and writer's guidelines free.

Nonfiction Book excerpts, essays, general interest, historical/nostalgic, how-to, humor, inspirational, interview/profile, new product, opinion, personal experience, photo feature, travel. Buys 15-20 mss/year. Query. Length: 500-3,500 words. Pays $50-350 for assigned articles; $25-250 for unsolicited articles.

Reprints: Send tearsheet or photocopy of article or typed ms with rights for sale noted and information about when and where the article previously appeared. Pays 100% of amount paid for an original article.

Photos: State availability of photos with submission. Reviews contact sheets, transparencies, 5×7 prints. Offers $5-25/photo. Captions, model releases, identification of subjects required.

Tips: *"Treks & Journeys* is particularly interested in articles on new destinations that are 'off the beaten path,' recreational opportunities, budget travel for both short-term and long-term stays, and environmentally responsible tourism experiences."

VACATIONS, Vacation Publications, Inc., 1502 Augusta, Houston TX 77057. (713)974-6903. Fax:(713)974-0445. Publisher: Alan Fox. Quarterly magazine. *"Vacations* provides a practical, money oriented guide to vacations for real travelers. Focus is on domestic destinatons." Estab. 1987. Circ. 46,738. This magazine did not respond to our request for information. Query before submitting.

VIA, (formerly *Motorland*), California State Automobile Assn., 150 Van Ness Ave., San Francisco CA 94102. (415)565-2451. Contact: Lynn Ferrin, editor. 20% freelance written. Bimonthly magazine specializing in northern California and the West, with occasional stories on world-wide travel, especially in the September "cruise" section. Also, traffic safety and motorists' consumer issues. "Our magazine goes to members of the AAA in northern California, Nevada and Utah. Our surveys show they are an upscale audience, well-educated and widely traveled. We like our travel stories to be finely crafted, evocative and personal, but we also include nitty gritty details to help readers arrange their own travel to the destinations covered." Estab. 1917. Circ. 2,400,000. **Pays on acceptance.** Byline usually given. Offers 25% kill fee. Buys first rights; occasional work-for-hire assignments. Editorial lead time 2 months. Submit seasonal material 6 months in advance. Usually reports in 1 month on queries. Writer's guidelines for #10 SASE.

Nonfiction: Travel. Special issue: Cruise issue (September/October). Buys 15-20 mss/year. Prefers to see finished mss with SASE from writers new to them. Length: 500-2,000 words. Pays $150-700. Sometimes pays expenses of writers on assignment.

Photos: State availability of photos with submission. Reviews 35mm and 4×5 transparencies. Offers $50-400/photo. Model releases, identification of subjects required. Buys first-time rights.

Tips: "We do not like to receive queries via fax or e-mail unless the writer does not expect a reply. We are looking for beautifully written pieces that evoke a destination. We purchase less than 1% of the material submitted. Send SASE with all queries and mss."

VOYAGEUR, The Magazine of Carlson Hospitality Worldwide, Pace Communications, 1301 Carolina St., Greensboro NC 27401. Editor: Jaci H. Ponzoni. 90% freelance written. In room magazine for Radisson hotels and affiliates. *"Voyageur* is an international magazine published quarterly for Carlson Hospitality Worldwide and distributed in the rooms of Radisson Hotels, Radisson SAS Hotels, Radisson Edwardian Hotels, Radisson Seven Seas Cruises, and Country Inns & Suites by Carlson throughout North and South America, Europe, Australia, Asia and the Middle East. All travel related stories must be in destinations where Radisson or Country Inns & Suites have hotels." Estab. 1992. Circ. 160,500. **Pays on acceptance.** Publishes ms an average of 2 months after acceptance. Offers 25% kill fee. Buys first North American serial rights. Editorial lead time 4 months. Submit seasonal material 6 months in advance. Reports in 1 month. Sample for $5. Writer's guidelines for #10 SASE.

• *Voyageur* was recently redesigned. Obtaining a current sample copy is strongly recommended.

Nonfiction: Travel. The *Cover Story* is an authoritative yet personal profile of a destination where Radisson has a major presence, featuring a mix of standard and off-the-beaten path activities and sites including sightseeing, recreation, restaurants, shopping and cultural attractions. Length: 1,100-1,500 words plus two mini-sidebars. *Our World* brings to life the spectrum of a country's or region's; arts and culture, including performing, culinary, visual and folk arts. The successful article combines a timely sample of cultural activities for travelers with a sense of the destination's unique spirit or personality as reflected in the arts. Must be a region where Radisson has a major presence. Length: 1,200 words plus two 75-word mini-sidebars. Query with published clips. Length: 1,500 words maximum. Pays $800-1,000. Sometimes pays expenses of writers on assignment.

Photos: State availability of photos with submission. Reviews contact sheets, transparencies, prints. Negotiates payment individually. Model releases and identification of subjects required. Buys one-time rights.

Columns/Departments: In The Bag (place-specific shopping story with cultural context and upscale attitude), 600-800 words and 50-word mini-sidebar; Good Sport (action-oriented, first person focusing on travel involving sports such as biking, kayaking, scuba diving, hiking or sailing), 600-800 words plus 50-word mini-sidebar; Travel Talk (expert view of trials, tribulations and joys of travel with practical, problem-solving advice), 350-400 words; Business Wise (insights into conducting business internationally) 350-400 words with 50-word mini-sidebar. Buys 24 mss/year. Query with published clips. Pays $300-500.

• The editor notes that she is particularly interested in seeing queries for the regular departments.

Tips: "We look for authoritative, energetic and vivid writing to inform and entertain business and leisure travelers, and we are actively seeking writers with an authentic European, Asian, South American or Australian perspective. Travel stories should be authoritative yet personal."

WESTERN RV NEWS, 42070 SE Locksmith Lane, Sandy OR 97055. (503)668-5660. Fax: (503)668-6387. Editor: Elsie Hathaway. 75% freelance written. Monthly magazine for owners of recreational vehicles. Estab. 1966. Pays on publication. Publishes ms an average of 6 months after acceptance. Byline given. Buys first rights and second serial (reprint) rights. Accepts simultaneous submissions. Reports in 1 month. Sample copy and writer's guidelines for 9×12 SAE with 5 first-class stamps. Guidelines for #10 SASE. Request to be put on free temporary mailing list for publication.

Nonfiction: How-to (RV oriented, purchasing considerations, maintenance), humor (RV experiences), new product (with ancillary interest to RV lifestyle), personal experiences (varying or unique RV lifestyles) technical (RV systems or hardware), travel. "No articles without an RV slant." Buys 100 mss/year. Submit complete ms. Length: 250-1,200 words. Pays $15-100.

Reprints: Send photocopy of article or typed ms with rights for sale noted and information about when and where the article previously appeared. Pays 60% of amount paid for an original article.

Photos: Send photos with submission. Prefer b&w. Offers $5-10/photo. Captions, model releases, identification of subjects required. Buys one-time rights.

Fillers: Encourage anecdotes, RV related tips and short humor. Length: 50-250 words. Pays $5-25.

Tips: "Highlight the RV lifestyle! Western travel (primarily NW destinations) articles should include information about the availability of RV sites, dump stations, RV parking and accessibility. Thorough research and a pleasant, informative writing style are paramount. Technical, how-to, and new product writing is also of great interest to us. Photos definitely enhance the possibility of article acceptance."

‡**WESTWAYS, The Magazine for Southern California**, Auto Club of Southern California, 2601 S. Figueroa, Los Angeles CA 90007. Fax: (213)741-3033. Editor: Susan LaTempa. Contact: Richard Stayton. 95% freelance written. "*Westways* is a monthly travel magazine for Southern Californians. It publishes travel features by writers from a variety of disciplines and covers destinations in the U.S. and internationally." Estab. 1909. Circ. 350,000. **Pays on acceptance.** Byline given. Offers 25-50% kill fee. Editorial lead time 18 months. Submit seasonal material 18 months in advance. Reports in 6 months on queries; 2 weeks on assigned mss. Does not review unsolicited manuscripts.

Nonfiction: Annual great drives, travel and art, and family travel themes issues. No destination stories based on a writer's single trip to the place described. Buys 50 mss/year. Query with published clips. Length: 600-2,500 words. Pays 50¢-$1/word. Pays the expenses of writers on assignment.

Photos: "Freelancers should not concern themselves with photography. We assign professional photographers."

Columns/Departments: Weekender (weekend travel in Southern California), 1,500 words; Good Sports (outdoor recreation), 1,700 words; Food Souvenirs (memoir and recipe from Western travel), 400 words plus recipe. Arts (September); Religion (December); Great Drives (February); Family (May). Buys 30 mss/year. Query with published clips. Pays 50¢/word.

Tips: "We are most interested in writers with a special expertise to bring to the travel experience, i.e., architecture, theater, snow boarding, etc."

WOMEN'S

Women have an incredible variety of publications available to them. A number of titles in this area have been redesigned to compete in the crowded marketplace. Many have stopped publishing fiction and are focusing more on short, human interest nonfiction articles. Magazines that also use material slanted to women's interests can be found in the following categories: Business and Finance; Child Care and Parental Guidance; Contemporary Culture; Food and Drink; Gay and Lesbian Interest; Health and Fitness; Hobby and Craft; Home and Garden; Relationships; Religious; Romance and Confession; and Sports.

ALLURE, Condé Nast, 360 Madison Ave., New York NY 10017. (212)880-2341. Fax: (212)370-1949. E-mail: allure@a ol.com. Articles Editor: Tom Prince. Monthly magazine. "*Allure* looks at the complex role beauty plays in the culture and analyzes the trends in cosmetics, skincare, fashion, haircare, fitness, health and more." Estab. 1991. Circ. 731,500. Call or write for guidelines, include SASE.

Nonfiction: Most beauty articles are written inhouse. Reflections section most open to freelancers. "Read and become *very* familiar with the magazine." Query before submitting.

‡**AMERICAN WOMAN**, GCR Publishing, 1700 Broadway, 34th Floor, New York NY 10019-5905. (212)541-7100. Fax: (212)245-1241. Editor-in-Chief: Lynn Varacalli. Managing Editor: Sandy Kosherick. 50% freelance written. Magazine published 7 times/year for "women in their 20s, 30s, 40s, single and married, dealing with relationships and self-help." Estab. 1990. Circ. 138,000. Pays on publication. Publishes ms an average of 2 months after acceptance. Byline given. Offers 25% kill fee. Buys one-time and second serial (reprint) rights. Submit seasonal material 5 months in advance. Accepts simultaneous submissions. Reports in 1 month. Sample copy for $2.99. Writer's guidelines for #10 SASE.

Nonfiction: Book excerpts, self-help, inspirational, interview/profile, personal experience, true life drama. "No poetry, recipes or fiction." Buys 40 mss/year. Query with published clips. Length: 750-1,900 words. Pays $300-900 for assigned articles; $200-500 for unsolicited articles. Pays for phone, mailings, faxes, transportation costs of writers on assignment.

Reprints: Send photocopy and information about when and where the article previously appeared. Pays $200-400.

Photos: State availability of photos with submission. Reviews contact sheets, transparencies, prints. Offers $100-175/photo. Captions, model releases, identification of subjects required. Buys one-time rights.

Tips: "We are always interested in true-life stories and stories of inspiration—women who have overcome obstacles in their lives, trends (new ideas in dating, relationships, places to go, new ways to meet men), articles about health, beauty, diet, self-esteem, fun careers, and money-saving articles (on clothes, beauty, vacations, mail order, entertainment)."

BLACK ELEGANCE, Lifestyles of Today's Black Women, 475 Park Ave., South, New York NY 10016. (212)689-2830. Fax:(212)889-7933. Editor-in-Chief: Sonia Alleyne. Published 9 times a year. "*Black Elleyance* is edited for the contemporary American Black Woman consumer. The editorial content focuses on aspects of elegant living; hair, beauty, fashion and fashion accessories, personal fitness, cooking and entertaining, careers, leisure, amusements, cultural pursuits, books, investments and financial management, travel/lodging, transportation, parenting, and homes, gardens and furnishings, and profiles of interesting personalities." Estab. 1986. Circ. 369,640. This magazine did not respond to our request for information. Query before submitting.

BRIDAL GUIDE, Globe Communications Corp., 3 E. 54th St., 15th Floor, New York NY 10022. (212)838-7733. Fax: (212)308-7165. Editor-in-Chief: Diane Forden. Travel Editor: Laurie Bain Wilson. Contact: Denise Schipani, senior editor. 50% freelance written. Prefers to work with experienced/published writers. A bimonthly magazine covering relationships, sexuality, fitness, wedding planning, psychology, finance, travel. "Please do not send queries concerning beauty and fashion, since we produce them in-house. We do not accept personal wedding essays, fiction, or poetry." Reports in 3 months. Sample copy for $4.95 and SASE with 4 first-class stamps. Writer's guidelines available.
Nonfiction: Queries only, accompanied by published clips. All correspondence accompanied by an SASE will be answered (response time is within 8 weeks). Length: 1,500-3,000 words. Pays 30¢ and up/word. **Pays on acceptance.** Buys 100 mss/year.
Photos: Lisa del Altomare, art director; Andrea Amadio, associate art director. Stephen Wilder, associate art director. Photography and illustration submissions should be sent to the art department.
Columns/Departments: Regular columns include finance, sex and health, new products, etiquette, relationships, travel, entertaining, food. Welcome queries from men who are engaged or married for Groom with a View essay end page.

‡BRIDE AGAIN, The Only Magazine Designed for Second Time Brides, 1240 N. Jefferson Ave., Suite G, Anaheim CA 92807. (714)632-7000. Fax: (714)632-5405. Contact: Beth Reed Ramirez, editor. Quarterly magazine for the second time bride. "*Bride Again* is targeted primarily to women ages 35-45 and secondarily to those 45 and over. They have been married at least once before, and most likely have children from a previous marriage or will be marrying someone with children. They have a career and income of over $45,000 per year, and are more mature and sophisticated than the 26-year-old first-time bride." Estab. 1997. Circ. 200,000. **Pays on acceptance.** Byline given. Buys all rights. Writer's guidelines for #10 SASE.
Nonfiction: Essays, how-to, humor, inspirational, interview/profile, personal experience. "Topics can be on, but not limited to: remarriage, blending families, becoming a stepmother, combining households, dealing with children in the wedding party, children—his, mine and ours; joint custody, dealing with difficult ex-spouses, real dresses for real women, legal aspects of remarriage, pre- and post-nuptual agreements, alternatives to the wedding veil, unusual wedding and/or honeymoon locations." Send complete ms. *No queries, please.* Length: 1,500-2,000 words. Pays 35¢/word.
Photos: Send photos with submission. Reviews transparencies. Negotiates payment individually. Buys all rights.
Columns/Departments: Finances, Blending Families, Wedding Plans: Problems & Solutions, Unusual Honeymoon Locations, Beauty for Ages 30+/40+/50+, Remarriage, Fashion; all 800-1,000 words. Book reviews (on the feature topics listed above), 250 words. Send complete ms. Pays 35¢/word.
Fiction: Publishes novel excerpts.

‡CHATELAINE, 777 Bay St., #800, Toronto, Ontario M5W 1A7 Canada. E-mail: editors@chatelaine.com. Contact: Senior Editor, Articles. Monthly magazine. "*Chatelaine* is edited to Canadian women ages 25-55, their changing attitudes and lifestyles. Emphasis is on food, fashion, beauty and home decoration. Other key editorial ingredients include parenting, health, finance, crafts, social issues and trends, high profile personalities, politics and original fiction. Regular departments include Health Centre, Parents & Kids, GreenScene, Gardening and Free For The Asking, advice columns covering medicine, law, finance and careers." **Pays on acceptance.** Byline given. Offers 25-100% kill fee. Buys first and electronic rights. Reports in 2 months on queries. Guidelines for #10 SASE with IRCs.
Nonfiction: Seeks "agenda-setting reports on national issues and trends as well as pieces on health, careers, personal finance and other facts of Canadian life." Buys 50 mss/year. Query or query with published clips. Length: 1,000-2,500 words. Pays $1,000-2,500. Pays expenses of writers on assignment.
Columns/Departments: Length: 500-1,000 words. Query or query with published clips. Pays $500-750.
Fiction: Caroline Connell. Query.
Fillers: Buys 30/year. Length: 200-500 words. Pays $250-350.

COMPLETE WOMAN, For All The Women You Are, Associated Publications, Inc., 875 N. Michigan Ave., Chicago IL 60611-1901. (312)266-8680. Editor: Bonnie L. Krueger. Contact: Martha Carlson, associate editor. 90% freelance written. Bimonthly magazine of general interest for women. Areas of concern are love life, health, fitness, emotions, etc. Estab. 1980. Circ. 350,000. Pays on publication. Publishes ms an average of 5 months after acceptance. Byline given. Buys first North American serial, second serial (reprint) and simultaneous rights. Submit seasonal material 5 months in advance. Accepts simultaneous submissions. Reports in 2 months. Guidelines for #10 SASE.
  • The editor reports a need for more relationship stories.

Nonfiction: Book excerpts, general interest, how-to, humor, inspirational, interview/profile, new product, personal experience, photo feature. "We want self-help articles written for today's woman. Articles that address dating, romance, sexuality and relationships are an integral part of our editorial mix, as well as inspirational and motivational pieces." Buys 60-100 mss/year. Query with published clips, or send complete ms. Length: 800-2,000 words. Pays $80-400. Sometimes pays expenses of writers on assignment.
Reprints: Send tearsheet or photocopy of article or short story or send typed ms with rights for sale noted and information about when and where the article previously appeared.
Photos: Send photos with submission. Reviews 2¼ or 35mm transparencies and 5×7 prints. Offers $35-75/photo. Captions, model releases, identification of subjects required. Buys one-time rights.
Poetry: Avant-garde, free verse, light verse, traditional. Nothing over 30 lines. Buys 50 poems/year. Submit maximum 5 poems. Pays $10.

‡CONDÉ NAST BRIDE'S, Condé Nast, 140 E. 45th St., 39th Floor, New York NY 10017. (212)880-2518. Managing Editor: Sally Kiobridge. Editor-in-Chief: Millie Martini-Bratten. Contact: Features or travel editors. Bimonthly magazine for the first- or second-time bride, her family and friends, the groom and his family and friends. Circ. 400,000. **Pays on acceptance.** Byline given. Offers 25% kill fee. Buys all rights. Editorial lead time 8 months. Accepts simultaneous submissions. Reports in 2 months on queries. Writer's guidelines for #10 SASE.
Nonfiction: Buys 6-7 mss/year. Query with published clips. Length: 2,000 words. Pays 50¢-$1/word. Pays expenses of writers on assignment.
Columns/Departments: Length: 750 words. Buys 20 mss/year. Query with published clips. Pays 50¢-$1.
Tips: "We look for good, helpful relationship pieces that will help a newlywed couple adjust to marriage. Wedding planning articles are usually written by experts or depend on a lot of interviews with experts. Writers must have a good idea of what we would and would not do: Read the 3 or 4 most current issues. What separates us from the competition is quality—writing, photographs, amount of information."

COSMOPOLITAN, The Hearst Corp., 224 W. 57th St., New York NY 10019. (212)649-2000. Contact: Catherine Romano, deputy editor-in-chief. 90% freelance written. Monthly magazine for 18- to 35-year-old single, married, divorced women—all working. "*Cosmopolitan* is edited for young women for whom beauty, fashion, fitness, career, relationships and personal growth are top priorities. Nutrition and food, travel, personal finance, home/lifestyle and celebrities are other interests reflected in the editorial lineup." Estab. 1886. Circ. 2,573,100. **Pays on acceptance.** Byline given. Offers 10-15% kill fee. Buys all magazine rights and occasionally negotiates first North American rights. Submit seasonal material 6 months in advance. Reports in 1 week on queries; 3 weeks on mss. Sample copy for $2.50. Writer's guidelines for #10 SASE.
• Ranked as one of the best markets for freelance writers in *Writer's Yearbook* magazine's annual "Top 100 Markets," January 1997.
Nonfiction: Book excerpts, how-to, humor, opinion, personal experience and anything of interest to young women. Buys 350 mss/year. Query with published clips or send complete ms. Length: 500-3,500 words. Pays $2,000-3,500 for features; $1,000-1,500 for short pieces. Pays expenses of writers on assignment.
Columns/Departments: Buys 45 mss/year. Length: 750 words. Pays $650-1,300.
Reprints: Accepts previously published submissions appearing in minor publications. Send tearsheet of article, typed ms with rights for sale noted and information about when and where the article previously appeared. Pays 100% of amount paid for an original article.
Fiction: Betty Kelly. Condensed novels, humorous, novel excerpts, romance. Buys 18 mss/year. Query. Length: 750-3,000 words.
• *Cosmopolitan* no longer accepts short stories.
Fillers: Irene Copeland. Facts. Buys 240/year. Length: 300-1,000 words.
Tips: "Combine information with entertainment value, humor and relatability." Needs "information- and emotion- and fun-packed relationship and sex service stories; first-person stories that deal with women's issues; essays from both men and women on topics that most women either relate to or are curious about." This editorial team headed American *Marie Claire* until September 1997.

COUNTRY WOMAN, Reiman Publications, P.O. Box 643, Milwaukee WI 53201. (414)423-0100. Managing Editor: Kathy Pohl. 75-85% written by readers. Willing to work with new/unpublished writers. Bimonthly magazine. "*Country Woman* is for contemporary rural women of all ages and backgrounds and from all over the U.S. and Canada. It includes a sampling of the diversity that makes up rural women's lives—love of home, family, farm, ranch, community, hobbies, enduring values, humor, attaining new skills and appreciating present, past and future all within the context of the lifestyle that surrounds country living." Estab. 1970. **Pays on acceptance.** Byline given. Buys first North American serial, one-time and second serial (reprint) rights. Submit seasonal material 5 months in advance. Reports in 2 months on queries; 3 months on mss. Sample copy for $2. Writer's guidelines for #10 SASE.
Nonfiction: General interest, historical/nostalgic, how-to (crafts, community projects, decorative, antiquing, etc.), humor, inspirational, interview/profile, personal experience, photo/feature packages profiling interesting country women—all pertaining to a rural woman's interest. Articles must be written in a positive, light and entertaining manner. Query. Length: 1,000 words maximum.
Reprints: Send typed ms with rights for sale noted and information about when and where the material previously appeared. Payment varies.

Photos: Send color photos with query or ms. Reviews 35mm or 2¼ transparencies or excellent-quality color prints. Uses only excellent quality color photos. No b&w. "We pay for photo/feature packages." Captions, model releases and identification of subjects required. Buys one-time rights.

Columns/Departments: Why Farm Wives Age Fast (humor), I Remember When (nostalgia) and Country Decorating. Buys 10-12 mss/year (maximum). Query or send complete ms. Length: 500-1,000 words. Pays $50-125.

Fiction: Main character *must* be a country woman. All fiction must have a country setting. Fiction must have a positive, upbeat message. Includes fiction in every issue. Would buy more fiction if stories suitable for our audience were sent our way. Query or send complete ms. Length: 750-1,000 words. Pays $90-125.

Poetry: Traditional, light verse. "Poetry must have rhythm and rhyme! It must be country-related. Always looking for seasonal poetry." Buys 30 poems/year. Submit maximum 6 poems. Length: 5-24 lines. Pays $10-25.

Tips: "We have recently broadened our focus to include 'country' women, not just women on farms and ranches. This allows freelancers a wider scope in material. Write as clearly and with as much zest and enthusiasm as possible. We love good quotes, supporting materials (names, places, etc.) and strong leads and closings. Readers relate strongly to where they live and the lifestyle they've chosen. They want to be informed and entertained, and that's just exactly why they subscribe. Readers are busy—not too busy to read—but when they do sit down, they want good writing, reliable information and something that feels like a reward. How-to, humor, personal experience and nostalgia are areas most open to freelancers. Profiles, to a certain degree, are also open. Be accurate and fresh in approach."

ESSENCE, 1500 Broadway, New York NY 10036. (212)642-0600. Editor-in-Chief: Susan L. Taylor. Executive Editor: Linda Villarosa. Editor-at-Large: Valerie Wilson Wesley. Monthly magazine. "*Essence* is the magazine for today's Black women. Edited for career-minded, sophisticated and independent achievers, *Essence*'s editorial is dedicated to helping its readers attain their maximum potential in various lifestyles and roles. The editorial content includes career and educational opportunities; fashion and beauty; investing and money management; health and fitness; parenting; information on home decorating and food; travel; cultural reviews; fiction; and profiles of achievers and celebrities." Estab. 1970. Circ. 1 million. **Pays on acceptance.** Makes assignments on one-time serial rights basis. 3 month lead time. Pays 25% kill fee. Byline given. Submit seasonal material 6 months in advance. Reports in 2 months. Sample copy for $3.25. Writer's guidelines free.

• Ranked as one of the best markets for freelance writers in *Writer's Yearbook*'s annual "Top 100 Markets," January 1996.

Nonfiction: Buys 200 mss/year. Query only; word length will be given upon assignment. Pays $500 minimum. Also publishes novel and nonfiction book excerpts.

Reprints: Send tearsheet of article, information about when and where the article previously appeared. Pays 50% of the amount paid for an original article.

Photos: Janice Wheeler, art director. State availability of photos with query. Pays $100 for b&w page; $300 for color page. Captions and model release required. "We particularly would like to see photographs for our travel section that feature Black travelers."

Columns/Departments: Query department editors: Living (home, food, lifestyle, travel, consumer information): Corliss Hill and Tara Roberts; Entertainment: Gordon Chambers; Health & Fitness: Ziba Kashef; Travel: Tara Roberts. Query only, word length will be given upon assignment. Pays $100 minimum.

Fiction: Martha Southgate, editor. Publishes novel excerpts.

Tips: "Please note that *Essence* no longer accepts unsolicited mss for fiction, poetry or nonfiction, except for the Brothers, Windows, Back Talk and Interiors columns. So please only send query letters for nonfiction story ideas."

FAMILY CIRCLE MAGAZINE, Gruner & Jahr, 375 Lexington Ave., New York NY 10017-5514. (212)499-2000. Editor-in-Chief: Susan Ungaro. 70% freelance written. Magazine published 17 times/year. "We are a national women's magazine which covers many stages of a woman's life, along with her everyday concerns about social, family and health issues. Query should stress the unique aspects of an article and expert sources; we want articles that will help our readers or make a difference in how they live." Usually buys all print rights. Offers 20% kill fee. Byline given. **Pays on acceptance.** Reports in 2 months.

• Ranked as one of the best markets for freelance writers in *Writer's Yearbook* magazine's annual "Top 100 Markets," January 1997.

Nonfiction: Nancy Clark, deputy editor. Women's interest subjects such as family and personal relationships, children, physical and mental health, nutrition, self-improvement and profiles of ordinary women doing extraordinary things for her community or the nation for 'Women Who Make a Difference' series. "We look for well-written, well-reported stories told through interesting anecdotes and insightful writing. We want well-researched service journalism on all subjects." Query. Length: 1,000-2,500 words. Pays $1/word.

Tips: "Query letters should be concise and to the point. Also, writers should keep close tabs on *Family Circle* and other women's magazines to avoid submitting recently run subject matter."

FIRST FOR WOMEN, Bauer Publishing Co., P.O. Box 1648, 270 Sylvan Ave., Englewood Cliffs NJ 07632. (201)569-6699. Fax: (201)569-6264. E-mail: firstfw@aol.com. Magazine published 18 times/year. Contact: Teresa Hagen, executive editor. "*First for Women* speaks directly to a woman about her real-life needs, concerns and interests. *First* provides an equal combination of service editorial (family, kids, health, food and home) with personal lifestyle and general interest topics (personal health, fitness, nutrition, beauty, fashion and contemporary issues) for the '30-something' woman." Estab. 1989. Circ. 1,282,600. **Pays on acceptance.** Byline given. Offers 20% kill fee.

Non-fiction: Buys 300 articles (1,200-word features and 550- to 750-word short pieces). Query before submitting. No e-mail queries. Pays $1/word. Feature sections more open to freelancers.

Reprints: Send photocopy of article and information about when and where the article previously appeared. Payment negotalbe, but less than amount paid for an original article. Buys first North American serial rights.

FLARE MAGAZINE, 777 Bay St., 5th Floor, Toronto, Ontario M5W 1A7 Canada. (416)596-5453. Fax: (416)596-5184. E-mail: editors@flare.com. Contact: Liza Finlay, managing editor. Canada's monthly fashion magazine for English-speaking, working women ages 18-39. **Pays on acceptance**. Byline given. Offers 50% kill fee. Buys first North American serial and electronic rights. Writer's guidelines free.

• Ranked as one of the best markets for freelance writers in *Writer's Yearbook*'s annual "Top 100 Markets," January 1997.

Nonfiction: Fashion, beauty, health and fitness, career, sex. Length: 1,200-2,000 words. Pays $1/word. Pays expenses of writers on assignment.

Reprints: Accepts previously published submissions.

Columns/Departments: 700 words. Pays $1/word.

Fillers: Length: 700 words minimum. Pays $1/word.

Tips: "Know our demographics."

GLAMOUR, Condé Nast, 350 Madison Ave., New York NY 10017. (212)880-8800. Fax: (212)880-6922. E-mail: glamourmag@aol.com. Contact: Ruth Whitney, editor-in-chief. 75% freelance written. Works with a small number of new/unpublished writers each year. Monthly magazine for college-educated women, 18-35 years old. "*Glamour* is edited for the contemporary American woman, it informs her of the trends, recommends how she can adapt them to her needs, and motivates her to take action. Over half of *Glamour*'s editorial content focuses on fashion, beauty and health, as well as coverage of personal relationships, career, travel, food and entertainment." Estab. 1939. Circ. 2,300,000. **Pays on acceptance**. Offers 20% kill fee. Publishes ms an average of 1 year after acceptance. Byline given. Reports in 3 months. Writer's guidelines for #10 SASE.

Nonfiction: Pamela Erens, articles editor. "Editorial approach is 'how-to' with articles that are relevant in the areas of careers, health, psychology, interpersonal relationships, etc. We look for queries that are fresh and include a contemporary, timely angle. Fashion, beauty, travel, food and entertainment are all staff-written. We use 1,000-word opinion essays for our Viewpoint section. Our His/Hers column features generally stylish essays on relationships or comments on current mores by male and female writers in alternate months." Pays $1,000 for His/Hers mss; $500 for Viewpoint mss. Buys first North American serial rights. Buys 10-12 mss/issue. Query "with letter that is detailed, well-focused, well-organized, and documented with surveys, statistics and research; personal essays excepted." Short articles and essays (1,500-2,000 words) pay $1,000 and up; longer mss (2,500-3,000 words) pay $1,500 minimum. Sometimes pays the expenses of writers on assignment.

Reprints: Send information about when and where the article previously appeared. Payment varies.

Tips: "We're looking for sharply focused ideas by strong writers and are constantly raising our standards. We are interested in getting new writers, and we are approachable, mainly because our range of topics is so broad. We've increased our focus on male-female relationships."

GOOD HOUSEKEEPING, Hearst Corp., 959 Eighth Ave., New York NY 10019. (212)649-2000. Editor-in-Chief: Ellen Levine. Deputy Editor: Diane Salvatore. Prefers to work with published/established writers. Monthly magazine. "*Good Housekeeping* is edited for the 'New Traditionalist.' Articles which focus on food, fitness, beauty, and child care draw upon the resources of the Good Housekeeping Institute. Editorial includes human interest stories, articles that focus social issues, money management, health news, travel, and "The Better Way," an 8-page hard-fact guide to better living." Circ. 5,000,000. **Pays on acceptance**. Buys first North American serial rights. Pays 25% kill fee. Byline given. Submit seasonal material 6 months in advance. Reports in 2 months. For sample copy call (800)925-0485. Writer's guidelines for #10 SASE.

Nonfiction: Diane Salvatore, deputy editor. Deborah Pike, health editor. Consumer, social issues, dramatic narrative, nutrition, work, relationships, psychology, trends. Buys 4-6 mss/issue. Query. Length: 1,500-2,500 words. Pays $1,500 + on acceptance for full articles from new writers. Pays $250-350 for local interest and travel pieces of 2,000 words. Pays expenses of writers on assignment.

Photos: Scott Yardley, art director. Maya MacMillan, photo editor. Photos purchased on assignment mostly. Pays $100-350 for b&w; $200-400 for color photos. Query. Model releases required.

Columns/Departments: The Better Way, editor: Lisa Benenson (consumer advice, how-to, shopping strategies, money savers, health). Profiles editor: Diane Baroni (inspirational, activist or heroic women), 300-600 words. My Problem and How I Solved It editor Sandra Lee (as told-to format), 2,000 words. Query. Pays $1/word for items 300-600 words.

Fiction: Lee Quarfoot, fiction editor. Uses original short fiction and condensations of novels that can appear in one issue. Looks for reader identification. "We get 1,500 unsolicited mss/month. A freelancer's odds are overwhelming, but we do look at all submissions." Send complete mss. Manuscripts will not be returned. Responds only on acceptance. Length: 1,500 words (short-shorts); novel according to merit of material; average 5,000-word short stories. Pays $1,000 minimum for fiction from new writers.

• Ranked as one of the best markets for fiction writers in *Writer's Digest* magazine's last "Fiction 50."

Tips: "Always send a SASE and clips. We prefer to see a query first. Do not send material on subjects already covered in-house by the Good Housekeeping Institute—these include food, beauty, needlework and crafts."

‡HARPER'S BAZAAR, The Hearst Corp., 1700 Broadway, New York, NY 10019. (212)903-5300. Fax: (212)265-8579. Publisher: Jeannette Chang. Contact: Eve MacSweeney, features director. *"Harper's Bazaar* is a monthly specialist magazine for women who love fashion and beauty. It is edited for sophisticated women with exceptional taste. *Bazaar* offers ideas in fashion and beauty, and reports on issues and interests relevant to the lives of modern women." Estab. 1867. Circ. 711,000. Pays on publication. Byline given. Offers 25% kill fee. Buys worldwide rights. Reports in 2 months on queries.
Nonfiction: Buys 36 mss/year. Query with published clips. Length: 2,000-3,000 words. Pays $2/word. Pays writer with contributor copies or other premiums rather than a cash payment.
Columns/Departments: Length: 500-700 words. Pays $2/word.

LADIES' HOME JOURNAL, Meredith Corporation, 125 Park Ave., 20th Floor, New York NY 10017-5516. (212)557-6600. Publishing Director/Editor-in-Chief: Myrna Blyth. 50% freelance written. Monthly magazine focusing on issues of concern to women 30-45. They cover a broader range of news and political issues than many other women's magazines. *"Ladies' Home Journal* is for active, empowered women who are evolving in new directions. It addresses informational needs with highly focused features and articles on a variety of topics including beauty and fashion, food and nutrition, health and medicine, home decorating and design, parenting and self-help, personalities and current events." Circ. 5,000,000. **Pays on acceptance.** Offers 25% kill fee. Rights bought vary with submission. Reports on queries within 3 months with SASE. Writer's guidelines for #10 SASE, Attention: Writer's Guidelines on envelope.
  ● Ranked as one of the best markets for freelance writers in *Writer's Yearbook* magazine's annual "Top 100 Markets," January 1997.
Nonfiction: Submissions on the following subjects should be directed to the editor listed for each: investigative reports, news-related features, psychology/relationships/sex (Pam O'Brien, features editor); medical/health (Elena Rover, health editor); celebrities/entertainment (Melina Gerosa, entertainment editor); travel stories (Karyn Dabaghian, associate editor). Query with published clips. Length: 2,000-3,000 words. Pays $2,000-4,000. Pays expenses of writers on assignment.
Photos: State availability of photos with submission. Offers variable payment for photos accepted with ms. Captions, model releases and identification of subjects required. Rights bought vary with submission. (*LHJ* arranges for its own photography almost all the time.)
Columns/Departments: Query the following editor or box for column ideas. A Woman Today (Box WT); Woman to Woman (Box WW); Parents' Journal (Mary Mohler, senior editor); Pet News (Shana Aborn, associate features editor). Pays $750-2,000.
Fiction: Mary Mohler, editor, books and fiction. Only short stories and novels submitted by an agent or publisher will be considered. Buys 12 mss/year. Does not accept poetry of any kind.
  ● Ranked as one of the best markets for fiction writers in the last *Writer's Digest*'s annual "Fiction 50."

McCALL'S, Gruner & Jahr, 375 Lexington Ave., New York NY 10017-5514. (212)499-2000. Editor: Sally Koslow. Contact: Cathy Cavender, executive editor. 90% freelance written. Monthly. "Study recent issues. Our publication carefully and conscientiously serves the needs of the woman reader—concentrating on matters that directly affect her life and offering information and understanding on subjects of personal importance to her." Circ. 5 million. **Pays on acceptance.** Publishes ms an average of 6 months after acceptance. Offers 20% kill fee. Byline given. Buys exclusive or First North American rights. Reports in 2 months. Writer's guidelines for #10 SASE.
Nonfiction: The editors are seeking meaningful stories of personal experience, fresh slants for self-help and relationship pieces, and well-researched action-oriented articles and narratives dealing with social problems concerning readers. Topics must have broad appeal, but they must be approached in a fresh, new, you-haven't-read-this-elsewhere way. *"McCall's* buys 200-300 articles/year, many in the 1,500-2,000-word length. Pays $1/word. These are on subjects of interest to women: health, personal narratives, celebrity biographies and autobiographies, etc. Almost all features on food, fashion, beauty and decorating are staff-written." Sometimes pays the expenses of writers on assignment.
Tips: "Query first. Use the tone and format of our most recent issues as your guide. Address submissions to executive editor unless otherwise specified."

MADEMOISELLE, Condé Nast, 350 Madison Ave., New York NY 10017. Contact: Katherine Brown Weissman, executive editor or Faye Haun, managing editor. 95% freelance written. Prefers to work with published/established writers. Columns are written by columnists; "sometimes we give new writers a 'chance' on shorter, less complex assignments." Monthly magazine for women age 18-31. *"Mademoiselle* is edited for a woman in her twenties. It focuses on the decade when she is starting out in life as an independent adult and experiencing being on her own for the first time. Editorial offers advice on fashion, beauty, relationships, work and self-discovery." Circ. 1.2 million. Buys first North American serial rights. **Pays on acceptance**; rates vary.
Nonfiction: Particular concentration on articles of interest to the intelligent young woman 18-31, including personal relationships, health, careers, trends, and current social problems. Send health queries to Brenda DeKoker. Send entertainment queries to Jeanie Pyun. Query with published clips and SASE. Length: 1,000-2,000 words.
Photos: Cindy Searight, creative director. Commissioned work assigned according to needs. Photos of fashion, beauty, travel. Payment ranges from no-charge to an agreed rate of payment per shot, job series or page rate. Buys all rights. Pays on publication for photos.
Tips: "We are looking for timely, well-researched manuscripts."

MARIE CLAIRE, Hearst Corp., 250 W. 55th St., New York NY 10019. (212)649-4450. Fax: (212)541-4295. E-mail: marieclaire@hearst.com. Editor-in-chief: Glenda Bailey. Executive Editor: Jenny Barnett. Contact: Brett Mirsky, associate editor. "*Marie Claire* is a monthly lifestyle magazine with a focus on beauty and fashion. It covers a broad range of topics such as world issues, entertaining, celebrity profiles and decorating." American *Marie Claire* was launched in September, 1994. There are currently 22 other international editions. The magazine aims to provide a great read on everything from world issues to intimate advice, fashion, beauty and service." Estab. 1994. Circ. 500,000. **Pays on acceptance**. Publishes ms an average of 5 months after acceptance. Byline given. Offers 25% kill fee. Makes work-for-hire assignments. Editorial lead time 3 months. Submit seasonal material 6 months in advance. Accepts simultaneous submissions. Reports in 3 weeks on queries. Sample copy for $5. Writer's guidelines free.
Nonfiction: Book excerpts, exposé, general interest, humor, personal experience. Does not want to see fiction, personal essays. Buys 50 mss/year. Query with published clips. Length: 500-3,000 words. Pays $1-1.50/word. Sometimes pays expenses of writers on assignment.
Photos: State availability of photos with submission. Reviews contact sheets, negatives, prints. Negotiates payment individually. Model releases, identification of subjects required.
Columns/Departments: Women of the world (the lead feature in every edition, an issue addressing women of another country or culture, but somehow relatable to an American woman as well); first person (personal and dramatic stories, always written from the female subject's point of view); true lives (may be written in first or third person, male or female, discussing a non-traditional lifestyle or unusual experience); emotional issues (relationship/sex related stories, provocative and newsy); working (career issues women face at work, at home, or in relationships); love life (any facet of love, sex, marriage and dating); review (movies, music, books, celebrities, TV, etc.).

MIRABELLA, A Hachette Filipacchi Magazines, Inc. Publication, 1633 Broadway, New York NY 10019. (212)767-5800. Publisher: Audrey Daniels-Arnold. Bimonthly magazine. "*Mirabella* is a fashion and beauty magazine that serves as the busy woman's guide to the good life. In addition to journalistic pieces and profiles, *Mirabella* provides extensive coverage on fashion and beauty, investigative reporting on health, and reflections on personal subjects." Estab. 1989. Circ. 31,480. This magazine did not respond to our request for information. Query before submitting.

MODERN BRIDE, 249 W. 17th St., New York NY 10011. (212)337-7096. Fax: (212)367-8342. Website: http://www.modernbride.com. Editor: Cele Lalli. Executive Editor: Mary Ann Cavlin. "*Modern Bride* is designed as the bride-to-be's guide to planning her wedding, honeymoon, and first home or apartment. Issues cover: (1) bridal fashion (including attendants and mother-of-the-bride), travel trousseau and lingerie; (2) home furnishings (tableware, furniture, linens, appliances, housewares, coverings, accessories, etc.); (3) honeymoon travel (covering the United States, Canada, Mexico, the Bahamas, the Caribbean, Europe and Asia). Additional regular features include personal and beauty care, wedding gifts, etiquette, marital relations, financial advice, and shopping information." **Pays on acceptance.** Offers 25% kill fee. Buys first periodical rights. Reports in 1 month.
Nonfiction: Book excerpts, general interest, how-to, personal experience. Buys 60 mss/year. Query with published clips. Length: 500-2,000 words. Pays $600-1,200.
Reprints: Send tearsheet of article or short story. Pays 50% of amount paid for an original article.
Columns/Departments: Geri Bain, editor. Travel.
Poetry: Free verse, light verse and traditional. Buys very few. Submit maximum 6 poems.

MS. MAGAZINE, MacDonald Communications, Inc., 135 W. 50th St., 16th Floor, New York NY 10020. (212)445-6162. Fax: (212)586-7441. E-mail: ms@echonyc.com. Contact: Marcia Gillespie, editor-in-chief. Executive Editors: Barbara Findlen, Gloria Jacobs. 85% freelance written. Bimonthly magazine on women's issues and news. Estab. 1972. Circ. 200,000. Byline given. Offers 20% kill fee. Buys first North American serial rights. Reports in 1-2 months. Sample copy for $6. Writer's guidelines for #10 SASE.
  • Ranked as one of the best markets for freelance writers in *Writer's Yearbook* magazine's annual "Top 100 Markets," January 1997. This magazine was recently sold to MacDonald Communications.
Nonfiction: International and national (US) news, the arts, books, popular culture, feminist theory and scholarship, ecofeminism, women's health, spirituality, political and economic affairs. Photo essays. Buys 4-5 features (3,000 words) and 4-5 short pieces (500 words)/year. Pays $1/word. Query with published clips. Length: 300-3,000 words. Pays expenses of writers on assignment.
Reprints: Send tearsheets of article or typed ms with rights for sale noted and information about when and where the article previously appeared. Pays 50% of amount paid for an original article.
Photos: State availability of photos with submission. Model releases and identification of subjects required. Buys one-time rights.
Columns/Departments: Buys 4-5 mss/year. Length: up to 3,000 words. Pays $1/word.
Tips: Needs "international and national women's news, investigative reporting, personal narratives, humor, world-class fiction and poetry, and prize-winning journalists and feminist thinkers."

NEW WOMAN MAGAZINE, K-III Magazines, 2 Park Ave., New York NY 10016. (212)545-3600. Editor-in-Chief: Betsy Carter. Contact: Sharlene Breakey, managing editor. Monthly magazine. Estab. 1970. Circ. 1,300,000. **Pays on acceptance.** Byline given. Offers variable kill fee. Buys first North American serial, first, one-time and electronic rights. Editorial lead time 5 months. Submit seasonal material 5 months in advance. Accepts simultaneous submissions. Reports in 3 months. Writer's guidelines for #10 SASE.

Nonfiction: Advice on relationships/sex and psychology, health news, book excerpts, essays, exposé, general interest, humor, interview/profile, opinion, personal experience, small travel pieces. Buys over 20 mss/year. Query with published clips. Length: 500-2,500 words. Pays variable rates. Pays expenses of writers on assignment.
Columns/Departments: Contact: Sharlene Breakey.

PLAYGIRL, 801 Second Ave., New York NY 10017. (212)661-7878. Fax: (212)697-6343. Editor-in-Chief: Judy Cole. Contact: Patrice Baldwin, managing editor. 75% freelance written. Prefers to work with published/established writers. Monthly magazine. "*Playgirl* addresses the needs, interests and desires of women 18 years of age and older. We provide something no other American women's magazine can: an uninhibited approach to exploring sexuality and fantasy that empowers, enlightens and entertains. We publish features articles of all sorts: interviews with top celebrities; essays and humor pieces on sexually related topics; first-person accounts of sensual adventures; articles on the latest trends in sex, love, romance and dating; and how-to stories that give readers sexy news they can use. We also publish erotic fiction—from a woman's perspective or from an empathic, sex-positive male point of view—and reader fantasies. The common thread—besides, of course, good, lively writing and scrupulous research—is a fresh, open-minded, inquisitive attitude." Circ. 500,000. Pays within 6 weeks of acceptance. Publishes ms an average of 3 months after acceptance. Byline given. Offers 20% kill fee. Buys all rights. Submit seasonal material 6 months in advance. Accepts simultaneous submissions, if so noted. Reports in 1 month on queries; 3 months on mss. Writer's guidelines for #10 SASE.
Nonfiction: Humor for the modern woman/man, exposés (related to women's issues), interview (Q&A format with major show business celebrities), articles on sexuality, medical breakthroughs, relationships, coping, careers, insightful, lively articles on current issues, investigative pieces particularly geared to *Playgirl*. Average issue: 3 articles; 1 celebrity interview. Buys 6 mss/issue. Query with published clips. Length: 1,000-2,500 words. Pays $300-1,000. Sometimes pays expenses of writers on assignment.
Fiction: Publishes novel excerpts.
Tips: "Best bet for first-time writers: Fantasy Forum. No phone calls please."

RADIANCE, The Magazine for Large Women, Box 30246, Oakland CA 94604. (510)482-0680. E-mail: radmag2 @aol.com. Website: http://www.radiancemagazine.com. Editor: Alice Ansfield. 95% freelance written. Quarterly magazine "that encourages and supports women *all* sizes of large to live fully now, to stop putting their lives on hold until they lose weight." Estab. 1984. Circ. 10,000. Pays on publication. Publishes ms an average of 12-20 months after acceptance. Byline given. Offers $25 kill fee. Buys one-time and second serial (reprint) rights. Submit seasonal material at least 1 year in advance. Accepts previously published submissions. Reports in 4 months. Sample copy for $3.50. Writer's guidelines for #10 SASE.
Nonfiction: Book excerpts (related to large women), essays, exposé, general interest, historical/nostalgic, how-to (on health/well-being/fashion/fitness, etc.), humor, inspirational, interview/profile, opinion, personal experience, photo feature, travel. "No diet successes or articles condemning people for being fat." Query with published clips. Length: 1,000-2,500 words. Pays $35-100. Sometimes pays writers with contributor copies or other premiums.
Photos: State availability of photos with submission. Offers $15-50/photo. Captions and identification of subjects preferred. Buys one-time rights.
Columns/Departments: Up Front and Personal (personal profiles of women from all areas of life); Health and Well-Being (physical/emotional well-being, self care, research); Expressions (features on artists who celebrate the full female figure); Images (designer interviews, color/style/fashion, features); Inner Journeys (spirituality, personal experiences, interviews); Perspectives (cultural and political aspects of being in a larger body); On the Move (women active in all kinds of sports, physical activities); Young Activists (bringing size awareness and esteem to the younger generation); Travel. Buys 60 mss/year. Query with published clips. Length: 1,000-3,500 words. Pays $50-100.
Fiction: Condensed novels, ethnic, fantasy, historical, humorous, mainstream, novel excerpts, romance, science fiction, serialized novels, slice-of-life vignettes relating somehow to large women. "No woman-hates-self-till-meets-man-type fiction!" Buys 15 mss/year. Query with published clips. Length: 800-2,500 words. Pays $35-100.
Poetry: Reflective, empowering, experiential. Related to women's feelings and experience, re: their bodies, self-esteem, acceptance. "We want well-crafted poems; prefer unrhymed; not preachy poetry." Buys 30 poems/year. Length: 4-45 lines. Pays $10-15.
Tips: "We welcome talented, sensitive, responsible, open-minded writers. We profile women from all walks of life who are all sizes of large, of all ages and from all ethnic groups and lifestyles. We welcome writers' ideas on interesting large women from across the US and abroad. We're an open, size-positive magazine that documents and celebrates body acceptance. *Radiance* is one of the major forces working for size acceptance. We want articles to address all areas of vital importance in women's lives. Please read a copy of *Radiance* before writing for us."

REDBOOK MAGAZINE, 224 W. 57th St., New York NY 10019. Senior Editors: Pamela Lister and Susan Gifford. Deputy Editor: Toni Gerber Hope. Health Editor: Andrea Bauman. Fiction Editor: Dawn Raffel. Contact: Any of editorial assistants listed on masthead. 90% freelance written. Monthly magazine. "*Redbook* addresses young married women between the ages of 25 and 44. Most of our readers are married with children 12 and under; over 60 percent work outside the home. The articles entertain, educate and inspire our readers to confront challenging issues. Each article must be timely and relevant to *Redbook* readers' lives." Estab. 1903. Circ. 3,200,000. **Pays on acceptance.** Publishes ms an average of 6 months after acceptance. Rights purchased vary with author and material. Reports in 3 months. Writer's guidelines for #10 SASE.
Nonfiction: Contact: Articles Department. Subjects of interest: social issues, parenting, sex, marriage, news profiles,

true crime, dramatic narratives, money, psychology, health. Query with published clips. Length: articles, 2,500-3,000 words; short articles, 1,000-1,500 words. "Please review at least the past six issues of *Redbook* to better understand subject matter and treatment." Enclose SASE for response.

Fiction: Contact: Fiction Department. "Of the 20,000 unsolicited manuscripts that we receive annually, we buy less than five. We also find many more stories that are not necessarily suited to our needs but are good enough to warrant our encouraging the author to send others. *Redbook* looks for fresh, well-crafted stories that reflect some aspect of the experiences and interests of our readers; it's a good idea to read several issues to get a feel for what we buy. No unsolicited novels or novellas, please." Payment begins at $1,000 for short stories. Please include SASE with all stories.

● Ranked as one of the best markets for fiction writers in *Writer's Digest*'s last annual "Fiction 50."

Tips: "Most *Redbook* articles require solid research, well-developed anecdotes from on-the-record sources, and fresh, insightful quotes from established experts in a field that pass our 'reality check' test."

‡**SELF**, 350 Madison Ave., 23rd Floor, New York NY 10017. Executive Editor: Judith Daniels. Monthly magazine for women ages 22-45. "*Self* is a magazine about total well-being. It is edited for active, professional women who are interested in improving the quality of their lives and the world they live in. The magazine provides a balanced approach to attain individual satisfaction with information on beauty, health, fitness, psychology, food, fashion, culture, career, politics and the environment." **Pays on acceptance**. Byline given. Buys one-time rights. Accepts simultaneous submissions. Reports in 1 month on queries. Sample copy free. Writer's guidelines for #10 SASE.

Nonfiction: Needs major pieces on health, nutrition, psychology, fitness, family relationships and sociological issues. Buys 40 mss/year. Query with published clips. Length: 1,500-5,000 words. Pays $1-2/word.

Columns/Departments: Needs short, news-driven items on health, nutrition, money, jobs, love/sex, mind/body, fitness, travel. Length: 300-1,000 words. Buys 50 mss/year. Query with published clips. Pays $1-2/word.

Tips: "Our articles contain a lot of factual information—and related anecdotes; most rely on the advice and opinion of experts. We don't publish articles on entertainment or celebrities. Our readers seek very focused and useful information about their interests."

VOGUE, Condé Nast, 350 Madison Ave., New York NY 10017. (212)880-8905. E-mail: voguemail@aol.com. Contact: Susan Morrison, features editor. Monthly magazine. "*Vogue* mirrors the changing roles and concerns of women, covering not only evolutions in fashion, beauty and style, but the important issues and ideas of the arts, health care, politics and world affairs." Estab. 1892. Circ. 1,136,000. **Pays on acceptance**. Byline given. Offers 25% kill fee. Reports in 3 months on queries. Writer's guidelines for #10 SASE.

● Ranked as one of the best markets for freelance writers in *Writer's Yearbook* magazine's annual "Top 100 Markets," January 1997.

Nonfiction: "Needs fresh voices on unexpected topics." Buys 5 unsolicited mss/year. Query with published clips. Length: 2,500 words maximum. Pays $1-2/word.

Tips: "Sophisticated, surprising and compelling writing a must." Please note: *Vogue* accepts *very* few unsolicited manuscripts. Most stories are generated in-house and are written by staff.

WOMAN'S DAY, 1633 Broadway, New York NY 10019. (212)767-6000. Fax: (212)767-5610. Deputy Editor: Maureen McFadden. 75% or more of articles freelance written. "*Woman's Day* is written and edited for the contemporary woman. *Woman's Day* editorial package covers the various issues that are inportant to women today. Editorial features are devoted to information on Food & Nutrition, Health & Fitness, Beauty & Fashion, as well as the traditional values of Home, Family and Children. The changing needs of women are also addressed with articles that focus on Careers, Money Management, Law, and Relationships." 17 issues/year. Circ. 6,000,000. Pays 25% kill fee. Byline given. **Pays on acceptance.** Reports in 1 month or less on queries. Submit detailed queries.

● Ranked as one of the best markets for freelance writers in *Writer's Yearbook* magazine's annual "Top 100 Markets," January 1997.

Nonfiction: Uses articles on all subjects of interest to women—family life, childrearing, education, homemaking, money management, careers, family health, work and leisure activities. Also interested in fresh, dramatic narratives of women's lives and concerns. "These must be lively and fascinating to read." Length: 500-2,200 words, depending on material. Payment varies depending on length, type, writer, and whether it's for regional or national use, but rates are high. Pays a bonus fee in addition to regular rate for articles based on writer's idea (as opposed to assigned story.) Bonus fee is an additional 20% of fee (up to $500). Pays the expenses of writers on confirmed assignment. "We no longer accept unsolicited manuscripts—and cannot return or be responsible for those that are sent to us."

Columns/Departments: "We welcome short (850 words), spirited essays on controversial topics for Back Talk page. Submit completed essays only, no queries, with SASE. Pays $2,000.

Fillers: Neighbors columns also pay $75/each for brief practical suggestions on homemaking, childrearing and relationships. Address to the editor of the section.

Tips: "Our primary need is for ideas with broad appeal that can be featured on the cover. These include diet stories, organizing tips and money saving information. We're buying more short pieces."

WOMAN'S LIFE, A Publication of Woman's Life Insurance Society, (formerly *Review*), 1338 Military St., P.O. Box 5020, Port Huron MI 48061-5020. (313)985-5191, ext. 29. Fax: (810)985-6881. Editor: Janice U. Whipple. Contact: Patricia J. Samar, director of communications. 30% freelance written. Works only with published/established writers. Quarterly magazine published for a primarily female-membership to help them care for themselves and their families. Estab. 1892. Circ. 32,000. Pays on publication. Publishes ms an average of 1 year after acceptance. Byline given. Not copyrighted. Buys one-time, simultaneous and second serial (reprint) rights. Submit seasonal material 6 months in advance. Accepts simultaneous submissions. Reports in 1 year (usually less). Sample copy for 9 × 12 SASE with 4 first-class stamps. Writer's guidelines for #10 SASE.

Nonfiction: Looking primarily for general interest stories for women aged 25-44 regarding physical, mental and emotional health and fitness; and financial/fiscal health and fitness. "We would like to see more creative financial pieces that are directed at women. Also interested in creative interesting stories about marketing life insurance and annuities to the women's market." Buys 4-10 mss/year. Send complete ms. Length: 1,000-2,000 words. Pays $150-500/ms.

Reprints: Send tearsheet or photocopy of article or send typed ms with rights for sale noted and information about when and where ms previously appeared. Pays 15% of amount paid for an original article.

Photos: Only interested in photos included with ms. Model release and identification of subjects required.

Tips: "We have begun more clearly defining the focus of our magazine. We receive FAR TOO MANY stories from people who clearly ignore the information in this listing and/or our writer's guidelines. No more stories about Tippy the Spotted Pig, please!"

WOMAN'S WORLD, The Woman's Weekly, Heinrich Bauer North America Inc., 270 Sylvan Ave., Englewood Cliffs NJ 07632. Fax: (201)569-3584. Editor-in-Chief: Stephanie Saible. Contact: Irene Daria or Sarah Hutter. 95% freelance written. Weekly magazine covering "human interest and service pieces of interest to family-oriented women across the nation. *Woman's World* is a women's service magazine. It offers a blend of Fashion, Food, Parenting and Beauty coupled with the true-life features and human interest stories." **Pays on acceptance.** Publishes ms an average of 4 months after acceptance. Buys first North American serial rights for 6 months. Submit seasonal material 4 months in advance. Reports in 6 weeks on queries; 2 months on mss. Writer's guidelines for #10 SASE.

Nonfiction: Dramatic personal women's stories and articles on self-improvement, medicine and health topics; pays $500 for 1,000 words. Features include Emergency (real life drama); My Story; Medical Miracle; Triumph; Courage; My Guardian Angel; Happy Ending (queries to Sarah Hutter). Also service stories on parenting, marriage, and work (queries to Irene Daria).

Fiction: Deborah Purcell, fiction editor. Short story, romance and mainstream of 1,600 words and mini-mysteries of 1,100 words. "Each of our stories has a light romantic theme and can be written from either a masculine or feminine point of view. Women characters may be single, married or divorced. Plots must be fast moving with vivid dialogue and action. The problems and dilemmas inherent in them should be contemporary and realistic, handled with warmth and feeling. The stories must have a positive resolution." Not interested in science fiction, fantasy, historical romance or foreign locales. No explicit sex, graphic language or seamy settings. Specify "short story" on envelope. Always enclose SASE. Reports in 2-4 months. No phone queries. Pays $1,000 on acceptance for North American serial rights for 6 months. "The 1,100 word mini-mysteries may feature either a 'whodunnit' or 'howdunnit' theme. The mystery may revolve around anything from a theft to murder. However, we are not interested in sordid or grotesque crimes. Emphasis should be on intricacies of plot rather than gratuitous violence. The story must include a resolution that clearly states the villain is getting his or her come-uppance." Submit complete mss. Specify "mini mystery" on envelope. Enclose SASE. Stories slanted for a particular holiday should be sent at least 6 months in advance. No phone queries.

Tips: "Come up with good queries. Short queries are best. We have a strong emphasis on well-researched material. Writers must send research with ms including book references and phone numbers for double checking. The most frequent mistakes made by writers in completing an article for us are sloppy, incomplete research, not writing to the format, and not studying the magazine carefully enough beforehand."

‡**WORKING WOMAN**, A MacDonald Communications, Inc. Publication, 135 W. 50th St., 16th Floor, New York NY 10020. (212)445-6100. Fax:(212)586-7449. Publisher: Barbara J. Litrell. Editor: Nancy Smith. Contact: Articles Department. Magazine published 10 times a year. "*Working Woman* reports on news, trends, information, people and ideas as they impact women in business. Professional/managerial women turn to *Working Women* as their key resource for managing the complexities of business today, from small business to the new corporate structure." Estab. 1978. Circ. 22,758. **Pays on acceptance.** Responds in 2 months.

Nonfiction: Articles on all aspects of the career woman's professional and private life. "Our readers are managers, professionals and business owners at midcareer and up. We are particularly interested in profiles of women that reflect larger social and business trends." Query with published clips. Length: 2,000-3,000 words. Pay varies.

Columns/Departments: Length: 1,200-1,400 words. Pay varies.

MARKETS THAT WERE listed in the 1997 edition of *Writer's Market* but do not appear this year are listed in the General Index with a notation explaining why they were omitted.

Trade, Technical and Professional Journals

Many writers who pick up a *Writer's Market* for the first time do so with the hope of selling an article or story to one of the popular, high-profile consumer magazines found on newsstands and in bookstores. Many of those writers are surprised to find an entire world of magazine publishing that exists outside the realm of commercial magazines and that they may have never known about—trade journals. Writers who *have* discovered trade journals have found a market that offers the chance to publish regularly in subject areas they find interesting, editors who are typically more accessible than their commercial counterparts and pay rates that rival those of the big-name magazines.

Trade journal is the general term for any publication focusing on a particular occupation or industry. Other terms used to describe the different types of trade publications are business, technical and professional journals. They are read by truck drivers, brick layers, farmers, fishermen, heart surgeons—let's not forget butchers, bakers, and candlestick makers—and just about everyone else working in a trade or profession. Trade periodicals are sharply angled to the specifics of the professions they report on. They offer business-related news, features and service articles that will foster their readers' professional development. A teacher reads *Learning* to keep up with developments in lesson plans and classroom management. Readers of *Beverage World* are looking for the latest news and information about the beverage industry.

Trade magazine editors tell us their readers are a knowledgeable and highly interested audience. Writers for trade magazines have to either possess knowledge about the field in question or be able to report it accurately from interviews with those who do. Writers who have or can develop a good grasp of a specialized body of knowledge will find trade magazine editors who are eager to hear from them. And since good writers with specialized knowledge are a somewhat rare commodity, trade editors tend, more than typical consumer magazine editors, to cultivate ongoing relationships with writers. If you can prove yourself as a writer who "delivers," you will be paid back with frequent assignments and regular paychecks.

An ideal way to begin your foray into trade journals is to write for those that report on your present profession. Whether you've been teaching dance, farming or working as a paralegal, begin by familiarizing yourself with the magazines that serve your occupation. After you've read enough issues to have a feel for the kinds of pieces they run, approach the editors with your own article ideas. If you don't have experience in a profession but can demonstrate an ability to understand (and write about) the intricacies and issues of a particular trade that interests you, editors will still be willing to hear from you.

Photographs help increase the value of most stories for trade journals. If you can provide photos, mention that in your query or send copies. Since selling photos with a story usually means a bigger paycheck, it is worth any freelancer's time to develop basic camera skills.

Query a trade journal as you would a consumer magazine. Most trade editors like to discuss an article with a writer first and will sometimes offer names of helpful sources. Mention any direct experience you may have in the industry in your cover letter. Send a resume and clips if they show you have some background or related experience in the subject area. Read each listing carefully for additional submission guidelines.

To stay abreast of new trade magazines starting up, watch for news in *Folio* and *Advertising Age* magazines. Another source for information about trade publications is the *Business Publica-*

tion Advertising Source, published by Standard Rate and Data Service (SRDS) and available in most libraries. Designed primarily for people who buy ad space, the volume provides names and addresses of thousands of trade journals, listed by subject matter.

Information on trade publications listed in the previous edition but not included in this edition of *Writer's Market*, can be found in the General Index.

ADVERTISING, MARKETING AND PR

Trade journals for advertising executives, copywriters and marketing and public relations professionals are listed in this category. Those whose main focus is the advertising and marketing of specific products, such as home furnishings, are classified under individual product categories. Journals for sales personnel and general merchandisers can be found in the Selling and Merchandising category.

AMERICAN DEMOGRAPHICS, American Demographics, Inc., P.O. Box 68, Ithaca NY 14851-0068. (607)273-6343. Fax: (607)273-3196. E-mail: editors@demographics.com. Editor-in-Chief: Diane Crispell. Managing Editor: Nancy Ten Kate. Contact: Diane Crispell, executive editor. 25% freelance written. Works with a small number of new/unpublished writers each year. Monthly magazine for business executives, market researchers, media and communications people, public policymakers. Estab. 1978. Circ. 35,000. Pays on publication. Publishes ms 4 months after acceptance. Buys all rights. Submit seasonal material 6 months in advance. Reports in 6 months. Include self-addressed stamped postcard to know ms arrived safely. Sample copy for $10 and 9×11 SAE. Guidelines for #10 SASE.
Nonfiction: General interest (on demographic trends, implications of changing demographics, profile of business using demographic data); how-to (on the use of demographic techniques, psychographics, understand projections, data, apply demography to business and planning). No anecdotal material. Pay varies, depending on experience, length and content of article, etc. Sometimes pays the expenses of writers on assignment.
Tips: "Writer should have clear understanding of specific population trends and their implications for business and planning. The most important thing a freelancer can do is to read the magazine and be familiar with its style and focus."

ART DIRECTION, Advertising Trade Publications, Inc., 456 Glenbrook Rd., Stamford CT 06906-1800. (203)353-1441. Fax: (203)353-1371. Editor: Dan Barron. 10% freelance written. Prefers to work with published/established writers. Monthly magazine emphasizing advertising design for art directors of ad agencies (corporate, in-plant, editorial, freelance, etc.). Circ. 8,933. Pays on publication. Buys one-time rights. Reports in 3 months. Sample copy for $4.50.
Nonfiction: How-to articles on advertising campaigns. Pays $100 minimum.

‡COSMETIC/PERSONAL CARE PACKAGING, O&B Communications, 3 Paoli Plaza, Paoli PA 19301. (610)647-8585. Fax: (610)647-8565. E-mail: cpcpkg@aol.com. Contact: Jim Wagner, editor. Managing Editor: Lisa Bonnell. 15% freelance written. Bimonthly magazine. CPC covers the marketing of fragrance, cosmetics and toiletries and how packaging delivers the brand message. Estab. 1996. Circ. 8,000. Pays within 30 days on invoice. Publishes ms an average of 2 months after acceptance. Byline given. Buys all rights. Editorial lead time 3 months. Submit seasonal material 3 months in advnace. Sample copy free. Writer's guidelines not available.
Nonfiction: How-to (how a package concept was designed), interview/profile, new product, technical. No general marketing articles, products older than 6 months. Buys 10 mss/year. Query. Length: 500-1,600 words. Pay varies. Pays expenses of writers on assignment.
Photos: Send photos with submission. Reviews contact sheets, transparencies. Offers no additional payment for photos accepted with ms. Captions required. Buys one-time rights.

DECA DIMENSIONS, 1908 Association Dr., Reston VA 22091. (703)860-5000. Fax: (703)860-4013. E-mail: decainc @aol.com(sub:CarolLund). Website: http://www.DECA.org. Editor: Carol Lund. 30% freelance written. Bimonthly magazine covering professional development, business, vocational training. "*Deca Dimensions* is the membership magazine for the Association of Marketing Students—primarily ages 16-20 in all 50 states and Canada. The magazine is delivered through the classroom. Students are interested in developing professional, leadership and career skills." Estab. 1947. Circ. 145,000. Pays on publication. Byline given. Buys first rights and second serial (reprint) rights. Editorial lead time 3 months. Submit seasonal material 4 months in advance. Accepts simultaneous submissions. Sample copy free.
Nonfiction: Essays, general interest, how-to (get jobs, start business, plan for college, etc.), interview/profile (business

---

‡   THE DOUBLE DAGGER before a listing indicates that the listing is new in this edition. New markets are often more receptive to freelance submissions.

leads), personal experience (working). Buys 4 mss/year. Send complete ms. Length: 800-1,000 words. Pays $125 for assigned articles; $100 for unsolicited articles.

Reprints: Send photocopy of article and information about when and where the article previously appeared. Pays 85% of amount paid for an original article.

Photos: State availability of photos with submission. Reviews negatives, transparencies, prints. Offers $15-25/photo. Captions required. Buys one-time rights.

Columns/Departments: Professional Development leadership. Buys 4 mss/year. Send complete ms. Pays $75-100. Length: 200-500 words.

Fillers: Anecdotes, facts, short humor. Length: 400-600 words. Pays $25-50.

MARKETING TOOLS, Information-based Tactics and Techniques, American Demographics, 127 W. State St., Ithaca NY 14850. Fax: (607)273-3196. E-mail: editors@marketingtools.com. Editor: Claudia Montague. 85% freelance written. Magazine published 10 times/year. "*Marketing Tools* is a magazine for professionals who deal with customer information—consumer and business-to-business. Our focus is on the technology used to gather, analyze, and act on customer data, as opposed to the data itself." Estab. 1994. Circ. 20,000. **Pays on acceptance**. Publishes ms an average of 2 months after acceptance. Byline given. Offers 50% kill fee. Rights shared with author. Editorial lead time 5 months. Submit seasonal material 1 year in advance. Sample copy for 9×12 SAE. Writer's guidelines for #10 SASE.

Nonfiction: Book excerpts, essays, how-to, interview/profile, new product, technical. Buys 100 mss/year. Query with published clips. Length: 750-4,000 words. Pays $200-700. Sometimes pays expenses of writers on assignment.

Reprints: Send typed ms with rights for sale noted and information about when and where the article previously appeared. Pay negotiable.

Photos: State availability of photos with submission. Reviews prints. Negotiates payment individually. Captions, model releases, identification of subjects required. Buys one-time rights.

Columns/Departments: Marketing Research (collecting, analyzing data); Database/Direct Marketing (collecting, managing, using data); Business-to-business (special concerns of B2B companies); all 1,500 words. Buys 50 mss/year. Query. Pays $350-400.

Tips: "Well-written queries from writers with some knowledge/experience in database or direct marketing are always welcome. Do NOT telephone to pitch a story idea. We stipulate in our writer's agreement that we reserve the right to reproduce work electronically—i.e., to upload it to our website."

MEDIA INC., Pacific Northwest Media, Marketing and Creative Services News, P.O. Box 24365, Seattle WA 98124-0365. (206)382-9220. Fax: (206)382-9437. E-mail: mediaindx@aol.com. Website: www.media-inc.com. Publisher: Richard K. Woltjer. Contact: Darcy Reinhart, editor. 20% freelance written. Monthly tabloid covering Northwest US media, advertising, marketing and creative-service industries. Audience is Northwest ad agencies, marketing professionals, media and creative-service professionals. Estab. 1987. Circ. 10,000. Byline given. Reports in 1 month. Sample copy for 9×12 SAE with 6 first-class stamps.

Tips: "It is best if writers live in the Pacific Northwest and can report on local news and events in Media Inc.'s areas of business coverage."

‡POTENTIALS IN MARKETING, Lakewood Publications, 50 S. Ninth St., Minneapolis MN 55402. (612)340-4922. Editor: Margaret Kaeter. Associate Editor: Paul Nolan. 25% freelance written. Magazine published monthly. "We reach marketing executives in Fortune 1000 companies. The focus is integrated marketing with a promotion marketing slant." Estab. 1970. Circ. 50,000. **Pays on acceptance**. Byline given. Offers 50% kill fee. Buys first rights, all rights or makes work-for-hire assignments. Editorial lead time 2 months. Submit seasonal material 2 months in advance. Reports in 2 weeks on queries; 1 month on mss. Sample copy free.

Nonfiction: How-to, interview/profile, new product, opinion, personal experience. Buys 15 mss/year. Query. Length: 1,500-3,000 words. Pays $300-1,000 for assigned articles; $100-500 for unsolicited articles. Sometimes pays expenses of writers on assignment.

Photos: State availability of photos with submission. Reviews transparencies. Negotiates payment individually. Model releases required. Buys one-time rights.

Columns/Departments: On The Edge (cutting edge business and marketing ideas); Cybermarketing (computers in marketing); Business-To-Business Marketing (case studies and how-to). Length: 1,500 words. Buys 12 mss/year. Query. Pays $100-500.

Tips: "Inside information detailing the 'how' and success of marketing campaigns is a sure way to get our attention. Expert, how-to pieces on off-beat marketing strategies and tactics are great, too."

RESPONSE TV, The Information Leader for the Electronic Merchandising Industry, Advanstar Communications, 201 E. Sandpointe, Suite 600, Santa Ana CA 92707. (714)513-8400. Fax: (714)513-8482. E-mail: rtvdave@aol.com. Website: http://www.advanstar.com. Editor: David Nagel. 30% freelance written. Monthly magazine covering direct response television. "We look for business writers with experience in advertising, marketing, direct marketing, telemarketing, TV production, cable TV industry and home shopping." Estab. 1992. Circ. 21,000. **Pays on acceptance.** Byline given. Offers 50% kill fee. Buys all rights. Editorial lead time 2 months. Reports in 2 weeks on queries, 1 month on mss. Write or e-mail for sample copy.

Nonfiction: General interest, interview/profile, opinion, technical, case studies. Buys 25 mss/year. Query with published clips. Most freelance work is assigned by editor. Send résumé and sample clips to be considered for assignments. Length:

2,000-3,000 words. Pays 25¢/word plus phone expenses. Sometimes pays expenses of writers on assignment.

Reprints: Rarely accepts previously published submissions. Send tearsheet of article or short story or typed ms with rights for sale noted.

Photos: State availability of photos with submission. Reviews contact sheets, negatives, transparencies. Negotiates payment individually. Model releases, identification of subjects required. Buys one-time rights.

Columns/Departments: New media (interactive advertising and merchandising), 200 words; International, 200 words; Legal (advertising and marketing law), 800 words. Buys 12 mss/year. Query with published clips. Pays $300.

Tips: "Familiarity with topics such as home shopping, direct response TV, internet commerce and infomercials. General interest in advertising and marketing."

SIGNCRAFT, The Magazine for the Commercial Sign Shop, SignCraft Publishing Co., Inc., P.O. Box 60031, Fort Myers FL 33906. (941)939-4644. Editor: Tom McIltrot. 10% freelance written. Bimonthly magazine of the sign industry. "Like any trade magazine, we need material of direct benefit to our readers. We can't afford space for material of marginal interest." Estab. 1980. Circ. 19,500. Pays on publication. Publishes ms an average of 9 months after acceptance. Byline given. Offers negotiable kill fee. Buys first North American serial or all rights. Reports in 1 month. Sample copy and writer's guidelines for $3.

Nonfiction: Interviews, profiles. "All articles should be directly related to quality commercial signs. If you are familiar with the sign trade, we'd like to hear from you." Buys 20 mss/year. Query with or without published clips. Length: 500-2,000 words. Pays up to $250.

Reprints: Accepts previously published submissions.

‡SIGNS OF THE TIMES, The Industry Journal Since 1906, ST Publications, Dept. WM, 407 Gilbert Ave., Cincinnati OH 45202-2285. (513)421-2050. Fax: (513)421-5144. E-mail: djohnson@stpubs.com. Website: http://www.signweb.com. Contact: Darek Johnson, editor. 15-30% freelance written. "We are willing to use more freelancers." Monthly magazine special buyer's guide between November and December issues. Estab. 1906. Circ. 16,000. Pays on publication. Publishes ms an average of 3 months after acceptance. Byline given. Buys variable rights. Accepts simultaneous and previously published submissions. Reports in 3 months. Free sample copy and writer's guidelines for 9×12 SAE with 10 first-class stamps.

● This publication is looking for more business-related articles and short profiles.

Nonfiction: Historical/nostalgic (regarding the sign industry); how-to (carved signs, goldleaf, etc.); interview/profile (focusing on either a signshop or a specific project); photo feature (query first); and technical (sign engineering, etc.). Nothing "nonspecific on signs, an example being a photo essay on 'signs I've seen.' We are a trade journal with specific audience interests." Buys 15-20 mss/year. Query with clips. Pays $150-500. Sometimes pays the expenses of writers on assignment.

Reprints: Send photocopy of article or typed ms with rights for sale noted and information about when and where the article previously appeared. Payment is negotiated.

Photos: Send photos with ms. "Sign industry-related photos only. We sometimes accept photos with funny twists or misspellings."

Fillers: Open to queries; request rates.

ART, DESIGN AND COLLECTIBLES

The businesses of art, art administration, architecture, environmental/package design and antiques/collectibles are covered in these listings. Art-related topics for the general public are located in the Consumer Art and Architecture category. Antiques and collectibles magazines for enthusiasts are listed in Consumer Hobby and Craft. (Listings of markets looking for freelance artists to do artwork can be found in *Artist's and Graphic Designer's Market*, Writer's Digest Books.)

ADOBE MAGAZINE, Adobe Systems Inc., 411 First Ave. S., Seattle WA 98104-2871. Fax: (206)470-7106. E-mail: editor@adobe.com. Editor-in-Chief: Christine Yarrow. Contact: Tamis Nordling, editor. 60% freelance written. Quarterly magazine covering graphic design, publishing, Adobe software. "Mission: To help users of Adobe products get their work done better and faster, and to entertain, educate, and inspire along the way." Estab. 1989. Circ. 600,000. **Pays on acceptance.** Publishes ms an average of 3 months after acceptance. Byline given. Offers 25% kill fee. Buys all rights. Editorial lead time 5 months. Sample copy free on request.

Nonfiction: How-to, humor, interview/profile, technical. Buys 60-70 mss/year. Query with published clips. *No unsolicited mss.* Length: 500-2,500 words. Pays $300-1,500.

Columns/Departments: How-to (technical guide to problem solving), 1,500-3,000 words. Pay varies.

‡AIRBRUSH ACTION MAGAZINE, Airbrush Action, Inc., 1985 Swarthmore Ave., Lakewood NJ 08701. (908)364-2111. Fax: (908)367-5908. E-mail: cstieglitz@monmouth.com. Contact: Joseph Lasala, editor/art director. Managing Editor: Robert Sumski. 80% freelance written. Bimonthly magazine. "*Airbrush Action* is the airbrush magazine covering the spectrum of airbrush applications: illustration, t-shirt airbrushing, fine art, automotive and sign painting, hobby/craft applications, wall murals, fingernails, body airbrushing, artist profiles, reviews and more." Estab. 1985. Circ. 60,000. Pays in 30 days. Publishes ms an average of 6 months after acceptance. Byline given. Offers 50% kill fee. Buys all rights. Editorial lead time 6 months. Submit seasonal material 6 months in advance. Accepts simultaneous submissions. Sample copy and writer's guidelines free.

Nonfiction: How-to, humor, inspirational, interview/profile, new product, personal experience, technical. Nothing unrelated to airbrush. Query with published clips. Pays 10¢/word. Sometimes pays expenses of writers on assignment.
Photos: Send photos with submission. Negotiates payment individually. Captions, model releases and identification of subjects required. Buys all rights.
Columns/Departments: Query with published clips.

‡AIRBRUSH MAGAZINE, Airbrush Magazine Inc. 3676 Cosby Hwy., Cosby TN 37722. (423)487-2168. Fax: (423)487-3026. E-mail: airmagzin@aol.com. Editor: Bill Jones. Contact: Laura Harris, publisher. 10% freelance written. Quarterly magazine covering airbrush art. "*Airbrush Magazine* is a step-by-step, how-to magazine that focuses on easy-to-understand articles." Estab. 1994. Circ. 35,000. Pays on publication. Byline given. Buys one-time rights. Editorial lead time 3 months. Submit seasonal material 3 months in advance. Accepts simultaneous submissions. Sample copy for $2. Writer's guidelines free.

Nonfiction: How-to (airbrush art). Buys 10 mss/year. Send complete ms. Length: 250-1,000 words. Pays $150-300.
Photos: State availability of or send photos with submission. Reviews transparencies. Negotiates payment individually. Captions, identification of subjects required. Buys one-time rights.

ANTIQUEWEEK, Mayhill Publications Inc., P.O. Box 90, Knightstown IN 46148-0090. (765)345-5133. Fax: (800)695-8153. E-mail: antiquewk@aol.com. Website: http://www.antiqueweek.com. Central Edition Editor: Tom Hoepf. Eastern Edition Editor: Connie Swaim. Genealogy Editor: Shirley Richardson. 80% freelance written. Weekly tabloid on antiques, collectibles and genealogy with 2 editions: Eastern and Central. "*AntiqueWeek* has a wide range of readership from dealers and auctioneers to collectors, both advanced and novice. Our readers demand accurate information presented in an entertaining style." Estab. 1968. Circ. 64,000. Pays on publication. Byline given. Buys first and second serial (reprint) rights. Submit seasonal material 1 month in advance. Free sample copy. Writer's guidelines for #10 SASE.

Nonfiction: Historical/nostalgic, how-to, interview/profile, opinion, personal experience, antique show and auction reports, feature articles on particular types of antiques and collectibles. Buys 400-500 mss/year. Query with or without published clips, or send complete ms. Length: 1,000-2,000 words. Pays $50-150.
Reprints: Send typed ms with rights for sale noted and information about when and where the article previously appeared. Pays 50% of amount paid for an original article.
Photos: Send photos with submission. Identification of subjects required.
Columns/Departments: Insights (opinions on buying, selling and collecting antiques), 500-1,000 words; Your Ancestors (advice, information on locating sources for genealogists). Buys 150 mss/year. Query. Length: 500-1,500 words. Pays $25-50.
Tips: "Writers should know their topics thoroughly. Feature articles must be well-researched and clearly written. An interview and profile article with a knowledgeable collector might be the break for a first-time contributor. As we move toward the year 2000, there is much more interest in 20th-century collectibles. *Antiqueweek* also seeks articles that reflect the lasting popularity of traditional antiques."

APPLIED ARTS, 885 Don Mills Rd., Suite 324, Toronto, Ontario M3C 1V9 Canada. (416)510-0909. Fax: (416)510-0913. E-mail: app-edit@interlog.com. Website: http://www.interlog.com/~app.arts. Editor: Sara Curtis. 50% freelance written. Magazine published 7 times/year covering graphic design, advertising, photography and illustration. Estab. 1986. Circ. 12,000. **Pays on acceptance.** Byline given. Buys first North American serial rights. Reports in 2 months on queries. Sample copy for 10×13 SAE with $1.70 Canadian postage or 4 IRCs.

Nonfiction: Portfolio/profile, technical (computers and the applied arts), trade articles about graphic design, advertising, photography and illustration. Buys 18-20 mss/year. Query with published clips. Length: 500-2,500 words. Pays 50-60¢/word (Canadian).
Photos: Offers no additional payment for photos accepted with ms. Buys one-time rights.
Tips: "It helps if writers have some familiarity with the communication arts field and graphics technology. Writers should include a solid selection of published articles. Ideas of most interest include specific recent advertising or design projects—print, video, multimedia or combined—preferably with a Canadian angle. Take time to read back issues of the magazine before querying."

THE APPRAISERS STANDARD, New England Appraisers Association, 5 Gill Terrace, Ludlow VT 05149-1003. (802)228-7444. E-mail: llt44@ludl.tds.net. Publisher/Editor: Linda L. Tucker. 50% freelance written. Works with a small number of new/unpublished writers each year. Bimonthly publication on the appraisals of antiques, art, collectibles, jewelry, coins, stamps and real estate. "The writer should be extremely knowledgeable on the subject, and the article should be written with appraisers in mind, with prices quoted for objects, good pictures and descriptions of articles being written about." Estab. 1980. Circ. 1,300. Pays on publication. Publishes ms an average of 1 year after acceptance. Byline given, with short bio to establish writer's credibility. Buys first and simultaneous rights. Submit seasonal material

2 months in advance. Accepts simultaneous submissions. Reports in 1 month on queries, 2 months on mss. Sample copy for 9×12 SAE with 78¢ postage. Writer's guidelines for #10 SASE.

Nonfiction: Interview/profile, personal experience, technical, travel. "All geared toward professional appraisers." Query with or without published clips, or send complete ms. Length: 700 words. Pays $50.

Reprints: Send typed ms with rights for sale noted and information about when and where the article previously appeared. Pays 100% of amount paid for an original article.

Photos: Send photos with submission. Reviews negatives and prints. Offers no additional payment for photos accepted with ms. Identification of subjects required. Buys one-time rights.

Tips: "Interviewing members of the association for articles, reviewing, shows and large auctions are all ways for writers who are not in the field to write articles for us."

‡**ART BUSINESS NEWS**, Advanstar Communications Inc., 270 Madison Ave., New York NY 10016. (203)656-3402. Editor-in-Chief: Johanna O'Melia. 25% freelance written. Prefers to work with published/established writers. Monthly trade tabloid covering news relating to the art and picture framing industry. Circ. 31,000. Pays on publication. Publishes ms an average of 3 months after acceptance. Byline given. Buys first-time rights. Submit seasonal material 2 months in advance. Accepts simultaneous submissions. Reports in 3 months. Sample copy for $5 and 12×16 SAE.

Nonfiction: News in art and framing field; interview/marketing profiles (of dealers, publishers and suppliers in the art industry); new products; articles focusing on small business people—framers, art gallery management, art trends; how-to (occasional article on "how-to frame" accepted). Buys 8-20 mss/year. Length: 2,500 words maximum. Query first. Pays $75-300. Sometimes pays the expenses of writers on assignment. Photography useful.

Tips: "We have more opportunity for shorter, hard news items and news features."

ARTS MANAGEMENT, 110 Riverside Dr., Suite 4E, New York NY 10024. (212)579-2039. Editor: A.H. Reiss. Magazine published 5 times/year for cultural institutions. 2% freelance written. Estab. 1962. Circ. 6,000. Pays on publication. Byline given. Buys all rights. Query. Reports in 2 months. Writer's guidelines for #10 SASE.

● Mostly staff-written; uses very little outside material.

Nonfiction: Short articles, 400-900 words, tightly written, expository, explaining how art administrators solved problems in publicity, fund raising and general administration; actual case histories emphasizing the how-to. Also short articles on the economics and sociology of the arts and important trends in the nonprofit cultural field. Must be fact-filled, well-organized and without rhetoric. Pays 2-4¢/word. No photographs or pictures.

‡**CMYK MAGAZINE**, Aroune-Freigen, 1101 Clay St., San Francisco CA 94408. (415)673-5869. Fax: (415)346-6536. E-mail: cmykcurt@aol.com. Contact: Curtis Clarkson, editor. 90% freelance written. Quarterly magazine. "*CMYK* publishes the very best work from *student* art directors, designers, illustrators and photographers. *CMYK* is distributed to art schools, ad agencies and design firms. Our readers are students and pros." Estab. 1996. Circ. 20,000. **Pays on acceptance.** Byline given. Buys all rights. Editorial lead time 6 weeks. Submit seasonal material 1 month in advance. Accepts simultaneous submissions. Sample copy for $9. Writers' guidelines free.

Nonfiction: Essays, how-to, inspirational, interview/profile, opinion, personal experience. Buys 15 mss/year. Query with published clips. Length: 800-1,700 words. Pays $150-200. Sometimes pays expenses of writers on assignment.

Photos: State availability of photos with submission. Reviews negatives. Negotiates payment individually. Identification of subjects required. Rights purchased vary.

Columns/Departments: Query with published clips. Pays $150-200.

CONTEMPORARY STONE DESIGN, Business News Publishing Co., 299 Market St., Third Floor, Saddle Brook NJ 07663. (201)291-9001. Fax: (201)291-9002. E-mail: stoneworld@aol.com. Website: http://www.stoneworld.com. Publisher: Alex Bachrach. Contact: Michael Reis, editor. Quarterly magazine covering the full range of stone design and architecture—from classic and historic spaces to current projects. Estab. 1995. Circ. 14,000. Pays on publication. Publishes ms an average of 3 months after acceptance. Byline given. Buys first rights only. Submit seasonal material 6 months in advance. Reports in 3 weeks. Sample copy for $10.

Nonfiction: Overall features on a certain aspect of stone design or specific articles on individual architectural projects. Interview/profile of a prominent architect/designer or firm. Photo feature, technical, architectural design. Buys 8 mss/year. Query with published clips. Length: 1,500-3,000 words. Pays $6/column inch. Pays expenses of writers on assignment.

Photos: State availability of photos with submission. Reviews transparencies and prints. Pays $10/photo accepted with ms. Captions and identification of subjects required. Buys one-time rights.

Columns/Departments: Upcoming Events (for the architecture and design community); Stone Classics (featuring historic architecture); Q&A session with a prominent architect or designer. 1,500-2,000 words. Pays $6/inch.

Tips: "The visual aspect of the magazine is key, so architectural photography is a must for any story. Cover the entire project, but focus on the stonework and how it relates to the rest of the space. Architects are very helpful in describing their work and often provide excellent quotes. As a relatively new magazine, we are looking for freelance submissions and are open to new feature topics. This is a narrow subject, however, so it's a good idea to speak with an editor before submitting anything."

COREL MAGAZINE, Omray Inc., 9801 Anderson Mill Rd., Suite 207, Austin TX 78750. (512)250-1700. Fax: (512)250-1016. E-mail: scottc@corelmag.com. Website: http://www.corelmag.com. Editor: Scott Campbell. 80-90%

freelance written. Monthly magazine. "*Corel Magazine* is edited for users of CorelDraw, Photo-Paint, and other graphics software from Corel Corp. and third parties. Focus is on step-by-step tutorials, technical and product solutions, and real-world graphic design. Targeted to graphic design professionals and business presentation graphics users." Circ. 40,000. Byline given. Offers $50 kill fee. Buys first North American serial rights. Editorial lead time 10 weeks. Submit seasonal material 3 months in advance. Reports in 2 weeks on queries; 1 month on mss. Sample copy free on request.

Nonfiction: How-to (graphics and text explaining how to create image or effect with Corel software), new product, personal experience, technical, product reviews, tips and tricks. Buys 180 mss/year. Query. Length: 500-2,500 words. Pays $150-750 for assigned articles; $50-500 for unsolicited articles. Sometimes pays expenses of writers on assignment.

Photos: Most artwork will be computer-generated. Send photos with submission. Offers no additional payment for photos accepted with ms.

Columns/Departments: In the Box (review/how-to), 1,500 words plus art. Query. Pays $150-500.

HOW, The Bottomline Design Magazine, F&W Publications, Inc., 1507 Dana Ave., Cincinnati OH 45207-1005. (513)531-2222. Fax: (513)531-2902. E-mail: howedit@aol.com. Website: http://www.howdesign.com. Editor: Kathleen Reinmann. 75% freelance written. Bimonthly graphic design and illustration business journal. "*HOW* gives a behind-the-scenes look at not only *how* the world's best graphic designers and illustrators conceive and create their work, but *why* they did it that way. We also focus on the *business* side of design—how to run a profitable studio." Estab. 1985. Circ. 38,000. **Pays on acceptance.** Byline given. Buys first North American serial rights. Reports in 6 weeks. Sample copy for cover price plus $1.50 (cover price varies per issue). Writer's guidelines for #10 SASE.

Nonfiction: Interview/profile, business tips, new products, environmental graphics, digital design. Special issues: Self-Promotion Annual (September/October); Business Annual (November/December); International Annual of Design (March/April); Paper/Stock Photography (May/June); Digital Design Annual (July/August). No how-to articles for beginning artists or fine-art-oriented articles. Buys 40 mss/year. Query with published clips and samples of subject's work (artwork or design). Length: 1,200-1,500 words. Pays $250-700. Sometimes pays expenses of writers on assignment.

Photos: State availability of artwork with submission. Reviews 35mm or larger transparencies (dupes only). May reimburse mechanical photo expenses. Captions are required. Buys one-time rights.

Columns/Departments: Marketplace (focuses on lucrative fields for designers/illustrators); Production (ins, outs and tips on production); Interactivity (behind the scenes of electronically produced design projects); Software Review and Workspace (takes an inside look at the design of creatives' studios). Buys 20 mss/year. Query with published clips. Length: 1,000-2,000 words. Pays $150-400.

Tips: "We look for writers who can recognize graphic designers on the cutting-edge of their industry, both creatively and business-wise. Writers must have an eye for detail, and be able to relay *HOW*'s step-by-step approach in an interesting, concise manner—without omitting any details. Showing you've done your homework on a subject—and that you can go beyond asking 'those same old questions'—will give you a big advantage."

LETTER ARTS REVIEW, 1624 24th Ave. SW, Norman OK 73072. (405)364-8794. Fax: (405)364-8914. E-mail: letterarts@netplus.net. Website: http://www.letterarts.com. Publisher/Editor: Karyn L. Gilman. 98% freelance written. Eager to work with new/unpublished writers with calligraphic expertise and language skills. Quarterly magazine on lettering and related book arts, both historical and contemporary in nature. Estab. 1982. Circ. 5,500. Pays on publication. Publishes ms an average of 9 months after acceptance. Byline given. Offers 20% kill fee. Buys first rights. Reports in 3 months. Sample copy for 9×12 SAE with 7 first-class stamps. Free writer's guidelines.

Nonfiction: Interview/profile, opinion, contemporary, historical. Buys 50 mss/year. Query with or without published clips, or send complete ms. Length: 1,000-2,000 words. Pays $50-200 for assigned articles; $25-200 for unsolicited articles. Sometimes pays the expenses of writers on assignment.

Photos: State availability of photos with submission. Reviews contact sheets, negatives, transparencies and prints. Pays agreed upon cost. Captions and identification of subjects required. Buys one-time rights.

Columns/Departments: Book Reviews, Viewpoint (critical), 500-1,500 words; Ms. (discussion of manuscripts in collections), 1,000-2,000 words; Profile (contemporary calligraphic figure), 1,000-2,000 words. Query. Pays $50-200.

Tips: "*Letter Arts Review*'s primary objective is to encourage the exchange of ideas on calligraphy and the lettering arts—its past and present as well as trends for the future. Historical research, typography, graphic design, fine press and artists' books, and other related aspects of the lettering arts are welcomed. Third person is preferred, however first person will be considered if appropriate. Writer should realize that this is a specialized audience."

THE MIDATLANTIC ANTIQUES MAGAZINE, Monthly Guide to Antiques, Art, Auctions & Collectibles, Henderson Newspapers, Inc., P.O. Box 908, Henderson NC 27536-0908. (919)492-4001. Fax: (919)430-0125. Editor: Lydia Stainback. 65% freelance written. Monthly tabloid covering antiques, art, auctions and collectibles. "The *MidAtlantic* reaches dealers, collectors, antique shows and auction houses primarily on the East Coast, but circulation includes 48 states and Europe." Estab. 1984. Circ. 14,000. Pays on publication. Byline given. Buys first rights. Submit seasonal material 6 months in advance. Reports in 1 month on queries; 2 months on mss. Sample copy and writer's guidelines for 10×13 SAE with 10 first-class stamps.

Nonfiction: Book excerpts, historical/nostalgic, how-to (choose an antique to collect; how to sell your collection; how to identify market trends), interview/profile, personal experience, photo feature, technical. Buys 20-30 mss/year. Query. Length: 800-2,000 words. Pays $50-125. Trade for advertising space. Rarely pays expenses of writers on assignment.

Photos: Send color photos with submission. Offers no additional payment for photos accepted with ms. Identification of subjects required. Buys one-time rights.

Tips: "Please contact by mail first, but a writer may call with specific ideas after initial contact. Looking for writers who have extensive knowledge in specific areas of antiques. Articles should be educational in nature. We are also interested in how-to articles, i.e., how to choose antiques to collect; how to sell your collection and get the most for it; looking for articles that focus on future market trends. We want writers who are active in the antiques business and can predict good investments. (Articles with photographs are given preference.) We are looking for people who are not only knowledgeable, but can write well."

AUTO AND TRUCK

These publications are geared to automobile, motorcycle and truck dealers; professional truck drivers; service department personnel; or fleet operators. Publications for highway planners and traffic control experts are listed in the Government and Public Service category.

‡**AUTO GLASS JOURNAL**, Grawin Publications, Inc., 303 Harvard E., Suite 101, P.O. Box 12099, Seattle WA 98102-0099. (206)322-5120. Editor: Jeff Martin. 10% freelance written. Prefers to work with published/established writers. Monthly magazine for the auto glass replacement industry. Includes step-by-step glass replacement procedures for current model cars and business management, industry news and trends. Estab. 1953. Circ. 5,700. **Pays on acceptance.** Publishes ms an average of 5 months after acceptance. No byline given. Buys all rights. Reports in 5 months. Sample copy for 6×9 SAE with 3 first-class stamps. Writer's guidelines for #10 SASE.
Nonfiction: Articles relating to auto glass and general business management. Buys 12-20 mss/year. Query with published clips. Length: 1,000-1,500 words. Pays $50-200, with photos.
Photos: State availability of photos. Reviews b&w contact sheets and negatives. Payment included with ms. Captions required. Buys all rights.

AUTOMOTIVE COOLING JOURNAL, National Automotive Radiator Service Association, P.O. Box 97, E. Greenville PA 18041. (215)541-4500. Fax: (215)679-4977. E-mail: narsa@aol.com. Editor: Wayne Juchno. Contact: Richard Krisher, managing editor. 20% freelance written. Monthly magazine. "The *ACJ* is targeted to the cooling system and air conditioning service shop owner and operator. Its mission is to provide these independent business people with information they need about service, management, marketing, regulation, environment and industry trends." Estab. 1956. Circ. 10,000. **Pays on acceptance.** Publishes ms an average of 3 months after acceptance. Byline given. Editorial lead time 3 months. Submit seasonal material 6 months in advance. Accepts simultaneous submissions. Reports in 2 months on mss; 1 month on queries.
Nonfiction: Interview/profile, new product, photo feature, technical. Buys 12 mss/year. Query with published clips. Length: 1,000-5,000 words. Pays $100-500 for assigned articles; $100-300 for unsolicited articles. Sometimes pays expenses of writers on assignment.
Reprints: Accepts previously published submissions. Payment is negotiable.
Photos: State availability of photos with submission. Reviews contact sheets. Negotiates payment individually. Captions, model releases, identification of subjects required. Buys one-time rights.

BUSINESS VEHICLE MANAGEMENT, Bobit Publishing Company, 2512 Artesia Blvd., Redondo Beach CA 90278. (310)376-8788. Fax: (310)374-7878. E-mail: bvm@aol.com. Editor/Publisher: Ed Bobit. Contact: Michelle Bowman, executive editor. 15% freelance written. Quarterly magazine covering small-fleet industry companies with 30 or fewer vehicles. "*Business Vehicle Management* is created as a quarterly directed to management decision-makers to educate, inform and provide resource knowledge in all phases of vehicle and business operations and management." Estab. 1995. Circ. 250,000. Pays on publication. Publishes ms an average of 6 months after acceptance. No byline. Buys all rights. Editorial lead time 6 months. Submit seasonal material 6 months in advance. Reports in 6 weeks on queries; 2 months on mss. Sample copy for $10. Writer's guidelines for #10 SASE.
Nonfiction: How-to, humor, interview/profile, photo feature, technical. Buys 10-12 mss/year. Query with published clips. Length: 1,000-3,000 words. Pays $0-300. Sometimes pays expenses of writers on assignment.
Photos: Send photos with submission. Reviews 4×5 transparencies. Offers no additional payment for photos accepted with ms. Captions, identification of subjects required. Buys all rights.
Fillers: Gags to be illustrated by cartoonist, newsbreaks, short humor. Length: 50-150 words. Pays $0-50.
Tips: "Know it in advance. Read several back issues to get an idea of our style and content."

NEW ENGLAND MECHANIC, P.O. Box M, Franklin MA 02038. (508)528-6211. Managing Editor: M. Zingraff. 40% freelance written. Bimonthly newspaper covering automotive repair, testing, maintenance. "Our slant on technical information is both for advanced technician and apprentice. We cover news on laws and regulations, some management information and profiles of shops and wholesales. Estab. 1996. Circ. 5,000. **Pays on acceptance**. Byline given. Offers 50% kill fee on assignments only. Buys one-time or second serial (reprint) rights. Editorial lead time 1 month. Reports in 2 months. Writer's guidelines for #10 SASE.
Nonfiction: General interest, how-to, interview/profile, technical. Buys 18 mss/year. Query with published clips. Length: 500-1,500 words. Pays $100-200 for assigned articles; $35-100 for unsolicited articles.
Reprints: Accepts previously published submissions.

Photos: State availability of photos with submission. Reviews contact sheets, 3×5 or larger prints. Pays $25 for first photo, $10 for each additional photo. Captions, identification of subjects required. Buys one-time rights.
Fillers: Facts. Buys 6 fillers/year. Length: 50-150 words. Pays $25-50.

O&A MARKETING NEWS, KAL Publications Inc., 532 El Dorado St., Suite 200, Pasadena CA 91101. Fax: (818)683-0969. Editor: Kathy Laderman. 10% freelance written. Bimonthly tabloid. "*O&A Marketing News* is editorially directed to people engaged in the distribution, merchandising, installation and servicing of gasoline, oil, TBA, quick lube, carwash, convenience store, alternative fuel and automotive aftermarket products in the 13 Western states." Estab. 1966. Circ. 8,000. Pays on publication. Publishes ms an average of 3 months after acceptance. Byline sometimes given. Not copyrighted. Buys one-time rights. Editorial lead time 1 month. Accepts simultaneous submissions. Reports in 1 month on mss. Sample copy for $3.
Nonfiction: Exposé, interview/profile, photo feature, industry news. Buys 20 mss/year. Send complete ms. Length: 100-10,000 words. Pays per column inch typeset.
Photos: State availability of photos with submission. Reviews contact sheets, prints (5×7 preferred). Offers $5/photo. Identification of subjects required. Buys one-time rights.
Fillers: Gags to be illustrated by cartoonist, short humor. Buys 7/year. Length: 1-200 words. Pays per column inch.
Tips: "Seeking Western industry news. We're always seeking more stories covering the more remote states such as Montana, Idaho, and Hawaii—but any timely, topical *news* oriented stories will be considered."

‡**OLD CARS**, Krause Publications, 700 E. State St., Iola WI 54990. (715)445-2214. Fax: (715)445-4087. Contact: John A. Gunnell, editorial director; Chad Elmore, news director. 60% freelance written. Weekly tabloid covering old cars. Estab. 1971. Circ. 100,000. Pays in the month after publication date. Buys perpetual but non-exclusive rights. For sample copy call circulation deparment. Writer's guidelines for #10 SASE.
Nonfiction: How-to, technical, auction prices realized lists. Buys 1,000-1,200 mss/year. Send complete ms. Length: 400-1,000 words. Pays 3¢/word.
Reprints: Accepts previously published submissions.
Photos: Pays $5/photo. Offers no additional payment for photos accepted with ms.
Tips: "Ninety percent of our material is done by a small group of regular contributors. Many new writers break in here, but we are *usually overstocked* with material and *never* seek nostalgic or historical pieces from new authors. Our big need is for well-written items that fit odd pieces in a tabloid page layout. Budding authors should try some short, catchy items that help us fill odd-ball 'news holes' with interesting writing. Authors with good skills can work up to longer stories. A weekly keeps us too busy to answer mail and phone calls. The best queries are 'checklists' where we can quickly mark a 'yes' or 'no' to article ideas."

OVERDRIVE, The Magazine for the American Trucker, Randall Publishing Co./Overdrive, Inc., P.O. Box 3187, Tuscaloosa AL 35403-3187. (205)349-2990. Fax: (205)750-8070. E-mail: longton@overdriveonline.com. Website: http://www.overdriveonline.com. Editorial Director: Linda Longton. Managing Editor: Deborah Lockridge. 15% freelance written. Monthly magazine for independent truckers. Estab. 1961. Circ. 115,800. Pays on publication. Publishes ms an average of 2 months after acceptance. Byline given. 10% kill fee. Buys all North American rights. Reports in 2 months. Sample copy and writers' guidelines for 9×12 SASE.
Nonfiction: Essays, exposé, how-to (truck maintainance and operation), interview/profile (successful independent truckers), personal experience, photo feature, technical. All must be related to independent trucker interest. Query with or without published clips, or send complete ms. Length: 500-2,000 words. Pays $100-600 for assigned articles; $50-500 for unsolicited articles.
Photos: Send photos with submission. Reviews transparencies and 5×7 prints. Offers $25-50/photo. Identification of subjects required. Buys all rights.
Tips: "Talk to independent truckers. Develop a good knowledge of their concerns as small business owners, truck drivers and individuals. We prefer articles that quote experts, people in the industry and truckers to first-person expositions on a subject. Get straight facts. Look for good material on truck safety, on effects of government regulations, and on rates and business relationships between independent truckers, brokers, carriers and shippers."

REFRIGERATED TRANSPORTER, Tunnell Publications, P.O. Box 66010, Houston TX 77266. (713)523-8124. Fax: (713)523-8384. Editor: Gary Macklin. 5% freelance written. Monthly. Byline given. Pays on publication. Reports in 1 month.
Nonfiction: "Articles on fleet management and maintenance of vehicles, especially the refrigerated van and the refrigerating unit, shop tips, loading or handling systems—especially for frozen or refrigerated cargo, new equipment specifications, conversions of equipment for better handling or more efficient operations. Prefers articles with illustrations obtained from fleets operating refrigerated trucks or trailers." Pays variable rate, $100/printed page and up.

‡**ROAD KING MAGAZINE, For the Professional Driver**, Hammock Publishing, Inc., 3322 West End Ave. #700, Nashville TN 37203. (615)385-9745. Fax: (615)386-9349. E-mail: roadking@hammock.com. Editor: Tom Berg. Managing Editor: Bill Hudgins. 80% freelance written. "*Road King* is published bimonthly for long-haul truckers. It celebrates the lifestyle and work and profiles interesting and/or successful drivers. It also reports on subjects of interest to our audience, including outdoors, vehicles, music and trade issues." Estab. 1963. Circ. 229,900. **Pays on acceptance**. Publishes ms an average of 4 months after acceptance. Byline given. Offers 50% kill fee. Buys first North American

serial rights or electronic rights. Editorial lead time 3 months. Submit seasonal material 4 months in advance. Reports in 2 months on queries. Sample copy for 9×12 SAE and 5 first-class stamps. Writer's guidelines for #10 SASE.

Nonfiction: How-to (trucking-related), humor, interview/profile, new product, photo feature, technical, travel. "No fiction, poetry." Buys 20 mss/year. Query with published clips. Length: 850-2,000 words. Pay is negotiable. Sometimes pays expenses of writers on assignment.

Photos: State availability of photos with submission. Reviews contact sheets. Negotiates payment individually. Model releases and identification of subjects required. Buys negotiable rights.

Columns/Departments: Lead Driver (profile of outstanding trucker), 800-1,000 words; Between Loads (travel destination), 1,000-1,200 words. Buys 6-10 mss/year. Query. Pay is negotiable.

Fillers: Anecdotes, facts, gags to be illustrated by cartoonist, short humor. Length: 100-250 words. Pays $50.

TOW-AGE, P.O. Box M, Franklin MA 02038-0822. Editor: J. Kruza. For readers who run their own towing service business. 5% freelance written. Prefers to work with published/established writers. Published every 6 weeks. Estab. 1960. Circ. 18,000. Buys all rights; usually reassigns rights. **Pays on acceptance.** Accepts simultaneous submissions. Reports in 1 month. Sample copy for $5. Writer's guidelines for #10 SASE.

Nonfiction: Articles on business, legal and technical information for the towing industry. "Light reading material; short, with punch." Informational, how-to, personal, interview, profile. Buys about 18 mss/year. Query or submit complete ms. Length: 600-800 words. Pays $50-150. Spot news and successful business operations. Length: 300-800 words. Technical articles. Length: 400-1,000 words. Pays expenses of writers on assignment.

Photos: Black and white 8×10 photos purchased with or without mss, or on assignment. Pays $25 for first photo; $10 for each additional photo in series. Captions required.

TRUCK WEST, Southam Business Communications, 1450 Don Mills Rd., Don Mills, Ontario M3B 2X7 Canada. (416)442-2268. Fax: (416)442-2092. E-mail: pcancilla@southam.ca. Editor: Patricia Cancilla. 10% freelance written. Monthly tabloid. "We write for the owner/operator audience in particular, as well as cover issues concerning fleets, truck manufacturers, legislators, etc." Estab. 1989. Circ. 22,000. Pays on publication. Publishes ms an average of 1 month after acceptance. Byline given. Not copyrighted. Makes work-for-hire assignments. Editorial lead time 1 month. Submit seasonal material 3 months in advance. Accepts simultaneous submissions. Reports in 1 month on queries. Sample copy and writer's guidelines free.

Nonfiction: Exposé, how-to (i.e., maintain your truck), interview/profile, new product, opinion, personal experience, technical. No product testimonials. Buys 15 mss/year. Query with published clips. Length: 300-1,500 words. Pays 25¢/word minimum. Sometimes pays expenses of writers on assignment.

Photos: State availability of photos with submission. Reviews transparencies, prints. Negotiates payment individually. Captions, identification of subjects required. Buys one-time rights.

Columns/Departments: News Briefs (new regulations, etc.), 500-800 words; Profiles (industry leaders), 1,000-1,500 words; Features (change monthly, i.e., tires, brakes, etc.), 1,000-1,500 words. Buys 5 mss/year. Query with published clips. Pays 25¢/word minimum.

‡TRUCKING TIMES, Herrmeyer Publishing, 2413A Center St., Cedar Falls IA 50613. (319)277-8332. Fax: (319)277-8950. E-mail: ttol@ttol.com. Editor: Richard Pratt. 25% freelance written. "*Trucking Times* is a bimonthly trade publication exclusively for manufacturers, dealers, installers and distributors of aftermarket light-truck accessories. Orienting pieces to the trade is key." Estab. 1989. Circ. 13,000. Pays on publication. Publishes ms an average of 4 months after acceptance. Byline sometimes given. Buys all rights or makes work-for-hire assignments. Editorial lead time 4 months. Submit seasonal material 6 months in advance. Reports in 3 weeks on queries; 2 months on mss. Sample copy free.

Nonfiction: How-to (installation of accessories, etc.), interview/profile, new product, opinion, photo feature, technical. "No retail pieces (like Truckin')." Buys 6-8 mss/year. Query with published clips. Length: 100-2,000 words. Pays $200-2,000. Sometimes pays expenses of writers on assignment.

Photos: State availability of photos or send photos with submission (preferred). Reviews 5×2 transparencies or 4×6 prints. Negotiates payment individually. Captions and identification of subjects required. Buys all rights.

Columns/Departments: Buys 4 mss/year. Query with published clips. Pays $100-1,000.

Tips: "Be straightforward. Sell to the entire market, not just rich kids or yuppies."

WARD'S AUTO WORLD, Intertec Publishing Corp., 3000 Town Center, Suite 2750, Southfield MI 48075. (810)357-0800. Fax: (810)357-0810. E-mail: wards@wardsauto.com. Website: http://www.wardsauto.com. Editor-in-Chief: David C. Smith. Contact: Michael Arnholt, managing editor. 10% freelance written. Monthly magazine. "*Ward's Auto World* is written for all disciplines in the auto industry, with a special slant toward engineers." Estab. 1965. Circ. 105,000. Pays 1 month after acceptance. Byline given. Kill fee varies. Buys all rights. Reports in 1 month. Sample copy and writer's guidelines for 8×10 SAE with 5 first-class stamps.

Nonfiction: Essays, general interest, international automotive news, interview, new product, opinion, personal experience, photo feature, technical. Few consumer type articles. No nostalgia or personal history stories (like "My Favorite Car"). Buys 5-10 mss/year. Query. Phone queries OK. Length: 500-2,500 words. Pays $250-1,000. Sometimes pays expenses of writers on assignment.

Photos: State availability of or send photos with submission. Negotiates payment individually. Identification of subjects required. Buys one-time rights.

Columns/Departments: Drew Winter, executive editor. Assignment only. Buys 12-24 mss/year. Pays $200-400.

Tips: "*Ward's Auto World* is a business newsmagazine with strong emphasis on reporting and writing. It is 90% staff-written, though uses a stable of solid freelancers."

WESTERN CANADA HIGHWAY NEWS, Craig Kelman & Associates, 3C-2020 Portage Ave., Winnipeg, Manitoba R3J 0K4 Canada. (204)885-7798. Fax: (204)889-3576. Managing Editor: Terry Ross. 30% freelance written. Quarterly magazine. "The official magazine of the Alberta, Saskatchewan and Manitoba trucking associations." Estab. 1995 (formerly *Manitoba Highway News*). Circ. 4,000. Pays on publication. Publishes ms an average of 2 months after acceptance. Byline given. Buys one-time rights. Editorial lead time 3 months. Submit seasonal material 3 months in advance. Accepts simultaneous submissions. Reports in 2 months on queries; 4 months on mss. Sample copy for 10×13 SAE with $1 IRC. Writer's guidelines free.
Nonfiction: Essays, general interest, how-to (run a trucking business), interview/profile, new product, opinion, personal experience, photo feature, technical, profiles in excellence (bios of trucking or associate firms enjoying success). Buys 10-12 mss/year. Query. Length: 500-3,000 words. Pays 18-25¢/word. Sometimes pays expenses of writers on assignment.
Reprints: Send photocopy of article or short story and information about when and where the article previously appeared. Pays 60% of amount paid for an original article.
Photos: State availability of photos with submission. Reviews 4×6 prints. Identification of subjects required. Buys one-time rights.
Columns/Departments: Safety (new safety innovation/products), 500 words; Trade Talk (new products), 300 words. Query. Pays 18-25¢/word.
Tips: "Our publication is fairly time-sensitive re: issues affecting the trucking industry in Western Canada. Current 'hot' topics are international trucking (NAFTA-induced changes), deregulation, driver fatigue, health and safety, alcohol and drug testing legislation/programs and national/international highway systems."

AVIATION AND SPACE

In this section are journals for aviation business executives, airport operators and aviation technicians. Publications for professional and private pilots are in the Consumer Aviation section.

AG-PILOT INTERNATIONAL MAGAZINE, Graphics Plus, P.O. Box 1607, Mt. Vernon WA 98273-1607. (360)336-9737. Fax: (360)336-2506. E-mail: agpilot@cnw.com. Editor/Publisher: Tom J. Wood. Contact: Krista Madlung. Monthly magazine emphasizing agricultural aviation, aerial firefighting, forestry spraying. 10% freelance written. Estab. 1978. Pays on publication. Publishes ms an average of 3 months after acceptance. Buys all rights. Byline given. Reports in 2 months. Sample copy for $3 and 9×12 SAE with 7 first-class stamps. Writer's guidelines for #10 SASE.
Nonfiction: Exposé (of EPA, OSHA, FAA, NTSB or any government function concerned with this industry), general interest, historical, humor, interview (of well-known ag/aviation person), new product, personal experience, photo feature. Sometimes pays expenses of writers on assignment. Buys 20 mss/year. Send complete ms. Length: 500-10,000 words. Pays $100-200.
Reprints: Accepts previously published submissions.
Photos: Send photos with submission. Reviews 4×5 transparencies, 5×7 prints. Offers no additional payment for photos accepted with ms. Captions required.
Columns/Departments: Good Old Days (ag/aviation history), 500-700 words. Buys 10 mss/year. Send complete ms. Pays $50-150.
Poetry: Interested in all ag-aviation-related poetry. Buys 10 poems/issue. Submit maximum 2 at one time. Length: 24-72 lines. Pays $25-50.
Fillers: Short jokes, short humor and industry-related newsbreaks. Length: 40-100 words. Pays $15-20.
Tips: "Writers should be witty and knowledgeable about the crop dusting aviation world. Material *must* be agricultural/aviation-oriented."

‡AIR CARGO WORLD, Journal of Commerce/Economist Group, 1230 National Press Bldg., Washington DC 20045. (202)783-1148. Fax: (202)783-2550. Editor: Paul Page. 70% freelance written. Monthly magazine covering air cargo industry, including airline-related and logistics issues. "We are an international monthly aimed at top executives in the air cargo and related industries. We strive for independent, sophisticated business journalism." Estab. 1948. Circ. 25,000. Pays on publication. Publishes ms an average of 2 months after acceptance. Byline given. Buys first and second serial (reprint) rights. Editorial lead time 2 months. Submit seasonal material 3 months in advance. Reports in 1 month on mss. Sample copy and writer's guidelines free.
Nonfiction: Book excerpts, exposé, how-to (shipping), interview/profile, new product, opinion, technical. Buys 28 mss/year. Query with published clips. Length: 900-3,000 words. Pays $400-800. Sometimes pays expenses of writers on assignment.
Tips: "Show a sophisticated knowledge of business concerns. Be topical and show the implications of contemporary events on long-term decision making."

‡GSE TODAY, P.O. Box 480, Hatch NM 87937. Fax: (505)267-1920. Managing Editor: Dixie Binning. 50% freelance written. Bimonthly magazine. "Our readers are those aviation professionals who are involved in ground support—the equipment manufacturers, the suppliers, the ramp operators, ground handlers, airport and airline managers. We cover issues of interest to this community—deicing, ramp safety, equipment technology, pollution, etc." Estab. 1993. Circ. 15,000. Pays on publication. Publishes ms an average of 2 months after acceptance. Buys all rights. Editorial lead time 2 months. Accepts unsolicited mss. Reports in 3 weeks on queries; 3 months on mss. Sample copy for 9×11 SAE with 5 first-class stamps.

Nonfiction: How-to (use or maintain certain equipment), interview/profile, new products, personal experience (from ramp operators), technical aspects of ground support equipment and issues, industry events, meetings, new rules and regulations. Buys 12-20 mss/year. Send complete ms. Length: 400-3,000 words. Pays 25¢/published word.

Reprints: Send photocopy or typed ms with rights for sale noted and information about when and where the article previously appeared. Pays 50% of the amount paid for an original article.

Photos: Send photos with submissions. Reviews 5×7 prints. Offers no additional payment for photos accepted with ms. Identification of subjects required. Buys all rights.

Tips: "Write about subjects that relate to ground services. Write in clear and simple terms—personal experience is always welcome. If you have an aviation background or ground support experience, let us know."

MOUNTAIN PILOT, 7009 S. Potomac St., Englewood CO 80112-4209. (303)397-7600. Fax: (303)397-7619. E-mail: ehuber@winc.usa.com. Publisher/Editor: Edward D. Huber. 50% freelance written. Bimonthly magazine on mountain flying performance, aviation and aerospace in the West. Considers anything on mountain flying or destination. Also camping at mountain airstrips. Estab. 1985. Circ. 15,000. Pays on publication. Publishes ms an average of 6 months after acceptance. Byline given. Offers $25 kill fee. Buys all rights. Submit seasonal/holiday material 6 months in advance. Sample copy available. Writing and photographic guidelines available.

Nonfiction: Editorial material focuses on mountain performance—flying, safety and education. Regular features include: aviation experiences, technology, high-altitude maintenance and flying, cold-weather tips and pilot techniques. Buys 18-35 mss/year. Send cover letter with copy of ms, Mac or DOS file saved as text only, unformed ASCII, or in QuarkXPress (Mac) on 3½-inch floppy diskette (telephonic submissions (303)397-6987), author's bio and photo. Length: 800-2,000 words. Pay starts at $50/published page (includes text and photos).

Reprints: Send tearsheet or photocopy of article or short story and information about when and where the article previously appeared.

Photos: Send photos with submission (copies acceptable for evaluation). Credit line given.

Columns/Departments: Mountain airports, lodging, survival, mountain flying, travel, product news and reviews, industry news. *Mountain Pilot* purchases first serial rights. May consider second serial reprint rights; query.

BEAUTY AND SALON

AMERICAN SALON, Advanstar, 270 Madison Ave., New York NY 10016. (212)951-6600. Fax: (212)481-6562. Website: http://www.hairnet.com. Editor: Lorraine Korman. Contact: Amanda Hathaway, managing editor. 5% freelance written. Monthly magazine covering "business stories of interest to salon owners and stylists, distributors and manufacturers of professional beauty products." Estab. 1876. Circ. 132,000. **Pays on acceptance**. Publishes ms an average of 3 months after acceptance. Byline given. Offers 50% kill fee. Buys first North American serial rights. Editorial lead time 3 months. Sample copy and writer's guidelines free.

Nonfiction: Query. Length: 250-1,000 words. Pays $300-500.

Reprints: Send typed ms with rights for sale noted. Payment negotiable.

COSMETICS, Canada's Business Magazine for the Cosmetics, Fragrance, Toiletry and Personal Care Industry, Maclean Hunter Publishing Ltd., 777 Bay St., 5th Floor, Toronto, Ontario M5W 1A7 Canada. (416)596-5817. Fax: (416)596-5179. E-mail: rawood@mhpublishing.com. Website: http://www.mhbizlink.com.cosmetics. Editor: Ronald A. Wood. 35% freelance written; "99.9% of freelance articles are assigned by the editor to writers whose work he is familiar with and who have a broad knowledge of this industry as well as contacts, etc." Bimonthly magazine. "Our main reader segment is the retail trade—department stores, drugstores, salons, estheticians—owners and cosmeticians/beauty advisors; plus manufacturers, distributors, agents and suppliers to the industry." Estab. 1972. Circ. 13,000. **Pays on acceptance**. Publishes ms an average of 3 months after acceptance. Byline given. Offers 50% kill fee. Buys all rights. Editorial lead time 4 months. Submit seasonal material 4 months in advance. Reports in 1 month. Sample copy for $6 (Canadian) and 8% GST.

Nonfiction: General interest, interview/profile, photo feature. Buys 60 mss/year. Query. Length: 250-1,200 words. Pays 25¢/word. Sometimes pays expenses of writers on assignment.

Photos: Send photos with submission. Reviews transparencies (2½ up to 8×10) and prints (4×6 up to 8×10). Offers no additional payment for photos accepted with ms. Captions, model releases and identification of subjects required. Buys all rights.

Columns/Departments: Behind the Scenes (brief profile of person not directly involved with major industry firms), 300 words and portrait photo. Buys 28 mss/year, "all assigned on a regular basis from correspondents and columnists that we know personally from the industry." Pays 25¢/word.

Tips: "Must have broad knowledge of the Canadian cosmetics, fragrance and toiletries industry and retail business."

DERMASCOPE MAGAZINE, The Encyclopedia of Aesthetics, Geneva Corporation, 3939 E. Hwy. 80, #408, Mesquite TX 75150. Fax: (214)686-5901. E-mail: dermascope@aol.com. Website: http://www.dermascope.com. Editor:

Saundra Wallens. Bimonthly magazine. "Our magazine is a source of practical advice and continuing education for skin care and body and spa therapy professionals. Our main readers are salon, day spa and destination spa owners, managers or technicians." Estab. 1976. Circ. 10,000. Pays on publication. Publishes ms an average of 6 months after acceptance. Byline given. Buys all rights. Editorial lead time 6 months. Submit seasonal material 9 months in advance. Reports in 2 months. Sample copy and writer's guidelines free.

Nonfiction: Book excerpts, general interest, historical/nostalgic, how-to, inspirational, personal experience, photo feature, technical. Buys 6 mss/year. Query with published clips. Length: 700-2,000 words. Pays $50-250.

Photos: State availability of photos with submission. Reviews 4×5 prints. Offers no additional payment for photos accepted with ms. Captions, model releases, identification of subjects required. Buys all rights.

Tips: "Write from the practitioner's point of view. Step-by-step how to's that show the skin care and body and spa therapist practical methodology are a plus. Would like more business and finance ideas, applicable to the industry."

NAILPRO, The Magazine for Nail Professionals, Creative Age Publications, 7628 Densmore Ave., Van Nuys CA 91406. Fax: (818)782-7450. E-mail: nailpro@aol.com. Website: http://nailpro. Editor: Linda Lewis. 75% freelance written. Monthly magazine "written for manicurists and nail technicians working in full-service salons or nails-only salons. It covers technical and business aspects of working in and operating a nail-care service, as well as the nail-care industry in general." Estab. 1989. Circ. 47,000. **Pays on acceptance.** Publishes ms 6 months after acceptance. Byline given. Offers 50% kill fee. Buys one-time, second serial (reprint), simultaneous or all rights. Editorial lead time 3 months. Submit seasonal material 3 months in advance. Accepts simultaneous submissions. Reports in 6 weeks. Sample copy for $2 and $8\frac{1}{2} \times 11$ SASE.

Nonfiction Book excerpts, how-to, humor, inspirational, interview/profile, personal experience, photo feature, technical. No general interest articles or business articles not geared to the nail-care industry. Buys 50 mss/year. Query. Length: 1,000-3,000 words. Pays $150-350.

Reprints: Send typed ms with rights for sale noted and information about when and where the article previously appeared. Pays 50-75% of amount paid for an original article.

Photos: Send photos with submission. Reviews transparencies and prints. Negotiates payment send individually. Model releases and identification of subjects required. Buys one-time rights.

Columns/Departments: Building Business (articles on marketing nail services/products), 1,500-3,000 words; Shop Talk (aspects of operating a nail salon), 1,500-3,000 words; Hollywood File (nails in the news, movies or TV), 1,000-1,500 words. Buys 50 mss/year. Query. Pays $200-300.

NAILS, Bobit Publishing, 2512 Artesia Blvd., Redondo Beach CA 90278-3296. (310)376-8788. Fax: (310)376-9043. E-mail: nailsmag@bobit.com. Website: http://nailsmag.com. Editor: Cyndy Drummey. Contact: Erika Kotite, managing editor. 10% freelance written. Monthly magazine. "*NAILS* seeks to educate on new techniques and products, nail anatomy and health, customer relations, working safely with chemicals, salon sanitation, and the business aspects of running a salon." Estab. 1983. Circ. 55,000. **Pays on acceptance.** Byline given. Buys all rights. Submit seasonal material 4 months in advance. Reports in 3 months on queries. Sample copy and writer's guidelines free for #10 SASE.

Nonfiction: Historical/nostalgic, how-to, inspirational, interview/profile, personal experience, photo feature, technical. "No articles on one particular product, company profiles or articles slanted towards a particular company or manufacturer." Buys 20 mss/year. Query with published clips. Length: 1,200-3,000 words. Pays $200-500. Sometimes pays expenses of writers on assignment.

Photos: State availability of photos with submission. Reviews contact sheets, transparencies and prints (any standard size acceptable). Offers $50-200/photo. Captions, model releases and identification of subjects required. Buys all rights.

Tips: "Send clips and query; *do not send unsolicited manscripts*. We would like to see ideas for articles on a unique salon or a business article that focuses on a specific aspect or problem encountered when working in a salon. The Modern Nail Salon section, which profiles nail salons and full-service salons, is most open to freelancers. Focus on an innovative business idea or unique point of view. Articles from experts on specific business issues—insurance, handling difficult employees, cultivating clients—are encouraged."

SKIN INC. MAGAZINE, The Complete Business Guide for Face & Body Care, Allured Publishing Corp., 362 S. Schmale Rd., Carol Stream IL 60188. (630)653-2155. Fax: (630)653-2192. Publisher/Editor: Marian Raney. Contact: Melinda Taschetta-Millane, managing editor. 30% freelance written. Magazine published 8 times/year. "Manuscripts considered for publication that contain original and new information in the general fields of skin care and makeup, dermatological and esthetician-assisted surgical techniques. The subject may cover the science of skin, the business of skin care and makeup and plastic surgeons on healthy (i.e. non-diseased) skin. Subjects may also deal with raw materials, formulations and regulations concerning claims for products and equipment." Estab. 1988. Circ. 12,000. Pays on publication. Publishes ms an average of 6 months after acceptance. Byline given. No kill fee. Buys all rights. Editorial lead time 6 months. Submit seasonal material 1 year in advance. Reports in 1 week on queries; 1 month on mss. Sample copy and writer's guidelines free.

Nonfiction: General interest, how-to, interview/profile, personal experience, technical. Buys 6 mss/year. Query with published clips. Length: 2,000 words. Pays $100-300 for assigned articles; $50-250 for unsolicited articles.

Photos: State availability of photos with submission. Reviews 3×5 prints. Offers no additional payment for photos accepted with ms. Captions, model releases, identification of subjects required. Buys one-time rights.

Columns/Departments: Dollars & Sense (tips and solutions for managing money), 2,000-2,500 words; Person to Person (managing personnel), 2,000-2,500 words; Marketing for the 90s (marketing tips for salon owners), 2,000-2,500

words; Retail for Profit (retailing products and services in the salon environment), 2,000-2,500 words. Query with published clips. Pays $50-250.
Fillers: Facts, newsbreaks. Buys 6 mss/year. Length: 250-500 words. Pays $50-100.
Tips: Have an understanding of the skin care industry.

BEVERAGES AND BOTTLING

Manufacturers, distributors and retailers of soft drinks and alcoholic beverages read these publications. Publications for bar and tavern operators and managers of restaurants are classified in the Hotels, Motels, Clubs, Resorts and Restaurants category.

AMERICAN BREWER, The Business of Beer, Box 510, Hayward CA 94543-0510. (415)538-9500. Fax: (510)538-7644. Website: www.ambrew.com. Publisher: Bill Owens. 100% freelance written. Magazine published 5 times/year covering micro-breweries. Estab. 1986. Circ. 20,000. Pays on publication. Publishes ms an average of 4 months after acceptance. Byline given. Buys one-time rights. Reports in 2 weeks on queries. Sample copy for $5.
Nonfiction: Business humor, opinion, travel. Query. Length: 1,500-2,500 words. Pays $50-250 for assigned articles.
Reprints: Send tearsheet or photocopy of article.

BEVERAGE WORLD, Strategic Business Communications, 226 W. 26th St., New York NY 10001. (212)822-5930. Fax: (212)822-5931. E-mail: bevworld@aol.com. Editor: Havis Dawson. Monthly magazine on the beverage industry. Estab. 1882. Circ. 35,000. **Pays on acceptance.** Publishes ms an average of 2 months after acceptance. Byline given. Buys all rights. Submit seasonal material 2 months in advance. Accepts simultaneous submissions. Free sample copy and writer's guidelines.
Nonfiction: How-to (increase profit/sales), interview/profile, technical. Buys 15 mss/year. Query with published clips. Length: 1,000-2,500 words. Pays $250/printed page. Sometimes pays expenses of writers on assignment.
Reprints: Send tearsheet, photocopy or typed ms with rights for sale noted and information about when and where the article previously appeared. Pays $250/printed page.
Photos: State availability of photos with submission. Reviews contact sheets. Captions required. Buys one-time rights.
Columns/Departments: Buys 5 mss/year. Query with published clips. Length: 750-1,000 words. Pay varies, $150/minimum.
Tips: "Background in beverage production and marketing a real plus. Business and/or technical writing experience *a must*. Please submit on paper; do not call."

MASSACHUSETTS BEVERAGE BUSINESS, New Beverage Publications Inc., 55 Clarendon St., Boston MA 02116. (617)423-7200. Fax: (617)482-7163. Executive Editor: P.S. Stone. 100% freelance written. Monthly magazine covering beverage alcohol industry. Estab. 1934. Circ. 7,800. Pays on publication. Publishes ms an average of 2 months after acceptance. Byline given. Offers $250-350 kill fee. Buys one-time rights or makes work-for-hire assignments. Editorial lead time 2 months. Submit seasonal material 3 months in advance. Accepts simultaneous submissions.
● *Massachusetts Beverage Business* is expanding its editorial coverage to include cigars, store design, ancillary products, etc.
Nonfiction: General interest, new product, technical, travel. Buys 96 mss/year. Send complete ms. Length: 1,200-3,000 words. Pays $200-300. Sometimes pays expenses of writers on assignment.
Reprints: Send typed ms with rights for sale noted and information about when and where the article previously appeared. Pays 20% of amount paid for an original article.
Photos: Send photos with submission. Reviews negatives, transparencies. Offers no additional payment for photos accepted with ms. Buys one-time rights.

‡MODERN BREWERY AGE, Business Journals, Inc., 50 Day St., Norwalk CT 06854. Fax: (203)852-8175. Editor: Peter V.K. Reid. 5% freelance written. "*Modern Brewery Age* is a bimonthly trade journal focused on the business of making and selling beer. The readership is made up of professionals in the brewing industry, and articles must reflect that level of expertise. Estab. 1933. Circ. 7,000. Pays on publication. Publishes ms an average of 2 months after acceptance. Byline given. Offers 20% kill fee. Buys first rights and second serial (reprint) rights. Editorial lead time 3 months. Reports in 2 months. Sample copy free.
Nonfiction: Historical/nostalgic, interview/profile, technical. No anecdotal essays about beer. Buys 6 mss/year. Query with published clips. Length: 1,000-4,000 words. Pays $200-500. Pays expenses of writers on assignment.
Photos: State availability of photos with submission. Reviews negatives and 5×7 prints. Negotiates payment individually. Captions required. Buys one-time rights.
Columns/Departments: Buys 6 mss/year. Query with published clips. Pays $100-250.
Tips: "Know something about brewing. Send clips showing aptitude for trade writing."

TEA & COFFEE TRADE JOURNAL, Lockwood Trade Journal Co., Inc., 130 W. 42nd St., Suite 1050, New York NY 10036. (212)391-2060. Fax: (212)827-0945. E-mail: teacof@aol.com. Editor: Jane Phillips McCabe. 50% freelance written. Prefers to work with published/established writers. Monthly magazine covering the international coffee and tea market. "Tea and coffee trends are analyzed; transportation problems, new equipment for plants and packaging are featured." Estab. 1901. Circ. 10,000. Pays on publication. Publishes ms an average of 2 months after acceptance. Byline given. Makes work-for-hire assignments. Submit seasonal material 1 month in advance. Accepts simultaneous submissions. Reports in 4 months. Free sample copy.

Nonfiction: Exposé, historical/nostalgic, interview/profile, new product, photo feature, technical. Special issue includes the Coffee Market Forecast and Review (January). "No consumer-related submissions. I'm only interested in the trade." Buys 60 mss/year. Query. Length: 750-1,500 words. Pays $5.50/published inch 4 months after publication.

Photos: State availability of photos with submission. Reviews contact sheets, negatives, transparencies and prints. Pays $5.50/published inch. Captions and identification of subjects required. Buys one-time rights.

Columns/Departments: Specialties (gourmet trends); Transportation (shipping lines). Buys 36 mss/year. Query. Pays $5.50/published inch.

VINEYARD & WINERY MANAGEMENT, P.O. Box 231, Watkins Glen NY 14891-0231. (607)535-7133. Fax: (607)535-2998. E-mail: vandwm@aol.com. Website: http://www.wines.com/vwm-online. Editor: J. William Moffett. 80% freelance written. Bimonthly trade magazine of professional importance to grape growers, winemakers and winery sales and business people. Estab. 1975. Circ. 4,500. Pays on publication. Byline given. Buys first North American serial rights and occasionally simultaneous rights. Reports in 3 weeks on queries; 1 month on mss. Sample copy free. Writer's guidelines for #10 SASE.

Nonfiction: How-to, interview/profile, technical. Subjects are technical in nature and explore the various methods people in these career paths use to succeed, and also the equipment and techniques they use successfully. Business articles and management topics are also featured. The audience is national with western dominance. Buys 30 mss/year. Query. Length: 300-5,000 words. Pays $30-1,000. Pays some expenses of writers on some assignments.

Photos: State availability of photos with submission. Reviews contact sheets, negatives and transparencies. Identification of subjects required. "Black and white often purchased for $20 each to accompany story material; 35mm and/or 4×5 transparencies for $50 and up; 6/year of vineyard and/or winery scene related to story. Query."

Tips: "We're looking for long-term relationships with authors who know the business and write well. Electronic submissions preferred; query for formats."

WINES & VINES, 1800 Lincoln Ave., San Rafael CA 94901-1298. Fax: (415)453-2517. Editor: Philip E. Hiaring. 10-20% freelance written. Works with a small number of new/unpublished writers each year. Monthly magazine for everyone concerned with the grape and wine industry including winemakers, wine merchants, growers, suppliers, consumers, etc. Estab. 1919. Circ. 4,500. Buy first North American serial or simultaneous rights. **Pays on acceptance.** Publishes ms an average of 3 months after acceptance. Special issues: Winetech (January); Vineyard (February); State-of-the-Art (March); Brandy/Specialty Wines, (April); Export-import (May); Enological (June); Statistical (July); Merchandising (August); Marketing (September); Equipment and Supplies (November); Champagne (December). Submit special issue material 3 months in advance. Reports in 2 months. Sample copy for 11×14 SAE with 7 first-class stamps. Free writer's guidelines.

Nonfiction: Articles of interest to the trade. "These could be on grape growing in unusual areas; new winemaking techniques; wine marketing, retailing, etc." Interview, historical, spot news, merchandising techniques and technical. No stories with a strong consumer orientation against trade. Author should know the subject matter, i.e., know proper grape growing/winemaking terminology. Buys 3-4 ms/year. Query. Length: 1,000-2,500 words. Pays 5¢/word. Sometimes pays the expenses of writers on assignment.

Reprints: Send typed ms with rights for sale noted and information about where the article appeared.

Photos: Pays $10 for 4×5 or 8×10 b&w photos purchased with mss. Captions required.

Tips: "Ours is a trade magazine for professionals. Therefore, we do not use 'gee-whiz' wine articles."

BOOK AND BOOKSTORE

Publications for book trade professionals from publishers to bookstore operators are found in this section. Journals for professional writers are classified in the Journalism and Writing category.

BLOOMSBURY REVIEW, A Book Magazine, Dept. WM, Owaissa Communications Co., Inc., 1762 Emerson St., Denver CO 80218-1012. (303)863-0406. Fax: (303)863-0408. E-mail: bloomsb@aol.com. Publisher/Editor-in-chief: Tom Auer. Editor/Associate Publisher: Marilyn Auer. Contact: Lori Kranz, associate editor. 75% freelance written. Bimonthly tabloid covering books and book-related matters. "We publish book reviews, interviews with writers and poets, literary essays and original poetry. Our audience consists of educated, literate, *non-specialized* readers." Estab. 1980. Circ. 50,000. Pays on publication. Publishes ms an average of 4 months after acceptance. Byline given. Buys first or one-time rights. Reports in 4 months. Sample copy for $4 and 9×12 SASE. Writer's guidelines for #10 SASE.

Nonfiction: Essays, interview/profile, book reviews. "Summer issue features reviews, etc., about the American West. *We do not publish fiction.*" Buys 60 mss/year. Query with published clips or send complete ms. Length 800-1,500 words. Pays $10-20. Sometimes pays writers with contributor copies or other premiums "if writer agrees."

Reprints: Considered but not encouraged. Send photocopy of article and information about when and where the article previously appeared. Pays 100% of amount paid for an original article.

Photos: State availability of photos with submissions. Reviews prints. Offers no additional payment for photos accepted with ms. Buys one-time rights.

Columns/Departments: Book reviews and essays. Buys 6 mss/year. Query with published clips or send complete ms. Length: 500-1,500 words. Pays $10-20.

Poetry: Ray Gonzalez, poetry editor. Avant-garde, free verse, haiku, light verse, traditional. Buys 20 poems/year. Submit up to 5 poems at one time. Pays $5-10.

Tips: "We appreciate receiving published clips and/or completed manuscripts. Please—no rough drafts. Book reviews should be of new books (within 6 months of publication)."

THE HORN BOOK MAGAZINE, The Horn Book, Inc., 11 Beacon St., Suite 1000, Boston MA 02108. (617)227-1555. (800)325-1170. Fax: (617)523-0299. E-mail: info@hbook.com. Editor: Roger Sutton. 10% freelance written. Prefers to work with published/established writers. Bimonthly magazine covering children's literature for librarians, booksellers, professors, teachers and students of children's literature. Estab. 1924. Circ. 21,500. Pays on publication. Publishes ms an average of 4 months after acceptance. Byline given. Submit seasonal material 6 months in advance. Accepts simultaneous submissions. Reports in 2 weeks on queries; 1 month on mss. Guidelines available upon request.

Nonfiction: Interview/profile (children's book authors and illustrators); topics of interest to the children's bookworld. Writers should be familiar with the magazine and its contents. Buys 20 mss/year. Query or send complete ms. Length: 1,000-2,800 words. Honorarium paid upon publication.

Tips: "Writers have a better chance of breaking in to our publication with a query letter on a specific article."

LOS ANGELES TIMES BOOK REVIEW, Times Mirror, Times Mirror Square, Los Angeles CA 90053. (213)237-7778. Fax: (213)237-4712. Website: http://www.LATIMES.com. Editor: Steve Wasserman. Deputy Editor: Tom Curen. 90% freelance written. Weekly tabloid reviewing current books. Estab. 1881. Circ. 1,500,000. Pays on publication. Publishes ms an average of 3 weeks after acceptance. Byline given. Offers variable kill fee. Buys first North American serial rights. No unsolicited book reviews or requests for specific titles to review. "Query with published samples— book reviews or literary features." Buys 500 mss/year. Length: 200-1,500 words. Pay varies; approximately 35¢/word.

QUILL & QUIRE, Canada's Magazine of Book News & Reviews, Key Publishers, 70 The Esplanade, Suite 210, Toronto, Ontario M5E 1R2 Canada. (416)360-0044. Fax: (416)955-0794. E-mail: quill@hookup.net. Editor: Scott Anderson. Monthly tabloid covering Canadian book industry. "Our readers are primarily booksellers, librarians, publishers and writers." Estab. 1935. Circ. 7,000. **Pays on acceptance.** Publishes ms an average of 1 month after acceptance. Offers 50% kill fee. Buys all rights. Editorial lead time 2 months. Submit seasonal material 2 months in advance. Reports in 1 month on queries; 2 months on mss. Sample copy for $4.75 (Canadian).

Nonfiction: Essays, interview/profile, opinion, technical, business, book reviews. Buys hundreds of mss/year. Query. Length: 250-3,000 words. Pays $45-1,000 (Canadian). Sometimes pays writers with contributor copies or other premiums. Pays expenses of writers on assignment.

Photos: State availability of photos with submission. Reviews contact sheets. Offers $100-300/photo.

Columns/Departments: Carol Toller, news editor. Writers' Bloc (issues of interest to writers); Terms of Trade (issues relating to book trade in Canada); Circulating (issues relating to librarianship in Canada); all 850-1,000 words. Buys 36 mss/year. Query. Pays $100 (Canadian) minimum.

‡SMALL PRESS MAGAZINE, The Magazine of Independent Publishing, The Jenkins Group, 121 E. Front St., Traverse City MI 49684. (616)933-0445. Fax: (616)933-0448. E-mail: mlink@smallpress.com. Executive Editor: Mardi Link. Assistant Editor: Phil Murphy. 25% freelance written. "*Small Press* is a bimonthly trade journal for small and independent publishing companies. We focus on marketing, promoting and producing books and how independent publishers can compete in this competitive industry. We also run profiles of successful publishers, an awards section and book reviews." Estab. 1982. Circ. 11,500. Pays on publication. Publishes ms an average of 2 months after acceptance. Byline given. Buys first North American serial rights or second serial (reprint) rights or makes work-for-hire assignments. Editorial lead time 2 months. Submit seasonal material 4 months in advance. Accepts simultaneous submissions. Reports in 3 weeks on queries; 1 month on mss. Writer's guidelines for #10 SASE.

Nonfiction: Book excerpts, exposé, essays, how-to, interview/profile. "No consumer-oriented stories. We are a trade magazine for publishers." Buys 20 mss/year. Query with published clips or send complete ms. Length: 900-2,500 words. Pays $200-500. Pays writers with a subscription or bio for book excerpts. Sometimes pays expenses of writers on assignment.

Photos: State availability of photos with submission. Reviews contact sheets and prints. Offers no additional payment for photos accepted with ms. Captions and identification of subjects required. Buys all rights.

Columns/Departments: Buys 10 mss/year. Query with published clips or send complete ms. Pays $25-100.

THE WOMEN'S REVIEW OF BOOKS, The Women's Review, Inc., Wellesley College, Wellesley MA 02181-8259. (617)283-2555. Website: http://www.wellesley.edu/WCW/CRW/WROB/welcome.html. Editor: Linda Gardiner. Monthly newspaper. "Feminist review of recent trade and academic titles by and about women. Reviews recent nonfiction books, primarily." Estab. 1983. Circ. 16,000. Pays on publication. Publishes ms an average of 2 months after acceptance. Byline given. Offers $50 kill fee. Buys first North American serial rights. Editorial lead time 2 months. Reports in 2 months. Sample copy free on request.

Nonfiction: Book reviews only. No articles considered. Query. No unsolicited mss. Buys 200 mss/year. Query with published clips. Pays 12¢/word. Sometimes pays expenses of writers on assignment.

Tips: "Only experienced reviewers for national media are considered. Reviewers must have expertise in subject of book under review. Never send unsolicited manuscripts."

BRICK, GLASS AND CERAMICS

These publications are read by manufacturers, dealers and managers of brick, glass and ceramic retail businesses. Other publications related to glass and ceramics are listed in the Consumer Art and Architecture and Consumer Hobby and Craft sections.

‡GLASS MAGAZINE, For the Architectural Glass Industry, National Glass Association, Suite 302, 8200 Greensboro Dr., McLean VA 22102-3881. (703)442-4890. Fax: (703)442-0630. Managing Editor-in-Chief: Stan McKenna. 25% freelance written. Prefers to work with published/established writers. Monthly magazine covering the architectural glass industry. Circ. 16,500. **Pays on acceptance.** Publishes ms an average of 3-6 months after acceptance. Byline given. Kill fee varies. Buys first rights only. Reports in 2 months. Sample copy for $5 and 9×12 SAE with 10 first-class stamps. Free writer's guidelines.
Nonfiction: Interview/profile (of various glass businesses; of industry people or business owners); and technical (about glazing processes). Buys 15 mss/year. Query with published clips. Length: 1,000 words minimum. Pays $150-300.
  • They are doing more inhouse writing; freelance cut by half.
Photos: State availability of photos.
Tips: "Do *not* send in general glass use stories. Research the industry first, then query."

STAINED GLASS, Stained Glass Association of America, 6 SW Second St., #7, Lee's Summit MO 64063. Fax: (816)524-9405. E-mail: sgmagaz@kcnet.com. Website: http://www.artglassworld.com/mag/sglass/sgkass.html. Editor: Richard Gross. 70% freelance written. Quarterly magazine. "Since 1906, *Stained Glass* has been the official voice of the Stained Glass Association of America. As the oldest, most respected stained glass publication in North America, *Stained Glass* preserves the techniques of the past as well as illustrates the trends of the future. This vital information, of significant value to the professional stained glass studio, is also of interest to those for whom stained glass is an avocation or hobby." Estab. 1906. Circ. 5,000. Pays on publication. Publishes ms an average of 6 months after acceptance. Byline given. Buys one-time rights. Editorial lead time 3 months. Submit seasonal material 6 months in advance. Accepts simultaneous submissions. Reports in 3 months. Sample copy and writer's guidelines free.
Nonfiction: How-to, humor, interview/profile, new product, opinion, photo feature, technical. Strong need for technical and how to create architectural type stained glass. Glass etching, use of etched glass in stained glass compositions, framing. Buys 9 mss/year. Query or send complete ms but must include photos or slides—very heavy on photos. Pays $25/page. Sometimes pays expenses of writers on assignment.
Reprints: Accepts previously published submissions from non-stained glass publications only. Send tearsheet of article. Pay negotiable.
Photos: Send slides with submission. Reviews 4×5 transparencies. Pays $75 for non-illustrated. Pays $125 plus 3 copies for line art or photography. Identification of subjects required. Buys one-time rights.
Columns/Departments: Teknixs (technical, how-to, stained and glass art), word length varies by subject. Buys 4 mss/year. Query or send complete ms, but must be illustrated.
Tips: "Writers should be extremely well versed in the glass arts. Photographs are extremely important and must be of very high quality. Very sight-oriented magazine. Submissions without photographs or illustrations are seldom considered unless something special and writer states that photos are available. However, prefer to see with submission."

‡US GLASS, METAL & GLAZING, Key Communications Inc., P.O. Box 569, Garrisonville VA 22463. Editor: Helen Price. 25% freelance written. Monthly magazine for companies involved in the auto glass and flat glass trades. Estab. 1966. Circ. 23,000. Pays on publication. Publishes ms an average of 3 months after acceptance. Byline given. Buys all rights. Editorial lead time 3 months. Submit seasonal material 2 months in advance. Accepts simultaneous submissions. Reports in 1 month on queries; 2 months on mss. Sample copy and writer's guidelines for $10.
Nonfiction: Helen Price. How-to, new product, technical. Buys 12 mss/year. Query with published clips. Pays $300-600 for assigned articles. Sometimes pays expenses of writers on assignment.
Photos: State availability of photos with submission. Reviews contact sheets. Offers no additional payment for photos accepted with ms. Captions, identification of subjects required. Buys first North American rights.

BUILDING INTERIORS

Owners, managers and sales personnel of floor covering, wall covering and remodeling businesses read the journals listed in this category. Interior design and architecture publications may be found in the Consumer Art, Design and Collectibles category. For journals aimed at other construction trades see the Construction and Contracting section.

THE PAINT DEALER, Dedicated to the Retail Paint Market, Mugler Publications, 111A N. Kirkwood Rd., St. Louis MO 63122. (314)984-0800. Fax: (314)984-0866. E-mail: primecoat@aol.com. Website: http://www.paintdealer.c

om. Contact: Mike Matthews, editor. Associate Editor: Jerry Rabushka. Monthly magazine "for retail paint store owners and paint/sundry buyers in larger chains. Topics covered are new products and how to use them, how to sell, how to manage or operate store, laws and regulations that affect architectural paint industry." Estab. 1992. Circ. 26,000 (U.S. and Canada). Pays on publication. Byline sometimes given. Buys one-time rights. Editorial lead time 3 months. Reports in 3 weeks on queries; 2 months on mss. Sample copy for $3. Writer's guidelines for #10 SASE.

Nonfiction: How-to, new product, technical, store management. Query with published clips. Length: 750-2,000 words. Pays $50-250. Sometimes pays expenses of writers on assignment.

Reprints: Accepts previously published submissions.

Photos: Send photos with submission. Offers no additional payment for photos accepted with ms.

Tips: "We are very specifically targeted and follow a pre-planned editorial calendar. Unsolicited manuscripts probably won't fit in. Best to check first. Frankly, we don't use a lot of freelancers but welcome inquiries."

PWC, Painting & Wallcovering Contractor, Finan Publishing Co. Inc., 8730 Big Bend Blvd., St. Louis MO 63119-3730. (314)961-6644. Fax: (314)961-4809. E-mail: jbeckner@finan.com. Website: http://www.paintstore.com. Editor: Jeffery Beckner. 90% freelance written. Bimonthly magazine. "*PWC* provides news you can use: information helpful to the painting and wallcovering contractor in the here and now." Estab. 1928. Circ. 30,000. Pays 30 days after acceptance. Publishes ms an average of 1 month after acceptance. Byline given. Kill fee determined on individual basis. Buys first North American serial rights. Editorial lead time 2 months. Submit seasonal material 2 months in advance. Accepts simultaneous submissions. Reports in 2 weeks. Sample copy free.

Nonfiction: Essays, exposé, how-to (painting and wallcovering), interview/profile, new product, opinion personal experience. Buys 40 mss/year. Query with published clips. Length: 1,500-2,500 words. Pays $300 minimum. Pays expenses of writers on assignment.

Reprints: Send photocopy of article and information about when the article appeared. Negotiates payment.

Photos: State availability of or send photos with submission. Reviews contact sheets, negatives, transparencies and prints. Offers no additional payment for photos accepted with ms. Identification of subjects required. Buys one-time and all rights.

Columns/Departments: Anything of interest to the small businessman, 1,250 words. Buys 2 mss/year. Query with published clips. Pays $50-100.

Tips: "We almost always buy on assignment. The way to break in is to send good clips; I'll try and give you work."

‡REMODELING, Hanley-Wood, Inc., One Thomas Circle NW, Suite 600, Washington DC 20005. (202)452-0800. Fax: (202)785-1974. E-mail: cweber@hanley-wood.com. Website: http://www.remodeling.hw.net. Editor-in-Chief: Paul Deffenbaugh. 10% freelance written. Monthly magazine covering residential and light commercial remodeling. "We cover the best new ideas in remodeling design, business, construction and products." Estab. 1985. Circ. 98,000. Pays on publication. Publishes ms an average of 3 months after acceptance. Byline given. Offers 5¢/word kill fee. Buys first North American serial rights. Reports in 1 month. Free sample copy and writer's guidelines.

Nonfiction: Interview/profile, small business trends, new product, technical. Buys 6 mss/year. Query with published clips. Length: 250-1,000 words. Pays 50¢/word. Sometimes pays the expenses of writers on assignment.

Photos: State availability of photos with submission. Reviews slides, 4×5 transparencies and 8×10 prints. Offers $25-100/photo. Captions, model releases and identification of subjects required. Buys one-time rights for print and electronic format.

Tips: "We specialize in service journalism for remodeling contractors. Knowledge of the industry is essential."

‡WALLS & CEILINGS, Dept. WM, 3225 S. MacDill Ave., Suite 129-242, Tampa FL 33629-8171. (813)254-1800. Fax: (813)980-3982. Editor: Greg Campbell. 20% freelance written. Monthly magazine for contractors involved in lathing and plastering, drywall, acoustics, fireproofing, curtain walls, movable partitions together with manufacturers, dealers, and architects. Estab. 1938. Circ. 20,000. Pays on publication. Byline given. Publishes ms an average of 4-6 months after acceptance. Buys all rights within trade. Submit seasonal material 4 months in advance. Accepts simultaneous and previously published submissions. Send tearsheet or photocopy of article or typed ms with rights for sale noted and information about when and where the article previously appeared. For reprints pays 50% of the amount paid for an original article. Reports in 6 months. Sample copy for 9×12 SAE with $2 postage. Writer's guidelines for #10 SASE.

Nonfiction: How-to (drywall and plaster construction and business management), technical. Buys 20 mss/year. Query or send complete ms. Length: 1,000-1,500 words. Pays $50-200. Sometimes pays the expenses of writers on assignment.

Photos: Send photos with submission. Reviews contact sheets, negatives, transparencies and prints. Photos required for ms acceptance, with captions and identification of subjects. Buys one-time rights.

BUSINESS MANAGEMENT

These publications cover trends, general theory and management practices for business owners and top-level business executives. Publications that use similar material but have a less technical slant are listed in the Consumer Business and Finance section. Journals for middle management, including supervisors and office managers, appear in the Management and Supervision section.

Those for industrial plant managers are listed under Industrial Operations and under sections for specific industries, such as Machinery and Metal. Publications for office supply store operators are included in the Office Environment and Equipment section.

ACCOUNTING TECHNOLOGY, Faulkner & Gray (Division of Thompson Professional Publishing), 11 Penn Plaza, New York NY 10001. (212)967-7000. Fax: (212)629-7885. Website: http://www.electronicaccountant.com or http://www.faulknergray.com. Editor: Robert W. Scott. Contact: Mike Cohn, senior editor. 10% freelance written. Magazine published 11 times/year. "*Accounting Technology* is a high quality magazine dedicated to a simple editorial charter. We show our readers how to make more money by applying technology. Our writers must have a background in technology or accounting and a clear readable writing style." Estab. 1984. Circ. 30,000. Pays on publication. Publishes ms an average of 3 months after acceptance. Offers 25% kill fee. Buys first North American, second serial (reprint) rights and electronic rights. Editorial lead time 3 months. Reports in 6 weeks. Sample copy and writer's guidelines free.
Nonfiction: How-to, review. Buys 50 mss/year. Query with published clips; no unsolicited mss. Pays $150-3,000.
Columns/Departments: By assignment only, 2,000 words. Buys 40 mss/year. Query with published clips. Pays $400.

ACCOUNTING TODAY, Faulkner & Gray, 11 Penn Plaza, New York NY 10001. (212)967-7000. Editor: Rick Telberg. Biweekly newspaper. "*Accounting Today* is the newspaper of record for the accounting industry." Estab. 1987. Circ. 35,000. Pays on publication. Publishes ms an average of 1 month after acceptance. Byline given. Buys all rights. Editorial lead time 2 weeks. Reports in 1 month. Sample copy for $5.
Nonfiction: Book excerpts, essays, exposé, how-to, interview/profile, new product, technical. Buys 35 mss/year. Query with published clips. Length: 500-1,500 words. Pays 25-50¢/word for assigned articles. Pays expenses of writers on assignment.
Photos: State availability of photos with submission. Negotiates payment individually.

ACROSS THE BOARD, The Conference Board Magazine, The Conference Board, 845 Third Ave., New York NY 10022. Fax: (212)980-7014. E-mail: atb@conference-board.org. Editor: A.J. Vogl. 60-70% freelance written. Monthly magazine covering general management. "Our audience is primarily senior executives of large American companies." Estab. 1976. Circ. 30,000. Pays on publication. Publishes ms an average of 3 months after acceptance. Byline given. Offers 33% kill fee. Buys first North American serial rights. Editorial lead time 3 months. Accepts simultaneous submissions. Reports in 3 weeks on queries; 2 weeks on mss. Sample copy and writer's guidelines free.
Nonfiction: Book excerpts, essays, how-to, opinion, personal experience. Buys 40 mss/year. Query with published clips, or send complete ms. Length: 2,500-3,500 words. Pays $800-1,000. Sometimes pays expenses of writers on assignment.
Reprints: Send tearsheet or photocopy of article or short story and information about when and where the article previously appeared.
Photos: State availability of photos with submission.
Columns/Departments: Soundings (strong opinions on subjects of pertinence to our readers), 600-800 words. Pays $100-200.

COMMUNICATION BRIEFINGS, Capitol Publications, Inc., Dept. WM, 1101 King St., Suite 110, Alexandria VA 22314. (703)548-3800. Fax: (703)684-2136. Website: http://www.combriefings.com. Editor: Jack Gillespie. Managing Editor: Joe McGavin. 15% freelance written. Prefers to work with published/established writers. Monthly newsletter covering business communication and business management. "Most readers are in middle and upper management. They comprise public relations professionals, editors of company publications, marketing and advertising managers, fund raisers, directors of associations and foundations, school and college administrators, human resources professionals, and other middle managers who want to communicate better on the job." Estab. 1980. Circ. 60,000. **Pays on acceptance.** Publishes ms an average of 3 months after acceptance. Byline given sometimes on Bonus Items and on other items if idea originates with the writer. Buys one-time rights. Submit seasonal material 2 months in advance. Reports in 1 month. Sample copy and writer's guidelines for #10 SAE and 2 first-class stamps.
Nonfiction: "Most articles we buy are 'how-to,' consisting of practical ideas, techniques and advice that readers can use to improve business communication and management. Areas covered: writing, speaking, listening, employee communication, human relations, public relations, interpersonal communication, persuasion, conducting meetings, advertising, marketing, fund raising, telephone techniques, teleconferencing, selling, improving publications, handling conflicts, negotiating, etc. Because half of our subscribers are in the nonprofit sector, articles that appeal to both profit and nonprofit organizations are given priority." *Short Items:* Articles with one or two brief tips that can stand alone.

MARKET CONDITIONS are constantly changing! If this is 1999 or later, buy the newest edition of *Writer's Market* at your favorite bookstore or order directly from Writer's Digest Books.

Length: 40-70 words. *Articles:* A collection of tips or ideas that offer a solution to a communication or management problem or that show a better way to communicate or manage. Examples: "How to produce slogans that work," "The wrong way to criticize employees," "Mistakes to avoid when leading a group discussion," and "5 ways to overcome writer's block." Length: 125-150 words. *Bonus Items:* In-depth pieces that probe one area of communication or management and cover it thoroughly. Examples: "Producing successful special events," "How to evaluate your newsletter," and "How to write to be understood." Length: 1,300 words. Buys 30-50 mss/year. Pays $20-50 for 40- to 150-word pieces; Bonus Items, $300. Pays expenses of writers on assignment.

Reprints: Previously published submissions "must be rewritten to conform to our style."

Tips: "Our readers are looking for specific, practical ideas and tips that will help them communicate better both within their organizations and with outside publics. Most ideas are rejected because they are too general or too elementary for our audience. Our style is down-to-earth and terse. We pack a lot of useful information into short articles. Our readers are busy executives and managers who want information dispatched quickly and without embroidery. We omit anecdotes, lengthy quotes and long-winded exposition. The writer has a better chance of breaking in at our publication with short articles and fillers since we buy only six major features (bonus items) a year. We require queries on longer items and bonus items. Writers may submit short tips (40-70 words) without querying. The most frequent mistakes made by writers completing an article for us are failure to master the style of our publication and to understand our readers' needs."

CONVENTION SOUTH, Covey Communications Corp., 2001 W. First St., P.O. Box 2267, Gulf Shores AL 36547-2267. (334)968-5300. Fax: (334)968-4532. E-mail: info@conventionsouth.com. Contact: Kristen McIntosh, managing editor. Editor: J.Talty O'Connor. 50% freelance written. Monthly tabloid for meeting planners who plan events in the South. Topics relate to the meetings industry—how to articles, industry news, destination spotlights. Estab. 1983. Circ. 10,000. Pays on publication. Publishes ms an average of 2 months after acceptance. Byline given. Buys first rights or second serial (reprint) rights. Editorial lead time 3 months. Submit seasonal/holiday material 2 months in advance. Accepts simultaneous submissions. Reports in 2 months on queries. Sample copy free. Writer's guidelines for #10 SASE.

Nonfiction: How-to (relative to meeting planning/travel), interview/profile, photo feature, technical, travel. Buys 50 mss/year. Query. Length: 1,250-3,000 words. Pays $75-150. Pays in contributor copies or other premiums if arranged in advance. Sometimes pays expenses of writers on assignment.

Reprints: Accepts previously published submissions.

Photos: Send photos with submission. Reviews 5×7 prints. Offers no additional payment for photos accepted with ms. Captions and identification of subjects required. Buys one-time rights.

Columns/Departments: How-tos (related to meetings), 700 words. Buys 12 mss/year. Query with published clips. Payment negotiable.

Tips: "Know who our audience is and make sure articles are appropriate for them."

‡**CREDIT UNION EXECUTIVE, CUNA & Affiliates' Management Journal**, Credit Union National Association, Inc., P.O. Box 431, Madison WI 53701-0431. (608)231-4081. Fax: (608)231-4370. Associate Editor: Mary Mink. Contact: Leigh Gregg, editor. 50% freelance written. Bimonthly magazine. "This publication is directed toward CEO's and senior management of large, sophisticated, leading-edge credit unions. It features articles on management, human resources, lending, marketing, technology and finance, written in a business-like, no-nonsense tone. We're a trade journal." Estab. 1963. Circ. 3,300. **Pays on acceptance**. Publishes ms 4 months after acceptance. Byline given. Makes work-for-hire assignments so CUNA has all rights. Editorial lead time 5 months. Reports in 1 month. Sample copy and writer's guidelines free.

Nonfiction: How to manage operations and functions of credit unions, issues of importance to credit unions and financial industry. No first-person, humor, product promotions. Case studies are OK. Buys 12-15 mss/year. Query with published clips. Length: 650 words for smaller articles, 1,800-2,000 for major features. Pays $500-600 for assigned articles. "We don't pay technical experts or vendors who are seeking wider exposure of their ideas to CU's. They get contributor's copies." Sometimes pays expenses of writers on assignment (usually phone expenses for interviews).

Tips: "Learn about credit unions before you call. Phone queries are OK. We use a lot of how-to articles geared to people running credit unions, not to the consumer or members of credit unions."

‡**EXPANSION MANAGEMENT MAGAZINE, Growth Strategies for Companies On the Move**, New Hope Communications, 9500 Nall, Suite 400, Overland Park KS 66207. (913)381-4800. Fax: (913)381-8858. Editor: Jack Wimer. Contact: Bill King, managing editor. 75% freelance written. Bimonthly magazine covering economic development. Estab. 1986. Circ. 41,000. **Pays on acceptance**. Publishes ms 1 month after acceptance. Byline given. Buys all rights and makes work-for-hire assignments. Editorial lead time 2 months. Sample copy for $7. Writer's guidelines free.

Nonfiction: *Expansion Management* presents articles and industry reports examining relocation trends, strategic planning, work force hiring, economic development agencies, relocation consultants and state, province and county reviews and profiles to help readers select future expansions and relocation sites." Buys 120 mss/year. Query with published clips. Length: 1,000-1,500 words. Pays $200-400 for assigned articles. Sometimes pays the expenses of writers on assignment.

Photos: Send photos with submission. Offers no additional payment for photos accepted with ms. Captions required. Buys one-time rights.

Tips: "Send clips first, then call me."

‡EXPORT TODAY, Trade Communications, Inc., 733 15th St. NW, Washington DC 20005. Fax: (202)483-5966. E-mail: julie@exporttoday.com. Editor: Barry Lynn. Contact: Erika Murphy. 25% freelance written. "Monthly magazine covering international trade and business for upper level executives at North American companies that actively export products or services or invest directly in overseas markets." Estab. 1985. Circ. 80,000. Pays within a month of publication. Byline given. Buys all rights. Editorial lead time 2 months. Submit seasonal material 1 month in advance. Reports in 2 weeks on queries; 1 month on mss. Sample copy for $3 (checks payable to *Export Today*).
Nonfiction: How-to (international business, finance, transportation). Buys 25 mss/year. Query with published clips. Length: 2,000 words. Pays $500-750. Pays writers with contributor copies or other premiums if the writer is in the business of trade and stands to benefit from the publication of an article in our magazine.
Photos: State availability of photos with submission. Reviews transparencies. Negotiates payment individually. Identification of subjects required. Buys one-time rights.
Columns/Departments: Query with published clips. Pays $250 minimum.
Tips: "Know the details of international business from the perspective of the businessperson."

‡HARVARD BUSINESS REVIEW, 60 Harvard Way, Boston MA 02163. (617)495-6800. Fax: (617)496-8145. E-mail: hbr_editorial@hbsp.harvard.edu. Editor: Nan Stone. Bimonthly magazine for senior and upper-middle managers. Circ. 209,300. **Pays on acceptance**. Byline given. Offers 40-50% kill fee. Buys all rights. Accepts previously published submissions. Reports in 1 month. Writer's guidelines for #10 SASE.
Nonfiction: Buys 36 mss/year. Query. Length: 5,000 minimum words. Pay $100 and 8 contributor's copies.
Columns/Departments: Buys 30 mss/year. Query. Pay varies. Length: 3,000 minimum words.
Fillers: Length: 2,500 minimum words. Pay varies.
Tips: "We are looking for first-rate thinkers in the area of general management. Articles generally should be supported by detailed research/case studies."

HR MAGAZINE, Society for Human Resource Management, 606 N. Washington St., Alexandria VA 22314. (703)548-3440. Fax: (703)836-0367. E-mail: hrmag@shrm.org. Website: http://www.shrm.org. Editor: Leon Rubis. Monthly magazine covering human resource professions "with special focus on business news that affects the workplace including court decisions, legislative actions and government regulations." Estab. 1950. Circ. 78,000. **Pays on acceptance.** Publishes ms an average of 4 months after acceptance. Byline given. Buys first North American, first, one-time, all or world rights or makes work-for-hire assignments. Writer's guidelines free.
Nonfiction: Interview/profile, new product, opinion, personal experience, technical. Buys 20-30 mss/year. Query. Length: 700-2,200 words. Pays expenses of writers on assignment.
Photos: State availability of photos with submission. Reviews contact sheets. Model releases and identification of subjects required. Buys electronic rights.

HR NEWS, Society for Human Resource Management, 606 N. Washington St., Alexandria VA 22314. (703)548-3440. Fax: (703)836-0367. E-mail: hrnews@shrm.org. Website: http://www.shrm.org. Editor: Leon Rubis. Monthly tabloid covering human resource professions "with special focus on business news that affects the workplace including court decisions, legislative actions and government regulations." Estab. 1982. Circ. 78,000. Pays on publication. Publishes ms an average of 1 month after acceptance. Byline given. Buys first or one-time rights or makes work-for-hire assignments. Editorial lead time 2 months. Reports in 1 month on queries. Sample copy and writer's guidelines free.
Nonfiction: Interview/profile, business trends. Buys 8-12 mss/year. Query with published clips. Length: 300-1,000 words. Sometimes pays expenses of writers on assignment.
Photos: State availability of photos with submission. Reviews contact sheets, any prints. Negotiates payment individually. Captions and identification of subjects required. Buys one-time rights.
Tips: "Experienced business/news writers should send some clips and story ideas for our file of potential writers in various regions and for various subjects. Local/state business news or government actions affecting HR management of potentially national interest is an area open to freelancers."

‡JOURNAL OF ACCOUNTANCY, American Institution of CPAs, 201 Plaza 3, Harborside Financial Center, Jersey City NJ 07311. Editor: Colleen Katz. Managing Editor: Elizabeth Uva. Contact: Sarah Cobb, manuscript editor. 10% freelance written. Monthly magazine. "The Journal is published as a teaching tool for CPAs in public practice and in business and industry. Any business problem encountered by them is a good subject for the J of A as long as it is clearly stated and the solution given. Actual case studies are desired." Estab. 1897. Circ. 350,000. **Pays on acceptance**. Publishes ms an average of 3 months after acceptance. Byline given. Offers 25% kill fee. Buys all rights. Editorial lead time 4 months. Reports in 2 weeks on queries; 2 months on mss. Sample copy and writer's guidelines free.
Nonfiction: How-to, technical, business solutions. No non-business or non-CPA-related pieces. Buys 12-20 mss/year. Query with published clips and final ms. Length: 1,000-2,000 words. Pays $1,000-2,000. Sometimes pays expenses of writers on assignment.
Photos: State availability of photos with submission. Reviews transparencies. Negotiates payment individually. Identification of subjects required. Buys one-time rights.
Tips: "We want practical, how-to, implementation articles, based on CPAs' experience in solving companies' problems in areas such as financial reporting, mgt. accounting, cost management, benefits/compensation, technology, human resources, that is, teaching models."

‡MAY TRENDS, George S. May International Company, 303 S. Northwest Hwy., Park Ridge IL 60068-4255. (708)825-8806. Fax: (708)825-7937. Editor: Rosalind J. Angell. 20% freelance written. Works with a small number of new/unpublished writers each year. Free magazine published 1-2 times/year for owners and managers of small and medium-sized businesses, hospitals and nursing homes, trade associations, Better Business Bureaus, educational institutions and newspapers. Estab. 1966. Circ. 30,000. Buys all rights. Byline given. Pays on publication. Publishes ms an average of 6 months after acceptance. Returns rejected material immediately. Reports in 2 months. Sample copy for 9×12 SAE with 4 first-class stamps.

Nonfiction: "We prefer articles dealing with how to solve problems of specific industries (manufacturers, wholesalers, retailers, service businesses, small hospitals and nursing homes) where contact has been made with key executives whose comments regarding their problems may be quoted. We want problem solving articles, *not* success stories that laud an individual company. We like articles that give the business manager concrete suggestions on how to deal with specific problems—i.e., 'five steps to solve . . .,' 'six key questions to ask when . . .,' and 'four tell-tale signs indicating . . . .' Focus is on marketing, economic and technological trends that have an impact on medium- and small-sized businesses, not on the 'giants'; automobile dealers coping with existing dull markets; and contractors solving cost-inventory problems. Will consider material on successful business operations and merchandising techniques." Buys up to 10 mss/year. Query or submit complete ms. Length: 2,000-3,000 words. Pays $250-500.

Tips: Query letter should tell "type of business and problems the article will deal with. We specialize in the problems of small (20-100 employees, $800,000-10,000,000 volume) businesses (manufacturing, wholesale, retail and service), plus medium and small health care facilities. We are now including nationally known writers in each issue—writers like the Vice Chairman of the Federal Reserve Bank, CEO of Chrysler, CEO of Microsoft; titles like the Chairman of the Joint Committee on Accreditation of Hospitals; and Canadian Minister of Export. Frequent mistakes: 1) writing for big business, rather than small; and 2) using language that is too academic."

‡MINI-STORAGE MESSENGER, MiniCo., Inc., 2531 W. Dunlap Ave., Phoenix AZ 85021. (602)870-1711. Fax: (602)861-1094. E-mail: messenger@minico.com. Contact: Tricia van Zelst, managing editor. 90% freelance written. Monthly magazine. "The Mini-Storage Messenger is written for owners and managers of self-storage facilities to help them run their business on a day-to-day basis. Topics include marketing, management, legal and operations." Estab. 1979. Circ. 6,000. **Pays on acceptance.** Publishes ms an average of 3 months after acceptance. Byline given. Offers 25% kill fee. Buys first rights and second serial (reprint) rights. Editorial lead time 4 months. Submit seasonal material 4 months in advance. Sample copy and writer's guidelines free.

Nonfiction: How-to (anything related to self-storage, e.g., how to market your facility); interview/profile. Buys 72 mss/year. Query. Length: 2,000-2,500 words. Pays $200-350 for assigned articles; $50-350 for unsolicited articles.

Columns/Departments: Finance, Legal, Management, Marketing, Operations. Length: 800-1,000 words. Buys 48 mss/year. Query. Pays $50-350.

Tips: "The *Mini-Storage Messenger* is very how-to oriented. Our intention is to help managers/owners run all aspects of their business. Step-by-step approaches, 10 tips, etc. are succinct and very appropriate articles. Articles should be specific to self-storage with real-life examples."

‡MINORITY BUSINESS ENTREPRENEUR (MBE), 3528 Torrance Blvd., Suite 101, Torrance CA 90503. (310)540-9398. Fax: (310)792-8263. E-mail: mbewbe@ix.netcom.com. Editor: Jeanie M. Barnett. Managing Editor: Lauren L. Bechen. 50% freelance written. Bimonthly magazine covering minority and women business ownership and development. Estab. 1984. Circ. 40,000. Pays on publication. Byline given. Buys first North American serial rights. Editorial lead time 3 months. Reports in 3 weeks on queries. Sample copy for $9½ \times 12½$ SASE and 7 first-class stamps. Writer's guidelines free.

Nonfiction: Interview/profile. Nothing unrelated to minority or women's business. Buys 4-6 mss/year. Query with published clips. Length: 750-1,000 words. Pays $0-300. Sometimes pays expenses of writers on assignment.

NATIONAL HOME CENTER NEWS, International News & Analysis for the Retail Home Improvement Industry, Lebhan-Friedman Inc., 425 Park Ave., New York NY 10022. (212)256-5107. Fax: (212)756-5295. Editor: Don Longo. Managing Editor: Lisa Gither Huh. Contact: John Caulfield, executive editor. 5% freelance written. Biweekly tabloid. "Articles require a broad in-depth knowledge of the retail home improvement market. Issues consist of a mix of news (company expansion, executive movement, financial developments), trends (customer service, consumer research, etc.) and merchandising (product category reports)." Estab. 1974. Circ. 53,000. Pays on publication. Publishes ms 1 month after acceptance. Byline given. Kill fee negotiated. Buys all rights. Editorial lead time 3 months. Submit seasonal material 3 months in advance. Reports ASAP. Sample copy for 11×14 SAE with 3 first-class stamps.

Nonfiction: How-to, interview/profile, photo feature, product trends. Buys 48 mss/year. Query with or without published clips. Length: 500-1,000 words. Pays $300-500. Sometimes pays expenses of writers on assignment.

Photos: State availability of photos with submission. Reviews contact sheets, negatives, transparencies, 5×7 prints. Negotiates payment individually. Buys all rights.

‡NORTHEAST EXPORT, A Magazine for New England Companies Exporting to the World, Laurentian Business Publishing, 404 Chestnut St., Suite 201, Manchester NH 03101-1831. (603)626-6354. Fax: (603)626-6359. Editor: Anita Becker. 80% freelance written. Bimonthly business-to-business magazine. "*Northeast Export* is the only publication directly targeted at New England's $21 billion export business community. All stories relate only to issues affecting New England exporters and feature only new exporters as profiles and examples. No unsolicited material."

Estab. 1997. Circ. 12,500. Pays on publication. Byline given. Offers 10% kill fee. Buys all rights. Editorial lead time 2 months. Sample copy free.

Nonfiction: Interview/profile, new product, industry trends/analysis. "We will not take unsolicited articles. Query first with clips." Buys 18-20 mss/year. Query with published clips. Length: 700-3,510 words. Pay varies.

Photos: State availability of photos with submission or send photos with submission. Reviews 2¼ transparencies and 5×7 prints. Negotiates payment individually. Captions, model releases and identification of subjects required. Buys one-time rights.

Tips: "We're interested in freelancers with a knowledge of business writing and magazine style, especially those with contacts in the New England manufacturing/exporting community."

‡OREGON BUSINESS, Oregon Business Media, 610 SW Broadway, Suite 200, Portland OR 97205. Fax: (503)221-6544. Website: http://www.oregonbusiness.com. Editor: Kathy Dimond. Contact: Shirleen Holt, managing editor. 30% freelance written. Monthly magazine covering business in Oregon. "Stories are designed to help Oregon companies grow. We accept *only* stories about Oregon businesses, issues and trends. No unsolicited mss." Estab. 1981. Circ. 19,490. Pays on publication. Publishes ms an average of 2 months after acceptance. Byline given. Buys first North American serial and electronic rights. Editorial lead time 2 months. Submit seasonal material 2 months in advance. Accepts simultaneous submissions. Reports in 1 month. Sample copy $4. Writer's guidelines for #10 SASE.

Nonfiction: How-to, interview/profile, new product. No non-Oregon pieces or fiction. Buys 40 mss/year. Query with published clips. Length: 500-3,000 words. Pays $325 minimum. Sometimes pays expenses of writers on assignment.

Photos: State availability of photos with submission. Reviews 2×3 transparencies. Offers $85-450/photo. Identification of subjects required. Buys one-time rights.

‡PROFESSIONAL COLLECTOR, Cadmus Custom Publishing, 101 Huntington Ave., 13th Floor, Boston MA 02199-7603. (617)424-7700. Fax: (617)437-7714. E-mail: procollector@cadmuscustom.com. Editor: Michael Buller. Contact: Leeann Boyer, managing editor. 90% freelance written. Quarterly magazine covering debt collection business/lifestyle issues. "We gear our articles directly to the debt collectors, not their managers." Estab. 1993. Circ. 135,000. Pays on publication. Byline given. Buys first North American serial rights. Editorial lead time 4 months. Submit seasonal material 4 months in advance. Sample copy and writer's guidelines free.

Nonfiction: Book excerpts, general interest, how-to (tips on good collecting), humor, interview/profile, new product, legal issues for collectors/FDCPA, business/industry issues dealing with debt collectors. Buys 10-15 mss/year. Query with published clips. Length: 750-2,000 words. Pays 50¢-$1/word for assigned articles. Sometimes pays expenses of writers on assignment.

Photos: State availability of photos with submission. Reviews contact sheets and 3×5 prints. Negotiates payment individually. Captions, model releases and identification of subjects required. Buys one-time rights.

Columns/Departments: Collectors & the Courts (collections legal issues), 750-1,000 words; Industry Roundup (issues within industry), 750-1,000 words; Tips, 750-1,000 words; Q&A (questions & answers for collectors), 1,500 words. Buys 15-20 mss/year. Query with published clips. Pays 50¢-$1/word.

Tips: "It helps to have extensive insider knowledge about the debt collection industry."

RECORDS MANAGEMENT QUARTERLY, Association of Records Managers and Administrators, Inc., 310 Appomattox Dr., Brentwood TN 37027. Editor: Ira A. Penn, CRM, CSP. 10% freelance written. Eager to work with new/unpublished writers. Quarterly professional journal covering records and information management. Estab. 1967. Circ. 12,000. Pays on publication. Publishes ms an average of 6 months after acceptance. Byline given. Buys all rights. Accepts simultaneous submissions. Reports in 1 month on mss. Sample copy $16. Free writer's guidelines.

Nonfiction: Professional articles covering theory, case studies, surveys, etc., on any aspect of records and information management. Buys 20-24 mss/year. Send complete ms. Length: 2,500 words minimum. Pays $50-300 "stipend"; no contract.

Photos: Send photos with ms. Offers no additional payment for photos. Prefers b&w prints. Captions required.

Tips: "A writer *must* know our magazine. Most work is written by practitioners in the field. We use very little freelance writing, but we have had some and it's been good. A writer must have detailed knowledge of the subject he/she is writing about. Superficiality is not acceptable."

‡RENTAL MANAGEMENT, American Rental Association, 1900 19th St., Moline IL 61265. Editor: Brian R. Alm. Managing Editor: Tamera Dawson. 30% freelance written. This is a monthly business magazine for the equipment rental industry worldwide (*not* property, real estate, appliances, furniture or cars), emphasizing management topics in particular but also marketing, merchandising, technology, etc. Estab. 1970. Circ. 15,500. **Pays on acceptance**. Publishes ms an average of 3 months after acceptance. Byline sometimes given. Buys first North American serial rights. Editorial lead time 2 months. Submit seasonal material 3 months in advance. Does not report on unsolicited work unless being considered for publication. Sample copy for 9×12 SAE and 6 first-class stamps.

Nonfiction: Small-business management and marketing. Buys 4-5 mss/year. Query with published clips. Length: 300-2,000 words. Pay is negotiated. Sometimes pays expenses of writers on assignment.

Photos: State availability of photos with submission. Reviews contact sheets, negatives, 35mm or 2¼ transparencies and any size prints. Negotiates payment individually. Identification of subjects required. Buys one-time rights.

Columns/Departments: "We are adequately served by existing columnists and have a long waiting list of others to use pending need." Buys 20 mss/year. Query with published clips. Pay is negotiated.

Tips: "Show me you can write maturely, cogently and fluently on management matters of direct and compelling interest to the small-business owner or manager in a larger operation; no sloppiness, no unexamined thoughts, no stiffness or affectation—genuine, direct and worthwhile English."

‡**RETAIL INFO SYSTEMS NEWS, Where retail management shops for technology**, Edgell Communications, 1 W. Hanover Ave., Randolph NJ 07869. Editor: Mark Frantz. 60% freelance written. Monthly magazine. "Readers are functional managers/executives in all types of retail and consumer goods firms. They are making major improvements in company operations and in alliances with customers/suppliers." Estab. 1988. Circ. 18,500. Pays on publication. Byline sometimes given. Buys first rights and second serial (reprint) rights. Editorial lead time 2-3 months. Submit seasonal material 3 months in advance. Sample copy for 11×15 SAE with 6 first-class stamps. Guidelines for #10 SAE.
Nonfiction: How-to, interview/profile, technical. Buys 100 mss/year. Query with published clips. Length: 1,200-2,400 words. Pays $500 maximum for assigned articles. Sometimes pays in contributor copies as negotiated. Sometimes pays expenses of writers on assignment.
Photos: Send photos with submission. Reviews contact sheets, negatives, transparencies and prints. Offers no additional payment for photos accepted with ms. Identification of subjects required. Buys one-time rights plus reprint, if applicable.
Tips: "Case histories about companies achieving substantial results using advanced management practices and/or advanced technology are best intro."

SECURITY DEALER, PTN Publishing Co., 445 Broad Hollow Rd., Melville NY 11747. (516)845-2700. Fax: (516)845-7109. Editor: Susan A. Brady. 25% freelance written. Monthly magazine for electronic alarm dealers, burglary and fire installers, with technical, business, sales and marketing information. Circ. 25,000. Pays 3 weeks after publication. Publishes ms an average of 4 months after acceptance. Byline sometimes given. Buys first North American serial rights. Accepts simultaneous submissions.
Nonfiction: How-to, interview/profile, technical. No consumer pieces. Query or send complete ms. Length: 1,000-3,000 words. Pays $300 for assigned articles; $100-200 for unsolicited articles. Sometimes pays the expenses of writers on assignment.
Photos: State availability of photos with submission. Reviews contact sheets and transparencies. Offers $25 additional payment for photos accepted with ms. Captions and identification of subjects required.
Columns/Departments: Closed Circuit TV, Access Control (both on application, installation, new products), 500-1,000 words. Buys 25 mss/year. Query. Pays $100-150.
Tips: "The areas of our publication most open to freelancers are technical innovations, trends in the alarm industry and crime patterns as related to the business as well as business finance and management pieces."

‡**SMALL BUSINESS NEWS, Philadelphia/South Jersey edition**, Small Business News, 325 Chestnut St., Suite #1116, Philadelphia PA 19106. (215)923-6395. Fax: (215)923-5059. Website: http://www.sbnpub.com. Editor: Darrell L. Browning. 30% freelance written. Monthly magazine covering regional businesses with 500 employees or less. "We publish business articles showing, *by example*, how smaller businesses grow, avoid mistakes, turn their companies around, use innovation and creativity or engage in new trends to meet business objectives." Estab. 1988. Circ. 27,000. Pays on publication. Byline given. Offers 30% kill fee. Buys all rights. Editorial lead time 2 months. Submit seasonal material 2 months in advance. Sample copy for $2. Writer's guidelines for #10 SASE
Nonfiction: How-to (save on employee turnover, avoid telephone fraud, etc.), opinion (industry trends). No fiction or book reviews. Query with 3 published clips. Length: 350-1,500 words. Pays $150-500.
Tips: "We publish *regional* business news combined with practical advice for owning and operating enterprises having 500 or less employees."

‡**SMALL BUSINESS NEWS, Pittsburgh edition**, Small Business News, Inc. 800 Vinial St., Suite B-208, Pittsburgh PA 15060. (412)321-6050. Fax: (412)321-6058. E-mail: sbnpubpi@interramp.com. Editor: Daniel Bates. 5% freelance written. Monthly regional tabloid. "We provide information and insight designed to help companies grow. Our focus is on local companies and their successful business strategies, with the ultimate goal of educating entrepreneurs. Our target audience is business owners and other top executives." Estab. 1992. Circ. 26,000. Pays on publication. Publishes ms an average of 3 months after acceptance. Byline given. Buys all rights and makes work-for-hire assignments. Editorial lead time 2 months. Submit seasonal material 4 months in advance. Reports in 1 month on queries. Sample copy for $3. Writer's guidelines free.
Nonfiction: Book excerpts, how-to, interview/profile, opinion. Annual Golf, Human Resources and Continuing Education Guide. "No basic profiles about 'interesting' companies or stories about companies with no ties to Pittsburgh." Query with published clips. Length: 250-1,000 words. Pays $150-300 for assigned articles.
Photos: State availability of photos with submission. Reviews negatives and transparencies. Negotiates payment individually. Identification of subjects required. Buys one-time rights or all rights.
Tips: "Call the editor and set up a meeting for submission guidelines."

‡**THE STATE JOURNAL**, The State Journal Corp., 904 Virginia St. E., Charleston WV 25301. (304)344-1630. Fax: (304)345-2721. E-mail: sjeditor@aol.com. Editor: Jack Bailey. 30% freelance written. "We are a biweekly journal dedicated to providing stories of interest to the business community in West Virginia." Estab. 1984. Circ. 12,000. Pays on publication. Publishes ms an average of 2 months after acceptance. Byline given. Buys first rights. Editorial lead

time 2 months. Submit seasonal material 4 months in advance. Reports in 3 weeks on queries; 2 months on mss. Sample copy and writer's guidelines for #10 SASE.
Nonfiction: General interest, interview/profile, new product, opinion, all business related. Buys 150 mss/year. Query. Length: 250-1,500 words. Pays $50. Sometimes pays expenses of writers on assignment.
Photos: State availability of photos with submission. Reviews contact sheets. Offers $15/photo. Captions required. Buys one-time rights.
Columns/Departments: Business related, slanted toward West Virginia. Buys 25 mss/year. Query. Pays $50.

CHURCH ADMINISTRATION AND MINISTRY

Publications in this section are written for clergy members, church leaders and teachers. Magazines for lay members and the general public are listed in the Consumer Religious section.

CHILDREN'S MINISTRY, Group Publishing Inc., 2890 N. Monroe Ave., Loveland CO 80538. (303)669-3836. Editor: Christine Yount. Contact; Barbara Beach, departments editor. 73% freelance written. Bimonthly magazine of practical articles for Christian adults who work with children from birth to 6th grade. "The magazine's purpose is to supply practical ideas to help adults encourage children to grow spiritually." Estab. 1991. Circ. 50,000. **Pays on acceptance.** Byline given. Buys all rights. Editorial lead time 6 months. Submit seasonal material 5 months in advance. Reports in 2 months. Sample copy for $2 and 9×12 SAE. Writer's guidelines for #10 SASE.
Nonfiction: How-to (practical, quick teaching ideas—games, crafts, devotional). No "preachy" articles. Query with or without published clips. Length: 50-1,200 words. Pays $25-100. Sometimes pays other than cash payments to reviewers. Sometimes pays expenses of writers on assignment.
Photos: State availability of photos with submission. Reviews contact sheets and prints. Offers $50-75/photo. Buys one-time rights.
Columns/Departments: Preschool Page (hints, songs, Bible activities), 50-125 words; Group Games, 125 words; Seasonal Specials, 125 words; Nursery Notes (help for nursery workers), 125 words; 5-Minute Messages (Scripture based, fun), 125 words; For Parents Only (ideas for parent self-help, communication with children), 125 words. Buys 50 mss/year. Send complete ms. Pays $25.
Tips: "Potential authors should be familiar with children's ministry and its style. Most successful authors are ones who have experience working with children in the church. We like new ideas with 'ah-hahs.' "

CREATOR MAGAZINE, Bimonthly Magazine of Balanced Music Ministries, Church Music Associates Inc., P.O. Box 64775, Tucson AZ 85728. (520)888-0600. Fax: (520)577-4969. E-mail: creatormag@aol.com. Editor: Marshall Sanders. 35% freelance written. Bimonthly magazine. "All readers are church music choir directors. Content focuses on the spectrum of worship styles from praise and worship to traditional to liturgical. All denominations subscribe. Articles on worship, choir rehearsal, handbells, children's/youth choirs, technique, relationships, etc." Estab. 1978. Circ. 6,000. Pays on publication. Publishes ms an average of 3 months after acceptance. Byline given. Buys first rights, one-time rights or second serial (reprint) rights; occasionally buys no rights. Editorial lead time 3 months. Submit seasonal material 4 months in advance. Accepts simultaneous submissions, if so noted. Sample copy for 9×12 SAE with 5 first-class stamps. Writer's guidelines free.
Nonfiction: Essays, how-to (be a better church musician, choir director, rehearsal technician, etc.), humor (short personal perspectives), inspirational, interview/profile (call first), new product (call first), opinion, personal experience, photo feature, religious, technical (choral technique). Special issues: July/August is directed toward adult choir members, rather than directors. Buys 20 mss/year. Query or send complete ms. Length: 1,000-10,000 words. Pays $30-75 for assigned articles; $30-60 for unsolicited articles. Pays expenses of writers on assignment.
Reprints: Accepts previously published submissions.
Photos: State availability of or send photos with submission. Reviews negatives, 8×10 prints. Offers no additional payment for photos accepted with ms. Captions appreciated. Buys one-time rights.
Columns/Departments: Hints & Humor (music ministry short ideas, anecdotes [cute] ministry experience), 75-250 words; Inspiration (motivational ministry stories), 200-500 words; Children/Youth (articles about specific choirs), 1,000-5,000 words. Buys 15 mss/year. Query or send complete ms. Pays $20-60.
Tips: "Request guidelines and stick to them. If theme is relevant and guidelines are followed, we will probably publish."

THE JOURNAL OF ADVENTIST EDUCATION, General Conference of SDA, 12501 Old Columbia Pike, Silver Spring MD 20904-6600. (301)680-5075. Fax: (301)622-9627. E-mail: 74617.1231@compuserve. Editor: Beverly J. Rumble. Bimonthly (except skips issue in summer) professional journal covering teachers and administrators in SDA school system. Estab. 1939. Circ. 7,500. Pays on publication. Publishes ms 1 year after acceptance. Byline given. Buys first rights. Editorial lead time 3 months. Reports in 6 weeks on queries; 4 months on mss. Sample copy for 10×12 SAE with 5 first-class stamps. Writer's guidelines free on request.
Nonfiction: Book excerpts, essays, how-to, personal experience, photo feature, religious, education. Theme issues have assigned authors. "No brief first-person stories about Sunday Schools." Query. Length: 1,000-1,500 words. Pays $25-100.
Reprints: Send tearsheet or photocopy of article and information about when and where the article previously appeared.
Photos: State availability of photos or send photos with submission. Uses mostly b&w. Reviews prints. Negotiates

payment individually. Captions required. Buys one-time rights.

LEADERSHIP, A Practical Journal for Church Leaders, Christianity Today, Inc., 465 Gundersen Dr., Carol Stream IL 60188. (630)260-6200. Fax: (630)260-0114. E-mail: LeaderJ@aol.com. Website: http://www.christianity.net/leadership. Editor: Kevin A. Miller. 75% freelance written. Works with a small number of new/unpublished writers each year. Quarterly magazine. Writers must have a "knowledge of and sympathy for the unique expectations placed on pastors and local church leaders. Each article must support points by illustrating from real life experiences in local churches." Estab. 1980. Circ. 70,000. **Pays on acceptance.** Publishes ms an average of 6 months after acceptance. Byline given. Buys first North American serial rights. Submit seasonal material 6 months in advance. Reports in 6 weeks on queries; 2 months on mss. Sample copy for $3. Free writer's guidelines.
Nonfiction: How-to, humor, personal experience. "No articles from writers who have never read our journal." Buys 50 mss/year. Send complete ms. Length: 100-5,000 words. Pays $75-375. Sometimes pays expenses of writers on assignment.
Reprints: Send photocopy of article and information about when and where the article previously appeared. Pays 50% of amount paid for an original article.
Photos: State availability of photos with submission. Offers no additional payment for photos accepted with ms. Identification of subjects required. Buys one-time rights.
Columns/Departments: To Illustrate (short stories or analogies that illustrate a biblical principle), 100 words. Buys 25 mss/year. Send complete ms. Pays $25-50. To Quip (clean, funny humor that makes a point), 100 words. Buys 12 mss/year. Send complete ms. Pays $25-35.

PASTORAL LIFE, Society of St. Paul, P.O. Box 595, Canfield OH 44406-0595. Fax: (216)533-1076. Editor: Anthony Chenevey, SSP. 66% freelance written. Works with new/unpublished writers. Monthly magazine emphasizing priests and those interested in pastoral ministry. Estab. 1953. Circ. 2,000. Buys first rights only. Byline given. Pays on publication. Publishes ms an average of 4 months after acceptance. Reports in 1 month. Sample copy and writer's guidelines for 6×9 SAE with 4 first-class stamps.
Nonfiction: "*Pastoral Life* is a professional review, principally designed to focus attention on current problems, needs, issues and important activities related to all phases of pastoral work and life." Query with outline before submitting ms. "New contributors are expected to include, in addition, a few lines of personal data that indicate academic and professional background." Buys 30 unsolicited mss/year. Length: 2,000-3,000 words. Pays 4¢/word minimum.

THE PREACHER'S MAGAZINE, Nazarene Publishing House, E. 10814 Broadway, Spokane WA 99206-5003. Editor: Randal E. Denny. Assistant Editor: Cindy Osso. 15% freelance written. Works with a small number of new/unpublished writers each year. Quarterly resource for ministers, Wesleyan-Arminian in theological persuasion." Circ. 18,000. Pays on publication. Publishes ms an average of 9 months after acceptance. Byline given. Buys first serial, second serial (reprint) and simultaneous rights. Submit seasonal material 9 months in advance. Writer's guidelines for #10 SASE.
Nonfiction: How-to, humor, inspirational, opinion, personal experience, all relating to aspects of ministry. No articles that present problems without also presenting answers to them or not relating to pastoral ministry. Buys 48 mss/year. Send complete ms. Length: 700-2,500 words. Pays 3½¢/word.
Reprints: Send photocopy of article or typed ms with rights for sale noted and information about when and where the article previously appeared. Pays 100% of amount paid for an original article.
Photos: Send photos with ms. Reviews 35mm transparencies, b&w prints. Model release, identification of subjects required. Buys one-time rights.
Columns/Departments: Stories Preachers Tell Each Other (humorous).
Fiction: Publishes novel excerpts.
Fillers: Anecdotes, short humor. Buys 10/year. Length: 400 words maximum. Pays 3½¢/word.
Tips: "Writers for the *Preacher's Magazine* should have insight into the pastoral ministry, or expertise in a specialized area of ministry. Our magazine is a highly specialized publication aimed at the minister. Our goal is to assist, by both scholarly and practical articles, the modern-day minister in applying Biblical theological truths."

‡PREACHING, Preaching Resources, Inc., Dept. WM, P.O. Box 369, Jackson TN 38302. (901)668-9948. Fax: (901)668-9633. E-mail: 74114.275@compuserve.com. Website: http://www.preaching.com. Editor: Dr. Michael Duduit. Contact: Mark Johnson, managing editor. 75% freelance written. Bimonthly magazine. "All articles must deal with preaching. Most articles used offer practical assistance in preparation and delivery of sermons, generally from an evangelical stance." Estab. 1985. Circ. 10,000. Pays on publication. Publishes ms an average of 1 year after acceptance. Byline given. Buys first rights. Submit seasonal material 1 year in advance. Reports in 4 months. Sample copy for $3.50. Writer's guidelines for SASE.
Nonfiction: How-to (preparation and delivery of sermon, worship leadership). Special issues: Personal Computing in Preaching (September-October); materials/resources to assist in preparation of seasonal preaching (November-December, March-April). Buys 18-24 mss/year. Query. Length: 1,000-2,000 words. Pays $35-50.
Photos: Send photos with submission. Reviews prints. Offers no additional payment for photos accepted with ms. Captions, model releases and identification of subjects required. Buys one-time rights.
Fillers: Buys 10-15/year. "Buys only completed cartoons." Art must be related to preaching. Pays $25.
Tips: "Most desirable are practical, 'how-to' articles on preparation and delivery of sermons."

‡THE PRIEST, Our Sunday Visitor, Inc., 200 Noll Plaza, Huntington IN 46750-4304. (219)356-8400. Fax: (219)356-8472. Editor: Father Owen F. Campion. Associate Editor: George P. Foster. 80% freelance written. Monthly magazine. "We run articles that will aid priests in their day-to-day ministry. Includes items on spirituality, counseling, administration, theology, personalities, the saints, etc." **Pays on acceptance.** Byline given. Not copyrighted. Buys first North American serial rights. Editorial lead time 3 months. Submit seasonal material at least 4 months in advance. Reports in 2 weeks on queries; 1 month on mss. Sample copy and writer's guidelines free.
Nonfiction: Essays, historical/nostalgic, humor, inspirational, interview/profile, opinion, personal experience, photo feature, religious. Buys 96 mss/year. Send complete ms. Length: 1,500-5,000 words. Pays $300 minimum for assigned articles; $50 minimum for unsolicited articles.
Photos: Send photos with submission. Reviews transparencies and prints. Negotiates payment individually. Captions and identification of subjects required. Buys one-time rights.
Columns/Departments: Viewpoint (whatever applies to priests and the Church), 1,000 words. Buys 36 mss/year. Send complete ms. Pays $50-100.
Tips: "Say what you have to say in an interesting and informative manner and stop. Freelancers are most often published in 'Viewpoints.' Please do not stray from the magisterium of the Catholic Church."

YOUR CHURCH, Helping You With the Business of Ministry, Christianity Today, Inc., 465 Gundersen Dr., Carol Stream IL 60188. (630)260-6200. Fax: (630)260-0114. E-mail: yceditor@aol.com. Website: http://www.christianity.net/yc. Editor: Richard Doebler. 70% freelance written. Bimonthly magazine. "Articles pertain to the business aspects of ministry pastors are called upon to perform: administration, purchasing, management, technology, building, etc." Estab. 1955. Circ. 150,000. **Pays on acceptance.** Publishes ms an average of 4 months after acceptance. Byline given. Buys one-time rights. Submit seasonal material 5 months in advance. Accepts simultaneous submissions. Reports in 1 month on queries; 2 months on mss. Sample copy and writer's guidelines for 9×12 SAE with 5 first-class stamps.
Nonfiction: How-to, new product, technical. Buys 25 mss/year. Send complete ms. Length: 900-1,500 words. Pays about 12½¢/word.
Reprints: Send photocopy of article and information about when and where the article previously appeared. Pays 30% of the amount paid for an original article.
Photos: State availability of photos with submission. Reviews 4×5 transparencies and 5×7 or 8×10 prints. Offers no additional payment for photos accepted with ms. Captions, model releases and identification of subjects required. Buys one-time rights.
Tips: "The editorial is generally geared toward brief and helpful articles dealing with some form of church business. Concise, bulleted points from experts in the field are typical for our articles."

CLOTHING

‡APPAREL INDUSTRY MAGAZINE, The Industry's Voice Since 1946, Shore-Varrone, Inc., 6255 Barfield Rd., Suite 200, Atlanta GA 30328-4300. (404)252-8831. Fax: (404)252-4436. E-mail: Andree_Conrad@svi.ccmail.compuserve.com. Editor: Andree Conrad. Senior Editor: Faye Musselman. 50% freelance written. Monthly magazine covering apparel manufacturing (not fashion) and management topics for apparel industry. "*Apparel Industry* just completed its 50th year of existence. It is one of the most respected business-to-business trade publications in the country, having won Neal Awards and many other prestigious prizes. Articles are always assigned. We are looking for first-rate business writers all over the country who have the skills and the interest to write about high-tech apparel manufacturing today. Please send clips showing ability to write for trade publications." Estab. 1946. Circ. 18,600. Pays on publication. Publishes ms an average of 3 months after acceptance. Byline given. Offers 50% kill fee. Buys first North American serial and second serial (reprint) rights. Editorial lead time 3 months. Submit seasonal material 3 months in advance. Accepts previously published submissions. Sample copy for $3.
Nonfiction: Technical. Query with published clips. *No unsolicited mss.* Sometimes pays expenses of writers on assignment.
Photos: Negotiates payment individually. Captions and identification of subjects required.
Tips: "Absolutely no unsolicited mss. will be considered. The magazine has too specific a focus for the editors to hope that freelancers could hit upon an article idea without editorial guidance. Writers who live in a town where apparel is manufactured may have a strike against them, having witnessed the ups and downs of the manufacturer in a period when much apparel manufacturing has moved offshore. Also, adverse publicity has tended to cloud perception of an industry which is actually very high-tech and continues to provide rewarding, interesting careers to highly creative individuals both here and abroad."

ATI, America's Textiles International, Billian Publishing Co., 2100 Powers Ferry Rd., Atlanta GA 30339. (770)955-5656. Fax: (770)952-0669. Website: http://www.billian.com/textile. Editor: James Burroughs. 10% freelance written. Monthly magazine covering "the business of textile, apparel and fiber industries with considerable technical focus on products and processes. No puff pieces pushing a particular product." Estab. 1887. Pays on publication. Byline given. Buys first North American serial rights.
Nonfiction: Technical, business. "No PR, just straight technical reports." Buys 10 mss/year. Query. Length: 500 words minimum. Pays $200/published page. Sometimes pays expenses of writers on assignment.

Photos: Send photos with submission. Reviews prints. Offers no additional payment for photos accepted with ms. Captions required. Buys one-time rights.

BOBBIN, Bobbin Media, 1110 Shop Rd., P.O. Box 1986, Columbia SC 29202-1986. (803)771-7500. Fax: (803)799-1461. Website: http://www.bobbin.com. Editor-in-Chief: Susan Black. 25% freelance written. Monthly magazine for CEO's and top management in apparel and sewn products manufacturing companies. Circ. 18,000. Pays on publication. Byline given. Buys all rights. Reports in 6 weeks. Free sample copy and writer's guidelines.
Columns/Departments: Trade View, R&D, Information Strategies, Personnel Management, Labor Forum, NON-Apparel Highlights, Fabric Notables, West Coast Report.
Tips: "Articles should be written in a style appealing to busy top managers and should in some way foster thought or new ideas, or present solutions/alternatives to common industry problems/concerns. CEOs are most interested in quick read pieces that are also informative and substantive. Articles should not be based on opinions but should be developed through interviews with industry manufacturers, retailers or other experts, etc. Sidebars may be included to expand upon certain aspects within the article. If available, illustrations, graphs/charts, or photographs should accompany the article."

‡EMB-EMBROIDERY/MONOGRAM BUSINESS, Miller Freeman Inc., 13760 Noel Rd., #500, Dallas TX 75240. (972)239-3060. E-mail: lhowle@mfi.com. Contact: LoLa Howle, editor. 30% freelance written. Monthly magazine covering computerized embroidery and digitizing design. "Readable, practical business and/or technical articles that show our readers how-to succeed in their profession." Estab. 1994. Circ. 20,100. **Pays on acceptance.** Publishes ms an average of 3 months after accceptance. Byline given. Buys one-time rights or all rights. Editorial lead time 2 months. Submit seasonal material 4 months in advance. Accepts simultaneous submissions. Reports in 3 weeks on queries; 1 month on mss. Sample copy for $7. Writer's guidelines not available.
Nonfiction: How-to (embroidery, sales, marketing, design, general business info), new product, photo feature, technical (computerized embroidery). No PR fluff on a manufacturer. Buys 4-6 mss/year. Query. Length: 800-2,500 words. Pays $200-600 for assigned articles; $200-400 for unsolicited articles. Sometimes pays expenses of writers on assignment.
Photos: Send photos with submission. Reviews transparencies, prints. Negotiates payment individually. Buys one-time or all rights.

IMPRINTING BUSINESS, WFC, Inc., 3000 Hadley Rd., South Plainfield NJ 07080. (908)769-1160. Fax: (908)769-1171. Website: http://www.wfcinc.com. Editor: Bruce Sachenski. Monthly magazine for persons in imprinted garment industry and screen printing. Circ. 23,000. Pays on publication. Publishes ms an average of 3 months after acceptance. Byline given. Buys one-time rights. Submit seasonal/holiday material 3 months in advance. Reports in 2 months. Sample copy for $10.
Nonfiction: How-to, new product, photo feature, technical, business. Buys 3 mss/year. Send complete ms. Length: 1,500-3,500 words. Pays $200-500 for assigned articles.
Reprints: Accepts previously published submissions. Pay varies.
Photos: Send photos with submission. Reviews contact sheets. Offers no additional payment for photos accepted with ms. Identification of subjects required.
Tips: "We need general business stories, advertising, shop management, etc."

MR MAGAZINE, The Magazine of Menswear Retailing, Business Journals, Inc., 50 Day St., Norwalk CT 06854. (203)853-6015. Fax: (203)852-8175. Editor: Karen Alberg Grossman. Contact: Noelle Cleary, managing editor. 20% freelance written. Magazine published 8 times/year covering "up-to-the-minute coverage of menswear industry and retailers." Estab. 1990. Circ. 30,000. Pays on publication. Publishes ms an average of 2 months after acceptance. Byline given. Buys all rights. Editorial lead time 2 months. Submit seasonal material 2 months in advance. Reports in 1 month. Sample copy for $3.50 (if available). Writer's guidelines free on request.
Nonfiction: Humor, interview/profile, new product, opinion, personal experience (all dealing with men and menswear). Editorial calendar available. Buys 25-30 mss/year. Query with published clips or send complete ms. Length: 500-2,000 words. Pays $150-750. Sometimes pays expenses of writers on assignment.
Reprints: Send typed ms with rights for sale noted and information about when and where the article previously appeared. Pays discounted rate, negotiable.
Photos: Send photos with submission. Reviews transparencies or prints. Offers no additional payment for photos accepted with ms. Identification of subjects required. Buys all rights.

TEXTILE RENTAL, Uniform and Linen Service Management Trends, Textile Rental Services Association of America, 1130 E. Hallandale Beach Blvd., Suite B, Hallandale FL 33009. (954)457-7555. Fax: (954)457-3890. E-mail: srbiller@aol.com. Website: http://www.trsa.org. Editor: Christine Seaman. Contact: Steven R. Biller, managing editor. 25% freelance written. Monthly magazine covering management and trends for uniform and linen rental executives. "*Textile Rental* covers government, environment, labor, workplace safety, regulatory compliance, computer technology, the economy, plant operations, strategic management, marketing, sales and service." Byline usually given. Offers negotiable kill fee. Editorial lead time 3 months. Submit seasonal material 4 months in advance. Reports in 1 month on queries; 2-3 months on mss. Sample copy free on request. Writer's guidelines for #10 SASE.
Nonfiction: Historical/nostalgic, how-to, inspirational, interview/profile, new product, technical. Buys 10-12 mss/year. Query with published clips. Length: 1,000-5,000 words. Pays $50-400. Pays in contributor copies at writer's request. Sometimes pays expenses of writers on assignment.

Reprints: Send typed ms with rights for sale noted and information about when and where the article previously appeared. Pay negotiable.

Photos: Reviews contact sheets. Negotiates payment individually. Captions and identification of subjects preferred. Buys one-time rights.

Fillers: Anecdotes, facts, gags to be illustrated by cartoonist, newsbreaks, short humor. Buys 25-30/year. Length: 150-500 words. Pays $35-100.

COIN-OPERATED MACHINES

‡VENDING TIMES, 1375 Broadway, New York NY 10018. (212)302-4700. Fax: (212)221-3311. Editor: Tim Sanford. Monthly magazine for operators of vending machines. Estab. 1960. Circ. 15,450. Pays on publication. Buys all rights. "We will discuss in detail the story requirements with the writer." Sample copy for $5.

Nonfiction: Feature articles and news stories about vending operations; practical and important aspects of the business. "We are always willing to pay for good material." Query. Payment negotiable.

CONFECTIONERY AND SNACK FOODS

These publications focus on the bakery, snack and candy industries. Journals for grocers, wholesalers and other food industry personnel are listed in Groceries and Food Products.

‡CONFECTIONER, APC, American Publishing Corp., 3108 Sowell Dr., Plano TX 75093. (972)758-0522. Fax: (972)758-0523. E-mail: treats@onramp.net. Contact: Lisbeth Echeandia, editor. 80% freelance written. Bimonthly magazine covering the confectionery and snack food industry. Estab. 1916. Circ. 13,571. Pays on publication. Byline given. Buys all rights. Editorial lead time 1 month. Submit seasonal material 2 months in advance. Accepts simultaneous submissions. Sample copy and writer's guidelines free.

Nonfiction: How-to, interview/profile, new product, opinion, technical. Buys 15 mss/year. Send complete ms. Length: 1,000-2,000 words. Pays 30-35¢/word. Sometimes pays expenses of writers on assignment.

Photos: State availability of photos with submission. Offers no additional payment for photos accepted with ms. Captions required. Buys all rights.

Tips: "Call the editor and ask for editorial calendar; discuss potential work; send samples."

PACIFIC BAKERS NEWS, 180 Mendell St., San Francisco CA 94124-1740. (415)826-2664. Publisher: C.W. Soward. 30% freelance written. Eager to work with new/unpublished writers. Monthly business newsletter for commercial bakeries in the western states. Estab. 1961. Pays on publication. No byline given; uses only 1-paragraph news items.

Nonfiction: Uses bakery business reports and news about bakers. Buys only brief "boiled-down news items about bakers and bakeries operating only in Alaska, Hawaii, Pacific Coast and Rocky Mountain states. We welcome clippings. We need monthly news reports and clippings about the baking industry and the donut business. No pictures, jokes, poetry or cartoons." Length: 10-200 words. Pays 10¢/word for news and 6¢ for clips (words used).

CONSTRUCTION AND CONTRACTING

Builders, architects and contractors learn the latest industry news in these publications. Journals targeted to architects are also included in the Consumer Art and Architecture category. Those for specialists in the interior aspects of construction are listed under Building Interiors.

ABERDEEN'S CONCRETE CONSTRUCTION, The Aberdeen Group, 426 S. Westgate St., Addison IL 60101. (630)543-0870. Fax: (630)543-5399. E-mail: cceditor@woenet.com. Website: http://www.supernetwork.net. Managing Editor: Anne Balogh. 20% freelance written. "A monthly how-to magazine for concrete contractors. It also covers job stories and new equipment in the industry." Estab. 1956. Circ. 80,000. **Pays on acceptance.** Publishes ms an average of 3 months after acceptance. Byline given. Editorial lead time 2 months. Submit seasonal material 3 months in advance. Reports in 2 weeks on queries; 1 month on mss. Sample copy free.

Nonfiction: How-to, new product, personal experience, photo feature, technical, job stories. Buys 7-10 mss/year. Query. Length varies. Pays $250 or more for assigned articles; $200 minimum for unsolicited articles. Pays expenses of writers on assignment.

Photos: State availability of photos with submission. Reviews contact sheets, negatives, transparencies, prints. Negotiates payment individually. Captions required. Buys one-time rights.

Tips: "Must have a good understanding of concrete construction industry. How-to stories only accepted from experts. Job stories must cover procedures, materials, and equipment used as well as the scope of the project."

AUTOMATED BUILDER, CMN Associates, Inc., P.O. Box 120, Carpinteria CA 93014-0120. (805)684-7659. Fax: (805)684-1765. E-mail: abmag@autbldrmag.com. Website: http://www.autbldrmag.com. Editor-in-Chief: Don Carlson.

15% freelance written. Monthly magazine specializing in management for industrialized (manufactured) housing and volume home builders. Estab. 1964. Circ. 25,000. **Pays on acceptance.** Publishes ms an average of 3 months after acceptance. Buys first North American serial rights. Phone queries OK. Reports in 2 weeks. Free sample copy and writer's guidelines.

Nonfiction: Case history articles on successful home building companies which may be 1) production (big volume) home builders; 2) mobile home manufacturers; 3) modular home manufacturers; 4) prefabricated (panelized) home manufacturers; 5) house component manufacturers; or 6) special unit (in-plant commercial building) manufacturers. Also uses interviews, photo features and technical articles. "No architect or plan 'dreams'. Housing projects must be built or under construction." Buys 15 mss/year. Query. Length: 500-1,000 words maximum. Pays $300 minimum.

Photos: Purchased with accompanying ms. Query. No additional payment. Wants 4×5, 5×7 or 8×10 glossies or 35mm or larger color transparencies (35mm preferred). Captions required.

Tips: "Stories often are too long, too loose; we prefer 500 to 750 words. We prefer a phone query on feature articles. If accepted on query, article usually will not be rejected later."

‡BUILDING & REMODELING NEWS, The Local Magazine for the Professional Builder/Remodeler, S.R. Sound, Inc., 600-C Lake St., Ramsey NJ 07446. (201)327-1600. Fax: (201)327-3185. Editor: Reneé Rewiski. 90% freelance written. "Local montly magazine for professionals in the residential construction trade. Provides need-to-know information about products, materials and techniques, plus business how-to." Estab. 1987. Circ. 55,000. Pays on publication. Publishes ms an average of 3 months after acceptance. Byline given. Rights negotiated individually. Editorial lead time 3 months. Submit seasonal material 6 months in advance. Reports in 2 months on queries; 6 months on mss. Sample copy and writer's guidelines free.

Nonfiction: Book excerpts, how-to, interview/profile, new product, opinion, personal experience, technical. "No general business. Articles must be construction industry specific." Query. Length: 800-2,400 words. Pays $200-500 for assigned articles; $50-250 for unsolicited articles.

Photos: State availability of photos with submission. Reviews 3×5 prints. Negotiates payment individually. Captions required. Buys all rights.

Columns/Departments: Marketing, Management, Accounting. Length: 750 words. Send complete ms. Pays $50-250.

Fillers: Anecdotes. Buys 2/year. Length: 250-750 words. Pays $50.

Tips: "Be industry specific. Must know and understand what contractor—not homeowner—needs to know about the subject. How-tos are always desired. Circulation is Northeast (Maine through Virginia), so subject must be described as used in a specific geographic area."

CAM MAGAZINE, Construction Association of Michigan, 500 Stephenson Hwy., Suite 400, Troy MI 48083. (810)585-1000. Fax: (810)972-1001. Editor: Phyllis L. Brooks. 5% freelance written. Monthly magazine. "*CAM Magazine* is devoted to the growth and progress of individuals and companies serving and servicing the construction industry. It provides a forum on new construction industry technology and practices, current information on new construction projects, products and services, and publishes information on industry personnel changes and advancements." Estab. 1978. Circ. 4,300. Pays on publication. Byline given. Buys all rights. Editorial lead time 2 months. Submit seasonal material 3 months in advance. Sample copy free.

Nonfiction: Construction-related only. Buys 3 mss/year. Query with published clips. Length: 1,000-2,000 words. Pays $250-500.

Photos: Send photos with submission. Reviews contact sheets, negatives, transparencies and prints. Offers no additional payment for photos accepted with ms. Buys one-time rights.

Fiction: Publishes novel excerpts.

Tips: "Anyone having *current* knowledge or expertise on some of our featured topics is welcomed to submit articles. Recent experience or information on a construction-related issue or new trends and innovations, is also helpful."

CONSTRUCTION EQUIPMENT GUIDE, 2627 Mt. Carmel Ave., Glenside PA 19038-0156. (800)523-2200. Fax: (215)885-2910. E-mail: cegglen@aol.com. Editor: Beth Baker. 25-30% freelance written. Biweekly newspaper. "We are looked at as the primary source of information in the construction industry by equipment manufacturers, sellers and users. We cover the Midwest, Northeast and Southeast states with our 3 editions published biweekly. We give the latest news on current construction projects, legislative actions, political issues, mergers and acquisitions, new unique applications of equipment and in-depth features." Estab. 1957. Circ. 80,000. Pays on publication. Publishes ms an average of 1 month after acceptance. Byline given. Offers 100% kill fee. Buys all rights. Editorial lead time varies. Accepts simultaneous submissions. Sample copy and writer's guidelines free.

Nonfiction: General interest, historical/nostalgic, how-to (winterizing construction equipment, new methods of construction applications), interview/profile, new product, personal experience, photo feature, technical. Buys 150 mss/year. Query with published clips. Length: 150-600 words. Negotiates payment individually. Pays expenses of writers on assignment.

Photos: Send photos with submission. Negotiates payment individually. Captions, identification of subjects required.

Columns/Departments: Equipment Auctions (photo coverage only with captions). Query. Pays $60 and expenses.

Tips: "Keep an eye out for commercial construction in your area. Take note of the name of the contractors on site. Then give us a call to see if you should follow up with a full story and photos. Pay attention to large and small jobs right around you. Read articles in *Construction Equipment Guide* to learn what information is important to our readers, who are mostly equipment users, sellers and makers."

CONSTRUCTION MARKETING TODAY, The Aberdeen Group, 426 S. Westgate St., Addison IL 60101. (708)543-0870. Fax: (708)543-3112. E-mail: rbrown@wocnet.com. Website: http://www.cmarket.net. Managing Editor: Ross Brown. 25% freelance written. Monthly tabloid. "Our readers are manufacturers of construction equipment and building materials. Specifically, our readers are marketing people and top execs at those companies. The magazine carries business news, marketing case studies and marketing how-to articles. The magazine does not have heavily technical content, so writers need not be knowledgeable of the industry. Business writing and company profile writing experience are a plus." Estab. 1990. Circ. 4,000. Pays on publication. Byline given. Buys first rights and simultaneous rights. Editorial lead time 2 months. Pay varies. Reports in 5 weeks on queries; 2 months on mss. Sample copy free.
Nonfiction: Exposé, how-to (marketing), interview/profile, opinion, personal experience, business news, marketing trends. "No stories aimed at contractors or stories that show no relevancy to the industry." Buys 15 mss/year. Query with published clips. Length: 800-3,000 words. Pays $250. Pays in contributor's copies if "author is an industry consultant or has a service he is trying to sell to our readers, or he works for a manufacturing company." Sometimes pays expenses of writers on assignment.
Reprints: Occasionally accepts previously published submissions. Send tearsheet, photocopy of article or typed ms with rights for sale noted and information about when and where the article previously appeared.
Photos: State availability of photos with submission. Reviews contact sheets. Negotiates payment individually. Captions and identification of subjects required. Buys all rights.
Tips: "Show that you have a grasp of what the magazine is about. We are not a technical how-to magazine geared to contractors, as most construction publications are. We have a unique niche. We are targeted to manufacturers marketing to contractors. We are looking for stories that have a fresh and intriguing look, that are entertaining to read, that are relevant to our readers, that are informative and that show an attention to detail in the reporting. Page one news, inside features, company profiles, industry marketing trends and marketing how-to stories are most open to freelancers. Stories should be tailored to our industry."

CONSTRUCTION SPECIFIER, 601 Madison St., Alexandria VA 22314-1791. (703)684-0300. Fax: (703)684-0465. E-mail: ascott@csinet.org. Editor: Anne Scott. 50% freelance written. Works with a small number of new/unpublished writers each year. Monthly professional society magazine for architects, engineers, specification writers and project managers. Estab. 1949. Circ. 19,000. Pays on publication. Publishes ms an average of 3 months after acceptance. Deadline: 90 days preceding publication on the 1st of each month. Buys world serial rights. Accepts previously published submissions. Send information about when and where the article previously appeared. Does not pay for reprints. Query for electronic submissions. "Call or write first." Model release, author copyright transferral requested. Sample copy for 9×12 SAE with 6 first-class stamps. Writer's guidelines for #10 SASE.
Nonfiction: Articles on selection and specification of products, materials, practices and methods used in non-residential construction projects, specifications as related to construction design, plus legal and management subjects. Query. Length: 2,500-3,500 words maximum. Pays up to 15¢/published word (negotiable), plus art. Pays minor expenses of writers on assignment, to an agreed upon limit.
Photos: Photos desirable in consideration for publication; line art, sketches, diagrams, charts and graphs also desired. Full color transparencies may be used; 8×10 glossies, 3¼ slides preferred. Payment negotiable.
Tips: "Make sure articles are technical and nonproprietary."

COST CUTS, The Enterprise Foundation, American City Bldg., 10227 Wincopin Circle, Suite 500, Columbia MD 21044-3400. (410)964-1230. Fax: (410)964-1918. Website: http://www.enterprisefoundation.org. Editor: Deborah Young. Quarterly newsletter. "*Cost Cuts* provides technical information on housing and related community services to low-income housing practitioners, raises awareness of the issues and approaches to housing low-income people and provides information on reducing costs in low-income housing development." Estab. 1983. Circ. 8,000. Pays on publication. Byline given. Buys one-time rights. Submit seasonal material 3 months in advance. Reports in 1 month. Sample copy for 9×12 SASE with 2 first-class stamps. Writer's guidelines for #10 SASE.
Nonfiction: How-to, interview/profile, technical. "No personal experience of do-it-yourselfers in single-family homes. We want articles concerning high production of low-income housing." Query with published clips. Length: 1,600-1,800 words. Pays $50-200 for assigned articles; $200 maximum for unsolicited articles.
Reprints: Send tearsheet of article, typed ms with rights for sale noted and information about when and where the article previously appeared.
Photos: Send photos with submission. Reviews contact sheets and 3×5 and 5×7 prints. Captions and identification of subjects required. Buys one-time rights.
Fillers: Facts, newsbreaks. Buys 20/year. Length: 100-500 words. Pays $25-50.
Tips: "The Foundation's mission is to see that all low-income people in the United States have the opportunity for fit and affordable housing and to move up and out of poverty into the mainstream of American life. Freelancers must be conscious of this context. Articles must include case studies of specific projects where costs have been cut. Charts of cost comparisons to show exactly where cuts were made are most helpful."

‡FABRICS & ARCHITECTURE, Industrial Fabrics Association International, 1801 County Rd. B, Roseville MN 55113. (612)222-2508. Fax: (612)222-6966. Contact: Bruce N. Wright, RA, editor. 25% freelance written. Bimonthly

magazine covering architecture, landscape architecture and architectural graphics which incorporate industrial and technical fabrics and membranes. Estab. 1989. Circ. 13,000. Pays on publication. Publishes ms an average of 3 months after acceptance. Byline given. Editorial lead time 6 months.
Nonfiction: Interview/profile, new product, photo feature, technical. Buys 10-12 mss/year. Query. Length: 500-700 words for short features, 1,200-1,500 words for longer features. Pays $75-100 for shorter, $200-250 for longer.
Tips: "Review past issues to gain a better understanding of the specialized market. When submitting story proposals, identify source(s) of high-quality photographs of building projects."

‡**HARD HAT NEWS**, Lee Publications, Inc., 6113 State Highway 5, Palatine Bridge NY 13428. (518)673-3237. Fax: (518)673-2381. Editor: Mary Hilton. 5% freelance written. Biweekly tabloid covering heavy construction, equipment, road and bridge work. "Writers should focus on jobsite stories in the Northeast. Our readers are contractors and heavy construction workers involved in excavation, highways, bridges, utility construction and underground construction." Estab. 1980. Circ. 23,000. Byline given. Not copyrighted. Editorial lead time 1 month. Submit seasonal material 1 month in advance. Accepts simultaneous submissions. Sample copy and writer's guidelines free.
Nonfiction: Interview/profile, new product, opinion, photo feature, technical. "No finished projects—we only look at job sites in progress." Send complete ms. Length: 50-1,200 words. Pays $1/inch. Sometimes pays expenses of writers on assignment.
Reprints: Accepts previously published submissions.
Photos: Send photos. Reviews 5×7 prints. Offers $5/photo. Captions and identification of subjects required.
Columns/Departments: New Products (user benefits); Open Houses (who was there); Association Meetings (coverage of national issues); all columns 50-600 words.
Fillers: Anecdotes, facts, newsbreaks, short humor, heavy construction, dirt moving, highway/bridge. Length: 25-100 words. Pays $1/inch.
Tips: "Visit the job site! Talk to the person in charge. Take photos of equipment—get manufacturer's name and model number and operator's name. Make it local—Northeast region."

JOINERS' QUARTERLY, Journal of Timber Framing & Traditional Joinery, Fox Maple Press, Inc., P.O. Box 249, Brownfield ME 04010. (207)935-3720. Fax: (207)935-4575. E-mail: foxmaple@nxi.com. Managing Editor: Laurie LaMountain. Contact: Steve K. Chappell, editor. 75% freelance written. Quarterly magazine covering traditional building, timber framing, natural and sustainable construction. Estab. 1982. Circ. 10,000. Pays on publication. Publishes ms an average of 9 months after acceptance. Byline given. Buys all rights. Editorial lead time 9 months. Submit seasonal material 6 months in advance. Accepts simultaneous submissions. Reports in 1 month on queries; 2 months on mss. Sample copy for $4.50. Writer's guidelines for #10 SASE.
Nonfiction: Historical/nostalgic (building techniques), how-to (timber frame, log build, sustainable materials, straw building), inspirational (craftsmanship), new product, technical (alternative building techniques). Buys 12 mss/year. Query. Length: 500-2,500 words. Pays $50 per published page. Sometimes pays expenses of writers on assignment.
Reprints: Send photocopy of article or short story and information about when and where the article previously appeared. Pays 50-100% of amount paid for an original article.
Photos: Send photos with submission. Reviews transparencies and prints. Offers no additional payment for photos accepted with ms. Identification of subjects required. Buys all rights.
Tips: "We're looking for articles on sustainable construction, especially from a timber framing aspect. Architects, builders and owner/builders are our primary readers and writers. We also like to feature natural and historical home building techniques such as straw/clay, roof thatching, sod home, etc."

PACIFIC BUILDER & ENGINEER, Vernon Publications Inc., 3000 Northup Way, Suite 200, Bellevue WA 98004. (206)827-9900. Fax: (206)822-9372. E-mail: pacbuilder@aol.com. Editor: Carl Molesworth. Editorial Director: Michele Andrus Dill. 44% freelance written. Biweekly magazine covering non-residential construction in the Northwest and Alaska. "Our readers are construction contractors in Washington, Oregon, Idaho, Montana and Alaska. The feature stories in *PB&E* focus on ongoing construction projects in our coverage area. They address these questions: What is the most significant challenge to the general contractor? What innovative construction techniques or equipment are being used to overcome the challenges?" Estab. 1902. Circ. 14,500. Pays on publication. Publishes ms an average of 2 months after acceptance. Byline given. Buys first North American serial and second serial (reprint) rights. Editorial lead time 6 weeks. Submit seasonal material 2 months in advance. Reports in 2 months on queries; 6 weeks on mss. Sample copy for $7. Writer's guidelines for #10 SASE.
Nonfiction: How-to, new product, photo feature. "No non-construction stories; no residential construction articles; no construction stories without a Northwest or Alaska angle." Buys 18 mss/year. Query with published clips. Length: 750-2,000 words. Pays $100-200. Sometimes pays expenses of writers on assignment.
Photos: State availability of photos with submission. Reviews contact sheets, transparencies. Offers $15-125/photo. Captions and identification of subjects and equipment required. Buys one-time rights.
Tips: "Find an intriguing, ongoing construction project in our five-state region. Talk to the general contractor's project manager to see what he/she thinks is unusual, innovative or exciting about the project to builders. Then go ahead and query us. If we haven't already covered the project, there's a possibility that we may assign a feature. Be prepared to tour the site, put on a hard hat and get your boots dirty."

PERMANENT BUILDINGS & FOUNDATIONS (PBF), R.W. Nielsen Co., P.O. Box 11067, 5245 N. Kensington, Kansas City MO 64119. (816)453-0590. Fax: (816)453-0591. E-mail: rnielsen@pbf.org. Website: http://www.pbf.org. Managing Editor: Carolyn R. Nielsen. Contact: Roger W. Nielsen, editor. 25% freelance written. Magazine published 7 times/year. "*PBF* readers are contractors who build residential, commercial and industrial buildings. Editorial focus is on materials that last: concrete and steel—and new technologies to build solid, energy efficient structures—insulated concrete and tilt-up, waterproofing, underpinning, roofing—and the business of contracting and construction." Estab. 1989. Circ. 35,000. Pays on publication. Byline given. Buys first North American serial rights. Editorial lead time 1 month. Submit seasonal material 2 months in advance. Reports in 2 weeks on queries; 2 months on mss. Sample copy for #10 SASE. Writer's guidelines free on request.

Nonfiction: General interest, how-to (construction methods, management techniques), humor, interview/profile, new product, technical, book reviews, tool reviews. Buys 10 mss/year. Query. Length: 500-1,500 words. Pays $150-750 for assigned articles; $50-500 for unsolicited articles. Sometimes pays expenses of writers on assignment.

Photos: State availability of photos with submission. Reviews contact sheets. Offers no additional payment for photos accepted with ms. Captions, model releases, identification of subjects required. Buys one-time rights.

Columns/Departments: Marketing Tips, 250-500 words; Q&A (solutions to contractor problems), 200-500 words. Query. Pays $50-500.

Fillers: Anecdotes, gags to be illustrated by cartoonist, short humor. Length: 30-500 words. Pays $25-250.

ROOFER MAGAZINE, Construction Publications, Inc., 12734 Kenwood Lane, #73, Ft. Myers FL 33907. (813)489-2929. E-mail: roofmag@pagenet.com. Editor: Angela Williamson. 10% freelance written. Eager to work with new/unpublished writers. Monthly magazine covering the roofing industry for roofing contractors. Estab. 1981. Circ. 25,000. Pays on publication. Publishes ms an average of 5 months after acceptance. Byline given. Buys first and second serial (reprint) rights. Submit seasonal material 4 months in advance. Reports in 2 months. Sample copy and writer's guidelines for SAE with 6 first-class stamps.

Nonfiction: Profiles of roofing contractors (explicit guidelines available), humorous pieces; other ideas welcome. Buys 5-10 mss/year. Query in writing. Length: approximately 1,500 words. Pays $125-250 (average: $175).

Photos: Send photos with completed mss; color slides are preferred. Identification of subjects required. "We purchase photographs for specific needs, but those that accompany an article are not purchased separately. The price we pay in the article includes the use of the photos. Always searching for photos of unusual roofs or those with a humorous slant."

Tips: "Contractor profiles are our most frequent purchase from freelance writers and a favorite to our readers. Our guidelines explain exactly what we are looking for and should help freelancers select the right person to interview. We provide sample questions to ask about the topics we would like discussed the most. For those submitting queries about other articles, we prefer substantial articles (no fillers please). Slant articles toward roofing contractors. We have little use for generic articles that can appear in any business publication and give little consideration to such material submitted."

‡SHOPPING CENTER WORLD, Intertec Publishing Corp., 6151 Powers Ferry Rd., Atlanta GA 30339-2941. (404)955-2500. Fax: (404)955-0400. E-mail: tdefranks@mindspring.com. Website: http://www.InternetReview.com. Editor: Teresa DeFranks. 75% freelance written. Prefers to work with published/established writers. Monthly magazine. "Material is written with the shopping center developer, owner, manager and shopping center tenant in mind." Estab. 1972. Pays on publication. Publishes ms an average of 3 months after acceptance. Byline given. Buys all rights. Query for electronic submissions. Reports in 2 months. Sample copy for $10.

Nonfiction: Interview/profile, new product, opinion, photo feature, technical. Buys 50 mss/year. Query with published clips or send complete ms. Length: 750-3,000 words. Pays $75-500. Sometimes pays expenses of writers on assignment.

Photos: State availability of photos with submission. Reviews 4×5 transparencies and 35mm slides. Offers no additional payment for photos. Model releases and identification of subjects required. Buys one-time rights.

Tips: "We are always looking for talented writers to work on assignment. Writers with real estate writing and business backgrounds have a better chance. Industry trends and state reviews are all freelance written on an assignment basis. Most assignments are made to those writers who are familiar with the magazine's subject matter and have already reviewed our editorial calendar of future topics."

UNDERGROUND CONSTRUCTION, (formerly *Pipeline & Utilities Construction*), Oildom Publishing Co. of Texas, Inc., P.O. Box 219368, Houston TX 77218-9368. (281)558-6930. Fax: (281)558-7029. E-mail: rcarpen@undergro undinfo.com. Website: http://www.undergroundinfo.com. Editor: Robert Carpenter. 15% freelance written. Monthly magazine covering underground oil and gas pipeline, water and sewer pipeline, cable construction for contractors and owning companies. Circ. 34,500. Buys first North American serial rights. Publishes ms an average of 3 months after acceptance. Reports in 1 month. Sample copy for SASE.

Nonfiction: How-to, job stories. Query with published clips. Length: 1,000-2,000 words. Pays $3-500 "unless unusual expenses are incurred in getting the story." Sometimes pays the expenses of writers on assignment.

Photos: Send photos with ms. Reviews color prints and slides. Captions required. Buys one-time rights.

Tips: "We supply guidelines outlining information we need." The most frequent mistake made by writers in completing articles is unfamiliarity with the field.

DENTAL

DENTAL ECONOMICS, PennWell Publishing Co., P.O. Box 3408, Tulsa OK 74101-3400. (918)835-3161. Fax: (918)831-9804. E-mail: markh@pennwell.com. Website: http://www.dentaleconomics.com. Publisher: Lyle Hoyt. Contact: Joseph Blaes, editor. 10% freelance written. Monthly dental trade journal. "Our readers are actively practicing dentists who look to us for current practice-building, practice-administrative and personal finance assistance." Estab. 1911. Circ. 110,000. **Pays on acceptance.** Publishes ms an average of 4 months after acceptance. Byline given. Buys first rights. Reports in 2 months. Free sample copy and writer's guidelines.
Nonfiction: General interest, how-to. "No human interest and consumer-related stories." Buys 10 mss/year. Query. Length: 750-3,500 words. Pays $150-500 for assigned articles; $75-350 for unsolicited articles. Sometimes pays the expenses of writers on assignment.
Photos: State availability of photos with submission. Reviews contact sheets. Model releases and identification of subjects required. Buys one-time rights.
Tips: "How-to articles on specific subjects such as practice-building, financial management and collections should be relevant to a busy, solo-practice dentist."

PROOFS, The Magazine of Dental Sales and Marketing, PennWell Publishing Co., P.O. Box 3408, Tulsa OK 74101-3400. (918)835-3161. Fax: (918)831-9804. E-mail: maryg@pennwell.com. Editor: Mary Elizabeth Good. Assistant Editor: Julie Harris. Contact: Mary Elizabeth Good. 5% freelance written. Magazine published 10 times/year. "*Proofs* is the only publication of the dental trade, for dental dealers, sales forces and key marketing personnel of manufacturers. It publishes news of the industry (not the profession), personnel changes and articles on how to sell dental equipment and merchandise and services that can be provided to the dentist-customer." Estab. 1917. Circ. 7,000. Pays on publication. Byline given. Buys first North American serial rights. Editorial lead time 1 month. Reports in 2 weeks on queries. Sample copy and writer's guidelines free.
Nonfiction: General interest, historical/nostalgic, how-to, interview/profile, opinion, personal experience. "No articles written for dentist-readers." Buys 15 mss/year. Query or send complete ms. Length: 400-1,250. Pays $100-200.
Photos: Either state availability of photos with submission or send photos with submission. Reviews minimum size 3½×5 prints. Now uses color photographs. Offers no additional payment for photos accepted with ms. Identification of subjects required. Buys one-time rights.
Tips: "Learn something about the dental industry and how it operates. We have no interest in manufacturers who sell only direct. We do not want information on products and how they work, but will take news items on manufacturers' promotions involving products. Most interested in stories on how to sell *in the dental industry*; industry personnel feel they are 'unique' and not like other industries. In many cases, this is true, but not entirely. We are most open to feature articles on selling, supply-house operations, providing service."

RDH, The National Magazine for Dental Hygiene Professionals, PennWell Publishing Co., P.O. Box 3306, Tulsa OK 74101. (918)831-9742. Fax: (918)831-9804. E-mail: markh@pennwell.com. Website: http://www.pennwell.c om. Editor: Mark Hartley. 30% freelance written. Monthly magazine covering information relevant to dental hygiene professionals as business-career oriented individuals. "Dental hygienists are highly trained, licensed professionals; most are women. They are concerned with ways to develop rewarding careers, give optimum service to patients and to grow both professionally and personally." Circ. 67,000. Usually pays 30 days after acceptance. Publishes ms an average of 4 months after acceptance. Byline given. Buys first serial rights. Reports in 1 month on queries and mss. Sample copies and writer's guidelines available.
Nonfiction: Essays, general interest, interview/profile, personal experience, photo feature, technical. "We are interested in any topic that offers broad reader appeal, especially in the area of personal growth (communication, managing time, balancing career and personal life). No undocumented clinical or technical articles; how-it-feels-to-be-a-patient articles; product-oriented articles (unless in generic terms); anything cutesy-unprofessional." Length: 1,500-3,000 words. Pays $200-350 for assigned articles; $50-200 for unsolicited articles. Sometimes pays expenses of writers on assignment.
Photos: Covers are shot on location across US.
Tips: "Freelancers should have a feel for the concerns of today's business-career woman—and address those interests and concerns with practical, meaningful and even motivational messages. We want to see good-quality manuscripts on both personal growth and lifestyle topics. For clinical and/or technical topics, we prefer the writers be members of the dental profession. New approaches to old problems and dilemmas will always get a close look from our editors. *RDH* is also interested in manuscripts for our feature section. Other than clinical information, dental hygienists are interested in all sorts of topics—finances, personal growth, educational opportunities, business management, staff/employer relations, communication and motivation, office rapport and career options. Other than clinical/technical articles, *RDH* maintains an informal tone. Writing style can easily be accommodated to our format."

DRUGS, HEALTH CARE AND MEDICAL PRODUCTS

CANADIAN PHARMACEUTICAL JOURNAL, 21 Concourse Gate #13, Nepean, Ontario K2E 754 Canada. (613)727-1364. Fax: (613)727-3757. E-mail: cpj@cyberus.ca. Editor: Andrew Reinboldt. Works with a small number of new/unpublished writers each year. Monthly journal for pharmacists. Estab. 1868. Circ. 13,038. Pays after editing.

Publishes ms an average of 6 months after acceptance. Buys first serial rights. Reports in 2 months. Free sample copy and writer's guidelines.

Nonfiction: Relevant to Canadian pharmacy. Publishes continuing education, pharmacy practice, education and legislation, how-to; historical. Length: 200-400 words (for news notices); 800-1,500 words (for articles). Query. Payment is contingent on value. Sometimes pays expenses of writers on assignment.

Photos: Color and b&w 5×7 glossies purchased with mss. Captions, model releases required.

Tips: "Query with complete description of proposed article, including topic, sources (in general), length, payment requested, suggested submission date, and whether photographs will be included. It is helpful if the writer has read a *recent* copy of the journal; we are glad to send one if required. References should be included where appropriate (this is vital where medical and scientific information is included). Send three copies of each manuscript. Author's degree and affiliations (if any) and writing background should be listed."

‡INDEPENDENT LIVING PROVIDER, The Sales & Service Magazine for HME Dealers, Equal Opportunity Publications, Inc., 1160 E. Jericho Turnpike, Suite 200, Huntington NY 11743. (516)421-9478. Fax: (516)421-0359. Contact: Anne Kelly, editor. 75% freelance written. Bimonthly magazine on home health care, rehabilitation, and disability issues as they relate to the home medical equipment (HME) dealer. *Independent Living Provider* magazine is written for home care dealers to enhance their business through knowledge of health care issues, sales and marketing strategies and service to clients." Estab. 1968. Circ. 35,000. Pays on publication. Byline given. Buys First North American serial rights. Reports in 3 months. Sample copy and writer's guidelines free.

Nonfiction: Business, interview/profile, health care, new product, disability, chronic illness. Buys 40 mss/year. Query. Length: 500-1,500 words. Pays 10¢/word.

Photos: Send photos with submission. Reviews prints. Offers $15/photo. Prefers 35mm color slides. Captions, identification of subjects required. Buys all rights.

Tips: "The best way to have a manuscript published is to first send a detailed query on a subject related to home health care and home dealers. We also need articles on innovative ways that home health care dealers are meeting their clients needs, as well as profiles of successful dealers."

‡OPTICAL PRISM, Canada's Optical Goods & Services Magazine, Vezcom, Inc., 31 Hastings Dr., Unionville, Ontario L3R 4Y5 Canada. (905)475-9343. Fax: (905)477-2821. E-mail: prism@istar.ca. Editor: Allan Vezina. 90% freelance written. Trade journal published 9 times/year covering the Canadian optical industry for "optometrists, opticians, ophthalmologists and optical suppliers and their sales staffs. Material covers clinical papers, practice management, contact lenses (clinical and practical), marketing, selling, motivation and merchandising." Estab. 1983. Circ. 7,400. **Pays on acceptance.** Publishes ms an average of 4 months after acceptance. Byline given. Not copyrighted. Buys one-time rights or second serial (reprint) rights. Editorial lead time 2 months. Submit seasonal material 3 months in advance. Accepts previously published submissions "with permission of original publisher in writing." Reports in 1 week. Sample copy and writer's guidelines free.

Nonfiction: How-to, inspirational, interview/profile, new product, technical. "No U.S.-specific material. We try to concentrate on the Canadian market." Buys 35-40 mss/year. Query. Length: 500-10,000 words. Pays 50-500 (Canadian).

Photos: Send photos with submission. Reviews transparencies and prints. Offers no additional payment for photos accepted with ms. Captions, model releases and indentification of subjects required. Buys one-time rights.

Tips: "Send query with detailed outline of the article along with the 'slant' to be taken, if any."

‡OPTI-COURIER, Opti-Courier, Ltd., 158 Fisher Rd., Huntington Valley PA 19006. (215)938-1739. Editor: Linda Herman. 65% freelance written. Monthly magazine. "*Opti-Courier* is a zany publication that addresses optical practitioners and salespeople. Serious subjects such as technical articles and business suggestions are addressed, but always kept on the wild and crazy side." Estab. 1994. Circ. 26,000. Pays on publication. Publishes ms an average of 2 months after acceptance. Byline given. Buys all rights and makes work-for-hire assignments. Editorial lead time 3 months. Submit seasonal material 4 months in advance. Reports in 6 weeks on queries; 2 months on mss. Sample copy free.

Nonfiction: General interest, how-to (optical), humor, interview/profile, new product, personal experience, photo feature, technical, business. Buys 100 mss/year. Query. Length: 800-1,000 words. Pays $50-100. Sometimes pays expenses of writers on assignment.

Photos: Send photos with submission. Reviews b&w prints. Negotiates payment individually. Identification of subjects required. Buys one-time rights.

Columns/Departments: Various optically-related columns. Buys 15 mss/year. Query. Pays $50-100.

Fillers: Facts, gags to be illustrated by cartoonist, short humor, cartoons, crossword puzzles, recipes. Buys 100/year.

Tips: "Be familiar with the optical, or at least the business world. Offer the small-business person tips in a crazy, fun way. Do not send over-photocopied, fly-specked submissions that have clearly made the rounds. Clear copy is greatly appreciated. If you don't know anything about optical, go out and talk to someone in the business before writing anything. *You must know the differences among the 3 O's.*"

EDUCATION AND COUNSELING

Professional educators, teachers, coaches and counselors—as well as other people involved in training and education—read the journals classified here. Many journals for educators are nonprofit forums for professional advancement; writers contribute articles in return for a byline and contributor's copies. *Writer's Market* includes only educational journals that pay freelancers for articles. Education-related publications for students are included in the Consumer Career, College and Alumni; and Teen and Young Adult sections. Listings in the Childcare and Parental Guidance and Psychology and Self-Improvement sections of Consumer Magazines may also be of interest.

‡**ARTS & ACTIVITIES**, Publishers' Development Corporation, Dept. WM, 591 Camino de la Reina, Suite 200, San Diego CA 92108-3104. (619)297-5352. Fax: (619)297-5353. Editor: Maryellen Bridge. 95% freelance written. Eager to work with new/unpublished writers. Monthly (except July and August) art education magazine covering art education at levels from preschool through college for educators and therapists engaged in arts and crafts education and training. Estab. 1932. Circ. 24,000. Pays on publication. Publishes ms an average of 9-12 months after acceptance. Byline given. Buys first North American serial rights. Submit seasonal material 6 months in advance. Reports in 3 months. Sample copy for 9×12 SAE with 8 first-class stamps. Writer's guidelines for #10 SASE.
Nonfiction: Historical/nostalgic (arts, activities, history); how-to (classroom art experiences, artists' techniques); interview/profile (of artists); opinion (on arts activities curriculum, ideas on how to do things better, philosophy of art education); personal experience in the art classroom ("this ties in with the how-to, we like it to be *personal*, no recipe style"); articles on exceptional art programs. Buys 80-100 mss/year. Length: 200-2,000 words. Pays $35-150.
 • Editors here are seeking more materials for upper elementary and secondary levels on printmaking, ceramics, 3-dimensional design, weaving, fiber arts (stitchery, tie-dye, batik, etc.), crafts, painting and multicultural art.
Tips: "Frequently in unsolicited manuscripts, writers obviously have not studied the magazine to see what style of articles we publish. Send for a sample copy to familiarize yourself with our style and needs. The best way to find out if his/her writing style suits our needs is for the author to submit a manuscript on speculation. We prefer an anecdotal style of writing, so that readers will feel as though they are there in the art room as the lesson/project is taking place. Also, good quality photographs of student artwork are important. We are a *visual* art magazine!"

THE ATA MAGAZINE, The Alberta Teachers' Association, 11010 142nd St., Edmonton, Alberta T5N 2R1 Canada. (403)453-2411. Fax: (403)455-6481. E-mail: postmaster@teachers.ab.ca. Website: http://www.teachers.ab.ca. Editor: Tim Johnston. Contact: Raymond Gariepy, managing editor. 50% freelance written. Quarterly magazine covering education. Estab. 1920. Circ. 39,500. Pays on publication. Publishes ms an average of 2 months after acceptance. Byline given. Offers kill fee of $75. Buys one-time rights. Editorial lead time 2 months. Submit seasonal material 2 months in advance. Accepts simultaneous submissions. Reports in 2 months. Sample copy and writer's guidelines free on request.
Nonfiction: Education-related topics. Length: 750-1,250 words. Pays $75-150. Sometimes pays expenses of writers on assignment.
Photos: Send photos with submission. Reviews 4×6 prints. Negotiates payment individually. Captions required. Negotiates rights.

CLASS ACT, Class Act, Inc., P.O. Box 802, Henderson KY 42420. E-mail: mthurman@hcc-uky.campus.mci.net. Editor: Susan Thurman. 75% freelance written. Educational newsletter published 9 times/year covering English/language arts education. "Our writers must know English as a classroom subject and should be familiar with writing for teens. If you can't make your manuscript interesting to teenagers, we're not interested." Estab. 1993. Circ. 300. **Pays on acceptance.** Publishes ms an average of 6 months after acceptance. Byline given. Offers 100% kill fee. Buys all rights. Editorial lead time 2 months. Submit seasonal material 3 months in advance. Accepts simultaneous submissions. Reports in 1 month. Sample copy for $3. Writer's guidelines for #10 SASE.
Nonfiction: How-to (games, puzzles, assignments relating to English education). "NO Masters theses; no esoteric articles; no poetry; no educational theory or jargon." Buys 15 mss/year. Send complete ms. Length: 100-2,000 words. Pays $10-40.
Columns/Departments: Writing assignments (innovative, thought-provoking for teens), 500 words; puzzles, games (English education oriented), 200 words; teacher tips (bulletin boards, time-saving devices), 100 words. Send complete ms. Pays $10-40.
Fillers: Teacher tips. Pays $10.
Tips: "Please know the kind of language used by junior/senior high students. Don't speak above them. Also, it helps to know what these students *don't* know, in order to explain or emphasize the concepts. Clip art is sometimes used but is not paid extra for. We like material that's slightly humorous while still being educational. Especially open to innovative writing assignments; educational puzzles and games and instructions on basics. Again, be familiar with this age group."

DANCE TEACHER NOW, The Practical Magazine of Dance, SMW Communications, Inc., 3101 Poplarwood Court, #310, Raleigh NC 27604-1010. Fax: (919)872-6888. E-mail: danceeditor@aol.com. Website: http://www.dance-teacher.com. Editor: K.C. Patrick. 80% freelance written. Magazine published 10 times/year. "Our readers are professional dance educators, business persons and related professionals in all forms of dance. Estab. 1979. Circ. 8,000. Pays on publication. Publishes ms an average of 3 months after acceptance. Byline given. Negotiates rights and permission to reprint on request. Submit seasonal/holiday material 6 months in advance. Reports in 3 months. Sample copy for 9×12 SAE with 6 first-class stamps. Free writer's guidelines by mail or on website.

Nonfiction: How-tos (teach, business), interview/profile, new product, personal experience, photo feature. Special issues: Summer Programs (February); Music & More; (July/August); Costumes and Production Preview (November); College/Training Schools (December). No PR or puff pieces. All articles must be well researched. Buys at least 50 mss/year. Query first. Length: 1,500-3,500 words. Pays $100-400.

Reprints: Occasionally buys previously published submissions. Send typed ms with rights for sale noted and information about when and where the article previously appeared.

Photos: Send photos with submission. Reviews contact sheets, negatives, transparencies and prints. Limited budget.

Columns/Departments: Practical Tips (how-tos or updates, 100-350 words. Pays $25/published tip. Free Calendar Listings (auditions/competitions/workshops), 50 words.

Tips: "Read several issues—particularly seasonal. Stay within writer's guidelines."

‡**EARLY CHILDHOOD NEWS, The Journal of Professional Development**, Peter Li, Inc., 330 Progress Rd., Dayton OH 45449. Fax: (937)847-5910. Editor: Tim Bete. 95% freelance written. Bimonthly magazine. "All articles must promote the professional development of those who work with children in child care settings." Estab. 1988. Circ. 30,000. Pays on publication. Publishes ms an average of 2 months after acceptance. Byline given. Buys first and second serial (reprint) rights. Editorial lead time 2 months. Submit seasonal material 4 months in advance. Accepts simultaneous and previously published submissions. Sample copy for $3. Writer's guidelines for #10 SASE.

Nonfiction: How-to (working with children), opinion, professional research-based development articles. No non-research-based activity articles. Buys 40 mss/year. Send complete ms. Length: 600-3,000 words. Pays $75-200.

Photos: Send photos with submission. Reviews 3×5 prints. Offers no additional payment for photos accepted with ms. Model releases and identification of subjects required. Buys one-time rights.

Columns/Departments: Parent Handout (reproducible newsletter for parents); Back Page ("warm and fuzzy" editorial). Length: 600 words. Buys 12 mss/year. Send complete ms. Pays $75-100.

Tips: "Have experience working in child care settings or an advanced degree in early childhood education."

EDUCATION IN FOCUS, Books for All Times, Inc., Box 2, Alexandria VA 22313. (703)548-0457. Editor: Joe David. Semiannual newsletter covering educational issues. Pays on publication. Buys first, one-time and second serial (reprint) rights. Negotiates rights to include articles in books. Accepts simultaneous submissions. Reports in 1 month. Query with SASE.

Nonfiction: "We are looking for articles that expose the failures and discuss the successes of education."

INSTRUCTOR MAGAZINE, Scholastic, Inc., 555 Broadway, New York NY 10012-3199. Website: http://scholastic.com/Instructor. Editor-in-Chief: Mickey Revenaugh. Publishing Coordinator: Joan Tashman. Eager to work with new/unpublished writers, especially teachers. Monthly magazine emphasizing elementary education. Estab. 1891. Circ. 275,000. **Pays on acceptance.** Publishes ms an average of 1 year after acceptance. Byline given. Buys all rights. Submit seasonal material 6 months in advance. Reports in 1 month on queries; 2 months on mss. Sample copy for $3. Writer's guidelines for SASE; mention *Writer's Market*.

Nonfiction: How-to articles on elementary classroom practice—practical suggestions and project reports. Occasionally publishes first-person accounts of classroom experiences. Buys 100 mss/year. Query. Length: 400-2,000 words. Pays $25-75 for short items; $125-400 for articles and features. Send all queries Attention: manuscripts editor.

Photos: Send photos with submission. Reviews 4×5 transparencies and prints. Offers no additional payment for photos accepted with ms. Model releases, identification of subjects required. Buys all rights.

Columns/Departments: Idea Notebook (quick teacher tips and ideas, seasonal activities, bulletin boards and crafts); At the End of the Day (first person essays by teachers). Buys 100 mss/year. Query with SASE. Length: 50-1,000 words. Pays $30-100.

Tips: "How-to articles should be kept practical, with concrete examples whenever possible. Writers should keep in mind that our audience is elementary teachers."

LEARNING, 3515 W. Market St., Greensboro NC 27403. Fax: (910)547-1590. E-mail: learning@vcom1.com. Website: http://www.learning.com. Publisher: Annie Galvin Teich. 60% freelance written by teachers and other experts in education. Bimonthly magazine covering educational topics for teachers in grades K-6. Estab. 1972. Circ. 200,000. **Pays on acceptance.** Buys all rights. Submit seasonal material 9 months in advance. Reports in up to 9 months. Sample copy for $4.95. Free writer's guidelines with SASE.

● *Learning* has become more selective; submissions must meet the format.

Nonfiction: "We publish manuscripts that describe innovative, practical teaching strategies." How-to (classroom management and hints for teaching in all curriculum areas); personal experience (from teachers in grades K-6); profile (with teachers in unusual or innovative teaching situations). Strong interest in articles that deal with discipline, teaching,

ALWAYS CHECK the most recent copy of a magazine for the address and editor's name before you send in a query or manuscript.

motivation and working with parents. Buys 250 mss/year. Query. Length: 500-3,500 words. Pays $15-350.
Tips: "We are looking for innovative ideas and practices as well as first-hand personal accounts of dramatic successes—or failures—with a lesson to be drawn. No theoretical or academic papers. We are also interested in examples of especially creative classrooms and teachers. Emphasis on professionalism will increase: top teachers telling what they do best and how."

‡MEDIA & METHODS, American Society of Educators, 1429 Walnut St., Philadelphia PA 19102. (215)563-3501. Fax: (215)587-9706. Editorial Director: Michele Sokoloff. Bimonthly trade journal published during the school year about educational products, equipment, multimedia technologies and programs for K-12 schools. Readership: Librarians and media specialists. Estab. 1963. Circ. 42,000. Pays on publication. Publishes ms an average of 3 months after acceptance. Byline given. Buys first North American serial rights. Free sample copy and writer's guidelines.
Nonfiction: How-to, practical, new product, case studies, technical. Must send query letter, outline or call editor. Do not send ms. Length: 600-1,200 words. Pays $75-200.
Photos: State availability of photos with submission. Reviews 3×5 prints. Offers no additional payment for photos accepted with ms. Captions and identification of subjects required. Buys one-time rights.

SCHOOL ARTS MAGAZINE, 50 Portland St., Worcester MA 01608-9959. Fax: (508)753-3834. Editor: Eldon Katter. 85% freelance written. Monthly magazine (September-May), serving arts and craft education profession, K-12, higher education and museum education programs written by and for art teachers. Estab. 1901. Pays on publication. Publishes ms an average of 3 months "if timely; if less pressing, can be 1 year or more" after acceptance. Buys all rights. Reports in 3 months. Free sample copy and writer's guidelines.
Nonfiction: Articles on art and craft activities in schools. Should include description and photos of activity in progress, as well as examples of finished artwork. Query or send complete ms. Length: 600-1,400 words. Pays $30-150.
Tips: "We prefer articles on actual art projects or techniques done by students in actual classroom situations. Philosophical and theoretical aspects of art and art education are usually handled by our contributing editors. Our articles are reviewed and accepted on merit and each is tailored to meet our needs. Keep in mind that art teachers want practical tips, above all—more hands-on information than academic theory. Write your article with the accompanying photographs in hand." The most frequent mistakes made by writers are "bad visual material (photographs, drawings) submitted with articles, or a lack of complete descriptions of art processes; and no rationale behind programs or activities. Familiarity with the field of art education is essential."

TEACHING TOLERANCE, The Southern Poverty Law Center, 400 Washington Ave., Montgomery AL 36104. (205)264-0286. Fax: (205)264-3121. Editor: Jim Carnes. 50% freelance written. Semiannual magazine. "*Teaching Tolerance* is dedicated to helping K-12 teachers promote tolerance and understanding between widely diverse groups of students. Includes articles, teaching ideas, and reviews of other resources available to educators." Estab. 1991. Circ. 150,000. **Pays on acceptance.** Byline given. Buys all rights. Editorial lead time 6 months. Submit seasonal material 6 months in advance. Sample copy and writer's guidelines free.
Nonfiction: Features, essays, how-to (classroom techniques), personal classroom experiences, photo features. "No jargon, rhetoric or academic analysis. No theoretical discussions on the pros/cons of multicultural education." Buys 6-8 mss/year. Query with published clips. Length: 1,000-3,000 words. Pays $500-3,000 maximum. Sometimes pays expenses of writers on assignment.
Photos: State availability of photos with submission. Reviews contact sheets and transparencies. Offers no additional payment for photos accepted with ms. Captions and identification of subjects required. Buys one-time rights.
Columns/Departments: Essays (personal reflection, how-to, school program), 400-800 words; Idea Exchange (special projects, successful anti-bias activities), 400 words; Between the Lines, (using literature to teach tolerance), 1,200 words; Student Writings (Short essays dealing with diversity, tolerance & justice), 300-500 words. Buys 8-12 mss/year. Pays $100-1,000. Query with published clips.
Tips: "We want lively, simple, concise writing. The writing style should be descriptive and reflective, showing the strength of programs dealing successfully with diversity by employing clear descriptions of real scenes and interactions, and by using quotes from teachers and students. We ask that prospective writers study previous issues of the magazine and writer's guidelines before sending a query with ideas. Most open to articles that have a strong classroom focus. We are interested in approaches to teaching tolerance and promoting understanding that really work—approaches we might not have heard of. We want to inform our readers; we also want to inspire and encourage them. We know what's happening nationally; we want to know what's happening in your neighborhood classroom."

TEACHING K-8, The Professional Ideabook for Teachers, Early Years, Inc., 40 Richards Ave., 7th Floor, Norwalk CT 06854-2319. (203)855-2650. Fax: (203)855-2656. E-mail: teachingk8@aol.com. Publisher: Allen Raymond. Contact: Patricia Broderick, editorial director. 90% freelance written. Monthly magazine published September through May, covering classroom teaching of K-8. Estab. 1970. Pays on publication. Publishes ms an average of 7 months after acceptance. Byline given. Buys all rights. Submit seasonal material 6 months in advance. Reports in 2 months. Sample copy for $3 and 9×12 SAE with 10 first-class stamps. Writer's guidelines for #10 SASE. "Do not fax queries."
Nonfiction: Classroom curriculum material. Send complete ms. Length: 1,200 words. Pays $50 maximum.
Photos: Offers no additional payment for photos. Model releases and identification of subjects required.
Tips: "We do not accept queries, only complete manuscripts. Manuscripts should be specifically oriented to a successful

teaching strategy, idea, project or program. Broad overviews of programs or general theory manuscripts are not usually the type of material we select for publication. Because of the definitive learning level we cover (pre-school through grade eight) we try to avoid presenting general groups of unstructured ideas. We prefer classroom-tested ideas and techniques. Read several issues and thoroughly familiarize yourself with the types of articles we use."

‡TECHniques, Making Educational and Career Connections, American Vocational Associations, 1410 King St., Alexandria VA 22314. E-mail: avahq@avaonline.org. Editor: Ann Dykman. Contact: Marlene Lozada, associate editor. 10% freelance written. Magazine published 8 times/year covering education with an emphasis on career preparation. "*TECHniques* has no 'slant.' We aim for an objective, journalistic treatment of issues. Readers are high school and community college teachers, administrators and counselors and also state education department or labor department employees." Estab. 1926. Circ. 40,000. Pays on publication. Publishes ms an average of 3 months after acceptance. Byline given. Offers 25% kill fee. Buys first North American serial rights and second serial (reprint) rights. Editorial lead time 3 months. Submit seasonal material 2 months in advance. Reports in 1 week on queries; 3 months on mss. Sample copy for $4.50. Writer's guidelines for #10 SASE.
Nonfiction: Book excerpts, general interest, how-to (teach, manage, setup a new school, implement educational reform), humor, interview/profile, opinion, personal experience, photo feature. No scholarly or technical articles. Buys 8-10 mss/year. Query with published clips or send complete ms. Length: 750-3,500 words. Pays $200-1,000. Sometimes pays expenses of writers on assignment.
Reprints: Occasionally accepts previously published material.
Photos: State availability of photos with submission. Reviews contact sheets, 2¼×2¼ transparencies, 4×6 prints. Negotiates payment individually. Model releases, identification of subjects required. Buys one-time rights.
Columns/Departments: Forum (opinion on issues), 750 words; Book reviews (subjects should relate to education or labor trends), 500-1,000 words. Query with published clips. Pays $50-150.
Tips: "Suggest story ideas, don't be cute, don't use exclamation points anywhere. Be enthusiastic, be professional—expect a 'round 2' of questions and requests for additional info."

TECHNOLOGY & LEARNING, 600 Harrison St., San Francisco CA 94107. Fax: (415)908-6604. E-mail: editors@techlearning.com. Website: http://www.techlearning.com. Editor-in-Chief: Judy Salpeter. 50% freelance written. Works with a small number of new/unpublished writers each year. Monthly magazine published during school year emphasizing elementary through high school educational technology topics. Estab. 1980. Circ. 80,000. Pays on publication. Publishes ms an average of 8 months after acceptance. Buys all rights. Submit seasonal material 6 months in advance. Reports in 3-5 months. Sample copy for 8×10 SAE with 6 first-class stamps. Writer's guidelines for #10 SASE.
Nonfiction: "We publish manuscripts that describe innovative ways of using technology in the classroom as well as articles that discuss controversial issues in computer education." Interviews, brief technology-related activity ideas and longer featurettes describing fully-developed and tested classroom ideas. Buys 20 mss/year. Query. Length: 800 words for software reviews; 1,500-2,500 words for major articles. Pays $150 or more for reviews; $400 or more for articles. Educational software reviews are assigned through editorial offices. "If interested, send a letter telling us of your areas of interest and expertise as well as the computer(s) and other equipment you have available to you." Pays expenses of writers on assignment.
Photos: State availability of photos with query.
Tips: "The talent that goes into writing our shorter hands-on pieces is different from that required for features (e.g., interviews, issues pieces, etc.). Write whatever taps your talent best. A frequent mistake is taking too 'novice' or too 'expert' an approach. You need to know our audience well and to understand how much they know about computers. Also, too many manuscripts lack a definite point of view or focus or opinion. We like pieces with clear, strong, well thought-out opinions."

TODAY'S CATHOLIC TEACHER, 330 Progress Rd., Dayton OH 45449-2386. (937)847-5900. Fax: (937)847-5910. Editor: Mary C. Noschang. 40% freelance written. Works with a small number of new/unpublished writers each year. For administrators and teachers concerned with Catholic schools and education in general. Estab. 1967. Circ. 50,000. Pays after publication. Publishes ms an average of 3 months after acceptance. Byline given. Buys all rights. Phone queries OK. Submit seasonal material 3 months in advance. Reports in 4 months. Sample copy for $3. Writer's guidelines for #10 SASE; mention *Writer's Market* in request.
Nonfiction: How-to (based on experience, particularly for teachers to use in the classroom to supplement curriculum, philosophy with practical applications); interview (of practicing educators, educational leaders); personal experience (classroom happenings other educators can learn from); a few profiles (of educational leaders). Buys 40-50 mss/year. Submit complete ms. Length: 800-2,000 words. Pays $150-250.
Reprints: Send typed ms with rights for sale noted and information about when and where the article appeared.
Photos: State availability of photos with ms. Possible additional payment for color or b&w glossy prints or transparencies. Buys one-time rights. Captions preferred; model releases required.
Tips: "We prefer articles that are of interest or practical help to educators—educational trends, teaching ideas, curriculum-related material, administration suggestions; articles teachers can use in classrooms to teach current topics, etc."

UNIVERSITY AFFAIRS, Association of Universities and Colleges of Canada, 600-350 Albert St., Ottawa, Ontario K1R 1B1 Canada. (613)563-1236. Fax: (613)563-9745. E-mail: pberkowi@aucc.ca. Website: http://www.aucc.ca. Editor: Christine Tausig Ford. Associate Editor: Peggy Berkowitz. 25% freelance written. Tabloid published 10 times/year.

"For university faculty and administrators across Canada, *University Affairs* contains news, issues and commentary about higher education and research." Estab. 1959. Circ. 29,000. **Pays on acceptance.** Byline given. Buys first or all rights. Editorial lead time 3 months. Reports in 6 weeks on queries; 2 months on mss. Sample copy free.
  • *University Affairs* is looking for greater analysis and more issues-oriented articles related to "hot" topics in higher education.
Nonfiction: Essays, general interest, interview/profile, opinion, photo feature. Buys 25 mss/year. Query with published clips. Length: 1,000-1,800 words. Pays $400-1,200 (Canadian).
Photos: State availability of photos with submission. Reviews contact sheets, negatives, transparencies, prints. Negotiates payment individually. Captions, model releases, identification of subjects required. Buys one-time rights.
Columns/Departments: Around the Universities (short articles about research or teaching achievements or "firsts"), 200 words. Query with published clips. Pay $50-75 (Canadian).
Tips: "Read the publication before contacting me. Have a solid understanding of both my needs and the subject matter involved. Be accurate, check facts, and make sure your writing is high quality. Look for the human interest angle. Put yourself in place of the readers—what makes your story meaningful for them."

WONDERFUL IDEAS, P.O. Box 64691, Burlington VT 05406-4691. 1-(800)92-IDEAS. Fax: (201)376-9382. E-mail: nancy@wonderful.com. Editor: Nancy Segal Janes. 40% freelance written. Newsletter published 5 times/year. "*Wonderful Ideas* provides elementary and middle school teachers with creative and thought-provoking math activities, games, and lessons, with a focus on manipulatives and problem solving. Teacher-written and classroom-tested, these activities are designed to challenge students, while drawing strong connections between mathematical concepts and concrete problems. Book reviews and relationships of activities to NCTM Standards are also included." Estab. 1989. Circ. 1,700. Pays on publication. Publishes ms an average of 6 months after acceptance. Byline given. Buys all rights. Editorial lead time 3 months. Submit seasonal material 3 months in advance. Accepts simultaneous submissions. Reports in 1 month on queries; 3 months on mss. Sample copy and writer's guidelines free.
Nonfiction: Ideas for teaching elementary and middle school mathematics. Buys 10-15 mss/year. Query. Length: 900 words. Pays $20-60.
Reprints: Photocopy of article or short story and information about when and where the article previously appeared. Pays 100% of amount paid for an original article.
Columns/Departments: Wonderful Materials (review of new math materials and books), 700 words. Buys 3 mss/year. Query. Pays $20-60.

ELECTRONICS AND COMMUNICATION

These publications are edited for broadcast and telecommunications technicians and engineers, electrical engineers and electrical contractors. Included are journals for electronic equipment designers and operators who maintain electronic and telecommunication systems. Publications for appliance dealers can be found in Home Furnishings and Household Goods.

‡AMERICA'S NETWORK, Advanstar Communications, 201 Sandpointe Ave., Suite 600, Santa Ana CA 92707. (714)513-8400. Fax: (714)513-8634. Website: http://www.americasnetwork.com. Editor: Mary Slepicka. Managing Editor: David Kopf. 25% freelance written. Published twice monthly covering the public telecommunications network. "*America's Network* evaluates emerging technologies from a business-case perspective for those who conceive, design and run America's public network." Estab. 1909. Circ. 57,000. Pays on publication. Byline given. Offers $100 kill fee. Buys all rights. Editorial lead time 2 months. Submit seasonal material 2 months in advance. Reports in 1 month on queries; 2 weeks on mss. Sample copy for $4.95 (call (800)346-0085, ext 477). Writer's guidelines free (call (714)513-8422).
Nonfiction: Technical, market research. No news or business pieces. Buys 35 mss/year. Query with published clips. Length: 1,500-3,000 words. Pays 50¢/word for "high-tech" and 35¢/word for "low-tech" articles.
Photos: State availability of photos with query or send photos with submission. Reviews transparencies and prints. Offers no additional payment for photos accepted with ms. Captions, model releases and identification of subjects required. Buys one-time rights or all rights.
Tips: "Send full résumé with technical writing/engineering experience. We keep a file of potential writers."

CANADIAN ELECTRONICS, Action Communications Inc., 135 Spy Court, Markham, Ontario L3R 5H6 Canada. (905)477-3222. Fax: (905)477-4320. Editor: Tim Gouldson. 5% freelance written. Bimonthly tabloid covering electronics engineering. Estab. 1985. Circ. 25,000. Pays on publication. Publishes ms an average of 2 months after acceptance. Byline given. Buys first Canadian rights. Editorial lead time 2 months. Reports in 1 week on queries; 1 month on mss. Sample copy free.
Nonfiction: New product, technical. Feature articles on selected subjects. No consumer electronics. Buys 3 mss/year. Query with published clips. Length: 500-700 words. Pays $200-400. Sometimes pays expenses of writers on assignment.
Photos: Send photos with submission. Negotiates payment individually. Captions, identification of subjects required. Buys one-time rights.

‡**COMMUNICATIONS NEWS**, Nelson Publishing, 2504 N. Tamiami Trail, Nokomis FL 34275. (941)966-9521. Fax: (941)966-2590. E-mail: nelpub@ix.netcom.com. Website: http://www.comnews.com. Editor: Ripley Hotch. Contact: Features Editor. 40% freelance written. Monthly magazine covering communications networks with "controlled circulation for data and voice communications, specifically network managers. Solutions-oriented for end users of networking software and equipment at medium-sized to large organizations." Estab. 1966. Circ. 80,000. **Pays on acceptance**. Publishes ms an average of 2 months after acceptance. Byline given. Offers 25% kill fee. Buys first rights. Editorial lead time 3 months. Reports in 2 weeks on queries.
Nonfiction: Interview/profile, new product, networking solutions. Buys 30 mss/year. Query with published clips. Length: 200-1,400 words. Pays $100-1,200. Pays expenses of writers on assignment.
Photos: Send photos with submission. Reviews transparencies. Negotiates payment individually. Identification of subjects required. Buys one-time rights.
Tips: "All submissions and initial contacts should be written. We advise checking our website for latest editorial calendar and guidelines."

COMMUNICATIONS QUARTERLY, P.O. Box 465, Barrington NH 03825-0465. Phone/Fax: (603)664-2515. E-mail: commquart@aol.com or 72127.745@compuserve.com. Publisher: Richard Ross. Editor: Terry Littlefield. 80% freelance written. Quarterly publication on theoretical and technical aspects of amateur radio and RF communication industry technology. Estab. 1990. Circ. 10,000. Pays on publication. Publishes ms an average of 6 months after acceptance. Byline given. Buys first rights. Reports in 1 month. Writer's guidelines for #10 SASE.
Nonfiction: "Interested in technical and theory pieces on all aspects of amateur radio and the RF communications industry. State-of-the-art developments are of particular interest to our readers. No human interest stories or articles related to the cable TV or broadcast industries." Query or send complete ms. Pays $40/published page.
Reprints: Sometimes accepts previously published submissions. Send photocopy of article and information about when and where the article previously appeared. Pays 100% of amount paid for an original article.
Photos: Send photos with submission. Reviews 5×7 prints. Offers no additional payment for photos accepted with ms. Captions and identification of subjects required. Buys one-time rights.
Tips: "We are looking for writers with knowledge of the technical or theoretical aspects of the amateur radio and communication industries. Our readers are interested in state-of-the-art developments, high-tech construction projects and the theory behind the latest technologies."

‡**DEALERSCOPE CONSUMER ELECTRONICS MARKETPLACE**, North American Publishing Co., 401 N. Broad St., Philadelphia PA 19108. E-mail: editordcem@napco.com. Editor: Janet Pinkerton. Contact: Michael McGann, managing editor. 20% freelance written. Monthly tabloid covering consumer electronics and major appliances. "We're very new-product oriented. We want to know all the ins and outs, including pricing and ship dates." Estab. 1922. Circ. 37,000. Pays on publication. Publishes ms an average of 2 months after acceptance. Byline given. Offers 100% kill fee. Buys first North American serial rights. Editorial lead time 2 months. Submit seasonal material 2 months in advance. Reports in 1 month. Sample copy and writer's guidelines free.
Nonfiction: Product round-ups. Special issues: Annual gold book issue. No first-person articles or product reviews. Buys 12-14 mss/year. Query. Length: 400-1,200 words. Pays $200-650 for assigned articles; $200-400 for unsolicited articles. Sometimes pays expenses of writers on assignment.
Photos: Send photos with submission. Reviews transparencies. Offers no additional payment for photos accepted with ms. Captions and identification of subjects required. Buys one-time rights.
Columns/Departments: Product roundups (product blurb with notes), 200-350 words. Query. Pays $200.
Tips: "Be sparse, yet insightful. Words are at a premium in our publication."

‡**ELECTRONIC DISTRIBUTION TODAY**, Custom Media, Inc., P.O. Box 23069, Chagrin Falls OH 44023. (216)543-9451. Fax: (216)543-9764. E-mail: edtmag@aol.com. Editor: Edward J. Walter. 20% freelance written. Bimonthly magazine "reaches industrial (not consumer) distributors of electronic parts and equipment. It features sales and management articles, case histories, operations, promotion/advertising, and merchandising." Estab. 1991. Circ. 6,500. Pays on publication. Publishes ms an average of 3 months after acceptance. Byline given. Buys first North American serial rights. Editorial lead time 1 month. Reports in 2 weeks on queries; 1 month on mss. Sample copy free.
Nonfiction: Interview/profile. Buys 6-10 mss/year. Query. Length: 500-1,500 words. Pays $500-1,500. Sometimes pays expenses of writers on assignment.
Photos: State availability of photos with submission. Reviews contact sheets. Offers $50/photo. Captions and identification of subjects required. Buys one-time rights.

ELECTRONIC SERVICING & TECHNOLOGY, The Professional Magazine for Electronics and Computer Servicing, CQ Communications, P.O. Box 12487, Overland Park KS 66282-2487. Phone/fax: (913)492-4857. E-mail: cpersedit@aol.com. Contact: Conrad Persson, editor. Managing Editor: Kirstie Wickham. 80% freelance written. Monthly magazine. "*Electronic Servicing & Technology* is edited for service technicians, field service personnel, and avid servicing enthusiasts, who service audio, video and computer equipment." Estab. 1950. Circ. 30,000. Pays on publication. Publishes ms an average of 4 months after acceptance. Byline given. Buys one-time rights. Editorial lead time 2 months. Accepts simultaneous submissions. Reports in 1 month on queries; 2 months on mss. Sample copy and guidelines free.
Nonfiction: How-to, new product, technical. Buys 40 mss/year. Query or send complete ms. Pays $300.
Reprints: Send typed ms with rights for sale noted and information about when and where the article previously

appeared.

Photos: Send photos with submission. Offers no additional payment for photos accepted with ms. Buys one-time rights.

Columns/Departments: Business Corner (business tips); Computer Corner (computer servicing tips); Video Corner (understanding/servicing TV and video); all 1,000-2,000 words. Buys 30 mss/year. Query or send complete ms. Pays $100-300.

Tips: "Writers should have a strong background in electronics, especially consumer electronics servicing."

‡**EMEDIA PROFESSIONAL**, (formerly *CD-ROM Professional*), Pemberton Press/Online Inc., 649 Massachusetts Ave., Suite 4, Cambridge MA 02139. (617)492-0268. Fax: (617)492-3159. E-mail: stephenn@onlineinc.com. Website: http://www.onlineinc.com/emedia. Editor: David R. Guenette. Contact: Stephen Nathans, associate editor. 70% freelance written. Monthly magazine covering CD-ROM, DVD, CD-recordable, multimedia, electronic publishing. Practical business, professional orientation. Estab. 1987. Circ. 22,000. Pays on publication. Publishes ms an average of 3 months after acceptance. Byline given. Kill fee varies. Buys first North American serial and second serial (reprint) rights. Editorial lead time 3-4 months. Reports in 1-2 months. Sample copy and writer's guidelines free.

Nonfiction: Interview/profile, new product, technical. Buys 108 mss/year. Length: 1,500-4,500 words. Pays $600-1,500.

Photos: State availability of photos with submissions. Reviews transparencies, prints. Offers no additional payment for photos accepted with ms. Captions required. Buys one-time rights.

Columns/Departments: Pays $600.

‡**RADIO WORLD INTERNATIONAL**, Industrial Marketing Advisory Services, 5827 Columbia Pike, 3rd Floor, Falls Church VA 22041-9811. (703)998-7600. Fax: (703)998-2966. Editor-in-chief: Alan Carter. Editor: T. Carter Ross. Contact: Angela Novak, managing editor. Managing Editor Latin America: Rogelio Ocampo. European Editor: Marguerite Clark. 50% freelance written. Monthly trade newspaper "covering radio station technology, regulatory news, business and management developments outside the US. Articles should be geared toward engineers, producers and managers." Estab. 1990. Circ. 20,000. Pays on publication. Byline given. Buys worldwide serial rights. Reports in 3 weeks.

Nonfiction: New products, technical, regulatory and management news, programming trend pieces. Buys 100 mss/year. Query with published clips. Length: 750-1,000 words. Pays 20¢/word. Sometimes pays expenses of writers on assignment.

Photos: Send photos with submission. Captions and identification of subjects required. Buys all rights.

Columns/Departments: User reports (field reports from engineers on specific equipment); radio management; studio/audio issues, 750-1,000 words. Buys 50/year. Query. Pays 20¢/word.

Fillers: Newsbreaks. Buys 50/year. Length: 100-500 words.

Tips: "Our news and feature sections are the best bets for freelancers. Focus on radio station operations and the state of the industry worldwide."

RADIO WORLD NEWSPAPER, IMAS Publishing, Suite 310, 5827 Columbia Pike, Falls Church VA 22041. (703)998-7600. Fax: (703)998-2966. E-mail: 74103.7435@compuserve.com. Editor-in-Chief: Lucia Cobo. Managing Editor: Paul J. McLane. News Editor: Matt Spangler. Contact: Al Peterson, technical editor. 50% freelance written. Bimonthly newspaper on radio station technology and ownership concerns. "Articles should be geared toward radio station engineers, producers, technical people and managers. The approach should be more how-to than theoretical, although emerging technology may be approached in a more abstract way." Estab. 1976. Pays on publication. Publishes ms an average of 2 months after acceptance. Byline given. Buys first North American serial rights plus right to publish in monthly international and annual directory supplements. Submit seasonal material 2 months in advance. Reports in 2 months.

Nonfiction: Exposé, historical/nostalgic, how-to (radio equipment maintenance and repair), humor, interview/profile, new product, opinion, personal experience, photo feature, technical. Length: 750-1,250 words. Pays $75-200. Pays in contributor copies or other premiums "if they request it, and for one special feature called Workbench." Sometimes pays expenses of writers on assignment.

Reprints: Send tearsheet or typed ms with rights for sale noted and information about when and where the article previously appeared. Pay varies.

Photos: Send photos with submission. Reviews 3×5 or larger prints. Identification of subjects required. Buys one-time rights.

Columns/Departments: Chris Joaquim, Buyers Guide editor. Buyers Guide User Reports (field reports from engineers on specific pieces of radio station equipment). Query. Length: 750-1,250 words.

Fillers: Newsbreaks, short humor. Buys 6/year. Length: 500-1,000 words. Pays $25-75.

Tips: "I frequently assign articles by phone. Sometimes just a spark of an idea can lead to a story assignment or publication. The best way is to have some radio station experience and try to think of articles other readers would benefit from reading."

‡**RELIGIOUS BROADCASTING**, National Religious Broadcasters, 7839 Ashton Ave., Manassas VA 20109. (703)330-7000. Fax: (703)330-6996. E-mail: ssmith@nrb.com. Editor: Ron J. Kopczick. Managing Editor: Sarah E. Smith. Contact: Christine L. Pryor, associate editor. 70% freelance written. Monthly magazine also with an online version. "*Religious Broadcasting* is the trade journal for the industry and the official voice of National Religious Broadcasters, a nonprofit association." Estab. 1969. Circ. 9,000. Pays on publication. Publishes ms an average of 3

months after acceptance. Byline given. Buys first rights and second serial (reprint) rights. Editorial lead time 6 months. Submit seasonal material 6 months in advance. Accepts simultaneous submissions. Reports in 2 weeks on queries; 1 month on mss. Sample copy and writer's guidelines free.

Nonfiction: Book excerpts, historical/nostalgic, humor, inspirational, interview/profile, new product, personal experience, photo feature, religious, technical. No opinion, essay. Buys 30 mss/year. Send complete ms. Length: 2,000-3,000 words. Pays $75-150 for assigned articles; pays contributor's copies for unsolicited articles. Sometimes pays expenses of writers on assignment.

Reprints: Accepts previously published submissions.

Photos: Send photos with submission. Reviews 5×7 prints. Negotiates payment individually. Captions, identification of subjects required. Buys one-time rights.

Columns/Departments: Sarah Smith, managing editor. Targeting Technology (broadcast equipment); Sales Spot (broadcast sales); Practical Programming (broadcast production); all 750 words. Acquires 10 mss/year. Send complete ms. Pays in contributor's copies.

Tips: "Talk to local religious broadcasters and become familiar with their issues and concerns. Interview local broadcasters who are impacting their communities. Become an expert in one small facet of broadcasting."

ENERGY AND UTILITIES

People who supply power to homes, businesses and industry read the publications in this section. This category includes journals covering the electric power, natural gas, petroleum, solar and alternative energy industries.

‡**ALTERNATIVE ENERGY RETAILER**, Zackin Publications, Inc., P.O. Box 2180, Waterbury CT 06722-2180. (203)755-0158. Fax: (203)755-3480. Editorial Director: John Florian. 5% freelance written. Prefers to work with published/established writers. Monthly magazine on selling home hearth products—chiefly solid fuel and gas-burning appliances. "We seek detailed how-to tips for retailers to improve business. Most freelance material purchased is about retailers and how they succeed." Estab. 1980. Circ. 10,000. Pays on publication. Publishes ms an average of 2 months after acceptance. Buys first North American serial rights. Submit seasonal material 4 months in advance. Reports in 2 weeks on queries. Sample copy for 9×12 SAE with 4 first-class stamps. Writer's guidelines for #10 SASE.

● Submit articles that focus on hearth market trends and successful sales techniques.

Nonfiction: How-to (improve retail profits and business know-how), interview/profile (of successful retailers). No "general business articles not adapted to this industry." Buys 10 mss/year. Query. Length: 1,000 words. Pays $200.

Photos: State availability of photos. Pays $25-125 maximum for 5×7 b&w prints. Reviews color transparencies. Identification of subjects required. Buys one-time rights.

Tips: "A freelancer can best break into our publication with features about readers (retailers). Stick to details about what has made this person a success."

‡**ELECTRIC PERSPECTIVES**, Edison Electric Institute, 701 Pennsylvania Ave. NW, Washington DC 20004. (202)508-5714. E-mail: ericbcm@eei.org. Website: http://www.eei.org. Editor: Eric R. Blume. 20% freelance written. Bimonthly magazine for executives and managers in investor-owned electric utilities. Estab. 1976. Circ. 20,000. **Pays on acceptance of final draft.** Publishes ms an average of 3 months after acceptance. Byline given. Offers 20% kill fee. Buys first rights or makes work-for-hire assignments. Editorial lead time 4 months. Submit seasonal material 4 months in advance. Accepts simultaneous submissions. Reports in 6 weeks on queries; 2 months on mss. Sample copy for $5. Writer's guidelines free.

Nonfiction: Business, essays, historical/nostalgic, photo feature, technical. Buys 5 mss/year. Query. Length: 2,000-5,000 words. Pays $1,200 for assigned articles; $800 for unsolicited articles.

Photos: Send photos with submission. Reviews transparencies, 3×5 prints. Negotiates payment individually. Model releases, identification of subjects required. Buys one-time rights.

Columns/Departments: End-Use Technology Review (electrotechnologies at work), 2,000 words; Regulatory Review (utility regulation), 2,000 words; Financial Review (financial subjects), 2,000 words; Statistical Review (utility statistics and analysis). Buys 2 mss/year. Pays $400-1,000.

Tips: "Must develop idea and have a style that will hold the interest of intelligent electric-utility decision maker—CEO or chief engineer or vice president of customer service or corporate pilot. Send abstract or outline first. We're looking for feature articles on hot topics for the electric-utility industry. New angles, rather than restatements of basic utility themes."

ELECTRICAL APPARATUS, The Magazine of Electromechanical & Electronic Application & Maintenance, Barks Publications, Inc., 400 N. Michigan Ave., Chicago IL 60611-4198. (312)321-9440. Editorial Director: Elsie Dickson. Senior Editor: Kevin N. Jones. Monthly magazine for persons working in electrical and electronic maintenance, chiefly in industrial plants, who install and service electrical motors, transformers, generators, controls and related equipment. Estab. 1967. Circ. 17,000. **Pays on acceptance.** Publishes ms an average of 3 months after acceptance. Byline given. Buys all rights unless other arrangements made. Reports in 1 week on queries; 1 month on mss. Sample copy for $4.

Nonfiction: Technical. Length: 1,500-2,500. Pays $250-500 for assigned articles plus authorized expenses.
Tips: "All feature articles are assigned to staff and contributing editors and correspondents. Professionals interested in appointments as contributing editors and correspondents should submit résumé and article outlines, including illustration suggestions. Writers should be competent with a camera, which should be described in résumé. Technical expertise is absolutely necessary, preferably an E.E. degree, or practical experience. We are also book publishers and some of the material in *EA* is now in book form, bringing the authors royalties. Also publishes an annual directory, subtitled *ElectroMechanical Bench Reference*."

‡**HOME ENERGY**, Energy Auditor and Retrofitter, Inc., 2124 Kittredge St., Berkeley CA 94704. (510)486-6048. Fax: (510)486-4673. E-mail: homeenergy@envirolink.org. Editor: Steven Bodzin. Managing Editor: John Nagiecki. 80% freelance written. Bimonthly magazine. "We provide practical information for professionals in residential energy conservation and home energy auditing." Estab. 1984. Circ. 3,500 (readership 12,000). Pays on publication. Publishes ms an average of 2 months after acceptance. Byline given. Buys one-time rights and electronic rights. Editorial lead time 2 months after acceptance. Submit seasonal material 4 months in advance. Accepts simultaneous submissions. Reports in 3 weeks on queries; 1 month on mss. Sample copy for 9×12 SAE with 4 first-class stamps. Writer's guidelines for #10 SASE.
Nonfiction: How-to (install, repair or maintain HVAC, analyze energy use, implement conservation measures), new product (HVAC, insulation). No articles that promote products rather than offering a critical view. Buys 10-15 mss/year. Query. Length: 2,000-3,500 words. Pays 20¢/word to $300. Sometimes pays expenses of writers on assignment.
Reprints: Accepts previously published submissions.
Photos: State availability of photos with submission. Reviews contact sheets, 35mm transparencies, 3×5 prints. Offers no additional payment for photos accepted with ms. Captions required. Buys one-time rights.
Columns/Departments: Trends (developments and other short reports that affect residential energy use), 1,000 words. Buys 15-20 mss/year. Send complete ms. Pays 20¢/word.
Tips: "Know the technology you are covering and make article interesting and readable for an informed consumer."

‡**INDEPENDENT ENERGY, The Power Industry's Business Magazine**, Penn Well Publishing Co., 1421 S. Sheridan Rd., Tulsa OK 74112. (918)832-9377. E-mail: johna@pennwell.com. Contact: John Anderson, managing editor. Magazine is published 10 times a year and covers Global Power Project development and financing. "The core readership is high-level executives involved in the building and funding of large-scale power plants worldwide." Estab. 1971. Circ. 10,500. Pays on publication. Publishes ms an average of 3 months after acceptance. Byline given. Buys all rights. Editorial lead time 4 months. Submit seasonal material 3 months in advance. Accepts simultaneous submissions. Reports in 3 weeks on queries; 1 month on mss. Sample copy and writer's guidelines free.
Nonfiction: Technical (business or finance). Buys 35 mss/year. Query with published clips. Length: 1,000-2,400 words. Pays $250-1,200. Sometimes pays expenses of writers on assignment.
Photos: State availability of photos with submission. Reviews prints. Offers no additional payment for photos accepted with ms. Identification of subjects required. Buys all rights.
Columns/Departments: Michael T. Burr, senior editor. Global Markets News Briefs (updates on power projects and markets), 100-500 words; Contract Updaters (contract signings), 50-100 words. Send complete ms. Pays $50-250.
Tips: "Call one of the editors to discuss what the magazine needs and what you have in mind. Don't be bashful. We're always looking for new correspondents. If you know about business journalism, you can probably write for us."

‡**THE JOURNAL OF PETROLEUM MARKETING**, MacFadden Trade Publishing, L.L.C., 233 Park Ave. S, 6th Floor, New York NY 10003. E-mail: 102363.1711@compuserve.com. Editor: John Callanan. Managing Editor: Mary Power. 20% freelance written. Monthly magazine. "*JPM* is edited for operators of wholesale petroleum distribution companies and retail petroleum marketers. All editorial is geared toward helping marketers run more profitable businesses and comply with government regulations." Estab. 1988. Circ. 25,000. Pays on publication. Byline given. Buys first, one-time, second serial (reprint) rights or makes work-for-hire assignments. Editorial lead time 2 months. Sample copy free.
Nonfiction: Interview/profile, new product. Buys 3 mss/year. Query with published clips. Length: 1,800-2,400 words. Pays $500. Pays writers with contributor copies or other premiums for industry experts or suppliers' trade-outs.
Photos: Send photos with submission. Reviews transparencies and prints. Negotiates payment individually. Identification of subjects required. Buys one-time or all rights.

NATIONAL PETROLEUM NEWS, 2101 S. Arlington Heights Rd., Suite 150, Arlington Heights IL 60005. (847)427-9512. Fax: (847)427-2041. Website: http://www.aip.com/npn-net. Editor: Don Smith. 3% freelance written. Prefers to work with published/established writers. Monthly magazine for decision-makers in the oil marketing and convenience store industry. Estab. 1909. Circ. 11,000. Rights purchased vary with author and material; usually buys all rights. Pays on acceptance if done on assignment. Publishes ms an average of 2 months after acceptance. "The occasional freelance copy we use is done on assignment." Query.
● This magazine is particularly interested in articles on international industry-related material.
Nonfiction: Material related directly to developments and issues in the oil marketing and convenience store industry and "how-to" and "what-with" case studies. "No unsolicited copy, especially with limited attribution regarding information in story." Buys 3-4 mss/year. Length: 2,000 words maximum. Pays $50-150/printed page. Sometimes pays expenses of writers on assignment.

Reprints: Send typed ms on disk with rights for sale noted and information about when and where the article appeared.
Photos: Pays $150/printed page. Payment for b&w photos "depends upon advance understanding."

‡PUBLIC POWER, Dept. WM, 2301 M St. NW, Washington DC 20037-1484. (202)467-2948. Fax: (202)467-2910. Editor/Publisher: Jeanne Wickline LaBella. 60% freelance written. Prefers to work with published/established writers. Bimonthly. Estab. 1942. **Pays on acceptance.** Publishes ms an average of 3 months after acceptance. Byline given. Query for electronic submissions. Reports in 6 months. Free sample copy and writer's guidelines.
Nonfiction: Features on municipal and other local publicly owned electric utilities. Pays $400 and up.
Photos: Reviews transparencies, slides and prints.

RELAY MAGAZINE, Florida Municipal Electric Association, P.O. Box 10114, Tallahassee FL 32302-2114. (904)224-3314. Editor: Stephanie Wolanski. 5% freelance written. Monthly magazine. "Must be electric utility-oriented, or must address legislative issues of interest to us." Estab. 1942. Circ. 2,100. Pays on publication. Byline given. Not copyrighted. Buys first North American serial, one-time and second serial (reprint) rights. Accepts simultaneous submissions. Send photocopy of article or typed ms with rights for sale noted and information about when and where article previously appeared. Reports in 3 months.
Nonfiction: Interview/profile, technical and electric innovations. Query first; no articles that haven't been pre-approved. Length: 3-6 pages double-spaced. Pays $50.
Reprints: Accepts previously published submissions. Query first.
Photos: State availability of photos with submission. Pay and rights purchased vary. Captions and identification of subjects required. Query first.

ENGINEERING AND TECHNOLOGY

Engineers and professionals with various specialties read the publications in this section. Publications for electrical, electronics and telecommunications engineers are in Electronics and Communication. Magazines for computer professionals are in the Information Systems.

‡CANADIAN CONSULTING ENGINEER, Southam Magazine Group Ltd., 1450 Don Mills Rd., Don Mills, Ontario M3B 2X7 Canada. (416)445-6641. E-mail: skneisel@southam.ca. Editor: Sophie Kneisel. 20% freelance written. Bimonthly magazine covering consulting engineering in private practice. Estab. 1958. Circ. 8,900. Pays on publication. Publishes ms an average of 2 months after acceptance. Byline given depending on length of story. Offers 50% kill fee; $200 minimum. Buys first North American serial rights. Editorial lead time 6 months. Reports in 2 months on queries. Sample copy free.
Nonfiction: Historical, new product, technical. Buys 8-10 mss/year. Query with published clips. Length: 300-1,500 words. Pays $200-500 for assigned articles; $100-400 for unsolicited articles. Sometimes pays expenses of writers on assignment.
Photos: State availability of photos with submission. Negotiates payment individually. Buys one-time rights.
Columns/Departments: Export (selling consulting engineering services abroad); Management (managing consulting engineering businesses); On-Line (trends in AEC systems). Length: 800 words. Buys 4 mss/year. Query with published clips. Pays $250-400.

‡MECHANICAL ENGINEERING, American Society of Mechanical Engineers, Dept. WM, 345 E. 47th St., New York NY 10017. (212)705-7782. Fax: (212)705-7841. E-mail: memag@asme.org. Website: http://memagazine.org. Editor: John Falcioni. 20% freelance written. Monthly magazine on mechanical process and design. "We publish general interest articles for graduate mechanical engineers on high-tech topics." Circ. 135,000. **Pays on acceptance.** Byline sometimes given. Kill fee varies. Buys first rights. Submit seasonal material 4 months in advance. Reports in 6 weeks. Writer's guidelines for SASE.
Nonfiction: Historical, interview/profile, new product, photo feature, technical. Buys 25 mss/year. Query with or without published clips or send complete ms. Length: 1,500-3,500 words. Pays $500-1,500.
Photos: Send photos with submission. Reviews transparencies and prints. Offers no additional payment for photos accepted with ms. Captions and identification of subjects required. Buys one-time rights.

‡MILITARY & AEROSPACE ELECTRONICS, The newspaper for decision makers in the changing worldwide military/aerospace industry, Penn Well Publishing, 10 Tara Blvd., 5th Floor, Nashva NH 03062. (603)891-9117. Fax: (603)891-0514. E-mail: jkeller@pennwell.com. Editor: John Keller. 20% freelance written. Monthly tabloid. M&AE covers design issues and enabling technologies for the military and aerospace electronic design engineers and engineering managers, with an emphasis on open-system standards and commercial off-the-shelf components. Estab. 1989. Circ. 41,000. Pays on publication. Byline given. Offers 50% kill fee. Buys all rights. Editorial lead time 2 months. Submit seasonal material 2 months in advance. Sample copy and writer's guidelines free.
Nonfiction: Exposé, how-to, new product, technical. Buys 24 mss/year. Query. Length: 500-3,000 words. Pays $100-2,000. Sometimes pays expenses of writers on assignment.
Photos: Send photos with submission. Reviews transparencies and prints. Offers no additional payment for photos

accepted with ms. Captions required. Buys all rights.

Columns/Departments: Special Report (in-depth applications), 3,000 words; Technology Focus (indepth technologies), 3,000 words; Analysis (varied slants), 1,500 words. Buys 20 mss/year. Query. Pays $100-2,000.

Tips: "It's easy: get me on the phone and we'll talk."

MINORITY ENGINEER, An Equal Opportunity Career Publication for Professional and Graduating Minority Engineers, Equal Opportunity Publications, Inc., 1160 E. Jericho Turnpike, Suite 200, Huntington NY 11743. (516)421-9421. Fax: (516)421-0359. E-mail: edpub@aol.com. Website: http://www.cop.com. Editor: James Schneider. 60% freelance written. Prefers to work with published/established writers. Triannual magazine covering career guidance for minority engineering students and minority professional engineers. Estab. 1969. Circ. 17,000. Pays on publication. Publishes ms an average of 6 months after acceptance. Byline given. Buys first rights. Accepts simultaneous submissions. Sample copy and writer's guidelines for 9 × 12 SAE with 5 first-class stamps.

Nonfiction: Book excerpts; articles (on job search techniques, role models); general interest (on specific minority engineering concerns); how-to (land a job, keep a job, etc.); interview/profile (minority engineer role models); new product (new career opportunities); opinion (problems of ethnic minorities); personal experience (student and career experiences); technical (on career fields offering opportunities for minority engineers). "We're interested in articles dealing with career guidance and job opportunities for minority engineers." Query or send complete ms. Length: 1,000-1,500 words. Sometimes pays expenses of writers on assignment. Pays 10¢/word.

Reprints: Send information about when and where the article previously appeared. Pays 100% of amount paid for an original article.

Photos: Prefers 35mm color slides but will accept b&w. Captions and identification of subjects required. Buys all rights. Pays $15. Cartoons accepted. Pays $25.

Tips: "Articles should focus on career guidance, role model and industry prospects for minority engineers. Prefer articles related to careers, not politically or socially sensitive."

‡PROGRESSIVE ENGINEER, Buck Mountain Publishing Co., P.O. Box 20305, Roanoke VA 24018. (540)772-2225. Fax: (540)776-0871. Contact: Tom Gibson, editor. 75% freelance written. Bimonthly magazine. "*Progressive Engineer* is written for all disciplines of engineers in the Mid-Atlantic region (VA, NC, MD, WV, DC). We take a less technical slant than most engineering magazines and cover the engineers behind the technology as well as the technology itself. Promotes the profession of engineering by writing about engineers, projects and related activities." Estab. 1997. Circ. 40,000. Pays on publication. Publishes ms an average of 4 months after acceptance. Byline given. Offers $25 kill fee. Buys first North American serial rights and second serial (reprint) rights. Editorial lead time 6 months. Accepts simultaneous submissions. Reports in 3 weeks on queries; 1 month on mss. Sample copy and writer's guidelines free.

Nonfiction: Book excerpts, expose, general interest, historical/nostalgic, how-to, interview/profile, new product, technical, travel. Buys 50 mss/year. Query with published clips. Length: 750-2,500 words. Pays $150-350. Sometimes pays expenses of writers on assignment.

Reprints: Accepts previously published submissions.

Photos: State availability of photos with submission. Reviews contact sheets, transparencies, prints. Offers $25-100. Captions, identification of subjects required. Buys one-time rights.

Columns/Departments: Profiles (individual engineers), 800 words; Issues (affecting engineers), 1,500 words; Travel, Places to Visit (see technology in action), 1,000 words. Query with published clips. Pays $150-225.

Tips: "If you know of an engineer doing something interesting or unique in your area, we'd like to hear about it."

SENSORS, The Journal of Applied Sensor Technology, Helmers Publishing, Inc., 174 Concord St., Peterborough NH 03458. (603)924-9631. Fax: (603)924-2076. E-mail: editors@sensorsmag.com. Website: http://www.sensorsmag.com. Editor: Dorothy Rosa. 5% freelance written. Monthly magazine covering electrical and mechanical engineering. "To provide timely, authoritative technical information on the integration of sensors—via data acquisition hardware and software—into subassemblies, manufacturing and process control systems, and products." Estab. 1984. Circ. 70,000. **Pays on acceptance.** Publishes ms an average of 6 months after acceptance. Byline given. Buys first North American serial rights, all rights or makes work-for-hire assignments. Editorial lead time 6 months. Query for electronic submissions. Reports in 1 month on queries; 2 months on mss. Sample copy and writer's guidelines free on request.

Nonfiction: Technical, new product, opinion. Special issue: Data acquisition (June). Buys 3 mss/year. Query. Length: 800-2,400 words. Pay negotiable. Sometimes pays expenses of writers on assignment.

Photos: Send photos with submission. Reviews prints. Offers no additional payment for photos accepted with ms. Caption, model releases and identification of subjects required. Buys one-time rights. *No* cartoons.

‡WOMAN ENGINEER, An Equal Opportunity Career Publication for Graduating Women and Experienced Professionals, Equal Opportunity Publications, Inc., 1160 E. Jericho Turnpike, Suite 200, Huntington NY 11743. (516)421-9478. Fax: (516)421-0359. Editor: Anne Kelly. 60% freelance written. Works with a small number of new/unpublished writers each year. Triannual magazine covering career guidance for women engineering students and professional women engineers. Estab. 1968. Circ. 16,000. Pays on publication. Publishes ms an average of 3-12 months after acceptance. Byline given. Buys First North American serial rights. Reports in 3 months. Free sample copy and writer's guidelines.

Nonfiction: "Interested in articles dealing with career guidance and job opportunities for women engineers. Looking for manuscripts showing how to land an engineering position and advance professionally. We want features on job-search techniques, engineering disciplines offering career opportunities to women; companies with career advancement opportunities for women; problems facing women engineers and how to cope with such problems; and role-model profiles of successful women engineers, especially in government, military and defense-related industries." Query. Length: 1,000-2,500 words. Pays 10¢/word.

Photos: Prefers color slides but will accept b&w. Captions and identification of subjects required. Buys all rights. Pays $15.

Tips: "We will be looking for shorter manuscripts (800-1,000 words) on job-search techniques and first-person 'As I See It.'"

ENTERTAINMENT AND THE ARTS

The business of the entertainment/amusement industry in arts, film, dance, theater, etc, is covered by these publications. Journals that focus on the people and equipment of various music specialties are listed in the Music section, while art and design business publications can be found in Art, Design and Collectibles. Entertainment publications for the general public can be found in the Consumer Entertainment section.

AMUSEMENT BUSINESS, Billboard Publications, Inc., P.O. Box 24970, Nashville TN 37202. (615)321-4269. Fax: (615)327-1575. Managing Editor: Linda Deckard. 25% freelance written. Works with a small number of new/unpublished writers each year. Weekly tabloid emphasizing hard news of the amusement, sports business, and mass entertainment industry for top management. Circ. 15,000. Pays on publication. Publishes ms an average of 3 weeks after acceptance. Byline sometimes given; "it depends on the quality of the individual piece." Buys all rights. Submit seasonal/holiday material 3 weeks in advance. Sample copy for 11 × 14 SAE with 5 first-class stamps.
  • *Amusement Business* is placing an increased emphasis on international developments and looking for shorter news stories.

Nonfiction: How-to (case history of successful advertising campaigns and promotions); interviews (with leaders in the areas we cover highlighting appropriate problems and issues of today, i.e., insurance, alcohol control, etc.). Likes lots of financial support data: grosses, profits, operating budgets and per-cap spending. Also needs lots of quotes. No personality pieces or interviews with stage stars. Buys 50-100 mss/year. Query. Phone queries OK. Length: 400-700 words.

Photos: State availability of photos with query. Captions and model release required. Buys all rights.

Columns/Departments: Auditorium Arenas; Fairs; Parks & Attractions; Food Concessions; Merchandise; Promotion; Carnivals; Talent & Touring; Management Changes; Sports; Profile; Eye On Legislation; Commentary and International News.

Tips: "There will be more and more emphasis on financial reporting of areas covered. Submission must contain the whys and whos, etc., and be strong enough that others in the same field will learn from it and not find it naive. We will be increasing story count while decreasing story length."

‡**BACK STAGE WEST, The Performing Arts Weekly**, BPI Communications, 5055 Wilshire Blvd., 6th Floor, Los Angeles CA 90036. (213)525-2356. Fax: (213)965-1340. Editor: Robert Kendt. Managing Editor: J. Brenna Guthrie. 50% freelance written. Weekly trade tabloid covering "the craft and business of acting on the West Coast. We print very specific, nuts-and-bolts advice and features on issues and people with an impact on performers' livelihood and art. We take actors and their struggles seriously but not without humor; mainly, we provide information and insight for a tough career." Estab. 1994. Circ. 12,536. Pays on publication. Publishes ms an average of 1 month after acceptance. Byline given. Offers 50% kill fee. Makes work-for-hire assignments. Editorial lead time 2 months. Submit seasonal material 4 months in advance. Reports in 2 weeks on queries "We prefer pitches and samples, not submissions." Sample copy for 10 × 13 SAE and $1.01 postage.

Nonfiction: Exposé, how-to, interview/profile, personal experience, photo feature, technical, theatre reviews (West Coast). Special issues on agents, comedy, dance, singing, commercial casting, acting training, young performers, theater rental space, speech and voiceover. No advertorial, agenda-tainted pieces, complaints. Buys 600 mss/year. Query with published clips. Length: 300-3,000 words. Pays $15-400. Sometimes pays expenses of writers on assignment.

Photos: Reviews 5 × 7 prints. Offers $50-75 per photo shoot. Identification of subjects required. Makes work-for-hire assignments.

Columns/Departments: The Craft (specific acting tips), 800-1,100 words; Actor's Actor (critical appreciation/profile of actor), 500-700 words; Profile, 1,100 words. Buys 120 mss/year. Query with published clips. Pays $50-75.

Fiction: Nothing but excerpts from plays in production. Buys 12 mss/year, but does not pay. Query with information about play's production history or future. Length: 2,000-2,700 words.

Tips: "This is a trade paper for performers on the West Coast, so we need writers who know the territory but can put their agenda aside and be relatively objective. An excellent way to break in is by reviewing West Coast theater; it's low-risk for both us and the writers, and it's a great intro to a writer's point of view, and lots of stories spin off from that. I'm especially interested in pitches on 'The Craft' column—very specific, very juicy information on a certain acting craft issue."

‡**BILLBOARD, The International News Weekly of Music and Home Entertainment**, Dept. WM, 1515 Broadway, New York NY 10036. (212)764-7300; or 5055 Wilshire Blvd., Beverly Hills CA 90036. (213)273-7040. Editor-in-Chief: Timothy White. L.A. Bureau Chief: Craig Rosen. Weekly music trade magazine. Pays on publication. Buys all rights. *No queries from freelance writers.*
Nonfiction: "Correspondents are appointed to send in spot amusement news covering phonograph record programming by broadcasters and record merchandising by retail dealers." Concert reviews, interviews with artists, and stories on video software (both rental and merchandising).

BOXOFFICE MAGAZINE, RLD Publishing Co., 6640 Sunset Blvd., Suite 100, Hollywood CA 90028-7159. (213)465-1186. Fax: (213)465-5049. E-mail: boxoff@earthlink.net. Website: http://www.boxoffice.com. Editor-in-Chief: Ray Greene. 15% freelance written. Monthly business magazine about the motion picture industry for members of the film industry: theater owners, film producers, directors, financiers and allied industries. Estab. 1920. Circ. 8,000. Pays on publication. Publishes ms an average of 4 months after acceptance. Byline given. Buys all rights, including electronic publishing. Submit seasonal material 4 months in advance. Send typed ms with rights for sale noted. Sample copy for $5.50.
Nonfiction: Investigative, interview, profile, new product, photo feature, technical. "We are a general news magazine about the motion picture industry and are looking for stories about trends, developments, problems or opportunities facing the industry. Almost any story will be considered, including corporate profiles, but we don't want gossip or celebrity coverage." Query with published clips. Length: 800-2,500 words. Pays 10¢/word or set price.
Photos: State availability of photos. Pays $10 maximum for 8 × 10 b&w prints. Captions required.
Tips: "Request a sample copy, indicating you read about *Boxoffice* in *Writer's Market*. Write a clear, comprehensive outline of the proposed story and enclose a résumé and clip samples. We welcome new writers but don't want to be a classroom; know how to write. We look for 'investigative' articles."

CALLBOARD, Monthly Theatre Trade Magazine, Theatre Bay Area, 657 Mission St., #402, San Francisco CA 94105. (415)957-1557. Fax: (415)957-1556. E-mail: tba@best.com. Website: http://www.theatrebayarea.org/. Editor: Belinda Taylor. 50% freelance written. Monthly magazine for theater. "We publish news, views, essays and features on the Northern California theater industry. We also include listings, audition notices and job resources." Estab. 1976. Circ. 5,000. Pays on publication. Publishes ms an average of 4 months after acceptance. Byline given. Offers 50% kill fee. Buys first rights. Editorial lead time 1 month. Submit seasonal material 2 months in advance. Accepts simultaneous submissions. Reports in 1 month on queries. Sample copy for $5.
Nonfiction: Book excerpts, essays, personal experience, technical (theater topics only), features. No reviews. *No profiles of actors.* Buys 12-15 mss/year. Query with published clips. Length: 800-2,000 words. Pays $100-200 for assigned articles. Pays other for unsolicited articles. Pays $35-75 for department articles. Sometimes pays expenses of writers on assignment (phone calls and some travel).
Reprints: Send tearsheet of article or typed ms with rights for sale noted and information about when and where the article previously appeared. Pays 25% of amount paid for an original article.
Photos: State availability of photos with submission. Reviews contact sheets or 5 × 7 prints. Offers no additional payment for photos accepted with ms. Identification of subjects required. Buys one-time rights.

‡**FUNWORLD**, International Association of Amusement Parks, 1448 Duke St., Alexandria VA 22314. (703)836-4800. Fax: (703)836-4801. E-mail: tayers@iaapa.org. Website: http://www.iaapa.org. Managing Editor: Tiffany Ayers. 80% freelance written. Monthly magazine covering the amusement industry for park owners and operators. Circ. approximately 8,000. Pays on publication. Publishes ms an average of 3 months after acceptance. Byline given. Buys all rights. Editorial lead time 2 months. Submit seasonal material 2 months in advance. Accepts simultaneous and previously published submissions. Sample copy and writer's guidelines free.
Nonfiction: How-to (training programs, etc.), interview/profile. Buys 65 mss/year. Query with published clips. Length: 1,500-3,500 words. Pays 20-30¢/word. Sometimes pays expenses of writers on assignment.
Photos: State availability of photos with submission. Reviews transparencies and prints. Offers no additional payment for photos accepted with ms. Identification of subjects required. Buys all rights.
Columns/Departments: Query with published clips. Pays 20-30¢/word.

THE HOLLYWOOD REPORTER, 5055 Wilshire Blvd., Los Angeles CA 90036-4396. (213)525-2000. Fax: (213)525-2377. Website: http://www.hollywoodreporter.com. Publisher/Editor-in-Chief: Robert J. Dowling. Editor: Alex Ben Block. Editorial Director of Special Issues: Randall Tierney. Contact: Matthew King, managing editor. Daily is 10% freelance written. Specials are 90% freelance written. Daily entertainment trade publication emphasizing indepth analysis and news coverage of creative and business aspects of film, TV, theater and music production. Estab. 1930. Circ. 23,000. Publishes ms an average of 1 week after acceptance for daily, 1 month for special issues. Query first.
Tips: "Short articles fit our format best. The most frequent mistake made by writers in completing an article for us is that they are not familiar with our publication. We are a business publication; we don't want celebrity gossip."

STAGE DIRECTIONS, The Practical Magazine of Theater, *SMW* Communications, Inc., 3101 Poplarwood, Suite 310, Raleigh NC 27604. Fax: (919)872-6888. E-mail: stagedir@aol.com. Website: http://www.stage-directions.com. Editor: Neil Offen. 25% freelance written. Magazine published 10 times/year covering theater: community, regional and academic. "*Stage Directions* covers a full range of theater—productions, design, management and marketing.

Articles are based on problem-solving." Estab. 1988. Circ. 4,500. Pays on publication. Publishes ms an average of 3 months after acceptance. Byline given. Buys all rights. Editorial lead time 6 months. Submit seasonal material 6 months in advance. Accepts simultaneous submissions, if so noted. Reports in 3 weeks on queries. Sample copy for 9×12 SAE with 2 first-class stamps. Writer's guidelines free.

Nonfiction: How-to, new product, personal experience, photo feature, technical. Buys 24 mss/year. Special issues: Sets and Scenery (September); Costumes (February); Summer Learning (January); Light, Sound, Special Effects (March). Query. Length: 350-1,000 words. Pays 10¢/word. Sometimes pays expenses of writers on assignment.

Reprints: Send typed ms with rights for sale noted and information about when and where the article previously appeared. Pays 50% of the amount paid for an original article.

Photos: State availability of photos with submission and describe. Reviews contact sheets, 2×2 transparencies and 5×7 prints. Offers $20/photo. Captions, model releases and identification of subjects required. Buys one-time rights.

Tips: "We are very receptive to new writers, but they must give evidence of quality writing and ability to follow through. Keep story focused and upbeat as you describe a theatrical problem-solving experience or situation. Use quotes from participants/experts."

FARM

The successful farm writer focuses on the business side of farming. For technical articles, editors feel writers should have a farm background or agricultural training, but there are opportunities for the general freelancer too. The following farm publications are divided into seven categories, each specializing in a different aspect of farming: equipment; crops and soil management; dairy farming; livestock; management; miscellaneous; and regional.

Agricultural Equipment

DEALER @ APPLICATOR, (formerly *Custom Applicator*), Vance Publishing Corp., 6263 Poplar Ave., Suite 540, Memphis TN 38119. (901)767-4020. Fax: (901)767-4026. Editor: Rob Wiley. 50% freelance written. Works with a small number of new/unpublished writers each year. Magazine for firms that sell and custom apply agricultural fertilizer and chemicals. Estab. 1957. Circ. 16,100. **Pays on acceptance.** Publishes ms an average of 2 months after acceptance. Buys all rights. Free sample copy and writer's guidelines.

Nonfiction: "We need articles on spray/dry chemical delivery technology related to the agriculture industry. We are seeing an incredible jump in computer-related technology and software packages for farm and custom application management that need reviewing. And we always need 'people' stories, interviews of actual dealers & applicators." Length: 750-1500 words. Must have color photos. Pays 20¢/word.

Reprints: Send typed ms with rights for sale noted and information about when and where the article previously appeared. Payment negotiable.

Photos: Accepts b&w glossy prints, prefers color. Color slides accepted for cover photos. Pays extra for cover shots.

Tips: "Our audience doesn't need to decipher 'computerese' or 'tech lingo' so make it readable; for a general audience. Conciseness sells here. A story without photos will not be published, so plan that into your work. Our readers are looking for methods to increase efficiency and stay abreast of new government regulations, so accuracy is important."

Crops and Soil Management

CITRUS & VEGETABLE MAGAZINE, 7402 N. 56th St., Suite 560, Tampa FL 33617-7737. (813)980-6386. Fax: (813)980-2871. Editor: Gordon Smith. Contact: Scott Emerson, managing editor. Monthly magazine on the citrus and vegetable industries. Estab. 1938. Circ. 12,000. Pays on publication. Publishes ms an average of 1 month after acceptance. Byline given. Kill fee varies. Buys exclusive first rights. Query first. Reports in 2 months on queries. Free sample copy and writer's guidelines.

Nonfiction: Book excerpts (if pertinent to relevant agricultural issues); how-to (grower interest—cultivation practices, etc.); new product (of interest to Florida citrus or vegetable growers); personal experience; photo feature. Buys 20 mss/ year. Query with published clips or send complete ms. Length: approximately 1,200 words. Pays about $200.

Photos: Send photos with submission. Reviews 5×7 prints. Prefers color slides. Offers $15 minimum/photo. Captions and identification of subjects required. Buys first rights.

Columns/Departments: Citrus Summary (news to citrus industry in Florida: market trends, new product lines), Vegetable Vignettes (new cultivars, anything on trends or developments within vegetable industry of Florida). Send complete ms.

Tips: "Show initiative—don't be afraid to call whomever you need to get your information for story together—accurately and with style. Submit ideas and/or completed manuscript well in advance. Focus on areas that have not been widely written about elsewhere in the press. Looking for fresh copy. Have something to sell and be convinced of its value. Become familiar with the key issues, key players in the citrus industry in Florida. Have a specific idea in mind for a news or feature story and try to submit manuscript at least one month in advance of publication."

GRAIN JOURNAL, Grain Publications, Inc., 2490 N. Water St., Decatur IL 62526. (217)877-8660. Fax: (217)877-9660. E-mail: ed@grainnet.com. Website: http://www.grainnet.com. Editor: Ed Zdrojewski. 10% freelance written. Bimonthly magazine covering grain handling and merchandising. "*Grain Journal* serves the North American grain industry, from the smallest country grain elevators and feed mills to major export terminals." Estab. 1972. Circ. 12,000. Pays on publication. Publishes ms an average of 2 months after acceptance. Byline sometimes given. Buys first rights. Editorial lead time 2 months. Submit seasonal material 2 months in advance. Accepts simultaneous submissions. Sample copy free.
Nonfiction: How-to, interview/profile, new product, technical. Query. Length: 750 words maximum. Pays $100.
Photos: Send photos with submission. Reviews contact sheets, negatives, transparencies, 3×5 prints. Offers $50-100/photo. Captions and identification of subjects required. Buys one-time rights.
Tips: "Call with your idea. We'll let you know if it is suitable for our publication."

‡**GRAINEWS**, Farm Business Communications (A division of United Grain Growers), P.O. Box 6600, Winnipeg, Manitoba R3G 3G7 Canada. (204)944-5587. Fax: (204)944-5416. Managing Editor: Andy Sirski. Assistant to the Editor: David Bedard. 80% freelance written. Newspaper published 16 times/year covering agriculture/agribusiness. **Pays on acceptance.** Publishes ms an average of 1 month after acceptance. Byline given. Buys all rights. Editorial lead time 1 month. Submit seasonal material 1 month in advance. Accepts previously published submissions. Reports in 2 weeks on queries. Sample copy free.
Nonfiction: Indepth how-to articles on various aspects of farming, general interest, historical/nostalgic, humor, new product, opinion, personal experience, technical. "Every article should be written from the farmer's perspective." Query. Pays $150 for assigned articles; $25 for unsolicited articles. Sometimes pays expenses of writers on assignment.
Photos: State availability of photos with submission. Offers no additional payment for photos accepted with ms. Captions and identification of subjects required. Buys one-time rights.
Poetry: Andy Sirski, editor. Traditional. Pays $25.
Tips: "We want writers who are farmers. We love 'how-to' articles on farm-related repairs, etc. Ask yourself how your story will help or entertain other farmers, and if it doesn't, don't send it. Don't send anything from June-August. It's our slowest time. The spring is best."

ONION WORLD, Columbia Publishing, 2809A Fruitvale Blvd., P.O. Box 1467, Yakima WA 98907-1497. (509)248-2452. Fax: (509)248-4056. Editor: D. Brent Clement. 50% freelance written. Monthly magazine covering the world of onion production and marketing for onion growers and shippers. Estab. 1985. Circ. 5,500. Pays on publication. Publishes ms an average of 1 month after acceptance. Byline given. Not copyrighted. Buys first North American serial rights. Submit seasonal material 1 month in advance. Accepts simultaneous submissions. Reports in 1 month. Sample copy for 9×12 SAE with 5 first-class stamps.
Nonfiction: General interest, historical/nostalgic, interview/profile. Buys 60 mss/year. Query. Length: 1,200-1,500 words. Pays $75-150 for assigned articles.
  • Columbia Publishing also produces *Fresh Cut, Packer/Shipper, The Tomato Magazine, Potato Country* and *Carrot Country.*
Reprints: Send photocopy of article and information about when and where the article previously appeared. Pays 50% of amount paid for an original article.
Photos: Send photos with submission. Offers no additional payment for photos accepted with ms unless it's a cover shot. Captions, identification of subjects required. Buys all rights.
Tips: "Writers should be familiar with growing and marketing onions. We use a lot of feature stories on growers, shippers and others in the onion trade—what they are doing, their problems, solutions, marketing plans, etc."

Dairy Farming

DAIRY GOAT JOURNAL, P.O. Box 10, 128 E. Lake St., Lake Mills WI 53551. (414)648-8285. Fax: (414)648-3770. Editor: Dave Thompson. 50% freelance written. Monthly. "We are looking for clear and accurate articles about dairy goat owners, their herds, cheesemaking, and other ways of marketing products. Some readers own two goats; others own 1,500 and are large commercial operations." Estab. 1917. Circ. 8,000, including copies to more than 70 foreign countries. Pays on publication.
Nonfiction: Information on personalities and on public issues affecting dairy goats and their owners. How-to articles with plenty of practical information. Health and husbandry articles should be written with appropriate experience or academic credentials. Buys 100 mss/year. Query with published clips. Makes assignments. Length: 750-2,500 words. Pays $50-150. Pays expenses of writers on assignment.
Photos: Color or b&w. Vertical or horizontal for cover. Goats and/or people. Pays $100 maximum for 35mm slides for covers; $20 to $70 for inside use or for b&w. Accurate identification of all subjects required.
Tips: "We love good articles about dairy goats and will work with beginners, if you are cooperative."

THE WESTERN DAIRYMAN, Dept. WM, P.O. Box 819, Corona CA 91718-0819. (909)735-2730. Fax: (909)735-2460. E-mail: westdairy2@aol.com. Editor: Dennis Halladay. 10% freelance written. Prefers to work with published/established writers. Monthly magazine dealing with large herd commercial dairy industry. *Rarely* publishes information about non-Western producers or dairy groups and events. Estab. 1922. Circ. 19,000. Pays on acceptance or publication.

Publishes ms an average of 3 months after acceptance. Byline given. Buys first North American serial rights. Submit seasonal material 3 months in advance. Reports in 1 month. Sample copy for 9 × 12 SAE with 4 first-class stamps.

Nonfiction: Interview/profile, new product, opinion, industry analysis. Special issues: Computers (February); Herd Health (August); Feeds and Feeding (May); Barns and Equipment (November). "No religion, nostalgia, politics or 'mom and pop' dairies." Query or send complete ms. Length: 300-5,000 words. Pays $100-300.

Reprints: Seldom accepts previously published submissions. Send information about when and where the article previously appeared. Pays 50% of amount paid for an original article.

Photos: Send photos with query or ms. Reviews b&w contact sheets and 35mm or 2¼ × 2¼ transparencies. Pays $25 for b&w; $50-100 for color. Captions and identification of subjects required. Buys one-time rights.

● Photos are now a more critical part of story packages.

Tips: "Pretend you're an editor for a moment; would you want to buy a story without any artwork? Neither would I. Writers often don't know modern commercial dairying and they forget they're writing for an audience of *dairymen*. Publications are becoming more and more specialized. You've really got to know who you're writing for and why they're different."

Livestock

THE BRAHMAN JOURNAL, Sagebrush Publishing Co., Inc., P.O. Box 220, Eddy TX 76524-0220. Phone/fax: (817)859-5451. Editor: Joe Ed Brockett. 10% freelance written. Monthly magazine covering Brahman cattle. Estab. 1971. Circ. 4,000. Pays on publication. Publishes ms an average of 2 months after acceptance. Byline given. Not copyrighted. Buys first North American serial, one-time and second serial (reprint) rights or makes work-for-hire assignments. Submit seasonal/holiday material 3 months in advance. Sample copy for 9 × 12 SAE with 5 first-class stamps.

Nonfiction: General interest, historical/nostalgic, interview/profile. Special issues: Herd Bull (July); Texas (October). Buys 3-4 mss/year. Query with published clips. Length: 1,200-3,000 words. Pays $100-250.

Reprints: Send typed ms with rights for sale noted. Pays 50% of amount paid for an original article.

Photos: Photos needed for article purchase. Send photos with submission. Reviews 4 × 5 prints. Offers no additional payment for photos accepted with ms. Captions required. Buys one-time rights.

CANADIAN GUERNSEY JOURNAL, Canadian Guernsey Association, 368 Woolwich St., Guelph, Ontario N1H 3W6 Canada. (519)836-2141. Fax: (519)824-9250. Editor: V.M. Macdonald. 10% freelance written. Bimonthly magazine covering diary farming and especially Guernsey cattle. Estab. 1905. Circ. 400. Pays on publication. Publishes ms an average of 3 months after acceptance. Byline given. Buys one-time rights. Editorial lead time 2 months. Sample copy for $5.

Nonfiction: How-to, humor, new product, personal experience, technical. Buys 2-4 mss/year. Query. Length: 400-2,000 words. Pays $25-150.

Reprints: Send tearsheet, photocopy or typed ms with rights for sale noted and information about when and where the article previously appeared. Payment negotiable.

Photos: Send photos with submission. Negotiates payment individually. Buys one-time rights.

Columns/Departments: Buys 2 mss/year. Pays $25-150.

FEED LOT MAGAZINE, Feed Lot Limited Partnership, P.O. Box 850, Dighton KS 67839. (316)397-2838. Editor: Robert A. Strong. 40% freelance written. Bimonthly magazine. "The editorial information content fits a dual role: large feedlots and their related cow/calf, operations, and large 500+ cow/calf, stocker operations. The information covers all phases of production from breeding, genetics, animal health, nutrition, equipment design, research through finishing fat cattle. *Feed Lot* publishes a mix of new information and timely articles which directly effect the cattle industry." Estab. 1993. Circ. 12,000. Pays on publication. Publishes ms an average of 2 months after acceptance. Byline given. Offers 50% kill fee. Buys all rights. Editorial lead time 2 months. Submit seasonal material 6 months in advance. Reports in 1 month. Sample copy and writer's guidelines for $1.50.

Nonfiction: Interview/profile, new product (cattle-related). Send complete ms. Length: 100-400 words. Pays 10¢/word.

Reprints: Send tearsheet or typed ms with rights for sale noted and information about when and where the article previously appeared. Pays 50% of amount paid for an original article.

Photos: State availability of or send photos with submission. Reviews contact sheets. Negotiates payment individually. Captions, model releases required. Buys all rights.

Tips: "Know what you are writing about—have a good knowledge of the subject."

LLAMAS MAGAZINE, The International Camelid Journal, Clay Press, Inc., P.O. Box 100, Herald CA 95638. (209)223-0469. Fax: (209)223-0466. E-mail: claypress@aol.com. Editor: cheryl Dal Porto. Magazine published 7 times/ year covering llamas, alpacas, camels, vicunas and guanacos. Estab. 1979. Circ. 6,000. Pays on publication. Publishes ms an average of 4 months after acceptance. Byline given. Buys first rights, second serial (reprint) rights and makes work-for-hire assignments. Submit seasonal material 6 months in advance. Reports in 1 month. Free sample copy. Writer's guidelines for 8½ × 11 SAE with $2.90 postage.

Nonfiction: How-to (on anything related to raising llamas), humor, interview/profile, opinion, personal experience, photo feature, travel (to countries where there are camelids). "All articles must have a tie-in to one of the camelid species." Buys 30 mss/year. Query with published clips. Length: 1,000-5,000 words. Pays $50-300 for assigned articles; $50-250 for unsolicited articles. May pay new writers with contributor copies. Sometimes pays expenses of writers on assignment.

Reprints: Send tearsheet of article and information about when and where the article previously appeared. Pays 10-25% of amount paid for an original article.

Photos: State availability of or send duplicate photos with submission. Reviews transparencies, 5×7 prints. Offers $25-100/photo. Captions, model releases and identification of subjects required. Buys one-time rights.

Fillers: Anecdotes, gags, short humor. Buys 25/year. Length: 100-500 words. Pays $25-50.

Tips: "Get to know the llama folk in your area and query us with an idea. We are open to any and all ideas involving llamas, alpacas and the rest of the camelids. We are always looking for good photos. You must know about camelids to write for us."

NATIONAL CATTLEMEN, National Cattlemen's Beef Association, 5420 S. Quebec St., Greenwood Village CO 80111-1904. (303)694-0305. Fax: (303)770-6921. E-mail: hd@ncanet.org. Website: http://www.cowtown.org/. Editor: Heather Draper. Monthly trade journal on the beef-cattle industry. "We deal extensively with animal health, price outlook, consumer demand for beef, costs of production, emerging technologies, developing export markets, marketing and risk management." Estab. 1988. Circ. 40,000. Pays on publication. Byline given. "Buys one-time rights but requires non-compete agreements." Sample copy for 9×12 SAE.

Nonfiction: How-to (cut costs of production, risk management strategies), new product (emerging technologies), opinion, technical (emerging technologies, animal health, price outlook). Query with published clips. Length: 1,000-1,300 words. Sidebars encouraged. Pays $200-300 for assigned articles.

Photos: Send photos with submission. Reviews negatives, transparencies. Identification of subjects required.

SHEEP! MAGAZINE, P.O. Box 10, 128 E. Lake St., Lake Mills WI 53551. (414)648-8285. Fax: (414)648-3770. Editor: Dave Thompson. 50% freelance written. Prefers to work with published/established writers. Monthly magazine. "We're looking for clear, concise, useful information for sheep raisers who have a few sheep to a 1,000 ewe flock." Estab. 1980. Circ. 15,000. Pays on publication. Byline given. Offers $30 kill fee. Buys all rights. Makes work-for-hire assignments. Submit seasonal material 3 months in advance. Free sample copy and writer's guidelines.

Nonfiction: Book excerpts; information (on personalities and/or political, legal or environmental issues affecting the sheep industry); how-to (on innovative lamb and wool marketing and promotion techniques, efficient record-keeping systems or specific aspects of health and husbandry). Health and husbandry articles should be written by someone with extensive experience or appropriate credentials (i.e., a veterinarian or animal scientist); profiles (on experienced sheep producers who detail the economics and management of their operation); features (on small businesses that promote wool products and stories about local and regional sheep producers' groups and their activities); new products (of value to sheep producers; should be written by someone who has used them); technical (on genetics, health and nutrition); first-person narratives. Buys 80 mss/year. Query with published clips or send complete ms. Length: 750-2,500 words. Pays $45-150. Pays expenses of writers on assignment.

Reprints: Send tearsheet or photocopy of article. Pays 40% of amount paid for an original article.

Photos: Color—vertical compositions of sheep and/or people—for cover. Use only b&w inside magazine. Black and white, 35mm photos or other visuals improve chances of a sale. Pays $100 maximum for 35mm color transparencies; $20-50 for 5×7 b&w prints. Identification of subjects required. Buys all rights.

Tips: "Send us your best ideas and photos! We love good writing!"

Management

FARM & COUNTRY, Ontario's Commercial Farmer Trade Journal, Agricultural Publishing Co., 1 Yonge St., Suite 1504, Toronto, Ontario M5E 1E5 Canada. (416)364-5324. Fax: (416)364-5857. E-mail: agpub@inforamp.net. Managing Editor: John Muggeridge. 25% freelance written. Tabloid published 18 times/year covering agriculture. Estab. 1935. Circ. 52,000. Pays on publication. Publishes ms an average of 1 month after acceptance. Not copyrighted. Buys first rights and one-time rights. Editorial lead time 2 weeks. Submit seasonal material 1 month in advance. Reports in 1 month. Sample copy and writer's guidelines free.

Nonfiction: Book excerpts, essays, exposé, general interest, historical/nostalgic, how-to, humor, interview/profile, new product, opinion, personal experience, photo feature, technical, travel. Buys 200 mss/year. Query with published clips. Length: 500-1,000 words. Pays $100-400 (Canadian).

Reprints: Send tearsheet, photocopy or typed ms with rights for sale noted and information about when and where the article previously appeared. Pays $7/column inch.

Photos: Send photos with submission. Reviews 2¼×2¼ transparencies and 4×5 prints. Offers $10-300 (Canadian)/photo. Captions, identification of subjects required. Buys one-time rights.

Columns/Departments: Opinion, humour, how-to (all dealing with agriculture), 700 words. Buys 75 mss/year. Query with published clips. Pays $100-200 (Canadian).

NEW HOLLAND NEWS, (formerly *Ford New Holland News*), P.O. Box 1895, New Holland PA 17557-0903. Fax: (717)355-3600. Editor: Gary Martin. 50% freelance written. Works with a small number of new/unpublished writers each year. Magazine published 8 times/year on agriculture; designed to entertain and inform farm families. Estab. 1960.

Pays on acceptance. Publishes ms an average of 6 months after acceptance. Byline given. Offers negotiable kill fee. Buys first North American serial, one-time and second serial (reprint) rights. Submit seasonal material 6 months in advance. Reports in 2 months. Sample copy and writer's guidelines for 9 × 12 SAE with 2 first-class stamps.

Nonfiction: "We need strong photo support for articles of 1,200-1,700 words on farm management and farm human interest." Buys 40 mss/year. Query. Pays $600-800. Sometimes pays the expenses of writers on assignment.

Reprints: Accepts previously published submissions.

Photos: Send photos with query when possible. Reviews color transparencies. Pays $50-300, $500 for cover shot. Captions, model release and identification of subjects required. Buys one-time rights.

Tips: "We thrive on good article ideas from knowledgeable farm writers. The writer must have an emotional understanding of agriculture and the farm family and must demonstrate in the article an understanding of the unique economics that affect farming in North America. We want to know about the exceptional farm managers, those leading the way in agriculture. We want new efficiencies and technologies presented through the real-life experiences of farmers themselves. Use anecdotes freely. Successful writers keep in touch with the editor as they develop the article."

SMALL FARM TODAY, The How-to Magazine of Alternative and Traditional Crops, Livestock, and Direct Marketing, Missouri Farm Publishing, Inc., Ridge Top Ranch, 3903 W. Ridge Trail Rd., Clark MO 65243-9525. (573)687-3525. Fax: (573)687-3148. Editor: Ron Macher. Contact: Paul Berg, managing editor. Bimonthly magazine "for small farmers and small-acreage landowners interested in diversification, direct marketing, alternative crops, horses, draft animals, small livestock, exotic and minor breeds, home-based businesses, gardening, vegetable and small fruit crops." Estab. 1984 as *Missouri Farm Magazine*. Circ. 12,000. Pays 60 days after publication. Publishes ms an average of 6 months after acceptance. Byline given. Buys first serial and nonexclusive reprint rights (right to reprint article in an anthology). Submit seasonal/holiday material 4 months in advance. Reports in 3 months. Sample copy for $3. Writer's guidelines available.

Nonfiction: Practical and how-to (small farming, gardening, alternative crops/livestock). Query letters recommended. Length: 1,200-2,600 words. Pays 3½¢/word.

Reprints: Send information about when and where the article previously appeared. Pays 58% of amount paid for an original article.

Photos: Send photos with submission. Offers $6 for inside photos and $10 for cover photos. Captions required. Pays $4 for negatives or slides. Buys one-time rights and nonexclusive reprint rights (for anthologies).

Tips: "Topic must apply to the small farm or acreage. It helps to provide more practical and helpful information without the fluff."

Miscellaneous

‡**BEE CULTURE**, P.O. Box 706, Medina OH 44256-0706. Fax: (216)725-5624. E-mail: bculture@aol.com. Website: http://www.airoot.com. Editor: Mr. Kim Flottum. 50% freelance written. Monthly magazine for beekeepers and those interested in the natural science of honey bees. Publishes environmentally-oriented articles relating to honey bees or pollination. Estab. 1873. Buys first North American serial rights. Pays on both publication and acceptance. Publishes ms an average of 4 months after acceptance. Reports in 1 month. Sample copy for 9 × 12 SAE with 5 first-class stamps. Free writer's guidelines.

Nonfiction: Interested in articles giving new ideas on managing bees. Also looking for articles on honey bee/environment connections or relationships. Also uses success stories about commercial beekeepers. No "how I began beekeeping" articles. No highly advanced, technical and scientific abstracts or impractical advice. Length: 2,000 word average. Pays $30-50/published page—on negotiation.

Reprints: Send photocopy of article or short story and information about when and where the article previously appeared. Pays 50% of amount paid for an original article.

Photos: Sharp b&w photos (pertaining to honey bees, honey plants or related to story) purchased with mss. Can be any size, prints or enlargements, but 4 × 5 or larger preferred. Pays $7-10/picture.

Tips: "Do an interview story on commercial beekeepers who are cooperative enough to furnish accurate, factual information on their operations. Frequent mistakes made by writers in completing articles are that they are too general in nature and lack management knowledge."

Regional

AGRI-TIMES NORTHWEST, J/A Publishing Co., 206 SE Court, P.O. Box 189, Pendleton OR 97801. (541)276-7845. Fax: (541)276-7964. Editor: Virgil Rupp. Managing Editor: Jim Eardley. 50% freelance written. Biweekly newspaper on agriculture in western Idaho, eastern Oregon and eastern Washington. "News, features about regional farmers/agribusiness *only*." Estab. 1983. Circ. 3,000. Pays on 15th of month after publication. Publishes ms an average of 1 month after acceptance. Byline given. Buys one-time rights. Submit seasonal material 1 month in advance. Accepts simultaneous submissions. Reports in 1 month. Sample copy for 50¢ and 8 × 10 SAE with 4 first-class stamps. Writer's guidelines for #10 SASE.

Nonfiction: How-to (regional farming and ranching), humor (regional farming and ranching), interview/profile (regional farmers/ranchers), photo feature (regional agriculture), technical (regional farming and ranching). Buys 50 mss/

year. Query with or without published clips, or send complete ms. Length: 750 words maximum. Pays 75¢/column inch.
Reprints: Send typed ms with rights for sale noted and information about when and where the article previously appeared. Pays 100% of amount paid for an original article.
Photos: Send photos with submission. Reviews contact sheets, negatives and prints. Offers $5-10/photo. Captions and identification of subjects required. Buys one-time rights.
Columns/Departments: Agri-Talk (quips, comments of farmers/ranchers). Buys 50 mss/year. Send complete ms. Length: 100 words maximum. Pays 75¢ per column inch.
Tips: "Focus on our region's agriculture. Be accurate."

ARKANSAS FARMER, 28 Fontaine Cove, Pontotoc MS 38863. Phone/fax: (601)489-1777. E-mail: eadorris@aol.c om. Editor: Eva Ann Dorris. 20% freelance written. Monthly tabloid covering agriculture, commercial farmers and ranchers doing business in Arkansas. Estab. 1985. Circ. 11,700. Pays on publication. Byline given. Negotiable kill fee. Submit seasonal/holiday material 6 weeks in advance. Reports in 3 weeks on queries; 1 month on mss. Sample copy for 9×13 SAE with 3 first class stamps.
Nonfiction: How-to (farming or ranching only), interview/profile (farmer, rancher, agribusiness or legislator), new product, technical (farm oriented products or method). No general interest pieces without relevance to farming. Buys 15-20 mss/year. Query with or without published clips, or send complete ms. Length: 500-1,000 words. Pays $75 without photos, $100 with usable color prints.
Reprints: Accepts previously published submissions. Send information about when and where the article previously appeared. Payment negotiable.
Photos: State availability of photos with submission. Reviews contact sheets and 3×5 or larger prints. Offers $5-20/photo. Captions and identification of subjects required. Buys rights to any Rural Press USA publication.
Tips: "Query with good ideas that will be of interest to Arkansas farmers and ranchers. We serve their interests *only*. Keep manuscripts short (15-25 inches maximum). Photos are helpful."

FARM FOCUS, Fundy Group Publications, P.O. Box 128, 2 Second St., Yarmouth, Nova Scotia B5A 4B1 Canada. (902)742-7111. Fax: (902)742-2311. Editor: Heather Jones. 50-60% freelance written. Bimonthly newspaper covering agriculture of interest in Atlantic Canada. Estab. 1972. Circ. 9,000. Pays on publication. Publishes ms an average of 1 month after acceptance. Byline given. Offers $20-25 kill fee. Buys first North American serial, first or second serial (reprint) rights. Editorial lead time 1 month. Submit seasonal material 1 month in advance. Reports in 2 weeks on queries; 1 month on mss. Sample copy free.
Nonfiction: Humor, opinion. Buys 1 mss/year. Query. Length: 1,500 words maximum. Pays per column inch. Pays copies for special columns. Pays expenses of writers on assignment.
Reprints: Send typed ms with rights for sale noted and information about when and where the article previously appeared. Pays 3¢/word for reprints.
Photos: State availability of or send photos with submission. Reviews negatives, transparencies, prints (b&w and color). Offers $10-20/photo. Captions required. Buys one-time rights.
Fiction: Buys 1-2 mss/year. Query. Length: 1,500 words maximum. Pays per column inch.
Tips: "Call with an idea/ideas of your own. Do not ask if any work is available."

FARMWEEK, Mayhill Publications, Inc., P.O. Box 90, Knightstown IN 46148-1242. (317)345-5133. Fax: (800)318-1055. E-mail: farmwk@aol.com. Editor: Nancy Searfoss. Associate Editor: Amy McKenzie. 5% freelance written. Weekly newspaper that covers agriculture in Indiana, Ohio and Kentucky. Estab. 1955. Circ. 35,000. Pays on publication. Byline given. Buys first rights. Submit seasonal material 1 month in advance. Reporting time varies; up to 1 year. Free sample copy and writer's guidelines.
Nonfiction: General interest (agriculture), interview/profile (ag leaders), new product, photo feature (Indiana, Ohio, Kentucky agriculture). "We don't want first-person accounts or articles from states outside Indiana, Kentucky, Ohio (unless of general interest to all farmers and agribusiness)." Query with published clips. Length: 500-1,500 words. Pays $50 maximum. Sometimes pays expenses of writers on assignment.
Photos: State availability of photos with submission. Reviews contact sheets and 4×5 and 5×7 prints. Offers $10 maximum/photo. Identification of subjects required. Buys one-time rights.
Tips: "We want feature stories about farmers and agribusiness operators in Indiana, Ohio and Kentucky. How do they operate their business? Keys to success? etc. Best thing to do is call us first with idea, or write. Could also be a story about some pressing issue in agriculture nationally that affects farmers everywhere."

FLORIDA GROWER AND RANCHER, The Oldest Spokesman For Florida Agriculture, Meister Publishing Co., 1555 Howell Branch Rd., Suite C-204, Winter Park FL 32789. (407)539-6552. Editor: Frank Garner. 10% freelance written. Monthly magazine "edited for the Florida farmer with commercial production interest primarily in citrus, vegetables, and other ag endeavors. Our goal is to provide articles which update and inform on such areas as production, ag financing, farm labor relations, technology, safety, education and regulation." Estab. 1907. Circ. 14,500. Pays on publication. Byline given. Buys all rights. Editorial lead time 2 months. Submit seasonal material 3 months in advance. Reports in 1 month. Sample copy for 9×12 SAE with 5 first class stamps. Writer's guidelines free.
Nonfiction: Interview/profile, photo feature, technical. Query with published clips. Length: 750-1,000 words. Pays $150-250.
Photos: Send photos with submission.

THE LAND, Minnesota's Ag Publication, Free Press Co., P.O. Box 3169, Mankato MN 56002-3169. E-mail: theland@ic.mankato.mn.us. Editor: Randy Frahm. 50% freelance written. Weekly tabloid "covering farming in Minnesota. Although we're not tightly focused on any one type of farming, our articles must be of interest to farmers. In other words, will your article topic have an impact on people who live and work in rural areas?" Estab. 1976. Circ. 40,000. **Pays on acceptance.** Publishes ms an average of 3 months after acceptance. Byline given. Buys first North American serial rights. Editorial lead time 1 month. Submit seasonal material 2 months in advance. Reports in 3 weeks on queries; 2 months on mss. Prefer to work with Minnesota writers. Writer's guidelines for #10 SASE.
Nonfiction: General interest (ag), how-to, interview/profile, personal experience, technical. Buys 15-40 mss/year. Query. Length: 500-1,500 words. Pays $25 minimum for assigned articles.
Photos: State availability of photos with submission. Reviews contact sheets. Negotiates payment individually. Buys one-time rights.
Tips: "Be enthused about rural Minnesota life and agriculture and be willing to work with our editors. We try to stress relevance." Most open to feature articles.

MAINE ORGANIC FARMER & GARDENER, Maine Organic Farmers & Gardeners Association, RR 2, Box 594, Lincolnville ME 04849. (207)763-3043. Editor: Jean English. 40% freelance written. Prefers to work with published/ established local writers. Quarterly magazine covering organic farming and gardening for urban and rural farmers and gardeners and nutrition-oriented, environmentally concerned readers. "*MOF&G* promotes and encourages sustainable agriculture and environmentally sound living. Our primary focus is organic farming, gardening and forestry, but we also deal with local, national and international agriculture, food and environmental issues." Estab. 1976. Circ. 10,000. Pays on publication. Publishes ms an average of 8 months after acceptance. Byline and bio given. Buys first North American serial, one-time, first serial or second serial (reprint) rights. Submit seasonal material 1 year in advance. Accepts simultaneous submissions. Reports in 2 months. Sample copy for $2 and SAE with 7 first-class stamps. Free writer's guidelines.
Nonfiction: Book reviews; how-to based on personal experience, research reports, interviews. Profiles of farmers, gardeners, plants. Information on renewable energy, recycling, nutrition, health, non-toxic pest control, organic farm management and marketing. "We use profiles of New England organic farmers and gardeners and news reports (500-1,000 words) dealing with US/international sustainable ag research and development, rural development, recycling projects, environmental and agricultural problems and solutions, organic farms with broad impact, cooperatives and community projects." Buys 30 mss/year. Query with published clips or send complete ms. Length: 1,000-3,000 words. Pays $20-150.
Reprints: Send typed ms with rights for sale noted and information about when and where the article previously appeared. Pays 50% of amount paid for an original article.
Photos: State availability of b&w photos with query; send 3×5 b&w photos with ms. Captions, model releases, identification of subjects required. Buys one-time rights.
Tips: "We are a nonprofit organization. Our publication's primary mission is to inform and educate, but we also want readers to enjoy the articles."

‡**N.D. REC/RTC MAGAZINE**, N.D. Association of RECs, P.O. Box 727, Mandan ND 58554-0727. (701)663-6501. Fax: (701)663-3745. Editor: Kent Brick. 10% freelance written. Prefers to work with published/established writers. Monthly. "Our magazine goes to the 75,000 North Dakota families who get their electricity from rural electric cooperatives. We cover lifestyle, energy use, farm and family matters, and other features of importance to this state. Of course, we represent the views of our statewide association." Estab. 1954. Circ. 78,000. Pays on publication; **pays on acceptance for assigned features**. Publishes ms average of 6 months after acceptance. Byline given. Buys first North American serial rights. Submit seasonal material 6 months in advance. Reports in 2 months. Sample copy for 9×12 SAE with 6 first-class stamps.
• *N.D. REC/RTC* reports a need for articles with greater emphasis on matters pertaining to equipment for the home and family issues related to money, parenting, personal health, small business and telecommunications.
Nonfiction: Exposé (subjects of ND interest dealing with rural electric, rural enterprises, rural lifestyle); historical/ nostalgic (ND events or people only); how-to (save energy, weatherize homes, etc.); interview/profile (on great leaders of the rural electric program, rural and small town America); opinion. Buys 10-12 mss/year. Pays $100-500. Pays expenses of writers on assignment.
Reprints: Send photocopy of article or short story or typed ms with rights for sale noted. Pays 25% of amount paid for an original article.
Photos: "Good quality photos accompanying ms improve chances for sale."
Fiction: Historical. "No fiction that does not relate to our editorial goals." Buys 2-3 mss/year. Length: 400-1,200 words. Pays $100-300. Reprints novel excerpts.
Tips: "Write about a North Dakotan—one of our rural residents who has done something notable in the ag/energy/ rural electric/rural lifestyle areas."

OHIO FARMER, 1350 W. Fifth Ave., Columbus OH 43212. (614)486-9637. Editor: Tim White. 40% freelance written. Magazine for Ohio farmers and their families published 15 issues/year (monthly April-December; biweekly January-March). Estab. 1848. Circ. 60,000. Usually buys all rights. Pays on publication. Publishes ms an average of 2 months after acceptance. Reports in 2 months. Sample copy for $1, SAE with 4 first-class stamps. Free writer's guidelines.
• This magazine is part of Farm Progress Co. State Farm magazine group.

Nonfiction: Technical and on-the-farm stories. Buys informational, how-to and personal experience. Buys 20 mss/year. Submit complete ms. Length: 600-700 words. Pays $400.
Photos: Offers no additional payment for photos purchased with ms. Send transparencies.
Tips: "Freelance submissions must be of a technical agricultural nature. We are actively seeking journalists with a good understanding of production and technical aspects of ag for freelance assignments."

PENNSYLVANIA FARMER, Farm Progress Publications, P.O. Box 4475, Gettysburg PA 17325. (717)334-4300. Fax: (717)334-3120. Editor: John Vogel. 20% freelance written. Monthly farm business magazine "oriented to providing readers with ideas to help their businesses and personal lives." Estab. 1877. Circ. 57,000. Pays on publication. Publishes ms an average of 3 months after acceptance. Buys first-time rights. Submit seasonal material 3 months in advance. Accepts simultaneous submissions. Reports in 1 month. Writer's guidelines for #10 SASE.
Nonfiction: Humor, inspirational, technical. No stories without a strong tie to Mid-Atlantic farming. Buys 15 mss/year. Query. Length: 500-1,000 words. Pays $50-150. Sometimes pays the expenses of writers on assignment.
Photos: Send photos with submission. Reviews 35mm transparencies. Pays $25-300 for each color photo accepted with ms. Captions and identification of subjects required.

‡TODAY'S FARMER, MFA Incorporated, 201 Ray Young Dr., Columbia MO 65201. (314)876-5252. Editor: Chuck Lay. Managing Editor: Tom Montgomery. Contact: Chuck Lay. 50% freelance written. Company publication. Magazine published 10 times/year "owned and published by MFA Incorporated, an agricultural cooperative. We examine techniques and issues that help farmers and ranchers better meet the challenges of the present and future." Estab. 1908. Circ. 46,000. **Pays on acceptance.** Publishes ms an average of 2 months after acceptance. Byline given. Offers 100% kill fee. Publication not copyrighted. Buys first North American serial rights. Editorial lead time 2 months. Submit seasonal material at least 3 months in advance. Sample copy for $1. Writer's guidelines available by phone.
Nonfiction: How-to (ag technical), interview/profile, photo feature, technical. "No fiction, articles on MFA competitors, or subjects outside our trade territory (Missouri, Iowa, Arkansas)." Buys 30 mss/year. Query with published clips. Length: 1,000-2,000 words. Pays $200 minimum (features). Sometimes pays expenses of writers on assignment.
Photos: Send photos with submission. Reviews contact sheets. Negotiates payment individually. Identification of subjects required. Buys one-time rights.
Tips: "Freelancers can best approach us by knowing our audience (farmers/ranchers who are customers of MFA) and knowing their needs. We publish traditional agribusiness information that helps farmers do their jobs more effectively. Know the audience. We edit for length, AP style."

WYOMING RURAL ELECTRIC NEWS, P.O. Box 380, Casper WY 82602-0380. (307)234-6152. Fax: (307)234-4115. Editor: Kris Wendtland. 10% freelance written. Monthly magazine for audience of small town residents, vacation-home owners, farmers and ranchers. Estab. 1955. Circ. 31,400. Byline given. Pays on publication. Publishes ms an average of 1 month after acceptance. Buys one-time rights. Submit seasonal material 2 months in advance. Reports in 3 months. Sample copy for SAE with 3 first-class stamps.
Nonfiction and Fiction: Wants science articles with question/answer quiz at end—test your knowledge. Buys electrical appliance articles. No nostalgia. No sad stories. Articles welcome that put present and/or future in positive light. Submit complete ms. Buys 4-10 mss/year. Length: 500-800 words. Pays $25-45.
Reprints: Sometimes buys reprints. Send tearsheet or photocopy of article or short story and information about when and where the article previously appeared.
Photos: Pays up to $40 for cover photos. Color only.
Tips: "Study an issue or two of the magazine to become familiar with our focus and the type of freelance material we're using. We're always looking for positive humor. Always looking for fresh, new writers, original perspectives. Submit entire manuscript. Don't submit a regionally set story from some other part of the country. Photos and illustrations (if appropriate) are always welcomed."

FINANCE

These magazines deal with banking, investment and financial management. Publications that use similar material but have a less technical slant are listed under the Consumer Business and Finance section.

‡AMERICA'S COMMUNITY BANKER, (formerly *Savings & Community Banker*), Suite 400, 900 19th St. NW, Washington DC 20006. (202)857-3100. Fax: (202)857-5581. E-mail: jnoe@acbankers.org. Website: http://www.acbankers.org. Editor: Jeffrey Noe. 25% freelance written. Monthly magazine. "*America's Community Banker* is written for senior managers and executives of community financial institutions. The magazine covers all aspects of financial institution management, with an emphasis on strategic business issues and trends. Recent features have included check imaging, fair lending, trends in mortgage finance and developing an investor regulations program." Circ. 14,000. **Pays on acceptance.** Publishes ms an average of 2 months after acceptance. Byline given. Offers 20% kill fee. Buys first North American serial rights. Editorial lead time 2-3 months. Submit seasonal material 6 months in advance. Query for electronic submissions. Reports in 1 month on queries. Sample copy and writer's guidelines free.

Nonfiction: How-to (articles on various aspects of a financial institution's operations). "Articles must be well-researched and backed up by a variety of sources, preferably senior managers of financial institutions or experts associated with the banking industry." Buys 6 mss/year. Query with published clips. Length: 1,500 words. Pays $500. Sometimes pays expenses of writers on assignment.

Photos: Send photos with submission. Reviews contact sheets, transparencies and prints. Negotiates payment individually. Identification of subjects required. Buys one-time rights.

Columns/Departments: Nationwide News (news items on banking and finance), 100-500 words; Operations Update (items on particular operational issues for financial institutions, such as marketing, retail banking or data processing), 100-500 words. Buys 25 mss/year. Query with published clips. Pays $100.

Tips: "The best way to develop a relationship with *America's Community Banker* is through our two departments, Nationwide News and Operations Update. If writers can prove themselves reliable there first, major feature assignments may follow."

BUYSIDE, Ideas For Today's Money Managers, Buyside, Ltd., P.O. Box 1329, Sonoma CA 95476. (707)935-9200. Fax: (707)935-9300. E-mail: lkeyson@buyside.com. Managing Editor: Lauren Keyson. 100% freelance written. Monthly magazine covering stocks and investment ideas. Estab. 1994. Circ. 30,000. Pays on publication. Publishes ms an average of 2 months after acceptance. Byline given. Offers 50% kill fee. Buys first rights. Editorial lead time 1 month. Submit seasonal material 3 months in advance. Accepts simultaneous submissions. Sample copy and writer's guidelines free.

Nonfiction: Opinion, financial (buyside, sellside). Buys 80 mss/year. Query. Length: 750-3,000 words. Pays $375-3,000. Pays expenses of writers on assignment.

Photos: Query first. Reviews contact sheets, negatives, 4×5 transparencies, 3×5 prints. Offers $50-500/photos. Negotiates payment individually. Buys one-time rights.

Columns/Departments: Take Five (financial humor), 500 words; Small Cap, 500 words. Query.

Fiction: Humorous (financial). Buys 12 mss/year. Query. Length: 450-500 words. Pays $375-500.

Tips: "Be knowledgeable about a particular industry—keep abreast of news, make contacts with analysts, heads of companies and investor relation firms. Know the investment thesis and secular reason for writing on the industry."

‡EQUITIES MAGAZINE INC., 160 Madison Ave., 3rd Floor, New York NY 10016. (212)213-1300. Editor: Robert J. Flaherty. 50% freelance written. "We are a monthly financial magazine covering the fastest-growing companies in the world. We study the management of companies and act as critics reviewing their performances. We aspire to be 'The Shareholder's Friend'. We want to be a bridge between quality public companies and sophisticated investors." Estab. 1951. Circ. 15,000. Pays on publication. Publishes ms an average of 2 months after acceptance. Byline given. Buys first and reprint rights. Sample copy for 9×12 SAE with 5 first-class stamps.

Nonfiction: New product, technical. Buys 30 mss/year. "We must know the writer first as we are careful about whom we publish. A letter of introduction with résumé and clips is the best way to introduce yourself. Financial writing requires specialized knowledge and a feel for people as well, which can be a tough combination to find." Query with published clips. Length: 300-1,500 words. Pays $150-750 for assigned articles, more for very difficult or investigative pieces. Carries guest columns by famous money managers who are not writing for cash payments, but to showcase their ideas and approach. Pays expenses of writers on assignment.

Photos: Send photos with submission. Reviews contact sheets, negatives, transparencies and prints. Offers no additional payment for photos accepted with ms. Identification of subjects required.

Columns/Departments: Pays $25-75 for assigned items only.

Tips: "Anyone who enjoys analyzing a business and telling the story of the people who started it, or run it today, is a potential *Equities* contributor. But to protect our readers and ourselves, we are careful about who writes for us. Business writing is an exciting area and our stories reflect that. If a writer relies on numbers and percentages to tell his story, rather than the individuals involved, the result will be numbingly dull."

THE FEDERAL CREDIT UNION, National Association of Federal Credit Unions, P.O. Box 3769, Washington DC 20007-0269. (703)522-4770. Fax: (703)524-1082. (Do not query by fax.) E-mail: tfcu@nafcunet.org. Website: http://www.nafcunet.org. Editor: Patrick M. Keefe. Contact: Robin Johnston, managing editor. 25% freelance written. "Looking for writers with financial, banking or credit union experience, but will work with inexperienced (unpublished) writers based on writing skill. Published bimonthly, *The Federal Credit Union* is the official publication of the National Association of Federal Credit Unions. The magazine has a unique focus among credit union publications, one which is well-suited to the large institutions that make up its primary reader base. Its editorial concentrates on Washington, D.C., and the rapidly changing regulatory and legislative environment affecting credit unions. More importantly, it covers how this environment will affect credit union strategy, operations, management, technology, and human resources."

WRITER'S MARKET is now available on CD-ROM. Streamline your market searches with *Writer's Market: the Electronic Edition.*

Estab. 1967. Circ. 10,203. Pays on publication. Publishes ms an average of 3 months after acceptance. Byline given. Buys first North American serial rights. Submit seasonal material 5 months in advance. Accepts simultaneous submissions. Reports in 2 months. Sample copy for 10×13 SAE with 5 first-class stamps. Writer's guidelines for #10 SASE.
Nonfiction: Query with published clips and SASE. Length: 1,200-2,000 words. Query. Pays $200-800.
Reprints: Send ms with rights for sale noted and information about when and where the article previously appeared.
Photos: Send photos with submission. Reviews 35mm transparencies and 5×7 prints. Offers no additional payment for photos accepted with ms. Model releases and identification of subjects required. Buys all rights.
Tips: "Provide résumé or listing of experience pertinent to subject. Looking only for articles that focus on events in Congress, regulatory agencies or technological developments applicable to financial institutions."

NAPFA ADVISOR, The Newsletter for Fee-Only Financial Advisors, National Association of Personal Financial Advisors, 355 West Dundee Rd., Suite 200, Buffalo Grove IL 60089. (708)537-7723. Fax: (301)365-1539. Editor: Margery Wasserman. Contact: Peter Phillips, managing editor. 60% freelance written. Monthly newsletter. "*NAPFA Advisor* publishes practice management and investment strategy articles targeted to fee-only financial advisors. Topics that relate to comprehensive financial planning geared to the practitioner are desired. Readers range from sole practitioners to members of larger firms." Estab. 1985. Circ. 1,000. Pays on publication. Publishes ms an average of 3 months after acceptance. Byline given. Buys first North American serial, first, one-time or second serial (reprint) rights. Editorial lead time 2 months. Submit seasonal material 3 months in advance. Accepts simultaneous submissions. Reports in 3 months on queries. Sample copy for 9×12 SAE with 4 first-class stamps.
Nonfiction: Reviews of financial planning books and software programs, financial planning issues, practice management tips. Buys 50 mss/year. Query. Length: 750-2,000 words. Pays 20¢/word up to $300.
Reprints: Send tearsheet of article. Pays 50% of amount paid for an original article.
Photos: State availability of photos with submission. Reviews 5×7 prints. Offers no additional payment for photos accepted with ms. Captions, model releases, identification of subjects required. Buys one-time rights.
Columns/Departments: Practice Profile (assigned), 1,700-2,000 words; Book Reviews (fee-only planning perspective), 750-1,500 words; Software Reviews (fee-only planning perspective), 750-1,500 words. Pays 20¢/word up to $300.
Tips: "All writing must be directed to the financial practitioner, not the consumer. Freelancers who are interested in writing for *NAPFA Advisor* will have a strong background in financial planning, investment, and practice management issues and will understand the differences between fee-only, fee-based, fee and commission, and commission-based financial planning."

FISHING

NORTHERN AQUACULTURE, Harrison House Publishers, 4611 William Head Rd., Victoria, British Columbia V9B 5T7 Canada. (604)478-9209. Fax: (604)478-1184. West Coast Editor: Peter Chettleburgh. 50% freelance written. Works with a small number of new/unpublished writers each year. Monthly trade paper covering aquaculture in Canada and northern US. Estab. 1985. Circ. 4,000. Pays on publication. Publishes ms an average of 3 months after acceptance. Byline given. Buys first North American serial rights. Submit seasonal material 5 months in advance. Reports in 3 weeks. Sample copy for 9×12 SAE with $2 IRCs. Free writer's guidelines.
Nonfiction: How-to, interview/profile, new product, opinion, photo feature. Buys 20-24 mss/year. Query. Length: 200-1,500 words. Pays 15¢/word for articles. May pay writers with contributor copies if writer requests. Sometimes pays the expenses of writers on assignment.
Photos: Send photos with submission. Reviews 5×7 prints. Captions required. Buys one-time rights.

‡PACIFIC FISHING, Salmon Bay Communications, 1515 NW 51st St., Seattle WA 98107. (206)789-5333. Fax: (206)784-5545. Editor: Brad Warren. 75% freelance written. Works with some new/unpublished writers. Monthly business magazine for commercial fishermen and others in the West Coast commercial fishing industry. "*Pacific Fishing* views the fisherman as a small businessman and covers all aspects of the industry, including harvesting, processing and marketing." Estab. 1979. Circ. 11,000. Pays on publication. Publishes ms an average of 2 months after acceptance. Byline given. Offers 10-15% kill fee on assigned articles deemed unsuitable. Buys one-time rights. Reports in 2 months. Sample copy and writer's guidelines for 9×12 SAE with 10 first-class stamps.
Nonfiction: Interview/profile, technical (usually with a business hook or slant). "Articles must be concerned specifically with *commercial* fishing. We view fishermen as small businessmen and professionals who are innovative and success-oriented. To appeal to this reader, *Pacific Fishing* offers 4 basic features: technical, how-to articles that give fishermen hands-on tips that will make their operation more efficient and profitable; practical, well-researched business articles discussing the dollars and cents of fishing, processing and marketing; profiles of a fisherman, processor or company with emphasis on practical business and technical areas; and in-depth analysis of political, social, fisheries management and resource issues that have a direct bearing on West Coast commercial fishermen." Buys 20 mss/year. Query noting whether photos are available, and enclosing samples of previous work. Length varies. One-paragraph news items to 3,000-word features. Payment varies. Sometimes pays the expenses of writers on assignment.
  ● Editors here are putting more focus on local and international seafood marketing, technical coverage of gear and vessels.
Reprints: Send photocopy of article and information about when and where the article previously appeared. Pays 100%

of the amount paid for an original article.

Photos: "We need good, high-quality photography, especially color, of West Coast commercial fishing. We prefer 35mm color slides. Our rates are $200 for cover; $50-100 for inside color; $25-50 for b&w and $10 for table of contents."

Tips: "Because of the specialized nature of our audience, the editor strongly recommends that freelance writers query the magazine in writing with a proposal. We enjoy finding a writer who understands our editorial needs and satisfies those needs, a writer willing to work with an editor to make the article just right. Most of our shorter items are staff written. Our freelance budget is such that we get the most benefit by using it for feature material."

WESTCOAST FISHERMAN, Westcoast Publishing Ltd., 1496 West 72 Ave., Vancouver, British Columbia V6P 3C8 Canada. (604)266-8611. Fax: (604)266-6437. E-mail: wcoast@west-coast.com. Website: http://www.west-coast.com. Contact: Kevin MacDonell, managing editor. 25% freelance written. Monthly trade journal covering commercial fishing in British Columbia. "We're a non-aligned magazine dedicated to the people in the B.C. commercial fishing industry. Our publication reflects and celebrates the individuals and communities that collectively constitute B.C. fishermen." Estab. 1986. Pays on publication. Publishes ms an average of 3 months after acceptance. Byline given. Buys first and one-time rights. Reports in 2 months.

Nonfiction: Interview/profile, photo feature, technical. Buys 30-40 mss/year. Query with or without published clips, or send complete ms. Length: 250-2,500 words. Pays $25-450.

Reprints: Send photocopy of article or typed ms with rights for sale noted and information about when and where the article previously appeared. Pays 100% of amount paid for an original article.

Photos: Send photos with submission. Reviews contact sheets, negatives, transparencies and 5×7 prints. Offers $5-100/photo. Identification of subjects required. Buys one-time rights.

Poetry: Avant-garde, free verse, haiku, light verse, traditional. "We use poetry written by or for West Coast fishermen." Buys 6 poems/year. Length: 1 page. Pays $25.

FLORISTS, NURSERIES AND LANDSCAPERS

Readers of these publications are involved in growing, selling or caring for plants, flowers and trees. Magazines geared to consumers interested in gardening are listed in the Consumer Home and Garden section.

FLORIST, The FTD Association, 29200 Northwestern Hwy., Southfield MI 48034. (313)355-9300. Fax: (810)948-6420. E-mail: flormag@ix.netcom.com. Editor-in-Chief: William P. Golden. Contact: Barbara Koch, managing editor. 5% freelance written. Monthly magazine for retail flower shop owners, managers and floral designers. Other readers include floriculture growers, wholesalers, researchers and teachers. Circ. 26,000. **Pays on acceptance.** Publishes ms an average of 2 months after acceptance. Buys one-time rights. Pays 10-25% kill fee. Reports in 1 month.

Nonfiction: Articles should pertain to marketing, merchandising, financial management or personnel management in a retail flower shop. Also, giftware, floral and interior design trends. No general interest, fiction or personal experience. Buys 5 unsolicited mss/year. Query with published clips. Length: 1,200-1,500 words. Pays $200-400.

Photos: State availability of photos with query. Pays $10-25 for 5×7 b&w photos or color transparencies. Buys one-time rights.

Tips: "Business management articles must deal specifically with retail flower shops and their unique merchandise and concerns. Send samples of published work with query. Suggest several ideas in query letter."

GROWERTALKS, Ball Publishing, 335 N. River St., P.O Box 9, Batavia IL 60510. (630)208-9080. Fax: (630)208-9350. E-mail: growertalk@aol.com. Website: http://www.growertalks.com. Managing Editor: Chris Beytes. 50% freelance written. Monthly magazine. "*GrowerTalks* serves the commercial greenhouse grower. Editorial emphasis is on floricultural crops: bedding plants, potted floral crops, foliage and fresh cut flowers. Our readers are growers, managers and owners. We're looking for writers who've had experience in the greenhouse industry." Estab. 1937. Circ. 10,500. Pays on publication. Publishes ms an average of 6 months after acceptance. Byline given. Buys first North American serial rights. Editorial lead time 4 months. Submit seasonal material 6 months in advance. Reports in 1 month. Sample copy and writer's guidelines free.

Nonfiction: How-to (time- or money-saving projects for professional flower/plant growers); interview/profile (ornamental horticulture growers); personal experience (of a grower); technical (about growing process in greenhouse setting). "No articles that promote only one product." Buys 36 mss/year. Query. Length: 1,200-1,600 words. Pays $125 minimum for assigned articles; $75 minimum for unsolicited articles. Sometimes pays in other premiums or contributor copies.

Photos: State availability of photos with submission. Reviews 2½×2½ slides and 3×5 prints. Negotiates payment individually. Captions, model releases and identification of subjects required. Buys one-time rights.

Tips: "Discuss magazine with ornamental horticulture growers to find out what topics that have or haven't appeared in the magazine interest them."

THE GROWING EDGE, New Moon Publishing Inc., 215 SW Second, Suite 201, P.O. Box 1027, Corvallis OR 97339-1027. (541)757-2511. Fax: (541)757-0028. E-mail: tcoene@peak.org. Website: http://www.teleport.com/~tomal

ex. Editor: Amy Knutson. 85% freelance written. Bimonthly magazine signature covering indoor and outdoor high-tech gardening techniques and tips. Estab. 1980. Circ. 20,000. Pays on publication. Publishes ms an average of 3 months after acceptance. Byline given. Buys first serial and reprint rights. Submit seasonal material at least 6 months in advance. Reports in 3 months. Sample copy for $7. Writer's guidelines for #10 SASE.

Nonfiction: Book excerpts and reviews relating to high-tech gardening, general interest, how-to, interview/profile, personal experience, technical. Query first. Length: 500-2,500 words. Pays 10¢/published word.

Reprints: Send tearsheet, photocopy or typed ms with rights for sale noted and information about when and where the article previously appeared. Payment negotiable.

Photos: Pays $175/color cover photos; $25-50/inside photo. Pays on publication. Credit line given. Buys first and reprint rights.

Tips: Looking for more hydroponics articles and information which will give the reader/gardener/farmer the "growing edge" in high-tech gardening and farming on topics such as high intensity grow lights, water conservation, drip irrigation, advanced organic fertilizers, new seed varieties and greenhouse cultivation.

LANDSCAPE DESIGN, Adams/Green Industry Publishing, 68860 Perez Rd., Suite J, Cathedral City CA 92234. (760)770-4370. Fax: (760)770-8019. Website: http://www.aip.com. Editor: Nancy Sappington. 35% freelance written. Monthly magazine. "*Landscape Design* features topics such as site amenities, plant materials, irrigation, erosion control, paving concepts and water features. Also, features large and small projects, designer profiles and problem-solving techniques and design methodologies." Estab. 1987. Circ. 14,000. Pays on publication. Publishes ms an average of 3 months after acceptance. Byline given. Buys all rights. Editorial lead time 1 month. Submit seasonal material 3 months in advance. Accepts simultaneous submissions. Sample copy and writer's guidelines free.

Nonfiction: Book excerpts, essays, how-to, new product, opinion, personal experience, photo feature, technical. Special issues: Trends in Land Planning (November); Planting for Color (December). No product endorsements. Buys 8 mss/year. Send complete ms. Length: 1,000-3,000 words. Pays $50-275.

Reprints: Accepts previously published submissions.

Photos: Send photos with submission. Reviews 35mm or 4×5 transparencies, prints. Offers no additional payment for photos accepted with ms. Captions required. Buys one-time rights.

Tips: "Request an editorial calendar—choose topics that might be of interest to our readers and pitch them in one or two paragraphs."

LINK MAGAZINE, Wholesale Florists and Florist Suppliers of America, P.O. Box 639, Vienna VA 22183. (703)242-7000. Fax: (703)319-1647. E-mail: ceo@wffsa.org. Editor: Lisa Gough. 1% freelance written. Monthly magazine. "*Link Magazine* covers floral and business issues that help WF & FSA members run their companies more effectively." Estab. 1978. Circ. 1,800. **Pays on acceptance.** Publishes ms an average of 2 months after acceptance. Byline given. Buys first North American serial rights. Editorial lead time 2 months. Submit seasonal material 4 months in advance. Accepts simultaneous submissions. Reports in 1 month. Sample copy for 8½×11 SAE with 7 first-class stamps.

Nonfiction: General interest (business, economics), technical (floriculture). Buys 5-10 mss/year. Query. Length: 1,500-2,500 words. Pays $200.

Reprints: Send typed ms with rights for sale noted and information about when and where the article previously appeared. Payment negotiable.

Photos: State availability of photos with submission. Offers no additional payment for photos accepted with ms. Captions, model releases and identification of subjects required. Buys one-time rights.

Tips: Looking for "business articles centering on new laws, new management techniques, new technology or family business issues are most desirable. Learn something about *Link*'s audience. Articles that are too broad aren't accepted."

ORNAMENTAL OUTLOOK, Your Connection To The South's Horticulture Industry, Meister Publishing Co., 1555 Howell Branch Rd., Suite C204, Winter Park FL 32789. (407)539-6552. Fax: (407)539-6544. Editor: Kris Sweet. 50% freelance written. Monthly magazine. "*Ornamental Outlook* is written for commercial growers of ornamental plants in Florida. Our goal is to provide interesting and informative articles on such topics as production, legislation, safety, technology, pest control, water management and new varieties as they apply to Florida growers." Estab. 1991. Circ. 12,500. Pays 30 days after publication. Publishes ms an average of 4 months after acceptance. Byline given. Buys all rights. Editorial lead time 2 months. Submit seasonal material 3 months in advance. Reports in 1-3 months. Sample copy for 9×12 SAE with 5 first-class stamps. Writer's guidelines free.

Nonfiction: Interview/profile, photo feature, technical. "No first-person articles. No word-for-word meeting transcripts or all-quote articles." Query with published clips. Length: 750-1,000 words. Pays $250/article including photos.

Photos: Send photos with submission. Reviews contact sheets, transparencies and prints. Offers $50-100/photo. Captions and identification of subjects required. Buys one-time rights.

Tips: "I am most impressed by written queries that address specific subjects of interest to our audience, the *Florida* grower of *commercial* horticulture. Our biggest demand is for features, about 1,000 words, that follow subjects listed on our editorial calendar (which is sent with guidelines). Do not send articles of national or consumer interest."

TREE CARE INDUSTRY MAGAZINE, National Arborist Association, P.O. Box 1094, Amherst NH 03031-1094. (800)733-2622. (603)673-3311. E-mail: 76142.462@compuserve.com. Website: http://newww.com/org/naa. Editor: Mark Garvin. 50% freelance written. Monthly magazine covering tree care and landscape maintenance. Estab. 1990. Circ. 27,500. Pays within 30 days of publication. Publishes ms an average of 3 months after acceptance. Byline given.

Buys first North American serial rights. Editorial lead time 10 weeks. Submit seasonal material 3 months in advance. Reports in 2 weeks on queries; 2 months on mss. Sample copy for 9×12 SAE with 6 first-class stamps. Writer's guidelines free on request.

Nonfiction: Book excerpts, general interest, historical/nostalgic, humor, interview/profile, new product, personal experience, technical. Buys 40 mss/year. Query with published clips Length: 900-3,500 words. Payment negotiable. Sometimes pays expenses of writers on assignment.

Photos: Send photos with submission. Reviews prints. Negotiates payment individually. Captions, identification of subjects required. Buys one-time rights.

Columns/Departments: Management Exchange (business management-related), 1,200-1,800 words; Industry Innovations (inventions), 1,200 words; From The Field (OP/ED from practitioners), 1,200 words. Buys 40 mss/year. Send complete ms. Pays $100 and up.

Tips: "Preference is given to writers with background and knowledge of the tree care industry; our focus is relatively narrow. Preference is also given to photojournalists willing to work on speculation."

TURF MAGAZINE, P.O. Box 391, 50 Bay St., St. Johnsbury VT 05819. (802)748-8908. Fax: (802)748-1866. E-mail: turf@together.net. Publishers: Francis Carlet and Dan Hurley. Editor: David G. Cassidy. 40% freelance written. "Our readers are professional turf grass managers: superintendents of grounds for golf courses, cemeteries, athletic fields, parks, recreation fields, lawn care companies, landscape contractors/architects." Estab. 1977. Four regional editions: North, South, Central and West; with a combined national circulation of 58,000. Pays on publication. Byline given. Buys all rights or makes work-for-hire assignments. Submit seasonal material 3 months in advance. Reports in 3 months. Sample copy for 10×13 SAE with 8 first-class stamps.

Nonfiction: How-to, interview/profile, opinion, technical. "We use on-the-job type interviews with good b&w photos that combine technical information with human interest." Buys 80 mss/year. Query with clips or send complete ms. Pays $100 for columns; $200 minimum for feature stories. Often pays expenses of writers on assignment.

Reprints: Send photocopy of article and information about when and where the article previously appeared. Pays $250-350.

Photos: Send photos with ms. Payment for photos is included in payment for articles. Reviews b&w prints. Needs a variety of photos with the story. Also seeking color transparencies for cover.

Tips: "Turf scoops and high profile articles preferred."

GOVERNMENT AND PUBLIC SERVICE

Listed here are journals for people who provide governmental services at the local, state or federal level or for those who work in franchised utilities. Journals for city managers, politicians, bureaucratic decision makers, civil servants, firefighters, police officers, public administrators, urban transit managers and utilities managers are listed in this section.

THE CALIFORNIA HIGHWAY PATROLMAN, California Association of Highway Patrolmen, 2030 V Street, Sacramento CA 95818-1730. (916)452-6751. Editor: Carol Perri. 60% freelance written. Monthly magazine covering CHP info, California history, history of vehicles and/or transportation. "Our readers are either uniformed officers or pro-law enforcement." Estab. 1937. Circ. 20,000. Pays on publication. Publishes ms an average of 9 months after acceptance. Byline given. Buys one-time rights. Submit seasonal material 6 months in advance. Accepts simultaneous submissions. Reports in 1 month on queries, up to 3 months on mss. Sample copy for 9×12 SAE with 5 first-class stamps. Writer's guidelines for #10 SASE.

Nonfiction: General interest, historical/nostalgic, humor, interview/profile, photo feature, technical, travel. "No 'how you felt when you received a ticket (or survived an accident)!' No fiction." Buys 80-100 mss/year. Query with or without published clips, or send complete ms. No telephone queries. Length: 750-3,000 words. Pays 5¢/word or $50 minimum.

Reprints: Send tearsheet or photocopy of article telling when and where the article previously appeared.

Photos: State availability of photos with submission. Send photos (or photocopies of available photos) with submission. Reviews prints. Offers $5/photo. Captions and identification of subjects required. Returns all photos. Buys one-time rights.

• Articles with accompanying photos receive preference.

CHIEF OF POLICE MAGAZINE, National Association of Chiefs of Police, 3801 Biscayne Blvd., Miami FL 33137. (305)573-0070. Executive Editor: Jim Gordon. Bimonthly trade journal for law enforcement commanders (command ranks). Circ. 13,500. **Pays on acceptance.** Publishes ms an average of 6 months after acceptance. Byline given. Buys first rights. Submit seasonal material 6 months in advance. Accepts simultaneous submissions. Reports in 2 weeks. Sample copy for $3 and 9×12 SAE with 5 first-class stamps. Writer's guidelines for #10 SASE.

Nonfiction: General interest, historical/nostalgic, how-to, humor, inspirational, interview/profile, new product, personal experience, photo feature, religious, technical. "We want stories about interesting police cases and stories on any law enforcement subject or program that is positive in nature. No exposé types. Nothing anti-police." Buys 50 mss/year. Send complete ms. Length: 600-2,500 words. Pays $25-75 for assigned articles; $10-50 for unsolicited articles. Payment includes publication on the organization's website at editor's discretion. Sometimes (when pre-requested) pays expenses of writers on assignment.

Reprints: Accepts previously published submissions.

Photos: Send photos with submission. Reviews 5×6 prints. Pays $5-10 for b&w; $10-25 for color. Captions required. Buys one-time rights.

Columns/Departments: New Police (police equipment shown and tests), 200-600 words. Buys 6 mss/year. Send complete ms. Pays $5-25.

Fillers: Anecdotes, short humor, law-oriented cartoons. Buys 100/year. Length: 100-1,600 words. Pays $5-25.

Tips: "Writers need only contact law enforcement officers right in their own areas and we would be delighted. We want to recognize good commanding officers from sergeant and above who are involved with the community. Pictures of the subject or the department are essential and can be snapshots. We are looking for interviews with police chiefs and sheriffs on command level with photos."

CORRECTIONS FORUM, Partisan Publishing Inc., 320 Broadway, Bethpage NY 11714. Fax: (516)942-5968. Editor: Thomas Kapinos. 60% freelance written. Magazine published 6 times/year covering prison and jail management. Estab. 1992. Circ. 11,000. Pays on publication. Publishes ms an average of 2 months after acceptance. Byline given. Editorial lead time 3 months. Submit seasonal material 3 months in advance. Accepts simultaneous submissions. Reports in 1 month on queries; 6 months on unsolicited mss. Sample copy for 9×12 SAE with 5 first-class stamps.

Nonfiction: How-to (as done by peers successfully), interview/profile, new product, technical. Buys 10 mss/year. Query. Length: 750-2,000 words. Pays $200 for assigned articles; $150 for unsolicited articles.

Reprints: Accepts previously published submissions.

Photos: Send photos with submission. Offers no additional payment for photos accepted with ms. Captions, identification of subjects required. Buys all rights.

Filler: Anecdotes, gags to be illustrated by cartoonist, newsbreaks, short humor. Buys 3/year.

Tips: Looking for interesting treatment of common themes, in-depth technology treatment for industry members, brief, thorough coverage of complex topics.

FIRE CHIEF, Intertec Publishing Corp., 35 E. Wacker Dr., Suite 700, Chicago IL 60601. (312)726-7277. Fax: (312)726-0241. E-mail: firechfmag@connectinc.com. Website: http://www.argusinc.com. Editor: Scott Baltic. 90% freelance written. Monthly. "*Fire Chief* is the management magazine of the fire service, addressing the administrative, personnel, training, prevention/education, professional development and operational issues faced by chiefs and other fire officers, whether in paid, volunteer or combination departments." Estab. 1956. Circ. 45,000. Pays on publication. Publishes ms an average of 6 months after acceptance. Byline given. Offers 50% kill fee. Buys first, one-time, second serial (reprint) or all rights. Editorial lead time 2 months. Submit seasonal material 4 months in advance. Reports in 1 month on queries; 2 months on mss. Sample copy and writer's guidelines free.

Nonfiction: How-to, technical. Buys 50-60 mss/year. Query with published clips. Length: 1,500-8,000 words. Pays $50-400. Sometimes pays expenses of writers on assignment.

Photos: State availability of photos with submissions. Reviews transparencies, prints. Negotiates payment individually. Captions, identification of subjects required. Buys one-time or reprint rights.

Tips: "Writers who are unfamiliar with the fire service are very unlikely to place anything with us. Many pieces that we reject are either too unfocused or too abstract. We want articles that help keep fire chiefs well informed and effective at their jobs."

FIREHOUSE MAGAZINE, PTN Publishing, 445 Broad Hollow Rd., Suite 21, Melville NY 11747. (516)845-2700. Fax: (516)845-7109. Editor-in-Chief: Harvey Eisner. Contact: Jeff Barrington, executive editor. 85% freelance written. Works with a small number of new/unpublished writers each year. Monthly magazine. "*Firehouse* covers major fires nationwide, controversial issues and trends in the fire service, the latest firefighting equipment and methods of firefighting, historical fires, firefighting history and memorabilia. Fire-related books, fire safety education, hazardous materials incidents and the emergency medical services are also covered." Estab. 1976. Circ. 127,000. Pays on publication. Byline given. Exclusive submissions only. Sample copy for 9×12 SAE with 7 first-class stamps. Writer's guidelines free.

Nonfiction: Book excerpts (of recent books on fire, EMS and hazardous materials); historical/nostalgic (great fires in history, fire collectibles, the fire service of yesteryear); how-to (fight certain kinds of fires, buy and maintain equipment, run a fire department); technical (on almost any phase of firefighting, techniques, equipment, training, administration); trends (controversies in the fire service). No profiles of people or departments that are not unusual or innovative, reports of nonmajor fires, articles not slanted toward firefighters' interests. No poetry. Buys 100 mss/year. Query with or without published clips, or send complete ms. Length: 500-3,000 words. Pays $50-400 for assigned articles; $50-300 for unsolicited articles. Sometimes pays expenses of writers on assignment.

Photos: Send photos with query or ms. Pays $15-45 for b&w prints; $20-200 for transparencies and color prints. Cannot accept negatives. Captions and identification of subjects required.

Columns/Departments: Training (effective methods); Book Reviews; Fire Safety (how departments teach fire safety to the public); Communicating (PR, dispatching); Arson (efforts to combat it). Buys 50 mss/year. Query or send complete ms. Length: 750-1,000 words. Pays $100-300.

Tips: "Read the magazine to get a full understanding of the subject matter, the writing style and the readers before sending a query or manuscript. Send photos with manuscript or indicate sources for photos. Be sure to focus articles on firefighters."

FOREIGN SERVICE JOURNAL, Dept. WM, 2101 E St. NW, Washington DC 20037-2990. (202)338-8244. Fax: (202)338-6820. Editor: Karen Krebsbach. 75% freelance written. Monthly magazine for Foreign Service personnel and others interested in foreign affairs and related subjects. Estab. 1924. Pays on publication. Publishes ms an average of 3 months after acceptance. Byline given. Buys first North American serial rights. Reports in 1 month. Sample copy for $3.50 and 10×12 SAE with 6 first-class stamps. Writer's guidelines for SASE.
Nonfiction: Uses articles on "diplomacy, professional concerns of the State Department and Foreign Service, diplomatic history and articles on Foreign Service experiences. Much of our material is contributed by those working in the profession. Informed outside contributions are welcomed, however." Query. Buys 15-20 unsolicited mss/year. Length: 1,000-4,000 words. Offers honoraria.
Fiction: Publishes short stories about foreign service life in the annual August fiction issue.
Tips: "We're more likely to want your article if it has something to do with diplomacy or U.S. foreign policy."

HEADWAY, (formerly *National Minority Politics*), 13555 Bammel N. Houston, Suite 227, Houston TX 77066. (281)444-4265. Fax: (281)583-9534. Website: http://www.headwaymag.com. Editor: Gwenevere Daye Richardson. 10-15% freelance written. Monthly award-winning opinion and news magazine taking a moderate to conservative political approach. Estab. 1988. Circ. 15,000. Pays on publication. Publishes ms an average of 1 month after acceptance. Byline given. Buys one-time rights. Editorial lead time 2 months. Submit seasonal material 2 months in advance. Accepts simultaneous submissions. Reports in 1 month on queries. Sample copy and writer's guidelines for $2.
Nonfiction: Exposé, interview/profile, commentary and features on national political topics. "These topics can be, but are not limited to, those considered traditionally 'minority' concerns, but prefer a broad view or analysis of national or regional political elections, trends, issues, and economic issues as well." Buys approximately 24 mss/year. Query with published clips. Length: 750-1,000 words. Pays $150-250 for assigned articles; $100 for unsolicited mss.
Columns/Departments: The Nation (commentaries on national issues), 750-1,000 words; features, 1,000-1,500 words; Speaking Out, (personal commentary), 750-1,000 words.
Fillers: Political cartoons. Pays $25.
Tips: "Submissions must be well-written, timely, have depth and take an angle not generally available in national newspapers and magazines. Since our magazine takes a moderate to conservative approach, we prefer not to receive commentaries which do not fall in either of these categories."

THE JOURNAL OF SAFE MANAGEMENT OF DISRUPTIVE AND ASSAULTIVE BEHAVIOR, Crisis Prevention Institute, Inc., 3315-K N. 124th St., Brookfield WI 53005. Fax: (414)783-5906. E-mail: cpi@execpc.com. Editor: Diana B. Kohn. 20% freelance written. Quarterly journal covering safe management of disruptive and assaultive behavior. "Our audience is human service and business professionals concerned about workplace violence issues. *CPI* is the world leader in violence prevention training." Estab. 1992. Circ. 8,000. Estab. 1992. Pays on publication. Publishes ms an average of 6 months after acceptance. Byline given. Offers 50% kill fee. Buys one-time and second serial (reprint) rights. Editorial lead time 6 months. Submit seasonal material 3 months in advance. Reports in 1 month on queries. Sample copy and writer's guidelines free.
Nonfiction: Interview/profile, new product, opinion, personal experience, research. Inquire for editorial calendar. Buys 30-40 mss/year. Query. Length: 1,500-3,000 words. Pays $50-300 for assigned articles; $50-100 for unsolicited mss.
Reprints: Accepts previously published submissions.
Tips: "Writers can inquire more about what our company does and how our resources fit in the marketplace. We can provide them with a good background on CPI if they write or e-mail us."

LAW AND ORDER, Hendon Co., 1000 Skokie Blvd., Wilmette IL 60091. (847)256-8555. Fax: (847)256-8574. E-mail: 71171.1344@compuserve.com. Editor: Bruce W. Cameron. 90% freelance written. Prefers to work with published/established writers. Monthly magazine covering the administration and operation of law enforcement agencies, directed to police chiefs and supervisors. Estab. 1952. Circ. 38,000. Pays on publication. Publishes ms an average of 6 months after acceptance. Byline given. Buys first North American serial rights. Submit seasonal material 3 months in advance. Reports in 1 month. Sample copy for 9×12 SAE. Free writer's guidelines.
Nonfiction: General police interest; how-to (do specific police assignments); new product (how applied in police operation); technical (specific police operation). Special issues: Buyers Guide (January); Communications (February); Training (March); International (April); Administration (May); Small Departments (June); Mobile Patrol (July); Equipment (August); Weapons (September); Police Science (November); Community Relations (December). No articles dealing with courts (legal field) or convicted prisoners. No nostalgic, financial, travel or recreational material. Buys 150 mss/year. Length: 2,000-3,000 words. Query; no simultaneous queries. Pays 10¢/word for professional writers; 5¢/word for others.
Photos: Send photos with ms. Reviews transparencies and prints. Identification of subjects required. Buys all rights.
Tips: "*L&O* is a respected magazine that provides up-to-date information that police chiefs can use. Writers must know their subject as it applies to this field. Case histories are well received. We are upgrading editorial quality—stories *must* show some understanding of the law enforcement field. A frequent mistake is not getting photographs to accompany article."

LAW ENFORCEMENT TECHNOLOGY, PTN Publishing Co., 445 Broad Hollow Rd., #21, Melville NY 11747. (516)845-2700. Fax: (516)845-2797. Editor: Tricia McGlone. 50% freelance written. Monthly magazine covering police management and technology. Estab. 1974. Circ. 35,000. Pays on publication. Publishes ms an average of 6 months after acceptance. Byline given. Offers 25% kill fee. Buys first North American serial rights. Editorial lead time 6 months. Submit seasonal material 6 months in advance. Reports in 1 month on queries; 2 months on mss. Sample copy for SAE with 6 first-class stamps. Writer's guidelines for #10 SASE.

Nonfiction: Book excerpts, how-to, humor, interview/profile, photo feature, police management and training. Buys 15 mss/year. Query. Length: 800-1,800 words. Pays $75-300 for assigned articles.

Reprints: Send typed ms with rights for sale noted and information about when and where the article previously appeared. Payment negotiable.

Photos: Send photos with submission. Reviews contact sheets, transparencies, 5×7 or 8×10 prints. Offers no additional payment for photos accepted with ms. Captions required. Buys one-time rights.

Fiction: Adventure, condensed novels, historical, humorous, mystery, novel excerpts, slice-of-life vignettes, suspense, (all must be police oriented). Buys 4 mss/year. Send complete ms. Length: 1,000-2,000 words. Pays $150-300.

Tips: "Writer should have background in police work or currently work for a police agency. Most of our articles are technical or supervisory in nature. Please query first after looking at a sample copy."

PLANNING, American Planning Association, 122 S. Michigan Ave., Suite 1600, Chicago IL 60603. (312)431-9100. Fax: (312)431-9985. E-mail: slewis@planning.org. Website: http://www.planning.org. Editor: Sylvia Lewis. 25% freelance written. Monthly magazine emphasizing urban planning for adult, college-educated readers who are regional and urban planners in city, state or federal agencies or in private business or university faculty or students. Estab. 1972. Circ. 30,000. Pays on publication. Publishes ms an average of 3 months after acceptance. Buys all rights. Byline given. Reports in 2 months. Sample copy and writer's guidelines for 9×12 SAE with 5 first-class stamps.

Nonfiction: Exposé (on government or business, but topics related to planning, housing, land use, zoning); general interest (trend stories on cities, land use, government); how-to (successful government or citizen efforts in planning, innovations, concepts that have been applied); technical (detailed articles on the nitty-gritty of planning, zoning, transportation but no footnotes or mathematical models). Also needs news stories up to 400 words. "It's best to query with a fairly detailed, one-page letter. We'll consider any article that's well written and relevant to our audience. Articles have a better chance if they are timely and related to planning and land use and if they appeal to a national audience. All articles should be written in magazine feature style." Buys 2 features and 1 news story/issue. Length: 500-2,000 words. Pays $100-900. "We pay freelance writers and photographers only, not planners."

Photos: "We prefer that authors supply their own photos, but we sometimes take our own or arrange for them in other ways." State availability of photos. Pays $25 minimum for 8×10 matte or glossy prints and $200 for 4-color cover photos. Captions required. Buys one-time rights.

POLICE, Bobit Publishing Co., 2512 Artesia Blvd., Redondo Beach CA 90278. (310)376-8788. Fax: (310)798-4598. E-mail: police@bobit.com. Website: http://www.policemagazine.com. 90% freelance written. Monthly magazine covering topics related to law enforcement officers at all levels. Estab. 1968. Circ. 55,000. Pays on publication. Publishes ms an average of 3 months after acceptance. Buys all rights. Submit theme material 3 months in advance. Sample copy for $2. Writer's guidelines for #10 SAE with 2 first-class stamps.

Nonfiction: General interest, interview/profile, new product, personal experience, technical. Buys 30 mss/year. Query or send complete ms. Length: 2,000-3,000 words. Pays $250-350.

Photos: Send photos with submission. Reviews color transparencies. Captions required. Buys all rights.

Columns/Departments: The Beat (entertainment section—humor, fiction, first-person drama, professional tips); The Arsenal (weapons, ammunition and equipment used in the line of duty); Fit For Duty (fitness, nutrition, mental health life style changes); Officer Survival (theories, skills and techniques used by officers for street survival); Behind the Wheel (traffic investigation/accident investigation); Point of Law (highlights current changes and application of constitutional law). Buys 50 mss/year. Query or send complete ms. Length: 1,000-2,500 words. Pays $75-250.

Tips: "You are writing for police officers—people who live a dangerous and stressful life. Study the editorial calendar—yours for the asking—and come up with an idea that fits into a specific issue. We are actively seeking talented writers."

POLICE AND SECURITY NEWS, DAYS Communications, Inc., 15 Thatcher Rd., Quakertown PA 18951-2503. (215)538-1240. Fax: (215)538-1208. Editor: James Devery. 40% freelance written. Bimonthly tabloid on public law enforcement and private security. "Our publication is designed to provide educational and entertaining information directed toward management level. Technical information written for the expert in a manner that the non-expert can understand." Estab. 1985. Circ. 20,964. Pays on publication. Publishes ms an average of 2 months after acceptance. Byline given. Buys first North American serial rights. Accepts simultaneous submissions. Sample copy and writer's guidelines for 9×12 SAE with $1.93 postage.

Nonfiction: Al Menear, articles editor. Exposé, historical/nostalgic, how-to, humor, interview/profile, opinion, personal experience, photo feature, technical. Buys 12 mss/year. Query. Length: 200-4,000 words. Pays 10¢/word. Sometimes pays in trade-out of services.

Reprints: Accepts previously published submissions.

Photos: State availability of photos with submission. Reviews 3×5 prints. Offers $10-50/photo. Buys one-time rights.

Fillers: Facts, newsbreaks, short humor. Buys 6/year. Length: 200-2,000 words. Pays 10¢/word.

POLICE TIMES, American Federation of Police & Concerned Citizens, Inc., 3801 Biscayne Blvd., Miami FL 33137. (305)573-0070. Fax: (305)573-9819. Executive Editor: Jim Gordon. 80% freelance written. Eager to work with new/unpublished writers. Quarterly magazine covering "law enforcement (general topics) for men and women engaged in law enforcement and private security, and citizens who are law and order concerned." Circ. 55,000. **Pays on acceptance.** Publishes ms an average of 6 months after acceptance. Byline given. Buys second serial (reprint) rights. Submit seasonal material 4 months in advance. Accepts simultaneous submissions. Sample copy for $2.50 and 9×12 SAE with 3 first-class stamps. Writer's guidelines for #10 SASE.

Nonfiction: Book excerpts; essays (on police science); exposé (police corruption); general interest; historical/nostalgic; how-to; humor; interview/profile; new product; personal experience (with police); photo feature; technical—all police-related. "We produce a special edition on police killed in the line of duty. It is mailed May 15 so copy must arrive six months in advance. Photos required." No anti-police materials. Buys 50 mss/year. Send complete ms. Length: 200-4,000 words. Pays $5-50 for assigned articles; $5-25 for unsolicited articles. Payment includes right to publish on organization's website.

Reprints: Accepts previously published submissions.

Photos: Send photos with submission. Reviews 5×6 prints. Offers $5-25/photo. Identification of subjects required. Buys all rights.

Columns/Departments: Legal Cases (lawsuits involving police actions); New Products (new items related to police services); Awards (police heroism acts). Buys variable number of mss/year. Send complete ms. Length: 200-1,000 words. Pays $5-25.

Fillers: Anecdotes, facts, newsbreaks, cartoons, short humor. Buys 100/year. Length: 50-100 words. Pays $5-10. Fillers are usually humorous stories about police officer and citizen situations. Special stories on police cases, public corruptions, etc., are most open to freelancers.

‡SUPERINTENDENT'S PROFILE & PRODUCE-SERVICE DIRECTORY, Profile Publications, 3300 LaFayette Rd., Jamesville NY 13078. Editor/Publisher: Jim Cropper. Prefers to work with published/established writers. Monthly magazine "specifically published for every highway superintendent, public works director, and D.O.T. official in New York State, including every village, city, town and county." Estab. 1978. Circ. 2,600. Bylines given for excellent material. Submit seasonal material 3 months in advance. Sample copy for $2 and 9×12 SAE with 5 first-class stamps.

Nonfiction: Interview/Profiles of Highway Superintendents or Public Works Directors in NYS highlighting their departmental operations, and any innovative techniques used in a variety of municipal tasks. Length: 2 full, 8½×11, pages typed single-spaced in 10 point type. Pays $150 for full-length ms. All mss edited to fit magazine format. Sometimes pays expenses of writers on assignment.

Reprints: Send tearsheet of previously published article or ms for consideration.

Photos: Subject matter must pertain to highway or public works. Reviews b&w 5×7s or contact sheets. Pays $5-10. Captions and identification of subjects required. All rights for use of photos granted to publisher if accepted.

Tips: "We are New York State's most widely read publication among highway, public works and D.O.T. professionals. Although we can't pay high rates, we will only consider high quality work. Articles should be written as objectively as possible, and should provide thorough reliable source identification, and content specifically suited to the highway and public works industry."

TRANSACTION/SOCIETY, Bldg. 4051, Rutgers University, New Brunswick NJ 08903. (908)445-2280 ext. 83. Fax: (908)445-3138. E-mail: horowitz@transaction.pub. Website: www.transactionpub.com. Editor: Irving Louis Horowitz. Publisher: Mary E. Curtis. 10% freelance written. Prefers to work with published/established writers. Bimonthly magazine for social scientists (policymakers with training in sociology, political issues and economics). Estab. 1962. Circ. 45,000. Buys all rights. Byline given. Pays on publication. Publishes ms an average of 6 months after acceptance. Reports in 3 months. Sample copy and writer's guidelines for 9×12 SAE with 5 first-class stamps.

Nonfiction: Andrew McIntosh, managing editor. "Articles of wide interest in areas of specific interest to the social science community. Must have an awareness of problems and issues in education, population and urbanization that are not widely reported. Articles on overpopulation, terrorism, international organizations. No general think pieces." Query. Payment for assigned articles only; *no payment for unsolicited articles.*

Photos: Douglas Harper, photo editor. Pays $200 for photographic essays done on assignment or upon publication.

Tips: "Submit an article on a thoroughly unique subject, written with good literary quality. Present new ideas and research findings in a readable and useful manner. A frequent mistake is writing to satisfy a journal, rather than the intrinsic requirements of the story itself. Avoid posturing and editorializing."

YOUR VIRGINIA STATE TROOPER MAGAZINE, Virginia State Police Association, 6944 Forest Hill Ave., Richmond VA 23225. Editor: Rebecca V. Jackson. 30% freelance written. Triannual magazine covering police topics for troopers and special agents (state police), non-sworn members of the department and legislators. Estab. 1974. Circ. 5,000. **Pays on acceptance.** Publishes ms an average of 3 months after acceptance. Byline given. Buys first North American serial, one-time rights and all rights on assignments. Submit seasonal material 4 months in advance. Accepts simultaneous submissions. Reports in 2 months. No sample copies.

Nonfiction: Exposé (consumer or police-related); general interest; fitness/health; tourist (VA sites); historical/nostalgic; how-to; book excerpts/reports (law enforcement related); humor, interview/profile (notable police figures); technical (radar); other (recreation). Buys 55-60 mss/year. Query with clips or send complete ms. Length: 2,500 words. Pays $250 maximum/article (10¢/word). Sometimes pays expenses of writers on assignment.

Reprints: Send typed ms with rights for sale noted and information about when and where the article previously appeared.

Photos: Send photos with ms. Pays $50 maximum for several 5×7 or 8×10 b&w glossy prints to accompany ms.

Cutlines and model releases required. Buys one-time rights.

Cartoons: Send copies. Pays $20. Buys one-time rights. Buys 20 cartoons/year.

GROCERIES AND FOOD PRODUCTS

In this section are publications for grocers, food wholesalers, processors, warehouse owners, caterers, institutional managers and suppliers of grocery store equipment. See the section on Confectionery and Snack Foods for bakery and candy industry magazines.

‡**AIRLINE, SHIP & CATERING ONBOARD SERVICES**, International Publishing of America, P.O. Box 470067, Celebration FL 34747. (407)397-0200. Fax: (407)397-2222. E-mail: onboardmag@aol.com. Editor: A. Morton. Contact: J. Mark Barfield, assistant editor. 70% freelance written. Bimonthly tabloid "contains new articles about the passsenger service departments of the transportation industries, their personnel and news dealing with industry innovations, new products, government regulations in airline, ship, railroad catering, duty free, onboard entertainment and ship supplier industries." Estab. 1968. Circ. 3,400. Pays on publication. Publishes ms an average of 3 months after acceptance. Byline given. Buys all rights. Editorial lead time 1 month. Submit seasonal material 6 months in advance. Reports in 1 month. Sample copy and writer's guidelines free.

Nonfiction: Articles must pertain to the audience described above. Buys 30 mss/year. Query. Length: 1,000-2,000 words. Pays 10-20¢/word. Sometimes pays expenses of writers on assignment.

Photos: Send photos with submission. Reviews transparencies, prints. Offers no additional payment for photos accepted with ms; negotiates payment individually. Identification of subjects required. Buys all rights.

Columns/Departments: Catering, Cuty Free, Associations (pertaining to specific industries), all 1,000-2,000 words. Buys 15 mss/year. Query. Pays 10-20¢/word.

Tips: "Send samples of your writing; request an assignment."

CANADIAN GROCER, Maclean-Hunter Ltd., Maclean Hunter Building, 777 Bay St., Toronto, Ontario M5W 1A7 Canada. (416)596-5772. Fax: (416)593-3162. E-mail: gcondon@mhpublishing.com. Website: http://www.mhbizlink. com/grocer. Assistant Editor: Julie Cooper. Contact: George H. Condon, editor. 20% freelance written. Prefers to work with published/established writers. Monthly magazine about supermarketing and food retailing for Canadian chain and independent food store managers, owners, buyers, executives, food brokers, food processors and manufacturers. Estab. 1886. Circ 18,500. **Pays on acceptance.** Publishes an average of 2 months after acceptance. Byline given. Buys first Canadian rights. Submit seasonal material 2 months in advance. Reports in 2 months. Sample copy for $5.

Nonfiction: Interview (Canadian trendsetters in marketing, finance or food distribution); technical (store operations, equipment and finance); news features on supermarkets. "Freelancers should be well versed on the supermarket industry. We don't want unsolicited material. Writers with business and/or finance expertise are preferred. Know the retail food industry and be able to write concisely and accurately on subjects relevant to our readers: food store managers, senior corporate executives, etc. A good example of an article would be 'How a dairy case realignment increased profits while reducing prices, inventory and stock-outs.' " Query with clips of previously published work. Phone queries OK. Pays 30¢/word. Pays expenses of writers on assignment.

Reprints: Send typed ms with rights for sale noted and information about when and where the article previously appeared. Pays 50% of amount paid for an original article.

Photos: State availability of photos. Pays $10-25 for prints or slides. Captions preferred. Buys one-time rights.

Tips: "Suitable writers will be familiar with sales per square foot, merchandising mixes and efficient consumer response."

‡**CORRECTIONAL FOODSERVICE**, International Publishing Co. of America, P.O. Box 470067, Celebration FL 34747. (407)397-0200. Fax: (407)397-2222. E-mail: correctmag@aol.com. Editor: A. Morton. Contact: J. Mark Barfield, assistant editor. 70% freelance written. "Bimonthly magazine for foodservice professionals employed in prisons, jails and other correctional institutions in the U.S. and Canada. It is directed to federal, state, county and city correctional facilities, as well as private caterers and contract feeders who serve the market. Each issue contains a feature editorial about correctional foodservice techniques, equipment, practitioners and other important issues." Estab. 1991. Circ. 5,000. Pays on publication. Publishes ms an average of 3 months after acceptance. Byline given. Buys all rights. Editorial lead time 1 month. Submit seasonal material 6 months in advance. Reports in 1 month. Sample copy and writer's guidelines free.

Nonfiction: Articles must pertain to the audience described above. Buys 30 mss/year. Query. Length: 1,000-2,000 words. Pays 10-20¢/word. Sometimes pays expenses of writers on assignment. Send photos with submission. Reviews transparencies, prints. Offers no additional payment for photos accepted with ms; negotiates payment individually. Identification of subjects required. Buys all rights.

Columns/Departments: Personnel Management, Waste Management, New Products, all 1,000-2,000 words. Buys 15 mss/year. Query. Pays 10-20¢/word.

Tips: "Send samples of writing; request an assignment."

‡**DISTRIBUTION CHANNELS, AWMA's Magazine for Candy, Tobacco, Grocery and General Merchandise Marketers**, American Wholesale Marketers Association, 1128 16th St. NW, Washington DC 20036. (202)463-

2124. Fax: (202)467-0559. E-mail: jillk@awmanet.org. Managing Editor: Jill Kosko. 75% freelance written. Magazine published 10 times/year. "We cover trends in candy, tobacco, groceries, beverages and other product categories found in convenience stores, grocery stores and drugstores, plus distribution topics. Contributors should have prior experience writing for the food industry. Editorial includes a mix of columns, departments and features (2-6 pages). We also cover AWMA programs." Estab. 1948. Circ. 10,000. **Pays on acceptance**. Publishes ms an average of 2 months after acceptance. Byline given. Editorial lead time 4 months.
Nonfiction: How-to, interview/profile, technical, industry trends; also technical and profiles of distribution firms or manufacturers. No comics, jokes, poems or other fillers. Buys 80 mss/year. Query with published clips. Length: 1,200-3,600 words. Pays $200-800. Sometimes pays industry members who author articles. Pays expenses of writers on assignment.
Photos: Authors must provide artwork (with captions) with articles.
Tips: "We're looking for reliable, accurate freelancers with whom we can establish a long-term working relationship. We need writers who understand this industry. We accept very few articles on speculation. Most are assigned."

FDM (FOOD DISTRIBUTION MAGAZINE), Products and Promotions for Mainstream Distribution, 213 N. Belcher Rd., Clearwater FL 34625. Fax: (813)724-6303. E-mail: fooddismag@aol.com. Editor: Steve Germain. 40% freelance written. Monthly magazine. "We are looking for pieces of interest to supermarket buyers, food distributors, and gourmet and specialty food stores. Quality writing, interesting and informative articles." Estab. 1958. Circ. 35,000. Pays on publication. Publishes ms an average of 2 months after acceptance. Byline given. Buys all rights. Editorial lead time 2-4 months. Submit seasonal material 4 months in advance. Reports in 2 months. Sample copy for $5.
• *Food Distribution* is looking to use more freelancers from across the nation, and is particularly interested in retailer profile features and indepth looks at specialty food retail operations.
Nonfiction: Humor, new product, photo feature. Buys 3-10 mss/year. Query with published clips. Length: 1,000-3,000 words. Pay negotiable. Often pays expenses of writers on assignment.
Reprints: Send information about when and where the article appeared. Pays negotiable rate.
Photos: Send color photos with submission. Reviews transparencies, prints. Negotiates payment individually. Buys one-time rights or all rights.
Tips: Query first with clips. Send color photos with story.

‡FOOD & SERVICE, Texas Restaurant Association, P.O. Box 1429, Austin TX 78767-1429. (512)472-3666. Fax: (512)472-2777. Editor: Olivia Carmichael Solis. 40% freelance written. Bimonthly magazine. "As the official publication of the Texas Restaurant Association, Food & Service targets restaurateurs and foodservice professionals. The magazine's focus is on informing readers of profitable industry practices, trends, legislative issues and actions, employee concerns and new products." Estab. 1941. Circ. 6,000. Pays on publication. Publishes ms an average of 2 months after acceptance. Byline given. Buys first rights. Editorial lead time 2 months. Submit seasonal material 3 months in advance. Reports in 3 weeks on queries; 1 month on mss. Writer's guidelines free.
Nonfiction: Interview/profile, new product, technical. No human interest, restaurant reviews, recipe stories or wine articles. Buys 12 mss/year. Query with published clips. Length: 1,000-2,000 words. Pays $200-500. Sometimes pays expenses of writers on assignment.
Reprints: Accepts previously published submissions.
Columns/Departments: Creative Marketing (creative restaurant marketing ideas), 1,000 words. Buys 6 mss/year. Query with published clips. Pays $200-300.

FOODSERVICE DIRECTOR, Bill Communications, 355 Park Ave. S., New York NY 10010. (212)592-6533. Fax: (212)592-6539. Contact: Walter J. Schruntek, editor. Managing Editor: Karen Weisberg. News Editor: Jeff Hirschfeld. 20% freelance written. Monthly tabloid on non-commercial foodservice operations for operators of kitchens and dining halls in schools, colleges, hospitals/health care, office and plant cafeterias, military, airline/transportation, correctional institutions. Estab. 1988. Circ. 45,000. Pays on publication. Byline sometimes given. Offers 25% kill fee. Buys all rights. Submit seasonal material 3 months in advance. Accepts simultaneous submissions. Free sample copy.
Nonfiction: How-to, interview/profile. Buys 60-70 mss/year. Query with published clips. Length: 700-900 words. Pays $250-500. Sometimes pays the expenses of writers on assignment.
Photos: Send photos with submission. Reviews transparencies. Offers no additional payment for photos accepted with ms. Identification of subjects required. Buys all rights.
Columns/Departments: Equipment (case studies of kitchen/serving equipment in use), 700-900 words; Food (specific category studies per publication calendar), 750-900 words. Buys 20-30 mss/year. Query. Pays $250-500.

FRESH CUT MAGAZINE, The Magazine for Value-added Produce, Columbia Publishing, P.O. Box 1467, Yakima WA 98907. (509)248-2452. Fax: (509)248-4056. E-mail: columbia@wolfenet.com. Editor: Ken Hodge. 40% freelance written. Monthly magazine covering minimally processed fresh fruits and vegetables, packaged salads, etc. "We want informative articles about processing produce. We also want stories about how these products are sold at retail, in restaurants, etc." Estab. 1993. Circ. 9,500. Pays on publication. Publishes ms an average of 2 months after acceptance. Byline given. Buys all rights. Editorial lead time 2 months. Submit seasonal material 3 months in advance. Reports in 1 month on queries; 2 months on mss. Sample copy for 9×12 SASE. Writer's guidelines for #10 SASE.
Nonfiction: Historical/nostalgic, new product, opinion, technical. Buys 20-40 mss/year. Query with published clips.

Special issues: Retail issue (May 97); Foodservice issue (August 97). Pays $5/column inch for assigned articles; $75-125 for unsolicited articles.
Photos: Send photos with submission. Reviews transparencies. Offers no additional payment for photos accepted with ms. Identification of subjects required. Buys one-time rights.
Columns/Departments: Packaging; Food Safety; Processing/engineering. Buys 20 mss/year. Query. Pays $125-200.
Fillers: Facts. Length: 300 words maximum. Pays $25-50.

GOURMET NEWS, United Publications, 106 Lafayette St., Box 1056, Yarmouth ME 04096. (207)846-0600. Fax: (207)846-0657. E-mail: jfriedrick@gourmetnews.com. Editor: Joanne Friedrick. 5% freelance written. "We are a monthly business newspaper covering the gourmet food industry. Our readers are gourmet food retailers and distributors, and articles should be written with them in mind. We do not write about gourmet restaurants." Estab. 1991. Circ. 22,000. Pays on publication. Publishes ms an average of 2 months after acceptance. Byline given. Offers $50 kill fee. Buys first rights. Editorial lead time 2 months. Reports in 4 months on queries.
Nonfiction: Features on trends and issues. Buys 2-3 mss/year. Query. No unsolicited mss. Length: 800-2,000 words. Pays $200-450.
Photos: State availability of photos with submissions. Reviews transparencies, prints. Offers no additional payment for photos accepted with ms.
Tips: "If you are a proven writer with proven skills, I will consider assigning articles to you. If you are relatively new in journalism, be prepared to pitch a specific story with a news angle, such as a trend in gourmet foods (growth of teas, organic foods) or an issue."

HEALTH FOODS BUSINESS, PTN Publishing Co., 2 University Plaza, Suite 204, Hackensack NJ 07601. (201)487-7800. Fax: (201)487-1061. Editor: Gina Geslewitz. 70% freelance written. Monthly magazine covering health foods. "The business magazine for natural products retailers." Estab. 1953. Circ. 12,600. Pays on publication. Publishes ms an average of 3 months after acceptance. Byline given. Buys first North American serial rights. Editorial lead time 4 months. Submit seasonal material 3 months in advance. Reports in 1 month on queries. Sample copy for $3. Writer's guidelines free on request.
Nonfiction: Store profile. Query. Pays $100-200.
Photos: State availability of photos with submissions.
Tips: "We are always looking for well-written store profiles with lots of detailed information, but new writers should always query first to receive writer's guidelines and other directions."

‡HEALTHCARE FOOD SERVICE, International Publishing Co. of America, P.O. Box 470067, Celebration FL 34747. (407)397-0200. Fax: (407)397-2222. E-mail: correctmag@aol.com. Editor: A. Morton. Contact: J. Mark Barfield, assistant editor. 70% freelance written. Bimonthly tabloid "for foodservice professionals employed in U.S. and Canadian hospitals, nursing homes, hospices and treatment centers; contract caterers and restaurant and cafeteria operators providing services to those health care facilities; and companies who supply goods or services to those foodservice professionals. Each issue contains feature editorials about health care foodservice techniques, dietary concerns, equipment, health care foodservice practitioners and other issues of importance." Estab. 1991. Circ. 12,600. Pays on publication. Publishes ms an average of 3 months after acceptance. Byline given. Buys all rights. Editorial lead time 1 month. Submit seasonal material 6 months in advance. Reports in 1 month. Sample copy and writer's guidelines free.
Nonfiction: Articles must pertain to the audience described above. Buys 30 mss/year. Query. Length: 1,000-2,000 words. Pays 10-20¢/word. Sometimes pays expenses of writers on assignment.
Photos: Send photos with submission. Reviews transparencies, prints. Offers no additional payment for photos accepted with ms; negotiates payment individually. Identification of subjects required. Buys all rights.
Columns/Departments: Personnel Management, Waste Management, New Products, all 1,000-2,000 words. Buys 15 mss/year. Query. Pays 10-20¢/word.
Tips: "Send samples of writing; request an assignment."

PACKER/SHIPPER, Columbia Publishing, P.O. Box 1467, Yakima WA 98907. (509)248-2457. Fax: (509)248-4056. E-mail: columbia@wolfenet.com. Editor: Ken Hodge. 75-100% freelance written. Magazine published 8 times/year covering packing, shipping and marketing fresh fruit and vegetables. Estab. 1992. Circ. 8,900. Pays on publication. Publishes ms an average of 2 months after acceptance. Byline given. Buys all rights. Editorial lead time 2 months. Submit seasonal material 3 months in advance. Accepts simultaneous submissions. Reports in 2 weeks on queries; 2 months on mss. Sample copy for 9×12 SASE.
Nonfiction: Historical/nostalgic, interview/profile, new product, opinion, technical. Buys 10-12 mss/year. Query. Length: 750-1,200 words. Pays $125-300 for assigned articles; $75-125 for unsolicited articles.
Photos: State availability of photos with submissions. Reviews contact sheets, transparencies, prints. Offers no additional payment for photos accepted with ms. Captions, identification of subjects required. Buys one-time rights.
Columns/Departments: Machinery; Sanitation/food safety; Marketing/packaging. Buys 70 mss/year. Query. Pays $125-200.
Fillers: Facts. Length: 100-300 words. Pays $25-50.

‡PRODUCE MERCHANDISING, Vance Publishing Corp., 10901 W. 84th Terrace, Lenexa KS 66214. (913)438-8700. Fax: (913)438-0691. E-mail: 103423.1660@compuserve.com. Editor: Elaine Symanski. Contact: Janice L. Mc-

Call, managing editor. 33% freelance written. Monthly. "The magazine's editorial purpose is to provide information about promotions, merchandising and operations in the form of ideas and examples. *Produce Merchandising* is the only monthly journal on the market that is dedicated solely to produce merchandising information for retailers." Circ. 12,000. **Pays on acceptance**. Publishes ms an average of 5 months after acceptance. Byline given. Buys all rights. Editorial lead time 2-3 months. Reports in 2 weeks on queries. Sample copy free. Writer's guidelines for #10 SASE.
Nonfiction: How-to, interview/profile, new product, photo feature, technical (contact the managing editor for a specific assignment). Buys 48 mss/year. Query with published clips. Length: 1,000-1,500 words. Pays $200-600. Pays expenses of writers on assignment.
Photos: State availability of photos with submission or send photos with submission. Reviews color slides and 3×5 or larger prints. Offers no additional payment for photos accepted with ms. Captions, model releases and identification of subjects required. Buys all rights.
Columns/Departments: Contact managing editor for a specific assignment. Buys 30 mss/year. Query with published clips. Pays $200-450.
Tips: "Send in clips and contact the managing editor with specific story ideas. Story topics are typically outlined up to a year in advance."

PRODUCE NEWS, 2185 Lemoine Ave., Fort Lee NJ 07024-6003. Fax: (201)592-0809. Editor: Gordon Hochberg. 10-15% freelance written. Works with a small number of new/unpublished writers each year. Weekly magazine for commercial growers and shippers, receivers and distributors of fresh fruits and vegetables, including chain store produce buyers and merchandisers. Estab. 1897. Pays on publication. Publishes ms an average of 2 weeks after acceptance. Deadline is 2 weeks before Thursday press day. Reports in 1 month. Sample copy and writer's guidelines for 10×13 SAE with 4 first-class stamps.
Nonfiction: News stories (about the produce industry). Buys profiles, spot news, coverage of successful business operations and articles on merchandising techniques. Query. Pays $1/column inch minimum for original material. Sometimes pays expenses of writers on assignment.
Photos: Black and white glossies. Pays $8-10/photo.
Tips: "Stories should be trade-oriented, not consumer-oriented. As our circulation grows in the next year, we are interested in stories and news articles from all fresh-fruit-growing areas of the country."

QUICK FROZEN FOODS INTERNATIONAL, E.W. Williams Publishing Co., Suite 305, 2125 Center Ave., Fort Lee NJ 07024-5898. (201)592-7007. Fax: (201)592-7171. Editor: John M. Saulnier. 20% freelance written. Works with a small number of new writers each year. Quarterly magazine—"every phase of frozen food manufacture, retailing, food service, brokerage, transport, warehousing, merchandising. Especially interested in stories from Europe, Asia and emerging nations." Circ. 13,700. Pays on publication. Publishes ms an average of 3 months after acceptance. Byline given. Offers kill fee; "if satisfactory, we will pay promised amount. If bungled, half." Buys all rights, but will relinquish any rights requested. Submit seasonal material 6 months in advance. Sample copy for $10.
Nonfiction: Book excerpts, general interest, interview/profile, new product (from overseas), personal experience, photo feature, technical, travel. No articles peripheral to frozen food industry such as taxes, insurance, government regulation, safety, etc. Buys 20-30 mss/year. Query or send complete ms. Length: 500-4,000 words. Pays 7¢/word or by arrangement. "We will reimburse postage on articles ordered from overseas."
Photos: "We prefer photos with all articles." State availability of photos or send photos with accompanying ms. Pays $10 for 5×7 color or b&w prints (contact sheet if many shots). Captions and identification of subject required. Buys all rights. Release on request.
Columns/Departments: News or analysis of frozen foods abroad. Buys 20 columns/year. Query. Length: 500-1,500 words. Pays by arrangement.
Fillers: Newsbreaks. Length: 100-500 words. Pays $5-20.
Tips: "We are primarily interested in feature materials (1,000-3,000 words with pictures). We are now devoting more space to frozen food company developments in Pacific Rim and East European countries. Stories on frozen food merchandising and retailing in foreign supermarket chains in Europe, Japan, China, Korea and Australia/New Zealand are welcome. National frozen food production profiles are also in demand worldwide. A frequent mistake is submitting general interest material instead of specific industry-related stories."

‡SCHOOL FOODSERVICE & NUTRITION, American School Food Service Association, 1600 Duke St., 7th Floor, Alexandria VA 22314. Fax: (703)739-3915. E-mail: pfitzgerald@asfsa.org. Editor: Patricia L. Fitzgerald. 25% freelance written. Magazine published 11 times/year covering school foodservice, child nutrition and noncommercial foodservice. "Members/readers range from district directors who manage multi-million-dollar budgets to part-time line workers. Magazine presents information on how-to-do jobs, innovative practices and trends, strategies for improving participation and the bottom line. Has a very business-like, how-to approach, but with a lively, active voice and tone." Estab. 1946. Publishes ms an average of 6 months after acceptance. Byline given. Makes work-for-hire assignments. Editorial lead time 3 months. Submit seasonal material 6 months in advance. Reports in 3 months on queries; 4 months on mss. Sample copy and writer's guidelines free.
Nonfiction: How-to, interview/profile, technical. Assigns 11-15 mss/year. Query with published clips. Length: 1,500-3,200 words. Pays $400-800.
Photos: State availability of photos with submission. Offers no additional payment for photos accepted with ms. Captions and identification of subjects required. Buys one-time rights.

Tips: "Know the market and audience. *Always* query first. Request a copy of editorial calendar and base ideas on upcoming topics. We're a small shop and reviews and phone call returns can be slow. *Don't* hound!"

SEAFOOD LEADER, Waterfront Press Co., 5305 Shilshole Ave., NW, #200, Seattle WA 98107. (206)789-6506. Fax: (206)789-9193. E-mail: wfpress@net.com. Managing Editor: Rob Lovitt. Contact: Peter Redmayne, editor. 20% freelance written. Works with a small number of new/unpublished writers each year. Bimonthly journal on the seafood business. Estab. 1980. Circ. 15,000. Pays on publication. Publishes ms an average of 3 months after acceptance. Byline given. Buys first rights and second serial (reprint) rights. Accepts simultaneous submissions. Reports in 1 month on queries; 2 months on mss. Sample copy for $4 with 9×12 SAE.
Nonfiction: General seafood interest, marketing/business, historical/nostalgic, interview/profile, opinion, photo feature. Each of *Seafood Leader's* 6 issues has a slant: Retail/Aquaculture (January/February), Buyer's Guide (March/April), International (May/June), Foodservice/Restaurant (July/August), Seafood Catalog (September/October) and Shrimp/Alaska (November/December). Each issue also includes stories outside of the particular focus, particularly shorter features and news items. No recreational fishing; no first person articles. Buys 12-15 mss/year. Query with or without published clips, or send complete ms. Length: 1,000-2,500 words. Pays 15-25¢/word published depending upon amount of editing necessary. Sometimes pays expenses of writers on assignment.
Reprints: Send tearsheet or photocopy of article, typed ms with rights for sale noted and information about when and where the article previously appeared. Pays 50% of amount paid for an original article.
Photos: State availability of photos with submission. Reviews contact sheets and transparencies. Offers $50/inside color photo, $100 for cover. Buys one-time rights.
Fillers: Newsbreaks. Buys 10-15/year. Length: 100-250 words. Pays $50-100.
Tips: "*Seafood Leader* is steadily increasing in size and has a growing need for full-length feature stories and special sections. Articles on innovative, unique and aggressive people or companies involved in seafood are needed. Writing should be colorful, tight and fact-filled, always emphasizing the subject's formula for increased seafood sales. Readers should feel as if they have learned something applicable to their business."

TODAY'S GROCER, (formerly *Florida Grocer*), F.G. Publications, Inc., P.O. Box 430760, South Miami FL 33243-0760. (305)441-1138. Fax: (305)661-6720. Editor: Dennis Kane. 3% freelance written. "*Today's Grocer* is a 19,500-circulation monthly trade newspaper, serving members of the food industry in Florida, Georgia, Alabama, North and South Carolina. Our publication is edited for chain and independent food store owners and operators as well as members of allied industries." Estab. 1956. **Pays on acceptance.** Byline given. Buys all rights. Submit seasonal material 3 months in advance. Reports in 2 months. Sample copy for 10×14 SAE with 10 first-class stamps.
Nonfiction: Book excerpts, exposé, general interest, humor, features on supermarkets and their owners, new product, new equipment, photo feature, video. Buys variable number of mss/year. Query with or without published clips or send complete ms. Payment varies.
Photos: State availability of photos with submission. Terms for payment on photos "included in terms of payment for assignment."
Tips: "We prefer feature articles on new stores (grand openings, etc.), store owners, operators; food manufacturers, brokers, wholesalers, distributors, etc. We also publish a section in Spanish and also welcome the above types of materials in Spanish (Cuban)."

HOME FURNISHINGS AND HOUSEHOLD GOODS

Readers rely on these publications to learn more about new products and trends in the home furnishings and appliance trade. Magazines for consumers interested in home furnishings are listed in the Consumer Home and Garden section.

APPLIANCE SERVICE NEWS, 110 W. Saint Charles Rd., P.O. Box 789, Lombard IL 60148-0789. Fax: (708)932-9552. Editor: William Wingstedt. Monthly magazine for professional service people whose main interest is repairing major and/or portable household appliances—service shop owner, service manager or service technician. Estab. 1950. Circ. 32,000. Buys all rights. Byline given. Pays on publication. Accepts simultaneous submissions. Reports in 1 month. Sample copy for $3.
Nonfiction: James Hodl, associate editor. "Our main interest is in technical articles about appliances and their repair. Material should be written in a straightforward, easy-to-understand style. It should be crisp and interesting, with high informational content. Our main interest is in the major and portable appliance repair field. We are not interested in retail sales." Query. Pays $200-300/feature.
Photos: Pays $20 for b&w photos used with ms. Captions required.

HOME FURNISHINGS EXECUTIVE, National Home Furnishings Association, P.O. Box 2396, High Point NC 27261. (910)883-1650. Fax: (910)883-1195. E-mail: hfexec@aol.com. Editor: Trisha L. McBride. 75% freelance written. Monthly magazine covering the home furnishings industry. "We hope that home furnishings retailers view our magazine as a profitability tool. We want each issue to help them make money or save money." Estab. 1927. Circ. 12,000. **Pays on acceptance.** Publishes ms an average of 6 weeks after acceptance. Byline given. Offers 20% kill fee. Buys first

North American serial rights. Editorial lead time 6 weeks. Reports in 1 month on queries; 6 weeks on mss. Sample copy and writer's guidelines for #10 SASE.

Nonfiction: Book excerpts, interview/profile, new product. Buys 55 mss/year. Query with published clips. Length: 300-2,000 words. Pays $50-750. Sometimes pays expenses of writers on assignment.

Photos: State availability of photos with submission. Reviews transparencies. Negotiates payment individually. Identification of subjects required. Buys one-time rights.

Columns/Departments: Executive Tipsheet (short "in box" items of interest—trend analysis, etc.), 250-300 words; On Managing Well (point-by-point articles on how retailers can manage their people better), 1,500 words; Advertising (how small retailers can create effective, low-cost advertising), 1,500 words. Query. Pays $50-500.

Fillers: Anecdotes, facts, newsbreaks, short humor. Buys about 15/year. Length: 50-200 words. Pays $10-25.

Tips: "Our readership includes owners of small 'ma and pa' furniture stores, executives of medium-sized chains (two to ten stores), and the executives of big chains (e.g., Heilig-Meyers), which have hundreds of stores."

HOME LIGHTING & ACCESSORIES, P.O. Box 2147, Clifton NJ 07015. (201)779-1600. Fax: (201)779-3242. Website: http://www.homelighting.com. Editor: Linda Longo. 25% freelance written. Prefers to work with published/established writers. Monthly magazine for lighting showrooms/department stores. Estab. 1923. Circ. 10,000. Pays on publication. Publishes ms an average of 6 months after acceptance. Buys first rights. Submit seasonal material 6 months in advance. Reports in 2 months. Sample copy for 9×12 SAE with 4 first-class stamps.

Nonfiction: Interview (with lighting retailers); personal experience (as a businessperson involved with lighting); profile (of a successful lighting retailer/lamp buyer); technical (concerning lighting or lighting design). Special issues: Outdoor (March); tribute to Tiffany's (August). Buys less than 6 mss/year. Query. Pays $60/published page. Sometimes pays the expenses of writers on assignment.

Reprints: Send tearsheet of article and information about when and where the article previously appeared.

Photos: State availability of photos with query. Offers no additional payment for 5×7 or 8×10 b&w glossy prints. Pays additional $90 for color transparencies used on cover. Captions required.

Tips: "We don't need fillers—only features. Deadline for all editorial is two months prior to publication."

‡**WINDOW FASHIONS, Design and Education Magazine**, G&W McNamara Publishing, Inc., 4225 White Bear Pkwy., Suite 400, St. Paul MN 55110. (612)293-1544. Fax: (612)653-4308. E-mail: bcarlson@dac.mail.net. Website: http://www.gwmcnamara.com. Editor: Kathleen Stoehr. 50% freelance written. Monthly magazine "dedicated to the advancement of the window fashions industry, *Window Fashions* magazine provides comprehensive information on design and business principles, window fashion aesthetics and product applications. The magazine serves the window treatment industry, including designers, retailers, dealers, specialty stores, workrooms, manufacturers, fabricators and others associated with the field of interior design." Estab. 1981. Circ. 22,000. Pays on publication. Publishes ms an average of 3 months after acceptance. Byline given. Offers 25% kill fee. Buys all rights. Editorial lead time 2-3 months. Submit seasonal material at least 3 months in advance. Reports in 3 months on queries if SASE is included. Sample copy for $5.

Nonfiction: How-to (window fashion installation), interview/profile (of designers), new product, photo feature, technical, and other specific topics within the field. "No broad topics not specific to the window fashions industry." Buys 24 mss/year. Query with published clips. Length: 800-1,500 words. Pays $150 minimum for assigned articles.

Reprints: Will consider if printed in a newsletter or used in a very small distribution area. Send tearsheet of article or short story or typed ms with rights for sale noted and information about when and where the article previously appeared. Pay negotiable.

Photos: State availability of photos with submission. Reviews 2×3, 4×6 or 8×10 transparencies, slides and prints (at least 4×6). Offers no additional payment for photos accepted with ms. Captions required. Buys all rights and release for publication, anthology, promotional use, etc.

Columns/Departments: Buys 24-36 mss/year. Query with published clips.

Tips: "The most helpful experience is if a writer has knowledge of interior design or, specifically, window treatments. We already have a pool of generalists, although we welcome clips from writers who would like to be considered for assignments. Our style is professional business writing—no flowery prose. Articles tend to be to the point, as our readers are busy professionals who read for information, not for leisure. Most of all we need creative ideas and approaches to topics in the field of window treatments and interior design. A writer needs to be knowledgeable in the field because our readers would know if information were inaccurate."

HOSPITALS, NURSING AND NURSING HOMES

In this section are journals for medical and nonmedical nursing home personnel, clinical and hospital staffs and medical laboratory technicians and managers. Journals publishing technical material on medical research and information for physicians in private practice are listed in the Medical category.

JOURNAL OF CHRISTIAN NURSING, Nurses Christian Fellowship, a division of Inter-Varsity Christian Fellowship, 430 E. Plaza Dr., Westmont IL 60559. (630)887-2500. Fax: (630)887-2520. E-mail: jcn@ivpress.com.

Editor: Judith Allen Shelly. Contact: Melodee Yohe, Managing Editor. 30-40% freelance written. Quarterly professional journal/magazine covering spiritual care, ethics, crosscultural issues, etc. "Our target audience is Christian nurses in the US and is nondenominational in character. We are prolife in position. We strive to help Christian nurses view nursing practice through the eyes of faith. Articles must be relevant to Christian nursing and consistent with our statement of faith." Estab. 1984. Circ. 10,000. Pays on publication. Publishes ms 1-2 years after acceptance. Byline given unless subject matter requires pseudonym. Offers 50% kill fee. Not copyrighted. Buys first rights; second serial (reprint) rights, rarely; all rights, only multiple-authored case studies. Editorial lead time up to 2 years. Submit seasonal material 1 year in advance. Reports in 1 month on queries; 2 months on mss. Sample copy for $5 (sub price $19.95/year) and SAE with 4 first-class stamps. Writers guidelines for #10 SASE.

Nonfiction: How-to, humor, inspirational, interview/profile, opinion, personal experience, photo feature, religious. All must be appropriate for Christian nurses. Poetry not accepted. No purely academic articles, subjects not appropriate for Christian nurses, devotionals, Bible study. Buys 20-30 mss/year. Send complete ms. Length: 6-12 pages (typed, double spaced). Pays $25-80 and up to 8 complimentary copies.

Reprints: Occasionally accepts previously published submissions. Send tearsheet or photocopy of article or short story and information about when and where the article previously appeared.

Photos: State availability of photos or send photos with submission. Offers no additional payment for photos accepted with ms. Model releases and identification of subjects required. No rights purchased; all photos returned.

Columns/Departments: Book Reviews (Resources). No payment for Book Reviews.

Tips: "Unless an author is a nurse, it will be unlikely that he/she will have an article accepted—unless they write a very interesting story about a nurse who is involved in creative ministry with a strong faith dimension."

JOURNAL OF NURSING JOCULARITY, The Humor Magazine for Nurses, JNJ Publishing, Inc., P.O. Box 40416, Mesa AZ 85274. (602)835-6165. E-mail: 73314.3032@compuserve.com. Website: http://www.jocularity.com. Editor: Fran London, RN, MS. 75% freelance written. Quarterly magazine covering nursing and medical humor. "*Journal of Nursing Jocularity* is read by health care professionals. Published manuscripts pertain to the lighter side of health care, from the perspective of the health care provider." Estab. 1990. Circ. 20,000. Pays on publication. Publishes ms an average of 1 year after acceptance. Buys one-time rights. Editorial lead time 1 year. Submit seasonal material 1 year in advance. Accepts simultaneous submissions. Reports in 2 months on queries; 3 months on mss. Sample copy for $2. Writer's guidelines for 9×10 SAE with 2 first-class stamps.

Nonfiction: Essays, historical/nostalgic, humor, interview/profile, opinion, personal experience, *current* research on therapeutic use of humor. "Our readers are primarily active nurses. Our focus is *insider humor*." Buys 4-8 mss/year. Length: 500-1,500 words. Pays $5 and up. Sometimes pays expenses of writers on assignment.

Reprints: Send typed ms with rights for sale noted and information about when and where the article previously appeared.

Photos: State availability of photos with submission. Model releases required. Buys one-time rights.

Columns/Departments: Stories from the Floor (anecdotes—true nursing experiences), 16-200 words; Call Lites (health care jokes with insider edge), 16-200 words; Student Nurse Cut-Ups (anecdotes—true student nurse experiences), 16-150 words; Liven Up (anecdotes using humor therapeutically at work), 50-200 words. Pays *JNJ* T-shirt.

Fiction: Humorous, slice-of-life vignettes. Buys 30 mss/year. Query or send complete ms. Length: 500-1,500 words. Pays $5 and up.

Poetry: Avant-garde, free verse, haiku, light verse, traditional, songs and cheers. Buys 4-6 poems/year. Submit maximum 3 poems. Pays $5.

Fillers: Anecdotes, gags to be illustrated by cartoonist, short humor. Length: 16-200 words. Pays JNJ T-shirt.

Tips: "Our readers are primarily working nurses. *JNJ*'s focus is insider humor—the kind only a health care provider understands. *Very few* non-health care providers have been able to submit material that rings true. We do not publish material written from a patient's point of view."

LONG TERM CARE, The Ontario Nursing Home Assoc., 345 Renfrew Dr., Suite 102-202, Markham, Ontario L3R 9S9 Canada. (905)470-8995. Fax: (905)470-9595. Assistant Editor: Tracey Ann Schofield. Contact: Heather Lang-Runtz, editor. Quarterly magazine covering "practical articles of interest to staff working in a long term care setting (nursing home, retirement home); professional issues; information must be applicable to a Canadian setting; focus should be on staff and for resident well-being." Estab. 1990. Circ. 4,600. Pays on publication. Publishes ms an average of 4 months after acceptance. Byline given. Buys one-time rights. Editorial lead time 3 months. Submit seasonal material 5 months in advance. Reports in 3 months. Sample copy and writer's guidelines free.

Nonfiction: General interest, how-to (practical, of use to long term care practitioners), inspirational, interview/profile. No personal experience, product-oriented, historical articles. Query with published clips. Length: 800-1,500 words. Pays up to $1,000.

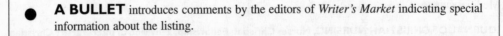

● **A BULLET** introduces comments by the editors of *Writer's Market* indicating special information about the listing.

Reprints: Send photocopy of article or short story and information about when and where the article previously appeared.

Photos: Send photos with submission. Reviews contact sheets, 5×5 prints. Offers no additional payment for photos accepted with ms. Captions, model releases required. Buys one-time rights.

Columns/Departments: Resident Health (nursing, rehabilitation, food services); Resident Life (activities, volunteers, spiritual and pastoral care); Environment (housekeeping, laundry, maintenance, safety, landscape and architecture, staff health and well being); all 800 words. Query with published clips. Pays up to $1,000.

Tips: "Articles must be positive, upbeat, and contain helpful information that staff and managers working in the long term care field can use. Focus should be on staff and resident well being. Articles that highlight new ways of doing things are particularly useful. Please call the editor to discuss ideas. Must be applicable to Canadian settings."

NURSEWEEK, California's Largest Newspaper and Career Guide for Nurses, California Nursing Review, 1156-C Aster Ave., Sunnyvale CA 94086. (408)249-5877. Fax: (408)249-3756. E-mail: ed@nurseweek.com. Website: http://www.nurseweek.com. Managing Editor: Whitney Wood. 25% freelance written. Biweekly nursing newspaper for greater L.A., Orange County and S.F. areas with 6 additional statewide issues throughout year. Estab. 1989. Circ. 100,000 metro; 210,000+ statewide. Pays on publication. Byline given. Offers kill fee, which may vary. Buys all rights. Submit seasonal material 6 months in advance. Reports in 3 months. Sample copy and writer's guidelines for 9×12 SAE with 2 first class stamps.

Nonfiction: News, workplace, socio-economic, interview/profile, personal experience, technical (continuing education articles) and travel, all nursing related. "Open to new ideas. No articles unrelated to nursing." Buys 120 mss/year. Query with published clips. Length: 300-2,500 words. Pays $100-500 for assigned articles; $75-300 for unsolicited articles. Pays expenses of writers on assignment.

Photos: State availability of photos with submission. Reviews transparencies and prints. Captions, model releases and identification of subjects required; no exceptions. Buys one-time rights.

Columns/Departments: After Hours (what nurses do in their off hours); Newsmaker (profile of a distinguished nurse or health care leader), 1,000-1,400 words. Query with published clips. Pays $100-500.

Tips: "We prefer queries to submissions. Keep the audience in mind; we are more focused and clinically oriented than consumer health publications. Strongly urge writers to read several issues before inquiring. Features and news items relevant to registered nurses are the best areas for freelancers."

NURSING98, Springhouse Corporation, 1111 Bethlehem Pike, P.O. Box 908, Springhouse PA 19477-0908. (215)646-8700. Fax: (215)653-0826. E-mail: nursing@springnet.com. Website: http://www.springnet.com. Contact: Pat Wolf, Editorial Dept. Administrator. Clinical Director: Patricia Nornhold. Managing Editor: Jane Benner. 100% freelance written by nurses. Monthly magazine "written by nurses for nurses; we look for practical advice for the direct caregiver that reflects the author's experience." Estab. 1971. Circ. 353,318. Pays on publication. Publishes ms an average of 18 months after acceptance. Byline given. Offers 50% kill fee. Buys all rights. Submit seasonal material 8 months in advance. "Any form acceptable, but focus must be nursing." Prefers submissions on disk in any program. Reports in 2 weeks on queries; 3 months on mss. Sample copy for $4. Call 800-617-1717, ext. 300 for free writers' guidelines. Guidelines also available on our website.

Nonfiction: Book excerpts, exposé, how-to (specifically as applies to nursing field), inspirational, new product, opinion, personal experience, photo feature. No articles from patients' point of view, humor articles, poetry, etc. Buys 100 mss/year. Query. Length: 100 words minimum. Pays $50-400 for feature articles.

Reprints: Accepts previously published submissions.

Photos: State availability of photos with submission. Offers no additional payment for photos accepted with ms. Model releases required. Buys all rights.

HOTELS, MOTELS, CLUBS, RESORTS AND RESTAURANTS

These publications offer trade tips and advice to hotel, club, resort and restaurant managers, owners and operators. Journals for manufacturers and distributors of bar and beverage supplies are listed in the Beverages and Bottling section.

BARTENDER MAGAZINE, Foley Publishing, P.O. Box 158, Liberty Corner NJ 07938. (908)766-6006. Fax: (908)766-6607. E-mail: barmag@aol.com. Website: http://www.bartender.com. Editor: Jaclyn M. Wilson. Contact: Raymond P. Foley, publisher. Quarterly magazine emphasizing liquor and bartending for bartenders, tavern owners and owners of restaurants with full-service liquor licenses. 100% freelance written. Prefers to work with published/established writers; eager to work with new/unpublished writers. Circ. 147,000. Pays on publication. Publishes ms an average of 3 months after acceptance. Buys first serial, first North American serial, one-time, second serial (reprint), all or simultaneous US rights. Byline given. Submit seasonal material 3 months in advance. Accepts simultaneous submissions. Reports in 2 months. Sample copies for 9×12 SAE with 4 first-class stamps.

Nonfiction: General interest, historical, how-to, humor, interview (with famous bartenders or ex-bartenders), new products, nostalgia, personal experience, unique bars, opinion, new techniques, new drinking trends, photo feature,

profile, travel, bar sports or bar magic tricks. Send complete ms. Length: 100-1,000 words.
Reprints: Send tearsheet of article and information about when and where the article previously appeared. Pays 25% of amount paid for an original article.
Photos: Send photos with ms. Pays $7.50-50 for 8×10 b&w glossy prints; $10-75 for 8×10 color glossy prints. Caption preferred and model release required.
Columns/Departments: Bar of the Month; Bartender of the Month; Drink of the Month; Creative Cocktails; Bar Sports; Quiz; Bar Art; Wine Cellar; Tips from the Top (from prominent figures in the liquor industry); One For The Road (travel); Collectors (bar or liquor-related items); Photo Essays. Query. Length: 200-1,000 words. Pays $50-200.
Fillers: Clippings, jokes, gags, anecdotes, short humor, newsbreaks, anything relating to bartending and the liquor industry. Length: 25-100 words. Pays $5-25.
Tips: "To break in, absolutely make sure that your work will be of interest to all bartenders across the country. Your style of writing should reflect the audience you are addressing. The most frequent mistake made by writers in completing an article for us is using the wrong subject."

BED & BREAKFAST, The Business of Innkeeping, Virgo Publishing Inc., Box 5400, Scottsdale AZ 85261. (602)990-1101. Fax: (602)675-8109. E-mail: cecileb@vpico.com. Website: http://www.vpico.com. Managing Editor: Cecile Blaine. 20% freelance written. Bimonthly magazine covering the bed-and-breakfast and innkeeping industries with regard to innkeepers. "Articles must be thoroughly researched, and we prefer that the author have some experience or expertise in the industry." Estab. 1994. Circ. 15,000. Pays on publication. Publishes ms 4 months after acceptance. Byline given. Buys first North American serial rights. Editorial lead time 4 months. Submit seasonal material 6 months in advance. Reports in 2 weeks on queries; 1 month on mss. Sample copy for 9×12 SASE.
Nonfiction: Book excerpts, interview/profile, new product, personal experience, technical. Buys 12 mss/year. Query with or without published clips. Length: 800-3,500 words. Pays $200 maximum for assigned articles. Pays expenses of writers on assignment.
Reprints: Send photocopy of article or short story and information about when and where the article previously appeared.
Photos: Send photos, slides or transparencies with submission. Negotiates payment individually. Model releases and identification of subjects required. Buys one-time rights.
Columns/Departments: Buys 6 mss/year. Pays $200 maximum.

‡CAMP MANAGEMENT, Camp Resources, Inc., 1415 N. Dayton St., Chicago IL 60622. (312)266-1716. Fax: (312)266-1887. E-mail: campmngt@aol.com. Contact: Jenny Beeh, Elisa Kronish, Kellee Van Keuren, editors. 25% freelance written. Bimonthly magazine covering children's summer camps. "As a magazine for camp professionals, *Camp Management* is designed to be a valuable resource, offering practical tips and solutions, news from the field and profiles of successful programs. We aim to be a forum for the camp community." Estab. 1994. Circ. 8,000. Pays on publication. Publishes ms an average of 3 months after acceptance. Byline given. Buys first rights, one-time rights or makes work-for-hire assignments. Editorial lead time 2 months. Submit seasonal material 4 months in advance. Accepts simultaneous submissions. Reports in 3 weeks on queries; 1 month on mss. Sample copy and writer's guidelines free.
Nonfiction: Essays, how-to, humor, inspirational, interview/profile, new product, personal experience, photo feature, technical, any issues affecting camp programs (i.e., education, safety, child development, staff, legal, financial, etc.). "We look for articles that offer practical, in-the-field information and hands-on ideas. We do not publish scholarly or academic theory pieces on the summer camp industry." Buys 12 mss/year. Query with published clips. Length: 500-3,000 words. Pays $100-500. Sometimes pays expenses of writers on assignment.
Reprints: Accepts previously published submissions.
Photos: State availability of photos with submission. Reviews contact sheets, transparencies, prints. Negotiates payment individually. Captions, model releases, identification of subjects required. Buys one-time rights.
Columns/Departments: Kellee Van Keuren, editor. Kidology (practical insights into child development issues); Earth Etiquette (environmental issues); Safe & Sound (camp health issues); all 1,500 words. Buys 12 mss/year. Query with published clips. Pays $25-300.
Fiction: Elisa Kronish, editor. Adventure, ethnic, historical, humorous, mainstream, slice-of-life vignettes. "Longer pieces of fiction that are not camp related are not accepted. We run very little fiction—only occasional short, relevant, entertaining pieces on camp or camp life." Buys 1 mss/year. Send complete ms. Length: 100-1,500 words. Pasy $100-500.
Tips: "We are interested in any submissions that summer camp directors (our readers) would find helpful, interesting or entertaining in their pursuit of providing quality camp programs for children. Please send queries, clips or manuscripts: we are open to a wide range of topics and offer a quick turnaround on ideas. Remember: camp is a *fun* business."

‡CHEF, The Food Magazine for Professionals, Talcott Communications Corp., 20 N. Wacker Dr., Suite 3230, Chicago IL 60606. (312)849-2220. Fax: (312)849-2174. E-mail: chefmag@aol.com. Contact: Brent T. Frei, editor-in-chief. Managing Editor: Joseph Mooney. 20% freelance written. Monthly magazine covering mid- to upscale foodservice. "*Chef* is the one magazine that communicates food production to a commercial, professional audience in a meaningful way." Circ. 38,000. Pays on publication. Byline given. Offers 10% kill fee. Buys first North American serial rights and second serial (reprint) rights. Editorial lead time 2 months. Submit seasonal material 4 months in advance. Reports in 3 weeks on queries; 2 months on mss. Sample copy free. Writer's guidelines not available.
Nonfiction: Book excerpts, essays, expose, general interest, historical/nostalgic, how-to (create a dish or perform a

technique), humor, inspirational, interview/profile, new product, opinion, personal experience, photo feature, technical, travel. Buys 24-36 mss/year. Query. Length: 750-1,500 words. Pays $200-300. Sometimes pays expenses of writers on assignment.

Reprints: Accepts previously published submissions.

Photos: State availability of photos with submission. Reviews transparencies. Negotiates payment individually. Captions, identification of subjects required. Buys one-time rights.

Columns/Departments: Taste (modern versions of classic dishes), 750 words; Plate (professional chef profiles), 1,000-1,200 words; Savor (themed recipes), 1,000-1,200 words Buys 12-18 mss/year. Query. Pays $200-300.

Tips: "Always query first, *after* you've read our magazine. Tell us how your idea can be used by our readers to enhance their businesses in some way."

CULINARY TRENDS, Dedicated to the World of Culinary Arts, Culinary Publications, Inc., 6285 E. Spring St., Long Beach CA 90808. (714)826-9188. Fax: (714)826-0333. Editor: Fred Mensinga. Contact: Linda Mensinga, art director. 50% freelance written. Quarterly magazine. "Our primary audience is chefs, restaurant owners, caterers, hotel managers, and anyone interested in cooking and food!" Pays on publication. Publishes ms an average of 4 months after acceptance. Byline given. Buys first or one-time rights. Editorial lead time 4 months. Sample copy for $7.

Nonfiction: How-to (cooking techniques), humor, interview/profile, opinion, photo feature, articles on restaurants must include photos and recipes. Buys 12 mss/year. Query with published clips. Length: 700-3,000 words. Pays $100-300.

Photos: Send photos with submission. Reviews transparencies, prints. Offers no additional payment for photos accepted with ms. Captions required. Buys one-time rights.

Columns/Departments: Wine (selling wine), 700 words. Buys 4 mss/year. Query with published clips. Pays $0-100.

Tips: "We like to get stories about restaurants with the focus on the chef and the food. Quality color or transparencies or slides are essential along with recipes."

‡EL RESTAURANTE MEXICANO, P.O. Box 2249, Oak Park IL 60303-2249. (708)445-9454. Fax: (708)445-9477. Contact: Kathleen Furore, editor. Bimonthly magazine covering Mexican restaurants. "*El Restaurante Mexicano* offers features and business-related articles that are geared specifically to owners and operators of Mexican, Tex-Mex and Southwestern cuisine restaurants." Estab. 1997. Circ. 12,000. Pays on publication. Publishes ms an average of 3 months after acceptance. Byline given. Buys first North American serial rights. Responds in 1 month. Sample copy free. Writer's guidelines not available.

Nonfiction: Stories about unique Mexican restaurants and about business issues that affect Mexican restaurant owners. "No specific knowledge of food or restaurants is needed; the key qualification is to be a good reporter who knows how to slant a story toward the Mexican restaurant operator." Buys 15-20 mss/year. Query with published clips. Length: 1,200-1,800 words. Pays $225. Pays expenses of writers on assignment.

FLORIDA HOTEL & MOTEL JOURNAL, The Official Publication of the Florida Hotel & Motel Association, Accommodations, Inc., P.O. Box 1529, Tallahassee FL 32302-1529. (904)224-2888. Fax: (904)222-FHMA. Editor: Mrs. Jayleen Woods. Contact: Janet Litherland, associate editor. 10% freelance written. Prefers to work with published/established writers. Magazine published 10 times/year for managers in every licensed hotel, motel and resort in Florida. Estab. 1978. Circ. 7,000. Pays on publication. Publishes ms an average of 2 months after acceptance. Byline given. Offers $50 kill fee. Buys all rights and makes work-for-hire assignments. Submit seasonal material 2 months in advance. Reports in 6 weeks. Sample copy and writer's guidelines for 9×12 SAE with 4 first-class stamps.

Nonfiction: General interest (business, finance, taxes); historical/nostalgic (old Florida hotel reminiscences); how-to (improve management, housekeeping procedures, guest services, security and coping with common hotel problems); humor (hotel-related anecdotes); inspirational (succeeding where others have failed); interview/profile (of unusual hotel personalities); new product (industry-related and non brand preferential); photo feature (queries only); technical (emerging patterns of hotel accounting, telephone systems, etc.); travel (transportation and tourism trends only—no scenics or site visits); property renovations and maintenance techniques. "We would like to run more humorous anecdotes on hotel happenings than we're presently receiving." Buys 10-12 mss/year. Query with proposed topic and clips of published work. Length: 750-2,500 words. Pays $75-250 "depending on type of article and amount of research." Sometimes pays expenses of writers on assignment.

Reprints: Send tearsheet of article and information about when and where the article previously appeared. Pays flat fee of $55.

Photos: Send photos with ms. Pays $25-100 for 4×5 color transparencies; $10-15 for 5×7 b&w prints. Captions, model release and identification of subjects required.

Tips: "We prefer feature stories on properties or personalities holding current membership in the Florida Hotel and Motel Association. Membership and/or leadership brochures are available (SASE) on request. We're open to articles showing how hotel management copes with energy systems, repairs, renovations, new guest needs and expectations. The writer may have a better chance of breaking in at our publication with short articles and fillers because the better a writer is at the art of condensation, the better his/her feature articles are likely to be."

FOOD & SERVICE, Texas Restaurant Association, P.O. Box 1429, Austin TX 78767-1429. (512)472-3666 (in Texas, 1-800-395-2872). Fax: (512)472-2777. E-mail: osolis@tramail.org. Website: http://www.txrestaurant.org. Editor: Olivia Carmichael Solis. 40% freelance written. Magazine published 7 times/year providing business solutions to Texas restaurant owners and operators. Estab. 1941. Circ. 6,000. Pays on publication. Reports in 1 month. Byline given. Buys first

rights. Pay varies. Sample copy and editorial calendar for 11 × 14 SAE with 6 first-class stamps. Free writer's guidelines.
Nonfiction: Features must provide business solutions to problems in the restaurant and food service industries. Topics vary but always have business slant; usually particular to Texas. No restaurant critiques, human interest stories or seasonal copy. Quote members of the Texas Restaurant Association; substantiate with facts and examples. Query in writing. Length: 1,500-2,500 words, features; shorter articles sometimes used; product releases, 300-word maximum. Payment rates vary.
Reprints: Send tearsheet or photocopy of article and information about when and where the article previously appeared. Pays 50% of amount paid for an original article.
Photos: State availability of photos, but photos usually assigned.

FOODSERVICE AND HOSPITALITY, Kostuch Publications, 23 Lesmill Rd., Don Mills, Ontario M3B 3P6 Canada. (416)447-0888. Fax: (416)447-5333. E-mail: rcaira@foodservice.ca. Website: http://www.foodserviceworld.com. Editor: Rosanna Caira. Associate Editor: Carolyn Cooper. 40-50% freelance written. Monthly magazine covering restaurant and hotel trade. Estab. 1968. Circ. 25,000. Pays on publication. Byline given. Buys first North American serial rights. Editorial lead time 3 months. Submit seasonal material 2 months in advance. Sample copy and writer's guidelines free.
Nonfiction: How-to, new product. No case studies. Buys 30-50 mss/year. Query with or without published clips. Length: 700-1,500 words. Pays 30-35¢ for assigned articles. Sometimes pays expenses of writers on assignment.
Photos: Send photos with submission. Offers $30-75/photo.

INNKEEPING WORLD, P.O. Box 84108, Seattle WA 98124. Fax: (206)362-7847. Editor/Publisher: Charles Nolte. 75% freelance written. Eager to work with new/unpublished writers. Magazine published 10 times/year emphasizing the hotel industry worldwide. Estab. 1979. Circ. 2,000. **Pays on acceptance.** Publishes ms an average of 2 months after acceptance. Buys all rights. No byline. Submit seasonal material 1 month in advance. Reports in 1 month. Sample copy and writer's guidelines for 9 × 12 SAE with 3 first-class stamps.
Nonfiction: Managing—interviews with successful hotel managers of large and/or famous hotels/resorts (600-1,200 words); Marketing—interviews with hotel marketing executives on successful promotions/case histories (300-1,000 words); Sales Promotion—innovative programs for increasing business (100-600 words); Food Service—outstanding hotel restaurants, menus and merchandising concepts (300-1,000 words); and Guest Relations—guest service programs, management philosophies relative to guests (200-800 words). Pays $100 minimum or 20¢/word (whichever is greater) for main topics. Other topics—advertising, cutting expenses, guest comfort, hospitality, ideas, reports and trends, special guestrooms, staff relations. Length: 50-500 words. Pays 20¢/word. "If a writer asks a hotel for a complimentary room, the article will not be accepted, nor will *Innkeeping World* accept future articles from the writer."
Tips: "We need more in-depth reporting on successful sales promotions—results-oriented information."

‡PIZZA TODAY, The Monthly Professional Guide To Pizza Profits, ProTech Publishing and Communications, Inc., P.O. Box 1347, New Albany IN 47151. (812)949-0909. Fax: (812)941-9711. Executive Editor: Robert T. Jordan. Contact: Kevin Nickols, managing editor or Bruce Allar, assignment editor. 25% freelance written. Prefers to work with published/established writers. Monthly magazine for the pizza industry, covering trends, features of successful pizza operators, business and management advice, etc. Estab. 1983. Circ. 40,000. Pays on publication. Publishes ms an average of 2 months after acceptance. Byline given. Offers 10-30% kill fee. Buys all and negotiable rights. Submit seasonal/holiday material 3 months in advance. Query for electronic submissions. "All articles must be supplied on a 3½-inch disk and accompanied by a hard copy. Most major wordprocessor formats accepted; else submit in ASCII format." Reports in 2 months on queries; 3 weeks on mss. Sample copy and writer's guidelines for 10 × 13 SAE with 6 first-class stamps. No phone calls, please.
Nonfiction: Interview/profile, new product, entrepreneurial slants, time management, pizza delivery, employee training. No fillers, fiction, humor or poetry. Buys 40-60 mss/year. Query with published clips. Length: 750-2,500 words. Pays $50-125/page. Sometimes pays expenses of writers on assignment.
Photos: Send photos with submission. Reviews contact sheets, negatives, 4 × 5 transparencies, color slides and 5 × 7 prints. Offers $5-25/photo. Captions required.
Tips: "We would like to receive nutritional information for low-cal, low-salt, low-fat, etc., pizza. Writers must have strong pizza business and foodservice background."

‡QSR, The Magazine of Quick Service Restaurant Success, Journalistic, Inc., 4905 Pine Cone Dr., Suite 2, Durham NC 27707. Fax: (919)489-4767. E-mail: lea@jayi.com. Contact: Lea Davis Paul, editor. 90% freelance written. Bimonthly magazine covering the quick-service segment of the restaurant industry. Estab. 1997. **Pays on acceptance.** Publishes ms an average of 6 weeks after acceptance. Byline given. Offers 25% kill fee. Buys all rights and makes work-for-hire assignments. Editorial lead time 2 months. Reports in 3 weeks on queries; 1 month on mss. Sample copy and writer's guidelines free.
Nonfiction: Book excerpts, expose, interview/profile, new product, industry reports, industry news analysis. No religious, essays, humor, inpsirational or travel. Buys 120 mss/year. Query with published clips. Length: 1,800-2,500 words. Pays $5-500. Sometimes pays expenses of writers on assignment.
Photos: Send photos with submission. Reviews prints. Offers no additional payment for photos accepted with ms. Captions, identification of subjects required. Buys one-time rights.
Columns/Departments: Management (news analysis, profiles, interviews, book reviews), 800-1,100 words; Service

in America (customer service), 800-1,100 words; Short Order (brief news analysis), 400-600 words. Buys 75 mss/year. Query with published clips. Pays $75-250.

Tips: "The most successful writers for *QSR* will (1) be familiar with the quick service restaurant industry and able to report on it with minimal direction, and (2) be able to apply literary journalism techniques to their writing."

THE WISCONSIN RESTAURATEUR, Wisconsin Restaurant Association, #300, 31 S. Henry, Madison WI 53703. (608)251-3663. Fax: (608)251-3666. Website: http://www.warmag@wiscrest.org. Editor: Sonya Knecht Bice. 20% freelance written. Eager to work with new/unpublished writers. Bimonthly magazine emphasizing restaurant industry, particularly Wisconsin, for restaurateurs, hospitals, institutions, food service students, etc. Estab. 1933. Circ. 4,000. **Pays on acceptance** or publication, varies. Publishes ms an average of 6 months after acceptance. Buys all rights or first rights. Editorial lead time 2 months. Pays 10% kill fee or $10. Byline given. Submit seasonal/holiday material 3 months in advance. Reports in 3 weeks. Sample copy and writer's guidelines for 9×12 SASE.

Nonfiction: Historical/nostalgia, how-to, humor, inspirational interview/profile, new product, opinion, personal experience, photo feature articles. "All must relate to foodservice. Need more in-depth articles. No features on nonmember restaurants." Buys 6 mss/year. Query with "copyright clearance information and a note about the writer in general." Phone queries OK. Length: 1,000-5,000 words. Pays $100 minimum for assigned articles; $25 minimum for unsolicited articles. Pays other than cash payment when requested.

Reprints: Send tearsheet of article and information about when and where it previously appeared. Payment negotiable.

INDUSTRIAL OPERATIONS

Industrial plant managers, executives, distributors and buyers read these journals. Some industrial management journals are also listed under the names of specific industries. Publications for industrial supervisors are listed in Management and Supervision.

COMPRESSED AIR, 253 E. Washington Ave., Washington NJ 07882-2495. Fax: (908)689-3095. E-mail: camag@ingersoll-rand.com. Website: http://www.ingersoll-rand.com/compair. Editor/Publications Manager: Tom McAloon. 75% freelance written. Magazine published 8 times/year emphasizing applied technology and industrial management subjects for engineers and managers. "*Compressed Air* is looking for articles that inform our readers of technological innovations in the workplace and at home, enhance our readers' ability to manage their professional lives, and increase our readers' awareness of their surroundings and history. Potential authors should be guided by the fact that we prefer articles that tell our readers 'why,' instead of 'how-to.' " Estab. 1896. Circ. 145,000. Buys all rights. Publishes ms an average of 6 months after acceptance. Reports in 2 months. Free sample copy; mention *Writer's Market* in request.

Nonfiction: "Articles must be reviewed by experts in the field." Buys 56 mss/year. Query with published clips. Pays negotiable fee. Sometimes pays expenses of writers on assignment.

Photos: State availability of photos in query. Payment for slides, transparencies and glossy prints is included in total purchase price. Captions required. Buys all rights.

Tips: "We are presently looking for freelancers with a track record in industrial/technology/management writing. Editorial schedule is developed in the summer before the publication year and relies heavily on article ideas from contributors. Résumé and samples help. Writers with access to authorities preferred; we prefer interviews over library research. The magazine's name doesn't reflect its contents. We suggest writers request sample copies."

‡PEM PLANT ENGINEERING & MAINTENANCE, Clifford/Elliot Ltd., 3228 S. Service Rd., 2nd Floor, West Wing, Burlington, Ontario L7N 3H8 Canada. (905)634-2100. Fax: (905)634-2238. E-mail: rr@industrialsourcebook.com. Website: www.industrialsourcebook.com. Contact: Rae Robb, editor. 30% freelance written. Bimonthly magazine looking for "informative articles on issues that affect plant floor operations and maintenance." Circ. 18,500. Pays on publication. Publishes ms an average of 3 months after acceptance. Byline given. Buys one-time rights. Editorial lead time 4 months. Submit seasonal material 4 months in advance. Accepts simultaneous submissions. Reports in 3 weeks on queries; 1 month on mss. Sample copy and writer's guidelines free.

Nonfiction: How-to (how-to keep production downtime to a minimum, how-to better operate an industrial operation); new product; technical. Buys 6 mss/year. Query with published clips. Length: 750-4,000 words. Pays $500-1,400 (Canadian). Sometimes pays expenses of writers on assignment.

Reprints: Sometimes accepts previously published submissions.

Photos: State availability of photos with submission. Reviews transparencies and prints. Negotiates payment individually. Captions required. Buys one-time rights.

Tips: "Information can be found at our website. Call us for sample issues, ideas, etc."

‡PROCESSING MAGAZINE, Putman Publishing Co., 301 E. Erie St., Chicago IL 60611. (312)644-2020. Fax: (312)644-0380. E-mail: trbmain@aol.com. Editor: Tim Burke. 5% freelance written. Monthly tabloid. "*Processing* is the foremost new product guide in North America. Its readers are senior engineers and managers of manufacturing facilities across the spectrum of the process industries. It is colorful, eye-catching, concise and often wry." Estab. 1987. Circ. 105,000. No byline. Makes work-for-hire assignments. Editorial lead time 3 months. Accepts simultaneous and previously published submissions. Sample copy for 12×16 SASE.

Nonfiction: Interview/profile, new product, technical. "No general interest, consumer stuff." Buys 1-2 mss/year. Send complete ms with photos. Length: 250-750 words. Payment negotiated individually.
Photos: Send photos with submission. Reviews transparencies and prints. Negotiates payment individually. Captions, model releases and identification of subjects required.
Tips: "Ideal writers have chemical, food and petroleum processing industry knowledge, work on a Mac (and can send disk), and have photos (we won't publish without them)."

QUALITY DIGEST, 40 Declaration Dr., Suite 100C, Chico CA 95973. (916)893-4095. Fax: (916)893-0395. E-mail: editorial@qualitydigest.com. Website: http://www.qualitydigest.com. Editor: Scott M. Paton. 75% freelance written. Monthly trade magazine covering quality improvement. Estab. 1981. Circ. 50,000. **Pays on acceptance.** Byline given. Buys all rights. Submit seasonal material 4 months in advance. Accepts simultaneous submissions. Reports in 3 months. Free sample copy and writer's guidelines.
Nonfiction: Book excerpts, how-to implement quality programs, etc., interview/profile, opinion, personal experience, technical. Buys 25 mss/year. Query with or without published clips or send complete ms. Length: 2,000-3,000 words. Pays $200-600. Pays in contributor copies for unsolicited mss. Sometimes pays expenses of writers on assignment.
Reprints: Send tearsheet of article.
Photos: Send photos with submission. Reviews any size prints. Offers no additional payment for photos accepted with ms. Captions, model releases and identification of subjects required. Buys one-time rights.
Tips: "Please be specific in your articles. Explain what the problem was, how it was solved and what the benefits are. Tell the reader how the technique described will benefit him or her."

‡RUBBER & PLASTICS NEWS, Crain Communications Inc., 1725 Merriman Rd., Suite 300, Akron OH 44313. (330)836-9180. Fax: (330)836-2831. Contact: Edward Noga, editor or Bruce Meyer, managing editor. Weekly tabloid covering rubber product manufacturers. "We specialize in hard news (expansions, acquisitions, layoffs, etc.)." Estab. 1971. Circ. 16,000. Pays on publication. Byline given. Buys all rights (including for use on internet and for use by other Crain Publications) and makes work-for-hire assignments. Reports in 1 month on queries. Writer's guidelines not available.
Nonfiction: Exposé, interview/profile, new product, basic news stories. Buys 10-20 mss/year. Query with published clips. Pays $12/inch published.
Photos: State availability of photos with submission. Reviews prints. Negotiates payment individually. Identification of subjects required. Buys all rights.
Tips: "We would like to increase our use of stringers/freelancers to keep eye out for news in their area and do stories on assigned basis."

WEIGHING & MEASUREMENT, Key Markets Publishing Co., P.O. Box 5867, Rockford IL 61125. (815)636-7739. Fax: (815)636-7741. Editor: David M. Mathieu. Bimonthly magazine for users of industrial scales and meters. Estab. 1914. Circ. 15,000. **Pays on acceptance.** Buys all rights. Offers 20% kill fee. Byline given. Reports in 2 weeks. Sample copy for $2.
Nonfiction: Interview (with presidents of companies); personal opinion (guest editorials on government involvement in business, etc.); profile (about users of weighing and measurement equipment); technical. Buys 25 mss/year. Query on technical articles; submit complete ms for general interest material. Length: 750-1,500 words. Pays $125-200.

INFORMATION SYSTEMS

These publications give computer professionals more data about their field. Consumer computer publications are listed under Personal Computers.

ACCESS TO WANG, The Independent Magazine for Wang System Users, New Media Publications, 10711 Burnet Rd., Suite 305, Austin TX 78758. Fax: (512)873-7782. E-mail: 75730.2465@compuserve.com. Editor: Richard Zelade. 75% freelance written. Monthly magazine providing how-to articles for users of Wang computer systems, Wang office automation software, and coexistence and migration applications. Estab. 1984. Circ. 10,000. Pays 30 days after publication. Publishes ms an average of 2 months after acceptance. Byline given. Offers $25 kill fee. Buys first North American serial rights. Editorial lead time 3 months. Submit seasonal material 4 months in advance. Sample copy and writer's guidelines free.
Nonfiction: How-to, new product, technical, computer reviews, computer product reviews. Buys 50 mss/year. Query. Length: 1,500-2,000 words. Pays $200 for assigned articles; $100 for unsolicited articles.
Photos: Send photos with submissions. Reviews 3×5 transparencies, prints. Offers no additional payment for photos accepted with ms. Captions, model releases, identification of subjects required. Buys all rights.
Columns/Departments: Special Report (varies from month to month), 2,000-2,500. Buys 12 mss/year. Query. Pays $150.
Tips: "Writer must have computer experience specific to Wang computers. Also must have networking, Unix, programming, or similar experience. First step: call for the editorial calendar."

AS/400 SYSTEMS MANAGEMENT, Adams Trade Press, 2101 S. Arlington Heights Rd., Suite 150, Arlington Heights IL 60005. (847)427-9512. Fax: (847)427-2006. E-mail: 73222.3344@compuserve.com. Website: http://www.hot

link400.com. Editor: Wayne Rhodes. 10% freelance written. Works with a small number of new/unpublished writers. Monthly magazine covering applications of IBM minicomputers (AS/400 and RS/6000) in business. Estab. 1973. Circ. 55,000. Pays on publication. Publishes ms an average of 3 months after acceptance. Byline given. Buys all rights. Submit seasonal material 4 months in advance. Reports in 3 months on queries. Sample copy for 9×12 SAE with 4 first-class stamps. Writer's guidelines sent via fax or e-mail.

Nonfiction: How-to (use the computer in business), technical (organization of a data base or file system). "A writer who submits material to us should be well versed in computer applications and in writing for business publications. No material on large-scale computer equipment." No poetry. Buys 8 mss/year. Query. Length: 1,500 words.

Tips: "Frequent mistakes are not understanding the audience and not having read past issues of the magazine."

CANADIAN COMPUTER RESELLER, The News Magazine for Value-Added Reselling, Maclean Hunter, 777 Bay St., 5th Floor, Toronto, Ontario M5W 1A7 Canada. (416)596-5000. Fax: (416)593-3166. E-mail: ccr@inforamp. net. Editor: Alison Eastwood. 70% freelance written. Biweekly magazine covering computer reseller industry. Estab. 1988. Circ. 15,000. **Pays on acceptance.** Publishes ms an average of 1 month after acceptance. Byline given. Buys negotiable rights. Editorial lead time 2 months. Sample copy free.

Nonfiction: Interview/profile, new product, technical. Buys 24 mss/year. Query with published clips. Length: 800-3,000 words. Pays $400-800 for assigned articles.

Photos: State availability of photos with submission. Reviews slides or 4×6 prints. Prefers color. Negotiates payment individually. Identification of subjects required. Buys negotiable rights.

Columns/Departments: Small Business (tips for small resellers and system integratory profiles of successful small businesses), 800 words. Buys 6 mss/year. Query with published clips. Pays $400.

Tips: "Writers need familiarity with technology, specifically with issues that relate to resellers and system integrators. Call before submitting any stories."

THE C/C++ USERS JOURNAL, Miller Freeman, Inc., 1601 W. 23rd, Suite 200, Lawrence KS 66046. (913)841-1631. Fax: (913)841-2624. E-mail: mbriand@mfi.com. Website: http://www.cuj.com. Editor: P.J. Plauger. Contact: Marc Briand. 90% freelance written. Monthly magazine "written for professional C and C++ programmers. Articles are practical, advanced, and code-intensive. Authors are *always* professional C and C++ programmers." Estab. 1988. Circ. 40,000. Pays on publication. Publishes ms an average of 5 months after acceptance. Byline given. Offers $150 kill fee. Buys all rights. Editorial lead time 4 months. Reports in 1 month on queries. Sample copy and writer's guidelines free.

Nonfiction: Technical. Buys 90-110 mss/year. Query. Length: 500 words minimum. Pay varies.

Reprints: Send electronically readable ms with rights for sale noted.

CIRCUIT CELLAR INK, The Computer Applications Journal, 4 Park St., Vernon CT 06066. (860)875-2199. Fax: (860)872-2204. E-mail: ken.davidson@circellar.com. Website: http://www.circellar.com. Editor: Kenneth Davidson. 99% freelance written. Monthly magazine. "Most of our articles are written by engineers for engineers. They deal with the lower level details of computer hardware and software design. Most articles deal with dedicated, embedded processors rather than desktop computers." Estab. 1988. Circ. 45,000. Pays on publication. Publishes ms an average of 6 months after acceptance. Byline given. Offers $100 kill fee. Buys first rights. Editorial lead time 2 months. Submit seasonal material 3 months in advance. Reports in 1 month. Sample copy and writer's guideline free.

Nonfiction: New product, technical. Buys 40 mss/year. Send complete ms. Length: 1,000-5,000 words. Pays $50/page.

Photos: Send photos with submissions. Reviews transparencies, slides, 3×5 prints. Offers no additional payment for photos accepted with ms. Captions required. Buys one-time rights.

Tips: "Contact editor with address, phone number, fax number, e-mail address, and article subject interests. Will send an author's guide."

COMPUTER GRAPHICS WORLD, PennWell Publishing Company, 10 Tara Blvd., 5th Floor, Nashua NH 03062-2801. (603)891-9160. Fax: (603)891-0539. E-mail: stevep@pennwell.com. Website: www.cgw.com. Editor: Stephen Porter. 60% freelance written. Monthly magazine. "*Computer Graphics World* specializes in covering computer-aided 3D modeling, animation, and visualization and their uses in engineering, science, and entertainment applications." Estab. 1978. Circ. 70,000. **Pays on acceptance.** Publishes ms an average of 4 months after acceptance. Byline given. Offers 20% kill fee. Buys all rights. Editorial lead time 4 months. Submit seasonal material 3 months in advance. Sample copy free.

Nonfiction: General interest, how-to (how-to create quality models and animations), interview/profile, new product, opinion, technical, user application stories. "We do not want to run articles that are geared to computer programmers. Our focus as a magazine is on users involved in specific applications." Buys 40 mss/year. Query with published clips. Length: 1,200-3,000 words. Pays $500 minimum. Sometimes pays expenses of writers on assignment.

Columns/Departments: Reviews (offers hands-on review of important new products), 750 words; and Application Stories (highlights unique use of the technology by a single user), 800 words. Buys 36-40 mss/year. Query with published clips. Pays $100-500.

Tips: "Freelance writers will be most successful if they have some familiarity with computers and know how to write from a user's perspective. They do not need to be computer experts, but they do have to understand how to explain the impact of the technology and the applications in which a user is involved. Both our feature section and our application story section are quite open to freelancers. The trick to winning acceptance for your story is to have a well-developed idea that highlights a fascinating new trend or development in computer graphics technology or profiles a unique and fascinating use of the technology by a single user or a specific class of users."

‡**DBMS**, Miller Freeman, Dept. WM, 411 Borel Ave., San Mateo CA 94402-32522. (415)358-9500. Fax: (415)358-9855. E-mail: cparkes@mfi.com. Website: http://www.dbmsmag.com. Executive Editor: Clara Parkes. 60% freelance written. Monthly magazine covering client/server, internet/intranet database applications and technology. "Our readers are database developers, consultants, VARs, programmers in MIS/DP departments and serious users." Estab. 1988. Circ. 90,000. **Pays on acceptance.** Publishes ms 3 months after acceptance. Byline given. Offers 33% kill fee. Buys all rights. Query for electronic submissions. Reports in 6 weeks on queries. Samply copy for 9×12 SAE with 8 first-class stamps.
Nonfiction: Technical. Buys 40-50 mss/year. Query with published clips. Length: 750-4,000 words. Pays $300-1,000.
Photos: Publishes screen shots.
Tips: "New writers should submit clear, concise queries of specific article subjects and ideas. *Read the magazine* to get a feel for the kind of articles we publish. This magazine is written for a highly technical computer database developer, consultant and user readership. We need technical and strategic features that inform this audience of new trends, software and techniques."

‡**DESKTOP ENGINEERING, Complete Computer Resource for Engineers**, Helmers Publishing, 174 Concord St., Peterborough NH 03458. (603)924-9631. Fax: (603)924-4004. E-mail: de-editors@helmers.com. Editor: Anthony J. Lockwood. Senior Editor: Vinoy Laughner. 90% freelance written. Monthly magazine covering microcomputer hardware/software for engineers. Estab. 1995. Circ. 55,000. **Pays on acceptance.** Publishes ms an average of 4 months after acceptance. Byline given. Buys all rights. Editorial lead time 3 months. Reports in 6 weeks on queries; 6 months on mss. Sample copy and writer's guidelines free.
Nonfiction: How-to, new product, technical, reviews. "No fluff." Buys 120 mss/year. Query. Length: 750-3,000 words. Pays 60¢/word for assigned articles. Negotiates fee for unsolicited articles. Sometimes pays expenses of writers on assignment.
Photos: Send photos with submission. Negotiates payment and rights purchased individually. Captions required.
Columns/Departments: Product Briefs (new products), 50-100 words; Reviews (software, hardware, books), 500-1,500 words. Buys 30 mss/year. Query. Pay varies.
Tips: "Call the editor or e-mail him for submission tips."

DESKTOP PUBLISHERS JOURNAL, Business Media Group, 462 Boston St., Topsfield MA 01983. (508)887-2246. Fax: (508)887-6117. E-mail: edit@dtpjournal.com. Website: http://www.dtpjournal.com. Editor-in-Chief: Barry Harrigan. Contact: Linda Lee. 80% freelance written. Monthly magazine covering desktop publishing, graphic design, electronic publishing, prepress and Internet/web publishing. Estab. 1987. Circ. 100,000. Pays 45 days after acceptance. Publishes ms an average of 4 months after acceptance. Byline given. Kill fee. Buys all rights. Editorial lead time 4 months. Reports in 1 month on queries. Sample copy for $4. Writer's guidelines for #10 SASE.
Nonfiction: How-to (use and apply DTP hardware, software and special techniques), interview/profile, new product, personal experience (within narrow limits), technical. Buys 60 mss/year. Query with published clips. Length: 750-3,000 words. Rates negotiated based on article length and complexity of topic.
Columns/Departments: Digital Imaging, Paper, Color, Alternative Media, Internet Issues, Web Watch, Legalese, Business, Type, Design, Product Reviews, FPO (opinion), Prepress and Printing, (all helping readers to understand and apply existing and emerging technologies in their work as desktop publishers), 750-1,500 words. Buys 100 mss/year. Query with published clips. Rates negotiated based on topic and complexity.
Tips: "Writers should have a clear understanding of the needs of electronic publishing professionals and what they need to know to work faster, smarter and more professionally. Familiarity with the desktop publishing industry is essential, as is some technical knowledge of the ways DTP hardware and software are used. Departments are the easiest way to break in, although we're always looking for new writers for feature-length articles."

DIGITAL AGE, OpenVMS•UNIX•Windows NT, Cardinal Business Media Inc., 1300 Virginia Dr., Suite 400, Fort Washington PA 19034. (215)643-8000. Fax: (215)643-4827. E-mail: simpsoncm@cardinal.com or hengymo@cardinal.com. Editor-in-Chief: Charlie Simpson. 30% freelance written. Monthly magazine. "*Digital Age* includes information about VAX, Alpha and open systems hardware and software, specifically how Digital and related technology can be integrated in multivendor enfironments. Areas of focus include OpenVMS, UNIX, Windows NT, networking and client-server computing." Estab. 1982. Circ. 50,000. Pays on publication. Publishes ms an average of 3 months after acceptance. Byline given. Buys all rights and makes work-for-hire assignments. Editorial lead time 3 months. Sample copy and writer's guidelines free.
Nonfiction: Interview/profile, new product, opinion, technical. Buys 20 mss/year. Query with published clips. Length: 500-2,000 words. Pays $100-800.
Photos: State availability of photos with submission. Reviews transparencies, 3×5 prints. Offers no additional payment for photos accepted with ms. Captions, model releases, identification of subjects required. Buys all rights.
Columns/Departments: Industry Watch (industry news), 500 words; Case By Case (case study solutions), 800-1,000 words; Product Watch (hands-off product review), 500 words; Directions (look at corporate strategy of prominent or new companies), 500-800 words. Buys 6 mss/year. Query. Pays $0-300.
Tips: "Queries should reflect topics listed on editorial calendar. Writers should have a background in technical writing

and be knowledgeable about the computer industry in general and Digital Equipment Corp. specifically."

‡**ENT, The Independent Newspaper for Windows NT Enterprise Computing**, Cardinal Business Media, 1300 Virginia Dr., Suite 400, Ft. Washington PA 19034. (215)643-8000. Fax: (215)643-3901. E-mail: gillenam@cardinal.com. Editor: Al Gillen. Managing Editor: Roseann McGrath Brooks. 50% freelance written. Trade journal published 18 times/ year. "Our publication provides enterprise solutions for managers of Windows NT systems. Our readers are high-level information technology managers who require business and technology information specifically in large-scale Windows NT-oriented computing environments." Estab. 1995. Circ. 80,000. Pays on publication. Publishes ms an average of 2 months after acceptance. Byline sometimes given. Buys all rights. Editorial lead time 2 months. Reports in 2 weeks on queries; 2 months on mss. Sample copy and writer's guidelines free.
Nonfiction: How-to (Windows NT usage tips), new product. Nothing unrelated to Windows NT. Buys 2 mss/year. "We *assign* freelance articles. We rarely take unsolicited stories." Query with published clips. Length: 500-1,500 words. Pays $200-1,100 for assigned articles; $200-800 for unsolicited articles.
Photos: Send photos with submission. Reviews transparencies. "We mostly use screen shots on disk." Offers no additional payment for photos accepted with ms. Captions and identification of subjects required. Buys all rights.
Tips: "Become familiar with horizontal trade publications in general and Windows NT in particular. A writer should call first and introduce him- or herself and explain why he or she would like to write for us."

ENTERPRISE SYSTEMS JOURNAL, Cardinal Business Media, 12225 Greenville Ave., Suite 700, Dallas TX 75243. (972)669-9000. Fax: (972)669-9909. E-mail: 76130.221@compuserve.com. Website: http://www.esj.com. Managing Editor: Debbie English. Contact: Keri Williams, editorial assistant. 100% freelance written. Monthly magazine. "*Enterprise Systems Journal* is a technical publication geared to I/S professionals involved in IBM host-based enterprise-wide computing." Estab. 1985. Circ. 85,000. Pays on publication. Publishes ms an average of 6 months after acceptance. Byline given. Buys all rights and makes work-for-hire assignments. Editorial lead time 4 months. Accepts simultaneous submissions. Writer's guidelines free.
Nonfiction: How-to (mainframe systems-related), personal experience (mainframe user stories). No high-level overviews or basic tutorials. Buys approximately 100 mss/year. Query. Length: 1,500-2,500 words. Pays $150/page. Sometimes pays expenses of writers on assignment.
Photos: State availability of photos with submission. Offers no additional payment for photos accepted with ms. Buys one-time rights.
Tips: "*ESJ* readers are technically savvy mainframe computer professionals. Our writers must demonstrate technical knowledge at least equal to our readers."

GOVERNMENT COMPUTER, Hum Communications Ltd., 202-557 Cambridge St. S., Ottawa Ontario K1S 4J4 Canada. (613)237-4862. Fax: (613)746-7227. E-mail: editor@hum.com. Website: http://www.hum.com. Editor: Tim Lougheed. 60% freelance written. Monthly magazine covering use and management of computers in Canadian public sector. Estab. 1991. Circ. 13,500. Pays on publication. Publishes ms an average of 10 weeks after acceptance. Byline given. Offers 10% kill fee. Buys first rights or second serial (reprint) rights. Editorial lead time 3 months. Reports in 3 weeks on queries; 2 months on mss. Sample copy for 10 × 12 SASE.
Nonfiction: Book excerpts, essays, how-to, humor, interview/profile, new product, opinion, personal experience, technical. Buys 30 mss/year. Query with published clips. Length: 750-3,000 words. Pays $75-500. Sometimes pays expenses of writers on assignment.
Reprints: Accepts previously published submissions.
Photos: State availability of photos with submissions. Negotiates payment individually. Captions, identification of subjects required. Buys one-time rights.

‡**GOVERNMENT COMPUTER NEWS**, 8601 Georgia Ave., Suite 300, Silver Spring MD 20910. E-mail: editoria@ gen.com. Chief Editor: Thomas Temin. Published biweekly for government information technology managers. **Pays on acceptance**. Byline given. Kill fee varies. Buys all rights. Reports in 1 month. Sample copy free. Writer's guidelines for #10 SASE.
Nonfiction: Buys 30 mss/year. Query. Length: 700-1,200 words. Pays $800-2,000. Pays expenses of writers on assignment.
Columns/Departments: Length: 400-600 words. Buys 75 mss/year. Query. Pays $250-400.
Fillers: Buys 10/year. Length: 300-500 words. Pays $250-450.
Tips: Needs "technical case histories of applications of computers to governmental missions and trends in information technology."

HP PROFESSIONAL, The Magazine For Hewlett-Packard Enterprise Computing, Cardinal Business Media Inc., 1300 Virginia Dr., Suite 400, Fort Washington PA 19034. (215)643-8000. Fax: (215)643-4827. E-mail: simpsoncm @cardinal.com or schwartzdr@cardinal.com or thompsonga@cardinal.com. Website: http://www.hppro.com. Editor-in-Chief: Charlie Simpson. 30% freelance written. Monthly magazine. "*HP Professional*'s mission is to assist managers with strategic planning and purchasing decisions by providing unbiased reporting and analysis on the use and integration of the HP9000 UNIX systems and servers, HP workstations, PCs, LANs and the HP 3000 business systems—all in multiplatform computing environments." Estab. 1987. Circ. 30,000. Pays on publication. Publishes ms an average of 3 months after acceptance. Byline given. Buys all rights and makes work-for-hire assignments. Editorial lead time 3 months. Sample copy free.

Nonfiction: Interview/profile, new product, opinion, technical. Buys 20 mss/year. Query with published clips. Length: 500-2,000 words. Pays $100-800.

Photos: State availability of photos with submission. Reviews negatives. Offers no additional payment for photos accepted with ms. Captions, model releases, identification of subjects required. Buys all rights.

Columns/Departments: And Another Thing . . (opinion on current computer trend or event), 800 words; INsites (case study solutions), 800-1,000 words; Product Watch (hands-off product review), 500 words; Strategic Directions (look at corporate strategy of prominent or new companies), 500 words. Buys 6 mss/year. Query. Pays $0-300.

Fillers: Newsbreaks. Buys 6/year. Length: 100-500 words. Pays $0-200.

Tips: "Queries should reflect topics listed on the editorial calendar. Writers should have a background in technical writing and be knowledgeable about the computer industry in general and Hewlett-Packard specifically."

ID SYSTEMS, The Magazine of Automated Data Collection, Helmers Publishing, Inc., 174 Concord St., Peterborough NH 03458. (603)924-9631. Fax: (603)924-7408. E-mail: editors@idsystems.com. Website: http://www.idsystems.com. Managing Editor: Mark Reynolds. Contact: Roberta Bell, editor. 20% freelance written. Monthly magazine about automatic identification technologies. Circ. 75,000. **Pays on acceptance.** Byline given. Buys all rights. Reports in 2 months on queries. Free sample copy and writer's guidelines.

Nonfiction: Application stories, technical tutorials. "We want articles we have assigned, not spec articles." Buys 36 mss/year. Query with published clips. Length: 1,200 words. Pays $300.

Photos: Send photos with submission. Reviews contact sheets, transparencies (35mm) and prints. Offers no additional payment for photos accepted with ms. Identification of subjects required. Rights vary article to article.

Tips: "Send letter, résumé and clips. If background is appropriate, we will contact writer as needed. We give detailed instructions."

‡INFORMATION WEEK, 600 Community Dr., Manhasset NY 11030. E-mail: pkrass@cmp.com. Managing Editor: Peter Krass. Weekly magazine for information systems managers. **Pays on acceptance**. Byline given. Offers 25% kill fee. Buys first North American serial rights. Reports in 1 month. Sample copy free. Writer's guidelines for #10 SASE.

Nonfiction: Buys 104 mss/year. Query with published clips. Length: 1,500-2,500 words. Pays $1/word. Pays expenses of writers on assignment.

Reprints: Accepts previously published submissions.

Fiction: Buys 10 mss/year. Length: 500 words. Pays $1/word.

Tips: Needs "feature articles on technology trends—all with a business angle. We look at implementations by users, new products, management issues, intranets, the Internet, web, networks, PCs, objects, workstations, sewers, etc. Our competitors are tabloids—we're better written, more selective and more analytical."

JOURNAL OF INFORMATION ETHICS, McFarland & Co., Inc., Publishers, Box 611, Jefferson NC 28640. (910)246-4460. Fax: (910)246-5018. Editor: Robert Hauptman, LRS, 720 Fourth Ave. S., St. Cloud State University, St. Cloud MN 56301. (320)255-4822. Fax: (320)255-4778. All ms queries to Editor. 90% freelance written. Semiannual scholarly journal. "Addresses ethical issues in all of the information sciences with a deliberately interdisciplinary approach. Topics range from electronic mail monitoring to library acquisition of controversial material. The journal's aim is to present thoughtful considerations of ethical dilemmas that arise in a rapidly evolving system of information exchange and dissemination." Estab. 1992. Circ. 500. Pays on publication. Publishes ms an average of 9 months after acceptance. Byline given. Buys all rights. Submit seasonal material 8 months in advance. Sample copy for $21. Writer's guidelines free.

Nonfiction: Essays, opinion, book reviews. Buys 10 mss/year. Send complete ms. Length: 500-3,500 words. Pays $25.

Tips: "Familiarize yourself with the many areas subsumed under the rubric of information ethics, e.g., privacy, scholarly communication, errors, peer review, confidentiality, e-mail, etc."

MICROSTATION WORLD, Bentley Systems, 690 Pennsylvania Dr., Exton PA 19353. (610)458-2958. Fax: (610)458-1060. E-mail: rachael.dalton@bentley.com. Website: http://www.bentley.com. Editor: Rachael Dalton. Project Editor: Peter Haapaniemi. 80% freelance written. Quarterly magazine. "*MicroStation World* magazine serves the information needs of managers, engineers and users of the various MicroStation software products. The magazine presents high-level user profiles, serves as the forum for the discussion of computer-aided design in the enterprise, articulates the latest executive issues, and provides in-depth profiles of Independent Software Developers. This kind of information, when balanced with clear application stories, news about the industry, and new Bentley products and services, will help executives maximize the effectiveness of technology." Estab. 1995. Circ. 120,000. Pays on publication. Publishes ms an average of 6 months after acceptance. Byline given. Buys all rights. Editorial lead time 2 months. Accepts simultaneous submissions. Reports in 3 weeks on queries; 1 month on mss. Sample copy free.

Nonfiction: How-to (managing technology), new product (CAD industry), technical (companies using CAD), MicroStation CAD software-related stories. Buys 20 mss/year. Query with published clips. Length: 1,000-5,000 words. Pays $200-1,700. Sometimes pays expenses of writers on assignment.

Reprints: Send tearsheet or photocopy of article or short story and information about when and where the article previously appeared.

Photos: State availability of photos with submission. Reviews contact sheets, transparencies. Model releases, identification of subjects required.

Columns/Departments: Executive Insider (information to assist executives manage technology), 300 words. Buys 24 mss/year. Query with published clips. Pays $10-500.

Tips: "Address technology as it impacts management. *MicroStation World* helps executives understand and implement 3D CAD technology through interesting profiles and descriptions of companies and individuals using MicroStation."

‡NETSCAPE WORLD, Web Publishing, an IDG business unit, 501 Second St., San Francisco CA 94107. (415)243-4188. Fax: (415)267-1732. E-mail: nweditors@wpi.com. Website: http://www.netscapeworld.com. Contact: Mark Cappel, editor. 90% freelance written. Monthly website. "The ideal author for *Netscape World* is a web developer or webmaster who wants to share his tricks, tips and techniques with his peers." Estab. 1996. Circ. 125,000. Pays on publication. Publishes ms an average of 1 month after acceptance. Byline given. Offers 10% kill fee. Buys first rights. Editorial lead time 3 months. Reports in 2 weeks on queries; 1 month on mss. Sample copy on web.

Nonfiction: Book excerpts, how-to, new product, technical. Buys 150 mss/year. Query with published clips Length: 1,000 words minimum. Pays $400-1,250.

Photos: State availability of photos with submission. Reviews 35mm transparencies. Offers no additional payment for photos accepted with ms. Captions, model releases, identification of subjects required. Buys one-time rights.

Columns/Departments: Many technical columns offering how-to information, 1,250 words. Buys 40 mss/year. Query with published clips. Pays $400-500.

Tips: "You must be a nerd, or at least have latent nerd tendencies."

NETWORK MAGAZINE, Strategies and Solutions for the Network Professional, (formerly *LAN Magazine*), Miller Freeman/United News & Media, 600 Harrison St., San Francisco CA 94107. (415)905-2200. Fax: (415)905-2587. E-mail: networkmag@mfi.com. Website: http://www.networkmag.com. Editor: Allen Zeichick. Contact: Hanna Hurley, executive editor. 60% freelance written. Monthly magazine covering computer networking. Estab. 1986. Circ. 82,500. Pays on publication. Publishes ms an average of 3 months after acceptance. Byline given. Offers $500 kill fee. Buys first rights. Editorial lead time 4 months. Submit seasonal material 4 months in advance. Reports in 3 weeks on queries; 1 month on mss. Sample copy for $4.95 on newsstand. Writer's guidelines free.

Nonfiction: Technical. Buys 50 mss/year. Query with published clips. Length: 3,800-4,200 words. Pays $1,600.

NETWORK WORLD, Network World Publishing, 161 Worcester Rd., Framingham MA 01701. (508)875-6400. Fax: (508)820-1103. E-mail: pdesmond@nww.com. Website: http://www.nwfusion.com. Editor-in-Chief: John Gallant. Contact: Paul Desmond, features editor. 25% freelance written. Weekly tabloid covering data, voice and video communications networks (including news and features on communications management, hardware and software, services, education, technology and industry trends) for senior technical managers at large companies. Estab. 1986. Circ. 150,000. Pays on publication. Byline given. Offers negotiable kill fee. Buys all rights. Submit all material 2 months in advance. Reports in 5 months. Free sample copy and writer's guidelines.

Nonfiction: Exposé, general interest, how-to (build a strong communications staff, evaluate vendors, choose a value-added network service), humor, interview/profile, opinion, technical. Editorial calendar available. "Our readers are users: avoid vendor-oriented material." Buys 100-150 mss/year. Query with published clips. Length: 500-2,500 words. Pays $600 minimum.

Photos: Send photos with submission. Reviews 35mm, 2¼ and 4×5 transparencies and b&w prints (prefers 8×10 but can use 5×7). Captions, model releases and identification of subjects required. Buys one-time rights.

Tips: "We look for accessible treatments of technological, managerial or regulatory trends. It's OK to dig into technical issues as long as the article doesn't read like an engineering document. Feature section is most open to freelancers. Be informative, stimulating, controversial and technically accurate. Take a stand."

NEWS/400, Duke Communications International, 221 E. 29th St., Loveland CO 80538. (970)663-4700. Fax: (970)663-3285. E-mail: editors@news400.com. Website: http://www.news400.com. Editorial Director: Dale Agger. 40% freelance written. Magazine published 14 times/year. "Programming, networking, IS management, technology for users of IBM AS/400 platform." Estab. 1982. Circ. 30,000 (international). Pays on publication. Publishes ms an average of 3 months after acceptance. Byline given. Offers 50% kill fee. Buys first, second serial (reprint) and all rights. Editorial lead time 4 months. Submit seasonal material 4 months in advance. Reports in 3 weeks on queries; 5 weeks on mss. Writer's guidelines available online.

Nonfiction: Book excerpts, opinion, technical. Buys 70 mss/year. Query. Length: 1,500-3,500 words. Pays 17-50¢/word. Pays in copies upon request of author. Sometimes pays expenses of writers on assignment.

Reprints: Accepts previously published submissions, if published in a noncompeting market. Send photocopy of story. Payment negotiable.

Photos: State availability of photos with submission. Offers no additional payment for photos accepted with ms.

Columns/Departments: Dialog Box (computer industry opinion), 1,500 words; Load'n'go (complete utility). Buys 24 mss/year. Query. Pays $250-1,000.

Tips: "Be familiar with IBM AS/400 computer platform."

RESELLER MANAGEMENT, Cahners Publishing Co., 275 Washington St., Newton MA 02158. (617)558-4723. Fax: (617)558-4757. E-mail: wbwadsworth@rm.cahners.com. Website: http://www.resellermgmt.com. Editor: Anthony Strattner. 65% freelance written. Monthly magazine. "*Reseller Management*'s readers are managers in the Value Added

Reseller Channel for computer products, charged with supervising, planning, and often executing reseller strategies. *Reseller Management*'s mission is a practical handbook for value added resellers. Virtually all editorial should be 'actionable.' Readers should generally be able to make a job-related decision or take a job-related action based on articles." Circ. 85,000. **Pays on acceptance.** Byline given. Kill fee varies. Buys all rights or makes work-for-hire assignments. Editorial lead time 4 months. Writer's guidelines free.
Nonfiction: How-to, interview/profile, new product, opinion, technical. Buys 60 mss/year. Query. Length: 2,000 words maximum. Pays 70-80¢/word. Pays expenses of writers on assignment when agreed upon in advance.
Reprints: Accepts previously published submissions.
Photos: State availability of photos. Offers no additional payment for photos accepted with ms.
Columns/Departments: Flat fee, varies.
Tips: "Think of all assignments as a package of elements. Look for sidebar opportunities. Pull out pieces of the main text. Create lists of action items. Look for mini-case history opportunities (one per package is usually right) at 300 words. Key Questions in Approaching Assignments: How does this story topic impact a VAR's business and the VAR community? What specific opportunities and perils exist for VARs relative to the topic? What quantifiable data elements support/disprove the above questions? What do VARs say, pro and con about the issue? What advice do they offer? What do vendors and experts say and what advice do they offer? What specific how-to guidelines should VARs follow to best deal with this particular story topic and exploit the relevant opportunity? How should the assignment be broken into multiple elements to present the material in keeping with the magazine's packaging goals?"

SOFTWARE HOME PAGE, (formerly *Software Quarterly*), IBM Corp. 5 W. Kirkwood Blvd., Roanoke TX 76299-0001. (817)962-5823. Fax: (817)962-7218. E-mail: bonziman@unet.ibm.com. Website: http://www.software.ibm.com. Editor: Melissa Cox. 100% freelance written. Online magazine covering advanced software and networking. "Requires knowledge of computer/networking industry and software technologies." Estab. 1996. Circ. 1,000,000. Pays on publication. Publishes 3-6 weeks after acceptance. Buys all rights or makes work-for-hire assignments. Editorial lead time 1 month.
Nonfiction: How-to, interview/profile, technical. Query with published clips. Length: 700 words. Pays $1/word. Pays expenses of writers on assignment.

SUN WORLD ONLINE, IDG's Web Magazine for Unix Professionals, IDG, 501 Second St., San Francisco CA 94107. (415)267-4518. Fax: (415)267-1732. E-mail: carolyn@sunworld.com. Website: http://www.sun.com/sunworldonline. (Prefers correspondence by e-mail.) Editor: Carolyn Wong. 20% freelance written. Monthly web magazine. "We are a product and how-to magazine for Unix professionals with an emphasis on Sun. *Sunworld Online* is written to be accessible to a semi-technical audience." Estab. 1989. Circ. 50,000. **Pays on acceptance.** Publishes ms an average of 1 month after acceptance. Byline given. Offers 50% kill fee. Buys first North American serial rights and nonexclusive all other and international rights. Editorial lead time 3 months. Submit seasonal material 3 months in advance. Query for electronic submissions. Reports in 3-4 weeks on queries; 1 month on mss.
Nonfiction: Technical, technical features, emphasis on practical issues, selections. Buys 15 mss/year. Query. Length: 1,500-5,000 words. Pays $250-2,000. Sometimes pays expenses of writers on assignment.
Photos: State availability of photos with submission. Negotiates payment individually. Captions required. Buys all rights.
Columns/Departments: Seek columnists with hands-on experience. Query. Pays $500-750.
Tips: "We need authors who have Risc workstations, work experience/expertise in a particular field relevant to the topics being discussed, who can write a well organized, readable article, meet a deadline, and know what they're talking about."

‡SYS ADMIN, R&D Publications, Inc., 1601 W. 23rd St., Suite 200, Lawrence KS 66046. (913)841-1631. E-mail: aankerholz@mfi.com. Website: http://www.samag.com. Editor: Ralph Barker. Contact: Amber Ankerholz. 90% freelance written. Monthly magazine. "*Sys Admin* is written for UNIX systems administrators. Articles are practical and technical. Our authors are practicing UNIX systems administrators." Estab. 1992. Circ. 20,000. Pays on publication. Publishes ms an average of 6 months after acceptance. Byline given. Kill fee $150. Buys all rights. Editorial lead time 4 months. Query for electronic submissions. Reports in 1 month on queries. Sample copy and writer's guidelines free.
Nonfiction: Technical. Buys 40-60 mss/year. Query. Length: 1,000 words minimum. Pay varies.

UNISPHERE, The Magazine for Unisys Users, Cardinal Business Media Inc.12225 Greenville Ave., Suite 700, Dallas TX 75243. (972)669-9000. Fax: (972)669-9909. E-mail: 73430.2347@compuserve.com. Website: http://www.cardinal.com. Managing Editor: Renee McKeon. 30% freelance written. Monthly magazine. "*Unisphere* provides information for IS management and technical professionals in Unisys host-based enterprises. Each issue includes a cover story or comprehensive focus section on significant new products, trends and strategies in the industry. Regular features and technical articles cover client/server computing, networking, storage management, etc." Estab. 1981. Circ. 15,000. Pays on publication. Publishes ms an average of 2 months after acceptance. Byline given. Buys all rights and makes work-for-hire assignments. Editorial lead time 3 months. Reports in 2 weeks on queries; 1 month on mss (sooner if possible). Sample copy and writer's guidelines free.
Nonfiction: How-to (computer industry), interview/profile, new product, opinion, technical. Nothing about vendor products that is self-serving or promotional. Special issues: Year 2000 issue (December). Buys 25 mss/year. Query. Length: 800-2,500 words. Pays $120/page or as agreed in advance. Sometimes pays expenses of writers on assignment.

Photos: State availability of photos with submission. Offers no additional payment for photos accepted with ms. Captions, model releases, identification of subjects required.

Tips: "Stay informed about news and product releases in the Unisys market."

‡**WINDOWS DEVELOPER'S JOURNAL**, Miller Freeman, Inc., Suite 200, 1601 W. 23rd St., Lawrence KS 66046. (913)841-1631. Fax: (913)841-2624. E-mail: wdletter@mfi.com. Website: http://www.wdj.com. Editor: Ron Burk. Contact: Ann Brocker, managing editor. 90% freelance written. Monthly magazine. "*WDJ* is written for advanced Windows programmers. Articles are practical, advanced, code-intensive, and not product-specific. We expect our authors to be working Windows programmers." Estab. 1990. Circ. 23,000. **Pays on acceptance.** Publishes ms an average of 6 months after acceptance. Byline given. Kill fee $150. Buys all rights. Editorial lead time 3 months. Query for electronic submissions. Reports in 2 weeks on queries. Sample copy and writer's guidelines free.

Nonfiction: Technical. Buys 70-80 mss/year. Query. Length: varies. Pay varies.

‡**WINDOWS NT MAGAZINE**, Duke Communications International, Inc., 221 E. 29th St., Loveland CO 80539-0447. (970)663-4700. Website: http://www.winntmag.com. Editor: Mark Smith. Managing Editor: Karen Forster. Article Acquisitions Coordinator: Dina Haun. 90% freelance written. Monthly magazine "giving NT professionals explanations, techniques, insights and ideas that help them do their job." Estab. 1995. Circ. 75,000. Pays on publication. Publishes ms an average of 3 months after acceptance. Byline given. Offers $100 kill fee. Buys all rights. Editorial lead time 3 months. Submit seasonal material 3 months in advance. Sample copy and writer's guidelines free.

Nonfiction: How-to (use a technology to solve a problem). No articles related to a product promoted by the writer. Buys 300 mss/year. Query or send complete ms. Length: 1,500-3,000 words. Pays 25¢/word. Sometimes pays expenses of writers on assignment.

Photos: State availability of photos with submission. Identification of subjects required.

WINDOWS TECH JOURNAL, PennWell Publishing Company, Ten Tara Blvd., 5th Floor, Nashua NH 03062. (603)891-0123. E-mail: 70262.2051@compuserve.com. Executive Editor: Kevin D. Weeks. 95% freelance written. Monthly magazine. "The publication contains tools and techniques for Windows programmers; it covers component based development." Estab. 1992. Circ. 25,000. Pays on publication. Publishes ms an average of 4 months after acceptance. Byline given. Kill fee based on article length and content. Buys all rights. Editorial lead time 4 months. Submit seasonal material 5 months in advance. Reports in 6 weeks on queries; 1 month on mss. Sample copy and writer's guidelines free.

Nonfiction: How-to (programming how-tos in Windows environment), new product/reviews (we assign reviews; do not submit), technical (programming). "We are not a user magazine; articles must be about Windows programming." Buys 130 mss/year. Query. Length: 2,500-5,000 words. Pay determined by length and content; $75 minimum.

Tips: "Our magazine is a highly technical resource for Windows programmers and developers. Freelancers should call for a copy of our editorial calendar and writer's guidelines. If they have an idea to fit in the editorial calendar, then query the executive editor, Kevin Weeks, via regular mail or e-mail. We are interested in articles about Delphi, Visual Basic, C, C++, Access."

X-RAY MAGAZINE, Publishing Workgroup & Multimedia Technology for Quark Users, X-Ray Publishing Ventures International, 2700 15th St., San Francisco CA 94110. (415)861-9258. Fax: (415)642-7422. E-mail: editor@xraymag.com. Editor: Heather Speirs. 90% freelance written. Bimonthly magazine. "Topics must be of interest to users of Quark software (QuarkXPress Quark Publishing System, etc.)." Estab. 1995. Circ.250,000. Pays within 30 days of publication. Publishes ms an average of 2 months after acceptance. Byline given. Buys all rights. Editorial lead time 4 months. Accepts simultaneous submissions. Reports in 2 weeks on queries. Sample copy for 8½×11 SAE with 6 first-class stamps.

Nonfiction: General interest, how-to (Quark/Quark-related software), new product, opinion, technical. Buys 50-60 mss/year. Query with published clips, preferably by e-mail. Length: 1,200-4,000 words. Pays $300-1,500. Sometimes pays expenses of writers on assignment.

Photos: State availability of photos with submission. Reviews contact sheets, negatives, transparencies, prints. Negotiates payment individually. Identification of subjects required. Buys one-time rights.

Columns/Departments: In The Trenches/Editorial, Design & Production (hands-on, how-to articles) 1,250-1,500 words; On a Budget (being frugal), 1,250-1,500 words; Xclamation Point! (first-person/opinion) 1,100 words. Query with publishing clips, preferably by e-mail. Buys 25-30 mss/year. Pays $350-450.

INSURANCE

BUSINESS & HEALTH, Solutions in Managed Care, Medical Economics Publishing Co., 5 Paragon Dr., Montvale NJ 07645-1742. (201)722-2490. Fax: (201)573-8979. E-mail: b&h@medec.com. Editor: Richard Service. Managing Editor: Helen Lippman. 90% freelance written. Monthly magazine. "*B&H* carries articles about how employers can cut their health care costs and improve the quality of care they provide to workers. We also write about health care policy at the federal, state and local levels." Estab. 1983. Circ. 52,000. **Pays on acceptance.** Publishes ms an average of 2 months after acceptance. Byline given. Offers 20% kill fee. Buys all rights. Editorial lead time 2 months. Submit seasonal material 4 months in advance. Reports in 3 months. Sample copy for 9×12 SAE with 6 first-class stamps. Writer's guidelines for #10 SASE.

Nonfiction: How-to (cut health care benefits costs, provide better care); case studies (of successful employer-led efforts); trend piece on broad issues such as 24-hour coverage or benefits for retirees. Buys approx. 50 mss/year. Query with published clips. Length: 2,000-3,500 words. Pays $1,000-1,700 for features, plus expenses of writers on assignment.

Columns/Departments: Primarily staff-written but will consider queries.

Tips: "Please be familiar with *B&H* and follow writer's guidelines. Articles should combine a business angle with a human interest approach and address both cost-containment and quality of care. Include cost-benefit analysis data and material for charts or graphs whenever possible."

FLORIDA UNDERWRITER, National Underwriter Co., 9887 Fourth St., N., Suite 230, St. Petersburg FL 33702-2488. (813)576-1101. Contact: James E. Seymour, editor. Editorial Director: Ian Mackenzie. 20% freelance written. Monthly magazine. "*Florida Underwriter* covers insurance for Florida insurance professionals: producers, executives, risk managers, employee benefit administrators. We want material about any insurance line, Life & Health or Property & Casualty, but *must* have a Florida tag—Florida authors preferred." Estab. 1984. Circ. 10,000. Pays on publication. Publishes ms an average of 3 months after acceptance. Byline given. Buys all rights. Submit seasonal material 3 months in advance. Accepts simultaneous submissions. Reports in 1 month. Free sample copy and writer's guidelines.

Nonfiction: Essay, exposé, historical/nostalgic, how-to, interview/profile, new product, opinion, technical. "We don't want articles that aren't about insurance for insurance people or those that lack Florida angle. No puff pieces. Note: Most non-inhouse pieces are contributed gratis by industry experts." Buys 6 mss/year. Query with or without published clips, or send complete ms. Length: 500-1,500 words. Pays $50-150 for assigned articles; $25-100 for unsolicited articles. "Industry experts contribute in return for exposure." Sometimes pays expenses of writers on assignment.

Reprints: Send tearsheet or photocopy of article or typed ms with rights for sale noted and information about when and where the article previously appeared. Pays 40% of amount paid for an original article.

Photos: State availability of photos with submission. Send photos with submission. Reviews 5×7 prints. Offers no additional payment for photos accepted with ms. Identification of subjects required.

GEICO DIRECT, K.L. Publications, 2001 Killebrew Dr., Suite 105, Bloomington MN 55425-1879. Editor: Bernadette Baczynski. 60% freelance written. Semiannual magazine published for the Government Employees Insurance Company (GEICO) policyholders. Estab. 1988. Circ. 2,000,000. **Pays on acceptance**. Byline given. Buys first North American serial rights. Reports in 2 months. Writer's guidelines for #10 SASE.

Nonfiction: Americana, home and auto safety, car care, financial, lifestyle, travel. Query with published clips. Length: 1,000 words. Pays $350-500.

Photos: Reviews 35mm transparencies. Payment varies.

Columns/Departments: Moneywise, 50+, Your Car. Query with published clips. Length: 500-600 words. Pays $175-350.

Tips: "We prefer work from published/established writers, especially those with specialized knowledge of the insurance industry, safety issues and automotive topics."

JEWELRY

THE DIAMOND REGISTRY BULLETIN, 580 Fifth Ave., #806, New York NY 10036. (212)575-0444. Fax: (212)575-0722. E-mail: diamond58@aol.com. Editor-in-Chief: Joseph Schlussel. 50% freelance written. Monthly newsletter. Estab. 1969. Pays on publication. Buys all rights. Submit seasonal material 1 month in advance. Accepts simultaneous submissions. Reports in 3 weeks. Sample copy for $5.

Nonfiction: Prevention advice (on crimes against jewelers); how-to (ways to increase sales in diamonds, improve security, etc.); interview (of interest to diamond dealers or jewelers). Submit complete ms. Length: 50-500 words. Pays $75-150.

Reprints: Accepts previously published submissions.

Tips: "We seek ideas to increase sales of diamonds. We also have interest in diamond mining."

THE ENGRAVERS JOURNAL, 26 Summit St., P.O. Box 318, Brighton MI 48116. (810)229-5725. Fax: (810)229-8320. E-mail: editor@engraversjournal.com. Website: http://www.engravers.com. Co-Publisher: Michael J. Davis. Managing Editor: Rosemary Farrell. 15% freelance written. "We are eager to work with published/established writers as well as new/unpublished writers." Magazine published 10 times/year covering the recognition and identification industry (engraving, marking devices, awards, jewelry, and signage.) "We provide practical information for the education and advancement of our readers, mainly retail business owners." Estab. 1975. **Pays on acceptance.** Publishes ms an average of 1 year after acceptance. Byline given "only if writer is recognized authority." Buys one-time rights and makes work-for-hire assignments. Reports in 2 weeks. Writer's guidelines free. Sample copy to "those who send writing samples with inquiry."

Nonfiction: General interest (industry-related); how-to (small business subjects, increase sales, develop new markets, use new sales techniques, etc.); technical. No general overviews of the industry. Query with writing samples "published or not, or send samples and résumé to be considered for assignments on speculation." Length: 1,000-5,000 words. Pays $100-500 for assigned articles; $50 for unsolicited articles.

Reprints: Accepts previously published submissions.

Photos: Send photos with query. Pays variable rate. Captions, model release, identification of subjects required.

Tips: "Articles should always be down to earth, practical and thoroughly cover the subject with authority. We do not want the 'textbook' writing approach, vagueness, or theory—our readers look to us for sound practical information. We use an educational slant, publishing both trade-oriented articles and general business topics of interest to a small retail-oriented readership."

‡FASHION ACCESSORIES, S.C.M. Publications, Inc., 65 W. Main St., Bergenfield NJ 07621-1696. (201)384-3336. Fax: (201)384-6776. Publisher: Samuel Mendelson. Monthly newspaper covering costume or fashion jewelry. Published for executives in the manufacturing, wholesaling and retail volume buying of fashion jewelry and accessories. Estab. 1951. Circ. 10,000. **Pays on acceptance.** Byline given. Not copyrighted. Buys first rights. Submit seasonal material 3 months in advance. Sample copy for $2 and 9×12 SAE with 4 first-class stamps.

Nonfiction: Essays, general interest, historical/nostalgic, how-to, humor, interview/profile, new product, travel. Buys 20 mss/year. Query with published clips. Length: 1,000-2,000 words. Pays $100-300.

Photos: Send photos with submission. Reviews 4×5 prints. Offers no additional payment for photos accepted with ms. Identification of subjects required. Buys one-time rights.

Columns/Departments: Fashion Report (interviews and reports of fashion news), 1,000-2,000 words.

Tips: "We are interested in anything that will be of interest to costume jewelry buyers."

JOURNALISM AND WRITING

Journalism and writing magazines cover both the business and creative sides of writing. Writing publications offer inspiration and support for professional and beginning writers. Although there are many valuable writing publications that do not pay, we list those that pay for articles.

AUTHORSHIP, National Writers Association, 1450 S. Havana, Suite 424, Aurora CO 80012. (303)751-7844. Editor: Sandy Whelchel. Bimonthly magazine covering writing articles only. "Association magazine targeted to beginning and professional writers. Covers how-to, humor, marketing issues." Estab. 1950s. Circ. 4,000. **Pays on acceptance.** Byline given. Buys first North American serial or second serial (reprint) rights. Editorial lead time 3 months. Submit seasonal material 6 months in advance. Accepts simultaneous submissions. Reports in 2 months on queries. Sample copy for #10 SASE.

Nonfiction: Writing only. Poetry (November/December). Buys 25 mss/year. Query or send complete ms. Length: 900 words. Pays $10 or discount on memberships and copies.

Photos: State availability of photos with submission. Reviews 5×7 prints. Offers no additional payment for photos accepted with ms. Model releases and identification of subjects required. Buys one-time rights.

Reprints: Accepts previously published submissions.

Tips: "Members of National Writers Association are given preference."

BOOK DEALERS WORLD, North American Bookdealers Exchange, P.O. Box 606, Cottage Grove OR 97424. Phone/fax: (541)942-7455. Editorial Director: Al Galasso. 50% freelance written. Quarterly magazine covering writing, self-publishing and marketing books by mail. Circ. 20,000. Pays on publication. Publishes ms an average of 3 months after acceptance. Byline given. Buys first serial and second serial (reprint) rights. Accepts simultaneous submissions. Reports in 1 month. Sample copy for $3.

Nonfiction: Book excerpts (writing, mail order, direct mail, publishing); how-to (home business by mail, advertising); interview/profile (of successful self-publishers). Positive articles on self-publishing, new writing angles, marketing, etc. Buys 10 mss/year. Send complete ms. Length: 1,000-1,500 words. Pays $25-50.

Reprints: Send typed ms with rights for sale noted and information about when and where the article previously appeared. Pays 80% of amount paid for an original article.

Columns/Departments: Print Perspective (about new magazines and newsletters); Self-Publisher Profile (on successful self-publishers and their marketing strategy). Buys 20 mss/year. Send complete ms. Length: 250-1,000 words. Pays $5-20.

FOR EXPLANATION of symbols, see the Key to Symbols and Abbreviations. For unfamiliar words, see the Glossary.

Fillers: Fillers concerning writing, publishing or books. Buys 6/year. Length: 100-250 words. Pays $3-10.
Tips: "Query first. Get a sample copy of the magazine."

BYLINE, P.O. Box 130596, Edmond OK 73013-0001. (405)348-5591. E-mail: bylinemp@aol.com. Website: http://www.bylinemag.com. Editor/Publisher: Marcia Preston. Contact: Kathryn Fanning, managing editor. 80-90% freelance written. Eager to work with new/unpublished writers. Monthly magazine for writers and poets. "We stress encouragement of beginning writers." Estab. 1981. **Pays on acceptance**. Publishes ms an average of 3 months after acceptance. Byline given. Buys first North American serial rights. Reports in 2 months or less. Sample copy for $4 postpaid. Writer's guidelines for #10 SASE.
Nonfiction: How-to, humor, inspirational, personal experience, *all* connected with writing and selling. Read magazine for special departments. Buys approximately 100 mss/year. Prefers queries; will read complete mss. Length: 1,500-1,800 words for features. Usually pays $50 for features. Needs short humor on writing (300-600 words). Pays $15-25 on acceptance.
Fiction: General fiction of high quality. Send complete ms: 2,000-4,000 words preferred. Pays $100.
Poetry: Betty Shipley, poetry editor. Any style, on a writing theme. Preferred length: 4-30 lines. Pays $5-10 on acceptance, plus free issue.
Tips: "We'd like to see more 1,500 to 1,800-word features on how to write better, market better, etc."

‡CANADIAN AUTHOR, Canadian Authors Association, Box 8029, 1225 Wonderland Rd., N, London, Ontario N6G 4X1 Canada. Fax: (519)473-4450. E-mail: wwkidlit@netcom.ca. Contact: Welwyn Wilton Katz, editor. 100% freelance written. Quarterly magazine. "*Canadian Author* is Canada's oldest literary magazine, by and for writers of all genres, and both journalistic and literary writers." Estab. 1919. Circ. 3,000. Pays on publication. Publishes ms an average of 6 months after acceptance. Byline given. Buys first North American rights, second serial (reprint) rights and makes work-for-hire assignments. Sample copy for $5. Writer's guidelines for #10 SAE and IRC.
Nonfiction: How-to (on writing, selling; the specifics of the different genres—what they are and how to write them); informational (the writing scene—who's who and what's what); interview (with Canadian writers, mainly leading ones, but also those with a story that can help others write and sell more often); opinion. No new product (software, books for writers); personal, lightweight writing experiences; no fillers. Send complete ms. Length: 900-3,000 words. Pays $20-65/printed page.
Photos: State availability of photos with query. Captions, model releases, identification of subjects required. Buys one-time rights.
Fiction: Literary fiction only, no genre. Buys 4 mss/year. Send complete ms. Length: 2,000-3,000 words. Pays $125.
Poetry: High quality. Avant garde, free verse, haiku, traditional. Buys 20 poems/year. Pays $20-30/printed page.

CANADIAN WRITER'S JOURNAL, P.O. Box 5180, New Liskeard, Ontario P0J 1P0 Canada. Fax: (705)647-8366. E-mail: dranchuk@aol.com. Accepts well-written articles by inexperienced writers. Quarterly magazine for writers. Estab. 1985. Circ. 350. 75% freelance written. Pays on publication. Publishes ms an average of 9 months after acceptance. Byline given. Reports in 2 months. Sample copy for $4 and $1 postage. Writer's guidelines for #10 SAE and IRC.
• *Canadian Writer's Journal* has a new owner and a new address.
Nonfiction: How-to articles for writers. Buys 50-55 mss/year. Query optional. Length: 500-2,000 words. Pays about $5/published magazine page.
Reprints: Send typed ms with rights for sale noted and information about when and where the article previously appeared. Pays 100% of amount paid for an original article.
Fiction: Requirements currently being met by annual contest. SASE for rules.
Poetry: Short poems or extracts used as part of articles on the writing of poetry. Annual poetry contest. Wind Song Column uses some short poems. Consult guidelines for details.
Tips: "We prefer short, tightly written, informative how-to articles. U.S. writers note that U.S. postage cannot be used to mail from Canada. Obtain Canadian stamps, use IRCs or send small amounts in cash."

EDITOR & PUBLISHER, 11 W. 19th St., New York NY 10011-4234. Fax: (212)929-1259. Website: http://www.mediainfo.com/edpub. Executive Editor: John Consoli. Contact: George Garneau, senior editor. 10% freelance written. Weekly magazine for newspaper publishers, editors, executives, employees and others in communications, marketing, advertising, etc. Estab. 1884. Circ. 25,000. Pays on publication. Publishes ms an average of 2 months after acceptance. Buys first serial rights. Reports in 2 months. Sample copy for $2.25.
Nonfiction: Uses newspaper business articles and news items; also newspaper personality features and printing technology. Query by fax.
Tips: "Freelancer may sell electronic or print rights elsewhere after publication in *E&P*, but we reserve the right to make articles printed in *E&P* available online for research purposes."

FICTION WRITER'S GUIDELINE, The Newsletter of Fiction Writer's Connection (FWC), P.O. Box 4065, Deerfield Beach FL 33442-4065. (954)426-4705. E-mail: bcamenson@aol.com. Editor: Blythe Camenson. 50% freelance written. Monthly newsletter covering how-to for fiction writers. "*Fiction Writer's Guideline* takes an upbeat approach to encourage writers, but doesn't shy away from the sometimes harsh realities of the publishing industry." Estab. 1993. Circ. 1,000. Pays on publication. Publishes ms an average of 3 months after acceptance. Byline given. Buys first, one-time or second serial (reprint) rights. Editorial lead time 1 month. Submit seasonal material 3 months in advance. Accepts simultaneous submissions. Reports in 2 weeks on queries; 1 month on mss. Sample copy for $3.50. Writer's guidelines for #10 SASE.

Nonfiction: General interest, how-to (the business and craft of writing fiction), interview/profile (of agents, editors, and authors), new product, short book reviews (how-to books for writers). Buys 30 mss/year. Length: 200-1,500 words. Pays $1-25. Sometimes pays expenses of writers on assignment. Send complete ms.

Reprints: Send typed ms with rights for sale noted and information about when and where the article previously appeared.

Columns/Departments: Advice From An Agent/Editor (how to approach, what they're looking for, advice to fiction writers), 1,500 words; "Writing Tips" (specific advice on style and structure), 400 words. Buys 12 mss/year. Query. Pays $1-25.

Fillers: Anecdotes, facts, newsbreaks; all to do with the business or craft of writing fiction. Buys 50/year. Length: 20-100 words. Pays $1-10.

Tips: Looking for "interviews with agents or editors. Our guidelines include specific questions to ask. Query or call first to make sure your choice hasn't already been interviewed. We also need a monthly cover article on some aspect of writing fiction, from specific tips for different categories/genres, to handling viewpoint, characterization, dialogue, etc. Also fillers. Request sample copy to see the format."

‡FREELANCE, Saskatchewan Writers Guild, Box 3986, Regina, Saskatchewan S4P 3R9. Editor: April Davies. 25% freelance written. Literary magazine published 6 times/year covering writing. "*FreeLance* is the membership newsmagazine of the Saskatchewan Writers Guild. It publishes literary news, news about members, a Saskatchewan literary events calendar, markets and resources information, news on new books by members, updates on SWG programs, articles on the craft or business of writing and literary issues, and comments on these." No poetry or fiction. Estab. 1969. Circ. 800. Pays on publication. Publishes ms an average of 2-4 months after acceptance. Byline given. Buys first North American serial or second serial (reprint) rights. Editorial lead time 1 month. Accepts previously published submissions. Reports in 1 month on queries; 3 months on mss. Sample copy free.

Nonfiction: Essays (on the craft of writing); how-to (craft or business of writing); new product (writing-related); opinion (literary issues); technical (craft of writing); reports on writers' conferences, colonies, workshops, etc. Buys 25 mss/year. Send complete ms. Length: 600-1,000 words. Pays $40/published page.

Photos: Send photos with submissions. Reviews prints. Offers $10 (based on publication size). Captions required. Buys one-time rights.

MAINE IN PRINT, Maine Writers and Publishers Alliance, 12 Pleasant St., Brunswick ME 04011. (207)729-6333. Fax: (207)725-1014. Editor: Lisa Holbrook. Monthly newsletter for writers, editors, teachers, librarians, etc., focusing on Maine literature and the craft of writing. Estab. 1975. Circ. 5,000. Pays on publication. Publishes ms an average of 2 months after acceptance. Byline given. Buys one-time rights. Editorial lead time 1 month. Accepts simultaneous submissions. Reports in 2 weeks on queries; 1 month on mss. Sample copy and writer's guidelines free.

Nonfiction: Essays, how-to (writing), interview/profile, technical writing. No creative writing, fiction or poetry. Buys 20 mss/year. Query with published clips. Length: 400-1,500 words. Pays $25-75 for assigned articles.

Reprints: Send tearsheet of article or short story and information about when and where the article previously appeared. Pays $25 for reprints.

Photos: State availability of photos with submission. Offers no additional payment for photos accepted with ms.

Columns/Departments: Front-page articles (writing related), 500-1,500 words. Buys 20 mss/year. Query. Pays $25 minimum.

Tips: "Become a member of Maine Writers & Publishers Alliance. Become familiar with Maine literary scene."

NEW WRITER'S MAGAZINE, Sarasota Bay Publishing, P.O. Box 5976, Sarasota FL 34277-5976. (941)953-7903. E-mail: newriters@aol.com. Editor: George J. Haborak. 95% freelance written. Bimonthly magazine. "*New Writer's Magazine* believes that *all* writers are *new* writers in that each of us can learn from one another. So, we reach pro and non-pro alike." Estab. 1986. Circ. 5,000. Pays on publication. Byline given. Buys first rights. Reports in 2 weeks on queries; 1 month on mss. *Writer's Market* recommends allowing 2 months for reply. Sample copy for $3. Writer's guidelines for #10 SASE.

Nonfiction: General interest, how-to (for new writers), humor, interview/profile, opinion, personal experience (with pro writer). Buys 50 mss/year. Send complete ms. Length: 700-1,000 words. Pays $10-50.

Photos: Send photos with submission. Reviews 5×7 prints. Offers no additional payment for photos accepted with ms. Captions required.

Fiction: Experimental, historical, humorous, mainstream, slice-of-life vignettes. "Again, we do *not* want anything that does not have a tie-in with the writing life or writers in general." Buys 2-6 mss/year. "We offer a special fiction contest held each year with cash prizes." Send complete ms. Length: 700-800 words. Pays $20-40.

Poetry: Free verse, light verse, traditional. Does not want anything *not* for writers. Buys 10-20 poems/year. Submit maximum 3 poems. Length: 8-20 lines. Pays $5 maximum.

Fillers: Anecdotes, facts, newsbreaks, short humor. Buys 5-15/year. Length: 20-100 words. Pays $5 maximum. Cartoons, writing lifestyle slant. Buys 20-30/year. Pays $10 maximum.

Tips: "Any article *with photos* has a good chance, especially an *up close and personal* interview with an established professional writer offering advice, etc."

OHIO WRITER, Poets League of Greater Cleveland, P.O. Box 91801, Cleveland OH 44101. Editor: Ron Antonucci. 75% freelance written. Bimonthly magazine covering writing and Ohio writers. Estab. 1987. Pays on publication. Publishes ms an average of 4 months after acceptance. Byline given. Buys one-time rights and second serial (reprint) rights. Editorial lead time 4 months. Submit seasonal material 4 months in advance. Reports in 1 month. Sample copy for $2.50. Writer's guidelines for SASE.
Nonfiction: Essays, how-to, humor, inspirational, interview/profile, opinion, personal experience—"all must relate to the writing life or Ohio writers, or Ohio publishing scene." Buys 24 mss/year. Send complete ms. Length: 1,000-2,000 words. Pays $25 minimum, up to $50 for lead article; other payment under arrangement with writer.
Reprints: Send photocopy of article or typed ms with rights for sale noted and information about when and where the article previously appeared. Pays 50% of amount paid for an original article.
Columns/Departments: Subjectively Yours (opinions, controversial stance on writing life), 1,500 words; Reviews (Ohio writers, publishers or publishing), 500 words; Focus On (Ohio publishing scene, how to write/publish certain kind of writing, e.g., travel). Buys 6 mss/year. Send complete ms. Pays $25-50; $5/book review.
Tips: "Profiles and interviews of writers who live in Ohio are always needed."

POETS & WRITERS, 72 Spring St., 3rd Floor, New York NY 10012. Fax: (212)226-3963. E-mail: editor@pw.org. Website: http://www.pw.org. Editor: Daryln Brewer. 100% freelance written. Bimonthly professional trade journal for poets and fiction writers. No poetry or fiction. Estab. 1973. Circ. 58,000. **Pays on acceptance** of finished draft. Publishes ms an average of 4 months after acceptance. Byline given. Offers 20% kill fee. Buys first North American serial and first rights or makes work-for-hire assignments. Editorial lead time 1 year. Submit seasonal material 1 year in advance. Reports in 6 weeks on mss. Sample copy for $3.95 to Circulation Dept. Writer's guidelines for #10 SASE.
Nonfiction: Personal essays about literature, how-to (craft of poetry or fiction writing), interview/profile with poets or fiction writers (no Q&A), regional reports of literary activity, reports on small presses, service pieces about publishing trends. Buys 35 mss/year. Query with published clips or send complete ms. "We do *not* accept submissions by fax or e-mail." Length: 1,500-3,600 words.
Photos: State availability of photos with submission. Reviews b&w prints. Offers no additional payment for photos accepted with ms.
Columns/Departments: Literary and publishing news, 500-600 words; profiles of emerging and established poets and fiction writers, 2,400-3,600 words; regional reports (literary activity in US), 1,800-3,600 words. Query with published clips, or send complete ms. Pays $100-300.

RISING STAR, 47 Byledge Rd., Manchester NH 03104. Phone/fax: (603)623-9796. Editor: Scott E. Green. 50% freelance written. Bimonthly newsletter on science fiction and fantasy markets for writers and artists. Estab. 1980. Circ. 150. Pays on publication. Publishes ms an average of 3 months after acceptance. Byline given. Not copyrighted. Buys first rights. Accepts simultaneous submissions. Reports in 1 month on queries. Sample copy for $1.50 and #10 SASE. Free writer's guidelines. Subscription $7.50 for 6 issues, payable to Scott Green.
Nonfiction: Book excerpts, essays, interview/profile, opinion. Buys 8 mss/year. Query. Length: 500-900 words. Pays $3 minimum.
Reprints: Send tearsheet or typed ms with rights for sale noted and information about when and where the article previously appeared. Pays $5.

ST. LOUIS JOURNALISM REVIEW, 470 E. Lockwood, Room 414, St. Louis MO 63119. (314)968-5905. Fax: (314)963-6104. Editor/Publisher Emeritus: Charles L. Klotzer. Contact: Edward Bishop, editor. 80% freelance written. Prefers to work with published/established writers. Monthly tabloid newspaper critiquing St. Louis media, print, broadcasting, TV and cable primarily by working journalists and others. Also covers issues not covered adequately by dailies. Occasionally buys articles on national media criticism. Estab. 1970. Circ. 4,000. Buys all rights. Byline given. Sample copy for $2.50.
Nonfiction: "We buy material which analyzes, critically, St. Louis metro area media and, less frequently, national media institutions, personalities or trends." No taboos. Pays the expenses of writers on assignment subject to prior approval.
Reprints: Send tearsheet of article or short story. Pays 10% of amount paid for an original article.

SCAVENGER'S NEWSLETTER, 519 Ellinwood, Osage City KS 66523-1329. (913)528-3538. E-mail: foxscav1@jc. net. (No e-mail submissions; queries OK). Editor: Janet Fox. 15% freelance written. Eager to work with new/unpublished writers. Monthly newsletter covering markets for science fiction/fantasy/horror/mystery materials especially with regard to the small press. Estab. 1984. Circ. 950. **Pays on acceptance.** Publishes ms an average of 8 months after acceptance. Byline given. Not copyrighted. Buys one-time rights. Accepts simultaneous submissions. Reports in 1 month if SASE included. Sample copy for $2.50. Writer's guidelines for #10 SASE.
Nonfiction: Essays, general interest, how-to (write, sell, publish science fiction/fantasy/horror/mystery), humor, interview/profile (writers, artists in the field), opinion. Buys 12-15 mss/year. Send complete ms. Length: 1,000 words maximum. Pays $4.
Reprints: Send information about when and where the article previously appeared. Pays 100% of amount paid for an original article.
Fiction: "Seeking a few (4-6) outstanding pieces of flash fiction to 1,200 words in the genre of SF/fantasy/horror/mystery. Looking for work that uses poetry techniques to make a short piece seem like a complete story." Pays $4.

Poetry: Avant-garde, free verse, haiku, traditional. All related to science fiction/fantasy/horror/mystery genres. Buys 24 poems/year. Submit maximum 3 poems. Length: 10 lines maximum. Pays $2.
Tips: "Because this is a small publication, it has occasional overstocks. We're especially looking for science fiction/ flash fiction/fantasy/horror/mystery."

SMALL PRESS REVIEW, P.O. Box 100, Paradise CA 95967. Editor: Len Fulton. Monthly for "people interested in small presses and magazines, current trends and data; many libraries." Circ. 3,500. Byline given. Reports in 2 months. Free sample copy.
Nonfiction: News, short reviews. Uses spot news, historical, think pieces. Accepts 50-200 mss/year. Length: 100-200 words. "Query if you're unsure."

TODAY'S $85,000 FREELANCE WRITER, (formerly *The Prolific Freelancer*), BSK Communications and Associates, P.O. Box 554, Oradell NJ 07649. (201)262-3277. Fax: (201)599-2635. E-mail: bskcom@tiac.net. Website: http:// www.tiac.net/users/bskcom. Editor: Brian S. Konradt. 95% freelance written. Bimonthly magazine covering commercial freelance writing as a part-time/full-time business. "*Today's $85,000 Freelance Writer* magazine helps writers build a high-profit, home-based writing/consulting business and write for local/national businesses, industries and commercial markets." Estab. 1997. Circ. 3,000. Pays on acceptance for columnists; pays on publication for contributors. Publishes ms an average of 6 months after acceptance. Byline given. Buys first North American serial rights only. Editorial lead time 2 months. Submit seasonal material 4 months in advance. Reports in 1 month on queries; 2 months on mss. Sample copy for $5. Writer's guidelines for #10 SASE or free at website.
Nonfiction: General interest, how-to, new product, technical. Buys 40 mss/year. Accepts queries only. Query with published clips or call to discuss article ideas. Length: 200-2,500 words. Pays 5¢/word for contributors; pays 10¢/word for regular columnists, plus contributor's copies.
Photos: State availability of photos with query. Reviews prints. Offers $15-30/photo. Identification of subjects required. Buys one-time rights.
Columns/Departments: Internet Marketing (how to market your writing business on the Internet), 500-2,500 words; Second Profit Ventures (secondary sources of income via writing), 500-1,000 words; Writing Competent Copy (how to write different types of copy for clients), 1,000-2,500 words; Baiting and Tackling Techniques (how to use different marketing strategies to get clients), 500-1,000 words; Client Communications (how to educate new and existing clients), 500-2,500 words.
Fillers: Facts, newsbreaks, business briefs. Buys 20/year. Length: 100-500 words. Pays $5-15.
Tips: "We help writers write for top-paying clients of local/national businesses, industries and commercial markets— not for publications. We want articles that show writers how to launch a high-profit commercial freelance writing/ consulting business, how to get clients, how to set their fees, how to write various types of copy, how to prepare promotional material, and a lot more."

THE WRITER, 120 Boylston St., Boston MA 02116-4615. Website: http://www.channel1.com/the writer/. Editor-in-Chief/Publisher: Sylvia K. Burack. 20-25% freelance written. Prefers to buy work of published/established writers. Monthly. Estab. 1887. **Pays on acceptance.** Publishes ms an average of 8 months after acceptance. Buys first serial rights. Sample copy for $3.50.
Nonfiction: Practical articles for writers on how to write for publication, and how and where to market manuscripts in various fields. Considers all submissions promptly. No assignments. Length: 2,000 words maximum.
Reprints: Occasionally buys previously published submissions from the *New York Times* and *Washington Post* book review sections. Send tearsheet or photocopy of article and information about when and where the article previously appeared.
Tips: "New types of publications and our continually updated market listings in all fields will determine changes of focus and fact."

WRITER'S DIGEST, 1507 Dana Ave., Cincinnati OH 45207. (513)531-2222. Fax: (513)531-1843. E-mail: writersdig @juno.com. Submissions Editor: Amanda Boyd. 90% freelance written. Monthly magazine about writing and publishing. "Our readers write fiction, poetry, nonfiction, plays and all kinds of creative writing. They're interested in improving their writing skills, improving their ability to sell their work and finding new outlets for their talents." Estab. 1920. Circ. 225,000. **Pays on acceptance.** Publishes ms an average of 1 year after acceptance. Buys first North American serial rights for one-time editorial use, possible electronic posting, microfilm/microfiche use and magazine promotional use. Pays 20% kill fee. Byline given. Submit seasonal material 8 months in advance. Reports in 2 months. Sample copy for $3.50 ($3.70 in Ohio). Writer's guidelines for #10 SASE.
  ● Ranked as one of the best markets for freelance writers in *Writer's Yearbook* magazine's annual "Top 100 Markets," January 1997.
Nonfiction: "Our mainstay is the how-to article—that is, an article exploring some technique of how to write or sell more of what you write. For instance, how to write compelling leads and conclusions, how to improve your character descriptions, how to become more efficient and productive. We like plenty of examples, anecdotes and $$$ in our articles—so other writers can actually see what's been done successfully by the author of a particular piece. We like our articles to speak directly to the reader through the use of the first-person voice. Don't submit an article on what five book editors say about writing mysteries. Instead, submit an article on how you cracked the mystery market and how our readers can do the same. But don't limit the article to your experiences; include the opinions of those five

editors to give your article increased depth and authority.'' General interest (about writing); how-to (writing and marketing techniques that work); inspirational; interview and profile (query first); new product; personal experience (marketing and freelancing experiences). ''We can always use articles on fiction and nonfiction technique, and solid articles on poetry or scriptwriting are always welcome. No articles titled 'So You Want to Be a Writer,' and no first-person pieces that ramble without giving a lesson or something readers can learn from in the sharing of the story.'' Buys 90-100 mss/year. Queries are preferred. Length: 500-3,000 words. Pays 15-40¢/word minimum. Sometimes pays expenses of writers on assignment.

Reprints: Accepts previously published submissions from noncompeting markets. Send tearsheet or photocopy of article, noting rights for sale and when and where the article previously appeared.

Photos: Used only with interviews and profiles. State availability of photos or send contact sheet with ms. Captions required.

Columns/Departments: Chronicle (first-person narratives about the writing life; length: 1,200-1,500 words); The Writing Life (length: 50-500 words); and Tip Sheet (short items that offer solutions to writing and freelance business-related problems that writers commonly face). Humor is welcome for Chronicle and Writing Life. Buys approximately 150 articles/year for Writing Life and Tip Sheet sections. Send complete ms.

Poetry: Light verse about ''the writing life''—joys and frustrations of writing. ''We are also considering poetry other than short light verse—but still related to writing, publishing, other poets and authors, etc.'' Buys an average of 1 an issue. Submit poems in batches of 1-5. Length: 2-20 lines. Pays $10-50/poem.

Fillers: Anecdotes and short humor, primarily for use in The Writing Life column. Uses up to 4/issue. Length: 50-250 words.

WRITER'S FORUM, Writer's Digest School, 1507 Dana Ave., Cincinnati OH 45207. (513)531-2222. Editor: Amanda Boyd. 100% freelance written. Quarterly newsletter covering writing techniques, marketing and inspiration for students enrolled in fiction and nonfiction writing courses offered by Writer's Digest School. Estab. 1970. Circ. 13,000. **Pays on acceptance.** Publishes ms an average of 6 months after acceptance. Byline given. Buys first serial or second serial (reprint) rights. Submit seasonal/holiday material 4 months in advance. Accepts simultaneous submissions. Reports in 6 weeks. Free sample copy.

Nonfiction: How-to (write or market short stories, or articles, novels and nonfiction books); articles that will motivate beginning writers. Buys 12 mss/year. Prefers complete mss to queries. ''If you prefer to query, please do so by mail, not phone.'' Length: 500-1,000 words. Pays $10-25.

Reprints: Accepts previously published submissions.

WRITER'S YEARBOOK, 1507 Dana Ave., Cincinnati OH 45207. (513)531-2222. Fax: (513)531-1843. E-mail: writersdig@juno.com. Submissions Editor: Amanda Boyd. 90% freelance written. Newsstand annual for freelance writers, journalists and teachers of creative writing. ''Please note that the *Yearbook* is a 'best of' format. That is, we are reprinting the best writing about writing published in the last year: articles, fiction and book excerpts. The *Yearbook* uses little original material, so do not submit queries or original manuscripts. We will, however, consider already-published material for possible inclusion.'' Estab. 1929. **Pays on acceptance.** Publishes ms an average of 6 months after acceptance. Offers 20% kill fee. Byline given. Buys reprint rights. ''If you don't want your manuscript returned, indicate that on the first page of the manuscript or in a cover letter.''

Reprints: ''In reprints, we want articles that reflect the current state of writing in America: trends, inside information, and money-saving and money-making ideas for the freelance writer. We try to touch on the various facets of writing in each issue of the *Yearbook*—from fiction to poetry to playwriting, and any other endeavor a writer can pursue. How-to articles—that is, articles that explain in detail how to do something—are very important to us. For example, you could explain how to establish mood in fiction, how to improve interviewing techniques, how to write for and sell to specialty magazines, or how to construct and market a good poem. We are also interested in the writer's spare time—what she/he does to retreat occasionally from the writing wars, where and how to refuel and replenish the writing spirit. 'How Beats the Heart of a Writer' features interest us, if written warmly, in the first person, by a writer who has had considerable success. We also want interviews or profiles of well-known bestselling authors, always with good pictures. Articles on writing techniques that are effective today are always welcome. We provide how-to features and information to help our readers become more skilled at writing and successful at selling their writing.'' Buys 15-20 mss (reprints only)/year. Send tearsheet or photocopy of article, noting rights for sale and when and where the article previously appeared. Length: 750-4,500 words. Pays 5¢/word minimum.

Photos: Interviews and profiles must be accompanied by high-quality photos. Reviews b&w photos only, depending on use. Captions required.

Fillers: Interested in funny, weird, wacky or otherwise offbeat incidents for our annual ''Year in Revue'' roundup. Send us the clip reporting the incident, indicate date and source. Pays $20 finder's fee.

‡WRITING THAT WORKS, The Business Communications Report, (formerly *Writing Concepts*), 7481 Huntsman Blvd., Suite 720, Springfield VA 22153-1648. Editor/Publisher: John De Lellis. Monthly newsletter. ''Our readers are company writers, editors, communicators and executives who write as part of their job. They want specific, practical advice on business writing and editing.'' Estab. 1983. Pays within 30 days of acceptance. Publishes ms an average of 2 months after acceptance. Byline sometimes given. Buys all rights. Editorial lead time 2 months. Reports in 3 weeks on queries. Two sample copies for $2 and #10 SASE.

• *Writing That Works* does *not* use material on how to get published or on freelancing.

Nonfiction: Practical, short, how-to articles geared to company writers, editors, publication staff and communicators. Buys 130 mss/year. Length: 100-500 words. Pays $30-150.

Columns/Departments: Publications Management, Quick Tips (useful sources, tips on writing and editing, PR and marketing, and communications/publications); Writing Techniques (*business* writing for organization staffers); Style Matters (business editing for organization staffers); PR and Marketing; Online Publishing (practical techniques for web, online and electronic publishing).

Tips: "Format your copy to follow *Writing That Works* style. Include addresses, phone numbers and prices for products/services mentioned in articles"

‡**WRITTEN BY, The Journal of the Writers Guild of America, west**, 7000 W. Third St., Los Angeles CA 90048. (213)782-4522. Fax: (213)782-4802. E-mail: writtenby@wga.org. Contact: Lisa Chambers, editor. 25% freelance written. Monthly magazine. "*Written By* is the premier magazine written by and for America's screen and TV writers. We focus on the craft of screenwriting and cover all aspects of the entertainment industry from the perspective of the writer. We are read by all screenwriters and most entertainment executives." Estab. 1987. Circ. 12,500. **Pays on acceptance.** Publishes ms an average of 2 months after acceptance. Byline given. Offers 25% kill fee. Buys first rights and electronic rights. Editorial lead time 2 months. Submit seasonal material 4 months in advance. Accepts simultaneous submissions. Reports in 2 months. Sample copy for $5. Writer's guidelines free.

Nonfiction: Essays, historical/nostalgic, humor, technical. No "how to break into Hollywood," "how to write scripts"-type beginner pieces. Buys 5-8 mss/year. Query with published clips. Length: 500-2,500 words. Pays $500-1,500 for assigned articles; $100-800 for unsolicited articles. Sometimes pays expenses of writers on assignment.

Reprints: Accepts previously published submissions.

Photos: State availability of photos with assignment. Reviews contact sheets. Negotiates payment individually. Captions, model releases, identification of subjects required. Buys one-time rights.

Tips: "The writer must *always* keep in mind that our audience is made up primarily of working writers who are inside the business, therefore all articles need to have an 'insider' feel and not be written for those who are still trying to break in to Hollywood. We prefer submissions on diskette."

LAW

While all of these publications deal with topics of interest to attorneys, each has a particular slant. Be sure that your subject is geared to a specific market—lawyers in a single region, law students, paralegals, etc. Publications for law enforcement personnel are listed under Government and Public Service.

THE ALTMAN WEIL PENSA REPORT TO LEGAL MANAGEMENT, Altman Weil Pensa Publications, 1100 Commerce Dr., Racine WI 53406. (414)886-1304. Fax: (414)886-1139. E-mail: jameswilber@counsel.com. Website: http://www.altmanweil.com. Editor: James Wilber. 15-20% freelance written. Works with a small number of new/unpublished writers each year. Monthly newsletter covering law office management, purchases (equipment, insurance services, space, etc.) and technology. Estab. 1974. Circ. 2,200. Pays on publication. Publishes ms an average of 6 months after acceptance. Byline given. Buys all rights; sometimes second serial (reprint) rights. Reports in 1 month on queries; 3 months on mss. Sample copy for #10 SASE.

Nonfiction: How-to (buy, use, repair), interview/profile, new product. "Looking especially for practical, "how-to" articles on law office management and technology." Buys 12 mss/year. Query. Submit a sample of previous writing. Length: 500-2,500 words. Pays $125/published page.

Reprints: Send photocopy of article or typed ms with rights for sale noted plus diskette, and information about when and where the article previously appeared. Pays 50% of amount paid for an original article.

BENCH & BAR OF MINNESOTA, Minnesota State Bar Association, 514 Nicollet Ave., Suite 300, Minneapolis MN 55402-1021. (612)333-1183. Fax: (612)333-4927. Editor: Judson Haverkamp. 10% freelance written. Magazine published 11 times/year. "Audience is mostly Minnesota lawyers. *Bench & Bar* seeks reportage, analysis, and commentary on trends and issues in the law and the legal profession, especially in Minnesota. Preference to items of practical/human interest to professionals in law." Estab. 1931. Circ. 15,000. **Pays on acceptance.** Publishes ms an average of 3 months after acceptance. Byline given. Buys first North American serial rights and makes work-for-hire assignments. Reports in 1 month. Sample copy for 9×12 SAE with 4 first-class stamps. Writer's guidelines free.

Nonfiction: General interest, historical/nostalgic, how-to (how to handle particular types of legal, ethical problems in office management, representation, etc.), humor, interview/profile, technical/legal. "We do not want one-sided opinion pieces or advertorial." Buys 4-5 mss/year. Query with published clips or send complete ms. Length: 1,500-3,000 words. Pays $300-800. Sometimes pays expenses of writers on assignment.

Photos: State availability of photos with submission. Reviews 5×7 or larger prints. Offers $25-100/photo upon publication. Model releases and identification of subjects required. Buys one-time rights.

‡**CALIFORNIA LAWYER**, Dept. WM, 1210 Fox Plaza, 1390 Market St., San Francisco CA 94102. (415)252-0500. Fax: (415)252-0288. E-mail: tema_goodwin@dailyjournal.com. Editor: Peter Allen. Managing Editor: Tema Goodwin.

80% freelance written. Monthly magazine of law-related articles and general-interest subjects of appeal to lawyers and judges. Estab. 1928. Circ. 135,000. **Pays on acceptance.** Publishes ms an average of 3 months after acceptance. Byline given. Buys first rights; publishes only original material. Accepts simultaneous submissions. Reports in 2 weeks on queries; 3 weeks on mss. *Writer's Market* recommends allowing 2 months for reply. Sample copy and writer's guidelines on request with SASE.

Nonfiction: General interest, news and feature articles on law-related topics. "We are interested in concise, well-written and well-researched articles on issues of current concern, as well as well-told feature narratives with a legal focus. We would like to see a description or outline of your proposed idea, including a list of possible sources." Buys 36 mss/year. Query with published clips if available. Length: 400-3,500 words. Pays $200-1,800.

Photos: Louise Kollenbaum, photo editor. State availability of photos with query letter or ms. Reviews prints. Identification of subjects and releases required.

Columns/Departments: Legal Technology, Short News, Legal Culture, Books. Query with published clips if available. Length: 750-1,500 words. Pays $200-600.

CORPORATE LEGAL TIMES, 3 E. Huron St., Chicago IL 60611. (312)654-3500. E-mail: jking@gsteps.com. Editor: Jennifer E. King. 50% freelance written. Monthly tabloid. "*Corporate Legal Times* is a monthly national magazine that gives general counsel and inhouse attorneys information on legal and business issues to help them better manage corporate law departments. It routinely addresses changes and trends in law departments, litigation management, legal technology, corporate governance and in-house careers. Law areas covered monthly include: environmental, intellectual property, international, and labor and employment. All stories need to be geared toward the inhouse attorney's perspective." Estab. 1991. Circ. 40,000. Pays on publication. Publishes ms an average of 3 months after acceptance. Byline given. Buys all rights. Editorial lead time 3 months. Submit seasonal material 6 months in advance. Reports in 3 weeks on queries. Sample copy for $9 × 12$ SAE with 8 first-class stamps. Writer's guidelines for #10 SASE.

Nonfiction: Interview/profile, technical, news about legal aspects of business issues and events. Buys 12-25 mss/year. Query with published clips. Length: 500-3,000 words. Pays $300-1,500. Freelancers should state availability of photos with submission.

Photos: Reviews color transparencies, b&w prints. Offers $25-150/photo. Identification of subjects required. Buys all rights.

Tips: "Our publication targets general counsel and inhouse lawyers. All stories need to speak to them—not to the general attorney population. Query with clips and a list of potential inhouse sources. Non-paid, contributed articles from law firm attorneys are accepted only if there is an inhouse attorney co-author."

‡JOURNAL OF COURT REPORTING, National Court Reporters Association, 8224 Old Courthouse Rd., Vienna VA 22182. (703)556-6272. Fax: (703)556-6291. E-mail: msic@nerahq.org. Editor: Benjamin M. Rogner, Ph.D. 20% freelance written. Monthly (except tri-monthly Aug/Sept/Oct). "The *Journal of Court Reporting* has two complementary purposes: to communicate the activities, goals and mission of its publisher, the National Court Reporters Association; and, simultaneously, to seek out and publish diverse information and views on matters significantly related to the information/court reporting profession." Estab. 1905. Circ. 34,000. **Pays on acceptance.** Publishes ms an average of 3 months after acceptance. Byline given. Buys one-time rights and makes work-for-hire assignments. Editorial lead time 3 months. Accepts simultaneous submissions. Sample copy for $5. Writer's guidelines free.

Nonfiction: Essays, historical/nostalgic, how-to, interview/profile, new product, technical. Buys 10 mss/year. Query. Length: 1,200 words. Pays $55-400. Sometimes pays expenses of writers on assignment.

Reprints: Accepts previously published submissions.

Photos: State availability of photos with submission. Offers no additional payment for photos accepted with ms. Captions, model releases and identification of subjects required. Buys one-time rights.

‡LAW PRACTICE MANAGEMENT—the Magazine of the Section of Law Practice Management of the American Bar Association, P.O. Box 11418, Columbia SC 29211-1418. Managing Editor/Art Director: Delmar L. Roberts. Editorial contact for freelance submissions: Mark A. Robertson, articles editor, Robertson & Williams, 3033 N.W. 63rd St., Suite 160, Oklahoma City OK 73116-3607. 10% freelance written. Magazine published 8 times/year for the practicing lawyer and law practice administrator. Estab. 1975. Circ. 20,883 (BPA). Rights purchased vary with author and material. Usually buys all rights. Byline given. Pays on publication. Publishes ms an average of 8 months after acceptance. Query. Sample copy for $8 plus $2 postage/handling (make check payable to American Bar Association). Free writer's guidelines. Returns rejected material in 3 months, if requested.

Nonfiction: "We assist the practicing lawyer in operating and managing his or her office by providing relevant articles and departments written in a readable and informative style. Editorial content is intended to aid the lawyer by conveying management methods that will allow him or her to provide legal services to clients in a prompt and efficient manner at reasonable cost. Typical topics of articles include fees and billing; client/lawyer relations; computer hardware/software; mergers; retirement/disability; marketing; compensation of partners and associates; legal data base research; and use of paralegals." No elementary articles on a whole field of technology, such as, "why you need computers in the law office." Typical articles pay $300-500.

Photos: Pays $50-60 for b&w photos purchased with mss; $50-100 for color; $400-500 for cover transparencies.

Tips: "We have a theme for each issue with two to three articles relating to the theme. We also publish thematic issues occasionally in which an entire issue is devoted to a single topic. The March and November/December issues each year are devoted to law practice technology."

THE LAWYERS WEEKLY, The Newspaper for the Legal Profession in Canada, Butterworth (Canada) Inc., 75 Clegg Rd., Markham, Ontario L6G IA1 Canada. (905)479-2665. Fax: (905)479-3758. E-mail: tlw@butterworths.ca. Editor: Jordan Furlong. 30% freelance written. "We will work with any *talented* writer of whatever experience level." Tabloid published 48 times/year covering Canadian law and legal affairs for a "sophisticated up-market readership of lawyers." Estab. 1983. Circ. 7,000/week; 22,500 once per month. Pays on publication. Publishes ms within 1 month after acceptance. Byline given. Offers 50% kill fee. Usually buys all rights. Submit seasonal material 6 weeks in advance. Accepts simultaneous submissions. Reports in 1 month. Sample copy for $8 (Canadian) with 9×12 SAE.

Nonfiction: Exposé, general interest (law), how-to (professional), humor, interview/profile (Canadian lawyers and judges), opinion, technical, news, case comments. "We try to wrap up the week's legal events and issues in a snappy informal package. We especially like news stories with photos or illustrations. We are always interested in feature or newsfeature articles involving current legal issues, but contributors should keep in mind our audience is trained in *English/Canadian common law*—not US law. That means most US-focused stories will generally not be accepted. No routine court reporting or fake news stories about commercial products. Buys 200-300 mss/year. Query or send complete ms. Length: 700-1,500 words. Payment negotiable in Canadian dollars. Sometimes pays the expenses of writers on assignment.

Photos: State availability of photos with query letter or ms. Reviews b&w and color contact sheets, negatives and 5×7 prints. Identification of subjects required. Buys one-time rights.

Fillers: Clippings, newsbreaks. Length: 50-200 words. Pays $10 minimum.

Tips: "Freelancers can best break into our publication by submitting news, features, and accounts of unusual or bizarre legal events. A frequent mistake made by writers is forgetting that our audience is intelligent and learned in law. They don't need the word 'plaintiff' explained to them." No unsolicited mss returned without SASE (or IRC to US or non-Canadian destinations). "No U.S. postage on SASEs, please!"

LEGAL ASSISTANT TODAY, James Publishing, Inc., 3520 Cadillac Ave., Suite E, Costa Mesa CA 92626. (714)755-5450. Fax: (714)751-5508. E-mail: editorlat@earthlink.net. Contact: Robert Sperber, managing editor. Executive Editor: Leanne Cazares. Bimonthly magazine "geared toward all legal assistants/paralegals throughout the country, regardless of specialty (litigation, corporate, bankruptcy, environmental law, etc.). How-to articles to help paralegals do their jobs more effectively are most in demand, as is career and salary information, and timely news and trends pieces." Estab. 1983. Circ. 17,000. **Pays on acceptance.** Publishes ms an average of 3 months after acceptance. Byline given. Usually buys all rights. Editorial lead time 10 weeks. Submit seasonal material 3 months in advance. Accepts simultaneous submissions. Reports in 1 month on queries; 2 months on mss. Sample copy and writer's guidelines free.

● *Legal Assistant Today* needs much more practitioner, "how-to" articles, noting that readers want articles on how to do their jobs better and faster.

Nonfiction: How-tos for paralegals, issues affecting the paralegal profession, profiles of new products for law office, opinion on legal topics (paralegal), personal experience of paralegals on the job. "Each issue has a theme: litigation support, research and discovery, corporate services. Since ours is a national magazine, we limit regional or local stories (except for the news)." Buys 36 mss/year. Query with published clips. Length: 2,000-4,000 words. (News, profiles shorter.) Pays $100 minimum. "Pay is negotiated per assignment; pay can be *substantially* more depending on experience and length and quality of manuscript." Pays expenses of writers on assignment.

Photos: Send photos with submission. Reviews prints. Negotiates payment individually. Identification of subjects required. Buys one-time rights.

Columns/Departments: "Last Laugh"—humorous piece on legal world; 1,000-1,200 words. Pays $75-100.

Fillers: Anecdotes, facts, newsbreaks and short humor "pertaining to paralegals." Pay negotiated.

Tips: "We prefer writers with previous experience working in a law office or writing for legal publications who have some understanding of what paralegals would find interesting or useful. Writers must understand our audience. There is some opportunity for investigative journalism as well as the usual features, profiles and news. How-to articles are especially desired. If you are a great writer who can interview effectively, and really dig into the topic to grab the readers' attention, we need you! We are open to ideas (queries), but also assign selected topics: News: brief, hard news topics regarding paralegals (or trend pieces on the profession); Profiles: paralegals who've worked on fascinating cases, etc.; Features: presents information to help paralegals advance in their careers."

THE NATIONAL LAW JOURNAL, New York Law Publishing Company, Dept. WM, 345 Park Ave. S., New York NY 10010. (212)741-8300. Fax: (212)696-1875. E-mail: nljeds@ljextra.com. Editor: Ben Gerson. Managing Editor: Patrick Oster. Contact: Adam Klein (articles), Anthony Paonita (news). 25-50% freelance written. Weekly newspaper for the legal profession. Estab. 1978. Circ. 40,000. Pays on publication. Publishes ms an average of 1 month after acceptance. Byline given. Kill fee varies. Buys all rights. Reports in 3 weeks on queries; 5 weeks on mss. Sample copy for $2 and 9×12 SAE with 2 first-class stamps.

Nonfiction: News, exposé (on subjects of interest to lawyers); interview/profile (of lawyers or judges of note); nonfiction book excerpts. "The bulk of our freelance articles are short, spot-news stories on local court decisions, lawsuits and lawyers; often, these come from legal affairs writers on local newspapers. Pays $25-150. We also buy longer pieces, 1,500-2,000-word profiles of prominent lawyers or legal trend stories. No articles without a legal angle, but we like to see good, idiomatic writing, mostly free of legal jargon." Buys 50-100 mss/year. Query with published clips or send complete ms. Pays $500. Sometimes pays the expenses of writers on assignment.

Columns/Departments: "For those who are not covering legal affairs on a regular basis, a good way into *The National Law Journal* is through our Exhibit A feature. Every week we print a sort of reporter's notebook on some proceeding currently underway in a courtroom or a short profile. The feature is stylistically and thematically quite flexible—we've even run pieces about lawyers' hangouts, mini-travelogues, and television reviews. It runs about 1,800 words and pays $250. We also use op-ed pieces on subjects of legal interest, many of which come from freelancers. Writers interested in doing an op-ed piece should query first. Pays $150. We have a legal section with an alternating topic each week (i.e. Banking Law, Legal Tech etc.). The section is written by contributing attorneys, usually from firms with multiple offices and typically not paid. Articles are submitted at 2,000 words."

THE PENNSYLVANIA LAWYER, Pennsylvania Bar Association, P.O. Box 186, 100 South St., Harrisburg PA 17108-0186. (717)238-6715. Fax: (717)238-7182. Executive Editor: Marcy Carey Mallory. Contact: Donald C. Sarvey, editorial director. Managing Editor: Sherri Kimmel. 25% freelance written. Prefers to work with published/established writers. Bimonthly magazine published as a service to the legal profession. Estab. 1978. Circ. 27,000. **Pays on acceptance.** Publishes ms an average of 6 months after acceptance. Byline given. Buys generally first rights, occasionally one-time rights or second serial (reprint) rights. Submit seasonal material 6 months in advance. Simultaneous submissions discouraged. Reports in 6 weeks. Sample copy and writer's guidelines for #10 SAE with 3 first-class stamps.
Nonfiction: General interest, how-to, interview/profile, new product, law-practice management, personal experience. All features *must* relate in some way to Pennsylvania lawyers or the practice of law in Pennsylvania. Buys 8-10 mss/ year. Query. Length: 600-1,500 words. Terms negotiable.

STUDENT LAWYER, American Bar Association, 750 N. Lake Shore Dr., Chicago IL 60611. (312)988-6048. Fax: (312)988-6281. E-mail: abastulawyer@abanet.org. Website: http://www.abanet.org/lsd. Editor: Stephanie Johnston. 99% freelance written. Works with a small number of new writers each year. Monthly magazine (September-May). Estab. 1972. Circ. 33,000. **Pays on acceptance.** Buys first serial and second serial (reprint) rights. Byline given. Submit seasonal material 4 months in advance. Reports in 6 weeks. Publishes ms an average of 3 months after acceptance. Sample copy for $4. Free writer's guidelines.
Nonfiction: Features cover legal education and careers and social/legal subjects. Also profiles (prominent persons in law-related fields); opinion (on matters of current legal interest); essays (on legal affairs); interviews. Query. Length: 3,000-4,000 words. Pays $450-900 for features. Covers some writer's expenses. *No* fiction, please!
Columns/Departments: Briefly (short stories on unusual and interesting developments in the law); Legal Aids (unusual approaches and programs connected to teaching law students and lawyers); Esq. (brief profiles of people in the law); End Note (short pieces on a variety of topics; can be humorous, educational, outrageous); Pro Se (opinion slot for authors to wax eloquent on legal issues); Et Al. (column for short features that fit none of the above categories). Buys 4-8 mss/issue. Length: 1,200-1,500 words. Pays $200-350.
Tips: "*Student Lawyer* actively seeks good new reporters and writers eager to prove themselves. Legal training definitely not essential; writing talent is. The writer should not think we are a law review; we are a feature magazine with the law (in the broadest sense) as the common denominator. Find issues of national scope and interest to write about; be aware of subjects the magazine—and other media—have already covered and propose something new. Write clearly and well. Expect to work with editor to polish manuscripts to perfection."

LEATHER GOODS

‡**SHOE RETAILING TODAY**, National Shoe Retailers Association, Suite 255, 9861 Broken Land Pkwy., Columbia MD 21046-1151. (410)381-8282. Fax: (410)381-1167. Editor: Carol Blank. Bimonthly newsletter covering footwear/ accessory industry. Estab. 1972. Circ. 4,000-5,000. Byline given. Buys one-time rights. Submit seasonal material 3 months in advance. Reports in 3 months. Call for sample copy.
Nonfiction: How-to, interview/profile, new product, technical. Pays $50-100 for assigned articles.
Photos: State availability of photos with submission. Offers no additional payment for photos accepted with ms. Buys one-time rights.

LIBRARY SCIENCE

Librarians read these journals for advice on promotion and management of libraries, library and book trade issues and information access and transfer. Be aware of current issues such as censorship, declines in funding and government information policies. For journals on the book trade see Book and Bookstore.

‡**CHURCH MEDIA LIBRARY MAGAZINE**, 127 Ninth Ave. N., Nashville TN 37234. (615)251-2752. Fax: (615)251-5607. Editor: Floyd B. Simpson. Quarterly magazine for adult leaders in church organizations and people interested in library work (especially church library work). Estab. 1891. Circ. 30,000. Pays on publication. Buys all, first serial and second serial (reprint) rights. Byline given. Reports in 1 month. Free sample copy and writer's guidelines.
Nonfiction: "We are primarily interested in articles that relate to the development of church libraries in providing media and services to support the total program of a church and in meeting individual needs. We publish how-to accounts

of services provided, promotional ideas, exciting things that have happened as a result of implementing an idea or service; human interest stories that are library-related; and media training (teaching and learning with a media mix). Articles should be practical for church library staffs and for teachers and other leaders of the church." Buys 10-15 mss/issue. Query. Pays 5½¢/word.

Reprints: Send photocopy of article or typed ms with rights for sale noted. Pays 75% of the amount paid for an original article.

LUMBER

SOUTHERN LUMBERMAN, Greysmith Publishing, Inc., P.O. Box 681629, Franklin TN 37068-1629. (615)791-1961. Fax: (615)790-6188. E-mail: grey@edge.net. Editor: Nanci P. Gregg. 20-30% freelance written. Works with a small number of new/unpublished writers each year. Monthly trade journal for the sawmill industry. Estab. 1881. Circ. 13,000. Pays on publication. Publishes ms an average of 3 months after acceptance. Byline given. Buys first North American rights. Submit seasonal material 6 months in advance. Reports in 1 month on queries; 2 months on mss. Sample copy for $3 and 9×12 SAE with 5 first-class stamps. Writer's guidelines for #10 SASE.

Nonfiction: How-to (sawmill better), interview/profile, equipment analysis, technical. Sawmill features. Buys 10-15 mss/year. Query with or without published clips, or send complete ms. Length: 500-2,000 words. Pays $150-350 for assigned articles; $100-250 for unsolicited articles. Sometimes pays expenses of writers on assignment.

Reprints: Send tearsheet or photocopy of article and information about when and where the article previously appeared. Pays 25-50% of amount paid for an original article.

Photos: Send photos with submission. Reviews transparencies, 4×5 color prints. Offers $10-25/photo. Captions and identification of subjects required. Always looking for news feature types of photos featuring forest products, industry materials or people.

Tips: "Like most, we appreciate a clearly-worded query listing merits of suggested story—what it will tell our readers they need/want to know. We want quotes, we want opinions to make others discuss the article. Best hint? Find an interesting sawmill operation owner and start asking questions—I bet a story idea develops. We need color photos too. Find a sawmill operator and ask questions—what's he doing bigger, better, different. We're interested in new facilities, better marketing, improved production."

MACHINERY AND METAL

AMERICAN METAL MARKET, Chilton Publications, A Unit of the Walt Disney Co., 825 Seventh Ave., New York NY 10019. (212)887-8550. Fax: (212)887-8520. E-mail: 74521.3225@compuserve.com. Website: http://www.amm.com. Editor: Michael G. Botta. Contact: Bob Manas, managing editor. 5% freelance written. Daily newspaper. "Bible of the metals industry. Covers production and trade of ferrous, nonferrous, and scrap metals. Read by senior executives. Focus on *breaking* news and price information." Estab. 1882. Circ. 11,000. Pays on publication per inch used in publication. Publishes ms an average of 1 month after acceptance. Byline given. Buys all rights and electronic rights. Editorial lead time 1 month. Reports in 2 weeks on queries. Sample copy and writer's guidelines free.

Nonfiction: Publishes roughly 45 special issues/year. Query. Pays $7/in.

Photos: Send photos with submission. Reviews 5×7 prints. Negotiates payment individually. Identification of subjects required. Buys all rights.

Tips: "Contact Bob Manas, managing editor, directly with story ideas. Primarily we are interested in purchasing *breaking* news items. Clear all stories with news desk (Manas) in advance. Unsolicited articles submitted at writer's risk. Contact Chuck Berry, senior editor, special issues, to discuss upcoming topics."

MANUFACTURING SYSTEMS, Chilton Publications, 191 S. Gary Ave., Carol Stream IL 60188. (630)665-1000. Fax: (630)462-2225. E-mail: kparker@chilton.com. Website: http://www.manufacturingsystems.com. Editor: Kevin Parker. Monthly magazine. "*Manufacturing Systems* is about the use of information technology to improve productivity in discrete manufacturing and process industries." Estab. 1984. Circ. 105,000. Pays on publication. Publishes ms an average of 3 months after acceptance. Byline sometime given. Buys first North American serial rights. Editorial lead time 2 months. Submit seasonal material 4 months in advance. Sample copy and writer's guidelines free.

Nonfiction: Interview/profile, new product, technical. Buys 9 mss/year. Send complete ms. Length: 1,200-2,000 words. Pays $1,200-1,500. Pays expenses of writers on assignment.

Photos: Send photos with submission. No additional payment for photos. Captions required.

MODERN MACHINE SHOP, 6915 Valley Ave., Cincinnati OH 45244-3029. (513)527-8800. Fax: (513)527-8801. E-mail: malbert@gardnerweb.com. Website: http://www.gardnerweb.com. Executive Editor: Mark Albert. 15% freelance written. Monthly. Estab. 1928. Pays 1 month following acceptance. Publishes ms an average of 6 months after acceptance. Byline given. Reports in 1 month. Call for sample copy. Writer's guidelines for #10 SASE.

Nonfiction: Uses only articles dealing with all phases of metalworking, manufacturing and machine shop work, with photos. "Ours is an industrial publication, and contributing authors should have a working knowledge of the metalworking industry. We regularly use contributions from machine shop owners, engineers, other technical experts, and suppliers to the metalworking industry. Almost all of these contributors pursue these projects to promote their own commercial interests." Buys 5 or fewer unsolicited mss/year. Query. Length: 1,000-3,500 words. Pays current market rate.

Tips: "Articles that review basic metalworking/machining processes, especially if they include a rethinking or re-evaluation of these processes in light of today's technical trends, are always welcome."

‡NICKEL, The Magazine Devoted to Nickel and Its Applications, Nickel Development Institute, 214 King St. W., Suite 510, Toronto, Ontario M5H 3S6 Canada. (416)591-7999. Fax: (416)591-7987. E-mail: jborland@nidi.org. Editor: James S. Borland. 30% freelance written. Quarterly magazine covering the metal nickel and all of its applications. Estab. 1985. Circ. 34,000. **Pays on acceptance**. Publishes ms an average of 3 months after acceptance. Byline given. Buys first rights. Accepts previously published submissions. Send tearsheet of article or typed ms with rights for sale noted and information about when and where the article previously appeared. For reprints, pays 50% of the amount paid for an original article. Reports in 1 month. Sample copies and writer's guidelines free from Nickel Development Institute Librarian.

Nonfiction: Semi-technical. Buys 20 mss/year. Query. Length: 50-1,000 words. Pays competitive rates, by negotiation. Sometimes pays expenses of writers on assignment.

Reprints: Send tearsheet of article or short story and information about when and where the article previously appeared.

Photos: State availability of photos with submission. Offers competitive rates by negotiation. Captions, model releases and identification of subjects required.

Tips: "Write to Librarian, Nickel Development Institute, for two free copies of *Nickel* and study them. Know something about nickel's 300,000 end uses. Be at home in writing semitechnical material. Then query the editor with a story idea in a one-page letter—no fax queries or phone calls. Complete magazine is open, except Technical Literature column."

‡ORNAMENTAL AND MISCELLANEOUS METAL FABRICATOR, National Ornamental And Miscellaneous Metals Association, 804-10 Main St., Suite E, Forest Park GA 30050. Fax: (404)363-2857. E-mail: nomma 2@aol.com. Editor: Todd Daniel. 20% freelance written. Bimonthly trade magazine "to inform, educate and inspire members of the ornamental and miscellaneous metalworking industry." Estab. 1959. Circ. 11,000. Pays when article actually received. Byline given. Buys one-time rights. Editorial lead time 2 months. Submit seasonal material 2 months in advance. Query for electronic submissions. Reports in 1 month on queries. Sample copy for 9×12 SAE and 6 first-class stamps. Writer's guidelines for $1.

Nonfiction: Book excerpts, essays, exposé, general interest, historical/nostalgic, how-to, humor, inspirational, interview/profile, new product, opinion, personal experience, photo feature, technical. Buys 5-7 mss/year. Query. Length: 1,200-2,000 words. Pays $200 for assigned articles; $50 minimum for unsolicited articles. Sometimes pays expenses of writers on assignment.

Reprints: Send typed ms with rights for sale noted (on disk). Pays 100% of amount paid for an original article.

Photos: State availability of photos with submission. Reviews contact sheets, negatives, transparencies, prints. May offer additional payment for photos accepted with ms. Model releases required.

Tips: "Make article relevant to our industry. Don't write in passive voice."

33 METALPRODUCING, Penton Publishing Inc., 1100 Superior Ave., Cleveland OH 44114. (216)696-7000. Fax: (216)931-9524. E-mail: 74512.3437@compuserve.com. Editor: Wallace D. Huskonen. 50% freelance written. Monthly magazine covering producing metal mill products from ore/scrap. "The mission of *33 Metalproducing* is to provide timely, authoritative and useful information on domestic and global trends in the metalproducing industry (SIC 33) for operating management engineers, and other management personnel." Estab. 1962. Circ. 18,000. Pays on publication. Publishes ms an average of 1 month after acceptance. Byline given. Editorial lead time 2 months. Reports in 2 weeks on queries; 1 month on mss. Sample copy and writer's guidelines free.

Nonfiction: Book excerpts, interview/profile, technical. Buys 20 mss/year. Query with published clips. Length: 750-3,000 words. Pays $100-1,000.

Photos: State availability of photos with submissions. Reviews contact sheets, negatives, transparencies, prints. Offers no additional payment for photos accepted with ms. Captions, identification of subjects required. Buys all rights.

Tips: "A freelance writer should demonstrate ability to use the language of metalproducing in producing features for *33MP*."

MAINTENANCE AND SAFETY

‡BREATHING AIR DIGEST, Sub-Aquatics, Inc., Publications Division, 8855 E. Broad St., Reynoldsburg OH 43068. (614)864-1235. Fax: (614)864-0071. Editor: Richard Lauer. Managing Editor: William McBride. 25% freelance written. Magazine published semiannually. "Our audience is primarily those involved with the production, handling, and use of high-pressure pure breathing air, particularly fire and safety departments, dive stores, etc. We are interested in articles of 500-1,500 words related to tips, experiences, technology and applications." Estab. 1989. Circ. 12,000. Pays on publication. Publishes ms an average of 1 year after acceptance. Byline given. Buys first and one-time rights. Editorial lead time 1 year. Accepts simultaneous submissions. Reports in 6 weeks on queries; 2 months on mss. Sample copy for 9×12 SAE and 2 first-class stamps.

Nonfiction: How-to, new product, personal experience, photo feature, technical. "We are not interested in brand-specific promotional material." Buys 3-6 mss/year. Send complete ms. Length: 500-1,500 words. Pays $50-70.
Photos: Send photos with submission. Reviews negatives, transparencies and prints. Offers no additional payment for photos accepted with ms. Buys one-time rights.
Columns/Departments: Pays $50-70.

BRUSHWARE, Centaur, Inc., Route 3, Box 165, Huddleston VA 24104. (540)297-1517. Editor: Leslie W. Neff. Publisher: Carl H. Wurzer. 100% freelance written. Bimonthly magazine covering brush, applicator, mop industry. "General management articles are what we look for. Writers who can do plant profiles of our industry." Estab. 1898. Circ. 1,800. **Pays on acceptance.** Publishes ms an average of 4 months after acceptance. Byline given. Offers 100% kill fee. Buys second serial (reprint) rights or makes work-for-hire assignments. Editorial lead time 4 months. Accepts simultaneous submissions.
Nonfiction: General interest, plant profiles with photos. Buys 20 mss/year. Query with or without published clips. Length: 800-2,000 words. Pays $500-1,000 for assigned articles; $25-100 for unsolicited articles. Pays expenses of writers on assignment.
Reprints: Accepts previously published submissions.
Photos: State availability of photos with submissions. Reviews 4×6 prints. Negotiates payment individually. Captions, identification of subjects required. Buys one-time rights.

‡CANADIAN OCCUPATIONAL SAFETY, Clifford/Elliot Ltd., 3228 S. Service Rd., 2nd Floor, West Wing, Burlington, Ontario L7N 3H8 Canada. (905)634-2100. Fax: (905)634-2238. E-mail: jr@industrialsourcebook.com. Website: http://www.industrialsourcebook.com. Editor: Jackie Roth. Contact: Matt Green, assistant editor. 40% freelance written. Bimonthly magazine. "We want informative articles dealing with issues that relate to occupational health and safety." Estab. 1989. Circ. 12,000. Pays on publication. Publishes ms an average of 3 months after acceptance. Byline given. Buys one-time rights. Editorial lead time 4 months. Submit seasonal material 4 months in advance. Accepts simultaneous and previously published submissions. Reports in 3 weeks on queries; 1 month on mss. Sample copy and writer's guidelines free.
Nonfiction: How-to, interview/profile. Buys 6-8 mss/year. Query with published clips. Length: 750-3,500 words. Pays $400-1,000 (Canadian). Sometimes pays expenses of writers on assignment.
Photos: State availability of photos with submission. Reviews transparencies. Negotiates payment individually. Captions required. Buys one-time rights.
Tips: "There are facts about COS on our company website. There is also plenty of h&s info on the Internet. Finally, it doesn't hurt to call us directly with possible ideas."

CLEANING AND MAINTENANCE MANAGEMENT, The Magazine for Today's Building Cleaning Maintenance/Housekeeping Executive, National Trade Publications, Inc., 13 Century Hill Dr., Latham NY 12110-2197. (518)783-1281. Fax: (518)783-1386. E-mail: anne@cleannet.com. Website: http://cleannet.com. Managing Editor: Dominic Tom. Monthly national trade magazine covering building cleaning maintenance/housekeeping operations in larger institutions such as hotels, schools, hospitals, office buildings, industrial plants, recreational and religious buildings, shopping centers, airports, etc. Articles must be aimed at managers of on-site building/facility cleaning staffs or owners/managers of contract cleaning companies. Estab. 1963. Circ. 42,000. Pays on publication, with invoice. Byline given. Buys all rights. Reports in 2 weeks. Sample copy and writer's guidelines for 9×12 SAE with 8 first-class stamps.
Nonfiction: Articles on: discussions of facility-wide systems for custodial operations/cleaning tasks; systemwide analysis of custodial task cost-effectiveness and staffing levels; the organization of cleaning tasks on an institution-wide basis; recruitment, training, motivation and supervision of building cleaning employees; the cleaning of buildings or facilities of unusual size, type, design, construction or notoriety; interesting case studies; or advice for the successful operation of a contract cleaning business. Buys 6-12 mss/year. Length: 500-1,500 words. Pays $50-200. Please query.
Photos: State availability of photos. Prefer color or b&w prints, rates negotiable. Captions, model releases and identification of subjects required.
Tips: Chances of acceptance are directly proportional to the article's relevance to the professional, on-the-job needs and interests of facility/custodial managers or contract building cleaners.

CLEANING BUSINESS, P.O. Box 1273, Seattle WA 98111. (206)622-4241. Fax: (206)622-6876. E-mail: wgriffin@seanet.com. Website: http://www.cleaningconsultants.com. Publisher: William R. Griffin. Associate Editor: Jim Saunders. 80% freelance written. Quarterly magazine. "We cater to those who are self-employed in any facet of the cleaning and maintenance industry and seek to be top professionals in their field. *Cleaning Business* is published for self-employed cleaning professionals, specifically carpet, upholstery and drapery cleaners; janitorial and maid services; window washers; odor, water and fire damage restoration contractors. Our readership is small but select. We seek concise, factual articles, realistic but definitely upbeat." Circ. 6,000. Pays 1 month after publication. Publishes ms an average of 3 months after acceptance. Byline given. Buys first serial, second serial (reprint) and all rights or makes work-for-hire assignments. Submit seasonal material 6 months in advance. Reports in 3 months. Sample copy for $3 and 8×10 SAE with 3 first-class stamps. Writer's guidelines for #10 SASE.
Nonfiction: Exposé (safety/health business practices); how-to (on cleaning, maintenance, small business management); humor (clean jokes, cartoons); interview/profile; new product (must be unusual to rate full article—mostly obtained from manufacturers); opinion; personal experience; technical. Special issues: "What's New?" (February). No "wordy

articles written off the top of the head, obviously without research, and needing more editing time than was spent on writing." Buys 40 mss/year. Query with or without published clips. Length: 500-3,000 words. Pays $5-80. ("Pay depends on amount of work, research and polishing put into article much more than on length.") Pays expenses of writers on assignment with prior approval only.

Photos: State availability of photos or send photos with ms. Pays $5-25 for "smallish" b&w prints. Captions, model release and identification of subjects required. Buys one-time rights and reprint rights. "Magazine size is 8½×11—photos need to be proportionate. Also seeks full-color photos of relevant subjects for cover."

Columns/Departments: "Ten regular columnists now sell four columns per year to us. We are interested in adding Safety & Health and Fire Restoration columns (related to cleaning and maintenance industry). We are also open to other suggestions—send query." Buys 36 columns/year; department information obtained at no cost. Query with or without published clips. Length: 500-1,500 words. Pays $15-85.

Fillers: Jokes, gags, anecdotes, short humor, newsbreaks, cartoons. Buys 40/year. Length: 3-200 words. Pays $1-20.

Tips: "We are constantly seeking quality freelancers from all parts of the country. A freelancer can best break in to our publication with fairly technical articles on how to do specific cleaning/maintenance jobs; interviews with top professionals covering this and how they manage their business; and personal experience. Our readers demand concise, accurate information. Don't ramble. Write only about what you know and/or have researched. Editors don't have time to rewrite your rough draft. Organize and polish before submitting."

INTERACTIVE TECHNOLOGIES, INC., 2266 N. Second St., North St. Paul MN 55109. (612)773-4696. Fax: (612)779-4879. E-mail: iti20@skypoint.com. Website: www.securitypro.com. Senior Editor: Joe Moses. Monthly magazines covering "applications of wireless security systems, written for dealers and installers." **Pays on acceptance.** Publishes ms an average of 4 months after acceptance. Byline sometimes given. Buys first rights or makes work-for-hire assignments. Editorial lead time varies. Submit seasonal material 6 months in advance. Writer's guidelines for #10 SASE.

● This listing differs from others. Interactive Technologies, Inc., is a wireless security company seeking articles on their products which they then place in appropriate trade journals. "We pay for the article ($300-400), and we worry about getting it published."

Nonfiction: How-to, interview/profile, new product, photo feature, technical. No unsolicited mss. No non-wireless installations. Buys 8-12 mss/year. Query with published clips. Length: 1,200-2,500 words. Pays $300-400. Sometimes pays expenses of writers on assignment.

Photos: State availability of photos with submission. Reviews 4×6 prints. Negotiates payment individually. Model releases, identification of subjects required. Buys one-time rights.

Tips: "We're looking for technical articles and profiles of dealers who install our wireless security products. Go through the Yellow Pages and find an ITI security dealer and tell him/her you want to write a story on a noteworthy wireless installation they've done. Then send a query."

PEST CONTROL MAGAZINE, 7500 Old Oak Blvd., Cleveland OH 44130. (216)243-8100. Fax: (216)891-2675. E-mail: pestcon@en.com. Website: http://www2.c4systm.com/PestControl. Editor: Jerry Mix. Monthly magazine for professional pest control operators and sanitarians. Estab. 1933. Circ. 20,000. Buys all rights. Buys 12 mss/year. Pays on publication. Submit seasonal material 2 months in advance. Reports in 1 month. Query or submit complete ms.

Nonfiction: Business tips, unique control situations, personal experience (stories about pest control operations and their problems). Must have trade or business orientation. No general information type of articles desired. Buys 3 unsolicited mss/year. Length: 1,000 words. Pays $150-500 minimum.

Columns/Departments: Regular columns use material oriented to this profession. Length: 2,000 words.

Photos: No additional payment for photos used with mss. Pays $50-500 for 8×10 color or transparencies.

‡SAFETY & HEALTH, National Safety Council, 1121 Apring Lake Dr., Itasca IL 60143. Fax: (630)775-2285. Website: http:www.nsc.org/pubs/sh.htm. Contact: Carrie Fearn, editor. 90% freelance written. Monthly association magazine. "Our audience is safety and health professionals. *Safety & Health* is the flagship publication of the National Safety Council, reporting on safety, health and environmental issues that affect the workplace." Circ. 40,000. Pays on publication. Publishes ms an average of 3 months after acceptance. Byline given. Offers 25% kill fee. Buys second serial (reprint) rights. Editorial lead time 3 months.

Nonfiction: How-to, interview/profile, technical. Buys 72 mss/year. Query with published clips. Length: 1,500-2,000 words. Pays $600-1,200.

Columns/Departments: Query with published clips. Payment varies.

SAFETY COMPLIANCE LETTER, with OSHA Highlights, Bureau of Business Practice, 24 Rope Ferry Rd., Waterford CT 06386. (860)442-4365. Fax: (800)437-3150. E-mail: michele_rubin@prenhall.com. Website: http://www.bbpnews.com. Editor: Michele Rubin. Publisher: James O'Shea. 75% freelance written. Bimonthly newsletter covering occupational safety and health. Publishes interview-based how-to and success stories for personnel in charge of safety and health in manufacturing/industrial environments. Circ. 15,000. Pays on acceptance after editing. Publishes ms an average of 3 months after acceptance. No byline given. Buys all rights. Reports in 1 month. Sample copy and writer's guidelines for SASE.

Nonfiction: How-to comply with particular occupational safety/health standards and changes in OSHA regulations. Only accepts articles that are based on an interview with a safety manager, safety consultant, occupational physician, or OSHA expert. Buys 48 mss/year. Query. Length: 750-1,200 words. Pays 15-20¢/word.

SECURITY SALES, Management Resource for the Professional Installing Dealer, Bobit Publishing, 2512 Artesia Blvd., Redondo Beach CA 90278-3296. (310)376-8788. Fax: (310)376-9043. E-mail: bobitpub@aol.com. Editor/Publisher: Jason Knott. Senior Editor: Vi Pangelinan. Contact: Amy Jones, executive editor. 5% freelance written. Monthly magazine "covers technology, management and marketing designed to help installing security dealers improve their businesses. Closed-circuit TV, burglary and fire equipment, integrated systems and access control systems are main topics." Estab. 1979. Circ. 23,940. Pays on publication. Publishes ms an average of 6 months after acceptance. Byline sometimes given. Buys all rights or one-time rights. Editorial lead time 2 months. Submit seasonal material 4 months in advance. Accepts simultaneous submissions. Sample copy free.
Nonfiction: How-to, technical. "No generic business operations articles. Submissions must be specific to security and contain interviews with installing dealers." Buys 6-10 mss/year. Send complete ms. Length: 800-1,500 words. Pays $50 minimum.
Reprints: Send typed ms with rights for sale noted and information about when and where the article previously appeared.
Photos: Send photos with submission. Reviews prints. Offers no additional payment for photos accepted with ms. Captions, model releases, identification of subjects required.
Tips: "Case studies of specific security installations with photos and diagrams are needed. Interview dealers who installed system and ask how they solved specific problems, why they chose certain equipment, cost of job, etc."

MANAGEMENT AND SUPERVISION

This category includes trade journals for middle management business and industrial managers, including supervisors and office managers. Journals for business executives and owners are classified under Business Management. Those for industrial plant managers are listed in Industrial Operations.

HR BRIEFING, Bureau of Business Practice, 24 Rope Ferry Rd., Waterford CT 06386. (860)442-4365, ext. 275. Editor: Valerie Bolden-Barrett. 75% freelance written. Eager to work with new/unpublished writers. Semimonthly newsletter emphasizing all aspects of personnel practices for HR managers in all types and sizes of companies, both white collar and industrial. **Pays on acceptance.** Publishes ms an average of 5 months after acceptance. Buys all rights. Submit seasonal material 4 months in advance. Reports in 1 month. Sample copy and writer's guidelines for 10×13 SAE with 2 first class stamps.
Nonfiction: Interviews with personnel managers or human resource professionals on topics of current interest in the personnel field. Buys 30 mss/year. Query with brief, specific outline. Length: 800-1,500 words.
Tips: "We're looking for concrete, practical material on how to solve problems. We're providing information about trends and developments in the field. We don't want filler copy. It's very easy to break in. Include your phone number with your query so we can discuss the topic. Send for guidelines first, though, so we can have a coherent conversation."

HUMAN RESOURCE EXECUTIVE, LRP Publications Magazine Group, 747 Dresher Rd., P.O. Box 980, Dept. 500, Dresher PA 19044. (215)784-0910. Fax: (215)784-0870. E-mail: dshadovitz@lrp.com. Website: http://www.workindex.com. Editor: David Shadovitz. 30% freelance written. "Monthly magazine serving the information needs of chief human resource professionals/executives in companies, government agencies and nonprofit institutions with 500 or more employees." Estab. 1987. Circ. 45,000. **Pays on acceptance.** Publishes ms an average of 2 months after acceptance. Byline given. Offers 50% kill fee on assigned stories. Buys first and all rights including reprint rights. Reports in 1 month. Sample copy for 10×13 SAE with 2 first-class stamps. Writer's guidelines for #10 SAE with 1 first-class stamp.
Nonfiction: Book excerpts, interview/profile. Buys 16 mss/year. Query with published clips. Length: 1,700-2,000 words. Pays $200-850. Sometimes pays expenses of writers on assignment.
Photos: State availability of photos with submission. Reviews contact sheets. Offers no additional payment for photos accepted with ms. Identification of subjects required. Buys first and repeat rights.

‡INCENTIVE, Managing & Marketing Through Motivation, Bill Communications, 355 Park Ave. S., New York NY 10010. (212)592-6458. Fax: (212)592-6459. E-mail: jjincent@aol.com. Editor: Jennifer Juergens. Contact: Joan Steinauer, managing editor. 20% freelance written. Monthly magazine concerning "motivating through the use of merchandise and travel, managing employees and motivating workers." Estab. 1891. Circ. 40,000. Pays on publication. Publishes ms an average of 3 months after acceptance. Byline given. Offers $100 kill fee. Buys one-time rights. Editorial lead time 3 months. Submit seasonal material 3 months in advance. Accepts simultaneous submissions. Reports in 1 month. Sample copy free.
Nonfiction: Book excerpts, how-to (motivate), inspirational, interview/profile, new product, travel. Buys 15 mss/year. Query with published clips. Length: 500-1,500 words. Pays $400-2,000. Sometimes pays the expenses of writers on assignment.
Photos: State availability of photos with submission.
Columns/Departments: Query. Pays $100-500.

MANAGE, 2210 Arbor Blvd., Dayton OH 45439. (513)294-0421. Fax: (513)294-2374. Website: http://www.cris.com/~nma1/index.html. Editor-in-Chief: Douglas E. Shaw. 60% freelance written. Works with a small number of new/unpublished writers each year. Quarterly magazine for first-line and middle management and scientific/technical managers. Estab. 1925. Circ. 40,000. **Pays on acceptance.** Publishes ms an average of 6 months after acceptance. Buys North American magazine rights with reprint privileges; book rights remain with the author. Reports in 3 months. Sample copy and writer's guidelines for 9×12 SAE with 3 first-class stamps.

Nonfiction: "All material published by *Manage* is in some way management-oriented. Most articles concern one or more of the following categories: communications, executive abilities, human relations, job status, leadership, motivation and productivity and professionalism. Articles should be specific and tell the manager how to apply the information to his job immediately. Be sure to include pertinent examples, and back up statements with facts. *Manage* does not want essays or academic reports, but interesting, well-written and practical articles for and about management." Buys 6 mss/issue. Phone queries OK. Submit complete ms. Length: 600-1,000 words. Pays 5¢/word.

Tips: "Keep current on management subjects; submit timely work. Include word count on first page of manuscript."

‡MANAGEMENT REVIEW, The American Management Association Magazine, American Management Association, 1601 Broadway, New York NY 10019-7420. Fax: (212)903-8083. E-mail: mgmtreview@amanet.org. Website: http://www.amanet.org. Editor: Martha H. Peak. Monthly magazine covering "Hands On" management issues for top/middle managers. "*Management Review* is the global membership magazine of the American Management Association, dedicated to broadening managers' know-how through insightful reporting of management trends and tips on how to manage more effectively." Estab. 1923. Circ. 75,000. Pays on publication. Byline given. Buys first worldwide rights. Editorial lead time 3-4 months. Submit seasonal material 3-4 months in advance. Reports in 4-5 weeks on queries. Sample copy for $5. Writer's guidelines free.

Nonfiction: Business stories only. Buys 24 mss/year. Query. Length: 1,200-2,000 words.

Photos: State availability of photos with submission. Captions and identification of subjects required.

Tips: "Submissions in writing ONLY. No fax. No cold calls."

‡MOBILITY, Employee Relocation Council, 1720 N St., NW, Washington DC 20036. (202)857-0857. Fax: (202)659-8631. E-mail: mobility@erc.org. Website: http://www.erc.org. Editor: Jerry Holloman. Contact: Christine M. Wilson, managing editor. 10% freelance written. Monthly magazine covering corporate employee relocation, human resources, real estate, technology. "*Mobility* is published by an association of corporations that transfer their own employees and anyone providing services to those moving families or administrators. Diverse industry groups include corporate representatives, brokers, appraisers, household goods companies, etc." Estab. 1980. Circ. 12,000. **Pays on acceptance.** Publishes ms an average of 2 months after acceptance. Byline given. Offers 25% kill fee. Buys first North American serial rights. Editorial lead time 2 months. Submit seasonal material 3 months in advance. Reports as soon as possible. Sample copy for $5. Writer's guidelines free.

Nonfiction: Interview/profile, relocation, human resources, real estate, technology. Special issues: Human Resources (March); Technology (June). Buys 4-6 mss/year. Query with published clips. Length: 2,000-3,000 words. Pays $1,000. Sometimes pays expenses of writers on assignment.

Reprints: Send photocopy of article or short story and information about when and where the article previously appeared.

Photos: Send photos with submission. Reviews transparencies. Identification of subjects required. Buys one-time rights.

Tips: "Writers may wish to view website http://www.erc.org. Be familiar with related topic areas."

SALES MANAGER'S BULLETIN, The Bureau of Business Practice, 24 Rope Ferry Rd., Waterford CT 06386-0001. Fax: (860)442-4365. Editor: Paulette S. Kitchens. 33% freelance written. Prefers to work with published/established writers. Semimonthly newsletter for sales managers and salespeople interested in getting into sales management. Estab. 1917. **Pays on acceptance.** Publishes ms an average of 6 months after acceptance. Submit seasonal material 6 months in advance. Original interview-based material only. No byline. Buys all rights. Reports in 1 month. Sample copy and writer's guidelines for SAE with 2 first-class stamps.

Nonfiction: How-to (motivate salespeople, cut costs, create territories, etc.); interview (with working sales managers who use innovative techniques); technical (marketing stories based on interviews with experts). "No articles on territory management, saving fuel in the field, or public speaking skills. Break into this publication by reading the guidelines and sample issue. Follow the directions closely and chances for acceptance go up dramatically. One easy way to start is with an interview article ('Here's what sales executives have to say about . . .'). Query is vital to acceptance. Send a simple note explaining briefly the subject matter, the interviewees, slant, length, and date of expected completion, accompanied by a SASE." No unqueried mss. Length: 800-1,000 words. Pays 12-15¢/word.

Tips: "Freelancers should always request samples and writer's guidelines, accompanied by SASE. Requests without SASE are discarded immediately. Examine the sample, and don't try to improve on our style. Write as we write. Don't 'jump around' from point to point and don't submit articles that are too chatty and with not enough real information. The more time a writer can save the editors, the greater his or her chance of a sale and repeated sales, when queries may no longer be necessary. We will focus more on selling more product, meeting intense competition, customer relations/partnerships, and sales forecasting."

SECURITY MANAGEMENT BULLETIN: Protecting People, Property & Assets, Bureau of Business Practice, 24 Rope Ferry Rd., Waterford CT 06386. Fax: (860)437-3150. E-mail: alex_vaughn@prenhall.com. Website: http://

www.bbpnews.com. Editor: Alex Vaughn. 75% freelance written. Eager to work with new/unpublished writers. Biweekly newsletter "slanted toward security directors, primarily industrial, retail and service businesses, but others as well." Circ. 3,000. Pays when article assigned to future issue. Buys all rights. Free sample copy and writer's guidelines.

Nonfiction: Interview (with security professionals only). "Articles should be tight and specific. They should deal with new security techniques or new twists on old ones." Buys 2-5 mss/issue. Query. Phone queries OK. Length: 750-1,000 words. Pays 15¢/word and up.

SUPERVISION, 320 Valley, Burlington IA 52601-5513. Fax: (319)752-3421. Publisher: Michael S. Darnall. Editor: Barbara Boeding. 95% freelance written. Monthly magazine for first-line foremen, supervisors and office managers. Estab. 1939. Circ. 2,620. Pays on publication. Publishes ms an average of 6 months after acceptance. Buys all rights. Reports in 1 month. Sample copy and writer's guidelines for 9×12 SAE with 4 first-class stamps; mention *Writer's Market* in request.

Nonfiction: How-to (cope with supervisory problems, discipline, absenteeism, safety, productivity, goal setting, etc.); personal experience (unusual success story of foreman or supervisor). No sexist material written from only a male viewpoint. Include biography and/or byline with ms submissions. Author photos requested. Buys 12 mss/issue. Query. Length: 1,500-1,800 words. Pays 4¢/word.

Tips: "Following AP stylebook would be helpful." Uses no advertising. Send correspondence to Editor.

TRAINING MAGAZINE, The Human Side of Business, Lakewood Publications, 50 S. Ninth St., Minneapolis MN 55402. (612)333-0471. Fax: (612)333-6526. E-mail: training@lakewoodpub.com. Website: www.trainingsupersite.com. Editor: Jack Gordon. Contact: Chris Lee, managing editor. 10% freelance written. Monthly magazine. "Our core readers are managers and professionals who specialize in employee training and development (e.g., corporate training directors, VP-human resource development, etc.). We have a large secondary readership among managers of all sorts who are concerned with improving human performance in their organizations. We take a businesslike approach to training and employee education." Estab. 1964. Circ. 56,000. **Pays on acceptance.** Publishes ms an average of 3 months after acceptance. Byline given. Buys first North American serial and second serial (reprint) rights. Reports in 2 weeks on queries; 2 months on mss. Sample copy for 10×13 SAE with 4 first-class stamps. Writer's guidelines for #10 SASE.

Nonfiction: Essays; exposé; how-to (on training, management, sales, productivity improvement, etc.); humor; interview/profile; new product; opinion; photo feature; technical (use of audiovisual aids, computers, etc.). "No puff, no 'testimonials' or disguised ads in any form." Buys 15 mss/year. Query. Length: 200-3,000 words. Pays $50-900.

Photos: State availability of photos with submission. Reviews transparencies, prints. Negotiates payment individually. Identification of subjects required. Buys first rights and limited reprint rights.

Columns/Departments: Training Today (news briefs, how-to tips, reports on pertinent research, trend analysis, etc.), 400 words. Buys 12 mss/year. Query. Pays $50-125.

Tips: "Send an intriguing query that demonstrates writing ability, as well as some insight into the topic you propose to cover. Then be willing to submit the piece on spec."

MARINE AND MARITIME INDUSTRIES

MARINE MECHANIC, Middle Coast Publishing, Inc., P.O. Box 2522, Iowa City IA 52244. (319)339-1877. Editor: Tim Banse. 50% freelance written. Bimonthly magazine covering marine engine repair. Estab. 1995. Circ. 10,000. Pays on publication. Byline given. Editorial lead time 6 months.

Nonfiction: How-to, new product, technical. Buys 10 mss/year. Query with published clips. Length: 500-2,000 words. Pays $50-1,000. Sometimes pays expenses of writers on assignment.

Reprints: Accepts previously published submissions.

Photos: State availability of photos with submission. Negotiates payment individually.

Columns/Departments: Pays $100-500.

OCEAN NAVIGATOR, Marine Navigation & Ocean Voyaging, Navigator Publishing Corp., 18 Danforth St., Portland ME 04101. (207)772-2466. Fax: (207)772-2879. E-mail: 76452.3245@compuserve.com. Editor: Tim Queeney. Bimonthly magazine covering marine navigation and ocean voyaging. Estab. 1985. Circ. 40,600. Pays on publication. Byline given. Accepts simultaneous submissions. Writer's guidelines available on request.

Nonfiction: How-to, personal experience (voyaging stories), technical. "Send outline or send complete ms." Pays 15¢/word.

Reprints: Send typed ms or photocopy of article or short story with rights for sale noted and information about when and where the article previously appeared.

Photos: Send photos with submission. Offers $50-75/photo; $400 for cover photo.

‡PROFESSIONAL MARINER, Journal of Professional Seamanship, Navigator Publishing, 18 Danforth St., Portland ME 04101. (207)772-2466. Fax: (207)772-2879. Editor: Evan True. 50% freelance written. Bimonthly magazine covering professional seamanship and maritime industry news. Estab. 1993. Circ. 22,000. Pays on publication. Byline given. Buys all rights. Editorial lead time 3 months. Accepts simultaneous submissions. Sample copy and writer's guidelines free.

Nonfiction: For professional mariners on vessels and ashore. Seeks submissions on industry regulations, towing, piloting, technology, engineering, business maritime casualties and feature stories about the maritime industry. Does accept "sea stories" and personal professional experiences as correspondence pieces. Buys 15 mss/year. Query. Length varies: short clips to long profiles/features. Pays 15¢/word. Sometimes pays expenses of writers on assignment.
Photos: Send photos and photo captions with submission. Reviews slides and prints. Negotiates payment individually. Identification of subjects required. Buys one-time rights.

MEDICAL

Through these journals physicians, therapists and mental health professionals learn how other professionals help their patients and manage their medical practices. Publications for nurses, laboratory technicians and other medical personnel are listed in the Hospitals, Nursing and Nursing Home section. Publications for drug store managers and drug wholesalers and retailers, as well as hospital equipment suppliers, are listed with Drugs, Health Care and Medical Products. Publications for consumers that report trends in the medical field are found in the Consumer Health and Fitness categories.

CARDIOLOGY WORLD NEWS, MPE Communications, Inc, 2338 Immokalee Rd., #168, Naples FL 34110. (941)513-9142. Fax: (941)513-9143. Editor: Karla Wheeler. 75% freelance written. Prefers to work with published/established writers. Quarterly magazine. "We need short news articles *for cardiologists* on any aspect of our field—diagnosis, treatment, risk factors, etc." Estab. 1985. **Pays on acceptance.** Publishes ms an average of 2 months after acceptance. Byline given "for special reports and feature-length articles." Offers 20% kill fee. Buys first North American serial rights. Reports in 2 months. Sample copy for $1. Free writer's guidelines with #10 SASE.
Nonfiction: New product and technical (clinical). No fiction, fillers, profiles of doctors or poetry. Query with published clips. Length: 250-1,200 words. Pays $50-300; $50/column for news articles. Pays expenses of writers on assignment.
Photos: State availability of photos with query. Pays $50/photo. Rough captions, model release and identification of subjects required. Buys one-time rights.
Tips: "Submit written news articles of 250-500 words on speculation with basic source material (not interview notes) for fact-checking. We demand clinical or writing expertise for full-length feature. Clinical cardiology conventions/symposia are the best source of news and feature articles."

EMERGENCY, The Journal of Emergency Services, 2512 Artesia Blvd., Redondo Beach CA 90278. (310)376-8788. Fax: (310)798-4598. E-mail: emg@bobit.com. Editor: Vari MacNeil. 100% freelance written. Works with a small number of new/unpublished writers each year. Monthly magazine. "Our readership is primarily composed of EMTs, paramedics and other EMS personnel. We prefer a professional, semi-technical approach to prehospital subjects." Estab. 1969. Circ. 30,000. Pays on publication. Publishes ms an average of 4 months after acceptance. Byline given. Buys all rights (revert to author after 3 months). Submit seasonal material 6 months in advance. Reports in 2 months. Sample copy for $3. Writer's guidelines for #10 SASE.
Nonfiction: Semi-technical how-to (on treating prehospital emergency patients), interview/profile, new techniques, opinion, photo feature. "We do not publish cartoons, term papers, product promotions disguised as articles or overly technical manuscripts." Buys 60 mss/year. Query with published clips. Length 1,500-3,000 words. Pays $100-400.
Photos: If possible, send photos with submission. Reviews color transparencies and b&w prints. Photos accepted with mss increase payment. Offers $30/photo without ms; $100 for cover photos. Captions and identification of subjects required. All medics pictured must be using universal precautions (gloves, etc.).
Columns/Departments: Open Forum (opinion page for EMS professionals), 750-800 words; Skills Primer (basic skills, how-to, with photos), 1,000-2,000 words; Rescue Call (covers a specific rescue or technique); Drug Watch (focuses on one particular drug a month). Buys 10 mss/year. Query first. Pays $50-300.
Fillers: Facts, newsbreaks. Buys 10/year. Length: 500 words maximum. Pays $0-75.
Tips: "Writing style for features and departments should be knowledgeable and lively with a clear theme or story line to maintain reader interest and enhance comprehension. The biggest problem we encounter is dull, lifeless term-paper-style writing with nothing to pique reader interest. Keep in mind we are not a textbook, but all technical articles must be well referenced with footnotes within the text. We follow AP style. Accompanying photos are a plus. We appreciate a short, one-paragraph biography on the author."

ALWAYS ENCLOSE a self-addressed, stamped envelope (SASE) with all your queries and correspondence.

‡**FIRE-RESCUE MAGAZINE**, (formerly *Rescue*), Jems Communications, P.O. Box 2789, Carlsbad CA 92018-2789. (619)431-9797. Fax: (619)431-8176. Managing Editor: Jeff Berend. 60% freelance written. Monthly magazine covering both the technical side and excitement of being a firefighter and rescuer. Estab. 1988. Circ. 50,000. Pays on publication. Byline given. Buys first North American and one-time rights. Submit seasonal material 6 months in advance. Query for electronic submissions (prefers diskette to accompany ms). Reports in 3 weeks on queries; 2 months on mss. Sample copy and writer's guidelines for 9×12 SAE with 5 first-class stamps.

Nonfiction: How-to, incident review/report, new product, opinion, photo feature, technical. Special issues: Fire suppression, incident command, vehicle extrication, rescue training, mass-casualty incidents, water rescue/major issues facing the fire service. Buys 15-20 mss/year. Query first with published clips or send complete ms. Length: 1,000-3,000 words. Pays $125-250. Sometimes pays the expenses of writers on assignment.

Photos: Send photos with submission. Reviews contact sheets, negatives, 2×2 and 35mm transparencies and 5×7 prints. Offers $35-125/photo. Buys one-time rights.

Tips: "Read our magazine, spend some time with a fire department. We focus on all aspects of fire and rescue. Emphasis on techniques and new technology, with color photos as support."

HEALTHPLAN, American Association of Health Plans, (formerly *HMO*), 1129 20th St. NW, Suite 600, Washington DC 20036. (202)778-3250. Fax: (202)331-7487. E-mail: jcook@aahp.org. Website: http://www.aahp.org. Editor: Susan Pisano. Contact: Diana Madden, managing editor. 75% freelance written. Bimonthly magazine. "*Healthplan* is geared toward senior administrative and medical managers in HMOs, PPOs, and similar health plans. Articles must ask 'why' and 'how' and answer with examples. Articles should inform and generate interest and discussion about topics on anything from patient care to regulatory issues." Estab. 1990. Circ. 7,000. Pays within 30 days of acceptance of article in final form. Publishes ms an average of 2 months after acceptance. Byline given. Offers 30% kill fee. Buys all rights. Editorial lead time 2 months. Submit seasonal material 2 months in advance. Accepts simultaneous submissions. Reports in 1 month on queries. Sample copy and writer's guidelines free.

Nonfiction: How-to (how industry professionals can better operate their health plans), opinion. "We do not accept stories that promote products." Buys 20 mss/year. Query. Length: 1,800-2,500 words. Pays 50¢/word minimum. Pays phone expenses of writers on assignment.

Photos: State availability of photos with submission. Reviews contact sheets. Offers no additional payment for photos accepted with ms. Buys all rights.

Columns/Departments: Information Technology (case study or how-to), 1,800 words; Chronic Care (case studies), 1,800 words; Preventive Care (case study or discussion of public health), 1,800 words; The Market (market niches for HMOs—with examples), 1,800 words. Buys 6 mss/year. Query with published clips. Pays 35-50¢/word.

Tips: "Follow the current health care debate. Look for health plan success stories in your community; we like to include case studies on everything from patient care to provider relations to regulatory issues so that our readers can learn from their colleagues. Our readers are members of our trade association and look for advice and news. Topics relating to the quality of health plans are the ones most frequently assigned to writers, whether a feature or department."

JEMS, The Journal of Emergency Medical Services, Jems Communications, Suite 200, 1947 Camino Vida Roble, Carlsbad CA 92008-2789. (619)431-9797. Fax: (619)431-8176. E-mail: lauren.ostrow@mosby.com. Website: http://www.jems.com. Executive Editor: Keith Griffiths. Contact: Lauren Simon Ostrow, senior editor. 80% freelance written. Monthly magazine directed to personnel who serve the pre-hospital emergency medicine industry: paramedics, EMTs, emergency physicians and nurses, administrators, EMS consultants, etc. Estab. 1980. Circ. 45,000. Pays on publication. Publishes ms an average of 6 months after acceptance. Byline given. Buys all North American serial rights. Submit seasonal material 6 months in advance. Free sample copy and writer's guidelines.

Nonfiction: Essays, general interest, how-to, continuing education, humor, interview/profile, new product, opinion, photo feature, technical. Buys 50 mss/year. Query. Length: 750-3,000 words. Pays $125-500.

Photos: State availability of photos with submission. Buys one-time rights.

Columns/Departments: "Columns and departments are staff-written with the exception of commentary on EMS issues and practices." Length: 1,000 words maximum.

Tips: "We are trying to build a cadre of EMS providers nationwide to submit news tips and write news stories. Fee is $10-50. It's a good way to attract the editors' attention."

MANAGED CARE, A Guide for Physicians, Stezzi Communications, Inc., 301 Oxford Valley Rd., Suite 1105A, Yardley PA 19067. (215)321-5480. Fax: (215)321-6670. E-mail: stezzicomm@aol.com. Website: http://www.stezzi.com/. Editor: Timothy Kelley. Managing Editor: John Marcille. 75% freelance written. Monthly magazine. "We emphasize practical, usable information that helps the physician or HMO administrator cope with the ever more complex array of options, challenges and hazards that accompanies the rapidly changing health care industry. Our regular readers understand that 'health care reform' isn't a piece of legislation; it's an evolutionary process that's already well under way. But we hope to help our readers also keep the faith that led them to medicine in the first place." Estab. 1992. Circ. 80,000. **Pays on acceptance.** Publishes ms an average of 1 month after acceptance. Byline given. Offers 20% kill fee. Buys all rights. Editorial lead time 3 months. Submit seasonal material 4 months in advance. Reports in 3 weeks on queries; 2 months on mss. Sample copy free.

Nonfiction: Book excerpts, general interest, how-to (deal with requisites of managed care, such as contracts with health plans, affiliation arrangements, relationships with staffers, computer needs, etc.), technical. Also considered occasionally are personal experience, opinion, interview/profile and humor pieces, *but these must have a strong managed care angle*

and draw upon the insights of (if they are not written by) *a knowledgeable MD or other managed care professional.* Don't waste those stamps on "A Humorous View of My Recent Gall Bladder Operation." Buys 35 mss/year. Query. Length: 1,000-3,000 words. Pays $1,000-1,500 for assigned articles; $100-1,000 for unsolicited articles. Pays expenses of writers on assignment.
Photos: State availability of photos with submissions. Reviews contact sheets, negatives, transparencies, prints. Negotiates payment individually. Buys one-time rights.
Columns/Departments: Paul Wynn, senior editor. News/Commentary (usually staff-written, but factual anecdotes involving managed care's effect on providers are welcome; either idea or manuscript can be bought. 100-300 words. Pays $50-100.
Tips: "We're looking for reliable freelancers who can write for our audience with our approach, so 'breaking in' may yield assignments. Do this by writing impeccably and with flair, and try to reflect the interests and perspective of the practicing physician or the active managed care executive. (Cardinal rule: The reader is busy, with many things vying for his/her reading time. Be sprightly, but don't waste our readers' time.)"

MEDICAL ECONOMICS, 5 Paragon Dr., Montvale NJ 07645. (201)358-7500. Fax: (201)573-0867. E-mail: nancy_meehan@medec.com. Website: http://www.medec.com. Contact: Nancy J. Meehan, outside copy chief. 2% freelance written. Biweekly magazine. Circ. 192,000. **Pays on acceptance.** Byline given. Offers 25% kill fee. Buys first world publication rights. Reports in 1 month on queries. Sample copy free.
Nonfiction: Articles about private physicians in innovative, pioneering and/or controversial situations affecting medical care delivery, patient relations or malpractice prevention/litigation; personal finance topics. Buys 40-50 mss/year. Query with published clips. Length: 1,500-3,000 words. Pays $1,200-2,500 for assigned articles. Pays expenses of writers on assignment.
Tips: "We look at health care issues from the perspective of practicing physicians."

MEDICAL IMAGING, The Business Magazine for Technology Management, 10 Risho Ave, East Providence RI 02916. (401)434-1050. Fax: (401)434-1090. E-mail: mtierney@healthtechnet.com. Website: http://www.sspubs.com. Editor: Jack Spears. Contact: Mary Tierney, editor. 5% freelance written. Monthly magazine covering diagnostic imaging equipment. Estab. 1986. Circ. 18,000. Pays on publication. Publishes ms an average of 2 months after acceptance. Byline given. Offers 50% kill fee. Buys all rights. Editorial lead time 2 months. Responds to query letters "as soon as possible." Sample copy for $10 prepaid. Writer's guidelines for #10 SASE.
Nonfiction: Interview/profile, technical. "No general interest/human interest stories about healthcare. Articles *must* deal with our industry, diagnostic imaging." Buys 6 mss/year. Query with published clips. Length: 1,500-2,500 words. Pays approximately 25¢/word. Sometimes pays expenses of writers on assignment.
Photos: State availability of photos with submission. Reviews negatives. Offers no additional payment for photos accepted with ms "unless assigned separately." Model releases, identification of subjects required. Buys all rights.
Tips: "Send a letter with an interesting story idea that is applicable to our industry, diagnostic imaging. Then follow up with a phone call. Areas most open to freelancers are features and technology profiles. You don't have to be an engineer or doctor but you have to know how to talk and listen to them."

THE NEW PHYSICIAN, 1982 Association Dr., Reston VA 20191. Editor: Amy Myers-Payne. 40% freelance written. Magazine published 9 times/year for medical students, interns, residents and educators. Circ. 25,000. **Pays on acceptance.** Publishes an average of 3 months after acceptance. Accepts simultaneous and previously published submissions. Send photocopy of article and information about when and where the article previously appeared. For reprints, pay varies. Publishes novel excerpts. Reports in 2 months. Sample copy for 10×13 SAE with 5 first-class stamps. Writer's guidelines for SASE.
Nonfiction: Articles on social, political, economic issues in medical education/health care. Buys about 12 features/year. Query or send complete ms. Length: 800-3,000 words. Pays 25-50¢/word with higher fees for selected pieces. Pays some expenses of writers on assignment.
Tips: "Although we are published by an association (the American Medical Student Association), we are not a 'house organ.' We are a professional magazine for readers with a progressive view on health care issues and a particular interest in improving medical education and the health care system. Our readers demand sophistication on the issues we cover. Freelancers should be willing to look deeply into the issues in question and not be satisfied with a cursory review of those issues."

OPTICAL PRISM, VezCom Inc., 31 Hastings Dr., Unionville Ontario L3R 4Y5 Canada. (905)475-9343. Fax: (905)477-2821. E-mail: prism@istar.ca. Editor: Allan K. Vezina. 90% freelance written. Magazine published 9 times/year "covering a wide variety of material including contact lens fitting, eyeglass and contact lens dispensing, practice management, marketing and merchandising articles, as well as wholesale and retail 'success stories.' " Estab. 1983. Circ. 7,500. **Pays on acceptance.** Publishes ms an average of 4 months after acceptance. Offers 100% kill fee. Buys first, one-time and second serial (reprint) rights. Editorial lead time 4 months. Submit seasonal material 5 months in advance. Accepts simultaneous submissions. Reports in 2 weeks on story outlines; 1 month on mss. Sample copy free.
Nonfiction: Essays, exposé, general interest, historical/nostalgic, how-to (fit contact lens types, fit eyeglasses, grind lenses, etc.), humor, inspirational, interview/profile, new product (full article only), personal experience, photo feature, technical. Buys 30-35 mss/year. Send complete ms, story outline. Length: 1,500-10,000 words. Pays 15¢/word to a maximum of $500 (Canadian).

Reprints: Pays 3¢/word to a maximum of $200 (Canadian). Send tearsheet of article or short story or typed ms with rights for sale noted, and information about when and where the article previously appeared.

Photos: Send photos with submission. Reviews transparencies. Offers no additional payment for photos accepted with ms. Captions, model releases, identification of subjects required. Buys one-time rights.

Tips: "Writers should remember they are writing for doctors of optometry and doctors of medicine—therefore, standards should be very high to reflect the educational backgrounds of the readers."

PHYSICIAN'S MANAGEMENT, Advanstar Communications, 7500 Old Oak Blvd., Cleveland OH 44130. (216)243-8100. Fax: (216)891-2683. E-mail: advedhc@en.com. Editor-in-Chief: Bob Feigenbaum. Prefers to work with published/established writers. Monthly magazine emphasizing finances, investments, malpractice, socioeconomic issues, estate and retirement planning, small office administration, practice management, computers and taxes for primary care physicians in private practice. Estab. 1960. Circ. 120,000. **Pays on acceptance.** Publishes ms an average of 6 months after acceptance. Submit seasonal material 5 months in advance. Reports in 1 month. Sample copy for $10. Writer's guidelines for #10 SASE.

Nonfiction: *"Physician's Management* is a practice management/economic publication, not a clinical one." Publishes how-to articles (limited to medical practice management); informational (when relevant to audience); personal experience articles (if written by a physician). No fiction, clinical material, or soap opera articles. Length: 2,000-2,500 words. Query with SASE. Pays $125/3-column printed page. Use of charts, tables, graphs, sidebars and photos strongly encouraged. Sometimes pays expenses of writers on assignment. Buys all rights to articles and graphics.

Tips: "Talk to doctors first about their practices, financial interests, and day-to-day nonclinical problems and then query us. Also, the ability to write a concise, well-structured and well-researched magazine article is essential."

PHYSICIAN'S PRACTICE DIGEST, 100 S. Charles St., 13th Floor, Baltimore MD 21201. (410)539-3100. Fax: (410)539-3188. E-mail: ppd@clark.net. Website: http://www.rothnet.com/ppd. Editor: Cathy Canning. 75% freelance written. Bimonthly magazine. "Magazine is about physician practice management, the business of medicine and health care. Readers are primarily in solo practice or small groups. Not a clinical publication." Estab. 1990. Circ. 80,000. Pays 1 month after submission. Publishes ms an average of 2 months after acceptance. Byline given. Offers 25% kill fee. Buys one-time rights. Editorial lead time 3 months. Submit seasonal material 6 months in advance. Sample copy and writer's guidelines free.

• *Physician's Practice Digest* reports a need for local news stories from the following states: KY, MI, TN, SC, NC, GA, MD, VA, DC. Articles should cover topics such as physician networks, merger activity between doctors, between hospitals, etc.

Nonfiction: How-to, interview/profile, opinion. "Anything related to health reform is hot now—managed care, reimbursement. No clinical articles." Buys 40 mss/year. Query with published clips. Length: 500-2,500 words. Rates are negotiable. Pays phone expenses.

Reprints: Send typed ms with rights for sale noted and information about when and where the article previously appeared.

Photos: State availability of photos with submission. Reviews transparencies. Negotiates payment individually. Captions, model releases and identification of subjects required. Buys one-time rights.

Columns/Departments: Office Technology (computers, software, simulators, etc.), 500 words; Malpractice (reform, arbitration, etc.), 500 words; Managed Care (contracting, UR, guidelines, Marketing, Law, Insurance, etc.), 500 words. Query with published clips. Pays 25-50¢/word.

Tips: "It's absolutely essential to read the magazine. We *do not* run clinical articles. We're trying to help our readers cope while the health care industry undergoes radical transformation. We welcome ideas and information that will help the physician better manage the practice. Read the magazine! Think about what the reader *needs to know.* Look for health care trends and find the angle that affects physicians."

‡PHYSICIAN'S SUCCESSFUL PRACTICE: FOCUS ON MANAGED CARE, MPE Communications, Inc., 2338 Immokalee Rd., #168, Naples FL 34110. (941)513-9142. Fax: (941)513-9143. E-mail: kscomm@naples.net. Contact: Karla Wheeler, editor. 75% freelance written. Prefers to work with published/established writers. Quarterly magazine distributed to 125,000 primary care physicians. *"Physician's Successful Practice* provides managed care news and practice management tips for doctors. We need short news items and features containing practical information to help doctors maximize success in their practice." Estab. 1980. **Pays on acceptance.** Publishes ms an average of 2 months after acceptance. Byline given for feature articles only. Offers 20% kill fee. Buys first North American serial rights. Reports in 2 months. Sample copy for $1. Writer's guidelines for #10 SASE.

Nonfiction: Nuts-and-bolts articles only. No fiction, fillers, profiles of doctors or poetry. Query with published clips. Length: 250-1,200 words. Pays $50-300. Pays expenses of writers on assignment.

Tips: Query first via mail, fax or e-mail.

‡PHYSICIANS' TRAVEL & MEETING GUIDE, Quadrant HealthCom, Inc., 105 Raider Blvd., Belle Mead NJ 08052. Fax: (908)874-6096. Contact: Bea Riemschneider, editor-in-chief. Managing Editor: Susann Tepperberg. 60% freelance written. Monthly magazine covering travel for physicians and their families. *Physicians' Travel & Meeting Guide* supplies continuing medical education events listings and extensive travel coverage of international and national destinations. Circ. 135,000. **Pays on acceptance.** Byline given. Buys first North American serial rights. Submit seasonal material 4-6 months in advance. Reports in 3 months.

Nonfiction: Photo feature, travel. Buys 25-35 mss/year. Query with published clips. Length: 450-3,000 words. Pays $150-1,000 for assigned articles.

Photos: State availability of photos with submission. Send photos with submission. Reviews 35mm or 4×5 transparencies. Captions and identification of subjects required. Buys one-time rights.

PODIATRY MANAGEMENT, P.O. Box 750129, Forest Hills NY 11375. (718)897-9700. Fax: (718)896-5747. E-mail: gcfg37a@prodigy.com. Website: http://www.podiatryMGT.com. Publisher: Scott C. Borowsky. Editor: Barry Block, DPM, J.D. Managing Editor: Martin Kruth. Magazine published 9 times/year. "Aims to help the doctor of podiatric medicine to build a bigger, more successful practice, to conserve and invest his money, to keep him posted on the economic, legal and sociological changes that affect him." Estab. 1982. Circ. 13,000. Pays on publication. Byline given. Buys first North American serial and second serial (reprint) rights. Submit seasonal material 4 months in advance. Accepts simultaneous submissions. Reports in 2 weeks. Sample copy for $3 and 9×12 SAE. Writer's guidelines for #10 SASE.

Nonfiction: General interest (taxes, investments, estate planning, recreation, hobbies); how-to (establish and collect fees, practice management, organize office routines, supervise office assistants, handle patient relations); interview/profile about interesting or well-known podiatrists; and personal experience. "These subjects are the mainstay of the magazine, but offbeat articles and humor are always welcome." Send tax and financial articles to Martin Kruth, 5 Wagon Hill Lane, Avon, CT 06001. Buys 25 mss/year. Query. Length: 1,000-2,500 words. Pays $150-600.

Reprints: Send photocopy of article. Pays 33% of amount paid for an original article.

Photos: State availability of photos. Pays $15 for b&w contact sheet. Buys one-time rights.

STITCHES, The Journal of Medical Humour, 16787 Warden Ave., R.R. #3, Newmarket, Ontario L3Y 4W1 Canada. (905)853-1884. Fax: (905)853-6565. Editor: Simon Hally. 90% freelance written. Magazine published 11 times/year covering humor for physicians. "*Stitches* is read primarily by physicians in Canada. Stories with a medical slant are particularly welcome, but we also run a lot of non-medical material. It must be funny and, of course, brevity is the soul of wit." Estab. 1990. Circ. 43,000. Pays on publication. Publishes ms 6 months after acceptance. Byline given. Offers 50% kill fee. Buys first North American serial rights. Editorial lead time 2 months. Submit seasonal material 3 months in advance. Reports in 6 weeks on queries; 2 months on mss. Sample copy free.

● *Stitches* also publishes a quarterly, *Stitches, The Leisure Journal for Dentists*.

Nonfiction: Humor, personal experience. Buys 20 mss/year. Send complete ms. Length: 100-2,000 words. Pays $35-750 (Canadian).

Fiction: Humorous. Buys 30 mss/year. Send complete ms. Length: 100-2,000 words. Pays $35-750 (Canadian).

Poetry: Humorous. Buys 5 poems/year. Submit maximum 5 poems. Length: 2-20 lines. Pays $20-100.

Fillers: Gags to be illustrated by cartoonist, short humor. Pay negotiable.

Tips: "Due to the nature of humorous writing, we have to see a completed manuscript, rather than a query, to determine if it is suitable for us. Along with a short cover letter, that's all we require."

STRATEGIC HEALTH CARE MARKETING, Health Care Communications, 11 Heritage Lane, P.O. Box 594, Rye NY 10580. (914)967-6741. E-mail: healthcomm@aol.com. Editor: Michele von Dambrowski. 75% freelance written. Prefers to work with published/established writers. "Will only work with unpublished writer on a 'stringer' basis initially." Monthly newsletter covering health care marketing and management in a wide range of settings including hospitals and medical group practices, home health services and managed care organizations. Emphasis is on strategies and techniques employed within the health care field and relevant applications from other service industries. Estab. 1984. Pays on publication. Publishes ms an average of 2 months after acceptance. Byline given. Offers 25% kill fee. Buys first North American serial rights. Reports in 1 month. Sample copy for 9×12 SAE with 3 first-class stamps. Guidelines sent with sample copy only.

● *Strategic Health Care Marketing* is specifically seeking writers with expertise/contacts in managed care, integrated delivery systems and demand management.

Nonfiction: How-to, interview/profile, new product, technical. Buys 50 mss/year. Query with published clips. No unsolicited mss. Length: 700-3,000 words. Pays $100-500. Sometimes pays expenses of writers on assignment with prior authorization.

Photos: State availability of photos with submissions. (Photos, unless necessary for subject explanation, are rarely used.) Reviews contact sheets. Offers $10-30/photo. Captions and model releases required. Buys one-time rights.

Tips: "Writers with prior experience on business beat for newspaper or newsletter will do well. We require a sophisticated, indepth knowledge of health care reform issues and impact. This is not a consumer publication—the writer with knowledge of both health care and marketing will excel. Interviews or profiles are most open to freelancers. Absolutely no unsolicited manuscripts; any received will be returned or discarded unread."

UNIQUE OPPORTUNITIES, The Physician's Resource, U O Inc., Suite 1236, 455 S. Fourth Ave., Louisville KY 40202. Fax: (502)587-0848. E-mail: bettuo@aol.com. Editor: Mollie Vento Hudson. Contact: Bett Coffman, associate editor. 45% freelance written. Bimonthly magazine covering physician relocation and career development. "Published for physicians interested in a new career opportunity. It offers physicians useful information and first-hand experiences to guide them in making informed decisions concerning their first or next career opportunity. It provides regular features and columns about specific aspects of the search process." Estab. 1991. Circ. 80,000 physicians. **Pays on acceptance.** Publishes ms an average of 2 months after acceptance. Byline given. Offers 33% kill fee. Buys first North American serial rights. Editorial lead time 3 months. Submit seasonal material 6 months in advance. Reports in 2 months on queries. Sample copy for 9 × 12 SAE with 6 first-class stamps. Writer's guidelines for #10 SASE.

Nonfiction: Opinion (on issues relating to physician recruitment), practice options and information of interest to physicians in career transition. Buys 12 mss/year. Query with published clips. Length: 1,500-3,500 words. Pays $750-1,500. Sometimes pays expenses of writers on assignment.

Photos: State availability of photos with submission. Negotiates payment individually. Model releases and identification of subjects required. Buys one-time rights.

Columns/Departments: Remarks (opinion from physicians and industry experts on physician career issues), 500-1,000 words; Physician Profiles (doctors with unusual or interesting careers), 500 words. Buys up to 6 mss/year. Query with published clips. Pays $250-500.

Tips: "Submit queries via letter with ideas for articles that directly pertain to physician career issues, such as specific or unusual practice opportunities, relocation or practice establishment subjects, etc. Feature articles are most open to freelancers. Physician sources are most important, with tips and advice from both the physicians and business experts. Physicians like to know what other physicians think and do and appreciate suggestions from other business people."

MUSIC

Publications for musicians and for the recording industry are listed in this section. Other professional performing arts publications are classified under Entertainment and the Arts. Magazines featuring music industry news for the general public are listed in the Consumer Entertainment and Music sections. (Markets for songwriters can be found in *Songwriter's Market*, Writer's Digest Books.)

CHURCH MUSICIAN TODAY, (formerly *The Church Musician*), 127 Ninth Ave. N., Nashville TN 37234. (615)251-2961. Fax: (615)251-2614 or 5951. Editor: Jere Adams. 20% freelance written. Works with a small number of new/unpublished writers each year; eager to work with new/unpublished writers. Monthly publication for church music leaders. Estab. 1950. Circ. 16,000. Buys all rights. **Pays on acceptance.** Publishes ms an average of 1 year after acceptance. Reports in 2 months. Sample copy for 9 × 12 SAE with 3 first-class stamps.

• *Church Musician Today* has gone from a quarterly to a monthly and no longer uses fiction or poetry.

Nonfiction: Leadership and how-to features, success stories and articles on Protestant church music. "We reject material when the subject of an article doesn't meet our needs. And they are often poorly written, or contain too many 'glittering generalities' or lack creativity. We're interested in success stories; a 'this-worked-for-me' type of story." Length: maximum 1,300 words. Pays up to 5½¢/word, 6¢ on diskette.

Reprints: Send photocopy of article or typed ms with rights for sale noted and information about when and where the article previously appeared.

Photos: Purchased with mss; related to mss content only. "We use color photos."

Fillers: Short humor. Church music slant. No clippings. Pays $5-15.

Tips: "I'd advise a beginning writer to write about his or her experience with some aspect of church music; the social, musical and spiritual benefits from singing in a choir; a success story about their instrumental group; a testimonial about how they were enlisted in a choir—especially if they were not inclined at first. A writer might speak to hymn singers—what turns them on and what doesn't. Some might include how music has helped them to talk about Jesus as well as sing about Him. We prefer most of these experiences be related to the church, of course, although we include many articles by writers whose affiliation is other than Baptist. A writer might relate his experience with a choir of blind or deaf members. Some people receive benefits from working with unusual children—retarded, or culturally deprived, emotionally unstable, and so forth. First choice for material will relate to music, worship, music administration, music education, worship planning, hymnody trends, worship trends, prominent music personalities, important music issues, music technology, drama, devotionals and book reviews on music/worship. *Church Musician Today* is the primary music administration periodical for ministers of music."

RECORDING, The Magazine for the Recording Musician, Music Maker Publications, 5412 Idylwild Trail, Suite 100, Boulder CO 80301. (303)516-9118. Fax: (303)516-9119. E-mail: recordin@idt.net. Editor: Nicholas Batzdorf. 90% freelance written. Monthly magazine covering technical and practical information to help musicians make better recordings. Estab. 1987. Circ. 30,000. Pays on publication. Publishes ms an average of 4 months after acceptance. Byline given. Kill fee negotiable. Buys all rights. Editorial lead time 3 months. Accepts simultaneous submissions. Reports in 2 weeks on queries. Writer's guidelines free.

Nonfiction: Book excerpts, how-to (record, or get the most from your recording equipment), opinion, technical. Buys 65 mss/year. Query. Length: 1,000-4,500 words. Pays $100 and up. Sometimes pays expenses of writers on assignment.

Photos: State availability of photos with submission. Reviews transparencies, prints. Negotiates payment individually. Buys one-time rights.

Columns/Departments: Fade Out (guest editorial), 1,000 words; Digital Diary (digital recording tips), 2,000 words. Buys 36 mss/year. Query. Pays $100 and up.

Tips: Query by phone or mail.

‡**SONGWRITER'S MONTHLY, The Stories Behind Today's Songs**, 332 Eastwood Ave., Feasterville PA 19053. Phone/fax: (215)953-0952. E-mail: a1foster@aol.com. Contact: Allen Foster, editor. 20% freelance written. Monthly magazine covering songwriting. Estab. 1992. Circ. 2,500. **Pays on acceptance.** Publishes ms an average of 6 months after acceptance. Byline given. Offers 100% kill fee. Buys first rights or one-time rights. Editorial lead time 3 months. Submit seasonal material 6 months in advance. Reports in 2 weeks on queries, 1 month on mss. Sample copy free. Writer's guidelines for #10 SASE.
Nonfiction: How-to (write better songs, get a deal, etc.), technical. No interviews or reviews. Buys 36 mss/year. Query. Length: 300-1,200 words. Pays 1-2¢/word.
Photos: State availability of photos with submission. Reviews prints. Offers no additional payment for photos accepted with ms. Identification of subjects required.
Fillers: Anecdotes, facts, newsbreaks, short humor. Buys 60/year. Length: 25-300 words. Pays $0-5.
Tips: "All writers should have some hands-on experience in the music business."

STUDIO SOUND, Miller Freeman Entertainment Ltd., 8 Montague Close, London Bridge, London SE1 9UR United Kingdom. (+)71-620-3636. Fax: (+)44 71-401-8036. Editor: Tim Goodyer. 80% freelance written. Monthly magazine covering "all matters relating to pro audio—music recording, music for picture, post production—reviews and feature articles." Estab. 1959. Circ. 20,000 worldwide. Pays on publication. Byline given. Offers 20% kill fee. Buys first rights. Editorial lead time 3 months. Accepts simultaneous submissions.
Nonfiction: Historical/nostalgic, how-to, interview/profile, new product, opinion, personal experience, photo feature. No company profiles. Buys 80 mss/year. Send complete ms. Length: 850-4,000 words. Pays $150 minimum. Sometimes pays expenses of writers on assignment.
Photos: State availability of photos with submission. Reviews 35mm transparencies and 5×7 prints. Negotiates payment individually. Identification of subjects required. Buys one-time rights.

OFFICE ENVIRONMENT AND EQUIPMENT

‡**MANAGING OFFICE TECHNOLOGY**, Penton Publishing, 1100 Superior Ave., Cleveland OH 44114. (216)696-7000. Fax: (216)931-9769. E-mail: lromei@penton.com. Website: http://www.penton.com. Editor: Lura Romei. 20% freelance written. *Managing Office Technology* is committed to providing quality office automation solutions and product information to its readers in mid-size and large companies in an authoritative, accurate, and timely presentation. Estab. 1956. Circ. 120,000. **Pays on acceptance.** Editorial lead time 5-6 months after acceptance. Byline given. Buys first North American serial rights. Editorial lead time 6 months. Query for electronic submissions. Reports in 2 months. Sample copy and writer's guidelines free.
Nonfiction: How-to. Buys 10 mss/year. Query. Length: 1,200-2,500 words. Pays $300-600 for assigned articles; $100-400 for unsolicited articles. Sometimes pays expenses of writers on assignment.
Photos: State availability of photos with submissions. Reviews contact sheets, transparencies, prints. Offers no additional payment for photos accepted with ms. Captions, identification of subjects required. Buys one-time rights.

MODERN OFFICE TECHNOLOGY, Penton Publishing, Dept. WM, 1100 Superior Ave., Cleveland OH 44114-2501. (216)696-7000. Fax: (216)931-9769. E-mail: lromei@penton.com. Contact: Lura K. Romei, editor. Production Manager: Gina Runyon-McKenna. 10-20% freelance written. Monthly magazine covering office automation for corporate management and personnel, financial management, administrative and operating management, systems and information management, managers and supervisors of support personnel and purchasing. Estab. 1956. Circ. 61,000. **Pays on acceptance.** Publishes ms an average of 6 months after acceptance. Byline given. Buys first and one-time rights. Reports in 3 months. Sample copy and writer's guidelines for 9×12 SAE with 4 first-class stamps.
Nonfiction: New product, opinion, technical. Query with or without published clips or send complete ms. Length: open. Pays $300-600 for assigned articles; $250-400 for unsolicited articles. Pays expenses of writers on assignment.
Photos: Send photos with submission. Reviews contact sheets, 4×5 transparencies and prints. Consult editor. Captions, identification of subjects required. Buys one-time rights.
Tips: "Submitted material should always present topics and ideas on issues that are clearly and concisely defined. Material should describe problems and solutions. Writer should describe benefits to reader in tangible results whenever possible."

‡**THE SECRETARY**®, Stratton Publishing & Marketing, Inc., 2800 Shirlington Rd., Suite 706, Arlington VA 22206. Publisher: Debra J. Stratton. Managing Editor: Susan L. Fitzgerald. 90% freelance written. Magazine published 9 times/ year covering the secretarial profession. Estab. 1946. Circ. 44,000. Pays on publication or "mostly unpaid." Publishes ms an average of 6-18 months after acceptance. Byline given. Kill fee negotiable. Buys first rights. Editorial lead time 3 months. Submit seasonal material 5 months in advance. Accepts simultaneous submissions. Query for electronic submissions. For electronic (IBM) PC-compatible, Word Perfect or ASCII on disk. Reports in 2-3 months. Sample copy $3 through (816)891-6600 ext. 235. Writer's guidelines free.
Nonfiction: Book excerpts, general interest, how-to (buy and use office equipment, advance career, etc.), interview/ profile, new product, personal experience. Buys 6-10 mss/year. Query. Length: 2,000 words. Pays $250 minimum for assigned articles; $0-75 minimum for unsolicited articles. Pays expenses of writers on assignment.

Reprints: Send tearsheet of article or typed ms with rights for sale noted (on disk, preferred) and information about when and where the article previously appeared.

Photos: Send photos with submission. Reviews transparencies and prints. Negotiable payment for photos accepted with ms. Identification of subjects required. Buys one-time rights.

Columns/Departments: Product News (new office products, non promotional), 500 words maximum; Random Input (general interest—career, woman's, workplace issues), 500 words maximum; First Person (first-hand experiences from secretaries), 800 words. Send complete ms.

Tips: "We're in search of articles addressing travel; meeting and event-planning; office recycling programs; computer hardware and software; workplace issues; international business topics. Must be appropriate to secretaries."

PAPER

BOXBOARD CONTAINERS, Intertec Publishing Co., Dept. WM, 29 N. Wacker Dr., Chicago IL 60606-3298. (312)726-2802. Fax: (312)726-2574. Editor: Greg Kishbaugh. Managing Editor: Robin Litwin. Monthly magazine covering box and carton manufacturing for corrugated box, folding carton, setup box manufacturers internationally emphasizing technology and management. Circ. 15,000. Pays on publication. Byline given. Buys first North American serial rights. Submit seasonal material 2 months in advance. Reports in 1 month. Free sample copy.

Nonfiction: How-to, interview/profile, new product, opinion, personal experience, photo feature, technical. Buys 10 mss/year. Query. Length: 2,000-6,000 words. Pays $75-350 for assigned articles; $75-250 for unsolicited articles. Sometimes pays expenses of writers on assignment.

Photos: Send photos with submission. Reviews 35mm, 4×5 and 6×6 transparencies and 8×10 prints. Offers no additional payment for photos accepted with ms. Captions, model releases, identification of subjects required. Buys one-time rights.

Tips: Features are most open to freelancers.

‡THE PAPER STOCK REPORT, News and Trends of the Paper Recycling Markets, McEntee Media Corp., 13727 Holland Rd., Cleveland OH 44142. (216)362-7979. Editor: Ken McEntee. Biweekly newsletter covering "market trends, news in the paper recycling industry. Audience is interested in new innovative markets, applications for recovered scrap paper as well as new laws and regulations impacting recycling." Estab. 1990. Circ. 2,000. Pays on publication. Publishes ms an average of 1 month after acceptance. Byline given. Buys first or all rights. Editorial lead time 2 months. Submit seasonal material 2 months in advance. Accepts simultaneous submissions. Reports in 1 month on queries. Sample copy for #10 SAE with 55¢ postage.

Nonfiction: Book excerpts, essays, exposé, general interest, historical/nostalgic, interview/profile, new product, opinion, technical, all related to paper recycling. Buys 0-13 mss/year. Send complete ms. Length: 250-1,000 words. Pays $50-250 for assigned articles; $25-250 for unsolicited articles. Pays expenses of writers on assignment.

Reprints: Accepts previously published submissions.

Photos: State availability of photos with submissions. Reviews contact sheets. Negotiates payment individually. Identification of subjects required.

Tips: "Article must be valuable to readers in terms of presenting new market opportunities or cost-saving measures."

‡RECYCLED PAPER NEWS, Independent Coverage of Environmental Issues in the Paper Industry, McEntee Media Corporation, 13727 Holland Rd., Brook Park OH 44142. (216)362-7979. Fax: (216)362-6553. E-mail: 71241.2763@compuserve.com. Editor: Ken McEntee. 10% freelance written. Monthly newsletter. "We are interested in any news impacting the paper recycling industry as well as other environmental issues in the paper industry, i.e., water/air pollution, chlorine-free paper, forest conservation, etc., with special emphasis on new laws and regulations." Estab. 1990. Pays on publication. Publishes ms an average of 2 months after acceptance. Buys first or all rights. Editorial lead time 1 month. Submit seasonal material 1 month in advance. Accepts simultaneous submissions. Reports in 2 months. Sample copy for 9×12 SAE and 55¢ postage. Writer's guidelines for #10 SASE.

Nonfiction: Book excerpts, essays, interview/profile, new product, opinion, personal experience, technical, new business, legislation, regulation, business expansion. Buys 0-5 mss/year. Query with published clips. Length: 100-5,000 words. Pays $10-500. Pays writers with contributor copies or other premiums by prior agreement.

Reprints: Accepts previously published submissions.

Columns/Departments: Query with published clips. Pays $10-500.

Tips: "We appreciate leads on local news regarding recycling or composting, i.e., new facilities or businesses, new laws and regulations, unique programs, situations that impact supply and demand for recyclables, etc. International developments are also of interest."

PETS

Listed here are publications for professionals in the pet industry—pet product wholesalers, manufacturers, suppliers, and retailers, and owners of pet specialty stores, grooming businesses, aquarium retailers and those interested in the pet fish industry. Publications for pet owners are listed in the Consumer Animal section.

GROOM & BOARD H.H. Backer Associates Inc., 20 E. Jackson Blvd., Suite 200, Chicago IL 60604-2383. (312)663-4040. Fax: (312)663-5676. E-mail: petage@aol.com. Editor: Karen Long MacLeod. 90% freelance written. Magazine published 9 times/year. "*Groom & Board* is the only national trade publication for pet-care professionals, including pet groomers, boarding kennel operators and service-oriented veterinarians. Features emphasize professional development, including progressive business management, animal handling procedures, emerging business opportunities and profiles of successful pet-care operations. Estab. 1980. Circ. 16,431. **Pays on acceptance.** Publishes ms an average of 3 months after acceptance. Byline given. Buys first North American serial, one-time, or exclusive to industry. Sample copy available.

Nonfiction: How-to (groom specific breeds of pets, run business, etc.), interview/profile (successful grooming and/or kennel operations), technical. No consumer-oriented articles or stories about a single animal (animal heroes, grief, etc.). Buys 40 mss/year. Query by phone after 3 pm CST. Length: 1,000-2,000 words. Pays $100-400 for assigned articles; $70-125 for unsolicited articles. Sometimes pays expenses of writers on assignment.

Photos: Reviews slides, transparencies, 5×7 color glossy prints. Captions, identification of subjects required. Buys one-time rights.

PET AGE, The Magazine for the Professional Retailer, H.H. Backer Associates, Inc., 20 E. Jackson Blvd., Suite 200, Chicago IL 60604-2383. (312)663-4040. Fax: (312)663-5676. E-mail: petage@aol.com. Editor: Karen Long MacLeod. 90% freelance written. Prefers to work with published/established writers. Monthly magazine for pet/pet supplies retailers, covering the complete pet industry. Estab. 1971. Circ. 22,000. **Pays on acceptance.** Publishes ms an average of 6 months after acceptance. Byline given. Buys first North American serial, one-time, or exclusive industry rights. Submit seasonal material 6 months in advance. Sample copy available.

Nonfiction: Profile (of a successful, well-run pet retail operation), how-to, business management, technical—all trade-related. Query by phone after 3 pm CST. Query with the name and location of a pet operation you wish to profile and why it would make a good feature. No general retailing articles or consumer-oriented pet articles. Buys 120 mss/year. Length: 1,000-2,500 words. Pays $200-500 for assigned articles. Sometimes pays the expenses of writers on assignment.

Photos: Reviews slides, transparencies, 5×7 color glossy prints. Captions, identification of subjects required. Buys one-time rights.

Tips: "This is a business publication for busy people, and must be very informative in easy-to-read, concise style. Articles about animal care or business practices should have the pet-retail angle or cover issues specific to this industry."

PET BUSINESS, 7-L Dundas Circle, Greensboro NC 27407. (910)292-4047. Executive Editor: Rita Davis. 30% freelance written. "Our monthly news magazine reaches retailers, distributors and manufacturers of pet products. Groomers, veterinarians and serious hobbyists are also represented." Estab. 1973. Circ. 18,000. Pays on publication. Publishes ms an average of 2 months after acceptance. Byline given. Buys first rights. Submit seasonal/holiday material 3 months in advance. Reports in 4 months. Sample copy for $3. Writer's guidelines for SASE.

Nonfiction: "Articles must be well-researched and pertain to major business trends in the pet industry. Research, legislative and animal behavior reports are of interest. All data must be attributed. Articles should be business-oriented, not intended for the pet owner market. Send query or complete ms." Length: 250-2,000 words. Pays 12¢/word.

Photos: Send color slides, transparencies or prints with submission. Offers $20/photo. Buys one-time rights.

Tips: "We are open to national and international news of the pet industry written in standard news format, or well-researched, business- or trend-oriented feature articles."

THE PET DEALER, PTN Publishing Co., 445 Broad Hollow Rd., Melville NY 11747. (516)845-2700. Fax: (516)845-2797. Editorial Director: Mark Hawver, (516)845-2700, ext. 247. 70% freelance written. Prefers to work with published/established writers, but works with new/unpublished writers. "We want writers who are good reporters and clear communicators with a good command of the English language." Monthly magazine emphasizing merchandising, marketing and management for owners and managers of pet specialty stores, departments, and pet groomers and their suppliers. Estab. 1949. Circ. 20,500. Pays on publication. Byline given. Submit seasonal material 4 months in advance. Reports in 3 months. Sample copy for $5 and 8×10 SAE with 10 first-class stamps.

Nonfiction: How-to (store operations, administration, merchandising, marketing, management, promotion and purchasing). Consumer pet articles—lost pets, best pets, humane themes—*not* welcome. Emphasis is on *trade* merchandising and marketing of pets and supplies. Buys 2-4 unsolicited mss/year. Query; queries without SASE will not be answered. Length: 1,000-2,000 words. Pays $50-125.

Reprints: Send typed ms with rights for sale noted and information about when and where the article previously appeared. Pays 1-10% of amount paid for an original article.

Photos: Submit undeveloped color photo material with ms. No additional payment for 5×7 b&w glossy prints. Buys one-time rights. Will give photo credit for photography students. Also seeking cover art: original illustrated animal portraits (paid).

Fillers: Publishes cartoons (unpaid).

Tips: "We're interested in store profiles outside the New York, New Jersey, Connecticut and Pennsylvania metro areas. Photos are of key importance and should include a storefront shot. Articles focus on new techniques in merchandising or promotion, and overall trends in the pet industry. Want to see more articles from retailers and veterinarians with retail operations. Submit query letter first, with writing background summarized; include samples. We seek one-to-one, interview-type features on retail pet store merchandising. Indicate the availability of the proposed article, and your willingness to submit on exclusive or first-in-the-trade-field basis."

PET PRODUCT NEWS, Fancy Publications, P.O. Box 6050, Mission Viejo CA 92690. (714)855-8822. Fax: (714)855-3045. Editor: Stacy N. Hackett. 70% freelance written. Monthly magazine. "*Pet Product News* covers business/legal and economic issues of importance to pet product retailers, suppliers and distributors, as well as product information and animal care issues. We're looking for straightforward articles on the proper care of dogs, cats, birds, fish and exotics (reptiles, hamsters, etc.) as information the retailers can pass on to new pet owners." Estab. 1947. Circ. 25,000. Pays on publication. Byline given. Offers $50 kill fee. Buys first North American serial rights. Editorial lead time 3 months. Submit seasonal material 4 months in advance. No multiple submissions. Reports in 2 weeks on queries. Sample copy for $4.50. Writer's guidelines free.
Nonfiction: General interest, interview/profile, new product, photo feature, technical. "No cute animal stories or those directed at the pet owner." Buys 150 mss/year. Query. Length: 500-1,500 words. Pays $175-350.
Columns/Departments: "Retail News" (timely news stories about business issues affecting pet retailers), 800-1,000 words; "Industry News" (news articles representing coverage of pet product suppliers, manufacturers, distributors and associations), 800-1,000 words; Dog & Cat (products and care of), 1,000-1,500 words; Fish & Bird (products and care of) 1,000-1,500 words; Small Mammals (products and care of), 1,000-1,500 words. Buys 120 mss/year. Query first. Pays $150-300.
Tips: "Be more than just an animal lover. You have to know about health, nutrition and care. Product and business articles are told in both an informative and entertaining style. Go into pet stores, talk to the owners and see what they need to know to be better business people in general, who have to deal with everything from balancing the books and free trade agreements to animal rights activists. All sections are open, but you have to be extremely knowledgeable on the topic, be it taxes, management, profit building, products, nutrition, animal care or marketing."

PLUMBING, HEATING, AIR CONDITIONING AND REFRIGERATION

SNIPS MAGAZINE, 1949 N. Cornell Ave., Melrose Park IL 60160. (708)544-3870. Fax: (708)544-3884. Editor: Nick Carter. 2% freelance written. Monthly magazine for sheet metal, warm air heating, ventilating, air conditioning and roofing contractors. Estab. 1932. Publishes ms an average of 3 months after acceptance. Buys all rights. "Write for detailed list of requirements before submitting any work."
Nonfiction: Material should deal with information about contractors who do sheet metal, warm air heating, air conditioning, ventilation and metal roofing work; also about successful advertising campaigns conducted by these contractors and the results. Length: under 1,000 words unless on special assignment. Pays 5¢/word for first 500 words; 2¢/word thereafter.
Photos: Pays $5 each for small snapshot pictures, $10 each for usable 8×10 pictures.

PRINTING

‡AMERICAN INK MAKER, PTN Publishing, 445 Broad Hollow Rd., Melville NY 11747. (516)845-2700. Editor: Linda M. Casatelli. Associate Editor: Melissa Martilotto. 80% freelance written. Monthly magazine covering printing ink. Estab. 1922. Circ. 6,000. Pays on publication. Publishes ms an average of 2 months after acceptance. Byline given. Buys first rights. Editorial lead time 3 months. Accepts simultaneous submissions. Reports in 2 weeks on queries; 1 month on mss. Sample copy and writer's guidelines free.
Nonfiction: Interview/profile, technical. "No P.R./puff pieces." Buys 30 mss/year. Query. Length: 2,000-3,500 words. Pays $400-800 for assigned articles; $300-500 for unsolicited articles. Pays writers with contributor copies or other premiums for consultants wanting ads. Sometimes pays expenses of writers on assignment.
Photos: State availability of photos with submission. Reviews contact sheets, negatives, transparencies or prints. Offers no additional payment for photos accepted with ms. Captions and identification of subjects required. Buys one-time rights.
Columns/Departments: International News (segment of market), 1,500 words. Buys 12-18 mss/year. Query. Pays $350-600.
Fillers: Management. Buys 4/year. Length: 1,500-2,500 words. Pays $300-500.
Tips: "Offer to do an assigned piece as a trial."

HIGH VOLUME PRINTING, Innes Publishing Co., P.O. Box 7280, Libertyville IL 60048. Fax: (847)247-8855. Editor: Catherine M. Stanulis. Estab. 1982. 35% freelance written. Eager to work with new/unpublished writers. Bimonthly magazine for book, magazine printers, large commercial printing plants with 20 or more employees. Aimed at telling the reader what he needs to know to print more efficiently and more profitably. Circ. 41,000. Pays on publication. Publishes ms an average of 9 months after acceptance. Byline given. Buys first and second serial rights. Reports in 2 months. Writer's guidelines, sample articles provided.

• Printing industry/technology knowledge is a *must!*

Nonfiction: How-to (production techniques); new product (printing, auxiliary equipment, plant equipment); photo feature (case histories featuring unique equipment); technical (product research and development); shipping; publishing distribution methods. No product puff. Buys 12 mss/year. Query. Length: 700-3,000 words. Pays $50-300.

Reprints: Accepts previously published articles from noncompetitive or regional publications only. Send photocopy of article along with information about when and where the article previously appeared. Pays 50% of their fee for an original article.

Photos: Send photos with ms. Pays $25-150 for any size color transparencies and prints. Captions, model release, and identification of subjects required.

Tips: "Feature articles covering actual installations and industry trends are most open to freelancers. Be familiar with the industry, spend time in the field, and attend industry meetings and trade shows where equipment is displayed. We would also like to receive clips and shorts about printing mergers."

‡**MODERN REPROGRAPHICS**, P.O. Box 2249, Oak Park IL 60303. (708)445-9454. Fax: (708)445-9477. E-mail: edavis@modrepto.com. Editor: Ed Avis. 60% freelance written. Bimonthly magazine. "Modern Reprographics is for people who do large-format reproduction, such as blueprints, color posters, etc. Articles are geared towards blueprint shops, service bureaus, and in-plant repro departments and help them find new markets and do their work better." Estab. 1993. Circ. 8,000. Pays on publication. Publishes ms an average of 1 month after acceptance. Byline given. Offers 25% kill fee. Buys first North American serial rights. Editorial lead time 2 months. Reports in 3 weeks on queries; 1 month on mss. Sample copy for 11×14 SAE with 5 first-class stamps.

Nonfiction: How-to, interview/profile (blueprint shop owner, e.g.), new product, personal experience, technical, new markets. Buys 15 mss/year. Query with published clips. Length: 800-2,000 words. Pays $150. Sometimes pays expenses of writers on assignment.

Reprints: Send typed ms with rights for sale noted and information about when and where the article previously appeared. For reprints, pays 75% of the amount paid for an original article.

Photos: State availability of photos with submission. Captions and identification of subjects required. Buys one-time rigths.

Tips: "Writers can best break in with a profile of an interesting, innovative reprographics shop or department. Profiles should have a 'hook,' and some historical background on the shop or department. We are picky about technical articles, so please query first. All articles are written in language that non-reprographers can understand."

‡**NEW ENGLAND PRINTER & PUBLISHER**, Pine Services Corp., 10 Tech Circle, Natick MA 01760-0015. (508)655-8700. Fax: (508)655-2586. E-mail: pboeing@pine.org. Contact: Peter A. Boeing, managing editor. 90% freelance written. Monthly magazine covering printing and graphic arts. Estab. 1938. Circ. 4,200. Pays on publication. Publishes ms an average of 3 months after acceptance. Byline given. Buys one-time rights. Editorial lead time 3 months. Submit seasonal material 3 months in advance. Accepts simultaneous submissions. Sample copy for 9×12 SAE with 3 first-class stamps.

Nonfiction: Historical/nostalgic, how-to, interview/profile, technical. Query with published clips. Length: 1,000-3,800 words. Pays $0-350.

Reprints: Accepts previously published submissions.

Photos: State availability of photos with submission. Reviews 4×5 prints. Offers $0-100/photo. Buys one-time rights.

PERSPECTIVES, International Publishing Management Association (IPMA), 1205 W. College St., Liberty MO 64068-3733. (816)781-1111. Fax: (816)781-2790. E-mail: laaron@ipma.org. Website: http://www.ipma.org. Editor: Susan Murphy. 40% freelance written. Monthly trade newsletter covering "inhouse print and mail departments are faced with competition from commercial printers and facilities management companies. Writers must be pro-insourcing and reflect that this industry is a profitable profession." Estab. 1986. Circ. 2,300; twice a year it reaches 5,000. Pays on publication. Publishes ms an average of 2 months after acceptance. Byline given. Buys all rights. Editorial lead time 2 months. Reports in 1 month. Sample copy for 9×12 SAE.

Nonfiction: Interview/profile, new product, technical, general management. Payment negotiated individually. Sometimes pays expenses of writers on assignment.

Reprints: Send photocopy of article and information about when and where the article previously appeared.

Photos: State availability of photos with submission. Reviews contact sheets, 5×7 prints. Offers no additional payment for photos accepted with ms. Captions required. Buys one-time rights.

Columns/Departments: Executive Insight (management, personnel how-tos, employment law), 650-1,500 words. Buys 12 mss/year. Query with published clips.

Tips: "A knowledge of the printing industry is helpful. Articles with concrete examples or company/individual profiles work best."

PRINT & GRAPHICS/PRINTING JOURNAL, 30 E. Padonia Rd., Suite 504, Timonium MD 21093. (410)628-7826. Fax: (410)628-7829. E-mail: spencecom1@aol.com. Publisher: Kaj Spencer. Contact: Henry Mortimer, editor. 10% freelance written. Eager to work with new/unpublished writers. Monthly tabloid of the commercial printing industry for owners and executives of graphic arts firms. Estab. 1980. Circ. 20,000. **Pays on acceptance.** Publishes ms an average of 2 months after acceptance. Byline given. Buys one-time rights. Accepts simultaneous submissions. Reports in 2 months. Sample copy for $2.

Nonfiction: Book excerpts, historical/nostalgic, how-to, interview/profile, new product, opinion, personal experience, photo feature, technical. "All articles should relate to graphic arts management or production." Buys 20 mss/year. Query with published clips. Length: 750-2,000 words. Pays $100-250.

Reprints: Send photocopy of article and information about when and where the article previously appeared. Pays $150 flat fee. Publishes trade book excerpts.

Photos: State availability of photos. Pays $25-75 for 5×7 b&w prints. Captions, identification of subjects required.

QUICK PRINTING, PTN Publishing, 445 Broadhollow Rd., Melville NY 11747. (516)845-2700. Fax: (516)249-5774. E-mail: ptngrafnet@aol.com. Publisher: William Lewis. Associate Editor: Mary Waters. Contact: Gerald Walsh, editor. 10% freelance written. Monthly magazine covering the quick printing industry. "Our articles tell quick printers how they can be more profitable. We want art or photography to illustrate points made." Estab. 1977. Circ. 62,000. Pays on publication. Publishes ms an average of 4 months after acceptance. Byline given. Buys first North American serial or all rights. Submit seasonal material 6 months in advance. Reports in 1 month. Sample copy for $5 and 9×12 SAE with 7 first-class stamps. Writer's guidelines for #10 SASE.

Nonfiction: How-to (on marketing products better or accomplishing more with equipment); new product; opinion (on the quick printing industry); personal experience (from which others can learn); technical (on printing). *No generic business articles*, or articles on larger printing applications. Buys 10-15 mss/year. Send complete ms. Length: 1,500-3,000 words. Pays $150 and up.

Photos: State availability of photos with submission. Reviews transparencies, prints. Offers no additional payment for photos accepted with ms. Captions and identification of subjects required.

Tips: "The use of digital publishing systems by quick printers is of increasing interest. Show a knowledge of the industry. Try visiting your local quick printer for an afternoon to get to know about us. When your articles make a point, back it up with examples, statistics, and dollar figures. We need good material in all areas, including equipment/software user profiles. Technical articles are most needed, but they must be accurate. No promotional pieces for a certain industry supplier."

‡SERIF, THE MAGAZINE OF TYPE & TYPOGRAPHY, Quixote Digital Typography, 1105 W. Chicago Ave., Suite 156, Oak Park IL 60302. (708)788-1501. Fax: (708)788-1530. E-mail: serif@quixote.com. Editor: D.A. Hosea. 80-100% freelance written. Quarterly magazine "covering the full spectrum of type and typography from classical to radical." Estab. 1994. Circ. 2,000. Pays on publication. Byline given. Buys first North American serial rights and the option to reprint in book form. Editorial lead time 6 months. Accepts simultaneous and previously published submissions. Sample copy for 9×12 SASE and 6 first-class stamps. Writer's guidelines for #10 SASE.

Nonfiction: Book excerpts, essays, exposé, general interest, historical/nostalgic, how-to, humor, interview/profile, new product, opinion, personal experience, photo feature, technical. Buys 12 mss/year. Send complete ms. Length: 500-5,000 words. Pays 20¢/word.

Photos: Send photos with submission. Reviews negatives and transparencies. Offers no additional payment for photos accepted with ms. Captions required. Buys one-time rights.

Tips: "Just because we haven't published something similar is no indication of disinterest."

PROFESSIONAL PHOTOGRAPHY

Journals for professional photographers are listed in this section. Magazines for the general public interested in photography techniques are in the Consumer Photography section. (For listings of markets for freelance photography use *Photographer's Market*, Writer's Digest Books.)

THE COMMERCIAL IMAGE, PTN Publishing Co., 445 Broad Hollow Rd., Melville NY 11747. (516)845-2700. Fax: (516)845-7109. Editor: Steven Shaw. Contact: Jennifer Sznurkowski, assistant editor. 50% freelance written. Monthly tabloid covering commercial photography. Pays on publication. Byline given. Buys one-time rights. Editorial lead time 3 months. Submit seasonal material 3 months in advance. Sample copy and writer's guidelines free on request.

Nonfiction: Interview/profile, technical. Buys 10 mss/year. Query with published clips. Length: 1,000-2,000 words. Pays $75/printed page.

Photos: Send photos with submission. Reviews 8×10 transparencies and prints. Offers no additional payment for photos accepted with ms. Captions, model releases, identification of subjects required. Buys one-time rights.

‡NEWS PHOTOGRAPHER, National Press Photographers Association, Inc., 1446 Conneaut Ave., Bowling Green OH 43402. (419)352-8175. Fax: (419)354-5435. E-mail: jgordon@bgnet.bgsu.edu. Editor: James R. Gordon. Published 13 times/year. "*News Photographer* magazine is dedicated to the advancement of still and television news photography. The magazine presents articles, interviews, profiles, history, new products, electronic imaging and news related to the practice of photojournalism." Estab. 1946. Circ. 11,000. **Pays on acceptance**. Publishes ms an average of 4 months after acceptance. Byline given. Offers 100% kill fee. Buys one-time rights. Editorial lead time 2 months. Submit seasonal material 2 months in advance. Accepts simultaneous and previously published submissions. Reports in 1 month. Sample copy for 9×12 SAE and 3 first-class stamps. Writer's guidelines free.

Nonfiction: Historical/nostalgic, how-to, interview/profile, new product, opinion, personal experience, photo feature, technical. Buys 10 mss/year. Query. Length: 1,500 words. Pays $300. Pays expenses of writers on assignment.
Photos: State availability of photos with submission. Reviews negatives, 35mm transparencies and 8×10 prints. Negotiates payment individually. Captions and identification of subjects required. Buys one-time rights.
Columns/Departments: Query.

PHOTO EDITORS REVIEW, Photo Editors International, 1201 Montego #4, Walnut Creek CA 94598. Phone/fax: (510)935-9735. Publisher/Photo Editor: Bob Shepherd. Bimonthly newsletter for professional photo editors and magazine photographers. Estab. 1994. Circ. 5,000. **Pays on acceptance.** Byline given. Offers 25% kill fee. Buys first North American serial, first, one-time or simultaneous rights. Editorial lead time 3 months. Submit seasonal material 4 months in advance. Accepts simultaneous submissions. Reports in 1 month on queries; 2 months on mss. Sample copy for $3 and #10 business envelope with 2 first-class stamps. Writer's guidelines for #10 SASE.
Nonfiction: Photo critiques from the editor's point of view and how-to photo features; legal and photo editing advice from professional photo editors. Buys 12-18 mss/year. Query. Length: 750-1,500 words. Pays up to $200 for assigned articles; up to $100 for unsolicited articles.
Reprints: Accepts previously published submissions.
Photos: Send photos with submission. (Remember, your submissions are unsolicited submissions. Although we will take every reasonable precaution to safeguard your photos, we cannot guarantee their safe return. Therefore, only send copies of originals.) Reviews contact sheets, 3½×5 to 8×10 prints. Offers $50/photo. Captions, model releases, identification of subjects required. Buys one-time rights.
Columns/Departments: Photo critiques, 750-1,500 words; legal (the photo editor and the law), 750-1,500 words; how-to photo features, 750-1,500 words. Buys 12-18 mss/year. Query. Pays $100-200.
Tips: "We are a trade publication that caters to the needs of professional photo editors; therefore, marketable photos that exhibit universal themes will be given top priority. We look for five characteristics by which we judge photographic materials: sharp exposure (unless the image was intended as a soft-focus shot), impact, easily identifiable theme or subject, emphasis of the theme or subject, and simplicity."

PHOTO LAB MANAGEMENT, PLM Publishing, Inc., 1312 Lincoln Blvd., Santa Monica CA 90401. (310)451-1344. Fax: (310)395-9058. E-mail: carolynplm@earthlink.net. Contact: Carolyn Ryan, editor. Associate Editor: Marquita Thomas. 75% freelance written. Monthly magazine covering process chemistries and equipment, digital imaging, and marketing/administration for photo lab owners, managers and management personnel. Estab. 1979. Circ. 21,000. Pays on publication. Publishes ms an average of 3 months after acceptance. Byline and brief bio given. Buys first North American serial rights. Reports on queries in 6 weeks.
Nonfiction: Personal experience (lab manager); technical; management or administration. Buys 40-50 mss/year. Query with brief bio. Length: 1,200-1,800 words. Payment negotiable.
Photos: Reviews 35mm color transparencies and 4-color prints suitable for cover. "We're looking for outstanding cover shots of photofinishing images."
Tips: "Our departments are written inhouse and we don't use 'fillers.' Send a query if you have some background in the industry or have a specific news story relating to photo processing or digital imaging. This industry is changing quickly due to computer technology, so articles must be cutting edge. Business management articles must focus on a photo lab approach and not be generic. Writers must have photofinishing knowledge."

THE PHOTO REVIEW, 301 Hill Ave., Langhorne PA 19047-2819. (215)757-8921. Fax: (215)757-6421. Editor: Stephen Perloff. 50% freelance written. Quarterly magazine on photography with reviews, interviews and articles on art photography. Estab. 1976. Circ. 2,500. Pays on publication. Publishes ms an average of 3 months after acceptance. Byline given. Buys one-time rights. Accepts simultaneous submissions. Reports in 1 month on queries; 2 months on mss. Sample copy for 9×12 SAE with 6 first-class stamps. Writer's guidelines for #10 SASE.
Nonfiction: Essays, historical/nostalgic, interview/profile, opinion. No how-to articles. Buys 10-15 mss/year. Query. Pays $25-200.
Reprints: Send tearsheet, photocopy or typed ms with rights for sale noted and information about when and where the article previously appeared. Payment varies.
Photos: Send photos with submission. Reviews 8×10 prints. Offers no additional payment for photos accepted with ms. Captions and identification of subjects required. Buys one-time rights.

PHOTOGRAPHIC PROCESSING, PTN Publishing Co., 445 Broad Hollow Rd., Melville NY 11747. (516)845-2700. Fax: (516)845-2797. Editor: Bill Schiffner. 30-40% freelance written. Monthly magazine covering photographic (commercial/minilab) and electronic processing markets. Estab. 1965. Circ. 23,000. Pays on publication. Publishes ms an average of 4 months after acceptance. Byline given. Offers $75 kill fee. Editorial lead time 3 months. Submit seasonal material 3 months in advance. Accepts simultaneous submissions. Sample copy and writer's guidelines free.
Nonfiction: How-to, interview/profile, new product, photo processing/digital imaging features. Buys 30-40 mss/year. Query with published clips. Length: 1,500-2,200 words. Pays $250-350 for assigned articles; $200-300 for unsolicited articles.
Photos: Send photos with submission. Reviews 4×5 transparencies, 4×6 prints. Offers no additional payment for photos accepted with ms. Captions required. Buys one-time rights. Looking for digitally manipulated covers.
Columns/Departments: Surviving in the 90s (business articles offering tips to labs on how make their businesses

run better), 1,500-1,800 words; Productivity Focus (getting more productivity out of your lab). Buys 10 mss/year. Query with published clips. Pays $150-200.

THE RANGEFINDER, 1312 Lincoln Blvd., Santa Monica CA 90401. (310)451-8506. Fax: (310)395-9058. Website: http://www.rangefinder_network.com. Contact: Bill Hurten, editor. Associate Editor: Marquita Thomas. Monthly magazine emphasizing professional photography. Circ. 50,000. Pays on publication. Publishes ms an average of 9 months after acceptance. Byline given. Buys first North American serial rights. Submit seasonal material 4 months in advance. Reports in 6 weeks. Sample copy for $3.50. Writer's guidelines for SASE.
Nonfiction: How-to (solve a photographic problem, such as new techniques in lighting, new poses or set-ups), profile, technical. "Articles should contain practical, solid information. Issues should be covered in-depth. Look thoroughly into the topic." Buys 5-7 mss/issue. Query with outline. Length: 800-1,200 words. Pays $100/published page.
Photos: State availability of photos with query. Captions preferred; model release required.
Tips: "Exhibit knowledge of photography. Introduce yourself with a well-written letter and a great story idea."

REAL ESTATE

AFFORDABLE HOUSING FINANCE, Business Communication Services, 657 Mission St., Suite 502, San Francisco CA 94105. (415)546-7255. Fax: (415)546-0954. E-mail: ahf@housingfinance.com. Editor: Andre Shashaty. Contact: Robert Freedman, associate editor. 20% freelance written. Bimonthly magazine. "We are a nuts-and-bolts magazine written for developers of affordable housing. Not generally interested in articles aimed at realtors or home buyers." Estab. 1992. Circ. 6,000. **Pays on acceptance.** Publishes ms an average of 1 month after acceptance. Byline given. Offers 50% kill fee. Buys all rights including electronic rights. Accepts simultaneous submissions. Reports in 1 month. Sample copy for 9×12 SAE with $2.16 postage. Writer's guidelines free.
Nonfiction: How-to, interview/profile (developer or financier), new product (new financing services), case studies of innovative affordable housing projects. Special issues: Rehab, Renovation and Repositioning, seniors housing, and tax exempt bond financing. "We have a very knowledgeable reader base in terms of housing finance—articles need to have hard news angle and skip the basics." Buys 10-20 mss/year. Query with published clips. Length: 500-2,000. Pays 25-45¢/word. Pays expenses of writers on assignment.
Reprints: Accepts previously published submissions. Payment varies.
Photos: State availability of photos with submission. Reviews prints. Offers additional payment for photos accepted with ms. Captions required. Buys all rights.
Tips: "Best to see sample copy before submitting. Writers with a strong background in business writing are welcome to query."

AREA DEVELOPMENT MAGAZINE, Sites and Facility Planning, Halcyon Business Publications, Inc., 400 Post Ave., Westbury NY 11590. (516)338-0900. Fax: (516)338-0100. Managing Editor: Pam Karr. Contact: Geraldine Gambale, editor. 80% freelance written. Prefers to work with published/established writers. Monthly magazine covering corporate facility planning and site selection for industrial chief executives worldwide. Estab. 1965. Circ. 42,000. Pays on publication. Publishes ms an average of 2 months after acceptance. Byline given. Buys all rights. Reports in 3 months. Free sample copy. Writer's guidelines for #10 SASE.
Nonfiction: How-to (experiences in site selection and all other aspects of corporate facility planning); historical (if it deals with corporate facility planning); interview (corporate executives and industrial developers); and related areas of site selection and facility planning such as taxes, labor, government, energy, architecture and finance. Buys 60 mss/year. Query. Length: 800-1,200 words. Pays 25¢/word. Sometimes pays expenses of writers on assignment.
Photos: State availability of photos with query. Reviews transparencies. Captions, identification preferred. Negotiates payment individually.

BUSINESS FACILITIES, Group C Communications, Inc., 121 Monmouth St., P.O. Box 2060, Red Bank NJ 07701. (908)842-7433. Fax: (908)758-6634. E-mail: peterson@groupc.com. Website: http://www.busfac.com. Contact: Eric Peterson, editor. Managing Editor: Mary Ellen McCandless. 30% freelance written. Prefers to work with published/established writers. Monthly magazine covering corporate expansion, economic development and commercial and industrial real estate. "Our audience consists of corporate site selectors and real estate people; our editorial coverage is aimed at providing news and trends on the plant location and corporate expansion field." Estab. 1967. Circ. 40,000. Pays on publication. Publishes ms an average of 2 months after acceptance. Byline given. Buys all rights. Reports in 2 weeks. Sample copy and writer's guidelines for SASE.
● Magazine is currently overstocked, and will be accepting fewer pieces for the near future.
Nonfiction: General interest, how-to, interview/profile, personal experience. No news shorts or clippings; feature material only. Buys 12-15 mss/year. Query. Length: 1,000-3,000 words. Pays $200-1,000 for assigned articles; $200-600 for unsolicited articles. Sometimes pays the expenses of writers on assignment.
Photos: State availability of photos with submission. Reviews contact sheets, transparencies, 8×10 prints. Payment negotiable. Captions, identification of subjects required. Buys one-time rights.
Tips: "First, remember that our reader is a corporate executive responsible for his company's expansion and/or relocation decisions and our writers have to get inside that person's head in order to provide him with something that's helpful in

his decision-making process. And second, the biggest turnoff is a telephone query. We're too busy to accept them and must require that all queries be put in writing. Submit major feature articles only; all news departments, fillers, etc., are staff-prepared. A writer should be aware that our style is not necessarily dry and businesslike. We tend to be more casual and a writer should look for that aspect of our approach."

CANADIAN PROPERTY MANAGEMENT, Mediaedge Communications Inc., 5255 Yonge St., Suite 1000, North York, Ontario M2N 6P4 Canada. (416)512-8186. E-mail: janel@mediaedge.com. Website: http://www.mediaedge.ca. 10% freelance written. Magazine published 8 times/year covering Canadian commercial, industrial, institutional (medical and educational), residential properties. "*Canadian Property Management* magazine is a trade journal supplying building owners and property managers with Canadian industry news, case law reviews, technical updates for building operations and events listings. Feature building and professional profile articles are regular features." Estab. 1985. Circ. 14,500. Pays on publication. Publishes ms an average of 3 months after acceptance. Byline given. Buys all rights. Editorial lead time 2 months. Submit seasonal material 2 months in advance. Accepts simultaneous submissions, if so noted. Reports in 3 weeks on queries; 2 months on mss. Sample copy for $5, subject to availability. Writer's guidelines free on request.
Nonfiction: Interview/profile, technical. "No promotional articles (e.g., marketing a product or service geared to this industry)!" Query with published clips. Length: 700-1,200 words. Pays an average of 35¢/word.
Reprints: Accepts previously published submissions.
Photos: State availability of photos with submission. Reviews transparencies, 3×5 prints. Offers no additional payment for photos accepted with ms. Captions, model releases, identification of subjects required.
Tips: "We do not accept promotional articles serving companies or their products. Freelance articles that are strong, information-based pieces that serve the interests and needs of property managers and building owners stand a better chance of being published. Proposals and inquiries with article ideas are appreciated the most. A good understanding of the real estate industry (management structure) is also helpful for the writer."

‡**CANADIAN REALTOR NEWS**, The Canadian Real Estate Association, 344 Slater St., 1600 Canada Building, Ottawa, Ontario K1R 7Y3 Canada. (613)237-7111. Fax: (613)234-2567. E-mail: jmccarthy@crea.ca. Editor: James McCarthy. 10-30% freelance written. Monthly tabloid (10 times a year) for licensed real estate professionals. Estab. 1955. Circ. 72,000. Pays on publication. Publishes ms an average of 1 month after acceptance. Byline given. Buys one-time rights and electronic rights for website. Editorial lead time 1 month. Sample copy for SAE.
Nonfiction: How-to (sell/manage real estate sales), interview/profile. Query. Length: 400-1,000 words. Pays $200-500. Sometimes pays expenses of writers on assignment.
Reprints: Accepts previously published submissions (except from competitors).
Photos: Negotiates payment individually. Identification of subjects required. Buys one-time rights. Reproduction with credit (not for profit).
Tips: "Call with suggested topics."

COMMERCIAL INVESTMENT REAL ESTATE JOURNAL, Commercial Investment Real Estate Institute, 430 N. Michigan Ave., Suite 600, Chicago IL 60611-4092. (312)321-4460. Fax: (312)321-4530. E-mail: csimpson@cirei.mhs .compuserve.com. Website: http://www.ccim.com. Editor and Publisher: Catherine Simpson. 10% freelance written. Bimonthly magazine. "*CIERJ* offers practical articles on current trends and business development ideas for commercial investment real estate practitioners." Estab. 1982. Circ. 10,000. **Pays on acceptance**. Publishes ms an average of 4 months after acceptance. Byline given. Offers 25% kill fee. Buys all rights. Editorial lead time 4 months. Submit seasonal material 4 months in advance. Reports in 2 weeks on queries; 1 month on mss. Sample copy for 9×12 SAE with 5 first-class stamps. Writer's guidelines for #10 SASE.
Nonfiction: Book excerpts, how-to, personal experience, technical. Buys 6 mss/year. Query with published clips. Length: 2,000-3,500 words. Pays $1,000-2,000. Sometimes pays expenses of writers on assignment.
Photos: Send photos with submission. Reviews prints. Offers no additional payment for photos accepted with ms. Buys all rights.
Tips: "Always query first with a detailed outline and published clips. Authors should have a background in writing on real estate or business subjects."

‡**THE COOPERATOR, The Co-op and Condo Monthly**, Manhattan Cooperator Publications, Inc., 301 E. 45th St., 17E, New York NY 10017. (212)697-1318. Fax: (212)682-7369. E-mail: diana@cooperator.com. Executive Editor: Victoria Chesler. Contact: Diana Mosher, executive editor. 20% freelance written. Monthly tabloid covering real estate. "*The Cooperator* covers condominium and cooperative issues in New York and beyond. It is read by unit owners and shareholders, board members and managing agents. We have just become a national publication and are interested in receiving articles from states outside of New York." Estab. 1980. Circ 60,000. Pays on publication. Publishes ms an average of 3 months after acceptance. Byline given. Buys all rights and makes work-for-hire assignments. Submit seasonal material 3 months in advance. Reports in 2 weeks on queries. Sample copy free. Writer's guidelines not available.
Nonfiction: Opinion. Buys 20 mss/year. Query with published clips. Length: 800-1,500 words. Pays $150-250.
Photos: State availability of photos with submission.

‡**THE DEALMAKER**, TKO, P.O. Box 2630, Mercerville NJ 08690. (609)587-6200. Fax: (609)587-3511. E-mail: deal.makers@property.com. Editor: Ann O'Neal. Managing Editor: Chris Gel. 10% freelance written. Weekly newsletter

covering "commercial real estate brokers, developers, management companies and investors." Estab. 1979. Circ. 6,100. Pays on publication. Publishes ms an average of 2 months after acceptance. Byline given. Offers 25% kill fee. Buys first North American serial rights. Editorial lead time 2 months. Accepts simultaneous submissions. Reports in 2 months on queries. Sample copy and writer's guidelines free.
Nonfiction: Interview/profile. Buys 8 mss/year. Query. Length: 2,000 words minimum. Pay varies.
Photos: State availability of photos with submission. Offers no additional payment for photos accepted with ms. Captions and identification of subjects required. Buys one-time rights.

JOURNAL OF PROPERTY MANAGEMENT, Institute of Real Estate Management, P.O. Box 109025, Chicago IL 60610-9025. (312)329-6058. Fax: (312)661-0217. E-mail: mevans@irem.org. Website: http://www.irem.org. Executive Editor: Mariwyn Evans. 30% freelance written. Bimonthly magazine covering real estate management. "The *Journal* has a feature/information slant designed to educate readers in the application of new techniques and to keep them abreast of current industry trends." Circ. 23,000. **Pays on acceptance.** Publishes ms an average of 3 months after acceptance. Byline given. Buys all rights. Reports in 6 weeks on queries; 1 month on mss. Free sample copy and writer's guidelines.
Nonfiction: How-to, interview, technical (building systems/computers), demographic shifts in business employment and buying patterns, marketing. "No non-real estate subjects, personality or company, humor." Buys 8-12 mss/year. Query with published clips. Length: 1,200-1,500 words. Sometimes pays the expenses of writers on assignment.
Reprints: Send photocopy of article or short story. Pays 35% of amount paid for an original article.
Photos: State availability of photos with submission. Reviews contact sheets. May offer additional payment for photos accepted with ms. Model releases, identification of subjects required. Buys one-time rights.
Columns/Departments: Kent Wadsworth, associate editor. Insurance Insights, Tax Issues, Investment and Finance Insights, Legal Issues. Buys 6-8 mss/year. Query. Length: 500-750 words.

MANAGERS REPORT: The Only National Trade Journal Serving Condominiums and Property Management, Ivor Thomas and Associates, 1700 Southern Blvd., West Palm Beach FL 33406. (407)687-4700. Fax: (407)687-9654. E-mail: mgrreport@aol.com. Editor: Ivor Thomas. Managing Editor: Marcia Thomas. Contact: Lisa Pinder, associate editor. 40% freelance written. Monthly magazine covering condominiums and property management. Estab. 1987. Circ. 20,000. **Pays on acceptance.** Buys second serial (reprint) rights. Editorial lead time 3 months. Submit seasonal material 4 months in advance. Accepts simultaneous submissions. Sample copy and writers guidelines free.
Nonfiction: How-to, interview/profile, new product, opinion, personal experience, photo feature, technical. Buys 120 mss/year. Query. Length: 50-3,000 words. Pays $25 (200-400 words); $75 (400-1,000 words); $150 (1,000-2,000 words).
Reprints: Accepts previously published submissions. Send typed ms with rights for sale noted.
Photos: Send photos with submission. Reviews contact sheets, negatives, prints. Offers $5-50/photo. Identification of subjects required. Buys all rights.
Poetry: Light verse, humorous relating to condominiums. Buys 12 poems/year. Submit maximum 12 poems at one time. Pays $10-50.
Fillers: Anecdotes, facts, gags to be illustrated by cartoonist, newsbreaks, short humor. Buys 60/year. Length: 6-50 words. Pays $10-50.
Tips: "We want to get more technical information. We need a layman's description of: e.g., how an air conditioner really cools air. We would like maintenance remedies: e.g., what is the best thing to be done for cracked pavement in a parking lot. Consult the reader response in the magazine for maintenance categories. We ask that our advertisers be used exclusively for research. Our readers are extrememly interested in knowing such things as the difference between latex and acrylic paint and when you use one or the other. We find that the more specific and technical the better. This also applies to interviews. Interviews are to gather good technical information. Legal, administrative maintenance. See our guidelines for primer questions. We would like interviews with pictures of individuals and/or associations. 95% of our interviews are done by phone. We would like to have regular correspondents in different areas of the country."

‡MULTIFAMILY EXECUTIVE, MGI Publications, 301 Oxford Valley Rd., Suite 903A, Yardley PA 19067. Fax: (215)321-5122. E-mail: mgipubs@aol.com. Editor: Edward J. McNeill, Jr., Contact: Jodi A. Bromberg, managing editor. 35% freelance written. Magazine published 8 times/year. "We target senior level executives in the multifamily housing industry—builders, developers, owners and managers." Circ. 25,000. Pays on publication. Publishes ms an average of 2 months after acceptance. Byline given. Buys first North American serial rights. Editorial lead time 3 months after acceptance. Submit seasonal material 4 months in advance. Reports in 2 months on queries. Sample copy for 9×12 SAE with 8 first-class stamps. Writer's guidelines free.
Nonfiction: Book excerpts, how-to, interview/profile, new product, opinion. Buys 15-20 mss/year. Query with published clips. Length: 750-1,500 words. Pays $100-1,000 for assigned articles; $100-500 for unsolicited articles. Sometimes pays expenses of writers on assignment.
Photos: State availability of photos with submission. Reviews transparencies. Negotiates payment individually. Model releases, identification of subjects required. Buys all rights.
Columns/Departments: Financial, Legal, Senior Housing, Affordable Housing (all written to an advanced level of multifamily executives); all 750-850 words. Buys 8 mss/year. Query with published clips. Pays $100-400.

‡NATIONAL RELOCATION & REAL ESTATE, RIS Publishing Inc., 50 Water St., Norwalk CT 06854. (203)855-1234. Fax: (203)852-7208. Editor: Lisa Prince. 30-50% freelance written. Bimonthly magazine covering residential real estate and corporate relocation. "Our readers are professionals within the relocation and real estate industries; therefore, we require our writers to have sufficient knowledge of the workings of these industries in order to ensure depth and accuracy in reporting." Estab. 1980. Circ. 33,000. Pays on publication. Byline sometimes given. Offers 20-50% kill fee. Buys all rights. Editorial lead time 4 months. Reports in 2 weeks on queries. Sample copy free.

Nonfiction: Exposé, how-to (use the Internet to sell real estate, etc.), interview/profile, new product, opinion, technical. Query with published clips. Length: 250-1,500 words. Pays $125-1,000. Pays writers with contributor copies or other premiums upon prior written agreement. Sometimes pays expenses of writers on assignment.

Photos: Send photos with submission. Reviews transparencies. Offers no additional payment for photos accepted with ms. Captions required.

Columns/Departments: Query with published clips. Pays $125-1,000.

Tips: "All queries must be done in writing. Phone queries are unacceptable. Any clips or materials sent should indicate knowledge of the real estate and relocation industries. In general, we are open to all knowledgeable contributors."

‡**PLANTS SITES & PARKS, The Corporate Advisor for Relocation Strategies**, BPI Communications Inc., 49 Music Square W., Nashville TN 37203. (800)561-5681. Fax: (615)329-4733. E-mail: info@bpicom.com. Website: www.bizsites.com. Editor: Ken Ibold. 35% freelance written. Bimonthly magazine covering business, especially as it involves site locations. Estab. 1974. Circ. 40,500. **Pays on acceptance.** Publishes ms an average of 1 month after acceptance. Byline given. Negotiable kill fee. Buys all rights. Editorial lead time 3-4 months. Reports in 1 month on queries. Sample copy and writer's guidelines free.

Nonfiction: Book excerpts, real estate, labor, industry, finance topics geared toward manufacturing executives. Buys 25-30 mss/year (total for features *and* columns/departments). Query with published clips. Length: 1,000-7,000 words. Pays $300 minimum for assigned articles. Pays expenses of writers on assignment.

Photos: State availability of photos with submission. Negotiates payment individually. Captions required. Rights negotiable.

Columns/Departments: Regional Review (profile business climate of each state), 1,000-5,000 words; Industry Outlook (trend stories on specific industries), 5,000-7,500 words; Global Market (business outlook for specific overseas areas), 2,000-5,000 words. Buys 25-30 mss/year (total for columns/departments and features). Query with published clips. Pays $300-2,000.

RESOURCES AND WASTE REDUCTION

‡**THE AMERICAN OIL & GAS REPORTER**, National Publisher's Group, P.O. Box 343, Derby KS 67037-0343. Editor: Bill Campbell. Contact: Tim Beims, special sections editor. 20% freelance written. Monthly magazine covering "cutting-edge technologies used in oil and gas exploration and production, with an emphasis on independent E&P companies. We also report on legislative and regulatory issues of importance to independent oilmen. Articles must be written to the industry, and about the industry." Estab. 1958. Circ. 13,540. Pays on publication. Publishes ms an average of 2 months after acceptance. Byline given. Offers 50% kill fee. Buys first rights. Editorial lead time 4 months. Submit seasonal material 4 months in advance. Accepts simultaneous submissions. Reports in 6 weeks on queries; 4 months on mss. Sample copy and writer's guidelines free.

Nonfiction: Interview/profile, technical. No blatantly promotional pieces, opinion, historical. Buys 24 mss/year. Query with published clips. Length: 1,500-2,300 words. Pays $200-750. Pays expenses of writers on assignment.

Tips: "Please send a *brief* abstract proposing a technical topic. Particularly interested in advanced technologies (geophysics, computer applications, 3- and 4-D seismic, subsea/offshore development, horizontal/multi-lateral drilling, etc.) with good case study applications."

‡**COMPOSTING NEWS, The Latest News in Composting and Scrap Wood Management**, McEntee Media Corporation, 13727 Holland Rd., Brook Park OH 44142. (216)362-7979. Fax: (216)362-6553. E-mail: 71241.2763@compuserve.com. Editor: Ken McEntee. 5% freelance written. Monthly newsletter. "We are interested in any news impacting the composting industry including new laws, regulations, new facilities/programs, end-uses, research, etc." Estab. 1992. Circ. 1,000. Pays on publication. Publishes ms an average of 1 month after acceptance. Buys first or all rights. Editorial lead time 1 month. Submit seasonal material 1 month in advance. Accepts simultaneous and previously published submissions. Reports in 2 months. Sample copy for 9×12 SAE and 55¢ postage. Writer's guidelines for #10 SASE.

Nonfiction: Book excerpts, essays, interview/profile, new product, opinion, personal experience, technical, new business, legislation, regulation, business expansion. Buys 0-5 mss/year. Query with published clips. Length: 100-5,000 words. Pays $10-500. Pays writers with contributor copies or other premiums by prior agreement.

Columns/Departments: Query with published clips. Pays $10-500.

Tips: "We appreciate leads on local news regarding composting, i.e., new facilities or business, new laws and regulations, unique programs, situations that impact supply and demand for composting. International developments are also of interest."

‡**EROSION CONTROL, The Journal for Erosion and Sediment Control Professionals**, Forester Communications, Inc., 5638 Hollister Ave., Suite 301, Santa Barbara CA 93117. (805)681-1300. Fax: (805)681-1312. E-mail: erosion@ix.netcom.com. Editor: John Trotti. 60% freelance written. Bimonthly magazine covering all aspects of erosion prevention and sediment control. "*Erosion Control* is a practical, hands-on, 'how-to' professional journal. Our readers

are civil engineers, landscape architects, builders, developers, public works officials, road and highway construction officials and engineers, soils specialists, farmers, landscape contractors and others involved with any activity that disturbs significant areas of surface vegetation." Estab. 1994. Circ. 17,000. Pays on publication. Publishes ms an average of 3 months after acceptance. Byline given. Buys all rights. Editorial lead time 4 months. Submit seasonal material 3 months in advance. Reports in 2 weeks. Accepts simultaneous submissions. Sample copy and writer's guidelines free.

Nonfiction: Photo feature, technical. Buys 15 mss/year. Query with published clips. Length: 3,000-4,000 words. Pays $350-650. Sometimes pays expenses of writers on assignment.

Photos: Send photos with submission. Reviews transparencies, prints. Offers no additional payment for photos accepted with ms. Captions, model releases, identification of subjects required. Buys all rights.

Tips: "Writers should have a good grasp of technology involved, good writing and communication skills, unbounded curiousity and no hidden agenda."

MSW MANAGEMENT, The Journal for Municipal Solid Waste Professionals, Forester Communications, Inc., 5638 Hollister Ave., Suite 301, Santa Barbara CA 93117. (805)681-1300. Fax: (805)681-1312. E-mail: erosion@ix.n etcom.com. Editor: John Trotti. 70% freelance written. Bimonthly magazine. "*MSW Management* is written for *public sector* solid waste professionals—the people working for the local counties, cities, towns, boroughs and provinces. They run the landfills, recycling programs, composting, incineration. They are responsible for all aspects of garbage collection and disposal; buying and maintaining the associated equipment; and designing, engineering and building the waste processing facilities, transfer stations and landfills." Estab. 1991. Circ. 24,000. Pays on publication. Byline given. Buys all rights. Editorial lead time 4 months. Submit seasonal material 4 months in advance. Accepts simultaneous submissions. Reports in 6 weeks on queries; 2 months on mss. Sample copy and writer's guidelines free.

Nonfiction: Photo feature, technical. "No rudimentary, basic articles written for the average person on the street. Our readers are experienced professionals with years of practical, in-the-field experience. Any material submitted that we judge as too fundamental will be rejected." Buys 15 mss/year. Query. Length: 3,000-4,000 words. Pays $350-650. Sometimes pays expenses of writers on assignment.

Photos: Send photos with submission. Reviews transparencies, prints. Offers no additional payment for photos accepted with ms. Captions, model releases, identification of subjects required. Buys all rights.

Tips: "We're a small company, easy to reach. We're open to any and all ideas as to possible editorial topics. We endeavor to provide the reader with usable material, and present it in full color with graphic embellishment whenever possible. Dry, highly technical material is edited to make it more palatable and concise. Most of our feature articles come from freelancers. Interviews and quotes should be from public sector solid waste managers and engineers—*not* PR people, *not* manufacturers. Strive to write material that is 'over the heads' of our readers. If anything, attempt to make them 'reach.' Anything submitted that is too basic, elementary, fundamental, rudimentary, etc. cannot be accepted for publication."

‡REMEDIATION MANAGEMENT, Forester Communications, 5638 Hollister Ave. #301, Santa Barbara CA 93117. Phone/fax: (805)681-1300. E-mail: erosion@ix.netcom.com. Editor: John Trotti. 50% freelance written. "The magazine is read by environmental restoration professionals who have the projects (PRPs) or those who perform the remediation tasks (assessment, engineering, construction and treatment." Estab. 1995. Circ. 17,000. Pays on publication. Publishes ms an average of 2 months after acceptance. Byline given. Buys all rights. Editorial lead time 4 months. Accepts simultaneous submissions. Reports in 2 weeks on queries. Sample copy and writer's guidelines free.

Nonfiction: Photo feature, technical. Buys 15 mss/year. Query. Length: 3,000-4,000 words. Pays $350-650. Pays expenses of writers on assignment.

Photos: Send photos with submission. Reviews transparencies and prints. Offers no additional payment for photos accepted with ms. Captions and identification of subjects required. Buys negotiable rights.

Columns/Departments: Query.

Tips: "Display a good grasp of the technology involved, good writing and communications skills, unbounded curiosity and have no hidden agenda."

‡WORLD WASTES MAGAZINE, The Independent Voice, Intertec Publishing, 6151 Powers Ferry Rd. NW, Atlanta GA 30339-2941. (770)955-2500. Fax: (770)618-0349. E-mail: pverbaas@mindspring.com. Editor: Bill Wolpin. Contact: Patti Verbanas, managing editor. 90% freelance written. Monthly magazine. "*World Wastes* reaches individuals and firms engaged in the removal and disposal of solid/hazardous wastes. This includes: refuse contractors; landfill operators; municipal, county and other government officials; recyclers and handlers of secondary materials; major generators of waste, such as plants and chain stores; engineers, architects and consultants; manufacturers and distributors of equipment; universities, libraries and associations; and legal, insurance and fianncial firms allied to the field. Readers include: owners, presidents, vice-presidents, directors, superintendents, engineers, managers, supervisors, consultants, purchasing agents and commissioners." Estab. 1958. Circ. 38,000. Pays on publication. Publishes ms an average of 4 months after acceptance. Byline given. Buys all rights. Editorial lead time 2 months. Submit seasonal material 6 months in advance. Reports in 1 week on queries; 1 month on mss. Sample copy and writer's guidelines free.

Nonfiction: How-to (practical information on improving solid waste management, i.e., how to rehabilitate a transfer station, how to improve recyclable collection, how to manage a landfill, etc.), interview/profile (of prominent persons in the solid waste industry). "No feel-good 'green' articles about recycling. Remember our readers are not the citizens but the governments and private contractors. No 'why you should recycle' articles." Buys over 50 mss/year. Query. Length: 700-1,500 words. Pays $75 flat rate to $150/printed page. Sometimes pays expenses of writers on assignment.

Photos: Send photos with submission. Reviews contact sheets, negatives, transparencies, prints. Offers no additional payment for photos accepted with ms. Identification of subjects required.

Tips: "Read the magazine and understand our audience. Write useful articles with sidebars that the readers can apply to their jobs. Use the Associated Press style book. Freelancers can send in queries or manuscripts or can fax a letter of interest (including qualifications/resume) in possible assignments. Writers must be deadline-oriented."

SELLING AND MERCHANDISING

Sales personnel and merchandisers interested in how to sell and market products successfully consult these journals. Publications in nearly every category of Trade also buy sales-related materials if they are slanted to the product or industry with which they deal.

THE AMERICAN SALESMAN, 320 Valley, Burlington IA 52601-5513. Fax: (319)752-3421. Publisher: Michael S. Darnall. Editor: Barbara Boeding. Monthly magazine for distribution through company sales representatives. Estab. 1955. Circ. 1,500. Publishes ms an average of 4 months after acceptance. Sample copy and writer's guidelines for 6×9 SAE with 3 first-class stamps; mention *Writer's Market* in request.

Nonfiction: Sales seminars, customer service and follow-up, closing sales, sales presentations, handling objections, competition, telephone usage and correspondence, managing territory, new innovative sales concepts. No sexist material. Written from a salesperson's viewpoint. Public relations articles or case histories reviewed. Length: 900-1,200 words. Uses no advertising. Follow AP Stylebook. Include biography and/or byline with ms submissions. Author photos used. Send correspondence to Editor.

ANSOM, Army Navy Store and Outdoor Merchandiser, PTN Publishing Co., 2 University Plaza, Suite 204, Hackensack NJ 07601. (201)487-7800. Fax: (201)487-1061. Editor: Paul Bubny. 20% freelance written. Monthly tabloid covering army/navy and outdoor product retailing (camping, hunting, fishing and related outdoor sports). Estab. 1949. Circ. 12,300. Pays on publication. Publishes ms an average of 2 months after acceptance. Byline given. Buys one-time rights. Editorial lead time 6 weeks. Submit seasonal material 3 months in advance. Reports in 1 week on queries; 1 month on mss. Writer's guidelines free.

Nonfiction: Book excerpts, how-to (merchandise various products, manage a retail operation), interview/profile, new product, technical. Buys 6-9 mss/year. Send complete ms. Length: 800-4,000 words. Pays $125-250 for assigned articles; $75-125 for unsolicited articles. Sometimes pays expenses of writers on assignment.

Reprints: Accepts previously published submissions, if non-competing market. Send typed ms with rights for sale noted and information about when and where the article previously appeared.

Photos: Send photos with submission. Reviews 5×8 prints, color slides. Negotiates payment individually. Captions, identification of subjects required. Buys one-time rights.

Columns/Departments: Legal Advisor (legal issues for small business owners), 1,000-1,200 words; Business Insights (general management topics of interest to small business owners), 1,000-1,500 words. Buys 12-18 mss/year. Send complete ms. Pays $75-175.

Tips: "Approach the editor either with subject matter that fits in with the magazine's specific area of concern, or with willingness to take on assignments that fit magazine's editorial scope."

ART MATERIALS TODAY, The Retailer's Guide to Success, F&W Publications, 1507 Dana Ave., Cincinnati OH 45207. (513)531-2690 ext. 422. Fax: (513)531-2902. E-mail: amtedit@aol.com. Editor: Cristine Antolik. Contact: Todd Tedesco, managing editor. 60-70% freelance written. Bimonthly magazine. "*Art Materials Today* is written for art material retailers. Offers practical business advice, industry news and information, merchandising tips, techniques and new products." Estab. 1993. Circ. 10,500. **Pays on acceptance.** Publishes ms an average of 4 months after acceptance. Byline given. Offers 20% kill fee. Buys first North American serial rights. Editorial lead time 5 months. Submit seasonal material 4 months in advance. Accepts simultaneous submissions. Reports in 1 month. Sample copy for 10×13 SAE with 5 first-class stamps. Writer's guidelines for #10 SASE.

Nonfiction: How-to, humor, interview/profile, investigative reports, new product, opinion. Buys 30 mss/year. Query with published clips or send complete ms. Length: 1,000-2,000 words. Pays $150-350. Sometimes pays expenses of writers on assignment.

Reprints: Accepts previously published submissions from non-competing markets. Send photocopy of article and information about when and where the article previously appeared. Pays 20% of amount paid for an original article.

Photos: Send photos with submission. Reviews 4×5 transparencies, 3½×5 prints. Offers no additional payment for photos accepted with ms. Captions required. Buys one-time rights.

Columns/Departments: What's Hot (top selling industry products), 1,500 words; Etc. (inspirational/humorous tidbits about business/industry), 1,000 words; Merchandising, 1,500 words; Finance, 1,500 words; Marketing, 1,500 words. Buys 20 mss/year. Query with published clips or send complete ms. Pays $75-350.

Tips: "Know the retail industry in general. Some art knowledge is helpful."

BALLOONS AND PARTIES MAGAZINE, Festivities Publications, 815 Harris St., Jacksonville FL 32206. (904)634-1902. Fax: (904)633-8764. Publisher/Editor: Debra Paulk. 10% freelance written. Monthly international trade journal for professional party decorators and for gift delivery businesses. Estab. 1986. Circ. 7,000. Pays on publication. Publishes ms an average of 3 months after acceptance. Byline given. Buys all rights. Submit seasonal material 6 months in advance. Reports in 6 weeks. Sample copy for 9×12 SAE.

Nonfiction: Interview/profile, photo feature, technical, craft. Buys 12 mss/year. Query with or without published clips, or send complete ms. Length: 500-1,500 words. Pays $100-300 for assigned articles; $50-200 for unsolicited articles. Sometimes pays expenses of writers on assignment.

Reprints: Send typed ms with rights for sale noted and information about when and where the article previously appeared. Length: up to 2,500 words. Pays 10¢/word.

Photos: Send photos with submission. Reviews 2×2 transparencies, 3×5 prints. Captions, model releases, identification of subjects required. Buys all rights.

Columns/Departments: Great Ideas (craft projects using balloons, large scale decorations), 200-500 words. Send complete ms with photos.

Tips: "Show unusual, lavish, and outstanding examples of balloon sculpture, design and decorating and other craft projects. Offer specific how-to information. Be positive and motivational in style."

‡CARD TRADE, Krause Publications, 700 E. State St., Iola WI 54990. (715)445-2214. Fax: (715)445-4087. E-mail: card.trade@krause.com. Editor: Kevin Isaacson. Contact: Scott Kelnhofer, managing editor. 20% freelance written. Monthly magazine covering the sports collectible industry. "We're looking for experts in small business retailing and related sales." Estab. 1994. Circ. 12,000. Pays on publication. Buys perpetual but non-exclusive rights. Editorial lead time 1 month.

Nonfiction: How-to (retail advice), new product. Buys 6-10 mss/year. Query. Length: 1,00-2,500 words. Pays $125-400.

Columns/Departments: Buys 30 mss/year. Query. Pays $125-200.

CHRISTIAN RETAILING, Strang Communications, 600 Rinehart Road, Lake Mary FL 32746. (407)333-0600. Fax: (407)333-7133. E-mail: mford@strang.com. Website: http://www.strang.com. Managing Editor: Marcia Ford. 60% freelance written. Magazine published 20 times/year covering issues and products of interest to Christian vendors and retail stores. "Our editorial is geared to help retailers run a successful business. We do this with product information, industry news and feature articles." Estab. 1958. Circ. 9,500. Pays on publication. Publishes ms an average of 5 months after acceptance. Bylines sometimes given. Kill fee varies. Buys all rights. Submit seasonal material 5 months in advance. Reports in 2 months. Sample copy for $3. Writer's guidelines for #10 SASE.

Nonfiction: How-to (any articles on running a retail business—books, gifts, music, video, clothing of interest to Christians), new product, religious, technical. Buys 36 mss/year. Send complete ms. Length: 700-2,000 words. Pays $200-340. Sometimes pays expenses of writers on assignment.

Reprints: Send photocopy of article and information about when and where the article previously appeared. Pay varies.

Photos: State availability of photos with submission. Reviews contact sheets, transparencies, prints. Usually offers no additional payment for photos accepted with ms. Captions required. Buys one-time rights.

Columns/Departments: Industry News; Book News; Music News; Video Update; Product Spectrum; Gift News.

Fillers: Cartoon, illustrations, graphs/charts.

Tips: "Visit Christian bookstores and see what they're doing—the products they carry, the issues that concern them. Then write about it!"

COLLEGE STORE, National Association of College Stores, 500 E. Lorain, Oberlin OH 44074. (216)775-7777. Fax: (216)775-4769. E-mail: rstevens@nacs.org. Website: www.nacs.org. Editor: Ronald D. Stevens. 50% freelance written. Bimonthly association magazine. "*College Store* is the journal of record for the National Association of College Stores and serves its members by publishing information and expert opinion on all phases of college store retailing." Estab. 1923. Circ. 7,200. **Pays on acceptance**. Byline given. Buys first rights. Editorial lead time 3 months. Submit seasonal material 6 months in advance. Accepts simultaneous submissions. Reports in 1 month. Sample copy free. Writer's guidelines not available.

• *College Store* celebrates its 75th anniversary, January 1998.

Nonfiction: Historical/nostalgic, how-to, interview/profile, personal experience, technical (unique attributes of college stores/personnel). "Articles must have clearly defined connection to college stores and collegiate retailing." Buys 24 mss/year. Query with published clips. Length: 1,500-3,000 words. Pays $400 minimum for assigned articles; $200 minimum for unsolicited articles. Sometimes pays expenses of writers on assignment.

Reprints: Send tearsheet or photocopy of article or short story or typed ms with rights for sale noted. Pay negotiable.

Photos: Send photos with submission. Reviews 2¼×2¼ transparencies, 5×7 prints. Negotiates payment individually. Captions, identification of subjects required. Buys one-time rights.

Columns/Departments: Buys 12 mss/year. Query with published clips. Pays $200-400.

Tips: "It's best if writers work (or have worked) in a college store. Articles on specific retailing successes are most open to freelancers—they should include information on how well an approach worked and the reasons for it, whether they are specific to a campus or region, etc."

THE CRAFTS REPORT, The Business Journal for the Crafts Industry, 300 Water St., P.O. Box 1992, Wilmington DE 19899. (302)656-2209. Fax: (302)656-4894. E-mail: tcrmag@aol.com. Website: http://www.craftsreport.com/. Editor: Bernadette Smedile Finnerty. 50% freelance written. Monthly magazine. "Our readers are professional craft artists, retailers, show promoters, from beginners to established professionals. We publish articles that help them market and sell their work, keep track of finances, inspire their creativity or anything else that will help them enhance their livelihood in craft." Estab. 1975. Circ. 20,000. Pays on publication. Publishes ms an average of 4 months after acceptance. Byline given. Offers $50 kill fee. Buys first North American serial rights. Editorial lead time 4 months. Sample copy for $5. Writer's guidelines for #10 SASE.

Nonfiction: Inspirational, interview/profile, new product (no pay), opinion, personal experience, photo feature. Special issues: Shows and Fairs (April); Bridal (May). No how-to or fluff. Buys 36 mss/year. Query with published clips. Length: 1,500-3,000 words. Pays 20¢/word maximum for assigned articles; 13¢/word maximum for unsolicited articles. Sometimes pays expenses of writers on assignment.

Photos: Send photos with submission. Reviews transparencies, 3×5 prints. Offers no additional payment for photos accepted with ms. Identification of subjects required.

Columns/Departments: Noelle Backer, associate editor. Craft Show Reviews (for the benefit of buyers and craft artists to choose shows to participate in), 700-900 words; Profiles (unusual crafts/success stories), 900 words; Crafting Your Business (business/management how-to), 900 words. Buys 6 mss/year. Query with published clips. Pays $75-200.

Tips: "First person and point of view articles are a good way to break in. For columns and features, we're looking for well-researched, in-depth material. Research plans must be outlined in the query letter. Well-researched articles are a must. Know what you're asking to write about and prove it in your query letter. Queries are considered more seriously than unsolicited manuscripts. Also, we're looking for more coverage of craft shows in the Midwest."

EDUCATIONAL DEALER, Fahy-Williams Publishing, Inc., 171 Reed St., P.O. Box 1080, Geneva NY 14456-8080. (315)789-0458. Fax: (315)781-6820. Editor: J. Kevin Fahy. 50% freelance written. Magazine published 5 times/year. "Slant should be toward educational supply *dealers*, not teachers or educators, as most commonly happens." Estab. 1973. Circ. 12,500. Pays on publication. Byline given. Buys one-time rights. Accepts simultaneous submissions. Reports in 3 weeks on queries; 3 months on mss. Sample copy for $3.

Nonfiction: Practical how-tos on merchandising, marketing, retailing, customer service, managing people, etc. Buys 10 mss/year. Query. Length: 1,500 words minimum. Pays $50 minimum.

Reprints: Send photocopy of article.

Photos: Send photos with submission. Reviews contact sheets. Offers no additional payment for photos accepted with ms. Identification of subjects required. Buys one-time rights.

Tips: "Our special features section is most open to freelancers. Become familiar with the educational supply industry, which is growing quickly. While the industry is a large one in terms of dollars spent on school supply products, it's a 'small' one in terms of its players and what they're doing. Everyone knows everyone else; they belong to the same organizations: NSSEA and EDSA. We are accepting more freelance material."

EVENTS BUSINESS NEWS, S.E.N. Inc., 523 Route 38, Suite 207, Cherry Hill NJ 08002. (609)488-5255. Fax: (609)488-8324. Contact: Jake O'Brien, editor. 20% freelance written. Bimonthly glossy magazine covering special events across North America, including festivals, fairs, auto shows, home shows, trade shows, etc. Covers 15 categories of shows/events. Byline given. Buys first rights. Submit seasonal material 3 months in advance. Sample copy and writers guidelines free.

Nonfiction: How-to, interview/profile, event review, new product. Special issues: annual special event directory, covering over 38,000 events. No submissions unrelated to selling at events. Query. Length: 400-750 words. Pays $2.50/column inch.

Reprints: Send photocopy of article and information about when and where the article previously appeared.

Photos: Send photos with submission. Reviews contact sheets. Offers $20/photo. Captions required. Buys one-time rights.

Columns/Departments: Five columns monthly (dealing with background of event, vendors or unique facets of industry in North America). Query with published clips. Length: 400-700 words. Pays $3column in.

‡GIFTWARE NEWS, Talcott Corp., 112 Adrossan, P.O. Box 5398, Deptford NJ 08096. (609)227-0798. Editor: Anthony DeMasi. 55% freelance written. Monthly magazine covering gifts, collectibles, and tabletops for giftware retailers. Estab. 1976. Circ. 45,000. Pays on publication. Publishes ms an average of 2 months after acceptance. Byline given. Buys all rights. Submit seasonal/holiday material 4 months in advance. Reports in 2 months on mss. Sample copy for $5.

Nonfiction: How-to (sell, display), new product. Buys 50 mss/year. Send complete ms. Length: 1,500-2,500 words. Pays $150-250 for assigned articles; $75-100 for unsolicited articles.

Photos: Send photos with submission. Reviews 4×5 transparencies and 5×7 prints. Offers no additional payment for photos accepted with ms. Identification of subjects required.

Columns/Departments: Stationery, giftbaskets, collectibles, holiday merchandise, tabletop, wedding market and display—all for the gift retailer. Buys 36 mss/year. Send complete ms. Length: 1,500-2,500 words. Pays $75-200.

Tips: "We are not looking so much for general journalists but rather experts in particular fields who can also write."

‡THE MUSIC & SOUND RETAILER, The Newsmagazine for Musical Instruments and Sound Product Merchandising, Testa Communications, 25 Willowdale Ave., Port Washington NV 11050. (516)767-2500. Fax: (516)883-5371. E-mail: msrctailer@testa.com. Editor: Adam Remson. Contact: David Feete, assistant editor. 25% freelance written. Monthly tabloid. "We are a news magazine covering business trends in the musical instrument industry.

We cover only the combon segment (not band and orchestra or piano) and come at it with a bit of irreverance and humor." Estab. 1983. Circ. 11,000. Pays on publication. Publishes ms an average of 2 months after acceptance. Byline given. Offers 50% kill fee. Buys all rights. Editorial lead time 2 months. Sample copy free. Writer's guidelines not available.

Photos: State availability of photos with submission. Offers no additional payment for photos accepted with ms. Buys one-time rights.

Columns/Departments: Buys 10 mss/year. Query. Pays $150-300.

PARTY & PAPER RETAILER, 4Ward Corp, 70 New Canaan Ave., Norwalk CT 06850. (203)845-8020. Editor-in-Chief: Trisha McMahon Drain. 90% freelance written. Monthly magazine for "every aspect of how to do business better for owners of party and fine stationery shops. Tips and how-tos on display, marketing, success stories, merchandising, operating costs, etc." Estab. 1986. Circ. 25,000. Pays on publication. Offers 15% kill fee. Buys first North American serial rights. Editorial lead time 2 months. Submit seasonal material 6 months in advance. Reports in 2 months. Sample copy for $5

Nonfiction: Book excerpts, how-to (retailing related). No articles written in the first person. Buys 100 mss/year. Query with published clips. Length: 800-1,800 words. Pay "depends on topic, word count expertise, deadline." Pays telephone expenses of writers on assignment.

Reprints: Send tearsheet or photocopy of article and information about when and where the article previously appeared.

Photos: State availability of photos with submission. Reviews transparencies. Negotiates payment individually. Captions, identification of subjects required. Buys one-time rights.

Columns/Departments: Shop Talk (successful party/stationery store profile), 1,800 words; Storekeeping (selling, employees, market, running store), 800 words; Cash Flow (anything finance related), 800 words; On Display (display ideas and how-to). Buys 30 mss/year. Query with published clips. Pay varies.

PROFESSIONAL SELLING, 24 Rope Ferry Rd., Waterford CT 06386-0001. (860)442-4365. Fax: (860)437-1593. Editor: Paulette S. Kitchens. 33% freelance written. Prefers to work with published/established writers. Bimonthly newsletter for sales professionals covering industrial, wholesale, high-tech and financial services sales. "*Professional Selling* provides field sales personnel with both the basics and current information that can help them better perform the sales function." Estab. 1917. **Pays on acceptance.** Publishes ms an average of 6 months after acceptance. No byline given. Buys all rights. Submit seasonal material 6 months in advance. Reports in 1 month. Sample copy and writer's guidelines for #10 SAE with 2 first-class stamps.

Nonfiction: How-to (successful sales techniques); interview/profile (interview-based articles). "We buy only interview-based material." Buys 12-15 mss/year. Written queries only; no unsolicited mss. Length: 800-1,000 words. Pays 12-15¢/word.

Tips: "*Professional Selling* includes four-pages (Sales Spotlight) devoted to a single topic of major importance to sales professionals. Only the lead article for each section is open to freelancers. Lead article must be based on an interview with an actual sales professional. Freelancers may occasionally interview sales managers, but the slant must be toward field sales, *not* management."

‡PROSALES, Hanley-Wood, Inc., One Thomas Circle, Suite 600, Washington DC 20005. (202)452-0800. Fax: (202)785-1974. E-mail: hkanter@hanley-wood.com. Editor: Greg Brooks. Contact: Hilary Kanter, managing editor. 30% freelance written. Monthly magazine covering construction supply dealers. Estab. 1989. Circ. 40,000. **Pays on acceptance**. Publishes ms an average of 4 months after acceptance. Byline given. Offers 25% kill fee. Buys all rights. Editorial lead time 6 months. Submit seasonal material 6 months in advance. Reports in 2 months on queries; 3 months on mss. Sample copy free.

Nonfiction: Interview/profile, new product, personal experience, technical. Buys 70 mss/year. Query with published clips. Length: 500-2,000 words. Pays $300-1,200. Sometimes pays expenses of writers on assignment.

Photos: State availability of photos with submission. Offers no additional payment for photos accepted with ms. Identification of subjects required. Buys all rights.

SALES AND MARKETING STRATEGIES & NEWS, Hughes Communications, 211 W. State St., Rockford IL 61101. Fax: (815)963-7773. Managing Editor: Bruce Ericson. Contact: Kristi Nelson, senior editor. Tabloid published 8 times/year covering brand marketing, promotion, incentives, sales automation, sales training, integrated marketing, meetings, p.o.p., trade show marketing. Estab. 1991. Circ. 65,000. Pays on publication. Publishes ms 3 months after acceptance. Byline given. Offers 15% kill fee. Buys first North American serial rights. Editorial lead time 4 months. Sample copy and writer's guidelines free.

Nonfiction: How-to, technical. Buys 120 mss/year. Query. Length: 500-900 words. Pays $150-300 for assigned articles. Expert writers are given a bio at end of story. Sometimes pays expenses of writers on assignment.

Photos: Send photos with submission. Reviews transparencies and prints. Offers no additional payment for photos accepted with ms. Identification of subjects required.

‡VIDEO STORE MAGAZINE, Advanstar Communications, 201 E. Sandpointe Ave. #600, Santa Ana CA 92707. (714)513-8465. Fax: (714)513-8403. E-mail: vstore@aol.com. Editor: Thomas K. Arnold. Contact: Marion Flanagan, executive editor. 35% freelance written. "We are a weekly business magazine for the home video industry. Our primary readers are the nation's video retailers. We focus on industry news and retailing trends." Estab. 1979. Circ. 45,000.

Pays on publication. Publishes ms an average of 1 month after acceptance. Byline given. Offers 50% kill fee. Buys first North American serial rights. Submit seasonal material 1 month in advance. Reports in 2 weeks on queries; 1 month on mss. Sample copy for 11×14 SAE and 3 first-class stamps.

Nonfiction: How-to (features on retailing, merchandising and management). Buys 30 mss/year. Query or query with published clips. Length: 1,600-2,400 words. Pays $400. Pays expenses of writers on assignment.

Photos: State availability of photos with submission. Reviews contact sheets. Offers $50/photo. Captions, model releases and identification of subjects required. Buys one-time rights.

Tips: "Be familiar with video stores and with the video business. Read our magazine and talk to video retailers about their concerns and needs. We need more management-type features; product stories are best handled by staff."

SPORT TRADE

Retailers and wholesalers of sports equipment and operators of recreation programs read these journals. Magazines about general and specific sports are classified in the Consumer Sports section.

AMERICAN FIREARMS INDUSTRY, AFI Communications Group, Inc., 2455 E. Sunrise Blvd., 9th Floor, Ft. Lauderdale FL 33304-3118. Fax: (954)561-4129. Articles Editor: R.A. Legmeister. 10% freelance written. Works with writers specifically in the firearms trade. Monthly magazine specializing in the sporting arms trade. Estab. 1973. Circ. 60,000. Pays on publication. Publishes ms an average of 1 month after acceptance. Buys all rights. Reports in 2 weeks.

Nonfiction: Publishes informational, technical and new product articles. No general firearms subjects. Query. Length: 900-1,500 words. Pays $150-300. Sometimes pays expenses of writers on assignment.

Photos: Reviews 8×10 color glossy prints. Manuscript price includes payment for photos.

‡BICYCLE RETAILER & INDUSTRY NEWS, Miller Freeman Publishing, 502 W. Cordova, Santa Fe NM 87501. (505)988-5099. Fax: (505)988-7224. E-mail: msani@aol.com. Managing Editor: Michael Gamstetler. Contact: Marc Sani, editor. 10% freelance written. Tabloid published 18 times/year covering bicycle industry. Very news-oriented. Estab. 1991. Circ. 14,500. **Pays on acceptance.** Publishes ms an average of 2 weeks after acceptance. Byline given. Buys all rights. Accepts simultaneous submissions. Reports in 3 days on queries. Sample copy and writer's guidelines free.

Nonfiction: Interview/profile, new product, technical. No travel, nostalgia, essays, humor. Buys 50-60 mss/year. Query. Length: 1,200 words. Pays up to $600 for assigned articles; 20¢/word for unsolicited articles.

Reprints: Accepts previously published submissions.

Photos: Offers $50/photo. Negotiates payment individually. Identification of subjects required. Buys one-time rights.

FITNESS MANAGEMENT, Issues and Solutions in Fitness Services, Leisure Publications, Inc., 215 S. Highway 101, Suite 110, P.O. Box 1198, Solana Beach CA 92075-0910. (619)481-4155. Fax: (619)481-4228. E-mail: fitmgt@cts.com. Website: http://www.fitnessworld.com. Co-Publisher: Edward H. Pitts. Contact: Ronale Tucker, editor. 50% freelance written. Monthly magazine. "Readers are owners, managers and program directors of physical fitness facilities. *FM* helps them run their enterprises safely, efficiently and profitably. Ethical and professional positions in health, nutrition, sports medicine, management, etc., are consistent with those of established national bodies." Estab. 1985. Circ. 26,000. Pays on publication. Publishes ms an average of 5 months after acceptance. Byline given. Pays 50% kill fee. Buys all rights (all articles published in *FM* are also published and archived on its website). Submit seasonal material 6 months in advance. Reports in 3 months. Sample copy for $5. Writer's guidelines for #10 SASE.

Nonfiction: Book excerpts (prepublication); how-to (manage fitness center and program); new product (no pay); photo feature (facilities/programs); technical; other (news of fitness research and major happenings in fitness industry). No exercise instructions or general ideas without examples of fitness businesses that have used them successfully. Buys 50 mss/year. Query. Length: 750-2,000 words. Pays $60-300 for assigned articles. Pays expenses of writers on assignment.

Photos: Send photos with submission. Reviews contact sheets, 2×2 and 4×5 transparencies; prefers glossy prints, 5×7 to 8×10. Offers $10-25/photo. Captions, model releases required.

Tips: "We seek writers who are expert in a business or science field related to the fitness-service industry or who are experienced in the industry. Be current with the state of the art/science in business and fitness and communicate it in human terms (avoid intimidating academic language; tell the story of how this was learned and/or cite examples or quotes of people who have applied the knowledge successfully)."

GOLF COURSE NEWS, The Newspaper for the Golf Course Industry, United Publications Inc., P.O. Box 997, 102 Lafayette St., Yarmouth ME 04096. (207)846-0600. Fax: (207)846-0657. Managing Editor: Mark Leslie.

FOR INFORMATION on setting your freelance fees, see How Much Should I Charge?

Contact: Hal Phillips, editor. 15% freelance written. Monthly tabloid "written with the golf course superintendent in mind. Our readers are superintendents, course architects and builders, owners and general managers." Estab. 1989. Circ. 25,000. **Pays on acceptance.** Publishes ms an average of 2 months after acceptance. Byline given. Buys first North American serial rights. Editorial lead time 1 month. Submit seasonal material 2 months in advance. Reports in 2 weeks on queries; 2 months on mss. Free sample copy and writer's guidelines.

Nonfiction: Book excerpts, general interest, interview/profile, new product, opinion, photo feature. "No how-to articles." Buys 24 mss/year. Query with published clips. Length: 500-1,000 words. Pays $200. Sometimes pays expenses of writers on assignment.

Photos: Send photos with submission. Reviews negatives, transparencies, prints. Offers no additional payment for photos accepted with ms. Identification of subjects required. Buys one-time rights.

Columns/Departments: On the Green (innovative ideas on the golf course), 500-800 words; Shop Talk (in the maintenance facility). Buys 4 mss/year. Query with published clips. Pays $200-500.

Tips: "Keep your eye out for news affecting the golf industry. Then contact us with your story ideas. We are a national paper and accept both national and regional interest articles. We are interested in receiving features on development of golf projects. We also have an edition covering the golf industry in the Asia-Pacific retion—aptly called *Golf Course News Asia-Pacific* published four times per year—April, June, September and November."

‡**IDEA TODAY**, The International Association of Fitness Professionals, Dept. WM, 6190 Cornerstone Court E., Suite 204, San Diego CA 92121. (619)535-8979. Fax: (619)535-8234. E-mail: hannont@ideafit.com. Contact: Therese Hannon, assistant editor. Editor: Patricia A. Ryan. Executive Editor: Diane Lofshult. 70% freelance written. Magazine published 10 times/year "for fitness professionals—aerobics instructors, one-to-one trainers and studio and health club owners—covering topics such as aerobics, nutrition, injury prevention, entrepreneurship in fitness, fitness-oriented research and exercise programs." Estab. 1984. Circ. 23,000. **Pays on acceptance.** Publishes ms an average of 4 months after acceptance. Byline given. Buys all rights. Accepts simultaneous submissions. Reports in 2 months on queries. Sample copy for $4.

Nonfiction: How-to, technical. No general information on fitness; our readers are pros who need detailed information. Buys 15 mss/year. Query. Length: 1,000-3,000 words. Pay varies.

Photos: State availability of photos with submission. Offers no additional payment for photos with ms. Model releases required. Buys all rights.

Columns/Departments: Exercise Science (detailed, specific info; must be written by expert), 750-1,500 words; Industry News (short reports on research, programs and conferences), 150-300 words; Fitness Handout (exercise and nutrition info for participants), 750 words. Buys 80 mss/year. Query. Length: 150-1,500 words. Pay varies.

Tips: "We don't accept fitness information for the consumer audience on topics such as why exercise is good for you. Writers who have specific knowledge of, or experience working in, the fitness industry have an edge."

INLINE RETAILER & INDUSTRY NEWS, Sports & Fitness Publishing, 2025 Pearl St., Boulder CO 80302. (303)440-5111. Fax: (303)440-3313. E-mail: rebroida@aol.com. Website: http://www.s2.com/inline. Editor: Rebecca Broida. 15% freelance written. Monthly tabloid covering the in-line skating industry. "*InLine Retailer* is a business magazine dedicated to spotting new trends, products and procedures that will help in-line retailers and manufacturers keep a competitive edge." Estab. 1992. Circ. 8,000. Pays on publication. Publishes ms an average of 1 month after acceptance. Byline given. Offers 30% kill fee. Buys first North American serial rights. Editorial lead time 2 months. Submit seasonal material 4 months in advance. Reports in 2 weeks on queries. Sample copy for $5.

• *Inline Retailer* reports that it is looking for more writers with a background in business, particularly sporting goods, to help write news pieces providing insight or analysis into the in-line industry.

Nonfiction: How-to, interview/profile, new product, technical. Buys 30 mss/year. Query with published clips. Length: 500-2,000 words. Pays 15¢/word minimum for assigned articles; 10¢/word for unsolicited articles. Sometimes pays expenses of writers on assignment.

Columns/Departments: Retailer Corner (tips for running an in-line retail store), 1,000-1,200 words; First Person (insights from high-level industry figures), 1,200-1,500 words. Buys 20 mss/year. Query with published clips or send complete ms. Pays 15-20¢/word.

Tips: "It's best to write us and explain your background in either the sporting goods business or in-line skating. Mail several clips and also send some ideas that you think would be suitable for our readers. The features and Retailer Corner sections are the ones we typically assign to freelancers. Writers should have solid reporting skills, particularly when it comes to getting subjects to disclose technology, news or tips that they may be unwilling to do without some prodding."

‡**NSGA RETAIL FOCUS**, National Sporting Goods Association, 1699 Wall St., Suite 700, Mt. Prospect IL 60056-5780. (708)439-4000. Fax: (708)439-0111. E-mail: nsga1699@aol.com. Publisher: Thomas G. Drake. Editor: Brent L. Heathcott. 75% freelance written. Works with a small number of new/unpublished writers each year. "*NSGA Retail Focus* serves as a monthly trade journal for presidents, CEOs and owners of more than 22,000 retail sporting goods firms." Estab. 1948. Circ. 9,000. Pays on publication. Publishes ms an average of 1 month after acceptance. Byline given. Offers 50% kill fee. Buys first rights and second serial (reprint) rights. Submit seasonal material 3 months in advance. Query for electronic submissions. Sample copy for 9×12 SAE with 5 first-class stamps.

Nonfiction: Essays, interview/profile, photo feature. "No articles written without sporting goods retail businesspeople in mind as the audience. In other words, no generic articles sent to several industries." Buys 50 mss/year. Query with published clips. Pays $75-500. Sometimes pays the expenses of writers on assignment.

Photos: State availability of photos with submission. Reviews contact sheets, negatives, transparencies and 5×7 prints. Payment negotiable. Buys one-time rights.

Columns/Departments: Personnel Management (succinct tips on hiring, motivating, firing, etc.); Tax Advisor (simplified explanation of how tax laws affect retailer); Sales Management (in-depth tips to improve sales force performance); Retail Management (detailed explanation of merchandising/inventory control); Advertising (case histories of successful ad campaigns/ad critiques); Legal Advisor; Computers; Store Design; Visual Merchandising; all 1,500 words. Buys 50 mss/year. Query. Length: 1,000-1,500 words. Pays $75-300.

POOL & SPA NEWS, Leisure Publications, 3923 W. Sixth St., Los Angeles CA 90020-4290. (213)385-3926. Fax: (213)383-1152. E-mail: psn@poolspanews.com. Website: http://poolspaworld.com. Editor-in-Chief: Anne Blakey. 15-20% freelance written. Semimonthly magazine emphasizing news of the swimming pool and spa industry for builders, retail stores and service firms. Estab. 1960. Circ. 17,000. Pays on publication. Publishes ms an average of 2 months after acceptance. Buys all rights. Reports in 2 weeks. Sample copy for $5 and 9×12 SAE with 10 first-class stamps.

Nonfiction: Interview, profile, technical. Length: 500-2,000 words. Pays 5-14¢/word. Pays expenses of writers on assignment.

Photos: Pays $10/b&w photo used.

‡SPORTING GOODS BUSINESS, SGB, Miller Freeman Inc., One Penn Plaza, New York NY 10119-1198. (800)288-1463. Fax: (212)279-4454. Website: http://www.sgblink.com. Editor: Chris McEvoy. Managing Editor: Leigh Gallagher. 25% freelance written. Tabloid published 18 times/year covering sports business and sporting goods product and retail. "Must have good grasp of sports business, retailing, vendor/retail terminology." Estab. 1966. Circ. 30,000. Pays on publication. Publishes ms less than 1 month after acceptance. Byline given. Offers 50-100% kill fee. Buys one-time rights. Editorial lead time 1 month.

Nonfiction: Interview/profile, new product, technical, business/investigative. Buys 60 mss/year. Query with published clips. Length: 900-1,500 words. Pays $350-500. Sometimes pays expenses of writers on assignment.

Photos: Assigned writers are typically asked to request art from interviewees.

Columns/Departments: Scoreboard (sports business/product news from Wall Street), 1,000 words. Buys 36 mss/year. Query with published clips.

Tips: Wants writer with a "good knowledge of the sports industry and a solid foundation as a business, product and trend writer, someone easy to work with who goes the extra yard when reporting." Must work on short lead time.

THOROUGHBRED TIMES, Thoroughbred Times Company, Inc., 496 Southland Dr., P.O. Box 8237, Lexington KY 40533. (606)260-9800. Editor: Mark Simon. 10% freelance written. Weekly tabloid "written for professionals who breed and/or race thoroughbreds at tracks in the U.S. Articles must help owners and breeders understand racing to help them realize a profit." Estab. 1985. Circ. 23,000. Pays on publication. Publishes ms an average of 1 month after acceptance. Byline given. Offers 50% kill fee. Buys all rights. Submit seasonal material 2 months in advance. Reports in 2 weeks.

Nonfiction: General interest, historical/nostalgic, interview/profile, technical. Buys 52 mss/year. Query. Length: 500-2,500 words. Pays 10-20¢/word. Sometimes pays expenses of writers on assignment.

Photos: State availability of photos with submission. Reviews prints. Offers $25/photo. Identification of subjects required. Buys one-time rights.

Tips: "We are looking for farm stories and profiles of owners, breeders, jockeys and trainers."

‡WHITETAIL BUSINESS, Krause Publications, Inc., 700 E. State St., Iola WI 54990. (715)445-2214, ext. 425. Fax: (715)445-4087. Website: http://www.krause.com. Contact: Dave Natzke, editor. Managing editor: Patrick Durkin. Bimonthly magazine. "*Whitetail Business* targets the hunting industry's driving force, the white-tailed deerhunting market. Archery, modern firearm and muzzleloader retail dealers make their largest profit from whitetail hunters, and *Whitetail Business* devotes itself to this largest profit category." Estab. 1997. Circ. 8,000. **Pays on acceptance.** Byline given. Offers $50 kill fee. Buys first North American serial rights. Editorial lead time up to 1 year. Submit seasonal material up to 1 year in advance. Sample copy and writer's guidelines free.

Nonfiction: New product, personal experience, technical. No humor. Query with or without published clips. Length: 400-1,500 words. Pays $200-350.

Photos: State availability of photos with submission. Reviews transparencies. Offers $25-300/photo. Identification of subjects required. Buys one-time rights.

Columns/Departments: Archery, Firearms/Muzzleloaders, Retail Management (all dealing with white-tailed deer hunting); all 400 words. Buys 25 mss/year. Query with published clips. Pays $250 maximum.

Fillers: Anecdotes. Length: 100 words maximum. Pasy $25 maximum.

Tips: "Keep it short."

STONE, QUARRY AND MINING

COAL PEOPLE MAGAZINE, Al Skinner Inc., Dept. WM, 629 Virginia St. W., P.O. Box 6247, Charleston WV 25362. (304)342-4129. Fax: (304)343-3124. Editor/Publisher: Al Skinner. Contact: Christina Karawan, managing editor.

50% freelance written. Monthly magazine. "Most stories are about people or historical—either narrative or biographical on all levels of coal people, past and present—from coal execs down to grass roots miners. Most stories are upbeat—showing warmth of family or success from underground up!" Estab. 1976. Circ. 11,000. Pays on publication. Publishes ms an average of 3 months after acceptance. Byline given. Buys first rights, second serial (reprint) rights and makes work-for-hire assignments. Submit seasonal material 2 months in advance. Reports in 3 months. Sample copy for 9×12 SAE with 10 first-class stamps.

Nonfiction: Book excerpts (and film if related to coal), historical/nostalgic (coal towns, people, lifestyles), humor (including anecdotes and cartoons), interview/profile (for coal personalities), personal experience (as relates to coal mining), photo feature (on old coal towns, people, past and present). Special issues: calendar issue for more than 300 annual coal shows, association meetings, etc. (January); surface mining/reclamation award (July); Christmas in Coal Country (December). No poetry, fiction or environmental attacks on the coal industry. Buys 32 mss/year. Query with published clips. Length: 5,000 words. Pays $75.

Reprints: Send photocopy of article and information about when and where the article previously appeared.

Photos: Send photos with submission. Reviews contact sheets, transparencies, 5×7 prints. Captions, identification of subjects required. Buys one-time reprint rights.

Columns/Departments: Editorials—anything to do with current coal issues (non-paid); Mine'ing Our Business (bull pen column—gossip—humorous anecdotes), Coal Show Coverage (freelance photojournalist coverage of any coal function across the US). Buys 10 mss/year. Query. Length: 300-500 words. Pays $15.

Fillers: Anecdotes. Buys 10/year. Length: 300 words. Pays $15.

Tips: "We are looking for good feature articles on coal people, towns, companies—past and present, color slides (for possible cover use) and b&w photos to complement stories. Could also use a few news writers to take photos and do journalistic coverage on coal events across the country. Slant stories more toward people and less on historical. More faces and names than old town, company store photos. Include more quotes from people who lived these moments!" The following geographical areas are covered: Eastern Canada; Mexico; Europe; China; Russia; Poland; Australia; as well as US states: Alabama, Tennessee, Virginia, Washington, Oregon, North and South Dakota, Arizona, Colorado, Alaska and Wyoming.

DIMENSIONAL STONE, Dimensional Stone Institute, Inc., Suite I, 6300 Variel Ave., Woodland Hills CA 91367. Fax: (818)704-6500. E-mail: trademags@earthlink.net. Website: http://www.infotile.com.au. Editor: Hal Wolkowitz. 25% freelance written. Monthly international magazine covering dimensional stone use for managers of producers, importers, contractors, fabricators and specifiers of dimensional stone. Estab. 1985. Circ. 15,849. Pays on publication. Publishes ms an average of 2 months after acceptance. Byline given. Buys first rights or second serial (reprint) rights. Reports in 1 month. Sample copy for 9×12 SAE with 11 first-class stamps.

Nonfiction: Interview/profile, technical, only on users of dimensional stone. Special issues: Technology (September); Remodeling and Renovation (November). Buys 6-7 mss/year. Send complete ms. Length: 1,000-3,000 words. Pays $100 maximum. Sometimes pays expenses of writers on assignment.

Reprints: Send tearsheet of article and information about when and where the article previously appeared.

Photos: Send photos with submission. Reviews transparencies, slides, prints. Publication produced using desktop publishing with scanning capabilities. Offers no additional payment for photos accepted with ms. Identification of subjects required.

Tips: "Articles on outstanding commercial and residential uses of dimensional stone are most open to freelancers. For queries, fax editor. Editors work in Microsoft Word on Macintosh system, so copy delivered on disk is appreciated."

‡MINE REGULATION REPORTER, Pasha Publications, #1000, 1616 N. Fort Myer Dr., Arlington VA 22209. (703)528-1244. Editor: Wayne Barber. 5% freelance written. Biweekly newsletter covering health, safety and environmental issues that relate to mine operations. Estab. 1989. Pays on publication. Publishes ms an average of 1 week after acceptance. Offers $25 kill fee. Buys all rights. Accepts simultaneous submissions. Query for electronic submissions, which are preferred. Free sample copy.

Nonfiction: Interview/profile, new product, technical. Buys 2 mss/year. Query. Pays $12.50/published inch—minimum 5 inches. Sometimes pays expenses of writers on assignment.

Tips: "Just give us the facts." Stories wanted on safety, health or environmental issues, such as in the mining industry.

‡PIT & QUARRY, Advanstar Communications, 7500 Old Oak Blvd., Cleveland OH 44130. (216)891-2607. Fax: (216)891-2675. E-mail: pitquar@en.com. Editor: Mark S. Kuhar. Managing Editor: Kyle Nichol. 20-30% freelance written. Monthly magazine covering nonmetallic minerals, mining and crushed stone. Audience has "knowledge of construction-related markets, mining, minerals processing, etc." Estab. 1918. Circ. 25,000. **Pays on acceptance**. Publishes ms an average of 6 months after acceptance. Byline given. Buys first North American serial rights. Editorial lead time 6 months. Accepts simultaneous submissions. Reports in 1 month on queries; 4 months on mss. Sample copy for 9×12 SAE and 4 first-class stamps. Writer's guidelines free.

Nonfiction: How-to, interview/profile, new product, technical. No humor or inspirational articles. Buys 12-15 mss/year. Query. Length: 1,200-2,500 words. Pays $250-700 for assigned articles; $250-500 for unsolicited articles. Pays writers with contributor copies or other premiums for simple news items, etc. Sometimes pays expenses of writers on assignment.

Photos: State availability of photos with submission or send photos with submission. Offers no additional payment for photos accepted with ms. Model releases and identification of subjects required. Buys one-time rights.

Columns/Departments: Environmental, economics. Length: 700 words. Buys 5-10 mss/year. Query. Pays $250-300.
Tips: "Be familiar with quarry operations (crushed stone or sand and gravel), not coal or metallic minerals mining. Know construction markets. We need more West Coast-focused stories."

STONE REVIEW, National Stone Association, 1415 Elliot Place NW, Washington DC 20007. (202)342-1100. Fax: (202)342-1100. E-mail: fatlee@cais.com. Editor: Frank Atlee. Bimonthly magazine "designed to be a communications forum for the crushed stone industry. Publishes information on industry technology, trends, developments and concerns. Audience is quarry operations/management, and manufacturers of equipment, suppliers of services to the industry." Estab. 1985. Circ. 4,000. Pays on publication. Publishes ms an average of 3 months after acceptance. Byline given. Negotiable kill fee. Buys one-time rights. Accepts simultaneous submissions. Reports in 1 month. Sample copy for 9×12 SAE with 3 first-class stamps.
Nonfiction: Technical. Query with or without published clips, or send complete ms. Length: 1,000-2,500 words. "Note: We have no budget for freelance material, but I'm willing to secure payment for right material."
Reprints: Send tearsheet, photocopy or typed ms with information about when and where the article previously appeared. Payment negotiable.
Photos: State availability of photos with query, then send photos with submission. Reviews contact sheets, negatives, transparencies, prints. Offers no additional payment for photos accepted with ms. Identification of subjects required. Buys one-time rights.
Tips: "At this point, most features are written by contributors in the industry, but I'd like to open it up. Articles on unique equipment, applications, etc., are good, as are those reporting on trends (e.g., there is a strong push on now for environmentally sound operations). Also interested in stories on family-run operations involving three or more generations."

STONE WORLD, Business News Publishing Company, 299 Market St., Third Floor, Saddle Brook NJ 07663. (201)291-9001. Fax: (201)291-9002. E-mail: stoneworld@aol.com. Website: http://www.stoneworld.com. Publisher: John Sailer. Contact: Michael Reis, editor. Monthly magazine on natural building stone for producers and users of granite, marble, limestone, slate, sandstone, onyx and other natural stone products. Estab. 1984. Circ. 18,000. Pays on publication. Publishes ms an average of 6 months after acceptance. Byline given. Buys first rights or second serial (reprint) rights. Submit seasonal material 6 months in advance. Reports in 2 months. Sample copy for $10.
Nonfiction: How-to (fabricate and/or install natural building stone), interview/profile, photo feature, technical, architectural design, artistic stone uses, statistics, factory profile, equipment profile, trade show review. Publishes technical book excerpts. Buys 10 mss/year. Query with or without published clips, or send complete ms. Length: 600-3,000 words. Pays $4/column inch. Pays expenses of writers on assignment.
Reprints: Send photocopy of article or typed ms with rights for sale noted and information about when and where the article previously appeared. Pays 50% of amount paid for an original article.
Photos: State availability of photos with submission. Reviews transparencies, prints. Pays $10/photo accepted with ms. Captions, identification of subjects required. Buys one-time rights.
Columns/Departments: News (pertaining to stone or design community); New Literature (brochures, catalogs, books, videos, etc., about stone); New Products (stone products); New Equipment (equipment and machinery for working with stone); Calendar (dates and locations of events in stone and design communities). Query or send complete ms. Length: 300-600 words. Pays $4/inch.
Tips: "Articles about architectural stone design accompanied by professional color photographs and quotes from designing firms are often published, especially when one unique aspect of the stone selection or installation is highlighted. We are also interested in articles about new techniques of quarrying and/or fabricating natural building stone."

TRANSPORTATION

These publications are for professional movers and people involved in transportation of goods. For magazines focusing on trucking see also Auto and Truck.

DISTRIBUTION, The Transportation & Business Logistics Magazine, Chilton Co., One Chilton Way, Radnor PA 19089. (610)964-4244. Fax: (610)964-4381. E-mail: jthomas@chilton.net. Website: http://www.chilton.net/distr. Editor: Jim Thomas. Contact: Jodi Melbin, managing editor. 50% or more freelance written. Monthly magazine. "Our audience is the companies that require transportation professionals. Stories revolve around ways—or programs—that improve distribution logistics processes within industries, as well as the use of carriers, forwarders and third-party companies." Estab. 1901. Circ. 70,000. **Pays on acceptance.** Publishes ms an average of 3 months after acceptance. Buys one-time rights. Editorial lead time 2 months. Sample copy for #10 SASE.
Nonfiction: General interest, how-to, interview/profile, technical, travel (to see departments). Buys 36 mss/year. Query with published clips. Length: 1,200-1,500 words. Pays $300-650.
Photos: Send photos with submissions. Reviews contact sheets, transparencies, prints. Negotiates payment individually. Identification of subjects required.
Columns/Departments: Global Report (global ports, DCs etc.), 500-750 words. Buys 12-20 mss/year. Query. Pays $300-650.
Tips: "Query letter with background and already published articles related to field. Most articles are assigned, so we

are interested in getting writers experienced in business writing. We are developing writer's guidelines."

‡ITS WORLD, Technology and applications for intelligent transportation systems, Advanstar Communication, Inc., 859 Willamette St., Eugene OR 97401-6806. Fax: (541)344-3514. E-mail: its@itsworld.com. Contact: Nancy Johnson, editor. 20% freelance written. Bimonthly tabloid covering intelligent transporation systems (the application of communications and computer technologies to surface transportation). Estab. 1996. Circ. 18,000. **Pays on acceptance.** Publishes ms an average of 3 months after acceptance. Byline given. Buys first rights or all rights. Editorial lead time 4 months. Reports in 6 weeks on queries; 1 month on mss. Sample copy and writer's guidelines free.
Nonfiction: How-to (applications of technology), interview/profile, technical. Buys 12 mss/year. Query with published clips. Length: 1,500-3,000 words. Pays $500-650. Sometimes pays expenses of writers on assignment.
Photos: Send photos with submission. Reviews 2×2 transparencies, prints. Negotiates payment individually. Captions, identification of subjects required. Buys one-time ro all rights.
Columns/Departments: World Watch (trends, activities and market opportunities in intelligent transportation systems in a country or region outside the U.S.), 1,250 words. Buys 2 mss/year. Query with published clips. Pays $500-650.
Tips: "Expertise in surface transportation and/or the application of advanced technologies (telecommunications, computers, etc.) to surface transportation is a must. Writers who demonstrate this through published works and other background information will be given highest consideration."

‡SHIPPING DIGEST, The National Shipping Weekly of Export Transportation, Geyer McAllister Publications Inc., 51 Madison Ave., New York NY 10010. (212)689-4411. Fax: (212)683-7929. E-mail: edit@shippingdigest.com. Website: http://www.shippingdigest.com. Editor: Jim Dow. 20% freelance written. Weekly magazine "read by executives responsible for exporting US goods to foreign markets. Emphasis is on services offered by ocean, surface and air carriers, their development and trends; port developments; trade agreements; government regulation; electronic data interchange." Pays on publication. Publishes ms an average of 1 month after acceptance. Byline given. Buys first rights. Reports in 2 months. Free sample copy and writer's guidelines.
Nonfiction: Interview/profile. Query. Length: 800-1,500 words. Pays $150-350.
Reprints: Send photocopy of article or short story and information about when and where the article previously appeared.
Photos: State availability of photos with submission. Reviews contact sheets and 5×7 prints. Offers no payment for photos accepted with ms. Identification of subjects required. Buys one-time rights.

TAXI NEWS, Chedmount Investments Ltd., 38 Fairmount Crescent, Toronto, Ontario M4L 2H4 Canada. (416)466-2328. Fax: (416)466-4220. Editor: Bill M'Ouat. 100% freelance written. Monthly tabloid covering taxicab industry. "We don't care about your biases/philosophy, but they must be clear to the reader. You must know what you are writing about and be able to back up opinions with facts. We are an independent newspaper covering news and views of a specific industry so you will be writing for a knowledgeable audience, while we also require stories, news items to be understandable to a wider, general audience." Estab. 1985. Circ. 10,300. Pays on publication. Publishes ms an average of 2 months after acceptance. Byline given. Offers 50% kill fee or $50 (Canadian). Buys all rights. Editorial lead time 2 months. Submit seasonal material 3 months in advance. Accepts simultaneous submissions. Reports in 2 weeks on queries; 1 month on mss. Sample copy for #10 SASE and Canadian stamp.
Nonfiction: Exposé, general interest, historical/nostalgic, how-to, humor, interview/profile, opinion, personal experience, photo feature. Buys 50 mss/year. Query or send complete ms. Length: 50-800 words. Pays $25-200 (Canadian).
Reprints: Accepts previously published submissions.
Photos: Send photos with submission. Reviews 3×5 prints. Offers $10-25/photo (Canadian). Captions, identification of subjects required. Buys all rights.
Columns/Departments: Have regular columnists, but will publish guest columns. Buys 36 mss/year. Query or send complete ms. Pays $100 (Canadian).
Tips: "We cover Toronto very well. Occasionally we'll use out-of-town material if it is A) well-written and/or B) of direct applicability to our readers' working lives e.g. tips (new) on avoiding robberies/violence—how to save money, new regulatory approaches, cab drivers helping people (gratuitous kindness...), etc. Don't get us sued."

TRAVEL

Travel professionals read these publications to keep up with trends, tours and changes in transportation. Magazines about vacations and travel for the general public are listed in the Consumer Travel section.

CORPORATE MEETINGS & INCENTIVES, Adams/Laux Publishing, 60 Main St., Maynard MA 01754. (508)448-8211. Editor: Barbara Scofidio. Contact: Barbara Scofidio. 75% freelance written. Monthly magazine covering meetings and incentive travel. "Our cover stories focus on issues of interest to senior execs—from customer service to encouraging innovation—and the integral role meetings play in achieving these goals." Circ. 36,000. Pays 30 days after acceptance. Offers 33% kill fee. Buys first North American serial rights and electronic rights. Editorial lead time 3 months. Submit seasonal material 4 months in advance. Sample copy for SAE with $1.50 postage. Writer's guidelines for #10 SASE.

Nonfiction: Interview/profile, travel with a meetings angle. Special issue: Golf (April). Buys 30 mss/year. Query with published clips. Length: 2,000-4,000 words. Pays 50¢/word. Sometimes pays expenses of writers on assignment.
Reprints: Accepts simultaneous submissions.
Photos: State availability of photos with submissions. Reviews contact sheets, transparencies, prints. Negotiates payment individually. Identification of subjects required. Buys one-time rights.
Columns/Departments: Buys 24 mss/year. Query. Pays $250-500.
Tips: "Looking for strong business writers with experience writing about employee motivation, quality programs, incentive programs—ways that companies improve productivity. Best to send relevant clips with a letter after taking a look at the magazine."

‡**DESTINATIONS, The Magazine of North American Motorcoach Tours & Travel**, American Bus Association, 1100 New York Ave. NW, Suite 1050, Washington DC 20005. (202)842-1645. Contact: Veronica Chao, editor-in-chief. 70% freelance written. Monthly magazine. "*Destinations* covers the cities, regions, attractions, and themed tours appropriate for bus groups. Its audience is the people who plan and run motorcoach tours." Estab. 1979. Circ. 6,000. **Pays on acceptance.** Publishes ms an average of 1 month after acceptance. Byline given. Buys one-time rights. Editorial lead time 15 weeks. Submit seasonal material 6 months in advance. Sample copy for $5.75. Writers' guidelines for #10 SASE.
Nonfiction: Interview/profile, photo feature, travel. No personal accounts of bus travel or travel outside the US and Canada. Buys 48-75 mss/year. Query with published clips. Length: 700-2,500 words. Pays $60/ms page. Sometimes pays expenses of writers on assignment.
Photos: State availability of photos with submission. Offers $25-200/photo. Identification of subjects required. Buys one-time rights.

RV BUSINESS, Affinity Group, Inc., 2575 Vista del Mar Dr., Ventura CA 93001. (800)765-1912. Fax: (805)667-4484. Editor-in-Chief: Sherman Goldenberg. Editor: John Sullaway. 50% freelance written. Monthly magazine. "*RV Business* caters to a specific audience of people who manufacture, sell, market, insure, finance, service and supply, components for recreational vehicles." Estab. 1972. Circ. 15,000. **Pays on acceptance.** Publishes ms an average of 2 months after acceptance. Byline given. Offers kill fee. Buys first North American serial rights. Editorial lead time 3 months. Reports in 2 months. Sample copy and writer's guidelines free.
Nonfiction: New product, photo feature, industry news and features. "No general articles without specific application to our market." Buys 300 mss/year. Query with published clips. Length: 125-2,200 words. Pays $35-800. Sometimes pays expenses of writers on assignment.
Photos: Send photos with submission. Reviews 35mm transparencies. Offers $25-50/photo. Captions, identification of subjects required. Buys one-time rights.
Columns/Departments: Top of the News (RV industry news), 75-400 words; Retailers (RV dealer news), 75-400 words; Features (indepth industry features), 800-2,000 words. Buys 300 mss/year. Query. Pays $25-800.
Tips: "Query. Send one or several ideas and a few lines letting us know how you plan to treat it/them. We are always looking for good authors knowledgeable in the RV industry or related industries. Change of editorial focus requires more articles that are brief, factual, hard hitting and business oriented. Review other publications in the field, including enthusiast magazines."

SPECIALTY TRAVEL INDEX, Alpine Hansen, 305 San Anselmo Ave., #313, San Anselmo CA 94960. (415)455-1643. Fax: (415)459-4974. E-mail: spectrav@ix.netcom.com. Website: http://www.specialtytravel.com. Editor: C. Steen Hansen. Contact: Risa Weinreb, editor. 90% freelance written. Semiannual magazine covering adventure and special interest travel. Estab. 1980. Circ. 45,000. Pays on publication. Byline given. Buys one-time rights. Editorial lead time 3 months. Submit seasonal material 3 months in advance. Writer's guidelines on request.
Nonfiction: How-to, new product, personal experience, photo feature, travel. Buys 15 mss/year. Query. Length: 1,250 words. Pays $200 minimum.
Reprints: Send tearsheet of article. Pays 100% of amount paid for an original article.
Photos: State availability of photos with submission. Reviews 35mm transparencies, 5×7 prints. Negotiates payment individually. Captions, identification of subjects required.

MARKETS THAT WERE listed in the 1997 edition of *Writer's Market* but do not appear this year are listed in the General Index with a notation explaining why they were omitted.

Scriptwriting

Everyone has a story to tell, something to say. In telling that story as a play, movie, TV show or educational video you have selected that form over other possibilities. Scriptwriting makes some particular demands, but one thing remains the same for authors of novels, nonfiction books and scripts: you'll learn to write by rewriting. Draft after draft your skills improve until, hopefully, someone likes your work enough to hire you.

Whether you are writing a video to train doctors in a new surgical technique, alternative theater for an Off-Broadway company or you want to see you name on the credits of the next Harrison Ford movie, you must perfect both writing and marketing skills. A successful scriptwriter is a talented artist and a savvy business person. But marketing must always be secondary to writing. A mediocre pitch for a great script will still get you farther than a brilliant pitch for a mediocre script. The art and craft of scriptwriting lies in successfully executing inspiration.

Writing a script is a private act. Polishing it may involve more people as you ask friends and fellow writers to take a look at it. Marketing takes your script public in an effort to find the person willing to give the most of what you want, whether it's money, exposure or control, in return for your work.

There are accepted ground rules to presenting and marketing scripts. Following those guidelines will maximize your chances of getting your work before an audience.

Presenting your script professionally earns a serious consideration of its content. Certain types of scripts have a definite format and structure. An educational video written in a one-column format, a feature film much longer than 120 pages or an hour-long TV show that peaks during the first 20 minutes indicates an amateur writer. There are several sources for correct formats, including *The Writer's Digest Book of Manuscript Formats*, by Buchman and Groves and *The Complete Guide to Script Formats*, by Cole and Haig.

Submission guidelines are similar to those for other types of writing. The initial contact is a one-page query letter, with a brief synopsis and a few lines as to your credits or experience relevant to the subject of your script. Never send a complete manuscript until it is requested. Almost every script sent to a producer, studio, or agent must be accompanied by a release form. Ask the producer or agent for his form when invited to submit the complete script. Always include a self-addressed stamped envelope if you want your work returned; a self-addressed stamped postcard will do for acknowledgement or reply if you do not need your script returned.

Most writers break in with spec scripts, written "for free," which serve as calling cards to show what they can do. These scripts plant the seeds of your professional reputation by making the rounds of influential people looking to hire writers, from advertising executives to movie moguls. Good writing is more important than a specific plot. Make sure you are sending out your best work; a first draft is not a finished product. Have several spec scripts completed, as a producer will often decide that a story is not right for him, or a similar work is already in production, but want to know what else you have. Be ready for that invitation.

Writing a script is a matter of learning how to refine your writing so that the work reads as a journey, not a technical manual. The best scripts have concise, visceral scenes that demand to be presented in a specific order and accomplish definite goals.

Educational videos have a message that must be expressed economically and directly, engaging the audience in an entertaining way while maintaining interest in the topic. Theatrical plays are driven by character and dialogue that expose a thematic core and engender enthusiasm or involvement in the conflict. Cinematic screenplays, while more visually-oriented, are a series of discontinuous scenes stacked to illuminate the characters, the obstacles confronting them and the resolution they reach.

A script is a difficult medium—written words that sound natural when spoken, characters that are original yet resonate with the audience, believable conflicts and obstacles in tune with the end result. One theater added to their listing the following tip: "Don't write plays. Write novels, short stories, anything but plays. But if you *must* write plays. . . ." If you are compelled to present your story visually, be aware of the intense competition. Hone it, refine it, keep working on it until it can be no better, then look for the best home you can find. That's success.

BUSINESS AND EDUCATIONAL WRITING

"It's no longer the plankton of the filmmaking food chain," says Kirby Timmons, creative director of the video production company CRM Films. Scripts for corporate training, business management and education videos have become as sophisticated as those designed for TV and film, and they carry the additional requirement of conveying specific content. With an audience that is increasingly media literate, anything that looks and feels like a "training film" will be dead in the water. The trick is to produce a script that engages, compels *and* informs about the topic, whether it's customer relations, listening skills or effective employee management, while staying on a tight budget.

This can create its own challenges, but is an excellent way to increase your skills and exercise your craft. Good scriptwriters are in demand in this field. There is a strong emphasis on producing a polished complete script before filming begins, and a writer's involvement doesn't end until the film is "in the can."

A remarkably diverse industry, educational and corporate video is a $18-25 billion business, compared to theatrical films and TV, estimated at $5 billion. And there is the added advantage that opportunities are widespread, from large local corporations to small video production houses in your area. Larger companies often have inhouse video production companies, but others rely on freelance writers. Your best bet would be to find work with companies that specialize in making educational and corporate video while at the same time making yourself known to the creative directors of inhouse video staffs in large corporations. Advertising agencies are also a good source of work, as they often are asked by their clients for help in creating films and use freelance writers and producers.

Business and educational video is a market-driven industry, with material created either in response to a general need or a specific demand. The production company usually identifies a subject and finds the writer. As such, there is a perception that a spec script will not work in this media. While it is true that, as in TV and theatrical films, a writer's spec script is rarely produced, it is a good résumé of qualifications and sample of skills. It can get you other work even though it isn't produced. Your spec script should demonstrate a knowledge of this industry's specific format. For the most part video scripts are written in two-columns, video on the left, audio on the right. Computer software is available to format the action and dialogue; *The Writer's Digest Guide to Manuscript Formats* also covers the basics of video script format.

Aside from the original script, another opportunity for the writer is the user's guide that often accompanies a video. If you are hired to create the auxiliary material you'll receive a copy of the finished video and write a concurrent text for the teacher or implementor to use.

Networking is very important. There is no substitute for calling companies and finding out what is in your area. Contact local training and development companies and find out who they serve and what they need. It pays to join professional organizations such as the Association of Visual Communicators and the Association for Training and Development, which offer seminars and conventions. Making the rounds at a business convention of video producers with your business card could earn you a few calls and invitations to submit writing samples.

Budgets are tighter for educational or corporate videos than for theatrical films. You'll want to work closely with the producer to make sure your ideas can be realized within the budget.

Your fee will vary with each job, but generally a script written for a production house such as CRM in a subject area with broad marketability will pay $5,000-7,000. A custom-produced video for a specific company will usually pay less. The pay does not increase exponentially with your experience; large increases come if you choose to direct and produce as well as write.

With the expansion of cable TV-based home shopping opportunities, direct response TV (informercials) is an area with increasing need for writers to create the scripts that sell the products. Production companies are located across the country, and more are popping up as the business grows. Pay can range from $5,000-18,000, depending on the type, length and success of the program. *The Hollywood Scriptwriter* (P.O. Box 10277, Burbank CA 91510, (818)845-5525, http://www.hollywoodscriptwriter.com.) published a three-part series on direct response scriptwriting, discussing structure, format and marketing, which is available for $8.

The future of business and educational video lies in interactive media or multimedia. Interactive media combines computer and video technology to create a product that doesn't have to progress along a linear path. Videos that offer the viewer the opportunity to direct the course of events hold exciting possibilities for corporate training and educational applications. Writers will be in high demand as stories offer dozens of choices in storylines. Interactive video will literally eat up pages of script as quickly as a good writer produces them. A training session may last only 20 minutes, but the potential untapped story lines could add up to hours worth of script that must be written, realized and made available. From training salespeople to doctors, or teaching traffic rules to issues in urbanization, corporate and educational video is about to undergo a tremendous revolution.

Information on business and educational script markets listed in the previous edition but not included in this edition of *Writer's Market*, can be found in the General Index.

‡**ARNOLD AND ASSOCIATES PRODUCTIONS, INC.**, 1204 16th Ave. S., Nashville TN 37212. (615)329-2800. President: John Arnold. Executive Producers: Deirdre Say, James W. Morris and Peter Dutton. Produces material for the general public (entertainment/motion pictures) and for corporate clients (employees/customers/consumers). Buys 10-15 scripts/year. Works with 3 writers/year. Buys all rights. Accepts previously produced material. Reports in 1 month.
Needs: Films (35mm), videotape. Looking for "upscale image and marketing programs." Dramatic writing for "name narrators and post scored original music; and motion picture. $5-6 million dollar budget. Dramatic or horror." Query with samples or submit completed script. Makes outright purchase of $1,000.
Tips: Looking for "upscale writers who understand corporate image production, and motion picture writers who understand story and dialogue."

A/V CONCEPTS CORP., 30 Montauk Blvd., Oakdale NY 11769-1399. (516)567-7227. Fax: (516)567-8745. Contact: P. Solimene or L. Solimene. Produces supplementary materials for elementary-high school students, either on grade level or in remedial situations. Estab. 1971. 100% freelance written. Buys 25 scripts/year from unpublished/unproduced writers. Employs video, book and personal computer media. Reports in 1 month on outline, 6 weeks on final scripts. Buys all rights. Sample copy for 9×12 SAE with 5 first-class stamps.
Needs: Interested in original educational computer (disk-based) software programs for Apple II family, IBM, Macintosh. Main concentration in language arts, mathematics and reading. "Manuscripts must be written using our lists of vocabulary words and meet our readability formula requirements. Specific guidelines are devised for each level. Student activities required. Length of manuscript and subjects will vary according to grade level for which material is prepared. Basically, we want material that will motivate people to read." Pays $300 and up.
Tips: "Writers must be creative and highly disciplined. We are interested in high interest/low readability materials."

BOSUSTOW MEDIA GROUP, 20326 Ruston Rd., Woodland Hills CA 91364-5643. (818)999-5929. E-mail: bosusto w@earthlink.net. Website: http://home.earthlink.net/~bosustow. Owner: Tee Bosustow. Estab. 1983. Produces material for corporate, TV and home video clients. Reports in 2 weeks on queries.
Needs: Tapes, cassettes, videotapes. "Unfortunately, no one style, etc., exists. We produce a variety of products, a good deal of it children's programming." Submit synopsis/outline and résumé only. Pays agreed-upon fee.

CRM FILMS, 1801 Avenue of the Stars, #715, Los Angeles CA 90067-5802. Fax: (310)789-5392. E-mail: 70206.454@c ompuserve.com. Website: www.crm.com. Creative Director: Kirby Timmons. Estab. 1960. Material for business and organizational training departments. Buys 2-4 scripts/year. Works with 6-8 writers/year. Buys all rights and interactive training rights. No previously produced material. Reports in 1 month. Catalog for 10×13 SAE with 4 first-class stamps. Query with résumé and script sample of writer's work in informational or training media. Makes outright purchase of $4,000-7,000, or in accordance with Writers Guild standard. "We accept WGA standard one-page informational/interactive agreement which stipulates *no* minimum but qualifies writer for pension and health coverage."

Needs: Videotapes, multimedia kits. "CRM is looking for short (10- 20-minute) scripts on management topics such as communication, decision making, team building and customer service. No 'talking heads,' prefer drama-based, awareness approach as opposed to 'how-to' style, but will on occasion produce either. 'New Workplace' training will be bigger this year; 'change' is always a hot topic."
Tips: "Know the *specific* training need which your idea or script fulfills! Recent successes relate real-life events as basis for organizational or team learning—The Challenger incident to illustrate how groupthink can negatively impact team decisions, for example. Other titles document the challenges of the 'New Workplace,' change and empowerment."

‡EDUCATIONAL VIDEO NETWORK, 1401 19th St., Huntsville TX 77340. (409)295-5767. Fax: (409)294-0233. E-mail: evn@swweb.net. Website: http://www.edvidnet.com. President: Debbie Henke. Contact: Anne Russell, executive editor. Estab. 1953. Produces material for junior high, senior high, college and university audiences. Works with "perhaps 10 third-party scripts/year." Buys all rights or pays royalty on gross retail and wholesale. Accepts previously produced material. Reports in 1-2 months. Free catalog and writer's guidelines.
Needs: Video for educational purposes. Query. Royalty varies.
Tips: "Educational video productions fall into two basic divisions. First are the curriculum-oriented programs that teachers in the various academic disciplines can use to illustrate or otherwise enhance textbook material in their subjects. Such programs should either be introductory overviews or concentrate on specific segments of lesson plans. Curriculum-oriented recent titles: *Monuments of Paris*; *The Internet: Cruising the Information Superhighway*; *Acids, Bases, and Salts*. Guidance & Development recent titles: *Teenage Alcohol Abuse, Teenage Conflict Resolution, 1st Aid & CPR, How to Get the Job You Want*. The second type of educational program deals with guidance and personal development areas. These programs need to reflect enough edutainment values to keep visually-sophisticated teens engaged while providing the real and valuable information that could help students with school and life. Recent titles: *Efficient Time Management, Making the Grade, Developing Your Self Esteem*, and *Dealing with Anger*. EVN is always looking for writers/producers who can write and illustrate for educational purposes."

EFFECTIVE COMMUNICATION ARTS, INC., P.O. Box 250, Wilton CT 06897-0250. (203)761-8787. (203)761-0568. President: David Jacobson. Estab. 1965. Produces films, videotapes and interactive materials. Has produced more than 75 video-based interactive multimedia programs for physician, nurse and health-care audiences. In addition, produces corporate training and marketing materials. Prefers to work with established writers. 80% freelance written. Buys approximately 12 scripts/year. Buys all rights. Reports in 1 month.
Needs: Multimedia kits, television shows/series, videotape presentations, interactive CD-ROM MPEG multimedia, D.V.D. Currently producing both custom and generic interactive programs. Submit interactive design, script and résumé. Makes outright purchase. Pays expenses of writers on assignment.
Tips: "Interactive design skills are increasingly important."

THE FILM HOUSE INC., 130 E. Sixth St., Cincinnati OH 45202. (513)381-2211. President: Ken Williamson. Estab. 1973. Audience is corporate communications and television commercials. Buys 5 scripts/year. Works with 3 writers/year. Buys all rights. No previously published material. Reoprts in 1 month on queries. Query with résumé.
Needs: Films, videotapes. Corporate, training and new product video. Writing assignments on a project basis only.
Tips: "We hire only seasonal, experienced writers on a freelance, per project basis. If interested send only a résumé."

HAYES SCHOOL PUBLISHING CO., INC., 321 Pennwood Ave., Wilkinsburg PA 15221-3398. (412)371-2373. Fax: (412)371-6408. President: Clair N. Hayes III. Estab. 1940. Produces material for school teachers and principals, elementary through high school. Also produces charts, workbooks, teacher's handbooks, posters, bulletin board material and reproducible blackline masters (grades K-12). 25% freelance written. Prefers to work with published/established writers. Buys 5-10 scripts/year from unpublished/unproduced writers. 100% of scripts produced are unagented submissions. Buys all rights. Reports in 3 months. Catalog for SAE with 3 first-class stamps. Writer's guidelines for #10 SAE with 2 first-class stamps.
Needs: Educational material only. Particularly interested in foreign language material and educational material for elementary school level. Query. Pays $25 minimum.

‡INTERACTIVE ARTS, 3200 Airport Ave., Santa Monica CA 90405. (213)390-9466. Fax: (310)390-7525. Vice President: David Schwartz. Estab. 1985. Audience is general public; theme parks; museums; college and high school students; corporate and industrial clients. Buys 4-5 scripts and 10 treatments/year. Works with 5-6 writers/year. Buys all rights. Reports in 2 weeks.
Needs: Multimedia (computer), interactive videodiscs, videotapes, educational/science documentaries, theme park

---

 THE DOUBLE DAGGER before a listing indicates that the listing is new in this edition. New markets are often more receptive to freelance submissions.

films. "Our needs vary from consumer multimedia titles to museum projects and from educational/scientific documentaries to theme park projects." Queries desired from California residents only.

JIST WORKS, INC., 720 N. Park Ave., Indianapolis IN 46202. (317)264-3767. Fax: (317)264-3763. E-mail: jistworks @aol.com. Website: http://www.jistworks.com. Video Production Manager: Kelli Lawrence. Estab. 1981. Produces career counseling, motivational materials (youth to adult) that encourage good planning and decision making for a successful future. Buys 7-10 scripts/year. Works with 2-3 writers/year. Buys all rights. Accepts previously produced material. Reports in 2 months. Catalog free. Query with synopsis. Makes outright purchase of $500 minimum.
Needs: Videotapes, multimedia kits. 15-30 minute video VHS tapes on job search materials and related markets.
Reprints: "We need writers for long formats, such as scripts and instructor's guides, as well as short formats for catalogs, press releases, etc. We pay a royalty on finished video productions. We repackage, market, duplicate and take care of all other expenses when we acquire existing programs. Average sell price is $139. Producer gets a percentage of this and is not charged for any costs. Contact us, in writing, for details."

MOTIVATION MEDIA INC., 1245 Milwaukee Ave., Glenview IL 60025-2499. (847)297-4740. Fax: (847)297-6829. E-mail: kevin.kivikko@motivationmedia.com. Website: http://www.motivationmedia.com. Vice President/Creativity: Kevin Kivikko. Produces customized meeting, training and marketing material for presentation to salespeople, customers, shareholders, corporate/industrial employees and distributors. 90% freelance written. Buys 50 scripts/year. Prefers to work with published/established writers. 100% unagented submissions. Buys all rights. Reports in 1 month.
Needs: Material for all audiovisual media—particularly marketing-oriented (sales training, sales promotional, sales motivational) material. Produces sales meeting programs, training videotapes, print collateral, audio programs and interactive multimedia. Software should be AV oriented. Query with samples and résumé. Pay is commensurate with scope of assignment and writer's qualifications and experience. Pays expenses of writers on assignment.

PALARDO PRODUCTIONS, 1807 Taft Ave., Suite 4, Hollywood CA 90028. Phone/fax: (213)469-8991. Director: Paul Ardolino. Estab. 1971. Produces material for youth ages 13-35. Buys 3-4 scripts/year. Buys all rights. Reports in 2 weeks on queries; 1 month on scripts.
Needs: Multimedia kits, tapes and cassettes, videotapes. "We are seeking comedy feature scripts involving technology and coming of age; techno-shortform projects." Submit synopsis/outline and résumé. Pays in accordance with Writers Guild standards.
Tips: "Do not send a complete script—only synopsis of four pages or less *first*."

CHARLES RAPP ENTERPRISES, INC., 1650 Broadway, New York NY 10019. (212)247-6646. President: Howard Rapp. Estab. 1954. Produces materials for firms and buyers. Works with 5 writers/year. "Work as personal manager/ agent in sales." Accepts previously produced material. Reports in 1 month on queries; 2 months on submissions. Submit résumé or sample of writing. Pays in accordance with Writers Guild standards.
Needs: Videotapes, treatments, scripts.

ROUSER COMPANY PRESENTATION RESOURCES, 208 W. Magnolia Ave., Knoxville TN 37917. Fax: (423)546-8303. E-mail: rouserco@conc.tdsnet.com. General Manager: Martin Rouser. Estab. 1932. Audience is corporate dealer network, end users. Buys 3 scripts/year. Works with 2 writers/year. Buys first rights. Accepts previously produced material. Reports in 1 month on queries and submissions. Query. Makes outright purchase.
Needs: Charts, videotapes, filmstrips (silent and sound), overhead transparencies, slides, tapes and cassettes. Corporate meeting opener multi-image module for the marine industry.

SPENCER PRODUCTIONS, INC., 736 West End Ave., New York NY 10025. (212)865-8829. General Manager: Bruce Spencer. Executive Producer: Alan Abel. Produces material for high school students, college students and adults. Occasionally uses freelance writers with considerable talent. Reports in 1 month.
Needs: Prerecorded tapes and cassettes. Satirical material only. Query. Pay is negotiable.

TALCO PRODUCTIONS, 279 E. 44th St., New York NY 10017-4354. (212)697-4015. Fax: (212)697-4827. President: Alan Lawrence. Vice President: Marty Holberton. Estab. 1968. Produces variety of material for TV, radio, business, trade associations, nonprofit organizations, public relations (chiefly political and current events), etc. Audiences range from young children to senior citizens. 20-40% freelance written. Buys scripts from published/produced writers only. Buys all rights. No previously published material. Reports in 3 weeks on queries. *Does not accept unsolicited mss.*
  ● Talco reports that it is doing more public relations-oriented work: print, videotape and radio.
Needs: Films (16, 35mm), slides, radio tapes and cassettes, videotape. "We maintain a file of writers and call on those with experience in the same general category as the project in production. We do not accept unsolicited manuscripts. We prefer to receive a writer's résumé listing credits. If his/her background merits, we will be in touch when a project seems right." Makes outright purchase/project and in accordance with Writers Guild standards (when appropriate). Sometimes pays expenses of writers on assignment.
Tips: "Concentration is now in TV productions. Production budgets will be tighter."

ED TAR ASSOCIATES, INC., 230 Venice Way, Venice CA 90291. (310)306-2195. Fax: (310)306-0654. Estab. 1972. Audience is dealers, salespeople, public. Buys all rights. No previously produced material. Makes outright purchase.

Needs: Films (16, 35mm), videotapes, slides, tapes, business theater and live shows, TV infomercials. "We are constantly looking for *experienced* writers of corporate, product and live show scripts. Send résumé and samples."

TEL-AIR INTERESTS, INC., 1755 NE 149th St., Miami FL 33181. (305)944-3268. Fax: (305)944-1143. E-mail: telair@aol.com. President: Grant H. Gravitt. Produces material for groups and theatrical and TV audiences. Buys all rights. Submit résumé.
Needs: Documentary films on education, travel and sports. Produces films and videotape. Makes outright purchase.

ULTITECH, INC., Foot of Broad St., Stratford CT 06497. (203)375-7300. Fax/BBS: (203)375-6699. E-mail: comcowic@meds.com. Website: http://www.meds.com. President: William J. Comcowich. Estab. 1993. Designs, develops and produces online services and interactive communications programs including video, multimedia, expert systems, software tools, computer-based training and audience response meetings. Specializes in medicine, science and technology. Prefers to work with published/established writers with video, multimedia and medical experience. 90% freelance written. Buys writing for approximately 15-20 programs/year. Electronic submissions onto BBS. Buys all rights. Reports in 1 month.
Needs: Currently producing about 10 interactive programs for medical audiences. Submit résumé and complete script. Makes outright purchase. Pays expenses of writers on assignment.
Tips: "Interactive media for learning and entertainment is a growing outlet for writers—acquiring skills for interactive design and development will pay back in assignments."

VISUAL HORIZONS, 180 Metro Park, Rochester NY 14623. (716)424-5300. Fax: (716)424-5313. E-mail: 73730.2512@compuserve.com. Website: http://www.btb.com/vh. President: Stanley Feingold. Produces material for general audiences. Buys 5 programs/year. Reports in 5 months. Free catalog.
Needs: Business, medical and general subjects. Produces silent and sound filmstrips, multimedia kits, slide sets, videotapes. Query with samples. Payment negotiable.
Tips: "We offer materials to help our audience make powerful presentations, train staff or customers, sell products or services and inspire audiences."

‡WIDGET PRODUCTIONS, LTD., 120 Duane St., #8, New York NY 10007. (212)285-1447. Contact: Terry Krueger. Audience is US/international TV. Buys 6 scripts/year. Works with 10 writers/year. Buys all rights. Accepts previously produced material. Reports in 1 month on queries and submissions. Query with synopsis. Makes outright purchase of $500-3,000, dependent on 30, 60, 120 second format.
Needs: Films (16mm), videotapes, tapes and cassettes. 30, 60, 120 second Direct Response TV commercials. Occasionally 30 minute (28-30 minute).
Tips: "DR is increasing slant toward direct selling and simple story."

WILLOW ASSOCIATES, 4061 Glendenning Rd., Downers Grove IL 60515-2228. (630)969-1982. Principal: William H. Holt, Jr. Estab. 1988. Audience is corporate communications. Buys 1 script/year. Works with 4 writers/year. Submissions not returned. Reports in 2 months on queries and submissions. Query.
Needs: Films (16mm), videotapes, slides, tapes and cassettes. Short, corporate communications, training topics.

PLAYWRITING

TV and movies are visual media where the words are often less important than the images. Writing plays uses different muscles, different techniques. Plays are built on character and dialogue—words put together to explore and examine characters.

The written word is respected in the theater by producer, cast, director and even audience, to a degree unparalleled in other formats. While any work involving so many people to reach its final form is in essence a collaboration, it is presided over by the playwright and changes can be made only with her approval, a power many screenwriters can only envy. If a play is worth producing, it will be produced "as is."

Counterbalancing the greater freedom of expression are the physical limitations inherent in live performance: a single stage, smaller cast, limited sets and lighting and, most importantly, a strict, smaller budget. These conditions affect not only what but also how you write.

Start writing your play by reading. Your local library has play anthologies. Check the listings in this section for play publishers such as Baker's Plays and Samuel French. Reading gives you a feel for how characters are built, layer by layer, word by word, how each interaction presents another facet of a character. Exposition must mean something to the character, and the story must be worth telling for a play to be successful.

There are plenty of books, seminars and workshops to help you with the writing of your play.

The development of character, setting, dialogue and plot are skills that will improve with each draft. The specific play format is demonstrated in *The Complete Book of Script Formats*, by Cole and Haig and *The Writer's Digest Book of Manuscript Formats*, by Buchman and Groves.

Once your play is finished you begin marketing it, which can take as long (or longer) than writing it. Before you begin you must have your script bound (three brads and a cover are fine) and copyrighted at the Copyright Office of the Library of Congress or registered with the Writers Guild of America. Write either agency and ask for information and an application.

Your first goal will be to get at least a reading of your play. You might be lucky and get a small production. Community theaters or smaller regional houses are good places to start. Volunteer at a local theater. As prop mistress or spotlight operator you will get a sense of how a theater operates, the various elements of presenting a play and what can and cannot be done, physically as well as dramatically. Personal contacts are important. Get to know the literary manager or artistic director of local theaters, which is the best way to get your script considered for production. Find out about any playwrights' groups in your area through local theaters or the drama departments of nearby colleges and universities. Use your creativity to connect with people that might be able to push your work higher.

Contests can be a good way to get noticed. Many playwriting contests offer as a prize at least a staged reading and often a full production. Once you've had a reading or workshop production, set your sights on a small production. Use this as a learning experience. Seeing your play on stage can help you view it more objectively and give you the chance to correct any flaws or inconsistencies. Incorporate any comments and ideas from the actors, director or even audience that you feel are on the mark into revisions of your script.

Use a small production also as a marketing tool. Keep track of all the press reviews, any interviews with you, members of the cast or production and put together a "press kit" for your play that can make the rounds with the script.

After you've been produced you have several directions to take your play. You can aim for a larger commercial production; you can try to get it published; you can seek artistic grants. After you have successfully pursued at least one of those avenues you can look for an agent. Choosing one direction does not rule out pursuing others at the same time. *The Dramatists Sourcebook*, published annually by Theatre Communications Group (355 Lexington Ave., New York NY 10017) lists opportunities in all these areas. The Dramatists Guild (234 W. 45th St., New York NY 10036) has three helpful publications: a bimonthly newsletter with articles, news and up-to-date information and opportunities; a quarterly journal; and an annual directory, a resource book for playwrights listing theaters, agents, workshops, grants, contests, etc.

Good reviews in a smaller production can get you noticed by larger theaters paying higher royalties and doing more ambitious productions. To submit your play to larger theaters you'll put together a submission package. This will include a one-page query letter to the literary manager or dramaturg briefly describing the play. Mention any reviews and give the number of cast members and sets. You will also send a two- to three-page synopsis, a ten-page sample of the most interesting section of your play, your résumé and the press kit you've assembled. Do not send your complete manuscript until it is requested.

You can also explore publishing your play. *Writer's Market* lists many play publishers. When your script is published your play will make money while someone else does the marketing. You'll be listed in a catalog that is sent out to hundreds or thousands of potential performance spaces—high schools, experimental companies, regional and community theaters—for possible production. You'll receive royalty checks for both performance fees and book sales. In contacting publishers you'll want to send your query letter with the synopsis and reviews.

There are several sources for grants. Some are federal or state, but don't overlook sources closer to home. The category "Arts Councils and Foundations" in Contests and Awards in this book lists a number of sources. On the national level contact the NEA Theater Program Fellowship for Playwrights (1100 Pennsylvania Ave. NW, Washington DC 20506). State arts commissions are another possible source, and also offer opportunities for involvement in programs where you can meet fellow playwrights. Some cities have arts and cultural commissions that offer grants for local artists. PEN publishes a comprehensive annual book, *Grants and Awards Available to American Writers* that also includes a section for Canadian writers. The latest edition is available from the PEN American Center (568 Broadway, New York NY 10012).

Once you have been produced on a commercial level, your play has been published or you have won an important grant, you can start pursuing an agent. This is not always easy. Fewer agents represent playwrights alone—there's more money in movies and TV. No agent will represent an unknown playwright. Having an agent does *not* mean you can sit back and enjoy the ride. You will still need to get out and network, establishing ties with theaters, directors, literary managers, other writers, producers, state art agencies and publishers, trying to get your work noticed. You will have some help, though. A good agent will have personal contacts that can place your work for consideration at a higher level than your efforts alone might.

There is always the possibility of moving from plays to TV and movies. There is a certain cachet in Hollywood surrounding successful playwrights. The writing style will be different—more visually oriented, less dependent on your words. The money is better, but you will have less command over the work once you've sold that copyright. It seems to be easier for a playwright to cross over to movies than for a screenwriter to cross over to plays.

Writing can make you feel isolated, even when your characters are so real to you they seem to be in the room as you write. Sometimes the experience and companionship of other playwrights is what you need to get you over a particular hurdle in your play. Membership and service organizations such as The Dramatists Guild, The International Women's Writing Guild and local groups such as the Playwright's Center in Minneapolis and the Northwest Playwright's Guild in Seattle can help you feel still a part of this world as you are off creating your own.

Information on playwriting markets listed in the previous edition but not included in this edition of *Writer's Market*, can be found in the General Index.

ACTORS THEATRE OF LOUISVILLE, 316 W. Main St., Louisville KY 40202-4218. (502)584-1265. Producing Director: Jon Jory. Estab. 1964. Produces approximately 20 new plays of varying lengths/year. Professional productions are performed for subscription audience from diverse backgrounds. Agented submissions only for full-length plays; open submissions to National Ten-Minute Play Contest (plays 10 pages or less). Reports in 9 months on submissions, mostly in the fall. Buys variable rights. Offers variable royalty.
Needs: "We are interested in full-length, one-act and ten-minute plays and in plays of ideas, language, humor, experiment and passion."

ALABAMA SHAKESPEARE FESTIVAL, 1 Festival Dr., Montgomery AL 36117-4605. Website: www.asf.net. Artistic Director: Kent Thompson. Contact: Eric Schmiedl, literary associate. Produces 14 plays/year. Inhouse productions, general audience, children audience. Reports in 1 year. Pays royalty. Unsolicited scripts accepted for the Southern Writers' Project only.
Needs: "Through the Southern Writers' Project, ASF develops works by Southern writers, works that deal with the South and/or African-American themes, and works that deal with Southern and/or African-American history."

ALLEYWAY THEATRE, 1 Curtain Up Alley, Buffalo NY 14202-1911. Fax: (716)852-2266. E-mail: alleywayth.com. Dramaturg: Joyce Stilson. Estab. 1980, competition 1990. Produces 4 full-length, 10-15 short plays/year. Submit complete ms. Reports in 6 months. Buys first production, credit rights. Pays 7% royalty plus travel and accommodations for opening.
● Alleyway Theatre also sponsors the Maxim Mazumdar New Play Competition. See the Contest & Awards section for more information.
Needs: "Theatrical" work as opposed to mainstream TV.
Tips: Sees a trend toward social issue-oriented works.

AMELIA MAGAZINE, 329 "E" St., Bakersfield CA 93304. (805)323-4064. Editor: Frederick A. Raborg, Jr. Estab. 1983. Publishes 1 play/year. Submit complete ms. Reports in 2 months. Buys first North American serial rights only. Pays $150 plus publication as winner of annual Frank McClure One-Act Play Award. Guidelines for SASE.
Needs: "Plays with virtually any theme or concept. We look for excellence within the one-act, 45-minute running time format. We welcome the avant-garde and experimental. We do not object to the erotic, though not pornographic. Fewer plays are being produced on Broadway, but the regionals seem to be picking up the slack. That means fewer equity stages and more equity waivers."

‡**AMERICAN MUSIC FESTIVAL**, 123 S. Broad St., Suite 1820, Philadelphia PA 19109. (215)893-1570. Fax: (215)893-1570. Artistic Director: Ben Levit. Estab. 1983. Produces 4 musicals/year. Professional productions for young minded audiences 20s-60s. Submit script and tape of music. Reports in 6 months. Pays royalty.
Needs: Music-driven music theater/opera pieces, varied musical styles, experimental work. Seven in orchestra, 10-14 cast, 28×40 stage.
Tips: Innovative topics and use of media, music, technology a plus. Sees trends of arts in technology (interactive theater, virtual reality, sound design); works are shorter in length (1-1½ hours with no intermissions or 2 hours with intermission).

AMERICAN STAGE FESTIVAL, 14 Court St., Nashua NH 03060. Fax: (603)889-2336. Artistic Director: Matthew Parent. Estab. 1975. "The ASF is a central New England LORT theater (professional equity company) with a 10-month season (March-December) for an audience of all ages, interests, education and sophistication levels." Query with synopsis. Produces 20% musicals, 80% nonmusicals. Nine are mainstage and ten are children's productions; 20% are originals. Royalty option and subsequent amount of gross: optional.
• This theater is looking for more comedies and mysteries—works with broad appeal.
Needs: "The Festival can do comedies, musicals and dramas. However, the most frequent problems are bolder language and action than a general mixed audience will accept. Prefer not to produce plays with strictly urban themes. We have a 40-foot proscenium stage with 30-foot wings, but no fly system and a thrust, black-box theater. Length: mainstage: 2-3 acts; children's productions: 50 minutes. Cast: 8 or fewer.
Tips: "We've just opened a second performance space, a 277-seat thrust theater and expanded our season from a summer series only, to year-round theater in two spaces."

AN CLAIDHEAMH SOLUIS/CELTIC ARTS CENTER, P.O. Box 861778, Los Angeles CA 90086-1778. (213)462-6844. Artistic Director: Sean Walsh. Estab. 1985. Produces 6 plays/year. Equity 99-seat plan. Query with synopsis. Reports in 6 months. Rights acquired vary. Pays $25-50.
Needs: Scripts of Celtic interest (Scottish, Welsh, Irish, Cornish, Manx, Breton). "This can apply to writer's background or subject matter. We are particularly concerned with works that relate to the survival of ethnic cultures and traditions, especially those in danger of extinction."

‡**APPLE TREE THEATRE**, 595 Elm Pl., Suite 210, Highland Park IL 60035. (847)432-8223. Artistic Director: Eileen Boevers. Estab. 1983. Produces 5 plays/year. "Professional productions intended for an adult audience mix of subscriber base and single-ticket holders. Our subscriber base is extremely theater-savvy and intellectual. Submit query and synopsis and tapes for musicals. Reports in 4 months. Royalty varies. Rights obtained vary. Return SASE submissions only if requested. "We produce a mixture of musicals, dramas, classical, contemporary and comedies. Length: 90 minutes-2½ hours. Small space, unit set required. No fly space, 3¼ thrust stage. Maximum actors: 15.
Tips: "No farces or large-scale musicals. Theaters need small shows with one-unit sets due to financial concerns. Also note the desire for non-linear pieces that break new ground. Please do not submit unsolicited manuscripts—send letter and description; if we want more, we will request it."

ARDEN THEATRE COMPANY, 40 N. 2nd St., Philadelphia PA 19106. (215)922-8900. Website: http://www.libertyn et.org/~arden. Artistic Directors: Terrence J. Nolen, Aaron Posner. Estab. 1988. Produces 5 plays/year. Query with synopsis. Reports in 6 months. Pays 5% royalty.
Needs: Full-length, adaptations and musicals. Flexible in terms of cast size.

‡**ARKANSAS REPERTORY THEATRE**, P.O. Box 110, Little Rock AR 72203-0110. (501)378-0445. Artistic Director: Cliff Fannin Baker. Submissions: Brady Mooy, literary manager. Estab. 1976. Produces 11-12 plays/year. "Professional productions for adult audiences. No kids' shows please." Submit query and synopsis only. Reports in 6 months. Keeps 5% rights for 5 years. Payment depends on the script, number of performances, if it was commissioned, which stage it's produced on. "We produce plays for a general adult audience. We do everything from intense dramas to farce. We don't produce much international work. Only full-length plays. We look for shows with less than 10 characters, but we have done epics as well. With a unit set, if possible."
Tips: "No one-acts or children's shows. Smaller casts are preferred."

‡**ARTISTS REPERTORY THEATRE**, 1111 S.W. Tenth Ave., Portland OR 97205. (503)294-7374. Fax: (503)294-7370. E-mail: allen@artistsrep.org. Website: http://www.europa.com/artistsrep/. Contact: Allen Nause, artistic director. Estab. 1982. Produces 8 plays/year. Plays performed in professional theater. With a subscriber-based audience. Reports in 6 months. Pays royalty. Send synopsis, sample and résumé. No unsolicited mss accepted.
Needs: "Full-length, hard-hitting, emotional, intimate, actor-oriented shows with small casts (rarely exceeds 10-13, usually 2-7). Language and subject matter are not a problem."
Tips: "No one-acts or children's scripts."

‡**ASOLO THEATRE COMPANY**, 5555 N. Tamiami Trail., Sarasota FL 34234. (941)351-9010. Fax: (941)351-5796. Website: http://www.sarasota-online.com/asolo. Contact: Bruce E. Rodgers, associate artistic director. Estab. 1960. Produces 7-8 plays/year. 10% freelance written. A LORT theater with 2 intimate performing spaces. No unsolicited scripts. Send a letter with 1-page synopsis, 1 page of dialogue and SAE. Reports in 8 months. Negotiates rights and payment.

Needs: Play must be *full length*. "We operate with a resident company in rotating repertory. We have a special interest in adaptations of great literary works."

BAILIWICK REPERTORY, 1229 W. Belmont Ave., Chicago IL 60657-3205. (773)883-1090. Contact: Literary Department. Executive Director: David Zak. Estab. 1982. Produces 5 mainstage plays (classic and newly commissioned) each year; 5 new full-length in New Directions series; 50 1-acts in annual Directors Festival; pride performance series (gay and lesbian plays, poetry), includes one acts, poetry, workshops, and staged adaptations of prose. Submit year-round. "Our audience is a typical Chicago market. Our plays are highly theatrical and politically aware." One acts should be submitted *before* April 1. (One-act play fest runs July-August). Reports in 9 months for full-length only. Pays 6% royalty.
Needs: "We need daring scripts that break the mold. Large cast or musicals are OK. Creative staging solutions are a must."
Tips: "Know the rules, then break them creatively and *boldly*! Please send SASE for manuscript submission guidelines before you submit."

‡BAKER'S PLAYS PUBLISHING CO., Dept. WM, 100 Chauncy St., Boston MA 02111-1783. (617)482-1280. Fax: (617)482-7613. Editor: John B. Welch. Contact: Ray Pape. Estab. 1845. 80% freelance written. Plays performed by amateur groups, high schools, children's theater, churches and community theater groups. 75% of scripts unagented submissions. Works with 2-3 unpublished/unproduced writers annually. Submit complete script with news clippings, résumé. Submit complete cassette of music with musical submissions. Publishes 18-25 straight plays and musicals, all originals. Pay varies; makes outright purchase price to split in production fees; 10% book royalty. Reports in 2-6 months.
Needs: "We are finding strong support in our new division—plays from young authors featuring contemporary pieces for high school production."
Tips: "We are particularly interested in adaptation of lesser-known folk tales from around the world. Also of interest are plays which feature a multicultural cast and theme. Collections of one-act plays for children and young adults tend to do very well. Also, high school students: Write for guidelines for our High School Playwriting Contest."

‡MARY BALDWIN COLLEGE THEATRE, Mary Baldwin College, Staunton VA 24401. (703)887-7192. Contact: Virginia R. Francisco. Estab. 1842. Produces 5 plays/year. 10% freelance written. 75% of scripts are unagented submissions. Works with 0-1 unpublished/unproduced writer annually. An undergraduate women's college theater with an audience of students, faculty, staff and local community (adult, conservative). Query with synopsis. Reports in 1 year. Buys performance rights only. Pays $10-50/performance.
Needs: Full-length and short comedies, tragedies, musical plays, particularly for young women actresses, dealing with women's issues both contemporary and historical. Experimental/studio theater not suitable for heavy sets. Cast should emphasize women. No heavy sex; minimal explicit language.
Tips: "A perfect play for us has several roles for young women, few male roles, minimal production demands, a concentration on issues relevant to contemporary society, and elegant writing and structure."

BARTER THEATRE, P.O. Box 867, Abingdon VA 24212-0867. (540)628-2281. Fax: (540)628-4551. Artistic Director: Richard Rose. Estab. 1933. Produces 14 plays/year. Play performed in residency at 2 facilities, a 500-seat proscenium theater and a smaller 150-seat flexible theater. "Our plays are intended for diversified audiences of all ages." Submit synopsis and dialogue sample only to: Richard Rose, artistic director. Reports in 6 months. Royalty negotiable.
   • Barter Theatre has premiered fifteen new works over the past three years. One of the premieres was optioned for Broadway for the 1995-96 season. In 1997 Barter will take one of its productions off-Broadway.
Needs: "We are looking for good plays, comedies and dramas, that entertain and are relevant; plays that comment on the times and mankind; plays that are universal. We prefer casts of 4-12, single or unit set. Hard language can be a factor."

‡BERKELEY REPERTORY THEATRE, 2025 Addison, Berkeley CA 94704. (510)204-8901. Fax: (510)841-7711. E-mail: litman@berkeleyrep.org. Website: http://www.berkeleyrep.org. Artistic Director: Sharon Ott. Contact: Tony Kelly, literary manager. Produces 6 plays/year. Agented submissions or a brief description of the play—an account of what the play is about; a production and publication history of the play; a list of other works with production and publication history; an account of other recognition (grants, awards, etc.); the first 20 pages of the script; a SASE if material is to be returned; a self-addressed stamped postcard if acknowledgement of receipt of script is desired.
Tips: "We are attracted to plays that explore the complexity of contemporary society, that demand the theater as their form of expression, and that compel our audience toward a significant examination of how and why we live our lives as we do. We are partial toward work in which the language is used for expressing complex ideas in a complex way rather than simply as a vehicle for human psychology. Plays need not be large or small in terms of cast-size or setting, but should be expansive in their theatrical vision of the world."

BOARSHEAD THEATER, 425 S. Grand Ave., Lansing MI 48933. (517)484-7800. Artistic Director: John Peakes. Estab. 1966. Produces 8 plays/year (6 mainstage, 2 Young People's Theater productions inhouse). Mainstage Actors' Equity Association company; also Youth Theater—touring to schools by our intern company. Query with one-page synopsis, cast list (with descriptions), 5-10 pages of representative dialogue, *SASE*. Reports on query and synopsis in 1 month. Full scripts (when requested) in 3-8 months. Pays royalty for mainstage productions.

Needs: Thrust stage. Cast usually 8 or less; ocassionally up to 12-14. Prefer staging which depends on theatricality rather than multiple sets. Send plays re Young People's Theater % Education Director. No musicals considered. One-acts only for Young People's Theater.

‡**BORDERLANDS THEATER**, P.O. Box 2791, Tucson AZ 85702. (520)882-8607. Producing Director: Barclay Goldsmith. Estab. 1986. Produces 3-5 plays/year. Productions are professional. Query and synopsis. Reports in 3-6 months. Pays royalty.
Tips: "The mission of Borderlands Theater is to present theater which reflects and leads to an understanding of the multi-racial/multi-ethnic diversity of the border region."

‡**BRISTOL RIVERSIDE THEATRE**, P.O. Box 1250, Bristol PA 19007. (215)785-6664. Fax: (215)785-2762. Producing Artistic Director: Susan D. Atkinson. Contact: David Abers, assistant to the artistic director. Estab. 1986. "Due to a backlog of submitted scripts, we will not be accepting any new scripts until summer, 1997."

CALIFORNIA THEATER CENTER, P.O. Box 2007, Sunnyvale CA 94087. (408)245-2978. Fax: (408)245-0235. E-mail: whudd@ix.netcom.com. Literary Manager/Resident Director: Will Huddleston. Estab. 1976. Produces 15 plays/year. "Plays are for young audiences in both our home theater and for tour." Query with synopsis. Reports in 6 months. Negotiates set fee.
Needs: All plays must be suitable for young audiences, must be around 1 hour in length. Cast sizes vary. Many shows require touring sets.
Tips: "Almost all new plays we do are for young audiences, one-acts with fairly broad appeal, not over an hour in length, with mixed casts of two to eight adult, professional actors. We read plays for all ages, though plays for kindergarten through fourth grade have the best chance of being chosen. Plays with memorable music are especially looked for, as well as plays based upon literary works or historical material young people know from school. Serious plays written in the style of psychological realism must be especially well written. Satires and parodies are difficult for our audiences unless they are based upon material familiar to children. Anything "cute" should be avoided. In the summer we seek large cast plays that can be performed entirely by children in our Summer Conservatory programs. We particularly look for plays that can do well in difficult venues, such as high school gymnasiums, multi-purpose rooms, etc."

‡**CENTER THEATER ENSEMBLE**, (formerly Center Theater), 1346 W. Devon Ave., Chicago IL 60660. (773)508-0200. Artistic Director: Daniel S. LaMorte. Estab. 1984. Produces approximately 4 plays/year. "We run professional productions in our Chicago 'off-Loop' theaters for a diverse audience. We also hold an international play contest annually. For more info send SASE to Dale Calandra, Literary Manager." *Agented submissions only.* Reports in 3 months.
● This theater has recently established a playwright-in-residence program and professional seminars in playwriting and screenwriting.

‡**THE CHANGING SCENE**, 1527½ Champa St., Denver CO 80202. (303)893-5775. Producing/Artistic Director: Alfred Brooks. Estab. 1968. Produces 8-10 plays/year. Submit complete ms. Reports in 6 months. Pays 3% royalty. "The prime consideration is freshness." Limitations: small cast, few props, no set changes.
Tips: "Nothing written for a camera, i.e., with 17 scenes in the first act. Sit coms are already well taken care of. We prefer non-realistic, experimental work."

‡**THE CHANGING SCENE THEATER**, 1527½ Champa St., Denver CO 80202. Director: Alfred Brooks. Contact: Maxine Munt, literary manager. Year-round productions in theater space. Cast may be made up of both professional and amateur actors. For public audience; age varies, but mostly youthful and interested in taking a chance on new and/or experimental works. No limit to subject matter or story themes. Emphasis is on the innovative. "Also, we require that the playwright be present for at least one performance of his work, if not for the entire rehearsal period. We have a small stage area, but are able to convert to round, semi-round or environmental. Prefer to do plays with limited sets and props." Two and three acts only.
Needs: Produces 8-10 nonmusicals a year; all are originals. 90% freelance written. 65% of scripts produced are unagented submissions. Works with 3-4 unpublished/unproduced writers annually. "We do not pay royalties or sign contracts with playwrights. We function on a performance-share basis of payment. Our theater seats 76; the first 50 seats go to the theater; the balance is divided among the participants in the production. The performance-share process is based on the entire production run and not determined by individual performances. We do not copyright our plays." Send complete script. Reporting time varies; usually several months.

MARKET CONDITIONS are constantly changing! If this is 1999 or later, buy the newest edition of *Writer's Market* at your favorite bookstore or order directly from Writer's Digest Books.

Recent Production: *Under Construction*, by Lenore Blumenfeld.

Tips: "We are experimental: open to young artists who want to test their talents and open to experienced artists who want to test new ideas/explore new techniques. Dare to write 'strange and wonderful' well-thought-out scripts. We want upbeat ones. Consider that we have a small performance area (24' × 31') when submitting."

CHARLOTTE REPERTORY THEATRE, 201 S. College St., Suite 2040, Charlotte NC 28244. (704)375-4796. Fax: (704)333-0224. Literary Manager: Claudia Carter Covington. Literary Associate: Carol Bellamy. Estab. 1976. Produces 13 plays/year. "We are a not-for-profit regional theater." Submit complete script with SASE. Reports in 3 months. Writers receive free plane fare and housing for festival.

Needs: "Need full-length scripts not previously produced professionally. No limitations in cast, props, staging, etc. No children's plays or musicals."

CHILDREN'S STORY SCRIPTS, Baymax Productions, 2219 W. Olive Ave., Suite 130, Burbank CA 91506-2648. (818)563-6105. Fax: (818)563-2968. Editor: Deedra Bébout. Estab. 1990. "Our audience consists of children, grades K-8 (5-13-year-olds)." Send complete script with SASE. Reports in 1 month. Licenses all rights to story; author retains copyright. Pays graduated royalty based on sales.

Needs: "We add new titles as we find appropriate stories. We look for stories which are fun for kids to read, involve a number of readers throughout, and dovetail with school subjects. This is a must! Not life lessons . . . school subjects."

Tips: "The scripts are not like theatrical scripts. They combine dialogue and prose narration, à la Readers Theatre. If a writer shows promise, we'll work with him. Our most important goal is to benefit children. We want stories that bring alive subjects studied in classrooms. Facts must be worked unobtrusively into the story—the story has to be fun for the kids to read. Send #10 SASE for guidelines with samples. We do not respond to submissions without SASE."

CHILDSPLAY, INC., P.O. Box 517, Tempe AZ 85280. (602)350-8101. Fax: (602)350-8584. Artistic Director: David P. Saar. Estab. 1978. Produces 5-6 plays/year. "Professional: Touring and in-house productions for youth and family audiences." Submit synopsis, character descriptions and 7- 10-page dialogue sample. Reports in 6 months. "On commissioned work we hold a small percentage of royalties for 3-5 years." Pays royalty of $20-35/performance (touring) or pays $3,000-8,000 commission.

Needs: Seeking *theatrical* plays on a wide range of contemporary topics. Touring shows: 5-6 actors; van-size. Inhouse: 6-10 actors; no technical limitations.

Tips: No traditionally-handled fairy tales. "Theater for young people is growing up and is able to speak to youth and adults. The material *must* respect the artistry of the theater and the intelligence of our audience. Our most important goal is to benefit children. If you wish your materials returned send SASE."

CINCINNATI PLAYHOUSE IN THE PARK, Dept. WM, P.O. Box 6537, Cincinnati OH 45206-0537. (513)345-2242. Fax: (513)345-2254. E-mail: theater1@tso.cin.ix.net. Website: http://www.cincyplay.com. Contact: Charles Towers, associate artistic director. Estab. 1960. Produces original works and previously produced plays. Nonprofit LORT theater, producing 11 plays/year in two spaces—a 629-seat thrust stage and a 220-seat, three-sided arena. "The audience is a broad cross-section of people from all over the Ohio, Kentucky and Indiana areas, from varied educational and financial bases." Write for guidelines for Lois and Richard Rosenthal New Play Prize to submit previously unproduced, new plays for consideration.

• See the playwriting section of Contests and Awards for more information on the Rosenthal New Play Prize.

CIRCUIT PLAYHOUSE/PLAYHOUSE ON THE SQUARE, 51 S. Cooper, Memphis TN 38104. (901)725-0776. Artistic Director: Jackie Nichols. Produces 16 plays/year. 100% freelance written. Professional plays performed for the Memphis/Mid-South area. Member of the Theatre Communications Group. 100% of scripts unagented submissions. Works with 1 unpublished/unproduced writer/year. Contest held each fall. Submit complete script. Reports in 6 months. Buys percentage of royalty rights for 2 years. Pays $500.

Needs: All types; limited to single or unit sets. Cast of 20 or fewer.

Tips: "Each play is read by three readers through the extended length of time a script is kept. Preference is given to scripts for the southeastern region of the U.S."

‡CITIARTS THEATRE, 1975 Diamond Blvd., A-20, Concord CA 94520. (510)798-1300. Fax: (510)676-5726. E-mail: willowsth@aol.com. Managing Director: Andrew Holtz. Estab. 1974. Produces 6 plays/year. Query with synopsis. Reports in 3 months. Pays standard royalty.

Needs: Small plays and musicals that are popular, rarely produced, or new. Certain "stylized plays or musicals which have a contemporary edge to them (e.g., *Les Liasons Dangereuses, La Bete, Candide*)." Cast size no larger than 13; most casts around 5-7. "We are not interested in one-character pieces. If work is a musical, we do not recommend those requiring a band of larger than 7 pieces."

Tips: "Our audiences want light entertainment, comedies and musicals."

CITY THEATRE COMPANY, 57 S. 13th St., Pittsburgh PA 15203. Fax: (412)431-5535. Producing Director: Marc Masterson. Associate Artistic Director/Literary Manager: Richard Keitel. Produces 5 full productions/year. "We are a small professional theater, operating under an Equity contract, and committed to plays of ideas and substance relevant to contemporary American values and cultures. Our seasons are innovative and challenging, both artistically and socially.

We perform in a 225-seat thrust or proscenium stage, playing usually seven times a week, each production running one month or more. We have a committed audience following." Query with synopsis or submit through agent. Obtains no rights. Pays 5-6% royalty. Reports in 6 months.

Needs: "No limits on style or subject, but we are most interested in theatrical plays that have something to say about the way we live. No light comedies or TV-issue dramas." Normal cast limit is 7. Plays must be appropriate for small space without flies.

Tips: "Our emphasis is on new and recent American plays."

I.E. CLARK PUBLICATIONS, P.O. Box 246, Schulenburg TX 78956-0246. (409)743-3232. Contact: Donna Cozzaglio. Estab. 1956. Publishes 15 plays/year for educational theater, children's theater, religious theater, regional professional theater and amateur community theater. 20% freelance written. Publishes 3-4 scripts/year, unagented submissions. Submit complete script, 1 at a time with SASE. Reports in 6 months. Buys all available rights; "We serve as an agency as well as a publisher." Pays standard book and performance royalty, amount and percentages dependent upon type and marketability of play. Catalog for $3. Writer's guidelines for #10 SASE.

Needs: "We are interested in plays of all types—short or long. Audiotapes of music or videotapes of a performance are requested with submissions of musicals. We require that a play has been produced (directed by someone other than the author); photos, videos, and reviews of the production are helpful. No limitations in cast, props, staging, etc. Plays with only one or two characters are difficult to sell. We insist on literary quality. We like plays that give new interpretations and understanding of human nature. Correct spelling, punctuation and grammar (befitting the characters, of course) impress our editors."

Tips: Publishes plays only. "Entertainment value and a sense of moral responsibility seem to be returning as essential qualities of a good play script. The era of glorifying the negative elements of society seems to be fading rapidly. Literary quality, entertainment value and good craftsmanship rank in that order as the characteristics of a good script in our opinion. 'Literary quality' means that the play must—in beautiful, distinctive, and un-trite language—say something; preferably something new and important concerning man's relations with his fellow man or God; and these 'lessons in living' must be presented in an intelligent, believable and creative manner. Plays for children's theater are tending more toward realism and childhood problems, but fantasy and dramatization of fairy tales are also needed."

‡CLASSIC STAGE COMPANY, 136 E. 13th St., New York NY 10003. (212)677-4210. Artist Director: David Esbjornson. Estab. 1967. Produces 2 plays/year. Query and synopsis plus 10 pages sample dialogue. Reports in 3 months. Pay varies.

Needs: "Translations and adaptations of classics only with no more than eight actors. No new plays."

Tips: Only classic text-based adaptations are read.

COAST TO COAST THEATER COMPANY, P.O. Box 3855, Hollywood CA 90078. (818)782-1212. Fax: (818)782-1931. Artistic Director: Bryan W. Simon. Contact: Douglas Coler. Estab. 1989. Produces 2-3 plays/year. Equity and equity waiver theater. Query with synopsis. Responds if interested. Buys West Coast, Midwest or East Coast rights, depending on location of production. Pays 5% royalty, makes outright purchase of $100-250, or pays per performance.

Needs: Full-length off-beat comedies or dramas with small casts, simple sets.

CONTEMPORARY DRAMA SERVICE, Meriwether Publishing Ltd., P.O. Box 7710, Colorado Springs CO 80933. (303)594-4422. Editor-in-Chief: Arthur Zapel. Associate Editors: Theodore Zapel, Rhonda Wray. Estab. 1969. Publishes 50-60 plays/year. "We publish for the secondary school market and colleges. We also publish for mainline liturgical churches—drama activities for church holidays, youth activities and fundraising entertainments. These may be plays, musicals or drama-related books." Query with synopsis or submit complete script. Reports in 6 weeks. Obtains either amateur or all rights. Pays 10% royalty or negotiates purchase.

● Contemporary Drama Service is now looking for play or musical adaptations of classic children's stories, for example: *Wizard of Oz, Rumpelstiltskin, Wind in the Willows, Winnie the Pooh*, etc.

Needs: "Most of the plays we publish are one acts, 15-45 minutes in length. We also publish full-length two-act or three-act plays. We prefer comedies. Musical plays must have name appeal either by prestige author, prestige title adaptation or performance on Broadway or TV. Comedy sketches, monologues and 2-character plays are welcomed. We prefer simple staging appropriate to high school, college or church performance. We like playwrights who see the world positively and with a sense of humor. Offbeat themes and treatments are accepted if the playwright can sustain a light touch and not take himself or herself too seriously. In documentary or religious plays we look for good research and authenticity. We are publishing many scenebooks for actors (which can be anthologies of great works excerpts), scenebooks on special themes and speech and theatrical arts textbooks. We are especially interested in authority-books on a variety of theater-related subjects."

Tips: Contemporary Drama Service is looking for creative books on: comedy writing, staging amateur theatricals and Christian youth activities.

THE COTERIE, 2450 Grand Ave., Kansas City MO 64108-2520. (816)474-6785. Fax: (816)474-7112. Artistic Director: Jeff Church. Estab. 1979. Produces 7-8 plays/year. "Plays produced at Hallmark's Crown Center in downtown Kansas City in the Coterie's resident theater (capacity 240). A typical performance run is one month in length." Query with synopsis, résumé, sample scene; submit complete script only if an established playwright in youth theater field. Reports in 6 months. "We retain some rights on commissioned plays." Pays royalty per performance and flat fee.

Needs: "We produce plays which are universal in appeal; they may be original or adaptations of classic or contemporary literature. Typically, not more than 12 in a cast—prefer 5-9 in size. No fly space or wing space."

Tips: "No couch plays. Prefer plays by seasoned writers who have established reputations. Groundbreaking and exciting scripts from the youth theater field welcome. It's perfectly fine if your play is a little off-center." Trends in the field that writers should be mindful of: "Make certain your submitted play to us is *very* theatrical and not cinematic. Writers need to see how far the field of youth and family theater has come—the interesting new areas we're going—before sending us your query or manuscript."

CREATIVE PRODUCTIONS, INC., 2 Beaver Place, Aberdeen NJ 07747. (908)566-6985. Artistic Director: Walter L. Born. Produces 2 musicals/year. Non-equity, professional, nonprofit company with year-round productions. "We use musicals where performers are an integrated company of traditional and non-traditional individuals for the broad spectrum of viewers." Query with synopsis. Reports in 1 month. Buys rights to perform play for specified number of performances. Fee negotiable.

Needs: Original musicals with upbeat themes adaptable to integrated company of traditional and non-traditional performers. Maximum cast of 12, sets can't fly, facilities are schools, no mammoth sets or multiple scene changes, 90 minutes maximum run time.

Tips: No "blue" material, pornographic, obscene language. Submit info on any performances. Demo tape (musicals), vocal/piano score, plus list of references on users of their material to confirm bio info.

CREEDE REPERTORY THEATRE, P.O. Box 269, Creede CO 81130-0269. (719)658-2541. Director: Richard Baxter. Estab. 1966. Produces 6 plays/year. Plays performed for a summer audience. Query with synopsis. Reports in 1 year. Royalties negotiated with each author—paid on a per performance basis.

Needs: One-act children's scripts. Special consideration given to plays focusing on the cultures and history of the American West and Southwest.

Tips: "We seek new adaptations of classical or older works as well as original scripts."

CROSSLEY THEATRES/ACTORS CO-OP, 1760 N. Gower, Hollywood CA 90028. (213)462-8460. Artistic Director: Robin Strand. Main Stage: AEA 99 seat theater plan; September-June, 5-6 plays; Second Stage: AEA 99 seat theater plan, primarily for developing new material including full-length plays, one acts, readings, musical revues. Query with synopsis. Reports in 10 weeks. Pays per performance.

Needs: "We seek material with large themes written with intelligence. No abuse stories (substance, family, etc.) unless moral or philosophical dilemma is investigated (i.e., Equus); no family dramas unless dramatic conflict transcends mere venting of hurt feelings (i.e., 1918)." Prefers casts of 12 or less (doubling is OK). Prefers minimum set changes.

Tips: "The Crossley Theatre and the Crossley Terrace Theatre are located on church grounds so there are some language restrictions. The Actors Co-op has received much critical acclaim including 77 Drama-Logue Awards and three L.A. Drama Critics Circle Awards in the last six years."

‡CROSSROADS THEATRE COMPANY, 7 Livingston Ave., New Brunswick NJ 08904. (908)249-5581. Artistic Director: Ricardo Khan. Estab. 1978. Stages five full professional productions, plus an end-of-the-year festival of play readings intended for all audiences. Submit query, synopsis and ten-page dialogue sample. Reports in 9 months. Pays royalty.

Needs: Full-length plays, one-acts, translations, adaptations, musicals, cabaret/revues. Especially interested in African-American, African and West Indian issue-oriented, experimental plays. No limitations.

Tips: "Please be patient in awaiting a response."

‡DETROIT REPERTORY THEATRE, 13103 Woodrow Wilson, Detroit MI 48238-3686. (313)868-1347. Artistic Director: Bruce Millan. Estab. 1957. Produces 4 plays/year. Professional theater, 194 seats operatinge on A.E.A. SPT contract Detroit metropolitan area. Submit complete ms. Reports in 3-6 months. Pays royalty.

Needs: Cast limited to no more than 7 characters.

Tips: Wants issue-oriented works. No musicals or one-act plays.

DINER THEATRE, 2015 S. 60th St., Omaha NE 68106. (402)553-4715. Fax: (402)553-4715. Artistic Director: Doug Marr. Estab. 1983. Produces 5 plays/year. Professional productions, general audience. Query with synopsis. Reports in 2 months on submissions. Pays $15-30/performance.

Needs: Comedies, dramas, musicals—original unproduced works. Full length, all styles/topics.

DORSET THEATRE FESTIVAL, Box 519, Dorset VT 05251-0519. (802)867-2223. Fax: (802)867-0144. E-mail: theatre@sover.net. Website: http://www.genghis.com/theatre.htm. Artistic Director: Jill Charles. Estab. 1976. Produces 5 plays/year, 1 a new work. "Our plays will be performed in our Equity summer stock theatre and are intended for a sophisticated community." Agented submissions only. Reports in 3-6 months. Rights and compensation arranged on an individual basis.

Needs: "Looking for full-length contemporary American comedy or drama. Limited to a cast of six."

Tips: "Language and subject matter appropriate to general audience."

DRAMATIC PUBLISHING, 311 Washington, Woodstock IL 60098. (815)338-7170. Fax: (815)338-8981. E-mail: 75712.3621@compuserve.com. Website: http://www.dramaticpublishing.com. Editor: Linda Habjan. Publishes paperback acting editions of original plays, adaptations and translations. Publishes 50-70 titles/year. Receives 500-1,000 queries and 500-1,000 mss/year. Pays 10% royalty on scripts; performance royalty varies. Publishes play 6-8 months after acceptance of ms. Accepts simultaneous submissions. Reports in 1 month on queries, 2 months on proposals, 6 months on mss. Catalog and ms guidelines free on request.

• Dramatic Publishing is seeking more material for the high school market, especially comedy.

Fiction: Interested in playscripts appropriate for children, middle and high schools, colleges, community, stock and professional theaters. Send full ms.

Recent Fiction Title: *Indiscretions*, by Jean Cocteau, translated by Jeremy Sams.

‡**DRAMATICS MAGAZINE**, 3368 Central Pkwy., Cincinnati OH 45225. (513)559-1996. Fax: (513)559-0012. E-mail: pubs@one.net. Website: http://www.etassoc.org. Editor: Don Corathers. Estab. 1929. Publishes 5 plays/year. For high school theater students and teachers. Submit complete ms. Reports in 3 months. Buys first North American serial rights only. Accepts previously published plays. Send tearsheet, photocopy or typed ms with rights for sale noted and information about when and where the work previously appeared. For reprints, pays 50% of the amount paid for an original piece. Purchases one-time publication rights only for $100-400.

Needs: "We are seeking one-acts to full-lengths that can be produced in an educational theater setting. We don't publish musicals."

Tips: "No melodrama, farce, children's theater, or cheap knock-offs of TV sitcoms or movies. Fewer writers are taking the time to learn the conventions of theater—what makes a piece work on stage, as opposed to film and television—and their scripts show it."

EAST WEST PLAYERS, 4424 Santa Monica Blvd., Los Angeles CA 90029. (213)660-0366. Fax: (213)666-0896. E-mail: ewplayers@earthlink.net. Website: http://www.earthlink.net/~ewplayers. Contact: Ken Narasaki, literary manager. Artistic Director: Tim Dang. Estab. 1965. Produces 5 plays/year. Professional theater performing under Equity 99-seat contract, presenting plays which explore the Asian-Pacific or Asian-American experience. Query with synopsis. Reports in 3 months on submissions. Pays royalty against percentage of box office.

Needs: "Whether dramas, comedies or performance art or musicals, all plays must either address the Asian-American experience or have a special resonance when cast with Asian-American actors."

• East West Players also holds a competition from January 1 through April 1. Send SASE for guidelines.

ELDRIDGE PUBLISHING CO., P.O. Box 1595, Venice FL 34284. (941)496-4679. Fax: (941)493-9680. E-mail: info@histage.com. Website: http://www.histage.com (general) and http://www.95church.com (religious). Editor: Susan Shore. Estab. 1906. Publishes 50-60 new plays/year for junior high, senior high, church and community audience. Query with synopsis (acceptable) or submit complete ms (preferred). Please send cassette tapes with any musicals. Reports in 2 months. Buys all rights. Pays 50% royalties and 10% copy sales. Makes outright purchase of $200-500. Writer's guidelines for #10 SASE.

Needs: "We are most interested in full-length plays and musicals for our school and community theater market. Nothing lower than junior high level, please. We always love comedies but also look for serious, high caliber plays reflective of today's sophisticated students. We also need one-acts and plays for children's theater. In addition, in our religious market we're always searching for holiday or any time plays."

Tips: "Submissions are welcomed at any time but during our fall season; response will definitely take two months. Authors are paid royalties twice a year. They receive complimentary copies of their published plays, the annual catalog and 50% discount if buying additional copies."

‡**THE ENSEMBLE STUDIO THEATRE**, 549 W. 52nd St., New York NY 10019. (212)247-4982. Fax: (212)664-0041. Artistic Director: Curt Dempster. Contact: Eileen Myers, literary manager. Estab. 1971. Produces 250 projects/year for off-off Broadway developmental theater. 100-seat house, 60-seat workshop space. Do not fax mss or résumés. Submit complete ms. Reports in 3 months. Standard production contract: mini contract with Actors' Equity Association or letter of agreement. Pays $80-1,000.

Needs: Full-length plays with strong dramatic actions and situations and solid one-acts, humorous and dramatic, which can stand on their own. Musicals also accepted; send tape of music. No verse-dramas or elaborate costume dramas.

Tips: Submit work September-April. "We are dedicated to developing new American plays."

ENSEMBLE THEATRE OF CINCINNATI, 1127 Vine St., Cincinnati OH 45248. (513)421-3555. Fax: (513)421-8002. Contact: D. Lynn Meyers, producing artistic director. Produces 14 plays/year. Professional-year round theater. Query and sysnopsis, submit complete ms or submit through agent. Reports in 5 months. Pays 5-10% royalty.

• Ensemble Theatre of Cincinnati has increased its number of productions from 8 to 14 plays/year.

Needs: Dedicated to good writing, any style.

EUREKA THEATRE COMPANY, 330 Townsend, Suite 210, San Francisco CA 94107. (415)243-9899. Fax: (415)243-0789. Literary Manager: Samuel Zap. Estab. 1972. Produces 3-5 fully-staged plays/year. Plays performed in professional-AEA, year-round for socially involved adult audiences. Query with synopsis. Reports in 3 months. Rights negotiated. Pays negotiable royalty/commission.

• The *Eureka* no longer accepts unsolicited scripts. Send letter of inquiry, synopsis, scene sample (15 pages maximum) and résumé.

Needs: "The mission of the Eureka Theatre Company continues to be to present productions of plays of honesty and integrity which address the concerns and realities of the time and place in which we live. We want to continue the Eureka tradition of entertaining and provoking our audiences as we present them with the urgency of dealing with the diversity and the opportunities of the society in which we live and work. In these final years of the twentieth century, we see it as an imperative to sum up this waning millenium even as we examine and question the next."

Tips: "No one-acts (although we would consider a collection and short works by a single writer or collective); no light-hearted musicals. We are tired of being told 'this is the next *Angels in America*.' We want plays which reflect the cultural diversity of the area in which we live and work. Remember, you are writing for the live stage, *not* for film or TV."

FLORIDA STUDIO THEATRE, 1241 N. Palm Ave., Sarasota FL 34236. (941)366-9017. Fax: (941)955-4137. Associate Director: Chris Angermann. Produces 7 established and 6 new plays/year. "FST is a professional not-for-profit theater." Plays are produced in 170-seat mainstage and 100-seat cabaret theater for subscription audiences (primarily). FST operates under a small professional theater contract of Actor's Equity. Query with synopsis. Reports in 2 months on queries; 6 months on mss. Pays $200 for workshop production of new script.

Needs: Contemporary plays, musical reviews, character plays. Prefer casts of no more than 8 and single sets on mainstage, 3-4 in cabaret.

Tips: "We are looking for material for our Cabaret Theatre—musical revues, one-two character musicals, one-character shows. All should be in two acts and run no longer than 90 minutes, including a 10- 15-minute intermission."

THE FOOTHILL THEATRE COMPANY, P.O. Box 1812, Nevada City CA 95959. (916)265-9320. Artistic Director: Philip Charles Sneed. Estab. 1977. Produces 6-9 plays/year. "We are a professional theater company operating under an Actors' Equity Association contract for part of the year, and performing in the historic 246-seat Nevada Theatre (built in 1865) and at an outdoor amphitheatre on the north shore of Lake Tahoe. The audience is a mix of locals and tourists." Query with synopsis or submit complete script. Reports in 6 months or less. Buys negotiable rights. Pay varies.

Needs: "We are most interested in plays which speak to the region and its history, as well as to its current concerns. No melodramas. Theatrical, above all." No limitations.

Tips: "Avoid the cliché at all costs, and don't be derivative; we're interested in a unique and unassailable vision."

FOUNTAIN THEATRE, 5060 Fountain Ave., Los Angeles CA 90029. (213)663-2235. Fax: (213)663-1629. Artistic Directors: Deborah Lawlor, Stephen Sachs. Contact: Simon Levy, dramaturg. Estab. 1990. Produces both a theater and dance season. Produced at Fountain Theatre (99-seat equity plan). Query through agent or recommendation of theater professional. Query with synopsis to: Simon Levy, producing director/dramaturg. Reports in 6 months. Rights acquired vary. Pays royalty.

Needs: Original plays, adaptations of American literature, "material that incorporates dance or language into text with unique use and vision."

THE FREELANCE PRESS, P.O. Box 548, Dover MA 02030-2207. (508)785-8250. Managing Editor: Narcissa Campion. Estab. 1984. Publishes 4 plays/year for children/young adults. Submit complete ms with SASE. Reports in 4 months. Pays 2-3% royalty. Pays 10% of the price of each script and score.

Needs: "We publish original musical theater to be performed by young people, dealing with issues of importance to them. Also adapt 'classics' into musicals for 8- to 16-year-old age groups to perform." Large cast; flexible.

SAMUEL FRENCH, INC., 45 W. 25th St., New York NY 10010. (212)206-8990. Fax: (212)206-1429. Editor: William Talbot. Estab. 1830. Subsidiaries include Samuel French Ltd. (London); Samuel French (Canada) Ltd. (Toronto); Samuel French, Inc. (Hollywood); Baker's Plays (Boston). Publishes paperback acting editions of plays. Averages 50-70 titles/year. Receives 1,500 submissions/year, mostly from unagented playwrights. 10% of publications are from first-time authors; 20% from unagented writers. Pays 10% royalty on retail price. Publishes play an average of 6 months after acceptance. Accepts simultaneous submissions. Allow *minimum* of 4 months for reply. Catalog set $4.50. Manuscript submission guidelines $4.

Nonfiction: Acting editions of plays.

Tips: "Broadway and Off-Broadway hit plays, light comedies and mysteries have the best chance of selling to our firm. Our market is comprised of theater producers—both professional and amateur—actors and students. Read as many plays as possible of recent vintage to keep apprised of today's market; write plays with good female roles; and be one hundred percent professional in approaching publishers and producers."

GEORGE STREET PLAYHOUSE, 9 Livingston Ave., New Brunswick NJ 08901. (908)846-2895. Website: http://www.swirftweare.com/georgestreet. Producing Artistic Director: Gregory Hurst. Literary Manager: Tricia Roche. Produces 7 plays/year. Professional regional theater (LORT C). No unsolicited scripts. Agent or professional recommendation only. Reports on scripts in 8-10 months. We also accept synopsis, dialogue sample and demo tape.

Needs: Full-length dramas, comedies and musicals with a fresh perspective on society. Prefers cast size under 9. Also presents 40-minute social issue-plays appropriate for touring to school-age children; cast size limited to 4-5 actors.

Tips: "We produce up to four new plays and one new musical each season. It is our firm belief that theater reaches the mind via the heart and the funny bone. Our work tells a compelling, personal, human story that entertains, challenges and stretches the imagination."

THE GOODMAN THEATRE, 200 S. Columbus Ave., Chicago IL 60603. (312)443-3811. Fax: (312)263-6004. E-mail: staff@goodman-theatre.org. Website: http://www.goodman~theatre.org. Artistic Director: Robert Falls. Director of New Play Development: Susan V. Booth. Estab. 1925. Produces 9 plays/year. "The Goodman is a professional, not-for-profit theater producing both a mainstage and studio series for its subscription-based audience. The Goodman does not accept unsolicited scripts from playwrights or agents, nor will it respond to synopses of plays submitted by playwrights, unless accompanied by a stamped, self-addressed postcard. The Goodman may request plays to be submitted for production consideration after receiving a letter of inquiry or telephone call from recognized literary agents or producing organizations." Reports in 6 months. Buys variable rights. Pay is variable.
Needs: Full-length plays, translations, musicals; special interest in social or political themes.

‡GREAT AMERICAN HISTORY THEATRE, 30 E. Tenth St., St. Paul MN 55101. (612)292-4323. Fax: (612)292-4322. Artistic Director: Ron Peluso. Estab. 1978. Produces 6-7 plays/year. Thrust stage; 597 seats. "Our performances are intended for mainstream audiences." Query with synopsis. Reports in 2 weeks on synopsis; 2 months on scripts. Buys production rights. Pays variable royalty. "We commission new works, amount to be negotiated."
Needs: "We provide audiences with a mirror to the lives of the people of Minnesota and the Midwest, and a window to other people and times. We do this by commissioning, producing and touring plays that dramatize the history, folklore and social issues of its own region and other locales. We limit our cast sizes to no larger than ten and we prefer pieces that can be staged simply."

‡GRETNA THEATRE, P.O. Box 578, Mt. Gretna PA 17064. (717)964-3322. Producing Director: Harvey Seifter. Estab. 1977. "Plays are performed at a professional equity theater during summer." Query with synopsis. "Include character breakdown with script's production history, plus five pages." Reports in 4-6 weeks. Rights negotiated. Royalty negotiated (6-12%).
Needs: "We produce full-length plays for a summer audience—subject, language and content are important."
Tips: "No one-acts." Special interest in new musicals; comedy is popular.

GRIMPENMIRE PRESS, 162 N. 17th St., Springfield OR 97477. E-mail: grimpenmir@aol.com. Associate Editor: Toni Rakestraw. Publishes 20 titles/year. Receives 30-40 queries and 30 mss/year. 80% of plays from first-time authors; 90% unagented writers. Pays 50% royalty on retail script sales, 70% royalty on production. No advances. Publishes book 1 year after acceptance of ms. Accepts simultaneous submissions. Reports in 6 months on queries and 10 months on mss. Book catalog and ms guidelines free on request.
Fiction: Plays. "We want material suitable for community and regional theater, nothing too offensive (strong language and content must be an integral part of plot/story). Submit synopsis with SASE.
Recent Fiction Title: *In Escher's Garden*, by James L. Schempp (play).
Tips: Audiences are community and regional theater goers composed of wide variety of ages and levels of sophistication. "We're a good starting point for playwrights. We're small, personal, and have a fast turn around. We want authors who are willing to work with us for the benefit of all of us."

‡THE GROUP (Seattle Group Theatre), 305 Harrison St., Seattle WA 98109. (206)441-9480. Fax: (206)441-9839. Artistic Director: José Carrasquillo. Contact: Tlaloc Rivas, literary intern. Estab. 1978. Produces 5 plays/year. "Plays are performed in our 197-seat theater—The Carlton Playhouse. Intended for a multiethnic audience. Professional, year-round theater." Query with synopsis, sample pages of dialogue and SASE for reply. No phone calls. Reports in 6-8 weeks. Rights obtained varies per production. Royalty varies.
Needs: "We look for scripts suitable for multiethnic casting that deal with social, cultural and political issues relevant to the world today."

HEUER PUBLISHING CO., 233 Dows Bldg., Box 248, Cedar Rapids IA 52406-0248. (319)364-6311. Fax: (319)364-1771. E-mail: editor@hitplays.com. Website: http://www.hitplays.com. Owner/Editor: C. Emmett McMullen. Estab. 1928. Publishes plays and musicals for junior and senior high school and church groups. Query with synopsis or submit complete script. Reports in 2 months. Purchases amateur rights only. Pays royalty or makes outright purchase.
Needs: "One-, two- and three-act plays and musicals suitable for middle, junior and senior high school productions. Preferably comedy or mystery/comedy with a large number of characters and minimal set requirements. Please avoid controversial or offensive subject matter. "

‡HIPPODROME STATE THEATRE, 25 SE Second Place, Gainesville FL 32601. (904)373-5968. Fax: (352)371-9130. E-mail: hipp@afn.org. Dramaturg: Website: http://hipp.gator.net. Tamerin Corn. Estab. 1973. Produces 7 productions. Plays are performed on one main stage (266 seats) for a subscriber audience. Query with synopsis and SASE; professional recommendation and agent submission preferred. Response: 6-10 months.
Needs: "We accept plays of any genre or subject matter. We're looking for writers with fresh, original voices whose résumés reflect their professional work." Cast should not exceed 8; staging flexible, but should be appropriate for thrust stage. "We do not accept unsolicited scripts and usually produce only one or two new works per season." Plese send query letter and synopsis only—*no* scripts until we request them (it helps us respond more efficiently). Prefer résumé and professional references. Please include a SASE for reply.
Tips: "We have received many plays that have a sit-com style of humor. We are *not* interested in this genre. We enjoy comedies but have a need for those that are more 'witty.' Our audiences seem to enjoy classics also."

HORIZON THEATRE COMPANY, P.O. Box 5376, Station E, Atlanta GA 30307. (404)523-1477. Website: www.mi ndspring.com/~horizonco/. Artistic Director: Lisa Adler. Estab. 1983. Produces 4 plays/year. Professional productions. Query with synopsis and résumé. Reports in 1-2 years. Buys rights to produce in Atlanta area. Pays 6-8% royalty or $50-75/performance.
Needs: "We produce contemporary plays with realistic base, but which utilize heightened visual or language elements. Interested in comedy, satire, plays that are entertaining and topical, but also thought provoking. Also particular interest in plays by women or with Southern themes." No more than 10 in cast.
Tips: "No plays about being in theater or film; no plays without hope; no plays that include playwrights as leading characters; no all-male casts; no plays with all older (50 plus) characters."

INTIMAN THEATRE, P.O. Box 19760, Seattle WA 98119. (206)269-1901. Fax: (206)269-1928. E-mail: intiman@scn .org. Website: http://www.seattlesquare.com/Intiman. Artistic Director: Warner Shook. Contact: Literary Manager. Estab. 1972. Produces 6 plays/year. LORT C Regional Theater in Seattle. Query with synopsis. Reports in 6 months. Prefers agented submissions.
Needs: Well-crafted dramas and comedies by playwrights who fully utilize the power of language and character relationships to explore enduring themes. Prefers character-driven plays.
Tips: "Our play development program conducts four readings per year of previously unproduced plays."

JD PRODUCTIONS, 425 S. Hubbard Lane, #372, Louisville KY 40207. (502)893-9412. Artistic Director: Jolene DeLory. Estab. 1994. Produces 6-8 plays/year for community, semiprofessional, professional, dinner theater, possible traveling troupe. All audiences, including children. Query with synopsis or submit complete ms. Reports in 6 weeks. Obtains all rights. Pays negotiable royalty, 50% minimum, depending on type of material.
Needs: Plays, musical revues, full-length, (2 hours and short). Open to all subjects at this time, directed toward all audiences, including children.
Tips: "Audiences are gravitating back toward classics, or plays that resemble classics. They like the older plays, especially mystery and comedy and older musicals (or shows with that tone). I am also looking for short plays and musical revues for my own theater group."

JEWEL BOX THEATRE, 3700 N. Walker, Oklahoma City OK 73118-7099. (405)521-1786. Fax: (405)525-6562. Artistic Director: Charles Tweed. Estab. 1986. Produces 6 plays/year. Amateur productions. For 3,000 season subscribers and general public. Submit complete script. Reports in 4 months. Pays $500 contest prize.
Needs: Send SASE for entry form during September-October. We produce dramas, comedies and musicals. Only two- or three-act plays can be accepted. Our theater is in-the-round, so we adapt plays accordingly." Deadline: mid-January.

JEWISH REPERTORY THEATRE, 1395 Lexington Ave., New York NY 10128. (212)415-5550. Fax: (212)415-5575. E-mail: jrep@echonyc.com. Website: http://www.jrt.org. Artistic Director: Ran Avni. Estab. 1974. Produces 4 plays, 15 readings/year. New York City professional off-Broadway production. Submit complete script with SASE. Reports in 1 month. First production/option to move to Broadway or off-Broadway. Pays royalty.
Needs: Full-length only. Straight plays, musicals. Must have some connection to Jewish life, characters, history. Maximum 7 characters. Limited technical facilities.
Tips: No biblical plays.

KUMU KAHUA, 46 Merchant St., Honolulu HI 96813. (808)536-4222. Fax: (808)536-4226. Artistic Director: Dennis Carroll. Estab. 1971. Produces 5 productions, 3-4 public readings/year. "Plays performed at new Kumu Kahua Theatre, flexible 120-seat theater, for community audiences." Submit complete script. Reports in 4 months. Pays royalty of $50/ performance; usually 14 performances of each production.
Needs: "Plays must have some interest for local audiences, preferably by being set in Hawaii or dealing with some aspect of the Hawaiian experience. Prefer small cast, with simple staging demands."
Tips: "We need time to evaluate scripts (our response time is four months)."

LIVE OAK THEATRE, 719 Congress Ave., Austin TX 78701. (512)472-5143. Fax: (512)472-7199. Contact: Michael Hankin. Estab. 1982. Professional theater produces 6 plays/season. "Strong commitment to and a history of producing new work." Pays royalty. Reports in late summer.
Needs: Full length, translations, adaptations, musicals (especially comedies).
Tips: Also sponsors annual new play awards.

THE LOFT PRODUCTION COMPANY, P.O. Box 173405, Tampa FL 33672. (813)275-9400. Fax: (813)222-1057. Artistic Director: Mr. Kelly Smith. Estab. 1987. Produces 6 plays/year. Amateur/professional productions. Performed at the Off-Center Theater-Tampa Bay Performing Arts Center. Diverse adult audiences. Query with synopsis or submit complete ms. $5 reading fee per submission. Submissions *not* returned. Reports in 6 months. Buys performance rights. Pays $500-1,000 royalty.
Needs: All genres, topics, styles and lengths. Prefers small cast (2-8) with minimal technical requirements.
Tips: "We look for cutting edge or alternative pieces. Nothing is taboo with us."

MAGIC THEATRE, INC., Bldg. D, Fort Mason, San Francisco CA 94123. (415)441-8001. Fax: (415)771-5505. E-mail: magicthtre@aol.com. Website: http://www.members.aol.com/magicthtre. Artistic Director: Mame Hunt. Estab.

1967. Produces 6 plays/year plus numerous co-productions. Regional theater. Query with synopsis. Reports in 4 months. Pays royalty or per performance fee.

Needs: "Plays that are innovative in theme and/or craft, cutting-edge political concerns, intelligent comedy. Full-length only, strong commitment to multicultural work

Tips: "Not interested in classics, conventional approaches and cannot produce large-cast plays."

MANHATTAN THEATRE CLUB, 453 W. 16th St., New York NY 10011-5896. Director of Play Development: Kate Loewald. Produces 8 plays/year. Two-theater performing arts complex classified as off-Broadway, using professional actors. No unsolicited scripts. No queries. Reports in 6 months.

Needs: "We present a wide range of new work, from this country and abroad, to a subscription audience. We want plays about contemporary problems and people. Comedies are welcome. Multiple set shows are discouraged. Average cast is eight."

MERIWETHER PUBLISHING LTD. (Contemporary Drama Service), Dept. WM, 885 Elkton Dr., Colorado Springs CO 80907-3557. President: Mark Zapel. Executive Editor: Arthur L. Zapel. Estab. 1969. "We publish how-to materials in book and video formats. We are interested in materials for middle school, high-school and college level students only. Our Contemporary Drama Service division publishes 60-70 plays/year." 80% written by unpublished writers. Buys 40-60 scripts/year from unpublished/unproduced writers. 90% of scripts are unagented submissions. Reports in 1 month on queries; 2 months on full-length mss. Query with synopsis/outline, résumé of credits, sample of style and SASE. Catalog available for $2 postage. Offers 10% royalty or makes outright purchase.

Needs: Book mss on theatrical arts subjects, especially books of short scenes for amateur and professional actors. "We are now looking for scenebooks with special themes: 'scenes for young women,' 'comedy scenes for two actors', etc. These need not be original, provided the compiler can get letters of permission from the original copyright owner. We are interested in all textbook candidates for theater arts subjects. Christian children's activity book mss also accepted. We will consider elementary level religious materials and plays, but no elementary level children's secular plays. Query. Pays royalty; sometimes makes outright purchase.

Tips: "We publish a wide variety of speech contest materials for high-school students. We are publishing more full length play scripts and musicals based on classic literature or popular TV shows, provided the writer includes letter of clearance from the copyright owner. Our educational books are sold to teachers and students at college and high-school levels. Our religious books are sold to youth activity directors, pastors and choir directors. Our trade books are directed at the public with a sense of humor. Another group of buyers is the professional theater, radio and TV category. We will be especially interested in full length (two- or three-act) plays with name recognition, either the playwright or the adaptation source. We are not interested in unknown playwrights for full length plays but will consider their works in one-act formats.

MERRIMACK REPERTORY THEATRE, Dept. WM, 50 E. Merrimack St., Lowell MA 01852-1205. (508)454-6324. Fax: (508)934-0166. Producing Artistic Director: David G. Kent. Contact: Emma Fried. Estab. 1979. Produces 7 plays/year. Professional LORT D. Agented submissions and letters of inquiry only. Reports in 6 months.

Needs: All styles and genres. "We are a small 372-seat theater—with a modest budget. Plays should be good stories, with strong dialogue, real situations and human concerns. Especially interested in plays about American life and culture."

MILL MOUNTAIN THEATRE, Market Square, Center in Square, Roanoke VA 24011-1437. (703)342-5730. Fax: (540)342-5745. Website: http://www.intrlink.com/MMT. Executive Director: Jere Lee Hodgin. Literary Manager: Jo Weinstein. Produces 8 established plays, 10 new one-acts and 2 new full-length plays/year. "Some of the professional productions will be on the main stage and some in our alternative Theater B. We no longer accept full-length unsolicited scripts, only one-act plays, 25-35 minutes." Send letter, synopsis and 10 pages of sample dialogue. Reports in 8 months. Payment negotiable on individual play. Send SASE for play contest guidelines; cast limit 15 for play and 24 for musicals. Do not include loose stamps or money.

Needs: "We are interested in plays with racially mixed casts, but not to the exclusion of others. We are constantly seeking one-act plays for 'Centerpieces', our lunch time program of script-in-hand productions. Playing time should be between 25-35 minutes. Cast limit 6."

Tips: "Subject matter and character variations are open, but gratuitous language and acts are not acceptable unless they are artistically supported. A play based on large amounts of topical reference or humor has a very short life. Be sure you have written a play and not a film script."

MIXED BLOOD THEATRE COMPANY, 1501 S. Fourth St., Minneapolis MN 55454. (612)338-0937. Artistic Director: Jack Reuler. Estab. 1975. Produces 3-6 plays/year. "Plays are produced on our main stage for adult audiences."

FOR EXPLANATION of symbols, see the Key to Symbols and Abbreviations. For unfamiliar words, see the Glossary.

Query and synopsis. Reports in 6 months. Pays $2,000/run plus a royalty if successful.

Needs: Comedies, dramas. "Open." We will do plays larger than 8 characters and requiring a full set and challenging production values; however, we do have a budget. Be realistic in light of today's financial circumstances.

Tips: "History plays rarely do well with us. Shows with a sports theme are usually of interest. Comedies always welcome."

THE NATIONAL PLAYWRIGHTS CONFERENCE/NEW DRAMA FOR MEDIA PROJECT AT THE EUGENE O'NEILL THEATER CENTER, 234 W. 44th St., Suite 901, New York NY 10036-3909. (212)382-2790. Fax: (212)921-5538. E-mail: acthuman@aol.com. Artistic Director: Lloyd Richards. Contact: Mary F. McCabe, managing director. Estab. 1965. Develops staged readings of 9-12 stage plays, 2-3 screenplays or teleplays/year. "We accept unsolicited scripts with no prejudice toward either represented or unrepresented writers. Our theater is located in Waterford, Connecticut, and we operate under an Equity LORT contract. We have three theaters: Barn—250 seats, Amphitheater—300 seats, Instant Theater—150 seats. Submission guidelines for #10 SASE with 2 first-class stamps in the fall. Complete bound, professionally unproduced, original plays are eligible (no adaptations). Decision by late April. Pays stipend plus room, board and transportation. We accept script submissions September 15-December 1 of each year. Conference takes place during July each summer."

• Scripts are selected on the basis of talent, not commercial potential.

Needs: "We use modular sets for all plays, minimal lighting, minimal props and no costumes. We do script-in-hand readings with professional actors and directors. Our focus is on new play/playwright development."

‡THE NEW AMERICAN THEATER CENTER, 118 N. Main St., Rockford IL 61101. (815)963-9454. Fax: (815)963-7215. Associate Artistic Director: Richard Raether. Produces a spectrum of American and international work in 10-month season. "The New American Theater Center is a professional equity theater company performing on two stages, a thrust stage with 282-seat house and a 100-seat house theater in the round. It is located in a predominantly middle-class Midwestern town." Submit synopsis with SASE. *No* full scripts. Pays royalty based on number of performances.

Needs: No limitations, prefer contemporary pieces. Open to format, etc. No opera.

Tips: "We look for new work that addresses contemporary issues; we do not look for work of any one genre or production style."

‡NEW PLAYS INCORPORATED, P.O. Box 5074, Charlottesville VA 22905. (804)979-2777. E-mail: patwhitton@aol.com. Artistic Director: Patricia Whitton. Estab. 1964. Publishes 3-6 plays/year. Publishes for children's or youth theaters. Submit complete ms or for adaptations, query first. Reports in 2 months or longer. Buys all semi-professional and amateur rights in U.S. and Canada. Pays 50% royalty.

Needs: I have eclectic taste—plays must have quality and originality in whatever genres, topics, styles or lengths the playwright chooses."

Tips: "No adaptations of stuff that has already been adapted a million times, e.g., *Tom Sawyer*, *A Christmas Carol*, or plays that sound like they've been written by the guidance counselor. There will be more interest in youth theater productions with moderate to large casts (15+). Plays must have been produced, directed by someone other than the author or author's spouse."

NEW PLAYWRIGHTS' PROGRAM, The University of Alabama, P.O. Box 870239, Tuscaloosa AL 35487-0239. (205)348-9032. Fax: (205)348-9048. E-mail: pcastagn@woodsquad.as.ua.edu. Director/Dramaturg: Dr. Paul C. Castagno. Endowed by Gallaway Fund, estab. 1982. Produces at least 1 new play/year. Mainstage and second stage, University Theatre, The University of Alabama. Submit synopsis or complete ms, August-March. Playwrights may submit potential workshop ideas for consideration. Reports in 6 months. Accepts scripts in various forms: new dramaturgy to traditional. Recent MFA playwriting graduates (within 1 year) may be given consideration for ACTF productions. Send SASE. Stipends competitive with or exceed most contests.

Needs: Southern themes; dramas with dance.

NEW STAGE THEATRE, 1100 Carlisle, Jackson MS 39202. (601)948-0143. Fax: (601)948-3538. Artistic Director: John Maxwell. Estab. 1965. Produces 9 plays/year. "Professional productions, 8 mainstage, 1 in our 'second space.' We play to an audience comprised of Jackson, the state of Mississippi and the Southeast." Query with synopsis. Reports in 6 weeks. Exclusive premiere contract upon acceptance of play for mainstage production. Pays royalty of 5-8% or $25-60/performance.

Needs: Southern themes, contemporary issues, small casts (5-8), single set plays.

• The New Stage no longer accepts children's theater.

NEW YORK STATE THEATRE INSTITUTE, 155 River St., Troy NY 12180. (518)274-3200. Fax: (518)274-3815. Producing Artistic Director: Patricia Di Benedetto Snyder. Produces 4-5 plays/year. Professional regional productions for adult and family audiences. Submit query with synopsis. Reports in 1 month on synopsis. Pay varies.

NEW YORK THEATRE WORKSHOP, 79 E. Fourth St., New York NY 10003. (212)780-9037. Fax: (212)460-8996. Artistic Director: James C. Nicola. Literary Manager: Mandy Mishell. Estab. 1979. Produces 3-4 full productions; approximately 50 readings/year. Plays are performed off-Broadway, Equity LOA contract theater. Audience is New

York theater-going audience and theater professionals. Query with synopsis and 10-page sample scene. Reports in 5 months. Option to produce commercially; percentage of box office gross from commercial and percentage of author's net subsidiary rights within specified time limit from our original production. Pays fee because of limited run, with additional royalty payments; for extensions; $1,500-2,000 fee range.

• The New York Theatre Workshop offers Van Lier Playwrighting Fellowships for emerging writers of color based in New York City. Address inquiries to Chion Miyagaura, Artistic Associate.

Needs: Full-length plays, one acts, translations/adaptations, music theater pieces; proposals for performance projects. Socially relevant issues, innovative form and language, minority issues. Plays utilizing more than 8 actors usually require outside funding.

Tips: No overtly commercial, traditional, Broadway-type musicals.

NINE O'CLOCK PLAYERS, 1367 N. St. Andrews Place, Los Angeles CA 90028-8592. (213)469-1973. Estab. 1928. Contact: Artistic Director. Produces 2 plays/year. "Plays produced at Assistance League Playhouse by resident amateur and semi-professional company. All plays are musical adaptations of classical children's literature. Plays must be appropriate for children ages 4-12." Query with synopsis. Reports in 1 month. Pays negotiable royalty or per performance.

Needs: "Plays must have at least 9-15 characters and be 75 minutes long. Productions are done on a proscenium stage in classical theater style. All plays must have humor, music and good moral values. No audience participation improvisational plays."

‡NORTHLIGHT THEATRE, 9501 Skokie Blvd., Skokie IL 60077. (847)679-9501. Artistic Director: Russell Vandenbroucke. Estab. 1975. Produces 5 plays/year. "We are a professional, Equity theater, LORT D. We have a subscription base of over 6,000, and have a significant number of single ticket buyers." Query with synopsis and SASE. Reports in 3 months. Buys production rights plus royalty on future mountings. Pays royalty and fee to playwright that is a guarantee against royalties.

Needs: "Full-length plays, translations, adaptations, musicals. Interested in plays of 'ideas,' plays that are passionate and/or hilarious, stylistic exploration, intelligence and complexity. Generally looking for cast size of eight or less, but there are always exceptions made for the right play."

Tips: "Please, do not try to do what television and film do better! Also, no domestic realism."

ODYSSEY THEATRE ENSEMBLE, 2055 S. Sepulveda Blvd., Los Angeles CA 90025. (310)477-2055. Fax: (310)444-0455. Director of Literary Programs: Jan Lewis. Estab. 1965. Produces 9 plays/year. Plays performed in a 3-theater facility. "All three theaters are Equity 99-seat theater plan. We have a subscription audience of 4,000 for a nine-play main season, and they are offered a discount on our rentals and co-productions. Remaining seats are sold to the general public." Query with résumé, synopsis, cast breakdown and 8-10 pages of sample dialogue and cassette if a musical. Scripts must be securely bound. Reports in 1 month on queries; 6 months on scripts. Buys negotiable rights. Pays 5-7% royalty. Does *not* return scripts without SASE.

Needs: "Full-length plays only with either an innovative form and/or provocative subject matter. We desire highly theatrical pieces that explore possibilities of the live theater experience. We are seeking full-length musicals and some plays with smaller casts (2-4). We are not reading one-act plays or light situation comedies. We are seeking Hispanic material for our resident Hispanic unit as well as plays from all cultures and ethnicities."

OLD GLOBE THEATRE, P.O. Box 2171, San Diego CA 92112-2171. (619)231-1941. Artistic Director: Jack O'Brien. Estab. 1935. Produces 12 plays/year. "Performs professional productions, some heading to Broadway for sophisticated, mature audiences." Query and synopsis with SASE. Accepts mostly agented submissions. Reports in 8 months. Obtains negotiable rights. Pays 100% royalty.

Needs: "We prefer smaller casts and ingenuous economic staging requirements."

Tips: "No gratuitous gutter language or immature, poorly structured plays. Nothing too influenced by TV sitcoms or movie-of-the-week melodramas. Avoid weak use of language. Show, don't tell, but if you tell, tell well."

OLDCASTLE THEATRE COMPANY, Box 1555, Bennington VT 05201-1555. (802)447-0564. Artistic Director: Eric Peterson. Produces 6 plays/year. Plays are performed in the new Bennington Center for the Arts, by a professional Equity theater company (in a May-October season) for general audiences, including residents of a three-state area and tourists during the vacation season. Submit complete ms. Reports in 6 months. Pays by negotiation with the playwright. A not-for-profit theater company.

Needs: Produces classics, musicals, comedy, drama, most frequently American works. Usual performance time is 2 hours.

OMAHA THEATER COMPANY FOR YOUNG PEOPLE, (formerly Emmy Gifford Children's Theater), 3504 Center St., Omaha NE 68105. (402)345-4849. Artistic Director: James Larson. Produces 6 plays/year. "Our target audience is children, preschool-high school and their parents." Query with synopsis and SASE. Reports in 9 months. Royalty negotiable.

Needs: "Plays must be geared to children and parents (PG rating). Titles recognized by the general public have a stronger chance of being produced." Cast limit: 25 (8-10 adults). No adult scripts.

Tips: "Unproduced plays may be accepted only after a letter of inquiry (familiar titles only!)."

‡ **EUGENE O'NEILL THEATER CENTER, NATIONAL MUSIC THEATER CONFERENCE,**, 234 W. 44th St., New York NY 10036. Fax: (212)921-5538. Artistic Director: Paulette Haupt. Associate Director: Michael Nassar. Developmental process for new music theater works Creative artists in residence with artistic staff and Equity company of actors/singers Public and private readings, script in hand, piano only. Stipend, room and board. For guidelines and application deadlines, send SASE to address above

THE OPEN EYE THEATER, P.O. Box 204, Denver NY 12421. Phone/fax: (607)326-4986. Producing Artistic Director: Amie Brockway. The Open Eye is a not-for-profit professional theater company working in New York City since 1972, in the rural villages of Delaware County, NY since 1991, and on tour. The theater specializes in the development of new plays for multi-generational audiences (children ages 8 and up, and adults of all ages). Ensemble plays with music and dance, culturally diverse and historical material, myth, folklore, and stories with universal themes are of interest. Program includes readings, developmental workshops, and fully staged productions.
Tips: Send one-page letter with one-paragraph plot synopsis, cast breakdown and setting, résumé and SAE. "We will provide the stamp and contact you *if we want to see the script*."

OREGON SHAKESPEARE FESTIVAL ASSOCIATION, P.O. Box 158, Ashland OR 97520. (541)482-2111. Fax: (541)482-0446. Website: http://www.mind.net\osf\. Director of Literary Development and Dramaturgy: Doug Langworthy. Estab. 1935. Produces 11 plays/year. The Angus Bowmer Theater has a thrust stage and seats 600. The Black Swan is an experimental space and seats 150. The Elizabethan Outdoor Theatre seats 1,200 (stages almost exclusively Shakespearean productions there, mid-June-September). Professional recommendation only. Response in 6 months. Negotiates individually for rights with the playwright's agent. "Most plays run within our ten-month season for 6-10 months, so royalties are paid accordingly."
Needs: "A broad range of classic and contemporary scripts. One or two fairly new scripts/season. Also a play readings series which focuses on new work. Plays must fit into our ten-month rotating repertory season. Black Swan shows usually limited to ten actors." No one-acts. Small musicals OK. Submissions from women and minority writers are strongly encouraged.
Tips: "We're always looking for a good comedy which has scope. We tend to prefer plays with a literary quality. We want plays to explore the human condition with language, metaphor and theatricality. We encourage translations of foreign plays as well as adaptations of non-dramatic material."

JOSEPH PAPP PUBLIC THEATER, 425 Lafayette St., New York NY 10003. (212) 539-8500. Producer: George C. Wolfe. Estab. 1964. Produces 12 plays/year. Professional productions. Query with synopsis and 10-page sample. Reports in 1 month on query; 6 months on scripts.
Needs: All genres, no one-acts.

PEOPLE'S LIGHT & THEATRE COMPANY, 39 Conestoga Rd., Malvern PA 19355. (610)647-1900. Co-Artistic Directors: Abigail Adams, Stephen Novelli. Estab. 1974. Produces 5-6 plays/year. LORT theater, general audience. Query with synopsis with 10 page dialogue sample. Reports in 6 months. Pays negotiable royalty.
Needs: Full length, *and* plays for family audiences; no musicals. Cast of 8-10 maximum. Prefers single set.

PIER ONE THEATRE, P.O. Box 894, Homer AK 99603. (907)235-7333. Website: http://www.alaska.net/~umbell. Artistic Director: Lance Petersen. Estab. 1973. Produces 5-8 plays/year. "Plays to various audiences for various plays—e.g. children's, senior citizens, adult, family, etc. Plays are produced on Kemai Peninsula." Submit complete script. Reports in 3 months. Pays $25-125/performance.
Needs: "No restrictions—willing to read *all* genres. However, for the near future, our New Works program will present work by Alaskan playwrights and work of specific Alaskan interest."
Tips: "We prefer to have the whole script to evaluate."

PIONEER DRAMA SERVICE, INC., P.O. Box 4267, Englewood CO 80155-4267. (303)779-4035. Fax: (303)779-4315. E-mail: piodrama@aol.com. Website: http://www.earthlink.net/~pioneerdrama/. Publisher: Steven Fendrich. Submissions Editor: Lynne Zborowski. Estab. 1963. Publishes approximately 30 new plays/year. Plays are performed by schools, colleges, community theaters, recreation programs, churches and professional children's theaters for audiences of all ages. Query preferred; unsolicited scripts with proof of production accepted. Reports in 2 weeks on queries, in 4 months on scripts. Retains all rights. Pays on royalty basis. All submissions automatically entered in Shubert Fendrich Memorial Playwriting Contest. Guidelines for SASE.
Needs: "We have a new Social Awareness section, and are looking for submissions in this area." Also musicals, comedies, mysteries, dramas, melodramas and children's theater (plays to be done by adult actors for children). Two-acts up to 90 minutes; children's theater, 1 hour. Prefers many female roles, simple sets. "Plays need to be appropriate for amateur groups." Prefers secular plays.
Tips: Interested in adaptations of classics of public domain works appropriate for children and teens. Also plays that deal with social issues for teens and preteens.

□**PLAYERS PRESS, INC.**, P.O. Box 1132, Studio City CA 91614-0132. Editorial Vice President: Robert W. Gordon. "We deal in all entertainment areas and handle publishable works for film and television as well as theater. Performing arts books, plays and musicals. All plays must be in stage format for publication." Also produces scripts for video and material for cable television. 80% freelance written. 20-30 scripts/year unagented submissions; 5-15 books also unagented. Works with 1-10 unpublished/unproduced writers annually. Query. "Include #10 SASE, reviews and proof of production. All play submissions must have been produced and should include a flier and/or program with dates of performance." Reports in 1 month on queries; 1 year on mss. Buys negotiable rights. "We prefer all area rights." Pays variable royalty according to area; approximately 10-75% of gross receipts. Also makes outright purchase of $100-25,000 or $5-5,000/performance.

Needs: "We prefer comedies, musicals and children's theater, but are open to all genres. We will rework the script after acceptance. We are interested in the quality, not the format. Performing Arts Books that deal with theater how-to are of strong interest."

Tips: "Send only material requested. Do not telephone."

PLAYS, The Drama Magazine for Young People, 120 Boylston St., Boston MA 02116-4615. Editor: Sylvia K. Burack. Contact: Elizabeth Preston, managing editor. Estab. 1941. Publishes approximately 75 one-act plays and dramatic program material each school year to be performed by junior and senior high, middle grades, lower grades. "Scripts should follow the general style of *Plays*. Stage directions should not be typed in capital letters or underlined. No incorrect grammar or dialect." Desired lengths are: junior and senior high—15-20 double-spaced pages (20-30 minutes playing time); middle grades—10-15 pages (15-20 minutes playing time); lower grades—6-10 pages (8-15 minutes playing time). Buys all rights. Pays "good rates on acceptance." Query first for adaptations. Reports in 2-3 weeks. Sample copy $3.50. Send SASE for specification sheet.

Needs: "Can use comedies, farces, melodramas, skits, mysteries and dramas, plays for holidays and other special occasions, such as Book Week; adaptations of classic stories and fables; historical plays; plays about black history and heroes; puppet plays; folk and fairy tales; creative dramatics; and plays for conservation, ecology or human rights programs."

‡PLAYWRIGHTS HORIZONS, 416 W. 42nd St., New York NY 10036. (212)564-1235. Artistic Director: Tim Sanford. Estab. 1971. Produces 6 plays/year. Plays performed "off-Broadway for a literate, urban, subscription audience." Send complete ms with author bio. Send plays to Sonya Soloieski, Literary Director; musicals Attn: Musical Theatre Program. Reports in 6 months. Negotiates for future rights. Pays outright sum, and then percentage after a certain run.

Needs: "We are looking for new, full-length plays and musicals by American authors."

Tips: "No adaptations, children's theater, biographical or historical plays, or relationship sit-coms. We look for plays with a strong sense of language and a clear dramatic action that truly use the resources of the theater. Minority authors are encouraged."

PLAYWRIGHTS PREVIEW PRODUCTIONS, 17 E. 47th St., New York NY 10017. (212)421-1380. Fax: (212)421-1387. E-mail: dsheppard@tuna.net. Artistic Director: Frances Hill. Literary Manager: David Sheppard. Estab. 1983. Produces 2-3 plays/year. Professional productions off or off off-Broadway—throughout the year. General audience. Submit complete script, one play only. Reports in 4 months. If produced, option for 6 months. Pays royalty.

Needs: Both one-act and full-length; generally 1 set or styled playing dual. Good imaginative, creative writing. Cast limited to 3-7.

Tips: "We tend to reject 'living-room' plays. We look for imaginative settings. Be creative and interesting with intellectual content. All submissions should be bound. Send SASE. We are looking for plays with ethnic backgrounds."

PLAYWRIGHTS THEATRE OF NEW JERSEY, 33 Green Village Rd., Madison NJ 07940. (201)514-1787. Producing Artistic Director: John Pietrowski. Artistic Director: Joseph Megel. Literary Manager: Kate McAteer. Estab. 1986. Produces 1-3 productions, 8 staged readings and sit-down readings/year. "We operate under a letter of agreement (LOA with LORT Rules) with Actors' Equity Association for all productions. Readings are held under a staged reading code." Submit complete ms. Short bio and production history required. Reports in 6-12 months. "For productions we ask the playwright to sign an agreement that gives us exclusive rights to the play for the production period and for 30 days following. After the 30 days we give the rights back with no strings attached, except for commercial productions. We ask that our developmental work be acknowledged in any other professional productions." Pays $500 for productions, $150 for staged readings. Scripts accepted September 1-April 30 only.

Needs: Any style or length; full length, one acts, musicals.

Tips: "We are looking for plays in the early stages of development—plays that take on important personal and social issues in a theatrical manner. Plays go through a three-step development process: a roundtable (inhouse reading), a public concert reading and then a workshop production."

POPE THEATRE COMPANY, 262 S. Ocean Blvd., Manalapan FL 33462. (561)585-3404. Fax: (561)588-4708. Producing Artistic Director: Louis Tyrrell. Estab. 1987. Produces 7 plays/year (5 during the regular season, 2 in the summer). "We are a fully professional (LOA) theater. We attract an audience comprised of both local residents and seasonal visitors. Many, but by no means all, of our subscribers are retirees." Agented submissions only. Reports in 6 months. Buys production rights only. Pays 6-10% royalty. "A SASE is required if a playwright wants a script returned."

Needs: "We produce new American plays. We prefer to do Florida premieres of thought-provoking, socially-conscious, challenging plays. Our stage is relatively small, which prevents us from producing works with a large cast."

‡**PRIMARY STAGES COMPANY, INC.**, 584 Ninth Ave., New York NY 10036. (212)333-7471. Fax: (212)333-2025. Contact: Andrew Leynse, literary manager. Artistic Director: Casey Childs. Estab. 1983. Produces 4 plays, 6 workshops/year. All plays are produced professionally off-Broadway at Primary Stages Theatre, 354 W. 45th St. *Agented submissions only.* Reports in 6 months. "If Primary Stages produces the play, we ask for the right to move it for up to six months after the closing performance." Writers paid $1,155 for production.
Needs: "We are looking for highly theatrical works that were written exclusively with the stage in mind. We do not want TV scripts or strictly realistic plays."
Tips: No "living room plays, disease-of-the-week plays, back-porch plays, father/son work-it-all-out-plays, etc."

THE QUARTZ THEATRE, 392 Taylor, Ashland OR 97520-3058. (503)482-8119. Artistic Director: Dr. Robert Spira. Estab. 1973. Produces several video films/year. Send 3 pages of dialogue and personal bio. Reports in 2 weeks. Pays 5% royalty after expenses.
Needs: "Any length, any subject, with or without music. We seek playwrights with a flair for language and theatrical imagination."
Tips: "We look at anything. We do not do second productions unless substantial rewriting is involved. Our theater is a stepping stone to further production. Our playwrights are usually well-read in comparative religion, philosophy, psychology, and have a comprehensive grasp of human problems. We seek the 'self-indulgent' playwright who pleases him/herself first of all."

‡**JONATHAN REINIS PRODUCTIONS, THEATRE ON THE SQUARE**, 450 Post St., San Francisco CA 94102. (415)433-6461. Estab. 1982. Produces 3 plays/year. Professional productions. 700-3,000 seats. All Equity or union actors. General audience. Agented submissions only. Reports in 2 months. Subsidiary rights negotiable. Pays 6% royalty for musicals, 8-10% for plays.
Needs: Musicals, dramas, comedies.
Tips: "No dreary, depressing ideological plays. Dance has become much more important. Younger generations (stomp, etc.) are leaning to performance art. Be flexible."

‡**DUDLEY RIGGS THEATRES**, 1586 Burton, St. Paul MN 55108. (612)332-6620. Artistic Director: Dudley Riggs. Estab. 1961. Produces 7-8 plays/year. "Comedy only! Revue and small musicals too. We have a wide range of audiences from teenage to seniors. We do some nonprofessional productions, but most are with a paid company and on a professional stage. Query and synopsis on longer works. Send full scripts for revue or musicals. Reports in 3 months. Obtains performance rights for our area and limited rights for touring. Each project is negotiated separately. Commissioned work on a percentage of ticket sales are common.
Needs: "We need revues of current events (social and political satire) and capsule musicals (3-7 actors). We have minimal staging—stage is 300 sq. ft. total—and a resident company of seven artists."
Tips: "No dramas, pageants, long-winded shows or large cast productions. There are too many dark plays, too few new musicals, and there's too much 'political correctness.' We only do comedy. It needs to be current or timeless and should be based on truth. There are no taboo subjects but they must have tasteful treatment."

SEATTLE REPERTORY THEATRE, 155 Mercer St., Seattle WA 98109. (206)443-2210. Artistic Director: Sharon Ott. Estab. 1963. Produces 9 plays/year: 6 mainstage, 3 second stage. Plays performed in Seattle, with occasional transfers elsewhere. Agented submissions only. Reports in 4-6 months. Buys percentage of future royalties. Pays royalty.
Needs: "The Seattle Repertory Theatre produces eclectic programming. We rarely produce plays with more than 15 people in the cast. We welcome a wide variety of writing."

‡**SECOND STAGE THEATRE**, P.O. Box 1807, Ansonia Station, New York NY 10023. (212)787-8302 Artistic Director: Carole Rothman. Estab. 1979. Produces 4 plays/year. Professional off-Broadway productions. Query with synopsis and ten-page writing sample or agented submission. Reports in 6 months. Pay varies.
Needs: "We need plays by living American authors that have a heightened language and unique view of the world, comedies, one-person shows and musicals for no more than 10 actors. Limited back-stage and no fly space, so scenic demands should be simple."
Tips: "No biographical plays, kitchen-sink realism, melodrama. Plays have lost a sense of theatricality in favor of cinematic realism. Yet those productions which have strongly succeeded in recent years harken back to strong theater and its ideals. Writers should be aware of this history. A simple twist or gimmick will not elevate an otherwise mundane play. A work should be infused with a certain eccentricism to be unique."

‡**SHAW FESTIVAL THEATRE**, P.O. Box 774, Niagara-on-the-Lake, Ontario L0S 1J0 Canada. Fax: (905)468-5438. Artistic Director: Christopher Newton. Estab. 1962. Produces 10 plays/year. "Professional summer festival operating three theaters (Festival: 861 seats; Court House: 316 seats; Royal George: 328 seats). We also host some music and some winter rentals. Mandate is based on the works of G.B. Shaw and his contemporaries. We prefer to hold rights for Canada and northeastern US, also potential to tour." Pays 5-6% royalty. Submit with SASE or SAE and IRCs, depending on country of origin.
Needs: "We operate an acting ensemble of up to 75 actors; this includes 14 actor/singers and we have sophisticated production facilities. During the summer season (April-October) the Academy of the Shaw Festival sometimes organizes workshops of new plays."

SOUTH COAST REPERTORY, P.O. Box 2197, Costa Mesa CA 92628-1197. (714)957-2602. Fax: (714)545-0391. Website: http://www.ocartsnet.org/scr/. Dramaturg: Jerry Patch. Literary Manager: John Glore. Estab. 1964. Produces 6 plays/year on mainstage, 5 on second stage. Professional nonprofit theater; a member of LORT and TCG. "We operate in our own facility which houses a 507-seat mainstage theater and a 161-seat second stage theater. We have a combined subscription audience of 21,000." Query with synopsis; scripts considered if submitted by agent. Reports in 4 months. Acquires negotiable rights. Pays negotiable royalty.
Needs: "We produce full lengths. We prefer well-written plays that address contemporary concerns and are dramaturgically innovative. A play whose cast is larger than 15-20 will need to be extremely compelling and its cast size must be justifiable."
Tips: "We don't look for a writer to write for us—he or she should write for him or herself. We look for honesty and a fresh voice. We're not likely to be interested in writers who are mindful of *any* trends. Originality and craftsmanship are the most important qualities we look for."

SOUTHERN APPALACHIAN REPERTORY THEATRE (SART), Mars Hill College, P.O. Box 620, Mars Hill NC 28754-0620. (704)689-1384. E-mail: sart@mhc.edu. Artistic Director: James W. Thomas. Asst. Managing Director: Dianne Chapman. Estab. 1975. Produces 6 plays/year. "Since 1975 the Southern Appalachian Repertory Theatre has produced 37 world premieres in the 166-seat Owen Theatre on the Mars Hill College campus. The theater's goals are quality, adventurous programming and integrity, both in artistic form and in the treatment of various aspects of the human condition. SART is a professional summer theater company whose audiences range from students to senior citizens." Reports in 1 year. It also conducts an annual Southern Appalachian Playwrights' Conference in which 5 playwrights are invited for informal readings of their new scripts. Deadline for submission is October 30 and conference is held the first weekend in April. If script is selected for production during the summer season, an honorarium is paid to the playwright. Enclose SASE for return of script.
Needs: Since 1975, one of SART's goals has been to produce at least one original play each summer season. To date, 37 original scripts have been produced. Plays by southern Appalachian playwrights or about southern Appalachia are preferred, but by no means exclusively. Complete new scripts welcomed.

STAGE ONE: The Louisville Children's Theatre, 5 Riverfront Plaza, Louisville KY 40202-3300. (502)589-5946. Fax: (502)588-5910. E-mail: kystage@aol.com. Producing Director: Moses Goldberg. Estab. 1946. Produces 6-7 plays/year. 20% freelance written; 15-20% unagented submissions (excluding work of playwright-in-residence). Plays performed by an Equity company for young audiences ages 4-18; usually does different plays for different age groups within that range. Submit complete script. Reports in 4 months. Pays negotiable royalty or $25-75/performance.
Needs: "Good plays for young audiences of all types: adventure, fantasy, realism, serious problem plays about growing up or family entertainment. Cast: ideally, twelve or less. Honest, visual potentiality, worthwhile story and characters are necessary. An awareness of children and their schooling is a plus. No campy material or anything condescending to children. Musicals if they are fairly limited in orchestration."

STAGE WEST, P.O. Box 2587, Fort Worth TX 76113. (817)924-9454. Fax: (817)926-8650. Artistic Director: Jerry Russell. Estab. 1979. Produces 8 plays/year. "We stage professional productions at our own theater for a mixed general audience." Query with synopsis. Reports in 6 months. Rights are negotiable. Pays 7% royalty.
Needs: "We want full-length plays that are accessible to a mainstream audience but possess traits that are highly theatrical. Cast size of ten or less and single or unit set are desired."

STEPPENWOLF THEATRE COMPANY, 1650 N. Halsted, Chicago IL 60614. (312)335-1888. Artistic Director: Martha Lavey. Dramaturg/Literary Manager: Michele Volansky. Estab. 1976. Produces 9 plays/year. 500 + 300 seat subscriber audience. Many plays produced by Steppenwolf have gone to Broadway. "We currently have 18,000 savvy subscribers." Query with synopsis, 10 pages sample dialogue. Agented submissions only or letter of recommendation from theater professional. Reports in 6 months. Buys first, second class and regional rights. Pays 6-8% royalty.
Needs: Wants all sorts of full-lengths with strong ensemble acting possibilities. "However, musicals are not our forté. Also, we've rarely produced one-acts and a 28-character play may be pushing it."
Tips: "Look to our history to know if your play is 'Steppenwolf material.' "

STUDIO ARENA THEATRE, 710 Main St., Buffalo NY 14201. (716)856-8025. Artistic Director: Gavin Cameron-Webb. Estab. 1965. Produces 8 plays/year. Professional productions. Agented submissions only. Reports in 6 months.
Needs: Full-length plays. No fly space.

‡**SUMMER NITE**, Northern Illinois University School of Theatre Arts, DeKalb IL 60115. (815)753-1600. Artistic Director: Gene Terruso. Estab. 1990. Produces 1 play/year. Summer equity company that premieres new works, previously unseen in Chicago, at the Bailiwick Arts Center. Query with synopsis and character breakdown. Reports in several months. Rights obtained are negotiable. Pays $1,000 minimum stipend.
Needs: Topical comedies and dramas, political pieces and musicals in the full-length form. "We cannot accept pieces that have been previously done in Chicago."

TADA!, 120 W. 28th St., New York NY 10001. (212)627-1732. Fax: (212)243-6736. E-mail: tada@ziplink.net. Website: http://www.tadatheater.com. Artistic Director: Janine Nina Trevens. Estab. 1984. Produces 2-4 plays/year. "TADA!

produces original musicals and plays performed by children at our 95-seat theater. Productions are for family audiences." Submit complete script and tape, if musical. Reports in 6 months. Pays 5% royalty or commission fee (varies).

• TADA! also sponsors a one-act play competition for their Spring Staged Reading Series. Works must be original, unproduced and unpublished one-acts. Plays may be geared toward teen audiences. Call for deadlines.

Needs: "Generally pieces run from 45-70 minutes. Must be enjoyed by children and adults and performed by a cast of children ages 8-17."

Tips: "No redone fairy tales or pieces where children are expected to play adults. Be careful not to condescend when writing for children's theater."

THE TEN-MINUTE MUSICALS PROJECT, P.O. Box 461194, West Hollywood CA 90046. (213)656-8751. Producer: Michael Koppy. Estab. 1987. Produces 1-10 plays/year. "Plays performed in Equity regional theaters in the US and Canada." Submit complete script, lead sheets and cassette. Deadline August 31; notification by December 15. Buys performance rights. Pays $250 royalty advance upon selection, against equal share of performance royalties when produced. Submission guidelines for #10 SASE.

Needs: Looking for complete short stage musicals playing between 7-14 minutes. Limit cast to 10 (5 women, 5 men).

‡THE THEATER AT MONMOUTH, P.O. Box 385, Monmouth ME 04259. (207)933-9999. Artistic Director: Michael O'Brien. Estab. 1970. Produces 5-6 titles/year. "We will accept submissions for children's theater (non-musical) productions based on classical fairy tales and children's stories. Productions are amateur and summer." Query and synopsis. Reports in 2 months. Pays $10-25/performance.

Needs: Children's theater (75 minutes or less), non-musical, with preference toward classical fairy tales and children's stories. Less than ten cast members. Very simple staging.

Tips: No full-length, new plays for adult audiences. No musicals.

‡THE THEATER OF NECESSITY, 11702 Webercrest, Houston TX 77048. (713)733-6042. Artistic Director: Philbert Plumb. Estab. 1981. Produces 4 plays/year. Plays are produced in a small professional theater. Submit complete script. Reports in 1 year. Buys performance rights. Pays standard royalties based on size of house for small productions or individual contracts for large productions (average $500/run). "We usually keep script on file unless we are certain we will never use it." Send SASE with script and #10 SASE for response.

Needs: "Any play in a recognizable genre must be superlative in form and intensity. Experimental plays are given an easier read. We move to larger venue if the play warrants the expense."

THEATRE & COMPANY, 20 Queen St. N., Kitchener, Ontario N2H 2G8 Canada. Fax: (519)571-9051. E-mail: stuartsw@wchat.on.ca. Website: http://www.cyg.net/~stamp. Artistic Director: Stuart Scadron-Wattles. Literary Manager: Wes Wikkerink. Estab. 1988. Produces 5 plays/year. Professional (non-equity) productions for a general audience. Query with synopsis and SAE with IRCs. Reports in 3 months. Pays $50-100/performance.

Needs: "One act or full length; comedy or drama; musical or straight; written from or compatible with a biblical world view." No cast above 10; prefers unit staging. Looking for small cast (less than 8) ensemble comedies.

• Theatre & Company is particularly interested in work by Canadians.

Tips: Looks for "non-religious writing from a biblical world view for an audience which loves the theater. Avoid current trends toward shorter scenes. Playwrights should be aware that they are writing for the stage—not television. We encourage audience interaction, using an acting ensemble trained in improvisation."

THEATRE AT LIME KILN, P.O. Box 663, Lexington VA 24450. (540)463-7088. Fax: (540)463-1082. E-mail: limekiln@cfw.com. Dramaturg: Eleanor Connor. Estab. 1983. Produces 7 plays/year. Professional outdoor summer theater. Audience is family oriented. Query with synopsis or submit complete ms. Reports in 4 months. Rights vary. Pay varies.

Needs: Full length, musical or straight. Material should reflect culture/issues/concerns of Appalachian region. Outdoor theater, limited sets. Cast of 9 or less preferred.

Tips: No urban angst. Smaller cast shows have a better chance of being produced.

‡THEATRE DE LA JEUNE LUNE, 105 N. First St., Minneapolis MN 55401-1411. (612)332-3968. Fax: (612)332-0048. Artistic Directors: Barbra Berlovitz Desbois, Vincent Garcieux, Robert Rosen, Dominique Serrand. Estab. 1979. Produces 2-3 plays/year. Professional nonprofit company producing September-June for general audience. Query with synopsis. Reports in 3 months. Pays royalty or per performance. No unsolicited scripts, please.

Needs: "All subject matter considered, although plays with universal themes are desired; plays that concern people of today. We are constantly looking for plays with large casts. Generally *not* interested in plays with 1-4 characters. No psychological drama or plays that are written alone in a room without the input of outside vitality and life."

Tips: "We are an acting company that takes plays and makes them ours; this could mean cutting a script or not heeding a writer's stage directions. We are committed to the performance in front of the audience as the goal of all the contributing factors; therefore, the actor's voice is extremely important."

THEATREVIRGINIA, 2800 Grove Ave., Richmond VA 23221-2466. Producing Artistic Director: George Black. Estab. 1955. Produces 5-8, publishes 0-1 new play/year. Query with synopsis and 15 page sample. Accepts agented submissions. Solicitations in 1 month for initial query, 3-8 months for script. Rights negotiated. Payment negotiated.

Needs: No one-acts; no children's theater.

‡**THEATREWORKS/USA**, 890 Broadway, New York NY 10003. (212)677-5959. Artistic Director: Jay Harnick. Estab. 1961. Produces 3-6 new productions/year. Professional Equity productions for young audiences. Query and synopsis or submit complete ms. Reports in 6 months. Pays 6% royalty.
Needs: "One-hour musicals or plays with music written for K-3rd or 3rd-7th grade age groups. Subjects: historical, biography, classic literature, fairy tales with specific point of view, contemporary literature. Limited to 5-6 actors and a portable set. Do not rely on lighting or special effects."
Tips: "No campy, 'fractured' fairy tales, shows specifically written to teach or preach, shows relying heavily on narrators or 'kiddy theater' filled with pratfalls, bad jokes and audience participation. Write smart. Kids see a lot these days, and they are sophisticated. Don't write down to them. They deserve a good, well-told story. Seeing one of our shows will provide the best description."

‡**UNICORN THEATRE**, 3820 Main St., Kansas City MO 64111. (816)531-PLAY. Fax: (816)531-0421. Producing Artistic Director: Cynthia Levin. Produces 6-8 plays/year. "We are a professional Equity Theatre. Typically, we produce plays dealing with contemporary issues." Send full script. Reports in 4-6 months.
Needs: Prefers contemporary (post-1950) scripts. Does not accept musicals, one-acts, or historical plays. Query (to Herman Wilson) with script, brief synopsis, bio, character breakdown, SASE if script is to be returned, SASP for acknowledgement of receipt is desired. A royalty/prize of $1,000 will be awarded the playwright of any play selected through this process, The National Playwright Award. This script receives production as part of the Unicorn's regular season.

‡**VENTANA PUBLICATIONS**, P.O. Box 191973, San Francisco CA 94119. (415)522-8989. Contact: Vicky Simmons, literary manager. Estab. 1991. Publishes 3-5 plays/year. Publishes for professional theaters and universities. Query and synopsis or enter contest. Reports in 3 months. "Ventana Publications has the exclusive right to sell/distribute selected play(s) on the basis of demand and opportunity for a period of two years from the date of publication, longer if author agrees." Pays 10% of book, 90% of production royalties plus copies.
Needs: "All lengths and genres. Plays must be produced or have significant accomplishment (contest winner, etc.)." No limitations.
Tips: "We are a small press; please query first."

VIGILANTE THEATRE CO., P.O. Box 507, Bozeman MT 59771-0507. (406)586-3897. Artistic Director: Brian V. Massman. Estab. 1982. Produces 1-2 plays/year. Plays by professional touring company that does productions by or about people and themes of the Northwest. "Past productions were concerned with homeless people, agriculture, literature by Northwest writers, one-company towns and spouse abuse in rural areas." Submit complete ms. Reports in 6 months. Pays $10-50/performance.
Needs: Produces full-length plays, small musicals and some one-acts. "Staging suitable for a small touring company and cast limited to four actors (two men, two women). Double casting actors for more play characters is also an option."
Tips: "No large musicals requiring orchestras and a chorus line. Although we prefer a script of some thematic substance, the company is very adept at comedy and would prefer the topic to include humor."

WALNUT STREET THEATRE, Ninth and Walnut Streets, Philadelphia PA 19107. (215)574-3550. Fax: (215)574-3598. Executive Director: Bernard Havard. Literary Manager: Beverly Elliott. Estab. 1809. Produces 5 mainstage and 5 studio plays/year. "Our plays are performed in our own space. WST has 3 theaters—a proscenium (mainstage), 1,052 seats; 2 studios, 79-99 seats. We have a subscription audience, second largest in the nation." Query with synopsis and 10 pages. Writer's must be members of the Dramatists' Guild. Reports in 5 months. Rights negotiated per project. Pays royalty (negotiated per project) or outright purchase.
Needs: "Full-length dramas and comedies, musicals, translations, adaptations and revues. The studio plays must have a cast of no more than four, simple sets."
Tips: "Bear in mind that on the mainstage we look for plays with mass appeal, Broadway-style. The studio spaces are our off-Broadway. No children's plays. Our mainstage audience goes for work that is entertaining and light. Our studio season is where we look for plays that have bite and are more provocative." Include SASE for return of materials.

WATERLOO COMMUNITY PLAYHOUSE, P.O. Box 433, Waterloo IA 50704-0433. (319)235-0367. Fax: (319)235-7489. Charles Stilwill, managing artistic director. Estab. 1917. Plays performed by Waterloo Community Playhouse with a volunteer cast. Produces 11 plays (7 adult, 4 children's); 1-2 musicals and 9-10 nonmusicals/year; 1-3 originals. 17% freelance written; most unagented submissions. Works with 1-3 unpublished/unproduced writers annually. "We are one of few community theaters with a commitment to new scripts. We do at least one and have done as many as four a year. We have 4,300 season members. Average attendance is 3,300. We do a wide variety of plays. Our public isn't going to accept nudity, too much sex, too much strong language. We don't have enough Black actors to do all-Black shows. Theater has done plays with as few as 2 characters, and as many as 98. On the main stage, we usually pay between $400 and $500. We also produce children's theater. Submit complete script. Please, no loose pages. Reports negatively within 1 year, but acceptance sometimes takes longer because we try to fit a wanted script into the balanced season. We sometimes hold a script longer than a year if we like it but cannot immediately find the right slot for it. In 1994 we did the world premiere of *The Ninth Step* which was written in 1989 and the year before we did the world premiere of *Grace Under Pressure*, written in 1984. We just did the world premiere of *A Tradition of Service* written in 1990."

Needs: "For our Children's Theater and our Adult Biannual Holiday (Christmas) show, we are looking for good adaptations of name children's stories or very good shows that don't necessarily have a name. We produce children's theater with both adult and child actors."

WEST COAST ENSEMBLE, P.O. Box 38728, Los Angeles CA 90038. (310)449-1447. Fax: (310)453-2254. Artistic Director: Les Hanson. Estab. 1982. Produces 6 plays/year. Plays performed at a theater in Hollywood. Submit complete script. Reports in 6-9 months. Obtains exclusive rights in southern California to present the play for the period specified. All ownership and rights remain with the playwright. Pays $25-45/performance.

Needs: Prefers a cast of 6-12.

Tips: "Submit the script in acceptable dramatic script format."

WESTBETH THEATRE CENTER, INC., 151 Bank St., New York NY 10014-2049. (212)691-2272. Fax: (212)924-7185. Producing Director: Arnold Engelman. Director, American Playwright Program: Craig Carlisle. Estab. 1977. Produces 10 readings and 6 productions/year. Professional off-Broadway theater. Obtains rights to produce as showcase with option to enter into full option agreement.

Needs: "Contemporary full-length plays. Production values (i.e., set, costumes, etc.) should be kept to a minimum." No period pieces. Limit 10 actors; doubling explained.

‡WILLOWS THEATRE COMPANY, 1975 Diamond Blvd., #A-20, Concord CA 94520. (510)798-1300. Artistic Director: Richard Elliott. "Professional productions for a suburban audience, 'safe' fare." Query and synopsis with SASE or agented submissions. Accepts new material in April and May only. Reports in 2 weeks on queries; 6 months on scripts. Pays royalty.

Needs: "Commercially viable, small-medium size musicals, plays with an edge. No more than 15 actors. Unit or simple sets with no fly space."

THE WOMEN'S PROJECT AND PRODUCTIONS, 55 West End Ave., New York NY 10023. (212)765-1706. Fax: (212)765-2024. Artistic Director: Julia Miles. Estab. 1978. Produces 3 plays/year. Professional Off-Broadway productions. Query with synopsis and 10 sample pages of dialogue. Reports in 1 month on queries.

Needs: "We are looking for full-length plays, written by women."

WOOLLY MAMMOTH THEATRE COMPANY, 1401 Church St. NW, Washington DC 20005-1903. (202)393-3939. Fax: (202)667-0904. E-mail: wollymamm@aol.com. Artistic Director: Howard Shalwitz. Literary Manager: Gary Oiler. Produces 5 plays/year. 50% freelance written. Produces professional productions for the general public in Washington DC. 2-3 scripts/year unagented submissions. Works with 1-2 unpublished/unproduced writers/year. Accepts unsolicited scripts. Reports in 6 months on scripts; very interesting scripts often take much longer. Buys first- and second-class production rights. Pays 5% royalty.

Needs: "We look only for plays that are highly unusual in some way. Also interested in multicultural projects. Apart from an innovative approach, there is no formula. One-acts are not used." Cast limit of 7.

WORCESTER FOOTHILLS THEATRE COMPANY, 100 Front St., Suite 137, Worcester MA 01608. (508)754-3314. Artistic Director: Marc P. Smith. Estab. 1974. Produces 7 plays/year. Full time professional theater, general audience. Query with synopsis. Reports in 3 weeks. Pays royalty.

Needs: "Produce plays for general audience. No gratuitous violence, sex or language. Prefer cast under 10 and single set. 30' proscenium with apron but no fly space."

SCREENWRITING

Practically everyone you meet in Los Angeles, from your airport cabbie on, is writing a script. It might be a feature film, movie of the week, TV series or documentary, but the sheer amount of competition can seem overwhelming. Some will never make a sale, while others make a decent living on sales and options without ever having any of their work produced. But there are those writers who make a living doing what they love and see their names roll by on the credits. How do they get there? How do *you* get there?

First, work on your writing. You'll improve with each script, so there is no way of getting around the need to write and write some more. It's a good idea to read as many scripts as you can get your hands on. Check your local bookstores and libraries. Script City (8033 Sunset Blvd., Suite 1500, Hollywood CA 90046, (800)676-2522) carries thousands of movie and TV scripts, classics to current releases, as well as books, audio/video seminars and software in their $2 catalog. Book City (Dept. 101, 308 N. San Fernando Blvd., Burbank CA 91502, (800)4-

CINEMA) has film and TV scripts in all genres and a large selection of movie books in their $2.50 catalog.

There are lots of books that will give you the "rules" of format and structure for writing for TV or film. Samuel French (7623 Sunset Blvd., Hollywood CA 90046 (213)876-0570) carries a number of how-to books and reference materials on these subjects. The correct format marks your script as a professional submission. Most successful scriptwriters will tell you to learn the correct structure, internalize those rules—and then throw them away and write intuitively.

Writing for TV

To break into TV you must have spec scripts—work written for free that serves as a calling card and gets you in the door. A spec script showcases your writing abilities and gets your name in front of influential people. Whether a network has invited you in to pitch some ideas, or a movie producer has contacted you to write a first draft for a feature film, the quality of writing in your spec script got their attention and that may get you the job.

It's a good idea to have several spec scripts, perhaps one each for three of the top five shows in the format you prefer to work in, whether it's sitcom (half-hour comedies), episodic (one hour series) or movie of the week (two hour dramatic movies). Perhaps you want to showcase the breadth of your writing ability; some writers have a portfolio of a few eight o'clock type shows (i.e., *Friends*, *Mad About You*, *Home Improvement*), a few nine-o'clock shows (i.e., *Ellen*, *Seinfeld*, *The X Files*) and one or two episodics (i.e., *Homicide*, *Law and Order*, *NYPD Blue*). These are all "hot" shows for writers and can demonstrate your abilities to create believable dialogue for characters already familiar to your intended readers. For TV and cable movies you should have completed original scripts (not sequels to existing movies) and you might also have a few for episodic TV shows.

In choosing the shows you write spec scripts for you must remember one thing: don't write a script for a show you want to work on. If you want to write for *NYPD Blue*, for example, you'll send a *Law and Order* script and vice versa. It may seem contradictory, but it is standard practice. It reduces the chances of lawsuits, and writers and producers can feel very proprietary about their show and their stories. They may not be objective enough to fairly evaluate your writing. In submitting another similar type of show you'll avoid those problems while demonstrating comparable skills.

In writing your TV script you must get *inside* the show and understand the characters' internal motivations. You must immerse yourself in how the characters speak, think and interact. Don't introduce new characters in a spec script for an existing show—write believable dialogue for the characters as they are portrayed. Be sure to choose a show that you like—you'll be better able to demonstrate your writing ability through characters you respond to.

You must also understand the external factors. How the show is filmed bears on how you write. Most sitcoms are shot on videotape with three cameras, on a sound stage with a studio audience. Episodics are often shot on film with one camera and include on-location shots. *Mad About You* has a flat, evenly-lit look and takes place in a limited number of locations. *Law and Order* has a gritty realism with varying lighting and a variety of settings from McCord's office to outside a bodega on East 135th.

Another important external influence in writing for TV is the timing of commercials in conjunction with the act structure. There are lots of sources detailing the suggested content and length of acts, but generally a sitcom has a teaser (short opening scene), two acts and a tag (short closing scene), and an episodic has a teaser, four acts and a tag. Each act closes with a turning point. Watching TV analytically and keeping a log of events will reveal some elements of basic structure. *Successful Scriptwriting*, by Wolff & Cox (Writer's Digest Books), offers detailed discussions of various types of shows.

Writing for the movies

With feature films you may feel at once more liberated and more bound by structure. An original movie script contains characters you have created, with storylines you design, allowing you more freedom than you have in TV. However, your writing must still convey believable dialogue and realistic characters, with a plausible plot and high-quality writing carried through the roughly 120 pages. The characters must have a problem that involves the audience. When you go to a movie you don't want to spend time watching the *second* worst night of a character's life. You're looking for the big issue that crystallizes a character, that portrays a journey with important consequences.

At the same time you are creating, you should also be constructing. Be aware of the basic three act structure for feature films. Scenes can be of varying lengths, but are usually no longer than three to three and a half pages. Some writers list scenes that must occur, then flesh them out from beginning to end, writing with the structure of events in mind. The beginning and climactic scenes are the easiest; it's how they get there from here that's difficult.

Many novice screenwriters tend to write too many visual cues and camera directions into their scripts. Your goal should be to write something readable, like a "compressed novella." Write succinct resonant scenes and leave the camera technique to the director and producer. In action/adventure movies, however, there needs to be a balance since the script demands more visual direction.

It seems to be easier for TV writers to cross over to movies. Cable movies bridge the two, and are generally less derivative and more willing to take chances with a higher quality show designed to attract an audience not interested in network offerings. Cable is also less susceptible to advertiser pullout, which means it can tackle more controversial topics.

Feature films and TV are very different and writers occupy different positions. TV is a medium for writers and producers; directors work for them. Many TV writers are also producers. In feature films the writers and producers work for the director and often have little or no say about what happens to the work once the script has been sold. For TV the writer pitches the idea; for feature films generally the producer pitches the idea and then finds a writer.

Marketing your scripts

If you intend to make writing your profession you must act professionally. Accepted submission practices should become second nature.

- The initial pitch is made through a query letter, which is no longer than one page with a one paragraph synopsis and brief summary of your credits if they are relevant to the subject of your script.
- Never send a complete manuscript until it is requested.
- Almost every script sent to a producer, studio or agent must be accompanied by a release form. Ask for that company's form when you receive an invitation to submit the whole script. Mark your envelope "release form enclosed" to prevent it being returned unread.
- Always include a self-addressed stamped envelope (SASE) if you want your work returned; a disposable copy may be accompanied by a self-addressed stamped postcard for reply.
- Allow four to six weeks from receipt of your manuscript before writing a follow-up letter.

When your script is requested, be sure it's written in the appropriate format. Unusual binding, fancy covers or illustrations mark an amateur. Three brass brads with a plain or black cover indicate a pro.

There are a limited number of ideas in the world, so it's inevitable that similar ideas occur to more than one person. Hollywood is a buyer's market and a release form states that pretty clearly. An idea is not copyrightable, so be careful about sharing premises. The written expression of that idea, however, can be protected and it's a good idea to do so. The Writers Guild of America can register scripts for television and theatrical motion pictures, series formats, storylines and step outlines. You need not be a member of the WGA to use this service. Copyrighting your work with the Copyright Office of the Library of Congress also protects your work from infringement. Contact either agency for more information and an application form.

If you are a writer, you should write—all the time. When you're not writing, read. There are numerous books on the art, craft and business of screenwriting. See the Publications of Interest at the end of *Writer's Market* for a few or check the catalogs of companies previously mentioned. The different industry trade papers such as *Daily Variety* and *Hollywood Reporter* can keep you in touch with the day to day news and upcoming events. Specialty newsletters such as *Hollywood Scriptwriter*, *Creative Screenwriting* and *New York Scriptwriter* offer tips from successful scriptwriters and agents. The *Hollywood Creative Directory* is an extensive list of production companies, studios and networks that also lists companies and talent with studio deals.

Computer services have various bulletin boards and chat hours for scriptwriters that provide contact with other writers and a chance to share information and encouragement.

It may take years of work before you come up with a script someone is willing to take a chance on. Those years need to be spent learning your craft and understanding the business. Polishing scripts, writing new material, keeping current with the industry and networking constantly will keep you busy. When you do get that call you'll be confident in your abilities and know that your hard work is beginning to pay off.

For information on some screenwriting markets not listed in *Writer's Market*, see the General Index.

‡**ABC PICTURES**, 2020 Ave. of Stars, #500, Los Angeles CA 90067. Contact: Kristen Arthur. Estab. 1995. Network and cable television. Buys 36 scripts/year. Works with 36 writers/year. Buys all rights. Reports in 1 month on queries. Query with synopsis. Pays in accordance with Writer's Guild standards.
Needs: Films (16mm and 35mm).
Tips: "We will only receive agented or lawyer submissions."

□**ALLIED ARTISTS, INC.**, 859 N. Hollywood Way, Suite 377, Burbank CA 91505. (818)594-4089. Vice President, Development: John Nichols. Estab. 1990. Produces material for broadcast and cable television, home video and film. Buys 3-5 scripts/year. Works with 10-20 writers/year. Buys first rights or all rights. Accepts previously produced material. Reports in 2 months on queries; 3 months on scripts. Submit synopsis/outline. Pays in accordance with Writers Guild standards (amount and method negotiable). Written queries only—*no phone pitches.*
Needs: Films, videotapes. Social issue TV special (30-60 minutes); special interest home video topics; instruction and entertainment; positive values feature screenplays.
Tips: "We are looking for positive, up-lifting dramatic stories involving real people situations. Future trend is for more reality-based programming, as well as interactive television programs for viewer participation."

‡**AMERICAN FILMWORKS**, 222 N. Canon Dr., Suite 201, Beverly Hills CA 90210. (310)288-0569. Contact: Rachelle Wyse. Works with 6 writers/year. Buys first or all rights. Accepts previously produced material. Reports in 3 months on queries. Query with synopsis. Pays in accordance with Writer's Guild standards.

‡**THE AMERICAN MOVING PICTURE COMPANY INC.**, 838 N. Doheny Dr., #904, Los Angeles CA 90069. (310)273-3838. C.E.O., President: William A. Levey. Estab. 1979. Theatrical motion picture audience. Buys screenplay rights and ancillaries. No previously produced material. Does not return submissions. Reports in 1 month. Query with synopsis. Pays in accordance with Writers Guild standards or more.
Needs: Films (35mm), commercial.

‡**AMERICAN ZOETROPE TELEVISION**, 9100 Wilshire Blvd., Suite 600, Beverly Hills CA 90212. Director of Development: Jodi Ticknor. Estab. 1975. Television audience. Buys 10 scripts/year. Works with 20 writers/year. Buys motion picture and television rights. Accepts previously produced material. Reports in 3 months on queries. Query with synopsis and résumé. Pays in accordance with Writer's Guild standards.
Needs: Filmstrips, sound. Action projects with male or female protagonists; disaster stories; projects with strong female leads: thrillers or women in jeopardy stories; teenagers in jeopardy stories of "bad girls" or "boys."

‡**ANASAZI PRODUCTIONS**, 100 Market St., Venice CA 90291. (310)314-4417. Contact: Peter Stelzer, vice president. Estab. 1990. General TV and film audience. Buys 1-3 scripts/year. Works with 5-10 writers/year. Buys all rights.

Accepts previously produced stage plays and books. Reports in 1 month on queries, 3 months on submissions. Query. Pays in accordance with Writer's Guild standards.

Needs: Films (35mm) and videotapes. Films (dramas and comedies). TV (true life stories, families in jeopardy).

ANGEL FILMS, 967 Highway 40, New Franklin MO 65274-9778. (573)698-3900. Fax: (573)698-3900. E-mail: euttland@aol.com. Vice President Production: Matthew Eastman. Estab. 1980. Produces material for feature films, television. Buys 10 scripts/year. Works with 20 writers/year. Buys all rights. Accepts previously published material (if rights available). Reports in 1 months on queries; 1-2 months on scripts. Query with synopsis. Makes outright purchase. Our company is a low-budget producer, which means people get paid fairly, but don't get rich."

Needs: Films (35mm), videotapes. "We are looking for projects that can be used to produce feature film and television feature film and series work. These would be in the areas of action adventure, comedy, horror, thriller, science fiction, animation for children." Also looking for direct to video materials.

Tips: "Don't copy others. Try to be original. Don't overwork your idea. As far as trends are concerned, don't pay attention to what is 'in.' By the time it gets to us it will most likely be on the way 'out.' And if you can't let your own grandmother read it, don't send it. If you wish material returned, enclose proper postage with all submissions. Send SASE for response to queries and return of scripts."

ANGEL'S TOUCH PRODUCTIONS, 22906 Calabash St., Woodland Hills CA 91364. Director of Development: Phil Nemy. Estab. 1986. Professional screenplays and teleplays. Send synopsis. Reports in 6 months. Rights negotiated between production company and author. Payment negotiated.

Needs: All types, all genres, only full-length teleplays and screenplays—no one-acts.

Tips: "We only seek feature film screenplays, television screenplays, and episodic teleplays. No phone calls!"

BARNSTORM FILMS, 73 Market St., Venice CA 90291. (310)396-5937. Contact: Josh Deighton. Estab. 1969. Produces feature films. Buys 2-3 scripts/year. Works with 4-5 writers/year.

Tips: Looking for strong, character-based commercial scripts. Not interested in science fiction or fantasy. Must send SASE with query letter. Query first, do not send script unless we request it!"

BOZ PRODUCTIONS, 7612 Fountain Ave., Los Angeles CA 90046. (213)876-3232. Fax: (213)876-3231. E-mail: boz51@aol.com. Director of Development: Steve Dandois. Estab. 1987. All audiences. Buys 3-5 scripts/year. Works with several writers/year. Buys all rights. Accepts previously produced material. Reports in 1 month on queries; 1-2 months on scripts. Query with synopsis and résumé. Pay varies.

Needs: Films (35mm). Feature-length film scripts or rights to real stories for MOW's.

CANVAS HOUSE FILMS, 3671 Bear St., #E, Santa Ana CA 92704. Producer: Mitch Teemley. Estab. 1994. General audience. Buys 2-3 scripts/year. Works with 10-15 writers/year. Buys first rights, all rights. Accepts previously produced material. Reports in 1 month on queries; 4 months on submissions. Query with detailed (2-4 page) synopsis and résumé or list of credits. Pays in accordance with Writers Guild standards.

Needs: Films (35mm). "Quality feature-length filmscripts—all types, but no lurid, 'hard-R'-rated material."

Tips: "Know proper formatting and story structure. There is a need for 'family' material that can appeal to *grown-ups* as well as children."

CINE/DESIGN FILMS, INC., P.O. Box 6495, Denver CO 80206. (303)777-4222. E-mail: jghusband@aol.com. Producer/Director: Jon Husband. Produces educational material for general, sales-training and theatrical audiences. 75% freelance written; 90% unagented submissions. "Original, solid ideas are encouraged." Rights purchased vary.

Needs: Films (16, 35mm). "Motion picture outlines in the theatrical and documentary areas. We are seeking theatrical scripts in the low-budget area that are possible to produce for under $1 million. We seek flexibility and personalities who can work well with our clients." Send 8-10-page outline before submitting ms. Pays $100-200/screen minute on 16mm productions. Theatrical scripts negotiable.

Tips: "Understand the marketing needs of film production today. Materials will not be returned."

CLARK FILM PRODUCTION CHARITY, INC., P.O. Box 773, Balboa CA 92661. President: Mr. Steven Clark. Estab. 1987. General audience. Buys 1 script/year. Works with 4 writers/year. Buys first rights. Accepts previously produced material. Reports in 6 months. Submit synopsis/outline. Pays in accordance with Writers Guild of America west standards.

Needs: Family-oriented, general audience materials.

Recent Production: "Currently working with King Kigel V, His Majesty the King of Rwanda, Africa, on a public service announcement through United Nations UNICEF for His Majesty's children and orphans with relief. Although now accepting general audience material, as always."

‡CODIKOW FILMS, 8899 Beverly Blvd., #719, Los Angeles CA 90048. (310)246-9388. Director of Development: Diana Williams. Estab. 1990. Buys 6 scripts/year. Works with 12 writers/year. Buys all rights. Accepts previously produced material. Reports in 1 month on submissions. Query or résumé. Pays in accordance with Writer's Guild standards.

Needs: Films (35mm). Commercial and independent screenplays; good writing—all subjects.

CPC ENTERTAINMENT, 840 N. Larrabee St., #2322, Los Angeles CA 90069. (310)652-8194. Fax: (310)652-4998. E-mail: 74151.1117@compuserve.com. Producer/Director: Peggy Chene. Vice President, Creative Affairs: Meri Howard. Development Associate: April Bourquin. Feature and TV. Buys 15 scripts/year. Works with 24 writers/year. Buys all rights. Recent production: "In the Eyes of a Stranger," CBS-TV thriller starring Richard Dean Anderson, CBS-TV. No previously produced material. Reports in 2 months on queries; 3 months on submissions. Query with 1 paragraph synopsis, 1 sentence premise and résumé. Outright purchase WGA minimum; and up.
  • CPC Entertainment is particularly looking for scripts of wider budget range, from low independent to high studio.
Needs: Needs feature and TV movie screenplays: small independent, or any budget for thrillers, true stories, action/adventure, character driven stories of any genre.

‡THE CRAMER COMPANY, 4605 Lankershim Blvd., Suite 617, North Hollywood CA 91602. (213)877-0150. Contact: Grady Hall, head of development. Estab. 1989. Buys 5-10 scripts/year. Works with 40-50 writers/year. Buys TV/film rights, life rights, magazine and newspaper article rights. Accepts previously produced material. Reports in 1-3 months. Query with synopsis and résumé. Pays in accordance with Writer's Guild standards. "For certain life rights and newspaper/magazine rights, we option stories, then pay network rates for material upon production."
Needs: "Looking for screenplays for television movies, especially from established/produced writers. Also, interested in finding interesting, compelling true-life stories, either published previously (newspapers, magazines, etc.) or where we can purchase the life rights of a subject and adapt stories (in conjunction with the writer who brings the material to our attention.)."
Tips: "We especially like compelling human-interest stories which bring a fresh perspective to a particular contemporary issue. Female leads are important to TV. Right now, we're steering clear of all but the most exceptional period pieces. Audience considerations are important in getting something on the air, but we don't think that means projects have to be gratuitous or overly sensational. We're looking for intelligent projects that we can find a place for on TV."

DAYDREAM PRODS., INC., 8969 Sunset Blvd., Los Angeles CA 90069. (310)285-9677. Estab. 1995. Buys 2 scripts/year. Works with 3-4 writers/year. Buys all rights. No previously produced material. Reports in 3 months on submissions. Query with synopsis. Pays in accordance with Writer's Guild standards.
Needs: Films (35mm).

EARTH TRACKS PRODUCTIONS, 4809 Avenue N, Suite 286, Brooklyn NY 11234. Contact: David Krinsky. Estab. 1985. Produces material for independent studios. Buys 1-3 scripts/year. Buys all rights. No books, no treatments, no plays, no articles. *Only* completed movie scripts. Reports in 6 weeks on queries.
  • This producer notes a high rate of inappropriate submissions. Please read and follow guidelines carefully.
Needs: Commercial, well-written, low budget, high concept scripts in the drama, dark comedy and thriller genres. No other genre scripts. Query with 1-page synopsis and SASE. No treatments. *Do not send any scripts unless requested.*
Tips: "Writers should be flexible and open to suggestions. Material with interest (in writing) from a known actor/director is a *major plus* in the consideration of the material. Any submissions of more than two pages will *not* be read or returned. We have recently reorganized and are only seeking quality, *low budget* scripts for inhouse production. Controversial, with strong lead characters (dialogue), are preferred." (Examples: 'Natural Born Killers,' 'From Dusk Till Dawn,' 'Pulp Fiction.') Do not send queries by certified/registered mail. They will be rejected. Note: Due to new postal regulations requested scripts are no longer returned. We do not have personnel to send to post office to wait on line to return your scripts. Sorry. They can no longer be dropped in mailboxes for return. Writers who want their scripts and insist their scripts be returned must pay a fee for our time and labor of $15 per script. No exceptions."

‡EMPIRE PICTURES, INC., 9100 Wilshire Blvd., #600, Beverly Hills CA 90212. Contact: Deanna Fuller, development coordinator. Estab. 1996. Buys 5 scripts/year. Works with 10 writers/year. Rights purchased depend on the property. No previously produced material. Reports in 1 month. Query with synopsis. Pay depends on property.
Needs: Films (35mm). "We are looking for material to produce into feature length films for theatrical release."

ENTERTAINMENT PRODUCTIONS, INC., 2118 Wilshire Blvd., Suite 744, Santa Monica CA 90403. (310)456-3143. Fax: (310)456-8950. Producer: Edward Coe. Contact: Story Editor. Estab. 1971. Produces films for theatrical and television (worldwide) distribution. Reports in 1 month only if SASE enclosed.
Needs: Screenplay originals. Query with synopsis and SASE. Price negotiated on a project-by-project basis. Writer's release in any form will be acceptable.
Tips: "State why script has great potential."

‡EPIPHANY PRODUCTIONS INC., 10625 Esther Ave., Los Angeles CA 90064. President: Scott Frank. Estab. 1983. Film and TV audiences. Buys 12 scripts/year. Works with 18 writers/year. Buys all rights. No previously produced material. Reports in 3 months on submissions. Query with synopsis.

GAMARA PICTURES, 6943 Hazeltine, #14, Van Nuys CA 91405. Producer/Director: Dali Moyzes. Intended for all audiences. Buys 4 scripts/year. Works with 4-8 writers/year. Buys all rights. Reports in 6 months. Query with complete script, résumé and SASE and standard release form. Pays in accordance with WGA standards.
Needs: Films (35mm). Feature film screenplays and TV sitcoms—any subject—for future possible production.

Tips: "Please send by special 4th class mail (printed matter)—about $1.50. Copy script on both sides of the paper or on the back of an old script; be environmentally friendly, save trees."

‡**RON GILBERT ASSOCIATES**, 4500 Wilshire Blvd., 2nd Floor, Los Angeles CA 90010. Contact: Corinne Olivo, vice president of development. Estab. 1985. Material for network television and some cable television movies. Buys 4 scripts/year. Works with 20 writers/year. Buys all rights or theatrical rights only. Accepts previously produced material (plays or documentaries only). Reports in 1 month on queries, 2 months on submissions. Catalog for #10 SASE. Send query with synopsis and résumé. Pays in accordance with Writer's Guild standards. Some options of non-union written material will be purchased for under $5,000 for one year.
Needs: Films (35mm).
Tips: "The television networks love true stories. However, television writers should keep in mind that the networks are now open to fictional stories, but each network has very specific guidelines for material. They all want strong roles for women between the ages of 18-35. This female lead is a victim who usually becomes the heroine and saves the day in the end. The networks want suspenseful stories that will keep the audience from changing the channel. This is the kind of material we are looking for to produce for the television networks."

GOLDEN QUILL, GQ-NY, 65 Bleecker St., 12th Floor, New York NY 10012; GQ-LA, 8899 Beverly Blvd., Suite 702, Los Angeles CA 90048. Executive Vice President: Hassan Ildari. Contact: Brenda White (Los Angeles); Christine Buckley (New York). Estab. 1991. Buys 3 scripts/year. Works with 6 writers/year. Reports in 3 weeks. Query with synopsis and SASE. Makes outright purchase.
Needs: Films (35mm). Currently seeking serious dramatic material.

‡**GRADE A PICTURE CO.**, 11718 Barrington Court, Suite 411, Los Angeles CA 90049. Contact: Andy Cohen. Estab. 1996. All audiences. Buys 5 scripts/year. Works with 25 writers/year. Buys all rights. Accepts previously produced material. Reports in 1 month. Query with synopsis. Pays in accordance with Writer's Guild standards.
Needs: Films (35mm). Looking for well-written, well-developed, completed feature film scripts only.

‡**GREEN GRASS BLUE SKY COMPANY**, 10700 Ventura Blvd., Studio City CA 91604. (818)763-4182. Contact: Frank Catalano, president. Estab. 1997. General audience. Buys all rights. Accepts previously produced material. Reports in 2 months on queries. Query or send completed script and résumé. Pay varies depending upon project.
Needs: Films.

‡**BETH GROSSBARD PRODUCTIONS**, 6915 Donna Ynez Lane, Pacific Palisades CA 90272. Contact: Beth Grossbard, producer. Estab. 1994. Buys 6 scripts/year. Works with 20 writers/year. First rights and true life story rights. No previously produced material. Reports in 2 months on queries; 3 months on submissions. Query with synopsis, treatment/outline and completed script. Pays in accordance with Writer's Guild standards.
Needs: Films (35mm).
Tips: "Looking for unique, high-concept stories; family dramas; true stories; strong (never been done before) historical pieces; women's issues; social issues."

EDWARD D. HANSEN, INC., 437 Harvard Dr., Arcadia CA 91006-2639. Phone/fax: (818)447-3168. President: Ed Hansen. Supervisor, Literary Development: Buck Flower. Estab. 1973. Theatrical, TV and home video markets comprise our audience. Optioned, purchased, marketed and/or produced 6 screenplays in 1996. Reports in 3 months.
Needs: Looking for scripts for feature films, movies of the week and home videos: all genres. Query with synopsis and SASE for release form. Pays in accordance with Writers Guild standards. Professional assistance available for novel or play adaptations, concept development and certain properties not "ready to shoot" that contain unique characters or an extremely marketable storyline.
• Edward D. Hansen reports an increased need for films in the low range, $150,000-2 million, and for scripts with over $20 million, real "star" vehicles, but very few requests for in-between budgets.
Tips: "Don't try to tap into a trend. By the time you get it done, it's gone. What comes around goes around. In the last year, we've been asked for scripts at the highest end ($20 million +) and at the lowest end $150,000. Very few requests for film productions between $2-20 million. More important than ever to have money or an actor *attached* to a spec script."

‡**HBO PICTURES**, 2049 Century Park E., Suite 3600, Los Angeles CA 90067. (310)201-9302. Story Editor: Bettina Moss. Buys 30 scripts/year. Works with 20 writers/year. Buys all rights. Accepts previously produced material. Reports in 1 month on queries. Query with synopsis. Payment varies.
Needs: Features for TV.

‡**HILL/FIELDS ENTERTAINMENT**, 4500 Wilshire Blvd., Los Angeles CA 90010. Contact: Lori Bradbard, manager of development. Estab. 1980. Buys 10 scripts/year. Works with 10 writers/year. Buys all rights. Reports in 1 month on queries, 3 months on submissions. Query with synopsis. Pays in accordance with Writer's Guild standards.
Needs: Film loops, films. Material for television movies, i.e., "stories that will appeal to men and women of all ages with relatable, sympathetic protagonists and easy-to-promote high-concepts."

INTERNATIONAL HOME ENTERTAINMENT, 1440 Veteran Ave., Suite 650, Los Angeles CA 90024. (213)460-4545. Assistant to the President: Jed Leland, Jr. Estab. 1976. Buys first rights. Reports in 2 months. Query. Pays in accordance with Writers Guild standards.
   • Looking for material that is international in scope.
Tips: "Our response time is faster on average now (3-6 weeks), but no replies without a SASE. *No unsolicited scripts.*We do not respond to unsolicited phone calls."

‡THE KAUFMAN COMPANY, 11340 W. Olympic Blvd., Suite 100, Los Angeles CA 90064. Contact: Sophia Xixis, director of development. Estab. 1990. Intended for all audiences. Buys 5-10 scripts/year. Works with 10 writers/year. Buys all rights. Reports in 2-3 weeks on queries, 2-3 months on submissions. Query with synopsis. Pays in accordance with Writer's Guild standards.
Needs: We option screenplays and manuscripts for television, cable and film.

KJD TELEPRODUCTIONS, 30 Whyte Dr., Voorhees NJ 08043. (609)751-3500. Fax: (609)751-7729. E-mail: mactoday@ios.com. President: Larry Scott. Estab. 1989. Broadcast audience. Buys 6 scripts/year. Works with 3 writers/year. Buys all rights. No previously produced material. Reports in 1 month. Catalog free. Query. Makes outright purchase.
Needs: Films, videotapes, multimedia kits.

‡LANCASTER GATE ENTERTAINMENT, 4702 Hayvenhurst Ave., Encino CA 91436. (818)995-6000. Director of Development: Brian K. Schlichter. Estab. 1989. Theatrical and television. Works with dozens of writers/year. Rights purchased negotiable. No previously produced material. Reports in 1 month on queries. Query. Pays in accordance with Writer's Guild standards.
Needs: Films (35mm-70mm). Feature and television scripts.

‡DAVID LANCASTER PRODUCTIONS, 3356 Bennett Dr, Los Angeles CA 90068-1704. Head of Production: Amy Krell. Estab. 1985. Feature films audience. Buys 8-10 scripts/year. Works with 18-25 writers/year. Buys film and TV rights. No previously produced material. Reports in 2-3 weeks on queries. Query with synopsis.
Needs: Action oriented screenplays, dramas with an edge.
Tips: "Please do not call us. We will reply only to queries accompanied by a SASE. Absolutely no unrequested screenplays accepted—we will refuse delivery on all unsolicited material."

RON LEVINSON PRODUCTIONS, 7201 Raintree Circle, Culver City CA 90230. (310)559-2470. Fax: (310)559-7244. TV and film material. Buys first and all rights. Submissions through agents or with release.

LIGHTVIEW ENTERTAINMENT, 11901 Santa Monica Blvd., Suite 571, Los Angeles CA 90025. Fax: (310)820-3670. E-mail: Lightview@aol.com. Producer: Laura McCorkindale. Estab. 1991. Options 20 scripts/year. Purchase price negotiable. Mail a 1-2 page detailed synopsis with SASE to the attention of Hollie Lobosky. "We will respond via mail within 1 month to let you know if we want to see your screenplay. If we request your screenplay after reading synopsis, please allow 3 months for a second response."
Needs: Feature film screenplays. "Our films range from smaller budget intelligent, artistic independent films to big budget commercial studio films. All genres."
Tips: "Take time writing your synopses and be detailed! Synopses should be as well written as your screenplay and should include the genre of the story. Be sure it is at least one page—but not more than two! Although we are looking for all types of screenplays, we are especially drawn to inspirational stories that enlighten and entertain. *We do not accept unsolicited phone calls*, so please correspond only through the mail." Please do *not* e-mail your synopsis; use e-mail only to follow up on the status of your project.

‡LONGBOW PRODUCTIONS, 4181 Sunswept Dr., Studio City CA 91604. Estab. 1990. Television networks, cable and feature films. Buys 3-5 scripts/year. Works with 6-8 writers/year. Payment negotiated on a per project basis. No previously produced material. Reports in 1 month on queries, 2 months on submissions. Prefers material repped by an agent; query and synopsis form gets quickest response. Payment negotiated on per project basis.
Needs: Two hour TV and feature films. Any genre with good characters and great story, from true-story to sci-fi.
Tips: "Think "G" rated to mild "R" for us—no gratuitous violence, etc. Make sure if you send a script, it is properly formatted and no longer than 100-125 pages in length."

‡□LEE MAGID PRODUCTIONS, P.O. Box 532, Malibu CA 90265. (213)463-5998. President: Lee Magid. Produces material for all markets: adult, commercial—even musicals. 90% freelance written. 70% of scripts produced are un-agented submissions. Works with many unpublished/unproduced writers. Buys all rights or will negotiate. No previously produced material. Does not return unsolicited material.
Needs: Films, sound filmstrips, phonograph records, television shows/series and videotape presentations. Currently interested in film material, either for video (television) or theatrical. "We deal with cable networks, producers, live-stage productions, etc." Works with musicals for cable TV. Prefers musical forms for video comedy. "We're interested in comedy material. Forget drug-related scripts." Submit synopsis/outline and résumé. Pays royalty, in accordance with Writers Guild standards, makes outright purchase or individual arrangement depending on author.

☐**MEDIACOM DEVELOPMENT CORP.**, P.O. Box 6331, Burbank CA 91510-6331. (818)594-4089. Director/ Program Development: Felix Girard. Estab. 1978. 80% freelance written. Buys 8-12 scripts/year from unpublished/ unproduced writers. 50% of scripts produced are unagented submissions. Query with samples. Reports in 1 month. Buys all rights or first rights. Written query only. Please do not call.
Needs: Produces films, multimedia kits, tapes and cassettes, slides and videotape with programmed instructional print materials, broadcast and cable television programs. Publishes software ("programmed instruction training courses"). Negotiates payment depending on project. Looking for new ideas for CD-ROM titles.
Tips: "Send short samples of work. Especially interested in flexibility to meet clients' demands, creativity in treatment of precise subject matter. We are looking for good, fresh projects (both special and series) for cable and pay television markets. A trend in the audiovisual field that freelance writers should be aware of is the move toward more interactive video disc/computer CRT delivery of training materials for corporate markets."

‡**MEGA FILMS, INC.**, 6399 Wilshire Blvd., Suite 200, Los Angeles CA 90048. (213)966-2750. Vice President: Betsy Chory. Audience is women, ages 18-49. Buys all rights. Reports in 1 month on queries, 2 months on submissions. Query with synopsis, followed by a signed submission release. Pays in accordance with Writer's Guild standards.
Needs: Films (35mm). "Our primary focus is Movies for Television. We also look for feature, low-budget, independent film material."

MILWAUKEE FILMWORKS, 4218 Whitsett Ave., Suite 4, Studio City CA 91604. (818)762-9080. Fax: (310)278-2632. Contact: Douglas Gardner. Estab. 1991. Film and TV audience. Buys 2 scripts/year. Works with 3 writers/year. Buys screenplays-option. Accepts previously produced material. *Feature scripts only.* Returns submissions on a case to case basis. Reports in 4 months. Query with complete script. Pay varies in accordance with Writers Guild standards.

‡**MIRAMAX FILMS**, 375 Greenwich St., New York NY 10013. Story Editor: Jennifer Sherwood. Buys 30-40 scripts/ year. Works with 20-30 writers/year. Buys first or all rights. Accepts previously produced material. Reports in 1 months on queries, 2 months on submissions. Query with synopsis or completed script. Payment varies.
Needs: Films (35mm).
Tips: "Materials must be submitted through agent, lawyer or signed release form; no unsolicited materials accepted without above."

‡**MNC FILMS**, P.O. Box 16195, Beverly Hills CA 90209-2195. Estab. 1991. Feature film audience. Buys 2 scripts/ year. Works with 3 writers/year. Buys all rights or purchases option on screenplay. Accepts previously produced material. Reports in 2 months. Query with synopsis. Pays in accordance with Writers Guild standards (work for hire) or variable fee for option of material.
Needs: Film (35mm). Feature length films. "I'm looking for story-driven films with well-developed characters. Screenplays or books easily adaptable for lower budget (few locations, stunts, special effects)."
Tips: "In the past I have received many submissions from writers who do not pay attention to the type of material that I am looking for. I am looking for character driven stories with an emphasis on individuals and relationships."

MONAREX HOLLYWOOD CORPORATION, 9421½ W. Pico Blvd., Los Angeles CA 90035. (310)552-1069. President: Chris D. Nebe. Estab. 1978. Producers of theatrical and television motion pictures and miniseries; also international distributors. Buys 5-6 scripts/year. Buys all rights. Reports in 2 months.
Needs: "We are seeking action, adventure, comedy and character-oriented love stories, dance, horror and dramatic screenplays." First submit synopsis/outline with SASE. After review of the synopsis/outline, the screenplay will be requested. Pays in accordance with Writers Guild standards.
Tips: "We look for exciting visuals with strong characters and a unique plot."

MONTIVAGUS PRODUCTIONS, 13930 Burbank Blvd., Suite 100, Sherman Oaks CA 91401-5003. (818)782-1212. Fax: (818)782-1931. Contact: Douglas Coler, VP Creative Affairs. Estab. 1990. Buys 3 scripts/year. Works with 3-4 writers/year. Buys all rights. Query with synopsis only. Responds if interested in synopsis; 1 month on scripts. Encourages submissions from new and emerging writers. Also interested in novels, short stories and plays for adaptation to the big screen. Pays in accordance with Writers Guild standards. Also accepts plays for theatrical staging under it's stageWorks! program.
Needs: Films (35mm).
Tips: Looking for character-driven scripts; no big budget action films. Keep query short and to the point. Synopsis should be a half to three-quarters of a page. No longer. "Please don't tell me how funny, or how good or how exciting your script is. I'll find out. It's the story I want to know first." Unsolicited scripts will be returned unread. Proper script format a must. Coverage will be shared with the writer.

‡**MORROW-HEUS PRODUCTIONS**, 8800 Venice Blvd., #209, Los Angeles CA 90034. (310)815-9973. Contact: Paul Shrater, director of development. Estab. 1989. Intended for the worldwide film and television audience. Buys film and television option. Accepts previously produced material. Reports in 1 month. Send query with synopsis. Pays negotiated option (standard industry practice).
Needs: Films (35mm). Feature film, television mow, drama, comedy, romance, adventure, action, thriller, family.

‡MOVIE REPS INTERNATIONAL, 7135 Hollywood Blvd., #104, Los Angeles CA 90046. (213)876-4052. Head of Acquisitions: Dany Bohbot. Estab. 1989. US and foreign audiences. Buys 4 scripts/year. Works with 2 writers/year. Buys first or all rights. No previously produced material. Reports in 1 month on queries. Free catalog. Query with synopsis. Pays royalty or makes outright purchase.
Needs: Films (35mm). Feature film script, minimum 100 pages. Genres: action/thriller, romantic comedy, adventure, art type of film. Looking for: fresh ideas, no holds bar kind of script, extremely original.
Tips: Originality is key; and combine it with high concept.

NEW & UNIQUE VIDEOS, 2336 Sumac Dr., San Diego CA 92105. (619)282-6126. E-mail: videos@concentric.net. Website: http://www.concentric.net/~videos. Creative Director: Candace Love. Estab. 1982. General TV and videotape audiences. Buys 10-15 scripts/year. Buys first rights, all rights. No previously produced material. Reports in 1-2 months. Catalog for #10 SASE. Query with synopsis. Makes outright purchase, negotiable.
Needs: Videotapes.
Tips: "We are seeking unique slants on interesting topics in 60-90 minute special-interest videotape format, preferably already produced, packaged and ready for distribution. Currently distributed titles include 'Massage for Relaxation'; 'Ultimate Mountain Biking' and 'Full Cycle: World Odyssey.' No movies or movie treatments. We concentrate on sports, health and other educational home-video titles. Please study the genre and get an understanding of what 'special interest' means. Video distribution has become highly competitive. Doing adequate homework at the beginning will prevent heartache down the road. Study your market. Determine the need for (yet another?) video on your topic. The elements for success are: intensive market research, passion, humor, imagination and a timely or timeless quality."

OCEAN PARK PICTURES, 220 Main St., Venice CA 90291. (310)450-1220. Executive Producer: Tim Goldberg. Estab. 1989. All audiences. Buys 5 scripts/year. Works with 10 writers/year. Buys first or all rights. Accepts previously produced material. Reports in 1 month on queries; 2 months on scripts. Query with synopsis, complete script and résumé. Pay varies.
Needs: Film (35mm).
Tips: Less demand for heavy violence.

OK PRODUCTIONS, 1727 N. Fairfax Ave., Los Angeles CA 90046. E-mail: abcooper@address.net. Producer: A.B. (Bud) Cooper, Jr.. Estab. 1982. Mainstream theatrical feature and TV MOW audience. Buys 1 script/year (options 2-3). Works with 3-4 writers/year. Buys all rights. Reports in 1 month. Query or query with synopsis and signed standard release. Pays in accordance with Writer's Guild standards when appropriate or a percentage of production budget with stated minimum and maximum.
Needs: Film (35mm). Full-length feature films of all types except pornography and slasher. "Salute the human spirit. Observe man's struggle. Great stories, great characters."
Tips: "Inquire only about your best work. Finished screenplays only. Get form, format, grammar, spelling and punctuation as perfect as you can. Be entertaining. Show subtext and reveal it through writing. Don't *tell* it."

‡PARALLEL PICTURES, P.O. Box 985B, Hollywood CA 90078. New Projects Executive: Rick Tyler. Estab. 1988. "For a general audience, ages 16-45; depends on project. We produce for domestic as well as overseas audiences." Works with 3 writers/year. Buys all rights. No previously published material. Reports in 2 months on queries; 6 months on scripts.
Needs: Films (35mm). "We are looking for feature-length screenplays—action/adventure, romantic comedy. We accept all genres—very openminded. We love rare and new ideas." Submit a short synopsis of script or project with a release form. Makes outright purchase.
Tips: "Take risks. I see too many replicas and poor development. If I don't see a plan of action or direction by the first 30 pages, something is wrong. Plots make the movie. That doesn't mean having many plots. You can keep it simple. Also, 80 pages is not feature length. Please bind all material. We won't look at a script made up of loose papers. Don't call us. We will call you."

☐ TOM PARKER MOTION PICTURES, 3941 S. Bristol, #285, Santa Ana CA 92704. (714)545-2887. Fax: (714)545-9775. President: Tom Parker. Contact: Jennifer Phelps, script/development. Produces and distributes feature-length motion pictures worldwide for theatrical, home video, pay and free TV. Also produces short subject special interest films (30, 45, 60 minutes). Works with 5-10 scripts/year. Previously produced and distributed "Amazing Love Secret" (R), and "The Sturgis Story" (R). Reports in 6 months. "Follow the instructions herein and do not phone for info or to inquire about your script."
Needs: "Complete script *only* for low budget (under $1 million) "R" or "PG" rated action/thriller, action/adventure, comedy, adult romance (R), sex comedy (R), family action/adventure to be filmed in 35mm film for the theatrical and home video market. (Do not send TV movie scripts, series, teleplays, stage plays). *Very limited dialogue.* Scripts should be action-oriented and fully described. Screen stories or scripts OK, but no camera angles please. No heavy drama, documentaries, social commentaries, dope stories, weird or horror. Violence or sex OK, but must be well motivated with strong story line." Submit synopsis and description of characters with finished scripts. Makes outright purchase: $5,000-25,000. Will consider participation, co-production.
Tips: "Absolutely will not return scripts or report on rejected scripts unless accompanied by SASE."

‡**PERSISTENT PICTURES, INC.**, 8500 Melrose Ave., #210, Los Angeles CA 90069. (310)289-3670. Contact: Debby Barkan, creative associate. Estab. 1992. Intended for an adult feature film audience. Buys 3-5 scripts/year. Works with 5-7 writers/year. Buys first or all rights. Reports in 1 month on queries, 2 months on submissions. Send query with synopsis and résumé. Negotiates payment individually.
Needs: Films (35mm).

‡**PICTURE ENTERTAINMENT CORPORATION**, 9595 Wilshire Blvd., Suite 505, Beverly Hills CA 90212. (310)858-8300. President/CEO: Lee Caplin. Vice President Development: Sonia Mintz. Produces feature films for theatrical audience and TV audience. Buys 2 scripts/year. Works with 10 writers/year. Buys all rights. Reports on submissions in 2 months.
Needs: Films (35mm); videotapes. Feature scripts 100-120 pages. Submit completed script. "Pays on a deal by deal basis; some WGA, some not."
Tips: "Don't send derivitive standard material. Emphasis on unique plot and characters, realistic dialogue. *Discourage* period pieces, over-the-top comedy, graphic sex/violence, SciFi. *Encourage* action, action/comedy, thriller, thriller/comedy." No summaries or treatments; completed screenplays only.

POP/ART FILM FACTORY, 513 Wilshire Blvd., #215, Santa Monica CA 90401. Contact: Daniel Zirilli. Estab. 1990. Produces material for "all audiences/features films." Reports in 2 months. Query with synopsis. Pays on per project basis.
Needs: Film (35mm), documentaries, multimedia kits. "We are interested in producing 1 feature length film—$2 million budget or less. Hard-edged, independent."
Tips: "Be original. Do not play it safe."

□**PROMARK ENTERTAINMENT GROUP**, 3599 Cahuenga Blvd. W., Los Angeles CA 90026. (213)878-0404. Vice President Creative Affairs: Gil Adrienne Wishnick. Promark is a foreign sales company, producing theatrical films for the foreign market, domestic theatrical and cable as well as for video. Buys 8-10 scripts/year. Works with 8-10 writers/year. Buys all rights. Reports in 1 month on queries, 2 months on submissions. Query with synopsis. Makes outright purchase.
   ● Promark is concentrating on action-thrillers in the vein of *The Net* or *Marathon Man*. They are not looking for science fiction/action as much this year, as they have a rather full production slate for '97 with many sci-fi and techno-thrillers.
Needs: Film (35mm). "We are looking for screenplays in the action, action-adventure, thriller and science fiction/action genres. Our aim is to produce lower budget (3 million and under) films that have a solid, novel premise—a smart but smaller scale independent film."
Tips: "Check on the genres any potential production company accepts and slant your submissions accordingly. Do your homework before you send a query or call. Find out who to contact, what their title is and what the production company tends to make in terms of genre, budget and style. Find the address yourself—don't ask the production executive for it, for example. It's insulting to the executive to have to inform a caller of the company name or address."

THE PUPPETOON STUDIOS, P.O. Box 80141, Las Vegas NV 89180. Contact: Barbara Schimpf, vice president of production. Estab. 1987. "Broad audience." Works with 5 writers/year. Reports in 1 month on queries; 2 months on scripts. Query with synopsis. Submit complete script. A Submission Release *must* be included with all queries. Currently producing the animated feature, "Moby Dick: The Whale's Tale." SASE required for return of all materials. Pays in accordance with Writers Guild standards. No novels, plays, poems, treatments; no submissions on computer disk. No unsolicited unagented material. Must include release form.
Needs: Films (35mm). "We are seeking animation properties including presentation drawings and character designs. The more detailed drawings with animation scripts the better."

RED HOTS ENTERTAINMENT, 634 N. Glen Oaks Blvd., #374, Burbank CA 91502-1024. Director of Development: Chip Miller. Contact: Dan Pomeroy, Vice President Development. Estab. 1990. Buys 1 script/year. Works with 3-5 writers/year. Buys first rights, all rights, "short and long term options, as well." No previously produced material. Reports in 3 weeks on queries; 2 months on mss. Query with synopsis or submit complete ms. Pays in accordance with Writer's Guild standards. "Negotiable on writer's previous credits, etc."
Needs: Film loops (16mm), films (35mm), videotapes. "We are a feature film and television production company and have no audiovisual material needs."
Tips: "Best advice possible: originality, uniqueness, write from your instincts and *don't* follow trends."

‡**TIM REID PRODUCTIONS**, 1640 S. Sepulveda Blvd., Los Angeles CA 90025. (310)231-3400. Contact: Sherri G. Sneed, vice president, development. Estab. 1996. Produces 2 films/year. MOW's for network TV. Query with synopsis. Reports in 2-3 weeks on submissions. Buys film rights in perpetuity. Makes outright purchase of $40,000-75,000.
Needs: Multi-cultural TV movies with positive black images.
Tips: Does not want to see stereotypical urban dysfunctional garbage. "Our deal is with Procter & Gamble for a guarantee of 2 films/year with conservative family values."

□**ROUGH DIAMOND PRODUCTIONS**, 1424 N. Kings Rd., Los Angeles CA 90069. (213)848-2900. Producers: Julia Verdin, Brent Morris. Estab. 1995. Audience is general-adult; feature and cable films. Buys 1-2 scripts/year. Works with 6-7 writers/year. Buys film, video rights. Reports ASAP on queries; 2 months on submissions. Query with synopsis or completed script and résumé. Call first and request submission release form before sending in scripts.

‡**ROXABOXEN**, 4319 Keystone Ave., Culver City CA 90232. Contact: Diane Smith or Anna Mehji. Estab. 1985. Audiences are children 18+, young adult 21-32, general comedies. Buys 2-3 scripts/year. Works with 2-4 writers/year. Buys first rights, all rights or options. Accepts previously produced material. Reports in 1-2 months on queries. Query with synopsis or completed script. Makes outright purchase or options.
Needs: Films (35mm).
Tips: Strong character driven and well structured into 3-act formula where characters can have clear transitions and story archs.

‡**SAUCE ENTERTAINMENT, INC.**, 100 Varick St., 3rd Floor, New York NY 10013. (212)343-3000. Contact: Kenji Mitsuka, executive assistant to the producers. Estab. 1995. Buys 1-4 scripts/year. Works with 10 writers/year. Buys first or all rights. Reports in 1 month. Query with synopsis. Pays royalty or makes outright purchase in accordance with Writer's Guild standards.
Needs: Films (16mm, 35mm), videotapes, multimedia kits. Feature films (narrative or documentary, any genre).

THE SHELDON/POST COMPANY, 1437 Rising Glen Rd., Los Angeles CA 90069. Producers: David Sheldon, Ira Post. Estab. 1989. Produces theatrical motion pictures, movies and series for television. Options and acquires all rights. Reports in 2 months. Query with 1-2 page synopsis, 2-3 sample pages and SASE. "Do not send scripts or books. If the synopsis is of interest, you will be sent a release form to return with your manuscript. No telephone inquiries." Pays in accordance with Writers Guild standards. No advance payments.
Needs: "We look for all types of material, including women's stories, children's and family stories, suspense dramas, horror, sci-fi, thrillers, action-adventure." True stories should include news articles or other documentation.
Tips: "A synopsis should tell the entire story with all of the plot—including a beginning, a middle and an end. During the past three years, the producers have been in business with 20th Century Fox, Paramount Pictures, Columbia Pictures and currently have contracts with Hearst Entertainment. Most recent productions: "Grizzly Adams and the Legend of Dark Mountain" and "Secrets of a Small Town.""

SHORELINE PICTURES, 1901 Avenue of the Stars, #1800, Los Angeles CA 90067. (310)551-2060. Fax: (310)201-0729. E-mail: shoreline@shorelineentertainment.com. Website: http://www.directnet.com/pictures/. Contact: Brooke Driskill, creative executive. Estab. 1993. Mass audience. Buys 8 scripts/year. Works with 8 writers/year. Buys all rights. Reports in 1 month on submissions. Query.
Needs: Films (35, 70mm). Looking for "character-driven films that are commercial as well as independent. No exploitation or horror. Comedies and dramas, yes. Completed screenplays only. We are especially keen to find a comedy. Also looking for television movies. True stories with leading ladies are nice. Note, there is an audience for adult films as reflected in films like *The Piano*, *The Player*, *Crying Game*, *Joy Luck Club*, etc. Principal of our company co-produced *Glengarry Glen Ross*."

‡**DARRYL SILVER**, 15600 Morrison St., Sherman Oaks CA 91403. Contact: Darryl Silver. Estab. 1995. Feature and TV. Buys 7 scripts/year. Works with 15-25 writers/year. Buys all rights. No previously produced material. Reports in 1 month. Query with synopsis. Buys option first.
Needs: Films (35mm) and TV.

‡**LLOYD SILVERMAN PRODUCTIONS**, 11283 Canton Dr., Los Angeles CA 91604. (213)650-4880. President: Lloyd Silverman. Estab. 1990. Buys 1-3 scripts/year. Works with 15-25 writers/year. Buys first or all rights. No previously produced material. Reports in 1 month on queries. Query with synopsis. Makes outright purchase.
Needs: Films (35mm).
 ● Lloyd Silverman has several projects currently in development, including *Snow Falling on Cedars*, *V.R.*, and *Heavy Duty*. Television series in development include *Solomon's Mind* and *Crasher*.
Tips: Looking for compelling, compact, intelligent scripts.

SKYLARK FILMS, 1123 Pacific St., Santa Monica CA 90405. (310)396-5753. Fax: (310)396-5753. E-mail: skyfilm@aol.com. Contact: Brad Pollack. Estab. 1990. Buys 6 scripts/year. Buys first or all rights. Accepts previously produced material. Reports in 2-4 weeks on queries; 1-2 months on submissions. Query with synopsis. Option or other structures depending on circumstances. Pays in accordance with Writer's Guild standards.
Needs: Films (TV, cable, feature).
 ● Skylark Films is now seeking action, suspense, thrillers and science fiction.
Tips: "Generally, we look for the best material we can find, other than the horror genre. Particular new areas of focus are romantic comedy, true stories for TV mow's and low-budget quicky material. No response without SASE unless we want to see material. Will also look at material for ½ weekly television syndication possibilities."

SOUTH FORK PRODUCTIONS, P.O. Box 1935, Santa Monica CA 90406-1935. Fax: (310)829-5029. Producer: Jim Sullivan. Estab. 1980. Produces material for TV and film. Buys 2 scripts/year. Works with 4 writers/year. Buys all rights. No previously produced material. Send synopsis/outline and motion picture treatments, plus previous credits,

with SASE. No complete scripts. Pays in accordance with Writers Guild Standards.
   ● South Fork is currently looking for Irish-based scripts.
Needs: Films (16, 35mm), videotapes.
Tips: "Follow established formats for treatments. SASE for return."

□**STARLIGHT PICTURES**, 3655 S. Decatur Blvd., Suite 14-159, Las Vegas NV 89103. E-mail: ideamaster@aol.com. Development Executive: Brian McNeal. Estab. 1989. Mass audiences, all audiences, movie-going public, international. Buys 0-2 scripts/year. Works with 1-10 writers/year. Options 0-5 scripts/year. Rights purchased according to WGA signatory regulations; rights optioned and/or purchased are motion picture/television rights. No previously produced material. Reports in 1 year on queries; 18 months on mss. Query with synopsis and self-addressed stamped postcard. Do not send a script unless requested. Submission material MUST BE represented/agented by WGA signatory agent. All submissions claiming to be properly represented will be verified. No freelance material will be considered. Freelance material will promptly be returned unread (if accompanied by proper postage), or disposed of otherwise. Pays in accordance with Writer's Guild standards.
Needs: Motion pictures for worldwide theatrical, television, cable and video release. "Production slate for next 18 months is currently at its limits. We are not actively seeking new properties. After this 18-month period, it is probable we will seek outside literary material. All submitted WGA-agented queries will be kept on file, and under consideration."
Tips: "A good script will get our attention. Horror, mystery, adventure, melodrama, comedy, etc. These are all really sub-genres. If it's not a good script first, the sub-genres become incidental. Furthermore, writers should never write with budget in mind. All too often, writers tend to downplay their stories, substituting dramatic and seemingly-expensive elements with less-expensive locations and effects. This takes away from the true story, and makes the script less appealing. Writers forget producers are in the business of make-believe. Seemingly expensive elements don't always have to be expensive. Let us, the producers, worry about the budget. Whether the ultimate finances of the movie are $500,000 or $20 million, the logistics and planning of the film are our concern. Writers should dictate the script as they would like to see it on the screen. Their only concern should be the story, and they should write it as vigorously and dramatic as possible." Contact WGA for proper format and guidelines.

‡**STARMIST DEVELOPMENT, INC.**, P.O. Box 6006, Torrance CA 90504-0006. Fax: (310)322-7903. E-mail: lorimcata.crl.com. CEO: Arnold Lütz. Estab. 1995. Film, video and television audience. Buys 5-6 scripts/year. Buys all rights. Reports in 6 months. Completed script and treatment. Pays $1,000-100,000.
Needs: Also accepting original 35mm films and videotapes for distributor. Pays $100,000-300,000.
Tips: "Be patient. The movie industry is a slow beast, but the rewards are beautiful. Take your time writing your treatment and screenplay. We're looking for all types of material, including women's stories, suspense dramas, family stories, horror, sci-fi, thrillers, action-adventure and more. Enclose postage if you want your script returned."

□**STONEROAD PRODUCTIONS, INC.**, 11288 Ventura Blvd., #909, Studio City CA 91604. Contact: Story Department. Estab. 1992. Produces feature films for theaters, cable TV and home video. PG, R, and G-rated films. Buys/options 10-15 scripts/year. Works with 10 writers/year. Buys all rights; if published material, subsidiary rights. Accepts previously produced material. Reports in 1 month on queries if interested; 2 months requested on submissions. Query with SASE and synopsis. Pay varies greatly: option, outright purchase, wide range.
Needs: Films (35mm). All genres. Looking for good material from writers who have taken the time to learn the unique and difficult craft of scriptwriting.
Tips: "Interesting query letters intrigue us—and tell us something about the writer. Query letter should include a short 'log line' or 'pitch' encapsulating 'what this story is about' and the genre in just a few sentences. We look for strong stories and strong characters. We make movies that we would like to see. Producers are known for encouraging new (e.g. unproduced) screenwriters and giving real consideration to their scripts."

‡**STORYOPOLIS PRODUCTIONS**, 116 N. Robertson, #A, Los Angeles CA 90048. (310)358-2525. Contact: Fonda Snyder, senior vice president of production. Estab. 1994. Film/TV producer. Query and synopsis. Reports in 3 months. Options film/TV rights. Pay varies. Whole family entertainment, skewed sensibility or stories based on myth, fable, fairy tale.

STUDIO MERRYWOOD, (formerly The Merrywood Studio), 85 Putnam Ave., Hamden CT 06517-2827. Phone/fax: (203)407-1834. E-mail: merrywood@compuserve.com. Website: http://ourworld.compuserve.com/homepages/Merrywood. Contact: Raul daSilva, creative director. Estab. 1984. Produces animated motion pictures for entertainment audiences. "We are planning to severely limit but not close out freelance input. Will be taking roughly 5-7%. We will accept only material which we request from agent. Cannot return material or respond to direct queries."
   ● The Merrywood Studio is no longer producing children's animation of any kind.
Needs: Proprietary material only. Human potential themes woven into highly entertaining drama, high adventure, comedy. This is a new market for animation with only precedent in the illustrated novels published in France and Japan. Cannot handle unsolicited mail/scripts and will not return mail. Open to *agented* submissions of credit sheets, concepts and synopses only. Profit sharing depending upon value of concept and writer's following. Pays at least Writers Guild levels or better, plus expenses.
Tips: "This is *not a market for beginning writers*. Established, professional work with highly unusual and original

themes is sought. If you love writing, it will show and we will recognize it and reward it in every way you can imagine. We are not a 'factory' and work on a very high level of excellence."

‡**RONALD SUPPA PRODUCTIONS, INC.**, 3737 Ventura Canyon Ave., Sherman Oaks CA 91423. Vice President: Jolene Rae. Estab. 1975. Mass audience. Buys 6 scripts/year. Works with 6 writers/year. Buys all rights or motion picture, television and allied rights. No previously produced material. Submissions through agents or publishers only.

TALKING RINGS ENTERTAINMENT, P.O. Box 80141, Las Vegas NV 89180. President/Artistic Director: Arnold Leibovit. Contact: Barbara Schimpf, vice president, production. Estab. 1988. "Produces material for motion pictures and television. Works with 5 writers/year. Reports on submissions in 2 months. Only send complete scripts. No treatments, novels, poems or plays, no submissions on computer disk. Query with synopsis. A Submission Release *must* be included with all queries. Produced and directed "The Fantasy Film Worlds of George Pal," "The Puppetoon Movie." Currently producing a remake of "The Time Machine," "Off The Funny Pages," "Darkside of the Moon." SASE required for return of all materials. Pays in accordance with Writers Guild Standards.
Needs: Films (35mm), videotapes. No unsolicited unagented material. Must include release form.

U.S. FILM CORP., 2029 Century Park E., #1260, Los Angeles CA 90067. (310)475-4547. President: Robert Nau. Estab. 1993. Action audience. Buys 5 scripts/year. Works with 10 writers/year. Buys all rights. Reports in 1 month. Query with synopsis. Pays per negotiation.
Needs Films (35mm). Action adventure, thrillers—feature length.

‡**VIDEO-VISIONS**, #102, 10635 Wilshire Blvd., Los Angeles CA 90024-4530. Executive Producer: Christine Peres-Peña. Estab. 1986. "We produce material for children—educational as well as entertaining. I'm looking for writers to write a Sesame Street/puppet-like show for multi-ethnic TV with references to all cultures—folklore, myths, music, art, architecture, food, roots etc. It must have comedic elements. It should teach morality, principles, virtues, science, math, history etc." Buys 2-5 scripts/year. Buys all rights. Reports in 1 month on queries; 2 months on scripts. Catalog for 9×12 SAE.
Needs: Films (16, 35mm), videotapes. "We need children's programming, cartoons, educational programs (30 minutes)—fast action entertainment (1½ or 2 hours) and scripts that are dramatic experiences of women (and their relationships). Submit complete script. Makes outright purchase of $500-5,000 in accordance with Writers Guild standards. Looking for stories, material that relates to today's troubled youth; their family stories; terrible backgrounds/history; What motivates youngsters to behave violently; solutions stories to problems through the justice system, juvenile hall, boot camp, youth camps etc. Stories in neighborhood, homes, school, streets . . . .
Tips: "Looking for all kinds of material related to our troubled youth, women's problems, relationships and creative, multicultural, children's programming.

‡**WEINY BRO PRODUCTIONS**, 2121 Montana Ave., #4, Santa Monica CA 90403. Director of Development: Matthew Weinberg. Estab. 1994. Film/television audiences. Buys all rights. Accepts previously produced material. Reports in 2 months on submissions. Query with synopsis. Pays royalty.
Needs: Films (35mm, 16mm). Feature films, TV pilots.

WONDERLAND ENTERTAINMENT GROUP, 1712 Anacapa St., Santa Barbara CA 93101. Phone/fax: (805)569-0733. Head of Acquisitions: Diane Itier. Estab. 1989. Produces material for any audience. Buys 5 scripts/year. Works with 4 writers/year. Buys all rights. Accepts previously produced material. Reports in 1 month. Submit complete script and résumé. Pays in accordance with Writers Guild standards.
Needs: Films. "We are seeking any screenplay for full-length motion pictures."
Tips: "Be patient but aggressive enough to keep people interested in your screenplay."

‡**ZACHARY ENTERTAINMENT**, 273 S. Swall Dr., Beverly Hills CA 90211-2612. Fax: (310)289-9788. Development Associate: Adam Bresson. Estab. 1981. Audience is film goers of all ages, television viewers. Buys 8-10 scripts/year. Works with 50 writers/year. Rights purchased vary. Produced *The Tie That Binds*, feature film for Hollywood Pictures, a division of Walt Disney Studios. Reports in 2 weeks on queries; 3 months on submissions. Query with synopsis. Pay varies.
Needs: Films for theatrical, cable and network television release.
● Zachary Entertainment reports that it is doing more films for television including "Carriers" for CBS-TV.

MARKETS THAT WERE listed in the 1997 edition of *Writer's Market* but do not appear this year are listed in the General Index with a notation explaining why they were omitted.

Syndicates

Newspaper syndicates distribute columns, cartoons and other written material to newspapers around the country—and sometimes around the world. Competition for syndication slots is stiff. The number and readership of newspapers are dropping. With paper costs high, there are fewer pages and less money to spend in filling them. Coveted spots in general interest, humor and political commentary are held by big-name columnists such as Ellen Goodman, Bob Herbert and Cal Thomas. And multitudes of aspiring writers wait in the wings, hoping one of these heavy hitters will move on to something else and leave the spotlight open.

Although this may seem discouraging, there are in fact many areas in which less-known writers are syndicated. Syndicates are not looking for general interest or essay columns. What they are looking for are fresh voices that will attract readers. As consumer interests and lifestyles change, new doors are being opened for innovative writers capable of covering emerging trends.

Most syndicates distribute a variety of columns, cartoons and features. Although the larger ones are usually only interested in running ongoing material, smaller ones often accept short features and one-shots in addition to continuous columns. Specialized syndicates—those that deal with a single area such as business—often sell to magazines, trade journals and other business publications as well as to newspapers.

THE WINNING COMBINATION

In presenting yourself and your work, note that most syndicated columnists start out writing for local newspapers. Many begin as staff writers, develop a following in a particular area, and are then picked up by a syndicate. Before approaching a syndicate, write for a paper in your area. Develop a good collection of clips that you feel is representative of your best writing.

New ideas are paramount to syndication. Sure, you'll want to study the popular columnists to see how their pieces are structured (most are short—from 500-750 words—and really pack a punch), but don't make the mistake of imitating a well-known columnist. Syndicates are looking for original material that is timely, saleable and original. Do not submit a column to a syndicate on a subject it already covers. The more unique the topic, the greater your chances of having it picked up. Most importantly, be sure to choose a topic that interests you and one you know well.

APPROACHING MARKETS

Request a copy of a syndicate's writer's guidelines. It will give you information on current needs, submission standards and response times. Most syndicates prefer a query letter and about six sample columns or writing samples and a SASE. You may also want to include a client list and business card if available. If you have a particular area of expertise pertinent to your submission, mention this in your letter and back it up by sending related material. For highly specialized or technical matter, provide credentials to show you are qualified to handle the topic.

In essence, syndicates act as agents or brokers for the material they handle. Writing material is usually sold as a package. The syndicate will promote and market the work to newspapers (and sometimes to magazines) and keep careful records of sales. Writers usually receive 40-60% of gross receipts. Some syndicates may also pay a small salary or flat fee for one-shot items.

Syndicates usually acquire all rights to accepted material, although a few are now offering writers and artists the option of retaining ownership. In selling all rights, writers give up ownership and future use of their creations. Consequently, sale of all rights is not the best deal for writers, and has been the reason many choose to work with syndicates that buy less restrictive rights. Before signing a contract with a syndicate, you may want to go over the terms with an attorney or with an agent who has a background in law. The best contracts will usually offer the writer a percentage of gross receipts (as opposed to net receipts) and will not bind the writer for longer than five years.

THE SELF-SYNDICATION OPTION

Many writers choose to self-syndicate. This route allows you to retain all rights, and gives you the freedom of a business owner. But as a self-syndicated writer, you must also act as your own manager, marketing team and sales force. You must develop mailing lists, and a pricing, billing and collections structure.

Payment is usually negotiated on a case-by-case basis. Small newspapers may offer only $10-20 per column, but larger papers may pay much more (for more information on pay rates, see How Much Should I Charge? on page 56). The number of papers you deal with is only limited by your marketing budget and your tenacity.

If you self-syndicate, be aware that some newspapers are not copyrighted, so you should copyright your own material. It's less expensive to copyright columns as a collection than individually. For more information on copyright procedures, see Copyrighting Your Writing in the Business of Writing section.

CHANGES IN THE MARKETPLACE

The newspaper syndication business mirrors the newspaper business as a whole. Advertising revenues are down, sales are down, readership is down. As a result, the competition for syndicated columns is fierce—and doesn't seem to promise to ease any time soon. Recognizing this, we have limited our syndicate listings to the top eight. A complete listing of syndicates with contact names and the features they represent can be found in the *Editor & Publisher Syndicate Directory* (11 W. 19th St., New York NY 10011). The weekly magazine, *Editor & Publisher*, also has news articles about syndicates and can provide you with information about changes and events in the industry.

Information on syndicates listed in the previous edition but not included in this edition of *Writer's Market*, **can be found in the General Index.**

ANDREWS MCMEEL UNIVERSAL, (formerly Universal Press Syndicate), Dept. WM, 4520 Main St., 7th Floor, Kansas City MO 64111. (816)932-6600. Website: http://www.uexpress.com. Contact: Syndicate editorial. Estab. 1970. Buys syndication rights. Reports normally in 1 month. Return postage required.
Nonfiction: Looking for features and columns for daily and weekly newspapers. "Any material suitable for syndication in daily newspapers." Currently handling James J. Kilpatrick, Dear Abby, William F. Buckley and others. Payment varies according to contract.

CHRONICLE FEATURES, Dept. WM, Suite 1011, 870 Market St., San Francisco CA 94102. (415)777-7212. General Manager: Stuart Dodds. Contact: Susan Peters. Buys 3 features/year. Syndicates to daily newspapers in the US and Canada with representation overseas. Reports in 2 months.
Needs: Newspaper columns and features. "The writer should be guided by the concerns and aspirations of today's newspaper reader. We look for diverse viewpoints, originality of expression and, in special fields of interest, exceptional expertise." Preferred length: 750 words. Submit complete ms, brief cover letter and SASE. Pays 50% revenue from syndication. Currently syndicates Latino Spectrum by Roberto Rodriguez and Patrisia Gonzales (op-ed column); Earthweek by Steve Newman (planetary diary); Working Life by Deborah L. Jacobs, (workplace advice); Faces, by Kenny Waghorn (caricatures).
Tips: "We are seeking features that will be ongoing, not single articles or news releases. Examples of a proposed feature are more welcome than a query letter describing it. Conduct all correspondence by mail rather than phone."

COPLEY NEWS SERVICE, P.O. Box 190, San Diego CA 92112. (619)293-1818. Fax: (619)293-3233. Editorial Manager: Glenda Winders. Most stories produced by news bureaus or picked up from Copley newspapers; 15% freelance written on a one-time basis. Offers 200 features/week. Sells to newspapers and online services. Reports in 6 months. Buys first rights.

Needs: Comic strips, travel stories, newspaper columns on computer technology, new ideas. Query with clips of published work. Pays $100/story or negotiated monthly salary. Only responds to faxed or e-mailed queries to buy.

Tips: "Competition is keen, but we are always on the lookout for good writers and fresh ideas."

‡KING FEATURES SYNDICATE, 235 E. 45th St., New York NY 10017. (212)455-4000. Contact: Submissions Editor. Estab. 1920. 100% written by writers on contract. Buys 4 features/year. Syndicates to newspapers. Reports in 2 months. Buys first North American serial rights. Free writer's guidelines. Submit complete ms or column idea with five or six sample columns, with SASE.

Needs: Newspaper columns. Pays 50% author's percentage. Currently syndicates *Click & Clack Talk Cars*, by Tom and Ray Magliozzi (funny auto advice); *Hints From Heloise*, by Heloise (household hints); *Carl Rowan* (commentary). Does *not* buy one-shots.

Tips: "Try to sign up several newspapers on your own, the larger the better. Make sure they pay you something. Freebies don't count!"

LOS ANGELES TIMES SYNDICATE, Times Mirror Square, Los Angeles CA 90053. (213)237-7987. Syndicates to US and worldwide markets. Reports in 2 months. Usually buys first North American serial rights and world rights, but rights purchased can vary. Submit seasonal material 6 weeks in advance. Material ranges from 800-2,000 words.

Needs: Reviews continuing columns and comic strips for US and foreign markets. Send comics to Cathryn Irvine, promotion manager, columns to Tim Lange, managing editor. Also reviews single articles, series, magazine reprints, and book serials; send these submissions to Beth Barber (2 Park Ave., Suite 1802, New York NY 10016). Send complete ms. Pays 50% commission. Currently syndicates Art Buchwald, Dr. Henry Kissinger, Dr. Jeane Kirkpatrick, William Pfaff and Paul Conrad.

‡NEW YORK TIMES SYNDICATION SALES CORP., 122 E. 42nd St., New York NY 10168. (212)499-3300. President/Editor-in-Chief: Gloria Brown Anderson. Contact: Submissions Editor. Syndicates select one-shot articles of previously published submissions by a recognized author. Buys second serial (reprint) rights.

Needs: Previously published magazine and newspaper features of 750-1,500 words. Primarily trend, holiday and lifestyle features; and interviews with celebrities or notable personalities. Submission *must* have been published within the previous year by a recognized author. Payment to author varies. Send tearsheets of article. Photos are welcome with articles. Enclose SASE.

Tips: "Topics should cover universal markets and either be by a well-known writer or have an off-beat quality. Considers articles or columns from recognized writers."

TRIBUNE MEDIA SERVICES, 435 N. Michigan, Suite 1400, Chicago IL 60601. (312)222-4444. E-mail: mmathes@tribune.com. Website: http://www.comicspage.com. President: David D. Williams. Syndicate Editor: Mark Mathes. Syndicates to newspapers and electronic media. Reports in 1 month. Buys all rights, first North American serial rights or second serial (reprint) rights.

Needs: Newspaper columns, comic strips, internet-related content. Query with published clips. Currently syndicates the columns of Bob Greene, Andy Rooney, Dave Berry and Jacqueline Mitchard; and cartoons of Jeff MacNelly, Mike Peters and Dick Lecher.

Tips: "TMS is one of the largest syndicates of news, commentary, humor, comics and entertainment to newspaper, broadcast and multimedia. Most of our features are multi-year commitments with creators and we consequently buy few one-time freelance pieces."

‡UNITED FEATURE SYNDICATE, 200 Madison Ave., New York NY 10016. (212)293-8500. Syndicate Director: Sid Goldberg. Editorial Director: Diana Loevy. Executive Editor: Robert Levy. Managing Editor, Comic Art: Amy Lago. 100% contract writers. Supplies features to 1,700 US newspapers, plus Canadian and other international papers. Works with published writers. Query with 4-6 samples and SASE. Reports in 2 months.

Needs: Current columnists include Jack Anderson, Judith Martin, Donald Lambro, Martin Sloane. Comic strips include Peanuts, Nancy, Drabble, Marmaduke, Rose is Rose and Dilbert. Standard syndication contracts are offered for columns and comic strips.

Tips: "We buy the kind of writing similar to other major syndicates—varied material, well-known writers. The best way to break in to the syndicate market is for writers to latch on with a major newspaper and to develop a following. Also, cultivate new areas and try to anticipate trends."

MARKETS THAT WERE listed in the 1997 edition of *Writer's Market* but do not appear this year are listed in the General Index with a notation explaining why they were omitted.

Greeting Cards & Gift Ideas

How many greeting cards did you buy last year? Americans bought nearly seven and a half billion cards last year. That's according to figures published by The Greeting Card Association, a national trade organization representing the multi-billion dollar greeting card industry.

In fact, nearly 50% of all first class mail now consists of greeting cards. And, of course, card manufacturers rely on writers to supply them with enough skillfully crafted sentiments to meet the demand. The perfect greeting card verse is one that will appeal to a large audience, yet will make each buyer feel that the card was written exclusively for him or her.

Three greeting card companies dominate this industry; together, American Greetings, Hallmark and Gibson Greetings supply 85% of all cards sold. The other 15% are published by approximately 1,500 companies who have found success mainly by not competing head to head with the big three but by choosing instead to pursue niche markets—regional and special-interest markets that the big three either cannot or do not supply.

A PROFESSIONAL APPROACH TO MARKETS

As markets become more focused, it's important to keep current on specific company needs. Familiarize yourself with the differences among lines of cards by visiting card racks. Ask retailers which lines are selling best. You may also find it helpful to read trade magazines such as *Gifts and Decorative Accessories* and *Party and Paper Retailer*. These publications will keep you apprised of changes and events within the field, including seminars and trade shows.

Once you find a card line that appeals to you, write to the company and request its market list, catalog or submission guidelines (usually available for a SASE or a small fee). This information will help you determine whether or not your ideas are appropriate for that market.

Submission procedures vary among greeting card publishers, depending on the size and nature of the company. Keep in mind that many companies (especially the large ones) will not review your writing samples until you've signed and returned their disclosure contract or submission agreement, assuring them that your material is original and has not been submitted elsewhere.

Some editors prefer to see individual card ideas on 3×5 cards, while others prefer to receive a number of complete ideas on $8\frac{1}{2} \times 11$ bond paper. Be sure to put your best pieces at the top of the stack. Most editors do not want to see artwork unless it is professional, but they do appreciate conceptual suggestions for design elements. If your verse depends on an illustration to make its point or if you have an idea for a unique card shape or foldout, include a dummy card with your writing samples.

The usual submission includes from 5 to 15 card ideas and an accompanying cover letter, plus mechanical dummy cards, if necessary. Some editors also like to receive a résumé, client list and business card. Some do not. Be sure to check the listings and the company's writer's guidelines for such specifications before submitting material.

Payment for greeting card verse varies, but most firms pay per card or per idea; a handful pay small royalties. Some companies prefer to test a card first and will pay a small fee for a test card idea. In some instances, a company may even purchase an idea and never use it.

Greeting card companies will also buy ideas for gift products and may plan to use card material for a number of subsequent items. Licensing—the sale of rights to a particular character for a variety of products from mugs to T-shirts—is a growing part of the greetings industry. Because of this, however, note that most card companies buy all rights. We now include in this section markets for licensed product lines such as mugs, bumper stickers, buttons, posters and the like.

Greeting card writing—it's a changing industry

After seventeen years of active participation in the greeting card industry, I can tell you that the most important thing to understand is CHANGE! The industry that was once considered recession proof, because people would always buy a card even when they couldn't buy a gift, is beginning to fall flat in the marketplace. Part of the reason for this stems from the diverse lifestyles of consumers themselves.

Consumers today are sophisticated, educated, worldly-wise, and catapulting through the information age at record speeds. Since it's faster and easier to keep up with others via voice-mail or e-mail, part of the challenge of greeting card manufacturers is to entice those with very little time to stop, shop, and buy their product.

How can you entice those consumers? You can create the right words for them to easily express the thoughts they want to convey. You are their spokesperson, the one who can share their hearts and minds. Think long and hard about the person you imagine your card is going to. See them holding your words in their hand. Are they smiling? Laughing? Crying? If so, you have touched them—you have delivered the message.

How can you make sure an editor will be interested in your material? Shop! Shop! Shop! Make sure you are completely familiar with what's it in the marketplace today. Have you noticed the changes? Have you noticed there are fewer sing-songy rhymes and more conversational, heart-felt rhythms that speak softly to real life issues? Have you realized that writers are dealing with a world of changing lifestyle—divorce, remarriage, blended, stirred, shaken families, people coming out, going through, passing on? They're all your people. Speak to them in a language that sounds personal and warm, yet universal in appeal. Life is hitting them from all sides, from every media. It is no longer a rose-colored greeting card world. You need to provide the buffers, the soothers, the forms of expression that help them share kindness and individuality.

What will the experts tell you? First of all, they'll suggest you should know something about the publisher you're submitting material to. What kinds of cards do they publish? If they only seem to use short prose or funny one-liners, don't bother sending your heart-wrenching rhyme or your cute or juvenile ideas. If they only produce funny cards, don't send serious ones.

Be professional when you submit material. Always send a SASE if you want your material returned. Publishers are not responsible for paying return postage. Always send your ideas in small, manageable batches, preferably one idea per index card and about 10-15 ideas per batch. Try not to mix humor batches with non-humor batches. Always include your name and some kind of numbering system so you can keep a record of purchased items. Punctuate your pieces properly. Do not send simultaneous submissions. Make a plan for sending submissions, and when one batch is returned, check it over and then send it to the next publisher on your list. Keep it in circulation. If it gets rejected a number of

INSIDER REPORT, *Artl*

times, reevaluate the material and consider whether it is as strong as it could be or whether you should continue to send it. Maybe it's too much like something the publishers already have. Often, that's the main reason for rejection.

Remember your target audience. Women purchase the majority of greeting cards. Those women are young mothers, older housewives, professional career women, grandmothers, sisters and daughters. All of these women have one thing in common. They have very little time to shop for a greeting card. They need to find what they want as quickly as possible. If they have to spend too long searching for the right card, they will probably move on down the aisle and right out of the store. Remember too, your words must seem like a special note, yet appeal to an audience of 10,000 people. You have to say enough, but not too much so that the card is too limiting for a number of recipients; say something meaningful, yet not sappy; direct, yet loving. You are the artist weaving a beautiful thought. You are a missionary of the most important relationships people have.

Why do you get rejected?

Greeting card companies have banks filled with material they have tested over time and know will sell. Unless your ideas are unique or are truly a new slant on the relationship you're addressing, you won't make the sale. Should you send illustrations with your idea? No, not unless you're particularly good at illustration. If you have visual idea, you can write it in words or send stick figures to show it. If your words are clear enough, your idea will be understood without additional artwork. In humor, it can be especially helpful to send some kind of visual description, however.

What else should you think about? Try to find the holes in the product line you see in your local card store. What situations aren't being addressed that you feel should be? What age groups or social groups or types of people do you feel are absent from the card racks? Are you finding the right material for men? For kids? For someone who just suffered the loss of a job, a pet, a dream? Do you think the relationships you find on those shelves are being addressed in all the ways they could be? Are they too unrealistic? Are they too straightforward? Do they make all mothers out to be saints and all spouses more wonderful than words?

What could you do to make the industry sound more current, more up-to-the minute, or just more fun? How could you relate to the people in your life in new ways? How would you draw more customers to the card racks? As you answer some of those questions and support those answers with professional, quality writing, you'll find yourself well on your way to a challenging hobby or an exciting career.

—Karen Moore Artl has been a senior editor at both American Greetings and Gibson Greetings. She is currently the Creative Director of the seasonal relationship lines at Gibson. Her book on greeting card writing will be published by Writer's Digest Books in 1998.

Information of interest to writers wishing to know more about working with the greeting card industry is available from the Greeting Card Association (1200 G Street NW, Suite 760, Washington, DC 20005).

MANAGING YOUR SUBMISSIONS

Because you will be sending out many samples, you may want to label each sample. Establish a master card for each verse idea and record where and when each was sent and whether it was rejected or purchased. Keep all cards sent to one company in a batch and give each batch a number. Write this number on the back of your return SASE to help you match up your verses as they are returned.

Information on greeting card companies listed in the previous edition but not included in this edition of *Writer's Market* can be found in the General Index.

‡**ALLPORT EDITIONS INC.**, 532 NW 12th, Portland OR 97209. (503)223-7268. Fax: (503)223-9182. E-mail: info@allport.com. Contact: Creative Director. Estab. 1982. 5% freelance written. Receives 200 submissions/year. Submit seasonal/holiday material 15 months in advance. Reports in 1 month. Buys all rights. Pays on publication. Writer's guidelines for SAE. Market list issued one time only.
Needs: Informal, conventional, humorous, birthday. Prefers unrhymed verse ideas. Submit 10 ideas/batch.
Tips: "We typically look for a greeting to match an existing piece of artwork. When a writer submits sketches or ideas of what the art should be on the front of the card they have limited themselves for adaptability. Humor greetings are the exception. Those usually drive the artwork, and we are most likely to purchase them. The type of humor that works best is witty without being offensive. We have found that the sarcastic, poking-fun-at-the-recipient cards are often the ones people pick up, read and laugh about in stores, but they don't buy them for fear of offending someone."

AMBERLEY GREETING CARD CO., 11510 Goldcoast Dr., Cincinnati OH 45249-1695. (513)489-2775. Editor: Dave McPeek. Estab. 1966. 90% freelance written. Bought 200 freelance ideas/samples last year. Reports in 1 month. Material copyrighted. Buys all rights. **Pays on acceptance.** Guidelines for #10 SASE. Market list regularly revised.
● This company is now accepting alternative humor.
Needs: "Original, easy to understand, belly-laugh or outrageous humor. We sell to the 'masses, not the classes,' so keep it simple and to the point. Humor accepted in all captions, including general birthday, family birthday, get well, anniversary, thank you, friendship, etc. No non-humorous material needed or considered this year." Pays $150/card idea. Submit maximum 10 ideas/batch.
Tips: "Send SASE for our writer's guidelines before submitting. Amberley publishes humorous specialty lines in addition to a complete conventional line that is accented with humor. Since humor is our specialty, we are highly selective. Be sure your SASE has correct U.S. postage. Otherwise it will not be returned."

‡**AMERICAN GREETINGS**, Dept. WM, One American Rd., Cleveland OH 44144-2398. (216)252-7300. Creative Recruitment Dept: Leia Madden. No unsolicited material. "We are currently reviewing only humorous writing for our Humorous/Alternative card lines." Send letter of inquiry describing education or experience along with a #10 SASE for guidelines. Reports within 1 month. Buys all rights. **Pays on acceptance.**
Tips: "We're open to humorous verse, funny copy twists, and off-the-wall humor styles."

ARGUS COMMUNICATIONS, 200 E. Bethany, Allen TX 75002-3804. (972)390-6300. Editorial Coordinator: Beth Davis. 90% freelance written. Primarily interested in material for posters. Reports in 2 months. **Pays on acceptance.** Send for submission guidelines (send a #10 SASE) before submitting material.
● Argus Communications has expanded its markets and is focusing on three specific groups: education, general and Christian. By describing more clearly its specific targets, freelance writers should be able to select and write for the market(s) where they feel their strengths are. In return, Argus hopes it will be able to get better use out of the submissions it receives.
Needs: "We have three specific markets for which we buy editorial: (1) Education market: poster editorial for teachers to place in their classrooms that is positive, motivational, inspirational, thought-provoking and success-oriented. Also, poster editorial that encourages teamwork and conflict resolution, and editorial that reflects basic values such as honesty, integrity, kindness, trust, etc. (2) General market: poster and postcard editorial for teenagers through adults that is bright, timely and funny. The editorial should reflect current trends, lifestyles and attitudes. Humor and light sarcasm are the emphasis for this market. (3) Christian market: poster editorial for teenagers through adults that is positive, inspirational, motivational, encouraging or even humorous. The editorial should express basic Christian faith, beliefs and values.
Other Product Lines: Postcards, calendars (for the Christian market).
Tips: "Poster editorial is an at-a-glance, brief message that makes an impression, whether it is thought-provoking, humorous or inspirational. Our posters capture your attention with a creative mixture of humorous, dynamic and motivational editorial. We do not need any long poetry. Postcard editorial should express a simple 'me to you' message. Think of a new way to express a friendly hi, thinking of you, miss you, thank you or what's new."

‡**BARNSTORMING DESIGNS, LTD.**, 106 Pipe Meadow Way, Frederick MD 21702. (301)695-6091. Estab. 1988. 100% freelance written. Bought 30 ideas/samples last year. Submit seasonal/holiday material 9 months in advance. Buys all rights. **Pays on acceptance.** Offers royalties.
Needs: Announcements, invitations, holiday cards. "All cards and invitations mail in tubes. They come with objects, ribbons and confetti and coordinate with the design." Prefers either rhymed or unrhymed verse.
Tips: "Our invitations and cards are 'fun' and high impact. Copy must be the same and work well with the total design concept."

bePUZZLED, Mystery Jigsaw Puzzles, 1297 Blue Hills Ave., Bloomfield CT 06002. (860)242-0735. Fax: (860)286-8710. E-mail: malbepuzzd@aol.com. Contact: Mary Ann Lombard, CEO. Creative Director: Richard DeZinno. 100% freelance written. Estab. 1987. Pays on completion. Publishes ms an average of 9 months after acceptance. Byline given (sometimes pen name required). Buys all rights. Submit seasonal/holiday material 9 months in advance. Accepts simultaneous submissions. Reports in 2 weeks on queries, 3 months on mss. Writer's guidelines for SASE.

Reprints: Send photocopy of article or typed ms with rights for sale noted and information about when and where the article previously appeared.

Needs: Mystery jigsaw puzzle using short mystery stories for children and adults. Adventure, humorous, mainstream, mystery, suspense (*exact* subject within genre above is released to writers as available.) Buys 10 mss/year. Query. Length: 3,500-5,500 words. Pays $250-2,000.

Tips: "Writers must follow submission format as outlined in writer's guidelines. We incorporate short mystery stories and jigsaw puzzles into a game where the clues to solve the mystery are cleverly hidden in both the short story and the puzzle picture. Writer must be able to integrate the clues in the written piece to these to appear in puzzle picture. Playing one of our games helps to clarify how we like to 'marry' the story clues and the visual clues in the puzzle." Manuscripts may not be returned.

BLUE MOUNTAIN ARTS, INC., Dept. WM, P.O. Box 1007, Boulder CO 80306-1007. E-mail: bma@rmi.net. Contact: Editorial Staff. Estab. 1971. Buys 100 items/year. Reports in 10 weeks. Pays on publication. Writer's guidelines for #10 SASE. Enclose SASE with submission.

Needs: "We are interested in reviewing poetry and writings that would be appropriate for greeting cards, which means that they should reflect a message, feeling, or sentiment that one person would want to share with another. We'd like to receive sensitive, original submissions about love relationships, family members, friendships, philosophies, and any other aspect of life. Poems and writings for specific holidays (Christmas, Valentine's Day, etc.) and special occasions, such as graduation, birthdays, anniversary, and get well are also considered." Submit seasonal material at least 4 months in advance. Buys worldwide, exclusive rights, $200/poem; anthology rights $25.

Other Product Lines: Calendars, gift books, prints, mugs.

Tips: "We strongly suggest that you familiarize yourself with our products before submitting material, although we caution you not to study them too hard. We do *not* need more poems that sound like something we've already published. We're looking for poetry that expresses real emotions and feelings, so we suggest that you have someone specific in mind (a friend, relative, etc.) as you write. The majority of the poetry we publish *does not rhyme*. We do not wish to receive books, unless you are interested in having portions excerpted for greeting cards; nor do we wish to receive artwork or photography. We prefer that submissions be typewritten, one poem per page. Only a small portion of the freelance material we receive is selected each year, either for publication on a notecard or in a gift anthology, and the review process can also be lengthy, but please be assured that every manuscript is given serious consideration."

BRILLIANT ENTERPRISES, 117 W. Valerio St., Santa Barbara CA 93101-2927. President: Ashleigh Brilliant. Estab. 1967. Buys all rights. Submit words and art in black on 3½×3½ horizontal, thin white paper in batches of no more than 15. Reports "usually in 2 weeks." Catalog and sample set for $2.

Needs: Postcards. Messages should be "of a highly original nature, emphasizing subtlety, simplicity, insight, wit, profundity, beauty and felicity of expression. Accompanying art should be in the nature of oblique commentary or decoration rather than direct illustration. Messages should be of universal appeal, capable of being appreciated by all types of people and of being easily translated into other languages. Because our line of cards is highly unconventional, it is essential that freelancers study it before submitting. No topical references or subjects limited to American culture or puns." Limit of 17 words/card. Pays $50 for "complete ready-to-print word and picture design."

THE CALLIGRAPHY COLLECTION INC., 2604 NW 74th Place, Gainesville FL 32653. (352)375-8530. Fax: (352)374-9957. Owner: Katy Fischer. Reports in 6 months. Buys all rights. Pays on publication.

Needs: "Ours is a line of framed prints of watercolors with calligraphy." Conventional, humorous, inspirational, sensitivity, soft line. Prefers unrhymed verse, but will consider rhymed. Submit 3 ideas/batch. Pays $75-200/idea.

● The Calligraphy Collection has increased its payment rates.

Other Product Lines: Gift books, plaques, musical picture frames.

Tips: "Sayings for friendship are difficult to get. Bestsellers are humorous, sentimental and inspirational ideas—such as for wedding and family and friends. Our audience is women 20 to 50 years of age. Write something they would like to give or receive as a lasting gift. The most popular size has room for about 35 words. Our gift item is for everyday use rather than just a special occasion so we do not mention birthdays or mother's day for example. It is a gift to tell someone how much they mean to you. How important their friendship is or what is special about knowing them. We need to keep sayings below 60 words, below 35 words for the most popular size."

COLORS BY DESIGN, 7723 Densmore Ave., Van Nuys CA 91436. (818)376-1226. Creative Director: Jane Daly. Estab. 1985. 20% of material freelance written. Receives 500 submissions/year; bought 200 ideas/samples last year. Does not return submissions accompanied by SASE. Buys all rights. Pays on publication. Writer's guidelines/market list free. Market list regularly revised and available to writer on mailing list basis.

Needs: Announcements, informal, juvenile, conventional, humorous, invitations, soft line.

COMSTOCK CARDS, 600 S. Rock, Suite 15, Reno NV 89502-4115. Fax: (702)856-9406. Production Manager: David Delacroix. Estab. 1986. 35% freelance written. Receives 2,000 submissions/year; bought 150 freelance ideas/

samples last year. Submit seasonal/holiday material 1 year in advance. Reports in 5 weeks. Buys all rights. **Pays on acceptance.** Writer's guidelines/market list for SASE. Market list issued one time only.

Needs: Humorous, informal, invitations, "puns, put-downs, put-ons, outrageous humor aimed at a sophisticated, adult female audience. Also risqué cartoon cards. No conventional, soft line or sensitivity hearts and flowers, etc." Pays $50-75/card idea, cartoons negotiable.

Other Product Lines: Notepads, cartoon cards, invitations.

Tips: "Always keep holiday occasions in mind and personal me-to-you expressions that relate to today's occurrences. Ideas must be simple and concisely delivered. A combination of strong image and strong gag line make a successful greeting card. Consumers relate to themes of work, sex and friendship combined with current social, political and economic issues."

CREATE-A-CRAFT, P.O. Box 330008, Fort Worth TX 76163-0008. Estab. 1967. 5% freelance written. Receives 300 submissions/year; bought 2 freelance ideas/samples last year. Submit seasonal/holiday material 1 year in advance. "No phone calls from freelancers accepted. We deal through agents only. Submissions not returned even if accompanied by SASE." Buys all rights. Sample greeting cards $2.50 for #10 SASE.

Needs: Announcements, conventional, humorous, juvenile, studio. "Payment depends upon the assignment, amount of work involved, and production costs involved in project."

Tips: "Follow all directions given. Those who do not follow directions are not given any consideration. No phone calls, no faxes or unagented work accepted. No unsolicited material. Send letter of inquiry describing education and experience, or résumé with one sample first. We screen applicants and request samples from those who interest us."

‡**CREATIVE CHRISTIAN MINISTRIES**, P.O. Box 12624, Roanoke VA 24027. Editorial Director: Betty Robertson. Estab. 1985. 25% freelance written. Bought 12 ideas/samples last year. Submit seasonal/holiday material 6 months in advance. Reports in 3 months. Buys one time rights. **Pays on acceptance**. Writer's guidelines/market list for SAE.

Needs: Inspirational.

Other Product Lines: Plaques.

Tips: "Personalized message which touch the heart for mother, father, son, daughter, etc."

‡**CURRENT, INC.**, Box 2559, Colorado Springs CO 80901-2559. (719)594-4100. Submit to: Freelance Editors. Estab. 1950. 5-10% freelance written. Receives an estimated 1,500 submissions/year; bought 180 ideas/samples last year. Submit best humor ideas *only* for birthday, friendship, get well. Reports in 6 weeks. Buys all rights. **Pays on acceptance.** "Flat fee only; no royalty." Writer's guidelines for #10 SASE.

Needs: Humor. All occasion and woman-to-woman cards; 1-2 line puns and prose not too risque. Pays $100/idea.

Tips: "We are primarily looking for original humor of all forms, except risqué, off-color sentiments. 99% of our customers are women and 80% of them are married and have children under the age of 18. Writers need to keep in mind that this is the audience we are trying to reach. We pick up trends and create our own. We suggest that writers keep abreast of what's selling at retail. Don't send traditional short prose sentiments or off-color humor because we *don't* buy it. Read our direct mail catalog."

DAYSPRING CARDS, P.O. Box 1010, Siloam Springs AR 72761. (501)549-9303. Fax: (501)524-8959. E-mail: annw@outreach.mhs.compuserve.com. Freelance Editor: Ann Woodruff. Estab. 1971. Submit seasonal/holiday material 1 year in advance. Reports in 2 months. **Pays on acceptance.** Guidelines for #10 SASE.

Needs: Announcements, invitations, all major seasonal and special days, all major everyday cards—birthday, anniversary, get well, friendship, etc. Material must be usable for the Christian market. Prefer unrhymed verse.

Tips: "Study our line before submitting. We are looking for sentiments with relational, inspirational messages that minister love and encouragement to the receiver. We see greeting cards as more than tools for social expression and relationship building. We see greeting cards as tools to help Christians communicate their heart and God's heart to the hearts of others. We believe the ministry of DaySpring Cards will touch others in a positive way by bringing hope to those who are discouraged, encouragement to those who are burdened, love to those who are hurting, comfort to those who are weary, and a smile to those who are feeling down."

DUCK AND COVER PRODUCTIONS, P.O. Box 21640, Oakland CA 94620. Contact: Jim Buser. Estab. 1990. 50% freelance written. Receives 1,000 submissions/year. Bought 80 ideas/samples last year. Reports in 3 weeks. Buys all rights on novelty products. Pays on publication. Guidelines for #10 SAE with 2 first-class stamps.

Other Product Lines: Novelty buttons and magnets *only*. Pays $25/idea.

Tips: "We do best with original, intelligent statements that make fun of life in the neurotic '90s. Our target audience would be educated, aware, yet skeptical and anxious young adults; however, anyone with an offbeat sense of humor can enjoy our line. We sell to novelty stores, head shops, record stores, bookstores, sex shops, comic stores, etc. There are no taboos for our writers; we encourage them to be as weird and/or rude as possible. We feel buttons and magnets are commercial cousins to graffiti and there is a definite psychological spin to our line. Cerebral material that makes use of contemporary pop vocabulary is a plus. We do *not* want to see old cliches or slogans already in the market."

EPCONCEPTS, P.O. Box 363, Piermont NY 10968. (914)359-7137. Fax: (914)365-0841. Contact: Steve Epstein. Estab. 1983. 95% freelance written. Receives 1,200 submissions/year; bought 25 ideas/samples last year. Submit seasonal/holiday material 2 months in advance. Reports in 3 months. Buys one-time greeting card rights. Pays ½ on acceptance; ½ on publication. Writer's guidelines for #10 SASE.

Needs: Announcements, conventional, humorous, informal, inspirational, invitations, juvenile, studio, all holidays. Prefers unrhymed verse ideas. Submit 20 ideas/batch on 8½×11 paper; no index cards. Include #10 SASE for reply.

Other Product Lines: Post cards, buttons, mugs, work (jotting down ideas) pads.

Tips: "Humorous sells best; especially birthdays, anniversaries, friendship/love and light risqué. Target audience is ages 20-50, upscale and appreciative of photography, antiques, illustrations and cartoons. Trends can always include certain social and political phenomenons, e.g., Presidents, first ladies, etc."

EPHEMERA, INC., P.O. Box 490, Phoenix OR 97535. E-mail: ephemera@mind.net. Contact: Editor. Estab. 1979. 90% freelance written. Receives 2,000 submissions/year; bought 200 slogans for novelty buttons and magnets last year. Reports in 5 weeks. Buys all rights. Pays on publication. Writer's guidelines for self addressed stamped envelope. Complete full color catalog available for $2.

Needs: Novelty buttons and magnets. Provocative, irreverent and outrageously funny slogans. "We want concise, high impact gems of wit that would sell in trendy card and gift shops, bookstores, record shops, political and gay shops, adult stores, amusement parks, etc! We've been in business for over 17 years and we have a reputation as *the* publisher of the wackiest slogans." Pays $35/slogan.

Tips: We're looking for satirical slogans about current events, pop culture, political causes, the president, job attitudes, coffee, booze, pot, drugs, sexual come-ons and put-downs, aging, slacker angst, gays and lesbians. But please don't limit yourself to these topics! Make us laugh out loud!

‡GALLANT GREETINGS, Dept. WM, P.O. Box 308, Franklin Park IL 60131. E-mail: gallant-greetings@worldnet.att .net. Website: http://gallant-greetings.com. Vice President, Sales and Marketing: Chris Allen. 90% freelance written. Bought 500 freelance ideas last year. Reports in 3 months. Buys world greeting card rights. Guidelines for SASE.

Needs: Traditional and humorous greeting card verse. Submit 20 cards/batch.

GIBSON GREETINGS, INC., P.O. Box 371804, Cincinnati OH 45222-1804. Contact: Editorial Department. Estab. 1850. Reports in 2 months. Buys all rights. **Pays on acceptance**.

Needs: Will review all types of cards conventional, humorous, religious, juvenile, cute, alternative. Rhyme or prose. "The successful writer is able to help people express their feelings in 5 to 50 words, using language the average person can relate to." Send for needs list. Starter packet available for #10 SASE with 55¢ postage.

Tips: "The most common mistake freelancers make is to send us poems, 'advice' quotes, or jokes rather than greeting card sentiments. The best training you can give yourself is to read, read, read greeting cards and to study how-to-write-greeting card books."

‡GREAT SEVEN, INC., 3870 Del Amo Blvd., #503, Torrance CA 90503. (310)371-4555. Estab. 1984. 75% freelance written. Receives 40-60 submissions/year; bought 25 ideas/samples last year. Submit seasonal/holiday material 6 months in advance. Buys all rights. **Pays on acceptance.**

Other Product Lines: Stickers, rubber stamps, banners.

KATE HARPER DESIGNS, P.O. Box 2112, Berkeley CA 94702. Contact: Editor. Estab. 1993. Submit seasonal/holiday material 1 year in advance. Reports in 1 month. Pays flat fee for usage, not exclusive, $25 plus author's name credit. **Pays on acceptance**. Writer's guidelines/market list for SASE.

Needs: Humorous, informal, inspirational, everyday cards. Prefers unrhymed verse ideas. Submit 10 ideas/batch.

   • Ms. Harper notes she wants to see "more topics on current events—issues of the day we all struggle with."

Tips: "Quotes needed about work, family, love, kids, career, technology and marriage with a twist of humor. Something a working mom would laugh at and/or tips on how to have it all and still live to tell about it. Be adventurous and say what you really think in first person. Nothing cute or sweet. Avoid quotes about women and weight, PMS, diet, sex. Write as if you were talking to your best friend at the kitchen table. We seek out new and unknown writers with a zing. Avoid traditional ideas. Serious quotes also considered. Quotes must be 20 words or less. For front of card only."

INFINITY COLLECTIONS, 5020 53rd Place, Hyattsville MD 20781. Contact: Karmen A. Booker. Estab. 1990. 20% freelance written. Submit material 2 months in advance. Reports in 2 months. Purchases exclusive rights to sentiment, a flat fee with no further royalties. Pays on publication. Writer's guidelines for $2.

Needs: Inspirational. Submit 5-8 ideas/batch on 3×5 index cards with SASE. Include name, address, social security number and numeric or alphanumeric reference on each submission. Responds in 1 month. Pays $30/idea.

   • Infinity Collections has an increased need for freelance material.

Tips: "Infinity Collections is looking for Christian messages such as love, friendship, joy, peace, and encouragement with a me-to-you message. Cards that sell best are Happy Birthday, Friendship, Thank You, Graduation, Mother's Day and Christmas cards. Card buyers look for a personal touch in verse. Therefore, please have someone in mind (a friend, relative, etc.) as you write."

‡J-MAR, P.O. Box 23149, Waco TX 76702. (817)751-0100. Fax: (817)751-0054. Assistant Product Marketing Manager: Kelly Shivers. Estab. 1984. 25% freelance written. Receives 200 submissions/year; bought 7 ideas/samples last year.

Submit seasonal/holiday material 10 months in advance. All submissions filed. Reports in 2 months. Buys all rights. **Pays on acceptance**.

Needs: Inspirational, soft line, friendship, birthdays, motivational, family, get well, sympathy, encouragement, humor, juvenile, seasonal, christenings, pastor/church thank you. Prefers either rhymed or unrhymed verse ideas.

Other Product Lines: Bookmarks, gift books, greeting books, calendars, puzzles.

Tips: "J-Mar's target audience is the Christian market. J-Mar appreciates submissions focused on core inspirational Christian values, verses and themes. Submissions can include biblical references or verses, poems and/or text.

‡CAROLE JOY CREATIONS INC., 107 Mill Plain Rd., Danbury CT 06811. (203)798-2060. President: Carole Gellineau. Estab. 1985. 5% freelance written. Receives 100 submissions/year. Submit seasonal/holiday material 8 months in advance. Reports in 6 months. Buys all rights. Pays within 30 days of acceptance. Writer's guidelines free.

Needs: Conventional, inspirational, sensitivity, humorous, African-American. Prefers either rhymed or unrhymed verse.

Tips: "We are looking for traditional cards with a sensitivity to the African-American consumer."

KOGLE CARDS, INC., 1498 S. Lipan St., Denver CO 80223. (303)698-9007. President: Patricia Koller. Art Director: Marci Chambers. Estab. 1982. 40% freelance written. Receives 100 submissions/year; bought 80 ideas/samples last year. Submit seasonal/holiday material 18 months in advance. Reports in 1 month. Buys all rights. Pays on publication.

Needs: Humorous, business related. Rhymed or unrhymed verse ideas.

Tips: "We produce cards designed for the business community, in particular salespeople, real estate, travel, hairdresser, insurance and chiropractic."

‡LAURA LEIDEN CALLIGRAPHY, INC., P.O. Box 141-WM, Watkinsville GA 30677. (706)769-6989. Contact: Shelley. Estab. 1978. 99% freelance written. Receives 100 submissions/year; bought 35 ideas/samples last year. Submit seasonal/holiday material 1 year in advance. Returns submissions if requested, but frequently keeps for later consideration. Reports in 9 months. Buys all rights. **Pays on acceptance**. After first purchase, we can notify writers of our current needs.

Needs: Conventional, inspirational, poems for family members and about the joys and trials of raising kids. Prefers rhymed verse. Submit 6 ideas/batch.

Other Product Lines: Plaques.

Tips: "Trends now are heavily leaning on sentimental and nostalgic verses about and for family."

LOVE GREETING CARDS, INC., 1717 Opa Loca Blvd., Opa-Locka FL 33054. (305)685-5683. Fax: (305)685-8473. Contact: Norman Drittel. Estab. 1984. 75% freelance written. Receives 200-300 submissions/year; bought 400 ideas/samples last year. Submit seasonal/holiday material 6 months in advance. Reports in 1 month. Buys all rights. **Pays on acceptance**. Market list regularly revised.

Needs: Informal, juvenile, humorous, general.

 • Love Greeting Cards is expanding and looking for more freelance material this year.

Other Product Lines: Greeting cards, posters, books ($100-300), posters ($200-500).

Tips: "There's a great demand for animal cards, flowers and computer art for greeting cards."

MADISON PARK GREETINGS, 1407 11th Ave., Seattle WA 98122. (206)324-5711. Copywriting Coordinator: Renée Capps. Estab. 1984. 50% of material freelance written. Receives 100 submissions/year. Submit seasonal/holiday material 10 months in advance. Reports in 2 months. Pays on publication. Writer's guidelines/market list free. Market list is issued one time only.

Needs: Announcements, informal, studio, conventional, inspirational, sensitivity, humorous, invitations, soft line.

MILLIDAY GREETINGS, P.O. Box 708, Berea OH 44017-0708. Website: http://www.milliday.com. Owner: Robert Stein. Estab. 1991. 95% of material freelance written. "We do not wish to see seasonal/holiday material which is not related to our trademarks." We publish Milliday Twins ™ cards for famous persons and events. Reports in 2 months with SASE. Buys all rights. **Pays on acceptance**. Will send guidelines, song, Milliday Software ™, traditions list, and samples for $5 and a mailing label. Market list revised regularly.

Needs: "We are looking for cards that promote our Milliday, Milleversary, and Milliday Twins trademarks and which support the celebration of Milliday or Milleversary personal holidays. (A couple would celebrate their first Wedding Milleversary on the one thousandth day of their marriage, their second Milleversary at 2,000 days etc.)" Millidays or Milleversaries are celebrated for any notable event." Prefers unrhymed verse. Submit 10 cards/batch. "We are interested in reviewing personal and business greeting cards and postcards. We especially need 'professional to client' Milliday ™ and Milleversary ™ cards both general and specific as to profession. We pay $30 to $150 for cards, buttons, t-shirts and other flat designs. A Milliday celebration is often a surprise to the celebrant since it is not annual. Have the age and point of view of the celebrant(s) in mind as you write."

NOVO CARD PUBLISHERS, INC., 4513 N. Lincoln Ave., Chicago IL 60625. (312)769-6000. Art Directors: Sheri Cline, Tom Benjamin. Estab. 1923. 95% of material freelance written. Receives 500 submissions/year. Bought 350 ideas/samples last year. Submit seasonal/holiday material 8 months in advance. Reports in 2 months. Buys greeting card reproduction rights. Pays on publication. Writer's guidelines/market list for SASE.

Needs: Announcements, conventional, humorous, informal, inspirational, invitations, juvenile, sensitivity, soft line, studio.

OATMEAL STUDIOS, P.O. Box 138W3, Rochester VT 05767. (802)767-3171. Creative Director: Helene Lehrer. Estab. 1979. 85% freelance written. Buys 200-300 greeting card lines/year. **Pays on acceptance.** Reports within 6 weeks. Current market list for #10 SASE.
Needs: Birthday, friendship, anniversary, get well cards, etc. Also Christmas, Hanukkah, Mother's Day, Father's Day, Easter, Valentine's Day, etc. Will review concepts. Humorous material (clever and *very* funny) year-round. "Humor, conversational in tone and format, sells best for us." Prefers unrhymed contemporary humor. Current pay schedule available with guidelines.
Other Product Lines: Notepads, stick-on notes.
Tips: "The greeting card market has become more competitive with a greater need for creative and original ideas. We are looking for writers who can communicate situations, thoughts, and relationships in a funny way and apply them to a birthday, get well, etc., greeting and we are willing to work with them in targeting our style. We will be looking for material that says something funny about life in a new way."

PAINTED HEARTS & FRIENDS, 1222 N. Fair Oaks Ave., Pasadena CA 91103. Fax: (818)798-7385 (Attn.: Teri Willis). E-mail: teri@paintedhearts.com. Contact: Teri Willis. 20% freelance written. Receives 500-1,000 submissions/year. Submit seasonal/holiday material 3 months in advance. Pays on publication. Writer's guidelines/market list for 4×9 SASE. Market list regularly revised.
Needs: Announcements, conventional, humorous, inspirational, realistic, invitations, juvenile. Submit 12 ideas/batch.
Other Product Lines: Invitations, post cards, poster.
Tips: Watercolor cards sell best for this company. *No poetry or lengthy verse.*

PANDA INK GREETING CARDS, P.O. Box 5129, West Hills CA 91308-5129. (818)340-8061. Fax: (818)883-6193. Contact: Ruth Ann. Estab. 1981. 10-20% freelance written. Receives 100 submissions/year; bought 50 ideas/samples last year. Submit seasonal/holiday material 6 months in advance. Reports in 1 month. Buys first rights. **Pays on acceptance.** Writer's guidelines for SASE.
Needs: Conventional, humorous, juvenile, soft line, Judaic, ethnic. Prefers rhymed verse ideas. Submit 10 ideas/batch.
Tips: "No risqué, sarcasm, insulting. Need Jewish/Yiddish language in most cases. We now have a metaphysical line of cards."

PAPER MOON GRAPHICS, P.O. Box 34672, Los Angeles CA 90034. (310)287-3949. Fax: (310)287-2588. Contact: Creative Director. Estab. 1978. 90% freelance written. Receives 2,000 submissions/year; bought 250 ideas/samples last year. Submit seasonal/holiday material 7 months in advance. Reports in 2 months. Buys card, stationery, ad rights.
Needs: Humorous, alternative humor/risqué. Prefers unrhymed verse ideas. Submit 12-18 ideas/batch. No original art. Send transparencies, photocopies, etc. Enclose SASE for return of work.
Other Product Lines: Stationery.
Tips: "Humor cards sell best for female audience 19-45. Trends are changing daily—humor always sells."

C.M. PAULA COMPANY, 6049 Hi-Tek Court, Mason OH 45040. Contact: Editorial Supervisor. Estab. 1958. 10% freelance written. "Looking for humor *only* from previously published social-expression writers. Seasoned writers should submit published writing samples. If there is a match in style, we will then contact writers with assignments." Reports in 2-3 months. Buys all rights. **Pays on acceptance.**
Product Lines: Coffee mugs, key rings, stationery pads, magnets, dimensional statues and awards.
Tips: "Our needs are light humor—nothing risqué. A writer can get a quick idea of the copy we use by looking over our store displays. Please note—we do not publish greeting cards."

PLUM GRAPHICS INC., P.O. Box 136, Prince Station, New York NY 10012. (212)337-0999. President: Yvette Cohen. Estab. 1983. 100% freelance written. Bought 21 samples last year. Does not return samples unless accompanied by SASE. Reports in 4 months. Buys greeting card and stationery rights. Pays on publication. Guidelines sheet for SASE, "sent out about twice a year in conjunction with the development of new cards."
Needs: Humorous. "We don't want general submissions. We want them to relate to our next line." Prefers unrhymed verse. Greeting cards pay $40.
Tips: "Sell to all ages. Humor is always appreciated. We want short, to-the-point lines."

QUALITY ARTWORKS, 2262 N. Penn Rd., P.O. Box 369, Hatfield PA 19440-0369. Contact: Attention: Writer's Market submissions. Creative Director: Linda Tomezsko Morris. Estab. 1985. 10% freelance written. Reports in 2 months. Buys all rights. **Pays on acceptance.** Writer's guidelines/market list for #10 SASE.
Needs: Bookmarks, scrolls. Conventional, inspirational, sensitivity, soft line. Prefers unrhymed verse. Buys 6-24 poems/year, maximum 100 words, preferably 15-50, rhymed or unrhymed, to use on bookmarks and scrolls. Desires relationship and non-relationship themes about hope, encouragement, honor, respect, recovery, healing, forgiveness, reconciliation, redemption, beauty, joy and celebration of God's creations. Payment is negotiable.
Tips: "We are looking for sophisticated yet inspirational verse (directed toward women). The main emphasis of our business is bookmarks. Think of what touches your heart inwardly. The message must communicate to mass market clearly. Too much symbolism is discouraged. Write with the consumer in mind—mostly female, 40 and above."

RED FARM STUDIO, 1135 Roosevelt Ave., P.O. Box 347, Pawtucket RI 02862-0347. Fax: (401)728-0350. Contact: Production Coordinator. Estab. 1955. 100% freelance written. Receives 200 submissions/year; buys 100 ideas/samples per year. Reports in 2 months. Buys exclusive publishing rights. **Pays within 1 month of acceptance.** For verse guidelines send #10 SASE.

Needs: Everyday occasion, conservative humor and Christmas cards (including religious). "We are looking for heartfelt, sincere sentiments, often with a conversational tone, both serious and humorous. Religious verse is generally more formal, often incorporating Bible verse. No family headings (such as sister's birthday, etc.). Usually no longer than 4 lines." Submit any number of ideas/samples per batch. Pays $4/line of copy. Prose, short and long.

Tips: "We pride ourselves on a premier nautical line of everyday greeting cards and Christmas boxed cards as well as our traditional lines. We are buying less 'flowery' verse that is typical of greeting cards, and opting for more down-to-earth, conversational writing—things a sender would actually *say* to the recipient."

‡**RESTAURANT GREETING CARDS**, 8440 Runford Dr., Boynton Beach FL 33437-2723. (407)392-8985. Fax: (407)392-4174. Contact: Michael Tomasso. Estab. 1975. 75% freelance written. Receives 100 submissions/year; bought 10 ideas/samples last year. Submit seasonal/holiday material 8 months in advance. Reports in 3 months. Pays on publication. Market list available on mailing list basis.

Needs: Humorous (must be restaurant related). Prefers unrhymed verse.

Tips: "Target market is restaurants. Humorous greeting, birthday, thank you, sells well. Pizza delivery, Chinese delivery, bagel, bakery, deli. Be sure not to offend ethnicity of card subject."

ROCKSHOTS, INC., 632 Broadway, New York NY 10012. (212)420-1400. Fax: (212)353-8756. Editor: Bob Vesce. Estab. 1979. Buys 75 greeting card verse (or gag) lines/year. Reports in 2 months. Buys rights for greeting-card use. Writer's guidelines for SASE.

Needs: Humorous ("should be off-the-wall, as outrageous as possible, preferably for sophisticated buyer"); soft line; combination of sexy and humorous come-on type greeting ("sentimental is not our style"); and insult cards ("looking for cute insults"). No sentimental or conventional material. "Card gag can adopt a sentimental style, then take an ironic twist and end on an off-beat note." Submit no more than 10 card ideas/samples per batch. Send to Attention: Submissions. Pays $50/gag line. Prefers gag lines on 8×11 paper with name, address, and phone and social security numbers in right corner, or individually on 3×5 cards.

Tips: "Think of a concept that would normally be too outrageous to use, give it a cute and clever wording to make it drop-dead funny, and you will have commercialized a non-commercial message. It's always good to mix sex and humor. Our emphasis is definitely on the erotic. Hard-core eroticism is difficult for the general public to handle on greeting cards. The trend is toward 'light' sexy humor, even cute sexy humor. 'Cute' has always sold cards, and it's a good word to think of even with the most sophisticated, crazy ideas. 80% of our audience is female. Remember that your gag line will be illustrated by a photographer, so try to think visually. If no visual is needed, the gag line *can* stand alone, but we generally prefer some visual representation. It is a very good idea to preview our cards at your local store if this is possible to give you a feeling of our style."

MARCEL SCHURMAN CO., INC., 2500 N. Watney Way, Fairfield CA 94533. Contact: Editor. Estab. 1950. 20% freelance written. Receives 500 submissions/year; bought 50 freelance ideas/samples last year. Reports in 6 weeks. **Pays on acceptance.** Writer's guidelines for #10 SASE.

  • Marcel Schurman has a new humorous card line, Laffs by Marcel, which requires sophisticated, clever ideas.

Needs: Sentimental, contemporary, inspirational/support, romance, friendship, seasonal and everyday categories. Prefers unrhymed verse, but on juvenile cards rhyme is OK. Submit 10-15 cards in single batch. Send humor ideas *only* to: Laffs by Marcel (our *new* humor division).

Tips: "Historically, our nostalgic and art museum cards sell best. However, we are moving toward more contemporary cards and humor. Target market: upscale, professional, well-educated; average age 40; more female. Be *original*."

SNAFU DESIGNS, Box 16643, St. Paul MN 55116. (612)698-8581. Editor: Scott F. Austin. Estab. 1985. Reports in 6 weeks. Buys all rights. **Pays on acceptance.** "Before we send you our guidelines, please send us something that is representative of your sense of humor (include a SASE). We will send you our guidelines if we feel your humor is consistent with ours."

Needs: Humorous, informal, birthday, friendship, thank you, anniversary, congratulations, get well, new baby, Christmas, Valentine's Day. Prefers unrhymed verse. Submit no more than 10 ideas/batch. Pays $100/idea.

Tips: "We use clever ideas that are simple and concisely delivered and are aimed at a sophisticated adult audience. Off-the-wall humor that pokes fun at the human condition. Please do not submit anything cute."

‡**SOUL SEARCHER GREETING CARDS**, P.O. Box 3462, Mankato MN 56002-3462. Owner: Julie Johnson. Estab. 1995. 20% freelance written. Submit seasonal/holiday material 9 months in advance. Reports in 3 months. Buys all rights. Pays on publication. Writer's guidelines for #10 SASE.

Needs: Inspirational, upbeat, soulful. Prefers unrhymed verse ideas. Prefers 10-25 cards/batch.

Tips: "We prefer short verses for birthday, get well, sympathy, love, friendship and nonoccasion cards, etc. Send at least 10 verses that stimulate the mind, body and spirit!"

SUNRISE PUBLICATIONS, INC., P.O. Box 4699, Bloomington IN 47402-4699. (812)336-9900. Website: http://www.interart.com. Contact: Angeline R. Larimer, creative writer. Estab. 1974. 5% freelance written. Receives 600 submissions/year. Bought 15 ideas/samples last year. Reports in 3 months. Buys worldwide exclusive license in all commercial formats. **Pays on acceptance.** Writer's guidelines for #10 SASE. Market list issued one-time only.

Needs: Contemporary, humorous, informal, soft line. No "off-color humor or lengthy poetry. Generally, we like short one- or two-line captions, sincere or clever. Our customers prefer this to lengthy rhymed verse. Longer copy is used but should be conversational. Submit ideas for birthday, get well, friendship, wedding, baby congrats, sympathy, thinking of you, anniversary, belated birthday, thank you, fun and love. We also have strong seasonal lines that use traditional, humorous and inspirational verses. These seasons include Christmas, Valentine's Day, Easter, Mother's Day, Father's Day, Graduation, Halloween and Thanksgiving." Payment varies.

Tips: "Think always of the sending situation and both the person buying the card and its intended recipient. Most of our traditional versing is done inhouse. We continue to look for exceptionally fresh and lively or emotionally-compelling ideas. We avoid any put-downs or age slams, anything mean-spirited or lewd."

SYNCHRONICITY GREETING CARDS, 122 E. Texas Ave., #1016, Baytown TX 77520. (713)422-6326. Contact: Erin Leinad, submissions editor. Receives 600 submissions/year; bought 50 ideas/samples last year. Reports in 1 month. Pays by royalty agreement only (10% of net). Writer's guidelines/market list for SAE and $1.

Needs: Sweet, sexy and sassy greeting cards. Submit 10 ideas/batch.

Other Product Lines: Fine art post cards, posters, current events, T-shirts, mugs, political buttons.

Tips: "We are producing a line of black and white photo art postcards of park pavilions. Send us a beautiful shot and we may purchase it. We are always ready to laugh, cry—or both, and so are the card seekers we are trying to reach."

‡TED PRODUCTS, 398 Columbus Ave., #290, Boston MA 02116. (617)350-6439. Owner: Ted Levenson. Estab. 1995. 40% freelance written. Receives thousands of submissons/year; bought 100 ideas/samples last year. Submit seasonal/holiday material 6 months in advance. Pays on publication. Guidelines free. Market list regularly revised.

Other Product Lines: Plaques, T-shirts, novelty and gift items, wall decor, clocks, mirrors. Pays royalty or up to $200/idea.

UNIQUE GREETINGS, INC., P.O. Box 5783, Manchester NH 03108. (603)647-6777. Contact: Michael Normand. Estab. 1988. 10% freelance written. Receives 15 submissions/year. Submit seasonal/holiday material 1 year in advance. Reports in 6 weeks. Buys all rights. Writer's guidelines/market list for SASE. Market list regularly revised.

Needs: Watercolors, cute animals, flower scenes, etc. Prefers unrhymed verse. Submit 12 ideas/batch.

Tips: "General and Happy Birthday sell the best."

VAGABOND CREATIONS, INC., 2560 Lance Dr., Dayton OH 45409. (937)298-1124. Editor: George F. Stanley, Jr. 10% freelance written. Bought 10-15 ideas/samples last year. Submit seasonal/holiday material 6 months in advance. Reports in 1 week. Buys all rights. Ideas sometimes copyrighted. **Pays on acceptance.** Writer's guidelines for #10 SASE. Market list issued one time only.

Needs: Cute, humorous greeting cards (illustrations and copy) often with animated animals or objects in people-situations with short, subtle tie-in message on inside page only. No poetry. Pays $15-25/card idea.

WARNER PRESS, PUBLISHERS, 1200 E. Fifth St., P.O. Box 2499, Anderson IN 46018-9988. Communications Editor: Robin Fogle. Estab. 1880. 50% freelance written. Reports in 2 months. Buys all rights. **Pays on acceptance.** Must send #10 SASE for guidelines before submitting.

Needs: Religious themes; sensitive prose and inspirational verse for Sunday bulletins. Pays $20-35. Also accepts ideas for coloring and activity books. Submit 5 pieces/batch with SASE. Include words "Freelance Approval" below return address on submission.

  • Warner Press has restructured and no longer buys material for boxed cards, posters, or calendars. It still purchases longer poetry and devotional material for use on our Sunday bulletins.

WEST GRAPHICS, 115 California Dr., Burlingame CA 94010. (800)648-9378. Website: http://www.westgraphics.c om. Contact: Production Department. Estab. 1980. 80% freelance written. Receives 20,000 submissions/year; bought 100 freelance ideas/samples last year. Reports in 6 weeks. Buys greeting card rights. Pays 30 days after publication. Writer's guidelines/market list for #10 SASE.

Needs: "We are looking for outrageous adult humor that is on the cutting edge." Prefers unrhymed verse. Submit 20-30 ideas/batch. Pays $60-100.

Tips: "West Graphics is an alternative greeting card company which offers a diversity of humor from 'off the wall' to 'tastefully tasteless'. Our goal is to publish cards that challenge the limits of taste and keep people laughing. The majority of our audience is women in their 30s and 40s, ideas should be targeted to birthday sentiment."

MARKETS THAT WERE listed in the 1997 edition of *Writer's Market* but do not appear this year are listed in the General Index with a notation explaining why they were omitted.

Contests and Awards

The contests and awards listed in this section are arranged by subject. Nonfiction writers can turn immediately to nonfiction awards listed alphabetically by the name of the contest or award. The same is true for fiction writers, poets, playwrights and screenwriters, journalists, children's writers and translators. You'll also find general book awards, miscellaneous awards, arts council and foundation fellowships, and multiple category contests.

New contests and awards are announced in various writer's publications nearly every day. However, many lose their funding or fold—and sponsoring magazines go out of business just as often. We have contacted the organizations whose contests and awards are listed here with the understanding that they are valid through 1997. If you are using this section in 1998 or later, keep in mind that much of the contest information listed here will not be current. Requirements such as entry fees change, as do deadlines, addresses and contact names.

To make sure you have all the information you need about a particular contest, always send a self-addressed, stamped, business-sized envelope (#10 SASE) to the contact person in the listing before entering a contest. The listings in this section are brief, and many contests have lengthy, specific rules and requirements that we could not include in our limited space. Often a specific entry form must accompany your submission. A response with rules and guidelines will not only provide specific instructions, it will also confirm that the award is still being offered.

When you receive a set of guidelines, you will see that some contests are not for some writers. The writer's age, previous publication, geographic location and the length of the work are common matters of eligibility. Read the requirements carefully to ensure you don't enter a contest for which you are not qualified. You should also be aware that every year, more and more contests, especially those sponsored by "little" literary magazines, are charging entry fees.

Contest and award competition is very strong. While a literary magazine may publish ten short stories in an issue, only one will win the prize in a contest. Give yourself the best chance of winning by sending only your best work. There is always a percentage of manuscripts cast off immediately as unpolished, amateurish or wholly unsuitable for the competition.

To avoid first-round rejection, make certain that you and your work qualify in every way for the award. Some contests are more specific than others. There are many contests and awards for a "best poem," but some award only the best lyric poem, sonnet or haiku.

Winning a contest or award can launch a successful writing career. Take a professional approach by doing a little extra research. Find out who the previous winner of the award was by investing in a sample copy of the magazine in which the prize-winning article, poem or short story appeared. Attend the staged reading of an award-winning play. Your extra effort will be to your advantage in competing with writers who simply submit blindly.

If a contest or award requires nomination by your publisher, ask your publisher to nominate you. Many welcome the opportunity to promote a work (beyond their own, conventional means). Just be sure the publisher has plenty of time before the deadline to nominate your work.

Further information on funding for writers is available at most large public libraries. See the *Annual Register of Grant Support* (National Register Publishing Co., a division of Reed-Elsevier, *Foundations and Grants to Individuals* (Foundation Center, 79 Fifth Ave., New York NY 10003) and *Grants and Awards Available to American Writers* (PEN American Center, 568 Broadway, New York NY 10012). For more listings of contests and awards for fiction writers, see *Novel & Short Story Writer's Market* (Writer's Digest Books). *Poet's Market* (Writer's Digest Books) lists contests and awards available to poets. *Children's Writer's & Illustrator's Market* (Writer's

Digest Books) has a section of contests and awards, as well. Two more good sources for literary contests are *Poets & Writers* (72 Spring St., New York NY 10012), and the *Associated Writing Programs Newsletter* (Old Dominion University, Norfolk VA 23529). Journalists should look into the annual Journalism Awards Issue of *Editor & Publisher* magazine (11 W. 19th St., New York NY 10011), published in the last week of December. Playwrights should be aware of the newsletter put out by The Dramatists Guild, (234 W. 44th St., New York NY 10036).

Information on contests and awards listed in the previous edition but not included in this edition of *Writer's Market*, can be found in the General Index.

General

‡**AMERICAN BOOKSELLERS BOOK OF THE YEAR (ABBY)**, American Booksellers Association, 828 S. Broadway, Tarrytown NY 10591. (914)591-2665. Fax: (914)591-2720. E-mail: jperlst@bookweb.org. Award Director: Jill Perlstein. Offered annually to previously published adult and children's titles that booksellers (members of the ABA) most enjoyed handselling (recommending) to their customers. Nominations and winners are selected by ABA members. Awards are presented at the annual ABA convention. Prizes: $5,000 to each author (adult and children's), an engraved Tiffany glass prism; four books in each category are awarded with the title "Honor Book."

‡**THE ANISFIELD-WOLF BOOK AWARDS**, The Cleveland Foundation, 1401 Euclid Ave., Suite 1400, Cleveland OH 44115. (216)861-3810. Fax: (216)861-1729. "The Anisfield-Wolf Book Award annually honors books which contribute to our understanding or racism or our appreciation of the diversity of human culture published during the year of the award." Deadline: January 31. Guidelines for SASE. Prize: $10,000. Judged by five-member panel chaired by Dr. Henry Louis Gates of Harvard University and including Joyce Carol Oates, Rita Dove and Stephen Jay Gould. Any work addressing issues of racial bias or human diversity may qualify.

‡**BANTA AWARD**, Wisconsin Library Association, % Literary Awards Comm., 5250 E. Terrace Dr., Suite A-1, Madison WI 53704-8340. (608)245-3640. Fax: (608)245-3646. Offered annually to books published during the year preceding the award. The Literary Awards committee reviews all works by Wisconsin authors that are not edited, revised editions or written in foreign languages. They may be submitted to the committee or the committee can be notified in a letter from the publisher or author. Deadline: May. Prize: $500, a plaque given by the Banta Corporation Foundation, a presentation at the Annual Conference of the Wisconsin Library Association between late October and early November. Judged by a committee of nine members representing different types of libraries and one library trustee. Only open to writers born and raised in Wisconsin, or currently living in the state. This is only for works that contribute to the world of literature and ideas (adult, not children's). Textbooks are not considered.

BUNTING FELLOWSHIP, Radcliffe College, 34 Concord Ave., Cambridge MA 02138. (617)495-8212. Fax:(617)495-8136. E-mail: bunting_fellowships@radcliffe.harvard.edu. Website: http://www.radcliffe.edu/bunting. Contact: Fellowships Coordinator. "To support women of exceptional promise and demonstrated accomplishment who wish to pursue independent work in academic and professional fields and in the creative arts. Projects with public policy applications are especially encouraged. Applications will be judged on the quality and significance of the proposed project, the applicant's record of accomplishment, and on the difference the fellowship might make in advancing the applicant's career." Deadline varies. Call or write for application. Award is $33,000 stipend, plus office space and access to most resources at Harvard University and Radcliffe College. "The competition for writers is very high. We discourage writers who have not had publications or demonstrated a high level of accomplishment."

‡**DWAA ANNUAL WRITING COMPETITION**, Dog Writers Association of America, 31441 Santa Margarita Pkwy., #A163, Rancho Santa Margarita CA 92688. (714)589-9065. Contest Director: Betsy Sikora Siino. Entries must have appeared in print between September 2 and August 31. "Various categories and special awards are designed to reward excellence annually in the ever-growing field of dog writing." Deadline: September 3. Guidelines and entry forms available for SASE. Charges $12/submission, plus $1/each special award consideration. "The award for the various regular categories is the Maxwell Medallion. In addition, we offer several corporate-sponsored special awards consisting of cash grants and certificates, plaques or trophies." Authors retain all rights to their work, yet their signatures on the entry forms grant the association the right to reprint the material for publicity and anthology purposes. Any writer may enter, however the work must be related in some way to dogs, and it must be published work.

‡**EDITORS' BOOK AWARD**, Pushcart Press, P.O. Box 380, Wainscott NY 11975. (516)324-9300. President: Bill Henderson. Unpublished books. Deadline: September 15. "All mss must be nominated by an editor in a publishing house."

FRIENDS OF THE DALLAS PUBLIC LIBRARY AWARD, The Texas Institute of Letters, P.O. Box 298300, Fort Worth TX 76129. (Must be marked Attn: TCU Press). (817)921-7822. Fax: (817)921-7333. Website: http://www.tcu.

edu/til. Award Director: Judy Alter. Offered annually for submissions published January 1-December 31 of previous year to recognize the writer of the book making the most important contribution to knowledge. Deadline: January 2. Guidelines for SASE. Award: $1,000. Writer must have been born in Texas, have lived in the state at least 2 consecutive years at some time, or the subject matter of the book should be associated with the state.

‡**HAWAI'I AWARD FOR LITERATURE**, State Foundation on Culture and the Arts, 44 Merchant St., Honolulu HI 96813. (808)586-0306. Fax: (808)586-0308. E-mail: sfca@iav.com. Contest/Award Director: Hawai'i Literary Arts Council (Box 11213, Honolulu HI 96828-0213). "The annual award honors the lifetime achievement of a writer whose work is important to Hawai'i and/or Hawai'i's people." Deadline: November. Nominations are a public process; inquiries should be directed to the Hawai'i Literary Arts Council at address listed. Prize: a governor's reception and cash award. "Cumulative work is considered. Self nominations are allowed, but not usual. Fiction, poetry, drama, certain types of nonfiction, screenwriting and song lyrics are considered. The award is not intended to recognize conventional academic writing and reportage, nor is it intended to recognize more commercial types of writing."

LOUISIANA LITERARY AWARD, Louisana Library Association, P.O. Box 3058, Baton Rouge LA 70821. (504)342-4928. Fax: (504)342-3547. E-mail: LLA@pelican.state.lib.la.us. Contact: Literary Award Committee. Estab. 1909. Offered annually for work published during the preceding year related to Louisiana. Guidelines for SASE.

MATURE WOMEN'S GRANTS, The National League of American Pen Women, 1300 17th St., Washington DC 20036. (202)785-1997. Contact: Shirley Holden Helberg, national scholarship chairman. Offered every 2 years to further the 35+ age woman and her creative purposes in art, music and letters. Deadline: January 15, even numbered years. Award announced by July 15. Send letter stating age, background and purpose for the monetary award. Send SASE after August 1 in odd-numbered years for information. Charges $8 fee. Prize: $1,000 each in art, letters and music.

‡**MISSISSIPPI REVIEW PRIZE**, Mississippi Review, U.S.M. Box 5144, Hattiesburg MS 39406. (601)266-4321. Fax: (601)266-5757. E-mail: fb@netdoor.com. Contest Director: Frederick Barthelme. Offered annually for unpublished literary, short fiction and poetry. Charges $10/story, 2 stories maximum. Maximum 6,500 words (25 pages). $5/poem, limit 4 entries/author ($20). Prize: $1,000. $1,000 for fiction, $500 for poetry. Mississippi Review keeps first rights to publication. Contest limited to writers in the U.S.

MODERN LANGUAGE ASSOCIATION PRIZE FOR A FIRST BOOK, Modern Language Association, 10 Astor Place, New York NY 10003-6981. (212)614-6406. Fax: (212)533-0680. Contact: Richard Brod. Offered annually for the first book-length scholarly publication by a current member of the association. To qualify, a book must be a literary or linguistic study, a critical edition of an important work, or a critical biography. Studies dealing with literary theory, media, cultural history and interdisciplinary topics are eligible. Deadline: May 1. Guidelines for SASE. Prize: $1,000 and certificate.

NATIONAL BOOK AWARDS, National Book Foundation, Attn: National Book Awards, 260 Fifth Ave., Room 904, New York NY 10001. (212)685-0261. Fax: (212)213-6570. Executive Director: Neil Baldwin. Awards Coordinator: Kevin La Follette. Fiction, nonfiction and poetry—books by American authors nominated by publishers. Guidelines available June 1 of each year. Deadline: July 15.

JOHN NEWBERY MEDAL, American Library Association, 50 E. Huron St., Chicago IL 60611. (800)545-2433. E-mail: santon@ala.org. Website: http://www.ala.org/alsc.html. Contact: Stephanie Anton, program director. Offered annually to a US author for the most distinguished contribution to American literature for children published in the United States in the preceding year. Guidelines for SASE. Award: medal.

OHIOANA BOOK AWARDS, Ohioana Library Association, 65 S. Front St., Room 1105, Columbus OH 43215. (614)466-3831. Fax: (614)728-6974. E-mail: ohioana@winslo.ohio.gov. Editor: Barbara Maslekoff. Estab. 1929. Books published within the past year by Ohioans or about Ohio and Ohioans, articles about Ohio writers, artists, museums, reviews of Ohio books. Submit 2 copies of book on publication.

‡**THE PARIS REVIEW DISCOVERY PRIZE**, The Paris Review, 541 E. 72nd St., New York NY 10021. (212)861-0016. Offered annually to the best work of fiction or poetry published in *The Paris Review* that year by an emerging or previously published writer. Guidelines for SASE. Prize: $1,000. *The Paris Review* does not ordinarily distinguish between award submissions and regular submissions. The only candidates for awards are writers who have already been published by *The Paris Review*. The magazine retains one-time first serial rights for published works. Submissions must be accompanied by a SASE, must be unpublished and must be written in English.

‡**PEN CENTER WEST LITERARY AWARDS**, PEN Center West, 672 S. Lafayette Park Place, #41, Los Angeles CA 90057. (213)365-8500. Fax: (213)365-9616. E-mail: rit2writ@ix.netcom.com. Contact: Rachel J. Hall, administrative coordinator. Estab. 1952. Awards and $500 cash prizes offered for work published in previous calendar year. Deadline: 4 copies must be received by December 31. Open to writers living west of the Mississippi River. Award categories: fiction, nonfiction, poetry, drama, children's literature, screenplay, teleplay, journalism, criticism, translation.

PULITZER PRIZES, The Pulitzer Prize Board, 702 Journalism, Columbia University, New York NY 10027. (212)854-3841. Website: http://www.pulitzer.org/. Estab. 1917. Journalism in US newspapers (daily or weekly), and in letters, drama and music by Americans. Deadline: Feb. 1 (journalism); Mar. 1 (music and drama); July 1 and Nov. 1 (letters).

ROCKY MOUNTAIN ARTIST'S/ECCENTRIC BOOK COMPETITION, Hemingway Western Studies Center, Boise State University, 1910 University Dr., Boise ID 83725. (208)385-1999. Fax: (208)385-4373. E-mail: ttrusky@quartz.idbsu.edu. Contest Director: Tom Trusky. Offered annually "to publish multiple edition artist's books of special interest to Rocky Mountain readers. Topics must be public issues (race, gender, environment, etc.). Authors may hail from Topeka or Ulan Bator, but their books must initially have regional appeal." Deadline: September 1-December 1. Guidelines for SASE. Prize: $500, publication, standard royalties. First rights to Hemingway Center. Open to any writer/artist.

‡THE CARL SANDBURG LITERARY ARTS AWARDS, The Friends of the Chicago Public Library, 400 S. State St., 10S-7, Chicago IL 60605. (312)747-4907. Fax: (312)747-4077. Estab. 1979. Chicago (and metropolitan area) writers of published fiction, nonfiction, poetry and children's literature. Book must be published between June 1, 1997 and May 31, 1998. Deadline for submission: August 1.

‡THE SEATON AWARD, Kansas Quarterly/Arkansas Review, Dept. of English and Philosophy, Box 1890, State University AR 72467. (501)972-3043. Award Director: Norman Lavers. Offered annually to encourage Kansas writers. Prize: $1,000. Judged by the editors. First North American serial rights are acquired. Contest open to writers with a Kansas connection (born or raised, live or lived, attend or attended school, or in any context lived in Kansas for a minimum of one uninterrupted year). There is no application procedure. If work by the author, in any genre, is accepted for publication in Kansas Quarterly/Arkansas Review, the work is automatically in the running for the award.

SOCIETY OF MIDLAND AUTHORS AWARD, Society of Midland Authors, % P.O. Box 10419, Chicago IL 60610-0419. Offered annually for work published between January 1 and December 31. "Award for best work by writers of the 12 Midwestern states: IL, IN, IA, KS, MI, MN, MO, NB, ND, SD, WI and OH, and the stimulation of creative literary effort. Six categories: poetry, adult fiction, adult nonfiction, biography, juvenile fiction, juvenile nonfiction." Deadline: January 15, of year following publication. Guidelines for SASE. Money and plaque given at annual dinner in Chicago, in May.

‡TORONTO MUNICIPAL CHAPTER IODE BOOK AWARD, Toronto Municipal Chapter IODE, 40 St. Claire Ave. E., Toronto, Ontario M4T 1M9 Canada. (416)925-5078. Fax: (416)925-5127. Contact: IODE Education Committee. Offered annually to previously published books of historical interest to Canadians. Deadline: October 30. Prize: $1,000. Author and illustrator must reside in or around Toronto.

TOWSON STATE UNIVERSITY PRIZE FOR LITERATURE, College of Liberal Arts, Towson State University, Towson MD 21252. (410)830-2128. Award Director: Dean, College of Liberal Arts. Contact: Sue Ann Nordhoff-Klaus, administrative assistant. Estab. 1979. Book or book-length ms that has been accepted for publication, written by a Maryland author of no more than 40 years of age. Deadline: May 15.

SAUL VIENER PRIZE, American Jewish Historical Society, 2 Thornton Rd., Waltham MA 02154. Editor: Marc Lee Raphael. Estab. 1985. Offered every 2 years for work published within previous 2 years. "Award for outstanding scholarly work in American Jewish history." Deadline: February 15. Write/call Marc Lee Raphael. Prize: $500. Open to any writer.

WHITING WRITERS' AWARDS, Mrs. Giles Whiting Foundation, 1133 Avenue of the Americas, 22nd fl., New York NY 10036. Director: Gerald Freund. "The Foundation gives annually $30,000 each to up to ten writers of poetry, fiction, nonfiction and plays. The awards place special emphasis on exceptionally promising emerging talent." Direct applications and informal nominations are not accepted by the Foundation.

WORLD FANTASY AWARDS ASSOCIATION, 5 Winding Brook Dr., #1B, Guilderland NY 12084-9719. Website: http://farrsite.com/wfc/wfc6.htm. President: Peter Dennis Pautz. Estab. 1975. Previously published work recommended by previous convention attendees in several categories, including life achievement, novel, novella, short story, anthology, collection, artist, special award-pro and special award non-pro. Deadline: July 1. Works are recommended by attendees of current and previous 2 years' conventions, and a panel of judges. Winners determined by vote of panel.

Nonfiction

ABC-CLIO AMERICA: HISTORY AND LIFE AWARD, Organization of American Historians, 112 N. Bryan St., Bloomington IN 47408-4199. (812)855-9852. Fax: (812)855-0696. E-mail: awards@oah.indiana.edu. Website: http://www.indiana.edu/~oah. Contact: Award and Prize Committee Coordinator. Offered every two years for a previously published article to recognize and encourage scholarship in American history in the journal literature advancing new perspectives on accepted interpretations or previously unconsidered topics. Deadline: November 15 of even-numbered years. Guidelines for SASE. Prize: cash award and certificate.

AIP SCIENCE WRITING AWARDS IN PHYSICS & ASTRONOMY, American Institute of Physics, One Physics Ellipse, College Park MD 20740. (301)209-3090. Fax: (301)209-0846. E-mail: jwrather@aip.acp.org. Website: http://www.aip.org. Contact: Joan Wrather, manager Public Information Division. Offered annually for previously published work "to recognize and stimulate distinguished writing that improves the general public's understanding and appreciation of physics and astronomy." Deadlines: articles, booklets or books by professional journalists published between January 1-December 31 due February 6; articles, booklets or books intended for children up to 15 years published between July 1-June 30 due July 24; articles, booklets or books by physicists or astronomers published between May 1-April 30 due May 19. Guidelines for SASE. Prize: $3,000, inscribed Windsor chair, certificate and certificate to publisher.

ANTHEM ESSAY CONTEST, Ayn Rand Institute. Fax: (310)306-4925. E-mail: mail@aynrand.org. Website: http://www.aynrand.org. Contact: David Bombardier. Offered annually. Purpose of award is to encourage analytical thinking and excellence in writing, and to introduce students to the philosophic ideas of Ayn Rand. Deadline: April 1. Contact your English teacher or guidance counselor, or visit the website. Prizes: 1st-$1,000, 2nd-$200 (10) and 3rd-$100 (20). Open to 9th and 10th graders.

VINCENT ASTOR MEMORIAL LEADERSHIP ESSAY CONTEST, US Naval Institute, 118 Maryland Ave., Annapolis MD 21402-5035. (410)295-1058. Fax: (410)269-7940. Website: http://www.usni.org. Contact: Valry Fetrow. Essays on the topic of leadership in the sea services (junior officers and officer trainees). Deadline: February 15.

RAY ALLEN BILLINGTON PRIZE, Organization of American Historians, 112 N. Bryan St., Bloomington IN 47408-4199. (812)855-9852. Fax: (812)855-0696. Contact: Award and Prize Committee Coordinator. E-mail: awards@oah.indiana.edu. Website: http://www.indiana.edu/~oah. Offered every two years for the best book in American frontier history, defined as including the pioneer periods of all geographical areas and comparisons between American frontiers and others. Deadline: Oct. 1 of even-numbered years. Guidelines for SASE. Prize: cash award, certificate and medal.

THE BROSS PRIZE, Lake Forest College, 555 N. Sheridan, Lake Forest IL 60045. (847)735-5169. Fax: (847)735-6291. Contact: Professor Ron Miller. Offered every 10 years for unpublished work "to award the best book or treatise on the relation between any discipline or topic of investigation and the Christian religion." Deadline: September 1, 2000. Guidelines for SASE. Prize: Award varies depending on interest earned. Manuscripts awarded prizes become property of the college. Open to any writer.

ARLEIGH BURKE ESSAY CONTEST, US Naval Institute, 118 Maryland Ave., Annapolis MD 21402-5035. (410)295-1058. Fax: (410)269-7940. Website: http://www.usni.org. Contact: Valry Fetrow. Estab. 1873. Essay that advances professional, literary or scientific knowledge of the naval and maritime services. Deadline: December 1.

‡CANADIAN LIBRARY ASSOCIATION STUDENT ARTICLE CONTEST, Canadian Library Association, 200 Elgin St., Suite 602, Ottawa, Ontario K2P 1L5 Canada. (613)232-9625, ext. 318. Fax: (613)563-9895. Contest Director: Brenda Shields. Offered annually to "unpublished articles discussing, analyzing or evaluating timely issues in librarianship or information science." Deadline: March 15. Guidelines for SASE. Prizes: 1st-$150, publication in *Feliciter*, trip to CLA's annual conference; Runners-Up: $75 choice of CLA publications. Judged by a CLA panel. "Open to all students registered in or recently graduated from a Canadian library school, a library techniques program or faculty of education library program. Submissions may be in English or French."

CLIFFORD PRIZE, American Society for 18th Century Studies, Computer Center 108, Utah State University, Logan UT 84322-3730. Phone/fax: (801)797-4065. E-mail: uthomp@email.unc.edu. Website: http://www.usu.edu/~english/asecs.html. Executive Secretary: Dr. Jeffrey Smitten. Contact: James Thompson, Mary Sheriff (UNC-Chapel Hill). Offered annually for previously published work, "the best nominated article, an outstanding study of some aspect of 18th-century culture, interesting to any 18th-century specialist, regardless of discipline." Guidelines for SASE. Must submit 8 copies of the article. Prize: $500, certificate. Winners must be society members ($25-65 dues).

COAST GUARD ESSAY CONTEST, Naval Institute Essay and Photo Contests, 118 Maryland Ave., Annapolis MD 21402-5035. (410)268-6110. Fax: (410)269-7940. Website: http://www.usni.org. Contact: Valry Fetrow. Offered annually for original, analytical and/or interpretative, unpublished essays; maximum 3,000 words. Essays must discuss current issues and new directions for the Coast Guard. Deadline: June 1. Guidelines available. Prizes: $1,000, $750 and $500. Winning essays are published in December *Proceedings*. Open to anyone.

MORTON N. COHEN AWARD, Modern Language Association of America, 10 Astor Place, New York NY 10003-6981. (212)475-9500. Fax: (212)533-0680. E-mail: awards@mla.org. Contact: Richard Brod. Estab. 1989. Awarded in odd-numbered years for a previously published distinguished edition of letters. At least 1 volume of the edition must have been published during the previous 2 years. Prize: $1,000. Guidelines for #10 SASE. Deadline: May 1.

‡THE NATHAN COHEN AWARD FOR EXCELLENCE IN THEATRE CRITICISM, The Canadian theatre Critics Association, 250 Dundas St. W., Suite 700, Toronto, Ontario M5T 2Z5 Canada. (416)367-8896. Fax: (416)367-5992. E-mail: artemis@adeo.comm. Contact: Jeniva Berger. Offered annually to previously published theater criticism published between January 1-December 31. "The national award is presented annually to help recognize high critical standards and to give encouragement to those working professionally in the field of theater criticism. There are two categories: Long Review for reviews, profiles and other theatrical features of 1,000 words to a maximum of 4,000 words; and Short Review for reviews of up to 1,000 words." Deadline: April 1. Guidelines for SASE. Charges $10 fee. Prize: $500 and a framed certificate. "There is a different judge each year. Our judges have been renowned Canadian theater people—writers such as Timothy Findley, playwrights such as Sharon Pollock, and performers such as R.H. Thomson." Entrants must be Canadian or Canadian residents. Entries must have been published during the specified dates. Photocopies or originals of the published works should be submitted as proof, along with the name of the editor and the date of publication. If photocopies are submitted, they must be clearly legible and with numbered pages.

CARR P. COLLINS AWARD, The Texas Institute of Letters, P.O. Box 298300, Fort Worth TX 76129. (817)921-7822. Fax: (817)921-7333. Secretary-Treasurer: Judy Alter. Offered annually for work published January 1-December 31 of the previous year to recognize the best nonfiction book by a writer who was born in Texas or who has lived in the state for at least 2 consecutive years at 1 point or a writer whose work has some notable connection with Texas. Deadline: January 2. Guidelines for SASE. Prize: $5,000.

‡COLORADO PRIZE, Colorado Review/Center for Literary Publishing, 359 Eddy, Ft. Collins CO 80523. (970)491-5449. Fax: (970)491-5601. Contest Director: David Milofsky. Offered annually to an unpublished collection. Deadline: January 15. Guidelines for SASE. Charges $22 fee. Prize: $1,000 and publication of book.

‡COMPETITION FOR WRITERS OF B.C. (BRITISH COLUMBIA) HISTORY, B.C. Historical Federation, 7953 Rosewood St., Burnaby, British Columbia V5E 2H4 Canada. (604)522-2062. Contest Director: Mrs. Pixie McGeachie. Offered annually to books published during contest year "to promote the history of British Columbia." Deadline: December 31. Guidelines for SASE. Prizes: 1st-The Lieutenant Governor's Medal for Historical Writing and $300, 2nd-$200, 3rd-$100. All 3 winners also receive framed certificates. Open to any writer. Book must contain any facet of B.C. history. Submit 2 copies must be submitted to the contest and they become the property of the B.C. Historical Federation.

AVERY O. CRAVEN AWARD, Organization of American Historians, 112 N. Bryan St., Bloomington IN 47408-4199. (812)855-9852. Fax: (812)855-0696. E-mail: awards@oah.indiana.edu. Website: http://www.indiana.edu/~oah. Contact: Award and Prize Committee Coordinator. Offered annually for the most original book on the coming of the Civil War, the Civil War years, or the Era of Reconstruction, with the exception of works of purely military history. Deadline: October 1. Guidelines for SASE. Prize: cash award and certificate.

MERLE CURTI AWARD, Organization of American Historians, 112 N. Bryan St., Bloomington IN 47408-4199. (812)855-9852. Fax: (812)855-0696. E-mail: awards@oah.indiana.edu. Website: http://www.indiana.edu/~oah. Contact: Award and Prize Committee Coordinator. Offered annually for books in the field of American social history (even-numbered years) and intellectual history (odd-numbered years). Deadline: October 1. Guidelines for SASE. Prize: cash award, certificate and medal.

DEXTER PRIZE, Society for the History of Technology, History Dept., Auburn University, 310 Thach Hall, Auburn AL 36849. (334)844-6645. Fax: (334)844-6673. Contact: Society Secretary. Estab. 1968. For work published in the previous 3 years: for 1997—1994 to 96. "Award given to the best book in the history of technology." Deadline: April 15. Guidelines for SASE. Prize: $2,000 and a plaque from the Dexter Chemical Company.

‡ANNIE DILLARD AWARD IN NONFICTION, The Bellingham Review, M.S. 9053, Western Washington University, Bellingham WA 98225. Website: http://www.wwu.edu/~bkreview/. Contact: Mr. Robin Hemley. Unpublished essay on any subject and in any style. Submissions from January 2-March 1. Guidelines and entry fees for SASE. Prize: 1st-$500; 2nd-$250; 3rd-$100, plus publication and copies.

EDUCATOR'S AWARD, The Delta Kappa Gamma Society, P.O. Box 1589, Austin TX 78767. (512)478-5748. Fax: (512)478-3961. E-mail: societyd@onr.com. Executive Coordinator: Dr. Theresa Fechek. Offered annually for quality fiction published January-December of previous year. This award recognizes educational research and writings of women authors whose book may influence the direction of thought and action necessary to meet the needs to today's complex society. Deadline: Feb. 1. Guidelines for SASE. Prize: $1,500. The book must be written by 1-2 women who are citizens of any country in which The Delta Kappa Gamma Society Int'l is organized: Canada, Costa Rica, El Salvador, Finland, Germany Great Britain, Guatemala, Iceland, Mexico, The Netherlands, Norway, Puerto Rico, Sweden, United States.

WILFRED EGGLESTON AWARD FOR NONFICTION, Writers Guild of Alberta, 11759 Great Rd., Edmonton Alberta T5M 3K6 Canada. (403)422-8174. Fax: (403)422-2663. E-mail: writers@compusmart.ab.ca. Assistant Director: Darlene Diver. Nonfiction book published in current year. Must be an Alberta author.

‡THE ALFRED EINSTEIN AWARD, American Musicological Society, 201 S. 34th St., Philadelphia PA 19104. (215)898-8698. Fax: (216)573-3673. Contact: Alfred Einstein Award Committee. Offered annually for material previously published from June 1-May 31 of the previous year. "The Alfred Einstein Award will honor each year a musicological article of exceptional merit by a scholar in the early stages of his or her career who is a citizen or permanent resident of Canada or the US." Deadline: June 1. No entry form. "The committee will entertain nomination from any individual, including eligible authors, who are encouraged to nominate their own articles. Nominations should include: author's name, title of article, name and year of periodical where published." Prize: $400 and certificate. "The article must have been published during the preceding calendar year, in any country and in any language. The article must be written by a scholar in the early stages of his or her career, 'early stages' typically indicated by time from completion of Ph.D. degree or academic appointment at non-tenured level."

‡RALPH WALDO EMERSON AWARD, Phi Beta Kappa Society, 1811 Q St., N.W., Washington DC 20009. (202)265-3808. Fax: (202)986-1601. E-mail: lsurles@pbk.org. Award Director: Linda D. Surles. Offered annually for scholarly studies of the intellectual and cultural condition of man. Submissions are required to be published between May 1, 1997 and April 30, 1998. Deadline: April 30. Guidelines for SASE. Prize: $2,500. Judged by the Committee for the Ralph Waldo Emerson Award (seven members).

FOREIGN LANGUAGE BOOK AND FOREIGN LANGUAGE ARTICLE PRIZES, Organization of American Historians, 112 N. Bryan St., Bloomington IN 47408-4199. (812)855-9852. Fax: (812)855-0696. E-mail: awards@oah.in diana.edu. Website: http://www.indiana.edu/~oah. Contact: Award and Prize Committee Coordinator. Offered annually for the best book and the best article on American history that have been published in languages other than English. Eligible books or articles should be concerned with the past (recent or distant) or with issues of continuity and change. Entries should also be concerned with events or processes that began, developed, or ended in what is now the United States. Deadline: April 1. Guidelines for SASE. Prize: English translation and publication. Winning article will be printed in the *Journal of American History* and its author awarded a certificate and a $500 subvention for refining the article's English translation; winning book will receive $1,000 toward translation for publication in English, and the author will receive a certificate.

GEORGE FREEDLEY MEMORIAL AWARD, Theatre Library Association, Benjamin Rosenthal Library, Queens College, C.U.N.Y., 65-30 Kissena Blvd., Flushing NY 11367. (718)997-3799. Fax: (718)997-3753. E-mail: rlwqc@cuny vm.cuny.edu. Contact: Richard Wall, Book Awards Committee Chair. Estab. 1968. Book published in the United States within the previous calendar year on a subject related to live theatrical performance (including cabaret, circus, pantomime, puppetry, vaudeville, etc.). Eligible books may include biography, history, theory, criticism, reference or related fields. Prize: $250 and certificate to the winner; $100 and certificate for Honorable Mention. Submissions and deadline: Nominated books are requested from publishers; one copy should be received by each of three award jurors as well as the Chairperson by February 15 of the year following eligibility.

THE CHRISTIAN GAUSS AWARD, The Phi Beta Kappa Society, 1811 Q St. NW, Washington DC 20009-1696. (202)265-3808. Fax: (202)986-1601. E-mail: lsurles@pbk.org. Contact: Administrator, Phi Beta Kappa Book Awards. Estab. 1950. Works of literary criticism or scholarship published in the US during the 12-month period preceding the entry deadline, and submitted by the publisher. Books must have been published May 1, 1997-April 30, 1998. Deadline: April 30. Author must be a US citizen or resident. Prize: $2,500.

LIONEL GELBER PRIZE, Lionel Gelber Foundation, 112 Braemore Gardens, Toronto Ontario M6G 2C8 Canada. (416)652-1947 or (416)656-3722. Fax: (416)658-5205. E-mail: oomfpub@pathcom.com. Prize Manager: Meisner Publicity. The largest juried prize of its kind, the international Lionel Gelber Prize is awarded annually in Canada to the author of the year's most outstanding work of nonfiction in the field of international relations. Books must be published in English or English translation between September 1, 1997 and August 31, 1998. Deadline: May 31. Guidelines for SASE; however, the publisher must submit the title on behalf of the author. Prize: $50,000 (Canadian funds).

LOUIS GOTTSCHALK PRIZE 1997, American Society for 18th Century Studies, Computer Center 108, Utah State University, Logan UT 84322-3730. Phone/fax: (801)797-4065. E-mail: uthomp@email.unc.edu. Website: http:// www.usu.edu/~english/asecs.html. Executive Secretary: Jeffrey Smitten. Contact: James Thompson, Mary Sheriff (UNC-Chapel Hill). Offered annually for previously published (between January 1996 and December 1997) work. Purpose is to award outstanding historical or critical study on the 18th century. Deadline: November 15, 1997. Guidelines and form available for SASE. Publisher must send 5 copies for contest. Prize: $1,000 and certificate from ASECS. Judged by committee of distinguished members. Winners must be society members ($25-65 dues).

‡G.K. HALL AWARD FOR LIBRARY LITERATURE, American Library Association, 50 E. Huron St., Chicago IL 60611. (312)280-3247. Fax: (312)280-3257. Offered annually to previously published books that make an outstanding contribution to library literature. Deadline: December 1. Guidelines for SASE or e-mail awards@ala.org. Prize: $500 and framed citation.

THE ILLINOIS-NWSA MANUSCRIPT AWARD, National Women's Studies Association, 7100 Baltimore Ave., #301, College Park MD 20715. (301)403-0525. Fax: (301)403-4137. E-mail: nwsa@umail.umd.edu. Contact: Loretta Younger, national executive administrator. Offered annually for unpublished quality fiction. Presented for the best book-length ms in women's studies. Deadline: Jan. 31. Guidelines for SASE. Prize: $1,000 and publication by Univ. of Illinois

Press. Anthologies, essay collections, fiction, poetry and unrevised doctoral dissertations are ineligible.

‡THE OTTO KENKELDEY AWARD, American Musicological Society, 201 S. 34th St., Philadelphia PA 19104. (215)898-8698. Fax: (216)573-3673. Contact: James Haar, Music Dept., Hill Hall, University of North Carolina, Chapel Hill NC 27599-3320. Offered annually for material published during the previous year. "The Otto Kenkeldey Award will honor each year the work of musicological scholarship deemed to be the most distinguished of those published during the previous year in any language in any country by a scholar who is a citizen or permanent resident of Canada or the U.S. Nominations, including self-nominations and publications may be submitted to the chair of the committee. Nominations and submissions are not requested, but neither are they discouraged." Prize: $400 and certificate. "Works should be a major book, edition, or other piece of scholarship that best exemplifies the highest qualities of originality of interpretation, clarity of though, and communication. It should be a work of musicological scholarship."

THE KIRIYAMA PACIFIC RIM BOOK PRIZE, Kiriyama Pacific Rim Foundation and University of San Francisco Center for the Pacific Rim, University of San Francisco Center for the Pacific Rim, 2130 Fulton St., San Francisco CA 94117-1080. (415)422-5984. Fax: (415)422-5933. E-mail: pacrim@usfca.edu. Website: http://www.usfca.edu/pac_rim/kiriyama.html. Contest Director: Dr. Barbara Bundy. Offered for work published November 1-October 31 of the award year to promote books that will contribute to better understanding and increased cooperation throughout all areas of the Pacific Rim. Deadline: July 1. Prize: $30,000 to be divided equally between the publisher and author. Books must be submitted for entry by the publisher. Proper entry forms must be submitted.

KATHERINE SINGER KOVACS PRIZE, Modern Language Association of America, 10 Astor Place, New York NY 10003-6981. (212)614-6406. Fax: (212)533-0680. E-mail: awards@mla.org. Contact: Richard Brod. Estab. 1990. Offered annually for book in English on Latin American or Spanish literatures or cultures published in previous year. Authors need not be members of the MLA. Guidelines for #10 SASE. Prize: $1,000. Deadline: May 1.

RICHARD W. LEOPOLD PRIZE, Organization of American Historians, 112 N. Bryan St., Bloomington IN 47408-4199. (812)855-9852. Fax: (812)855-0696. E-mail: awards@oah.indiana.edu. Website: http://www.indiana.edu/~oah. Contact: Award and Prize Committee Coordinator. Offered every 2 years for the best book written by a historian connected with federal, state, or municipal government, in the areas of foreign policy, military affairs broadly construed, the historical activities of the federal government, or biography in one of the foregoing areas. The winner must have been employed in a government position for at least 5 years, and the publisher should include verification of this fact when a book is submitted. Deadline: September 1 of odd-numbered years. Prize: cash award and certificate.

JAMES RUSSELL LOWELL PRIZE, Modern Language Association of America, 10 Astor Place, New York NY 10003-6981. (212)475-9500. Fax: (212)533-6080. E-mail: awards@mla.org. Contact: Richard Brod. Offered annually for literary or linguistic study, or critical edition or biography published in previous year. Open to MLA members only. Guidelines for #10 SASE. Prize: $1,000. Deadline: March 1.

McLEMORE PRIZE, Mississippi Historical Society, P.O. Box 571, Jackson MS 39205-0571. (601)359-6850. Fax: (601)359-6975. Secretary: Elbert R. Hilliard. Estab. 1902. Scholarly book on a topic in Mississippi history/biography published in the year of competition (year previous to January 1 deadline). Deadline: January 1.

‡THE MACPHERSON PRIZE, Canadian Political Science Association, 1 Stewart St., #205, Ottawa, Ontario K1N 6H7 Canada. (613)564-4026. Fax: (613)230-2746. E-mail: cpsa@csse.ca. Contact: Michelle Hopkins. Contest offered every 2 years (even years) for the best book published in English or in French, in the field of political theory. Deadline: December 10. Guidelines for SASE. Prize: $750 and a set of the books submitted. The author must be either a Canadian citizen or a permanent resident (landed immigrant) who resides in Canada. Single-authored books only.

MARINE CORPS ESSAY CONTEST, Naval Institute Essay and Photo Contests, 118 Maryland Ave., Annapolis MD 21402-5035. (410)268-6110. Fax: (410)269-7940. Website: http://www.usni.org. Contact: Valry Fetrow. Offered annually for original, analytical and/or interpretative, unpublished essays; maximum 3,000 words. Essays must discuss current issues and new directions for the Marine Corps. Deadline: May 1. Guidelines available. Prizes: $1,000, $750 and $500. Winning essays published in November *Proceedings*. Open to anyone.

HOWARD R. MARRARO PRIZE and SCAGLIONE PRIZE FOR ITALIAN LITERARY STUDIES, Modern Language Association of America, 10 Astor Place, New York NY 10003-6981. (212)614-6406. Fax: (212)533-0680. E-mail: awards@mla.org. Contact: Richard Brod. Joint prize offered in even-numbered years for books or essays on any phase of Italian literature or comparative literature involving Italian, published in previous 2 years. Open to MLA members only. Guidelines for #10 SASE. Prize: $1,000. Deadline: May 1.

THE MAYFLOWER SOCIETY CUP COMPETITION, North Carolina Literary and Historical Association, 109 E. Jones St., Room 305, Raleigh NC 27601-2807. (919)733-7305. Contact: Rita Cashion, awards coordinator. Previously published nonfiction by a North Carolina resident. Deadline: July 15.

KENNETH W. MILDENBERGER PRIZE, Modern Language Association of America, 10 Astor Place, New York NY 10003-6981. (212)614-6406. Fax: (212)533-0680. E-mail: awards@mla.org. Contact: Richard Brod. Offered annually for a research publication from the previous year in the field of teaching foreign languages and literatures. Guidelines for #10 SASE. Prize: $500 and a year's membership in the MLA. Deadline: May 1. Author need not be member.

MLA PRIZE FOR A DISTINGUISHED SCHOLARLY EDITION, Modern Language Association of America, 10 Astor Place, New York NY 10003-6981. (212)614-6406. Fax: (212)533-0680. E-mail: awards@mla.org. Director of Special Projects: Richard Brod. Offered in odd-numbered years. Work published between 1995 and 1996 qualifies for the 1997 competition. To qualify for the award, an edition should be based on an examination of all available relevant textual sources; the source texts and the edited text's deviations from them should by fully described; the edition should employ editorial principles appropriate to the materials edited, and those principles should be clearly articulated in the volume; the text should be accompanied by appropriate textual and other historical contextual information; the edition should exhibit the highest standards of accuracy in the presentation of its text and apparatus; and the text and apparatus should be presented as accessibly and elegantly as possible. Deadline: May 1. Guidelines for SASE. Prize: $1,000 and certificate. Editor need not be a member of the MLA.

MLA PRIZE FOR INDEPENDENT SCHOLARS, Modern Language Association of America, 10 Astor Place, New York NY 10003-6981. (212)614-6406. Fax: (212)533-0680. E-mail: awards@mla.org. Contact: Richard Brod. Offered annually for book in the field of English or another modern language or literature published in previous year. Authors who hold tenured or tenured-track positions in higher education are not eligible. Authors do not need to be members of MLA to compete for this prize. Guidelines and application form for SASE. Prize: $1,000 and a year's membership in the MLA. Deadline: May 1.

NATIONAL JEWISH BOOK AWARD—AUTOBIOGRAPHY/MEMOIR, Sandra Brand and Arik Weintraub Award, Jewish Book Council, 15 E. 26th St., New York NY 10010. (212)532-4949. Director: Carolyn Starman Hessel. Offered annually to an author of an autobiography or a memoir of the life of a Jewish person.

NATIONAL JEWISH BOOK AWARD—CONTEMPORARY JEWISH LIFE, The Jewish Book Council, 15 E. 26th St., New York NY 10010. (212)532-4949. Contact: Carolyn Starman Hessel. Offered annually for a nonfiction work dealing with the sociology of modern Jewish life.

NATIONAL JEWISH BOOK AWARD—HOLOCAUST, Leon Jolson Award, Jewish Book Council, 15 E. 26th St., New York NY 10010. (212)532-4949. Contact: Carolyn Starman Hessel. Offered annually for a nonfiction book concerning the Holocaust. Deadline: September 1.

NATIONAL JEWISH BOOK AWARD—JEWISH CHRISTIAN RELATIONS, Chas. H. Revson Foundation Award, Jewish Book Council, 15 E. 26th St., New York NY 10010. (212)532-4949, ext. 297. Fax: (212)481-4174. President Arthur Kurzweil. Executive Director: Carolyn Starman Hessel. Offered for a nonfiction work detailing some aspect of Jewish-Christian relations.

‡**NATIONAL JEWISH BOOK AWARD—JEWISH HISTORY**, Gerrard and Ella Berman Award, Jewish Book Council, 15 E. 26th St., New York NY 10010. (212)532-4949 ext. 297. Director: Carolyn Starman Hessel. Offered annually for a book of Jewish history. Deadline: September 1.

NATIONAL JEWISH BOOK AWARD—JEWISH THOUGHT, Dorot Foundation Award, Jewish Book Council, 15 E. 26th St., New York NY 10010. (212)532-4949. Director: Carolyn Starman Hessel. Offered annually for a book dealing with some aspect of Jewish thought, past or present. Deadline: September 1.

NATIONAL JEWISH BOOK AWARD—SCHOLARSHIP, Sarah H. and Julius Kushner Memorial Award, Jewish Book Council, 15 E. 26th St., New York NY 10010. (212)532-4949. Director: Carolyn Starman Hessel. Offered annually for a book which makes an original contribution to Jewish learning. Deadline: September 1.

NATIONAL JEWISH BOOK AWARD—VISUAL ARTS, Anonymous Award, Jewish Book Council, 15 E. 26th St., New York NY 10010. (212)532-4949. Director: Carolyn Starman Hessel. Offered annually for a book about Jewish art. Deadline: September 1.

NATIONAL WRITERS ASSOCIATION NONFICTION CONTEST, The National Writers Association, Suite 424, 1450 S. Havana, Aurora CO 80012. (303)751-7844. Fax: (303)751-8593. E-mail: sandywrter@aol.com. Director: Sandy Whelchel. Annual contest "to encourage writers in this creative form and to recognize those who excel in nonfiction writing." Charges $18 fee. Deadline: December 31. Prizes: $200, $100, $50. Guidelines for #10 SASE.

THE FREDERIC W. NESS BOOK AWARD, Association of American Colleges and Universities, 1818 R St. NW, Washington DC 20009. (202)387-3760. Fax: (202)265-9532. Website: www.aacu-edu.org. Director for Membership: Peggy Neal. Offered annually for work previously published July 1-June 30 of the year in which it is being considered. "Each year the Frederic W. Ness Book Award Committee of the Association of American Colleges and Universities recognizes books which contribute to the understanding and improvement of liberal education." Deadline: August 15. Guidelines and entry forms for SASE. "Writers may nominate their own work; however, we send letters of invitation to publishers to nominate qualified books." Prize: Presentation at the association's annual meeting and $1,000. Transportation and one night hotel for meeting are also provided.

NEW JERSEY COUNCIL FOR THE HUMANITIES BOOK AWARD, New Jersey Council for the Humanities (NJCH), 28 W. State St., 6th Floor, New Brunswick NJ 08608. (609)695-4838. Fax: (609)695-4929. Coordinator: Erica Mosner. Offered annually for work previously published April 1-March 31 to honor a title by a New Jersey author or a New Jersey subject and to bring more exposure to humanities books that stimulate curiosity and enrich the general public's understanding of their world. Guidelines for SASE. "Publisher only must nominate the book, but author can call us and we will send the information directly to their publisher." Prize: $1,000 for the author, and title distributed to up to 100 libraries throughout New Jersey. Judged by NJCH's Book Award Committee.

NEW YORK STATE HISTORICAL ASSOCIATION MANUSCRIPT AWARD, P.O. Box 800, Cooperstown NY 13326-0800. (607)547-1481. Director of Publications: Dr. Wendell Tripp. Estab. 1973. Unpublished book-length monograph on New York State history. Deadline: January 20.

NORTH AMERICAN INDIAN PROSE AWARD, University of Nebraska Press, 327 Nebraska Hall, Lincoln NE 68588-0520. Fax: (402)472-0308. E-mail: gdunham@unlinfo.unl.edu. Editor, Native American Studies: Gary H. Dunham. Offered for the best new work by an American Indian writer. Prize: publication by the University of Nebraska Press with $1,000 advance. Guidelines for #10 SASE. Deadline: July 1.

NWSA GRADUATE SCHOLARSHIP IN LESBIAN STUDIES, National Women's Studies Association, 7100 Baltimore Ave., #301, College Park MD 20715. (301)403-0525. Fax: (301)403-4137. Offered annually for unpublished quality fiction awarded to a student who will be doing research for or writing a Master's thesis or Ph.D. dissertation in Lesbian Studies. Guidelines for SASE. Prize: $500.

ELI M. OBOLER MEMORIAL AWARD, American Library Association's Intellectual Freedom Round Table, 50 E. Huron St., Chicago IL 60611. (312)280-4224. Contact: Chairman. Offered every 2 years "to the author of an article (including a review), a series of thematically connected articles, a book, or a manual published on the local, state or national level, in English or in English translation. The works to be considered must have as their central concern one or more issues, events, questions or controversies in the area of intellectual freedom, including matters of ethical, political, or social concern related to intellectual freedom. The work for which the award is granted must have been published within the *two-year* period ending the December prior to the ALA Annual Conference at which it is granted." Deadline: December 1, 1997.

FRANK LAWRENCE AND HARRIET CHAPPELL OWSLEY AWARD, Southern Historical Association, Department of History, University of Georgia, Athens GA 30602-1602. (706)542-8848. Fax: (706)542-2455. Managing Editor: John B. Boles. Contact: Secretary-Treasurer. Estab. 1934. Offered in odd-numbered years for recognition of a distinguished book in Southern history published in even-numbered years. Publishers usually submit the books. Deadline: March 1.

LOUIS PELZER MEMORIAL AWARD, Organization of American Historians, 112 N. Bryan St., Bloomington IN 47408-4199. (812)855-9852. Fax: (812)855-0696. E-mail: awards@oah.indiana.edu. Website: http://www.indiana.edu/~oah. Contact: Award and Prize Committee Coordinator. Offered annually for the best essay in American history by a graduate student. The essay may be about any period or topic in the history of the United States, and the author must be enrolled in a graduate program at any level, in any field. Entries should not exceed 7,000 words and should be mailed to *Journal of American History*, 1125 E. Atwater, Indiana University, Bloomington, IN 47401. Deadline: November 30. Guidelines for SASE. Prize: cash award, medal, certificate and publication in the *Journal of American History*.

PEN/JERARD FUND, PEN American Center, 568 Broadway, New York NY 10012. (212)334-1660. Fax: (212)334-2181. E-mail: pen@echonyc.com. Contact: John Morrone. Estab. 1986. Biennial grant of $4,000 for American woman writer of nonfiction for a booklength work in progress in odd-numbered years. Guidelines for #10 SASE. Next award: 1999. Deadline: January 2.

PEN/MARTHA ALBRAND AWARD FOR FIRST NONFICTION, PEN American Center, 568 Broadway, New York NY 10012. (212)334-1660. Fax: (212)334-2181. E-mail: pen@echonyc.com. Coordinator: John Morrone. Offered annually for a first-published book of general nonfiction distinguished by qualities of literary and stylistic excellence. Eligible books must have been published in the calendar year under consideration. Authors must be American citizens or permanent residents. Although there are no restrictions on the subject matter of titles submitted, non-literary books will not be considered. Books should be of adult nonfiction for the general or academic reader. Deadline: December 15. Publishers, agents and authors themselves must submit 3 copies of each eligible title. Prize: $1,000 and a residence at the Johnson Studio Center, Johnson, Vermont.

PEN/SPIELVOGEL-DIAMONSTEIN AWARD, PEN American Center, 568 Broadway, New York NY 10012. (212)334-1660. Fax: (212)334-2181. E-mail: pen@echonyc.com. Coordinator: John Morrone. Offered for the best previously unpublished collection of essays on any subject by an American writer. "The $5,000 prize is awarded to preserve the dignity and esteem that the essay form imparts to literature." Authors must be American citizens or permanent residents. The essays included in books submitted may have been previously published in magazines, journals or anthologies, but must not have collectively appeared before in book form. Books will be judged on literary character and distinction of the writing. Publishers, agents, or the authors must submit 4 copies of each ms. Deadline: Dec. 15.

PERGAMON-NWSA GRADUATE SCHOLARSHIP IN WOMEN'S STUDIES, National Women's Studies Association, 7100 Baltimore Ave., #301, College Park MD 20715. (301)403-0525. Fax: (301)403-4137. Offered annually for unpublished quality fiction to award a student who will be doing research for or writing a Master's thesis or Ph.D. dissertation in the interdisciplinary field of women's studies. Guidelines for SASE. Prize: 1st-$1,000, 2nd-$500. Special preference given to NWSA members and to those whose research projects on women examine color or class.

‡PHI BETA KAPPA AWARD IN SCIENCE, Phi Beta Kappa Society, 1811 Q St., N.W., Washington DC 20009. (202)265-3808. Fax: (202)986-1601. E-mail: lsurles@pbk.org. Award Director: Linda D. Surles. Offered annually to outstanding contributions by scientists to the literature of science. Submissions are required to be published between May 1, 1997 and April 30, 1998. Deadline: April 30. Guidelines for SASE. Prize: $2,500. Judged by the Committee for the PBK Award in Science (5 members). Open to scientists only. No science writers.

PHI BETA KAPPA BOOK AWARDS, The Phi Beta Kappa Society, 1811 Q St. NW, Washington DC 20009-1696. (202)265-3808. Fax: (202)986-1601. Contact: Book Awards Administrator. Estab. 1776. Offered annually to recognize and honor outstanding scholarly books published in the US May 1, 1996-April 30, 1997 in the fields of the humanities, the social sciences, and the natural sciences and mathematics. Deadline: April 30. "Authors may request information, however books must be submitted by the publisher." Entrants must be U.S. citizens or residents.

COLIN L. POWELL JOINT WARFIGHTING ESSAY CONTEST, Naval Institute Essay and Photo Contests, 118 Maryland Ave., Annapolis MD 21402-5035. (410)268-6110. Fax: (410)269-7940. Website: http://www.usni.org. Contact: Valry Fetrow. Offered annually for original, analytical and/or interpretative, unpublished essays; maximum 3,000 words. Essays must discuss combat readiness in a joint context (key issues involving two or more services). Essays may be heavy in uni-service detail, but must have joint application in terms of tactics, strategy, weaponry, combat training, force structure, doctrine, operations, organization for combat, or interoperability of hardware, software and procedures. Deadline: April 1. Guidelines available. Prizes: $2,500, $2,000 and $1,000. Winning essays published in July *Proceedings*. Open to military professionals and civilians.

JAMES A. RAWLEY PRIZE, Organization of American Historians, 112 N. Bryan St., Bloomington IN 47408-4199. (812)855-9852. Fax: (812)855-0696. E-mail: awards@oah.indiana.edu. Website: http://www.indiana.edu/~oah. Contact: Award and Prize Committee Coordinator. Offered annually for a book dealing with the history of race relations in the US. Deadline: October 1. Guidelines for SASE. Prize: cash award and certificate.

‡PHILLIP D. REED MEMORIAL AWARD FOR OUTSTANDING WRITING ON THE SOUTHERN ENVIRONMENT, Southern Environmental Law Center, 201 W. Main St., Charlottesville VA 22902. (804)977-4090. Fax: (804)977-1483. Award Director: Cathryn McCue. Offered annually for pieces published in the previous calendar year "to encourage and promote writing about natural resources in the South as a way to focus attention on these environmental issues." Deadline: March. Guidelines for SASE. Prize: $1,000. Judged by "prominent writers (not necessarily nature writers) and members of our board of trustees." Open to any writer.

ELLIOTT RUDWICK PRIZE, Organization of American Historians, 112 N. Bryan St., Bloomington IN 47408-4199. (812)855-9852. Fax: (812)855-0696. E-mail: awards@oah.indiana.edu. Website: http://www.indiana.edu/~oah. Contact: Award and Prize Committee Coordinator. Offered every 2 years for a book on the experience of racial and ethnic minorities in the United States. Books on interactions between 2 or more minority groups, or comparing the experience of 2 or more minority groups are especially welcome. Deadline: Sept. 1 of even-numbered years. Guidelines for SASE. Prize: cash award and certificate. James A. Rawley Prize winners are ineligible for the Elliott Rudwick Prize.

THE CORNELIUS RYAN AWARD, The Overseas Press Club of America, 320 East 42 St., New York NY 10017. (212)983-4655. Fax: (212)983-4692. Manager: Sonya Fry. Offered annually for excellence in a nonfiction book on foreign affairs. Deadline: January 31. Guidelines for SASE. Generally publishers nominate the work, but writers may also submit in their own name. Charges $100 fee. Prize: certificate and $1,000. The work must be published and on the subject of foreign affairs.

THEODORE SALOUTOS AWARD, Dept. of History, Iowa State University, Ames IA 50011. Fax: (515)294-6390. E-mail: rdhurt@iastate.edu. Website: http://www.public.iastate.edu/~history_info/homepage.htm. Fax: (202)219-0391. Contact: R. Douglas Hurt, Dept. of History, Iowa State University, Ames, Iowa, 50011. Offered annually for best graduate paper submitted to Agricultural History. Deadline: December 31. Guidelines for SASE. Prize: Monetary award and publication in the journal. Award made at OAH annual meeting. Judged by committees composed of members of the Society. Open to any writer. Nominations can be made by authors or publishers or anyone else.

THE BARBARA SAVAGE "MILES FROM NOWHERE" MEMORIAL AWARD, The Mountaineers Books, 1001 SW Klickitat Way, Suite 201, Seattle WA 98134. (206)223-6303. Award Director: Margaret Foster. Offered in even-numbered years for previously unpublished book-length nonfiction personal adventure narrative. Narrative must be based on an outdoor adventure involving hiking, mountain climbing, bicycling, paddle sports, skiing, snowshoeing, nature, conservation, ecology, or adventure travel not dependent upon motorized transport. Subjects *not* acceptable include hunting, fishing, or motorized or competitive sports. Guidelines for 9×12 SASE. Prize: $3,000 cash award, a $12,000 guaranteed advance against royalties and publication by The Mountaineers. Deadline: October 1, 1998.
● More regional and conservation-oriented titles are preferred.

ALDO AND JEANNE SCAGLIONE PRIZE FOR STUDIES IN GERMANIC LANGUAGES, Modern Language Association of America, 10 Astor Place, New York NY 10003-6981. (212)614-6406. Fax: (212)533-0680. E-mail: awards@mla.org. Contact: Richard Brod. Offered in even-numbered years for outstanding scholarly work appearing in print in the previous two years and written by a member of the MLA, on the linguistics or literatures of the Germanic languages. Deadline: May 1. Guidelines for SASE. Prize: $1,000 and certificate presented at association's annual convention in December. Works of literary history, literary criticism, and literary theory are eligible. Books that are primarily translations are not.

ALDO AND JEANNE SCAGLIONE PRIZE FOR STUDIES IN SLAVIC LANGUAGES AND LITERA- TURES, Modern Language Association, 10 Astor Place, New York NY 10003-6981. (212)614-6406. Fax: (212)533-0680. E-mail: awards@mla.org. Contact: Richard Brod. Offered each odd-numbered year for books published in the previous 2 years. Books published in 1995 or 1996 are eligible for the 1997 award. Membership in the MLA is not required. Works of literary history, literary criticism, philology and literary theory are eligible, books that are primarily translations are not. Deadline: May 1. Guidelines for SASE. Prize: $1,000 and a certificate.

ALDO AND JEANNE SCAGLIONE PRIZE IN COMPARATIVE LITERARY STUDIES, Modern Language Association of America, 10 Astor Place, New York NY 10003-6981. (212)614-6406. Fax: (212)533-0680. E-mail: awards@mla.org. Contact: Richard Brod. Offered annually for outstanding scholarly work published in the preceding year in the field of comparative literary studies involving at least 2 literatures. Deadline: May 1. Prize: $1,000 and certificate. Judged by committee of the MLA. Writer must be a member of the MLA. Works of scholarship, literary history, literary criticism and literary theory are eligible. Books that are primarily translations are not.

ALDO AND JEANNE SCAGLIONE PRIZE IN FRENCH AND FRANCOPHONE STUDIES, 10 Astor Place, New York NY 10003-6981. (212)614-6406. Fax: (212)533-0680. E-mail: awards@mla.org. Contact: Richard Brod. Offered annually for work published in the preceding year that is an outstanding scholarly work in the field of French or francophone linguistic or literary studies. Prize: $1,000 and certificate. Judged by a committee of the MLA. Writer must be a member of the MLA. Works of scholarship, literary history, literary criticism and literary theory are eligible; books that are primarily translations are not. Deadline: May 1.

‡**SCHOLARSHIP IN JEWISH WOMEN'S STUDIES**, 7100 Baltimore Ave., #301, College Park MD 20715. (301)403-4137. Offered annually to a graduate student who is enrolled for the fall semester and whose area of research is Jewish Women's Studies. Guidelines for SASE. Prize: $500.

SCIENCE IN SOCIETY BOOK AWARDS, Canadian Science Writers' Association, P.O. Box 75, Station A, Toronto, Ontario M5W 1A2 Canada. Phone/fax: (416)928-0624. E-mail: cswa@interlog.com. Website: http://www.interl og.com/~cswa. Director: Andy F. Visser-deVries. Offered annually for a first edition work published January 1-December 31 of that year. Two awards: Children's Book Award and General Science Book Award, available for and to the general public with value in promoting greater understanding of science. Deadline: December 15. Guidelines for SASE. Prize: $1,000 and a plaque. Works entered become property of CSWA. Open to Canadian citizens or residents of Canada. Material published in Canada.

‡**SCIENCE WRITING AWARD IN PHYSICS AND ASTRONOMY BY SCIENTISTS**, American Institute of Physics, One Physics Ellipse, College Park MD 20740. (301)209-3090. Fax: (301)209-0846. E-mail: jwrather@aip.acp.o rg. Contest/Award Director: Joan Wrather. Offered annually to previously published entries appearing in print between May 1, 1997 and April 30, 1998 "to recognize and stimulate distinguished writing that improves the general public's

---

✝ **THE DOUBLE DAGGER** before a listing indicates that the listing is new in this edition. New markets are often more receptive to freelance submissions.

understanding and appreciation of physics and astronomy." Deadline: May 19 (unless it falls on a Saturday or Sunday). Guidelines available, SASE is not necessary. Prize: $3,000, a Windsor Chair and a certificate. Judged by a committee of distinguished scientists and journalists. Articles, booklets, or books must be intended for the general public by physicists, astronomers or members of AIP Member and Affiliated Societies.

‡**SCIENCE-WRITING AWARD IN PHYSICS AND ASTRONOMY**, American Institute of Physics, 1 Physics Ellipse, College Park MD 20740-3843. (301)209-3090. E-mail: jwrather@aip.acp.org. Website: http://www.aip.org. Contact: Joan Wrather. Previously published articles, booklets or books "that improve public understanding of physics and astronomy." Deadline: February 3 for professional writers; May 19 for physicists, astronomers or members of AIP member and affililated societies; July 25 for articles or books intended for children, preschool-15 years old.

MINA P. SHAUGHNESSY PRIZE, Modern Language Association of America, 10 Astor Place, New York NY 10003-6981. (212)614-6406. Fax: (212)533-0680. E-mail: awards@mla.org. Contact: Richard Brod. Offered annually for research publication (book or article) in the field of teaching English language, literature, rhetoric and composition published during preceding year. Guidelines for #10 SASE. Prize: $500 and a year's membership. Deadline: May 1.

FRANCIS B. SIMKINS AWARD, Southern Historical Association, Department of History, University of Georgia, Athens GA 30602-1602. (706)542-8848. Fax: (706)542-2455. Managing Editor: John B. Boles. Contact: Secretary-Treasurer. Estab. 1934. Offered in odd-numbered years for recognition of the best first book by an author in the field of Southern history over a 2-year period. The award is sponsored jointly with Longwood College. Longwood College supplies the cash amount and the certificate to the author(s) for this award. The SHA furnishes a certificate to the publisher. Deadline: March 1.

‡**THE SMILEY PRIZE**, Canadian Political Science Association, 1 Stewart St., #205, Ottawa, Ontario K1N 6H7 Canada. (613)564-4026. Fax: (613)230-2746. E-mail: cpsa@csse.ca. Contact: Michelle Hopkins. Offered every 2 years (even years) for the best book, in English or French, published in a field relating to the study of government and politics in Canada. Deadline: December 10. Prize: $750 and a set of the books submitted. Judged by three CPSA members. No textbooks, edited texts or collections of essays.

‡**CHARLES S. SYDNOR AWARD**, Southern Historical Association, Department of History, University of Georgia, Athens GA 30602. (706)542-8848. Fax: (706)542-2455. Contact: Secretary-Treasurer. Offered in even-numbered years for recognition of a distinguished book in Southern history published in odd-numbered years. Deadline: March 1.

AMAURY TALBOT PRIZE FUND FOR AFRICAN ANTHROPOLOGY 1997, Barclays Bank Trust Limited, Trust Management Office, V Group, Osborne Court, Gadbrook Park, Rudheath, Northwich Cheshire CW9 7UE England. Annual award for previously published nonfiction on anthropological research relating to Africa. Only works published in 1997 eligible. Preference given to those relating to Nigeria and then West Africa. All applications, together with 2 copies of the book, article or work in question, should be sent by January 31, 1998 to: Amaury Talbot Prize coordinator, Royal Anthropological Institute, 50 Fitzroy St., London W1P 5H5 England. The Institute undertakes the administration of the Prize on behalf of the Trustees, Bardays Bank Trust Company Limited. Entries will *not* be returned.

THE THEATRE LIBRARY ASSOCIATION AWARD, Theatre Library Association, Benjamin Rosenthal Library, Queens College, C.U.N.Y., 65-30 Kissena Blvd., Flushing NY 11367. (718)997-3799. Fax: (718)997-3753. E-mail: rlwqc@cunyvm.cuny.edu. Contact: Richard Wall, book awards committee chair. Estab. 1973. Book published in the United States within the previous calendar year on a subject related to recorded or broadcast performance (including motion pictures, television and radio). Eligible books may include biography, history, theory, criticism, reference or related fields. Prize: $250 and certificate to the winner; $100 and certificate for Honorable Mention. Submissions and deadline: Nominated books are requested from publishers; one copy should be received by each of three award jurors as well as the Chairperson by February 15 of the year following eligibility.

FREDERICK JACKSON TURNER AWARD, Organization of American Historians, 112 N. Bryan St., Bloomington IN 47408-4199. (812)855-9852. Fax: (812)855-0696. E-mail: awards@oah.indiana.edu. Website: http://www.indiana. edu/~oah. Contact: Award and Prize Committee Coordinator. Offered annually for an author's first book on some significant phase of American history and also to the press that submits and publishes it. The entry must comply with the following rules: 1) the work must be the first book-length study of history published by the author; 2) if the author has a Ph.D., he/she must have received it no earlier than seven years prior to submission of the manuscript for publication; 3) the work must be published in the calendar year before the award is given; 4) the work must deal with some significant phase of American history. Deadline: September 1. Guidelines for SASE. Prize: cash award, certificate and medal.

‡**TWELFTH PRIZE FOR BIBLIOGRAPHY**, International League of Antiquarian Booksellers, Hauptstrasse 19A, D-53604, Bad Honnef, Germany. Director: Konrad Meuschel. Offered every four years for work published or unpublished January 1, 1993-December 12, 1996 for the best work published or unpublished, of learned bibliography or of research into the history of the books or of typography, and books of general interest on the subject. Deadline: December 12, 1996. Guidelines for SASE. Prize: $10,000. Judged by 1) the President of the International League of Antiquarian Booksellers; 2) the Secretary of the Quadrennial Prize; 3) a member nominated by the League Committee; 4) three

persons whose bibliographical knowledge is generally recognized. These last three, chosen from countries speaking different languages, will be helped by specialists, appointed as necessary. Open to any writer.

‡**W.D. WEATHERFORD AWARD**, Berea College Appalachian Center and Hutchins Library, C.P.O. 2336, Berea KY 40404. (606)986-9341 ext 5140. Offered annually for outstanding published writing which best illustrates the problems, personalities and unique qualities of the Appalachian South between January 1-December 31. Deadline: December 31. Guidelines for SASE. Prize: $500. Judged by an independent committee from various parts of the Appalachian South. Entries must have been first published during the year for which the award is made and may be nominated by its publisher, a member of the award committee or any reader.

JON WHYTE ESSAY COMPETITION, Writers Guild of Alberta, 11759 Groat Rd., Edmonton, Alberta T5M 3K6 Canada. (403)422-8174. Fax: (403)422-2663. E-mail: writers@compusmart.ab.cq. Assistant Director: Darlene Diver. Offered annually for unpublished work. Essay competition on announced theme. Theme is announced May 1. Winner announced October 15. 2,800 words. Deadline: September 1. Guidelines for SASE. Charges $10 fee Canadian. Prize: $2,000 plus publication in 2 newspapers and radio readings. Must be Alberta resident.

‡**THE ELIE WIESEL ETHICS ESSAY CONTEST**, 1177 Avenue of the Americas, 36th Floor, New York NY 10036. Contest Director: Cicily Wilson. Offered annually to unpublished students. SASE for entry form and guidelines required. Prizes: 1st-$5,000; 2nd-$2,500; 3rd-$1,500; two honorable mentions-$500 each. Judged by Mr. Elie Wiesel and a committee drawn from the world of academe. "The Elie Wiesel Foundation for Humanity reserves the right to publish the winning essays in whole or in part. These essays may not be published elsewhere without written permission from the Foundation." Open to any student registered during the fall semester 1997 as a full-time junior or senior at an accredited 4-year college or university.

L. KEMPER AND LEILA WILLIAMS PRIZE, The Historic New Orleans Collection and Louisiana Historical Association, 533 Royal St., New Orleans LA 70130-2179. Website: http://www.hnoc.org. Director: Dr. Jon Kukla. Offered annually for the best published work on Louisiana history. Deadline: February 1. Prize: $1,500 and a plaque.

WORD IS ART, Austin Writers' League, 1501 West Fifth St., Suite E-2, Austin TX 78703. (512)499-8914. Fax: (512)499-0441. E-mail: awl@eden.com. Website: http://www.eden.com/~awl. Director: Angela Smith. Offered annually for previously published work between January 1 and December 31 to recognize the six best submissions on the subject of writing published in the *Austin Writer*. Entries are all published articles and poetry which appear over a calendar year in the *Austin Writer*. Prize: 6 $100 prizes. Open to any writer published in the *Austin Writer*.

Fiction

AIM MAGAZINE SHORT STORY CONTEST, P.O. Box 20554, Chicago IL 60620-0554. (312)874-6184. Fax: (216)543-2746. Managing Editor: Dr. Myron Apilado. Contact: Ruth Apilado, associate editor. Estab. 1974. Unpublished short stories (4,000 words maximum) "promoting brotherhood among people and cultures." Deadline: August 15.

‡**NELSON ALGREN SHORT STORY AWARDS**, *Chicago Tribune*, 435 N. Michigan Ave., Chicago IL 60611. Offered annually for previously unpublished stories between 2,500-10,000 words by American writers. Deadline: February 1. Guidelines for SASE. Prize: 1st-$5,000; $1,000 each to 3 runners-up. No phone calls please.

‡**AMERICAN SHORT FICTION PRIZES FOR FICTION**, American Short Fiction, Department of English, Parlin 108, U.T. Austin, Austin TX 78712. (512)471-1772. Contest Director: Joseph Kruppa. Offered annually to unpublished and published writers "to reward and recognize excellence in the writing of short fiction." Deadline: May 15. Charges $20 fee. Prizes: All entrants receive 1-year subscription to *ASF*, 1st-$1,000 and publication in *ASF*, 2nd-$500 and possible publication in *ASF*, 3rd-$200 and possible publication in *ASF*. Judged by the editor and editorial assistants of *ASF*. Entrants should enclose SASE if they want their ms returned.

ANNUAL SHORT STORY CONTEST, (formerly Penny Dreadful Short Story Contest), sub-TERRAIN Magazine, P.O. Box 1575, Bentall Centre, Vancouver, British Columbia V6C 2P7 Canada. (604)876-8710. Fax: (604)879-2667. Offered annually to foster new and upcoming writers. Deadline May 15. Guidelines for SASE. Charges $15 fee for first story, $5 for additional entries. Prize: $250 (Canadian), publication and subscription to sub-TERRAIN.

ANVIL PRESS INTERNATIONAL 3-DAY NOVEL WRITING CONTEST, Anvil Press, 204-A 175 E. Broadway, Vancouver, British Columbia V5T 1W2 Canada. (604)876-8710. Fax: (604)879-2667. E-mail: subter@pinc.com. Website: http://www.bc.books.ca. Contact: Brian Kaufman. Estab. 1988. Offered annually for the best novel written in 3 days (Labor Day weekend). Entrants return finished novels to Anvil Press for judging. Registration deadline: Friday before Labor Day weekend. Send SASE (IRC if from the US) for details. Charges $25 fee.

‡**BEST FIRST PRIVATE EYE NOVEL CONTEST**, St. Martins Press & The Private Eye Writers of America (PWA), 175 Fifth Ave., New York NY 10003. (212)674-5151. Fax: (212)254-4553. Offered annually for unpublished

writers "to encourage new voices in a timeless genre." Deadline: August 1. Guidelines for SASE. Prize: Publication by St. Martin's Press with a $10,000 advance against royalties. "Any writer may enter, but the submission must be a novel in which the main character is an independent investigator who is not a member of any law enforcement or government agency, and who receives a fee for his or her investigative services."

BRAZOS BOOKSTORE (HOUSTON) SHORT STORY AWARD, The Texas Institute of Letters, P.O. Box 298300, Fort Worth TX 76129. (817)921-7822. Fax: (817)921-7333. Director: Judy Alter. Offered annually for previously published work between January 1 and December 31 of year before award is given to recognize the best short story submitted to the competition. The story submitted must have appeared in print for the first time to be eligible. Deadline: January 2. Guidelines for SASE. Prize: $750. Writers must have been born in Texas, must have lived in Texas for at least two consecutive years or the subject matter of the work must be associated with Texas.

GEORGES BUGNET AWARD FOR FICTION (NOVEL), Writers Guild of Alberta, 11759 Groat Rd., Edmonton Alberta T5M 3K6 Canada. (403)422-8179. Fax: (403)422-2663. E-mail: writers@compusmart.ab.ca. Assistant Director: Darlene Diver. Offered annually for work previously published January 1-December 31 of the past year. Deadline: December 31. Guidelines for SASE. Prize: $500 and leatherbound copy of book. Must be an Alberta author.

‡RAYMOND CARVER SHORT STORY CONTEST, English Department, Humboldt State University, Arcata CA 95521. Contact: Coordinator. Offered annually for unpublished work. Deadline: November 1. Guidelines available for SASE. Charges $10/story fee. Prizes: 1st-$1,000 plus publication in *Toyon*, Humboldt State University's literary magazine; 2nd-$500; 3rd-$250. Contest open to any writer living in the US.

‡COTTONWOOD COOPERATIVE FICTION WRITERS FELLOWSHIP, P.O. Box 4530, Albuquerque NM 87196-4530. E-mail: cottonwd@unm.edu. Contest/Award Director: Charli Buono de Valdez. Offered annually for "writers who have never published a novel or collection of stories." Deadline: May 31. Guidelines for SASE. Charges $8 fee. Prize: $1,000. Open to any unpublished writer residing in Arizona, Colorado, New Mexico, Oklahoma, Texas or Utah.

DAVID DORNSTEIN MEMORIAL CREATIVE WRITING CONTEST FOR YOUNG ADULT WRITERS, The Coalition for the Advancement of Jewish Education, 261 W. 35th St., Floor 12A, New York NY 10001. (212)268-4210. Fax: (212)268-4214. E-mail: 500-8447@mcimail.com. Executive Director: Eliot Spack. Contest offered annually for unpublished short story based on a Jewish theme or topic. Deadline: December 31. Guidelines for SASE. Prize: $1,000 and publication in the *Jewish Education News*. Writer must prove age of 18-35 years old. Story must be based on Jewish theme, topic. Submit only 1 story each year.

‡STANLEY ELLSIN PRIZE FOR SHORT FICTION, *Colorado Review*/Center for Literary Publishing, 359 Eddy, Fort Collins CO 80523. (970)491-5449. Fax: (970)491-5601. E-mail: colorado_review@vihes.colostate.edu. Award Director: David Milofsky. Offered annually for short fiction by a writer who has never been published in a journal with a circulation more than 200. Deadline: May 5. Guidelines for SASE. Charges $12 fee. Prize: $500 and publication.

‡THE EVERGREEN CHRONICLES NOVELLA CONTEST, The Evergreen Chronicles, P.O. Box 8939, Minneapolis MN 55408. (612)823-6638. Contest Director: Jim Berg. Offered annually. Looking for an original novella by an emerging, unpublished gay, lesbian, bisexual, straight or transgendered writer. Deadline: September 30. Guidelines for SASE. Prizes: 1st-$500 and publication in special issue of *The Evergreen Chronicles*, 2nd-$100 and possible publication. Finalists are selected by Evergreen editorial staff, and guest judges select winners. First rights for winners are retained. Open to writers who have had no more than one novel or novella published. Manuscripts must in some way address the gay, lesbian, bisexual or transgender experience.

THE WILLIAM FAULKNER CREATIVE WRITING COMPETITION, The Pirate's Alley Faulkner Society, 632 Pirate's Alley, New Orleans LA 70116-3254. (504)586-1609. Contest Director: Joseph J. DeSalvo, Jr. Contact: Rosemary James, editor. Offered annually for unpublished mss to encourage publisher interest in a promising writer's novel, novella, short story, personal essay, poem or short story by a Louisiana high school student. Deadline: April 15. Guidelines for SASE. Charges entry fee: novel-$35; novella-$30; short story $25; personal essay-$25; individual poem-$25; high school short story $10. Prize: novel-$7,500; novella-$2,500; short story-$1,500; personal essay-$1,000; individual poem-$750; high school-$1,000; and expenses for trip to New Orleans for Faulkner Celebration. Excerpts published in Society's Literary Quarterly, *The Double Dealer Redux*. The Society retains the right to publish excerpts of longer fiction; short stories in toto. Judges are well known authors. Open to all U.S. residents.

ROBERT L. FISH MEMORIAL AWARD, Mystery Writers of America, Inc., 17 E. 47th St., 6th Floor, New York NY 10017. (212)888-8171. Fax: (212)888-8107. Website: http://www.mysterywriters.org/. Contact: Priscilla Ridgway. Offered annually for the best first mystery or suspense short story published in the previous year. Deadline: Dec. 1.

H.E. FRANCIS SHORT STORY AWARD, University of Alabama in Huntsville & Ruth Hindman Foundation, 2007 Gallatin St., Huntsville AL 35801. (205)539-3320. Fax: (205)533-6893. E-mail: htp@aol.com. Director: Patricia

Sammon. Offered annually for unpublished work. Deadline: December 31. Guidelines for SASE. Charges $15 reading fee. Prize: $1,000. Acquires first time publication rights.

THE JANET HEIDINGER KAFKA PRIZE, English Department, Susan B. Anthony Institute for Gender and Women's Studies, 538 Lattimore Hall, University of Rochester, Rochester NY 14627. Attention: Director SBA Center. Book-length fiction (novel, short story or experimental writing) by US woman citizen. Publishers must submit 4 copies. Deadline: February 28.

DRUE HEINZ LITERATURE PRIZE, University of Pittsburgh Press, 127 N. Bellefield Ave., Pittsburgh PA 15260. Series Editor: Ed Ochester. Estab. 1936. Collection of short fiction. Offered annually to writers who have published a book-length collection of fiction or a minimum of 3 short stories or novellas in commercial magazines or literary journals of national distribution. Does not return manuscripts. Guidelines for SASE (essential). Submit: July-August. Prize: $10,000.

ERNEST HEMINGWAY FOUNDATION PEN AWARD FOR FIRST FICTION, PEN American Center, 568 Broadway, New York NY 10012. E-mail: pen@echonyc.com. Contact: John Morrone. First-published novel or short story collection by an American author. Submit 3 copies. Deadline: December 15.

‡LORIAN HEMINGWAY SHORT STORY COMPETITION, Hemingway Days Festival, P.O. Box 993, Key West FL 33041-4045. (305)294-4440. Coordinators: Lorian Hemingway and Carol Shaughnessy. Estab. 1981. Unpublished short stories. Deadline: June 1. Charges $10 fee for each story postmarked by June 1, and $15 for each story postmarked by June 15; no stories will be accepted after June 15. Guidelines for SASE. Prize: 1st-$1,000 plus round trip airfare to Key West and accommodations during the subsequent year's Hemingway Days Writers' Workshop and Conference; 2nd and 3rd-$500 runner-up awards.

INTERNATIONAL IMITATION HEMINGWAY COMPETITION, PEN Center West, 672 S. La Fayette Park Place, Suite 41, Los Angeles CA 90057. (213)365-8500. Fax: (213)365-9616. E-mail: rit2writ@ix.netcom.com. Contact: Rachel Hall. Offered annually for unpublished one-page (500 words) parody of Hemingway. Must mention Harry's Bar and must be funny. Deadline: March 15. Winner receives round trip transportation for two to Florence, Italy and dinner at Harry's Bar & American Grill in Florence.

JAMES FELLOWSHIP FOR THE NOVEL IN PROGRESS, The Heekin Group Writer's & Education Fund, P.O. Box 1534, Sisters OR 97759. Phone/fax: (541)548-4147. E-mail: hgfhl/@aol.com. Director: Sarah Heekin Redfield. Offered annually for unpublished work. "Our writing fellowships program is designed to support the community of new and emerging writers." Deadline: December. Guidelines for SASE. Charges $25 fee. Prize: 2 awards of $3,000.

JAPANOPHILE ANNUAL SHORT STORY CONTEST, *Japanophile*, Box 223, Okemos MI 48864. (517)669-2109. E-mail: japanlove@aol.com. Website: http://www.voyager.net/japanophile. Director: Earl Snodgrass. Offered annually for unpublished work to encourage good fiction-writing that contributes to understanding of Japan and Japanese culture. Deadline: December 31. Guidelines for SASE. Charges $5 fee. Prize: $100, a certificate, and usually publication.

‡JAMES JONES FIRST NOVEL FELLOWSHIP, Wilkes University, English Department, Kirby Hall, Wilkes-Barre PA 18766. (717)831-4530. Contest Director: Patricia B. Heaman. Offered annually for unpublished novels, novellas and closely-linked short stories (all works-in-progress). "The award is intended to honor the spirit of unblinking honesty, determination and insight into modern culture exemplified by the late James Jones." Deadline: March 1. Guidelines for SASE. Charges $15 fee. Prize: $2,500. The competition is open to all American writers who have not previously published novels.

JESSE H. JONES AWARD, The Texas Institute of Letters, P.O. Box 298300, Fort Worth TX 76129. (817)921-7822. Fax: (817)921-7333. Director: Judy Alter. Offered annually for work previously published January 1-December 31 of year before award is given to recognize the writer of the best book of fiction entered in the competition. Deadline: January 2. Guidelines for SASE. Prize: $6,000. Judged by a panel selected by the TIL Council. To be eligible, a writer must have been born in Texas, or have lived in the state for at least two consecutive years at some time, or the subject matter of the work should be associated with the state.

‡AGA KHAN PRIZE FOR FICTION, *The Paris Review*, 541 E. 72nd St., New York NY 10021. (212)861-0016. Offered annually to the best previously unpublished short story published in *The Paris Review* that year. Guidelines for SASE. Prize: $1,000. *The Paris Review* does not ordinarily distinguish between award submissions and regular submissions. The only candidates for awards are writers who have already been published by *The Paris Review*. Submissions must be accompanied by SASE, unpublished and written in English.

LIBIDO SHORT FICTION CONTEST, *Libido*, 5318 N. Paulina St., Chicago IL 60640. Fax: (773)275-0752. E-mail: rune@mcs.com. Website: http://www.indro.com/libido. Contact: J.L. Beck, submissions editor. Erotic short fiction, 1,000-4,000 words. Deadline: Entries must be postmarked by no later than September 1. Only entries with SASE will be returned. Entries must clearly say "contest" on the envelope. Charges $15 fee. Prizes: 1st-$1,000 and publication in

Libido; 2nd-$200; 3rd through 5th-l-year subscriptions to *Libido*. Winners chosen by *Libido* editors. "Open to all sexual orientations, but winning stories will fit the general tone and style of *Libido*. Bonus points are awarded for accuracy of characterization, sense of style and humor, particularly the darker side." For issue with last year's winner, send $8.

LINES IN THE SAND SHORT FICTION CONTEST, LeSand Publications, 1252 Terra Nova Blvd., Pacifica CA 94044. (415)355-9069. Associate Editor: Barbara J. Less. Estab. 1992. Offered annually to encourage the writing of good, short fiction. Deadline: October 31. Guidelines for #10 SASE. Charges $5 fee. Prizes: 1st-$50; 2nd-$25; 3rd-$10; plus publication in January/February Awards edition.

LONG FICTION CONTEST, White Eagle Coffee Store Press, P.O. Box 383, Fox River Grove IL 60021. (708)639-9200. E-mail: wecspress@aol.com. Offered annually since 1993 for unpublished work to recognize and promote long short stories of 8,000-14,000 words (about 30-50 pages). Deadline: December 15. Guidelines for SASE. Charges $12 fee. A.E. Coppard Prize: $500 and publication plus 25 copies of chapbook. Open to any writer, no restrictions on materials. Sample of previous winner: $5.95, including postage.

‡**MARY McCARTHY PRIZE IN SHORT FICTION**, Sarabande Books, 2234 Dundee Rd., #200, Louisville KY 40205. (502)458-4028. Fax: (502)458-4065. E-mail: sarabandeb@aol.com. Contest Director: Sarah Gorham. Offered annually to award publication to an outstanding collection of stories or novellas. Submissions accepted January 1-February 15. Guidelines for SASE. Charges $15 fee. Prize: $2,000 publication (paper and cloth), standard royalty contract. All finalists considered for publication. Judged by nationally prominent writers.

MAGIC REALISM MAGAZINE SHORT-FICTION AWARD, Pyx Press, P.O. Box 922648, Sylmar CA 91392-2648. Award for works published in 1997. Entries must be original works of magic realism in English of less than 20,000 words. Only stories that first appeared in 1997 considered. Reprint rights must be available. Submit tearsheets/photocopies or published material; nothing in ms format will be considered. Entries not acknowledged or returned. Deadline: April 30, 1998. No fee. Winning entry announced in winter '98/'99 issue of *Magic Realism*. No limit on number of entries per author or publisher. Winning story published in chapbook form by Pyx Press. Winning author receives $150; publisher receives $50. Any individual may nominate their own or another's published work.

‡**THE MALAHAT REVIEW NOVELLA PRIZE**, The Malahat Review, Box 1700, Victoria, British Columbia V8W 2Y2 Canada. (250)721-8524. E-mail: malahat@uvic.ca. Contest Director: Derk Wynand. Offered every 2 years (even years). To promote unpublished novellas. Deadline: March 1. Guidelines for SASE. Charges $25 fee (includes a one-year subscription to *Malahat*, published quarterly). Prize: $400, plus payment for publication. ($25/page). Obtains first world rights. After publication rights revert to the author. Open to any writer.

MALICE DOMESTIC AWARD, Malice Domestic, % Pam Reed Bookstore, etc., 27 W. Washington St., Hagerstown MD 21740. (201)797-8896. Fax: (301)797-9453. Website: http://www.erols.com/malice. Director: Pam Reed. Offered annually for unpublished work. MALICE will award two grants to unpublished writers in the Malice Domestic genre at MALICE VIII in April '98. The competition is designed to help the next generation of Malice authors get their first work published and to foster quality Malice literature. Deadline: December 15. Guidelines for SASE. Prize: $500. Judged by Malice Domestic Board of Directors or their designated representatives. Writers must not have published a book in any field. Members of the Malice Domestic Board of Directors and their families are ineligible to apply. MALICE encourages applications from minority candidates.

MID-LIST PRESS FIRST SERIES AWARD FOR SHORT FICTION, Mid-List Press, 4324 12th Ave. S., Minneapolis MN 55407-3218. Open to any writer who has never published a book-length collection of short fiction (short stories, novellas); minimum 50,000 words. Submit entire ms beginning *after* March 31, and must be postmarked by July 1. Accepts simultaneous submissions. Charges $15 fee. No ms returned without SASE. Mss submitted without return envelope *must* include #10 SASE for notification. Will acknowledge receipt of ms only if self-addressed stamped postcard enclosed. Guidelines and entry form for SASE. Awards include publication and an advance against royalties.

MID-LIST PRESS FIRST SERIES AWARD FOR THE NOVEL, Mid-List Press, 4324-12th Ave. S., Minneapolis MN 55407-3218. Offered annually for unpublished novels to locate and publish quality manuscripts by first-time writers, particularly those mid-list titles that major publishers may be rejecting. Deadline: February 1. Guidelines for SASE. *Applicants should write, not call, for guidelines.* Charges $15 fee. Prize: $1,000 advance against royalties, plus publication. Judged by ms readers and editors of Mid-List Press; editors and publishers make final decisions. Open to any writer who has never published a *novel*.

MILKWEED NATIONAL FICTION PRIZE, Milkweed Editions, 430 First Ave. N., Suite 400, Minneapolis MN 55401. (612)332-3192. Fax: (612)332-6248. Contact: Elisabeth Fitz, first reader. Estab. 1986. Annual award for unpublished works. "Milkweed is looking for a novel, novella, or a collection of short stories. Manuscripts should be of high literary quality and must be double-spaced and between 150-400 pages in length." *Must* request contest guidelines, send SASE. Prize: Publication by Milkweed Editions and a cash advance of $2,000 on any royalties or other payment agreed upon in the contractual arrangement negotiated at the time of acceptance. Winner will be chosen from the manuscripts Milkweek accepts for publication each year. All manuscripts submitted to Milkweed will automatically be considered for the prize. Submission directly to the contest is no longer necessary. "Manuscript must be written in English. Writers should have previously published a book of fiction or three short stories (or novellas) in magazines/journals with national distribution." Catalog available on request for $1.50.

NATIONAL WRITERS ASSOCIATION NOVEL WRITING CONTEST, The National Writers Association, Suite 424, 1450 S. Havana, Aurora CO 80012. (303)751-7844. Fax:(303)751-8593. Director: Sandy Whelchel. Annual contest "to help develop creative skills, to recognize and reward outstanding ability and to increase the opportunity for the marketing and subsequent publication of novel manuscripts." Deadline: April 1. Guidelines for #10 SASE. Charges $35 fee. Prizes: 1st-$500; 2nd-$300; 3rd-$200.

NATIONAL WRITERS ASSOCIATION SHORT STORY CONTEST, The National Writers Association, Suite 424, 1450 S. Havana, Aurora CO 80012. (303)751-7844. Fax:(303)751-8593. Director: Sandy Whelchel. Annual contest "to encourage writers in this creative form and to recognize those who excel in fiction writing." Deadline: July 1. Guidelines for #10 SASE. Charges $15 fee. Prizes: $200, $100, $50, copy of *Writer's Market*.

‡NEPEAN PUBLIC LIBRARY ANNUAL SHORT STORY CONTEST, Nepean Public Library, 101 Centre-pointe Dr., Nepean, Ontario K2G 5K7 Canada. E-mail: steasdal@mail.library.on.com. Contest Director: Marlene Mc-Causland. Offered annually for unpublished short stories to encourage writing in the community." Deadline: March 31. Guidelines for SASE. Charges $5/story fee. Prizes: 1st-$500; 2nd-$250; 3rd-$100. Judged by 2 experienced writers/authors. "We retain the right to display and publish them at a later date. All other rights remain with the author." Open to residents of Ottawa-Carleton Regional Municipality, Ontario, age 18 and over.

NEW MUSE AWARD, Broken Jaw Press/M.A.P. Productions, Box 596 Station A, Fredericton, New Brunswick E3B 5A6 Canada. Contact: Joe Blades. Offered annually for unpublished poetry book mss (individual poems may have been previously published) to encourage development of booklength mss by poets without a first book published. Deadline: March 31. Guidelines for SASE (with Canadian postage or IRC). Charges $15 fee (all entrants receive copy of winning book upon publication). Prize: book publication on trade terms.

THE FLANNERY O'CONNOR AWARD FOR SHORT FICTION, The University of Georgia Press, 330 Research Dr., Athens GA 30602-4901. (706)369-6140. Fax: (706)369-6131. Contact: Jane Kobres, competition coordinator. Estab. 1981. Submission period: June-July 31. Charges $10 fee. Does not return mss. Manuscripts must be 200-275 pages long. Authors do not have to be previously published. Guidelines for SASE. Prize: $1,000 and publication.

HOWARD O'HAGER AWARD FOR SHORT FICTION, Writers Guild of Alberta, 11759 Groat Rd., Edmonton Alberta T5M 3K6 Canada. (403)422-8174. Fax: (403)422-2663. E-mail: writers@compusmart.ab.ca. Assistant Director: Darlene Diver. Short fiction book published in current year. Must be an Alberta author.

‡THE OHIO STATE UNIVERSITY PRESS PRIZE IN SHORT FICTION, Ohio State University Press and the MFA Program in Creative Writing at The Ohio State University, 180 Pressey Hall, 1070 Carmack Rd., Columbus OH 43210-1002. (614)292-6930. Fax: (614)292-2065. E-mail: bucy.4@osu.edu. Director: William Roorbach. Offered annually to published and unpublished writers. Accepts submissions in January only. Guidelines for SASE. Charges $20 fee. Prize: $1,500, publication, an invitation to Ohio State University to give a public reading and direct a creative writing workshop. "All writers in English, published or unpublished, may submit their work. No translations permitted unless the translated material is all the author's own. No employee or student of the university is eligible."

CHRIS O'MALLEY PRIZE IN FICTION, *The Madison Review*, Dept. of English, 600 N. Park St., Madison WI 53706. (608)263-3374. Contest Director: Ronald Kuka. Offered annually for previously unpublished work. Awarded to the best piece of fiction. Deadline: September 30. Prize: $500, plus publication in the spring issue of *The Madison Review*. All contest entries are considered as submissions to *The Madison Review*, the literary journal sponsoring the contest. No simultaneous submissions to other publications. Charges $3 fee.

PEN/FAULKNER AWARDS FOR FICTION, PEN/Faulkner Foundation, 201 East Capitol St., Washington DC 20003. (202)675-0345. Fax: (202)608-1719. E-mail: delaney@folger.edu. Website: http://www.folger.edu. Executive Director: Janice F. Delaney. Offered annually for published work in a calendar year for best book-length work of fiction by American citizen. Deadline: October 31. Prize: $15,000—one winner, 5,000—4 nominees. Judged by 3 writers of fiction (published); different each year.

PLAYBOY COLLEGE FICTION CONTEST, *Playboy*, 680 N. Lake Shore Dr., Chicago IL 60611. (312)751-8000. Website: http://www.playboy.com. Fiction Editor: Alice Turner. Annual award for unpublished short stories by registered students at a college or university. Submissions accepted September 1-January 1. Information in October issue or send SASE to College Fiction Contest, 730 Fifth Ave., New York NY 10019. Prizes: 1st-$3,000 and publication in *Playboy*; 2nd-$500; four runners-up-$200.

EDGAR ALLAN POE AWARD, Mystery Writers of America, Inc., 17 E. 47th St., New York NY 10017. (212)888-8171. Website: http://www.mysterywriters.org. Contact: Priscilla Ridgway. Entries must be produced/published in the year they are submitted. Deadline: December 1. Entries for the book categories are usually submitted by the publisher but may be submitted by the author or his agent.

PRISM INTERNATIONAL FICTION CONTEST, *Prism International*, University of British Columbia, Buch E462, 1866 Main Mall, Vancouver, British Columbia V6T 1Z1 Canada. (604)822-2514. Fax: (604)822-3616. E-mail: prism@unixg.ubc.ca. Website: http://www.arts.ubc.ca/crwr/prism/prism.html. Offered annually for previously unpublished fiction. Deadline: December 1. Maximum length: 25 pages. Story's title should appear on every page. Author's name and address must appear *only* on a separate cover page. Entry fee: $15 for one story, plus $5 for each additional story. Canadians pay in Canadian funds. Entry fee includes one year subscription. Works of translations are eligible. For complete guidelines, send #10 SASE with Canadian postage or #10 SAE with 1 IRC. Prizes: 1st-$2,000; 5 honorable mentions of $200 each, plus publication payment.

PROMETHEUS AWARD/HALL OF FAME, Libertarian Futurist Society, 89 Gebhardt Rd., Penfield NY 14526. (716)288-6137. E-mail: amonsen@aol.com or 74033.2607@compuserve.com. Website: http://www.libertarian.com/lfs/. Contact: Victoria Varga or Anders Monsen. Estab. 1979. Prometheus Award: pro-freedom, anti-authoritarian novel published during previous year. Hall of Fame: one classic libertarian novel at least 5 years old. Deadline: March 1.

QUARTERLY WEST NOVELLA COMPETITION, *Quarterly West*, 317 Olpin Union, University of Utah, Salt Lake City UT 84112. (801)581-3938. Estab. 1976. Offered biennially for 2 unpublished novellas. Charges $20 fee. Guidelines for SASE. Deadline: December 31 of even-numbered years. Prize: 2 winning writers receive $500 and publication in *Quarterly West*.

‡THOMAS H. RADDALL ATLANTIC FICTION PRIZE, Writers' Federation of Nova Scotia, 1809 Barrington St., #901, Halifax, Nova Scotia B3J 3K8 Canada. (902)423-8116. Fax: (902)422-0881. E-mail: writersl@fox.nstn.ca. Award Director: Jane Buss. Offered annually to fiction published during the year preceding the competition. The Prize "honors the best fiction writing by an Atlantic born (Nova Scotia, New Brunswick, Newfoundland, Prince Edward Island) or resident (1 year) writer. Deadline: 3rd Friday in April. Forward 4 copies of published book of fiction to the Writers' Federation of Nova Scotia. Prize: $5,000 (Canadian funds) and medal.

SIR WALTER RALEIGH AWARD, North Carolina Literary and Historical Association, 109 E. Jones St., Raleigh NC 27601-2807. (919)733-7305. Awards Coordinator: Rita Cashion. Previously published fiction by a North Carolina resident. Deadline: July 15.

HAROLD U. RIBALOW AWARD, Hadassah WZOA, 50 W. 58th St., New York NY 10019. Fax: (212)446-9521. Editor: Alan Tigay. Offered annually for an English-language book of fiction on a Jewish theme published January 1-December 31 in a calendar year. Deadline: April. Prize: $1,000. Books should be submitted by the publisher.

THE IAN ST. JAMES AWARDS, P.O. Box 60, Cranbrook, Kent TN17 2ZR United Kingdom (01580)212626. Fax: (01580)212041. Contact: Merric Davidson. Offered annually to unpublished short stories. Deadline: April 30. Guidelines for SASE with IRCs. Charges £6 fee or £10 if critique is required. Prizes: 1st-£2,000, 2nd-£1,000, 3rd-£500, seven honorable mentions-£200. Winning stories published in annual book. Runners-up (approximately 40) published in *The New Writer* magazine. Open to writers over 18 without a novel or novella published.

‡SEVENTEEN MAGAZINE FICTION CONTEST, 850 Third Ave., New York NY 10022. E-mail: seventeen@aol.com. Estab. 1948. Contact: Ben Schrank. Previously unpublished short stories from writers 13-21 years old. Deadline: April 30. Guidelines for SASE, or check the November issue. Prize: 1st-$1,000 and publication in the magazine; 2nd-$500; 3rd-$250; five honorable mentions-$50.

‡SOUTH CAROLINA FICTION PROJECT, South Carolina Arts Commission, 1800 Gervais St., Columbia SC 29201. (803)734-8696. Fax: (803)734-8526. Contest Director: Sara June Goldstein. Offered annually for unpublished fiction. Deadline: March 15. Guidelines for SASE. Prize: $500. Judged by a panel of professional writers. *The Post and Courier* newspaper (Charleston SC) purchases first publication rights. Open to any writer who is a legal resident of South Carolina, as well as writers residing in the state. 12 stories are selected for monthly publication.

THE SOUTHERN REVIEW/LOUISIANA STATE UNIVERSITY SHORT FICTION AWARD, Louisiana State University, 43 Allen Hall, Baton Rouge LA 70803. (504)388-5108. Fax: (504)388-5098. E-mail: bmacon@unixl.sncc.lsu.edu. Committee Chairman: Dave Smith. First collection of short stories by an American published in the US during previous year. Deadline: January 31. Publisher or author may enter by mailing 2 copies of the collection.

THE STAND MAGAZINE SHORT STORY COMPETITION, *Stand Magazine*, 179 Wingrove Rd., Newcastle on Tyne, NE4 9DA United Kingdom. (0191)-2733280. E-mail: dlatane@vcu.edu. Contact: Editors of *Stand Magazine*. "This biennial competition is an open international contest for unpublished writing in the English language intended to foster a wider interest in the short story as a literary form and to promote and encourage excellent writing in it." Deadline: June 30, 1997. "Please note that intending entrants enquiring from outside the UK should send International Reply Coupons, not stamps from their own countries. In lieu of an entry fee we ask for a minimum donation of £4 or

$8 US per story entered." Editorial inquiries and requests for entry form should be made with SASE to: Prof. David Latane, English Dept., VCU, Richmond, VA 23284-2005.

STORY'S SHORT STORY COMPETITION, Story, 1507 Dana Ave., Cincinnati OH 45207. (513)531-2690, ext. 268. Fax: (513)531-1843. Contact: Sandi Luppert, promotion manager. Offered annually for unpublished work. Deadline: October 31. Guidelines for SASE. Charges $10 fee. Prize: 1st-$1,000; 2nd-$500; 3rd-$250. On occasion, awards merchandise prizes from additional sponsors. Entries must not be under consideration at other publications. Writers are free to market them elsewhere after winners are announced. Story reserves the right to publish selected winners. Buys first North American rights.

‡STORY'S SHORT STORY THEME COMPETITION, Story, 1507 Dana Ave., Cincinnati OH 45207-9966. (513)531-2690, ext. 268. Fax: (513)531-1843. Contact: Sandi Luppert, promotion manager. Theme changes annually. Competition offered for unpublished work not under consideration at other publications. Charges $10 fee. Prize: 1st-$1,000; 2nd-$500; 3rd-$250. Story reserves the right to publish selected winners. Buys first North American rights. Guidelines for SASE. Deadline: May 1.

TARA FELLOWSHIP FOR SHORT FICTION, The Heekin Group Writer's & Education Fund, P.O. Box 1534, Sisters OR 97759. Phone/fax: (541)548-4147. E-mail: ltsfhl@aol.com. Director: Sarah Heekin Redfield. Offered annually for unpublished work. "Our writing fellowships program is designed to support the community of new and emerging writers." Deadline: December 1. Guidelines for SASE. Charges $25 fee. Prize: 2 for Tara Fellowship, $1,500. Reading panels—finalists judges are always publishers. Past judges: Gray Wolf Press, Soho Press, Riverhead Books, Browndeer Press, Hyperion Books for Children. 1997-98 publisher judges to be announced.

‡SYDNEY TAYLOR MANUSCRIPT COMPETITION, Association of Jewish Libraries, 1327 Wyntercreek Lane, Dunwoody GA 30338. (770)394-2060. E-mail: m-psand@mindspring.com. Award Director: Paula Sandfelder. Offered annually for unpublished authors. "Material should be a work of fiction in English, with universal appeal of Jewish content for readers aged 8-11 years. It should deepen the understanding of Judaism for all children, Jewish and non-Jewish, and reveal positive aspects of Jewish life. No short stories. Length: 64-200 pages." Deadline: January 15. Guidelines for SASE. Prize: $1,000. Judged by 5 ASL member librarians. Open to any unpublished writer of books.

STEVEN TURNER AWARD, The Texas Institute of Letters, P.O. Box 298300, Fort Worth TX 76129. (817)921-7822. Fax: (817)921-7333 (must be marked Attn: TCU Press). Website: http://www.tcu.edu/til. Director: Judy Alter. Offered annually for previously published work between January 1 and December 31 of year before. The award is given to recognize the writer of the best first book of fiction submitted. Deadline: January 2. Guidelines for SASE. Prize: $1,000. To be eligible, a writer must have been born in Texas, or have lived in the state for at least two consecutive years at some time, or the subject matter of the work should be associated with the state.

‡VERY SHORT FICTION AWARD, Glimmer Train Press, Inc., 710 SW Madison St., Suite 504, Portland OR 97205. (503)221-0836. Fax: (503)221-0837. Contest Director: Linda Davies. Annual award offered to encourage the art of the very short story. Contest opens April 1 and ends July 31; entry must be postmarked between these dates. Prizes: 1st-$1,200 and possible publication in Glimmer Train Stories; 2nd-$500; 3rd-$300. Charges $10/story fee. Word count must not exceed 2,000. First page of story to include name, address and phone number. "VSF AWARD" must be written on outside of envelope. Materials are not returned. Results will be mailed to entrants in November. Editor will telephone winners by November 1.

THE VIRTUAL PRESS ANNUAL WRITER'S CONTEST, The Virtual Press, 408 E. Division St., Shawano WI 54166. E-mail: contest@tvp.com. Website: http://tvp.com/ or www.tvpress.com. Contact: Roberta Stanek, editor. Offered annually for unpublished work to promote the writing of quality short fiction, fantasy, mystery and science fiction. Deadline: November 1. Guidelines for SASE. Charges $5 fee. Prize: 12 cash awards (4 per category): 1st-$75, 2nd-$50, 3rd-$25, 4th-$10, plus publication in annual anthology.

EDWARD LEWIS WALLANT BOOK AWARD, Department of English, Franklin & Marshall College, P.O. Box 3003, Lancaster PA 17604-3003. Contact: Dr. Sanford Pinsller. Estab. 1963. Offered for fiction with significance for the American Jew (novel or short stories) by an American writer (one who was born or educated in the United States) published during current year. Deadline: December 31.

WELLSPRING'S SHORT FICTION CONTEST, 4080 83rd Ave. N., Suite A, Brooklyn Park MN 55443. (612)566-6663. Contest Director: Meg Miller. Estab. 1988. Offered 2 times/year for previously unpublished short fiction to encourage the writing of well-crafted and plotted, meaningful short fiction. Deadlines: January 1, July 1. Guidelines for #10 SASE. Charges $12 fee. Prize: 1st-$100; 2nd-$75; 3rd-$25. $6 for sample copy.

‡EDITH WHARTON CITATION OF MERIT FOR FICTION WRITERS, New York State Writers Institute, University at Albany, HU 355, Albany NY 12222. (518)442-5620. Fax: (518)442-5621. E-mail: writer@poppa.fab.albany.edu. Award Director: Donald Faulkner, associate director. Offered every 2 years (odd years). "Upon the recommendation of an advisory panel of distinguished authors convened under the aegis of the New York State Writers Institute, the Governor of the State of New York awards the Edith Wharton Citation of Merit for Fiction Writers to a New York State author in recognition of a life-long body of work and artistic achievement. The recipient serves as New York State Author for two years to promote and encourage fiction writing within the state." Nominations may be submitted to the Writers Institute for consideration by the advisory panel. Prize: $10,000 and designation as New York State Author for two years. Judged by an advisory panel of distinguished authors chosen by the Writers Institute each time the Citation is awarded. Writers must be a New York State resident with a long and distinguished career as a fiction writer.

WINNERS' CIRCLE SHORT STORY CONTEST, Canadian Authors Association, Metropolitan Toronto Branch, 33 Springbank Ave., Scarborough, Ontario M1N 1G2 Canada. (416)698-8687. Fax: (416)698-8687. Contact: Bill Belfontaine. Contest to encourage writing of new short stories (1,500-3,500 words) which help Canadian authors to get published. Opens July 1 annually, closes November 30. Guidelines, entry form and free 24-page booklet, "How Best to Write for a Short Story Contest," for 90¢ SASE (SAE/IRC). No mss returned, but winner's list available for separate SASE (SAE/IRC). Winners announced to local and national media soon after judging, usually March of following year. Prizes: 5 cash winners (1st, $500; 4 others, $125 each). 10 or more Honorary Mentions. Winners and honorary mentions published in *Winners' Circle Anthology* and also receive official contest certificate. Entry fee $15/story, multiple submissions encouraged. All winners receive free copy of professionally published current *Winners' Circle Anthology*.

THOMAS WOLFE FICTION PRIZE, North Carolina Writers' Network, 3501 Hwy. 54 W., Studio C, Chapel Hill NC 27516. Fax: (919)929-0535. E-mail: nc_writers@unc.edu. Contact: Bobbie Collins-Perry, program & services director. Offered annually for unpublished work "to recognize a notable work of fiction—either short story or novel excerpt—while honoring one of North Carolina's best writers—Thomas Wolfe." Deadline: August 31. Guidelines for SASE. Charges $7 fee. Prize: $500 and potential publication. Past judges have included Anne Tyler, Barbara Kingsolver, C. Michael Curtis and Randall Kenan.

‡TOBIAS WOLFF AWARD IN FICTION, The Bellingham Review, M.S.9053, Western Washington University, Bellingham WA 98225. Website: http://www.wwu.edu/~bhreview/. Contact: Mr. Robin Hemley. Unpublished short story or novel except. Submissions from January 2-March 1. SASE for guidelines and fees. Prize: 1st-$500; 2nd-$250; 3rd-$100, plus publication and copies.

WRITERS' JOURNAL ANNUAL SHORT STORY CONTEST, Val-Tech Publishing, Inc., P.O. Box 25376, St. Paul MN 55125. (612)730-4280. Contact: Valerie Hockert. Estab. 1987. Unpublished short stories. Deadline: May 31. $5 fee.

WRITERS' JOURNAL FICTION CONTEST, Val-Tech Publishing, P.O. Box 25376, St. Paul MN 55125. (612)730-4280. Contact: Valerie Hockert. Offered annually for unpublished fiction. Deadline: December 31. Charges $5 fee.

Poetry

‡AKRON POETRY PRIZE, University of Akron Press, 374B Bierce Library, Akron OH 44325-1703. (330)972-5342. Fax: (330)972-6383. E-mail: press@uakron.edu. Website: http://www.uakron.edu/uapress. Contest Director: Elton Glaser. Annual contest for unpublished poetry. "The Akron Poetry Prize brings the public writers with original and compelling voices. Books must exhibit three essential qualities: mastery of language, maturity of feeling and complexity of thought." Deadline: Entries must be postmarked between May 15-June 30. Guidelines available online or for SASE. Charges $15. Winning poet receives $500 and publication of book. The University of Akron Press has the right to publish the winning manuscript, inherent with winning of the Poetry Prize. Open to poets writing in English.

ANHINGA PRIZE FOR POETRY, Anhinga Press, P.O. Box 10595, Tallahassee FL 32302. Phone/fax: (904)442-6323. Contact: Rick Campbell. Offered annually for a book-length collection of poetry by an author who has not published more than one book of poetry. "We use a well-known independent judge." Submit January 1-March 15. Guidelines for #10 SASE. Charges $20 fee. Prize: $2,000 and publication. Open to any writer writing in English.

ANNUAL INTERNATIONAL POETRY CONTEST, Poet's Study Club of Terre Haute, Indiana, 826 S. Center St., Terre Haute IN 47807. (812)234-0819. Contact: President of Poet's Study Club. Offered annually in 3 categories: Serious Poems, Light Verse, Haiku. Deadline: February 1. Guidelines for SASE. Prizes: 1st-$25 and 2nd-$15 in each category. Judged by competent writers who also often judge for our State Poetry Societies, etc. Open to any writer.

ANNUAL POETRY CONTEST, National Federation of State Poetry Societies, 1206 13th Ave., SE, St. Cloud MN 56304. Chairperson: Claire van Breemen Downes. Estab. 1959. Previously unpublished poetry. "Fifty categories. Flier lists them all." Deadline: March 15. Guidelines for #10 SASE. Charges fees. See guidelines for fees and prizes. All awards are announced in June. Top awards only (not honorable mentions) published the following June.

ARKANSAS POETRY AWARD, The University of Arkansas Press, 201 Ozark Ave., Fayetteville AR 72701. (501)575-3246. Fax: (501)575-6044. E-mail: uaprinfo@cavern.uark.edu. Website: http://www.uark.edu/campus-resour

ces/uaprinfo/public_html/. Award Director: Carolyn Brt. Estab. 1990. Offered for previously unpublished full-length poetry ms to recognize living US poets whose works have not been previously published or accepted for publication in book form and thus forward the Press's stated mission of "disseminating the fruits of creative activity." Deadline May 1. Charges $15 fee. Guidelines for #10 SASE. Award: publication of the collection by the University of Arkansas Press.

‡**ARVON INTERNATIONAL POETRY COMPETITION**, Kilnhurst, Kilnhurst Rd., TodMorden, Lancashire OL14 6AX England. (01144)01706 816582. Fax: (01144)01706 816359. Contest Director: David Pease. Offered every 2 years (odd years) to unpublished poems. Guidelines for SASE with IRCs. Charges £3.50 or $7 fee. Prizes: 1st-£5,000, 2nd-£500 (5 prizes), 3rd-£250 (10 prizes). Judged by a panel of 4 poets. Arvon has right to publish winning entries within one year of announcement. "Open to all poems on any subject and of any length written in the English language."

‡**BARNARD NEW WOMEN POETS PRIZE**, Barnard College, 3009 Broadway, New York NY 10027. (212)854-3453. Fax: (212)854-9478. Contest/Award Directors: Christopher Baswell and Claudia Rankine. Offered annually to publish a previously unpublished woman poet. Deadline: October 15. Guidelines for SASE. Charges $14.75, the cost of one book by a previous winner plus shipping. Prize: $1,500 and publication by Beacon Press. Open to any unpublished, woman poet.

‡**BLUESTEM POETRY AWARD**, The English Department, Emporia State University, 1200 Commercial, Box 4019, Emporia KS 66801. (316)341-5216. Fax: (316)341-5216. Award Director: Christopher Howell. Offered annually "to help a poet get published." Deadline: March 2, 1998. Guidelines for SASE. Charges $15 fee. Prize: $1,000 and a published book, both soft and hard cover. No full length, single author collections.

‡**THE FREDERICK BOCK PRIZE**, *Poetry*, 60 W. Walton St., Chicago IL 60610. (312)255-3703. Editor: Joseph Parisi. Offered annually for poems published in *Poetry* during the preceding twelve months (October through September). Guidelines for SASE. Prize: $300. Judged by the editors of *Poetry*. *Poetry* buys all rights to the poems published in the magazine. Copyrights are returned to the authors on request. Any writer may submit poems to *Poetry*. Only poems published in *Poetry* during the preceding year are considered for the annual prizes.

GEORGE BOGIN MEMORIAL AWARD, Poetry Society of America, 15 Gramercy Park S., New York NY 10003. (212) 254-9628. E-mail: poetsocy@panix.com. Website: http://www.poetrysociety.org. Contact: Award Director. Offered for a selection of 4-5 poems that reflects the encounter of the ordinary and the extraordinary, uses language in an original way, and takes a stand against oppression in any of its forms. Guidelines for #10 SASE. Guidelines subject to change. Deadline: December 19. Charges $5 fee for nonmembers. Prize: $500.

BRITTINGHAM PRIZE IN POETRY/FELIX POLLAK PRIZE IN POETRY, University of Wisconsin Press, 114 N. Murray St., Madison WI 53715. Contest Director: Ronald Wallace. Estab. 1985. Unpublished book-length mss of original poetry. Submissions must be *received* by the press *during* the month of September accompanied by a SASE for contest results. Prizes: $1,000 and publication of the *2 winning mss*. Guidelines for #10 SASE. Manuscripts will *not* be returned. Charges $15 fee, payable to University of Wisconsin Press. One entry fee covers both prizes.

‡**BUCKNELL SEMINAR FOR YOUNGER POETS**, Stadler Center for Poetry, Bucknell University, Lewisburg PA 17837. (717)524-1853. E-mail: sstyers@bucknell.edu. Website: http://www.bucknell.edu/departments/english/poetry _center/. Director: Cynthia Hogue. Assistant to the Director: Steven Styers. Offered annually. "The Seminar provides an extended opportunity for undergraduates to write and to be guided by established poets. It balances private time for writing, disciplined learning, and camaraderie among the 10 Fellows selected." Deadline: March 1. Guidelines for SASE. Prize: 10 fellowships provide tuition, room, board and spaces for writing during 4-week long seminar. Fellows are responsible for their own transportation. Only students from American colleges who have completed their sophomore, junior or senior years are eligible to apply.

GERALD CABLE POETRY COMPETITION, Silverfish Review Press, P.O. Box 3541, Eugene OR 97403-0541. (503)344-5060. Series Editor: Rodger Moody. To publish a poetry book by a deserving author who has yet to publish a full-length book. Submit September. Guidelines for SASE. Charges $15 reading fee. Prize: $1,000.

CLEVELAND STATE UNIVERSITY POETRY CENTER PRIZE, Cleveland State University Poetry Center, 1983 E. 24 St., Cleveland OH 44115-2440. (216)687-3986. Fax: (216)687-6943. Contact: Editor. Estab. 1962. Offered to identify, reward and publish the best unpublished book-length poetry ms submitted. Submissions accepted only December-February. Deadline: Postmarked on or before March 1. Charges $15 fee. "Submission implies willingness to sign contract for publication if manuscript wins." $1,000 prize for best ms. One or more of the other finalist mss may be published for standard royalty (no prize). Guidelines for SASE. Manuscripts are not returned.

‡**BERNARD F. CONNERS PRIZE FOR POETRY**, *The Paris Review*, 541 E. 72nd St., New York NY 10021. (212)861-0016. Offered annually to the finest previously unpublished poem over 200 lines published in *The Paris Review* that year. Guidelines for SASE. Prize: $1,000. Judged by *The Paris Review* editorial staff. *The Paris Review* does not ordinarily distinguish between award submissions and regular submissions. The only candidates for awards are writers who have already been published by *The Paris Review*. The magazine retains one-time first serial rights for

published works. Submissions must be accompanied by a self-addressed stamped envelope, must be unpublished and must be written in English.

CONTEMPORARY POETRY SERIES, University of Georgia Press, 330 Research Dr., Athens GA 30602. (706)369-6140. Coordinator: Jane Kobres. Offered 2 times/year. Two awards: for poets who have not had a full-length book of poems published (deadline in September), and poets with at least one full-length publication (deadline in January). Guidelines for SASE. Charges $10 fee.

BILLEE MURRAY DENNY POETRY AWARD, Lincoln College, 300 Keokuk St., Lincoln IL 62656. Contest Administrator: Janet Overton. Estab. 1981. Unpublished poetry. Deadline: May 31. Prizes: $1,000, $500, $250. Charges $10/poem fee (limit 3-$30). Send SASE for entry form.

‡MARIE LOUISE D'ESTERNAUX POETRY CONTEST, Brooklyn Poetry Circle, 2550 Independence Ave., #3U, Bronx NY 10463. Contact: Ruth M. Fowler. "Annual contest for previously unpublished poetry to encourage young people to study poetry, to write poetry and to enrich themselves and others." Deadline: April 15. Guidelines for SASE. Prize: 1st-$50; 2nd-$25.

ALICE FAY DI CASTAGNOLA AWARD, Poetry Society of America, 15 Gramercy Park S., New York NY 10003. (212)254-9628. E-mail: poetsocy@panix.com. Website: http://www.poetrysociety.org. Contact: Award Director. Manuscript in progress: poetry, prose or verse-drama. Guidelines for #10 SASE. Guidelines subject to change. Deadline: December 19. Prize: $1,000. Members only.

"DISCOVERY"/THE NATION, The Joan Leiman Jacobson Poetry Prizes, The Unterberg Poetry Center of the 92nd Street YM-YWHA, 1395 Lexington Ave., New York NY 10128. Estab. 1973. Open to poets who have not published a book of poems (chapbooks, self-published books included). Deadline: late January. Charges $5 fee. Write for complete competition guidelines, or call (212)415-5759.

MILTON DORFMAN POETRY PRIZE, Rome Art & Community Center, 308 W. Bloomfield St., Rome NY 13440. (315)336-1040. Fax: (315)336-1090. Contact: Maureen Murphy. Estab. 1990. "The purpose of the Milton Dorfman Poetry Prize is to offer poets an outlet for their craft. All submissions must be previously unpublished." Entries accepted: July 1-November 1. Guidelines for #10 SASE. Charges $3 fee per poem. Make checks payable to: Rome Art & Community Center. Prize: 1st-$500; 2nd-$200; 3rd-$100. Open to any writer. Include name, address and phone number.

‡EDITORS' PRIZE, Spoon River Poetry Review, Campus Box 4240, English Dept., Illinois State University, Normal IL 61790-4240. (309)438-7906. Fax: (309)438-5414. Contest Director: Lucia Cordell Getsi. Offered annually to unpublished poetry "to identify and reward excellence." Deadline: May 1. Guidelines for SASE. Charges $15/3 poem fee (entitles entrant to a year's subscription valued at $14). Prizes: 1st-$500, two $100 runner-up prizes, publication of first place, runners-up, honorable mention and selected finalist poems. Open to all writers.

‡VERNA EMERY POETRY COMPETITION, (formerly Verna Emery Poetry Prize), Purdue University Press, 1532 S. Campus Courts, Bldg. E, West Lafayette IN 47907-1532. (765)494-2038. Fax: (765)496-2442. Offered annually for a single-authored book of poetry. No translations. Deadline: April 15. Guidelines for SASE. Charges $15 entry fee. Prize: $500 cash upon publication plus royalty arrangements.

NORMA FARBER FIRST BOOK AWARD, Poetry Society of America, 15 Gramercy Park S., New York NY 10003. (212)254-9628. E-mail: poetsocy@panix.com. Website: http://www.poetrysociety.org. Contact: Award Director. First book of original poetry submitted by the publisher. Deadline: December 19. Charges $10/book fee. Guidelines for #10 SASE. Guidelines subject to change. Prize: $500.

THE 49th PARALLEL POETRY AWARD, The Bellingham Review, M.S. 9053, Western Washington University, Bellingham WA 98225. Contest Director: Robin Hemley. Estab. 1977. Unpublished poetry. Submit October 1-December 31. Send SASE for new guidelines and fees. Awards: 1st-$500, 2nd-$250, 3rd-$100, plus publication and copies.

GREEN LAKE CHAPBOOK PRIZE, Owl Creek Press, 2693 SW Camano Dr., Camano Island WA 98292. Contact: Rich Ives. Any combination of published and unpublished poems under 40 pages in length as long as the work has not previously appeared in book form (except anthologies). Guidelines for SASE. Include SASE for return of ms. Deadline: August 15. Charges $10 fee. Prize: Publication and $500 advance against royalties.

CECIL HEMLEY MEMORIAL AWARD, Poetry Society of America, 15 Gramercy Park S., New York NY 10003. (212)254-9628. E-mail: poetsocy@panix.com. Website: http://www.poetrysociety.org. Contact: Award Director. Unpublished lyric poem on a philosophical theme. Guidelines for #10 SASE. Deadline: December 19. Members only. Prize: $300.

‡THE BESS HOKIN PRIZE, *Poetry*, 60 W. Walton St., Chicago IL 60610. (312)255-3703. Editor, *Poetry*: Joseph Parisi. Offered annually for poems published in *Poetry* during the preceding twelve months (October through September).

Guidelines for SASE. Prize: $500. Judged by the editors of *Poetry*. *Poetry* buys all rights to the poems published in the magazine. Copyrights are returned to the authors on request. Any writer may submit poems to *Poetry*. Only poems published in *Poetry* during the preceding year are considered for the annual prizes.

INTERNATIONAL TANKA SPLENDOR AWARDS, AHA Books, P.O. Box 1250, Gualala CA 95445-1250. (707)882-2226. E-mail: ahabooks@mcn.org. Website: http://www.faximum.com/AHA!POETRY. Editor: Jane Reichhold. Estab. 1988. "The purpose of the contest is to acquaint writers with the Japanese poetry form, tanka and tanka sequences. By choosing 31 winners for publication in a chapbook, it is hoped that standards and examples will be set, re-evaluated, changed and enlarged. The genre is one of Japan's oldest, but the newest to English." Deadline: September 30. Guidelines for #10 SASE. Maximum 10 entries. No fee. Send SASE for winners list. 31 winning entries published in *Tanka Splendor*, which is given to the winners and then goes on sale for up to 3 years by AHA Books distribution.

RANDALL JARRELL POETRY PRIZE, North Carolina Writers' Network, 3501 Highway 54 West, Studio C, Chapel Hill NC 27516. Offered annually for unpublished work "to honor Randall Jarrell and his life at UNC-Greensboro by recognizing the best poetry submitted." Deadline: November 1. Guidelines for SASE. Charges $7 fee. Prize: $500, a public reading and reception and publication in *Parnassus: Poetry in Review*.

THE CHESTER H. JONES FOUNDATION NATIONAL POETRY COMPETITION, P.O. Box 498, Chardon OH 44024-9996. Estab. 1982. Offered annually for persons in the US, Canada and US citizens living abroad. Winning poems plus others, called "commendations," are published in a chapbook available from the foundation. Deadline: March 31. Charges $2 fee for first poem, $1 for each succeeding poem up to 10. Maximum 10 entries, no more than 32 lines each; must be unpublished. Prize: 1st-$1,000; 2nd-$750; 3rd-$500; 4th-$250; 5th-$100; several honorable mentions-$50. All commendations which are printed in the winners book receive $10. Winners receive the book free.

THE JUNIPER PRIZE, University of Massachusetts, Amherst MA 01003. (413)545-2217. Fax: (413)545-1226. Website: http://www.umass.edu/umpress. Contact: Chris Hammel. Estab. 1964. Subsequent book of poetry. Deadline: September 30. Charges $10 fee.

KALLIOPE'S ANNUAL SUE SANIEL ELKIND POETRY CONTEST, *Kalliope, a journal of women's art*, 3939 Roosevelt Blvd., Jacksonville FL 32205. (904)381-3511. Contact: Mary Sue Koeppel. Offered annually for unpublished work. "Poetry may be in any style and on any subject. Maximum poem length is 50 lines. Only unpublished poems and poems not submitted elsewhere are eligible." Deadline: November 1, 1997. Guidelines for SASE. Charges entry fee: $4/poem or 3 poems for $10. No limit on number of poems entered by any one poet. Prize: $1,000, publication of poem in *Kalliope*. The winning poem is published as are the finalists' poems. Copyright then returns to the authors.

‡**BARBARA MANDIGO KELLY PEACE POETRY AWARDS**, Nuclear Age Peace Foundation, 1187 Coast Village Rd., Suite 123, Santa Barbara CA 93108. Fax: (805)568-0466. E-mail: wagingpeace@hapf.org. Website: http://www.napf.org. Contact: Chris Pizzinat and Ruth Floyd. Offered annually for unpublished poems "to encourage poets to explore and illuminate some aspect of peace and the human spirit." Deadline: June 30. Guidelines for SASE. Charges $5 fee for 1-3 poems. No fee for youth entries. Prizes: Adult-$500, youth (13-18)-$250, youth (12 and under)-$250. Judged by a committee of poets chosen by the Nuclear Age Peace Foundation. The Nuclear Age Peace Foundation reserves the right to publish and distribute the award-winning poems. Open to any writer.

‡**THE GEORGE KENT PRIZE**, *Poetry*, 60 W. Walton St., Chicago IL 60610. (312)255-3703. Editor, *Poetry*: Joseph Parisi. Offered annually for poems by an Illinois author published in *Poetry* during the preceding twelve months (October through September). Guidelines for SASE. Prize: $500. Judged by the editors of *Poetry*. *Poetry* buys all rights to the poems published in the magazine. Copyrights are returned to the authors on request. Any writer may submit poems to *Poetry*. Only poems published in *Poetry* during the preceding year are considered for the annual prizes. This contest is open only to any resident of Illinois.

‡**(HELEN AND LAURA KROUT) MEMORIAL OHIOANA POETRY AWARD**, Ohioana Library Association, 65 S. Front St., Suite 1105, Columbus OH 43215. (614)466-3831. Fax: (614)728-6974. E-mail: ohioana@winslo.ohio.gov. Website: http://www.oplin.lib.oh.us/OHIOANA/. Contact: Linda R. Hengst. Offered annually "to an individual whose body of work has made, and continues to make, a significant contribution to the poetry and through whose work, interest in poetry has been developed." Deadline: December 31. Guidelines for SASE. Prize: $1,000. Recipieint must have been born in Ohio or lived in Ohio at least 5 years.

LAST POEMS POETRY CONTEST, sub-TERRAIN Magazine, P.O. Box 1575, Bentall Centre, Vancouver, British Columbia V6C 2P7 Canada. (604)876-8710. Fax: (604)879-2667. Offered annually for unpublished poetry that encapsulates the North American experience at the close of the 20th Century. Deadline: January 31. Guidelines for SASE. Charges $15 fee, 4 poem limit. Prize: $200, publication in spring issue and 4-issue subscription to sub-TERRAIN.

‡**THE JAMES LAUGHLIN AWARD**, The Academy of American Poets, 584 Broadway, Suite 1208, New York NY 10012-3250. (212)274-0343. Fax: (212)274-9427. E-mail: poets@artswire.org. Contact: India Amos. Offered annually to submissions under contract with publishers. Previously published entries must have come under contract between

April 30, 1997 and April 30, 1998. The purpose of the award is to recognize and support a poet's second book. Deadline: April 30. Guideline for SASE. Prize: $5,000 and at least 5,000 hardcover copies for distribution. Judged by a panel of three poets. Submissions must be in English by one poet, and it must be the poet's second book.

LEAGUE OF CANADIAN POETS AWARDS, National Poetry Contest, Canadian Poetry Chapbook Contest, Gerald Lampert Memorial Award, and Pat Lowther Memorial Award, 54 Wolseley St., 3rd Floor, Toronto, Ontario M5T 1A5 Canada. (416)504-1657. Fax: (416)703-0059. E-mail: league@ican.net. Website: http://www.swifty.com/lc/. Estab. 1966. Offered annually to promote new Canadian poetry/poets and also to recognize exceptional work in each category. Submissions to be published in the preceding year (awards), or previously unpublished (poetry contest, chapbook contest). Deadline: January 31. Deadline for chapbook contest: March 1. Enquiries from publishers welcome. Charge: $6/poem fee for contest, $12 for chapbook contest and $15 fee/title for each award. Open to Canadians living at home and abroad. The candidate must be a Canadian citizen or landed immigrant, although publisher need not be Canadian. For complete contest and awards rules, contact Edita Petrauskaite at address above.

‡**THE LEVINSON PRIZE**, *Poetry*, 60 W. Walton St., Chicago IL 60610. (312)255-3703. Editor, *Poetry*: Joseph Parisi. Offered annually for poems published in *Poetry* during the preceding twelve months (October through September). Guidelines for SASE. Prize: $500. Judged by the editors of *Poetry*. *Poetry* buys all rights to the poems published in the magazine. Copyrights are returned to the authors on request. Any writer may submit poems to *Poetry*. Only poems published in *Poetry* during the preceding year are considered for the annual prizes.

‡**THE LEVIS POETRY PRIZE**, Four Way Books, P.O. Box 607, Marshfield MA 02050. Phone/fax: (617)837-4887. Offered annually to all US poets in memory of poet Larry Levis. Submissions accepted January 1-April 30. For guidelines, send a SASE to: Four Way Books, P.O. Box 535, Village Station, New York NY 10014. Charges $15 fee. Prize: $2,000 and publication of a book-length collection of poems.

THE RUTH LILLY POETRY PRIZE, The Modern Poetry Association, 60 W. Walton St., Chicago IL 60610-3305. Contact: Joseph Parisi. Estab. 1986. Offered annually to poet whose accomplishments in the field of poetry warrant extraordinary recognition. No applicants or nominations are accepted. Deadline varies. Prize: $75,000.

LOCAL 7's ANNUAL NATIONAL POETRY COMPETITION, Santa Cruz/Monterey Local 7, National Writers Union, P.O. Box 2409, Aptos CA 95001-2409. Coordinator: Matt Friday. Offered annually for previously unpublished poetry to encourage the writing of poetry and to showcase unpublished work of high quality. Proceeds support the work of Local 7 of the National Writers Union. Deadline varies. Guidelines for #10 SASE. Charges $3/poem fee. Prize: 1st-$200; 2nd-$100; 3rd-$50.

LOUISIANA LITERATURE PRIZE FOR POETRY, *Louisiana Literature*, SLU—Box 792, Southeastern Louisiana University, Hammond LA 70402. (504)549-5022. Fax: (504)549-5021. E-mail: dhanson@selu.edu. Contest Director: Dr. David Hanson. Estab. 1984. Unpublished poetry. Deadline: February 16. Rules for SASE. Prize: $400. Entries considered for publication.

LYRIC POETRY AWARD, Poetry Society of America, 15 Gramercy Park, New York NY 10003. (212)254-9628. Fax: (212)673-2352. E-mail: poetsocy@panix.com. Website: http://www.poetrysociety.org. Director: Timothy Donnelly. Offered annually for unpublished work to promote excellence in the lyric poetry field. Deadline: December 19. Guidelines for SASE. Prize: $500.

‡**NAOMI LONG MADGETT POETRY AWARD**, Lotus Press, Inc., P.O. Box 21607, Detroit MI 48221. (313)861-1280. Fax: (313)861-4740. Contact: Constance Withers. Offered annually to recognize an outstanding unpublished poetry ms by an African-American. Entries accepted from February 1-April 1. Guidelines for SASE. Charges $15 fee. Prize: $500 and publication by Michigan State University Press. Open to any African-American poet.

‡**THE MALAHAT REVIEW LONG POEM PRIZE**, The Malahat Review, Box 1700, Victoria, British Columbia V8W 2Y2 Canada. E-mail: malahat@uvic.ca. Contact: Derk Wynand. Offered every 2 years to unpublished long poems. Deadline: March 1. Guidelines for SASE. Charges $25 fee (includes a one-year subscription to the *Malahat*, published quarterly.) Prize: $400, plus payment from publication ($25/page). Preliminary reading by editorial board; final judging by the editor and 2 recognized poets. Obtains first world rights. After publication rights revert to the author. Open to any writer.

THE LENORE MARSHALL POETRY PRIZE, (formerly The Lenore Marshall Prize), *The Nation* and The Academy of American Poets, 584 Broadway, #1208, New York NY 10012. (212)274-0343. E-mail: poets@artswire.org. Website: http://www.poets.org. Awards Administrator: India Amos. Book of poems published in US during previous year and nominated by the publisher. Prize: $10,000. Deadline: June 1. Query the Academy of American Poets for details.

LUCILLE MEDWICK MEMORIAL AWARD, Poetry Society of America, 15 Gramercy Park S., New York NY 10003. (212)254-9628. E-mail: poetsocy@panix.com. Website: http://www.poetrysociety.org. Contact: Award Director.

Original poem in any form or freedom on a humanitarian theme. Guidelines for #10 SASE. Guidelines subject to change. Prize: $500. Deadline: December 19. Members only.

MID-LIST PRESS FIRST SERIES AWARD FOR POETRY, Mid-List Press, 4324 12th Ave. S., Minneapolis MN 55407-3218. Estab. 1990. Offered annually for unpublished book of poetry to encourage new poets. Deadline: February 1. Guidelines for SASE. Charges $15 fee. Prize: publication and an advance against royalties. Judged by Mid-List's editors and ms readers. Winners are offered a contract at the conclusion of the judging. Contest is open to any writer who has never published a book of poetry. ("We do not consider a chapbook to be a book of poetry.")

‡VASSAR MILLER PRIZE IN POETRY, University of North Texas Press, % Scott Cairns, English Dept., Seattle Pacific University, Seattle WA 98119. (206)281-2000. Fax: (757)683-5746. E-mail: scairns@spu.edu. Series Editor: Scott Cairns. Offered annually for 50-80 p.p., original, unpublished poetry ms. Deadline: November 30. Guidelines for SASE. Charges $16 fee, payable to UNT Press. Prize: $500 and standard publication contract with UNT Press. A different final judge each year; past judges include Richard Howard, Cynthia MacDonald, Sydney Lea, Yusef Komunyakaa and Heather McHugh. Standard copyright in author's name when published.

MORSE POETRY PRIZE, Northeastern University English Deptment, 406 Holmes Hall, Boston MA 02115. (617)437-2512. Contact: Guy Rotella. Previously published poetry, book-length mss of first or second books. Charges $10/fee. Prize: Publication by Northeastern University Press and a $500 cash award.

‡KATHRYN A. MORTON PRIZE IN POETRY, Sarabande Books, 2234 Dundee Rd., Suite 200, Louisville KY 40205. (502)458-4028. Fax: (502)458-4065. E-mail: sarabandeb@aol.com. Contest Director: Sarah Gorham. Offered annually to award publication to an outstanding collection of poetry. Submissions accepted January 1-February 15. Guidelines for SASE. Charges $15 fee. Prize: $2,000, publication (paper and cloth), standard royalty contract. All finalists considered for publication. Judged by nationally prominent writers.

‡MUDFISH POETRY PRIZE, Mudfish/Box Turtle Press, 184 Franklin St., New York NY 10013. (212)219-9278. Editor: Jill Hoffman. Offered annually for unpublished poems. Deadline: December 12. Guidelines for SASE. Charges $10 for 3 poems; $2 each additional poem. Prize: $500 and publication. All entries considered for publication.

NATIONAL LOOKING GLASS POETRY CHAPBOOK COMPETITION, *Pudding Magazine: The International Journal of Applied Poetry*, 60 N. Main St., Johnstown OH 43031. (614)967-6060. Contest Director: Jennifer Bosveld. "To publish a collection of poems that represents our magazine's editorial slant: popular culture, social justice, psychological, etc. Poems might be themed or not." Two opportunities annually. Deadlines: June 30 and September 30. Guidelines for #10 SASE. Charges $10 fee. Prize: publication and 20 copies to the author plus wholesale rights.

‡NATIONAL POETRY BOOK AWARD, Salmon Run Press, P.O. Box 231081, Anchorage AK 99523. (907)688-4268. E-mail: mpep33A@prodigy.com. Contact: John Smelcer. Offered annually to previously published or unpublished poetry. "Each year we invite poets nationwide to send their 48-96 page poetry ms. After the deadline, our judge/staff selects one ms to become published in a run of no fewer than 500 copies." Deadline: December 30. Guidelines for SASE. Charges $10 fee. Prize: Publication of ms (minimum 500 copies), advertising in national literary magazines (*Poets & Writer*, etc.), arrangements for national reviews with approximately 50 promotional copies sent. Judges rotate each year. Author maintains all rights. Open to all poets.

THE NATIONAL POETRY SERIES, The Copernicus Society of America, P.O. Box G, Hopewell NJ 08525. (609)466-9712. Fax: (609)466-4706. Director: Daniel Halpern. Offered annually for unpublished work. The National Poetry Series was established to ensure the publication of five new books of poetry in America each year. Deadline: January 1-February 15. Guidelines for SASE. Charges $25 fee. Prize: Book publication and $1,000 award. Judged by five different judges, each a poet of national reputation. Judges are different each year. Open to any writer.

NATIONAL WRITERS ASSOCIATION POETRY CONTEST, The National Writers Association, Suite 424, 1450 S. Havana, Aurora CO 80012. (303)751-7844. Fax:(303)751-8593. Director: Sandy Whelchel. Annual contest "to encourage the writing of poetry, an important form of individual expression but with a limited commercial market." Charges $10 fee. Prizes: $100, $50, $25. Guidelines for #10 SASE.

HOWARD NEMEROV SONNET AWARD, *The Formalist: A Journal of Metrical Poetry*, 320 Hunter Dr., Evansville IN 47711. Contact: Mona Baer. Offered annually for an unpublished sonnet to encourage poetic craftsmanship and to honor the memory of the late Howard Nemerov, third US Poet Laureate and a masterful writer of sonnets. Deadline: June 15. Guidelines for SASE. Entry fee: $3/sonnet. Prize: $1,000 cash and publication in *The Formalist*; 11 other finalists also published. Acquires first North American serial rights for those sonnets chosen for publication. Upon publication all rights revert to the author. Open to the international community of writers.

‡NEW ENGLAND POETRY CLUB CONTESTS, New England Poetry Club, 11 Puritan Rd., Arlington MA 02139. Contest Director: Virginia Thayer. Offered annually to multiple categories of unpublished poetry. Deadline: June 30. Guidelines for SASE. No entry fee for club members. Charges $3/poem for non-club members. Prizes: $100-500, varies for each award. Judged by well-known poets and/or previous winners of Poetry Club awards. Some contests are only available to club members. No poem may be entered in more than one contest.

‡bp NICHOL CHAPBOOK AWARD, Phoenix Community Works Foundation, 316 Dupont St., Toronto, Ontario M5R 1V9 Canada. (416)964-7919. Award Director: Philip McKenna. Offered annually to a previously published chapbook (10-48 pp) of poetry in English, published in Canada during the year prior to the year of the award. Deadline: March 30. Guidelines for SASE. Prize: $1,000 (Canadian). Judged by two writers appointed by the Foundation. Open to any writer. Author or publisher may make submissions. Send 3 copies (nonreturnable), plus a short c.v. of the author.

‡THE FRANK O'HARA AWARD CHAPBOOK COMPETITION, Thorngate Road, Campus Box 4240, English Dept., Illinois State University, Normal IL 61790-4240. (309)438-7705. Fax: (309)438-5414. E-mail: jmelled@ilstu.edu. Director: Jim Elledge. Offered annually to published or unpublished poetry. "To recognize excellence in poetry by gays, lesbians and bisexuals. Entrants may be beginners, emerging poets or those with a national reputation. Poems may be formal, free verse, post-modern, prose poems, etc." Deadline: February 1. Guidelines for SASE. Charges $10/ms fee. Prize: $200 and publication of the winning ms; author also receives 25 copies of the chapbook. The winning ms is copyrighted by Thorngate Road in the poet's name. Open to any writer.

NATALIE ORNISH POETRY AWARD IN MEMORY OF WAYNE GARD, The Texas Institute of Letters, P.O. Box 298300, Fort Worth TX 76129. (817)921-7822. Fax: (817)921-7333 (must be marked Attn: TCU Press). Website: http://www.tcu.edu/til. Offered annually for previously published work between January 1 and December 31 of year before award is given to honor the writer of the best book of poems published during the previous year. Deadline: January 2. Guidelines for SASE. Prize: $1,000. Judged by a panel of three. Poet must have been born in Texas, have lived in the state at some time for at least two consecutive years, or subject matter is associated with the state.

GUY OWEN POETRY PRIZE, *Southern Poetry Review*, Advancement Studies, CPCC, Charlotte NC 28235. (704)330-6002. Award Director: Ken McLaurin. Estab. 1985. Offered annually for the best unpublished poem submitted in an open competition. Given in memory of Guy Owen, a poet, fiction writer and founder of *Southern Poetry Review*. Submit in April only—3-5 previously unpublished poems and SASE. Charges $8 fee that includes one year subscription to *SPR* to begin with the Winter issue, containing the winning poem. Prize: $500 and publication in *SPR*. All submissions considered for publication.

OWL CREEK POETRY PRIZE, Owl Creek Press, 2693 SW Camano Dr., Camano Island WA 98292. Any combination of published and unpublished poems over 50 pages in length as long as the work has not previously appeared in book form (except anthologies). Guidelines for SASE. Include SASE for return of ms. Deadline: February 15. Charges $15 fee. Prize: Publication and $750 advance against royalties.

PAT PARKER POETRY AWARD, National Women's Studies Association, 7100 Baltimore Ave., #301, College Park MD 20715. (301)403-0525. Fax: (301)403-4137. Offered annually for unpublished work. Awarded for an outstanding narrative poem or dramatic monologue by a Black, lesbian, feminist poet. Poems can be up to 50 lines and on a topic to the concerns of African American women, lesbians, and feminists, or the life and work of poet Pat Parker. Special preference will be given to poems that inspire, enlighten, or encourage. Submissions accepted May 1-July 31. Charges $21 fee. Guidelines for SASE. Prize: $250.

‡PAUMANOK POETRY AWARD, Visiting Writers Program, SUNY Farmingdale, Knapp Hall Farmingdale NY 11735. E-mail: brownml@snyfarvg.cc.farmingdale.edu. Website: http://www.farmingdale.edu/Engdept/paward.html. Acting Director, Visiting Writers Program: Margery L. Brown. Offered annually for published or unpublished poems. Send cover letter, 1-paragraph bio, 1-5 poems (name and address on each poem). Include SASE for notification of winners. (Send photocopies only; mss will not be returned.) Deadline: September 15. Charges $12 fee, payable to SUNY Farmingdale VWP. Prize: 1st-$1,000 plus expenses for a reading in 1996-97 series; 2 runners-up—$500 plus expenses for a reading in series.

‡PETERLOO POETS OPEN POETRY COMPETITION, 2 Kelly Gardens, Calstock, Cornwall PL18 9SA UK. Publication Director: Harry Chambers. Estab. 1971. "Annual competition for new (unpublished) poetry." Deadline: March 1. Entry fee indicated on rules/entry form. Awards consist of cash prizes and publication.

THE RICHARD PHILLIPS POETRY PRIZE, The Phillips Publishing Co., P.O. Box 121, Watts OK 74964. Contact: Richard Phillips, Jr. Offered annually to give a modest financial reward to emerging poets who have not yet established themselves sufficiently to generate appropriate compensation for their work. Deadline: Postmarked by January 31. Guidelines for SASE. Charges $15 fee. Prize: $1,000 and publication. Open to all poets. "There are no anthologies to buy. No strings attached. Simply put, the poet who enters the best manuscript will win the prize of $1,000 and will receive a check in that amount within 60 days of the deadline." Recent winners: Deborah Vallet (Atlanta GA) and Kathryn Presley (Somerville TX).

‡POET LORE NARRATIVE POETRY CONTEST, *Poet Lore*, The Writer's Center, 4508 Walsh St., Bethesda MD 20815. (301)654-8664. Directors: Phillip Jason, Geraldine Connolly. Estab. 1889. Offered annually for unpublished narrative poems of 100 lines or more. Deadline: November 30. Prize: $350 and publication in *Poet Lore*. "*Poet Lore* has first publication rights for poems submitted. All rights revert to the author after publication in *Poet Lore*."

THE POETRY CENTER BOOK AWARD, The Poetry Center, San Francisco State University, 1600 Holloway Ave., San Francisco CA 94132-9901. (415)338-3132. Fax: (415)338-0966. Award Director: Melissa Black. Estab. 1980. Offered annually for previously published books of poetry and chapbooks, appearing in year of the prize. "Prize given for an extraordinary book of American poetry." Deadline December 31. Guidelines for #10 SASE. Charges $10/book fee. Prize: $500 and an invitation to read in the Poetry Center Reading Series. Please include a cover letter noting author name, book title(s), name of person issuing check, and check number.

‡POETS AND PATRONS, INC. INTERNATIONAL NARRATIVE POETRY CONTEST, 2820 W. Birch-wood, Chicago IL 60045. Chairperson: Robert Mills. Deadline: September 1. *Must* send for rules after March 1.

POETS CLUB OF CHICAGO INTERNATIONAL SHAKESPEAREAN/PETRARCHAN SONNET CON-TEST, 130 Windsor Park Dr. C-323, Carol Stream IL 60188. Chairman: LaVone Holt. Estab. 1954. Deadline: September 1. Guidelines for SASE after March 1.

FELIX POLLAK PRIZE IN POETRY/BRITTINGHAM PRIZE IN POETRY, University of Wisconsin Press, 114 N. Murray St., Madison WI 53715. Contest Director: Ronald Wallace. Estab. 1994. Unpublished book length ms of original poetry. Submissions must be received by the press during the month of September (postmark is irrelevant) and must be accompanied by SASE for contest results. Prize: $1,000 and publication to the 2 best submissions. Guidelines for #10 SASE. Does not return mss. Charges $20 fee, payable to University of Wisconsin Press. One fee covers both competitions. Notification in February.

QUARTERLY REVIEW OF LITERATURE POETRY SERIES, 26 Haslet Ave., Princeton NJ 08540. (609)921-6976. "QRL Poetry Series is a book publishing series chosen from an open competition." Publishes 4-6 titles/year. Prize: $1,000, publication and 100 copies to each winner for a book of miscellaneous poems, a single long poem, a poetic play or a book of translations. Guidelines for SASE.

ROANOKE-CHOWAN AWARD FOR POETRY, North Carolina Literary and Historical Association, 109 E. Jones St., Room 305, Raleigh NC 27601-2807. (919)733-7305. Fax: (919)733-8807. Awards Coordinator: Rita Cashim. Previously published poetry by a resident of North Carolina. Deadline: July 15.

NICHOLAS ROERICH POETRY PRIZE, Story Line Press, Three Oaks Farm, Brownsville OR 97327-9718. (541)466-5352. Fax: (541)466-3200. E-mail: slp@ptinet.com. Contact: Jenny Root. Estab. 1988. Full-length book of poetry. Any writer who has not published a full-length collection (48 pages or more) in English is eligible. Deadline: October 15. Guidelines for SASE. Charges $20 fee. Prize: winner—$1,000, publication, a reading at the Nicholas Roerich Museum in New York. Runner-up—scholarship to Wesleyan Writers Workshop in Canada.

ANNA DAVIDSON ROSENBERG AWARD FOR POEMS ON THE JEWISH EXPERIENCE, Judah L. Magnes Museum, 2911 Russell St., Berkeley CA 94705. (510)549-6950. Website: http://jfed.org/Magnes/Magnes.htm. Contact: Paula Friedman. Offered annually for unpublished work to encourage poetry of/on/from the Jewish experience. Deadline for requesting mandatory entry forms is July 15; deadline for receipt of poems is August 31. Guidelines and entry form for SASE. Submissions must include entry form. Charges $2 fee for up to 4 poems. Prize: 1st-$100; 2nd-$50; 3rd-$25; $25-New/Emerging Poet Prize; $25-Youth Award; also, Senior Award and Honorable Mentions. All winners receive certificate, and selection of winning poems are read in an Awards Reading here. Open to any writer.

‡SALT HILL JOURNAL POETRY PRIZE, Salt Hill Journal/Syracuse University, English Dept., Syracuse University, Syracuse NY 13244. (315)443-2174. Contact: Michael Paul Thomas. Offered annually "to award the strongest contemporary poetry and to publish winners and honorable mentions." Deadline: May 1. Charges $5 fee. Prizes: 1st-$500, 2nd-$100. Winners and three honorable mentions receive publication. The entries are first read by graduate students and finalists are passed on to a judge who is a nationally recognized poet. Open to any writer.

‡SHELLEY MEMORIAL AWARD, Poetry Society of America, 15 Gramercy Park S., New York NY 10003. (212)254-9628. E-mail: poetsocy@panix.com. Website: http://www.poetrysociety.org. Contact: Award Director. Deadline: December 19. By nomination only to a living American poet. Prize: $2,000-6,000.

SLIPSTREAM ANNUAL POETRY CHAPBOOK COMPETITION, *Slipstream*, Box 2071, Niagara Falls NY 14301. (716)282-2616 after 5 P.M. EST. Website: http://wings.buffalo.edu/libraries/units/pl/slipstream. Director: Dan Si-coli. Offered annually to help promote a poet whose work is often overlooked or ignored. Deadline: December 1. Guidelines for SASE. Charges $10 fee. Prize: $500 and 50 copies of published chapbook. Judged by editors of Slipstream magazine. Open to any writer. Past winners have included Gerald Locklin, David Chorlton, Serena Fusek, Robert Cooperman, Sherman Alexie, Kurt Nimmo, Katharine Harer, Richard Amidon and Matt Buys.

PEREGRINE SMITH POETRY CONTEST, Gibbs Smith, Publisher, P.O. Box 667, Layton UT 84041. (801)544-2958. Fax: (801)544-5582. Poetry Editor: Gail Yngve. Offered annually for unpublished work. The purpose of this award is to recognize and publish a previously unpublished work. Deadline: April 30. "We only accept submissions during the month of April each year." Guidelines for SASE. Charges $15 fee. Prize: $500 and publication of the winning entry. Judged by Christopher Merrill. Open to any writer.

SNAKE NATION PRESS'S ANNUAL POETRY CONTEST, Snake Nation Press, 110 #2 W. Force St., Valdosta GA 31601. (912)219-8334. Contest Director: Roberta George. Editor: Nancy Phillips. Estab. 1989. Annual contest to give a wider audience to readable, understandable poetry. Deadline: March 15. Guidelines for #10 SASE. Charges $10 fee. Prize consists of $500, 50 copies and distribution. Open to everyone.

THE SOW'S EAR CHAPBOOK PRIZE, *The Sow's Ear Poetry Review*, 19535 Pleasant View Dr., Abingdon VA 24211-6827. (540)628-2651. Contest Director: Larry K. Richman. Estab. 1988. 24-26 pages of poetry. Submit March-April. Guidelines for #10 SASE. Charges $10 fee. Prize: 1st-$500, 50 copies and distribution to subscribers; 2nd-$100; 3rd-$100.

‡**THE SOW'S EAR POETRY PRIZE**, The Sow's Ear Poetry Review, 19535 Pleasant View Dr., Abingdon VA 24211-6827. (540)628-2651. Contest Director: Larry K. Richman. Estab. 1988. Previously unpublished poetry. Submit September-October. Guidelines for #10 SASE. Charges $2 fee/poem. Prizes: $500, $100, $50 and publication, plus publication for 20-25 finalists. All submissions considered for publication.

‡**SPRING AND FALL POETRY CHAPBOOK CONTESTS**, White Eagle Coffee Store Press, P.O. Box 383, Fox River Grove IL 60021-0383. (847)639-9200. Offered 2 times/year since 1991 to unpublished poetry chapbooks. Length: 20-24 pages. Deadlines: March 30 and September 30. Guidelines for SASE. Charges $10 fee. Prize: $200, publication and 25 copies of chapbook. Open to any writer. Previous winners include Timothy Russell, Becky Gould Gibson, Leilani Wright, Robert Joe Stout.

ANN STANFORD POETRY PRIZE, The Southern California Anthology, % Master of Professional Writing Program, WPH 404, U.S.C., Los Angeles CA 90089-4034. (213)740-3252. Contest Director: James Ragan. Estab. 1988. Previously unpublished poetry to honor excellence in poetry in memory of poet and teacher Ann Stanford. Include cover sheet with name, address and titles of the 5 poems entered. Deadline: April 15. Guidelines for #10 SASE. Charges $10 fee. Prize: 1st-$750; 2nd-$250; 3rd-$100. Winning poems are published in *The Southern California Anthology* and all entrants receive a free issue.

THE AGNES LYNCH STARRETT POETRY PRIZE, University of Pittsburgh Press, 127 N. Bellefield Ave., Pittsburgh PA 15260. (412)624-4110. Fax: (412)624-7380. Series Editor: Ed Ochester. Estab. 1936. First book of poetry for poets who have not had a full-length book published. Deadline: March and April only. Guidelines for SASE (essential). Prize: $3,000.

STEPHEN G. STEPHANSSON AWARD FOR POETRY, Writers Guild of Alberta, 11759 Groat Rd., Edmonton Alberta T5M 3K6 Canada. (403)422-8174. Fax: (403)422-2663. E-mail: writers@compusmart.ab.ca. Assistant Director: Darlene Diver. Poetry book published in current year. Must be an Alberta poet.

‡**STILL WATERS PRESS POETRY CHAPBOOK COMPETITIONS**, 459 S. Willow Ave., Galloway Township NJ 08201-4633. Website: http://www2.netcom.com/~salake/StillWatersPoetry.html. Contact: Shirley Lake Warren, founding editor. Two contests offered annually to unpublished chapbooks or previously published poems in chapbooks. Deadlines: February 28 (Women's Words) and September 30 (Winter). Guidelines for SASE. Charges $10 fee. Prizes: Publication with review distribution and publicity package, plus copies. Simultaneous submissions prohibited. Previous publication history and copyright permission required, if applicable. The Women's Words Competition is open to women only. The Winter Competition is open to women and men.

‡**THE EUNICE TIETJENS MEMORIAL PRIZE**, *Poetry*, 60 W. Walton St., Chicago IL 60610. (312)255-3703. Editor, *Poetry*: Joseph Parisi. Offered annually for poems published in *Poetry* during the preceding twelve months (October through September). Guidelines for SASE. Prize: $200. Judged by the editors of *Poetry*. *Poetry* buys all rights to the poems published in the magazine. Copyrights are returned to the authors on request. Any writer may submit poems to *Poetry*. Only poems published in *Poetry* during the preceding year are considered for the annual prizes.

‡**KATE TUFTS DISCOVERY AWARD FOR POETRY**, The Claremont Graduate School, 740 N. College Ave., Claremont CA 91711. (909)621-8974. Website: http://www.cgs.edu/common/tuftsent.html. Award Director: Jack Miles. Offered annually for poetry published in a first or very early book in English during the previous year. Guidelines and form for SASE. Entry form must accompany submission. Deadline: September 15. Prize: $5,000. Entrants must agree to reproduction rights and to be present at award ceremony.

‡**KINGSLEY TUFTS POETRY AWARD AT THE CLAREMONT GRADUATE SCHOOL**, The Claremont Graduate School, 740 N. College Ave., Claremont CA 91711. (909)621-8974. Website: http://www.egs.edu/common/tuftsent.html. Award Director: Jack Miles. Offered annually for poetry published in book form in English during the previous year. Also open to book-length mss that have not been published but were created in the year prior to the

award. In that case, poet must have publication credits. Guidelines and form for SASE. Entry form must accompany submission. Deadline: September 15. Prize: $50,000. Entrants must agree to reproduction rights and to be present at award ceremony and week's residency the Claremont Graduate School.

‡**UNION LEAGUE CIVIC AND ARTS POETRY PRIZE**, *Poetry*, 60 W. Walton St., Chicago IL 60610. (312)255-3703. Editor, *Poetry*, Joseph Parisi. Offered annually for poems published in *Poetry* during the preceding twelve months (October through September). Guidelines for SASE. Prize: $1,000. Judged by the editors of *Poetry*. *Poetry* buys all rights to the poems published in the magazine. Copyrights are returned to the authors on request. Any writer may submit poems to *Poetry*. Only poems published in *Poetry* during the preceding year are considered for the annual prizes.

‡**DANIEL VAROUJAN AWARD**, New England Poetry Club, 11 Puritan Rd., Arlington MA 02174. Contest Director: Virginia Thayer. Offered annually for "an unpublished poem worthy of Daniel Varoujan, a poet killed by the Turks at the onset of the first genocide of this century which decimated three-fourths of the Armenian population." Send poems in duplicate. $3 per poem entry. Deadline: June 31. Guidelines for SASE. Prize: $500. Open to any writer.

VERVE POETRY CONTEST, *VERVE* Magazine, P.O. Box 3205, Simi Valley CA 93093. Contest Director: Ron Reichick. Estab. 1989. Offered 2 times/year for previously unpublished poetry. "Fund raiser for *VERVE* Magazine which receives no grants and has no ties with any institutions." Deadlines: April 1 and October 1. Guidelines for #10 SASE. Charges $2/poem. Prizes: 1st-$100 and publication in *Verve*; 2nd-$50; 3rd-$25.

‡**THE BRONWEN WALLACE AWARD**, The Writers' Development Trust, 24 Ryerson Ave., Suite 201, Toronto, Ontario M5T 2P3 Canada. (416)504-8222. Fax: (416)504-9090. Contact: Administrator. Offered annually for unpublished poetry in even years, for unpublished short fiction in odd years. Deadline: early January. Guidelines available for #10 SASE. Prize: $1,000. Open to Canadian writers under 35 years old who have not yet published in book form.

THE ROBERT PENN WARREN POETRY PRIZE COMPETITION, Cumberland Poetry Review, P.O. Box 120128, Ackten Station, Nashville TN 37212. Contest/Award Director: Eva Touster. Offered annually for unpublished poems to encourage the writing of good poetry. Deadline: March 1. Guidelines for SASE. Charges $28 fee (includes a year's subscription to *Cumberland Party Review* which is $18 a year). Prize: 1st-$500, 2nd-$300, 3rd-$200 and Honorable Mention. Publication of winners in the Fall issue of *Cumberland Poetry Review*. Initial judging by the editors of *CPR*. The judge who makes the final decision is an internationally-known poet selected each year. All work submitted according to the published guidelines will be considered.

THE WASHINGTON PRIZE, The Word Works, Inc., P.O. Box 42164, Washington DC 20015. E-mail: wordworks@writer.org. Website: http://www.writer.org/wordwork/wordwrk1.htm. Contact: Miles David Moore. Offered annually to recognize a living American poet for an unpublished work of excellence, to help further his or her life as a writer, and to keep poetry alive in the United States. Contest open February 1-March 1 (postmark). Guidelines for SASE. Charges $15 fee. Prizes: $1,000 and publication; author gets 15% of the run. Open to all U.S. citizens.

‡**WHITE PINE PRESS POETRY PRIZE**, White Pine Press, 10 Village Square, Fredonia NY 14063. (716)672-5743. Fax: (716)672-4724. Offered annually for previously published or unpublished poets. Deadline: October 15. Guidelines for SASE. Charges $15 fee. Prize: $500 plus publication. "Initial screening is done by our in-house editorial staff. Finalists are judged by a poet of national reputation. If the winner is published by White Pine Press, we hold rights until the book is out of print; then rights revert to the author. With previously published work, the author is responsible for obtaining permission for publication by White Pine Press." Open to any writer who is a U.S. citizen.

‡**THE WALT WHITMAN AWARD**, The Academy of American Poets, 584 Broadway, Suite 1208, New York NY 10012-3250. (212)274-0343. Fax: (212)274-9427. E-mail: poets@artwire.com. Website: http://www.artswire.org/poets/page.html. Contact: India Amos. Offered annually to publish and support a poet's first book. Entries accepted from September 15-November 15. Guidelines for SASE. Charges $20 fee. Prize: $5,000, a residency for one month at the Vermont Studio Center, publication by Louisiana State University Press. Judged by an eminent poet. Submissions must be in English by a single poet. Translations are not eligible. Contestants must be living citizens of the US and neither published nor committed to publish a volume of poetry 40 pages or more in length in an edition of 500 or more copies.

‡**WALT WHITMAN CITATION OF MERIT FOR POETS**, New York State Writers Institute, University at Albany, NU 355, Albany NY 12222. (518)442-5620. Fax: (518)442-5621. E-mail: writers@poppa.fab.albany.edu. Contact: Donald Faulkner, associate director. Offered every 2 years (odd years). "Upon the recommendation of an advisory panel of distinguished poets convened under the aegis of the New York State Writers Institute, the Governor of the State of New York awards the Walt Whitman Citation of Merit to a New York State poet in recognition of a life-long body of work and artistic achievement. The recipient serves as New York State Poet for two years to promote and encourage poetry within the state." Nominations may be submitted to the Writers Institute for consideration by the advisory panel. Prize: $10,000 and designation as New York State Poet for two years. Judged by an advisory panel of distinguished poets chosen by the Writers Institute each time the Citation is awarded. Poet must be a New York State resident with a long and distinguished career as a published poet.

WICK POETRY CHAPBOOK SERIES "OPEN" COMPETITION, Wick Poetry Program Dept. of English, Kent State University, P.O. Box 5190, Kent OH 44242-0001. (330)672-2676. Fax: (330)672-3152. E-mail: wickpoet@kent.e du. Director: Maggie Anderson. Publication of a chapbook of poems by a poet currently living in Ohio who has not previously published a full-length book (48 or more pages, an edition of 500 or more copies). Deadline: October 31. Guidelines for SASE. Charges $5 entry fee. Prize: Publication of the chapbook by the Kent State University Press.

WICK POETRY CHAPBOOK SERIES "STUDENT" COMPETITION, Wick Poetry Program, Dept. of English, Kent State University, P.O. Box 5190, Kent OH 44242-0001. (330)672-2676. Fax: (330)672-3152. E-mail: wickpoet@ke nt.edu. Director: Maggie Anderson. Publication of a chapbook of poems by a poet currently enrolled in an Ohio college or university who has not previously published a full length book (48 or more pages; edition of 500 copies or more). Deadline: October 31. Guidelines for SASE. Prize: Publication of the chapbook by the Kent State University Press.

STAN AND TOM WICK POETRY PRIZE, Wick Poetry Program, Dept. of English, Kent State University, P.O. Box 5190, Kent OH 44242-0001. (330)672-2676. Fax: (330)672-3152. E-mail: wickpoet@kent.edu. Director: Maggie Anderson. First Book Prize open to anyone writing in English who has not previously published a full-length book of poems (a volume of 48 pages or more published in an edition of 500 or more copies). Deadline: May 1. Guidelines for SASE. Charges $10 entry fee. Prize: $1,000 prize and book publication by the Kent State University Press.

THE WILDWOOD PRIZE IN POETRY, Harrisburg Area Community College Alumni Association, A213E, 1 HACC Dr., Harrisburg PA 17110. (717)780-2487. Fax: (717)737-6489. Director: T.H.S. Wallace. Offered annually for unpublished poems to publish the best poetry being written in America. Deadline: November 30. Charges $5 entry fee (drawn to Harrisburg Area Community College) for 3 poems. Prize: $500 cash award and publication. Acquires First North American serial rights. The works must be no more than 100 lines, in English, no translations.

ROBERT H. WINNER MEMORIAL AWARD, Poetry Society of America, 15 Gramercy Park S., New York NY 10003. (212)254-9628. E-mail: poetsocy@panix.com. Website: http://www.poetrysociety.org. Contact: Award Director. "For a poet whose first book appeared when he was almost 50, recognizing and rewarding the work of someone in midlife. Open to poets over 40, still unpublished or with one book." Guidelines for #10 SASE. Guidelines subject to change. Charges $5 fee for nonmembers. Deadline: December 19. Prize: $2,500.

‡THE J. HOWARD AND BARBARA M.J. WOOD PRIZE, *Poetry*, 60 W. Walton St., Chicago IL 60610. (312)255-3703. Editor, *Poetry*: Joseph Parisi. Offered annually for poems published in *Poetry* during the preceding twelve months (October through September). Guidelines for SASE. Prize: $1,500. Judged by the editors of *Poetry*. *Poetry* buys all rights to the poems published in the magazine. Copyrights are returned to the authors on request. Any writer may submit poems to *Poetry*. Only poems published in *Poetry* during the preceding year are considered for the annual prizes.

THE WRITER MAGAZINE/EMILY DICKINSON AWARD, Poetry Society of America, 15 Gramercy Park S., New York NY 10003. (212)254-9628. E-mail: poetsocy@panix.com. Website: http://www.poetrysociety.org. Contact: Award Director. Poem inspired by Emily Dickinson, though not necessarily in her style. Guidelines for #10 SASE. Guidelines subject to change. Deadline: December 19. Members only. Prize: $100.

WRITERS' JOURNAL QUARTERLY POETRY CONTEST, Val-Tech Publishing, Inc., P.O. Box 25376, St. Paul MN 55125. (612)730-4280. Contact: Esther M. Leiper. Previously unpublished poetry. Deadlines: February 28, April 15, August 15, November 30. Charges $2 fee first poem; $1 each thereafter.

YALE SERIES OF YOUNGER POETS, Yale University Press, P.O. Box 209040, New Haven CT 06520-9040. Website: http://www.yale.edu/yup/. Contact: Richard Miller. First book of poetry by poet under the age of 40. Submit during February. Guidelines for SASE. Charges $15 fee. Winning manuscript is published by Yale University Press. The author receives royalties.

PHYLLIS SMART YOUNG PRIZES IN POETRY, *The Madison Review*, Dept. of English, 600 N. Park St., Madison WI 53706. (608)263-3374. Director: Ronald Kuka. Contact: Michelle Ephraim or Christine Grimando. Offered annually for previously unpublished work. "Awarded to the best poems submitted, out of a field of around 500 submissions yearly. The purpose of the prize is to award good poets." Submissions must consist of 3 poems. Deadline: September 30. Prize: $500; plus publication in the spring issue of *The Madison Review*. All contest entries are considered as submissions to *The Madison Review*, the literary journal sponsoring the contest. No simultaneous submissions to other publications. Charges $3 fee.

Playwriting and Scriptwriting

ALASKA NATIVE PLAYS CONTEST, University of Alaska Anchorage, 3211 Providence Dr., Anchorage AK 99508. (907)786-1794. Fax: (907)786-1799. E-mail: afdpe@uaa.alaska.edu. Website: http://www.uaa.alaska.edu. (Click Theatre; Click Native Plays). Contest Director: Dr. David Edgecombe. Offered annually for unpublished works "to encourage the writing, reading and production of plays with American Native (Indian) issues, themes and characters." Deadline: March 20. Guidelines for SASE. Prize: 1st-$500; 2nd-$200; 3rd-$100. "Any writer may enter—Native American writers are strongly encouraged."

‡**ALBERTA PLAYWRITING COMPETITION**, Alberta Playwrights' Network, 1134 Eighth Ave. SW, 2nd Floor, Calgary, Alberta T2P 1J5 Canada. Phone/Fax: (403)269-8564. E-mail: apn@nucleus.com. Annual competition for unproduced plays with one-act, full-length and Discovery categories. Discovery is open only to previously unproduced playwrights. Deadline: October 1. Charges $35 fee (Canadian funds). Prize for winner of each category: $1,500, written critique, workshop of winning play, reading of excerpt of winning play at Alberta Theatre Project's PlayRites festival. Judged by three anonymous professional playwrights, directors or dramaturges. Open only to residents of Alberta.

AMERICAN SHORTS, Florida Studio Theater, 1241 N. Palm Ave., Sarasota FL 34236. (941)366-9017. Fax: (941)955-4137. Offered annually for unpublished plays no more than 5 pages long on a theme that changes every year. Deadline varies. Send inquiry to above address or call Mark Griffin at extension #326 with inquiries. Prize: $500.

‡**ANNUAL ONE-ACT PLAY COMPETITION**, TADA!, 120 W. 28th St., New York NY 10001. (212)627-1732. Fax: (212)243-6736. Contact: Nina Trevens. Offered annually for unpublished work to encourage playwrights, composers and lyricists to develop new plays for young audiences. Deadline: varies each year, usually in early spring/late winter. For guidelines call Nina Trevens at (212)627-1732. Prize: cash prize and staged readings of winners. Must be material with a cast composed predominantly of children.

THE MARGARET BARTLE PLAYWRITING AWARD, Community Children's Theatre of Kansas City, 8021 E. 129th Terrace, Grandview MO 64030-2114. (816)761-5775. Award Director: E. Blanche Sellens. Estab. 1951. Offered annually for unpublished plays for elementary school audiences. "Our purpose is two-fold: to award a deserving author of a good, well-written play, and to produce the play royalty-free by one of our trouping units." Deadline: January 31. Guidelines for SASE. Prize: $500.

‡**BAY AREA PLAYWRIGHTS FESTIVAL**, The Playwrights Foundation, P.O. Box 460357, San Francisco CA 94117. (415)263-3986. E-mail: kentnich@aol.com. Contact: Jayne Wenger. Offered annually to unpublished plays to encourage development of a new work. Deadline: February 1. Guidelines for SASE. Prize: small stipend and a professionally staged reading. Judged by a committee of 7 theater professionals. Unproduced full-length plays only.

THE BEVERLY HILLS THEATRE GUILD-JULIE HARRIS PLAYWRIGHT AWARD COMPETITION, 2815 N. Beachwood Drive, Los Angeles CA 90068. (213)465-2703. Playwright Award Coordinator: Marcella Meharg. Estab. 1978. Original full-length plays, unpublished, unproduced and not currently under option. Application and guidelines required, available upon request with SASE. Submissions accepted with applications from August 1-November 1.

‡**ROBERT BONE MEMORIAL PLAYWRITING AWARD**, The Playwrights' Project, Sammons Center for the Arts, 3630 Harry Hines Blvd., #12, Dallas TX 75219. (214)497-1752. Contact: Raphael Parry, artistic director. Offered annually for full-length plays and musicals by residents of Arkansas, Arizona, Colorado, New Mexico, Oklahoma or Texas. Deadline: May 1. Submit script, synopsis, bio and SASE for acknowledgment of receipt; include cassette for musical. Entry fee: $15. Prize: $500.

‡**BORDER PLAYWRIGHTS PROJECT**, Borderlands Theater, P.O. Box 2791, Tucson AZ 85702. (520)882-8607. Fax: (520)882-7406. Offered annually to "unpublished, unproduced, full-length plays reflecting the culturally diverse realities of the Border region and the Border as a metaphor." Deadline: March 30. Guidelines for SASE. Prizes: 7-10 day residencies with public staged readings for three writers, plus an honorarium, travel and lodging. Plays may be in English, Spanish or bilingual. Special consideration will be given to Latino, Native American, African-American and Asian playwrights.

CALIFORNIA PLAYWRIGHTS COMPETITION, South Coast Repertory, P.O. Box 2197, Costa Mesa CA 92628. (714)957-2602. Fax: (714)545-0391. Literary Manager: John Glore. Offered every 2 years (odd years) for unpublished playwrights. Deadline: December 1 (odd years). Prizes: 1st-$3,000, 2nd-$2,000. Judged by the South Coast Repertory. Winning writers agree to grant SCR a short-term option to premiere winning plays. Open to any writer whose principal residence is in the state of California. Entries must be accompanied by a completed application (available after September 1 in contest years). "Project is currently being modified. Please call for information."

CALIFORNIA YOUNG PLAYWRIGHTS CONTEST, The Playwright Project, 1450 Frazee Rd., Suite 215, San Diego CA 92108. (619)298-9242. Fax: (619)298-9244. Contest Director: Deborah Salzer. Offered annually for previously unpublished plays by young writers to stimulate young people to create dramatic works, and to nurture promising young writers (under age 19). Deadline: April 1. Guidelines for SASE. Award consists of "professional production of 3-5 winning plays at the Old Globe Theatre in San Diego, plus royalty. All entrants receive detailed evaluation letter." Judged by theater professionals in the Southern California area. Scripts must be a minimum of 10 standard typewritten pages; send 2 copies. Writers must be California residents under age 19 as of the deadline date.

CEC JACKIE WHITE MEMORIAL NATIONAL CHILDREN'S PLAYWRITING CONTEST, Columbia Entertainment Company, 309 Parkade Blvd., Columbia MO 65202. (314)874-5628. Contact: Betsy Phillips. Estab. 1988. Offered annually for "top notch unpublished scripts for theater school use, to challenge and expand the talents of our students, ages 10-15. Should be a full length play with speaking roles for 20-30 characters of all ages with at least 10 roles developed in some detail." Deadline: June 1. Production and some travel expenses for 1st and 2nd place winners; cash award for 1st place. Guidelines for SASE. Entrants receive written evaluation. Charges $10 fee.

THE COLUMBUS SCREENPLAY DISCOVERY AWARDS, 433 N. Camden Dr., #600, Beverly Hills CA 90210. (310)288-1988. Fax: (310)288-0257. Monthly and annual contest "to discover new screenplay writers." Deadline: December 1. Charges $45 fee. Prize: options up to $10,000, plus professional development guidance and access to agents, producers, and studios. Judged by reputable industry professionals (producers, development executives, story analysts). Writer must give option to purchase if selected.

‡CONNECTIONS, Delaware Theatre Company, 200 Water St., Wilmington DE 19801. Offered every two years for the best new play dealing with interracial dynamics in America. Deadline: April 1. Guidelines for SASE. Prize: $10,000 and a reading of the winner's script at the Delaware Theatre Company.

CUNNINGHAM PRIZE FOR PLAYWRITING, The Theatre School, DePaul University, 2135 N. Kenmore, Chicago IL 60614. (773)325-7938. Fax: (773)325-7920. E-mail: lgoetsch@wppost.depaul.edu. Contact: Lara Goetsch. Offered annually for published or unpublished work "to recognize and encourage the writing of dramatic works which affirm the centrality of religion, broadly defined, and the human quest for meaning, truth and community." Deadline: December 1. Guidelines for SASE. Prize: $5,000. Judged by "a panel of distinguished citizens including members of the faculty of DePaul University, representatives of the Cunningham Prize Advisory Commitee, critics and others from the theater professions, chaired by John Ransford Watts, dean of the Theatre School." Open to writers whose residence is in the Chicago area, defined as within 100 miles of the Loop.

DAYTON PLAYHOUSE FUTUREFEST, The Dayton Playhouse, 1301 E. Siebenthaler Ave., Box 1957, Dayton OH 45414-5357. (937)277-0144. Fax: (937)227-9539. Managing Director: Tina McPhearson. Estab. 1983. "Three plays selected for full productions, three for readings at July 1997 FutureFest weekend; the six authors will be given travel and lodging to attend the festival. Judges view all productions and select a winner." Prizes: $1,000 and $100 to the other 5 playwrights. Guidelines for SASE. Guidelines can also be faxed. Deadline: September 30.

WALT DISNEY STUDIOS FELLOWSHIP PROGRAM, Walt Disney Studios, 500 S. Buena Vista St., Burbank CA 91521. (818)560-6894. Contact: Troy Nethercott. Offering approximately 12 positions for writers to work full-time developing their craft at Disney in feature film and television writing. Deadline: April 1-18, 1998. "Writing samples are required, as well as a résumé, completed application form and notarized standard letter agreement (available from the Program Administrator.)" A $33,000 salary for 1 year period beginning mid-October. Fellows outside of LA area will be provided with airfare and 1 month's accommodations. Open to all writers. Members of the WGA should apply through the Guild's Employment Access Department at (213)782-4648.

‡DRAMA FEST, Lodi Arts Commission, 125 S. Hutchins St., Suite D, Lodi CA 95240. (209)367-5442. Fax: (209)367-5461. Contact: Cyndi Olagaray. Offered every two years (even years). "To select 2 plays for award and production. One play is for children and the other for adult audiences. Plays must be unproduced/unpublished. Accepting submissions January 1-April 1. Guidelines for SASE. Prize: $1,000 plus production of plays during festival in August/September. Judged by a local panel with a background in drama. "We reserve the right for the winners to be unproduced and unpublished prior to festival debut performances." Open to any writer residing in the US.

DRURY COLLEGE ONE-ACT PLAY CONTEST, Drury College, 900 N. Benton Ave., Springfield MO 65802-3344. (417)873-7430. Contact: Sandy Asher. Estab. 1986. Offered in even-numbered years for unpublished and professionally unproduced plays. One play per playwright. Deadline: December 1. Guidelines for SASE.

DUBUQUE FINE ARTS PLAYERS ANNUAL ONE-ACT PLAYWRITING CONTEST, 1321 Tomahawk Dr., Dubuque IA 52003. (319)583-6748. Contest Coordinator: Jennie G. Stabenow. Annual competition since 1977 for previously unpublished, unproduced plays. Adaptations must be of playwright's own work or of a work in the public domain. No children's plays or musicals. No scripts over 35 pages or 40 minutes performance time. Two copies of ms required. Script Readers' review sheets available. "Concentrate on character, relationships, and a good story." Deadline: January 31. Guidelines for #10 SASE. Charges $10 fee for each play submitted. Prizes: $600, $300, $200, plus possible

---

ALWAYS ENCLOSE a self-addressed, stamped envelope (SASE) with all your queries and correspondence.

full production of play. Buys rights to first full-stage production and subsequent local video rights. Reports by June 30.

DAVID JAMES ELLIS MEMORIAL AWARD, Theatre Americana, Box 245, Altadena CA 91003. (818)683-1740. Contact: Playreading Committee. Offered annually for previously unpublished work to produce original plays of Americana background and history or by American authors. Deadline: February 1. "No entry necessary but we will send guidelines on request with SASE." Prize: $500.

EMERGING PLAYWRIGHT AWARD, Playwrights Preview Productions, 17 E. 47th St., New York NY 10017. Phone/fax: (212)289-2168. Contact: David Sheppard, Jr. Submissions required to be unpublished and unproduced in New York City. Send script, letter of introduction, production history, author's name résumé and SASE. Submissions accepted year-round. Plays selected in August and January for award consideration. Estab. 1983. Prize: $500 and New York showcase production. One play submission per person.

SHUBERT FENDRICH MEMORIAL PLAYWRITING CONTEST, Pioneer Drama Service, Inc., P.O. Box 4267, Englewood CO 80155. (303)779-4035. Fax: (303)779-4315. E-mail: piodrama@aol.com. Website: http://websites.earthli nk.net/~pioneerdrama/. Contact: Editorial Staff. Offered annually for unpublished but previously produced submissions to encourage the development of quality theatrical material for educational and community theater. Deadline: March 1. Guidelines for SASE. Prize: $1,000 royalty advance, publication. Rights acquired only if published. People already published by Pioneer Drama are not eligible.

THE FESTIVAL OF EMERGING AMERICAN THEATRE, The Phoenix Theatre, 749 N. Park Ave., Indianapolis IN 46202. (317)635-7529. Contact: Bryan Fonseca. Annual playwriting competition for previously unproduced full-length and one-act works. Submit script, 1-2 page synopsis, production history of play and author's bio/résumé. Include 9×12 SASE for return of script; #10 SASE if judge's critique desired. Guidelines for SASE. Charges $5 entry fee. Deadline: February 28. Announcement and notification of winners in May. First prize: $750 honorarium for full-length play, $325 for one-act.

FESTIVAL OF NEW WORKS, Plays-In-Progress, 615 Fourth St., Eureka CA 95501. (707)443-3724. Contact: Susan Bigelow-Marsh. Offered fall and spring for unpublished/unproduced submissions to give playwrights an opportunity to hear their work and receive audience feedback. Deadlines: August 1 and March 1. Guidelines for SASE. Award: staged reading. Open to any writer.

FMCT'S BIENNIAL PLAYWRIGHTS COMPETITION (MID-WEST), Fargo-Moorhead Community Theatre, P.O. Box 644, Fargo ND 58107-0644. (701)235-1901. Fax: (701)235-2685. E-mail: fmct@pol.org. Website: http://www.fargoweb.com/fmct. Contact: Cindy Snelling, director of education. Estab. 1988. Biennial contest (next contest will be held 1997-98). Submissions required to be unpublished, unproduced one-acts 30-50 minutes in length. Send SASE for contest rules. Deadline: July 1, 1997.

‡FULL-LENGTH PLAY COMPETITION, West Coast Ensemble, P.O. Box 38728, Los Angeles CA 90038. (310)449-1447. Fax: (310)453-2254. Contest/Award Director: Les Hanson. Offered annually for unpublished playwrights "to nurture, support and encourage." Deadline: December 31. Guidelines for SASE. Prize: $500 and presentation of play. Permission to present the play is granted if work is selected as finalist.

FUND FOR NEW AMERICAN PLAYS, J.F. Kennedy Center for the Performing Arts, Washington DC 20566. (202)416-8024. Fax: (202)416-8026. Manager: Max Woodward. Estab. 1988. Previously unproduced work. "Program objectives: to encourage playwrights to write, and nonprofit professional theaters to produce new American plays; to ease the financial burdens of nonprofit professional theater organizations producing new plays; to provide a playwright with a better production of the play than the producing theater would normally be able to accomplish." Deadline: March 16 (date changes from year to year). "Nonprofit theater organizations can mail in name and address to be placed on the mailing list." Prize: $10,000 for playwrights plus grants to theaters based on scripts submitted by producing theaters. A few encouragement grants of $2,500 are given to promising playwrights chosen from the submitted proposals. Submissions and funding proposals only through the producing theater.

JOHN GASSNER MEMORIAL PLAYWRITING COMPETITION, New England Theatre Conference, Inc., Department of Theatre, Northeastern University, 360 Huntington Ave., Boston MA 02115. E-mail: netc@world.std.com. Offered annually to unpublished full-length plays. Deadline: April 15. Guidelines for SASE. Charges $10 fee. Prizes: 1st-$1,000; 2nd-$500. Judged by a panel named by the NETC Executive Board. Open to all playwrights who are New England residents, and to any NETC number. Playwrights living outside New England may participate by joining NETC.

GREAT PLATTE RIVER PLAYWRIGHTS FESTIVAL, University of Nebraska at Kearney, Theatre Department, 905 W. 25th St., Kearney NE 68849. (308)865-8406. Fax: (308)865-8157. E-mail: greenj@platte.unk.edu. Contact: Jeffrey Green. Estab. 1988. Unpublished submissions. "Purpose of award is to develop original dramas and encourage playwrights to work in regional settings. There are five catagories: 1) Adult; 2) Youth (Adolescent); 3) Children's; 4) Musical Theater; 5) Native American. Entries may be drama or comedy." Deadline: April 1. Awards: 1st-$500; 2nd-$300; 3rd-$200; plus free lodging and a travel stipend. "The Festival reserves the rights to development and premiere production of the winning plays without payment of royalties." Contest open to entry by any writer "provided that the writer submits playscripts to be performed on stage—works in progress also acceptable. Works involving the Great Plains will be most favored. More than one entry may be submitted." SASE required for return of scripts. Selection announcement by July 31 only to writers who provide prepaid postcard or SASE.

PAUL GREEN PLAYWRIGHTS PRIZE, North Carolina Writers' Network, 3501 Hwy. 54 W., Studio C, Chapel Hill NC 27516. Fax: (919)929-0535. E-mail: nc_writers@unc.edu. Program & Services Director: Bobbie Collins-Perry. Offered annually for unpublished submissions to honor a playwright, held in recognition of Paul Green, North Carolina's dramatist laureate and Pulitzer Prize-winning playwright. Deadline: September 30. Guidelines for SASE. Charges $10 ($7.50 for NCWN members). Prize: $500 and potential production of play. Open to any writer.

‡HEART OF FILM FEATURE LENGTH SCREENPLAY AWARD, 1600 Nueces, Austin TX 78701. (512)478-4795. Fax: (512)478-6205. Website: http://www.Instar.com/Austinfilm. Directors: Barbara Morgan, Marsha Milam. Offered annually for unproduced screenplays. Sponsored by the Austin Film Festival and Heart of Film Screenwriters Conference, the competition is looking for quality screenplays to be read, at the finalist and semi-finalist levels, by a jury of producers, development executives and writers in order to offer unknown writers industry exposure. Two categories: Adults/Mature and Children/Family. Prizes: $3,500 for the winner of each category plus air fare and accommodations to attend the Austin Film Festival and Heart of Film Screenwriters Conference in October and participation in the Festival's Mentorship Program. Deadline: May 15. Entry fee: $35. Winners are announced October 3 during the AFF Awards Luncheon. The writer must hold rights when submitted. The script must be original work and must be 90-130 pages. Guidelines for SASE or call 1(800)310-FEST for more info.

HENRICO THEATRE COMPANY ONE-ACT PLAYWRITING COMPETITION, Henrico Recreation & Parks, P.O. Box 27032, Richmond VA 23273. (804)672-5115. Fax: (804)672-5284. Contest/Award Director: J. Larkin Brown. Offered annually for previously unpublished plays or musicals to produce new dramatic works in 1-act form. Deadline: July 1. Guidelines for SASE. Prize: winner $250; runner-up $125; Winning entries may be produced; videotape sent to author. "Scripts with small casts and simpler sets given preference. Controversial themes should be avoided."

HIGH SCHOOL PLAYWRITING CONTEST, Baker's Plays, 100 Chauncy St., Boston MA 02111-1783. (617)482-1280. Fax: (617)482-7613. Contest Director: Ray Pape. Offered annually for previously unpublished plays. "Open to any high school student. Plays must be accompanied by the signature of a sponsoring high school drama or English teacher, and it is recommended that the play receive a production or a public reading prior to the submission." Deadline: postmarked by January 31. Guidelines for #10 SASE. Prize: 1st-$500 and the play published by Baker's Plays; 2nd-$250 and Honorable Mention; 3rd-$100 and Honorable Mention. Write for more information.

‡HUDSON RIVER CLASSICS ANNUAL CONTEST, Hudson River Classics, Inc., P.O. Box 940, Hudson NY 12534. Phone/fax: (518)828-1329. Contest Director: W. Keith Hedrick. Offered annually for unpublished playwrights. Submit entries between March 1-June 1. Guidelines for SASE. Charges $5 fee. Prize: $500 and concert reading of winning play. Judges vary.

INTERNATIONAL ONE-PAGE PLAY COMPETITION, *Lamia Ink!*, P.O. Box 202, Prince St. Station, New York NY 10012. Contact: Cortland Jessup. Offered annually to encourage and promote performance writers and to challenge all interested writers. Interested in all forms of theater and performance writing in one page format. Deadline: March 15. No phone calls. Guidelines for SASE. Charges $1/one-page play. Maximum of 3 plays per author per competition. Prize: 1st-$200. Public reading given for top 12 in NYC. Publication in *Lamia Ink!*. If play has been previously published, playwright must have retained copyright. Prize: 1st-$200.

INTERNATIONAL PLAY CONTEST, Center Theater, 1346 W. Devon, Chicago IL 60660. (773)508-0200. Contact: Monica McCarthy. Offered annually for unpublished work to foster and encourage the growth of playwrights. Deadline: end of June. Guidelines for SASE. Charges $15 fee. Prize: 1st-$300 cash award and production option. "Responses only to those inquiries that include a SASE."

JEWEL BOX THEATRE PLAYWRIGHTING COMPETITION, Jewel Box Theatre, 3700 N. Walker, Oklahoma City OK 73118-7099. (405)521-1786. Contact: Charles Tweed. Estab. 1982. Two- or three-acts accepted or one-acts comprising an evening of theater. Deadline: January 15. Send SASE in October for guidelines. Prize: $500.

‡KEY WEST THEATRE FESTIVAL, Theatre Key West, P.O. Box 992, Key West FL 33041. (305)292-3725. Fax: (305)293-0845. Artistic Director: Joan McGillis. Offered annually to develop new unproduced plays. "We are particularly looking for one-act and full-length scripts, preferably with single sets and a maximum cast of eight. We are also looking for musicals and children's plays." Deadline: April 30. Guidelines for SASE. Inquiries may also be made via e-mail to theatrekw@aol.com. Prize: production, airfare and accommodations in Key West for part of the rehearsal period and the opening of the play. Judged by the artistic director and a panel of qualified readers. Scripts must be submitted by an agent or be accompanied by two letters of recommendation.

KUMU KAHUA/UHM THEATRE DEPARTMENT PLAYWRITING CONTEST, Kumu Kahua Theatre Inc./ University of Hawaii at Manoa, Department of Theatre and Dance, 1770 East-West Rd., Honolulu HI 96822. (808)956-

2588. Fax: (808)956-4226. Contact: Dennis Carroll. Offered annually for unpublished work to honor full-length and short plays. Deadline: January 1. Guidelines available every September. Prize: $500 (Hawaii Prize); $400 (Pacific Rim); $200 (Resident). First 2 categories open to residents and nonresidents. For Hawaii Prize, plays must be set in Hawaii or deal with some aspect of the Hawaiian experience. For Pacific Rim prize, plays must deal with Hawaii or the Pacific Islands, Pacific Rim or Pacific/Asian/American experience—short plays only considered in 3rd category!

L.A. DESIGNERS' THEATRE-COMMISSIONS, L.A. Designers' Theatre, P.O. Box 1883, Studio City CA 91614-0883. (213)650-9600. Fax: (818)985-9200. (818)769-9000 T.D.D. Contact: Richard Niederberg. Quarterly contest "to promote new work and push it onto the conveyor belt to filmed or videotaped entertainment." All submissions must be registered with copyright office and be unpublished by "major" publishers. Material will *not* be returned. Deadline: February 15, May 15, August 15, November 15. "No rules, no fees, no entry forms. Just present an idea that can be commissioned into a full work." Prize: A production or publication of the work in the Los Angeles market. "We only want 'first refusal.' If you are picked, we negotiate royalties with the writer." Open to any writer. Proposals for works not yet completed are encouraged.

LIVE OAK THEATRE'S BEST NEW AMERICAN PLAY AWARD, Live Oak Theatre, 719 Congress Ave., Austin TX 78701-3923. (512)472-5143. Fax: (512)472-7199. E-mail: liveoak@eden.com. Contact: Michael Hankin. Annual award for previously unpublished, unproduced, full-length plays. Deadline: April 1. Prize: $1,000, staged reading in annual Harvest Festival and possible production. Plays must not have had a professional (Equity) production and must be unencumbered upon submission. Open to US citizens and residents. Send script with $15 fee. SASE for return.

LOFT FEST—FESTIVAL OF SHORTS, The Loft Production Company, P.O. Box 173405, Tampa FL 33672. (813)275-9400. Fax: (813)222-1057. Contact: Mr. Kelly Smith. Offered annually for unpublished submissions. Six-week festival of theater. Accepting 10-minute plays and one-acts. All with simple to no set and small casts. Deadline: March 31. Send brief synopsis, character breakdown, set requirements and manuscripts. Award: Production of play and $50 for 10-minute play, $100 for one-acts. Charges $5 fee. Submissions are not returned. Open to any writer.

LOVE CREEK ANNUAL SHORT PLAY FESTIVAL, Love Creek Productions, % Granville, 79 Liberty Place, Weehawken NJ 07087-7014. Festival Manager: Cynthia Granville-Callahan. Estab. 1985. Annual festival for unpublished plays, unproduced in New York in the previous year under 40 minutes, at least 2 characters. "We established the Festival as a playwriting competition in which scripts are judged on their merits in performance." Deadline: September 30. Guidelines for #10 SASE. All entries must specify "festival" on envelope and must include letter giving permission to produce script, if chosen and stating whether equity showcase is acceptable. Cash price awarded to winner.

LOVE CREEK MINI FESTIVALS, Love Creek Productions, % Granville, 79 Liberty Place, Weehawken NJ 07087-7014. Festival Literary Manager: Cynthia Granville-Callahan. "The Mini Festivals are an outgrowth of our annual Short Play Festival in which we produce scripts concerning a particular issue or theme which our artistic staff selects according to current needs, interests and concerns of our members, audiences and playwrights submitting to our Short Play Festival throughout the year." Considers scripts unpublished, unproduced in New York City in past year under 40 minutes, at least 2 characters. Guidelines for #10 SASE. Submissions must list name of festival on envelope and must include letter giving permission to produce script, if chosen, and stating whether equity showcase is acceptable. Finalists receive a mini-showcase production in New York City. Winner receives a cash prize. Write for upcoming themes, deadlines ongoing. Fear of God: Religion in the 90s, Women Now Gay and Lesbian Festival. Will be presented again in 1997 along with others TBA.

‡THE LOW-BUDGET FEATURE PROJECT, Cyclone Entertainment Group/Cyclone Productions, 3412 Milwaukee, Suite 485, Northbrook IL 60062. (847)657-0446. Fax: (847-657-0446. Contact: Lee Alan. Offered annually. The Low-Budget Feature Project is a program designed to establish an avenue by which screenwriter's may obtain a feature film writing credit. The selected script is produced as a feature film. Deadline: April 1. Guidelines for SASE. Charges $50 entry fee. Prize: The winning applicant will be eligible to receive 5% of the film's profits, if any, until the films' copyright has expired or the film is sold. Judged by the production team and director-Lee Alan. Only after winner is selected do we enter into an additional rights agreement. Open to any writer.

MAXIM MAZUMDAR NEW PLAY COMPETITION, Alleyway Theatre, One Curtain Up Alley, Buffalo NY 14202-1911. (716)852-2600. Fax: (716)852-2266. E-mail: alleywayth,com. Website: http://www.alleyway.com. Dramaturg: Joyce Stilson. Estab. 1990. Annual competition. Full Length: not less than 90 minutes, no more than 10 performers. One-Act: less than 60 minutes, no more than 6 performers. Deadline: July 1. Finalists announced January 1. "Playwrights may submit work directly. There is no entry form. Annual playwright's fee $5; may submit one in each category, but pay only one fee. Please specify if submission is to be included in competition." Prize: full length—$400, travel plus lodging, production and royalties; one-act—$100, production plus royalties. "Alleyway Theatre must receive first production credit in subsequent printings and productions."

MIDWESTERN PLAYWRIGHTS FESTIVAL, University of Toledo and Toledo Rep Theatre, University of Toledo, Toledo OH 43606. (419)530-2202. Fax: (419)530-8439. Contact: John S. Kuhn. Offered annually for unpublished submissions to celebrate regional theater. Deadline: June 1. Guidelines for SASE. Prize: The winning playwright will receive $1,000, a staged reading and full production of the winning play in the Spring at the Toledo Repertoire Theatre. A stipend will also be provided for travel, room and board for the readings and for a two-week residency during production. Two other finalists will receive $350 and $150 and staged readings. Judged by members from both sponsoring organizations. Playwright must be an Ohio, Michigan, Illinois or Indiana resident. Submission must be an unpublished, full-length, two-act play, not produced professionally. Cast limit of ten, prefer one set, commercially producible play.

MILL MOUNTAIN THEATRE NEW PLAY COMPETITION, Mill Mountain Theatre, Center in the Square, 1 Market Square, 2nd Floor, Roanoke VA 24011-1437. (703)342-5730. Fax: (540)342-5745. Website: http://www.intrlink. com/MMT. Literary Manager: Jo Weinstein. Estab. 1985. Previously unpublished and unproduced plays for up to 10 cast members. Plays must be agent submitted—or have the recommendation of a director, literary manager or dramaturg. Deadline: January 1. Guidelines for SASE.

MIXED BLOOD VERSUS AMERICA, Mixed Blood Theatre Company, 1501 S. Fourth St., Minneapolis MN 55454. (612)338-0984. Contact: David B. Kunz. Estab. 1983. Theater company estab. 1975. "Mixed Blood Versus America encourages and seeks out the emerging playwright. Mixed Blood is not necessarily looking for scripts that have multi-racial casts, rather good scripts that will be cast with the best actors available." Open to all playwrights who have had at least one of their works produced or workshopped (either professionally or educationally). Only unpublished, unproduced plays are eligible for contest. Limit 2 submissions per playwright. No translations or adaptations. Guidelines for SASE. Deadline: March 15.

MRTW ANNUAL RADIO SCRIPT CONTEST, Midwest Radio Theatre Workshop, 915 E. Broadway, Columbia MO 65201. (314)874-5676. Contact: Sue Zizza. Estab. 1979. "To encourage the writing of radio scripts and to showcase both established and emerging radio playwrights. Some winning works are produced for radio and all winning works are published in the annual MRTW Scriptbook, the only one of its kind in this country." Deadline: November 15. Guidelines for SASE. "A cash award of $800 is split among the top 2-4 entries, depending on recommendation of the jurors. Winners receive free workshop registration. Those who receive honorable mention, as well as award-winning plays, are included in the scriptbook; a total of 10-16 are published annually. We acquire rights to publish the script in the scriptbook, distributed at cost, and to produce the script for air; all other rights retained by the author."

‡MUSICAL STAIRS, West Coast Ensemble, P.O. Box 38728, Los Angeles CA 90038. (310)449-1447. Fax: (310)453-2254. Award Director: Les Hanson. Offered annually for unpublished writers "to nurture, support and encourage musical creators." Deadline: June 30. Prize: $500 and presentation of musical. Judged by a panel of readers and artistic director. Permission to present the musical is granted if work is selected as finalist.

‡NANTUCKET SHORT PLAY COMPETITION AND FESTIVAL, Nantucket Theatrical Productions, Box 2177, Nantucket MA 02584. (508)228-5002. Contest Director: Jim Patrick. Offered annually for unpublished plays to "seek the highest quality of playwriting distilled into a short play format." Deadline: January 1. Charges $5 fee. Prize: $200 plus staged readings. Selected plays also receive staged readings. Judged by the artistic director plus a varying panel of theater or literary volunteers. "We acquire the right to give up to four staged readings within one calendar year of submission deadline." Plays must be less than 40 pages.

NATIONAL CANADIAN ONE-ACT PLAYWRITING COMPETITION, Ottawa Little Theatre, 400 King Edward Ave., Ottawa, Ontario K1N 7M7 Canada. (613)233-8948. Fax: (613)233-8027. Director: George Stonyk. Contact: Elizabeth Holden, office manager. Estab. 1913. "To encourage literary and dramatic talent in Canada." Submit January-May. Guidelines for #10 SASE with Canadian postage or #10 SAE with 1 IRC. Prize: $1,000, $700, $500.

‡NATIONAL HISPANIC PLAYWRITING CONTEST, Arizona Theatre Co. in affiliation with Centro Cultural Mexicano, P.O. Box 1631, Tucson AZ 85702. (520)884-8210. Contest Director: Rebecca Million. Offered annually for unproduced, unpublished playwrights. "The contest purports to recognize plays of theatrical and literary merit by Hispanic playwrights." Deadline: December 1. Guidelines for SASE. Prize: $1,000 and possible inclusion in ATC's Genesis New Play Reading Series. Judged by ATC's artistic staff and a representative of Centro Cultural Mexicano. Contest is open to all Hispanics currently residing in the United States, its territories, and/or Mexico.

NATIONAL PLAYWRIGHTS' AWARD, Unicorn Theatre, 3820 Main St., Kansas City MO 64111. (816)531-7529. Fax: (816)531-0421. Contact: Herman Wilson, literary assistant. Offered annually for previously unproduced work. "We produce contemporary original scripts, preferring scripts that deal with social concerns. However, we accept (and have produced) comedies." Guidelines for SASE. Prize: $1,000 in royalty/prize fee and mainstage production at the Unicorn as part of its regular season.

NATIONAL TEN-MINUTE PLAY CONTEST, Actors Theatre of Louisville, 316 W. Main St., Louisville KY 40202-4218. (502)584-1265. Fax: (502)561-3300. Literary Manager: Michael Bigelow Dixon. Estab. 1964. Previously unproduced (professionally) ten-minute plays (10 pages or less). "Entries must *not* have had an Equity or Equity-waiver production." Deadline: December 1. Prize: $1,000. Please write or call for submission guidelines.

‡NEW AMERICAN COMEDY FESTIVAL, Ukiah Players Theatre, 1041 Low Gap Rd., Ukiah CA 95482. (707)462-1210. Contact: Lesley Currier. Offered every 2 years for unpublished work to help playwrights develop their full-length

"...firmly committed to discovering and showcasing the best new voices in American fiction."

—Richard Currey

Since 1931, STORY has helped some of the finest writers of this century break into print. William Saroyan, Erskine Caldwell, Truman Capote, J.D. Salinger, Norman Mailer—to name just a few.

Today STORY is still taking chances, publishing cutting-edge stories other magazines are often too timid to touch, and introducing fresh new writing talent like Junot Díaz, Abraham Rodriguez, Jr., A.M. Homes and Susan Power.

Subscribe to STORY today—and begin enjoying the extraordinary literary magazine that commits itself to the up-and-coming.

GET YOUR WORK INTO THE RIGHT BUYERS' HANDS!

You work hard...and your hard work deserves to be seen by the right buyers. But in a constantly changing industry, it's not easy to know who those buyers are. That's why you need to keep up-to-date and on top with the most current edition of this indispensable market guide.

Keep ahead of these changes by ordering *1999 Writer's Market* today. You'll save the frustration of getting manuscripts returned in the mail. And of NOT submitting your work to new listings that you don't know exist. To order the upcoming 1999 edition, just complete the attached order card and return it with your payment or credit card information. Order now and you'll get the 1999 edition at the 1998 price—just $27.99—no matter how much the regular price may increase! *1999 Writer's Market* will be published and ready for shipment in September 1998.

Keep on top of the fast-changing industry and get a jump on selling your work with help from the *1999 Writer's Market*. Order today! You deserve it!

And NOW, keeping up is even easier — with the **NEW Electronic Edition of** *Writer's Market*!

NOW AVAILABLE! Writer's Market on CD-ROM!
The fastest, easiest way to locate your most promising markets!

Now you can get the same vital Writer's Market resources in a compact, searchable, electronic CD-ROM format. It's easier than ever to locate the information you need...when you need it. And, this electronic edition is expanded to offer you even more:

- Customize searches - set any parameters (by pay range, subject, state, or any other set of criteria)
- Submission Tracker - create and call up submissions records to see which publishers are past due answering your queries, or are late in paying
- *Writer's Encyclopedia, Third Edition* - get this handy reference tool on the CD — at no additional cost!
  (A $22.99 value, but yours FREE!)
- Writer's guidelines - many of the listings now include ALL the data you need to submit your work. No more writing for guidelines!

Order your CD today, or the combination book and CD package. And, don't forget to reserve your 1999 editions at the 1998 prices! Just complete the order card on the reverse and keep up with the publishing industry (and technology!) Order Today!

CD-ROM is designed to work with:
- Windows: 486DX/66 or higher; 8MB RAM; 256-color display; mouse; Windows 3.1 or later; MS-DOS 3.1 or later; 15MB available hard disk space; double-speed CD- ROM drive.

More Great Books to Help You Sell Your Work!

comedies into funnier, stronger scripts. Deadline: September 30 of odd-numbered years. Guidelines for SASE. Prize $1,000 each for 2 winning playwrights, also travel (up to $400) to Ukiah for 2-week festival, lodging and per diem.

‡**THE NEW HARMONY PROJECT CONFERENCE/LABORATORY**, The New Harmony Project, 613 N. East St., Indianapolis IN 46202. (317)464-9405. Fax: (317)635-4201. Executive Director: Jeffrey L. Sparks. Offered annually for either previously published or unpublished scripts. "The purpose of The New Harmony Project is to identify new theater and film scripts that emphasize the dignity of the human spirit and celebrate the worth of the human experience." Deadline: Mid-November. "Writers of selected scripts, along with writers-in-residence and a company of actors, directors and dramaturges, are brought to New Harmony, Indiana for two and one-half weeks in May. During this time, scripts are put through a series of rehearsals with actors and directors. Critique sessions are held with writers, actors and directors. Each fully-developed script is given a final reading with an audience of conference participants and special invited guests on the final weekend." Judged by a script search committee (comprised of Board members) and our artistic director. "We look for writers whose work reflects our philosophy and who we think would benefit from development at The New Harmony Project. We accept proposals on an open-call basis (with specified guidelines), then request scripts from selected writers. Of those scripts submitted, up to four are selected for full development, and up to three for limited development."

NEW PLAYS STAGED READING CONTEST, TADA! 120 W. 28th St., New York NY 10001, (212)627-1732. Fax: (212)243-6736. E-mail: tada@ziplink.net. Website: http://www.tadatheater.com. Contest Director: Janine Nina Trevens. Offered annually for unpublished and unproduced work to introduce the playwriting process to family audiences in a staged reading series featuring the winning entries. The cast must be predominantly children, the children are cast from the TADA! company and adult actors will be hired. The plays must be appropriate for children and teenage audiences. Deadline varies each year, usually in early spring/late winter. Please send cover letter and play with SASE for return. If the play is a musical, include a tape of the music. No application form necessary. Prize: $100-500 and staged reading held in TADA!'s theater. Grand Prize is a workshopped production. Contest is open.

‡**NEW VOICE SERIES**, Remembrance Through the Performing Arts, 3300 Bee Caves Rd., Suite 650, Austin TX 78746. (512)329-9118. Fax: (512)329-9118. Award Director: Marla Macdonald. Offered annually "to find talented playwrights who are in the early stages of script development. We develop these scripts on the page through a Work In Progress production." Deadline: December 1. Playwrights need to send script, bio and a script size SASE. Prize: free development of their play with our company plus free representation of their plays to theaters nationally for world premieres. Open to playwrights from Texas only.

NEW WOMEN PLAYWRIGHT'S FESTIVAL, Off Center Theater, P.O. Box 518, Tampa FL 33601. (813)222-1087. Fax: (813)222-1057. Contact: Karla Hartley. Offered annually for unpublished plays to encourage and produce female playwrights. Deadline: September 12. Charges $15 fee. Prize: 1st-$1,000 plus production; 2nd-$100 plus staged reading; 3rd-$50 plus choral reading. Judged by theatre staff. Open to women playwrights. Full-length comedies only.

DON AND GEE NICHOLL FELLOWSHIPS IN SCREENWRITING, Academy of Motion Picture Arts & Sciences, 8949 Wilshire Blvd., Beverly Hills CA 90211-1972. (310)247-3059. Website: http://www.oscars.org. Director: Greg Beal. Estab. 1985. Offered annually for unproduced screenplays to identify talented new screenwriters. Deadline: May 1. Charges $30 fee. Guidelines for SASE, available January 1-April 30. Prize: $25,000 fellowships (up to 5/year). Recipients announced late October. Open to writers who have not earned more than $1,000 writing for films or TV.

OFF-OFF-BROADWAY ORIGINAL SHORT PLAY FESTIVAL, 45 W. 25th St., New York NY 10010. Fax: (212)206-1429. Contact: William Talbot. Offered annually for unpublished work. "The Festival was developed in 1976 to bolster those theater companies and schools offering workshops, programs and instruction in playwriting. It proposes to encourage them by offering them and their playwrights the opportunity of having their plays seen by new audiences and critics, and of having them reviewed for publication." Deadline: late winter. Guidelines for SASE. Prize: "Presentation on NY stage before NY audiences and critics. Publication of selected plays by Samuel French, Inc." "No individual writer may enter on his/her own initiative. Entries must come from theater companies, professional schools or colleges which foster playwriting by conducting classes, workshops or similar programs of assistance to playwrights."

OGLEBAY INSTITUTE TOWNGATE THEATRE PLAYWRITING CONTEST, Oglebay Institute, Stifel Fine Arts Center, 1330 National Rd., Wheeling WV 26003. (304)242-7700. Fax: (304)242-7747. Director, Performing Arts Dept. Estab. 1976. Offered annually for unpublished works. Deadline: January 1. Guidelines for SASE. Prize: $300, limited-run production of play. "All full-length *non-musical* plays that have never been professionally produced or published are eligible." Winner announced May 31.

OPUS MAGNUM DISCOVERY AWARD, Christopher Columbus Society, 433 N. Camden Dr., #600, Beverly Hills CA 90210. (310)288-1881. Fax: (310)288-0257. Contact: Carlos de Abreu. Annual award to discover new authors with books/manuscripts that can be optioned for features or TV movies. Deadline: December 1. Guidelines for SASE. Charges $75 fee. Prize: Option moneys to winner, up to $10,000.

MILDRED & ALBERT PANOWSKI PLAYWRITING AWARD, Forest A. Roberts Theatre, Northern Michigan University, Marquette MI 49855-5364. (906)227-2553. Fax: (906)227-2567. Award Director: Dr. James A. Panowski.

Estab. 1978. Unpublished, unproduced, full-length plays. Scripts must be *received* on or before the Friday before Thanksgiving. Guidelines and application for SASE.

‡PERISHABLE THEATRE'S WOMEN'S PLAYWRITING FESTIVAL, P.O. Box 23132, Providence RI 02903. (401)331-2695. Fax: (401)331-7811. Festival Directors: Kathleen Jenkins and Vanessa Gilbert. Offered annually for unpublished plays to encourage women playwrights. Deadline: December 31. Guidelines for SASE. Prize: $250. Judged by the co-directors and the artistic director of the theater. Open to women playwrights exclusively.

ROBERT J. PICKERING AWARD FOR PLAYWRIGHTING EXCELLENCE, Coldwater Community Theater, % 89 Division, Coldwater MI 49036. (517)279-7963. Committee Chairperson: J. Richard Colbeck. Estab. 1982. Previously unproduced monetarily. "To encourage playwrights to submit their work, to present a previously unproduced play in full production." Deadline: end of year. Guidelines for SASE. Submit script with SASE. Prize: 1st-$300, 2nd-$100, 3rd-$50. "We reserve right to produce winning script."

PLAYHOUSE ON THE SQUARE NEW PLAY COMPETITION, Playhouse on the Square, 51 S. Cooper, Memphis TN 38104. Contact: Jackie Nichols. Submissions required to be unproduced. Deadline: April 1. Guidelines for SASE. Prize: $500 plus production.

THE PLAYWORKS FESTIVAL, University of Texas at El Paso, Theatre Arts Department, 500 W. University, El Paso TX 79968-0549. (915)747-7854. Fax: (915)747-5438. E-mail: mwright@utep.edu. Director: Michael Wright. Offered annually for 3 residencies in the program. Each writer-in-residence is expected to develop a new play during the 3-week residency through daily workshops. "We are especially interested in students of Hispanic-American or Native American origin." Deadline: January 31. Guidelines for SASE. Prize: "We pay travel and an honorarium, and provide housing." Open to undergraduate or graduate students.

PLAYWRIGHTS' CENTER JEROME PLAYWRIGHT-IN-RESIDENCE FELLOWSHIP, The Playwrights' Center, 2301 Franklin Ave. E, Minneapolis MN 55406. (612)332-7481. Fax: (612)332-6037. Lab Director: Elissa Adams. Estab. 1976. To provide emerging playwrights with funds and services to aid them in the development of their craft. Deadline: September 16. Open to playwrights only—may not have had more than 2 different fully staged productions of their works by professional theaters. Must spend fellowship year in Minnesota at Playwrights' Center.

PLAYWRIGHTS' CENTER McKNIGHT FELLOWSHIP, The Playwrights' Center, 2301 Franklin Ave. E, Minneapolis MN 55406. (612)332-7481. Fax: (612)332-6037. Lab Director: Elissa Adams. Estab. 1982. Recognition of playwrights whose work has made a significant impact on the contemporary theater. Deadline: January 16. Open to playwrights only. Must have had a minimum of two different fully staged productions by professional theaters. Must spend 1 month at Playwrights' Center. U.S. citizens or permanent residents only.

THE PLAYWRIGHTS' CENTER PLAYLABS, The Playwrights' Center, 2301 Franklin Ave. E, Minneapolis MN 55406. (612)332-7481. Fax: (612)332-6037. Lab Director: Elissa Adams. Assists in the development of unproduced or unpublished new plays. Deadline: December 16. US citizen/resident playwrights only; and must be available for entire pre-conference and conference.

PRINCESS GRACE AWARDS PLAYWRIGHT FELLOWSHIP, Princess Grace Foundation—USA, 150 E. 58th St., 21st Floor, New York NY 10155. (212)317-1470. Fax: (212)317-1473. Contact: Ms. Toby E. Boshak. Offered annually for unpublished submissions to support playwright through residency program with New Dramatists, Inc. located in New York City. A ten-week residence. Deadline: March 31. Guidelines for SASE. Award: $7,500 plus ten-week residency with New Dramatists, Inc. in New York City. Foundation looks to support aspiring young artists in America. Must be a US citizen or have US status. Under ordinary circumstances the candidate should be no more than 30 years of age at time of application.

‡PROMISING PLAYWRIGHT AWARD, Colonial Players, Inc. 98 Tower Dr., Stevensville MD 21666. (410)263-0533. Coordinator: Fran Marchand. Offered every 2 years for unpublished plays by residents of MD, VA, WV, PA, DE and DC "to encourage aspiring playwrights." Submissions accepted September 1-December 31 of even-numbered years. Guidelines for #10 SASE. Prize: $750 plus possible production of play.

‡PUTTIN' ON THE RITZ, ONE-ACT PLAY CONTEST, Puttin' On the Ritz, Inc., 915 White Horse Pike, Oaklyn NJ 08107. (609)858-5230. Contest Director: Alex Wilkie. Offered annually "to encourage playwrights by the production of their new works. We especially encourage playwrights from the New Jersey/Philadelphia region." Deadline: January 31. Prize: production of those works selected by the One-Act Play contest committee. "We receive about 125 plays, and of those, produce three or four." Plays that have been professionally produced will not be considered.

GWEN PHARIS RINGWOOD AWARD FOR DRAMA, Writers Guild of Alberta, 11759 Great Rd., Edmonton, Alberta T5M 3K6 Canada. (403)422-8174. Fax: (403)422-2663. E-mail: writers@compusmart.ab.ca. Contact: Darlene Diver. Drama book published in current year or script of play produced three times in current year in a community theater. Must be an Alberta playwright. Eligible plays must be registered with the WGA-APN Drama Award Production

Registry. Contact either the WGA head office, or the Alberta Playwrights' Network for registry forms.

RIVERFRONT PLAYHOUSE SCRIPTWRITING COMPETITION, Riverfront Playhouse, P.O. Box 105, Palo Cedro CA 96073; Playhouse: 1620 E. Cypress, Redding, CA 96002. (916)547-4801. Contest Director: Paul Robeson. "Offered annually for unpublished scripts to broaden the appreciation, awareness, and understanding of live theater by providing the environment for local talent to act, direct and creatively express themselves in the arts of the stage.The competition is designed to encourage and stimulate artistic growth among community playwrights. It provides playwrights the unique opportunity to mount and produce an original work at the *Riverfront Playhouse*." Deadline: December 2. Guidelines for SASE. Charges $25 fee. Prize: a reading, workshop and/or a full production of the winning entry. Cash prizes, as determined by the Board of Directors of the *Riverfront Playhouse*.

ROCHESTER PLAYWRIGHT FESTIVAL, Midwest Theatre Network, 5031 Tongen Ave. NW, Rochester MN 55901. (507)281-1472. Executive Director: Joan Sween. Offered for unpublished submissions to support emerging playwrights. No categories, but entries are considered for production by various types of theaters: community theater, dinner theater, issues theater, satiric/new theater, children's theater, musical theater. Entry form required. Guidelines and entry form for SASE. No fee for first entry. Subsequent entries by same author, $10 fee. Prize: full production, travel stipend, accomodations, cash prize. Open to any writer.

RICHARD RODGERS AWARDS IN MUSICAL THEATER, American Academy of Arts and Letters, 633 W. 155th St., New York NY 10032-7599. (212)368-5900. Fax: (212)491-4615. Executive Director: Virginia Dajani. Estab. 1978. The Richard Rodgers Awards subsidize full productions, studio productions and staged readings by nonprofit theaters in New York City of works by composers and writers who are not already established in the field of musical theater. Deadline: November 1. SASE for guidelines and application.

THE LOIS AND RICHARD ROSENTHAL NEW PLAY PRIZE, Cincinnati Playhouse in the Park, Box 6537, Cincinnati OH 45206. (513)345-2242. Fax: (513)345-2254. E-mail: theater1@tso.cin.ix.net. Website: http://www.cincyplay.com. Contact: Charles Towers, associate artistic director. Unpublished full-length plays only. Query first for guidelines. Complete scripts will not be accepted. Scripts must not have received a full-scale professional production. Deadline: October 15-February 1.

‡MORTON R. SARETT NATIONAL PLAYWRITING COMPETITION, University of Nevada-Las Vegas Theatre, 4505 Maryland Pkwy., P.O. Box 455036, Las Vegas NV 89154-5036. (702)895-3666. Contact: Corrine A. Bonate. Offered every 2 years (odd years) for "original, innovative, unpublished, unproduced, full-length plays in English on any subject." Deadline: mid-December. Guidelines for SASE. Prize: $3,000 and production by UNLV Theatre. Judged by professional playwrights, directors and educators. The winner must acknowledge in perpetuity the Morton R. Sarett Memorial Award in written form in the program of all productions of this play. Open to any writer.

‡THE SCREENWRITER'S PROJECT, Cyclone Entertainment Group/Cyclone Productions, 3412 Milwaukee, Suite 485, Northbrook IL 60062. (847)657-0446. Fax: (847)657-0446. E-mail: cycprod@aol.com. Contact: Lee Alan. Offered annually to give both experienced and first-time writers the opportunity to begin a career as a screenwriter. Deadline: August 1. Guidelines for SASE. Charges $30 fee. Prizes: three $5,000 grants. Judged by professional script readers and our director Lee Alan. Open to any writer.

SCRIPT SEARCH, (formerly Search For World Premiere), The Loft Production Company, P.O. Box 173405, Tampa FL 33672. (813)275-9400. Fax: (813)222-1057. Contact: Mr. Kelly Smith. Offered annually for unpublished full-length, original scripts for production. Simple to no sets, small casts. Accepting comedies, dramas, musicals and alternative theater pieces. Submit ms, brief synopsis, character/set breakdown. Charges $5 reading fee/submission. Submissions not returned. Award: 3-4 week production of play, $500-1,000 honorarium. Open to any writer.

SIENA COLLEGE INTERNATIONAL PLAYWRIGHTS COMPETITION, Siena College Department of Creative Arts/Theatre Program, 515 Loudon Rd., Loudonville NY 12211-1462. (518)783-2381. Fax: (518)783-4293. E-mail: maciag@siena.edu. Website: http://www.siena.edu. Contact: Gary Maciag, director of theatre. Offered every 2 years for unpublished plays "to allow students to explore production collaboration with the playwright. In addition, it provides the playwright an important development opportunity. Plays should be previously unproduced, unpublished, full-length, non-musicals and free of copyright and royalty restrictions. Plays should require unit set or minimal changes and be suitable for a college-age cast of 3-10. There is a required 6-week residency." Deadline: June 30 even-numbered years. Guidelines for SASE. Guidelines are available after November 1 in odd-numbered years. Prize: $2,000 honorarium; up to $1,000 to cover expenses for required residency; full production of winning script. Winning playwright must agree that the Siena production will be the world premiere of the play. Open to any writer.

‡DOROTHY SILVER PLAYWRITING COMPETITION, Jewish Community Center, 3505 Mayfield Rd., Cleveland Heights OH 44118. (216)382-4000, ext. 275. Fax: (216)382-5401. Contact: Elaine Rembrandt. Estab. 1948. All entries must be original works, not previously produced, suitable for a full-length presentation; directly concerned with the Jewish experience. Deadline: December 15. Cash award plus staged reading.

‡**SOUTH CAROLINA PLAYWRIGHTS' FESTIVAL**, Trustus Theatre, P.O. Box 11721, Columbia SC 29211. (803)771-9153. Estab. 1989. Offered annually for professionally unproduced work. "Full-length plays accepted. No musicals, children's shows, translations or adaptations." Cast limit 8, 1 set preferred. Submit January 1-February 1. Contact by phone between 1-6 pm. Guidelines for SASE. Prize: 1st-$500, full production, travel and housing for opening; 2nd-$250 plus staged reading; one acts $50 and late night readings. Submission procedure: application (available after September 1, 1998, two copies of synopsis, 1 copy of résumé, SASE.

SOUTHEASTERN THEATRE CONFERENCE NEW PLAY PROJECT, 461 King Richard Dr,. Murray KY 42701-9061. (502)762-5487. E-mail: jamesaye@aol.com. Contact: James I. Schempp. Offered annually for the discovery, development and publicizing of worthy new unproduced plays and playwrights. Eligibility limited to members of 10 state SETC Region: Alabama, Florida, Georgia, Kentucky, Missouri, North Carolina, South Carolina, Tennessee, Virginia, West Virginia. Submit March 1-June 1. Bound full-length or related one acts under single cover (one submission only). Send SASE with scripts for return. Guidelines available upon request. Prize: $1,000, staged reading at SETC Convention, expenses paid trip to convention and preferred consideration for National Playwrights Conference.

SOUTHERN APPALACHIAN PLAYWRIGHTS' CONFERENCE, Southern Appalachian Repertory Theatre, P.O. Box 620, Mars Hill NC 28754. (704)689-1384. Fax: (704)689-1211. Assistant Managing Director: Dianne J. Chapman. Offered annually for unpublished, unproduced plays to promote the development of new plays. Deadline: October 31. Guidelines for SASE. Prize: 5 playwrights are invited for informal readings in April, room and board provided. All plays are considered for later production with honorarium provided for the playwright.

‡**SOUTHERN PLAYWRIGHTS COMPETITION**, Jacksonville State University, 700 Pelham Rd. N., Jacksonville AL 36265-9982. (205)782-5411. Fax: (205)782-5441. E-mail: swhitton@jsucc.jsu.edu. Contact: Steven J. Whitton. Estab. 1988. Offered annually. "The Southern Playwrights Competition seeks to identify and encourage the best of Southern playwrighting." Deadline: February 15. Guidelines for SASE. Prize: $1,000 and a production of the play. Playwrights must be native to or resident of AL, AR, FL, GA, KY, LA, MO, NC. SC, TN, TX, VA or WV.

SOUTHWEST THEATRE ASSOCIATION NEW PLAY CONTEST, Southwest Theatre Association, Department of Theatre Arts, University of Texas at El Paso, 500 W. University, El Paso TX 79968-0549. (915)747-7854. Fax: (915)747-5438. Contact: Michael Wright. Annual contest for unpublished, unproduced work to promote the writing and production of new plays in the Southwest region. Deadline: March 16. Guidelines for SASE. Charges $10. Prize: $200 honorarium, a staged reading at the annual SWTA convention, publication in *Theatre Southwest*. Judged by the New Plays Committee of the Southwest Theatre Association. Open to all writers. No musicals or children's plays. Letter of recommendation suggested.

SPRING STAGED READING PLAY CONTEST, TADA!, 120 W. 28th St., New York NY 10001. (212)627-1732. Fax: (212)243-6736. E-mail: tada@ziplink.net. Website: http://www.tadatheater.com. Contest Director: Janine Nina Trevens. Offered annually for unpublished work to introduce the playwriting process to family audiences in a staged reading series featuring the winning entries. One-act plays to be appropriate for children or teenage or family audiences, cast to be mostly children 8-17. Deadline: varies yearly; usually late winter, early spring. Please send a cover letter and play with SASE for return, no application form necessary. Prize: $200 and a staged reading held in TADA!'s theater with TADA! cast and others hired by TADA! Contest is open. Plays must be appropriate for children or family audiences.

STAGES, P.O. Box 214820, Dallas TX 75221. (214)630-7722. Fax: (214)630-4468. Contact: Marilyn Pyeatt. Offered annually for unpublished and unproduced submissions to encourage playwriting, develop new works and showcase talent. Deadline: March 15. Guidelines for SASE. Prize: $100 honorarium and production. Judged by a committee of play-readers. Finalists are selected for readings (public) and final decision is made by committee, Executive Director and directors. Open to any writer.

STANLEY DRAMA AWARD, Dept. of Humanities, Wagner College, Staten Island NY 10301. Offered for original full-length plays, musicals or one-act play sequences that have not been professionally produced or received trade book publication. Presented as a memorial to Alma Timolat Stanley (Mrs. Robert C. Stanley). Deadline: September 1. Guidelines for SASE. Award: $2,000. Stage plays only.

MARVIN TAYLOR PLAYWRITING AWARD, Sierra Repertory Theatre, P.O. Box 3030, Sonora CA 95370-3030. (209)532-3120. Fax: (209)532-7270. E-mail: srt@mlode.com. Website: http://www.mlode.com/~nsierra/srt. Producing Director: Dennis Jones. Estab. 1981. Full-length plays. Deadline: August 31.

‡**TEXAS PLAYWRIGHT FESTIVAL**, Stages Repertory Theatre, 3201 Allen Pkwy., Suite 101, Houston TX 77019. (713)527-0240. Fax: (713)527-8669. Artistic Director: Rob Bundy. Offered annually to provide an outlet for unpublished Texas playwrights. Entries received from October 1-December 31. Guidelines for SASE. Prize: A reading by professional actors and a small stipend is awarded if available. Judged by the artistic director and his committee. Writer must be a current or previous resident of Texas, or the play must be set in Texas or have a Texas theme.

THEATER AT LIME KILN REGIONAL PLAYWRITING CONTEST, Theater at Lime Kiln, 14 S. Randolph St., Lexington VA 24450. (540)463-7088. Fax: (540)463-1082. E-mail: limekiln@cfw.com. Contact: Eleanor Connor.

Offered annually for unpublished work. "With this contest Lime Kiln seeks to encourage playwrights to create works about our region of the country. Material should be limited geographically to Appalachia (Virginia, Western North Carolina, West Virginia, Eastern Kentucky, Eastern Tennessee). Plays with music encouraged." Submit August 1-September 30. Guidelines for SASE. Prize: 1st-$1,000; 2nd-$500; possibility of staged reading. Open to all writers.

‡THEATRE BC'S ANNUAL CANADIAN NATIONAL PLAYWRITING COMPETITION, Theatre BC, 1005 Broad St., #307, Victoria, British Columbia V8W 2A1 Canada. (250)381-2443. Fax: (250)381-4419. E-mail: theatrebc@pacificcoast.net. Executive Director: Jim Harding. Offered annually to unpublished plays "to promote the development and production of new plays (previously unproduced) at all levels of theater. Categories: Full-Length (2 acts or longer); One Act (less than 60 minutes) and an open Special Merit (juror's discretion). Deadline: June. Guidelines for SASE or check Theatre BC's website: http://www.culturenet.ca/theatrebc/. Charges $35/entry and $25 (optional) for written critique. Prize: Full-Length-$1,500; One Act-$1,000; Special Merit-$750. Winners are also invited to new play workshops: 18 hours with a professional dramaturge, registrant actors and a public readings at provincial "Backstage" workshop (every November). Production and publishing rights remain with the playwright. However, copies of the final draft are retained for reference by TBC members. Any resident in Canada is eligible. All submissions are made under pseudonyms. E-mail inquiries welcome.

UNIVERSITY OF ALABAMA NEW PLAYWRIGHTS PROGRAM, P.O. Box 870239, Tuscaloosa AL 35487-0239. (205)348-9032. Fax: (205)348-9048. E-mail: pcastagn@woodsquad.as.ua.edu. Director/Dramaturg: Dr. Paul C. Castagno. Estab. 1982. Full-length plays for mainstage; experimental plays for B stage. Workshops and small musicals can be proposed. Queries responded to quickly. Stipends competitive with, or exceed, most contests. Development process includes readings, visitations, and possible complete productions with faculty director and dramaturg. Guidelines for SASE. Up to 6 months assessment time. Submit between August-March.

‡VENTANA PUBLICATIONS PLAY AWARD, Ventana Publications, P.O. Box 191973, San Francisco CA 94119. Contact: Vicky Simmons. Offered annually for "original one-act or full-length produced plays with significant accomplishments (for example, previous contest winners, plays that have had development and workshop at an established theater, etc.). Proof of production/acomplishment will be required. Deadline: February 15. Guidelines for SASE. Charges $10/entry. Prize(s): Publication with standard royalty contract. Open to any writer.

VERMONT PLAYWRIGHT'S AWARD, The Valley Players, P.O. Box 441, Waitsfield VT 05673. Award Director: Jennifer Howard. Offered annually for unpublished nonmusical, full-length play suitable for production by a community theater group to encourage development of playwrights in Vermont, New Hampshire and Maine. Deadline: February 1. Prize: $1,000. Must be a resident of Vermont, New Hampshire or Maine.

WEST COAST ENSEMBLE FULL-PLAY COMPETITION, West Coast Ensemble, P.O. Box 38728, Los Angeles CA 90038. Artistic Director: Les Hanson. Estab. 1982. Unpublished (in Southern California) plays. No musicals or children's plays for full-play competition. No restrictions on subject matter. Deadline: December 31.

JACKIE WHITE MEMORIAL NATIONAL CHILDREN'S PLAYWRITING CONTEST, Columbia Entertainment Co., 309 Parkade, Columbia MO 65202. (573)874-5628. Contest Director: Betsy Phillips. Offered annually for unpublished plays. "We are searching for good scripts suitable for audiences of all ages to be performed by the 35-40 students, grade 6-9, in our theater school." Deadline: June 1. Guidelines for SASE. Charges $10 entry fee. Prize: $250 and full production, plus travel expenses to come see production.

WICHITA STATE UNIVERSITY PLAYWRITING CONTEST, University Theatre, Wichita State University, Wichita KS 67260-0153. (316)689-3185. Fax: (316)689-3951. Contest Director: Professor Leroy Clark. Estab. 1974. Unpublished, unproduced full-length or 2-3 short plays of at least 90 minutes playing time. No musicals or children's plays. Deadline: February 15. Guidelines for SASE. Prize: production of winning play (ACTF) and expenses paid trip for playwright to see final rehearsals and/or performances. Contestants must be graduate or undergraduate students in a US college or university.

‡TENNESSEE WILLIAMS/NEW ORLEANS LITERARY FESTIVAL ONE-ACT CONTEST, The Creative Writing Workshop at the University of New Orleans, 5500 Prytania St., Suite 217, New Orleans LA 70115. (504)581-1144. Fax: (504)529-2430. Offered annually to unpublished and unproduced plays "to foster continuing interest in the playwriting field and to honor the creative spirit of America's greatest playwright, Tennessee Williams." Deadline: December 1. Guidelines for SASE or call the festival office. Charges $15/submission. Prize: $1,000, a staged reading at festival the year the prize is won and a full production the following year. The top 10 finalists are announced by a nationally released press announcement. All contestants are notified of the winner and finalists. Open to any writer. Length: 1 hour maximum.

WOMEN'S PLAYWRITING FESTIVAL, Perishable Theatre, P.O. Box 23132, Providence RI 02903. (401)331-2695. Fax: (401)331-7811. Website: http://www.ids.net/~as220/perishable/home.html. Contact: Kathleen Jenkins. Offered annually for unpublished/unproduced one acts by women, 10-30 minutes in length, 2 submissions per author. Deadline: December 31. SASE for guidelines. Prize: 3 winners of $200 each.

‡YOUNG CONNECTICUT PLAYWRIGHTS FESTIVAL, Maxwell Anderson Playwrights Series, P.O. Box 671, West. Redding CT 06896. (203)938-2770. Contact: Bruce Post. Offered annually for unpublished plays to offer recognition and encouragement to young playwrights. Deadline: February 15. Guidelines for SASE. Prize: An awards ceremony and professionally staged reading for 4 finalists. Open to any Connecticut resident aged 12-18.

YOUNG PLAYWRIGHTS FESTIVAL, Young Playwrights Inc., Suite 906, 321 W. 44th St., New York NY 10036. (212)307-1140. Fax: (212)307-1454. E-mail: writeaplay@aol.com. Artistic Director: Sheri M. Goldhirsch. Offered annually. Only stage plays accepted for submission (no musicals, screenplays or adaptations). "Writers age 18 or younger are invited to send scripts for consideration in the annual Young Playwrights Festival. Winning plays will be performed in professional Off Broadway production." Deadline: October 15. Contest/award rules and entry forms available for SASE. Entrants must be 18 or younger as of the annual deadline.

Journalism

AMY WRITING AWARDS, The Amy Foundation, P.O. Box 16091, Lansing MI 48901. (517)323-6233. Fax: (517)323-7293. Website: http://www.amyfound.org. President: James Russell. Estab. 1985. Nonfiction articles containing scripture published in the secular media. Deadline: January 31, for those from previous calendar year. Prize: $10,000, $5,000, $4,000, $3,000, $2,000 and 10 prizes of $1,000.

THE WHITMAN BASSOW AWARD, Overseas Press Club of America and AT&T, 320 East 42 St., Mezzanine, New York NY 10017. (212)983-4655. Fax: (212)983-4692. Manager: Sonya Fry. Offered annually for previously published best reporting in any medium on international environmental issues. Deadline: January 31. Charges $100 fee. Prize: certificate and $1,000. Work must be published by US-based publications or broadcast.

‡MIKE BERGER AWARD, Columbia University Graduate School of Journalism, 2950 Broadway, New York NY 10027-7004. (212)854-5984. Fax: (212)854-7837. Website: http://www.jrn.columbia.edu. Contact: Pilar Alayo. Offered annually honoring "human interest reporting about the daily life of New York City in the traditions of the late Meyer 'Mike' Berger." Deadline: February 15. Guidelines for SASE. Cash prize. Each entry must consist of FOUR copies of each of the following: 1) a letter from the editor indicating the scope of the reporter's work; 2) a brief biography of the reporter; 3) up to five clips published in 1996 that best typify the reporter's work.

‡THE WORTH BINGHAM PRIZE, The Worth Bingham Memorial Fund, 1616 H Street, N.W., 3rd Floor, Washington DC 20006. (202)737-3700. Fax: (202)737-0530. E-mail: susan@cfj.org. Award Director: Susan Talalay. Offered annually to articles published during the year of the award. "The Prize honors newspaper or magazine investigative reporting of stories of national significance where the public interest is being ill-served. Entries may include a single story, a related series of stories or up to three unrelated stories." Deadline: February 15. Award rules for SASE. Prize: $10,000. Judged by a three-person panel.

THE ERIC AND AMY BURGER AWARD, Overseas Press Club of America, 320 East 42 St., Mezzanine, New York NY 10017. (212)983-4655. Fax: (212)983-4692. Manager: Sonya Fry. Offered annually for previously published best reporting in any medium dealing with human rights. Deadline: January 31. Charges $100 fee. Prize: certificate and $1,000. Work must be published by U.S.-based publications or broadcast.

CANADIAN FOREST SERVICE-SAULT STE. MARIE JOURNALISM AWARD, Canadian Forest Service-Sault Ste. Marie/Natural Resources Canada, % CSWA, P.O. Box 75, Station A, Toronto, Ontario M5W 1A2 Canada. Phone/fax: (416)928-9624. E-mail: cswa@interlog.com. Website: http://www.interlog.com/~cswa. Contact: Andy F. Visser-deVries. Offered annually for work published January 1-December 31 of the previous year to recognize outstanding journalism that promotes public awareness of forests and issues surrounding forests in Ontario. Deadline: February 15. Guidelines for SASE. Prize: for 1 newspaper and for 1 magazine $750 and plaque each. Material becomes property of Canadian Forest Service. Does not return mss. Open to writers who have published in an Ontario publication.

RUSSELL L. CECIL ARTHRITIS MEDICAL JOURNALISM AWARDS, Arthritis Foundation, 1330 West Peachtree St. NW, Atlanta GA 30309-9901. (404)872-7100. Fax: (404)872-0457. E-mail: lnewbern@arthritis.org. Website: http://www.arthritis.org. Contact: Lisa M. Newbern. Estab. 1956. News stories, articles and radio/TV scripts on the subject of arthritis and the Arthritis Foundation published or broadcast for general circulation during the previous calendar year. Deadline: February 15.

HARRY CHAPIN MEDIA AWARDS, World Hunger Year, 505 Eighth Ave., 21st Floor, New York NY 10018-6582. (212)629-8850. Fax: (212)465-9274. E-mail: whyria@aol.com. Website: http://www.iglou.com/why. Coordinator: Jessica Keith. Estab. 1982. Critical issues of domestic and world hunger, poverty and development (newspaper, periodical, TV, radio, photojournalism, books). Prizes: $1,000-2,500. Deadline: February 18.

‡CORPORATE COVER-UP CONSPIRACY CONTEST, *Whistleblower Magazine* and Truth, Justice & American Way Society, P.O. Box 383, Cookeville TN 38503. (615)432-6046. Award Director: G.W. Brown. Offered annually "to expose stories such as nuclear plant conspiracies that mainstream media fear to touch." Deadline: January 1. "Sample issue with the type of story we are seeking: $4. Prize: $500, plus best of contest will be published in the April 1998 issue of the *Whistleblower*. "We claim the rights to published winning entries."

DART AWARD, Dart Foundation through Michigan State University's Victims and the Media Program, MSU School of Journalism, East Lansing MI 48824-1212. (511)432-2171. Fax: (517)355-7710. E-mail: bucquero@pilot.msu.edu. Website: http://www.journalism.msu.edu/victims.html. Director: Sue Carter. Asstistant Director: Bonnie Bucqueroux. Offered annually for previously published work to encourage treatment of victims and victim issues with compassion, dignity, and respect. Awarded for best newspaper feature on victim(s) of violence each year. Deadline: March 1. Guidelines for SASE. Prize: $10,000 to winning newspaper, shared with team. Open to all daily and weekly newspapers.

THE GREAT AMERICAN TENNIS WRITING AWARDS, *Tennis Week*, 341 Madison Ave., New York NY 10017. (212)808-4750. Fax: (212)983-6302. E-mail: kennisweek@tennisweek.com. Publisher: Eugene L. Scott. Contact: Heather Holland or Kim Kodl, managing editors. Estab. 1986. Category 1: unpublished ms by an aspiring journalist with no previous national byline. Category 2: unpublished ms by a non-tennis journalist. Category 3: unpublished ms by a tennis journalist. Categories 4-6: published tennis-related articles and one book award. Deadline: December 15.

O. HENRY AWARD, The Texas Institute of Letters, P.O. Box 298300, Fort Worth TX 76129. (817)921-7822. Fax: (817)921-7333 (must be marked Attn: TCU Press). Website: http://www.til.tcu.edu/. Director: Judy Alter. Offered annually for previously published work between January 1-December 31 of previous year to recognize the best-written work of journalism appearing in a magazine or weekly newspaper. Deadline: January 2. Guidelines for SASE. Prize: $500. Judged by a panel chosen by the TIL Council. Writers must have been born in Texas, have lived in Texas for at least two consecutive years at some time, or the subject matter of the work should be associated with Texas.

‡SIDNEY HILLMAN FOUNDATION, Unite, 1710 Broadway, New York NY 10019. (212)265-7000 ext 725. Fax: (212)582-3175. E-mail: jmort@uniteunion.org. Website: http://www.uniteunion.org. Contest Director: Jo-Ann Mort. Offered annually to previously published print, electronic and public policy books contributing to progressive social change that must have appeared in print during the year of the award. Deadline: January 17. Guidelines for SASE. Prize: $2,000 plus plaque. Judges: Hendrick Hertzberg, *The New Yorker*, Sara Fritz, *The Los Angeles Times*, Frank Snobuda, *The Washington Post*. Open to any writer.

INTERNATIONAL READING ASSOCIATION PRINT MEDIA AWARD, International Reading Association, P.O. Box 8139, Newark DE 19714-8139. (302)731-1600 ext. 215. Fax: (302)731-1057. Contact: Janet Butler. Estab. 1956. Recognizes outstanding reporting on reading and literacy by professional journalists. Deadline: January 15.

DONALD E. KEYHOE JOURNALISM AWARD, Fund for UFO Research, P.O. Box 277, Mt. Rainier MD 20712. (703)684-6032. Fax: (703)684-6032. Chairman: Richard Hall. Estab. 1979. Offered annually for the best article or story published or broadcast in a newspaper, magazine, TV or radio news outlet during the previous calendar year. Separate awards for print and broadcast media. Also makes unscheduled cash awards for published works on UFO phenomena research or public education.

‡HERB LAMPERT STUDENT WRITING AWARD, Canadian Science Writers' Association, P.O. Box 75, Station A, Toronto, Ontario M5W 1A2 Canada. (416)928-9624. E-mail: cswa@interlog.com. Contest/Award Director: Andy F. Visser-deVries. Offered annually to any student science writer who has an article published in a student or other newspaper or aired on a radio or TV station in Canada. Deadline: February 15. Guidelines for SASE. Prize: $750 for print and broadcast winners. Open to any Canadian resident or citizen.

‡ROBERT T. MORSE WRITER'S AWARD, American Psychiatric Association, 1400 K St. NW, Washington DC 20005. (202)682-6324. Fax: (202)682-6255. E-mail: emurphy@psych.org. Website: http://www.psych.org. Media Assistant: Erin Murphy. Offered annually for articles previously published August 1-July 31. Deadline: July 31. Send name and address—no envelope required. Prizes: $1,000 Honorarium and plaque to be presented at APA's Annual Meeting. Judges: 4 psychiatrists and 3 mental health professional communicators. "Anyone can be nominated, but no books! Just articles."

FRANK LUTHER MOTT-KAPPA TAU ALPHA RESEARCH AWARD IN JOURNALISM, University of Missouri, School of Journalism, Columbia MO 65211. (573)882-7685. E-mail: ktahq@showme.missouri.edu. Executive Director, Kappa Tau Alpha: Dr. Keith Sanders. For "best researched book in mass communication." Requires 6 copies. No forms required. Deadline: January 5. Award: $1,000.

NATIONAL AWARDS FOR EDUCATION REPORTING, Education Writers Association, 1331 H St. NW, #307, Washington DC 20005. (202)637-9700. Fax: (202)637-9707. Website: http://www.ewa.org. Executive Director: Lisa Walker. Estab. 1960. Offered annually for submissions published during the previous year. Categories are: 1) newspapers under 100,000 circulation; 2) newspapers over 100,000 circulation; 3) magazines excluding trade and institutional journals that are circulated to the general public; 4) special interest, institutional and trade publications; 5) television; and 6) radio. Write for more information. Deadline: mid-January. Charges $35 fee.

ALICIA PATTERSON JOURNALISM FELLOWSHIP, Alicia Patterson Foundation, 1730 Pennsylvania Ave. NW, Suite 850, Washington DC 20006. (202)393-5995. Fax: (301)951-8512. E-mail: apfengel@charm.net. Website: http://www.charm.net/~apfengel/home.html. Contact: Margaret Engel. Offered annually for previously published submissions to give 6-8 print journalists a year of in-depth research and reporting. Applicants must have 5 years of professional print journalism experience and be US citizens. Fellows write 4 magazine-length pieces for the *Alicia Patterson Reporter*, a quarterly magazine, during their fellowship year. Fellows must take a year's leave from their jobs, but may do other freelance articles during the year. Deadline: October 1. Write, call, fax or check website for applications. Prize: $30,000 stipend for calendar year.

THE POPE AWARD FOR INVESTIGATIVE JOURNALISM, The Pope Foundation, 211 W. 56 St., Suite 5H, New York NY 10019. Director: Catherine E. Pope. Offered annually to journalists who have been working for a minimum of 10 years. Deadline: November 15. Guidelines for SASE. Prize: 3 awards of $15,000 each.

PRINT MEDIA AWARD, International Reading Association, 800 Barksdale Rd., Newark DE 19714. (302)731-1600 ext. 293. Fax: (302)731-1057. Offered annually for previously published work between January 1 and December 31. Deadline: January 15. Guidelines for SASE. Prize: Announcement at annual convention. Limited to professional journalists.

THE MADELINE DANE ROSS AWARD, Overseas Press Club of America, 320 East 42 St., Mezzanine, New York NY 10017. (212)983-4655. Fax: (212)983-4692. Manager: Sonya Fry. Offered annually for previously published best foreign correspondent in any medium showing a concern for the human condition. Deadline: January 31. Charges $100 fee. Prize: certificate and $1,000. Work must be published by US-based publications or broadcast.

WILLIAM B. RUGGLES JOURNALISM SCHOLARSHIP, National Institute for Labor Relations Research, 5211 Port Royal Rd., Suite 510, Springfield VA 22151. (703)321-9820. Contact: David Kendrick. Estab. 1974. "To honor the late William B. Ruggles, editor emeritas of the Dallas Morning News, who coined the phrase 'Right to Work.' " Deadline: January 1-March 31. Prize: $2,000 scholarship. "We do reserve the right to reprint the material/excerpt from the essay in publicizing the award. Applicant must be a graduate or undergraduate student majoring in journalism in institutions of higher learning throughout the US."

SCIENCE IN SOCIETY JOURNALISM AWARDS, Canadian Science Writers' Association, P.O. Box 75, Station A, Toronto, Ontario M5W 1A2 Canada. Phone/fax: (416)960-9624. E-mail: cswa@interlog.com. Website: http://www.interlog.com/~cswa. Contact: Andy F. Visser-deVries. Offered annually for work published/aired January 1-December 31 of previous year to recognize outstanding contributions to science journalism in all media. Two newspaper, 2 magazine, 2 TV, 2 radio, 1 trade publication, student science writing award (Herb Lampert Student Writing Award). Deadline: January 31. Guidelines for SASE. Prize: $1,000 and a plaque. Material becomes property of CSWA. Does not return mss. Open to Canadian citizens or residents of Canada.

‡SCIENCE WRITING AWARD IN PHYSICS AND ASTRONOMY FOR JOURNALISTS, American Institute of Physics, One Physics Ellipse, College Park MD 20740. (301)209-3090. Fax: (301)209-0846. E-mail: jwrather@aip.acp.org. Contest/Award Director: Joan Wrather. Offered annually to previously published work appearing in print in 1997 "to recognize and stimulate distinguished writing that improves the general public's understanding and appreciation of physics and astronomy." Deadline: February 6 (unless it falls on Saturday or Sunday). Guidelines available, SASE is not necessary. Prize: $3,000, a Windsor Chair and a certificate. Entrants must be a journalist, and articles, booklets or books must be intended for the general public.

‡SUGARMAN FAMILY AWARD FOR JEWISH CHILDREN'S LITERATURE, District of Columbia Jewish Community Center, 1529 16th St. NW, Washington DC 20036. (202)518-9400 ext. 254. Fax: (202)518-9420. Award Director: Marcia F. Goldberg. Offered every 2 years to previously published entries appearing in print between January 1, 1997 and December 31, 1998 "to thank, encourage and inspire writers and illustrators of books for Jewish children. Deadline: December 31, 1998. Charges $25 fee. Prize: $750. Judged by a panel of 3 jurors. Entrants must live in the United States. Self-published books are not eligible.

‡PAUL TOBENKIN MEMORIAL AWARD, Columbia University Graduate School of Journalism, 2950 Broadway, New York NY 10027-7004. (212)854-5984. Fax: (212)854-7837. Website: http://www.jrn.columbia.edu/. Contact: Pilar Alayo. Offered annually honoring "outstanding achievement in the field of newspaper writing in the fight against racial and religious hatred, intolerance, discrimination and every form of bigotry, reflecting the spirit of Paul Tobenkin. Deadline: February 15. Guidelines for SASE. Cash prize. Each entry must consist of FOUR copies of each of the following: 1) a letter from the editor indicating the scope of the reporter's work; 2) a brief biography of the reporter; 3) up to five clips published in 1996 that best typify the reporter's work.

STANLEY WALKER JOURNALISM AWARD, The Texas Institute of Letters, P.O. Box 298300, Fort Worth TX 76129. (817)921-7822. Fax: (817)921-7333. Director: Judy Alter. Offered annually for work published January 1-December 31 of previous year to recognize the best writing appearing in a daily newspaper. Guidelines for SASE. Prize:

$1,000. Writer must have been born in Texas, or must have lived in the state for 2 consecutive years at some time, or the subject matter of the article must be associated with the state.

‡EDWARD WEINTAL PRIZE FOR DIPLOMATIC REPORTING, Georgetown University Inst. for the Study of Diplomacy, 1316 36th St. NW, Washington DC 20007. (202)965-5735 ext. 3010. Fax: (202)965-5811. Contest/Award Director: Charles Dolgas. Offered annually to honor previously published journalists whose work reflects initiative, hard digging and bold thinking in the coverage of American diplomacy and foreign policy. Deadline: mid-January. Writer should place name on award mailing list to receive notice of nominations being sought. Prize: $5,000. Judged by the Weintal committee. "Nominations are made by the editor on the basis of a specific story or series or on the basis of a journalist's overall news coverage."

Writing for Children and Young Adults

AMERICAN ASSOCIATION OF UNIVERSITY WOMEN AWARD, NORTH CAROLINA DIVISION, North Carolina Literary and Historical Association, 109 E. Jones St., Raleigh NC 27601-2807. (919)733-7305. Awards Coordinator: Rita Cashion. Previously published juvenile literature by a North Carolina resident. Deadline: July 15.

R. ROSS ANNETT AWARD FOR CHILDREN'S LITERATURE, Writers Guild of Alberta, 11759 Groat Rd., Edmonton, Alberta T5M 3K6 Canada. (403)422-8174. Fax: (403)422-2663. E-mail: writers@compusmart.ab.ca. Director: Darlene Diver. Children's book published in current year. Must be an Alberta author.

IRMA S. AND JAMES H. BLACK AWARD, Bank Street College of Education, 610 W. 112th St., New York NY 10025. (212)875-4452. Fax: (212)875-4558. E-mail: lindag@bnk1.bnkst.edu. Website: http://www.bnkst.edu/library/clib/isb.html. Award Director: Linda Greengrass. Estab. 1972. Offered annually for a book for young children, for excellence of both text and illustrations. Entries must have been published during the previous calendar year. Deadline for entries: January after book is published.

BOOK PUBLISHERS OF TEXAS AWARD FOR CHILDREN'S OR YOUNG PEOPLE'S BOOK, The Texas Institute of Letters, P.O. Box 298300 Fort Worth TX 76129. (817)921-7822. Fax: (817)921-7333 (must be marked Attn: TCU Press). Website: http://www.tcu.edu/til. . Director: Judy Alter. Offered annually for work published January 1-December 31 of previous year to recognize the best book for children or young people. Deadline: January 2. Guidelines for SASE. Prize: $250. Writer must have been born in Texas or have lived in the state for at least 2 consecutive years at 1 time, or the subject matter is associated with the state.

BOSTON GLOBE-HORN BOOK AWARD, *The Boston Globe*, 135 Morrissey Blvd, P.O. Box 2378, Boston MA 02107. Offered annually for previously published work in children's literature. Awards for original fiction or poetry, picture book, and nonfiction. Publisher submits entry. Prize: $500 in each category.

CHILDREN'S WRITER WRITING CONTESTS, *Children's Writer* Newsletter, 95 Long Ridge Rd., West Redding CT 06896. (203)792-8600. Fax: (203)792-8406. Contact: Mrs. Cheryl Delag, assistant editor. Offered 3 times/year to promote higher quality children's literature. "Each contest has its own theme. Our last 3 were (1) An early-reader humorous story for ages 4-8; to 750 words. (2) A folk or fairy tale for ages 8-12; to 850 words. (3) A science article for ages 6-8; to 850 words." Submissions must be unpublished. Deadline: Last Friday in February, June and October. Guidelines for SASE; put "Contest Request" in lower left of envelope. Charges $10 fee for nonsubscribers only, which is applicable against a subscription to *Children's Writer*. Prize: 1st—$100 or $1,000, a certificate and publication in *Children's Writer*; 2nd—$50 or $500, and certificate; 3rd-5th—$25 or $250 and certificates. One or two contests each year with the higher cash prizes also include $100 prizes plus certificates for 6th-12th places. Acquires first North American serial rights for grand prize winners and occasionally for second and third prize winners.

DELACORTE PRESS PRIZE FOR A FIRST YOUNG ADULT NOVEL, Delacorte Press, 1540 Broadway, New York NY 10036. (212)354-6500. Executive Editor: Wendy Lamb. Estab. 1983. Previously unpublished young adult fiction. Submissions: October 1-December 31. Guidelines for SASE. Prize: $1,500 cash, publication and $6,000 advance against royalties. Judged by editors of Delacorte.

JOAN FASSLER MEMORIAL BOOK AWARD, Association for the Care of Children's Health (ACCH), 7910 Woodmont Ave., #300, Bethesda MD 20814. (301)654-6549. Fax: (301)986-4553. E-mail: acch@clark.net. Website: http://acch.org. Contact: Jennifer Fincken, membership manager. Offered annually for work published in 1995 and 1996 to the author(s) of the trade book that makes the most distinguished contribution to a child's or young person's understanding of hospitalization, illness, disabling conditions, dying and death, and preventive care. Deadline: December 31. Send SASE for guidelines. Prize: $1,000 and a plaque.

‡GOLDEN KITE AWARDS, Society of Children's Book Writers and Illustrators (SCBWI), Suite 106, 22736 Vanowen St., West Hills CA 91307. (818)888-8771. E-mail: scbwi@juno.com. Website: www.scbwi.org. Coordinator: Sue

Alexander. Estab. 1973. Calendar year published children's fiction, nonfiction and picture illustration books by a SCBWI members only. Deadline: December 15.

HIGHLIGHTS FOR CHILDREN FICTION CONTEST, *Highlights for Children*, 803 Church St., Honesdale PA 18431-1824. Manuscript Coordinator: Beth Troop. Estab. 1946. Stories for children ages 2-12; category varies each year. Guidelines for SASE. Stories should be limited to 900 words for older readers, 500 words for younger readers. No crime or violence, please. Specify that ms is a contest entry. All entries must be postmarked January 1-February 28.

INTERNATIONAL READING ASSOCIATION CHILDREN'S BOOK AWARD, International Reading Association, P.O. Box 8139, 800 Barksdale Rd., Newark DE 19714-8139. (302)731-1600 ext. 221. Fax: (302)731-1057. E-mail: 75141.2005@compuserve.com. First or second book by an author who shows unusual promise in the children's book field. Categories: younger readers, ages 4-10; older readers, ages 10-16+, and informational book (ages 4-16+). Deadline: December 1.

JUVENILE LITERATURE AWARDS, Friends of American Writers, 15237 W. Redwood Lane, Libertyville IL 60048. Chairman: Kay O'Connor. Offered annually for previously published work from previous year for fiction or nonfiction. Deadline: December 31. Prize: $1,000. It must be the first, second or third book published by the author in the young people's categories of preschool, elementary, intermediate, or secondary school readership. The author must be a native of, or a current resident of, or have lived for five years in, or the setting of the book must be in one of these states . . . Arkansas, Illinois, Indiana, Iowa, Kansas, Michigan, Minnesota, Missouri, Nebraska, North Dakota, Ohio, South Dakota or Wisconsin.

‡MILKWEED PRIZE FOR CHILDREN'S LITERATURE, Milkweed Editions, First Ave. N., Suite 400, Minneapolis MN 55401. (612)332-3192. First Reader: Elisabeth Fitz. Annual prize for unpublished works. Estab. 1993. "Milkweed is looking for a novel or biography intended for readers aged 8-14. Manuscripts should be of high literary quality and must be double-spaced, 90-200 pages in length. The Milkweed Prize for Children's Literature will be awarded to the best manuscript for children ages 8-14 that Milkweed accepts for publication during each calendar year by a writer not previously published by Milkweed Editions. Prize: $2,000 advance on any royalties agreed upon at the time of acceptance. Must SASE for guidelines, both for regular children's submission policies and for the announcement of the restructured contest. Catalog for $1.50 postage.

‡THE NATIONAL CHAPTER OF CANADA IODE VIOLET DOWNEY BOOK AWARD, National Chapter of Canada IODE, 40 Orchard View Blvd., Suite 254, Toronto, Ontario M4R 1B9 Canada. (416)487-4416. Fax: (416)487-4417. Contest/Award Director: Marty Dalton. Offered annually to previously published children's books of at least 500 words. Entries must have appeared in print between January 1 and December 31. Deadline: January 31. Guidelines for SASE. Prize: $3,000 (Canadian funds). Judged by members of IODE. Entrants must be Canadian citizens.

SCOTT O'DELL AWARD FOR HISTORICAL FICTION, 1700 E. 56th St., #3906, Chicago IL 60637. (773)752-7880. Director: Zena Sutherland. Estab. 1981. Historical fiction book for children set in the Americas. Entries must have been published during previous year. Deadline: December 31.
  ● Katherine Paterson was the 1997 winner of this award for *Jip*, published by Lodestar.

PEN/NORMA KLEIN AWARD, PEN American Center, 568 Broadway, New York NY 10012. (212)334-1660. Fax: (212)334-2181. E-mail: pen@echonyc.com. Contact: John Morrone. Offered in odd-numbered years to recognize an emerging voice of literary merit among American writers of children's fiction. *Candidates may not nominate themselves.* Next award is 1999. Deadline: December 15, 1998. Guidelines for #10 SASE. Award: $3,000.

PRIX ALVINE-BÉLISLE, Association pour L'avancement des sciences et des techniques de la documentation, ASTED Inc., 3414 av. Parc #202, Montreal, Quebec, Canada. (514)281-5012. Fax: (514)281-8219. E-mail: info@asted.org. Website: http://www.asted.org. Director: Josée Valiquette. Offered annually for work published the previous year before the award to promote authors of French youth literature in Canada. Deadline: April 1. Prize: $500. "It is not the writers but the editors who send their books to us."

‡SCIENCE WRITING AWARD IN PHYSICS AND ASTRONOMY FOR CHILDREN, American Institute of Physics, One Physics Ellipse, College Park MD 20740. (301)209-3090. Fax: (301)209-0846. E-mail: jwrather@aip.ac p.org. Contest/Award Director: Joan Wrather. Offered annually to previously published entries appearing in print between

---

MARKET CONDITIONS are constantly changing! If this is 1999 or later, buy the newest edition of *Writer's Market* at your favorite bookstore or order directly from Writer's Digest Books.

July 1, 1997 and June 30, 1998, "to recognize and stimulate distinguished writing that improves the children's understanding and appreciation of physics and astronomy." Deadline: July 24 (unless it falls on a Saturday or Sunday). Guidelines available; SASE is not necessary. Prize: $3,000, a Windsor Chair and a certificate. Articles, booklets or books must be intended for children ages preschool to fifteen years old.

SILVER BAY AWARDS FOR CHILDREN'S LITERATURE, The Writer's Voice of the Silver Bay Association, Silver Bay NY 12874. (518)543-8833. Fax: (518)543-6733. Contact: Sharon Ofner. Offered annually for best unpublished children's ms set in the Adirondack Mountains, illustrated or non-illustrated. Deadline: February 1. Charges $25 fee. Prize: $1,000.

TEDDY AWARD FOR BEST CHILDREN'S BOOK, Austin Writers' League, 1501 West Fifth St., Suite E-2, Austin TX 78703. (512)499-8914. Fax: (512)499-0441. E-mail: awl@eden.com. Website: http://www.eden.com/~awl. Director: Angela Smith. Offered annually for work published January 1-December 31 to honor an outstanding book for children published by a member of the Austin Writers' League. Deadline: January 31. Guidelines for SASE. Charges $10 fee. Prize: $1,000 and trophy. Entrants must be Austin Writers' League members. Dues may accompany entry fee.

TEXAS BLUEBONNET AWARD, Texas Library Association's Texas Association of School Librarians and Children's Round Table, Suite 401, 3355 Bee Cave Rd., Austin TX 78746. (512)328-1518. Fax: (512)328-8852. E-mail: carolynr@txla.org. Website: http://www.txla.org. Contact: Patricia Smith. Published books for children recommended by librarians, teachers and students.

LAURA INGALLS WILDER MEDAL, American Library Association, 50 E. Huron St., Chicago IL 60611. (800)545-2433. E-mail: efitzsim@ala.org. Website: http://www.ala.org/alsc.html. Contact: E. Fitzsimons, deputy executive director. Offered triennially to an author or illustrator whose works have made a lasting contribution to children's literature. Guidelines for SASE. Award: medal.

(ALICE WOOD MEMORIAL) OHIOANA FOR CHILDREN'S LITERATURE, Ohioana Library Association, 65 Front St., Suite 1105, Columbus OH 43215. (614)466-3831. Fax: (614)728-6974. E-mail: ohioana@winslo.ohio.gov. Website: http://www.oplin.lib.ohio.us/ohioana/. Contact: Linda R. Hengst. Offered "to an author whose body of work has made, and continues to make, a significant contribution to literature for children or young adults." Prize: $1,000. Deadline: December 31. Nomination forms available for SASE. Recipient must have been born in Ohio or lived in Ohio at least 5 years.

WORK-IN-PROGRESS GRANT, Society of Children's Book Writers and Illustrators (SCBWI) and Judy Blume, 22736 Vanowen St., #106, West Hills CA 91307. E-mail: scbwi@juno.com. Website: http://www.scbwi.org. Two grants—one designated specifically for a contemporary novel for young people—to assist SCBWI members in the completion of a specific project. Deadline: March 1. Guidelines for SASE. Members only.

‡WRITING FOR CHILDREN COMPETITION, The Writers' Union of Canada, 24 Ryerson Ave., Toronto, Ontario M5T 2P3. (416)703-8982. E-mail: twuc@the-wire.com. Website: http://www.swifty.com/twuc. Competition Administrator: Kerry Lamond. Offered annually "to discover developing Canadian writers of unpublished children's/young-adult works." Deadline: April 23. "Visit our website: www.swifty.com/twuc. Charges $15/entry fee. Prize: $1,500. Open to Canadian citizens or landed immigrants who have not been published in book format and who do not currently have a contract with a publisher.

Translation

‡ASF TRANSLATION PRIZE, The American-Scandinavian Foundation, 725 Park Ave., New York NY 10021. (212)879-9779. Fax: (212)569-5385. Offered annually to a "translation of Scandinavian literature into English of a Nordic author born within last 200 years." Deadline: June 1, 1998. Guidelines for SASE. Prizes: $2,000, publication of an excerpt in an issue of Scandinavian Review and a commemorative bronze medallion; the Inger Sjöberg Prize of $500. "The Prize is for an outstanding English translation of poetry, fiction, drama or literary prose originally written in Danish, Finnish, Icelandic, Norwegian or Swedish that has not been previously published in the English language."

‡FELLOWSHIPS FOR TRANSLATORS, National Endowment for the Arts Literature Program, 1100 Pennsylvania Ave. NW, Washington DC 20506. (202)682-5428. Website: http://arts.enow.gov. Contact: Mark Allison, assistant, Heritage and Preservation. Published translators of exceptional talent.

SOEURETTE DIEHL FRASER TRANSLATION AWARD, The Texas Institute of Letters, P.O. Box 298300, Fort Worth TX 76129. (817)921-7822. Fax: (817)921-7333. Director: Judy Alter. Offered annually for work published January 1-December 31 of previous year to recognize the best translation of a literary book into English. Deadline: January 2. Guidelines for SASE. Prize: $1,000. Translator must have been born in Texas or have lived in the state for at least two consecutive years at some time.

GERMAN PRIZE FOR LITERARY TRANSLATION, American Translators Association, 1800 Diagonal Rd., Suite 220, Alexandria VA 22314. Fax: (703)683-6100. Website: http://atanet.org. Chair: Eric McMillan. Contact: Walter Bacak, executive director. Offered in odd-numbered years for previously published book translated from German to English. In even-numbered years, the Lewis Galentière Prize is awarded for translations other than German to English. Deadline April 15. Prize: $500, a certificate of recognition, and up to $500 toward expenses for attending the ATA Annual Conference.

‡THE HAROLD MORTON LONDON TRANSLATION AWARD, The Academy of American Poets, 584 Broadway, Suite 1208, New York NY 10012-3250. (212)274-0343. Fax: (212)274-9427. E-mail: poets@artswire.com. Website: http://www.poets.org. Contact: India Amos. Offered annually to recognize a published translation of poetry from any language into English. Deadline: December 31. Guidelines for SASE. Prize: $1,000. Judged by a noted translator. Translators must be living US citizens. Anthologies by a number of translators are ineligible.

‡LOCKERT LIBRARY OF POETRY IN TRANSLATION, Princeton University Press, 41 William St., Princeton NJ 08540. (609)452-4900. E-mail: rebrown@pupress.princeton.edu. Website: http://www.pupress.princeton.edu. Editor: Robert E. Brown. Book-length poetry translation of a single poet.

PEN/BOOK-OF-THE-MONTH CLUB TRANSLATION PRIZE, PEN American Center, 568 Broadway, New York NY 10012. (212)334-1660. Fax: (212)334-2181. E-mail: pen@echonyc.com. Contact: John Morrone. One award of $3,000 to a literary book-length translation into English published in the calendar year under consideration. (No technical, scientific or reference.) Deadline: December 15. Publishers, agents or translators may submit 3 copies of each eligible title.

PEN/RALPH MANHEIM MEDAL FOR TRANSLATION, PEN American Center, 568 Broadway, New York NY 10012. (212)334-1660. Fax: (212)334-2181. E-mail: pen@echonyc.com. Contact: John Morrone. Translators nominated by the PEN Translation Committee. Given every 3 years. Next award: 2000.

‡THE RAIZISS/DE PALCHI TRANSLATION AWARD, The Academy of American Poets, 584 Broadway, Suite 1208, New York NY 10012-3250. (212)274-0343. Fax: (212)274-9427. E-mail: poets@artswire.com. Website: http://www.poets.org. Contact: India Amos. Offered every 2 years (odd years) to recognize outstanding unpublished translations of modern Italian poetry into English. Accepts entries from September 1-November 1. Prize: $20,000 and a one-month residency at the American Academy in Rome. Judged by a panel of 3 poets/translators. Applicants must verify permission to translate the poems or that the poems are in the public domain. Open to any US citizen. Guidelines for SASE.

ALDO AND JEANNE SCAGLIONE PRIZE FOR TRANSLATION OF A LITERARY WORK, Modern Language Association of America, 10 Astor Place, New York NY 10003-6981. (212)614-6406. Fax: (212)533-0680. E-mail: awards@mla.org. Director of Special Projects: Richard Brod. Offered in even-numbered years for the translation of a book-length literary work and in odd-numbered years for a book-length work of literary history, literary criticism, philology or literary theory appearing in print during the pervious two years. Deadline: May 1. Guidelines for SASE. Prize: $1,000 and a certificate presented at the association's annual convention in December. Translators need not be members of the MLA.

‡UNGER AWARD, American Translators Association, 1800 Diagonal Rd., #220, Alexandria VA 22314. (703)683-6100. Fax: (703)683-6122. Award Director: Eric McMillan. Offered every 2 years (odd years) to previously published translations appearing in print January 1-December 31. The purpose of this award is to recognize outstanding translations from German into English. Deadline: May 15. Guidelines for SASE. Prize: $1,000, $500 toward conference expenses to accept the award, and certificate.

Multiple Writing Areas

AKRON MANUSCRIPT CLUB WRITER'S CONTEST, Akron Manuscript Club, Akron University, Falls Writer's Workshop & Taylor Memorial Library, P.O. Box 1101, Cuyahoga Falls OH 44223-0101. (216)923-2094. E-mail: mmlop @aol.com. Contact: M.M. LoPiccolo. Estab. 1929. Offered annually for previously unpublished stories to provide critique, encouragement and some financial help to authors in 3 categories. Deadline is always sometime in March. Guidelines for #10 SASE. Charges $25 entry/critique fee. Prize: 1st-certificate to $50, according to funding; 2nd and 3rd-certificates. Send no entry until you get current guidelines.

AMELIA STUDENT AWARD, *Amelia Magazine*, 329 E St., Bakersfield CA 93304. (805)323-4064. Editor: Frederick A. Raborg, Jr. Previously unpublished poems, essays and short stories by high school students, 1 entry per student; each entry should be signed by parent, guardian *or* teacher to verify originality. Deadline: May 15. No entry fee; however, if guidelines and sample are required, please send SASE with $3 handling charge.

‡ANNUAL FICTION AND POETRY CONTEST, Rambunctious Press, 1221 W. Pratt, Chicago IL 60626-4329. Contest Director: Mary Alberts. Estab. 1982. Unpublished short stories and poems. Deadline varies. Charges $3/story, $2/poem.

ANTIETAM REVIEW LITERARY AWARD, *Antietam Review*, 7 W. Franklin St., Hagerstown MD 21740-4804. Fax: (301)791-3132. Short fiction (up to 5,000 words) and poetry (up to 30 lines). Submissions accepted from June 1-September 1. Guidelines for SASE. Charges $10 reading fee/short story, $3/poem. Up to 5 entries at a time are permitted. First prize (fiction): $100, publication in *AR*, 2 copies of the magazine. First prize (poetry): $50, publication, plus 2 copies. ALL entries considered for publication. Open to natives or residents of MD, PA, VA, WV, DE and DC.

ARIZONA AUTHORS' ASSOCIATION ANNUAL NATIONAL LITERARY CONTEST, Arizona Authors' Association, 3509 E. Shea Blvd., #117, Phoenix AZ 85028-3339. (602)942-9602. E-mail: ggbenn@juno.com. Contact: Eileen Birin. Previously unpublished poetry, short stories, essays. Deadline: July 29. Charges $5 fee for poetry; $7 fee for short stories and essays.

‡ARTS AND LETTERS COMPETITION, Government of Newfoundland and Labrador Cultural Affairs Division, Box 1854, St. John's, Newfoundland A1C 5P9 Canada. (709)729-5253. Fax: (709)729-5952. Chairperson: Julia Pickard. Offered annually "to encourage creative talent of the residents of Newfoundland and Labrador. Senior Divison (19 years and older): poetry, fiction, nonfiction and dramatic scripts. Junior Division (12-18 years old): prose and poetry. All works are unpublished. Guidelines for SASE or call the Arts and Letters Competition office at (709)729-5253. Prizes, Senior Division: 1st-$600, 2nd-$300, 3rd-$150 for each category; Junior Division: 1st-$300, 2nd-$200, 3rd-$100 for each category. Rights remain with the author, but the first place winner is usually published in an annual booklet. Open to residents of province of Newfoundland and Labrador.

‡AWP AWARD SERIES, Associated Writing Programs, Tallwood House, Mail Stop 1E3, George Mason University, Fairfax VA 22030. (703)993-4301. Fax: (703)993-4302. Contest/Award Director: Gwyn McVay. Offered annually to foster new literary talent. Categories: poetry, short fiction, creative nonfiction, novel. Entries must be postmarked between January 1 and February 28. Guidelines for SASE. Charges $15 for nonmembers, $10 for members. Winners receive a cash honorarium (novel-$10,000; other categories-$2,000) and publication by a participating press. Open to all writers.

‡BAKELESS LITERARY PUBLICATION PRIZES, Bread Loaf Writers' Conference/Middlebury College, Middlebury College, Middleburg VT 05753. (802)443-5286. Fax: (802)443-2087. Contest Director: Michael Collier. Offered annually for unpublished authors of poetry, fiction and creative nonfiction. Submissions accepted January 1-March 1. Guidelines for SASE. Charges $10 fee. Prize: Publication of book length ms by University Press of New England and a Fellowship to attend the Bread Loaf Writers' Conference. Open to all writing in English who have not yet published a book in their entry's genre.

EMILY CLARK BALCH AWARD, *Virginia Quarterly Review*, 1 West Range, Charlottesville VA 22903. (804)924-3124. Fax:(804)924-1397. Editor: Staige D. Blackford. Best short story/poetry accepted and published by the *Virginia Quarterly Review* during a calendar year. No deadline.

CANADIAN AUTHORS ASSOCIATION ANNUAL CREATIVE WRITING AWARDS FOR HIGH SCHOOL, COLLEGE AND UNIVERSITY STUDENTS, Canadian Authors Association, Box 32219, 250 Harding Blvd. W, Richmond Hill, Ontario L4C 9R0 Canada. Fax: (905)737-2961. E-mail: bfarrar@learn.senecac.on.ca. To encourage creative writing of unpublished fiction and poetry by writers between ages 12-21. Deadline: Must be postmarked by Saturday, March 31, 1998. Must be secondary school, college or university student. Prizes of $500 and 4 honorable mentions in each category (best poem, best story). Send SAE and 1 IRC, or SASE in Canada for guidelines.

‡CANADIAN AUTHORS ASSOCIATION AWARDS PROGRAM, P.O. Box 419, Campbellford, Ontario K0L 1L0 Canada. (705)653-0323. Fax: (705)653-0593. Contact: Alec McEachern. Offered annually for short stories, historical fiction, books inspirational to young people, short stories for children and to promising writers under age 30. Deadlines vary. Guidelines for SASE. Prizes range from air travel for two to $10,000. Trustees appointed by the CAA select judges. Entrants must be Canadians by birth, naturalized Canadians or landed immigrants.

‡CANADIAN HISTORICAL ASSOCIATION AWARDS, Canadian Historical Association, 395 Wellington, Ottawa, Ontario K1A 0N3 Canada. (613)233-7885. Fax: (613)567-3110. Offered annually. Categories: regional history, Canadian history, history (not Canadian), women's history (published articles, English or French), doctoral dissertations. Deadlines vary. Guidelines for SASE. Prizes: certificates of merit-$1,000. Judged by Canadian Historical Associations committees. Open to Canadian writers.

THE CHELSEA AWARDS FOR POETRY AND SHORT FICTION, % Richard Foerster, Editor, P.O. Box 1040, York Beach ME 03910. Estab. 1958. Previously unpublished submissions. "Two prizes awarded for the best work of short fiction and for the best group of 4-6 poems selected by the editors in anonymous competitions." Deadline: June 15 for fiction; December 15 for poetry. Guidelines for SASE. Charges $10 fee (includes free subscription to

Chelsea). Checks made payable to Chelsea Associates, Inc. Prize: $750, winning entries published in *Chelsea*. Include SASE for notification of competition results. Does not return mss. *Note:* General submissions and other business should be addressed to the editor at *Chelsea*, P.O. Box 773, Cooper Station, New York, NY 10276.

CITY OF TORONTO BOOK AWARDS, City of Toronto, Corporate Communications, Toronto City Hall, Toronto, Ontario M5H 2N2 Canada. (416)392-0468. Fax: (416)392-7999. Offered annually for work published January 1-December 31 of previous year to honor authors of books of literary merit that are evocative of Toronto. Deadline: January 31. Guidelines for SASE. Prize: Total of $15,000 in prize money. Each finalist (usually 4-6) receives $1,000 and the winning author receives the remainder ($9,000-11,000). Fiction and nonfiction books for adults and/or children are eligible. Textbooks, reprints and mss are not eligible.

CNW/FLORIDA STATE WRITING COMPETITION, Florida Freelance Writers Association, Contest Administrator, P.O. Box A, North Stratford NH 03590. Contact: Dana Cassell, executive director. Annual contest. Deadline: March 15. Subject areas include: adult articles, adult short stories, writing for children, novels, nonfiction books; categories within these areas vary from year to year. Guidelines for #10 SASE. Entry fees vary from year to year; in 1996 were $5-10.

COLORADO BOOK AWARDS, Colorado Center for the Book, 2123 Downing, Denver CO 80205. (303)839-8320. Fax: (303)839-8319. E-mail: 103332.1376@compuserve.com. Website: http://www.aclin.org/~ccftb. Director: Megan Maguire. Offered annually for work published November/December of previous year or current calendar year. The purpose is to champion all Colorado authors and in particular to honor the award winners and a reputation for Colorado as a state whose people promote and support reading, writing and literacy through books. The categories are children, young adult, fiction, nonfiction & poetry. Guidelines for SASE. Charges $30 fee. Prize: $500 cash prize in each category and an annual dinner event where winners are honored. Judged by booksellers, librarians, authors. This award is for authors who reside or have resided in Colorado, or who have Colorado-based themes.

‡COMMONWEALTH CLUB OF CALIFORNIA BOOK AWARDS, 595 Market St., San Francisco CA 94105. (415)597-6700. Fax: (415)597-6729. E-mail: cwc@sirius.com. Website: http://www.sfgate.com/~common. Contest/Award Director: Jim Coplan. Estab. 1931. Offered annually for previously published submissions appearing in print January 1-December 31 of the previous year. "Purpose of award is the encouragement and production of literature in California. Categories include: fiction, nonfiction, poetry, first work of fiction, juvenile ages up to 10, juvenile 11-16, notable contribution to publishing and Californiana." Deadline: January 31. Guidelines for SASE. Can be nominated by publisher as well. Prize: Medals to be awarded at publicized event. "Work must be authored by California resident (or must have been a resident at time of publication)."

VIOLET CROWN BOOK AWARDS, Austin Writers' League, 1501 West Fifth St., Suite E-2, Austin TX 78703. (512)499-8914. Fax: (512)499-0441. E-mail: awl@eden.com. Website: http://www.eden.com.~awl. Director: Angela Smith. Offered annually for work published September 1-August 31 to honor three outstanding books published in fiction, nonfiction and literary categories by Austin Writers' League members. Deadline: August 31. Guidelines for SASE. Charges $10 fee. Prize: 3 $1,000 cash prizes and trophies. Entrants must be Austin Writers' League members. Membership dues may accompany entry fee.

CWW ANNUAL AWARDS COMPETITION, Council for Wisconsin Writers, P.O. Box 55322, Madison WI 53705. Offered annually for work published January 1-December 31 of previous year. Thirteen awards: major/life achievement, short fiction, scholarly book, short nonfiction, nonfiction book, juvenile fiction book, children's picture book, poetry book, fiction book, outdoor writing, nonfiction juvenile book, drama (produced), outstanding service to Wisconsin writers. Deadline: January 15. Guidelines for SASE. Charges entry fee: $25 for nonmembers, $10 for members. Prize: $500-1,000 and certificate. Open to Wisconsin residents.

THE DANCING JESTER PRESS "ONE NIGHT IN PARIS SHOULD BE ENOUGH" CONTEST, The Dancing Jester Press, 3411 Garth Rd., Suite 208, Baytown TX 77521. E-mail: djpress@aol.com. Contact: (Ms.) Shiloh Daniel. Offered annually for unpublished work to recognize excellence in poetics. Prize: 1st-the night of April 1, 1998 in Paris, France, all expenses paid; 2nd-chapbook publication; 3rd-a pair of "One Night in Paris Should Be Enough" T-shirts.

EDITORS' PRIZE, Missouri Review, 1507 Hillcrest Hall, University of Missouri, Columbia MO 65211. (573)882-4474. E-mail: moreview@showme.missouri.edu. Contact: Speer Morgan, Greg Michalson. Offered annually for unpublished fiction, essays or poetry. Deadline: October 15. Guidelines for SASE. Charges $15/entry; fee includes 1 year subscription. Prize: Fiction—$1,500 and publication; Essay—$1,000 and publication; Larry Levis Prize in poetry, prize amount to be announced, includes publication. Open to any writer.

FEMINIST WRITERS' CONTEST, Dept WM, Des Plaines/Park Ridge NOW, P.O. Box 2440, Des Plaines IL 60018. Contact: Contest Director. Estab. 1990. Categories: Fiction and nonfiction (3,000 or fewer words). Work should reflect feminist perspectives (should not endorse or promote sexism, racism, ageism, anti-lesbianism, etc.) Guidelines for SASE. Deadline: August 31. Charges $10 fee. Cash awards.

FOLIO, Department of Literature, American University, Washington DC 20016. Estab. 1984. Fiction, poetry, essays, interviews and b&w artwork. "We look for quality work and award an annual prize for best poem and best story published per year." Published twice annually. Manuscripts read September-March 15.

FRIENDS OF AMERICAN WRITERS AWARDS, Friends of American Writers, 6101 N. Sheridan Rd. East, Chicago IL 60660. (312)743-7323. Contest/Award Directors: Pearl Robbins (adult) and Kay O'Connor (juvenile), 15237 W. Redwood Lane, Libertyville IL 60048. (847)362-3782. Annual award for submissions published January 1-December 31 of each year. Two categories: adult and juvenile literature, fiction or nonfiction of literary quality. Deadline: December 1. $1,600 for 1st adult award and $1,000 2nd adult award. Juvenile $1,000 1st and $600 2nd. Entry forms and guidelines for #10 SASE.

GEORGETOWN REVIEW FICTION AND POETRY CONTEST, (formerly *Georgetown Review* Short Story and Poetry Contest), P.O. Box 6309, Southern Station, Hattiesburg MS 39406-6309. (601)583-6940. E-mail: jsfulmer@w hale.st.usm.edu. Website: http://www2.digimag.net/~georgetownreview/. Contact: John Fulmer. Deadline: October 1. Guidelines for SASE. Entry fee: $10/short story; $5/poem, $2 each additional poem. Prize: $1,000 for winning story; $500 for winning poem. Nine finalists receive publication and 1 year's subscription. Maximum length: 25 pages or 6,500 words. Previously published or accepted work ineligible. No mss returned.

‡GEORGIA STATE UNIVERSITY REVIEW WRITING CONTEST, Georgia State University Review, Georgia State University Plaza, Campus Box 1894, Atlanta GA 30303-3083. (404)651-4804. Fax: (404)651-1710. Contact: Editor. Offered annually "to publish the most promising work of up-and-coming writers of poetry (3-5 poems. None over 100 lines.) Fiction (10,000 word limit). Deadline: January 31. Guidelines for SASE. Charges $10 fee. Prize: $1,000 to winner of each category, plus a copy of winning issue to each paid submission. Fiction and poetry editors subject to change annually. Rights revert to writer upon publication.

THE GREENSBORO REVIEW LITERARY AWARD IN FICTION AND POETRY, *The Greensboro Review*, English Department, University of North Carolina-Greensboro, Greensboro NC 27412-5001. (910)334-5459. Fax: (910)334-3281. E-mail: clarkj@fagan.uncg.edu. Website: http://www.uncg.edu. Contact: Fiction or Poetry Editor. Estab. 1984. Annual award for fiction and poetry recognizing the best work published in the winter issue of *The Greensboro Review*. Deadline: September 15. Sample copy for $4.

HACKNEY LITERARY AWARDS, *Writing Today*, Box 549003/Birmingham-Southern College, Birmingham AL 35254. (205)226-4921. Fax: (205)226-3072. E-mail: bhopkins@bsc.edu. Website: http://www.bsc.edu/. Contact: Martha Andrews, director of special events. Estab. 1969. Offered annually for unpublished novel, short story (maximum 5,000 words) and poetry (50 line limit). Deadline: September 30 (novels), December 31 (short stories and poetry). Guidelines on website or for SASE. Charges $25 entry fee for novels, $10 for short story and poetry. Prize: $2,000 each category.

‡CHARLES JOHNSON AWARD FOR FICTION AND POETRY, Charles Johnson, Ricardo Cortez Cruz, Southern Illinois University, English Dept. 4503, Carbondale IL 62901-4503. (618)453-5321. E-mail: delacruz3@aol.com. Award Director: Ricardo Cortez Cruz. Offered annually for unpublished poets and fiction writers. "The contest seeks to support increased artistic and intellectual growth and encourage excellence and diversity in creative writing." Deadline: January 28. Guidelines for SASE. Prizes: $500 and a signed copy of a book by Charles Johnson. Only finalists are further notified. "Contest is open to all U.S. college students exploring issues relevant to minority and/or marginalized culture."

‡KINETICS-ANNUAL AFRICAN-AMERICAN WRITING CONTEST, Kinetics, P.O. Box 132067, Columbus OH 43213. Offered annually; unpublished submissions only. "The contest encourages fiction and nonfiction writing of an African-American bent. There are three categories: poetry, fiction and essay." Deadline: the day before Thanksgiving. Guidelines for SASE. Prizes: $75 first place; $50 second place; $25 third place. "Kinetics reserves the right to publish winners and other noted pieces in the *Kinetics Journal*. Kinetics also reserves editing rights." Open to any unpublished writer.

HENRY KREISEL AWARD FOR BEST FIRST BOOK, Writers Guild of Alberta, 11759 Groat Rd., Edmonton Alberta T5M 3K6 Canada. (403)422-8174. Fax: (403)422-2663. E-mail: writers@compusmart.ab.ca. Assistant Director: Darlene Diver. Book can be of any genre published in current year. It must be an Alberta author's first book.

‡LITERARY COMPETITION, Writers' Federation of New Brunswick, P.O. Box 37, Station A, Fredericton, New Brunswick E3B 4Y2 Canada. Phone/fax: (506)459-7228. Project Coordinator: Anna Mae Snider. Offered annually for unpublished fiction, nonfiction, poetry and children's literature. Also awarded: the Alfred Bailey Prize (for poetry ms), The Richards Prize (short novel, collection of short stories) and The Sheree Fitch Prize (writers 14-18 years old). Deadline: February 14. Guidelines for SASE. Charges $10 for members/students, $15 for nonmembers. Prizes: fiction, nonfiction, poetry, children's literature, 1st-$200, 2nd-$100, 3rd-$30; the Alfred Bailey Prize and the Richards Prize-$400 each; the Sheree Fitch Prize, 1st-$150, 2nd-$100, 3rd-$50. Judged by published writers from outside New Brunswick. The contest is open to New Brunswick residents only.

LITERATURE FELLOWSHIP, Artist Trust, 1402 Third Ave., Suite 404, Seattle WA 98101. (206)467-8734. Fax: (206)467-9633. E-mail: arttrust@eskimo.com. Website: http://www.halcyon.com/cqlew/. Executive Director: Marshel H. Paul. Contact: Olivia Taguinod, associate director. Offered every two years: 1995, 1997, 1999, etc. The literature fellowship is an award to a writer (fiction/poetry) in Washington State who is a practicing professional artist. Recipient must complete a community-based "Meet the Artist" event. Deadlines are in the summer and change depending on what creative disciplines are being awarded. Writers should send SASE two months before deadline. Recipients are chosen by a selection panel coordinated by staff. Prize: $5,000 ($4,500 upfront and $500 after the recipient completes a community event called "Meet the Artist"). Must be a resident of Washington State; must be 18 years or older; cannot be in a matriculated study program. Fiction writers and poets only.

AUDRE LORDE MEMORIAL PROSE PRIZE, National Women's Studies Association, 7100 Baltimore Ave., #301, College Park MD 20715. (301)403-0525. Fax: (301)403-4137. Offered annually for unpublished feminist writers who write fiction or prose. Submitted work should take up a topic of discourse found in the work of Lorde or seek to illustrate a condition, idea, or ideal inherent in her fiction or prose. Submissions accepted September 1-November 17. Guidelines for SASE. Prize: $250 to two winners.

‡MANITOBA LITERARY AWARDS, Manitoba Writers Guild, 206-100 Arthur St., Winnipeg, Manitoba R3B 1H3 Canada. (204)942-6134. Fax: (204)942-5754. E-mail: mbwriter@escape.ca. Website: http://www.mbwriter.mb.ca. Contact: Robyn Maharaj. Awards offered annually include: the McNally Robinson Book of the Year Award, the McNally Robinson Book for Young People Award, the John Hirsch Award for Most Promising Manitoba Writer, and two Book Publishers Awards. Awards offered biennially include: the Heaven Chapbook Prize and les Prix des caisse populaires. Deadline for books is December 1st. Books published between December 1-31 will be accepted until mid-January. Prizes: $250-2,500. Guidelines and submission forms available upon request. Open to Manitoba writers only.

MASTERS LITERARY AWARDS, Center Press, P.O. Box 16452, Encino CA 91416-6452. Contact: Gabriella Stone. Offered annually and quarterly for work published within 2 years (preferred) and unpublished work (accepted). Fiction: 15 page, maximum; Poetry: 5 pages or 150 lines, maximum; Nonfiction: 10 page, maximum. Deadlines: March 15, June 15th, August 15th, December 15. Guidelines for SASE. Charges $10 reading/administration fee. Prizes: 5 quarterly honorable mentions from which is selected one yearly Grand Prize of $1,000. "A selection of all winning entries will appear in our national literary publication." Center Press retains one time publishing rights to selected winners. Open to all writers.
   • The Grand Prize winner for 1997 was Scott Alejandro Sonders, for his novel *The Orange Messiah*.

THE MENTOR AWARD, *Mentor Newsletter*, P.O. Box 4382, Overland Park KS 66204-0382. Fax: (913)262-7290. Award Director: Maureen Waters. Estab. 1989. Offered annually to promote and encourage mentoring through unpublished feature articles, essays, book/movie reviews, interviews or short stories about mentoring-related subjects. Guidelines for #10 SASE. Charges $5 fee. Prize: $100. Writer must be at least 16 years old.

‡MIDLAND AUTHORS AWARD, Society of Midland Authors, P.O. Box 10419, Chicago IL 60610-0419. Annual awards for published fiction, nonfiction, poetry, biography, children's fiction and children's nonfiction. Authors must reside in the states of Illinois, Indiana, Iowa, Kansas, Michigan, Minnesota, Missouri, Nebraska, North Dakota, South Dakota, Wisconsin or Ohio. Guidelines for SASE. Deadline: January 15.

THE NEBRASKA REVIEW AWARDS IN FICTION AND POETRY, *The Nebraska Review*, FAB 212, University of Nebraska-Omaha, Omaha NE 68182-0324. (402)554-2880. (402)554-3436. E-mail: nereview@fa-cpacs.unomaha.edu. Contact: Susan Aizenberg (poetry), James Reed (fiction). Estab. 1973. Previously unpublished fiction and a poem or group of poems. Deadline: November 30. Charges $9 fee (includes a subscription to *The Nebraska Review*).

NEW MILLENNIUM WRITINGS AWARD, New Millennium Writings Journal, P.O. Box 2463, Knoxville TN 37901. (423)428-0389. Website: http://www.mach2.com/books or http://www.magamall.com. Director: Don Williams. Offered twice annually for unpublished fiction, poetry, essays or nonfiction prose, to encourage new fiction writers, poets and essayists and bring them to attention of publishing industry. Deadline: December 15, June 15. Guidelines for SASE. Charges $10 fee. Entrants receive an issue of *NMW* in which winners appear. Prize: Fiction-$1,000; Poetry-$750; Essay or nonfiction prose-$500 and publication of winners and runners-up, 25 honorable mentions listed.

‡NEW WRITERS AWARDS, Great Lakes Colleges Association, The Philadelphia Center, North American Building, 7th Floor, 121 S. Broad St., Philadephia PA 19107. Fax: (215)735-7373. E-mail: clark@philactr.edu. Award Director: Prof. Mark Andrew Clark. Offered annually to the best first book of poetry and the best first book of fiction among those submitted by publishers. Deadline: February 28. Guidelines for SASE. Prizes: Winning authors will be invited to tour the GLCA colleges, where they will participate in whatever activities they and the college deem appropriate. An honorarium of at least $300 will be guaranteed the author by each of the colleges they visit. Open to any first book of poetry or fiction submitted by a publisher.

‡NEW YORK UNIVERSITY PRESS PRIZES IN FICTION AND POETRY, New York University Press, 70 Washington Sq. S., New York NY 10012. (212)998-2575. Fax: (212)995-3833. Offered annually for unpublished writers "to support innovative, experimental and important fiction and poetry by authors whose work either has not yet appeared in book form or who remain unrecognized relative to the quality and ambition of their writing." Deadline: May 2. Guidelines for SASE. Prizes: Publication of the work by New York University Press plus a $1,000 honorarium for both the fiction and poetry winners. Open to any writer.

‡NIMROD, (formerly Nimrod, Arts and Humanities Council of Tulsa Prizes), The University of Tulsa, 600 S. College, Tulsa OK 74104-3189. (918)631-3080. Fax: (918)631-3033. E-mail: ringoldfl@centum.utulsa.edu. Website: http://www.51.umich.edu/~jringold/nimrod/nimrod.html. Editor: Francine Ringold. Unpublished fiction and poetry. Theme issue in the spring. *Nimrod*/Hardman Awards issue in the fall. For contest or theme issue guidelines send SASE. Charges $20 fee. $20 includes two issues. Deadline: April 17. Sample copies $10.

NORTH AMERICAN NATIVE AUTHORS FIRST BOOK AWARDS, The Greenfield Review Literary Center, P.O. Box 308, Greenfield Center NY 12833. (518)583-1440. Fax: (518)583-9741. Website: http://nativeauthors.com. Director: Joseph Bruchac. Offered annually for unpublished work in book form to recognize literary achievement in prose and in poetry by Native North American writers who have not yet published a book. Deadline: March 15. Guidelines for SASE. Prize: $500 plus publication by The Greenfield Review Press with a standard contract for royalties. Judged by a panel of established Native American writers. Only writers who are American Indian, Inuit, Aleut or Metis and who have not yet published a book.

KENNETH PATCHEN COMPETITION, Pig Iron Press, P.O. Box 237, Youngstown OH 44501. (330)747-6932. Fax: (330)747-0599. Website: http://WebScribe.com/Scribe/pig.htm. Contact: Bill Koch. Offered annually for unpublished poetry or fiction (except for individual works published in magazines/journals). Alternates annually between poetry (odd years) and fiction (even years). Deadline: December 31. Guidelines for SASE. Charges $10 fee. Prize: Trade Paperback publication in an edition of 1,000 copies, and $500.

QUINCY WRITER'S GUILD ANNUAL CREATIVE WRITING CONTEST, Quincy Writer's Guild, c/o Rev. Michael Barrett, P.O. Box 433, Quincy IL 62306-0433. Categories include serious poetry, light poetry, short story, fiction. Deadline: January 1-April 15. Charges $2/poem; $4/short story or article. "No identification should appear on manuscripts, but send a separate 3×5 card attached to each entry with name, address, phone number, word count, and title of work." Previously unpublished work. Cash prizes. Guidelines for SASE.

RHYME TIME CREATIVE WRITING COMPETITION, *Rhyme Time*, P.O. Box 2907, Decatur IL 62524. Award Director: Linda Hutton. Estab. 1981. Annual no-fee contest. Submit 1 typed poem, any style, any length. One winner will receive $25; one runner-up will receive a year's subscription to *Rhyme Time*. No poems will be published. Include SASE. Deadline: November 1.

‡MARY ROBERTS RINEHART FUND, MSN 3E4 English Department, George Mason University, 4400 University Dr., Fairfax VA 22030-4444. (703)993-1180. Contact: William Miller. Offered annually for unpublished authors. Grants by nomination to unpublished creative writers for fiction, poetry, drama, biography, autobiography or history with a strong narrative quality. Submissions are accepted for fiction and poetry in odd years, and nonfiction and drama in even years. Deadline: Nov. 30. Prize: varies, approximately $1,000. Submissions must include nominating letter from person in appropriate field.

ROM/CON, 1555 Washington Ave., San Leandro CA 94577. (415)357-5665. Director: Barbara N. Keenan. Awards for previously published material in 12 categories appearing in *Affaire de Coeur* magazine. Deadline: March 15. "Rom/Con Awards are given at the annual conference and are presented for the highest quality of writing in the Romance genre."

BRUCE P. ROSSLEY LITERARY AWARD, 96 Inc., P.O. Box 15558, Boston MA 02215. (617) 267-0543. Fax: (617)262-3568. Director: Vera Gold. Offered annually to give greater recognition to a writer of merit. In addition to writing, accomplishments in the fields of teaching and community service are considered. Deadline: September 30. Nominations are accepted from August 1 to September 30. Guidelines for SASE. Charges $10 fee. Prize: $1,000. Any writer in New England may be nominated, but the focus is merit and those writers who have been under-recognized.

‡SHORT GRAIN WRITING CONTEST, Grain Magazine, P.O. Box 1154, Regina Saskatchewan S4P 3B4 Canada. (306)244-2828. Fax: (306)244-0255. Fax: (306)244-0255. E-mail: grain.mag@sk.sympatico.ca. Website: http://www.sasknet.com/corporate/skwriter. Contest Director: J. Jill Robinson. Offered annually for unpublished dramatic monologues, postcard stories (narrative fiction) and prose (lyric) poetry. Maximum length for all entries: 500 words. Deadline: January 31. Guidelines for SAE and International Reply Coupons or Canadian stamps. Charges $20 fee for 2 entries, plus $5 for additional entries; U.S. and International entries: $20, plus $4 postage in U.S. funds (non-Canadian). Prizes: 1st-$500, 2nd-$300, 3rd-$200. All entrants receive a one year subscription to *Grain*. *Grain* purchases first Canadian serial rights only. Copyright remains with the author. Open to any writer. No fax or e-mail submissions.

‡SHORT PROSE COMPETITION FOR DEVELOPING WRITERS, The Writers' Union of Canada, 24 Ryerson Ave., Toronto, Ontario M5T 2P3 Canada. (416)703-8982. E-mail: twuc@the-wire.com. Competition Administrator:

Kerry Lamond. Offered annually "to discover developing Canadian writers of unpublished prose fiction and nonfiction." Deadline: November 3. "Visit our website at http://www.swifty.com/twuc." $25/entry fee. Prizes: 1st-$2,500, 2nd-$1,000. All members are professionally published book authors. The author agrees to permit publication of the winning piece in *Books in Canada* (a Canadian literary journal). Open to Canadian citizens or landed immigrants who have not been published in book format and who do not currently have a contract with a publisher.

SONORA REVIEW ANNUAL LITERARY AWARDS, *Sonora Review*, English Department, University of Arizona, Tucson AZ 85721. $500 Fiction Award given each Spring to the best previously unpublished short story. Deadline: December 1. Charges $10 or $12 one-year subscription fee. $500 Poetry Award given each Fall to the best previously unpublished poem. Four poems/5 page maximum submission. Deadline: July 1. Charges $10 or $12 one-year subscription fee. $150 nonfiction award given each fall to the best previously unpublished essay. Deadline: July 1. Charges $10 reading fee or $12 one-year subscription. For all awards, all entrants receive a copy of the issue in which the winning entry appears. No formal application form is required; regular submission guidelines apply. SASE required for return of ms. Guidelines for #10 SASE. For samples, send $6.

THE SOUTHERN PRIZE, *The Southern Anthology*, 2851 Johnston St., #123, Lafayette LA 70503. Director: R. Sebastian Bennett, Ph.D. Offered annually for unpublished fiction and poetry "to promote and reward outstanding fiction and poetry; to encourage both traditional and innovative forms." Deadline: May 30. Guidelines for SASE. Charges fee: $10/short fiction or novel excerpt (7500 word limit); or $10/set of 3 poems. Prize: $600 grand prize and publication. Six finalists published; stipend for top three finalists. Contest open to all writers writing in English. No form or genre restrictions. Submissions need not address "Southern" themes. *The Southern Anthology* encourages both traditional and avant-garde writing.

SOUTHWEST REVIEW AWARDS, Southern Methodist University, 307 Fondren Library West, P.O. Box 750374, Dallas TX 75275-0374. (214)768-1036. Fax: (214)768-1408. E-mail: swr@mail.suny.edu. Contact: Elizabeth Mills. Offered annually for fiction, nonfiction and poetry published in the magazine. "The $1,000 John H. McGinnis Memorial Award is given each year for fiction and nonfiction that has been published in the *Southwest Review* in the previous year. Stories or articles are not submitted directly for the award, but simply for publication in the magazine. The Elizabeth Matchett Stover Award, an annual prize of $150, is awarded to the author of the best poem or group of poems published in the magazine during the preceding year."

‡STONEFLOWER LITERARY CONTEST, Stoneflower Press, 1824 Nacogdoches, Suite 191, San Antonio TX 78209. E-mail: stoneflower@aol.com. Contest Director: Brenda Davidson-Shaddox. Offered annually to promote interest in writing/reading categories: short fiction and poetry. Deadline: March 31. Guidelines for SASE. Charges for fiction: $10/first story, $8/each additional story; poetry; $5/first poem, $3/each additional poem. Prizes: Fiction 1st-$75, 2nd-$25, copy of journal for honorable mentions; Poetry 1st-$50, 2nd-$10 copy of journal for honorable mentions. Open to any writer.

‡SUB-TERRAIN MAGAZINE AWARDS, *Sub-Terrain Magazine*, 175 E. Broadway, #204A, Vancouver, British Columbia V5T 1W2 Canada. (604)876-8710. Fax: (604)879-2667. Contest/Award Director: Brian Kaufman. Offered annually to unpublished novels, nonfiction, poems, short stories and photography. Contests include the Anvil Press International 3-Day Novel Writing Contest, Sub-Terrain Creative Nonfiction Writing Contest, The Not Quite the Cover of the Rolling Stone Award, Last Poems Poetry Contest and Moonless Night Short Story Contest. Deadlines vary. Charges $15 fee including a subscription to magazine; $25 for 3-Day-Novel Contest. Prizes: cash prize and publication. The winner of The 3-Day Novel Contest receives a cash prize and royalties. Judged by Sub-Terrain editorial collective: Brian Kaufman, Paul Pitre, Dennis E. Bolen, Bryan Wade, Hilary Green, Andrea Shearer, Ken Babstock, Tamas Dobozy, Suzanne Buffam. The magazine acquires one-time rights only. After publication rights revert to the author.

TENNESSEE WRITERS ALLIANCE LITERARY COMPETITION, Tennessee Writers Alliance, P.O. Box 120396, Nashville TN 37212. (615)385-3163. Contact: Literary Competition Director. Offered annually on rotating basis for unpublished short fiction, poetry, nonfiction (personal essay). Deadline varies. Guidelines for SASE. Charges $5 fee for members, $10 fee for non-member Tennessee residents. Prize: 1st-$500; 2nd-$250; 3rd-$100 and publication. Acquires right to publish once. Open to any member of Tennessee Writers Alliance and Tennessee residents. Membership open to all, regardless of residence, for $25/year, $15/year for students.

TMWC LITERARY CONTEST, Tennessee Mountain Writers, Inc., P.O. Box 4895, Oak Ridge TN 37831. Phone/fax: (423)482-6567. E-mail: tmw9@compuserve.com. Contact: Patricia Hope. Offered annually for unpublished work to give beginning writers an outlet for their work. Deadline: September 30. Guidelines for SASE. Charges $10 fee. Prize: 1st-$250; 2nd-$150; 3rd-$75.

WESTERN MAGAZINE AWARDS, Western Magazine Awards Foundation, Main Post Office, Box 2131, Vancouver, British Columbia V6B 3T8 Canada. (604)669-2844. Fax: (604)669-3717. Contact: Tina Baird. Offered annually for magazine work published January 1-December 31 of previous calendar year. Entry categories include business, culture, science, technology and medicine, entertainment, fiction, political issues, and much more. Write or phone for rules and entry forms. Deadline: February 1. Entry fee: $27 for work in magazines with circulation under 20,000; $35 for work in magazines with circulation over 20,000. Prize: $500. Applicant must be Canadian citizen, landed immigrant, or fulltime resident of Canada. The work must have been published in a magazine whose main editorial office is in Western Canada, the NW Territories and Yukon.

‡**WIND MAGAZINE CONTESTS**, Wind Publications, P.O. Box 24548, Lexington KY 40524. Contest Director: Charlie Hughes. Offered annually for unpublished poems, chapbooks and short stories. Deadlines: June 30 for poems, October 31 for chapbooks, April 30 for short stories. Guidelines for SASE. Charges $2/poem, $10/chapbook and short story. Prizes: $500 and publication in *Wind Magazine* for winning poem and short story, $100 plus 25 copies of published book for the winning chapbook. All finalists receive a one-year subscription to the magazine. Authors are responsible for copyright clearance on previously published poems. Open to all writers.

WRITERS AT WORK FELLOWSHIP COMPETITION, Writers at Work, P.O. Box 1146, Centerville UT 84014-5146. (801)292-9285. Website: http://www.ihi-env.com/watw.html. Contact: Dawn Marano. Offered annually for unpublished short stories, novel excerpts and poetry. Deadline: March 15. Guidelines for SASE. Charges $12 fee. Short stories or novel excerpts 20 double-spaced pages maximum; one story per entry. Poetry submissions limited to 6 poems, 10 pages maximum. No names on manuscript, please. Prize: $1,500, publication and partial conference tuition; $500, partial conference tuition.

‡**WRITER'S DIGEST NATIONAL SELF-PUBLISHED BOOK AWARDS**, *Writer's Digest*, 1507 Dana Ave., Cincinnati OH 45207-9966. (513)531-2690, ext. 268. Fax: (513)531-1843. Contact: Sandi Luppert, promotions manager. Offered annually for self-publishers to bring their books to the attention of publishers and editors. Categories: life stories, cookbooks, children's and young adult books, fiction, nonfiction and poetry. Charges entry fee. Guidelines for #10 SASE. Deadline: December 15.

WRITER'S DIGEST WRITING COMPETITION, *Writer's Digest*, 1507 Dana Ave., Cincinnati OH 45207-9966. (513)531-2690, ext. 268. Fax: (513)531-1843. Contact: Sandi Luppert. Contest in 67th year. Categories: Personal Essays, Feature Articles, Literary Short Stories, Mainstream/Genre Short Stories, Rhyming Poems, Non-Rhyming Poems, Stage Plays, Television/Movie Scripts and Children's Fiction and Nonfiction. Submissions must be unpublished. For guidelines send #10 SASE. Charges entry fee. Deadline: May 31.

Arts Councils and Foundations

ARTIST FELLOWSHIP, Alabama State Council on the Arts, 201 Monroe St., Montgomery AL 36130. (334)242-4076, ext. 226. Fax: (334)240-3269. E-mail: becky@arts.al.us. Literature Programs Manager: Becky Mullen. Offered every 2 years for previously published work based on achievement and quality of work. Artists may use funds to set aside time to create their art, improve their skills, or do what they consider most advantageous to enhance their artistic careers. Deadline: May 1. Call or write to request guidelines. Prize: $5,000 (2) or $10,000 (1) (most often 2 artists are chosen). Any legal resident of Alabama who has lived in state for 2 years prior to application.

ARTIST FELLOWSHIP AWARDS, Wisconsin Arts Board, 101 E. Wilson St. 1st Floor, Madison WI 53702. (608)264-8191. Fax: (608)267-0380. Director: Mark Fraire. Offered every 2 years to recognize the significant contributions of professional artists in Wisconsin, and intended to support continued artistic and professional development, enabling artists to create new work, complete work in progress, and pursue activities which contribute to their artistic growth. Deadline: September 15. SASE is not necessary. Contact WAB at (608)266-0190 to receive application materials. Applicants must reside in Wisconsin a minimum of 1 year prior to application and may not be fulltime students pursuing a degree in the fine arts.

‡**ARTISTS FELLOWSHIP**, Japan Foundation, 39th Floor, 152 W. 57th St., New York NY 10019. (212)489-0299. Fax: (212)489-0409. E-mail: chris_watanabe@jfny.org. Website: http://www.jfny.org/. Contact: Chris Watanabe. Offered annually. Deadline: December 1. "Contact us in September. Write or fax. Judged by committee at the Japan Foundation headquarters in Tokyo. Keep in mind that this is an international competition. Due to the breadth of the application pool only four artists are selected for awards in the US. Applicants need not submit a writing sample, but if one is submitted it must be brief. Three letters of recommendation must be submitted from peers. One letter will double as a letter of affiliation, which must be submitted by a *Japan-based* (not necessarily an ethnic Japanese) peer artist. The applicant must present a concise and cogent project objective and must be a professional writer/artist with accessible qualifications, i.e., a list of major works or publications."

ARTS RECOGNITION AND TALENT SEARCH, National Foundation for Advancement in the Arts, 800 Brickell Ave., Suite 500, Miami FL 33131. (305)377-1140 or (800)970-ARTS. Fax: (305)377-1149. E-mail: nfaa@nfaa.org. Programs Administration Director: Laura Padron. Estab. 1981. For achievements in dance, music (classical, jazz and vocal), photography, theater, visual arts and writing. Students fill in and return the application, available at every public and private high school around the nation, for cash awards of up to $3,000 each and scholarship opportunities worth more than $3 million. Deadline: early—June 1, regular—October 1. Charges $25 registration fee for June; $35 for October.

‡**ASSISTANCE TO ESTABLISHED WRITERS**, Nova Scotia Department of Education and Cultural Cultural Affairs Division, P.O. Box 578, Halifax, Nova Scotia B3J 2S9 Canada. (902)424-6389. Fax: (902)424-0710. Offered twice annually for unpublished submissions to assist the professional writer with the costs of completing the research or manuscript preparation for a project in which a trade publisher has expressed serious interest." Deadline: April 1 and October 1. Prize: Maximum of $2,000 (Canadian). Applicant must be a Canadian citizen or landed immigrant and must have had their principal residence in Nova Scotia for 12 consecutive months at the time of application. Applicant must be an experienced writer who writes for print or broadcast media, film or stage, who has been consistently published and/or produced in the media.

GEORGE BENNETT FELLOWSHIP, Phillips Exeter Academy, 20 Main St., Exeter NH 03833-2460. Coordinator, Selection Committee: Charles Pratt. Estab. 1968. Annual award of stipend, room and board "to provide time and freedom from material considerations to a person seriously contemplating or pursuing a career as a writer. Applicants should have a manuscript in progress which they intend to complete during the fellowship period." Guidelines for SASE. The committee favors writers who have not yet published a book with a major publisher. Deadline: December 1. Charges $5 fee. Residence at the Academy during the Fellowship period required.

BUSH ARTIST FELLOWSHIPS, The Bush Foundation, E-900 First National Bank Bldg., 332 Minnesota St., St. Paul MN 55101. (612)227-5222. Contact: Kathi Polley. Estab. 1976. Award for Minnesota, North Dakota, South Dakota, and western Wisconsin residents 25 years or older "to buy 12-18 months of time for the applicant to do his/her own work." Up to 15 fellowships/year, $36,000 each. Deadline: October. All application categories rotate on a two year cycle. Literature (fiction, creative nonfiction, poetry) and scriptworks (playwriting, screenwriting) will be offered next for the 1998 fellowships. Applications available August 1998.

CREATIVITY FELLOWSHIP, Northwood University, Alden B. Dow Creativity Center, Midland MI 48640-2398. (517)837-4478. Fax: (517)837-4468. E-mail: creativity@northwood.edu. Website: http://www.northwood.edu. Award Director: Carol B. Coppage. Estab. 1979. Ten-week summer residency for individuals in any field who wish to pursue new and creative ideas that have potential impact in their fields. No accommodations for family/pets. Deadline: December 31.

‡**DOCTORAL DISSERTATION FELLOWSHIPS IN JEWISH STUDIES**, National Foundation for Jewish Culture, 330 7th Ave., 21st Floor, New York NY 10001. (212)629-0500. Fax: (212)629-0508. Offered annually to students. Deadline varies, usually early January. Guidelines for SASE. Prize: a $6,000-$9,000 grant. Judged by a panel of scholarly experts in each field. Open to students who have completed their course work and need funding for research in order to write their dissertation thesis or a Ph.D. in a Jewish field of study.

‡**FELLOWSHIP-LITERATURE**, Alabama State Council on the Arts, 201 Monroe St., Montgomery AL 36130. (334)242-4076, ext. 226. Fax: (334)240-3269. Contact: Becky Mullen. Literature Fellowship offered on alternate, even-numbered years for previously published or unpublished work to set aside time to create and to improve skills. Two year Alabama residency requirement. Deadline: May 1. Guidelines available. Prize: $10,000 or $5,000.

‡**FELLOWSHIPS FOR CREATIVE WRITERS**, National Endowment for the Arts Literature Program, 1100 Pennsylvania Ave. NW, Washington DC 20506. (202)682-5428. Website: http://arts.endow.gov. Award Director: Gigi Bradford. Published creative writers of exceptional talent. Deadline: Fiction/Creative Nonfiction, March 17, 1997. Poetry: call or write for guidelines in January, 1998.

‡**FELLOWSHIPS (LITERATURE)**, RI State Council on the Arts, 95 Cedar St., Suite 103, Providence RI 02903. (401)277-3880. Fax: (401)521-1351. E-mail: ride0600@ride.ri.net. Website: http://www.modcult.brown.edu/RISCA/. Director: Randall Rosenbaum. Offered every two years for previously published or unpublished work. Deadline: April 1, 1997. Guidelines for SASE. Prize: $5,000 fellowship; $1,000 runner-up. Judged by peer review panel for first cut; final decisions are made by out-of-state judge in Literature. Rhode Island residents only.

‡**FLORIDA INDIVIDUAL ARTIST FELLOWSHIPS**, Florida Department of State, Division of Cultural Affairs, The Capitol, Tallahassee FL 32399-0250. (904)487-2980. Fax: (904)922-5259. Website: http://www.clos.state.fl.us. Contact: Valerie Ohlsson, arts consultant. Fellowship for Florida writers only. Prize: $5,000 each for fiction, poetry and children's literature. Deadline: January.

‡**GAP (GRANTS FOR ARTIST PROJECTS); FELLOWSHIP**, Artist Trust, 1402 Third Ave, Suite 404, Seattle WA 98101-2118. (206)467-8734. Fax: (206)467-9633. E-mail: arttrust@eskimo.com. Website: http://www.halcyon.com/cglew/. Executive Director: Marschel Paul. Fellowship offered as announced for either published or unpublished work. "The GAP is awarded to 30-50 artists, including writers, per year. The award is meant to help finance a specific project, which can be in very early stages or near completion. The Fellowship is awarded to eight artists per year; the award is made on the basis of work of the past five years. It is 'no-strings-attached' funding." Guidelines for SASE. Prize: GAP: up to $1,200. Fellowship: $5,000. Fulltime students not eligible. *Only Washington state residents are eligible.*

HEEKIN GROUP FOUNDATION WRITING FELLOWSHIPS PROGRAM, The Heekin Group Writers and Education Fund, P.O. Box 1534, Sisters OR 97759. (541)548-4147. Contest/Award Director: Sarah Heekin Redfield.

Offered annually for unpublished works. James Fellowship for the Novel in Progress (2), Tara Fellowship for Short Fiction (2); Mary Molloy Fellowship for Children's Working Novel (1); The Cuchulain Fellowship for Rhetoric (1). These 6 fellowships are awarded to beginning career writers for assistance in their literary pursuits. Deadline: December 1. Guidelines for SASE. Charges $25 fellowship application fee. Prize: James Fellowship: $3,000; Tara Fellowship: $1,500; Mary Molloy Fellowship: $2,000; Siobhan Fellowship: $2,000. Roster of finalist judges include Graywolf Press, SOHO Press, Dalkey Archive Press, The Ecco Press, Riverhead Books, Hyperion Books. Fellowships are available to those writers who are unpublished in the novel, short fiction and essay.

‡**THE HODDER FELLOWSHIP**, Princeton University Humanities Council, 122 E. Pyne, Princeton NJ 08544. (609)258-4713. Offered annually. "The Hodder Fellow typically has one or two works published and would be working on a new project at Princeton. The fellowship is designed to allow a humanist in the early stages of a career to pursue research while completing a project in the fields of literature and the arts." Deadline: November 15. Guidelines for SASE. Prize: Stipend for an academic year's stay in Princeton, currently $43,000. The work must be an independent project in the humanities.

IDAHO WRITER-IN-RESIDENCE, Idaho Commission on the Arts, Box 83720, Boise ID 83720-0008. (208)334-2119. Fax: (208)334-2488. E-mail: djosephy@lca.state.id.us. Program Coordinator: Diane Josephy Peavey. Estab. 1982. Offered every 3 years. Award of $8,000 for an Idaho writer, who over the three-year period reads his/her work throughout the state to increase the appreciation for literature. Deadline: spring, 1998; dates change. Guidelines for SASE. Open to any *Idaho* writer.

ILLINOIS ARTS COUNCIL ARTISTS FELLOWSHIP, James R. Thompson Center, 100 W. Randolph, Suite 10-500, Chicago IL 60601. (312)814-6750. Contact: Director of Artists Services. Offered every 2 years for previously published or unpublished work. "Submitted work must have been completed no more than four years prior to deadline. Artists fellowships are awarded to Illinois artists of exceptional talent to enable them to pursue their artistic goals; fellowships are offered in poetry and prose (fiction and creative nonfiction)." Deadline: September 1 of odd-numbered years. "Interested Illinois writers should write or call for information." Prize: $500 Finalist Award; $5,000 or $10,000 Artist's Fellowship. "Writer must be Illinois resident and not a degree-seeking student. Applicants for Poetry Fellowship can submit up to 15 pages of work in manuscript; prose fellowship applicants can submit up to 30 pages of work."

INDIVIDUAL ARTIST FELLOWSHIP, Oregon Arts Commission, 775 Summer St. NE, Salem OR 97310. (503)986-0086. Fax: (503)986-0260. E-mail: vincent.k.dunn@state.or.us. Website: http://www.das.state.or.us/OAC/. Contact: Vincent Dunn, assistant director. Offered in even-numbered years to reward achievement in the field of literature. Deadline: September 1. Guidelines for SASE. Prize: $3,000. "Writers must be Oregon residents 18 years and older. Degree candidate students not eligible."

INDIVIDUAL ARTIST FELLOWSHIP, Tennessee Arts Commission, 401 Charlotte Ave., Nashville TN 37243-0780. (615)741-1701. Fax: (615)741-8559. E-mail: aswanson@mail.state.tn.us. Website: http://www.arts.state.tn.us. Director: Alice Swanson. Offered annually for recognition for emerging literary artists. Deadline: First or 2nd Monday in January. Write to above address or call—guidelines too large for SASE—we will mail. Prize: $2,000 plus matching private funds—this year $1,000. Must be resident of Tennessee. 1998 poetry, 1999 prose, etc. Must have publication history.

INDIVIDUAL ARTIST FELLOWSHIP AWARD, Montana Arts Council, 316 N. Park Ave., Suite 252, Helena MT 59620. (406)444-6430. Contact: Fran Morrow. Offered annually to *Montana residents only*. Deadline: Fall.

INDIVIDUAL ARTISTS FELLOWSHIPS, Nebraska Arts Council, 3838 Davenport St., Omaha NE 68131-2329. (402)595-2122. Fax: (402)595-2334. Website: http://www.gps.kiz.ne.us/nac_web_site/nac.htm. Contact: Suzanne Wise. Estab. 1991. Offered every 3 years (literature alternates with other disciplines) to recognize exemplary achievements by originating artists in their fields of endeavor and supports the contributions made by Nebraska artists to the quality of life in this state. Deadline: November 15, 2000. "Generally, distinguished achievement awards are $5,000 and merit awards are $1,000-2,000. Funds available are announced in September prior to the deadline." Must be a resident of Nebraska for at least 2 years prior to submission date; 18 years of age; not enrolled in an undergraduate, graduate or certificate-granting program in English, creative writing, literature, or related field.

JOSEPH HENRY JACKSON AWARD, The San Francisco Foundation, Administered by Intersection for the Arts, 446 Valencia St., San Francisco CA 94103. (415)626-2787. Contact: Charles Wilmoth, program director. Estab. 1965. Offered annually for unpublished, work-in-progress fiction (novel or short story), nonfiction or poetry by author age 20-35, with 3-year consecutive residency in northern California or Nevada prior to submission. Deadline: November 15-January 31.

EZRA JACK KEATS MEMORIAL FELLOWSHIP, Ezra Jack Keats Foundation (funding) awarded through Kerlan Collection, University of Minnesota, 109 Walter Library, 117 Pleasant St. SE., Minneapolis MN 55455. (612)624-4576. Fax: (612)625-5525. E-mail: carrie.e.tahtamouuni~1@tcumn.edu. Website: http://160.94.230.174/kerlan. Curator, Kerlan Collection: Karen Hoyle. Contact: Carrie Tahtamouni, library assistant III. "To award a talented writer and/or illustrator of children's books who wishes to use Kerlan Collection for the furtherance of his or her artistic development." Deadline: early May. Guidelines for SASE. Prize: $1,500 for travel to study at Kerlan Collection. Judged by a committee of 4-5 members from varying colleges at University of Minnesota and outside the University. "Special consideration will be given to someone who would find it difficult to finance the visit to the Kerlan Collection."

KENTUCKY ARTS COUNCILS FELLOWSHIPS IN WRITING, Kentucky Arts Council, 31 Fountain Place, Frankfort KY 40601. (502)564-3757. Fax: (502)564-2839. Contact: Irwin Pickett. Offered in even-numbered years for development/artist's work. Deadline: September 1998. Guidelines for SASE (3 months before deadline). Award: $5,000. Must be Kentucky resident.

‡THE GERALD LOEB AWARDS, The John E. Anderson Graduate School of Management at UCLA, 110 Westwood Plaza, Suite F315, Box 951481, Los Angeles CA 90095-1481. (310)206-1877. Fax: (310)206-9830. E-mail: loeb@anderson.ucla.edu. Website: http://www.anderson.ucla.edu/media/loeb. Contact: Office of Communications. Consideration is limited to articles published in the previous calendar year. "To recognize writers who make significant contributions to the understanding of business, finance and the economy." Deadline: February 6. Charges $50 fee ($25 for small newspapers) Prize: $2,000 in each category. Winners in each category receive $1,000. Honorable mentions, when awarded, receive $500.

‡MONEY FOR WOMEN, Barbara Deming Memorial Fund, Inc., P.O. Box 40-1043, Brooklyn NY 11240-1043. Contact: Pam McAllister. "Small grants to individual feminists in the arts (artists, writers, poets, photographers) whose work addresses women's concerns and/or speaks for peace and justice from a feminist perspective." Deadlines: December 31 and June 30. Guidelines for SASE. Prize: grants up to $1,000: "The Fund does *not* give educational assistance, monies for personal study or loans, monies for dissertation or research projects, grants for group projects, business ventures, or emergency funds for hardships." Open to individual feminists in the arts. Applicants must be citizens of the US or Canada.
  ● The fund also offers two awards, the "Gerty, Gerty, Gerty in the Arts, Arts, Arts" for outstanding works by a lesbian and the "Fannie Lou Hamer Award" for work which combats racism and celebrates women of color.

‡NATIONAL MUSIC THEATER CONFERENCE, Eugene O'Neill Center, 234 W. 44th St., #901, New York NY 10036. (212)382-2790. Fax: (212)921-5538. Contest Director: Paulette Haupt. Associate Director: Michael Nassar. Offered annually to unpublished musicals or operas. "The O'Neill Theater Center is a developmental theater in which visions can be explored and risks can be taken that are not possible during production deadlines. The focus of the conference is on the creative process while a work is still in progress." Deadline: March 1. Application and guidelines for SASE. Charges $10 entry fee. Prize: Artists selected receive a stipend, room and board, and round trip transportation from New York to Connecticut, in addition to the developmental process provided by the O'Neill Theater Center. Open to any writer.

JAMES D. PHELAN LITERARY AWARD, The San Francisco Foundation, Administered by Intersection for the Arts, 446 Valencia St., San Francisco CA 94103. (415)626-2787. Contact: Charles Wilmoth, program director. Estab. 1965. Offered annually for unpublished, work-in-progress fiction, nonfiction, short story, poetry or drama by California-born author age 20-35. Deadline: November 15-January 31.

‡SCHOLARSHIP IN JEWISH WOMEN'S STUDIES, 7100 Baltimore Ave., College Park MD 20715. (301)403-4137. Offered annually to a graduate student who is enrolled for the fall semester and whose area of research is Jewish Women's Studies. Guidelines for SASE. Prize: $500.

SEATTLE ARTISTS PROGRAM, Seattle Arts Commission, 312 First Ave. N., 2nd Floor, Seattle WA 98119-4501. (206)684-7171. Fax: (206)684-7172. Seattle Artists Project Manager: Irene Gomez. Offered every 2 years. Next literary deadline will be in 1998. The Seattle Artists Program, commissions new works by professional artists in all disciplines. Visual artworks in 2 and 3 dimensions are commissioned each year. In alternate years, media, performing and literary artworks are commissioned. This is a biannual program, and the deadline date vary. Guidelines for SASE. Award amounts are $7,500 and $2,000. Decided through open, competitive peer-panel review process and subject to approval by the full Commission. Applicants must be residents of or maintain studio space in the city of Seattle, Washington. Established and emerging artists are eligible. Artists may not be commissioned in consecutive years through this program. Adaptations/translations are not accepted except if the content differs significantly from that of an original work.

STUDENT RESEARCH GRANT, the Society for the Scientific Study of Sex, Box 208, Mount Vernon IA 52314. (319)895-8407. Fax: (319)895-6203. Website: http://www.ssc.wisc.edu/ssss. Contact: Howard J. Ruppel, executive director. . Offered twice a year for unpublished works. "The student research grant award is granted twice yearly to help support graduate student research on a variety of sexually related topics." Deadline: February 1 and September 1. Rules and entry forms for SASE. Prize: $750. "Open to students pursuing graduate study."

‡UCROSS FOUNDATION RESIDENCY, 2836 US Highway 14-16E, Clearmont WY 82835. (307)737-2291. Fax: (307)737-2322. Contact: Sharon Dynak, executive director. Eight concurrent positions open for artists-in-residence in various disciplines (includes writers, visual artists, music, humanities) extending from 2 weeks-2 months. No charge for room, board or studio space. Deadline: March 1 for August-December program; October 1 for January-May program.

UTAH ORIGINAL WRITING COMPETITION, Utah Arts Council, 617 E. S. Temple, Salt Lake City UT 84102-1177. (801)533-5895. Fax: (801)533-6196. E-mail: glebeda@state.ut.us. Website: http://www.dced.state.ut.us/arts. Literary Coordinator: Guy Lebeda. Offered annually for unpublished work to recognize merits of literary writing of Utahns by national judges. Deadline: end of June. Write, phone or fax for guidelines. Prize: certificate and cash prizes of $200-1,000. Open to Utah citizens only.

WRITERS FELLOWSHIPS, NC Arts Council, Dept. of Cultural Resources, Raleigh NC 27601-2807. (919)733-2111. E-mail: dmcgill@ncacmail.dcr.state.nc.us. Literature Director: Deborah McGill. Offered every two years. "To serve writers of fiction, poetry, literary nonfiction and literary translation in North Carolina and to recognize the contribution they make to this state's creative environment." Deadline: November 1, 1998. Write for guidelines. We offer eleven $8,000 grants every two years. Writer must have been a resident of NC for at least a year and may not be enrolled in any degree-granting program at the time of application.

Miscellaneous

BOWLING WRITING COMPETITION, American Bowling Congress Publications, 5301 S. 76th St., Greendale WI 53129-1127. Fax: (414)421-7977. Editor: Bill Vint. Estab. 1935. Feature, editorial and news all relating to the sport of bowling. Deadline: December 1. Prize: First place in each division will carry a $300 award. In addition to the first place awards, others will be: News and Editorial-$225, $200, $175, $150, $75 and $50; Feature-$225, $200, $175, $150, $125, $100, $75, $50 and $50. There also will be five honorable mention certificates awarded in each category.

STEPHEN LEACOCK MEMORIAL AWARD FOR HUMOUR, Stephen Leacock Associates, P.O. Box 854, Orillia, Ontario L3V 6K8 Canada. (705)325-6546. Contest Director: Jean Dickson. Estab. 1947. For a book of humor published in previous year by a Canadian author. Include 10 copies of each entry and a b&w photo with bio. Deadline: December 31. Charges $25 fee. Prize: Stephen Leacock Memorial Medal and Laurentian Bank of Canada Award of $5,000.

‡REUBEN AWARD, National Cartoonists Society, P.O. Box 20267, New York NY 10023. (212)627-1550. "Outstanding Cartoonist of the Year." Winning cartoonists need not be NCS members.

WESTERN HERITAGE AWARDS, National Cowboy Hall of Fame & Western Heritage Center, 1700 NE 63rd, Oklahoma City OK 73111. (405)478-2250 ext. 221. Fax: (405)478-4714. Contact: Lynda Haller. Offered annually for excellence in representation of great stories of the American West published January 1-December 31 in a calendar year. Competition includes 7 literary categories: Nonfiction; Western Novel; Juvenile Book; Art Book; Short Story; Poetry Book; and Magazine Article. Deadline for entries: November 30.

CONTESTS AND AWARDS THAT WERE listed in the 1997 edition of *Writer's Market* but do not appear this year are listed in the General Index with a notation explaining why they were omitted.

Resources

Publications of Interest

In addition to newsletters and publications from local and national organizations, there are trade publications, books, and directories which offer valuable information about writing and about marketing your manuscripts and understanding the business side of publishing. Some also list employment agencies that specialize in placing publishing professionals, and some announce actual freelance opportunities.

TRADE MAGAZINES

ADVERTISING AGE, Crain Communications Inc., 740 N. Rush St., Chicago IL 60611. (312)649-5200. *Weekly magazine covering advertising in magazines, trade journals and business.*

AMERICAN JOURNALISM REVIEW, 8701 Adelphi Rd., Adelphi MD 20783. (301)431-4771. *10 issues/ year magazine for journalists and communications professionals.*

DAILY VARIETY, Daily Variety Ltd./Cahners Publishing Co., 5700 Wilshire Blvd., Los Angeles CA 90036. (213)857-6600. *Trade publication on the entertainment industry, with helpful information for screenwriters.*

EDITOR & PUBLISHER, The Editor & Publisher Co., 11 W. 19th St., New York NY 10011. (212)675-4380. *Weekly magazine covering the newspaper publishing industry.*

FOLIO, Cowles Business Media, 11 Riverbend Dr. South, P.O. Box 4949, Stamford CT 06907-0949. (203)358-9900. *Monthly magazine covering the magazine publishing industry.*

GIFTS & DECORATIVE ACCESSORIES, Geyer-McAllister Publications, Inc., 51 Madison Ave., New York NY 10010-1675. (212)689-4411. *Monthly magazine covering greeting cards among other subjects, with an annual buyer's directory in September.*

HORN BOOK MAGAZINE, 11 Beacon St., Boston MA 02108. (617)227-1555. *Bimonthly magazine covering children's literature.*

PARTY & PAPER RETAILER, 4 Ward Corp., 70 New Canaan Ave., Norwalk CT 06850. (203)845-8020. *Monthly magazine covering the greeting card and gift industry.*

POETS & WRITERS INC., 72 Spring St., New York NY 10012. (212)226-3586. *Bimonthly magazine, primarily for literary writers and poets.*

PUBLISHERS WEEKLY, Bowker Magazine Group, Cahners Publishing Co., 249 W. 17th St., 6th Floor, New York NY 10011. (212)645-0067. *Weekly magazine covering the book publishing industry.*

SCIENCE FICTION CHRONICLE, P.O. Box 022730, Brooklyn NY 11202-0056. (718)643-9011. *Monthly magazine for science fiction, fantasy and horror writers.*

TRAVELWRITER MARKETLETTER, The Waldorf-Astoria, Suite 1880, New York NY 10022. *Monthly newsletter for travel writers with market listings as well as trip information.*

THE WRITER, 120 Boylston St., Boston MA 02116. (617)423-3157. *Monthly writers' magazine.*

WRITER'S DIGEST, 1507 Dana Ave., Cincinnati OH 45207. (513)531-2222. *Monthly writers' magazine.*

WRITING FOR MONEY, Blue Dolphin Communications, Inc., 83 Boston Post Rd., Sudbury MA 01776. *Bimonthly freelance market reports.*

BOOKS AND DIRECTORIES

AV MARKET PLACE, R.R. Bowker, A Reed Reference Publishing Co., 121 Chanlon Rd., New Providence NJ 07974. (908)464-6800.

THE COMPLETE BOOK OF SCRIPTWRITING, by J. Michael Straczynski, Writer's Digest Books, 1507 Dana Ave., Cincinnati OH 45207. (513)531-2222.

THE COMPLETE GUIDE TO SELF PUBLISHING, by Marilyn and Tom Ross, Writer's Digest Books, 1507 Dana Ave., Cincinnati OH 45207. (513)531-2222.

COPYRIGHT HANDBOOK, R.R. Bowker, A Reed Reference Publishing Co., 121 Chanlon Rd., New Providence NJ 07974. (908)464-6800.

DRAMATISTS SOURCEBOOK, edited by Kathy Sova, Theatre Communications Group, Inc., 355 Lexington Ave., New York NY 10017. (212)697-5230.

EDITORS ON EDITING: What Writers Need to Know About What Editors Do, edited by Gerald Gross, Grove/Atlantic Press, 841 Broadway, New York NY 10003. *Forty essays by America's most distinguished trade book editors on the art and craft of editing*

GRANTS AND AWARDS AVAILABLE TO AMERICAN WRITERS, *19th Ed., PEN American Center, 568 Broadway, New York NY 10012. (212)334-1660.*

GUIDE TO LITERARY AGENTS, edited by Kirsten Holm, Writer's Digest Books, 1507 Dana Ave., Cincinnati OH 45207. (513)531-2222.

THE GUIDE TO WRITERS CONFERENCES, ShawGuides, Inc. Educational Publishers, Box 1295, New York NY 10023. (212)799-6464.

HOW TO WRITE IRRESISTIBLE QUERY LETTERS, by Lisa Collier Cool, Writer's Digest Books, 1507 Dana Ave., Cincinnati OH 45207. (513)531-2222.

THE INSIDER'S GUIDE TO INTERACTIVE WRITING AND PUBLISHING, by Anthony Tedesco, Paul Tedesco and Thomas Elia, 61 E. Eighth St., Suite 272, New York NY 10003. (212)353-0455; anthony@crispzine.com.

INTERNATIONAL DIRECTORY OF LITTLE MAGAZINES & SMALL PRESSES, edited by Len Fulton, Dustbooks, P.O. Box 100, Paradise CA 95967. (916)877-6110.

LITERARY MARKET PLACE and INTERNATIONAL LITERARY MARKET PLACE, R.R. Bowker, A Reed Reference Publishing Co., 121 Chanlon Rd., New Providence NJ 07974. (908)464-6800.

MAGAZINE WRITING THAT SELLS, by Don McKinney, Writer's Digest Books, 1507 Dana Ave., Cincinnati OH 45207. (513)531-2222.

MY BIG SOURCEBOOK, 66 Canal Center Plaza, Suite 200, Alexandria VA 22314-5507. (703)683-0683.

NATIONAL WRITERS UNION GUIDE TO FREELANCE RATES & STANDARD PRACTICE, by Alexander Kopelman, distributed by Writer's Digest Books, 1507 Dana Ave., Cincinnati OH 45207, (513)531-2222.

PROFESSIONAL WRITER'S GUIDE, edited by Donald Bower and James Lee Young, National Writers Press, Suite 424, 1450 S. Havana, Aurora CO 80012. (303)751-7844.

STANDARD DIRECTORY OF ADVERTISING AGENCIES, National Register Publishing, A Reed Reference Publishing Co., 121 Chanlon Rd., New Providence NJ 07974. (908)464-6800.

SUCCESSFUL SCRIPTWRITING, by Jurgen Wolff and Kerry Cox, Writer's Digest Books, 1507 Dana Ave., Cincinnati OH 45207. (513)531-2222.

THE WRITER'S GUIDE TO BOOK EDITORS, PUBLISHERS & LITERARY AGENTS, by Jeff Herman, Prima Publishing, Box 1260, Rocklin CA 95677-1260. (916)632-4400 .

THE WRITER'S GUIDE TO MAGAZINES EDITORS AND PUBLISHERS, by Judy Mandell, Prima Publishing, P.O. Box 1260BK, Rocklin CA 95677-1260. (916)632-4400.

THE WRITER'S LEGAL COMPANION, by Brad Bunnin and Peter Beren, Addison-Wesley Publishing Co., 1 Jacob Way, Reading MA 01867. (617)944-3700.

Organizations of Interest

BY ANDREW LUCYSZYN

Writing is a solitary exercise—it often leaves writers shut away by themselves. Writers' organizations can provide contact to the outside world, allowing you to connect with thousands of others who share the same goals, struggle with the same challenges and ask the same questions about editors, publishers and agents.

An organization's function varies according to its size and goals. Local groups tend to focus on assisting with the craft of writing through critique or reading sessions. National organizations often pursue goals that are wider in scope, such as negotiating collective bargaining agreements or health insurance coverage for members. Organizations offer diverse benefits, from helpful newsletters and workshops, to dependable databases of other writers' experiences in different markets, to highly prestigious awards. Members' contributions differ as well, ranging from who brings the doughnuts next week to hundreds of dollars in dues and meeting professional membership qualifications.

The Internet has given discussion groups a new platform on which to meet, and writers have taken full advantage of this common meeting ground. Some organizations operate only online with moderated forums, vast information resources and members from around the world. These groups have the advantage of instant communication and a wide array of opinions. However, they leave you staring at the computer in your den.

Whether you write nonfiction or science fiction, self-help or short stories, there are national organizations representing your field as a whole or representing their members in court. Hundreds more smaller, local groups are providing assistance from paragraph to paragraph. There is an organization—probably several—to suit your needs.

ACADEMY OF AMERICAN POETS, 584 Broadway, Suite 1208, New York NY 10012-3250. (212) 274-0343. Fax: (212) 274-9427. Website: http://www.poets.org. Contact: David Killeen. Estab. 1934. Dues: $25 minimum donation for lowest level of membership. "The Academy of American Poets was founded to support American poets at all stages of their careers and to foster the appreciation of contemporary poetry. The largest organization in the country dedicated specifically to the art of poetry, the Academy sponsors programs nationally. These include National Poetry Month; the most important collection of awards for poetry in the United States; a national series of public readings and residencies; and other programs that provide essential support to American poets, poetry publishers, and readers of poetry."

AMERICAN BOOK PRODUCERS ASSOCIATION, 160 Fifth Ave., Suite 625, New York NY 10010-7000. (212)645-2368. Estab. 1980. The American Book Producers Association is the trade association of independent book producers in the U.S. and Canada. Book producers provide all the services necessary for publication except sales and order fulfillment. They work with authors, agents, editors, designers, photographers, illustrators, typesetters and printers to deliver fully edited manuscripts with or without layouts; camera-ready mechanicals; film for a printer; or finished books. Book producers also assist in developing marketing plans.

AMERICAN MEDICAL WRITERS ASSOCIATION, 9650 Rockville Pike, Bethesda MD 20814-3998. (301)493-0003. Members of this organization are medical writers, editors, publishers, administrators, audiovisualists and pharmaceutical and public relations professionals concerned with effective communication about medicine and allied sciences. Awards for medical books and medical films are given; a conference is held annually.

AMERICAN SOCIETY OF JOURNALISTS AND AUTHORS (ASJA), 1501 Broadway, Suite 302, New York NY 10036. (212) 997-0947. Fax: (212) 768-7414. E-mail: asja@compuserve.com. Website: http://www.asja.org. Executive Director: Alexandra Owens. Dues: $25 application fee applied toward $100 one-time initiation fee upon acceptance; then $165 per year. "The American Society of Journalists and Authors is the nation's leading organization of independent, freelance nonfiction writers. It encourages high standards of nonfiction writing, takes a strong stand against practices denigrating the freelance writer's professional status, holds educational conferences and meetings, offers awards for outstanding accomplishments and examines issues that concern the freelance writer and the reading public. ASJA offers extensive benefits focusing on professional development, including regular confidential market information, meetings with editors and others in the field, an exclusive job referral service, seminars and workshops, discount services and, above all, the opportunity for members to explore professional issues and concerns with their peers. ASJA brings leadership in establishing professional and ethical standards, and in recognizing and encouraging the pursuit of excellence in nonfiction writing. ASJA publishes a monthly newsletter for its members, a 'Code of Ethics and Fair Practices,' an annual membership directory and books on writing. Only professional freelance writers of nonfiction for general audiences are eligible for membership. Qualifications: six full-length articles from national periodicals or major regional magazines or newspapers (e.g., New York Magazine, the Los Angeles Times); or two nonfiction books, or one book and a contract for a second; or a combination of these books and articles." 1,030 members. Information package free.

AMERICAN TRANSLATORS ASSOCIATION, 1800 Diagonal Rd., Suite 220, Alexandria VA 22314-0214. (703)683-6100. This international organization advocates improvement of professional standards and encourages professional training. The ATA Chronicle is a monthly publication for organization members. The American Translators Association convenes annually to exchange ideas and discuss common problems. 3,500 members.

ASIAN AMERICAN WRITERS' WORKSHOP, 37 St. Mark's Place, New York NY 10003. (212) 228-6718. Fax: (212) 228-7718. Website: http://www.panix.com/~aaww/. Estab. 1991. Dues: Individual-$35. Patron- $100. "The Asian American Writers' Workshop is dedicated to the creation, publication and distribution of Asian American literature. By forming a national network of writers, readers, editors, and publishers, we offer both artistic and professional support through readings, workshops, a literary journal, a literary news magazine, books, contests, and an Asian American bookstore. Membership includes a subscription to the APA Journal and TEN, as well as book discounts, a national writing workshop and reading series, locally held (New York City area) writing workshops and public readings, in-store gallery, and performance series."

ASSOCIATED WRITING PROGRAMS, Tallwood House MS1E3, George Mason University, Fairfax VA 22030. (703)993-4301. Fax: (703) 993-4302. Estab. 1967. Dues: $50 first year, then $30 annual renewal fee. "The Associated Writing Programs were created to represent the emerging presence of writers in colleges and universities. AWP's mission is to foster literary talent and achievement; to advocate the teaching of the craft of writing as a primary aspect of education; and to serve the creators and readers of contemporary writing. Students who want to major in creative writing can find appropriate colleges in the geographical areas of their choice by writing the Association. The Association publishes a newsletter, an annual anthology of student work, and a catalog describing 250 writing programs in the U.S. and Canada. A year's membership includes 6 issues of the AWP Chronicle and 7 issues of the AWP Job List; alternatively, members may opt to receive the Job List as e-mail. Members also receive a 33% discount on AWP Award Series entry fees, and an 18% discount on registration to the Annual Conference. AWP counts among its members 280 colleges and universities and 16,000 individual writers."

ASSOCIATION OF AUTHORS' REPRESENTATIVES, 10 Astor Pl., 3rd Floor, New York NY 10003. (212)353-3709. A voluntary professional organization for agents that resulted from the merger of Independent Literary Agents Association (ILAA) and Society of Authors' Representatives (SAR). This organization has a strong code of ethics—which the AAR enforces—for its members. AAR members are not allowed to charge reading fees for manuscripts. For a list of members and the code of ethics send $5 and an SAE with 2 first-class stamps.

ASSOCIATION OF DESK-TOP PUBLISHERS, 3401-A800 Adams Way, San Diego CA 92116-2429. (619)563-9714. This international association focuses primarily on reviews of hardware and software used in desktop publishing. A monthly newsletter publishes reviews, along with a calendar of events and other items of interest to freelance desktop publishers. More than 4,000 members.

AUSTIN WRITERS' LEAGUE, 1501 W. Fifth St., Suite E-2, Austin TX 78703. (512) 499-8914. Fax: (512) 499-0441. "The Austin Writers' League is the largest regional writing organization in Texas and the second largest in the nation. Whatever your interest—poetry, fiction, journalism, humor, academic, technical, business, advertising, public relations, juvenile, screen writing—you'll find support and information here. Open to anyone interested in writing." 1,600 members.

THE AUTHORS GUILD, 330 W. 42nd St., 29th Floor, New York NY 10036. (212)563-5904. A national professional organization made up of book authors and magazine writers. It is involved in issues such as free speech, copyright and taxes, and has represented the writer in such matters before Congress and in the courts. The Guild also provides writers with information about publishers' contract provisions for advances, royalties, subsidiary rights, etc. All Authors Guild members also belong to the Authors League of America, which comprises the Authors Guild and the Dramatists Guild. More than 6,500 members.

THE AUTHORS LEAGUE OF AMERICA, INC., 330 W. 42nd St., New York NY 10036. (212)564-8350. This professional organization comprises the Authors Guild's 6,500 book authors and magazine writers and the Dramatists Guild's 8,000 playwrights. The Guilds publish and distribute (to members only) the Dramatists Guild Quarterly and Newsletter and the Authors Guild Bulletin which, along with other printed materials, provide information on contract terms, copyright, libel and other legal and professional matters affecting writers.

CALIFORNIA WRITERS' CLUB, Ten affiliated branches located in Bakersfield (Membership: Barbara Nelson, (805) 366-5944); Berkeley (Membership: Julian Adams, (510) 845-4725); East Sierra (Membership: Rlee Peters, (619) 446-4825); High Desert (Meetings: Ruth Theodos, (619) 242-0330); Mount Diablo (Membership: Jenny Catalano, (510) 933-6301, Saggcat@aol.com); Peninsula (Membership: Christina Ashton, (415) 345-80230; Redwood (Membership: Barbara Truax, (415) 892-9639, BarbTruax@aol.com); Sacramento (Membership: Marilyn-Smith Murphy, (916) 726-7868); San Fernando Valley (Membership: Mary Terzian, (310) 822-1817, nayri@aol.com); South Bay (Membership: Beverly Morgan, (408) 629-6455. Dues: $20 entry fee, $37.50 annual dues; $525 lifetime membership. "Each branch meets monthly (except summertime) to hear writers, editors, teachers, publishers, and agents speak on the publishing industry. Some branches also hold workshops and critique groups. Each April, members from various branches gather for the annual All-Branch Meeting. In alternate years, the club sponsors a summer weekend conference covering all aspects of writing and publishing. Membership is open to all published writers, editors and photojournalists who meet the stated qualifications." Contact a local chairperson for membership requirements.

CANADIAN AUTHORS ASSOCIATION, 27 Doxsee Ave. N., Campbellford, Ontario, K0L 1L0, Canada. (705) 653-0323. Fax: (705)653-0593. E-mail: canauthedden.on.ca. Website: http://www.Canauthors.org/national.html. Contact: Alec McEachern. Estab. 1921. Dues: $115 plus GST ($123.05) per year. "The Canadian Authors Association is Canada's national organization for writers to support the development of writing and marketing skills, to promote networking among writers and to protect the interests of Canadian writers. Members meet in branches across Canada from Nova Scotia to British Columbia. Each year a writers conference is held which includes an awards dinner with over $25,000 in prestigious writing awards including cash, medals and trips. Our motto is 'Writers Helping Writers.' Members are writers, engaged in writing in any genre, who have produced a sufficient body of published work. Associate members are writers who have not yet produced sufficient material to qualify as a Member or wish to support Canadian writing. We suggest that writers attend branch meetings in a location near them to learn more about the CAA and then make a decision on applying for membership."

COPYWRITERS COUNCIL OF AMERICA, FREELANCE, Linick Bldg. 102, 7 Putter Lane, Middle Island NY 11953-0102. (516)924-8555.

THE DRAMATISTS GUILD, 234 W. 44th St., 11th Floor, New York NY 10036. (212)398-9366. A division of the Authors League of America, Inc., this organization includes playwrights, lyricists and composers as members. The Dramatists Guild contracts are considered the world's most comprehensive contracts for playwrights. This association publishes the Dramatists Guild Newsletter issued 10 times per year, and the Dramatists Quarterly. 8,000 members.

EDITORIAL FREELANCERS ASSOCIATION, 71 W. 23rd St., Suite 1504, New York NY 10010. (212)929-5400. This organization exists to advance professionalism, to exchange information and support, and to furnish benefits to its members. Activities include seminars and training workshops. The EFA's members work part-time and full-time in capacities such as writer, indexer and proofreader. 950 members.

EDUCATION WRITERS ASSOCIATION, 1331 H. NW, Suite 307, Washington DC 20036. (202)637-9700. Fax:(202) 637-9707. E-mail: ewaoffice@aol.com. Website: http://www.ewa/org. Estab. 1947. Dues: $50. The Education Writers Association is the national professional organization of education reporters, writers and editors whose goal is to improve education writing and reporting to the public. EWA holds several seminars for reporters, sponsors a fellowship program, gives reporters a chance to showcase their best work and compete for recognition and cash prizes, provides free publications put out by the organization. Active membership is open to working reporters or freelance writers who cover education for the general press, including newspapers, magazines, radio and television. Associate membership is open to reporters and writers for education organizations and institutions, public information officers and others interested in how education is reported. 800 members.

FREELANCE EDITORIAL ASSOCIATION, P.O. Box 380835, Cambridge MA 02238-0835. (617) 643-8626.

INDEPENDENT WRITERS OF CHICAGO, 7855 Gross Point Rd., Unit M, Skokie IL 60077. (847) 676-3784. Website: http://www.iwoc.org. President: Jim Kepler. "IWOC is an association of self-employed nonfiction writers in the Midwest, though primarily Chicago and suburbs. IWOC sponsors meetings 10 times a year, plus several half-day seminars at reasonable rates. Members also receive or have access to Writers Line, biennial rate survey, sample contracts and more. They serve large corporations, small businesses, and nonprofit organizations and represent a broad range of writing talents and specialties. Professional members are working freelance writers who have the skills and experience to meet client needs and expectations. These writers are available to companies or individuals searching for qualified communicators. Many IWOC writers offer a broad range of services, including design, desktop publishing, and Website authoring. Associate members are not currently employed as independent writers but who are interested in the business of writing."

INTERNATIONAL ASSOCIATION OF BUSINESS COMMUNICATORS, 1 Hallidie Plaza, Suite 600, San Francisco CA 94102. (415)433-3400. Website: http://www.iabc.com. "IABC is the leading resource for effective communication. Members are writers, editors, audiovisual specialists, and managers of communication and public relations programs for profit and not-for-profit organizations worldwide. We provide products, services, activities and networking opportunities to help people and organizations achieve excellence in public relations, employee communication, marketing communication, public affairs and other forms of communication. IABC specializes in helping people and organizations: make business sense of communication, think strategically about communication, measure and clarify the value of communication, build better relationships with stakeholders. Our products and services include: Communication World, an award-winning print magazine covering trends and issues; an annual international conference; Communication Bank, a comprehensive information service that provides how-to handbooks, customized information searches of electronic databases, IABC Research Foundation materials and information on award-winning programs; an accreditation program; a searchable electronic member database." 12,500 members.

INTERNATIONAL ASSOCIATION OF CRIME WRITERS INC., North American Branch, JAF Box 1500, New York NY 10116. (212)243-8966.

INTERNATIONAL ONLINE WRITERS ASSOCIATION (IOWA), Website: http:// www.project-iowa.org. Registration forms on website. No fee for membership. "IOWA offers help and services to writers around the world through shared ideas, workshops, critiques and professional advice. The organization is composed of a variety of writers from around the world." Sponsors monthly workshops online conducted by published authors and other professionals, weekly online critiques and frequent round robin collaboration sessions. Also maintains a library of essays, poems , short stories and novel chapters, plus an information resource library containing links to other writing resources.

INTERNATIONAL TELEVISION ASSOCIATION, 6311 N. O'Connor Rd., Suite 230, Irving TX 75039. (214)869-1112. The ITA is an organization of non-broadcast video professionals working in the areas of training films, educational materials and public service announcements. 7,500 members.

INTERNATIONAL WOMEN'S WRITING GUILD, Box 810, Gracie Station, New York NY 10028-0082. (212)737-7536. Website: http://www/iwwg.com. Executive Director: Hannelore Hahn. Estab. 1976. Dues: $35 ($45 outside U.S.) annually. "The International Women's Writing Guild is a network for the personal and professional empowerment of women through writing. It has engendered and supported the joyful camaraderie that comes from shared interests of a woman's writing community. Membership benefits include a bimonthly newsletter, health insurance at group rates, and writing services such as agents lists. IWWG offers workshops on every kind of writing and directs an annual week-long conference in August at Skidmore College, Saratoga Springs, New York. It is open to any woman regardless of portfolio."

THE LOFT, Pratt Community Center, 66 Malcolm Ave. SE, Minneapolis MN 55414. (612) 379-8999. Website: http:// www.tc.umn.edu/nlhome/m555/loft/index.html. Membership Director: Christina Erickson Putney. Dues: Individual-$40; Household-$50. "The mission of the Loft is to foster a writing community, the artistic development of individual writers, and an audience for literature. The Loft seeks to recognize and encourage cultural diversity and pluralism in its membership and in all of its programs. Since 1974, the Loft has steadily grown to become the largest, most comprehensive literary center in the nation. Now with a dedicated and professional staff, writers continue to play an integral leadership role as board members, teachers and administrators. Each year, over 50,000 people are served by the Loft through a wide range of workshops and classes, public readings, performances, contests and special events."

MYSTERY WRITERS OF AMERICA, INC., 17 E. 47th St., 6th Floor, New York NY 10017. Website: http:// www.bookwire.com/mwa/. President: Donald E. Westlake. Estab. 1945. Dues: $65 annual for U.S. members; $32.50 for writers based outside the U.S. "MWA was established for the purpose of promoting and protecting the interests and welfare of mystery writers and to increase the esteem and literary recognition given to the genre. The National Office maintains an extensive library of reference materials available through the mail. It handles inquiries and correspondence from American and foreign publishers, fellow writers organizations, motion picture and television producers, lecture agencies, the media, and various enterprises in the mystery field. MWA is available for advice on publishing problems. In addition, a permanent Grievance committee is on hand to field complaints, to provide support and guidance, and where possible to seek redress. Meetings are held each month by all chapters, dinner optional (Excepting July and August) at which prominent speakers discuss various aspects of criminology, publishing and other matters of interest and concern to authors. Courses, workshops, and seminars are conducted by MWA chapters, often with the participation of local colleges and universities, in which various committees, endeavor to promote and protect our legitimate interests. Annual activities include a convention, presentation of awards and publication of an anthology of members' work . The Edgar Allan Poe Awards Banquet is the highlight event of the year, attended by illustrious authors, guests, editors, publishers, television and motion picture producers from the U.S. and abroad. Attendance affords members an unparalleled opportunity to meet industry notables. The National organization's newsletter *The Third Degree* is published ten times a year, and local chapters also circulate their own bulletins and newsletters that focus on matters of interest to their membership." 2,600 members.

NATIONAL ASSOCIATION OF SCIENCE WRITERS, Box 294, Greenlawn NY 11740. (516)757-5664. Members of this professional organization are writers and editors who prepare scientific information for the layperson. Activities of the NASW include competitions and an annual joint meeting with the American Association for the Advancement of Science. NASW gives annual awards and distributes a Guide to Careers in Science Writing (single copies free for #10 SASE). The group also publishes a newsletter and the book Communicating Science ($3 prepaid per copy).

NATIONAL WRITERS ASSOCIATION, 1450 S. Havana, Suite 424, Aurora CO 80012. (303)751-7844. The National Writers Association has two categories of members: professional members, who have either been published in national magazines, had a book published on a royalty basis, or had a stageplay, screenplay or teleplay produced; and associate members who have a serious interest in writing. The NWA operates a 2,000-volume library and sponsors contests as well as a home study magazine writing course. It distributes to its members research reports on various aspects of writing, copyright, etc. Conferences are held yearly.

NATIONAL WRITERS UNION, 113 University Pl., 6th Floor, New York NY 10003. (212) 254-0279. Fax: (212) 254-0673. E-mail: nwu wu.org. Website: http://www.nwu.org/nwu. Contact: Bruce Hartford. Estab. 1983. Dues: Categorized on a sliding scare according to writing income: Under $5,000/year- $80/year; $5,000-$25,000/year- $132/year; over $25,000- $180/year. "The NWU is the trade union for freelance writers in all genres except film/video/radio. We participate in grievances, collective bargaining, offer contract advice, wage industry campaigns, oppose-censorship, defend free speech, provide health plans, engage in legislative and lobbying on behalf of creators, and much more. The Union works to raise rates and improve treatment of freelance writers by magazine and book publishers. It holds conferences on legal, economic, trade and craft issues affecting writers. The NWU is affiliated with the United Automobile Workers (UAW) and through them with the AFL-CIO. NWU has locals and organizing committees throughout the country. Our members include journalists, book authors, poets, copywriters, academic authors, cartoonists, and technical and business writers. The NWU has a Supporters Circle open to individuals or organizations who are not writers but wish to support the union." 4,500 members.

NEW DRAMATISTS, 424 W. 44th St., New York NY 10036. (212)757-6060.

PEN AMERICAN CENTER, 568 Broadway, New York NY 10012. (212)334-1660. Estab. 1921. "PEN American Center, the largest of nearly 130 Centers worldwide that compose International PEN, is a membership association of prominent literary writers and editors. As a major voice of the literary community, the organization seeks to defend the freedom of expression wherever it may be threatened, and to promote and encourage the recognition and reading of contemporary literature. All PEN members receive the quarterly PEN Newsletter and qualify for medical insurance at group rates. Members living near the Headquarters or Branches are invited to PEN events throughout the year. Membership in American PEN includes reciprocal privileges in foreign PEN Centers for those traveling abroad. The PEN Cafe, an on-line conversation and discussion group, is available to PEN members. Membership is by invitation of the Admission Committee after nomination by a PEN member. The standard qualification for a writer to join is publication of two or more books of a literary character, or one book generally acclaimed to be of exceptional distinction. Also eligible for membership are editors , translators, playwrights and literary essayists. Candidates for membership should be nominated by two current members of PEN, or may nominate themselves with the support of a current member."

PENNWRITERS, INC., 108 Jaspin Way, Canonsburg PA 15317. Contact: Joy Hopkins. Pennsylvania-based group divided into six regions. Dues: $35 for the first year, $25 annually thereafter. "There are small core groups in each region who meet for critiques, workshops, etc., and each region hosts workshops open to the entire group. We sponsor an annual conference with workshops, round tables, editors and agents. All events are reasonably priced. We also have an annual writing contest, library of books and tapes available to members through the mail, mail critique partners, and a bimonthly newsletter. We have writers in every genre and field imaginable." 500 members.

POETRY SOCIETY OF AMERICA, 15 Grammercy Park, New York NY 10003. (212)254-9628. Website: http://www.bookwire.com/psa/psa.html. Estab. 1910. Dues: $40 base membership fee, also various contributor levels and discounts. "The Poetry Society of America seeks to raise the awareness of poetry, deepen the understanding of it and encourage more people to read, listen and write poetry. Each year the PSA offers six to eight poetry seminars offering small audiences the opportunity to participate in a dialogue with some of America's best-known poets and to deepen their knowledge of contemporary and historical poetry. PSA presents a national series of readings including 'Tributes in Libraries' and 'Poetry in Public Places,' mounts poetry on mass transit vehicles through 'Poetry in Motion,' and broadcasts an educational poetry series on public television. The PSA also offers annual contests for poetry (many open to nonmembers), seminars and poetry festivals and publishes the PSA newsletter. Membership is open to all persons in sympathy with the mission of the Poetry Societry of America. Benefits include: free entrance to all PSA contests free of charge, discount admissions to PSA readings, peer workshops, a subscription to the PSA Journal, program calendars and invitations to readings and events, discounts on book purchases through the Grolier Poetry Book Shop. 2,000 members

POETS & WRITERS, 72 Spring St., New York NY 10012. (212)226-3586. Fax: (212) 226-3963. Website: http://www.pw.org. Estab. 1970. Dues: contributions of $50 or more entitle donors to membership in the Friends of Poets & Writers and a complimentary one-year subscription to *Poets & Writers* magazine. "Poets & Writers serves as an information clearing house and service organization for the nation's literary community. P&W Information Services offers additional resources to writers, including information on publishing opportunities, literary agents and funding sources. P&W also hosts publishing seminars to help writers understand the literary marketplace. In addition to maintaining biographical archives on poets and fiction writers, Poets & Writers provides a telephone service to people seeking either answers to questions of a general literary nature or the current address of a poet or writer listed in its publication, *A Directory of American Poets and Fiction Writers.* The organization also publishes *Poets & Writers Writer's Guide to Copyright, Author and Audience and Literary Agents,* as well as booklets on literary agents, copyright, literary bookstores and sponsors."

PUBLIC RELATIONS SOCIETY OF AMERICA, 33 Irving Pl., New York NY 10003. (212)995-2230. The largest public relations society in the world. PRSA provides its members with networking opportunities as well as opportunities for professional development. Members attend chapter meetings and an annual convention. They also receive the monthly newspaper, Tactics, which covers current strategies in public relations, and the quarterly magazine, Strategist, which deals with other public relations issues. 16,000 members.

ROMANCE WRITERS OF AMERICA, 13700 Veterans Memorial, Suite 315, Houston TX 77014-1073. (281) 440-6885. Fax: (281) 440-7510. Website: http://www. rwanational.com. President: Libby Hall. Dues: $10 new-member filing fee, $60 annually. "RWA is the world's largest non-profit genre organization, specializes in romance fiction. RWA's purpose is to promote excellence in the romance industry and to support all its writers, published and unpublished, help writers become published and establish careers in their writing field, provide continuing support for writers within the romance publishing industry, promote mutual support among members, promote and advocate an 'author-friendly' environment in the publishing industry, be a strong voice within the romance publishing, wholesaling, and retailing industries, strive to maintain and increase the market share of romance fiction. Each year RWA sends a Summit Team to meet with publishing industry officials to discuss issues of vital concern to authors, issues such as poor availability of print run, reserve against returns, and sell-through information; forced use of pseudonyms; erosion of author rights; erosion of author royalties; and other business practices our members feel are detrimental to an author's ability to earn a living." Sponsors an annual conference in July as well as regional conferences. 7,900 members with more than 150 local chapters.

SCIENCE FICTION AND FANTASY WRITERS OF AMERICA, INC., 5 Winding Brook Dr., #1B, Guilderland NY 12084. (518)869-5361. Website: http://www.sfwa.org/misc/sfwa_info.htm. Contact: Peter Dennis Pautz. Estab. 1965 Dues: $10 one-time fee, $50/year for active and associate members, $35/year for affiliate members. "SFWA is an organization of writers, artists, editors and other allied professionals in the science fiction and fantasy genres. Its purposes include to inform writers on professional matters, protect their interests, and help them deal effectively with agents, editors, anthologists, and producers in non-print media, as well as to encourage public interest in and appreciation for science fiction and fantasy literature. SFWA supports a Grievance Committee, legal counsel, a Speaker's Bureau and a Circulating Book Plan, which offers members access to new hardcover books. Various committees monitor contracts and royalty statements, maintain contact with other writers' organizations, set standards for author/agent relationships, and help members deal with the strange world of science fiction conventions. The minimum requirement for active membership is the professional publication (acceptance and payment) of three short stories or one full-length fiction book, while other professionals may join as affiliates. All members receive the quarterly SFWA Bulletin, annual membership directory, The SFWA Handbook, and copies of our model paperback and hardcover contracts. In addition, active, associate, and estate members receive the in-house newsletter, *The Forum.* Active members also may vote for officers and for the Nebula Awards." 1,800 members.

SEATTLE WRITERS ASSOCIATION, P.O. Box 33265, Seattle WA 98133. (206) 860-5207. President: Claudia McCormick. Estab. 1986. Dues: $30 annually. "SWA's sole purpose is to provide the tolls to succeed in the field of writing. We feature published and unpublished writers in fiction and nonfiction. Monthly meetings provide both published and aspiring writers the opportunity to connect with the critique group nearest them and build their own network. SWA offers newsletters, full manuscript review for longer works, marketing advice, agent recommendations and other support services, such as press releases and bookmarks to announce member's new publications." Sponsors the annual Winter Workshop (February) and Writers in Performance contest for short stories, articles, essays, children's stories, fiction and nonfiction book excerpts, poetry (May). Guidelines and membership information for SASE.

SOCIETY OF AMERICAN BUSINESS EDITORS & WRITERS, University of Missouri, School of Journalism, 76 Gannett Hall, Columbia MO 65211. (314)882-7862. Contact: Janine Latus-Musick. This is an organization of editors, teachers and writers of business journalism. SABEW offers its members a resume bank, so potential employers can have easy access to their qualifications; a 24-hour job hotline, with a recorded list of available jobs; and a CompuServe bulletin board, which contains organization news, job listings, selected articles from The Business Journalist and other reference materials. SABEW holds an annual convention. The organization recently created a contest to recognize overall excellence in newspaper business sections. 2,200 members.

SOCIETY OF AMERICAN TRAVEL WRITERS, 4101 Lake Boone Trail, Suite 201, Raleigh NC 27607. (919)787-5181. This organization is concerned with conservation, historic preservation and quality travel reporting. Members include writers, editors, photographers, broadcasters, travel film lecturers and public relations representatives. Annual awards are based on contributions to conservation, preservation and beautification.

SOCIETY OF CHILDREN'S BOOK WRITERS AND ILLUSTRATORS, 22736 Vanowen St., Suite 106, West Hills CA 91307. (818) 888-8760. Website: http://www.scbwi.org. President: Stephen Mooser. Executive Director: Lin

Oliver. Estab. 1968. Dues: $50 annually. "SCBWI is the only professional organization dedicated to serving the people who write, illustrate, or share a vital interest in children's literature. The SCBWI acts as a network for the exchange of knowledge between writers, illustrators, editors, publishers, agents, librarians, educators, booksellers and others involved with literature for young people. It sponsors an annual National Conference on writing and illustrating books and multimedia as well as dozens of regional conferences and events throughout the world. It also publishes a bimonthly newsletter, awards grants for works in progress, and provides many informational publications on the art and business of writing and selling written, illustrated and electronic material. The SCBWI also presents the annual Golden Kite Award for the best fiction and non-fiction books." 10,000 members.

SOCIETY OF PROFESSIONAL JOURNALISTS, 16 S. Jackson, Greencastle IN 46135. (317)653-3333. Website: http://www.spj.org. Estab. 1909. "The Society of Professional Journalists is the nation's largest and most broad-based journalism organization. SPJ is dedicated to encouraging the free practice of journalism; stimulating high standards of ethical behavior; and perpetuating a free press. Members seek continuing professional education, career services and support, journalism advocacy. The society has established several awards and holds a contest, as well as publishing *The Quill*, a monthly magazine, and other materials for the public. An annual meeting is held in the fall, and regional conferences take place every spring. To become a professional member, an applicant must, at the time of application, be principally engaged in journalism (more than 50% of working hours). Other memberships are available for retirees, college and post-college graduate students, high school students, associates and institutions." 13,500 members and 300 active chapters.

VOLUNTEER LAWYERS FOR THE ARTS, One E. 53rd St., 6th Floor, New York NY 10022. (212)319-2787. For legal advice from VLA, call their Lawline at (212)319-2910. This nationwide organization of lawyers offers free legal services to people in the creative arts, including writers, on matters related to practicing art. Eligibility for these services is determined by the writer's income; in some cases, even though writers qualify for free legal services, they are responsible for paying court costs. For information on free legal aid, or to locate branches in other cities, writers should contact one of the following: California Lawyers for the Arts, Fort Mason Center Building C, Room 255, San Francisco CA 94123, (415)775-7200; Lawyers for the Creative Arts, 213 W. Institute, Suite 411, Chicago IL 60610, (312)944-2787.

WOMEN IN COMMUNICATIONS, INC., Suite 417, 2101 Wilson Blvd., Arlington VA 22201. Women in Communications is a professional organization for women and men in all fields of communications. Its members work in advertising, communications education, film, magazines, newspapers, photojournalism, public relations, publishing, radio, technical writing and TV. There are 86 campus chapters and 80 professional chapters in addition to members-at-large. The organization publishes a national magapaper, *The Professional Communicator*, ten times per year; and a national directory of professional members biennially. A national professional conference is held annually. 12,000 members.

WRITERS ALLIANCE, 12 Skylark Lane, Stony Brook NY 11790. (516)751-7080. Dues: $10. The Writers Alliance sees itself as "the grass roots Authors Guild." It provides its members with market listings and information on publishing trends, publishes a newsletter, The Backup Street Irregular, and is a general support and information service for writers. Membership information is available for SASE. 360 members.

THE WRITER'S CENTER, 4508 Walsh St., Bethesda MD 20815-6006. (301) 654-8664. E-mail: postmaster@writer.org. Website: http://www.writer.org. Dues: General- $30; Family-$45; Student-$20. "The Writer's Center is a literary crossroads designed to encourage the creation and distribution of contemporary literature. To support these goals we offer a host of interrelated programs and services including: workshops in all genre, a gallery of books and journals, readings and conferences, publications, desktop publishing center, meeting and workspace, and information and communications center. The heart of our program is the more than 200 workshops we offer each year: informal, small groups where participants can share work with one another. We welcome all genres and levels of skill as well as the other arts." 2,200 members.

WRITERS CONNECTION, P.O. Box 24770, San Jose CA 95154-4770. (408) 445-3600. Fax: (408) 445-3609. E-mail: writerscxn@aol.com. Estab. 1983. Dues: $45 annually. "Writers Connection serves writers working in all genres of writing by providing information, inspiration, resources, motivation, and access to professionals in the publishing, film and TV, and multimedia industries. Members receive a monthly newsletter, discounts on Writers Connection's conferences, discounts on writing how-to and reference books, tapes, and special reports, and help with writing-related questions. Our newsletter features cutting-edge information including: listings of regional and national markets and opportunities, industry news, contests and book reviews; profiles of agents, editors, producers, publishers, and successful writers sharing tips, insights, and strategies for success; innovative columns covering fiction writing, scriptwriting, children's writing, writing interactive multimedia, business and technical writing, and online writing and resources; feature articles on writing techniques for different genres, ways to use your skills, marketing strategies, tips on managing yourself as a writer, ideas for writing with computers, inspiration to keep you writing." Sample copy $3.

We've just made getting your words published a little easier.

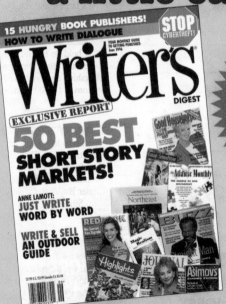

Order Form

☐ **YES!** Start my subscription to **Writer's Digest**, the magazine thousands of successful authors rely on for timely information and instruction in all areas of writing and getting published. I pay just $19.96 for 12 monthly issues...a savings of more than $15 off the newsstand price.

☐ I'm enclosing payment (or paying by credit card). Add an **extra issue** to my subscription FREE — 13 in all!

Charge my ☐ Visa ☐ MC

Acct. # _____ Exp. _____

Signature _____

☐ I prefer to be billed later.

NAME _____

ADDRESS _____

CITY _____ STATE _____ ZIP _____

Outside U.S. add $10 (includes GST in Canada) and remit in U.S. funds. Annual newsstand rate $35.88. Allow 4-6 weeks for first issue delivery.

SAVE MORE THAN $15!

YOUR MONTHLY GUIDE TO GETTING PUBLISHED

T8WM6

WRITERS GUILD OF ALBERTA, 11759 Groat Rd., Edmonton, Alberta, T5M 3K6, Canada. (403)422-8174.

WRITERS GUILD OF AMERICA, East Chapter: 555 W. 57th St., New York NY 10019, (212) 767-7800; West Chapter: 8955 Beverly Blvd., West Hollywood CA 90048, (310) 550-1000. Website: http://www.wga.org. Estab. 1933. Dues: $2,500. "The Writers Guild of America is the sole collective bargaining representative for writers in the motion picture, broadcast, cable, interactive and new media industries. It has numerous affiliation agreements with other U.S. and international writing organizations and is in the forefront of the debates concerning economic and creative rights for writers. The Employment Access Department works with producers, studio and network heads and writers to increase employment opportunities and the availability of writing assignments for writers who are Black, Latino, Asian/Pacific Islander, American Indian, women, over 40 or disabled. The Department of Industry Alliances furthers the cause of writers who work in fields other than traditional movies and television shows, with a particular emphasis on interactive, nonfiction entertainment, animation and informational films." The Guild also publishes a variety of publications for its members. Prospective members must accumulate units of writing credit according to Guild standards to meet admission requirements. A booklet listing the Guild's minimum rates for scripts of various lengths is available from either Guild for $3.55, which includes postage, plus applicable sales tax for residents of New York and California. The WGA also publishes a list of literary agencies who are signatory to the Manager's Basic Agreement, which is available for $2 and a SASE. WGA publishes a booklet, "Professional Writer's Teleplay/Screenplay Format," for about $4.28, which includes postage, plus applicable sales tax. A certified check, or a money order made out to Writers Guild of America should accompany any order. For administrative purposes only, the union is divided by the Mississippi River into the Writers Guild of America, East (WGAe) and the Writers Guild of America, West (WGAw). In all other respects it is a single union. 8,500 members.

Websites of Interest

The Internet provides a wealth of information for writers. The number of websites devoted to writing and publishing is vast and will continue to expand as the year progresses. Below is a short—and thus incomplete—list of websites that offer information and hypertext links to other pertinent sites relating to writing and publishing. Because the Internet is such an amorphous, evolving, mutable entity with website addresses launching, crashing and changing daily, some of these addresses may be obsolete by the time this book goes to print. But this list does give you a few starting points for your online journey. If, in the course of your electronic ventures, you find additional websites of interest, please let us know by e-mailing us at writersmarket@fw pubs.com.

AcqWeb: http://www.library.vanderbilt.edu/law/acqs/acqs.html
Although geared toward librarians and researchers, AcqWeb provides reference information useful to writers, such as library catalogs, bibliographic services, Books in Print, and other Web reference resources.

Amazon.com: http://www.amazon.com
Calling itself "Earth's Biggest Bookstore," Amazon.com has more than 2 million books available on their website at discounted prices, plus a personal notification service of new releases, reader reviews, bestseller and suggested book information.

Authorlink: http://www.authorlink.com
An information and news service for editors, literary agents and writers. Showcasing and matching quality manuscripts to publishers' needs, this site also contains interviews with editors and agents, publishing industry news, links and writer's guidelines.

Barnes and Noble Online: http://www.barnesandnoble.com
The world's largest bookstore chain's website contains 400,000 in-stock titles at discount prices as well as personalized recommendations, online events with authors and book forum access for members.

Book Zone: http://www.bookzone.com
A catalog source for books, audio books, and more, with links to other publishing opportunities, diversions and distractions, such as news, classifieds, contests, magazines, and trade groups.

Books A to Z: http://www.booksatoz.com
Information on publications services and leads to other useful websites, including areas for book research, production services, self-publishing, bookstores, organizations, and publishers.

Books and Writing Online: http://www.clark.net/pub/iz/Books/books.html
A collection of sources directing you to other sites on the net, this is a good place to jump to other areas on the Web with information pertaining to writing, literature and publishing.

BookWeb: http://www.ambook.org
This ABA site offers books news, markets, discussions groups, events, resources and other book-related information.

Bookwire: http://www.bookwire.com
A gateway to finding information about publishers, booksellers, libraries, authors, reviews and awards. Also offers information about frequently asked publishing questions and answers,

a calendar of events, a mailing list, and other helpful resources.

Children's Writing Resource Center: http://www.mindspring.com/~cbi

Presented by Children's Book Insider, The Newsletter for Children's Writers. Offers information on numerous aspects of publishing and children's literature, such as an InfoCenter, a Research Center, results of various surveys, and secrets on getting published.

Crisp: http://www.crispzine.com

Award-winning Bibliotech section features established fiction and poetry editors volunteering their creative and connective assistance to new "under35" writers, as well as multi-genre excerpts, interviews, information and inspiration for—and from—writers of all ages.

Editor & Publisher: http://www.mediainfo.com:80/edpub/ep/classi.htm

The Internet source for Editor & Publisher, *this site provides up-to-date industry news, with other opportunities such as a research area and bookstore, a calendar of events and classifieds.*

The Electronic Newsstand's Monster Magazine List: http://www.enews.com/monster

One of the largest directories of magazines on the Web. The Monster List not only provides links to their magazines, but also tracks the content of many major magazines on a continually updating basis. It also allows the user to customize their own newsstand to view only the magazines of their choice.

E-Talent.Net.Inc.: http://www.e-talentnet.com

A writer's service covering rights, critiques, publishing and other nuts and bolts aspects of the industry, including how to network and develop projects in most creative mediums from screenplays to novels to computer programs.

Inkspot: http://www.inkspot.com

An elaborate site that provides information about workshops, how-to information, copyright, quotations, writing tips, resources, contests, market information, publishers, booksellers, associations, mailing lists, newsletters, conferences, and more.

Internet Entertainment Network: http://HollywoodNetwork.com

Home to Showbiz Online.com, this site covers everything in Hollywood whether its dealmaking, music, screenwriting, or profiles of agents and Hollywood executives.

Internet Road Map to Books: http://www.bookport.com/b_roadmap.html

Leads to publishers' websites, resources for writers, book reviews, online editing, and other helpful areas.

Publishers' Catalogues Home Page: http://www.lights.com/publisher/index.html

A mammoth link collection of publishers around the world arranged geographically. This site is one of the most comprehensive directories on the Internet of publishers.

Ultimate Book List and Writer's Page: http://www.missouri.edu/~wleric/writehelp.html

Provides links and information on resources, references, authors, online writing, publishing, handouts, other websites of interest, prize winners and more.

The Write Page: http://www.writepage.com

Online newsletter for readers and writers of genre fiction, featuring information on authors, books about writing, new releases, organizations, conferences, websites, research, public service efforts writers can partake in, and writer's rights.

Glossary

Key to symbols and abbreviations is on page 3.

Advance. A sum of money a publisher pays a writer prior to the publication of a book. It is usually paid in installments, such as one-half on signing the contract; one-half on delivery of a complete and satisfactory manuscript. The advance is paid against the royalty money that will be earned by the book.

Advertorial. Advertising presented in such a way as to resemble editorial material. Information may be the same as that contained in an editorial feature, but it is paid for or supplied by an advertiser and the word "advertisement" appears at the top of the page.

All rights. See Rights and the Writer in the Minding the Details article.

Anthology A collection of selected writings by various authors or a gathering of works by one author

Assignment. Editor asks a writer to produce a specific article for an agreed-upon fee.

Auction. Publishers sometimes bid for the acquisition of a book manuscript that has excellent sales prospects. The bids are for the amount of the author's advance, advertising and promotional expenses, royalty percentage, etc. Auctions are conducted by agents.

B&W. Abbreviation for black and white photographs.

Backlist. A publisher's list of its books that were not published during the current season, but that are still in print.

Belles lettres. A term used to describe fine or literary writing—writing more to entertain than to inform or instruct.

Bimonthly. Every two months. See also *semimonthly.*

Bionote. A sentence or brief paragraph about the writer. Also called a "bio," it can appear at the bottom of the first or last page of a writer's article or short story or on a contributor's page.

Biweekly. Every two weeks.

Boilerplate. A standardized contract. When an editor says "our standard contract," he means the boilerplate with no changes. Writers should be aware that most authors and/or agents make many changes on the boilerplate.

Book packager. Draws all elements of a book together, from the initial concept to writing and marketing strategies, then sells the book package to a book publisher and/or movie producer. Also known as book producer or book developer.

Business size envelope. Also known as a #10 envelope, it is the standard size used in sending business correspondence.

Byline. Name of the author appearing with the published piece.

Category fiction. A term used to include all various labels attached to types of fiction. See also *genre.*

CD-ROM. Compact Disc-Read Only Memory. A computer information storage medium capable of holding enormous amounts of data. Information on a CD-ROM cannot be deleted. A computer user must have a CD-ROM drive to access a CD-ROM.

Chapbook. A small booklet, usually paperback, of poetry, ballads or tales.

Clean copy. A manuscript free of errors, cross-outs, wrinkles or smudges.

Clips Samples, usually from newspapers or magazines, of your *published* work.

Coffee table book. An oversize book, heavily illustrated.

Column inch. The amount of space contained in one inch of a typeset column.

Commercial novels. Novels designed to appeal to a broad audience. These are often broken down into categories such as western, mystery and romance. See also *genre.*

Commissioned work. See *assignment.*

Concept. A statement that summarizes a screenplay or teleplay—before the outline or treatment is written.

Contact sheet. A sheet of photographic paper on which negatives are transferred so you can see the entire roll of shots placed together on one sheet of paper without making separate, individual prints.

Contributor's copies. Copies of the issues of magazines sent to the author in which the author's work appears.

Cooperative publishing. See *co-publishing.*

Co-publishing. Arrangement where author and publisher share publication costs and profits of a book. Also known as *cooperative publishing.* See also *subsidy publisher.*

Copyediting. Editing a manuscript for grammar, punctuation and printing style, not subject content.

Copyright. A means to protect an author's work. See Copyright in the Minding the Details section.

Cover letter. A brief letter, accompanying a complete manuscript, especially useful if responding to an editor's request for a manuscript. A cover letter may also accompany a book proposal. A cover letter is *not* a query letter; see Targeting Your Ideas in the Getting Published section.

Derivative works. A work that has been translated, adapted, abridged, condensed, annotated or otherwise produced by altering a previously created work. Before producing a derivative work, it is necessary to secure the written permission of the copyright owner of the original piece.

Desktop publishing. A publishing system designed for a personal computer. The system is capable of typesetting, some illustration, layout, design and printing—so that the final piece can be distributed and/or sold.

Disk. A round, flat magnetic plate on which computer data may be stored.

Docudrama. A fictional film rendition of recent newsmaking events and people.

Dot-matrix. Printed type where individual characters are composed of a matrix or pattern of tiny dots. Near letter quality (see *NLQ*) dot-matrix submissions are generally acceptable to editors.

Electronic submission. A submission made by modem or on computer disk.

El-hi. Elementary to high school.

E-mail. Electronic mail. Mail generated on a computer and delivered over a computer network to a specific individual or group of individuals. To send or receive e-mail, a user must have an account with an online service, which provides an e-mail address and electronic mailbox.

Epigram. A short, witty sometimes paradoxical saying.

Erotica. Fiction or art that is sexually oriented.

Fair use. A provision of the copyright law that says short passages from copyrighted material may be used without infringing on the owner's rights.

Fax (facsimile machine). A communication system used to transmit documents over telephone lines.

Feature. An article giving the reader information of human interest rather than news. Also used by magazines to indicate a lead article or distinctive department.

Filler. A short item used by an editor to "fill" out a newspaper column or magazine page. It could be a timeless news item, a joke, an anecdote, some light verse or short humor, puzzle, etc.

First North American serial rights. See Rights and the Writer in the Minding the Details article.

Formula story. Familiar theme treated in a predictable plot structure—such as boy meets girl, boy loses girl, boy gets girl.

Frontlist. A publisher's list of its books that are new to the current season.

Galleys. The first typeset version of a manuscript that has not yet been divided into pages.

Genre. Refers either to a general classification of writing, such as the novel or the poem, or to the categories within those classifications, such as the problem novel or the sonnet. Genre fiction describes commercial novels, such as mysteries, romances and science fiction. Also called category fiction.

Ghostwriter. A writer who puts into literary form an article, speech, story or book based on another person's ideas or knowledge.

Glossy. A black and white photograph with a shiny surface as opposed to one with a non-shiny matte finish.

Gothic novel. A fiction category or genre in which the central character is usually a beautiful young girl, the setting an old mansion or castle, and there is a handsome hero and a real menace, either natural or supernatural.

Graphic novel. An adaptation of a novel in graphic form, long comic strip or heavily illustrated story, of 40 pages or more, produced in paperback form.

Hard copy. The printed copy of a computer's output.

Hardware. All the mechanically-integrated components of a computer that are not software. Circuit boards, transistors and the machines that are the actual computer are the hardware.

Home page. The first page of a World Wide Web document.

Honorarium. Token payment—small amount of money, or a byline and copies of the publication.

Hypertext. Words or groups of words in an electronic document that are linked to other text, such as a definition or a related document. Hypertext can also be linked to illustrations.

Illustrations. May be photographs, old engravings, artwork. Usually paid for separately from the manuscript. See also *package sale*.

Imprint. Name applied to a publisher's specific line or lines of books (e.g., Anchor Books is an imprint of Doubleday).

Interactive. A type of computer interface that takes user input, such as answers to computer-generated questions, and then acts upon that input.

Interactive fiction. Works of fiction in book or computer software format in which the reader determines the path the story will take. The reader chooses from several alternatives at the end of a "chapter," and thus determines the structure of the story. Interactive fiction features multiple plots and endings.

Internet. A worldwide network of computers that offers access to a wide variety of electronic resources. Originally a US Department of Defense project, begun in 1969.

Invasion of privacy. Writing about persons (even though truthfully) without their consent.

Kill fee. Fee for a complete article that was assigned but which was subsequently cancelled.

Lead time. The time between the acquisition of a manuscript by an editor and its actual publication.

Letter-quality submission Computer printout that looks typewritten.

Libel. A false accusation or any published statement or presentation that tends to expose another to public contempt, ridicule, etc. Defenses are truth; fair comment on a matter of public interest; and privileged communication—such as a report of legal proceedings or client's communication to a lawyer.

List royalty. A royalty payment based on a percentage of a book's retail (or "list") price. Compare *net royalty*.

Little magazine. Publications of limited circulation, usually on literary or political subject matter.

LORT. An acronym for League of Resident Theatres. Letters from A to D follow LORT and designate the size of the theater.

Magalog. Mail order catalog with how-to articles pertaining to the items for sale.

Mainstream fiction. Fiction that transcends popular novel categories such as mystery, romance and science fiction. Using conventional methods, this kind of fiction tells stories about people and their conflicts with greater depth of characterization, background, etc., than the more narrowly focused genre novels.

Mass market. Nonspecialized books of wide appeal directed toward a large audience. Smaller and more cheaply produced than trade paperbacks, they are found in many non-bookstore outlets, such as drug stores, supermarkets, etc.

Microcomputer A small computer system capable of performing various specific tasks with data it receives. Personal computers are microcomputers.

Midlist. Those titles on a publisher's list that are not expected to be big sellers, but are expected to have limited sales.

Midlist books are mainstream, not literary, scholarly or genre, and are usually written by new or unknown writers.

Model release. A paper signed by the subject of a photograph (or the subject's guardian, if a juvenile) giving the photographer permission to use the photograph, editorially or for advertising purposes or for some specific purpose as stated.

Modem. A device used to transmit data from one computer to another via telephone lines.

Monograph. A detailed and documented scholarly study concerning a single subject.

Multimedia. Computers and software capable of integrating text, sound, photographic-quality images, animation and video.

Multiple submissions Sending more than one poem, gag or greeting card idea at the same time. This term is often used synonymously with simultaneous submission.

Net royalty. A royalty payment based on the amount of money a book publisher receives on the sale of a book after booksellers' discounts, special sales discounts and returns. Compare list royalty.

Network. A group of computers electronically linked to share information and resources.

Newsbreak. A brief, late-breaking news story added to the front page of a newspaper at press time or a magazine news item of importance to readers.

NLQ. Near letter-quality print required by some editors for computer printout submissions. See also *dot-matrix*

Novelette. A short novel, or a long short story; 7,000 to 15,000 words approximately. Also known as a novella.

Novelization. A novel created from the script of a popular movie, usually called a movie "tie-in" and published in paperback.

Offprint. Copies of an author's article taken "out of issue" before a magazine is bound and given to the author in lieu of monetary payment. An offprint could be used by the writer as a published writing sample.

On spec. An editor expresses an interest in a proposed article idea and agrees to consider the finished piece for publication "on speculation." The editor is under no obligation to buy the finished manuscript.

One-shot feature. As applies to syndicates, single feature article for syndicate to sell; as contrasted with article series or regular columns syndicated.

One-time rights. See Rights and the Writer in the Minding the Details article.

Online Service. Computer networks accessed via modem. These services provide users with various resources, such as electronic mail, news, weather, special interest groups and shopping. Examples of such providers include America Online and CompuServe.

Outline. A summary of a book's contents in five to 15 double-spaced pages; often in the form of chapter headings with a descriptive sentence or two under each one to show the scope of the book. A screenplay's or teleplay's outline is a scene-by-scene narrative description of the story (10-15 pages for a ½-hour teleplay; 15-25 pages for a 1-hour teleplay; 25-40 pages for a 90-minute teleplay; 40-60 pages for a 2-hour feature film or teleplay).

Over-the-transom. Describes the submission of unsolicited material by a freelance writer.

Package sale. The editor buys manuscript and photos as a "package" and pays for them with one check.

Page rate. Some magazines pay for material at a fixed rate per published page, rather than per word

Parallel submission. A strategy of developing several articles from one unit of research for submission to similar magazines. This strategy differs from simultaneous or multiple submission, where the same article is marketed to several magazines at the same time.

Payment on acceptance. The editor sends you a check for your article, story or poem as soon as he decides to publish it.

Payment on publication. The editor doesn't send you a check for your material until it is published.

Pen name. The use of a name other than your legal name on articles, stories or books when you wish to remain anonymous. Simply notify your post office and bank that you are using the name so that you'll receive mail and/or checks in that name. Also called a pseudonym.

Photo feature. Feature in which the emphasis is on the photographs rather than on accompanying written material.

Plagiarism. Passing off as one's own the expression of ideas and words of another writer.

Potboiler. Refers to writing projects a freelance writer does to "keep the pot boiling" while working on major articles— quick projects to bring in money with little time or effort. These may be fillers such as anecdotes or how-to tips, but could be short articles or stories.

Proofreading. Close reading and correction of a manuscript's typographical errors.

Proscenium. The area of the stage in front of the curtain

Prospectus. A preliminary written description of a book or article, usually one page in length.

Pseudonym. See *pen name*.

Public domain. Material that was either never copyrighted or whose copyright term has expired.

Query. A letter to an editor intended to raise interest in an article you propose to write.

Release. A statement that your idea is original, has never been sold to anyone else and that you are selling the negotiated rights to the idea upon payment.

Remainders. Copies of a book that are slow to sell and can be purchased from the publisher at a reduced price. Depending on the author's book contract, a reduced royalty or no royalty is paid on remainder books.

Reporting time. The time it takes for an editor to report to the author on his/her query or manuscript.

Reprint rights. See Rights and the Writer in the Minding the Details article.

Round-up article. Comments from, or interviews with, a number of celebrities or experts on a single theme.

Royalties, standard hardcover book. 10% of the retail price on the first 5,000 copies sold; 12½% on the next 5,000; 15% thereafter.

Royalties, standard mass paperback book. 4 to 8% of the retail price on the first 150,000 copies sold.

Royalties, standard trade paperback book. No less than 6% of list price on the first 20,000 copies; 7½% thereafter.

Scanning. A process through which letter-quality printed text (see *NLQ*) or artwork is read by a computer scanner and converted into workable data.

Screenplay. Script for a film intended to be shown in theaters.

Self-publishing. In this arrangement, the author keeps all income derived from the book, but he pays for its manufacturing, production and marketing.

Semimonthly. Twice per month.

Semiweekly. Twice per week.

Serial. Published periodically, such as a newspaper or magazine.

Sidebar. A feature presented as a companion to a straight news report (or main magazine article) giving sidelights on human-interest aspects or sometimes elucidating just one aspect of the story.

Similar submission. See *parallel submission*.

Simultaneous submissions. Sending the same article, story or poem to several publishers at the same time. Some publishers refuse to consider such submissions. No simultaneous submissions should be made without stating the fact in your letter.

Slant. The approach or style of a story or article that will appeal to readers of a specific magazine. For example, a magazine may always use stories with an upbeat ending.

Slice-of-life vignette. A short fiction piece intended to realistically depict an interesting moment of everyday living.

Slides. Usually called transparencies by editors looking for color photographs.

Slush pile. The stack of unsolicited or misdirected manuscripts received by an editor or book publisher.

Software. The computer programs that control computer hardware, usually run from a disk drive of some sort. Computers need software in order to run. These can be word processors, games, spreadsheets, etc.

Speculation. The editor agrees to look at the author's manuscript with no assurance that it will be bought.

Style. The way in which something is written—for example, short, punchy sentences or flowing narrative.

Subsidiary rights. All those rights, other than book publishing rights included in a book contract—such as paperback, book club, movie rights, etc.

Subsidy publisher. A book publisher who charges the author for the cost to typeset and print his book, the jacket, etc. as opposed to a royalty publisher who pays the author.

Synopsis. A brief summary of a story, novel or play. As part of a book proposal, it is a comprehensive summary condensed in a page or page and a half, single-spaced. See also *outline*.

Tabloid Newspaper format publication on about half the size of the regular newspaper page, such as the *National Enquirer*.

Tagline. A caption for a photo or a comment added to a filler.

Tearsheet Page from a magazine or newspaper containing your printed story, article, poem or ad.

Trade. Either a hardcover or paperback book; subject matter frequently concerns a special interest. Books are directed toward the layperson rather than the professional.

Transparencies. Positive color slides; not color prints.

Treatment. Synopsis of a television or film script (40-60 pages for a 2-hour feature film or teleplay).

Unsolicited manuscript. A story, article, poem or book that an editor did not specifically ask to see.

User friendly. Easy to handle and use. Refers to computer hardware and software designed with the user in mind.

Vanity publisher. See *subsidy publisher*.

Word processor. A computer program, used in lieu of a typewriter, that allows for easy, flexible manipulation and output of printed copy.

World Wide Web (WWW). An Internet resource that utilizes hypertext to access information. It also supports formatted text, illustrations and sounds, depending on the user's computer capabilities.

Work-for-hire. See Copyright in the Minding the Details article.

YA. Young adult books.

Book Publishers Subject Index

This index will help you find publishers that consider books on specific subjects—the subjects you choose to write about. Remember that a publisher may be listed here under a general subject category such as Art and Architecture, while the company publishes *only* art history or how-to books. Be sure to consult each company's detailed individual listing, its book catalog and several of its books before you send your query or proposal. The page number of the detailed listing is provided for your convenience.

FICTION

Adventure: Ariadne 342; Atheneum Bks. for Yng. Rdrs. 98; Avon 100; Avon Flare 100; ‡b. dazzle 343; Bantam 102; ‡BDD Bks. For Yng. Rdrs. 102; ‡Bethany House 106; ‡Blue Sky Press 108; Book Creations 360; Bookcraft 109; ‡Books In Motion 110; Borealis 318; Caitlin 319; Camelot Books 117; Cave Books 121; Clarion 128; Compass Prod. 361; ‡Council for Indian Educ. 132; Davies, Robert 321; Denlingers 140; Dial Bks. for Yng. Rdrs. 140; Doubleday Adult 142; Dundurn 321; Fine, Donald I. 152; ‡General Licensing Co. 362; ‡Geringer, Laura 158; ‡Harkey 165; ‡HarperCollins Children's 166; HarperCollins 166; Holiday House 173; Houghton Mifflin Bks. for Children 175; Houghton Mifflin, Adult 175; Jones Univ., Bob 188; Landmine 350; Little, Brown, Children's 199; Lodestar 201; ‡Milkweeds for Yng. Rdrs. 213; ‡Minstrel 213; Mountaineers Books 217; ‡Nelson, Tommy 220; New Victoria 225; ‡Piñata 243; ‡Presidio 248; Pride 248; ‡Questar 252; Quintet 332; Quixote 253; Rain Dancer 253; Random House, Adult 255; Red Deer College 332; Review and Herald 257; Riverhead 259; ‡Severn House 334; Sierra Club 272; ‡Simon & Pierre 334; Snowapple 335; Soho Press 275; Turnstone 336; Vandamere 301; Weiss Assoc., Daniel 366; Whispering Coyote 308; ‡Willow Creek 311; Wordstorm Prod. 339; ‡Worldwide Library 340; Write Way 313; ‡Writers Press 314; Whitman, Albert 309

Comic Books: ‡Kitchen Sink 191

Confession: Doubleday Adult 142; ‡Harkey 165; Houghton Mifflin, Adult 175; Random House, Adult 255; Riverhead 259

Erotica: ‡Artemis 342; Blue Moon 108; ‡Book Enhancers 360; ‡Carroll & Graf 119; Circlet 127; ‡Delta Trade Paperbacks 139; Doubleday Adult 142; Ekstasis Editions 323; Gay Sunshine & Leyland 157; Houghton Mifflin, Adult 175; New Victoria 225; Orloff 232; Pride 248; Quintet 332; ‡Russian Hill 261; ‡Signet 272; ‡Triangle 290; Vandamere 301

Ethnic: Arcade 95; Arsenal Pulp 317; ‡Arte Publico 97; Atheneum Bks. for Yng. Rdrs. 98; Avalon 99; ‡Avisson 99; Avon Flare 100; Borealis 318; Branden 111; ‡Braziller, George 112; Bryant & Dillon 114; Can. Inst. of Ukrainian Studies 319; Carolina Wren 345; Chicago Spectrum 124; China Books 125; Coteau 320; ‡Council for Indian Educ. 132; ‡Derrynane 140; ‡Dial Press 141; Doubleday Adult 142; Dundurn 321; Ecco Press 146; Fine, Donald I. 152; Fjord 153; Four Walls Eight Windows 156; Gay Sunshine & Leyland 157; Harper Perennial 166; HarperCollins (Canada) 324; Holiday House 173; Houghton Mifflin Bks. for Children 175; Houghton Mifflin, Adult 175; Interlink 184; Just Us 189; Kaya 190; Lee & Low 195; Lincoln Springs 350; Little, Brown, Children's 199; Lollipop Power 350; Mage 207; Mercury House 210; Northland 228; ‡Piñata 243; Post-Apollo Press 354; Pride 248; Quintet 332; Quixote 253; Rain Dancer 253; Red Deer College 332; Riverhead 259; Royal Fireworks 260; ‡Russian Hill 261; ‡Snowapple 335; Soho Press 275; ‡Signet 272; Spinsters Ink 278; Stone Bridge 280; ‡Triangle 290; Turnstone 336; Univ. of Illinois 295; Univ. of Texas 298; Ward Hill 305; White Pine 309; YMAA Pub. Ctr. 358

Experimental: Arsenal Pulp 317; ‡Artemis 342; Atheneum Bks. for Yng. Rdrs. 98; ‡b. dazzle 343; Beach Holme 317; Black Heron Press 107; China Books 125; ‡Depth Charge 346; Doubleday Adult 142; Ekstasis Editions 323; Empyreal 323; Gay Sunshine & Leyland 157; Goose Lane 323; ‡Grove/Atlantic 163; ‡Harkey 165; HarperCollins (Canada) 324; ‡House of Anansi 325; ‡Lintel 350; Livingston Press 200; Mercury House 210; ‡New Directions 221; Post-Apollo Press 354; Pride 248; Quarry 331; Quixote 253; Rain Dancer 253; Random House, Adult 255; Red Deer College 332; Riverhead 259; Ronsdale 333; Smith, The 275; Snowapple 335; Stone Bridge 280; Third Side Press 287; Turnstone 336; Univ. of Illinois 295; York Press 340

Fantasy: Ace 86; ‡Artemis 342; Atheneum Bks. for Yng. Rdrs. 98; Avon 100; ‡Avon Science Fiction 100; ‡b. dazzle 343; Baen 101; Bantam 102; ‡BDD Bks. For Yng. Rdrs. 102; ‡Blue Sky Press 108; Blue Star 108; ‡Books In Motion 110; ‡Cartwheel 119; Circlet 127; Compass Prod. 361; Crossway Books 134; Davies, Robert 321; DAW 137; Del Rey 138; Dial Bks. for Yng. Rdrs. 140; Dundurn 321; ‡General Licensing Co. 362; ‡Geringer, Laura 158; ‡Greenwillow 161; ‡HarperCollins Children's 166; HarperCollins 166; Hollow Earth 173; Houghton Mifflin, Adult 175; Humanitas 326; Little, Brown, Children's

199; Lodestar 201; ‡Milkweeds for Yng. Rdrs. 213; ‡Minstrel 213; Naiad 218; New Victoria 225; ‡Orchard 232; Pride 248; Rain Dancer 253; Random House, Adult 255; Red Deer College 332; ‡ROC Books 259; St. Martin's 263; ‡Severn House 334; ‡Signet 272; ‡Simon & Schuster Bks. for Yng. Rdrs. 273; Snowapple 335; ‡Spectra 277; Stone Bridge 280; TOR 288; ‡Triangle 290; TSR 290; Warner Aspect 305; Warner Books 305; Whispering Coyote 308; Whitman, Albert 309; Write Way 313

Feminist: Ariadne 342; Arsenal Pulp 317; ‡Artemis 342; Bantam 102; ‡Bridge Works 113; Calyx 344; Carolina Wren 345; Chicago Spectrum 124; Circlet 127; Coteau 320; Denlingers 140; Dundurn 321; Empyreal 323; Firebrand 153; Fjord 153; Four Walls Eight Windows 156; Goose Lane 323; Harper Perennial 166; HarperCollins (Canada) 324; Houghton Mifflin, Adult 175; ‡House of Anansi 325; Interlink 184; ‡Kensington 190; Lincoln Springs 350; Little, Brown, Children's 199; Mage 207; Mercury House 210; Naiad 218; New Victoria 225; ‡Nightshade 226; Papier-Mache 236; Post-Apollo Press 354; Pride 248; Quarry 331; Riverhead 259; ‡Russian Hill 261; Snowapple 335; Soho Press 275; Spinsters Ink 278; Stone Bridge 280; Third Side Press 287; Turnstone 336

Gay/Lesbian: Arsenal Pulp 317; Bantam 102; ‡Braziller, George 112; Calyx 344; Carolina Wren 345; Circlet 127; ‡Curtis/Strongmen 135; Davies, Robert 321; Doubleday Adult 142; Empyreal 323; Firebrand 153; Gay Sunshine & Leyland 157; Houghton Mifflin, Adult 175; ‡House of Anansi 325; Little, Brown, Children's 199; Lollipop Power 350; Madwoman 351; Mercury House 210; Naiad 218; New Victoria 225; Post-Apollo Press 354; Pride 248; Quarry 331; Rising Tide 258; Riverhead 259; ‡Russian Hill 261; Spinsters Ink 278; Stone Bridge 280; ‡Stonewall Inn 281; Third Side Press 287; ‡Triangle 290

Gothic: ‡Artemis 342; Atheneum Bks. for Yng. Rdrs. 98; Dundurn 321; Ekstasis Editions 323; HarperCollins 166; Landmine 350; Lincoln Springs 350; Mercury House 210; Pride 248; ‡Triangle 290; TSR 290

Historical: ‡Alexander 88; Arcade 95; Ariadne 342; Atheneum Bks. for Yng. Rdrs. 98; ‡Avisson 99; ‡b. dazzle 343; Ballantine 101; Bantam 102; Beach Holme 317; Beacon Hill Press of KC 104; Beil, Frederic 105; Berkley Pub. Grp. 105; ‡Bethany House 106; ‡Blue Sky Press 108; Book Creations 360; Bookcraft 109; ‡Books In Motion 110; ‡Bookwrights 360; Borealis 318; Branden 111; ‡Bridge Works 113; Caitlin 319; Carolrhoda 119; ‡Chariot Children's Bks. 122; ‡Chariot/Victor 123; Chicago Spectrum 124; China Books 125; ‡Council for Indian Educ. 132; Counterpoint 132; Crossway Books 134; Databooks 136; Davies, Robert 321; Denlingers 140; ‡Derrynane 140; Dial Bks. for Yng. Rdrs. 140; Doubleday Adult 142; Dundurn 321; Ecco Press 146; Éditions La Liberté 322; Fine, Donald I. 152; ‡Forge 154; Friends United 157; Gay Sunshine & Leyland 157; ‡Geringer, Laura 158; Goose Lane 323; ‡Greenwillow 161; Harlequin 324; ‡HarperCollins Children's 166; HarperCollins 166; Harvest House 168; Hendrick-Long 170; Hiller Box Manufacturing 362; Holiday House 173; Houghton Mifflin Bks. for Children 175; Houghton Mifflin, Adult 175; Howells House 176; Kindred Prod. 327; Lincoln Springs 350; Little, Brown, Children's 199; Lodestar 201; Mage 207; ‡Milkweeds for Yng. Rdrs. 213; Nautical & Aviation 219; ‡New England 221; New Victoria 225; ‡One World 231; Orloff 232; Pelican 238; Philomel 242; Pineapple 243; ‡Presidio 248; Pride 248; Quintet 332; Rain Dancer 253; Random House, Adult 255; Red Deer College 332; Review and Herald 257; Riverhead 259; St. Martin's 263; ‡Sanders, J.S. 266; ‡Severn House 334; Sierra Club 272; ‡Signet 272; Silver Moon 365; ‡Simon & Schuster Bks. for Yng. Rdrs. 273; Snowapple 335; Soho Press 275; TOR 288; Tyndale House 292; Ward Hill 305; Weiss Assoc., Daniel 366; Whitman, Albert 309; Write Way 313; ‡Writers Press 314

Horror: ‡Artemis 342; Atheneum Bks. for Yng. Rdrs. 98; Bantam 102; ‡Books In Motion 110; Compass Prod. 361; Doubleday Adult 142; Dundurn 321; ‡Forge 154; ‡General Licensing Co. 362; ‡Harkey 165; Landmine 350; Leisure Books 196; Pride 248; Random House, Adult 255; ‡ROC Books 259; St. Martin's 263; ‡Severn House 334; ‡Signet 272; TOR 288; ‡Triangle 290; Warner Books 305; Weiss Assoc., Daniel 366; Write Way 313

Humor: Acme 342; American Atheist 91; Arcade 95; Ariadne 342; Atheneum Bks. for Yng. Rdrs. 98; Avon Flare 100; ‡b. dazzle 343; ‡BDD Bks. For Yng. Rdrs. 102; ‡Blue Sky Press 108; ‡Books In Motion 110; Camelot Books 117; Caitlin 319; ‡Cartwheel 119; Catbird 120; ‡Centennial 122; Chicago Spectrum 124; Clarion 128; Compass Prod. 361; ‡Council for Indian Educ. 132; Counterpoint 132; Davenport, May 136; Dial Bks. for Yng. Rdrs. 140; Doubleday Adult 142; Dundurn 321; ‡General Licensing Co. 362; ‡Geringer, Laura 158; ‡Greenwillow 161; ‡Harkey 165; ‡HarperCollins Children's 166; Hiller Box Manufacturing 362; Holiday House 173; Houghton Mifflin Bks. for Children 175; Houghton Mifflin, Adult 175; Key Porter 327; Little, Brown, Children's 199; ‡Little Tiger 200; Lodestar 201; ‡Milkweeds for Yng. Rdrs. 213; ‡Minstrel 213; New Victoria 225; ‡Nightshade 226; Orloff 232; Pelican 238; Post-Apollo Press 354; Pride 248; ‡Questar 252; Quixote 253; Rain Dancer 253; ‡Random House Bks. For Yng. Rdrs. 255; Red Deer College 332; Review and Herald 257; Riverhead 259; ‡Russian Hill 261; ‡Simon & Schuster Bks. for Yng. Rdrs. 273; SJL Pub. 274; ‡TSR 290; Turnstone 336; Vandamere 301; Whitman, Albert 309; ‡Willow Creek 311; Wordstorm Prod. 339

Juvenile: ‡Abbeville Kids 83; ‡Absey 85; American Diabetes Assoc. 92; Archway Paperbacks 96; Atheneum Bks. for Yng. Rdrs. 98; ‡b. dazzle 343; Bantam 102; ‡BDD Bks. For Yng. Rdrs. 102; ‡Blue Sky Press 108; Bookcraft 109; Borealis 318; Boyds Mills 111; Brown Bear 318; ‡Candlewick 117; Carolrhoda 119; ‡Cartwheel 119; ‡Chariot Children's Bks. 122; ‡Charlesbridge 123; Chicago Spectrum 124; ‡Chronicle Bks. for Children 126; Clarion 128; Cobblehill 129; Compass Prod. 361; Concordia 130; Coteau 320; ‡Council for Indian Educ. 132; Crossway Books 134; Davenport, May 136; Davies, Robert 321; Dawn 138; Dial Bks. for Yng. Rdrs. 140; Down East 142; Dundurn 321; Dutton Children's 145; Eakin Press/Sunbelt Media 145; Éditions La Liberté 322; Editions Phidal 322; Ekstasis Editions 323; ‡Farrar Straus & Giroux Bks for Yng Rdrs 151; Farrar, Straus & Giroux 151; Fiesta City 347; ‡Focus Pub. 154; Friends United 157; ‡General Licensing Co. 362; ‡Geringer, Laura 158; Godine, David R. 159; Green Bark 161; ‡Greenwillow 161; ‡Grolier 162; Grosset & Dunlap 162; Harcourt Brace, Children's 165; ‡HarperCollins Children's 166; HarperCollins (Canada) 324; Hendrick-Long 170; Heritage

House 325; Highsmith 172; Hiller Box Manufacturing 362; Holiday House 173; ‡Holt Bks. for Yng. Rdrs. 174; Houghton Mifflin Bks. for Children 175; ‡Hyperion Bks. for Children 179; Ideals Children's Books 180; Jones Univ., Bob 188; Just Us 189; Kindred Prod. 327; ‡Knopf And Crown Bks. For Yng. Rdrs. 191; Lee & Low 195; Lerner 196; ‡Les Éditions du Vermillon 327; ‡Levine, Arthur 196; Little, Brown, Children's 199; ‡Little Tiger 200; Living the Good News 200; Lodestar 201; Lollipop Power 350; Lorimer & Co., James 328; Lothrop, Lee & Shepard 202; McClanahan Book Co. 363; McElderry, Margaret K. 204; ‡Mariposa 208; Meadowbrook 210; Mega-Books 364; Milkweed 212; ‡Milkweeds for Yng. Rdrs. 213; ‡Minstrel 213; Morehouse 215; Morrow, William 215; Morrow Junior Books 216; ‡Nelson, Tommy 220; Northland 228; Orca 330; ‡Orchard 232; Pacific Educational 330; Pauline Books & Media 237; ‡Peachtree Children's 238; Peachtree 238; ‡Peel Prod. 353; Pelican 238; Philomel 242; ‡Piñata 243; Pippin 244; Pleasant Co. 245; Pride 248; ‡Puffin 251; ‡Questar 252; Quintet 332; Quixote 253; Rain Dancer 253; Raincoast 332; ‡Random House Bks. For Yng. Rdrs. 255; Random House, Inc. Juvenile Books 255; Red Deer College 332; Review and Herald 257; Ronsdale 333; Roussan 333; Royal Fireworks 260; Scholastic 268; Scholastic Canada 334; ‡Scholastic Press 268; ‡Seedling 270; ‡Sierra Club Bks. for Children 272; Silver Moon 365; ‡Simon & Schuster Bks. for Yng. Rdrs. 273; SJL Pub. 274; ‡Skinner 274; Soundprints 276; Speech Bin 277; Storm Peak 355; Thistledown 335; Tidewater Publishers 288; Tricycle 290; Tyndale House 292; Vanwell 338; ‡Victor 302; ‡Viking Children's Bks. 302; Walker & Co. 304; Ward Hill 305; Weiss Assoc., Daniel 366; Whispering Coyote 308; Whitman, Albert 309; Wisdom 312; Wordstorm Prod. 339; ‡Writers Press 314

Literary: ‡Algonquin 89; ‡Anvil 317; Arcade 95; Ariadne 342; Arsenal Pulp 317; ‡Arte Publico 97; ‡Avisson 99; Baker Books 101; Bantam 102; ‡Baskerville 103; Beach Holme 317; Beil, Frederic 105; Black Heron Press 107; Bookcraft 109; Borealis 318; ‡Braziller, George 112; ‡Bridge Works 113; Broadway Books 113; Cadmus Editions 344; Calyx 344; Can. Inst. of Ukrainian Studies 319; ‡Carroll & Graf 119; Catbird 120; Cave Books 121; Champion Books 122; Chicago Spectrum 124; China Books 125; Coffee House 129; Coteau 320; Counterpoint 132; Davenport, May 136; Davies, Robert 321; ‡Delta Trade Paperbacks 139; ‡Depth Charge 346; ‡Derrynane 140; ‡Dial Press 141; Doubleday Adult 142; Dundurn 321; Ecco Press 146; Ekstasis Editions 323; Empyreal 323; Eriksson, Paul S. 148; Faber & Faber 149; ‡Farrar Straus & Giroux Bks for Yng Rdrs 151; Fine, Donald I. 152; Fjord 153; Four Walls Eight Windows 156; ‡Geringer, Laura 158; Godine, David R. 159; Goose Lane 323; ‡Graywolf 160; ‡Greenwillow 161; ‡Grove/Atlantic 163; Gutter Press 324; ‡Harper Libros 165; Harper Perennial 166; ‡HarperCollins Children's 166; HarperCollins 166; HarperCollins (Canada) 324; Hollow Earth 173; Houghton Mifflin Bks. for Children 175; Houghton Mifflin, Adult 175; Hounslow 325; ‡House of Anansi 325; Howells House 176; Hyperion 179; Kaya 190; Knopf, Alfred A. 192; ‡Knopf And Crown Bks. For Yng. Rdrs. 191; Landmine 350; ‡Laurel Books 194; ‡Le Loup de Gouttière 327; ‡Les Éditions du Vermillon 327; Lincoln Springs 350; Little, Brown 199; Livingston Press 200; Lodestar 201; Longstreet 202; ‡MacMurray & Beck 207; ‡Macrae, John 207; Mage 207; ‡Main Street 207; ‡Mariner 208; Maritimes Arts Projects Productions 329; ‡Marlowe 209; Mercury House 210; ‡Moyer Bell 217; New Rivers 224; New York Univ. 225; NeWest Publishers 329; ‡Nightshade 226; ‡Noonday 227; ‡North Star 227; Norton, W.W. 229; Orloff 232; ‡Owl Books 234; Owl Creek 234; Passeggiata 237; Peachtree 238; Permanent Press/Second Chance 240; ‡Picador 242; Pineapple 243; Post-Apollo Press 354; Pride 248; Puckerbrush 354; Quarry 331; Rain Dancer 253; Red Deer College 332; Riverhead 259; Ronsdale 333; ‡Russian Hill 261; St. Martin's 263; ‡Sanders, J.S. 266; ‡Scribner 269; ‡Signet 272; ‡Simon & Pierre 334; ‡Smith, Gibbs 275; Smith, The 275; Snowapple 335; Soho Press 275; Somerville House 365; S. Methodist Univ. 277; ‡Still Waters 280; Stone Bridge 280; ‡Stonewall Inn 281; Stormline 355; Story Line 281; Summit Pub. Grp. 283; ‡Talese, Nan 284; Third Side Press 287; Thistledown 335; Turnstone 336; ‡Turtle Point 291; ‡Univ. Of Georgia 295; ‡Viking 302; ‡Vintage 303; White Pine 309; ‡Wyatt Book 314; Zoland 315

Mainstream/Contemporary: ‡Absey 85; Academy Chicago 85; ‡Alexander 88; ‡Algonquin 89; Arcade 95; Ariadne 342; ‡Arte Publico 97; Atheneum Bks. for Yng. Rdrs. 98; Avon Flare 100; Baker Books 101; Bantam 102; ‡BDD Bks. For Yng. Rdrs. 102; Berkley Pub. Grp. 105; ‡Bethany House 106; ‡Blue Sky Press 108; ‡Book Enhancers 360; Bookcraft 109; ‡Books In Motion 110; ‡Bookwrights 360; Caitlin 319; Camelot Books 117; ‡Chariot/Victor 123; Chicago Spectrum 124; ‡Chronicle Bks. for Children 126; Coteau 320; Davies, Robert 321; Dell 139; Denlingers 140; Dickens Press 346; Doubleday Adult 142; Dundurn 321; ‡Dunne, Thomas 144; Dutton 146; Eakin Press/Sunbelt Media 145; Ecopress 346; Éditions La Liberté 322; Ekstasis Editions 323; Fawcett Juniper 151; Fine, Donald I. 152; Fjord 153; ‡Forge 154; ‡General Licensing Co. 362; HarperCollins (Canada) 324; Houghton Mifflin, Adult 175; Howells House 176; Hyperion 179; Key Porter 327; Landmine 350; Lincoln Springs 350; Little, Brown 199; Lodestar 201; Longstreet 202; ‡Macrae, John 207; Mage 207; ‡Main Street 207; ‡Mariner 208; ‡Milkweeds for Yng. Rdrs. 213; Morrow, William 215; ‡Nightshade 226; ‡One World 231; Orloff 232; Pantheon 235; Paper Chase 235; Papier-Mache 236; Peachtree 238; Permanent Press/Second Chance 240; ‡Perspectives 240; Pineapple 243; Pippin 244; Pride 248; Quarry 331; Quintet 332; Rain Dancer 253; Random House, Adult 255; Red Deer College 332; Review and Herald 257; Riverhead 259; ‡Russian Hill 261; St. Martin's 263; Seven Stories 271; ‡Severn House 334; Sierra Club 272; ‡Signet 272; ‡Simon & Pierre 334; ‡Smith, Gibbs 275; Snowapple 335; Soho Press 275; Third Side Press 287; Turnstone 336; Univ. of Illinois 295; ‡Turtle Point 291; Univ. of Iowa 296; Univ. Press of Mississippi 299; ‡Viking 302; Villard Books 303; ‡Vintage 303; Warner Books 305; Wordstorm Prod. 339

Military/War: Naval Inst. 219; ‡Presidio 248

Multicultural: ‡Blue Sky Press 108; ‡Piñata 243

Multimedia: Serendipity 270

Mystery: Academy Chicago 85; ‡Alexander 88; Arcade 95; ‡Artemis 342; Atheneum Bks. for Yng. Rdrs. 98; Avalon 99; Avon 100; Avon Flare 100; Baker Books 101; Bantam 102; ‡BBD Bks. For Young Rdrs. 102; Berkley Pub. Grp. 105; Book Creations 360; ‡Book Enhancers 360; Bookcraft 109; ‡Books In Motion 110; Bryant & Dillon 114; ‡Carroll & Graf 119; ‡Cartwheel 119; ‡Centennial 122; Chicago Spectrum 124; Clarion 128; Compass Prod. 361; ‡Council for Indian Educ. 132;

‡Cumberland House 135; Davies, Robert 321; ‡Dead Letter 138; ‡Dell Publishing Island 139; Dial Bks. for Yng. Rdrs. 140; Doubleday Adult 142; Dundurn 321; ‡Dunne, Thomas 144; Fine, Donald I. 152; Fjord 153; ‡Forge 154; ‡Foul Play 155; Gay Sunshine & Leyland 157; ‡General Licensing Co. 362; ‡Greenwillow 161; ‡Harkey 165; HarperCollins 166; Harvest House 168; Hollow Earth 173; Houghton Mifflin Bks. for Children 175; Houghton Mifflin, Adult 175; ‡Kensington 190; Landmine 350; Lincoln Springs 350; Little, Brown, Children's 199; Lodestar 201; ‡McGregor 205; Mega-Books 364; ‡Minstrel 213; Mysterious Press 218; Naiad 218; ‡Nelson, Tommy 220; New Victoria 225; Norton, W.W. 229; Orloff 232; Owen, Richard C. 233; Permanent Press/Second Chance 240; Pocket Books 246; ‡Presidio 248; Pride 248; ‡Questar 252; Rain Dancer 253; Random House, Adult 255; ‡Random House Bks. For Yng. Rdrs. 255; Royal Fireworks 260; ‡Russian Hill 261; St. Martin's 263; Scholastic 268; ‡Scribner 269; ‡Severn House 334; ‡Signet 272; Silver Moon 365; ‡Simon & Pierre 334; ‡Simon & Schuster Bks. for Yng. Rdrs. 273; Snowapple 335; Soho Press 275; Spinsters Ink 278; Stone Bridge 280; ‡Stonewall Inn 281; Sudbury 282; Vandamere 301; ‡Walker & Co. 304; Warner Books 305; Whitman, Albert 309; Wordstorm Prod. 339; Write Way 313

Occult: ‡Artemis 342; Dundurn 321; Holmes Pub. Grp. 174; Llewellyn 200; Pride 248; Quintet 332; Rain Dancer 253; ‡Signet 272; Write Way 313

Picture Books: ‡Abbeville Kids 83; Austen Sharp 343; ‡b. dazzle 343; ‡BDD Bks. For Yng. Rdrs. 102; ‡Blue Sky Press 108; Boyds Mills 111; Carolrhoda 119; ‡Cartwheel 119; ‡Chariot Children's Bks. 122; ‡Charlesbridge 123; ‡Chronicle Bks. for Children 126; Cobblehill 129; Compass Prod. 361; Concordia 130; ‡Council for Indian Educ. 132; Doubleday Adult 142; Dundurn 321; Dutton Children's 145; ‡Farrar Straus & Giroux Bks for Yng Rdrs 151; Farrar, Straus & Giroux 151; ‡Focus Pub. 154; ‡Geringer, Laura 158; Green Bark 161; ‡Greenwillow 161; ‡Grolier 162; Grosset & Dunlap 162; Harcourt Brace, Children's 165; ‡Harkey 165; ‡HarperCollins Children's 166; HarperCollins (Canada) 324; Hiller Box Manufacturing 362; Holiday House 173; ‡Holt Bks. for Yng. Rdrs. 174; Houghton Mifflin Bks. for Children 175; ‡Humanics Children's 177; ‡Hyperion Bks. for Children 179; Ideals Children's Books 180; Key Porter 327; ‡Knopf And Crown Bks. For Yng. Rdrs. 191; Lee & Low 195; ‡Levine, Arthur 196; Little, Brown, Children's 199; ‡Little Tiger 200; Living the Good News 200; Lodestar 201; Lothrop, Lee & Shepard 202; McClanahan Book Co. 363; McElderry, Margaret K. .204; ‡Mariposa 208; Morehouse 215; ‡Nelson, Tommy 220; Northland 228; ‡North-South 228; Orca 330; ‡Orchard 232; Owl Books 364; ‡Peachtree Children's 238; ‡Peel Prod. 353; Philomel 242; ‡Piñata 243; Pippin 244; ‡Puffin 251; Quintet 332; Rain Dancer 253; Raincoast 332; ‡Random House Bks. For Yng. Rdrs. 255; Random House, Inc. Juvenile Books 255; Red Deer College 332; Scholastic 268; ‡Scholastic Press 268; ‡Silver Press 273; ‡Simon & Schuster Bks. for Yng. Rdrs. 273; Snowapple 335; ‡Tricycle 290; Whispering Coyote 308; Whitman, Albert 309; ‡Willow Creek 311; ‡Writers Press 314

Plays: Anchorage 94; ‡Anvil 317; Compass Prod. 361; Coteau 320; Dundurn 321; Ecco Press 146; Ekstasis Editions 323; Fiesta City 347; ‡Hill & Wang 172; Meriwether 211; Owen, Richard C. 233; Pacific Educational 330; Players 245; Playwrights Canada 331; Post-Apollo Press 354; Pride 248; Rain Dancer 253; Red Deer College 332; Riverhead 259; ‡Simon & Pierre 334; ‡Tambra 356; Unfinished Monument 337

Poetry (including chapbooks): ‡Absey 85; ‡Acropolis 86; ‡Ahsahta 342; ‡Anvil 317; ‡Arte Publico 97; ‡Asphodel 97; ‡Avisson 99; ‡b. dazzle 343; Beach Holme 317; ‡BOA 109; Boyds Mills 111; Cadmus Editions 344; Caitlin 319; Calyx 344; ‡Candlewick 117; Carolina Wren 345; Champion Books 122; Chatham 123; Cleveland State Univ. Poetry Center 345; Copper Canyon 131; ‡Council for Indian Educ. 132; Counterpoint 132; Dante Univ. Of America Press 136; ‡Depth Charge 346; Ecco Press 146; Ecrits Des Forges 322; Editions Du Noroît 322; Ekstasis Editions 323; ‡Focus Pub. 154; Gaff 348; ‡Graywolf 160; ‡Grove/Atlantic 163; Guernica Editions 323; Harper Perennial 166; High Plains 172; Hippocrene 172; Hippopotamus 325; ‡Hohm 173; Humanitas 326; Ideals Children's Books 180; Intertext 349; Jefferson Univ., Thomas 187; Jewish Publication 187; Kaya 190; Kroshka Books 193; ‡Le Loup de Gouttière 327; ‡Les Éditions du Vermillon 327; ‡Lintel 350; Livingston Press 200; March Street Press 208; Maritimes Arts Projects Productions 329; Meadowbrook 210; Milkweed 212; Morrow, William 215; ‡New Directions 221; New Rivers 224; New York Univ. 225; ‡Nightshade 226; ‡North Star 227; Norton, W.W. 229; Oberlin College 352; Ohio State Univ. 230; Orchises 232; Owl Creek 234; Passeggiata 237; ‡Piñata 243; Post-Apollo Press 354; ‡Pot Shard 354; Pride 248; Puckerbrush 354; Quarry 331; Rain Dancer 253; Red Deer College 332; Ronsdale 333; Royal Fireworks 260; ‡Smith, Gibbs 275; Smith, The 275; Snowapple 335; Sono Nis 335; ‡Still Waters 280; Stone Bridge 280; Stormline 355; Story Line 281; Thistledown 335; Tia Chucha 357; ‡Treasure 289; Turnstone 336; ‡Turtle Point 291; Unfinished Monument 337; ‡Univ. of Akron 293; Univ. of Arkansas 294; Univ. of California 294; ‡Univ. of Chicago 294; Univ. of Iowa 296; Univ. of Massachusetts 296; Univ. of North Texas 297; Univ. of Scranton 298; Vehicule 338; Wake Forest Univ. 304; ‡Wesleyan Univ. 308; Whispering Coyote 308; White Pine 309; Wisdom 312; ‡Yale Univ. 314

Regional: ‡Alexander 88; Beach Holme 317; Blair, John F. 107; Borealis 318; Down East 142; Eakin Press/Sunbelt Media 145; Goose Lane 323; Hendrick-Long 170; Interlink 184; ‡MacMurray & Beck 207; ‡Milkweeds for Yng. Rdrs. 213; ‡Nightshade 226; Northland 228; Pelican 238; Philomel 242; Pineapple 243; Raincoast 332; ‡Russian Hill 261; ‡Simon & Pierre 334; Stormline 355; Sunstone 283; Texas Christian Univ. 286; Thistledown 335; Tidewater Publishers 288; Univ. of Tennessee 298; Univ. Press of Colorado 299; Univ. Press of New England 300; Wisdom 312

Religious: ‡Artemis 342; Baker Books 101; Beacon Hill Press of KC 104; ‡Bethany House 106; Blue Star 108; Bookcraft 109; ‡Books In Motion 110; Branden 111; Broadman & Holman 113; ‡Chariot Children's Bks. 122; ‡Chariot/Victor 123; Compass Prod. 361; Concordia 130; Counterpoint 132; Crossway Books 134; Doubleday Adult 142; ‡Focus Pub. 154; Friends United 157; ‡Harkey 165; HarperCollins (Canada) 324; Harvest House 168; Hiller Box Manufacturing 362; Kindred Prod. 327; ‡Les Éditions du Vermillon 327; Lion Publishing 198; Living the Good News 200; Morehouse 215; Nelson, Thomas 220; ‡Nelson, Tommy 220; Pauline Books & Media 237; ‡Questar 252; Quintet 332; Rain Dancer 253; Resource Publications

365; Revell, Fleming H. 257; Review and Herald 257; ‡Riehle Found. 258; Riverhead 259; S. Methodist Univ. 277; Summit Pub. Grp. 283; Tyndale House 292; Unity 292; ‡Victor 302

Romance: ‡Avalon 99; Avon 100; Avon Flare 100; Bantam 102; Beacon Hill Press of KC 104; Berkley Pub. Grp. 105; ‡Bethany House 106; Bookcraft 109; Borealis 318; Bryant & Dillon 114; ‡Dell Publishing Island 139; Dial Bks. for Yng. Rdrs. 140; ‡Fanfare 151; ‡General Licensing Co. 362; ‡Harkey 165; Harlequin 324; Houghton Mifflin, Adult 175; Humanitas 326; ‡Kensington 190; Leisure Books 196; Lincoln Springs 350; ‡Love Spell 202; ‡Loveswept 203; ‡Milkweeds for Yng. Rdrs. 213; New Victoria 225; Pocket Books 246; Pride 248; ‡Questar 252; Rain Dancer 253; Scholastic 268; ‡Severn House 334; Silhouette 273; ‡Steeple Hill 279; Warner Books 305; Weiss Assoc., Daniel 366; Zebra Books 315

Science Fiction: Ace 86; ‡Alexander 88; ‡Artemis 342; Atheneum Bks. for Yng. Rdrs. 98; Avon 100; ‡Avon Science Fiction 100; Baen 101; Bantam 102; Berkley Pub. Grp. 105; ‡Book Enhancers 360; ‡Books in Motion 110; ‡Carroll & Graf 119; ‡Cartwheel 119; Chicago Spectrum 124; Circlet 127; Compass Prod. 361; DAW 137; Del Rey 138; Ekstasis Editions 323; ‡Farthest Star 151; Gay Sunshine & Leyland 157; ‡General Licensing Co. 362; ‡Harkey 165; HarperCollins 166; Hollow Earth 173; Landmine 350; Little, Brown, Children's 199; Lodestar 201; New Victoria 225; ‡Orchard 232; Owen, Richard C. 233; Pocket Books 246; Pride 248; Quarry 331; Rain Dancer 253; ‡ROC Books 259; Royal Fireworks 260; St. Martin's 263; ‡Severn House 334; ‡Signet 272; ‡Simon & Schuster Bks. for Yng. Rdrs. 273; SJL Pub. 274; ‡Spectra 277; Stone Bridge 280; TOR 288; ‡Triangle 290; TSR 290; Warner Aspect 305; Warner Books 305; Weiss Assoc., Daniel 366; ‡Wesleyan Univ. 308; Write Way 313

Short Story Collections: ‡Absey 85; ‡Algonquin 89; Arcade 95; Arsenal Pulp 317; ‡b. dazzle 343; Bookcraft 109; Borealis 318; ‡Bridge Works 113; Caitlin 319; Calyx 344; Champion Books 122; Chicago Spectrum 124; Chronicle 126; Circlet 127; Coffee House 129; Coteau 320; ‡Council for Indian Educ. 132; Counterpoint 132; ‡Delta Trade Paperbacks 139; Doubleday Adult 142; Dundurn 321; Ecco Press 146; Éditions La Liberté 322; Ekstasis Editions 323; Empyreal 323; Gay Sunshine & Leyland 157; ‡General Licensing Co. 362; Godine, David R. 159; Goose Lane 323; HarperCollins (Canada) 324; Houghton Mifflin, Adult 175; ‡House of Anansi 325; Humanitas 326; ‡Le Loup de Gouttière 327; ‡Les Éditions du Vermillon 327; Lincoln Springs 350; Livingston Press 200; Mage 207; Mercury House 210; Naiad 218; New Rivers 224; ‡North Star 227; Orloff 232; Owen, Richard C. 233; Owl Creek 234; Papier-Mache 236; Puckerbrush 354; Quarry 331; Quixote 253; Rain Dancer 253; Red Deer College 332; Resource Publications, 365; ‡Riehle Found. 258; Riverhead 259; Ronsdale 333; ‡Severn House 334; Snowapple 335; Somerville House 365; S. Methodist Univ. 277; Stone Bridge 280; ‡Triangle 290; TSR 290; Turnstone 336; Univ. of Illinois 295; Univ. of Missouri 296; ‡Vintage 303; White Pine 309; ‡Willow Creek 311; ‡Woman in the Moon 358; Zoland 315

Spiritual (New Age, etc.): ‡Acropolis 86; ‡Focus Pub. 154; Llewellyn 200; ‡Starburst 279; Wilshire 311; ‡Woman in the Moon 358

Sports: ‡Milkweeds for Yng. Rdrs. 213

Suspense: Arcade 95; Atheneum Bks. for Yng. Rdrs. 98; Avon 100; Avon Flare 100; Bantam 102; ‡BDD Bks. For Yng. Rdrs. 102; Berkley Pub. Grp. 105; Bookcraft 109; ‡Books In Motion 110; Bryant & Dillon 114; ‡Carroll & Graf 119; Chicago Spectrum 124; Clarion 128; DAW 137; ‡Dell Publishing Island 139; Denlingers 140; Dial Bks. for Yng. Rdrs. 140; Dickens Press 346; Doubleday Adult 142; Dundurn 321; ‡Dunne, Thomas 144; Fine, Donald I. 152; Fjord 153; ‡Forge 154; ‡Foul Play 155; Harlequin 324; HarperCollins 166; Houghton Mifflin Bks. for Children 175; Houghton Mifflin, Adult 175; Hounslow 325; Ivy League 349; ‡Kensington 190; Landmine 350; Leisure Books 196; Little, Brown, Children's 199; Lodestar 201; ‡McGregor 205; ‡Minstrel 213; Mysterious Press 218; ‡Orchard 232; ‡Presidio 248; Pocket Books 246; Pride 248; ‡Questar 252; Rain Dancer 253; Random House, Adult 255; Riverhead 259; ‡Russian Hill 261; St. Martin's 263; ‡Scribner 269; ‡Severn House 334; ‡Signet 272; Soho Press 275; TOR 288; Vandamere 301; ‡Walker & Co. 304; Warner Books 305; Wordstorm Prod. 339; Write Way 313

Translation: Catbird 120; Dante Univ. Of America Press 136; Fjord 153; Gay Sunshine & Leyland 157; Guernica Editions 323; ‡Hohm 173; Interlink 184; Italica 186; Mercury House 210; Passeggiata 237; Univ. Of California 294; Univ. of Nebraska 296; Univ. of Texas 298

Western: ‡Alexander 88; Atheneum Bks. for Yng. Rdrs. 98; Avalon 99; Avon 100; Bantam 102; Berkley Pub. Grp. 105; Book Creations 360; ‡Book Enhancers 360; Bookcraft 109; ‡Books In Motion 110; ‡Council for Indian Educ. 132; ‡Cumberland House 135; HarperCollins 166; ‡Jameson 187; Leisure Books 196; Lodestar 201; New Victoria 225; ‡Questar 252; Rain Dancer 253; Red Deer College 332; St. Martin's 263; TOR 288; Walker & Co. 304

Young Adult: Archway Paperbacks 96; Atheneum Bks. for Yng. Rdrs. 98; Bantam 102; ‡BDD Bks. For Yng. Rdrs. 102; Beach Holme 317; ‡Bethany House 106; Bookcraft 109; Borealis 318; Boyds Mills 111; Caitlin 319; ‡Candlewick 117; Chicago Spectrum 124; ‡Chronicle Bks. for Children 126; Cobblehill 129; Concordia 130; Coteau 320; Davenport, May 136; Dial Bks. for Yng. Rdrs. 140; Dundurn 321; Dutton Children's 145; ‡Edge 146; Éditions La Liberté 322; Eriako Assoc. 361; Farrar, Straus & Giroux 151; ‡Farrar Straus & Giroux Bks for Yng. Rdrs. 151; Fawcett Juniper 151; ‡Focus Pub. 154; ‡General Licensing Co. 362; ‡Geringer, Laura 158; Harcourt Brace, Children's 165; ‡Harkey 165; ‡HarperCollins Children's 166; HarperCollins (Canada) 324; Hendrick-Long 170; ‡Holt Bks. for Yng. Rdrs. 174; Houghton Mifflin Bks. for Children 175; ‡Hyperion Bks. for Children 179; Jones Univ., Bob 188; Just Us 189; ‡Knopf And Crown Bks. For Yng. Rdrs. 191; ‡Les Éditions du Vermillon 327; Little, Brown, Children's 199; Living the Good News 200; Lodestar 201; Lorimer & Co., James 328; McElderry, Margaret K. 204; ‡Mega-Books 364; Morehouse 215; ‡New England 221; Orca 330; Pacific Educational 330; ‡Peachtree Children's 238; Philomel 242; ‡Piñata 243; Pippin 244; Pride 248; ‡Puffin 251; ‡Questar 252; Rain Dancer

253; ‡Random House Bks. For Yng. Rdrs. 255; Random House, Inc. Juvenile Books 255; Red Deer College 332; Roussan 333; Scholastic 268; Scholastic Canada 334; ‡Simon & Schuster Bks. for Yng. Rdrs. 273; Snowapple 335; Speech Bin 277; Thistledown 335; TSR 290; Tyndale House 292; ‡Viking Children's Bks. 302; Walker & Co. 304; Ward Hill 305; Weiss Assoc., Daniel 366; ‡Writers Press 314

NONFICTION

Agriculture/Horticulture: American Press 93; ‡Barnegat Light 102; Bright Mountain 344; Camino Books 117; China Books 125; Counterpoint 132; Doubleday Adult 142; Dover Pub. 142; Down Home 143; Ecopress 346; ‡Haworth Press 169; Hoard, W.D. 348; Houghton Mifflin Bks. for Children 175; Houghton Mifflin, Adult 175; ‡Hungry Mind 178; Idyll Arbor 181; Iowa State Univ. 186; Key Porter 327; Libraries Unlimited 197; Lyons & Burford 203; Mountain House 352; Ohio Univ. 230; Parkway 236; ‡Prentice-Hall 247; ‡Purdue Univ. 251; Purich 331; Quixote 253; Rain Dancer 253; Stipes 280; Storey Publishing/Garden Way 281; Thunder Dog 357; Univ. of Alaska 293; Univ. of Idaho 295; Univ. of Nebraska 296; Univ. of North Texas 297; Weidner & Sons 307; Whitman, Albert 309; Windward 312; ‡Woodbridge 358

Alternative Lifestyles: Beach Holme 317; Sterling 279

Americana: ‡AGS 359; Adams Media 87; Addicus Books 87; ‡Ancestry 94; Ardsley House 96; ‡Arkansas Research 96; Atheneum Bks. for Yng. Rdrs. 98; Avanyu 99; Bantam 102; Berkshire House 106; Blair, John F. 107; Boston Mills 318; Bowling Green State Univ. 111; Branden 111; Brevet 112; Camino Books 117; Carol 118; Cave Books 121; Caxton Printers 121; ‡Centennial 122; Charles River Press 123; Children's Press 124; Clarion 128; Clear Light 128; Compass Prod. 361; Cornell Maritime 131; Creative Pub. 133; Crown Pub. Group 134; ‡Cumberland House 135; Databooks 136; Davenport, May 136; Denali 140; Denlingers 140; Doubleday Adult 142; Dover Pub. 142; Dowling Press 142; Down East 142; Down The Shore 346; Eakin Press/Sunbelt Media 145; Eastern Nat'l Assoc. 146; Ecco Press 146; Editions La Liberté 322; Elliott & Clark 147; Eriksson, Paul S. 148; ‡Excelsior Cee 149; ‡Fordham Univ. 154; ‡Fromm Int'l 157; General Pub. Grp. 158; Glenbridge 159; Godine, David R. 159; ‡Gulf 163; Harper Perennial 166; HarperCollins 166; Heyday 171; High Plains 172; Houghton Mifflin Bks. for Children 175; Houghton Mifflin, Adult 175; Howells House 176; Ideals Children's 180; Int'l Publishers 185; J & L Lee 186; Jefferson Univ., Thomas 187; Jenkins Group 362; JSA Publications 363; ‡Ketz, Louise 363; ‡KQED 192; Kroshka Books 193; Kurian Reference Books, George 363; Laing Comm. 363; Layla Prod. 363; Lehigh Univ. 195; Lexikos 196; Lincoln Springs 350; Lion Books 198; Longstreet 202; Lorien 350; Lyons & Burford 203; McDonald & Woodward 204; Macmillan General Ref. 206; ‡Main Street 207; Meyerbooks 351; Michigan State Univ. 212; Mosaic Press Miniature Books 352; Mountain House 352; ‡Mountain Press 216; Mustang Publishing 218; Mystic Seaport Museum 218; Ohio Univ. 230; Pacific Books 234; Parnassus 236; Pelican 238; Penguin Studio 239; ‡Peters, A.K. 241; Picton 243; Pleasant Co. 245; ‡Prentice-Hall 247; Pruett 250; ‡Purdue Univ. 251; Quill Driver/Word Dancer 252; Quintet 332; Quixote 253; Rain Dancer 253; Reference Press Inter'l. 256; ‡Reynolds, Morgan 258; Royal Fireworks 260; ‡Rutgers Univ. 261; Sachem Pub. Assoc. 365; ‡Sanders, J.S. 266; ‡Santa Monica 266; ‡Schiffer 267; Scholastic Canada 334; Sgt. Kirkland's 270; Shoreline 334; Silver Burdett 273; ‡Smith, Gibbs 275; Storm Peak 355; Texas Christian Univ. 286; ‡TwoDot 292; Univ. of Alaska 293; Univ. of Arizona 293; Univ. of Arkansas 294; ‡Univ. of Georgia 295; Univ. of Idaho 295; Univ. of Illinois 295; Univ. of Nebraska 296; Univ. of North Texas 297; Univ. of Oklahoma 297; Univ. of Tennessee 298; Univ. Press of Kentucky 299; Univ. Press of Mississippi 299; Univ. Press of New England 300; Upney Editions 338; Utah St. Univ. 300; Vandamere 301; Vanderbilt Univ. 301; Voyageur 304; Washington St. Univ. 305; Wayfarer 357; ‡Westcliffe 308; Westernlore 308; Wieser & Wieser 366; Wilderness Adventure Books 358; ‡Yale Univ. 314

Animals: ‡AGS 359; Adams Media 87; Alpine Pub. 90; Atheneum Bks. for Yng. Rdrs. 98; Autonomedia 99; ‡Backcountry 100; Ballantine 101; Barron's Educational Series 103; Blackbirch Press, Inc. 107; Carol 118; ‡Cartwheel 119; Cave Books 121; ‡Chronicle Bks. for Children 126; Compass Prod. 361; Crown Pub. Group 134; Denlingers 140; Doubleday Adult 142; Dover Pub. 142; ‡Dummies 144; Dutton Children's 145; Epicenter 148; Eriksson, Paul S. 148; Half Halt 163; Harper Perennial 166; HarperCollins 166; Holiday House 173; Houghton Mifflin Bks. for Children 175; Houghton Mifflin, Adult 175; ‡Howell Bk. House 176; ICS Books 180; Ideals Children's 180; Iowa State Univ. 186; Jones Univ., Bob 188; Kesend, Michael 191; Krieger Pub. 192; Little, Brown Children's 199; Lyons & Burford 203; McDonald & Woodward 204; ‡Macmillan Consumer Info. Grp. 206; Macmillan General Ref. 206; ‡Main Street 207; ‡Millbrook 213; ‡Mountain Press 216; Northland 228; Northword 228; Ohio Univ. 230; ‡Orchard 232; Pineapple 243; ‡Putnam's Sons 251; Rain Dancer 253; ‡Rainbow 254; ‡Random House Bks. For Yng. Rdrs. 255; Review and Herald 257; Seaside 269; ‡Seedling 270; ‡Signet 272; ‡Simon & Schuster Bks. for Yng. Rdrs. 273; Soundprints 276; Southfarm 277; Sterling 279; Storey Publishing/Garden Way 281; Totline Pub. 289; Trafalgar Sq. 289; Univ. of Alaska 293; Weidner & Sons 307; ‡Westcliffe 308; Whitman, Albert 309; ‡Willow Creek 311; Windward 312

Anthropology/Archaelogy: American Press 93; Autonomedia 99; Avanyu 99; ‡Baywood 104; Beacon Press 104; ‡Bergin & Garvey 105; Blackbirch Press 107; Cambridge Univ. 116; Cave Books 121; Children's Press 124; Clear Light 128; ‡Council for Indian Educ. 132; ‡Cummings & Hathaway 135; Denali 140; Doubleday Adult 142; Eagle's View 145; Evans & Co. 149; Filter Press 152; ‡Fordham Univ. 154; ‡Greenwood Press 161; ‡Greenwood Pub Grp 161; ‡Grosset 162; ‡Gulf 163; Heritage House 325; Horsdal & Schubart 325; Houghton Mifflin Bks. for Children 175; Houghton Mifflin, Adult 175; ‡House of Anansi 325; Howells House 176; ‡Icon 179; Inner Traditions Int'l 182; Insight 183; Jefferson Univ., Thomas 187; Johnson 188; Kent State Univ. 190; Knowledge, Ideas & Trends 192; Kroshka Books 193; Libraries Unlimited 197; Lone Pine 328; McDonald & Woodward 204; Macmillan General Ref. 206; Mage 207; Mayfield 210; ‡Millbrook 213; Minnesota Hist. Soc. Press 213; Natural Heritage/Natural History 329; Nelson-Hall 220; New York Univ. 225; Northland 228; Ohio Univ. 230; Parnassus 236; ‡Pendaya 353; Pennsylvania Hist. and Museum Comm. 239; Plenum 245; ‡Prentice-Hall 247; Quintet

332; Rain Dancer 253; Red Deer College 332; Review and Herald 257; ‡Rutgers Univ. 261; Sgt. Kirkland's 270; Stanford Univ. 278; Texas A&M Univ. 286; Univ. of Alaska 293; Univ. of Arizona 293; ‡Univ. of Chicago 294; ‡Univ. of Georgia 295; Univ. of Idaho 295; Univ. of Iowa 296; Univ. of Montreal 337; Univ. of Nebraska 296; Univ. of Nevada 297; Univ. of New Mexico 297; Univ. of Tennessee 298; Univ. of Texas 298; ‡Univ. Press of Florida 299; Vanderbilt Univ. 301; ‡Vintage 303; Washington St. Univ. 305; ‡Weatherhill 306; Westernlore 308; ‡Westview 308; White Cliffs Media 309; Whitman, Albert 309; ‡Yale Univ. 314

Art/Architecture:
‡Abbeville Kids 83; ‡Abbeville Press 83; ABC-CLIO 84; Aberdeen Group 84; Abrams 85; ACA Books 85; Allworth 89; American Press 93; Apollo Books 95; Art Direction 97; Asian Humanities 97; ‡Asphodel 97; Atheneum Bks. for Yng. Rdrs. 98; Avanyu 99; Balcony 343; Barron's Educational Series 103; Beil, Frederic 105; Blackbirch Press 107; Bowling Green State Univ. 111; Branden 111; ‡Braziller, George 112; Broadview 318; Bucknell Univ. 114; ‡Bullfinch 114; Calyx 344; Cambridge Univ. 116; Camino Books 117; Carol 118; Center for African-American Studies 345; Charlton 320; Children's Press 124; China Books 125; Chronicle 126; ‡Chronicle Bks. for Children 126; Clarkson Potter 128; Clear Light 128; Consultant Press 131; Counterpoint 132; Crown Pub. Group 134; ‡Da Capo Press 345; Davenport, May 136; Davies, Robert 321; Davis 137; Detselig 321; Doubleday Adult 142; Dover Pub. 142; ‡Dummies 144; Dundurn 321; Ecco Press 146; Elliott & Clark 147; Epicenter 148; Eriksson, Paul S. 148; Fairleigh Dickinson Univ. 150; Family Album 347; Flower Valley 347; ‡Fordham Univ. 154; ‡Foster, Walter 155; Four Walls Eight Windows 156; ‡Fromm Int'l 157; General Pub. Grp. 158; Godine, David R. 159; Goose Lane 323; ‡Grove/Atlantic 163; Guernica Editions 323; Gutter Press 324; ‡Harkey 165; Harper Perennial 166; HarperCollins 166; ‡Harvard Univ. 168; Hemingway Western Studies 348; High Plains 172; Holiday House 173; Hollow Earth 173; Holmes & Meier 173; Horsdal & Schubart 325; Houghton Mifflin Bks. for Children 175; Houghton Mifflin, Adult 175; Hounslow 325; Howells House 176; Hudson Hills 177; ‡Hungry Mind 178; ‡Icon 179; Ideals Children's 180; Italica 186; Jefferson Univ., Thomas 187; Kent State Univ. 190; Kesend, Michael 191; Lang, Peter 193; ‡Le Loup de Gouttière 327; Lehigh Univ. 195; Lerner 196; Libraries Unlimited 197; Little, Brown Children's 199; Lyons & Burford 203; McFarland & Co. 204; McGraw-Hill Companies, Prof. Bk. Grp. 205; Macmillan General Ref. 206; ‡Macrae, John 207; Mage 207; Mayfield 210; Meriwether 211; Minnesota Hist. Soc. Press 213; ‡Monacelli 214; Morrow, William 215; Mosaic Press Miniature Books 352; ‡Moyer Bell 217; Mystic Seaport Museum 218; Natural Heritage/Natural History 329; New York Univ. 225; North Light 227; Northland 228; Norton, W.W. 229; Ohio State Univ. 230; Ohio Univ. 230; Owen, Richard C. 233; ‡Owl Books 234; Pacific Educational 330; Parnassus 236; PBC Int'l 237; ‡Peel Prod. 353; Pelican 238; ‡Pendaya 353; Pennsylvania Hist. and Museum Comm. 239; Pogo 353; Post-Apollo Press 354; Prairie Oak 247; ‡Prentice-Hall 247; Professional Pub. 249; Pruett 250; Quarry 331; Quintet 332; ‡Race Point 354; Rain Dancer 253; Raincoast 332; Random House, Adult 255; Reference Press Int'l. 256; ‡Running Press 261; Sasquatch 267; ‡Schiffer 267; Scottwall Assoc. 355; Shoreline 334; ‡Smith, Gibbs 275; ‡Sound View 355; Sourcebooks 276; Sterling 279; Stoddart 335; Stone Bridge 280; Summit Pub. Grp. 283; Sunstone 283; ‡Talese, Nan 284; Tenth Avenue 366; Texas A&M Univ. 286; Totline Pub. 289; ‡Tricycle 290; ‡Turtle Point 291; Univ. of Alaska 293; Univ. of Alberta Press 337; Univ. of California 294; ‡Univ. of Chicago 294; ‡Univ. of Georgia 295; Univ. of Massachusetts 296; Univ. of Missouri 296; Univ. of New Mexico 297; Univ. of Scranton 298; Univ. of Tennessee 298; Univ. of Texas 298; ‡Univ. Press of Florida 299; Univ. Press of Mississippi 299; Univ. Press of New England 310; Upney Editions 338; Vanderbilt Univ. 301; ‡Visions 303; ‡Visions Comm. 357; Walch, J. Weston 304; Washington St. Univ. 305; ‡Watson-Guptill 306; ‡Weatherhill 306; ‡Wesleyan Univ. 308; ‡Westview 308; Whitman, Albert 309; ‡Whitson 309; Wiley, John 311; Williamson 311; ‡Yale Univ. 314; Zoland 315

Astrology/Psychic/New Age:
‡Acropolis 86; ‡America West Pub. 90; American Fed. 92; Austen Sharp 343; Bantam 102; Blue Star 108; Broadway Books 113; Cassandra Press 345; Celestial Arts 121; Crossing Press 134; ‡Emerald Wave 346; HarperCollins 166; Hay House 169; Holmes Pub. Grp. 174; Huntington House 179; In Print Pub. 349; Inner Traditions Int'l 182; Llewellyn 200; ‡Magickal Childe 351; ‡Marlowe 209; Ottenheimer 364; Penguin Studio 239; ‡Prometheus 249; Quest Books 252; Sterling 279; Swan-Raven 283; Valley of the Sun 300; Weiser, Samuel 307; Wild Flower 310; ‡Woman in the Moon 358

Audiocassettes:
Bantam 102; ‡Books in Motion 110; Course Crafters 361; Schirmer 268; Walch, J. Weston 304

Autiobiography:
Carolina Wren 345; Charles River Press 123; Clarkson Potter 128; Little, Brown 199; Norton, W.W. 229; Pantheon 235; Permanent Press/Second Chance 240; Soho Press 275; Storm Peak 355; Sudbury 282; Turnstone 336; Vehicle 338; Zondervan 315

Automotive:
Auto Book 343; Bonus Books 109; Fisher 153; Owen, Richard C. 233; ‡SAE Int'l 262; Systems Co. 284

Bibliographies:
Borgo 110; Family Album 347; Locust Hill 200; Scarecrow 267; ‡Whitson 309

Biography:
Academy Chicago 85; Adams Media 87; Addison Wesley Longman 87; ‡Alexander 88; ‡Algonquin 89; American Atheist 91; American Eagle 92; Apollo Books 95; Arcade 95; Arden 96; ‡Asphodel 97; Atheneum Bks. for Yng. Rdrs. 98; Avanyu 99; ‡Avisson 99; Avon 100; Balcony 343; Bantam 102; Barbour & Co. 102; Barricade 103; ‡Baskerville 103; Beil, Frederic 105; Berkshire House 106; ‡Bethany House 106; Blackbirch Graphics 360; Blackbirch Press 107; Bliss 343; Bonus Books 109; Bookcraft 109; Borgo 110; Bowling Green State Univ. 111; Branden 111; Brassey's 111; ‡Braziller, George 112; ‡Bridge Works 113; Bright Mountain 344; Broadway Books 113; Bryant & Dillon 114; Caitlin 319; Cambridge Univ. 116; Camino Books 117; Can. Plains Research 320; Carol 118; Carolina Wren 345; Carolrhoda 119; ‡Carroll & Graf 119; ‡Centennial 122; ‡Chariot Children's Bks. 122; ‡Chariot/Victor 123; Charles River Press 123; Chicago Spectrum 124; China Books 125; ‡Christian Literature 125; ‡Chronicle Bks. for Children 126; Citadel 128; Clarion 128; Clarkson Potter 128; Clear Light 128; ‡Council for Indian Educ. 132; Counterpoint 132; Creative Pub. 133; Creative Spark 361; ‡Crestwood 133; Cross Cultural 134; Crown Pub. Group 134; ‡Cummings & Hathaway 135; ‡Curtis/Strongmen 135;

‡Da Capo Press 345; Dante Univ. Of America Press 136; Databooks 136; Davidson, Harlan 137; Davies, Robert 321; Dee, Ivan R. 138; ‡Delta Trade Paperbacks 139; Denlingers 140; ‡Derrynane 140; Detselig 321; ‡Dial Press 141; ‡Dillon House 141; Discipleship Resources 141; Doubleday Adult 142; ‡Doubleday Religious 142; Dover Pub. 142; Dowling Press 142; Down Home 143; Dundurn 321; ‡Dunne, Thomas 144; Dutton 144; Eakin Press/Sunbelt Media 145; Eastern Nat'l Assoc. 146; Ecco Press 146; ECW Press 322; Éditions La Liberté 322; Ekstasis Editions 323; Elliott & Clark 147; Enslow 148; Epicenter 148; Eriksson, Paul S. 148; ‡Excelsior Cee 149; Faber & Faber 149; Family Album 347; Fine, Donald I. 152; ‡Fordham Univ. 154; Friends United 157; ‡Fromm Int'l 157; General Pub. Grp. 158; Giniger, K.S. 362; Godine, David R. 159; Goose Lane 323; ‡Grove/Atlantic 163; Guernica Editions 323; Gutter Press 324; Hancock House 164; ‡Harper Business 165; Harper Perennial 166; ‡Harperactive 166; HarperCollins 166; HarperCollins (Canada) 324; HarperSanFrancisco 167; Hastings 168; Hendrick-Long 170; Heritage House 325; High Plains 172; Hoard, W.D. 348; Holiday House 173; Holmes & Meier 173; Horsdal & Schubart 325; Houghton Mifflin Bks. for Children 175; Houghton Mifflin, Adult 175; Hounslow 325; ‡House of Anansi 325; Howells House 176; ‡Hungry Mind 178; ‡Hyperion Bks. for Children 179; I.A.A.S. Publishers 348; ‡Image Books 181; ‡Insignia 183; Int'l Publishers 185; Italica 186; J & L Lee 186; ‡Jameson 187; Jefferson Univ., Thomas 187; Jenkins Group 362; Jewish Publication 187; Jones Univ., Bob 188; Just Us 189; Kent State Univ. 190; Kesend, Michael 191; ‡Ketz, Louise 363; Key Porter 327; Kindred Prod. 327; ‡Knopf And Crown Bks. For Yng. Rdrs. 191; Knowledge, Ideas & Trends 192; Kregel Publications 192; Kroshka Books 193; Kurian Reference Books, George 363; Lake View 193; ‡Lamppost 363; Lang, Peter 193; Lawrence, Merloyd 194; Lehigh Univ. 195; Library of Virginia 350; Limelight 198; Lion Books 198; Lion Publishing 198; Little, Brown 199; Longstreet 202; McDonald & Woodward 204; ‡McGregor 205; McGuinn & McGuire 205; ‡Macmillan Bks. 205; Macmillan General Ref. 206; ‡Macrae, John 207; Madison Books 207; Mage 207; Maisonneuve 208; ‡Mariner 208; Masters Press 209; Mercury House 210; Minnesota Hist. Soc. Press 213; ‡Minstrel 213; Mitchell Lane 214; Morrow, William 215; Mosaic Press Miniature Books 352; ‡Mountain N'Air 216; ‡Moyer Bell 217; Mystic Seaport Museum 218; Naval Inst. 219; ‡New England 221; New Victoria 225; Nine Pines 329; Nodin 226; ‡Noonday 227; ‡North Point 227; ‡Northfield 227; Norton, W.W. 229; NTC/Contemporary Pub. 229; Ohio State Univ. 230; Ohio Univ. 230; ‡One World 231; Orca 330; Orchises 232; Oregon State Univ. 232; ‡Owl Books 234; Pacific Press 234; Pantheon 235; Papier-Mache 236; Partners in Publishing 353; Pauline Books & Media 237; Peachtree 238; Pelican 238; Pennsylvania Hist. and Museum Comm. 239; Permanent Press/Second Chance 240; ‡Peters, A.K. 241; ‡Picador 242; Pineapple 243; Pocket Books 246; Pride 248; Prima 249; ‡Prometheus 249; Pruett 250; Publicom 365; ‡Puffin 251; ‡Purdue Univ. 251; ‡Putnam's Sons 251; Quarry 331; Quill Driver/Word Dancer 252; Rain Dancer 253; ‡Rainbow 254; Random House, Adult 255; ‡Regan 256; Regnery Pub. 256; Republic of Texas 257; Revell, Fleming H. 257; Review and Herald 257; ‡Reynolds, Morgan 258; ‡Riehle Found. 258; ‡Rising Star 258; Riverhead 259; Rockbridge Pub. Co. 259; Ronsdale 333; Royal Fireworks 260; ‡Russian Hill 261; ‡Rutgers Univ. 261; Rutledge Hill 262; ‡SAE Int'l 262; ‡Safari 262; St. Martin's 263; ‡Sanders, J.S. 266; Sandlapper 266; Schirmer 268; Scottwall Assoc. 355; ‡Scribner 269; Seven Stories 271; Shoreline 334; Sibyl 271; ‡Signet 272; ‡Simon & Pierre 334; ‡Skinner 274; Soho Press 275; Sono Nis 335; Stoddart 335; Summit Pub. Grp. 283; Swedenborg Found. 284; ‡Talese, Nan 284; Taylor 285; Tenth Avenue 366; Texas State Hist. Assoc. 286; Thunder's Mouth 287; Times Books 288; Titan 336; Titan 336; ‡Twayne 291; 2M Comm. 366; ‡Umbrella 336; Unfinished Monument 337; Univ. of Alaska 293; Univ. of Arkansas 294; Univ. of Idaho 295; Univ. of Illinois 295; Univ. of Massachusetts 296; Univ. of Nebraska 296; Univ. of Nevada 297; Univ. of New Mexico 297; Univ. of North Texas 297; Univ. of Texas 298; Univ. Press of Kentucky 299; Univ. Press of Mississippi 299; Univ. Press of New England 300; Upney Editions 338; Utah St. Univ. 300; Vandamere 301; Vanderbilt Univ. 301; Vanwell 338; Vehicule 338; ‡Viking 302; ‡Vintage 303; Walker & Co. 304; Ward Hill 305; Warner Books 305; Washington St. Univ. 305; Watts Franklin 306; ‡Weatherhill 306; ‡Wesleyan Univ. 308; ‡Western Tanager 357; Westernlore 308; ‡Westview 308; White Cliffs Media 309; White-Boucke 357; Whitecap 339; Wiley, John 311; ‡Yale Univ. 314; Zoland 315; Zondervan 315

Booklets: Bureau for At-Risk Youth 115; Foreign Policy 154

Business/Economics: Abbott, Langer 84; Accent On Living 85; Adams Media 87; Adams-Blake 87; Adams-Hall 342; Addicus Books 87; Addison Wesley Longman 87; Aegis Publishing 88; AKTRIN 88; Allen Pub. 89; Allworth 89; Almar Press 90; Amacom 90; ‡America West Pub. 90; ‡American Bar Assoc. 91; ‡American College of Physician Executives 91; American Hospital 92; ‡American Inst. of CPAs 93; American Nurses 93; American Press 93; Atheneum Bks. for Yng. Rdrs. 98; ‡Auburn House 98; Autonomedia 99; ‡Avery Pub. Grp. 99; Avon 100; Bantam 102; Barricade 103; Barron's Educational Series 103; Berkley Pub. Group. 105; Betterway 106; Birch Lane 106; Bloomberg Press 107; BNA Books 109; Bonus Books 109; ‡Book Enhancers 360; Bookhaven 110; Brevet 112; Broadway Books 113; Bryant & Dillon 114; ‡Business & Legal Reports 115; Business McGraw-Hill 115; Butterworth-Heinemann 115; Cambridge Univ. 116; Can. Plains Research 320; Caradium Publishing 117; ‡Career Press 118; Carol 118; ‡Carroll & Graf 119; Carswell Thomson 320; Cato Inst. 120; Center for African-American Studies 345; China Books 125; Consultant Press 131; ‡Cumberland House 135; ‡Cummings & Hathaway 135; ‡Currency 135; Davidson, Harlan 137; Davies, Robert 321; Dearborn Financial 138; Detselig 321; Doubleday Adult 142; Drama Publishers 143; ‡Dummies 144; Dundurn 321; Eakin Press/Sunbelt Media 145; ‡Element 147; Engineering & Mgmt. 147; Eriako Assoc. 361; Eriksson, Paul S. 148; Fairleigh Dickinson Univ. 150; Fisher 153; ‡Forum 155; Free Press 156; ‡Gateway 157; Giniger, K.S. 362; Glenbridge 159; Great Quotations 160; ‡Greenwood Pub Grp 161; ‡Gulf 163; ‡Harper Business 165; ‡Harper Libros 165; Harper Perennial 166; HarperCollins 166; HarperCollins (Canada) 324; ‡Harvard Bus. School 167; ‡Harvard Univ. 168; Hastings 168; ‡Haworth Press 169; Health Comm. 169; Holmes & Meier 173; ‡Hoover's 174; Houghton Mifflin, Adult 175; Hounslow 325; Howells House 176; ‡HRD 176; I.A.A.S. Publishers 348; ‡ICC 179; ‡ILR 181; ‡Image Grafx 362; In Print Pub. 349; Insight 183; ‡Inter Trade 183; Intercultural 184; Int'l Found. Of Employee Benefit Plans 184; Int'l Publishers 185; Int'l Wealth 185; Iowa State Univ. 186; Jain 186; ‡Jamenair 349; ‡Jameson 187; Jenkins Group 362; Jewish Lights 187; Jist Works 188; ‡Ketz, Louise 363; Key Porter 327; Kroshka Books 193; Kurian Reference Books, George 363; Laing Comm. 363; Lang, Peter 193; Lawco 350; Libraries Unlimited 197; Lifetime Books 197; Lorimer

319; Carol 118; Cato Inst. 120; Celestial Arts 121; ‡Charlesbridge 123; Chicago Review 124; China Books 125; Church Growth Inst. 127; College Board 129; Compass Prod. 361; Corwin 131; Cottonwood 132; ‡Council for Indian Educ. 132; Course Crafters 361; Creative Spark 361; ‡Culture Concepts 321; ‡Cummings & Hathaway 135; Dante Univ. Of America Press 136; Davidson, Harlan 137; Davis 137; Denison & Co. 140; Detselig 321; Dickens Press 346; Discipleship Resources 141; Doubleday Adult 142; Dundurn 321; Eastern Press 346; Ecopress 346; Éditions La Liberté 322; Education Center 146; ETC Pub. 148; ‡Excelsior Cee 149; Free Spirit 157; Front Row Experience 348; ‡Gateway 157; ‡Gessler 158; ‡Greenwood Pub Grp 161; ‡Grosset 162; Group Pub. 162; Gryphon House 163; Gutter Press 324; Harcourt Brace Canada 324; Harper Perennial 166; Hay House 169; Heinemann 170; Highsmith 172; Hiller Box Manufacturing 362; Hi-Time 348; Houghton Mifflin, Adult 175; Howells House 176; ‡Humanics Learning 177; Humanics Pub. Grp. 177; ‡Hungry Mind 178; Hunter House 178; I.A.A.S. Pub. 348; Incentive 182; Insight 183; ‡Inter Trade 183; Intercultural 184; IRI/Skylight 186; ‡Jamenair 349; Jenkins Group 362; ‡Jossey-Bass/Pfeiffer 189; Kent State Univ. 190; ‡KQED 192; Kroshka Books 193; Kurian Reference Books, George 363; ‡Laurel Books 194; Leadership 195; ‡Learning Pub. 195; Les Éditions du Vermillon 327; Libraries Unlimited 197; Living the Good News 200; LRP Pub 203; Lucent 203; Macmillan General Ref. 206; ‡Main Street 207; Maisonneuve 208; ‡Management Tech. Inst. 351; ‡Mariner 208; Maupin House 209; Meriwether 211; Metamorphous 212; Milkweed 212; Modern Language Assoc. 214; Morehouse 215; Mountain House 352; Neal-Schuman 220; New Hope 221; New York Univ. 225; Nichols 226; ‡Noonday 227; Nova Press 229; Oasis Press 230; Octameron 230; Ohio State Univ. 230; Ohio Univ. 230; Optima 231; Oryx 233; Pacific Educ. 330; Paideia 353; Partners in Publishing 353; Peguis 330; Pencil Point 239; Peterson's 241; Phi Delta Kappa 242; ‡Pioneer Inst. 353; Planning/Comm. 245; Praeger 246; Prakken Pub. 354; ‡Prentice-Hall 247; ‡Preservation 247; Pride 248; Prometheus 249; Prufrock 250; Publicom 365; Publishers Res. Grp. 365; Quarry 331; Rain Dancer 253; ‡Rainbow 254; Reference Press Int'l. 256; Reference Service 256; Regnery Pub. 256; Reidmore 333; Religious Education 256; Resource Pub. 365; Review and Herald 257; ‡Revolutionary Press 355; ‡Rising Star 258; Riverhead 259; Royal Fireworks 260; ‡Rutgers Univ. 261; St. Anthony Messenger 263; ‡Schocken 268; Scholastic Prof. Books 268; ‡Scribner 269; Shoreline 334; Silver Moon 365; Social Science Educ. 275; South End 276; Speech Bin 277; Standard Pub. 278; ‡Starburst 279; ‡Stenhouse 279; Sugar Hill 356; Sulzburger & Graham 282; Teachers College 285; Texas Western Press 287; Thompson Educ. 336; Totline Pub. 289; ‡Treasure 289; ‡Umbrella 336; Univ. of Alaska 293; ‡Univ. of Chicago 294; Univ. of Montreal 337; Univ. of Ottawa 338; ‡Univ. of W. Ontario 338; Vandamere 301; Vanderbilt Univ. 301; Verso 339; ‡Vintage 303; Walch, J. Weston 304; Wall & Emerson 339; Weidner & Sons 307; ‡Westview 308; ‡Writers Press 314; ‡Wyndham Hall 314; ‡Yale Univ. 314

Entertainment/Games: Arden 96; Bonus Books 109; Cardoza 118; Chess 123; Dover Pub. 142; Drama Pub. 143; ‡Drew, Lisa 143; Facts On File 150; Gambling Times 348; General Pub. Grp. 158; ICS Books 180; Index Pub. Grp. 182; McFarland & Co. 204; ‡Macmillan Consumer Info. Grp. 206; ‡Minstrel 213; Piccadilly 243; Speech Bin 277; Standard Pub. 278; Sterling 279; Stuart, Lyle 282; Univ. of Nevada 297

Ethnic: ‡Arkansas Research 96; Arsenal Pulp 317; ‡Arte Publico 97; Avanyu 99; ‡Avisson 99; Balcony 343; Barricade 103; ‡Bethany House 106; Blackbirch Graphics 360; Bowling Green State Univ. 111; Broadview 318; Bryant & Dillon 114; Calyx 344; Camino Books 117; Can. Inst. of Ukrainian Stud. 319; Carol 118; Carolina Wren 345; Carolrhoda 119; Center for African-American Stud. 345; Charles River Press 123; Chicago Spectrum 124; Children's Press 124; China Books 125; Clarity Press 345; Clear Light 128; Commune-A-Key 129; Companion 130; ‡Council for Indian Educ. 132; Creative Spark 361; ‡Cummings & Hathaway 135; David, Jonathan 137; Davidson, Harlan 137; ‡Delta Trade Paperbacks 139; Denali 140; ‡Derrynane 140; Detselig 321; Discipleship Resources 141; Doubleday Adult 142; Eagle's View 145; Eakin Press/Sunbelt Media 145; Eastern Press 346; Epicenter 148; Eriako Assoc. 361; Evras 347; Fairleigh Dickinson Univ. 150; Feminist Press at CUNY 152; Filter Press 152; Fitzhenry & Whiteside 323; Guernica Editions 323; Hancock House 164; ‡Harper Libros 165; ‡Harvard Univ. 168; Heyday 171; Hippocrene 172; Holmes & Meier 173; Houghton Mifflin Bks. for Children 175; Houghton Mifflin, Adult 175; ‡Humanics Learning 177; ‡Hungry Mind 178; Hyperion Press (Canada) 326; I.A.A.S. Pub. 348; Indiana Univ. Press 182; Inner Traditions Int'l 182; Insight 183; Interlink 184; Int'l Pub. 185; Italica 186; Ivy League 349; Just Us 189; Kaya 190; ‡Knopf And Crown Bks. For Yng. Rdrs. 191; Kurian Reference Books, George 363; ‡Laurier 327; Lee & Low 195; Lerner 196; Libraries Unlimited 197; Lincoln Springs 350; Lion Books 198; Little, Brown Children's 199; Locust Hill 200; McDonald & Woodward 204; McFarland & Co. 204; ‡McGregor 205; Macmillan General Ref. 206; Mage 207; ‡Main Street 207; Maisonneuve 208; Mangajin 351; Mayfield 210; Mercury House 210; Michigan State Univ. 212; Middle Passage 351; ‡Millbrook 213; Minnesota Hist. Soc. Press 213; Mitchell Lane 214; Natural Heritage/Natural History 329; Naturegraph 219; New World 225; New York Univ. 225; NeWest Pub. 329; Nodin 226; Ohio Univ. 230; ‡One World 231; Pacific Educ. 330; Pacific View 235; Passeggiata 237; Pelican 238; ‡Piñata 243; Pruett 250; Purich 331; Rain Dancer 253; Raincoast 332; Reference Service 256; Reidmore 333; Riverhead 259; Royal Fireworks 260; ‡Rutgers Univ. 261; ‡Schocken 268; ‡Seal 269; Shoreline 334; ‡Signet 272; ‡Simon & Schuster Bks. for Yng. Rdrs. 273; South End 276; Stanford Univ. 278; Sterling 279; Stoddart 335; Stone Bridge 280; Summit Pub. Grp. 283; Temple Univ. 285; Texas A&M Univ. 286; Todd 288; Totline Pub. 289; Tuttle, Charles E. 291; 2M Comm. 366; Univ. of Alaska 293; Univ. of Arizona 293; ‡Univ. of Chicago 294; Univ. of Idaho 295; Univ. of Manitoba 337; Univ. of Massachusetts 296; Univ. of Nebraska 296; Univ. of Nevada 297; Univ. of New Mexico 297; Univ. of North Texas 297; Univ. of Oklahoma 297; Univ. of Tennessee 298; Univ. of Texas 298; Univ. Press of Kentucky 299; Univ. Press of Mississippi 299; ‡Vintage 303; Washington St. Univ. 305; ‡Wesleyan Univ. 308; ‡Westview 308; White Cliffs Media 309; White Pine 309; Whitman, Albert 309; Williamson 311; ‡Wyndham Hall 314; YMAA Pub. Ctr. 358

Fashion/Beauty: ‡Abbeville Press 83

Feminism: Carolina Wren 345; Feminist Press at CUNY 152; Firebrand 153; New Victoria 225; Publishers Assoc. 251; Spinsters Ink 278; Vehicule 338; Calyx 344

324; HarperCollins 166; HarperCollins (Canada) 324; ‡Harvard Univ. 168; Hemingway Western Studies 348; ‡Hill & Wang 172; Holmes & Meier 173; Horsdal & Schubart 325; Houghton Mifflin, Adult 175; ‡House of Anansi 325; Howells House 176; ‡Humanities Press 178; Huntington House 179; ‡Hyperion Bks. for Children 179; I.A.A.S. Pub. 348; ICS Books 180; Ide House 180; ‡ILR 181; Indiana Univ. Press 182; Insight 183; ‡Insignia 183; Interlink 184; Int'l City/County Mgmt. 184; Int'l Pub. 185; Jefferson Univ., Thomas 187; ‡Jossey-Bass/Pfeiffer 189; Key Porter 327; Kroshka Books 193; Kurian Reference Books, George 363; Lake View 193; Lang, Peter 193; ‡Laurel Books 194; Liberal Press 197; Lincoln Springs 350; Lion Books 198; Loompanics 202; Lorimer & Co., James 328; Macmillan General Ref. 206; Maisonneuve 208; Mangajin 351; ‡Mariner 208; ‡Marlowe 209; Mercury House 210; Message Co. 211; Michigan State Univ. 212; Milkweed 212; ‡Millbrook 213; Mountain House 352; ‡Moyer Bell 217; Naval Inst. 219; Nelson-Hall 220; New England Pub. Assoc. 364; New York Univ. 225; NeWest Pub. 329; Northern Illinois Univ. 227; Norton, W.W. 229; Ohio State Univ. 230; Oryx 233; Pantheon 235; Pelican 238; Pennsylvania Hist. and Museum Comm. 239; ‡Pioneer Inst. 353; Planners 245; Planning/Comm. 245; ‡PPI 246; Praeger 246; Prentice-Hall Canada 331; ‡Prentice-Hall 247; Prima 249; ‡Prometheus 249; Publishers Assoc. 251; ‡Purdue Univ. 251; Purich 331; Rain Dancer 253; Regnery Pub. 256; Reidmore 333; ‡Reynolds, Morgan 258; Riverhead 259; ‡Russian Hill 261; ‡Rutgers Univ. 261; Sachem Pub. Assoc. 365; ‡St. Martin's Scholarly & Ref. 263; ‡Sanders, J.S. 266; ‡Schocken 268; Sierra Club 272; SJL Pub. 274; Social Science Educ. 275; South End 276; Stanford Univ. 278; Stoddart 335; Stone Bridge 280; Summit Pub. Grp. 283; Teachers College 285; Temple Univ. 285; Texas A&M Univ. 286; Thompson Educ. 336; Thunder's Mouth 287; ‡Transnational 289; Univ. of Alaska 293; Univ. of Alberta Press 337; Univ. of Arkansas 294; ‡Univ. of Georgia 295; Univ. of Illinois 295; Univ. of Massachusetts 296; Univ. of Missouri 296; Univ. of Nebraska 296; Univ. of North Texas 297; Univ. of Oklahoma 297; Univ. of Ottawa 338; ‡Univ. Press of Florida 299; Univ. Press of Mississippi 299; Univ. Press of New England 300; Utah St. Univ. 300; Vanderbilt Univ. 301; Vehicule 338; Verso 301; Verso 339; ‡Vintage 303; Walch, J. Weston 304; Washington St. Univ. 305; Watts Franklin 306; Wayfinder 357; ‡Westview 308; Wilder Pub. Ctr. 310; ‡Wyndham Hall 314

Health/Medicine: Adams Media 87; Adams-Blake 87; Addicus Books 87; Addison Wesley Longman 87; ‡Allyn & Bacon 89; Almar Press 90; ‡America West Pub. 90; ‡American College of Physician Executives 91; American Diabetes Assoc. 92; American Hospital 92; American Nurses 93; American Press 93; ‡Amer. Psychiatric Press 93; Atheneum Bks. for Yng. Rdrs. 98; ‡Auburn House 98; ‡Avery Pub. Grp. 99; Avon 100; Ballantine 101; Bantam 102; Barricade 103; Barron's Educ. Series 103; ‡Baywood 104; Berkley Pub. Grp. 105; Blackbirch Press 107; Blue Poppy 108; Bonus Books 109; ‡Book Enhancers 360; Branden 111; Broadway Books 113; Brookline Books 114; Butterworth-Heinemann 115; ‡Butterworths Canada 319; Cambridge Educ. 116; Cambridge Univ. 116; Cardoza 118; Career 118; Carol 118; Cassandra Press 345; Cato Inst. 120; Celestial Arts 121; Cerier Book Dev., Alison Brown 361; ‡Chapters 122; Children's Press 124; China Books 125; Chronicle 126; ‡Chronimed 127; Commune-A-Key 129; Consumer Press 131; Crossing Press 134; Crown Pub. Grp. 134; ‡Cummings & Hathaway 135; Current Clinical Strategies 135; Davies, Robert 321; ‡Delta Trade Paperbacks 139; Detselig 321; Dimi 141; Doubleday Adult 142; Dover Pub. 142; ‡Dummies 144; Dundurn 321; ‡Element 147; ‡Emerald Wave 346; Emis, Inc. 347; Engineering & Mgmt. 147; Eriksson, Paul S. 148; Evans & Co. 149; Facts On File 150; Feminist Press at CUNY 152; Fisher 153; ‡Forge 154; Free Spirit 157; ‡Fromm Int'l 157; Giniger, K.S. 362; ‡Government Inst. 159; Graber Prod. 362; Graduate Group 160; ‡Grosset 162; Harbor 164; ‡Harper Libros 165; HarperCollins 166; HarperCollins (Canada) 324; Hastings 168; Hatherleigh Press 168; ‡Haworth Press 169; Hay House 169; Health Comm. 169; ‡Health Info. Pr. 169; ‡Henry, Joseph 171; Herbal Studies 348; ‡Hohm 173; Holmes Pub. Grp. 174; Houghton Mifflin, Adult 175; Hounslow 325; Human Kinetics 177; ‡Humanics Learning 177; Hunter House 178; I.A.A.S. Pub. 348; ICS Books 180; Idyll Arbor 181; Inner Traditions Int'l 182; ‡Innisfree 183; Insight 183; Int'l Found. Of Employee Benefit Plans 184; Int'l Medical 185; Ivy League 349; Jain 186; Jenkins Group 362; Jewish Lights 187; Jones Univ., Bob 188; Kali 350; ‡Kensington 190; Kesend, Michael 191; Key Porter 327; ‡KQED 192; Krieger Pub. 192; Kroshka Books 193; ‡Kumarian 193; Laing Comm. 363; ‡Lamppost 363; Lawrence, Merloyd 194; Libraries Unlimited 197; Lifetime Books 197; ‡Lippincott 198; ‡Lippincott-Raven 198; Llewellyn 200; McFarland & Co. 204; ‡Macmillan Bks. 205; Macmillan General Ref. 206; ‡Main Street 207; ‡Maradia 351; ‡Marcus 329; ‡Marlowe 209; Masters Press 209; Mayfield 210; Metamorphous 212; Meyerbooks 351; ‡Millbrook 213; Mosaic Press Miniature Books 352; ‡Muir, John 217; NASW Press 218; Naturegraph 219; New Harbinger 221; New York Univ. 225; Newjoy Press 225; ‡Northstone 330; Norton, W.W. 229; NTC/Contemporary Pub. 229; Ohio Univ. 230; Olson, C. 352; ‡One World 231; Open Road 231; Oryx 233; Ottenheimer 364; ‡Owl Books 234; Pacific Press 234; Pacific View 235; Pacific View 353; Peachtree 238; Pelican 238; Penguin Studio 239; PennWell 240; ‡Perspectives 240; ‡Peters, A.K. 241; ‡Pioneer Inst. 353; Plenum 245; ‡Practice Mgmt. 246; Precept 247; Prentice-Hall Canada 331; ‡Prentice-Hall 247; Prima 249; Productive 331; ‡Prometheus 249; ‡Putnam's Sons 251; Quest Books 252; ‡Race Point 354; Rain Dancer 253; Random House, Adult 255; ‡Rawson 255; Regnery Pub. 256; Review and Herald 257; ‡Rising Star 258; Riverhead 259; ‡Rodale 260; Running Press 261; ‡Rutgers Univ. 261; ‡San Francisco 266; ‡Santa Monica 266; ‡Schocken 268; ‡Scribner 269; ‡Seal 269; Shoreline 334; Sidran 271; ‡Signet 272; South End 276; S. Methodist Univ. 277; Speech Bin 277; ‡Starburst 279; Sterling 279; Stillpoint 280; Storm Peak 355; Success Pub. 282; Sulzberger & Graham 282; Summers 283; Summit Pub. Grp. 283; ‡Surrey 283; Swan-Raven 283; Systems Co. 284; ‡Talese, Nan 284; ‡Tarcher, Jeremy 285; Taylor 285; Temple Univ. 285; Ten Speed 286; Texas Western Press 287; Third Side Press 287; Times Books 288; Todd 288; ‡Tricycle 290; Tuttle, Charles E. 291; 2M Comm. 366; Unfinished Monument 337; Unity 292; Univ. of Alaska 293; Univ. of Montreal 337; Univ. Press of Mississippi 299; Vanderbilt Univ. 301; VGM Career Horizons 302; ‡Viking 302; ‡Vintage 303; ‡Visions 303; Volcano 303; Walch, J. Weston 304; Walker & Co. 304; Wall & Emerson 339; Warner Books 305; Weidner & Sons 307; Weiser, Samuel 307; Whitman, Albert 309; Wieser & Wieser 366; Wiley, John 311; Woodbine House 312; ‡Woodbridge 358; Woodland 313; ‡Workman 313; ‡Wyndham Hall 314; ‡Yale Univ. 314; YMAA Pub. Ctr. 358

Hi-Lo: Cambridge Educ. 116; ‡Crestwood 133; National Textbook 219

History: ‡AGS 359; ‡A&B 83; ‡Abbeville Press 83; ABC-CLIO 84; Academy Chicago 85; Adams Media 87; Addison Wesley Longman 87; ‡Alexander 88; ‡Algonquin 89; American Atheist 91; ‡Ancestry 94; Appalachian Mountain Club 95; Arcade 95; Ardsley House 96; ‡Arkansas Research 96; Aronson, Jason 96; Arsenal Pulp 317; Atheneum Bks. for Yng. Rdrs. 98; Autonomedia 99; Avanyu 99; ‡Avisson 99; Avon 100; Balcony 343; Bantam 102; Barricade 103; ‡Baylor Univ. 343; Beil, Frederic 105; Berkshire House 106; Birch Lane 106; Blackbirch Press 107; Bliss 343; Bookcraft 109; Borealis 318; Boston Mills 318; Bowling Green State Univ. 111; Branden 111; Brassey's 111; ‡Braziller, George 112; Brevet 112; ‡Bridge Works 113; Bright Mountain 344; Broadview 318; Broadway Books 113; Bryant & Dillon 114; Bucknell Univ. 114; Caitlin 319; Cambridge Univ. 116; Camino Books 117; Can. Inst. of Ukrainian Stud. 319; Can. Library Assoc. 319; Can. Plains Research 320; Carol 118; ‡Carroll & Graf 119; ‡Cartwheel 119; Catholic Univ. of America 120; ‡Centennial 122; Center for African-American Stud. 345; ‡Chariot/Victor 123; Charles River Press 123; Chatham 123; Chicago Review 124; Chicago Spectrum 124; Children's Press 124; China Books 125; Citadel 128; Clarion 128; Clear Light 128; Companion 130; Cornell Maritime 131; ‡Council for Indian Educ. 132; Counterpoint 132; Creative Pub. 133; Creative Spark 361; Cross Cultural 134; Crown Pub. Grp. 134; ‡Cumberland House 135; ‡Cummings & Hathaway 135; ‡Da Capo Press 345; Dante Univ. Of America Press 136; Databooks 136; Davidson, Harlan 137; Davies, Robert 321; Dee, Ivan R. 138; Denali 140; ‡Derrynane 140; Detselig 321; Dickens Press 346; ‡Dillon House 141; Discipleship Resources 141; Doubleday Adult 142; ‡Doubleday Religious 142; Dover Pub. 142; Down East 142; Down Home 143; Down The Shore 346; ‡Drew, Lisa 143; Dundurn 321; ‡Dunne, Thomas 144; Dutton Children's 145; Eagle's View 145; Eakin Press/Sunbelt Media 145; Eastern Nat'l Assoc. 146; Ecco Press 146; Éditions La Liberté 322; Eerdmans, William B. 146; ‡Elephant 147; Elliott & Clark 147; Epicenter 148; Eriksson, Paul S. 148; ETC Pub. 148; ‡Excelsior Cee 149; Faber & Faber 149; Facts On File 150; Fairleigh Dickinson Univ. 150; Family Album 347; Feminist Press at CUNY 152; Filter Press 152; Fine, Donald I. 152; Fitzhenry & Whiteside 323; ‡Fordham Univ. 154; Foreign Policy 154; ‡Fortress 155; ‡Forum 155; Four Walls Eight Windows 156; ‡Fromm Int'l 157; Gem Guides 158; Giniger, K.S. 362; Glenbridge 159; Golden West 159; Goose Lane 323; ‡Greenwood Pub Grp 161; ‡Grove/Atlantic 163; Guernica Editions 323; Gutter Press 324; Hancock House 164; Harper Perennial 166; HarperCollins 166; HarperCollins (Canada) 324; ‡Harvard Univ. 168; ‡Hellgate 170; Hendrick-Long 170; Heritage 171; Heritage House 325; Heyday 171; High Plains 172; ‡Hill & Wang 172; Hippocrene 172; Holiday House 173; Holmes & Meier 173; Horsdal & Schubart 325; Houghton Mifflin Bks. for Children 175; Houghton Mifflin, Adult 175; Hounslow 325; ‡House of Anansi 325; Howell Press 176; Howells House 176; ‡Humanities Press 178; ‡Hungry Mind 178; ‡Hyperion Bks. for Children 179; I.A.A.S. Pub. 348; ICS Pub. 180; Ide House 180; ‡ILR 181; Indiana Hist. Soc. 349; Indiana Univ. Press 182; Inner Traditions Int'l 182; ‡Insignia 183; Interlink 184; International Marine 185; Int'l Pub. 185; Italica 186; J & L Lee 186; ‡Jameson 187; Jefferson Univ., Thomas 187; Jewish Lights 187; Jewish Publication 187; Johnson 188; JJones Univ., Bob 188; JSA Publications 363; ‡Judaica 189; Kent State Univ. 190; Kesend, Michael 191; ‡Ketz, Louise 363; Kinseeker 191; ‡Knopf And Crown Bks. For Yng. Rdrs. 191; Knowledge, Ideas & Trends 192; ‡KQED 192; Krieger Pub. 192; Kroshka Books 193; Kurian Reference Books, George 363; Laing Comm. 363; Lake View 193; Lang, Peter 193; Laurel Books 194; Layla Prod. 363; Lehigh Univ. 195; Lerner 196; Lexikos 196; Liberal Press 197; Libraries Unlimited 197; Library of Virginia 350; Limelight 198; Lincoln Springs 350; Lion Books 198; Little, Brown 199; Little, Brown Children's 199; Livingston Press 200; Lone Pine 328; Longstreet 202; Lorien 350; Lorimer & Co., James 328; Lucent 203; ‡Lynx Images 328; McDonald & Woodward 204; McFarland & Co. 204; ‡McGregor 205; McGuinn & McGuire 205; ‡Macmillan Bks. 205; Macmillan General Ref. 206; ‡Macrae, John 207; Madison Books 207; Mage 207; Maisonneuve 208; ‡Mariner 208; Maritimes Arts Projects Productions 329; ‡Marlowe 209; Meyerbooks 351; Michigan State Univ. 212; Milkweed 212; ‡Millbrook 213; ‡Millenium 213; Minnesota Hist. Soc. Press 213; Morehouse 215; Morrow, William 215; Mosaic Press Miniature Books 352; Motorbooks 216; ‡Mountain Press 216; Mystic Seaport Museum 218; Natural Heritage/Natural History 329; Nautical & Aviation 219; Naval Inst. 219; ‡New England 221; New England Pub. Assoc. 364; New Victoria 225; New York Univ. 225; NeWest Pub. 329; Nodin 226; ‡North Point 227; Northern Illinois Univ. 227; Northland 228; Norton, W.W. 229; Ohio State Univ. 230; Ohio Univ. 230; Orca 330; ‡Orchard 232; Oregon State Univ. 232; Owen, Richard C. 233; ‡Owl Books 234; Pacific View 235; Pantheon 235; Parnassus 236; Passeggiata 237; ‡Peachtree Children's 238; Peachtree 238; Pelican 238; Pennsylvania Hist. and Museum Comm. 239; Permanent Press/Second Chance 240; Picton 243; Pineapple 243; ‡Planet Dexter 244; Pocket Books 246; Pogo 353; Praeger 246; Prairie Oak 247; ‡Prentice-Hall 247; ‡Presidio 248; Pride 248; Primer 354; ‡Prometheus 249; Pruett 250; Publishers Assoc. 251; ‡Puffin 251; ‡Purdue Univ. 251; Purich 331; Quarry 331; Quintet 332; Rain Dancer 253; Raincoast 332; Random House, Adult 255; ‡Random House Bks. For Yng. Rdrs. 255; Red Deer College 332; Regnery Pub. 256; Reidmore 333; Republic of Texas 257; Review and Herald 257; ‡Reynolds, Morgan 258; Riverhead 259; Rockbridge Pub. Co. 259; Ronsdale 333; Royal Fireworks 260; ‡Rutgers Univ. 261; Sachem Pub. Assoc. 365; St. Anthony Messenger 263; St. Bede's 263; ‡St. Martin's Scholarly & Ref. 263; ‡San Francisco 266; ‡Sanders, J.S. 266; Sandlapper 266; Sasquatch 267; ‡Schiffer 267; ‡Schocken 268; Scholastic Canada 334; Scottwall Assoc. 355; ‡Seaside 269; Sgt. Kirkland's 270; Shoreline 334; Silver Burdett 273; Silver Moon 365; ‡Simon & Schuster Bks. for Yng. Rdrs. 273; ‡Skinner 274; Social Science Educ. 275; Sono Nis 335; South End 276; S. Methodist Univ. 277; Southfarm 277; Stackpole 278; Stanford Univ. 278; Sterling 279; Stoddart 335; Storm Peak 355; Summit Pub. Grp. 283; Sunstone 283; ‡Talese, Nan 284; Tamarack 356; Taylor 285; Teachers College 285; Temple Univ. 285; Texas A&M Univ. 286; Texas State Hist. Assoc. 286; Texas Western Press 287; Tidewater Pub. 288; ‡Twayne 291; ‡Umbrella 336; United Church Publishing House 337; ‡Univ. of Akron 293; Univ. of Alaska 293; Univ. of Alberta Press 337; Univ. of Arkansas 294; Univ. of California 294; ‡Univ. of Georgia 295; Univ. of Idaho 295; Univ. of Illinois 295; Univ. of Iowa 296; Univ. of Manitoba 337; Univ. of Massachusetts 296; Univ. of Missouri 296; Univ. of Montreal 337; Univ. of Nebraska 296; Univ. of Nevada 297; Univ. of New Mexico 297; Univ. of North Texas 297; Univ. of Oklahoma 297; Univ. of Ottawa 337; Univ. of Tennessee 298; Univ. of Texas 298; ‡Univ. Press of Florida 299; Univ. Press of Kentucky 299; Univ. Press of Mississippi 299; Univ. Press of New England 300; Upney Editions 338; Utah St. Univ. 300; Vandamere 301; Vanderbilt Univ. 301; Vanwell 338; Vehicule 338; ‡Vestal 302; ‡Viking 302; ‡Voyageur 304; Walch, J. Weston 304; Ward Hill 305; Warner Books 305; Washington St. Univ. 305; Watts Franklin 306; Wayfinder 357; ‡Weatherhill 306; ‡Wesleyan Univ. 308; ‡Western Tanager

357; Westernlore 308; ‡Westview 308; Whitecap 339; Whitman, Albert 309; Wieser & Wieser 366; Wilderness Adventure Books 358; Wiley, John 311; ‡Writers Press 314; ‡Yale Univ. 314; Zondervan 315

Hobby: Adams Media 87; ‡Ancestry 94; ‡Arkansas Research 96; Berkshire House 106; Betterway 106; Blue Sky 343; Bonus Books 109; ‡Bookworks 360; Brewers 112; C&T Pub. 117; Carol 118; ‡Carstens 119; ‡Centennial 122; Charlton 320; Chicago Review 124; Children's Press 124; Collector 129; ‡Council for Indian Educ. 132; Crown Pub. Grp. 134; ‡Cumberland House 135; Davies, Robert 321; Dimi 141; Doubleday Adult 142; Dover Pub. 142; Dowling Press 142; Down Home 143; ‡Dummies 144; Eagle's View 145; Éditions La Liberté 322; Eriksson, Paul S. 148; ‡Excelsior Cee 149; Fox Chapel Publishing 156; ‡Gateway 157; Gem Guides 158; ‡Honor 174; Houghton Mifflin, Adult 175; ‡House Of Collectibles 176; Index Pub. Grp. 182; Interweave 185; Jenkins Group 362; JSA Publications 363; Kalmbach 189; Kesend, Michael 191; ‡KQED 192; Lark Books 194; Lifetime Books 197; Little, Brown Children's 199; Lyons & Burford 203; Macmillan General Ref. 206; ‡Millbrook 213; Mosaic Press Miniature Books 352; Mustang Publishing 218; No Starch 226; Norton, W.W. 229; Oak Knoll 229; Owl Books 364; Paper Chase 235; Parnassus 236; Productive 331; Quintet 332; Rain Dancer 253; ‡Rainbow 254; Reference Press Int'l. 256; Riverhead 259; ‡Rodale 260; ‡Schiffer 267; Scholastic Canada 334; ‡Seaworthy 269; Sono Nis 335; Stackpole 278; Sterling 279; Storey Publishing/Garden Way 281; Stuart, Lyle 282; Success Pub. 282; Sulzburger & Graham 282; Summit Pub. Grp. 283; ‡Vestal 302; Voyageur 304; Weidner & Sons 307; Weka Pub. 307; Whitman, Albert 309; Wieser & Wieser 366; ‡Willow Creek 311

House And Home: Betterway 106; Blue Sky 343; Bonus Books 109; Ortho 233; Pantheon 235; Sourcebooks 276; Sterling 279; Taylor 285; Warner Books 305

How-To: aatec 341; ‡Abbeville Press 83; Abbott, Langer 84; Aberdeen Group 84; ‡Absey 85; Accent On Living 85; Accent Publications 86; Adams Media 87; Adams-Blake 87; Addicus Books 87; ‡Alexander 88; Allen Pub. 89; Allworth 89; Almar Press 90; Alpine Pub. 90; Amacom 90; ‡American Bar Assoc. 91; American Correctional Assoc. 91; American Diabetes Assoc. 92; Amherst Media 94; ‡Ancestry 94; Andrews McMeel 95; Appalachian Mountain Club 95; ‡Arkansas Research 96; Art Direction 97; ASA 97; Auto Book 343; Avon 100; ‡b. dazzle 343; Ballantine 101; Bantam 102; ‡Barnegat Light 102; Barricade 103; Bentley, Robert 105; Berkley Pub. Grp. 105; ‡Bethany House 106; Betterway 106; Blackbirch Graphics 360; Bloomberg Press 107; Blue Sky 343; Bookcraft 109; Bookhaven 110; ‡Bookworks 360; ‡Bookwrights 360; ‡Bridge Learning Systems 344; ‡Bridge Street 344; ‡Bristol Fashion 113; Bryant & Dillon 114; Business McGraw-Hill 115; Butterworth-Heinemann 115; Cambridge Educ. 116; Camino Books 117; C&T Pub. 117; Caradium Publishing 117; Cardoza 118; ‡Career Press 118; Carol 118; Cassandra Press 345; CCC Pub. 121; ‡Centennial 122; Cerier Book Dev., Alison Brown 361; Chicago Review 124; Chicago Spectrum 124; China Books 125; Chosen Books 125; Christian Publications 125; ‡Chronimed 127; Church Growth Inst. 127; Clarkson Potter 128; College Board 129; Concordia 130; Consultant Press 131; Consumer Press 131; Corkscrew 345; Cornell Maritime 131; ‡Council for Indian Educ. 132; ‡Countryman 132; Countrysport 133; Craftsman 133; Crown Pub. Grp. 134; ‡Culture Concepts 321; ‡Cumberland House 135; Databooks 136; David, Jonathan 137; Davies, Robert 321; Dearborn Financial 138; Denlingers 140; Detselig 321; Dimi 141; Doubleday Adult 142; ‡Doubleday Religious 142; Dover Pub. 142; Dowling Press 142; Down Home 143; ‡Dummies 144; Eagle's View 145; Ecopress 346; Eriksson, Paul S. 148; ‡Excelsior Cee 149; Fairview 150; Fiesta City 347; Flower Valley 347; Focal 153; Focus on the Family 154; Fox Chapel Publishing 156; Gambling Times 348; Gay Sunshine & Leyland 157; Graduate Group 160; Graphic Arts Tech. Found. 160; Group Pub. 162; Gryphon House 163; Half Halt 163; Hamilton, Alexander 164; Hancock House 164; Hanser Gardner 164; ‡Harper Libros 165; Harper Perennial 166; HarperCollins 166; HarperSanFrancisco 167; Hastings 168; ‡Health Info. Pr. 169; Heinemann 170; Herbal Studies 348; Heritage 171; Heritage House 325; Hollow Earth 173; Houghton Mifflin, Adult 175; Hounslow 325; ‡House Of Collectibles 176; ‡Howell Bk. House 176; Human Kinetics 177; ‡Humanics Learning 177; Hyperion Press (Canada) 326; I.A.A.S. Pub. 348; ICS Books 180; ‡Image Books 181; ‡Image Grafx 362; In Print Pub. 349; Insight 183; ‡Inter Trade 183; International Marine 185; Int'l Wealth 185; Interweave 185; IRI/Skylight 186; Jain 186; ‡Jamenair 349; Jelmar 349; Jenkins Group 362; Jist Works 188; ‡Jossey-Bass/Pfeiffer 189; JSA Publications 363; Kalmbach 189; Kesend, Michael 191; ‡KQED 192; Laing Comm. 363; ‡Lamppost 363; ‡Laurier 327; Layla Prod. 363; Lifetime Books 197; Lion Books 198; Living the Good News 200; Llewellyn 200; Lone Eagle 201; Loompanics 202; McDonald & Woodward 204; McGraw-Hill Companies, Prof. Bk. Grp. 205; McGraw-Hill Ryerson 328; ‡McGregor 205; ‡Macmillan Bks. 205; ‡Macmillan Brands 206; ‡Macmillan Consumer Info. Grp. 206; Macmillan General Ref. 206; ‡Main Street 207; ‡Management Tech. Inst. 351; Masters Press 209; Maupin House 209; Maximum 210; Meadowbrook 210; Menasha Ridge 364; Meriwether 211; Message Co. 211; Metamorphous 212; Morrow, William 215; Motorbooks 216; ‡Mountain N'Air 216; ‡Mountain Press 216; Mountaineers Books 217; Mustang Publishing 218; Mystic Seaport Museum 218; Naturegraph 219; New Hope 221; No Starch 226; ‡Nolo 226; North Light 227; Nova Press 229; NTC/Contemporary Pub. 229; Oak Knoll 229; Oasis Press 230; Ohio Univ. 230; Olson, C. 352; Orchises 232; Ortho 233; Owl Books 364; Pacific Press 234; Paideia 353; Paladin 235; Paper Chase 235; Parrot 353; Partners in Publishing 353; Peachpit 238; ‡Peel Prod. 353; ‡Perspectives 240; Phi Delta Kappa 242; Piccadilly 243; Pineapple 243; ‡Planet Dexter 244; ‡PPI 246; Pride 248; Productive 331; PROMPT 250; Prufrock 250; Publicom 365; ‡Que 252; Quill Driver/Word Dancer 252; Quintet 332; ‡Race Point 354; Ragged Mountain 253; Rain Dancer 253; ‡Rainbow 254; Rainbow Pub. 254; Red Eye 355; Reference Press Int'l. 256; Resource Pub. 365; Revell, Fleming H. 257; ‡Revolutionary Press 355; Richboro 258; ‡Rising Star 258; Rocky Mountain 333; ‡Rodale 260; Royal Fireworks 260; ‡Running Press 261; ‡Safari 262; ‡Santa Monica 266; ‡Schiffer 267; Seaside 269; Self-Counsel 334; Sierra Club 272; ‡Signet 272; ‡Sourcebooks 276; Speech Bin 277; ‡Starburst 279; Steel Balls 355; Sterling 279; Stoddart 335; Stoeger 280; Stone Bridge 280; ‡Stoneydale 281; Storey Publishing/Garden Way 281; Stuart, Lyle 282; Success Pub. 282; Sulzburger & Graham 282; Summit Pub. Grp. 283; Sunstone 283; ‡Surrey 283; Systems Co. 284; ‡Tambra 356; ‡Tarcher, Jeremy 285; Taylor 285; Tech. Books for the Layperson 356; Ten Speed 286; Tenth Avenue 366; Thunder Dog 357; Tiare 287; Titan 336; Todd 288; ‡Tricycle 290; Turtle Press 291; 2M Comm. 366; ‡Visions 303; ‡Visions Comm. 357; ‡Watson-Guptill 306; ‡Weatherhill

306; Weiser, Samuel 307; Weka Pub. 307; Whitehorse 358; ‡Wiese, Michael 310; Wilderness Adventure Books 358; Wilderness Press 310; Wiley, John 311; Williamson 311; ‡Willow Creek 311; Wilshire 311; ‡Windsor 312; ‡Workman 313; Writer's Digest 314; YMAA Pub. Ctr. 358

Humanities: Asian Humanities 97; Borgo 110; Dante Univ. Of America Press 136; Feminist Press at CUNY 152; ‡Fordham Univ. 154; Free Press 156; ‡Greenwood Press 161; ‡Greenwood Pub Grp 161; Indiana Univ. Press 182; Lang, Peter 193; ‡Learning Pub. 195; Roxbury 260; ‡St. Martin's Scholarly & Ref. 263; Stanford Univ. 278; Univ. of Arkansas 294; ‡Whitson 309; Zondervan 315

Humor: Accent On Living 85; Adams Media 87; Andrews McMeel 95; Arsenal Pulp 317; ASA 97; Atheneum Bks. for Yng. Rdrs. 98; ‡b. dazzle 343; Ballantine 101; Bantam 102; Barbour & Co. 102; Birch Lane 106; Bonus Books 109; Bookcraft 109; Carol 118; Catbird 120; CCC Pub. 121; ‡Centennial 122; Chicago Spectrum 124; Citadel 128; Clarion 128; Clarkson Potter 128; Clear Light 128; Commune-A-Key 129; Compass Prod. 361; Corkscrew 345; ‡Council for Indian Educ. 132; Crown Pub. Grp. 134; ‡Cumberland House 135; Davenport, May 136; Davies, Robert 321; ‡Dell Trade Paperbacks 139; Detselig 321; Doubleday Adult 142; ‡Doubleday Religious 142; Dover Pub. 142; Dowling Press 142; Down Home 143; Epicenter 148; Eriksson, Paul S. 148; ‡Excelsior Cee 149; Fiesta City 347; Friends United 157; ‡General Licensing Co. 362; General Pub. Grp. 158; Great Quotations 160; ‡Gulf 163; ‡Harkey 165; Harper Perennial 166; HarperCollins 166; Hastings 168; Hoard, W.D. 348; Holiday House 173; ‡Honor 174; Houghton Mifflin Bks. for Children 175; Houghton Mifflin, Adult 175; Hounslow 325; ‡Hungry Mind 178; ICS Books 180; ‡Image Books 181; Jenkins Group 362; JSA Publications 363; Key Porter 327; Knowledge, Ideas & Trends 192; ‡KQED 192; ‡Lamppost 363; Layla Prod. 363; Limelight 198; Longstreet 202; ‡Main Street 207; Meadowbrook 210; Menasha Ridge 364; Meriwether 211; Mosaic Press Miniature Books 352; Mustang Publishing 218; New Leaf 224; NTC/Contemporary Pub. 229; Orchises 232; Owen, Richard C. 233; Paladin 235; Peachtree 238; Pelican 238; Piccadilly 243; ‡Pinnacle 244; Pocket Books 246; Price Stern Sloan 248; Pride 248; ‡Questar 252; Quixote 253; Ragged Mountain 253; Rain Dancer 253; ‡Rainbow 254; Raincoast 332; Random House, Adult 255; Red Deer College 332; Republic of Texas 257; Review and Herald 257; ‡Revolutionary Press 355; ‡Rising Star 258; Riverhead 259; Royal Fireworks 260; Rutledge Hill 262; ‡Sanders, J.S. 266; Sandlapper 266; Seaside 269; ‡Smith, Gibbs 275; Sound & Vision 335; ‡Spectacle Lane 355; Sterling 279; Stoddart 335; Stuart, Lyle 282; Summit Pub. Grp. 283; Titan 336; 2M Comm. 366; ‡Weatherhill 306; White-Boucke 357; ‡Willow Creek 311; Wordstorm Prod. 339; ‡Workman 313

Illustrated Book: ‡AGS 359; ‡A&B 83; ‡Abbeville Kids 83; ‡Abbeville Press 83; Abrams 85; Adams Media 87; Alpine Pub. 90; Amer. & World Geo. Pub. 359; Avanyu 99; ‡b. dazzle 343; Balcony 343; Ballantine 101; Bantam 102; Beil, Frederic 105; Betterway 106; Blackbirch Graphics 360; Blackbirch Press 107; Bliss 343; Boston Mills 318; Branden 111; ‡Braziller, George 112; Broadway Books 113; ‡Bullfinch 114; Can. Plains Research 320; C&T Pub. 117; Caxton Printers 121; ‡Charlesbridge 123; Chatham 123; ‡Chronicle Bks. for Children 126; Compass Prod. 361; ‡Council for Indian Educ. 132; Countrysport 133; ‡Cumberland House 135; Darlington Prod. 136; Databooks 136; Davies, Robert 321; Davis 137; Detselig 321; Dial Books for Yng. Rdrs. 140; Doubleday Adult 142; ‡Doubleday Religious 142; Dover Pub. 142; Down Home 143; Down The Shore 346; ‡Dummies 144; Dundurn 321; Eakin Press/Sunbelt Media 145; Elliott & Clark 147; Eriako Assoc. 361; ‡Falcon Press 150; ‡Fromm Int'l 157; ‡General Licensing Co. 362; General Pub. Grp. 158; Giniger, K.S. 362; Godine, David R. 159; Goose Lane 323; Great Quotations 160; ‡Grolier 162; ‡Gulf 163; Harper Perennial 166; ‡Health Info. Pr. 169; Heritage House 325; Hiller Box Manufacturing 362; Holiday House 173; ‡Holt Bks. for Yng. Rdrs. 174; Houghton Mifflin Bks. for Children 175; Houghton Mifflin, Adult 175; Hounslow 325; Howell Press 176; Howells House 176; Humanics Pub. Grp. 177; ‡Hunt & Thorpe 326; ‡Hyperion Bks. for Children 179; I.A.A.S. Pub. 348; ICS Books 180; Ideals Pubs. 181; ‡Image Books 181; Inst. of Police Tech. & Mgmt. 183; International Marine 185; Jefferson Univ., Thomas 187; Jenkins Group 362; Jewish Lights 187; Jewish Publication 187; ‡Judaica 189; Just Us 189; Kalmbach 189; Kesend, Michael 191; Key Porter 327; ‡Kitchen Sink 191; ‡KQED 192; Kurian Reference Books, George 363; Laing Comm. 363; ‡Lamppost 363; Lark Books 194; Layla Prod. 363; Lee & Low 195; Lexikos 196; Library of Virginia 350; Limelight 198; Living the Good News 200; Lodestar 201; Longstreet 202; Lothrop, Lee & Shepard 202; McDonald & Woodward 204; Macmillan General Ref. 206; Mage 207; ‡Main Street 207; Maritimes Arts Projects Productions 329; Minnesota Hist. Soc. Press 213; Mosaic Press Miniature Books 352; Mountain Automation 352; ‡New England 221; Northword 228; Ohio Univ. 230; Orca 330; ‡Orchard 232; Ottenheimer 364; Owen, Richard C. 233; Pelican 238; ‡Pendaya 353; Penguin Studio 239; Pennsylvania Hist. and Museum Comm. 239; Peter Pauper 241; Philomel 242; ‡Picador 242; Pogo 353; Pride 248; Publicom 365; ‡Puffin 251; ‡Que 252; ‡Questar 252; Quintet 332; Raincoast 332; Random House, Adult 255; Red Deer College 332; Reference Press Int'l. 256; ‡Regan 256; Royal Fireworks 260; Sandlapper 266; ‡Santa Monica 266; ‡Schiffer 267; Scottwall Assoc. 355; ‡Seaworthy 269; Shoreline 334; ‡Smith, Gibbs 275; Soundprints 276; Sourcebooks 276; Speech Bin 277; Sta-Kris 355; Standard Pub. 278; Stoddart 335; Tamarack 356; Tenth Avenue 366; Texas State Hist. Assoc. 286; Tidewater Pub. 288; Titan 336; Titan 336; Totline Pub. 289; ‡Treasure 289; Univ. of New Mexico 297; Vanderbilt Univ. 301; Verso 301; ‡Watson-Guptill 306; Wayfinder 357; ‡Weatherhill 306; ‡Westcliffe 308; Whitman, Albert 309; Wilderness Adventure Books 358; ‡Willow Creek 311; Windward 312; ‡Yale Univ. 314

Juvenile Books: ‡A&B 83; ‡Abbeville Kids 83; Abingdon 84; ‡Absey 85; Accent Publications 86; Adams Media 87; Addison Wesley Longman 87; American Diabetes Assoc. 92; Archway Paperbacks 96; ‡Arte Publico 97; Atheneum Bks. for Yng. Rdrs. 98; Augsburg 98; ‡b. dazzle 343; Baker Books 101; Barbour & Co. 102; Barron's Educ. Series 103; Behrman House 105; Beil, Frederic 105; Blackbirch Graphics 360; Blackbirch Press 107; Bookcraft 109; Borealis 318; Boyds Mills 111; Branden 111; Camino Books 117; ‡Candlewick 117; C&T Pub. 117; Carolrhoda 119; ‡Cartwheel 119; Chariot Children's Bks. 122; ‡Chariot/Victor 123; ‡Charlesbridge 123; Chicago Review 124; Chicago Spectrum 124; Child Welfare League Of America 124; Children's Press 124; China Books 125; ‡Chronicle Bks. for Children 126; Clarion 128; Cobblehill 129; Compass Prod. 361; Concordia 130; ‡Council for Indian Educ. 132; Creative Spark 361; ‡Crestwood 133; Davenport, May 136; David,

Jonathan 137; Davies, Robert 321; Dawn 138; Denison & Co. 140; Dial Books for Yng. Rdrs. 140; ‡Dillon House 141; Dover Pub. 142; Down East 142; Dundurn 321; Dutton Children's 145; Eakin Press/Sunbelt Media 145; Eastern Nat'l Assoc. 146; Éditions La Liberté 322; Eerdmans, William B. 146; Enslow 148; Eriako Assoc. 361; ‡Explorer's Guide 149; Facts On File 150; Fairview 150; Farrar, Straus & Giroux 151; Feminist Press at CUNY 152; Fiesta City 347; Focus on the Family 154; ‡Focus Pub. 154; Free Spirit 157; Friends United 157; ‡General Licensing Co. 362; Godine, David R. 159; Graber Prod. 362; ‡Grolier 162; Grosset & Dunlap 162; Group Pub. 162; Gryphon House 163; Harcourt Brace, Children's 165; ‡Harkey 165; ‡Harperactive 166; HarperCollins (Canada) 324; Hendrick-Long 170; Highsmith 172; Hiller Box Manufacturing 362; Holiday House 173; ‡Holt Bks. for Yng. Rdrs. 174; Houghton Mifflin Bks. for Children 175; Houghton Mifflin, Adult 175; Humanics Pub. Grp. 177; ‡Hunt & Thorpe 326; ‡Hyperion Bks. for Children 179; Hyperion Press (Canada) 326; I.A.A.S. Pub. 348; ICS Books 180; Ideals Children's 180; Incentive 182; Jewish Lights 187; Jewish Publication 187; Jones Univ., Bob 188; ‡Judaica 189; Just Us 189; Kali 350; Key Porter 327; ‡Knopf And Crown Bks. For Yng. Rdrs. 191; Laing Comm. 363; ‡Lamppost 363; Lark Books 194; Layla Prod. 363; Lee & Low 195; Lerner 196; ‡Les Éditions du Vermillon 327; Liguori 197; Little, Brown Children's 199; ‡Little Simon 199; Living the Good News 200; Lodestar 201; Lorimer & Co., James 328; Lothrop, Lee & Shepard 202; Lucent 203; McClanahan Book Co. 363; McElderry, Margaret K. 204; Mage 207; ‡Mariposa 208; Marlor 209; Meadowbrook 210; Messner 211; ‡Millbrook 213; ‡Minstrel 213; Mitchell Lane 214; ‡Moody 214; Morehouse 215; Morrow Junior Books 216; Mountaineers Books 217; ‡Muir, John 217; ‡Nelson, Tommy 220; ‡New England 221; New Hope 221; Nine Pines 329; Northword 228; Orca 330; ‡Orchard 232; Ottenheimer 364; Owl Books 364; Pacific Educ. 330; Pacific Press 234; Pacific View 235; Pacific View 353; Pauline Books & Media 237; ‡Peachtree Children's 238; Peachtree 238; Pelican 238; ‡Perspectives 240; Philomel 242; ‡Piñata 243; Pippin 244; ‡Planet Dexter 244; Players 245; Pleasant Co. 245; ‡PPI 246; Price Stern Sloan 248; Pride 248; ‡Prometheus 249; Prufrock 250; ‡Puffin 251; Quarry 331; ‡Questar 252; Quixote 253; Rain Dancer 253; ‡Rainbow 254; Raincoast 332; ‡Random House Bks. For Yng. Rdrs. 255; Random House, Inc. Juvenile Books 255; Red Deer College 332; Review and Herald 257; Ronsdale 333; ‡Rosen Pub. Grp. 260; Royal Fireworks 260; ‡Running Press 261; Sandlapper 266; Sasquatch 267; Scholastic Canada 334; Scholastic 268; ‡Scholastic Press 268; Scholastic Prof. Books 268; ‡Seedling 270; Sierra Club 272; ‡Sierra Club Bks. For Children 272; Silver Burdett 273; Silver Moon 365; ‡Silver Press 273; ‡Simon & Schuster Bks. for Yng. Rdrs. 273; SJL Pub. 274; ‡Skinner 274; ‡Smith, Gibbs 275; Soundprints 276; Speech Bin 277; Standard Pub. 278; Sterling 279; Stoddart 335; Storey Publishing/Garden Way 281; Summit Pub. Grp. 283; Tenth Avenue 366; Tidewater Pub. 288; Totline Pub. 289; ‡Treasure 289; ‡Tricycle 290; Twenty-First Century 291; Tyndale House 292; ‡Umbrella 336; ‡Univ. of Ok. Nat'l Res. Ctr. 357; Vanwell 338; ‡Victor 302; ‡Viking Children's Bks. 302; ‡Visions 303; ‡Visions Comm. 357; Volcano 303; Walker & Co. 304; Ward Hill 305; Watts Franklin 306; Whitecap 339; Whitman, Albert 309; Wiley, John 311; Williamson 311; ‡Willow Creek 311; Windward 312; ‡Writers Press 314; Zondervan 315; Jenkins Group 362

Labor/Management: Abbott, Langer 84; ‡Baywood 104; BNA Books 109; Drama Pub. 143; ‡FPMI 156; ‡Gulf 163; Hamilton, Alexander 164; ‡ILR 181; Intercultural 184; Int'l Pub. 185; Temple Univ. 285

Language and Literature: ABC-CLIO 84; Adams Media 87; Anchorage 94; Arsenal Pulp 317; ‡Arte Publico 97; Asian Humanities 97; ‡Avisson 99; Bantam 102; Barron's Educ. Series 103; Beil, Frederic 105; Borealis 318; Bowling Green State Univ. 111; ‡Braziller, George 112; ‡Bridge Works 113; Broadview 318; Brookline Books 114; Bryant & Dillon 114; Calyx 344; Can. Inst. of Ukrainian Stud. 319; Carol 118; Carolina Wren 345; Catholic Univ. of America 120; Chicago Spectrum 124; China Books 125; Clarion 128; Clarkson Potter 128; College Board 129; Coteau 320; Cottonwood 132; Counterpoint 132; Course Crafters 361; ‡CSLI 134; ‡Cummings & Hathaway 135; Dante Univ. Of America Press 136; Davenport, May 136; Davidson, Harlan 137; Davies, Robert 321; Dee, Ivan R. 138; Doubleday Adult 142; ‡Doubleday Religious 142; Dover Pub. 142; Down Home 143; Dundurn 321; ‡Duquesne Univ. 144; Eastern Press 346; Ecco Press 146; Éditions La Liberté 322; Education Center 146; ‡Excelsior Cee 149; Facts On File 150; Family Album 347; Feminist Press at CUNY 152; ‡Fordham Univ. 154; Four Walls Eight Windows 156; ‡Fromm Int'l 157; ‡Gessler 158; Goose Lane 323; ‡Graywolf 160; ‡Greenwood Pub Grp 161; ‡Grove/Atlantic 163; Guernica Editions 323; Gutter Press 324; ‡Harkey 165; Harper Perennial 166; HarperCollins (Canada) 324; ‡Harvard Univ. 168; Heinemann 170; Highsmith 172; Hippocrene 172; Hippopotamus 325; Houghton Mifflin Bks. for Children 175; Houghton Mifflin, Adult 175; ‡House of Anansi 325; Humanics Learning 177; Humanitas 326; ‡Hungry Mind 178; Indiana Univ. Press 182; Intertext 349; Italica 186; Jefferson Univ., Thomas 187; Jewish Publication 187; Kaya 190; Kent State Univ. 190; Lake View 193; Lang, Peter 193; Langenscheidt 194; ‡Laurier 327; ‡Le Loup de Gouttière 327; Lehigh Univ. 195; ‡Les Éditions du Vermillon 327; Libraries Unlimited 197; Lincoln Springs 350; Livingston Press 200; Locust Hill 200; Longstreet 202; ‡Macmillan Bks. 205; ‡Macmillan Consumer Info. Grp. 206; Macmillan General Ref. 206; ‡MacMurray & Beck 207; Mage 207; Maisonneuve 208; Mangajin 351; Maritimes Arts Projects Productions 329; Maupin House 209; Mayfield 210; Mercury House 210; Michigan State Univ. 212; Milkweed 212; Modern Language Assoc. 214; National Textbook 219; Neal-Schuman 219; New York Univ. 225; ‡Noonday 227; Norton, W.W. 229; Ohio State Univ. 230; Ohio Univ. 230; Optima 231; Oregon State Univ. 232; Oryx 233; ‡Owl Books 234; Passeggiata 237; Peguis 330; Pencil Point 239; ‡Picador 242; Post-Apollo Press 354; ‡Prentice-Hall 247; Pride 248; ‡Prometheus 249; Puckerbrush 354; ‡Purdue Univ. 251; Quarry 331; Rain Dancer 253; ‡Revolutionary Press 355; ‡Reynolds, Morgan 258; ‡Rising Star 258; Riverhead 259; Ronsdale 333; Roxbury 260; Royal Fireworks 260; Russian Info. Svces. 261; ‡Rutgers Univ. 261; ‡St. Martin's Scholarly & Ref. 263; ‡Sanders, J.S. 266; ‡Scribner 269; Serendipity 270; Sierra Club 272; ‡Signet 272; ‡Simon & Pierre 334; Smith, The 275; Stanford Univ. 278; Stoddart 335; Stone Bridge 280; Stormline 355; Story Line 281; Texas Christian Univ. 286; Texas Western Press 287; Totline Pub. 289; ‡Turtle Point 291; Twayne 291; Univ. of Alaska 293; Univ. of California 294; ‡Univ. of Chicago 294; ‡Univ. of Georgia 295; Univ. of Idaho 295; Univ. of Illinois 295; Univ. of Iowa 296; Univ. of Montreal 337; Univ. of Nebraska 296; Univ. of Nevada 297; Univ. of North Texas 297; Univ. of Oklahoma 297; Univ. of Ottawa 338; Univ. of Scranton 298; Univ. of Tennessee 298; Univ. of Texas 298; ‡Univ. Press of Florida 299; Univ. Press of Kentucky 299; Univ. Press of Mississippi 299; Utah St. Univ. 300; Vanderbilt Univ. 301; Vehicule 338; Verso 339; ‡Viking 302; ‡Vintage

303; Wadsworth 304; Wake Forest Univ. 304; Walch, J. Weston 304; ‡Weatherhill 306; Weidner & Sons 307; ‡Wesleyan Univ. 308; White Pine 309; Whitman, Albert 309; Writer's Digest 314; ‡Wuerz 340; ‡Yale Univ. 314; York Press 340; Zoland 315

Law: Allworth 89; ‡American Bar Assoc. 91; American Correctional Assoc. 91; Beacon Press 104; BNA Books 109; Butterworth-Heinemann 115; ‡Butterworths Canada 319; ‡C Q Books 115; Carswell Thomson 320; ‡Drew, Lisa 143; ‡Government Inst. 159; Graduate Group 160; Hamilton, Alexander 164; Indiana Univ. Press 182; Inst. of Police Tech. & Mgmt. 183; Lawyers & Judges 195; LRP Pub 203; ‡Macmillan Consumer Info. Grp. 206; Nolo 226; Norton, W.W. 229; Ohio State Univ. 230; Phi Delta Kappa 242; Planners 245; Purich 331; ‡Quorum 253; ‡Rothman, Fred B. 260; Self-Counsel 334; Summers 283; Temple Univ. 285; ‡Transnational 289; ‡Univ. of Chicago 294; Wiley, John 311

Literary Criticism: ‡Asphodel 97; Barron's Educ. Series 103; Borgo 110; Bucknell Univ. 114; Dundurn 321; Fairleigh Dickinson Univ. 150; Godine, David R. 159; Guernica Editions 323; Gutter Press 324; Hippopotamus 325; Holmes & Meier 173; ‡House of Anansi 325; Intertext 349; Lang, Peter 193; Maisonneuve 208; Maritimes Arts Projects Productions 329; NeWest Pub. 329; Northern Illinois Univ. 227; Passeggiata 237; ‡Picador 242; ‡Purdue Univ. 251; ‡Simon & Pierre 334; Smith, The 275; Stanford Univ. 278; Texas Christian Univ. 286; Univ. of Arkansas 294; Univ. of Massachusetts 296; Univ. of Missouri 296; Univ. of Tennessee 298; Univ. of Texas 298; Univ. Press of Mississippi 299; Wake Forest Univ. 304; York Press 340

Marine Subjects: ‡Bristol Fashion 113; Cornell Maritime 131; Gaff 348; Howell Press 176; International Marine 185; McGraw-Hill Companies, Prof. Bk. Grp. 205; Marlor 209; Mystic Seaport Museum 218; Sono Nis 335; Wescott Cove 307

Military/War: ‡AGS 359; Adams Media 87; ‡Algonquin 89; American Eagle 92; ‡Arkansas Research 96; Avon 100; Bantam 102; Blair, John F. 107; ‡Bookwrights 360; Brassey's 111; Carol 118; Charlton 320; Crown Pub. Grp. 134; ‡Cumberland House 135; ‡Cummings & Hathaway 135; ‡Da Capo Press 345; Darlington Prod. 136; Databooks 136; ‡Derrynane 140; Detselig 321; Doubleday Adult 142; Dundurn 321; Eakin Press/Sunbelt Media 145; Eastern Nat'l Assoc. 146; ‡Elephant 147; Fairleigh Dickinson Univ. 150; Fine, Donald I. 152; ‡Fordham Univ. 154; ‡Greenwood Pub Grp 161; Harper Perrennial 166; ‡Hellgate 170; Hippocrene 172; Houghton Mifflin, Adult 175; Howell Press 176; Howells House 176; I.A.A.S. Pub. 348; ‡Insignia 183; Jefferson Univ., Thomas 187; ‡Ketz, Louise 363; Key Porter 327; Kurian Reference Books, George 363; Libraries Unlimited 197; Lincoln Springs 350; McFarland & Co. 204; McGraw-Hill Ryerson 328; Macmillan General Ref. 206; Maisonneuve 208; ‡Mariner 208; Michigan State Univ. 212; Motorbooks 216; Natural Heritage/Natural History 329; Nautical & Aviation 219; Naval Inst. 219; New York Univ. 225; Ohio Univ. 230; Paladin 235; Penguin Studio 239; Praeger 246; ‡Presidio 248; ‡Putnam's Sons 251; Quintet 332; Reference Service 256; Regnery Pub. 256; Republic of Texas 257; ‡Reynolds, Morgan 258; Riverhead 259; Rockbridge Pub. Co. 259; Rutledge Hill 262; Sachem Pub. Assoc. 365; ‡Sanders, J.S. 266; ‡Schiffer 267; Sgt. Kirkland's 270; ‡Signet 272; Southfarm 277; Stackpole 278; Stoddart 335; Summit Pub. Grp. 283; Texas A&M Univ. 286; Univ. of Alaska 293; Univ. of Nebraska 296; Univ. of North Texas 297; Univ. Press of Kentucky 299; Vandamere 301; Vanwell 338; ‡Vintage 303; ‡Westview 308; Wieser & Wieser 366; Wiley, John 311; ‡Yale Univ. 314

Money/Finance: Accent On Living 85; Adams Media 87; Adams-Blake 87; Adams-Hall 342; Allen Pub. 89; Almar Press 90; ‡American Bar Assoc. 91; American Nurses 93; ‡Avery Pub. Grp. 99; Betterway 106; Bloomberg Press 107; Bonus Books 109; ‡Book Enhancers 360; Bookhaven 110; Broadway Books 113; Bryant & Dillon 114; Business McGraw-Hill 115; Cambridge Educ. 116; Caradium Publishing 117; ‡Career Press 118; Carol 118; Cato Inst. 120; Charlton 320; Consumer Press 131; ‡Cumberland House 135; ‡Cummings & Hathaway 135; Davies, Robert 321; Dearborn Financial 138; Detselig 321; Dimi 141; Doubleday Adult 142; ‡Dummies 144; Dundurn 321; Focus on the Family 154; ‡Gateway 157; Harper Perrennial 166; HarperCollins (Canada) 324; ‡Haworth Press 169; Hay House 169; Hensley, Virgil 171; ‡Hoover's 174; Houghton Mifflin, Adult 175; Hounslow 325; I.A.A.S. Pub. 348; Insight 183; ‡Inter Trade 183; Int'l Wealth 185; Jenkins Group 362; Key Porter 327; Kroshka Books 193; ‡Lamppost 363; Lifetime Books 197; McGraw-Hill Companies, Prof. Bk. Grp. 205; McGraw-Hill Ryerson 328; ‡McGregor 205; ‡Macmillan Consumer Info. Grp. 206; Macmillan General Ref. 206; ‡Main Street 207; ‡Moody 214; New World 225; New York Univ. 225; ‡Nolo 226; ‡Northfield 227; NTC/Contemporary Pub. 229; Oasis Press 230; Pilot 243; Planning/Comm. 245; Prentice-Hall Canada 331; ‡Prentice-Hall 247; Pride 248; Productive 331; Quill Driver/Word Dancer 252; ‡Rainbow 254; Reference Press Int'l. 256; ‡Reynolds, Morgan 258; ‡Signet 272; Sourcebooks 276; ‡Starburst 279; Steel Balls 355; Stoddart 335; Success Pub. 366; Sulzburger & Graham 282; Summit Pub. Grp. 283; Systems Co. 284; Ten Speed 286; ‡Times Business 288; Todd 288; ‡ULI 292; ‡Univ. of Chicago 294; Wiley, John 311; ‡Windsor 312

Multicultural: ABC-CLIO 84; Broadway Books 113; ‡Chronicle Bks. for Children 126; Facts On File 150; Feminist Press at CUNY 152; ‡Gessler 158; Pacific View 353; Guernica Editions 323; Highsmith 172; Intercultural 184; Judson 189; Lee & Low 195; ‡Mariposa 208; Mitchell Lane 214; ‡Oryx 233; Pacific View 235; ‡Piñata 243; ‡Rutgers Univ. 261; ‡Umbrella 336; Volcano 303; Ward Hill 305

Multimedia: Addison Wesley Longman 87; ‡Amer. Water Works 94; ‡Butterworths Canada 319; Cardoza 118; Duke 143; Ecopress 346; Group Pub. 162; ‡Gulf 163; ‡Harkey 165; ‡Harperactive 166; Jist Works 188; Liguori 197; ‡Lynx Images 328; McGraw-Hill Companies, Prof. Bk. Grp. 205; Macmillan General Ref. 206; Mountain Automation 352; Paideia 353; Paladin 235; Precept 247; Rain Dancer 253; Reference Press Int'l. 256; Review and Herald 257; ‡SAE Int'l 262; Serendipity 270; ‡Upstart 300; Wadsworth 304; Walch, J. Weston 304; ‡Wuerz 340; YMAA Pub. Ctr. 358

Music/Dance: Abingdon 84; American Catholic Press 342; American Press 93; ‡A-R 95; Ardsley House 96; Arsenal Pulp 317; Atheneum Bks. for Yng. Rdrs. 98; Betterway 106; Birch Lane 106; Bliss 343; Branden 111; Bucknell Univ. 114; Cambridge Univ. 116; Cambridge Univ. 116; Carol 118; ‡Cartwheel 119; Center for African-American Stud. 345; Centerstream

122; Chicago Spectrum 124; Children's Press 124; ‡Cummings & Hathaway 135; ‡Da Capo Press 345; Dance Horizons 136; ‡Delta Trade Paperbacks 139; Doubleday Adult 142; Dover Pub. 142; Dowling Press 142; ‡Dummies 144; Ecco Press 146; ECW Press 322; Éditions La Liberté 322; Fairleigh Dickinson Univ. 150; Fallen Leaf 347; Feminist Press at CUNY 152; General Pub. Grp. 158; Glenbridge 159; ‡Greenwood Pub Grp 161; Guernica Editions 323; Harper Perennial 166; HarperCollins 166; ‡Harvard Univ. 168; Houghton Mifflin Bks. for Children 175; Houghton Mifflin, Adult 175; ‡Humanics Learning 177; Indiana Univ. Press 182; Inner Traditions Int'l 182; JSA Publications 363; Krieger Pub. 192; Lang, Peter 193; Libraries Unlimited 197; Limelight 198; McFarland & Co. 204; ‡Macmillan Consumer Info. Grp. 206; Macmillan General Ref. 206; Mage 207; ‡Main Street 207; Mayfield 210; Meriwether 211; Mosaic Press Miniature Books 352; Nelson-Hall 220; New York Univ. 225; Norton, W.W. 229; Ohio Univ. 230; Owen, Richard C. 233; Pacific Educ. 330; Pelican 238; Pencil Point 239; Penguin Studio 239; Popular Culture Ink 246; Prima 249; ‡Pro/AM 249; Quarry 331; Quintet 332; Rain Dancer 253; Random House, Adult 255; Resource Pub. 365; ‡San Francisco 266; ‡Santa Monica 266; Scarecrow 267; Schirmer 268; ‡Simon & Pierre 334; Sound & Vision 335; Stipes 280; Tenth Avenue 366; Tiare 287; Titan 336; Titan 336; Totline Pub. 289; ‡Univ. of Chicago 294; Univ. of Illinois 295; Univ. of Iowa 296; Univ. of Nebraska 296; Univ. Press of Kentucky 299; Univ. Press of Mississippi 299; Univ. Press of New England 300; Vanderbilt Univ. 301; ‡Vestal 302; ‡Viking 302; Wadsworth 304; Walch, J. Weston 304; Walker & Co. 304; ‡Watson-Guptill 306; ‡Weatherhill 306; Weiser, Samuel 307; ‡Wesleyan Univ. 308; White Cliffs Media 309; White-Boucke 357; Whitman, Albert 309; Writer's Digest 314; ‡Yale Univ. 314

Nature/Environment: aatec 341; aatec 341; ABC-CLIO 84; Abrams 85; Adams Media 87; ‡Algonquin 89; ‡Amer. Water Works 94; Amwell 94; Appalachian Mountain Club 95; Arcade 95; Atheneum Bks. for Yng. Rdrs. 98; Autonomedia 99; ‡Backcountry 100; Bantam 102; Barricade 103; ‡Baywood 104; Beachway Press 104; Beacon Press 104; Berkshire House 106; Blackbirch Graphics 360; Blackbirch Press 107; Blair, John F. 107; Bliss 343; BNA Books 109; Boston Mills 318; Broadview 318; Can. Plains Research 320; Carol 118; Carolrhoda 119; ‡Cartwheel 119; Cave Books 121; ‡Chapters 122; Chatham 123; Chemtec 320; Children's Press 124; China Books 125; Chronicle 126; ‡Chronicle Bks. for Children 126; Clarion 128; Clarkson Potter 128; Clear Light 128; Cornell Maritime 131; ‡Council for Indian Educ. 132; Counterpoint 132; ‡Countryman 132; Crown Pub. Grp. 134; Dawn 138; Detselig 321; Dimi 141; Discipleship Resources 141; Doubleday Adult 142; Dover Pub. 142; Down East 142; Down Home 143; Down The Shore 346; ‡Dummies 144; Dundurn 321; Dutton Children's 145; Eakin Press/Sunbelt Media 145; Eastern Nat'l Assoc. 146; Ecopress 346; Éditions La Liberté 322; Ekstasis Editions 323; Elliott & Clark 147; ‡Emerald Wave 346; Epicenter 148; Eriksson, Paul S. 148; ‡Explorer's Guide 149; Faber & Faber 149; Facts On File 150; ‡Falcon Press 150; Filter Press 152; Fitzhenry & Whiteside 323; Four Walls Eight Windows 156; Gem Guides 158; Godine, David R. 159; Goose Lane 323; ‡Government Inst. 159; Great Quotations 160; ‡Grosset 162; Grosset & Dunlap 162; ‡Gulf 163; Hancock House 164; Harper Perennial 166; HarperCollins 166; HarperCollins (Canada) 324; Hay House 169; ‡Henry, Joseph 171; Heritage House 325; Heyday 171; High Plains 172; Horsdal & Schubart 325; Houghton Mifflin Bks. for Children 175; Houghton Mifflin, Adult 175; ‡Humanics Learning 177; ‡Hungry Mind 178; ICS Books 180; Ideals Children's 180; Inner Traditions Int'l 182; Innisfree 183; Insight 183; Jewish Lights 187; Johnson 188; Jones Univ., Bob 188; Kali 350; Kesend, Michael 191; Key Porter 327; ‡Knopf And Crown Bks. For Yng. Rdrs. 191; ‡KQED 192; Kroshka Books 193; Lark Books 194; Lawrence, Merloyd 194; Lerner 196; Lexikos 196; Little, Brown 199; Little, Brown Children's 199; Llewellyn 200; Lone Pine 328; Longstreet 202; Lorien 350; ‡Lynx Images 328; Lyons & Burford 203; McDonald & Woodward 204; Macmillan General Ref. 206; ‡Macrae, John 207; ‡Main Street 207; Maritimes Arts Projects Productions 329; Mercury House 210; Milkweed 212; ‡Millbrook 213; Mosaic Press Miniature Books 352; ‡Mountain N'Air 216; ‡Mountain Press 216; Mountaineers Books 217; ‡Muir, John 217; Natural Heritage/Natural History 329; Naturegraph 219; New England Cartographics 352; New Lexington 224; New World 225; New York Univ. 225; ‡North Point 227; Northland 228; Northword 228; Norton, W.W. 229; Noyes Data 229; Oasis Press 230; Ohio Univ. 230; Olson, C. 352; Orca 330; ‡Orchard 232; Oregon State Univ. 232; ‡Owl Books 234; Owl Books 364; Pacific Educ. 330; Pacific Press 234; Parnassus 236; Pineapple 243; ‡Planet Dexter 244; ‡Prentice-Hall 247; Primer 354; Pruett 250; ‡Putnam's Sons 251; Quintet 332; Ragged Mountain 253; Rain Dancer 253; ‡Rainbow 254; Raincoast 332; Random House, Adult 255; ‡Random House Bks. For Yng. Rdrs. 255; Red Deer College 332; Regnery Pub. 256; Review and Herald 257; Riverhead 259; Rocky Mountain 333; Ronsdale 333; ‡Rutgers Univ. 261; Sasquatch 267; Scholastic Canada 334; ‡Scribner 269; ‡Seal 269; ‡Sierra Club Bks. For Children 272; Sierra Club 272; Silver Burdett 273; ‡Simon & Schuster Bks. for Yng. Rdrs. 273; ‡Smith, Gibbs 275; Soundprints 276; South End 276; Stackpole 278; Stanford Univ. 278; ‡Starburst 279; Sterling 279; Stillpoint 280; Stipes 280; Stoddart 335; Storey Publishing/Garden Way 281; Summit Pub. Grp. 283; Systems Co. 284; ‡Tarcher, Jeremy 285; Ten Speed 286; Texas A&M Univ. 286; Texas Western Press 287; Thunder Dog 357; ‡Tide-Mark 287; Totline Pub. 289; ‡Tricycle 290; Univ. of Alaska 293; Univ. of Alberta Press 337; Univ. of Arizona 293; Univ. of Arkansas 294; Univ. of California 294; ‡Univ. of Georgia 295; Univ. of Idaho 295; Univ. of Iowa 296; Univ. of Massachusetts 296; Univ. of Nebraska 296; Univ. of Nevada 297; Univ. of North Texas 297; Univ. of Oklahoma 297; Univ. of Ottawa 338; Univ. of Texas 298; Univ. Press of Colorado 299; Univ. Press of New England 300; Upney Editions 338; Vanderbilt Univ. 301; ‡Venture 301; Verso 339; VGM Career Horizons 302; ‡Vintage 303; ‡Visions Comm. 357; Voyageur 304; Wadsworth 304; Walker & Co. 304; Washington St. Univ. 305; Watts Franklin 306; Wayfinder 357; ‡Weatherhill 306; Weidner & Sons 307; ‡Westcliffe 308; Whitecap 339; Whitman, Albert 309; Wieser & Wieser 366; Wilderness Adventure Books 358; Wilderness Press 310; Williamson 311; ‡Willow Creek 311; Windward 312; ‡Wuerz 340; Zoland 315; Hemingway Western Studies 348

Philosophy: ‡Acropolis 86; ‡Alba 88; American Atheist 91; Ardsley House 96; Aronson, Jason 96; Asian Humanities 97; Autonomedia 99; Bantam 102; Beacon Press 104; Blue Star 108; ‡Bridge Works 113; Broadview 318; Bucknell Univ. 114; ‡Bullfinch 114; Carol 118; Cassandra Press 345; Catholic Univ. of America 120; Clear Light 128; Counterpoint 132; Cross Cultural 134; ‡Cummings & Hathaway 135; Davidson, Harlan 137; Davies, Robert 321; Detselig 321; Doubleday Adult 142; Dover Pub. 142; Dundurn 321; ‡Duquesne Univ. 144; Eerdmans, William B. 146; ‡Element 147; ‡Emerald Wave 346; Facts On File 150; Fairleigh Dickinson Univ. 150; ‡Fordham Univ. 154; Glenbridge 159; ‡Greenwood Pub Grp 161; ‡Grosset

162; Guernica Editions 323; Gutter Press 324; ‡Harkey 165; Harper Perennial 166; HarperCollins 166; ‡Harvard Univ. 168; Hay House 169; ‡Hohm 173; Holmes Pub. Grp. 174; Houghton Mifflin, Adult 175; ‡House of Anansi 325; Humanics Pub. Grp. 177; ‡Humanities Press 178; ‡Hungry Mind 178; I.A.A.S. Pub. 348; ‡Image Books 181; Indiana Univ. Press 182; Inner Traditions Int'l 182; Inst. of Psychological Research 327; Int'l Pub. 185; Italica 186; Jefferson Univ., Thomas 187; Jewish Lights 187; ‡Judaica 189; Krieger Pub. 192; Kroshka Books 193; Kurian Reference Books, George 363; Lang, Peter 193; Larson/PBPF 194; ‡Laurel Books 194; ‡Le Loup de Gouttière 327; ‡Les Éditions du Vermillon 327; Libraries Unlimited 197; Lorien 350; ‡MacMurray & Beck 207; Maisonneuve 208; ‡Mariner 208; Mayfield 210; Mercury House 210; Michigan State Univ. 212; New York Univ. 225; Nicolas-Hays 352; Northern Illinois Univ. 227; ‡Northstone 330; Ohio State Univ. 230; Ohio Univ. 230; Omega 352; ‡Oneworld 330; Paulist Press 237; ‡Picador 242; Praeger 246; ‡Prentice-Hall 247; Pride 248; ‡Prometheus 249; ‡Purdue Univ. 251; Quest Books 252; Rain Dancer 253; ‡Rainbow 254; Regnery Pub. 256; Review and Herald 257; ‡Revolutionary Press 355; ‡Rising Star 258; Riverhead 259; St. Bede's 263; ‡St. Martin's Scholarly & Ref. 263; ‡Schocken 268; ‡Scribner 269; Somerville House 365; South End 276; Stone Bridge 280; ‡Stonewall Inn 281; Swan-Raven 283; Swedenborg Found. 284; ‡Talese, Nan 284; ‡Tarcher, Jeremy 285; Teachers College 285; Texas A&M Univ. 286; Turtle Press 291; Unity 292; Univ. of Alberta 337; ‡Univ. of Chicago 294; ‡Univ. of Georgia 295; Univ. of Illinois 295; Univ. of Massachusetts 296; Univ. of Montreal 337; Univ. of Ottawa 338; Univ. of Scranton 298; ‡Univ. Press of Florida 299; Vanderbilt Univ. 301; Verso 301; Verso 339; ‡Viking 302; ‡Vintage 303; Wadsworth 304; Wall & Emerson 339; Weiser, Samuel 307; ‡Wesleyan Univ. 308; Wisdom 312; ‡Wyndham Hall 314; ‡Yale Univ. 314; YMAA Pub. Ctr. 358

Photography: ‡AGS 359; ‡Abbeville Press 83; Allworth 89; Amherst Media 94; Atheneum Bks. for Yng. Rdrs. 98; Avanyu 99; Branden 111; Butterworth-Heinemann 115; Caitlin 319; ‡Carstens 119; Cave Books 121; Chronicle 126; Clarion 128; Clarkson Potter 128; Clear Light 128; Companion 130; Consultant Press 131; Crown Pub. Grp. 134; Doubleday Adult 142; Dover Pub. 142; Down Home 143; ‡Dummies 144; Elliott & Clark 147; Epicenter 148; Eriako Assoc. 361; Focal 153; General Pub. Grp. 158; Godine, David R. 159; Hollow Earth 173; Houghton Mifflin, Adult 175; Hounslow 325; Howells House 176; Hudson Hills 177; Humanitas 326; ICS Books 180; Jenkins Group 362; Key Porter 327; Kurian Reference Books, George 363; Layla Prod. 363; Lodestar 201; Longstreet 202; Minnesota Hist. Soc. Press 213; Motorbooks 216; Natural Heritage/Natural History 329; New York Univ. 225; Northland 228; Norton, W.W. 229; ‡Pendaya 353; Penguin Studio 239; Quarry 331; Quintet 332; Rain Dancer 253; Raincoast 332; Random House, Adult 255; Reference Press Int'l. 256; ‡Stonewall Inn 281; Stormline 355; Temple Univ. 285; Tenth Avenue 366; ‡Tide-Mark 287; Univ. of Iowa 296; Univ. of Nebraska 296; Univ. of New Mexico 297; ‡Univ. Press of Florida 299; Univ. Press of Mississippi 299; Warner Books 305; ‡Watson-Guptill 306; Wayfinder 357; ‡Weatherhill 306; ‡Westcliffe 308; Whitman, Albert 309; Wieser & Wieser 366; ‡Willow Creek 311; Writer's Digest 314; Zoland 315

Psychology: Active Parenting 86; Adams Media 87; Addicus Books 87; Addison Wesley Longman 87; ‡Alba 88; ‡Aletheia 88; ‡Alexander 88; ‡Allyn & Bacon 89; American Diabetes Assoc. 92; American Nurses 93; American Press 93; Aronson, Jason 96; Asian Humanities 97; Atheneum Bks. for Yng. Rdrs. 98; ‡Avisson 99; Avon 100; Bantam 102; Barricade 103; ‡Baywood 104; ‡Bethany House 106; ‡Bridge Works 113; Broadway Books 113; Brookline Books 114; Bucknell Univ. 114; Cambridge Univ. 116; Carol 118; Cassandra Press 345; Celestial Arts 121; Center for African-American Stud. 345; Cerier Book Dev., Alison Brown 361; Chicago Spectrum 124; Citadel 128; Commune-A-Key 129; Conari 130; Crown Pub. Grp. 134; ‡Cummings & Hathaway 135; ‡Da Capo Press 345; Davies, Robert 321; ‡Daybreak 138; Detselig 321; Dickens Press 346; Dimi 141; Doubleday Adult 142; Dutton 144; Éditions La Liberté 322; Eerdmans, William B. 146; Ekstasis Editions 323; ‡Element 147; ‡Emerald Wave 346; Emis, Inc. 347; Eriksson, Paul S. 148; Evans & Co. 149; Facts On File 150; Fairleigh Dickinson Univ. 150; Fairview 150; Free Spirit 157; ‡Fromm Int'l 157; Glenbridge 159; ‡Greenwood Press 161; ‡Greenwood Pub Grp 161; ‡Grosset 162; Guernica Editions 323; Harper Perennial 166; HarperCollins 166; HarperSanFrancisco 167; ‡Harvard Univ. 168; Hastings 168; Hatherleigh Press 168; ‡Haworth Press 169; Hay House 169; Health Comm. 169; ‡Health Info. Pr. 169; ‡Henry, Joseph 171; Houghton Mifflin, Adult 175; Human Kinetics 177; ‡Humanics Learning 177; Hyperion 179; I.A.A.S. Pub. 348; ‡Image Books 181; Inner Traditions Int'l 182; ‡Innisfree 183; Insight 183; Inst. of Psychological Research 327; ‡Jossey-Bass/Pfeiffer 189; Knowledge, Ideas & Trends 192; Krieger Pub. 192; Kroshka Books 193; Lang, Peter 193; Larson/PBPF 194; ‡Laurel Books 194; Lawrence, Merloyd 194; ‡Le Loup de Gouttière 327; Libraries Unlimited 197; Lifetime Books 197; Llewellyn 200; ‡Macmillan Bks. 205; Macmillan General Ref. 206; ‡MacMurray & Beck 207; ‡Main Street 207; Maisonneuve 208; ‡Management Tech. Inst. 351; Mayfield 210; Metamorphous 212; Nelson-Hall 220; New Harbinger 221; New Lexington 224; New World 225; New York Univ. 225; Nicolas-Hays 352; Nine Pines 329; Norton, W.W. 229; NTC/Contemporary Pub. 229; Ohio Univ. 230; ‡Oneworld 330; Ottenheimer 364; Paper Chase 235; Paradigm 236; Pauline Books & Media 237; ‡Perspectives 240; Plenum 245; Praeger 246; ‡Prentice-Hall 247; Pride 248; Prima 249; ‡Prometheus 249; Quest Books 252; Rain Dancer 253; ‡Rainbow 254; ‡Rawson 255; ‡Revolutionary Press 355; Riverhead 259; Safer Society 262; ‡Scribner 269; Sibyl 271; Sidran 271; ‡Signet 272; Sourcebooks 276; Stanford Univ. 278; ‡Starburst 279; Steel Balls 355; Stillpoint 280; Stoddart 335; Success Pub. 282; Sulzburger & Graham 282; Swedenborg Found. 284; ‡Tarcher, Jeremy 285; Third Side Press 287; Trilogy Books 290; Trilogy Books 290; ‡Twayne 291; 2M Comm. 366; Unity 292; ‡Univ. of Chicago 294; ‡Univ. of Georgia 295; Univ. of Montreal 337; Univ. of Nebraska 296; ‡Victor 302; ‡Vintage 303; ‡Visions 303; Walch, J. Weston 304; Warner Books 305; Weidner & Sons 307; Weiser, Samuel 307; ‡Westview 308; Wiley, John 311; Williamson 311; Wilshire 311; Wisdom 312; ‡Woodbridge 358; ‡Wyndham Hall 314; ‡Yale Univ. 314

Real Estate: Dearborn Financial 138; ‡Government Inst. 159; NTC/Contemporary Pub. 229; ‡Starburst 279; ‡ULI 292; ‡Univ. of Chicago 294

Recreation: Abrams 85; Accent On Living 85; Amer. & World Geo. Pub. 359; Appalachian Mountain Club 95; Atheneum Bks. for Yng. Rdrs. 98; ‡Backcountry 100; Beachway Press 104; Berkshire House 106; Betterway 106; Bliss 343; ‡Career Press 118; Carol 118; ‡Cartwheel 119; ‡Centennial 122; Chatham 123; Chronicle 126; Compass Prod. 361; ‡Council for

Indian Educ. 132; ‡Countryman 132; Crown Pub. Grp. 134; ‡Cumberland House 135; ‡Dawbert 346; Denali 140; Detselig 321; Discipleship Resources 141; Doubleday Adult 142; Down East 142; Down Home 143; ‡Dummies 144; Ecopress 346; Enslow 148; Epicenter 148; Eriksson, Paul S. 148; ‡Explorer's Guide 149; Facts On File 150; ‡Falcon Press 150; Gem Guides 158; Globe Pequot 159; Golden West 159; Harper Perennial 166; Heritage House 325; Heyday 171; Horsdal & Schubart 325; Houghton Mifflin Bks. for Children 175; Houghton Mifflin, Adult 175; ‡Howell Bk. House 176; Human Kinetics 177; ICS Books 180; Idyll Arbor 181; Jenkins Group 362; Johnson 188; Kroshka Books 193; Layla Prod. 363; Lion Books 198; Little, Brown Children's 199; Lone Pine 328; McFarland & Co. 204; ‡Macmillan Bks. 205; ‡Macmillan Consumer Info. Grp. 206; Macmillan General Ref. 206; Masters Press 209; Menasha Ridge 364; Meriwether 211; ‡Mountain N'Air 216; Mountaineers Books 217; ‡Muir, John 217; Mustang Publishing 218; Natural Heritage/Natural History 329; New England Cartographics 352; New York Niche Press 352; Ohio Univ. 230; Orca 330; ‡Out There 233; Paper Chase 235; Parnassus 236; Peachtree 238; Pelican 238; Primer 354; Pruett 250; Quintet 332; Ragged Mountain 253; Rain Dancer 253; ‡Rainbow 254; Raincoast 332; Riverhead 259; Rocky Mountain 333; ‡Running Press 261; Sasquatch 267; Scholastic Canada 334; Stackpole 278; ‡Starburst 279; Sterling 279; Stipes 280; Sulzburger & Graham 282; Summit Pub. Grp. 283; ‡Surrey 283; Ten Speed 286; Univ. of Idaho 295; ‡Venture 301; Voyageur 304; Wayfinder 357; ‡Western Tanager 357; Whitecap 339; Whitman, Albert 309; Wieser & Wieser 366; Wilderness Press 310; ‡Willow Creek 311; Windward 312; World Leisure 313

Reference: ‡AGS 359; Abbott, Langer 84; ABC-CLIO 84; Abingdon 84; ACA Books 85; Adams Media 87; Aegis Publishing 88; AKTRIN 88; ‡Alba 88; ‡Alexander 88; Allworth 89; ‡Allyn & Bacon 89; Alpine Pub. 90; Amacom 90; American Atheist 91; ‡American Bar Assoc. 91; American Correctional Assoc. 91; American Diabetes Assoc. 92; American Hospital 92; American Nurses 93; ‡Amer. Psychiatric Press 93; ‡Ancestry 94; Andrews McMeel 95; Apollo Books 95; Appalachian Mountain Club 95; Arden 96; Arkansas Research 96; ‡Arte Publico 97; Asian Humanities 97; Asphodel 97; Avanyu 99; ‡Avery Pub. Grp. 99; ‡Avisson 99; Baker Books 101; Ballantine 101; Barricade 103; Behrman House 105; Beil, Frederic 105; ‡Bethany House 106; Betterway 106; Blackbirch Graphics 360; Blackbirch Press 107; Bliss 343; Bloomberg Press 107; BNA Books 109; Bookcraft 109; Bookhaven 110; Borealis 318; Borgo 110; Bowling Green State Univ. 111; Branden 111; Brassey's 111; ‡Bridge Street 344; ‡Bridge Works 113; ‡Bristol Fashion 113; Broadway Books 113; Brookline Books 114; ‡Business & Legal Reports 115; Business McGraw-Hill 115; Butterworth-Heinemann 115; ‡Butterworths Canada 319; CQ Inc. 116; Cambridge Univ. 116; Can. Library Assoc. 319; Caradium Publishing 117; Cardoza 118; ‡Career Press 118; ‡Carroll & Graf 119; Carswell Thomson 320; Celestial Arts 121; Cerier Book Dev., Alison Brown 361; Charlton 320; Christian Publications 125; ‡Chronimed 127; College Board 129; Computer Science 130; ‡Computing McGraw-Hill 130; Consultant Press 131; Coteau 320; ‡Countryman 132; Creative Spark 361; Crown Pub. Grp. 134; ‡Cumberland House 135; ‡Cummings & Hathaway 135; Dante Univ. Of America Press 136; Darlington Prod. 136; Databooks 136; David, Jonathan 137; ‡Dawbert 346; Dearborn Financial 138; Denali 140; Detselig 321; Dickens Press 346; ‡Doubleday Religious 142; Drama Pub. 143; ‡Dummies 144; Dundurn 321; Earth-Love 346; Eckert, J.K. 361; Eerdmans, William B. 146; ‡Element 147; Emis, Inc. 347; Engineering & Mgmt. 147; Enslow 148; Evans & Co. 149; Evras 347; Facts On File 150; Fairleigh Dickinson Univ. 150; Fairview 150; ‡Falcon Press 150; Fallen Leaf 347; Ferguson, J.G. 152; ‡Fire Engineering 152; Focal 153; Foreign Policy 154; Friends United 157; ‡Fromm Int'l 157; Gambling Times 348; Giniger, K.S. 362; ‡Government Inst. 159; Graber Prod. 362; Graduate Group 160; Graphic Arts Tech. Found. 160; ‡Greenwood Press 161; ‡Greenwood Pub Grp 161; ‡Grolier 162; ‡Gulf 163; Hancock House 164; Harper Perennial 166; HarperCollins 166; HarperSanFrancisco 167; ‡Harvard Univ. 168; Hastings 168; Hatherleigh Press 168; ‡Haworth Press 169; ‡Health Info. Pr. 169; Heinemann 170; Herbal Studies 348; Heritage 171; Highsmith 172; Hiller Box Manufacturing 362; Hippocrene 172; Hoard, W.D. 348; Hollow Earth 173; Holmes & Meier 173; ‡Hoover's 174; ‡Howell Bk. House 176; ‡HRD 176; Human Kinetics 177; Hunter Publishing 178; ‡ICC 179; ‡Image Books 181; Index Pub. Grp. 182; ‡Insignia 183; Inst. of Police Tech. & Mgmt. 183; ‡Inter Trade 183; Intercultural 184; Int'l City/County Mgmt. 184; Int'l Found. Of Employee Benefit Plans 184; Int'l Medical 185; Int'l Pub. 185; J & L Lee 186; Jain 186; Jewish Lights 187; Jewish Publication 187; Jist Works 188; JSA Publications 363; ‡Judaica 189; ‡Ketz, Louise 363; Kinseeker 191; Knowledge, Ideas & Trends 192; Kregel Publications 192; Krieger Pub. 192; Kurian Reference Books, George 363; Laing Comm. 363; Lake View 193; Lang, Peter 193; Langenscheidt 194; ‡Laurier 327; Lawyers & Judges 195; Leadership 195; ‡Learning Pub. 195; Lehigh Univ. 195; Libraries Unlimited 197; Library of Virginia 350; Lifetime Books 197; Locust Hill 200; Lone Eagle 201; Longstreet 202; Loompanics 202; LRP Pub 203; McBooks 350; McFarland & Co. 204; ‡McGraw-Hill Companies, Prof. Bk. Grp. 205; McGraw-Hill Ryerson 328; ‡Macmillan Bks. 205; ‡Macmillan Brands 206; ‡Macmillan Consumer Info. Grp. 206; Macmillan General Ref. 206; Madison Books 207; Mangajin 351; Masters Press 209; Meadowbrook 210; ‡Medical Physics 210; Meriwether 211; Metamorphous 212; Meyerbooks 351; Michigan State Univ. 212; ‡Millenium 213; Minnesota Hist. Soc. Press 213; ‡Moyer Bell 217; Mystic Seaport Museum 218; Nautical & Aviation 219; Neal-Schuman 220; Nelson, Thomas 220; New England Pub. Assoc. 364; New Lexington 224; Nichols 226; No Starch 226; ‡Nolo 226; Norton, W.W. 229; NTC/Contemporary Pub. 229; Oasis Press 230; Octameron 230; Ohio Univ. 230; ‡Oneworld 330; ‡Orbis 232; Orchises 232; Oryx 233; Ottenheimer 364; Our Sunday Visitor 233; ‡Out There 233; Pacific Books 234; Pacific Educ. 330; Pacific View 235; Parkway 236; Parrot 353; Partners in Publishing 353; Peachpit 238; Pencil Point 239; Pennsylvania Hist. and Museum Comm. 239; PennWell 240; Phi Delta Kappa 242; Philosophy Documentation 242; Picton 243; Pineapple 243; Pocket Books 246; Popular Culture Ink 246; ‡Practice Mgmt. 246; Prakken Pub. 354; Precept 247; ‡Prentice-Hall 247; Pride 248; Productive 331; Professional Pub. 249; ‡Prometheus 249; PROMPT 250; Purich 331; ‡Que 252; Quill Driver/ Word Dancer 252; Quintet 332; ‡Race Point 354; Rain Dancer 253; Red Eye 355; Reference Press Int'l. 256; Reference Service 256; ‡Regan 256; Review and Herald 257; ‡Riehle Found. 258; ‡Rising Star 258; ‡Rosen Pub. Grp. 260; ‡Rothman, Fred B. 260; Russian Info. Svces. 261; ‡Rutgers Univ. 261; Rutledge Hill 262; Sachem Pub. Assoc. 365; ‡SAE Int'l 262; ‡St. Martin's Scholarly & Ref. 263; St. Martin's 263; Sandlapper 266; ‡Santa Monica 266; Scarecrow 267; ‡Schiffer 267; Schirmer 268; ‡Seaworthy 269; Self-Counsel 334; Serendipity 270; Shoreline 334; Sidran 271; ‡Signet 272; Silver Burdett 273; ‡Simon & Pierre 334; SJL Pub. 274; Sono Nis 335; ‡Sound View 355; Sourcebooks 276; Speech Bin 277; Standard Pub. 278; Sterling

279; Stoeger 280; Stone Bridge 280; Sulzburger & Graham 282; Summers 283; Tech. Books for the Layperson 356; Ten Speed 286; Texas State Hist. Assoc. 286; Tidewater Pub. 288; Todd 288; Tower 289; ‡Transnational 289; ‡Umbrella 336; Unity 292; Univ. of Alaska 293; Univ. of Idaho 295; Univ. of Illinois 295; Univ. of Montreal 337; Univ. of North Texas 297; ‡Univ. of Ok. Nat'l Res. Ctr. 357; Univ. of Ottawa 338; Univ. Press of Kentucky 299; Univ. Press of New England 300; Upney Editions 338; Utah St. Univ. 300; Vanderbilt Univ. 301; ‡Victor 302; ‡Visions Comm. 357; Walker & Co. 304; Wall & Emerson 339; ‡Watson-Guptill 306; Wayfinder 357; ‡Weatherhill 306; Weidner & Sons 307; Weka Pub. 307; ‡Westcliffe 308; ‡Westview 308; White-Boucke 357; Whitehorse 358; Wiley, John 311; Wisdom 312; Woodbine House 312; Wordware 313; ‡Wyndham Hall 314; ‡Yale Univ. 314; York Press 340; Zondervan 315

Regional: Adams Media 87; Addicus Books 87; ‡Alexander 88; ‡Algonquin 89; Almar Press 90; Amer. & World Geo. Pub. 359; Appalachian Mountain Club 95; ‡Arkansas Research 96; Arsenal Pulp 317; ‡Arte Publico 97; Austen Sharp 343; Avanyu 99; ‡Avisson 99; Balcony 343; ‡Barnegat Light 102; ‡Baylor Univ. 343; Berkshire House 106; Blair, John F. 107; Bliss 343; Blue Sky 343; Bonus Books 109; ‡Bookwrights 360; Borealis 318; Boston Mills 318; Bowling Green State Univ. 111; Bright Mountain 344; Brown Bear 318; Caitlin 319; Camino Books 117; Can. Plains Research 320; Carol 118; Cave Books 121; Caxton Printers 121; ‡Centennial 122; ‡Chapters 122; Chatham 123; Chicago Review 124; Chronicle 126; Clear Light 128; Compass Prod. 361; Cornell Maritime 131; Coteau 320; ‡Countryman 132; Creative Pub. 133; ‡Cumberland House 135; ‡Cummings & Hathaway 135; Databooks 136; Davidson, Harlan 137; Denali 140; Doubleday Adult 142; Down East 142; Down Home 143; Down The Shore 346; Dundurn 321; Eakin Press/Sunbelt Media 145; Ecco Press 146; ECW Press 322; Eerdmans, William B. 146; ‡Element 147; Epicenter 148; ‡Explorer's Guide 149; Family Album 347; Filter Press 152; Fitzhenry & Whiteside 323; ‡Fordham Univ. 154; Gem Guides 158; Globe Pequot 159; Golden West 159; Goose Lane 323; Guernica Editions 323; ‡Gulf 163; Hancock House 164; Harper Perennial 166; Hemingway Western Studies 348; Hendrick-Long 170; Heritage House 325; Heyday 171; High Plains 172; Hoard, W.D. 348; Horsdal & Schubart 325; Houghton Mifflin Bks. for Children 175; Houghton Mifflin, Adult 175; ‡Hungry Mind 178; Hunter Publishing 178; ‡Image Grafx 362; Indiana Hist. Soc. 349; Indiana Univ. Press 182; J & L Lee 186; ‡Jameson 187; Jenkins Group 362; Johnson 188; Johnston Assoc. Int'l. 349; Kent State Univ. 190; Kinseeker 191; Lahontan Images 350; Lexikos 196; Library of Virginia 350; Livingston Press 200; Lone Pine 328; Longstreet 202; Lorimer & Co., James 328; McBooks 350; McGraw-Hill Ryerson 328; ‡McGregor 205; ‡Macmillan Travel 206; Maritimes Arts Projects Productions 329; Maupin House 209; Menasha Ridge 364; Michigan State Univ. 212; Minnesota Hist. Soc. Press 213; Moon 215; ‡Mountain Press 216; Mountaineers Books 217; Natural Heritage/Natural History 329; New England Cartographics 352; ‡New England 221; New York Niche Press 352; New York Univ. 225; NeWest Pub. 329; Nodin 226; Northern Illinois Univ. 227; Northland 228; Ohio State Univ. 230; Ohio Univ. 230; Orca 330; Oregon State Univ. 232; ‡Out There 233; ‡Owl Books 234; Pacific Books 234; Pacific Educ. 330; Pacific View 235; Parkway 236; Parnassus 236; ‡Peachtree Children's 238; Pelican 238; Penguin Books Canada 331; Pennsylvania Hist. and Museum Comm. 239; Pineapple 243; Prentice-Hall Canada 331; Primer 354; Pruett 250; ‡Purdue Univ. 251; Quarry 331; Quill Driver/Word Dancer 252; Quixote 253; Raincoast 332; Red Deer College 332; Republic of Texas 257; ‡Rising Star 258; Riverhead 259; Rockbridge Pub. Co. 259; Rocky Mountain 333; Ronsdale 333; ‡Russian Hill 261; ‡Rutgers Univ. 261; ‡Sanders, J.S. 266; Sandlapper 266; Sasquatch 267; ‡Schiffer 267; Scottwall Assoc. 355; ‡Simon & Pierre 334; ‡Smith, Gibbs 275; Sono Nis 335; S. Methodist Univ. 277; Stormline 355; Summit Pub. Grp. 283; Sunstone 283; Tamarack 356; Temple Univ. 285; Texas A&M Univ. 286; Texas Christian Univ. 286; Texas Western Press 287; Tidewater Pub. 288; Turnstone 336; ‡TwoDot 292; ‡Univ. of Akron 293; Univ. of Alaska 293; Univ. of Alberta Press 337; Univ. of Arizona 293; ‡Univ. of Georgia 295; Univ. of Idaho 295; Univ. of Manitoba 337; Univ. of Missouri 296; Univ. of Nevada 297; Univ. of North Texas 297; Univ. of Oklahoma 297; Univ. of Ottawa 338; Univ. of Scranton 298; Univ. of Tennessee 298; Univ. of Texas 298; Univ. Press of Colorado 299; ‡Univ. Press of Florida 299; Univ. Press of Mississippi 299; Univ. Press of New England 300; Upney Editions 338; Utah St. Univ. 300; Valiant 357; Vandamere 301; Vanderbilt Univ. 301; Vanwell 338; Vehicule 338; ‡Vestal 302; ‡Voyageur 304; Walker & Co. 304; Washington St. Univ. 305; Wayfinder 357; ‡Westcliffe 308; ‡Western Tanager 357; Westernlore 308; Whitecap 339; Wilderness Adventure Books 358; Zoland 315

Religion: Abingdon 84; Accent On Living 85; Accent Publications 86; ‡Acropolis 86; Acta Pub. 86; ‡Alba 88; ‡Alexander 88; American Atheist 91; American Catholic Press 342; Aronson, Jason 96; Asian Humanities 97; Atheneum Bks. for Yng. Rdrs. 98; Augsburg 98; Baker Books 101; Bantam 102; Barbour & Co. 102; ‡Baylor Univ. 343; Beacon Hill Press of KC 104; Beacon Press 104; Behrman House 105; ‡Bethany House 106; Blue Star 108; Bookcraft 109; ‡Bookwrights 360; ‡Bridge Learning Systems 344; Broadman & Holman 113; Bucknell Univ. 114; Can. Inst. of Ukrainian Stud. 319; Cassandra Press 345; Catholic Univ. of America 120; ‡Chariot Children's Bks. 122; ‡Chariot/Victor 123; China Books 125; Chosen Books 125; ‡Christian Literature 125; Christian Publications 125; Church Growth Inst. 127; Compass Prod. 361; Concordia 130; Counterpoint 132; Creation House 133; Cross Cultural 134; ‡Cummings & Hathaway 135; David, Jonathan 137; Davies, Robert 321; ‡Daybreak 138; Detselig 321; Discipleship Resources 141; Doubleday Adult 142; ‡Doubleday Religious 142; Dover Pub. 142; Dundurn 321; ‡Duquesne Univ. 144; Eerdmans, William B. 146; ETC Pub. 148; Facts On File 150; ‡Focus Pub. 154; ‡Fordham Univ. 154; ‡Fortress 155; ‡Forum 155; Forward Movement 155; Franciscan Univ. 156; Friends United 157; Great Quotations 160; ‡Greenwood Pub Grp 161; ‡Grosset 162; Group Pub. 162; Guernica Editions 323; Harper Perennial 166; HarperCollins 166; HarperCollins (Canada) 324; HarperSanFrancisco 167; ‡Harvard Univ. 168; Harvest House 168; Hendrickson 171; Hensley, Virgil 171; Hiller Box Manufacturing 362; Hi-Time 348; ‡Hohm 173; Hollow Earth 173; Holmes Pub. Grp. 174; ‡Honor 174; Houghton Mifflin, Adult 175; ‡House Of Collectibles 176; ‡Humanities Press 178; ‡Hungry Mind 178; ‡Hunt & Thorpe 326; ICS Pub. 180; ‡Image Books 181; Indiana Univ. Press 182; Inner Traditions Int'l 182; ‡Innisfree 183; Italica 186; Jefferson Univ., Thomas 187; Jewish Lights 187; Jewish Publication 187; ‡Jossey-Bass/Pfeiffer 189; ‡Judaica 189; Judson 189; Kindred Prod. 327; ‡KQED 192; Kregel Publications 192; Kroshka Books 193; Kurian Reference Books, George 363; Lang, Peter 193; Larson/PBPF 194; Libraries Unlimited 197; Liguori 197; Lion Publishing 198; Living the Good News 200; ‡Macmillan Consumer Info. Grp. 206; Macmillan General Ref. 206; Mangajin 351; Mayfield

210; Meriwether 211; ‡Millenium 213; ‡Moody 214; Morehouse 215; Morrow, William 215; Nelson, Thomas 220; ‡Nelson, Tommy 220; New Hope 221; New Leaf 224; New World 225; New York Univ. 225; Nicolas-Hays 352; Nine Pines 329; ‡North Point 227; Norton, W.W. 229; Ohio Univ. 230; ‡One World 231; ‡Oneworld 330; ‡Orbis 232; Ottenheimer 364; Our Sunday Visitor 233; Pacific Press 234; Pauline Books & Media 237; Paulist Press 237; Pelican 238; ‡Prentice-Hall 247; ‡Preservation 247; ‡Prometheus 249; Publishers Assoc. 251; ‡Putnam's Sons 251; Quarry 331; ‡Questar 252; Rainbow Pub. 254; Random House, Adult 255; Regnery Pub. 256; Religious Education 256; Resource Pub. 365; Resurrection 257; Revell, Fleming H. 257; Review and Herald 257; ‡Riehle Found. 258; ‡Rising Star 258; Riverhead 259; ‡Rutgers Univ. 261; St. Anthony Messenger 263; St. Bede's 263; ‡St. Martin's Scholarly & Ref. 263; ‡Schocken 268; ‡Scribner 269; Servant 270; Shaw, Harold 271; Shoreline 334; Sibyl 271; ‡Skinner 274; Standard Pub. 278; Starburst 279; Stillpoint 280; Success Pub. 282; Summit Pub. Grp. 283; Swedenborg Found. 284; ‡Tarcher, Jeremy 285; Tuttle, Charles E. 291; Tyndale House 292; United Church Publishing House 337; Unity 292; ‡Univ. of Georgia 295; Univ. of Montreal 337; Univ. of Ottawa 338; Univ. of Scranton 298; Univ. of Tennessee 298; Vanderbilt Univ. 301; ‡Victor 302; ‡Visions 303; ‡Visions Comm. 357; Wadsworth 304; Weiser, Samuel 307; ‡Westview 308; Whitman, Albert 309; Wilshire 311; Wisdom 312; ‡Wyndham Hall 314; ‡Yale Univ. 314; Zondervan 315

Scholarly: ‡Baylor Univ. 343; ‡Baywood 104; Beacon Press 104; BNA Books 109; Borgo 110; Broadview 318; Bucknell Univ. 114; Cambridge Univ. 116; Can. Inst. of Ukrainian Stud. 319; Can. Plains Research 320; Center for African-American Stud. 345; Cross Cultural 134; Dante Univ. Of America Press 136; ‡Duquesne Univ. 144; Eastern Press 346; Fairleigh Dickinson Univ. 150; Focal 153; ‡Fordham Univ. 154; ‡Greenwood Press 161; ‡Greenwood Pub Grp 161; ‡Haworth Press 169; Hemingway Western Studies 348; ‡Icon 179; Indiana Univ. Press 182; Johnson 188; Kent State Univ. 190; Knopf, Alfred A. 192; Lake View 193; Lang, Peter 193; Lehigh Univ. 195; McFarland & Co. 204; Michigan State Univ. 212; Minnesota Hist. Soc. Press 213; Modern Language Assoc. 214; Nelson-Hall 220; New Lexington 224; Ohio State Univ. 230; Oregon State Univ. 232; Pacific Books 234; Passeggiata 237; Phi Delta Kappa 242; ‡Pioneer Inst. 353; ‡Prentice-Hall 247; Publishers Assoc. 251; ‡Purdue Univ. 251; Religious Education 256; ‡St. Martin's Scholarly & Ref. 263; St. Martin's 263; Scarecrow 267; Schirmer 268; Stanford Univ. 278; Texas Christian Univ. 286; Texas State Hist. Assoc. 286; Texas Western Press 287; ‡Twayne 291; ‡Univ. of Akron 293; Univ. of Alaska 293; Univ. of Alberta Press 337; Univ. of Arizona 293; Univ. of California 294; Univ. of Illinois 295; Univ. of Manitoba 337; Univ. of Missouri 296; Univ. of New Mexico 297; Univ. of Ottawa 338; Univ. of Scranton 298; Univ. of Tennessee 298; Univ. of Texas 298; ‡Univ. of W. Ontario 338; Univ. Press of Colorado 299; ‡Univ. Press of Florida 299; Univ. Press of Kentucky 299; Univ. Press of Mississippi 299; Utah St. Univ. 300; Vanderbilt Univ. 301; ‡Venture 301; ‡Wesleyan Univ. 308; Westernlore 308; ‡Westview 308; ‡Whitson 309; ‡Yale Univ. 314; York Press 340

Science/Technology: ABC-CLIO 84; Abrams 85; Adams Media 87; Addison Wesley Longman 87; Aegis Publishing 88; Almar Press 90; American Astronautical Soc. 91; American Eagle 92; American Nurses 93; American Press 93; ‡Amer. Water Works 94; Atheneum Bks. for Yng. Rdrs. 98; Bantam 102; ‡Battelle 103; Blackbirch Press 107; Butterworth-Heinemann 115; Cambridge Educ. 116; Cambridge Univ. 116; Carol 118; Carolrhoda 119; ‡Cartwheel 119; Cave Books 121; Chemtec 320; Children's Press 124; ‡Chronicle Bks. for Children 126; College Board 129; Counterpoint 132; Crown Pub. Grp. 134; ‡Da Capo Press 345; Databooks 136; Doubleday Adult 142; Dover Pub. 142; Dundurn 321; Dutton 144; Dutton Children's 145; Ecopress 346; Éditions La Liberté 322; Enslow 148; Faber & Faber 149; Facts On File 150; Focal 153; Four Walls Eight Windows 156; ‡Government Inst. 159; Graber Prod. 362; Graphic Arts Tech. Found. 160; ‡Grosset 162; Grosset & Dunlap 162; ‡Gulf 163; ‡Harkey 165; Harper Perennial 166; HarperCollins 166; ‡Health Info. Pr. 169; ‡Harvard Univ. 168; ‡Helix 170; ‡Henry, Joseph 171; Houghton Mifflin Bks. for Children 175; Houghton Mifflin, Adult 175; ‡House of Anansi 325; Howells House 176; ‡HRD 176; ‡Humanics Learning 177; Humanitas 326; Hungry Mind 178; Ideals Children's 180; Insight 183; Inst. of Psychological Research 327; Johnson 188; Kalmbach 189; ‡Ketz, Louise 363; ‡Knopf And Crown Bks. For Yng. Rdrs. 191; Krieger Pub. 192; Kroshka Books 193; ‡Kumarian 193; Kurian Reference Books, George 363; ‡Laurel Books 194; Lehigh Univ. 195; Lerner 196; Libraries Unlimited 197; ‡Lippincott 198; Little, Brown 199; Little, Brown Children's 199; Lorien 350; Lyons & Burford 203; McDonald & Woodward 204; McGraw-Hill Companies, Prof. Bk. Grp. 205; ‡Macmillan Bks. 205; Macmillan General Ref. 206; Message Co. 211; Messner 211; Metamorphous 212; ‡Millbrook 213; ‡Millenium 213; ‡Mountain Press 216; Naturegraph 219; Naval Inst. 219; Norton, W.W. 229; Noyes Data 229; Ohio Univ. 230; Oregon State Univ. 232; Owen, Richard C. 233; Owl Books 364; Pacific Educ. 330; Paladin 235; Parkway 236; Pencil Point 239; Penguin Studio 239; PennWell 240; ‡Peters, A.K. 241; ‡Planet Dexter 244; Plenum 245; ‡Practice Mgmt. 246; Precept 247; ‡Prentice-Hall 247; Professional Pub. 249; PROMPT 250; ‡Purdue Univ. 251; ‡Putnam's Sons 251; Quest Books 252; Rain Dancer 253; ‡Rainbow 254; ‡Random House Bks. For Yng. Rdrs. 255; Regnery Pub. 256; ‡Running Press 261; ‡Rutgers Univ. 261; ‡San Francisco 266; Scholastic Canada 334; ‡Scribner 269; Silver Burdett 273; Silver Moon 365; SJL Pub. 274; Sky 274; Somerville House 365; South End 276; Stanford Univ. 278; Sterling 279; Stipes 280; Stoddart 335; Sulzburger & Graham 282; Summit Pub. Grp. 283; Systems Co. 284; Ten Speed 286; Texas Western Press 287; Times Books 288; ‡Times Business 288; Totline Pub. 289; ‡Tricycle 290; Univelt 293; ‡Univ. of Akron 293; Univ. of Alaska 293; Univ. of Arizona 293; ‡Univ. of Chicago 294; Univ. of Texas 298; Verso 339; ‡Vintage 303; ‡Visions 303; ‡Visions Comm. 357; Wadsworth 304; Walch, J. Weston 304; Walker & Co. 304; Wall & Emerson 339; Watts Franklin 306; Weidner & Sons 307; Whitman, Albert 309; Wiley, John 311; Williamson 311; Windward 312; ‡Wuerz 340; ‡Wyndham Hall 314; ‡Yale Univ. 314

Self-Help: Accent On Living 85; Active Parenting 86; Adams Media 87; Addicus Books 87; Aegis Publishing 88; ‡Alexander 88; Allen Pub. 89; Almar Press 90; Amacom 90; American Diabetes Assoc. 92; ‡Arkansas Research 96; Atheneum Bks. for Yng. Rdrs. 98; Augsburg 98; ‡Avery Pub. Grp. 99; ‡Avisson 99; Avon 100; Baker Books 101; Ballantine 101; Bantam 102; Barricade 103; ‡Bethany House 106; Betterway 106; Blackbirch Graphics 360; Blue Poppy 108; Bonus Books 109; ‡Book Enhancers 360; Bookcraft 109; ‡Bookwrights 360; ‡Bridge Street 344; Bryant & Dillon 114; Business McGraw-Hill

115; Caradium Publishing 117; ‡Career Press 118; Carol 118; ‡Carroll & Graf 119; Cassandra Press 345; CCC Pub. 121; Celestial Arts 121; Cerier Book Dev., Alison Brown 361; Chicago Spectrum 124; China Books 125; Chosen Books 125; Christian Publications 125; ‡Chronimed 127; Clarkson Potter 128; Cliffs Notes 128; College Board 129; Commune-A-Key 129; Conari 130; Consumer Press 131; Creative Spark 361; Crown Pub. Grp. 134; ‡Curtis/Strongmen 135; Databooks 136; David, Jonathan 137; Davies, Robert 321; ‡Daybreak 138; ‡Dell Trade Paperbacks 139; Detselig 321; Dickens Press 346; Dimi 141; Doubleday Adult 142; ‡Doubleday Religious 142; Dowling Press 142; ‡Dummies 144; Dundurn 321; Dutton 144; Earth-Love 346; ‡Element 147; Eriksson, Paul S. 148; ‡Excelsior Cee 149; Fairview 150; Fine, Donald I. 152; Fisher 153; Focus on the Family 154; Free Spirit 157; Giniger, K.S. 362; Graber Prod. 362; Graduate Group 160; Great Quotations 160; Harbor 164; ‡Harkey 165; ‡Harper Libros 165; Harper Perennial 166; HarperCollins 166; HarperCollins (Canada) 324; HarperSanFrancisco 167; Harvest House 168; Hastings 168; Hatherleigh Press 168; Hay House 169; Health Comm. 169; ‡Health Info. Pr. 169; Herbal Studies 348; ‡Hohm 173; Holmes Pub. Grp. 174; Houghton Mifflin, Adult 175; Hounslow 325; Human Kinetics 177; Humanics Pub. Grp. 177; Hunter House 178; Huntington House 179; Hyperion 179; ‡Image Books 181; ‡Image Grafx 362; ‡Innisfree 183; Insight 183; ‡Inter Trade 183; Int'l Wealth 185; Ivy League 349; Jain 186; ‡Jamenair 349; Jewish Lights 187; Jist Works 188; ‡Jossey-Bass/Pfeiffer 189; ‡Kensington 190; Kesend, Michael 191; Key Porter 327; Knowledge, Ideas & Trends 192; Kroshka Books 193; ‡Lamppost 363; Lifetime Books 197; Liguori 197; Limelight 198; Living the Good News 200; Llewellyn 200; Loompanics 202; McDonald & Woodward 204; McGraw-Hill Companies, Prof. Bk. Grp. 205; ‡McGregor 205; ‡Macmillan Bks. 205; ‡Macmillan Consumer Info. Grp. 206; Macmillan General Ref. 206; ‡Main Street 207; ‡Management Tech. Inst. 351; ‡Marlowe 209; Masters Press 209; Metamorphous 212; Meyerbooks 351; ‡Moyer Bell 217; ‡Muir, John 217; Mustang Publishing 218; Nelson, Thomas 220; New Harbinger 221; New Leaf 224; New World 225; Newjoy Press 225; Nicolas-Hays 352; Nine Pines 329; ‡Nolo 226; ‡Northstone 330; Norton, W.W. 229; Nova Press 229; NTC/Contemporary Pub. 229; Ohio Univ. 230; Ottenheimer 364; Pacific Press 234; Paper Chase 235; Parrot 353; Partners in Publishing 353; Pauline Books & Media 237; Paulist Press 237; Peachtree 238; Pelican 238; ‡Perspectives 240; Peter Pauper 241; Planning/Comm. 245; ‡PPI 246; ‡Preservation 247; Pride 248; Prima 249; Productive 331; Publicom 365; ‡Putnam's Sons 251; Quest Books 252; Quixote 253; ‡Race Point 354; Rain Dancer 253; ‡Rainbow 254; Random House, Adult 255; ‡Rawson 255; ‡Regan 256; Resource Pub. 365; Resurrection 257; Revell, Fleming H. 257; Review and Herald 257; ‡Revolutionary Press 355; ‡Rising Star 258; Riverhead 259; ‡Rodale 260; ‡Rosen Pub. Grp. 260; Royal Fireworks 260; ‡Running Press 261; Rutledge Hill 262; ‡SAE Int'l 262; Safer Society 262; St. Martin's 263; ‡Seal 269; Self-Counsel 334; Servant 270; Shaw, Harold 271; Sibyl 271; Sidran 271; ‡Signet 272; SJL Pub. 274; ‡Skinner 274; Sourcebooks 276; Sta-Kris 355; ‡Starburst 279; Steel Balls 355; Stillpoint 280; Stoddard 335; Studio 4 Prod. 356; Success Pub. 282; Sulzburger & Graham 282; Summit Pub. Grp. 283; ‡Surrey 283; Swedenborg Found. 284; Systems Co. 284; ‡Tambra 356; ‡Tarcher, Jeremy 285; Tech. Books for the Layperson 356; Ten Speed 286; Third Side Press 287; Todd 288; ‡Tricycle 290; Trilogy Books 290; Turtle Press 291; Tuttle, Charles E. 291; Tyndale House 292; Unity 292; Valley of the Sun 300; ‡Victor 302; ‡Visions 303; ‡Visions Comm. 357; Volcano 303; Walker & Co. 304; ‡Weatherhill 306; Weiser, Samuel 307; White-Boucke 357; Wiley, John 311; Williamson 311; Wilshire 311; Wisdom 312; ‡Woodbridge 358; World Leisure 313; Zondervan 315

Sex: Blue Moon 108; Broadway Books 113

Social Sciences: Addison Wesley Longman 87; Broadview 318; C Q Press 116; Cambridge Educ. 116; ‡Dillon House 141; Eerdmans, William B. 146; Feminist Press at CUNY 152; Foreign Policy 154; Free Press 156; ‡Greenwood Press 161; ‡Greenwood Pub Grp 161; Indiana Univ. Press 182; Insight 183; Int'l Pub. 185; Lang, Peter 193; Messner 211; Nelson-Hall 220; New Lexington 224; Northern Illinois Univ. 227; Oryx 233; Plenum 245; Roxbury 260; ‡St. Martin's Scholarly & Reference 275; Stanford Univ. 278; Teachers College 285; Texas Western Press 287; Univ. of California 294; Univ. of Missouri 296; Verso 339; Wadsworth 304; Walch, J. Weston 304; ‡Whitson 309

Sociology: ‡Aletheia 88; ‡Allyn & Bacon 89; American Press 93; Arsenal Pulp 317; Atheneum Bks. for Yng. Rdrs. 98; Avanyu 99; Bantam 102; Barricade 103; ‡Baywood 104; ‡Bethany House 106; Branden 111; ‡Bridge Works 113; Broadview 318; Bucknell Univ. 114; Can. Inst. of Ukrainian Stud. 319; Can. Plains Research 320; Cato Inst. 120; Center for African-American Stud. 345; Child Welfare League Of America 124; China Books 125; Creative Spark 361; Cross Cultural 134; ‡Cummings & Hathaway 135; Davies, Robert 321; Detselig 321; Doubleday Adult 142; Dundurn 321; Éditions La Liberté 322; Eerdmans, William B. 146; Enslow 148; Eriksson, Paul S. 148; Evans & Co. 149; Fairleigh Dickinson Univ. 150; Fairview 150; FemFeminist Press at CUNY 152; ‡Fordham Univ. 154; Free Spirit 157; Glenbridge 159; ‡Greenwood Press 161; ‡Greenwood Pub Grp 161; ‡Grosset 162; Harper Perennial 166; HarperCollins 166; ‡Harvard Univ. 168; ‡Haworth Press 169; Hay House 169; ‡Hill & Wang 172; Houghton Mifflin, Adult 175; ‡House of Anansi 325; Howells House 176; ‡Humanities Press 178; ‡Hungry Mind 178; I.A.A.S. Pub. 348; ‡ILR 181; Insight 183; Jefferson Univ., Thomas 187; Knowledge, Ideas & Trends 192; Kroshka Books 193; ‡Kumarian 193; Lake View 193; Lang, Peter 193; ‡Laurel Books 194; ‡Learning Pub. 195; ‡Les Éditions du Vermillon 327; Libraries Unlimited 197; Lincoln Springs 350; ‡Lippincott 198; Lorimer & Co., James 328; McFarland & Co. 204; Macmillan General Ref. 206; ‡MacMurray & Beck 207; Mage 207; Maisonneuve 208; Mangajin 351; ‡Mariner 208; Mayfield 210; Messner 211; Metamorphous 212; NASW Press 218; Nelson-Hall 220; New York Univ. 225; Ohio State Univ. 230; Ohio Univ. 230; ‡One World 231; ‡Oneworld 330; ‡Owl Books 234; ‡Perspectives 240; ‡Pioneer Inst. 353; Planning/Comm. 245; Plenum 245; Praeger 246; ‡Prentice-Hall 247; ‡Purdue Univ. 251; Rain Dancer 253; ‡Rainbow 254; Random House, Adult 255; Regnery Pub. 256; ‡Rising Star 258; Riverhead 259; Roxbury 260; ‡Rutgers Univ. 261; ‡St. Martin's Scholarly & Ref. 263; South End 276; Stanford Univ. 278; Steel Balls 355; Stoddard 335; ‡Stonewall Inn 281; Success Pub. 366; Summit Pub. Grp. 283; Teachers College 285; Temple Univ. 285; Thompson Educ. 336; ‡Twayne 291; United Church Publishing House 337; Univ. of Alberta Press 337; Univ. of Arkansas 294; ‡Univ. of Chicago 294; ‡Univ. of Georgia 295; Univ. of Illinois 295; Univ. of Massachusetts 296; Univ. of Montreal 337; Univ. of Ottawa 338; Univ. of Scranton 298; Univ. Press of New England 300; Vehicule 338; ‡Venture 301; Verso 301; Verso 339; ‡Vintage 303; Wadsworth 304; Walch,

J. Weston 304; ‡Wesleyan Univ. 308; ‡Westview 308; Wilder Pub. Ctr. 310; ‡Wyndham Hall 314; ‡Yale Univ. 314

Software: Adams-Blake 87; ‡American Bar Assoc. 91; ‡Amer. Water Works 94; ‡A-R 95; Branden 111; ‡Bridge Learning Systems 344; Cardoza 118; Career 118; Cliffs Notes 128; Doubleday Adult 142; Duke 143; Eckert, J.K. 361; Family Album 347; ‡HRD 176; ‡Image Grafx 362; ‡Inter Trade 183; ‡Jamenair 349; Jist Works 188; Kroshka Books 193; Laing Comm. 363; ‡M & T 203; McGraw-Hill Companies, Prof. Bk. Grp. 205; Macmillan General Ref. 206; ‡Mega Media 351; MIS 214; National Textbook 219; Neal-Schuman 220; No Starch 226; Nova Press 229; Osbornemacgrawhill †Osborne/McGraw-Hill 233; Paideia 353; ‡Peters, A.K. 241; Philosophy Documentation 242; Planning/Comm. 245; Productive 331; ‡Que 252; Rain Dancer 253; Richboro 258; Royal Fireworks 260; SAS Inst. 267; Schirmer 268; Serendipity 270; Sugar Hill 356; Sulzburger & Graham 282; Summers 283; Sybex 284; Systemsware 356; Wadsworth 304; Walch, J. Weston 304; ‡Windsor 312

Spiritual: Bantam 102; ‡Bethany House 106; Brett Books 344; Creation House 133; Crossing Press 134; ‡Daybreak 138; ‡Doubleday Religious 142; ‡Focus Pub. 154; ‡Harper Libros 165; Harper Perennial 166; Hay House 169; Humanics Pub. Grp. 177; ‡Image Books 181; ‡Innisfree 183; Jewish Lights 187; ‡Northstone 330; ‡One World 231; ‡Putnam's Sons 251; ‡Rising Star 258; Riverhead 259; ‡Tarcher, Jeremy 285; Taylor 285

Sports: Adams Media 87; ‡Algonquin 89; American Press 93; Amwell 94; Archway Paperbacks 96; Atheneum Bks. for Yng. Rdrs. 98; ‡Avisson 99; Avon 100; Bantam 102; Barron's Educ. Series 103; Bentley, Robert 105; Blackbirch Press 107; Bonus Books 109; Bowling Green State Univ. 111; Brassey's 111; Broadway Books 113; Carol 118; Carolrhoda 119; ‡Cartwheel 119; ‡Centennial 122; Cerier Book Dev., Alison Brown 361; Charlton 320; Children's Press 124; Compass Prod. 361; Countrysport 133; Creative Spark 361; Crown Pub. Grp. 134; ‡Cumberland House 135; ‡Da Capo Press 345; Databooks 136; Doubleday Adult 142; Dover Pub. 142; Down East 142; Down Home 143; ‡Dummies 144; Eakin Press/Sunbelt Media 145; Ecopress 346; ECW Press 322; ‡Emerald Wave 346; Eriksson, Paul S. 148; Evras 347; Facts On File 150; Fine, Donald I. 152; Graber Prod. 362; Great Quotations 160; ‡Greenwood Pub Grp 161; Harper Perennial 166; HarperCollins 166; Heritage House 325; Holiday House 173; Houghton Mifflin Bks. for Children 175; Houghton Mifflin, Adult 175; Howell Press 176; Human Kinetics 177; ICS Books 180; Ideals Children's 180; Jewish Publication 187; Jones Univ., Bob 188; JSA Publications 363; Kali 350; Kesend, Michael 191; ‡Ketz, Louise 363; Key Porter 327; Lawco 350; Lerner 196; Lion Books 198; Little, Brown 199; Little, Brown Children's 199; Longstreet 202; Lyons & Burford 203; McBooks 350; McFarland & Co. 204; McGraw-Hill Companies, Prof. Bk. Grp. 205; McGraw-Hill Ryerson 328; ‡McGregor 205; ‡Macmillan Bks. 205; ‡Macmillan Consumer Info. Grp. 206; Macmillan General Ref. 206; Masters Press 209; Menasha Ridge 364; ‡Millbrook 213; Mosaic Press Miniature Books 352; Motorbooks 216; Mountaineers Books 217; Mustang Publishing 218; New York Univ. 225; ‡North Point 227; Norton, W.W. 229; NTC/Contemporary Pub. 229; Open Road 231; Orca 330; ‡Out There 233; Owen, Richard C. 233; ‡Owl Books 234; Paper Chase 235; Parnassus 236; Pelican 238; Penguin Books Canada 331; Prairie Oak 247; Prentice-Hall Canada 331; Pruett 250; ‡Putnam's Sons 251; Quintet 332; Ragged Mountain 253; ‡Rainbow 254; Raincoast 332; Random House, Adult 255; ‡Random House Bks. For Yng. Rdrs. 255; ‡Rising Star 258; ‡Safari 262; St. Martin's 263; ‡Santa Monica 266; Sasquatch 267; Scholastic Canada 334; ‡Seaworthy 269; ‡Signet 272; Silver Moon 365; SJL Pub. 274; ‡Spectacle Lane 355; Stackpole 278; Sterling 279; Stoddart 335; Stoeger 280; ‡Stoneydale 281; Summit Pub. Grp. 283; ‡Surrey 283; Taylor 285; Turtle Press 291; Univ. of Illinois 295; Univ. of Iowa 296; Univ. of Nebraska 296; Walker & Co. 304; Warner Books 305; White-Boucke 357; Whitman, Albert 309; Wieser & Wieser 366; Wilderness Adventure Books 358; ‡Willow Creek 311; Wilshire 311; Windward 312; ‡Workman 313

Technical: aatec 341; Abbott, Langer 84; Aberdeen Group 84; Adams-Blake 87; Aegis Publishing 88; ‡Allyn & Bacon 89; ‡American Bar Assoc. 91; ‡American College of Physician Executives 91; American Correctional Assoc. 91; American Eagle 92; American Hospital 92; ‡American Inst. of CPAs 93; American Nurses 93; American Press 93; American Society of Civil Engineers Press 93; ‡Amer. Water Works 94; ASA 97; Auto Book 343; ‡Baywood 104; ‡Baywood 104; Bentley, Robert 105; Bloomberg Press 107; Blue Poppy 108; ‡Book Enhancers 360; ‡Bookwrights 360; Branden 111; Brevet 112; ‡Bridge Learning Systems 344; Brookline Books 114; Business McGraw-Hill 115; Butterworth-Heinemann 115; Can. Plains Research 320; Cave Books 121; Chemtec 320; Chicago Spectrum 124; Computer Science 130; Cornell Maritime 131; Craftsman 133; ‡Cummings & Hathaway 135; Current Clinical Strategies 135; Darlington Prod. 136; Databooks 136; Drama Pub. 143; Duke 143; Eckert, J.K. 361; Engineering & Mgmt. 147; Evras 347; ‡Fire Engineering 152; Focal 153; ‡FPMI 156; ‡Government Inst. 159; Graphic Arts Tech. Found. 160; ‡Gulf 163; Hancock House 164; Hanser Gardner 164; Hatherleigh Press 168; Hoard, W.D. 348; Hollow Earth 173; ‡HRD 176; Human Kinetics 177; ‡ICC 179; Idyll Arbor 181; ‡Image Grafx 362; Index Pub. Grp. 182; Inst. of Police Tech. & Mgmt. 183; Int'l Found. Of Employee Benefit Plans 184; Interweave 185; Jelmar 349; Krieger Pub. 192; Kroshka Books 193; ‡Kumarian 193; Laing Comm. 363; Lake View 193; ‡Lippincott 198; Lone Eagle 201; ‡M & T 203; McFarland & Co. 204; McGraw-Hill Companies, Prof. Bk. Grp. 205; ‡Marshall & Swift 209; Maximum 210; ‡Medical Physics 210; Metal Powder Industries 211; Metamorphous 212; Michigan State Univ. 212; MIS 214; Neal-Schuman 220; Nichols 226; No Starch 226; Nova Press 229; Noyes Data 229; Orchises 232; Osbornemacgrawhill †Osborne/McGraw-Hill 233; Pacific Books 234; Parkway 236; Partners in Publishing 353; Peachpit 238; Pencil Point 239; Pennsylvania Hist. and Museum Comm. 239; PennWell 240; Planners 245; ‡Practice Mgmt. 246; Precept 247; Productive 331; Professional Pub. 249; PROMPT 250; Purich 331; ‡Que 252; Quintet 332; ‡Race Point 354; Reference Press Int'l. 256; Religious Education 256; ‡Rising Star 258; Royal Fireworks 260; ‡SAE Int'l 262; ‡Sams 265; ‡San Francisco 266; SAS Inst. 267; ‡Seaworthy 269; SJL Pub. 274; Sky 274; Sourcebooks 276; Stipes 280; Success Pub. 282; Sulzburger & Graham 282; Summers 283; Sybex 284; Systems Co. 284; Systemsware 356; Tech. Books for the Layperson 356; Texas Western Press 287; Tiare 287; ‡Transnational 289; ‡ULI 292; Univelt 293; Univ. of Alaska 293; Univ. of Idaho 295; ‡Vestal 302; ‡Visions 303; ‡Visions Comm. 357; Weidner & Sons 307; Weka Pub. 307; ‡Windsor 312; Wordware 313

Textbook: Abingdon 84; ACA Books 85; Active Parenting 86; ‡Alba 88; ‡Allyn & Bacon 89; Amacom 90; ‡American

There are seven **Writer's Digest School** courses to help you write better and sell more:

Novel Writing Workshop. A professional novelist helps you iron out your plot, develop your main characters, write the background for your novel, and complete the opening scene and a summary of your novel's complete story. You'll even identify potential publishers and write a query letter.

Marketing Your Nonfiction Book. You'll work with your mentor to create a book proposal that you can send directly to a publisher. You'll develop and refine your book idea, write a chapter-by-chapter outline of your subject, line up your sources of information, write sample chapters, and complete your query letter.

Writing & Selling Short Stories. Learn the basics of writing/selling short stories: plotting, characterization, dialogue, theme, conflict, and other elements of a marketable short story. Course includes writing assignments and one complete short story.

Writing & Selling Nonfiction Articles. Master the fundamentals of writing/selling nonfiction articles: finding article ideas, conducting interviews, writing effective query letters and attention-getting leads, and targeting your articles to the right publication. Course includes writing assignments and one complete article manuscript (and its revision).

Writing Your Life Stories. With the help of a professional writer you'll chronicle your life or your family's. Learn the important steps to documenting your history including researching and organizing your material, continuity, pacing and more!

Writer's Digest Criticism Service. Have your work evaluated by a professional writer before you submit it for pay. Whether you write books, articles, short stories or poetry, you'll get an objective review plus the specific writing and marketing advice that only a professional can provide.

The Elements of Effective Writing. Discover how to conquer the pesky grammar and usage problems that hold so many writers back. You'll refresh your basic English composition skills through step-by-step lessons and writing exercises to help steer your manuscripts clear of the rejection pile.

Mail this card today for FREE information!

College of Physician Executives 91; American Correctional Assoc. 91; American Hospital 92; American Nurses 93; ‡Amer. Psychiatric Press 93; Anchorage 94; Arden 96; Ardsley House 96; Art Direction 97; Asian Humanities 97; ‡Avisson 99; Baker Books 101; Barron's Educ. Series 103; Behrman House 105; Bliss 343; Blue Poppy 108; ‡Bookwrights 360; Bowling Green State Univ. 111; Branden 111; Brassey's 111; ‡Bridge Street 344; Broadview 318; Brookline Books 114; Butterworth-Heinemann 115; C Q Press 116; Cambridge Univ. 116; Can. Plains Research 320; Career 118; Center for African-American Stud. 345; Chemtec 320; China Books 125; Cliffs Notes 128; Computer Science 130; ‡Computing McGraw-Hill 130; Corwin 131; Cottonwood 132; Course Crafters 361; ‡CSLI 134; ‡Cummings & Hathaway 135; Current Clinical Strategies 135; Davidson, Harlan 137; Dearborn Financial 138; Dee, Ivan R. 138; Detselig 321; Dover Pub. 142; Drama Pub. 143; Duke 143; Eckert, J.K. 361; Eerdmans, William B. 146; Engineering & Mgmt. 147; ETC Pub. 148; ‡Excelsior Cee 149; ‡Fire Engineering 152; Focal 153; ‡Fordham Univ. 154; Foreign Policy 154; Free Press 156; Friends United 157; ‡Gessler 158; Graphic Arts Tech. Found. 160; ‡Greenwood Pub Grp 161; Group Pub. 162; ‡Gulf 163; Hanser Gardner 164; Harcourt Brace Canada 324; ‡Haworth Press 169; Hoard, W.D. 348; Howells House 176; Human Kinetics 177; ‡Humanities Press 178; I.A.A.S. Pub. 348; Idyll Arbor 181; ‡Image Grafx 362; Indiana Univ. Press 182; Inst. of Police Tech. & Mgmt. 183; Inst. of Psychological Research 327; Intercultural 184; Int'l City/County Mgmt. 184; Int'l Found. Of Employee Benefit Plans 184; Int'l Medical 185; Int'l Pub. 185; Jain 186; Jefferson Univ., Thomas 187; Jist Works 188; Kregel Publications 192; Krieger Pub. 192; ‡Kumarian 193; Laing Comm. 363; Lang, Peter 193; ‡Laurel Books 194; Leadership 195; ‡Learning Pub. 195; Liberal Press 197; Libraries Unlimited 197; ‡Lippincott 198; ‡Lippincott-Raven 198; ‡Management Tech. Inst. 351; Mangajin 351; Mayfield 210; ‡Medical Physics 210; Meriwether 211; Metal Powder Industries 211; Metamorphous 212; NASW Press 218; National Textbook 219; Neal-Schuman 220; Nelson-Hall 220; New Harbinger 221; Oasis Press 230; Optima 231; Orchises 232; Pacific Books 234; Pacific Educ. 330; Pacific View 235; Paideia 353; Paradigm 236; Partners in Publishing 353; Paulist Press 237; Pencil Point 239; ‡Peters, A.K. 241; Philosophy Documentation 242; Picton 243; ‡Practice Mgmt. 246; Precept 247; ‡Prentice-Hall 247; Professional Pub. 249; Prufrock 250; Publicom 365; Publishers Assoc. 251; Publishers Res. Grp. 365; Purich 331; Rainbow Pub. 254; Reidmore 333; Religious Education 256; Review and Herald 257; ‡Rosen Pub. Grp. 260; Roxbury 260; Royal Fireworks 260; ‡SAE Int'l 262; St. Bede's 263; St. Martin's 263; ‡San Francisco 266; Sandlapper 266; SAS Inst. 267; ‡Schiffer 267; Schirmer 268; Sibyl 271; Sidran 271; ‡Smith, Gibbs 275; Sourcebooks 276; Speech Bin 277; Stanford Univ. 278; Stipes 280; Sulzburger & Graham 282; Systems Co. 284; Systemsware 356; Tech. Books for the Layperson 356; Thompson Educ. 336; ‡Transnational 289; Univ. of Alaska 293; Univ. of Alberta Press 337; ‡Univ. of Chicago 294; Univ. of Idaho 295; Univ. of Montreal 337; Univ. of Ottawa 338; ‡Upstart 300; Utah St. Univ. 300; Vanderbilt Univ. 301; ‡Venture 301; VGM Career Horizons 302; ‡Visions 303; ‡Visions Comm. 357; Wadsworth 304; Wall & Emerson 339; ‡Watson-Guptill 306; Weidner & Sons 307; ‡Westview 308; White Cliffs Media 309; White Pine 309; Wisdom 312; Wordware 313; ‡Wuerz 340; ‡Wyndham Hall 314; ‡Yale Univ. 314; York Press 340; Zondervan 315

Translation: Aronson, Jason 96; ‡Arte Publico 97; Barron's Educ. Series 103; Brookline Books 114; Calyx 344; Can. Inst. of Ukrainian Stud. 319; Chatham 123; China Books 125; Citadel 128; Clarkson Potter 128; Counterpoint 132; Dante Univ. Of America Press 136; Davies, Robert 321; Doubleday Adult 142; Dover Pub. 142; Ecco Press 146; Eerdmans, William B. 146; ETC Pub. 148; Evras 347; Feminist Press at CUNY 152; ‡Fordham Univ. 154; Free Press 156; Goose Lane 323; Guernica Editions 323; ‡Gulf 163; Harper Perennial 166; Harvard Common 167; Hippopotamus 325; ‡Hohm 173; Holmes & Meier 173; Hounslow 325; Howells House 176; ‡Image Grafx 362; Indiana Univ. Press 182; Inst. of Psychological Research 327; Intercultural 184; Intertext 349; Jefferson Univ., Thomas 187; Johnson 188; Lang, Peter 193; Mage 207; Maisonneuve 208; Mangajin 351; Mercury House 210; ‡Millenium 213; Motorbooks 216; Mountaineers Books 217; Northern Illinois Univ. 227; Ohio Univ. 230; Pacific Books 234; Passeggiata 237; Paulist Press 237; ‡Peters, A.K. 241; Post-Apollo Press 354; Puckerbrush 354; Rain Dancer 253; ‡Rutgers Univ. 261; St. Bede's 263; Stone Bridge 280; Univ. of Alaska 293; Univ. of California 294; ‡Univ. of Chicago 294; Univ. of Massachusetts 296; Univ. of Montreal 337; Univ. of Nebraska 296; Univ. of Ottawa 338; Univ. of Texas 298; Vanderbilt Univ. 301; ‡Vintage 303; Wake Forest Univ. 304; White Pine 309; Zoland 315

Transportation: ‡AGS 359; ASA 97; Bentley, Robert 105; Boston Mills 318; Career 118; ‡Carstens 119; Howell Press 176; Iowa State Univ. 186; Kalmbach 189; Lerner 196; Motorbooks 216; Norton, W.W. 229; ‡Schiffer 267; Sono Nis 335; Success Pub. 282

Travel: Academy Chicago 85; ‡Alexander 88; Almar Press 90; Appalachian Mountain Club 95; Arcade 95; Atheneum Bks. for Yng. Rdrs. 98; ‡Barnegat Light 102; Barron's Educ. Series 103; Beachway Press 104; Blackbirch Press 107; Blair, John F. 107; Blue Sky 343; Camino Books 117; Cardoza 118; Carol 118; Carousel 345; Cave Books 121; Charles River Press 123; Chatham 123; Chicago Spectrum 124; China Books 125; Chronicle 126; ‡Compass 130; Compass Prod. 361; ‡Countryman 132; ‡Cumberland House 135; ‡Dawbert 346; Dimi 141; Doubleday Adult 142; Dover Pub. 42; Down Home 143; Down The Shore 346; ‡Dummies 144; Ecco Press 146; Ekstasis Editions 323; Epicenter 148; Eriako Assoc. 361; Eriksson, Paul S. 148; ‡Explorer's Guide 149; ‡Falcon Press 150; Gem Guides 158; Giniger, K.S. 362; Globe Pequot 159; Golden West 159; Graber Prod. 362; ‡Grove/Atlantic 163; ‡Gulf 163; Harper Perennial 166; HarperCollins 166; HarperCollins (Canada) 324; Harvard Common 167; Hastings 168; ‡Hellgate 170; Heyday 171; Hippocrene 172; Hollow Earth 173; Houghton Mifflin Bks. for Children 175; Houghton Mifflin, Adult 175; Hounslow 325; ‡Hungry Mind 178; Hunter Publishing 178; ICS Books 180; Interlink 184; Italica 186; Jain 186; Jenkins Group 362; Johnson 188; Johnston Assoc. Int'l. 349; Kesend, Michael 191; ‡KQED 192; Kurian Reference Books, George 363; Lone Pine 328; Lonely Planet 201; ‡Lynx Images 328; Lyons & Burford 203; McDonald & Woodward 204; Macmillan General Ref. 206; ‡Macmillan Travel 206; Mangajin 351; Marlor 209; Menasha Ridge 364; Mercury House 210; Moon 215; Mosaic Press Miniature Books 352; Mountain Automation 352; ‡Mountain N'Air 216; ‡Mountain Press 216; Mountaineers Books 217; ‡Muir, John 217; Mustang Publishing 218; New York Niche Press 352; New York Univ. 225; Newjoy Press 225; ‡North Point 227; Norton, W.W. 229; Ohio Univ. 230; Open Road 231; Orca 330;

Orca 330; ‡Out There 233; ‡Owl Books 234; Pacific View 235; Parnassus 236; Passport 237; Pelican 238; ‡Pendaya 353; Pennsylvania Hist. and Museum Comm. 239; Pilot 243; Primer 354; Pruett 250; ‡Putnam's Sons 251; Quarry 331; Quixote 253; Raincoast 332; Red Deer College 332; Riverhead 259; Rockbridge Pub. Co. 259; Rocky Mountain 333; Russian Info. Svces. 261; Rutledge Hill 262; ‡Sanders, J.S. 266; Sasquatch 267; ‡Seal 269; Seaside 269; Shoreline 334; Sierra Club 272; Soho Press 275; Stone Bridge 280; Storm Peak 355; Sulzburger & Graham 282; ‡Surrey 283; Tamarack 356; Todd 288; Turnstone 336; Upney Editions 338; ‡Voyageur 304; Wayfinder 357; Wescott Cove 307; ‡Westcliffe 308; Whitecap 339; Whitehorse 358; Whitman, Albert 309; Wieser & Wieser 366; Wilderness Adventure Books 358; ‡Workman 313; World Leisure 313; Zoland 315

True Crime: Academy Chicago 85; Addicus Books 87; Bantam 102; Berkley Pub. Grp. 105; ‡Carroll & Graf 119; ‡McGregor 205; Penguin Books Canada 331; ‡Pinnacle 244; St. Martin's 263; Stoddart 335

Women's Issues/Studies: ABC-CLIO 84; Adams Media 87; American Nurses 93; Arden 96; Arsenal Pulp 317; ‡Arte Publico 97; ‡Artemis 342; ‡Avisson 99; Baker Books 101; Bantam 102; Barricade 103; ‡Baylor Univ. 343; ‡Baywood 104; Beacon Press 104; ‡Bethany House 106; Blackbirch Graphics 360; Blackbirch Press 107; Bonus Books 109; ‡Book Enhancers 360; Bowling Green State Univ. 111; Broadview 318; Broadway Books 113; Bryant & Dillon 114; Calyx 344; Carol 118; Carolina Wren 345; Celestial Arts 121; Center for African-American Stud. 345; Charles River Press 123; Chicago Spectrum 124; China Books 125; Commune-A-Key 129; Companion 130; Conari 130; Consumer Press 131; Creative Spark 361; Crossing Press 134; ‡Cummings & Hathaway 135; Davidson, Harlan 137; Davies, Robert 321; Detselig 321; Doubleday Adult 142; Dowling Press 142; ‡Drew, Lisa 143; Dundurn 321; Epicenter 148; ‡Excelsior Cee 149; Fairleigh Dickinson Univ. 150; Feminist Press at CUNY 152; Filter Press 152; Focus on the Family 154; ‡Focus Pub. 154; ‡Forge 154; ‡Fortress 155; Goose Lane 323; Great Quotations 160; ‡Greenwood Pub Grp 161; ‡Grosset 162; ‡Harper Libros 165; Harper Perennial 166; HarperCollins (Canada) 324; ‡Harvard Univ. 168; Harvest House 168; ‡Haworth Press 169; Hay House 169; Health Comm. 169; Heinemann 170; Hensley, Virgil 171; ‡Hill & Wang 172; Holmes & Meier 173; Houghton Mifflin, Adult 175; ‡House of Anansi 325; ‡Hungry Mind 178; Hunter House 178; ICS Books 180; Ide House 180; ‡ILR 181; ‡Image Books 181; Indiana Univ. Press 182; Inner Traditions Int'l 182; ‡Innisfree 183; Insight 183; Int'l Pub. 185; Jewish Lights 187; Jewish Publication 187; Key Porter 327; Knowledge, Ideas & Trends 192; ‡Kumarian 193; Lake View 193; ‡Lamppost 363; ‡Learning Pub. 195; Liberal Press 197; Libraries Unlimited 197; Lincoln Springs 350; ‡Lippincott 198; Llewellyn 200; Locust Hill 200; Longstreet 202; Lorimer & Co., James 328; McFarland & Co. 204; Macmillan General Ref. 206; ‡MacMurray & Beck 207; Maisonneuve 208; ‡Management Tech. Inst. 351; Maritimes Arts Projects Productions 329; Mayfield 210; Mercury House 210; Michigan State Univ. 212; Milkweed 212; Minnesota Hist. Soc. Press 213; ‡Moody 214; New Hope 221; New World 225; New York Univ. 225; Nicolas-Hays 352; NTC/Contemporary Pub. 229; Ohio Univ. 230; ‡One World 231; Owen, Richard C. 233; Paideia 353; Paper Chase 235; Papier-Mache 236; Penguin Studio 239; Post-Apollo Press 354; ‡Pot Shard 354; Praeger 246; Publishers Assoc. 251; ‡Puffin 251; ‡Putnam's Sons 251; ‡Rainbow 254; Reference Service 256; Review and Herald 257; ‡Reynolds, Morgan 258; Riverhead 259; Royal Fireworks 260; ‡Rutgers Univ. 261; ‡St. Martin's Scholarly & Ref. 263; Scarecrow 267; ‡Schocken 268; ‡Seal 269; Shoreline 334; Sibyl 271; ‡Skinner 274; Sourcebooks 276; South End 276; Spinsters Ink 278; Steel Balls 355; Stone Bridge 280; Sulzburger & Graham 282; Summit Pub. Grp. 283; Swan-Raven 283; ‡Tarcher, Jeremy 285; Teachers College 285; Temple Univ. 285; Tenth Avenue 366; Texas A&M Univ. 286; Third Side Press 287; Thompson Educ. 336; Thunder Dog 357; Times Books 288; ‡Transnational 289; Trilogy Books 290; ‡Twayne 291; 2M Comm. 366; ‡Umbrella 336; United Church Publishing House 337; Univ. of Arizona 293; ‡Univ. of Chicago 294; Univ. of Idaho 295; Univ. of Manitoba 337; Univ. of Massachusetts 296; Univ. of Nebraska 296; Univ. of Oklahoma 297; Univ. of Ottawa 338; Univ. of Tennessee 298; Univ. of Texas 298; Univ. Press of Kentucky 299; Vanderbilt Univ. 301; Verso 301; Verso 339; ‡Victor 302; ‡Viking 302; ‡Vintage 303; ‡Visions 303; Volcano 303; ‡Westview 308; White Pine 309; Wiley, John 311; ‡Yale Univ. 314; Zoland 315

World Affairs: ABC-CLIO 84; Addison Wesley Longman 87; Beacon Press 104; Brassey's 111; ‡Bridge Street 344; ‡C Q Books 115; Clarity Press 345; Dee, Ivan R. 138; Family Album 347; ‡Hungry Mind 178; Lucent 203; McFarland & Co. 204; ‡Moyer Bell 217; ‡New England 221; Stoddart 335; Times Books 288; Univ. of Arizona 293; ‡Univ. Press of Florida 299

Young Adult: Archway Paperbacks 96; Atheneum Bks. for Yng. Rdrs. 98; ‡Avisson 99; Barron's Educ. Series 103; Blackbirch Graphics 360; Blackbirch Press 107; ‡Blue Heron 108; Cambridge Educ. 116; Cliffs Notes 128; Cobblehill 129; College Board 129; Davenport, May 136; Dial Books for Yng. Rdrs. 140; Dundurn 321; ‡Edge 146; Enslow 148; Facts On File 150; ‡General Licensing Co. 362; Group Pub. 162; Hendrick-Long 170; Highsmith 172; Holiday House 173; ‡Holt Bks. for Yng. Rdrs. 174; Jewish Publication 187; Jones Univ., Bob 188; Just Us 189; Little, Brown Children's 199; Living the Good News 200; Lodestar 201; Lucent 203; McElderry, Margaret K. 204; Mitchell Lane 214; Philomel 242; Pippin 244; ‡PPI 246; Price Stern Sloan 248; Random House, Inc. Juvenile Books 255; ‡Reynolds, Morgan 258; ‡Rosen Pub. Grp. 260; Scholastic 268; Silver Burdett 273; Speech Bin 277; Twenty-First Century 291; Tyndale House 292; ‡Umbrella 336; Walker & Co. 304; Ward Hill 305; Zondervan 315;

General Index

A double-dagger (‡) precedes listings that are new to this edition. Markets that appeared in the 1997 edition of *Writer's Market* but are not included in this edition are identified by a two-letter code explaining why the market was omitted: (**ED**)—Editorial Decision, (**NS**)—Not accepting Submissions, (**NR**)—No (or Late) Response to Listing Request, (**OB**)—Out of Business, (**RR**)—Removed by Market's Request, (**UC**)—Unable to Contact, (**RP**)—Business Restructured or Purchased, (**NP**)—No longer Pays or Pays in Copies Only, (**SR**)—Subsidy/Royalty Publisher, (**UF**)—Uncertain Future.